ROTHMANS FOOTBALL YEARBOOK 1991-92

EDITOR: JACK ROLLIN

QUEEN ANNE PRESS
MACDONALD & CO
LONDON and SYDNEY

A *Queen Anne Press* BOOK

© Rothmans Publications Ltd/Queen Anne Press

First published in Great Britain in 1991 by
Queen Anne Press, a division of
Macdonald & Co (Publishers) Ltd
165 Great Dover Street
London SE1 4YA

A member of Maxwell Macmillan Publishing Corporation

Cover photograph Left: Gudni Bergsson (Tottenham), right: Anders Limpar (Arsenal)
(*Colorsport*)

A CIP catalogue record for this book
is available from the British Library

ISBN 0–356–20164–3 (hardback)
0–356–19198–2 (paperback)

Typeset by BPCC Whitefriars Ltd,
Tunbridge Wells
Printed and bound in Great Britain by
BPCC Hazell Books, Aylesbury

CONTENTS

INTRODUCTION

The 22nd edition of *Rothmans Football Yearbook* has extended items on both domestic and international football. As last year, every one of the 92 Football League clubs has a full page photograph of the 1990–91 squad and there are again six pages devoted to each team. Newly promoted Barnet, the 93rd club, are also featured.

For the first time, transfer fees during 1990–91 are indicated in the section covering player moves. Although only tribunal fees are officially disclosed, others have been reproduced as those published at the time. Also each club has an item entitled 'Did You Know', relating to an historical fact of interest.

On the international scene, the directory of nations in FIFA now includes full addresses. The ongoing 1992 European Championship series is given full coverage with fixtures for the remaining games. Non-league football is well reported as is European club soccer. The return of English clubs to European fare is also given prominence.

With so many changes in the Laws of the Game having taken place in the last year or so, it has also been decided to include these again with the latest amendments documented.

The Editor would like to thank Maurice Golesworthy for historical notes on the clubs, as well as Alan Elliott for the Scottish section. Thanks are also due to John English, whose painstaking and conscientious reading of the proofs has been of invaluable assistance in the preparation of the book as well as editorial assistance from Mavis Suckling and Christine Forrest.

The Editor would also like to pay tribute to the various organisations who have helped to make this edition complete, especially Sheila Murphy of the Football League, Mike McNamara of The Football Association, and the secretaries of all the Football League and Scottish League clubs for their kind co-operation. The ready availability of Football League secretary David Dent and his staff to answer queries was as usual most appreciated especially Ian Cotton and Chris Hull and thanks are due in equal measure to the Scottish Football League.

ACKNOWLEDGEMENTS

The Editor would also like to express his appreciation of the following individuals and organisations for their co-operation; Mike Foster, Glynis Firth, Sandra Whiteside, Lorna Parnell, Debbie Birch (all from The Football League), David Barber and Steve Clark (The Football Association), David C. Thompson of The Scottish Football League, Bernard Turner (FA of Wales), Alan Dick, Malcolm Brodie, C. S. Allatt and Peter Hughes (English Schools FA), W. P. Goss (AFA), Ken Scott for GM Vauxhall Conference information, Rev. Nigel Sands, Edward Grayson, Andy Howland and Don Aldridge.

Mank thanks to Caroline North, Publishing Director at Queen Anne Press, for her support and encouragement during the year, and to her assistant Stephanie Bennett.

Finally, sincere thanks to Ken Webb and the production staff at BPCC Whitefriars for their efforts in the production of this book which was much appreciated in the final stages.

6

EDITORIAL

History shows that leaders of a revolution must be sure of their fellow dissidents. A puppet's string can easily be cut in any coup and in the battle between the Football Association and the Football League it could be said to have been an attempt at a *coup de grass*...

It was in April that the FA announced its intention of implementing an 18-team Super League in 1992–93 to benefit the England team. Some judged this to be an ill-timed move, deliberately designed to throw the 1991–92 season into such potential chaos that a Super League would be welcomed. By doing this they claimed that the goalposts had not only been moved, but the venue had been changed. Yet this was never a contest between the FA and the League, just the on-going attempts by the big clubs to distance themselves financially from the rest.

Throughout this discourse, scarcely any thought was given to the two most important ingredients of the professional game, namely the players and the spectators. It has been mischievously suggested that the Super League would need neither. As a cost-cutting exercise it has its merits. The 2036 Football League games during the 1990–91 produced an overall policing bill of £6.78 million. Wages and other heavy expenditure would also largely disappear, but presumably sponsorship would still be there and executive suites provided with videos of bygone games. Never mind the ball, let's get on with the game. Next thing you know, Tesco will be dispensing with its customers.

The Football League has been in existence for over 100 years. That in itself does not constitute sufficient argument for a continuance in the same form. Longevity can lead to senile decay. But the facts present a different picture. Despite the recession, the Football League showed a modest increase in attendances during 1990–91, for an unprecedented fifth successive season. The introduction of the play-off system has undoubtedly given the League competition a tremendous shot-in-the-arm and resulted in far fewer meaningless matches at the tail end of the season.

One strong criticism of the League is that it lacks leadership. The decision to revert to a 22-team First Division gave the Super League lobby powerful ammunition, but remember it was the clubs who voted for it in the first place.

Both the Italian Serie A and the West (sorry just) German Bundesliga have been put forward as models for a Super League. Yet the Italians have four teams relegated from it each season from 18 and the cream of the German national team plays in Italy anyway. Even with home advantage, the Italians failed to win the 1990 World Cup, something our clapped-out system managed to achieve 25 years ago. True the Germans won it last year, but only because their elite were playing in Italy, the most competitive league of all.

There were other sceptics who wondered just where the vast sums of money were to be derived from to fund a Super League. The FA's record of high level sponsorship has been unable to date to find a backer of sufficient wealth for the FA Cup. Television remains pie in the sky and only licensing offers obvious extra remuneration.

The FA has been considered an unlikely source of rebellion. But remember they have murmured approval at previous breakaway threats and in 1974 they decided that there were no longer any amateurs in the game. If they had been really serious about the England team they could have laid long-term plans to include their own in a Super League. The School of Excellence would provide the necessary raw material without it developing the bad habits of other League clubs.

Sensibly no League can be organised to solely benefit a national team. If the England side never played another match or one day was forced to become a quarter of a Great Britain set up, the game would still survive. But the facade of pretending this was designed for national benefit has now vanished.

What is clear is that a quarter of the clubs in the League might well gain in the short term, the remainder will certainly struggle and then there will be enforced changes of name to Aimless Wanderers, Nomadic Rovers and Cardboard City. Odd too, that the body which fostered the pyramid system for non-league football stands accused of virtually mummifying incentive to reach the top.

ROTHMANS FOOTBALL AWARDS

BARNET FOOTBALL CLUB became the 93rd Football League club when they won promotion from the GM Vauxhall Conference at the completion of the 1990–91 season. It ended a frustrating sequence of events for the North London club which had seen them finishing runners-up three times since 1986–87. Formed in 1888 they first played in the Olympian League but it was much later in their history that they created an impact winning the Athenian League a record seven times. In 1945–46 they won the Amateur Cup and 20 years later turned professional taking the Southern League title in their first season. Manager Barry Fry is in his second spell in charge of the club and succeeded in steering them to the championship despite transferring Phil Gridelet, Paul Harding, Andrew Clarke and David Regis to other Football League clubs during this momentous season.

MANCHESTER UNITED FOOTBALL CLUB crowned their return to European football by winning the Cup-Winners' Cup in style. Arguably the most pleasing aspect of their triumph came from their performances away from Old Trafford. Drawn at home in the first leg against Pecsi Munkas of Hungary, they were able to take a 2-0 lead into the return and won again 1-0. Fourth Division Wrexham put up a gallant performance in the second round but lost 5-0 on aggregate before the French club Montpellier presented United with their most serious opposition. At Old Trafford the first leg ended 1-1, but in France it was a different story as Alex Ferguson's team gave an outstanding performance to win 2-0. Legia Warsaw, who had knocked out Sampdoria, were made to look an ordinary side in Poland as United won 3-1 and the 1-1 second leg was academic. United then topped their season with a memorable and surprisingly easy 2-1 final success over Barcelona.

STEVE NORRIS became the first player in 20 years to notch up more than half of his team's goals in the Football League when scoring 30 of Halifax Town's 59 goals. At one stage in the season it seemed that he might well break the club's individual scoring record for one campaign, a feat achieved by Albert Valentine in 1934–35 when he registered 34 goals in the Third Division (North). But Steve Norris actually began the season playing for Carlisle United and when he joined Halifax on 5 October they were still searching for their first League goal! Eight days later the Yorkshire side broke their duck at Carlisle of all places, Norris grabbing one of the three Town goals that day. Thanks chiefly to his scoring prowess, Halifax did manage to finish two places off the bottom of the Fourth Division.

STUART PEARCE established himself as the most prolific scoring defender in the Football League for one season without the assistance of a penalty kick. His 16 League and Cup goals were well earned and provided an extra dimension to Nottingham Forest's attacking patterns. Of course several of his successful strikes came from ferocious free-kicks, none better revealed than in the FA Cup Final against Tottenham Hotspur. Stuart Pearce, a resolute full-back, came comparatively late into the Football League as he was over 21 when he was signed by Coventry City from Wealdstone, but he soon showed that he had lost nothing in his footballing education for this beginning. Since then he has forced himself into the England team and has captained his country. During one of the close season matches against New Zealand he scored the second full international goal of his career.

TEDDY SHERINGHAM enjoyed his most successful scoring season in 1990–91 finishing as the Football League's highest marksman with 33 goals for Millwall in the Second Division. He also took his total of goals in League games to 93 thus overhauling the total achieved by Derek Possee with 79 from 1967 to 1973. Apart from a short loan spell with Aldershot, Teddy Sheringham had played all his football with Millwall, the club he joined as an apprentice. In the summer of 1991 he joined Nottingham Forest for £2,000,000. Last season, during which he did not miss one League game, he also took his total of League games to over the 200 mark. It was also his first full season without being partnered by Tony Cascarino who had been transferred to Aston Villa. Sheringham responded by producing his best finishing power to come within four goals of Richard Parker's 37 achieved in the old Third Division Southern Section in 1926–27.

GRAHAM TAYLOR started his new career as England manager with an unbeaten record of 12 matches after taking over the role from Bobby Robson. For any manager of a national team fewer matches only produce greater pressure and the switch from club management can be a traumatic affair. For Graham Taylor there was the added responsibility of taking charge of a team which had just acquitted itself admirably in the 1990 World Cup. He had to continue the momentum built up by this improvement but at the same time stamp his own authority. He can be satisfied that his immediate targets have been met in such a fashion that the long term aims lie well within his grasp. He has already been more successful in the first dozen games than any of his predecessors.

MILESTONES DIARY 1990–91

June 1990

14   **Arthur Sandford, Football League** chief executive, asks **Gordon Taylor,** his opposite number at the **PFA,** to provide evidence to back his claim of over-reaction to the **Swindon Town** case and allegations that most **First Division** clubs are in **breach** of other **rules. Dario Gradi, seven years** with **Crewe** as **manager,** is given a **ten-year** contract. **Chelsea** coach Mick McGiven joins **Ipswich. Lucien Laurent, 82,** the first **World Cup** goalscorer in **1930,** enjoys watching the **1990** competition on **TV** in Besancon, France.

15   **Dave Beasant,** the **Chelsea** goalkeeper, is given permission to replace the injured **David Seaman** in the **England World Cup** squad. **Bournemouth** and **Sheffield Wednesday** may go to court over their possible demotion in view of Swindon's appeal.

17   **Manager Ian Bowyer** agrees to part company with **Hereford** over a **disagreement** about failing to re-sign his son **Gary.**

18   **Ray Harford** is appointed **caretaker** manager of **Wimbledon** after **Bobby Gould** refuses new contract.

19   **Frantisek Planicka, 86,** who kept goal for **Czechoslovakia** against **Italy** in the **1934 World Cup** in Rome is invited to see the **1990** re-match. **Folkestone** go into voluntary **liquidation.**

20   The **playing area** of the **Olympic Stadium** in **Rome** is to be cut into **306,000** pieces and **sold** at between **£50–£100** a piece after the **World Cup Final.**

21   **Swindon** drop **High Court action** and will abide by the decision of an **FA appeal panel.**

23   **Bryan Robson** to return to **England** with **achilles tendon trouble.**

25   **Bournemouth** and **Sheffield Wednesday** ready to drop action against the **Football League** who block **Chester's** move to **Macclesfield. Hibs** fans urged to close their accounts with the **Bank of Scotland** who are backing **Hearts takeover.**

27   **Everton** appoint former player **Jimmy Gabriel** as **coach.**

28   First change in **offside law** for **65 years** announced by FIFA: players **level** no longer offside.

29   **UEFA** leave decision to re-admit **English clubs** until **July 10. Football League** delay decision on **Chester City** moving to **Macclesfield.**

30   **Brian Tiler, Bournemouth's** former managing director is **killed** in a **car crash** in Italy, **manager Harry Redknapp** is **injured.**

July

2   **FA** cut **Swindon's** punishment; they can **stay** in **Division Two. Tranmere** are furious.

3   **Andy Linighan** moves from **Norwich** to **Arsenal** for **£1.25m. Football League** to continue to **investigate Swindon Town's** affairs.

4   **Italians** claim defeat against **Argentina** in the **World Cup** was due to an unlucky **17.** It was Italy's **17th match** at the **San Paolo Stadium, Naples;** it produced a goal for them in **17 minutes** from **Salvatore Schillaci** but **Roberto Donadoni,** who wore the **No. 17** shirt, missed the **fateful penalty. Hearts** pay **£750,000** to **Rangers** for **Derek Ferguson. Hereford** appoint **Colin Addison** as **manager.**

5   **Andy Townsend** moves from **Norwich** to **Chelsea** for **£1.2m** and **Dennis Wise** joins him from **Wimbledon** in a **£1.6m** deal.

6   **Frank McGarvey** is appointed **manager** of **Queen of the South.**

8   **West Germany** win the **World Cup** beating **Argentina 1-0** with a late **penalty. Two Argentines** are **sent off**: **Pedro Monzon** and **Gustavo Dezotti,** the **first** players dismissed in a **World Cup Final.**

9   **Alan Dicks** is appointed **manager** of **Fulham. Martin Edwards** stays as **Manchester United** chairman after five hour board meeting, but with **reduced shareholding. World Cup TV** audience reckoned to have been **31bn,** a record.

12   **Tony Coton** transferred from **Watford** to **Manchester City** for **£1m. Birmingham City** announce **computer membership** for **terraces. Chelsea** announce **five year extension** of **Commodore sponsorship. Chester** receive **League approval** for two year share of **Macclesfield's ground.**

13   **Hearts** call off takeover plans for **Hibernian.**

14   **Graham Taylor** starts work on his **four year term** as **England** manager.

15   **England** supporters **deported** from **Italy** during **World Cup** consider **legal action** against **Italian police** and **British Government.**

16   **Miguel Munoz,** former **Real Madrid** player and **Spanish national team manager** dies at **68.**

17   **Leeds United** must pay **£1m** to **Leicester City** for **Gary McAllister. Joe Jordan** turns down **Aston Villa's** approach as **manager.**

18   **Anatoly Byshovets** appointed **USSR manager. Glenn Hoddle (Monaco),** out of action for **nine months** with injured left knee, **may be on way back** to fitness.

19   The **English Schools FA,** founded **1904,** alter constitution to include girls. They will also **press the FA** to **alter their rules** to allow **boys and girls** to play together up to **age of 11. Tottenham** deny bid of **£12m** for **Paul Gascoigne** and **Gary Lineker** from **Juventus. Chelsea** given **planning permission** for **35,000 all-seater** stand at **Stamford Bridge** development.

20   **Lawrie McMenemy** appointed as **Graham Taylor's No.2.**

22   **John Sillett** signs **three year deal** to remain at **Coventry** as **manager** and will then retire. **Czech national** manager **Jozef Venglos,** a **Doctor** of **PE** and **Philosophy,** becomes **Aston Villa's manager.**

23   **Hooliganism** costs **QPR** an extension of their **£600,000 sponsorship** with **KLM** because of **Dutch** and **English fans'** misbehaviour.

24   **FIFA** may cut **Europe's World Cup** places in **1994** from **14 to 12.**

25 The **Football Association oppose** the **Football League's** intention to return to a **22-club First Division** and may not approve the idea.

26 **England manager Taylor** joins the **anti-22 club** First Division lobby. **Football League unable** to announce **sponsorship** of the **League Cup** by **National Power** and go ahead with the **first round draw**.

27 **Colchester** announce biggest **sponsorship** for a non-league club, a **six-figure fee** from **Holimarine** and **Pennant**.

29 **Football League** order **Swindon** to pay **£67,000** additional **transfer fees** for some previous deals. **Oxford City**, founded **1882**, but **out of action** since **1988**, will return this season in the **South Midlands League, Division One**.

30 **Rumbelows** agree **£5m four-year sponsorship** of the **League Cup**, following **National Power's** announcement of **£605m losses**.

31 **Aldershot** 'hopelessly insolvent' **wound-up** in the **High Court** with debts of **£490,000**. **Graham White** closes **Colne Dynamoes**, runaway winners of the **HFS Loans League**, after **abusive and threatening calls and letters** from supporters who wanted the club to play in the **GM Vauxhall Conference**. **Scarborough's Black Death vodka shirt advertising** is queried by **League**.

August

2 **Clubs** vote to **return** to a **22-club First Division** by **1991-92** and **increase League complement** to **94** by **1992-93 with two clubs** from the **GM Vauxhall Conference**. Only **Arsenal, Tottenham Hotspur** and **Manchester United oppose** the idea, but **conflict** with the **FA** seems inevitable. **Aldershot** hope to mount a fiscal **rescue package**. **Aston Villa** announce profit of **£895,000**. **Elton John** sells **Watford** to **Jack Petchey**, West Ham's vice-chairman for **£6m**. **Cost** of implementing **Lord Justice Taylor's** report could be **£400m**.

5 **Adrian Mings**, 21, **kick boxing champion** with **Chippenham Town** to have trials with **Wolves**.

6 **Gordon Taylor, chief executive** of the **PFA criticises** influx of **foreign players** into the **Football League**.

7 **Liverpool** announce **profit** of **£572,000** despite wages, bonus payments and expenses rising to around **£4m**. **Five employees** earn more than **£230,000**.

8 **Spencer Trethewy**, 19, a local **property developer** agrees to put **£200,000** into **Aldershot** over the next **12 months** in exchange for a **directorship** and **shareholding**, allowing the **winding-up order** to be **removed**. The **club** had had its **debts revised** to **£376,145**.

9 **First time** in **20 years** no Football League club has come before the **FA disciplinary committee**. **Sunderland** announce profit of over **£30,000**.

12 **Jim Bett** joins **Mo Johnston** in ending his **Scottish international** career. **ITV** acquire exclusive rights to **televise Manchester United** and **Aston Villa's European** games.

13 **Newport AFC** return to **Somerton Park** in a friendly to beat **Moreton-in-Marsh** their former **landlords 2-0** before a crowd of **2,354**.

14 Through **satellite** and more **conventional TV outlets**, armchair viewers could look forward to **115 live games** this season. **BSB** will have **70**, **ITV 21**. **Fourteen League clubs** are among those **breaking FA regulations** for **re-selling Cup Final tickets**. **Kenny Dalglish** finally **hangs up his boots** in a match with **Real Sociedad**. It is his **516th appearance** for the club. Previously he had made **324 appearances** for **Celtic**. His goals record: **172** for **Liverpool**, **167** for **Celtic**.

15 **Steve Perryman** resigns as **Brentford manager**.

16 **Roberto Falcao**, 36, appointed **coach** to **Brazil**. **Phil Holder** becomes **caretaker** manager at **Brentford**. **Luton** may **lift ban** on away fans in **1991-92**.

17 **Charity Shield** income since **1974** is estimated to have topped **£3m**.

18 Fans hoping to see **Kotor** play **Bokeljan** in **Yugoslavia's Third Division** discover a **circus** on the **pitch** and are allowed in **free** to watch it. **Scottish League Centenary** match attracts only **15,085** fans to **Hampden Park**. The **League** beat the **Scottish FA 1-0**. **Liverpool** and **Manchester United** share the **Charity Shield** in a **1-1** draw at **Wembley** watched by **66,558**.

20 **Joe Royle** the **Oldham Athletic manager** is appointed **part-time England Under-21 coach** under **Lawrie McMenemy**. Extended contracts for **managers**: **Graham Turner five years** at **Wolves, David Pleat three** at **Leicester**.

21 **Oxford United** watch **Aylesbury prisoner Paul Reynolds**, serving sentence for **armed robbery**. **Barclays** announce **£60,000** increase in **prize money** as part of **£7m deal** over **three years**: **£2.2m 1990-91**; **£2.3m 1991-92** and **£2.5m 1992-93**. **England** players to have new **Monday midday deadline** for reporting fit.

22 **Leeds United** face **expulsion** from **Football League** and the **FA** if there is **further misbehaviour** by **fans**. **Bryan Robson** will **miss** the **first three months** of the season after **second operation** on his **achilles tendon**. Vandals flood part of **Arsenal's Highbury ground**. **Oxford** announce **loss** of **£559,442**.

24 **Gate receipts** for **Barclays League** games in **1989-90** amounted to **£87.2m**, **£15m up** on previous season.

25 **Season's** opening **League games** produce crowds of **528,661**, the highest opening figures since **1981-82**. **Tottenham** record **1,250th win**, **Everton** their **1,200th defeat**. **Peter Shilton (Derby)** plays his **900th League game**. **Millwall** end run of **20 games** without a win. **Steve Bull (Wolves)** scores his **150th League and Cup goal** for **Wolves**. **Kevin Hodges** breaks **Plymouth record** with **471st appearance**. **Brentford draw** for the **700th time**, **Stockport** for the **800th**. **Fulham** concede their **4,500th goal**, **Torquay** their **3,900th**. **Exeter's 31 match unbeaten** League and Cup home record **ends**.

27 **Everton** goalkeeper **Neville Southall fined** week's wages for his goalmouth **sit-in** at half-time on **Saturday**.

28 **Bob Pearson** severs connection with **Millwall** after **15 years**.

29 **Peterborough United** fear **financial crisis**.

30 **Southall** spoken to by **police** for **alleged swearing** during game with **Coventry**. **Colin Murphy** appointed **youth coach** at **Leicester**. **Igor Belanov**, the **Soviet** international with **Borussia Moenchengladbach**, pays fine of **£7,500** for **shoplifting** rather than face **trial**. **Gordon Taylor** appoints **Steve Harrison**, his **former No.2** at **Watford** and **Peter Shilton** to his **part-time coaching staff**.

31 **Valery Lobanovsky, ex-Soviet World Cup** manager, takes over the **UAE**.

September

1 **Roy Wegerle** scores **32-second penalty** for **QPR**. **David Hirst (Sheffield Wednesday)** scores **four** goals, the first such total for the club since **Derek Dooley** in **March 1952**. **Guy Whittingham (Portsmouth) fractures** cheekbone in collision with colleague **Colin Clarke** and may **miss five games**. **Sheffield Wednesday** announce **loss** of **£1.7m**. **Robert Maxwell** puts **Derby County** up for **sale** at **£8m**.

3 **Graham Taylor** announces bulk of **Bobby Robson's World Cup squad** for his first game against **Hungary**. **Wales** will play **Belgium** at **Cardiff Arms Park**, Welsh Rugby HQ.

4 **Steve Bruce (Manchester United)** becomes **first Division One** player to be **sent off** for 'professional foul'. **Terry Butcher (Rangers)** faces **discipline** after allegations of an **incident** back in **June** against **Tunisia**.

5 The **Gulf Crisis** rules out proposed **England v West Germany** game in **Saudi Arabia**.

6 **Franz Beckenbauer** to join **Marseille** as **coach**. **Zenith Data Systems Cup winners** will collect **£100,000** this season. **Sheffield United** plan **£5m redevelopment** of **Bramall Lane**.

7 **Bristol Rovers'** application for **12,000 all-seater stadium** at **Mangotsfield** is **turned down** on green belt grounds. **FIFA** approve idea of **covered grounds** in **USA** for **World Cup** in **1994**.

8 **David Longhurst**, **25**, collapses and **dies** shortly before half-time during **York's** home game with **Lincoln**, the first **fatality** in a **League game** since **1927** when **Sam Wynne** died playing for **Bury v Sheffield United**. In **May 1969** referee **Roy Harper died** while in charge of **York v Halifax** game. **Charlton suffer a club record-equalling ninth** successive **defeat**. **Keith Edwards' (Huddersfield)** hat-trick includes his **250th League goal**.

10 **Alex Macdonald** sacked as manager of **Hearts**.

11 **Wales** lose **1-0** to **Denmark** in Copenhagen, **England's Under-21** beat **Hungary 3-1** and in **Scotland's Under-21** side in the **2-0 win** over **Romania** there is **Christian Dailly**, at **16 years 11 months** their youngest at this level.

12 **European Championship** sensation: **Faeroe Islands** beat **Austria 1-0** in **Sweden** in their first competitive international. **Scotland** edge **Romania** out **2-1** at Hampden Park watched by only **12,801** and **Northern Ireland** lose **2-0** to **Yugoslavia**. In friendlies, **Gary Lineker's 36th goal** for **England** in **59 games** is enough to finish **Hungary** at Wembley and the **Republic of Ireland's 1-0** win over **Morocco** in Dublin produces their **53rd goal** in **44 games** under **Jack Charlton** and **28th clean sheet**. **Preston** having talks with **Arab** backers. **Reading** are up for **sale**. **Blackpool** seek **£200m redevelopment**.

14 **Tony Ward**, who had left arm **amputated** after **motorcycle accident**, joins **Stevenage**. **Charlton** submit revised plans to **return** to **The Valley** for **1991-92**.

15 **Oldham's fifth successive win** equals their best start for **61 years**. **Charlton** suffer club record **tenth successive defeat**. **Martin Hicks** equals **Reading** record with **536th** senior appearance. **Maidstone's 6-1** win over **Scunthorpe** is their **record** League win. **Doncaster** goalkeeper **Paul Crichton** saves **one penalty kick three times** against **Rochdale**.

16 **Liverpool** beat **Manchester United 4-0** in televised game but **Ian Rush fails to score** against them for the **20th time**. **Alfred Riedl**, **Austria's Under-21** coach takes over from **Josef Hickersberger** who resigned after the **Faroes** farce. **Fire** destroys main stand at **Bath**.

17 **Kenny Jackett (Watford)** forced to **retire** with **knee injury**. **Scarborough's** plan to **sell ground** to help finance new stadium, **rejected** by **council**. **FA veto Scots** plan to revive **England v Scotland** game. **Bristol City** invite **Bristol Rovers** to share **Ashton Gate** after fire at **Twerton Park**. **Football League** write to **Tottenham** asking about reports of a **£1.1m loan** from **Robert Maxwell** and a conditional agreement of **£12m** cash injection through a **rights issue**. **League** also asking for **video recording** of an interview with **Maxwell** on the **Frost on Sunday** programme.

18 **Wrexham** can use only **seven** of the **13 players** on duty at **Blackpool** on Saturday, in their **Cup Winners' Cup** tie because of **UEFA regulations** on four 'foreign' players per team. **Dundee United's 3-1** win in **Iceland** is watched by **213 spectators**. **John Thomas**, **Preston** striker **breaks leg** after **25 seconds** against his former club **Bolton**. **Doncaster** equal best start to a season achieved first in **1946** with **fifth successive win**.

19 **Manchester United** and **Aston Villa** launch England's re-entry into Europe with **2-0** and **3-1 wins** respectively over **Pecsi Munkas** and **Banik Ostrava**. **Wrexham** survive in a **goalless** draw with **Lyngby**. **Joe Jordan**, who signed a three year contract with **Bristol City** six weeks ago is to join **Hearts**. **Nottingham Forest** to give trial to **Nestor Lorenzo**, **Argentine** World Cup player. **Leeds United** plan **£20m** re-vamp of **Elland Road** into **40,000** all-seater stadium. **Terry Hurlock (Rangers)** fined **£1,000** for selling **FA Cup Final tickets** at **Millwall** in excess of their face value.

20 **Jacek Ziober's 54th minute goal** for **Montpellier** gives **Bobby Robson** a **losing** return to Europe with **PSV**.

22 **Liverpool's** win of the **143rd Merseyside derby** at Goodison Park is their **tenth successive victory**. For the **sixth consecutive time** there is a **penalty** awarded in **Chelsea's match**. **Southend** suffer **first defeat** after **club record-breaking seven successive wins**. **Real Madrid** and **AC Milan** want to re-vamp later stages of **European cups** in **mini-leagues**. In the **GM Vauxhall Conference Gateshead** have **two sent off** and **lose 9-0** at home to **Sutton United**.

24 **Newcastle** announce **£16.5m** redevelopment **plan**. **Liverpool** will apply for a place in **Europe** next season after **favourable comments** by **Lennart Johansson**, **UEFA president**. **England** players in the **World Cup** received **£23,000** each in **bonuses** plus **£30,000** for **commercial ventures**. **Phil Holder**

appointed **manager** of **Brentford**. **Football supporters** could be asked to **pay levy** to help cost of **policing grounds**, according to a **chief superintendent**.

25 **Crystal Palace** record biggest **cup win** and **Southend** equal their record **defeat** in an **8-0** scoreline in the **Rumbelows Cup** at Selhurst Park. Lou Macari says he will pay **£1,000** fine if he can have the **ban lifted**. **Celtic** move into **Skol Cup Final** with **2-0 win** over **Dundee United**.

26 **Four goals** for **Paul Gascoigne (Tottenham Hotspur)** including penalty after **rare miss** from the spot by **Gary Lineker** in **5-0 win** over **Hartlepool** in the **Rumbelows**, which has produced **92 goals in 32 midweek games**. **Rangers** will face **Celtic** after their **1-0 Skol Cup win** over **Aberdeen**.

29 **Liverpool** beat their previous best season's start of **1978-79** with **seventh successive win**, taking overall run to **11**. **Leicester** suffer **seventh successive defeat**. Trevor Senior (Reading) scores **club record-breaking 167th League and Cup goal**. **Crystal Palace** achieve their **1,000th win, Aston Villa** suffer their **1,250th defeat**.

October

1 Censured **Tottenham physiotherapist David Butler** requests **personal hearing** from **FA** following **alleged remarks** to a referee while **treating** a **head injury** to **David Howells** two weeks prior to last Saturday.

2 **Rangers' six goals** complete a **10-0** whitewash of **Valletta**, but for **Glenavon** and **Derry** it's the **end of the road**. **FA** to investigate **brawl** which caused Monday's **abandonment** of the **Thamesside Trophy** game between **Chelmsford** and **Redbridge Forest**.

3 Both **Aston Villa** and **Manchester United** win on foreign soil **in Europe**, as do **Wrexham**. **Aberdeen, Dundee United** and **Hearts** are also **safely through**, but **Portadown, St Patrick's Athletic** and **Glentoran** are **out** along with **Bobby Robson's PSV Eindhoven**, **Portadown** conceding **eight goals** to **Porto**. Lou Macari pays his **£1,000 fine**. **Three players** are **sent off** at **Valley Parade**: **one** from **Bradford**, **two** from **Chester**.

4 **High Court** rule that **Tottenham** must pay **£900,000** to building company **Wimpey** for work **carried out** at White Hart Lane. **Port Vale axe** plans to **move ground**. **Adrian Shaw**, 24, **Chesterfield** retires with **knee injury**. **Alan Curbishley** appointed **Charlton coach** in place of **Mike Flanagan**. Home Secretary urged to introduce legislation **outlawing racist** and **abusive chants**.

5 **Peter Taylor, Brian Clough's** former assistant, **dies at 62**. **World's oldest ground Sandygate**, Sheffield home of **Hallam** and venue of **Boxing Day 1860** game between **Hallam** and **Sheffield FC (the oldest club)**, is **saved** as **£4,000** is raised to **secure 99-year lease**. **Salvatore Schillaci** has **Juventus** contract extended to 1993, salary increasing from **£170,000 to £475,000**.

6 **Liverpool's 12th** successive **League win** equals **First Division record** set up by **Everton 96 years ago**. **Portsmouth** suffer **1,000th defeat**, **Chelsea** record their **800th draw**. **West Ham** score **seven** against **Hull**. **Lincoln** register their **5,200th League goal**. **Dundee United's** game with **Dunfermline** is **abandoned** after 62 minutes because of **waterlogged pitch**.

8 **Jimmy Lumsden** confirmed as **Bristol City manager**. **Frank Stapleton**, 34, announces **retirement** from **international football**. Two Roma players, **Andrea Carnevale** and **Angelo Peruzzi** fail drugs tests. **Football Trust** will allocate **£137.5m** for **ground improvements**.

9 **Oleg Kuznetsov**, Soviet international, signs **five-year** contract with **Rangers** following transfer from **Dynamo Kiev** for **£1m**. **Sunderland** score **six Rumbelows Cup** goals at **Bristol City**. **Ian Rush** scores his **250th goal** for **Liverpool** in the **49th minute** against **Crewe**, his second of a **hat-trick**. **Nicky Banger** scores a **debut treble** for **Southampton**. FA confirm that **somersault throw-in** by **Changez Khan** of **Stafford Rangers** is **legitimate** and **approved by FIFA**.

10 **Faeroes fade 4-1** in Denmark. **Halifax**, goalless in the League, **score** against **Manchester United** in the **Rumbelows**, the second in the tie they **lose 5-2** on aggregate. **Manchester City** announce **profit of £384,784**, their sixth successive trading surplus. **Paraguay's Olimpia** win the **South American Cup**.

11 **Alfio 'Coco' Basile** is the new **Argentine manager**. **Beazer Homes League** crowds are **up by 21 per cent** this season, those in the **Vauxhall League** by **17 per cent**. **Football League** clear the **Robert Maxwell loan** to **Tottenham**.

12 **Football League** plan to back the **World Cup bid** for **1998** and the **Cardiff WRU** headquarters may stage a **European soccer final** this season. **Oxford United** try for yet another move, to a new **£12m** stadium, their **11th attempt**. **Torquay** equal their **best start** to a season in **tenth unbeaten game**.

13 **Millwall** suffer **first defeat** in ten League games losing **2-1** at **Middlesbrough**. **Wolves** draw for the **800th time**. **Halifax's** goal famine ends in the League after **729 minutes** as they **win 3-0** at **Carlisle**. **Northampton's 2,800th** League game ends in victory. **Scunthorpe** score **2,500th League goal**.

15 **Wrexham**, 40 minutes away from Manchester, must **start their journey** for the **Cup-Winners' Cup 24 hours before** the match because of **UEFA rules**. **FA** promote **bid** for **1996 European Championship** finals.

16 **England's Under-21's lose 1-0** to **Poland** before only **2,146** at **Tottenham**, the **lowest crowd** at this level for **five years**, but **Scotland** beat the **Swiss Under-21 team 4-2**.

17 A **Gary Lineker penalty** and another goal from his replacement **Peter Beardsley** overcome **Poland** at **Wembley** before **77,040**, **Wales** have a convincing **3-1 win** over **Belgium** and a **John Aldridge hat-trick** helps the **Republic** to beat **Turkey 5-0**. **Scotland** edge **Switzerland** out **2-1** but **Northern Ireland** are held **1-1** by **Denmark** on this **European Championship** night. **Egypt** sack **World Cup** coach **Mahmoud El-Gohary**.

18 After a **dispute** with the **League**, **Aston Villa** will be allowed to **keep** their **entire ITV fee** of around **£225,000** for the **Inter-Milan** game next Wednesday.

19 **Tottenham's shares** on the stock exchange are **suspended**. **Southend** turn down **'name-your-price' bid** from **Zurich Grasshoppers** for their **two groundsmen** after being impressed with the **Roots Hall pitch** in a **TV film**.

20 **Mass brawl** at **Old Trafford** of 21 **Manchester United** and **Arsenal** players, only **Arsenal** goalkeeper **David Seaman** is **not involved**. Liverpool's run of **eight successive** wins this season **ends** in a **1-1 draw** at **Norwich**. **Ian Rush** plays in his **500th** senior domestic game. **Luton** suffer their **1,000th defeat**. **Oldham** brreak **53-year-old** club record with **16th** unbeaten game. **Gordon Davies** scores his **155th League goal** for **Fulham** to overhaul **Bedford Jezzard's** club record. **Fastest goal** of the season: **Paul Jewell (Bradford)** in **18 seconds**. **Lineker's** deputy **Paul Walsh** scores a hat-trick for **Spurs**. **Seven players** are **sent off** in other League games.

22 The **FA charges Manchester United** and **Arsenal** with bringing the **game into disrepute**.

23 **Manchester United** take **three goals** off **Wrexham** in the **Cup-Winners' Cup**. **Arsenal** fine manager **George Graham** and **five players** two weeks' wages for the **Old Trafford affair**.

24 **Aston Villa** give **memorable display** in **exciting 2-0 first leg lead** over **Inter-Milan**, but **only Hearts** of the other British hopes **manage to win**, taking a **3-1 lead** over **Bologna**. **Rangers crash 3-0** in **Belgrade**, **Dundee United lose a goal** in Arnhem against **Vitesse** and **Aberdeen** are held **goalless** at home by **Legia Warsaw**. **Real Madrid's 9-1** win over **Tirol equals** their **highest score** in Europe for **29 years** and **Hugo Sanchez's four goals** equal the **quartet** achieved by **Ferenc Puskas** in the **1960 European Cup Final**.

25 **Costa Pereira**, 60, **Portugal's 1966 World Cup** goalkeeper **dies**. **Hamilton plan move** to **all-seater** stadium **next year**.

26 **Cardiff City** are **banned** from **buying** or **selling** players.

27 **Derby score** in a **first half** for the **first time** and register **initial win** this season. **QPR score** their **4,100th League** goal. **Liverpool, Tottenham, Arsenal** and **Crystal Palace** are unbeaten in **Division One** as are **Oldham** and **West Ham** in **Division Two** and **Torquay** in the **Fourth Division**. **Two late goals** by **Brian McClair** help **United** to **share six goals** with **City** in the **113th Mancunian** derby. **Tommy Tynan (Torquay)** scores **300th goal** of his career.

28 **Rangers** win the **Skol Cup**, beating **Celtic 2-1** after extra time before **62,817** at **Hampden Park**, but manager **Graeme Souness'** appearance on the pitch might lead to a **further ban** as he is already serving one.

29 **Irving Scholar** resigns as a **director** of **Tottenham Hotspur plc**, but stays as **club chairman**.

30 **Sheffield United** beat **Everton 2-1** in the **Rumbelows Cup**, the visitors having **Dave Watson sent off**.

31 **Manchester United** again **raise their game** to defeat **Liverpool 3-1** in the **Rumbelows Cup** at **Old Trafford**. **Colin Harvey** is **sacked** by **Everton**. **Gary Lineker** receives the **Stanley Matthews Fair Play Trophy** on behalf of the **England World Cup team**. **West Germany** allow **Luxembourg** to **score two late goals** but **win 3-2**. **German fans** cause before-the-match **vandalism**. **Darko Pancev** scores a **hat-trick** in **Yugoslavia's 500th** international, a **4-1** win over **Austria**. **Newcastle** launch **share issue** to supporters. **Wimbledon** may be able **to move** from **Plough Lane** if they **raise money** to **pay off a covenant** on the ground.

November

1 **Hearts** ordered to pay **£75,000** compensation to **Bristol City** for **Joe Jordan**. **Brighton** announce **plans** for new **£18m all-seater stadium** at a **site** as yet **unknown**. Romanian manager **Gheorghe Constantin** resigns. **Crystal Palace** announce trading **profit** of **£1.8m**. **Coventry abandon** hopes of signing **Uruguayan Jose Perdomo**. **Barcelona** poised **to sign Jan Molby** the **Liverpool** midfield player for **£1m**.

2 **Spencer Trethewy**, 19, **Aldershot's** financial saviour, is **suspended** as a **director** by **chairman Colin Hancock**. **Manchester United** become the **first club** in Britain to **insure** the **lives** of their **fans**. **Fulham's** future is **in doubt** after the **local council fail** to obtain a **compulsory purchase order** on **Craven Cottage**. A **cracked bone** in **Dave Beasant's finger** will cause him to **miss Chelsea's game** with **Aston Villa** tomorrow after **394 consecutive appearances** in four divisions with **Wimbledon, Newcastle** and **Chelsea**. He is **seven short** of **Harold Bell's record** of **401** for **Tranmere**.

3 **Crystal Palace concede two goals** in **19 minutes** at **Manchester United** and **lose** their **unbeaten record**. **Aston Villa** concede their **first goal** in **594 minutes** of **League** and **Cup** football. **Birmingham's 3,500th League** game increases **unsuccessful run** to **ten matches**. **Preston score** after **367 minutes**. **Torquay equal** a **30-year-old club record** with their **15th unbeaten game**.

4 **Liverpool end Tottenham's** unbeaten run with a **3-1 win** at **White Hart Lane**. **Bruce Grobbelaar** celebrates his **500th League** and **Cup** game for **Liverpool**. **Overall attendances** top **six million**, the average of **9,765** per game being compared with **9,325 last season**.

5 **FA insurers** facing **compensation claim** from **Manchester United** for **£100,000** for **injury** to **England captain Bryan Robson**. **Leeds** trying to **sign Bulgarian international Nikolai Iliev** from **Bologna**. **Action** brought by **Cabra Estates**, **landlords** of **Stamford Bridge** against **Chelsea**, dismissed in **High Court**. **Howard Kendall** returns to **Everton** as **manager** with **Colin Harvey** as his **assistant**.

6 **Graham Taylor** selects **32-year-old Gordon Cowans (Aston Villa)** in his squad for the game with the **Republic of Ireland**. **Southend** beat **Aldershot 10-1** in a **Leyland Daf Cup** tie, equalling their **record win** and inflicting the **Shots heaviest defeat**.

7 **Internazionale** destroy an inept, naive **Aston Villa 3-0** and their exit is accompanied by **defeats** for **Aberdeen, Hearts, Dundee United** while **Rangers** are held to a **draw**. Only **Manchester United survive** in **Europe** against **Wrexham**. **Chesterfield fail** to overturn a **£12,500 League fine** imposed for **postponing** a **Rumbelows tie** with **Hartlepool** because of a **virus infection**.

8 In an **Everton** back-room **clear-out**, only **Jimmy Gabriel** survives and will **coach** the **reserves**. **Villa** hope to sign **Ivo Stas** from **Banik Ostrava** for **£300,000**. **David Butler** the **Spurs physio** is **cleared** of **swearing** at a **referee**, his **defence assisted** by a **lip-reading expert** who studied a **video film**. The **PFA** will **appoint** a **new chairman** following **Garth Crooks'** forced **retirement** with **injury** at **Charlton**. **Marco Van Basten (AC Milan)** faces **double disciplinary** trouble: **sent off** on Wednesday against **FC**

Brugge and **awaiting** the **verdict** from last month's after-match **tunnel incident** against **Portugal. John Aldridge** fails in the **penalty shoot-out** in the **UEFA Cup** for **Real Sociedad** against **Partizan Belgrade. Robert Atkins, Minister for sport, approves** case for **one governing body. Colchester** unveil **plans** for **10,000 all-seater stadium** at **Ardleigh.**

9 **Brazil** complete **four successive games without scoring** drawing 0-0 with **Chile. Torquay** lose their **unbeaten record** at **Scarborough** to a **penalty goal** and have a **player sent off. Mark Lawrenson resigns** as **manager** of **Peterborough.**

10 **Four thousand rioting Millwall** and **West Ham fans** seriously **damage** the game's **image** again. **Molby** may stay **with Liverpool** after all. He **scores** a **penalty** in the **4-0 win** over **Luton,** their **21st League game without defeat. Aston Villa's** League goal famine ends after **five hours 45 minutes. Nestor Lorenzo,** Argentina's **World Cup** player **scores** on **Swindon debut,** their **first home goal** for **419 minutes. Bolton** achieve their **5,500th League goal, Bradford** their **4,800th. Gary Cooper** (Maidstone) converts **Maidstone's** first **penalty** for **13 months** then **misses** another. **Kettering's 1-0** win over **Colchester** in the **GM Vauxhall Conference** is watched by **5,020.**

11 **Dundee** win the **B & Q Centenary Cup** in Scotland, beating **Ayr 3-2** after **extra time. Manchester City** discover **seating damage** after **Leeds game.**

12 **Arsenal** have **two points deducted, Manchester United** one after the **FA disciplinary committee** deliberates on the **Old Trafford brawl.** Both clubs are **fined £50,000.**

13 **UEFA** applaud the **FA's action** and it could help **Liverpool's re-entry** into **Europe. England's Under-21 win 3-0** in the **Republic,** but **Scotland lose 2-0** at the same level in **Bulgaria.** The **Centenary** match for the **Irish League** with the **Football League** ends in a **1-1 draw** in **Belfast. St Mirren** sign **Spanish midfield player Victor** from **Sampdoria.**

14 With **Paul Gascoigne** on the **substitutes bench, England** draw **1-1** in **Dublin** with the **Republic** as do **Scotland** in **Bulgaria. Wales** win with an **Ian Rush goal** in **Luxembourg** and **Northern Ireland** draw **0-0** in **Austria. Coventry** sack **John Sillett** after his **wish not to have his contract renewed** at the end of the season and **appoint** Rangers' **Terry Butcher** as player-manager. Ex-England schoolboy **Gary Durrant** (Ipswich), **19,** quits through **injury.** No **'Faeroes'** for **San Marino;** they **lose 4-0** in **Switzerland.**

15 **Paul Reid** appointed player-manager of **Manchester City. Clayton Blackmore, sent off** against **Luxembourg** will have the **support** of the **opposing manager** and **player involved** in the **incident. Mark Lawrenson** joins **Corby** as a **player. Marco Van Basten** suspended for **four games** by **UEFA.**

16 **Peterborough** confirm **Dave Booth** as manager.

17 **Arsenal's defensive record** reaches **558 minutes without conceding** a goal, but **Sheffield United** are still searching for their **first League win** and have **not scored** for **529 minutes. Oldham's** run ends after **20 League games.** In the **FA Cup,** non-League successes for **Leek** who win **2-0** at **Scarborough, Chorley 2-1** over **Bury** and **Colchester 2-1** against **Reading. Top scorers: Aldershot 6-2** over **Tiverton** but they **also miss a penalty.**

19 **John Toshack** sacked by **Real Madrid.** His **64 game** record had yielded just **eight defeats. France's slush fund scandal** hits **Marseille,** three of whose **players** are detained by **police. Alan Roberts, 25, Lincoln** forward **retires** with **knee trouble.**

20 **Arsenal** and **Manchester United** decide **against an appeal** to the **FA** on **points deduction. Bryan Robson's testimonial** generates **£300,000** from a **41,658 crowd** against **Celtic, 3-1 winners. Robson** plays the **last 18 minutes. Hartlepool United** face **winding-up** order. **QPR** hoping to entice **Bobby Gould** to **link up** with **coach Don Howe.**

21 **Hayes** beat **Cardiff 1-0** in an **FA Cup replay** at **Brentford. Alfredo di Stefano** appointed **caretaker manager** of **Real Madrid.**

22 **All-seater compulsion** may be **put back** past the **1994-95** deadline for **First** and **Second Division** clubs. **Claude Bez, Bordeaux chairman,** steps down after being **charged with fraud. Bribery scandal** hits **Portugal. Robert Maxwell** threatens to **pull out** of soccer **unless** the **League apologise** over his **£1m** loan to **Spurs** chairman **Irving Scholar.**

23 **Van Basten's suspension** is **cut** to **two games** on appeal.

24 **Arsenal equal 43-year-old club record 17 games without defeat** in the **League,** but concede **first goal in 602 minutes. Sheffield United's** goal famine **stretches** to **619 minutes. Bradford's 3,300th League game** ends in a **draw. Doncaster record** their **1,000th League win. Jim McLean** celebrates **19 years** as **Dundee United manager** but they are **knocked off** the **top of the table** by **Aberdeen** beating them **3-2** at **Tannadice.**

25 **Rangers** snatch a **fortunate 2-1 win** over **Celtic** at **Parkhead** in front of **52,565** and **take over** the **Premier Division leadership.**

26 **Brian Marwood** appointed **PFA chairman. Chief Executive Gordon Taylor** voices concern over **trial by TV. Wigan** announce profit of **£200,000** but are losing **£3,000 a week, Scarborough's surplus** is **£203,565.** Five ex-East German internationals are included in **Germany's squad v Switzerland** for **December 19. Leeds** give trials to **Faroes** players **Alan Morkore** and **Jan Dam.**

27 **Manchester United** will offer **Ryan Giggs** a **five year contract** on **Thursday,** his **17th birthday.** The former **Cardiff schoolboy,** eligible for either **Wales** or **England,** is said to be the **finest prospect** since **George Best. Colin Lee** is replaced as **Watford manager** by **Steve Perryman.** The **Varsity match** will take place on **Boat Race day March 30** at **Craven Cottage. Macclesfield-**based **Chester's Leyland Daf attendance** of **409** is the **lowest** in their **106-year history.**

28 **Manchester United stun Arsenal** with a **6-2 Rumbelows Cup win** at **Highbury** and **Nottingham Forest** lose their **22-match unbeaten record** in the **competition** in a **5-4 defeat** at **Coventry. Reading** put up **entire first team squad for sale.**

29 **Brentford report loss of £351,016. Bury** put **all senior squad** on **offer. Coventry** appoint **Mick Mills** as **assistant manager. Dutch internationals Ruud Gullit** and **Frank Rijkaard score** as **AC Milan** beat **Sampdoria 2-0** in **Bologna** to keep the **European Super Cup.**

30   Two more **managerial sackings**: **Graham Carr** at **Blackpool** and **Allan Clarke** at **Lincoln**. Blackpool appoint **Carr's** assistant **Billy Ayre**. **Watford** appoint **Peter Shreeves** as **assistant manager**. **Coventry** first team **coach Dixie McNeil leaves** the club. The **French FA** propose to ban all **directors**, **players** and **coaches** found guilty in the **recent scandals** from one year to life. **Publisher John Madejski** agrees to take over **Reading** who have **debts** of **£700,000**.

December 1990

1   **Tottenham's team coach** is **wheel-clamped** during **lunchtime break** on way to **Chelsea**, then **towed away** with the **players' kit** inside. They **lose 3-2**. Despite **Vinny Jones** ending **Sheffield United's goal famine** after **669 minutes**, they are **beaten 2-1** at **Aston Villa**. **Nine goals** at **Leicester** where **City's 5-4 win** over **Newcastle reverses** the **scoreline** of the corresponding game at **Newcastle** last season. **Hattricks** for **David Kelly (Leicester)**, **Mick Quinn (Newcastle)** and a rare **treble** of **headed goals** from **Doncaster's Lee Turnbull**. **West Ham** extend **unbeaten** run to **21**. **Hull**, **second** from bottom of **Division Two**, **fail to score** for the **first time**.

2   **Arsenal** inflict **Liverpool's** first defeat in a comprehensive **3-0 win** at **Highbury**, the **Merseysiders' cautious team selection** and **approach** proving entirely **inappropriate** for the occasion.

3   **Major cup** competitions face **penalty shoot-outs** next season, **cutting out second replays**, because of **policing** requirements. **Newcastle's £8m share** issue raises only **£1.25m**.

4   **Steve McManaman**, 18, without **Liverpool senior experience**, is called up for **England's Under-21 squad**. **Oldham lose 6-1** to **Baltimore Blast** in a **six-a-side** exhibition game. **Graham Taylor** withdraws from further **expert commentating** on **ITV**. The **FA** report **6,300 new referees** against a **loss of 4,500** many of whom have **given up** because of **abuse** and **assaults**.

5   No goals in the **Under-21 game** with **Wales** at **Tranmere**. **Luton** beat **Liverpool 4-0** in the **Guinness Soccer Six** final.

6   **Salvatore Schillaci** of **Juventus** is **suspended** for **one match** for **threatening** to have **Bologna** striker **Fabbio Poli shot** for striking him. **Poli** is **banned** for **two games**. **Barcelona's Bulgarian** striker **Hristo Stoichkov** may be **banned** for **three months** for **stamping** on referee **Ildefonso Urizar's foot**.

7   **Driving rain** reduces **Scarborough's gate** against **Wrexham** to **625**, the **lowest ever** in **Division Four**. **Sheffield United** are **£3m** in debt.

8   **Liverpool's** match at **Nottingham Forest** is one of **29 League** and **Cup games called off** in England and Scotland because of **snow**. **Bryan Robson** successfully **returns** to League action as a **70th minute substitute** in **Manchester United's 1-1 draw** with **Leeds** at **Old Trafford**. **Arsenal's 1-1 draw** at **Luton** is their **19th game without defeat**, **West Ham** go **22** with a **1-0 win** at **Portsmouth**. **Arsenal captain Tony Adams** is **sent off** for a **professional foul**. **Barnet hold Northampton** to a **goalless draw** in the **FA Cup** and **Mark Biggins** scores **three** in **Woking's 5-1 win** over **Merthyr** who have **two players sent off**.

11   **Alan McLoughlin** joins **Southampton** from **Swindon** for **£1m**. **FA** anger **Manchester United** by **switching** their **third-round FA Cup tie** with **QPR** to **Monday 7 January** to allow **BSkyB** to **televise** it. **Neil Webb** is **sent off** in **England B** goalless game in **Algeria**, in appalling weather. He is only the **seventh England player** to be **dismissed above youth level** for **his country**, the others being: **Tony Cottee**, **Alan Ball**, **Alan Mullery**, **Trevor Cherry**, **Sammy Lee** and **Ray Wilkins**. **Stoichkov** is **banned** for **two months** and heavily **fined**. **Johan Cruyff** the **Barcelona manager** is **suspended** for **one match** for over-zealous protests. **Rift** between the **Football League** and the **FA** widens when the latter are **refused** permission to talk to **county associations**. **Grimsby** have **Tony Rees** and **Tom Watson sent off** at **Darlington** for **fighting each other** in a **Leyland Daf** game. **Bury** manager **Sam Ellis** agrees to become **Manchester City's first team coach**. **Sheffield United** fight back from being **two down** to **Oldham** in the **Zenith Data Systems Cup** to **win 7-2**. **Manchester United** expect to announce **debit** of **£3m**. **League clubs** can win **£100,000** in **prize-money** from the **Football Trust** for **inventive schemes** involving the **local community**.

12   **Mike Walsh** is appointed **manager** of **Bury**, stepping up from **assistant**. Hard-up **Tottenham** are to **increase prices**. **Barnet** beat **Northampton 1-0** in their **cup replay**, **Leek** and **Wycombe** draw **1-1** at home respectively with **Chester** and **Peterborough**. **Four Italian clubs**: **Atalanta**, **Bologna**, **Internazionale** and **Roma** reach the **UEFA Cup quarter-finals**.

13   Despite the **general impression** that **hooliganism** is a **past problem**, **policing costs** for **1989-90** rose by **42.5 percent** to **£6.82m** for **League games** alone in **England**, **Scotland** and the **GM Vauxhall Conference**. The **FA's proposal** for an **executive board** to govern the game **is at odds** with the **League joint arrangement**. **Africa** will get an **extra place** in the **1994 World Cup finals** at the **expense** of **Europe**. Moves for **wider goals** and **four periods of play** were **not followed up**. **Redbridge Forest's** merger with **Dagenham** is called off. The club was itself formed as an **amalgamation** of **Leytonstone** and **Ilford** with **Walthamstow Avenue**. **Andy Townsend (Chelsea)** leaves hospital after **swallowing his tongue** on **Wednesday** against **Swindon**.

15   **Arsenal** equal their **1947 best start** to a season in their **17th unbeaten game** and **20th overall** since League defeat. **Derby's 3,600th League game** produces **10 goals** and a **6-4 home defeat** against **Chelsea**. **Ian Rush** celebrates his **300th League game** for **Liverpool** with his **173rd goal** in the competition. **Arsenal's psychological advantage** over **Liverpool** continues to **evaporate**. An **injury-time equaliser** enables **Wimbledon** to **draw 2-2** at **Highbury**. **Liverpool's 2-0 win** over **Sheffield United** puts them **four points** ahead with a **game in hand**. **Celtic's** problems continue. **Dunfermline** beat them **2-1** at **Parkhead**.

17   **Gary Lineker** is awarded **FIFA's annual fair play prize** worth **£20,000** for **never being sent off** or **cautioned** during his **career**. **Nottingham council** want **Notts** and **Forest** to **ground-share** at a new **45,000 all-seater stadium** site south of the city.

18   **Peter Shilton's benefit** game at **Tottenham** watched by **12,181** bitterly cold fans sees an **England XI** beat an **Italia 90 side 4-0**. **Franz Beckenbauer** threatens to **quit Marseille**. **Oldham fined £8,000** for

arriving **late** at **West Bromwich**. A **last meeting** between **West** and **East Germany** in **Leipzig** is **called off** because of **crowd violence fears**. **Nuneaton Borough** are **wound up**.

19   Tony Adams is **jailed** for **nine months**, **five** of them **suspended** for a **drink-driving** offence, the **third player** thus imprisoned for **motoring offences** in recent years. **Jan Molby** (**Liverpool**) **three months** in October 1988 and **Mick Quinn** (when with **Portsmouth**) **21 days** in December **1986**. **England's** bid for the **1998 World Cup** officially launched. The **Iraqi Football Federation** annexes a **Kuwaiti club** and plans to **incorporate** the rest. **West Ham** include **six reserves** and **lose 5-1** on **Luton's artificial** surface in the **Zenith**. **Marco Van Basten** scores **five** as **Holland** beat **Malta 8-0** while **Emilio Butragueno** grabs **four goals** as **Spain** beat **Albania 9-0**.   A combined **German side** beats **Switzerland 4-0** in **Stuttgart**. The **PFA threaten** to take the **FA** to **court** over apparent **double standards** over **appeals** against **automatic suspension** when **television evidence** is **not permitted** to substantiate **players' cases**.

20   **Folkestone**, **reformed** in **August** seem **destined to fold** at last. **Exeter** chairman **Ivor Doble** is **suspended** for **12 months** and **fined** over **misconduct** in **connection** with **claims** to the **Football Trust**. **FA ban** referees **Graham Pooley** and **Mangel Singh** over **misinterpretation** of the **professional foul** after **sending off players** for **handball** respectively in **League** and **reserve team matches**.

21   **Oldham** move to the **top** of the **Second Division** beating **Plymouth 5-3**.

22   **Three players sent off** at **Tottenham** by referee **David Elleray**: **Ceri Hughes** (**Luton**), **Nayim** and **Pat Van Den Hauwe** (**Tottenham**) and **Luton** captain **John Dreyer** accuses **Gary Lineker** of **taking a dive**. **Eight others** are **sent off** in the **League** and **five** in **Scotland**. **Manchester City** fail to score for the **first time**. **Gary Shaw** (**Shrewsbury**) scores a **hat-trick** in **four minutes 32 seconds**. **Tommy Tynan** (**Torquay**) scores his **250th League goal**. **West Ham** lose **unbeaten run** in the **League** after **23 matches**, **1-0** at **Barnsley**. **Arsenal** create club **record** with **18th** undefeated game from **start** of the **season**. **Sheffield United** record **first League success** in **17 attempts** (**League record** is **25** by **Newport County 1970-71**).

23   **Three** players **dismissed** in the **Leicester v Watford** game and another at **Sunderland** take the **weekend's League** total to **15**, easily the **worst record** in the **League's history**. The **total number** of **dismissals** is **105**: **81 League**, **16 Rumbelows**, **4 FA Cup**, **4 Leyland Daf**.

26   **High winds** and **heavy rain** have dramatic effect on **Boxing Day attendances** which amount to **436,936** for the **38 surviving games**. **Liverpool** are **held 1-1** at **QPR**, but **Arsenal** beat **Derby 3-0** helped by a **wind-assisted clearance** from **goalkeeper David Seaman** which **bounces** in the **Derby penalty area**, is tipped **on to the bar** by **Martin Taylor** the **County goalkeeper**, only to see **Alan Smith** dive in to **head** the **third goal**.

27   **Sheffield United** changes hands as **Paul Woolhouse**, a director, **buys** the **club**. **Stoichkov ban** is **reduced** to **six weeks**.

28   **Diego Maradona** is voted **Italy's** most **hated man** in a newspaper poll which includes **Saddam Hussein**, **George Bush** and **Madonna**.

29   **Arsenal's 4-1 win** over **Sheffield United** puts them **within a point** of **Liverpool** and stretches their **unbeaten run** to **23 games**. **QPR** record **first win** in **11 attempts** thanks to a **penalty save** against **Sunderland** by **Jan Stejskal** in a **3-2 win**. **Shrewsbury draw** for the **500th time**.

30   **Crystal Palace** consolidate **third place** by beating **Liverpool** with a **Mark Bright** goal in the **42nd minute**, leaving the **champions one point ahead** of **Arsenal** with **only one game** in **hand**.

31   **Tottenham's annual meeting** is **adjourned**, much to the **annoyance** of **shareholders**.

January 1991

1   **Poor weather** again hits **attendances**, though there are **no postponements** in the **Football League**. In the **five o'clock TV game Paul Gascoigne** (**Tottenham Hotspur**) is **sent off** for **dissent** against **Manchester United**. **Booked five times** previously in the season, it is his **third career dismissal**. He is also the **first player** to be **sent off** in a **League fixture televised live**. **United** win **2-1**. **Liverpool** beat **Leeds United 3-0** before the **biggest crowd**: **36,975**. They stay **one point ahead** of **Arsenal**, **1-0 winners** at **Manchester City**. **Fastest goal** of the season: **Tony Thomas eight seconds** for **Tranmere Rovers** v **Southend United**.

2   **Referee Ken Redfern suspended** for **one match** for **failing to send off** a player for **serious foul play**. With the **Norwich City v Nottingham Forest** game **switched** to avoid **heavy holiday policing costs**, the **45 fixtures** over the **New Year** period attract **459,230 spectators**. **Forest** win **6-2**. **Rangers** beat **Celtic 2-0**.

3   **FIFA** may reduce **age limit** for **referees** in next **World Cup**.

4   **Financially** hit **Bordeaux** may be **automatically relegated** with **debts** of **£31m**.

5   **Tim Buzaglo's hat-trick** for **Woking** in their **4-2 win** at **West Bromwich Albion** leads the **FA Cup shocks**. But **Barnet crash 5-0** at **home** to **Portsmouth** for whom **Guy Whittingham** also hits **three**. **Aldershot** earn **replay** after **goalless draw** from 'home' tie switched to **West Ham**. **Newcastle United** field **youngest player** in their **cup history**: **16 year old Steve Watson** and beat **Derby 2-0**. **Liverpool** survive at **Blackburn**, only a bizarre **own goal** by **Mark Atkins** saving them in the **last minute** at **1-1**.

6   Some **300 fans** are arrested in **Italy** following **riots** in **Turin**, **Genoa** and **Florence**.

7   **Cameroon** appoint **Philippe Redon**, a **Frenchman** as **coach**. **French players** threaten **strike** over **freedom of contract** restrictions. **Graham Carr** becomes **Maidstone United manager** after **Keith Peacock** is **dismissed**.

8   **Brian Talbot** is **sacked** as **West Bromwich manager**. The **Liverpool** player **Steve McMahon** is **sent off** but the **Reds** beat **Blackburn 3-0**. He is the **third** to be **dismissed** in this tie: **Glenn Hysen** and **Kevin Moran** were **sent off** on **Saturday**. The **FA of Wales** want **offside law** changed after **successful trial** in the **Welsh League**; players are **not offside** if they **receive the ball** from their **own half** of the **field**.

9   **Football League** to **enquire** into **allegations** of **irregular payments** at **Chelsea**. **Keith Hackett** becomes

third referee overruled by the **authorities**, when his **dismissal** of **Keith Dublin (Watford)** is **reversed** to a **caution**. **Gordon Taylor** of the **PFA** expresses **concern** over number of **dismissals**.

10 **Manchester United** plan to follow **Tottenham** and **Millwall** on to the **Stock Market**. Despite an **operating profit** the club's **overall loss** is **£2,863,677**.

11 **Chelsea**, found **guilty** of **four counts** of **irregular payments**, are **fined £105,000** and may **contest** it in the **courts**.

12 With **Liverpool** and **Arsenal** held **goalless** at **Aston Villa** and **Tottenham** respectively, **Crystal Palace** move within **four points** of the **Anfield** club by **beating Sheffield United 1-0**. **Southampton's 4-3** win at **Luton** takes **goals total** between these two to **31** in **six encounters**. **Maidstone** have **three players sent off** as **Graham Carr** visits his old club **Northampton** in a **2-0 defeat**. In **Nottingham Forest's 3-0** win over **Coventry**, **Nigel Clough misses** from a **penalty** and **Stuart Pearce** has the retaken shot **saved** by **Steve Ogrizovic**. **David Booth** is dismissed by **Peterborough** after their **3-2 defeat** at **Carlisle**.

13 **Greek youth**, 16, **dies** after being **hit by rocket** before **AEK Athens v Olympiakos** game. **Real Madrid** have **two sent off** and **lose 3-0** at **Atletico Madrid**.

14 **FA express concern** over **George Courtney's interpretation** of the **professional foul** when **not dismissing** a player in the **Barnsley v Leeds FA Cup tie** at **Elland Road**. **Diego Maradona threatens** to **quit** if **Napoli** do not let him go at the **end of the year**. **Scunthorpe United** announce **loss of £232,000**.

16 **Italian League** beat the **Football League 3-0**. **West Ham** overcome **Aldershot 6-1** after their **opponents** are reduced to **ten men** in the cup replay.

17 **John Bond** replaces **Asa Hartford** as **Shrewsbury manager**.

19 **Harrow** referee **David Elleray** books **Sheffield United's Vinny Jones** after **five seconds** and **sends him off** in the **second half**. Among other **dismissals**, **Aldershot** and **Exeter City** each have **two sent off**. **Liverpool** are held **1-1 by Wimbledon**, but **Arsenal** stretch **unbeaten run** this season to **23 games** with a **1-0 win** over **Everton**. **Nine goal** game sees **Maidstone beat York 5-4**. **Bournemouth** announce **loss of £842,547**.

20 **Derby's televised game** with **Tottenham** is **marred** by **threats** of **demonstrations** against **chairman Robert Maxwell**. **Spurs win 1-0**.

21 **Police charges** will be **subsidised** by **£2.5m**.

22 **Chris Turner** appointed **Peterborough manager**. **Tony Cottee** scores all **four goals** for **Everton** in the **Zenith Data Systems Cup tie v Sunderland** which ends **4-1**.

23 **Referee Courtney** hits the headlines again in the **Rumbelows Cup tie** between **Manchester United** and **Southampton**. He **dismisses Jimmy Case** for a **trip** on **Bryan Robson 40 yards from goal** but **does not** show the **red card** to **Les Sealey**, the **United goalkeeper** for bringing down **Rod Wallace**. **Dave Mackay** resigns as **Birmingham City manager**.

24 **Video** helps clear **Neil Webb** of using **violent conduct** in the **England B** game with **Algeria**, but **TV companies** are to be **asked** by the **football authorities** to **edit close-ups** of players.

25 **Referee Courtney** will be **asked** by the **FA** to reconsider the **Case 'case'**. **Clayton Blackmore**, the **Manchester United** defender, is shaken by a **four match ban** imposed by **UEFA** for a **sending-off offence** against **Luxembourg** while playing for **Wales**. But **Luxembourg** will **support** his **appeal**.

26 **Brighton** hold **Liverpool 2-2** at **Anfield** in the **fourth round** of the **FA Cup**, while **Shrewsbury** beat **Wimbledon 1-0** and **Cambridge** succeed **2-0** against **Middlesbrough**. **Guy Whittingham** scores **four** in **Portsmouth's 5-1** win over **Bournemouth**. **Crewe's 1-0** win over **Rotherham** puts them into the **fifth round** for the **first time** since they reached the **semi-final** in **1888**. In the **Scottish Cup**, **Motherwell substitute Steve Kirk** sinks **Aberdeen** and **Airdrie edge out Hearts 2-1**. **Millwall** and **Sheffield Wednesday** share **eight goals**.

27 **Woking** go down bravely at **Everton 1-0**, collecting around **£90,000** for **switching their tie** to **Goodison Park**.

28 The **Football Trust** is to give **£7.73m** towards the **£27m** to meet the **cost** of the **Taylor report**. **Anfield** and **Ibrox** will benefit most. **Marseille** president **Bernard Tapie** is **banned for a year** over allegations of **bribing players** and **intimidating referees**. The **Kentish Cup** may be **axed** because **Belgium** have **refused** to **supply ammunition** for the **British Forces**. **Brian Grant** scores a **hat-trick** for **Ross County** in their **shock 6-2** win at **Queen of the South** in the **Scottish Cup**.

29 **David Pleat sacked** at **Leicester**. **Chelsea** chairman **Ken Bates resigned** from the **Management Committee** but will stand for **re-election**. **Tug-of-country** involving **Nigel Spackman**, an **Englishman** picked by **Scotland**, has his **international future suspended** while it is sorted out. **ITV drop plans** to **switch Liverpool v Arsenal** game.

30 **Leeds** and **Arsenal** draw their **cup replay 1-1**, **West Ham** take **five goals** off **Luton** in another replay and **Brighton** lose in **extra time 3-2** to **Liverpool**. **Sheffield Wednesday** beat **Millwall 2-0**. **Terry Dolan** appointed **Hull manager**.

31 **Relegation** from the **Premier Division** in **Scotland** is cancelled as **Falkirk's reorganisation plan** is **adopted**. Next term the **top division** will consist of **12 teams**, playing **44 matches**, the **First Division** will have **12** and the **Second Division 14**. **Promotion** and **relegation** will be **two up, two down**. **Vauxhall Motors** are told they can **carry on** despite the company's **withdrawal** of **sponsorship** for the **Vauxhall League**. **Lord Justice Taylor appeals** to clubs to **ground-share**. **English clubs** back scheme for **1998 World Cup** to be **staged in this country**.

February

1 **Cambridge United** extend **unbeaten run** to **13 League and Cup games** beating **Mansfield 2-1** for a **club record ninth successive win**.

2 **Arsenal's unbeaten League** run **ends** after **23 matches** and **26 overall** when they **lose 2-1** at **Chelsea**. **Nigel Pepper (York)** is **sent off** against **Darlington**, the **third time** he has been **dismissed** against **them** this season.

3 **Liverpool fail** to take over at the **top** of the **First Division** from **Arsenal** after a **1-1 draw** at **Manchester United** watched by **43,690.** But they are **8-13 favourites** for the title with **Arsenal 5-4.**

4 The **Rugby Football Union refuse Wimbledon's** plea to stage **games** at **Twickenham.**

5 **Northern Ireland** give a fine performance in **beating Poland 3-1** in a friendly. **England B win 1-0** against **Wales** in Swansea. **Home Affairs Select Committee** report on **policing** football **hooliganism** is **welcomed**. It makes **54** wide-ranging **recommendations. Roger Milla** virtually rules himself **out** of the **Cameroon** team v England after **allegedly demanding money.**

6 Two **Gary Lineker goals** including a penalty **defeat disappointing Cameroon**. The **Republic of Ireland** beat **Wales 3-0** in Wrexham, but substitute **Dimitri Kuznetsov** gives the **USSR victory** over **Scotland** at Hampden Park. The **FA turn down Southampton's appeal** over the **Jimmy Case sending-off** and **confirm** the **£1,000 fine** on **Arsenal** captain **Tony Adams** for a **gesture** at **Loftus Road** during the match with **Queens Park Rangers** last year.

7 **Lou Macari** appointed **Birmingham City manager. Paul Gascoigne's groin strain** may need an **operation**.

8 **Eight countries: England, Brazil, Chile, France, Switzerland, India, Morocco** and **Portugal** apply for the **1998 World Cup** finals. **Irving Scholar (Tottenham)** suggests a **winter break** of **two** or **three weeks.**

9 **Snow, ice** and **arctic** conditions **reduce** the **programme** to **four Football League** and **eight Scottish League** games, the **worst** list of postponements since **New Year's Day 1979** when only **three English** games survived. Appropriately perhaps, the **first goal** is scored on **Stirling's artificial surface. Liverpool beat Everton 3-1** in the **144th Merseyside** derby taking their **overall lead** to **53**, with **Everton** on **48** and **43** drawn.

10 **Manchester United** take a **2-1 lead** over **Leeds United** in the **Rumbelows Cup semi-final** first leg.

11 **League** officials start their bid to **gain a powerful voice** in the **overall control** of the game in the first of a **series of regional meetings** with **FA councillors.**

12 **League** to **sound out** referees over becoming **professional.**

13 **Diego Maradona linked** with **drug** and **sex ring. Cardiff** have **seven days** to **repay £255,000** owed to the **local council. League** to examine the **FA's national school** at **Lilleshall**. Only **28** of **81** graduates have played **League football.**

14 The **Association** of **Chief Police Officers** say that the **FA** had **agreed** in principle to at **least eight days' notice** for **re-arranged fixtures**, reviving **spectre** of **penalty shoot-outs** next season. **FA chief executive Graham Kelly** suggests that football **supporters** may be **consulted** on the game's **future** but favours **ground-sharing** by clubs. **Building contractors Jewson** are to **sponsor family** enclosures to the tune of **£1.2m** over **two years. Gordon Taylor** calls for **dismissals** to be sufficient **punishment** for **professional fouls. FA** are to propose that **deliberate handball** be included as **serious foul play** and want **clarification** of the **professional foul** in the **penalty area.**

15 **South Yorkshire police** admit **blunder** at **Rotherham** the previous month when **exit gates** remained **closed** as over **2,000 Stoke fans tried** to **leave.**

16 **Cambridge United** end **Sheffield Wednesday's 18-match unbeaten run** in registering their own **tenth successive win** with a **4-0 fifth round FA Cup win. Arsenal edge** out **Leeds 2-1** in the **third replay** of their **fourth round** tie. **Teddy Sheringham** scores all **four goals** for **Millwall** in a **4-1 win** over **Plymouth**, taking his total to **80** in the **League** for a **new club record** and with **98** overall, equals **John Calvey's record.**

17 The **USA's** hopes of a **professional outdoor league collapse.**

18 **Steve McMahon** (knee tendon) and **Ronnie Whelan** (broken leg) are **long-term injury casualties** for **Liverpool** now. **Maidstone United** plan an **£8m complex** at **Hollingbourne** near the M20. **Manchester United lose 2-1** to **Norwich** and still seek an **FA Cup win** over **City** after **85 years** of trying, suffering their **first defeat** in **21 League and Cup games.**

19 **Arsenal** captain **Adams injured** in **second reserve game** since being **released** from **prison** on the previous Thursday. **Notts County** are **losing £3,000** a week. **Rochdale** appoint their physio **Dave Sutton** as their **21st post-war record. League** may introduce **two-legged European-style Rumbelows Cup** to overcome replay date problems.

20 Two goals by **Tony Cottee** help **Everton** to **draw 4-4** after extra time with **Liverpool** in their **fifth-round FA Cup** replay. **Winding-up** proceedings taken **against Cardiff. Wimbledon's ground-sharing** hopes with **Queens Park Rangers** are **dashed** by the **Football Trust**, who say **both clubs would not qualify** for **ground improvement** payments.

21 **Maxwell Holmes**, the **Leeds director**, beats **Ken Bates** in the **election** to the **League's management committee. Brentford** goalkeeper **Graham Benstead** saves **three penalties** in a shoot-out in the **Leyland Daf Cup** to help his team **beat Wrexham 3-0. Rangers fined** a **record £23,000** by the **Scottish Football Association** after a rotating **advertising sign** displaying **Tennents name** was **not switched on** in the **Scottish Cup** third round tie the previous month. **Football Trust** to **help fund policing costs. Wealdstone's Lower Mead** Ground is **sold** to **Tesco** for **£6m.**

22 **Kenny Dalglish resigns** as **Liverpool manager**. Under his managership the **club won three League championship** titles and **two FA Cups** including the **double** in his **first season 1985-86. Ronnie Moran** becomes **caretaker.**

23 **Liverpool crash 3-1** on **Luton's artificial surface**, while **Arsenal** beat **Crystal Palace 4-0** to **lead** on a **goal difference of ten** better than the **Merseysiders. Tottenham** lose **5-1** at **Wimbledon** after only being **one down** with **19 minutes** to go.

24 In the **Rumbelows Cup semi-finals, Sheffield Wednesday win 2-0** in the first leg at **Chelsea** while **Manchester United** confirm a **place** in the **final** by winning **1-0** at **Leeds.**

25 **Bobby Gould** appointed **West Bromwich Albion** manager. **Nottingham Forest** force a **replay** with **Southampton** in the Cup with a **late equaliser. Millwall** receive **grant** of **£400,000** from **Lewisham council** towards a **new ground.**

26 **Tottenham Hotspur's AGM** reveals **depth of debt** that may require the **£10m sale** of **Gascoigne** and

Lineker. **Steve Bull's** two goals in **Wolverhampton Wanderers'** 3-1 win over **Port Vale** take him to **170**, levelling **him** with **Billy Hartill's** total and **24** behind **John Richards' League and Cup figure**. **Barcelona** coach **Johan Cruyff** is taken to **hospital** with a **suspected heart condition**.

27 **England** make only **£128,000** from the **World Cup. Cruyff** undergoes **successful operation. Sheffield Wednesday** complete **Rumbelows success** over **Chelsea** 3-1 at **Hillsborough**, and **Dave Watson** ends the **Merseyside marathon** with a goal for **Everton** against **Liverpool** in their fifth round second replay in the **FA Cup**, completing a **week of misery** at **Anfield. Graeme Souness** counts himself **out of the Liverpool** managerial stakes. **Adams** leads **Arsenal** to a **1-0 win** over **Shrewsbury** in the **fifth round**. League chief executive **Arthur Sandford** warns that clubs **aspiring to promotion** would have to **satisfy financial criteria**.

28 **Bobby Robson criticised** as being **'too soft'** to manage **PSV Eindhoven**, the **Dutch League leaders**. **Howard Wilkinson** signed new **five-year** contract as **Leeds manager. Wendy Toms** is selected as **first woman** to take an **official part** in a **League game** as **fourth official** for the **Bournemouth v Reading** game on **12 March**.

March

1 Annie Bassett resigns as **Birmingham City's chief executive** after eight months. **Alan Hansen retires** at **Liverpool**. Referee **George Courtney** has a **private meeting** with the **FA. Everton** receive **work permit** for **Polish** international **Robert Warzycha**.

2 On the **eve** of the **Liverpool–Arsenal** clash, their **chief rivals all falter: Crystal Palace** lose 3-1 at **Coventry**, **Leeds** 2-0 at **Southampton** and **Manchester United** similarly at home **to Everton** in front of **45,656** spectators. **Wimbledon** and **Tottenham** are held to **draws. Fourth Division** cellar dwellers **Halifax** concede two goals in three minutes at **Walsall**, lose goalkeeper **Jonathan Gould** with a **broken nose** but go on to **win 5-2. Rangers** lose 1-0 to **Aberdeen** at **Pittodrie**, their **lead reduced** to **six points** with the **Dons** playing **one game less. Hans Gillhaus** is the **last minute match winner**.

3 With **David Seaman's** sure handling and a **66th minute strike** by **Paul Merson**, **Arsenal** take a **three point lead** over **Liverpool** at **Anfield**. It was **Seaman's 17th clean sheet** in the League and **22nd overall**.

4 A **Nigel Jemson** hat-trick for **Nottingham Forest** dumps **Southampton** 3-1 in their **fifth round replay**. **West Ham's Trevor Morley** is stabbed in a **domestic row** at his home. **Chelsea's Ken Bates** calls for **government help** towards **policing** costs. They are expected to be **£7.5m** this season.

5 **FIFA applaud** the **Italian League's** decision to **employ full-time referees**. Troubled **Aldershot** have a **new chairman** in **Mike Gill-Anderson** replacing **Colin Hancock** who must concentrate on his **dental practice**.

6 **Brian McClair's first minute goal** for **Manchester United** against **Montpellier** is **cancelled out** by a **Lee Martin** own goal six minutes later. **Real Sociedad manager** John Toshack rules himself **out of the Anfield job. Cardiff, Swansea** and **Wrexham may be barred** from the **Welsh Cup** from **1992-93 unless they quit** the Football League. **Luton** announce loss of **£1m. Aston Villa** pay **£1m** for **Gary Penrice** (**Watford**). **George Graham** adds his name to the list of **non-Liverpool aspirants**.

7 **Frank McGarvey** is axed as **Queen of the South** manager. **Scottish FA** set to **drop cup replays** because of **increased league fixtures. FA Cup Final receipts** will **top £2m** this season for the **first time**.

8 **Tottenham** deny knowledge of a **£7m bid** from **Lazio** for **Paul Gascoigne**.

9 **Cambridge United** push **Arsenal** all the way at **Highbury** before **losing** 2-1 in the **sixth round** and a **Roy Keane goal** is enough for **Nottingham Forest** at **Norwich. Liverpool** win their **first post-Dalglish** game beating **Manchester City** 3-0 at **Maine Road** with the help of **two Jan Molby** penalties. **Revitalised Sheffield United** register **sixth successive win**. In the **Third Division**, **Bolton** stretch unbeaten run to **23 League games**. **Abel Resino**, goalkeeper of **Atletico Madrid** claims **world record 1,230 minutes** without conceding a goal after the **3-0** win against **Osasuna**.

10 **Gascoigne** rescues **Tottenham** with a **winner** in the **83rd minute** to defeat **Notts County** 2-1 in the **televised cup tie**.

11 The **farcically extended sixth round** ends with **West Ham** beating **Everton** 2-1 on the **satellite screened** game. **Wembley** will **stage** the **all-London semi-final** between **Arsenal** and **Tottenham. Gascoigne** undergoes **surgery** on **torn stomach muscles**.

12 **Glyn Hodges** the **Sheffield United** player **on loan** from **Crystal Palace** is **fined** by **manager Dave Bassett** for a **head-butting incident** on Saturday. **FIFA reduce age limit** for **referees** to **45** for the **1994 World Cup. Roger Palmer** scores his **150th League goal** in **Oldham's** 2-2 draw at **Swindon**.

13 **Terry Venables** mounts a **bid to takeover** the **Tottenham** club. **Portsmouth manager Frank Burrows** leaves by **mutual consent**, the **20th managerial casualty** of the season. **Hodges** is **charged** with **bringing the game into disrepute. Steve Watson's somersault throw-in** at **Newcastle** is **cleared** by the **FA. Clayton Blackmore** will be **supported** by **Roby Langers**, the **Luxembourg player** with whom he was involved in the **sending-off incident** on **14 November**, when he meets **UEFA disciplinary appeals committee**.

14 **Carlisle axe manager Clive Middlemass. Barnet, Colchester United, Kettering Town** and **Altrincham**, the chief candidates for a **League place** are **cleared** by **League officials** for suitable admission. The **FA** and **League agree** to **pay Luton** and **Oldham £100,000** each towards **replacing their artificial pitches. Alex Ferguson** receives a **£1,000 a week pay rise** by **Manchester United** as part of a **new four-year contract**.

15 **Gascoigne leaves hospital** with **Lazio's** bid now **confirmed** around a **world record £8.5m**.

16 **Liverpool** recover from **being a goal down** to **Sunderland** to **win 2-1. Sheffield United** make it **seven wins in a row. Abel Resino's record** ends at **1,275 minutes**.

17 **Arsenal beat Leeds** 2-0 in the **televised game** to regain **their goal difference lead**. Three players from **Rangers** and one from **Celtic** are **sent off** in **Celtic's 2-0 win** at **Parkhead**.

18 **Gascoigne's transfer moves** nearer with a **prospective five-year contract** worth **£400,000** a year **after tax**.

19 Manchester United win 2-0 in Montpellier to reach the semi-final. Reading forced to pay £265,118 by High Court after injuries to five policeman during crowd disturbances in a Reading v Bristol City match.

20 Lights fail at Marseille but they beat AC Milan 1-0 for a 2-1 aggregate European Cup win, and the Dynamo Dresden v Red Star Belgrade game is called off after crowd rioting in the 78th minute. Walsall are up for sale for the third time in five years. Jemson's equaliser for Forest halts Arsenal in a 1-1 Highbury draw.

21 Swansea part company with manager Terry Yorath. They have lost their last nine League games.

22 Venables' consortium attempt apparently collapses.

23 Liverpool's 7-1 win at Derby revives their championship hopes as Arsenal are held to a goalless draw at Norwich. Derby's was their 13th without a win. Frank Burrows takes over at Swansea. Barnet, Colchester and Kettering are level in the Conference.

24 Celtic beat Rangers 3-0, the losers having another player dismissed. Mark Hughes is the PFA's Player of the Year.

25 David Hay appointed manager of St Mirren.

26 Jim Smith resigns as manager of Newcastle United. Oxford United announce loss of more than £1m. England Under-21 beat the Republic of Ireland 3-0 while the Scots edge out Bulgaria 1-0.

27 Both England and Scottish seniors are held 1-1 by the Republic and Bulgaria respectively. But Wales do well to hold Belgium 1-1 in Brussels while Northern Ireland lose 4-1 in Yugoslavia. Glyn Hodges suspended for six matches and fined £1,000. Jim Smith joins Middlesbrough as coach. AC Milan banned from European competitions for a season after walking off the pitch during the floodlight failure at Marseille and refusing to return. Dresden are banned for two seasons. Red Star are fined £6,000 but are declared 3-0 winners of the tie.

28 Maradona's future in doubt after allegations of failing to pass a drugs test. Crystal Palace announce profit of £1,799,535. Wealdstone to share Vicarage Road with Watford next season. On transfer deadline day, less than £1m changes hands, but Peterborough make a record six signings.

29 West Ham draw 1-1 at Oldham in the top of the Second Division table clash. Both are level on points with Oldham ahead on goal difference. Maradona guilty of using cocaine. George Graham defends his goalkeeper Seaman, after Graham Taylor's criticism of the Arsenal player's performance for England.

30 Though Arsenal do not manage more than a 2-0 win at lowly Derby, Liverpool are well beaten 3-1 at Anfield by Queens Park Rangers, leaving the Gunners two points ahead as 3-1 on favourites for the championship. Neville Southall makes his 500th senior appearance in Everton's 2-2 draw with Aston Villa. Nottingham Forest debutant Tony Loughlan scores with his first touch after 36 seconds. The University match at Fulham ends goalless. Altrincham beat Barnet 4-1 for a Conference record 25 games without defeat. Atletico Madrid's goalkeeping hero Abel lets the ball slip through his arms as they draw 1-1 in Barcelona. Real Madrid's new coach Radomir Antic, once of Luton, starts with a 1-0 home defeat by Burgos.

31 The Genoa local derby is drawn goalless, but Sampdoria keep top spot in Italy after it.

April
1 A Matthew Le Tissier goal after four minutes is sufficient for Southampton to beat Liverpool at The Dell. Nottingham Forest win for the first time in nine League attempts, 2-0 against Sheffield United. Derby make it a club record 15 League games without a win by drawing 1-1 at QPR. Niall Quinn scores a hat-trick for Manchester City in the 3-1 win at Crystal Palace. In Exeter's 4-2 win at Rotherham, four goals are scored in the last four minutes. Ossie Ardiles watches his new Newcastle lose 2-0 at home to Bristol Rovers.

2 Charlton Athletic are given local council permission to return to The Valley. Terry Venables hopeful of a deal to take over Tottenham. FIFA announce record-breaking average TV audience of 513 million for the 1990 World Cup finals, with 26.7 billion people watching in 167 countries. Maradona flees to Argentina.

3 Arsenal complete a 5-0 demolition of Aston Villa to move five points clear of Liverpool.

4 Trevor Morley makes a successful come-back for West Ham reserves. Glenn Hoddle is the new boss of Swindon.

5 The FA's idea of an 18-team Super League starting 1992-93 threatens a revolution in the game. Jimmy Hill takes over the day-to-day running of Fulham.

6 After Arsenal's 2-0 win at Sheffield United, the bookmakers are refusing to take any more money on George Graham's team. Chelsea, 3-0 down at Stamford Bridge to Luton after 23 minutes draw 3-3 despite having Graeme Le Saux, one of their goalscorers sent off. Aberdeen close the gap on Rangers by beating Celtic 1-0, while the leaders are held goalless at Ibrox by Hibernian. Dundee United beat St Johnstone 2-1 in the Scottish Cup semi-final.

7 Gordon Taylor the PFA chief executive expresses serious reservations about the proposed Super-League. Crystal Palace beat Everton 4-1 after extra time to win the Zenith Data Systems Cup.

8 Football League president Bill Fox claims that the FA have 'hi-jacked' the First Division. Walsall announce record loss of £522,901. Justin Fashanu appointed player-coach of Southall. Barnet lose 3-2 at home to Kidderminster.

9 A Le Tissier equaliser salvages a point for Southampton in the 1-1 draw with Arsenal, but Liverpool are similarly held at home by Coventry. Motherwell clinch their first Scottish Cup Final place for 39 years by beating Celtic 4-2.

10   Manchester United have a convincing **3-1 win** in Warsaw against a **strangely inept Legia** in the first leg of their **semi-final. Barcelona,** for whom **Cruyff** returns to the **manager's bench,** lead Juventus 3-1. **Marseille** also **win 3-1** in **Moscow** against **Spartak** but **Bayern Munich** are **shaken** at home by **Red Star Belgrade** who take a **2-1 lead. No goals** in the **UEFA Cup** semi-finals. **Paul Gascoigne** returns for **61 minutes** in **Tottenham's 2-1 defeat** at Norwich. **Oldham** are held **goalless** at Leicester and **West Ham lose 1-0 at Brighton.** But **Sheffield Wednesday** beat **Blackburn 3-1.**

11   **The League, who acknowledge** themselves **powerless to prevent clubs** defecting are to **investigate** the FA's *Blueprint for Football,* but are **denied access** to it. The **Football Supporters Association** comes out **against** the **Super League. Brian Talbot** is **appointed Aldershot's manager** in place of **Len Walker** while **Carlisle appoint Aidan McCaffery.**

12   **The FA decide against challenging** the **Rotterdam venue** for the **Cup-Winners' Cup Final** after much thought. **All clubs in Europe** will be **allowed to field** at least **five foreign players** in **League matches** next year. **UEFA** have **done a deal** with the **EEC.**

13   **Liverpool win 5-4** at **Leeds** but only **after surrendering** a **four-goal lead. Lee Chapman** strikes **three times** for **United** and has **another disallowed** for **a foul on the goalkeeper.** After **11 games without defeat, QPR** lose **2-1** to **Sheffield United. Aldershot** win for the **first time** in **nine attempts. League attendances** are **47 spectators** per match **higher** than **last season,** goalscoring is **just 0.15** per game **better.**

14   **Paul Gascoigne stuns Arsenal** in the **FA Cup semi-final** at **Wembley** with a **blistering free-kick** in the **fifth minute** and the **Gunners** never recover, **losing 3-1** while in the other match, **referee Keith Hackett** sends off **West Ham's Tony Gale** for an **alleged professional foul** in the **26th minute** and **Nottingham Forest** romp to a **4-0 win.**

15   **Rangers** manager **Graeme Souness** is **tipped** to take over as **Liverpool manager.**

16   **Souness** moves to **Anfield** with a **five-year contract.**

17   **Arsenal** are **held 2-2** by **Manchester City** and **David Seaman** concedes his **16th goal of the season** equalling **Ray Clemence's effort** for **Liverpool** in **1978-79. West Ham** win with a **Morley goal** at **Ipswich** to go **top of Division Two,** but **Sheffield Wednesday lose** similarly **at Newcastle. Coventry** land **Football Trust grant** of **£2m. Cardiff** have a **winding-up order adjourned.**

18   **UEFA 'rebuild the Berlin Wall'** by **allowing four former East German clubs** to **play in Europe next season! Ian Porterfield** is **dismissed** at **Reading.**

19   **Liverpool** re-admitted to **Europe** after **six years. Walter Smith** appointed **Rangers boss.** Third Division leaders **Southend** beaten **2-0** at home by **Wigan. Legislation** creating **new criminal offences** of **invading the pitch, throwing missiles** and **shouting obscene or racist chants** at football matches **clears the Commons.**

20   After beating **Norwich 3-0,** Liverpool need only **draw with Crystal Palace** at **Anfield on Tuesday** to ensure **runners-up position** and a place in the **UEFA Cup. Derby** are **relegated** after **losing 2-1** at **Manchester City** who have **goalkeeper Tony Coton sent off** in the **34th minute. Nottingham Forest** hit **Chelsea** for **seven. GM Vauxhall leaders Colchester** draw **1-1** with **Altrincham** before a **crowd of 6,986.**

21   **John Sheridan** wins the **Rumbelows Cup** for **Sheffield Wednesday** with an **opportunist strike** from the **edge of the area** in the **37th minute** against **Manchester United.**

22   **Maurice Malpas** is named **Scottish Football Writers' Association Player of the Year.** The **Vauxhall League** will become the **Diadora League** next season after a **£400,000 deal** with the **Italian sports shoe** and **clothing makers. Jeremy Goss, Cypriot** born **England youth international** of **Norwich** will be **capped by Wales!**

23   **Arsenal** maintain their **three point lead** by beating **QPR 2-0.** Liverpool beat **Crystal Palace 3-0, Ian Rush** scoring the **300th goal** of his **career. David White** scores **four** of **Manchester City's goals** in the **5-1 win** at **Aston Villa. Zico** resigns as **Brazil's sports secretary. Millwall** given **green light** for a **proposed move** to a new **£15m all-seat** ground.

24   **Despite** being **held 1-1** by **Legia, Manchester United win** through to meet **Barcelona** in the **Cup-Winners' Cup Final** after the **Spaniards** lose **1-0** in a bad-tempered affair against **Juventus. Bayern concede** a **gift** and an **own goal** in the **2-2 draw** with **Red Star,** but **Marseille** are **not stretched** in **beating Spartak 2-1.** There will be another **all-Italian UEFA final** after **Roma** edge out **Brondby 2-1** and **Internazionale** beat **Sporting Lisbon 2-0. Forest** take **five goals** off **Norwich.** Third Division **Cambridge** win **fourth game** in **eight days.**

25   **Leeds United** consider using **No.13** instead of **No.3** after a **plague** of **injuries** to their **left-backs** this season. **Four** have been **side-lined. Millwall** will be awarded a **grant of £2.5m** by the **Football Trust.**

26   **Gascoigne's last game** for **Spurs** looks like being the **Cup Final. Colchester** lose **2-0** at **Telford.**

27   With **no First Division programme, England B** beat **Iceland** with a **Nigel Clough goal** and **18,224** benefit **Ray Kennedy** in his **testimonial** at **Highbury** when an **Arsenal XI** lose **3-1** to a **Liverpool** team. **West Ham crash 3-1** at **Blackburn,** but **Oldham** win **2-1** at **Ipswich** and **Sheffield Wednesday** beat **Barnsley 3-1. Teddy Sheringham** scores **another hat-trick** for **Millwall,** his **fourth** of the season. **Southend, Grimsby** and **Cambridge** all **win** in **Division Three** while **Fourth Division leaders Darlington** go **four points** clear after **winning 3-0** at **Northampton. League attendances** are now **down** on **average 23 spectators** per game. **Millwall Lionesses** beat **Doncaster Belles 1-0** in the **Women's Mycil FA Cup Final.**

29   **Gordon Strachan** is voted **Footballer of the Year** by the **Football Writers' Association. Barnet's 4-1 win** at **Wycombe** puts them **four points** ahead of **Altrincham** who have **two games in hand.**

30   **Arsenal's Kevin Campbell** salvages a point for **England Under-21** in the **2-2 draw** in **Turkey. Manchester United** may be **allowed** to play a **League game** after **11 May. Cambridge** hold **Southend** to a **goalless draw** at **Roots Hall** watched by **10,664. Altrincham** concede a **last minute goal** at **Slough drawing 3-3** while **Colchester** beat **Gateshead 3-0.**

May

1   Unconvincing **England win** in **Turkey** with a **scrambled goal** from **debutant Dennis Wise, Scotland leave it late** before **twice striking** in **San Marino**, the **Republic of Ireland** are **held by Poland** and **Northern Ireland unbelievably** by the **Faeroes. Wales** beat **Iceland 1-0** in a **friendly**.

2   The **1994 World Cup finals** may be **staged partly indoors. Altrincham** appear to have **blown their chances** of promotion by **losing 2-0** at home to **Northwich**.

3   In **1994 players** will have the **names** and **numbers** on the **front. Brian Clough** returns from **holiday** and **suspends reserve coach Archie Gemmill** for allowing his team to **throw away** the **Central League title** by losing **three out of four games**.

4   **Liverpool fail again**, this time losing **4-2** at **Chelsea** while **Arsenal kick-off** when all other games have ended and **draw 0-0** at **relegation-threatened Sunderland** in a **televised** affair. **Derby** with cares removed, **thrash Southampton 6-2** with **Paul Williams** scoring a **hat-trick** ending **run of 20 games without a win. Ian Wright** of **Crystal Palace** is another **treble shooter. Oldham lose 2-0** at **Notts County** but **go up** with **West Ham** who **draw 1-1** at **Selhurst Park** against **Charlton. Sheffield Wednesday** beat **Millwall 2-1. Southend** make it to the **Second Division** for the **first time** in their history after **winning 1-0** at **Bury. At** the **bottom** of the **Third Division, Crewe** and **Mansfield** are relegated and **Rotherham** hold only a **theoretical** chance of **surviving despite beating Cambridge 3-2**, the visitors' **first defeat in nine. Darlington lose** for the **first time** in 12 but **Hartlepool** extend their **unbeaten run** to **13. Aberdeen** set up a **grandstand finish** to the **Scottish championship** by **beating St Johnstone 2-1** while **Rangers** are **losing 3-0** at **Motherwell. The two contenders meet on Saturday. Barnet** clinch the **93rd spot** in the **Football League**.

6   **Liverpool's 2-1 afternoon defeat** against **Nottingham Forest**, covered by **television**, hands the **championship** to **Arsenal** whose **evening celebration** ends with a **3-1 win** over **Manchester United, Alan Smith** scoring a **hat-trick**; an **anti-climactic end** to the **title race, courtesy** of the **small screen**.

7   **Bobby Campbell** of **Chelsea** becomes the **27th managerial casualty** of the **season** when he **resigns. Millwall** win the **FA Youth Cup** beating **Sheffield Wednesday 3-0** on **aggregate** after a **goalless draw** at **The Den. Guiseley** win the **FA Vase replay**, beating **Gresley 3-1** following **Saturday's 4-4 draw**.

8   **Crowd trouble** mars the **first leg** of the **UEFA Cup Final** in **Milan** as **Inter** beat **Roma 2-0. Hamburg** may be **banned** from the **German Bundesliga** with **debts** of **£4.3m. Sheffield Wednesday clinch promotion** beating **Bristol City 3-1. Twenty-one leading clubs** agree in **principle** the **FA's plans** for a **Super League. Chelsea chairman Ken Bates** wants **nursery clubs** to be **permitted**.

9   The **Football League plan** to **fight** the **FA** over the **Super League plan**, pointing out the **likelihood** of **heavy fines** if clubs **break away**.

10   **George Graham** is named **Barclays Manager of the Year. Luton end away fan ban. Reading** appoint **Mark McGhee, Newcastle** forward, as **player-manager. Arsenal** unveil **bond issue** to **raise £20m** to improve **Highbury**.

11   The **League's 92nd season** ends with a **flourish** of **free-scoring** and **big crowds** after **no fewer** than **35 teams** had **theoretical chances** of **improving** their **various positions** in **29** of the **matches**. A **best-of-season 580,129** takes the **attendance figure** into **credit** for the **fifth successive term. Arsenal** lead the way **trouncing Coventry 6-1** with **Anders Limpar** scoring **three goals. Forest beat Leeds 4-3. Tony Lormor** scores **four** for **Lincoln. Luton** wriggle free, **Sunderland** just fail, **Oldham** snatch the **Second Division** with an **injury-time penalty** after going **2-0 down** to **Sheffield Wednesday** and **Cambridge** wrest the **Third Division title** from **Southend**, beaten by **Brentford. Notts County, Millwall, Brighton** and **Middlesbrough** reach the **play-offs** in **Division Two**, despite the **latter losing 1-0** at **Barnsley. West Bromwich** join already **relegated Hull** in **Division Three** after **failing to beat ten-man Bristol Rovers. Grimsby** edge **Bolton** out of **promotion** on **goal difference**, while **Tranmere, Brentford** and **Bury** make the **play-offs. Darlington** as **Fourth Division champions, Stockport** in **style** beating **Scunthorpe 5-0, Hartlepool** and **Peterborough** win **promotion, Blackpool, Burnley, Torquay** and even **Scunthorpe** making the **play-offs. In** Scotland, **Rangers** beat **Aberdeen** for their **41st title** with two **Mark Hateley goals. Wycombe** beat **Kidderminster 2-1** in the **FA Trophy Final**.

13   **Cardiff** may go **part-time. Jim Ryan** is **sacked** by **Luton, Gerry Francis** resigns at **Bristol Rovers**.

14   **Wimbledon** are to **move** into **Selhurst Park** with **Crystal Palace** next season.

15   **Manchester United** fully **deserve** to beat **Barcelona 2-1** in the **Cup-Winners' Cup Final** in **Rotterdam**, winning **more easily** than the score suggests. **Bordeaux** are **relegated** in **France** after **losing their appeal**.

16   The **principal aim** of the **Super League** to help the **England team** is **cast into doubt** when it emerges that **Bert Millichip** the chairman and **Graham Kelly** the **chief executive disagree** about its **22 or 18 club format**.

17   **Colin Addison** quits as **Hereford manager. Graham Paddon, Stoke's caretaker-manager** returns to **Portsmouth** in a **similar capacity** while they seek a **new manager**.

18   **Dramatic FA Cup Final** sees **Paul Gascoigne** commit **two fouls**, the second resulting in him being **carried off** with **ligament damage. Stuart Pearce whacks Forest** ahead from the **second free-kick** after **15 minutes**, but **referee Roger Milford** fails to notice **the wall being pulled apart. Tottenham** then dominate, **Paul Stewart equalises** from an angle after **54 minutes** and **Des Walker**, under pressure, **concedes an own goal** in the **fourth minute of extra time**. In the **Scottish Cup Final, Motherwell** beat **Dundee United 4-3** after **extra time**.

19   **Swansea** win the **Welsh Cup** for the **10th time** beating **Wrexham 2-0**.

20   **England B** beat **Switzerland 2-1** and the **2,036th and final League game** sees two cup winners, **Manchester United** and **Tottenham** draw **1-1** before **46,791** at **Old Trafford**. But **Spurs** could be in the **hands of receivers** next season and **Lazio** may pull out of the **Gascoigne deal**.

21   **Manchester United** aim to **raise £18m** by **floating** a **share issue. Clubs** will have to **pay more** for **police presence. England** beat the **USSR 3-1** in the **England Challenge Cup** at **Wembley**, only **23,789** turning up to watch. **Don Howe** is **sacked** as **QPR coach**.

22 **Stan Mortensen dies** at **69. Jack Charlton's 50th game** in charge of the **Republic of Ireland** ends in a **1-1 draw** against **Chile. The FA** had to pay **£225,000** for **Graham Taylor** when he **left Aston Villa. Nottingham Forest** announce plans for a **£12 million all-seat covered stadium. Inter** win the **UEFA Cup** despite **losing** the **second leg 1-0** to **Roma. Chris Nicholl dismissed** by **Southampton.** A **Gallup survey** commissioned by the **League** reveals **large majority** of **supporters** are **against** the **Super League, 68 per cent** in fact.

23 **Argentina** and the **USSR draw 1-1** in the **England Challenge Cup** at **Old Trafford. John Sillett** appointed **Hereford** manager. **Republic of Ireland** players will receive a **benefit** after **50 appearances.**

24 **Jim Smith** appointed **Portsmouth manager.**

25 A **draw** in a **bad-tempered game** is enough for **England** to **win** the **Challenge Cup;** fortunately for them, otherwise **Argentina** might have been able to **challenge someone** for it **next season. . .**

26 **Nottingham Forest** pay **£1.4m** for **Barnsley's Carl Tiler. Birmingham** win the **Leyland Daf Trophy** beating **Tranmere 3-2** before **58,756** at **Wembley,** more than **14,000** over the **crowd** for **England's game** with **Argentina.**

27 **England** start their **Under-21 tournament** in **Toulon** by beating **Senegal 2-1. UEFA** favour **licensing** scheme to **prevent financial collapse** of clubs.

28 **Scotland's Under-21's beat Poland 1-0. Dr Jozef Venglos** stands down as **Aston Villa manager. Gerry Francis** is **appointed** by **QPR. Cardiff** dismiss **Len Ashurst.**

29 **Wretched European Cup Final devoid** of **enterprise** and **expertise** ends as it should: **a penalty competition** in which **Red Star beat Marseille 5-3. Wales draw 0-0** with **Poland** and **England trounce Mexico 6-0** at **Under-21** level. **Dundee** plan takeover of **Dundee United.**

30 **Football League** say that an **independent survey** carried out by **Touche Ross, the accountants,** suggests that the **cost to clubs** and **supporters** of the **Super League breakaway** would be **£45m** over the **first five years. Brian Little** appointed **manager** of **Leicester City. Wales Under-21 win 2-1** in **Poland, Scotland draw 1-1** with the **French.**

31 **England Under-21's beat USSR 2-1. Ron Atkinson** rejects offer to **manage Aston Villa.**

June

1 An **own goal** gives **England victory** in **Sydney** against **Australia,** but the **Republic of Ireland** are held to a **1-1 draw** in **Boston** by the **USA.**

2 For the **first time promotion** from a division in the **Football League** is **decided on penalties. Torquay** gain a place in **Division Three** by **beating Blackpool 5-4** when their match had been **drawn 2-2** after extra time.

3 **Crowd figures** announced in **Italy** show an **increase** of **1.8m** to **10,150,000. Gate receipts** for the **First Division** rose to **£135m.** An **injury-time goal** from **Gary Lineker** sees **England beat New Zealand** in **Auckland. England's Under-21** side win the **Toulon tournament** for the **second year running** beating **France** with a **goal** from **Alan Shearer.**

4 **Kevin Durham,** 29, a **Barnet** forward **dies** of a **heart attack** in **Majorca.** Five top **English referees: George Courtney, Keith Hackett, Neil Midgley, Allan Gunn** and **Ray Lewis** will be **removed** from **FIFA's panel** because they are **over the new age limit. Brentford** sign **five-year sponsorship deal** with **KLM** worth **£250,000.**

5 **Wales** beat **World Cup holders Germany 1-0** at **Cardiff's National Stadium** to **head** their **European Championship qualifying group. The Germans** had been **unbeaten** in **16 games** over **16 months. Norway** beat **Italy 2-1. Autoglass** signs a **£600,000 deal** to **sponsor** what was the **Leyland Daf Cup,** over **three years.**

6 **Football League** give the **FA seven days' notice** to **abandon** their **Blueprint** or face **court action.** The **PFA** proposes a **compromise. Ron Atkinson resigns** as **Sheffield Wednesday manager. Notts County** manager **Neil Warnock turns down** chance of taking over **Chelsea. David Pleat** becomes **Luton** manager and his **former player Raddy Antic** becomes **manager** of **Real Madrid. Celebrations** for **Chile's first success** in the **Libertadores Cup** cause **nine deaths, 128 injuries** and many **arrests** after **Colo Colo** beat **Olimpia** of **Paraguay 3-0** before **65,000** in **Santiago. Tom Pendry,** chairman of the **House of Commons** all-party football committee **predicts further hardship** for **clubs over decision** to **increase police charges.**

7 **Ron Atkinson** becomes **Aston Villa manager** allegedly at **1m** over four years. **Norwich** break their **transfer record** by **paying £1m** for **Darren Beckford** from **Port Vale.** The **appointment** of an **administrator** will probably **save Halifax. Lazio** still hopeful of completing a deal for **Gascoigne.**

8 **England** beat **New Zealand 2-0** in **Wellington. Deliberate handball** will be **classed** as a **professional foul** and **goalkeepers** will **not be allowed** to **pat the ball forward** to get round the **four-step rule;** two **amendments** to the **laws of the game** passed at **Belfast's** meeting of the **International Board.**

10 **Arsenal** raise **nearly one-third** of the **£16.5m** required to **fund** the **conversion of Highbury** into a **37,000 all-seat** stadium. Both **Robert Maxwell** and **Alan Sugar** the **computer millionaire** are said to be **interested** in takeover bids for **Tottenham. Manchester United** shares on **offer** at **385p** go on the **stock market** at **335p** but fall to **308p. Scarborough,** the **worst supported** team in the **League** are to build a **creche** to **boost crowds.**

11 **Ian Porterfield** becomes **manager** of **Chelsea,** he was formerly **No.2** there before moving on. **Ian Branfoot** takes over at **Southampton,** eight years after leaving them.

12 **Lineker scores all England's goals** in their **4-2 win** over **Malaysia** in **Kuala Lumpur,** moving to **within four** of **Bobby Charlton's record 49 goals,** having **overtaken Jimmy Greaves'** total. **Forty-four MPs** call for the **League** and **FA** to **settle their differences,** but the **FA** will ask the **High Court** to **rule** on whether their plans are **legal. Tottenham** get **12 months' extension** of their **overdraft** by the **Midland Bank.**

13 **Most First Division clubs** plan to **inform** the **management committee** of the **Football League** of **their intention** to **resign** from the competition and **form** a **Premier League** from **1992–93.**

INDEX TO SOME OF THE MORE INTERESTING DIARY ITEMS

Appearances—
Peter Shilton, Kevin Hodges Aug. 25; Martin Hicks Sept. 15; Ian Rush Oct. 20, Dec. 15; Neville Southall Mar. 30; Bruce Grobbelaar Nov. 4; Faeroes Sept. 12.

Attendance figures—
Fine start Aug. 25; Vauxhall and Beazer Homes Oct. 11; Top million Nov. 4; Chester's lowest Nov. 27; Scarborough Dec. 7; Average up Apr. 13 – down Apr. 27; Final day boom May 11

Awards—
Gary Lineker Oct. 31, Dec. 17; Brian Clough OBE and Sir Bert Millichip in Queen's Birthday honours list in June. (See also Pages 952, 953, 954)

Big money moves—
Andy Linighan July 3; Andy Townsend and Dennis Wise July 5; Tony Coton July 12; Gary McAllister July 17; Oleg Kuznetsov Oct. 9; Alan McLoughlin Dec. 11 (see also late transfers pages 608–609)

Bleak weekend—
Record dismissals Dec. 23

Club milestones—
Exeter Aug. 25; Oldham Sept 15; Charlton Ath Sept. 15; Doncaster Sept. 18, Nov. 24; Southend Sept. 22, Sept. 25, Nov. 6; Aldershot Nov. 6; Liverpool Sept. 29; Oct. 6, Dec, 2; Crystal Palace Sept. 29; Aston Villa Sept. 29; Portsmouth Oct. 6; Torquay Oct. 12, Nov. 3; Luton Oct. 20; Arsenal Nov. 24; Dec. 15; Dec. 22, Feb. 2; Sheffield Utd Dec. 22; Crewe Jan. 26; Derby Apr. 1.

FA and FL—
FA against 22 Division 1 July 25; League vote Aug. 2; Row over county talk Dec. 11; PFA threat to FA Dec 19; League to examine Excellence Feb. 13; Super League Apr. 5; Gordon Taylor worried Apr. 7; Bill Fox Apr. 8; Supporters fear Apr. 11; League threaten FA May 9; June 6; FA rift May 16; Gallup Poll May 22; Cost of breakaway May 30; Break nears June 13

Football Trust—
Grounds Oct. 8; Grants Jan. 28 and Feb. 21 (see also Page 626).

Goalkeeping record—
Abel Resino Mar. 9; Mar. 16.

Goalscoring milestones—
Steve Bull Aug. 25, Feb. 26; Sheffield Wed Sept. 1; Keith Edwards Sept. 8; Maidstone Sept. 15; Trevor Senior Sept. 29; Ian Rush Oct. 9, Apr. 23; Halifax famine ends Oct. 13; Gordon Davies Oct. 20; Tommy Tynan Oct. 27, Dec. 22; Gary Lineker June 12; Teddy Sheringham Feb. 16; Roger Palmer Mar. 12.

Law changes—
Offside June 28; Wales Jan. 8; Handball Feb. 14; Board decisions June 8.

Money matters—
Aldershot July 31, Aug. 8; Derby sale Sept. 3; Zenith cash Sept. 6; Schillaci Oct. 5; Hallam ground Oct. 5; Tottenham share Oct. 19; Newcastle share Dec. 13, subsidy Jan. 21; Manchester Utd stock exchange Jan. 10, June 10; Chelsea fine Jan. 11; Cardiff problems Feb. 13, Apr. 17; Notts Co Feb. 19; Rangers Feb. 21; Millwall grant Feb. 25 and Apr. 25; Ken Bates plea Mar. 4; FA Cup Final receipts Mar. 7; Reading police payment Mar. 19; Arsenal bond issue May 10, June 10.

Profit and loss—
Oxford Utd Aug 22, Mar. 26; Liverpool Aug. 7; Sunderland Aug. 9; Charity Shield Aug. 18; Barclays Aug. 24; Sheffield Wed Sept. 3; Manchester City Oct. 10; Crystal Palace Nov. 1, Mar. 28; Scarborough Nov. 26; Brentford Nov. 29; Sheffield Utd Dec. 7; Manchester Utd Dec. 11; Scunthorpe Utd Jan. 14; Bournemouth Jan. 19; Luton Mar. 6; Walsall Apr. 18.

Scottish reorganisation—
Falkirk Jan. 31.

Sponsors—
Chelsea July 12; Colchester July 27; League Cup July 26; Rumbelows July 30; Barclays Aug. 21; Vauxhall Jan. 31; Jewson Feb. 14; Diadora Apr. 22.

Television—
European Aug. 12; Live fare Aug. 14; Villa keep fee Oct. 18; Editing plea Jan. 24; ITV drop plan Jan. 29.

UEFA—
Readmit English June 29; 'Berlin Wall' Apr. 18; Liverpool back Apr. 19.

World Cup—
Stars revisit June 14, 19; Cost of 'sods' June 20; Final farce July 8; Place cuts July 24; TV audience July 9, Apr. 2; England bonus Sept. 24; League 1998 bid Oct. 12; Launched Dec. 19; Africa Dec. 13; Referees age limit Jan. 3, Mar. 12; Clubs backing 1998 Jan. 31; 1998 again Feb. 8; England profit Feb. 27.

Youth—
Christian Dailly Sept. 11; Steve Watson Jan. 5.

FROM THE CHAPLAIN

The 1990–91 season was a quietly encouraging one for the chaplains in the game, as well as for those who welcome and support their ministry and seek to extend the chaplains' influence and involvement in the sport of professional football. Not only did it begin with over one-third of the clubs in the Football League now benefiting from the appointment of chaplains, but a second national conference held in October amply demonstrated just how valuable the chaplain's ministry within his club can be in many different ways. These vary from the high-profile role played by the former chaplain at Sheffield Wednesday in the wake of the Hillsborough disaster to the quiet, steady, on-going supportive care given to players, administrators and fans at a club during and after important and stressful times in their lives.

Further encouragement, and evidence of the ever-widening understanding and appreciation of the value of having a chaplain at a club, came as the season progressed and news filtered through of several more appointments being made at clubs which had not previously had a chaplain. In one or two instances this was in response to a letter circularised to all such clubs by the chairman of one of the First Division clubs which has long known and valued the work of the clergyman who serves them.

'On The Praying Staff'

Then again, though not for the first time, one of the Sunday newspaper colour supplements presented a serious, attractive and revealing article about the caring, pastoral role of the Football Chaplains, complete with several stunningly effective photos under the title of 'Let Us Play' (!) and an engaging sub-heading asserting that 'every club needs a man on the praying staff'!

Effective

Such publicity for the chaplains, while occasionally welcomed, is unusual, for these men are far removed from being status seekers. Their involvement is almost always low-key, undemonstrative, and usually well away from any limelight. But that of course is what makes it so effective, for, as one First Division manager said of his chaplain, 'He's my Heineken chaplain – he reaches parts of the club others cannot reach'.

Should any reader be interested in serving in such a capacity, or in making contact with a potential chaplain on behalf of his club, he is invited to write, in complete confidence of course, to Christians In Sport, PO Box 93, Oxford.

OFFICIAL CHAPLAINS TO FOOTBALL LEAGUE CLUBS

Rev Ernie Hume — Sheffield U
Rev John Bingham — Chesterfield
Rev Richard Chewter — Exeter C
Rev Alan Fisher — Bournemouth
Rev Andrew Taggart — Torquay U
Rev David Jeans — Sheffield W
Rev Nigel Sands — Crystal Palace
Very Rev Alan Warren — Leicester C
Rev Phillip Miller — Ipswich T
Rev Allen Bagshawe — Hull C
Rev Tony Adamson — Newcastle U
Rev Derek Cleave — Bristol C
Rev Brian Rice — Hartlepool U
Rev John Boyers — Watford
Rev Michael Chantry — Oxford U
Rev John Maxwell — Aldershot
Rev Michael Futers — Derby County
Very Rev Brandon Jackson — Lincoln C

Rev Dennis Hall — Wigan Ath
Rev William Hall — Middlesbrough
Rev Canon John Hestor — Brighton & HA
Rev Mervyn Terrett — Luton T
Rev Jim Rushton — Carlisle U
Rev Robert de Berry — Queen's Park Rangers
Rev Gary Piper — Fulham
Rev Tony Horsfall — Barnsley
Rev Barry Kirk — Reading
Rev Martin Short — Bradford C
Revs Roger Sutton and Justin Dennison — Manchester U
Rev Martin Butt — Walsall
Rev Kevin Tugwell — Cardiff C
Rev Steve Riley — Leeds U
Revs Alan Poulter and Robin Sutton — Tranmere R
Rev Neville Gallagher — Maidstone U
Rev Jeff Banks — Halifax T
Rev Paul Bennett — Swindon T

THE FOOTBALL LEAGUE

Featuring full details of each of the 93 clubs in the Football League.
Officials, statistics, 1990–91 team photo, full 1990–91 League record and career details of the players.

THE FOOTBALL LEAGUE OFFICIALS

Chief Executive
A. Sandford

President
W. Fox (*Blackburn Rovers*)

Life Vice-Presidents
L. C. Cearns
H. E. McGee
Sir John Smith CBE, JP, DL, Hon.LLD
Sir Arthur South
R. Wragg

Management Committee
P. D. Bloom (*Plymouth Argyle*)
R. T. Chase JP (*Norwich City*)
H. D. Ellis (*Aston Villa*)
J. Maxwell Holmes (*Leeds U*)
W. G. McKeag BA Cantab. (*Newcastle United*)
M. D. B. Sinclair (*York City*)
I. H. Stott (*Oldham Athletic*)

Life Members
Sir Matt Busby CBE, KCSG
E. M. Gliksten
N. J. Thomas
The Rt Hon Lord Westwood JP, FCIS
J. F. Wiseman
F. A. Would
R. Wragg

Secretary
David Dent

REVIEW OF THE SEASON

Consistency is an important factor in determining success and Arsenal had it during their impressive 1990–91 season which saw them win the League Championship. In 50 League and Cup matches they lost only three times and their solitary defeat in the First Division represented the best record for a title-winning team this century.

In wresting the championship back from Liverpool, Arsenal again found the Anfield side to be their chief rivals, though the ending was something of an anti-climactic affair in part due to the needs of televised football. On 4 May Liverpool began the day just three points behind the leaders, albeit with an inferior goal difference. That afternoon they lost 4-2 at Chelsea, where ironically Arsenal had suffered their lone reverse 2-1 on 2 February. Thus the Gunners were able to start their match at Sunderland in somewhat more relaxed fashion, kicking-off knowing the Stamford Bridge result.

Two days later there was a repeat performance before the cameras, though this time the small screen devotees witnessed Liverpool's further demise in a 2-1 defeat at Nottingham Forest which handed the championship to Arsenal. They were able to celebrate that evening in style, beating Manchester United 3-1.

Moreover there was more than a touch of irony over this fixture. Most of Arsenal's problems had been derived from their Old Trafford rivals. On 20 October they had been involved in a fracas which resulted in them being deducted two points and United one, as a consequence of the disgraceful scene which erupted at Old Trafford. Arsenal did win the game 1-0 only to find themselves with just a point from it.

Five weeks later United went to Highbury in the Rumbelows Cup and took a 3-0 lead by half-time. Arsenal pulled back two goals but Alex Ferguson's men responded with three further goals in a handsome 6-2 victory. Four days later manager George Graham had to face reigning champions Liverpool on the same ground under the gaze of the TV cameras. Naturally he did not have to motivate his players for such a game, but they would have been less than human if the after effects of shell-shock had not had some bearing on their performance.

But as it happened it was Liverpool's approach to the match which helped sweep away any self-doubts which might have lingered. Indeed the Merseysiders' cautious, over-defensive attitude was not right for the occasion. A bold, more imaginative attacking stance might well have caused Arsenal serious trouble. Arsenal won 3-0 and not only did Liverpool probably lose the psychological factor, it was arguably the moment that Kenny Dalglish decided to quit the managerial role.

It was Liverpool's first defeat in the League and the first time they had failed to score. They were only fitfully effective after this, often as brilliant as ever, just as frequently unsure and out of touch. Again their performances were judged against their own high standards and perhaps as such unfairly regarded. But their midfield lost the services of Steve McMahon and Ronnie Whelan in the second half of the season and Alan Hansen's absence throughout the campaign left the defence without its usual authority. Dalglish subsequently departed to be replaced temporarily by the No.2 Ronnie Moran until Graeme Souness was persuaded to leave Rangers and return to Anfield.

Meanwhile Graham was able to select a fairly settled team. Of the 19 players called upon, David Seaman, Lee Dixon, Nigel Winterburn and Steve Bould did not miss a game. Seaman had an outstanding first season at Highbury and at one stage seemed likely to concede fewer goals than any other goalkeeper in First Division history. Both full-backs attacked relentlessly whenever possible and Bould enjoyed the best season of his career. Skipper Tony Adams missed eight games having been jailed for a drink-driving offence but Paul Davis, Alan Smith and Paul Merson were only absent from at least part of a game on one occasion each. The Swedish import Anders Limpar lost the edge from his effervescent displays following injury, but had the satisfaction of scoring a hat-trick in the last game. Smith's unselfish leadership of the attack still gave him 23 League goals and he found a fine partner in the strong running Kevin Campbell, the latest in a long line of Arsenal discoveries.

Graham said that he felt the team needed more flair in attack but many other managers would have been happy to settle for much less up front that the Gunners possessed. Arsenal's only other defeat came in the semi-final of the FA Cup at Wembley against North London rivals Tottenham Hotspur. Spurs won 3-1 and deservedly so, in what was probably the Highbury team's poorest showing of the entire season.

Third placed Crystal Palace were there on 22 December after winning 2-0 at Manchester City and remained in the position. They were also able to return to Wembley, this time in the Zenith Data Systems Cup where they beat Everton 4-1 after extra time. The resurrec-

Nottingham Forest defender Des Walker (dark shirt, second right) is pressurized into heading into his own goal to give Tottenham Hotspur the winning goal in extra time during the 1991 FA Cup Final at Wembley. (Allsport)

tion of East Germany from the rubble of the Berlin Wall robbed them of a deserved place in Europe. Leeds United were inclined to be erratic. But from the end of October they had a run of 11 games without defeat before crashing 3-0 at Liverpool on New Year's Day.

Manchester City had several fine runs, 15 without defeat after losing the opening game at Tottenham 3-1 and in the last nine were beaten only in the Manchester derby. Peter Reid could derive much satisfaction from his first season as player-manager.

Neighbours Manchester United never really threatened in the League but reserved their best performances in cup games. They reached the Rumbelows Cup Final but gave a disappointing display in losing 1-0 to Sheffield Wednesday. However, they redeemed themselves on their return to Europe by taking the Cup-Winners' Cup, with flashes of the traditional fluency which epitomised United sides of other eras.

Wimbledon continued to confound their critics. They were as high as sixth as early as 8 December and had one run of ten games without defeat. Nottingham Forest, capable of producing the most attractive football in the First Division, had one spell of nine games without a win but finished with 20 goals in their last six before being well beaten by Spurs in the FA Cup Final. Tottenham's off-field problems inevitably filtered through to the pitch and they won only one of their last 15 League games. But they rose to the challenge of the Cup Final magnificently after losing Paul Gascoigne, who had masterminded their semi-final victory, to win 2-1.

Everton, with Howard Kendall restored at the helm, appeared in transition but lost just one of their last dozen and Chelsea's poor record in the second half of the season wiped out earlier successes which included five straight wins. Queens Park Rangers had seemed destined for relegation suffering eight successive defeats, before an impressive late run from mid-January which included a 3-1 win at Liverpool on 30 March.

Sheffield United seemed ever more likely to make a quick return to Division Two after failing to win any of their first 16 games and scoring just seven goals. But on 26 January they beat Derby County 1-0 to start a run of seven consecutive wins.

Two wins successively was the most Southampton managed at one spell and despite being eighth on 10 November had a below-mid-table look about them. Goalscoring was a problem for Norwich City. They achieved only 41 and in one run of six games scored just once and that produced a 1-0 win at Luton Town. Luton for their part escaped relegation even though in the nine matches before their last they had taken just two points. Above them Aston Villa looked vulnerable relying overmuch on David Platt's goalscoring. They reserved their best and worst performances in the UEFA Cup respectively in the home and away legs against Internazionale. Coventry City, too, were rarely decisive and won only once away from Highfield Road.

Derby County went down with Sunderland. Derby lost 6-4 at home to Chelsea on 15 December, the first of a club record 20 games without a win. Already relegated, they then beat Southampton 6-2. Sunderland's isolated victories were not enough though they did the double over Luton and had wins over Manchester United and Crystal Palace.

Oldham Athletic finally edged West Ham United out of the Second Division championship having been no lower than second all season and given the launch of 16 games without defeat. West Ham had a run of 21 without loss but were hit by injuries and only goalkeeper Ludek Miklosko played in every match. Third placed Sheffield Wednesday also made a fine start with 12 games undefeated. Top scorer David Hirst ended a barren spell with seven goals in the last five games and they fully deserved Rumbelows Cup success over Manchester United.

Notts County finished with seven successive wins and Millwall failed to capitalise on starting with nine games without defeat and Teddy Sheringham's 33 goals. Brighton went into the last game having scored just once in six attempts but made the play-offs along with Middlesbrough who suffered a similar goal drought scoring in only two of their last six.

Barnsley were on the fringe of the play-offs as were Bristol City at times and despite losing their last two games, Oxford's fortunes were transformed by a run of 15 without defeat. Newcastle United called upon the services of 36 players, Wolverhampton Wanderers won only two of their last 15 and went out of both cups quickly. The 11 players who started Bristol Rover's season off ended it! Of course there were changes during the term...

Ipswich Town drew 18 times, seven consecutively and Port Vale were unable to notch up more than two wins in a row. Charlton Athletic had made their escape by early March but Portsmouth were sliding into trouble at one stage until mid-April. Plymouth Argyle went nine games in mid-season without victory from mid-November to mid-January while by mid-March Blackburn Rovers slipped to 22nd. Watford were toiling until they had seven wins in the last 11 and Swindon Town lost 11 of their last 17. Leicester City managed to beat Oxford United 1-0 in the last game but West Bromwich Albion and Hull City went down. Albion were actually unbeaten in their last nine games! Hull were the last team in the League to fail to score when they lost 3-0 at Middlesbrough on 1 December but a token effort to revive ended in March.

Cambridge United topped the Third Division even though another fine FA Cup run led to a fixture backlog. They had to play ten games in April and lost just two of their last 13. Southend United gave away an enormous lead and in the last 12 matches scored only nine goals yet won four and drew three of them. Grimsby Town were never lower than third and survived a few late hiccups at home. Bolton Wanderers climbed from 23rd to second at one stage and Tranmere Rovers' best run saw six wins in a row in April. Brentford lost just one of the last six and Bury needed to beat Tranmere 2-1 to reach the play-offs; a lone victory from five.

Eighth was the highest Bradford City reached all season though Bournemouth were fifth at one time. Wigan Athletic lost two of their last three to rob themselves of a play-off chance and one success in seven caused similar late disappointment for Huddersfield Town. Birmingham City's poor scoring record was offset by success in the Leyland Daf Cup while seven consecutive defeats to mid-March hit Leyton Orient badly.

Notwithstanding several lapses, Stoke City were still third at the start of December but late in the season they suffered six successive defeats. Reading recorded just two wins in the last 14 and Exeter City did not recover from an early season spell of ten games without victory. Preston North End's last day win over Wigan was their first in eight but Shrewsbury Town won six of their last seven.

Chester City's move to Macclesfield hit attendances badly. Only 631 saw the Reading game on 5 March. Nine consecutive defeats cost Wales manager Terry Yorath his job at Swansea City and Fulham hovered dangerously close to relegation and in one spell of 12 games scored only five times. Crewe Alexandra, Rotherham United and Mansfield Town were relegated. Crewe made a brave effort with four wins in the last five and Rotherham, rock bottom for five months, managed to beat Cambridge 3-2 four days before being relegated. Mansfield's last win was on 6 April when they beat Reading 2-0.

For Darlington, return to the Football League brought further promotion. After losing 3-1 at Stockport County on 1 December they lost only three of 29 games and went top on 23 February. Stockport themselves won eight of their last nine, Hartlepool United were unbeaten in their last 14 dropping only four points and Peterborough United after making six transfer-deadline signings did enough to reach Third Division football again.

Blackpool, 20th on 20 October, lost only three times in the second half only to suffer defeat on the last day at Walsall which cost them promotion. Burnley also failed despite

Paul Merson (white sleeves) the Arsenal striker puts his team ahead in the crucial clash with Liverpool at Highbury on 2 December 1990. Arsenal won 3-0 and went on to regain the championship from their opponents. (Colorsport)

one defeat in the last ten and Torquay United's up and down form stabilised long enough to put them in the play-offs along with Scunthorpe United whose five straight wins in February and March proved significant.

Wretched support hindered Scarborough. One rainy evening in December only 625 turned up. Yet they almost made the play-offs. Northampton Town appeared to be coasting along but slumped in their last eight games and though Doncaster Rovers were also top at the turn of the year they finished eighth. Rochdale's promising start—only one reverse in 12—was not maintained and financially-hit Cardiff City took only three points from a possible 24 at the end.

Inconsistent Lincoln City generally lacked goals, only 22 being derived from the first 29 games, yet they beat Carlisle United 6-2 on the last day. Injury-hit Gillingham beat Doncaster 2-0 on the same programme, their first success in ten. Walsall had one sequence of 17 games where they scored only seven times and Hereford United never managed more than two consecutive wins in a row.

After 15 games without a win, Chesterfield won five on the trot in a run from November and Maidstone United went ten without success from the end of February. Carlisle United struggled from the turn of the year and the defence fell apart conceding 36 goals in one spell of 13 games. York City only managed to reach 18th place by mid-October and Halifax Town made the worst goalscoring start in Football League history failing to score in their first eight games. Aldershot's wretched season was relieved by a deserved goalless draw at West Ham in the FA Cup and Wrexham won only two of their last 12 to finish with the wooden spoon.

LIST OF REFEREES FOR SEASON 1991–92

Paul Alcock (S. Merstham, Surrey)
David Allison (Lancaster)
Gerald Ashby, (Worcester)
David Axcell, (Southend)
Mike Bailey, (Impington, Cambridge)
Keren Barrett, (Coventry)
Steven Bell, (Huddersfield)
Alan Bennett, (Sheffield)
Ray Bigger, (Croydon)
Martin Bodenham, (Looe, Cornwall)
Jim Borrett, (Harleston, Norfolk)
John Brandwood, (Lichfield, Staffs.)
Kevin Breen, (Liverpool)
Alf Buksh, (London)
Keith Burge, (Tonypandy)
Billy Burns, (Scarborough)
Vic Callow, (Solihull)
John Carter, (Christchurch)
Brian Coddington, (Sheffield)
Keith Cooper, (Pontypridd)
Keith Cooper, (Swindon)
George Courtney, (Spennymoor)
Ian Cruikshanks, (Hartlepool)
Paul Danson, (Leicester)
Alan Dawson, (Jarrowe)
John Deakin, (Llantwit Major, S. Glam.)
Roger Dilkes, (Mossley, Lancs.)
Phil Don, (Hanworth Park, Middlesex)
Paul Durkin, (Portland, Dorset)
David Elleray, (Harrow)
Tom Fitzharris, (Bolton)
Alan Flood, (Stockport)
Peter Foakes, (Clacton-on-Sea)
David Frampton, (Poole, Dorset)
Dermot Gallagher, (Banbury, Oxon.)
Rodger Gifford, (Llanbradach, Mid. Glam.)
Ron Groves, (Weston-Super-Mare)
Allan Gunn, (South Chailey, Sussex)
Keith Hackett, (Sheffield)
Bob Hamer, (Bristol)
Paul Harrison, (Oldham)
Robert Hart, (Darlington)
Ian Hemley, (Ampthill, Beds.)
Ian Hendrick, (Preston)
Brian Hill, (Kettering)
Terry Holbrook, (Walsall)

Mike James, (Horsham)
Peter Jones, (Loughborough)
John Key, (Sheffield)
Howard King, (Merthyr Tydfil)
John Kirby, (Sheffield)
Ray Lewis, (Gt. Bookham, Surrey)
John Lloyd, (Wrexham)
Stephen Lodge, (Barnsley)
Terry Lunt, (Ashton-in-Makerfield, Lancs)
Ken Lupton, (Stockton-on-Tees)
John Martin, (Nr. Alton, Hants.)
Neil Midgley, (Bolton)
Roger Milford, (Bristol)
Kelvin Morton, (Bury St. Edmunds)
John Moules, (Erith, Kent)
Bob Nixon, (West Kirkby, Wirrall)
Jim Parker, (Preston)
Roger Pawley, (Cambridge)
Mike Peck, (Kendal)
David Phillips, (Barnsley)
Michael Pierce, (Portsmouth)
Graham Poll, (Berkhamsted)
Graham Pooley, (Bishops Stortford)
Richard Poulain, (Huddersfield)
Ken Redfern, (Whitley Bay)
Mike Reed, (Birmingham)
Jim Rushton, (Stoke-on-Trent)
Paul Scoble, (Portsmouth)
Dave Shadwell, (Bromsgrove)
Lester Shapter, (Torquay)
Ray Shepherd, (Leeds)
Gurnam Singh, (Wolverhampton)
Arthur Smith, (Rubery, Birmingham)
Jeff Smith, (Stafford)
Paul Taylor, (Waltham Cross, Herts.)
Colin Trussell, (Liverpool)
Paul Vanes, (Warley, West Midlands)
Tony Ward, (London)
John Watson, (Whitley Bay)
Trevor West, (Hull)
Clive Wilkes, (Gloucester)
Alan Wilkie, (Chester-le-Street)
Gary Willard, (Worthing, W. Sussex)
Roger Wiseman (Borehamwood, Herts.)
Joe Worrall, (Warrington)
Philip Wright, (Northwich)

INTRODUCTION TO THE CLUB SECTION

The full page team photographs which appear on the first of each club's six pages in this section of the yearbook were taken at the beginning of the 1990–91 season, and therefore relate to the season covered by this edition's statistics.

The third and fourth pages of each club's section give a complete record of the League season for the club concerned, including date, venue, opponents, result, half-time score, League position, goalscorers, attendance and complete line-ups, including substitutes where used, for every League game in the 1990–91 season. These two pages also include consolidated lists of goalscorers for the club in League, Rumbelows Cup and FA Cup matches and a summary of results in the two main domestic cups. The full League history of the club, a complete list of major honours won and best placings achieved, and a note of the team's first and second choice colours appears on the second page of this section. The colours are checked with the clubs, but please note that second choice colours may vary during the season.

Note also that the League position shown after each League result is recalculated as at every Saturday night plus full holiday programmes, but the position after mid-week fixtures will not normally be updated. Please be advised that the attendance figures quoted for each League game are those which appeared in the Press at the time, whereas the attendance statistics published on pages 610 and 611 are those issued officially by the Football League after the season has been completed. However, the figures for each League game are those used by the Football League in its weekly bulletin, in conjunction with the *Sunday Telegraph* and Jack Rollin's column in that newspaper.

On the fourth page of each club's section, the total League appearances for the season are listed at the foot of each player's column. Substitutes are inserted as numbers 12 and 14 where they actually came on to play. The players taken off are respectively given an asterisk (*) and a dagger (†). But in order to give the chart a uniform appearance, where only one substitute has played the number 12 will have been used. Some clubs, Aston Villa for example, have used 13 as their second substitute number, but again for purposes of uniformity, they appear as 14.

In the totals at the foot of each column, substitute appearances are listed separately below the '+' sign, but have been amalgamated in the totals which feature in the player's historical section on the final page for each club. Thus these appearances include those as substitute.

The final pages for each club lists all the players included on the Football League's 'Retained' list, which is published at the end of May. Here you will find each player's height and weight, where known plus birthplace, birthdate and source, together with total League appearances and goals for each club he has represented. Full names of all other players retained including trainees, non-contract players and schoolboys are also given. In addition more club information is added on these pages including items of interest from the club's history and a list of previous managers.

Any transfers which take place between the publication of the League's Retained list and this book going to press will be included in the transfer section between pages 601 and 609, but the player's details will remain under the club which retained him at the end of the season. An asterisk * by a player's name on the fifth and sixth pages means that he was given a free transfer at the end of the 1990–91 season, a dagger † against a name means that he is a non-contract player, and a double dagger ‡ indicates that the player's registration was cancelled during the season. An § indicates either a Trainee or an Associated Schoolboy who has made Football League appearances.

The play-offs in the Football League are listed separately on pages 586 and 587. Appearances made by players in these play-offs will *not* be included in their career totals.

Two pages have been included for Barnet, the 93rd club in the Football League.

Editor's note: In the Scottish League, substitutes where used are listed as 12 and 14. The second player to be taken off is also picked out with a dagger.

32

ALDERSHOT 1990-91   *Back row (left to right):* Jerry Williams, Glen Burvill, Charlie Henry, Steve Wignall.
Centre row: Ian Stewart, Richard Dunwell, Peter Hucker, Ricky Cornish, Adrian Randall.
Front row: Leigh Cooper, Dale Banton, Mark Ogley, Steve Beeks, David Puckett, Kevan Brown. (Photograph: Eric Marsh)

Division 4 — **ALDERSHOT**

Recreation Ground, High St, Aldershot GU11 1TW. Telephone Aldershot (0252) 20211. Clubcall: 0898 121630. Aldershot Promotions (0252) 311992.

Ground capacity: 5000.

Record attendance: 19,138 v Carlisle U, FA Cup 4th rd (replay), 28 January 1970.

Record receipts: £22,949.66 v Sheffield W, Littlewoods Cup 2nd rd, 2nd leg, 3 October 1989.

Pitch measurements: 116yd × 72yd.

President: Arthur English.

Chairman: M. Gill-Anderson.

Directors: S. Banks, M. Davey, T. Gladwell.

Team Manager: Brian Talbot.

Hon. Doctor: A. Gillespie FRCS.

Secretary:

Team coach: Ian McDonald. *Physio:* Steve Wignall.

Marketing and Commercial Manager: R. Stone

Year Formed: 1926. *Turned Professional:* 1927. *Ltd Co.:* 1927.

Club Nickname: 'Shots'. *Club Chaplin:* Rev J. M. Maxwell.

Record League Victory: 8-1 v Gateshead, Division 4, 13 September 1958 – Marshall; Henry, Jackson; Mundy, Price, Gough; Walters, Stepney (3), Lacey (3), Matthews (2), Tyrer.

Record Cup Victory: 7-0 v Chelmsford, FA Cup, 1st rd, 28 November 1931 – Robb; Twine, McDougall (1); Norman Wilson, Gardiner, Middleton (1); Blackbourne, Stevenson (1), Thorn (3), Hopkins (1), Edgar. 7-0 v Newport (I of W), FA Cup, 2nd rd, 8 December 1945 – Reynolds; Horton, Sheppard; Ray, White, Summerbee; Sinclair, Hold (1), Brooks (5), Fitzgerald, Hobbs (1).

Record Defeat: 1–10 v Southend U, Leyland Daf Cup, Pr rd, 6 November 1990.

Most League Points (2 for a win): 57, Division 4, 1978–79.

Most League Points (3 for a win): 75, Division 4, 1983–84.

Most League Goals: 83, Division 4, 1963–64.

Highest League Scorer in Season: John Dungworth, 26, Division 4, 1978–79.

Most League Goals in Total Aggregate: Jack Howarth, 171, 1965–71 and 1972–77.

Most Capped Player: Peter Scott, 1 (10), Northern Ireland.

Most League Appearances: Murray Brodie, 461, 1970–83.

Record Transfer Fee Received: £150,000 from Wolverhampton W for Tony Lange, July 1989.

Record Transfer Fee Paid: £54,000 to Portsmouth for Colin Garwood, February 1980.

Football League Record: 1932 Elected to Division 3 (S); 1958–73 Division 4; 1973–76 Division 3; 1976–87 Division 4; 1987–89 Division 3; 1989– Division 4.

Honours: Football League: best season: 8th, Division 3, 1973–74. *FA Cup:* best season: 5th rd, 1932–33, 5th rd replay, 1978–79. *Football League Cup:* best season: 3rd rd replay, 1984–85.

Colours: Red shirts, royal blue trim, blue shorts with red trim, red stockings with royal blue trim. **Change colours:** All yellow.

ALDERSHOT 1990–91 LEAGUE RECORD

Match No.	Date	Venue	Opponents	Result	H/T Score	Lg. Pos.	Goalscorers	Attendance
1	Aug 25	A	Rochdale	L 0-4	0-0	—		1619
2	Sept 1	H	Scunthorpe U	W 3-2	2-0	15	Puckett (pen), Randall, Banton	2001
3	8	A	Wrexham	L 2-4	1-1	20	Kennedy (og), Cooper	2704
4	14	H	Northampton T	D 3-3	1-1	—	Puckett (pen), Williams, Randall	2741
5	18	H	Cardiff C	D 0-0	0-0	—		2310
6	22	A	Burnley	L 0-3	0-2	20		5517
7	29	H	Scarborough	D 2-2	0-1	20	Henry 2	1857
8	Oct 2	A	Hartlepool U	L 0-1	—			1916
9	6	A	Lincoln C	D 2-2	1-0	22	Burvill, Banton	2755
10	12	H	Torquay U	L 2-3	1-1	—	Henry, Randall	3289
11	19	H	Stockport Co	D 2-2	1-0	—	Puckett, Williams	2413
12	23	A	Gillingham	D 1-1	0-0	—	Puckett	3140
13	27	A	Walsall	D 2-2	0-2	23	Whitlock 2	3567
14	Nov 2	H	Halifax T	D 2-2	1-0	—	Williams, Randall	2686
15	10	A	Blackpool	L 2-4	1-4	23	Williams, Puckett	2065
16	24	H	Maidstone U	W 4-3	3-1	21	Puckett 2, Henry, Burvill	2146
17	Dec 1	A	Doncaster R	L 0-3	0-0	23		2093
18	15	H	Hereford U	W 1-0	1-0	20	Puckett	1783
19	21	A	York C	L 0-2	0-1	—		1749
20	29	H	Peterborough U	W 5-0	3-0	20	Cooper, Flower, Puckett 2, Randall	2363
21	Jan 1	A	Carlisle U	W 2-1	1-0	19	Puckett, Shepherd (og)	2978
22	12	A	Scunthorpe U	L 2-6	1-3	20	Puckett 2 (1 pen)	2727
23	19	H	Rochdale	D 2-2	2-1	20	Henry, Randall	1854
24	26	A	Northampton T	L 1-2	0-1	21	Henry	3800
25	Feb 1	A	Cardiff C	W 3-1	3-1	—	Henry, Puckett, Randall	1629
26	19	H	Darlington	L 0-2	0-1	—		1920
27	23	H	Blackpool	L 1-4	1-1	21	Puckett	2164
28	Mar 2	H	Doncaster R	D 1-1	0-0	21	Henry	1728
29	5	H	Wrexham	W 3-2	2-1	—	Henry 2, Puckett	1395
30	9	A	Hereford U	L 0-1	0-1	21		2275
31	12	H	Hartlepool U	L 1-5	1-4	—	Puckett	1579
32	16	A	Scarborough	L 0-2	0-2	22		1195
33	23	H	Lincoln C	L 0-3	0-1	22		1653
34	30	A	Darlington	L 1-3	0-1	23	Randall	4250
35	Apr 1	H	York C	L 0-1	0-0	24		1904
36	6	A	Peterborough U	L 2-3	1-2	24	Yanushevski, Henry	5543
37	8	A	Torquay U	L 0-5	0-2	—		2535
38	13	H	Carlisle U	W 3-0	2-0	24	Puckett 2, Henry	1818
39	16	H	Burnley	L 1-2	0-0	—	Puckett	2473
40	19	A	Stockport Co	L 2-3	1-2	—	Williams, Henry	4422
41	23	H	Chesterfield	W 1-0	1-0	—	Flower	1500
42	27	A	Gillingham	W 1-0	1-0	23	Puckett	2083
43	30	A	Chesterfield	L 0-1	0-1	—		2222
44	May 4	H	Walsall	L 0-4	0-0	24		1826
45	8	A	Maidstone U	D 1-1	0-1	—	Williams	1298
46	11	A	Halifax T	L 0-3	0-1	23		1428

Final League Position: 23

GOALSCORERS

League (61): Puckett 21 (3 pens), Henry 13, Randall 8, Williams 6, Banton 2, Burvill 2, Cooper 2, Flower 2, Whitlock 2, Yanushevski 1, own goals 2.
Rumbelows Cup (3): Puckett 3 (1 pen).
FA Cup (9): Henry 2, Puckett 2, Randall 2, Stewart 2, Williams 1.

Sheffield	Brown	Cooper	Ogley	Whitlock	Wignall	Coombs	Puckett	Banton	Henry	Randall	Murphy	Burvill	Williams	Stewart	Flower	Lange	Cornish	Hucker	Gray	Dunwell	Hopkins	Beeks	Yanushevski	Talbot	Reinelt	Halbert	Joyce	Coles	Match No.
1	2	3	4	5	6	7*	8	9	10	11	12																		1
1	2	3		5	6		8	9	10	11		4	7																2
1	2	3		5	6	14	8	9†	10	11		4*	7		12														3
1	2	3		5	6		8	9	10			4	7		11														4
1	2	3		5	6		8	9	10			4	12	7*	11														5
1	2	3		5	6	14	8	9*	10			4	12	7	11†														6
1	2	3		5	6		8	9*	10			4	12	7	11														7
1	2	3		5	6		8	9	10			4	7		11														8
1	2	3		5	6		8*	12	10			4	7	9	11														9
1	2	3		5	6		8	12	10			4	7	9	11*														10
1	2	3	14	5	6		8	12	10			4	7†	9	11*														11
1	2	3	7	5			8*	12	10			4		9	11	6													12
1	2	3	7	5			8		10			4		9	11	6													13
1	2	3	7	5			8		10			4	12	9*	11	6													14
1	2	3	12		6		8		10			4	7	9	11	5*													15
	2	3*		5	6		8		10			4	7	9	11			1		12									16
	2			5	6*		8	12	10			4	7	9	11		3	1											17
	2	3*		5	6		8		10			4	7	9	11	12		1											18
	2	3		5	6*		8	9	10			4	7		11	12		1											19
	2	3		5			8		10			4	7	9	11	6		1											20
	2	3		5			8		10			4	7	9	11	6		1											21
	2	3		5			8		10			4	7	9*	11	6		1	12										22
	2	3		5	14		8†		10			4	7	9*	11	6		1	12										23
	2	3	9	5			8		10			4	7		11	6		1											24
	2	3		5	6		8		10			4	7*	12	11			1	9										25
	2				6		8	9				4	7*	11	5		3	1	10	12									26
	2				6		8	9				4	12	7	11	5		1	10	3*									27
	2				6		8		10			4	7	9	11	5		1	3										28
	2	3			6		8	12	10			4	7	9*	11	5		1											29
	2	3	9*		6		8		10			4	7		11	5		1			12								30
	2	3			6		8		10			4	7	9	11	5		1											31
	2	3	6				8*		10			4	7	9	11†	5		1			14	12							32
	2	3	6				8*	12	10			4	7	9	11	5		1											33
		3			6		8		10	12			7	9	11*	5		1					2	4					34
	2	3					8		10	11*			7†	9	12	5		1			6			4	14				35
		3			6		8*		10				7	9	12	5		1					2	4	11				36
	2	3	14				8		10				7	12	11	5		1			6†			4	9*				37
	2		7				8		10					9	11	5	3				6			4					38
	2		7				8	14	10	12				9	11†	5	3				6			4*					39
	2		11		6		8		10					9	7	5	12	1			3			4*					40
	2		7		6		8		10			4		9	5			1	3		11								41
	2				6		8	9	10	12				7*	5			1	3		11			4					42
	2*		7		6		8	9	10†	12					5			1	3		11			4			14		43
		3			6		8	10	9†	12				7	5			1			11			4*	14			2	44
			4		6		8							7	9	5	3							10*	12	11		1	45
			4*		6†		8	9	10						5		3								12	11		1	46
15	40	33	31	28	14	1	46	13	41	34	1	34	37	33	30	2	7	27	3	—	9	—	6	10	3	—	3	2	

Substitute appearances (+): 3s, 1s, 2s, 8s, 2s, 2s, 7s, 2s, 3s, 2s, 2s, 2s, 1s, 1s, 2s, 2s, 3s

Fisher — Match No. 45(2) 46(2); Terry — Match No. 46(7); Tucker — Match No. 46(14).

Rumbelows Cup	First Round	Southend U (a)	1-2
		(h)	2-2
FA Cup	First Round	Tiverton T (h)	6-2
	Second Round	Maidstone U (h)	2-1
	Third Round	West Ham (h) (at West Ham)	0-0
		(a)	1-6

ALDERSHOT

Player and Position	Ht	Wt	Birth Date	Place	Source	Clubs	League App	Gls
Goalkeepers								
David Coles*	5 10	12 00	15 6 64	Wandsworth	Apprentice	Birmingham C	—	—
						Mansfield T	3	—
						Aldershot	120	—
						Newport Co (loan)	14	—
					HJK Helsinki	Crystal Palace	—	—
						Brighton & HA	1	—
						Aldershot	30	—
Peter Hucker	6 2	12 12	28 10 59	London	Apprentice	QPR	160	—
						Cambridge U (loan)	—	—
						Oxford U	66	—
						WBA (loan)	7	—
						Manchester U (loan)	—	—
						Millwall	—	—
						Aldershot	27	—
Steve Osgood†	6 0	12 00	20 1 62	Surrey	Farnborough	Aldershot	1	—
Defenders								
Kevan Brown	5 9	11 08	2 1 66	Andover		Southampton	—	—
						Brighton & HA	53	—
						Aldershot	110	2
Leigh Cooper	5 8	10 09	7 5 61	Reading	Apprentice	Plymouth Arg	323	15
						Aldershot	33	2
Ricky Cornish‡	5 11	11 05	1 11 70	Lewisham	Cambridge U	Aldershot	9	—
Alex Fisher§	5 11	12 08	30 1 73	Southampton	Trainee	Aldershot	2	—
John Flower	6 4	15 04	9 12 64	Northampton	Corby T	Sheffield U	—	—
						Aldershot	32	2
Tony Hopkins	5 9	11 05	17 2 71	Pontypool	Trainee	Newport Co	6	—
					Bristol C	Aldershot	10	—
Anthony Joyce†	5 11	11 00	24 9 71	Wembley	Trainee	QPR	—	—
						Aldershot	3	—
Mark Ogley	5 10	11 02	10 3 67	Barnsley	Apprentice	Barnsley	19	—
						Aldershot (loan)	8	—
						Carlisle U	33	1
						Aldershot	62	—
Jason Tucker§	5 11	11 00	3 2 73	Isleworth	Trainee	Aldershot	1	—
Des Vertannes‡			25 4 72	Hounslow	Trainee	Fulham	2	—
						Aldershot	—	—
Mark Whitlock	6 0	12 02	14 3 61	Portsmouth	Apprentice	Southampton	61	1
						Grimsby T (loan)	8	—
						Aldershot (loan)	14	—
						Bournemouth	99	1
						Reading	27	—
						Aldershot	29	2
Steve Wignall‡	5 11	12 01	17 9 54	Liverpool	Amateur	Liverpool	—	—
						Doncaster R	130	1
						Nottingham F (loan)	—	—
						Colchester U	281	22
						Brentford	67	2
						Aldershot	161	4
Viktor Yanushevski‡	5 11	11 05	23 1 60	Minsk	CSKA Moscow	Aldershot	6	1
Midfield								
Steve Beeks*	5 10	11 05	10 4 71	Ashford	Trainee	Aldershot	3	—
Billy Bone‡			4 10 71	Newcastle	Sunderland	Aldershot	—	—
Glen Burvill	5 9	10 10	26 10 62	Canning Town	Apprentice	West Ham U	—	—
						Aldershot	65	15
						Reading	30	—
						Fulham (loan)	9	2
						Aldershot	195	23
Charlie Henry	5 11	12 08	13 2 62	Acton	Apprentice	Swindon T	223	26
						Torquay U (loan)	6	1
						Northampton T (loan)	4	1
						Aldershot	81	18
Ian McDonald†	5 9	11 09	10 5 53	Barrow	Apprentice	Barrow	35	2
						Workington	42	4
						Liverpool	—	—
						Colchester U (loan)	5	2
						Mansfield T	56	4
						York C	175	29
						Aldershot	340	49

ALDERSHOT

Foundation: It was through the initiative of Councillor Jack White, a local newsagent who immediately captured the interest of the Town Clerk D. Llewellyn Griffiths, that Aldershot Town was formed in 1926. Having established a limited liability company under the chairmanship of Norman Clinton, an Aldershot resident and chairman of the Hampshire County FA they rented the Recreation Ground from the Aldershot Borough Council.

First Football League game: 27 August, 1932, Division 3(S), v Southend U (h) L 1-2 – Robb; Wade, McDougall; Lawson, Spence, Middleton; Proud, White, Gamble, Douglas, Fishlock (1).

Did you know: In season 1971–72 the Shots drew a total of 22 Fourth Division games including five in a row. Of those five games four were goalless draws.

Managers (and Secretary-managers)
Angus Seed 1927–37, Bill McCracken 1937–49, Gordon Clark 1950–55, Harry Evans 1955–59, Dave Smith 1959–71 (GM from 1967), Tommy McAnearney 1967–68, Jimmy Melia 1968–72, Tommy McAnearney 1972–81, Len Walker 1981–84, Ron Harris (GM) 1984–85, Len Walker 1985–91, Brian Talbot April 1991– .

Player and Position	Ht	Wt	Birth Date	Place	Source	Clubs	League App	Gls
Adrian Randall	5 11	11 00	10 11 68	Amesbury	Apprentice	Bournemouth	3	—
						Aldershot	107	12
Brian Talbot†	5 10	12 00	21 7 53	Ipswich	Apprentice	Ipswich T	177	25
						Arsenal	254	40
						Watford	48	8
						Stoke C	54	5
						WBA	74	5
						Fulham	5	1
						Aldershot	10	—
Peter Terry§	6 1	11 00	11 9 72	Edmonton	Trainee	Aldershot	1	—
Jerry Williams*	5 11	11 10	24 3 60	Didcot	Apprentice	Reading	309	17
						Gillingham	13	—
						Aldershot	67	7
Forwards								
Dale Banton*	5 8	11 00	15 5 61	Kensington	Apprentice	West Ham U	5	—
						Aldershot	106	47
						York C	138	48
						Walsall	10	—
						Grimsby T (loan)	8	1
						Aldershot	44	3
Paul Coombs	5 11	12 07	4 9 70	Bristol	QPR	Aldershot	16	1
Richard Dunwell‡	5 10	11 00	17 6 71	Islington	Millwall	Aldershot	1	—
Paul Halbert§	5 9	11 00	28 10 73	St Albans	Trainee	Aldershot	3	—
James Murphy*	5 10	12 04	17 11 71	Islington	Leyton Orient	Aldershot	3	—
David Puckett	5 7	10 05	29 10 60	Southampton	Apprentice	Southampton	95	14
						Nottingham F (loan)	—	—
						Bournemouth	35	14
						Stoke C (loan)	7	—
						Swansea (loan)	8	3
						Aldershot	113	50
Robert Reinelt§	5 10	11 05	11 3 74	Epping	Trainee	Aldershot	5	—
Ian Stewart	5 7	11 09	10 9 61	Belfast	Juniors	QPR	67	2
						Millwall (loan)	11	3
						Newcastle U	42	3
						Portsmouth	1	—
						Brentford (loan)	7	—
						Aldershot	101	—

Trainees
Bryant, Jamie A; Cleeve, David; Fisher, Alexander J; Halbert, Paul J; Higham, Paul; Laing, Andrew D; Parks, Wayne B; Payne, Simon J; Reinelt, Robert S; Roast, Bradley S; Spry, Nicholas; Terry, Peter E; Tucker, Jason J; Wright, Craig A.

**Non-Contract
McDonald, Ian C; Talbot, Brian E.

Associated Schoolboys
Birmingham, Michael J; Gandolfi, Neil F; Rogers, Sean.

**Non-Contract Players who are retained must be re-signed before they are eligible to play in League matches.

38

ARSENAL 1990–91 *Back row (left to right):* Gary Lewin (Physiotherapist), Pat Rice (Youth Team Coach), Brian Marwood, Gus Caesar, Lee Dixon, Kevin Campbell, Andy Linighan, Perry Groves, Alan Smith, Paul Merson, Paul Davis, Stewart Houston (First Team Coach), George Armstrong (Reserve Team Coach).
Front row: David Seaman, Craig McKernon, Nigel Winterburn, Anders Limpar, David O'Leary, Tony Adams, George Graham (Manager), Michael Thomas, Colin Pates, David Rocastle, Siggi Jonsson, Steve Bould, Alan Miller.

Division 1   ARSENAL

Arsenal Stadium, Highbury, London N5. Telephone 071-226 0304. Recorded information on 071-359 0131. Clubline: 0898 20 20 20.

Ground capacity: 45,000.

Record attendance: 73,295 v Sunderland, Div 1, 9 March 1935.

Record receipts: £233,595 v Everton, Littlewoods Cup semi-final, 24 February 1988.

Pitch measurements: 110yd × 71yd.

Chairman: P. D. Hill-Wood. *Vice-chairman:* D. Dein.

Directors: Sir Robert Bellinger CBE, DSC, R. G. Gibbs, C. E. B. L. Carr, R. C. S. Carr.

Managing Director: K. J. Friar.

Manager: George Graham. *Assistant Manager/Coach:* Stewart Houston.

Physio: Gary Lewin. *Reserve Coach:* George Armstrong. *Youth Coach:* Pat Rice.

Secretary: K. J. Friar. *Assistant Secretary:* David Miles. *Commercial Manager:* John Hazell. *Marketing Manager:* Phil Carling.

Year Formed: 1886. *Turned Professional:* 1891. *Ltd Co.:* 1893.

Previous Names: 1886, Dial Square; 1886–91, Royal Arsenal; 1891–1914, Woolwich Arsenal.

Club Nickname: 'Gunners'.

Previous Grounds: 1886–87, Plumstead Common; 1887–88, Sportsman Ground; 1888–90, Manor Ground; 1890–93, Invicta Ground; 1893–1913, Manor Ground; 1913, Highbury.

Record League Victory: 12-0 v Loughborough T, Division 2, 12 March 1900 – Orr; McNichol, Jackson; Moir, Dick (2), Anderson (1); Hunt, Cottrell (2), Main (2), Gaudie (3), Tennant (2).

Record Cup Victory: 11-1 v Darwen, FA Cup, 3rd rd, 9 January 1932 – Moss; Parker, Hapgood; Jones, Roberts, John; Hulme (2), Jack (3), Lambert (2), James, Bastin (4).

Record Defeat: 0-8 v Loughborough T, Division 2, 12 December 1896.

Most League Points (2 for a win): 66, Division 1, 1930–31.

Most League Points (3 for a win): 83, Division 1, 1990–91.

Most League Goals: 127, Division 1, 1930–31.

Highest League Scorer in Season: Ted Drake, 42, 1934–35.

Most League Goals in Total Aggregate: Cliff Bastin, 150, 1930–47.

Most Capped Player: Kenny Sansom, 77 (86), England.

Most League Appearances: David O'Leary, 522, 1975–91.

Record Transfer Fee Received: £1,250,000 from Crystal Palace for Clive Allen, August 1980.

Record Transfer Fee Paid: £1,300,000 to QPR for David Seaman, May 1990.

Football League Record: 1893 Elected to Division 2; 1904–13 Division 1; 1913–19 Division 2; 1919– Division 1.

Honours: Football League: Division 1 – Champions 1930–31, 1932–33, 1933–34, 1934–35, 1937–38, 1947–48, 1952–53, 1970–71, 1988–89, 1990–91; Runners-up 1925–26, 1931–32, 1972–73; Division 2 – Runners-up 1903–04. *FA Cup:* Winners 1929–30, 1935–36, 1949–50, 1970–71, 1978–79; Runners-up 1926–27, 1931–32, 1951–52, 1971–72, 1977–78, 1979–80. *Double Performed:* 1970–71. *Football League Cup:* Winners 1986–87; Runners-up 1967–68, 1968–69, 1987–88. **European Competitions:** *Fairs Cup:* 1963–64, 1969–70 (winners), 1970–71; *European Cup:* 1971–72; *UEFA Cup:* 1978–79, 1981–82, 1982–83; *European Cup-Winners' Cup:* 1979–80 (runners-up).

Colours: Red shirts with white sleeves, white shorts, red stockings. **Change colours:** Yellow shirts, navy blue shorts, yellow stockings.

ARSENAL 1990–91 LEAGUE RECORD

Match No.	Date		Venue	Opponents	Result		H/T Score	Lg. Pos.	Goalscorers	Atten- dance
1	Aug	25	A	Wimbledon	W	3-0	0-0	—	Merson, Smith, Groves	13,733
2		29	H	Luton T	W	2-1	1-1	—	Merson, Thomas	32,723
3	Sept	1	H	Tottenham H	D	0-0	0-0	3		40,009
4		8	A	Everton	D	1-1	0-0	5	Groves	29,919
5		15	H	Chelsea	W	4-1	0-0	2	Limpar, Dixon (pen), Merson, Rocastle	41,516
6		22	A	Nottingham F	W	2-0	1-0	2	Rocastle, Limpar	26,013
7		29	A	Leeds U	D	2-2	1-1	2	Limpar 2	30,085
8	Oct	6	H	Norwich C	W	2-0	2-0	2	Davis 2	36,048
9		20	A	Manchester U	W	1-0	1-0	2	Limpar	47,232
10		27	H	Sunderland	W	1-0	0-0	2	Dixon (pen)	38,539
11	Nov	3	A	Coventry C	W	2-0	0-0	2	Limpar 2	15,336
12		10	A	Crystal Palace	D	0-0	0-0	2		28,181
13		17	A	Southampton	W	4-0	3-0	2	Merson, Limpar, Smith 2	36,243
14		24	A	QPR	W	3-1	0-1	2	Merson, Smith, Campbell	18,555
15	Dec	2	H	Liverpool	W	3-0	1-0	—	Merson, Dixon (pen), Smith	40,419
16		8	A	Luton T	D	1-1	1-0	2	Smith	12,506
17		15	H	Wimbledon	D	2-2	2-1	2	Merson, Adams	30,163
18		23	A	Aston Villa	D	0-0	0-0	—		22,687
19		26	H	Derby Co	W	3-0	2-0	2	Smith 2, Merson	25,538
20		29	H	Sheffield U	W	4-1	0-1	2	Dixon (pen), Smith 2, Thomas	37,866
21	Jan	1	A	Manchester C	W	1-0	0-0	2	Smith	30,579
22		12	A	Tottenham H	D	0-0	0-0	2		34,753
23		19	H	Everton	W	1-0	0-0	1	Merson	35,349
24	Feb	2	A	Chelsea	L	1-2	0-0	1	Smith	29,094
25		23	H	Crystal Palace	W	4-0	2-0	1	O'Leary, Merson, Smith, Campbell	42,512
26	Mar	3	A	Liverpool	W	1-0	0-0	—	Merson	37,221
27		17	H	Leeds U	W	2-0	0-0	—	Campbell 2	26,218
28		20	H	Nottingham F	D	1-1	1-0	—	Campbell	34,152
29		23	A	Norwich C	D	0-0	0-0	2		20,131
30		30	A	Derby Co	W	2-0	1-0	1	Smith 2	18,397
31	Apr	3	H	Aston Villa	W	5-0	1-0		Campbell 2, Davis, Smith 2	41,868
32		6	A	Sheffield U	W	2-0	1-0	1	Campbell, Smith	26,920
33		9	A	Southampton	D	1-1	0-0	—	Smith	20,949
34		17	H	Manchester C	D	2-2	2-2	—	Campbell, Merson	38,412
35		23	H	QPR	W	2-0	0-0	—	Dixon (pen), Merson	42,393
36	May	4	A	Sunderland	D	0-0	0-0	1		22,606
37		6	H	Manchester U	W	3-1	2-0	—	Smith 3 (1 pen)	40,229
38		11	H	Coventry C	W	6-1	2-1	1	Peake (og), Limpar 3, Smith, Groves	41,039

Final League Position: 1

GOALSCORERS

League (74): Smith 23 (1 pen), Merson 13, Limpar 11, Campbell 9, Dixon 5 (5 pens), Davis 3, Groves 3, Rocastle 2, Thomas 2, Adams 1, O'Leary 1, own goal 1.
Rumbelows Cup (10): Groves 3, Smith 3, Adams 2, Merson 2.
FA Cup (9): Limpar 2, Smith 2, Adams 1, Campbell 1, Dixon 1, Merson 1, Thomas 1.

Seaman	Dixon	Winterburn	Thomas	Bould	Adams	Rocastle	Davis	Smith	Merson	Limpar	Groves	Campbell	Linighan	Hillier	Jonsson	O'Leary	Cole	Pates	Match No.
1	2	3	4	5	6	7	8	9	10	11*	12								1
1	2	3	4	5	6	7	8	9	10	11*	12								2
1	2	3	4	5	6	7	8	9	10*	11	12								3
1	2	3	4	5	6	7	8	9*	10	11	12								4
1	2	3	4	5†	6	7	8		10	11	9*	12	14						5
1	2	3	4	5	6	7*	8	12	10	11	9								6
1	2	3†		5	6	7	8	9	10*	11	12		14			4			7
1	2	3		5	6	7	8	9	10†	11*	12		14			4			8
1	2	3	4	5	6	7*	8	9	10	11	12								9
1	2	3	4	5	6	7*	8	9	10	11	12								10
1	2	3	4	5	6		8	9*	10	11	7†	12				14			11
1	2	3	4	5	6		8	14	10*	11†	12	9				7			12
1	2†	3	4	5	6		8	9	10	11	7*	12				14			13
1	2	3	4	5	6†		8	9	10	11	7*	12				14			14
1	2	3	4	5	6		8	9	10	11						7			15
1	2	3	4	5	6		8	9	10	11*	12					7			16
1	2	3*	4	5	6		8	9	10	11	7					12			17
1	2	3	4	5		12	8	9	10	11*	7		6						18
1	2	3	4	5		7*	8	9	10	11†		12	6			14			19
1	2	3†	4	5			8	9	10	11	7*		6			14	12		20
1	2	3	4	5			8	9	10	11*	12	6	14			7†			21
1	2	3	4	5			8†	9	10*	11	12	6	14			7			22
1	2	3	4	5†			8	9	10	11*	6	12	14			7			23
1	2	3	4	5†			8	9	10	11*	7	12	6			14			24
1	2	3	4	5		12	8	9	10*	11			6†			7	14		25
1	2	3	4	5	6*14	12		9	10		11†	8				7			26
1	2	3	4	5	6			9	10		11	8				7			27
1	2	3	4	5	6		8†	9	10*	14	12	11				7			28
1	2	3		5	6	4†	8	9		11*	12	10	14			7			29
1	2	3		5	6	7†	8	9	10	11*	12	4				14			30
1	2	3	14	5	6		8	9	10*	11	12	7	4†						31
1	2	3	14	5	6		8	9	10*	11†	12	7	4						32
1	2	3	14	5	6		8	9	12	11*	10	7	4†						33
1	2†	3	4	5	6		8	9	10*	12	11	7				14			34
1	2	3		5	6		8	9	10†	11*	12	7	4			14			35
1	2	3		5	6		8	9	10	11*	7		4			12			36
1	2	3	14	5	6		8	9	10	11†	7		4*			12			37
1	2	3		5	6		8	9	10†	11	12	7*14	4						38
38	38	38	27	38	30	13	36	35	36	36	32	13	15	7	9	2	11	— —	
			+4s			+3s	+1s	+2s	+1s	+2s		+19s	+7s	+3s	+7s	+10s	+1s	+1s	

Rumbelows Cup	Second Round	Chester C (a)	1-0	
		(h)	5-0	
	Third Round	Manchester C (a)	2-1	
	Fourth Round	Manchester U (h)	2-6	
FA Cup	Third Round	Sunderland (h)	2-1	
	Fourth Round	Leeds U (h)	0-0	
		(a)	1-1	
		(h)	0-0	
		(a)	2-1	
	Fifth Round	Shrewsbury T (a)	1-0	
	Sixth Round	Cambridge U (h)	2-1	
	Semi-final	Tottenham H (at Wembley)	1-3	

ARSENAL

Player and Position	Ht	Wt	Birth Date	Place	Source	Clubs	League App	Gls
Goalkeepers								
Allan Miller	6 2	13 08	29 3 70	Epping	Trainee	Arsenal	—	—
						Plymouth Arg (loan)	13	—
David Seaman	6 3	13 00	19 9 63	Rotherham	Apprentice	Leeds U	—	—
						Peterborough U	91	—
						Birmingham C	75	—
						QPR	141	—
						Arsenal	38	—
James Will			7 10 72	Turriff	Trainee	Arsenal	—	—
Defenders								
Tony Adams	6 1	13 03	10 10 66	London	Apprentice	Arsenal	214	18
Steve Bould	6 3	12 08	16 11 62	Stoke	Apprentice	Stoke C	183	6
						Torquay U (loan)	9	—
						Arsenal	87	2
Gus Caesar*	6 0	12 00	5 3 66	London	Apprentice	Arsenal	44	—
						QPR (loan)	5	—
Jim Carstairs*	6 0	12 05	29 1 71	Fife	Trainee	Arsenal	—	—
						Brentford (loan)	8	—
Lee Dixon	5 9	10 12	17 3 64	Manchester	Local	Burnley	4	—
						Chester C	57	1
						Bury	45	5
						Stoke C	71	5
						Arsenal	115	11
Craig Gaunt			31 3 73	Nottingham	Trainee	Arsenal	—	—
Charles Hartfield*	6 0	12 00	4 9 71	London	Trainee	Arsenal	—	—
Andy Linighan	6 3	12 06	18 8 62	Hartlepool	Smiths BC	Hartlepool U	110	4
						Leeds U	66	3
						Oldham Ath	87	6
						Norwich C	86	8
						Arsenal	10	—
Craig McKernon	5 9	11 00	23 2 68	Gloucester	Apprentice	Mansfield T	94	—
						Arsenal	—	—
Scott Marshall			1 5 73	Edinburgh	Trainee	Arsenal	—	—
Steve Morrow	6 0	11 03	2 7 70	Belfast	Trainee	Arsenal	—	—
						Reading (loan)	10	—
David O'Leary	6 1	13 02	2 5 58	London	Apprentice	Arsenal	522	10
Colin Pates	5 11	11 00	10 8 61	Mitcham	Apprentice	Chelsea	281	10
						Charlton Ath	38	—
						Arsenal	3	—
						Brighton & HA (loan)	17	—
Michael Thomas	5 10	12 04	24 8 67	Lambeth	Apprentice	Arsenal	153	23
						Portsmouth (loan)	3	—
Ken Webster			2 3 73	Hammersmith	Trainee	Arsenal	—	—
Nigel Winterburn	5 10	10 07	11 12 63	Coventry	Local	Birmingham C	—	—
						Oxford U	—	—
						Wimbledon	165	8
						Arsenal	129	3
Midfield								
Steve Clements			26 9 72	Slough	Trainee	Arsenal	—	—
Paul Davis	5 10	10 10	9 12 61	London	Apprentice	Arsenal	307	29
Mark Flatts			14 10 72	Islington	Trainee	Arsenal	—	—
David Hillier	5 10	11 06	19 12 69	Blackheath	Trainee	Arsenal	16	—
Siggi Jonsson	5 11	11 11	27 9 66	Akranes, Iceland	Akranes FC	Sheffield W	67	4
						Barnsley (loan)	5	—
						Arsenal	8	—
Matthew Joseph			30 9 72	Bethnal Green	Trainee	Arsenal	—	—

ARSENAL

Foundation: Formed by workers at the Royal Arsenal, Woolwich in 1886 they began as Dial Square (name of one of the workshops) and included two former Nottingham Forest players Fred Beardsley and Morris Bates. Beardsley wrote to his old club seeking help and they provided the new club with a full set of red jerseys and a ball. The club became known as the "Woolwich Reds" although their official title soon after formation was Woolwich Arsenal.

First Football League game: 2 September, 1893, Division 2, v Newcastle U (h) D 2-2 – Williams; Powell, Jeffrey; Devine, Buist, Howat; Gemmell, Henderson, Shaw (1), Elliott (1), Booth.

Did you know: In 1932–33 when Cliff Bastin created a Football League record for a winger by scoring 33 goals as an outside-left, he scored another four in the annual friendly against Racing Club de Paris which Arsenal won 5-2 in France.

Managers (and Secretary-managers)
Sam Hollis 1894–97, Tom Mitchell 1897–98, George Elcoat 1898–99, Harry Bradshaw 1899–1904, Phil Kelso 1904–08, George Morrell 1908–15, Leslie Knighton 1919–25, Herbert Chapman 1925–34, George Allison 1934–47, Tom Whittaker 1947–56, Jack Crayston 1956–58, George Swindin 1958–62, Billy Wright 1962–66, Bertie Mee 1966–76, Terry Neill 1976–83, Don Howe 1984–86, George Graham May 1986– .

Player and Position	Ht	Wt	Birth Date	Place	Source	Clubs	League App	Gls
Gary McKeown	5 10	11 07	19 10 70	Oxford	Trainee	Arsenal	—	—
Ray Parlour			7 3 73	Romford	Trainee	Arsenal	—	—
Kevin Richardson (To Real Sociedad Sept 1990)	5 9	11 02	4 12 62	Newcastle	Apprentice	Everton	109	16
						Watford	39	2
						Arsenal	96	5
David Rocastle	5 9	11 12	2 5 67	Lewisham	Apprentice	Arsenal	179	20
Forwards								
Kwame Ampadu	5 10	10 13	20 11 70	Bradford	Trainee	Arsenal	2	
						Plymouth Arg (loan)	6	1
						WBA (loan)	7	1
John Bacon			23 3 73	Dublin	Trainee	Arsenal	—	—
Kevin Campbell	6 0	13 01	4 2 70	Lambeth	Trainee	Arsenal	38	11
						Leyton Orient (loan)	16	9
						Leicester C (loan)	11	5
Andrew Cole	5 11	11 02	15 10 71	Nottingham	Trainee	Arsenal	1	—
Paul Dickov			1 11 72	Livingston	Trainee	Arsenal	—	—
Perry Groves	5 11	11 12	19 4 65	London	Apprentice	Colchester U	156	26
						Arsenal	142	20
Martin Hayes (To Celtic July 1990)	6 0	11 08	21 3 66	Walthamstow	Apprentice	Arsenal	102	26
Neil Heaney	5 9	11 01	3 11 71	Middlesbrough	Trainee	Arsenal	—	—
						Hartlepool U (loan)	3	—
Anders Limpar			24 9 65	Sweden	Cremonese	Arsenal	34	11
Paul Merson	5 10	11 09	20 3 68	London	Apprentice	Arsenal	125	38
						Brentford (loan)	7	
Alan Smith	6 3	12 10	21 11 62	Birmingham	Alvechurch	Leicester C	191	73
						Arsenal	150	67
						Leicester C (loan)	9	3

Trainees
Charlton, John L; Faulkner, Richard A; Fowler, Kevin A; Gooden, Ty M; Lee, Justin D; Read, Paul C; Selley, Ian; Shaw, Paul; Warden, Danny; Young, Stuart R.

Associated Schoolboys
Black, Michael J; Clarke, Albert; Hall, Graeme B; Hughes, Stephen J; McGowan, Gavin G; Rawlins, Matthew; Rose, Matthew.

Associated Schoolboys who have accepted the club's offer of a Traineeship/Contract
Brisset, Jason C; Clarke, Adrian J; Harford, Paul T; McArdle, Mark; Rust, Nicholas C.I; Swain, Joel T; Zumrutel, Sonner.

44

ASTON VILLA 1990-91 *Back row (left to right):* Peter Withe, Neil Cox, Andy Comyn, Lee Butler, Kent Nielsen, Nigel Spink, Ian Ormondroyd, Paul McGrath, Dave Richardson.
Centre row: Dennis Booth, Derek Mountfield, Gareth Williams, Dwight Yorke, Tony Cascarino, Mark Blake, Ivo Stas, Gordon Cowans, Jim Walker.
Front row: Tony Daley, Nigel Callaghan, Bernard Gallacher, David Platt, Dr Jozef Venglos (Manager), Stuart Gray, Chris Price, Kevin Gage.

Division 1   **ASTON VILLA**

Villa Park, Trinity Rd, Birmingham B6 6HE. Telephone 021-327 2299. Commercial Dept. 021-327 5399. Clubcall: 0898 121148. Ticketline: 0898 121848.

Ground capacity: 40,000.

Record attendance: 76,588 v Derby Co, FA Cup 6th rd, 2 March 1946.

Record receipts: £385,678 Everton v Norwich C, FA Cup semi-final, 15 April 1989.

Pitch measurements: 115yd × 75yd.

President: H. J. Musgrove. *Chairman:* H. D. Ellis.

Directors: J. A. Alderson, Dr D. H. Targett, P. D. Ellis.

Manager: Ron Atkinson. *Assistant Managers:* Dave Richardson. *First Team Coach:* Peter Withe.

Secretary: Steven Stride. *Coaches:* Dennis Booth and Bobby Downes.

Physio: Jim Walker. *Youth Coach:* Richard Money.

Commercial Manager: Abdul Rashid.

Year Formed: 1874. *Turned Professional:* 1885. *Ltd Co.:* 1896.

Previous Grounds: 1874–76, Aston Park; 1876–97, Perry Barr; 1897, Villa Park.

Club Nickname: 'The Villans'.

Record League Victory: 12-2 v Accrington S, Division 1, 12 March 1892 – Warner; Evans, Cox; Harry Devey, Jimmy Cowan, Baird; Athersmith (1), Dickson (2), John Devey (4), L. Campbell (4), Hodgetts (1).

Record Cup Victory: 13-0 v Wednesbury Old Ath, FA Cup, 1st rd, 30 October 1886 – Warner; Coulton, Simmonds; Yates, Robertson, Burton (2); R. Davis (1), A. Brown (3), Hunter (3), Loach (2), Hodgetts (2).

Record Defeat: 1-8 v Blackburn R, FA Cup, 3rd rd, 16 February 1889.

Most League Points (2 for a win): 70, Division 3, 1971–72.

Most League Points (3 for a win): 78, Division 2, 1987–88.

Most League Goals: 128, Division 1, 1930–31.

Highest League Scorer in Season: 'Pongo' Waring, 49, Division 1, 1930–31.

Most League Goals in Total Aggregate: Harry Hampton, 215, 1904–15 and Billy Walker, 213, 1919–34.

Most Capped Player: Peter McParland, 33 (34), Northern Ireland.

Most League Appearances: Charlie Aitken, 561, 1961–76.

Record Transfer Fee Received: £1,469,000 (£1,175,000 basic fee) from Wolverhampton W for Andy Gray, September 1979.

Record Transfer Fee Paid: £1,600,000 to Real Sociedad for Dalian Atkinson, June 1991.

Football League Record: 1888 Founder Member of the League; 1936–38 Division 2; 1938–59 Division 1; 1959–60 Division 2; 1960–67 Division 1; 1967–70 Division 2; 1970–72 Division 3; 1972–75 Division 2; 1975–87 Division 1; 1987–88 Division 2; 1988– Division 1.

Honours: Football League: Division 1 – Champions 1893–94, 1895–96, 1896–97, 1898–99, 1899–1900, 1909–10, 1980–81; Runners-up 1888–89, 1902–03, 1907–08, 1910–11, 1912–13, 1913–14, 1930–31, 1932–33, 1989–90; Division 2 – Champions 1937–38, 1959–60; Runners-up 1974–75, 1987–88; Division 3 – Champions 1971–72. *FA Cup:* Winners 1887, 1895, 1897, 1905, 1913, 1920, 1957; Runners-up 1892, 1924. *Double Performed:* 1896–97. *Football League Cup:* Winners 1961, 1975, 1977; Runners-up 1963, 1971. **European Competitions:** *European Cup:* 1981–82 (winners), 1982–83; *UEFA Cup:* 1975–76, 1977–78, 1983–84, 1990–91. *World Club Championship:* 1982–83; *European Super Cup:* 1982–83 (winners).

Colours: Claret shirts, blue trim, white shorts, claret and blue trim, blue stockings, claret trim. **Change colours:** White shirts, purple/black trim, black shorts, white stockings.

ASTON VILLA 1990–91 LEAGUE RECORD

Match No.	Date	Venue	Opponents	Result	H/T Score	Lg. Pos.	Goalscorers	Atten- dance
1	Aug 25	H	Southampton	D	1-1	1-1	—	Cascarino	29,542
2	Sept 1	A	Liverpool	L	1-2	1-1	18	Platt	38,061
3	5	A	Manchester C	L	1-2	0-0	—	Platt (pen)	30,199
4	8	H	Coventry C	W	2-1	1-0	13	Platt (pen), Cascarino	27,001
5	15	A	Derby Co	W	2-0	1-0	8	Daley, Platt	19,024
6	22	H	QPR	D	2-2	2-2	9	Mountfield, Ormondroyd	23,301
7	29	A	Tottenham H	L	1-2	1-1	11	Platt	34,939
8	Oct 6	H	Sunderland	W	3-0	1-0	9	Olney, Daley, Platt	26,017
9	20	A	Wimbledon	D	0-0	0-0	9		6646
10	27	H	Leeds U	D	0-0	0-0	8		24,219
11	Nov 3	A	Chelsea	L	0-1	0-1	9		23,555
12	10	H	Nottingham F	D	1-1	0-0	9	Nielsen	25,797
13	17	A	Norwich C	L	0-2	0-1	13		17,243
14	24	A	Luton T	L	0-2	0-1	13		10,071
15	Dec 1	H	Sheffield U	W	2-1	1-0	12	Platt, Price	21,713
16	15	A	Southampton	D	1-1	0-1	13	Platt (pen)	16,604
17	23	H	Arsenal	D	0-0	0-0	—		22,687
18	26	A	Everton	L	0-1	0-0	13		27,804
19	29	A	Manchester U	D	1-1	1-1	15	Pallister (og)	47,485
20	Jan 1	H	Crystal Palace	W	2-0	0-0	13	Platt 2 (1 pen)	25,523
21	12	H	Liverpool	D	0-0	0-0	13		40,026
22	19	A	Coventry C	L	1-2	0-0	14	Platt	15,751
23	Feb 2	H	Derby Co	W	3-2	1-1	13	Cowans (pen), Cascarino, Yorke	21,852
24	23	A	Nottingham F	D	2-2	0-1	13	Cascarino, Mountfield	22,036
25	Mar 2	A	Sheffield U	L	1-2	0-0	15	Mountfield	22,074
26	9	H	Luton T	L	1-2	0-2	16	Cascarino	20,587
27	16	H	Tottenham H	W	3-2	2-0	15	Platt 3	32,638
28	23	A	Sunderland	W	3-1	1-0	14	Cascarino 2, Platt	21,099
29	30	H	Everton	D	2-2	0-1	13	Platt, Olney	27,660
30	Apr 3	A	Arsenal	L	0-5	0-1	—		41,868
31	6	H	Manchester U	D	1-1	0-0	17	Cascarino	33,307
32	10	A	QPR	L	1-2	1-0	—	Platt	11,539
33	13	A	Crystal Palace	D	0-0	0-0	17		18,331
34	20	H	Wimbledon	L	1-2	1-1	17	Olney	17,001
35	23	A	Manchester C	L	1-5	0-2	—	Platt (pen)	24,168
36	May 4	A	Leeds U	L	2-5	1-2	17	Nielsen, Mountfield	29,188
37	8	H	Norwich C	W	2-1	1-1	—	Bowen (og), Yorke	16,697
38	11	H	Chelsea	D	2-2	1-2	17	Cascarino, Platt (pen)	27,866

Final League Position: 17

GOALSCORERS

League (46): Platt 19 (6 pens), Cascarino 9, Mountfield 4, Olney 3, Daley 2, Nielsen 2, Yorke 2, Cowans 1 (pen), Ormondroyd 1, Price 1, own goals 2.
Rumbelows Cup (8): Platt 3 (2 pens), Daley 2, Ormondroyd 2, Cascarino 1.
FA Cup (1): Gray 1.

Spink	Price	Gray	McGrath	Mountfield	Nielsen	Daley	Platt	Olney	Cowans	Cascarino	Gage	Gallacher	Yorke	Ormondroyd	Birch	Comyn	Blake	Butler	Callaghan	Penrice	Match No.
1	2	3	4	5	6	7	8	9	10	11											1
1	2	3	4	5	6	7	8		10	11	9										2
1	2	3	4	5*	6	7	8	12	10	11	9										3
1	2		4	5	6	7	8	9*	10	11		3	12								4
1	2	3	4	5	6	7	8		10	11	9										5
1	2	3	4	5	6	7	8	9*	10				12	11							6
1	2	3	4	5	6	7	8	9*	10				12	11							7
1	2	3	4	5	6	7	8	9†	10	14			12	11*							8
1	2	3		5	6	7	8		10	11			9*	12	4						9
1	2	3		5	6	7	8		10	11				9	4						10
1	2		4	5	6	7*	8		10	11		3	12	9							11
1	2	3	4	5	6	7	8	9	10	11											12
1	2	3	4	5	6	7	8	9	10	11											13
1	2	3	4	5†	6	7	8		10	11			14	12		9*					14
1	2	3	4		6	7	8	9*	10	12			11			5					15
1	2	3	4		6	7	8		10	11			14	9†	5*	12					16
1	2	3	4		6	7	8		10	11				9		5					17
1	2	3	4	5*	6	7	8		10	11			12	9							18
1	2	3	4	5	6	7*	8		10	11			9	12							19
	2	3	4	5	6		8		10	9			7	11				1			20
1	2		4		6		8		10	9	3		7			5				11	21
1	2	3	4		6		8		10	9	11†		14	12	7	5*					22
1	2	3	4	5	6	7			10	9	8		12				11*				23
1	2		4	5	6				10	9	3		7*	11		12	8				24
1	2	11	4	5	6			12	10	9	3		7	8*							25
1	2	3	4	5*	6†		8	12	10	9	14		7							11	26
1	2		4	5	6		8	12	10	9	3		7*							11	27
1	2		4	5	6		8		10	9	3						11			7	28
1	2		4	5	6*		8	12	10	9	3						11			7	29
1*	2		4	5			8		10	9	3					6	12			7	30
	2		4	5	6		8	7*	10	9	3		12	11				1			31
	2		4	5*	6		8	7	10	9	3			11				1	12		32
	2		4	5	6		8	7*	10	9	3			11				1	12		33
1	2			5	6	14	8	7	10	9	3			11†	4*	12					34
1	2		4		6	7	8	9	10	12	3					5*				11	35
1	2		4	5	6	7*	8		10	9	3		12							11	36
1	2		4	5	6		8		10	9	3		12				11*			7	37
1	2		4	5	6		8		10	9	3						11			7	38
34	38	22	35	32	37	22	35	13	38	33	20	2	8	13	6	9	6	4	2	9	
					+1s			+5s			+3s	+1s	+10s	+5s	+2s	+2s	+1s			+3s	

Rumbelows Cup	Second Round	Barnsley (h)	1-0
		(a)	1-0
	Third Round	Millwall (h)	2-0
	Fourth Round	Middlesbrough (h)	3-2
	Fifth Round	Leeds U (a)	1-4
FA Cup	Third Round	Wimbledon (h)	1-1
		(a)	0-1

ASTON VILLA

Player and Position	Ht	Wt	Birth Date	Birth Place	Source	Clubs	League App	Gls
Goalkeepers								
Lee Butler	6 2	14 02	30 5 66	Sheffield	Haworth Coll	Lincoln C	30	—
						Aston Villa	8	—
						Hull C (loan)	4	—
Glen Livingstone	6 2	14 01	13 10 72	Birmingham	Trainee	Aston Villa	—	—
Nigel Spink	6 1	14 06	8 8 58	Chelmsford	Chelmsford C	Aston Villa	283	—
Defenders								
Andy Comyn	6 1	12 00	2 8 68	Manchester	Alvechurch	Aston Villa	15	—
Darrell Duffy	5 11	11 00	18 1 71	Birmingham	Trainee	Aston Villa	1	—
Kevin Gage	5 9	11 02	21 4 64	Chiswick	Apprentice	Wimbledon	168	15
						Aston Villa	115	8
Bernard Gallacher*	5 8	11 02	22 3 67	Johnstone	Apprentice	Aston Villa	57	—
						Blackburn R (loan)	4	—
Craig Liddle‡	5 10	12 03	21 10 71	Perkinsville	Trainee	Aston Villa	—	—
Paul McGrath	6 0	13 02	4 12 59	Ealing	St Patrick's Ath	Manchester U	163	12
						Aston Villa	70	1
Derek Mountfield	6 1	12 07	2 11 62	Liverpool	Apprentice	Tranmere R	26	1
						Everton	106	19
						Aston Villa	88	9
Kent Nielsen	6 2	14 01	28 12 61	Frederiksberg	Brondby	Aston Villa	73	4
Chris Price	5 7	10 02	30 3 60	Hereford	Apprentice	Hereford U	330	27
						Blackburn R	83	11
						Aston Villa	108	2
Bryan Small	5 9	11 08	15 11 71	Birmingham	Trainee	Aston Villa	—	—
Ivo Stas	6 2	14 00	10 2 65	Ostrava	Banik Ostrava	Aston Villa	—	—
Midfield								
Mark Blake	5 11	12 03	16 12 70	Nottingham	Trainee	Aston Villa	16	—
						Wolverhampton W (loan)	2	—
Russell Bullivant	6 0	11 09	6 9 72	Birmingham	Trainee	Aston Villa	—	—
Gordon Cowans	5 9	10 07	27 10 58	Durham	Apprentice Bari	Aston Villa	286	42
						Aston Villa	105	7
Neil Cox	5 11	12 10	8 10 71	Scunthorpe	Trainee	Scunthorpe U	17	1
						Aston Villa	—	—
Richard Crisp	5 7	10 05	23 5 72	Wordsley		Aston Villa	—	—
Steve Froggatt	5 10	11 00	9 3 73	Lincoln	Trainee	Aston Villa	—	—
Stuart Gray	5 10	11 05	19 4 60	Withernsea	Local	Nottingham F	49	3
						Bolton W (loan)	10	—
						Barnsley	120	23
						Aston Villa	106	9
Forwards								
Nigel Callaghan	5 9	10 09	12 9 62	Singapore	Apprentice	Watford	222	41
						Derby Co	76	10
						Aston Villa	26	1
						Derby Co (loan)	12	1
						Watford (loan)	12	1
Martin Carruthers	5 11	11 07	7 8 72	Nottingham	Trainee	Aston Villa	—	—
Tony Cascarino	6 2	11 10	1 9 62	St Paul's Cray	Crockenhill	Gillingham	219	78
						Millwall	105	42
						Aston Villa	46	11
Tony Daley	5 9	10 05	18 10 67	Birmingham	Apprentice	Aston Villa	159	21
David Jones	5 9	11 04	6 5 71	Wrexham	Trainee	Aston Villa	—	—
Ian Olney	6 1	11 03	17 12 69	Luton	Trainee	Aston Villa	68	14

ASTON VILLA

Foundation: Cricketing enthusiasts of Villa Cross Wesleyan Chapel, Aston, Birmingham decided to form a football club during the winter of 1873–74. Football clubs were few and far between in the Birmingham area and in their first game against Aston Brook St. Mary's Rugby team they played one half rugby and the other soccer. In 1876 they were joined by a Scottish soccer enthusiast George Ramsay who was immediately appointed captain and went on to lead Aston Villa from obscurity to one of the country's top clubs in a period of less than 10 years.

First Football League game: 8 September, 1888, Football League, v Wolverhampton W, (a) D 1–1 – Warner; Cox, Coulton; Yates, H. Devey, Dawson; A. Brown, Green (1), Allen, Garvey, Hodgetts.

Did you know: When left-half Bob Iverson scored Aston Villa's fastest-ever League goal after ten seconds in a home game against Charlton Athletic, 3 December 1938, the only Charlton player to touch the ball was goalkeeper Sam Bartram.

Managers (and Secretary-managers)
George Ramsay 1884–1926*, W. J. Smith 1926–34*, Jimmy McMullan 1934–35, Jimmy Hogan 1936–44, Alex Massie 1945–50, George Martin 1950–53, Eric Houghton 1953–58, Joe Mercer 1958–64, Dick Taylor 1965–67, Tommy Cummings 1967–68, Tommy Docherty 1968–70, Vic Crowe 1970–74, Ron Saunders 1974–82, Tony Barton 1982–84, Graham Turner 1984–86, Billy McNeill 1986–87, Graham Taylor 1987–90, Dr. Jozef Venglos 1990–91, Ron Atkinson June 1991– .

Player and Position	Ht	Wt	Birth Date	Birth Place	Source	Clubs	League App	Gls
Ian Ormondroyd	6 4	13 07	22 9 64	Bradford	Thackley	Bradford C	87	20
						Oldham Ath (loan)	10	1
						Aston Villa	55	6
Mark Parrott	5 11	11 00	14 3 71	Cheltenham	Trainee	Aston Villa	—	—
Gary Penrice	5 7	10 00	23 3 64	Bristol	Mangotsfield	Bristol R	188	54
						Watford	43	18
						Aston Villa	12	—
David Platt	5 10	11 12	10 6 66	Chadderton	Chadderton	Manchester U	—	—
						Crewe Alex	134	55
						Aston Villa	121	50
Gareth Williams	5 10	11 08	12 3 67	Isle of Wight	Gosport	Aston Villa	12	—
Lee Williams	5 7	11 00	3 2 73	Birmingham	Trainee	Aston Villa	—	—
Dwight Yorke	5 10	11 12	3 12 71	Tobago	St Clairs CS	Aston Villa	20	2

Trainees
Boden, Christopher; Fenton, Graham A; Goodwin, Craig; Hedigan, Darren; Hoban, Neil A; Hodgson Shaun D; Ibrahim, Kevin A; McCallum, Matthew; McNamara, Phillip J; Morgan, Steven; Peachey, Wayne T; Pitcher, Steven; Travis, David L; Walker, Stephen L.

**Non-Contract
Davis, Neil

Associated Schoolboys
Accison, Keith R; Aston, Lee A; Boyce, Christopher; Brammeld, Craig G; Brown, Ian S; Burchell, Lee A; Clarke, Michael J; Creamer, Christopher P; Finney, Nicholas D.J; Grassby, Darren P; Green, James S; Haupt, Simon P; James, Stuart; Leek, Brian; Leonard, Matthew; Morris, Adam J; Oakes, Michael C; Rachel, Adam; Sutton, Liam R; Wiltshire, John M.

Associated Schoolboys who have accepted the club's offer of a Traineeship/Contract
Cowe, Steven M; Evans, Darren; Harrison, Garry M; Hutson, Otis M.F; King, Ian J; Pearce, Christopher J; Pearce, Dennis A; Scimeca, Ricardo; Williams, Graeme E.

**Non-Contract Players who are retained must be re-signed before they are eligible to play in League matches.

BARNET 1990–91   *Back row (left to right):* Gordon Ogbourne (Kit Manager), Frank Murphy, Richard Nugent, Roger Willis, Hakan Havrettin, Mick Bodley, Gary Phillips. Nicky Evans, Mark Flashman, Geoff Cooper, Gary Blackford, Gary Poole, David Tomlinson, Paul Wilson, Andy McDade (Physiotherapist). *Front row:* Mark Carter, Wayne Turner, Paul Richardson, David Howell, Edwin Stein, Stan Flashman (Chairman), Barry Fry (Manager), Tony Lynch, Kenny Lowe, Gary Bull. Duncan Horton, Kevin Durham (deceased).

Division 4   **BARNET**

Underhill Stadium, Barnet Lane, Barnet, Herts EN5 2BE.
Telephone 081-441 6932. Clubcall: 0898 121544.

Ground capacity: 9000.

Record attendance: 11,026 v Wycombe Wanderers. FA Amateur Cup 4th Round 1951–52.

Record Receipts: £31,202 v Portsmouth FA Cup 3rd Round 5th January 1991.

Pitch measurements: 113yd × 73yd.

Chairman: S. Flashman.

Managing Director: T. Hill.

Directors: J. Quill, L. Rose, L. Wise.

Manager: Barry Fry. *Assistant Manager:* Edwin Stein. *Physio:* Andy McDade.

Secretary: Bryan Ayres. *Commercial Manager:* .

Year Formed: 1888. *Turned Professional:* 1965. *Ltd Co:*

Club Nickname: The Bees.
Previous Names: 1906–19 Barnet Alston FC.

Previous Grounds: Queens Road (1888–1901) Totteridge Lane (1901–07).

Record Transfer Fee Received: £350,000 from Wimbledon for Andy Clarke, February 1991.

Record Transfer Fee Paid: £40,000 to Barrow for Kenny Lowe, January 1991 and £40,000 to Runcorn for Mark Carter, February 1991.

Football League Record: Promoted to Division 4 from GMVC 1991.

Honours: FA Amateur Cup Winners 1945–46, GM Vauxhall Conference Winners 1990–91.

FA Cup Best Season: Never past 3rd Round.

Colours: Amber shirts, Black shorts, black stockings.

Change Colours: White shirts, White shorts, White stockings.

Player and Position	Ht	Wt	Birth Date	Birth Place	Source	Clubs	League App	Gls
Goalkeepers								
Gary Phillips	6 0	14 00	20 9 61	St Albans	Barnet	WBA	—	—
						Brentford	143	—
						Reading	24	—
						Hereford U (loan)	6	—
						Barnet	—	—
Defenders								
Mickey Bodley	5 11	12 00	14 9 67	Hayes	Apprentice	Chelsea	6	1
						Northampton T	20	—
						Barnet	—	—
Geoff Cooper	5 10	11 00	27 12 60	Kingston	Bognor Regis	Brighton & H A	7	—
						Barnet	—	—
Gary Poole	6 0	11 00	11 9 67	Stratford	School	Tottenham H	—	—
						Cambridge U	43	—
						Barnet	—	—
Midfield								
Hakan Hayrettin			4 2 70	Enfield	Trainee	Leyton Orient	—	—
						Barnet	—	—
Forwards								
Gary Bull	5 9	11 07	12 6 66	West Bromwich	Southampton	—	—	
						Cambridge U	19	4
						Barnet	—	—
Roger Willis	6 1	11 06	17 6 67	Sheffield		Grimsby T	9	—
						Barnet	—	—

52

BARNSLEY 1990–91 *Back row (left to right)*: Brendan O'Connell, Mark Burton, Andy Saville, Ian Wardle, Phil Whitehead, Clive Baker, Mark Smith, Dean Connelly, Gary Fleming.

Centre row: John Benson (Chief Scout), John Deehan (First Team Coach), Steve Lowndes, Steve Cooper, Colin Hoyle, Carl Tiler, Gerry Taggart, Paul McGugan, Jim Dobbin, Joe Joyce, Eric Winstanley (Youth Team Coach), Mark Nile (Physiotherapist).

Front row: Colin Marshall, Ian Banks, Wayne Beaumont, Paul Cross, Mel Machin (Team Manager), Steve Agnew, Owen Archdeacon, Brian McCord, Mark Robinson.

Division 2   BARNSLEY

Oakwell Ground, Grove St, Barnsley. Telephone Barnsley (0226) 295353. Clubcall: 0898 121152. Commercial Office: 0226 286718. Fax: 0226 201000.

Ground capacity: 27,464 (15,000 under cover).

Record attendance: 40,255 v Stoke C, FA Cup 5th rd, 15 February 1936.

Pitch measurements: 110yd × 75yd.

President: Arthur Raynor. *Vice-presidents: Chairman:* J. A. Dennis.

Directors: C. B. Taylor (Vice-chairman), C. H. Harrison, M. R. Hayselden, R. F. Potter.

Team Manager: Mel Machin.

First Team Coach: John Deehan. *Physio:* Mark Nile.

Secretary: Michael Spinks. *Commercial Manager:* Gerry Whewall.

Year Formed: 1887. *Turned Professional:* 1888. *Ltd Co.:* 1899.

Previous Name: Barnsley St Peter's, 1887–89.

Club Nickname: 'The Tykes', 'Reds' or 'Colliers'.

Record League Victory: 9-0 v Loughborough T, Division 2, 28 January 1899 – Greaves; McCartney, Nixon; Porteous, Burleigh, Howard; Davis (4), Hepworth (1), Lees (1), McCullough (1), Jones (2). 9-0 v Accrington S, Division 3 (N), 3 February 1934 – Ellis; Cookson, Shotton; Harper, Henderson, Whitworth; Spence (2), Smith (1), Blight (4), Andrews (1), Ashton (1).

Record Cup Victory: 6-0 v Blackpool, FA Cup, 1st rd replay, 20 January 1910 – Mearns; Downs, Ness; Glendinning, Boyle (1), Utley; Bartrop, Gadsby (1), Lillycrop (2), Tufnell (2), Forman. 6-0 v Peterborough U, League Cup, 1st rd, 2nd leg, 15 September 1981 – Horn; Joyce, Chambers, Glavin (2), Banks, McCarthy, Evans, Parker (2), Aylott (1), McHale, Barrowclough (1).

Record Defeat: 0-9 v Notts Co, Division 2, 19 November 1927.

Most League Points (2 for a win): 67, Division 3 (N), 1938–39.

Most League Points (3 for a win): 74, Division 2, 1988–89.

Most League Goals: 118, Division 3 (N), 1933–34.

Highest League Scorer in Season: Cecil McCormack, 33, Division 2, 1950–51.

Most League Goals in Total Aggregate: Ernest Hine, 123, 1921–26 and 1934–38.

Most Capped Player: Eddie McMorran, 9 (15), Northern Ireland.

Most League Appearances: Barry Murphy, 514, 1962–78.

Record Transfer Fee Received: £1,400,000 from Nottingham F for Carl Tiler, April 1991.

Record Transfer Fee Paid: £175,000 to Barnet for Phil Gridelet, September 1990.

Football League Record: 1898 Elected to Division 2; 1932–34 Division 3 (N); 1934–38 Division 2; 1938–39 Division 3 (N); 1946–53 Division 2; 1953–55 Division 3 (N); 1955–59 Division 2; 1959–65 Division 3; 1965–68 Division 4; 1968–72 Division 3; 1972–79 Division 4; 1979–81 Division 3; 1981– Division 2.

Honours: Football League: best season: 3rd, Division 2, 1914–15, 1921–22; Division 3 (N) – Champions 1933–34, 1938–39, 1954–55; Runners-up 1953–54; Division 3 – Runners-up 1980–81; Division 4 – Runners-up 1967–68; Promoted 1978–79. *FA Cup:* Winners 1912; Runners-up 1910. *Football League Cup:* best season: 5th rd, 1981–82.

Colours: Red shirts, white trim, white shorts, red stockings. **Change colours:** White shirts, red shorts, white stockings.

BARNSLEY 1990–91 LEAGUE RECORD

Match No.	Date		Venue	Opponents	Result		H/T Score	Lg. Pos.	Goalscorers	Attendance
1	Aug 25		H	Brighton & HA	W	2-1	0-1	—	Cooper, Smith	6865
2	Sept	1	A	Millwall	L	1-4	0-2	14	Banks	10,114
3		8	H	Oldham Ath	L	0-1	0-0	19		11,257
4		15	A	Blackburn R	W	2-1	1-0	16	Saville, Rammell	7665
5		18	A	Notts Co	W	3-2	1-1	—	McCord, Saville, O'Connell	7195
6		22	H	Port Vale	D	1-1	0-1	11	Archdeacon (pen)	8533
7		29	A	Charlton Ath	L	1-2	0-0	14	Rammell	4379
8	Oct	2	H	Ipswich T	W	5-1	3-0	—	Taggart, Archdeacon, Rammell, Agnew, Saville	6930
9		6	H	Oxford U	W	3-0	0-0	7	Rammell, Saville, O'Connell	6776
10		13	A	Portsmouth	D	0-0	0-0	8		8701
11		20	A	WBA	D	1-1	0-0	8	Cooper	9577
12		23	H	Sheffield W	D	1-1	0-0	—	Rammell	23,079
13		27	H	Swindon T	W	5-1	1-0	6	O'Connell, Agnew 2 (1 pen), Rammell 2	7690
14	Nov	3	A	Middlesbrough	L	0-1	0-1	7		18,470
15		7	A	Bristol R	L	1-2	0-1	—	Banks	4563
16		10	H	Leicester C	D	1-1	0-0	9	O'Connell	8581
17		17	A	Newcastle U	D	0-0	0-0	8		15,548
18		24	H	Wolverhampton W	D	1-1	1-1	8	Saville	9267
19	Dec	1	A	Watford	D	0-0	0-0	8		7839
20		15	A	Brighton & HA	L	0-1	0-0	12		5829
21		22	H	West Ham U	W	1-0	1-0	8	Smith	10,348
22		26	A	Plymouth Arg	D	1-1	0-0	10	Rammell	5668
23		29	A	Hull C	W	2-1	0-0	8	Agnew, Deehan	7916
24	Jan	1	H	Bristol C	W	2-0	2-0	6	Rammell, Taggart	8961
25		12	H	Millwall	L	1-2	1-2	7	Agnew	7857
26		19	A	Oldham Ath	L	0-2	0-1	9		13,849
27		23	A	Leicester C	L	1-2	0-0	14	Smith	9027
28		26	H	Bristol R	W	1-0	1-0	—	Saville	6197
29	Mar	2	H	Watford	W	2-1	0-0	10	Saville, Rammell	6755
30		9	A	Wolverhampton W	W	5-0	3-0	10	Saville, Rammell, Stancliffe (og), Robinson, Agnew	15,671
31		16	H	Charlton Ath	D	1-1	0-1	10	O'Connell	6373
32		19	H	Portsmouth	W	4-0	2-0	—	Saville 2, Rimmer, Agnew	4921
33		23	A	Oxford U	L	0-2	0-0	9		4689
34		30	H	Plymouth Arg	W	1-0	1-0	9	Agnew (pen)	6142
35	Apr	1	A	West Ham U	L	2-3	2-0	9	Saville, O'Connell	24,607
36		6	H	Hull C	W	3-1	0-1	9	O'Connell 2, Rammell	6859
37		9	H	Notts Co	W	1-0	1-0	—	O'Connell	9801
38		13	A	Bristol C	L	0-1	0-1	9		12,081
39		15	A	Port Vale	W	1-0	0-0	—	Saville	6939
40		20	H	WBA	D	1-1	0-0	8	Deehan	9593
41		23	H	Blackburn R	L	0-1	0-1	—		8648
42		25	A	Ipswich T	L	0-2	0-1	—		7379
43		27	A	Sheffield W	L	1-3	1-1	9	Smith	30,693
44	May	4	A	Swindon T	W	2-1	2-1	8	Tiler, Smith	9070
45		7	H	Newcastle U	D	1-1	0-1	—	Smith	9543
46		11	H	Middlesbrough	W	1-0	0-0	8	Tiler	14,494

Final League Position: 8

GOALSCORERS

League (63): Rammell 12, Saville 12, O'Connell 9, Agnew 8 (2 pens), Smith 6, Archdeacon 2 (1 pen), Banks 2, Cooper 2, Deehan 2, Taggart 2, Tiler 2, McCord 1, Rimmer 1, Robinson 1, own goal 1.
Rumbelows Cup (1): Cooper 1.
FA Cup (1): Deehan 1.

Baker	Fleming	Taggart	McCord	Joyce	Smith	Banks	Cooper	Saville	Agnew	Archdeacon	Tiler	O'Connell	Robinson	Connelly	Rammell	Dobbin	Gridelet	Marshall	Deehan	Rimmer	Cross	Match No.
1	2	3	4	5	6	7	8	9	10	11												1
1	2	3	4	5		7	8	9*	10	11	6	12										2
1	2	3	4	5*			8	9	10	11	6	12	7									3
1	2	3	4	5			8*	9†		11	6	12	7	10	14							4
1	2*	3	4	5			8†	9	10	11	6	12	7		14							5
1	2†	3	4	5			8	9			6	12	7	10*	14							6
1	2	3	4	5			8†	9	10	11	6	12	7*		14							7
1		3	4	5	2			9	10	11*	6	7	12		8							8
1		3	4	5	2			9	10	11	6	7			8							9
1	5	3	4		2			9	10*	11	6	7		12	8							10
1	5	3	4	2	12	9		11			6	7		10	8*							11
1	5	3	4		2		9		11		6	7		10	8							12
1	5	3*	4	12	2		9	10	11		6	7			8							13
1	5	3	4	2*	12	9	10	11			6	7			8							14
1	5*	3	4		2	12	9	10	11		6	7			8							15
1	5	3	4		2	12	9	10*	11		6	7			8							16
1	5		4	3	2	9†				11	6	7	12	10*		8	14					17
1	5			8*	3	2	9			11	6	7	10		4		12					18
1	5		8	3	2		9*			11	6	7	12		10		4					19
1	5	3	4†		2*		9	10	11		6	7		12	8	14						20
1	4	3		5	2*		9	10	11		6	7		12	8†			14				21
1	4*	3		5	2		9	10	11		6	7			8			12				22
1	4	3		5	2		9	10	11		6	7			8*			12				23
1	4	3		5	2		9	10	11		6	7			8*			12				24
1	3		4†	5*	2		9	10	11		6	7		14	8			12				25
1	3		4*	5	2		9	10	11		6	7			8	12						26
1	4	3		5	2		9	10	11		6	7			8							27
1	4	3		5	2†		9	10	11		6	7	12		8*14							28
1	4	3†		5*	2		9	10	11		6	7			8	14			12			29
1	3		2		5	14		9	10	11	6	7†12			8*			4				30
1	3		2*			14		9	10	11	6	7	12		8			4		5†		31
1	3				2			9	10†11		6	7*	5		8	14		4	12			32
1	3		8†	2*			9	10	11		6	7	5		12	14		4				33
1	3				5			9	10	11	6	7			8	2		4				34
1	3				5			9	10	11	6	7	4		8†	2*		14	12			35
1	3				5			9	10	11	6	7	4*		8	2		12				36
1	3				5			9	10	11	6	7	4		8	2						37
1	4	3*			5			9	10	11	6	7	12		8	2†		14				38
1	3				5			9	10	11	6	7	2		12			8*	4			39
1	3				5			9	10†11		6	7	2*		12	14		8	4			40
1	3		14		5			9		11	6	7	2†		12	10		8*	4			41
1	3	12			5*	2		9	10	11	6	7			8†14			4				42
1	3	12	2†		5	4		9*	10	11	6	7			8			14				43
1	2	3			5	4		9	10	11	6	7			8*			12				44
1	2	3*			5	4		9	10	11	6	7			8			12				45
1	2	3			5	4		9	10		6	7	11		8							46
46	44	28	23	3	36	31	8	45	38	45	45	39	15	5	32	8	1	—	3	10	1	
	+	+			+	+	+						+	+	+	+	+	+	+	+	+	
	2s	1s			1s	2s	4s						6s	7s	4s	8s	6s	3s	1s	8s 5s	1s	

Rumbelows Cup   First Round   Wigan Ath (a)   1-0

                                          (h)   0-1

                Second Round   Aston Villa (a)   0-1

                                          (h)   0-1

FA Cup   Third Round   Leeds U (h)   1-1

                                          (a)   0-4

BARNSLEY

Player and Position	Ht	Wt	Birth Date	Place	Source	Clubs	League App	Gls
Goalkeepers								
Clive Baker	5 9	11 00	14 3 59	N Walsham	Amateur	Norwich C	14	—
						Barnsley	291	—
Phil Whitehead	6 2	13 00	17 12 69	Halifax		Halifax T	42	—
						Barnsley	—	—
						Halifax T (loan)	9	—
Defenders								
Paul Cross	5 7	9 06	31 10 65	Barnsley	Apprentice	Barnsley	115	—
Gary Fleming	5 9	11 07	17 2 67	Londonderry	Apprentice	Nottingham F	74	—
						Manchester C	14	—
						Notts Co (loan)	3	—
						Barnsley	56	—
Brian McCord	5 10	11 06	24 8 68	Derby	Apprentice	Derby Co	5	—
						Barnsley	40	2
Mark Smith	6 2	13 11	21 3 60	Sheffield	Apprentice	Sheffield W	282	16
						Plymouth Arg	82	6
						Barnsley	62	9
Gerry Taggart	6 1	12 03	18 10 70	Belfast	Trainee	Manchester C	12	1
						Barnsley	51	4
Carl Tiler	6 2	13 00	11 2 70	Sheffield	Trainee	Barnsley	71	3
Midfield								
Steve Agnew	5 9	10 06	9 11 65	Shipley	Apprentice	Barnsley	194	29
Ian Banks	5 11	12 12	9 1 61	Mexborough	Apprentice	Barnsley	164	37
						Leicester C	93	14
						Huddersfield T	78	17
						Bradford C	30	3
						WBA	4	—
						Barnsley	70	5
Wayne Bullimore	5 9	10 06	12 9 70	Sutton-in-Ashfield	Trainee	Manchester U	—	—
						Barnsley	—	—
Dino Connelly	5 9	10 08	6 1 70	Glasgow	Trainee	Arsenal	—	—
						Barnsley	9	—
Jim Dobbin	5 10	10 06	17 9 61	Dunfermline	Whitburn BC	Celtic	2	—
						Motherwell (loan)	2	—
						Doncaster R	64	13
						Barnsley	129	12
Phil Gridelet	5 11	12 00	30 4 67	Edgware	Barnet	Barnsley	4	—
Colin Marshall	5 5	9 05	1 11 69	Glasgow	Trainee	Barnsley	4	—
Mark Robinson	5 9	11 08	21 11 68	Manchester	Trainee	WBA	2	—
						Barnsley	67	3
Forwards								
Owen Archdeacon	5 7	11 00	4 3 66	Greenock	Gourock U	Celtic	76	7
						Barnsley	66	5
John Deehan	5 11	13 00	8 8 57	Solihull	Apprentice	Aston Villa	110	42
						WBA	47	5
						Norwich C	162	62
						Ipswich T	49	11
						Manchester C	—	—
						Barnsley	11	2
Colin Hoyle	5 11	12 03	15 1 72	Derby	Trainee	Arsenal	—	—
						Chesterfield (loan)	3	—
						Barnsley	—	—
Brendan O'Connell	5 10	10 09	12 11 66	London		Portsmouth		
						Exeter C	81	19
						Burnley	64	17
						Huddersfield T (loan)	11	1
						Barnsley	56	11

BARNSLEY

Foundation: Many clubs owe their inception to the church and Barnsley are among them, for they were formed in 1887 by the Rev. T. T. Preedy, curate of Barnsley St. Peter's and went under that name until a year after being admitted to the Second Division of the Football League in 1898.

First Football League game: 1 September, 1898, Division 2, v Lincoln C (a) L 0-1 – Fawcett; McArtney, Nixon; King, Burleigh, Porteous; Davis, Lees, Murray, McCullough, McGee.

Did you know: First elected to the Football League as members of the Second Division in 1898 Barnsley have completed more seasons in this Division than any other club. Their total is 55.

Managers (and Secretary-managers)
Arthur Fairclough 1898–1901*, John McCartney 1901–04*, Arthur Fairclough 1904–12, John Hastie 1912–14, Percy Lewis 1914–19, Peter Sant 1919–26, John Commins 1926–29, Arthur Fairclough 1929–30, Brough Fletcher 1930–37, Angus Seed 1937–53, Tim Ward 1953–60, Johnny Steele 1960–71 (continued as GM), John McSeveney 1971–72, Johnny Steele (GM) 1972–73, Jim Iley 1973–78, Allan Clarke 1978–80, Norman Hunter 1980–84, Bobby Collins 1984–85, Allan Clarke 1985–89, Mel Machin December 1989–   .

Player and Position	Ht	Wt	Birth Date	Place	Source	Clubs	League App	Gls
Andy Rammell	5 10	11 07	10 2 67	Nuneaton	Atherstone U	Manchester U	—	—
						Barnsley	40	12
Stuart Rimmer	5 7	9 04	12 10 64	Southport	Apprentice	Everton	3	—
						Chester C	114	67
						Watford	10	1
						Notts Co	4	2
						Walsall	88	31
						Barnsley	15	1
Andrew Saville	6 0	12 00	12 12 64	Hull	Local	Hull C	100	18
						Walsall	38	5
						Barnsley	60	15

Trainees
Burton, Mark A; Degnan, Lee A; Eaton, Barry; Firth, Lee; Hodgkinson, Neil A; Jackson, Michael; Liddell, Andrew M; Mercer, Mark S; Monaghan, Andrew; Morgan, Gregory D; Watson, David N; Wilkinson, Allan D; Winks, Corrie D.

Associated Schoolboys
Allison, Richard; Bennett, Troy; Bochenski, Simon; Brooke, David; Craft, Adrian; Dobson, Stephen P; Driver, Christopher; Fearon, Dean A; Gregory, Andrew; Guest, Ashley C; Hanby, Robert J; Jackson, Christopher D; Jebson, Carl M; Lumb, Richard M; Newsam, Andrew; Peacock, Dennis; Pettinger, Paul A; Shelley, Steven; Skelton, Ian S; Standish, Mark A; Walker, Allan; Widdowson, Steven; Yates, Kevin; Young, Shaun S.

BIRMINGHAM CITY 1990–91 *Back row (left to right):* Michael Burton, Mark Rutherford, John Deakin, Dennis Bailey, Greg Downs, Paul Tait, Andrew Harris, John Frain, Kevin Ashley.
Centre row: Dean Peer, Paul Masefield, Ian Clarkson, Simon Sturridge, Sean Francis, Nigel Gleghorn, Mark Yates, Matthew Fox.
Front row: Robert Hopkins, Doug Bell, Kevin Langley, Dean Williams, Trevor Matthewson, Martin Thomas, Phil Sproson, Vince Overson, Colin Gordon.

Division 3   BIRMINGHAM CITY

St Andrews, Birmingham B9 4NH. Telephone 021-772 0101/ 2689. Lottery office/Souvenir shop: 021 772 1245. Clubcall: 0898 121188. Fax: 021 766 7866. Club Soccer Shop: 021 766 8274.

Ground capacity: 26,113.

Record attendance: 66,844 v Everton, FA Cup 5th rd, 11 February 1939.

Record receipts: £116,372.50 v Nottingham Forest, FA Cup 5th rd, 20 February 1988.

Pitch measurements: 115yd × 75yd.

Directors: S. Kumar BA (Chairman), R. Kumar BSC (Vice-chairman), J. F. Wiseman, T. W. J. Edmonds, B. Kumar MSC.

General Manager: E. Partridge.

Manager: *. Physio:*   *. Commercial Manager:* Joan Hill.

Secretary: H. J. Westmancoat FFA, MBIM.

Year Formed: 1875. *Turned Professional:* 1885. *Ltd Co.:* 1888.

Previous Names: 1875–88, Small Heath Alliance; 1888, dropped 'Alliance'; became Birmingham 1905; became Birmingham City 1945.

Club Nickname: 'Blues'.

Previous Grounds: 1875, waste ground near Arthur St; 1877, Muntz St, Small Heath; 1906, St Andrews.

Record League Victory: 12-0 v Walsall T Swifts, Division 2, 17 December 1892 – Charnley; Bayley, Jones; Ollis, Jenkyns, Devey; Hallam (2), Walton (3), Mobley (3), Wheldon (2), Hands (2). 12-0 v Doncaster R, Division 2, 11 April 1903 – Dorrington; Goldie, Wassell; Beer, Dougherty (1), Howard; Athersmith (1), Leonard (3), McRoberts (1), Wilcox (4), Field (1). Aston. (1 og).

Record Cup Victory: 9-2 v Burton W, FA Cup, 1st rd, 31 October 1885 – Hedges; Jones, Evetts (1); F. James, Felton, A. James (1); Davenport (2), Stanley (4), Simms, Figures, Morris (1).

Record Defeat: 1-9 v Sheffield W, Division 1, 13 December 1930 and v Blackburn R, Division 1, 5 January 1895.

Most League Points (2 for a win): 59, Division 2, 1947–48.

Most League Points (3 for a win): 82, Division 2, 1984–85.

Most League Goals: 103, Division 2, 1893–94 (only 28 games).

Highest League Scorer in Season: Joe Bradford, 29, Division 1, 1927–28.

Most League Goals in Total Aggregate: Joe Bradford, 249, 1920–35.

Most Capped Player: Malcolm Page, 28, Wales.

Most League Appearances: Frank Womack, 491, 1908–28.

Record Transfer Fee Received: £975,000 from Nottingham F for Trevor Francis, February 1979.

Record Transfer Fee Paid: £350,000 to Derby Co for David Langan, June 1980.

Football League Record: 1892 elected to Division 2; 1894–96 Division 1; 1896–1901 Division 2; 1901–02 Division 1; 1902–03 Division 2; 1903–08 Division 1; 1908–21 Division 2; 1921–39 Division 1; 1946–48 Division 2; 1948–50 Division 1; 1950–1955 Division 2; 1955–65 Division 1; 1965–72 Division 2; 1972–79 Division 1; 1979–80 Division 2; 1980–84 Division 1; 1984–1985 Division 2; 1985–86 Division 1; 1986–89 Division 2; 1989– Division 3.

Honours: Football League: Division 1 best season: 6th, 1955–56; Division 2 – Champions 1892–93, 1920–21, 1947–48, 1954–55; Runners-up 1893–94, 1900–01, 1902–03, 1971–72, 1984–85. *FA Cup:* Runners-up 1931, 1956. *Football League Cup:* Winners 1963. *Leyland Daf Cup:* Winners 1991. **European Competitions:** *European Fairs Cup:* 1955–58, 1958–60 (runners-up), 1960–61 (runners-up), 1961–62.

Colours: Royal blue shirts, white shorts, blue stockings with white trim. **Change colours:** All yellow.

BIRMINGHAM CITY 1990–91 LEAGUE RECORD

Match No.	Date	Venue	Opponents	Result	H/T Score	Lg. Pos.	Goalscorers	Atten- dance
1	Aug 25	A	Cambridge U	W 1-0	0-0	—	Gleghorn	6338
2	Sept 1	H	Leyton Orient	W 3-1	2-0	3	Bailey, Hopkins, Moran	5847
3	8	A	Stoke C	W 1-0	0-0	2	Gleghorn	16,009
4	15	H	Bury	W 1-0	0-0	2	Peer	7344
5	18	H	Exeter C	D 1-1	1-0	—	Bailey	7703
6	22	A	Wigan Ath	D 1-1	0-0	3	Tait	3907
7	29	H	Preston NE	D 1-1	0-0	3	Bailey	7154
8	Oct 2	A	Fulham	D 2-2	2-1	—	Matthewson, Overson	4011
9	6	A	Reading	D 2-2	1-2	5	Matthewson, Sturridge	5695
10	13	H	Southend U	D 1-1	0-0	5	Sturridge	9333
11	20	H	Grimsby T	D 0-0	0-0	4		10,123
12	23	A	Crewe Alex	D 1-1	1-0	—	Gleghorn	4449
13	27	A	Shrewsbury T	L 1-4	0-2	7	Bailey	6050
14	Nov 3	H	Huddersfield T	L 1-2	0-1	11	Tait	7412
15	10	A	Chester C	W 1-0	0-0	8	Hopkins	2273
16	24	H	Bournemouth	D 0-0	0-0	10		7416
17	Dec 1	A	Swansea C	L 0-2	0-2	14		4896
18	15	H	Rotherham U	W 2-1	1-0	11	Tait, Overson	4734
19	21	A	Tranmere R	L 0-1	0-1	—		5034
20	26	H	Brentford	L 0-2	0-0	15		6612
21	29	H	Bolton W	L 1-3	0-0	16	Bailey	7318
22	Jan 1	A	Mansfield T	W 2-1	0-0	15	Gayle 2	3652
23	5	H	Bradford C	D 1-1	1-0	14	Frain (pen)	6315
24	12	A	Leyton Orient	D 1-1	0-1	14	Sturridge	4708
25	19	H	Cambridge U	L 0-3	0-2	15		5859
26	26	A	Bury	W 1-0	0-0	14	Sturridge	3009
27	Feb 2	A	Exeter C	W 2-0	0-0	12	Gayle 2	5154
28	5	H	Wigan Ath	D 0-0	0-0	—		5319
29	13	A	Bradford C	L 0-2	0-0	—		4776
30	16	A	Bournemouth	W 2-1	1-0	10	Sturridge, Mundee (og)	6330
31	23	H	Chester C	W 1-0	0-0	8	Dolan	6702
32	Mar 2	H	Swansea C	W 2-0	0-0	6	Sturridge, Rodgerson	6903
33	9	A	Rotherham U	D 1-1	0-1	8	Frain (pen)	5015
34	12	H	Fulham	W 2-0	1-0	—	Peer, Gleghorn	8083
35	16	A	Preston NE	L 0-2	0-1	10		5334
36	18	A	Southend U	L 1-2	1-0	—	Gleghorn	6328
37	23	H	Reading	D 1-1	1-0	11	Rodgerson	6795
38	30	A	Brentford	D 2-2	1-2	12	Frain, Gleghorn	6757
39	Apr 2	H	Tranmere R	W 1-0	0-0	—	Yates	7675
40	7	A	Bolton W	L 1-3	1-2	—	Gayle	11,280
41	13	H	Mansfield T	D 0-0	0-0	12		7635
42	16	H	Stoke C	W 2-1	2-1	—	Matthewson, Hopkins	6729
43	20	A	Grimsby T	D 0-0	0-0	11		8842
44	27	H	Crewe Alex	L 0-2	0-1	11		6429
45	May 4	H	Shrewsbury T	L 0-1	0-1	13		6256
46	11	A	Huddersfield T	W 1-0	0-0	12	Gayle	5195

Final League Position: 12

GOALSCORERS

League (45): Gayle 6, Gleghorn 6, Sturridge 6, Bailey 5, Frain 3 (2 pens), Hopkins 3, Matthewson 3, Tait 3, Overson 2, Peer 2, Rodgerson 2, Dolan 1, Moran 1, Yates 1, own goal 1.
Rumbelows Cup (1): Downs 1 (pen).
FA Cup (2): Aylott 1, Sturridge 1.

Thomas	Ashley	Downs	Frain	Overson	Matthewson	Peer	Bailey	Hopkins	Gleghorn	Tait	Sturridge	Fox	Moran	Clarkson	Rutherford	Aylott	Gordon	Gayle	Rodgerson	Dolan	Francis	Bell	Yates	O'Reilly	Robinson	Williams	Match No.
1	2	3	4	5	6	7	8	9	10	11*	12																1
1	2	3	4		6	7	8	9†	10	11*	12	5	14														2
1	2	3	4		6	7	8		10	11	12	5				9*											3
1		3	4	5	6	7	8		10	11	12			2		9*											4
1	3†	4			6	7	8	12	10	11			14	2		9*											5
1			4	5	3		8	7	10	11	12	9*		2		6											6
1	12	4	5	3	7	8	9		11				6	2		10*											7
1	10	4	5	3	7	8		11	9*	6	12			2													8
1			4	5	3	7	8	11	10			9		2													9
1			4	5	3	7	8	11	10			9		2													10
1			4	5	3	7	8	2	10	11*	9	12															11
1			4	5	3	7*	12	2	10	11	8					9											12
1	4		5	3	12	7	10	11†	8	6		2*	14			9											13
1	3*		5	6	7	12	2	10	11	8						9											14
1*	3	4	5	6	7	8	2	10	11		12					9											15
1	3	4	5	6	7	8	2*	10	11		12							9									16
1	3	4	5	6	7*	12	10	11			2					9		8									17
1	3†	4	5	6	14	12	10	11			2					9		8*	7								18
1		3	5	6	7*	8	10	11			2					9		12	4								19
1		3	5	6	7*	8	10	11	14		2†					9		12	4								20
1		4	5	3	7	12	10		11	6						9*		8	2								21
1		4	5	3	7	8	10			6						9		2	11								22
1		4	5	3	7	8*	10		12	6						9		2	11								23
1		4	5	3			10	7*	8	6	12					9		2	11								24
1		4	5	3	14		10	8	6*		2†					9			7	11	12						25
1		3	5	6	7	4	10	11								9		8	2								26
1			6	7	4	3	10	11		5						9		8	2								27
1			6	7	4	3	10	11		5						9†		8*	2	14	12						28
1		5	6	7	8	4*	10	11		3						9		2		12							29
1		3	5	6	7	8*	10	11			2					9		4	12								30
1		3	5	6	7		10	11			2					9		4	8								31
1		3	5	6	7*	12	10	11			2					9†		8	4	14							32
1		3	5	6	7	12	10	11			2					9†		8	4*	14							33
1		3	5	6	7	4	10	11			2					9		8									34
1		3	5	6	7	9	10*	11			12	2				8						4					35
1		3	5	6	7	11	10		12	2				9*		8						4					36
1		3	5	6	7		10	11	12	2						8*	9					4					37
1		3	5	6			10	11		2		12	9*			7	14						4†	8			38
1		3	5	6	7		10	11						9		2		4	8								39
1		3	5	6	7			11		10	12		8	3		2*	4							9			40
1		3	5	6	7	12	10	11		2						8†		4*	14						9		41
1		3	5	6		11	10			2				8*	12	7							4		9		42
1		3		6	7	12	11	10		2				8*		4							5		9		43
		3		6	7		11		10	2				8	12	4							5*		9	1	44
1		3	5†	6	14	12		11	10	2				8*		7	4								9		45
1		3	5	6	4			11	10	2						7							8		9		46
45	3	16	42	40	46	37	25	18	42	17	33	9	2	34	1	23	3	20	25	5	—	1	8	1	9	1	
	+					+	+	+						+	+	+	+	+	+	+	+	+	+		+		
	1s					3s	7s	5s						5s	2s	6s	3s	2s	2s	2s	2s	5s	3s		1s		

Rumbelows Cup First Round — Bournemouth (h) — 0-1

(a) — 1-1

FA Cup First Round — Cheltenham T (h) — 1-0

Second Round — Brentford (h) — 1-3

BIRMINGHAM CITY

Player and Position	Ht	Wt	Birth Date	Birth Place	Source	Clubs	League App	Gls
Goalkeepers								
Martin Thomas	6 1	13 00	28 11 59	Senghennydd	Apprentice	Bristol R	162	—
						Cardiff C (loan)	15	—
						Tottenham H (loan)	—	—
						Southend U (loan)	6	—
						Newcastle U (loan)	3	—
						Newcastle U	115	
						Middlesbrough (loan)	4	—
						Birmingham C	123	—
Dean Williams	6 0	11 07	5 1 72	Lichfield	Trainee	Birmingham C	4	
Defenders								
Ian Clarkson	5 11	12 00	4 12 70	Birmingham	Trainee	Birmingham C	66	—
Greg Downs	5 9	10 07	13 12 58	Carlton	Apprentice	Norwich C	169	7
						Torquay U (loan)	1	1
						Coventry C	146	4
						Birmingham C	17	—
Matthew Fox	6 0	13 00	13 7 71	Birmingham	Trainee	Birmingham C	14	—
Nigel Larkins			6 4 72	Burton-on-Trent	Trainee	Birmingham C	—	—
Paul Masefield	5 11	12 08	21 10 70	Birmingham	Trainee	Birmingham C	—	—
Trevor Matthewson	6 1	12 05	12 2 63	Sheffield	Apprentice	Sheffield W	3	—
						Newport Co	75	—
						Stockport Co	80	—
						Lincoln C	43	2
						Birmingham C	92	4
Vince Overson	6 0	13 00	15 5 62	Kettering	Apprentice	Burnley	211	6
						Birmingham C	182	3
Dean Peer	6 2	12 00	8 8 69	Dudley	Trainee	Birmingham C	86	6
Ian Rodgerson	5 8	11 05	9 4 66	Hereford	Local	Hereford U	100	6
						Cardiff C	99	4
						Birmingham C	25	2
Phil Sproson‡	6 0	12 00	13 10 59	Trent Vale	Amateur	Port Vale	426	33
						Birmingham C	12	—
Midfield								
Ian Atkins‡	6 0	12 03	16 1 57	Birmingham	Apprentice	Shrewsbury T	278	58
						Sunderland	77	6
						Everton	7	1
						Ipswich T	77	4
						Birmingham C	93	6
Doug Bell‡	5 11	12 01	5 9 59	Paisley	Cumbernauld	St Mirren	2	1
						Aberdeen	108	6
						Rangers	35	1
						St Mirren (loan)	4	—
						Hibernian	32	3
						Shrewsbury T	50	6
						Hull C (loan)	4	—
						Birmingham C	16	—
John Deakin*	5 8	10 08	29 6 66	Sheffield	Barnsley Apprentice	Doncaster R	23	—
						Grimsby T	—	—
					Shepshed C	Birmingham C	7	—
John Frain	5 7	11 10	8 10 68	Birmingham	Apprentice	Birmingham C	128	10
Andrew Harris	5 10	12 02	17 11 70	Birmingham	Trainee	Birmingham C	1	—
Robert Hopkins*	5 7	10 05	25 10 61	Birmingham	Apprentice	Aston Villa	3	1
						Birmingham C	123	21
						Manchester C	7	1
						WBA	83	11
						Birmingham C	50	9
Forwards								
Trevor Aylott	6 1	14 00	26 11 57	London	Apprentice	Chelsea	29	2
						QPR (loan)	—	—
						Barnsley	96	26
						Millwall	32	5
						Luton T	32	10
						Crystal Palace	53	12
						Barnsley (loan)	9	—
						Bournemouth	147	27
						Birmingham C	25	—

BIRMINGHAM CITY

Foundation: In 1875 cricketing enthusiasts who were largely members of Trinity Church, Bordesley, determined to continue their sporting relationships throughout the year by forming a football club which they called Small Heath Alliance. For their earliest games played on waste land in Arthur Street, the team included three Edden brothers and two James brothers.

First Football League game: 3 September, 1892, Division 2, v Burslem Port Vale (h) W5-1 – Charsley; Bayley, Speller; Ollis, Jenkyns, Devey; Hallam (1), Edwards (1), Short (1), Wheldon (2), Hands.

Did you know: Over 34 years have elapsed since a Birmingham City player scored a hat-trick in an FA Cup tie. On that occasion Alex Govan scored three goals in a 6-1 4th Round victory at Southend United.

Managers (and Secretary-managers)
Alfred Jones 1892–1908*, Alec Watson 1908–1910, Bob McRoberts 1910–15, Frank chRichards 1915–23, Bill Beer 1923–27, Leslie Knighton 1928–33, George Liddell 1933–39, Harry Storer 1945–48, Bob Brocklebank 1949–54, Arthur Turner 1954–58, Pat Beasley 1959–60, Gil Merrick 1960–64, Joe Mallett 1965, Stan Cullis 1965–70, Fred Goodwin 1970–75, Willie Bell 1975–77, Jim Smith 1978–82, Ron Saunders 1982–86, John Bond 1986–87, Garry Pendrey 1987–89, Dave Mackay 1989–1991, Lou Macari 1991.

Player and Position	Ht	Wt	Birth Date	Birth Place	Source	Clubs	League App	Gls
Dennis Bailey	6 0	11 01	13 11 65	Lambeth		Fulham	—	—
					Farnborough	Crystal Palace	5	1
						Bristol R (loan)	17	9
						Birmingham C	75	23
						Bristol R (loan)	6	1
Eamonn Dolan	5 10	12 03	20 9 67	Dagenham	Apprentice	West Ham U	15	3
						Bristol C (loan)	3	—
						Birmingham C	10	1
Sean Francis	5 10	11 09	1 8 72	Birmingham	Trainee	Birmingham C	3	—
John Gayle	6 4	13 01	30 7 64	Birmingham	Burton Albion	Wimbledon	20	2
						Birmingham C	22	6
Nigel Gleghorn	6 0	12 13	12 8 62	Seaham	Seaham Red Star	Ipswich T	66	11
						Manchester C	34	7
						Birmingham C	85	15
Colin Gordon	6 1	12 12	17 1 63	Stourbridge	Oldbury U	Swindon T	72	33
						Wimbledon	3	—
						Gillingham (loan)	4	2
						Reading	24	9
						Bristol C (loan)	8	4
						Fulham	17	2
						Birmingham C	26	3
						Hereford U (loan)	6	—
						Walsall (loan)	6	1
						Bristol R (loan)	4	—
Richie Moran‡			9 9 63	Maidstone	Fujita	Birmingham C	8	1
Mark Rutherford	5 11	11 00	25 3 72	Birmingham	Trainee	Birmingham C	5	
Simon Sturridge	5 8	10 00	9 12 69	Birmingham	Trainee	Birmingham C	90	19
Paul Tait	6 1	10 00	31 7 71	Sutton Coldfield	Trainee	Birmingham C	42	5
Mark Yates	5 11	11 09	24 1 70	Birmingham	Trainee	Birmingham C	52	6

Trainees
Adams, Carl A; Bignot, Marcus; Brown, Steven M; Casemore, Craig P; Coogan, Mark A; Dale, Andrew J; Devery, Brendon J; Duffy, Paul J; Foy, David L; Gray, Brian S; Green, Andrew P; Halford, John D; Higgins, Matthew P; Jones, Paul T; Naylor, Richard J; O'Connor, David W.P; Powell, Mark; Shevlin, Tomas; Wall, Mario K; Williams, Richard J.

**Non-Contract
Harrison, Mark

Associated Schoolboys
Black, Simon A; Bunch, James; Cooper, Kevin J; Cross, Robert B; Griffiths, Terence J; Hiles, Paul; Lewis, Craig S; Lucas, Jay; Palmer, Daniel S; Steadman, Richard D; Webb, Matthew; Weston, Richard.

Associated Schoolboys who have accepted the club's offer of a Traineeship/Contract
Aston, David E; Baker, Lewis M; McKeever, Scott J; Potter, Graham S; Robinson, Steven E; Scott, Richard P; Wratten, Adam P.

**Non-Contract Players who are retained must be re-signed before they are eligible to play in League matches.

BLACKBURN ROVERS 1990-91 *Back row (left to right):* Lee Richardson, Mark Atkins, Lee Gillespie, Terry Gennoe, Darren Collier, David May, Darren Donnelly.
Centre row: Jack Cunningham (Physiotherapist), Jim Furnell (Reserve/Youth Team Manager), Howard Gayle, Jason Wilcox, Craig Skinner, Keith Hill, Kevin Moran, Mike Duxbury, Neil Oliver, Lenny Johnrose, David Hall (Youth Team Coach), Sammy Chung (Chief Scout).
Front row: Paul Shepstone, Scott Sellars, Don Mackay (Manager), John Millar, Nicky Reid, Frank Stapleton, Chris Sulley, Tony Parkes (Assistant Manager), Alan Irvine, Simon Garner.

Division 2   BLACKBURN ROVERS

Ewood Park, Blackburn BB2 4JF. Telephone Blackburn (0254) 55432.

Ground capacity: 19,440.

Record attendance: 61,783 v Bolton W, FA Cup 6th rd, 2 March, 1929.

Record receipts: £85,510 v Liverpool, FA Cup 3rd rd, 5 January, 1991.

Pitch measurements: 115yd × 76yd.

Chairman: W. Fox. *Vice-chairman:* R. D. Coar BSC.

Directors: T. W. Ibbotson LLB, K. C. Lee, I. R. Stanners, G. R. Root FCMA.

Manager: Donald Mackay. *Assistant Manager:* Tony Parkes. *Reserve Team Manager:* Jim Furnell.

Physio: Jack Cunningham.

Commercial Manager: Ken Beamish.

Secretary: John W. Howarth FAAI.

Year Formed: 1875. *Turned Professional:* 1880. *Ltd Co.:* 1897.

Previous Name: Blackburn Grammar School OB.

Club Nickname: 'Blue and Whites'.

Previous Grounds: 1875, Brookhouse Ground; 1876, Alexandra Meadows; 1881, Leamington Road; 1890, Ewood Park.

Record League Victory: 9-0 v Middlesbrough, Division 2, 6 November 1954 – Elvy; Suart, Eckersley; Clayton, Kelly, Bell; Mooney (3), Crossan (2), Briggs, Quigley (3), Langton (1).

Record Cup Victory: 11-0 v Rossendale, FA Cup 1st rd, 13 October 1884 – Arthur; Hopwood, McIntyre; Forrest, Blenkhorn, Lofthouse; Sowerbutts (2), J. Brown (1), Fecitt (4), Barton (3), Birtwistle (1).

Record Defeat: 0-8 v Arsenal, Division 1, 25 February 1933.

Most League Points (2 for a win): 60, Division 3, 1974–75.

Most League Points (3 for a win): 77, Division 2, 1987–88, 1988–89.

Most League Goals: 114, Division 2, 1954–55.

Highest League Scorer in Season: Ted Harper, 43, Division 1, 1925–26.

Most League Goals in Total Aggregate: Simon Garner, 163, 1978–91.

Most Capped Player: Bob Crompton, 41, England.

Most League Appearances: Derek Fazackerley, 596, 1970–86.

Record Transfer Fee Received: £600,000 from Manchester C for Colin Hendry, November 1989.

Record Transfer Fee Paid: £700,000 to Barnsley for Steve Agnew, July 1991.

Football League Record: 1888 Founder Member of the League; 1936–39 Division 2; 1946–47 Division 1; 1947–57 Division 2; 1957–66 Division 1; 1966–71 Division 2; 1971–75 Division 3; 1975–79 Division 2; 1979–80 Division 3; 1980– Division 2.

Honours: Football League: Division 1 – Champions 1911–12, 1913–14; Division 2 – Champions 1938–39; Runners-up 1957–58; Division 3 – Champions 1974–75; Runners-up 1979–80. *FA Cup:* Winners 1884, 1885, 1886, 1890, 1891, 1928; Runners-up 1882, 1960. *Football League Cup:* Semi-final 1961–62. *Full Members' Cup:* Winners 1986–87.

Colours: Blue and white halved shirts, white shorts, blue stockings. **Change colours:** Yellow shirts, blue stripe, yellow shorts, blue stripe, yellow stockings.

BLACKBURN ROVERS 1990–91 LEAGUE RECORD

Match No.	Date	Venue	Opponents	Result		H/T Score	Lg. Pos.	Goalscorers	Attendance
1	Aug 25	A	Bristol C	L	2-4	1-0	—	Gayle 2	13,755
2	28	H	Hull C	W	2-1	1-0	—	Stapleton, Gayle	7337
3	Sept 1	H	Newcastle U	L	0-1	0-0	13		11,329
4	8	A	Ipswich T	L	1-2	1-0	18	Richardson	10,953
5	15	H	Barnsley	L	1-2	0-1	19	Stapleton	7665
6	18	H	Leicester C	W	4-1	1-0	—	Irvine, Atkins, Reid, Starbuck	6520
7	22	A	Portsmouth	L	2-3	0-1	17	Hill, Johnrose	7801
8	29	H	Brighton & HA	L	1-2	1-1	19	Johnrose	6027
9	Oct 3	A	Bristol R	W	2-1	0-1	—	Johnrose, Reid	5200
10	6	A	Oldham Ath	D	1-1	0-1	16	Johnrose	12,093
11	13	H	Watford	L	0-2	0-1	19		7060
12	20	H	Plymouth Arg	D	0-0	0-0	20		6267
13	24	A	West Ham U	L	0-1	0-1	—		20,003
14	27	A	Wolverhampton W	W	3-2	2-0	19	Stapleton 3	17,776
15	Nov 3	H	Millwall	W	1-0	0-0	17	Johnrose	7336
16	10	H	Sheffield W	W	1-0	1-0	12	Hill	13,437
17	17	A	WBA	L	0-2	0-1	16		6985
18	23	H	Port Vale	D	1-1	0-0	—	Johnrose	8061
19	Dec 1	A	Swindon T	D	1-1	0-1	14	Stapleton	8091
20	8	A	Hull C	L	1-3	0-2	16	Atkins	4166
21	15	H	Bristol C	L	0-1	0-0	16		7072
22	22	A	Middlesbrough	W	1-0	0-1	16	Moran (pen)	17,206
23	26	H	Notts Co	L	0-1	0-1	17		8648
24	29	H	Oxford U	L	1-3	0-1	18	Johnrose	6428
25	Jan 1	A	Charlton Ath	D	0-0	0-0	19		5558
26	12	A	Newcastle U	L	0-1	0-0	20		16,382
27	19	H	Ipswich T	L	0-1	0-0	21		8256
28	26	A	Leicester C	W	3-1	1-1	18	Livingstone, Gayle, Sulley (pen)	8167
29	Feb 9	H	Portsmouth	D	1-1	0-1	19	Sulley (pen)	7348
30	16	H	WBA	L	0-3	0-2	19		7695
31	Mar 2	H	Swindon T	W	2-1	1-0	21	Garner, Livingstone	6506
32	9	A	Port Vale	L	0-3	0-2	21		7004
33	12	H	Bristol R	D	2-2	1-0	—	Livingstone, Stapleton	5969
34	16	A	Brighton & HA	L	0-1	0-0	22		6468
35	19	A	Watford	W	3-0	1-0	—	Livingstone 2, Stapleton	6913
36	23	H	Oldham Ath	W	2-0	0-0	19	Livingstone 2	12,175
37	30	A	Notts Co	L	1-4	0-1	19	Stapleton	6831
38	Apr 1	H	Middlesbrough	W	1-0	0-0	18	Shepstone	8925
39	6	A	Oxford U	D	0-0	0-0	17		4767
40	10	A	Sheffield W	L	1-3	1-0	—	Irvine	23,139
41	13	H	Charlton Ath	D	2-2	2-1	19	Atkins, Livingstone	6714
42	20	A	Plymouth Arg	L	1-4	0-4	21	Stapleton	5122
43	23	A	Barnsley	W	1-0	1-0	—	Sulley	8648
44	27	H	West Ham U	W	3-1	3-1	17	Richardson, Atkins, Sellars	10,808
45	May 4	H	Wolverhampton W	D	1-1	1-1	18	Livingstone	9560
46	11	A	Millwall	L	1-2	1-1	19	May	11,318

Final League Position: 19

GOALSCORERS

League (51): Stapleton 10, Livingstone 9, Johnrose 7, Atkins 4, Gayle 4, Sulley 3 (2 pens), Hill 2, Irvine 2, Reid 2, Richardson 2, Garner 1, May 1, Moran 1 (pen), Sellars 1, Shepstone 1, Starbuck 1.
Rumbelows Cup (3): Hill 1, Johnrose 1, Stapleton 1.
FA Cup (1): Garner 1.

Gennoe	Atkins	Sulley	Irvine	Hill	Moran	Richardson	Millar	Stapleton	Shepstone	Gayle	Johnrose	Oliver	Collier	Reid	Dewhurst	Starbuck	Wilcox	Duxbury	Grew	Beglin	Garner	Gallacher	May	Skinner	Mimms	Sellars	Dobson	Livingstone	Match No.
1	2	3†	4	5	6	7	8	9	10*	11	12		14																1
	2	3	7	5		10	8	9*		11	12			1	4	6													2
	2	3		5	6	10	8*	9	12	7	11			1	4														3
	2	3		5		10	8	6	7*	12				1	4		9	11											4
	2			5	6	7	8	9		12				1	4		10	11	3*										5
	2		7	5	6	8	3	9						1	4		10	11											6
	2		7	5	6	8	3	9		12				1	4		10*	11											7
	2		7		6	8†	3		12			9		1	4	5	10	11*	14										8
	2		7		6	8	9		10					1	4	5	11	3											9
	2		7		6	12	8	9		10				1	4	5	14	11†	3*										10
			7		6	8	9		10						4	5	11	2	1	3									11
14			7†	6		8	9	12							4	5	11*	2	1	3	10								12
11			6	12	8	9		7							4	5	2*	1	3	10									13
11		5	6		8	9		7	12						4	14	2†	1	3	10*									14
11		5	6	14	8	9		7†	12	2					4		1	3	10*										15
11	14	5	6	4*	8	9	12	7†	10						2		1	3											16
11	12	5	6*	4	8	9		7	10						2		1		3										17
11	10	5		4	8	9		7	12	1						6*		3	2										18
11	10	5	6	4	8	9	12	7*		2†					1		14	3											19
2	11†	5	6	4	8	9		7	12	14					1		10*	3											20
2	3	5	6	7†	8	9	12		10	4					11*	1			14										21
2	3	5	6*	14		8		9	4	11	10†	12		1		7													22
2	3	5†	14		8	7	12	4	6*	11	10			1		9													23
2	3	5		9	8	7	12	4	6	11				1		10*													24
2	3		6	12	8	9	11	7*	10		4	5			1														25
2*			6	8	9	12	4	3		10													5	7	1	11			26
2	3*		8	7		4	10	5	12																1	11	6	9	27
2	3		8	7		4	10	5																	1	11	6	9	28
2	3	12	8	7*		4	10	5																	1	11	6	9	29
2	3	12	5*	8†	7	14	4		11	10															1	6	9		30
2†	3	11	14	4		8	7	12	10*										6					1	5	9			31
	3	11†	14	4	10	8	7	12	2										5	1				6	9*				32
	3†	14	4	11	10	8	7*	12	2										5	1				6	9				33
14		3	4	8	10	11	12	2†											5	1				6	9*				34
14		3	4	8	10	11	12	2†											5	1				6	9				35
14	3	6	4†	8	10	11	7*	2											5	1				9					36
14	3	6	4	8	10	11†	12	2											5	1				9*					37
12	3	7*	6	4	8	10	11	9	2										5	1									38
	3	7	6	4	8*	10	12	2											5	1			11	9					39
12	3*	7	4	8†	10	14	11	2											5	1				6	9				40
	3	7	8	11	10*	14	4	2†											5	1				6	9				41
2	7	5	8	3		10	4																	1	11	6	9		42
2	3	7	5	8		10	12	4																1	11*	6	9		43
2	3	7	5	8		10	12	4															1	11*	6	9			44
2	3	7	5	10	8		4															4	1	11	6	9			45
2	3	7	5	10*	8	14	4	12														4	12	1	11†	6			46
1	35	25	23	19	32	32	34	38	15	22	9	2	10	29	13	5	15	20	13	6	11	4	19	4	22	9	17	18	
	+7s	+4s	+3s		+6s			+10s	2s					+17s	1s		+1s				+1s	3s	2s	+1s		+3s			

Beckford—Match No. 34(7); 35(7*); 36(12), 37(7); Donnelly—Match No. 41(12); 46(9)

Rumbelows Cup	Second Round	Rotherham U (a)	1-1
		(h)	1-0
	Third Round	QPR (a)	1-2
FA Cup	Third Round	Liverpool (h)	1-1
		(a)	0-3

BLACKBURN ROVERS

Player and Position	Ht	Wt	Birth Date	Place	Source	Clubs	League App	Gls
Goalkeepers								
Darren Collier	6 0	12 06	1 12 67	Stockton	Middlesbrough	Blackburn R	27	—
Terry Gennoe	6 2	13 03	16 3 53	Shrewsbury	Bricklayers Sp	Bury	3	—
						Blackburn R (loan)	—	—
						Leeds U (loan)	—	—
						Halifax T	78	—
						Southampton	36	—
						Everton (loan)	—	—
						Crystal Palace (loan)	3	—
						Blackburn R	289	—
Lee Gillespie‡	6 0		15 1 72	Preston	Trainee	Blackburn R	—	—
Bobby Mimms	6 2	12 13	12 10 63	York	Apprentice	Halifax T	—	—
						Rotherham U	83	—
						Everton	29	—
						Notts Co (loan)	2	—
						Sunderland (loan)	4	—
						Blackburn R (loan)	6	—
						Manchester C (loan)	3	—
						Tottenham H	37	—
						Aberdeen (loan)	6	—
						Blackburn R	22	—
Defenders								
Mark Atkins	6 1	12 00	14 8 68	Doncaster	School	Scunthorpe U	48	2
						Blackburn R	129	17
Richard Brown			13 1 67	Nottingham	Ilkeston T	Sheffield W	—	—
					Kettering T	Blackburn R	—	—
						Maidstone U (loan)	3	—
Robert Dewhurst	6 3	13 01	10 9 71	Keighley	Trainee	Blackburn R	13	—
Tony Dobson	6 1	12 10	5 2 69	Coventry	Apprentice	Coventry C	54	1
						Blackburn R	17	—
Mike Duxbury	5 9	11 02	1 9 59	Accrington	Apprentice	Manchester U	299	6
						Blackburn R	22	—
Keith Hill	6 0	11 03	17 5 69	Bolton	Apprentice	Blackburn R	63	3
David May	6 0	12 00	24 6 70	Oldham	Trainee	Blackburn R	37	1
John Millar*	5 7	10 00	8 12 66	Lanark		Chelsea	11	—
						Northampton T (loan)	1	—
						Hamilton A (loan)	10	—
						Blackburn R	126	1
Kevin Moran	5 11	12 09	29 4 56	Dublin	Pegasus (Eire)	Manchester U	231	21
					Sporting Gijon	Blackburn R	51	3
Neil Oliver*	5 11	11 10	11 4 67	Berwick	Coldstream	Berwick R	93	—
						Blackburn R	6	—
Chris Sulley	5 8	10 00	3 12 59	Camberwell	Apprentice	Chelsea	—	—
						Bournemouth	206	3
						Dundee U	7	—
						Blackburn R	127	3
Midfield								
Lenny Johnrose	5 11	12 00	29 11 69	Preston	Trainee	Blackburn R	35	10
Nicky Reid	5 10	12 04	30 10 60	Ormston	Apprentice	Manchester C	217	2
						Blackburn R	153	8
Lee Richardson	5 11	11 00	12 3 69	Halifax	School	Halifax T	56	2
						Watford	41	1
						Blackburn R	38	2
Scott Sellars	5 7	9 10	27 11 65	Sheffield	Apprentice	Leeds U	76	12
						Blackburn R	172	28
Paul Shepstone	5 8	10 06	8 11 70	Coventry	Atherstone U	Coventry C	—	—
						Birmingham C	—	—
						Blackburn R	25	1

BLACKBURN ROVERS

Foundation: It was in 1875 that some Public School old boys called a meeting at which the Blackburn Rovers club was formed and the colours blue and white adopted. The leading light was John Lewis, later to become a founder of the Lancashire FA, a famous referee who was in charge of two FA Cup Finals, and a vice-president of both the FA and the Football League.

First Football League game: 15 September, 1888, Football League, v Accrington (h) D 5-5 – Arthur; Beverley, James Southworth; Douglas, Almond, Forrest; Beresford (1), Walton, John Southworth (1), Fecitt (1), Townley (2).

Did you know: In 1886 when they were particularly hard-up Rovers organised a draw with tickets at 6d (5p) each. First prize was a newly built cottage on the New Bank road valued at £140. Other prizes included a piano, watches, a sewing machine and a washing machine and wringing machine.

Managers (and Secretary-managers)
Thomas Mitchell 1884–96*, J. Walmsley 1896–1903*, R. B. Middleton 1903–25, Jack Carr 1922–26 (TM under Middleton to 1925), Bob Crompton 1926–30 (Hon. TM), Arthur Barritt 1931–36 (had been Sec. from 1927), Reg Taylor 1936–38, Bob Crompton 1938–41, Eddie Hapgood 1944–47, Will Scott 1947, Jack Bruton 1947–49, Jackie Bestall 1949–53, Johnny Carey 1953–58, Dally Duncan 1958–60, Jack Marshall 1960–67, Eddie Quigley 1967–70, Johnny Carey 1970–71, Ken Furphy 1971–73, Gordon Lee 1974–75, Jim Smith 1975–78, Jim Iley 1978, John Pickering 1978–79, Howard Kendall 1979–81, Bobby Saxton 1981–86, Don Mackay February 1987– .

Player and Position	Ht	Wt	Birth Date	Place	Source	Clubs	League App	Gls
Forwards								
Darren Donnelly	5 10	11 06	28 12 71	Liverpool	Trainee	Blackburn R	2	—
Simon Garner	5 9	11 12	23 11 59	Boston	Apprentice	Blackburn R	459	163
Howard Gayle	5 10	10 09	18 5 58	Liverpool	Local	Liverpool	4	1
						Fulham (loan)	14	—
						Birmingham C (loan)	13	1
						Newcastle U (loan)	8	2
						Birmingham C	33	8
						Sunderland	48	4
						Stoke C	6	2
						Blackburn R	112	29
Alan Irvine	5 9	11 03	12 7 58	Glasgow	Glasgow BC	Queen's Park	88	9
						Everton	60	4
						Crystal Palace	109	12
						Dundee U	24	3
						Blackburn R	52	3
Steve Livingstone	6 1	12 07	8 9 69	Middlesbrough	Trainee	Coventry C	31	5
						Blackburn R	18	9
Craig Skinner	5 10	11 00	21 10 70	Bury	Trainee	Blackburn R	7	—
Gardner Speirs‡	5 8	10 00	14 4 63	Airdrie	St Mirren BC	St Mirren	90	15
						Kilmarnock	5	—
						Dunfermline Ath	4	—
						Hartlepool U	1	—
						Blackburn R	—	—
Frank Stapleton*	6 0	13 01	10 7 56	Dublin	Apprentice	Arsenal	225	75
						Manchester U	223	60
						Ajax	4	—
						Derby Co	10	1
					Le Havre	Blackburn R	81	13
Jason Wilcox	5 10	11 06	15 7 71	Bolton	Trainee	Blackburn R	19	—

Trainees
Ainsworth, Gareth; Baah, Peter H; Beattie, James L; Butterworth, John; Cullen, Anthony S; Holt, Matthew J; Lyndsay, Scott W; McGarry, Ian J; O'Shaughnessy, Brendan J; Pickup, Jonathan J; Sixsmith, Alan L; Thorne, Peter L; Ward, Darren.

Associated Schoolboys
Ainscough, Paul B; Baxter, Lee S; Berry, James S; Davies, Gareth J; Gill, Wayne J; Goodall, Daniel J; Grunshaw, Steven J; Hitchen, Lee A; Hitchen, Steven J; Lowey, Simon P; McCrone, Christian P; McClean, James L; Man, Wai M; Metcalfe, Joshua H; Moss, Lee; Ormerod, Brett R; Paver, Mark J; Ridgway, Alec D; Scott, Andrew M; Sweeney, Damian; Thornton, Scott L.

70

BLACKPOOL 1990-91. *Back row (left to right):* Andy Gouck, Mark Taylor, Mike Davies, Dean Kay, Nigel Hawkins, Gordon Owen, Tony Rodwell. *Centre row:* Steve Redmond (Physiotherapist), Gary Briggs, Colin Methven, Dave Lancaster, Steve McIlhargey, Andy Garner, Paul Groves, Ian Gore, Neil Bailey (Youth Team Manager). *Front row:* Dave Burgess, David Eyres, Ryan James, Trevor Sinclair, Graham Carr (Manager), Billy Ayre (Assistant Manager), Gary Brook, Alan Wright, Mark Bradshaw.

Division 4 BLACKPOOL

Bloomfield Rd Ground, Blackpool FY1 6JJ. Telephone Blackpool (0253) 404331. Fax: 0253 405011.

Ground capacity: 9641.

Record attendance: 38,098 v Wolverhampton W, Division 1, 17 September 1955.

Record receipts: £72,949 v Tottenham H, FA Cup 3rd rd, 5 January 1991.

Pitch measurements: 111yd × 73yd.

President: C. A. Sagar BEM.

Chairman: Owen J. Oyston. *Vice-chairman:* G. Bloor.

Managing Director: David Hatton.

Directors: M. H. Melling, T. White, J. Wilde MBE, O. Oyston, J. Allitt, J. Crowther LLB. Mrs. V. Oyston.

Manager: Bill Ayre.

Secretary: Jean Mishelly.

Commercial Manager: Geoffrey Warburton.

Coach: *Physio:* Stephen Redmond.

Year Formed: 1887. *Turned Professional:* 1887. *Ltd Co.:* 1896.

Previous Name: 'South Shore' combined with Blackpool in 1899, twelve years after the latter had been formed on the breaking up of the old 'Blackpool St John's' club.

Club Nickname: 'The Seasiders'.

Previous Grounds: 1887, Raikes Hall Gardens; 1897, Athletic Grounds; 1899, Raikes Hall Gardens; 1899, Bloomfield Road.

Record League Victory: 7-0 v Preston NE (away), Division 1, 1 May 1948 – Robinson; Shimwell, Crosland; Buchan, Hayward, Kelly; Hobson, Munro (1), McIntosh (5), McCall, Rickett (1).

Record Cup Victory: 7-1 v Charlton Ath, League Cup, 2nd rd, 25 September 1963 – Harvey; Armfield, Martin; Crawford, Gratrix, Cranston; Lea, Ball (1), Charnley (4), Durie (1), Oakes (1).

Record Defeat: 1-10 v Small Heath, Division 2, 2 March 1901 and v Huddersfield T, Division 1, 13 December 1930.

Most League Points (2 for a win): 58, Division 2, 1929–30.

Most League Points (3 for a win): 86, Division 4, 1984–85.

Most League Goals: 98, Division 2, 1929–30.

Highest League Scorer in Season: Jimmy Hampson, 45, Division 2, 1929–30.

Most League Goals in Total Aggregate: Jimmy Hampson, 247, 1927–38.

Most Capped Player: Jimmy Armfield, 43, England.

Most League Appearances: Jimmy Armfield, 568, 1952–71.

Record Transfer Fee Received: £633,333 from Manchester C for Paul Stewart, March 1987.

Record Transfer Fee Paid: £116,666 to Sunderland for Jack Ashurst, October 1979.

Football League Record: 1896 Elected to Division 2; 1899 Failed re-election; 1900 Re-elected; 1900–30 Division 2; 1930–33 Division 1; 1933–37 Division 2; 1937–67 Division 1; 1967–70 Division 2; 1970–71 Division 1; 1971–78 Division 2; 1978–81 Division 3; 1981–85 Division 4; 1985–90 Division 3; 1990– Division 4.

Honours: Football League: Division 1 – Runners-up 1955–56; Division 2 – Champions 1929–30; Runners-up 1936–37, 1969–70; Division 4 – Runners-up 1984–85. *FA Cup:* Winners 1953; Runners-up 1948, 1951. *Football League Cup:* Semi-final 1962. *Anglo-Italian Cup:* Winners 1971; Runners-up 1972.

Colours: Tangerine shirts with navy and white trim, white shorts, tangerine stockings with white tops. **Change colours:** White shirts with navy and tangerine trim, tangerine shorts, tangerine stockings with navy and white tops.

BLACKPOOL 1990–91 LEAGUE RECORD

Match No.	Date		Venue	Opponents	Result	H/T Score	Lg. Pos.	Goalscorers	Atten- dance
1	Aug	25	A	Scunthorpe U	L 0-2	0-1	—		3024
2	Sept	1	H	Rochdale	D 0-0	0-0	21		3357
3		8	A	Northampton T	L 0-1	0-0	23		4300
4		15	H	Wrexham	W 4-1	2-1	14	Stant, Eyres, Phillips (og), Rodwell	3497
5		18	H	Burnley	L 1-2	0-2	—	Stant	4737
6		22	A	Chesterfield	D 2-2	1-1	17	Groves, Garner (pen)	3549
7		29	H	Hartlepool U	W 2-0	2-0	13	Eyres, Groves	3181
8	Oct	3	A	Scarborough	W 1-0	0-0	—	Groves	1713
9		6	A	Torquay U	L 1-2	0-2	12	Stant	2854
10		13	H	Darlington	L 1-2	0-1	15	Garner	4092
11		20	H	Gillingham	W 2-0	0-0	13	Stant, Eyres	3041
12		22	A	Stockport Co	D 0-0	0-0	—		4337
13		27	A	Halifax T	L 3-5	3-2	15	Rodwell 2, Stant	1945
14	Nov	3	H	Walsall	L 1-2	0-2	16	Groves	3233
15		10	H	Aldershot	W 4-2	4-1	16	Sinclair, Taylor, Garner (pen), Lancaster	2065
16		24	A	Doncaster R	L 0-1	0-1	18		2113
17	Dec	1	A	Hereford U	D 1-1	0-1	18	Bamber	2588
18		15	H	Maidstone U	D 2-2	1-1	18	Garner, Bamber	2341
19		23	A	Carlisle U	L 0-1	0-1	—		5195
20		26	H	Peterborough U	D 1-1	1-1	18	Garner	3658
21		29	H	Lincoln C	W 5-0	2-0	17	Groves 2 (1 pen), Bamber 2, Eyres	2519
22	Jan	1	A	York C	W 1-0	1-0	16	Horner	3115
23		12	A	Rochdale	L 1-2	1-0	17	Bamber	2621
24		19	H	Scunthorpe U	W 3-1	2-0	15	Bamber 2, Garner	2494
25		26	A	Wrexham	W 1-0	1-0	11	Garner (pen)	2393
26	Feb	5	H	Chesterfield	W 3-0	2-0	—	Bamber, Horner, Garner	2357
27		16	H	Doncaster R	W 2-0	0-0	10	Taylor, Horner	3533
28		23	A	Aldershot	W 4-1	1-1	9	Bamber 2, Garner 2	2164
29	Mar	2	A	Hereford U	W 3-0	1-0	7	Bamber 2, Richards	3636
30		9	A	Maidstone U	D 1-1	1-1	9	Richards	2253
31		12	H	Scarborough	W 3-1	2-1	—	Richards, Taylor, Bamber	3798
32		16	A	Hartlepool U	W 2-1	1-1	5	Horner, Rodwell	2840
33		19	A	Darlington	D 1-1	0-1	—	Willis (og)	4108
34		23	H	Torquay U	W 1-0	1-0	4	Bamber	4778
35		30	A	Peterborough U	L 0-2	0-1	7		7721
36	Apr	2	H	Carlisle U	W 6-0	3-0	—	Bamber 2, Horner, Groves (pen), Richards, Rodwell	5368
37		6	A	Lincoln C	W 1-0	1-0	4	Bamber	4003
38		13	H	York C	W 1-0	0-0	5	Groves	5086
39		17	H	Cardiff C	W 3-0	2-0	—	Groves, Horner, Rodwell	4813
40		20	A	Gillingham	D 2-2	1-1	5	Davies, Horner	3025
41		23	A	Burnley	L 0-2	0-0	—		18,395
42		27	H	Stockport Co	W 3-2	2-1	5	Eyres, Garner 2	8590
43		30	H	Halifax T	W 2-0	0-0	—	Rodwell, Groves	5883
44	May	2	A	Cardiff C	D 1-1	1-0	—	Garner (pen)	1793
45		7	H	Northampton T	W 2-1	2-0	—	Eyres, Groves	7298
46		11	A	Walsall	L 0-2	0-2	5		8051

Final League Position: 5

GOALSCORERS

League (78): Bamber 17, Garner 13 (4 pens), Groves 11 (2 pens), Horner 7, Rodwell 7, Eyres 6, Stant 5, Richards 4, Taylor 3, Davies 1, Lancaster 1, Sinclair 1, own goals 2.
Rumbelows Cup (1): Brook 1.
FA Cup (4): Groves 2, Garner 1, own goal 1.

McIlhargey	Gore	Bradshaw	Groves	Briggs	Wright M	Sinclair	Brook	Lancaster	Garner	Eyres	Taylor	Rodwell	Wright A	Stant	Davies	Hedworth	Horner	Smalley	Owen	Barber	Bamber	Richards	Gouck	Match No.
1	2	3†	4	5	6	7	8*	9	10	11	12	14												1
1	2		4	5	6	7	8	9*	10	11	12			3										2
1	2		4	5*	6	7		9	10	11†			14	3	8	12								3
1	6		4				14	9*	10	11		7	3		8†12		2	5						4
1	6		4				14	9	10	11		7	3		8†12		2*	5						5
1	6		4				8		10	11		7	3		9		2	5						6
1	6		4				8		10	11		7*	3		9	12	2	5						7
1	6		4				8		10	11		7	3		9		2	5						8
1			4				8		10*	11		7	3		9	12	2	5	6					9
1			4	5			14	8†	10	11		7	3		9	12	2		6*					10
1			4	5			8		10	11		7	3		9		2		6					11
1			4	5			8		10	11		7	3		9		2		6					12
1 14			4				8		10	11		7	3		9	12	2†	5	6*					13
1			4				14	8†	10	11	12	7	3		9*		2	5	6					14
1	6		4				9		8	10		11*	7	3		2	8	5	12					15
1	6		4	5			9*		10	11	12	7	3			2	8							16
	6		4	5			9		10			7	3			2	8			1	11			17
1	6		4	5			9		10			7	3			2	8*				11	12		18
	6		4	5			9		10	11*		7	3			2	8			1		12		19
1	6		4	5			9		10*14			7†	3			2	8				11	12		20
1	6		4	5			9			11		7	3			2	8				10			21
1	6		4	5			9 12			11*		7	3			2	8				10			22
1	6		4*	5			12			10 11		7	3			2	8				9			23
1	6		4							10	11	7	3		2	5	8				9			24
1	6		4							10	11	7	3		2	5	8				9			25
1	6		4				12			10 14	11†	7*	3		2	5	8				9			26
1	6		4				12			10	11	7*	3		2	5	8				9			27
1	6		4							10	11	7	3		2	5	8				9*12			28
1	6		4							10*	11	7	3		2	5	8				9	12		29
1	6		4	5						14	11	7†	3		2		8*				9	10 12		30
1	6		4	5							11	7	3		8		2				9	10		31
1	6		4	5						14	11†	7	3		2		8				9	10*12		32
1	6		4	5							11	7	3		2		8				9	10		33
1	6		4	5						14	11*	7†	3		2		8				9	10 12		34
1	6		4	5						14	11†	7	3		2		8*				9	10 12		35
1	6		4							11 14		7	3		2		5* 8				9	10 12†		36
1	6		4	5				2			11	7	3				8				9	10		37
1	6		4	5					12		11	7	3		2		8				9	10*		38
1	6		4	5					12		11	7	3		2		8				9*10			39
1	6		4	5					12	10*	11	7	3		2		8				9			40
1	6		4	5					12	14 10	11	7*	3		2		8				9†			41
1	6		4	5					12	10	11	7	3		2		8				9*			42
1	6		4	5						10	11	7	3		2		8				9*12			43
1	6		4	5					12	10	11	7	3		2		8				9*			44
1	6		4	5						10	11	7	3		2		8				9			45
1	6		4	5†					12	10	11 14	7	3		2		8				9*			46
44	40	1	46	30	3	19	3	7	34	30	13	43	45	12	30	20	39	6	—	2	23	16	—	
+			+	+	+	+	+	+	+	+	+				+			+			+	+		
1s			12s	1s	1s	2s	6s	6s	2s						7s			1s			6s	5s		

BLACKPOOL

Player and Position	Ht	Wt	Birth Date	Birth Place	Source	Clubs	League App	Gls
Goalkeepers								
Mark Gayle‡	6 0	12 00	21 10 69	Bromsgrove	Trainee	Leicester C	—	—
						Blackpool	—	—
Steve McIlhargey	6 0	11 07	28 8 63	Ferryhill	Blantyre Celtic	Walsall	—	—
						Rotherham U (loan)	—	—
						Blackpool	66	—
Defenders								
Gary Briggs	6 3	12 10	8 5 58	Leeds	Apprentice	Middlesbrough	—	—
						Oxford U	420	18
						Blackpool	47	2
Dave Burgess	5 10	11 02	20 1 60	Liverpool	Local	Tranmere R	218	1
						Grimsby T	69	—
						Blackpool	65	1
Steve Burns‡	5 11	12 00	28 10 68	Salford	Local	Blackpool	—	—
Shaun Elliott‡	6 0	11 10	26 1 58	Haltwhistle	Apprentice	Sunderland	321	12
						Norwich C	31	2
						Blackpool	67	—
Chris Hedworth	6 1	10 11	5 1 64	Newcastle	Apprentice	Newcastle U	9	—
						Barnsley	25	—
						Halifax T	38	—
						Blackpool	20	—
Philip Horner	6 1	12 07	10 11 66	Leeds	School	Leicester C	10	—
						Rotherham U (loan)	4	—
						Halifax T	72	4
						Blackpool	39	7
Ryan James*	5 9	11 07	3 12 71	Blackwood		Blackpool	—	—
Mark Murray			13 6 73	Manchester	Trainee	Blackpool	—	—
Midfield								
Mark Bradshaw	5 10	11 05	7 6 69	Ashton	Trainee	Blackpool	42	1
						York C (loan)	1	—
Michael Davies	5 8	10 00	19 1 66	Stretford	Apprentice	Blackpool	226	14
Ian Gore	5 11	12 04	10 1 68	Liverpool		Birmingham C	—	—
					Southport	Blackpool	96	—
Andy Gouck			8 6 72	Blackpool	Trainee	Blackpool	13	1
Paul Groves	5 11	11 05	28 2 66	Derby	Burton Alb	Leicester C	16	1
						Lincoln C (loan)	8	1
						Blackpool	65	12
Dean Kay*	5 10	11 00	25 8 71			Blackpool	—	—
Trevor Sinclair	5 10	11 02	2 3 73	Dulwich	Trainee	Blackpool	40	1
Alan Wright	5 4	9 04	28 9 71	Ashton Under Lyne		Blackpool	86	—
Forwards								
Dave Bamber	6 3	13 10	1 2 59	St Helens	Manchester Univ	Blackpool	86	29
						Coventry C	19	3
						Walsall	20	7
						Portsmouth	4	1
						Swindon T	106	31
						Watford	18	3
						Stoke C	43	8
						Hull C	28	5
						Blackpool	23	17
Gary Brook	5 10	12 04	9 5 64	Dewsbury	Frickley Ath	Newport Co	14	2
						Scarborough	64	15
						Blackpool	29	6
						Notts Co (loan)	1	—
						Scarborough (loan)	8	—
Tony Diamond*	5 10	10 04	23 8 68	Rochdale	Apprentice	Blackburn R	26	3
						Wigan Ath (loan)	6	2
						Blackpool	3	1

BLACKPOOL

Foundation: Old boys of St. John's School who had formed themselves into a football club decided to establish a club bearing the name of their town and Blackpool FC came into being at a meeting at the Stanley Arms Hotel in the summer of 1887. In their first season playing at Raikes Hall Gardens, the club won both the Lancashire Junior Cup and the Fylde Cup.

First Football League game: 5 September, 1896, Division 2, v Lincoln C (a) L 1-3 – Douglas; Parr, Bowman; Stuart, Stirzaker, Norris; Clarkin, Donnelly, R. Parkinson, Mount (1), J. Parkinson.

Did you know: Scottish international goalkeeper George Farm never missed an FA Cup tie in his 12 seasons with Blackpool. His total was 47 including three Finals.

Managers (and Secretary-managers)
Tom Barcroft 1903–33* (Hon. Sec.), John Cox 1909–11, Bill Norman 1919–23, Maj. Frank Buckley 1923–27, Sid Beaumont 1927–28, Harry Evans 1928–33 (Hon. TM), Alex "Sandy" Macfarlane 1933–35, Joe Smith 1935–58, Ronnie Suart 1958–67, Stan Mortensen 1967–69, Les Shannon 1969–70, Bob Stokoe 1970–72, Harry Potts 1972–76, Allan Brown 1976–78, Bob Stokoe 1978–79, Stan Ternent 1979–80, Alan Ball 1980–81, Allan Brown 1981–82, Sam Ellis 1982–89, Jimmy Mullen 1989–90, Graham Carr 1990, Bill Ayre December 1990– .

Player and Position	Ht	Wt	Birth Date	Place	Source	Clubs	League App	Gls
David Eyres	5 10	11 00	26 2 64	Liverpool	Rhyl	Blackpool	71	13
Andy Garner	6 0	12 01	8 3 66	Chesterfield	Apprentice	Derby Co	71	17
						Blackpool	124	32
Nigel Hawkins	5 9	10 07	7 9 68	Bristol	Apprentice	Bristol C	18	2
						Blackpool	7	—
Dave Lancaster	6 3	14 00	8 9 61	Preston	Colne Dynamoes	Blackpool	8	1
						Chesterfield (loan)	12	4
Gordon Owen*	5 8	10 09	14 6 59	Barnsley	Amateur	Sheffield W	48	5
						Rotherham U (loan)	9	—
						Doncaster R (loan)	9	—
						Chesterfield (loan)	6	2
						Cardiff C	39	14
						Barnsley	68	25
						Bristol C	53	11
						Hull C (loan)	3	—
						Mansfield T	58	8
						Blackpool	29	4
						Carlisle U (loan)	5	—
						Exeter C (loan)	4	—
Carl Richards	6 0	13 00	12 1 60	Jamaica	Enfield	Bournemouth	71	15
						Birmingham C	19	2
						Peterborough U	20	5
						Blackpool	38	8
Simon Robinson*			6 4 65	West Bromwich	Mansfield T	Blackpool	—	—
Tony Rodwell	5 11	11 02	26 8 62	Southport	Colne Dynamoes	Blackpool	45	7
Mark Taylor	5 7	10 00	20 11 64	Hartlepool	Local	Hartlepool U	47	4
						Crewe Alex (loan)	3	—
						Blackpool	109	41
						Cardiff C (loan)	6	3

Trainees
Bonner, Mark; Horsfield, Damien J; Morris, Neil A; Potter, Ian L; Proctor, Alistair; Stoddard, John A; Stoneman, Paul.
**Non-Contract
Leitch, Grant; Murphy, James A.
Associated Schoolboys
Birkman, Peter; Blacow, Iain C; Carroll, David; Hargreaves, Boyd M; Saddler, Ian D; Shaw, Richard E; Sheppard, James H; Thomson, Paul D; Woodhall, Alan C.
Associated Schoolboys who have accepted the club's offer of a Traineeship/Contract
Beech, Christopher S; Irvine, Jonathan A; Little, Glen; Mitchel, Neil; Trickett, Andrew.
**Non-Contract Players who are retained must be re-signed before they are eligible to play in League matches.

76

BOLTON WANDERERS 1990-91   *Back row (left to right):* Paul Hughes, Barry Cowdrill, Mark Came, Mark Winstanley, Paul Comstive, Alan Stubbs, Nicky Spooner.

Centre row: Phil Neal (Manager), Julian Darby, Gary Henshaw, Dean Crombie, Dave Felgate, Kevin Rose, Mike Jeffrey, Gary Brown, Neil Fisher, Mick Brown (Coach), Robbie Savage.

Front row: Ewan Simpson (Physiotherapist), David Reeves, Phil Brown, Tony Philliskirk, Stuart Storer, Steve Thompson, David Burke, Darren Oliver, Scott Green, Steve Carroll (Youth Team Coach).

Division 3   BOLTON WANDERERS

Burnden Park, Bolton BL3 2QR. Telephone Bolton (0204) 389200. Information Service: Bolton 21101. Commercial Dept. (0204) 24518.

Ground capacity: 29,000.

Record attendance: 69,912 v Manchester C, FA Cup 5th rd, 18 February 1933.

Record receipts: £53,931 v Everton, League Cup semi-final 2nd leg, 15 February 1977.

Pitch measurements: 113yd × 76yd.

President: Nat Lofthouse.

Chairman: G. Hargreaves.

Directors: P. A. Gartside, G. Ball, G. Seymour, G. Warburton, W. B. Warburton.

Team Manager: Phil Neal. *Coach:* Mick Brown.

Physio: E. Simpson.

Chief Executive & Secretary: Des McBain. *Commercial Manager:* T. Holland.

Year Formed: 1874. *Turned Professional:* 1880. *Ltd Co.:* 1895.

Previous Name: 1874–77, Christ Church FC; 1877 became Bolton Wanderers.

Club Nickname: 'The Trotters'.

Previous Grounds: Park Recreation Ground and Cockle's Field before moving to Pike's Lane ground 1881; 1895, Burnden Park.

Record League Victory: 8-0 v Barnsley, Division 2, 6 October 1934 – Jones; Smith, Finney; Goslin, Atkinson, George Taylor; George T. Taylor (2), Eastham, Milsom (1), Westwood (4), Cook. (1 og).

Record Cup Victory: 13-0 v Sheffield U, FA Cup, 2nd rd, 1 February 1890 – Parkinson; Robinson (1), Jones; Bullough, Davenport, Roberts; Rushton, Brogan (3), Cassidy (5), McNee, Weir (4).

Record Defeat: 0-7 v Manchester C, Division 1, 21 March 1936.

Most League Points (2 for a win): 61, Division 3, 1972–73.

Most League Points (3 for a win): 83, Division 3, 1990–91.

Most League Goals: 96, Division 2, 1934–35.

Highest League Scorer in Season: Joe Smith, 38, Division 1, 1920-21.

Most League Goals in Total Aggregate: Nat Lofthouse, 255, 1946–61.

Most Capped Player: Nat Lofthouse, 33, England.

Most League Appearances: Eddie Hopkinson, 519, 1956–70.

Record Transfer Fee Received: £340,000 from Birmingham C for Neil Whatmore, August 1981.

Record Transfer Fee Paid: £350,000 to WBA for Len Cantello, May 1979.

Football League Record: 1888 Founder Member of the League; 1899–1900 Division 2; 1900–03 Division 1; 1903–05 Division 2; 1905–08 Division 1; 1908–09 Division 2; 1909–10 Division 1; 1910–11 Division 2; 1911–33 Division 1; 1933–35 Division 2; 1935–64 Division 1; 1964–71 Division 2; 1971–73 Division 3; 1973–78 Division 2; 1978–80 Division 1; 1980–83 Division 2; 1983–87 Division 3; 1987–88 Division 4; 1988– Division 3.

Honours: Football League: Division 1 best season: 3rd, 1891–92, 1920–21, 1924–25; Division 2 – Champions 1908–09, 1977–78; Runners-up 1899–1900, 1904–05, 1910–11, 1934–35; Division 3 – Champions 1972–73. *FA Cup:* Winners 1923, 1926, 1929, 1958; Runners-up 1894, 1904, 1953. *Football League Cup:* Semi-final 1976–77. *Freight Rover Trophy:* Runners-up 1986. *Sherpa Van Trophy:* Winners 1989.

Colours: White shirts, navy blue shorts, red stockings, blue and white tops. **Change colours:** Red shirts, white shorts, red stockings.

BOLTON WANDERERS 1990–91 LEAGUE RECORD

Match No.	Date		Venue	Opponents	Result		H/T Score	Lg. Pos.	Goalscorers	Attendance
1	Aug 25		A	Shrewsbury T	W	1-0	0-0	—	Storer	4608
2	Sept	1	H	Bradford C	L	0-1	0-0	13		7031
3		8	A	Huddersfield T	L	0-4	0-2	17		5419
4		15	H	Crewe Alex	W	3-2	0-2	11	Philliskirk, Green, Darby	4933
5		18	H	Preston NE	L	1-2	0-1	—	Darby	5844
6		22	A	Brentford	L	2-4	1-1	18	Green, Reeves	5077
7		28	A	Wigan Ath	L	1-2	0-2	—	Philliskirk (pen)	4366
8	Oct	2	H	Mansfield T	D	1-1	0-1	—	Reeves	3631
9		6	H	Stoke C	L	0-1	0-0	23		8521
10		13	A	Bury	D	2-2	1-0	20	Thompson, Philliskirk (pen)	5634
11		20	A	Leyton Orient	W	1-0	1-0	18	Storer	4121
12		23	H	Rotherham U	D	0-0	0-0	—		4692
13		27	H	Swansea C	W	1-0	1-0	18	Philliskirk	4158
14	Nov	3	A	Chester C	W	2-0	0-0	16	Reeves, Philliskirk	2553
15		10	H	Reading	W	3-1	0-1	15	Thompson 2 (1 pen), Reeves	4648
16		24	A	Grimsby T	W	1-0	1-0	13	Green	6240
17	Dec	1	H	Tranmere R	W	2-1	2-1	6	Green, Philliskirk	6941
18		15	A	Fulham	W	1-0	0-0	5	Philliskirk	3466
19		22	H	Cambridge U	D	2-2	2-0	4	Storer, Thompson	5800
20		26	A	Southend U	D	1-1	0-0	5	Green	7539
21		29	A	Birmingham C	W	3-1	0-0	5	Philliskirk, Darby, Reeves	7318
22	Jan	1	H	Bournemouth	W	4-1	1-1	4	Darby, Comstive 2, Philliskirk (pen)	7639
23		12	A	Bradford C	D	1-1	0-0	5	Philliskirk	8764
24		19	H	Shrewsbury T	W	1-0	0-0	4	Thompson	6164
25	Feb	2	A	Preston NE	W	2-1	2-1	4	Philliskirk 2 (1 pen)	9844
26		5	H	Brentford	W	1-0	1-0	—	Evans (og)	6731
27		9	H	Huddersfield	D	1-1	0-1	3	Philliskirk	7947
28		13	H	Exeter C	W	1-0	1-0	—	Reeves	5532
29		16	H	Grimsby T	D	0-0	0-0	3		10,318
30		23	A	Reading	W	1-0	1-0	2	Cowdrill	5997
31	Mar	1	A	Tranmere R	D	1-1	0-0	—	Patterson	10,076
32		9	H	Fulham	W	3-0	2-0	2	Philliskirk 2 (1 pen), Patterson	7316
33		12	A	Mansfield T	L	0-4	0-0	—		3611
34		16	H	Wigan Ath	W	2-1	1-0	3	Reeves, Darby	7812
35		19	H	Bury	L	1-3	0-1	—	Green	9006
36		23	A	Stoke C	D	2-2	0-0	3	Darby, Storer	13,869
37		26	A	Exeter C	L	1-2	0-1	—	Reeves	4009
38		30	H	Southend U	W	1-0	0-0	3	Darby	10,666
39	Apr	2	A	Cambridge U	L	1-2	0-1	—	Philliskirk	7763
40		7	H	Birmingham C	W	3-1	2-1	—	Philliskirk, Darby, Cunningham	11,280
41		13	A	Bournemouth	L	0-1	0-1	3		7159
42		16	A	Crewe Alex	W	3-1	0-1	—	Philliskirk 2 (2 pens), Reeves	4419
43		20	H	Leyton Orient	W	1-0	0-0	3	Reeves	7926
44		27	A	Rotherham U	D	2-2	0-1	4	Cunningham 2	8045
45	May	4	A	Swansea C	W	2-1	1-1	4	Darby, Storer	4713
46		11	H	Chester C	W	1-0	1-0	4	Cunningham	12,826

Final League Position: 4

GOALSCORERS

League (64): Philliskirk 19 (7 pens), Reeves 10, Darby 9, Green 6, Storer 5, Thompson 5 (1 pen), Cunningham 4, Comstive 2, Patterson 2, Cowdrill 1, own goal 1.
Rumbelows Cup (9): Philliskirk 5 (2 pens), Darby 3, Stubbs 1.
FA Cup (7): Philliskirk 2, Comstive 1, Darby 1, Reeves 1, Storer 1, Thompson 1.

Felgate	Brown	Burke	Cowdrill	Came	Winstanley	Green	Thompson	Reeves	Philliskirk	Darby	Storer	Stubbs	Comstive	Crombie	Henshaw	Seagraves	Lee	Stevens	Patterson	Cunningham	Match No.
1	2	3	4*	5	6	7	8	9	10	11	12										1
1	2	3	4*	5†	6	7	8	9	10	11	12	14									2
1	2	3			6	4	8	9	10*11		7	5	12								3
1	2	3	5*		6	4	8	9	10	11	7	12									4
1	2	3				4	8	9	10	11	7	5			6						5
1	2	3				4	8	9	10		12		5	11*	6	7					6
1	2	3*			6	4	8	9	10	11	7		12			5					7
1	2	3			6	4	8	9	10	11	7					5					8
1	2	3*12			6	4	8	9†10		11						5	7	14			9
1	2	3			6	4	8	12	10	11	5						7		9*		10
1	2	3			6	4	8	9	10	11	5						7				11
1	2	3			6	4	8	9	10†11		5	12					7*14				12
1	2	3			6	4*	8	9†10		11	7	5	12				14				13
1	2	3			6	4	8	9	10	11	7					5					14
1	2	3			6	4	8	9	10*11		7		12			5					15
1	2	3			6	10*	8	9	11		7	4				5	12				16
1	2	3			6	8		9	10	11	7	4				5					17
1	2	3			6	4	8	9	10	11	7					5					18
1	2	3			6		8	9	10	11	7	4				5					19
1	2	3	5		6	12	8	9	10	11	7	4*									20
1	2	3	5		6	12	8	9	10	11†	7*14	4									21
1	2	3	5		6		8	9	10	11	7	4									22
1	2	3	5		6		8	9	10	11	7	4*							12		23
1	2	3			6	12	8	9	10	11*	7					5			4		24
1	2	3			6	7	8	9	10	11						5			4		25
1	2	3			6	7	8	9	10	11						5			4		26
1	2	3			6	7*	8	9	10	11			12			5			4		27
1	2	3			6	7	8	9	10	11						5			4		28
1	2	3			6	7*	8	9	10	11†		14	12			5			4		29
1	2	3			6	7	8	9	10	11						5			4		30
1	2	3			6	7	8	9	10	11						5			4		31
1	2	3			6	7	8	9	10	11						5			4		32
1	2	3			6	7	8	9	10†11			14	12			5			4*		33
1	2	3			6*	7	8	9	10	11		12				5			4		34
1	2	14	3†			7*	8	9	10	11	6	12				5			4		35
1	2	3				12	8	9	10	11	7		6			5			4*		36
1	2	3				12	8	9	10	11	7*		6			5			4		37
1	2	3				7	8		10	11	12		6			5			4*	9	38
1	2	3				7	8	12	10	11	14		6			5			4*	9†	39
1	2	3				7	8	12	10	11			6			5			4	9*	40
1		3	4			7†	8	12	10	11	2		6	14		5				9*	41
1	2	3	14			8		12	10	11	7		6			5			4†	9*	42
1	2	3	14			8		12	10	11	7*		6			5			4†	9	43
1	2	3				8		12	10	11	7		6			5			4*	9	44
1	2	3				8		12	10	11	7		6			5			4*	9	45
1	2	3			12	8		10	11	7			6			5			4*	9	46
46	45	13	35	8	32	33	45	36	43	45	30	16	12	2	1	32	4	1	18	9	
			+1s	+1s		+8s		+8s				+5s	+7s	+6s		+3s			+4s	+1s	

Rumbelows Cup First Round   Huddersfield T (a)   3-0
                                           (h)   2-1
             Second Round   Coventry C (a)   2-4
                                      (h)   2-3
FA Cup   First Round   Witton Alb (a)   2-1
             Second Round   Chesterfield (a)   4-3
             Third Round   Barrow (h)   1-0
             Fourth Round   Manchester U (a) 0-1

BOLTON WANDERERS

Player and Position	Ht	Wt	Birth Date	Birth Place	Source	Clubs	League App	Gls
Goalkeepers								
David Felgate	6 2	13 10	4 3 60	Bl Ffestiniog	Blaenau	Bolton W	—	—
						Rochdale (loan)	35	—
						Bradford C (loan)	—	—
						Crewe Alex (loan)	14	—
						Rochdale (loan)	12	—
						Lincoln C	198	—
						Cardiff C (loan)	4	—
						Grimsby T (loan)	12	—
						Grimsby T	12	—
						Rotherham U (loan)	—	—
						Bolton W	213	—
Kevin Rose	6 1	13 06	23 11 60	Evesham	Ledbury T	Lincoln C	—	—
					Ledbury T	Hereford U	268	—
						Bolton W	6	—
						Halifax T (loan)	—	—
						Carlisle U (loan)	11	—
						Rochdale (loan)	3	—
Defenders								
Phil Brown	5 11	11 06	30 5 59	South Shields	Local	Hartlepool U	217	8
						Halifax T	135	19
						Bolton W	137	5
David Burke	5 10	10 13	6 8 60	Liverpool	Apprentice	Bolton W	69	1
						Huddersfield T	189	3
						Crystal Palace	81	—
						Bolton W	14	—
Mark Came	6 0	12 13	14 9 61	Exeter	Winsford U	Bolton W	173	7
Barry Cowdrill	5 11	11 04	3 1 57	Birmingham	Sutton Coldfield	WBA	131	—
						Rotherham U (loan)	2	—
						Bolton W	118	4
Julian Darby	6 0	11 04	3 10 68	Bolton		Bolton W	200	26
Paul Hughes‡	5 9	11 06	19 12 68	Denton	Trainee	Bolton W	13	—
Phil Neal	5 11	12 02	20 2 51	Irchester	Apprentice	Northampton T	186	29
						Liverpool	455	41
						Bolton W	64	3
Darren Oliver	5 8	10 05	1 11 71	Liverpool		Bolton W	—	—
Mark Seagraves	6 1	12 10	22 10 66	Bootle	Local	Liverpool	—	—
						Norwich C (loan)	3	—
						Manchester C	42	—
						Bolton W	32	—
Nicky Spooner	5 8	11 00	5 6 71	Manchester	Trainee	Bolton W	—	—
Alan Stubbs	6 2	12 12	6 10 71	Kirkby	Trainee	Bolton W	23	—
Mark Winstanley	6 1	12 04	22 1 68	St Helens	Trainee	Bolton W	143	2
Midfield								
Gary Brown*	5 10	11 02	3 1 69	Beverley	Blackburn R	Bolton W	—	—
Paul Comstive	6 1	12 07	25 11 61	Southport	Amateur	Blackburn R	6	—
						Rochdale (loan)	9	2
						Wigan Ath	35	2
						Wrexham	99	8
						Burnley	82	17
						Bolton W	49	3
Neil Fisher	5 8	11 00	7 11 70	St Helens	Trainee	Bolton W	—	—
Gary Henshaw	5 9	11 08	18 2 65	Leeds	Apprentice	Grimsby T	50	9
						Bolton W	70	4
						Rochdale (loan)	9	1
Sammy Lee	5 7	10 01	7 2 59	Liverpool	Apprentice	Liverpool	197	13
						QPR	30	—
					Osasuna	Southampton	2	—
						Bolton W	4	—
Mark Patterson	5 6	10 10	24 5 65	Darwen	Apprentice	Blackburn R	101	20
						Preston NE	55	19
						Bury	42	10
						Bolton W	19	2
Bob Savage‡	5 7	11 01	8 1 60	Liverpool	Apprentice	Liverpool	—	—
						Wrexham (loan)	27	10
						Stoke C	7	—
						Bournemouth	82	18
						Bradford C	11	—
						Bolton W	87	11

BOLTON WANDERERS

Foundation: In 1874 boys of Christ Church Sunday School, Blackburn Street, led by their master Thomas Ogden, established a football club which went under the name of the school and whose president was Vicar of Christ Church. Membership was 6d (2cp). When their president began to lay down too many rules about the use of church premises, the club broke away and formed Bolton Wanderers in 1877, holding their earliest meetings at the Gladstone Hotel.

First Football League game: 8 September, 1888, Football League, v Derby C (h), L 3-6 – Harrison; Robinson, Mitchell; Roberts, Weir, Bullough, Davenport (2), Milne, Coupar, Barbour, Brogan (1).

Did you know: The lowest attendance for an FA Cup Final replay this century was 20,470 at Bolton in 1901 when Spurs beat Sheffield United 3-1. This was due largely to the railway's refusal to allow cheap excursion tickets to Bolton where the station was being rebuilt.

Managers (and Secretary-managers)
Tom Rawthorne 1874–85*, J. J. Bentley 1885–86*, W. G. Struthers 1886–87*, Fitzroy Norris 1887*, J. J. Bentley 1887–95*, Harry Downs 1895–96*, Frank Brettell 1896–98*, John Somerville 1898–1910, Will Settle 1910–15, Tom Mather 1915–19, Charles Foweraker 1919–44, Walter Rowley 1944–50, Bill Ridding 1951–68, Nat Lofthouse 1968–70, Jimmy McIlroy 1970, Jimmy Meadows 1971, Nat Lofthouse 1971 (then admin. man. to 1972), Jimmy Armfield 1971–74, Ian Greaves 1974–80, Stan Anderson 1980–81, George Mulhall 1981–82, John McGovern 1982–85, Charlie Wright 1985, Phil Neal December 1985– .

Player and Position	Ht	Wt	Birth Date	Place	Source	Clubs	League App	Gls
Steve Thompson	5 11	11 10	2 11 64	Oldham	Apprentice	Bolton W	333	49
Forwards								
Tony Cunningham	6 2	13 10	12 11 57	Jamaica	Stourbridge	Lincoln C	123	32
						Barnsley	42	11
						Sheffield W	28	5
						Manchester C	18	1
						Newcastle U	47	4
						Blackpool	71	17
						Bury	58	17
						Bolton W	9	4
Scott Green	6 0	11 12	15 1 70	Walsall	Trainee	Derby Co	—	—
						Bolton W	46	8
Mike Jeffrey	5 9	10 06	11 8 71	Liverpool	Trainee	Bolton W	13	—
Tony Philliskirk	6 1	11 03	10 2 65	Sunderland	Amateur	Sheffield U	80	20
						Rotherham U (loan)	6	1
						Oldham Ath	10	1
						Preston NE	14	6
						Bolton W	88	37
David Reeves	6 0	11 05	19 11 67	Birkenhead	Heswell	Sheffield W	17	2
						Scunthorpe U (loan)	4	2
						Scunthorpe U (loan)	6	4
						Burnley (loan)	16	8
						Bolton W	85	20
Ian Stevens*	5 9	12 00	21 10 66	Malta		Preston NE	11	2
						Stockport Co	2	—
					Lancaster C	Bolton W	47	7
Stuart Storer	5 11	11 08	16 1 67	Harborough		Mansfield T	1	—
						Birmingham C	8	—
						Everton	—	—
						Wigan Ath (loan)	12	—
						Bolton W	111	12

Trainees
Bentham, Nicholas J; Birks, Stephen J; Bragg, Lee E; Clarke, Christopher J; Coffey, Steven; Edge, Dean J; Fitzmaurice, Francis; Gerard, Steven M; Jones, Andrew E.J; Leedham, Paul; Lewin, Craig; Smith, Barry

Associated Schoolboys
Agnew, Neil; Antrobus, Wayne A; Archer, Daniel J; Fist, Dean T; Harrison, Craig A; Holden, Martin J; Howard, Steven R; Hughes, Lee A; Irlam, Ashley J; Livesey, Matthew D; Osmand, Marc; Sumner, Mark; Wall, Ryan J; Wiggans, Andrew.

BOURNEMOUTH 1990–91 *Back row (left to right):* George Lawrence, Denny Mundee, Matthew Holmes, Shaun Teale, Paul Mitchell, Paul Miller, Peter Shearer.
Centre row: Terry Shanahan (Assistant Manager), Efan Ekoku, Jamie Redknapp, Peter Guthrie, Trevor Aylott, John Williams, Paul Morrell, Stuart Morgan (Chief Scout), Tony Pulis (First Team Coach).
Front row: John Kirk (Trainer), Luther Blissett, Sean O'Driscoll, Kevin Bond (Captain), Gavin Peacock, David Coleman, John Dickens (Physiotherapist)
Photograph courtesy of Bob Armstrong Press Services.

Division 3   AFC BOURNEMOUTH

Dean Court Ground, Bournemouth. Telephone Bournemouth (0202) 395381. Fax: (0202) 309797.

Ground capacity: 11,375.

Record attendance: 28,799 v Manchester U, FA Cup 6th rd, 2 March 1957.

Record receipts: £33,723 v Manchester U, FA Cup 3rd rd, 7 January 1984.

Pitch measurements: 112yd × 75yd.

Chairman: P. W. Hayward JP.

Managing Director: **. Directors:** E. G. Keep, G. M. C. Hayward, B. E. Willis, C. W. Legg.

Secretary: K. R. J. MacAlister.

Manager: Harry Redknapp.

Coach: Tony Pulis. **Trainer:** J. Kirk. **Physio:** John Dickens.

Assistant. Manager: Terry Shanahan.

Commercial Manager: Arthur White.

Year Formed: 1899. **Turned Professional:** 1912. **Ltd Co.:** 1914.

Previous Names: Boscombe St Johns, 1890–99; Boscombe FC, 1899–1923; Bournemouth & Boscombe Ath FC, 1923–71.

Club Nickname: 'Cherries'.

Previous Grounds: 1899–1910, Castlemain Road, Pokesdown; 1910, Dean Court.

Record League Victory: 7-0 v Swindon T, Division 3 (S), 22 September 1956 – Godwin; Cunningham, Keetley; Clayton, Crosland, Rushworth; Siddall (1), Norris (2), Arnott (1), Newsham (2), Cutler (1). 10-0 win v Northampton T at start of 1939–40 expunged from the records on outbreak of war.

Record Cup Victory: 11-0 v Margate, FA Cup, 1st rd, 20 November 1971 – Davies; Machin (1), Kitchener, Benson, Jones, Powell, Cave (1), Boyer, MacDougall (9 incl. 1p), Miller, Scott (De Garis).

Record Defeat: 0-9 v Lincoln C, Division 3, 18 December 1982.

Most League Points (2 for a win): 62, Division 3, 1971–72.

Most League Points (3 for a win): 97, Division 3, 1986–87.

Most League Goals: 88, Division 3 (S), 1956–57.

Highest League Scorer in Season: Ted MacDougall, 42, 1970–71.

Most League Goals in Total Aggregate: Ron Eyre, 202, 1924–33.

Most Capped Player: Colin Clarke, 6 (30), Northern Ireland.

Most League Appearances: Ray Bumstead, 412, 1958–70.

Record Transfer Fee Received: £465,000 from Manchester C for Ian Bishop, August 1989.

Record Transfer Fee Paid: £210,000 to Gillingham for Gavin Peacock, August 1989.

Football League Record: 1923 Elected to Division 3 (S). Remained a Third Division club for record number of years until 1970; 1970–71 Division 4; 1971–75 Division 3; 1975–82 Division 4; 1982–87 Division 3; 1987–90 Division 2; 1990– Division 3.

Honours: Football League: Division 3 – Champions 1986–87; Division 3 (S) – Runners-up 1947–48. Promotion from Division 4 1970–71 (2nd), 1981–82 (4th). FA Cup: best season: 6th rd, 1956–57. Football League Cup: best season: 4th rd, 1962, 1964. Associate Members' Cup: Winners 1984.

Colours: Red and black striped shirts, white shorts, white stockings. **Change colours:** Blue and black striped shirts, white shorts, white stockings.

AFC BOURNEMOUTH 1990–91 LEAGUE RECORD

Match No.	Date		Venue	Opponents	Result	H/T Score	Lg. Pos.	Goalscorers	Atten- dance
1	Aug	25	A	Brentford	D 0-0	0-0	—		5669
2	Sept	1	H	Bury	D 1-1	1-0	16	O'Driscoll	5285
3		8	A	Wigan Ath	L 0-2	0-1	21		2159
4		15	H	Stoke C	D 1-1	0-0	20	Blissett (pen)	6374
5		18	H	Bradford C	W 3-1	1-1	—	Teale, Blissett (pen), Oliver (og)	4942
6		22	A	Exeter C	L 0-2	0-2	17		6145
7		29	H	Fulham	W 3-0	1-0	12	Bond, Blissett, Ekoku	5855
8	Oct	2	A	Reading	L 1-2	1-0	—	Mundee	5300
9		5	A	Southend U	L 1-2	1-1	—	Ekoku	5255
10		20	H	Crewe Alex	D 1-1	0-1	19	Blissett (pen)	5548
11		23	A	Huddersfield T	W 3-1	2-0	—	Teale, Blissett, Peacock	5373
12		27	A	Preston NE	D 0-0	0-0	19		4953
13		30	H	Tranmere R	W 1-0	1-0	—	Jones	6268
14	Nov	3	H	Shrewsbury T	W 3-2	2-2	10	Blissett, Peacock 2	5561
15		10	H	Rotherham U	W 4-2	2-0	5	Peacock, Blissett 3 (2 pens)	5442
16		24	A	Birmingham C	D 0-0	0-0	7		7416
17	Dec	1	A	Chester C	D 0-0	0-0	8		1103
18		14	H	Swansea C	W 1-0	1-0	—	Blissett (pen)	5031
19		22	A	Grimsby T	L 0-5	0-2	11		5651
20		26	H	Mansfield T	D 0-0	0-0	10		5280
21		29	H	Leyton Orient	D 2-2	0-0	11	Miller, Teale	6139
22	Jan	1	A	Bolton W	L 1-4	1-1	14	Blissett (pen)	7639
23		12	A	Bury	W 4-2	1-0;	13	Holmes, Blissett, Lawrence, Ekoku	2761
24		19	H	Brentford	W 2-0	0-0	10	Teale, O'Driscoll	7167
25	Feb	2	A	Bradford C	L 0-3	0-2	14		4914
26		5	H	Exeter C	W 2-1	1-1	—	Jones, Blissett	4982
27		16	H	Birmingham C	L 1-2	0-1	14	Watson	6330
28		23	A	Rotherham U	D 1-1	0-1	13	Jones	4107
29		27	A	Stoke C	W 3-1	0-0	—	Jones, Lawrence, Blissett	7797
30	Mar	2	H	Chester C	W 1-0	0-0	10	Blissett (pen)	4669
31		5	H	Wigan Ath	L 0-3	0-2	—		4662
32		9	A	Swansea C	W 2-1	0-1	7	Pulis, Mundee	3086
33		12	H	Reading	W 2-0	0-0	—	Jones 2	5921
34		16	A	Fulham	D 1-1	0-0	8	Jones	4085
35		18	A	Tranmere R	L 0-1	0-1	—		5418
36		23	H	Southend U	W 3-1	1-1	8	Blissett, Prior (og), Watson	7421
37		30	A	Mansfield T	D 1-1	1-1	9	Holmes	2663
38	Apr	2	H	Grimsby T	W 2-1	1-1	—	Jones, Cooke	7021
39		6	A	Leyton Orient	L 0-2	0-1	9		4289
40		13	H	Bolton W	W 1-0	1-0	8	Cooke	7159
41		16	H	Cambridge U	L 0-1	0-0	—		7156
42		20	A	Crewe Alex	W 2-0	1-0	8	Blissett 2	2892
43		24	A	Cambridge U	L 0-4	0-3	—		6433
44		27	H	Huddersfield T	W 3-1	0-1	8	Watson, Blissett, Bond	6888
45	May	2	H	Preston NE	D 0-0	0-0	—		7064
46		11	A	Shrewsbury T	L 1-3	0-0	9	Morrell	5016

Final League Position: 9

GOALSCORERS

League (58): Blissett 19 (8 pens), Jones 8, Peacock 4, Teale 4, Ekoku 3, Watson 3, Bond 2, Cooke 2, Holmes 2, Lawrence 2, Mundee 2, O'Driscoll 2, Miller 1, Morrell 1, Pulis 1, own goals 2.
Rumbelows Cup (3): Blissett 2, Aylott 1.
FA Cup (7): Jones 3, Brooks 1, Ekoku 1, Fereday 1, Teale 1.

Guthrie	Mitchell	Morrell	Teale	Shearer	Bond	O'Driscoll	Peacock	Aylott	Holmes	Blissett	Coleman	Ekoku	Redknapp	Lawrence	Mundee	Miller	Peyton	Brooks	Jones	Fereday	Pulis	Watson	Wood	Cooke	Morris	Match No.
1	2	3	4	5	6*	7	8	9	10	11†	12	14														1
1	2	3	4	5	6*	7	8	9	10†	11		12	14													2
1		3	4	5†	6	7		9	12	11	10			8*	14	2										3
1		3	4	5	6	2	8	9	10	11			12			7*										4
1		3	4	5†	6	2	8	9*	10	11	14	12				7										5
1			4		6	5	8	9	10	11		3	12			7*	2									6
1			4		6	5	8	9*	10	11		3	12			7	2									7
1		3*	4		6	5†	8		10	11	14	9				7	2	12								8
			5	4	6		8	14	10*	11†	3	9				7	2	12	1							9
		3	4		6	5	8	9	10	11			12	7†			2*	1	14							10
		3	4		6	5	8		10	11			12	7*	2	1	9									11
		3	4		6	5	8		10†	11	12	14			2	1	7*	9								12
		3	4		6	5	8		7*	11			12		2	1	10	9								13
		3	4		6	5	8		7	11					2	1	10	9								14
		3	4			5	8		7	11	6				2	1	10	9								15
		3	4			5	8		7†	11	6	12	14	2	1	10	9*									16
		3	4			5			7*	11	8	12		2	1	10	9	6								17
		3	4			5			7	11		12	6	2	1	10	9	8*								18
		3	4			5			7	11	14	12		6	2	1	10†	9*	8							19
		3	4			5			12	11		14	8	7	2	1	10†	9	6*							20
			4			5			7	11	9		10	6	2	1		12	3	8*						21
			4			5			7	11	9		10	6	2	1		12	3	8*						22
		3	4	12	5				7	11		14	10		2	1		9	8†	6*						23
		3	4	2	6				7	11	12	10			1		9*	8	5							24
1		3	4		6				7*	11		10	14		8	9†	2		5	12						25
1		3	4		6				12	11		10*	14		8	9	2†		5	7						26
		3	4		6				8	11		10*	12		1	9	2		5	7						27
		3	4		6				8	11	12	2			1	9		10*	5	7						28
		3	4		6				8*	11	12	2			1	9		10	5	7						29
		3	4		6				8	11	12	10	2		1	9*			5	7						30
		3	4		6				8	11†	12	14	2		1	9		10*	5	7						31
		3	4	10	6				11*			12	2		1		8	9	5	7						32
		3	4	8	6						12	2*	1		9	10	11		5	7						33
		3	4	10	6				11			12		1	9	8*	2		5	7						34
		3	4	8	6				11			12		1	9	10*	2		5	7						35
		3	4	2	6				10	11		12		1	9	8			5	7*						36
		3	4	2	6†				10	11		12		1	9				5	7	8*	14				37
		3	4	2	6				10*	11				1	9	12			5	7	8					38
		3	4	2	6				10	11				1	9				5	7	8					39
		3	4	2	6				10	11	9*			1		12			5	7	8					40
		3	4	2	6				10	11				1	9				5	7	8					41
		3	4	2	6				10	11	14			1	9*	12			5	7†	8					42
		3	4	2	6				14	11*	9			1	12	10			5	7	8†					43
		3	4	2	6				10	11*	14			1	9	12			5	7	8†					44
		3	4	2	6				10	11	12			1	9				5	7*	8					45
		3	4		6				10	11	12		14	1	9	2		7*	5		8†					46
10	2	42	46	5	29	45	15	8	38	45	4	5	5	17	16	14	36	12	30	17	12	23	20	10	—	
					+1s	+1s			+1s	+4s				+3s	+15s4s	+17s5s	+2s		+1s	+3s	+1s	+3s		+1s	+1s	

Rumbelows Cup	First Round	Birmingham C (a)	1-0
		(h)	1-1
	Second Round	Millwall (h)	0-0
		(a)	1-2
FA Cup	First Round	Gillingham (h)	2-1
	Second Round	Hayes (h)	1-0
	Third Round	Chester C (a)	3-2
	Fourth Round	Portsmouth (a)	1-5

AFC BOURNEMOUTH

Player and Position	Ht	Wt	Birth Date	Birth Place	Source	Clubs	League App	Gls
Goalkeepers								
Peter Guthrie	6 1	12 13	10 10 61	Newcastle	Weymouth	Tottenham H	—	—
						Swansea C (loan)	14	—
						Charlton Ath (loan)	—	—.
					Barnet	Bournemouth	10	—
Gerry Peyton	6 2	13 09	20 5 56	Birmingham	Atherstone T	Burnley	30	—
						Fulham	345	—
						Southend U (loan)	10	—
						Bournemouth	202	—
Defenders								
Kevin Bond	6 0	13 07	22 6 57	London	Apprentice	Bournemouth	—	—
						Norwich C	142	12
					Seattle S	Manchester C	110	11
						Southampton	140	6
						Bournemouth	88	3
Paul Morrell	5 11	13 05	23 3 61	Poole	Weymouth	Bournemouth	298	7
Shaun Teale	6 0	13 07	10 3 64	Southport	Weymouth	Bournemouth	100	4
Alex Watson	6 0	10 12	6 4 68	Liverpool	Apprentice	Liverpool	4	—
						Derby Co (loan)	5	—
						Bournemouth	23	3
John Williams	6 1	13 12	3 10 60	Liverpool	Amateur	Tranmere R	173	13
						Port Vale	50	2
						Bournemouth	117	9
Midfield								
Shaun Brooks	5 7	11 00	9 10 62	London	Apprentice	Crystal Palace	54	4
						Orient	148	26
						Bournemouth	121	13
David Coleman	5 7	10 08	8 4 67	Salisbury		Bournemouth	50	2
						Colchester U (loan)	6	1
Wayne Fereday	5 9	11 00	16 6 63	Warley	Apprentice	QPR	197	21
						Newcastle U	33	—
						Bournemouth	18	—
Ian Hedges			5 2 69	Bristol	Gloucester C	Bournemouth	—	—
Paul Mitchell			20 10 71	Bournemouth	Trainee	Bournemouth	2	—
David Morris†	5 11	12 00	19 11 71	Plumstead	Trainee	Bournemouth	1	—
Sean O'Driscoll	5 8	11 03	1 7 57	Wolverhampton	Alvechurch	Fulham	148	13
						Bournemouth (loan)	19	1
						Bournemouth	300	17
Tony Pulis	5 10	11 08	16 1 58	Newport	Apprentice Happy Valley, HK	Bristol R	85	3
						Bristol R	45	2
						Newport Co	77	—
						Bournemouth	74	3
						Gillingham	16	—
						Bournemouth	15	1
Keith Rowland			1 9 71	Portadown	Trainee	Bournemouth	—	—
Forwards								
Luther Blissett	5 11	12 00	1 2 58	Jamaica		Watford	246	95
						AC Milan	30	5
						Watford	127	44
						Bournemouth	121	56
Richard Cooke	5 6	9 00	4 9 65	Islington	Apprentice	Tottenham H	11	2
						Birmingham C (loan)	5	—
						Bournemouth	72	16
						Luton T	17	1
						Bournemouth	10	2

AFC BOURNEMOUTH

Foundation: There was a Bournemouth FC as early as 1875, but the present club arose out of the remnants of the Boscombe St John's club (formed 1890). The meeting at which Boscombe FC came into being was held at a house in Gladstone Road in 1899. They began by playing in the Boscombe and District Junior League.

First Football League game: 25 August, 1923, Division 3(S), v Swindon T (a), L 1-3 – Heron; Wingham, Lamb; Butt, C. Smith, Voisey; Miller, Lister (1), Davey, Simpson, Robinson.

Did you know: When Bournemouth became the first Fourth Division side to beat the Wolves in an FA Cup, 4th round tie, 26 January 1957, Reg Cutler brought the woodwork crashing down in the sixth minute after he had collided with a post. A seven-minute hold-up followed while the goal was re-erected. Just before half-time Reg scored the only goal.

Managers (and Secretary-managers)
Vincent Kitcher 1914–23*, Harry Kinghorn 1923–25, Leslie Knighton 1925–28, Frank Richards 1928–30, Billy Birrell 1930–35, Bob Crompton 1935–36, Charlie Bell 1936–39, Harry Kinghorn 1939–47, Harry Lowe 1947–50, Jack Bruton 1950–56, Fred Cox 1956–58, Don Welsh 1958–61, Bill McGarry 1961–63, Reg Flewin 1963–65, Fred Cox 1965–70, John Bond 1970–73, Trevor Hartley 1974–78, John Benson 1975–78, Alec Stock 1979–80, David Webb 1980–82, Don Megson 1983, Harry Redknapp November 1983–

Player and Position	Ht	Wt	Birth Date	Place	Source	Clubs	League App	Gls
Efan Ekoku	6 1	12 00	8 6 67	Manchester	Sutton U	Bournemouth	20	3
Matt Holmes	5 7	10 07	1 8 69	Luton		Bournemouth	68	5
						Cardiff C (loan)	1	—
Andy Jones	5 11	13 06	9 1 63	Wrexham	Rhyl	Port Vale	90	49
						Charlton Ath	66	15
						Port Vale (loan)	17	3
						Bristol C (loan)	4	1
						Bournemouth	33	8
George Lawrence	5 10	12 02	14 9 62	London	Apprentice	Southampton	10	1
						Oxford U (loan)	15	4
						Oxford U	63	21
						Southampton	68	11
						Millwall	28	4
						Bournemouth	67	5
Denny Mundee	5 10	11 00	10 10 68	Swindon	Apprentice	QPR	—	—
						Swindon T	—	—
						Bournemouth	33	2
						Torquay U (loan)	9	—
Peter Shearer	6 0	11 06	4 2 67	Birmingham	Apprentice	Birmingham C	4	—
						Rochdale	1	—
					Cheltenham T	Bournemouth	43	5

Trainees
Berry, Trevor J; Bibbo, Salvatore; Bradford, Lee T; Butcher, Gareth L; Case, Andrew J; Elliott, Steven M; Ferris, Eamon R; Lovell, Matthew W; MacAuley, Philip P; Mean, Scott; Phillips, Brett S; Shanahan, John A; Smith, Paul; Worsfold, Paul S; Zumrutel, Ender.

**Non-Contract
Masters, Neil B; Morris, David K.

Associated Schoolboys
Barfoot, Stuart J; Eastland, Robert L; Hill, Lee D; Jones, Mark D; Jones, Stephen M; Ormerod, Mark I; Pashen, Lee M; Pitts, Richard L; Richards Carl D; Rodgers, Alan P; Stone, Phillip K; Taylor, Mark R; Town, David E.

Associated Schoolboys who have accepted the club's offer of a Traineeship/Contract
Kerr, Stuart P; Wake, Nathan.

**Non-Contract Players who are retained must be re-signed before they are eligible to play in League matches.

BRADFORD CITY 1990-91 *Back row (left to right):* Neil Woods, Scott Bairstow, Peter Jackson, Gavin Oliver, Lee Sinnott, Brian Tinnion, Sean McCarthy, Mark Leonard, Brian Mitchell.

Centre row: Steve Smith (Youth Coach), Greg Abbott, David Campbell, Lee Duxbury, Michael McHugh, Paul Tomlinson, Mark Evans, Martin Pattison, Mark Stuard, Tony Adcock, Craig Taylor, Bryan Edwards (Physiotherapist).

Front row: Kevin Megson, Mark Ellis, Andy Clarkson, Paul Jewell, John Docherty (Manager), Leighton James (Coach), Des Wroe, Karl Goddard, Alan Davies, Mark Jules.

Division 3   BRADFORD CITY

Valley Parade Ground, Bradford BD8 7DY. Telephone Bradford (0274) 306062 (Office); (0274) 307050 (Ticket Office).

Ground capacity: 14,814.

Record attendance: 39,146 v Burnley, FA Cup 4th rd, 11 March 1911.

Record receipts: £59,250 v Tottenham H, FA Cup 3rd rd, 7 January 1989.

Pitch measurements: 110yd × 76yd.

Chairman: D. Simpson. *Vice-chairman:* D. Thompson FCA.

Directors: P. Wilkowski, D. Taylor FCA, M. WOODHEAD. *Associate Directors:* M. Smith, M. Scott, P. Brearley.

Manager: John Docherty. *Assistant-Manager:* Bob Pearson.

Youth Coach: Leighton James. *Physio:* Brian Edwards. *Youth Coach:* Steve Smith.

Secretary: Terry Newman. *Chief Commercial Executive:* Keith Hanvey.

Year Formed: 1903. *Turned Professional:* 1903. *Ltd Co.:* 1908.

Club Nickname: 'The Bantams'.

Record League Victory: 11-1 v Rotherham U, Division 3 (N), 25 August 1928 – Sherlaw; Russell, Watson; Burkinshaw (1), Summers, Bauld; Harvey (2), Edmunds (3), White (3), Cairns, Scriven (2).

Record Cup Victory: 11-3 v Walker Celtic, FA Cup, 1st rd (replay), 1 December 1937 – Parker; Rookes, McDermott; Murphy, Mackie, Moore; Bagley (1), Whittingham (1), Deakin (4 incl. 1p), Cooke (1), Bartholomew (4).

Record Defeat: 1-9 v Colchester U, Division 4, 30 December 1961.

Most League Points (2 for a win): 63, Division 3 (N), 1928–29.

Most League Points (3 for a win): 94, Division 3, 1984–85.

Most League Goals: 128, Division 3 (N), 1928–29.

Highest League Scorer in Season: David Layne, 34, Division 4, 1961–62.

Most League Goals in Total Aggregate: Bobby Campbell, 121, 1981–84, 1984–86.

Most Capped Player: Harry Hampton, 9, Northern Ireland.

Most League Appearances: Cec Podd, 502, 1970–84.

Record Transfer Fee Received: £850,000 from Everton for Stuart McCall, June 1988.

Record Transfer Fee Paid: £290,000 to Newcastle U for Peter Jackson, October 1988.

Football League Record: 1903 Elected to Division 2; 1908–22 Division 1; 1922–27 Division 2; 1927–29 Division 3 (N); 1929–37 Division 2; 1937–61 Division 3; 1961–69 Division 4; 1969–72 Division 3; 1972–77 Division 4; 1977–78 Division 3; 1978–82 Division 4; 1982–85 Division 3; 1985–90 Division 2; 1990– Division 3.

Honours: Football League: Division 1 best season: 5th, 1910–11; Division 2 – Champions 1907–08; Division 3 – Champions 1984–85; Division 3 (N) – Champions 1928–29; Division 4 – Runners-up 1981–82. *FA Cup:* Winners 1911 (first holders of the present trophy). *Football League Cup:* best season: 5th rd, 1965, 1989.

Colours: Amber shirts with thin claret stripe, claret shorts, amber stockings. **Change colours:** White shirts, black shorts, white stockings.

BRADFORD CITY 1990–91 LEAGUE RECORD

Match No.	Date	Venue	Opponents	Result	H/T Score	Lg. Pos.	Goalscorers	Atten- dance
1	Aug 25	H	Tranmere R	L	1-2	0-1	—	McCarthy	7970
2	Sept 1	A	Bolton W	W	1-0	0-0	11	Duxbury	7031
3	8	H	Reading	W	2-1	1-0	9	Tinnion (pen), Babb	7034
4	15	A	Grimsby T	D	1-1	0-1	8	Stuart	7960
5	18	A	Bournemouth	L	1-3	1-1	—	Leonard	4942
6	22	H	Swansea C	L	0-1	0-0	12		7724
7	29	A	Leyton Orient	L	1-2	0-1	17	Jewell	3761
8	Oct 3	H	Chester C	W	2-1	0-0	—	Duxbury, Leonard	5519
9	6	H	Brentford	L	0-1	0-1	16		6402
10	13	A	Exeter C	D	2-2	1-1	16	McCarthy, Stuart	4517
11	20	A	Mansfield T	W	1-0	1-0	16	Jewell	3582
12	24	H	Stoke C	L	1-2	0-0	—	McCarthy	8086
13	27	H	Wigan Ath	W	2-1	1-1	13	McCarthy 2	6803
14	Nov 3	A	Rotherham U	W	2-0	0-0	12	Oliver, James	6057
15	10	H	Preston NE	W	2-1	0-1	10	Tinnion (pen), Leonard	7440
16	24	A	Crewe Alex	D	0-0	0-0	12		3644
17	Dec 2	A	Huddersfield T	W	2-1	0-1	—	James, Sinnott	9697
18	15	H	Cambridge U	L	0-1	0-0	10		6354
19	22	H	Shrewsbury T	L	2-4	2-1	13	Tracey, Torpey	5722
20	26	A	Fulham	D	0-0	0-0	13		3029
21	28	A	Southend U	D	1-1	0-1	—	Jewell	6767
22	Jan 1	H	Bury	W	3-1	2-0	11	Torpey, Duxbury 2	7174
23	5	A	Birmingham C	D	1-1	0-1	10	Adcock	6315
24	12	H	Bolton W	D	1-1	0-0	12	Torpey	8764
25	18	A	Tranmere R	L	1-2	0-1	—	Torpey	6508
26	26	H	Grimsby T	L	0-2	0-0	15		8314
27	Feb 2	H	Bournemouth	W	3-0	2-0	13	Tracey, Tinmon (pen), Oliver	4914
28	13	H	Birmingham C	W	2-0	0-0	—	McCarthy 2	4776
29	23	A	Preston NE	W	3-0	2-0	10	Babb, Torpey, McCarthy	6878
30	Mar 3	H	Huddersfield T	D	2-2	2-0	—	Oliver, McCarthy	9569
31	12	A	Chester C	L	2-4	0-1	—	Babb 2	1303
32	16	H	Leyton Orient	W	4-0	1-0	13	Tinnion 2 (1 pen), Babb 2	5059
33	20	H	Exeter C	W	3-0	2-0	—	Torpey, McCarthy, Jewell	5328
34	23	A	Brentford	L	1-6	1-4	13	Duxbury	5601
35	26	H	Crewe Alex	W	2-0	1-0	—	Oliver, McCarthy	5163
36	30	H	Fulham	D	0-0	0-0	11		6207
37	Apr 2	A	Shrewsbury T	L	0-1	0-0	—		3090
38	6	H	Southend U	W	2-1	1-0	11	Torpey, McCarthy	5846
39	13	A	Bury	D	0-0	0-0	11		5285
40	20	H	Mansfield T	W	1-0	1-0	12	Babb	6307
41	27	A	Stoke C	L	1-2	1-2	12	Babb	6946
42	30	A	Reading	W	2-1	1-0	—	James (pen), McCarthy	1934
43	May 4	A	Wigan Ath	L	0-3	0-2	11		3267
44	7	A	Cambridge U	L	1-2	1-1	—	Leonard	8679
45	9	A	Swansea C	W	2-0	1-0	—	Babb, Oliver	2126
46	11	H	Rotherham U	W	1-0	0-0	8	Babb	6354

Final League Position: 8

GOALSCORERS

League (62): McCarthy 13, Babb 10, Torpey 7, Duxbury 5, Oliver 5, Tinnion 5 (4 pens), Jewell 4, Leonard 4, James 3 (1 pen), Stuart 2, Tracey 2, Adcock 1, Sinnott 1.
Rumbelows Cup (7): McCarthy 2 (1 pen), Abbott 1, James 1, Leonard 1, Oliver 1, own goal 1.
FA Cup (1): Jewell 1.

Tomlinson	Mitchell	Tinnion	James	Oliver	Sinnott	Abbott	Duxbury	McCarthy	Leonard	Stuart	Adcock	Jewell	Megson	Babb	Torpey	Tracey	Reid	McHugh	Evans	Match No.
1	2	3	4	5	6	7	8	9	10	11*12										1
1	2	3	4	5	6	7	8	9	10	11*	12									2
1	2	3	4	5	6		7		10	11	9	8*12								3
1	2	3*	4	5	6	8	7	9	10	11		12								4
1	2	3	4	5	6	8	7	9	10	11										5
1	2	3	4	5	6	8	7*	9	10	11		12								6
1	2	3	4	5	6†	8*	7	9	10	11		14	12							7
1	2	3	4	5			7	9	10	11	8		6							8
1	2	3	4†	5	6		7	9	10	11	8*14	12								9
1	2	3	4*	5	6	12	7	9	10	11	8									10
1		2	5	6	4			9	10	11	8	7	3							11
1	2		4	5	6		7	9	10	11	8		3							12
1	2		4	5	6		7	9	11*10	8	12	3								13
1		4	5	6	2	7	9		10	8	11	3								14
1	11	4	5	6	2	7	9	12	10*	8		3								15
1		3	4	5	6	2	7	9		8		10	11							16
1		3	4	5	6	2	7	9		8		10	11							17
1		3	4	5	6	2	7	9		8		10	11							18
1	14	3	4	5	6	2	7	9*	12	8†		10	11							19
1		3	4	5	6	2	7	9		8		10	11							20
1		3	4	5	6	2	7		9	8		10	11							21
1		3	4	5	6	2	7		9	8		10	11							22
1		3	4	5		2	6		8	7	11	9	10							23
1		3	4	5	6	2	7	9		8		10	11							24
1		3	4	5	6	2	7	9		8		12	10	11*						25
1	14	3	4	5	6	2	7	9*		8†	12	10	11							26
1		3	2	5	6		4	7		8			9	10	11					27
1		3	2*	5	6		4	7		8		9†10	11	12	14					28
1		3	2	5	6		4	7		8			9	10	11					29
1		3	2	5	6		4	7		8			9	10	11					30
1		3	2	5	6	14	4	7		8†		9	10	11*12						31
1		3	2	5	6		4	7		8			9	10	11					32
1	12	3	2	5	6*		4	7		8			9	10	11					33
1		3	2	5	6		4	7		8			9	10	11					34
1		3	2	5	6		4	7		8			9	10	11					35
		3	2	5	6	14	4	7	12	8			9*10	11†					1	36
		3	2	5	6	8	4	7					9	10	11				1	37
		3	2	5	6		4	7		8			9	10	11				1	38
1		3	2	5	6		4	7		8			9	10	11					39
1		3	2	5	6		4	7		8			9	10	11					40
1		3	2	5	6	12	4	7		8			9	10*	11					41
1	3		2	5	6		4	7		8			9	10	11					42
1	14	3†	2	5	6		4	7	12	8			9	10*	11					43
1	8	3	2	5	6		4	7	10				9		11					44
1	8	3	2	5	6		4	7	10				9		11					45
1	8	3	2	5	6	14	4	7	10*	11			9	12						46
43	16	41	46	46	44	21	45	42	15	13	8	35	3	27	28	16	14	—	3	
			+4s		+5s		+3s				+2s	+3s	+1s	+7s	+1s		+2s	+1s		

Rumbelows Cup	First Round	Bury (h)	2-0
		(a)	2-3
	Second Round	Luton T (a)	1-1
		(h)	1-1
	Third Round	Tottenham H (a)	1-2
FA Cup	First Round	Shrewsbury T (h)	0-0
		(a)	1-2

BRADFORD CITY

Player and Position	Ht	Wt	Birth Date	Place	Source	Clubs	League App	Gls
Goalkeepers								
Mark Evans	6 0	11 08	24 8 70	Leeds	Trainee	Bradford C	11	—
Paul Tomlinson	6 2	12 10	22 2 64	Brierley Hill	Amateur	Sheffield U	37	—
						Birmingham C (loan)	11	—
						Bradford C	164	—
Defenders								
Philip Babb	6 0	12 03	30 11 70	Lambeth		Millwall	—	—
						Bradford C	34	10
Scott Bairstow	6 1		1 6 72	Bradford		Bradford C	—	—
Andy Clarkson*			24 2 72	Leeds	Trainee	Bradford C	—	—
Brian Mitchell	6 2	13 00	30 7 63	Stonehaven	King Street	Aberdeen	65	1
						Bradford C	158	9
Gavin Oliver	6 0	12 10	6 9 62	Felling	Apprentice	Sheffield W	20	—
						Tranmere R (loan)	17	1
						Brighton & HA (loan)	16	—
						Bradford C	217	7
Martin Pattison*	6 0	11 07	21 7 71	Bradford	Trainee	Bradford C	—	—
Lee Sinnott	6 1	12 07	12 7 65	Aldridge	Apprentice	Walsall	40	2
						Watford	78	2
						Bradford C	173	6
Craig Taylor*	5 11	11 00	10 12 70	Leeds	Trainee	Bradford C	—	—
Brian Tinnion	6 0	11 05	23 2 68	Newcastle	Apprentice	Newcastle U	32	2
						Bradford C	92	11
Derek Wroe‡			19 9 70	Stockport	Trainee	Bradford C	—	—
Midfield								
Greg Abbott	5 9	10 07	14 12 63	Coventry	Apprentice	Coventry C	—	—
						Bradford C	281	38
David Campbell	5 9	10 09	2 6 65	Eglington	Oxford BC (NI)	Nottingham F	41	3
						Notts Co (loan)	18	2
						Charlton Ath	30	1
						Plymouth Arg (loan)	1	—
						Bradford C	35	4
						Shamrock R (loan)	—	—
Lee Duxbury	5 10	11 07	7 10 69	Skipton	Trainee	Bradford C	58	6
						Rochdale (loan)	10	—
Craig Lawford§			25 11 72	Dewsbury	Trainee	Bradford C	1	—
Wesley Reid	5 8	11 03	10 9 68	Lewisham	Trainee	Arsenal	—	—
						Millwall	6	—
						Bradford C	16	—
Forwards								
Robbie James	5 11	13 00	23 3 57	Swansea	Apprentice	Swansea C	394	99
						Stoke C	48	6
						QPR	87	4
						Leicester C	23	—
						Swansea C	90	16
						Bradford C	46	3
Paul Jewell	5 8	10 08	28 9 64	Liverpool	Apprentice	Liverpool	—	—
						Wigan Ath	137	35
						Bradford C	107	12
Mark Jules*	5 9		5 9 71	Bradford	Trainee	Bradford C	—	—

BRADFORD CITY

Foundation: Bradford was a rugby stronghold around the turn of the century but after Manningham RFC held an archery contest to help them out of financial difficulties in 1903, they were persuaded to give up the handling code and turn to soccer. So they formed Bradford City and continued at Valley Parade. Recognising this as an opportunity of spreading the dribbling code in this part of Yorkshire, the Football League immediately accepted the new club's first application for membership of the Second Division.

First Football League game: 1 September, 1903, Division 2, v Grimsby T (a), L 0-2 – Seymour; Wilson, Halliday; Robinson, Millar, Farnall; Guy, Beckram, Forrest, McMillan, Graham.

Did you know: Newly formed Bradford City were elected members of the Football League (Second Division) in 1903 before they had got a team together. They were promoted in only their fifth season.

Managers (and Secretary-managers)
Robert Campbell 1903–05, Peter O'Rourke 1905–21, David Menzies 1921–26, Colin Veitch 1926–28, Peter O'Rourke 1928–30, Jack Peart 1930–35, Dick Ray 1935–37, Fred Westgarth 1938–43, Bob Sharp 1943–46, Jack Barker 1946–47, John Milburn 1947–48, David Steele 1948–52, Albert Harris 1952, Ivor Powell 1952–55, Peter Jackson 1955–61, Bob Brocklebank 1961–64, Bill Harris 1965–66, Willie Watson 1966–69, Grenville Hair 1967–68, Jimmy Wheeler 1968–71, Bryan Edwards 1971–75, Bobby Kennedy 1975–78, John Napier 1978, George Mulhall 1978–81, Roy McFarland 1981–82, Trevor Cherry 1982–87, Terry Dolan 1987–89, Terry Yorath 1989–90, John Docherty March 1990–   .

Player and Position	Ht	Wt	Birth Date	Place	Source	Clubs	League App	Gls
Mark Leonard	5 11	11 10	27 9 62	St Helens	Witton A	Everton	—	—
						Tranmere R (loan)	7	—
						Crewe Alex	54	15
						Stockport Co	73	24
						Bradford C	138	29
Sean McCarthy	6 0	12 02	12 9 67	Bridgend	Bridgend	Swansea C	91	25
						Plymouth Arg	70	19
						Bradford C	42	13
Michael McHugh	5 11	11 00	3 4 71	Donegal		Bradford C	1	—
Mark Stuart	5 8	11 02	15 12 66	Hammersmith	QPR schoolboy	Charlton Ath	107	28
						Plymouth Arg	57	11
						Ipswich T (loan)	5	2
						Bradford C	13	2
Stephen Torpey	6 2	12 11	8 12 70	Islington	Trainee	Millwall	7	—
						Bradford C	29	7
Darren Treacy	5 10	12 09	6 9 70	Lambeth	Trainee	Millwall	7	—
						Bradford C	16	2

Trainees
Crabtree, Anthony M; Cressey, Matthew A; Coy, Paul T; Delahaye, Stephen T; Howe, Jeremy; Inch, Simon M; Lawford, Craig B; McGinley, Martin G; Margerison, Lee; Quigley, Adrian K; Richards, Dean I; Smith, Darren P; Sykes, Matthew J; Tomkinson, Alan P; White, Jonathan G.

Associated Schoolboys
Bentley, Christopher; Blair, David A; Carss, Anthony J; Elam, Lee P.G; Fitton, Christian J; Gibson, Jamie A; Graystone, Neil J; Hamilton, Derick V; Harris, Robert D; Higgins, Kevin T; Lobley, Hayden S; Lynch, Michael; McFatter, Robin; Mangan, Mark A; Morton, Philip; Quigley, David J; Richardson, Christopher; Rickerby, Jason M; Stabb, Christopher J; Stuttard, Andrew J; Sunderland, Andrew D; Sutcliffe, Adrian; Tomlinson, Graeme M; Vincent, Paul R; Walsh, Lee.

Associated Schoolboys who have accepted the club's offer of a Traineeship/Contract
Owen, Gary J; Partridge, Scott M; Wilson, Richard J.

94

BRENTFORD 1990–91 *Back row (left to right):* Kevin Godfrey, Simon Ratcliffe, Keith Millen, Terry Evans, Graham Benstead, Jamie Bates, Gary Blissett, Dean Holdsworth.

Centre row: Joe Gadston (Youth Team Manager), Robert Peters, Allan Cockram, Jason Cousins, Ashley Bayes, Stuart Cash, Fergus Moore, Khotso Moabi, Roy Clare (Physiotherapist).

Front row: Mark Fleming, Paul Buckle, Garry Brooke, Keith Jones, Phil Holder (Manager), Richard Cadette, Neil Smillie, Andy Driscoll, Eddie May.

Division 3

BRENTFORD

Brentford FC

Griffin Park, Braemar Rd, Brentford, Middlesex TW8 0NT.
Telephone 081-847 2511. Commercial Dept: 081-560 6062.
Press Office: 081-574 3047. Clubcall: 0898 121108.

Ground capacity: 11,405.

Record attendance: 39,626 v Preston NE, FA Cup 6th rd,
5 March 1938.

Record receipts: £55,002 v Liverpool, Milk Cup 2nd rd,
5 October 1983.

Pitch measurements: 111yd × 74yd.

President: W. Wheatley. *Life Vice-president:* F. Edwards.

Chairman: M. M. Lange. *Vice-chairman:* E. J. Radley-Smith.

Directors: R. J. J. Blindell LLB, D. Tana, G. V. Potter.

Chief Executive: K. A. Loring.

Manager: Phil Holder. *Asst. Manager:* Wilf Rostron.

Physio: Roy Clare.

Youth Team Manager: Joe Gadston.

Community Liaison Officer: Martyn Spong.

Secretary: Polly Kates.

Press Officer/Programme Editor: Eric White (081-574 3047).

Year Formed: 1889. *Turned Professional:* 1899. *Ltd Co.:* 1901.

Club Nickname: 'The Bees'.

Previous Grounds: 1889–91, Clifden Road; 1891–95, Benns
Fields, Little Ealing; 1895–98, Shotters Field; 1898–1900, Cross
Road, S. Ealing; 1900–04, Boston Park; 1904, Griffin Park.

Record League Victory: 9-0 v Wrexham, Division 3, 15 October 1963 – Cakebread; Coote,
Jones; Slater, Scott, Higginson; Summers (1), Brooks (2), McAdams (2), Ward (2), Hales
(1). (1 og).

Record Cup Victory: 7-0 v Windsor & Eton (away), FA Cup, 1st rd, 20 November 1982 –
Roche; Rowe, Harris (Booker), McNichol (1), Whitehead, Hurlock (2), Kamara, Bowles,
Joseph (1), Mahoney (3), Roberts.

Record Defeat: 0-7 v Swansea T, Division 3 (S), 8 November 1924 and v Walsall, Division 3
(S), 19 January 1957.

Most League Points (2 for a win): 62, Division 3 (S), 1932–33 and Division 4, 1962–63.

Most League Points (3 for a win): 76, Division 3, 1990–91.

Most League Goals: 98, Division 4, 1962–63.

Highest League Scorer in Season: Jack Holliday, 38, Division 3 (S), 1932–33.

Most League Goals in Total Aggregate: Jim Towers, 153, 1954–61.

Most Capped Player: John Buttigieg, Malta.

Most League Appearances: Ken Coote, 514, 1949–64.

Record Transfer Fee Received: £350,000 from QPR for Andy Sinton, March 1989.

Record Transfer Fee Paid: £167,000 to Hibernian for Eddie May, July 1989.

Football League Record: 1920 Original Member of Division 3; 1921–33 Division 3 (S);
1933–35 Division 2; 1935–47 Division 1; 1947–54 Division 2; 1954–62 Division 3 (S);
1962–63 Division 4; 1963–66 Division 3; 1966–72 Division 4; 1972–73 Division 3;
1973–78 Division 4; 1978– Division 3.

Honours: Football League: Division 1 best season: 5th, 1935–36; Division 2 – Champions
1934–35; Division 3 (S) – Champions 1932–33; Runners-up 1929–30, 1957–58; Division 4 –
Champions 1962–63. *FA Cup:* best season: 6th rd, 1938, 1946, 1949, 1989. *Football League
Cup:* best season: 4th rd, 1982–83. *Freight Rover Trophy* – Runners-up 1985.

Colours: Red and white striped shirts, black shorts, red stockings with black tops. **Change
colours:** All blue.

BRENTFORD 1990–91 LEAGUE RECORD

Match No.	Date	Venue	Opponents	Result	H/T Score	Lg. Pos.	Goalscorers	Attendance
1	Aug 25	H	Bournemouth	D	0-0	0-0	—	5669
2	Sept 1	A	Mansfield T	W	2-0	0-0	6	Smillie, Godfrey	2511
3	8	H	Chester C	L	0-1	0-0	11		4812
4	15	A	Swansea C	D	2-2	0-1	13	Bates, Jones (pen)	4127
5	18	A	Rotherham U	D	2-2	0-1	—	Holdsworth, Smillie	4298
6	22	H	Bolton W	W	4-2	1-1	9	May, Brooke, Jones, Holdsworth	5077
7	29	H	Grimsby T	W	1-0	1-0	8	Jones	5951
8	Oct 2	A	Preston NE	D	1-1	0-0	—	Godrey	5025
9	6	A	Bradford C	W	1-0	1-0	6	Godfrey	6402
10	14	H	Cambridge U	L	0-3	0-0	—		6833
11	20	H	Huddersfield T	W	1-0	0-0	6	May	5509
12	23	A	Reading	W	2-1	1-0	—	Gayle, Holdsworth	6562
13	26	A	Tranmere R	L	1-2	0-0	—	Holdsworth (pen)	7173
14	Nov 4	H	Southend U	L	0-1	0-1	—		8021
15	10	H	Bury	D	2-2	0-0	7	Blissett, Cockram	5303
16	24	A	Exeter C	D	1-1	1-1	9	Blissett	3826
17	Dec 2	H	Leyton Orient	W	1-0	0-0	—	Godfrey	7383
18	16	A	Stoke C	D	2-2	1-1	—	Cadette, Smillie	10,995
19	23	H	Wigan Ath	W	1-0	1-0	—	Blissett (pen)	6495
20	26	A	Birmingham C	W	2-0	0-0	3	Blissett 2	6612
21	29	A	Crewe Alex	D	3-3	1-2	3	Blissett, Cadette, Cockram	3636
22	Jan 1	H	Shrewsbury T	W	3-0	1-0	3	Blissett (pen), Gayle, Cockram	7064
23	12	H	Mansfield T	D	0-0	0-0	4		6064
24	19	A	Bournemouth	L	0-2	0-0	6		7167
25	26	H	Swansea C	W	2-0	0-0	4	Blissett, Jones	5373
26	Feb 2	A	Rotherham U	L	1-2	1-0	5	Jones	5540
27	5	A	Bolton W	L	0-1	0-1	—		6731
28	16	H	Exeter C	W	1-0	0-0	5	Millen	5118
29	23	A	Bury	D	1-1	0-0	7	Cadette	2956
30	Mar 3	A	Leyton Orient	W	2-1	0-1	—	Cadette, Holdsworth	5136
31	9	H	Stoke C	L	0-4	0-0	6		7249
32	12	H	Preston NE	W	2-0	0-0	—	Bates, Blissett	4856
33	16	A	Grimsby T	L	0-2	0-2	9		6685
34	19	A	Cambridge U	D	0-0	0-0	—		4931
35	23	H	Bradford C	W	6-1	4-1	6	Oliver (og), Evans, Jones, Cadette 2, Gayle	5601
36	30	H	Birmingham C	D	2-2	2-1	8	Ratcliffe, Blissett	6757
37	Apr 1	A	Wigan Ath	L	0-1	0-0	8		2160
38	6	H	Crewe Alex	W	1-0	1-0	8	Fleming	5066
39	13	A	Shrewsbury T	D	1-1	0-0	9	Ratcliffe	2841
40	16	H	Fulham	L	1-2	0-1	—	Rostron	7839
41	20	A	Huddersfield T	W	2-1	1-1	10	Peters, Gayle	6489
42	23	A	Fulham	W	1-0	1-0	—	Rostron	6765
43	27	H	Reading	W	1-0	0-0	6	Millen	6398
44	30	A	Chester C	W	2-1	2-0	—	Gayle, Evans	1275
45	May 4	H	Tranmere R	L	0-2	0-2	6		7341
46	11	A	Southend U	W	1-0	0-0	6	Gayle	9666

Final League Position: 6

GOALSCORERS

League (59): Blissett 10 (2 pens), Cadette 6, Gayle 6, Jones 6 (1 pen), Holdsworth 5 (1 pen), Godfrey 4, Cockram 3, Smillie 3, Bates 2, Evans 2, May 2, Millen 2, Ratcliffe 2, Rostron 2, Brooke 1, Fleming 1, Peters 1, own goal 1.
Rumbelows Cup (4): Bates 1, Evans 1, Godfrey 1, Jones 1 (pen).
FA Cup (9): Holdsworth 3, Blissett 2, Jones 2, Godfrey 1, May 1.

Benstead	Cousins	Fleming	Millen	Bates	Buckle	Jones	May	Holdsworth	Godfrey	Smillie	Cadette	Brooke	Evans	Cockram	Ratcliffe	Cash	Gayle	Parks	Blissett	Rostron	Carstairs	Goodyear	Peters	Match No.
1	2	3	4	5	6	7	8	9	10*	11	12													1
1	2	3	4	5	6	7	8		10	11	9*	12												2
1		3†	4	2	6	7	8		10	11		9*	5	12	14									3
1			4	2	6†	7	8	9*	10	11	14	12	5		3									4
1			4	2	6*	7	8	9	10†	11	14	12	5		3									5
1			4	2		7	8	9	10†	11	14	6*	5	12	3									6
1	5		4	2		7	8		10	11	9	6			3									7
1	5		4	2		7	8		10	11	9	6			3									8
1	5		4	2	14	7	8		10	11	9*	6†		12	3									9
1	2		4	5		7	8		10	11	9*	6†		12	3	14								10
1	2			5		7	8		10	11		6*	12	4	3	9								11
1				2		7	8	9	10	11		5		4	3	6								12
	12		2			7	8	9*	10	11		5		4	3	6		1						13
1			4			7	8		10	11	6*	5		2	3	9		12						14
1		3	4			7	8	9	10†	11		5	14	2		6*	12							15
1		3	4			7	8	9*	12	11		5	6	2		10								16
1		3*	4	12	6	7		9†	8	11		5		2		14	10							17
1	5	3	4		6	7			8*	11	9			2		12	10							18
1		3	4		6	7			8	11	9*	5		2		12	10							19
1		3	4		6†	7			8*	11	9*	5	14	2		12	10							20
1		3	4		6†	7			8*	11	9	5	14	2		12	10							21
1		3	4		6	7	12	9*				5	8	2		11	10							22
1			4		6	7		9*		11		5	12	2		8	10		3					23
1			4		6	7			11	9		5	12	2		8*	10		3					24
1			4	12	6	7†			11	9		5	14	2		8	10		3*					25
1		3	4		6	7*	14	12	11	9		5		2		8†	10							26
1		3	4		6	7	14	8	11	9*		5		2		12	10†							27
1			4		6†	7	9		11	12		5	14	2			10*		8	3				28
1			4		6	7		10	11	9*		5	8	2		12			14	3†				29
1			4		6†	7		9	12	11	10	5	8*	2					14	3				30
1	4				6†	7		9		11	10*	5	8	2		12			14	3				31
1			4		6	7		9*		11†12		5	14	2			10		8	3				32
1			4		6*	7		14	11	9		5		2		12	10†		8	3				33
1			4			7		9*11		10		5		2		8	12		6	3				34
1			4	14		7		10	11		9*	5		2		6	12		8	3†				35
1			4			7		9*11		12		5		2		6	10		8		3			36
1	11†		4			7		9		12		5	14	2		6	10*		8		3			37
1		3			4	11	7	9*		12			14	2		6†	10		8		5			38
1		3			4	11		9	12				7*	2		6	10		8		5			39
1		3	4			7		9	11			5	12	2		10*			8		6			40
1		3	4			7		9				5		2		10			8		6	11		41
1		3	4			7		9	12			5		2		10*			8		6	11		42
1		4	3			7		9	12	14		5	6*			10			8		2	11†		43
1		4	3			7		9				5				11	10	6			2	8		44
1		4	3			7		9	12			5		2		11†	10	14			6*	8		45
1		4	3			7			12	11		5		2		9	10	8				6*		46
45	8	18	31	30	24	45	16	27	26	33	19	8	36	7	34	11	23	1	22	18	8	10	6	
	+	+	+		+	+	+	+	+	+			+	+		+			+	+				
	1s	2s	2s		1s	3s	6s	3s	9s	3s			13s4s			10s			4s	4s				

Rumbelows Cup First Round Hereford U (h) — 2-0
   (a) — 0-1
  Second Round Sheffield W (a) — 1-2
   (h) — 1-2
FA Cup First Round Yeovil (h) — 5-0
  Second Round Birmingham C (a) — 3-1
  Third Round Oldham Ath (a) — 1-3

BRENTFORD

Player and Position	Ht	Wt	Birth Date	Place	Source	Clubs	League App	Gls
Goalkeepers								
Laurence Batty*	6 0	13 07	15 2 64	London	Farense	Fulham	9	—
						Crystal Palace (loan)	—	—
						Brentford	—	—
Ashley Bayes			19 4 72	Lincoln	Trainee	Brentford	1	—
Graham Benstead	6 1	13 07	20 8 63	Aldershot	Apprentice	QPR	—	—
						Norwich C (loan)	1	—
						Norwich C	15	—
						Colchester U (loan)	18	—
						Sheffield U (loan)	8	—
						Sheffield U	39	—
						Brentford	45	—
Defenders								
Jamie Bates	6 1	12 12	24 2 68	London	Trainee	Brentford	130	5
John Buttigieg*	6 0	11 13	5 10 63	Sliema	Sliema W	Brentford	40	—
						Swindon T (loan)	3	—
Jason Cousins	6 0	11 06	4 10 70	Hillingdon	Trainee	Brentford	21	—
Terry Evans	6 5	15 01	12 4 65	London	Hillingdon B	Brentford	174	15
Mark Fleming	5 9	10 11	11 8 69	Hammersmith	Trainee	QPR	3	—
						Brentford	35	1
Marcus Gayle	6 2	12 13	27 9 70	Hammersmith	Trainee	Brentford	45	6
Clive Goodyear*	6 0	11 04	15 1 61	Lincoln	Local	Luton T	90	4
						Plymouth Arg	106	5
						Wimbledon	26	—
						Brentford	10	—
Simon Line	6 0	13 00	1 11 71	York	Trainee	Crystal Palace	—	—
						Brentford	—	—
Keith Millen	6 2	12 04	26 9 66	Croydon	Juniors	Brentford	228	12
Rob Peters	5 8	11 02	18 5 71	Kensington	Trainee	Brentford	8	1
Simon Ratcliffe	5 11	11 09	8 2 67	Davyhulme	Apprentice	Manchester U	—	—
						Norwich C	9	—
						Brentford	82	5
Wilf Rostron	5 7	11 11	29 9 56	Sunderland	Apprentice	Arsenal	17	2
						Sunderland	76	17
						Watford	317	22
						Sheffield W	7	—
						Sheffield U	36	3
						Brentford	22	2
Midfield								
Paul Buckle	5 8	10 08	16 12 70	Hatfield	Trainee	Brentford	37	—
Allan Cockram*	5 8	10 08	8 10 63	Kensington	Local	Tottenham H	2	—
						Bristol R	1	—
					St Albans	Brentford	90	14
Keith Jones	5 9	10 11	14 10 65	Dulwich	Apprentice	Chelsea	52	7
						Brentford	163	12
Khotso Moabi‡			13 12 71	Swaziland	Trainee	Brentford	—	—
Neil Smillie	5 6	10 07	19 7 58	Barnsley	Apprentice	Crystal Palace	83	7
						Brentford (loan)	3	—
						Brighton & HA	75	2
						Watford	16	3
						Reading	39	—
						Brentford	107	10
Forwards								
Paul Birch	6 0	12 05	3 12 68	Reading	Trainee	Arsenal	—	—
						Portsmouth	—	—
						Brentford	18	2

BRENTFORD

Foundation: Formed as a small amateur concern in 1889 they were very successful in local circles. They won the championship of the West London Alliance in 1893 and a year later the West Middlesex Junior Cup before carrying off the Senior Cup in 1895. After winning both the London Senior Amateur Cup and the Middlesex Senior Cup in 1898 they were admitted to the Second Division of the Southern League.

First Football League game: 28 August, 1920, Division 3, v Exeter C (a), L 0-3 – Young; Rosier, Hodson; Amos, Levitt, Elliott; Henery, Morley, Spredbury, Thompson, Smith.

Did you know: No club has achieved a 100% home record in any Football League season since Brentford won all 21 of their Division 3(S) games in 1929-30.

Managers (and Secretary-managers)
Will Lewis 1900–03*, Dick Molyneux 1903–06, W. G. Brown 1906–08, Fred Halliday 1908–26 (only secretary to 1922), Ephraim Rhodes 1912–15, Archie Mitchell 1921–22, Harry Curtis 1926–49, Jackie Gibbons 1949–52, Jimmy Blain 1952–53, Tommy Lawton 1953, Bill Dodgin Snr 1953–57, Malcolm Macdonald 1957–65, Tommy Cavanagh 1965–66, Billy Gray 1966–67, Jimmy Sirrel 1967–69, Frank Blunstone 1969–73, Mike Everitt 1973–75, John Docherty 1975–76, Bill Dodgin Jnr 1976–80, Fred Callaghan 1980–84, Frank McLintock 1984–87, Steve Perryman 1987–90, Phil Holder September 1990– .

Player and Position	Ht	Wt	Birth Date	Birth Place	Source	Clubs	League App	Gls
Gary Blissett	6 1	11 13	29 6 64	Manchester	Altrincham	Crewe Alex	122	39
						Brentford	150	41
Richard Cadette	5 8	11 07	21 3 65	Hammersmith	Wembley	Orient	21	4
						Southend U	90	48
						Sheffield U	28	7
						Brentford	76	19
						Bournemouth (loan)	8	1
Andy Driscoll	5 7	10 13	21 10 71	Staines	Trainee	Brentford	13	2
Kevin Godfrey	5 10	10 11	24 2 60	Kennington	Apprentice	Leyton Orient	285	63
						Plymouth Arg (loan)	7	1
						Brentford	88	14
Dean Holdsworth	5 11	11 04	8 11 68	London	Trainee	Watford	16	3
						Carlisle U (loan)	4	1
						Port Vale (loan)	6	2
						Swansea C (loan)	5	1
						Brentford (loan)	7	1
						Brentford	69	29
Eddie May (To Falkirk)	5 9	12 00	30 8 67	Edinburgh	Hutchison Vale	Dundee U	—	—
						Hibernian	109	10
						Brentford	47	10

Trainees
Brady, Christopher J; Burton, Jamie R; Clubb, Matthew C; Dickson, Christopher M; Dunkley, Kerry; Grace, Darren M; Hynes, Michael C; Ivers, Mark A; Jagroop, Mark A; Mason, Neil; Price, Paul J; Sparks, Christopher J; Thomas, Lee; Tripp, Daniel E; Turner, Mark; Webb, Paul A.

Associated Schoolboys
Bradshaw, Ian; Carey, John D.T; Christophe, Stephen J; Cleary, Kevin J; Cole, George; Daldy, Neil F; De Sousa, Charles R; Goodliffe, Jason; Hills, Jamie J; Swayle, Daniel B; Wright, Simon.

Associated Schoolboys who have accepted the club's offer of a Traineeship/Contract
Aouf, Tamer; Bunce, Nathan; Hutchings, Carl E; Johnson, Michael; Ravenscroft, Craig A.

BRIGHTON & HOVE ALBION 1990–91 *Back row (left to right)*: David Coldwell, Paul McCarthy, Perry Digweed, Nicky Bissett, Brian McKenna, Wayne Stemp, Steve Gatting.

Centre row: Larry May (Reserve Coach), John Robinson, Derek McGrath, Chris Lyons, John Crumplin, Adrian Owers, Gary Chivers, Stuart Munday, Lee Cormack, Ted Streeter (Youth Development Officer).

Front row: Malcolm Stuart (Physiotherapist), Garry Nelson, Mark Barham, Dean Wilkins, Barry Lloyd (Manager), Robert Codner, Ian Chapman, Steve Penney, Martin Hinshelwood (Coach).

Division 2   **BRIGHTON & HOVE ALBION**

Goldstone Ground, Old Shoreham Rd, Hove, Sussex BN3 7DE.
Telephone Brighton (0273) 739535. Commercial Dept: (0273)
778230. Recorded information (team & ticket news etc):
Seagull Line 0898 800609.

Ground capacity: 17,677.

Record attendance: 36,747 v Fulham, Division 2, 27 December
1958.

Pitch measurements: 112yd × 75yd.

Chairman: D. C. Sizen. *Vice-chairman:* R. A. Bloom. *President:*
G. A. Stanley.

Directors: P. F. Kent, T. H. Appleby, B. E. Clarke, J. L. Campbell, W. A. Archer, D.
Sullivan.

Manager: Barry Lloyd.

Secretary: Steve Rooke. *Chief Executive:* Ron Pavey.

Coach: Martin Hinshelwood. *Physio:* Malcolm Stuart.

Marketing Manager: Terry Gill. *Lottery Manager:* Dave Treagus.

Year Formed: 1900. *Turned Professional:* 1900. *Ltd Co.:* 1904.

Previous Name: Brighton & Hove Rangers. *Previous Grounds:* 1900, Withdean; 1901,
County Ground; 1902, Goldstone Ground.

Club Nickname: 'The Seagulls'.

Record League Victory: 9-1 v Newport C, Division 3 (S), 18 April 1951 – Ball; Tennant
(1p), Mansell (1p); Willard, McCoy, Wilson; Reed, McNichol (4), Garbutt, Bennett (2),
Keene (1). 9-1 v Southend U, Division 3, 27 November 1965 – Powney; Magill, Baxter;
Leck, Gall, Turner; Gould (1), Collins (1), Livesey (2), Smith (3), Goodchild (2).

Record Cup Victory: 10-1 v Wisbech, FA Cup, 1st rd, 13 November 1965 – Powney; Magill,
Baxter; Collins (1), Gall, Turner; Gould, Smith (2), Livesey (3), Cassidy (2), Goodchild (1).
(1 og).

Record Defeat: 0-9 v Middlesbrough, Division 2, 23 August 1958.

Most League Points (2 for a win): 65, Division 3 (S), 1955–56 and Division 3, 1971–72.

Most League Points (3 for a win): 84, Division 3, 1987–88.

Most League Goals: 112, Division 3 (S), 1955–56.

Highest League Scorer in Season: Peter Ward, 32, Division 3, 1976–77.

Most League Goals in Total Aggregate: Tommy Cook, 113, 1922-29.

Most Capped Player: Steve Penney, 17, Northern Ireland.

Most League Appearances: 'Tug' Wilson, 509, 1922–36.

Record Transfer Fee Received: £900,000 from Liverpool for Mark Lawrenson, August 1981.

Record Transfer Fee Paid: £500,000 to Manchester U for Andy Ritchie, October 1980.

Football League Record: 1920 Original Member of Division 3; 1921–58 Division 3 (S);
1958–62 Division 2; 1962–63 Division 3; 1963–65 Division 4; 1965–72 Division 3; 1972–73
Division 2; 1973–77 Division 3; 1977-79 Division 2; 1979–83 Division 1; 1983–87 Division
2; 1987–88 Division 3; 1988– Division 2.

Honours: Football League: Division 1 best season: 16th 1979–80; Division 2 – Runners-up
1978–79; Division 3 (S) – Champions 1957–58; Runners-up 1953–54, 1955–56; Division 3 –
Runners-up 1971–72, 1976–77, 1987–88; Division 4 – Champions 1964–65. *FA Cup:*
Runners-up 1982–83. *Football League Cup:* best season: 5th rd, 1978–79.

Colours: Blue and white striped shirts, blue shorts with red trim, blue stockings. **Change
colours:** White shirts with red patterned check, red shorts, red stockings with blue and white
trim.

BRIGHTON & HOVE ALBION 1990–91 LEAGUE RECORD

Match No.	Date		Venue	Opponents	Result		H/T Score	Lg. Pos.	Goalscorers	Atten- dance
1	Aug	25	A	Barnsley	L	1-2	1-0	—	Nelson	6885
2	Sept	1	H	Wolverhampton W	D	1-1	0-1	20	Small (pen)	9820
3		8	A	Watford	W	1-0	0-0	15	Nelson	7847
4		15	H	Charlton Ath	W	3-2	1-1	10	Small, Codner, Wilkins	8281
5		19	H	Portsmouth	W	3-2	3-1	—	Small, Codner, Wilkins	9117
6		22	A	Bristol C	L	1-3	0-2	10	Small	11,522
7		29	A	Blackburn R	W	2-1	1-1	7	Byrne, Reid (og)	6027
8	Oct	3	H	Sheffield W	L	0-4	0-2	—		10,379
9		6	H	Swindon T	D	3-3	3-1	11	Gatting, Small, Byrne	7940
10		13	A	WBA	D	1-1	1-0	11	Byrne	9833
11		20	A	Oxford U	L	0-3	0-1	12		4733
12		24	H	Hull C	W	3-1	1-0	—	Byrne, Wilkins, Walker	5354
13		27	A	Middlesbrough	L	2-4	2-3	11	Wilkins, Small	7532
14	Nov	3	A	Ipswich T	W	3-1	2-0	9	Byrne, Small 2 (1 pen)	11,437
15		10	H	Plymouth Arg	W	3-2	1-1	8	Barham, Small, Codner	7305
16		17	A	West Ham U	L	1-2	1-0	9	Small	23,082
17		24	H	Millwall	D	0-0	0-0	9		9638
18	Dec	1	A	Oldham Ath	L	1-6	0-2	12	Wilkins	11,426
19		15	H	Barnsley	W	1-0	0-0	10	Barham	5829
20		22	A	Port Vale	W	1-0	0-0	7	Small	6750
21		26	A	Bristol R	L	0-1	0-1	9		6936
22	Jan	1	A	Notts Co	L	1-2	1-2	11	Gurinovich	8276
23		12	A	Wolverhampton W	W	3-2	2-1	10	Wade, Codner, Barham	12,788
24		16	H	Newcastle U	W	4-2	1-0	—	Wade 4	7684
25		19	H	Watford	W	3-0	2-0	6	Small (pen), Codner 2 (1 pen)	8339
26	Feb	2	A	Charlton Ath	W	2-1	1-0	6	Small (pen), Codner	7178
27		20	H	Leicester C	W	3-0	1-0	—	Small, Wilkins, Wade	6455
28		23	A	Plymouth Arg	L	0-2	0-2	6		5384
29		27	A	Newcastle U	D	0-0	0-0	—		12,692
30	Mar	2	H	Oldham Ath	L	1-2	0-1	6	Chivers	9496
31		9	A	Millwall	L	0-3	0-2	9		9824
32		13	A	Sheffield W	D	1-1	0-1	—	Byrne	23,969
33		16	H	Blackburn R	W	1-0	0-0	7	Chivers	6468
34		20	A	WBA	W	2-0	1-0	—	Nelson 2	6676
35		23	A	Swindon T	W	3-1	1-1	4	Walker, Codner (pen), Nelson	7342
36		30	A	Bristol R	W	3-1	2-1	4	Byrne 2, Walker	6276
37	Apr	3	H	Port Vale	L	1-2	1-1	—	Chivers	9733
38		6	A	Leicester C	L	0-3	0-2	6		8444
39		10	H	West Ham U	W	1-0	1-0	—	Byrne	11,904
40		13	H	Notts Co	D	0-0	0-0	5		9864
41		16	A	Portsmouth	L	0-1	0-1	—		12,271
42		20	H	Oxford U	L	0-3	0-1	6		8118
43		23	H	Bristol C	L	0-1	0-0	—		7738
44		27	A	Hull C	W	1-0	0-0	6	Barham	4037
45	May	4	A	Middlesbrough	L	0-2	0-0	7		18,054
46		11	H	Ipswich T	W	2-1	1-0	6	Small (pen), Wilkins	12,281

Final League Position: 6

GOALSCORERS

League (63): Small 15 (5 pens), Byrne 9, Codner 8 (2 pens), Wilkins 7, Wade 6, Nelson 5, Barham 4, Chivers 3, Walker 3, Gatting 1, Gurinovich 1, own goal 1.
Rumbelows Cup (1): Small 1.
FA Cup (7): Barham 2, Byrne 2, Small 2 (1 pen), Gurinovich 1.

Digweed	Crumplin	Bromage	Wilkins	McCarthy	Chivers	Nelson	Barham	Small	Codner	Walker	Robinson	Meola	Chapman	Gatting	Byrne	Owers	McKenna	Wade	Gurinovich	McGrath	Stemp	Pates	Iovan	Beeney	Bissett	Match No.
1	2	3	4*	5	6	7	8	9	10	11	12															1
	2		4	5	6	7		9	10	11	8	1	3													2
1	2		4	5	6	8	7	9	10	11				3												3
1	2		4	5		8	7*	9	10	11	12		6	3												4
1	2		4	5		7*	8	9	10	11	12		6	3†	14											5
1	2		4	5		7*	8	9	10	11	12		6	3												6
1	2		4	5	3	7		9	10	11			6		8											7
1	2		4	5	6	7*		9	10	11	12			3	8											8
1	2		4	5	6	7		9	10	11				3	8											9
1	2		4	5	6	7		9		11				3	8	10										10
1	2		4	5†	6	7*		9		11	12		14	3	8	10										11
1	2		4		6	7		9	10	11			5	3	8											12
	2*		4		6	7		9	10	11			5	3	8		1	12								13
1	2		4		6	7		9	10	11			3	5	8											14
1	2		4		6	7		9	10	11			3	5	8											15
1	2		4		6	7		9	10	11			3	5	8											16
1	2		4	3	6	7		9	10	11				5	8											17
1	12		4	6		2		7	9	10	11*		3	5	8†			14								18
1	3		4	6		2	12	7	9	10	11			5	8*											19
1	3		4	6		2		7	9	10	11			5					8							20
1	2		4	6		12		7	9	10	11*		3†	5					8	14						21
1	3		4	6		2	7		9	10	11			5					8							22
1	2		4*	5	6	7		9	10	11	12			3	8											23
1	2		4	5	6	7		9	10	11				3	8											24
1	2		4	5	6	7		9†	10	11	14			3	12			8*								25
1	2		4	5	6	7		9	10	11				3	8											26
1	2		4					9*	10	11	7		6	3	8			12				5				27
1	2		4			7*			10	11	12		6	3	8			9†	14	5						28
1	2		4	5					10	11	7		6	3	8			9				5				29
1	2		4	6				9*	10	11	7			3	8			12				5				30
1	2*		4	6				9	10		7			3	8				11			5				31
1	2		4	6	14			9†	10	11*	7		12	3	8							5				32
1	2		4	6	14	9†		10	11	7*	12		12	3	8							5				33
1	2		4	6	9			10	11	7				3	8							5				34
1	2		4	6	9			10	11	7*				3	8			12				5				35
1	2		4	6	9			10	11	7				3	8*			12				5				36
1	2		4	6	9			10	11	7*				3	8			12				5				37
1	2		4	6	9*			10	11	7				3	8			12				5				38
1	2		4	6	12			7*	9	10	11			3	8							5				39
1	2		4	6				7	9	10	11			3	8							5				40
1	2		4†	6	12	7*		9	10	11				3	8							5	14			41
	2		4	6	12	7†		9*	10	11				3	8							5	14	1		42
1	2		4	6		7		9	10	11				3	8							5				43
	2		4	6	12	7		9*		11				3	8							5		1	10	44
1	2		4	6	12	7		9*		11			14	3†	8							5			10	45
1	2		4			7		9	10	11			14	3	8*			12				5			6†	46
42	45	1	46	21	39	12	32	39	42	45	13	1	15	43	34	2	1	5	3	1	2	17	—	2	3	

Substitute appearances: +1s (Chivers) · +11s (Small) · +2s (Chapman) · +8s (Gatting) · +4s 1s (Byrne / Owers) · +6s 1s 4s (Wade / Gurinovich / McGrath) · +2s (Pates)

Rumbelows Cup	First Round	Northampton T (h)	0-2
		(a)	1-1
FA Cup	Third Round	Scunthorpe U (h)	3-2
	Fourth Round	Liverpool (a)	2-2
		(h)	2-3

BRIGHTON & HOVE ALBION

Player and Position	Ht	Wt	Birth Date	Place	Source	Clubs	League App	Gls
Goalkeepers								
Mark Beeney	6 4	13 00	30 12 67	Pembury		Gillingham	2	—
						Maidstone U	50	—
						Aldershot (loan)	7	—
						Brighton & HA	2	—
Perry Digweed	6 0	11 04	26 10 59	London	Apprentice	Fulham	15	—
						Brighton & HA	155	—
						WBA (loan)	—	—
						Charlton Ath (loan)	—	—
						Newcastle U (loan)	—	—
						Chelsea (loan)	3	—
Brian McKenna*	6 0	13 12	30 1 72	Dublin	Home Farm	Brighton & HA	1	—
Defenders								
Nicky Bissett	6 2	12 10	5 4 64	Fulham	Barnet	Brighton & HA	48	6
Russel Bromage	5 11	11 05	9 11 59	Stoke	Apprentice	Port Vale	347	13
						Oldham Ath (loan)	2	—
						Bristol C	46	1
						Brighton & HA	1	—
						Maidstone U (loan)	3	—
Ian Chapman	5 8	11 05	31 5 70	Brighton		Brighton & HA	89	—
Gary Chivers	5 11	11 05	15 5 60	Stockwell	Apprentice	Chelsea	133	4
						Swansea C	10	—
						QPR	60	—
						Watford	14	—
						Brighton & HA	136	12
Steve Gatting*	5 11	11 11	29 5 59	Park Royal	Apprentice	Arsenal	58	5
						Brighton & HA	316	19
Stefan Iovan			23 8 60	Rumania	Steaua	Brighton & HA	2	—
Robert Isaac‡	5 11	12 07	30 11 65	Hackney	Apprentice	Chelsea	9	—
						Brighton & HA	30	—
Chris Lyons*	5 10	11 06	30 8 72	Stepney	Trainee	Brighton & HA	—	—
Paul McCarthy	6 0	13 06	4 8 71	Cork	Trainee	Brighton & HA	24	—
Stuart Munday	5 11	11 00	28 9 72	London	Trainee	Brighton & HA	—	—
Greg O'Dowd	5 10	10 00	16 3 73	Dublin	Trainee	Brighton & HA	—	—
Wayne Stemp	5 11	11 02	9 9 70	Epsom	Trainee	Brighton & HA	4	—
Midfield								
Mark Barham	5 7	11 00	12 7 62	Folkestone	Apprentice	Norwich C	177	23
						Huddersfield T	27	1
						Middlesbrough	4	—
						WBA	4	—
						Brighton & HA	49	6
David Coldwell*	5 11	11 09	31 1 72	Crawley	Trainee	Brighton & HA	—	—
John Crumplin	5 8	11 10	26 5 67	Bath	Bognor	Brighton & HA	114	4
Igor Gurinovich†			5 3 60	Minsk	Dynamo Minsk	Brighton & HA	4	1
Derek McGrath	5 5	10 01	21 1 72	Dublin	Trainee	Brighton & HA	6	—
Adrian Owers*	5 8	10 02	26 2 65	Danbury	Apprentice	Southend U	27	—
					Chelmsford C	Brighton & HA	40	4
						Gillingham (loan)	10	—
Steve Penney*	5 9	10 04	16 1 64	Ballymena	Ballymena U	Brighton & HA	138	15
John Robinson	5 10	11 05	29 8 71	Rhodesia	Trainee	Brighton & HA	20	—
Dean Wilkins	5 8	11 08	12 7 62	Hillingdon	Apprentice	QPR	6	—
						Brighton & HA	2	—
						Orient (loan)	10	—
					Zwolle	Brighton & HA	179	17

BRIGHTON & HOVE ALBION

Foundation: After barely two seasons in existence, a professional club named Brighton United, consisting mostly of Scotsmen, was forced to disband in 1900. The club's manager John Jackson determined to keep the professional game alive in the town and initiated the movement which led to the formation of Brighton & Hove Rangers that same year.

First Football League game: 28 August, 1920, Division 3, v Southend U (a), L 0-2 – Hayes; Woodhouse, Little; Hall, Comber, Bentley; Longstaff, Ritchie, Doran, Rodgerson, March.

Did you know: Irish International Jack Doran was the first player to score as many as five goals for Brighton in a Football League game. He achieved this feat when Brighton beat Northampton Town 7-0 in 1921-22.

Managers (and Secretary-managers)
John Jackson 1901–05, Frank Scott-Walford 1905–08, John Robson 1908–14, Charles Webb 1919–47, Tommy Cook 1947, Don Welsh 1947–51, Billy Lane 1951–61, George Curtis 1961–63, Archie Macaulay 1963–68, Fred Goodwin 1968–70, Pat Saward 1970–73, Brian Clough 1973–74, Peter Taylor 1974–76, Alan Mullery 1976–81, Mike Bailey 1981–82, Jimmy Melia 1982–83, Chris Catlin 1983–86, Alan Mullery 1986–87, Barry Lloyd January 1987–.

Player and Position	Ht	Wt	Birth Date	Birth Place	Source	Clubs	League App	Gls
Forwards								
John Byrne	6 0	12 04	1 2 61	Manchester	Apprentice	York C	175	55
						QPR	126	30
					Le Havre	Brighton & HA	38	9
Robert Codner	5 11	11 05	23 1 65	Walthamstow	Dagenham	Leicester C	—	—
					Barnet	Brighton & HA	115	18
Garry Nelson	5 10	11 04	16 1 61	Southend	Amateur	Southend U	129	17
						Swindon T	79	7
						Plymouth Arg	74	20
						Brighton & HA	144	47
						Notts Co (loan)	2	—
David Savage	5 11	10 04	30 7 73	Dublin	Kilkenny C	Brighton & HA	—	—
Mike Small	6 0	13 05	2 3 62	Birmingham		Luton T	3	—
						Peterborough U (loan)	4	1
				PAOK Salonika	Brighton & HA	39	15
Bryan Wade	5 8	11 05	25 6 63	Bath	Trowbridge T	Swindon T	60	19
						Swansea C	36	5
					Haverfordwest	Brighton & HA	11	6
Clive Walker	5 8	11 04	26 5 57	Oxford	Apprentice	Chelsea	198	60
						Sunderland	50	10
						QPR	21	1
						Fulham	109	29
						Brighton & HA	45	3

Trainees
Barrett, Michael; Bennett, Peter J.P; Funnell, Simon P; Lockhart, Jonathan; Logan, William P; McCann, Alan M.T; McDonald, Charles S; Nimmo, Andrew K; Reid, Philip C; Rush, Spencer; Sheriff, Mark; Smith, Timothy; Williams, Jamie P.

Associated Schoolboys
Aylward, Adam C; Dale, Stephen P; Jones, Duncan K; Peters, Gary J; Smith, Daniel K.

Associated Schoolboys who have accepted the club's offer of a Traineeship/Contract
Myall, Stuart T; Oliva, Umberto; Pryce-Jones, Liam; Simmonds, Daniel B; Tuck, Stuart G.

BRISTOL CITY 1990–91 *Back row (left to right)*: Cameron Toshack. Matt Bryant. Paul Mardon. Wayne Allison. Mark Aizlewood. Murray Jones. Ronnie McQuilter. Dave Rennie.

Centre row: Micky Mellon. Louie Donowa. Darren Keeling. Chris Honor. Andy Leaning. Ronnie Sinclair. Steve Weaver. Nicky Morgan. Bob Taylor. Glenn Humphries. Jason Eaton.

Front row: Gary Shelton. Andy Llewellyn. John Bailey. Rob Newman. Dave Smith. Gerry Mitchell. Mark Madge. Simon Darlaston. Junior Bent. Andy May.

Division 2   BRISTOL CITY

Ashton Gate, Bristol BS3 2EJ. Telephone Bristol (0272) 632812 (5 lines). Clubcall: 0898 121176.

Ground capacity: 25,271.

Record attendance: 43,335 v Preston NE, FA Cup 5th rd, 16 February 1935.

Record receipts: £97,777.50 v Chelsea, FA Cup 4th round, 27 January 1990.

Pitch measurements: 115yd × 75yd.

Chairman: L. J. Kew. *Vice-chairman:* W. I. Williams.

Directors: O. W. Newland, P. Manning, M. Fricker, K. Sage, D. Coller. *Commercial Manager:* John Cox.

Manager: Jimmy Lumsden. *Assistant Manager:* Tony Taylor.

Physio: Buster Footman. *Football Secretary:* Jean Harrison. *Commercial Manager:* John Cox.

Year Formed: 1894. *Turned Professional:* 1897. *Ltd Co.:* 1897. BCFC (1982) PLC.

Previous Name: Bristol South End 1894–97.

Club Nickname: 'Robins'.

Previous Grounds: 1894, St John's Lane; 1904, Ashton Gate.

Record League Victory: 9-0 v Aldershot, Division 3 (S), 28 December 1946 – Eddols; Morgan, Fox; Peacock, Roberts, Jones (1); Chilcott, Thomas, Clark (4 incl. 1p), Cyril Williams (1), Hargreaves (3).

Record Cup Victory: 11-0 v Chichester C, FA Cup, 1st rd, 5 November 1960 – Cook; Collinson, Thresher; Connor, Alan Williams, Etheridge; Tait (1), Bobby Williams (1), Atyeo (5), Adrian Williams (3), Derrick. (1 og).

Record Defeat: 0-9 v Coventry C, Division 3 (S), 28 April 1934.

Most League Points (2 for a win): 70, Division 3 (S), 1954–55.

Most League Points (3 for a win): 91, Division 3, 1989–90.

Most League Goals: 104, Division 3 (S), 1926–27.

Highest League Scorer in Season: Don Clark, 36, Division 3 (S), 1946–47.

Most League Goals in Total Aggregate: John Atyeo, 314, 1951–66.

Most Capped Player: Billy Wedlock, 26, England.

Most League Appearances: John Atyeo, 597, 1951–66.

Record Transfer Fee Received: £600,0000 from Norwich C for Rob Newman, June 1991.

Record Transfer Fee Paid: £235,000 to St Mirren for Tony Fitzpatrick, July 1979.

Football League Record: 1901 Elected to Division 2; 1906–11 Division 1; 1911–22 Division 2; 1922–23 Division 3 (S); 1923-24 Division 2; 1924–27 Division 3 (S); 1927–32 Division 2; 1932–55 Division 3 (S); 1955–60 Division 2; 1960–65 Division 3; 1965–76 Division 2; 1976–80 Division 1; 1980–81 Division 2; 1981–82 Division 3; 1982–84 Division 4; 1984–90 Division 3; 1990– Division 2.

Honours: Football League: Division 1 – Runners-up 1906–07; Division 2 – Champions 1905–06; Runners-up 1975–76; Division 3 (S) – Champions 1922–23, 1926–27, 1954–55; Runners-up 1937–38; Division 3 – Runners-up 1964–65, 1989–90. *FA Cup:* Runners-up 1909. *Football League Cup:* Semi-final 1970–71, 1988–89. *Welsh Cup:* Winners 1934. *Anglo-Scottish Cup:* Winners 1977–78. *Freight Rover Trophy:* Winners 1985–86; Runners-up 1986–87.

Colours: Red shirts, white shorts, red stockings. **Change colours:** Yellow shirts, green shorts, yellow stockings.

BRISTOL CITY 1990–91 LEAGUE RECORD

Match No.	Date		Venue	Opponents	Result	H/T Score	Lg. Pos.	Goalscorers	Attendance
1	Aug	25	H	Blackburn R	W 4-2	0-1	—	Aizlewood, Taylor 2, Morgan	13,755
2	Sept	2	A	Swindon T	W 1-0	1-0	—	Bent	12,249
3		8	H	Plymouth Arg	D 1-1	1-0	5	Morgan	14,283
4		15	A	WBA	L 1-2	0-2	9	Newman	12,081
5		22	H	Brighton & HA	W 3-1	2-0	8	Smith, Taylor 2	11,522
6		29	H	Newcastle U	W 1-0	1-0	5	Smith	15,858
7	Oct	3	A	Leicester C	L 0-3	0-1	—		9815
8		6	A	Wolverhampton W	L 0-4	0-2	12		17,891
9		13	H	West Ham U	D 1-1	0-0	13	Morgan	16,838
10		20	H	Oldham Ath	L 1-2	1-2	13	Morgan	14,031
11		24	A	Millwall	W 2-1	0-1	—	Horne (og), Aizlewood	10,335
12		27	A	Port Vale	L 2-3	1-2	13	Smith (pen), Allison	7451
13	Nov	3	H	Watford	W 3-2	1-0	11	Allison 2, Falconer (og)	11,576
14		10	A	Oxford U	L 1-3	1-2	13	Shelton	6834
15		17	H	Hull C	W 4-1	1-0	10	May, Newman, Morgan, Shelton	9346
16		24	A	Ipswich T	D 1-1	0-1	11	Taylor	10,037
17	Dec	1	H	Charlton Ath	L 0-1	0-1	13		10,984
18		8	H	Sheffield W	D 1-1	1-1	12	Shirtliff (og)	11,254
19		15	A	Blackburn R	W 1-0	0-0	9	Newman	7072
20		22	A	Notts Co	L 2-3	1-1	11	Bent, Smith	6586
21		26	H	Portsmouth	W 4-1	1-1	8	Morgan 2, Shelton, Rennie	11,892
22		29	H	Middlesbrough	W 3-0	1-0	7	May, Morgan, Allison	14,023
23	Jan	1	A	Barnsley	L 0-2	0-2	9		8961
24		12	H	Swindon T	L 0-4	0-1	9		16,169
25		19	A	Plymouth Arg	L 0-1	0-0	12		8074
26		26	A	Bristol R	L 2-3	2-2	13	Scott (pen), Newman	7054
27	Feb	2	H	WBA	W 2-0	1-0	9	Morgan, Taylor	11,492
28		16	A	Hull C	W 2-1	0-1	8	May, Newman	5212
29		23	H	Oxford U	W- 3-1	2-1	8	Shelton 2, Taylor	10,938
30	Mar	2	A	Charlton Ath	L 1-2	1-2	9	Smith	5477
31		5	H	Bristol R	W 1-0	0-0	—	Donowa	22,227
32		9	H	Ipswich T	W 4-2	2-1	5	Taylor 2, Shelton, Morgan	11,474
33		12	H	Leicester C	W 1-0	0-0	—	Taylor	13,297
34		16	A	Newcastle U	D 0-0	0-0	5		13,578
35		20	A	West Ham U	L 0-1	0-0	—		22,951
36		23	H	Wolverhampton W	D 1-1	0-0	7	Bryant	15,499
37		30	A	Portsmouth	L 1-4	0-1	8	Morgan	10,418
38	Apr	1	H	Notts Co	W 3-2	1-1	7	Allison, Donowa, Shelton	13,466
39		6	A	Middlesbrough	L 1-2	1-1	8	Taylor	13,846
40		13	H	Barnsley	W 1-0	1-0	7	Newman	12,081
41		20	A	Oldham Ath	L 1-2	0-0	9	Newman	14,086
42		23	A	Brighton & HA	W 1-0	0-0	—	Shelton	7738
43		27	H	Millwall	L 1-4	0-0	8	Morgan	16,741
44	May	4	H	Port Vale	D 1-1	1-0	9	Rennie	11,555
45		8	A	Sheffield W	L 1-3	0-1	—	Allison	31,706
46		11	A	Watford	W 3-2	0-0	9	Morgan, Newman, Donowa	13,029

Final League Position: 9

GOALSCORERS

League (68): Morgan 13, Taylor 11, Newman 8, Shelton 8, Allison 6, Smith 5 (1 pen), Donowa 3, May 3, Aizlewood 2, Bent 2, Rennie 2, Bryant 1, Scott 1 (pen), own goals 3.
Rumbelows Cup (5): Morgan 4, Smith 1.
FA Cup (1): Allison 1.

Sinclair	Llewellyn	Aizlewood	May	Shelton	Rennie	Donowa	Newman	Taylor	Morgan	Smith	Bent	Allison	Humphries	Bailey	Leaning	Scott	Bryant	Mardon	Match No.
1	2	3	4	5	6	7	8	9	10	11									1
1	2	3	4	5	6		8	9	10*	11	7	12							2
1	2	3	4	5	6		8	9*	10	11	7	12							3
1	2	3	4	5	6		8	9*	10	11	7	12							4
1	2	3	4	5	6		8	9	10*	11	7	12							5
1	2	3	4	5	6		8	9	10	11	7								6
1	2	3	4	5	6		8	9	10	11*	7	12							7
1		3	4	5	6	7	2	9	10	11		8*	12						8
	2		4	7	5	6	8	9	10	11		3		1					9
	2		4	7	5	6†14	8	9*	10	11	12	3		1					10
1	2		4	7	5	6	8	12	10*	11	9	3							11
1	2		4	7	5	6 12	8		10	11	9	3*							12
1	2		4	7	5	6 12	8		10	11*	9	3							13
1	2		4	7	5	6 14	8	12	10*	11	9	3†							14
1	2	3	4	5	6		8		10	11	7	9							15
1	2	3	4	5	6		8	12	10	11	7	9*							16
1	2	3	4	5	6		8	9	10†11	7*12	14								17
1	2		4	5	6		8	9	10	11	7*12				3				18
1	2		4	5	6		8	9	10	11	7				3				19
	2		4	5	6		8	9	10*11	7	12				3	1			20
	2 14		4	5	6		8	9*10	11	7†12					3	1			21
	2 6		4	5	7*12	8		10	11	9					3	1			22
	2 6		4	5	7 14	8 12	10*11	9							3†	1			23
	2 6		4	5	7 14	8 12	10*11	9							3†	1			24
	2 6		4		7*12	8		10	11	9					3	1	5		25
	2 6		4		7	8	9	10	11*12						3	1	5		26
	2 6		4	7		8	9	10*11	12						3	1	5		27
	2 6		4	7	12	8	9	10	11*						3	1	5		28
	2 6		4	7		8	9	10	11						3	1	5		29
	2 6†	4	7	14		8	9*10	11	12						3	1	5		30
	2 6	4†	7	14	11	8	9*10	12							3	1	5		31
	2 6	4* 7		11	8	9	10	12							3	1	5		32
	2 6	4	7†	11	8	9	10*14	12							3	1	5		33
	2 6	4	7	14	8	9	10*11†	12							3	1	5		34
	2 6	4	7	11*	8	9	10								3	1	5		35
	2† 6	4	7	11	8	9	10*	14	12						3	1	5		36
	2* 6	4	7 14	11	8	9	10†	12							3	1	5		37
	2 6	4	7	11	8	9	10*	12							3	1	5		38
	6* 2	7	4	11†	8	9	14	10							3	1	5 12		39
	2		4	7	8	9	11	10							3	1	5	6	40
	2 6	4†	7	8	9*12	14	10								3	1	5	11	41
	2* 6	12	7	8	11	10	9								3	1	5	4	42
	2 6		7	8	11	10	12 9								3	1	5	4*	43
	6 2	7	4	12	8	11*10	9								3	1	5		44
	6 2	7*4	12	8		10	11 9								3	1	5		45
	2 6	4	7	12	8		10	11*	9						3	1	5		46
17	42	41	44	43	29	11	46	34	43	32	15	18	1	6	29	27	22	6	
	+	+		+	+		+	+	+	+	+						+		
	1s	1s		3s	13s		5s	1s	2s	5s	19s 1s						1s		

Rumbelows Cup First Round WBA (a) 2-2
                                        (h) 1-0
                    Second Round Sunderland (a) 1-0
                                        (h) 1-6
FA Cup Third Round Norwich C (a) 1-2

BRISTOL CITY

Player and Position	Ht	Wt	Birth Date	Place	Source	Clubs	League App	Gls
Goalkeepers								
Andy Leaning	6 1	13 07	18 5 62	York	Rowntree M	York C	69	—
						Sheffield U	21	—
						Bristol C	54	—
Ron Sinclair	5 10	11 09	19 11 64	Stirling	Apprentice	Nottingham F	—	—
						Wrexham (loan)	11	—
						Sheffield U (loan)	—	—
						Leeds U (loan)	—	—
						Derby Co (loan)	—	—
						Leeds U	8	—
						Halifax T (loan)	14	—
						Bristol C	44	—
Steve Weaver	5 11	10 02	5 5 72	Bristol	Trainee	Bristol C	—	—
Defenders								
John Bailey	5 8	11 03	1 4 57	Liverpool	Apprentice	Blackburn R	120	1
						Everton	171	3
						Newcastle U	40	—
						Bristol C	80	1
Matthew Bryant	6 1	12 11	21 9 70	Bristol	Trainee	Bristol C	22	1
						Walsall (loan)	13	—
Robert Edwards	6 0	11 06	1 7 73	Kendal		Carlisle U	48	5
						Bristol C	—	—
Chris Honor	5 9	10 09	5 6 68	Bristol	Apprentice	Bristol C	60	1
						Torquay U (loan)	3	—
						Hereford U (loan)	3	—
						Swansea C (loan)	2	—
Darren Keeling‡			29 11 71	Bristol	Trainee	Bristol C	—	—
Andy Llewellyn	5 7	11 12	26 2 66	Bristol	Apprentice	Bristol C	237	3
Ron McQuilter‡	6 2	12 01	24 12 70	Glasgow		Bristol C	—	—
Mark Madge‡			31 12 71	Bristol	Trainee	Bristol C	—	—
Paul Mardon	6 0	11 10	14 9 69	Bristol	Trainee	Bristol C	42	—
						Doncaster (loan)	3	—
Rob Newman	6 2	12 00	13 12 63	London	Apprentice	Bristol C	394	52
Andy Paterson			5 5 72	Glasgow		Bristol C	—	—
Martin Scott	5 8	9 10	7 1 68	Sheffield	Apprentice	Rotherham U	94	3
						Nottingham F (loan)	—	—
						Bristol C	27	1
Midfield								
Mark Aizlewood	6 0	12 08	1 10 59	Newport	Apprentice	Newport Co	38	1
						Luton T	98	3
						Charlton Ath	152	9
						Leeds U	70	3
						Bradford C	39	1
						Bristol C	42	2
Simon Darlaston‡			30 12 71	Gloucester	School	Bristol C	—	—
Andy May	5 8	11 00	26 2 64	Bury	Apprentice	Manchester C	150	8
						Huddersfield T	114	5
						Bolton W (loan)	10	2
						Bristol C	45	3
Michael Mellon	5 8	11 03	18 3 72	Paisley	Trainee	Bristol C	9	—
David Rennie	6 0	12 00	29 8 64	Edinburgh	Apprentice	Leicester C	21	1
						Leeds U	101	5
						Bristol C	77	6
Gary Shelton	5 7	11 03	21 3 58	Nottingham	Apprentice	Walsall	24	—
						Aston Villa	24	7
						Notts Co (loan)	8	—
						Sheffield W	198	18
						Oxford U	65	1
						Bristol C	86	17

BRISTOL CITY

Foundation: The name Bristol City came into being in 1897 when the Bristol South End club, formed three years earlier, decided to adopt professionalism and apply for admission to the Southern League after competing in the Western League. The historic meeting was held at The Albert Hall, Bedminster. Bristol City employed Sam Hollis from Woolwich Arsenal as manager and gave him £40 to buy players. In 1901 they merged with Bedminster, another leading Bristol club.

First Football League game: 7 September, 1901, Division 2, v Blackpool (a) W 2-0 – Moles; Tuft, Davies; Jones, McLean, Chambers; Bradbury, Connor, Boucher, O'Brien (2), Flynn.

Did you know: The last time City scored 100 League goals in a season they could only finish 14th in the Table. This was in the Third Division 1962-63 when only champions Northampton Town scored more goals than the City.

Managers (and Secretary-managers)
Sam Hollis 1897–99, Bob Campbell 1899–1901, Sam Hollis 1901–05, Harry Thickett 1905–10, Sam Hollis 1911–13, George Hedley 1913–15, Jack Hamilton 1915–19, Joe Palmer 1919–21, Alex Raisbeck 1921–29, Joe Bradshaw 1929–32, Bob Hewison 1932–49 (under suspension 1938–39), Bob Wright 1949–50, Pat Beasley 1950–58, Peter Doherty 1958–60, Fred Ford 1960–67, Alan Dicks 1967–80, Bobby Houghton 1980–82, Roy Hodgson 1982, Terry Cooper 1982–88 (Director from 1983), Joe Jordan 1988–90, Jimmy Lumsden October 1990– .

Player and Position	Ht	Wt	Birth Date	Place	Source	Clubs	League App	Gls
Forwards								
Wayne Allison	6 1	12 06	16 10 68	Huddersfield		Halifax T	84	23
						Watford	7	—
						Bristol C	37	6
Junior Bent	5 5	10 06	1 3 70	Huddersfield	Trainee	Huddersfield T	36	6
						Burnley (loan)	9	3
						Bristol C	21	2
Gary Campbell	6 0	11 08	25 8 72	Glasgow	Trainee	Bristol C	—	—
Louie Donowa	5 9	11 00	24 9 64	Ipswich	Apprentice	Norwich C	62	11
						Stoke C (loan)	4	1
					Coruna Willem II	Ipswich T	23	1
						Bristol C	24	3
Jason Eaton‡	5 10	11 00	29 1 69	Bristol	Trowbridge	Bristol R	3	—
						Bristol C	13	1
Nicky Morgan	5 10	12 08	30 10 59	East Ham	Apprentice	West Ham U	21	2
						Portsmouth	95	32
						Stoke C	88	21
						Bristol C	51	17
David Smith	6 0	11 00	25 6 61	Sidcup	Welling U	Gillingham	104	10
						Bristol C	79	9
Bob Taylor	5 10	11 02	3 2 67	Horden	Horden CW	Leeds U	42	9
						Bristol C	88	46
Gerard Mitchell‡			6 8 72	Motherwell	Trainee	Bristol C	—	—

Trainees
Benton, Stephen K; Clifford, Steven A; Cook, Anthony C; Cutler, Mark A; Fox, Andrew D; Giles, Christopher P.J; Griffiths, Craig M; Hogg, Andrew; Kennedy, Paul; Mark, Jonathan; O'Brien, Paul S; Smith, Graham J; Souch, Mark; Terry, Paul; Vernon, Deion A; Watkins, Jason.

Associated Schoolboys
Bailey, Andrew; Barclay, Dominic A; Britten, Anthony P; Brown, Scott; Cameron, Scott A; Clark, Lee; Cook, Shane; Curtis, Matthew; Donaldson, Michael I; Edwards, Duncan; Farrow, Marcus W; Freeman, Lewis G.E; Graham, Delmar; Grasso, Santino; Gregg, Edward J; Hewitt, Richard D; Levett, Simon; Maynard, Neil K; Poulson, Robert; Poulton, Craig; Powell, Nicholas J; Smith, Michael G; Westlake, Andrew E; Williams, Simon K; Wilson, Justin.

Associated Schoolboys who have accepted the club's offer of a Traineeship/Contract
Bessel, Wayne; Durbin, Gary; Milson, Paul J; Skidmore, Robert; Wyatt, Michael.

112

BRISTOL ROVERS 1990–91 *Back row (left to right):* Bob Bloomer, Geoff Twentyman, David Mehew, Devon White, Steve Yates, Bill Clark, Ian Hazel, Andy Reece.
Centre row: Ray Kendall (Kit Manager), Vaughan Jones, Mark Hewitson, Paul Nixon, Ian Willmott, Gavin Kelly, Brian Parkin, Marcus Browning, Adrian Boothroyd, Tony Pounder, Christian McClean, Roy Dolling (Physiotherapist).
Front row: Phil Purnell, Ian Alexander, Ian Holloway, Graham Muxworthy (Youth Coach). Des Bulpin (Reserve Team Manager). Gerry Francis (Manager). Carl Saunders, Tony Sealy.

Division 2 **BRISTOL ROVERS**

1883

Twerton Park, Twerton, Bath. Telephone: 0272 352508. Training ground: 0272 861743. Match day ticket office: 0225 312327. Offices: 199 Two Mile Road, Kingswood, Bristol BS15 1AZ.

Ground capacity: 9813.

Record attendance: 38,472 v Preston NE, FA Cup 4th rd, 30 January 1960.

Record receipts: £23,275 v Southampton, FA Cup 4th rd, 28 January 1978.

Pitch measurements: 112yd × 75yd.

President: Marquis of Worcester.

Vice-Presidents: Dr W. T. Cussen, A. I. Seager, H. E. L. Brown.

Chairman: D. H. A. Dunford. *Vice-chairman:*

Directors: R. Craig, G. M. H. Dunford, V. Stokes, R. Andrews.

Manager: Martin Dobson. *Assistant Manager:*

Coach: Des Bulpin. *Physio:* Roy Dolling. *Commercial Manager:* A. Wood.

Secretary: R. C. Twyford. *Office Manager:* Mrs Angela Mann.

Year Formed: 1883. *Turned Professional:* 1897. *Ltd Co.:* 1896.

Previous Names: 1883, Black Arabs; 1884, Eastville Rovers; 1897, Bristol Eastville Rovers; 1898, Bristol Rovers.

Club Nickname: 'Pirates'.

Previous Grounds: Purdown, Three Acres, Ashley Hill, Rudgeway, Eastville.

Record League Victory: 7-0 v Brighton & HA, Division 3 (S), 29 November 1952 – Hoyle; Bamford, Geoff Fox; Pitt, Warren, Sampson; McIlvenny, Roost (2), Lambden (1), Bradford (1), Peterbridge (2). (1 og). 7-0 v Swansea T, Division 2, 2 October 1954 – Radford; Bamford, Watkins; Pitt, Muir, Anderson; Petherbridge, Bradford (2), Meyer, Roost (1), Hooper (2). (2 og). 7-0 v Shrewsbury T, Division 3, 21 March 1964 – Hall; Hillard, Gwyn Jones; Oldfield, Stone (1), Mabbutt; Jarman (2), Brown (1), Biggs (1p), Hamilton, Bobby Jones (2).

Record Cup Victory: 6-0 v Merthyr Tydfil, FA Cup, 1st rd, 14 November 1987 – Martyn; Alexander (Dryden), Tanner, Hibbitt, Twentyman, Jones, Holloway, Meacham (1), White (2), Penrice (3) (Reece), Purnell.

Record Defeat: 0-12 v Luton T, Division 3 (S), 13 April 1936.

Most League Points (2 for a win): 64, Division 3 (S), 1952–53.

Most League Points (3 for a win): 93, Division 3, 1989–90.

Most League Goals: 92, Division 3 (S), 1952–53.

Highest League Scorer in Season: Geoff Bradford, 33, Division 3 (S), 1952–53.

Most League Goals in Total Aggregate: Geoff Bradford, 245, 1949–64.

Most Capped Player: Neil Slatter, 10 (22), Wales.

Most League Appearances: Stuart Taylor, 545, 1966–80.

Record Transfer Fee Received: £1,000,000 from Crystal Palace for Nigel Martyn, November 1989.

Record Transfer Fee Paid: £100,000 to Birmingham C for Stewart Barrowclough, July 1979.

Football League Record: 1920 Original Member of Division 3; 1921–53 Division 3 (S); 1953–62 Division 2; 1962–74 Division 3; 1974–81 Division 2; 1981–90 Division 3; 1990– Division 2.

Honours: Football League: Division 2 best season: 6th, 1955–56, 1958–59; Division 3 (S) – Champions 1952–53; Division 3 – Champions 1989–90; Runners-up 1973–74. *FA Cup:* best season: 6th rd, 1950–51, 1957–58. *Football League Cup:* best season: 5th rd, 1970–71, 1971–72.

Colours: Blue and white quartered shirts, white shorts, blue stockings with two white rings on top. **Change colours:** White shirts, black shorts, white stockings.

BRISTOL ROVERS 1990–91 LEAGUE RECORD

Match No.	Date		Venue	Opponents	Result		H/T Score	Lg. Pos.	Goalscorers	Atten-dance
1	Aug	25	A	Leicester C	L	2-3	0-2	—	White, Jones	13,648
2	Sept	1	H	Charlton Ath	W	2-1	1-0	11	White, Mehew	5357
3		8	A	Wolverhampton W	D	1-1	1-1	14	Holloway	17,912
4		15	H	Hull C	D	1-1	1-0	17	Mehew	4734
5		22	A	Ipswich T	L	1-2	0-0	18	Saunders	11,084
6		29	A	Notts Co	L	2-3	1-2	20	Saunders, Holloway (pen)	6563
7	Oct	3	H	Blackburn R	L	1-2	1-0	—	White	5200
8		6	H	Sheffield W	L	0-1	0-1	22		6413
9		13	A	Swindon T	W	2-0	1-0	21	Pounder, Holloway (pen)	11,494
10		20	A	Middlesbrough	W	2-1	0-1	18	White, Holloway (pen)	18,589
11		24	H	Oxford U	W	1-0	1-0	—	Holloway (pen)	5526
12		27	H	Portsmouth	L	1-2	1-1	18	White	6500
13	Nov	3	A	WBA	L	1-3	1-2	19	White	10,997
14		7	H	Barnsley	W	2-1	1-0	—	Mehew, Pounder	4563
15		10	H	Port Vale	W	2-0	1-0	11	Nixon, Mehew	5661
16		17	A	Watford	D	1-1	1-0	14	Drysdale (og)	8285
17		24	H	Oldham Ath	W	2-0	1-0	10	Mehew, White	6542
18	Dec	1	A	Millwall	D	1-1	0-0	9	Mehew	9291
19		15	H	Leicester C	D	0-0	0-0	13		5791
20		22	H	Newcastle U	D	1-1	0-0	13	Saunders	6643
21		26	A	Brighton & HA	W	1-0	1-0	11	Saunders	6936
22		29	A	Plymouth Arg	D	2-2	2-2	10	Saunders 2	8469
23	Jan	1	H	West Ham U	L	0-1	0-0	10		7932
24		12	A	Charlton Ath	D	2-2	1-1	11	Saunders, White	5606
25		19	H	Wolverhampton W	D	1-1	1-1	13	Saunders	6042
26		26	H	Bristol C	W	3-2	2-2	10	Mehew 2, Saunders	7054
27	Feb	2	A	Hull C	L	0-2	0-1	11		5302
28		16	H	Watford	W	3-1	1-1	10	Holloway, White, Saunders	5736
29		23	H	Port Vale	L	2-3	0-3	10	Alexander, Saunders	7166
30		26	A	Barnsley	L	0-1	0-1	—		6197
31	Mar	2	H	Millwall	W	1-0	0-0	11	Sealy	5587
32		5	A	Bristol C	L	0-1	0-0	—		22,227
33		9	A	Oldham Ath	L	0-2	0-0	12		12,775
34		12	A	Blackburn R	D	2-2	0-1	—	Holloway, Saunders	5969
35		16	H	Notts Co	D	1-1	1-0	12	Clark	4878
36		20	H	Swindon T	W	2-1	1-1	—	Saunders, Sealy	6123
37		23	A	Sheffield W	L	1-2	0-0	12	Saunders	25,074
38		30	H	Brighton & HA	L	1-3	1-2	14	Reece	6276
39	Apr	1	A	Newcastle U	W	2-0	0-0	12	Sealey, White	17,509
40		6	H	Plymouth Arg	D	0-0	0-0	12		5668
41		10	H	Ipswich T	W	1-0	1-0	—	Sealy	4983
42		20	H	Middlesbrough	W	2-0	1-0	11	Saunders (pen), Bailey	5722
43		27	A	Oxford U	L	1-3	1-3	11	White	6744
44	May	4	A	Portsmouth	L	1-3	1-2	12	Saunders	9410
45		8	A	West Ham U	L	0-1	0-1	—		23,054
46		11	H	WBA	D	1-1	0-0	13	Pounder	7595

Final League Position: 13

GOALSCORERS

League (56): Saunders 16 (1 pen), White 11, Mehew 8, Holloway 7 (4 pens), Sealy 4, Pounder 3, Alexander 1, Bailey 1, Clark 1, Jones 1, Nixon 1, Reece 1, own goal 1.
Rumbelows Cup (2): Alexander 1, Twentyman 1.
FA Cup (0).

Parkin	Alexander	Twentyman	Yates	Mehew	Jones	Holloway	Reece	White	Saunders	Pounder	Hazel	Bloomer	Nixon	McClean	Purnell	Kelly	Sealy	Gordon	Clark	Willmott	Boothroyd	Bailey	Match No.
1	2	3	4	5*	6	7	8	9	10	11	12												1
1	2	3	4	5*	6	7	8	9	10	11		12											2
1	2	3	4	5*	6	7	8	9	10	11	12												3
1	2	3	4	5	6	7	8	9	10	11													4
1		3	4	5	6	7	8*	9	10	11	2	12											5
1	2	3	4	5	6	7	8	9	10*	11		12											6
1	2	3	4	5*	6	7	8	9		11			10		12								7
1	2*	3	4	5	6	7	8	9		11†			10	14	12								8
1	14	3	4	12	6	7	8	9		10		2†	5*		11								9
1		3	4	12	6	7	8	9		10		2	5*		11								10
1		3	4	12	6	7	8	9		10		2	5*		11								11
1	14	3	4	12	6	7	8	9		10		2†	5*		11								12
1		3	4	12	6	7	8	9		10*		2	5		11								13
1	2	3	4	5	6	7	8†	9	10			14	11*		12								14
1	2	3	4	5	6	7	8	9	12	10		11*											15
1	2	3	4	5	6	7	8	9	12	10		11*											16
1	2	3	4	5	6	7	8†	9	10	11*			14	12									17
1	2	3	4	5	6	7	8	9	10	11													18
1	2	3	4	5	6	7	8	9	10	11													19
1	2	3	4	5*	6	7	8	9	10	11		12											20
1	2	3	4	5	6	7	8	9	10	11*		12											21
1		3	4	5*	6	7	8	9	10	11		2	12										22
1		3	4	5*	6	7	8	9	10	11		2	12										23
	2†	3	4	5*	6	7	8	9	10	11			14			1	12						24
	2	3	4	5*	6	7	8	9	10	11						1	12						25
	2*	3	4	5	6	7	8	9	10	11						1	12						26
	2	3	4†	5*	6	7	8	9	10	11			14			1	12						27
1	2	3	4	5*	6	7	8	9	10	11							12						28
1	2	3	4	5*	6	7	8	9	10	11							12						29
1	2	3	4	5*	6	7	8	9†	10	11							12	14					30
1	2	3	4	5	6	7	8	9	10	11*							12						31
1	2*	3		5	6	7	8	9	10	11									4	12			32
1		3	14			7	8	9	10	11*	5†						12		4	6	2		33
1	2	3		5*		7	8†	9	10	11							12	14	4	6			34
1	2	3	12		6	7	8	9	10	11*							5		4				35
1	2	3	12		6	7	8		10	11							5	9*	4				36
1	2	3			6	7	8	9	10	11*							5	12	4				37
1	2	3	12		6	7	8	9	10	14							5*		4			11†	38
1	2	3			6	7	8	9	10	12							5		4			11*	39
1	2	3			6	7	8	9	10	12							5*		4		14	11†	40
1	2	3	12		6	7	8	9	10	14							5*		4			11†	41
	2	3	12		6	7	8	9	10							1	5*		4			11	42
	2	3			6	7	8	9	10	12						1	5*		4			11	43
	2	3	14	5	6	7	8	9	10	12					11*	1			4†				44
1	2	3	4		6	7	8	9	10	11	12										5*		45
1	2*	3	4	5†	6	7	8	9	10	11	12										14		46
39	37	46	33	30	44	46	46	45	36	39	2	7	10	—	6	7	9	1	13	2	2	6	
	+	+	+			+	+	+	+	+	+	+	+		+	+	+		+	+	+	+	
	2s		1s	11s		2s	6s	4s	6s	6s	2s	3s				9s	3s	1s	1s	1s			

Rumbelows Cup	First Round	Torquay U (h)	1-2
		(a)	1-1
FA Cup	Third Round	Crewe Alex (h)	0-2

BRISTOL ROVERS

Player and Position	Ht	Wt	Birth Date	Place	Source	Clubs	League App	Gls
Goalkeepers								
Gavin Kelly	6 0	12 13	29 9 68	Beverley		Hull C	11	—
						Bristol R (loan)	—	—
						Bristol R	7	—
Brian Parkin	6 3	13 00	12 10 65	Birkenhead	Local	Oldham Ath	6	—
						Crewe Alex (loan)	12	—
						Crewe Alex	86	—
						Crystal Palace (loan)	—	—
						Crystal Palace	20	—
						Bristol R	69	—
Defenders								
Bob Bloomer	5 10	11 06	21 6 66	Sheffield		Chesterfield	141	15
						Bristol R	13	—
Adrian Boothroyd	5 8	10 12	8 2 77	Bradford	Trainee	Huddersfield T	10	—
						Bristol R	3	—
Billy Clark	6 0	12 03	19 5 67	Christchurch	Local	Bournemouth	4	—
						Bristol R	56	2
Vaughan Jones	5 8	11 11	2 9 59	Tonyrefail	Apprentice	Bristol R	101	3
						Newport Co	68	4
						Cardiff C	11	—
						Bristol R	267	9
Geoff Twentyman	6 1	13 02	10 3 59	Liverpool	Chorley	Preston NE	98	4
						Bristol R	219	5
Ian Willmott	5 10	12 06	10 7 68	Bristol	Weston Super Mare	Bristol R	20	—
Steven Yates	5 11	12 06	29 1 70	Bristol	Trainee	Bristol R	113	—
Midfield								
Ian Alexander	5 8	10 07	26 1 63	Glasgow	Leicester Juv	Rotherham U	11	—
					Pezoporikos	Motherwell	24	2
						Morton	7	1
						Bristol R	191	4
Ian Hazel	5 10	10 04	1 12 67	London	Apprentice	Wimbledon	7	—
						Bristol R (loan)	3	—
						Bristol R	14	—
Mark Hewitson*	5 8	10 10	27 2 71	Oxford	Trainee	Oxford U	—	—
						Bristol R	—	—
Ian Holloway	5 7	9 12	12 3 63	Kingswood	Apprentice	Bristol R	111	14
						Wimbledon	19	2
						Brentford (loan)	13	2
						Brentford	16	—
						Torquay U (loan)	5	—
						Bristol R	179	26
Andy Reece	5 11	12 04	5 9 62	Shrewsbury	Willenhall	Bristol R	171	11
Forwards								
Marcus Browning	5 11	12 00	22 4 71	Bristol	Trainee	Bristol R	1	—
Christian McClean*	6 4	14 00	17 10 63	Colchester	Clacton	Bristol R	51	6
David Mehew	5 11	11 07	29 10 67	Camberley		Leeds U	—	—
						Bristol R	161	51
Paul Nixon	5 10	11 03	23 09 63	Seaham	New Zealand	Bristol R	44	6
Tony Pounder	5 8	11 00	11 3 66	Yeovil	Weymouth	Bristol R	45	3
Philip Purnell	5 8	10 02	16 9 64	Bristol	Mangotsfield	Bristol R	141	22
Carl Saunders	5 8	10 12	25 11 64	Marston Green	Local	Stoke C	164	23
						Bristol R	58	21

BRISTOL ROVERS

Foundation: Bristol Rovers were formed at a meeting in Stapleton Road, Eastville, in 1883. However, they first went under the name of the Black Arabs (wearing black shirts). Changing their name to Eastville Rovers in their second season, they won the Gloucestershire Senior Cup in 1888–89. Original members of the Bristol & District League in 1892, this eventually became the Western League and Eastville Rovers adopted professionalism in 1897.

First Football League game: 28 August, 1920, Division 3, v Millwall (a) L 0-2 – Stansfield; Bethune, Panes; Boxley, Kenny, Steele; Chance, Bird, Sims, Bell, Palmer.

Did you know: Rovers have beaten a First Division Manchester United side in both of the principle Cup competitions – 4-0 in the FA Cup, 3rd round (at Eastville), 7 January 1956, and 2-1 in League Cup, 3rd round, replay, (at Old Trafford), 11 October 1972.

Managers (and Secretary-managers)
Alfred Homer 1899–1920 (continued as secretary to 1928), Ben Hall 1920–21, Andy Wilson 1921–26, Joe Palmer 1926–29, Dave McLean 1929–30, Albert Prince-Cox 1930–36, Percy Smith 1936–37, Brough Fletcher 1938–49, Bert Tann 1950–68 (continued as GM to 1972), Fred Ford 1968–69, Bill Dodgin Snr 1969–72, Don Megson 1972–77, Bobby Campbell 1978–79, Harold Jarman 1979–80, Terry Cooper 1980–81, Bobby Gould 1981–83, David Williams 1983–85, Bobby Gould 1985–87, Gerry Francis 1987–91, Martin Dobson July 1991–.

Player and Position	Ht	Wt	Birth Date	Birth Place	Source	Clubs	League App	Gls
Tony Sealy*	5 8	11 08	7 5 59	London	Apprentice	Southampton	7	—
						Crystal Palace	24	5
						Port Vale (loan)	17	6
						QPR	63	18
						Port Vale (loan)	6	4
						Fulham (loan)	5	1
						Fulham	20	9
						Leicester C	39	7
						Bournemouth (loan)	13	2
					Braga	Brentford	12	4
						Swindon T	—	—
						Bristol R	37	7
Devon White	6 3	14 00	2 3 64	Nottingham	Arnold T	Lincoln C	29	4
					Boston U	Bristol R	167	43

Trainees
Archer, Lee; Bourne, Richard M; Chenoweth, Paul; Elliott, Dean M; Gurney, Andrew R; Hervin, Mark P; Maddison, Lee R; Owen, Craig P; Proudfoot, Jamie R; Stewart, William M.P; Thomas, Spencer; Tovey, Paul W; Upshall, Jason F.

Associated Schoolboys
Brockwell, Jamie S; Dampier, Steven M; Davies, Steven; French, Jonathan; Harrington, Mark P; Harris, Paul; Maddison, Neil R; Marsh, Andrew J; Micciche, Marco; Robottom Karl D; Rogers, Stuart; Wills, Andrew K.

Associated Schoolboys who have accepted the club's offer of a Traineeship/Contract
Bennett, Anthony P; Crossey, Scott; Impey, Scott; Paul, Martin L; Smith, Ian S; Stewart, Andrew W.

118

BURNLEY 1990–91 *Back row (left to right):* Peter Mumby, Andy Farrell, Paul France, David Williams, Ian Measham, Chris Pearce, Neil Howarth, Steve Davis, Jason Withe.
Centre row: Jimmy Holland (Physiotherapist), George Bray (Trainer), Joe Jakub, Ray Deakin, John Smyth, Ron Futcher, Paul McKay, Jason Hardy, Danny Sonner, John Deary, Graham Lawrie, Neil Grewcock, Arthur Bellamy (Youth Coach).
Front row: Nigel Smith, Roger Eli, John Francis, Frank Casper (Manager), Jimmy Mullen (Assistant Manager), Winston White, Ian Bray, David Hamilton.

Division 4   **BURNLEY**

Turf Moor, Burnley BB10 4BX. Telephone Burnley (0282)
27777. Clubcall: 0898 121153.
Ground capacity: 20,912.
Record attendance: 54,775 v Huddersfield T, FA Cup 3rd rd,
23 February 1924.
Record receipts; £63,988 v Sheffield W, FA Cup 6th rd,
12 March 1983.
Pitch measurements: 115yd × 73yd.
Chairman: F. J. Teasdale.
Vice-chairman: Dr R. D. Iven MRCS (Eng), LRCP (Lond), MRCGP.
Directors: B. Dearing LLB, B. Rothwell JP, C. Holt,
R. Blakeborough.
Manager: Frank Casper. *Assistant Manager:* Jimmy Mullen.
Secretary: Albert Maddox. *Youth Team Coach:* Harry Wilson.
Commercial Manager: Mrs Joyce Pickles. *Physio:* Jimmy Holland.
Year Formed: 1882. *Turned Professional:* 1883. *Ltd Co.:* 1897.
Previous Name: 1881–82, Burnley Rovers.
Club Nickname: 'The Clarets'.
Previous Grounds: 1881, Calder Vale; 1882, Turf Moor.
Record League Victory: 9-0 v Darwen, Division 1, 9 January 1892 – Hillman; Walker,
McFettridge, Lang, Matthew, Keenan, Nicol (3), Bowes, Espie (1), McLardie (3), Hill (2).
Record Cup Victory: 9-0 v Crystal Palace, FA Cup, 2nd rd (replay) 10 February 1909 –
Dawson; Barron, McLean; Cretney (2), Leake, Moffat; Morley, Ogden, Smith (3), Abbott
(2), Smethams (1). 9-0 v New Brighton, FA Cup, 4th rd, 26 January 1957 – Blacklaw;
Angus, Winton; Seith, Adamson, Miller; Newlands (1), McIlroy (3), Lawson (3),
Cheesebrough (1), Pilkington (1). 9-0 v Penrith FA Cup, 1st rd, 17 November 1984 –
Hansbury; Miller, Hampton, Phelan, Overson (Kennedy), Hird (3 incl. 1p), Grewcock (1),
Powell (2), Taylor (3), Biggins, Hutchison.
Record Defeat: 0-10 v Aston Villa, Division 1, 29 August 1925 and v Sheffield U, Division
1, 19 January 1929.
Most League Points (2 for a win): 62, Division 2, 1972–73.
Most League Points (3 for a win): 80, Division 3, 1981–82.
Most League Goals: 102, Division 1, 1960–61.
Highest League Scorer in Season: George Beel, 35, Division 1, 1927–28.
Most League Goals in Total Aggregate: George Beel, 178, 1923–32.
Most Capped Player: Jimmy McIlroy, 51 (55), Northern Ireland.
Most League Appearances: Jerry Dawson, 522, 1907–28.
Record Transfer Fee Received: £300,000 from Everton for Martin Dobson, August 1974,
and from Derby Co for Leighton James, November 1975.
Record Transfer Fee Paid: £165,000 to QPR for Leighton James, September 1978.
Football League Record: 1888 Original Member of the Football League; 1897–98 Division
2; 1898–1900 Division 1; 1900–13 Division 2; 1913–30 Division 1; 1930–47 Division 2;
1947–71 Division 1; 1971–73 Division 2; 1973–76 Division 1; 1976–80 Division 2; 1980–82
Division 3; 1982–83 Division 2; 1983–85 Division 3; 1985– Division 4.
Honours: Football League: Division 1 – Champions 1920–21, 1959–60; Runners-up 1919–
20, 1961–62; Division 2 – Champions 1897–98, 1972–73; Runners-up 1912–13, 1946–47;
Division 3 – Champions 1981–82. Record 30 consecutive Division 1 games without defeat
1920–21. *FA Cup:* Winners 1913–14; Runners-up 1946–47, 1961–62. *Football League Cup:*
semi-final 1960–61, 1968–69, 1982–83. *Anglo Scottish Cup:* Winners 1978–79. *Sherpa Van
Trophy:* Runners-up 1988. **European Competitions;** *European Cup:* 1960–61. *European Fairs
Cup:* 1966–67.
Colours: Claret shirts with sky blue sleeves, white shorts and stockings. **Change colours:** All
white with claret facings.

BURNLEY 1990–91 LEAGUE RECORD

Match No.	Date		Venue	Opponents	Result		H/T Score	Lg. Pos.	Goalscorers	Attendance
1	Aug	25	H	Lincoln C	D	2-2	1-1	—	Deary, Jakub	6106
2	Sept	1	A	Darlington	L	1-3	1-2	19	Futcher	3671
3		8	H	Scarborough	W	2-1	0-1	14	Futcher, Grewcock	4723
4		14	A	Stockport Co	D	2-2	2-0	—	Futcher 2 (1 pen)	3523
5		18	A	Blackpool	W	2-1	2-0	—	Mumby, Deary	4737
6		22	H	Aldershot	W	3-0	2-0	3	Jakub, Mumby, Francis (pen)	5517
7		28	A	Carlisle U	D	1-1	0-1	—	Edwards (og)	5205
8	Oct	2	H	Northampton T	W	3-0	0-0	—	Terry (og), Francis, Eli	6271
9		6	H	York C	D	0-0	0-0	2		6808
10		13	A	Hereford U	L	0-3	0-0	9		3688
11		20	A	Peterborough U	L	2-3	2-3	9	Futcher 2	5102
12		23	H	Maidstone U	W	2-1	2-0	—	Davis, Futcher	5567
13		27	H	Rochdale	W	1-0	1-0	6	White	7971
14	Nov	3	A	Wrexham	W	4-2	1-0	2	Jakub, Francis, Mumby 2	3997
15		10	A	Walsall	L	0-1	0-0	3		5710
16		24	H	Halifax T	W	2-1	0-0	3	Mumby, Francis	6620
17	Dec	1	H	Cardiff C	W	2-0	0-0	3	Deary, Francis	6348
18		15	A	Gillingham	L	2-3	0-3	4	Deary, Futcher (pen)	3687
19		22	H	Hartlepool U	W	4-0	2-0	2	Francis 2, Deary, Davis	8514
20		29	A	Torquay U	L	0-2	0-1	5		4210
21	Jan	1	H	Scunthorpe U	D	1-1	1-0	5	Francis	8557
22		12	H	Darlington	W	3-1	2-0	6	Davis, Futcher, Francis	8491
23		19	A	Lincoln C	L	0-1	0-0	6		4167
24		26	H	Stockport Co	W	3-2	2-1	5	Deary, Futcher, Eli	8946
25	Feb	16	A	Halifax T	W	2-1	0-1	4	Francis 2 (1 pen)	4755
26		23	H	Walsall	W	2-0	0-0	3	Grewcock, Eli	7783
27		26	A	Doncaster R	L	1-2	1-0	—	Deary	3080
28	Mar	1	A	Cardiff C	L	0-3	0-3	—		3591
29		5	A	Chesterfield	L	1-2	0-1	—	White	4022
30		9	H	Gillingham	D	2-2	0-1	6	Futcher (pen), Davis	6459
31		12	A	Northampton T	D	0-0	0-0	—		3710
32		16	H	Carlisle U	W	2-1	0-1	6	Farrell 2	6635
33		19	H	Hereford U	W	2-1	0-1	—	Futcher, Eli	5716
34		23	A	York C	L	0-2	0-2	6		4407
35		26	A	Scarborough	W	1-0	1-0	—	Francis	2373
36		30	H	Chesterfield	L	0-1	0-0	5		8373
37	Apr	1	A	Hartlepool U	D	0-0	0-0	4		4967
38		6	H	Torquay U	D	1-1	0-0	7	Futcher (pen)	6661
39		13	A	Scunthorpe U	W	3-1	0-0	7	Futcher, Eli, Davis	4449
40		16	A	Aldershot	W	2-1	0-0	—	Eli 2	2473
41		20	H	Peterborough U	W	4-1	4-1	6	Eli 2, Futcher 2 (1 pen)	10,018
42		23	H	Blackpool	W	2-0	0-0	—	Eli, Futcher (pen)	18,395
43		27	A	Maidstone U	L	0-1	0-1	6		3130
44		30	H	Doncaster R	W	1-0	0-0	—	Futcher	10,410
45	May	4	A	Rochdale	D	0-0	0-0	6		7344
46		11	H	Wrexham	W	2-0	1-0	6	Francis 2	10,161

Final League Position: 6

GOALSCORERS

League (70): Futcher 18 (6 pens), Francis 14 (2 pens), Eli 10, Deary 7, Davis 5, Mumby 5, Jakub 3, Farrell 2, Grewcock 2, White 2, own goals 2.
Rumbelows Cup (3): Futcher 1, Hamilton 1, Mumby 1.
FA Cup (5): White 2, Francis 1, Mumby 1, own goal 1.

Pearce	France	Bray	Deary	Farrell	Davis	Mumby	Futcher	Francis	Jakub	Grewcock	Hamilton	White	Deakin	Measham	Pender	Eli	Williams	Smith	Sonner	Lancashire	Match No.
1	2*	3	4	5	6	7†	8	9	10	11	12	14									1
1		3†	4	5	6	12	8	9	10			2	7*	11	14						2
1			4	5	6	7	8	9	10*12	11				3	2						3
1			4	14	6	7†	8*	9	10	12	11			3	2	5					4
1			4	12	6		8	9	10			11	7*	3	2	5					5
1			4		6		8	9	10			11	7*	3	2	5	12				6
1			4	11	6		8	9	10				7	3	2	5					7
1			4	11	6		8	9	10				7	3	2	5*12					8
1			4	5	6		8*14	9	10	12			7	3	2		11†				9
1			4	11*	6		8	14	9	10	12		7†	3	2	5					10
1			4	11	6			8	9	10			7*	3	2	5	12				11
1			4		6	12	8	9	10	11*			7	3	2	5					12
1			4		6	12	8*	9	10	11			7	3	2	5					13
1			4		6		8	9	10	11			7	3	2	5					14
1			4		6		8	9	10	11*			7	3	2	5	12				15
1			4	12	6		8	9	10	11			7	3	2	5*					16
1			4	12	6		8	14	9	10			7†	3	2	5*					17
1			4	5	6		8	9	10	11			7	3	2						18
1			4	12	6	14	8	9	10	11†			7	3	2	5*					19
1			4		6		8	9	10	11			7*	3	2	5	12	1			20
1			4	12	6		8	9	10	11			7*	3	2	5					21
1			4		6		8	9	10				7	3	2	5	12	11*			22
1			4		6		8	9	10	11				3	2	5	12		7*		23
1			4	7	6		8		10	11				3	2	5	9				24
			4	7	6		8		10	11				3	2	5	9	1			25
			4	5	6		8		10	11			7	3	2		9	1			26
1	12		4	7	6		8		10	11†		14		3	2	5*	9				27
1			4	7†	6	12	8		10	11		14		3	2	5	9*				28
1			4		6		8	9	10	12	11†	7		3	2	5					29
1			4		6		8*	9	10	11			7	3	2	5	12				30
1			4		6		8	9	10		11		7	3	2	5					31
1			4	14	6		8	9	10	11†			7*	3	2	5	12				32
1			4	7	6		8	9	10					3	2	5	11				33
1			4	7	6	12		9	10			8*		3	2	5	11				34
1			4	7	6		8	9	10			11		3	2	5					35
1			4	7	6	11*	8	9	10					3	2	5	12				36
1			4	7	6	11*	8	9	10	12				3	2	5					37
1	14		4	7	6		8	9	10	11*			3†		2	5	12				38
1		3	4	7	6		8	9*10						2	5	11		12			39
1		3	4	7	6		8	9	10					2	5	11					40
1		3	4	7	6		8*	9	10	12	14			2	5†11						41
1		3	4	7	6		8	9	10					2	5	11					42
1		3*	4	7	6		8	9	10	12				2	5	11					43
1		3	4	7	6		8	9	10					2	5	11					44
1		3	4†	7	6		8	9*10	12	14				2	5	11					45
1		3		7	6		8	9	10	8	4*			2	5			11	12		46
43	1	10	43	30	46	15	30	45	46	21	8	26	37	44	40	15	3	2	1	—	

Substitute appearances: +1s +1s · +7s · +5s +4s · +9s +3s +3s · +1s · +11s · +1s +1s

Rumbelows Cup	First Round	Stockport Co (a)	2-0
		(h)	0-1
	Second Round	Nottingham F (a)	1-4
		(h)	0-1
FA Cup	First Round	Stafford R (a)	3-1
	Second Round	Stoke C (h)	2-0
	Third Round	Manchester C (h)	0-1

BURNLEY

Player and Position	Ht	Wt	Birth Date	Place	Source	Clubs	League App	Gls
Goalkeepers								
Chris Pearce	6 0	11 04	7 8 61	Newport	Apprentice	Wolverhampton W	—	—
						Blackburn R	—	—
						Rochdale (loan)	5	—
						Barnsley (loan)	—	—
						Rochdale	36	—
						Port Vale	48	—
						Wrexham	25	—
						Burnley	167	—
David Williams	6 0	12 00	18 9 68	Liverpool	Trainee	Oldham Ath	—	—
						Burnley	17	—
Defenders								
Ian Bray	5 8	11 05	6 12 62	Neath	Apprentice	Hereford U	108	4
						Huddersfield T	89	1
						Burnley	11	—
Steve Davis	6 0	12 07	26 7 65	Birmingham	Apprentice	Stoke C	—	—
						Crewe Alex	145	1
						Burnley	147	11
Ray Deakin*	5 8	11 01	19 6 59	Liverpool	Apprentice	Everton	—	—
						Port Vale	23	6
						Bolton W	105	2
						Burnley	213	6
Roger Eli	5 10	12 00	11 9 65	Bradford	Apprentice	Leeds U	2	—
						Wolverhampton W	18	—
						Cambridge U	—	—
						Crewe Alex	27	1
						York C	4	1
						Bury	2	—
						Burnley	55	10
Paul France	6 1	11 08	10 9 68	Huddersfield	Trainee	Huddersfield T	11	—
						Cobh Ramblers (loan)	—	—
						Bristol C	—	—
						Burnley	2	—
Graham Lawrie	5 8	10 12	4 9 71	Aberdeen	Keith	Burnley	—	—
Paul McKay	5 8	10 05	28 1 71	Banbury	Trainee	Burnley	12	—
Ian Measham	5 11	11 08	14 12 64	Barnsley	Apprentice	Huddersfield T	17	—
						Lincoln C (loan)	6	—
						Rochdale (loan)	12	—
						Cambridge U	46	—
						Burnley	110	1
John Pender	6 0	12 07	19 11 63	Luton	Apprentice	Wolverhampton W	117	3
						Charlton Ath	41	—
						Bristol C	83	3
						Burnley	40	—
John Smyth*	5 10	11 00	28 4 70	Dundalk	Dundalk	Liverpool	—	—
						Burnley	—	—
Midfield								
John Deary	5 10	11 11	18 10 62	Ormskirk	Apprentice	Blackpool	303	43
						Burnley	84	9
Andy Farrell	5 11	11 00	7 10 65	Colchester	School	Colchester U	105	5
						Burnley	154	11
David Hamilton	5 6	10 00	7 11 60	South Shields	Apprentice	Sunderland	—	—
						Blackburn R	114	7
						Cardiff C (loan)	10	—
						Wigan Ath	103	7
						Chester C	28	—
						Burnley	11	—

BURNLEY

Foundation: The majority of those responsible for the formation of the Burnley club in 1881 were from the defunct rugby club Burnley Rovers. Indeed, they continued to play rugby for a year before changing to soccer and dropping "Rovers" from their name. The changes were decided at a meeting held in May 1882 at the Bull Hotel.

First Football League game: 8 September, 1888, Football League, v PNE (a), L 2-5 – Smith; Lang, Bury, Abrams, Friel, Keenan, Brady, Tait, Poland (1), Gallocher (1), Yates.

Did you know: Burnley enjoyed a run of 10 Second Division victories in season 1912–13. Leading scorer Bert Freeman netted 14 goals in these games ending with four in a 5-1 win over Leicester Fosse.

Managers (and Secretary-managers)
Arthur F. Sutcliffe 1893–96*, Harry Bradshaw 1896–99*, Ernest Magnall 1899–1903*, Spen Whittaker 1903–10, R. H. Wadge 1910*, John Haworth 1910–24, Albert Pickles 1925–32, Tom Bromilow 1932–35, Alf Boland 1935–39*, Cliff Britton 1945–48, Frank Hill 1948–54, Alan Brown 1954–57, Billy Dougall 1957–58, Harry Potts 1958–70 (GM to 1972), Jimmy Adamson 1970–76, Joe Brown 1976–77, Harry Potts 1977–79, Brian Miller 1979–83, John Bond 1983–84, John Benson 1984–85, Martin Buchan 1985, Tommy Cavanagh 1985–86, Brian Miller 1986–89, Frank Casper January 1989– .

Player and Position	Ht	Wt	Birth Date	Place	Source	Clubs	League App	Gls
Jason Hardy	5 8	10 00	14 12 69		Trainee	Burnley	40	1
Neil Howarth			15 11 71	Farnworth	Trainee	Burnley	1	—
Joe Jakub	5 6	9 06	7 12 56	Falkirk	Apprentice	Burnley	42	—
						Bury	265	27
					AZ 67	Chester C	42	1
						Burnley	92	8
Mark Monington	5 8	11 00	21 10 70	Bilsthorpe	School	Burnley	21	1
Nigel Smith*	5 7	10 04	21 12 69	Leeds	Leeds U	Burnley	13	—
Forwards								
John Francis	5 8	11 02	21 11 63	Dewsbury	Emley	Sheffield U	42	6
						Burnley	64	18
Ron Futcher	6 0	12 10	25 9 56	Chester	Apprentice	Chester	4	—
						Luton T	120	40
						Manchester C	17	7
					Minnesota	Barnsley	19	6
					Portland	Oldham Ath	65	30
					NAC Breda	Bradford C	42	18
					Tulsa	Port Vale	52	20
						Burnley	57	25
Neil Grewcock*	5 6	11 03	26 4 62	Leicester	Shepshed C	Leicester C	8	1
						Gillingham (loan)	13	1
						Gillingham	21	3
						Burnley	202	27
Graham Lancashire§			19 10 72	Blackpool	Trainee	Burnley	1	—
Peter Mumby	5 9	11 05	22 2 69	Bradford	Trainee	Leeds U	6	—
						Shamrock R (loan)	—	—
						Burnley	45	9
Danny Sonner			9 1 72	Wigan	Wigan Ath	Burnley	2	—

Trainees
Douglas, Paul A; Frankum, Noel K; Hill, Dennis J; Hilton, Matthew R; Isherwood, Alvin L; King, Andrew R; Lancashire, Graham; Murray Paul G; Pemberton, Paul M; Rahman, Jamalur; Robinson, Lee A; Seals, Taras; Shiels, Matthew K; Vaughan, Paul; Wallace, Simon P.

Associated Schoolboys
Arthur, Paul M; Backhouse, Steven J; Carrington, David J; Ingham, Damian P; McCaffery, Stephen P; McCluskey, Anthony; Mullin, John; Palmer, Carl E; Pearson, Scott J; Taylor, Matthew J.

Associated Schoolboys who have accepted the club's offer of a Traineeship/Contract
Lawson, Andrew P; Livesey, David; Parry, Christopher M; Ryder, Damian M.

BURY 1990–91 *Back row (left to right):* Mandy Johnson (Physiotherapist). Andy Feeley. Chris Withe. Charlie Bishop. Kevin Hulme. John McGinlay. Wilf McGuinness (Coach).

Centre row: Jack Chapman (Assistant Manager). David Lee. Colin Greenall. Paul Atkin. Gary Kelly. Tony Cunningham. Peter Valentine. Mark Patterson. Mick Walsh (Manager).

Front row: Roger Stanislaus. Phil Parkinson. Andy Hill. Sam Ellis. Alan Knill. Liam Robinson. Ronnie Mauge.

Division 3 **BURY**

Gigg Lane, Bury BL9 9HR. Telephone 061-764 4881/2.
Commercial Dept. 061-705 2144. Clubcall: 0898 121197.
Community Programme: 061-797 5423. Social Club: 061-764
6771.

Ground capacity: 8500.

Record attendance: 35,000 v Bolton W, FA Cup 3rd rd,
9 January 1960.

Record receipts: £22,200 v Nottingham F, League Cup quarter-
final, 17 January 1978.

Pitch measurements: 112yd × 72yd.

President:

Chairman: T. Robinson. *Vice-chairman:* Canon J. R. Smith MA.

Directors: C. H. Eaves, I. Pickup, J. Smith, A. Noonan, F. Mason.

Manager: Mike Walsh. *Assistant Manager:* Jack Chapman.

Reserve Coach: . *Physio:* Mandy Johnson.

Secretary: John Heap. *Commercial Manager:* Neville Neville.

Year Formed: 1885. *Turned professional:* 1885. *Ltd Co.:* 1897. **Club Nickname:** 'Shakers'.

Club Sponsors: MacPherson Paints.

Record League Victory: 8-0 v Tranmere R, Division 3, 10 January 1970 – Forrest; Tinney,
Saile; Anderson, Turner, McDermott; Hince (1), Arrowsmith (1), Jones (4), Kerr (1),
Grundy. (1 og).

Record Cup Victory: 12-1 v Stockton, FA Cup, 1st rd (replay), 2 February 1897 –
Montgomery; Darroch, Barbour; Hendry (1), Clegg, Ross (1); Wylie (3), Pangbourn, Millar
(4), Henderson (2), Plant. (1 og).

Record Defeat: 0-10 v Blackburn R, FA Cup, preliminary round, 1 October 1887 and v
West Ham U, Milk Cup, 2nd rd, 2nd leg, 25 October 1983.

Most League Points (2 for a win): 68, Division 3, 1960–61.

Most League Points (3 for a win): 84, Division 4, 1984–85.

Most League Goals: 108, Division 3, 1960–61.

Highest League Scorer in Season: Craig Madden, 35, Division 4, 1981–82.

Most League Goals in Total Aggregate: Craig Madden, 129, 1978–86.

Most Capped Player: Bill Gorman, 11 (13), Eire and (4), Northern Ireland.

Most League Appearances: Norman Bullock, 506, 1920–35.

Record Transfer Fee Received: £250,000 from Sheffield U for Jamie Hoyland, July 1990.

Record Transfer Fee Paid: £175,000 to Shrewsbury T for John McGinlay, July 1990.

Football League Record: 1894 Elected to Division 2; 1895–1912 Division 1; 1912–24
Division 2; 1924–29 Division 1; 1929–57 Division 2; 1957–61 Division 3; 1961–67 Division
2; 1967–68 Division 3; 1968–69 Division 2; 1969–71 Division 3; 1971–74 Division 4; 1974–
80 Division 3; 1980–85 Division 4; 1985– Division 3.

Honours: Football League: Division 1 best season: 4th, 1925–26; Division 2 – Champions
1894–95; Runners-up 1923–24; Division 3 – Champions 1960–61; Runners-up 1967–68. *FA
Cup:* Winners 1900, 1903. *Football League Cup:* Semi-final 1963.

Colours: White shirts, navy blue shorts, navy stockings. **Change colours:** Red shirts, white
shorts, red stockings.

BURY 1990–91 LEAGUE RECORD

Match No.	Date	Venue	Opponents	Result	H/T Score	Lg. Pos.	Goalscorers	Attendance
1	Aug 25	H	Chester C	W 2-1	2-1		Patterson, McGinlay (pen)	2628
2	Sept 1	A	Bournemouth	D 1-1	0-1	7	Cunningham	5285
3	8	H	Rotherham U	W 3-1	2-0	3	Cunningham, Patterson, Mauge	2988
4	15	A	Birmingham C	L 0-1	0-0	7		7344
5	18	A	Swansea C	W 2-1	1-1	—	Cunningham, Mauge	3505
6	22	H	Mansfield T	W 1-0	1-0	6	Mauge	2620
7	29	H	Crewe Alex	L 1-3	0-1	7	Mauge	3201
8	Oct 2	A	Shrewsbury T	D 1-1	0-0	—	McGinlay (pen)	3258
9	6	A	Cambridge U	D 2-2	1-0	8	Patterson, Lee	3886
10	13	H	Bolton W	D 2-2	0-1	7	Patterson, Knill	5634
11	20	H	Reading	W 2-1	2-1	5	Parkinson, Stanislaus	2807
12	23	A	Fulham	L 0-2	0-0	—		3439
13	27	A	Southend U	L 1-2	1-1	9	Parkinson	4001
14	Nov 3	H	Tranmere R	W 3-0	1-0	6	Mauge, McGinlay 2	3776
15	10	A	Brentford	D 2-2	0-0	6	Lee, Patterson	5303
16	24	H	Stoke C	D 1-1	0-0	8	McGinlay	5118
17	Dec 1	A	Wigan Ath	W 2-1	1-0	5	Lee, Cunningham	2861
18	15	H	Exeter C	W 3-1	2-1	4	Mauge, Lee, Valentine	2370
19	22	A	Huddersfield T	L 1-2	1-0	5	Bishop	4841
20	29	H	Preston NE	W 3-1	1-1	7	Patterson, Cunningham, Robinson	5404
21	Jan 1	A	Bradford C	L 1-3	0-2	9	Lee	7174
22	5	A	Grimsby T	W 1-0	1-0	8	Cunningham	6249
23	12	H	Bournemouth	L 2-4	0-1	8	Robinson 2	2761
24	19	A	Chester C	L 0-1	0-0	9		1421
25	26	H	Birmingham C	L 0-1	0-0	11		3009
26	Feb 2	H	Swansea C	W 1-0	0-0	9	Lee	2135
27	5	A	Mansfield T	W 1-0	1-0	—	Hulme	1921
28	16	A	Stoke C	D 2-2	0-1	8	Hulme 2	9885
29	19	H	Leyton Orient	W 1-0	1-0	—	Lee (pen)	2207
30	23	H	Brentford	D 1-1	0-0	6	Hulme	2956
31	Mar 2	A	Wigan Ath	D 2-2	1-0	5	Hulme, Cunningham	2967
32	5	A	Rotherham U	W 3-0	0-0	—	Kearney, Lee, Cunningham	3658
33	9	A	Exeter C	L 0-2	0-1	4		3590
34	12	H	Shrewsbury T	W 2-1	1-0	—	Lee 2	2417
35	16	A	Crewe Alex	D 2-2	1-1	4	Cunningham, McGinlay	3384
36	19	H	Bolton W	W 3-1	1-0	—	McGinlay 3	9006
37	23	H	Cambridge U	W 3-1	1-1	4	Lee 3 (1 pen)	3342
38	30	A	Leyton Orient	L 0-1	0-1	6		3514
39	Apr 1	H	Huddersfield T	W 2-1	1-0	5	Hulme, Stanislaus	6318
40	6	A	Preston N E	D 1-1	0-1	5	Hulme	5641
41	9	H	Grimsby T	W 3-2	1-1	—	Valentine, Lee 2	4748
42	13	H	Bradford C	D 0-0	0-0	4		5285
43	20	A	Reading	L 0-1	0-1	6		3081
44	27	H	Fulham	D 1-1	1-1	7	Robinson	3217
45	May 4	H	Southend U	L 0-1	0-0	7		4254
46	11	A	Tranmere R	W 2-1	1-1	7	Bishop, Sheron	9081

Final League Position: 7

GOALSCORERS

League (67): Lee 15 (2 pens), Cunningham 9, McGinlay 9 (2 pens), Hulme 7, Mauge 6, Patterson 6, Robinson 4, Bishop 2, Parkinson 2, Stanislaus 2, Valentine 2, Kearney 1, Knill 1, Sheron 1.
Rumbelows Cup (3): Cunningham 1, Mauge 1, Valentine 1.
FA Cup (1): Mauge 1.

Kelly	Hill	Stanislaus	Mauge	Valentine	Greenall	Lee	Parkinson	Cunningham	McGinlay	Patterson	Knill	Robinson	Hulme	Atkin	Bishop	Feeley	Price	Kearney	Bradley	Sheron	Match No.
1	2	3	4	5	6	7	8	9	10	11											1
1	2*	3	4	5		7	10†	9		11	6	8	12	14							2
1		3	4*	5		7	10	9		11	6	8		12	2						3
1		3	4	5	12	7	10	9†14		11	6*	8			2						4
1		3	4		5	7	10	9†14		11	6	8			2*12						5
1		3	4		5	7	10	9	12	11	6	8*			2						6
1	14		4	5	3	7	8	9*10		11	6†12				2						7
1		3	4	5	6*	7†	8	9	10	11	12			14	2						8
1	2	3	4	5		7	8	9	10	11	6										9
1	2	3	4	5		7	8	9	10	11	6										10
1	2	3	4	5		7	8		10	11	6	9									11
1	2	3	4	5		7	8		10*11		6	9†12			14						12
1	2	3		5*		7†	8		10	11	6	9	12	4	14						13
1	2	3†	4	5		7	8		10	11*	6	9	12		14						14
1	2	3	4†	5		7*	8	12	10	11	6	9			14						15
1	2	3†	4	5		7*	8	12	10	11	6	9			14						16
1	2		4	5		7	8	12	10*11		6	9				3					17
1	2	14	4	5		7	8	9	12	11	6†10*					3					18
1		3	4	5			8	9	12	11		10			6	7†	2*14				19
1		3		5		7*	8	9	12	11	6†10				4	14	2				20
1	3*			5		7	8	9		11		10			6	4	2	12			21
1		3		5	12	7	10	9		11		8			6*	4	2				22
1		3		5	6	7	10	9	12			8			4*11		2				23
1		3		5	6	7*		9				8	12		4	11	2	10			24
1		3		5	6	7	10	9				8	12		11*	2		4			25
1		3		5	6	7	10	9				8	11		12	2*		4			26
1		3		5*	6	7	10	9		12		8	11			2		4			27
1		3		5	6	7	10	9				8	11			2		4			28
1		3		5	6	7	10	9				8	11			2		4			29
1		3		5	6	7	10	9				8	11			2		4			30
1				5	6	7	10	9				8	11		3	2		4			31
1	14			5	6	7*10		9	12			8	11		3	2†		4			32
1	14				6	7	10	9	12		5	8	11*		3	2†		4			33
1	2				6	7	11	9	10		5	8			3			4			34
1	2	14		5	6	7	11†	9	10*			8	12		3			4			35
1	2	12		5	6	7	11	9	10			8*			3			4			36
1	2	12		5	6	7	11*	9	10			8			3			4			37
1		3	4	5	6	7	10					8	9		2			11			38
1		3	4	5	6	7	10					8	9*		2			11	12		39
1		3	4	5	6	7	10					8	9*	2†14				11	12		40
1		3	4	5	6	7	10					8	9*		2			11	12		41
1		3	4*	5	6	7	10					8	9		2			11	12		42
1		3	4	5	6	7						8	9	10*	2	12		11			43
1		3	4	5	6	7	10					8	9		2			11			44
1		3	4*	5	6	7	10					8	9		2			11	12		45
1		3		5	6	7	10					4	9		2	12		11		8*	46
46	12	40	26	42	29	45	44	30	16	22	19	41	17	8	25	20	1	22	—	1	

Subs: +4s +3s +2s +3s +9s +1s +2s +7s +3s +4s +7s +2s +1s +4s

Rumbelows Cup First Round Bradford C (a)	0-2
(h)	3-2
FA Cup First Round Chorley (a)	1-2

BURY

Player and Position	Ht	Wt	Birth Date	Birth Place	Source	Clubs	League App	Gls
Goalkeepers								
Aidan Davison*	6 1	13 02	11 5 68	Sedgefield	Billingham Syn	Notts Co	1	—
						Leyton Orient (loan)	—	—
						Bury	—	—
						Chester C (loan)	—	—
						Blackpool (loan)	—	—
Gary Kelly	5 10	12 03	3 8 66	Fulwood	Apprentice	Newcastle U	53	—
						Blackpool (loan)	5	—
						Bury	84	—
Defenders								
Paul Atkin*	6 0	12 04	3 9 69	Nottingham	Trainee	Notts Co	—	—
						Bury	21	1
Charlie Bishop	6 0	12 01	16 2 68	Nottingham	Apprentice	Stoke C	—	—
						Watford	—	—
						Bury	114	6
Shaun Dunn*	6 2	11 10	19 1 71	North Shields		Blackpool	—	—
						Bury	—	—
Colin Greenall	5 10	11 06	30 12 63	Billinge	Apprentice	Blackpool	183	9
						Gillingham	62	4
						Oxford U	67	2
						Bury (loan)	3	—
						Bury	31	—
Mark Kearney	5 10	11 00	12 6 62	Ormskirk	Marine	Everton	—	—
						Mansfield T	250	29
						Bury (loan)	13	1
						Bury	9	—
Alan Knill	6 2	10 09	8 10 64	Slough	Apprentice	Southampton	—	—
						Halifax T	118	6
						Swansea C	89	3
						Bury	63	2
Gareth Price*	5 10	11 00	21 2 70	Swindon	Trainee	Mansfield T	—	—
						Bury	4	—
Mark Simms*			17 10 70	Southport	Blackburn R			
					Preston NE	Bury	—	—
Roger Stanislaus	5 9	12 11	2 11 68	Hammersmith	Trainee	Arsenal	—	—
						Brentford	111	4
						Bury	44	2
Peter Valentine	5 10	12 00	16 4 63	Huddersfield	Apprentice	Huddersfield T	19	1
						Bolton W	68	1
						Bury	244	10
Mick Walsh	6 0	12 00	20 6 56	Manchester		Bolton W	177	4
						Everton	20	—
						Norwich C (loan)	5	—
						Burnley (loan)	3	—
					Ft Lauderdale	Manchester C	4	—
						Blackpool	153	5
						Bury	—	—
Midfield								
Pat Bradley	5 10	12 03	27 4 72	Sydney	Trainee	Bury	1	—
Andy Feeley*	5 10	12 07	30 9 61	Hereford	Apprentice	Hereford U	51	3
						Chelsea (loan)	—	—
					Trowbridge T	Leicester C	76	—
						Brentford	67	—
						Bury	57	2

BURY

Foundation: A meeting at the Waggon & Horses Hotel, attended largely by members of Bury Wesleyans and Bury Unitarians football clubs, decided to form a new Bury club. This was officially formed at a subsequent gathering at the Old White Horse Hotel, Fleet Street, Bury on April 24, 1885.

First Football League game: 1 September, 1894, Division 2, v Manchester C (h) W 4-2 – Lowe; Gillespie, Davies; White, Clegg, Ross; Wylie, Barbour (2), Millar (1), Ostler (1), Plant.

Did you know: One of the most astonishing scoring feats by a Bury player was that by George Jones in their Third Division championship-winning season of 1970-71. On Saturday 5 December, he scored four of his side's goals in a 5-1 League victory at Reading and followed this a week later by scoring a goal in only 10 seconds against Notts County in an FA Cup tie at Gigg Lane.

Managers (and Secretary-managers)
  T. Hargreaves 1887*, H. S. Hamer 1887–1907*, Archie Montgomery 1907–15, William Cameron 1919–23, James Hunter Thompson 1923–27, Percy Smith 1927–30, Arthur Paine 1930–34, Norman Bullock 1934–38, Jim Porter 1944–45, Norman Bullock 1945–49, John McNeil 1950–53, Dave Russell 1953–61, Bob Stokoe 1961–65, Bert Head 1965–66, Les Shannon 1966–69, Jack Marshall 1969, Les Hart 1970, Tommy McAnearney 1970–72, Alan Brown 1972–73, Bobby Smith 1973–77, Bob Stokoe 1977–78, David Hatton 1978–79, Dave Connor 1979–80, Jim Iley 1980–84, Martin Dobson 1984–89, Sam Ellis 1989–90, Mike Walsh December 1990–.

Player and Position	Ht	Wt	Birth Date	Place	Source	Clubs	League App	Gls
Asa Hartford‡	5 7	11 04	24 10 50	Clydebank	Amateur	WBA	213	18
						Manchester C	185	22
						Nottingham F	3	—
						Everton	81	6
						Manchester C	75	7
						Norwich C	28	2
						Bolton W	81	8
						Stockport Co	45	—
						Oldham Ath	7	—
						Shrewsbury T	25	—
						Bury	—	—
Dave Lee	5 8	10 02	5 11 67	Manchester	Schools	Bury	206	34
Philip Parkinson	5 10	10 11	1 12 67	Chorley	Apprentice	Southampton	—	—
						Bury	113	5
Forwards								
Ian Bennett*	5 9	11 00	12 2 72	Birmingham		Bury	—	—
Andy Gayle*	5 8	11 02	17 9 70	Manchester	Trainee	Oldham Ath	1	—
						Crewe Alex	1	—
						Bury	—	—
Kevin Hulme	5 10	11 09	2 12 67	Farnworth	Radcliffe Bor	Bury	48	8
						Chester C (loan)	4	—
Ron Mauge	5 10	11 00	10 3 69	Islington	Trainee	Charlton Ath	—	—
						Fulham	50	2
						Bury	29	6
Liam Robinson	5 6	11 04	29 12 65	Bradford	School	Nottingham F	—	—
						Huddersfield T	21	2
						Tranmere R (loan)	4	3
						Bury	207	73

Trainees
Anderson, Lee C; Denny, Steven; Emmett, Darren; Greenhalgh, Laurence L; Hughes, Ian; Kent, Daniel; Wagstaff, Andrew P.

Associated Schoolboys
Adams, Daniel B; Booth, Gary M; Brown, Stuart I; Chadwick, Craig; Higgins, Saul J; Millington, Michael D; Mulville, Jason; Nash, Sean P; Palfrey, Ian A; Steele, Winfield J.J; Unsworth, Lee P; Wallace, Richard E; Williamson, Paul J.

Associated Schoolboys who have accepted the club's offer of a Traineeship/Contract
Calderbank, Darren P; Wilkinson, Lee.

CAMBRIDGE UNITED 1990-91 *Back row (left to right):* Mike Cook, Gary Woolf, Stephen Lewis, John Vaughan, Mike Cheetham, Shaun Harrington.
Centre row: Graham Scarff (Youth Team Manager), Roy Johnson (Physiotherapist), Phil Chapple, Liam Daish, Gary Clayton, Steve Claridge, Dion Dublin, Steve Welsh,
Richard Wilkins, John Taylor, Norman Proctor (Chief Scout).
Front row: Chris Leadbitter, Jamie Kearns, Lee Philpott, Tony Dennis, John Beck (Manager), Gary Johnson (Assistant Manager), Laurie Ryan, Alan Kimble, Andy Fensome,
Colin Bailie.

Division 2   **CAMBRIDGE UNITED**

Abbey Stadium, Newmarket Rd, Cambridge. Telephone Teversham (0223) 241237. Clubcall: 0898 446700.

Ground capacity: 9998.

Record attendance; 14,000 v Chelsea, Friendly, 1 May 1970.

Record receipts: £62,391 v Sheffield W, FA Cup 5th rd, 16 February 1991.

Pitch measurements: 110yd × 74yd.

President: D. A. Ruston.

Chairman: R. H. Smart. *Vice-chairman:* D. A. Ruston.

Directors: G. Harwood, J. Howard, C, Howlett, R. Hunt, G. Lowe, R. Smith.

Team Manager: John Beck. *Assistant Manager:* Gary Johnson.

Physio: Roy Johnson. *Youth Coach:* Graham Scarff.

Secretary: Steve Greenall. *Commercial Manager:* John Holmes. *Stadium Manager:* Ian Darler.

Year Formed: 1919. *Turned Professional:* 1946. *Ltd Co.:* 1948.

Club Nickname: 'United'.

Previous Name: Abbey United until 1949.

Record League Victory: 6-0 v Darlington, Division 4, 18 September 1971 – Roberts; Thompson, Akers, Guild, Eades, Foote, Collins (1p), Horrey, Hollett, Greenhalgh (4), Phillips. (1 og). 6-0 v Hartlepool, Division 4, 11 February 1989 – Vaughan; Beck, Kimble, Turner, Chapple (1), Daish, Clayton, Holmes, Taylor (3 incl. 1p), Bull (1), Leadbitter (1).

Record Cup Victory: 5-1 v Bristol C, FA Cup, 5th rd, second replay, 27 February 1990 – Vaughan; Fensome, Kimble, Bailie (O'Shea), Chapple, Daish, Cheetham (Robinson), Leadbitter (1), Dublin (2), Taylor (1), Philpott (1).

Record Defeat: 0-6 v Aldershot, Division 3, 13 April 1974 and v Darlington, Division 4, 28 September 1974 and v Chelsea, Division 2, 15 January 1983.

Most League Points (2 for a win): 65, Division 4, 1976–77.

Most League Points (3 for a win): 86, Division 3, 1990–91.

Most League Goals: 87, Division 4, 1976–77.

Highest League Scorer in Season: David Crown, 24, Division 4, 1985–86.

Most League Goals in Total Aggregate: Alan Biley, 74, 1975–80.

Most Capped Player: Tom Finney, 7 (15), Northern Ireland.

Most League Appearances: Steve Spriggs, 416, 1975–87.

Record Transfer Fee Received: £350,000 from Derby Co for Alan Biley, January 1980.

Record Transfer Fee Paid: £140,000 to Northampton T for George Reilly, November 1979.

Football League Record: 1970 Elected to Division 4; 1973–74 Division 3; 1974–77 Division 4; 1977–78 Division 3; 1978–84 Division 2; 1984–85 Division 3; 1985–90 Division 4; 1990–91 Division 3; 1991- Division 2.

Honours: Football League: Division 2 best season: 8th, 1979–80; Division 3 – Champions 1990–91; Runners-up 1977–78; Division 4 – Champions 1976–77. *FA Cup:* best season: 6th rd, 1989–90, 1990–91. *Football League Cup:* 4th rd, 1980–81.

Colours: Yellow shirts, black shorts, black and yellow stockings. **Change colours:** All sky blue with amber and black trim.

CAMBRIDGE UNITED 1990–91 LEAGUE RECORD

Match No.	Date		Venue	Opponents	Result		H/T Score	Lg. Pos.	Goalscorers	Atten-dance
1	Aug	25	H	Birmingham C	L	0-1	0-0	—		6338
2	Sept	1	A	Fulham	W	2-0	1-0	9	Claridge, Chapple	4145
3		9	H	Southend U	L	1-4	0-1	—	Cheetham	4790
4		15	A	Reading	D	2-2	0-0	16	Cheetham, Kimble (pen)	4276
5		18	A	Mansfield T	D	2-2	0-0	—	Cheetham, Taylor	2450
6		21	H	Chester C	D	1-1	1-0	—	Dublin	3687
7		29	A	Exeter C	W	1-0	1-0	13	Dublin	4227
8	Oct	2	H	Leyton Orient	W	1-0	0-0	—	Philpott	4991
9		6	H	Bury	D	2-2	0-1	10	Kimble (pen), Chapple	3886
10		14	A	Brentford	W	3-0	0-0	—	Claridge 2, Kimble (pen)	6833
11		20	A	Stoke C	D	1-1	1-0	8	Dublin	12,673
12		23	H	Wigan Ath	L	2-3	0-1	—	Taylor, Wilkins	4626
13		27	H	Rotherham U	W	4-1	3-0	6	Dublin, Robinson (og), Taylor 2	4142
14	Nov	3	A	Swansea C	D	0-0	0-0	8		3902
15		10	A	Huddersfield T	L	1-3	0-1	13	Claridge	4917
16		24	H	Shrewsbury T	W	3-1	2-0	6	Daish, Taylor, Kimble	3632
17		30	H	Crewe Alex	L	3-4	2-1	—	Dublin, Claridge, Dennis	4729
18	Dec	15	A	Bradford C	W	1-0	0-0	8	Chapple	6354
19		22	A	Bolton W	D	2-2	0-2	8	Chapple, Dublin	5800
20		26	H	Tranmere R	W	3-1	3-0	6	Cheetham, Bailie, Dublin	4547
21		29	H	Grimsby T	W	1-0	0-0	6	Dublin	5922
22	Jan	1	A	Preston NE	W	2-0	1-0	5	Dublin, Taylor	5256
23		12	H	Fulham	W	1-0	0-0	3	Taylor	5087
24		19	A	Birmingham C	W	3-0	2-0	3	Wilkins, Taylor, Dublin (pen)	5859
25	Feb	1	H	Mansfield T	W	2-1	1-1	—	Taylor, Dublin	5094
26		23	H	Huddersfield T	D	0-0	0-0	4		5602
27	Mar	1	A	Crewe Alex	L	1-3	1-1	—	Chapple	3484
28		12	A	Leyton Orient	W	3-0	0-0	—	Claridge, Cheetham, Taylor	4292
29		16	H	Exeter C	W	1-0	1-0	6	Dennis	4833
30		19	H	Brentford	D	0-0	0-0	—		4931
31		23	A	Bury	L	1-3	1-1	9	Dublin	3342
32		25	A	Chester C	W	2-0	1-0	—	Taylor 2	1015
33		29	A	Tranmere R	L	0-2	0-0	—		11,079
34	Apr	2	H	Bolton W	W	2-1	1-0	—	Philpott, Taylor	7763
35		6	A	Grimsby T	L	0-1	0-1	7		8550
36		9	H	Reading	W	3-0	1-0	—	Leadbitter, Cheetham, Dublin (pen)	5825
37		13	H	Preston NE	D	1-1	1-0	7	Dublin	6262
38		16	A	Bournemouth	W	1-0	0-0	—	Philpott	7156
39		18	A	Shrewsbury T	W	2-1	1-0	—	Claridge 2	2571
40		20	H	Stoke C	W	3-0	0-0	4	Claridge, Cheetham, Dublin	5743
41		24	H	Bournemouth	W	4-0	3-0	—	Bailie, Taylor, Claridge 2	6433
42		27	A	Wigan Ath	W	1-0	1-0	3	Dublin	3273
43		30	A	Southend U	D	0-0	0-0	—		10,664
44	May	4	A	Rotherham U	L	2-3	2-2	3	Philpott, Law (og)	5402
45		7	H	Bradford C	W	2-1	1-1	—	Wilkins, Sinnott (og)	8679
46		11	H	Swansea C	W	2-0	2-0	1	Claridge, Philpott	9023

Final League Position: 1

GOALSCORERS

League (75): Dublin 16 (2 pens), Taylor 14, Claridge 12, Cheetham 7, Chapple 5, Philpott 5, Kimble 4 (3 pens), Wilkins 3, Bailie 2, Dennis 2, Daish 1, Leadbitter 1, own goals 3.
Rumbelows Cup (4): Leadbitter 2, Cheetham 1, Dublin 1.
FA Cup (12): Taylor 5, Dublin 4, Kimble 1 (pen), Leadbitter 1, Philpott 1.

Vaughan	Fensome	Kimble	Bailie	Chapple	O'Shea	Cheetham	Wilkins	Dublin	Taylor	Philpott	Claridge	Leadbitter	Dennis	Daish	Cook	Berryman	Sheffield	Kearns	Clayton	Welsh	Match No.
1	2	3	4†	5	6	7	8	9	10*	11	12	14									1
1	2	3	4†	5	6	7	8	9	12	10	11*	14									2
1	2	3	4*	5	6	7	8	9	14	12	10†	11									3
1	2	3	4	5		7	8	9	12	10	11*			6							4
1	2	3	4*	5		7	11	9†	14	12	10		8	6							5
1	2	3		5		7	4	9	12	11	10*		8	6							6
1	2	3		5		7	4	9	10	11*	12		8	6							7
1	2*	3		5	12	7	4	9	10	11			8	6							8
1	2	3	12	5	6	7	4*	9	10	11			8								9
1		3	14	5	2	7*	4†	9	10	11	12		8	6							10
1		3	14	5	2	7*	4	9	10	11	12		8†	6							11
1		3	12	5	2	7	4	9	10	11			8*	6							12
1	2	3	8	5		7*	4	9	10	11	12			6							13
1	2	3		5		7	4	9	10	11			8	6							14
1	2†	3	8	5			4*	9	10	11	7	14	12	6							15
1	2	3	4	5	12			9	10	11*	7†	8	14	6							16
1	2	3	4	5				9	10	11	7*	8	12	6							17
1	2	3	4	5	6	7	8	9	10	11											18
1	2	3	4	5	6	7	8	9	10	11*	12										19
1	2	3	4	5	6	7†	8	9	10	11*	12	14									20
1	2	3*	4	5	6	7	8	9	10†	11	12	14									21
1	2	3	4	5	6	7	8	9	10	11											22
1	2	3		5	6	7	8	9	10	11		4									23
1	2	3		5	6	7†	8	9	10	11*	12	4	14								24
1	2	3		5	6	7	8	9	10	11		4									25
1	2	3		5	6	7	8	9	10	11		4									26
1	2*	3		5	6	7	8	9	10	11	12	4†	14								27
1	2†	3	4	5	6	7	8	9	10	11*	12	14									28
		3	2*	5	6	7	8	9	10	11	12	4			1						29
		3		5	6	7	8	9	10*	14	12	11†	4				1		2		30
		3		5	6	7	8	9	10	11*	12	4				1			2		31
1		3		5	6	7	8	9	10	14	12	11†	4*						2		32
1		3*		5	6	7†	8	9	10	14	12	11	4						2		33
1		3		5	6	7	8	9	10	11		4							2		34
1		3	14	5	6	7	8	9	10*	11	12	4							2†		35
1	2		4	5	6	7	8	9	10	11		3									36
1	2	3	4	5	6	7†		9	10*	11	12	8	14								37
1	2	3	4	5	6	7		9	10	11		8*	12								38
1	2	3	4	5	6	14	12	10*	11†	9	8	7									39
1	2		4	5	6	7	8†	12	10*	11	9	3	14								40
1	2	3	4	5	6	7†	8	9	11*	10	12	14									41
1	2	3	4	5	6	7	8	9	11*	12†	10	14									42
1	2	3	4†	5	6	7	8	9	12	10	11*	14									43
1	2†	3	4	5	6	7*	8	9	11	10	12							14			44
1	2	3	4	5	6	7	8	9	11	10											45
1	2	3*	4	5	6†	7	8	9	11	10	12								14		46
43	36	43	27	43	39	42	41	44	37	36	16	30	6	13	1	1	2	1	5	—	

| | | | + | | + | + | | + | + | + | + | + | + | | + | | | | + | + | |
| | | | 5s | | 1s | 2s | | 2s | 3s | 9s | 14s | 9s | 14s | | 1s | | | | 1s | 1s | |

Rumbelows Cup	First Round	Walsall (a)		2-4	
		(h)		2-1	
FA Cup	First Round	Exeter C (a)		2-1	
	Second Round	Fulham (a)		0-0	
		(h)		2-1	
	Third Round	Wolverhampton W (a)		1-0	
	Fourth Round	Middlesbrough (h)		2-0	
	Fifth Round	Sheffield W (h)		4-0	
	Sixth Round	Arsenal (a)		1-2	

CAMBRIDGE UNITED

Player and Position	Ht	Wt	Birth Date	Place	Source	Clubs	League App	Gls
Goalkeepers								
Paul Bastock†	5 8	10 00	19 5 70	Leamington	Trainee	Coventry C	—	—
						Cambridge U	12	—
Steve Berryman*			26 12 66	Blackburn		Hartlepool U	1	—
						Exeter C	—	—
						Cambridge U	1	—
John Vaughan	5 10	13 01	26 6 64	Isleworth	Apprentice	West Ham U	—	—
						Charlton Ath (loan)	6	—
						West Ham U	—	—
						Bristol R (loan)	6	—
						Wrexham (loan)	4	—
						Bristol C (loan)	2	—
						Fulham	44	—
						Bristol C (loan)	3	—
						Cambridge U	118	—
Defenders								
Colin Bailie	5 11	10 11	31 3 64	Belfast	Apprentice	Swindon T	107	4
						Reading	84	1
						Cambridge U	91	3
Phil Chapple	6 2	12 07	26 11 66	Norwich	Apprentice	Norwich C	—	—
						Cambridge U	140	14
Liam Daish	6 2	13 05	23 9 68	Portsmouth	Apprentice	Portsmouth	1	—
						Cambridge U	83	2
Andy Fensome	5 8	11 02	18 2 69	Northampton	Trainee	Norwich C	—	—
						Newcastle U (loan)	—	—
						Cambridge U	60	—
Jamie Kearns‡			28 10 71	Hammersmith	Trainee	Cambridge U	1	—
Alan Kimble	5 8	11 00	6 8 66	Poole		Charlton Ath	6	—
						Exeter C (loan)	1	—
						Cambridge U	208	20
Fergus O'Donohue			7 10 69	Cork	Cork C	Cambridge U	—	—
Danny O'Shea	6 0	12 08	26 3 63	Kennington	Apprentice	Arsenal	6	—
						Charlton Ath (loan)	9	—
						Exeter C	45	2
						Southend U	118	12
						Cambridge U	66	—
Steve Welsh†	6 0	12 03	19 4 68	Glasgow	Army	Cambridge U	1	—
Midfield								
Michael Cheetham	5 11	11 05	30 6 67	Amsterdam	Army	Ipswich T	4	—
						Cambridge U	80	17
Gary Clayton	5 11	12 08	2 2 63	Sheffield	Apprentice Burton Alb	Rotherham U	—	—
						Doncaster R	35	5
						Cambridge U	107	7
						Peterborough (loan)	4	—
Mike Cook*	5 9	10 12	18 10 68	Coventry	Trainee	Coventry C	—	—
						York C (loan)	6	1
						Cambridge U	17	1
						York C (loan)	6	—
Lee Philpott	5 9	10 06	21 2 70	Barnet	Trainee	Peterborough U	4	—
						Cambridge U	87	10
Matthew Proctor			4 10 72	Bury St Edmunds	Trainee	Cambridge U	—	—
Richard Wilkins	6 0	12 00	28 5 65	London	Haverhill R	Colchester U	152	22
						Cambridge U	41	3

CAMBRIDGE UNITED

Foundation: The football revival in Cambridge began soon after World War II when the Abbey United club (formed 1919) decided to turn professional and in 1949 changed their name to Cambridge United. They were competing in the United Counties League before graduating to the Eastern Counties League in 1951 and the Southern League in 1958.

First Football League game: 15 August, 1970, Division 4, v Lincoln C (h) D 1-1 – Roberts; Thompson, Meldrum (1), Slack, Eades, Hardy, Leggett, Cassidy, Lindsey, McKinven, Harris.

Did you know: After Andy Sinton scored two goals for United against Burnley, 26 March 1983, they played 79 consecutive League games in none of which any of their players was able to score more than a single goal. Then Steve Pyle got two against Swansea City, 1 March 1985.

Managers (and Secretary-managers)
Bill Whittaker 1949–55, Gerald Williams 1955, Bert Johnson 1955–59, Bill Craig 1959–60, Alan Moore 1960–63, Roy Kirk 1964–66, Bill Leivers 1967–74, Ron Atkinson 1974–78, John Docherty 1978–83, John Ryan 1984–85, Ken Shellito 1985, Chris Turner 1985–90, John Beck January 1990–.

Player and Position	Ht	Wt	Birth Date	Birth Place	Source	Clubs	League App	Gls
Forwards								
Steve Claridge	5 11	11 08	10 4 66	Portsmouth	Fareham	Bournemouth	7	1
					Weymouth	Crystal Palace	—	—
						Aldershot	62	19
						Cambridge U	50	16
Tony Dennis†	5 7	10 02	1 12 63	Eton	Slough	Cambridge U	55	7
Mark Dobie			8 11 63	Carlisle	Gretna	Cambridge U	—	—
Dion Dublin	6 0	12 04	22 4 69	Leicester		Norwich C	—	—
						Cambridge U	113	37
Chris Leadbitter	5 9	10 07	17 10 67	Middlesbrough	Apprentice	Grimsby T	—	—
						Hereford U	36	1
						Cambridge U	113	11
Laurie Ryan‡	5 9	10 12	15 10 63	Watford	Dunstable	Cambridge U	51	13
John Taylor	6 2	11 12	24 10 64	Norwich	Local	Colchester U	—	—
					Sudbury	Cambridge U	125	41

Trainees
Banthorpe, Alec N.A; Bussell, Harvey G.W; Giles, Stephen P; Hayes, Marc; Merrick, Simon; Robinson, David J; Rowett, Gary; Sinclair, Colin N; Stay, Daryl

**Non-Contract
Dennis, John A; Welsh, Stephen.
**Non-Contract Players who are retained must be re-signed before they are eligible to play in League matches.

136

CARDIFF CITY 1990-91 *Back row (left to right):* Neil Matthews, Alan Lewis, Gavin Ward, Roger Hansbury, Gareth Abraham, Chris Pike, Nathan Blake. *Centre row:* Stephen Hookings, Damon Searle, Chris Fry, Jason Perry, John Morgan, Leigh Barnard, Mark Jones, Pat Heard. *Front row:* Jeff Chandler, Lee Stephens, Chris Summers, Roger Gibbins, Cohen Griffith, Ian Rodgerson, Ray Daniel.

Division 4   CARDIFF CITY

Ninian Park, Cardiff CF1 8SX. Telephone Cardiff (0222) 398636. Commercial Office: (0222) 220516.

Ground capacity: 19,300.

Record attendance: 61,566, Wales v England, 14 October 1961.

Club record: 57,893 v Arsenal, Division 1, 22 April 1953.

Record receipts: £50,517.75 v QPR, FA Cup, 3rd rd, 6 January 1990.

Pitch measurements: 114yd × 78yd.

President:

Chairman: J. A. Clemo.

Directors: L. Clemo, R. P. Maughan.

Secretary: Eddie Harrison.

First team coach: Eddie May. *Commercial Manager:* C. Davies

Physio: Jimmy Goodfellow.

Year Formed: 1899. *Turned Professional:* 1910. *Ltd Co.:* 1910.

Previous Names: 1899–1902, Riverside; 1902–08, Riverside Albion; 1908, Cardiff City.

Club Nickname: 'Bluebirds'.

Previous Grounds: Riverside, Sophia Gardens, Old Park and Fir Gardens. Moved to Ninian Park, 1910.

Record League Victory: 9-2 v Thames, Division 3 (S), 6 February 1932 – Farquharson; E. L. Morris, Roberts; Galbraith, Harris, Ronan; Emmerson (1), Keating (1), Jones (1), McCambridge (1), Robbins (5).

Record Cup Victory: 8-0 v Enfield, FA Cup, 1st rd, 28 November 1931 – Farquharson; Smith, Roberts; Harris (1), Galbraith, Ronan; Emmerson (2), Keating (3); O'Neill (2), Robbins, McCambridge.

Record Defeat: 2-11 v Sheffield U, Division 1, 1 January 1926.

Most League Points (2 for a win): 66, Division 3 (S), 1946–47.

Most League Points (3 for a win): 86, Division 3, 1982–83.

Most League Goals: 93, Division 3 (S), 1946–47.

Highest League Scorer in Season: Stan Richards, 30, Division 3 (S), 1946–47.

Most League Goals in Total Aggregate: Len Davies, 128, 1920–31.

Most Capped Player: Alf Sherwood, 39 (41), Wales.

Most League Appearances: Phil Dwyer, 471, 1972–85.

Record Transfer Fee Received: £215,000 from Portsmouth for Jimmy Gilligan, October 1989.

Record Transfer Fee Paid: £180,000 to San Jose Earthquakes for Godfrey Ingram, September 1982.

Football League Record: 1920 Elected to Division 2; 1921–29 Division 1; 1929–31 Division 2; 1931–47 Division 3 (S); 1947–52 Division 2; 1952–57 Division 1; 1957–60 Division 2; 1960–62 Division 1; 1962–75 Division 2; 1975–76 Division 3; 1976–82 Division 2; 1982–83 Division 3; 1983–85 Division 2; 1985–86 Division 3; 1986–88 Division 4; 1988–90 Division 3; 1990– Division 4.

Honours: Football League: Division 1 – Runners-up 1923–24; Division 2 – Runners-up 1920–21, 1951–52, 1959–60; Division 3 (S) – Champions 1946–47; Division 3 – Runners-up 1975–76, 1982–83; Division 4 – Runners-up 1987–88. *FA Cup:* Winners 1926–27 (only occasion the Cup has been won by a club outside England); Runners-up 1925. *Football League Cup:* Semi-final 1965–66. *Welsh Cup:* Winners 20 times. *Charity Shield:* 1927. European Competitions: *European Cup-Winners' Cup:* 1964–65, 1965–66, 1967–68, 1968–69, 1969–70, 1970–71, 1971–72, 1973–74, 1974–75, 1976–77, 1977–78, 1988–89.

Colours: Blue shirts, white shorts, blue stockings. **Change colours:** All yellow.

CARDIFF CITY 1990–91 LEAGUE RECORD

Match No.	Date		Venue	Opponents	Result		H/T Score	Lg. Pos.	Goalscorers	Attendance
1	Aug	25	H	Scarborough	D	0-0	0-0	—		3819
2	Sept	1	A	Hartlepool U	W	2-0	0-0	6	Griffith, Pike	2800
3		8	H	Torquay U	D	3-3	1-2	6	Griffith, Pike 2 (1 pen)	3656
4		15	A	Lincoln C	D	0-0	0-0	9		3152
5		18	A	Aldershot	D	0-0	0-0	—		2310
6		22	H	Stockport Co	D	3-3	3-0	11	Griffith, Pike, Gibbins	3608
7		29	A	Scunthorpe U	W	2-0	0-0	8	Pike 2 (1 pen)	2573
8	Oct	2	H	Rochdale	L	0-1	0-0	—		3391
9		5	H	Wrexham	W	1-0	1-0	—	Pike	3452
10		13	A	York C	W	2-1	0-0	5	Blake 2	2596
11		20	A	Hereford U	D	1-1	1-0	7	Jones	5782
12		23	H	Doncaster R	L	0-2	0-1	—		3891
13		27	H	Peterborough U	D	1-1	1-0	9	Pike	2940
14	Nov	3	A	Maidstone U	L	0-3	0-2	9		2010
15		10	H	Chesterfield	W	2-1	1-1	9	Gibbins, Pike	2019
16		24	A	Gillingham	L	0-4	0-0	11		2793
17	Dec	1	A	Burnley	L	0-2	0-0	13		6348
18		15	H	Walsall	L	0-2	0-1	16		2017
19		21	A	Northampton T	D	0-0	0-0	—		3033
20		26	H	Carlisle U	W	3-1	1-0	14	Pike, Taylor 2	2281
21		29	H	Halifax T	W	1-0	0-0	12	Taylor	2903
22	Jan	1	A	Darlington	L	1-4	0-3	13	Griffith	3151
23		12	H	Hartlepool U	W	1-0	1-0	11	Griffith	2619
24		26	H	Lincoln C	L	0-1	0-1	14		2513
25	Feb	1	H	Aldershot	L	1-3	1-3	—	Gibbins	1629
26		15	H	Gillingham	W	2-0	1-0	—	Gibbins, Pike (pen)	2170
27		19	A	Scarborough	W	2-1	1-1	—	Griffith 2	1192
28		23	A	Chesterfield	D	0-0	0-0	14		3065
29		26	A	Stockport Co	D	1-1	0-1	—	Blake	3376
30	Mar	1	H	Burnley	W	3-0	3-0	—	Heard, Pike (pen), Griffith	3591
31		9	A	Walsall	D	0-0	0-0	12		3950
32		12	A	Rochdale	D	0-0	0-0	—		1569
33		16	H	Scunthorpe U	W	1-0	0-0	12	Pike (pen)	2873
34		19	H	York C	W	2-1	1-1	—	Heard, Barnard	2620
35		22	A	Wrexham	L	0-1	0-1	—		1787
36		30	A	Carlisle U	L	2-3	0-1	11	Matthews, Blake	2264
37	Apr	1	H	Northampton T	W	1-0	1-0	11	Campbell (og)	4805
38		6	A	Halifax T	W	2-1	1-0	11	Pike, Heard	1364
39		10	A	Torquay U	L	1-2	0-1	—	Gibbins	3341
40		13	H	Darlington	L	0-1	0-0	12		4544
41		17	A	Blackpool	L	0-3	0-2	—		4813
42		20	H	Hereford U	L	0-2	0-2	12		2845
43		27	A	Doncaster R	D	1-1	1-1	13	Heath	2227
44	May	2	H	Blackpool	D	1-1	0-1	—	Griffith	1793
45		4	A	Peterborough U	L	0-3	0-1	13		6642
46		11	H	Maidstone U	D	0-0	0-0	13		2011

Final League Position: 13

GOALSCORERS

League (43): Pike 14 (5 pens), Griffith 9, Gibbins 5, Blake 4, Heard 3, Taylor 3, Barnard 1, Heath 1, Jones 1, Matthews 1, own goal 1.
Rumbelows Cup (6): Griffith 5, Pike 1.
FA Cup (0).

Hansbury	Rodgerson	Daniel	Barnard	Abraham	Perry	Jones	Griffith	Gibbins	Pike	Heard	Blake	Chandler	Matthews	Lewis	Searle	Fry	Morgan	Summers	Baddeley	Stephens	De Mange	Taylor	Russell	Toshack	Heath	MacDonald	Unsworth	Ward	Match No.
1	2	3	4	5	6	7†	8	9	10*	11	12		14																1
1	2	3	4	5*	6	7	8	9	10	11	12																		2
1	2	3	4		6	7	8	9	10	11				5															3
1	2	3	4		6	7*	8	9	10†	11				5	12	14													4
1	2	3	4		6	7	8	9		11				5	10														5
1	2	3	4		6		8	9	10	11				5	7														6
1	2	3	4		6	7*	8	9	10	11	12			5															7
1	2	3	4		6	7	8	9	10†	11*	12			5	14														8
1	2	3	4		6	7*	8	9	10	11	12			5															9
1	2	3*	4		6	7	8	9	10	11				5†	12	14													10
1	2	3	4		6	7*	8	9	12	11	10			5															11
1	2	3	4		6	7	8	9*		11	10			5	12														12
1	2*	3	4		6	7	8		10		9†			5	11	12	14												13
1			4		6	7	8	9	10	11	12		2	5*	3†			14											14
1			4		6	7	8	9	10	11			2	5	3														15
1	9				6	7*	8			11†			2	3	12	4	14	5	10										16
1					6	7*	8	9	10	11			2	5	3		14					12	4†						17
1					6			9	10	11	4		2	5	3	12						8	7*						18
1					6		8*	9	10	11	4		2	5	3	12						4	7						19
1					12		8	9	10	11	4		2	5	3							6	7						20
1					12		8	9	10	11	4		2	5	3	14						6†	7						21
1					6	2*	8	9	10	11†	4			5	3	12		14					7						22
1					6	2	8	9		11	4			5	3	10							7						23
1			5		6*	8	9	10		11	4		2	3	12								7						24
1	6		5			8	9	12		10	4		2*	11	3								7						25
1	6		5			8	9	10	11		4		2	3									7						26
1	6		5			8	9	10	11	4			2	12	3	7*													27
1	6		5			8	9	10	11	4			2		3	7*					12								28
1	6		5			8	9	10	11	4			2		3	7													29
1	6		5			8	9	10	11	4			2		3	7													30
1	6		5			8	9	10	11	4			2		3	7													31
1	6		5			8*	9	10	11	4			2		3	7									12				32
1	6		5			8	9	10	11*	4			2	14	3	7†									12				33
1	6		5			8	9	10	11	4			2		3	7*									12				34
1	6†		5			8	9	10	11	4			2	14	3	12						7*							35
1			5			8	9		11	4			2		3						6				7	10			36
1			5			8	9		11	4			2		3						6				7	10			37
1	12		5			8	9	10	11				2		3						4				7*	6			38
1	12		5			8	9	10*	11†				2	14	3						4				7	6			39
1						8	9	10	11				2	5	3						4				7	6			40
1			5			12	9	10	11*	8†			2	14	3						4				7	6			41
1			5			12	9	10	11	8†			2*	14	3						4				7	6			42
1			5			8	9	10*		12			2	11	3						4				7	6			43
1			5			8	9	10*		11†			2	6	3	12	14				4				7				44
1			5			8	9	10		11			2	6	3	12					4				7*				45
1†			5	4		8	9	10		11			6	3	9*		2								7		12	14	46
46	14	13	26	2	43	20	43	43	37	38	33	—	36	16	34	14	1	—	2	1	15	6	3	1	11	8	—	—	
			+2s			+2s	+2s		+2s				+7s	+1s	+1s	+11s	+1s	+9s	+3s	+3s	+2s				+3s	+1s	+1s		

Rumbelows Cup	First Round	Mansfield T (a)	1-1
		(h)	3-0
	Second Round	Portsmouth (h)	1-1
		(a)	1-3
FA Cup	First Round	Hayes (h)	0-0
		(a)	0-1

CARDIFF CITY

Player and Position	Ht	Wt	Birth Date	Place	Source	Clubs	League App	Gls
Goalkeepers								
Roger Hansbury	5 11	12 00	26 1 55	Barnsley	Apprentice	Norwich C	78	—
						Bolton W (loan)	—	—
						Cambridge U (loan)	11	—
						Orient (loan)	—	—
					Eastern Ath	Burnley	83	—
						Cambridge U	37	—
						Birmingham C	57	—
						Sheffield U (loan)	5	—
						Wolverhampton W (loan)	3	—
						Colchester U (loan)	4	—
						Cardiff C	81	—
Gavin Ward	6 2	12 12	30 6 70	Sutton Coldfield		Shrewsbury T	—	—
						WBA	—	—
						Cardiff C	3	—
Defenders								
Gareth Abraham	6 4	12 11	13 2 69	Merthyr Tydfil	Trainee	Cardiff C	72	4
Lee Baddeley§			12 7 74	Cardiff		Cardiff C	2	—
Nathan Blake	5 10	12 00	27 1 72	Newport	Trainee	Cardiff C	46	4
Pat Heard	5 9	11 05	17 3 60	Hull	Apprentice	Everton	11	—
						Aston Villa	24	2
						Sheffield W	25	3
						Newcastle U	34	2
						Middlesbrough	25	2
						Hull C	80	5
						Rotherham U	44	7
						Cardiff C	38	3
Steve Hookings*	5 11	10 12	4 8 72	Cardiff	Trainee	Cardiff C	—	—
Allan Lewis	6 2	12 10	31 5 71	Pontypridd	Trainee	Cardiff C	38	—
Neil Matthews	6 0	11 07	3 12 67	Manchester	Apprentice	Blackpool	76	1
						Cardiff C	37	1
Jason Perry	5 11	10 04	2 4 70	Newport		Cardiff C	83	—
Damon Searle	5 11	10 05	26 10 71	Cardiff	Trainee	Cardiff C	35	—
Midfield								
Leigh Barnard*	5 8	11 07	29 10 58	Worsley	Apprentice	Portsmouth	79	8
						Peterborough U (loan)	4	—
						Swindon T	217	21
						Exeter C (loan)	6	2
						Cardiff C	63	9
Roger Gibbins	5 10	11 09	6 9 55	Enfield	Apprentice	Tottenham H	—	—
						Oxford U	19	2
						Norwich C	48	12
					N England	Cambridge U	100	12
						CardiffC	139	17
						Swansea C	35	6
						Newport Co	79	9
						Torquay U	33	5
					Newport Co	Cardiff C	93	6
Mark Jones	5 8	9 12	26 9 61	Berinsfield	Apprentice	Oxford U	129	7
						Swindon T	40	9
						Cardiff C	22	1
Jon Morgan*	5 8	10 01	10 7 70	Cardiff	Trainee	Cardiff C	55	3
Lee Stephens*	5 7	10 03	30 9 71	Cardiff	Trainee	Cardiff C	3	—
Jamie Unsworth§			1 5 73	Bury	Trainee	Cardiff C	1	—

CARDIFF CITY

Foundation: Credit for the establishment of a first class professional football club in such a rugby stronghold as Cardiff, is due to members of the Riverside club formed in 1899 out of a cricket club of that name. Cardiff became a city in 1905 and in 1908 the local FA granted Riverside permission to call themselves Cardiff City.

First Football League game: 28 August, 1920, Division 2, v Stockport C (a) W 5-2 – Kneeshaw; Brittain, Leyton; Keenor (1), Smith, Hardy; Grimshaw (1), Gill (2), Cashmore, West, Evans (1).

Did you know: Of the three men who have each scored five goals for Cardiff in a League game only one is a Welshman – Walter Robbins (see under 'Record League Victory.') The other two – Hughie Ferguson and Jim Henderson were Scots.

Managers (and Secretary-managers)
Davy McDougall 1910–11, Fred Stewart 1911–33, Bartley Wilson 1933–34, B. Watts-Jones 1934–37, Bill Jennings 1937–39, Cyril Spiers 1939–46, Billy McCandless 1946–48, Cyril Spiers 1948–54, Trevor Morris 1954–58, Bill Jones 1958–62, George Swindin 1962–64, Jimmy Scoular 1964–73, Frank O'Farrell 1973–74, Jimmy Andrews 1974–78, Richie Morgan 1978–82, Len Ashurst 1982–84, Jimmy Goodfellow 1984, Alan Durban 1984–86, Frank Burrows 1986–89, Len Ashurst 1989–91.

Player and Position	Ht	Wt	Birth Date	Birth Place	Source	Clubs	League App	Gls
Forwards								
Jeff Chandler‡	5 7	10 01	19 6 59	Hammersmith	Apprentice	Blackpool	37	7
						Leeds U	26	2
						Bolton W	157	36
						Derby Co	46	10
						Mansfield T (loan)	6	—
						Bolton W	24	4
						Cardiff C	25	—
Chris Fry*	5 9	9 06	23 10 69	Cardiff	Trainee	Cardiff C	55	1
Cohen Griffith	5 10	10 08	26 12 62	Georgetown	Kettering T	Cardiff C	83	18
Philip Heath*	5 9	12 02	24 11 64	Stoke	Apprentice	Stoke C	156	17
						Oxford U	37	1
						Cardiff C	11	1
Steve Lynex‡	5 7	11 10	23 1 58	West Bromwich	Apprentice Shamrock R	WBA	—	—
						Birmingham C	46	10
						Leicester C	213	57
						Birmingham C (loan)	10	2
						WBA	29	3
						Cardiff C	62	2
Chris Pike	6 2	12 07	19 10 61	Cardiff	Barry T	Fulham	42	4
						Cardiff C (loan)	6	2
						Cardiff C	80	32
Chris Summers*	5 11	11 02	6 1 72	Cardiff	Trainee	Cardiff C	3	—
Cameron Toshack†	6 2	12 00	7 3 70	Cardiff	Trainee	Swansea C	—	—
						Bristol C	—	—
						Cardiff C	4	—

Trainees
Baddeley, Lee M; Donovan, Jason M; Dore, Craig A; Gameson, Lee J; Gee, Andrew N; Jones, Nathan J; Marriott, Paul W; Parsons, Andrew K; Popham, Philip H; Semark, Robin H; Speake, Jason W; Unsworth, Jamie J.

Non-Contract
Toshack, John C.

Associated Schoolboys
Bellamy, Nicholas M; Graham, Ben; James, Philip; Jones, Ian; Keepin, Andrew W; Metcalfe, Mark; Phelps, David J; Street, Daniel C; Walker, Lee; Williams, Morgan D; Young, Scott.

Associated Schoolboys who have accepted the club's offer of a Traineeship/Contract
Bird, Anthony; Callaway, Nilsson, A.D; Crocker, Matthew; Curtis, Julian; Gorman, Andrew P; Hainsworth, Darren J; Sime, Leighton R.

**Non-Contract Players who are retained must be re-signed before they are eligible to play in League matches.

CARLISLE UNITED 1990–91 *Back row (left to right)*: Tony Shepherd, Robert Edwards, Mike Graham, Ian Taylor, Jason Priestley, Dave Miller, Ian Dalziel, John Halpin. *Centre row*: Simon Jeffels, Paul Fitzpatrick, Darren Edmondson, Richard Sendall, Paul Proudlock, Keith Walwyn, Craig Goldsmith, Steve Norris, Nigel Saddington, John Holliday, Alex Jones. *Front row*: Peter Hampton (Assistant Manager/Physiotherapist), Eric Gates, Michael Bennett, Clive Middlemass (Manager), Andrew Jenkins (Chairman), Derek Walsh, Eamonn Elliott, Aidan McCaffery (Coach), David Wilkes (Football in Community Supervisor).

Division 4   **CARLISLE UNITED**

Brunton Park, Carlisle CA1 1LL. Telephone Carlisle (0228) 26237. Commercial Dept: (0228) 24014.

Record attendance: 27,500 v Birmingham C, FA Cup 3rd rd, 5 January 1957 and v Middlesbrough, FA Cup 5th rd, 7 February 1970.

Record receipts: £75,988.50 v Liverpool, FA Cup 3rd 7 January 1989.

Ground capacity: 18,506.

Pitch measurements: 117yd × 78yd.

President: J. C. Monkhouse. *Vice-presidents:* J. Johnstone JP, T. L. Sibson, Dr T. Gardner MB, CHB.

Chairman: H. A. Jenkins. *Vice-chairman:* J. R. Sheffield.

Directors: R. S. Liddell, T. A. Bingley, C. J. Vasey, J. B. Lloyd, A. Liddell, A. Hodgkinson.

Team Manager: Aidan McCaffery. *Assistant Manager:* Peter Hampton.

Coach: . *Physio:* Peter Hampton.

Commercial Manager: Frank Layton.

Club Secretary: Miss Alison Moore.

Year Formed: 1903. *Ltd Co.:* 1921.

Previous Grounds: 1903–5, Milholme Bank; 1905–9, Devonshire Park; 1909– Brunton Park.

Previous Name: Shaddowgate United.

Club Nickname: 'Cumbrians' or 'The Blues'.

Record League Victory: 8-0 v Hartlepools U, Division 3 (N), 1 September 1928 – Prout; Smiles, Cook; Robinson (1) Ross, Pigg; Agar (1), Hutchison (1), McConnell (4), Ward (1), Watson. 8-0 v Scunthorpe United, Division 3 (N), 25 December 1952 – MacLaren; Hill, Scott; Stokoe, Twentyman, Waters; Harrison (1), Whitehouse (5), Ashman (2), Duffett, Bond.

Record Cup Victory: 6-1 v Billingham Synthonia, FA Cup, 1st rd, 17 November 1956 – Fairley; Hill, Kenny; Johnston, Waters, Thompson; Mooney, Broadis (1), Ackerman (2), Garvie (3), Bond.

Record Defeat: 1-11 v Hull C, Division 3 (N), 14 January 1939.

Most League Points (2 for a win): 62, Division 3 (N), 1950–51.

Most League Points (3 for a win): 80, Division 3, 1981–82.

Most League Goals: 113, Division 4, 1963–64.

Highest League Scorer in Season: Jimmy McConnell, 42, Division 3 (N), 1928–29.

Most League Goals in Total Aggregate: Jimmy McConnell, 126, 1928–32.

Most Capped Player: Eric Welsh, 4, Northern Ireland.

Most League Appearances: Alan Ross, 466, 1963–79.

Record Transfer Fee Received: £275,000 from Vancouver Whitecaps for Peter Beardsley, April 1981.

Record Transfer Fee Paid: £120,000 to York C for Gordon Staniforth, October 1979.

Football League Record: 1928 Elected to Division 3 (N); 1958–62 Division 4; 1962–63 Division 3; 1963–64 Division 4; 1964–65 Division 3; 1965–74 Division 2; 1974–75 Division 1; 1975–77 Division 2; 1977–82 Division 3; 1982–86 Division 2; 1986–87 Division 3; 1987– Division 4.

Honours: Football League: Division 1 best season: 22nd, 1974–75; Promoted from Division 2 (3rd) 1973–74; Division 3 – Champions 1964–65; Runners-up 1981–82; Division 4 – Runners-up 1963–64. *FA Cup:* 6th rd 1974–75. *Football League Cup:* Semi-final 1969–70.

Colours: Blue shirts, white shorts, blue stockings. **Change colours:** Red shirts, white shorts, red stockings.

CARLISLE UNITED 1990–91 LEAGUE RECORD

Match No.	Date		Venue	Opponents	Result		H/T Score	Lg. Pos.	Goalscorers	Atten-dance
1	Aug	25	H	Doncaster R	L	2-3	1-2	—	Walwyn, Shepherd	4218
2	Sept	1	A	Peterborough U	D	1-1	1-1	17	Norris	3675
3		8	H	Maidstone U	W	1-0	1-0	12	Edwards (pen)	3808
4		15	A	Hereford U	L	2-4	0-2	16	Proudlock, Edwards	2773
5		17	A	Stockport Co	L	1-3	0-1	—	Norris	3118
6		22	H	Hartlepool U	W	1-0	0-0	15	Gates	3303
7		27	H	Burnley	D	1-1	1-0	—	Walwyn	5205
8	Oct	2	A	Gillingham	L	1-2	1-2	—	Walwyn	3022
9		6	A	Walsall	D	1-1	1-0	16	Gates	4248
10		13	H	Halifax T	L	0-3	0-3	18		3697
11		20	H	Chesterfield	W	1-0	1-0	16	Gates	3029
12		24	A	Scarborough	D	1-1	0-1	—	Shepherd	1329
13		27	A	Torquay U	L	0-3	0-0	19		3269
14	Nov	3	H	Lincoln C	D	0-0	0-0	19		3095
15		10	H	York C	W	1-0	0-0	18	Gates	2888
16		24	A	Rochdale	W	1-0	0-0	15	Gates	1733
17	Dec	1	A	Wrexham	L	0-3	0-2	17		1682
18		15	H	Northampton T	W	4-1	2-0	15	Proudlock, Walwyn, Gates, Jeffels	2873
19		23	H	Blackpool	W	1-0	1-0	—	Edwards (pen)	5195
20		26	A	Cardiff C	L	1-3	0-1	15	Jeffels	2281
21		29	H	Scunthorpe U	L	0-2	0-0	16		2971
22	Jan	1	H	Aldershot	L	1-2	0-1	18	Miller	2978
23		5	A	Darlington	L	1-3	0-1	18	Shepherd	3726
24		12	H	Peterborough U	W	3-2	1-1	15	Jeffels, Halpin, Gates	2744
25		19	A	Doncaster R	L	0-4	0-0	17		2447
26		26	H	Hereford U	L	0-1	0-1	18		2572
27	Feb	2	H	Stockport Co	W	1-0	0-0	17	Barras (og)	2750
28		5	A	Hartlepool U	L	1-4	0-2	—	Edwards (pen)	2670
29		16	H	Rochdale	D	1-1	0-0	17	Miller	2505
30		23	A	York C	L	0-2	0-0	17		2002
31		26	H	Darlington	L	0-2	0-1	—		2896
32	Mar	2	H	Wrexham	W	2-0	0-0	17	Lillis, Gates	2207
33		9	A	Northampton T	D	1-1	0-1	17	Proudlock	3216
34		12	H	Gillingham	L	0-4	0-2	—		2633
35		16	A	Burnley	L	1-2	1-0	18	Proudlock	6635
36		19	A	Halifax T	D	1-1	1-1	—	Edwards (pen)	1004
37		23	H	Walsall	L	0-3	0-0	18		2433
38		30	H	Cardiff C	W	3-2	1-0	18	Shepherd, Proudlock 2	2264
39	Apr	2	A	Blackpool	L	0-6	0-3	—		5368
40		6	H	Scunthorpe U	L	0-3	0-3	18		1909
41		13	A	Aldershot	L	0-3	0-2	19		1818
42		20	A	Chesterfield	L	1-4	1-2	20	Shepherd (pen)	2708
43		27	H	Scarborough	W	4-1	2-0	21	Sendall, Miller, Fyfe 2	1762
44	May	1	A	Maidstone U	D	0-0	0-0	—		1111
45		4	H	Torquay U	W	3-1	1-0	20	Fyfe, Miller, Sendall	2176
46		11	A	Lincoln C	L	2-6	1-2	20	Proudlock, Shepherd (pen)	2333

Final League Position: 20

GOALSCORERS

League (47): Gates 8, Proudlock 7, Shepherd 6 (2 pens), Edwards 5 (4 pens), Miller 4, Walwyn 4, Fyfe 3, Jeffels 3, Norris 2, Sendall 2, Halpin 1, Lillis 1, own goal 1.
Rumbelows Cup (3): Fitzpatrick 1, Proudlock 1, Walwyn 1.
FA Cup (0).

Priestley	Miller	Edwards	Graham	Jones	Fitzpatrick	Walsh	Shepherd	Walwyn	Gates	Proudlock	Goldsmith	Norris	Sendall	Methven	Jeffels	Edmondson	Fyfe	Owen	Thorpe	Bennett	Siddall	Elliott	Wilkes	Halpin	Dalziel	Holliday	Lillis	Armstrong	Match No.
1	2	3	4	5	6	7*	8	9	10†	11	12	14																	1
1	2	3	4†	5	6	7	8	9	10*	11		14	12																2
1	2	3	4		6*	7	8	9*	10	11			12	5															3
1	2	3	4		6*	7	8		10†	11	12	14	9	5															4
1	2	3			6	7	8		10*	11	12	9	5	4															5
1	2	3			6	7	8	12	10	11		9*	5	4															6
1	2	3			6	7	8	9	10	11			5	4															7
1	2	3			6	7	8	9	10	11			5	4															8
1	2	3			6	7	8	9	10	11			5	4															9
1	2	3			6†	7	8	9*	10	11			5	4	12	14													10
1	2	3			6	7	8		10*	11			5	4	12	9													11
1	2†	3			6	7	8	9*	12	10			5	4		11	14												12
1		3			6	7	8		10	11			5	4	2*	9	12												13
1		3	4		6	7	8	12	10	11*			5		2	9													14
1			4	5	6	7	8	9	10						2	11			3										15
			4	5	6	7	8	9	10	11					2				3		1								16
		3		5	2		8	9	10	11	14	12			6	7*					1			4†					17
	6	3		5		7	8	9	10	11					4	2					1								18
	6	3		5	12	7*	8	9	10	11					4	2					1								19
	6	3		5	12		8	9*	10	11					4	2	14	7*			1								20
	7†	3		5			8	9*	10	11					4	2	14	6			1			12					21
	7	3		5	6		8	9	10*	11					4	2		12			1								22
	2	3		5	6		8	9*	10†	7			12		4						1			11	14				23
	2	3		5	6		8	9*	10	7			12		4						1			11					24
	8	3		5	6†			9*	10	7					4	2	12	14			1			11					25
	2	3		5				9	10*	7					4	6	12				1			11	8				26
	2	3	4	5			8		10*	12	9				6						1			11	7				27
	2	3	4*	5			8		10	12	9				6						1			11	7				28
	7	3	4		6		8		10						9	2					1			11	5				29
	7	3	4		6		8		12	10					9*	2†	14				1			11	5				30
	2	3	4		6		8		10	7*					9†	14				5	1	12		11					31
	2	3	4		6		8		10	7						12				5	1			11				9*	32
	2	3	4		6		8		10*	7						12					1			11	5			9	33
	2	3	4		6*		8		10†	7					9	12	14				1			11	5				34
1	2	3	4†	14			8	12		7					6	5	10							11				9*	35
1	2	3			4		8			7					6	5	10							11				9*	36
1	2			4†			8	12		7*					6	5	10	14						11	3				37
1	2			4			8			7					6	5	10							11	3				38
1	2			4			8			7					6	5†	10	14						11	3		12		39
1	2			4			8*	12		7					6	5	14							11	3	10			40
			4	5				9	12	7					6	8†	14			10	1	2*		11	3				41
			4	5	2*			9†	10	7					6	8	14				1			11	3		12		42
			4	5				9	10	7					6	8					1			11*	3		12	2	43
			4	5				9	10	7					6	8					1			11	3			2	44
			4	5				9	10	7					6	8					1			11	3			2	45
1			4*	5				9	10	7					6	8					1			11	3		12	2	46
22	41	36	13	26	29	19	43	20	33	43	—	2	15	12	21	30	8	4	6	16	24	3	—	18	13	1	4	4	
			+3s		+1s	+2s	+5s	+2s	+4s	+3s	+10s				+1s	+8s	+1s	+7s	+1s		+1s	+1s	+3s					+2s	

Rumbelows Cup	First Round	Scunthorpe U (h)		1-0
		(a)		1-1
	Second Round	Derby Co (h)		1-1
		(a)		0-1
FA Cup	First Round	Wigan Ath (a)		0-5

CARLISLE UNITED

Player and Position	Ht	Wt	Birth Date	Place	Source	Clubs	League App	Gls
Goalkeepers								
Jason Priestley	5 11	12 02	25 10 70	Leeds	Trainee	Carlisle U	22	—
						Hartlepool U (loan)	16	—
Barry Siddall	6 1	14 02	12 9 54	Ellesmere Port	Apprentice	Bolton W	137	—
						Sunderland	167	—
						Darlington (loan)	8	—
						Port Vale	81	—
						Blackpool (loan)	7	—
						Stoke City	20	—
						Tranmere R (loan)	12	—
						Manchester C (loan)	6	—
						Blackpool	110	—
						Stockport Co	21	—
						Hartlepool U	11	—
						WBA	—	—
						Carlisle U	24	—
Ian Taylor	6 1	12 00	25 11 67	Doncaster	Bridlington T	Carlisle U	—	—
Defenders								
Lee Armstrong§			19 10 72	Workington	Trainee	Carlisle U	6	—
Mike Bennett*	5 7	10 00	24 12 62	Bolton	Apprentice	Bolton W	65	1
						Wolverhampton W	6	—
						Cambridge U	76	—
						Bradford C	—	—
						Preston NE	86	1
						Carlisle U	17	—
Ian Dalziel	5 8	11 10	24 10 62	South Shields	Apprentice	Derby Co	22	4
						Hereford U	150	8
						Carlisle U	79	2
Darren Edmondson	6 0	12 02	4 11 71	Coniston	Trainee	Carlisle U	31	—
Eamon Elliot*	5 5	9 09	27 8 71	Belfast	Trainee	Carlisle U	4	—
Mike Graham	5 9	11 07	24 2 59	Lancaster	Apprentice	Bolton W	46	—
						Swindon T	141	1
						Mansfield T	133	1
						Carlisle U	100	2
John Holliday	6 4	11 00	13 3 70	Penrith		Carlisle U	1	—
Simon Jeffels	6 1	11 08	18 1 66	Barnsley	Apprentice	Barnsley	42	—
						Preston NE (loan)	1	—
						Carlisle U	50	3
Alex Jones	6 2	12 08	27 11 64	Blackburn	Apprentice	Oldham Ath	9	—
						Stockport Co (loan)	3	—
						Preston NE	101	3
						Carlisle U	62	4
David Miller	5 11	11 02	8 1 64	Burnley	Apprentice	Burnley	32	3
						Crewe Alex (loan)	3	—
					Colne Dyn	Tranmere R	29	1
						Preston NE	58	2
						Burnley (loan)	4	—
						Carlisle U	83	7
Nigel Saddington*	6 1	12 06	9 12 65	Sunderland		Doncaster R	6	—
						Sunderland	3	—
						Carlisle U	97	16
Midfield								
Paul Fitzpatrick	6 4	11 10	5 10 65	Liverpool	Local	Tranmere R	—	—
						Liverpool	—	—
						Preston NE	—	—
						Bolton W	14	—
						Bristol C	44	7
						Carlisle U	109	4
						Preston NE (loan)	2	—
John Halpin*	5 10	11 07	15 11 61	Broxburn	Celtic BC	Celtic	7	—
						Sunderland (loan)	—	—
						Carlisle U	153	17
Tony Shepherd	5 9	10 07	16 11 66	Glasgow	Celtic BC	Celtic	28	3
						Bristol C (loan)	3	—
						Carlisle U	75	8
Derek Walsh	5 7	11 05	24 10 67	Hamilton	Apprentice	Everton	1	—
						Hamilton A	2	—
						Carlisle U	82	6

CARLISLE UNITED

Foundation: Carlisle United came into being in 1903 through the amalgamation of Shaddongate United and Carlisle Red Rose. The new club was admitted to the Second Division of the Lancashire Combination in 1905–06, winning promotion the following season.

First Football League game: 25 August, 1928, Division 3(N), v Accrington S (a) W 3-2 – Prout; Coulthard, Cook; Harrison, Ross, Pigg; Agar, Hutchison, McConnell (1), Ward (1), Watson. 1 o.g.

Did you know: Alan Ashman was the first player to score a hat-trick in his League debut for United. Ashman, who later became manager, performed this feat in a 4-0 win at Rochdale, 18 August 1951.

Managers (and Secretary-managers)
H. Kirkbride 1904–05*, McCumiskey 1905–06*, J. Houston 1906–08*, Bert Stansfield 1908–10, J. Houston 1910–12, D. Graham 1912–13, George Bristow 1913–30, Billy Hampson 1930–33, Bill Clarke 1933–35, Robert Kelly 1935–36, Fred Westgarth 1936–38, David Taylor 1938–40, Howard Harkness 1940–45, Bill Clark 1945–46*, Ivor Broadis 1946–49, Bill Shankly 1949–51, Fred Emery 1951–58, Andy Beattie 1958–60, Ivor Powell 1960–63, Alan Ashman 1963–67, Tim Ward 1967–68, Bob Stokoe 1968–70, Ian MacFarlane 1970–72, Alan Ashman 1972–75, Dick Young 1975–76, Bobby Moncur 1976–80, Martin Harvey 1980, Bob Stokoe 1980–85, Bryan "Pop" Robson 1985, Bob Stokoe 1985–86, Harry Gregg 1986–87, Cliff Middlemass 1987–91, Aidan McCaffery April 1991– .

Player and Position	Ht	Wt	Birth Date	Birth Place	Source	Clubs	League App	Gls
David Wilkes†	5 8	10 02	10 3 64	Barnsley	Apprentice	Barnsley	17	2
						Halifax (loan)	4	—
					Hong Kong H	Stockport Co	8	—
					Hong Kong H	Carlisle U	1	—
Forwards								
Tony Fyfe	6 2	12 00	23 2 62	Carlisle		Carlisle U	48	12
						Scarborough (loan)	6	1
						Halifax T	16	—
						Carlisle	16	3
Eric Gates	5 6	10 08	28 6 55	Ferryhill	Apprentice	Ipswich T	296	73
						Sunderland	181	43
						Carlisle U	38	8
Craig Goldsmith*	5 7	11 03	27 8 63	Peterborough	Blackstones	Peterborough U	46	6
						Carlisle U	30	1
Paul Proudlock	5 10	11 00	25 10 65			Hartlepool U	15	—
						Middlesbrough	5	1
						Carlisle U	95	16
Richard Sendall	5 10	11 06	10 7 67	Stamford	Apprentice	Watford	—	—
						Blackpool	11	—
						Carlisle U	73	12
						Cardiff C (loan)	4	—
Keith Walwyn‡	6 1	13 02	17 2 56	Jamaica	Winterton	Chesterfield	3	2
						York C	245	119
						Blackpool	69	16
						Carlisle U	62	15

Trainees
Armstrong, Lee W; Bell, Robert J; Caig, Antony; Cranston, Nicholas G; Graham, Calum I; Nugent, Richard; Parker, Gary A; Potts, Craig; Reay, Simon; Thomson, Marcus E; Thorpe, Jeffrey R; Townsley, Derek J.

**Non-Contract
Wilkes, David A.

Associated Schoolboys
Dalton Neil J; Gawith, Anthony L; Gray, Alan M; Otway, Paul; Prokas, Richard; Wilson, Graeme J.

Associated Schoolboys who have accepted the club's offer of a Traineeship/Contract
Brown, Paul B; McKechnie, Michael; Prins, Jason; Scott, Alan.

**Non-Contract Players who are retained must be re-signed before they are eligible to play in League matches.

148

CHARLTON ATHLETIC 1990-91   *Back row (left to right):* Steve Crane, Paul Bacon, Spencer Barham, Paul Mortimer, Andy Jones, Steve MacKenzie, Darren Pitcher, Gordon Watson.
Centre row: Steve Brown, Stuart Balmer, Tommy Caton, Lee Harrison, Bob Bolder, Mike Salmon, Simon Webster, Jason Lee, Rosario Franco.
Front row: Garth Crooks, Scott Minto, Mark Reid, Andy Peake, Colin Walsh, Robert Lee, Steve Gritt, Mark Tivey.

Division 2   CHARLTON ATHLETIC

The Valley, Floyd Road, Charlton, London SE7 8BL.
Telephone: 081-293-4567.

Ground capacity: 12,300.

Record attendance: 75,031 v Aston Villa, FA Cup 5th rd, 12 February 1938 (at The Valley).

Record receipts: £114,618.70 v Liverpool (at Selhurst Park), Division 1, 23 January 1988.

Pitch measurements:.

President: R. D. Collins.

Chairman: R. N. Alwen. *Vice-chairman:* M. J. Norris.

Directors: R. D. Collins, D. G. Ufton, M. A. Simons, R. A. Murray.

General Manager: Arnie Warren.

Commercial Manager: Andy Bryant.

Player-coaches: Alan Curbishley and Steve Gritt. *Physio:* Jimmy Hendry.

Company Secretary: Chris Parkes. *Reserve team coach:* Keith Peacock.

Year Formed: 1905. *Turned Professional:* 1920. *Ltd Co.:* 1919.

Club Nickname: 'Addicks', 'Robins' or 'Valiants'.

Previous Grounds: 1906, Siemen's Meadow; 1907, Woolwich Common; 1909, Pound Park; 1913, Horn Lane; 1919, The Valley; 1923, Catford (The Mount); 1924, The Valley; 1985 Selhurst Park; 1991 The Valley.

Record League Victory: 8-1 v Middlesbrough, Division 1, 12 September 1953 – Bartram; Campbell, Ellis; Fenton, Ufton, Hammond; Hurst (2), O'Linn (2), Leary (1), Firmani (3), Kiernan.

Record Cup Victory: 7-0 v Burton A, FA Cup, 3rd rd, 7 January 1956 – Bartram; Campbell, Townsend; Hewie, Ufton, Hammond; Hurst (1), Gauld (1), Leary (3), White, Kiernan (2).

Record Defeat: 1-11 v Aston Villa, Division 2, 14 November 1959.

Most League Points (2 for a win): 61, Division 3 (S), 1934–35.

Most League Points (3 for a win): 77, Division 2, 1985–86.

Most League goals: 107, Division 2, 1957–58.

Highest League Scorer in Season: Ralph Allen, 32, Division 3 (S), 1934–35.

Most League Goals in Total Aggregate: Stuart Leary, 153, 1951–62.

Most Capped Player: John Hewie, 19, Scotland.

Most League Appearances: Sam Bartram, 582, 1934–56.

Record Transfer Fee Received: £600,000 from Sheffield W for Paul Williams, August 1990.

Record Transfer Fee Paid: £600,000 to Chelsea for Joe McLaughlin, August 1989.

Football League Record: 1921 Elected to Division 3 (S); 1929–33 Division 2; 1933–35 Division 3 (S); 1935–36 Division 2; 1936–57 Division 1; 1957–72 Division 2; 1972–75 Division 3; 1975–80 Division 2; 1980–81 Division 3; 1981–86; Division 2; 1986–90 Division 1; 1990– Division 2.

Honours: Football League: Division 1 – Runners-up 1936–37; Division 2 – Runners-up 1935–36, 1985–86; Division 3 (S) – Champions 1928–29, 1934–35; Promoted from Division 3 (3rd) 1974–75, 1980–81. *FA Cup:* Winners 1947; Runners-up 1946. *Football League Cup:* best season: 4th rd, 1962–63, 1964–65, 1978–79, 1986–87. *Full Members Cup:* Runners-up 1987.

Colours: Red shirts, white shorts, red stockings. **Change colours:** All blue.

150

CHARLTON ATHLETIC 1990–91 LEAGUE RECORD

Match No.	Date	Venue	Opponents	Result	H/T Score	Lg. Pos.	Goalscorers	Attendance
1	Aug 25	H	Swindon T	L	1-2	1-2	—	Reid	7524
2	Sept 1	A	Bristol R	L	1-2	0-1	23	Lee	5357
3	8	H	Sheffield W	L	0-1	0-0	24		7407
4	15	A	Brighton & HA	L	2-3	1-1	24	Watson, Crooks	8281
5	18	A	Oldham Ath	D	1-1	1-1	—	Watson	13,176
6	22	H	Millwall	D	0-0	0-0	23		11,735
7	29	H	Barnsley	W	2-1	0-0	21	Pitcher, Watson	4379
8	Oct 2	A	Wolverhampton W	L	0-3	0-1	—		14,363
9	6	A	Port Vale	D	1-1	0-0	21	Caton (pen)	6706
10	13	H	Leicester C	L	1-2	0-2	22	Dyer	6000
11	20	H	Watford	L	1-2	1-0	24	Lee	5892
12	24	A	Newcastle U	W	3-1	2-0	—	MacKenzie, Lee, Reid (pen)	14,016
13	27	A	West Ham U	L	1-2	0-0	23	Dyer	24,019
14	30	A	Notts Co	D	2-2	0-0	—	Lee, Watson	5067
15	Nov 3	H	Plymouth Arg	L	0-1	0-1	23		5239
16	10	A	Middlesbrough	W	2-1	1-0	23	Lee, Caton (pen)	17,998
17	17	H	Oxford U	D	3-3	1-2	23	Watson 2, Lee	4928
18	24	H	Portsmouth	W	2-1	2-0	23	Lee, Watson	5513
19	Dec 1	A	Bristol C	W	1-0	1-0	20	Lee	10,984
20	15	A	Swindon T	D	1-1	1-0	20	Mortimer	7396
21	22	H	Hull C	W	2-1	1-1	17	Hockaday (og), Lee	4989
22	26	A	WBA	L	0-1	0-1	18		9305
23	29	A	Ipswich T	D	4-4	1-2	17	Peake, Mortimer, Dyer, Caton (pen)	11,719
24	Jan 1	H	Blackburn R	D	0-0	0-0	18		5558
25	12	A	Bristol R	D	2-2	1-1	17	Mortimer, Dyer	5606
26	19	A	Sheffield W	D	0-0	0-0	18		22,318
27	22	H	Notts Co	W	3-1	2-0	—	Mortimer 2, Peake	4516
28	Feb 2	H	Brighton & HA	L	1-2	0-1	16	Dyer	7178
29	16	A	Oxford U	D	1-1	0-1	17	Lee	4726
30	23	H	Middlesbrough	L	0-1	0-1	18		5510
31	Mar 2	H	Bristol C	W	2-1	2-1	18	Dyer 2	5477
32	9	A	Portsmouth	W	1-0	1-0	16	Peake	8235
33	12	H	Wolverhampton W	W	1-0	0-0	—	Grant	6853
34	16	A	Barnsley	D	1-1	1-0	13	Grant	6373
35	20	A	Leicester C	W	2-1	0-0	—	Pitcher (pen), Mortimer	8363
36	23	H	Port Vale	L	0-1	0-0	14		5222
37	30	H	WBA	W	2-0	1-0	11	Pitcher (pen), Lee	5686
38	Apr 1	A	Hull C	D	2-2	0-0	13	Lee, Gorman	5689
39	6	H	Ipswich T	D	1-1	0-0	13	Lee	6443
40	10	A	Millwall	L	1-3	0-1	—	Wilson	15,241
41	13	A	Blackburn R	D	2-2	1-2	14	Wilson, Leaburn	6714
42	16	H	Oldham Ath	D	1-1	1-1	—	Mortimer	5367
43	20	A	Watford	L	1-2	0-2	14	Gorman	10,178
44	27	H	Newcastle U	W	1-0	0-0	13	Peake	7234
45	May 4	H	West Ham U	D	1-1	1-1	14	Minto	16,137
46	11	A	Plymouth Arg	L	0-2	0-1	16		6816

Final League Position: 16

GOALSCORERS

League (57): Lee 13, Dyer 7, Mortimer 7, Watson 7, Peake 4, Caton 3 (3 pens), Pitcher 3 (2 pens), Gorman 2, Grant 2, Reid 2 (1 pen), Wilson 2, Crooks 1, Leaburn 1, MacKenzie 1, Minto 1, own goal 1.
Rumbelows Cup (2): Minto 1, Watson 1.
FA Cup (1): Dyer 1.

Bolder	Gritt	Reid	Peake	Webster	Caton	Lee	MacKenzie	Walsh	Crooks	Mortimer	Jones	Pitcher	Watson	Minto	Balmer	Salmon	Dyer	Wilder	Curbishley	Leaburn	Kernaghan	Grant	Gorman	Wilson	Bacon	Salako	Match No.
1	2†	3	4	5	6	7	8	9	10*	11	12	14															1
1	2	3	4	5	6	7	8	9*10		11†12	14																2
1	3		4	5	6	7	8	9	12			11	2	10*													3
1			4	5	6†	7	8	9	12			11*	2	10	3	14											4
	12		4	5	6	7	8†11					9	2	10*	3	14	1										5
			4	5	6	7	8	11				9	2	10	3		1										6
			4	5	6	7	8	11				9	2	10	3		1										7
			4	5	6	7	8	9	12				2	10	3		1	11*									8
		3	4	5	6	7	8	12				2	10	11*			1	9									9
		3	4	5	6	7	8	11†12					10*14		2		1	9									10
		3	4	5		7	8		12				10	11	6	1		9*	2								11
1		3	4	5		7	8					2	10	11*	6			9	12								12
1		3	4	5		7	8					2	10	11	6			9									13
1		3	4	5		7	8					2	10	11	6			9									14
1		3	4	5†	6	7	8					2	10	11*14				9	12								15
1		3	4	5	6	7			10			2		11				9	8								16
1	3†		4	5	6	7			10			2	14	11				9*	8	12							17
1			4		6	7			11			2	10	3	5			9	8								18
1			4		6	7			11			2	10	3	5			9	8								19
1			4		6	7*			11			2	10	3	5			9	8	12							20
1			4		6	7			11			2	10	3	5			9	8								21
1			4	5	6	7		11				2	10	3				9*	8	12							22
1		3	4	5	6	7			11			2		10				9	8*12								23
1		3	4	5	6	7			11			2	14	10†				9*	8	12							24
1	12		4	5		7			11			2	14	3	6			9	8*10†								25
1			4	5		7			11			2		3				9	8	10	6						26
1			4	5		7			11			2		3				9	8	10	6						27
1			4	5		7			11			2	12	3				9	8	10*	6						28
1	12		4	5		7			11			2		3	14			9†	8*10		6						29
1	12		4		7				11			2		3	6			9	8*10		5						30
1		3	4	5		7			10			2		11				9		12	6	8*					31
1	8	3	4	5		7			10			2		11				9			6						32
1	8*	3	4	5		7			10			2		11				9			6	12					33
1	12	3	4	5		7			10			2		11				9			6	8*					34
1		3	4	5		7			10			2		11				9			6	8					35
1		3	4	5		7			10			2		11				9	12		6	8*					36
1		3*	4	5		7			10			2		11					9		6	8	12				37
1		4†		5		7			10			2		3	14			9*			6	8	12	11			38
1				5		7			10			2		3	6				4	12		8		9*11†14			39
1			4	5		7			10			2		3	6			14	9			8*12		11†			40
1			4	5			14		10			2		3	6			7	9			8*12		11†			41
1			4	5					10			2		3	6		12	7	9			8*		11			42
1			4	5			14		10			2		3	6		8	7	9*				12	11†			43
1		3	4	5		7			10			2		11	6		8*		12				9†14				44
1		3	4	5†		7			10			2		11	6		8	14	12			9*					45
1	12	3	4		7*				10			5		11	6		9†		8			14				2	46
39	5	23	45	40	20	43	15	10	2	32	5	42	18	42	19	7	34	1	20	11	13	11	2	6	—	1	
	+	+						+	+			+	+	+	+		+		+	+		+	+	+	+		
	5s	1s						3s	5s			2s	2s	4s	1s		5s		5s	9s		1s	6s	1s	1s		

Rumbelows Cup	Second Round	Leyton Orient (h)		2-2
		(a)		0-1
FA Cup	Third Round	Everton (h)		1-2

CHARLTON ATHLETIC

Player and Position	Ht	Wt	Birth Date	Place	Source	Clubs	League App	Gls
Goalkeepers								
Bob Bolder	6 3	14 06	2 10 58	Dover	Dover	Sheffield W	196	—
						Liverpool	—	—
						Sunderland	22	—
						Luton T (loan)	—	—
						Charlton Ath	176	—
Lee Harrison*	6 2	12 02	12 9 71	Billericay	Trainee	Charlton Ath	—	—
Mike Salmon	6 2	13 00	14 7 64	Leyland	Local	Blackburn R	1	—
						Chester C (loan)	16	—
						Stockport Co	118	—
						Bolton W	26	—
						Wrexham (loan)	17	—
						Wrexham	83	—
						Charlton Ath	7	—
Matthew Watts*			7 10 72	Kettering	Rothwell T	Charlton Ath	—	—
Defenders								
Paul Bacon	5 9	10 04	20 12 70	London	Trainee	Charlton Ath	1	—
Stuart Balmer	6 1	12 04	20 6 69	Falkirk	Celtic	Charlton Ath	24	—
Spencer Barham*	5 9	10 05	14 8 72	Essex	Trainee	Charlton Ath	—	—
Anthony Barness	5 10	10 12	25 3 72	London	Trainee	Charlton Ath	—	—
Steve Brown			13 5 72	Brighton	Trainee	Charlton Ath	—	—
Tommy Caton	6 2	13 00	6 10 62	Liverpool	Apprentice	Manchester C	165	8
						Arsenal	81	2
						Oxford U	53	3
						Charlton Ath	57	5
Steve Gritt	5 9	10 10	31 10 57	Bournemouth	Apprentice	Bournemouth	6	3
						Charlton Ath	347	24
						Walsall	20	1
						Charlton Ath	12	—
Scott Minto	5 10	10 00	6 8 71	Cheshire	Trainee	Charlton Ath	69	3
Darren Pitcher	5 9	12 02	12 10 69	London	Trainee	Charlton Ath	44	3
						Galway U (loan)	—	—
Mark Reid	5 8	11 05	15 9 61	Kilwinning	Celtic BC	Celtic	124	5
						Charlton Ath	211	15
Andy Salako			8 11 72	Nigeria	Trainee	Charlton Ath	1	—
Simon Webster	6 0	11 07	20 1 64	Earl Shilton	Apprentice	Tottenham H	3	—
						Exeter C (loan)	26	—
						Norwich C (loan)	—	—
						Huddersfield T	118	4
						Sheffield U	37	3
						Charlton Ath	40	—
Midfield								
Alan Curbishley	5 11	11 10	8 11 57	Forest Gate	Apprentice	West Ham U	85	5
						Birmingham C	130	11
						Aston Villa	36	1
						Charlton Ath	63	6
						Brighton & HA	116	13
						Charlton Ath	25	—
Rosario Franco*	5 10	11 00	22 12 71	London	Trainee	Charlton Ath	—	—
Paul Mortimer	5 11	11 03	8 5 68	London	Fulham	Charlton Ath	113	17
Andy Peake	5 10	12 00	1 11 61	Market Harborough	Apprentice	Leicester C	147	13
						Grimsby T	39	4
						Charlton Ath	157	5
Colin Walsh	5 9	10 11	22 7 62	Hamilton	Apprentice	Nottingham F	139	32
						Charlton Ath	89	11
						Peterborough U (loan)	5	1
						Middlesborough (loan)	13	1

CHARLTON ATHLETIC

Foundation: Although formed in 1905 by members of such clubs as East Street Mission, Blundell Mission, and Charlton Reds, Charlton Athletic did not really make their presence felt until adopting professionalism and joining the Southern League in 1920. Before that, they had played in such competitions as the Lewisham, Southern Suburban and London Leagues.

First Football League game: 27 August, 1921, Division 3(S), v Exeter C (h) W 1-0 – Hughes; Mitchell, Goodman; Dowling (1), Hampson, Dunn; Castle, Bailey, Halse, Green, Wilson.

Did you know: After Charlton won the FA Cup in 1947 manager Jimmy Seed dropped the trophy and broke the top off the lid. A garage did a temporary repair before a Town Hall reception after which a silversmith did a professional job.

Managers (and Secretary-managers)
Walter Rayner 1920–25, Alex MacFarlane 1925–28, Albert Lindon 1928, Alex MacFarlane 1928–32, Albert Lindon 1932–33, Jimmy Seed 1933–56, Jimmy Trotter 1956–61, Frank Hill 1961–65, Bob Stokoe 1965–67, Eddie Firmani 1967–70, Theo Foley 1970–74, Andy Nelson 1974–79, Mike Bailey 1979–81, Alan Mullery 1981–82, Ken Craggs 1982, Lennie Lawrence 1982–91.

Player and Position	Ht	Wt	Birth Date	Birth Place	Source	Clubs	League App	Gls
Daniel Wareham	5 10	10 08	29 12 72	Kent	Trainee	Charlton Ath	—	—
Forwards								
Steve Crane‡	5 10	11 00	3 6 72	Orsett	Trainee	Charlton Ath	—	—
Garth Crooks‡	5 8	12 01	10 3 58	Stoke	Apprentice	Stoke C	147	48
						Tottenham H	125	48
						Manchester U (loan)	7	2
						WBA	40	16
						Charlton Ath	56	15
Alex Dyer	5 11	11 12	14 11 65	West Ham	Apprentice	Watford	—	—
						Blackpool	108	19
						Hull C	60	14
						Crystal Palace	17	2
						Charlton Ath	35	7
Paul Gorman	5 9	12 02	18 9 68	Macclesfield	Trainee	Doncaster R	16	2
					Fisher Ath	Charlton Ath	8	2
Kim Grant	5 10	10 12	25 9 72	Ghana	Trainee	Charlton Ath	12	2
Carl Leaburn	6 3	12 12	30 3 69	Lewisham	Apprentice	Charlton Ath	80	4
						Northampton T (loan)	9	—
Robert Lee	5 8	10 12	1 2 66	West Ham	ABTA	Charlton Ath	252	46
Mark Tivey	5 9	10 00	10 2 71	London	Trainee	Charlton Ath	—	—

Trainees
Antoine, Richard B; Darlington, Jermaine C; Julian, Martin J; Nguyen, The V; Primus, Linvoy S; Secker, John R.
Associated Schoolboys
Bailey, Richard; Bakes, Sean; Burt, Leslie; Dixon, Franklyn; Jackson, James T; Lee, Dean J.
Associated Schoolboys who have accepted the club's offer of a Traineeship/Contract
Appiah, Sam K; Gray, Andrew J; Mills, Daniel R; Newton, Shaun; Sturgess, Paul C.

154

CHELSEA 1990–91 *Back row (left to right):* Damian Matthew, Graham Stuart, Gareth Hall, Erland Johnsen, Kerry Dixon, Andy Townsend, Steve Clarke, Graeme Le Saux, Kevin McAllister.

Centre row: Frank Sibley (Reserve Team Coach), Bob Ward (Physiotherapist), Jason Cundy, David Lee, Roger Freestone, Dave Beasant, Kevin Hitchcock, Kenneth Monkou, Alan Dickens, Gwyn Williams (Assistant Manager), Dave Collyer (Youth Team Coach).

Front row: John Bumstead, Dennis Wise, Peter Nicholas, Bobby Campbell (Manager), Gordon Durie, Tony Dorigo, Kevin Wilson.

Division 1   **CHELSEA**

Stamford Bridge, London SW6. Main Office/Box Office Telephone 071-385 5545. Clubcall: 0898 121159. Ticket News and Promotions: 0898 121011. Fax: 071 381 4831.

Ground capacity: 43,900 (21,500 covered).

Record attendance: 82,905 v Arsenal, Division 1, 12 Oct 1935.

Record receipts: £212,894 v Arsenal, Division 1, 30 September 1989.

Pitch measurements: 114yd × 71yd.

President: G. M. Thomson.

Chairman: K. W. Bates. *Vice-chairman:*

Directors: C. Hutchinson (Managing), Y. S. Todd, S. S. Tollman.

Team Manager: Ian Porterfield. *Assistant. Manager:* Gwyn Williams.

Physio: Bob Ward. *Reserve Team Manager:* Eddie Niedzwiecki.

Company Secretary/Director: Yvonne Todd. *Match Secretary:* Keith Lacy. *Commercial Manager:* John Shaw.

Year Formed: 1905. *Turned Professional:* 1905. *Ltd Co.:* 1905.

Club Nickname: 'The Blues'.

Record League Victory: 9-2 v Glossop N E, Division 2, 1 September 1906 – Byrne; Walton, Miller; Key (1), McRoberts, Henderson; Moran, McDermott (1), Hilsdon (5), Copeland (1), Kirwan (1).

Record Cup Victory: 13-0 v Jeunesse Hautcharage, ECWC, 1st rd 2nd leg, 29 September 1971 – Bonetti; Boyle, Harris (1), Hollins (1p), Webb (1), Hinton, Cooke, Baldwin (3), Osgood (5), Hudson (1), Houseman (1).

Record Defeat: 1-8 v Wolverhampton W, Division 1, 26 September 1953.

Most League Points (2 for a win): 57, Division 2, 1906–07.

Most League Points (3 for a win): 99, Division 2, 1988–89.

Most League Goals: 98, Division 1, 1960–61.

Highest League Scorer in Season: Jimmy Greaves, 41, 1960–61.

Most League Goals in Total Aggregate: Bobby Tambling, 164, 1958–70.

Most Capped Player: Ray Wilkins, 24 (84), England.

Most League Appearances: Ron Harris, 655, 1962–80.

Record Transfer Fee Received: £925,000 from Everton for Pat Nevin, July 1988.

Record Transfer Fee Paid: £1,600,000 to Wimbledon for Dennis Wise, July 1990.

Football League Record: 1905 Elected to Division 2; 1907–10 Division 1; 1910–12 Division 2; 1912–24 Division 1; 1924–30 Division 2; 1930–62 Division 1; 1962–63 Division 2; 1963–75 Division 1; 1975–77 Division 2; 1977–79 Division 1; 1979–84 Division 2; 1984–88 Division 1; 1988–89 Division 2; 1989– Division 1.

Honours: Football League: Division 1 – Champions 1954–55; Division 2 – Champions 1983–84, 1988–89; Runners-up 1906–7, 1911–12, 1929–30, 1962–63, 1976–77. *FA Cup:* Winners 1970; Runners-up 1914–15, 1966–67. *Football League Cup:* Winners 1964–65; Runners-up 1971–72. *Full Members' Cup:* Winners 1985–86. *Zenith Data Systems Cup:* Winners 1989-90.

European Competitions: *European Fairs Cup:* 1958–60, 1965–66, 1968–69; *European Cup-Winners' Cup:* 1970–71 (winners), 1971–72.

Colours: Royal blue with red and white trim on collar and right cuff, royal blue with red and white trim on left leg, blue stockings. **Change colours:** Red and white shirts, white shorts, red trim, white stockings.

CHELSEA 1990–91 LEAGUE RECORD

Match No.	Date		Venue	Opponents	Result		H/T Score	Lg. Pos.	Goalscorers	Atten- dance
1	Aug 25		H	Derby Co	W	2-1	1-0	—	Lee, Nicholas	24,652
2		28	A	Crystal Palace	L	1-2	0-1	—	Dorigo	27,101
3	Sept 1		A	QPR	L	0-1	0-1	13		19,813
4		8	H	Sunderland	W	3-2	2-1	9	Dixon, Wilson, Wise (pen)	19,424
5		15	A	Arsenal	L	1-4	0-0	13	Wilson	41,516
6		22	H	Manchester C	D	1-1	0-1	12	Wilson	20,924
7		29	H	Sheffield U	D	2-2	2-1	13	Wilson 2	19,873
8	Oct 6		A	Southampton	D	3-3	2-1	13	Clarke, Wilson, Wise (pen)	16,911
9		20	H	Nottingham F	D	0-0	0-0	14		22,403
10		27	A	Liverpool	L	0-2	0-2	15		38,463
11	Nov 3		H	Aston Villa	W	1-0	1-0	11	Le Saux	23,555
12		10	H	Norwich C	D	1-1	1-1	11	Wise (pen)	16,925
13		17	A	Wimbledon	L	1-2	0-1	14	Durie	10,773
14		25	A	Manchester U	W	3-2	2-1	—	Pallister (og), Townsend, Wise (pen)	37,836
15	Dec 1		H	Tottenham H	W	3-2	2-0	9	Dixon, Bumstead, Durie	33,478
16		8	H	Crystal Palace	W	2-1	1-1	9	Stuart, Durie	21,558
17		15	A	Derby Co	W	6-4	3-1	7	Dixon 2, Durie 2, Wise, Le Saux	15,057
18		22	H	Coventry C	W	2-1	0-0	6	Townsend, Wise	16,317
19		26	A	Leeds U	L	1-4	0-1	7	Dixon	30,893
20		29	A	Luton T	L	0-2	0-0	8		11,050
21	Jan 1		H	Everton	L	1-2	1-1	8	Wilson	18,351
22		12	H	QPR	W	2-0	1-0	7	Durie 2	19,255
23		19	A	Sunderland	L	0-1	0-0	9		20,038
24	Feb 2		H	Arsenal	W	2-1	0-0	9	Stuart, Dixon	29,094
25		9	A	Manchester C	L	1-2	0-2	9	Wise	25,116
26		16	H	Wimbledon	D	0-0	0-0	9		13,378
27	Mar 2		A	Tottenham H	D	1-1	1-1	9	Durie	26,168
28		9	H	Manchester U	W	3-2	1-1	8	Durie, Dorigo, Monkou	22,818
29		16	A	Sheffield U	L	0-1	0-0	8		20,581
30		23	H	Southampton	L	0-2	0-1	9		13,391
31		30	H	Leeds U	L	1-2	0-2	9	Le Saux	17,585
32	Apr 1		A	Coventry C	L	0-1	0-0	10		14,272
33		6	H	Luton T	D	3-3	1-3	10	Le Saux, Stuart, Wise (pen)	12,603
34		13	A	Everton	D	2-2	0-1	11	Dixon 2	19,526
35		17	A	Norwich C	W	3-1	2-0	—	Wise, Durie 2	12,301
36		20	A	Nottingham F	L	0-7	0-3	10		20,305
37	May 4		H	Liverpool	W	4-2	2-0	10	Dixon 2, Wise (pen), Durie	32,266
38		11	A	Aston Villa	D	2-2	2-1	10	Cundy, Stuart	27,866

Final League Position: 11

GOALSCORERS

League (58): Durie 12, Dixon 10, Wise 10 (6 pens), Wilson 7, Le Saux 4, Stuart 4, Dorigo 2, Townsend 2, Bumstead 1, Clarke 1, Cundy 1, Lee 1, Monkou 1, Nicholas 1, own goal 1.
Rumbelows Cup (18): Dixon 4, Durie 3, Townsend 3, Wilson 2, Wise 2 (2 pens), Lee 1, Le Saux 1, McAllister 1, Stuart 1.
FA Cup (1): Dixon 1.

Beasant	Hall	Dorigo	Townsend	Johnsen	Lee	Wise	Nicholas	Dixon	Wilson	Le Saux	McAllister	Cundy	Bumstead	Monkou	Dickens	Clarke	Durie	Hitchcock	Stuart	Matthew	Mitchell	Sinclair	Myers	Burley	Pearce	Match No.
1	2	3	4	5	6	7	8	9	10	11*	12															1
1	2	3	4	5	6	7	8	9	10	11*	12															2
1	2	3	4		6	7	8	9	10	11		5														3
1	2	3	4		6	7	8†	9	10	11*	12	5	14													4
1	2	3	7		6		8*	9	10		12	5	11†	4	14											5
1		3	4	5*	12		8	9	10	11	7			6		2										6
1		3	4	5		7	8	9	10	11				6		2										7
1		3	4	5		7	8	9		11	12			6		2	10*									8
1		3	4	5		7	8†	9*11			12		14	6		2	10									9
1		3	4	5	11		8*	9	14	7	12			6		2†	10									10
	2	3	4	5		7		9	11	12				6*	8		10	1								11
	2	3	4	6		7		9	11	12		5			8*		10	1								12
	2	3	4	6		7	8*	9	11	12		5					10	1								13
1	2		4		11			9	3		12	5		6	8		10*		7							14
1	2	3	4		11	7		9				5		6	8		10									15
1	2		4		11			9	3			5		6	8		10		7							16
1	2	3	4			7	8	9		11*	12	5	14	6†			10									17
1	2	3	4			7	8	9		11	12	5		6*			10									18
1	2	3*	4		6	7		9		11	12	5			8		10									19
1	2		4*		6	7		9	10	11	12	5	14		8†	3										20
1	2		4		6	7*		9	10	11	12	5				3										21
1	2	3	4			7		9		11		5		6	8		10									22
1	2	3	4			7		9		11†	12	5	14	6	8*		10									23
1	2	3	4			7*		9†		11	12	5	14	6	8		10									24
1	2*	3	4			7		9	10†	11	12	5	14	6	8											25
1		3	4*			7		9		11	12	5		6	8	2	10									26
1		3	4		14	7†		9		11*	12	5		6	8	2	10									27
1		3	4			7		9		11		5		6	8	2	10									28
1		3	4			7		9*		11	12	5		6	8	2	10									29
1		3	4			7		9*		11	12	5		6	8	2	10									30
1		3	4			7		9		11		5		6	8	2	10									31
1		3	4			7		9		11		5		6	8	2	10									32
1	2		4		6	7		9	10*	11	12	5			8	3										33
1	2		4	12		7		9	10*	11		5		6	8	3										34
1	2		4			7		9	10	11		5		6	8	3										35
1	2	11	4	5		7		9†	10					6	8	3*				12			14			36
1		3	4			7*		9	10	11	12	5		6	8	2	10									37
1		3	4			7		9	10	11	12	5†	14	6	8*	2	10									38
35	24	31	34	6	17	33	11	33	17	24	5	28	8	27	13	17	24	3	17	6	1	4	—	—	—	
					+4s	+1s				+5s	+4s	+8s	+1s	+5s			+3s	+1s	+2s	+2s			+3s	+1s	+1s	

Rumbelows Cup

	Second Round	Walsall (a)	5-0
		(h)	4-1
	Third Round	Portsmouth (h)	0-0
		(a)	3-2
	Fourth Round	Oxford U (a)	2-1
	Fifth Round	Tottenham H (h)	0-0
		(a)	3-0
	Semi-final	Sheffield W (h)	0-2
		(a)	1-3
FA Cup	Third Round	Oxford U (h)	1-3

CHELSEA

Player and Position	Ht	Wt	Birth Date	Place	Source	Clubs	League App	Gls
Goalkeepers								
Dave Beasant	6 4	13 00	20 3 59	Willesden	Edgware T	Wimbledon	340	—
						Newcastle U	20	—
						Chelsea	95	—
Roger Freestone	6 2	12 03	19 8 68	Newport		Newport Co	13	—
						Chelsea	42	—
						Swansea C (loan)	14	—
						Hereford U (loan)	8	—
Kevin Hitchcock	6 1	12 02	5 10 62	Custom House	Barking	Nottingham F	—	—
						Mansfield T (loan)	14	—
						Mansfield T	168	—
						Chelsea	14	—
						Northampton T (loan)	17	—
Jason Winters	6 0	11 08	15 9 71	Oatham	Trainee	Chelsea	—	—
Defenders								
Darren Barnard	5 9	11 00	30 11 71	Rinteln	Workingham	Chelsea	—	—
Steve Clarke	5 9	11 02	29 8 63	Saltcoats	Beith Jnrs	St Mirren	151	6
						Chelsea	132	5
Jason Cundy	6 1	13 10	12 11 69	Wimbledon	Trainee	Chelsea	29	1
Roy Davies‡	5 6	9 06	19 8 71	Cardiff	Trainee	Chelsea	—	—
Tony Dorigo	5 10	10 00	31 12 65	Melbourne	Apprentice	Aston Villa	111	1
						Chelsea	146	11
Gareth Hall	5 8	10 07	20 3 69	Croydon		Chelsea	73	1
Giles Jacobs*			8 2 72	Hounslow	Trainee	Chelsea	—	—
						Aldershot (loan)	—	—
Erland Johnsen	6 0	12 10	5 4 67	Fredrikstad	Bayern Munich	Chelsea	24	—
David Lee	6 3	14 00	26 11 69	Kingswood	Trainee	Chelsea	71	6
Graeme Le Saux	6 0	12 00	17 10 68	Jersey		Chelsea	36	5
Kenneth Monkou	6 0	12 09	29 11 64	Surinam	Feyenoord	Chelsea	63	2
Ian Pearce§			7 5 74	Bury St Edmunds	School	Chelsea	1	—
Frank Sinclair	5 8	11 02	3 12 71	Lambeth	Trainee	Chelsea	4	—
Midfield								
John Bumstead‡	5 7	10 05	27 11 58	Rotherhithe	Apprentice	Chelsea	339	38
Craig Burley	6 1	11 07	24 9 71	Ayr	Trainee	Chelsea	1	—
Alan Dickens	5 11	12 01	3 9 64	Plaistow	Apprentice	West Ham U	192	23
						Chelsea	38	1
Damien Matthew	5 11	10 10	23 9 70	Islington	Trainee	Chelsea	10	—
Andy Myers§			3 11 73	Hounslow	Trainee	Chelsea	3	—
Andy Townsend	5 11	12 07	23 7 63	Maidstone	Weymouth	Southampton	83	5
						Norwich C	71	8
						Chelsea	34	2
Dennis Wise	5 6	9 05	15 12 66	Kensington		Wimbledon	135	27
						Chelsea	33	10
Forwards								
Kerry Dixon	6 0	13 00	24 7 61	Luton	Apprentice Dunstable	Tottenham H	—	—
						Reading	116	51
						Chelsea	300	142
Gordon Durie	6 0	12 00	6 12 65	Paisley	Hill O'Beath	East Fife	81	26
						Hibernian	47	14
						Chelsea	123	51
Kevin McAllister	5 5	11 00	8 11 62	Falkirk		Falkirk	64	18
						Chelsea	106	7
						Falkirk (loan)	6	3

CHELSEA

Foundation: Chelsea may never have existed but for the fact that Fulham rejected an offer to rent the Stamford Bridge ground from Mr. H. A. Mears who had owned it since 1904. Fortunately he was determined to develop it as a football stadium rather than sell it to the Great Western Railway and got together with Frederick Parker, who persuaded Mears of the financial advantages of developing a major sporting venue. Chelsea FC was formed in 1905, and when admission to the Southern League was denied, they immediately gained admission to the Second Division of the Football League.

First Football League game: 2 September, 1905, Division 2, v Stockport C (a) L 0-1 – Foulke; Mackie, McEwan; Key, Harris, Miller; Moran, J.T. Robertson, Copeland, Windridge, Kirwan.

Did you know: The only season in which the aggregate of attendances at Stamford Bridge for Football League matches exceeded 1m was when they won the Championship in 1954–55. The biggest gate that season was 75,043 v Wolves, 9 April.

Managers (and Secretary-managers)
John Tait Robertson 1905–07, David Calderhead 1907–33, A. Leslie Knighton 1933–39, Billy Birrell 1939–52, Ted Drake 1952–61, Tommy Docherty 1962–67, Dave Sexton 1967–74, Ron Suart 1974–75, Eddie McCreadie 1975–77, Ken Shellito 1977–78, Danny Blanchflower 1978–79, Geoff Hurst 1979–81, John Neal 1981–85 (Director to 1986), John Hollins 1985–88, Bobby Campbell 1988–91, Ian Porterfield June 1991–

Player and Position	Ht	Wt	Birth Date	Birth Place	Source	Clubs	League App	Gls
David Mitchell	6 1	11 08	13 6 62	Scotland		Rangers	26	6
					Feyenoord	Chelsea	7	—
						Newcastle (loan)	2	1
Eddie Newton	5 11	11 02	13 12 71	Hammersmith	Trainee	Chelsea	—	—
Graham Stuart	5 8	11 06	24 10 70	Tooting	Trainee	Chelsea	21	5
Colin West (To Dundee Aug 1990)	5 7	11 00	19 9 67	Middlesbrough	Apprentice	Chelsea	16	4
						Partick T (loan)	24	10
						Swansea C (loan)	14	3
Kevin Wilson	5 7	10 10	18 4 61	Banbury	Banbury U	Derby Co	122	30
						Ipswich T	98	34
						Chelsea	130	39

Trainees
Bradley, James J; Chatfield, Ian R; Colgan, Nicholas V; Davies, Jeremy; Faulkner, Lee; Forrester, Romon C; James, Andrew; Myers, Andrew; Rowe, Ezekiel B.

Associated Schoolboys
Barnes, Steven L; Bowder, Stanley R; Carbon, Vincent; Christie, Terry W; Collins, Kevin J; Duberry, Michael W; Godfrey, Christopher P; Ho, Wai K; Hughes, John P; Luckett, Colin A; Marskell, Ben; Mendes, Hillyard A; Parfitt, Mike; Parsons, John; Pearce, Ian A; Roukin, Jason, D; Sakala, Landilani; Sloan, Craig S; Sullivan, Mark J; Yates, Paul S.

Associated Schoolboys who have accepted the club's offer of a Traineeship/Contract
Goddard, Ryan N.J; Izzet, Mustafa; McLennan, Jason D; Martin, Steven M; Metcalfe, Christian W; Norman, Craig T; Shipperley, Neil J; Skiverton, Terence J.

CHESTER CITY 1990-91 *Back row (left to right):* Gary Bennett, Spencer Whelan, Chris Lightfoot, Barry Butler, Billy Stewart, Graham Abel, Alan Reeves, David Pugh, Neil Ellis, Joe Hinnigan (Physiotherapist), Tony Allan (Secretary).

Front row: Martin Lane, Brian Croft, Carl Dale, Graham Barrow (Assistant Manager), Harry McNally (Manager), Mr RH Crofts (Chairman), Sean Lundon, Robert Painter, Roger Preece.

Division 3   **CHESTER CITY**

The Stadium, Sealand Rd, Chester CH1 4LW. Telephone Chester (0244) 371376, 371809. Cityline (Ticket and Travel Information) (0244) 373829.

Ground: Moss Rose Ground, London Road, Macclesfield.

Ground capacity: 10,000.

Record attendance: 20,500 v Chelsea, FA Cup 3rd rd (replay), 16 January, 1952.

Record receipts: £30,609 v Sheffield W, FA Cup 4th rd, 31 January 1987.

Pitch measurements: 110yd × 80yd.

Club Patron: Duke of Westminster.

President: Reg Rowlands.

Chairman: R. H. Crofts.

Directors: P. Russell, W. D. MacDonald, N. A. MacLennon, H. McNally.

Team Manager: Harry McNally. *Assistant Manager:* Graham Barrow.

Secretary: R. A. Allan. *Physio:* Joe Hinnigan. *Commercial Manager:* Miss A. Walker

Year Formed: 1884. *Turned Professional:* 1902. *Ltd Co.:* 1909.

Previous Name: Chester until 1983.

Club Nickname: 'Blues'.

Previous Grounds: Faulkner Street; Old Showground; 1904, Whipcord Lane; 1906, Sealand Road.

Record League Victory: 12-0 v York C, Division 3 (N), 1 February 1936 – Middleton; Common, Hall; Wharton, Wilson, Howarth; Horsman (2), Hughes, Wrightson (4), Cresswell (2), Sargeant (4).

Record Cup Victory: 6-1 v Darlington, FA Cup, 1st rd, 25 November 1933 – Burke; Bennett, Little; Pitcairn, Skitt, Duckworth; Armes (3), Whittam, Mantle (2), Cresswell (1), McLachlan.

Record Defeat: 2-11 v Oldham Ath, Division 3 (N), 19 January 1952.

Most League Points (2 for a win): 56, Division 3 (N), 1946–47 and Division 4, 1964–65.

Most League Points (3 for a win): 84, Division 4, 1985–86.

Most League Goals: 119, Division 4, 1964–65.

Highest League Scorer in Season: Dick Yates, 36, Division 3 (N), 1946–47.

Most League Goals in Total Aggregate: Gary Talbot, 83, 1963–67 and 1968–70.

Most Capped Player: Bill Lewis, 7 (30), Wales.

Most League Appearances: Ray Gill, 408, 1951–62.

Record Transfer Fee Received: £300,000 from Liverpool for Ian Rush, May 1980.

Record Transfer Fee Paid: £84,000 to Tranmere R for Eddie Bishop, December 1990.

Football League Record: 1931 Elected Division 3 (N); 1958–75 Division 4; 1975–82 Division 3; 1982–86 Division 4; 1986– Division 3.

Honours: Football League: Division 3 best season: 5th, 1977–78; Division 3 (N) – Runners-up 1935–36; Division 4 – Runners-up 1985–86. *FA Cup:* best season: 5th rd, 1976–77, 1979–80. *Football League Cup:* Semi-final 1974–75. *Welsh Cup:* Winners 1908, 1933, 1947. *Debenhams Cup:* Winners 1977.

Colours: Royal blue shirts, white shorts, blue stockings, white trim. **Change colours:** Gold black shorts, black stockings.

CHESTER CITY 1990–91 LEAGUE RECORD

Match No.	Date	Venue	Opponents	Result	H/T Score	Lg. Pos.	Goalscorers	Attendance
1	Aug 25	A	Bury	L	1-2	1-2	—	Pugh	2628
2	Sept 1	H	Exeter C	L	1-2	0-1	22	Abel (pen)	1377
3	18	A	Brentford	W	1-0	0-0	15	Painter	4812
4	15	H	Leyton Orient	W	2-0	0-0	9	Bennett, Painter	1716
5	18	H	Stoke C	D	1-1	0-1	—	Ellis	3579
6	21	A	Cambridge U	D	1-1	0-1	—	Butler	3687
7	29	H	Huddersfield T	L	1-2	1-1	14	Charlton (og)	1540
8	Oct 3	A	Bradford C	L	1-2	0-0	—	Abel (pen)	5519
9	6	A	Tranmere R	W	2-1	1-0	14	Pugh, Abel (pen)	6642
10	13	H	Grimsby T	L	1-2	0-2	15	Dale	1875
11	20	H	Shrewsbury T	W	3-2	1-0	15	Bennett, Morton, Dale	1431
12	23	A	Preston NE	D	0-0	0-0	—		5465
13	27	A	Crewe Alex	W	3-1	2-1	12	Morton 2, Pugh (pen)	4262
14	Nov 3	H	Bolton W	L	0-2	0-0	15		2553
15	10	H	Birmingham C	L	0-1	0-0	16		2273
16	24	A	Swansea C	L	0-1	0-0	17		3361
17	Dec 1	A	Bournemouth	D	0-0	0-0	19		1103
18	15	A	Mansfield T	L	0-1	0-1	19		1919
19	22	H	Southend U	W	1-0	0-0	19	Dale	1523
20	26	A	Rotherham U	L	1-2	0-0	19	Butler	3547
21	29	A	Fulham	L	1-4	0-1	19	Dale	3084
22	Jan 12	A	Exeter C	D	1-1	1-1	19	Bishop	4008
23	19	H	Bury	W	1-0	0-0	18	Bishop	1421
24	26	A	Leyton Orient	L	0-1	0-1	19		3437
25	Feb 2	A	Stoke C	W	3-2	1-0	18	Dale, Bishop 2	11,037
26	23	A	Birmingham C	L	0-1	0-0	18		6702
27	26	H	Wigan Ath	L	1-2	0-1	—	Bishop	914
28	Mar 2	A	Bournemouth	L	0-1	0-0	19		4669
29	5	H	Reading	W	1-0	0-0	—	Butler	631
30	9	H	Mansfield T	W	1-0	1-0	18	Morton	1157
31	12	H	Bradford C	W	4-2	1-0	—	Morton, Dale 2, Lightfoot	1303
32	16	A	Huddersfield T	D	1-1	0-1	17	Lightfoot	5337
33	20	A	Grimsby T	L	0-2	0-1	—		6012
34	23	H	Tranmere R	L	0-2	0-1	18		2705
35	25	H	Cambridge U	L	0-2	0-1	—		1015
36	30	H	Rotherham U	L	1-2	0-1	18	Butler	1079
37	Apr 2	A	Southend U	D	1-1	1-0	—	Bishop	6190
38	6	H	Fulham	W	1-0	1-0	18	Morton	1047
39	13	A	Reading	D	2-2	1-1	18	Painter, Bishop	2707
40	16	A	Wigan Ath	L	0-2	0-2	—		2131
41	20	A	Shrewsbury T	L	0-1	0-1	19		2952
42	23	H	Swansea C	W	2-1	1-1	—	Bennett, Butler	852
43	27	H	Preston NE	D	1-1	1-0	18	Abel (pen)	1351
44	30	H	Brentford	L	1-2	0-2	—	Dale	1275
45	May 4	H	Crewe Alex	W	3-1	3-0	18	Morton, Dale 2	3126
46	11	A	Bolton W	L	0-1	0-1	19		12,826

Final League Position: 19

GOALSCORERS

League (46): Dale 10, Bishop 7, Morton 7, Butler 5, Abel 4 (4 pens), Bennett 3, Painter 3, Pugh 3 (1 pen), Lightfoot 2, Ellis 1, own goal 1.
Rumbelows Cup (5): Croft 2, Abel 1 (pen), Ellis 1, own goal 1.
FA Cup (11): Dale 4, Croft 2, Painter 2, Abel 1 (1 pen), Bennett 1, Bertschin 1.

Stewart	Preece	Lundon	Butler	Abel	Lane	Pugh	Barrow	Bennett	Dale	Croft	Ellis	Lightfoot	Painter	Reeves	Morton	Barber	Withe	Whelan	Bertschin	Bishop	Brightwell	Match No.
1	2	3	4	5	6	7*	8	9	10	11	12											1
1	2	3*		5	6	7	8	12	10	11	9	4										2
1	2		4	5	6	3	8	7	10	11†		9*	12	14								3
1	2		4	5	6	3	8	7	10	11		9										4
1	2		4	5	6	3	8	7	10	11	12	9*										5
1	2	12	4		6	3	8	7	10*	11	5	9										6
1	2		4	5	6	3	8†	7	10	11		9*	12	14								7
1	2		4	5	6	3		7	10	11		9	12	8*								8
1	2	8*	4	5	6	3		7	10	11		9†	12	14								9
1	2	8*	4		6	3		7	10	11		5†	12	14	9							10
	2		4	5	6			7	10	11		8*	12		9	1	3					11
	2		4	5	6			7	10	11		8*	12	14	9	1	3†					12
	2*		4	5	6	3		7	10	11		8	12		9	1						13
1			4	5	6	3		7	10	11	12	8*	2†	9				14				14
1	2*		4	5	6	3		7	10	11	12	8		9								15
1			4	5	6	3		7	10*	11	12	8	2					9				16
1			4	5	6	3		7	10*	12		8	2	11				9				17
1	2	5	3				8	12	7	11		4	6		10*			9				18
1	2	5	3	12			8*		7	11		4	6	14	10†			9				19
1	2	5	3	8†					7	11	12	4	6		10*			9				20
1	2	5	3				8	7	10	11		4	12					9*	6			21
1	7	5	3					12	10	11*		4	8		9			2	6			22
1	2	5	3	12			8		10	11		4	6		9*			7				23
1	2	5	3	12			8		10	11		4	6		9*			7				24
1	2	5			6		8	12	10	11		4	3		9*			7				25
1	2	5†	14		6		8		10	11*		4	3	12				9	7			26
1	2	5			6		8		10	11		4	3	12				9*	7			27
1	2				6		8		10*	11		4	3	12			5	9	7			28
1	2	14			6		8	12		11†		4	3		10		5	9*	7			29
1	2	11			6	12	8		10			4	3		9		5*		7			30
1	2	11		5	6		8		10			4	3		9				7			31
1	2	11		5	6†	14		10	12			4	8*		9		3		7			32
1	2	11		5				7	10	8		4	6		9		3					33
1	2	11		5		14		10	8*			4	6†		9		3		12	7		34
1	2	11		5		3		10	12			4	6*		9				7	8		35
1	2	8		3				11	10	12		4	6*		9				7	5		36
	2	8		3	6			12		11*		4	14		9	1	10			7	5†	37
	2	8		3	6†	12			11			4	14		9	1	10*			7	5	38
	2	8	6*	3					10	12		4	11		9	1				7	5	39
	2	8	6*14	3					10	12		4	11		9	1				7	5†	40
	2	8	6	5	3	14			10*	12		4	11		9	1	7†					41
1	2	7	5	6	3				10*	11		4	8		9		12					42
1	2	7	5	6	3				10	11†	14	4	8		9*		12					43
1	2	7	5	6	3				10	11*	12	4	8		9							44
1	2	7	6	3					10	14	11†	4	8		9*		5			12		45
1	2*	7	6	3					10	11		4	8†	14	9		5			12		46
38	**35**	**4**	**42**	**29**	**38**	**33**	**20**	**23**	**41**	**31**	**13**	**33**	**34**	**3**	**31**	**8**	**2**	**9**	**14**	**19**	**6**	
		+1s	+1s		+2s	+4s			+7s	+3s	+7s	+8s	+4s	+8s	+7s	+3s			+2s	+5s		

Rumbelows Cup	First Round	Preston NE (a)	0-2
		(h)	5-1
	Second Round	Arsenal (h)	0-1
		(a)	0-5
FA Cup	First Round	Doncaster R (h)	2-2
		(a)	2-1
	Second Round	Leek T (a)	1-1
		(h)	4-0
	Third Round	Bournemouth (h)	2-3

CHESTER CITY

Player and Position	Ht	Wt	Birth Date	Place	Source	Clubs	League App	Gls
Goalkeepers								
Andy Gill‡	6 0	13 00	28 9 70	Manchester	Trainee	Preston NE	—	—
						Chester C	—	—
Billy Stewart	5 11	11 07	1 1 65	Liverpool	Apprentice	Liverpool	—	—
						Wigan Ath	14	—
						Chester C	186	—
Defenders								
Graham Abel	6 2	13 00	17 9 60	Runcorn	Runcorn	Chester C	219	19
Barry Butler	6 2	13 00	4 6 62	Farnworth	Atherton T	Chester C	196	9
Joe Hinnigan	6 0	12 00	3 12 55	Liverpool	S Liverpool	Wigan Ath	66	10
						Sunderland	63	4
						Preston NE	52	8
						Gillingham	103	7
						Wrexham	29	1
						Chester C	54	2
Martin Lane*	5 9	11 04	12 4 61	Altrincham	Amateur	Manchester U	—	—
						Chester C	175	3
						Coventry C	3	—
						Wrexham (loan)	6	—
						Chester C	99	—
Alan Reeves*	6 0	12 00	19 11 67	Birkenhead		Norwich C	—	—
						Gillingham (loan)	18	—
						Chester C	40	2
Spencer Whelan	6 1	11 13	17 9 71	Liverpool	Liverpool	Chester C	11	—
Midfield								
Graham Barrow	6 2	13 07	13 6 54	Chorley	Altrincham	Wigan Ath	179	36
						Chester C	162	13
Eddie Bishop	5 8	11 07	28 11 62	Liverpool	Runcorn	Tranmere R	76	19
						Chester C	19	7
Chris Lightfoot	5 11	11 00	1 4 70	Wimwick	Trainee	Chester C	129	11
Sean Lundon‡	5 10	10 10	7 3 69	Liverpool	Apprentice	Chester C	56	4
Robert Painter	5 11	11 00	26 1 71	Ince	Trainee	Chester C	84	8
Roger Preece	5 9	10 12	9 6 69	Much Wenlock	Apprentice	Coventry C	—	—
						Wrexham	110	12
						Chester C	35	—
David Pugh	5 10	11 02	19 9 64	Liverpool	Runcorn	Chester C	72	6
Karl Senior§			3 9 72	Northwich	School	Chester C	1	—

CHESTER CITY

Foundation: All students of soccer history have read about the medieval games of football in Chester, but the present club was not formed until 1884 through the amalgamation of King's School Old Boys with Chester Rovers. For many years Chester were overshadowed in Cheshire by Northwich Victoria and Crewe Alexandra who had both won the Senior Cup several times before Chester's first success in 1894–95.

First Football League game: 2 September, 1931, Division 3(N), v Wrexham (a) D 1-1 – Johnson; Herod, Jones; Keeley, Skitt, Reilly; Thompson, Ranson, Jennings (1), Cresswell, Hedley.

Did you know: In season 1976–77 Chester went through four rounds of the FA Cup without conceding a goal before Kenny Hibbitt scored when Chester were beaten 1-0 at Wolverhampton.

Managers (and Secretary-managers)
Charlie Hewitt 1930–36, Alex Raisbeck 1936–38, Frank Brown 1938–53, Louis Page 1953–56, John Harris 1956–59, Stan Pearson 1959–61, Bill Lambton 1962–63, Peter Hauser 1963–68, Ken Roberts 1968–76, Alan Oakes 1976–82, Cliff Sear 1982, John Sainty 1982–83, John McGrath 1984, Harry McNally June 1985–   .

Player and Position	Ht	Wt	Birth Date	Birth Place	Source	Clubs	League App	Gls
Forwards								
Gary Bennett	6 1	12 06	20 9 63	Liverpool		Wigan Ath	20	3
						Chester C	126	36
						Southend U	42	6
						Chester C	38	4
Keith Bertschin*	6 1	11 08	25 8 56	Enfield	Barnet	Ipswich T	32	8
						Birmingham C	118	29
						Norwich C	114	29
						Stoke City	88	29
						Sunderland	36	7
						Walsall	55	9
						Chester C	19	—
Brian Croft	5 9	10 10	27 9 67	Chester		Chester C	59	3
						Cambridge U	17	2
						Chester C	82	3
Carl Dale	6 0	12 00	29 4 66	Colwyn Bay	Bangor C	Chester C	116	41
Neil Ellis	6 0	12 00	30 4 69	Bebington	Bangor C	Chester C	21	1
Neil Morton	5 10	11 00	21 12 68	Congleton	Trainee	Crewe Alex	31	1
					Northwich Vic	Chester C	34	7

Trainees
Brooks, Philip; Carroll, Lee J; Cranmer, Martin L.A; Cunniffe, Matthew P; Edwards, David A; Evans, Gary N; Fletcher, Gary C; Limbert, Mark; Lord, Jeremy J; McQuillan, Mathew M; Senior, Karl R.

Associated Schoolboys
Atkinson, Eric J; Barthorpe, Darren J; Dixon, Neil; Evans, Thomas P; Hillman, Mark; Ingman, David J; Jeanrenaud, Paul; Roberts, Daniel L; Roberts Joel H; Stevenson, Keith D; White, David J; Wilson, Nicholas K.

Associated Schoolboys who have accepted the club's offer of a Traineeship/Contract
O'Hara, Paul J.

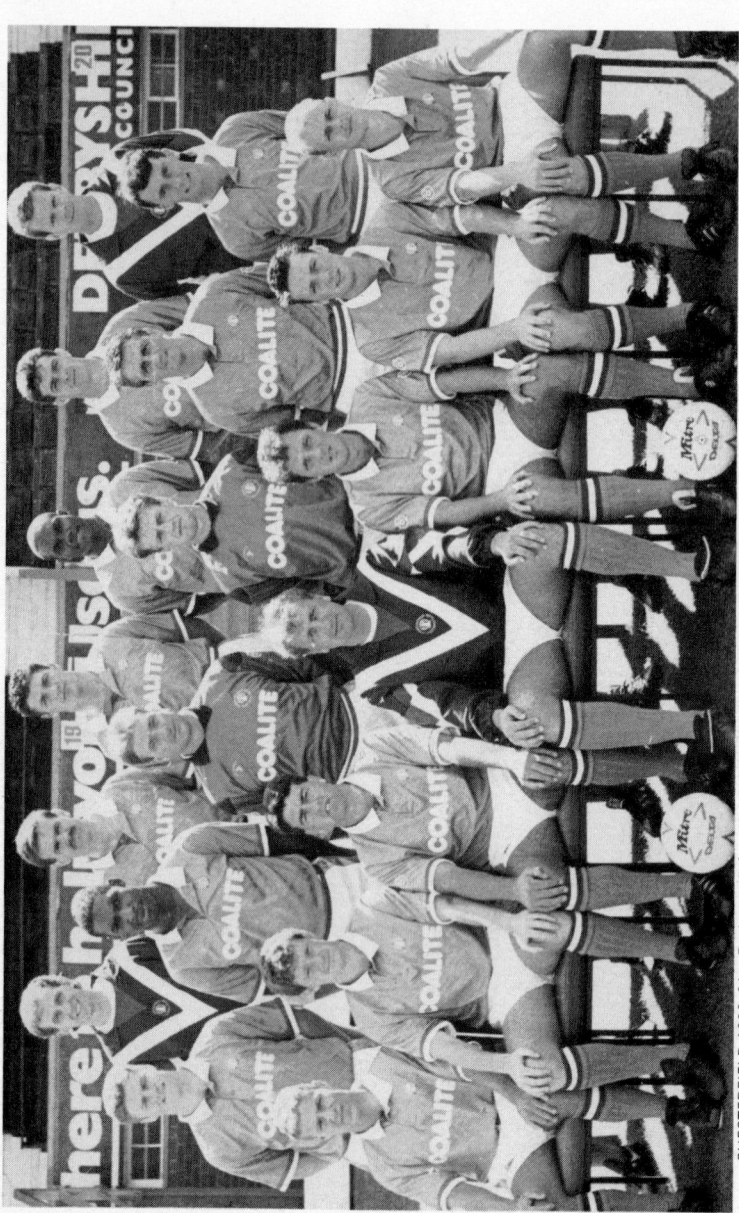

CHESTERFIELD 1990–91 *Back row (left to right)*: Dave Rushbury (Physiotherapist), Dave Waller, Tony Brien, Calvin Plummer, Lee Rogers, Chris McMenemy (Assistant Manager).
Centre row: Sean Dyche, Andy Morris, Mick Leonard, Mike Allison, Nigel Hart, Jamie Hewitt.
Front row: Andy Rolph, Adrian Shaw, Bryn Gunn, Paul Hart (Manager), John Ryan, Lee Francis, Steven Williams.

Division 4   **CHESTERFIELD**

Recreation Ground, Chesterfield S40 4SX. Telephone Chesterfield (0246) 209765. Commercial Dept: (0246) 231535.

Ground capacity: 11,638.

Record attendance: 30,968 v Newcastle U, Division 2, 7 April 1939.

Record receipts: £32,410 v Sheffield U, Division 3, 25 March 1989.

Pitch measurements: 112yd × 72yd.

President: His Grace the Duke of Devonshire MC, DL, JP.

Vice-president: P. C. J. T. Kirkman.

Chairman: J. N. Lea. *Vice-chairman:* B. W. Hubbard.

Associate Directors: J. A. Plant, R. F. Pepper.

Team Manager: Chris McMenemy.

Physio: Dave Rushbury. *Assistant Manager:* Chris McMenemy.

Secretary: Bob Pepper. *Commercial Manager:* Jim Brown.

Year Formed: 1866. *Turned Professional:* 1891. *Ltd Co:* 1871.

Club Nickname: 'Blues' or 'Spireites'.

Record League Victory: 10-0 v Glossop, Division 2, 17 January 1903 – Clutterbuck; Thorpe, Lerper; Haig, Banner, Thacker; Tomlinson (2), Newton (1), Milward (3), Munday (2), Steel (2).

Record Cup Victory: 5-0 v Wath Ath (away), FA Cup, 1st rd, 28 November 1925 – Birch; Saxby, Dennis; Wass, Abbott, Thompson; Fisher (1), Roseboom (1), Cookson (2), Whitfield (1), Hopkinson.

Record Defeat: 0-10 v Gillingham, Division 3, 5 September 1987.

Most League Points (2 for a win): 64, Division 4, 1969–70.

Most League Points (3 for a win): 91, Division 4, 1984–85.

Most League Goals: 102, Division 3 (N), 1930–31.

Highest League Scorer in Season: Jimmy Cookson, 44, Division 3 (N), 1925–26.

Most League Goals in Total Aggregate: Ernie Moss, 161, 1969–76, 1979–81 and 1984–86.

Most Capped Player: Walter McMillen, 4 (7), Northern Ireland.

Most League Appearances: Dave Blakey, 613, 1948–67.

Record Transfer Fee Received: £200,000 from Wolverhampton W for Alan Birch, August 1981.

Record Transfer Fee Paid: £150,000 to Carlisle U for Phil Bonnyman, March 1980.

Football League Record: 1899 Elected to Division 2; 1909 failed re-election; 1921–31 Division 3 (N); 1931–33 Division 2; 1933–36 Division 3 (N); 1936–51 Division 2; 1951–58 Division 3 (N); 1958–61 Division 3; 1961–70 Division 4; 1970–83 Division 3; 1983–85 Division 4; 1985–89 Division 3; 1989– Division 4.

Honours: Football League: Division 2 best season: 4th, 1946–47; Division 3 (N) – Champions 1930–31, 1935–36; Runners-up 1933–34; Division 4 – Champions 1969–70, 1984–85. *FA Cup:* best season: 5th rd, 1932–33, 1937–38, 1949–50. *Football League Cup:* best season: 4th rd, 1964–65. *Anglo-Scottish Cup:* Winners 1980–81.

Colours: Blue shirts, white shorts, white stockings. **Change colours:** Yellow shirts, green shorts, yellow stockings.

CHESTERFIELD 1990–91 LEAGUE RECORD

Match No.	Date	Venue	Opponents	Result		H/T Score	Lg. Pos.	Goalscorers	Attendance
1	Aug 25	H	Hartlepool U	L	2-3	0-2	—	Gunn (pen), Morris	3821
2	Sept 1	A	Scarborough	L	0-1	0-0	23		1990
3	3	H	Hereford U	W	1-0	1-0	17	Brien	3183
4	15	A	Torquay U	L	0-2	0-0	21		2468
5	19	A	Lincoln C	D	1-1	0-0	—	Plummer	2855
6	22	H	Blackpool	D	2-2	1-1	19	Brien, Morris	3549
7	29	A	Wrexham	D	1-1	1-0	18	Morris	2147
8	Oct 2	H	York C	D	2-2	0-2	—	Williams D, Morris	3572
9	6	H	Northampton T	D	0-0	0-0	19		3826
10	13	A	Rochdale	L	0-3	0-1	20		2492
11	20	A	Carlisle U	L	0-1	0-1	21		3029
12	23	H	Scunthorpe U	W	1-0	1-0	—	Caldwell	3371
13	27	H	Doncaster R	W	2-1	2-1	16	Francis, Caldwell	4389
14	Nov 3	A	Peterborough U	L	1-2	0-1	18	Cordner	4225
15	10	A	Cardiff C	L	1-2	1-1	19	Cooke	2019
16	25	H	Walsall	D	2-2	1-1	—	Caldwell, Lemon	3687
17	Dec 1	H	Gillingham	D	1-1	0-0	20	Albiston	3468
18	15	A	Halifax T	L	1-2	0-2	21	Plummer	1415
19	22	A	Darlington	L	0-1	0-0	23		2925
20	29	H	Stockport Co	D	1-1	0-1	22	Brien	4307
21	Jan 1	A	Maidstone U	L	0-1	0-1	22		1793
22	12	A	Scarborough	L	0-1	0-1	23		3217
23	19	A	Hartlepool U	L	0-2	0-1	23		2134
24	26	H	Torquay U	D	1-1	1-0	23	Benjamin	2921
25	Feb 2	H	Lincoln C	D	1-1	0-1	23	McGugan	3588
26	5	A	Blackpool	L	0-3	0-2	—		2357
27	16	A	Walsall	L	0-3	0-1	23		3995
28	23	H	Cardiff C	D	0-0	0-0	23		3065
29	Mar 2	A	Gillingham	W	1-0	1-0	23	Ryan	3095
30	5	H	Burnley	W	2-1	1-0	—	Turnbull 2	4022
31	9	H	Halifax T	W	2-1	0-1	22	Williams, S, Turnbull	3565
32	12	A	York C	W	2-0	1-0	—	Lancaster, Williams S	1751
33	16	H	Wrexham	W	2-1	0-0	20	Gunn, Williams S	3368
34	19	H	Rochdale	D	1-1	0-0	—	Williams S	3048
35	23	A	Northampton T	L	0-2	0-1	21		3379
36	30	A	Burnley	W	1-0	0-0	19	Lancaster	8373
37	Apr 1	H	Darlington	D	2-2	1-2	19	Turnbull 2 (1 pen)	4602
38	6	A	Stockport Co	L	1-3	1-3	20	Turnbull	3044
39	13	H	Maidstone U	L	1-2	0-0	21	Lancaster	3040
40	17	A	Hereford U	W	3-2	1-1	—	Lemon, Turnbull, Caldwell	1750
41	20	H	Carlisle U	W	4-1	2-1	18	Ryan, Lancaster, Turnbull 2 (2 pens)	2708
42	23	A	Aldershot	L	0-1	0-1	—		1500
43	27	A	Scunthorpe U	L	0-3	0-0	20		3046
44	30	H	Aldershot	W	1-0	1-0	—	Dyche	2222
45	May 4	A	Doncaster R	W	1-0	1-0	16	Plummer	2649
46	11	H	Peterborough U	D	2-2	2-0	18	Plummer, Dyche	8837

Final League Position: 18

GOALSCORERS

League (47): Turnbull 9 (3 pens), Caldwell 4, Lancaster 4, Morris 4, Plummer 4, Williams S 4, Brien 3, Dyche 2, Gunn 2 (1 pen), Lemon 2, Ryan 2, Albiston 1, Benjamin 1, Cooke 1, Cordner 1, Francis 1, McGugan 1, Williams D 1.
Rumbelows Cup (3): Morris 3.
FA Cup (6): Caldwell 2, Barnes 1, Cooke 1, Morris 1, own goal 1.

Leonard	Francis	Rogers	Dyche	Brien	Gunn	Plummer	Hewitt	Rolph	Cooke	Morris	Shaw	Ryan	Williams D	Allison	Hart	Lemon	Caldwell	Boyd	Cordner	Barnes	Albiston	Godfrey	Benjamin	McGugan	Turnbull	Lancaster	Williams S	Match No.
1	2*	3	4	5	6	7	8	9	10	11	12																	1
1	2	3	4	5	6	7*	8	9		11			10														12	2
	2*	3		5	6	7	8	9	10				11	1	12	4												3
	2			5	6	7	8	9	10*		12		11	1	3	4												4
	2	12		5	6	7	8	9	10*				11	1	3	4												5
	2*	12		5	6	7	8	9	10				11	1	3	4												6
	2	12		5	6	7	8	9	10*	11				1	3	4												7
	2	14		5	6	7	8*	9	10†		12		11	1	3	4												8
	2			5	6	7		9	10				11	1	3	4	8											9
	2	9†		5	6	7			12				11	1	3	4	8		14	10*								10
	2	12		5	6	7			10				9	1	3	4	8										11*	11
	2	11		5	6	7			10				9	1	3	4	8											12
	2	14	11	5	6	7			10				9†	1	3	4	8*										12	13
	2	9	11*	5	6	7			10					1	3	4		12	14								8†	14
	2*	11	12	5	6	7			10					1	3	4	8				9							15
	11	2		5	6	7			10					1	3	4	8										9	16
	11		5	2	12	7			10*	14				1	6	4	8		3								9†	17
	2		7	5	6	9	12		10	11*			8	1		4			3									18
1	2		7	5		9	11					8			6	4	10*	12	3									19
1	2		7	5		9	11	10				3			6	4	8*	12										20
1	2		7	5		9	11	12				3			6	4		8*			10†	14						21
1	2		7	5		9	11	12				3			6	4					10*					8		22
1	2†12		7*	5		9	11		6	10		3				4					14					8		23
1			7	5	2	9	11		10			3				4						8	6					24
1			7	5	2	9	11		10*			3				4	12					8	6					25
1			7	5	2	9	11		14			3				4*10†					8	6				12		26
1			7	5	2	9	11†12					3				4	10*				14	6	8					27
1			7	5	2	8	11	12								4					9	6	10				3*	28
1			7	5	2	8†11						3*				4					14	6	10	9	12			29
1			7	5	2	8*11						3				4						6	10	9	12			30
1			7	5	2		11		12			3				4						6	10	9			8*	31
1			7	5	2		11		12			3				4						6	10	9			8*	32
1			7	5	2		11					3				4						6	10	9			8	33
1			7	5	2		11					3				4						6	10	9			8	34
1	14		7	5	2		11		12			3†				4						6	10	9			8*	35
1	2	5				11	6					3				4	7						10	9			8	36
1	2	5	12			11*						3				4	7					6	10	9			8	37
1		5		2	12	11		9†				3				4	7					14	6	10			8*	38
1		3	14	5	2	12	11									4	8*					6	10	9			7†	39
1	14	5	7	2†		11	12					3				4	8*					6	10	9				40
1	14	5	7*	2		11	12					3				4†	8					6	10	9				41
1	4	5	7	14	2	11	12					3										9	6†10*				8	42
1	4	5	7	2		9	11	12				3*					8†						6	10		14		43
1	4	5	7	2		9	11					3					8						6	10				44
1	4	5	7	2		9	11					3					8*						6	10		12		45
1		5	7	2	12	9	11	4				3					8†					14	6	10*				46
30	26	31	22	41	34	23	42	7	19	11	—	38	4	16	18	39	22	—	1	1	3	2	5	22	19	12	18	
	+	+	+	+	+	+	+	+	+	+	+	+	+		+		+	+	+				+			+		
	3s	3s	6s	2s	2s	4s	1s	8s	1s	4s	1s	1s	1s		1s		1s	1s	3s				6s			7s		

Rumbelows Cup	First Round	Hartlepool U (h)	1-2
		(a)	2-2
FA Cup	First Round	Spennymoor U (h)	3-2
	Second Round	Bolton W (h)	3-4

CHESTERFIELD

Player and Position	Ht	Wt	Birth Date	Place	Source	Clubs	League App	Gls
Goalkeepers								
Mike Allison‡	5 11	11 08	17 3 66	Elderslie	Horwich RMI	Chesterfield	16	—
Mike Astbury‡	5 10	13 08	22 1 64	Leeds	Apprentice	York C	48	—
						Peterborough U (loan)	4	—
						Darlington	38	—
						Chester C	5	—
						Chesterfield	8	—
Mick Leonard	6 1	12 04	9 5 59	Carshalton	Epsom & Ewell	Halifax T	69	—
						Notts Co	204	—
						Chesterfield	92	—
						Halifax T (loan)	3	—
Defenders								
Arthur Albiston‡	5 7	11 05	14 7 57	Edinburgh	Apprentice	Manchester U	379	6
						WBA	43	2
						Dundee	10	—
						Chesterfield	3	1
Tony Brien	6 0	12 00	10 2 69	Dublin	Apprentice	Leicester C	16	1
						Chesterfield	115	7
Lee Francis	5 10	10 11	24 10 69	Walthamstow	Trainee	Arsenal	—	—
						Chesterfield (loan)	2	—
						Chesterfield	29	1
Bryn Gunn	6 2	13 07	21 8 58	Kettering	Apprentice	Nottingham F	131	1
						Shrewsbury T (loan)	9	—
						Walsall (loan)	6	—
						Mansfield T (loan)	5	—
						Peterborough U	131	14
						Chesterfield	82	10
Jamie Hewitt	5 10	10 08	17 5 68	Chesterfield	School	Chesterfield	212	11
Paul McGugan	6 3	13 07	17 7 64	Glasgow	Eastercraigs	Celtic	47	2
						Barnsley	49	2
						Chesterfield	22	1
Lee Rogers	5 10	12 00	21 10 66	Doncaster	Doncaster R	Chesterfield	169	—
John Ryan	5 10	11 07	18 2 62	Oldham	Apprentice	Oldham Ath	77	8
						Newcastle U	28	1
						Sheffield W	8	1
						Oldham Ath	23	—
						Mansfield T	62	1
						Chesterfield	82	6
Midfield								
Sean Dyche	6 0	12 04	28 6 71	Kettering	Trainee	Nottingham F	—	—
						Chesterfield	50	4
Adrian Shaw‡	5 10	11 07	13 4 66	Easington	Apprentice	Nottingham F	—	—
						Halifax T	100	1
						York C	5	—
						Chesterfield	50	3
Steven Williams	5 11	11 06	18 7 70	Mansfield		Mansfield T	11	—
						Chesterfield	36	5
Forwards								
Chris Benjamin§	5 11	13 00	5 12 72	Sheffield	Trainee	Chesterfield	11	1
Charlie Boyd‡	5 6	9 04	20 9 69	Liverpool	Trainee	Liverpool	—	—
						Chesterfield	1	—
Dave Caldwell	5 10	10 08	31 7 60	Aberdeen	Inverness Caley	Mansfield T	157	57
						Carlisle U (loan)	4	—
						Swindon T (loan)	5	—
						Chesterfield	68	17
						Torquay U	24	4
					Overpelt	Torquay U	17	6
					Overpelt	Chesterfield	23	4
John Cooke	5 8	11 00	25 4 62	Salford	Apprentice	Sunderland	55	4
						Carlisle U (loan)	6	2
						Sheffield W	—	—
						Carlisle U	106	11
						Stockport Co	58	7
						Chesterfield	20	1

CHESTERFIELD

Foundation: Chesterfield are fourth only to Stoke, Notts County and Nottingham Forest in age for they can trace their existence as far back as 1866, although it is fair to say that they were somewhat casual in the first few years of their history playing only a few friendlies a year. However, their rules of 1871 are still in existence showing an annual membership of 2s (10p), but it was not until 1891 that they won a trophy (the Barnes Cup) and followed this a year later by winning the Sheffield Cup, Barnes Cup and the Derbyshire Junior Cup.

First Football League game: 2 September, 1899, Division 2, v Sheffield W (a) L 1-5 – Hancock; Pilgrim, Fletcher; Ballantyne, Bell, Downie; Morley, Thacker, Gooing, Munday (1), Geary.

Did you know: In season 1933–34 Chesterfield enjoyed a run of 10 Division 3(N) wins after losing 1-0 at Accrington 2 September until losing 2-1 at Newcastle 11 November.

Managers (and Secretary-managers)
E. Russell Timmeus 1891–95*, Gilbert Gillies 1895–1901, E. F. Hind 1901–1902, Jack Hoskin 1902–1906, W. Furness 1906–07, George Swift 1907–10, G. H. Jones 1911–13, R. L. Weston 1913–17, T. Callaghan 1919, J. J. Caffrey 1920–22, Harry Hadley 1922, Harry Parkes 1922–27, Alec Campbell 1927, Ted Davison 1927–32, Bill Harvey 1932–38, Norman Bullock 1938–45, Bob Brocklebank 1945–48, Bobby Marshall 1948–52, Ted Davison 1952–58, Duggie Livingstone 1958–62, Tony McShane 1962–67, Jimmy McGuigan 1967–73, Joe Shaw 1973–76, Arthur Cox 1976–80, Frank Barlow 1980–83, John Duncan 1983–87, Kevin Randall 1987–88, Paul Hart 1988–91, Chris McMenemy April 1991–   .

Player and Position	Ht	Wt	Birth Date	Birth Place	Source	Clubs	League App	Gls
Scott Cordner§	6 1	12 04	3 8 72	Grimsby	Trainee	Chesterfield	4	1
Paul Godfrey‡	5 7	10 03	27 9 72	Derby	Trainee	Chesterfield	2	—
Paul Lemon	5 10	11 07	3 6 66	Middlesbrough	Apprentice	Sunderland	107	15
						Carlisle U (loan)	2	—
						Walsall (loan)	2	—
						Reading (loan)	3	—
						Chesterfield	39	2
Andy Morris	6 5	15 07	17 11 67	Sheffield		Rotherham U	7	—
						Chesterfield	110	17
Calvin Plummer*	5 8	10 07	14 2 63	Nottingham	Apprentice	Nottingham F	12	2
						Chesterfield	28	7
						Derby Co	27	3
						Barnsley	54	6
						Nottingham F	8	2
						Derry C (loan)	—	—
						Plymouth Arg	23	1
						Chesterfield	71	12
Andy Rolph*	5 6	10 00	28 10 69	Birmingham	Trainee	Birmingham C	—	—
						Chesterfield	36	1
Lee Turnbull	6 0	11 09	27 9 67	Teesside	Local	Middlesbrough	16	4
						Aston Villa	—	—
						Doncaster R	123	21
						Chesterfield	19	9
Dave Waller	5 10	10 00	20 12 63	Urmston	Local	Crewe Alex	168	55
						Shrewsbury T	11	3
						Chesterfield	119	53

Trainees
Bell, Scott A; Benjamin, Christopher; Clark, Philip; Cordner, Scott; Goldring, Mark; Harper, Marcus J; Holder, Mark S; Lewis, Andrew R; Payne, Karl; Pell, Steven M; Robinson, Robert A; Russell, Keith D; Thompson, Justin J; Whitehead, Scott A; Wilkinson, Gareth B.

Associated Schoolboys
Evans, Lee J; Goodwin, Robert; Hamilton, Michael J; Hickton, Grant C; Houghton, Darren C; Pearson, Michael R; Pick, Ashley C; Pilgrim, David J; Smith, Mark; Tomlinson, Ronald J; Wilcockson, Andrew.

COVENTRY CITY 1990–91 *Back row (left to right):* Brian Borrows, Andrew Pearce, Steve Ogrizovic, Brian Kilcline, Keith Waugh, Lloyd McGrath, Keith Thompson. *Centre row:* Paul Edwards, Howard Clark, Tony Dobson, Kevin MacDonald, Cyrille Regis, Steve Livingstone, Peter Billing, Jose Perdomo, Dougie McGuire. *Front row:* Trevor Peake, Dean Emerson, Kevin Drinkell, Terry Paine (Reserve Team Coach), John Sillett (Team Manager), George Dalton (Physiotherapist), David Smith. Michael Gynn, David Speedie, Kevin Gallacher.

Division 1   COVENTRY CITY

Highfield Road Stadium, King Richard Street, Coventry CV2 4FW. Telephone Coventry (0203) 257171. Telex: 312132, answer back code COV AFC. Fax: 0203 630318.

Ground capacity: 26,218.

Record attendance: 51,455 v Wolverhampton W, Division 2, 29 April 1967.

Record receipts: £177,271.55 v Nottingham F, Littlewoods Cup Semi-final 2nd leg, 25 February 1990.

Pitch measurements: 112yd × 76yd.

Life President: Derrick H. Robbins.

Chairman: J. Poynton. *Vice-chairman:*

Directors: M. F. French FCA, J. F. W. Reason, D. W. Richardson.

Managing Director: G. W. Curtis.

Secretary: G. P. Hover.

Player-manager: Terry Butcher. *Assistant Manager:* Mick Mills. *Physio:* G. Dalton.

Year Formed: 1883. *Turned Professional:* 1893. *Ltd Co.:* 1907.

Previous Names: 1883–98, Singers FC; 1898, Coventry City FC.

Club Nickname: 'Sky Blues'.

Previous Grounds: Binley Road, 1883–87; Stoke Road, 1887–99; Highfield Road, 1899–.

Record League Victory: 9-0 v Bristol C, Division 3 (S), 28 April 1934 – Pearson; Brown, Bisby; Perry, Davidson, Frith; White (2), Lauderdale Bourton (5), Jones (2), Lake.

Record Cup Victory: 7-0 v Scunthorpe U, FA Cup, 1st rd, 24 November 1934 – Pearson; Brown, Bisby; Mason, Davidson, Boileau; Birtley (2), Lauderdale (2), Bourton (1), Jones (1), Liddle (1).

Record Defeat: 2-10 v Norwich C, Division 3 (S), 15 March 1930.

Most League Points (2 for a win): 60, Division 4, 1958–59 and Division 3, 1963–64.

Most League Points (3 for a win): 63, Division 1, 1986–87.

Most League Goals: 108, Division 3 (S), 1931–32.

Highest League Scorer in Season: Clarrie Bourton, 49, Division 3 (S), 1931–32.

Most League Goals in Total Aggregate: Clarrie Bourton, 171, 1931–37.

Most Capped Player: Dave Clements, 21 (48), Northern Ireland.

Most League Appearances: George Curtis, 486, 1956–70.

Record Transfer Fee Received: £1,250,000 from Nottingham F for Ian Wallace, July 1980.

Record Transfer Fee Paid: £900,000 to Dundee U for Kevin Gallacher, January 1990.

Football League Record: 1919 Elected to Division 2; 1925–26 Division 3 (N); 1926–36 Division 3 (S); 1936–52 Division 2; 1952–58 Division 3 (S); 1958–59 Division 4; 1959–64 Division 3; 1964–67 Division 2; 1967– Division 1.

Honours: Football League: Division 1 best season: 6th, 1969–70; Division 2 – Champions 1966–67; Division 3 – Champions 1963–64; Division 3 (S) – Champions 1935–36; Runners-up 1933–34; Division 4 – Runners-up 1958–59. *FA Cup:* Winners 1986–87. *Football League Cup:* best season: Semi-final 1980–81, 1989–90. **European Competitions:** *European Fairs Cup:* 1970–71.

Colours: Sky blue and white striped shirts with navy blue trim, navy blue shorts with sky blue and white trim, sky blue stockings. **Change colours:** All yellow.

COVENTRY CITY 1990–91 LEAGUE RECORD

Match No.	Date		Venue	Opponents	Result		H/T Score	Lg. Pos.	Goalscorers	Attendance
1	Aug	25	A	Manchester U	L	0-2	0-0	—		46,715
2		29	H	Everton	W	3-1	2-0	—	Speedie, Gallacher, Dobson	12,902
3	Sept	1	H	Nottingham F	D	2-2	0-0	7	Kilcline (pen), Borrows (pen)	12,630
4		8	A	Aston Villa	L	1-2	0-1	11	Borrows	27,001
5		15	H	Wimbledon	D	0-0	0-0	15		8925
6		22	A	Luton T	L	0-1	0-1	17		8336
7		29	H	QPR	W	3-1	2-0	12	Livingstone 2, Gynn	9890
8	Oct	6	A	Manchester C	L	0-2	0-0	14		26,198
9		20	H	Southampton	L	1-2	1-1	16	Borrows (pen)	10,040
10		27	A	Sheffield U	W	1-0	0-0	12	Borrows (pen)	17,978
11	Nov	3	H	Arsenal	L	0-2	0-0	16		15,336
12		10	A	Sunderland	D	0-0	0-0	14		20,101
13		17	H	Liverpool	L	0-1	0-0	15		22,571
14		24	H	Leeds U	D	1-1	0-1	16	Gallacher	16,183
15	Dec	1	A	Crystal Palace	L	1-2	0-1	17	Regis	17,052
16		8	A	Everton	L	0-1	0-0	18		17,472
17		15	H	Manchester U	D	2-2	1-1	18	Gallacher, Regis	17,106
18		22	A	Chelsea	L	1-2	0-0	18	Gallacher	16,317
19		26	H	Tottenham H	W	2-0	0-0	16	Gallacher, Gynn	22,731
20		29	H	Norwich C	W	2-0	0-0	16	Borrows (pen), Speedie	12,039
21	Jan	1	A	Derby Co	D	1-1	1-1	16	Regis	15,741
22		12	A	Nottingham F	L	0-3	0-0	16		18,344
23		19	H	Aston Villa	W	2-1	0-0	15	Gynn, Speedie	15,751
24	Feb	2	A	Wimbledon	L	0-1	0-0	15		3981
25		23	H	Sunderland	D	0-0	0-0	16		10,453
26	Mar	2	H	Crystal Palace	W	3-1	1-0	16	Peake, Kilcline 2	10,891
27		9	A	Leeds U	L	0-2	0-1	17		28,880
28		13	H	Luton T	W	2-1	0-1	—	Borrows, Pearce	9521
29		16	A	QPR	L	0-1	0-1	16		9510
30		23	H	Manchester C	W	3-1	2-0	15	Regis, Gynn, Gallacher	13,198
31		30	A	Tottenham H	D	2-2	2-1	15	Smith, Gallacher	29,033
32	Apr	1	H	Chelsea	W	1-0	0-0	12	Gynn	14,272
33		6	A	Norwich C	D	2-2	1-1	11	Gallacher, Gynn	11,550
34		9	A	Liverpool	D	1-1	1-1	—	Gynn	31,063
35		13	H	Derby Co	W	3-0	0-0	9	Gallacher 2, Woods	11,961
36		20	A	Southampton	L	1-2	0-2	14	Gynn	15,461
37	May	4	H	Sheffield U	D	0-0	0-0	14		17,312
38		11	A	Arsenal	L	1-6	1-2	16	Gallacher	41,039

Final League Position: 16

GOALSCORERS
League (42): Gallacher 11, Gynn 8, Borrows 6 (4 pens), Regis 4, Kilcline 3 (1 pen), Speedie 3, Livingstone 2, Dobson 1, Peake 1, Pearce 1, Smith 1, Woods 1.
Rumbelows Cup (15): Gallacher 5, Livingstone 5, Regis 3, Gynn 1, Speedie 1.
FA Cup (3): Gynn 2, Kilcline 1.

Ogrizovic	Borrows	Edwards	McGrath	Kilcline	Peake	Gallacher	Dobson	Speedie	Drinkell	Smith	Regis	MacDonald	Clark	Gynn	Thompson	Perdomo	Livingstone	Titterton	Emerson	Billing	Butcher	Sutton	Hurst	Fleming	Woods	Pearce	Robson	Sansom	Match No.
1	2	3*	4	5	6	7	8†	9	10	11	12	14																	1
1	2	3	4	5	6	7	8	9	10	11*			12																2
1	2	3	4*	5	6	7	11†	9	10		12					8	14												3
1	2	3	4†	5	6	7	14	9	10*		12					8	11												4
1	2	3		5	6	7		9	10	11*		14				8			4†12										5
1	2	3†		5	6	7*		9	10	11		4				8	12	14											6
1	2	3		5	6	7				12	9	4		8					11*10										7
1	2	3		5	6	7				12	9	8*		4			11†10	14											8
1	2			6	7	3†	8			12	9	11*		4			10	14	5										9
1	2	3			6	7		8		11	9			4			10		5										10
1	2	3			6			10		11	9			8		7			4	5									11
1	2	3			6			10		11	9			8		7			4	5									12
1	2	3	7		6	11		10*		12	9			8					5	4									13
1	2	3	7*		6	11†		8		12	9			10		14			5	4									14
1	2	3	14		6	7		8		12	9			11†		10			5	4*									15
1	2	3	10		6	7		8	9	11				4					5										16
1	2	3	4*		6	7			10	11	9			8		12			5										17
1	2	3			6	7		10	12	11*	9			8					4	5									18
1	2	3			6	7		10		11	9			8					4		5								19
1	2	3			6	7		10*12		11	9			8					4		5								20
1	2	3	5		6	7				11	9			8					10	4									21
1	2			5	6		3		7	11*	9			8		12	10		4										22
1	2	3	4		6			10		11	9	7		8						5									23
	2		5					10	11	9	7*			8			6		4		1		3	12					24
1	2	3		5	6			10*11		9	7†			8			4						14	12					25
1	2		5	6	10*			11	9		12	8		4					3				7						26
1	2	14	5†		10			11	9*			8		4					3			7	6	12					27
1	2	3			6	10			11	9			8		4								7	5					28
1	2	3			6	10			11	9			8										7	5	4				29
1	2				6	10			11	9			8										7	5	4	3			30
1	2				6	10	12		11	9*			8		14								7	5	4†	3			31
1	2				6	10			11	9			8		4								7	5	3				32
1	2	7†			6	10	12		11	9*			8		4									5	3				33
1	2				6	10			11	9*			8		4								7	5	3				34
1	2				6	10			11	9			8		4								7	5	3				35
1	2				6	10			11	9			8		4	5							7		3				36
1	2				6	10			11	9			8		4								7	5	3				37
1	2	12			6	10			11	9			8		4								7	5	3*				38
37	38	22	12	14	36	32	5	18	11	30	31	7	—	35	—	4	6	—	20	15	6	1	3	—	12	11	3	9	
+	+					+		+	+	+	+	+				+			+	+	+				+	+		+	
1s	2s					1s		4s	6s	3s	2s	2s				1s			4s	1s	4s				1s	2s		1s	

Rosario — Match No. 33(14), 34(12).

Rumbelows Cup	Second Round	Bolton W (h)	4-2
		(a)	3-2
	Third Round	Hull C (h)	3-0
	Fourth Round	Nottingham F (h)	5-4
	Fifth Round	Sheffield W (h)	0-1
FA Cup	Third Round	Wigan Ath (h)	1-1
		(a)	1-0
	Fourth Round	Southampton (h)	1-1
		(a)	0-2

COVENTRY CITY

Player and Position	Ht	Wt	Birth Date	Place	Source	Clubs	League App	Gls
Goalkeepers								
Trevor Barefield*			18 9 71	Long Hanborough	Trainee	Coventry C	—	—
Tim Clarke	6 3	13 07	19 9 68	Stourbridge	Halesowen	Coventry C	—	—
Steve Ogrizovic	6 5	15 00	12 9 57	Mansfield	ONRYC	Chesterfield	16	—
						Liverpool	4	—
						Shrewsbury T	84	—
						Coventry C	278	1
Defenders								
Peter Billing	6 2	12 07	24 10 64	Liverpool	S Liverpool	Everton	1	—
						Crewe Alex	88	1
						Coventry C	33	—
Martyn Booty	5 8	12 01	30 5 71	Kirby Muxloe	Trainee	Coventry C	—	—
Brian Borrows	5 10	10 12	20 12 60	Liverpool	Amateur	Everton	27	—
						Bolton W	95	—
						Coventry C	228	9
Terry Butcher†	6 4	14 0	28 12 58	Singapore	Amateur	Ipswich T	271	16
						Rangers	127	9
						Coventry C	6	—
Howard Clark	5 11	11 01	19 9 68	Coventry	Apprentice	Coventry C	20	1
Paul Edwards	5 11	11 00	25 12 63	Birkenhead	Altrincham	Crewe Alex	86	6
						Coventry C	31	—
Chris Greenman	5 10	11 06	22 12 68	Bristol	School	Coventry C	—	—
Tony Harwood*	5 11	13 11	20 12 70	Chatham	Trainee	Coventry C	—	—
Brian Kilcline	6 2	12 00	7 5 62	Nottingham	Apprentice	Notts Co	158	9
						Coventry C	173	28
Lee Middleton*	5 9	11 09	10 9 70	Nuneaton	Trainee	Coventry C	2	—
Trevor Peake	6 0	12 09	6 7 57	Nuneaton	Nuneaton Bor	Lincoln C	171	7
						Coventry C	276	6
Andrew Pearce	6 4	13 00	20 4 66	Bradford	Halesowen	Coventry C	11	1
Kenny Sansom	5 6	11 08	26 9 58	Camberwell	Apprentice	Crystal Palace	172	3
						Arsenal	314	6
						Newcastle U	20	—
						QPR	36	—
						Coventry C	9	—
David Titterton	5 11	12 09	25 9 71	Hatton	Trainee	Coventry C	2	—
Midfield								
Dean Emerson	5 10	11 07	27 12 62	Salford	Local	Stockport Co	156	7
						Rotherham U	55	8
						Coventry C	93	—
Mick Gynn	5 5	10 10	19 8 61	Peterborough	Apprentice	Peterborough U	156	33
						Coventry C	198	27
Lee Hurst	6 0	11 09	21 9 70	Nuneaton	Trainee	Coventry C	4	—
Kevin MacDonald	6 1	12 06	22 12 60	Inverness	Inverness Caley	Leicester C	138	8
						Liverpool	40	1
						Leicester C (loan)	3	—
						Rangers (loan)	3	—
						Coventry C	31	—
						Cardiff C (loan)	8	—
Lloyd McGrath	5 9	10 06	24 2 65	Birmingham	Apprentice	Coventry C	138	3
Jose Perdomo‡	5 9	12 00	6 1 65	Uruguay	Genoa	Coventry C	4	—
David Smith	5 8	10 02	29 3 68	Gloucester	Apprentice	Coventry C	124	14
Karl Wilson	5 9	10 12	19 11 73	Dublin		Coventry C	—	—
Forwards								
Paul Dadson‡			15 11 71	Farnham		Coventry C	—	—
Kevin Drinkell	5 11	12 06	18 8 60	Grimsby	Apprentice	Grimsby T	270	89
						Norwich C	121	50
						Rangers	36	12
						Coventry C	37	5
Kevin Gallacher	5 7	9 11	23 11 66	Clydebank	Duntocher BC	Dundee U	131	27
						Coventry C	47	14

COVENTRY CITY

Foundation: Workers at Singer's cycle factory formed a club in 1883. The first success of Singers' FC was to win the Birmingham Junior Cup in 1891 and this led in 1894 to their election to the Birmingham and District League. Four years later they changed their name to Coventry City and joined the Southern League in 1908 at which time they were playing in blue and white quarters.

First Football League game: 28 August, 1920, Division 2, v Rotherham C (a) W 3-2 – Mitchell; Chaplin, Laurence; Fenwick, Hanney, Hadley (1); Dougall, Mercer (1), Parker, Nash, Gibson (1).

Did you know: In a Division 3(S) game, 4 March 1933, Coventry City led QPR 7-0 at half-time and there was no further scoring in the second half.

Managers (and Secretary-managers)
H. R. Buckle 1909–10, Robert Wallace 1910–13*, Frank Scott-Walford 1913–15, William Clayton 1917–19, H. Pollitt 1919–20, Albert Evans 1920–24, Jimmy Kerr 1924–28, James McIntyre 1928–31, Harry Storer 1931–45, Dick Bayliss 1945–47, Billy Frith 1947–48, Harry Storer 1948–53, Jack Fairbrother 1953–54, Charlie Elliott 1954–55, Jesse Carver 1955–56, Harry Warren 1956–57, Billy Frith 1957–61, Jimmy Hill 1961–67, Noel Cantwell 1967–72, Bob Dennison 1972–81 (became GM), Dave Sexton 1981–83, Bobby Gould 1983–84, Don Mackay 1985–86, George Curtis 1986–87 (became MD), John Sillett 1987–90, Terry Butcher November 1990– .

Player and Position	Ht	Wt	Birth Date	Birth Place	Source	Clubs	League App	Gls
Matthew Jenkins‡	5 7	10 07	6 6 72	Leamington Spa	Trainee	Coventry C	—	—
Doug McGuire‡	5 8	11 00	6 9 67	Bathgate	Celtic BC	Celtic	2	—
						Sunderland (loan)	1	—
						Coventry C	4	—
Craig Middleton	5 9	11 00	10 9 70	Nuneaton	Trainee	Coventry C	1	—
Cyrille Regis*	6 0	13 06	9 2 58	Mariapousoula	Hayes	WBA	237	82
						Coventry C	238	47
Robert Rosario	6 3	12 01	4 3 66	Hammersmith	Hillingdon Bor	Norwich C	126	18
						Wolverhampton W (loan)	2	1
						Coventry C	2	—
Ray Woods	5 11	11 00	7 6 65	Birkenhead	Apprentice	Tranmere R	7	2
					Colne D	Wigan Ath	28	3
						Coventry C	12	1

Trainees
Bickley, Jason L; Bufton, Warren R; Carr, Gerard J; Crews, Barry W; Davies, Martin L; Dickson, Darren M; Fleming, Terence M; French, Alun K; Kirk, Nicholas T; McNeil, Richard L; Procter, David; Smith, Ricky; Stephenson, Michael J; Storer, Darran; Upton, Richard M; Young, Boyd.

**Non-Contract
Butcher, Terry I.

Associated Schoolboys
Barnwell, Jamie; Blake, Timothy A; Chadwick, Luke D; Coleman, Daniel; Keeling, Tommy L; Mitchell, Peter J; Rogers, Lee; Savage, Christopher J.

Associated Schoolboys who have accepted the club's offer of a Traineeship/Contract
Carmichael, David; O'Brien, Paul W; Williams, Stephen D.

**Non-Contract Players who are retained must be re-signed before they are eligible to play in League matches.

178

CREWE ALEXANDRA 1990–91 *Back row (left to right)*: Martin Disley, Steve Walters, Paul Clayton, Paul Fishenden, Andy Gunn, Jason Smart, Rob Edwards, Aaron Callaghan.

Centre row: Morace Masser (Kit Manager), Dale Jasper, Andy Sussex, Chris Curran, Dean Greygoose, Paul Edwards, Chris Cutler, Tony Naylor, Neil Lennon, Kenny Swain (Assistant Manager and Player).

Front row: Phil Blakemore (Physiotherapist), Aidan Murphy, Darren Foreman, Rob Jones, Dario Gradi (Manager), Craig Hignett, Dave McKearney, Mark Gardiner, Peter Muirhead.

Photo by courtesy of Steve Finch L.R.P.S.

Division 4   CREWE ALEXANDRA

Football Ground, Gresty Rd, Crewe. Telephone Crewe (0270) 213014.

Ground capacity: 7200.

Record attendance: 20,000 v Tottenham H, FA Cup 4th rd, 30 January 1960.

Record receipts: £24,556 v Chelsea, FA Cup 3rd rd replay, 10 January 1990.

Pitch measurements: 112yd × 74yd.

President: N. Rowlinson.

Chairman: J. Bowler. *Vice-chairman:* J. McMillan.

Directors: K. Potts, H. Smith, D. Rowlinson, R. Clayton.

Manager: Dario Gradi. *Coach/Assistant Manager:* Kenny Swain.

Secretary/Commercial Manager: Mrs Gill Palin.

Year Formed: 1877. *Turned Professional:* 1893. *Ltd Co.:* 1892.

Club Nickname: 'Railwaymen'.

Record League Victory: 8-0 v Rotherham U, Division 3 (N), 1 October 1932 – Foster; Pringle, Dawson; Ward, Keenor (1), Turner (1); Gillespie, Swindells (1), McConnell (2), Deacon (1), Weale (1).

Record Cup Victory: 5-0 v Druids, FA Cup, 1st rd, 15 October 1887 – Hickton; Conde, Cope; Bayman, Halfpenny, Osborne (1); Pearson, Payne (1), Price (1), Tinsley, Ellis. (2 scorers unknown.)

Record Defeat: 2-13 v Tottenham H, FA Cup 4th rd replay, 3 February 1960.

Most League Points (2 for a win): 59, Division 4, 1962–63.

Most League Points (3 for a win): 78, Division 4, 1988–89.

Most League Goals: 95, Division 3 (N), 1931–32.

Highest League Scorer in Season: Terry Harkin, 35, Division 4, 1964–65.

Most League Goals in Total Aggregate: Bert Swindells, 126, 1928–37.

Most Capped Player: Bill Lewis, 12 (30), Wales.

Most League Appearances: Tommy Lowry, 436, 1966–78.

Record Transfer Fee Received: £300,000 from Coventry C for Paul Edwards, March 1990.

Record Transfer Fee Paid: £80,000 to Barnsley for Darren Foreman, March 1990.

Football League Record: 1892 Original Member of Division 2; 1896 Failed re-election; 1921 Re-entered Division 3 (N); 1958–63 Division 4; 1963–64 Division 3; 1964–68 Division 4; 1968–69 Division 3; 1969–89 Division 4; 1989–91 Division 3; 1991– Division 4.

Honours: Football League: Division 2 best season: 10th, 1892–93. *FA Cup:* best season: semi-final 1888. *Football League Cup:* best season: 3rd rd, 1974–75, 1975–76, 1978–79.

Colours: Red shirts, white shorts, red stockings. **Change colours:** Blue shirts, white or blue shorts, white stockings.

CREWE ALEXANDRA 1990–91 LEAGUE RECORD

Match No.	Date		Venue	Opponents	Result	H/T Score	Lg. Pos.	Goalscorers	Atten- dance
1	Aug	25	H	Fulham	D 1-1	0-0	—	Gardiner	4143
2	Sept	1	A	Southend U	L 2-3	1-1	17	Sussex, Hignett	2994
3		8	H	Grimsby T	L 1-2	0-2	22	Gardiner	3265
4		15	A	Bolton W	L 2-3	2-0	23	Jasper, Sussex	4933
5		18	A	Reading	L 1-2	0-2	—	McKearney	3663
6		21	H	Tranmere R	L 2-3	2-2	—	Gardiner, Naylor	4267
7		29	A	Bury	W 3-1	1-0	22	Gardiner, Edwards R, Hignett	3201
8	Oct	2	H	Stoke C	L 1-2	0-1	—	Foreman	7200
9		6	H	Wigan Ath	W 1-0	0-0	20	Rose	3771
10		13	A	Swansea C	L 1-3	1-2	21	Sussex	3888
11		20	A	Bournemouth	D 1-1	1-0	21	Sussex	5548
12		23	H	Birmingham C	D 1-1	0-1	—	Sussex	4449
13		27	H	Chester C	L 1-3	1-2	22	Gardiner (pen)	4262
14	Nov	3	A	Mansfield T	W 3-1	1-0	21	Gardiner, Sussex 2	2701
15		9	A	Shrewsbury T	L 0-1	0-0	—		4461
16		24	H	Bradford C	D 0-0	0-0	22		3644
17		30	A	Cambridge U	W 4-3	1-2	—	Clayton, Lennon, Hignett, Ward	4729
18	Dec	15	H	Huddersfield T	D 1-1	0-1	20	Clayton	2590
19		22	A	Leyton Orient	L 2-3	2-3	21	Edwards R, Sussex	3901
20		26	H	Preston NE	D 2-2	1-1	20	Gardiner, Murphy	4405
21		29	H	Brentford	D 3-3	2-1	21	Gardiner 2, Jones	3636
22	Jan	1	A	Exeter C	L 0-3	0-1	21		4023
23		12	H	Southend U	L 0-2	0-1	22		3595
24		19	A	Fulham	L 1-2	0-1	23	Lennon	3477
25	Feb	1	H	Reading	W 1-0	1-0	—	Doyle	3358
26		4	A	Tranmere R	L 0-2	0-1	—		5120
27		22	H	Shrewsbury T	L 1-2	0-0	—	Edwards R	3940
28	Mar	1	H	Cambridge U	W 3-1	1-1	—	Sussex, Hignett, Doyle	3484
29		9	A	Huddersfield T	L 1-3	0-2	21	Hignett	5429
30		13	A	Stoke C	L 0-1	0-0	—		15,455
31		16	H	Bury	D 2-2	1-1	23	Edwards R, Sussex	3384
32		19	H	Swansea C	W 3-0	1-0	—	Hignett 2 (1 pen), Gardiner	2622
33		23	A	Wigan Ath	L 0-1	0-0	22		2426
34		26	A	Bradford C	L 0-2	0-1	—		5163
35		30	A	Preston NE	L 1-5	0-2	23	Sussex	4852
36	Apr	1	H	Leyton Orient	D 3-3	1-1	23	Edwards R 2, Lennon	3048
37		6	A	Brentford	L 0-1	0-1	24		5066
38		9	A	Rotherham U	D 1-1	1-1	—	Scott	4141
39		13	H	Exeter C	D 1-1	0-0	23	Murphy	3099
40		16	H	Bolton W	L 1-3	1-0	—	Edwards R	4419
41		20	H	Bournemouth	L 0-2	0-1	24		2892
42		23	A	Grimsby T	W 1-0	0-0	—	Hignett	7166
43		27	A	Birmingham C	W 2-0	1-0	23	Edwards R 2	6429
44		30	H	Rotherham U	W 3-1	3-0	—	Hignett 3	4086
45	May	4	A	Chester C	L 1-3	0-3	23	Hignett	3126
46		11	H	Mansfield T	W 3-0	1-0	22	Edwards R 2, Hignett	2648

Final League Position: 22

GOALSCORERS

League (62): Hignett 13 (1 pen), Edwards R 11, Sussex 11, Gardiner 10 (1 pen), Lennon 3, Clayton 2, Doyle 2, Murphy 2, Foreman 1, Jasper 1, Jones 1, McKearney 1, Naylor 1, Rose 1, Scott 1, Ward 1.
Rumbelows Cup (4): Sussex 4.
FA Cup (8): Hignett 2, Callaghan 1, Carr 1, Gardiner 1, McKearney 1, Sussex 1, Ward 1.

Rumbelows Cup	First Round	Grimsby T (a)	1-2
		(h)	1-0
	Second Round	Liverpool (a)	1-5
		(h)	1-4

Greygoose	Jones	Callaghan	Smart	Swain	McKearney	Walters	Murphy	Hignett	Gardiner	Sussex	Naylor	Foreman	Jasper	Lennon	Carr	Gunn	Clayton	Rose	Edwards R	Gabbiadini	Ward	Edwards P	Curran	Doyle	Moore	Beresford	Scott	Gorton	Match No.
1	2	3	4	5*	6	7	8	9	10	11	12																		1
1	2*	3	4	5	6	7	8	9	10	11	12																		2
1	2*	3	4	5	6	7	12	9	10	11	8†	14																	3
1	2	3	4	5	6			9	10	11	12	8*	7†	14															4
1	2		4	5	6			9	10	11	12	8*	7	3															5
1	2	12	4	5	6			9	10	11	8†			3	7*	14													6
1		12	4	5				9	10	11			7	2	3			6	8*										7
1	14	12	4	5				9	10†	11		8*	7	2	3			6											8
1		10	4	5				9		11		12	7	2	3			6	8*										9
1	9	3	4	5*	14			12	10	11				8	7†	2		6											10
1	14	3		5	9			7†	10	11		8*			2	4		6	12										11
1		3		5	9			7†	10	11		8*			2	4	14	6	12										12
1		3		5	9			7	10	11		8*			2	4	14	6†	12										13
1	3			5	9			12	10	11			7*		2	4		14	6†		8								14
	2†	5		6	3			12	10				7	14	4		11	8								9*	1		15
			4	2	3	12		10		9			7	6*	5		8		11				1						16
			4	6	2			7		9			3	5	10		8		11				1						17
	3	6*	4	2	14			7		9	8			5	11		12†	10					1						18
	10	3	4†	2	14			7*	12	9				5	11	6	8						1						19
	12	3		2	4		7	10	9				6		5	11		8*					1						20
	8*	3		2	4		7	10	9				6		5	11		12					1						21
	8†	3		2	4		7	10	9				6		5	11*	14	12					1						22
1		4	2	3			8*	10	9				7		5	11		6†12			8								23
1		4	2	3				8	9			7†	6	5	11*			14	10	12									24
1	14	4	2	3				8	12	9		7	6†	5	11*			10											25
1		4	2	3			14	8*	12	9		7	6	5	11			10†											26
		4	2	3			14	8	10	9		7†	6*	5		12		1	11										27
		3	4	2				8	10	9			6	5	12				7*11	1									28
		3	4	2	14		7	8	10	9†			6	5*	12				11	1									29
		3	4	2	14		7†	8*	10	9			6	5	11				12	1									30
1	2	3	4				8	7	12	10	9		6	5*	11														31
1	2	3*	4	12	5		7†	8	10	9			6		14	11													32
1	2	3	4	7	10		8		9				6	5	12	11*													33
1	2	3	4	7			8		9				6	5*	12	10†11		14											34
1	2		4	3			12†	9		14	6	5	8	10*11												7			35
1	2	5	4	3			7		9	12	6		8*	11												10			36
1	2	5	4	3			7		9	12	6		8*	11												10			37
	2	5	4	3	14		7		9	8†	6*	12		11												10	1		38
	2	5	4	3			7		9	14	6	12	8	11†												10*	1		39
	2	5	4	3*			12		9	8†	6	7	14	11												10	1		40
1	2	5	4	3†			12		9	8	6*	7	14	11												10			41
1	2	3	4		14		8	6†	9	12			7	5		11*										10			42
1	2	3	4				8	6	9			7	5		11										10				43
1	2	3	4				8*	6	9	12	14	7	5		11										10†				44
1	2	3*	4	12			8	6	9			7	5	14	11										10†				45
1	2	3	4		14		8	6				7†	5		9*	11									10				46
31	29	35	37	39	23	3	13	31	30	44	5	7	23	32	32	1	16	15	21	1	4	9	1	6	—	3	12	3	

+ +   + +   + + + + + + + +   + + +

3s 4s   2s 8s 1s 3s 7s 3s   9s 2s 2s 2s 4s 2s 6s 2s 8s 1s   3s 1s 1s

Garvey — Match No. 46(12).

FA Cup

	First Round	Lincoln C (a)	4-1
	Second Round	Atherstone (h)	1-0
	Third Round	Bristol R (a)	2-0
	Fourth Round	Rotherham U (h)	1-0
	Fifth Round	West Ham U (a)	0-1

CREWE ALEXANDRA

Player and Position	Ht	Wt	Birth Date	Birth Place	Source	Clubs	League App	Gls
Goalkeepers								
Paul Edwards	5 11	11 08	22 2 65	Liverpool	St Helens T	Crewe Alex	27	—
Andy Gorton‡	5 11	11 04	23 9 66	Salford		Oldham Ath	26	—
						Stockport Co (loan)	14	—
						Tranmere R (loan)	1	—
						Stockport Co	34	—
						Lincoln C	20	—
					Glossop	Oldham Ath	—	—
						Crewe Alex	3	—
Dean Greygoose	5 11	11 05	18 12 64	Thetford	Apprentice	Cambridge U	26	—
						Orient (loan)	—	—
						Lincoln C (loan)	6	—
						Orient	1	—
						Crystal Palace	—	—
						Crewe Alex	142	—
Defenders								
Aaron Callaghan	5 11	11 02	8 10 66	Dublin	Apprentice	Stoke C	7	—
						Crewe Alex (loan)	8	—
						Oldham Ath	16	2
						Crewe Alex	121	6
Darren Carr	6 0	12 07	4 9 68	Bristol		Bristol R	30	—
						Newport Co	9	—
						Sheffield U	13	1
						Crewe Alex	36	—
Chris Curran	6 1	12 06	6 1 71	Manchester	Trainee	Crewe Alex	5	—
Rob Jones	5 11	11 00	5 11 71	Wrexham	Trainee	Crewe Alex	67	2
Neil Lennon	5 9	11 06	25 6 71	Lurgan	Trainee	Manchester C	1	—
						Crewe Alex	34	3
David McKearney	5 10	11 02	20 6 68	Crosby		Bolton W	—	—
						Crewe Alex	48	2
Jason Smart	6 0	12 00	15 2 69	Rochdale	Trainee	Rochdale	117	4
						Crewe Alex	78	2
Kenny Swain	5 9	11 07	28 1 52	Birkenhead	Wycombe W	Chelsea C	119	26
						Aston Villa	148	2
						Nottingham F	112	2
						Portsmouth	113	—
						WBA (loan)	7	1
						Crewe Alex	125	1
Midfield								
Martin Disley			24 6 71	Ormskirk		Crewe Alex	1	—
Craig Hignett	5 10	10 08	12 1 70	Whiston		Crewe Alex	74	21
Dale Jasper	6 0	11 07	14 1 64	Croydon	Apprentice	Chelsea	10	—
						Brighton & HA	49	6
						Crewe Alex	104	2
Aidan Murphy	5 10	10 10	17 9 67	Manchester	Apprentice	Manchester U	—	—
						Lincoln C (loan)	2	—
						Oldham Ath (loan)	—	—
						Crewe Alex	106	12
Colin Rose	5 8	10 09	22 1 72	Winsford	Trainee	Crewe Alex	17	1
Steve Walters	5 10	11 08	9 1 72	Plymouth	Trainee	Crewe Alex	57	2
Forwards								
Paul Clayton*	5 11	11 03	4 1 65	Dunstable	Apprentice	Norwich C	13	—
						Darlington	22	3
						Crewe Alex	60	12
Bob Colville‡	5 10	12 00	27 4 63	Nuneaton	Rhos U	Oldham Ath	32	4
						Bury	11	1
						Stockport Co	71	20
						York C	24	—
						Crewe Alex	—	—
Chris Cutler‡	5 11	11 00	7 4 64	Manchester	Amateur	Bury	23	3
						Crewe Alex	140	24
Robert Edwards†	5 8	11 07	23 2 70	Manchester	Trainee	Crewe Alex	43	12

CREWE ALEXANDRA

Foundation: Crewe Alexandra played cricket and probably rugby before they decided to form a football club in 1877. Whether they took the name "Alexandra" from a pub where they held their meetings, or whether it was after Princess Alexandra, is a matter of conjecture. Crewe's first trophy was the Crewe and District Cup in 1887 and it is worth noting that they reached the semi-finals of the FA Cup the following year.

First Football League game: 3 September, 1892, Division 2, v Burton Swifts (a) L 1-7 – Hickton; Moore, Cope; Linnell, Johnson, Osborne; Bennett, Pearson (1), Bailey, Barnett, Roberts.

Did you know: In their record-breaking 1931–32 season Crewe scored 36 goals in one spell of only seven consecutive home League games. More than half of this total was scored by Harry Deacon(10) and Ted Sweeney(9).

Managers (and Secretary-managers)
W. C. McNeill 1892–94*, J. G. Hall 1895–96*, 1897 R. Roberts* (1st team sec.), J. B. Bromerley 1898–1911* (continued as Hon. Sec. to 1925), Tom Bailey 1925–38, George Lillicrop 1938–44, Frank Hill 1944–48, Arthur Turner 1948–51, Harry Catterick 1951–53, Ralph Ward 1953–55, Maurice Lindley 1955–58, Harry Ware 1958–60, Jimmy McGuigan 1960–64, Ernie Tagg 1964–71 (continued as secretary to 1972), Dennis Viollet 1971, Jimmy Melia 1972–73, Ernie Tagg 1974, Harry Gregg 1975–78, Warwick Rimmer 1978–79, Tony Waddington 1979–81, Arfon Griffiths 1981–82, Peter Morris 1982–83, Dario Gradi June 1983– .

Player and Position	Ht	Wt	Birth Date	Birth Place	Source	Clubs	League App	Gls
Paul Fishenden‡	6 0	10 12	2 8 63	Hillingdon	Local	Wimbledon	75	25
						Fulham (loan)	3	—
						Millwall (loan)	3	—
						Orient (loan)	4	—
						Crewe Alex	81	25
Mark Gardiner	5 10	10 07	25 12 66	Cirencester	Apprentice	Swindon T	10	1
						Torquay U	49	4
						Crewe Alex	97	26
Steve Garvey§			22 11 73	Tameside	Trainee	Crewe Alex	1	—
Andrew Gunn	6 0	12 01	2 2 71	Barking	Trainee	Watford	—	—
						Crewe Alex	4	—
John Moore‡	6 0	11 11	1 10 66	Consett	Apprentice	Sunderland	16	1
						St Patricks Ath (loan)	—	—
						Newport Co (loan)	2	—
						Darlington (loan)	2	1
						Mansfield T (loan)	5	1
						Rochdale (loan)	10	2
						Hull C	14	1
						Sheffield U (loan)	5	—
					Utrecht	Shrewsbury T	8	1
						Crewe Alex	1	—
Tony Naylor	5 8	10 08	29 3 67	Manchester	Droylsden	Crewe Alex	16	1
Tony Rigby*	5 7	10 08	10 8 72	Ormskirk	Trainee	Crewe Alex	—	—
Andy Sussex	6 0	11 06	23 11 64	Enfield	Apprentice	Leyton Orient	144	17
						Crewe Alex	102	24
Jason Withe‡			16 8 71	Liverpool	WBA	Burnley	—	—
						Crewe Alex	—	—

Trainees
Congerton, Lee D; Duffy, Christopher J; Garvey, Stephen H; Howard, Shane; Hughes, Anthony B; Jackson, Michael J; Keen, Ryan H; Malone, Michael P; Rushton, Paul; Sorvel, Neil S; Stephenson, Ashlyn R; Wall, Justin W; Watson, Nicholas; Whalley, Gareth; Williams, Philip P; Woodward, Andrew S.

**Non-Contract
Edwards, Robert; Mayfield, Alexander.

Associated Schoolboys
Brown, Adrian C; Brown, Scott; Byrne, Liam; Carroll, Kevin T; Ceradlo, Mark; Chapman, Iain A; Corcoran, Matthew L; Cox, Paul J; Dawson, Douglas A; Dootson, Warren; Fairclough, Andrew; Frazer, Stuart A; Gunn, Benjamin J; Hawtin, Dale C; Keen, Anthony M; Lewis, John E; Lister, Daniel; McCauley, Andrew; Murphy, Daniel B; Murray, Thomas O; Nichols, Matthew; Ouslem, Joseph A; Parker, Justin N; Pope, Stephen A; Rivers, Mark A; Tierney, Francess

Associated Schoolboys who have accepted the club's offer of a Traineeship/Contract
Adebola, Dele; Byrne, Christopher; Meeson, Christopher A; Williams, Carwyn.

**Non-Contract Players who are retained must be re-signed before they are eligible to play in League matches.

184

CRYSTAL PALACE 1990–91 *Back row (left to right):* Eddie McGoldrick, Phil Barber, Jeff Hopkins, Alan Pardew, Andy Thorn, Mark Bright, Geoff Thomas, Rudi Hedman, Garry Thompson, Glyn Hodges.
Centre row: David West (Physiotherapist), Spike Hill (Kit Manager), Simon Line, Alex Dyer, Jamie Moralee, Andy Woodman, Nigel Martyn, Perry Suckling, Gareth Southgate, Simon Osborn, Mark Dennis, Gary O'Reilly, Alan Smith (Assistant Manager), Ian Branfoot (1st Team Coach).
Front row: Simon Rodger, David Stevens, Darren Carr, John Humphrey, Eric Young, Steve Coppell (Manager), Andy Gray, Ian Wright, David Whyte, Ricky Newman, Richard Shaw, John Salako.

Division 1   CRYSTAL PALACE

Selhurst Park, London SE25 6PU. Telephone 081-653 4462. Lottery Office: 081-771 9502. Souvenir Shop: 081-653 5584. Fax: 081-771 5311. Clubline: 0898 400 333. Palace Ticket Line: 0898 400 333. Palace Publications: 081-771 8299. Fax: 081-653 6312.

Ground capacity: 29,949.

Record attendance: 51,482 v Burnley, Division 2, 11 May 1979.

Record receipts: £268,000 v Arsenal, Division 1, 10 November 1990.

Pitch measurements: 110yd × 74yd.

President: S. Stephenson.

Chairman: R. G. Noades.

Directors: R. Anderson, B. Coleman OBE, A. S. C. De Souza, G. Geraghty, S. Hume-Kendall, M. E. Lee, G. Lucking, P. H. N. Norman, K. A. Sinclair, Chief B. O. Umunna.

Team Manager: Steve Coppell. *Assistant Manager:* Alan Smith. *Coach:* *Physio:* David West.

Company Secretary: Doug Miller. *Club Secretary:* Mike Hurst. *Assistant Secretary:* Terry Byfield. *Marketing Manager:* Tony Willis.

Year Formed: 1905. *Turned Professional:* 1905. *Ltd Co.:* 1905.

Club Nickname: 'The Eagles'.

Club Sponsor: Tulip Computers.

Commercial Manager: Graham Drew.

Previous Grounds: 1905, Crystal Palace; 1915, Herne Hill; 1918, The Nest; 1924, Selhurst Park.

Record League Victory: 9-0 v Barrow, Division 4, 10 October 1959 – Rouse; Long, Noakes; Truett, Evans, McNichol; Gavin (1), Summersby (4 incl. 1p), Sexton, Byrne (2), Colfar (2).

Record Cup Victory: 8–0 v Southend U, Rumbelows League Cup, 2nd rd (1st leg), 25 September 1990 – Martyn; Humphrey (Thompson (1)), Shaw, Pardew, Young, Thorn, McGoldrick, Thomas, Bright (3), Wright (3), Barber (Hodges (1)).

Record Defeat: 0–9 v Liverpool, Division 1, 12 September 1990.

Most League Points (2 for a win): 64, Division 4, 1960–61.

Most League Points (3 for a win): 81, Division 2, 1988–89.

Most League Goals: 110, Division 4, 1960–61.

Highest League Scorer in Season: Peter Simpson, 46, Division 3 (S), 1930–31.

Most League Goals in Total Aggregate: Peter Simpson, 154, 1930–36.

Most Capped Player: Paddy Mulligan, 14 (50), Eire; Ian Walsh, 14 (18), Wales; Peter Nicholas, 14 (72) Wales.

Most League Appearances: Jim Cannon, 571, 1973–88.

Record Transfer Fee Received: £800,000 (nett) from Arsenal for Kenny Sansom, August 1980.

Record Transfer Fee Paid: £1,000,000 to Bristol Rovers for Nigel Martyn, November 1989.

Football League Record: 1920 Original Members of Division 3; 1921–25 Division 2; 1925–58 Division 3 (S); 1958–61 Division 4; 1961–64 Division 3; 1964–69 Division 2; 1969–73 Division 1; 1973–74 Division 2; 1974–77 Division 3; 1977–79 Division 2; 1979–81 Division 1; 1981–89 Division 2; 1989– Division 1.

Honours: Football League: Division 1 best season: 3rd 1990–91; Division 2 – Champions 1978–79; Runners-up 1968–69; Division 3 – Runners-up 1963–64; Division 3 (S) – Champions 1920–21; Runners-up 1928–29, 1930–31, 1938–39; Division 4 – Runners-up 1960–61. *FA Cup:* best season: Runners-up 1989–90. *Football League Cup:* best season; 5th rd, 1968–69, 1970–71. *Zenith Data Systems Cup:* Winners: 1991.

Colours: Red and blue shirts, red shorts, red stockings. **Change colours:** All red or all blue.

CRYSTAL PALACE 1990–91 LEAGUE RECORD

Match No.	Date		Venue	Opponents	Result		H/T Score	Lg. Pos.	Goalscorers	Atten-dance
1	Aug	25	A	Luton T	D	1-1	1-1	—	Young	9583
2		28	H	Chelsea	W	2-1	1-0	—	Gray (pen), Wright	27,101
3	Sept	1	H	Sheffield U	W	1-0	1-0	4	Thompson	16,831
4		8	A	Norwich C	W	3-0	2-0	2	Barber, Wright, Salako	15,306
5		15	H	Nottingham F	D	2-2	1-0	4	Shaw, Thomas	20,545
6		22	A	Tottenham H	D	1-1	0-1	5	Thomas	34,859
7		29	A	Derby Co	W	2-0	1-0	4	Wright, Bright	15,202
8	Oct	6	H	Leeds U	D	1-1	0-0	4	Thomas	21,676
9		20	A	Everton	D	0-0	0-0	4		24,504
10		27	H	Wimbledon	W	4-3	1-1	4	Thomas, Humphrey, Gray, Bright	17,220
11	Nov	3	A	Manchester U	L	0-2	0-2	4		45,724
12		10	H	Arsenal	D	0-0	0-0	4		28,181
13		17	A	QPR	W	2-1	1-0	4	Wright 2	14,360
14		24	A	Southampton	W	3-2	2-2	4	Wright 2, Bright	15,851
15	Dec	1	H	Coventry C	W	2-1	1-0	3	Bright, Gray	17,052
16		8	A	Chelsea	L	1-2	1-1	4	Thorn	21,558
17		16	H	Luton T	W	1-0	1-0		Bright	15,579
18		22	A	Manchester C	W	2-0	1-0	3	Pointon (og), Wright	25,321
19		26	H	Sunderland	W	2-1	0-0	3	Salako, Bright	15,560
20		30	H	Liverpool	W	1-0	1-0	—	Bright	26,280
21	Jan	1	A	Aston Villa	L	0-2	0-0	3		25,523
22		12	A	Sheffield U	W	1-0	0-0	3	Bright	17,139
23		19	H	Norwich C	L	1-3	0-1	3	Bright	17,201
24	Feb	2	A	Nottingham F	W	1-0	0-0	3	Young	17,045
25		16	H	QPR	D	0-0	0-0	3		16,006
26		23	A	Arsenal	L	0-4	0-2	3		42,512
27	Mar	2	A	Coventry C	L	1-3	0-1	3	Wright	10,891
28		9	H	Southampton	W	2-1	0-0	3	Thomas 2	14,529
29		16	H	Derby Co	W	2-1	0-0	3	Gray (pen), Wright	14,752
30		23	A	Leeds U	W	2-1	1-1	3	Wright, Salako	28,556
31		30	A	Sunderland	L	1-2	0-1	3	Pardew	19,704
32	Apr	1	H	Manchester C	L	1-3	0-2	3	Salako	18,001
33		13	H	Aston Villa	D	0-0	0-0	3		18,331
34		17	H	Tottenham H	W	1-0	1-0	3	Young	26,285
35		20	H	Everton	D	0-0	0-0	3		16,439
36		23	A	Liverpool	L	0-3	0-1	—		36,767
37	May	4	A	Wimbledon	W	3-0	0-0	3	Wright 3	10,002
38		11	H	Manchester U	W	3-0	1-0	3	Wright, Salako 2	25,301

Final League Position: 3

GOALSCORERS

League (50): Wright 15, Bright 9, Salako 6, Thomas 6, Gray 4 (2 pens), Young 3, Barber 1, Humphrey 1, Pardew 1, Shaw 1, Thompson 1, Thorn 1, own goal 1.
Rumbelows Cup (11): Bright 4, Wright 3, Hodges 1, Salako 1, Thompson 1, Young 1.
FA Cup (2): Salako 1, Wright 1.

Martyn	Humphrey	Shaw	Gray	Young	Thorn	Barber	Thomas	Salako	Wright	Hodges	Dennis	Thompson	Bright	Hedman	Pardew	McGoldrick	Collymore	Bodin	Osborn	Southgate	Match No.
1	2	3	4	5	6	7	8	9	10	11*12											1
1	2	3	4	5	6	12	8	7	10	11*		9									2
1	2	3	4	5	6	12	8	7	10	11*		9†	14								3
1	2	3	4	5	6	11	8	7	10			9									4
1	2	3		5	6	11*	8	7	10	12		9	14		4†						5
1	2	3		5	6	11	8		10			9*12			4	7					6
1	2	3		5	6*11		8		10	12		9			4	7					7
1	2	3	12	5	6	11	8		10			9			4*	7					8
1	2	3	12	5	6	11*	8	7	10			9			4						9
1	2	3	4	5	6	12	8	7	10	11*			9								10
1	2	3	4	5	6	11	8	7	10				9								11
1	2	3	4	5	6	11*	8	7	10				9			12					12
1	2	3	4	5	6	11*	8	7	10				9			12					13
1	2	3	4	5	6		8	7	10*				9		12	11					14
1	2	3	4	5			8	7	10		6*		9		12	11					15
1	2	3	4	5	6		8	7	10		12		9			11*					16
1	2	3	4	5	6		8	7	10				9			11					17
1	2	3	4	5	6		8	7	10				9			11					18
1	2	3	4	5	6		8	7	10				9			11					19
1	2	3	4	5	6		8	7	10				9			11					20
1	2	3	4	5*	6		8	7	10		12		9			11					21
1	2	3	4	5	6		8	7	10				9			11					22
1	2	3	4	5	6	12	8	7	10				9			11*					23
1	2	3	4	5		11	8	7	10				9		6						24
1	2	3	4*	5	6	11†	8	7	10				9		12	14					25
1	2	3	4	5		11*	8	7	10				9		6	12					26
1	2	3	4	5	6	12	8	7	10				9			11*					27
1	2	3	4		6	12	8	7	10			5*	9			11					28
1	2	3	4	5	6		8	7	10				9		12	11*					29
1	2	3	4	5	6		8	7	10				9			11					30
1	2	3	4	5	6		8	7	10				9			11*	12				31
1	2	3	4	5	6		8	7	10				9			11*	12				32
1	2	3		5	6		8	7	10				9		4	11*	12				33
1	2			5	6		8	7*10					9†		4	11	12	3	14		34
1	2			5	6		8	7	10				9		4†	11*12		3	14		35
1	2				6		8	7	10				14		4	11	12	3*	9†	5	36
1	2			5	6		8	7	10				9*		4	11	12	3			37
1	2		12	5	6		8	7	10				9			11*		3	4		38
38	38	36	27	34	34	13	38	35	38	5	—	8	29	1	15	21	—	5	2	1	
			+		+					+		+	+		+	+	+	+			
			3s		6s					2s	1s	3s	3s		4s	5s	6s	2s			

Rumbelows Cup	Second Round	Southend U (h)		8-0
		(a)		2-1
	Third Round	Leyton Orient (h)		0-0
		(a)		1-0
	Fourth Round	Southampton (a)		0-2
FA Cup	Third Round	Nottingham F (h)		0-0
		(a)		2-2
		(a)		0-3

CRYSTAL PALACE

Player and Position	Ht	Wt	Birth Date	Place	Source	Clubs	League App	Gls
Goalkeepers								
Nigel Martyn	6 2	14 00	11 8 66	St Austell	St Blazey	Bristol R	101	—
						Crystal Palace	63	—
Perry Suckling	6 1	11 02	12 10 55	Leyton	Apprentice	Coventry C	27	—
						Manchester C	39	—
						Crystal Palace	56	—
						West Ham U (loan)	6	—
Andrew Woodman	6 1	12 04	11 8 71	Denmark Hill	Trainee	Crystal Palace	—	—
Defenders								
Mark Dennis‡	5 9	10 08	2 5 61	Streatham	Apprentice	Birmingham C	130	1
						Southampton	95	2
						QPR	28	—
						Crystal Palace	9	—
Rudi Hedman†	6 3	12 00	16 11 64	London	Local	Colchester U	176	10
						Crystal Palace	18	—
						Leyton Orient (loan)	5	—
Jeff Hopkins	6 1	11 11	14 4 64	Swansea	Apprentice	Fulham	219	4
						Crystal Palace	70	2
John Humphrey	5 10	11 01	31 1 61	Paddington	Apprentice	Wolverhampton W	149	3
						Charlton Ath	194	3
						Crystal Palace	38	1
Gary O'Reilly*	5 11	12 00	21 3 61	Isleworth	Amateur	Tottenham H	45	—
						Brighton & HA	79	3
						Crystal Palace	70	2
						Birmingham C (loan)	1	—
Simon Rodger	5 9	11 07	3 10 71	Shoreham	Trainee	Crystal Palace	—	—
Richard Shaw	5 9	11 08	11 9 68	Brentford	Apprentice	Crystal Palace	74	1
						Hull C (loan)	4	—
Gareth Southgate	5 10	11 12	3 9 70	Watford	Trainee	Crystal Palace	1	—
Andy Thorn	6 0	11 05	12 11 66	Carshalton	Apprentice	Wimbledon	107	2
						Newcastle U	36	2
						Crystal Palace	51	2
Tony Witter	6 1	12 07	12 8 65	London	Grays Ath	Crystal Palace	—	—
Eric Young	6 2	13 00	25 3 60	Singapore	Slough T	Brighton & HA	126	10
						Wimbledon	99	9
						Crystal Palace	34	3
Midfield								
Phil Barber	5 11	12 06	10 6 65	Tring	Aylesbury U	Crystal Palace	234	35
Paul Bodin	6 0	12 01	13 9 64	Cardiff	Chelsea	Newport Co	—	—
						Cardiff C	57	3
					Bath C	Newport Co	6	1
						Swindon T	93	9
						Crystal Palace	5	—
Darren Carr‡	5 7	10 04	4 11 69	Birmingham	Burton Alb	Crystal Palace	—	—
Andy Gray	5 11	13 03	22 2 64	Lambeth	Dulwich H	Crystal Palace	98	27
						Aston Villa	37	4
						QPR	11	2
						Crystal Palace	65	10
Eddie McGoldrick	5 10	12 00	30 4 65	London	Nuneaton	Northampton T	107	9
						Crystal Palace	69	—
Ricky Newman	5 10	11 00	5 8 70	Guildford		Crystal Palace	—	—
Simon Osborn	5 10	11 04	19 1 72	New Addington	Trainee	Crystal Palace	4	—
Alan Pardew	5 10	11 00	18 7 61	Wimbledon	Yeovil	Crystal Palace	120	8
David Stevens‡	5 11	11 00	19 10 70	Plumstead	Trainee	Crystal Palace	—	—
Geoff Thomas	5 10	10 07	5 8 64	Manchester	Local	Rochdale	11	1
						Crewe Alex	125	20
						Crystal Palace	136	18

CRYSTAL PALACE

Foundation: There was a Crystal Palace club as early as 1861 but the present organisation was born in 1905 after the formation of a club by the company that controlled the Crystal Palace (the building that is), had been rejected by the FA who did not like the idea of the Cup Final hosts running their own club. A separate company had to be formed and they had their home on the old Cup Final ground until 1915.

First Football League game: 28 August, 1920, Division 3, v Merthyr T (a) L 1-2 – Alderson; Little, Rhodes; McCracken, Jones, Feebury; Bateman, Conner, Smith, Milligan (1), Whibley.

Did you know: Palace's most prolific scorer, Peter Simpson, netted a hat-trick on his debut for the club in September 1929, and during the following season scored a total of 10 League and Cup hat-tricks including one six and two fours.

Managers (and Secretary-managers)
John T. Robson 1905–07, Edmund Goodman 1907–25 (had been secretary since 1905 and afterwards continued in this position to 1933). Alec Maley 1925–27, Fred Maven 1927–30, Jack Tresadern 1930–35, Tom Bromilow 1935–36, R. S. Moyes 1936, Tom Bromilow 1936–39, George Irwin 1939–47, Jack Butler 1947–49, Ronnie Rooke 1949–50, Charlie Slade and Fred Dawes (joint managers) 1950–51, Laurie Scott 1951–54, Cyril Spiers 1954–58, George Smith 1958–60, Arthur Rowe 1960–62, Dick Graham 1962–66, Bert Head 1966–72 (continued as GM to 1973), Malcolm Allison 1973–76, Terry Venables 1976–80, Ernie Walley 1980, Malcolm Allison 1980–81, Dario Gradi 1981, Steve Kember 1981–82, Alan Mullery 1982–84, Steve Coppell June 1984– .

Player and Position	Ht	Wt	Birth Date	Birth Place	Source	Clubs	League App	Gls
Forwards								
Mark Bright	6 0	11 00	6 2 62	Stoke	Leek T	Port Vale	29	10
						Leicester C	42	6
						Crystal Palace	180	74
Stan Collymore	6 4	13 01	22 1 71	Stone	Stafford R	Crystal Palace	6	—
Jamie Moralee	6 1	11 01	2 12 71	Wandsworth	Trainee	Crystal Palace	—	—
John Salako	5 9	11 00	11 2 69	Nigeria	Trainee	Crystal Palace	115	8
						Swansea C (loan)	13	3
Garry Thompson	6 1	14 00	7 10 59	Birmingham	Apprentice	Coventry C	134	38
						WBA	91	39
						Sheffield W	36	7
						Aston Villa	60	17
						Watford	34	8
						Crystal Palace	20	3
David Whyte	5 9	10 06	20 4 71	Greenwich		Crystal Palace	—	—
Ian Wright	5 11	11 11	3 11 63	Woolwich	Greenwich B	Crystal Palace	217	84

Trainees
Brazier, Paul D; Cutler, Scott S; Finnan, Anthony O; Glass, James R; Gordon, Dean D; Halpin, Mark; Harding, Benjamin; Holman, Mark B; McCall, Stuart; McPherson, Andrew; Myatt, John; Oliva, Umberto; Pepper, Mark J; Rollison, Simon A; Thomas, Scott P; Tomlin, Darren M; Watts, Grant S.

**Non-Contract
Hedman, Rudolph G.

Associated Schoolboys
Bell, Stuart J; Cripps, Paul; Cyrus, Andrew; Harris, Jason A; Hilderly, Clifford; Little, Glen; Monger, Adam J; Needham, James; Powell, Richard; Roberts, Christopher; Robertson, Simon; Thompson, Anthony M; Trafford, Andrew D; Wade, Tom; Wareing, Paul A; White, Craig.

Associated Schoolboys who have accepted the club's offer of a Traineeship/Contract
Clark, Timothy C; Sparrow, Paul.

**Non-Contract Players who are retained must be re-signed before they are eligible to play in League matches.

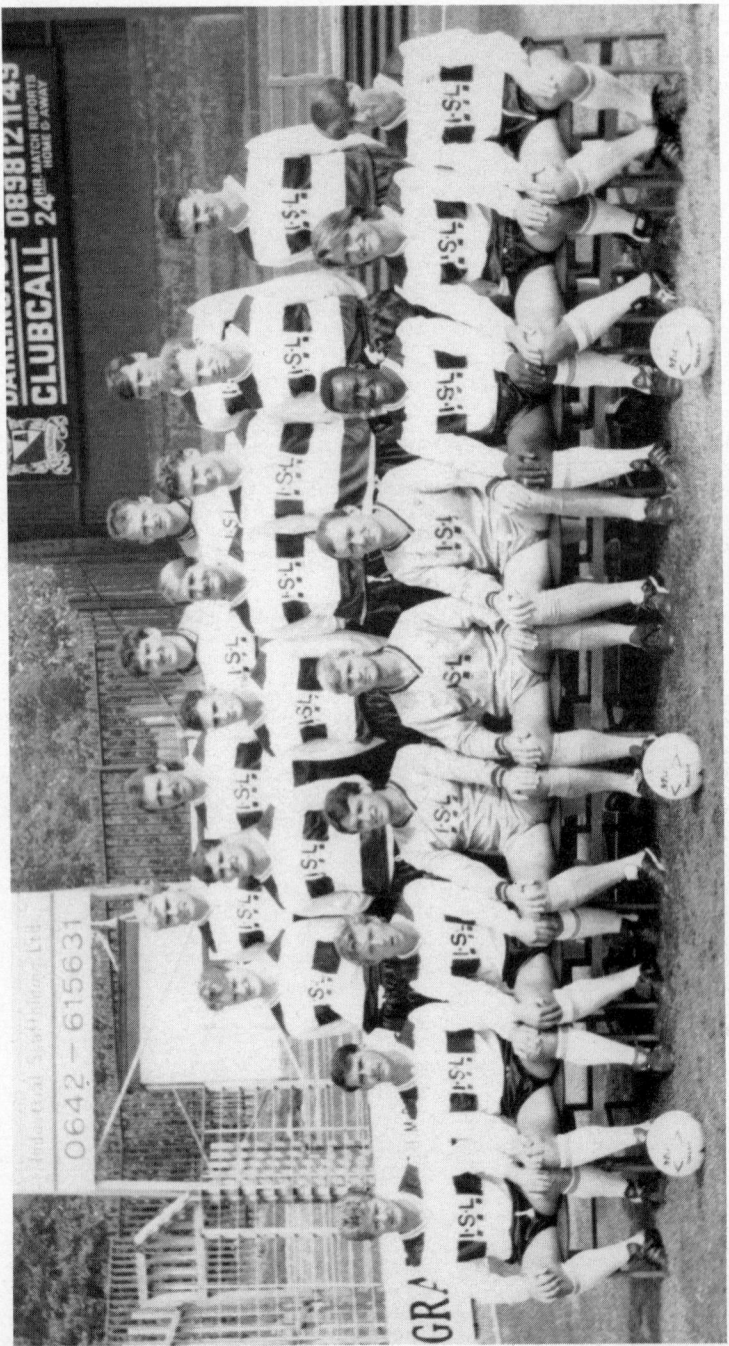

DARLINGTON 1990–91 *Back row (left to right):* David Cork, Mick Tait, Mark Prudhoe, Matthew Coddington, Phil Linacre.
Centre row: Drew Coverdale, Gary Coatsworth, Jim Willis, Kevan Smith, Michael Trotter, David Corner, John Borthwick.
Front row: Les McJannet, Andy Toman, David Geddis, Frank Gray (Assistant Manager), Brian Little (Manager), Tony McAndrew (Youth Team Coach), Steve Mardenborough,
Gary Gill, Paul Emson.

Division 3   **DARLINGTON**

Feethams Ground, Darlington. Telephone Darlington (0325) 465097, 467712. Commercial Dept: (0325) 481212.

Ground capacity: 10,000.

Record attendance: 21,023 v Bolton W, League Cup 3rd rd, 14 November 1960.

Record receipts: £25,016 v Middlesbrough, Division 3, 8 November 1986

Pitch measurements: 110yd × 74yd.

President: J. L. T. Moore.

Chairman: R. Corden. *Vice-chairman:* A. Noble.

Directors: J. Brockbank.

Manager: Frank Gray. *Chief Executive:* T. D. Hughes.

Secretary: Brian Anderson. *Commercial Manager:*

Coach/Assistant Manager: . *Physio:* Drew Coverdale.

Year Formed: 1883. *Turned Professional:* 1908. *Ltd Co.:* 1891.

Club Nickname: 'The Quakers'.

Record League Victory: 9-2 v Lincoln C, Division 3 (N), 7 January 1928 – Archibald; Brooks, Mellen; Kelly, Waugh, McKinnell; Cochrane (1), Gregg (1), Ruddy (3), Lees (3), McGiffen (1).

Record Cup Victory: 7-2 v Evenwood T, FA Cup, 1st rd, 17 November 1956 – Ward; Devlin, Henderson; Bell (1p), Greener, Furphy; Forster (1), Morton (3), Tulip (2), Davis, Moran.

Record Defeat: 0-10 v Doncaster R, Division 4, 25 January 1964.

Most League Points (2 for a win): 59, Division 4, 1965–66.

Most League Points (3 for a win): 85, Division 4, 1984–85.

Most League Goals: 108, Division 3 (N), 1929–30.

Highest League Scorer in Season: David Brown, 39, Division 3 (N), 1924–25.

Most League Goals in Total Aggregate: Alan Walsh, 90, 1978–84.

Most Capped Player: None.

Most League Appearances: Ron Greener, 442, 1955–68.

Record Transfer Fee Received: £150,000 from Barnsley for David Currie, February 1988.

Record Transfer Fee Paid: £40,000 to Hartlepool U for Andy Toman, July 1989.

Football League Record: 1921 Original Member Division 3 (N); 1925–27 Division 2; 1927–58 Division 3 (N); 1958–66 Division 4; 1966–67 Division 3; 1967–85 Division 4; 1985–87 Division 3; 1987–89 Division 4; 1989–90 GM Vauxhall Conference; 1990–91 Division 4; 1991– Division 3.

Honours: Football League: Division 2 best season: 15th, 1925–26; Division 3 (N) – Champions 1924–25; Runners-up 1921–22; Division 4 Champions 1990–91 – Runners-up 1965–66. *FA Cup:* best season: 3rd rd, 1910–11, 5th rd, 1957–58. *Football League Cup:* best season: 5th rd, 1967–68. GM Vauxhall Conference Champions 1989–90.

Colours: All white. **Change colours:** All yellow.

DARLINGTON 1990–91 LEAGUE RECORD

Match No.	Date	Venue	Opponents	Result	H/T Score	Lg. Pos.	Goalscorers	Attendance
1	Aug 25	A	Gillingham	L 0-1	0-0	—		3730
2	Sept 1	H	Burnley	W 3-1	2-1	11	Gray (pen), Gill, McJannet	3671
3	8	A	Walsall	D 2-2	2-1	9	Gray, Gill	4348
4	15	H	Halifax T	W 3-0	1-0	4	Cork, McJannet, Gill	2992
5	18	H	York C	D 0-0	0-0	—		3582
6	22	A	Wrexham	D 1-1	1-0	8	Borthwick	1908
7	29	A	Doncaster R	W 1-0	1-0	5	Cork	3695
8	Oct 2	H	Peterborough U	L 0-1	0-0	—		3748
9	6	H	Hereford U	W 3-1	0-0	5	Cork, Burke, Trotter	3376
10	13	A	Blackpool	W 2-1	1-0	3	Borthwick, Gill	4092
11	20	A	Maidstone U	W 3-2	0-1	2	Cork, Borthwick, Toman	2077
12	23	H	Northampton T	D 1-1	1-0	—	Gray (pen)	4882
13	27	H	Scunthorpe U	D 0-0	0-0	2		3852
14	Nov 3	A	Rochdale	D 1-1	1-1	4	O'Shaughnessy (og)	2881
15	10	H	Hartlepool U	L 0-1	0-1	5		5713
16	24	A	Lincoln C	W 3-0	2-0	4	Gill (pen), Smith, Ellison	2182
17	Dec 1	A	Stockport Co	L 1-3	1-2	6	Coatsworth	2938
18	15	H	Torquay U	W 3-0	1-0	5	Borthwick, Toman, Coverdale	2997
19	22	H	Chesterfield	W 1-0	0-0	4	Gill	2925
20	29	A	Scarborough	D 1-1	1-0	4	Coverdale	2408
21	Jan 1	H	Cardiff C	W 4-1	3-0	3	McJannet, Cork, Willis, Tait	3151
22	5	H	Carlisle U	W 3-1	1-0	1	Coverdale, Linacre, Smith	3726
23	12	A	Burnley	L 1-3	0-2	2	Linacre	8491
24	26	A	Halifax T	D 0-0	0-0	4		1658
25	29	H	Gillingham	D 1-1	0-0	—	Willis	2882
26	Feb 2	A	York C	W 1-0	1-0	3	Borthwick	2925
27	5	H	Wrexham	W 1-0	1-0	—	Gill	3279
28	19	A	Aldershot	W 2-0	1-0	—	Ellison, Borthwick	1920
29	23	A	Hartlepool U	D 0-0	0-0	1		6100
30	26	A	Carlisle U	W 2-0	1-0	—	Borthwick, Linacre	2896
31	Mar 2	H	Stockport Co	W 1-0	0-0	1	Mardenborough	4046
32	5	H	Walsall	W 1-0	0-0	—	Tait	3971
33	9	A	Torquay U	L 1-2	0-0	1	Ellison	3078
34	12	A	Peterborough U	D 2-2	0-1	1	Cork, Smith	8362
35	16	H	Doncaster R	D 1-1	0-1	1	Toman	4410
36	19	H	Blackpool	D 1-1	1-0	—	Smith	4108
37	23	A	Hereford U	D 1-1	0-0	1	McJannet	2462
38	30	H	Aldershot	W 3-1	1-0	1	Gray 2 (2 pens), Borthwick	4250
39	Apr 1	A	Chesterfield	D 2-2	2-1	1	Francis (og), Cork	4602
40	6	H	Scarborough	W 2-1	0-1	1	Toman, Borthwick	3962
41	9	H	Lincoln C	D 1-1	0-0	—	Gill	4241
42	13	A	Cardiff C	W 1-0	0-0	1	Matthews (og)	4544
43	20	H	Maidstone U	D 1-1	0-1	1	Toman	4150
44	27	A	Northampton T	W 3-0	3-0	1	Borthwick, Cook, Trotter	4884
45	May 4	A	Scunthorpe U	L 1-2	0-1	1	Gray (pen)	5769
46	11	H	Rochdale	W 2-0	1-0	1	Cork, Gray (pen)	9160

Final League Position: 1

GOALSCORERS

League (68): Borthwick 10, Cork 8, Gill 8 (1 pen), Gray 7 (6 pens), Toman 5, McJannet 4, Smith 4, Coverdale 3, Ellison 3, Linacre 3, Tait 2, Trotter 2, Willis 2, Burke 1, Coatsworth 1, Cook 1, Mardenborough 1, own goals 3.
Rumbelows Cup (4): Cork 2, Borthwick 1, Gray (1 pen).
FA Cup (1): Gill 1.

Prudhoe	McJannet	Gray	Trotter	Smith	Corner	Geddis	Toman	Borthwick	Cork	Tait	Mardenborough	Emson	Gill	Burke	Coatsworth	Ellison	Coverdale	Willis	Linacre	Cook	Evans	Match No.
1	2	3	4†	5	6	7*	8	9	10	11	12	14										1
1	2	3	14	5	6	12	8	9	10†	11			7*	4								2
1	2	3	14	5	6	12	8	9	10	11			7*	4†								3
1	2	3		5	6		8	9	10	11			7	4								4
1	2	3		5	6	12	8	9*	10	11			7	4								5
1	2	3		5	6	12	8	9	10*	11		14	7†	4								6
1	2	3		5	6	12	8	9	10†	11		14	7	4*								7
1	2	3		5	6		8	9	10	11	12		7*	4								8
1	2†	3	14	5*	6		8	9	10	11	12			4	7							9
1		3	14	5	6	12	8	9*	10†	11		2		4	7							10
1		3		5		12	8	9*	10	11		2		4	7	6						11
1		3		5		12	8	9	10	11		2		4*	7	6						12
1		3		5	6	4	8	9	10	11		2		12	7*							13
1		3*		5	6	12	8	9	10	11		2	7	4								14
1	2			5	6		8	9*	10	11			7			3	12	4				15
1	2		14	5			8	9	12	11			7†			3	10*	4	6			16
1			14	5			8	9†	10	11			7		2*	3	12	4	6			17
1		3	14	5		12	8	9		11			7		2†		10*	4	6			18
1	2	3*		5			8	9	10	11	12		7					4	6			19
1	2	3*		5		12	8	9	10	11			7					4	6			20
1	2	3†		5			8	9	10*	11		14	7				12	4	6			21
1	2	3		5			8	9		11			7				10	4	6			22
1	2	3	12	5			8	9		11			7				10	4	6*			23
1	2	3	7	5	14		8	9*		11					12		10	4	6†			24
1	2	3	12	5	14		8	9		11			7				10*	4	6†			25
1	2	3	12	5			8†	9		11			7		14		10*	4	6			26
1	2	3	8	5				9	12	11			7		14		10†	4	6*			27
1	2	3	8	5				9	12	11			7				10*	4	6			28
1	2	3	8	5				9	12	11			7		14		10†	4	6*			29
1	2	3		5	6		8	9		11			7				10	4				30
1	2	3		5	6		8	9		11			7†		14	12	10*	4				31
1	2	3	12	5			8	9		11			7†		14		10*	4	6			32
1	2	3	12	5			8	9		11			7*		14		10†	4	6			33
1	2	3		5			8	9	10*	11			7		12			4	6			34
1	2	3	14	5			8	9	10	11			7†					4	6*			35
1	2	3		5	6		8	9	10†	11			7*		14	12		4				36
1	2	3		5			8	9*	12	11			7		14		10†	4	6			37
1	2	3		5	6*		8	9	10	11	12							4		7		38
1	2	3*		5	6		8	9	10	11	12							4		7		39
1	2	3		5			8	9	10	11								4	6	7		40
1	2	3*		5			8	9	10	11	12							4	6	7		41
1	2	3*		5			8	9	10	11	12							4	6	7		42
1	2	3		5			8	9	10	11	12							4*	6	7		43
1	2	3		5	6		8	9	10*	11							12	4		7		44
1	2†	3	12	5			8	9	10	11					14			4	6*	7		45
1		3*		5			8	9	10	11	12	2						4	6	7		46
46	38	43	11	46	13	2	43	46	31	45	17	12	36	5	6	9	14	28	6	9	—	

Substitutes: +1s 13s 2s 11s 3s 18s 2s 6s 4s 2s 2s 1s

Rumbelows Cup	First Round	Blackpool (h)	0-0
		(a)	1-1
	Second Round	Swindon T (h)	3-0
		(a)	0-4
FA Cup	First Round	York C (h)	1-1
		(a)	0-1

DARLINGTON

Player and Position	Ht	Wt	Birth Date	Birth Place	Source	Clubs	League App	Gls
Goalkeepers								
Matt Coddington	6 1	11 05	17 9 69	Lytham St Annes	Trainee	Middlesbrough	—	—
						Bury (loan)	—	—
						Halifax T (loan)	—	—
						Darlington	—	—
Mark Prudhoe	6 0	12 12	8 11 63	Washington	Apprentice	Sunderland	7	—
						Hartlepool U (loan)	3	—
						Birmingham C	1	—
						Walsall	26	—
						Doncaster R (loan)	5	—
						Sheffield W (loan)	—	—
						Grimsby T (loan)	8	—
						Hartlepool U (loan)	13	—
						Bristol C (loan)	3	—
						Carlisle U	34	—
						Darlington	58	—
Defenders								
Gary Coatsworth	6 1	11 06	7 10 68	Sunderland		Barnsley	6	—
						Darlington	12	1
David Corner	6 2	12 13	15 5 66	Sunderland	Apprentice	Sunderland	33	1
						Cardiff C (loan)	6	—
						Peterborough U (loan)	9	—
						Leyton Orient	4	—
						Darlington	15	—
Drew Coverdale	5 11	10 06	20 9 69	Teesside	Trainee	Middlesbrough	—	—
						Darlington	16	3
Allan Evans	6 1	12 13	12 10 56	Dunfermline	Dunfermline U	Dunfermline Ath	98	14
						Aston Villa	380	51
						Leicester C	14	—
						Darlington	1	—
Frank Gray†	5 10	11 10	27 10 54	Glasgow	Apprentice	Leeds U	193	17
						Nottingham F	81	5
						Leeds U	142	10
						Sunderland	146	8
						Darlington	43	7
Martin Griffiths‡			11 9 71	Teeside	Bristol C	Darlington	—	—
Les McJannet	5 8	10 04	2 8 61	Cumnock		Mansfield T	74	—
					Matlock T	Scarborough	34	—
						Darlington	65	5
Kevan Smith	6 3	12 02	13 12 59	Yarm	Stockton	Darlington	245	11
						Rotherham U	59	4
						Coventry C	6	—
						York C	31	5
						Darlington	46	4
Michael Trotter	6 3	12 02	27 10 69	Hartlepool	Trainee	Middlesbrough	—	—
						Doncaster R (loan)	3	—
						Darlington	24	2
Jimmy Willis	6 2	12 04	12 7 68	Liverpool	Blackburn R	Halifax T	—	—
						Stockport Co	10	—
						Darlington	78	4
Midfield								
Paul Emson‡	5 10	11 00	22 10 58	Lincoln	Brigg T	Derby C	127	13
						Grimsby T	97	15
						Wrexham	49	5
						Darlington	48	5
Gary Gill	5 10	11 09	28 11 64	Middlesbrough	Apprentice	Middlesbrough	77	2
						Hull C (loan)	1	—
						Darlington	36	8
Steve Marden-borough	5 8	11 00	11 9 64	Birmingham	Apprentice	Coventry C		
						Wolverhampton W	9	1
						Cambridge U (loan)	6	—
						Swansea C	36	7
						Newport Co	64	11
						Cardiff C	32	1
						Hereford U	27	—
						Darlington	35	1

DARLINGTON

Foundation: A football club was formed in Darlington as early as 1861 but the present club began in 1883 and reached the final of the Durham Senior Cup in their first season, losing to Sunderland in a replay after complaining that they had suffered from intimidation in the first. The following season Darlington won this trophy and for many years were one of the leading amateur clubs in their area.

First Football League game: 27 August, 1921, Division 3(N), v Halifax T (h) W 2-0 – Ward; Greaves, Barbour; Dickson (1), Sutcliffe, Malcolm; Dolphin, Hooper (1), Edmunds, Wolstenholme, Winship.

Did you know: Darlington were one of the first clubs to play two League games over a week-end when in January 1974 they drew 1-1 with Stockport County on Saturday and 0-0 with Torquay United on Sunday – both games at home.

Managers (and Secretary-managers)
Tom McIntosh 1902–11, W. L. Lane 1911–12*, Dick Jackson 1912–19, Jack English 1919–28, Jack Fairless 1928–33, George Collins 1933–36, George Brown 1936–38, Jackie Carr 1938–42, Jack Surtees 1942, Jack English 1945–46, Bill Forrest 1946–50, George Irwin 1950–52, Bob Gurney 1952–57, Dick Duckworth 1957–60, Eddie Carr 1960–64, Lol Morgan 1964–66, Jimmy Greenhalgh 1966–68, Ray Yeoman 1968–70, Len Richley 1970–71, Frank Brennan 1971, Ken Hale 1971–72, Allan Jones 1972, Ralph Brand 1972–73, Dick Conner 1973–74, Billy Horner 1974–76, Peter Madden 1976–78, Len Walker 1978–79, Billy Elliott 1979–83, Cyril Knowles 1983–87, Dave Booth 1987–89, Brian Little 1989–1991, Frank Gray June 1991–.

Player and Position	Ht	Wt	Birth Date	Birth Place	Source	Clubs	League App	Gls
Mick Tait	5 11	12 05	30 9 56	Wallsend	Apprentice	Oxford U	64	23
						Carlisle U	106	20
						Hull C	33	3
						Portsmouth	240	30
						Reading	99	9
						Darlington	45	2
Andy Toman	5 10	11 09	7 3 62	Northallerton	Bishop Auckland	Lincoln C	24	4
						Hartlepool U	112	28
						Darlington	43	5
Forwards								
John Borthwick	6 0	10 12	24 3 64	Hartlepool		Hartlepool U	117	15
						Darlington	46	10
David Cork	5 9	11 08	28 10 62	Doncaster	Apprentice	Arsenal	7	1
						Huddersfield T	110	25
						WBA (loan)	4	—
						Scunthorpe U	15	—
						Darlington	34	8
Tony Ellison			13 1 73	Bishop Auckland	Trainee	Darlington	13	3
David Geddis	6 0	11 08	12 3 58	Carlisle	Apprentice	Ipswich T	43	5
						Luton T (loan)	13	4
						Aston Villa	47	12
						Luton T (loan)	4	—
						Barnsley	45	24
						Birmingham C	46	18
						Brentford (loan)	4	—
						Shrewsbury T	39	11
						Swindon T	10	3
						Darlington	13	—
Phil Linacre*	6 0	11 00	17 5 62	Middlesbrough	Apprentice	Coventry C	—	—
						Hartlepool U	82	17
					Newcastle Blue Star			
						Darlington	8	3

Trainees
Cooper, Richard P; Filer, Simon; Gregan, Sean M; Ravenhall, Vincent; Shaw, Simon R; Weightman, Jason D.

**Non-Contract
Gary, Francis T.

Associated Schoolboys
Blake, Robert J; Carter, Stuart; Casey, Mark; Christie, Ross; Hack, Benjamin C; Malsbury, Gary; Middleton, James; Scott, Ryan; Theakston, Justin

Associated Schoolboys who have accepted the club's offer of a Traineeship/Contract
Cooper, Paul; Dalgarno, Scott A; Scollett, Matthew.

DERBY COUNTY 1990–91 *Back row (left to right):* Roy McFarland (Assistant Manager), Phil Gee, Michael Forsyth, Nick Pickering, Kevin Francis, Peter Shilton, Mark Wright, Martin Taylor, Mick Harford, Ted McMinn, Trevor Hebberd, Paul Williams, Gordon Guthrie (Physiotherapist). *Front row:* Mark Patterson, Steve Hayward, Jonathan Davidson, Mel Sage, Dean Saunders, Arthur Cox (Manager), Gary Micklewhite, Steve Cross, Geraint Williams, Craig Ramage, Robert Briscoe.

Division 2 — **DERBY COUNTY**

Baseball Ground, Shaftesbury Crescent, Derby DE3 8NB.
Telephone Derby (0332) 40105. Ramtique Sports Shop: (0332) 292081. Clubcall: 0898 121187.

Ground capacity: 24,000 (16,000 seats).

Record attendance: 41,826 v Tottenham H, Division 1, 20 September 1969.

Record receipts: £135,789 v West Ham U, Littlewoods Cup, 5th rd (replay), 24 January 1990.

Pitch measurements: 110yd × 75yd.

President:

Chairman: I. R. Maxwell MC. *Vice-chairman:* I. R. C. Maxwell.

Managing Director: A. S. Webb.

Directors: F. W. Fern, J. N. Kirkland, W. Hart, G. Glossop, C. R. Charlton, C. M. McKerrow, B. E. Fearn, M. McGarry.

Manager: Arthur Cox. *Assistant Manager:* Roy McFarland.

Physio: Gordon Guthrie.

Secretary: Michael Dunford. *Marketing Manager:* C. Tunnicliffe. (Tel. 0332 40105).

Year Formed: 1884. *Turned Professional:* 1884. *Ltd Co.:* 1896.

Club Nickname: 'The Rams'.

Previous Grounds: 1884–95, Racecourse Ground; 1895, Baseball Ground.

Record League Victory: 9-0 v Wolverhampton W, Division 1, 10 January 1891 – Bunyan; Archie Goodall, Roberts; Walker, Chalmers, Roulston (1); Bakewell, McLachlan, Johnny Goodall (1), Holmes (2), McMillan (5). 9-0 v Sheffield W, Division 1, 21 January 1899 – Fryer; Methven, Staley; Cox, Archie Goodall, May; Oakden (1), Bloomer (6), Boag, McDonald (1), Allen. (1 og).

Record Cup Victory: 12-0 v Finn Harps, UEFA Cup, 1st rd 1st leg, 15 September 1976 – Moseley; Thomas, Nish, Rioch (1), McFarland, Todd (King), Macken, Gemmill, Hector (5), George (3), James (3).

Record Defeat: 2-11 v Everton, FA Cup 1st rd, 1889–90.

Most League Points (2 for a win): 63, Division 2, 1968–69 and Division 3 (N), 1955–56 and 1956–57.

Most League Points (3 for a win): 84, Division 3, 1985–86 and Division 3, 1986–87.

Most League Goals: 111, Division 3 (N), 1956–57.

Highest League Scorer in Season: Jack Bowers, 37, Division 1, 1930–31 and Ray Straw, 37 Division 3 (N), 1956–57.

Most League Goals in Total Aggregate: Steve Bloomer, 292, 1892–1906 and 1910–14.

Most Capped Player: Peter Shilton, 34 (125), England.

Most League Appearances: Kevin Hector, 486, 1966–78 and 1980–82.

Record Transfer Fee Received: £2,900,000 from Liverpool for Dean Saunders, July 1991.

Record Transfer Fee Paid: £1,000,000 to Oxford U for Dean Saunders, October 1988.

Football League Record: 1888 Founder Member of the Football League; 1907–12 Division 2; 1912–14 Division 1; 1914–15 Division 2; 1915–21 Division 1; 1921–26 Division 2; 1926–53 Division 1; 1953–55 Division 2; 1955–57 Division 3 (N); 1957–69 Division 2; 1969–80 Division 1; 1980–84 Division 2; 1984–86 Division 3; 1986–87 Division 2; 1987–91 Division 1; 1991– Division 2.

Honours: Football League: Division 1 – Champions 1971–72, 1974–75; Runners-up 1895–96, 1929–30, 1935–36; Division 2 – Champions 1911–12, 1914–15, 1968–69, 1986–87; Runners-up 1925–26; Division 3 (N) Champions 1956–57; Runners-up 1955–56. *FA Cup:* Winners 1945–46; Runners-up 1897–98, 1898–99, 1902–03. *Football League Cup:* Semi-final 1967–68. *Texaco Cup:* 1971–72. **European Competitions:** *European Cup:* 1972–73, 1975–76; *UEFA Cup:* 1974–75, 1976–77.

Colours: White shirts with black collar and red flash on sleeve, black shorts with red flash on one side, white stocking, black turnover. **Change colours:** Red and black striped shirts, red shorts, red and black stockings.

DERBY COUNTY 1990–91 LEAGUE RECORD

Match No.	Date		Venue	Opponents	Result		H/T Score	Lg. Pos.	Goalscorers	Atten-dance
1	Aug	25	A	Chelsea	L	1-2	0-1	—	Saunders	24,652
2		29	H	Sheffield U	D	1-1	0-0	—	Saunders	18,011
3	Sept	1	H	Wimbledon	D	1-1	0-1	16	Saunders (pen)	12,469
4		8	A	Tottenham H	L	0-3	0-1	19		29,614
5		15	H	Aston Villa	L	0-2	0-1	20		19,024
6		22	A	Norwich C	L	1-2	0-0	19	Patterson	13,258
7		29	H	Crystal Palace	L	0-2	0-1	20		15,202
8	Oct	6	A	Liverpool	L	0-2	0-1	20		37,076
9		20	H	Manchester C	D	1-1	0-1	19	Saunders	17,884
10		27	A	Southampton	W	1-0	1-0	20	Harford	16,328
11	Nov	3	H	Luton T	W	2-1	1-0	19	Saunders (pen), Callaghan	15,008
12		10	H	Manchester U	D	0-0	0-0	19		21,115
13		17	A	Leeds U	L	0-3	0-2	19		27,868
14		24	H	Nottingham F	W	2-1	1-1	17	Ramage, Saunders	21,729
15	Dec	1	A	Sunderland	W	2-1	1-0	14	Saunders, Harford	21,212
16		15	H	Chelsea	L	4-6	1-3	15	Saunders 2, Hebberd, Micklewhite	15,057
17		23	H	QPR	D	1-1	0-1	—	Saunders	16,429
18		26	A	Arsenal	L	0-3	0-2	17		25,538
19		29	A	Everton	L	0-2	0-0	18		25,361
20	Jan	1	H	Coventry C	D	1-1	1-1	18	Harford	15,741
21		12	A	Wimbledon	L	1-3	0-0	18	Harford	4724
22		20	H	Tottenham H	L	0-1	0-1	—		17,747
23		26	A	Sheffield U	L	0-1	0-0	19		18,390
24	Feb	2	A	Aston Villa	L	2-3	1-1	20	Harford, Sage	21,852
25		23	H	Norwich C	D	0-0	0-0	20		14,102
26	Mar	2	H	Sunderland	D	3-3	2-3	20	Saunders 3 (1 pen)	16,027
27		16	A	Crystal Palace	L	1-2	0-0	20	Micklewhite	14,752
28		23	H	Liverpool	L	1-7	1-3	20	Saunders (pen)	20,531
29		30	H	Arsenal	L	0-2	0-1	20		18,397
30	Apr	1	A	QPR	D	1-1	1-0	20	Harford	12,036
31		10	A	Nottingham F	L	0-1	0-0	—		25,109
32		13	A	Coventry C	L	0-3	0-0	20		11,961
33		16	A	Manchester U	L	1-3	1-1	—	Williams P	32,776
34		20	A	Manchester C	L	1-2	0-1	20	Harford	24,037
35		23	H	Leeds U	L	0-1	0-1	—		12,666
36	May	4	H	Southampton	W	6-2	3-1	20	Williams P 3 (1 pen), Saunders 2, Phillips	11,680
37		8	H	Everton	L	2-3	1-1		Harford (pen), Saunders	12,403
38		11	A	Luton T	L	0-2	0-1	20		12,889

Final League Position: 20

GOALSCORERS

League (37): Saunders 17 (4 pens), Harford 8 (1 pen), Williams P 4 (1 pen), Micklewhite 2, Callaghan 1, Hebberd 1, Patterson 1, Phillips 1, Ramage 1, Sage 1.
Rumbelows Cup (10): Harford 3, Saunders 3, Ramage 2, Micklewhite 1, own goal 1.
FA Cup (0).

Shilton	Sage	Forsyth	Williams G	Wright	Davidson	Micklewhite	Saunders	Harford	Ramage	Williams P	Patterson	Hebberd	Watson	Francis	Callaghan	Cross	Gee	Pickering	Briscoe	Kavanagh	Taylor	McMinn	Wilson	Phillips	Hayward	Match No.
1	2	3	4	5	6	7	8	9	10	11*	12															1
1	2	3	4	5		7	8	9	6	11		10														2
1	2	3	4	5		7*	8	9	10†	11		12	6	14												3
1	2	3	4	5		7*	8	9	10†	11	14	12	6													4
1		3	4	5		7	8	9		11	2	10	6													5
1	12	3	4	5	11	7†	8	9		2*	10		6	14												6
1	2	3	4	5		7*	8	9		10		12	6		11											7
1	2	6	4	5		7	8	9	10	3					11											8
1	2	6	4	5		7	8	9	10*			12			11	3										9
1	2	6	4	5		7	8	9	10						11	3										10
1	2	6	4	5		7	8		10						11	3	9									11
1	2*	6	4	5		7	8	9	10						11	3		12								12
1		6	4	5		7	8	9	10*		14	12			11	3†		2								13
1		6	4*	5		7	8	9	12		3	10			11			2								14
1		6		5			8	9	4	2		10			11	3		7								15
1	2	6		5		7	8	9	4*	12		10			11	3										16
1	2	6		5		7	8	9	12	4†	10*				11	3		14								17
	2	6		5	12	7*	8	9	10	4†					11	3		14		1						18
	2	6		5		7†	8	9	10*	4					11	3		12	14	1						19
	2	6		5	12		8	9	10	4*					11	3		7		1						20
1	2			5	12		8	9	4			10		7		3*		11	6							21
1	2		4	5		7*	8	9	12			10				3		11	6							22
1	2	6	4	5		7	8	9	10							3						11				23
1	2	6	4	5		7	8	9	10							3						11				24
1	2	6	4	5		7	8	9	12							3						11*	10			25
1	2	6	4	5		7	8	9								3						11	10			26
1	2	6	4	5		7	8			11						3						9	10			27
1	2	6	4	5		7	8	9	12							3						11	10*			28
1	2	6	4	5		7	8	9								3						11	10			29
1	2	6	4	5		7	8	9								3		11					10			30
1	2	6	4	5†		7	8	9	12							3					14	11*	10			31
1	2	6	4	5		7	8	9								3						11	10			32
	2	6	4	5		7	8	9	11							3				1			10			33
	2		4	5		7	8	9		11	12			14		3		6†		1			10*			34
	2	3*	4	5		7†	8	9	10	12	14									1		11		6		35
1	2	3	4	5*		7	8	9	10									12				11		6		36
	2		4	5		7†	8	9	10	12										1		11	3*	6	14	37
1	2	3	4	5		7	8	9	10*	6	12			14								11†				38
31	33	35	31	37	2	35	38	36	15	17	6	12	5	—	12	19	1	12	2	5	7	13	11	3	—	
+1s			+3s						+2s	+2s	5s	9s		2s				2s	1s	1s	1s	6s			1s	

Rumbelows Cup	Second Round	Carlisle (a)	1-1
		(h)	1-0
	Third Round	Sunderland (h)	6-0
	Fourth Round	Sheffield W (a)	1-1
		(h)	1-2
FA Cup	Third Round	Newcastle U (a)	0-2

DERBY COUNTY

Player and Position	Ht	Wt	Birth Date	Birth Place	Source	Clubs	League App	Gls
Goalkeepers								
Peter Shilton	6 0	14 00	18 9 49	Leicester	Apprentice	Leicester C	286	1
						Stoke C	110	—
						Nottingham F	202	—
						Southampton	188	—
						Derby Co	144	—
Martin Taylor	5 11	12 04	9 12 66	Tamworth	Mile Oak R	Derby Co	10	—
						Carlisle U (loan)	10	—
						Scunthorpe U (loan)	8	—
Defenders								
Robert Briscoe	5 8	10 13	4 9 69	Derby	Trainee	Derby Co	13	1
Jonathan Davidson	5 8	11 11	1 3 70	Cheadle	Trainee	Derby Co	11	—
Mike Forsyth	5 11	12 02	20 3 66	Liverpool	Apprentice	WBA	29	—
						Derby Co	191	4
Mark Patterson	5 10	11 05	13 9 68	Leeds	Trainee	Carlisle U	22	—
						Derby Co	21	1
Justin Phillips	6 3	14 07	17 12 71	Derby	Trainee	Derby Co	3	1
Steve Round	5 10	11 00	9 11 70	Buxton	Trainee	Derby Co	—	—
Mel Sage	5 8	10 04	24 3 64	Gillingham	Apprentice	Gillingham	132	5
						Derby Co	123	4
Mark Wright	6 3	12 01	1 8 63	Dorchester	Amateur	Oxford U	10	—
						Southampton	170	7
						Derby Co	144	10
Midfield								
Steve Cross	5 10	11 05	22 12 59	Wolverhampton	Apprentice	Shrewsbury T	262	34
						Derby Co	69	3
Steve Hayward	5 10	11 07	8 9 71	Walsall	Trainee	Derby Co	4	—
Trevor Hebberd	6 0	11 04	19 6 58	Winchester	Apprentice	Southampton	97	7
						Bolton W (loan)	6	—
						Leicester C (loan)	4	1
						Oxford U	260	37
						Derby Co	81	10
Jason Kavanagh	5 9	11 00	23 11 71	Birmingham	Birmingham C Schoolboys	Derby Co	11	—
Ted McMinn	6 0	12 11	28 9 62	Castle Douglas	Glenafton Ath	Queen of South	62	5
						Rangers	63	4
					Seville	Derby Co	67	5
Gary Micklewhite	5 7	10 04	21 3 61	Southwark	Apprentice	Manchester U	—	—
						QPR	106	11
						Derby Co	202	29
Nick Pickering	6 0	12 02	4 8 63	Newcastle	Apprentice	Sunderland	179	18
						Coventry C	78	9
						Derby Co	44	3
Steve Taylor	5 8	10 04	10 1 70	Holbrook	Trainee	Derby Co	—	—
Peter Weston	5 7	10 12	13 2 74	Stoke	Trainee	Derby Co	—	—
Geraint Williams	5 7	10 06	5 1 62	Treorchy	Apprentice	Bristol R	141	8
						Derby Co	238	7
Paul Williams	5 11	12 00	26 3 71	Burton	Trainee	Derby Co	29	5
						Lincoln C (loan)	3	—
Ian Wilson*	5 7	10 10	27 3 58	Aberdeen	Elgin C	Leicester C	285	17
						Everton	34	1
					Besiktas	Derby Co	11	—

DERBY COUNTY

Foundation: Derby County was formed by members of the Derbyshire County Cricket Club in 1884, when football was booming in the area and the cricketers thought that a football club would help boost finances for the summer game. To begin with, they sported the cricket club's colours of amber, chocolate and pale blue, and went into the game at the top immediately entering the FA Cup.

First Football League game: 8 September, 1888, Football League, v Bolton W (a) W 6-3 – Marshall; Latham, Ferguson, Williamson; Monks, W. Roulstone; Bakewell (2), Cooper (2), Higgins, H. Plackett, L. Plackett (2).

Did you know: When Derby clinched the Second Division championship with a 1-0 win at Millwall, 12 April 1969, they wore red shirts and black shorts loaned to them by the home club. They had intended playing in all-white but Millwall had also decided on that strip.

Managers (and Secretary-managers)
Harry Newbould 1896–1906, Jimmy Methven 1906–22, Cecil Potter 1922–25, George Jobey 1925–41, Ted Magner 1944–46, Stuart McMillan 1946–53, Jack Barker 1953–55, Harry Storer 1955–62, Tim Ward 1962–67, Brian Clough 1967–73, Dave Mackay 1973–76, Colin Murphy 1977, Tommy Docherty 1977–79, Colin Addison 1979–82, Johnny Newman 1982, Peter Taylor 1982–84, Roy McFarland 1984, Arthur Cox May 1984– .

Player and Position	Ht	Wt	Birth Date	Birth Place	Source	Clubs	League App	Gls
Forwards								
Martyn Chalk	5 6	10 00	30 8 69	Louth	Louth U	Derby Co	—	—
Phil Gee	5 9	10 04	19 12 64	Pelsall	Gresley R	Derby Co	105	25
Mick Harford	6 2	12 09	12 2 59	Sunderland	Lambton St BC	Lincoln C	115	41
						Newcastle U	19	4
						Bristol C	30	11
						Birmingham C	92	25
						Luton T	139	57
						Derby Co	52	12
Craig Ramage	5 9	11 08	30 3 70	Derby	Trainee	Derby Co	29	2
						Wigan Ath (loan)	10	2
Dean Saunders	5 8	10 06	21 6 64	Swansea	Apprentice	Swansea C	49	12
						Cardiff C (loan)	4	—
						Brighton & HA	72	21
						Oxford U	59	22
						Derby Co	106	42
Kris Sleeuwenhoek	5 7	10 00	2 10 71	Oldham	Wolves Schoolboys	Derby Co	—	—
Robert Straw	5 9	11 08	4 11 70	Derby	Trainee	Derby Co	—	—
John Symonds‡	5 11	11 07	3 9 70	Coventry	Trainee	Derby Co	—	—

Trainees
Allen, Craig; Blount, Mark; Carsley, Lee K; Clarke, Mark A; Darkes, Craig J; Hillyer, Jamie A; Lewis, Colin A; Moore, Michael T; Smith, Matthew J; Sturridge, Dean C; Thomson, Jon M; Wilkinson, Robert N; Wilson, Kevin P.

**Non-Contract
White, Jason G.

Associated Schoolboys
Davies, William; Filik, Robert; Flindall, Andrew M; Glover, Richard; Johnson, Brian A; Joseph, Marc; McDermott, Thomas; McHugh, Edward T; Matthews, Martin; Rafferty, Brian; Rutter, James; Tunstall, Jamie A; Warren, Matthew T.J; White, Alan; Wood, Mark; Wrack, Darren; Wright, Nicholas J.
Associated Schoolboys who have accepted the club's offer of a Traineeship/Contract
Anderson, Wayne S; Burton, Michael; Geddis, Stewart R; Stallard, Mark; Wood, Mark.
**Non-Contract Players who are retained must be re-signed before they are eligible to play in League matches.

202

DONCASTER ROVERS 1990–91 *Back row (left to right):* Dave Blakey (General Manager), Eric Brailsford (Physiotherapist), Colin Douglas, Andy Holmes, David Jones, Paul Crichton, Mark Samways, John Muir, Brendan Ormsby, Lee Boyle, Jim Golze (Youth Team Coach). *Centre row:* Shane Reddish, Kevin Noteman, Rufus Brevett, Max Nicholson, Steve Beaglehole (Assistant Manager), Billy Bremner (Manager), Lee Turnbull, David Harle, Eddie Gormley, Grant Morrow. *Front row:* Chris Redhead, Mark Rankine, Mark Place, Vince Brockie, Steve Adams, John Stiles.

Division 4   DONCASTER ROVERS

Belle Vue Ground, Doncaster. Telephone Doncaster (0302) 539441.

Ground capacity: 7794.

Record attendance: 37,149 v Hull C, Division 3 (N), 2 October 1948.

Record receipts: £22,000 v QPR, FA Cup 3rd rd, 5 January 1985.

Pitch measurements: 110yd × 76yd.

Chairman: J. J. Burke. *Vice-chairman:* K. Chappell.

Directors: J. Ryan, M. J. H. Collett, W. Turner.

Manager: Billy Bremner. *Assistant Manager:* Steve Beaglehole.

General Manager: Dave Blakey.

Secretary: Mrs K. J. Oldale. *Physio:* Eric Brailsford. *Youth Team Coach:* Jim Golze.

Doncaster Rovers Football Club Ltd.
(Founded 1879)

Year Formed: 1879. *Turned Professional:* 1885. *Ltd Co.:* 1905 and 1920.

Club Nickname: 'Rovers'.

Previous Grounds: 1880–1916, Intake Ground; 1920–22, Benetthorpe Ground; 1922, Low Pasture, Belle Vue.

Record League Victory: 10-0 v Darlington, Division 4, 25 January 1964 – Potter; Raine, Meadows; Windross (1), White, Ripley (2); Robinson, Book (2), Hale (4), Jeffrey, Broadbent (1).

Record Cup Victory: 7-0 v Blyth Spartans, FA Cup, 1st rd, 27 November 1937 – Imrie; Shaw, Rodgers; McFarlane, Bycroft, Cyril Smith; Burton (1), Kilourhy (4), Morgan (2), Malam, Dutton.

Record Defeat: 0-12 v Small Heath, Division 2, 11 April 1903.

Most League Points (2 for a win): 72, Division 3 (N), 1946–47.

Most League Points (3 for a win): 85, Division 4, 1983–84.

Most League Goals: 123, Division 3 (N), 1946–47.

Highest League Scorer in Season: Clarrie Jordan, 42, Division 3 (N), 1946–47.

Most League Goals in Total Aggregate: Tom Keetley, 180, 1923–29.

Most Capped Player: Len Graham, 14, Northern Ireland.

Most League Appearances: Fred Emery, 417, 1925–36.

Record Transfer Fee Received: £200,000 from Leeds U for Ian Snodin, May 1985.

Record Transfer Fee Paid: £60,000 to Stirling Albion for John Philliben, March 1984.

Football League Record: 1901 Elected to Division 2; 1903 Failed re-election; 1904 Re-elected; 1905 Failed re-election; 1923 Re-elected to Division 3 (N); 1935–37 Division 2; 1937–47 Division 3 (N); 1947–48 Division 2; 1948–50 Division 3 (N); 1950–58 Division 2; 1958–59 Division 3; 1959–66 Division 4; 1966–67 Division 3; 1967–69 Division 4; 1969–71 Division 3; 1971–81 Division 4; 1981–83 Division 3; 1983–84 Division 4; 1984–88 Division 3; 1988– Division 4.

Honours: Football League: Division 2 best season: 7th, 1901–02; Division 3 (N) Champions 1934–35, 1946–47, 1949–50; Runners-up 1937–38, 1938–39; Division 4 – Champions 1965–66, 1968–69; Runners-up 1983–84. Promoted 1980–81 (3rd). *FA Cup:* best season: 5th rd, 1951–52, 1953–54, 1954–55, 1955–56. *Football League Cup:* best season: 5th rd, 1975–76.

Colours: Home: White shirts red trim, white shorts red quarter, white stockings, red turnover. Away: Green shirts with white trim, green shorts white quarter, green stockings white turnovers. **Change colours:** All green.

DONCASTER ROVERS 1990–91 LEAGUE RECORD

Match No.	Date		Venue	Opponents	Result		H/T Score	Lg. Pos.	Goalscorers	Atten- dance
1	Aug	25	A	Carlisle U	W	3-2	2-1	—	Noteman, Jones, Muir	4218
2	Sept	1	H	Wrexham	W	3-1	2-1	1	Muir, Noteman, Ormsby	2101
3		8	A	Halifax T	W	1-0	0-0	1	Jones	2394
4		15	A	Rochdale	W	3-0	2-0	1	Muir 2, Gormley	2607
5		18	H	Walsall	W	2-0	1-0	—	Muir 2	3925
6		22	A	York C	L	1-3	0-1	1	Noteman	3742
7		29	H	Darlington	L	0-1	0-1	2		3695
8	Oct	2	A	Torquay U	L	0-1	0-1	—		3312
9		7	A	Scarborough	L	1-2	0-1	—	Brockie (pen)	2156
10		13	H	Hartlepool U	D	2-2	1-0	7	Muir 2	2801
11		20	H	Lincoln C	W	1-0	0-0	5	Grayson	2968
12		23	A	Cardiff C	W	2-0	1-0	—	Gormley (pen), Grayson	3891
13		27	A	Chesterfield	L	1-2	1-2	4	Muir	4389
14	Nov	3	H	Gillingham	D	1-1	0-1	6	Rankine	2502
15		10	A	Peterborough U	D	1-1	0-0	6	Grayson	4691
16		24	H	Blackpool	W	1-0	1-0	5	Grayson	2113
17	Dec	1	H	Aldershot	W	3-0	0-0	4	Turnbull 3	2093
18		15	H	Scunthorpe U	D	1-1	1-0	3	Turnbull	3963
19		21	A	Stockport Co	D	0-0	0-0	—		3347
20		26	H	Maidstone U	W	3-0	1-0	1	Brevett 2 (1 pen), Grayson	2717
21		29	H	Hereford U	W	3-1	2-0	1	Noteman, Ormsby, Muir	3170
22	Jan	1	A	Northampton T	D	0-0	0-0	1		5270
23		12	A	Wrexham	L	1-2	0-1	4	Harle	1850
24		19	H	Carlisle U	W	4-0	0-0	3	Gormley 2, Morrow, Brevett	2447
25		25	H	Rochdale	W	1-0	1-0	—	Noteman	3436
26	Feb	2	H	Walsall	L	0-1	0-0	2		3805
27		5	H	York C	D	2-2	0-0	—	Turnbull 2 (1 pen)	2916
28		16	A	Blackpool	L	0-2	0-0	3		3533
29		22	H	Peterborough U	L	0-2	0-0	—		2995
30		26	H	Burnley	W	2-1	0-1	—	Brockie (pen), Muir	3080
31	Mar	2	A	Aldershot	D	1-1	0-0	3	Harle (pen)	1728
32		8	H	Scunthorpe U	L	2-3	1-3	—	Whitehurst, Muir	4015
33		16	A	Darlington	D	1-1	1-0	7	Ormsby	4410
34		24	H	Scarborough	L	0-2	0-1	—		2734
35		30	A	Maidstone U	W	1-0	1-0	8	Rankine	1512
36	Apr	1	H	Stockport Co	W	1-0	0-0	7	Ashurst	3372
37		6	A	Hereford U	D	1-1	1-1	8	Noteman	2013
38		13	H	Northampton T	W	2-1	1-0	8	Gormley, Muir	2939
39		16	A	Hartlepool U	D	1-1	0-0	—	Ormsby	3365
40		20	A	Lincoln C	D	0-0	0-0	9		3363
41		23	H	Halifax T	L	1-2	1-1	—	Ormsby (pen)	2360
42		27	H	Cardiff C	D	1-1	1-1	10	Noteman	2227
43		30	A	Burnley	L	0-1	0-0	—		10,410
44	May	4	H	Chesterfield	L	0-1	0-1	11		2649
45		7	H	Torquay U	D	1-1	1-1	—	Adams	1642
46		11	A	Gillingham	L	0-2	0-1	11		2653

Final League Position: 11

GOALSCORERS

League (56): Muir 13, Noteman 7, Turnbull 6 (1 pen), Gormley 5 (1 pen), Grayson 5, Ormsby 5 (1 pen), Brevett 3 (1 pen), Brockie 2 (2 pens), Harle 2 (1 pen), Jones 2, Rankine 2, Adams 1, Ashurst 1, Morrow 1, Whitehurst 1.
Rumbelows Cup (3): Brockie 1 (pen), Jones 1, Muir 1.
FA Cup (3): Gormley 1, Noteman 1, Rankine 1.

Crichton	Rankine	Brevett	Holmes	Ormsby	Douglas	Gormley	Stiles	Muir	Jones D	Noteman	Harle	Mardon	Turnbull	Brockie	Morrow	Adams	Place	Grayson	Jones M	Ashurst	Samways	Reddish	Rowe	Parsley	Whitehurst	Smalley	Bennett	Cullen	Match No.
1	2	3	4	5	6	7	8	9	10	11																			1
1	2	3	4	5	6	7*	8	9	10	11	12																		2
1	2	3	4	5	6	7	8	9	10	11																			3
1	2	3	4		6	7	8	9	10	11		5																	4
1	2	3	4		6	7	8†	9	10*	11		5	12		14														5
1	2	3	4		6	7	8*	9		11	12	5†	10		14														6
1	2	3	4	5	6	7†	8	9		11			12		14	10*													7
1	2	3	4	5	6	7	8	9		11					10*	12													8
1	2	3	4†	5	6	7	8	9		11	12		14			10*													9
1	2	3		5	6	7	8	9		11	12							4	10*										10
1	2	3		5	6	7	8	9		11								4	10										11
1	2	3		5	6	7	8	9		11								4	10										12
1	2	3		5	6*	7	8	9		11			12					4	10										13
1	2	3		5	6	7	8	9		11			12					4	10*										14
1	2	3		5	6	7	8	14		11*			12					9	10†	4									15
1	2	3		5	6	7		9		11			8					10		4									16
1	2	3		5	6		8	9		11			7					10		4									17
1	2	3		5	6	7		9		11			12	8				10*		4									18
	2	3		5	6	12	8	9		11			7					10*		4	1								19
	2	3		5	6		8	9		11			7					10		4	1								20
	2	3		5	6	12	8	9		11			7*					10		4	1								21
	2	3		5	6	12	8	9*		11			7					10		4	1								22
	2	3		5	6	12	8*	9		11			7	14				10†		4	1								23
	2	3		5	6		8	9		11†			7	14				10*	12	4	1								24
	2*	3		5	6		8	9		11			7	14				10	12†	4	1								25
		3		5	6	7	8	9*	10†	11		2	12							4	1	14							26
		3		5	6	7	8*	9		11		2	12					10		4	1								27
		3	7	5	6	12		9*		11			14					10		4	1	2	8†						28
	7*	3	12	5	6		8	9		11			14					10†		4	1					2			29
		3		5	6	12	8			11			7	14				10*		4	1	2†			9				30
		3	2†	5	6	12	8*	10		11			7							4	1	14			9				31
		3		5	6	12	8*	10		11			7							4	1	2			9				32
1		3		5	6	12	8	10*		11			7							4					9	2			33
1	10	3		5	6	12	8*			11			7							4					9	2			34
	11	3		5	6	12	8*	10					7†	14						4	1				9	2			35
	11	3		5	6	7	8	10												4	1				9	2			36
	11	3		5	6	12	8	10*					7†							4	1				9	2			37
			4	5	6	12	8			11			14					10†			1	3	7*		9	2			38
			4	5	6	7	8	10		11											1	3			9	2			39
			10	5	6	12	8	9		11			7†		14					4	1	3*				2			40
		3	7	5	6	14	8	10		11†										4	1	12			9	2*			41
		3	7	5	6*	12	8	10												4	1	11			9	2			42
		3	7	5	6	12	8	10							9*					4	1	11				2			43
		3	7	5	6	12	8†	10							14					4	1	11*				2	9		44
		3	7	5	6			10†		11					14					4	1	8*		12	9	2			45
			7	5	6										14						1	3		12	9	2*		4	46
20	40	27	10	43	46	32	37	35	7	41	16	3	13	1	9	2	1	17	5	29	26	9	3	2	13	14	1	1	
	+				+		+	+	+	+			+	+	+	+		+				+	+	+		+			
	1s				8s		4s	6s	1s	6s			6s	6s	5s	3s		6s				2s	1s	1s		1s			

Limber — Match No. 46(8); Holland — Match No. 46(10†); Nicholson — Match No. 46(11).

Rumbelows Cup	First Round	Rotherham U (h)	2-6
		(a)	1-2
FA Cup	First Round	Chester C (a)	2-2
		(h)	1-2

DONCASTER ROVERS

Player and Position	Ht	Wt	Birth Date	Birth Place	Source	Clubs	League App	Gls
Goalkeepers								
Paul Crichton	6 1	12 05	3 10 68	Pontefract	Apprentice	Nottingham F	—	—
						Notts Co (loan)	5	—
						Darlington (loan)	5	—
						Peterborough U (loan)	4	—
						Darlington (loan)	3	—
						Swindon T (loan)	4	—
						Rotherham U (loan)	6	—
						Torquay U (loan)	13	—
						Peterborough U	47	—
						Doncaster R	20	—
Chris Neville‡	6 0	11 10	20 10 70	Cambridge	Trainee	Ipswich T	1	—
						Doncaster R	—	—
Mark Samways	6 0	11 12	11 11 68	Doncaster	Trainee	Doncaster R	95	—
						Leeds U (loan)	—	—
Defenders								
Jack Ashurst‡	6 0	12 04	12 10 54	Renton	Apprentice	Sunderland	140	4
						Blackpool	53	3
						Carlisle U	194	2
						Leeds U	89	1
					Bridlington	Doncaster R	73	1
						Doncaster R	29	1
Lee Boyle			22 1 72	North Shields	Ipswich T	Doncaster R	—	—
Vincent Brockie*	5 8	10 10	2 2 69	Greenock	Trainee	Leeds U	2	—
						Doncaster R	54	7
David Cullen§			10 1 73	Durham	Trainee	Doncaster R	1	—
Colin Douglas	6 1	11 00	9 9 62	Hurtford	Celtic BC	Celtic	—	—
						Doncaster R	212	48
						Rotherham U	83	4
						Doncaster R	137	4
Andy Holmes*	6 1	12 12	7 1 69	Stoke	Apprentice	Stoke C	8	—
						Doncaster R	11	—
Brendan Ormsby	5 11	11 09	1 10 60	Birmingham	Apprentice	Aston Villa	117	4
						Leeds U	46	5
						Shrewsbury T (loan)	1	—
						Doncaster R	43	5
Mark Place‡	5 11	10 08	16 11 69		Trainee	Mansfield T	15	—
						Doncaster R	1	—
Shane Reddish	5 10	11 10	5 5 71	Bolsover	Mansfield T	Doncaster R	12	—
Paul Smalley‡	5 11	11 00	17 11 66	Nottingham	Apprentice	Notts Co	118	—
						Scunthorpe U	86	1
						Blackpool (loan)	6	—
						Leeds U	—	—
						Doncaster R	14	—
Midfield								
Eddie Gormley	5 7	10 07	23 10 68	Dublin	Bray W	Tottenham H	—	—
						Chesterfield (loan)	4	—
						Motherwell (loan)	—	—
						Shrewsbury T (loan)	—	—
						Doncaster R	40	5
David Harle	5 9	10 07	15 8 63	Denaby	Apprentice	Doncaster R	61	3
						Exeter C	43	6
						Doncaster R	83	17
						Leeds U	3	—
						Bristol C (loan)	8	—
						Bristol C	15	2
						Scunthorpe U	89	10
						Peterborough U	22	2
						Doncaster R	32	2
Mark Rankine	5 10	11 01	30 9 69	Doncaster	Trainee	Doncaster R	140	17
Chris Redhead	5 8	9 12	19 9 71	Newcastle	Trainee	Doncaster R	—	—
Brian Rowe			24 10 71	Sunderland	Trainee	Doncaster R	4	—
John Stiles	5 9	10 12	6 5 64	Manchester	Vancouver W	Leeds U	65	2
						Doncaster R	79	2

DONCASTER ROVERS

Foundation: In 1879 Mr. Albert Jenkins got together a team to play a game against the Yorkshire Institution for the Deaf. The players stuck together as Doncaster Rovers joining the Midland Alliance in 1889 and the Midland Counties League in 1891.

First Football League game: 7 September, 1901, Division 2, v Burslem Port Vale (h) D 3-3 – Eggett; Simpson, Layton; Longden, Jones, Wright; Langham, Murphy, Price, Goodson (2), Bailey (1).

Did you know: Rovers record breaking goalscoring feats of 1946–47 tend to overshadow the fact that in 1934–35 they scored 21 goals in one run of five games with Albert Turner getting 10 of them including five in a 7-1 win over New Brighton.

Managers (and Secretary-managers)
Arthur Porter 1920–21*, Harry Tufnell 1921–22, Arthur Porter 1922–23, Dick Ray 1923–27, David Menzies 1928–36, Fred Emery 1936–40, Bill Marsden 1944–46, Jackie Bestall 1946–49, Peter Doherty 1949–58, Jack Hodgson and Sid Bycroft (joint managers) 1958, Jack Crayston 1958–59 (continued as Sec-Man to 1961), Jackie Bestall (TM) 1959–60, Norman Curtis 1960–61, Danny Malloy 1961–62, Oscar Hold 1962–64, Bill Leivers 1964–66, Keith Kettleborough 1966–67, George Raynor 1967–68, Lawrie McMenemy 1968–71, Maurice Setters 1971–74, Stan Anderson 1975–78, Billy Bremner 1978–85, Dave Cusack 1985–87, Dave Mackay 1987–89, Billy Bremner July 1989– .

Player and Position	Ht	Wt	Birth Date	Birth Place	Source	Clubs	League App	Gls
Forwards								
Steve Adams*	5 8	10 12	7 5 59	Sheffield	Worksop T	Scarborough	48	5
						Doncaster R	35	2
Craig Bennett§			29 8 73	Doncaster	Trainee	Doncaster R	2	—
Nicholas Gallagher‡			28 1 71	Boston		Doncaster R	1	—
Simon Holland‡			26 3 73	Sunderland	Trainee	Doncaster R	1	—
David Jones	6 3	14 04	3 7 64	Harrow		Chelsea	—	—
						Bury	1	—
						Leyton Orient	2	—
						Burnley	4	—
						Ipswich T	—	—
						Doncaster R	40	14
Mark McKay‡			12 11 67	Edinburgh		Doncaster R	1	—
Grant Morrow	5 10	11 07	4 10 70	Glasgow	Rowntree M	Doncaster R	21	3
John Muir	6 2	14 06	26 4 63	Sedgley	Dudley T	Doncaster R	55	17
Max Nicholson			3 10 71	Leeds	Trainee	Doncaster R	3	—
Kevin Noteman	5 10	10 09	15 10 69	Preston	Trainee	Leeds U	1	—
						Doncaster R	72	10
Billy Whitehurst	6 0	13 00	10 6 59	Thurnscoe	Mexborough	Hull C	193	47
						Newcastle U	28	7
						Oxford U	40	4
						Reading	17	8
						Sunderland	17	3
						Hull C	36	5
						Sheffield U	22	2
						Stoke C (loan)	3	—
						Doncaster R	13	1

Trainees
Almunshi, Haidar M; Armstrong, Stephen; Bennett, Craig; Cullen, David J; Holland, Simon L.D; Limber, Nicholas; McKenzie, Roger M; Roberts, Jamie S; White, Stuart; Worboys, Gavain A.

Associated Schoolboys
Batty, Richard; Bell, Lynden; Buxton, Nick G; Cairns, Luke; Clegg, Christopher G; Fretwell, Adam; Grant, Leon A; Harmer, Russell; Hodgson, Leigh A; Keegan, Craig; Long, James; McMillan, Jamie; Maxfield, Scott; Nixon, Russell S; Oliver, Jonathan; Oliver, Mark A; Otter, Stephen P; Perkins, Sean P; Robinson, Antony; Woods, Gary.

Associated Schoolboys who have accepted the club's offer of a Traineeship/Contract
Edmonds, Christopher J; Soar, Mark; Sykes, Paul R; Thew, Lee.

208

EVERTON 1990–91   *Back row (left to right):* Kevin Sheedy, Norman Whiteside, Jason Kearton, Martin Keown, Neville Southall, Dave Watson, John Ebbrell, Graham Smith.
Centre row: Paul Power, Mike Lyons, Mike Newell, Graeme Sharp, Neil McDonald, Ray Atteveld, Andy Hinchcliffe, Peter Beagrie, Les Helm, Jimmy Gabriel.
Front row: Ian Snodin, Mike Milligan, Kevin Ratcliffe, Colin Harvey, Pat Nevin, Stuart McCall, Tony Cottee.

Division 1   **EVERTON**

Goodison Park, Liverpool L4 4EL. Telephone 051-521 2020. Match ticket information: 051-523 6642. Match information: 0898 121599 Clubcall 0898 121199. Dial-a-seat service: 051-525 1231.

Ground capacity: 41,366 (29,500 seats).

Record attendance: 78,299 v Liverpool, Division 1, 18 September 1948.

Record receipts: £207,780 v Liverpool, FA Cup, 5th rd, 21 February 1988.

Pitch measurements: 112yd × 78yd.

Chairman: Sir Philip D. Carter CBE.

Directors: A. W. Waterworth, D. H. Pitcher, K. M. Tamlin, D. A. B. Newton, Dr D. M. Marsh, W. Kenright.

Manager: Howard Kendall. *Assistant Manager:* Colin Harvey.

Physio: Chris Goodson. *Coach:*

Reserve Team Coach: Jimmy Gabriel.

Chief Executive & Secretary: Jim Greenwood.

Marketing Manager: Derek Johnston. *Sales Promotion Manager:* Nigel Coates.

Year Formed: 1878. *Turned Professional:* 1885. *Ltd Co.:* 1892.

Previous Name: St Domingo FC, 1878–79.

Club Nickname: 'The Toffees'.

Previous Grounds: 1878, Stanley Park; 1882, Priory Road; 1884, Anfield Road; 1892, Goodison Park.

Record League Victory: 9-1 v Manchester C, Division 1, 3 September 1906 – Scott; Balmer, Crelley; Booth, Taylor (1), Abbott (1); Sharp, Bolton (1), Young (4), Settle (2), George Wilson. 9-1 v Plymouth Arg, Division 2, 27 December 1930 – Coggins; Williams, Cresswell; McPherson, Griffiths, Thomson; Critchley, Dunn, Dean (4), Johnson (1), Stein (4).

Record Cup Victory: 11-2 v Derby Co, FA Cup, 1st rd, 18 January 1890 – Smalley; Hannah, Doyle; Kirkwood (3), Holt, Parry; Latta, Brady (3), Geary (2), Chadwick, Millward (3).

Record Defeat: 4-10 v Tottenham H, Division 1, 11 October 1958.

Most League Points (2 for a win): 66, Division 1, 1969–70.

Most League Points (3 for a win): 90, Division 1, 1984–85.

Most League Goals: 121, Division 2, 1930–31.

Highest League Scorer in Season: William Ralph 'Dixie' Dean, 60, Division 1, 1927–28 (All-time League record).

Most League Goals in Total Aggregate: William Ralph 'Dixie' Dean, 349, 1925–37.

Most Capped Player: Kevin Ratcliffe, 56, Wales.

Most League Appearances: Ted Sagar, 465, 1929–53.

Record Transfer Fee Received: £2,750,000 from Barcelona for Gary Lineker, July 1986.

Record Transfer Fee Paid: £2,000,000 to West Ham U for Tony Cottee, July 1988.

Football League Record: 1888 Founder Member of the Football League; 1930–31 Division 2; 1931–51 Division 1; 1951–54 Division 2; 1954– Division 1.

Honours: Football League: Division 1 – Champions 1890–91, 1914–15, 1927–28, 1931–32, 1938–39, 1962–63, 1969–70, 1984–85, 1986–87; Runners-up 1889–90, 1894–95, 1901–02, 1904–05, 1908–09, 1911–12, 1985–86; Division 2 Champions 1930–31; Runners-up 1953–54. *FA Cup:* Winners 1906, 1933, 1966, 1984; Runners-up 1893, 1897, 1907, 1968, 1985, 1986, 1989. *Football League Cup:* Runners-up 1976–77, 1983–84. *League Super Cup:* Runners-up 1986. *Simod Cup:* Runners-up 1989. *Zenith Data Systems Cup:* Runner-up 1991. **European Competitions:** *European Cup:* 1963–64, 1970–71. *European Cup-Winners' Cup:* 1966–67, 1984–85 (winners). *European Fairs Cup:* 1962–63, 1964–65, 1965–66. *UEFA Cup:* 1975–76, 1978–79, 1979–80.

Colours: Royal blue shirts with white collar and white trim on sleeve, white shorts with blue trim, blue stockings with white dicing on turnover. **Change colours:** All yellow.

EVERTON 1990–91 LEAGUE RECORD

Match No.	Date	Venue	Opponents	Result	H/T Score	Lg. Pos.	Goalscorers	Atten- dance
1	Aug 25	H	Leeds U	L	2-3	0-2	—	Nevin, Ebbrell	34,412
2	29	A	Coventry C	L	1-3	0-2	—	Nevin	12,902
3	Sept 1	A	Manchester C	L	0-1	0-1	20		31,456
4	8	H	Arsenal	D	1-1	0-0	20	Newell	29,919
5	15	A	Sunderland	D	2-2	2-2	18	Sharp, Newell	25,004
6	22	H	Liverpool	L	2-3	0-2	18	Hinchcliffe, McCall	39,847
7	29	H	Southampton	W	3-0	2-0	18	Cottee 2, Ebbrell	23,093
8	Oct 7	A	Nottingham F	L	1-3	1-1	—	McDonald	25,790
9	20	H	Crystal Palace	D	0-0	0-0	18		24,504
10	27	A	Luton T	D	1-1	0-1	18	Nevin	10,047
11	Nov 3	H	QPR	W	3-0	1-0	17	Newell, Nevin, McDonald	22,352
12	10	A	Sheffield U	D	0-0	0-0	17		21,447
13	18	H	Tottenham H	D	1-1	1-1	—	McCall	28,716
14	24	A	Wimbledon	L	1-2	0-1	18	Sheedy (pen)	6411
15	Dec 1	H	Manchester U	L	0-1	0-0	18		32,400
16	8	H	Coventry C	W	1-0	0-0	15	McCall	17,472
17	16	A	Leeds U	L	0-2	0-2	—		27,775
18	22	A	Norwich C	L	0-1	0-1	16		14,294
19	26	H	Aston Villa	W	1-0	0-0	15	Sharp	27,804
20	29	H	Derby Co	W	2-0	0-0	14	Newell, Nevin	25,361
21	Jan 1	A	Chelsea	W	2-1	1-1	11	Sharp, Cundy (og)	18,351
22	13	H	Manchester C	W	2-0	2-0	—	Beagrie, Sheedy	22,774
23	19	A	Arsenal	L	0-1	0-0	12		35,349
24	Feb 2	H	Sunderland	W	2-0	0-0	12	Sheedy, Beagrie	23,124
25	9	A	Liverpool	L	1-3	1-1	12	Nevin	25,116
26	23	H	Sheffield U	L	1-2	1-1	12	Cottee	28,148
27	Mar 2	A	Manchester U	W	2-0	2-0	11	Newell, Watson	45,656
28	16	A	Southampton	W	4-3	2-1	11	Watson, Milligan, Newell, Cottee	15,410
29	23	H	Nottingham F	D	0-0	0-0	11		23,078
30	30	A	Aston Villa	D	2-2	1-0	10	Warzycha 2	27,660
31	Apr 1	H	Norwich C	W	1-0	0-0	9	Newell	20,485
32	10	H	Wimbledon	L	1-2	1-1	—	Cottee	14,590
33	13	H	Chelsea	D	2-2	1-0	10	Cottee, Ebbrell	19,526
34	20	A	Crystal Palace	D	0-0	0-0	13		16,439
35	24	A	Tottenham H	D	3-3	1-1	—	Nevin, Stewart (og), Cottee	21,675
36	May 4	H	Luton T	W	1-0	0-0	11	Cottee	19,809
37	8	A	Derby Co	W	3-2	1-1	—	Cottee 2, Sheedy	12,403
38	11	A	QPR	D	1-1	1-1	9	Nevin	12,508

Final League Position: 9

GOALSCORERS

League (50): Cottee 10, Nevin 8, Newell 7, Sheedy 4 (1 pen), Ebbrell 3, McCall 3, Sharp 3, Beagrie 2, McDonald 2, Warzycha 2, Watson 2, Hinchcliffe 1, Milligan 1, own goals 2.
Rumbelows Cup (12): Cottee 4, Sharp 3, McDonald 2, Ebbrell 1, Nevin 1, own goal 1.
FA Cup (9): Cottee 2, Ebbrell 2, Sharp 2, Watson 2, Sheedy 1.

Southall	McDonald	Hinchcliffe	Keown	Watson	Milligan	Nevin	McCall	Sharp	Newell	Ebbrell	Sheedy	Atteveld	Ratcliffe	Whiteside	Cottee	Beagrie	Snodin	Youds	Warzycha	Barlow	Jenkins	Match No.
1	2	3	4	5	6	7	8*	9	10	11	12											1
1	2*	3	4	5	8	7		9	10	6		11†12	14									2
1		3	2	5	6	7		9	10	8	11*12	4										3
1		3		5	6	7	8*	9	10	11		2	4	12								4
1		3		5	6	7	8	9	10	11		2	4									5
1	14	3		5	6†	7	8	9	10*11			2	4	12								6
1	6	3		5		7	8	9*12	11			2	4	10								7
1	6	3		5		7*	8	9	12	11		2	4	10								8
1	6	3†14		5		7	8	9	12	11		2	4*	10								9
1	6		3	5		7	8	9		11		2	4	10								10
1	6		3	5		7	8		9	10		2	4		11							11
1	6		3	5		7	8		9	11	10*	2	4		12							12
1	6†		5			14	8	9	12	3	11	2	4		10	7*						13
1	2		5			14	8	9*10	3	11	7	4	6†12									14
1	2		5			7	8	12	9	3*11	6	4	10									15
1	2	3	5	6	7	8	12	9	14	11†		4	10*									16
1	2	3	5	14	8	9†10	6*			7	4	12	11									17
1	2	11	3†	5	7	12	9	6		8		4	10*	14								18
1	8	3	14	5	7*	9	12	6	10			4	11†	2								19
1	2	3	5	7	8	9	12	6	10			4	11*									20
1	2	3	5	7	8	9		6	10			4	11									21
1	2	3	5	7	8	9		6	10			4	12	11*								22
1	2	14	5†	6*	7	8	9	3	10			4	12	11								23
1	2		5	6*	7	8	9	3	10			4	12	11								24
1	2		5	6	7	8	9	3	10			4	12	11*								25
1	2	3	6	5	7	14	8	9*12	11			4†	10									26
1	2	3	6	5	7†	8	9*10	11		14		4	12									27
1	2	6	5	11	7*	8	9	3	14			4	10†12									28
1	14	2	5†	6	11*	9	12	3	8			4	10	7								29
1	2	3	5	6	12	8	9		11*			4	10	7								30
1	2	3	5	6	12	8		9	14	11†		10	4	7*								31
1	2†	3	5	6*	9	8				4	10	11	14	7	12							32
1		4	5	7	8	9*	6	11	3	10	2	12										33
1		4	5†	7	8	9	6	11	3	10*14	2	12										34
1	3	5		9	8		6	12	4	10	11	2*	7									35
1	3	5		8	9	2	6	4	10	11	7											36
1	5		9	8	12	3	6	2	4	10	11	7*										37
1	5†12	7	8	9	2	6	4	10*11	14	3												38
38	27	21	21	32	16	31	33	24	20	34	20	17	35	1	20	14	1	5	7	—	1	
+		+		+	+		+	+	+	+	+	+	+	+	+			+	+	+		
2s		3s		1s	6s		3s	9s	2s	2s	3s	1s	1s	9s	3s			3s	1s	2s		

Rumbelows Cup	Second Round	Wrexham (a)	5-0
		(h)	6-0
	Third Round	Sheffield U (a)	1-2
FA Cup	Third Round	Charlton Ath (a)	2-1
	Fourth Round	Woking (a) (at Everton)	1-0
	Fifth Round	Liverpool (a)	0-0
		(h)	4-4
		(h)	1-0
	Sixth Round	West Ham U (a)	1-2

EVERTON

Player and Position	Ht	Wt	Birth Date	Birth Place	Source	Clubs	League App	Gls
Goalkeepers								
Jason Kearton	6 1	11 10	9 7 69	Ipswich (Australia)	Brisbane Lions	Everton	—	—
Neville Southall	6 1	12 01	16 9 58	Llandudno	Winsford	Bury	39	—
						Everton	329	—
						Port Vale (loan)	9	—
Defenders								
Andy Hinchcliffe	5 10	12 10	5 2 69	Manchester	Apprentice	Manchester C	112	8
						Everton	21	1
Iain Jenkins§			24 11 72	Prescot	Trainee	Everton	1	—
Martin Keown	6 1	12 04	24 7 66	Oxford	Apprentice	Arsenal	22	—
						Brighton & HA (loan)	23	1
						Aston Villa	112	3
						Everton	44	
Neil McDonald	5 11	11 04	2 11 65	Newcastle	Wallsend BC	Newcastle U	180	24
						Everton	85	4
Kevin Ratcliffe	5 11	12 07	12 11 60	Mancot	Apprentice	Everton	350	2
Dave Watson	6 0	11 12	20 11 61	Liverpool	Amateur	Liverpool	—	—
						Norwich C	212	11
						Everton	165	14
Mark Wright*	5 9	10 08	29 1 70	Manchester	Trainee	Everton	1	—
						Blackpool (loan)	3	—
						Huddersfield T (loan)	10	1
Edward Youds	6 0	11 00	3 5 70	Liverpool	Trainee	Everton	8	—
						Cardiff C (loan)	1	—
						Wrexham (loan)	20	2
Midfield								
Ray Atteveld	5 10	12 00	8 9 66	Amsterdam	Haarlem	Everton	38	1
John Ebbrell	5 7	9 12	1 10 69	Bromborough	FA School	Everton	57	3
Marcus Ebdon*	5 9	11 00	17 10 70	Pontypool	Trainee	Everton	—	—
Stuart McCall	5 6	10 01	10 6 64	Leeds	Apprentice	Bradford C	238	37
						Everton	103	6
Mike Milligan	5 8	11 00	20 2 67	Manchester	Apprentice	Oldham Ath	162	17
						Everton	17	1
Neil Sang*	5 9	10 07	23 5 72	Liverpool	Trainee	Everton	—	—
Kevin Sheedy	5 9	10 11	21 10 59	Builth Wells	Apprentice	Hereford U	51	4
						Liverpool	3	—
						Everton	258	66
Ian Snodin	5 7	8 12	15 8 63	Rotherham	Apprentice	Doncaster R	188	25
						Leeds U	51	6
						Everton	96	2
Norman Whiteside	6 0	12 08	7 5 65	Belfast	Apprentice	Manchester U	206	47
						Everton	29	9
Forwards								
Stuart Barlow	5 10	11 00	16 7 68	Liverpool		Everton	2	—
Peter Beagrie	5 8	9 10	28 11 65	Middlesbrough	Local	Middlesbrough	33	2
						Sheffield U	84	11
						Stoke C	54	7
						Everton	36	2
Tony Cottee	5 8	11 04	11 7 65	West Ham	Apprentice	West Ham U	212	92
						Everton	92	36
Pat Nevin	5 6	10 00	6 9 63	Glasgow	Gartcosh U	Clyde	73	17
						Chelsea	193	36
						Everton	92	14

EVERTON

Foundation: St. Domingo Church Sunday School formed a football club in 1878 which played at Stanley Park. Enthusiasm was so great that in November 1879 they decided to expand membership and changed the name to Everton playing in black shirts with a white sash and nicknamed the "Black Watch". After wearing several other colours, royal blue was adopted in 1901.

First Football League game: 8 September, 1888, Football League, v Accrington (h) W 2-1 – Smalley; Dick, Ross; Holt, Jones, Dobson; Fleming (2), Waugh, Lewis, E. Chadwick, Farmer.

Did you know: Everton was the first club to notch up 10 or more away wins in three consecutive League seasons. They achieved this in seasons 1984–85, 85–86, 86–87 – all in Division One.

Managers (and Secretary-managers)
W. E. Barclay 1888–89*, Dick Molyneux 1889–1901*, William C. Cuff 1901–18*, W. J. Sawyer 1918–19*, Thomas H. McIntosh 1919–35*, Theo Kelly 1936–48, Cliff Britton 1948–56, Ian Buchan 1956–58, Johnny Carey 1958–61, Harry Catterick 1961–73, Billy Bingham 1973–77, Gordon Lee 1977–81, Howard Kendall 1981–87, Colin Harvey 1987–90, Howard Kendall November 1990–   .

Player and Position	Ht	Wt	Birth Date	Birth Place	Source	Clubs	League App	Gls
Mike Newell	6 0	11 00	27 1 65	Liverpool	Amateur	Liverpool	—	—
						Crewe Alex	3	—
						Wigan Ath	72	25
						Luton T	63	18
						Leicester C	81	21
						Everton	55	14
Gary Powell*	5 10	10 02	2 4 69	Holylake	Trainee	Everton	—	—
						Lincoln C (loan)	11	—
						Scunthorpe U (loan)	4	1
						Wigan Ath (loan)	14	4
Phil Quinlan			17 4 71	Madrid	Trainee	Everton	—	—
						Huddersfield T (loan)	8	2
Graeme Sharp	6 1	11 08	16 10 60	Glasgow	Eastercraigs	Dumbarton	40	17
						Everton	322	111
Robert Warzycha			20 6 63	Poland	Gornik Zabrze	Everton	8	2

Trainees
Bayley, Andrew J; Christian, Darren; Coy, Chilton S; Doolan, John; Dulson, Craig T; Gouldstone, David A; Jenkins, Iain; Kenny, William; Langton, Edward P; McDonough, Michael; Moore, Neil; Norris, Barry; Priest, Christopher; Sharrock, Mark; Unsworth, David G; Walsh, Ian J; Wilson, David J; Woods, Kenneth.

Associated Schoolboys
Agiadis, Nicholas; Ball, Stephen M; Brennan, Jonathon W; Brown, Paul R; Donnachie, John; Dreslin, John C; Emery, Richard; Holcroft, Peter I; Leeming, Daniel J; Loupe, Kevin A; McGarry, Kevin, L; McMahon, Alan D; Maughan, David W; Owen, Phillip G; Powell, Mark A; Price, Christopher; Price, Gregory T; Roberts, Sean M; Ryan, Terence J; Smith, Alex P; Smith, David L; Smith, Dean A; Speare, James P.V; Weathers, Andrew W; Williams, Neil W; Woodhouse, Lee J; Woods, Matthew J.

Associated Schoolboys who have accepted the club's offer of a Traineeship/Contract
Carridge, John J; Grant, Anthony J; Jones, Terence P; Renforth, Glenn L; Ruffer, Carl J; Tait, Paul.

EXETER CITY 1990–91   *Back row (left to right):* Paul Batty, Paul Eshelby, Lee Rogers, Jonathon Brown, Tony Frankland, Andy Wright, Steve Harrower, Andrew Tibbenham.
Centre row: Terry Cooper (Manager), Ben Rowe, Mick Tanner, Richard Dryden, Kevin Miller, Richard Young, Steve Berryman, Mark Cooper, Jim McNichol, Gordon Hobson.
Front row: Brian McDermott, Scott Hiley, Tom Kelly, Shaun Taylor, Clive Whitehead (Coach), Danny Bailey, Steve Neville (Assistant Manager).

Division 3   EXETER CITY

St James Park, Exeter EX4 6PX. Telephone Exeter (0392) 54073.

Ground capacity: 17,086.

Record attendance: 20,984 v Sunderland, FA Cup 6th rd (replay), 4 March 1931.

Record receipts: £32,007 v Newcastle U, FA Cup 5th rd replay, 18 February 1981.

Pitch measurements: 114yd × 73yd.

President: W. C. Hill.

Chairman:

Directors: L. G. Vallance, A. W. Gooch, S. Dawe, G. Vece.

Manager: Terry Cooper. *Coach/Assistant Manager:* Steve Neville.

Secretary: M. A. Holladay. *Company Secretary:* A. R. Trump.

Commercial Manager: Mike Lewis.

Year Formed: 1904. *Turned Professional:* 1908. *Ltd Co.:* 1908.

Club Nickname: 'The Grecians'.

Record League Victory: 8-1 v Coventry C, Division 3 (S), 4 December 1926 – Bailey; Pollard, Charlton; Pullen, Pool, Garrett; Purcell (2), McDevitt, Blackmore (2), Dent (2), Compton (2). 8-1 v Aldershot, Division 3 (S), 4 May 1935 – Chesters; Gray, Miller; Risdon, Webb, Angus; Jack Scott (1), Wrightson (1), Poulter (3), McArthur (1), Dryden (1). (1 og).

Record Cup Victory: 9-1 v Aberdare, FA Cup 1st rd, 26 November 1927 – Holland; Pollard, Charlton; Phoenix, Pool, Gee; Purcell (2), McDevitt, Dent (4), Vaughan (2), Compton (1).

Record Defeat: 0-9 v Notts Co, Division 3 (S), 16 October 1948 and v Northampton T, Division 3 (S), 12 April 1958.

Most League Points (2 for a win): 62, Division 4, 1976–77.

Most League Points (3 for a win): 89, Division 4, 1989–90.

Most League Goals: 88, Division 3 (S), 1932–33.

Highest League Scorer in Season: Fred Whitlow, 33, Division 3 (S), 1932–33.

Most League Goals in Total Aggregate: Tony Kellow, 129, 1976–78, 1980–83, 1985–88.

Most Capped Player: Dermot Curtis, 1 (17), Eire.

Most League Appearances: Arnold Mitchell, 495, 1952–66.

Record Transfer Fee Received: £105,000 from Blackpool for Tony Kellow, November 1978.

Record Transfer Fee Paid: £65,000 to Blackpool for Tony Kellow, March 1980.

Football League Record: 1920 Elected Division 3; 1921–58 Division 3 (S); 1958–64 Division 4; 1964–66 Division 3; 1966–77 Division 4; 1977–84 Division 3; 1984–90 Division 4; 1990– Division 3.

Honours: Football League: Division 3 best season: 8th, 1979–80; Division 3 (S) – Runners-up 1932–33; Division 4 – Champions 1989–90; Runners-up 1976–77. *FA Cup:* best season: 6th rd replay, 1931. *Football League Cup:* never beyond 4th rd. *Division 3 (S) Cup:* Winners 1934.

Colours: Red and white striped shirts, black shorts, red stockings with white stripes. **Change colours:** Blue and white.

EXETER CITY 1990–91 LEAGUE RECORD

Match No.	Date	Venue	Opponents	Result	H/T Score	Lg. Pos.	Goalscorers	Attendance
1	Aug 25	H	Reading	L 1-3	1-1	—	Hobson	5694
2	Sept 1	A	Chester C	W 2-1	1-0	14	Hiley, Bailey	1377
3	8	H	Swansea C	W 2-0	1-0	8	Neville, Hobson (pen)	4719
4	15	A	Mansfield T	W 2-0	1-0	4	Dryden, Hobson	2355
5	18	A	Birmingham C	D 1-1	0-1	—	Dryden	7703
6	22	H	Bournemouth	W 2-0	2-0	5	Dryden 2	6145
7	29	H	Cambridge U	L 0-1	0-1	6		4227
8	Oct 2	A	Huddersfield T	L 0-1	0-0	—		4317
9	6	A	Preston NE	L 0-1	0-1	9		4716
10	13	H	Bradford C	D 2-2	1-1	12	Hobson (pen), Neville	4517
11	20	H	Tranmere R	D 0-0	0-0	12		5045
12	23	A	Southend U	L 1-2	1-1	—	Taylor	4280
13	27	A	Fulham	L 2-3	2-1	16	Hobson (pen), Dryden	4523
14	Nov 3	H	Grimsby T	D 0-0	0-0	18		4647
15	10	A	Leyton Orient	L 0-1	0-0	18		3785
16	24	H	Brentford	D 1-1	1-1	19	Kelly (pen)	3826
17	Dec 1	H	Stoke C	W 2-0	0-0	18	Neville, Eshelby	5377
18	15	A	Bury	L 1-3	1-2	18	Morgan	2370
19	22	H	Rotherham U	W 2-0	0-0	18	Cooper, Morgan	3752
20	26	A	Wigan Ath	L 1-4	0-3	18	Tankard (og)	2045
21	29	A	Shrewsbury T	D 2-2	0-1	18	Marshall, Cooper	3179
22	Jan 1	H	Crewe Alex	W 3-0	1-0	16	Marshall, Cooper 2	4023
23	12	A	Chester C	D 1-1	1-1	17	Dryden	4008
24	19	A	Reading	L 0-1	0-0	17		5123
25	26	H	Mansfield T	W 2-0	1-0	16	Hobson, Neville	3432
26	Feb 2	H	Birmingham C	L 0-2	0-0	17		5154
27	5	A	Bournemouth	L 1-2	1-1	—	Morgan	4982
28	13	A	Bolton W	L 0-1	0-1	—		5532
29	16	A	Brentford	L 0-1	0-0	17		5118
30	23	H	Leyton Orient	W 2-0	2-0	17	Cooper, Hiley	3216
31	26	A	Swansea C	W 3-0	0-0	—	Neville 3	2385
32	Mar 2	A	Stoke C	L 1-2	1-1	16	Cooper (pen)	8536
33	9	H	Bury	W 2-0	1-0	16	Cooper 2 (1 pen)	3590
34	13	H	Huddersfield T	D 2-2	0-0	—	Cooper, Neville	3625
35	16	A	Cambridge U	L 0-1	0-1	16		4833
36	20	A	Bradford C	L 0-3	0-2	—		5328
37	23	H	Preston NE	W 4-0	0-0	16	Rowbotham, Neville, Jones 2	3525
38	26	H	Bolton W	W 2-1	1-0	—	Marshall, Rowbotham	4009
39	30	H	Wigan Ath	W 1-0	1-0	15	Taylor	4510
40	Apr 1	A	Rotherham U	W 4-2	0-0	14	Jones, Taylor, Neville, Hobson	3701
41	13	A	Crewe Alex	D 1-1	0-0	15	Rowbotham	3099
42	20	A	Tranmere R	L —1	0-1	16		5178
43	27	H	Southend U	L 1-2	1-1	16	Cooper	4941
44	30	H	Shrewsbury T	W 3-0	1-0	—	Neville, Taylor, Boughey	2763
45	May 4	H	Fulham	L 0-1	0-1	15		3799
46	11	A	Grimsby T	L 1-2	0-2	16	Cooper	14,225

Final League Position: 16

GOALSCORERS

League (58): Cooper 11 (2 pens), Neville 11, Hobson 7 (3 pens), Dryden 6, Taylor 4, Jones 3, Marshall 3, Morgan 3, Rowbotham 3, Hiley 2, Bailey 1, Boughey 1, Eshelby 1, Kelly 1 (pen), own goal 1.
Rumbelows Cup (1): Dryden 1.
FA Cup (1): Neville 1.

Miller	Hiley	Dryden	Rogers	Taylor	Cooper	Hobson	Bailey	McDermott	Neville	Whitehead	Batty	Frankland	Young	Eshelby	Kelly	Brown	Rowe	Marshall	Cawley	Morgan	Owen	O'Toole	Jones	McNichol	Rowbotham	Boughey	Match No.
1	2	3	4	5	6†	7	8*	9	10	11	12	14															1
1	2	3	4	5	6*	7	12	9†	10	11	8	14															2
1	2	3	4	5	6	7	8	9	10	11*		12															3
1	2	3	4	5	6	7	8	9*	10	11	12																4
1	2	3	4	5	6	7	8	9	10	11																	5
1	2	3	4	5	6		8	9	10	11		7*	12														6
1	2	3	4	5	6	7	8	9*	10	11†		12	14														7
1	2	3	4	5	6	7	8	9*	10	11†		12	14														8
1	2	3	4	5	6		8						9	12	11	7	10*										9
1	2	3	4	5	6	7	8		10				9*	12	11												10
1	2	3	4	5	6	7	8		10					12	11*			9									11
1	2	3	4	5	6	7	8		10					12	11*14			9†									12
1	2	3	4	5	6	7	8		10					9	11												13
1	2	3	4	5	6	7	8		10					11	12			9*									14
1	2	3	4*	5	6	7	8		10					11	9	12											15
1	2	3*		5	6				10		8		12		11			7	4	9							16
1	2	3		5	6		8		10						11			7	4	9							17
1	2	3		5	6		8		10									7	4	9	11						18
1	2	3		5	6		8		10						11	7		4	9								19
1	2	3		5	6	10							8		11	7	12	4*	9								20
1	2	3		5	6	10								12	7	4		11	9*	8							21
1	2*	3		5	6	9			10					12		4		11				8	7				22
1	2	3		5	6	9			10							4		11	12			8*	7				23
1	2	3		5	6	9							7†12	4	14	11*		10				8					24
1	2	3		5	6	9							7*	4				11				8	10				25
1	2			5	6				10							7*	3	11	4	12		8	9				26
1	2			5	6				10							12	3	11	4*	7		8	9				27
1	2			5	6	8			10*							12	3	11	7				9	4			28
1	2	10		5	6	8										12	3	11	7*				9	4			29
1	2	7		5	6	8			10								3	11					9	4			30
1	2	7			6	8*			10		5	12					3	11					9	4			31
1	2	7		5	6				10		8*						3	11	9					4	12		32
1	2	7		5	6	8			10*		8						3	11	9					4	12		33
1	2	7		5	6	8			10								3	11	9					4			34
1	2		7	5	6	8			10								3	12	11*				9	4			35
1	2	14		5	6	8					7						3	11	10*				9	4†12			36
1	2	4		5	6	8			10				9				3	11				12			7*		37
1	2	4		5	6	8			10				9				3	11							7		38
1	2	4		5	6	8			10*								3	11	12						7	9	39
1	2	4†		5	6	8				12			14				3	11	10						7*	9	40
1	2	4		5	6*	8				12			14				3	11	10†						7	9	41
1	2	4		5		8				12						6*	3	11	10						7	9	42
1	2	4		5	6				10				12				3	11*	8						7	9	43
1	2	4		5	6†	8			10				14				3	11	12						7*	9	44
1	2	4		5		8			10†				6				3*	11	14				12		7	9	45
1	2	4		5	6†	8				12							3	11	9*				7		14	10	46
46	46	41	16	45	42	37	17	8	35	8	9	—	3	9	13	26	1	31	7	14	4	6	16	9	9	8	
			+				+		+		+	+	+	+	+	+	+	+	+		+		+	+			
			1s				1s		5s		2s	3s	4s	9s	9s	3s	1s	1s	3s				4s	4s			

Rumbelows Cup   First Round   Notts Co (h)   1-1
    (a)   0-1
FA Cup   First Round   Cambridge U (h)   1-2

EXETER CITY

Player and Position	Ht	Wt	Birth Date	Birth Place	Source	Clubs	League App	Gls
Goalkeepers								
Kevin Miller	6 1	12 10	15 3 69	Falmouth	Newquay	Exeter C	77	—
Defenders								
Jon Brown	5 10	11 03	8 9 66	Barnsley	Denaby U	Exeter C	29	—
Peter Cawley	6 4	13 00	15 9 65	London	Chertsey	Wimbledon	1	—
						Bristol R (loan)	10	—
						Fulham (loan)	5	—
						Bristol R	3	—
						Southend U	7	1
						Exeter C	7	—
Richard Dryden	6 0	11 02	14 6 69	Stroud		Bristol R	13	—
						Exeter C	92	13
						Manchester C (loan)	—	—
Tony Frankland	6 1	10 07	11 10 72	Greenwich		Exeter C	7	—
Tom Kelly	5 10	11 10	28 3 64	Bellshill	Hibernian	Hartlepool U	15	—
						Torquay U	120	—
						York C	35	2
						Exeter C	34	3
Jim McNichol*	6 0	12 10	9 6 58	Glasgow	Apprentice	Ipswich T	—	—
						Luton T	15	—
						Brentford	155	22
						Exeter C	87	10
						Torquay U	124	13
						Exeter C	42	8
Lee Rogers‡	5 11	12 07	8 4 67	Bristol	Apprentice	Bristol C	30	—
						Hereford U (loan)	13	—
						York C (loan)	7	—
						Exeter C	78	—
Shaun Taylor	6 1	13 00	26 3 63	Plymouth	Bideford	Exeter C	200	16
Clive Whitehead‡	5 11	11 06	24 11 55	Birmingham	Northfield J	Bristol C	229	10
						WBA	168	6
						Wolverhampton W (loan)	2	—
						Portsmouth	65	2
						Exeter C	46	5
Midfield								
Paul Batty‡	5 7	10 07	9 1 64	E Dington	Apprentice	Swindon T	108	7
						Chesterfield	26	—
						Exeter C	111	11
						Cambridge U (loan)	—	—
Mark Cooper	5 8	11 04	18 12 68	Wakefield	Trainee	Bristol C	—	—
						Exeter C	47	11
						Southend U (loan)	5	—
Steven Harrower‡	5 8	11 01	9 10 61	Exeter	Local	Exeter C	187	10
Scott Hiley	5 9	10 07	27 9 68	Plymouth	Trainee	Exeter C	144	8
Steve Neville	5 9	11 00	18 9 57	Walthamstow	Apprentice	Southampton	5	1
						Exeter C	93	22
						Sheffield U	49	6
						Exeter C (loan)	33	17
						Exeter C	59	10
						Bristol C	134	40
						Exeter C	120	39
Darren Rowbotham	5 10	11 05	22 10 66	Cardiff	Trainee	Plymouth Arg	46	2
						Exeter C	113	46
Ben Rowe‡	5 7	10 00	1 10 70	Hull	Bristol C	Exeter C	12	2
Forwards								
Gordon Hobson	5 9	10 07	27 11 57	Sheffield	Sheffield RGRS	Lincoln C	272	73
						Grimsby T	52	18
						Southampton	33	8
						Lincoln C	61	22
						Exeter C	37	7
Murray Jones	6 4	14 00	7 10 64	Bexley	Carshalton	Crystal Palace	—	—
						Bristol C	—	—
						Doncaster R (loan)	5	—
						Exeter C	20	3

EXETER CITY

Foundation: Exeter City was formed in 1904 by the amalgamation of St. Sidwell's United and Exeter United. The club first played in the East Devon League and then the Plymouth & District League. After an exhibition match between West Bromwich Albion and Woolwich Arsenal was held to test interest as Exeter was then a rugby stronghold, Exeter City decided at a meeting at the Red Lion Hotel to turn professional in 1908.

First Football League game: 28 August, 1920, Division 3, v Brentford (h) W 3-0 – Pym; Coleburne, Feebury (1p); Crawshaw, Carrick, Mitton; Appleton, Makin, Wright (1), Vowles (1), Dockray.

Did you know: In the period beginning 17 October 1931 and ending 13 September 1933 centre-forward Fred Whitlow scored nine League hat-tricks for the City while none of his team mates got even one.

Managers (and Secretary-managers)
Arthur Chadwick 1910–22, Fred Mavin 1923–27, Dave Wilson 1928–29, Billy McDevitt 1929–35, Jack English 1935–39, George Roughton 1945–52, Norman Kirkman 1952–53, Norman Dodgin 1953–57, Bill Thompson 1957–58, Frank Broome 1958–60, Glen Wilson 1960–62, Cyril Spiers 1962–63, Jack Edwards 1963–65, Ellis Stuttard 1965–66, Jock Basford 1966–67, Frank Broome 1967–69, Johnny Newman 1969–76, Bobby Saxton 1977–79, Brian Godfrey 1979–83, Gerry Francis 1983–84, Jim Iley 1984–85, Colin Appleton 1985–87, Terry Cooper May 1988–.

Player and Position	Ht	Wt	Birth Date	Birth Place	Source	Clubs	League App	Gls
Brian McDermott‡	5 8	9 12	8 4 61	Slough	Apprentice	Arsenal	61	12
						Fulham (loan)	3	—
						Oxford U	24	2
						Huddersfield T (loan)	4	1
						Cardiff C	51	8
						Exeter C	68	4
Gary Marshall	5 11	10 10	20 4 64	Bristol	Shepton Mallet	Bristol C	68	7
						Torquay U (loan)	7	1
						Carlisle U	21	2
						Scunthorpe U	41	3
						Exeter C	32	3
Trevor Morgan	6 1	13 01	30 9 56	Forest Gate	Leytonstone	Bournemouth	53	13
						Mansfield T	12	6
						Bournemouth	88	33
						Bristol C	32	8
						Exeter C	30	9
						Bristol R	55	24
						Bristol C	19	8
						Bolton W	77	17
						Colchester U	32	12
						Exeter C	17	3
Andy Tibenham‡	5 5	9 09	9 1 71	Sheffield	Denaby U	Exeter C	—	—
Andy Wright*	5 9	10 06	23 11 71	Plymouth	Trainee	Exeter C	—	—
Richard Young‡	6 3	13 07	31 12 68	Nottingham	Apprentice	Notts Co	35	5
						Southend U	9	—
						Exeter C	49	10

Trainees
Annunziata, Lee J; Day, James A; Redwood, Toby R.B; Taylor, Craig.

Associated Schoolboys
Allen, Stephen J.A; Cullen, Marc R; Fairchild, Neil; Grylls, Casey B.H.V; Hines, Christopher J; Hutchings, Mark; Lafferty, Philip R; Locke, Zak W; Murch, Stephen; Page, Mark J; Parsons, Timothy J; Pears, Richard J; Phillips, Martin J; Plumb, Gareth L; Povey, Craig T; Powell, Shane M; Reed, Dean; Rice, Gary J; Rodwell, Andrew; Sercombe, Kevin J; Smith, Jason L; Turvey, Mark A.

FULHAM 1990–91 *Back row (left to right):* Shaun Gore, Gavin Nebbeling, Steve Milton, Jim Stannard, Laurence Batty, Glen Thomas, Justin Skinner, Peter Scott. *Front row:* John Marshall, Clive Walker, Francis Joseph, Martin Pike, Mark Newson, Jeff Eckhardt, Michael Cole, Mark Kelly, Richard Langley.

Division 3   FULHAM

Craven Cottage, Stevenage Rd, Fulham, London SW6. Telephone 071-736 6561. Pools Office: 071-736 4634. Clubcall: 0898 121198.

Ground capacity: 18,304.

Record attendance: 49,335 v Millwall, Division 2, 8 October 1938.

Record receipts: £80,247 v Chelsea, Division 2, 8 October 1983.

Pitch measurements: 110yd × 75yd.

Chairman: Jimmy Hill.

Directors: W. F. Muddyman (Vice-chairman), C. A. Swain, A. Muddyman.

Manager: Alan Dicks. *Assistant Manager:* T. Wilson.

Coach: Ray Lewington. *Physio:* Glen Hunter. *Youth Development Officer:* Sid Rudgley. *Community Scheme Organiser:* Tom Enefer. *Youth Team Coach:* Terry Bullivant.

Club Secretary: Mrs Janice O'Doherty.

Commercial Manager: Dominic Ostrowski.

Year Formed: 1879. *Turned Professional:* 1898. *Ltd Co.:* 1903. *Reformed:* 1987.

Club Nickname: 'Cottagers'.

Previous Name: 1879–88, Fulham St Andrew's.

Previous Grounds: 1879 Star Road, Fulham; c.1883 Eel Brook Common, 1884 Lillie Road; 1885 Putney Lower Common; 1886 Ranelagh House, Fulham; 1888 Barn Elms, Castelnau; 1889 Purser's Cross (Roskell's Field), Parsons Green Lane; 1891 Eel Brook Common; 1891 Half Moon, Putney; 1895 Captain James Field, West Brompton; 1896 Craven Cottage.

Record League Victory: 10-1 v Ipswich T, Division 1, 26 December 1963 – Macedo; Cohen, Langley; Mullery (1), Keetch, Robson (1); Key, Cook (1), Leggat (4), Haynes, Howfield (3).

Record Cup Victory: 6-0 v Wimbledon (away), FA Cup, 1st rd (replay), 3 December 1930 – Iceton; Gibbon, Lilley; Oliver, Dudley, Barrett; Temple, Hammond (1), Watkins (1), Gibbons (2), Penn (2). 6-0 v Bury, FA Cup, 3rd rd, 7 January 1938 – Turner; Bacuzzi, Keeping; Evans, Dennison, Tompkins; Higgins, Worsley, Rooke (6), O'Callaghan, Arnold.

Record Defeat: 0-10 v Liverpool, League Cup 2nd rd, 1st leg, 23 September 1986.

Most League Points (2 for a win): 60, Division 2, 1958–59 and Division 3, 1970–71.

Most League Points (3 for a win): 78, Division 3, 1981–82.

Most League Goals: 111, Division 3 (S), 1931–32.

Highest League Scorer in Season: Frank Newton, 43, Division 3 (S), 1931–32.

Most League Goals in Total Aggregate: Gordon Davies, 158, 1978–84, 1986–91.

Most Capped Player: Johnny Haynes, 56, England.

Most League Appearances: Johnny Haynes, 594, 1952–70.

Record Transfer Fee Received: £333,333 from Liverpool for Richard Money, May 1980.

Record Transfer Fee Paid: £150,000 to Orient for Peter Kitchen, February 1979, and to Brighton & HA for Teddy Maybank, December 1979.

Football League Record: 1907 Elected to Division 2; 1928–32 Division 3 (S); 1932–49 Division 2; 1949–52 Division 1; 1952–59 Division 2; 1959–68 Division 1; 1968–69 Division 2; 1969–71 Division 3; 1971–80 Division 2; 1980–82 Division 3; 1982–86 Division 2; 1986– Division 3.

Honours: Football League: Division 1 best season: 10th, 1959–60; Division 2 – Champions 1948–49; Runners-up 1958–59; Division 3 (S) – Champions 1931–32; Division 3 – Runners-up 1970–71. *FA Cup:* Runners-up 1974–75. *Football League Cup:* best season: 5th rd, 1967–68, 1970–71.

Colours: White shirts red and black trim, black shorts, white stockings red and black trim. **Change colours:** All red.

FULHAM 1990–91 LEAGUE RECORD

Match No.	Date		Venue	Opponents	Result	H/T Score	Lg. Pos.	Goalscorers	Attendance
1	Aug 25	A		Crewe Alex	D 1-1	0-0	—	Marshall	4143
2	Sept 1	H		Cambridge U	L 0-2	0-1	21		4145
3	8	A		Shrewsbury T	D 2-2	0-1	20	Pike, Haag	2929
4	15	H		Huddersfield T	D 0-0	0-0	19		3853
5	18	H		Wigan Ath	L 1-2	1-1	—	Thomas	3041
6	22	A		Preston NE	L 0-1	0-0	23		4691
7	29	A		Bournemouth	L 0-3	0-1	24		5855
8	Oct 2	H		Birmingham C	D 2-2	1-2	—	Brazil, Rosenior	4011
9	6	H		Rotherham U	W 2-0	2-0	22	Rosenior, Davies	3498
10	13	A		Stoke C	L 1-2	0-1	23	Rosenior	12,394
11	20	A		Swansea C	D 2-2	0-2	22	Brazil (pen), Davies	4500
12	23	H		Bury	W 2-0	0-0	—	Newson, Knill (og)	3439
13	27	H		Exeter C	W 3-2	1-2	20	Pike, Davies 2	4523
14	Nov 4	A		Leyton Orient	L 0-1	0-1	—		6163
15	10	A		Southend U	D 1-1	0-1	20	Brazil	5808
16	24	H		Tranmere R	L 1-2	0-1	20	Davies	4194
17	Dec 1	A		Reading	L 0-1	0-1	21		4073
18	15	H		Bolton W	L 0-1	0-0	22		3466
19	22	A		Mansfield T	D 1-1	1-0	23	Eckhardt	2838
20	26	H		Bradford C	D 0-0	0-0	23		3029
21	29	H		Chester C	W 4-1	1-0	20	Skinner 2, Scott, Brazil	3084
22	Jan 1	A		Grimsby T	L 0-3	0-0	20		7492
23	12	A		Cambridge U	L 0-1	0-0	20		5087
24	19	H		Crewe Alex	W 2-1	1-0	20	Eckhardt, Davies	3477
25	26	A		Huddersfield T	L 0-1	0-1	20		4369
26	Feb 2	A		Wigan Ath	L 0-2	0-1	20		2258
27	5	H		Preston NE	W 1-0	0-0	—	Stant	2750
28	16	A		Tranmere R	D 1-1	1-1	20	Stant	5211
29	23	H		Southend U	L 0-3	0-2	20		5113
30	Mar 2	H		Reading	D 1-1	1-1	20	Stant	4475
31	9	A		Bolton W	L 0-3	0-2	20		7316
32	12	A		Birmingham C	L 0-2	0-1	—		8083
33	16	H		Bournemouth	D 1-1	0-0	20	Talbot	4085
34	19	H		Stoke C	L 0-1	0-0	—		3131
35	23	A		Rotherham U	L 1-3	0-3	23	Scott	3188
36	30	A		Bradford C	D 0-0	0-0	22		6207
37	Apr 1	H		Mansfield T	W 1-0	0-0	20	Stant	3555
38	6	A		Chester C	L 0-1	0-1	22		1047
39	9	H		Shrewsbury T	W 4-0	0-0	—	Skinner 2 (1 pen), Baker, Marshall	3415
40	13	H		Grimsby T	D 0-0	0-0	20		5464
41	16	A		Brentford	W 2-1	1-0	—	Haag, Stant	7839
42	20	H		Swansea C	D 1-1	0-0	20	Haag	4208
43	23	H		Brentford	L 0-1	0-1	—		6765
44	27	A		Bury	D 1-1	1-1	21	Pike	3217
45	May 4	A		Exeter C	W 1-0	1-0	21	Skinner (pen)	3799
46	11	H		Leyton Orient	D 1-1	0-1	21	Onwere (pen)	6590

Final League Position: 21

GOALSCORERS

League (41): Davies 6, Skinner 5 (2 pens), Stant 5, Brazil 4 (1 pen), Haag 3, Pike 3, Rosenior 3, Eckhardt 2, Marshall 2, Scott 2, Baker 1, Newson 1, Onwere 1 (pen), Talbot 1, Thomas 1, own goal 1.
Rumbelows Cup (1): Joseph 1.
FA Cup (3): Brazil 1 (pen), Davies 1, Pike 1.

Batty	Newson	Pike	Skinner	Eckhardt	Thomas	Baker	Kelly	Joseph	Milton	Marshall	Cole	Scott	Stannard	Ferney	Haag	Brazil	Davies	Rosenior	Langley	Cobb	North	Morgan	Gray	Nebbeling	Stant	Parks	Finch	Talbot	Match No.
1	2	3	4	5	6	7	8	9	10*	11	12																		1
1	2	3	14	6	5	8*	7	9†	10	11	12	4																	2
	2	3	14	6	5	8	7		12	11			1	4†	9*	10													3
	2	3		6	5	8	7			11			1	4	9	10*	12												4
	2	3	8	6	5		7†	14		11			1	4*	9	10	12												5
	2	3	14	6*	5		7		12	11		4†	1		9	10	8												6
	2	3		5	6†		7			11		4*	1		8	10	12	9	14										7
	2	3		5†			7			11			1	4	8*10		12	9	14	6									8
	2	3					7			11			1	4	12	10	8*	9		6	5								9
	2	3					7		14	11			1	4*		10	8†	9		12	5	6							10
	2	3					7		11*				1	4		10	8	9		12	5	6							11
	2	3	12				7*	14					1	4		10	11†	9		8	5	6							12
	2	3	4				14	7					1		12	10	11*	9		8†	5	6							13
	2	3	4†				14	7	9*				1		12	10	11				5	6							14
	2	3	4				7						8	1		10	11				5	6	9						15
	2	3†12					7	14					8	1	4*	10	11				5	6	9						16
	2	3	4				7		8	12				1		10		9			5	6	11*						17
	2	12	14	4	3			8†		11*			1		10	7	9				5	6							18
	2	7*		4	3					11			1		10	12	9				5	6							19
	2	7	14	4†	3					11			1		10	12	9*				5	6							20
		11		4	2	3				12	9		8	1		10	7				5	6*							21
		9		4	6	3				12	2†		8	1	11*	10	7				5							14	22
		9	4*	8	3	7				11	2			1		12	10				5		6						23
		11		4	9	3				12			8	1		10	7*				5	2	6						24
		11		4	9	3				12	8†			1	14	10	7*				5	2	6						25
		11		4	9						8	3		1	14	10	7*				5	2	6†						26
		11		4	8							3		1	6	12	10	7*			5	2			9				27
		11		4	8							3		1	6	12	10	7*	14		5				2†	9			28
				3	8	2				12	11		4	1		10	7*				5	6			9				29
	2	3			8					7*11		4			10	12					5	6			9	1			30
	2	3								7		4			10	12		14*		6	11				9	1	5†	8	31
		3	11	4						7			8	1		10	12				5	2			9*			6	32
		3	11	4						7*			8	1		10	12				5	2			9			6	33
		11†		4	3					7*			8	1		10	12	14			5	2			9			6	34
		11		4	3					9†14			8	1		12	10	7			5	2						6*	35
		3	11	4	6					7			8*	1		12	10				5	2			9				36
		3	11	4	6					7			8	1		12	10				5	2			9*				37
		3	11†14	4	6					7			8*	1		12	10				5	2			9				38
		6	11	4		3	12			7			8*	1		10					5	2			9				39
		6	11	4		3		12		7				1		10	14				5	2†			9				40
		11		4	6					7				1		10	3				5	2			9				41
		11		4	6					7				1		10	3*	12			5	2			9				42
		11		4	14	6				12	7			1		10*	3				5	2			9				43
		11		4	3	6				7				1		10					12	5	2*		9				44
	2	11		4	3*	6				7			8	1		10					12	5			9†				45
	2	11		4†	3	6				7			8*	1		10					12	5			9				46
2	31	45	24	28	32	5	17	2	12	34	—	23	42	12	12	41	19	11	—	4	38	32	3	5	19	2	1	5	

```
         +   +   +   +   +   +   +   +   +           +   +   +   +       +   +                       +
        1s  8s  1s  2s  1s  1s  2s 11s1s  2s         2s 11s1s 11s      4s  7s                      1s
```

Onwere — Match No. 40(8*) 41(8) 42(8) 43(8†) 44(8) 45(14) 46(14).

Rumbelows Cup	First Round	Peterborough U (h)	1-2
		(a)	0-2
FA Cup	First Round	Farnborough (h)	2-1
	Second Round	Cambridge U (h)	0-0
		(a)	1-2

FULHAM

Player and Position	Ht	Wt	Birth Date	Birth Place	Source	Clubs	League App	Gls
Goalkeepers								
Tony Parks*	5 11	10 08	26 1 63	Hackney	Apprentice	Tottenham H	37	—
						Oxford U (loan)	5	—
						Gillingham (loan)	2	—
						Brentford	71	—
						QPR (loan)	—	—
						Fulham	2	—
Jim Stannard	6 0	13 06	6 10 62	London	Local	Fulham	41	—
						Charlton Ath (loan)	1	—
						Southend U (loan)	17	—
						Southend U	92	—
						Fulham	177	1
Defenders								
Jeff Eckhardt	5 11	11 06	7 10 65	Sheffield		Sheffield U	74	2
						Fulham	141	7
Martin Ferney	5 11	12 04	8 11 71	Lambeth	Trainee	Fulham	14	—
John Finch	6 1	11 12	5 7 66	Lambeth	Dorking	Fulham	1	—
Shaun Gore*	6 4	13 01	21 9 68	London		Fulham	26	—
						Halifax T (loan)	15	—
Richard Langley*	5 7	11 05	20 3 65	London	Cor Cas	Fulham	50	—
Simon Morgan	5 11	12 07	5 9 66	Birmingham		Leicester C	160	3
						Fulham	32	—
Gavin Nebbeling	6 0	12 04	15 5 63	Johannesburg	Arcadia S	Crystal Palace	151	8
						Northampton T (loan)	11	—
						Fulham	42	—
Mark Newson	5 10	12 06	7 12 60	Stepney	Apprentice Maidstone U	Charlton Ath	—	—
						Bournemouth	177	23
						Fulham	47	1
Stacey North	6 2	12 06	25 11 64	Luton	Apprentice	Luton T	25	—
						Wolverhampton W (loan)	3	—
						WBA	98	—
						Fulham	38	—
Martin Pike	5 9	11 04	21 10 64	South Shields	Apprentice	WBA	—	—
						Peterborough U	126	8
						Sheffield U	129	5
						Tranmere R (loan)	2	—
						Bolton W (loan)	5	1
						Fulham	66	5
Steve Rocastle			8 11 71	Lewisham	Norwich C	Fulham	—	—
Glen Thomas	6 0	11 06	6 10 67	London	Apprentice	Fulham	119	3
Mark Tucker	5 11	11 07	27 4 72	Woking	Trainee	Fulham	—	—
Midfield								
Graham Baker	5 9	10 08	3 12 58	Southampton	Apprentice	Southampton	113	22
						Manchester C	117	19
						Southampton	60	9
						Aldershot (loan)	7	2
						Fulham	6	1
Gary Cobb	5 8	11 05	6 8 68	Luton	Apprentice	Luton T	9	—
						Northampton T (loan)	1	—
						Swansea C (loan)	5	—
						Fulham	11	—
Mark Kelly	5 8	10 06	7 10 66	Blackpool		Shrewsbury T	—	—
						Cardiff C	105	2
						Fulham	18	—
Ray Lewington	5 6	11 08	7 9 56	Lambeth	Apprentice Vancouver W	Chelsea	85	4
						Wimbledon (loan)	23	—
						Fulham	174	20
						Sheffield U	36	—
						Fulham	60	1
John Marshall	5 10	11 04	18 8 64	Surrey	Apprentice	Fulham	265	23
Udo Onwere	6 0	11 03	9 11 71	Hammersmith	Trainee	Fulham	7	1
Peter Scott	5 8	10 10	1 10 63	London	Apprentice	Fulham	238	26
Justin Skinner	6 0	11 03	30 1 69	London	Apprentice	Fulham	135	23

FULHAM

Foundation: Churchgoers were responsible for the foundation of Fulham, which first saw the light of day as Fulham St. Andrew's Church Sunday School FC in 1879. They won the West London Amateur Cup in 1887 and the championship of the West London League in its initial season of 1892–93. The name Fulham had been adopted in 1888.

First Football League game: 3 September, 1907, Division 2, v Hull C (h) L 0-1 – Skene; Ross, Lindsay; Collins, Morrison, Goldie; Dalrymple, Freeman, Bevan, Hubbard, Threlfall.

Did you know: Syd 'Carnera' Gibbons is one of a small number of centre-halves since World War 1 to score a hat-trick in a Football League game. He performed this feat for Fulham in a 3-3 draw with Southampton at Craven Cottage, 3 November 1934.

Managers (and Secretary-managers)
Harry Bradshaw 1904–09, Phil Kelso 1909–24, Andy Ducat 1924–26, Joe Bradshaw 1926–29, Ned Liddell 1929–31, Jim MacIntyre 1931–34, Jim Hogan 1934–35, Jack Peart 1935–48, Frank Osborne 1948–64 (was secretary-manager or GM for most of this period), Bill Dodgin Snr 1949–53, Duggie Livingstone 1956–58, Bedford Jezzard 1958–64 (GM for last two months), Vic Buckingham 1965–68, Bobby Robson 1968, Bill Dodgin Jnr 1969–72, Alec Stock 1972–76, Bobby Campbell 1976–80, Malcolm Macdonald 1980–84, Ray Harford 1984–86, Ray Lewington 1986–90, Alan Dicks July 1990–

Player and Position	Ht	Wt	Birth Date	Place	Source	Clubs	League App	Gls
Forwards								
Gary Brazil	5 11	9 13	19 9 62	Tunbridge Wells	Apprentice	Crystal Palace	—	—
						Sheffield U	62	9
						Port Vale (loan)	6	3
						Preston NE	166	58
						Mansfield T (loan)	—	—
						Newcastle U	23	2
						Fulham	42	4
Michael Cole*	5 11	11 04	3 9 66	Stepney	Amateur	Ipswich T	38	3
						Port Vale (loan)	4	1
						Fulham	48	4
Gordon Davies*	5 7	10 12	3 8 55	Merthyr	Merthyr T	Fulham	247	113
						Chelsea	13	6
						Manchester C	31	9
						Fulham	147	45
Kelly Haag	6 0	12 03	6 10 70	Enfield	Trainee	Brentford	5	—
						Fulham	23	3
Julian Hails			20 11 67	Lincoln		Fulham	—	—
Francis Joseph‡	5 10	12 00	6 3 60	Kilburn	Hillingdon B	Wimbledon	51	14
						Brentford	110	44
						Wimbledon (loan)	5	1
						Reading	11	2
						Bristol R (loan)	3	—
						Aldershot (loan)	10	2
						Sheffield U	13	3
						Gillingham	18	1
						Crewe Alex	16	2
						Fulham	4	—
Steve Milton	6 0	12 07	13 4 63	London	Apprentice Whyteleafe	West Ham U	—	—
						Fulham	57	9
Phil Stant	6 1	12 07	13 10 62	Bolton	Camberley Army	Reading	4	2
						Hereford U	89	38
						Notts Co	22	6
						Blackpool (loan)	12	5
						Lincoln C (loan)	4	—
						Huddersfield T (loan)	5	1
						Fulham	19	5

Trainees
Baranowski, Frank M; Brodrick, Darren; Gayle, Anthony; Humphreys, Gavin D; Hurdle, Agustus A.J; Jamfy, Kwabena; Kelly, Paul L.M; Lewis, Karl J; Lewis, Leon J; Morgan, Michael I; O'Connor, Daniel T; Rudgley, Simon P; Sheldrick, Paul C; Sugrue, James S; Tabi, Jonas A.

Associated Schoolboys
Andrews, Nicholas; Bartley, Carl; Dafedjiaiye, Matthew; Hawkins, Benjamin J; Johns, Jason; McMahon, James; Paine, Darren; Power, James S; Smith, David P; Smith, Desmond L; Warner, Carl A; Webb, Christopher M.

Associated Schoolboys who have accepted the club's offer of a Traineeship/Contract
Armitage, James A; Jupp, Duncan A; Moorhouse, Gary P; Murphy, Gary J; Omogbehin, Colin; Richards, Jonathan I; Whitaker, Andrew T; Wright, Stuart J.

226

GILLINGHAM 1990–91 *Back row (left to right)*: David Crown, Steve Lovell, Ivan Haines, Ron Hillyard (Assistant Manager), Harvey Lim, Peter Heritage, Tim O'Shea, Joseph Dunne.

Centre row: Javed Mughal (Physiotherapist), David Jordan, Lee Palmer, Mike Trusson, Brian Clarke, Peter Beadle, Alan Walker, Buster Collins, Malcolm Machin (Youth Team Manager).

Front row: Peter Johnson, Mark Dempsey, Tony Eeles, Paul Haylock, Damien Richardson (Manager), Billy Manuel, Ian Docker, Garry Kimble, Mark O'Connor.
Picture courtesy of the Chatham News and Standard.

Division 4   **GILLINGHAM**

Priestfield Stadium, Gillingham. Telephone Medway (0634) 51854/576828. Commercial Office: 51462.

Ground capacity: 19,581.

Record attendance: 23,002 v QPR, FA Cup 3rd rd 10 January 1948.

Record receipts: £35,070 v Everton, FA Cup 4th rd, 2nd replay, 4 February 1984.

Pitch measurements: 114yd × 75yd.

President: J. W. Leech. *Vice-presidents:* G. B. Goodere, G. V. W. Lukehurst.

Chairman: M. G. Lukehurst. *Vice-chairman:* Rt. Hon. Earl Henry Sondes.

Directors: P. H. Giles FCA, G. Trevor Carney. A. Smith, B. Baker.

Manager: Damien Richardson. *Assistant Manager:* Ron Hillyard.

Player Coach: Ron Hillyard. *Physio:* Javed Mughal.

Chief Executive/Company Secretary: Barry Bright. *Commercial Manager:* John Letley.

Year Formed: 1893. *Turned Professional:* 1894. *Ltd Co.:* 1893.

Club Nickname: 'The Gills'.

Previous Name: New Brompton, 1893–1913.

Record League Victory: 10-0 v Chesterfield, Division 3, 5 September 1987 – Kite; Haylock, Pearce, Shipley (2) (Lillis), West, Greenall (1), Pritchard (2), Shearer (2), Lovell, Elsey (2), David Smith (1).

Record Cup Victory: 10-1 v Gorleston, FA Cup, 1st rd, 16 November 1957 – Brodie; Parry, Hannaway; Riggs, Boswell, Laing; Payne, Fletcher (2), Saunders (5), Morgan (1), Clark (2).

Record Defeat: 2-9 v Nottingham F, Division 3 (S), 18 November 1950.

Most League Points (2 for a win): 62, Division 4, 1973–74.

Most League Points (3 for a win): 83, Division 3, 1984–85.

Most League Goals: 90, Division 4, 1973–74.

Highest League Scorer in Season: Ernie Morgan, 31, Division 3 (S), 1954–55 and Brian Yeo, 31, Division 4, 1973–74.

Most League Goals in Total Aggregate: Brian Yeo, 135, 1963–75.

Most Capped Player: Tony Cascarino, 3 (33), Republic of Ireland.

Most League Appearances: John Simpson, 571, 1957–72.

Record Transfer Fee Received: £250,000 from Bournemouth for Gavin Peacock, August 1989.

Record Transfer Fee Paid: £102,500 to Tottenham H for Mark Cooper, October 1987.

Football League Record: 1920 Original Member of Division 3; 1921 Division 3 (S); 1938 Failed re-election; Southern League 1938–44; Kent League 1944–46; Southern League 1946–50; 1950 Re-elected to Division 3 (S); 1958–64 Division 4; 1964–71 Division 3; 1971–74 Division 4; 1974–89 Division 3; 1989– Division 4.

Honours: Football League: Division 3 best season: 4th, 1978–79, 1984–85; Division 4 – Champions 1963–64; Runners-up 1973–74. *FA Cup:* best season: 5th rd, 1969–70. *Football League Cup:* best season: 4th rd, 1964.

Colours: Royal blue shirts white trim, white shorts blue trim, white stockings. **Change colours:** Black and white striped shirts, black shorts, black stockings.

GILLINGHAM 1990–91 LEAGUE RECORD

Match No.	Date		Venue	Opponents	Result		H/T Score	Lg. Pos.	Goalscorers	Atten- dance
1	Aug	25	H	Darlington	W	1-0	0-0	—	Lovell (pen)	3730
2		31	A	Torquay U	L	1-3	0-0	—	Lovell (pen)	3072
3	Sept	8	H	Hartlepool U	W	3-0	1-0	4	Lovell 2, Heritage	3155
4		15	A	Scarborough	L	1-2	1-1	10	Lovell	1499
5		19	A	Hereford U	D	1-1	1-0	—	Heritage	2632
6		22	H	Maidstone U	L	0-2	0-2	14		8004
7		29	A	York C	D	1-1	0-0	14	Docker	2259
8	Oct	2	H	Carlisle U	W	2-1	2-1	—	Lovell 2 (1 pen)	3022
9		6	H	Rochdale	D	2-2	0-0	11	Lovell 2	3316
10		13	A	Scunthorpe U	L	0-1	0-1	13		2357
11		20	A	Blackpool	L	0-2	0-0	15		3041
12		23	H	Aldershot	D	1-1	0-0	—	Walker	3140
13		27	H	Wrexham	L	2-3	1-1	17	Docker, Carpenter	3077
14	Nov	3	A	Doncaster R	D	1-1	1-0	17	Lovell	2502
15		9	A	Halifax T	W	2-1	0-1	—	Crown, Trusson	1708
16		24	H	Cardiff C	W	4-0	0-0	14	O'Connor Crown, Walker, Docker	2793
17	Dec	1	A	Chesterfield	D	1-1	0-0	15	Lovell	3468
18		15	H	Burnley	W	3-2	3-0	11	Crown 3	3687
19		22	A	Lincoln C	D	1-1	1-1	11	Lovell	2685
20		26	H	Walsall	W	1-0	0-0	10	Lovell	3695
21		29	H	Northampton T	D	0-0	0-0	10		4934
22	Jan	1	A	Stockport Co	D	1-1	1-1	10	Beadle	2859
23		11	H	Torquay U	D	2-2	0-1	—	Crown, Uzzell (og)	4329
24		25	H	Scarborough	D	1-1	0-0	—	Beadle	3756
25		29	A	Darlington	D	1-1	0-0	—	Crown	2882
26	Feb	2	H	Hereford U	W	2-1	1-1	10	Walker, O'Connor	3223
27		15	A	Cardiff C	L	0-2	0-1	—		2170
28		22	H	Halifax T	W	1-0	0-0	—	Crown	2800
29		26	H	Peterborough	L	2-3	1-0	—	Trusson, Beadle	3088
30	Mar	2	H	Chesterfield	L	0-1	0-1	14		3095
31		9	A	Burnley	D	2-2	1-0	15	Lovell, Crown	6459
32		12	A	Carlisle U	W	4-0	2-0	—	Beadle 2, Lovell, Crown	2633
33		16	H	York C	D	0-0	0-0	14		3056
34		19	H	Scunthorpe U	D	1-1	0-0	—	Trusson (pen)	2324
35		23	A	Rochdale	W	3-1	0-1	12	Beadle 2, Kimble	1654
36		30	A	Walsall	D	0-0	0-0	14		3074
37	Apr	1	H	Lincoln C	D	2-2	2-2	13	Crown, Walker	3765
38		6	A	Northampton T	L	1-2	1-1	15	Trusson (pen)	2993
39		13	A	Stockport C	L	1-3	1-1	15	Lovell	3001
40		16	A	Peterborough U	L	0-2	0-1	—		5831
41		20	H	Blackpool	D	2-2	1-1	15	Palmer, Lovell	3025
42		24	A	Maidstone U	L	1-3	1-2	—	Lovell	2935
43		27	A	Aldershot	L	0-1	0-1	16		2083
44		30	A	Hartlepool U	L	0-1	0-1	—		3782
45	May	4	A	Wrexham	L	0-3	0-0	17		1231
46		11	H	Doncaster R	W	2-0	1-0	15	O'Connor, Lovell	2653

Final League Position: 15

GOALSCORERS

League (57): Lovell 19 (3 pens), Crown 11, Beadle 7, Trusson 4 (2 pens), Walker 4, Docker 3, O'Connor 3, Heritage 2, Carpenter 1, Kimble 1, Palmer 1, own goal 1.
Rumbelows Cup (1): Lovell 1.
FA Cup (1): Crown 1.

Hillyard	Dunne	Manuel	Clarke	Walker	O'Shea	O'Connor	Trusson	Lovell	Heritage	Johnson	Kimble	Beadle	Haines	Palmer	Docker	Lim	Crown	McDonald	Eeles	Dempsey	Carpenter	West	Harle	Gleasure	Hague	Owers	Jordan	Butler	Match No.
1	2	3	4	5	6*	7	8	9	10†	11	12	14																	1
1	2†	3		5	14	7	8	9		11	12	10*	4	6															2
1	2*			5	6	7	8	9	10	11			4	3	12														3
1	2			5	6	7*	8	9	10	11			4	12	3														4
	2			5	6	7	8	9	10*	11			4	12	3	1													5
	2†			5	6	7	8	9	10*	11			4	3	14	1		12											6
	6*			5		7	8	9	10	11			4	3	12	1		2											7
	6			5		7*		9	10	11			4	12	3	8	1	2											8
	6			5		7		9		11		14	4*	10†	3	8	1	2	12										9
	6	3		5		7*		9	10	11			4	12	8	1		2†	14										10
	3	4†		5		7	6*	9	14	11				12	8	1	10	2											11
	3			5		7	6	9	14	11			4*	12	8	1	10	2†											12
	3			5		7		9	14	11			4*	6	8	1	10	2†	12										13
	3	4		5		7	6	9	12	11					8	1	10*	2											14
	4	3		5		7	6	9		11					8	1	10	2											15
	11	3	4	5		7	6	9							8	1	10	2											16
	11	3	4	5	2	7	6	9							8	1	10												17
	12	3	4	5	2	7	6	9	14	11†					8	1	10*												18
	11*	3	4		2	7	6	9	14	12					8	1	10†							5					19
	11	3	4	5	2	7	6	9							8	1	10												20
	11	3	4	5	2	7	6	9						12	8*	1	10												21
	11	3	4	5	2	7*	6	9						12	8	1	10												22
	11*		4	5	2		6	9	14					7	8	1	10				12	3†							23
	11†	3	4	5	2	7*		9	14					6	8	1	10				12								24
	11	3	4	5	2		6	9						7	8*	1	10				12								25
	11†	3	4	5	2	7		9	14				6	12	8*	1	10												26
		3	4	5	2†	7	6	9	14	11*	12				8	1	10												27
		3	4	5	2	7	6*	9		11				12	8	1	10												28
		3	4†	5	2	7*	6	9		11				12	8	1	10		14										29
		3		5	2*	12	6	9		11†				8	7	1	10		14		4								30
	2*	3		5	12	7	6	9		11			4		8	1	10				1								31
	2	3		5†	12	7	6	9		11			4		8	1	10				1					14			32
	2*	3				7	6	9		11	12		4		8	1	10								5				33
	2	3		5	9	7	6			11*	12		4		8	1	10												34
	2*	3		5	11	7	6	9					4	12	8	1	10												35
	7*			5	2		6	9		11			4	12	8	1	10					3							36
	2*			5		7	6	9		11			4	12	8	1	10†					3				14			37
	2	14		5			6†	9		11			4	7*	8	1					12	3				10			38
	14		4	5			6*	9†		11					8	1				7	2	3				10	12		39
	12		4	5		7	6	9		11					8	1					2	3*				10			40
	14			5		7	6			11†					8	1					2	3			4*	10	12	9	41
	12			5		7*	6			11					8	1					2	3			4	10		9	42
	12			5		7	6			11†					8	1					2	3*	14		4	10		9	43
	14			5	12		6†			11*					8	1					2	3	7		4	10		9	44
	3			5	2					11				7†	8	1	10				12	14			4	6*		9	45
				5	2	3†				11			4	7*	8	1	10				14	12				6		9	46
4	25	31	20	44	26	39	39	46	8	22	23	12	12	18	26	39	29	10	1	—	6	1	1	3	6	9	—	6	
	+1s	+7s		+3s	+2s			+7s	+2s	+11s	+10s			+3s	+5s			+1s			+5s	+2s	+3s		+1s		+1s	+1s +2s	

Rumbelows Cup   First Round   Shrewsbury T (h)   1-0
                                               (a)   0-2
FA Cup   First Round   Bournemouth (a)   1-2

GILLINGHAM

Player and Position	Ht	Wt	Birth Date	Birth Place	Source	Clubs	League App	Gls
Goalkeepers								
Ron Hillyard*	5 11	11 04	31 3 53	Rotherham	Amateur	York C	61	—
						Hartlepool U (loan)	23	—
						Bury (loan)	—	—
						Brighton & HA (loan)	—	—
						Gillingham	563	—
Harvey Lim	6 0	13 07	30 8 67	Halesworth	Apprentice	Norwich C	—	—
						Plymouth Arg (loan)	—	—
						Gillingham	43	—
Defenders								
Tony Butler	6 1	11 07	28 9 72	Stockport	Trainee	Gillingham	6	—
Brian Clarke	6 3	13 08	10 10 68	Eastbourne	School	Gillingham	33	—
Ian Docker*	5 8	11 02	12 9 69	Gravesend	Trainee	Gillingham	87	3
Paul Hague	6 2	12 06	16 9 72	Durham	Trainee	Gillingham	7	—
Ivan Haines*	5 9	10 12	14 9 68	Chatham		Gillingham	51	—
Peter Johnson*	5 9	11 00	5 10 58	Harrogate	Apprentice	Middlesbrough	43	—
						Newcastle U	16	—
						Bristol C (loan)	20	—
						Doncaster R	12	—
						Darlington	89	2
						Crewe Alex	8	—
						Exeter C	5	—
						Southend U	126	3
						Gillingham	69	2
Billy Manuel	5 5	10 00	28 6 69	Hackney	Apprentice	Tottenham H	—	—
						Gillingham	87	5
Eliot Martin	5 8	10 06	27 9 72	Plumstead	Trainee	Gillingham	—	—
Tim O'Shea	5 11	11 04	12 11 66	London	School	Tottenham H	3	—
						Newport Co (loan)	10	—
						Leyton Orient	9	1
						Gillingham	82	2
Lee Palmer	6 0	12 04	19 9 70	Gillingham	Trainee	Gillingham	61	4
Brendan Place‡			13 12 65	Dublin	Athlone T	Gillingham	4	—
Alan Walker	6 1	12 07	17 12 59	Mossley	Telford U	Lincoln C	75	4
						Millwall	92	8
						Gillingham	111	6
Midfield								
Austin Berkley	5 9	10 10	28 1 73	Dartford	Trainee	Gillingham	—	—
Richard Carpenter	5 11	12 00	30 9 72	Sheppey	Trainee	Gillingham	9	1
Mark Dempsey	5 7	10 09	10 12 72	Dublin	Trainee	Gillingham	2	—
Joe Dunne	5 9	11 00	25 5 73	Dublin	Trainee	Gillingham	26	—
Tony Eeles	5 7	9 12	15 11 70	Chatham	Trainee	Gillingham	42	2
Michael Harle§	6 0	12 00	31 10 72	Lewisham	Trainee	Gillingham	2	—
Steve Thompson‡			17 2 72	Manchester	Trainee	Gillingham	2	—
Mike Trusson	5 10	12 04	26 5 59	Northolt	Apprentice	Plymouth Arg	73	15
						Stoke C (loan)	—	—
						Sheffield U	126	31
						Rotherham U	124	19
						Brighton & HA	37	2
						Gillingham	64	6
Forwards								
Andrew Arnott	6 1	12 06	18 10 73	Chatham	Trainee	Gillingham	—	—
Peter Beadle	6 0	11 12	13 5 72	London	Trainee	Gillingham	34	9
Paul Burke	5 6	10 00	8 8 72	Camberwell	Trainee	Gillingham	—	—

GILLINGHAM

Foundation: The success of the pioneering Royal Engineers of Chatham excited the interest of the residents of the Medway Towns and led to the formation of many clubs including Excelsior. After winning the Kent Junior Cup and the Chatham District League in 1893, Excelsior decided to go for bigger things and it was at a meeting in the Napier Arms, Brompton, in 1893 that New Brompton FC came into being as a professional concern, securing the use of a ground in Priestfield Road.

First Football League game: 28 August, 1920, Division 3, v Southampton (h) D 1-1 – Branfield; Robertson, Sissons; Battiste, Baxter, Wigmore; Holt, Hall, Gilbey (1), Roe, Gore.

Did you know: In December 1924, when the Gills were involved in four FA Cup replays with Barrow before losing 2-1 at New Cross, they played nine League and Cup games in 19 days.

Managers (and Secretary-managers)
W. Ironside Groombridge 1896–1906* (previously financial secretary), Steve Smith 1906–08, W. I. Groombridge 1908–19*, George Collins 1919–20, John McMillan 1920–23, Harry Curtis 1923–26, Albert Hoskins 1926–29, Dick Hendrie 1929–31, Fred Maven 1932–37, Alan Ure 1937–38, Bill Harvey 1938–39, Archie Clark 1939–58, Harry Barratt 1958–62, Freddie Cox 1962–65, Basil Hayward 1966–71, Andy Nelson 1971–74, Len Ashurst 1974–75, Gerry Summers 1975–81, Keith Peacock 1981–87, Paul Taylor 1988, Keith Burkinshaw 1988–89, Damien Richardson May 1989– .

Player and Position	Ht	Wt	Birth Date	Birth Place	Source	Clubs	League App	Gls
David Crown	5 10	11 04	16 2 58	Enfield	Walthamstow A			
						Brentford	46	8
						Portsmouth	28	2
						Exeter C (loan)	7	3
						Reading	88	15
						Cambridge U	106	45
						Southend U	113	61
						Gillingham	30	11
Lindon Guscott‡			29 3 72	London	Trainee	Gillingham	2	—
David Jordan*	6 0	11 07	26 10 71	Gillingham	Trainee	Gillingham	2	—
Garry Kimble*	5 8	11 00	6 8 66	Poole		Charlton Ath	9	1
						Exeter C (loan)	1	—
						Cambridge U	41	2
						Doncaster R	65	1
						Fulham	3	—
						Maidstone U	—	—
						Gillingham	48	1
Steve Lovell	5 9	12 03	16 7 60	Swansea	Apprentice	Crystal Palace	74	3
						Stockport Co (loan)	12	—
						Millwall	146	44
						Swansea C (loan)	2	1
						Gillingham	178	75
Mark O'Connor	5 7	10 02	10 3 63	Rochdale	Apprentice	QPR	3	—
						Exeter C (loan)	38	1
						Bristol R	80	10
						Bournemouth	128	12
						Gillingham	56	4

Trainees
Cropper, Nicholas M; Ealham, Lee P; Gethin, Barry; Giemza, Stefan; Golden, Paul T; Harle, Michael J. L; Harrison, Stuart J; Smale, Justin P; Wood, Simon; Wren, Nicholas J.

Associated Schoolboys
Bernini, Scott; Brookes, James; Carcary, Murray J; Christou, Christopher B; Connelly, Paul; Egan, Gareth P; Gardner, Lee D; Hake, Kevin S; Massey, Simon; Maxted, Daniel R; Napier, Carl A; Smith, Gary J; Stevens, Justin G; Verrall, Damon F; Williams, Kevin J; Wilson, Paul A.F.

Associated Schoolboys who have accepted the club's offer of a Traineeship/Contract
Hunt, Kevin; Newman, Terry R; Russell, Steven J; Trott, Robin F.

232

GRIMSBY TOWN 1990-91 *Back row (left to right):* Peter Jellitt (Physiotherapist), Chris Hargreaves, Mark Lever, Andy Tillson, Ian Knight, Steve Sherwood, Paul Reece, Keith Alexander, John Cockerill, Roger Willis, Gary Birtles, Arthur Mann (Youth Team Coach).
Front row: Paul Agnew, Tony Rees, Shaun Cunnington, Tommy Watson, Alan Buckley (Manager), Gary Childs, John McDermott, Dave Gilbert, Kevin Jobling.

Division 2 — **GRIMSBY TOWN**

Blundell Park, Cleethorpes, South Humberside DN35 7PY.
Telephone Cleethorpes (0472) 697111. Clubcall: 0898 121576.
Ground capacity: 18,496.
Record attendance: 31,651 v Wolverhampton W, FA Cup 5th
rd, 20 February 1937.
Record receipts: £44,137 v Norwich C, Milk Cup 5th rd.
16 January 1985.
Pitch measurements: 111yd × 74yd.
Presidents: T. J. Lindley, T. Wilkinson.
Chairman: P. W. Furneaux. *Vice-chairman:* W. H. Carr.
Directors: P. W. Furneaux (Chairman), T. Aspinall, G. W.
Duffield, G. Lamming, J. Mager.
Manager: Alan Buckley. *Assistant Manager:* Arthur Mann.
Coach:
Company Secretary: I. Fleming. *Lottery Director:* T. E. Harvey.
Physio: Peter Jellett.
Year Formed. 1878. *Turned Professional:* 1890. *Ltd Co.:* 1890.
Previous Name: Grimsby Pelham.
Club Nickname: 'The Mariners'.
Previous Grounds: Clee Park; Abbey Park.
Record League Victory: 9-2 v Darwen, Division 2, 15 April 1899 – Bagshaw; Lockie, Nidd;
Griffiths, Bell (1), Nelmes; Jenkinson (3), Richards (1), Cockshutt (3), Robinson, Chadburn
(1).
Record Cup Victory: 8-0 v Darlington, FA Cup, 2nd rd, 21 November 1885 – G. Atkinson;
J. H. Taylor, H. Taylor; Hall, Kimpson, Hopewell; H. Atkinson (1), Garnham, Seal (3),
Sharman, Monument (4).
Record Defeat: 1-9 v Arsenal, Division 1, 28 January 1931.
Most League Points (2 for a win): 68, Division 3 (N), 1955–56.
Most League Points (3 for a win): 83, Division 3, 1990–91.
Most League Goals: 103, Division 2, 1933–34.
Highest League Scorer in Season: Pat Glover, 42, Division 2, 1933–34.
Most League Goals in Total Aggregate: Pat Glover, 182, 1930–39.
Most Capped Player: Pat Glover, 7, Wales.
Most League Appearances: Keith Jobling, 448, 1953–69.
Record Transfer Fee Received: £300,000 from Everton for Paul Wilkinson, March 1985.
Record Transfer Fee Paid: £110,000 to Watford for James Gilligan, July 1985.
Football League Record: 1892 Original Member Division 2; 1901–03 Division 1; 1903
Division 2; 1910 Failed re-election; 1911 re-elected Division 2; 1920–21 Division 3; 1921–26
Division 3 (N); 1926–29 Division 2; 1929–32 Division 1; 1932–34 Division 2; 1934–48
Division 1; 1948–51 Division 2; 1951–56 Division 3 (N); 1956–59 Division 2; 1959–62
Division 3; 1962–64 Division 2; 1964–68 Division 3; 1968–72 Division 4; 1972–77 Division
3; 1977–79 Division 4; 1979–80 Division 3; 1980–87 Division 2; 1987–88 Division 3; 1988–
90 Division 4; 1990–91 Division 3; 1991– Division 2.
Honours: Football League: Division 1 best season: 5th, 1934–35; Division 2 – Champions
1900–01, 1933–34; Runners-up 1928–29; Division 3 (N) – Champions 1925–26, 1955–56;
Runners-up 1951–52; Division 3 – Champions 1979–80; Runners-up 1961–62; Division 4 –
Champions 1971–72; Runners-up 1978–79; 1989–90. *FA Cup:* Semi-finals, 1936, 1939.
Football League Cup: best season: 5th rd, 1979–80, 1984–85. *League Group Cup:* Winners
1981–82.
Colours: Black and white vertical striped shirts, black shorts with red triangular panel on
side, white stockings with red band on turnover. **Change colours:** All blue.

GRIMSBY TOWN 1990–91 LEAGUE RECORD

Match No.	Date		Venue	Opponents	Result		H/T Score	Lg. Pos.	Goalscorers	Atten- dance
1	Aug	25	A	Preston NE	W	3-1	2-0	—	Gilbert (pen), Hargreaves, Woods	6372
2	Sept	1	H	Wigan Ath	W	4-3	1-2	1	Childs, Hargreaves, Woods 2	5162
3		8	A	Crewe Alex	W	2-1	2-0	1	Woods, Cockerill	3265
4		15	H	Bradford C	D	1-1	1-0	3	Oliver (og)	7960
5		18	H	Huddersfield T	W	4-0	1-0	—	Rees, Watson, Cockerill 2	6158
6		22	A	Shrewsbury T	W	2-1	0-0	1	Woods, Watson	2904
7		29	A	Brentford	L	0-1	0-1	2		5951
8	Oct	2	H	Rotherham U	W	2-1	2-0	—	Lever, Woods	6923
9		6	H	Swansea C	W	1-0	1-0	2	Gilbert	5974
10		13	H	Chester C	W	2-1	2-0	1	Woods, Bennett (og)	1875
11		20	A	Birmingham C	D	0-0	0-0	1		10,123
12		23	H	Leyton Orient	D	2-2	1-1	—	Woods, Knight	6660
13		27	H	Stoke C	W	2-0	0-0	2	Watson, Childs	10,799
14	Nov	3	A	Exeter C	D	0-0	0-0	1		4647
15		10	A	Tranmere R	W	2-1	0-1	2	Cunnington, Gilbert	6140
16		24	H	Bolton W	L	0-1	0-1	2		6240
17	Dec	1	H	Mansfield T	W	2-0	0-0	2	Gilbert 2 (1 pen)	5350
18		15	H	Southend U	L	0-2	0-2	2		8126
19		22	H	Bournemouth	W	5-0	2-0	2	Rees 2, Cunnington, Gilbert 2 (1 pen)	5651
20		26	A	Reading	L	0-2	0-1	2		3045
21		29	A	Cambridge U	L	0-1	0-0	2		5922
22	Jan	1	H	Fulham	W	3-0	0-0	2	Rees, Hargreaves, Childs	7492
23		5	H	Bury	L	0-1	0-1	2		6249
24		12	A	Wigan Ath	L	0-2	0-2	2		2868
25		19	H	Preston NE	W	4-1	2-0	2	Lever, Rees 2, Childs	5391
26		26	A	Bradford C	W	2-0	0-0	1	Watson, Gilbert	8314
27	Feb	2	A	Huddersfield T	D	1-1	0-1	2	Watson	6571
28		5	H	Shrewsbury T	W	1-0	0-0	—	Watson	5683
29		16	A	Bolton W	D	0-0	0-0	2		10,318
30		23	H	Tranmere R	L	0-1	0-0	3		6375
31	Mar	2	A	Mansfield T	D	1-1	0-0	3	Rees	3502
32		9	H	Southend U	W	1-0	1-0	3	Gilbert	9689
33		12	H	Rotherham U	W	4-1	2-0	—	Rees 2, Dempsey (og), Woods	5542
34		16	H	Brentford	W	2-0	2-0	2	Woods 2	6685
35		20	H	Chester C	W	2-0	1-0	—	Woods, Watson	6012
36		23	A	Swansea C	D	0-0	0-0	2		3203
37		30	H	Reading	W	3-0	3-0	1	Cockerill 2, Gilbert (pen)	7219
38	Apr	2	A	Bournemouth	L	1-2	1-1	—	Watson	7021
39		6	H	Cambridge U	W	1-0	1-0	1	Gilbert (pen)	8550
40		9	A	Bury	L	2-3	1-1	—	Rees, Gilbert (pen)	4748
41		13	A	Fulham	D	0-0	0-0	2		5464
42		20	H	Birmingham C	D	0-0	0-0	2		8842
43		23	H	Crewe Alex	L	0-1	0-0	—		7166
44		27	A	Leyton Orient	W	2-0	1-0	2	Birtles, Watson	4306
45	May	4	A	Stoke C	D	0-0	0-0	2		11,832
46		11	H	Exeter C	W	2-1	2-0	3	Cockerill 2	14,225

Final League Position: 3

GOALSCORERS

League (66): Gilbert 12 (6 pens), Woods 12, Rees 10, Watson 9, Cockerill 7, Childs 4, Hargreaves 3, Cunnington 2, Lever 2, Birtles 1, Knight 1, own goals 3.
Rumbelows Cup (2): Gilbert 1, Hargreaves 1.
FA Cup (0).

Sherwood	McDermott	Jobling	Tillson	Knight	Cunnington	Childs	Gilbert	Woods	Cockerill	Hargreaves	Rees	Watson	Alexander	Lever	Birtles	Agnew	Baraclough	Croft	Futcher	Smith	Match No.
1	2	3	4	5	6	7	8	9	10	11											1
1	2	3	4	5*	6	7		11	10	8†	9	12	14								2
1	2	3	4		6	7*	8	11	10		9	12		5							3
1	2	3	4		6		8	11*	10		9	7		5	12						4
1	2	3	4		6		8	11	10		9	7		5							5
1	2	3	4		6		8	11	10	9		7		5							6
1	2	3	4*	14	6		8	11	10	12	9	7		5†							7
1	2	3	4		6		8	11*	10	12	9	7		5							8
1	2	3	4		6		8	11	10		9	7		5							9
1	2	3	4		6		8	11	10		9	7		5							10
1	2	3	4		6	12	8	11	10		9	7*		5							11
1	2	3*	4	14	6	7	8	11		12	9	10		5†							12
1	2	3	4		6	7	8	11			9	10		5							13
1		3	4	14	6	7†	8	11	10	12	9*	2		5							14
1		3	4		6		8	11	10	12		7		5	9*	2					15
1	2	3	4	5	6	12	8	11	10		9†	7*	14								16
1	2	3	4	5	6	7	8	11	10		9										17
1	2*	3	4		6		8	11	10	12	9	7†		5	14						18
1	2				6	7	8	11	10		9			5	4	3					19
1	2	12			6	7†	8	11	10		9*			5	4	3	14				20
1	2	7			6	12	8	11	10*		9			5	4†	3	14				21
1	2	10			6	7	8	11			9*	12		5	4	3					22
1	2	10	14		6	7	8	11			9	12		5	4†	3*					23
1	2	3			6	7	8*	11			9	10		5	4†				14	12	24
1	2				6	7	8	11		12	9*	10		5		3			4		25
1	2	3			6	7	8	11			9	10		5					4		26
1	2	3			6	7	8*	11			9	10		5	12				4		27
1	2	3			6	7	8	11*			9	10		5	12				4		28
1	2	3			6	7	8	11*			9	10		5	12				4		29
1	2	3			6	7	8	11	14	12	9	10*		5†					4		30
1	2	3			6	7	8				9	10		5	11				4		31
1	2	3			6	7*	8	14	10		9	12		5	11†				4		32
1	2	3			6		8	12	10		9	7		5	11*				4		33
1	2	3			6		8	11	10		9	7		5					4		34
1	2	3			6		8	11	10		9	7		5					4		35
1	2	3			6		8	11	10		9	7†		5	12				4	14*	36
1	2	3			6	12	8	11†	10		9	7	14	5*					4		37
1	2	3			6		8	11†	10		9	7*	14	5	12				4		38
1	2	3			6		8		10		9	7		5					4	11	39
1	2	3			6		8	11	10		9	7†	14	5*	12				4		40
1	2	3			6		8	11	10		9*	7	12	5					4		41
1	2	3			6	12	8	11	10		9†	7*	14	5					4		42
1	2	3			6		8	11	10	12		7†	14	5	9				4*		43
1	2	3			6†		8	11*	10	12		7	14	5	9				4		44
1	2	3			6		8	11	10			7	12	5	9*				4		45
1	2	3			6		8	11	10		9*	7	12	5					4		46
46	43	44	18	4	46	20	44	42	34	8	36	36	—	40	15	6	1	—	22	1	
	+		+		+		+	+	+		+	+		+	+	+	+		+		
	1s		4s		5s		2s	1s	10s		5s	1s		8s	1s	3s	1s		10s		

Rumbelows Cup	First Round	Crewe Alex (h)	2-1
		(a)	0-1
FA Cup	First Round	Blackpool (a)	0-2

GRIMSBY TOWN

Player and Position	Ht	Wt	Birth Date	Place	Source	Clubs	League App	Gls
Goalkeepers								
Paul Reece	5 11	12 07	16 7 68	Nottingham	Kettering	Grimsby T	29	—
Steve Sherwood	6 4	14 07	10 12 53	Selby	Apprentice	Chelsea	16	—
						Brighton & HA (loan)	—	—
						Millwall (loan)	1	—
						Brentford (loan)	62	—
						Watford	211	1
						Grimsby T	155	—
Defenders								
Paul Agnew	5 9	10 04	15 8 65	Lisburn	Cliftonville	Grimsby T	161	3
Paul Futcher	6 0	12 03	25 9 56	Chester	Apprentice	Chester	20	—
						Luton T	131	1
						Manchester C	37	—
						Oldham Ath	98	1
						Derby Co	35	—
						Barnsley	230	—
						Halifax T	15	—
						Grimsby T	22	—
Ian Knight	6 2	12 04	26 10 66	Hartlepool	Apprentice	Barnsley	—	—
						Sheffield W	21	—
						Scunthorpe U (loan)	2	—
						Grimsby T	17	2
Mark Lever	6 3	12 05	29 3 70	Beverley	Trainee	Grimsby T	116	6
John McDermott	5 7	10 07	3 2 69	Middlesbrough		Grimsby T	161	1
Geoff Stephenson†	5 7	11 00	28 4 70	Tynemouth	Trainee	Grimsby T	21	—
Midfield								
Gary Childs	5 7	10 08	19 4 64	Birmingham	Apprentice	WBA	3	—
						Walsall	131	17
						Birmingham C	55	2
						Grimsby T	69	9
John Cockerill	6 0	12 07	12 7 61	Cleethorpes	Stafford R	Grimsby T	97	18
Gary Croft§			17 2 74	Burton-on-Trent	Trainee	Grimsby T	1	—
Shaun Cunnington	5 8	10 04	4 1 66	Bourne	Amateur	Wrexham	199	12
						Grimsby T	149	8
Kevin Jobling	5 9	10 13	1 1 68	Sunderland	Apprentice	Leicester C	9	—
						Grimsby T	125	6
Tommy Watson	5 8	10 10	29 9 69	Liverpool	Trainee	Grimsby T	97	14
Forwards								
Garry Birtles*	6 0	12 00	27 7 56	Nottingham	Long Eaton U	Nottingham F	87	32
						Manchester U	58	11
						Nottingham F	125	38
						Notts Co	63	9
						Grimsby T	61	9
David Gilbert	5 4	10 04	22 6 63	Lincoln	Apprentice	Lincoln C	30	1
					Boston U	Scunthorpe U	1	—
						Northampton T	120	21
						Grimsby T	100	25
Chris Hargreaves	5 10	10 13	12 5 72	Cleethorpes	Trainee	Grimsby T	37	5
Tony Rees	5 9	11 13	1 8 64	Merthyr Tydfil	Apprentice	Aston Villa	—	—
						Birmingham C	95	12
						Peterborough U (loan)	5	2
						Shrewsbury T (loan)	2	—
						Barnsley	31	3
						Grimsby T	71	23

GRIMSBY TOWN

Foundation: Grimsby Pelham FC as they were first known, came into being at a meeting held at the Wellington Arms in September 1878. Pelham is the family name of big landowners in the area, the Earls of Yarborough. The receipts for their first game amounted to 6s. 9d. (approx. 39p). After a year, the club name was changed to Grimsby Town.

First Football League game: 3 September, 1892, Division 2, v Northwich Victoria (h) W 2-1 – Whitehouse; Lundie, T. Frith; C. Frith, Walker, Murrell; Higgins, Henderson, Brayshaw, Riddoch (2), Ackroyd.

Did you know: In season 1933–34, when Grimsby Town won the Second Division championship, they had no less than seven players who appeared in every League game. They were Kelly, Jacobson, Hall, Betmead, Buck, Bestall and Craven.

Managers (and Secretary-managers)
H. N. Hickson 1902–20*, Haydn Price 1920, George Fraser 1921–24, Wilf Gillow 1924–32, Frank Womack 1932–36, Charles Spencer 1937–51, Bill Shankly 1951–53, Billy Walsh 1954–55, Allenby Chilton 1955–59, Tim Ward 1960–62, Tom Johnston 1962–64, Jimmy McGuigan 1964–67, Don McEvoy 1967–68, Bill Harvey 1968–69, Bobby Kennedy 1969–71, Lawrie McMenemy 1971–73, Ron Ashman 1973–75, Tom Casey 1975–76, Johnny Newman 1976–79, George Kerr 1979–82, David Booth 1982–85, Mike Lyons 1985–87, Bobby Roberts 1987–88, Alan Buckley June 1988– .

Player and Position	Ht	Wt	Birth Date	Place	Source	Clubs	League App	Gls
Mark Smith	5 11	11 05	19 12 61	Sheffield		Sheffield U	—	—
					Gainsborough Tr	Scunthorpe U	1	—
					Kettering	Rochdale	27	7
						Huddersfield T	96	11
						Grimsby T	11	—
Neil Woods	6 1	12 12	30 7 66	York	Apprentice	Doncaster R	65	16
						Rangers	3	—
						Ipswich T	27	5
						Bradford C	14	2
						Grimsby T	44	12

Trainees
Blake, Robert; Burns, Stuart I; Croft, Gary; Drury, Robert J; Ford, Matthew; Handyside, Peter D; Hunter, Christopher; Penny, Christian; Stacey, Christopher L; Talbot, Kyle; Waiton, Steven M.

**Non-Contract
Mann, Neil; Stephenson, Geoffrey.

Associated Schoolboys
Bacon, Daniel J; Barratt, Mark A; Bowman, Steven; Dunlop, Simon A; Greenacre, Neil D; Holberry, Robert N; Lambert, Darren K.

**Non-Contract Players who are retained must be re-signed before they are eligible to play in League matches.

238

HALIFAX TOWN 1990-91   *Back row (left to right):* Billy Barr, Paul Donnelly, Tony Gregory, Dominic Naylor, Brian Butler, Derek Hall, Paul Fleming, Terry McPhillips.
Centre row: Mark Hans (Kit Manager), Phil Horner, Tony Fyfe, Nick Richardson, Jonathan Gould, David Brown, Chris Hedworth, Mitch Cook, David Evans, Ray Swires (Physiotherapist)

Front row: Dean Martin, Tommy Graham (Player-coach), Paul Futcher, Brian Taylor (Assistant Manager), Jim McCalliog (Manager), Graham Broadbent, Shaun Smith, Craig Fleming.

Division 4   **HALIFAX TOWN**

Shay Ground, Halifax HX1 2YS. Offices: 7 Clare Road, Halifax HX1 2HX. Telephone Halifax (0422) 53423/43381. Ground: 0422 361582 (Match day only), Fax: (0422) 349487.

Ground capacity: 8049.

Record attendance: 36,885 v Tottenham H, FA Cup 5th rd, 15 February 1953.

Record receipts: £27,000 v Manchester U, League Cup, 2nd rd, 1st leg, 26 September 1990.

Pitch measurements: 110yd × 70yd.

President: John S. Crowther. *Vice-president:* F. Hinchliffe.

Chairman: S. J. Brown. *Vice-chairman:* D. Greenwood.

Associate Directors: B. J. Boulton, G. Butler, J. Hallett, I. R. Stewart, C. Swift, D. Newiss.

Manager: Jim McCalliog. *Assistant Manager:* Brian Taylor. *Physio:* R. Swires.

Youth Team Coach: Arthur Graham.

General Manager/Secretary: Bev. Fielding. *Promotion and Marketing Executive:* Angela Harrison.

Commercial Manager: Paul Kendall.

Year Formed: 1911. *Turned Professional:* 1911. *Ltd Co.:* 1911.

Club Nickname: 'The Shaymen'.

Previous Grounds: Sandhall and Exley.

Record League Victory: 6-0 v Bradford PA, Division 3 (N), 3 December 1955 – Johnson; Griffiths, Ferguson; Watson, Harris, Bell; Hampson (2), Baker (3), Watkinson (1), Capel, Lonsdale. 6-0 v Doncaster R, Division 4, 2 November 1976 – Gennoe; Trainer, Loska (Bradley), McGill, Dunleavy (1), Phelan, Hoy (2), Carroll (1), Bullock (1), Lawson (1), Johnston.

Record Cup Victory: 7-0 v Bishop Auckland, FA Cup 2nd rd (replay), 10 January 1967 – White; Russell, Bodell; Smith, Holt, Jeff Lee; Taylor (2), Hutchison (2), Parks (2), Atkins (1), McCarthy.

Record Defeat: 0-13 v Stockport Co, Division 3 (N), 6 January, 1934.

Most League Points (2 for a win): 57, Division 4, 1968–69.

Most League Points (3 for a win): 60, Division 4, 1982–83.

Most League Goals: 83, Division 3 (N), 1957–58.

Highest League Scorer in Season: Albert Valentine. 34, Division 3 (N), 1934–35.

Most League Goals in Total Aggregate: Ernest Dixon, 129, 1922–30.

Most Capped Player: None.

Most League Appearances: John Pickering, 367, 1965–74.

Record Transfer Fee Received: £250,000 from Watford for Wayne Allison, July 1989.

Record Transfer Fee Paid: £50,000 to Hereford U for Ian Juryeff, September 1990.

Football League Record: 1921 Original Member of Division 3 (N); 1958–63 Division 3; 1963–69 Division 4; 1969–76 Division 3; 1976– Division 4.

Honours: Football League: Division 3 best season: 3rd, 1970–71; Division 3(N) – Runners-up 1934–35; Division 4 – Runners-up 1968–69. *FA Cup:* best season; 5th rd, 1932–33, 1952–53. *Football League Cup:* best season: 4th rd, 1964.

Colours: Sky blue and white shirts, white shorts, sky blue stockings. **Change colours:** Yellow and black shirts, blue and yellow shorts, yellow stockings.

HALIFAX TOWN 1990–91 LEAGUE RECORD

Match No.	Date	Venue	Opponents	Result	H/T Score	Lg. Pos.	Goalscorers	Atten-dance
1	Aug 25	H	Stockport Co	D	0-0	0-0	—		2362
2	Sept 1	A	Lincoln C	L	0-1	0-1	18		2947
3	8	H	Doncaster R	L	0-1	0-0	22		2394
4	15	A	Darlington	L	0-3	0-1	23		2992
5	18	A	Peterborough U	L	0-2	0-1	—		3082
6	21	H	Torquay U	L	0-1	0-1	—		1447
7	29	A	Northampton T	L	0-1	0-0	24		2977
8	Oct 6	H	Scunthorpe U	D	0-0	0-0	24		1468
9	13	A	Carlisle U	W	3-0	3-0	24	Barr, Norris, Graham	3697
10	20	A	York C	D	3-3	0-1	24	Norris 2, Graham	2601
11	23	H	Hereford U	L	0-4	0-1	—		1762
12	27	H	Blackpool	W	5-3	2-3	24	Norris (pen), Ellis, Graham, Gregory, Juryeff	1945
13	Nov 2	A	Aldershot	D	2-2	0-1	—	Norris 2	2686
14	9	H	Gillingham	L	1-2	1-0	—	Dobson	1708
15	24	A	Burnley	L	1-2	0-0	24	Juryeff	6620
16	Dec 1	A	Walsall	L	1-3	1-2	24	Norris	4153
17	15	H	Chesterfield	W	2-1	2-0	24	Norris (pen), Ellis	1415
18	21	H	Rochdale	W	2-0	1-0	—	Butler, Martin	1831
19	26	A	Scarborough	L	1-4	1-1	23	Norris	1327
20	29	A	Cardiff C	L	0-1	0-0	23		2903
21	Jan 1	H	Hartlepool U	L	1-2	1-1	24	Norris	1707
22	12	H	Lincoln C	D	1-1	0-1	24	Broadbent	1447
23	18	A	Stockport Co	L	1-5	0-3	—	Norris	4030
24	26	H	Darlington	D	0-0	0-0	24		1658
25	Feb 1	H	Peterborough U	D	1-1	1-0	—	Richardson	1133
26	5	A	Torquay U	L	1-3	0-1	—	Norris	2223
27	16	H	Burnley	L	1-2	1-0	24	Norris	4755
28	22	A	Gillingham	L	0-1	0-0	—		2800
29	27	A	Maidstone U	L	1-5	1-3	—	Norris (pen)	1020
30	Mar 2	H	Walsall	W	5-2	1-2	24	Norris 3 (2 pens), Juryeff 2	1464
31	9	A	Chesterfield	L	1-2	1-0	24	Norris	3565
32	12	A	Wrexham	W	2-1	0-1	—	Juryeff, Norris	1263
33	15	H	Northampton T	W	2-1	2-0	—	Norris 2	1347
34	19	H	Carlisle U	D	1-1	1-1	—	Juryeff	1004
35	23	A	Scunthorpe U	D	4-4	1-1	24	Richardson, Norris 2 (1 pen), Ellis	3134
36	26	H	Wrexham	W	2-0	0-0	—	Norris 2	1429
37	30	H	Scarborough	L	1-2	0-1	22	Norris	1623
38	Apr 1	A	Rochdale	D	1-1	1-0	22	Juryeff	2040
39	6	H	Cardiff C	L	1-2	0-1	22	Juryeff	1364
40	13	A	Hartlepool U	L	1-2	0-0	22	Norris (pen)	3185
41	16	H	Maidstone U	W	3-2	2-0	—	Ellis, Richardson, Juryeff	1002
42	19	H	York C	W	2-1	1-1	—	Norris, Evans	1421
43	23	A	Doncaster R	W	2-1	1-1	—	Cooper, Norris (pen)	2360
44	27	A	Hereford U	L	0-1	0-1	22		1820
45	30	A	Blackpool	L	0-2	0-0	—		5883
46	May 11	H	Aldershot	W	3-0	1-0	22	Patterson, Flower (og), Norris	1428

Final League Position: 22

GOALSCORERS

League (59): Norris 30 (8 pens), Juryeff 9, Ellis 4, Graham 3, Richardson 3, Barr 1, Broadbent 1, Butler 1, Cooper 1, Dobson 1, Evans 1, Gregory 1, Martin 1, Patterson 1, own goal 1.
Rumbelows Cup (4): Evans 1, Fyfe 1, Gregory 1, Richardson 1.
FA Cup (5): Juryeff 2, Norris 2, Graham 1.

Brown	Fleming P	Cook	Evans	Fleming C	Futcher	Butler	Graham	McPhillips	Fyfe	Hall	Gregory	Donnelly	Broadbent	Richardson	Juryeff	Barr	Martin	Norris	Ellis	Gould	Dobson	Leonard	Cooper	Gore	Whitehead	Megson	Patterson	Hutchinson	Match No.
1	2	3	4	5	6	7	8	9	10	11																			1
1	2	3	4	5		6		9	10	11	7	8*12																	2
1	2	3	4	5	6	7	11	9*12					10	8															3
1	2	3†	4	5	6	7	11*		10					14	12	8	9												4
1	2*		4	5	6		8				3	7		11	10	9	12												5
1			4	5	6		14				3†	7	8	12	10*	9	2	11											6
1	2		4	5	6	8			12			7	14		10*	9	3†11												7
1	2		4	5	6	11	10				7				9	3		8											8
1	2		4	5	6	11	10				7				9	3		8											9
1	2		4	5	6		10				7				9	3		8	11										10
1	2†		4	5	6	14	10*12				7				9	3		8	11										11
			4	5	6	2			10		7				9	3		8	11	1									12
	2		4	5		10*	6				7				9	3	12	8	11	1									13
			4	5	6						7*11			12	9	2		8	3	1		10							14
	2		4	5	6	12	10								9	3	7	8	11*	1									15
			4	5	6	2	10								9	3	7	8	11	1									16
	2		4	5	6	7	10								9	3		8	11	1									17
	2	10	4	5		7	6								9	3	12	8	11*	1									18
	2	10	4	5		7	6*								9	3	11	8	12	1									19
	2	10	4	5		7									9	3	6	8	11	1									20
	2	10	4	5		7							12		9	3	6	8	11*	1									21
	2	10	4	5		7	6						9			3*		8	11	1			12						22
	2	10†	4	5		7	6						14		9	3*		8	11	1			12						23
	2	3	4	5		6					7				9	10		8	11	1									24
		3		5		6					7		10		9	2	4	8	11	1									25
		3		5		6				11	7		10*		9	2	4	8	12	1									26
	2	3		5					10		7*		12		9		6	8		1				11	4				27
	2	3	4	5		10				11					9		8	7		1			6						28
	2	3	4	5		10				11					9		8	7		1			6						29
	2		4	5		10								7	9	3	11	8	12	1*			6						30
	2		4	5										10	9	3	11	8	7				6	1					31
	2		4	5										10*	9	3	11	8	7				12	6	1				32
	2		4	5										10	9	3	11	8	7					6	1				33
	2	14	4	5										10*	9	3†11		8	7				12	6	1				34
	2		4	5										10		3	11	8	7					9	6	1			35
	2		4	5		12					7*			10		3	11	8						9	6	1			36
	2	4*	5			12								10		3	11	8						9	6	1	7		37
	2		5		10										9	3	4	8		11				6	1	7			38
	2		4	5		12								10*	9	3	6	8		11					1	7			39
	2		4	5		12								10		3	6	8	11	1			9			7*			40
	2		4	5										10	9	3	6	8	7*	1			11				12		41
	2		4	5										10	9*		6	8	7	1			11				12	3	42
	2		4	5										10	12	11	8			1			9	6			7	3*	43
	2		4	5						14				10	12	11	8			1			9	6			7†	3*	44
			4	5	3									10	2		8	11	1				9	6		7*12			45
	2*		4	5						14				10	3		8	11†	1				9			7			46
11	39	16	42	46	15	19	23	3	3	8	11	8	3	23	34	34	26	39	27	23	1	3	13	15	9	5	3	3	

Substitute appearances: +1s · +7s · +2s +1s · +1s +3s +4s +3s · +3s +2s · +3s · +4s · +3s

Griffiths — Match No. 46(6); German — Match No. 46(12).

Rumbelows Cup	First Round	Lincoln C (h)	2-0	
		(a)	0-1	
	Second Round	Manchester U (h)	1-3	
		(a)	1-2	
FA Cup	First Round	Wrexham (h)	3-2	
	Second Round	Rotherham U (a)	1-1	
		(h)	1-2	

HALIFAX TOWN

Player and Position	Ht	Wt	Birth Date	Birth Place	Source	Clubs	League App	Gls
Goalkeepers								
David Brown‡	6 1	12 08	28 1 57	Hartlepool	Horden CW	Middlesbrough	10	—
						Plymouth Arg (loan)	5	—
						Oxford U	21	—
						Bury	146	—
						Preston NE	74	—
						Scunthorpe U (loan)	5	—
						Halifax T	38	—
Jonathan Gould	6 1	12 07	18 7 68	London	Derby Co	Halifax T	23	—
Defenders								
Billy Barr	5 11	11 07	21 1 69	Halifax	Trainee	Halifax T	133	7
Brian Butler	5 6	10 08	4 7 66	Salford	Apprentice	Blackpool	74	5
						Stockport Co	32	2
						Halifax T	56	4
David Evans	5 11	12 05	20 5 58	West Bromwich	Apprentice	Aston Villa	2	—
						Halifax T	218	9
						Bradford C	223	3
						Halifax T	42	1
Paul Fleming	5 7	10 00	6 9 67	Halifax		Halifax T	139	1
Ian Hutchinson§	5 8	11 05	7 11 72	Teeside	Trainee	Halifax T	3	—
Shaun Smith‡	5 10	11 00	9 4 71	Leeds	Trainee	Halifax T	7	—
Midfield								
Mitch Cook*	5 10	12 00	15 10 61	Scarborough	Scarborough	Darlington	34	4
						Middlesbrough	6	—
						Scarborough	81	10
						Halifax T	54	2
						Scarborough (loan)	9	1
						Darlington (loan)	9	1
Graham Cooper†	5 10	10 09	18 11 65	Huddersfield	Local	Huddersfield T	74	13
						Wrexham	63	16
						York C (loan)	2	—
						Halifax T	17	1
Paul Donnelly	5 8	10 00	23 12 71	Liverpool	Trainee	Halifax T	13	—
Craig Fleming	6 0	11 07	6 10 71	Calder	Trainee	Halifax T	57	—
David German§			16 10 73	Sheffield	Sheffield W	Halifax T	1	—
Tommy Graham	5 9	11 09	31 3 58	Glasgow	Arthurlie	Aston Villa	—	—
						Barnsley	38	13
						Halifax T	71	17
						Doncaster R	11	2
						Scunthorpe U	109	21
						Scarborough	111	11
						Halifax T	44	4
Tony Gregory	5 8	10 10	21 3 68	Doncaster	Apprentice	Sheffield W	18	1
						Halifax T	12	1
Neil Griffiths§	6 0	12 03	4 9 72	Halifax	Trainee	Halifax T	1	—
Derek Hall‡	5 8	11 02	5 1 65	Manchester	Apprentice	Coventry C	1	—
						Torquay U (loan)	10	2
						Torquay U	45	4
						Swindon T	10	—
						Southend U	123	15
						Halifax T	49	4
Dean Martin*	5 10	10 02	9 9 67	Halifax	Local	Halifax T	153	7
Dominic Naylor‡	5 9	11 07	12 8 62	Watford	Trainee	Watford	—	—
						Halifax T	6	1
Jamie Paterson§	5 5	9 07	26 4 73	Dumfries	Trainee	Halifax T	6	1
Nick Richardson	6 0	12 07	11 4 67	Halifax	Local	Halifax T	60	9

HALIFAX TOWN

Foundation: The idea of a soccer club in a Rugby League stronghold was first mooted by a Mr. A. E. Muir who soon interested Joe McClelland (who became secretary-manager of the new club) and Dr. A. H. Muir their first chairman. Following correspondence in *The Halifax Evening Courier* the club was formed at a meeting at the Saddle Hotel in May 1911.

First Football League game: 27 August, 1921, Division 3(N), v Darlington (a) L 0-2 – Haldane; Hawley, Mackrill; Hall, Wellock, Challinor; Pinkey, Hetherington, Woods, Dent, Phipps.

Did you know: In season 1923–24 Halifax Town held First Division Manchester City to two draws in the FA Cup 2nd round (4th rnd modern equivalent) – 2-2 at Maine Road and 0-0 at the Shay before going down 3-0 in a 2nd replay at Old Trafford.

Managers (and Secretary-managers)
A. M. Ricketts 1911–12*, Joe McClelland 1912–30, Alec Raisbeck 1930–36, Jimmy Thomson 1936–47, Jack Breedon 1947–50, William Wootton 1951–52, Gerald Henry 1952–54, Willie Watson 1954–56, Billy Burnikell 1956, Harry Hooper 1957–62, Willie Watson 1964–66, Vic Metcalfe 1966–67, Alan Ball Snr 1967–70, George Kirby 1970–71, Ray Henderson 1971–72, George Mulhall 1972–74, Johnny Quinn 1974–76, Alan Ball Snr 1976–77, Jimmy Lawson 1977–78, George Kirby 1978–81, Mick Bullock 1981–84, Mick Jones 1984–86, Bill Ayre 1986–90, Jim McCalliog April 1990– .

Player and Position	Ht	Wt	Birth Date	Birth Place	Source	Clubs	League App	Gls
Forwards								
Graham Broadbent‡	6 0	12 07	20 12 58	Halifax	Emley	Halifax T	32	3
Mark Ellis	5 9	10 09	6 1 62	Bradford	Trinity Ath	Bradford C	218	30
						Halifax T	30	4
Ian Juryeff	5 11	12 00	24 11 62	Gosport	Apprentice	Southampton	2	—
						Mansfield T (loan)	12	5
						Reading (loan)	7	1
						Leyton Orient	111	44
						Ipswich T (loan)	2	—
						Halifax T	17	7
						Hereford U	28	4
						Halifax T	34	9
Terry McPhillips‡	5 10	11 00	1 10 68	Manchester	Trainee	Liverpool	—	—
						Halifax T	93	28
						Northampton T (loan)	1	—
Kevin Megson	5 11	11 00	1 7 71	Halifax	Trainee	Bradford C	27	—
						Halifax T	5	—
Steve Norris	5 9	10 08	22 9 61	Coventry	Telford	Scarborough	45	13
						Notts Co (loan)	1	—
						Carlisle U	29	5
						Halifax T	39	30

Trainees
Armstrong, Leighton J; Ash, Graham M; Fisher, Warren J; German, David; Gibson, Wayne E; Griffiths, Neil; Hutchinson, Ian N; Millward, Paul T; Niblo, Jonathan W; Paterson, Jamie R; Richardson, Joseph C; Shaw, Peter A; Stoney, Jarrod P; Tindall, Jonathan D; Warnes, Andrew M; Yates, Sean A.

**Non-Contract
Cooper, Graham.

Associated Schoolboys
Hook, Stephen J; Radio, Leano.

**Non-Contract Players who are retained must be re-signed before they are eligible to play in League matches.

244

HARTLEPOOL UNITED 1990–91 *Back row (left to right):* Steven Fletcher, Paul Baker, Chris Errington, Rob McKinnon, Ian Bennyworth.
Top Centre row: John Craggs (Coach), Alan Lamb, Garry Macdonald, Mick Smith, Keith Nobbs, Gary Henderson (Physiotherapist), Andy Davies, Steve Tupling, Kenny Davies, Ian Dunbar, John Tinkler, Bryan Robson (Assistant Manager).
Front Centre row: Alan Murray (Chief Executive), Austin Elliott (Director), Garry Gibson (Chairman), Cyril Knowles (Manager), Dr D Russell (Club Doctor), David Jukes (Director), Roland Boyes MP (Vice President), Alan Bamford (Director).
Front row: Paul Olsson, Don Hutchison, Paul Dalton, Brian Honour, Joe Allon.

Division 3   HARTLEPOOL UNITED

The Victoria Ground, Clarence Road, Hartlepool. Telephone Hartlepool (0429) 272584. Commercial Dept: (0429) 222077. Fax: 0429 863007.

HUFC
1 9 0 8
HARTLEPOOL UNITED
FOOTBALL CLUB LTD
VICTORIA GROUND
HARTLEPOOL
CLEVELAND TS24 8BZ
TEL. 0429-272584
FAX 0429-863007

Ground capacity: 9607.

Record attendance: 17,426 v Manchester U, FA Cup 3rd rd, 5 January 1957.

Record receipts: £42,300 v Tottenham H, Rumbelows Cup, 2nd rd 2nd leg, 9 October 1990.

Pitch measurements: 110yd × 75yd.

President: E. Leadbitter.

Chairman: G. Gibson. *Vice-chairman:* A. Bamford.

Directors: D. Dukes, A. Elliott.

Manager: Alan Murray. *Assistant Manager:*

Chief Executive: K. D. Green. *Sponsorship Manager:*

Coach: John Craggs. *Physio:* Gary Henderson.

Year Formed: 1908. *Turned Professional:* 1908. *Ltd Co.:* 1908.

Club Nickname: 'The Pool'.

Previous Names: Hartlepools United until 1968; Hartlepool until 1977.

Record League Victory: 10-1 v Barrow, Division 4, 4 April 1959 – Oakley; Cameron, Waugh; Johnson, Moore, Anderson; Scott (1), Langland (1), Smith (3), Clark (2), Luke (2). (1 og).

Record Cup Victory: 6-0 v North Shields, FA Cup, 1st rd, 30 November 1946 – Heywood; Brown, Gregory; Spelman, Lambert, Jones; Price, Scott (2), Sloan (4), Moses, McMahon.

Record Defeat: 1-10 v Wrexham, Division 4, 3 March 1962.

Most League Points (2 for a win): 60, Division 4, 1967–68.

Most League Points (3 for a win): 82, Division 4, 1990–91.

Most League Goals: 90, Division 3 (N), 1956–57.

Highest League Scorer in Season: William Robinson, 28, Division 3 (N), 1927–28.

Most League Goals in Total Aggregate: Ken Johnson, 98, 1949–64.

Most Capped Player: Ambrose Fogarty, 1 (11), Eire.

Most League Appearances: Wattie Moore, 447, 1948–64.

Record Transfer Fee Received: £175,000 from Liverpool for Don Hutchison, November 1990.

Record Transfer Fee Paid: £20,000 to Manchester U for Paul Dalton, May 1989.

Football League Record: 1921 Original Member of Division 3 (N); 1958–68 Division 4; 1968–69 Division 3; 1969–91 Division 4; 1991– Division 3.

Honours: Football League: Division 3 best season: 22nd, 1968–69; Division 3 (N) – Runners-up 1956–57. *FA Cup:* best season: 4th rd, 1954–55, 1977–78, 1988–89. *Football League Cup,* best season: 4th rd, 1974–75.

Colours: Sky blue, navy blue and white squared shirts, navy blue shorts, sky blue stockings. **Change colours:** All yellow.

HARTLEPOOL UNITED 1990–91 LEAGUE RECORD

Match No.	Date		Venue	Opponents	Result		H/T Score	Lg. Pos.	Goalscorers	Atten-dance
1	Aug	25	A	Chesterfield	W	3-2	2-0	—	Tupling, Baker, Fletcher	3821
2	Sept	1	H	Cardiff C	L	0-2	0-0	12		2800
3		8	A	Gillingham	L	0-3	0-1	19		3155
4		18	H	Rochdale	D	2-2	1-0	—	Dalton, O'Shaughnessy (og)	5725
5		22	A	Carlisle U	L	0-1	0-0	22		3303
6		29	A	Blackpool	L	0-2	0-2	23		3181
7	Oct	2	H	Aldershot	W	1-0	1-0	—	Allon	1916
8		6	H	Maidstone U	W	1-0	1-0	15	Dalton	2069
9		13	A	Doncaster R	D	2-2	0-1	17	Place (og), Allon	2801
10		16	H	York C	L	0-1	0-1	—		2746
11		20	A	Wrexham	D	2-2	1-0	17	Smith, Honour	1733
12		23	H	Peterborough U	W	2-0	2-0	—	Allon, Baker	2190
13		27	H	Hereford U	W	2-1	1-0	10	Allon (pen), Olsson	2135
14	Nov	3	A	Northampton T	L	2-3	1-1	14	Fletcher, Baker	3342
15		10	A	Darlington	W	1-0	1-0	12	Allon	2888
16		24	H	Scarborough	W	2-0	1-0	9	Baker, Tinkler	2122
17	Dec	1	A	Torquay U	W	1-0	0-0	7	Allon	2835
18		15	H	Lincoln C	W	2-0	2-0	6	Allon 2	2055
19		22	A	Burnley	L	0-4	0-2	8		8514
20	Jan	1	A	Halifax T	W	2-1	1-1	7	Allon 2	1707
21		12	A	Cardiff C	L	0-1	0-1	9		2619
22		19	H	Chesterfield	W	2-0	1-0	7	Allon, Tupling	2134
23		26	A	York C	D	0-0	0-0	8		3075
24		29	H	Stockport	W	3-1	2-1	—	Baker, Allon 2	2384
25	Feb	5	H	Carlisle U	W	4-1	2-0	—	Allon 2 (1 pen), Honour, Dalton	2670
26		16	A	Scarborough	L	0-2	0-0	7		1804
27		23	H	Darlington	D	0-0	0-0	8		6100
28		26	A	Scunthorpe U	L	1-2	0-0	—	Allon (pen)	2220
29	Mar	2	H	Torquay U	D	0-0	0-0	9		2209
30		9	A	Lincoln C	L	1-3	0-2	11	Allon	2575
31		12	A	Aldershot	W	5-1	4-1	—	Dalton 3, Allon, Tinkler	1579
32		16	H	Blackpool	L	1-2	1-1	10	McKinnon	2840
33		23	A	Maidstone U	W	4-1	0-0	9	Honour 2, Dalton, Baker	1462
34		26	H	Walsall	W	2-1	2-0	—	Allon 2	2556
35		29	A	Stockport Co	W	3-1	1-0	—	Baker, Allon 2	5217
36	Apr	1	H	Burnley	D	0-0	0-0	6		4967
37		6	A	Walsall	W	1-0	0-0	6	Allon	2758
38		9	H	Scunthorpe U	W	2-0	0-0	—	Dalton, Baker	2840
39		13	H	Halifax T	W	2-1	0-0	4	Baker, Allon	3185
40		16	H	Doncaster R	D	1-1	0-0	—	MacPhail	3365
41		20	H	Wrexham	W	2-1	2-0	4	Allon, Baker	3077
42		23	A	Rochdale	D	0-0	0-0	—		1686
43		27	A	Peterborough	D	1-1	0-0	4	Allon	7636
44		30	H	Gillingham	W	1-0	1-0	—	Allon	3782
45	May	4	A	Hereford U	W	3-1	2-0	3	Baker, Dalton 2	2387
46		11	H	Northampton T	W	3-1	1-1	3	Dalton, Allon, Baker	6957

Final League Position: 3

GOALSCORERS

League (67): Allon 28 (3 pens), Baker 12, Dalton 11, Honour 4, Fletcher 2, Tinkler 2, Tupling 2, McKinnon 1, MacPhail 1, Olsson 1, Smith 1, own goals 2.
Rumbelows Cup (5): Allon 2, Baker 1, Dalton 1, Honour 1.
FA Cup (3): Allon 3.

Cox	Olsson	McKinnon	Tinkler	Smith	Bennyworth	Allon	Tupling	Baker	Fletcher	Dalton	Honour	Nobbs	Duggan	Hutchison	MacPhail	Shotton	MacDonald	Dunbar	Davies, K	Lamb	Heaney	Poole	Gabbiadini	Nesbitt	Davies, A	Match No.
1	2	3	4	5*	6	7	8	9	10	11	12															1
1	2†	3	4		6	7	8	9	14	11*	12	10			5											2
1	2	3	4†		6	7	8	12	9*	11	10			14	5											3
1	2	3	4		6	7	8	9		11*	10	12			5											4
1	2	3	4		6	7	8	9		11*	10				5	12										5
1	2	3	4		6†	7	8*	9		11	12	10		14	5											6
1		3			6	7	8	9		11	10	2	4		5											7
1		3			6	7*	8	9	12	11	10	2	4		5											8
1	14	3	4†	5*	6	7	8	9		11	10	2				12										9
1	4	3		5	6*	7	8	9	12		10	2		14		11†										10
1	4	3		5†		7	8	9	12	11*	10	2		14	6											11
1	4	3			6	7	14	9*	12	11	10	2†		8	5											12
1	4	3			6	7		9		11*	10	2		8	5			12								13
1	4	3			6	7		9	12	11*	10	2		8	5											14
1	4	3	14		6	7	8	9	12	11*	10	2†			5											15
1	2	3	4			7		9*	12	11	10			8	5	14			6†							16
1	2	3	4		6	7		9		11	10				5									8		17
1	2	3			6	7	8	9	12	11*	10	4			5											18
1	4	3	14			7	8	9*		11	10†	2			5						12				6	19
1	4	3			6	7	8	9*		11	10	2			5						12					20
1	4	3	14		6	7	8*	9		11†	10	2			5						12					21
1	4†	3	14		6	7	8	9		11*	10	2			5						12					22
1	4	3			6	7	8	9		12	10	2			5						11*					23
1	4	3			6	7	8	9		12	10	2*			5						11†				14	24
1	4*	3			6†	7	8	9		11	10	2			5						12				14	25
1	4	3	12		6	7	8	9		11*	10	2			5											26
1		3	4		6	7	8	9		11	10	2			5											27
1		3	4	11	6	7	8	9*		12	10	2†			5						14					28
1		3	4		6	7	8	9	12	11*	10	2			5											29
1		3	4	5	6	7	8	9	12	11*	10	2														30
1			4	5	6	7	8	9†	12	11*	10	2					3	14								31
1		3	4	5	6	7	8	9	12	11*	10	2														32
1		3	4	5	6	7	8	9		11	10	2														33
1		3	4	5*	6	7	8	9	12	11	10	2														34
		3	4		6	7	8	9	12	11*	10	2			5							1				35
		3	4		6	7	8	9		11	10	2			5							1				36
		3	4		6	7	8	9		11*	10	2			5							1	12			37
		3	4		6	7	8	9		11	10	2			5							1				38
	14	3	4		6	7	8†	9		11*	10	2			5							1	12			39
		3	4		6	7	8	9		11*	10	2			5							1	12			40
	8	3	4*		6†	7	14	9		11	10	2			5							1	12			41
	4	3				7	8	9		11	6				5							1	10		2	42
	8	3			6	7	4	9		11	10	2			5							1				43
	8	3			6	7	4	9		11	10	2			5							1				44
	8	3			6	7	4	9		11	10	2			5							1				45
	8	3			6	7	4	9		11	10	2			5							1				46
34	29	45	23	11	42	46	40	43	5	40	39	38	2	7	42	—	1	—	1	—	2	12	1	1	2	

Substitute appearances:
+2s   +3s +1s +1s   +2s +3s +9s +6s +3s +2s   +4s   +1s +1s +2s +2s +4s +1s   +4s   +2s

Rumbelows Cup	First Round	Chesterfield (a)	2-1
		(h)	2-2
	Second Round	Tottenham H (a)	0-5
		(h)	1-2
FA Cup	First Round	Runcorn (a)	3-0
	Second Round	Wigan Ath (a)	0-2

HARTLEPOOL UNITED

Player and Position	Ht	Wt	Birth Date	Birth Place	Source	Clubs	League App	Gls
Goalkeepers								
Brian Cox*	6 1	13 10	7 5 61	Sheffield	Apprentice	Sheffield W	22	—
						Huddersfield T	213	—
						Mansfield T	54	—
						Hartlepool U	34	—
Rob Moverley‡	6 3	12 00	16 1 69	Batley	Trainee	Bradford C	—	—
						Hartlepool U	29	—
Defenders								
Ian Bennyworth	6 0	12 07	15 1 62	Hull	Apprentice	Hull C	1	—
					Gainsborough Tr	Scarborough	89	3
					Nuneaton Bor	Hartlepool U	70	2
Andy Davies	6 0	11 06	6 6 72	Wolverhampton	Trainee	Torquay U	13	—
						Hartlepool U	4	—
Rob McKinnon	5 11	11 01	31 7 66	Glasgow	Rutherglen G	Newcastle U	1	—
						Hartlepool U	224	6
						Manchester U (loan)	—	—
John MacPhail	6 0	12 03	7 12 55	Dundee	St Columba's	Dundee	68	—
						Sheffield U	135	7
						York C	142	24
						Bristol C	26	1
						Sunderland	130	22
						Hartlepool U	42	1
Keith Nobbs	5 10	11 10	19 9 61	Bishop Auckland	Apprentice	Middlesbrough	1	—
						Halifax T	87	1
					Bishop Auckland	Hartlepool U	212	1
Mick Smith	6 1	11 09	28 10 58	Sunderland	Lambton St BC	Lincoln C	25	—
						Wimbledon	205	14
						Aldershot (loan)	7	—
					Seaham Red	Hartlepool U	47	6
Midfield								
Paul Dalton	5 11	11 07	25 4 67	Middlesbrough	Brandon U	Manchester U	—	—
						Hartlepool U	108	24
Kenneth Davies*	6 0	11 00	22 12 70	Stockton	Trainee	Hartlepool U	6	—
Brian Honour	5 7	12 05	16 2 64	Horden	Apprentice	Darlington	74	4
					Peterlee	Hartlepool U	224	15
Mark Nesbitt			11 1 72	Doncaster R	Trainee	Middlesbrough	—	—
						Hartlepool U	1	—
Paul Olsson	5 8	10 11	24 12 65	Hull	Apprentice	Hull C	—	—
						Exeter C (loan)	8	—
						Exeter C	35	2
						Scarborough	48	5
						Hartlepool U	54	3
John Shotton‡	5 8	10 06	17 8 71	Hartlepool	Trainee	Manchester U	—	—
						Hartlepool U	1	—
John Tinkler	5 8	11 07	24 8 68	Trimdon		Hartlepool U	131	7
Steve Tupling	6 0	12 08	11 7 64	Wensleydale	Apprentice	Middlesbrough	—	—
						Carlisle U (loan)	1	—
						Darlington	111	8
						Newport Co	33	2
						Cardiff C	5	—
						Torquay U (loan)	3	—
						Exeter C (loan)	9	1
						Hartlepool U	68	3

HARTLEPOOL UNITED

Foundation: The inspiration for the launching of Hartlepool United was the West Hartlepool club which won the FA Amateur Cup in 1904–05. They had been in existence since 1881 and their Cup success led in 1908 to the formation of the new professional concern which first joined the North-Eastern League. In those days they were Hartlepools United and won the Durham Senior Cup in their first two seasons.

First Football League game: 27 August, 1921, Division 3(N), v Wrexham (a) W 2-0 – Gill; Thomas, Crilly; Dougherty, Hopkins, Short; Kessler, Mulholland (1), Lister (1), Robertson, Donald.

Did you know: On the occasion that Hartlepool's ground record was created (5 January 1957) they fought back from 3-0 down to draw level with the star studded Manchester United side before the visitors won 4-3. Manchester United were League Champions for the second successive season in 1956–57.

Managers (and Secretary-managers)
Alfred Priest 1908–12, Percy Humphreys 1912–13, Jack Manners 1913–20, Cecil Potter 1920–22, David Gordon 1922–24, Jack Manners 1924–27, Bill Norman 1927–31, Jack Carr 1932–35 (had been player-coach since 1931), Jimmy Hamilton 1935–43, Fred Westgarth 1943–57, Ray Middleton 1957–59, Bill Robinson 1959–62, Allenby Chilton 1962–63, Bob Gurney 1963–64, Alvan Williams 1964–65, Geoff Twentyman 1965, Brian Clough 1965–67, Angus McLean 1967–70, John Simpson 1970–71, Len Ashurst 1971–74, Ken Hale 1974–76, Billy Horner 1976–83, Johnny Duncan 1983, Mike Docherty 1983, Billy Horner 1984–86, John Bird 1986–88, Bobby Moncur 1988–89, Cyril Knowles 1989–91, Alan Murray May 1991– .

Player and Position	Ht	Wt	Birth Date	Birth Place	Source	Clubs	League App	Gls
Forwards								
Joe Allon	5 11	11 02	12 11 66	Gateshead		Newcastle U	9	2
						Swansea C	34	11
						Hartlepool U	112	50
Paul Baker	6 1	12 10	5 1 63	Newcastle	Bishop Auckland	Southampton	—	—
						Carlisle U	71	11
						Hartlepool U	168	54
Paul Clark*			3 2 72	Consett	Trainee	Hartlepool U	—	—
Ian Dunbar‡	5 9	10 03	6 6 71	Newcastle		Hartlepool U	3	—
Steve Fletcher			26 6 72	Hartlepool	Trainee	Hartlepool U	14	2
Ricardo Gabbiadini	6 0	13 05	11 3 70	Newport	Trainee	York C	1	—
						Sunderland	1	—
						Blackpool (loan)	5	3
						Brighton & HA (loan)	1	—
						Grimsby T (loan)	3	1
						Crewe Alex (loan)	2	—
						Hartlepool U	5	—
Alan Lamb‡	5 10	11 12	30 10 70	Gateshead		Nottingham F	—	—
						Hereford U (loan)	10	2
						Hartlepool U	14	—
Gary MacDonald‡	6 0	12 01	26 3 62	Middlesbrough	Apprentice	Middlesbrough	53	5
						Carlisle U	9	—
						Darlington	162	35
						Stockport Co	1	—
						Hartlepool U	18	1
Nicky Southall			28 1 72	Teeside		Hartlepool U	—	—

Trainees
Brewis, Stephen L; Edwards, Paul G; Jones, Steven; Lester, Jason M; McGuckin, Thomas I; Potter, Steven; Walton, Charles A; Watson, Mark.

HEREFORD UNITED 1990–91   *Back row (left to right):* Mark Davies. Stephen McElroy. Mark Sutton. Leigh Harris.
Standing: John Layton. Gary Stevens. Richard Jones. Jon Narbett. Darren Peacock. Marcus Priday. Russell Bradley. Ian Juryeff. Tony Elliott. Paul Wheeler. Chris Hemming.
Paul Tester. Peter Isaac (Physiotherapist).
Seated: Colin Addison (Manager). Shane Jones. Colin Robinson. Mark A. Jones. Mel Pejic. Ian Benbow. Mark Jones. Steve Devine. Bobby Smith (Assistant Manager).
Front row: Paul Burton. Gareth Davies.

Division 4　　　　　　　**HEREFORD UNITED**

Edgar Street, Hereford. Telephone Hereford (0432) 276666.
Commercial Dept: (0432) 273155.

Ground capacity: 13,777.

Record attendance: 18,114 v Sheffield W, FA Cup 3rd rd,
4 January 1958.

Record receipts: £72,840 v Manchester U, FA Cup 4th rd,
28 January 1990.

Pitch measurements: 111yd × 74yd.

Chairman: P. S. Hill FRICS. *Vice-chairman:* M. B. Roberts.

Directors: D. H. Vaughan, A. J. Phillips, G. C. E. Hales,
H. A. R. Cotterell, J. W. T. Duggan.

Manager: John Sillett. *Assistant Manager:*

Physio: Colin Taylor.

Secretary: David Vaughan. *Commercial Manager:* Paul Roberts.

Year Formed: 1924. *Turned Professional:* 1924. *Ltd Co.:* 1939.

Club Nickname: 'United'.

Record League Victory: 6-0 v Burnley (away), Division 4, 24 January 1987 – Rose;
Rodgerson, Devine, Halliday, Pejic, Dalziel, Harvey (1p), Wells, Phillips (3), Kearns (2),
Spooner.

Record Cup Victory: 6-1 v QPR, FA Cup, 2nd rd, 7 December 1957 – Sewell; Tomkins,
Wade; Masters, Niblett, Horton (2p); Reg Bowen (1), Clayton (1), Fidler, Williams (1),
Cyril Beech (1).

Record Defeat: 0-6 v Rotherham U, Division 4, 29 April 1989.

Most League Points (2 for a win): 63, Division 3, 1975–76.

Most League Points (3 for a win): 77, Division 4, 1984–85.

Most League Goals: 86, Division 3, 1975–76.

Highest League Scorer in Season: Dixie McNeil, 35, 1975–76.

Most League Goals in Total Aggregate: Stewart Phillips, 93, 1980–88, 1990–1.

Most Capped Player: Brian Evans, 1 (7), Wales.

Most League Appearances: Mel Pejic, 397, 1980–91.

Record Transfer Fee Received: £200,000 from QPR for Darren Peacock, December 1990.

Record Transfer Fee Paid: £50,000 to Halifax T for Ian Juryeff, December 1989.

Football League Record: 1972 Elected to Division 4; 1973–76 Division 3; 1976–77 Division
2; 1977–78 Division 3; 1978– Division 4.

Honours: Football League: Division 2 best season: 22nd, 1976–77; Division 3 – Champions
1975–76; Division 4 – Runners-up 1972–73. *FA Cup:* best season: 4th rd, 1971–72, 1976–77,
1981–82, 1989–90. *Football League Cup:* best season: 3rd rd, 1974–75. *Welsh Cup:* Winners,
1990.

Colours: White shirts, black shorts, white stockings. **Change colours:** All red.

HEREFORD UNITED 1990–91 LEAGUE RECORD

Match No.	Date		Venue	Opponents	Result		H/T Score	Lg. Pos.	Goalscorers	Attendance
1	Aug	25	H	Northampton T	L	1-2	0-1	—	Jones R	3187
2	Sept	1	H	York C	W	2-0	0-0	10	Juryeff, Phillips	2422
3		8	A	Chesterfield	L	0-1	0-1	15		3183
4		15	H	Carlisle U	W	4-2	2-0	8	Narbett 3 (1 pen), Goddard	2773
5		19	H	Gillingham	D	1-1	0-1	—	Bradley	2632
6		22	A	Walsall	D	0-0	0-0	12		4558
7		29	H	Stockport Co	D	0-0	0-0	12		2619
8	Oct	3	A	Lincoln C	D	1-1	0-0	—	Phillips	2205
9		6	A	Darlington	L	1-3	0-0	13	Narbett	3376
10		13	H	Burnley	W	3-0	0-0	11	Narbett, Millar, Wheeler	3688
11		20	H	Cardiff C	D	1-1	0-1	12	Wheeler	5782
12		23	A	Halifax T	W	4-0	1-0	—	Phillips 3, Millar	1762
13		27	A	Hartlepool U	L	1-2	0-1	11	Phillips	2135
14	Nov	3	H	Scarborough	D	3-3	0-1	11	Tester, Narbett, Peacock	3017
15		10	A	Maidstone U	D	1-1	0-1	13	Jones M A	1938
16		24	H	Peterborough U	D	0-0	0-0	13		2148
17	Dec	1	H	Blackpool	D	1-1	1-0	14	Lowndes	2588
18		15	A	Aldershot	L	0-1	0-1	17		1783
19		22	H	Scunthorpe U	W	2-0	0-0	12	Dobson, Phillips	2218
20		26	A	Wrexham	W	2-1	1-1	11	Robinson, Phillips	2109
21		29	A	Doncaster R	L	1-3	0-2	14	Robinson	3170
22	Jan	1	H	Torquay U	D	0-0	0-0	14		3409
23		12	A	York C	L	0-1	0-0	16		1942
24		19	A	Northampton T	L	0-3	0-1	18		3577
25		26	A	Carlisle U	W	1-0	1-0	15	Tester	2572
26		30	H	Rochdale	W	2-0	0-0	16	Narbett (pen), Wheeler	2014
27	Feb	2	A	Gillingham	L	1-2	1-1	13	Brain	3223
28		6	H	Walsall	D	0-0	0-0	—		1947
29		23	H	Maidstone U	W	4-0	1-0	15	Hemming, Wheeler, Brain, Bradley	2390
30	Mar	2	A	Blackpool	L	0-3	0-1	16		3636
31		9	H	Aldershot	W	1-0	1-0	13	Brain	2275
32		13	H	Lincoln C	L	0-1	0-0	—		2195
33		16	A	Stockport Co	L	2-4	0-1	15	Pejic, Narbett (pen)	2569
34		19	A	Burnley	L	1-2	1-0	—	Phillips	5716
35		23	H	Darlington	D	1-1	0-0	17	Narbett (pen)	2462
36		30	H	Wrexham	W	1-0	0-0	16	Phillips	2521
37	Apr	1	A	Scunthorpe U	L	0-3	0-2	17		3001
38		6	H	Doncaster R	D	1-1	1-1	16	Brain	2013
39		13	A	Torquay U	D	1-1	0-1	16	Brain	3238
40		17	H	Chesterfield	L	2-3	1-1	—	Heritage, Tester	1750
41		20	A	Cardiff C	W	2-0	2-0	16	Brain, Narbett (pen)	2845
42		27	H	Halifax T	W	1-0	1-0	15	Brain	1820
43		30	A	Rochdale	L	1-2	1-0	—	Brain	1166
44	May	4	H	Hartlepool U	L	1-3	0-2	15	Narbett (pen)	2387
45		7	A	Peterborough U	L	0-3	0-2	—		7433
46		11	A	Scarborough	L	1-2	0-1	17	Jones S	1093

Final League Position: 17

GOALSCORERS

League (53): Narbett 11 (6 pens), Phillips 10, Brain 8, Wheeler 4, Tester 3, Bradley 2, Millar 2, Robinson 2, Dobson 1, Goddard 1, Hemming 1, Heritage 1, Jones M A 1, Jones R 1, Jones S 1, Juryeff 1, Lowndes 1, Peacock 1, Pejic 1.
Rumbelows Cup (1): Phillips 1.
FA Cup (2): Narbett 1, Pejic 1.

Wood	Jones MA	Devine	Jones R	Peacock	Pejic	Robinson	Narbett	Juryeff	Wheeler	Tester	Phillips	Bradley	Goddard	Gordon	Benbow	Millar	Lowndes	Hemming	Jones S	Burton	Dobson	Brain	Heritage	Elliott	Mitchell	Vaughan	Match No.
1	2	3	4	5	6	7	8	9	10†	11*	12	14															1
1	2	3	6	5	4	7†	8	9	10*	11	12	14															2
1	2	3		5	6	12	8	9	14	11*	10	4	7†														3
1	2	3		5	4	12	8		14	11*	10	6	7	9†													4
1	2			5	4	7*	8		14	11†10			6	3	9	12												5
1	2	3		5	4	12	8		14	11†10*			6	7	9													6
1	2	3		5	6	12	8		14	11	10*	4†	7	9													7
1	2	6	7		4	12	8			11*	10	5	3	9													8
1	2	6†	7		4	12	8		14	11	10*	5	3	9													9
1	2	6	7		4		8		14		12	10†	5	3*		9	11										10
1	2*	3	7	5	4		8		14		12	10†	6			9	11										11
1	2		7	5	4	12	8		14	3	10*	6				9†11											12
1	2		7	5	4	12	8		14	3*10		6				9†11											13
1	2		7	5	4	12	8		14	3	10	6				9†11*											14
1	2		7	5	4	12	8		9*	3	10						11	6									15
1	2*		7	9	4	11	8		10†	3		5						6	12	14							16
1	2		7	5	4	9†	8		14	3							11	6*12			10						17
1	2		7	5	4		8		14	12	9	6					11	3*			10†						18
1	2	3	6		4		8				11	9	5				7					10					19
1	2	3	6		4	12	8				11	9	5				7*					10					20
1	2	3	6		4	7	8*				11	9	5						12†			10	14				21
1	2	3	6		4	7	14				11	9	5						12			10†	8*				22
1	2	3	6		4	7	8		10*	11		9	5						12								23
1	2	3	6		4	7	8		10*	11		9	5			12											24
1	2	3	6		4	7	8		10	11		9	5														25
1	2	3	6*		4	7	8		10	11	9†	5							12			14					26
1	2	3	6		4	7	8*		10	11		5						14	12			9†					27
1	2	3	6		4	7*	8		10	11		5										9	12				28
1	2	3	6†		4*14				10	11		5						8	12			7	9				29
1	2	3	6		4		8		14	11		5					7†					9†10					30
1	2	3	6		4	12	8		10†11		14	5										7*	9				31
1	2	3	6*		4	12	8		10†11		14	5										7	9				32
1	2	5			4	6	8		12	3	10					7*						11	9				33
	2	5	7		4	6	8		12	3	10											11*	9	1			34
	2	3	6		4	12	8		11	10		5					7					9*		1			35
	2	3	6		4		8		12	11	10	5					7					9*		1			36
	2	3	6		4	12	8*		11	10†		5				7			14			9		1			37
1	2	3	6		4	10	8†		12	11		5							14			7	9*				38
1	2	3	6		4	12	8		11	10†		5							14			7*	9				39
1	2†	3	6		4		8		11			5				7			14			10*	9			12	40
1	2	3	6		4		8		11	12		5				7			14			10†	9*				41
1	2	3	6		4		8		11*	9†		5				7			14			10				12	42
1	2	3	6		4		8					5				7*	10	11				9				12	43
1	2*	3	6		4		8		11	10		5					12					7	9				44
1	2	3	6		4		8		12	11	10	5*										7	9				45
	2	4	6		5	12	8*		14								7	10†				11	9	1		3	46
41	46	38	40	15	46	16	44	3	13	41	31	39	8	6	—	5	16	5	3	1	6	20	17	5	—	1	
									+19s		+20s	+3s	+6s	+2s	+1s		+1s	+1s	+15s	+1s		+2s	+1s		+3s		

Rumbelows Cup First Round Brentford (a) 0-2
                                       (h) 1-0

FA Cup First Round Peterborough U (h) 1-1
                                       (a) 1-2

HEREFORD UNITED

Player and Position	Ht	Wt	Birth Date	Birth Place	Source	Clubs	League App	Gls
Goalkeepers								
Tony Elliott	6 0	12 12	30 11 69	Nuneaton		Birmingham C	—	—
						Hereford U	57	—
Mark Priday*	6 0	11 12	16 10 71	Knighton	Trainee	Hereford U	3	—
George Wood	6 3	14 00	26 9 52	Douglas	East Stirling	East Stirling	44	1
						Blackpool	117	—
						Everton	103	—
						Arsenal	60	—
						Crystal Palace	192	—
						Cardiff C	67	—
						Blackpool (loan)	15	—
						Hereford U	41	—
Defenders								
Russell Bradley	6 0	12 05	28 3 66	Birmingham		Nottingham F	—	—
						Hereford U (loan)	12	1
						Hereford	74	3
Steve Devine	5 9	10 07	11 12 64	Strabane	Apprentice	Wolverhampton W	—	—
						Derby Co	11	—
						Stockport Co	2	—
						Hereford U	208	3
Karl Goddard	5 9	10 10	29 12 67	Leeds	Apprentice	Manchester U	—	—
						Bradford C	73	—
						Exeter C (loan)	1	—
						Colchester U (loan)	16	1
						Hereford U	8	1
Chris Hemming*	5 11	11 02	13 4 66	Newcastle	School	Stoke C	93	2
						Wigan Ath (loan)	4	—
						Hereford U	41	3
Mark A. Jones*	5 8	10 12	22 10 61	Warley	Apprentice	Aston Villa	24	—
						Brighton & HA	9	—
						Birmingham C	34	—
						Shrewsbury T	—	—
						Hereford U	156	2
Mel Pejic	5 9	10 08	27 4 59	Chesterton	Local	Stoke C	1	—
						Hereford U	397	13
Midfield								
Ian Benbow‡	5 10	11 00	9 1 69	Hereford	Trainee	Hereford U	83	4
Mark Jones*	5 8	10 01	4 1 68	Brownhills	Apprentice	Walsall	8	—
						Exeter C (loan)	5	—
						Hereford U	42	8
Richard Jones	5 11	11 01	26 4 69	Pontypool		Newport Co	41	1
						Hereford U	97	5
Shane Jones§	5 9	10 02	8 11 72	Tredegar	Trainee	Hereford U	33	1
Jon Narbett	5 10	10 08	21 11 68	Birmingham	Apprentice	Shrewsbury T	26	3
						Hereford U	116	23
Nigel Vaughan	5 5	8 10	20 5 59	Caerleon	Apprentice	Newport Co	224	32
						Cardiff C	149	42
						Reading (loan)	5	1
						Wolverhampton W	93	10
						Hereford U	1	—
Forwards								
Simon Brain	5 6	10 08	31 3 66	Evesham	Cheltenham T	Hereford U	22	8
Paul Burton§	5 9	10 01	6 8 73	Hereford		Hereford U	4	1
Peter Heritage	6 1	13 00	8 11 60	Bexhill	Hythe T	Gillingham	57	11
						Hereford U	18	1

HEREFORD UNITED

Foundation: A number of local teams amalgamated in 1924 under the chairmanship of Dr. E. W. Maples to form Hereford United and joined the Birmingham Combination. They graduated to the Birmingham League four years later.

First Football League game: 12 August, 1972, Division 4, v Colchester U (a) L 0-1 – Potter; Mallender, Naylor; Jones, McLaughlin, Tucker; Slattery, Hollett, Owen, Radford, Wallace.

Did you know: While Dixie McNeil holds Football League goalscoring records for Hereford their most prolific scorer was Charlie Thompson. Signed from Sheffield United in 1947 he scored 184 goals in over 450 Southern League games up to 1958. He scored eight when they beat Thynnes 11-0 in an FA Cup tie.

Managers (and Secretary-managers)
Eric Keen 1939, George Tranter 1948–49, Alex Massie 1952, George Tranter 1953–55, Joe Wade 1956–62, Ray Daniels 1962–63, Bob Dennison 1963–67, John Charles 1967–71, Colin Addison 1971–74, John Sillett 1974–78, Mike Bailey 1978–79, Frank Lord 1979–82, Tommy Hughes 1982–83, Johnny Newman 1983–87, Ian Bowyer 1987–90, Colin Addison 1990–91, John Sillett May 1991– .

Player and Position	Ht	Wt	Birth Date	Place	Source	Clubs	League App	Gls
Steve Lowndes	5 10	10 13	17 6 60	Cwmbran	Amateur	Newport Co	208	39
						Millwall	96	16
						Barnsley	116	20
						Hereford U	17	1
Ian Mitchell*			1 10 71	Tredegar	Merthyr	Hereford U	3	—
Stewart Phillips*	6 0	11 07	30 12 61	Halifax	Amateur	Hereford U	293	83
						WBA	15	4
						Swansea C	20	1
						Hereford U	37	10
Colin Robinson*	5 10	10 12	15 5 60	Birmingham	Mile Oak R	Shrewsbury T	194	41
						Birmingham C	37	6
						Hereford U	64	6
Paul Tester*	5 8	10 12	10 3 59	Stroud	Cheltenham T	Shrewsbury T	98	12
						Hereford U (loan)	4	—
						Hereford U	114	14
Paul Wheeler*	5 11	11 03	3 1 65	Caerphilly	Apprentice Aberaman	Bristol R	—	—
						Cardiff C	101	10
						Hull C	5	—
						Hereford U	54	12

Trainees
Burton, Paul S; Davies, Gareth M; Davis, Mark J; Harris, Leigh J; Jones, Shane G; McElroy, Stephen L; Parker, Paul A; Seaward, Sean M; Sutton, Mark J.

Associated Schoolboys
Averis, Kevin; Dorrington, Shane; Morris, Elliott W; Pugh, Christian A; Rogers, Allen B; Rudge, Nicholas D; Sims, Robert G.

HUDDERSFIELD TOWN 1990-91 *Back row (left to right):* Andy Duggan, Iffy Onuora, Lee Martin, Ken O'Doherty, Steve Hardwick, Graham Mitchell, Iwan Roberts.
Centre row: Chris Marsden, Simon Trevitt, Mike Cecere, Peter Withe (Assistant Manager), Robert Wilson, Kieran O'Regan, Gary Barnett.
Front row: Mick Byrne, Neil Parsley, Kevin Donovan, Eoin Hand (Manager), Simon Charlton, Dudley Lewis, Mark Smith.

Division 3   HUDDERSFIELD TOWN

© 1973

Leeds Rd, Huddersfield HD1 6PE. Telephone (0484) 420335/6. Commercial Dept: (0484) 534867. Recorded Information: (0898) 121635.

Ground capacity: 32,000.

Record attendance: 67,037 v Arsenal, FA Cup 6th rd, 27 February 1932.

Record receipts: £52,607 v Newcastle U, Division 2, 7 May, 1984.

Pitch measurements: 115yd × 75yd.

Chairman: K. S. Longbottom. *Vice-chairman:* D. G. Headey.

Directors: C. Senior, C. Hodgkinson, J. B. Buckley, F. L. Thewlis.

Manager: Eoin Hand. *Assistant Manager:*

Coach: George Mulhall.

Secretary: C. D. Patzelt. *Commercial Manager:* Tony Flynn. *Chief Executive:* Paul Fletcher.

Physio: Gary Williams.

Year Formed: 1908. *Turned Professional:* 1908. *Ltd Co.:* 1908.

Club Nickname: 'The Terriers'.

Record League Victory: 10-1 v Blackpool, Division 1, 13 December 1930 – Turner; Goodall, Spencer; Redfern, Wilson, Campbell; Bob Kelly (1), McLean (4), Robson (3), Davies (1), Smailes (1).

Record Cup Victory: 7-1 v Chesterfield (away), FA Cup, 3rd rd, 12 January 1929 – Turvey; Goodall, Wadsworth; Evans, Wilson, Naylor: Jackson (1), Kelly, Brown (3), Cumming (2), Smith. (1 o.g.).

Record Defeat: 1-10 v Manchester C, Division 2, 7 November 1987.

Most League Points (2 for a win): 66, Division 4, 1979–80.

Most League Points (3 for a win): 82, Division 3, 1982–83.

Most League Goals: 101, Division 4, 1979–80.

Highest League Scorer in Season: Sam Taylor, 35, Division 2, 1919–20; George Brown, 35, Division 1, 1925–26.

Most League Goals in Total Aggregate: George Brown, 142, 1921–29 and Jimmy Glazzard, 142, 1946–56.

Most Capped Player: Jimmy Nicholson, 31 (41), Northern Ireland.

Most League Appearances: Billy Smith, 520, 1914–34.

Record Transfer Fee Received: £250,000 from Reading for Craig Maskell, July 1990.

Record Transfer Fee Paid: £275,000 to Watford for Iwan Roberts, August 1990.

Football League Record: 1910 Elected to Division 2; 1920–52 Division 1; 1952–53 Division 2; 1953–56 Division 1; 1956–70 Division 2; 1970–72 Division 1; 1972–73 Division 2; 1973–75 Division 3; 1975–80 Division 4; 1980–83 Division 3; 1983–88 Division 2; 1988– Division 3.

Honours: Football League: Division 1 – Champions 1923–24, 1924–25, 1925–26; Runners-up 1926–27, 1927–28, 1933–34; Division 2 – Champions 1969–70; Runners-up 1919–20, 1952–53; Division 4 – Champions 1979–80. *FA Cup:* Winners 1922; Runners-up 1920, 1928, 1930, 1938. *Football League Cup:* Semi-final, 1967–68.

Colours: Blue and white striped shirts, white shorts, white stockings. **Change colours:** Red/black striped shirts, black shorts, black stockings.

HUDDERSFIELD TOWN 1990–91 LEAGUE RECORD

Match No.	Date	Venue	Opponents	Result	H/T Score	Lg. Pos.	Goalscorers	Attendance
1	Aug 25	H	Southend U	L	1-2	1-1	—	Wilson	5219
2	Sept 1	A	Swansea C	L	0-1	0-0	23		4787
3	8	H	Bolton W	W	4-0	2-0	12	Roberts, Edwards 3	5419
4	15	A	Fulham	D	0-0	0-0	14		3853
5	18	A	Grimsby T	L	0-4	0-1	—		6158
6	22	H	Reading	L	0-2	0-0	20		4689
7	29	A	Chester C	W	2-1	1-1	18	Donovan, Roberts	1540
8	Oct 2	H	Exeter C	W	1-0	0-0	—	Onuora	4317
9	6	H	Leyton Orient	W	1-0	1-0	11	Jackson	4686
10	13	A	Rotherham U	W	3-1	1-1	8	Onuora, O'Regan (pen), Roberts	6120
11	20	A	Brentford	L	0-1	0-0	11		5509
12	23	H	Bournemouth	L	1-3	0-2	—	O'Regan	5373
13	27	H	Mansfield T	D	2-2	1-1	14	Smith, Wilson	4413
14	Nov 3	A	Birmingham C	W	2-1	1-0	13	Roberts, O'Regan (pen)	7412
15	10	A	Cambridge U	W	3-1	1-0	9	Roberts, Marsden, O'Regan (pen)	4817
16	24	A	Preston NE	D	1-1	1-0	11	Onuora	4646
17	Dec 2	H	Bradford C	L	1-2	1-0	—	Onuora	9697
18	15	A	Crewe Alex	D	1-1	1-0	14	Barnett	2590
19	22	H	Bury	W	2-1	0-1	10	O'Regan (pen), Roberts	4841
20	29	A	Stoke C	L	0-2	0-1	14		11,869
21	Jan 1	H	Wigan Ath	W	1-0	0-0	13	O'Regan	4887
22	5	A	Tranmere R	L	0-2	0-1	13		5626
23	12	H	Swansea C	L	1-2	1-1	15	Stant	4052
24	19	A	Southend U	W	1-0	1-0	14	Smith	5509
25	26	H	Fulham	W	1-0	1-0	10	Marsden	4369
26	Feb 2	H	Grimsby T	D	1-1	1-0	11	Marsden	6571
27	9	A	Bolton W	D	1-1	1-0	11	Haylock	7947
28	16	H	Preston NE	W	1-0	1-0	9	Marsden	5504
29	19	A	Shrewsbury T	D	0-0	0-0	—		2821
30	23	A	Cambridge U	D	0-0	0-0	9		5602
31	26	A	Tranmere R	W	2-1	0-1	—	Onuora, Haylock	4889
32	Mar 3	A	Bradford C	D	2-2	0-2	—	Roberts 2	9569
33	9	H	Crewe Alex	W	3-1	2-0	5	Swain (og), Roberts, Onuora	5429
34	13	A	Exeter C	D	2-2	0-0	—	Haylock 2	3625
35	16	H	Chester C	D	1-1	1-0	7	O'Regan	5337
36	19	H	Rotherham U	W	4-0	1-0	—	Marsden, Roberts, O'Regan (pen), Maguire	4576
37	23	A	Leyton Orient	L	0-1	0-0	7		3292
38	26	A	Reading	W	2-1	2-1	—	Edwards, Roberts	4231
39	30	H	Shrewsbury T	W	2-1	2-1	5	Roberts, Onuora	5684
40	Apr 1	A	Bury	L	1-2	0-1	6	Quinlan	6318
41	6	H	Stoke C	W	3-0	1-0	6	O'Regan (pen), Quinlan, Wright	6520
42	13	A	Wigan Ath	D	1-1	1-0	6	Roberts	4642
43	20	H	Brentford	L	1-2	1-1	7	O'Regan (pen)	6489
44	27	A	Bournemouth	L	1-3	1-0	10	O'Regan (pen)	6888
45	May 4	A	Mansfield T	D	0-0	0-0	10		2507
46	11	H	Birmingham C	L	0-1	0-0	11		5195

Final League Position: 11

GOALSCORERS

League (57): Roberts 13, O'Regan 11 (8 pens), Onuora 7, Marsden 5, Edwards 4, Haylock 4, Quinlan 2, Smith 2, Wilson 2, Barnett 1, Donovan 1, Jackson 1, Maguire 1, Stant 1, Wright 1, own goal 1.
Rumbelows Cup (1): O'Regan 1.
FA Cup (2): Onuora 1, Roberts 1.

Hardwick	Trevitt	Parsley	Marsden	Mitchell	Lewis	O'Regan	Wilson	Roberts	Smith	Barnett	Edwards	Campbell	Jackson	Onuora	Charlton	Donovan	Martin	O'Doherty	Stant	Haylock	Maguire	Kelly	Ireland	Wright	Quinlan	Match No.
1	2	3	4	5	6	7	8	9	10	11*	12															1
1	2	3	4	5	6†	7	8	9	14	11*	12	10														2
1	2	3	4*	5		7	12	9	10		8		6	11												3
1	2	3	4	5		7	14	9	10	12	8†		6	11*												4
1	2*	3	4	5		7		9	10		8		6	11	12											5
1			4	5		7	2	9	10		8		6	11	3											6
1				5		7	2	9	10	8	12		6	11	3	4*										7
1			4	5		7	2	9	10	11*	8		6	12	3											8
1			4	5		7	2		10	11	8		6	9	3											9
1			4	5		7	2	9	10		8		6	11	3											10
1			4	5		7	2	9	10	8	12		6	11*	3											11
1	14		4	5		7	2	9	10	11†	8*		6	12	3											12
1	2	12	4	5		7	8	9	10				6*	11	3											13
1	2		4	5	6	7	8	9	10					11	3											14
1	2		4	5		7	8	9	10				6	11	3											15
1	2		4	5		7	8	9	10				6	11	3											16
1	2		4	5		7	8	9	10*12				6	11	3											17
			4	5		7	2	9	10					11	3	8	1	6								18
	2		4	5		7	8	9	10					11	3		1	6								19
	2	3*		5		7	12	9	10				6	11		8	1	4								20
	2			5		7	8	9	10*				6	11	3	12	1	4								21
1	2		8	5		7	14	9		11*			6†	12					4	10						22
1	2		4	5		7	8	9	12					11	3				6*	10						23
1	2		4	5		7	8	9		11			6	12	3					10*						24
1	2		4	5		7	8	9		11			6	12	3					10*						25
1	2		4	5		7	8*	9		11			6	12	3					10						26
1	2		4	5		7		9		11			6	8	3					10*	12					27
1	2		4	5		7	8†	9		11			6	12	3					10*		14				28
1	2		4	5		7	8	9		11			6	12	3					10*						29
1	2		4	5		7	8	9		11				12	3	6				10*						30
1	2		4	5		7	8*	9		11				10	3	6				12						31
1	2		4	5		7		9		11			6	8	3					10						32
1	2		4	5		7		9		11			6	8	3					10*		12				33
1	2		4	5		7		9		11*12			6	8	3					10						34
1	2		4	5	14	7		9		11*			6	8	3†				12	10						35
1	2		4	5	3	7	14	9		11†			6	8					12	10*						36
1	2		4	5		7	8	9					6	11					12	10*				3		37
1	2		4	5		7		9	10*	11			6	8					12					3		38
1	2		4	5		7		9	10*	11			6	8										3	12	39
1	2		4	5	14	7		9†		11*	12		6	8										3	10	40
1	2		4	5		7				11	12		6	8*	9									3	10	41
1	2		4	5		7		9		11*12			6	8										3	10	42
1	2		4	5		7		9		11*			6	8								12		3	10	43
1	2		4	5		7		9					6	12								8*	11	3	10	44
1	2		4	5		7		9					6	12	14							8†	11*	3	10	45
1	2		4	5		7		9		12			6	11								8†	14	3	10*	46
42	38	6	43	46	4	46	25	44	29	19	10	1	38	32	29	4	4	8	5	9	1	3	3	10	7	
	+2s		+2s				+4s		+3s	+3s	+8s			+11s	+1s	+2s				+3s	+3s	+1s	+3s	+1s		

Rumbelows Cup	First Round	Bolton W (h)	0-3
		(a)	1-2
FA Cup	First Round	Altrincham (a)	2-1
	Second Round	Blackpool (h)	0-2

HUDDERSFIELD TOWN

Player and Position	Ht	Wt	Birth Date	Birth Place	Source	Clubs	League App	Gls
Goalkeepers								
Steve Hardwick*	5 11	13 00	6 9 56	Mansfield	Amateur	Chesterfield	38	—
						Newcastle U	92	—
						Oxford U	156	—
						Crystal Palace (loan)	3	—
						Sunderland (loan)	6	—
						Huddersfield T	109	—
Lee Martin	5 11	11 08	9 9 68	Huddersfield	Trainee	Huddersfield T	47	—
Defenders								
David Campbell			13 9 69	Dublin	Bohemians	Huddersfield T	1	—
Simon Charlton	5 7	10 11	25 10 71	Huddersfield	Trainee	Huddersfield T	33	—
Jon Dyson			18 12 71	Mirfield	School	Huddersfield T	—	—
Peter Jackson	6 1	12 06	6 4 61	Bradford	Apprentice	Bradford C	278	24
						Newcastle U	60	3
						Bradford C	58	5
						Huddersfield T	38	1
Dudley Lewis	5 10	10 09	17 11 62	Swansea	Apprentice	Swansea C	230	2
						Huddersfield T	34	—
Graham Mitchell	6 0	11 05	16 2 68	Shipley	Apprentice	Huddersfield T	163	2
Ken O'Doherty	6 0	12 00	30 3 63	Dublin	UCD	Crystal Palace	42	—
						Huddersfield T	63	1
Neil Parsley	5 10	10 11	25 4 66	Liverpool	Witton Alb	Leeds U	—	—
						Chester C (loan)	6	—
						Huddersfield T	8	—
						Doncaster R (loan)	3	—
Simon Trevitt	5 11	11 02	20 12 67	Dewsbury	Apprentice	Huddersfield T	132	1
Midfield								
John Kelly	5 10	10 09	20 10 60	Bebbington	Cammellaird	Tranmere R	64	9
						Preston NE	130	27
						Chester C	85	17
						Swindon T	7	1
						Oldham Ath	52	6
						Walsall	39	1
						Huddersfield T (loan)	10	—
						Huddersfield T	4	—
Chris Marsden	5 11	10 12	3 1 69	Sheffield	Trainee	Sheffield U	16	1
						Huddersfield T	89	8
Kieran O'Regan	5 9	10 08	9 11 63	Cork	Tranmore Ath	Brighton & HA	86	2
						Swindon T	26	1
						Huddersfield T	119	16
Mark Wilson*			12 10 71	Barnsley	Rotherham U	Huddersfield T	—	—
Robert Wilson	5 10	11 11	5 6 61	Kensington	Apprentice	Fulham	175	34
						Millwall	28	12
						Luton T	24	1
						Fulham	47	4
						Huddersfield T	57	8
Forwards								
Gary Barnett	5 6	9 13	11 3 63	Stratford	Apprentice	Coventry C	—	—
						Oxford U	45	9
						Wimbledon (loan)	5	1
						Fulham (loan)	2	1
						Fulham	180	30
						Huddersfield	22	1
Brian Byrne			23 3 72	Dublin	Trainee	Huddersfield T	—	—
Jason Byrne*			16 5 72	Dublin	Trainee	Huddersfield T	—	—
Mick Byrne (To Shamrock R. Sept 1990)	5 11	12 03	14 1 60	Dublin	Shamrock R	Huddersfield T	56	11
						Shelbourne (loan)	—	—

HUDDERSFIELD TOWN

Foundation: A meeting, attended largely by members of the Huddersfield & District FA, was held at the Imperial Hotel in 1906 to discuss the feasibility of establishing a football club in this rugby stronghold. However, it was not until a man with both the enthusiasm and the money to back the scheme came on the scene, that real progress was made. This benefactor was Mr. Hilton Crowther and it was at a meeting at the Albert Hotel in 1908, that the club formally came into existence with a capital of £2,000 and joined the North-Eastern League.

First Football League game: 3 September, 1910, Division 2, v Bradford PA (a) W 1-0 – Mutch; Taylor, Morris; Beaton, Hall, Bartlett; Blackburn, Wood, Hamilton (1), McCubbin, Jee.

Did you know: Between a defeat by Swindon Town, 1 February 1913, and Arsenal, 27 February 1932, Huddersfield were undefeated at home in the FA Cup. During this spell they played 25 home ties, winning 24 and drawing 1.

Managers (and Secretary-managers)
Fred Walker 1908–10, Richard Pudan 1910–12, Arthur Fairclough 1912–19, Ambrose Langley 1919–21, Herbert Chapman 1921–25, Cecil Potter 1925–26, Jack Chaplin 1926–29, Clem Stephenson 1929–42, David Steele 1943–47, George Stephenson 1947–52, Andy Beattie 1952–56, Bill Shankly 1956–59, Eddie Boot 1960–64, Tom Johnston 1964–68, Ian Greaves 1968–74, Bobby Collins 1974–75, Tom Johnston 1975–77 (GM), 1977–78, Mike Buxton 1978–86, Steve Smith 1986–87, Malcolm Macdonald 1987–88, Eoin Hand June 1988–.

Player and Position	Ht	Wt	Birth Date	Birth Place	Source	Clubs	League App	Gls
Kevin Donovan	5 7	10 10	17 12 71	Halifax	Trainee	Huddersfield T	7	1
Keith Edwards	5 8	10 03	16 7 57	Stockton		Sheffield U	70	29
						Hull C	132	57
						Sheffield U	191	114
						Leeds U	38	6
						Aberdeen	9	2
						Hull C	55	29
						Stockport Co	27	10
						Huddersfield T (loan)	10	4
						Huddersfield T	18	4
						Plymouth Arg (loan)	3	1
Gary Haylock	6 0	11 12	31 12 70	Bradford	Trainee	Huddersfield T	12	4
						Shelbourne (loan)	—	—
Mark Hurst‡	5 10	11 02	18 8 70	Derby	Trainee	Nottingham F	—	—
						Huddersfield T	—	—
Simon Ireland			23 11 71	Barnstaple	School	Huddersfield T	6	—
Peter Maguire*	5 8	9 10	11 9 69	Holmfirth	Trainee	Leeds U	2	—
						Huddersfield T	7	1
						Stockport (loan)	2	—
Iffy Onuora	5 10	11 10	28 7 67	Glasgow		Huddersfield T	63	10
Iwan Roberts	6 3	12 05	26 6 68	Banour		Watford	63	9
						Hunddersfield T	44	13

Trainees
Billy, Christopher A; Booth, Andrew D; Brennan, Anthony; Collins, Simon; Dysart, John; Forest, Marc S; Johnson, Matthew L; Kelly, Kevin; Mooney, Thomas; Stocchero, Daniel M; Thomas, Robert S; Thompson, Paul; Wallace, David A.

**Non-Contract
Gledhill, Richard.

Associated Schoolboys
Aspinall, Brendan J; Baldry, Simon; Barret, Anthony M; Brown, Mark E; Cramp, Richard J; Crowther, Matthew J; Crowther, Paul; Donaldson, Stephen; Eastwood, Stephen; Hansgate, Paul M; Hart, Andrew C; Hedden, Matthew P; Johnson, Dean C; Lumb, Gavin J; Marsh, Richard J; Midwood, Michael A; Moorehouse, Robert J; Rayne, Dean E; Thompson, Andrew J; Walker, David C; Wood, Michael J.
Associated Schoolboys who have accepted the club's offer of a Traineeship/Contract
Rowe, Rodney C; Whitehead, Scot.
**Non-Contract Players who are retained must be re-signed before they are eligible to play in League matches.

HULL CITY 1990–91 *Back row (left to right):* Mike Smith, Jeigh Jenkinson, Richard Jobson, Neil Buckley, Dave Cleminshaw, Iain Hesford, Rob Gawthorpe, Dave Bamber, Peter Swan, David Mail, Andy Payton.
Centre row: Mike Docherty, Tom Wilson (Secretary), Gerry Flynn, Mark Calvert, Steve Doyle, Nicky Brown, Malcolm Shotton (Youth Team Coach), Russ Wilcox, Lee Warren, Tony Finnigan, Jeff Radcliffe (Physiotherapist), Dale Roberts.
Front row: Ken De Mange, Ian McParland, Wayne Jacobs, Leigh Palin, Richard Cheetham (Chairman), Stan Ternent, Martin Fish (Vice Chairman), Garreth Roberts, Paul Hunter, Les Thompson, Gwyn Thomas.

Division 3   **HULL CITY**

Boothferry Park, Hull HU4 6EU. Telephone Hull (0482) 51119. Commercial Manager: (0482) 566050. Football in the Community Office: 0482 565088. Fax: 0482 565752.

Ground capacity: 17,932.

Record attendance: 55,019 v Manchester U, FA Cup 6th rd, 26 February 1949.

Record receipts: £79,604 v Liverpool FA Cup, 5th rd, 18 February 1989.

Pitch measurements: 112yd × 73yd.

President: T. C. Waite FIMI, MIRTE. *Honorary Vice-president:* H. Bermitz.

Vice-presidents: R. Beercock, K. Davis, N. Howe, R. Booth, A. Fetiveau, W. Law.

Chairman: R. M. Cheetham. *Vice-chairman:* M. W. Fish FCA.

Directors: D. Robinson, J. Johnson BA, DPA, G. H. C. Needler MA, FCA, C. M. Thorpe LL.B., M. G. ST, Quinton BA, MBA.

Manager: Terry Dolan. *Assistant Manager:* Jeff Lee.

Reserve Team Manager: Tom Wilson. *Physio:* Jeff Radcliffe, MCSP, SRP.

Secretary: Frank Boughton, FMI.PUR.M. *Commercial Manager:* Simon Cawkill. *Stadium Manager:* John Cooper.

Ticket Office/Gate Manager: Wilf Rogerson. *Hon, Medical Officers:* G. Hoyle, MBCHB, FRCS, Dr. B. Kell, MBBS.

Year Formed: 1904. *Turned Professional:* 1905. *Ltd Co.:* 1905.

Club Nickname: 'The Tigers'.

Previous Grounds: 1904, Boulevard Ground (Hull RFC); 1905, Anlaby Road (Hull CC); 1944/5 Boulevard Ground; 1946, Boothferry Park.

Record League Victory: 11-1 v Carlisle U, Division 3 (N), 14 January 1939 – Ellis; Woodhead, Dowen; Robinson (1), Blyth, Hardy; Hubbard (2), Richardson (2), Dickinson (2), Davies (2), Cunliffe (2).

Record Cup Victory: 8-2 v Stalybridge Celtic (away), FA Cup, 1st rd, 26 November 1932 – Maddison; Goldsmith, Woodhead; Gardner, Hill (1), Denby; Forward (1), Duncan, McNaughton (1), Wainscoat (4), Sargeant (1).

Record Defeat: 0-8 v Wolverhampton W, Division 2, 4 November 1911.

Most League Points (2 for a win): 69, Division 3, 1965–66.

Most League Points (3 for a win): 90, Division 4, 1982–83.

Most League Goals: 109, Division 3, 1965–66.

Highest League Scorer in Season: Bill McNaughton, 39, Division 3 (N), 1932–33.

Most League Goals in Total Aggregate: Chris Chilton, 195, 1960–71.

Most Capped Player: Terry Neill, 15 (59), Northern Ireland.

Most League Appearances: Andy Davidson, 520, 1952–67.

Record Transfer Fee Received: £400,000 from Sunderland for Tony Norman, December 1988.

Record Transfer Fee Paid: £200,000 to Leeds U for Peter Swan, March 1989.

Football League Record: 1905 Elected to Division 2; 1930–33 Division 3 (N); 1933–36 Division 2; 1936–49 Division 3 (N); 1949–56 Division 2; 1956–58 Division 3 (N); 1958–59 Division 3; 1959–60 Division 2; 1960–66 Division 3; 1966–78 Division 2; 1978–81 Division 3; 1981–83 Division 4; 1983–85 Division 3; 1985–91 Division 2; 1991– Division 3.

Honours: Football League: Division 2 best season: 3rd, 1909–10; Division 3 (N) – Champions 1932–33, 1948–49; Division 3 – Champions 1965–66; Runners-up 1958–59; Division 4 – Runners-up 1982–83. *FA Cup:* best season: Semi-final, 1930. *Football League Cup:* best season: 4th, 1973–74, 1975–76, 1977–78. *Associate Members' Cup:* Runners-up 1984.

Colours: Black and amber vertical stripes, amber sleeve shirts, black shorts, black/amber stockings. **Change colours:** Green and white shirts, white shorts, green trim, green stockings.

HULL CITY 1990–91 LEAGUE RECORD

Match No.	Date		Venue	Opponents	Result		H/T Score	Lg. Pos.	Goalscorers	Attendance
1	Aug	25	H	Notts Co	L	1-2	1-1	—	Payton	7385
2		28	A	Blackburn R	L	1-2	0-1	—	Mail	7337
3	Sept	1	A	Sheffield W	L	1-5	1-2	24	Payton	23,673
4		8	H	Swindon T	D	1-1	0-0	23	Buckley	5240
5		15	A	Bristol R	D	1-1	0-1	22	Swan	4734
6		19	A	Millwall	D	3-3	2-1	—	Payton 2, Palin	9446
7		22	H	WBA	D	1-1	1-1	21	Payton	5953
8		29	H	Port Vale	W	3-2	1-0	18	Palin (pen), Payton 2	5185
9	Oct	2	A	Watford	W	1-0	1-0	—	Swan	6448
10		6	A	West Ham U	L	1-7	1-2	17	Hockaday	19,472
11		13	H	Oldham Ath	D	2-2	1-0	17	Palin (pen), Payton	8676
12		20	H	Wolverhampton W	L	1-2	0-1	21	Payton	7144
13		24	A	Brighton & HA	L	1-3	0-1	—	Bamber	5354
14		27	A	Plymouth Arg	L	1-4	1-1	21	Bamber	5039
15	Nov	3	H	Newcastle U	W	2-1	1-0	20	Jacobs, Swan	8375
16		10	H	Ipswich T	D	3-3	1-0	21	Payton 2, McParland	5294
17		17	A	Bristol C	L	1-4	0-1	22	Finnigan	9346
18		23	H	Leicester C	W	5-2	3-1	—	Payton 2, Swan 2, Palin (pen)	5855
19	Dec	1	A	Middlesbrough	L	0-3	0-0	23		17,024
20		8	H	Blackburn R	W	3-1	2-0	19	Swan 2, Payton	4166
21		15	A	Notts Co	L	1-2	0-1	22	Swan	5537
22		22	A	Charlton Ath	L	1-2	1-1	22	Payton	4989
23		26	H	Oxford U	D	3-3	1-0	23	Swan 2, Payton	5103
24		29	H	Barnsley	L	1-2	0-0	24	Palin	7916
25	Jan	1	A	Portsmouth	L	1-5	0-2	24	Payton	8004
26		12	H	Sheffield W	L	0-1	0-1	24		10,907
27		19	A	Swindon T	L	1-3	0-2	24	Payton	7297
28	Feb	2	H	Bristol R	W	2-0	1-0	24	Swan, Buckley	5302
29		16	H	Bristol C	L	1-2	1-0	24	Payton	5212
30		23	A	Ipswich T	L	0-2	0-1	24		9900
31	Mar	2	H	Middlesbrough	D	0-0	0-0	24		6828
32		9	A	Leicester C	W	1-0	0-0	23	Payton	8386
33		12	H	Watford	D	1-1	0-0	—	Wilcox	5815
34		16	H	Port Vale	D	0-0	0-0	23		6105
35		20	A	Oldham Ath	W	2-1	1-0	—	Swan, Payton	12,626
36		23	H	West Ham U	D	0-0	0-0	23		9558
37		30	A	Oxford U	L	0-1	0-1	23		4591
38	Apr	1	H	Charlton Ath	D	2-2	0-0	23	Hunter, Payton (pen)	5689
39		6	A	Barnsley	L	1-3	1-0	24	Payton	6859
40		10	A	WBA	D	1-1	1-1	—	Payton	10,356
41		13	H	Portsmouth	L	0-2	0-0	24		4871
42		16	H	Millwall	D	1-1	1-0	—	Payton	4102
43		20	A	Wolverhampton W	D	0-0	0-0	24		9313
44		27	H	Brighton & HA	L	0-1	0-0	24		4037
45	May	4	H	Plymouth Arg	W	2-0	1-0	24	Thompson, Hunter	3175
46		11	A	Newcastle U	W	2-1	1-0	24	Walmsley, Thompson	17,940

Final League Position: 24

GOALSCORERS

League (57): Payton 25 (1 pen), Swan 12, Palin 5 (3 pens), Bamber 2, Buckley 2, Hunter 2, Thompson 2, Finnigan 1, Hockaday 1, Jacobs 1, McParland 1, Mail 1, Walmsley 1, Wilcox 1.
Rumbelows Cup (1): Swan 1.
FA Cup (2): Buckley 1, McParland 1.

Hesford	Buckley	Jacobs	Jobson	Mail	Finnigan	Roberts	Payton	Swan	Palin	Thomas	Bamber	Hunter	De Mange	Brown	Thompson	Doyle	McParland	Wilcox	Hockaday	Atkinson	Ngata	Shotton	Jenkinson	Waites	Calvert	Warren	Smith	Dearden	Match No.
1	2	3*	4	5	6	7	8	9†	10	11	12	14																	1
1	2	3	4	5	6	7†	8	9	10	11*	12	14																	2
1	5	3		4	6	7	8	9†	10	11	12	14	2*																3
1	5	3*		4	6		8†	9	10				2		7	11	12	14											4
1	5	3		4*	6		8	9	10						7	11	12	2											5
1	5			4			8†		10			14			12	3	11	9	6	2		7*							6
1	5			4			8		10		12	14				3	11*	9	6	2		7†							7
1	5			4			8	9	10	11						3	12		6	2		7							8
1	5			4			8	9	10	11			7			3			6	2									9
1	5			4*			8	9	10	11			7			3	12		6	2†		14							10
1		3		4			8		10	11*			7	9					6	2		5	12						11
1		3		4			8		10	11			7	9					6*	2		5	12						12
1		3		4			8		10	11*				9	7				6†	2		5	12	14					13
1		3		4			8		10				7*	9			11		6	2		5	12						14
1		3		4	7		8	9	10								11*	12	6	2		5							15
1		3		4	7*		8		10	11				9			6			2		5	12						16
1		3		4	7		8		10							9*	11	2	6			5	12						17
1		3		4	7		8	9	10									5	6*	2			12		11				18
1		3		4	7		8	9	10				14					5	6†	2			12		11*				19
1				4	7		8	9†	10				14			3		5	6	2			12		11*				20
1				4	7		8	9	10				14			3		5†	6	2			12		11*				21
1	5				7*		8	9	10		12					3			6	2				11	4				22
1	5						8	9	10							3	12		6	2				11	4*	7			23
1	5	3					8	9	10				7				12		6	2				11	4*				24
1	5	3			12		8	9	10			4	14				7†		6	2*		6		11					25
	5	3					10	9				4			8†		12	11	6			14				7*		1	26
	5	3					10	9				4			12		7†	11	6*			14					1		27
	5	3					8	9	10			4					11		6			12				7*	1		28
	5	3					8	9	10			14						4*	6			12				7†			29
	5	3					8	9				14		12			4		6			11†			10	7*			30
	3†			5			8	9	10			14				4	7		6			12				11*			31
				5			8	9	10						3	4	7		6							11			32
				5			8	9	10*						3	4	7		6			12				11			33
				5			8	9							3	4	7		6			12				10*	11		34
		4		5			8	9							3		7	10	6							11			35
		4		5			8	9							3		7	10	6			12				11*			36
		4		5			8	9							3*		7	12	6			14	10†			11			37
		4		5†			8	9				12			3		7*	10	6			14				11			38
1		4		5			8	9				7			3†		10	14	6			12				11*			39
1		4		5			8	9							6		7	10*				12				11			40
1		4		5			8	9					2			7	10	12	6	3						11*			41
1				5†			8	9	10			14				4	2	12	6			11	7*						42
1				5			8		10		12			9†		4	2*		14	6		11		7					43
1				5			8*	9	10			14				4	2†		12	6		11		7					44
		6		5					10						3		4	2*	9			11					8	7 12	45
	14	2		5					10						3		4					11					8	7 12	46

Totals:

| 31 | 30 | 19 | 2 | 35 | 15 | 8 | 43 | 38 | 35 | 10 | 6 | 6 | 5 | 2 | 19 | 11 | 7 | 24 | 35 | 14 | 1 | 26 | 12 | 10 | 7 | 15 | 4 | 3 | |

Substitute appearances (+):
1s · · · · 1s 3s · · · 1s 3s 12s 1s · 1s 1s · · 9s 7s · 2s 9s · · 14s · 2s

Wright—Match No. 29(1) 30(1) 31(1) 32(1) 33(1) 34(1); Butler—Match No. 35(1) 36(1) 37(1) 38(1); Norton—Match No. 26(2) 27(2) 28(2) 29(2) 30(2) 31(2) 32(2) 33(2) 34(2) 35(2) 36(2) 37(2) 38(2) 39(2) 40(2); Hobson—Match No. 40(3) 42(3) 43(3) 44(3); Wilson—Match No. 45(1) 46(1); Allison—Match No. 46(6†); Walmsley—Match No. 46(9*).

Rumbelows Cup	Second Round	Wolverhampton W (a)	0-0
		(h)	1-1
	Third Round	Coventry C (a)	0-3
FA Cup	Third Round	Notts Co (h)	2-5

HULL CITY

Player and Position	Ht	Wt	Birth Date	Birth Place	Source	Clubs	League App	Gls
Goalkeepers								
David Cleminshaw	6 1	12 09	1 11 70	South Cave	Trainee	Hull C	—	—
Robert Gawthorpe*			18 8 71	Hull	Trainee	Hull C	—	—
Iain Hesford	6 2	13 12	4 3 60	Zambia	Apprentice	Blackpool	202	—
						Sheffield W	—	—
						Fulham (loan)	3	—
						Notts Co (loan)	10	—
						Sunderland	97	—
						Hull C	91	—
Steve Wilson§			24 4 74	Hull	Trainee	Hull C	2	—
Defenders								
Neil Allison§			20 10 73	Hull	Trainee	Hull C	1	—
Nicky Brown	6 0	12 03	16 10 66	Hull	Local	Hull C	61	2
Neil Buckley	6 2	13 06	25 9 68	Hull	Trainee	Hull C	55	3
						Burnley (loan)	5	—
Gary Hobson§			12 11 72	North Ferriby	Trainee	Hull C	4	—
David Hockaday	5 10	10 09	9 11 57	Billingham	Amateur	Blackpool	147	24
						Swindon T	245	6
						Hull C	35	1
Wayne Jacobs	5 9	10 02	3 2 69	Sheffield	Apprentice	Sheffield W	6	—
						Hull C	104	4
David Mail	5 11	11 12	12 9 62	Bristol	Apprentice	Aston Villa	—	—
						Blackburn R	206	4
						Hull C	36	1
Malcolm Shotton	6 3	13 12	16 2 57	Newcastle	Apprentice	Leicester C	—	—
						Nuneaton Bor	—	—
						Oxford U	263	12
						Portsmouth	10	—
						Huddersfield T	16	1
						Barnsley	66	6
						Hull C	42	2
Paul Waites	5 10	12 08	24 1 71	Hull	Trainee	Hull C	11	—
Russell Wilcox	6 0	11 10	25 3 64	Hemsworth	Apprentice	Doncaster R	1	—
						Cambridge U	—	—
					Frickley	Northampton T	138	9
						Hull C	31	1
Midfield								
Graeme Atkinson	5 10	10 02	11 11 71	Hull	Trainee	Hull C	29	1
Mark Calvert	5 9	11 05	11 9 70	Newcastle	Trainee	Hull C	12	—
Mark Cooper*			12 10 71	Hull	Trainee	Hull C	—	—
Ken De Mange	5 9	11 10	3 9 64	Dublin	Home Farm	Liverpool	—	—
						Scunthorpe U (loan)	3	2
						Leeds U	15	1
						Hull C	68	2
Gerry Flynn‡	5 10	11 00	28 3 72	Belfast	Bangor	Hull C	—	—
Herry Ngata†			24 8 71	New Zealand		Hull C	14	—
Leigh Palin	5 9	10 03	12 9 65	Worcester	Apprentice	Aston Villa	—	—
						Shrewsbury T (loan)	2	—
						Nottingham F	—	—
						Bradford C	71	10
						Stoke C	19	3
						Hull C	44	6
Andy Payton	5 9	10 06	23 10 66	Burnley		Hull C	134	48
Garreth Roberts*	5 5	10 08	15 11 60	Hull	Apprentice	Hull C	414	47
Peter Swan	6 0	11 12	28 9 66	Leeds	Local	Leeds U	49	11
						Hull C	80	24
Gwyn Thomas*	5 7	11 05	26 9 57	Swansea	Apprentice	Leeds U	89	3
						Barnsley	201	17
						Hull C	22	—

HULL CITY

Foundation: The enthusiasts who formed Hull City in 1904 were brave men indeed. More than that they were audacious for they immediately put the club on the map in this Rugby League fortress by obtaining a three-year agreement with the Hull Rugby League club to rent their ground! They had obtained quite a number of conversions to the dribbling code, before the Rugby League forbade the use of any of their club grounds by Association Football clubs. By that time, Hull City were well away having entered the FA Cup in their initial season and the Football League, Second Division after only a year.

First Football League game: 2 September, 1905, Division 2, v Barnsley (h) W 4-1 – Spendiff; Langley, Jones; Martin, Robinson, Gordon (2); Rushton, Spence (1), Wilson (1), Howe, Raisbeck.

Did you know: In 1920–21 Hull City played four consecutive FA Cup ties without conceding a goal before losing 1-0 at home to Preston North End. Their goalkeeper in these games was Billy Mercer who went on to win League Championship and FA Cup runners-up medals with Huddersfield Town.

Managers (and Secretary-managers)
James Ramster 1904–05*, Ambrose Langley 1905–13, Harry Chapman 1913–14, Fred Stringer 1914–16, David Menzies 1916–21, Percy Lewis 1921–23, Bill McCracken 1923–31, Haydn Green 1931–34, John Hill 1934–36, David Menzies 1936, Ernest Blackburn 1936–46, Major Frank Buckley 1946–48, Raich Carter 1948–51, Bob Jackson 1952–55, Bob Brocklebank 1955–61, Cliff Britton 1961–70 (continued as GM to 1971), Terry Neill 1970–74, John Kaye 1974–77, Bobby Collins 1977–78, Ken Houghton 1978–79, Mike Smith 1979–82, Bobby Brown 1982, Colin Appleton 1982–84, Brian Horton 1984–88, Eddie Gray 1988–89, Colin Appleton 1989, Stan Ternent 1989–91, Terry Dolan February 1991 .

Player and Position	Ht	Wt	Birth Date	Place	Source	Clubs	League App	Gls
Lee Warren	6 0	11 13	28 2 69	Manchester	Trainee	Leeds U	—	—
						Rochdale	31	1
						Hull C	53	—
						Lincoln C (loan)	3	1
Forwards								
Paul Hunter	6 0	12 09	30 8 68	Kirkcaldy	Leven Royal Colts	East Fife	164	56
						Hull C	27	5
Leigh Jenkinson	6 0	12 02	9 7 69	Thorne	Trainee	Hull C	62	1
						Rotherham U (loan)	7	—
Ian McParland	5 8	10 08	4 10 61	Edinburgh	Ormiston Pr	Notts Co	221	69
						Hull C	47	7
						Walsall (loan)	11	6
Michael Smith*	5 8	10 09	19 12 68	Hull		Hull C	19	1
Les Thompson*	5 10	11 00	23 9 68	Cleethorpes		Hull C	35	4
						Scarborough (loan)	3	1
David Walmsley§			23 11 72	Hull	Trainee	Hull C	1	1

Trainees
Allison, Neil J; Britt, Peter J; Gallagher, Mark; Garbutt, Alan C; Greenwood, Roger D.M; Hobson, Gary; Holleron, Kevin; Horsley, Richard C; Ledingham, Marc L; Morrow, Keith P; Noonan, Lee; Proctor, David N; Thompson, Ross M; Vincent, Steven B; Walmsley, David G; Welburn, Paul A; Whincup, Kirk R; Willingham, Mark J; Wilson, Stephen L.

**Non-Contract
Ngata, Heremaia.

Associated Schoolboys
Bennett, Darren P; Burke, Neil; Edeson, Matthew K; McKenzie, Jonathan; Salter, Alan; Smith, Carl A; Stowe, Dean; White, Richard C.

Associated Schoolboys who have accepted the club's offer of a Traineeship/Contract
Boughen, Mark R; Fisher, Steven L; Hopkin, Matthew C; Houghton, Nicholas N; Lowthorpe, Adam; Said, Lee S; Shirtliff, Mark A.

****Non-Contract Players who are retained must be re-signed before they are eligible to play in League matches.

IPSWICH TOWN 1990–91   *Back row (left to right):* Lee Honeywood, Phil Mitchell, Steve Palmer, Brian Gayle, Chris Swailes, Gavin Johnson, David Gregory, Gary Durrant, Andy Banks.
Centre row: Louie Donowa, Simon Milton, Neil Thompson, Tony Humes, Craig Forrest, Phil Parkes, Phil Whelan, David Lowe, Gary Thompson, Ian Redford.
Front row: Mick Stockwell, David Linighan, Glenn Pennyfather, Romeo Zondervan, Jason Dozzell, Frank Yallop, Chris Kiwomya, David Hill.

Division 2   **IPSWICH TOWN**

Portman Road, Ipswich, Suffolk IP1 2DA. Telephone Ipswich (0473) 219211 (4 lines). Sales & Marketing Dept: (0473) 212202.

Ground capacity: 31,000.

Record attendance: 38,010 v Leeds U, FA Cup 6th rd, 8 March 1975.

Record receipts: £105,950 v AZ 67 Alkmaar, UEFA Cup Final 1st leg, 6 May 1981.

Pitch measurements: 112yd × 70yd.

Chairman: J. Kerr MBE.

Directors: H. R. Smith, J. M. Sangster, K. H. Brightwell, J. Kerridge, D. Sheepshanks, P. M. Cobbold.

Manager: John Lyall. *Assistant Manager:* Charlie Woods.

First Team Coach: Peter Trevivian. *Reserve Coach:*

Physio: D. Bingham. *Youth Team Coach:* Bryan Klug.

Secretary: David C. Rose.

Commercial Manager: R. Powell.

Year Formed: 1878. *Turned Professional:* 1936. *Ltd Co.:* 1936.

Club Nickname: 'Blues' or 'Town'.

Record League Victory: 7-0 v Portsmouth, Division 2, 7 November 1964 – Thorburn; Smith, McNeil; Baxter, Bolton, Thompson; Broadfoot (1), Hegan (2), Baker (1), Leadbetter, Brogan (3). 7-0 v Southampton, Division 1, 2 February 1974 – Sivell; Burley, Mills (1), Morris, Hunter, Beattie (1), Hamilton (2), Viljoen, Johnson, Whymark (2), Lambert (1) (Woods). 7-0 v WBA, Division 1, 6 November 1976 – Sivell; Burley, Mills, Talbot, Hunter, Beattie (1), Osborne, Wark (1), Mariner (1) (Bertschin), Whymark (4), Woods.

Record Cup Victory: 10-0 v Floriana, European Cup, Prel. rd, 25 September 1962 – Bailey; Malcolm, Compton; Baxter, Laurel, Elsworthy (1); Stephenson, Moran (2), Crawford (5), Phillips (2), Blackwood.

Record Defeat: 1-10 v Fulham, Division 1, 26 December 1963.

Most League Points (2 for a win): 64, Division 3 (S), 1953–54 and 1955–56.

Most League Points (3 for a win): 83, Division 1, 1981–82.

Most League Goals: 106, Division 3 (S), 1955–56.

Highest League Scorer in Season: Ted Phillips, 41, Division 3 (S), 1956–57.

Most League Goals in Total Aggregate: Ray Crawford, 203, 1958–63 and 1966–69.

Most Capped Player: Allan Hunter, 47 (53), Northern Ireland.

Most League Appearances: Mick Mills, 591, 1966–82.

Record Transfer Fee Received: £725,000 from Glasgow Rangers for Terry Butcher, August 1986.

Record Transfer Fee Paid: £330,000 to Manchester C for Brian Gayle, January 1990.

Football League Record: 1938 Elected to Division 3 (S); 1954–55 Division 2; 1955–57 Division 3 (S); 1957–61 Division 2; 1961–64 Division 1; 1964–68 Division 2; 1968–86 Division 1; 1986– Division 2.

Honours: Football League: Division 1 – Champions 1961–62; Runners-up 1980–81, 1981–82; Division 2 – Champions 1960–61, 1967–68; Division 3 (S) – Champions 1953–54, 1956–57. *FA Cup:* Winners 1977–78. *Football League Cup:* best season: Semi-final 1981–82, 1984–85, *Texaco Cup:* 1972–73. **European Competitions:** *European Cup:* 1962–63. *European Cup-Winners' Cup:* 1978–79. *UEFA Cup:* 1973–74, 1974–75, 1975–76, 1977–78, 1979–80, 1980–81 (winners), 1981–82, 1982–83.

Colours: Blue shirts, white shorts, blue stockings. **Change colours:** All orange.

IPSWICH TOWN 1990–91 LEAGUE RECORD

Match No.	Date		Venue	Opponents	Result		H/T Score	Lg. Pos.	Goalscorers	Atten- dance
1	Aug 25		H	Sheffield W	L	0-2	0-2	—		17,284
2		28	A	Swindon T	L	0-1	0-0	—		10,817
3	Sept 1		A	WBA	W	2-1	0-1	15	Humes, Thompson	10,318
4		8	H	Blackburn R	W	2-1	0-1	10	Gregory, Stockwell	10,953
5		15	A	Millwall	D	1-1	1-0	12	Kiwomya	12,604
6		19	A	West Ham U	L	1-3	1-0	—	Milton	18,764
7		22	H	Bristol R	W	2-1	0-0	12	Gayle, Kiwomya	11,084
8		29	H	Watford	D	1-1	0-0	11	Gayle	11,351
9	Oct 2		A	Barnsley	L	1-5	0-3	—	Thompson (pen)	6930
10		6	A	Plymouth Arg	D	0-0	0-0	13		5935
11		13	H	Port Vale	W	3-0	1-0	12	Milton 2, Stockwell	10,369
12		20	H	Newcastle U	W	2-1	2-0	9	Gayle, Milton	15,567
13		23	A	Oldham Ath	L	0-2	0-0	—		13,170
14		27	A	Leicester C	W	2-1	2-0	8	Stockwell 2	11,053
15	Nov 3		H	Brighton & HA	L	1-3	0-2	10	Stockwell	11,437
16		10	A	Hull C	D	3-3	0-1	10	Dozzell, Redford, Kiwomya	5294
17		17	H	Notts Co	D	0-0	0-0	11		10,778
18		24	H	Bristol C	D	1-1	1-0	12	Dozzell	10,037
19	Dec 1		A	Wolverhampton W	D	2-2	2-1	11	Dozzell, Redford	15,803
20		8	H	Swindon T	D	1-1	0-0	9	Redford (pen)	9358
21		15	H	Sheffield W	D	2-2	2-1	11	Milton, Redford	19,333
22		21	A	Portsmouth	D	1-1	1-0	—	Palmer	7010
23		26	H	Middlesbrough	L	0-1	0-0	13		12,508
24		29	H	Charlton Ath	D	4-4	2-1	13	Stockwell, Thompson, Dozzell, Milton	11,719
25	Jan 1		A	Oxford U	L	1-2	0-1	14	Thompson	5103
26		12	H	WBA	W	1-0	0-0	13	Whitton	11,036
27		19	A	Blackburn R	W	1-0	0-0	11	Whitton	8256
28	Feb 2		H	Millwall	L	0-3	0-2	14		13,338
29		23	H	Hull C	W	2-0	1-0	12	Goddard 2	9900
30	Mar 2		A	Wolverhampton	D	0-0	0-0	13		13,350
31		9	A	Bristol C	L	2-4	1-2	15	Dozzell, Goddard	11,474
32		16	A	Watford	D	1-1	0-1	17	Linighan	7732
33		18	H	Port Vale	W	2-1	1-0	—	Glover (og), Thompson	5820
34		22	H	Plymouth Arg	W	3-1	1-0	—	Morgan (og), Goddard 2	9842
35		30	A	Middlesbrough	D	1-1	1-0	15	Linighan	15,140
36	Apr 2		H	Portsmouth	D	2-2	1-1	—	Dozzell, Thompson (pen)	11,314
37		6	A	Charlton Ath	D	1-1	0-0	14	Linighan	6443
38		10	A	Bristol R	L	0-1	0-1	—		4983
39		13	H	Oxford U	D	1-1	1-1	16	Kiwomya	9135
40		17	H	West Ham U	L	0-1	0-1	—		20,290
41		20	A	Newcastle U	D	2-2	2-1	15	Kiwomya 2	17,638
42		25	A	Barnsley	W	2-0	1-0	—	Kiwomya, Goddard	7379
43		27	H	Oldham Ath	L	1-2	0-1	15	Kiwomya	12,332
44	May 4		H	Leicester C	W	3-2	0-1	13	Houghton, Gayle, Kiwomya	11,347
45		7	A	Notts Co	L	1-3	0-2	—	Humes	6902
46		11	A	Brighton & HA	L	1-2	0-1	14	Kiwomya	12,281

Final League Position: 14

GOALSCORERS

League (60): Kiwomya 10, Dozzell 6, Goddard 6, Milton 6, Stockwell 6, Thompson 6 (2 pens), Gayle 4, Redford 4 (1 pen), Linighan 3, Humes 2, Whitton 2, Gregory 1, Houghton 1, Palmer 1, own goals 2.
Rumbelows Cup (4): Redford 2, Kiwomya 1, Milton 1.
FA Cup (2): Dozzell 2.

Forrest	Yallop	Thompson	Stockwell	Gayle	Linighan	Lowe	Humes	Redford	Kiwomya	Zondervan	Dozzell	Gregory	Palmer	Milton	Hill	Johnson	Whitton	Goddard	Houghton	Parkes	Match No.
1	2	3*	4	5	6	7	8	9	10	11	12										1
1	2	3†	4	5	6	7	8	10*	9	11		12	14								2
1	2	3	4	5	6	7†	8		11	9	10*	14	12								3
1	2	3	4	5	6		8†	10	9*			7	14	11	12						4
1	2		4	5	6		8	10	9		7		11		3						5
1	2	12	4	5	6*		8	10	9		7		11		3						6
1	2	12	4	5	6		8*	10	9		7		11		3						7
1	2	12	4	5	6		8	10	3		7*		11	9							8
1	2	3	4	5	6		8	10	7				11	9							9
1	2		4	5	6		8	10	3		7		11	9							10
1	2		4	5	6		8	10*	3		7		11	9	12						11
1	2		4	5	6		8†	10	3		7*	14	11	9	12						12
1	2	12	4	5	6		8	10	3		7*		11	9							13
1	2		4	5	6	7*	8	3	12		10		11	9							14
1	2	12	4	5	6		8	10	3		14	7†	11	9*							15
1	2	11	4	5	6		8	10	3	7				9							16
1	2	11	4	5	6		8	10	3	7				9							17
1	2	11	4	5	6		3	8	10		7			9							18
1	2		4		6		3	8	10*		7		11	12	9	5					19
1	2		4†		6	14	3	8*	10		7		11	12	9	5					20
1	2	3	4	5		7	8		10	12	6		11	9*							21
1	2	3	4	5		7	8		10	12	6		11*	9							22
1	2	3	4	5		7	9	8	10	12	6*		11								23
1	2	3	4*	5		7	9	8	10	12	6		11								24
1	2	3	4	5†		7	9	7	10	12	6		11*	14							25
1	2	3	4	5		7*	12	11	8†	10	6		14				9				26
1	2	3	4			7*	8		10		6		11	12		5	9				27
1	2	3	4	5		7*	14	8	10		6†		11				9	12			28
1	2	3	4*	5	6		7		10	12			11				9	8			29
1	2	3	4	5			12	7	10		6		11*				9	8			30
1	2*	3	4	5			7		10		6		11	12			9	8			31
1	2	3	4	6	5		11		10		7						9	8			32
1	2	3	4	6	5		12	11*	10		7						9	8			33
1	2	3	4	6	5		11		10		7						9	8			34
1	2	3	4	6	5		12	11	10		7						9*	8			35
1	2	3	4	6	5		11	9*	10		7							8	12		36
1	2	3	4	6	5		11*	12	10		7							8	9		37
1	2	3	4	6	5	7*		12	11	10								8	9		38
1	2	3	4	6	5		11		7	10								8	9		39
1	14	3	4	6	5		2†	11*	7	10			12					8	9		40
1	2	3	4	6	5		11		7	10							9	8			41
1	2	3		6	5		11		7	10			4	9				8			42
1	2	3		6	5	14	11		7*		12	4†	9					8	10		43
	2	3	4	6	5		11		7				9					8	10	1	44
	2	3	4	6	5	9	11		7				10					8	10	1	45
			4	6	5	2	11		7				9	3				8	10	1	46
43	44	33	44	33	45	12	15	23	34	33	27	14	18	27	18	5	10	18	7	3	
+	+					+	+	+	+	+	+	+	+					+	+		
1s	5s					1s	1s	3s	3s	1s	3s	7s	5s	4s	5s	2s		1s	1s		

Rumbelows Cup Second Round Shrewsbury T (a) — 1-1
                                    (h) — 3-0
                Third Round Southampton (h) — 0-2
FA Cup Third Round Southampton (a) — 2-3

IPSWICH TOWN

Player and Position	Ht	Wt	Birth Date	Birth Place	Source	Clubs	League App	Gls
Goalkeepers								
Ron Fearon	6 0	11 12	19 11 60	Romford	Apprentice	QPR	—	—
						Reading	61	—
					Sutton	Ipswich T	28	—
						Brighton & HA (loan)	7	—
Craig Forrest	6 4	12 03	20 9 67	Vancouver	Apprentice	Ipswich T	116	—
						Colchester U (loan)	11	—
Phil Parkes	6 3	15 01	8 8 50	Sedgeley	Amateur	Walsall	52	—
						QPR	344	—
						West Ham U	344	—
						Ipswich	3	—
Defenders								
Jason Dozzell	6 2	12 04	9 12 67	Ipswich	School	Ipswich T	246	34
Brian Gayle	6 1	12 07	6 3 65	London		Wimbledon	83	3
						Manchester C	55	3
						Ipswich T	53	4
Lee Honeywood	5 8	10 10	3 8 71	Chelmsford	Trainee	Ipswich T	—	—
Tony Humes	5 11	10 10	19 3 66	Blyth	Apprentice	Ipswich T	115	10
Gavin Johnson	6 0	11 01	10 10 70	Ipswich	Trainee	Ipswich T	17	—
David Linighan	6 2	10 12	9 1 65	Hartlepool	Local	Hartlepool U	91	5
						Leeds U (loan)	—	—
						Derby Co	—	—
						Shrewsbury T	65	1
						Ipswich T	127	5
Neil Thompson	6 0	13 07	2 10 63	Beverley	Apprentice	Nottingham F	—	—
						Hull C	31	—
						Scarborough	87	15
						Ipswich T	83	9
Phil Whelan	6 4	14 01	7 8 72	Stockport		Ipswich T	—	—
Frank Yallop	5 11	11 03	4 4 64	Watford	Apprentice	Ipswich T	238	4
Midfield								
Andy Bernal	5 10	12 05	16 7 66	Canberra		Ipswich T	9	—
David Gregory	5 10	11 03	23 1 70	Sudbury	Trainee	Ipswich T	27	1
David Hill	5 9	10 03	6 6 66	Nottingham	Local	Scunthorpe U	140	10
						Ipswich T	61	—
						Scunthorpe U (loan)	9	1
Simon Milton	5 9	11 09	23 8 63	London	Bury St Edmunds	Ipswich T	115	27
						Exeter C (loan)	2	3
						Torquay U (loan)	4	1
Philip Mitchell*	5 11	11 07	3 6 68	Belfast	Linfield, Ards	Ipswich T	—	—
Steve Palmer	6 1	12 07	31 3 68	Brighton	Cambridge Univ	Ipswich T	28	1
Glenn Pennyfather	5 8	10 10	11 2 63	Billericay	Apprentice	Southend U	238	36
						Crystal Palace	34	1
						Ipswich T	8	1
Ian Redford	5 10	11 08	5 4 60	Dundee	Errol R	Dundee	85	34
						Rangers	172	23
						Dundee U	101	20
						Ipswich T	68	8
Mike Stockwell	5 6	10 02	14 2 65	Chelmsford	Apprentice	Ipswich T	173	13
Romeo Zondervan	5 9	10 02	4 3 59	Surinam	Den Haag	Twente Enschede	—	—
						WBA	84	5
						Ipswich T	246	13

IPSWICH TOWN

Foundation: Considering that Ipswich Town only reached the Football League in 1938, many people outside of East Anglia may be surprised to learn that this club was formed at a meeting held in the Town Hall as far back as 1878 when Mr. T. C. Cobbold, MP, was voted president. Originally it was the Ipswich Association FC to distinguish it from the older Ipswich Football Club which played rugby. These two amalgamated in 1888 and the handling game was dropped in 1893.

First Football League game: 27 August, 1938, Division 3(S), v Southend U (h) W 4-2 – Burns; Dale, Parry; Perrett, Fillingham, McLuckie; Williams, Davies (1), Jones (2), Alsop (1), Little.

Did you know: When Ipswich were held to a 1-1 draw by Gateshead at Portman Road in the FA Cup, 3rd rnd in January 1952 they had recalled goalkeeper Mick Burns for what proved to be his last game. He had joined the club in 1938 and was aged 43 years 7 months.

Managers (and Secretary-managers)
Mick O'Brien 1936–37, Scott Duncan 1937–55 (continued as secretary), Alf Ramsey 1955–63, Jackie Milburn 1963–64, Bill McGarry 1964–68, Bobby Robson 1969–82, Bobby Ferguson 1982–87, Johnny Duncan 1987–90, John Lyall May 1990– .

Player and Position	Ht	Wt	Birth Date	Place	Source	Clubs	League App	Gls
Forwards								
Gary Durrant‡	5 10	11 03	6 11 71	Lowestoft	Trainee	Ipswich T	—	—
Paul Goddard	5 8	12 00	12 10 59	Harlington	Apprentice	QPR	70	23
						West Ham U	170	54
						Newcastle U	61	19
						Derby Co	49	15
						Millwall	20	1
						Ipswich T	19	6
Chris Kiwomya	5 10	10 05	2 12 69	Huddersfield		Ipswich T	92	17
David Lowe	5 11	11 00	30 8 65	Liverpool	Apprentice	Wigan Ath	188	40
						Ipswich T	120	36
Gary Thompson	6 0	11 04	7 9 72	Ipswich		Ipswich T	—	—
Steve Whitton	6 0	12 07	4 12 60	East Ham	Apprentice	Coventry C	74	21
						West Ham U	39	6
						Birmingham C (loan)	8	2
						Birmingham C	95	28
						Sheffield W	32	4
						Ipswich	10	2

Trainees
Betts, Simon R; Cook, Adam; Devine, Declan P; Durrant, Lee R; Gray, Simon R; Gregory, Neil R; Harrison, Gary D; Nicholls, Darren; Pearn, Steven; Shaw, Marcus; Smedley, Martin; Smith, Kevin L; Tanner, Adam D.

Associated Schoolboys
Byrne, Steven; Dalrymple, Craig I; Dolby, Gavin P; Elliott, Lee; Kessler, Carl J; Mansfield, Graham P; Morin, Gareth N; Mortley, Peter R; Portrey, Simon D; Pryke, Damian A; Scowcroft, James B; Vaughan, Antony J; Ward, Lee J; Watson, Mark R; Weston, Kenneth; Weston, Mathew.

Associated Schoolboys who have accepted the club's offer of a Traineeship/Contract
Cotterell, Leo S; Eason, Jeremy J; Morgan, Philip J; Powley, Darren L.

LEEDS UNITED 1990–91   *Back row (left to right):* Chris O'Donnell. Chris Kamara. Vinny Jones. John Pearson. Lee Chapman. John McClelland. Peter Haddock. Andy Williams.
Centre row: Alan Sutton (Physiotherapist). Gary McAllister. Simon Grayson. Dylan Kerr. John Luckie. Mervyn Day. Chris Whyte. Mike Whitlow. Mel Sterland. Michael Hennigan (Coach).
Front row: Bobby Davison. Chris Fairclough. Gary Speed. Glynn Snodin. Howard Wilkinson (Manager). Gordon Strachan. Jim Beglin. Imre Varadi. David Batty. (Copyright LUFC.)

Division 1   **LEEDS UNITED**

Elland Road, Leeds LS11 0ES. Telephone Leeds (0532) 716037 (4 lines). Ticket Office: 710710. Fax: 706560.

Ground capacity: 40,176.

Record attendance: 57,892 v Sunderland, FA Cup 5th rd (replay), 15 March 1967.

Record receipts: £146,483, FA Cup semi-final replay, Everton v West Ham U, 16 April 1980.

Pitch measurements: 117yd × 76yd.

President: The Right Hon The Earl of Harewood LLD.

Chairman: L. Silver OBE. *Vice-chairman:* P. J. Gilman. *Deputy Chairman:* J. W. G. Marjason. *Managing Director:* W. J. Fotherby.

Directors: R. Barker MCIT, MBIM, Coun. M. J. Bedford, E. Carlile, Coun. M. Feldman, G. M. Holmes BSC (ECON), Coun. A. Hudson, R. P. Ridsdale.

Manager: Howard Wilkinson. *Assistant Manager:* Mike Hennigan.

Company Secretary: N. Pleasants.

Coaches: Mike Hennigan, Peter Gunby, Dick Bate. *Physio:* Alan Sutton.

Commercial Manager: Bob Baldwin.

Year Formed: 1919, as Leeds United after disbandment (by FA order) of Leeds City (formed in 1904). *Turned Professional:* 1920. *Ltd Co.:* 1920.

Club Nickname: 'United'.

Record League Victory: 8-0 v Leicester C, Division 1, 7 April 1934 – Moore; George Milburn, Jack Milburn; Edwards, Hart, Copping; Mahon (2), Firth (2), Duggan (2), Furness (2), Cochrane.

Record Cup Victory: 10-0 v Lyn (Oslo), European Cup, 1st rd 1st leg, 17 September 1969 – Sprake; Reaney, Cooper, Bremner (2), Charlton, Hunter, Madeley, Clarke (2), Jones (3), Giles (2) (Bates), O'Grady (1).

Record Defeat: 1-8 v Stoke C, Division 1, 27 August 1934.

Most League Points (2 for a win): 67, Division 1, 1968–69.

Most League Points (3 for a win): 85, Division 2, 1989–90.

Most League Goals: 98, Division 2, 1927–28.

Highest League Scorer in Season: John Charles, 42, Division 2, 1953–54.

Most League Goals in Total Aggregate: Peter Lorimer, 168, 1965–79 and 1983–86.

Most Capped Player: Billy Bremner, 54, Scotland.

Most League Appearances: Jack Charlton, 629, 1953–73.

Record Transfer Fee Received: £825,000 from Everton for Ian Snodin, January 1987.

Record Transfer Fee Paid: £1,700,000 to Southampton for Rodney and Ray Wallace, July 1991.

Football League Record: 1920 Elected to Division 2; 1924–27 Division 1; 1927–28 Division 2; 1928–31 Division 1; 1931–32 Division 2; 1932–47 Division 1; 1947–56 Division 2; 1956–60 Division 1; 1960–64 Division 2; 1964–82 Division 1; 1982–90 Division 2; 1990– Division 1.

Honours: Football League: Division 1 – Champions 1968–69, 1973–74; Runners-up 1964–65, 1965–66, 1969–70, 1970–71, 1971–72; Division 2 – Champions 1923–24, 1963–64, 1989–90; Runners-up 1927–28, 1931–32, 1955–56. *FA Cup:* Winners 1972; Runners-up 1965, 1970, 1973. *Football League Cup:* Winners 1967–68. **European Competitions:** *European Cup:* 1969–70, 1974–75 (runners-up). *European Cup-Winners' Cup:* 1972–73 (runners-up). *European Fairs Cup:* 1965–66, 1966–67 (runners-up), 1967–68 (winners), 1968–69, 1970–71 (winners). *UEFA Cup:* 1971–72, 1973–74, 1979–80.

Colours: All white. **Change colours:** All yellow.

LEEDS UNITED 1990–91 LEAGUE RECORD

Match No.	Date		Venue	Opponents	Result		H/T Score	Lg. Pos.	Goalscorers	Atten- dance
1	Aug	25	A	Everton	W	3-2	2-0	—	Fairclough, Speed, Varadi	34,412
2		28	H	Manchester U	D	0-0	0-0			29,172
3	Sept	1	H	Norwich C	W	3-0	2-0	2	Chapman 2, Varadi	25,684
4		8	A	Luton T	L	0-1	0-1	6		10,185
5		15	H	Tottenham H	L	0-2	0-0	9		31,342
6		23	A	Sheffield U	W	2-0	0-0	—	Pearson, Strachan	26,078
7		29	H	Arsenal	D	2-2	1-1	8	Chapman, Strachan (pen)	30,085
8	Oct	6	A	Crystal Palace	D	1-1	0-0	8	Speed	21,676
9		20	H	QPR	L	2-3	2-2	11	Whyte, Chapman	27,443
10		27	A	Aston Villa	D	0-0	0-0	9		24,219
11	Nov	3	H	Nottingham F	W	3-1	2-0	7	Chapman, Strachan (pen), McAllister	30,409
12		11	A	Manchester C	W	3-2	2-0	—	Chapman, Shutt, Strachan	27,782
13		17	H	Derby Co	W	3-0	2-0	5	Chapman, Strachan, Speed	27,868
14		24	A	Coventry C	D	1-1	1-0	5	Chapman	16,183
15	Dec	1	H	Southampton	W	2-1	2-0	5	Fairclough, Shutt	29,341
16		8	A	Manchester U	D	1-1	0-0	5	Sterland	40,927
17		16	H	Everton	W	2-0	2-0	—	Strachan (pen), Shutt	27,775
18		23	A	Sunderland	W	1-0	0-0	—	Sterland	23,773
19		26	H	Chelsea	W	4-1	1-0	4	Sterland, Chapman 2, Whitlow	30,893
20		29	H	Wimbledon	W	3-0	3-0	3	Chapman, Speed, Sterland	29,292
21	Jan	1	A	Liverpool	L	0-3	0-2	4		36,975
22		12	A	Norwich C	L	0-2	0-1	4		17,786
23		19	H	Luton T	W	2-1	1-0	4	Strachan (pen), Fairclough	27,010
24	Feb	2	A	Tottenham H	D	0-0	0-0	4		32,253
25	Mar	2	A	Southampton	L	0-2	0-1	4		16,585
26		9	H	Coventry C	W	2-0	1-0	4	Davison, Whyte	28,880
27		17	A	Arsenal	L	0-2	0-0	—		26,218
28		23	H	Crystal Palace	L	1-2	1-1	4	Speed	28,556
29		30	A	Chelsea	W	2-1	2-0	4	Shutt, Fairclough	17,585
30	Apr	2	H	Sunderland	W	5-0	3-0	—	Chapman 2, Shutt, Speed 2	28,132
31		6	A	Wimbledon	W	1-0	1-0	4	Chapman	6800
32		10	H	Manchester C	L	1-2	1-1	—	McAllister	28,757
33		13	H	Liverpool	L	4-5	0-4	4	Chapman 3, Shutt	31,460
34		17	A	QPR	L	0-2	0-0	—		10,998
35		23	A	Derby Co	W	1-0	1-0	—	Shutt	12,666
36	May	4	H	Aston Villa	W	5-2	2-1	4	Price (og), Chapman 2, Whyte, Shutt	29,188
37		8	H	Sheffield U	W	2-1	1-0	—	Sterland, Shutt	28,978
38		11	A	Nottingham F	L	3-4	1-2	4	Chapman 2, Shutt	25,067

Final League Position: 4

GOALSCORERS

League (65): Chapman 21, Shutt 10, Speed 7, Strachan 7 (4 pens), Sterland 5, Fairclough 4, Whyte 3, McAllister 2, Varadi 2, Davison 1, Pearson 1, Whitlow 1, own goal 1.
Rumbelows Cup (13): Chapman 4, Speed 3, McAllister 2, Fairclough 1, Strachan 1, Whyte 1, own goal 1.
FA Cup (7): Chapman 3, McAllister 1, Sterland 1, Strachan 1 (pen), own goal 1.

Lukic	Sterland	Snodin	Batty	Fairclough	Whyte	Strachan	Varadi	Chapman	McAllister	Speed	Kamara	Haddock	Whitlow	Jones	Pearson	Shutt	Williams	Davison	McClelland	Match No.
1	2	3	4	5	6	7	8*	9	10	11†	12	14								1
1	2	12	4	5	6	7	8	9	10	11*		3								2
1	2	3*	4	5	6	7	8	9	10†	11		14	12							3
1	2	3†	4		6	7	12	9	10	14		5	11		8*					4
1	2	12	4	5	6	7	8	9	10	11*		14	3†							5
1	2		4	5	6	7	8*	9	10	11		3			12					6
1	2	11*	4	5	6	7		9	10		12	3				8				7
1	2		4	5	6	7		9	10	11		3				8				8
1	2	3	4	5	6	7		9	10*	11	12					8†	14			9
1	2		4	5	6	7		9	10	11		3				8				10
1	2	12	4	5	6	7		9	10	11		3				8*				11
1	2		4	5	6	7		9	10	11		3			12	8*				12
1	2		4	5	6	7		9	10	11		3				8				13
1	2		4	6	5	7		9	10	11		3†	14		12	8*				14
1	2		4	5	6	7		9*	10†	11		3			12	8	14			15
1	2		4	5	6	7		9	10	11		3				8				16
1	2	12	4	5	6	7		9	10	11*		3				8				17
1	2	12	4	5	6	7		9	10	11		3*				8				18
1	2	3	4	5	6	7		9	10	11*					12	8				19
1	2	3*	4	5	6	7		9	10	11	12				14	8†				20
1	2	3*	4	5	6	7		9	10	11	12				14	8†				21
1	2	3	4	5	6	7		9	10	11*	12				14	8†				22
1	2	3*	4	5	6	7		9	10	11					12	8				23
1	2	12		5	6	7		9†	10	11		3		4	14*	8				24
1	2		4	5	6			9	10	11		3				8	7*	12		25
1	2		4	5	6	7		9	10	11		3			12	8*				26
1	2		4	5	6	7		9	10	11		3			12	8*				27
1	2		4	5	6	7		9	10†	11		3			14	8*		12		28
1	2		4	5	6	7*		9	10	11		3				8		12		29
1	2		4		6	7		9	10	11		3				8			5	30
1	2		4		6	7		9	10	11		3				8*		12	5	31
1	2		4		6			9	10	11		3				8	7*	12	5	32
1	2		4	5	6	7		9	10	11		3				8				33
1	2		4	5	6	7		9	10	11		3*				8		12		34
1	2	3*	4	5	6	7		9	10	11						8		12		35
1	2	3	4	5	6			9	10	11						8	7*	12		36
1	2	3	4	5	6			9	10	11						8	7			37
1	2	3	4	5	6	7*		9	10	11						8		12		38
38	38	14	37	34	38	34	5	38	38	35	5	10	14	1	4	25	5	2	3	
		+6s				+1s				+3s	+2s	+5s	+4s		+9s	+3s	+7s	+3s		

Rumbelows Cup	Second Round	Leicester C (a)		0-1
		(h)		3-0
	Third Round	Oldham Ath (h)		2-0
	Fourth Round	QPR (a)		3-0
	Fifth Round	Aston Villa (h)		4-1
	Semi-final	Manchester U (a)		1-2
		(h)		0-1
FA Cup	Third Round	Barnsley (a)		1-1
		(h)		4-0
	Fourth Round	Arsenal (a)		0-0
		(h)		1-1
		(a)		0-0
		(h)		1-2

LEEDS UNITED

Player and Position	Ht	Wt	Birth Date	Place	Source	Clubs	League App	Gls
Goalkeepers								
Mervyn Day	6 2	15 01	26 6 55	Chelmsford	Apprentice	West Ham U	194	—
						Orient	170	—
						Aston Villa	30	—
						Leeds U	225	—
						Coventry C (loan)	—	—
Neil Edwards*	5 8	11 02	5 12 70	Aberdare	Trainee	Leeds U	—	—
						Huddersfield T (loan)	—	—
John Lukic	6 4	13 07	11 12 60	Chesterfield	Apprentice	Leeds U	146	—
						Arsenal	223	—
						Leeds U	38	—
Tony O'Dowd			6 7 70	Dublin	Shelbourne	Leeds U	—	—
						Kilkerry (loan)	—	—
Defenders								
Jim Beglin	5 11	11 00	29 7 63	Dublin	Shamrock R	Liverpool	64	2
						Leeds U	19	—
						Plymouth Arg (loan)	5	—
						Blackburn R (loan)	6	—
Len Curtis			2 1 73	Dublin		Leeds U	—	—
Chris Fairclough	5 11	11 02	12 4 64	Nottingham	Apprentice	Nottingham F	107	1
						Tottenham H	60	5
						Leeds U	87	12
Peter Haddock	5 11	11 05	9 12 61	Newcastle	Apprentice	Newcastle U	57	—
						Burnley (loan)	7	—
						Leeds U	118	1
Nikolai Iliev‡			31 3 64	Sofia	Bologna	Leeds U	—	—
Dylan Kerr	5 11	12 05	14 1 67	Valetta	Arcadia Shepherds	Leeds U	8	—
Jason Longstaff*	5 10	12 03	8 2 71	Leeds	Trainee	Leeds U	—	—
John McClelland	6 2	13 05	7 12 55	Belfast	Portadown	Cardiff C	4	1
					Bangor	Mansfield	125	8
						Rangers	96	4
						Watford	184	3
						Leeds U	6	—
						Watford (loan)	1	—
Steven Nicholson‡			20 10 71	Leeds	Trainee	Leeds U	—	—
Chris O'Donnell*	5 9	12 00	26 5 68	Newcastle	Apprentice	Ipswich T	14	—
						Northampton T (loan)	1	—
						Leeds U	1	—
Grenville Shorte‡	6 1	12 08	14 10 70	Leeds	Trainee	Leeds U	—	—
Mel Sterland	5 10	12 10	1 10 61	Sheffield	Apprentice	Sheffield W	279	37
						Rangers	9	3
						Leeds U	80	10
Chris Whyte	6 1	11 10	2 9 61	London	Amateur	Arsenal	90	8
						Crystal Palace (loan)	13	—
					Los Angeles	WBA	84	7
						Leeds U	38	3
Midfield								
David Batty	5 7	10 07	2 12 68	Leeds	Trainee	Leeds U	132	1
Darren Edmonds*	5 9	11 06	12 4 71	Watford	Trainee	Leeds U	—	—
Simon Grayson	5 11	10 11	16 12 69	Ripon	Trainee	Leeds U	2	—
Chris Kamara	6 1	12 00	25 12 57	Middlesbrough	Apprentice	Portsmouth	63	7
						Swindon T	147	21
						Portsmouth	11	—
						Brentford	152	28
						Swindon T	87	6
						Stoke C	60	5
						Leeds U	18	1
Gary McAllister	5 10	9 06	25 12 64	Motherwell	Fir Park BC	Motherwell	59	6
						Leicester C	201	47
						Leeds U	38	2
Glynn Snodin	5 6	9 05	14 2 60	Rotherham	Apprentice	Doncaster R	309	61
						Sheffield W	59	1
						Leeds U	94	10
Gary Speed	5 9	10 06	8 9 69	Hawarden	Trainee	Leeds U	64	10
Gordon Strachan	5 6	10 03	9 2 57	Edinburgh		Dundee	60	13
						Aberdeen	183	55
						Manchester U	160	33
						Leeds U	91	26

LEEDS UNITED

Foundation: Immediately the Leeds City club (founded in 1904) was wound up by the FA in October 1919, following allegations of illegal payments to players, a meeting was called by a Leeds solicitor, Mr. Alf Masser, at which Leeds United was formed. They joined the Midland League playing their first game in that competition in November 1919. It was in this same month that the new club had discussions with the directors of a virtually bankrupt Huddersfield Town who wanted to move to Leeds in an amalgamation. But Huddersfield survived even that crisis.

First Football League game: 28 August, 1920, Division 2, v Port Vale (a) L 0-2 – Down; Duffield, Tillotson; Musgrove, Baker, Walton; Mason, Goldthorpe, Thompson, Lyon, Best.

Did you know: Leeds United did not concede a single goal in their first six appearances in the European Cup in 1969–70. Then George Connelly got one after only 45 seconds when Celtic beat them 1-0 in the first Semi-final 1st leg at Leeds.

Managers (and Secretary-managers)
Dick Ray 1919–20, Arthur Fairclough 1920–27, Dick Ray 1927–35, Bill Hampson 1935–47, Willis Edwards 1947–48, Major Frank Buckley 1948–53, Raich Carter 1953–58, Bill Lambton 1958–59, Jack Taylor 1959–61, Don Revie 1961–74, Brian Clough 1974, Jimmy Armfield 1974–78, Jock Stein 1978, Jimmy Adamson 1978–80, Allan Clarke 1980–82, Eddie Gray 1982–85, Billy Bremner 1985–88, Howard Wilkinson October 1988–   .

Player and Position	Ht	Wt	Birth Date	Place	Source	Clubs	League App	Gls
Mike Whitlow	5 11	12 01	13 1 68	Northwich	Witton Alb	Leeds U	67	3
Russell Wigley			9 1 72	Cardiff	Trainee	Leeds U	—	—
Andy Williams	6 0	11 09	29 7 62	Birmingham	Solihull	Coventry C	9	—
						Rotherham U	87	13
						Leeds U	46	3
Forwards								
Lee Chapman	6 3	13 00	5 12 59	Lincoln	Amateur	Stoke C	99	34
						Plymouth Arg (loan)	4	—
						Arsenal	23	4
						Sunderland	15	3
						Sheffield W	149	63
					Niort	Nottingham F	48	15
						Leeds U	59	33
Bob Davison	5 8	11 08	17 7 59	South Shields	Seaham CW	Huddersfield T	2	—
						Halifax T	63	29
						Derby Co	206	83
						Leeds U	89	31
Darryl Franklin*	5 5	10 06	1 3 71	Caerphilly	Trainee	Leeds U	—	—
Michael Knop*			29 12 71	Northwich	Trainee	Leeds U	—	—
John Pearson	6 2	13 02	1 9 63	Sheffield	Apprentice	Sheffield W	105	24
						Charlton Ath	61	15
						Leeds U	99	12
						Rotherham U (loan)	11	5
Carl Shutt	5 10	11 10	10 10 61	Sheffield	Spalding U	Sheffield W	40	16
						Bristol C	46	10
						Leeds U	51	16
Imre Varadi	5 8	11 01	8 7 59	Paddington	Letchworth GC	Sheffield U	10	4
						Everton	26	6
						Newcastle U	81	39
						Sheffield W	76	33
						WBA	32	9
						Manchester C	65	26
						Sheffield W	22	3
						Leeds U	19	4

Trainees
Ball, Stephen; Billy, Marlon; Crosby, Andrew K; Flear, Christopher R; Gallagher, John; Hayward, Darren F; Henderson, Damian R; Hepworth, Richard; Little, Patrick; Morgan, Ross G; Mulrain, Steven; Nicholls, Ryan R; O'Hara, Gary J; Philpott, Marcus; Preston, Mark R; Stoker, Gareth.

Associated Schoolboys
Bowman, Robert A; Cotterall, Nathan P; Doherty, Gerald A; Falk, Darren L; Flanagan, Matthew J; Ford, Mark S; Grimston, Andrew; Holmes, Damien L; Hoyle, Michael S; Linskell, Francis; Littlewood, Martin; Lynam, Gary M; Metcalf, Dennis; Owen, Alun H; Parrott, Ben; Sibson, Andrew; Sullivan, Christopher J.

Associated Schoolboys who have accepted the club's offer of a Traineeship/Contract
Byrne, Alexander M; Couzens, Andrew J; Daly, Kevin T; Hill, Stephen H; Oliver, Simon J; Tinkler, Mark R; Tobin, Stephen R; Whelan, Noel D.

280

LEICESTER CITY 1990-91 *Back row (left to right):* Taff Davies (Kit Manager), Mark Geeson (Physiotherapist), Paul Reid. Paul Kitson. Des Linton. Steven Holden. Steve Walsh. Carl Muggleton. Russell Hoult. Martin Hodge. Tony James. David Oldfield. Richard Smith. Gary Hyde. Ricky Hill. Bobby Roberts (Coach).
Centre row: Rob Johnson. Marc North. Tony Spearing. Colin Gibson. Tommy Wright. David Kelly. Gordon Lee (Manager). Ali Mauchlen (Player-Coach). Gary Mills. Kevin Russell. Paul Ramsey. Scott Oakes.
Front row: Andy Jeffrey. Gary Fitzpatrick. Ian Baraclough. Jason Peake.

Division 2   **LEICESTER CITY**

City Stadium, Filbert St, Leicester LE2 7FL. Telephone Leicester (0533) 555000. Clubcall: 0898 121185.

Ground capacity: 31,000.

Record attendance: 47,298 v Tottenham H, FA Cup 5th rd, 18 February 1928.

Record receipts: £123,695 v Nottingham F, Littlewoods Cup, 4th rd, 30 November 1988.

Pitch measurements: 112yd × 75yd.

President: K. R. Brigstock.

Chairman: Martin George. *Vice-Chairman:* T. Smeaton.

Directors: J. M. Elsom FCA, R. W. Parker, J. E. Sharp, T. W. Shipman, W. K. Shooter FCA.

Manager: Brian Little. *Coach/Assistant Manager:* Gordon Lee.

Secretary: Alan Bennet.

Youth Coach: Colin Murphy.

Physio: Mark Geeson. *PRO:* Alan Birchenall. *Commercial Manager:* Peter Hill.

Year Formed: 1884.

Club Nickname: 'Fiberts' or 'Foxes'.

Previous Grounds: 1884, Victoria Park; 1887, Belgrave Road; 1888, Victoria Park; 1891, Filbert Street.

Previous Name: 1884–1919, Leicester Fosse.

Record League Victory: 10-0 v Portsmouth, Division 1, 20 October 1928 – McLaren; Black, Brown; Findlay, Carr, Watson; Adcock, Hine (3), Chandler (6), Lochhead, Barry (1).

Record Cup Victory: 8-1 v Coventry C (away), League Cup, 5th rd, 1 December 1964 – Banks; Sjoberg, Norman (2); Roberts, King, McDerment; Hodgson (2), Cross, Goodfellow, Gibson (1), Stringfellow (2). (1 og).

Record Defeat: 0-12 (as Leicester Fosse) v Nottingham F, Division 1, 21 April 1909.

Most League Points (2 for a win): 61, Division 2, 1956–57.

Most League Points (3 for a win): 70, Division 2, 1982–83.

Most League Goals: 109, Division 2, 1956–57.

Highest League Scorer in Season: Arthur Rowley, 44, Division 2, 1956–57.

Most League Goals in Total Aggregate: Arthur Chandler, 259, 1923–35.

Most Capped Player: Gordon Banks, 37 (73), England.

Most League Appearances: Adam Black, 528, 1920–35.

Record Transfer Fee Received: £1,050,000 from Everton for Gary Lineker, July 1985.

Record Transfer Fee Paid: £500,000 to Everton for Wayne Clarke, July 1989.

Football League Record: 1894 Elected to Division 2; 1908–09 Division 1; 1909–25 Division 2; 1925–35 Division 1; 1935–37 Division 2; 1937–39 Division 1; 1946–54 Division 2; 1954–55 Division 1; 1955–57 Division 2; 1957–69 Division 1; 1969–71 Division 2; 1971–78 Division 1; 1978–80 Division 2; 1980–81 Division 1; 1981–83 Division 2; 1983–87 Division 1; 1987– Division 2.

Honours: Football League: Division 1 – Runners-up 1928–29; Division 2 – Champions 1924–25, 1936–37, 1953–54, 1956–57, 1970–71, 1979–80; Runners-up 1907–08. *FA Cup:* Runners-up 1949, 1961, 1963, 1969. *Football League Cup:* Winners 1964; Runners-up 1965. **European Competitions:** *European Cup-Winners' Cup:* 1961–62.

Colours: Blue shirts, white shorts, white stockings. **Change colours:** Red shirts, black shorts, black stockings.

LEICESTER CITY 1990–91 LEAGUE RECORD

Match No.	Date	Venue	Opponents	Result	H/T Score	Lg. Pos.	Goalscorers	Attendance
1	Aug 25	H	Bristol R	W 3-2	2-0	—	Kelly, Alexander (og), Wright	13,648
2	28	A	Oldham Ath	L 0-2	0-0	—		13,099
3	Sept 1	A	Port Vale	L 0-2	0-0	16		8840
4	8	H	West Ham U	L 1-2	0-1	20	Mills	14,605
5	15	A	Plymouth Arg	L 0-2	0-1	20		6336
6	18	A	Blackburn R	L 1-4	0-1	—	Oldfield	6520
7	22	H	Sheffield W	L 2-4	1-2	22	Oldfield, Kelly	16,156
8	29	A	Middlesbrough	L 0-6	0-4	23		16,178
9	Oct 3	H	Bristol C	W 3-0	1-0	—	James, Kelly 2	9815
10	6	H	Notts Co	W 2-1	1-0	19	Oldfield, Kelly	13,597
11	13	A	Charlton Ath	W 2-1	2-0	14	Balmer (og), James	6000
12	20	A	Portsmouth	L 1-3	0-1	17	Mills	9286
13	24	H	Swindon T	D 2-2	0-1	—	Mauchlen, North	9592
14	27	H	Ipswich T	L 1-2	0-2	20	Kelly (pen)	11,053
15	Nov 3	A	Oxford U	D 2-2	1-2	21	Wright, Kelly	5371
16	10	A	Barnsley	D 1-1	0-0	22	Wright	8581
17	17	H	Wolverhampton W	W 1-0	1-0	21	Kelly	16,574
18	23	A	Hull C	L 2-5	1-3	—	North, Reid	5855
19	Dec 1	H	Newcastle U	W 5-4	2-1	19	Fenwick, Kelly 3 (1 pen), Oldfield	11,045
20	15	A	Bristol R	D 0-0	0-0	18		5791
21	23	H	Watford	D 0-0	0-0	—		16,920
22	26	A	Millwall	L 1-2	0-1	20	Oldfield	6686
23	Jan 1	H	WBA	W 2-1	0-1	20	Walsh, James	12,210
24	12	H	Port Vale	D 1-1	0-1	19	Oldfield	9307
25	19	A	West Ham U	L 0-1	0-1	20		21,652
26	26	H	Blackburn R	L 1-3	1-1	21	Kelly	8167
27	Feb 2	H	Plymouth Arg	W 3-1	2-1	19	Wright, Kelly, James	8172
28	20	A	Brighton & HA	L 0-3	0-1	—		6455
29	23	H	Barnsley	W 2-1	0-0	17	James, Peake	9027
30	Mar 2	A	Newcastle U	L 1-2	0-2	22	Wright	13,575
31	5	A	Wolverhampton W	L 1-2	1-1	—	Gibson	15,707
32	9	H	Hull C	L 0-1	0-0	22		8386
33	12	A	Bristol C	L 0-1	0-0	—		13,297
34	16	H	Middlesbrough	W 4-3	0-2	20	Oldfield, Walsh, James, Russell	8324
35	20	H	Charlton Ath	L 1-2	0-0	—	Mortimer (og)	8363
36	23	A	Notts Co	W 2-0	2-0	20	Mills, Russell (pen)	11,532
37	30	H	Millwall	L 1-2	0-0	21	Kelly	10,783
38	Apr 1	A	Watford	L 0-1	0-0	21		10,078
39	6	H	Brighton & HA	W 3-0	2-0	21	Wright, Russell, Mills	8444
40	10	H	Oldham Ath	D 0-0	0-0	—		11,846
41	13	A	WBA	L 1-2	1-1	22	Russell	13,991
42	20	H	Portsmouth	W 2-1	1-0	20	Walsh, Russell	10,509
43	24	A	Sheffield W	D 0-0	0-0	—		31,308
44	27	A	Swindon T	L 2-5	2-3	22	James, Wright	10,404
45	May 4	A	Ipswich T	L 2-3	1-0	23	Reid, Mills (pen)	11,347
46	11	H	Oxford U	W 1-0	1-0	22	James	19,011

Final League Position: 22

GOALSCORERS

League (60): Kelly 14 (2 pens), James 8, Oldfield 7, Wright 7, Mills 5 (1 pen), Russell 5 (1 pen), Walsh 3, North 2, Reid 2, Fenwick 1, Gibson 1, Mauchlen 1, Peake 1, own goals 3.
Rumbelows Cup (1): Kelly 1 (pen).
FA Cup (1): James 1.

Appearance / team-sheet grid (shirt numbers per match; * and † denote substitutions). Because of the density of this grid, some middle/right-hand column placements are approximate.

Muggleton	Mills	Johnson	Mauchlen	Walsh	Paris	Wright	North	Oldfield	Davies	Kelly	James	Hill	Reid	Kitson	Ramsey	Hodge	Spearing	Hooper	Linton	Gavin	Fenwick	Peake	Gibson	Madden	Smith	Russell	Match No.
1	2	3*	4	5	6	7	8	9	10†	11	12	14															1
1	2	3	4	5	6*	7	8	9†	10	11	12	14															2
1	2	3	4	5	6†	7*	8	9	10	11		14	12														3
1	2	3	4*	5			8		10	11	6	7†12	9	14													4
	2			5		7	12	8	10*11	6		4	9†			14	1	3									5
	10	2		5	12	7		9	14	11	6	8†			4		1	3*									6
	10	2*	5	12	14	6	9		11		7†	8			4		3	1									7
	10	2	5	3	7		9†		11*	6	14	8			4			1	12								8
	10	2*	5	3	7	12	9		11	6		8			4			1									9
	10	2*	5	3	7	12	9		11	6		8			4			1									10
	10	2		3	7	5*	9†		11	6		8			4			1	12	14							11
	10	2		3	7	5	9		11	6	12	8			4*			1									12
	10	14	2		3†	7	5	9		11	6	12	8			4*			1									13
	10		2	5		7	3†	9*		11		4	8	12	14			1			6						14
	10		2	5*		7	3	12		11		4	8†	9				1			6	14					15
	10		2			7	8			11	6	4		9		3	1			5							16
	10	9†	2			7*	8	12		11	6	4	14			3	1			5							17
	10	9*	2			7	8	12		11	6	4	14			3†	1			5							18
	10	4	2	5	12	14	3	8†		11		9					1			6	7*						19
	10		2	5		12				11	14	8	7	4†		3	1		9*	6							20
1	10			5	12		2	9*		11		8	7	4						6		3					21
1		2	5	4	7	6	9			11	8*10									12		3					22
1	10		2	5		7	4	9		11	6	8										3					23
1	10		2	5		7†	4	9		11	6		8*					14		12		3					24
1	10		2			12	4	9		11	6		8†					7*	3		5	14					25
1	10		2			7	4	9		11	6		8						3		5	6					26
1	10*		2			7	4	9		11	6		8						12		3	5					27
1	10	4				7	2	9		11	6		8						3				5				28
1	10	4	5			7	2	9*		11	6			12					8		3						29
1	10	4	5			7	2	9*		11	6		14	12					8†		3						30
1	10	4	5			7	2	9†		11	6		14	12	8*						3						31
1	10	4	5			7	2	12		11	6				9*	8					3						32
1	10	4	5			7	2	9		11*	6		14	12	8						3†						33
1	10	4	5			7	2	9			6		8	12							3*					11	34
1	10	4	5			7	2	9			6		12		3*											11	35
1	10*	4	5			7		9		14	6		12	8		2					3					11†	36
1	10	4	5			7	2	9†		14	6			8		12					3*					11	37
1	10	4	5			7		9		14	6	12		8†	3	2										11*	38
	10	4*		7			12	9		6	8	2	1			5					3†		14	11			39
	10	14		5*		7	12			8	6	4†	9		1	3	2									11	40
	10	14		5		7†	12			8	6	4	9		1	3	2									11*	41
	10	14	4	5		7*	2	12		8	6	9			1	3										11†	42
	10		4	5		7	2	12		8	6	9			1	3										11*	43
	10		4	5		7	2	12		8	6	9			1	3*										11	44
	10			5		7	2	9*		8	6	4			1	3					12					11	45
	10		4*	5		7	2			11	6	9	12		1	3									8		46
22	45	8	40	35	10	40	35	32	5	41	35	19	24	2	20	10	16	14	5	1	8	4	17	3	2	13	
	+4s			+3s	+4s	+4s	+10s1s	+3s	+3s	+7s	+9s	+5s	+4s		+1s		+3s	+2s			+4s	+1s			+2s		

Rumbelows Cup — Second Round — Leeds U (h) — 1-0
(a) — 0-3
FA Cup — Third Round — Millwall (a) — 1-2

LEICESTER CITY

Player and Position	Ht	Wt	Birth Date	Birth Place	Source	Clubs	League App	Gls
Martin Hodge	6 2	13 07	4 2 59	Southport	Apprentice	Plymouth Arg	43	—
						Everton	25	—
						Preston NE (loan)	44	—
						Oldham Ath (loan)	4	—
						Gillingham (loan)	4	—
						Sheffield W	197	—
						Leicester C	75	—
Russell Hoult	6 4	13 02	22 11 72	Leicester	Trainee	Leicester C	—	—
Carl Muggleton	6 1	11 13	13 9 68	Leicester	Apprentice	Leicester C	25	—
						Chesterfield (loan)	17	—
						Blackpool (loan)	2	—
						Hartlepool U (loan)	8	—
						Stockport Co (loan)	4	—
						Liverpool (loan)	—	—
Paul O'Connor‡	5 11	12 10	17 8 71	Easington	Trainee	Leicester C	—	—
Defenders								
Colin Gibson	5 8	10 08	6 4 60	Bridport	Apprentice	Aston Villa	185	10
						Manchester U	79	9
						Port Vale (loan)	6	2
						Leicester C	18	1
Tony James	6 3	14 00	27 6 67	Sheffield	Gainsborough T			
						Lincoln C	29	—
						Leicester C	69	10
Andy Jeffrey*	5 10	11 00	15 1 72	Bellshill	Trainee	Leicester C	—	—
Des Linton	6 1	11 13	5 9 71	Birmingham	Trainee	Leicester C	10	—
Richard Smith	6 0	12 00	3 10 70	Leicester	Trainee	Leicester C	8	—
						Cambridge U (loan)	4	—
Tony Spearing*	5 9	10 12	7 10 64	Romford	Apprentice	Norwich C	69	—
						Stoke C (loan)	9	—
						Oxford U (loan)	5	—
						Leicester C	73	1
Steve Walsh	6 3	14 00	3 11 64	Fulwood	Local	Wigan Ath	126	4
						Leicester C	152	15
Midfield								
Billy Davies (To Dunfermline Ath. Oct 1990)	5 5	9 08	31 5 64	Glasgow	Pollok U BC Elfsborg	Rangers	11	1
						St Mirren	74	5
						Leicester C	6	—
Gary Fitzpatrick*	5 10	10 06	5 8 71	Birmingham	Trainee	Leicester C	1	—
Ricky Hill	5 11	13 00	5 3 59	London	Apprentice Le Havre	Luton T	436	54
						Leicester C	26	—
Gary Hyde*	6 0	9 07	28 12 69	Wolverhampton	Trainee	Darlington	38	3
						Leicester C	—	—
Rob Johnson	5 6	9 12	22 2 62	Bedford	Apprentice	Luton T	97	1
						Lincoln C (loan)	4	—
						Leicester C	25	—
Des Lyttle‡	5 9	12 00	24 9 71	Wolv'hampton	Trainee	Leicester C	—	—
Ally Mauchlen	5 7	10 05	29 6 60	Kilwinning	Irvine Meadow	Kilmarnock	120	10
						Motherwell	76	4
						Leicester C	219	10
Gary Mills	5 8	11 05	11 11 61	Northampton	Apprentice Seattle S Seattle S	Nottingham F	58	8
						Derby Co	18	1
						Nottingham F	79	4
						Notts Co	75	8
						Leicester C	87	9
Scott Oakes	5 10	9 12	5 8 72	Leicester	Trainee	Leicester C	2	—
Jason Peake	5 9	11 05	29 9 71	Leicester	Trainee	Leicester C	8	1
Paul Ramsey	5 11	13 00	3 9 62	Derry	Apprentice	Leicester C	290	13
Darren Williams	5 10	10 05	15 12 68	Birmingham	Trainee	Leicester C	10	2
						Lincoln C (loan)	9	—
						Chesterfield (loan)	5	1
Forwards								
Ian Baraclough	6 1	11 02	4 12 70	Leicester	Trainee	Leicester C	—	—
						Wigan Ath (loan)	9	2
						Grimsby T (loan)	4	—

LEICESTER CITY

Foundation: In 1884 a number of young footballers who were mostly old boys of Wyggeston School, held a meeting at a house on the Roman Fosse Way and formed Leicester Fosse FC. They collected 9d (less than 4p) towards the cost of a ball, plus the same amount for membership. Their first professional, Harry Webb from Stafford Rangers, was signed in 1888 for 2s 6d (12p) per week, plus travelling expenses.

First Football League game: 1 September, 1894, Division 2, v Grimsby T (a) L 3-4 – Thraves; Smith, Bailey; Seymour, Brown, Henrys; Hill, Hughes, McArthur (1), Skea (2), Priestman.

Did you know: Arthur Chandler is best remembered for his goalscoring feats but he was also the first player to make 100 consecutive League and Cup appearances for the club – a milestone he reached in October 1925.

Managers (and Secretary-managers)
William Clark 1896–97, George Johnson 1898–1907*, James Blessington 1907–09, Andy Aitken 1909–11, J. W. Bartlett 1912–14, Peter Hodge 1919–26, William Orr 1926–32, Peter Hodge 1932–34, Andy Lochhead 1934–36, Frank Womack 1936–39, Tom Bromilow 1939–45, Tom Mather 1945–46, Johnny Duncan 1946–49, Norman Bullock 1949–55, David Halliday 1955–58, Matt Gillies 1959–68, Frank O'Farrell 1968–71, Jimmy Bloomfield 1971–77, Frank McLintock 1977–78, Jock Wallace 1978–82, Gordon Milne 1982–86, Bryan Hamilton 1986–87, David Pleat 1987–91, Brian Little May 1991   .

Player and Position	Ht	Wt	Birth Date	Place	Source	Clubs	League App	Gls
Steven Holden	6 0	11 13	4 9 72	Luton	Trainee	Leicester C	—	—
David Kelly	5 11	10 10	25 11 65	Birmingham	Alvechurch	Walsall	147	63
						West Ham U	41	7
						Leicester C	54	21
Paul Kitson	5 11	10 12	9 1 71	Co Durham	Trainee	Leicester C	20	—
Marc North*	5 10	11 00	25 9 66	Ware	Apprentice	Luton T	18	3
						Lincoln C (loan)	4	—
						Scunthorpe U (loan)	5	2
						Birmingham C (loan)	5	1
						Grimsby T	67	17
						Leicester C	71	9
David Oldfield	6 0	12 02	30 5 68	Perth, Aust	Apprentice	Luton T	29	4
						Manchester C	26	6
						Leicester C	62	12
Paul Reid	5 5	10 02	19 1 68	Warley	Apprentice	Leicester C	150	21
Kevin Russell	5 8	10 10	6 12 66	Portsmouth	Apprentice	Brighton & HA	—	—
						Portsmouth	4	1
						Wrexham	84	43
						Leicester C	23	5
						Peterborough U (loan)	7	3
						Cardiff C (loan)	3	—
Tommy Wright	5 7	9 10	10 1 66	Fife	Apprentice	Leeds U	81	24
						Oldham Ath	112	23
						Leicester C	85	10

Trainees
Byrne, Thomas A; Cameron, Darren J; Foley, Dean T; Gallagher, Gordon P; Grace, Gary I; Haughton, Warren A; Kane, Liam B.D; Lewis, Neil A; Mogg, Lewis R; Moore, Christian; Newcombe, Simon B; Thorpe, Anthony L; Vassell, Robert A; Williams, Martin K.

Associated Schoolboys
Baines, Matthew P; Davey, Tim; Hallam, Craig D; James, Scott; Kerr, Christopher J; Kerr, Matthew; King, Darryl J; McKenzie, Donald O; Murphy, Benjamin; Nimblette, Wayne C; Stanton, Wayne; Talbott, Cory R.

Associated Schoolboys who have accepted the club's offer of a Traineeship/Contract
Bedder, Matthew J; Blyth, Ian; Bunting, Nathan J; Clines, James; Crane, Adrian P; Eustace, Scott D; Joachim, Julian K; Thompson, Ian T.

LEYTON ORIENT 1990–91 *Back row (left to right)*: Greg Berry, Mark Cooper, Paul Newell, Paul Heald, John Sitton, Adrian Whitbread.
Centre row: John Gorman (Youth Coach), Wayne Burnett, Keith Day, Terry Howard, Carl Hoddle, Kevin Nugent, Chris Zoricich, Steve Castle, Danny Carter, Andy Sayer, Bill Songhurst (Physiotherapist).
Front row: Kevin Dickenson, Kevin Hales, Lee Harvey, Peter Eustace (Assistant Manager), Frank Clark (Manager), Geoff Pike, Alan Hull, Steve Baker.

Division 3　　　　　　　　　　　　**LEYTON ORIENT**

Leyton Stadium, Brisbane Road, Leyton, London E10 5NE.
Telephone 081-539 2223/4. Clubcall: 0898 121150.

Ground capacity: 18,869 (7,171 seats).

Record attendance: 34,345 v West Ham U, FA Cup 4th rd,
25 January 1964.

Record receipts: £87,867.92 v West Ham U, FA Cup 3rd rd,
10 January 1987.

Pitch measurements: 110yd × 80yd.

Chairman: T. Wood OBE.

Managing Director: Frank Clark.

Directors: A. Pincus, D. L. Weinrabe, H. Linney, M. Pears.

Manager: Frank Clark. *Coach/Assistant Manager:* Peter Eustace. *Physio:* Bill Songhurst.

Secretary: Miss Carol Stokes. *Asst. Sec.:* Mrs Sue Tilling. *Commercial Manager:* Frank
Woolf.

Year Formed: 1881. *Turned Professional:* 1903. *Ltd Co.:* 1906.

Club Nickname: 'The O's'.

Previous Names: 1881–86, Glyn Cricket and Football Club; 1886–88, Eagle Football Club;
1888–98, Orient Football Club; 1898–1946, Clapton Orient; 1946–66, Leyton Orient; 1966–
87, Orient.

Previous Grounds: Glyn Road, 1884–96; Whittles Athletic Ground, 1896–1900; Millfields
Road, 1900–30; Lea Bridge Road, 1930–37.

Record League Victory: 8-0 v Crystal Palace, Division 3 (S), 12 November 1955 – Welton;
Lee, Earl; Blizzard, Aldous, McKnight; White (1), Facey (3), Burgess (2), Heckman,
Hartburn (2). 8-0 v Rochdale, Division 4, 20 October 1987 – Wells; Howard, Dickenson,
Smalley, Day, Hull, Hales, Castle (Sussex), Shinners, Godfrey (Harvey), Comfort. 8-0 v
Colchester U, Division 4, 15 October 1988 – Wells; Howard, Dickenson, Hales (1p), Day
(1). Sitton (1), Baker (1), Ward, Hull (3). Juryeff, Comfort (1).

Record Cup Victory: 9-2 v Chester, League Cup, 3rd rd, 15 October 1962 – Robertson;
Charlton, Taylor; Gibbs, Bishop, Lea; Deeley (1), Waites (3), Dunmore (2), Graham (3),
Wedge.

Record Defeat: 0-8 v Aston Villa, FA Cup 4th rd, 30 January 1929.

Most League Points (2 for a win): 66, Division 3 (S), 1955–56.

Most League Points (3 for a win): 75, Division 4, 1988–89.

Most League Goals: 106, Division 3 (S), 1955–56.

Highest League Scorer in Season: Tom Johnston, 35, Division 2, 1957–58.

Most League Goals in Total Aggregate: Tom Johnston, 121, 1956–58, 1959–61.

Most Capped Player: John Chiedozie, 8 (10), Nigeria.

Most League Appearances: Peter Allen, 432, 1965–78.

Record Transfer Fee Received: £600,000 from Notts Co for John Chiedozie, August 1981.

Record Transfer Fee Paid: £175,000 to Wigan Ath for Paul Beesley, October 1989.

Football League Record: 1905 Elected to Division 2; 1929–56 Division 3 (S); 1956–62
Division 2; 1962–63 Division 1; 1963–66 Division 2; 1966–70 Division 3; 1970–82 Division
2; 1982–85 Division 3; 1985–89 Division 4; 1989– Division 3.

Honours: Football League: Division 1 best season: 22nd, 1962–63; Division 2 – Runners-up
1961–62; Division 3 – Champions 1969–70; Division 3 (S) – Champions 1955–56; Runners-
up 1954–55. *FA Cup:* Semi-final 1977–78. *Football League Cup:* best season: 5th rd, 1963.

Colours: Red shirts with black and white bars, white shorts, red stockings. **Change colours:**
Yellow shirts, blue shorts, yellow stockings.

LEYTON ORIENT 1990–91 LEAGUE RECORD

Match No.	Date	Venue	Opponents	Result	H/T Score	Lg. Pos.	Goalscorers	Attendance
1	Aug 25	H	Swansea C	W 3-0	0-0	—	Sayer, Harvey, Castle	4206
2	Sept 1	A	Birmingham C	L 1-3	0-2	8	Sayer	5847
3	8	H	Mansfield T	W 2-1	1-0	5	Castle, Harvey	3703
4	15	A	Chester C	L 0-2	0-0	10		1716
5	17	A	Tranmere R	L 0-3	0-2	—		5510
6	22	H	Rotherham U	W 3-0	0-0	10	Castle 2 (1 pen), Berry	3493
7	29	H	Bradford C	W 2-1	1-0	9	Castle 2	3761
8	Oct 2	A	Cambridge U	L 0-1	0-0	—		4991
9	6	A	Huddersfield T	L 0-1	0-1	12		4686
10	13	H	Shrewsbury T	W 3-2	3-1	10	Harvey, Achampong, Nugent	4394
11	20	H	Bolton W	L 0-1	0-1	13		4121
12	23	A	Grimsby T	D 2-2	1-1	—	Carter, Achampong	6660
13	27	A	Reading	W 2-1	0-0	10	Nugent, Carter	4513
14	Nov 4	H	Fulham	W 1-0	1-0	—	Berry	6163
15	10	H	Exeter C	W 1-0	0-0	4	Nugent	3785
16	24	A	Wigan Ath	W 2-1	2-1	4	Berry, Nugent	2260
17	Dec 2	A	Brentford	L 0-1	0-0	—		7383
18	15	H	Preston NE	W 1-0	1-0	3	Achampong	3282
19	22	H	Crewe Alex	W 3-2	3-2	3	Carter, Howard, Berry	3901
20	29	A	Bournemouth	D 2-2	0-0	4	Castle, Achampong	6139
21	Jan 1	H	Stoke C	L 0-2	0-1	7		6371
22	12	H	Birmingham C	D 1-1	1-0	9	Castle	4708
23	26	H	Chester C	W 1-0	1-0	8	Castle	3437
24	Feb 2	H	Tranmere R	W 4-0	1-0	6	Bart-Williams, Pike, Castle, Cooper	4313
25	5	A	Rotherham U	D 0-0	0-0	—		4056
26	19	A	Bury	L 0-1	0-1	—		2207
27	23	A	Exeter C	L 0-2	0-2	12		3216
28	Mar 3	H	Brentford	L 1-2	1-0	—	Cooper	5136
29	9	A	Preston NE	L 1-2	1-0	15	Bart-Williams	3651
30	12	H	Cambridge U	L 0-3	0-0	—		4292
31	16	A	Bradford C	L 0-4	0-1	15		5059
32	19	A	Shrewsbury T	L 0-3	0-0	—		2236
33	23	H	Huddersfield T	W 1-0	0-0	15	Nugent	3292
34	30	H	Bury	W 1-0	1-0	16	Cooper	3514
35	Apr 1	A	Crewe Alex	D 3-3	1-1	16	Cooper 2, Taylor	3048
36	6	H	Bournemouth	W 2-0	1-0	15	Bond (og), Carter	4289
37	9	H	Southend U	L 0-1	0-1	—		6306
38	13	A	Stoke C	W 2-1	0-1	14	Cooper 2	7957
39	16	A	Mansfield	D 3-3	2-2	—	Castle, Cooper 2	2050
40	20	A	Bolton W	L 0-1	0-0	13		7926
41	23	H	Wigan Ath	D 1-1	0-0	—	Tomlinson	2613
42	27	H	Grimsby T	L 0-2	0-1	14		4306
43	30	A	Swansea C	D 0-0	0-0	—		2132
44	May 4	H	Reading	W 4-0	1-0	12	Carter, Berry, Castle (pen), Howard	2648
45	7	A	Southend U	D 1-1	0-0	—	Day	8760
46	11	A	Fulham	D 1-1	1-0	13	Howard	6590

Final League Position: 13

GOALSCORERS

League (55): Castle 12 (2 pens), Cooper 9, Berry 5, Carter 5, Nugent 5, Achampong 4, Harvey 3, Howard 3, Bart-Williams 2, Sayer 2, Day 1, Pike 1, Taylor 1, Tomlinson 1, own goal 1.
Rumbelows Cup (9): Castle 3 (1 pen), Nugent 3, Berry 2, Harvey 1.
FA Cup (8): Castle 3, Pike 2, Carter 1, Howard 1, Nugent 1.

Heald	Baker	Howard	Sitton	Day	Hales	Harvey	Castle	Nugent	Sayer	Berry	Carter	Achampong	Whitbread	Pike	Zoricich	Hull	Dickenson	Cooper	Bart-Williams	Newell	Fee	Hoddle	Taylor	Cobb	Tomlinson	Hackett	Otto	Match No.
1	2	3	4	5	6†	7	8	9	10	11*	12	14																1
1	2	3	4			7	8*	9	10	11†	12	14	5	6														2
1	2	3	4			7	8	9	10	11*	12		5	6														3
1	2	3	4			7	8	9	10*	11	12		5	6														4
1	2	3	4			7*	8	9		11	10	12	5	6														5
1	2	3	4				8	9	10	11		7*12	5	6														6
1	2	3	4				8	9		11		7 10	5	6														7
1		3	4	14			8	9	12	11†	7	10*	5	6	2													8
1		3	4			11	8	9			7	10*	5	6	2	12												9
1		3	4			11*	8	9	12		7	10	5	6	2													10
1		3		4		11	8	9		12	7	10*	5	6	2													11
1		3		4			8	9		11*	7	10	5	6	2			12										12
1		3		4		12	8	9		11	7	10*	5	6	2													13
1	2	3	14	4†		10*	8	9		11	7	12	5	6														14
1	2	3	4			10	8	9		11*	7	12	5	6														15
1	2	3	4			10†	8	9		11*	7	12	5	6	14													16
1	2	3				10	8	9			7	11*	5	6	4			12										17
1	2	3	4				8	9		11*	7	10	5	6														18
1	2	3	4			12	8	9		11*	7	10	5	6														19
1	2	3	4			11*	8	9			7	10	5	6	12													20
1	2	3	4			12	8	9		11*	7	10	5	6														21
1	2	3	4			12†	8	9		11*	7	10	5	6	14													22
1	2	3		5		11	8			12	7	10*	4	9			6†14											23
1	12	3	2			11	8			10	7†		5	4			6 14	9*										24
1	2	3				11*	8			10†	7	12	5	4	9		6 14											25
	2	3	4			10	8			9	7		5*11				6 12		1									26
12		3	4				8			10	7	11	5				6* 9	2	1									27
	2	3	4†			11*	8			10	7		5	6				9 12	1	14								28
		3		14		11*	8				7	12	5	6			2†	9 10	1	4								29
		3					8	12			7	11	5	6	2			9 10*	1	4								30
		3		14			8	12			7	11	5†	6	2			9 10*	1	4								31
		3		5			8	9			7	11		6	2	12		10*	1	4								32
		3		4			8	9	12	6*	7	11	5		2			10	1									33
1		3		4			8	9†		7*11	5		2			10	6					12 14						34
1		3		4		8*	9			7	11†	5		2			10	6					12 14					35
1		3		4			8	9		7	11	5		2			10*	6					12					36
1		3		4			8		9*	7	11	5		2			10	6						12				37
1	2	3		4	14	12	8	9	11†	7*		5					10	6										38
1	2	3		4		7	8	9	11			5					10	6										39
1	2	3		4	14	11*	8†	9	12			5	7				10	6										40
1		3	14	4		8			11*		7	5†	2				10	6						9 12				41
1		3	5	4			8		11		7		2				10	6						9				42
1		3		4	6	8	9		11	7			2				10									5		43
1		3		4		8	9		11	7			2				10*	6						12		5		44
1		3		4		8	9		11	7			2				10	6								5		45
1		3		4		8	9		11	7			2				10*	6								5	12	46
38	23	46	22	21	3	21	45	33	6	32	38	25	38	30	24	—	6	18	19	8	4	—	—	2	—	4	—	
	+		+	+	+		+	+	+	+			+	+	+		+	+	+	+				+		+		
2s			2s	3s	2s	5s			5s	3s	4s	9s			4s		2s	1s	4s	2s		1s	2s	3s	2s	1s	1s	

Rumbelows Cup

First Round	Maidstone U (a)		2-2
	(h)		4-1
Second Round	Charlton Ath (a)		2-2
	(h)		1-0
Third Round	Crystal Palace (a)		0-0
	(h)		0-1

FA Cup

First Round	Southend U (h)		3-2
Second Round	Colchester U (a)		0-0
	(h)		4-1
Third Round	Swindon T (h)		1-1
	(a)		0-1

LEYTON ORIENT

Player and Position	Ht	Wt	Birth Date	Birth Place	Source	Clubs	League App	Gls
Goalkeepers								
Paul Heald	6 2	12 05	20 8 68	Wath on Dearne	Trainee	Sheffield U	—	—
						Leyton Orient	103	—
Paul Newell	6 1	11 05	23 2 69	Greenwich	Trainee	Southend U	15	—
						Leyton Orient	8	—
Defenders								
Adam Baker			1 6 72	Newham	Trainee	Leyton Orient	—	—
Keith Day	6 1	11 00	29 11 62	Grays	Aveley	Colchester U	113	12
						Leyton Orient	149	7
Kevin Dickenson	5 6	10 06	24 2 62	London	Apprentice	Tottenham H	—	—
						Charlton Ath	75	1
						Leyton Orient	184	3
Warren Hackett			16 12 71	Newham	Tottenham H	Leyton Orient	4	—
Kevin Hales	5 7	10 04	13 1 61	Dartford	Apprentice	Chelsea	20	2
						Leyton Orient	261	22
Lee Harvey	5 11	11 07	21 12 66	Harlow	Local	Leyton Orient	150	19
Terry Howard	6 1	11 07	26 2 66	Stepney	Amateur	Chelsea	6	—
						Crystal Palace (loan)	4	—
						Chester C (loan)	2	—
						Leyton Orient	190	19
Mark O'Neill			4 10 72	Dublin	Trainee	Leyton Orient	—	—
John Sitton*	6 0	12 02	21 10 59	Hackney	Apprentice	Chelsea	13	—
						Millwall	45	1
						Gillingham	107	5
						Leyton Orient	170	7
Adrian Whitbread	6 2	11 13	22 10 71	Epping	Trainee	Leyton Orient	46	—
Midfield								
Steve Baker	5 5	10 05	2 12 61	Newcastle	Apprentice	Southampton	73	—
						Burnley (loan)	10	—
						Leyton Orient	112	6
Chris Bart-Williams§			16 6 74	Freetown	Trainee	Leyton Orient	21	2
Wayne Burnett			4 9 71	Lambeth	Trainee	Leyton Orient	3	—
Steve Castle	5 11	12 05	17 5 56	Ilford	Apprentice	Leyton Orient	206	45
Carl Hoddle*	6 0	11 00	8 3 67	Harlow	Bishop's Stortford			
						Leyton Orient	28	2
Lloyd Moncur*	5 10	11 02	16 9 71	Newham	Trainee	Leyton Orient	—	—
Geoff Pike*	5 6	11 00	28 9 56	Clapton	Apprentice	West Ham U	291	32
						Notts Co	82	17
						Leyton Orient	44	1
Keith Sharman	6 2	12 00	6 11 71	London	Trainee	Leyton Orient	—	—
Chris Zoricich†	5 11	11 10	3 5 69	New Zealand		Leyton Orient	28	—
Forwards								
Kenny Achampong	5 9	10 10	26 6 66	London	Apprentice	Fulham	81	15
						West Ham U (loan)	—	—
						Charlton Ath	10	—
						Leyton Orient	34	4
Greg Berry	5 11	12 00	5 3 71	Essex	East Thurrock	Leyton Orient	44	6
Danny Carter	5 11	11 12	29 6 69	Hackney	Billericay	Leyton Orient	74	10
Paul Cobb			13 12 72	Thurrock	Purfleet	Leyton Orient	4	—
Mark Cooper	6 1	13 00	5 4 67	Watford	Apprentice	Cambridge U	71	17
						Tottenham H	—	—
						Shrewsbury T (loan)	6	2
						Gillingham	49	11
						Leyton Orient	75	24

LEYTON ORIENT

Foundation: There is some doubt about the foundation of Leyton Orient, and, indeed, some confusion with clubs like Leyton and Clapton over their early history. As regards the foundation, the most favoured version is that Leyton Orient was formed originally by members of Homerton Theological College who established Glyn Cricket Club in 1881 and then carried on through the following winter playing football. Eventually many employees of the Orient Shipping Line became involved and so the name Orient was chosen in 1888.

First Football League game: 2 September, 1905, Division 2, v Leicester Fosse (a) L 1-2 – Butler; Holmes, Codling; Lamberton, Boden, Boyle; Kingaby (1), Wootten, Leigh, Evenson, Bourne.

Did you know: Peter Kitchen created the club's record for most goals in a season of FA Cup games with a total of seven in 1977–78. He also scored one in the League Cup and his total of eight for these two competitions is also a club record.

Managers (and Secretary-managers)
Sam Omerod 1905–06, Ike Ivenson 1906, Billy Holmes 1907–22, Peter Proudfoot 1922–29, Arthur Grimsdell 1929–30, Peter Proudfoot 1930–31, Jimmy Seed 1931–33, David Pratt 1933–34, Peter Proudfoot 1935–39, Tom Halsey 1939, Billy Wright 1939–45, Billy Hall 1945, Billy Wright 1945–46, Charlie Hewitt 1946–48, Neil McBain 1948–49, Alec Stock 1949–56, 1956–58, 1958–59, Johnny Carey 1961–63, Benny Fenton 1963–64, Dave Sexton 1965, Dick Graham 1966–68, Jimmy Bloomfield 1968–71, George Petchey 1971–77, Jimmy Bloomfield 1977–81, Paul Went 1981, Ken Knighton 1981, Frank Clark May 1982– .

Player and Position	Ht	Wt	Birth Date	Birth Place	Source	Clubs	League App	Gls
Alan Hull*	5 9	11 00	4 9 62	Rochford	Barking	Leyton Orient	79	16
Kevin Nugent	6 1	12 04	10 4 69	Edmonton	Trainee	Leyton Orient	58	8
						Cork C (loan)	—	—
Ricky Otto			9 11 67	London	Dartford	Leyton Orient	1	—
Andy Sayer	5 9	10 12	6 6 66	Brent	Apprentice	Wimbledon	58	15
						Cambridge U (loan)	5	—
						Fulham	53	15
						Leyton Orient	21	3
						Sheffield U (loan)	3	—
Michael Tomlinson§			15 9 72	Lambeth	Trainee	Leyton Orient	1	1

Trainees
Bart-Williams, Christopher; Lakin, Barry; McCarthy, John I; O'Hanlon, George T; Patience, Brett J; Sheikh, Azzaz B.M; Stephenson, Andrew; Thompson, David C; Tomlinson, Michael L; Warne, Colin.

**Non-Contract
Welsh, Alexander; Zoricich, Christopher V.

Associated Schoolboys
Bird, Robert J; Colinson, David J; Gilby, Frank S; Howard, Anthony; Okai, Stephen P; Rayment, Stuart; Ross, Anthony; Smith, Murray H; Trott, Ian J; Wedlock, Grant.

Associated Schoolboys who have accepted the club's offer of a Traineeship/Contract
Beckett, Nathan J; Denny, Neil R; Fowler, Lee P; McDermott, Dean P; Ramage, Andrew; Rolls, George E; Sweetman, Nicholas E; Warren, Mark W.

**Non-Contract Players who are retained must be re-signed before they are eligible to play in League matches.

LINCOLN CITY 1990–91 *Back row (left to right):* Matthew Dickins, Paul Dobson, Matthew Carmichael, Sean Dunphy, Jason Lee, Ian Bowling, Keith Alexander, Tony Lormor, Grant Brown, Paul Ward, Mark Wallington.
Centre row: David Clarke, Neil Smith, John Schofield, Shane Nicholson, Gerry Brook (Physiotherapist), Steve Thompson (Manager), Dean Crombie (Assistant Manager), Steve Stout, Graham Bressington, David Puttnam, Paul Smith.
Front row: Adrian Barker, Dean West, Steve Parkinson, Jamie Hardwick, Stuart Mulhill, Stuart Diamond, Mark Hunt.

Division 4 — LINCOLN CITY

Sincil Bank, Lincoln LN5 8LD. Telephone Lincoln (0522) 522224 and 510263. Fax: (0522) 520564. Executive Club: (0522) 532634.

Ground capacity: 11,500.

Record attendance: 23,196 v Derby Co, League Cup 4th rd, 15 November 1967.

Record receipts: £34,843.30 v Tottenham H, Milk Cup 2nd rd, 26 October 1983.

Pitch measurements: 110yd × 75yd.

Hon. Life Presidents: V. C. Withers, D. W. L. Bocock.

President: H. Dove.

Chairman: K. J. Reames. *Vice-chairman:* M. B. Pryor.

Directors: G. R. Davey (Managing), R. Staples, H. C. Sills.

Hon. Consultant Surgeon: Mr Brian Smith. *Hon. Club Doctor:* Nick Huntley.

Secretary: G. R. Davey.

Manager: Steve Thompson. *Assistant Manager:*

Physio: Adrian Davies. *Commercial Manager:* Wayne Jenner.

Year Formed: 1883. *Turned Professional:* 1892. *Ltd Co.:* 1892.

Club Nickname: 'The Red Imps'.

Previous Grounds: 1883, John O'Gaunt's; 1894, Sincil Bank.

Record League Victory: 11-1 v Crewe Alex, Division 3 (N), 29 September 1951 – Jones; Green (1p), Varney; Wright, Emery, Grummett (1); Troops (1), Garvey, Graver (6), Whittle (1), Johnson (1).

Record Cup Victory: 8-1 v Bromley, FA Cup, 2nd rd, 10 December 1938 – McPhail; Hartshorne, Corbett; Bean, Leach, Whyte (1); Hancock, Wilson (1), Ponting (3), Deacon (1), Clare (2).

Record Defeat: 3-11 v Manchester C, Division 2, 23 March 1895.

Most League Points (2 for a win): 74, Division 4, 1975–76.

Most League Points (3 for a win): 77, Division 3, 1981–82.

Most League Goals: 121, Division 3 (N), 1951–52.

Highest League Scorer in Season: Allan Hall, 42, Division 3 (N), 1931–32.

Most League Goals in Total Aggregate: Andy Graver, 144, 1950–55 and 1958–61.

Most Capped Player: David Pugh, 3 (7), Wales and George Moulson, 3, Eire.

Most League Appearances: Tony Emery, 402, 1946–59.

Record Transfer Fee Received: £180,000 from Newcastle U for Mick Harford, December 1980.

Record Transfer Fee Paid: £60,000 to Southampton for Gordon Hobson, September 1988, £60,000 to Sheffield U for Alan Roberts, October 1989, and £60,000 to Leicester C for Grant Brown, January 1990.

Football League Record: 1892 Founder member of Division 2. Remained in Division 2 until 1920 when they failed re-election but also missed seasons 1908–09 and 1911–12 when not re-elected. 1921–32 Division 3 (N); 1932–34 Division 2; 1934–48 Division 3 (N); 1948–49 Division 2; 1949–52 Division 3 (N); 1952–61 Division 2; 1961–62 Division 3; 1962–76 Division 4; 1976–79 Division 3; 1979–81 Division 4; 1981–86 Division 3; 1986–87 Division 4; 1987–88 GM Vauxhall Conference; 1988– Division 4.

Honours: Football League: Divison 2 best season: 5th, 1901–02; Division 3 (N) – Champions 1931–32, 1947–48, 1951–52; Runners-up 1927–28, 1930–31, 1936–37; Division 4 – Champions 1975–76; Runners-up 1980–81. *FA Cup:* best season: 1st rd of Second Series (5th rd equivalent), 1886–87, 2nd rd (5th rd equivalent), 1889–90, 1901–02. *Football League Cup:* best season: 4th rd, 1967–68. GM Vauxhall Conference Champions – 1987–88.

Colours: Red and white striped shirts, black shorts, red stockings with white trim. **Change colours:** All blue.

LINCOLN CITY 1990–91 LEAGUE RECORD

Match No.	Date		Venue	Opponents	Result		H/T Score	Lg. Pos.	Goalscorers	Attendance
1	Aug	25	A	Burnley	D	2-2	1-1	—	Brown, Smith P	6106
2	Sept	1	H	Halifax T	W	1-0	1-0	7	Schofield	2947
3		15	H	Cardiff C	D	0-0	0-0	12		3152
4		19	H	Chesterfield	D	1-1	0-0	—	Puttnam	2855
5		22	A	Scunthorpe U	L	1-2	1-1	16	Warren	2844
6		29	A	Maidstone U	L	1-4	0-1	19	Casey	2190
7	Oct	3	H	Hereford U	D	1-1	0-0	—	Smith P	2205
8		6	H	Aldershot	D	2-2	0-1	20	Smith P 2	2755
9		13	A	Peterborough U	L	0-2	0-1	19		4766
10		20	A	Doncaster R	L	0-1	0-0	20		2968
11		24	H	Rochdale	L	1-2	1-1	—	Nicholson	1974
12		27	H	Northampton T	W	3-1	0-1	21	Nicholson (pen), Smith P, Casey	3352
13	Nov	3	A	Carlisle U	D	0-0	0-0	22		3095
14		10	A	Stockport Co	L	0-4	0-2	22		2644
15		24	H	Darlington	L	0-3	0-2	23		2182
16	Dec	1	H	Scarborough	W	2-0	1-0	21	Schofield, Smith P	2204
17		15	A	Hartlepool U	L	0-2	0-2	22		2055
18		22	H	Gillingham	D	1-1	1-1	24	Puttnam	2685
19		29	A	Blackpool	L	0-5	0-2	24		2519
20	Jan	1	H	Wrexham	D	0-0	0-0	23		2527
21		5	H	Walsall	W	2-1	1-0	22	Casey, Dobson	2500
22		12	A	Halifax T	D	1-1	1-0	22	Davis	1447
23		19	H	Burnley	W	1-0	0-0	22	Carmichael	4167
24		26	A	Cardiff C	W	1-0	1-0	19	Alexander	2513
25	Feb	2	H	Chesterfield	D	1-1	1-0	19	Casey	3588
26		19	A	Walsall	D	0-0	0-0	—		3582
27		23	H	Stockport Co	L	0-3	0-1	20		3257
28		26	A	York C	L	0-1	0-0	—		1808
29	Mar	2	A	Scarborough	L	0-3	0-2	20		1432
30		5	A	Torquay U	W	1-0	0-0	—	Puttnam	2330
31		9	H	Hartlepool U	W	3-1	2-0	19	Lormor 2, Puttnam	2575
32		13	A	Hereford U	W	1-0	0-0	—	Lormor	2195
33		16	H	Maidstone U	W	2-1	1-1	16	Alexander, Lormor	2583
34		20	H	Peterborough U	L	0-2	0-1	—		5542
35		23	A	Aldershot	W	3-0	1-0	16	Nicholson (pen), Lee, Alexander	1653
36		26	H	York C	W	2-1	1-1	—	Davis, Lee	2564
37		30	H	Torquay U	W	3-2	0-0	13	Schofield, Puttnam, Stoutt	3315
38	Apr	1	A	Gillingham	D	2-2	2-2	12	Lormor, Puttnam	3765
39		6	H	Blackpool	L	0-1	0-1	14		4003
40		9	A	Darlington	D	1-1	0-0	—	Lormor	4241
41		13	A	Wrexham	D	2-2	1-0	14	Lormor 2	1269
42		17	H	Scunthorpe U	L	1-2	0-0	—	Nicholson (pen)	3212
43		20	H	Doncaster R	D	0-0	0-0	14		3363
44		27	A	Rochdale	D	0-0	0-0	14		1481
45		30	A	Northampton T	D	1-1	1-1	—	Lee	2544
46	May	11	H	Carlisle U	W	6-2	2-1	14	Lormor 4, Carmichael, West D	2333

Final League Position: 14

GOALSCORERS

League (50): Lormor 12, Puttnam 6, Smith P 6, Casey 4, Nicholson 4 (3 pens), Alexander 3, Lee 3, Schofield 3, Carmichael 2, Davis 2, Brown 1, Dobson 1, Stoutt 1, Warren 1, West D 1.
Rumbelows Cup (1): Davis 1.
FA Cup (1): Lormor 1.

Wallington	Casey	Nicholson	Brown	Stoutt	Davis	Schofield	Smith P	Puttnam	Smith N	Lormor	Clarke	Carmichael	Powell	Rawcliffe	Warren	Sims	Bressington	Wilson	Bowling	Stant	Scott	Alexander	Dobson	Crombie	West G	Lee	Ward	Dickins	Match No.
1	2	3	4	5	6	7	8	9	10	11																			1
1	2	5	4		6	7	8	11	10	9*	3	12																	2
1	2	5	4		6	7	8	11	10		3		9																3
1	2	5	4	3	6	7*	8	11	10				9		12														4
1	2	5	4	3	6		8	11	10*		12		9			7													5
1	2	14	4	5	6†	7	8	11	10*	12	3		9																6
1	2		4	11†	6	7	12	14		9*	3		8				5	10											7
1	2		4		6	7		9		11	3*		8		12		5	10											8
1	2	14	4		6	12	9	11		7	3†		8				5*	10											9
1	2	11	4	12	6	7	9	14		3			8				10*	5†											10
1	2	3	4		6	7	9	11		12			8				5*	10											11
1	2	3	4	5	6	7	9	11					8				10												12
1	2	3	4	5	6	7	9	11					8					10											13
1		3	4	5	6	7	9	11					8				2	10											14
	2	3	4	5	6*	7	8		11								12	10	1		9								15
12	11		4	2	6	7	8		10		3						5*		1			9†14							16
	10	4*	2		6	7	8	12			3						5		1			9†14	11						17
	2		4		6	7	8	10		12	3						5		1			9*	11						18
	2	10	4†		6	7	8	9		12	3*14						5		1				11						19
	2	3				7	10	8	4			6					5		1			9	11						20
	2	3			6	7	10	8	4								5		1			12	11	9*					21
	2	3			6	7	8	12			4	10					5		1			14	11†	9*					22
	2	3			6*	7	8	12			4	10					5		1				11	9					23
	2	3				7	8	10*			4	6					5		1				11	9	12				24
	2	3				7	8				4	6					10		1			12	11	9*	5				25
	2	3				7	8				4	5	12				10*		1				11	9	6				26
	2	3				7	8	10			4*		12				6		1				11	9	5				27
	2*			5		7	8	11			4	3	6				10		1			12	9						28
	2*					7	8	11			4	3	6				5		1				10						29
12		3			6	7	2	10			4		8				5		1			11*				9			30
1	12	3			6*	7	2	10			4		8				5					11				9			31
1		3	14		6	7	2	10*			4		8				5					11	12†			9			32
1		3	7	12	6		2	10			4		8†				5					11				9			33
1		3	8	12	6	7	2	10			4						5					11*				9			34
1		3	8	14	6*	7	2	10			4	12					5					11†				9			35
1		3	8	12	6	7	2	10			4						5					11					9*		36
1		3	6	14		7	2	10			4	12					5					11†			8		9*		37
1		3	6			7	2	10			4	11					5									9	8		38
1		6	3			7	2	10	12		4	9					5					11*			8				39
		3	6			7	2	10			4	11					5								8	9		1	40
		3	6			7	2	10			4	11					5								8	9		1	41
		3	6	12		7	2	10			4						5					11*			8	9		1	42
		3	6	12		7	2	10			4	11					5								8	9*		1	43
		3*	6	8		7	2	10	12		4	11					5									9		1	44
		3	6	14		7	2	10†			4	11					5					12			8	9*		1	45
			4	8		7	2	11	10†		4	6					5									9	5	1	46

23	26	38	32	15	29	41	45	38	9	31	14	20	11	—	2	5	36	3	16	4	1	21	9	—	3	17	9	7	
+	+		+	+	+	+	+	+	+	+	+				+	+		+				+	+	+	+				
3s	2s		10s 1s	1s	1s	5s	3s	3s	1s	6s					1s	1s		1s				5s	2s	1s	1s				

West, D — Match No. 46(3).

Rumbelows Cup	First Round	Halifax T (a)	0-2
		(h)	1-0
FA Cup	First Round	Crewe Alex (h)	1-4

LINCOLN CITY

Player and Position	Ht	Wt	Birth Date	Place	Source	Clubs	League App	Gls
Goalkeepers								
Ian Bowling	6 3	14 08	27 7 65	Sheffield	Gainsborough T			
						Lincoln C	24	—
						Hartlepool U (loan)	1	—
Matt Dickins†	6 4	14 00	3 9 70	Sheffield	Trainee	Sheffield U	—	—
						Leyton Orient (loan)	—	—
						Lincoln C	7	—
Mark Wallington*	6 1	14 11	17 9 52	Grantham	Amateur	Walsall	11	—
						Leicester C	412	—
						Derby Co	67	—
						Lincoln C	87	—
Defenders								
Grant Brown	6 0	11 12	19 11 69	Sunderland	Trainee	Leicester C	14	—
						Lincoln C	66	3
Paul Casey	5 8	10 06	6 10 61	Rinteln	Apprentice	Sheffield U	25	1
					Boston U	Lincoln C	49	4
Dean Crombie*	6 0	11 12	9 8 57	Lincoln	Ruston Sp	Lincoln C	33	—
						Grimsby T	320	3
						Reading (loan)	4	—
						Bolton W	95	1
						Lincoln C	1	—
Sean Dunphy	6 3	13 05	5 11 70	Rotherham	Trainee	Barnsley	6	—
						Lincoln C		—
Shane Nicholson	5 10	11 06	3 6 70	Newark	Trainee	Lincoln C	104	5
Steve Sims‡	6 1	14 04	2 7 57	Lincoln	Apprentice	Leicester C	79	3
						Watford	152	4
						Notts Co	85	5
						Watford	19	1
						Aston Villa	41	—
						Lincoln City	5	—
Stephen Stoutt	5 8	11 06	5 4 64	Halifax	Local	Huddersfield T	6	—
						Wolverhampton W	94	5
						Grimsby T	3	1
						Lincoln C	46	1
Steve Thompson	6 1	14 04	28 7 55	Sheffield	Boston U	Lincoln C	154	8
						Charlton Ath	95	—
						Leicester C	—	—
						Sheffield U	20	1
						Lincoln C	27	—
Dean West§			5 12 72	Wakefield	Leeds U	Lincoln C	1	1
Midfield								
Graham Bressington	6 0	12 06	8 7 66	Eton	Wycombe W	Lincoln C	110	3
David Clarke	5 10	11 00	3 12 64	Nottingham	Apprentice	Notts Co	123	7
						Lincoln C	81	6
Peter Rawcliffe‡	5 6	10 02	8 12 63	Grimsby	Louth U King's Lynn	Grimsby T	22	2
						Lincoln C	1	—
Alan Roberts‡	5 9	10 00	8 12 64	Newcastle	Apprentice	Middlesbrough	38	2
						Darlington	119	19
						Sheffield U	36	2
						Lincoln C	10	—
Jon Schofield	5 11	11 03	16 5 65	Barnsley	Gainsborough T	Lincoln C	100	7
Neil Smith	5 10	10 12	10 2 70	Warley	Trainee Redditch	Shrewsbury T	1	—
						Lincoln C	16	—
Paul Ward	5 11	12 05	15 9 63	Bedlington	Apprentice	Chelsea	—	—
						Middlesbrough	76	1
						Darlington	124	9
						Leyton Orient	31	1
						Scunthorpe U	55	6
						Lincoln C	9	—

LINCOLN CITY

Foundation: Although there was a Lincoln club as far back as 1861, the present organisation was formed in 1883 winning the Lincolnshire Senior Cup in only their fourth season. They were Founder members of the Midland League in 1889 and that competition's first champions.

First Football League game: 3 September, 1892, Division 2, v Sheffield U (a) L 2–4 – W. Gresham; Coulton, Neill; Shaw, Mettam, Moore; Smallman, Irving (1), Cameron (1), Kelly, J. Gresham.

Did you know: When they won the championship of Division 3(N) in 1947–48, Jimmy Hutchinson scored over three times more goals than any other player – a total of 32 in the League including two hat-tricks. Geoff Marlow was second highest scorer with 10.

Managers (and Secretary-managers)
David Calderhead 1900–07, John Henry Strawson 1907–14 (had been secretary), George Fraser 1919–21, David Calderhead Jnr. 1921–24, Horace Henshall 1924–27, Harry Parkes 1927–36, Joe McClelland 1936–46, Bill Anderson 1946–65 (GM to 1966), Roy Chapman 1965–66, Ron Gray 1966–70, Bert Loxley 1970–71, David Herd 1971–72, Graham Taylor 1972–77, George Kerr 1977–78, Willie Bell 1977–78, Colin Murphy 1978–85, John Pickering 1985, George Kerr 1985–87, Peter Daniel 1987, Colin Murphy 1987–90, Allan Clarke 1990, Steve Thompson November 1990– .

Player and Position	Ht	Wt	Birth Date	Place	Source	Clubs	League App	Gls
Forwards								
Keith Alexander	6 4	13 06	14 11 58	Nottingham	Barnet	Grimsby T	83	26
						Stockport Co	11	—
						Lincoln C	23	3
Matt Carmichael	6 2	11 07	13 5 64	Singapore	Army	Lincoln C	52	7
Paul Dobson	5 9	10 06	17 12 62	Hartlepool	Amateur	Newcastle U		
						Hartlepool U	31	8
					Horden	Hartlepool U	80	24
						Torquay U	77	38
						Doncaster R	24	10
						Scarborough	61	22
						Halifax T (loan)	1	1
						Hereford U (loan)	6	1
						Lincoln C	10	1
Jason Lee	6 3	13 08	9 5 71	London	Trainee	Charlton Ath	1	—
						Stockport Co (loan)	2	—
						Lincoln C	17	3
Tony Lormor	6 1	12 03	29 10 70	Ashington	Trainee	Newcastle U	8	3
						Norwich C (loan)	—	—
						Lincoln C	55	20
David Puttnam	5 10	11 09	3 2 67	Leicester	Leicester U	Leicester C	7	—
						Lincoln C	66	7
Keith Scott	6 3	12 00	10 6 67	London	Leicester U	Lincoln C	16	2
Paul Smith	5 11	10 09	9 11 64	Rotherham	Apprentice	Sheffield U	36	1
						Stockport Co (loan)	7	5
						Port Vale	44	7
						Lincoln C	107	21

Trainees
Davis, Jason, M; Hardwick, James; Harrison, Richard C; Hurford, Lee R; McCormick, Craig L; Mulhall, Stuart; West, Dean.

**Non-Contract
Dickins, Matthew.

Associated Schoolboys
Barker, Adrian; Brown, Michael A; Foster, Jonathon; Fraser, Gregory A; Morgan, James.

**Non-Contract Players who are retained must be re-signed before they are eligible to play in League matches.

298

LIVERPOOL 1990–91 *Back row (left to right):* Ray Houghton, Alec Watson, Mike Hooper, Gary Gillespie, Bruce Grobbelaar, Ian Rush, Glenn Hysen.
Centre row: Ronnie Moran (Chief Coach), Ronnie Rosenthal, Steve Staunton, Gary Ablett, Jan Molby, Barry Venison, David Burrows, Roy Evans (First Team Coach).
Front row: John Barnes, Steve Nicol, Alan Hansen, Kenny Dalglish (Manager), Ronnie Whelan, Steve McMahon, Peter Beardsley.

Division 1   LIVERPOOL

Anfield Road, Liverpool 4. Telephone 051-263 2361. Clubcall: 0898 121184. Ticket and Match Information: 051-260 9999 (24-hour service) or 051-260 8680 (office hours) or 0898 12 1584 for Ticket Call.

Ground Capacity: 39,772.

Record attendance: 61,905 v Wolverhampton W, FA Cup 4th rd, 2 February 1952.

Record receipts: £227,351 v QPR, FA Cup, 6th rd replay, 14 March 1990.

Pitch measurements: 110yd × 75yd.

Chairman: N. White, FSCA. *Vice-chairman:* S. T. Moss JP, DL.

Directors: Sir J. W. Smith CBE, JP, DL, HON. LLD, S. C. Reakes JP, J. T. Cross, R. Paisley OBE, MSC (HON), G. A. Ensor LLB, D. R. Moores.

Vice-presidents: C. J. Hill, H. E. Roberts, W. D. Corkish FCA.

Team Manager: Graeme Souness. *Coach:* Ron Moran.

Chief Executive/General Secretary: Peter Robinson.

Commercial Manager: K. Addison.

Year Formed: 1892. *Turned Professional:* 1892. *Ltd Co.:* 1892.

Club Nickname: 'Reds' or 'Pool'.

Record League Victory: 10-1 v Rotherham T, Division 2, 18 February 1896 – Storer; Goldie, Wilkie; McCarthy, McQueen, Holmes; McVean (3), Ross (2), Allan (4), Becton (1), Bradshaw.

Record Cup Victory: 11-0 v Stromsgodset Drammen, ECWC 1st rd 1st leg, 17 September 1974 – Clemence; Smith (1), Lindsay (1p), Thompson (2), Cormack (1), Hughes (1), Boersma (2), Hall, Heighway (1), Kennedy (1), Callaghan (1).

Record Defeat: 1-9 v Birmingham C, Division 2, 11 December 1954.

Most League Points (2 for a win): 68, Division 1, 1978–79.

Most League Points (3 for a win): 90, Division 1, 1987–88.

Most League Goals: 106, Division 2, 1895–96.

Highest League Scorer in Season: Roger Hunt, 41, Division 2, 1961–62.

Most League Goals in Total Aggregate: Roger Hunt, 245, 1959–69.

Most Capped Player: Emlyn Hughes, 59 (62), England.

Most League Appearances: Ian Callaghan, 640, 1960–78.

Record Transfer Fee Received: £3,200,000 from Juventus for Ian Rush, June 1986.

Record Transfer Fee Paid: £2,900,000 to Derby Co for Dean Saunders, July 1991.

Football League Record: 1893 Elected to Division 2; 1894–95 Division 1; 1895–96 Division 2; 1896–1904 Division 1; 1904–05 Division 2; 1905–54 Division 1; 1954–62 Division 2; 1962– Division 1.

Honours: Football League: Division 1 – Champions 1900–01, 1905–06, 1921–22, 1922–23, 1946–47, 1963–64, 1965–66, 1972–73, 1975–76, 1976–77, 1978–79, 1979–80, 1981–82, 1982–83, 1983–84, 1985–86, 1987–88, 1989–90 (Liverpool have a record number of 18 League Championship wins); Runners-up 1898–99, 1909–10, 1968–69, 1973–74, 1974–75, 1977–78, 1984–85, 1986–87, 1988–89, 1990–91; Division 2 – Champions 1893–94, 1895–96, 1904–05, 1961–62. *FA Cup:* Winners 1965, 1974, 1986, 1989; Runners-up 1914, 1950, 1971, 1977, 1988; *Football League Cup:* Winners 1981, 1982, 1983, 1984; Runners-up 1977–78, 1986–87. *League Super Cup:* Winners 1985–86. **European Competitions:** *European Cup:* 1964–65, 1966–67, 1973–74, 1976–77 (winners), 1977–78 (winners), 1978–79, 1979–80, 1980–81 (winners), 1981–82, 1982–83, 1983–84 (winners), 1984–85 (runners-up); *European Cup-Winners' Cup:* 1965–66 (runners-up), 1971–72, 1974–75; *European Fairs Cup:* 1967–68, 1968–69, 1969–70, 1970–71; *UEFA Cup:* 1972–73 (winners), 1975–76 (winners); *Super Cup:* 1977 (winners), 1978; *World Club Championship:* 1981 (runners-up).

Colours: All red with white markings. **Change colours:** Racing green with white markings.

LIVERPOOL 1990–91 LEAGUE RECORD

Match No.	Date		Venue	Opponents	Result	H/T Score	Lg. Pos.	Goalscorers	Attendance
1	Aug	25	A	Sheffield U	W 3-1	0-0	—	Barnes, Houghton, Rush	27,009
2		28	H	Nottingham F	W 2-0	0-0	—	Rush, Beardsley	33,663
3	Sept	1	H	Aston Villa	W 2-1	1-1	1	Beardsley, Barnes	38,061
4		8	A	Wimbledon	W 2-1	2-0	1	Barnes, Whelan	12,364
5		16	H	Manchester U	W 4-0	3-0	1	Beardsley 3, Barnes	35,726
6		22	A	Everton	W 3-2	2-0	1	Beardsley 2, Barnes (pen)	39,847
7		29	A	Sunderland	W 1-0	1-0	1	Houghton	31,107
8	Oct	6	H	Derby Co	W 2-0	1-0	1	Houghton, Beardsley	37,076
9		20	A	Norwich C	D 1-1	1-1	1	Gillespie	21,275
10		27	H	Chelsea	W 2-0	2-0	1	Rush, Nicol	38,463
11	Nov	4	A	Tottenham H	W 3-1	1-0	—	Rush 2, Beardsley	35,003
12		10	H	Luton T	W 4-0	3-0	1	Rush 2, Molby (pen), Beardsley	35,207
13		17	A	Coventry C	W 1-0	0-0	1	Beardsley	22,571
14		24	H	Manchester C	D 2-2	0-0	1	Rush, Rosenthal	37,849
15	Dec	2	A	Arsenal	L 0-3	0-1	—		40,419
16		15	H	Sheffield U	W 2-0	0-0	1	Barnes, Rush	33,516
17		22	H	Southampton	W 3-2	2-1	1	Rosenthal 2, Houghton	31,894
18		26	A	QPR	D 1-1	0-0	1	Barnes	17,848
19		30	A	Crystal Palace	L 0-1	0-1	—		26,280
20	Jan	1	H	Leeds U	W 3-0	2-0	1	Barnes, Rosenthal, Rush	36,975
21		12	A	Aston Villa	D 0-0	0-0	1		40,026
22		19	A	Wimbledon	D 1-1	1-0	2	Barnes	35,030
23	Feb	3	A	Manchester U	D 1-1	1-1	—	Speedie	43,690
24		9	H	Everton	W 3-1	1-1	1	Molby, Speedie 2	38,127
25		23	H	Luton T	L 1-3	1-0	2	Molby (pen)	12,032
26	Mar	3	A	Arsenal	L 0-1	0-0	—		37,221
27		9	A	Manchester C	W 3-0	2-0	2	Molby 2 (2 pens), Barnes	35,150
28		16	H	Sunderland	W 2-1	2-1	1	Rush, Owers (og)	37,582
29		23	A	Derby Co	W 7-1	3-1	1	Molby (pen), Barnes 2, Rush, Nicol 2, Houghton	20,531
30		30	H	QPR	L 1-3	0-2	2	Molby (pen)	37,251
31	Apr	1	A	Southampton	L 0-1	0-1	2		20,255
32		9	H	Coventry C	D 1-1	1-1	—	Rush	31,063
33		13	A	Leeds U	W 5-4	4-0	2	Houghton, Molby (pen), Speedie, Barnes 2	31,460
34		20	H	Norwich C	W 3-0	2-0	2	Barnes, Houghton, Rush	37,065
35		23	H	Crystal Palace	W 3-0	1-0	—	Rush, Barnes, McGoldrick (og)	36,767
36	May	4	A	Chelsea	L 2-4	0-2	2	Speedie, Rosenthal	32,266
37		6	A	Nottingham F	L 1-2	0-1	—	Molby (pen)	26,151
38		11	H	Tottenham H	W 2-0	1-0	2	Rush, Speedie	36,192

Final League Position: 2

GOALSCORERS

League (77): Barnes 16 (1 pen), Rush 16, Beardsley 11, Molby 9 (8 pens), Houghton 7, Speedie 6, Rosenthal 5, Nicol 3, Gillespie 1, Whelan 1, own goals 2.
Rumbelows Cup (10): Rush 5, Houghton 2, Gillespie 1, McMahon 1, Staunton 1.
FA Cup (13): Rush 5, Beardsley 2, McMahon 2, Barnes 1, Houghton 1, Staunton 1, own goal 1.

Grobbelaar	Hysen	Burrows	Nicol	Whelan	Molby	Gillespie	Houghton	Rush	Barnes	McMahon	Rosenthal	Venison	Beardsley	Ablett	Staunton	McManaman	Carter	Speedie	Hooper	Marsh	Match No.
1	2	3	4	5	6*	7	8	9	10	11	12										1
1	2	3		5		6	8	9	10	11	12	4	7*								2
1	2		4	5		6	8	9	10	11		7	3								3
1	2	3	4	5	8	6		9	10	11			7								4
1	2	3	4	5		6	8	9	10	11			7								5
1	2	3		5		6	8	9	10	11		4	7								6
1	2	3	4	5		6	8	9	10	11			7								7
1		3	4	5		6	8	9	10	11		7	2								8
1	2	3	4			6	8	9	10	11		5*	7		12						9
1	2	3	4		14	6	8	9	10*	11†	12		7		5						10
1	2	3	4		7	6		9	10*	11		12	8	5							11
1	2	3	4†		10	6	8	9		11	12	7*	5	14							12
1	2	3	4	5		6	8	9		11		7	10								13
1	2	3		5	14	6†	8	9	10	11*†	12		7	4							14
1	2	3	4	5	11*	6	14	9	10		12	8†		7							15
1	2	3	4	5		6	8	9	10	11			7*		12						16
1	2	3	4			6	8	9	10	11			7		5						17
1	2	3	4			6	8	9	10	11			7		5						18
1	2	3	4	5		6	8*	9	10	11	12		7								19
1	2	3	4			6	8	9	10	11			7		5						20
1	2	3	4		8	6		9	10	11	12				5		7*				21
1		3	4		8*	6		9	10	11	12			2	5		7				22
1	2	3	4	5	12			9	10	11*			6	8			7				23
1	2	3	4	5†	11			10				9	12	6	8	14	7*				24
	2		4	5			8	9	10			3	7	6	11*		12		1		25
1	2	3	4	5	11*		8	9	10				7	6			12				26
1	2	3	4	5			8	9*	10		12		7	6				11			27
	2	3	4	5			8	9	10				7*	6	12			11	1		28
	2	3	4	5*	11		8	9	10				7	6	12				1		29
	2	3	4	5	11		8	9			12		7	6	10*				1		30
	2	14	4	5	11†		8	9	10				7	6	3*		12		1		31
	2		4	5	11		8†	9	10				7	6	3*	14	12		1		32
	2	6	4	5			8	9	10				7		3			11	1		33
1		3	4	5	11		8	9	10				7	2	6						34
1		3	4	5	11		8	9	10				7	2	6						35
1		3	4	5	2†		8	9	10		12		7		6	14*	11				36
1		3	4	5			8	9	10				7*	2	6			11	12		37
1	5	3†	4				8	9	10*		12			2	6	14		11		7	38
31	32	34	35	14	22	30	31	37	35	22	4	6	24	23	20	—	2	8	7	1	
					+1s	+3s	+1s				+12s		+3s	+4s	+2s	+3s		+4s		+1s	

Rumbelows Cup	Second Round	Crewe Alex (h)	5-1
		(a)	4-1
	Third Round	Manchester U (a)	1-3
FA Cup	Third Round	Blackburn R (a)	1-1
		(h)	3-0
	Fourth Round	Brighton & HA (h)	2-2
		(a)	3-2
	Fifth Round	Everton (h)	0-0
		(a)	4-4
		(a)	0-1

LIVERPOOL

Player and Position	Ht	Wt	Birth Date	Place	Source	Clubs	League App	Gls
Goalkeepers								
Bruce Grobbelaar	6 1	13 00	6 10 57	Durban	Vancouver W	Crewe Alex	24	1
						Vancouver W	—	—
						Liverpool	369	—
Michael Hooper	6 2	13 05	10 2 64	Bristol	Local	Bristol C	1	—
						Wrexham (loan)	20	—
						Wrexham	14	—
						Liverpool	37	—
						Leicester C (loan)	14	—
Defenders								
Gary Ablett	6 0	11 04	19 11 65	Liverpool	Apprentice	Liverpool	95	1
						Derby Co (loan)	6	—
						Hull C (loan)	5	—
David Burrows	5 8	11 00	25 10 68	Dudley	Apprentice	WBA	46	1
						Liverpool	82	—
John Carroll*	6 1	11 08	13 10 71	Dublin	Home Farm	Liverpool	—	—
David Collins	6 1	12 10	30 10 71	Dublin	Trainee	Liverpool	—	—
Gary Gillespie	6 2	12 07	5 7 60	Stirling	School	Falkirk	22	—
						Coventry C	172	6
						Liverpool	156	14
Alan Hansen‡	6 1	13 00	13 6 55	Alloa	Sauchie BC	Partick T	86	6
						Liverpool	434	8
Steve Hollis	5 10	11 06	22 8 72	Liverpool	Trainee	Liverpool	—	—
Glenn Hysen	6 1	12 08	30 10 59	Gothenburg	Fiorentina	Liverpool	67	1
Barry Jones	6 0	12 00	30 6 70	Liverpool	Prescot T	Liverpool	—	—
Steve Nicol	5 10	12 00	11 12 61	Irvine	Ayr U BC	Ayr U	70	7
						Liverpool	242	34
Steve Staunton	5 11	11 02	19 1 69	Drogheda	Dundalk	Liverpool	65	—
						Bradford C (loan)	8	—
Barry Venison	5 10	11 09	16 8 64	Consett	Apprentice	Sunderland	173	2
						Liverpool	97	—
Midfield								
Warren Godfrey	5 11	11 02	31 3 72	Liverpool	Trainee	Liverpool	—	—
Steve Harkness	5 9	10 11	27 8 71	Carlisle	Trainee	Carlisle U	13	—
						Liverpool	—	—
Ray Houghton	5 8	11 04	9 1 62	Glasgow	Amateur	West Ham U	1	—
						Fulham	129	16
						Oxford U	83	10
						Liverpool	117	20
Craig Johnston	5 8	10 13	8 12 60	Johannesburg	Sydney C	Middlesbrough	64	16
						Liverpool	190	30
Marc Kenny	5 11	11 00	17 9 73	Dublin	Trainee	Liverpool	—	—
Kevin Lampkin	5 10	11 08	20 12 72	Liverpool	Trainee	Liverpool	—	—
Steve McMahon	5 9	11 08	20 8 61	Liverpool	Apprentice	Everton	100	11
						Aston Villa	75	7
						Liverpool	189	28
Jan Molby	6 1	14 07	4 7 63	Denmark	Ajax	Liverpool	157	34
Jamie Redknapp	5 11	11 08	25 6 73	Barton-on-Sea	Trainee	Bournemouth	13	—
						Liverpool	—	—
Jamie Robinson	6 1	12 03	26 2 72	Liverpool	Trainee	Liverpool	—	—
Nick Tanner	6 1	13 10	24 5 65	Bristol	Mangotsfield	Bristol R	107	3
						Liverpool	4	—
						Norwich C (loan)	6	—
						Swindon T (loan)	7	—
Ronnie Whelan	5 9	10 13	25 9 61	Dublin	Home Farm	Liverpool	312	44
Forwards								
John Barnes	5 11	12 00	7 11 63	Jamaica	Sudbury Court	Watford	233	65
						Liverpool	140	61
Peter Beardsley	5 8	11 07	18 1 61	Newcastle	Wallsend BC	Carlisle U	102	22
					Vancouver W	Manchester U	—	—
					Vancouver W	Newcastle U	147	61
						Liverpool	131	46

LIVERPOOL

Foundation: But for a dispute between Everton FC and their landlord at Anfield in 1892, there may never have been a Liverpool club. This dispute persuaded the majority of Evertonians to quit Anfield for Goodison Park, leaving the landlord, Mr. John Houlding, to form a new club. He originally tried to retain the name "Everton" but when this failed, he founded Liverpool Association FC on 15 March, 1892.

First Football League game: 2 September, 1893, Division 2, v Middlesbrough (a) W 2-0 – McOwen; Hannah, McLean; Henderson, McQue (1), McBride; Gordon, McVean (1), M. McQueen, Stott, H. McQueen.

Did you know: Liverpool's run of 24 games without defeat in the Football League Cup between 27 August 1980, when they lost 1-0 at Bradford, and 15 February 1983, when they went down 1-0 at Burnley, is a record for this competition.

Managers (and Secretary-managers)
W. E. Barclay 1892–96, Tom Watson 1896–1915, David Ashworth 1920–22, Matt McQueen 1923–28, George Patterson 1928–36 (continued as secretary), George Kay 1936–51, Don Welsh 1951–56, Phil Taylor 1956–59, Bill Shankly 1959–74, Bob Paisley 1974–83, Joe Fagan 1983–85, Kenny Dalglish 1985–91, Graeme Souness April 1991

Player and Position	Ht	Wt	Birth Date	Birth Place	Source	Clubs	League App	Gls
Jimmy Carter	5 10	10 04	9 11 65	London	Apprentice	Crystal Palace	—	—
						QPR	—	—
						Millwall	110	11
						Liverpool	5	—
Tony Cousins	5 9	11 10	25 8 69	Dublin	Dundalk	Liverpool	—	—
Wayne Harrison*	5 8	10 07	15 11 67	Stockport	Apprentice	Oldham Ath	5	1
						Liverpool	—	—
						Oldham Ath (loan)	1	—
						Crewe Alex (loan)	3	1
Don Hutchison	6 2	11 04	9 5 71	Gateshead	Trainee	Hartlepool U	24	2
						Liverpool	—	—
Steve McManaman	5 11	10 02	11 2 72	Liverpool	School	Liverpool	2	—
Mike Marsh	5 8	10 14	21 7 69	Liverpool	Kirkby T	Liverpool	5	—
Russell Payne	5 10	11 08	8 7 70	Wigan	Skelmersdale	Liverpool	—	—
Ronny Rosenthal	5 10	11 12	11 10 63	Haifa	Standard Liege	Luton T	—	—
						Liverpool	24	12
Ian Rush	6 0	12 06	20 10 61	St Asaph	Apprentice	Chester	34	14
						Liverpool	224	139
						Juventus	29	7
						Liverpool	97	41
David Speedie	5 7	11 00	20 2 60	Glenrothes	Amateur	Barnsley	23	—
						Darlington	88	21
						Chelsea	162	47
						Coventry C	122	31
						Liverpool	12	6

Trainees
Brownbill, Barry K; Deery, Michael A; Dennis, Wayne A; Fox, Michael J; Gandy, Ian; Gelling, Stuart; Hagan, Kevin K; Holcroft, Robert J; Horrigan, Ian R; Howard, Andrew P; Kelly, Johnathan J; McAree, Rodney; Matteo, Dominic; Matthews, Anthony; Roscoe, Andrew R; Russell, Alexander J; Walsh, Stephen J.

Associated Schoolboys
Brenchley, Scott A; Brunskill, Iain R; Cain, Adam G; Darwin, William J; Dixon, Kenneth J; Embleton, Daniel C; Fitzpatrick, Kevin; Frodsham, Ian T; Joyce, Paul C; Li, Christian; McMullen, Andrew S; Makinson, Steven; Meredith, Graham; Murphy, John J; Nicholson, John; Pickthall, Carl J; Prescott, Mark; Rogers, Jason L; Snape, Paul F; Stannard, John F; Van Zyl, John E.

Associated Schoolboys who have accepted the club's offer of a Traineeship/Contract
Brydon, Lee; Fowler, Robert B; Jones, Stuart J; Stalker, Mark E; Whittaker, Stuart.

304

LUTON TOWN 1990-91 *Back row (left to right):* Richard Cooke. Paul Gray. Marvin Johnson. Kurt Nogan. Richard Harvey. Jason Rees.
Centre row: George Ley (Coach). John Moore (Coach). Julian James. Ceri Hughes. Iain Dowie. Andy Petterson. Alec Chamberlain. Graham Rodger. Darron McDonough.
John Faulkner (Assistant Manager). Dave Galley (Physiotherapist).
Front row: David Beaumont. Tim Breacker. John Dreyer. Jim Ryan (Manager). David Preece. Kingsley Black. Lars Elstrup. (Copyright Apex Photography.)

Division 1   LUTON TOWN

Kenilworth Road Stadium, 1 Maple Rd, Luton, Beds. LU4 8AW. Telephone, Offices: Luton (0582) 411622; Credit Hotline (0582) 30748 (24 hrs); Banqueting: (0582) 411526.

Ground capacity: 13,023.

Record attendance: 30,069 v Blackpool, FA Cup 6th rd replay, 4 March 1959.

Record receipts: £77,000 v Oxford U, Littlewoods Cup semi-final, 28 February 1988.

Pitch measurements: 110yd × 72yd.

President: E. Pearson.

Chairman: P. Nelkin.

General Manager/Secretary: Bill J. Tomlins.

Directors: D. Kohler, R, Smith, P. Collins, E. S. Pearson, N. Terry, C. J. Hudson, H. Richardson.

Commercial Manager: Wendy Grzybowska.

Manager: David Pleat.

Coaches: John Faulkner, John Moore and George Ley.

Physio: Dave Galley.

Year Formed: 1885. ***Turned Professional:*** 1890. ***Ltd Co.:*** 1897.

Club Nickname: 'The Hatters'.

Previous Grounds: 1885, Excelsior, Dallow Lane; 1897, Dunstable Road; 1905, Kenilworth Road.

Record League Victory: 12-0 v Bristol R, Division 3 (S), 13 April 1936 – Dolman; Mackey, Smith; Finlayson, Nelson, Godfrey; Rich, Martin (1), Payne (10), Roberts (1), Stephenson.

Record Cup Victory: 9-0 v Clapton, FA Cup, 1st rd (replay after abandoned game), 30 November 1927 – Abbott; Kingham, Graham; Black, Rennie, Fraser; Pointon, Yardley (4), Reid (2), Woods (1), Dennis (2).

Record Defeat: 0-9 v Small Heath, Division 2, 12 November 1898.

Most League Points (2 for a win): 66, Division 4, 1967–68.

Most League Points (3 for a win): 88, Division 2, 1981–82.

Most League Goals: 103, Division 3 (S), 1936–37.

Highest League Scorer in Season: Joe Payne, 55, Division 3 (S), 1936–37.

Most League Goals in Total Aggregate: Gordon Turner, 243, 1949–64.

Most Capped Player: Mal Donaghy, 58 (70), Northern Ireland.

Most League Appearances: Bob Morton, 494, 1948–64.

Record Transfer Fee Received: £1,000,000 from QPR for Roy Wegerle, December 1989.

Record Transfer Fee Paid: £850,000 to Odense for Lars Elstrup, August 1989.

Football League Record: 1897 Elected to Division 2; 1900 Failed re-election; 1920 Division 3; 1921 Division 3 (S); 1937–55 Division 2; 1955–60 Division 1; 1960–63 Division 2; 1963–65 Division 3; 1965–68 Division 4; 1968–70 Division 3; 1970–74 Division 2; 1974–75 Division 1; 1975–82 Division 2; 1982– Division 1.

Honours: *Football League:* Division 1 best season: 7th, 1986–87; Division 2 – Champions 1981–82; Runners-up 1954–55, 1973–74; Division 3 – Runners-up 1969–70; Division 4 – Champions 1967–68; Division 3 (S) – Champions 1936–37; Runners-up 1935–36. *FA Cup:* Runners-up 1959. *Football League Cup:* Winners 1987–88; Runners-up 1988–89. *Simod Cup:* Runners-up 1988.

Colours: White shirts with navy and orange trim, navy shorts, white stockings. **Change colours:** All Orange.

Special Loupe system for deaf and blind in our handicapped area. Soccer Line, 0839 664466 for latest news and views about Luton Town, 44p per min. peak, 33p per min. off peak.

LUTON TOWN 1990–91 LEAGUE RECORD

Match No.	Date	Venue	Opponents	Result		H/T Score	Lg. Pos.	Goalscorers	Attendance
1	Aug 25	H	Crystal Palace	D	1-1	1-1	—	Dowie	9583
2	29	A	Arsenal	L	1-2	1-1	—	Elstrup	32,723
3	Sept 1	A	Southampton	W	2-1	2-1	8	Elstrup 2	14,878
4	4	H	Manchester U	L	0-1	0-1	—		12,576
5	8	H	Leeds U	W	1-0	1-0	8	Black	10,185
6	15	A	QPR	L	1-6	0-1	11	Hughes	10,186
7	22	H	Coventry C	W	1-0	1-0	7	Dowie	8336
8	29	H	Norwich C	W	3-1	0-1	6	Elstrup 3	12,794
9	Oct 20	A	Sunderland	L	0-2	0-2	8		20,025
10	27	H	Everton	D	1-1	1-0	7	Elstrup	10,047
11	Nov 3	A	Derby Co	L	1-2	0-1	8	Black	15,008
12	10	A	Liverpool	L	0-4	0-3	13		35,207
13	17	A	Manchester C	D	2-2	0-2	12	Dowie, Dreyer (pen)	9564
14	24	H	Aston Villa	W	2-0	1-0	9	Black, Elstrup	10,071
15	Dec 1	A	Nottingham F	D	2-2	1-1	10	Elstrup 2	16,498
16	8	H	Arsenal	D	1-1	0-1	11	Dreyer (pen)	12,506
17	16	A	Crystal Palace	L	0-1	0-1	—		15,579
18	22	A	Tottenham H	L	1-2	1-1	12	Dowie	27,007
19	26	H	Sheffield U	L	0-1	0-0	12		10,004
20	29	H	Chelsea	W	2-0	0-0	12	Cundy (og), Black	11,050
21	Jan 1	A	Wimbledon	L	0-2	0-1	14		4521
22	12	H	Southampton	L	3-4	2-2	15	Elstrup, James, Dreyer (pen)	9021
23	19	A	Leeds U	L	1-2	0-1	16	Elstrup	27,010
24	Feb 2	H	QPR	L	1-2	1-0	16	Black	8479
25	23	H	Liverpool	W	3-1	0-1	15	Black, Dowie 2	12,032
26	Mar 2	H	Nottingham F	W	1-0	0-0	14	Dowie	9577
27	5	A	Manchester C	L	0-3	0-3	—		20,404
28	9	A	Aston Villa	W	2-1	2-0	13	Mountfield (og), Pembridge	20,587
29	13	A	Coventry C	L	1-2	1-0	—	Rodger	9521
30	16	H	Norwich C	L	0-1	0-1	14		8604
31	23	A	Manchester U	L	1-4	1-1	18	Preece	41,752
32	30	A	Sheffield U	L	1-2	1-0	18	Elstrup	18,487
33	Apr 1	H	Tottenham H	D	0-0	0-0	18		11,322
34	6	A	Chelsea	D	3-3	3-1	18	Elstrup, Farrell, Black	12,603
35	13	H	Wimbledon	L	0-1	0-0	18		8219
36	20	H	Sunderland	L	1-2	1-1	18	Rodger	11,157
37	May 4	A	Everton	L	0-1	0-0	18		19,809
38	11	H	Derby Co	W	2-0	1-0	18	Harford (og), Elstrup	12,889

Final League Position: 18

GOALSCORERS

League (42): Elstrup 15, Black 7, Dowie 7, Dreyer 3 (3 pens), Rodger 2, Farrell 1, Hughes 1, James 1, Pembridge 1, Preece 1, own goals 3.
Rumbelows Cup (2): Black 1, Harvey 1.
FA Cup (4): Elstrup 2, Black 1, Farrell 1.

Chamberlain	Breacker	James	McDonough	Beaumont	Dreyer	Elstrup	Preece	Dowie	Hughes	Black	Rees	Harvey	Nogan	Johnson	Williams	Farrell	Pembridge	Rodger	Holsgrove	Telfer	Match No.
1	2	3	4	5	6	7	8	9	10*	11	12										1
1	2	3†	4	5	6	7	8	9	10	11*	12	14									2
1	2	3	4†	5	6	7	8	9	10	11*	14	12									3
1	2		4*	5	6	7	8	9	10	11	12	3†	14								4
1	2	3		5	6	7	8†	9	10	11*	4			12	14						5
1	2	3	14	5	6	7	8	9*10		11	4†			12							6
1	2	12		5	6	7*	8	9	10	11	4	3									7
1	2			5	6	7	8	9	10	11		3			4						8
1		14		5	6	7	8	9	10†11*12			3		2	4						9
1				5	6	7*	8	9	10	11	12	3		2	4						10
1		14		5	6	7	8	9*10†11				3	12	2	4						11
1				5	6	7	8	9	10*11			3		2	4	12					12
1		14		5	6	7†	8	9	10*11			3		2	4	12					13
1				5	6	7	8	9	10	11		3		2	4						14
1				5	12	6	7	8	9	10*11			3		2	4					15
1				5		6	7	8	9	11	10*	3		2	4	12					16
1				5	10*	6	7	8	9	11†14		3		2	4	12					17
1				5†14	6	7*	8	9	10	11		3		2	4	12					18
1				5	14	6	7	8	9	10*11		3†		2	4	12					19
1	12	5		6	7	8			11	10	3		2*	4			9				20
1	14	5		6	7	8	12		11	10*	3		2†			9	4				21
1	2	5	10*	6	7	8	12		11		3					14	9	4†			22
1	2	5		6	7		12		11	8*	3					4	9	10			23
1		5	2	3		8	9		11			7		4			10*	6	12		24
1	3*		4	6	7	8	9		11	12				2			10	5			25
1	3		4	6	7	8	9		11					2			10	5			26
1	3		4	6	7	8	9*		11					2	12		10	5			27
1	3		4	6	7	8	9		11					2			10	5			28
1	3	4*	6	7	8	9		11					2	12			10	5			29
1	3†	4	6	7	8	9		11	14				2*	12			10	5			30
1		4*	6	7	8			11	12	3			2			9	10	5			31
1	14		4†	6	7	8			11*				2			9	10	5			32
1	14		6	7*	8			11	4†	3	12		2			9	10	5			33
1	14	4	6	7	8			11			3	12	2			9*10†		5			34
1		4*	6	7	8			11	12	3			2			9	10	5			35
1	2*14	4	6	7	8			11	12	3						9†10		5			36
1	14	4	2	6	7	8			11	9*	3						10	5†	12		37
1	14	5	2	6	7	8			11		4†	3	12			9*10					38
38	8	10	21	29	38	37	37	26	17	37	11	26	1	24	15	11	18	14	—	—	
		+	+	+				+		+	+	+	+	+	+		+	+			
		7s	5s	4s				3s		10s	3s	8s	2s	1s	9s		1s	1s			

Rumbelows Cup Second Round Bradford C (h) 1-1
                              (a) 1-1
FA Cup Third Round Sheffield U (a) 3-1
            Fourth Round West Ham U (h) 1-1
                              (a) 0-5

LUTON TOWN

Player and Position	Ht	Wt	Birth Date	Birth Place	Source	Clubs	League App	Gls
Goalkeepers								
Alec Chamberlain	6 2	13 00	20 6 64	March	Ramsey T	Ipswich T	—	—
						Colchester U	184	—
						Everton	—	—
						Tranmere R (loan)	15	—
						Luton T	82	—
Andy Petterson	6 1	14 04	26 9 69	Freemantle		Luton T	—	—
						Swindon T (loan)	—	—
Richard Watkiss*	5 10	11 08	22 11 71	Hitchin	Trainee	Luton T	—	—
Defenders								
Tim Allpress	6 0	12 00	27 1 71	Hitchin	Trainee	Luton T	1	—
Dave Beaumont	5 10	11 05	10 12 63	Edinburgh	'S' Form	Dundee U	89	3
						Luton T	67	—
John Dreyer	6 0	11 10	11 6 63	Alnwick	Wallingford T	Oxford U	60	2
						Torquay U (loan)	5	—
						Fulham (loan)	12	2
						Luton T	94	6
Ken Gillard	5 9	11 08	30 4 72	Dublin	Trainee	Luton T	—	—
Richard Harvey	5 9	11 10	17 4 69	Letchworth	Apprentice	Luton T	72	—
Matthew Jackson	6 1	12 12	19 10 71	Leeds	School	Luton T	—	—
						Preston NE (loan)	4	—
Marvin Johnson	5 11	11 06	29 10 68	Wembley	Apprentice	Luton T	63	—
Mark Pembridge	5 7	11 01	29 11 70	Merthyr	Trainee	Luton T	18	1
Graham Rodger	6 2	11 11	1 4 67	Glasgow	Apprentice	Wolverhampton W	1	—
						Coventry C	36	2
						Luton T	16	2
Darren Salton	6 1	12 01	16 3 72	Edinburgh	Trainee	Luton T	—	—
Kevin Shanley	5 11	11 11	8 9 70	Ireland	Trainee	Luton T	—	—
Midfield								
Kingsley Black	5 8	10 11	22 6 68	Luton	School	Luton T	123	26
Sean Farrell	6 1	12 08	28 2 69	Watford	Apprentice	Luton T	21	1
						Colchester U (loan)	9	1
Ceri Hughes	5 9	11 06	26 2 71	Pontypridd	Trainee	Luton T	18	1
Julian James	5 10	11 11	22 3 70	Tring	Trainee	Luton T	41	2
Darron McDonough	5 11	12 06	7 11 62	Antwerp	Apprentice	Oldham Ath	183	14
						Luton T	96	5
Mark McGonagle*	5 5	10 11	9 2 72	Luton	Trainee	Luton T	—	—
Michael O'Brien	5 10	11 04	28 11 70	Dublin	Trainee	Luton T	—	—
David Preece	5 5	10 00	28 5 63	Bridgnorth	Apprentice	Walsall	111	5
						Luton T	184	6
Jason Rees	5 5	9 08	22 12 69	Pontpridd	Trainee	Luton T	35	—
Alan Richards*	6 1	12 00	1 10 71	Preston		Luton T	—	—
Ian Scott‡	5 10	11 05	25 11 68	Luton	Apprentice	Luton T	—	—
Paul Telfer	5 9	10 02	21 10 71	Edinburgh	Trainee	Luton T	1	—
Aaron Tighe	5 9	10 09	11 7 69	Banbury	Apprentice	Luton T	—	—
						Leicester C (loan)	—	—
Steve Williams*	5 11	10 11	12 7 58	London	Apprentice	Southampton	278	18
						Arsenal	95	4
						Luton T	40	1
Forwards								
Stuart Brown*	5 10	12 08	19 9 71	Cambridge		Luton T	—	—
Gary Crawshaw*	5 8	10 08	4 2 71	Reading	Trainee	Luton T	—	—

LUTON TOWN

Foundation: Formed by an amalgamation of two leading local clubs, Wanderers and Excelsior a works team, at a meeting in Luton Town Hall in April 1885. The Wanderers had three months earlier changed their name to Luton Town Wanderers and did not take too kindly to the formation of another Town club but were talked around at this meeting. Wanderers had already appeared in the FA Cup and the new club entered in its inaugural season.

First Football League game: 4 September, 1897, Division 2, v Leicester Fosse (a) D 1-1 – Williams; McCartney, McEwen; Davies, Stewart, Docherty; Gallacher, Coupar, Birch, McInnes, Ekins (1).

Did you know: When Luton notched up their 8-2 win over Sunderland at Kenilworth Road, 19 November 1955, the Wearsiders were First Division leaders. Luton scored four goals in each half, the first four in a nine-minute spell. Bob Morton got a hat-trick.

Managers (and Secretary-managers)
Charlie Green 1901–28*, George Thomson 1925, John McCartney 1927–29, George Kay 1929–31, Harold Wightman 1931–35, Ted Liddell 1936–38, Neil McBain 1938–39, George Martin 1939–47, Dally Duncan 1947–58, Syd Owen 1959–60, Sam Bartram 1960–62, Bill Harvey 1962–64, George Martin 1965–66, Allan Brown 1966–68, Alec Stock 1968–72, Harry Haslam 1972–78, David Pleat 1978–86, John Moore 1986–87, Ray Harford 1987–89, Jim Ryan 1900–91, David Pleat June 1991– .

Player and Position	Ht	Wt	Birth Date	Place	Source	Clubs	League App	Gls
Lars Elstrup	5 11	11 11	24 3 63	Roby, Denmark	OB Odense	Luton T	60	19
David Gormley	5 6	10 09	5 8 72	Dublin		Luton T	—	—
Paul Gray‡	5 9	11 08	28 1 70	Portsmouth	Trainee	Luton T	7	1
Paul Holsgrove	6 1	12 00	26 8 69	Wellington	Trainee	Aldershot	3	—
						Wimbledon (loan)	—	—
						WBA (loan)	—	—
					From Wokingham	Luton T	1	—
Kurt Nogan	5 10	11 01	9 9 70	Cardiff	Trainee	Luton T	19	2

Trainees
Campbell, Jamie; Cooper, David B.E; Elliott, Andrew; Hancock, Paul J; Holtham, Matthew D; Lawford, John S; Murray, Paul A; Newman, Paul S; Rogers, Lee; Rutherford, Ian S; Sutton, Robert A; Thompson, Darren J.

Associated Schoolboys
Campbell, Lee A; Cheeseman, Mark J; Fleet, Matthew J; Goodridge, Steven J; Harvey, Neil D; Hutchinson, Gary J; Jukes, Andrew; McLaren, Paul A; Mann, David J; Watkins, Neil S; Woolgar, Matthew.

Associated Schoolboys who have accepted the club's offer of a Traineeship/Contract
Brittain, Vincent J; Goodfellow, Scott; Hartson, John; Philp, Richard W.

310

MAIDSTONE UNITED 1990–91   *Back row (left to right):* Frank Brooks (Trainer), Ken Steggles (Physiotherapist), Liburd Henry, Darren Davis, Darren Oxbrow, Stuart Weaver,
Jason Lillis, Nicky Johns, Mark Golley, Gary Moore, Karl Elsey, Clive Walker (Assistant Manager), Ron Gee (Kit Manager).
Centre row:
Front row: Paul Rumble, Mark Gall, Lawrence Osborne, Matthew Toms, Graham Carr (Team Manager), Paul Haylock, Bradley Sandeman, Tony Sorrell, Chris Pullan.

Division 4   **MAIDSTONE UNITED**

Watling Street, Dartford, Kent DA2 6EN. Telephone (0622) 754403.

Ground capacity: 5250.

Record attendance: (at The Stadium, London Road, Maidstone): 10,591 v Charlton Ath., FA Cup 3rd rd replay, 15 January 1979.

Pitch measurement: 110yd × 75yd.

Manager: Graham Carr. *Coach:* Tommy Taylor.

Directors: J. C. Thompson (Chairman), G. Pearson, D. Berry, Dr M. J. Frank (Club Doctor), R. J. Gilbert.

Secretary: W. T. Williams. *Physio:* Ken Steggles.

Year Formed: 1897.

Club Nickname: 'Stones'.

Previous Leagues: East Kent, Thames & Medway Combination, Kent, Corinthian, Athenian, Isthmian, Southern, GM Vauxhall Conference.

Record League Victory: 6–1 v Scunthorpe U, Division 4, 15 September 1990 – Beeney; Roast, Rumble (1), Berry, Golley, Madden (Henry), Pritchard, Osborne, Charlery (2), Butler (2), Sorrell (1).

Record Defeat: 1-4 v Colchester U, Division 4, 26 September 1989.

Most League Points (3 for a win): 73, Division 4, 1989–90.

Most League Goals: 77, Division 4, 1989–90.

Highest League Scorer in Season: Steve Butler, 21, Division 4, 1989–90.

Most League Goals in Total Aggregate: Steve Butler, 41, Division 4, 1989–91.

Most Capped Player: None.

Most League Appearances: Mark Golley, 81, 1989–91.

Football League Record: 1989 Promoted to Division 4.

Honours: Football League: best season: 5th, Division 4, 1989–90. *FA Cup:* Never past 3rd rd. *Football League Cup:* Never past 1st rd.

Record Transfer Fee Received: £300,000 from Wimbledon for Warren Barton, June 1990.

Record Transfer Fee Paid: £40,000 to Watford for Liburd Henry, July 1990.

Colours: Gold shirts, black shorts, black stockings with gold trim.

MAIDSTONE UNITED 1990–91 LEAGUE RECORD

Match No.	Date	Venue	Opponents	Result	H/T Score	Lg. Pos.	Goalscorers	Attendance
1	Aug 25	A	York C	W 1-0	1-0	—	Butler	2357
2	Sept 1	H	Northampton T	L 1-3	0-0	13	Pritchard	2049
3	8	A	Carlisle U	L 0-1	0-1	18		3808
4	15	H	Scunthorpe U	W 6-1	3-0	7	Sorrell, Charlery 2, Butler 2, Rumble	1778
5	22	A	Gillingham	W 2-0	2-0	6	Pritchard, Osborne	8004
6	29	H	Lincoln C	W 4-1	1-0	4	Charlery 3, Sorrell	2190
7	Oct 1	A	Stockport Co	L 0-1	0-0	—		3207
8	6	A	Hartlepool U	L 0-1	0-1	10		2069
9	13	H	Walsall	L 1-3	1-1	12	Osborne	2329
10	20	H	Darlington	L 2-3	1-0	14	Gall, Butler	2077
11	23	A	Burnley	L 1-2	0-2	—	Butler	5567
12	27	A	Scarborough	W 2-0	0-0	14	Cooper, Osborne	1402
13	31	H	Wrexham	L 0-2	0-1	—		1668
14	Nov 3	H	Cardiff C	W 3-0	2-0	12	Berry 2, Butler	2010
15	10	H	Hereford U	D 1-1	1-0	14	Cooper (pen)	1938
16	24	A	Aldershot	L 3-4	1-3	16	Butler, Gall, Osborne	2146
17	Dec 1	H	Peterborough U	W 2-0	0-0	12	Gall, Butler	1920
18	15	A	Blackpool	D 2-2	1-1	14	Butler, Gall	2341
19	22	H	Torquay U	D 2-2	0-2	13	Butler 2	2062
20	26	A	Doncaster R	L 0-3	0-1	16		2717
21	29	A	Rochdale	L 2-3	1-1	18	Gall, Charlery	1778
22	Jan 1	H	Chesterfield	W 1-0	1-0	17	Butler	1793
23	12	A	Northampton T	L 0-2	0-0	18		3710
24	19	H	York C	W 5-4	4-2	16	Butler 3, Charlery, Wimbleton	1846
25	26	A	Scunthorpe U	D 2-2	1-1	16	Charlery, Butler	2703
26	Feb 23	A	Hereford U	L 0-4	0-1	18		2390
27	27	H	Halifax T	W 5-1	3-1	—	Cooper, Butler, Gall 3 (1 pen)	1020
28	Mar 2	A	Peterborough U	L 0-2	0-1	18		4623
29	9	H	Blackpool	D 1-1	1-1	18	Butler	2253
30	13	A	Stockport Co	L 2-3	0-1	—	Butler, Charlery	1412
31	16	A	Lincoln C	L 1-2	1-1	19	Gall	2583
32	20	A	Walsall	D 0-0	0-0	—		2475
33	23	H	Hartlepool U	L 1-4	0-0	19	Butler (pen)	1462
34	30	H	Doncaster R	L 0-1	0-1	20		1512
35	Apr 2	A	Torquay U	D 1-1	1-0	—	Sorrell	2456
36	6	H	Rochdale	L 0-1	0-0	21		1340
37	9	A	Wrexham	D 2-2	1-1	—	Henry, Stebbing	1029
38	13	A	Chesterfield	W 2-1	0-0	18	Henry, Sandeman	3040
39	16	A	Halifax T	L 2-3	0-2	—	Gall, Moore	1002
40	20	A	Darlington	D 1-1	1-0	19	Sorrell	4150
41	24	H	Gillingham	W 3-1	2-1	—	Oxbrow, Butler (og), Sorrell	2935
42	27	H	Burnley	W 1-0	1-0	17	Gall (pen)	3130
43	May 1	H	Carlisle U	D 0-0	0-0	—		1111
44	4	H	Scarborough	L 0-1	0-0	19		1277
45	8	H	Aldershot	D 1-1	1-0	—	Elsey	1298
46	11	A	Cardiff C	D 0-0	0-0	19		2011

Final League Position: 19

GOALSCORERS

League (66): Butler 20 (1 pen), Gall 11 (2 pens), Charlery 9, Sorrell 5, Osborne 4, Cooper 3 (1 pen), Berry 2, Henry 2, Pritchard 2, Elsey 1, Moore 1, Oxbrow 1, Rumble 1, Sandeman 1, Stebbing 1, Wimbleton 1, own goal 1.
Rumbelows Cup (3): Butler 2, Charlery 1.
FA Cup (5): Butler 2, Gall 2, Osborne 1.

Johns	Roast	Rumble	Berry	Golley	Madden	Pritchard	Elsey	Charley	Butler	Lillis	Sorrell	Gall	Beeney	Osborne	Cooper	Henry	Stebbing	Oxbrow	Gilbert	Bromage	Wimbleton	Brown	Sandeman	Kevan	Haylock	Pullan	Davis	Moore	Match No.
1	2	3	4	5	6	7*	8	9	10†	11	12	14																	1
1	2	3	4	5	6	7	8	9*10		11†12		14																	2
	2	3	4	5	6†	7		9	10	12	11		1	8*14															3
	2	3	4	5	6*	7		9	10		11		1	8		12													4
	2	3	4	5	6	7*		9	10	12	11		1	8															5
	2	3	4	5	6†			9*10		7	11		1	8	14	12													6
	2	3	4	5	6				10	7*11			1	8		12	9												7
1	2	3	4	5	6	7*		9	10	12	11†			8				14											8
1	2*	3	4	5		7†		9	10	12	11			8	14		6												9
		3	4	5				9*10		11	7		1	2†	14	12	8	6											10
		3*	4	5				9	14	10	7†		1	8	11	12	6	2											11
			4*	5				9	14	10	12	7†	1	8	3	11	2	6											12
	2			5*			8	14	10	12	7		1	9	3	11	6†	4											13
	2			5			8		10	7			1	9	3	11	4	6											14
	2			5		12	8	10*		7		14	1	9	3	11†	4	6											15
1				2		11†	8	14	10	7*	12			9	3	5	4	6											16
1	2		4	5			8		10	12	7*			9	3	6	11												17
	2		4	5			8	14	10†12		7*		1	9	3	6	11												18
1	2		4	5			8	12	10		7			9	11*	3	6												19
1	2	14	4	5			8	12	10*		7			9	11	3†	6												20
1	2	3	4	5	6†		8	10*			7			9	11		14	12											21
		3	4	5			8	9*10			7		1	2	11	6	12												22
1	2†		4	5	7		8	9*10		12				11		6	14	3											23
1			4	5			8		9	10				11	2	7		3	6										24
1			4	5			8		9	10	12			11	2	7*		3	6										25
1	2*							9	10		6		12	11	3		5		4			7	8						26
1						12	8	10			7*	9		11	3		5		4			2	6						27
1								9	10		6*	7	12	11	3	14	5		4			2	8†						28
1			4				3	7	10		8	9	12	11	6*	5			2										29
			4				6	9	10		8	7	1	3		11	5		2										30
			6				4	9	10		8	7	1	3		11	5						2						31
			6				4	9	10		8	7	1	3		5	11				2								32
			6				4	9	10		7	1	12	3†	11	5		8*	2	14									33
1		3				12		9*10		7	6			11	4		8		2				5						34
1		3						9*10		7	6		12	11	4		8		2				5						35
1		3				12		9*10		6	7			11	4		8		2				5						36
1		3				12		10		7	6		9	11	4		8		2				5*						37
1		3						10		7	6		9	11	4		8		2				5						38
1		3						10		7	6		9*11		4		8		2				5	12					39
1		3	4				9	10		7*	6			11	5		8		2				12						40
1		3						10		7	6		9	11	4		8		2				5						41
1		3						10		7	6		9*11		4		8		2				5	12					42
1		3				12		10*		7	6		9	11	4		8		2				5						43
1		3	14			10		7		6*			9	11	4		8		2				5†12						44
1		3	5			10*		7		6			9	11	4		8		2				12						45
1		3	6			10		7					9	11	4		8		2				5						46
29	16	26	25	32	10	8	26	22	32	10	25	29	17	33	22	25	30	29	2	3	2	3	20	3	16	—	11	—	
	+1s			+4s	+1s	+2s	+7s			+9s	+2s	+5s		+4s	+5s	+5s	+3s	+1s	+2s						+1s		+5s		

Rumbelows Cup — First Round — Leyton Orient (h) 2-2, (a) 1-4

FA Cup — First Round — Torquay U (h) 4-1; Second Round — Aldershot (a) 1-2

MAIDSTONE UNITED

Player and Position	Ht	Wt	Birth Date	Birth Place	Source	Clubs	League App	Gls
Goalkeepers								
Nicky Johns	6 2	11 05	8 6 57	Bristol	Minehead	Millwall	50	—
						Tampa Bay R	—	—
						Sheffield U (loan)	1	—
						Charlton Ath	288	—
						QPR	10	—
						Maidstone U	42	—
Defenders								
Les Berry‡	6 2	11 13	4 5 56	Plumstead	Apprentice	Charlton Ath	358	11
						Brighton & HA	23	—
						Gillingham (loan)	11	—
						Gillingham	20	—
						Maidstone U	63	2
Gary Breen†			12 12 73	London	Charlton Ath	Maidstone U	—	—
Darren Davis	6 0	11 00	5 2 67	Sutton Ashfield	Apprentice	Notts Co	92	1
						Lincoln C	102	4
						Maidstone U	11	—
Billy Gilbert‡	5 11	12 00	10 11 59	Lewisham	Apprentice	Crystal Palace	237	3
						Portsmouth	140	—
						Colchester U	27	—
						Maidstone U	4	—
Paul Haylock	5 8	11 00	24 3 63	Lowestoft	Apprentice	Norwich C	155	3
						Gillingham	152	—
						Maidstone U	16	—
Darren Oxbrow	6 1	12 06	1 9 69	Ipswich	Trainee	Ipswich T	—	—
						Maidstone U	54	1
Jesse Roast	6 1	12 07	16 3 64	Barking	Barking	Maidstone U	32	—
Paul Rumble	5 11	11 05	14 3 69	Hemel Hempstead	Trainee	Watford	—	—
						Scunthorpe U (loan)	8	1
						Maidstone U	50	3
Gary Stebbing	5 9	11 00	11 8 65	Croydon	Apprentice	Crystal Palace	102	3
						Southend U (loan)	5	—
					KV Ostend	Maidstone U	39	1
Midfield								
Karl Elsey*	5 10	12 00	20 11 58	Swansea	Pembroke B	QPR	7	—
						Newport Co	123	15
						Cardiff C	59	5
						Gillingham	128	13
						Reading	44	3
						Maidstone U	72	5
Steve Galliers*	5 6	9 07	21 8 57	Fulwood	Chorley	Wimbledon	155	10
						Crystal Palace	13	—
						Wimbledon	146	5
						Bristol C (loan)	9	—
						Bristol C	68	6
						Maidstone U	8	—
Mark Golley	6 1	13 00	28 10 62	Beckenham	Sutton U	Maidstone U	81	3
David Madden	6 0	11 03	6 1 63	London	Apprentice	Southampton	—	—
						Bournemouth (loan)	5	—
						Arsenal	2	—
						Charlton Ath	20	1
						Reading	9	1
						Crystal Palace	27	5
						Birmingham C (loan)	5	1
						Maidstone U	10	—
Chris Pullan*	5 8	10 12	14 12 67	Durham	School	Watford	12	—
						Halifax T (loan)	5	1
						Maidstone U	1	—

MAIDSTONE UNITED

Foundation: First appeared as Maidstone Invicta in December 1891 playing in the Maidstone & District League and the Kent League before changing name to Maidstone United in 1897. Then employed part-time professionals until reverting to amateur status in 1927, Re-adopted professionalism when joining the Southern League in 1971.

First Football League game: 19 August, 1989, Division 4, v Peterborough U (a) L 0-1 – Beeney; Barton (Stebbing), Cooper, Berry, Golley, Pearce, Lillis (Charlery), Elsey, Sorrell, Butler, Gall.

Did you know: As a non-League club Maidstone reached the 3rd round of the FA Cup five times in the post-war period. Only two other non-League clubs can better this record – Altrincham and Yeovil – seven times each

Managers (and Secretary-managers)
Ken Spurgeon 1971, Roy Houghton 1971–72, Ernie Morgan 1972–73, Robin Stepney 1973–75, Terry Adlington 1975–77, Barry Watling 1977–80, Bill Williams 1980–85, Barry Fry 1985–86, Bill Williams 1980–85, Barry Fry 1985–86, Bill Williams 1986–87 (Continued as General Manager), John Still 1987–89, Keith Peacock 1989–91, Craham Carr January 1991– .

Player and Position	Ht	Wt	Birth Date	Birth Place	Source	Clubs	League App	Gls
Bradley Sandeman	5 10	10 08	24 2 70	Northampton	Trainee	Northampton T	58	3
						Maidstone U	20	1
Tony Sorrell	5 10	12 04	17 10 66	Bromchurch	Bishops Stortford	Maidstone U	55	8
Forwards								
Mark Gall	5 10	12 00	14 5 63	Brixton	Greenwich Bor	Maidstone U	75	29
Liburd Henry	5 11	11 00	29 8 67	Dominica	Leytonstone/ Ilford	Watford	10	1
						Halifax T (loan)	5	—
						Maidstone U	30	2
Jason Lillis	5 11	11 10	1 10 69	Chatham	Trainee	Gillingham	29	3
						Maidstone U	52	14
						Carlisle U (loan)	4	1
Gary Moore†			29 12 68	Greenwich		Maidstone U	5	1
Lawrence Osborne	5 10	11 07	20 10 67	London	Apprentice	Arsenal	—	—
						Newport Co	15	—
					Redbridge F	Maidstone U	37	4
Howard Pritchard‡	5 10	12 07	18 10 58	Cardiff	Apprentice	Bristol C	38	2
						Swindon T	65	11
						Bristol C	119	22
						Gillingham	88	20
						Walsall	45	7
						Maidstone U	33	6

Trainees
Brewer, Mark A; Heath, Dean M; Johnston, Daniel E; King, Richard C; Mas, Bartolome W.P; Mearns, John F; Paris, Spencer P.C; Sinclair, Robert A; Toms, Matthew; Weaver, Stuart N; Wilson-Head, Robert S.

Associated Schoolboys
Britt, James J; Carr, Russell E; Everitt, James E.

MANCHESTER CITY 1990–91   *Back row (left to right):* Neil Pointon, Niall Quinn, Colin Hendry, Paul Lake, David White.
Centre row: Tony Book (Reserve-Youth Team Coach), Roy Bailey (Medical Trainer), Gary Megson, Jason Beckford, Andy Dibble, Andy Hill, Tony Coton, Mark Brennan, Mark Ward, Sam Ellis (First Team Coach).
Front row: Wayne Clarke, Ian Brightwell, Adrian Heath, Peter Reid (Manager), Steve Redmond, Alan Harper, Clive Allen.

Division 1   **MANCHESTER CITY**

Maine Road, Moss Side, Manchester M14 7WN. Telephone 061-226 1191/2. Ticket Office: 061-226 2224. Development Office: 061-226 3143. Clubcall: 0898 121191. Ticketcall: 0898 121591.

Ground capacity: 44,055.

Record attendance: 84,569 v Stoke C, FA Cup 6th rd, 3 March 1934 (British record for any game outside London or Glasgow).

Record receipts: £239,476. Everton v Liverpool, Milk Cup Final replay, 28 March 1984.

Pitch measurements: 118yd × 76yd.

Chairman: P. J. Swales. *Vice-charman:* F. Pye.

Directors: I. L. G. Niven, C. B. Muir OBE, M. T. Horwich, W. C. Adams, A. Thomas, G. Doyle, W. A. Miles, B. Turnbull, J. Greibach.

Secretary: Bernard Halford. *Commercial Manager:* P. Critchley.

General Manager: Jimmy Frizzell. *Player-manager:* Peter Reid.

Assistant Manager: Sam Ellis. *Medical Trainer:* Roy Bailey.

Year Formed: 1887 as Ardwick FC; 1894 as Manchester City.

Turned Professional: 1887 as Ardwick FC. *Ltd Co.:* 1894. *Club Nickname:* Blues The Citizens.

Previous Names: 1887–94, Ardwick FC (formed through the amalgamation of West Gorton and Gorton Athletic, the latter having been formed in 1880).

Previous Grounds: 1880–81, Clowes Street; 1881–82, Kirkmanshulme Cricket Ground; 1882–84, Queens Road; 1884–87, Pink Bank Lane; 1887–1923, Hyde Road (1894–1923, as City); 1923, Maine Road.

Record League Victory: 10-1 Huddersfield T, Division 2, 7 November 1987 – Nixon; Gidman, Hinchliffe, Clements, Lake, Redmond, White (3), Stewart (3), Adcock (3), McNab (1) Simpson.

Record Cup Victory: 10-1 v Swindon T, FA Cup, 4th rd, 29 January 1930 – Barber; Felton, McCloy; Barrass, Cowan, Heinemann; Toseland, Marshall (5), Tait (3), Johnson (1), Brook (1).

Record Defeat: 1-9 v Everton, Division 1, 3 September 1906.

Most League Points (2 for a win): 62, Division 2, 1946–47.

Most League Points (3 for a win): 82, Division 2, 1988–89.

Most League Goals: 108, Division 2, 1926–27.

Highest League Scorer in Season: Tommy Johnson, 38, Division 1, 1928–29.

Most League Goals in Total Aggregate: Tommy Johnson, 158, 1919–30.

Most Capped Player: Colin Bell, 48, England.

Most League Appearances: Alan Oakes, 565, 1959–76.

Record Transfer Fee Received: £1,700,000 from Tottenham H for Paul Stewart, June 1988.

Record Transfer Fee Paid: £1,437,500 to Wolverhampton W for Steve Daley, September 1979 (£1,150,000 basic fee).

Football League Record: 1892 Ardwick elected founder member of Division 2; 1894 Newly-formed Manchester C elected to Division 2; Division 1 1899–1902, 1903–09, 1910–26, 1928–38, 1947–50, 1951–63, 1966–83, 1985–87, 1989–; Division 2 1902–03, 1909–10, 1926–28, 1938–47, 1950–51, 1963–66, 1983–85, 1987–89.

Honours: Football League: Division 1 – Champions 1936–37, 1967–68; Runners-up 1903–04, 1920–21, 1976–77; Division 2 – Champions 1898–99, 1902–03, 1909–10, 1927–28, 1946–47, 1965–66; Runners-up 1895–96, 1950–51, 1987–88. *FA Cup:* Winners 1904, 1934, 1956, 1969; Runners-up 1926, 1933, 1955, 1981. *Football League Cup:* Winners 1970, 1976; Runners-up 1973–74. **European Competitions:** *European Cup:* 1968–69. *European Cup-Winners' Cup:* 1969–70 (winners), 1970–71. *UEFA Cup:* 1972–73, 1976–77, 1977–78, 1978–79.

Colours: Sky blue shirts, dark blue collar, white shorts, navy blue stockings. **Change colours:** Alternate maroon and white striped shirts with fine blue stripe between, England neckline with button down neck, integral shadow diamond weave, maroon shorts with 1½" blue stripe and white stripe, maroon stockings with sky blue diamond on turnover.

MANCHESTER CITY 1990–91 LEAGUE RECORD

Match No.	Date		Venue	Opponents	Result	H/T Score	Lg. Pos.	Goalscorers	Atten-dance
1	Aug	25	A	Tottenham H	L 1-3	1-1	—	Quinn	33.501
2	Sept	1	H	Everton	W 1-0	1-0	14	Heath	31,456
3		5	H	Aston Villa	W 2-1	0-0	—	Ward (pen), Pointon	30,199
4		8	A	Sheffield U	D 1-1	0-0	7	White	21,895
5		15	A	Norwich C	W 2-1	2-0	6	Quinn, Brennan	26,247
6		22	A	Chelsea	D 1-1	1-0	6	Ward (pen)	20,924
7		29	A	Wimbledon	D 1-1	0-0	7	Allen	6158
8	Oct	6	H	Coventry C	W 2-0	0-0	5	Harper, Quinn	26,198
9		20	A	Derby Co	D 1-1	1-0	5	Ward (pen)	17,884
10		27	H	Manchester U	D 3-3	2-1	5	White 2, Hendry	36,427
11	Nov	3	A	Sunderland	D 1-1	0-1	5	White	23,137
12		11	H	Leeds U	L 2-3	0-2	—	Ward (pen), White	27,782
13		17	A	Luton T	D 2-2	2-0	7	White, Redmond	9564
14		24	A	Liverpool	D 2-2	0-0	7	Ward (pen), Quinn	37,849
15	Dec	1	H	QPR	W 2-1	1-0	6	Quinn 2	25,080
16		15	H	Tottenham H	W 2-1	0-1	6	Redmond, Ward (pen)	31,263
17		22	H	Crystal Palace	L 0-2	0-1	8		25,321
18		26	A	Southampton	L 1-2	1-1	8	Quinn	16,029
19		29	A	Nottingham F	W 3-1	2-1	7	Quinn 2, Clarke	24,937
20	Jan	1	H	Arsenal	L 0-1	0-0	7		30,579
21		13	A	Everton	L 0-2	0-2	—		22,774
22		19	H	Sheffield U	W 2-0	1-0	8	Ward 2	25,741
23	Feb	2	A	Norwich C	W 2-1	2-0	8	Quinn, White	15,194
24		9	H	Chelsea	W 2-1	2-0	7	Megson, White	25,116
25	Mar	2	A	QPR	L 0-1	0-1	8		12,376
26		5	H	Luton T	W 3-0	3-0	—	Quinn 2, Allen (pen)	20,404
27		9	H	Liverpool	L 0-3	0-2	5		33,150
28		16	H	Wimbledon	D 1-1	1-1	6	Ward (pen)	21,089
29		23	A	Coventry C	L 1-3	0-2	7	Allen	13,198
30		30	H	Southampton	D 3-3	0-0	7	Allen, Brennan, White	23,163
31	Apr	1	A	Crystal Palace	W 3-1	2-0	6	Quinn 3	18,001
32		6	H	Nottingham F	W 3-1	3-0	6	Ward (pen), Quinn, Redmond	25,169
33		10	A	Leeds U	W 2-1	1-1	—	Hill, Quinn	28,757
34		17	A	Arsenal	D 2-2	2-2	—	Ward (pen), White	38,412
35		20	H	Derby Co	W 2-1	1-0	4	Quinn, White	24,037
36		23	A	Aston Villa	W 5-1	2-0	—	White 4, Brennan	24,168
37	May	4	A	Manchester U	L 0-1	0-1	5		45,286
38		11	H	Sunderland	W 3-2	2-2	5	Quinn 2, White	39,194

Final League Position: 5

GOALSCORERS

League (64): Quinn 20, White 16, Ward 11 (9 pens), Allen 4 (1 pen), Brennan 3, Redmond 3, Clarke 1, Harper 1, Heath 1, Hendry 1, Hill 1, Megson 1, Pointon 1.
Rumbelows Cup (5): Allen 2, Beckford 1, Harper 1, Hendry 1.
FA Cup (3): Allen 1, Hendry 1, Quinn 1.

Coton	Brightwell I	Pointon	Harper	Hendry	Lake	White	Reid	Quinn	Heath	Ward M	Redmond	Allen	Dibble	Brennan	Beckford	Megson	Clarke	Hill	Hughes	Margetson	Match No.
1	2	3	4	5*	6	7	8	9	10†	11	12	14									1
1	2	3	4	5	8	7	6	9	10	11											2
	2	3		5	8*	7	6	9	10	11	12		1	4							3
1	2	3	8	5		7	6	9*	10	11	12			4							4
1	2	3	8	5		7	6*	9	10	11	12	14		4†							5
1	2	3	8	5		7*	6†	9	10	11	12	14		4							6
1	2	3	4	5		7†		9	8*	11	6	12				10	14				7
1	2	3	10	5		7*	4†	9	8	11	6	12		14							8
1	14	3*	2	5		7	4	9†	8	11	6	12				10					9
1	12	3	2	5		7	4*	9	8	11	6					10					10
1		3	2	5		7	4	9	8	11*	6	12				10					11
1	14	3	2†	5		7	4*	9	8	11	6	12				10					12
1	2	3	4	5		7*		9	8	11	6					10					13
	2	3		5		7	4	9	8*	11	6	12	1			10					14
	2	3		5		7	4	9	8	11	6		1			10					15
1	2	3		5		7	4	9	8*	11	6					10	12				16
1	2*	3		5		7	4	9	8	11	6					10	12				17
1	2	3	12	5		7	4	9		11	6					10	8*				18
1	2	3		5		7	4	9	8*	11	6					10	12				19
1	2	3		5		7	4	9		11	6					10	8				20
1	2	3	12	5*		7	4	9	8	11	6			14		10†					21
1	2	3		5		7	4	9		11	6			8		10					22
1	2	3	4	5		7		9	12	11	6			8*		10					23
1	2	3	4	5		7		9	12	11	6			8*		10					24
1	2	3	12	5		7	4†		8	11*	6			14		10					25
1	2†	3	12	5		7	4*	9		11	6			8		10	14				26
1	2	3		5		7	4	9	12	11	6			8		10*					27
1	2		10	5		7	4	9	12	11	6			8*			3				28
1	2		10			7	4	9	5	11	6			8			3				29
1	2		10			7	4	9	5	11	6			8			3				30
1	2	3	10			7	4	9	5	11	6			8							31
1	2	3*	10			7	4	9	5	11	6			8			12				32
1	2	3	10			7		9	5	11	6			8				4			33
1	2	3	10			7		9	5	11	6			8				4			34
1		3	10	5		7	12	9	4	11*	6			8				2			35
1		3	10	5		7		9	4	11	6			8				2			36
.		3	10	5		7	14	9	4	11*	6			8†	12			2		1	37
		3	10	5		7		9	4	11*	6			8	12			2		1	38
33	30	35	25	32	3	38	28	38	31	36	35	8	3	12	—	19	3	7	—	2	
			+3s	+4s			+2s		+4s			+2s		+12s		+4s	+2s	+4s	+1s	+1s	

Rumbelows Cup — Second Round — Torquay U (a) — 4-0

(h) — 0-0

Third Round — Arsenal (h) — 1-2

FA Cup — Third Round — Burnley (a) — 1-0

Fourth Round — Everton (a) — 2-1

Fifth Round — Notts Co (a) — 0-1

MANCHESTER CITY

Player and Position	Ht	Wt	Birth Date	Birth Place	Source	Clubs	League App	Gls
Goalkeepers								
Tony Coton	6 1	11 08	19 5 61	Tamworth	Mile Oak	Birmingham C	94	—
						Hereford U (loan)	—	—
						Watford	233	—
						Manchester C	35	—
Andy Dibble	6 2	13 07	8 5 65	Cwmbran	Apprentice	Cardiff C	62	—
						Luton T	30	—
						Sunderland (loan)	12	—
						Huddersfield T (loan)	5	—
						Manchester C	72	—
						Aberdeen (loan)	5	—
						Middlesbrough (loan)	19	—
Martyn Margetson	6 0	13 10	8 9 71	West Glamorgan	Trainee	Manchester C	2	—
Defenders								
Colin Hendry	6 1	12 02	7 12 65	Keith	Islavale	Dundee	41	2
						Blackburn R	102	22
						Manchester C	57	4
Andy Hill	5 11	12 00	20 1 65	Maltby	Apprentice	Manchester U	—	—
						Bury	264	10
						Manchester C	8	1
Mark Peters	5 11	10 10	6 7 72	St Asaph	Trainee	Manchester C	—	—
Neil Pointon	5 10	11 00	28 11 64	Warsop Vale	Apprentice	Scunthorpe U	159	2
						Everton	102	5
						Manchester C	35	1
Steve Redmond	5 11	12 13	2 11 67	Liverpool	Apprentice	Manchester C	204	6
John Wills*			7 11 71	Chester	Trainee	Manchester C	—	—
Midfield								
Mark Brennan	5 10	10 13	4 10 65	Rossendale	Apprentice	Ipswich T	168	19
						Middlesbrough	65	6
						Manchester C	16	3
David Brightwell	6 1	13 05	7 1 71	Lutterworth		Manchester C	—	—
						Chester C (loan)	6	—
Ian Brightwell	5 10	11 07	9 4 68	Lutterworth	Trainee	Manchester C	136	14
Sean Harkin			3 12 73	Birmingham	Trainee	Manchester C	—	—
Alan Harper	5 8	10 09	1 11 60	Liverpool	Apprentice	Liverpool	—	—
						Everton	127	4
						Sheffield W	35	—
						Manchester C	50	1
Michael Hughes	5 6	10 08	2 8 71	Larne	Carrick R	Manchester C	2	—
Paul Kelly	5 8	11 07	6 3 71	Urmston	Trainee	Manchester C	—	—
Paul Lake	6 0	12 02	28 10 68	Manchester	Trainee	Manchester C	108	7
Steve Lomas			18 1 74	Hanover	Trainee	Manchester C	—	—
Gary Megson	5 10	11 06	2 5 59	Manchester	Apprentice	Plymouth Arg	78	10
						Everton	22	2
						Sheffield W	123	13
						Nottingham F	—	—
						Newcastle U	24	1
						Sheffield W	110	12
						Manchester C	60	2
Mike Quigley	5 6	9 04	2 10 70	Manchester	Trainee	Manchester C	—	—
Peter Reid	5 8	10 07	20 6 56	Huyton	Apprentice	Bolton W	225	23
						Everton	159	8
						QPR	29	1
						Manchester C	48	1
Garry Sliney	5 10	12 03	2 9 73	Dublin		Manchester C	—	—
Michael Wallace	5 8	10 02	5 10 70	Farnworth	Trainee	Manchester C	—	—
Mark Ward	5 6	9 12	10 10 62	Prescot	Apprentice Northwich V	Everton	—	—
						Oldham Ath	84	12
						West Ham U	165	12
						Manchester C	55	14

MANCHESTER CITY

Foundation: Manchester City was formed as a Limited Company in 1894 after their predecessors Ardwick had been forced into bankruptcy. However, many historians like to trace the club's lineage as far back as 1880 when St. Mark's Church, West Gorton added a football section to their cricket club. They amalgamated with Gorton Athletic in 1884 as Gorton FC. Because of a change of ground they became Ardwick in 1887.

First Football League game: 3 September, 1892, Division 2, v Bootle (h) W 7-0 – Douglas; McVickers, Robson; Middleton, Russell, Hopkins; Davies (3), Morris (2), Angus (1), Weir (1), Milarvie.

Did you know: City delayed the kick-off of their game at Everton in 1928 through their late arrival. However, they were level (1-1) at the interval and won 6-2 with Tom Johnson scoring five goals. This eased the pain of their subsequent fine.

Managers (and Secretary-managers)
Joshua Parlby 1893–95*, Sam Omerod 1895–1902, Tom Maley 1902–06, Harry Newbould 1906–12, Ernest Magnall 1912–24, David Ashworth 1924–25, Peter Hodge 1926–32, Wilf Wild 1932–46 (continued as secretary to 1950), Sam Cowan 1946–47, John "Jock" Thomson 1947–50, Leslie McDowall 1950–63, George Poyser 1963–65, Joe Mercer 1965–71 (continued as GM to 1972), Malcolm Allison 1972–73, Johnny Hart 1973, Ron Saunders 1973–74, Tony Book 1974–79, Malcolm Allison 1979–80, John Bond 1980–83, John Benson 1983, Billy McNeill 1983–86, Jimmy Frizzell 1986–87 (continued as GM), Mel Machin 1987–89, Howard Kendall 1990, Peter Reid November 1990–   .

Player and Position	Ht	Wt	Birth Date	Place	Source	Clubs	League App	Gls
Forwards								
Clive Allen	5 10	12 03	20 5 61	London	Apprentice	QPR	49	32
						Arsenal	—	—
						Crystal Palace	25	9
						QPR	87	40
						Tottenham H	105	60
					Bordeaux	Manchester C	50	14
Jason Beckford	5 9	12 04	14 2 70	Manchester	Trainee	Manchester C	20	1
						Blackburn R (loan)	4	—
Wayne Clarke	6 0	11 08	28 2 61	Wolverhampton	Apprentice	Wolverhampton W	148	30
						Birmingham C	92	38
						Everton	57	18
						Leicester C	11	1
						Manchester C	16	1
						Shrewsbury T (loan)	7	6
						Stoke C (loan)	9	3
Simon Dyer*			7 10 71	Swansea	Trainee	Manchester C	—	—
Adrian Heath	5 6	10 01	11 1 61	Stoke	Apprentice	Stoke C	95	16
						Everton	226	71
					Espanol	Aston Villa	9	—
						Manchester C	47	3
Niall Quinn	6 4	12 04	6 10 66	Dublin	Eire Youth	Arsenal	67	14
						Manchester C	47	24
Mike Sheron	5 9	11 03	11 1 72	Liverpool	Trainee	Manchester C		
						Bury (loan)	5	1
Ashley Ward	6 1	11 07	24 11 70	Middleton	Trainee	Manchester C	1	
						Wrexham (loan)	4	2
David White	6 1	12 09	30 10 67	Manchester		Manchester C	188	44
Darren Wilson*			30 9 71	Manchester		Manchester C	—	—

Trainees
Beirne, Michael A; Bibby, Richard; Davies, Allan; Flitcroft, Gary W; Foster, John C; Foster, Matthew R; Kerr, David W; Lewis, Ian R; Locke, Stuart J; McCullough, Ronald K; Mike, Adrian R; Mulvey, Eamon M.

Associated Schoolboys
Beech, Christopher; Booth, Scott C; Brennan, Steven J; Creighton, Mark G; Davis, Leon; Dowe, Julian W.W.L; Downer, Lee J; Dunbar, Christopher; Evans, Gareth J; Hughes, Robert M; Kilcommons, Laurence S; McDonnell, John M; Roe, David; Samuel, Gavin; Seymour, Andrew; Smith, Ian R; Turner, David E; Walker, David A; Winter, Paul E.

Associated Schoolboys who have accepted the club's offer of a Traineeship/Contract
Edghill, Richard A; Ingram, Rae; Lydiate, Joseph L; McDowell, Stephen A; McHugh, Darren R; Sharpe, John J; Smith, Daniel S; Thomas, Scott L.

322

MANCHESTER UNITED 1990-91 *Back row (left to right):* Mal Donaghy, Lee Sharpe, Viv Anderson, Les Sealey, Jim Leighton, Mike Phelan, Neil Webb, Steve Bruce. *Centre row:* Jim McGregor (Physiotherapist), Archie Knox (Assistant Manager), Colin Gibson, Brian McClair, Russell Beardsmore, Clayton Blackmore, Paul Ince, Ralph Milne, Norman Davies (Kit Manager). *Front row:* Danny Wallace, Denis Irwin, Mark Robins, Bryan Robson, Alex Ferguson (Manager), Mark Hughes, Gary Pallister, Lee Martin.

Division 1   **MANCHESTER UNITED**

Old Trafford, Manchester M16 0RA. Telephone 061-872 1661. Ticket and Match Information: 061-872 0199. Membership enquiries: 061-872 5208. Souvenir shop: 061-872 3398.

Ground capacity: 50,726.

Record attendance: 76,962 Wolverhampton W v Grimsby T, FA Cup semi-final. 25 March 1939.

Club record: 70,504 v Aston Villa, Division 1, 27 December 1920.

Record receipts: £232,173.70 v Nottingham F, FA Cup 6th rd, 18 March 1989.

Pitch measurements: 116yd × 76yd.

President: Sir Matt Busby CBE, KCSG.

Vice-presidents: J. A. Gibson, W. A. Young, J. G. Gulliver, R. L. Edwards.

Chairman/Chief Executive: C. M. Edwards.

Directors: J. M. Edelson, R. Charlton CBE, E. M. Watkins LL.M., A. M. Midani, N. Burrows, R. L. Olive, M. Knighton.

Manager: Alex Ferguson. *Coaches:* Jim Ryan, Bryan 'Pop' Robson.

Secretary: Kenneth Merrett. *Commercial Manager:* D. A. McGregor.

Physio: Jim McGregor.

Year Formed: 1878 as Newton Heath LYR; 1902, Manchester United.

Turned Professional: 1885. *Ltd Co.:* 1907.

Previous Name: Newton Heath, 1880–1902.

Club Nickname: 'Red Devils'.

Previous Grounds: 1880–93, North Road, Monsall Road; 1893, Bank Street; 1910, Old Trafford (played at Maine Road 1941–49).

Record League Victory: 10-1 v Wolverhampton W, Division 2, 15 October 1892 – Warner; Mitchell, Clements; Perrins, Stewart (3), Erentz; Farman (1), Hood (1), Donaldson (3), Carson (1), Hendry (1).

Record Cup Victory: 10-0 v RSC Anderlecht, European Cup, Prel. rd (2nd leg), 26 September 1956 – Wood; Foulkes Byrne; Colman, Jones, Edwards; Berry (1), Whelan (2), Taylor (3), Viollet (4), Pegg.

Record Defeat: 0-7 v Blackburn R, Division 1, 10 April 1926 and v Aston Villa, Division 1, 27 December 1930 and v Wolverhampton W. Division 2, 26 December 1931.

Most League Points (2 for a win): 64, Division 1, 1956–57.

Most League Points (3 for a win): 81, Division 1, 1987–88.

Most League Goals: 103, Division 1, 1956–57 and 1958–59.

Highest League Scorer in Season: Dennis Viollet, 32, 1959–60.

Most League Goals in Total Aggregate: Bobby Charlton, 199, 1956–73.

Most Capped Player: Bobby Charlton, 106, England.

Most League Appearances: Bobby Charlton, 606, 1956–73.

Record Transfer Fee Received: £1,800,000 from Barcelona for Mark Hughes, August 1986.

Record Transfer Fee Paid: £2,300,000 to Middlesbrough for Gary Pallister, August 1989.

Football League Record: 1892 Newton Heath elected to Division 1; 1894–1906 Division 2; 1906–22 Division 1; 1922–25 Division 2; 1925–31 Division 1; 1931–36 Division 2; 1936–37 Division 1; 1937–38 Division 2; 1938–74 Division 1; 1974–75 Division 2; 1975– Division 1.

Honours: Football League: Division 1 – Champions 1907–8, 1910–11, 1951–52, 1955–56, 1956–57, 1964–65, 1966–67; Runners-up 1946–47, 1947–48, 1948–49, 1950–51, 1958–59, 1963–64, 1967–68, 1979–80, 1987–88. Division 2 – Champions 1935–36, 1974–75; Runners-up 1896–97, 1905–06, 1924–25, 1937–38. *FA Cup:* Winners 1909, 1948, 1963, 1977, 1983, 1985, 1990; Runners-up 1957, 1958, 1976, 1979. *Football League Cup:* 1982–83 (Runners-up), 1990–91 (Runners-up). **European Competitions:** *European Cup:* 1956–57 (s-f), 1957-58 (s-f), 1965–66 (s-f), 1967–68 (winners), 1968–69 (s-f). *European Cup-Winners' Cup:* 1963–64, 1977–78, 1983–84, 1990–91 (winners). *European Fairs Cup:* 1964–65. *UEFA Cup:* 1976–77, 1980–81, 1982–83, 1984–85.

Colours: Red shirts, white shorts, black stockings. **Change colours:** Royal blue on white shirts, navy/royal blue shorts, navy stockings.

MANCHESTER UNITED 1990–91 LEAGUE RECORD

Match No.	Date	Venue	Opponents	Result	H/T Score	Lg. Pos.	Goalscorers	Atten-dance
1	Aug 25	H	Coventry C	W 2-0	0-0	—	Bruce, Webb	46,715
2	28	A	Leeds U	D 0-0	0-0	—		29,172
3	Sept 1	A	Sunderland	L 1-2	0-1	6	McClair	26,105
4	4	A	Luton T	W 1-0	1-0	—	Robins	12,576
5	8	H	QPR	W 3-1	1-0	3	McClair, Robins 2	43,427
6	16	A	Liverpool	L 0-4	0-3	—		35,726
7	22	H	Southampton	W 3-2	1-1	3	McClair, Blackmore, Hughes	41,228
8	29	H	Nottingham F	L 0-1	0-1	5		46,766
9	Oct 20	H	Arsenal	L 0-1	0-1	7		47,232
10	27	A	Manchester C	D 3-3	1-2	6	Hughes, McClair 2	36,427
11	Nov 3	H	Crystal Palace	W 2-0	2-0	6	Webb, Wallace	45,724
12	10	A	Derby Co	D 0-0	0-0	6		21,115
13	17	H	Sheffield U	W 2-0	0-0	6	Bruce, Hughes	45,903
14	25	H	Chelsea	L 2-3	1-2	—	Wallace, Hughes	37,836
15	Dec 1	A	Everton	W 1-0	0-0	7	Sharpe	32,400
16	8	H	Leeds U	D 1-1	0-0	7	Webb	40,927
17	15	A	Coventry C	D 2-2	1-1	9	Hughes, Wallace	17,106
18	22	A	Wimbledon	W 3-1	0-1	7	Bruce 2 (2 pens), Hughes	9744
19	26	H	Norwich C	W 3-0	0-0	6	Hughes, McClair 2	39,801
20	29	H	Aston Villa	D 1-1	1-1	6	Bruce (pen)	47,485
21	Jan 1	A	Tottenham H	W 2-1	1-1	5	Bruce (pen), McClair	29,399
22	12	H	Sunderland	W 3-0	3-0	5	Hughes 2, McClair	45,934
23	19	A	QPR	D 1-1	0-1	5	Phelan	18,544
24	Feb 3	H	Liverpool	D 1-1	1-1	—	Bruce (pen)	43,690
25	26	A	Sheffield U	L 1-2	0-0	—	Blackmore (pen)	27,570
26	Mar 2	H	Everton	L 0-2	0-2	5		45,656
27	9	A	Chelsea	L 2-3	1-1	6	Hughes, McClair	22,818
28	13	A	Southampton	D 1-1	0-1	—	Ince	15,701
29	16	A	Nottingham F	D 1-1	1-0	5	Blackmore	23,859
30	23	H	Luton T	W 4-1	1-1	5	Bruce 2, Robins, McClair	41,752
31	30	A	Norwich C	W 3-0	2-0	5	Bruce 2 (pen), Ince	18,282
32	Apr 2	H	Wimbledon	W 2-1	0-1	—	Bruce, McClair	36,660
33	6	A	Aston Villa	D 1-1	0-0	5	Sharpe	33,307
34	16	H	Derby Co	W 3-1	1-1	—	Blackmore, McClair, Robson	32,776
35	May 4	H	Manchester C	W 1-0	1-0	6	Giggs	45,286
36	6	A	Arsenal	L 1-3	0-2	—	Bruce (pen)	40,229
37	11	A	Crystal Palace	L 0-3	0-1	6		25,301
38	20	H	Tottenham H	D 1-1	1-0	—	Ince	46,791

Final League Position: 6

GOALSCORERS

League (58): Bruce 13 (7 pens), McClair 13, Hughes 10, Blackmore 4 (1 pen), Robins 4, Ince 3, Wallace 3, Webb 3, Sharpe 2, Giggs 1, Phelan 1, Robson 1.
Rumbelows Cup (21): Hughes 6, Sharpe 6, Blackmore 2, Bruce (2 pens), McClair 2, Anderson 1, Wallace 1, Webb 1.
FA Cup (4): Hughes 2, McClair 2.

Sealey	Irwin	Donaghy	Bruce	Phelan	Pallister	Webb	Ince	McClair	Hughes	Blackmore	Beardsmore	Robins	Anderson	Sharpe	Martin	Wallace	Robson	Walsh	Ferguson	Giggs	Whitworth	Wratten	Bosnich	Kontchelskis	Match No.
1	2	3	4	5	6	7	8	9	10	11															1
1	2	3	4	5	6	7	8*	9	10	11	12														2
1	2	3*	4	5	6	7	8	9	10†	11	12	14													3
1	2	14	4	5	6	7	8	9	12	3	11†	10*													4
1	2		4	5	6	7	8	9		3	11	10													5
1	2	14	4	5	6†	7	8*	9	10	3	12	11													6
1	2†	3		5	6	7		9	10	11	12	8*	4	14											7
1	2	4		5	6	7	8	9	12	3	11†	10*		14											8
1	2†		4	5	6	7	8	9	10	3		12		11*	14										9
1	2		4		6	7	8	9	10	5				11*	3	12									10
1	2		4	5	6	7	8	9		3				11	12	10*									11
1	2†	14	4	5	6	7	8	9	10	3				11*	12										12
1	2*		4	5	6	7	8	9	10	3				11	12										13
1	2		4	5†	6	7	8	9	10	3*		14		12	11										14
1	2		4	5	6	14	8†	9	10	3				7*	12	11									15
1	2*	14	4	5†	6		8	9	10	3				7	11	12									16
1		14	4	5	6	7	8†	9	10	2				3*	11	12									17
1		3	4	5	6	11	8	9	10	2*				12			7								18
1	2	14	4	12	6	5	8	9	10	3						11†	7*								19
1	2		4	12	6	5	8	9	10	3						11	7*								20
1	2†		4	5*	6	7	8	9	10	3		12		11		14									21
1	2		4	12	6	5*	8†	9	10	3		14				11	7								22
1	2	6	4	5		8		9	10	11				7*	12	14	3†								23
1	2		4	5†	6		8*	9	10	3				11	14	12	7								24
	2	5		6	4†	8	9		10		12	3		11			7*	1	14						25
1	2†	5			6		8	9	10	12		7		3*	11				4	14					26
1		4		5	6		8	9	10	2*				11	3	12	7								27
1	2†	4		5	6		8	9	10	3		14		7*	12	11									28
1	2	12	4	5	6		8	9	10	3*				11			7								29
1	2		4	5	6			9	10	3		12		11		8*	7								30
1	2*		4	5	6	9	8	12	10	3		14			11†		7								31
	2	3	4†	5	6	7	8	9	10	12				11*				1	14						32
1	2	3	4	5*	6		8	9	10	12				11			7								33
	2	3	4		6	5*	8	12	10			9		11			7						1		34
	2	12	4	5	6		8	9	10	3							7	1			11*				35
		6	4	2		5	8	9	10*	3	12			11			7†						1	14	36
	2	3	4		6*	5	8	12	9†					11	10			1	14					7	37
	2†	14	4	5	6		8	9	10	3	12			11*			7	1							38
31	33 +1s	17 +8s	31	30 +3s	36	31 +1s	31	34 +2s	29 +2s	35	5 +7s	7 +12s	1	20 +3s	7 +7s	13 +6s	15 +2s	5	2 +3s	1 +1s	1 +2s	—	2	1	

Rumbelows Cup	Second Round	Halifax T (a)	3-1
		(h)	2-1
	Third Round	Liverpool (h)	3-1
	Fourth Round	Arsenal (a)	6-2
	Fifth Round	Southampton (a)	1-1
		(h)	3-2
	Semi-final	Leeds U (h)	2-1
		(a)	1-0
	Final	Sheffield W (at Wembley)	0-1
FA Cup	Third Round	QPR (h)	2-1
	Fourth Round	Bolton W (h)	1-0
	Fifth Round	Norwich C (a)	1-2

MANCHESTER UNITED

Player and Position	Ht	Wt	Date	Place	Source	Clubs	League App	Gls
Mark Bosnich†	6 2	13 07	13 1 72	Sydney, Australia		Manchester U	3	—
Jim Leighton	6 1	12 08	24 7 58	Johnstone	Dalry T	Aberdeen	300	—
						Manchester U	73	—
						Arsenal (loan)	—	—
Michael Pollitt*	6 3	13 03	29 2 72	Farnworth	Trainee	Manchester U	—	—
						Oldham Ath (loan)	—	—
Les Sealey	6 1	12 08	29 9 57	Bethnal Green	Apprentice	Coventry C	158	—
						Luton T	207	—
						Plymouth Arg (loan)	6	—
						Manchester U (loan)	2	—
						Manchester U	31	—
Gary Walsh	6 1	12 12	21 3 68	Wigan		Manchester U	35	—
						Airdrie (loan)	3	—

Defenders

Player and Position	Ht	Wt	Date	Place	Source	Clubs	League App	Gls
Derek Brazil	6 0	12 00	14 12 68	Dublin	Rivermount BC	Manchester U	2	—
						Oldham Ath (loan)	1	—
Steve Bruce	6 0	12 06	31 12 60	Newcastle	Apprentice	Gillingham	205	29
						Norwich C	141	14
						Manchester U	124	20
Brian Carey	6 3	11 13	31 5 68	Cork	Cork C	Manchester U	—	—
						Wrexham (loan)	3	—
Mal Donaghy	5 10	12 07	13 9 57	Belfast	Larne	Luton T	410	16
						Manchester U	69	—
						Luton T (loan)	5	—
Tony Gill‡	5 9	10 00	6 3 68	Bradford	Apprentice	Manchester U	10	1
Dennis Irwin	5 7	9 07	31 10 65	Cork	Apprentice	Leeds U	72	1
						Oldham Ath	167	4
						Manchester U	34	—
Jason Lydiate	5 11	12 07	29 10 71	Manchester	Trainee	Manchester U	—	—
Lee Martin	5 11	11 05	5 2 68	Hyde		Manchester U	71	1
Sean McAuley	5 10	10 11	23 6 72	Sheffield	Trainee	Manchester U	—	—
Gary Pallister	6 4	13 00	30 6 65	Ramsgate	Billingham	Middlesbrough	156	5
						Darlington (loan)	7	—
						Manchester U	71	3
Alan Tonge*	5 8	11 11	25 2 72	Bury	Trainee	Manchester U	—	—
Neil Whitworth	6 2	12 06	12 4 72	Ince		Wigan Ath	2	—
						Manchester U	1	—

Midfield

Player and Position	Ht	Wt	Date	Place	Source	Clubs	League App	Gls
Russell Beardsmore	5 6	8 10	28 9 68	Wigan	Apprentice	Manchester U	56	4
Clayton Blackmore	5 9	11 03	23 9 64	Neath	Apprentice	Manchester U	139	16
Anthony Costa*	5 4	9 10	6 12 71	Rhymney Valley	Trainee	Manchester U	—	—
Adrian Doherty	5 8	10 06	10 6 73	Strabane	School	Manchester U	—	—
Darren Ferguson	5 10	10 04	9 2 72	Glasgow	Trainee	Manchester U	5	—
Paul Ince	5 11	11 06	21 10 67	Ilford	Trainee	West Ham U	72	7
						Manchester U	57	3
Craig Lawton	5 7	10 03	5 1 72	Mancot	Trainee	Manchester U	—	—
Ralph Milne*	5 9	12 00	13 5 61	Dundee	School	Dundee U	179	44
						Charlton Ath	22	—
						Bristol C	30	6
						Manchester U	23	3
						West Ham U (loan)	—	—
Mike Phelan	5 11	12 03	24 9 62	Nelson	Apprentice	Burnley	168	9
						Norwich C	156	9
						Manchester U	71	2
Bryan Robson	5 11	11 12	11 1 57	Chester-Le-Street	Apprentice	WBA	197	39
						Manchester U	289	68
Roger Sallis*	5 7	10 04	22 3 72	Derby	Trainee	Manchester U	—	—
Lee Sharpe	5 11	11 04	27 5 71	Birmingham	Trainee	Torquay U	14	3
						Manchester U	63	3
Paul Sixsmith	5 10	10 12	22 9 71	Bolton	Trainee	Manchester U	—	—
Kieran Toal	5 8	11 01	14 12 71	Manchester	Trainee	Manchester U	—	—
Neil Webb	6 1	13 02	30 7 63	Reading	Apprentice	Reading	72	22
						Portsmouth	123	34
						Nottingham F	146	47
						Manchester U	43	5

MANCHESTER UNITED

Foundation: Manchester United was formed as comparatively recently as 1902 after their predecessors, Newton Heath, went bankrupt. However, it is usual to give the date of the club's foundation as 1878 when employees of the Lancashire and Yorkshire Railway Company formed Newton Heath L and YR. Cricket and Football Club. They won the Manchester Cup in 1886 and as Newton Heath FC were admitted to the Second Division in 1892.

First Football League game: 3 September, 1892, Division 1, v Blackburn R (a) L 3–4 – Warner; Clements, Brown; Perrins, Stewart, Erentz; Farman (1), Coupar (1), Donaldson (1), Carson, Mathieson.

Did you know: When David Herd scored four goals for Manchester United against Sunderland, 26 November 1966, his first three were against different goalkeepers – Jimmy Montgomery, Charlie Hurley and John Parke in that order. United went on to win 5-0.

Managers (and Secretary-managers)
Ernest Magnall 1900–12, John Robson 1914–21, John Chapman 1921–26, Clarence Hildrith 1926–27, Herbert Bamlett 1927–31, Walter Crickmer 1931–32, Scott Duncan 1932–37, Jimmy Porter 1938–44, Walter Crickmer 1944–45*, Matt Busby 1945–69 (continued as GM then Director), Wilf McGuinness 1969–70, Frank O'Farrell 1971–72, Tommy Docherty 1972–77, Dave Sexton 1977–81, Ron Atkinson 1981–86, Alex Ferguson November 1986–

Player and Position	Ht	Wt	Birth Date	Birth Place	Source	Clubs	League App	Gls
David Wilson*	5 9	10 10	20 3 69	Burnley	Apprentice	Manchester U	4	—
						Charlton Ath (loan)	7	2
						Lincoln C (loan)	3	—
Paul Wratten	5 7	9 13	29 11 70	Middlesbrough	Trainee	Manchester U	2	—
Forwards								
Ryan Giggs	5 11	9 09	29 11 73	Cardiff	School	Manchester U	2	1
Deiniol Graham	5 10	10 05	4 10 69	Cannock	Trainee	Manchester U	2	—
Mark Hughes	5 8	12 05	1 11 63	Wrexham	Apprentice	Manchester U	89	37
					Barcelona	Manchester U	106	37
Andrej Kontchelskist	5 10	12 04	23 1 69	Kirovograd	Donetsk	Manchester U	1	—
Brian McClair	5 9	12 02	8 12 63	Airdrie	Apprentice	Aston Villa		
						Motherwell	39	15
						Celtic	145	99
						Manchester U	151	52
Giuliano Maiorana	5 9	11 08	18 4 69	Cambridge	Histon	Manchester U	7	—
Mark Robins	5 7	10 01	22 12 69	Ashton-under-Lyme	Apprentice	Manchester U	46	11
Danny Wallace	5 4	10 06	21 1 64	London	Apprentice	Southampton	255	64
						Manchester U	45	6

Trainees
Brameld, Marcus J; Burke, Raphael E; Davies, Simon I; Gordon, Mark; Gough, Paul; McKee, Colin; McReavie, Alan S; Noone, Andrew C; Potts, Leslie A; Sharples, John B; Shields, James J; Smyth, Peter W; Switzer, George; Taylor, Leonard A; Telford, Colin L; Wilkinson, Ian M.

**Non-Contract
Bosnich, Mark J; Kontchelskis, Andrej.

Associated Schoolboys
Appleton, Michael A; Badoo, Mark O; Barnes, Lee M; Christopher, Anton; Cooke, Terence J; Edwards, Marc; Eyre, Richard P; Gardner, David S; Gibson, Paul R; Hall, Stephen; Hart, Ian M; Irving, Richard J; Johnson, David A; Lacey, Nicholas; McDonald, Robert; Mitten, Paul J; Monaghan, Matthew S; Murdoch, Colin J; Mustoe, Neil; Neville, Philip J; O'Donnell, Gerard; Parkin, Daniel J; Phillips, David; Ryan, Mark; Stott, Steven B; Twynham, Gary S; Wearden, Andrew M; Westwood, Ashley M; Whittam, Phillip R.

Associated Schoolboys who have accepted the club's offer of a Traineeship/Contract
Beckham, David R.J; Brown, Karl D; Butt, Nicholas; Dean, Craig; Gillespie, Keith R; Neville, Gary A; O'Kane, John A; Rawlinson, Mark D; Roberts, Joseph; Savage, Robert W; Scholes, Paul; Thornley, Benjamin L.

**Non-Contract Players who are retained must be re-signed before they are eligible to play in League matches.

328

MANSFIELD TOWN 1990–91 *Back row (left to right):* Graham Leishman. Steve Chambers. Mark Smalley. Andy Beasley. Jason Pearcey. Mark Kearney. Paul Brogan. David Hodges.

Centre row: Kevin Randall (Youth Development). David Hunt. Steve Charles. Kevin Gray. Tony Lowery. Ian Stringfellow. Malcolm Murray. Wayne Davidson. Wayne Fairclough. John Newman (Chief Scout). Dennis Pettitt (Physiotherapist).

Front row: Jason Milner. Steve Mills. Steve Prindiville. Steve Wilkinson. Billy Dearden (Assistant Manager). George Foster (Player-Manager). Ian Hathaway. Kevin Kent. Trevor Christie. Damien O'Brien.

Division 4   MANSFIELD TOWN

Field Mill Ground, Quarry Lane, Mansfield. Telepone Manfield (0623) 23567. Commercial Office: 0623 658070. Fax: 0623 25014

Ground capacity: 10,468.

Record attendance: 24,467 v Nottingham F, FA Cup 3rd rd, 10 January 1953.

Record receipts: £46,915 v Sheffield W, FA Cup 3rd rd, 5 January 1991.

Pitch measurements: 115yd × 72yd.

Chairman: J. W. Pratt. *Vice-chairman:*

Directors: G. Hall (Managing), J. A. Brown.

Player-manager: George Foster. *Assistant Manager/Coach:* Bill Dearden.

Coach: Bill Dearden. *Physio:* Dennis Pettitt. *Community Scheme Organiser:* D. Bentley Tel: 0623 25197.

Secretary: J. D. Eaton. *Commercial Manager:* J. Slater.

Year Formed: 1910. *Turned Professional:* 1910. *Ltd Co.:* 1921.

Previous Name: Mansfield Wesleyans 1891–1910.

Club Nickname: 'The Stags'.

Record League Victory: 9-2 v Rotherham U, Division 3 (N), 27 December 1932 – Wilson; Anthony, England; Davies, S. Robinson, Slack; Prior, Broom, Readman (3), Hoyland (3), Bowater (3).

Record Cup Victory: 8-0 v Scarborough (away), FA Cup, 1st rd, 22 November 1952 – Bramley; Chessell, Bradley; Field, Plummer, Lewis; Scott, Fox (3), Marron (2), Sid Watson (1), Adam (2).

Record Defeat: 1-8 v Walsall, Division 3 (N), 19 January 1933.

Most League Points (2 for a win): 68, Division 4, 1974–75.

Most League Points (3 for a win): 81, Division 4, 1985–86.

Most League Goals: 108, Division 4, 1962–63.

Highest League Scorer in Season: Ted Harston, 55, Division 3 (N), 1936–37.

Most League Goals in Total Aggregate: Harry Johnson, 104, 1931–36.

Most Capped Player: John McClelland, 6 (53), Northern Ireland.

Most League Appearances: Rod Arnold, 440, 1970–83.

Record Transfer Fee Received: £500,000 from Middlesbrough for Simon Coleman, September 1989.

Record Transfer Fee Paid: £80,000 to Leicester C for Steve Wilkinson, September 1989.

Football League Record: 1931 Elected to Division 3 (S); 1932–37 Division 3 (N); 1937–47 Division 3 (S); 1947–58 Division 3 (N); 1958–60 Division 3; 1960–63 Division 4; 1963–72 Division 3; 1972–75 Division 4; 1975–77 Division 3; 1977–78 Division 2; 1978–80 Division 3; 1980–86 Division 4; 1986–91 Division 3; 1991– Division 4.

Honours: Football League: Division 2 best season: 21st, 1977–78; Division 3 – Champions 1976–77; Division 4 – Champions 1974–75; Division 3 (N) – Runners-up 1950–51. *FA Cup:* best season: 6th rd, 1968–69. *Football League Cup:* best season: 5th rd, 1975–76. *Freight Rover Trophy:* Winners 1986–87.

Colours: Amber shirts with blue trim, blue shorts, amber stockings. **Change colours:** Green shirt, white shorts, white stockings.

MANSFIELD TOWN 1990–91 LEAGUE RECORD

Match No.	Date		Venue	Opponents	Result		H/T Score	Lg. Pos.	Goalscorers	Attendance
1	Aug	25	A	Wigan Ath	W	2-0	0-0	—	Charles, Stringfellow	2032
2	Sept	1	H	Brentford	L	0-2	0-0	12		2511
3		8	A	Leyton Orient	L	1-2	0-1	16	Leishman	3703
4		15	H	Exeter C	L	0-2	0-1	21		2355
5		18	H	Cambridge U	D	2-2	0-0	—	O'Shea (og), Christie	2450
6		22	A	Bury	L	0-1	0-1	21		2620
7		29	H	Southend U	L	0-1	0-0	23		2120
8	Oct	2	A	Bolton W	D	1-1	1-0	—	Fairclough	3631
9		6	A	Shrewsbury T	W	3-0	1-0	18	Christie, Kent, Fairclough	2587
10		13	H	Preston NE	L	0-1	0-1	19		3225
11		20	H	Bradford C	L	0-1	0-1	20		3582
12		22	A	Tranmere R	L	2-6	1-1	—	Christie, Charles	5996
13		27	A	Huddersfield T	D	2-2	1-1	23	Kent, Christie	4413
14	Nov	3	H	Crewe Alex	L	1-3	0-1	23	Kent	2701
15		10	H	Swansea C	W	2-0	0-0	23	Wilkinson 2	2200
16		24	A	Rotherham U	D	1-1	1-0	23	Charles	3729
17	Dec	1	A	Grimsby T	L	0-2	0-0	23		5350
18		15	H	Chester C	W	1-0	1-0	21	Christie	1919
19		22	H	Fulham	D	1-1	0-1	22	Wilkinson	2838
20		26	A	Bournemouth	D	0-0	0-0	21		5280
21		29	A	Reading	L	1-2	0-0	23	Fairclough	4100
22	Jan	1	H	Birmingham C	L	1-2	0-0	23	Charles	3652
23		12	A	Brentford	D	0-0	0-0	23		6064
24		19	H	Wigan Ath	D	1-1	1-0	21	Christie	2166
25		26	A	Exeter C	L	0-2	0-1	21		3432
26	Feb	1	A	Cambridge U	L	1-2	1-1	—	Gray	5094
27		5	H	Bury	L	0-1	0-1	—		1921
28		23	A	Swansea C	W	2-1	1-1	22	Christie, Wilkinson	3354
29	Mar	2	H	Grimsby T	D	1-1	0-0	22	Kent	3502
30		5	H	Stoke C	D	0-0	0-0	—		2941
31		9	A	Chester C	L	0-1	0-1	22		1157
32		12	H	Bolton W	W	4-0	0-0	—	Wilkinson, Fairclough 2, Christie	3611
33		15	A	Southend U	L	1-2	1-0	—	Wilkinson	5400
34		19	A	Preston NE	L	1-3	1-2	—	Christie	3245
35		23	H	Shrewsbury T	W	2-1	1-0	20	Wilkinson, Fairclough	2524
36		26	A	Stoke C	L	1-3	0-1	—	Smalley	9113
37		30	H	Bournemouth	D	1-1	1-1	20	Wilkinson	2663
38	Apr	1	A	Fulham	L	0-1	0-0	—		3555
39		6	H	Reading	W	2-0	1-0	20	Christie, Wilkinson	2498
40		13	A	Birmingham C	D	0-0	0-0	21		7635
41		16	H	Leyton Orient	D	3-3	2-2	—	Wilkinson, Ford, Stringfellow	2050
42		20	A	Bradford	L	0-1	0-1	22		6307
43		23	H	Rotherham U	L	1-2	1-0	—	Wilkinson	4041
44		27	H	Tranmere R	L	0-2	0-0	24		2393
45	May	4	H	Huddersfield T	D	0-0	0-0	24		2507
46		11	A	Crewe Alex	L	0-3	0-1	24		2648

Final League Position: 24

GOALSCORERS

League (42): Wilkinson 11, Christie 10, Fairclough 6, Charles 4, Kent 4, Stringfellow 2, Ford 1, Gray 1, Leishman 1, Smalley 1, own goal 1.
Rumbelows Cup (1): Charles 1.
FA Cup (3): Charles 1, Kearney 1, Wilkinson 1.

Beasley	Murray	Kearney	Clark	Foster	Smalley	Kent	Chambers	Wilkinson	Stringfellow	Charles	Hodges	Gray	Fairclough	Leishman	Christie	Chapman	Hathaway	Prindiville	Lowery	Withe	Ling	Pearcey	Spooner	Smith	Ford	Fee	Holland	Match No.
1	2	3	4	5	6	7	8	9	10	11																		1
1	2	3	4*	5	6	7	8	9	10	11	12																	2
1	2	3	4	5		7	8		10	11		6*	9	12															3
1	2	3	4	5		7	8	10*		11†14		6	12	9															4
1	2	3		5	6	7	8	9		11			10	12	4*														5
1	2	3	4	5		7	8	9	10*			11	6	12															6
1		3	4	5	6	7	2	9	10*	8			11	12															7
1	7	3	4	5	6		2			8			11		9	10													8
1	2	3	4	5	6	7	8						11		9	10													9
1	2	3	4	5	6				14	8			11†12		9	10	7*											10
1	2	3	4	5	6	7†				8			14	11*12	9	10												11
1	2*	3	4	5	6	7				8			12	11	9	10												12
1	2	3	4*	5	6	7	14			8			11†12		9	10												13
1	2	3	4	5	6	7		9†14		8*			11	12		10												14
1	2	3	4	5		7		9	10	8			6	11														15
1	2	3	4	5		7		9	10	8			6	11														16
1	2*	3	4	5		7	14	9†10		8			6	11	12													17
1	2	3	4	5		7		9		8			6	11		10												18
1	2	3	4	5		7		9		8			6	11		10												19
1	2		4	5		7		9	12	8			6	11		10*		3										20
1	2		4	5		7		9		8			6	11		10		3										21
1	2		4	5		7		9*12		8			6	11		10		3										22
1	2†		4	5			12	9*	8				6	11		10		7	14	3								23
1			4	5			12	9*	3				6	8		10		7	2	11								24
1		4†	5	6			9		3				8		10	12	14	11	2	7*								25
1			5			4	10			8			6	11*	9	12		2	3	7								26
1			5			4	12	10*	8			6			9	11		2	3	7								27
			5	3	7	2	10			8			6	11		9		4		1								28
1	14		5	3	7	2	10			8			6	11*	9†	12		4										29
1	3		5		7	2*10				8			6	11	12	9		4										30
1	3		5		7	2	10*			8			6	11	12	9		4										31
1	3		5*	6	7	2	10			8			12	11		9		4										32
1	3		5	6	7	2	10	12		8				11*		9		4										33
1	11			3	7	2	10	5*	8				6			9	12	4										34
1			5			2	10			8			6	11		9		3			4	7	8					35
1	5			3		2	10	12					6	11		9*					4	8	7					36
1						2	10	12					6	11		9*		3			4	8	7	5				37
1						2	10		12				6	11		9		3			4	7*	8	5				38
						2	10			8			6	11		9		3	1		4		7	5				39
						2	10	12		8			6*11			9		3	1		4		7	5				40
					6	2	10	11								9		3	1		4	8	7	5				41
1					6†	2*10	12		8				11			9				14	3		4		7	5		42
1			5			2	10						11			9		12			3		4	8*	7	6		43
1	14					2†10		8*					5	11		9					3		4	12	7	6		44
1	8					2*10		9	12				5	11							3		4		7	6		45
1						2	10	9	12				5	11							3		4		7	6*	8	46
42	28	20	24	34	21	27	30	36	15	36	—	28	41	1	33	6	6	4	5	21	3	4	12	6	12	10	1	
	+							+	+	+		+	+		+		+	+	+				+					
	2s							2s	3s	9s		3s	2s		3s		10s	2s			4s	2s	2s		1s			

Rumbelows Cup First Round Cardiff C (h) 1-1
(a) 0-3
FA Cup First Round Preston NE (a) 1-0
Second Round York C (h) 2-1
Third Round Sheffield W (h) 0-2

MANSFIELD TOWN

Player and Position	Ht	Wt	Birth Date	Birth Place	Source	Clubs	League App	Gls
Goalkeepers								
Andy Beasley	6 2	12 01	5 2 64	Sedgley	Apprentice	Luton T	—	—
						Mansfield T	85	—
						Gillingham (loan)	—	—
						Peterborough U (loan)	7	—
						Scarborough (loan)	4	—
Jason Pearcey	6 1	13 05	23 7 71	Leamington Spa	Trainee	Mansfield T	10	—
Defenders								
Wayne Fairclough	5 10	9 12	27 4 68	Nottingham	Apprentice	Notts Co	71	—
						Mansfield T	54	6
Greg Fee	6 1	12 00	24 6 64	Halifax		Bradford C	7	—
					Boston U	Sheffield W	26	—
						Preston NE (loan)	15	—
						Northampton T (loan)	1	—
						Leyton Orient (loan)	5	—
						Mansfield T	10	—
George Foster	5 10	11 02	26 9 56	Plymouth	Apprentice	Plymouth Arg	212	6
						Torquay U (loan)	6	3
						Exeter C (loan)	28	—
						Derby Co	30	—
						Mansfield T	339	—
Malcolm Murray	5 11	11 02	26 7 64	Buckie	Buckie T	Hearts	27	—
						Hull C	11	—
						Mansfield T	58	—
Steve Prindiville*	5 9	11 04	26 12 68	Harlow	Apprentice	Leicester C	1	—
						Chesterfield	43	1
						Mansfield T	28	—
Mark Smalley*	5 11	11 06	2 1 65	Newark	Apprentice	Nottingham F	3	—
						Birmingham C (loan)	7	—
						Bristol R (loan)	10	—
						Leyton Orient	64	4
						Mansfield T	49	2
Chris Withe	5 10	11 03	25 9 62	Liverpool	Apprentice	Newcastle U	2	—
						Bradford C	143	2
						Notts Co	80	3
						Bury	31	1
						Chester C (loan)	2	—
						Mansfield T (loan)	11	—
						Mansfield T	10	—
Midfield								
Steve Chambers	5 10	10 10	20 7 68	Worksop	Apprentice	Sheffield W	—	—
						Mansfield T	57	—
Steve Charles	5 9	10 07	10 5 60	Sheffield	Sheffield Univ	Sheffield U	123	10
						Wrexham	113	37
						Mansfield T	174	30
Martin Clark	5 9	10 11	13 10 68	Uddington	Hamilton A	Clyde	51	2
						Nottingham F	—	—
						Falkirk (loan)	3	1
						Mansfield T (loan)	14	1
						Mansfield T	24	—
Gary Ford	5 8	11 10	8 2 61	York	Apprentice	York C	366	52
						Leicester C	16	2
						Port Vale	75	12
						Walsall (loan)	13	2
						Mansfield T	12	1
Kevin Gray	6 0	13 00	7 1 72	Sheffield	Trainee	Mansfield T	48	1
Paul Holland			8 7 73	Lincoln	School	Mansfield T	1	—
David Hunt*	5 11	13 09	17 4 59	Leicester	Apprentice	Derby Co	5	—
						Notts Co	336	28
						Aston Villa	13	—
						Mansfield T	22	—
Tony Lowery*	5 9	11 01	6 7 61	Wallsend	Ashington	WBA	1	—
						Walsall (loan)	6	1
						Mansfield T	252	19
						Walsall (loan)	6	—
Jason Milner‡			6 5 72	Worksop	Trainee	Mansfield T	—	—

MANSFIELD TOWN

Foundation: Many records give the date of Mansfield Town's formation as 1905. But the present club did not come into being until 1910 when the Mansfield Wesleyans (formed 1891) and playing in the Notts and District League, decided to spread their wings and changed their name to Mansfield Town, joining the new Central Alliance in 1911.

First Football League game: 29 August, 1931, Division 3(S), v Swindon T (h) W 3-2 – Wilson; Clifford, England; Wake, Davis, Blackburn; Gilhespy, Readman (1), Johnson, Broom (2), Baxter.

Did you know: Town's initial victory over a First Division side was against West Ham United, 26 February 1969, when they won 3-0 in an FA Cup 5th round tie at Field Mill. The visitors included such stars as Bobby Moore, Martin Peters, Geoff Hurst and Trevor Brooking.

Managers (and Secretary-managers)
John Baynes 1922–25, Ted Davison 1926–28, Jack Hickling 1928–33, Henry Martin 1933–35, Charlie Bell 1935, Harold Wightman 1936, Harold Parkes 1936–38, Jack Poole 1938–44, Lloyd Barke 1944–45, Roy Goodall 1945–49, Freddie Steele 1949–51, George Jobey 1952–53, Stan Mercer 1953–55, Charlie Mitten 1956–58, Sam Weaver 1958–60, Raich Carter 1960–63, Tommy Cummings 1963–67, Tommy Eggleston 1967–70, Jock Basford 1970–71, Danny Williams 1971–74, Dave Smith 1974–76, Peter Morris 1976–78, Billy Bingham 1978–79, Mick Jones 1979–81, Stuart Boam 1981–83, Ian Greaves 1983–89, George Foster February 1989– .

Player and Position	Ht	Wt	Birth Date	Birth Place	Source	Clubs	League App	League Gls
Steve Spooner	5 10	12 00	25 1 61	Sutton	Apprentice	Derby Co	8	—
						Halifax T	72	13
						Chesterfield	93	14
						Hereford U	84	19
						York C	72	11
						Rotherham U	19	1
						Mansfield T	12	—
Forwards								
Keith Cassells‡	5 10	11 12	10 7 57	London	Wembley T	Watford	12	—
						Peterborough U (loan)	8	—
						Oxford U	45	13
						Southampton	19	4
						Brentford	86	28
						Mansfield T	163	52
Gary Castledine			27 3 70	Dumfries		Mansfield T	—	—
Trevor Christie*	6 2	12 00	28 2 59	Newcastle	Apprentice	Leicester C	31	8
						Notts Co	187	64
						Nottingham F	14	5
						Derby Co	65	22
						Manchester C	9	3
						Walsall	99	22
						Mansfield T	92	24
Wayne Davidson	5 9	11 00	7 12 68	Wallsend		Mansfield T	—	—
Graham Leishman‡	5 9	10 07	6 4 68	Manchester	Irlam T	Mansfield T	27	3
Ian Stringfellow	5 9	10 02	8 5 69	Nottingham	Apprentice	Mansfield T	106	18
Steve Wilkinson	6 0	10 12	1 9 68	Lincoln	Apprentice	Leicester C	9	1
						Rochdale (loan)	—	—
						Crewe Alex (loan)	5	2
						Mansfield T	76	26

Trainees
Hall, Geoffrey; Jones, Adam; Jordan, Jonathon P; Morgan, Peter C; Mowbray, Graham S; Parkins, Christopher J; Perkins, Christopher P; Shaw, Paul; Tucker, Mark C; Wilson, Kevin.

Associated Schoolboys
Holland, Paul; Marrows, Dean; Morgan, James K; Stark, Wayne R.

Associated Schoolboys who have accepted the club's offer of a Traineeship/Contract
Cann, Scott A; Crookes, Dominic D; Doughty, Stephen J; Foster, Stephen; Johnson, Carl; Langton, Mark D; Smith, Dean R; Timmons, Christopher B; Ward, Darren.

334

MIDDLESBROUGH 1990-91 *Back row (left to right):* Jimmy Phillips, Trevor Putney, Stephen Pears, Kevin Poole, John Wark, Martin Russell
Centre row: David Nish (First Team Coach), Nicky Mohan, Simon Coleman, Ian Baird, Gary Parkinson, Tony Mowbray, Colin Cooper, Owen McGee, Colin Todd (Manager).
Front row: Alan Kernaghan, Paul Kerr, John Hendrie, Robbie Mustoe, Stuart Ripley, Bernie Slaven, Mark Proctor, Gary Hamilton, Mark Burke.

Division 2   MIDDLESBROUGH

Ayresome Park, Middlesbrough, Cleveland TS1 4PB. Telephone Middlesbrough (0642) 819659/815996. Commercial Dept. (0642) 826664. Clubcall: 0898 121181. Fax: 0642 820244.

Ground capacity; 26,500.

Record attendance: 53,596 v Newcastle U, Division 1, 27 December 1979.

Record receipts: £102,530 v Notts Co, Division 2, semi-final play-off 1st leg, 19 May 1991.

Pitch measurements: 114yd × 73yd.

Chairman: M. C. Henderson.

Directors: G. Fordy, S. Gibson, R. Corbidge.

Chief Executive/Secretary: Keith Lamb.

*Manager:*Lennie Lawrence. *Coach:*

Physio: Tommy Johnson.

Youth Development Officer: Ron Bone. *Marketing Manager:* Mitch Hatfield. *Press & PRO:* Clive Armitage.

Year Formed: 1876. *Turned Professional:* 1889; became amateur 1892, and professional again, 1899. *Ltd Co:* 1892.

Club Nickname: 'The Boro'.

Previous Grounds: 1877, Old Archery Ground, Linhorpe Road; 1903, Ayresome Park.

Record League Victory: 9-0 v Brighton & HA, Division 2, 23 August 1958 – Taylor; Bilcliff, Robinson; Harris (2 pens), Phillips, Walley; Day, McLean, Clough (5), Peacock (2), Holliday.

Record Cup Victory: 9-3 v Goole T, FA Cup, 1st rd, 9 January 1915 – Williamson; Haworth, Weir; Davidson, Cook, Malcolm; Wilson, Carr (3), Elliott (3), Tinsley (3), Davies.

Record Defeat: 0-9 v Blackburn R, Division 2, 6 November 1954.

Most League Points (2 for a win): 65, Division 2, 1973–74.

Most League Points (3 for a win): 94, Division 3, 1986–87.

Most League Goals: 122, Division 2, 1926–27.

Highest League Scorer in Season: George Camsell, 59, Division 2, 1926–27 (Second Division record).

Most League Goals in Total Aggregate: George Camsell, 326, 1925–39.

Most Capped Player: Wilf Mannion, 26, England.

Most League Appearances: Tim Williamson, 563, 1902–23.

Record Transfer Fee Received: £2,300,000 from Manchester United for Gary Pallister, August 1989.

Record Transfer Fee Paid: £700,000 to Manchester U for Peter Davenport, November 1988.

Football League Record: 1899 Elected to Division 2; 1902–24 Division 1; 1924–27 Division 2; 1927–28 Division 1; 1928–29 Division 2; 1929–54 Division 1; 1954–66 Division 2; 1966–67 Division 3; 1967–74 Division 2; 1974–82 Division 1; 1982–86 Division 2; 1986–87 Division 3; 1987–88 Division 2; 1988–89 Division 1; 1989– Division 2.

Honours: Football League: Division 1 best season : 3rd, 1913–14. Division 2 – Champions 1926–27, 1928–29, 1973–74; Runners-up 1901–02. Division 3 – Runners-up 1966–67, 1986–87. *FA Cup:* best season: 6th rd, 1935–36, 1946–47, 1969–70, 1974–75, 1976–77, 1977–78; old last eight 1900–01, 1903–04. *Football League Cup:* Semi-final 1975–76. *Amateur Cup:* Winners 1895, 1898, *Anglo-Scottish Cup:* Winners 1975–76.

Colours: Red shirts, white shorts, red stockings. **Change colours:** All sky blue.

MIDDLESBROUGH 1990–91 LEAGUE RECORD

Match No.	Date		Venue	Opponents	Result	H/T Score	Lg. Pos.	Goalscorers	Attendance
1	Aug	25	H	West Ham U	D 0-0	0-0	—		20,680
2	Sept	1	A	Plymouth Arg	D 1-1	1-0	17	Slaven	6266
3		8	H	Notts Co	W 1-0	0-0	11	Wark	17,380
4		15	H	Swindon T	W 3-1	0-1	7	Slaven 2, Mustoe	9127
5		17	A	Port Vale	L 1-3	1-0	—	Russell	7880
6		22	H	Oldham Ath	L 0-1	0-0	15		19,363
7		29	H	Leicester C	W 6-0	4-0	9	Phillips, Hendrie, Kerr 2, Slaven, Baird	16,174
8	Oct	3	A	Newcastle U	D 0-0	0-0	—		17,023
9		6	A	Watford	W 3-0	2-0	8	Mowbray, Baird 2	8057
10		13	H	Millwall	W 2-1	0-0	6	Rae (og), Hendrie	20,277
11		20	H	Bristol R	L 1-2	1-0	7	Kerr	18,589
12		23	A	Wolverhampton W	L 0-1	0-0	—		17,285
13		27	A	Brighton & HA	W 4-2	3-2	7	Slaven 3, Baird	7532
14	Nov	3	H	Barnsley	W 1-0	1-0	5	Kerr	18,470
15		6	A	WBA	W 1-0	0-0	—	Slaven	10,521
16		10	H	Charlton Ath	L 1-2	0-1	4	Baird	17,998
17		17	A	Portsmouth	W 3-0	1-0	4	Slaven, Baird, Stevens (og)	8433
18		24	A	Oxford U	W 5-2	2-2	4	Baird 3 (2 pens), Slaven, Mustoe	5262
19	Dec	1	H	Hull C	W 3-0	0-0	3	Baird, Slaven, Kerr	17,024
20		15	A	West Ham U	D 0-0	0-0	4		23,705
21		22	A	Blackburn R	L 0-1	0-1	4		17,206
22		26	A	Ipswich T	W 1-0	0-0	3	Baird	12,508
23		29	A	Bristol C	L 0-3	0-1	4		14,023
24	Jan	1	H	Sheffield W	L 0-2	0-1	5		22,869
25		12	H	Plymouth Arg	D 0-0	0-0	5		14,198
26		19	A	Notts Co	L 2-3	2-2	5	Baird, Ripley	9316
27	Feb	2	H	Swindon T	W 2-0	2-0	5	Mustoe, Slaven	14,588
28		19	H	WBA	W 3-2	0-0	—	Slaven, Mustoe, Rees (og)	15,334
29		23	A	Charlton Ath	W 1-0	1-0	4	Slaven	5510
30		26	H	Portsmouth	L 1-2	0-1	—	Parkinson (pen)	15,922
31	Mar	2	A	Hull C	D 0-0	0-0	4		6828
32		9	H	Oxford U	D 0-0	0-0	4		14,029
33		12	H	Newcastle U	W 3-0	2-0	—	Slaven 2, Walsh	18,250
34		16	A	Leicester C	L 3-4	2-0	4	Putney, Phillips, McGee	8324
35		20	A	Millwall	D 2-2	0-2	—	Kerr, Mowbray	10,371
36		23	H	Watford	L 1-2	0-0	5	Baird	14,583
37		30	H	Ipswich T	D 1-1	0-1	6	Mowbray	15,140
38	Apr	1	A	Blackburn R	L 0-1	0-0	6		8925
39		6	H	Bristol C	W 2-1	1-1	5	Ripley 2	13,846
40		9	H	Port Vale	W 4-0	1-0	—	Baird, Ripley, Russell, Wark	15,053
41		13	A	Sheffield W	L 0-2	0-0	6		30,598
42		20	A	Bristol R	L 0-2	0-1	7		5722
43		27	H	Wolverhampton W	W 2-0	1-0	7	Ripley, Hendrie	16,447
44	May	4	H	Brighton & HA	W 2-0	0-0	6	Coleman, Ripley	18,054
45		7	A	Oldham Ath	L 0-2	0-2	—		14,213
46		11	A	Barnsley	L 0-1	0-0	7		14,494

Final League Position: 7

GOALSCORERS

League (66): Slaven 16, Baird 14 (2 pens), Kerr 6, Ripley 6, Mustoe 4, Hendrie 3, Mowbray 3, Phillips 2, Russell 2, Wark 2, Coleman 1, McGee 1, Parkinson 1 (pen), Putney 1, Walsh 1, own goals 3.
Rumbelows Cup (9): Mustoe 3, Slaven 3, Hendrie 1, Kerr 1, Mowbray 1.
FA Cup (2): Baird 1, Kerr 1.

Pears	Cooper	Phillips	Mowbray	Kernaghan	Wark	Slaven	Mustoe	Baird	Proctor	Hendrie	Ripley	Russell	Kerr	McGee	Putney	Coleman	Parkinson	Walsh	Dibble	Arnold	Pollock	Match No.
1	2	3	4	5	6	7	8	9	10	11												1
1	2	3	4	5	6	7	8			11	9	10										2
1	2	3	4	5	6	7*	8	12		11	9	10										3
1	2	3	4	5	6	7	8	12		11	9	10*										4
1	2	3	4	5	6	7*	8	12		11	9	10										5
1	2	3	4	5	6	7	8	9		11	12	10*										6
1	2	3	4	5†	6	12	8	9		11	7*	10	14									7
1	2	3	4	5	6	7	8	9		11		10										8
1	2	3	4	5	6	7	8	9		11		10										9
1	2	3	4	5	6	7	8	9		11		10										10
1	2	3	4	5	6*	7	8	9		11		10	12									11
1	2	3	4	5		7	8	9		11	6*	10	12									12
1	2	3	4	5	6	7	8	9		11†14	10*		12									13
1	2	3	4	5		7	8	9*		11	12	10	6									14
1	2	3	4	5†		7	8	9		11	12	10	6*14									15
1	2	3	4	5		7*	8	9		11	12	10	6									16
1	2	3	4	5	6	7	8*	9	14	11†12	10											17
1	2	3	4	5†	6	7	8	9	14	11	12	10*										18
1	2	3	4		6†	7	8	9*14	11	12	10				5							19
1	2		4		6	7	8	9		11*12	10	3			5							20
1	2	3	4		6	7	8	9		11	12	10*			5							21
1	2	3	4		8	7		9	6	11	12	10*			5							22
1	2	3	4		7	8		9	6	11		10			5							23
1	2	3	4		8	7		9	6*	11	12	10			5							24
1	2†	3	4		7	8*	9		11	12	10	14		6	5							25
1		3	4		8	12		9		7	11*		10†		6	5	2	14				26
1		3	4		8	7	10	9		11*12		6			2	5			1			27
		3	4		8	7	10	9		11		6			2	5			1			28
		3	4		8	7	10†9	14	11*12			6			2	5			1			29
		3	4		8	7	10	9		11*12		6			2	5			1			30
		3	4		8	7	10	9		11*12		6			2	5			1			31
	3		4		8	7	10	9		11	12	2	6*		5				1			32
	3		4		8†7	10	9		11	12	2	6		5*	1	14						33
	3		4		8	7	10*	9		11	12	2	6		5			1				34
	3		4		8	7	10	9		11	12	2	6		5*	1						35
	3		4		8†7	10	9		11*	5	2	6		14	1	12						36
	2	3	4		7	10	9	14	12	11	6†	5	8*	1								37
	2	3	4		7	10	9	8	6	11	5			1								38
	3		4		7*10	9	8	6	11	5	2	12	1									39
	3	4	14	12	10†	9	8	6*11	7	5	2	1										40
	3	4		12	10	9	8	6*11	7	5	2	1										41
	3	14	4	12	10†	9	8	6	11	7*	5	2	1									42
	2	3	4		7	12	8	9	11	6*	10†	5		1		14						43
	2	3	4*	7	12	9	8	10†11	14	6	5	1										44
	2	3	4	7		9	8	10	11	6	5	1										45
	2	3	4	7		9	8	10	11	6	5	1										46
27	32	44	40	23	31	41	39	41	13	40	22	10	20	6	20	18	10	10	19	—	—	

Substitute appearances:

+ + + + + + + + + + + +   +   + +
1s 1s 5s 2s 3s 5s 1s 17s 1s 4s 2s 3s 1s   3s   2s 1s

Rumbelows Cup	First Round	Tranmere R (h)	1-1
		(a)	2-1
	Second Round	Newcastle U (h)	2-0
		(a)	0-1
	Third Round	Norwich C (h)	2-0
	Fourth Round	Aston Villa (a)	2-3
FA Cup	Third Round	Plymouth Arg (h)	0-0
		(a)	2-1
	Fourth Round	Cambridge U (a)	0-2

MIDDLESBROUGH

Player and Position	Ht	Wt	Birth Date	Birth Place	Source	Clubs	League App	Gls
Goalkeepers								
Stephen Pears	6 0	12 11	22 1 62	Brandon	Apprentice	Manchester U	4	—
						Middlesbrough (loan)	12	—
						Middlesbrough	205	—
Kevin Poole	5 10	11 10	21 7 63	Bromsgrove	Apprentice	Aston Villa	28	—
						Northampton T (loan)	3	—
						Middlesbrough	34	—
						Hartlepool U (loan)	12	—
Defenders								
Simon Coleman	6 0	10 08	13 3 68	Worksop		Mansfield T	96	7
						Middlesbrough	55	2
Colin Cooper	5 10	10 00	28 2 67	Durham		Middlesbrough	188	6
Lee Crosby			23 1 72	Hartlepool	Trainee	Middlesbrough	—	—
Owen McGee	5 7	10 07	20 4 70	Teesside	Trainee	Middlesbrough	21	1
Nicky Mohan	6 2	12 00	6 10 70	Middlesbrough	Trainee	Middlesbrough	28	—
Tony Mowbray	6 1	12 02	22 11 63	Saltburn	Apprentice	Middlesbrough	331	25
Gary Parkinson	5 10	11 11	10 1 68	Middlesbrough	Amateur	Everton		
						Middlesbrough	171	5
Jim Phillips	6 0	12 07	8 2 66	Bolton	Apprentice	Bolton W	108	2
						Rangers	25	—
						Oxford U	79	8
						Middlesbrough	56	2
Mark Sunley‡			13 10 71	Stockton		Middlesbrough	—	—
Midfield								
Gary Hamilton	5 8	11 02	27 12 65	Glasgow	Apprentice	Middlesbrough	229	25
Dan Holmes			13 6 72	Clophill	Trainee	Middlesbrough	—	—
Robert Lake			13 10 71	Stockton	Trainee	Middlesbrough	—	—
Robbie Mustoe	5 10	10 08	28 8 68	Oxford		Oxford U	91	10
						Middlesbrough	41	4
Jamie Pollock§			16 2 74	Stockton	Trainee	Middlesbrough	1	—
Mark Proctor	5 10	12 08	30 1 61	Middlesbrough	Apprentice	Middlesbrough	109	12
						Nottingham F	64	5
						Sunderland (loan)	5	—
						Sunderland	112	19
						Sheffield W	59	4
						Middlesbrough	73	4
Trevor Putney	5 7	10 11	11 2 61	Harold Hill	Brentwood W	Ipswich T	103	8
						Norwich C	82	9
						Middlesbrough	48	1
Martin Russell	5 9	10 05	27 4 67	Dublin	Apprentice	Manchester U	—	—
						Birmingham C (loan)	5	—
						Leicester C	20	—
						Norwich C (loan)	—	—
						Scarborough	51	9
						Middlesbrough	11	2
John Wark	5 10	11 07	4 8 57	Glasgow	Apprentice	Ipswich T	296	94
						Liverpool	70	28
						Ipswich T	89	23
						Middlesbrough	32	2
Forwards								
Dale Anderson‡	6 0	10 07	23 8 70	Darlington	Trainee	Darlington	15	—
						Middlebrough	—	—
Ian Arnold			4 7 72	Durham City	Trainee	Middlesbrough	2	—
Ian Baird	6 0	12 09	1 4 64	Southampton	Apprentice	Southampton	17	3
						Cardiff C (loan)	12	6
						Southampton	5	2
						Newcastle U (loan)	5	1
						Leeds U	85	33
						Portsmouth	20	1
						Leeds U	77	17
						Middlesbrough	63	19

MIDDLESBROUGH

Foundation: The story of how the idea of a Middlesbrough football club was first mooted at a tripe supper at the Corporation Hotel in 1875 is well known locally. But the club was formally established at a meeting in the Talbot Hotel the following year and is one of the oldest clubs in the North East.

First Football League game: 2 September, 1899, Division 2, v Lincoln C (a) L 0-3 – Smith; Shaw, Ramsey; Allport, McNally, McCracken; Wanless, Longstaffe, Gettins, Page, Pugh.

Did you know: George Camsell was this club's top scorer in no less than 10 successive seasons 1926–36. His best goalscoring run was 29 goals in 12 consecutive League games in his record-breaking 1926–27 season.

Managers (and Secretary-managers)
John Robson 1899–1905, Alex Massie 1905–06, Andy Aitken 1906–09, J. Gunter 1908–10*, Andy Walker 1910–11, Tom McIntosh 1911–19, James Howie 1920–23, Herbert Bamlett 1923–26, Peter McWilliam 1927–34, Wilf Gillow 1934–44, David Jack 1944–52, Walter Rowley 1952–54, Bob Dennison 1954–63, Raich Carter 1963–66, Stan Anderson 1966–73, Jack Charlton 1973–77, John Neal 1977–81, Bobby Murdoch 1981–82, Malcolm Allison 1982–84, Willie Maddren 1984–86, Bruce Rioch 1986–90, Colin Todd 1990–91, Lennie Lawrence July 1991– .

Player and Position	Ht	Wt	Birth Date	Birth Place	Source	Clubs	League App	Gls
Alan Comfort‡	5 7	11 02	8 12 64	Aldershot	Apprentice	QPR	—	—
						Cambridge U	63	5
						Leyton Orient	150	47
						Middlesbrough	15	2
Paul Hanford			4 1 72	Middlesbrough	Trainee	Middlesbrough	—	—
John Hendrie	5 7	11 04	24 10 63	Lennoxtown	Apprentice	Coventry C	21	2
						Hereford U (loan)	6	—
						Bradford C	173	46
						Newcastle U	34	4
						Leeds U	27	5
						Middlesbrough	41	3
Alan Kernaghan	6 2	12 12	25 4 67	Otley	Apprentice	Middlesbrough	146	11
						Charlton Ath (loan)	13	—
Stuart Ripley	5 11	12 06	20 11 67	Middlesbrough	Apprentice	Middlesbrough	210	23
						Bolton W (loan)	5	1
Lee Roxby‡			18 10 71	Stockton	Trainee	Middlesbrough	—	—
Bernie Slaven	5 11	10 10	13 11 60	Paisley		Morton	22	1
						Airdrie	2	—
						Q of the S	2	—
						Albion R	42	27
						Middlesbrough	251	98
Lee Tucker*			14 9 71	Middlesbrough	Trainee	Middlesbrough	—	—

Trainees
Colhoun, Trevor A; Collett, Andrew A; Devine, Michael; Ferguson, Mark; Green, Scott; Keavney, David G; Lauderdale, Neil C; Livingstone, Steven J; McDowell, Roddy; Martin, Steven; Martin, Steven; Melling, Paul; Napier, Stephen; Peverell, Nicholas J; Pollock, Jamie; Templeman, Richard J; Waller, Michael A; White, Neil; Young, Michael S.

Associated Schoolboys
Devers, Peter; Dixon, Steven K; Dwyer, Paul J; Gate, Paul; Hood, James W; Johnson, Ian; McGargle, Stephen; Maughan, Neil G; Norton, Paul; Ripley, Andrew I; Sumberbell, Mark.

Associated Schoolboys who have accepted the club's offer of a Traineeship/Contract
Barron, Michael J; Illman, Neil D; Lee, Anthony S; Maddick, Kevin A; Roberts, Ben J; Taylor, Mark S; Todd, Andrew.

MILLWALL 1990-91 *Back row (left to right):* Malcolm Allen, Darren Treacy, Phil Babb, Teddy Sheringham, Stephen Torpey, David Thompson, Mick McCarthy, Keith Stevens, Manus Magill, Steve Wood, Ken Cunningham.
Centre row: Steve Harrison (Youth Team Coach), Peter Melville (Physiotherapist), John McGlashan, Paul Stephenson, Alan McLeary, Brian Horne, Pete* Hucker, Keith Branagan, Paul Goddard, Terry Hurlock, Wesley Reid, Tom Walley (Youth Team Coach), Ian Evans (Reserve Team Coach).
Front row: Darren Thompson, Gary Waddock, Jimmy Carter, Sean Sparham, Ian Dawes, Bruce Rioch (Manager), Ian McNeill (Assistant Manager), Les Briley, Darren Morgan, Kevin O'Callaghan, Alan Dowson, Nicky Coleman, Alex Rae, Ansell Henry.

Division 2   MILLWALL

The Den, Cold Blow Lane, London SE14 5RH. Telephone 071-639 3143, Commercial Dept: 071-639 4590. Credit Card Bookings 071-277 6877.

Ground capacity: 19,222.

Record Attendance: 48,672 v Derby Co, FA Cup 5th rd, 20 February 1937.

Record Receipts: £106,839 v West Ham U, Division 2, 10 November 1990.

Pitch measurements: 112yd × 74yd.

President: Lord Mellish.

Chairman: R. I. Burr. *Vice-chairman:* P. W. Mead. *Directors:* J. D. Burnige, B. E. Mitchell, P. M. Mead, D. Sullivan.

Chief Executive Secretary: G. I. S. Hortop.

Manager: Bruce Rioch. *Assistant Manager:* Ian McNeill.

Coach: Steve Harrison.

Commercial Manager: W. W. Neil.

Physio: Peter Melville. *Chief Scout:* Allen Batsford.

Year Formed: 1885. *Turned Professional:* 1893. *Ltd Co.:* 1894.

Previous Names: 1885, Millwall Rovers; 1889, Millwall Athletic.

Club Nickname: 'The Lions'.

Previous Grounds: 1885, Glengall Road, Millwall; 1886, Back of 'Lord Nelson'; 1890, East Ferry Road; 1901, North Greenwich; 1910, The Den.

Record League Victory: 9-1 v Torquay U, Division 3 (S), 29 August 1927 – Lansdale; Tilling, Hill; Amos, Bryant (3), Graham; Chance, Hawkins (3), Landells (1), Phillips (2), Black. 9-1 v Coventry C, Division 3 (S), 19 November 1927 – Lansdale; Fort, Hill; Amos, Collins (1), Graham; Chance, Landells (4), Cock (2), Phillips (2), Black.

Record Cup Victory: 7-0 v Gateshead, FA Cup, 2nd rd, 12 December 1936 – Yuill; Ted Smith, Inns; Brolly, Hancock, Forsyth; Thomas (1), Mangnall (1), Ken Burditt (2), McCartney (2), Thorogood (1).

Record Defeat: 1-9 v Aston Villa, FA Cup 4th rd, 28 January 1946.

Most League Points (2 for a win): 65, Division 3 (S), 1927–28 and Division 3, 1965–66.

Most League Points (3 for a win): 90, Division 3, 1984–85.

Most League Goals: 127, Division 3 (S), 1927–28.

Highest League Scorer in Season: Richard Parker, 37, Division 3 (S), 1926–27.

Most League Goals in Total Aggregate: Teddy Sheringham, 93, 1984–91.

Most Capped Player: Eamonn Dunphy, 22 (23), Eire.

Most League Appearances: Barry Kitchener, 523, 1967–82.

Record Transfer Fee Received: £1,500,000 from Aston Villa for Tony Cascarino, March 1990.

Record Transfer Fee Paid: £800,000 to Derby Co for Paul Goddard, December 1989.

Football League Record: 1920 Original Members of Division 3; 1921 Division 3 (S); 1928–34 Division 2; 1934–38 Division 3 (S); 1938–48 Division 2; 1948–58 Division 3 (S); 1958–62 Division 4; 1962–64 Division 3; 1964–65 Division 4; 1965–66 Division 3; 1966–75 Division 2; 1975–76 Division 3; 1976–79 Division 2; 1979–85 Division 3; 1985–88 Division 2; 1988–90 Division 1; 1990– Division 2.

Honours: Football League: Division 2 – Champions 1987–88; Division 3 (S) – Champions 1927–28, 1937–38; Runners-up 1952–53; Division 3 – Runners–up 1965–66, 1984–85; Division 4 – Champions 1961–62; Runners-up 1964–65. *FA Cup:* Semi-final 1900, 1903, 1937 (first Division 3 side to reach semi-final). *Football League Cup:* best season: 5th rd, 1973–74, 1976–77. *Football League Trophy:* Winners 1982–83.

Colours: Blue shirts, white shorts, blue stockings. **Change colours:** Yellow shirts, black shorts, black stockings.

MILLWALL 1990–91 LEAGUE RECORD

Match No.	Date		Venue	Opponents	Result	H/T Score	Lg. Pos.	Goalscorers	Attendance
1	Aug	25	A	Watford	W 2-1	1-0	—	Allen 2	11,541
2	Sept	1	H	Barnsley	W 4-1	2-0	3	Allen, Rae, Carter, Sheringham	10,114
3		8	A	Newcastle U	W 2-1	1-0	3	Allen, Sheringham	23,922
4		15	H	Ipswich T	D 1-1	1-1	3	Rae	12,604
5		19	H	Hull C	D 3-3	1-2		Sheringham, Carter, Waddock	9446
6		22	A	Charlton Ath	D 0-0	0-0	5		11,735
7		30	A	Swindon T	D 0-0	0-0	—		11,667
8	Oct	3	H	Portsmouth	W 2-0	0-0	—	Rae, Sheringham	10,393
9		6	H	WBA	W 4-1	2-0	4	Sheringham 3, Rae	10,718
10		13	A	Middlesbrough	L 1-2	0-0	4	Rae	20,277
11		20	A	Notts Co	W 1-0	1-0	4	O'Callaghan	7599
12		24	H	Bristol C	L 1-2	1-0	—	Waddock	10,335
13		27	H	Sheffield W	W 4-2	0-2	4	Carter, Sheringham, Allen, Rae	12,863
14	Nov	3	A	Blackburn R	L 0-1	0-0	4		7336
15		7	H	Oxford U	L 1-2	1-0	—	Allen	7681
16		10	H	West Ham U	D 1-1	0-0	6	Stephenson	20,591
17		17	A	Plymouth Arg	L 2-3	0-2	6	Sheringham, Rae	6542
18		24	A	Brighton & HA	D 0-0	0-0	6		9638
19	Dec	1	H	Bristol R	D 1-1	0-0	6	Sheringham	9291
20		15	H	Watford	L 0-2	0-2	7		8910
21		22	A	Wolverhampton W	L 1-4	1-2	9	Sheringham	14,504
22		26	H	Leicester C	W 2-1	1-0	7	Sheringham 2 (1 pen)	6686
23		29	H	Oldham Ath	D 0-0	0-0	9		10,010
24	Jan	1	A	Port Vale	W 2-0	2-0	8	Sheringham, Goodman	8418
25		12	A	Barnsley	W 2-1	2-1	6	Sheringham (pen), Rae	7857
26		19	H	Newcastle U	L 0-1	0-1	7		11,478
27	Feb	2	A	Ipswich T	W 3-0	2-0	7	Sheringham, Goodman, Rae	13,338
28		16	H	Plymouth Arg	W 4-1	1-1	6	Sheringham 4	8388
29		24	A	West Ham U	L 1-3	1-1	—	Goodman	20,503
30		27	A	Oxford U	D 0-0	0-0	—		4570
31	Mar	2	A	Bristol R	L 0-1	0-0	7		5587
32		9	H	Brighton & HA	W 3-0	2-0	6	Goodman, Briley, Sheringham	9824
33		12	A	Portsmouth	D 0-0	0-0	—		7826
34		16	H	Swindon T	W 1-0	0-0	6	O'Callaghan	8894
35		20	H	Middlesbrough	D 2-2	2-0	—	Thompson, Goodman	10,371
36		23	A	WBA	W 1-0	0-0	6	Sheringham	9116
37		30	A	Leicester C	W 2-1	0-0	5	Sheringham 2	10,783
38	Apr	3	H	Wolverhampton W	W 2-1	1-1	—	Stevens, Sheringham	13,780
39		6	A	Oldham Ath	D 1-1	1-0	4	Allen	13,434
40		10	H	Charlton Ath	W 3-1	1-0	—	Sheringham 3	15,241
41		13	H	Port Vale	L 1-2	1-1	4	Thompson	10,860
42		16	A	Hull C	D 1-1	0-1	—	Kerr	4102
43		20	H	Notts Co	L 1-2	0-1	4	Kerr	10,162
44		27	A	Bristol C	W 4-1	0-1	5	Sheringham 3, Thompson	16,741
45	May	4	A	Sheffield W	L 1-2	0-1	5	Sheringham	30,278
46		11	H	Blackburn R	W 2-1	1-1	5	Sheringham (pen), Rae	11,318

Final League Position: 5

GOALSCORERS

League (70): Sheringham 33 (3 pens), Rae 10, Allen 7, Goodman 5, Carter 3, Thompson 3, Kerr 2, O'Callaghan 2, Waddock 2, Briley 1, Stephenson 1, Stevens 1.
Rumbelows Cup (2): Sheringham 2.
FA Cup (6): Rae 2, Sheringham 2, Stephenson 2.

Branagan	Stevens	Dawes	Morgan	Wood	McLeary	Carter	Allen	Sheringham	Rae	Briley	Waddock	Horne	Stephenson	Cunningham	McGlashan	O'Callaghan	McCarthy	Goddard	Dowson	Goodman	Thompson	Fillery	Kerr	McGinlay	Match No.
1	2	3	4	5	6	7	8	9	10*	11	12														1
	2	3	4	5	6	7	8	9	10	11		1													2
	2	3	4	5	6	7	8	9	10*	11	12	1													3
	2	3	4	5	6	7	8	9	10	11		1													4
	2	3	4	5	6	7	8	9			10	1	11												5
	2		4*	5	6	7	8	9			10	1	11		3	12									6
	2	3	4	5	6	7	8	9	10*		11	1	12												7
	2	3		5	6	7	8*	9	10		4	1	12	11											8
		3		5	6	7	8	9	10		4	1			2	11									9
	2	3		5	6	7	8*	9	10		4	1	12	11											10
	2			5	6	7		9	10		8	1			3	11	4								11
	2			5	6	7	12	9	10*		8	1			3	11	4								12
1	2	3		5	6	7	8	9	10		4					11									13
1	2	3	12	5	6	7	8†	9	10		4					11*	14								14
1	2	3		5	6	7	8	9†	10		4*			12		11	14								15
	2	3		5	6	7	8*	9	10		4	1				11		12							16
	2	3		5	6	7		9	10		4	1		11						8					17
	2				6	7		9	10	11	4	1				3	5			8					18
	2			12	6	7		9	10	11	4	1				3	5*			8					19
	2			5	6	7*		9			4	1	12	10	11					8	3				20
	2	3		5	6	12	8	9	10	11	4	1	7*												21
	2	3		5	6	7	8*	9	10	11	4	1						12							22
	2	3		5	6	7	8*	9	10	11	4	1						12							23
	2	3		5	6			9	10	11	4	1								8					24
	2	3		5	6			9	10	11	4	1	7*	12						8					25
	2	3		5	6			9	10	11*	4	1	7†	14		12				8					26
		3			6			9	10		4	1	7		2	11				8	5				27
1		3			6			9	10		4		7		2	11				8	5				28
		3			6	12		9	10		4*	1	7		2	11				8	5				29
1	2	3			6			9	10	11	4		7				5			8					30
1	2	3			6*			9	10†	11	4		7	14			5			8	12				31
1	2	3			6			9	10	11	4		7	12			5*			8					32
1	2	3			6			9	10	11	4		7				5			8					33
1	2	3			6			9	10	11*			7				5	12		8	4				34
1	2	3			6			9	10	11*			7				5	12		8	4				35
1	2	3			6			9	10				7				5	12		8	4	11*			36
1	2	3			6			9	10†				7	14			5	12		8*	4		11		37
1	2	3*			6			9		10			7				5	12		8	4		11		38
1	2	3			6*	8†		9		10			7				5	12		14	4		11		39
1	2	3			6			9		10			7*				5	12		8	4		11		40
1	2	3			6†			9	14	10			7				5	12		8*	4		11		41
1*	2	3						9	10				7				5	12	6		4		11	8	42
	2	3					14	9	10		4*	1	12	11†			6				5		7	8	43
	2	3						9		11	4	1	7				6			8	5		10		44
	2	3						9	12	11*	4	1	7				6			8	5		10		45
	2	3					12	9	10		4†	1	7		6*	14				8	5			11	46
18	42	40	7	24	41	23	18	46	37	21	37	28	25	21	4	9	11	4	1	20	16	1	10	2	
		+1s	+1s	+1s	+1s	+3s			+2s		+3s		+5s	+2s	+4s	+11s	+1s			+2s			+3s	+1s	

Rumbelows Cup	Second Round	Bournemouth (a)		0-0
		(h)		2-1
	Third Round	Aston Villa (a)		0-2
FA Cup	Third Round	Leicester C (h)		2-1
	Fourth Round	Sheffield W (h)		4-4
		(a)		0-2

MILLWALL

Player and Position	Ht	Wt	Birth Date	Birth Place	Source	Clubs	League App	Gls
Goalkeepers								
Keith Branagan	6 1	13 02	10 7 66	Fulham		Cambridge U	110	—
						Millwall	34	—
						Brentford (loan)	2	—
John Donegan	6 0	13 01	19 5 71	Cork	Kilkenny	Millwall	—	—
Carl Emberson	6 1	12 11	13 7 73	Epsom	Trainee	Millwall	—	—
Brian Horne	5 11	13 13	5 10 67	Billericay	Apprentice	Millwall	163	—
Defenders								
Nicky Coleman*	5 10	11 12	6 5 66	Crayford	Apprentice	Millwall	88	—
						Swindon T (loan)	13	4
Ken Cunningham	5 11	11 02	28 6 71	Dublin		Millwall	28	—
Ian Dawes	5 7	11 11	22 2 63	Croyden	Apprentice	QPR	229	3
						Millwall	108	5
Alan Dowson*	5 8	10 06	17 6 70	Gateshead	Trainee	Millwall	1	—
						Fulham (loan)	4	—
Mark Foran	6 4	13 12	30 10 73	Aldershot	Trainee	Millwall	—	—
Mick McCarthy	6 2	12 12	7 2 59	Barnsley	Apprentice	Barnsley	272	7
						Manchester C	140	2
						Celtic	48	—
					Lyon	Millwall	18	—
Alan McLeary	5 11	10 08	6 10 64	London	Apprentice	Millwall	273	5
Sean Sparham‡	5 7	10 10	4 12 68	Bexley		Millwall	28	—
						Brentford (loan)	5	1
David Thompson	6 3	12 07	20 11 68	N'humberland	Trainee	Millwall	64	6
Steve Wood	6 0	11 09	2 2 63	Bracknell	Apprentice	Reading	219	9
						Millwall	103	—
Midfield								
Les Briley	5 6	11 00	2 10 56	Lambeth	Apprentice	Chelsea	—	—
						Hereford U	61	2
						Wimbledon	61	2
						Aldershot	157	3
						Millwall	227	13
Terry Hurlock (To Rangers. Aug 1990)	5 9	13 02	22 9 58	Hackney	Leytonstone	Brentford	220	18
						Reading	29	—
						Millwall	104	8
Paul Kerr	5 8	11 04	9 6 64	Portsmouth	Apprentice	Aston Villa	24	3
						Middlesbrough	125	13
						Millwall	10	2
Darren Morgan	5 6	9 05	5 11 67	Camberwell	Apprentice	Millwall	43	2
						Bradford C (loan)	2	—
						Peterborough U (loan)	5	—
Keith Stevens	6 0	12 05	21 6 64	Merton	Apprentice	Millwall	288	4
Gary Waddock	5 9	12 07	17 3 62	Kingsbury	Apprentice	QPR	203	8
					Charleroi	Millwall	58	2
Forwards								
Malcolm Allen	5 8	10 06	21 3 67	Deiniolen	Apprentice	Watford	39	5
						Aston Villa (loan)	4	—
						Norwich C	35	8
						Millwall	29	9
Sean Devine	5 10	12 00	6 9 72	Lewisham	Trainee	Millwall	—	—
Jon Goodman	5 11	12 10	2 6 71	Walthamstow	Bromley	Millwall	23	5
John Humphrey	5 11	12 09	2 7 69	Guildford	Leatherhead	Millwall	—	—

MILLWALL

Foundation: Formed in 1885 as Millwall Rovers by employees of Morton & Co, a jam and marmalade factory in West Ferry Road. The founders were predominantly Scotsmen. Their first headquarters was the The Islanders pub in Tooke Street, Millwall. Their first trophy was the East End Cup in 1887.

First Football League game: 28 August, 1920, Division 3, v Bristol R (h) W 2-0 – Lansdale; Fort, Hodge; Voisey (1), Riddell, McAlpine; Waterall, Travers, Broad (1), Sutherland, Dempsey.

Did you know: In 1929–30 Millwall were twice held to a draw in historic Cup ties with the famous Corinthians – 2-2 at the old Cup Final ground at Sydenham and 1-1 at The Den, before winning 5-1 at Stamford Bridge. The total attendance was over 136,000.

Managers (and Secretary-managers)
Willie Henderson 1894–95*, John Beveridge 1895–1907* (continued as secretary until 1915), Fred Kidd 1907–08, George Saunders 1908–09, Herbert Lipsham 1913–19, Robert Hunter 1919–33, Bill McCracken 1933–36, Charlie Hewitt 1936–40, Bill Voisey 1940–44, Jack Cock 1944–48, Charlie Hewitt 1948–56, Ron Gray 1956–57, Jimmy Seed 1958–59, Reg Smith 1959–61, Ron Gray 1961–63, Billy Gray 1963–66, Benny Fenton 1966–74, Gordon Jago 1974–77, George Petchey 1978–80, Peter Anderson 1980–82, George Graham 1982–86, John Docherty 1986–90, Bob Pearson 1990, Bruce Rioch April 1990–   .

Player and Position	Ht	Wt	Birth Date	Birth Place	Source	Clubs	League App	Gls
John McGinlay	5 9	11 06	8 4 64	Inverness	Elgin C	Shrewsbury T	60	27
						Bury	25	9
						Millwall	2	—
Manus Magill‡	6 0	11 07	2 8 71	Ballymena		Millwall	—	—
John McGlashan	6 1	12 00	3 6 67	Dundee	Dundee Violet	Montrose	68	11
						Millwall	8	—
Kevin O'Callaghan*	5 8	11 04	19 10 61	London	Apprentice	Millwall	20	3
						Ipswich T	115	3
						Portsmouth	87	16
						Millwall	76	14
Alex Rae	5 9	11 00	30 9 69	Glasgow	Bishopbriggs	Falkirk	83	20
						Millwall	39	10
Teddy Sheringham	5 8	12 04	2 4 66	Highams Park	Apprentice	Millwall	220	93
						Aldershot (loan)	5	—
Paul Stephenson	5 10	10 09	2 1 68	Newcastle	Apprentice	Newcastle U	61	1
						Millwall	65	4

Trainees
Bedford, Roy D; Dickson, Hugh J; Dolby, Tony C; Franklin, Jeffery T; Lee, Brian R; Manning, Paul J; Owen, Daniel; Roberts, Andrew J; Rogerson, Colin C; Walker, Lee M.D.

Associated Schoolboys
Bull, Steven; Button, Marlon L; Curry, Paul; Francis, Dean; French, Jermaine; Gordon, Neville; Hatcher, Kevin T; Irving, Paul R; McIntyre, Ian S; Martin, Matthew D; Miller, Steven W; Morey, Robert; Morgan, Vaughan A; Munyenya, Daniel; Nixon, Andrew W; Pike, David; Pitcher, Geoffrey; Porter, Adam J; Ross, Ian; Spaine, Vidal E; Thatcher, Ben D; Whitehouse, Christopher J; Willis, Ben S.

Associated Schoolboys who have accepted the club's offer of a Traineeship/Contract
Beard, Mark; Chapman, Daniel G; Knight, Glen; McArthur, Frank P; Middleton, Mathew J; Okyere-Darkoh, Joseph; Smith, Brett R.

NEWCASTLE UNITED 1990–91 *Back row (left to right):* Kevin Dillon, Mick Quinn, Neil Simpson, Steve Howey, Darren Bradshaw, John Anderson. *Centre row:* Derek Wright (Physiotherapist). Lee Clark, Mark Stimson, Bjorn Kristensen, Tommy Wright, John Burridge, Kevin Scott, Liam O'Brien, Mark McGhee. Bobby Saxton (First Team Coach).
Front row: Gary Brazil, Kevin Brock, Paul Sweeney, Billy Askew, Jim Smith (Manager), Roy Aitken, John Gallacher, Ray Ranson, Scott Sloan.

Division 2   NEWCASTLE UNITED

St James' Park, Newcastle-upon-Tyne NE1 4ST. Telephone 091-232 8361. Promotions/Commercial Manager: 091-232 2285. Ticket Office Hotline: 091-261 1571. Club Shop: 091-261 6357. Club Shop Answering Service: 091-232 4080. Football in the Community Scheme: 091-261 9715. Harveys Restaurant: 091-222 1860. Club Fax: 091-232 9875. Clubcall: 0898 121590. Clubcall Ticket Line: 0898 121190.

Ground capacity: 33,508.

Record attendance: 68,386 v Chelsea, Division 1, 3 Sept 1930.

Record receipts: £157,153 v Sunderland, Division 2 play-off, semi-final, 16 May 1990.

Pitch measurements: 115yd × 75yd.

President: Stan Seymour.

Vice-presidents: James Rush AFC, John Hall.

Chairman: George R, Forbes.

Vice-chairman: Peter G. Mallinger.

Directors: W. Gordon McKeag, Bob Young, Russell Cushing, Douglas Hall. *Associate Director:* Trevor Bennett.

Manager: Ossie Ardiles. *Assistant. Manager:* Tony Galvin.

Coaches: Colin Suggett and Derek Fazackerley. *Physio:* Derek Wright.

General Manager/Secretary: R. Cushing.

Assistant Secretary: K. Slater. *Commercial Manager:* G. McDonnell.

Year Formed: 1881. *Turned Professional:* 1889. *Ltd Co.:* 1890.

Club Nickname: 'Magpies'.

Previous Names: Stanley 1881; Newcastle East End 1882–1892.

Previous Grounds: South Byker, 1881; Chillingham Road, Heaton, 1886 to 1892.

Record League Victory: 13-0 v Newport Co, Division 2, 5 October 1946 – Garbutt; Cowell, Graham; Harvey, Brennan, Wright; Milburn (2), Bentley (1), Wayman (4), Shackleton (6), Pearson.

Record Cup Victory: 9-0 v Southport (at Hillsborough) FA Cup, 4th rd, 1 February 1932 – McInroy; Nelson, Fairhurst; McKenzie, Davidson, Weaver (1); Boyd (1), Jimmy Richardson (3), Cape (2), McMenemy (1), Lang (1).

Record Defeat: 0-9 v Burton Wanderers, Division 2, 15 April 1895.

Most League Points (2 for a win): 57, Division 2, 1964–65.

Most League Points (3 for a win): 80, Division 2, 1983–84 and Division 2, 1989–90.

Most League Goals: 98, Division 1, 1951–52.

Highest League Scorer in Season: Hughie Gallacher, 36, Division 1, 1926–27.

Most League Goals in Total Aggregate: Jackie Milburn, 178, 1946–57.

Most Capped Player: Alf McMichael, 40, Northern Ireland.

Most League Appearances: Jim Lawrence, 432, 1904–22.

Record Transfer Fee Received: £2,000,000 from Tottenham H for Paul Gascoigne, July 1988.

Record Transfer Fee Paid: £850,000 to Wimbledon for Dave Beasant, June 1988 and £850,000 to Wimbledon for Andy Thorn, August 1988.

Football League Record: 1893 Elected to Division 2; 1898–1934 Division 1; 1934–48 Division 2; 1948–61 Division 1; 1961–65 Division 2; 1965–78 Division 1; 1978–84 Division 2; 1984–89 Division 1; 1989– Division 2.

Honours: Football League: Division 1 – Champions 1904–05, 1906–07, 1908–09, 1926–27; Division 2 – Champions 1964–65; Runners-up 1897–98, 1947–48. *FA Cup:* Winners 1910, 1924, 1932, 1951, 1952, 1955; Runners-up 1905, 1906, 1908, 1911, 1974. *Football League Cup:* Runners-up 1975–76. *Texaco Cup:* Winners 1973–74, 1974–75. **European Competitions:** *European Fairs Cup:* 1968–69 (winners), 1969–70, 1970–71 *UEFA Cup:* 1977–78. *Anglo-Italian Cup:* Winners 1973.

Colours: Black and white striped shirts, black shorts, black stockings. **Change colours:** Canary shirts, green shorts, canary stockings.

NEWCASTLE UNITED 1990–91 LEAGUE RECORD

Match No.	Date		Venue	Opponents	Result	H/T Score	Lg. Pos.	Goalscorers	Attendance
1	Aug	25	H	Plymouth Arg	W 2-0	1-0	—	Kristensen, Quinn	23,984
2	Sept	1	A	Blackburn R	W 1-0	0-0	5	O'Brien	11,329
3		8	H	Millwall	L 1-2	0-1	8	Quinn	23,922
4		15	A	Port Vale	W 1-0	0-0	5	Quinn	10,025
5		18	A	Sheffield W	D 2-2	1-1	—	McGhee 2	30,628
6		22	H	West Ham U	D 1-1	1-1	7	McGhee	25,462
7		29	A	Bristol C	L 0-1	0-1	10		15,858
8	Oct	3	H	Middlesbrough	D 0-0	0-0	—		17,023
9		6	H	Portsmouth	W 2-1	1-0	9	Quinn 2	17,682
10		13	A	Oxford U	D 0-0	0-0	9		6820
11		20	A	Ipswich T	L 1-2	0-2	10	Quinn (pen)	15,567
12		24	H	Charlton Ath	L 1-3	0-2	—	Brock	14,016
13		27	H	WBA	D 1-1	0-1	12	O'Brien	14,774
14	Nov	3	A	Hull C	L 1-2	0-1	16	McGhee	8375
15		10	A	Wolverhampton W	L 1-2	1-1	19	Clark	18,721
16		17	H	Barnsley	D 0-0	0-0	19		15,548
17		24	H	Watford	W 1-0	0-0	16	Quinn (pen)	13,774
18	Dec	1	A	Leicester C	L 4-5	1-2	16	Quinn 3, O'Brien	11,045
19		16	A	Plymouth Arg	W 1-0	0-0	—	Peacock	7845
20		22	A	Bristol R	D 1-1	0-0	15	Gaynor	6643
21		26	H	Swindon T	D 1-1	1-1	15	Quinn	17,003
22		29	H	Notts Co	L 0-2	0-0	16		17,557
23	Jan	1	A	Oldham Ath	D 1-1	0-0	15	Quinn	14,550
24		12	H	Blackburn R	W 1-0	0-0	14	Mitchell	16,382
25		16	A	Brighton & HA	L 2-4	0-1	—	Quinn, Brock	7684
26		19	A	Millwall	W 1-0	1-0	15	Peacock	11,478
27	Feb	2	H	Port Vale	W 2-0	1-0	12	Peacock, Quinn	14,602
28		23	H	Wolverhampton W	D 0-0	0-0	13		18,612
29		27	H	Brighton & HA	D 0-0	0-0	—		12,692
30	Mar	2	H	Leicester C	W 2-1	2-0	12	McGhee, Sloan	13,575
31		9	A	Watford	W 2-1	1-0	11	Anderson, Quinn	10,018
32		12	A	Middlesbrough	L 0-3	0-2	—		18,250
33		16	H	Bristol C	D 0-0	0-0	11		13,578
34		23	A	Portsmouth	W 1-0	1-0	11	Brock	9607
35		30	A	Swindon T	L 2-3	1-1	13	Peacock, Quinn	9309
36	Apr	1	H	Bristol R	L 0-2	0-0	14		17,509
37		6	A	Notts Co	L 0-3	0-0	16		7806
38		10	H	Oxford U	D 2-2	1-1	—	Hunt, Melville (og)	10,004
39		13	H	Oldham Ath	W 3-2	2-0	13	Peacock, Hunt, Brock	16,615
40		17	H	Sheffield W	W 1-0	1-0	—	Brock	18,330
41		20	H	Ipswich T	D 2-2	1-2	12	Stimson, Quinn	17,638
42		24	H	West Ham U	D 1-1	1-0	—	Peacock	24,195
43		27	A	Charlton Ath	L 0-1	0-0	12		7234
44	May	4	A	WBA	D 1-1	0-1	11	Quinn	16,706
45		7	A	Barnsley	D 1-1	1-0	—	Peacock	9534
46		11	H	Hull C	L 1-2	0-1	11	Clark	17,940

Final League Position: 11

GOALSCORERS

League (49): Quinn 18 (2 pens), Peacock 7, Brock 5, McGhee 5, O'Brien 3, Clark 2, Hunt 2, Anderson 1, Gaynor 1, Kristensen 1, Mitchell 1, Sloan 1, Stimson 1, own goal 1.
Rumbelows Cup (1): Anderson 1.
FA Cup (4): Quinn 2, McGhee 1, Stimson 1.

Burridge	Scott	Sweeney	Aitken	Kristensen	Ranson	Dillon	Anderson	Quinn	Howey	O'Brien	McGhee	Brock	Fereday	Simpson	Bradshaw	Gourlay	Gallacher	Clark	Robinson	Sloan	Appleby	Askew	Roche	Watson, S	Stimson	Gaynor	Peacock	Mitchell	Match No.
1	2	3	4	5	6	7	8	9	10	11																			1
1	2	3	4	5	6	7	8	9			12	11	10*																2
1	2	3	4	5	6	7*	8	9			12	11†	10	14															3
1	2		4	5	6	7*	3	9		11	10	8†	12	14															4
1	2			5	6	7	3	9			10	8	11	12	4*														5
1	2		4	5	6	7	3*	9			14	10	8†	11	12														6
1	2		4	5	6			9				10		8*	3	7	11†	12	14										7
1	2	3	4	5*	6	7		9		11	10	8						12											8
1	2	3	4		6	7*	5	9		11	10	8						12											9
1	2		4		6		5	9		11	10	8	7*		3			12											10
1	2	3	4	10	14		5	9		11*		8	7		6†			12											11
1	2	14	4*	5	6		3†		9	11	10	8						12		7									12
1	2	3			5	6			12	11	10		9†			8	7*	4	14										13
1	2	3			6		5		11	10			9*			7	8	4	12										14
1	2				6		5	9		11*	10				3	4		7	8	12									15
1	2				6		3	9		11		8	12		4*			7					10	5					16
1	2		4	5	6			9		11	8	10						3							7				17
1	2		4	5				9		8	12	10						3					7*	6					18
1	5		4	6†	14		2	9	12	11								7*						3	10		8		19
1	5		4	6	12		2	9		7	11*													3	10		8		20
1	5		4	6	8	11	2	9	12		7†							10*						3			8		21
1	5		4*	6	10	11	2	9	12		7†							14						3			8		22
1	5		4	6	2			9	12		7							10					11*	3			8		23
1			4	6	2	7	5	9			12												11	3		8	10		24
1			4	6	5	10	2	9			7							12					11	3			8*		25
1			4	6	2	7*	5	9			11		12										10	3			8		26
1			4	6	2	7	5	9			11												10	3			8		27
1	5		4	6	2	7		9			12	11†											14	3			8		28
1	5		4	6	2	7		9			12	11											10	3			8*		29
1	5		4	6				9		2	10	11				7*								3			8		30
1	5		4	6				2†	9	7	10*	11												3			8		31
1	5		4	6				9		7	11†							12						3			8*		32
1	5		4	6				9	10†12	14	11												2				8*		33
1	5		4	6		7		9		14	10*11†												2	3			8		34
1	5		4			7	6	9			11												2	3			8		35
1	5		4	14		7†	6	9			12	11											2	3			8		36
1	5		4	6		7*		9		10†11							12						2	3			8		37
1	5				6			9		11						7	12						4	2	3		8		38
1	5				6			9		11						7	12						4	2	3		8		39
	5				6			9	12	14			11					7†					4	2	3		8		40
	5				6			9	12	14			11					7					4†	2	3		8		41
	5				6			9		4			11					7						2			8		42
	5				6			9	12	4			11					7†					14	2			8		43
	5				6			9	12	4								7					11	2†			8		44
	5				6			9	12	4								7					14	2			8		45
	5				6			9		4			11					7						2			8		46
39	42	8	32	39	24	19	27	43	3	23	17	36	6	1	6	2	1	13	—	11	1	1	5	22	23	4	27	2	
		+	+	+				+	+	+	+	+	+	+				+	+	+				+	+	+			
		1s	1s	3s				8s	10s	4s	2s	2s	3s	1s				6s	3s	5s				1s	3s	2s			

Makel—Match No. 44(14) 45(11) 46(12); Moran—Match No. 28(10*); Hunt—Match No. 31(12) 32(10) 33(7) 34(12) 35(10) 36(10*) 37(14) 38(10*) 39(10*) 40(10*) 41(10*) 42(10) 43(10*) 44(10*) 45(10*) 46(10*); Watson, J—Match No. 46(14); Neilson—Match No. 31(14) 32(2) 33(3); Elliott—Match No. 32(14) 42(3) 43(3) 44(3) 45(3†) 46(3†); Srnicek—Match No. 40(1) 41(1) 42(1) 43(1) 44(1) 45(1) 46(1)

Rumbelows Cup	Second Round	Middlesbrough (a)	0-2
		(h)	1-0
FA Cup	Third Round	Derby Co (h)	2-0
	Fourth Round	Nottingham F (h)	2-2
		(a)	0-3

NEWCASTLE UNITED

Player and Position	Ht	Wt	Birth Date	Birth Place	Source	Clubs	League App	Gls
Goalkeepers								
John Burridge*	5 11	12 11	3 12 51	Workington	Apprentice	Workington	27	—
						Blackpool	134	—
						Aston Villa	65	—
						Southend U (loan)	6	—
						Crystal Palace	88	—
						QPR	39	—
						Wolverhampton W	74	—
						Derby Co (loan)	6	—
						Sheffield U	109	—
						Southampton	62	—
						Newcastle U	67	—
Pavel Srnicek	6 2	14 9	10 3 68	Ostrava	Banik Ostrava	Newcastle U	7	—
Tommy Wright	6 1	13 05	29 8 63	Belfast	Linfield	Newcastle U	23	—
						Hull C (loan)	6	—
Defenders								
John Anderson	5 11	11 06	7 11 59	Dublin	Apprentice	WBA	—	—
						Preston NE	51	—
						Newcastle U	299	14
Matthew Appleby	5 10	11 02	16 4 72	Middlesbrough	Trainee	Newcastle U	1	—
Darren Bradshaw	5 10	11 03	19 3 67	Sheffield	Matlock T	Chesterfield	18	—
						York C	59	3
						Newcastle U	19	—
Tony Cole	6 0	11 04	18 .9 72	Gateshead	School	Newcastle U	—	—
Robbie Elliott	5 10	10 13	25 12 73	Newcastle	Trainee	Newcastle U	6	—
Bjorn Kristensen	6 1	12 05	10 10 63	Malling	Aarhus	Newcastle U	78	4
Philip Mason	5 6	10 07	3 12 71	Consett	Trainee	Newcastle U	—	—
Alan Neilson	5 11	11 07	26/9/72	Wegburg	Trainee	Newcastle U	3	—
Michael Parkinson	5 7	11 04	8 6 71	Sunderland	Trainee	Newcastle U	—	—
Ray Ranson	5 9	11 12	12 6 60	St Helens	Apprentice	Manchester C	183	1
						Birmingham C	137	—
						Newcastle U	74	1
David Roche	5 11	12 01	13 12 70	Newcastle	Trainee	Newcastle U	10	—
Kevin Scott	6 2	11 06	17 12 66	Easington		Newcastle U	120	5
Mark Stimson	5 11	11 00	27 12 67	Plaistow		Tottenham H	2	—
						Leyton Orient (loan)	10	—
						Gillingham (loan)	18	—
						Newcastle U	60	2
Steve Watson	6 0	12 07	1 4 74	North Shields	Trainee	Newcastle U	24	—
Midfield								
Roy Aitken	6 0	12 00	24 11 58	Irvine	Celtic BC	Celtic	483	40
						Newcastle U	54	1
Billy Askew	5 5	10 10	2 10 59	Lumley	Apprentice	Middlesbrough	12	—
						Blackburn R (loan)	—	—
						Hull C	253	19
						Newcastle U	6	—
						Shrewsbury T (loan)	5	—
Kevin Brock	5 9	10 12	9 9 62	Middleton Stoney	Apprentice	Oxford U	246	26
						QPR	40	2
						Newcastle U	103	9
Lee Clark	5 7	11 07	27 10 72	Wallsend	Trainee	Newcastle U	19	3
Kevin Dillon*	6 0	12 07	18 12 59	Sunderland	Apprentice	Birmingham C	186	15
						Portsmouth	215	45
						Newcastle U	62	—
Archie Gourlay	5 8	10 00	29 6 69	Greenock		Morton	2	—
						Newcastle U	3	—
						Morton (loan)	4	—
Lee Makel	5 10	9 10	11 1 73	Sunderland	Trainee	Newcastle U	3	—
Liam O'Brien	6 1	13 03	5 9 64	Dublin	Shamrock R	Manchester U	31	2
						Newcastle U	72	9
Gavin Peacock	5 7	11 00	18 11 67	Kent		QPR	17	1
						Gillingham	70	11
						Bournemouth	56	8
						Newcastle U	27	7
Neil Simpson	5 10	11 06	15 11 61	London	Middlefield W	Aberdeen	206	19
						Newcastle U	4	—

NEWCASTLE UNITED

Foundation: It stemmed from a newly formed club called Stanley in 1881. In October 1882 they changed their name to Newcastle East End to avoid confusion with Stanley in Co. Durham. Shortly afterwards another club Rosewood merged with them. Newcastle West End had been formed in August 1882 and they played on a ground which is now St. James' Park. In 1889, West End went out of existence after a bad run and the remaining committee men invited East End to move to St. James' Park. They accepted and at a meeting in Bath Lane Hall in 1892, changed their name to Newcastle United.

First Football League game: 2 September, 1893, Division 2, v Royal Arsenal (a) D 2-2 – Ramsay; Jeffery, Miller; Crielly, Graham, McKane; Bowman, Crate (1), Thompson, Sorley (1), Wallace. Graham and not Crate scored according to some reports.

Did you know: Newcastle have fielded more Scottish than English internationals. Among the 23 men who appeared for them in five FA Cup finals in seven years 1904–11 were 11 Scots, but there were also six Geordies – Colin Veitch, Jackie Carr, George Jobey, John Rutherford, Jimmy Stewart and Dave Willis.

Managers (and Secretary-managers)
Frank Watt 1895–32 (continued as secretary to 1932), Andy Cunningham 1930–35, Tom Mather 1935–39, Stan Seymour 1939–47 (Hon-manager), George Martin 1947–50, Stan Seymour 1950–54 (Hon-manager), Duggie Livingstone 1954–56, Stan Seymour (Hon-manager 1956–58), Charlie Mitten 1958–61, Norman Smith 1961–62, Joe Harvey 1962–75, Gordon Lee 1975–77, Richard Dinnis 1977, Bill McGarry 1977–80, Arthur Cox 1980–84, Jack Charlton 1984, Willie McFaul 1985–88, Jim Smith 1988–91, Ossie Ardiles March 1991–

Player and Position	Ht	Wt	Birth Date	Birth Place	Source	Clubs	League App	Gls
Paul Sweeney (To St Johnstone. March 1991)	5 7	10 00	10 1 65	Glasgow	St Kentigerns Acad	Raith R Newcastle U	205 36	8 —
Alan Thompson	6 0	12 05	22 12 73	Newcastle	Trainee	Newcastle U	—	—
John Watson§	5 9	10 10	14 4 74	South Shields	Trainee	Newcastle U	1	—
Forwards								
John Gallacher	5 10	10 08	26 1 69	Glasgow		Falkirk Newcastle U	18 29	5 6
Steve Howey	6 1	10 09	26 10 71	Sunderland	Trainee	Newcastle U	12	—
Andy Hunt	6 0	11 07	9 6 70	Thurrock	Kettering T	Newcastle U	16	2
Mark McGhee*	5 10	12 00	25 5 57	Glasgow	Apprentice	Bristol C Morton Newcastle U Aberdeen Hamburg Celtic Newcastle U	— 64 28 164 30 88 67	37 5 63 7 27 24
Mick Quinn	5 9	13 00	2 5 62	Liverpool	Apprentice	Derby Co Wigan Ath Stockport Co Oldham Ath Portsmouth Newcastle U	— 69 63 80 121 88	19 39 34 54 50
David Robinson	6 0	13 02	27 11 69	Newcastle	Trainee	Newcastle U Peterborough U	5 7	— 3
Scott Sloan	5 10	11 06	14 12 67	Wallsend	Ponteland	Berwick R Newcastle U	61 16	20 1

Trainees
Cornish, Darren; English, Michael; Heron, Thomas; Lewis, Stephen; Milner, John F; Morton, Graeme F; Reay, Simon; Watson, John I.

Associated Schoolboys
Alderson, Richard; Appleby, Richard D; Armstrong, Alun; Baldwin, Shaun T; Dinning, Tony; Foster, Gary H; Geddes, Paul A; Gower, Mark S; Murray, Nathan A; Pouton, Alan; Stokoe, Graham L; Ternent, Neill S.

NORTHAMPTON TOWN 1990–91 *Back row (left to right)*: Bradley Sandeman, Paul Wilson, Michael Bell, Matt Tarry, Steve Berry, Wayne Williams, Julian Capone, Kevin Wilkin, Stephen Hall.
Centre row: Dennis Casey (Physiotherapist), David Johnson, Darren Wood, Matt Carr, Terry Angus, Peter Gleasure, Darren Watts, Irvin Gernon, Steve Terry, Darren Collins, Greg Campbell, Steve Brown, Brian Carnaby (Youth Coach).
Front row: Theo Foley (Manager), Martin Singleton, Stuart Beavon, Adrian Thorpe, Trevor Quouw, Phil Chard, David Scope, Bobby Barnes, Joe Kiernan (Assistant Manager).

Division 4   **NORTHAMPTON TOWN**

County Ground, Abington Avenue, Northampton NN1 4PS. Telephone Northampton (0604) 234100. Commercial Dept: (0604) 234100. Information Line: 0898 700275.

Ground capacity: 11,907.

Record attendance: 24,523 v Fulham, Division 1, 23 April 1966.

Record receipts: £47,292.40 v Coventry C, FA Cup 3rd rd, 6 January 1990.

Pitch measurements: 112yd × 75yd.

Chairman: M. McRitchie. *Vice-chairman:*

Directors: D. Kerr, M. Church, R. Church, B. Hancock.

Company Secretary: Philip Mark Hough.

Manager: Theo Foley.

Coach: Clive Walker.

Physio: Dennis Casey. *General Commercial Manager:* Mark Underwood.

Year Formed: 1897. *Turned Professional:* 1901. *Ltd Co.:* 1901.

Club Nickname: 'The Cobblers'.

Record League Victory: 10-0 v Walsall, Division 3 (S), 5 November 1927 – Hammond; Watson, Jeffs; Allen, Brett, Odell; Daley, Smith (3), Loasby (3), Hoten (1), Wells (3).

Record Cup Victory: 9-1 v Metropolitan Police, FA Cup, 1st rd, 28 November 1931 – Hammond; English, Fred Dawes; Dowsey, O'Dell, Davies; Scott, Riches (1), Bowen (2), Albert Dawes (3), Wells (2). (1 og).

Record Defeat: 0-11 v Southampton, Southern League, 28 December 1901.

Most League Points (2 for a win): 68, Division 4, 1975–76.

Most League Points (3 for a win): 99, Division 4, 1986–87.

Most League Goals: 109, Division 3, 1962–63 and Division 3 (S), 1952–53.

Highest League Scorer in Season: Cliff Holton, 36, Division 3, 1961–62.

Most League Goals in Total Aggregate: Jack English, 135, 1947–60.

Most Capped Player: E. Lloyd Davies, 12 (16), Wales.

Most League Appearances: Tommy Fowler, 521, 1946–61.

Record Transfer Fee Received: £265,000 from Watford for Richard Hill, July 1987.

Record Transfer Fee Paid: £85,000 to Manchester C for Tony Adcock, January 1988.

Football League Record: 1920 Original Member of Division 3; 1921 Division 3 (S); 1958–61 Division 4; 1961–63 Division 3; 1963–65 Division 2; 1965–66 Division 1; 1966–67 Division 2; 1967–69 Division 3; 1969–76 Division 4; 1976–77 Division 3; 1977–87 Division 4; 1987–90 Division 3; 1990– Division 4.

Honours: Football League: Division 1 best season: 21st, 1965–66; Division 2 – Runners-up 1964–65; Division 3 – Champions 1962–63; Division 3 (S) – Runners-up 1927–28, 1949–50; Division 4 – Champions 1986–87; Runners-up 1975–76. *FA Cup:* best season: 5th rd, 1933–34, 1949–50, 1969–70. *Football League Cup:* best season: 5th rd, 1964–65, 1966–67.

Colours: Yellow shirts, solid claret strip on right hand side, yellow shorts, claret trim, yellow stockings, with claret hoops. **Change colours:** Dark blue shirts, blue trim, dark blue shorts with white triangle, dark blue stockings with white tops.

NORTHAMPTON TOWN 1990–91 LEAGUE RECORD

Match No.	Date		Venue	Opponents	Result	H/T Score	Lg. Pos.	Goalscorers	Attendance
1	Aug	25	A	Hereford U	W 2-1	1-0	—	Wilkin, Barnes	3187
2	Sept	1	A	Maidstone U	W 3-1	0-0	2	Wilson, Wood, Thorpe	2049
3		8	H	Blackpool	W 1-0	0-0	2	Barnes	4300
4		14	A	Aldershot	D 3-3	1-1	—	Wilkin, Barnes, Beavon	2741
5		18	A	Scarborough	D 1-1	0-1	—	Barnes (pen)	1525
6		22	H	Peterborough U	L 1-2	0-2	4	Barnes	5573
7		29	H	Halifax T	W 1-0	0-0	3	Collins	2977
8	Oct	2	A	Burnley	L 0-3	0-0	—		6271
9		6	A	Chesterfield	D 0-0	0-0	7		3826
10		13	H	Stockport Co	W 1-0	0-0	4	Chard	3927
11		19	H	Walsall	W 5-0	2-0	—	Barnes, Terry, Campbell 2, Chard	4055
12		23	A	Darlington	D 1-1	0-1	—	Barnes	4882
13		27	A	Lincoln C	L 1-3	1-0	5	Terry	3352
14	Nov	3	H	Hartlepool U	W 3-2	1-1	3	Wilson 2, Beavon (pen)	3342
15		9	H	Wrexham	W 1-0	0-0	—	Barnes	3855
16		24	A	York C	W 1-0	0-0	2	Barnes	2202
17	Dec	1	H	Rochdale	W 3-2	1-2	1	Chard 2, Beavon (pen)	3809
18		15	H	Carlisle U	L 1-4	0-2	1	Campbell	2873
19		21	H	Cardiff C	D 0-0	0-0	—		3033
20		29	A	Gillingham	D 0-0	0-0	3		4934
21	Jan	1	H	Doncaster R	D 0-0	0-0	4		5270
22		12	H	Maidstone U	W 2-0	0-0	3	Adcock, Barnes	3710
23		19	H	Hereford U	W 3-0	1-0	2	Chard, Beavon (pen), Angus	3577
24		26	H	Aldershot	W 2-1	1-0	1	Adcock, Beavon (pen)	3800
25	Feb	1	H	Scarborough	L 0-2	0-2	—		4058
26		5	A	Peterborough U	L 0-1	0-0	—		5952
27		15	H	York C	W 2-1	1-1	—	Angus, Barnes	2685
28		23	A	Wrexham	W 2-0	2-0	2	Terry, Barnes	1790
29	Mar	2	A	Rochdale	D 1-1	0-0	2	Beavon (pen)	1890
30		5	A	Scunthorpe U	L 0-3	0-3	—		2852
31		9	H	Carlisle U	D 1-1	1-0	2	Campbell	3216
32		12	H	Burnley	D 0-0	0-0	—		3710
33		15	A	Halifax T	L 1-2	0-2	—	Brown	1347
34		23	A	Chesterfield	W 2-0	1-0	3	Chard, Beavon (pen)	3379
35		26	A	Torquay U	D 0-0	0-0	—		2373
36		30	H	Scunthorpe U	W 2-1	1-1	3	Terry, Beavon (pen)	3728
37	Apr	1	A	Cardiff C	L 0-1	0-1	3		4805
38		6	H	Gillingham	W 2-1	1-1	3	Berry, Chard	2993
39		9	A	Stockport Co	L 0-2	0-1	—		3707
40		13	A	Doncaster R	L 1-2	0-1	6	Beavon	2939
41		16	H	Torquay U	L 1-4	1-0	—	Adcock	2678
42		20	A	Walsall	D 3-3	1-0	7	Barnes, Beavon, Terry	3345
43		27	H	Darlington	L 0-3	0-3	7		4884
44		30	H	Lincoln C	D 1-1	1-1	—	Berry	2544
45	May	7	A	Blackpool	L 1-2	0-2	—	Terry	7298
46		11	A	Hartlepool U	L 1-3	1-1	10	Brown	6957

Final League Position: 10

GOALSCORERS

League (57): Barnes 13 (1 pen), Beavon 10 (7 pens), Chard 7, Terry 6, Campbell 4, Adcock 3, Wilson 3, Angus 2, Berry 2, Brown 2, Wilkin 2, Collins 1, Thorpe 1, Wood 1.
Rumbelows Cup (4): Wilkin 2, Barnes 1 (pen), Brown 1.
FA Cup (4): Barnes 2, Beavon 1, Campbell 1.

Gleasure	Chard	Wilson	Terry	Scully	Wood	Beavon	Wilkin	Berry	Barnes	Brown	Thorpe	Angus	Sandeman	Bell	Beresford	Collins	Johnson	Campbell	Williams	Fee	Gernon	Scope	Hitchcock	Evans	Adcock	Quow	Match No.
1	2	3	4	5	6	7	8*	9	10	11	12																1
1	2	3	4	5	6*	7	8	9	10	11	12																2
1	2	3	4	5		7	8†	9*	10	11	12	6	14														3
1	2	3†	4	5		7	8	9*	10	11	12	6	14														4
1	2	3	4	5		7	8	9*	10	11	12	6†	14														5
1	2	3	4	5		7	8	9†	10	11	12	6*	14														6
	2	3	4	5		7	8†	12	10	11*		6		9	1	14											7
	2	3	4	5		7		12	11	10		6		9†	1		8*	14									8
	2	3	4	5		7		12	11	10	14	6		9†	1		8*										9
	2	3	4	5		7		9†	10	11		6	14		1		8*	12									10
	2	3	4	5		7			10	11	12	6		9*	1		8										11
	2	3	4	5		7*		12	10		14	6		9†	1	11	8										12
	2	3	4	5		7			10		14	6*		9†	1	12	11	8									13
	2	3	4			7		12	10			6†		9*	1	14	11	8	5								14
	2	3	4	5		7			12	10	11			9†	1	14	8	6*									15
	2	3	4	5		7			10	11*	9	6			1		12	8									16
	2	3*	4			7			10	11	9	6			1	14	12	8			5						17
	2	3	4			7		9		11*	10	6†			1	12	8		5		14						18
	2	3	4			7			10	11		6		9	1		8	5*	12								19
	2	3	4			7			10	11		6		12			8		5				1		9*		20
	2		4			7		12	10	11		6		8†		3			5			14	1		9*		21
	2		4			7			10	11		6		8		3			5*		12				9		22
	2	3	4			7			10	11	12	6		8*					5				1		9		23
	2	3	4			7			10	11	8	6		12					5*				1		9		24
	2	3	4			7		12†	10	11		6	14	8					5*				1		9		25
	2	3	4			7			10*	11	12	6	14	8					5†				1		9		26
	2	3	4			7			10	11	12	6		8*					5				1		9		27
	2	3	4						10	11	12	6	14	8					5†				1		9*	7	28
	2	3	4			7			10*	11	12	6	14	8					5				1		9†		29
	2	3	4			7			10*	11		6		8†				12	5				1		9	14	30
	2	3	4			7			10*	11		6		8†			14	9	12				1		5		31
	2	3	4			7			10*	11	8	6					14	9	12				1		5†		32
	2	3	4			7			10	11	8†	6					14	9	12				1		5*		33
	2	3	4			7			10	11		6					5	8					1		9		34
	2	3	4			7			10	11		6					8						1		9	5	35
	2	3	4			7			10	11		6					12	8					1		9	5*	36
1	2	3	4			7		12	10	11		6†					14	8*							9	5	37
1	2	3	4			7		6	10*	11†		8					14	12							9	5	38
1	2	3	4			7		11	9	6	10*						14	8	12						5†		39
1	2	3	4			7		11	12	5	9	6					10†	14	8*								40
1	2	3	4			7		11	10	12	8	6									5*				9		41
1	2	3†	4			7		11	10	12	8*	6					14				5				9		42
1	2	3†	4			7		8	10	11†	5*	6					14		12						9		43
1		3	4					8	10			6	14			11	12	2			5*				9	7†	44
1		3	4					7*	10	11		6	14			12		2			5†				9	8	45
1		3†	4					10	11	12		6					8	14			7	2			9*	5	46
16	43	44	46	15	2	41	7	20	42	37	12	42	—	22	13	3	8	20	10	1	8	3	17	2	20	12	

subs: 2s · 7s · 1s · 3s · 15s · 5s · 6s · 5s · 17s · 5s · 4s · 4s · 1s · 1s

Rumbelows Cup	First Round	Brighton & HA (a)	2-0
		(h)	1-1
	Second Round	Sheffield U (h)	0-1
		(a)	1-2
FA Cup	First Round	Littlehampton (a)	4-0
	Second Round	Barnet (a)	0-0
		(h)	0-1

NORTHAMPTON TOWN

Player and Position	Ht	Wt	Birth Date	Birth Place	Source	Clubs	League App	Gls
Goalkeepers								
Peter Gleasure	5 11	12 13	8 10 60	Luton	Apprentice	Millwall	55	—
						Northampton T (loan)	11	—
						Northampton T	333	—
						Gillingham (loan)	3	—
Defenders								
Terry Angus			14 1 66	Coventry	VS Rugby	Northampton T	42	2
Matt Carr*	6 3		30 10 71	Middlesbrough	Trainee	Northampton T	—	—
Irving Gernon	6 2	12 01	30 12 62	Birmingham	Apprentice	Ipswich T	76	—
						Northampton T (loan)	9	—
						Gillingham	35	1
						Reading	25	—
						Northampton T	20	1
Stephen Hall*			28 10 71	Hartlepool	Trainee	Northampton T	—	—
David Johnson	5 10	11 02	10 3 67	Northampton	Irthlingborough .D	Northampton T	32	—
Steve Terry	6 1	13 03	14 6 62	Clapton	Apprentice	Watford	160	14
						Hull C	62	4
						Northampton T	63	8
Wayne Williams*	5 11	11 09	17 11 63	Telford	Apprentice	Shrewsbury T	221	7
						Northampton T	55	1
Paul Wilson	5 10	10 12	2 8 68	Bradford	Trainee	Huddersfield T	15	—
						Norwich C	—	—
						Northampton T	125	5
Darren Wood	6 1	12 08	22 10 68	Derby	Trainee	Chesterfield	67	3
						Reading	32	2
						Northampton	2	1
Midfield								
Stuart Beavon	5 6	10 04	30 11 58	Wolverhampton	Apprentice	Tottenham H	4	—
						Notts Co (loan)	6	—
						Reading	396	44
						Northampton T	41	10
Michael Bell			15 11 71	Newcastle	Trainee	Northampton T	34	—
Steve Berry*	5 7	11 06	4 4 63	Gosport	Apprentice	Portsmouth	28	2
						Aldershot (loan)	7	—
						Sunderland	35	2
						Newport Co	60	6
						Swindon T	4	—
						Aldershot	48	6
						Northampton T	102	7
Julian Capone*			3 6 72	Bedford	Trainee	Northampton T	—	—
Philip Chard	5 8	11 03	16 10 60	Corby	Nottingham F	Peterborough U	172	18
						Northampton T	115	27
						Wolverhampton W	34	5
						Northampton T	72	9
Trevor Quow	5 7	10 12	28 9 60	Peterborough	Apprentice	Peterborough U	203	17
						Gillingham	79	3
						Northampton T	61	2
Forwards								
Tony Adcock	5 10	12 04	27 2 63	Bethnal Green	Apprentice	Colchester U	210	98
						Manchester C	15	5
						Northampton T	72	30
						Bradford C	38	6
						Northampton T	21	3

NORTHAMPTON TOWN

Foundation: Formed in 1897 by school teachers connected with the Northampton and District Elementary Schools' Association, they survived a financial crisis at the end of their first year when they were £675 in the red and became members of the Midland League – a fast move indeed for a new club. They achieved Southern League membership in 1901.

First Football League game: 28 August, 1920, Division 3, v Grimsby T (a) L 0-2 – Thorpe; Sproston, Hewison; Jobey, Tomkins, Pease; Whitworth, Lockett, Thomas, Freeman, MacKechnie.

Did you know: When the Cobblers won promotion from the Fourth Division in 1975–76 all 15 of their most regular players found the net, including goalkeeper Alan Starling who scored from a penalty – the only goal of his extensive League career.

Managers (and Secretary-managers)
Arthur Jones 1897–1907*, Herbert Chapman 1907–12, Walter Bull 1912–13, Fred Lessons 1913–19, Bob Hewison 1920–25, Jack Tresadern 1925–30, Jack English 1931–35, Syd Puddefoot 1935–37, Warney Cresswell 1937–39, Tom Smith 1939–49, Bob Dennison 1949–54, Dave Smith 1954–59, David Bowen 1959–67, Tony Marchi 1967–68, Ron Flowers 1968–69, Dave Bowen 1969–72 (continued as GM and secretary to 1985 when joined the board), Billy Baxter 1972–73, Bill Dodgin Jnr 1973–76, Pat Crerand 1976–77, Bill Dodgin Jnr 1977, John Petts 1977–78, Mike Keen 1978–79, Clive Walker 1979–80, Bill Dodgin Jnr 1980–82, Clive Walker 1982–84, Tony Barton 1984–85, Graham Carr 1985–90, Theo Foley May 1990– .

Player and Position	Ht	Wt	Birth Date	Birth Place	Source	Clubs	League App	Gls
Bobby Barnes	5 7	10 05	17 12 62	Kingston	Apprentice	West Ham U	43	5
						Scunthorpe U (loan)	6	—
						Aldershot	49	26
						Swindon T	45	13
						Bournemouth	14	—
						Northampton T	80	31
Steve Brown	5 9	10 12	6 7 66	Northampton	Irthlingborough .D	Northampton T	61	3
Greg Campbell	5 11	11 05	13 7 65	Portsmouth	Apprentice	West Ham U	5	—
						Brighton & HA (loan)	2	—
						Plymouth Arg	35	6
						Northampton T	25	4
Darren Collins‡	5 11	12 00	24 5 67	Winchester	Petersfield U	Northampton T	51	9
David Scope	5 8	10 12	10 5 67	Newcastle	Blyth Sp	Northampton T	14	—
Adrian Thorpe	5 6	11 00	20 11 63	Chesterfield	Heanor T	Bradford C	17	1
						Tranmere R (loan)	5	3
						Notts Co	59	9
						Walsall	27	1
						Northampton T	40	4
Kevin Wilkin			1 10 67	Cambridge	Cambridge C	Northampton T	9	2

Trainees
Ashdjian, John A; Baalham, Shane; Barron, Daniel; Burnham Jason J; Colkin, Lee; Hallcro, Darren; Hallcro, Wayne; Hanson, David; Harrold, Russell M; Kiernan, Daniel J; Kitchin, Lee; Parker, Sean; Underwood, Simon S; Waldock, Casey K.C; Waring, James M; Watts, Darren J; Wright, Graeme.

Associated Schoolboys
Bingham, Matthew J; Curry, Simon; Knight, Stuart A; Tero, Mark J; Willis, Ian.

Associated Schoolboys who have accepted the club's offer of a Traineeship/Contract
Lamb, Paul D; Parsons, Mark C.

358

NORWICH CITY 1990-91 *Back row (left to right):* Andy Theodosiou, Adrian Pennock, John Polston, Tim Sherwood, Ian Butterworth, Paul Blades, Lee Power.
Centre row: Dave Stringer (Manager), Tim Sheppard (Physiotherapist), Henrik Mortensen, Colin Woodthorpe, Daryl Sutch, Dean Coney, Bryan Gunn, Jonathar Sheffield.
Mark Walton, Robert Rosario, Ian Culverhouse, Jason Minett, Mark Bowen, Mike Walker (Reserve Team Manager), David Williams (Assistant Manager').
Front row: Robert Ullathorne, Robert Fleck, Jeremy Goss, David Smith, David Phillips, Ian Crook, Dale Gordon, Ruel Fox.

Division 1   **NORWICH CITY**

Carrow Road, Norwich NR1 1JE. Telephone Norwich (0603) 612131. Commercial Dept: (0603) 615011. Box Office: (0603) 761661. Clubcall: 0898 121144. Match Information Line: 0898 121514.

NORWICH CITY FC

Ground capacity: 24,284.

Record attendance: 43,984 v Leicester C, FA Cup 6th rd, 30 March 1963.

Record receipts: £126,395 v West Ham U, FA Cup 6th rd (replay), 22 March 1989.

Pitch measurements: 114yd × 74yd.

President: G. C. Watling.

Chairman: Robert T. Chase JP. *Vice-chairman:* J. A. Jones.

Directors: F. J. Kennedy, B. W. Lockwood, G. A. Paterson, A. Scholes DMS, IPFA.

Manager: Dave Stringer. *Assistant Manager/Coach:* Dave Williams.

Commercial Manager: Ray Cossey.

Physio: Tim Sheppard MCSP, SRP.

Secretary: A. R. W. Neville.

Year Formed: 1902. *Turned Professional:* 1905. *Ltd Co.:* 1905.

Club Nickname: 'The Canaries'.

Previous Grounds: 1902, Newmarket Road; 1908–35, The Nest, Rosary Road.

Record League Victory: 10-2 v Coventry C, Division 3 (S), 15 March 1930 – Jarvie; Hannah, Graham; Brown, O'Brien, Lochhead (1); Porter (1), Anderson, Hunt (5), Scott (2), Slicer (1).

Record Cup Victory: 8-0 v Sutton U, FA Cup, 4th rd, 28 January 1989 – Gunn; Culverhouse, Bowen, Butterworth, Linighan, Townsend (Crook), Gordon, Fleck (3), Allen (4), Phelan, Putney (1).

Record Defeat: 2-10 v Swindon T, Southern League, 5 September 1908.

Most League Points (2 for a win): 64, Division 3 (S), 1950–51.

Most League Points (3 for a win): 84, Division 2, 1985–86.

Most League Goals: 99, Division 3 (S), 1952–53.

Highest League Scorer in Season: Ralph Hunt, 31. Division 3 (S), 1955–56.

Most League Goals in Total Aggregate: Johnny Gavin, 122, 1945–54, 1955–58.

Most Capped Player: Martin O'Neill, 18 (64), Northern Ireland.

Most League Appearances: Ron Ashman, 592, 1947–64.

Record Transfer Fee Received: £1,250,000 from Arsenal for Andy Linighan, July 1990.

Record Transfer Fee Paid: £925,000 to Port Vale for Darren Beckford, June 1991.

Football League Record: 1920 Original Member of Division 3; 1921 Division 3 (S): 1934–39 Division 2; 1946–58 Division 3 (S); 1958–60 Division 3; 1960–72 Division 2; 1972–74 Division 1; 1974–75 Division 2; 1975–81 Division 1; 1981–82 Division 2; 1982–85 Division 1; 1985–86 Division 2; 1986– Division 1.

Honours: Football League: Division 1 best season: 4th, 1988–89; Division 2 – Champions 1971–72, 1985–86. Division 3 (S) – Champions 1933–34; Division 3 – Runners-up 1959–60. *FA Cup:* Semi-finals 1959, 1989. *Football League Cup:* Winners 1962, 1985; Runners-up 1973, 1975.

Colours: Yellow shirts green trim, green shorts yellow trim, yellow stockings. **Change colours:** White shirts green trim, white shorts green trim, white stockings.

NORWICH CITY 1990–91 LEAGUE RECORD

Match No.	Date		Venue	Opponents	Result	H/T Score	Lg. Pos.	Goalscorers	Attendance
1	Aug	25	H	Sunderland	W 3-2	2-0	—	Gordon, Sherwood, Fox	17,247
2		28	A	Southampton	L 0-1	0-0	—		17,706
3	Sept	1	A	Leeds U	L 0-3	0-2	15		25,684
4		8	H	Crystal Palace	L 0-3	0-2	17		15,306
5		15	A	Manchester C	L 1-2	0-2	17	Fleck	26,247
6		22	H	Derby Co	W 2-1	0-0	16	Phillips, Fox	13,258
7		29	H	Luton T	L 1-3	1-0	17	Gordon	12,794
8	Oct	6	A	Arsenal	L 0-2	0-2	17		36,048
9		20	A	Liverpool	D 1-1	1-1	17	Fox	21,275
10		27	A	QPR	W 3-1	2-0	16	Power 2, Phillips	11,103
11	Nov	3	H	Sheffield U	W 3-0	1-0	12	Sherwood, Jones (og), Phillips	14,806
12		10	A	Chelsea	D 1-1	1-1	12	Gordon	16,925
13		17	A	Aston Villa	W 2-0	1-0	9	Crook, Fox	17,243
14		24	A	Tottenham H	L 1-2	1-1	11	Crook	33,942
15	Dec	1	H	Wimbledon	L 0-4	0-4	13		12,324
16		8	H	Southampton	W 3-1	1-1	10	Phillips, Ruddock (og), Bowen	11,705
17		15	A	Sunderland	W 2-1	0-1	10	Sherwood, Gordon	18,693
18		22	H	Everton	W 1-0	1-0	9	Polston	14,294
19		26	A	Manchester U	L 0-3	0-0	9		39,801
20		29	A	Coventry C	L 0-2	0-0	9		12,039
21	Jan	2	H	Nottingham F	L 2-6	1-2	—	Sherwood, Fleck	17,043
22		12	H	Leeds U	W 2-0	1-0	11	Sherwood, Gordon	17,786
23		19	A	Crystal Palace	W 3-1	1-0	10	Goss, Fleck 2	17,201
24	Feb	2	H	Manchester C	L 1-2	0-2	10	Polston	15,194
25		23	A	Derby Co	D 0-0	0-0	10		14,102
26	Mar	2	A	Wimbledon	D 0-0	0-0	10		4041
27		16	A	Luton T	W 1-0	1-0	10	Sherwood	8604
28		23	H	Arsenal	D 0-0	0-0	10		20,131
29		30	H	Manchester U	L 0-3	0-2	11		18,282
30	Apr	1	A	Everton	L 0-1	0-0	13		20,485
31		6	H	Coventry C	D 2-2	1-1	13	Sherwood, Fleck	11,550
32		10	H	Tottenham H	W 2-1	1-1	—	Power, Crook	19,014
33		17	H	Chelsea	L 1-3	0-2	—	Polston	12,301
34		20	A	Liverpool	L 0-3	0-2	15		37,065
35		24	A	Nottingham F	L 0-5	0-2	—		17,641
36	May	4	H	QPR	W 1-0	0-0	13	Gordon	13,469
37		8	A	Aston Villa	L 1-2	1-1	—	Gordon	16,697
38		11	A	Sheffield U	L 1-2	1-2	15	Polston	21,019

Final League Position: 15

GOALSCORERS

League (41): Gordon 7, Sherwood 7, Fleck 5, Fox 4, Phillips 4, Polston 4, Crook 3, Power 3, Bowen 1, Goss 1, own goals 2.
Rumbelows Cup (5): Goss 2, Crook 1, Fleck 1, Sherwood 1.
FA Cup (7): Fleck 3, Gordon 2, Mortensen 1, Rosario 1.

Gunn	Blades	Bowen	Butterworth	Polston	Sherwood	Gordon	Fox	Crook	Rosario	Phillips	Fleck	Goss	Minett	Culverhouse	Power	Sutch	Smith	Mortensen	Walton	Ullathorne	Sutton	Woodthorpe	Match No.
1	2	3	4	5	6	7	8	9	10	11													1
1	2	3	4	5	6	7	8*	9†	10	11	12		14										2
1	2	3†	4	5	6	7	8*		10	11	12	9	14										3
1	2	3	4	5	6†	7	12		10*	11	8	9	14										4
1	5	3	4		6	7	10	9		11		8		2									5
1	5	3	4		6	7	10	9		11		8		2									6
1	5†	3	4		9	7*	10	6		11		8	14	2	12								7
1	5	3	4		9	7	10	6		11		8*		2	12								8
1	5	3	4		9	7	10	6		11				2	8								9
1	5	3	4		9	7	10*	6		11	12			2	8								10
1	5	3	4		9	7	10	6		11				2	8								11
1	5	3	4		9	7	10	6		11*	12			2	8								12
1	5	3	4		9	7	10	6		11	12			2	8*								13
1	5	3	4		9	7	10	6		11	12			2	8*								14
1	5	3	4		9	7	10	6†		11	12		14	2	8*								15
1		3	4	5	9	7	10*	6		11		8		2	12								16
1		3	4	5	9	7		6	10	11				2	8								17
1		3	4	5	9	7		6	10	11	12			2	8*								18
1		3	4	5	9	7	10	6		11				2	8*	12							19
1		3	4	5	9	7	10*	6		11		8		2	12								20
1		3	4	5	9	7		6	10	11		8		2									21
1		3	4	5	9	7	10	6		11		8		2									22
1		3	4	5	9	7	10	6		11		8		2									23
1		3	4	5	9*	7		6		11		8		2				10	12				24
1		4	3	5	9	7	12	6*		11		8		2		10							25
1		4	3	5	9	7				11		8	10	2			6						26
1		4	3	5	9	7		6		11		8	10	2									27
1		4	3	5	9	7	10	6		11		8		2									28
1		4	3	5	9	7	10	6		11		8		2									29
1		4	3	5	9*		10	6		11		8	7	2				12					30
1		3	4	5	9	7	12			11		8	6	2	10*								31
1		3	4	5	9	7*12		6		11		8		2	10								32
1		3	4	5	9	7	12	6		11		8		2	10*								33
1		3	4	5	9		10			11		8	6	2		7							34
			4	5	9†	12	10	14		11		8*	6	2		7			1	3			35
		3	4	5	9	7	10			11		8*	6	2					1		12		36
		3	4	5	9	7		10*		11		8	6	2					1		12		37
		3		5		7		10		11		8	6†	2				14	12	1	9*	4	38
34	21	37	31	27	37	35	23	31	9	38	23	14	—	34	13	2	2	—	4	2	—	1	
					+1s		+5s	+1s			+6s	+5s	+2s		+3s	+2s	+1s	+3s			+2s		

Rumbelows Cup	Second Round	Watford (h)	2-0	
		(a)	3-0	
	Third Round	Middlesbrough (a)	0-2	
FA Cup	Third Round	Bristol C (h)	2-1	
	Fourth Round	Swindon T (h)	3-1	
	Fifth Round	Manchester U (h)	2-1	
	Sixth Round	Nottingham F (h)	0-1	

NORWICH CITY

Player and Position	Ht	Wt	Birth Date	Birth Place	Source	Clubs	League App	Gls
Goalkeepers								
Bryan Gunn	6 2	13 13	22 12 63	Thurso	Invergordon BC	Aberdeen	15	—
						Norwich C	175	—
Jon Sheffield	5 11	11 07	1 2 69	Bedworth		Norwich C	1	—
						Aldershot (loan)	26	—
						Ipswich T (loan)	—	—
						Cambridge U (loan)	2	—
Mark Walton	6 2	13 13	1 6 69	Merthyr	Swansea C	Luton T	—	—
						Colchester U	40	—
						Norwich C	5	—
Defenders								
Paul Blades	6 0	10 12	5 1 65	Peterborough	Apprentice	Derby Co	166	1
						Norwich C	21	—
Mark Bowen	5 8	11 13	7 12 63	Neath	Apprentice	Tottenham H	17	2
						Norwich C	134	11
Ian Butterworth	6 1	12 10	25 1 64	Nantwich	Apprentice	Coventry C	90	—
						Nottingham F	27	—
						Norwich C	153	2
Ian Culverhouse	5 10	11 02	22 9 64	B Stortford	Apprentice	Tottenham H	2	—
						Norwich C	192	—
Adrian Pennock	6 0	12 04	27 3 71	Ipswich	Trainee	Norwich C	1	—
John Polston	5 11	11 00	10 6 68	London	Apprentice	Tottenham H	24	1
						Norwich C	27	4
Andy Theodosiou*	6 0	12 10	30 10 70	Stoke Newington	Tottenham H	Norwich C	—	—
Robert Ullathorne	5 7	10 07	11 11 71	Wakefield	Trainee	Norwich C	2	—
Colin Woodthorpe	5 11	11 08	13 1 69	Ellesmere Pt	Apprentice	Chester C	155	6
						Norwich C	1	—
Midfield								
Steve Ball	6 0	12 01	2 9 69	Colchester	Trainee	Arsenal	—	—
						Colchester U	4	—
						Norwich C	—	—
Ian Crook	5 8	10 06	18 1 63	Romford	Apprentice	Tottenham H	20	1
						Norwich C	149	10
Dale Gordon	5 10	11 08	9 1 67	Gt Yarmouth	Apprentice	Norwich C	191	27
Jeremy Goss	5 9	10 09	11 5 65	Cyprus	Amateur	Norwich C	55	3
Jason Minett	5 10	10 02	2 8 71	Peterborough	Trainee	Norwich C	2	—
David Phillips	5 10	11 02	29 7 63	Wegberg	Apprentice	Plymouth Arg	73	15
						Manchester C	81	13
						Coventry C	100	8
						Norwich C	76	8
Tim Sherwood	6 1	11 04	6 2 69	St Albans	Trainee	Watford	32	2
						Norwich C	64	10
David Smith	5 9	11 12	26 12 70	Liverpool	Trainee	Norwich C	4	—
Daryl Sutch	6 0	12 00	11 9 71	Lowestoft	Trainee	Norwich C	4	—
Forwards								
Dean Coney	6 0	13 04	18 9 63	Dagenham	Apprentice	Fulham	211	56
						QPR	48	7
						Norwich C	17	1
Robert Fleck	5 8	11 08	11 8 65	Glasgow	Possil Y M	Partick Th	2	1
						Rangers	85	29
						Norwich C	107	29
Ruel Fox	5 6	10 00	14 1 68	Ipswich	Apprentice	Norwich C	76	9

NORWICH CITY

Foundation: Formed in 1902, largely through the initiative of two local schoolmasters who called a meeting at the Criterion Cafe, they were shocked by an FA Commission which in 1904 declared the club professional and ejected them from the FA Amateur Cup. However, this only served to strengthen their determination. New officials were appointed and a professional club established at a meeting in the Agricultural Hall in March 1905.

First Football League game: 28 August, 1920, Division 3, v Plymouth A (a) D 1-1 – Skermer; Gray, Gadsden; Wilkinson, Addy, Martin; Laxton, Kidger, Parker, Whitham (1), Dobson.

Did you know: After holding First Division Leeds to a 3-3 draw in the FA Cup in 1934-35 Norwich had their legs pulled about their nickname. So they took a couple of canaries to Leeds for the replay and presented them to the club before beating them 2-1.

Managers (and Secretary-managers)
John Bowman 1905–07, James McEwen 1907–08, Arthur Turner 1909–10, Bert Stansfield 1910–15, Major Frank Buckley 1919–20, Charles O'Hagan 1920–21, Albert Gosnell 1921–26, Bert Stansfield 1926, Cecil Potter 1926–29, James Kerr 1929–33, Tom Parker 1933–37, Bob Young 1937–39, Jimmy Jewell 1939, Bob Young 1939–45, Cyril Spiers 1946–47, Duggie Lochhead 1945–50, Norman Low 1950–55, Tom Parker 1955–57, Archie Macaulay 1957–61, Willie Reid 1961–62, George Swindin 1962, Ron Ashman 1962–66, Lol Morgan 1966–69, Ron Saunders 1969–73, John Bond 1973–80, Ken Brown 1980–87, Dave Stringer December 1987– .

Player and Position	Ht	Wt	Birth Date	Place	Source	Clubs	League App	Gls
Henrik Mortensen	5 10	11 07	12 2 68	Odder, Denmark	Aarhus	Norwich C	18	—
Lee Power	5 11	11 02	30 6 72	Lewisham	Trainee	Norwich C	17	3
Chris Sutton§			10 3 73	Nottingham	Trainee	Norwich C	2	—
Robert Taylor*	6 0	11 07	30 4 71	Norwich	Trainee	Norwich C	—	—
						Leyton Orient	3	1

Trainees
Brown, Nicholas J; Bugg, Philip E; Burrows, Peter M; Church, Phillip R; Collins, Sean C; Ewens, David T; Hamilton, John T; Johnson, Andrew J; Mortimer, Philip D; Sutton, Christopher R; Wooding, Timothy D.

**Non-Contract
Williams, David M.

Associated Schoolboys
Carey, Shaun P; Cleveland, Darren L; Crowfoot, Darren L; Gibb, Alistair S; Hall, Darren D; Harrington, Justin D; Herd, Stuart A.L; Irvine, Alexander P; Kreft, Stacey J; Mellon, Richard C; Nicholls, Ryan J; Oldbury, Marcus J; Prior, Adam G; Ruse, Barry O; Wright, Jonathan.

Associated Schoolboys who have accepted the club's offer of a Traineeship/Contract
Akinbiyi, Adeola; Cureton, Jamie; Eadie, Darren M; Ewins, Scott R; Marshall, Andrew J; Roberts, Glyn S; Snowling, Scott.

**Non-Contract Players who are retained must be re-signed before they are eligible to play in League matches.

364

NOTTINGHAM FOREST 1990–91 *Back row (left to right):* Roy Keane, Garry Parker, Darren Wassall, Brian Rice, Ian Woan, Brett Williams, Steve Hodge. *Centre row:* Archie Gemmill (Coach), Franz Carr, Steve Chettle, Steve Sutton, Mark Crossley, Terry Wilson, Tommy Gaynor, Liam O'Kane (Coach). *Front row:* Nigel Clough, Brian Laws, Des Walker, Brian Clough (Manager), Stuart Pearce, Nigel Jemson, Gary Crosby.

Division 1   **NOTTINGHAM FOREST**

City Ground, Nottingham NG2 5FJ. Telephone Nottingham (0602) 822202. Information Desk: 821122.

Commercial Manager: 820444.

Ground capacity: 31,920 (15,114 seats).

Record attendance: 49,945 v Manchester U, Division 1, 28 October 1967.

Record receipts: £186,000 v Tottenham H, Littlewoods Cup 5th rd, 17 January 1990.

Pitch measurements: 115yd × 78yd.

Chairman: M. Roworth. *Vice-chairman:* F. T. C. Pell FCA.

Directors: G. E. Macpherson JP, F. Reacher, J. F. Hickling, I. I. Korn, J. M. Smith, C. Wootton.

Manager: Brian Clough OBE. *Assistant Manager:* Ron Fenton.

Secretary: P. White. *Commercial Manager:* Dave Pullan.

Coach: Liam O'Kane. *Physio:* G. Lyas.

Year Formed: 1865. *Turned Professional:* 1889. *Ltd Co.:* 1982.

Club Nickname: 'Reds'.

Previous Grounds: 1865, Forest Racecourse; 1879, The Meadows; 1880, Trent Bridge Cricket Ground; 1882, Parkside, Lenton; 1885, Gregory, Lenton; 1890, Town Ground; 1898, City Ground.

Record League Victory: 12-0 v Leicester Fosse, Division 1, 12 April 1909 – Iremonger; Dudley, Maltby; Hughes (1), Needham, Armstrong; Hooper (3), Marrison, West (3), Morris (2), Spouncer (3 incl. 1p).

Record Cup Victory: 14-0 v Clapton (away), FA Cup, 1st rd, 17 January 1891 – Brown; Earp, Scott; A. Smith, Russell, Jeacock; McCallum (2), 'Tich' Smith (1), Higgins (5), Lindley (4), Shaw (2).

Record Defeat: 1-9 v Blackburn R, Division 2, 10 April 1937.

Most League Points (2 for a win): 70, Division 3 (S), 1950–51.

Most League Points (3 for a win): 74, Division 1, 1983–84.

Most League Goals: 110, Division 3 (S), 1950–51.

Highest League Scorer in Season: Wally Ardron, 36, Division 3 (S), 1950–51.

Most League Goals in Total Aggregate: Grenville Morris, 199, 1898–1913.

Most Capped Player: Martin O'Neill, 36 (64), Northern Ireland.

Most League Appearances: Bob McKinlay, 614, 1951–70.

Record Transfer Fee Received: £1,500,000 from Manchester U for Neil Webb, August 1989.

Record Transfer Fee Paid: £1,400,000 to Barnsley for Carl Tiler, April 1991.

Football League Record: 1892 Elected to Division 1; 1906–07 Division 2; 1907–11 Division 1; 1911–22 Division 2; 1922–25 Division 1; 1925–49 Division 2; 1949–51 Division 3 (S); 1951–57 Division 2; 1957–72 Division 1; 1972–77 Division 2; 1977– Division 1.

Honours: Football League: Division 1 – Champions 1977–78; Runners-up 1966–67, 1978–79; Division 2 – Champions 1906–07, 1921–22; Runners-up 1956–57; Division 3 (S) – Champions 1950–51. *FA Cup:* Winners 1898, 1959; Runners-up 1991. *Anglo-Scottish Cup:* Winners 1976–77; *Football League Cup:* Winners 1977–78, 1978–79, 1988–89, 1989–90; Runners-up 1979–80. *Simod Cup:* Winners 1989. **European Competitions:** *Fairs Cup:* 1961–62, 1967–68. *European Cup:* 1978–79 (winners), 1979–80 (winners), 1980–81. *Super Cup:* 1979–80 (winners), 1980–81 (runners-up). *World Club Championship:* 1980–81 (runners-up). *UEFA Cup:* 1983–84, 1984–85.

Colours: Red shirts, white shorts, red stockings. **Change colours:** White shirts, black shorts, white stockings.

NOTTINGHAM FOREST 1990–91 LEAGUE RECORD

Match No.	Date	Venue	Opponents	Result	H/T Score	Lg. Pos.	Goalscorers	Atten-dance
1	Aug 25	H	QPR	D 1-1	0 1	—	Jemson (pen)	21,619
2	28	A	Liverpool	L 0-2	0-0	—		33,663
3	Sept 1	A	Coventry C	D 2-2	0-0	17	Jemson 2 (1 pen)	12,630
4	8	H	Southampton	W 3-1	1-1	10	Wilson, Jemson 2	18,559
5	15	A	Crystal Palace	D 2-2	0-1	12	Pearce 2	20,545
6	22	H	Arsenal	L 0-2	0-1	14		26,013
7	29	A	Manchester U	W 1-0	1-0	9	Pearce	46,766
8	Oct 7	H	Everton	W 3-1	1-1	—	Hodge 2, Jemson	25,790
9	20	A	Chelsea	D 0-0	0-0	6		22,403
10	27	H	Tottenham H	L 1-2	1-0	10	Clough	27,347
11	Nov 3	A	Leeds U	L 1-3	0-2	10	Jemson	30,409
12	10	A	Aston Villa	D 1-1	0-0	10	Carr	25,797
13	17	H	Sunderland	W 2-0	1-0	8	Chettle, Clough	22,757
14	24	A	Derby Co	L 1-2	1-1	10	Chettle	21,729
15	Dec 1	H	Luton T	D 2-2	1-1	11	Carr, Clough	16,498
16	15	A	QPR	W 2-1	0-0	11	Clough, Pearce	10,156
17	22	A	Sheffield U	L 2-3	0-0	11	Keane, Pearce	20,394
18	26	H	Wimbledon	W 2-1	2-1	11	Pearce, Keane	16,221
19	29	H	Manchester C	L 1-3	1-2	11	Gaynor	24,937
20	Jan 2	A	Norwich C	W 6-2	2-1	—	Wilson, Clough, Polston (og), Keane 2, Crosby	17,043
21	12	H	Coventry C	W 3-0	0-0	9	Pearce, Clough, Keane	18,344
22	19	A	Southampton	D 1-1	1-1	11	Clough	16,044
23	Feb 2	H	Crystal Palace	L 0-1	0-0	11		17,045
24	16	A	Sunderland	L 0-1	0-1	11		20,394
25	23	H	Aston Villa	D 2-2	1-0	11	Clough, Hodge	22,036
26	Mar 2	A	Luton T	L 0-1	0-0	12		9577
27	16	H	Manchester U	D 1-1	0-1	13	Wilson	23,859
28	20	A	Arsenal	D 1-1	0-1	—	Jemson	34,152
29	23	A	Everton	D 0-0	0-0	12		23,078
30	30	A	Wimbledon	L 1-3	1-1	14	Loughlan	6392
31	Apr 1	H	Sheffield U	W 2-0	1-0	11	Gaynor 2	25,308
32	6	A	Manchester C	L 1-3	0-3	14	Pearce	25,169
33	10	H	Derby Co	W 1-0	0-0	—	Keane	25,109
34	20	H	Chelsea	W 7-0	3-0	11	Keane 2, Parker, Woan, Clough, Pearce 2	20,305
35	24	H	Norwich C	W 5-0	2-0	—	Glover, Clough, Pearce, Crosby, Woan	17,641
36	May 4	A	Tottenham H	D 1-1	1-0	8	Clough	30,891
37	6	H	Liverpool	W 2-1	1-0	—	Clough (pen), Woan	26,151
38	11	H	Leeds U	W 4-3	2-1	8	Parker 2, Clough 2	25,067

Final League Position: 8

GOALSCORERS

League (65): Clough 14 (1 pen), Pearce 11, Jemson 8 (2 pens), Keane 8, Gaynor 3, Hodge 3, Parker 3, Wilson 3, Woan 3, Carr 2, Chettle 2, Crosby 2, Glover 1, Loughlan 1, own goal 1.
Rumbelows Cup (11): Clough 3, Jemson 2, Parker 2, Chettle 1, Crosby 1, Keane 1, Pearce 1.
FA Cup (20): Pearce 4, Jemson 3 (1 pen), Parker 3, Clough 2, Crosby 2, Hodge 2, Keane 2, Charles 1, Wilson 1.

Crossley	Laws	Williams	Walker	Chettle	Hodge	Crosby	Parker	Clough	Jemson	Carr	Wassall	Keane	Starbuck	Wilson	Pearce	Gaynor	Rice	Charles	Woan	Loughlan	Glover	Gemmill	Match No.
1	2	3	4	5*	6	7	8	9	10	11	12												1
1	2	3	4	5		7	8	9	10					6		11							2
1	2	3	4	5	6*		8	9	10	11		7		12									3
1	2*		4	5			8	9	10	7	12	11†		6	3			14					4
1	2		4	5			8	9	10			7		6	3	11*12							5
1	2		4	5		7	8	9	10			6			3	11							6
1	2		4	5		7	8	9	10			6			3	11							7
1	2		4	5	6	7	8	9*10				11			3	12							8
1	2		4	5	6	10	12		9	7		11	8*	3									9
1	2		4	5	6	7	8	9	10			11			3								10
1	2			5		7	8*	9	10	4	6	12		3	11†			14					11
1	2		4	5		7	8	9	10	11		6			3								12
1	2		4	5	6*	7	11		9	10		8	12		3								13
1	2		4	5	6*	7	11		9	10		8	12		3								14
1	2		4	5		11	8	9	10*	7		6	12		3								15
1	2		4	5		11	8	9	10	7		6			3								16
1	2		4	5		11	8	9	10*	7		6	12		3								17
1	2		4	5	6†		11	9	10*	7		8	12	14	3								18
1	2		4	5		14	11†	9		7		8*12	6		3	10							19
1	2		4	5		11	10	9		7		8		6*	3			12					20
1	2		4	5		10	11	9		7*14	6	12	8†	3									21
1	2	3	4	5	12	10	11	9		7*		6	8										22
1			4	5	6	7	11	9				10		8	3		2						23
1	2		4	5	12	14	11	9				10	7†	8	3	6*							24
1	2		4	5	6	7	11*	9				10		8	3		12						25
1			4	5		6		9	10			7		8	3		2	11					26
1	2		4	5		7	11	9	10			6		8	3								27
1	2		4	5		7	11	9	10			6		8	3								28
1	3		4			7	11	9	10		5	6	12	8*			2						29
1			4	5		11		9		6	8†				3*	2	12	7	10	14			30
1			4	5		8		9		6		3	10	2	11	7							31
1			4	5			9		6		3	7	2	11	10	8							32
1	12		4	5			9		6		3	7*	2	11	10	8							33
1			4	5	7	8	9		6		3		2	11	10								34
1	12		4	5	7	8	9†		6		3		2*11	10	14								35
1	2		4	5	7	8	9	12	6*	3			11	10									36
1	2		4	5	6	7	8	9			3		11	10									37
1	2		4	5	6	7	8	9	12		3*		11	10									38
38	30	4	37	37	12	27	35	37	22	13	3	35	3	13	33	9	—	9	9	2	8	2	

```
        +          + +  +     +       +     + +         + +  +     +
        2s         2s 2s 1s   1s      4s    9s 2s       2s 1s 1s 3s 2s
```

Rumbelows Cup Second Round	Burnley (h)	4-1
	(a)	1-0
Third Round	Plymouth Arg (a)	2-1
Fourth Round	Coventry C (a)	4-5
FA Cup Third Round	Crystal Palace (a)	0-0
	(h)	2-2
	(h)	3-0
Fourth Round	Newcastle U (a)	2-2
	(h)	3-0
Fifth Round	Southampton (a)	1-1
	(h)	3-1
Sixth Round	Norwich C (a)	1-0
Semi-final	West Ham U (at Villa Park)	4-0
Final	Tottenham H (at Wembley)	1-2

NOTTINGHAM FOREST

Player and Position	Ht	Wt	Birth Date	Birth Place	Source	Clubs	League App	League Gls
Goalkeepers								
Mark Crossley	6 0	13 09	16 6 69	Barnsley		Nottingham F	48	—
						Manchester U (loan)		—
Leigh Hawkes	6 0	11 13	30 11 73	Romford	Trainee	Nottingham F	—	—
Andrew Marriott	6 0	12 07	11 10 70	Nottingham	Trainee	Arsenal	—	—
						Nottingham F	—	—
						WBA (loan)	3	—
						Blackburn R (loan)	2	—
						Colchester U (loan)	10	—
Mark Smith	6 1	13 09	2 1 73	Birmingham	Trainee	Nottingham F	—	—
Steve Sutton	6 1	13 07	16 4 61	Hartington	Apprentice	Nottingham F	199	—
						Mansfield T (loan)	8	—
						Derby Co (loan)	14	—
						Coventry C (loan)	1	—
Defenders								
Craig Boardman	6 0	11 08	30 11 70	Barnsley	Trainee	Nottingham F	—	—
Gary Bowyer	6 0	12 13	22 6 71	Manchester		Hereford U	14	2
						Nottingham F	—	—
Ray Byrne	6 1	11 02	4 7 72	Newry	Newry	Nottingham F	—	—
Stuart Cash	5 11	11 10	5 9 65	Tipton	Halesowen	Nottingham F	—	—
						Rotherham U (loan)	8	1
						Brentford (loan)	11	—
Gary Charles	5 9	10 13	13 4 70	London		Nottingham F	12	—
						Leicester C (loan)	8	—
Steve Chettle	6 1	12 00	27 9 68	Nottingham	Apprentice	Nottingham F	117	5
Martin Fancutt	5 8	10 08	15 10 73	Derby	Trainee	Nottingham F	—	—
Jason Fletcher*	5 11	11 10	29 9 69	Nottingham	Trainee	Nottingham F	—	—
Philip Gilchrist	6 0	11 12	25 8 73	Stockton	Trainee	Nottingham F	—	—
Chris Hope	6 0	11 01	14 11 72	Sheffield	Darlington	Nottingham F	—	—
Ian Kilford	5 10	10 05	6 10 73	Bristol	Trainee	Nottingham F	—	—
Brian Laws	5 10	11 05	14 10 61	Wallsend	Apprentice	Burnley	125	12
						Huddersfield T	56	1
						Middlesbrough	107	12
						Nottingham F	92	4
Barrett Noble	5 9	10 07	6 2 74	Sheffield	Trainee	Nottingham F	—	—
Stuart Pearce	5 10	12 09	24 4 62	Shepherds Bush	Wealdstone	Coventry C	51	4
						Nottingham F	206	34
Des Walker	5 11	11 03	26 11 65	Hackney	Apprentice	Nottingham F	231	—
Darren Wassall	5 11	11 09	27 6 68	Edgbaston		Nottingham F	13	—
						Hereford U (loan)	5	—
						Bury (loan)	7	1
Brett Williams	5 10	11 11	19 3 68	Dudley	Apprentice	Nottingham F	25	—
						Stockport Co (loan)	2	—
						Northampton T (loan)	4	—
						Hereford U (loan)	14	—
Midfield								
Gary Crosby	5 7	9 11	8 5 64	Sleaford	Lincoln U Grantham	Lincoln C	7	—
						Nottingham F	90	8
Scot Gemmill	5 10	10 01	2 1 71	Paisley	School	Nottingham F	4	—
Steve Hodge	5 7	9 12	25 10 62	Nottingham	Apprentice	Nottingham F	123	30
						Aston Villa	53	12
						Tottenham H	45	7
						Nottingham F	82	20
Stephen Howe	5 7	10 04	6 11 73	Annitsford	Trainee	Nottingham F	—	—
Roy Keane	5 10	11 03	10 8 71	Cork	Cobh Ramblers	Nottingham F	35	8
Anthony Loughlan	6 0	12 03	19 1 70	Surrey	Leicester U	Nottingham F	2	1
Alan Mahood	5 8	9 12	26 3 73	Kilwinning	Bonnyton Th	Morton	8	—
						Nottingham F	—	—
Thorvaldur Orlygsson	5 11	10 08	2 8 66	Odense	Akureyri	Nottingham F	12	1
Garry Parker	5 10	11 00	7 9 65	Oxford	Apprentice	Luton T	42	3
						Hull C	84	8
						Nottingham F	97	16
Brian Rice	6 0	11 10	11 10 63	Glasgow	Whitburn Central	Hibernian	84	11
						Nottingham F	91	9
						Grimsby T (loan)	4	—
						WBA (loan)	3	—
						Stoke C (loan)	18	

NOTTINGHAM FOREST

Foundation: One of the oldest football clubs in the world, Nottingham Forest was formed at a meeting in the Clinton Arms in 1865. Known originally as the Forest Football Club, the game which first drew the founders together was "shinney" a form of hockey. When they determined to change to football in 1865, one of their first moves was to buy a set of red caps to wear on the field.

First Football League game: 3 September, 1892, Division 2, v Everton (a) D 2-2 – Brown; Earp, Scott; Hamilton, A. Smith, McCracken; McCallum, W. Smith, Higgins (2), Pike, McInnes.

Did you know: Forest once played successive FA Cup ties in the same round at Newcastle. In 1920-21 they sold their ground rights to Newcastle for a minimum of £2,000 in the 1st Round and after drawing 1-1 they were beaten at St. James's Park 2-0 in the replay.

Managers (and Secretary-managers)
Harry Radford 1889–97*, Harry Haslam 1897–1909*, Fred Earp 1909–12, Bob Masters 1912–25, John Baynes 1925–29, Stan Hardy 1930–31, Noel Watson 1931–36, Harold Wightman 1936–39, Billy Walker 1939–60, Andy Beattie 1960–63, John Carey 1963–68, Matt Gillies 1969–72, Dave Mackay 1972, Allan Brown 1973–75, Brian Clough January 1975– .

Player and Position	Ht	Wt	Birth Date	Place	Source	Clubs	League App	Gls
Mark A Smith	5 9	10 04	16 12 64	Bellshill	St Mirren BC	Queen's Park	82	7
						Celtic	6	1
						Dunfermline Ath	53	6
						Stoke C (loan)	2	—
						Nottingham F	—	—
						Mansfield T (loan)	7	—
Steven Stone	5 9	11 03	20 8 71	Gateshead	Trainee	Nottingham F	—	—
Mark Telford			17 12 71	South Shields	Trainee	Notts Co	—	—
						Nottingham F	—	—
Terry Wilson	6 0	10 10	8 2 69	Broxburn	Apprentice	Nottingham F	99	9
Ian Woan	5 10	11 09	14 12 67	Wirral	Runcorn	Nottingham F	12	3
Forwards								
Darren Barry	5 10	11 08	5 3 73	Cork	Trainee	Nottingham F	—	—
Steven Bell	5 11	11 09	4 12 73	Middlesbrough	Trainee	Nottingham F	—	—
Franz Carr	5 7	10 12	24 9 66	Preston	Apprentice	Blackburn R	—	—
						Nottingham F	131	17
						Sheffield W (loan)	12	—
						West Ham U (loan)	3	—
Nigel Clough	5 9	11 04	19 3 66	Sunderland	AC Hunters	Nottingham F	235	86
Tommy Gaynor	6 1	13 02	29 1 63	Limerick	Limerick	Doncaster R	33	7
						Nottingham F	53	10
						Newcastle U (loan)	4	1—
Lee Glover	5 10	12 01	24 4 70	Kettering	Trainee	Nottingham F	28	4
						Leicester C (loan)	5	1
						Barnsley (loan)	8	—
Nigel Jemson	5 10	11 10	10 8 69	Preston	Trainee	Preston NE	32	8
						Nottingham F	41	12
						Bolton W (loan)	5	—
						Preston NE (loan)	9	2
Neil Lyne	6 1	12 04	4 4 70	Leicester	Leicester U	Nottingham F	—	—
						Walsall (loan)	7	—
						Shrewsbury T (loan)	16	6
Stephen McLoughlin*	5 10	10 09	21 11 69	Nottingham	Trainee	Nottingham F	—	—
Dale Pearce	5 11	10 11	6 10 73	Newcastle	Trainee	Nottingham F	—	—
Philip Starbuck	5 10	10 13	24 11 68	Nottingham	Apprentice	Nottingham F	36	2
						Birmingham C (loan)	3	—
						Hereford U (loan)	6	—
						Blackburn R (loan)	6	1
Luke Yates	5 6	11 01	19 3 74	Sandwell	Trainee	Nottingham F	—	—

Trainees
Forrest, Cuan F; Kaminsky, Jason M.G.S; Mallabar, Gavin W; Mitchell, Andrew J.

Associated Schoolboys
Brooks, Mark L; Corry, Stephen; Drury, Nathan; Gilmore, Craig; Guinan, Stephen; Hughes, Luke; McMahon, Sam K; Porteous, Jason; Rookyard, Carl; Smith, Richard; Smith, Stephen; Statham, Mark A; Taylor, Michael; Thom, Stuart P; Walker, Justin; Woolford, Stephen.

Associated Schoolboys who have accepted the club's offer of a Traineeship/Contract
Armstrong, Steven C; Glasser, Neil; Helliwell, Craig; McGregor, Paul A; Marshall, Lee; Ring, Gerard; Warner, Vance J; Wright, Dale C.

NOTTS COUNTY 1990–91   *Back row (left to right):* Craig Finch, Shaun Browne, Paul Cox, Don O'Riordan, Richard Walker, Mark Telford, Antony Thompson, Steven Aldridge, Mark Wells.
Centre row: Mick Jones (Assistant Manager), Phil Stant, Charlie Palmer, Dean Yates, Steve Cherry, Kevin Blackwell, Craig Short, Gary Lund, Nicky Platnauer, Dave Wilson (Physiotherapist).
Front row: Phil Robinson, David Norton, Tommy Johnson, Phil Turner, Derek Pavis (Chairman), Neil Warnock (Manager), Mark Draper, Kevin Bartlett, Dean Thomas, Gary Chapman.

Division 1   **NOTTS COUNTY**

County Ground, Meadow Lane, Nottingham NG2 3HJ.
Telephone Nottingham (0602) 861155. Clubcall: 0898 121101.
Football in the Community: 863656. County '75: 864718.
Supporters Club: 866802.

Ground capacity: 21,097.

Record attendance: 47,310 v York C, FA Cup 6th rd, 12 March 1955.

Record receipts: £63,505 v Everton, FA Cup 6th rd, 10 March 1984.

Pitch measurements: 114yd × 74yd.

Chairman: D. C. Pavis. *Vice-chairman:* J. Mounteney.

Directors: W. A. Hopcroft, M. Pavis, P. Jackson, D. Ward, F. Sherwood.

Team Manager: Neil Warnock. *Commerical Manager:* Miss S. Shaw.

Coach: Mick Jones.

Chief Executive: N. E. Hook MCIM. AMLD.

Physio: David Wilson BA, MCSP, DIPTP, GRAD DIP PHYS SRP.

Year Formed: 1862 *(see Foundation).*

Turned Professional: 1885. *Ltd Co.:* 1888.

Club Nickname: 'Magpies'.

Previous Grounds: 1862, The Park; 1864, The Meadows; 1877, Beeston Cricket Ground; 1880, Castle Ground; 1883, Trent Bridge; 1910, Meadow Lane.

Record League Victory: 11-1 v Newport C, Division 3 (S), 15 January 1949 – Smith; Southwell, Purvis; Gannon, Baxter, Adamson; Houghton (1), Sewell (4), Lawton (4), Pimbley, Johnston (2).

Record Cup Victory: 15-0 v Rotherham T (at Trent Bridge), FA Cup, 1st rd, 24 October 1885 – Sherwin; Snook, H. T. Moore; Dobson (1), Emmett (1), Chapman; Gunn (1), Albert Moore (2), Jackson (3), Daft (2), Cursham (4). (1 og).

Record Defeat: 1-9 v Blackburn R, Division 1, 16 November, 1889 and v Aston Villa, Division 1, 29 September, 1888 and v Portsmouth, Division 2, 9 April, 1927.

Most League Points (2 for a win): 69, Division 4, 1970–71.

Most League Points (3 for a win): 87, Division 3, 1989–90.

Most League Goals: 107, Division 4, 1959–60.

Highest League Scorer in Season: Tom Keetley, 39, Division 3 (S), 1930–31.

Most League Goals in Total Aggregate: Les Bradd, 124, 1967–78.

Most Capped Player: Harry Cursham, 8, England, Martin O'Neill, 8 (64), Northern Ireland.

Most League Appearances: Albert Iremonger, 564, 1904–26.

Record Transfer Fee Received: £350,000 from Tottenham H for John Chiedozie, August 1984.

Record Transfer Fee Paid: £600,000 to Orient for John Chiedozie, August 1981.

Football League Record: 1888 Founder Member of the Football League; 1893–97 Division 2; 1897–1913 Division 1; 1913–14 Division 2; 1914–20 Division 1; 1920–23 Division 2; 1923–26 Division 1; 1926–30 Division 2; 1930–31 Division 3 (S); 1931–35 Division 2; 1935–50 Division 3 (S); 1950–58 Division 2; 1958–59 Division 3; 1959–60 Division 4; 1960–64 Division 3; 1964–71 Division 4; 1971–73 Division 3; 1973–81 Division 2; 1981–84 Division 1; 1984–85 Division 2; 1985–90 Division 3; 1990–91 Division 2; 1991– Division 1.

Honours: Football League: Division 1 best season: 3rd, 1890–91, 1900–01; Division 2 – Champions 1896–97, 1913–14, 1922–23; Runners-up 1894–95, 1980–81; Division 3 (S) – Champions 1930–31, 1949–50; Runners-up 1936–37; Division 3 – Runners-up 1972-73; Division 4 – Champions 1970–71; Runners-up 1959–60. *FA Cup:* Winners 1893–94; Runners-up 1890–91. *Football League Cup:* best season: 5th rd, 1963–64, 1972–73, 1975–76.

Colours: Black and white broad striped shirts, amber sleeve and neck trim, black shorts with white side flash, black stockings with white and amber trim. **Change colours:** All sky blue.

NOTTS COUNTY 1990–91 LEAGUE RECORD

Match No.	Date	Venue	Opponents	Result	H/T Score	Lg. Pos.	Goalscorers	Attendance
1	Aug 25	A	Hull C	W 2-1	1-1	—	Palmer, Lund	7385
2	Sept 1	H	Oxford U	W 3-1	1-1	4	Johnson, Lund, Melville (og)	6393
3	8	A	Middlesbrough	L 0-1	0-0	7		17,380
4	15	H	Portsmouth	W 2-1	1-0	4	Draper, Thomas	6451
5	18	H	Barnsley	L 2-3	1-1	—	Robinson, Lund	7195
6	22	A	Watford	W 3-1	3-1	6	Platnauer, Dublin (og), Bartlett	7973
7	29	H	Bristol R	W 3-2	2-1	3	Yates, Thomas, Robinson	6563
8	Oct 1	A	Port Vale	W 1-0	0-0	—	Johnson (pen)	7723
9	6	A	Leicester C	L 1-2	0-1	5	Johnson	13,597
10	13	H	Wolverhampton W	D 1-1	0-1	5	Thomas	12,833
11	20	H	Millwall	L 0-1	0-1	6		7599
12	23	A	Plymouth Arg	D 0-0	0-0	—		6651
13	27	A	Oldham Ath	L 1-2	0-0	9	Regis	12,940
14	30	H	Charlton Ath	D 2-2	0-0	—	Balmer (og), Bartlett	5067
15	Nov 3	A	West Ham U	L 0-1	0-0	8		10,871
16	10	H	WBA	W 4-3	3-1	7	Bartlett 2, Regis, Draper (pen)	8162
17	17	A	Ipswich T	D 0-0	0-0	7		10,778
18	24	H	Swindon T	D 0-0	0-0	7		6113
19	Dec 1	A	Sheffield W	D 2-2	0-2	7	Draper (pen), Bartlett	23,474
20	15	H	Hull C	W 2-1	1-0	5	Regis, Bartlett	5537
21	22	H	Bristol C	W 3-2	1-1	5	Regis 2, Draper	6586
22	26	A	Blackburn R	W 1-0	1-0	5	Bartlett	8648
23	29	A	Newcastle U	W 2-0	0-0	5	Bartlett, Draper (pen)	17,557
24	Jan 1	H	Brighton & HA	W 2-1	2-1	4	Bartlett, McCarthy (og)	8276
25	12	A	Oxford U	D 3-3	2-1	4	Robinson, Turner, Yates	5358
26	19	H	Middlesbrough	W 3-2	2-2	4	Draper, Regis, Johnson	9316
27	22	A	Charlton Ath	L 1-3	0-2	—	Regis	4516
28	Feb 2	H	Portsmouth	L 1-2	0-1	4	Johnson	12,680
29	23	A	WBA	D 2-2	1-1	5	Bartlett 2	11,068
30	Mar 2	H	Sheffield W	L 0-2	0-1	5		15,546
31	12	H	Port Vale	D 1-1	0-1	—	Johnson	6305
32	16	A	Bristol R	D 1-1	0-1	8	Johnson	4878
33	19	A	Wolverhampton W	W 2-0	2-0	—	Johnson, Bartlett	12,375
34	23	H	Leicester C	L 0-2	0-2	8		11,532
35	30	H	Blackburn R	W 4-1	1-0	7	Bartlett, Johnson 3	6831
36	Apr 1	A	Bristol C	L 2-3	1-1	8	Johnson, O'Riordan	13,466
37	6	H	Newcastle U	W 3-0	0-0	7	Regis 2, Short Chris	7806
38	9	A	Barnsley	L 0-1	0-1	—		9801
39	13	A	Brighton & HA	D 0-0	0-0	8		9864
40	16	H	Watford	W 1-0	0-0	—	Paris	6168
41	20	A	Millwall	W 2-1	1-0	5	Yates, Regis	10,162
42	23	A	Swindon T	W 2-1	1-0	—	Yates, Johnson	7853
43	27	H	Plymouth Arg	W 4-0	1-0	4	Draper, Regis 3 (1 pen)	7370
44	May 4	A	Oldham Ath	W 2-0	1-0	4	Regis, Johnson	12,311
45	7	H	Ipswich T	W 3-1	2-0	—	Johnson 2 (1 pen), Regis	6902
46	11	A	West Ham U	W 2-1	2-0	4	Draper 2	26,551

Final League Position: 4

GOALSCORERS

League (76): Johnson 16 (2 pens), Regis 15 (1 pen), Bartlett 13, Draper 9 (3 pens), Yates 4, Lund 3, Robinson 3, Thomas 3, O'Riordan 1, Palmer 1, Paris 1, Platnauer 1, Short Chris 1, Turner 1, own goals 4.
Rumbelows Cup (5): Johnson 3 (1 pen), Bartlett 1, Robinson 1.
FA Cup (9): Lund 2, O'Riordan 2, Turner 2, Bartlett 1, Short Craig 1, own goal 1.

Cherry	Palmer	Platnauer	Short Craig	Yates	Robinson	Thomas	Draper	Bartlett	Lund	Johnson	Norton	Brook	Chapman	Turner	Regis	Harding	Short Chris	O'Riordan	Nelson	Paris	Davis	Match No.
1	2	3	4	5	6	7	8	9*	10	11	12											1
1	4	3		5	6	7	8	9	10	11	2											2
1	4	3		5	6	7	8	9	10	11	2*	12										3
1	2	3	4	5	6	7	8	9	10	11*			12									4
1	2	3	4	5	6	7	8	9	10	11												5
1	2	3	4	5	6	7	8*	9	10	11				12								6
1	2	3	4	5	6	7*	8	9	10	11†				12	14							7
1	2	3	4	5	6	7	8*	9	10	11				12								8
1	2	3	4	5	6	7	12	9	10	11†				8*	14							9
1	2	3	4	5	6	7	12	9†	10	11*				8	14							10
1	2	3*	4	5	6	7	12	9†	10	11				8	14							11
1	2		4	5	6	7	11	9	10					8		3						12
1	2	3	4	5	6	7	8*	9	10	11†				14	12							13
1	2	3	4	5	6*	7	8	9	10	11†				14	12							14
1	2		4	5		7	11	9					12	8	10	3		6*				15
1	2		4	5	12	7	11†	9						8	10	3*		6	14			16
1	2		4	5		7	11	9						8	10	3		6				17
1	2		4	5		7	11	9						8	10*	3		6	12			18
1	2		4	5		7	11	9						8	10	3		6				19
1	2		4	5		7	11	9						8	10	3		6				20
1	2		4	5		7	11	9					12	8	10	3		6*				21
1	2		4	5		7	11	9						8	10	3		6				22
1			4	5		7	11	9		8*	2				10	3	12	6				23
1			4	5		7	11	9						8	10	3	2	6				24
1	2		4	5	3	7	11	9*						8	10	12		6				25
1	2		4	5	3	7	11	9						8	10	12		6*				26
1	2		4	5	6	7	11*	9						8	10	3						27
1	2		4	5		7	11*	9					12	8	10	3		6†	14			28
1	2		4	5			11*	9	10†				12	8	14	3		6	7			29
1	2		4	5		7	11*	9					12	8	10	3		6				30
1	2		4	5		7	11	9	10†				12	8	14	3*		6				31
1			4	5		7	11†	9	10					8	14	3*	2	6			12	32
1			4	5		7		9		11				8	10		2	6		3		33
1	12		4	5		7	14	9		11				8	10		2*	6		3†		34
1			4	5		7	10	9†		11				8	14	12	2	6*		3		35
1			4	5		7	10	9		11				8			2	6		3		36
1	5		4			7	10	9					12	8	11	3*	2	6				37
1	5		4			7	10	9*					12	8	11	3	2	6†			14	38
1	5		4			7	10	9*		11				8	12		2	6		3		39
1	2		4	5		7*	10			11			12	8	9			6		3		40
1	2		4	5		7	10			11*			12	8	9			6		3		41
1	2		4	5		7	10	14		11*			12	8	9†			6		3		42
1	2		4	5		7	10*	14		11†			12	8	9			6		3		43
1	2		4	5		7	10*	14		11†				8	9	12		6		3		44
1	2		4			7*	10			11				8	9	12	5	6		3		45
1	2		4*				10			11				8	9	7	5	6		3	12	46
46	39	13	43	41	18	44	41	37	16	29	3	—	—	35	26	20	11	31	—	13	—	

```
 +                 +  +              +  +       +  +  +  +  +  +           +  +  +
1s                1s 4s 3s          8s 1s 1s 6s 3s 11s 4s    4s          2s 2s 2s
```

Rumbelows Cup	First Round	Exeter C (a)	1-1
		(h)	1-0
	Second Round	Oldham Ath (h)	1-0
		(a)	2-5
FA Cup	Third Round	Hull C (a)	5-2
	Fourth Round	Oldham Ath (h)	2-0
	Fifth Round	Manchester C (h)	1-0
	Sixth Round	Tottenham H (a)	1-2

NOTTS COUNTY

Player and Position	Ht	Wt	Birth Date	Place	Source	Clubs	League App	Gls
Goalkeepers								
Kevin Blackwell‡	5 11	12 10	21 12 58	Luton	Boston U	Barnet	—	—
						Scarborough	44	—
						Notts Co	—	—
Steve Cherry	5 11	11 00	5 8 60	Nottingham	Apprentice	Derby Co	77	—
						Port Vale (loan)	4	—
						Walsall	71	—
						Plymouth Arg	73	—
						Chesterfield (loan)	10	—
						Notts Co	110	—
Paul Dolan	6 4	13 05	16 4 66	Ottawa	Vancouver W	Notts Co	—	—
Defenders								
Paul Cox	5 11	11 12	1 1 72	Nottingham	Trainee	Notts Co	—	—
Steven Hodder	5 9	11 03	18 10 71	Sheffield	Nottingham F	Notts Co	—	—
David Norton	5 7	11 03	3 3 65	Cannock	Apprentice	Aston Villa	44	2
						Notts Co	27	1
						Rochdale (loan)	9	—
						Hull C (loan)	15	—
Charlie Palmer	5 11	12 03	10 7 63	Aylesbury	Apprentice	Watford	10	1
						Derby Co	51	2
						Hull C	70	1
						Notts Co	88	6
Alan Paris	5 11	10 12	15 8 64	Slough	Slough T	Watford	—	—
						Peterborough U	137	2
						Leicester C	88	3
						Notts Co	15	1
Nicky Platnauer	5 10	12 12	10 6 61	Leicester	Bedford T	Bristol R	24	7
						Coventry C	44	6
						Birmingham C	28	2
						Reading (loan)	7	—
						Cardiff C	115	6
						Notts Co	57	1
Chris Short	5 10	12 02	9 5 70	Munster		Scarborough	43	1
						Manchester U (loan)	—	—
						Notts Co	15	1
Craig Short	6 0	11 04	25 6 68	Bridlington	Pickering T	Scarborough	63	7
						Notts Co	87	2
Dean Thomas	5 9	11 08	19 12 61	Bedworth	Nuneaton Bor	Wimbledon	57	8
					Dusseldorf	Northampton T	74	11
						Notts Co	54	4
Anthony Thompson			1 7 72	Mansfield	Trainee	Notts Co	—	—
Richard Walker			9 11 71	Derby	Trainee	Notts Co	—	—
Dean Yates	6 1	10 04	26 10 67	Leicester	Apprentice	Notts Co	267	31
Midfield								
Steve Aldridge			4 9 71	Basford		Notts Co	—	—
Shaun Browne			3 11 71	Nottingham	Nottingham F	Notts Co	—	—
Gary Chapman	5 10	12 00	1 5 64	Leeds		Bradford C	5	—
						Notts Co	25	4
						Mansfield T (loan)	6	—
Mark Draper	5 10	10 00	11 11 70	Derbyshire	Trainee	Notts Co	99	15
Paul Harding	5 10	12 05	6 3 64	Mitcham	Barnet	Notts Co	24	—
Don O'Riordan	6 0	11 12	14 5 57	Dublin	Apprentice	Derby Co	6	1
						Doncaster R (loan)	2	—
					Tulsa	Preston NE	158	8
						Carlisle U	84	18
						Middlesbrough	41	2
						Grimsby T	86	14
						Notts Co	91	4
						Mansfield T (loan)	6	—
Philip Robinson	5 9	10 10	6 1 67ᶠ	Stafford	Apprentice	Aston Villa	3	1
						Wolverhampton W	71	8
						Notts Co	65	5
						Birmingham C (loan)	9	1
Eddie Snook	5 7	10 01	18 10 68	Washington	Apprentice	Notts Co	—	—

NOTTS COUNTY

Foundation: For many years the foundation date of the Football League's oldest club was given as 1862 and the club celebrated its centenary in 1962. However, the researches of Keith Warsop have since shown that the club was on a very haphazard basis at that time, playing little more than practice matches. The meeting which put it on a firm footing was held at the George IV Hotel in December 1864, when they became known as the Notts Football Club.

First Football League game: 15 September, 1888, Football League, v Everton (a) L 1-2 – Holland; Guttridge, McLean; Brown, Warburton, Shelton; Hodder, Harker, Jardine, Moore (1), Wardle.

Did you know: Notts County have competed in every FA Cup competition since 1877 – a record. They drew their initial game 1-1 against the Sheffield club at Trent Bridge, but lost the replay 3-0.

Managers (and Secretary-managers)
Edwin Browne 1883–93*, Tom Featherstone 1893*, Tom Harris 1893–13*, Albert Fisher 1913–27, Horace Henshall 1927–34, Charlie Jones 1934–35, David Pratt 1935, Percy Smith 1935–36, Jimmy McMullan 1936–37, Harry Parkes 1938–39, Tony Towers 1939–42, Frank Womack 1942–43, Major Frank Buckley 1944–46, Arthur Stollery 1946–49, Eric Houghton 1949–53, George Poyser 1953–57, Tommy Lawton 1957–58, Frank Hill 1958–61, Tim Coleman 1961–63, Eddie Lowe 1963–65, Tim Coleman 1965–66, Jack Burkitt 1966–67, Andy Beattie (GM 1967), Billy Gray 1967–68, Jimmy Sirrel 1969–75, Ron Fenton 1975–77, Jimmy Sirrel 1978–82 (continues as GM to 1984), Howard Wilkinson 1982–83, Larry Lloyd 1983–84, Richie Barker 1984–85, Jimmy Sirrel 1985–87, John Barnwell 1987–88, Neil Warnock January1989– .

Player and Position	Ht	Wt	Birth Date	Birth Place	Source	Clubs	League App	Gls
Phil Turner	5 8	10 13	12 2 62	Sheffield	Apprentice	Lincoln C	241	19
						Grimsby T	62	8
						Leicester C	24	2
						Notts Co	98	9
Mark Wells			15 10 71	Leicester	Trainee	Notts Co	—	—
Forwards								
Kevin Bartlett	5 9	10 12	12 10 62	Portsmouth	Apprentice	Portsmouth	3	—
					Fareham	Cardiff C	82	25
						WBA	37	10
						Notts Co	54	21
Craig Finch			21 12 71	Burton-on-Trent	Trainee	Notts Co	—	—
Tommy Johnson	5 10	10 00	15 1 71	Newcastle	Trainee	Notts Co	87	38
Gary Lund	5 11	11 00	13 9 64	Grimsby	School	Grimsby T	60	24
						Lincoln C	44	13
						Notts Co	138	40
Scott Machin‡	6 0	12 00	29 9 70	Leicester	Trainee	Notts Co	—	—
Dave Regis	6 3	13 00	3 6 64	Paddington	Barnet	Notts Co	37	15

Trainees
Barrow, Lee A; Blatherwick, Steven S; Brough, John R; Crossland, Daniel; Harmon, Darren J; Hill, Philip W; Johnson, Michael O; Moore, James W; Patterson, Gary; Powell, Darren L; Rogers, Kevin A; Saunders, Darren D; Sherlock, Paul G; Simpson, Michael; Slawson, Stephen M; Walker, James B; Ward, Richard.

**Non-Contract
Blackwell, Kevin P.

Associated Schoolboys
Abbey, Paul A; Armeni, Christopher; Clark, Andrew D; Dodson, Matthew J; Freeman, Matthew C; Gallagher, Thomas D; Hawkins, Andrew; Henry, Alvin M; Huckerby, Darren C; Lawley, Edward W.H; Marshall, Daniel J; Needham, Ben; Ridgway, Ian D; Rigby, Malcolm R.

Associated Schoolboys who have accepted the club's offer of a Traineeship/Contract
Galloway, Michael A; Horseman, Brian G; Smith, Paul A; Wells, Iain D.

**Non-Contract Players who are retained must be re-signed before they are eligible to play in League matches.

OLDHAM ATHLETIC 1990–91 *Back row (left to right)*: Neil Redfearn, David Currie, Paul Warhurst, Willie Donachie, Paul Kane.
Centre row: Ronnie Evans (Kit Manager), Bill Urmson (Coach), Gunnar Halle, John Keeley, Paul Moulden, Jon Hallworth, Richard Jobson, Frank Bunn, Ian Liversedge (Physiotherapist).
Front row: Roger Palmer, Andy Barlow, Ian Marshall, Earl Barrett, Joe Royle (Manager), Rick Holden, Nick Henry, Andy Ritchie, Neil Adams.

Division 1   **OLDHAM ATHLETIC**

Boundary Park, Oldham. Telephone 061-624 4972. Commercial Dept: 061-652 0966. Clubcall: 0898 121142.

Ground capacity: 19,432.

Record attendance: 47,671 v Sheffield W, FA Cup 4th rd. 25 January 1930.

Record receipts: £82,320 v West Ham U, Littlewoods Cup semi-final first leg, 14 February 1990.

Pitch measurements: 110yd × 74yd.

President: R. Schofield.

Chairman & Chief Executive: I. H. Stott, ***Vice-chairman:*** D. A. Brierley.

Directors: G. T. Butterworth, R. Adams, D. R. Taylor, P. Chadwick, J. Slevin, N. Holden.

Manager: Joe Royle.

Secretary: Terry Cale. ***Commercial Manager:*** Alan Hardy.

Player-coach: Willie Donachie. ***Coach:*** Billy Urmson.

Physio: Ian Liversedge.

Year Formed: 1895. ***Turned Professional:*** 1899. ***Ltd Co.:*** 1906.

Previous Name: 1895, Pine Villa; 1899, Oldham Athletic.

Club Nickname: 'The Latics'.

Previous Ground: Sheepfoot Lane; 1905, Boundary Park.

Record League Victory: 11-0 v Southport, Division 4, 26 December 1962 – Hollands; Branagan, Marshall; McCall, Williams, Scott; Ledger (1), Johnstone, Lister (6), Colquhoun (1), Whitaker (3).

Record Cup Victory: 10-1 v Lytham, FA Cup, 1st rd, 28 November 1925 – Gray; Wynne, Grundy; Adlam, Heaton, Naylor (1), Douglas, Pynegar (2), Ormston (2), Barnes (3), Watson (2).

Record Defeat: 4-13 v Tranmere R, Division 3 (N), 26 December 1935.

Most League Points (2 for a win): 62, Division 3, 1973–74.

Most League Points (3 for a win): 88, Division 2, 1990–91.

Most League Goals: 95, Division 4, 1962–63.

Highest League Scorer in Season: Tom Davis, 33, Division 3 (N), 1936–37.

Most League Goals in Total Aggregate: Roger Palmer, 138, 1980–91.

Most Capped Player: Albert Gray, 9 (24), Wales.

Most League Appearances: Ian Wood, 525, 1966–80.

Record Transfer Fee Received: £1,000,000 from Everton for Mike Milligan, August 1990.

Record Transfer Fee Paid: £600,000 to Everton for Mike Milligan, June 1991.

Football League Record: 1907 Elected to Division 2; 1910–23 Division 1; 1923–35 Division 2; 1935–53 Division 3 (N); 1953–54 Division 2; 1954–58 Division 3 (N); 1958–63 Division 4; 1963–69 Division 3; 1969–71 Division 4; 1971–74 Division 3; 1974–91 Division 2; 1991–Division 1.

Honours: *Football League:* Division 1 – Runners-up 1914–15; Division 2 – Champions 1990–91; Runners-up 1909–10; Division 3 (N) – Champions 1952–53; Division 3 – Champions 1973–74; Division 4 – Runners-up 1962–63. *FA Cup:* Semi-final 1913, 1989–90. *Football League Cup:* Runners-up 1990.

Colours: All blue with red piping. **Change colours:** All red with blue piping.

OLDHAM ATH 1990–91 LEAGUE RECORD

Match No.	Date	Venue	Opponents	Result	H/T Score	Lg. Pos.	Goalscorers	Atten- dance
1	Aug 25	A	Wolverhampton W	W 3-2	1-1	—	Marshall 3	20,864
2	28	H	Leicester C	W 2-0	0-0	—	Marshall, Ritchie	13,099
3	Sept 1	H	Portsmouth	W 3-1	2-0	1	Holden R, Kuhl (og), Warhurst	11,657
4	8	A	Barnsley	W 1-0	0-0	1	Marshall	11,257
5	15	H	Oxford U	W 3-0	0 0	1	Marshall, Barrett, Redfearn	12,429
6	18	H	Charlton Ath	D 1-1	1-1	—	Redfearn	13,176
7	22	A	Middlesbrough	W 1-0	0-0	1	Palmer	19,363
8	29	A	WBA	D 0-0	0-0	1		13,782
9	Oct 2	H	Swindon T	W 3-2	1-1	—	Moulden, Holden R, Redfearn (pen)	12,575
10	6	H	Blackburn R	D 1-1	1-0	1	Moulden	12,093
11	13	A	Hull C	D 2-2	0-1	2	Henry, Redfearn	8676
12	20	A	Bristol C	W 2-1	2-1	1	Adams 2	14,031
13	23	H	Ipswich T	W 2-0	0-0	—	Moulden, Currie	13,170
14	27	H	Notts Co	W 2-1	0-0	1	Redfearn, Ritchie	12,940
15	Nov 3	A	Sheffield W	D 2-2	2-0	1	Henry, Currie	34,845
16	10	H	Watford	W 4-1	3-1	1	Ritchie 2 (1 pen), Redfearn, Henry	12,410
17	17	A	Port Vale	L 0-1	0-0	1		11,384
18	24	A	Bristol R	L 0-1	0-0	2		6542
19	Dec 1	A	Brighton & HA	W 6-1	2-0	2	Henry, Marshall 2, Adams, Redfearn, Ritchie	11,426
20	15	H	Wolverhampton W	W 4-1	1-1	2	Barrett, Ritchie, Palmer 2	11,587
21	21	H	Plymouth Arg	W 5-3	2-2	—	Redfearn 2, Palmer 2, Barrett	11,296
22	26	A	West Ham U	L 0-2	0-1	2		24,950
23	29	A	Millwall	D 0-0	0-0	2		10,010
24	Jan 1	H	Newcastle U	D 1-1	0-0	2	Stimson (og)	14,550
25	12	A	Portsmouth	W 4-1	2-1	2	Holden R, Palmer, Marshall 2	10,840
26	19	A	Barnsley	W 2-0	1-0	2	Marshall, Ritchie	13,849
27	Feb 2	A	Oxford U	L 1-5	0-3	2	Adams	5411
28	16	H	Port Vale	W 2-0	0-0	2	Redfearn, Jobson	12,630
29	23	H	Watford	D 1-1	1-0	2	Redfearn	8230
30	Mar 2	A	Brighton & HA	W 2-1	1-0	2	Ritchie 2	9496
31	9	H	Bristol R	W 2-0	0-0	1	Redfearn, Ritchie	12,775
32	12	A	Swindon T	D 2-2	0-0	—	Ritchie, Palmer	8193
33	16	H	WBA	W 2-1	1-1	1	Palmer 2	12,584
34	20	H	Hull C	L 1-2	0-1	—	Ritchie (pen)	12,626
35	23	A	Blackburn R	L 0-2	0-0	1		12,175
36	29	H	West Ham U	D 1-1	0-0	—	Ritchie (pen)	16,932
37	Apr 1	A	Plymouth Arg	W 2-1	1-0	1	Ritchie, Adams	8852
38	6	H	Millwall	D 1-1	0-1	2	Ritchie	13,434
39	10	A	Leicester C	D 0-0	0-0	—		11,846
40	13	A	Newcastle U	L 2-3	0-2	2	Holden R, Marshall	16,615
41	16	A	Charlton Ath	D 1-1	1-1	—	Adams	5367
42	20	H	Bristol C	W 2-1	0-0	2	Marshall, Redfearn (pen)	14,086
43	27	A	Ipswich T	W 2-1	1-0	2	Marshall 2	12,332
44	May 4	A	Notts Co	L 0-2	0-1	2		12,311
45	7	H	Middlesbrough	W 2-0	2-0	—	Marshall, Holden R	14,213
46	11	H	Sheffield W	W 3-2	0-1	1	Marshall, Bernard, Redfearn (pen)	18,809

Final League Position: 1

GOALSCORERS

League (83): Marshall 17, Ritchie 15 (3 pens), Redfearn 14 (3 pens), Palmer 9, Adams 6, Holden R 5, Henry 4, Barrett 3, Moulden 3, Currie 2, Bernard 1, Jobson 1, Warhurst 1, own goals 2.
Rumbelows Cup (5): Currie 2, Holden R 1, Moulden 1, Redfearn 1 (pen).
FA Cup (3): Redfearn 2 (2 pens), Adams 1.

Hallworth	Warhurst	Barlow	Redfearn	Barrett	Holden A	Adams	Ritchie	Marshall	Donachie	Holden R	Palmer	Moulden	Henry	Jobson	Currie	Fillery	Williams	Brazil	Kane	Halle	Bernard	Match No.
1	2	3	4	5	6	7†	8	9	10*	11	12	14										1
1	2	3	10	5	6*	7	8	9		11	12		4									2
1	2	3	10	5		7*	8	9		11			4	6	12							3
1	2	3	10	5			8*	9		11	12	14	4	6	7†							4
1	2	3	10	5		7*		9		11	12	14	4	6	8†							5
1	2	3	10	5		14		9		11	7	8*	4†	6	12							6
1	2	3	10*	5		7	8	12		11		14	4	6	9†							7
1		3	10	5			12		2	11	7	8	4	6	9*							8
1	2†	3	10	5			8*	9		11	7	14	4	6	12							9
1	6	3	10	5			8	9	2*	11	7		4		12							10
1		3	10	5		14	8†	9		11	12		4	6	7	2*						11
1	2	3	10	5		7		9		11	12		4	6	8*							12
1	2	3	10	5		7†		9*	14	11	12		4	6	8							13
1	2	3	10	5		7		9*		11	12		4	6	8							14
1	2	3	10*	5		7	8	9		11			4	6	9	12						15
1	2	3	10	5		7	8	9		11*	12		4	6								16
1	2*	3	10	5		7	8	9†	14	11			4	6	12							17
1	12	3	10	5		7*	8	9		11†		14	4	6				2				18
1	2	3	10	5		7*	8	9†	14	11			4	6	12							19
1	2*	3	10	5		7	8	9		11	12		4	6								20
1	2	3	10	5		7	8	9		11			4	6								21
1	2	3	10	5		7*	8	9		11			4	6	12							22
1	2	3	10	5		7*	8	9		11	12		4	6								23
1	2†	3	10	5		7	8*	9		11	12	14	4	6								24
1	2	3	10	5		7	8	9		11			4	6								25
1	2	3	10	5		7	8	9		11			4	6								26
1	2	3	10	5			8	9		11†	12	14	4	6					7*			27
1		3	10	5		7†	8	9		11*			4	6	12				14	2		28
1		3	10	5			8*	9		11			4	6	12				7	2		29
1		3	10	5			8	9		11			4	6					7	2		30
1		3	10	5			8	9†		11	12	14	4	6					7*	2		31
1		3	10	5			8	9*		11	12	14	4	6					7†	2		32
1		3	10	5			8	9		11	12		4	6					7	2*		33
1		3	10	5			8	9		11	12	14	4	6					7†	2*		34
1		3	10	5			8	9		11	12	14	4*	6					7	2†		35
1	14	3	10†	5		7	8	9*		11			4	6	12					2		36
1	9	3	10	5		7	8			11			4	6					12	2*		37
1	9	3	10†	5		7*	8			11			4	6	12				14	2		38
1	9	3	12	5		7†	8*		14	11			4	6					10	2		39
1	9†	3	12	5			8		14	11	7		4	6					10	2*		40
1	12	3	10	5		7†	8*	9		11			4	6					14	2		41
1	8	3	10	5		7		9		11			4	6	12					2*		42
1	8	3	12	5		7*		9		11			4	6					10	2		43
1		3	8	5		7*		9		11		14	4	6	10				12	2†		44
1		3		5		7		9		11	10		4	6	12					2*	8	45
1		3	12	5		7†		9		11	10		4	6					14	2*	8	46
46	30	46	41	46	2	21	29	25	12	42	20	11	43	43	16	1	—	1	12	17	2	
	+				+	+	+	+		+			+	+	+	+	+	+	+			
	3s				4s	10s	2s	1s		5s			9s	13s	1s	11s	1s	2s	5s			

Rumbelows Cup — Second Round — Notts Co (a) — 0-1
    (h) — 5-2
    Third Round — Leeds U (a) — 0-2
FA Cup — Third Round — Brentford (h) — 3-1
    Fourth Round — Notts Co (a) — 0-2

OLDHAM ATHLETIC

Player and Position	Ht	Wt	Birth Date	Place	Source	Clubs	League App	Gls
Goalkeepers								
Jon Hallworth	6 2	12 10	26 10 65	Stockport	School	Ipswich T	45	—
						Swindon T (loan)	—	—
						Bristol R (loan)	2	—
						Fulham (loan)	—	—
						Oldham Ath	77	—
John Keeley	6 1	14 02	27 7 61	Plaistow	Apprentice Chelmsford	Southend U	54	—
						Brighton & HA	138	—
						Oldham Ath	—	—
Andy Rhodes (To Dunfermline Ath July 1990)	6 0	12 00	23 8 64	Doncaster	Apprentice	Barnsley	36	—
						Doncaster R	106	—
						Oldham Ath	69	—
Defenders								
Andy Barlow	5 9	11 01	24 11 65	Oldham		Oldham Ath	219	3
Earl Barrett	5 10	11 00	28 4 67	Rochdale	Apprentice	Manchester C	3	—
						Chester C (loan)	12	—
						Oldham Ath	154	5
Willie Donachie	5 9	11 03	5 10 51	Glasgow	Juniors	Manchester C	351	2
					Portland T	Norwich C	11	—
					Portland T	Burnley	60	3
						Oldham Ath	169	3
Jason Fisk‡			18 9 71	Hull	Trainee	Oldham Ath	—	—
Gunnar Halle	5 11	11 02	11 8 65	Oslo	Lillestrom	Oldham Ath	17	—
Wayne Heseltine	5 9	11 06	3 12 69	Bradford	Trainee	Manchester U	—	—
						Oldham Ath	1	—
Andy Holden	6 1	13 00	14 9 62	Flint	Rhyl	Chester C	100	17
						Wigan Ath	49	4
						Oldham Ath	21	4
Darren Huyton‡			26 9 71	Ashton	School	Oldham Ath	—	—
Richard Jobson	6 1	12 02	9 5 63	Hull	Burton A	Watford	28	4
						Hull C	221	17
						Oldham Ath	44	1
Ian Marshall	6 1	12 12	20 3 66	Liverpool	Apprentice	Everton	15	1
						Oldham Ath	102	24
Paul Warhurst	6 1	14 00	26 9 69	Stockport	Trainee	Manchester C	—	—
						Oldham Ath	67	2
Midfield								
Paul Bernard§	5 11	11 08	30 12 72	Edinburgh	Trainee	Oldham Ath	2	1
Mike Fillery	5 11	13 00	17 9 60	Mitcham	Apprentice	Chelsea	161	32
						QPR	97	9
						Portsmouth	64	6
						Oldham Ath	2	—
						Millwall (loan)	1	—
Chris Halstead‡			23 12 71	Burnley	School	Oldham Ath	—	—
Nick Henry	5 6	9 08	21 2 69	Liverpool	Trainee	Oldham Ath	107	4
Paul Kane	5 8	9 09	20 6 65	Edinburgh	Salvesen BC	Hibernian	247	33
						Oldham Ath	17	—
Norman Kelly (To Dunfermline Ath March 1991)	5 8	11 00	10 10 70	Belfast	Trainee	Oldham Ath	2	—
						Wigan Ath (loan)	4	—
Neil Redfearn	5 10	12 04	20 6 65	Dewsbury	Apprentice	Nottingham F	—	—
						Bolton W	35	1
						Lincoln C (loan)	10	1
						Lincoln C	90	12
						Doncaster R	46	14
						Crystal Palace	57	10
						Watford	24	3
						Oldham Ath	62	16
Ian Thompstone	6 0	11 03	17 1 71		Trainee	Manchester C	1	1
						Oldham Ath	—	—
Forwards								
Neil Adams	5 8	10 08	23 11 65	Stoke	Local	Stoke C	32	4
						Everton	20	—
						Oldham Ath (loan)	9	—
						Oldham Ath	58	10

OLDHAM ATHLETIC

Foundation: It was in 1895 that John Garland, the landlord of the Featherstall and Junction Hotel, decided to form a football club. As Pine Villa they played in the Oldham Junior League. In 1899 the local professional club Oldham County, went out of existence and one of the liquidators persuaded Pine Villa to take over their ground at Sheepfoot Lane and change their name to Oldham Athletic.

First Football League game: 9 September, 1907, Division 2, v Stoke (a) W 3-1 – Hewitson; Hodson, Hamilton; Fay, Walders, Wilson; Ward, W. Dodds (1), Newton (1), Hancock, Swarbrick (1).

Did you know: Oldham would have won the Football League Championship on goal average in 1914-15 if they had only drawn at Liverpool in their final game, but they lost 2-0 and Everton took the title.

Managers (and Secretary-managers)
David Ashworth 1906–14, Herbert Bamlett 1914–21, Charlie Roberts 1921–22, David Ashworth 1923–24, Bob Mellor 1924–27, Andy Wilson 1927–32, Jimmy McMullan 1933–34, Bob Mellor 1934–45 (continued as secretary to 1953), Frank Womack 1945–47, Billy Wootton 1947–50, George Hardwick 1950–56, Ted Goodier 1956–58, Norman Dodgin 1958–60, Jack Rowley 1960–63, Les McDowall 1963–65, Gordon Hurst 1965–66, Jimmy McIlroy 1966–68, Jack Rowley 1968–69, Jimmy Frizzell 1970–82, Joe Royle July 1982–

Player and Position	Ht	Wt	Birth Date	Place	Source	Clubs	League App	Gls
Frankie Bunn	5 11	10 06	6 11 62	Birmingham	Apprentice	Luton T	59	9
						Hull C	95	23
						Oldham Ath	78	26
David Currie	5 11	12 09	27 11 62	Stockton	Local	Middlesbrough	113	31
						Darlington	76	33
						Barnsley	80	30
						Nottingham F	8	1
						Oldham Ath	27	2
Rick Holden	5 11	12 07	9 9 64	Skipton		Burnley	1	—
						Halifax T	67	12
						Watford	42	8
						Oldham Ath	87	14
Scott McGarvey‡	6 0	11 05	22 4 63	Glasgow	Apprentice	Manchester U (loan)	25	3
						Wolverhampton W	13	2
						Portsmouth	23	6
						Carlisle U (loan)	10	3
						Carlisle U	25	8
						Grimsby T	50	7
						Bristol C	26	9
						Oldham Ath	4	1
						Wigan Ath (loan)	3	—
Paul Moulden	5 10	11 00	6 9 67	Farnworth	Apprentice	Manchester C	64	18
						Bournemouth	32	13
						Oldham Ath	32	3
Roger Palmer	5 10	11 00	30 1 59	Manchester	Apprentice	Manchester C	31	9
						Oldham Ath	420	138
Andy Ritchie	5 9	11 11	28 11 60	Manchester	Apprentice	Manchester U	33	13
						Brighton & HA	89	23
						Leeds U	136	40
						Oldham Ath	136	63
Gary Williams*	5 8	10 11	8 6 63	Bristol	Apprentice	Bristol C	100	1
						Portsmouth	—	—
						Swansea C	6	—
						Bristol R	—	—
						Oldham Ath	61	12

Trainees
Bamber, Neil S; Bernard, Paul R.J; Bradshaw, Gary; Challender, Gregory L; Everingham, Nicholas P; Gerrard, Paul W; Hall, David T; Kenton, Andrew M; Lockley, Richard J; Makin, Christopher; Mayo, Jonathon P; Miller, Peter D; Miller, Robert J; Vigon, Adam M.S; Wilson, Gregory J.

Associated Schoolboys
Adams, Christian; Beresford, David; Berry, Matthew; Boden, Matthew Liam T; Booth, J; Frost, John A; Graham, Alan A; Hilton, Robert C; Knapman, Steven C; Owen, Jonathon K; Pemberton, Martin C; Quinn, Dean S; Serrant, Carl; Smith, Howard; Smith, Matthew C; Speak, Matthew I; Street, John P; Swinnerton, David C; Thorp, Matthew C; Walker, Ian S; Woods, Andrew N.

Associated Schoolboys who have accepted the club's offer of a Traineeship/Contract
Eyre, John R; Hoolickin, Anthony P; Rickers, Paul S.

OXFORD UNITED 1990-91 *Back row (left to right):* Graham Waters, Phil Heath, Richard Hill, Paul Kee, Ceri Evans, Andrew Melville, Alan Judge, Matthew McDonnell, Paul Simpson, Paul Evans.

Centre row: Darren Jackson, Paul Byrne, David Fogg (Coach), David Penney, Michael Ford, John Clinkard (Physiotherapist), Lee Nogan, John Durnin, David Moss (Coach), Joey Beauchamp, Jonathon Muttock.

Front row: Les Phillips, Stephen McClaren, Mark Stein, Steve Foster, Brian Horton (Manager), Martin Foyle, Mickey Lewis, Les Robinson, Garry Smart.

Division 2 **OXFORD UNITED**

OXFORD UNITED F.C.

Manor Ground, Headington, Oxford. Telephone Oxford (0865) 61503. Supporters Club: (0865) 63063. Clubcall: 0898 121172. Fax: (0865) 741820.

Ground capacity: 11,622.

Record attendance: 22,750 v Preston NE, FA Cup 6th rd, 29 February 1964.

Record receipts: £71,304 v Aston Villa, Milk Cup semi-final, 12 March 1986.

Pitch measurements: 110yd × 75yd.

President: The Duke of Marlborough.

Managing Director: P. D. McGeough.

Directors: G. E. Coppock, J. A. Hunt, Miss G. N. A. Maxwell, A. Ramsey, P. Reeves.

Manager: Brian Horton. *Coach:* David Moss.

Physio: John Clinkard.

Secretary: Mick Brown.

Year Formed: 1893. *Turned Professional:* 1949. *Ltd Co.:* 1949.

Club Nickname: 'The U's'.

Previous Names: 1893, Headington; 1894, Headington United; 1960, Oxford United.

Previous Grounds: 1893–94 Headington Quarry; 1894–98 Wootten's Field; 1898–1902 Sandy Lane Ground; 1902–09 Britannia Field; 1909–10 Sandy Lane; 1910–14 Quarry Recreation Ground; 1914–22 Sandy Lane; 1922–25 The Paddock Manor Road; 1925–Manor Ground.

Record League Victory: 7-0 v Barrow, Division 4, 19 December 1964 – Fearnley; Beavon, Quartermann; Ron Atkinson (1), Kyle, Jones; Morris, Booth (3), Willey (1), Graham Atkinson (1), Harrington (1).

Record Cup Victory: 6-0 v Gillingham, League Cup, 2nd rd (1st leg), 24 September 1986 – Judge; Langan, Trewick, Phillips (Brock), Briggs, Shotton, Houghton (1), Aldridge (4 incl. 1p), Charles (Leworthy), Hebberd, Slatter. (1 og).

Record Defeat: 0-6 v Liverpool, Division 1, 22 March 1986.

Most League Points (2 for a win): 61, Division 4, 1964–65.

Most League Points (3 for a win): 95, Division 3, 1983–84.

Most League Goals: 91, Division 3, 1983–84.

Highest League Scorer in Season: John Aldridge, 30, Division 2, 1984–85.

Most League Goals in Total Aggregate: Graham Atkinson, 77, 1962–73.

Most Capped Player: Ray Houghton, 12 (41), Eire and Neil Slatter, 12 (22), Wales.

Most League Appearances: John Shuker, 478, 1962–77.

Record Transfer Fee Received: £1,000,000 from Derby Co for Dean Saunders, October 1988.

Record Transfer Fee Paid: £285,000 to Gillingham for Colin Greenall, February 1988.

Football League Record: 1962 Elected to Division 4; 1965–68 Division 3; 1968–76 Division 2; 1976–84 Division 3; 1984–85 Division 2; 1985–88 Division 1; 1988– Division 2.

Honours: Football League: Division 1 best season: 18th, 1985–86, 1986–87; Division 2 – Champions 1984–85; Division 3 – Champions 1967–68, 1983–84; Division 4 – Promoted 1964–65 (4th). *FA Cup:* best season: 6th rd, 1963-64 (record for 4th Division club). *Football League Cup:* Winners 1985–86.

Colours: Gold, navy blue trim, navy blue shorts, navy stockings. **Change colours:** All red.

OXFORD UNITED 1990–91 LEAGUE RECORD

Match No.	Date	Venue	Opponents	Result	H/T Score	Lg. Pos.	Goalscorers	Atten- dance
1	Aug 25	H	Port Vale	W 5-2	2-1	—	Foster 2, Stein 2, Simpson (pen)	4838
2	Sept 1	A	Notts Co	L 1-3	1-1	10	Phillips	6393
3	8	H	WBA	L 1-3	0-2	16	Foyle	5225
4	15	A	Oldham Ath	L 0-3	0-0	18		12,429
5	18	A	Plymouth Arg	D 2-2	0-0	—	Foyle, Stein	5859
6	22	H	Swindon T	L 2-4	2-2	20	Penney, Foyle	7961
7	29	H	Wolverhampton W	D 1-1	1-1	22	Simpson	7418
8	Oct 3	A	West Ham U	L 0-2	0-2	—		18,125
9	6	A	Barnsley	L 0-3	0-0	23		6776
10	13	H	Newcastle U	D 0-0	0-0	23		6820
11	20	H	Brighton & HA	W 3-0	1-0	22	Simpson 3	4733
12	24	A	Bristol R	L 0-1	0-1	—		5526
13	27	A	Watford	D 1-1	0-0	22	Stein	7521
14	Nov 3	H	Leicester C	D 2-2	2-1	22	Simpson, Foyle	5371
15	7	A	Millwall	W 2-1	0-1	—	Sheringham (og), Foyle	7681
16	10	H	Bristol C	W 3-1	2-1	20	Simpson 2, Foyle	6834
17	17	A	Charlton Ath	D 3-3	2-1	20	Magilton, Mortimer (og), Nogan	4928
18	24	H	Middlesbrough	L 2-5	2-2	20	Stein, Nogan	5262
19	Dec 1	A	Portsmouth	D 1-1	0-1	22	Durnin	6902
20	15	A	Port Vale	L 0-1	0-1	23		5963
21	22	H	Shefield W	D 2-2	1-2	23	Simpson 2	6061
22	26	A	Hull C	D 3-3	0-1	24	Magilton, Durnin, Stein	5103
23	29	A	Blackburn R	W 3-1	1-0	19	Durnin, Foster, Nogan	6428
24	Jan 1	H	Ipswich T	W 2-1	1-0	17	Magilton (pen), Durnin	5103
25	12	H	Notts Co	D 3-3	1-2	16	Durnin, Stein, Melville	5358
26	19	A	WBA	L 0-2	0-1	19		8017
27	Feb 2	H	Oldham Ath	W 5-1	3-0	17	Magilton 2, Foyle, Lewis, Nogan	5411
28	16	H	Charlton Ath	D 1-1	1-0	18	Foyle	4726
29	23	A	Bristol C	L 1-3	1-2	19	Nogan	10,938
30	27	H	Millwall	D 0-0	0-0	—		4570
31	Mar 2	H	Portsmouth	W 1-0	0-0	15	Melville	5226
32	5	A	Swindon T	D 0-0	0-0	—		9058
33	9	A	Middlesbrough	D 0-0	0-0	17		14,029
34	13	H	West Ham U	W 2-1	1-0	—	Simpson, Durnin	8225
35	16	A	Wolverhampton W	D 3-3	0-3	14	Melville, Stein, Simpson	11,357
36	23	H	Barnsley	W 2-0	0-0	15	Foyle, Ford	4689
37	30	H	Hull C	W 1-0	1-0	12	Durnin	4591
38	Apr 1	A	Sheffield W	W 2-0	0-0	11	Durnin, Simpson	28,682
39	6	H	Blackburn R	D 0-0	0-0	11		4767
40	10	A	Newcastle U	D 2-2	1-0	—	Simpson 2	10,004
41	13	A	Ipswich T	D 1-1	1-1	10	Simpson	9135
42	17	H	Plymouth Arg	D 0-0	0-0	—		4295
43	20	A	Brighton & HA	W 3-0	1-0	10	Durnin, Evans, Foyle	8118
44	27	H	Bristol R	W 3-1	3-1	10	Simpson, Magilton, Jones (og)	6744
45	May 4	H	Watford	L 0-1	0-0	10		8437
46	11	A	Leicester C	L 0-1	0-1	10		19,011

Final League Position: 10

GOALSCORERS

League (69): Simpson 17 (1 pen), Foyle 10, Durnin 9, Stein 8, Magilton 6 (1 pen), Nogan 5, Foster 3, Melville 3, Evans 1, Ford 1, Lewis 1, Penney 1, Phillips 1, own goals 3.
Rumbelows Cup (8): Foyle 3, Foster 2, Magilton 1, Melville 1, Simpson 1.
FA Cup (5): Foyle 2, Durnin 1, Magilton 1, Nogan 1.

Judge	Robinson	Ford	Phillips	Foster	Melville	Evans	Lewis	Foyle	Stein	Simpson	Kee	Jackson	Penney	Nogan	Smart	Walker	McClaren	Durnin	Magilton	Beauchamp	Veysey	Byrne	Gardner	Match No.
1	2	3	4	5	6	7	8	9	10	11														1
	2	3	4	5	6		8	9	10	11	1	7*	12											2
	2	3	4	5	6	7	8	9	10	11	1													3
	2	3	4	5	6		8	9	10	11	1	7*		12										4
	2	3	4	5*	6		8	9	10	11	1	7		12										5
	2	3	4		6		8	9	10	11	1	7	12	5*										6
	2	3	4		6		8	9	10	11		5				1	7*12							7
	2	3	4		6		8*	9	10	11		5	12			1			7					8
1	2*	3†	4	5	6	14	8		10	11		9						12	7					9
1	2		4	5	6		3	9		8	11								7	10				10
1	2		4	5	6		3	9		8	11	1							7	10				11
	2			5	6	3	4	9		8	11	1		12					7	10*				12
	2			5	6	3	4	9		8	11	1		10					7					13
	2			5	6	3	4	9		8	11	1		10					7					14
	2			5	6		4	9		8	11	1		10	3				7					15
	2	12		5	6	3	4	9		8	11	1		10*					7					16
	2			5	6	3	4	9		8	11	1		10					7					17
	2			5	6	3	4	9		8	11	1		10					7					18
	2			5	6		4*	9		8	11			12	10†	3		14		7		1			19
	2			5	6	3	4			8*11			12	10				9	7		1			20
	2	8*		5	6	3	4†			11			12	10			14	9	7		1			21
	2			5	6	3				8*11			12	10			4	9	7		1			22
	2	8		5	6					11				10	3		4	9	7		1			23
	2	8		5	6					11				10	3		4	9	7		1			24
	2	8*		5	6			12		11				10	3		4	9	7		1			25
	2	8		5	6			12		11				10	3		4*	9	7		1			26
	2	8		5	6		9	4		11				10	3				7		1			27
	2	8*		5	6		9	4	12	11				10	3				7		1			28
	2	14	8	5	6		9†	4	12	11				10	3*				7		1			29
	2	3	8	5	6		9	4		11*				10	12				7		1			30
	2	3	8	5	6		9*	4		11				10	12				7		1			31
	2	3	8	5	6		9	4		11				10*	12				7		1			32
	2	3	8	5	6		9	4		11				10					7		1			33
	2	3	8	5	6		9	4		11				10					7		1			34
	2	3	8	5	6		9	4*12		11				10					7		1			35
	2	3		5	6		4	9		11				10					7		1	8		36
	2	3		5	6		4	9		11				10					7		1	8		37
	2	3		5	6		4	9		11				8				10	7		1			38
	2	3		5	6		4	9	12	11				8*				10	7		1			39
	2	3		5	6		4	9		11				8*				10	7		1		12	40
		3		5	6		4	9		11				8	2			10	7*		1		12	41
		3		6	5			9	10	11				8	2					7	1		4	42
		3		6	5			9	7	11				8	2			10			1		4	43
1	2	3		6	5		7	9*11						8				10	4				12	44
1	2	3		6	5		7	9		11				8				10*	4				12	45
1	2	3			6		7	9		11				14				8	5†	10*	4		12	46
6	43	27 +1s	24 +1s	38	46	17 +1s	34	36 +6s	28	46	13	4 +1s	3 +6s	29 +3s	14 +1s	2	6 +1s	20 +6s	37	4	25 +5s	2	2	

Rumbelows Cup	First Round	Reading (a)	1-0
		(h)	2-1
	Second Round	Port Vale (a)	2-0
		(h)	0-0
	Third Round	West Ham U (h)	2-1
	Fourth Round	Chelsea (h)	1-2
FA Cup	Third Round	Chelsea (a)	3-1
	Fourth Round	Tottenham H (a)	2-4

OXFORD UNITED

Player and Position	Ht	Wt	Birth Date	Birth Place	Source	Clubs	League App	Gls
Goalkeepers								
Alan Judge*	5 11	11 06	15 5 60	Kingsbury	Amateur	Luton T	11	—
						Reading (loan)	33	—
						Reading	44	—
						Oxford U	80	—
						Lincoln C (loan)	2	—
						Cardiff C (loan)	8	—
Paul Kee	6 3	12 12	8 11 69	Belfast	Ards	Oxford U	34	—
Ken Veysey	5 11	11 08	8 6 67	Hackney		Torquay U	72	—
						Oxford U	25	—
Defenders								
Ceri Evans	6 1	14 02	2 10 63	Christchurch	Otaga Univ, Worcester Coll (Oxford)	Oxford U	46	3
Paul Evans	5 7	11 01	16 3 72	Shrewsbury	Trainee	Oxford U	—	—
Stuart Fisher	5 11	11 06	21 3 73	Oxford	Trainee	Oxford U	—	—
Mike Ford	5 11	12 05	9 2 66	Bristol		Leicester C	—	—
					Devizes	Cardiff C	145	13
						Oxford U	69	4
Steve Foster	6 0	14 00	24 9 57	Portsmouth	Apprentice	Portsmouth	109	6
						Brighton HA	172	6
						Aston Villa	15	3
						Luton T	163	11
						Oxford U	73	7
Paul Harwood	5 7	10 08	12 1 73	Oxford	Trainee	Oxford U	—	—
Darren Jackson	6 1	12 08	24 9 71	Bristol	Trainee	Oxford U	6	—
Andy Melville	6 1	12 06	29 11 68	Swansea	School	Swansea C	175	22
						Oxford U	46	3
Jon Muttock	6 2	13 00	23 12 71	Oxford	Trainee	Oxford U	1	—
Gary Smart	5 9	11 03	29 4 64	Totnes	Wokingham	Oxford U	72	—
Midfield								
Paul Byrne	5 9	11 06	30 6 72	Dublin	Trainee	Oxford U	5	—
Richard Hill*	6 0	12 04	20 9 63	Hinckley		Leicester C	—	—
					Nuneaton	Northampton T	86	46
						Watford	4	—
						Oxford U	63	13
Mickey Lewis	5 8	12 07	15 2 65	Birmingham	School	WBA	24	—
						Derby Co	43	1
						Oxford U	115	2
Steve McClaren	5 7	9 08	3 5 61	Fulford	Apprentice	Hull C	178	16
						Derby Co	25	—
						Lincoln C (loan)	8	—
						Bristol C	61	2
						Oxford U	29	—
Jim Magilton	5 10	12 07	6 5 69	Belfast	Apprentice	Liverpool	—	—
						Oxford U	37	6
Les Phillips	5 8	10 06	7 1 63	London	Apprentice	Birmingham C	44	3
						Oxford U	161	9
Les Robinson	5 8	11 05	1 3 67	Mansfield		Mansfield T	15	—
						Stockport Co	67	3
						Doncaster R	82	12
						Oxford U	44	—
Graham Waters‡	5 8	11 02	5 11 71	St Austell	Trainee	Oxford U	—	—

OXFORD UNITED

Foundation: There had been an Oxford United club around the time of World War I but only in the Oxfordshire Thursday League and there is no connection with the modern club which began as Headington in 1893, adding "United" a later. Playing first on Quarry Fields and subsequently Wootten's Fields, they owe much to a Dr. Hitchings for their early development.

First Football League game: 18 August, 1962, Division 4, v Barrow (a) L 2-3 – Medlock; Beavon, Quartermain; R. Atkinson, Kyle, Jones; Knight, G. Atkinson (1), Houghton (1), Cornwell, Colfar.

Did you know: Oxford United were drawn at home in eight successive FA Cup ties 1963-65, including all six in 1963–64 when they became the first Fourth Division side to reach the Sixth Round.

Managers (and Secretary-managers)
Harry Thompson 1949–58 (Player Manager 1949-51), Arthur Turner 1959–69 (continued as GM to 1972), Ron Saunders 1969, Gerry Summers 1969–75, Mick Brown 1975–79, Bill Asprey 1979–80, Ian Greaves 1980–82, Jim Smith 1982–85, Maurice Evans 1985–88, Mark Lawrenson 1988, Brian Horton October 1988–   .

Player and Position	Ht	Wt	Birth Date	Place	Source	Clubs	League App	Gls
Forwards								
Chris Allen	5 11	12 02	18 11 72	Oxford	Trainee	Oxford U	—	—
Joey Beauchamp	5 11	11 03	13 3 71	Oxford	Trainee	Oxford U	8	—
John Durnin	5 10	11 10	18 8 65	Liverpool	Waterloo Dock	Liverpool	—	—
						WBA (loan)	5	2
						Oxford U	87	25
Martin Foyle	5 10	11 02	2 5 63	Salisbury	Amateur	Southampton	12	1
						Blackburn R (loan)	—	—
						Aldershot	98	35
						Oxford U	126	36
Matthew Keeble	5 5	9 12	8 9 72	Chipping Norton	Trainee	Oxford U	—	—
Matt McDonnell	5 10	10 10	10 4 71	Reading	Trainee	Oxford U	—	—
Lee Nogan	5 10	11 00	21 5 69	Cardiff	Apprentice	Oxford U	42	5
						Brentford (loan)	11	2
						Southend U (loan)	6	1
David Penney	5 8	10 07	17 8 64	Wakefield	Pontefract	Derby Co	19	—
						Oxford U	38	3
						Swansea C (loan)	12	3
Paul Simpson	5 6	11 11	26 7 66	Carlisle	Apprentice	Manchester C	118	18
						Oxford U	113	34
Mark Stein	5 3	9 02	28 1 66	Capetown, SA		Luton T	54	19
						Aldershot (loan)	2	1
						QPR	33	4
						Oxford U	75	17

Trainees
Caine, Michael F; Didcock, Tristan S ; Druce, Mark A; Holmes, Keith N; Kelly, Leighton J; McLean, Richard G; Maciak, Michael; Mutchell, Robert D; Tavinor, Stephen J; Wallbridge, Andrew J; Wanless, Paul S; Wild, Robert P.

Associated Schoolboys
Bastable, Gary J; Border, Benjamin J; Byles, Paul J; Francis, Stephen M; Godfrey, Russell L; Goodall, Grant S; Gordon, Ian P; Greig, Neil J; Keane, Paul; Lidster, Darren; Lyford, Neil R; McGregor, Christian N; Maciak, Jason; Matthews, Gary P; Purnell, Rhydian M; Watts, Darren W.

Associated Schoolboys who have accepted the club's offer of a Traineeship/Contract
Bayliss, Gary J; Conneely, Michael; Ford, Robert J; Girolami, Adriano; Maisey, Darren; Morrisey, Terry; Stevens, Greg R.

388

PETERBOROUGH UNITED 1990–91 *Back row (left to right):* Noel Luke, Garry Butterworth, Dale Watkins, Kevin Bremner, Mark Hine, Phil Crosby, Milton Graham. *Centre row:* David Robinson, Paul Culpin, Keith Oakes, Paul Bradshaw, George Berry, Steve Osborne, Gerry McElhinney (Youth Team Manager). *Front row:* Bill Harvey (Physiotherapist), Mark Lawrenson (Manager), David Riley, Mick Halsall, Dave Booth (Assistant Manager), Darrin Clark, Worrell Sterling.

Division 3   **PETERBOROUGH UNITED**

London Road Ground, Peterborough PE2 8AL. Telephone Peterborough (0733) 63947.

Ground capacity: 28,000.

Record attendance: 30,096 v Swansea T, FA Cup 5th rd, 20 February 1965.

Record receipts: £51,315 v Brighton & HA, 5th rd, 15 February 1986.

Pitch measurements: 112yd × 76yd.

President: C. W. Swift OBE.

Chairman: J. F. Devaney. *Vice-chairman:* M. C. Lewis.

Directors: M. G. Cook, FCA, A. Devaney (Miss), J. T. Dykes, A. Palkovich. *Chief Executive/Company Secretary:* M. B. Devaney (Mrs).

General Manager:

Manager: Chris Turner. *Assistant Manager:* Lil Fuccillo.

Managing Director/Secretary: Arnold V. Blades.

Physio: Keith Oakes.

Commercial Manager: J. Hill.

Year Formed: 1934. *Turned Professional:* 1934. *Ltd Co.:* 1934.

Club Nickname: 'The Posh'.

Record League Victory: 8-1 v Oldham Ath, Division 4, 26 November 1969 – Drewery; Potts, Noble; Conmy, Wile, Wright; Moss (1), Price (3), Hall (4), Halliday, Robson.

Record Cup Victory: 6–0 v Redditch, FA Cup, 1st rd (replay), 22 November 1971 – Drewery; Carmichael, Brookes; Oakes, Turner, Wright; Conmy, Price (1), Hall (2), Barker (2), Robson (1).

Record Defeat: 1-8 v Northampton T, FA Cup 2nd rd (2nd replay), 18 December, 1946.

Most League Points (2 for a win): 66, Division 4, 1960–61.

Most League Points (3 for a win): 82, Division 4, 1981–82.

Most League Goals: 134, Division 4, 1960–61.

Highest League Scorer in Season: Terry Bly, 52, Division 4, 1960–61.

Most League Goals in Total Aggregate: Jim Hall, 122, 1967–75.

Most Capped Player: Tony Millington, 8 (21), Wales.

Most League Appearances: Tommy Robson, 482, 1968–81.

Record Transfer Fee Received: £110,000 from Blackpool for Bob Doyle, July 1979.

Record Transfer Fee Paid: £100,000 to Halifax T for David Robinson, July 1989.

Football League Record: 1960 Elected to Division 4; 1961–68 Division 3, when they were demoted for financial irregularities; 1968–74 Division 4; 1974–79 Division 3; 1979–91 Division 4; 1991– Division 3.

Honours: Football League: Division 3 best season: 4th, 1977–78; Division 4 – Champions 1960–61, 1973–74. *FA Cup:* best season: 6th rd, 1965. *Football League Cup:* Semi-final 1966.

Colours: Royal blue shirts, white shorts, white stockings, two royal blue bars. **Change colours:** White shirts, royal blue trim, white shorts, royal blue trim, royal blue stockings, two white bars.

PETERBOROUGH UNITED 1990–91 LEAGUE RECORD

Match No.	Date	Venue	Opponents	Result	H/T Score	Lg. Pos.	Goalscorers	Attendance
1	Aug 25	A	Wrexham	D	0-0 0-0	—		2863
2	Sept 1	H	Carlisle U	D	1-1 1-1	16	Bremner (pen)	3675
3	8	A	Scunthorpe U	D	1-1 0-1	16	Russell	3028
4	15	H	Walsall	D	0-0 0-0	15		4099
5	18	H	Halifax T	W	2-0 1-0	—	Culpin, Russell	3082
6	22	A	Northampton T	W	2-1 2-0	5	Russell, Culpin	5573
7	29	H	Torquay U	L	1-2 1-0	10	Culpin	3160
8	Oct 2	A	Darlington	W	1-0 0-0	—	Culpin	3748
9	6	A	Stockport Co	L	1-2 1-1	9	Luke	2924
10	13	H	Lincoln C	W	2-0 1-0	8	Culpin, Sterling	4766
11	20	H	Burnley	W	3-2 3-2	6	Culpin, Luke, Berry (pen)	5102
12	23	A	Hartlepool U	L	0-2 0-2	—		2190
13	27	A	Cardiff C	D	1-1 0-1	8	Hine	2940
14	Nov 3	H	Chesterfield	W	2-1 1-0	7	Berry, Hine	4225
15	10	H	Doncaster R	D	1-1 0-0	8	Bremner (pen)	4691
16	24	A	Hereford U	D	0-0 0-0	6		2148
17	Dec 1	A	Maidstone U	L	0-2 0-0	8		1920
18	15	H	York C	W	2-0 0-0	8	Culpin, Sterling	3335
19	21	H	Scarborough	W	2-0 0-0	—	Culpin, Riley	3237
20	26	A	Blackpool	D	1-1 1-1	7	Culpin	3658
21	29	A	Aldershot	L	0-5 0-3	7		2363
22	Jan 2	H	Rochdale	D	1-1 1-0	—	Sterling	3687
23	12	A	Carlisle U	L	2-3 1-1	8	Sterling 2	2744
24	19	H	Wrexham	D	2-2 0-0	9	Sterling 2	3208
25	26	A	Walsall	W	1-0 0-0	7	Skipper (og)	4438
26	Feb 1	A	Halifax T	D	1-1 0-1	—	Riley	1133
27	5	H	Northampton T	W	1-0 0-0	—	Halsall	5952
28	22	A	Doncaster R	W	2-0 0-0	—	Osborne, Halsall	2995
29	26	A	Gillingham	W	3-2 0-1	—	Halsall, Hine, Riley	3088
30	Mar 2	H	Maidstone U	W	2-0 1-0	4	Oakes, Riley	4623
31	9	A	York C	W	4-0 3-0	3	Riley 2, Hine, Robinson DJ	2511
32	12	H	Darlington	D	2-2 1-0	—	Robinson DJ, Halsall	8362
33	15	A	Torquay U	D	0-0 0-0	—		2800
34	20	A	Lincoln C	W	2-0 1-0	—	Riley, Robinson DJ	5542
35	23	H	Stockport Co	D	0-0 0-0	2		7047
36	30	H	Blackpool	W	2-0 1-0	2	Berry, Gavin	7721
37	Apr 3	A	Scarborough	L	1-3 1-3	—	Gavin	2141
38	6	H	Aldershot	W	3-2 2-1	2	Oakes, Gavin, Cooper	5543
39	13	A	Rochdale	W	3-0 1-0	2	Burns (og), Halsall 2	2384
40	16	A	Gillingham	W	2-0 1-0	—	Sterling, Gavin	5831
41	20	A	Burnley	L	1-4 1-4	3	Oakes	10,018
42	23	H	Scunthorpe U	D	0-0 0-0	—		5774
43	27	H	Hartlepool U	D	1-1 0-0	3	Berry (pen)	7636
44	May 4	H	Cardiff C	W	3-0 1-0	5	Robinson DA, Bremner, Culpin	6642
45	7	H	Hereford U	W	3-0 2-0	—	Berry (pen), Sterling, Gavin	7433
46	11	A	Chesterfield	D	2-2 0-2	4	Robinson DA, Berry	8837

Final League Position: 4

GOALSCORERS

League (67): Culpin 10, Sterling 9, Riley 7, Berry 6 (3 pens), Halsall 6, Gavin 5, Hine 4, Bremner 3 (2 pens), Oakes 3, Robinson DJ 3, Russell 3, Luke 2, Robinson DA 2, Cooper 1, Osborne 1, own goals 2.
Rumbelows Cup (6): Bremner 3, Culpin 1, Sterling 1, own goal 1.
FA Cup (7): Culpin 2, Halsall 2, Riley 2, Sterling 1.

Dearden	Luke	Crosby	Halsall	Robinson DA	Berry	Sterling	Oakes	Bremner	Riley	Butterworth	Osborne	Watkins	McElhinney	Culpin	Hine	Russell	Bradshaw	Hill	Clayton	Danzey	Morgan	Gavin	Charlery	Costello	Cooper	Pope	Robinson DJ	Match No.
1	2	3	4	5	6	7	8	9	10*	11	12																	1
1	2	3	4			7	8	9		11	10*	5		6	12													2
1	2	3	4			7		9		11		5*		6	12	8	10											3
1	2	3	4			7		9		11		5*		6	12	8	10											4
1	2	3	4			7		9		11	12			6	10*	8	5											5
1	2	3	4			7		9*14		11	12			6	10†	8	5											6
1	2	3	4		12	7		9*14	5	11				6†10		8												7
	2	3	4		14	7		9*11			12			6	10†	8	5	1										8
	2	3	4			7		9*11			12			6	10	8	5	1										9
	2	3	4			7	5	9*	12 14	11				6	10†		8	1										10
	2	3	4			7	5	9	12	11				6	10*		8	1										11
	2†	3	4			7	5	9	14	11	12			6	10*		8	1										12
	2	3	4			7	5	9	12	11				6	10*		8	1										13
	2	3	4			7	5	9	12	11				6	10*		8	1										14
	2	3	4			7	5	9	10*	11	12			6			8	1										15
	2	3	4		12	7	5	9	10	11*				6			8	1										16
	2		4		3	7	5	9	10	11 12			14	6*			8	1										17
	2	3	4			7	5	9		11				6	10		8	1										18
	2	3	4			7*	5	9†	14	11	12			6	10		8	1										19
	2	3	4		6	7	5	9		11					10		8	1										20
	2	3	4		6	7	5	9		11*	12				10		8	1										21
	2	3	4		6	7	5	9		11	12				10*		8	1										22
	2	3	4		6	7	5	9		11					10		8	1										23
	2	3	4		6	7	5	9	12	11*					10		8	1										24
	7	6	4		11	9	5		3						10		8	1	2									25
	7	6	4		11	9	5		3						10*		8	1	2	12								26
	7	6	4		11	9	5		3						10		8	1	2									27
	7	6	4		12 11	9	5		3		10						8	1	2*									28
	7	6	4		2 11	9	5		3								8	1									10	29
	7	6	4		2 11	9	5		3		12						8	1									10*	30
	7	6	4		2 11	9	5		3								8	1									10	31
	7	6	4		2 11	9*	5		3		12						8	1									10	32
	7	6	4		2 11	9	5		3								8	1									10	33
	7	6	4		2 11	9	5		3								8	1									10	34
	7	6	4		2 11	9	5		3		12						8	1									10*	35
	7	6	4		2 11	9†	5		3									1			8*	10	12	14				36
	7†	6	4		2 11	9*	5		3									1			8	10	12	14				37
	7	6	4		2 11	9	5		3									1			8*12	10						38
	7	6	4		2 11	9	5		3		12							1			8	10*						39
	7	6	4		2 11	9*	5		3				14					1			8	10†	12					40
	8	6	4		2 11†		5	9	3		12							1				10*	7	14				41
	11	6	4	5	2	7		9	3									1			8†	10*	12	14				42
	11	6	4	5	2	7		9	3		12							1			8	4*10						43
	11	6	4	5	2	7		9†	3		12		14					1			8	10*						44
	11	6	4	5	2	7		9*	3		12				10†			1			8	14						45
	11	6	4	5	2	7		9*	3		12		14					1			8	10†						46
7	45	45	45	6	28	46	27	13	35	46	3	5	20	21	33	7	39	1	4	—	5	10	2	3	2	1	7	
					+4s		+4s	+6s			+16s	+4s		+7s			+1s				+1s	+1s	+2s	+2s	+4s	+1s		

Rumbelows Cup

First Round	Fulham (a)	2-1	
	(h)	2-0	
Second Round	QPR (a)	1-3	
	(h)	1-1	

FA Cup

First Round	Hereford U (a)	1-1	
	(h)	2-1	
Second Round	Wycombe W (a)	1-1	
	(h)	2-0	
Third Round	Port Vale (a)	1-2	

PETERBOROUGH UNITED

Player and Position	Ht	Wt	Birth Date	Birth Place	Source	Clubs	League App	Gls
Paul Bradshaw*	6 3	13 04	28 4 56	Altrincham	Apprentice	Blackburn R	78	—
						Wolverhampton W	200	—
					Vancouver W	WBA	8	—
						Bristol R	5	—
						Newport Co	23	—
						WBA	6	—
						Peterborough U	39	—
Edward Herbert‡			9 10 68	Peterborough	Market Deeping	Peterborough U	—	—
Defenders								
George Berry*	6 0	13 04	19 11 57	Rostrup, W Germ	Apprentice	Wolverhampton W	124	4
						Stoke C	237	27
						Doncaster R (loan)	1	—
						Peterborough U	32	6
Phil Crosby	5 9	10 08	9 11 62	Leeds	Apprentice	Grimsby T	39	1
						Rotherham U	183	2
						Peterborough U	87	—
Paul Hill§			28 1 73	Nottingham	Trainee	Peterborough U	1	—
Gerry McElhinney*	6 1	13 10	19 9 56	Londonderry	Distillery	Bolton W	109	2
						Rochdale (loan)	20	1
						Plymouth Arg	91	2
						Peterborough U	87	1
Keith Oakes*	5 10	12 02	3 7 56	Bedworth	Apprentice	Peterborough U	62	2
						Newport Co	232	27
						Gillingham	86	7
						Fulham	76	3
						Peterborough U	97	9
David Robinson	6 0	12 03	14 1 65	Cleveland	Billingham	Hartlepool U	66	1
						Halifax T	72	1
						Peterborough U	51	6
Chris Swailes	6 1	12 11	19 10 70	Gateshead	Trainee	Ipswich T	—	—
						Peterborough U	—	—
Midfield								
Garry Butterworth	5 8	10 11	8 9 69	Peterborough	Trainee	Peterborough U	105	3
Gary Cooper	5 8	11 03	20 11 65	Edgware	Fisher Ath	Maidstone U	60	7
						Peterborough U	6	1
Milton Graham‡	5 10	12 04	2 11 62	Tottenham	Local	Bournemouth	73	12
						Chester C	129	11
						Peterborough U	15	2
Mick Halsall	5 10	11 04	21 7 61	Bootle	Apprentice	Liverpool	—	—
						Birmingham C	36	3
						Carlisle U	92	11
						Grimsby T	12	—
						Peterborough U	178	21
Noel Luke	5 11	10 11	28 12 64	Birmingham	School	WBA	9	1
						Mansfield T	50	9
						Peterborough U	206	27
Neil Pope†	5 9	12 10	9 10 72	Ashton	Cambridge U	Peterborough U	2	—
Forwards								
Kevin Bremner	5 9	12 05	7 10 57	Banff	Keith	Colchester U	95	31
						Birmingham C (loan)	4	1
						Wrexham (loan)	4	1
						Plymouth Arg (loan)	5	1
						Millwall	96	33
						Reading	64	22
						Brighton & HA	128	36
						Peterborough U	17	3

PETERBOROUGH UNITED

Foundation: The old Peterborough & Fletton club, founded in 1923, was suspended by the FA during season 1932–33 and disbanded. Local enthusiasts determined to carry on and in 1934 a new professional club Peterborough United was formed and entered the Midland League the following year.

First Football League game: 20 August, 1960, Division 4, v Wrexham (h) W 3-0 – Walls; Stafford, Walker; Rayner, Rigby, Norris; Halls, Emery (1), Bly (1), Smith, McNamee (1).

Did you know: Jim Hall and Peter Price each scored hat-tricks for Peterborough in the same League games – v Oldham Athletic, November 26, 1969, and v Barrow, October 9, 1971. Between those two dates no other club side achieved this distinction.

Managers (and Secretary-managers)
Jock Porter 1934–36, Fred Taylor 1936–37, Vic Poulter 1937–38, Sam Madden 1938–48, Jack Blood 1948–50, Bob Gurney 1950–52, Jack Fairbrother 1952–54, George Swindin 1954–58, Jimmy Hagan 1958–62, Jack Fairbrother 1962–64, Gordon Clark 1964–67, Norman Rigby 1967–69, Jim Iley 1969–72, Noel Cantwell 1972–77, John Barnwell 1977–78, Billy Hails 1978–79, Peter Morris 1979–82, Martin Wilkinson 1982–83, John Wile 1983–86, Noel Cantwell 1986–88 (continued as GM), Mick Jones 1988–89, Mark Lawrenson 1989–90, Chris Turner January 1991– .

Player and Position	Ht	Wt	Birth Date	Place	Source	Clubs	League App	Gls
Ken Charlery	6 1	12 07	28 11 64	Stepney	Fisher Ath	Maidstone U	59	11
						Peterborough U	4	—
Peter Costello	6 0	11 07	31 10 69	Halifax	Trainee	Bradford C	20	2
						Rochdale	34	10
						Peterborough U	5	—
Paul Culpin†	5 10	11 10	8 2 62	Kirby Muxloe		Leicester C	—	—
					Nuneaton	Coventry C	9	2
						Northampton T	63	23
						Peterborough U	40	12
Michael Danzey‡	6 1	12 12	8 2 71	Widnes	Trainee	Nottingham F		
						Chester C (loan)	2	—
						Peterborough U	1	—
Pat Gavin	6 0	12 00	5 6 67	Hammersmith	Hanwell T	Gillingham	13	7
						Leicester C	3	—
						Gillingham (loan)	34	1
						Peterborough U	11	5
Steve Osborne*	5 10	11 11	3 3 69	Middlesbrough	South Bank	Peterborough U	60	7
David Riley	5 7	10 10	8 12 60	Northampton	Keyworth U	Nottingham F	12	2
						Darlington (loan)	6	2
						Peterborough U (loan)	12	2
						Port Vale	76	11
						Peterborough U	56	12
Worrell Sterling	5 8	10 08	8 6 65	Bethnal Green	Apprentice	Watford	94	14
						Peterborough U	104	17
Dale Watkins†	5 8	11 05	4 11 71	Peterborough	Trainee	Peterborough U	10	—

Trainees
Allen, Daniel; Collins, David J; Curtis, Hamish; Herrick, Mark J; Hill, Paul J; Hyatt, Lee C; Jones, Timothy P; McInerney, Ian; Matthews, Michael; Murray, Marc; O'Connor, Jason; Roberts, Shaun; Simpson, Craig G.

**Non-Contract
Culpin, Paul; Pope, Neil.

Associated Schoolboy
Rice, Alan J.

**Non-Contract Players who are retained must be re-signed before they are eligible to play in League matches.

394

PLYMOUTH ARGYLE 1990–91   *Back row (left to right):* Owen Pickard, Mark Fiore, Mark Damerell, Adrian Burrows, Adam King, Steve Morgan, Danis Salman, Kenny Brown.

Centre row: Alan Gillett, Andy Morrison, Andy Thomas, Nicky Marker, Dave Walter, Rhys Wilmot, Robbie Turner, Paul Robinson, Kevin Summerfield, Malcolm Musgrove.

Front row: Paul Rowe, Kevin Hodges, Martin Barlow, Darren Garner, David Kemp, Paul Adcock, Paul Smith, Jason Rowbotham, David Byrne.

Division 2   **PLYMOUTH ARGYLE**

Home Park, Plymouth, Devon PL2 3DQ. Telephone Plymouth (0752) 562561-2-3. *Marketing Department:* 0752 569597. Lottery Shop: 561041. Pilgrim Shop: 0752 558292

Ground capacity: 25,000.

Record attendance: 43,596 v Aston Villa, Division 2, 10 October1936.

Record receipts: £96,989.57 v Derby Co, FA Cup 6th rd, 10 March 1984.

Pitch measurements: 112yd × 75yd.

President: S. J. Rendell.

Chairman: P. D. Bloom.

Directors: R. Burroughs ARICS, G. E. Jasper, D. Forshaw, C. Hartley.

Manager: David Kemp. *Coach:* Alan Gillett.

Secretary: Graham Little. *Commercial Manager:* S. Soutter.

Physio: E. Salmon.

Year Formed: 1886. *Turned Professional:* 1903. *Ltd Co.:* 1903.

Club Nickname: 'The Pilgrims'.

Previous Name: 1886–1903, Argyle Athletic Club.

Record League Victory: 8-1 v Millwall, Division 2, 16 January 1932 – Harper; Roberts, Titmuss; Mackay, Pullan, Reed; Grozier, Bowden (2), Vidler (3), Leslie (1), Black (1). (1 og).

Record Cup Victory: 6-0 v Corby T, FA Cup, 3rd rd, 22 January 1966 – Leiper; Book, Baird; Williams, Nelson, Newman; Jones (1), Jackson (1), Bickle (3), Piper (1), Jennings.

Record Defeat: 0-9 v Stoke C, Division 2, 17 December 1960.

Most League Points (2 for a win): 68, Division 3 (S), 1929–30.

Most League Points (3 for a win): 87, Division 3, 1985–86.

Most League Goals: 107, Division 3 (S), 1925–26 and 1951–52.

Highest League Scorer in Season: Jack Cock, 32, Division 3 (S), 1925–26.

Most League Goals in Total Aggregate: Sammy Black, 180, 1924–38.

Most Capped Player: Moses Russell, 20 (23), Wales.

Most League Appearances: Kevin Hodges, 512, 1978–91.

Record Transfer Fee Received: £250,000 from Everton for Gary Megson, February 1980 and £250,000 from Bradford C for Sean McCarthy, July 1990.

Record Transfer Fee Paid: £170,000 to Sheffield W for Mark Smith, January 1987.

Football League Record: 1920 Original Member of Division 3; 1921–30 Division 3 (S); 1930–50 Division 2; 1950–52 Division 3 (S); 1952–56 Division 2; 1956–58 Division 3 (S); 1958–59 Division 3; 1959–68 Division 2; 1968–75 Division 3; 1975–77 Division 2; 1977–86 Division 3; 1986– Division 2.

Honours: Football League: Division 2 best season: 4th, 1931–32, 1952–53; Division 3 (S) – Champions 1929–30, 1951–52; Runners-up 1921–22, 1922–23, 1923–24, 1924–25, 1925–26, 1926–27 (record of six consecutive years); Division 3 – Champions 1958–59; Runners-up 1974–75, 1985–86. *FA Cup:* best season: semi-final 1983–84. *Football League Cup:* Semi-final 1965, 1974.

Colours: Green and white striped shirts, black shorts, white stockings green tops. **Change colours:** Yellow shirts, green shorts, yellow stockings.

PLYMOUTH ARGYLE 1990–91 LEAGUE RECORD

Match No.	Date		Venue	Opponents	Result		H/T Score	Lg. Pos.	Goalscorers	Attendance
1	Aug	25	A	Newcastle U	L	0-2	0-1	—		23,984
2		28	H	Watford	D	1-1	1-0	—	Thomas	7734
3	Sept	1	H	Middlesbrough	D	1-1	0-1	19	Thomas	6266
4		8	A	Bristol C	D	1-1	0-1	17	Thomas	14,283
5		15	H	Leicester C	W	2-0	1-0	14	Hodges, Pickard	6336
6		18	H	Oxford U	D	2-2	0-0	—	Burrows, Thomas	5859
7		22	A	Wolverhampton W	L	1-3	1-3	16	Turner	15,137
8		29	A	Portsmouth	L	1-3	1-0	17	Thomas	8636
9	Oct	2	H	WBA	W	2-0	1-0	—	Thomas, Fiore	5617
10		6	H	Ipswich T	D	0-0	0-0	15		5935
11		13	A	Sheffield W	L	0-3	0-2	16		23,489
12		20	A	Blackburn R	D	0-0	0-0	16		6267
13		23	H	Notts Co	D	0-0	0-0	—		6651
14		27	H	Hull C	W	4-1	1-1	14	Morrison, Salman 2, Turner	5039
15	Nov	3	A	Charlton Ath	W	1-0	1-0	12	Turner	5239
16		10	A	Brighton & HA	L	2-3	1-1	14	Turner, Barlow	7305
17		17	H	Millwall	W	3-2	2-0	12	Robinson 2, Marker (pen)	6542
18		24	H	West Ham U	L	0-1	0-0	13		11,490
19	Dec	1	A	Port Vale	L	1-5	1-2	15	Ampadu	6717
20		8	A	Watford	L	0-2	0-0	17		6361
21		16	H	Newcastle U	L	0-1	0-0	—		7845
22		21	A	Oldham Ath	L	3-5	2-2	—	Edwards, Brown 2	11,296
23		26	H	Barnsley	D	1-1	0-0	19	Morgan	5668
24		29	H	Bristol R	D	2-2	2-2	20	Jones (og), Turner	8469
25	Jan	1	A	Swindon T	D	1-1	0-0	22	Turner	9736
26		12	A	Middlesbrough	D	0-0	0-0	21		14,198
27		19	H	Bristol C	W	1-0	0-0	17	Robinson	8074
28	Feb	2	A	Leicester C	L	1-3	1-2	21	Marker	8172
29		16	A	Millwall	L	1-4	1-1	22	Garner	8388
30		23	H	Brighton & HA	W	2-0	2-0	21	Morgan, Burrows	5384
31	Mar	2	H	Port Vale	W	2-0	0-0	19	Turner 2	5145
32		5	A	West Ham U	D	2-2	0-1	—	Turner 2	18,933
33		13	A	WBA	W	2-1	1-1	—	Hodges, Turner	8673
34		16	H	Portsmouth	D	1-1	1-0	18	Brown (pen)	6586
35		19	H	Sheffield W	D	1-1	0-0	—	Morgan	7806
36		22	A	Ipswich T	L	1-3	0-1	—	Fiore	9842
37		30	A	Barnsley	L	0-1	0-1	18		6142
38	Apr	1	H	Oldham Ath	L	1-2	0-1	19	Fiore	8852
39		6	A	Bristol R	D	0-0	0-0	20		5668
40		9	H	Wolverhampton W	W	1-0	0-0	—	Hodges	7618
41		13	H	Swindon T	D	3-3	2-1	18	Morrison, Salman, Viveash (og)	6712
42		17	A	Oxford U	D	0-0	0-0	—		4295
43		20	A	Blackburn R	W	4-1	4-0	17	Burrows 2, Turner 2	5122
44		27	A	Notts Co	L	0-4	0-1	20		7370
45	May	4	A	Hull C	L	0-2	0-1	21		3175
46		11	H	Charlton Ath	W	2-0	1-0	18	Pitcher (og), Turner	6816

Final League Position: 18

GOALSCORERS

League (54): Turner 14, Thomas 6, Burrows 4, Brown 3 (1 pen), Fiore 3, Hodges 3, Morgan 3, Robinson 3, Salman 3, Marker 2 (1 pen), Morrison 2, Ampadu 1, Barlow 1, Edwards 1, Garner 1, Pickard 1, own goals 3.
Rumbelows Cup (4): Thomas 2, Fiore 1, Salman 1.
FA Cup (1): Marker 1 (pen).

Wilmot	Brown	Morgan	Marker	Burrows	Hodges	Byrne	Morrison	Turner	Thomas	Fiore	Pickard	King	Robinson	Adcock	Summerfield	Salman	Barlow	Walter	Ampadu	Evans	McAllister	Edwards	Clement	Garner	Meade	Damerell	Cross	Cooper	Match No.
1	2	3	4	5	6	7	8	9	10	11*12																			1
1	2	3	4	5	6	7*	8	9	10			11	12																2
1	2	3	4	5	6	7	8*	9	10			11		12															3
1	2	3	4	5	6	7		9	10	8	11																		4
1	2	3†	4	5	6	7	14	9	10	8	11*12																		5
1	2	3*	4	5	6	7		9	10	8		12		11															6
1	2		4	5	6	7		9	10	8		12	11* 3																7
1 , 2		3	4	5	6	7		9	10	8*		12		11															8
1	2	3	4	5	6	7		9	10	8		11																	9
1	2	3	4	5	6	7*		9	10	8		12		11															10
1	2	3	4	5	6	7	14	9	10*	8	12	11†																	11
1	2	3	4	5	6	12	11	9	10	8*						7													12
1	2	3	4	5	6		11	9	10	8						7													13
	2	3	4	5			11	9	10*	8			12			6	7	1											14
	2	3	4	5	14	12	11	9		8†						6	7	1	10*										15
1	2	3	4	5	14	12	11†	9		8						6	7		10*										16
1	2	3	4	5	11			8		9						6	7		10										17
1	2	3	4	5	11		14	8		9†12						6	7		10*										18
1	2	3	4†	5	11		14	8		9*						6	7		10 12										19
1	2	3		5	11			8		9*						6	7		10 12		4								20
1	2	3		5			9	8 12 11		10*						6	7				4								21
1	2	3		5	7		9	8	11*							6					4		10				12		22
1	2†	3		5	7		9	8	11*							6 12					4		10 14						23
		3		5	8		11	9					12			6	7	1			4		10* 2						24
		3		5	8		11	9								10					4		2						25
	2	3	4	5	8		11	9								6	7	1											26
	2	3	4	5	8		11						9 10			6	7	1											27
	2	3	4	5	8		11						9 10†			6	7*	1					12	14					28
	2	3	4	5	8		10						9			6	7*	1						11 12					29
1	2	3	4	5	8*		10	9		11						6	7						12						30
1		3	4	5	8			9		11						6	7		10		2								31
1	2	3	4	5	8			9		11						6	7		10										32
1	2	3	4	5	8		14	9		11						6	7*		10†				12						33
1	2	3	4	5	8		10	9		11*						6	7						12						34
1	2	3	4	5	8		10	9		11						6	7												35
1	2	3	4	5	8†		10	9		11						6	7*						14	12					36
1	2	3	4	5	8*		10	9		11							7†				6		14 12						37
1	2	3	4	5	8†		10	9		11						6 12					7*		14						38
1	2	3	4	5	8		10	9		11						6											7		39
1	2	3	4	5	8		10	9		11						6							12	7*					40
1	2	3*	4		8		10	9		11						6							12	7†			5 14		41
1	2		4	5	8†		10	9		11						6							12	7*			3 14		42
1	2		4	5	8†		10	9		11						6 12								7*			3 14		43
	2			5	8†			9		11		10 12				14	1		7				6				3		44
	2		4	5			10	9		11			8			6 12	1							7*			3		45
1	2		4	5	10†		9			11			8*			6	7		12				3				14		46
36	43	40	39	45	40	11	27	39	14	38	4	4	7	9	1	35	25	10	6	1	7	3	8	5	2	—	6	—	
		+	+	+						+	+	+				+			+	+			+	+	+	+	+		
		2s	3s	5s					3s	4s	4s	3s				5s			3s	1s			8s	3s	4s	1s	3s		

Tallon — Match No. 44(4*)

Rumbelows Cup	Second Round	Wimbledon (h)		1-0
		(a)		2-0
	Third Round	Nottingham F (h)		1-2
FA Cup	Third Round	Middlesbrough (a)		0-0
		(h)		1-2

PLYMOUTH ARGYLE

Player and Position	Ht	Wt	Birth Date	Birth Place	Source	Clubs	League App	Gls
Goalkeepers								
David Walter	6 3	13 03	3 9 64	Barnstable	Bideford T	Exeter C	44	—
						Plymouth Arg (loan)	—	—
						Plymouth Arg	10	—
Rhys Wilmot	6 1	12 00	21 2 62	Newport	Apprentice	Arsenal	8	—
						Hereford U (loan)	9	—
						Orient (loan)	46	—
						Swansea C (loan)	16	—
						Plymouth Arg (loan)	17	—
						Plymouth Arg	82	—
Defenders								
John Brimacombe‡	5 11	11 10	25 11 58	Plymouth	Liskeard/ Saltash	Plymouth Arg	98	3
Julian Broddle (To St Mirren Dec 1990)	5 9	11 03	1 11 64	Laughton	Apprentice	Sheffield U	1	—
						Scunthorpe U	144	32
						Barnsley	77	4
						Plymouth Arg	9	—
						Bradford C (loan)	—	—
Kenny Brown	5 8	11 06	11 7 67	Barking	Apprentice	Norwich C	25	—
						Plymouth Arg	126	4
Adrian Burrows	5 11	11 12	16 1 59	Sutton	Local	Mansfield T	78	5
						Northampton T	88	4
						Plymouth Arg	220	10
						Southend U (loan)	6	—
Andy Clement	5 8	11 00	12 11 67	Cardiff	Apprentice	Wimbledon	26	—
						Bristol R (loan)	6	—
						Newport Co (loan)	5	1
					Woking	Plymouth Arg	16	—
Ryan Cross	5 11	11 00	11 10 72	Plymouth	Trainee	Plymouth Arg	7	—
Nick Marker	6 1	13 00	3 5 65	Exeter	Apprentice	Exeter C	202	3
						Plymouth Arg	151	10
Paul Maxwell	5 11	11 00	15 7 73	Plymouth	Trainee	Plymouth Arg	—	—
Steve Morgan	5 11	13 00	19 9 68	Oldham	Apprentice	Blackpool	144	10
						Plymouth Arg	40	3
Andy Morrison	5 11	12 00	30 7 70	Inverness	Trainee	Plymouth Arg	54	3
Jason Rowbotham	5 9	11 00	3 1 69	Cardiff	Trainee	Plymouth Arg	9	—
Danis Salman	5 10	11 08	12 3 60	Cyprus	Apprentice	Brentford	325	8
						Millwall	93	4
						Plymouth Arg	46	3
Darren Tallon‡			1 6 72	Glasgow	Trainee	Plymouth Arg	1	—
Midfield								
Mark Clode	5 6	9 06	24 2 73	Plymouth	Trainee	Plymouth Arg	—	—
Mark Edworthy	5 7	9 08	24 12 72	Barnstaple	Trainee	Plymouth Arg	—	—
Mark Fiore	5 10	11 10	18 11 69	Southwark	Trainee	Wimbledon	1	—
						Plymouth Arg	50	4
Darren Garner	5 6	11 01	10 12 71	Plymouth	Trainee	Plymouth Arg	7	1
Kevin Hodges	5 8	10 00	12 6 60	Bridport	Apprentice	Plymouth Arg	512	81
Adam King	5 11	11 12	4 10 69	Hillingdon	Trainee	West Ham U	—	—
						Plymouth Arg	16	—
						Bristol R (loan)	—	—
Paul Smith*	5 10	11 02	18 9 71	South Brent	Trainee	Plymouth Arg	—	—
Andy Thomas‡	6 0	10 10	16 12 62	Oxford	Apprentice	Oxford U	116	32
						Fulham (loan)	4	2
						Derby Co (loan)	1	—
						Newcastle U	31	6
						Bradford C	23	5
						Plymouth Arg	50	18

PLYMOUTH ARGYLE

Foundation: The Plymouth Argyle Association Football Club developed out of the Argyle Athletic club which was formed in 1886 at a meeting in Argyle Terrace, Mutley. Plymouth was a rugby stronghold, but servicemen brought soccer to the town and it spread quickly. At first Argyle Athletic Club played both soccer and rugby in colours of green and black. The rugby section was eventually disbanded, and after a number of exhibition games had satisfied the locals of the feasibility of running a professional club, Plymouth Argyle was formed in 1903.

First Football League game: 28 August, 1920, Division 3, v Norwich C (h) D 1-1 – Craig; Russell, Atterbury; Logan, Dickinson, Forbes; Kirkpatrick, Jack, Bowler, Heeps (1), Dixon.

Did you know: At Christmas 1960 Argyle lost 6-4 at Charlton but the following day beat the Londoners 6-4 at Home Park with Wilf Carter becoming the first Argyle player to score five goals in a League game.

Managers (and Secretary-managers)
Frank Brettell 1903–05, Bob Jack 1905–06, Bill Fullerton 1906–07, Bob Jack 1910–38, Jack Tresadern 1938–47, Jimmy Rae 1948–55, Jack Rowley 1955–60, Neil Dougall 1961, Ellis Stuttard 1961–63, Andy Beattie 1963–64, Malcolm Allison 1964–65, Derek Ufton 1965–68, Billy Bingham 1968–70, Ellis Stuttard 1970–72, Tony Waiters 1972–77, Mike Kelly 1977–78, Malcolm Allison 1978–79, Bobby Saxton 1979–81, Bobby Moncur 1981–83, Johnny Hore 1983–84, Dave Smith 1984–88, Ken Brown 1988–90, David Kemp March 1990– .

Player and Position	Ht	Wt	Birth Date	Place	Source	Clubs	League App	Gls
Forwards								
Paul Adcock	5 8	10 02	2 5 72	Ilminster	Trainee	Plymoth Arg	12	—
Martin Barlow	5 7	10 03	25 6 71	Barnstable	Trainee	Plymouth Arg	32	1
David Cooper‡	5 10	11 10	23 6 71	London	Trainee	Wimbledon	—	—
						Plymouth Arg	3	—
Mark Damerell	5 9	11 00	31 7 65	Plymouth	St Blazey	Plymouth Arg	5	—
Mike Evans	6 0	11 02	1 1 73	Plymouth	Trainee	Plymouth Arg	4	—
Raphael Meade‡	5 10	11 09	22 11 62	Islington	Apprentice Sporting	Arsenal	41	14
					Lisbon	Dundee U	11	4
						Luton T	4	—
						Ipswich T	1	—
					Odense	Plymouth Arg	5	—
Owen Pickard	5 10	11 03	18 11 69	Barnstaple	Trainee	Plymouth Arg	14	1
Paul Robinson	6 4	14 07	21 2 71	Nottingham	Notts Co, Bury	Scarborough	20	3
						Plymouth Arg	11	3
Paul Rowe‡	5 10	10 12	1 8 71	Wadebridge	Trainee	Plymouth Arg	—	—
Rob Turner	6 3	14 01	18 9 66	Easington	Apprentice	Huddersfield T	1	—
						Cardiff C	39	8
						Hartlepool U (loan)	7	1
						Bristol R	26	2
						Wimbledon	10	—
						Bristol C	52	12
						Plymouth Arg	39	14

Trainees
Balsdon, Mark A; Bull, Leighton J; Jones, Stephen A; Richardson, Harry S; Roberts, Kevin P; Widger, Andrew; Wotton, Garry L.
Associated Schoolboys
Daley, Ryan P; Hellings, Mark; Hutchinson, James; King, Simon; Lockyer, Adam J; Morgan, James A; Rutouski, Yan; Twiddy, Christopher

400

PORTSMOUTH 1990–91 *Back row (left to right):* Warren Neill, Warren Aspinall, Guy Whittingham.
Centre row: Lee Russell, Gary Stevens, Alan Knight, Graeme Hogg, Andy Gosney, Colin Clarke, Mark Chamberlain.
Front row: Steve Wigley, Kenny Black, Gavin Maguire, Mick Fillery, Martin Kuhl, Micky Hazard, Mark Kelly, John Beresford.

Division 2   **PORTSMOUTH**

Fratton Park, Frogmore Rd, Portsmouth PO4 8RA. Telephone Portsmouth (0705) 731204. Commercial Dept: (0705) 827111. Ticket Office: (0705) 750825. Lottery Office: (0705) 825016. Clubcall: 0898 338383.

Ground capacity: 26,352.

Record attendance: 51,385 v Derby Co, FA Cup 6th rd, 26 February 1949.

Record receipts: £173,000 v Tottenham H, FA Cup 5th rd, 16 February 1991.

Pitch measurements: 116yd × 73yd.

Chairman: J. A. Gregory. *Vice-chairman:* D. K. Deacon.

Directors: M. H. Gregory, R. Stainton, J. W. Sloan, J. P. R. Prevost FCA., D. Deacon, B. Henson, P. Britten.

Team Manager: Jim Smith. *Coach:* Steve Wicks.

Club Secretary: P. Weld. *Marketing Manager:*

Physio: N. Sillett. *Youth Team Coach:* K. Todd.

Year Formed: 1898. *Turned Professional:* 1898. *Ltd Co.:* 1898.

Club Nickname: 'Pompey'.

Record League Victory: 9-1 v Notts Co, Division 2, 9 April 1927 – McPhail; Clifford, Ted Smith; Reg Davies (1), Foxall, Moffat; Forward (1), Mackie (2), Haines (3), Watson, Cook (2).

Record Cup Victory: 7-0 v Stockport Co, FA Cup, 3rd rd, 8 January 1949 – Butler; Rookes, Ferrier; Scoular, Flewin, Dickinson; Harris (3), Barlow, Clarke (2), Phillips (2), Froggatt.

Record Defeat: 0-10 v Leicester C, Division 1, 20 October 1928.

Most League Points (2 for a win): 65, Division 3, 1961–62.

Most League Points (3 for a win): 91, Division 3, 1982–83.

Most League Goals: 91, Division 4, 1979–80.

Highest League Scorer in Season: Billy Haines, 40, Division 2, 1926–27.

Most League Goals in Total Aggregate: Peter Harris, 194, 1946–60.

Most Capped Player: Jimmy Dickinson, 48, England.

Most League Appearances: Jimmy Dickinson, 764, 1946–65.

Record Transfer Fee Received: £915,000 from AC Milan for Mark Hateley, June 1984.

Record Transfer Fee Paid: £450,000 to QPR for Colin Clarke, June 1990.

Football League Record: 1920 Original Member of Division 3; 1921 Division 3 (S); 1924–27 Division 2; 1927–59 Division 1; 1959–61 Division 2; 1961–62 Division 3; 1962–76 Division 2; 1976–78 Division 3; 1978–80 Division 4; 1980–83 Division 3; 1983–87 Division 2; 1987–88 Division 1; 1988– Division 2.

Honours: Football League: Division 1 – Champions 1948–49, 1949–50; Division 2 – Runners-up 1926–27, 1986–87; Division 3 (S) – Champions 1923–24; Division 3 – Champions 1961–62, 1982–83. *FA Cup:* Winners 1939; Runners-up 1929, 1934. *Football League Cup:* best season: 5th rd, 1960–61, 1985–86.

Colours: Blue shirts, white shorts, red stockings. **Change colours:** red shirts, black shorts, red stockings.

PORTSMOUTH 1990–91 LEAGUE RECORD

Match No.	Date		Venue	Opponents	Result	H/T Score	Lg. Pos.	Goalscorers	Atten-dance
1	Aug	25	H	WBA	D 1-1	0-1	—	Whittingham	12,008
2		29	A	West Ham U	D 1-1	1-1	—	Whittingham	20,835
3	Sept	1	A	Oldham Ath	L 1-3	0-2	18	Whittingham	11,657
4		8	H	Port Vale	L 2-4	1-1	21	Aspinall (pen), Kelly	8835
5		15	A	Notts Co	L 1-2	0-1	21	Chamberlain	6451
6		19	A	Brighton & HA	L 2-3	1-3	—	Kuhl 2 (1 pen)	9117
7		22	H	Blackburn R	W 3-2	1-0	19	Stevens, Clarke, Wigley	7801
8		29	H	Plymouth Arg	W 3-1	0-1	16	Clarke 2, Kuhl	8636
9	Oct	3	A	Millwall	L 0-2	0-0	—		10,393
10		6	A	Newcastle U	L 1-2	0-1	20	Anderson (og)	17,682
11		13	H	Barnsley	D 0-0	0-0	20		8701
12		20	H	Leicester C	W 3-1	1-0	14	Aspinall, Clarke, Black	9286
13		23	A	Watford	W 1-0	1-0	—	Aspinall	8274
14		27	A	Bristol R	W 2-1	1-1	10	Clarke, Stevens	6500
15	Nov	3	H	Wolverhampton W	D 0-0	0-0	13		14,574
16		10	A	Swindon T	L 0-3	0-2	16		8621
17		17	H	Middlesbrough	L 0-3	0-1	18		8433
18		24	A	Charlton Ath	L 1-2	0-2	19	Clarke	5513
19	Dec	1	H	Oxford U	D 1-1	1-0	21	Whittingham	6902
20		8	H	West Ham U	L 0-1	0-0	22		12,045
21		15	A	WBA	D 0-0	0-0	21		7856
22		21	H	Ipswich T	D 1-1	0-1	—	Clarke	7010
23		26	A	Bristol C	L 1-4	1-1	22	Clarke	11,892
24		29	A	Sheffield W	L 1-2	0-1	23	Whittingham	22,885
25	Jan	1	H	Hull C	W 5-1	2-0	21	Chamberlain, Beresford, Kuhl 2 (1 pen), Whittingham	8004
26		12	H	Oldham Ath	L 1-4	1-2	22	Kuhl (pen)	10,840
27		19	A	Port Vale	L 2-3	2-1	22	Whittingham 2	6314
28	Feb	2	H	Notts Co	W 2-1	1-0	22	Kuhl (pen), Wigley	12,680
29		9	A	Blackburn R	D 1-1	1-0	22	Clarke	7348
30		23	A	Swindon T	W 2-1	2-1	20	Whittingham, Wigley	8889
31		26	A	Middlesbrough	W 2-1	1-0	—	Aspinall, Kuhl (pen)	15,922
32	Mar	2	A	Oxford U	L 0-1	0-0	20		5226
33		9	H	Charlton Ath	L 0-1	0-1	20		8235
34		12	H	Millwall	D 0-0	0-0	—		7826
35		16	A	Plymouth Arg	D 1-1	0-1	19	Kuhl	6586
36		19	A	Barnsley	L 0-4	0-2	—		4921
37		23	H	Newcastle U	L 0-1	0-1	21		9607
38		30	H	Bristol C	W 4-1	1-0	20	Clarke 3 (1 pen), Whittingham	10,418
39	Apr	2	A	Ipswich T	D 2-2	1-1	—	Kuhl 2 (1 pen)	11,314
40		6	H	Sheffield W	W 2-0	1-0	18	Whittingham, Kuhl (pen)	10,390
41		13	H	Hull C	W 2-0	0-0	17	Russell, Kuhl (pen)	4871
42		16	H	Brighton & HA	W 1-0	1-0	—	Murray	12,271
43		20	A	Leicester C	L 1-2	0-1	18	Wigley	10,509
44		27	H	Watford	L 0-1	0-0	19		10,074
45	May	4	H	Bristol R	W 3-1	2-1	16	Beresford, Wigley, Whittingham	9410
46		11	A	Wolverhampton W	L 1-3	0-1	17	Clarke	12,570

Final League Position: 17

GOALSCORERS

League (58): Clarke 13 (1 pen), Kuhl 13 (8 pens), Whittingham 12, Wigley 5, Aspinall 4 (1 pen), Beresford 2, Chamberlain 2, Stevens 2, Black 1, Kelly 1, Murray 1, Russell 1, own goal 1.
Rumbelows Cup (6): Clarke 2, Aspinall 1, Chamberlain 1, Neill 1, Whittingham 1.
FA Cup (11): Whittingham 7, Clarke 2, Aspinall 1, Chamberlain 1.

Knight	Neill	Beresford	Fillery	Symons	Maguire	Wigley	Stevens	Clarke	Whittingham	Chamberlain	Powell	Kelly	Kuhl	Black	Hogg	Aspinall	Gosney	Murray	Awford	Gale	Butters	Anderson	Daniel	Russell	Match No.
1	2	3	4	5*	6	7†	8	9	10	11	12	14													1
1	2	3	4		6	7	8	9	10	11			5												2
1	2	3*	4		6	7	8	9	10	11†		14	5	12											3
1	2	3			6	7	8	9		11†	12	14	4		5	10*									4
1	2	3			6	7	8	9		11	12		4		5*	10									5
	2	3			6†	7	8	9		11*			4		5	10	1	12	14						6
	2	3				7	8	9		11*			4	6	5†	10	1	12	14						7
	2	3			14	7	8	9			12		4	6		10	1	11*	5†						8
	2	3			5	7	8	9			12		4	6		10	1	11*							9
	2	3			5	7	8	9			12		4	6		10†	1	11*	14						10
	2	3†			5	7*	8	9			12		4	11		10	1	14						6	11
	2	3			6	7	8	9			12		4*	11		10	1				5				12
	2	3			6	7	8	9					4	11		10	1				5				13
	2	3			6	7	8	9					4	11		10	1				5				14
	2	3			6		8	9			12	14	4	11*		10	1				5			7†	15
	2	3†			6	7	8	9*		11	12		4			10	1		14		5				16
		3				7	8	9		11		14	4			10*	1	12			6		2	5†	17
1		3				7*	8	9	10	11			4†	6				14	2		5			12	18
1	2	3					8	9*	10	11	12		4					6			5	7			19
1	2	3			12		8	9	10	11			4					6			5	7*			20
1	2	3					8	9		11			4			10		6			5	7			21
1	2	3					8*12	9		11			4			10		6			5	7			22
1	2	3					8	9		11	12		4			10*		6			5	7†14			23
1*	2	3				7	8	9	10	11			8	5		4		6†			12	14			24
	2	3				7	8	9	10	11			8	5		4	1	6							25
	2†	3			6	7	8	9*	10	11			8	5		4	1	12						14	26
	2	3			6	7	8	9	10	11			8	5		4	1								27
	2	3			6	7	8	9	10	11			8	5		4	1								28
	2	3				7	8	9	10	11			8	5		4*	1	12						6	29
	2*	3			6	7	8	9	10	11			8	5		4	1							12	30
		3			6	7	8	9	10	11			8	5		4	1	9						2	31
	2	3			6	7	8	9	10	11			8	5		4*	1								32
	2	3			6	7	8	9	10	11*			8	5			1	4			12				33
					6	7	8	9	10		12		8	5		4	1				11*	3	2		34
					6	7	2*	9	10				8	5		4	1	12			11	3			35
					6	7	12	9	14				8	5		4	1	10	2*		11†	3	6		36
1					6	7	12	9					8	14	5	4†		10			11*	3	2		37
1	12				6	7	10	9					8†14			4					5	11*	3	2	38
1	12				6	7	10	9					8	14		4†					5	11*	3	2	39
1	12				6	7	10	9					8	14		4*					5	11	3	2	40
1	11				6	7	10	9					8			4					5	3	2		41
1	11*				6	7	10	9					8†	14		4					5	12	3	2	42
1	11				6	7	10	9					8	14		4†					5	12	3*	2	43
1	11				6*	7	10	9					8	12		4					5	3	2		44
1	11					7	10	9					8		6	4*		12			5	14	3†	2	45
1	11					7	10	9†					8		6	4		12			5*14	3	2	46
22	30	39	3	1	22	39	31	38	34	22	—	2	41	14	20	32	24	17	8	2	23	13	13	16	
		+			+	+		+	+	+	+		+		+	+	+	+			+	+	+		
		3s			1s	2s		4s	3s	3s	8s		7s		1s	8s	6s	1s			7s	1s	3s		

Rumbelows Cup	Second Round	Cardiff C (a)	1-1
		(h)	3-1
	Third Round	Chelsea (a)	0-0
		(h)	2-3
FA Cup	Third Round	Barnet (a)	5-0
	Fourth Round	Bournemouth (h)	5-1
	Fifth Round	Tottenham H (h)	1-2

PORTSMOUTH

Player and Position	Ht	Wt	Birth Date	Birth Place	Source	Clubs	League App	Gls
Goalkeepers								
Andy Gosney	6 4	13 05	8 11 63	Southampton	Apprentice	Portsmouth	47	—
Alan Gough	5 10	12 01	10 3 71	Watford	Shelbourne	Portsmouth	—	—
Alan Knight	6 1	13 02	3 7 61	Ballham	Apprentice	Portsmouth	401	—
Defenders								
Andy Awford	5 9	11 09	14 7 72	Worcester	Trainee	Portsmouth	18	—
Guy Butters	6 3	13 00	30 10 69	Hillingdon	Trainee	Tottenham H	35	1
						Southend U (loan)	16	3
						Portsmouth	23	—
Shaun Gale	6 0	11 06	8 10 69	Reading	Trainee	Portsmouth	3	—
Jason Hall*	5 6	10 04	28 10 70	Epping	Trainee	Portsmouth	—	—
Graeme Hogg	6 1	12 12	17 6 64	Aberdeen	Apprentice	Manchester U	83	1
						WBA (loan)	7	—
						Portsmouth	100	2
Gavin Maguire	5 10	11 08	24 11 67	Hammersmith	Apprentice	QPR	40	—
						Portsmouth	70	—
Warren Neill	5 8	11 10	21 11 62	Acton	Apprentice	QPR	181	3
						Portsmouth	110	—
Gary Stevens	6 0	12 00	30 3 62	Hillingdon	Apprentice	Brighton & HA	133	2
						Tottenham H	147	6
						Portsmouth	52	3
Kit Symons	6 1	11 09	5 3 71	Basingstoke	Trainee	Portsmouth	4	—
Chris White*	5 11	11 10	11 12 70	Chatham	Trainee	Portsmouth	—	—
Midfield								
John Beresford	5 5	10 04	4 9 66	Sheffield	Apprentice	Manchester C	—	—
						Barnsley	88	5
						Portsmouth	72	2
Kenny Black	5 9	12 01	29 11 63	Stenhousemuir	Linlithgow Rose	Rangers	22	1
						Motherwell	17	—
						Hearts	178	15
						Portsmouth	62	3
Chris Burns			9 11 67	Manchester	Cheltenham T	Portsmouth	—	—
Mark Chamberlain	5 8	10 07	19 11 61	Stoke	Apprentice	Port Vale	96	17
						Stoke C	112	17
						Sheffield W	66	8
						Portsmouth	91	14
Ray Daniel	5 10	11 00	10 12 64	Luton	Apprentice	Luton T	22	4
						Gillingham (loan)	5	—
						Hull C	58	3
						Cardiff C	56	1
						Portsmouth	14	—
Lee Darby*	6 0	11 06	20 9 69	Salford		Portsmouth	1	—
Stuart Doling	5 6	10 06	28 10 72	Newport, IOW	Trainee	Portsmouth	—	—
Lee Gosling*	5 10	11 07	5 3 70	Basingstoke	Trainee	Portsmouth	—	—
Martin Kuhl	5 11	11 13	10 1 65	Frimley	Apprentice	Birmingham C	111	5
						Sheffield U	38	4
						Watford	4	—
						Portsmouth	113	23
Lee Russell	5 11	11 04	3 9 69	Southampton	Trainee	Portsmouth	24	1
Micky Turner*	5 10	12 07	15 10 71	Cuckfield	Trainee	Portsmouth	—	—
Forwards								
Darren Anderton	6 0	11 07	3 3 72	Southampton	Trainee	Portsmouth	20	—

PORTSMOUTH

Foundation: At a meeting held in his High Street, Portsmouth offices in 1898, solicitor Alderman J. E. Pink and five other business and professional men agreed to buy some ground close to Goldsmith Avenue for £4,950 which they developed into Fratton Park in record breaking time. A team of professionals was signed up by manager Frank Brettell and entry to the Southern League obtained for the new club's September 1899 kick-off.

First Football League game: 28 August, 1920, Division 3, v Swansea T (h) W 3-0 – Robson; Probert, Potts; Abbott, Harwood, Turner; Thompson, Stringfellow (1), Reid (1), James (1), Beedie.

Did you know: Best-ever start to a season by a goalkeeper in the Football League is that of Tom Newton in season 1922–23. He did not concede a goal in Portsmouth's first eight games, but was then beaten by a dramatic first-minute goal by Plymouth Argyle's Jack Fowler in a 2-1 defeat at Fratton Park.

Managers (and Secretary-managers)
Frank Brettell 1898–1901, Bob Blyth 1901–04, Richard Bonney 1905–08, Bob Brown 1911–20, John McCartney 1920–27, Jack Tinn 1927–47, Bob Jackson 1947–52, Eddie Lever 1952–58, Freddie Cox 1958–61, George Smith 1961–70, Ron Tindall 1970–73 (GM to 1974), John Mortimore 1973–74, Ian St. John 1974–77, Jimmy Dickinson 1977–79, Frank Burrows 1979–82, Bobby Campbell 1982–84, Alan Ball 1984–89, John Gregory 1989–90, Frank Burrows 1990 1991, Jim Smith June 1991–   .

Player and Position	Ht	Wt	Birth Date	Place	Source	Clubs	League App	Gls
Warren Aspinall	5 9	12 05	13 9 67	Wigan	Apprentice	Wigan Ath	51	22
						Everton	7	—
						Aston Villa	44	14
						Portsmouth	76	15
Colin Clarke	5 11	12 10	30 10 62	Newry	Apprentice	Ipswich T	—	—
						Peterborough U	82	18
						Gillingham (loan)	8	1
						Tranmere R	45	22
						Bournemouth	46	26
						Southampton	82	36
						Bournemouth (loan)	4	2
						QPR	46	11
						Portsmouth	42	13
Mark Kelly	5 8	9 10	27 11 69	Sutton		Portsmouth	49	2
						Tottenham H (loan)	—	—
Andy McFarlane			30 11 66	Wolverhampton	Cradley T	Portsmouth	—	—
Shaun Murray	5 8	11 02	7 2 70	Newcastle	Trainee	Tottenham H	—	—
						Portsmouth	25	1
Darryl Powell	6 0	12 03	15 11 71	London	Trainee	Portsmouth	11	—
Mike Ross	5 6	9 13	2 9 71	Southampton	Trainee	Portsmouth	1	—
Guy Whittingham	5 10	11 12	10 11 64	Evesham	Yeovil,Army	Portsmouth	79	35
Steve Wigley	5 9	10 05	15 10 61	Ashton	Curzon Ashton	Nottingham F	82	2
						Sheffield U	28	1
						Birmingham C	87	4
						Portsmouth	97	9

Trainees
Askham, Paul N; Cheverton, Darren L; Daughtry, Paul W; Knott, Alan; O'Brien, Simon; Owen, Christian P; Perrett, Russell; Price, Benjamin; Tierling, Lee A; Watts, Christian J; Wiseman, Simon L; Young, Roy E.

Associated Schoolboys
Anstey, Craig D; Brown, Lee P; Burton, Deon J; Coe, Douglas G; Cornwall, Martin I; Cunningham, Aaron M; Fazakerley, Jacob K; Fitches, Ben; Foster, Adam, Gardner, Christopher D; Gilbert, Greig F; Haycock, Matthew; Headington, Marcus J; Hearn, Mathew C; Hussey, Mathew; Igoe, Samuel G; Jones, Gary; Lewis, David J; Loveridge, Jon S; Mosedale, Anthony J; O'Mahony, Sean S; Osbourne, Steven A; Renyard, Nathan R.E; Rowe, David J; Sanger, Jon D; Scaddan, Richard J; Sherrington, James D; Spake, Daniel; Sparks, Richard J; Steeves, Jamie S; Stewart, Paul T.

Associated Schoolboys who have accepted the club's offer of a Traineeship/Contract
Bromige, Glyn J; Burton, Nicholas J; Green, Bjay; Ogburn, Mark; Sutton, Graham W.

PORT VALE 1990-91 *Back row (left to right):* Dean Glover, Robbie Earle, Neil Aspin, Ron Jepson, Tim Parkin, Gary West, Paul Millar, Kevin Finney, Darren Beckford, Simon Mills.

Centre row: John Rudge (Manager), Steve Hunt (Youth Team Coach), Robert Myatt, Alan Webb, Mark Grew, Matt Booth, Trevor Wood, Darren Hughes, Gary McKinstry, Jim Joyce (Physiotherapist), Mike Pejic (Team Coach).

Front row: Brian Mills, John Jeffers, Nicky Cross, Gary Ford, Ray Walker (Captain), Ron Atkinson, Andy Porter, Derek Swann, John Johnston, Ryan Kidd.

Division 2 **PORT VALE**

Vale Park, Burslem, Stoke-on-Trent. Telephone Stoke-on-Trent (0782) 814134. Commercial Dept: (0782) 835524. Clubcall: 0898 121636. Fax: 834981.

Ground capacity: 20,950.

Record attendance: 50,000 v Aston Villa, FA Cup 5th rd, 20 February 1960.

Record receipts: £92,658 v Derby Co, FA Cup 3rd rd, 7 January 1990.

Pitch measurements: 116yd × 76yd.

President: J. Burgess.

Chairman: W. T. Bell TECH. ENG, MIMI.

Executive Director: .

Directors: D. P. McGrath, N. C. Tizley, I. McPherson, A. Belfield.

Manager: John Rudge.

Secretary: A. R. Waterhouse. *Commercial Manager:*

Coach: Mike Pejic. *Physio:* R. Gray.

Year Formed: 1876. *Turned Professional:* 1885. *Ltd Co.:* 1911.

Club Nickname: 'Valiants'.

Previous Name: Burslem Port Vale; became Port Vale, 1913.

Previous Grounds: 1876, Limekin Lane, Longport; 1881, Westport; 1884, Moorland Road, Burslem; 1886, Athletic Ground, Cobridge; 1913, Recreation Ground, Hanley; 1950, Vale Park.

Record League Victory: 9-1 v Chesterfield, Division 2, 24 September 1932 – Leckie; Shenton, Poyser; Sherlock, Round, Jones; McGrath, Mills, Littlewood (6), Kirkham (2), Morton (1).

Record Cup Victory: 7-1 v Irthlingborough (away), FA Cup, 1st rd, 12 January 1907 – Matthews; Dunn, Hamilton; Eardley, Baddeley, Holyhead; Carter, Dodds (2), Beats, Mountford (2), Coxon (3).

Record Defeat: 0-10 v Sheffield U, Division 2, 10 December 1892 and v Notts Co, Division 2, 26 February 1895.

Most League Points (2 for a win): 69, Division 3 (N), 1953–54.

Most League Points (3 for a win): 88, Division 4, 1982–83.

Most League Goals: 110, Division 4, 1958–59.

Highest League Scorer in Season: Wilf Kirkham 38, Division 2, 1926–27.

Most League Goals in Total Aggregate: Wilf Kirkham, 154, 1923–29, 1931–33.

Most Capped Player: Sammy Morgan, 7 (18), Northern Ireland.

Most League Appearances: Roy Sproson, 761, 1950–72.

Record Transfer Fee Received: £925,000 from Norwich C for Darren Beckford, June 1991.

Record Transfer Fee Paid: £200,000 to Middlesbrough for Dean Glover, February 1989, and £200,000 to Leeds U for Neil Aspin, July 1989.

Football League Record: 1892 Original Member of Division 2, Failed re-election in 1896; Re-elected 1898; Resigned 1907; Returned in Oct, 1919, when they took over the fixtures of Leeds City; 1929–30 Division 3 (N); 1930–36 Division 2; 1936–38 Division 3 (N); 1938–52 Division 3 (S); 1952–54 Division 3 (N); 1954–57 Division 2; 1957–58 Division 3 (S); 1958–59 Division 4; 1959–65 Division 3; 1965–70 Division 4; 1970–78 Division 3; 1978–83 Division 4; 1983–84 Division 3; 1984–86 Division 4; 1986–89 Division 3; 1989– Division 2.

Honours: Football League: Division 2 best season: 5th, 1930–31; Division 3 (N) – Champions 1929–30, 1953–54; Runners-up 1952–53; Division 4 – Champions 1958–59; Promoted 1969–70 (4th). *FA Cup:* Semi-final 1954, when in Division 3. *Football League Cup:* never past 2nd rd.

Colours: White shirts with black shading, black shorts, white stockings with black rings. **Change colours:** All yellow.

PORT VALE 1990–91 LEAGUE RECORD

Match No.	Date	Venue	Opponents	Result	H/T Score	Lg. Pos.	Goalscorers	Atten-dance
1	Aug 25	A	Oxford U	L	2-5	1-2	—	Jeffers, Earle	4838
2	28	H	Wolverhampton W	L	1-2	1-2	—	Beckford (pen)	12,349
3	Sept 1	H	Leicester C	W	2-0	0-0	12	Earle, Beckford	8840
4	8	A	Portsmouth	W	4-2	1-1	9	Cross, Earle, Beckford 2	8835
5	15	H	Newcastle U	L	0-1	0-0	15		10,025
6	17	H	Middlesbrough	W	3-1	0-1	—	Beckford 2, Earle	7880
7	22	A	Barnsley	D	1-1	1-0	9	Beckford	8533
8	29	A	Hull C	L	2-3	0-1	13	Gibson, Cross	5185
9	Oct 1	H	Notts Co	L	0-1	0-0	—		7723
10	6	H	Charlton Ath	D	1-1	1-0	14	Beckford	6706
11	13	A	Ipswich T	L	0-3	0-1	15		10,369
12	20	A	Sheffield W	D	1-1	0-1	15	Gibson	24,527
13	22	H	WBA	L	1-2	1-2	—	Walker (pen)	8824
14	27	H	Bristol C	W	3-2	2-1	17	Walker 2 (1 pen), Beckford	7451
15	Nov 3	A	Swindon T	W	2-1	0-1	15	Ford, Beckford	7714
16	10	A	Bristol R	L	0-2	0-1	18		5661
17	17	H	Oldham Ath	W	1-0	0-0	15	Beckford	11,384
18	23	A	Blackburn R	D	1-1	0-0	—	Walker (pen)	8061
19	Dec 1	H	Plymouth Arg	W	5-1	2-1	10	Jeffers, Ford, Beckford 2, Walker	6717
20	15	H	Oxford U	W	1-0	1-0	8	Beckford	5953
21	22	H	Brighton & HA	L	0-1	0-0	10		6750
22	26	A	Watford	L	1-2	0-1	12	Earle	8084
23	29	A	West Ham U	D	0-0	0-0	12		23,603
24	Jan 1	H	Millwall	L	0-2	0-2	12		8418
25	12	A	Leicester C	D	1-1	0-1	15	Earle	9307
26	19	H	Portsmouth	W	3-2	1-2	14	Aspin, Glover, Beckford	6314
27	Feb 2	A	Newcastle U	L	0-2	0-1	15		14,602
28	16	A	Oldham Ath	L	0-2	0-0	16		12,630
29	23	H	Bristol R	W	3-2	3-0	15	Millar, Beckford, Walker (pen)	7166
30	26	A	Wolverhampton W	L	1-3	1-2	—	Earle	15,919
31	Mar 2	A	Plymouth Arg	L	0-2	0-0	16		5145
32	9	H	Blackburn R	W	3-0	2-0	14	Beckford 3 (1 pen)	7004
33	12	A	Notts Co	D	1-1	1-0	—	Beckford	6305
34	16	H	Hull C	D	0-0	0-0	15		6105
35	18	H	Ipswich T	L	1-2	0-1	—	Van der Laan	5820
36	23	A	Charlton Ath	W	1-0	0-0	16	Van der Laan	5222
37	30	H	Watford	D	0-0	0-0	16		6661
38	Apr 3	A	Brighton & HA	W	2-1	1-1	—	Beckford, Van der Laan	9733
39	6	H	West Ham U	L	0-1	0-0	15		9658
40	9	A	Middlesbrough	L	0-4	0-1	—		15,053
41	13	A	Millwall	W	2-1	1-1	15	Van der Laan, Beckford	10,860
42	15	H	Barnsley	L	0-1	0-0	—		6939
43	27	H	WBA	D	1-1	1-0	16	Earle	13,650
44	May 4	A	Bristol C	D	1-1	0-1	17	Earle	11,555
45	6	H	Sheffield W	D	1-1	0-0	—	Earle	13,317
46	11	H	Swindon T	W	3-1	2-1	15	Earle, Mills B 2	7713

Final League Position: 15

GOALSCORERS

League (56): Beckford 22 (2 pens), Earle 11, Walker 6 (4 pens), Van der Laan 4, Cross 2, Ford 2, Gibson 2, Jeffers 2, Mills B 2, Aspin 1, Glover 1, Millar 1.
Rumbelows Cup (0).
FA Cup (3): Beckford 2, Walker 1 (pen).

Grew	Mills	Hughes	Walker	Aspin	Glover	Ford	Earle	Cross	Beckford	Jeffers	Porter	Millar	Wood	Jepson	Parkin	Gibson	Agboola	Platnauer	Van der Laan	Webb	Mills, B	Kent	Match No.
1	2	3	4	5	6	7*	8	9†	10	11	12		14										1
	2†	3	4	5	6	7	8	9	10	11	12		14*	1									2
	2	3	4	5	6	7*	8	9†	10	11	12			1	14								3
	2		4	5	6		8	9	10	11	7			1		3							4
	2		4	5	6	11*	8	9	10	3	7			1	12								5
	2		4	5	6	11	8	9	10	3	7			1									6
	2		4	5	6	11	8	9	10	3	7			1									7
	2		4	5	6	7		9	10	11	8			1		3							8
	2		4	5	6	14	8	9*	10	11	7			1	12	3†							9
	2		4	5	6	12	8	9	10	11	7			1		3*							10
	2	3	4	5	6	7		12	10	11†	8			1	9*	14							11
	2	3	4	5		7		9	10	12	8			1		6	11*						12
	2	3	4	5		7		9	10	12	8			1		6	11*						13
	2	3*	4	5		7		12	10	11	8			1	9	6							14
	2	3	4*	5		7	9	12	10†	11	8			1	14	6							15
	2	3	4	5		7	9	12	10	11	8*			1		6							16
	2	3*	4	5		7	12	9	10	11	8			1		6							17
	2		4	5		7	12	9	10	11	8			1		6	3*						18
	2		4	5		7	8		10	11				1	9	6	3						19
	2		4	5		7	8		10	11				1	9	6	3						20
	2*		4	5		7	8	12	10	11				1	9	6	3						21
	4		2		6	14	8	12†	10*	11	7			1	9	5	3						22
	4		2		6		8		10	11	7			1	9	5	3						23
	4		2		6	12	8		10	11	7*		14	1	9†	5	3						24
12	4		2		6		8		10*	11	7			1	9	5	3						25
12	4		2		6	7	8		10	11				1	9*	5	3						26
	2		4	5	6		8		10	11	7	12		1	9*		3						27
	2		4	5	6	14	8		10	11†	7	12		1*	9		3						28
1	4		2		6	7	8		10	11	9*					5	3	12					29
1	4		2		6	7	8		10	11	9*					5	3	12					30
1	2		4	5	6	14	8		10	11	7†				9*		3	12					31
1	2		4	5	6	11*	8		10		7				9		3	12					32
1	2		4	5	6	11*	8		10		7				9†		14	12	3				33
1	2		4	5	6	11	8				7				9			3	10*	12			34
1	2		4	5	6	11*	8				7				9			3	10	12			35
1	2		4	5	6		8		10	11	9*							3	12			7	36
1	2	11			6		8		10		12					5		3	9	4*		7	37
1	2		4		6		8		10	11						5		3	9			7	38
1	2		4		6		8		10	11*	12					5		3	9			7	39
1	2		4	14	6†		8		10	11	12					5		3	9			7*	40
1	2	12	4				8		10	11						5		3*	9	6		7	41
	2	3	4				8		10	11*	12			1		5			9	6		7	42
	2	3	4		6		8		10	11				1		5			9			7	43
	2	3	4		6	10	8			11	12			1		5*			9			7	44
	2	3	4	5	6		8		10	11				1					9			7	45
	2	3	4	5	6		8		10*	11				1				12	9			7	46
14	39	16	45	40	41	22	34	14	43	29	36	8	32	11	28	5	9	14	10	4	1	11	
	+	+		+		+	+	+		+	+	+		+	+	+		+				+	
	2s	1s		1s		8s	1s	5s		2s	4s	9s		4s	1s	1s		8s				1s	

Rumbelows Cup	Second Round	Oxford U (h)	0-2
		(a)	0-0
FA Cup	Third Round	Peterborough U (h)	2-1
	Fourth Round	Manchester C (h)	1-2

PORT VALE

Player and Position	Ht	Wt	Birth Date	Birth Place	Source	Clubs	League App	Gls
Goalkeepers								
Mark Grew	5 11	12 08	15 2 58	Bilston	Amateur	WBA	33	—
						Wigan Ath (loan)	4	—
						Notts Cu (loan)	—	—
						Leicester C	5	—
						Oldham Ath (loan)	5	—
						Ipswich T	6	—
						Fulham (loan)	4	—
						WBA (loan)	1	—
						Derby Co (loan)	—	—
						Port Vale	138	—
						Blackburn R (loan)	13	—
Trevor Wood	6 0	12 06	3 11 68	Jersey	Apprentice	Brighton & HA	—	—
						Port Vale	37	—
Defenders								
Neil Aspin	6 0	12 03	12 4 65	Gateshead	Apprentice	Leeds U	207	5
						Port Vale	83	1
Matt Booth*	6 0	11 09	10 12 70	Stoke	Trainee	Port Vale	—	—
Dean Glover	5 10	11 11	29 12 63	Birmingham	Apprentice	Aston Villa	28	—
						Sheffield U (loan)	5	—
						Middlesbrough	50	5
						Port Vale	107	5
Darren Hughes	5 11	10 11	6 10 65	Prescot	Apprentice	Everton	3	—
						Shrewsbury T	37	1
						Brighton & HA	26	2
						Port Vale	142	2
Ryan Kidd	6 0	11 07	6 10 71	Heywood	Trainee	Port Vale	—	—
Rob Myatt‡			21 11 72	Stoke	Trainee	Port Vale	—	—
Tim Parkin	6 2	13 03	31 12 57	Penrith	Apprentice Malmo Almondsbury G	Blackburn R	13	—
						Bristol R	206	12
						Swindon T	110	6
						Port Vale	41	1
Alan Webb	5 10	12 00	1 1 63	Wellington	Apprentice	WBA	24	—
						Lincoln C (loan)	11	—
						Port Vale	187	2
Gary West	6 2	12 07	25 8 64	Scunthorpe	Apprentice	Sheffield U	75	1
						Lincoln C	83	4
						Gillingham	52	3
						Port Vale	17	1
						Lincoln C (loan)	3	—
						Gillingham (loan)	1	—
Paul West	5 11	11 00	22 6 70		Alcester T	Port Vale	—	—
Midfield								
Robbie Earle	5 9	10 10	27 1 65	Newcastle, Staffs	Amateur	Stoke C	—	—
						Port Vale	294	77
Kevin Finney*	6 0	12 00	19 10 69	Newcastle-U-Lyme	Apprentice	Port Vale	37	1
John Johnston‡			21 3 72	Bangor	Trainee	Port Vale	—	—
Simon Mills	5 8	11 04	16 8 64	Sheffield	Apprentice	Sheffield W	5	—
						York C	99	5
						Port Vale	148	6
Andy Porter	5 9	11 02	17 9 68	Manchester	Trainee	Port Vale	97	2
Ray Walker	5 10	12 00	6 7 81	North Shields	Apprentice	Aston Villa	23	—
						Port Vale (loan)	15	1
						Port Vale	215	21

PORT VALE

Foundation: Formed in 1876 as Port Vale, adopting the prefix 'Burslem' in 1884 upon moving to that part of the city. It was dropped in 1911.

First Football League game: 3 September, 1892, Division 2, v Small Heath (a) L 1–5 – Frail; Clutton, Elson; Farrington, McCrindle, Delves; Walker, Scarratt, Bliss (1), Jones. (Only 10 men).

Did you know: Port Vale's championship-winning margin of 11 points in Division 3(N) in 1953–54 was a record for that division. This was the season in which they suffered only three defeats.

Managers (and Secretary-managers)
Sam Gleaves 1896–1905*, Tom Clare 1905–11, A. S. Walker 1911–12, H. Myatt 1912–14, Tom Holford 1919–24 (continued as trainer), Joe Schofield 1924–30, Tom Morgan 1930–32, Tom Holford 1932–35, Warney Cresswell 1936–37, Tom Morgan 1937–38, Billy Frith 1945–46, Gordon Hodgson 1946–51, Ivor Powell 1951, Freddie Steele 1951–57, Norman Low 1957–62, Freddie Steele 1962–65, Jackie Mudie 1965–67, Sir Stanley Matthews (GM) 1965–68, Gordon Lee 1968–74, Roy Sproson 1974–77, Colin Harper 1977, Bobby Smith 1977–78, Dennis Butler 1978–79, Alan Bloor 1979, John McGrath 1980–83, John Rudge March 1984–   .

Player and Position	Ht	Wt	Birth Date	Birth Place	Source	Clubs	League App	Gls
Forwards								
Paul Atkinson‡	5 9	10 02	19 1 66	Chester-Le-Street	Apprentice	Sunderland	60	5
						Port Vale	4	3
						Hartlepool U (loan)	11	1
Darren Beckford	6 1	11 01	12 5 67	Manchester	Apprentice	Manchester C	11	—
						Bury (loan)	12	5
						Port Vale (loan)	11	4
						Port Vale	167	68
Nicky Cross	5 9	11 04	7 2 61	Birmingham	Apprentice	WBA	105	15
						Walsall	109	45
						Leicester C	58	15
						Port Vale	61	15
John Jeffers	5 10	11 10	5 10 68	Liverpool	Trainee	Liverpool	—	—
						Port Vale	86	3
Kevin Kent	5 11	11 00	19 3 65	Stoke	Apprentice	WBA	2	—
						Newport Co	33	1
						Mansfield T	229	36
						Port Vale	11	—
Gary McKinstry	5 9	10 08	7 1 72	Banbridge	Portadown	Port Vale	—	—
Paul Millar	6 2	12 07	16 1 66	Belfast	Portadown	Port Vale	40	5
						Hereford U (loan)	5	2
Brian Mills	5 9	10 10	26 12 71	Stone	Trainee	Port Vale	2	2
Derek Swann‡			24 10 66	Dublin	Bohemians	Port Vale	—	—
Robin Van der Laan	5 11	12 05	5 9 68	Schiedam	Wageningen	Port Vale	18	4

Trainees
Banks, Ian G; Bedson, Nicholas S; Beeby, Matthew; Bennett, Tony; Blake, Martin G; Boswell, Christopher W; Brown, Saxton; Burbridge, Nigel J; Craig, Nikolas; Dyas, Mark W; Gillard, Christopher; Harrison, Michael; Lovatt, Gregory; Mitchell, Richard D; Royall, Adam; Rushton, David; Shea, Gareth D.

Associated Schoolboys
Collins, Andrew J; Corden, Simon W; Harrison, Adam P; Hughes, Simon D; Johnson, Mark; Lymer, Gareth D.J; Ormiston, Christopher J; Shemilt, Andrew; Tweats, Timothy A.

Associated Schoolboys who have accepted the club's offer of a Traineeship/Contract
Brown, Christopher E; Byrne, Paul T; McCarthy, Anthony M; Mountford, Wayne; Palmer, Shane M; Parris, Mark; Stirk, Mark A.

412

PRESTON NORTH END 1990–91 *Back row (left to right):* Steve Senior, Bob Atkins, Adrian Hughes, Roy Tunks, Alan Kelly, Simon Farnworth, Tony Hancock, Mike Flynn, Jeff Wrightson.

Centre row: Warren Joyce, Martin James, Steven Anderton, Gary Swann, Neil Williams, Nigel Greenwood, Graham Shaw, Mick Rathbone, Dave Thompson.

Front row: Matt Lambert, Graham Easter, Ian Bogie, Walter Joyce (Youth Development Officer), Les Chapman (Team Manager), Steve Harper, Nathan Peel, Steven Greaves.

Division 3   **PRESTON NORTH END**

Deepdale, Preston PR1 6RU. Telephone Preston (0772) 795919. Answerphone (0772) 709170. Commercial Dept: (0772) 795465/795156. Pitch Hire: (0772) 705468. Community Office: (0772) 704275.

Ground capacity: 15,120.

Record attendance: 42,684 v Arsenal, Division 1, 23 April 1938.

Record receipts: £54,000 v Burnley, Sherpa Van Trophy, Northern Final, second leg, 19 April 1988.

Pitch measurements: 110yd × 72yd. (Artificial surface.)

President: Tom Finney OBE, JP.

Vice President: T. C. Nicholson JP, FCIOB.

Chairman: Keith W. Leeming.

Vice-chairmen: J. T. Garratt, M. J. Woodhouse.

Directors: E. Griffith BVSC, MRCVS (Company Secretary), J. E. Wignall, J. T. Worden.

Manager: Les Chapman. *Asst. Manager:*

Physio: Andy Jones.

Secretary: D. J. Allan. *General Manager:* Paul Agnew.

Year Formed: 1881. *Turned Professional:* 1885. *Ltd Co.:* 1893.

Club Nicknames: 'The Lilywhites' or 'North End'.

Record League Victory: 10-0 v Stoke, Division 1, 14 September 1889 – Trainer; Howarth, Holmes; Kelso, Russell (1), Graham; Gordon, Jimmy Ross (2), Nick Ross (3), Thomson (2), Drummond (2).

Record Cup Victory: 26-0 v Hyde, FA Cup, 1st rd, 15 October 1887 – Addision; Howarth, Nick Ross; Russell (1), Thomson (5), Graham (1); Gordon (5), Jimmy Ross (8), John Goodall (1), Dewhurst (3), Drummond (1).

Record Defeat: 0-7 v Blackool, Division 1, 1 May 1948.

Most League Points (2 for a win): 61, Division 3, 1970–71.

Most League Points (3 for a win): 90, Division 4, 1986–87.

Most League Goals: 100, Division 2, 1927–28 and Division 1, 1957–58.

Highest League Scorer in Season: Ted Harper, 37, Division 2, 1932–33.

Most League Goals in Total Aggregate: Tom Finney, 187, 1946–60.

Most Capped Player: Tom Finney, 76, England.

Most League Appearances: Alan Kelly, 447, 1961–75.

Record Transfer Fee Received: £765,000 from Manchester C for Michael Robinson, June 1979.

Record Transfer Fee Paid: £125,000 to Norwich C for Mike Flynn, December 1989.

Football League Record: 1888 Founder Member of League; 1901–04 Division 2; 1904–12 Division 1; 1912–13 Division 2; 1913–14 Division 1; 1914–15 Division 2; 1919–25 Division 1; 1925–34 Division 2; 1934–49 Division 1; 1949–51 Division 2; 1951–61 Division 1; 1961–70 Division 2; 1970–71 Division 3; 1971–74 Division 2; 1974–78 Division 3; 1978–81 Division 2; 1981–85 Division 3; 1985–87 Division 4; 1987– Division 3.

Honours: Football League: Division 1 – Champions 1888–89 (first champions), 1889–90; Runners-up 1890–91, 1891–92, 1892–93, 1905–06, 1952–53, 1957–58; Division 2 – Champions 1903–04, 1912–13, 1950–51; Runners-up 1914–15, 1933–34; Division 3 – Champions 1970–71; Division 4 – Runners-up 1986–87. *FA Cup:* Winners 1889, 1938; Runners-up 1888, 1922, 1937, 1954, 1964. *Double Performed:* 1888–89. *Football League Cup:* best season: 4th rd, 1963, 1966, 1972, 1981.

Colours: White shirts, navy blue shorts, white stockings. **Change colours:** All yellow.

414

PRESTON NORTH END 1990–91 LEAGUE RECORD

Match No.	Date		Venue	Opponents	Result		H/T Score	Lg. Pos.	Goalscorers	Attendance
1	Aug	25	H	Grimsby T	L	1-3	0-2	—	Joyce	6372
2	Sept	1	A	Reading	D	3-3	1-2	19	Joyce, Peel, Senior	4228
3		8	H	Tranmere R	L	0-4	0-2	24		5648
4		14	A	Southend U	L	2-3	1-0	—	Joyce, Thomas (pen)	4614
5		18	A	Bolton W	W	2-1	1-0	—	James, Bogie (pen)	5844
6		22	H	Fulham	W	1-0	0-0	15	Hughes	4691
7		29	A	Birmingham C	D	1-1	0-0	16	Bogie	7154
8	Oct	2	H	Brentford	D	1-1	0-0	—	Swann	5025
9		6	H	Exeter C	W	1-0	1-0	13	Bogie	4716
10		13	A	Mansfield T	W	1-0	1-0	11	Rathbone	3225
11		20	A	Rotherham U	L	0-1	0-0	14		4599
12		23	H	Chester C	D	0-0	0-0	—		5465
13		27	H	Bournemouth	D	0-0	0-0	15		4953
14	Nov	3	A	Wigan Ath	L	1-2	1-2	17	Greenwood	4728
15		10	A	Bradford C	L	1-2	1-0	17	Bogie	7440
16		24	H	Huddersfield T	D	1-1	0-1	18	Joyce	4646
17	Dec	1	H	Shrewsbury T	W	4-3	2-0	17	Bogie 2, Wrightson, Swann	4515
18		15	A	Leyton Orient	L	0-1	0-1	17		3282
19		22	H	Stoke C	W	2-0	1-0	17	Swann 2	7532
20		26	A	Crewe Alex	D	2-2	1-1	17	Bogie, Shaw	4405
21		29	A	Bury	L	1-3	1-1	17	Mooney	5404
22	Jan	1	H	Cambridge U	L	0-2	0-1	18		5256
23		12	H	Reading	L	1-2	0-1	18	Swann	4470
24		19	A	Grimsby T	L	1-4	0-2	19	Mooney	5391
25		26	H	Southend U	W	2-1	1-0	18	Shaw, Wrightson	4351
26	Feb	2	H	Bolton W	L	1-2	1-2	19	Wrightson	9844
27		5	A	Fulham	L	0-1	0-0	—		2750
28		16	A	Huddersfield T	L	0-1	0-1	19		5504
29		23	H	Bradford C	L	0-3	0-2	19		6878
30	Mar	2	A	Shrewsbury T	W	1-0	1-0	18	Shaw	2989
31		9	H	Leyton Orient	W	2-1	0-1	19	Shaw, Thompson	3651
32		12	A	Brentford	L	0-2	0-0	—		4856
33		16	H	Birmingham C	W	2-0	1-0	18	Cartwright, Joyce	5334
34		19	A	Mansfield T	W	3-1	2-1	—	Jepson 2, Joyce (pen)	3245
35		23	A	Exeter C	L	0-4	0-0	17		3525
36		26	H	Swansea C	W	2-0	0-0	—	Shaw 2	3491
37		30	H	Crewe Alex	W	5-1	2-0	17	Joyce, Shaw, Bogie, Thompson, James	4852
38	Apr	1	A	Stoke C	W	1-0	0-0	17	Shaw	11,524
39		6	H	Bury	D	1-1	1-0	17	Shaw	5641
40		13	A	Cambridge U	D	1-1	0-1	17	Joyce	6262
41		16	A	Swansea C	L	1-3	1-1	—	Senior	2507
42		20	H	Rotherham U	L	1-2	0-0	17	Flynn	4069
43		27	A	Chester C	D	1-1	0-1	17	Joyce	1351
44	May	2	A	Bournemouth	D	0-0	0-0	—		7064
45		7	A	Tranmere R	L	1-2	1-0	—	Ashcroft	6006
46		11	H	Wigan Ath	W	2-1	0-1	17	Jepson, Shaw	5917

Final League Position: 17

GOALSCORERS

League (54): Shaw 10, Joyce 9 (1 pen), Bogie 8 (1 pen), Swann 5, Jepson 3, Wrightson 3, James 2, Mooney 2, Senior 2, Thompson 2, Ashcroft 1, Cartwright 1, Flynn 1, Greenwood 1, Hughes 1, Peel 1, Rathbone 1, Thomas 1 (pen).
Rumbelows Cup (3): Swann 2, Shaw 1.
FA Cup (0).

Farnworth	Senior	Swann	Greaves	Flynn	Wrightson	Williams	Joyce	Thomas	Shaw	Harper	Peel	Bogie	James	Hughes	Kelly	Fee	Rathbone	Greenwood	Ashcroft	Mooney	Easter	Thompson	Jepson	Cartwright	Lambert	Eaves	Kerfoot	Jackson	Match No.
1	2	3	4	5	6	7	8	9	10	11*12																			1
1	2	3		5	6	7*10	9		12	8†	4	11	14																2
1	2	3			6	7	10	9		8*12	4	11	5																3
	2*	8			6	3	11	9	10		7	12	5	1	4														4
1		11			6	2	7	9*10	12	8	3	5	4																5
1		10			6	2	7	9		8	11	5	4	3															6
1	2	11			6	7	10	9		8	3	5*	4	12															7
1	2	11			6	7*10	9	12	8	3	5	4																	8
1	2	11			6	10	9		8	7	5	4	3																9
1	2	11			6	14*10	9	12	8	7	5†	4	3																10
1	2	11	12	6	10	9	7*	8	3	5	4																		11
1		11	2	5	6	10	7	8	3	9*	4	12																	12
1		11	2	6	10	7	8	3	5	4	9																		13
1	2	11	4	6	10	7	8*	3	5†	12	9	14																	14
	2	7*	4†	6	11	10	12	8	14	5	1	3	9																15
	2	10		6	4	9	7*12	8	11	5	1	3																	16
	2	10		6	4	9	11	8	5	1	3	7																	17
	2	10	12	6	14	4	9	11	8	5	1	3†	7*																18
	2	11	4	6	3	9	10	8	5	1	7																		19
	2	11	4	6	3	9	10	8	5	1	7																		20
	2	11	4	6	3†	9	10	12	14	8	5*	1	7																21
	2	11	4	6	9	10	12	14	8†	5*	1	3	7																22
	2	11	4	6†	9	10*14	1	5	3	12	7	8																	23
	2	11	4	6	9	10	8	1	5	3	7																		24
		11	4	6	9	10	8	3	1	5	2	7																	25
1		11	5	6	2	10	8	12	3	4	9	7*																	26
1		11	5	6	2	10	8*12	3	4	9	7																		27
1	2	11	5	6	3	10	8†12	14	4	7*	9																		28
1		11	5	6	3	10	8*	2	4	12	7	9																	29
1	2	11	5	6	10	3	4	7	9	8																			30
1	2	5	6	10	12	3	4	11	7	9*	8																		31
1	2	5	10	11	4	6†	12	7	8	3*	9	14																	32
1	2	5	6	4	10	11	3	7	9	8																			33
1	2	5	6	4	10	11	3	7	9	8																			34
1	2	5	6	4	10	11	8†	3	12	7*	9	14																	35
	2	5	6	4	10	11	8	3	1	7	9																		36
	2	5	6†	4	10*11	8	3	1	7	9	12	14																	37
	2	5	6	4	10	11	8	3	1	12	7*	9																	38
	2	6	4	10	11	8	3	1	12	7*	9	5																	39
	2	6	4	10	11	3	1	7	9	8	5																		40
	2	6	4	10	11	12	3	1	7	9	8*14	5†																	41
	2	6	5	4	10*11	8	3	1	12	7	9																		42
	2	6	5	4	10†11	12	3	1	14	7*	9	8																	43
	2	5	4	10	11	3	1	9	7	8	6																		44
	2	5	4	10*11	14	12	3	1	9†	7	8	6																	45
	2	5	4	10	11	8†	3	1	9*	7	12	4	6	14															46
23	38	30	2	33	40	11	42	5	44	27	1	28	34	25	23	15	11	3	6	9	1	21	13	13	4	1	—	3	
				+2s	+2s					+9s	+9s	+3s	+3s	+1s				+2s	+2s	+8s			+1s	+1s	+1s	+2s	+1s	+1s	

Rumbelows Cup First Round Chester C (h) 2-0
(a) 1-5

FA Cup First Round Mansfield T (h) 0-1

PRESTON NORTH END

Player and Position	Ht	Wt	Birth Date	Birth Place	Source	Clubs	League App	Gls
Goalkeepers								
Simon Farnworth	6 0	11 10	28 10 63	Chorley	Apprentice	Bolton W	113	—
						Stockport Co (loan)	10	—
						Tranmere R (loan)	7	—
						Bury	105	—
						Preston NE	23	—
Alan Kelly	6 2	12 05	11 8 68	Preston		Preston NE	119	—
Roy Tunks*	6 1	13 11	21 1 51	Wuppertal	Apprentice	Rotherham U	138	—
						York C (loan)	4	—
						Ipswich T (loan)	—	—
						Newcastle U (loan)	—	—
						Preston NE	277	—
						Wigan Ath	245	—
						Hartlepool U	5	—
						Preston NE	25	—
Defenders								
Bob Atkins	6 0	12 02	16 10 62	Leicester	Local	Sheffield U	40	3
						Preston NE	200	5
Richard Cunningham*	6 0	11 06	31 3 72	Hawarden	Trainee	Preston NE	—	—
Neil Edmonds‡	5 8	10 08	18 10 68	Accrington	Trainee	Oldham Ath	5	—
						Rochdale	43	8
						Preston NE	—	—
Mike Flynn	6 0	11 00	23 2 69	Oldham	Trainee	Oldham Ath	40	1
						Norwich C	—	—
						Preston NE	58	2
Adrian Hughes	6 2	12 12	19 12 70	Billinge	Trainee	Preston NE	85	3
Matthew Lambert	6 0	12 06	28 9 71	Morecambe	Trainee	Preston NE	5	—
Mike Rathbone*	5 10	11 12	6 11 58	Birmingham	Apprentice	Birmingham C	20	—
						Blackburn R	273	2
						Preston NE	91	4
Steve Senior	5 8	11 04	15 5 64	Sheffield	Apprentice	York C	168	6
						Darlington (loan)	5	—
						Northampton T	4	—
						Wigan Ath	109	3
						Preston NE	38	2
Jeff Wrightson	5 11	11 00	18 5 68	Newcastle	Apprentice	Newcastle U	4	—
						Preston NE	129	3
Midfield								
Steven Anderton*	5 8	11 05	2 10 69	Lancaster	Trainee	Preston NE	1	—
Ian Bogie	5 7	10 02	6 12 67	Newcastle	Apprentice	Newcastle U	14	—
						Preston NE	79	12
Lee Cartwright§	5 8	10 06	19 9 72	Rossendale	Trainee	Preston NE	14	1
Graham Easter‡	5 7	10 07	26 9 69	Epsom	Trainee	WBA	—	—
						Huddersfield T	—	—
						Crewe Alex	3	—
						Preston NE	1	—
David Eaves§	5 11	11 07	13 2 73	Blackpool	Trainee	Preston NE	3	—
Steve Greaves‡	5 9	11 03	17 1 70	London	Trainee	Fulham	1	—
						Waterford (loan)	—	—
						Brighton & HA (loan)	—	—
						Preston NE	2	—
Martin James	5 10	11 07	18 5 71	Formby	Trainee	Preston NE	37	2
Warren Joyce	5 9	11 11	20 1 65	Oldham	Local	Bolton W	184	17
						Preston NE	148	29
Sammy McIlroy*	5 10	11 08	2 8 54	Belfast	Apprentice	Manchester U	342	57
						Stoke C	133	14
						Manchester C	13	1
						Bury	43	6
					Modling	Bury	57	2
						Preston NE	20	—
Gary Swann	5 9	11 02	11 4 62	York	Apprentice	Hull C	186	9
						Preston NE	170	32
David Thompson	5 11	12 04	27 5 62	Manchester	Local	Rochdale	155	13
						Manchester U (loan)	—	—
						Notts Co	55	8
						Wigan Ath	108	14
						Preston NE	21	2
Neil Williams	5 11	11 04	23 10 64	Waltham Abbey	Apprentice	Watford	—	—
						Hull C	91	10
						Preston NE	95	5

PRESTON NORTH END

Foundation: North End Cricket and Rugby Club which was formed in 1863, indulged in most sports before taking up soccer in about 1879. In 1881 they decided to stick to football to the exclusion of other sports and even a 16–0 drubbing by Blackburn Rovers in an invitation game at Deepdale, a few weeks after taking this decision, did not deter them for they immediately became affiliated to the Lancashire FA.

First Football League game: 8 September, 1888, Football League, v Burnley (h) W 5-2 – Trainer; Haworth, Holmes; Robertson, W. Graham, J. Graham; Gordon (1), Ross (2), Goodall, Dewhurst (2), Drummond.

Did you know: During 1947–48 Preston became the only club ever to play successive away FA Cup ties in different rounds on the same ground. A 1-0 victory over Manchester City was followed by a 4-1 defeat by Manchester United. Both games at Maine Road.

Managers (and Secretary-managers)
Charlie Parker 1906–15, Vincent Hayes 1919–23, Jim Lawrence 1923–25, Frank Richards 1925–27, Alex Gibson 1927–31, Lincoln Hayes 1931–1932 (run by committee 1932–36), Tommy Muirhead 1936–37, (run by committee 1937–49), Will Scott 1949–53, Scot Symon 1953–54, Frank Hill 1954–56, Cliff Britton 1956–61, Jimmy Milne 1961–68, Bobby Seith 1968–70, Alan Ball Sr 1970–73, Bobby Charlton 1973–75, Harry Catterick 1975–77, Nobby Stiles 1977–81, Tommy Docherty 1981, Gordon Lee 1981–83, Alan Kelly 1983–85, Tommy Booth 1985–86, Brian Kidd 1986, John McGrath 1986–90, Les Chapman May 1990– .

Player and Position	Ht	Wt	Birth Date	Place	Source	Clubs	League App	Gls
Forwards								
Lee Ashcroft§	5 10	11 00	7 9 72	Preston	Trainee	Preston NE	14	1
Nigel Greenwood	5 11	12 00	27 11 66	Preston	Apprentice	Preston NE	45	14
						Bury	110	25
						Preston NE	10	1
Tony Hancock†	6 1	12 12	31 1 67	Manchester	Stockport Georgians	Stockport Co	22	5
						Burnley	17	—
						Preston NE	—	—
Steve Harper*	5 10	11 05	3 2 69	Stoke	Trainee	Port Vale	28	2
						Preston NE	77	10
Ronnie Jepson	6 1	13 02	12 5 63	Stoke	Nantwich	Port Vale	22	—
						Peterborough U (loan)	18	5
						Preston NE	14	3
Jason Kerfoot§	5 8	10 10	17 4 73	Preston	Trainee	Preston NE	1	—
Nathan Peel	6 1	12 07	17 5 72	Blackburn	Trainee	Preston NE	10	1
Graham Shaw	5 8	10 01	7 6 67	Newcastle	Apprentice	Stoke C	99	18
						Preston NE	75	15
John Thomas*	5 8	11 03	5 8 58	Wednesbury		Everton	—	—
						Tranmere R (loan)	11	2
						Halifax T (loan)	5	—
						Bolton W	22	6
						Chester	44	20
						Lincoln C	67	20
						Preston NE	78	38
						Bolton W	73	31
						WBA	18	1
						Preston NE	16	4

Trainees
Ashcroft, Lee; Bagnall, John A; Burrow, David R; Burton, Simon P; Cartwright, Lee; Christie, David; Close, Jamie T; Critchley, Adam D; Dalgarno, Alan W; Eaves, David M.C; Finney, Stephen K; Flitcroft, David J; Hindle, Paul J; Kerfoot, Jason J.T; McCullough, Gary; O'Connor, Kerry J; Rapsey, Jason A; Schofield, Christopher; Siddall, Adam M; Veitch, Stephen D; Williams, Christopher J.

**Non-Contract
Chapman, Leslie; Hancock, Anthony E; Johnson, Steven E; Nixon, Craig G.

Associated Schoolboys
Alder, Joseph; Arnold, Lee; Baker, Alistair M; Banks, Andrew M; Booker, Geoffrey S; Borland, John R; Borwick, Christopher S; Boustead, Steven G; Brandes, Christopher M; Crellin, Simon A; Duffell, Paul; Garratt, Leroy; Ginocchio, Mark; Hallsworth, Martin J; Hassall, Andrew R; Holland, Christopher J; Kilbane, Kevin D; Linford, Paul R; McMenemy, Paul J; Molyneux, Steven B; Moylon, Craig; Parkinson, Christopher; Parkinson, Stuart G; Poole, David J; Squires, James A; Sumner, Craig R; Taylor, Thomas P; Wilson, Dean R; Wright, James C.

Associated Schoolboys who have accepted the club's offer of a Traineeship/Contract
Allardyce, Craig S; England, Kieran J; Hall, Andrew B; Heavey, Paul A; Iles, Thomas W.S; Raywood, Matthew J; Rimmer, Christopher E; Sheridan, Brian J.

**Non-Contract Players who are retained must be re-signed before they are eligible to play in League matches.

418

QUEENS PARK RANGERS 1990-91   *Back row (left to right)*: Roy Wegerle, Les Ferdinand, Mark Falco, Tony Roberts, Brian Law, Dominic Iorfa, Alen McDonald.
Centre row: Justin Channing, Mike Varney (Consultant Physiotherapist), George Smith (Youth Team Coach), Les Boyle (Youth Team Trainer), Don Howe (Chief Coach), Ron Berry (Kit Manager), Roger Cross (Reserve Team Coach), Brian Morris (Club Physiotherapist), David Bardsley.
Front row: Ray Wilkins, Simon Barker, Clive Wilson, Paul Parker, Danny Maddix, Andy Sinton, Ken Sansom.

Division 1   QUEEN'S PARK RANGERS

South Africa Road, W12 7PA. Telephone 081-743 0262. Box Office: 081-749 5744. Supporters Club: 081-749 6771. Club Shop: 081-749 6862. Marketing: 081-740 8737.

Ground capacity: 23,480 (23,000 covered).

Record attendance: 35,353 v Leeds U, Division 1, 27 April 1974.

Record receipts: £114,743 v Tottenham H, Division 1, 12 January 1985.

Pitch measurements: 112yd × 72yd.

Chairman: R. C. Thompson.

Directors: (Corporate): C. B. Berlin (Managing): R. B. Copus (Club); A Chandler, P. D. Ellis, A. Ingham, B. Rowe.

Chief Coach: Gerry Francis. *Assistant Coach:*

Secretary: Miss S. F. Marson. *Marketing Manager:* B. Rowe.

Reserve Team Coach: Roger Cross.

Physio: Brian Morris.

Year Formed: 1885 *(see Foundation).* **Turned Professional:** 1898. **Ltd Co.:** 1899.

Club Nicknames: 'Rangers' or 'Rs'. *Previous Name:* 1885–87, St Jude's.

Previous Grounds: 1885 *(see Foundation),* Welford's Fields; 1888–99; London Scottish Ground, Brondesbury, Home Farm, Kensal Rise Green, Gun Club Wormwood Scrubs, Kilburn Cricket Ground; 1899, Kensal Rise Athletic Ground; 1901, Latimer Road, Notting Hill; 1904, Agricultural Society, Park Royal; 1907, Park Royal Ground; 1917, Loftus Road; 1931, White City; 1933, Loftus Road; 1962, White City; 1963, Loftus Road.

Record League Victory: 9-2 v Tranmere R, Division 3, 3 December 1960 – Drinkwater; Woods, Ingham; Keen, Rutter, Angell; Lazarus (2), Bedford (2), Evans (2), Andrews (1), Clark (2).

Record Cup Victory: 8-1 (away) v Bristol R (away), FA Cup, 1st rd, 27 November 1937 – Gilfillan; Smith, Jefferson; Lowe, James, March; Cape, Mallett, Cheetham (3), Fitzgerald (3) Bott (2). 8-1 v Crewe Alex, Milk Cup, 1st rd, 3 October 1983 – Hucker; Neill, Dawes, Waddock (1), McDonald (1), Fenwick, Micklewhite (1), Stewart (1), Allen (1), Stainrod (3), Gregory.

Record Defeat: 1-8 v Mansfield T, Division 3, 15 March 1965 and v Manchester U, Division 1, 19 March 1969.

Most League Points (2 for a win): 67, Division 3, 1966–67.

Most League Points (3 for a win): 85, Division 2, 1982–83.

Most League Goals: 111, Division 3, 1961–62.

Highest League Scorer in Season: George Goddard, 37, Division 3 (S), 1929–30.

Most League Goals in Total Aggregate: George Goddard, 172, 1926–34.

Most Capped Player: Don Givens, 26 (56), Eire.

Most League Appearances: Tony Ingham, 519, 1950–63.

Record Transfer Fee Received: £1,300,000 from Arsenal for David Seaman, May 1990.

Record Transfer Fee Paid: £1,000,000 to Luton T for Roy Wegerle, December 1989.

Football League Record: 1920 Original Members of Division 3; 1921 Division 3 (S); 1948–52 Division 2; 1952–58 Division 3 (S); 1958–67 Division 3; 1967–68 Division 2; 1968–69 Division 1; 1969–73 Division 2; 1973–79 Division 1; 1979–83 Division 2; 1983– Division 1.

Honours: Football League: Division 1 – Runners-up 1975–76; Division 2 – Champions 1982–83; Runners-up 1967–68, 1972–73; Division 3 (S) – Champions 1947–48; Runners-up 1946–47; Division 3 – Champions 1966–67. *FA Cup:* Runners-up 1982. *Football League Cup:* Winners 1966–67; Runners-up 1985–86. (In 1966–67 won Division 3 and Football League Cup.) **European Competition:** *UEFA Cup:* 1976–77, 1984–85.

Colours: Blue and white hooped shirts, white shorts, white stockings. **Change colours:** Red and black hooped shirts, black shorts, black stockings with 4 red bands at top.

QUEEN'S PARK RANGERS 1990–91 LEAGUE RECORD

Match No.	Date	Venue	Opponents	Result	H/T Score	Lg. Pos.	Goalscorers	Atten- dance
1	Aug 25	A	Nottingham F	D	1-1	1-0	—	Wegerle	21,619
2	29	H	Wimbledon	L	0-1	0-0	—		9762
3	Sept 1	H	Chelsea	W	1-0	1-0	11	Wegerle (pen)	19,813
4	8	A	Manchester U	L	1-3	0-1	15	Wegerle (pen)	43,427
5	15	H	Luton T	W	6-1	1-0	7	Wegerle 2, Sinton, Wilkins, Falco, Parker	10,186
6	22	A	Aston Villa	D	2-2	2-2	8	Sinton, Wegerle (pen)	23,301
7	29	A	Coventry C	L	1-3	0-2	10	Ferdinand	9890
8	Oct 6	H	Tottenham H	D	0-0	0-0	11		21,405
9	20	A	Leeds U	W	3-2	2-2	10	Wilkins, Wegerle 2	27,443
10	27	H	Norwich C	L	1-3	0-2	11	Wegerle (pen)	11,103
11	Nov 3	A	Everton	L	0-3	0-1	13		22,352
12	10	A	Southampton	L	1-3	1-1	15	Falco	15,957
13	17	H	Crystal Palace	L	1-2	0-1	16	Wegerle	14,360
14	24	H	Arsenal	L	1-3	1-0	19	Wegerle (pen)	18,555
15	Dec 1	A	Manchester C	L	1-2	0-1	19	Sinton	25,080
16	8	A	Wimbledon	L	0-3	0-1	19		5358
17	15	H	Nottingham F	L	1-2	0-0	19	Wegerle (pen)	10,156
18	23	A	Derby Co	D	1-1	1-0	—	Wegerle	16,429
19	26	H	Liverpool	D	1-1	0-0	19	Falco	17,848
20	29	H	Sunderland	W	3-2	1-1	17	Maddix, Wegerle (pen), Falco	11,072
21	Jan 1	A	Sheffield U	L	0-1	0-1	19		21,158
22	12	A	Chelsea	L	0-2	0-1	19		19,255
23	19	H	Manchester U	D	1-1	1-0	18	Falco	18,544
24	Feb 2	A	Luton T	W	2-1	0-1	18	Ferdinand 2	8479
25	16	A	Crystal Palace	D	0-0	0-0	18		16,006
26	23	H	Southampton	W	2-1	2-0	18	Ferdinand 2	11,009
27	Mar 2	H	Manchester C	W	1-0	1-0	17	Ferdinand	12,376
28	16	H	Coventry C	W	1-0	1-0	17	Ferdinand	9510
29	23	A	Tottenham H	D	0-0	0-0	17		30,860
30	30	A	Liverpool	W	3-1	2-0	16	Ferdinand, Wegerle, Wilson	37,251
31	Apr 1	H	Derby Co	D	1-1	0-1	16	Wegerle (pen)	12,036
32	6	A	Sunderland	W	1-0	0-0	12	Tillson	17,899
33	10	H	Aston Villa	W	2-1	0-1	—	Allen, Tillson	11,539
34	13	H	Sheffield U	L	1-2	1-1	12	Allen	18,801
35	17	H	Leeds U	W	2-0	0-0	—	Wegerle, Barker	10,998
36	23	H	Arsenal	L	0-2	0-0	—		42,393
37	May 4	A	Norwich C	L	0-1	0-0	12		13,469
38	11	H	Everton	D	1-1	1-1	12	Wegerle	12,508

Final League Position: 12

GOALSCORERS

League (44): Wegerle 18 (8 pens), Ferdinand 8, Falco 5, Sinton 3, Allen 2, Tillson 2, Wilkins 2, Barker 1, Maddix 1, Parker 1, Wilson 1.
Rumbelows Cup (6): Ferdinand 2, Barker 1, Falco 1, Maddix 1, Wegerle 1.
FA Cup (1): Maddix 1.

Roberts	Bardsley	Sansom	Channing	McDonald	Maddix	Wilkins	Wilson	Falco	Wegerle	Sinton	Barker	Ferdinand	Parker	Stejskal	Allen	Law	Herrera	McCarthy	Iorfa	Caesar	Meaker	Tillson	Peacock	Brevett	Match No.
1	2	3	4	5	6	7*	8	9†	10	11	12	14													1
1	2	3	4*	5	6	7	8	9	10†	11	12	14													2
1	2	3		6	5	7	8	9	10	11			4												3
1	2	3		5	6*	7	8	9	10	11	12		4												4
1	2	3		5	6	7	8	9*	10	11	12		4												5
1	2	3		5	6	7	8		10	11		9	4												6
1	2†	3*	14	5	6	7	8		10	11	12	9	4												7
1	2	3		5	6	7	12		10	11	8	9*	4												8
	2	3		5	6	7	12		10	11	8	9*	4	1											9
	2	3	14	5†	6	7	12		10	11	8	9*	4	1											10
	2	3		5	6*	7	12	9	10	11	8		4	1											11
	2*	3		5	6	7		9	10	11	8		4	1	12										12
1	2	3		5		7		9	10	11	8		4			6									13
1	2	3				7		9*	10	11	8				12	6	4			5					14
1	2	3				7			10	11	8				12	6	4	9*		5					15
1	2	3			6	7		9	10	11	8				12		4*			5					16
	2*	3			6	7	4	9	10	11	8			1	12					5					17
	2	3			6	7		9	10	11	8			1								4	5		18
	2	3			6	7		9	10	11	8			1								5	4		19
	2	3			6	7		9	10*	11	8			1						5	12	4			20
	2	3			6	7		9	10	11*	8			1							12	4	5		21
	2	3			6	7	4†	9	10*	11	8			1							12	14	5		22
	2	3			6	7		9		11	8	10*		1	12							4	5		23
	2	3			6	7				11*	8	10		1	9						12	4	5		24
	2	3			6	7		9*		11	8	10		1	12							4	5		25
	2	3			6	7		9		11	8	10		1								4	5		26
	2	3			6	7		9*		11	8	10		1							12	4	5		27
	2	3			6	7			10	11	8	9*		1							12	4	5		28
	2				6	7			10	11	8	9		1								4	5	3	29
	2				6	7	14		10*	11†	8	9		1							12	4	5	3	30
	2*				6	7			10	11	8	12		1	9†						14	4	5	3	31
	2				6	7			10	11	8	9		1								4	5	3	32
	2				6	7			10	11	8*	9†	12	1							14	4	5	3	33
	2*				6	7			10†	11	8	12		1	9						14	4	5	3	34
	2			9	6†	7			10	11	8			1								4	5	3	35
	2			9	6†	7			10	11	8	12		1							14	4*	5	3	36
	2				6*	7			10	11	8	4		1	9						12		5	3	37
	2			5	6*	7			10	11	8	4		1	12								9	3	38

```
12 38 28  3 17 32 38 11 17 35 38 31 15 13 26  4  3  3  1  1  5  —  18 19 10
          +              + +        + + +        +           + +        + +
         2s             2s 3s      4s 3s 4s     6s          1s 5s      8s 1s
```

Rumbelows Cup	Second Round	Peterborough U (h)		3-1
		(a)		1-1
	Third Round	Blackburn R (h)		2-1
	Fourth Round	Leeds U (h)		0-3
FA Cup	Third Round	Manchester U (a)		1-2

QUEEN'S PARK RANGERS

Player and Position	Ht	Wt	Birth Date	Birth Place	Source	Clubs	League App	Gls
Goalkeepers								
Peter Caldwell			5 6 72	Dorchester	Trainee	QPR	—	—
Tony Roberts	6 0	12 00	4 8 69	Bangor	Trainee	QPR	18	—
Jan Stejskal	6 3	12 00	15 1 62	Czechoslovakia	Sparta	QPR	26	—
Defenders								
David Bardsley	5 10	10 06	11 9 64	Manchester	Apprentice	Blackpool	45	—
						Watford	100	7
						Oxford U	74	7
						QPR	69	1
Rufus Brevett	5 8	11 00	24 9 69	Derby	Trainee	Derby Co	—	—
						Doncaster R	109	3
						QPR	10	—
Justin Channing	5 10	11 03	19 11 68	Reading	Apprentice	QPR	53	4
Roberto Herrera	5 7	10 06	12 6 70	Torbay	Trainee	QPR	6	—
Brian Law	6 2	11 10	1 1 70	Merthyr	Apprentice	QPR	20	—
Alan McCarthy	5 11	12 10	11 1 72	London	Trainee	QPR	2	—
Alan McDonald	6 2	12 07	12 10 63	Belfast	Apprentice	QPR	219	8
						Charlton Ath (loan)	9	—
Danny Maddix	5 11	11 00	11 10 67	Ashford	Apprentice	Tottenham H	—	—
						Southend U (loan)	2	—
						QPR	106	6
Darren Peacock	6 2	12 06	3 2 68	Bristol	Apprentice	Newport Co	28	—
						Hereford U	59	4
						QPR	19	—
Karl Ready	6 1	12 00	14 8 72	Neath		QPR	—	—
Andy Tillson	6 2	12 07	30 6 66	Huntingdon	Kettering	Grimsby T	105	5
						QPR	19	2
Paul Vowels			26 8 71	Neath	Trainee	QPR	—	—
Midfield								
Simon Barker	5 9	11 00	4 11 64	Farnworth	Apprentice	Blackburn R	182	35
						QPR	88	5
Steven Crocker*			23 3 72	London	Trainee	QPR	—	—
David Macciochi			14 9 72	Harlow	Trainee	QPR	—	—
David McEnroe	5 8	10 10	19 8 72	Dublin	Trainee	QPR	—	—
Michael Meaker	5 11	11 05	18 8 71	Greenford	Trainee	QPR	8	—
Paul Parker	5 7	10 09	4 4 64	Essex	Apprentice	Fulham	153	2
						QPR	125	1
Michael Rutherford	5 9	11 10	6 6 72	Sidcup	Trainee	QPR	2	—
Andy Sinton	5 7	10 07	19 3 66	Newcastle	Apprentice	Cambridge U	93	13
						Brentford	149	28
						QPR	86	12
Ray Wilkins	5 8	11 02	14 9 56	Hillingdon	Apprentice	Chelsea	179	30
						Manchester U	160	7
						AC Milan	73	2
					Paris St Germain	Rangers	70	2
						QPR	61	3
Clive Wilson	5 7	10 00	13 11 61	Manchester	Local	Manchester C	98	9
						Chester C (loan)	21	2
						Manchester C (loan)	11	—
						Chelsea	81	5
						QPR	13	1

QUEEN'S PARK RANGERS

Foundation: There is an element of doubt about the date of the foundation of this club, but it is believed that in either 1885 or 1886 it was formed through the amalgamation of Christchurch Rangers and St. Jude's Institute FC. The leading light was George Wodehouse, whose family maintained a connection with the club until comparatively recent times. Most of the players came from the Queen's Park district so this name was adopted after a year as St. Jude's Institute.

First Football League game: 28 August, 1920, Division 3, v Watford (h) L 1-2 – Price; Blackman, Wingrove; McGovern, Grant, O'Brien; Faulkner, Birch (1), Smith, Gregory, Middlemiss.

Did you know: QPR played a 'home' Division 3(S) game at Highbury, 1 March 1930, when their ground was closed because of spectator trouble. They beat Coventry City 3-1 in front of a crowd which was at least three times above their average.

Managers (and Secretary-managers)
James Cowan 1906–13, James Howie 1913–20, Ted Liddell 1920–24, Will Wood 1924–25 (had been secretary since 1903), Bob Hewison 1925–30, John Bowman 1930–31, Archie Mitchell 1931–33, Mick O'Brien 1933–35, Billy Birrell 1935–39, Ted Vizard 1939–44, Dave Mangnall 1944–52, Jack Taylor 1952–59, Alec Stock 1959–65 (GM to 1968), Jimmy Andrews 1965, Bill Dodgin Jnr 1968, Tommy Docherty 1968, Les Allen 1969–70, Gordon Jago 1971–74, Dave Sexton 1974–77, Frank Sibley 1977–78, Steve Burtenshaw 1978–79, Tommy Docherty 1979–80, Terry Venables 1980–84, Gordon Jago 1984, Alan Mullery 1984, Frank Sibley 1984–85, Jim Smith 1985–88, Trevor Francis 1988–90, Don Howe 1990–91, Gerry Francis June 1991– .

Player and Position	Ht	Wt	Birth Date	Place	Source	Clubs	League App	Gls
Forwards								
Bradley Allen	5 7	10 00	13 9 71	Harold Wood	Schoolboys	QPR	11	2
Maurice Doyle	5 8	10 07	17 10 69	Ellesmere Port	Trainee	Crewe Alex	8	2
						QPR	—	—
						Crewe Alex (loan)	7	2
						Wolverhampton W (loan)	—	—
Mark Falco	6 0	12 00	22 10 60	Hackney	Apprentice	Tottenham H	174	67
						Chelsea (loan)	3	—
						Watford	33	14
						Rangers	14	5
						QPR	87	27
Les Ferdinand	5 11	13 05	18 12 66	London	Hayes	QPR	30	10
						Brentford (loan)	3	—
						Besiktas (loan)	.	
Andrew Impey	5 8	10 06	13 9 71	Hammersmith	Yeading	QPR	—	—
Dominic Iorfa	6 1	12 12	1 10 68	Lagos	Antwerp	QPR	7	—
Roy Wegerle	5 8	10 02	19 3 64	South Africa	Tampa Bay R	Chelsea	23	3
						Swindon T (loan)	7	1
						Luton T	45	10
						QPR	54	24

Trainees
Bircham, Stephen; Bixby, Michael E; Bromage, Raymond P; Brown, Stewart M; Duong, Vinh-Tam; Finlay, Darren J; Freedman, Douglas A; Gallen, Stephen J; McArdle, Martin P.G; Magill, Robert D; Parker, Thomas G.P; Peacock, John S; Wilkinson, Gary R.

Associated Schoolboys
Brazier, Matthew R; Challis, Trevor M; Cook, Anthony M; Cooper, Paul; Cross, John R; Flitter, Matthew; Gallen, Kevin A; Goodwin, Lee; Hurst, Richard A; Mahoney-Johnson, Michael A; Mark, Robert J; Marsden, David J; Monteath, Jonathan; Plummer, Christopher S; Siddons, James J; Spencer, Darren A; Waring, Ian A; White, Dene; Wilson, Ross E.

Associated Schoolboys who have accepted the club's offer of a Traineeship/Contract
Bryan, Marvin L; Davey, Joe L; Dichio, Daniele; Dickinson, Steven D; Graham, Mark R; Jackson, Stephen; Millard, Martyn L.

424

READING 1990–91 *Back row (left to right)*: John Haselden (Coach/Physio), Floyd Streete, Michael Conroy, Trevor Senior, Steve Francis, Phil Burns, Martin Hicks (Captain), Adrian Williams, Scott Taylor, Eddie Niedzwiecki.
Centre row: Linden Jones, Steve Moran, Craig Maskell, Michael Gilkes, Ian Porterfield, George Friel, Keith Knight, Michael Gooding, Steve Richardson.
Front row: David Leworthy, Keith McPherson.

Division 3 **READING**

Elm Park, Norfolk Road, Reading. Telephone Reading (0734) 507878.

Ground capacity: 13,200.

Record attendance: 33,042 v Brentford, FA Cup 5th rd, 19 February 1927.

Record receipts: £70,693.79 v Arsenal, FA Cup 3rd rd, 10 January 1987.

Pitch measurements: 112yd × 77yd.

Life President: J. H. Brooks.

Chairman: John Madejski. *Managing Director:* M. J. Lewis.

Directors: G. Denton.

Manager: Mark McGhee.

Coach: Stewart Henderson.

Physio: John Haselden.

Marketing Manager: Joanne Venner.

Secretary: Jayne E. Hill.

Year Formed: 1871. *Turned Professional:* 1895. *Ltd Co.:* 1895.

Club Nickname: 'The Royals'.

Previous Grounds: 1871, Reading Recreation; Reading Cricket Ground; 1882, Coley Park; 1889, Caversham Cricket Ground; 1896, Elm Park.

Record League Victory: 10-2 v Crystal Palace, Division 3 (S), 4 September 1946 – Groves; Glidden, Gulliver; McKenna, Ratcliffe, Young; Chitty, Maurice Edelston (3), McPhee (4), Barney (1), Deverell (2).

Record Cup Victory: 6-0 v Leyton, FA Cup, 2nd rd, 12 December 1925 – Duckworth; Eggo, McConnell; Wilson, Messer, Evans; Smith (2), Braithwaite (1), Davey (1), Tinsley, Robson (2).

Record Defeat: 0-18 v Preston NE, FA Cup 1st rd, 1893–94.

Most League Points (2 for a win): 65, Division 4, 1978–79.

Most League Points (3 for a win): 94, Division 3, 1985–86.

Most League Goals: 112, Division 3 (S), 1951–52.

Highest League Scorer in Season: Ronnie Blackman, 39, Division 3 (S), 1951–52.

Most League Goals in Total Aggregate: Ronnie Blackman, 156, 1947–54.

Most Capped Player: Billy McConnell, 8, Northern Ireland.

Most League Appearances: Martin Hicks, 500, 1978–91.

Record Transfer Fee Received: £325,000 from Watford for Trevor Senior, July 1987.

Record Transfer Fee Paid: £250,000 to Leicester C for Steve Moran, November 1987 and £250,000 to Huddersfield T for Craig Maskell, August 1990.

Football League Record: 1920 Original Member of Division 3; 1921–26 Division 3 (S); 1926–31 Division 2; 1931–58 Division 3 (S); 1958–71 Division 3; 1971–76 Division 4; 1976–77 Division 3; 1977–79 Division 4; 1979–83 Division 3; 1983–84 Division 4; 1984–86 Division 3; 1986–88 Division 2; 1988– Division 3.

Honours: Football League: Division 2 best season: 13th, 1986–87; Division 3 – Champions 1985–86. Division 3 (S) – Champions 1925–26; Runners-up 1931–32, 1934–35, 1948–49, 1951–52; Division 4 – Champions 1978–79. *FA Cup:* Semi-final 1927. *Football League Cup:* best season: 4th rd, 1965, 1966, 1978. *Simod Cup:* Winners 1987–88.

Colours: Navy and white diagonal striped shirts, navy blue shorts, navy blue stockings.
Change colours: All gold.

READING 1990–91 LEAGUE RECORD

Match No.	Date	Venue	Opponents	Result		H/T Score	Lg. Pos.	Goalscorers	Atten- dance
1	Aug 25	A	Exeter C	W	3-1	1-1	—	Moran, Senior, Maskell	5694
2	Sept 1	H	Preston NE	D	3-3	2-1	5	Moran 2, Friel	4228
3	8	A	Bradford C	L	1-2	0-1	10	Maskell	7034
4	15	H	Cambridge U	D	2-2	0-0	12	Senior, Maskell	4276
5	18	H	Crewe Alex	W	2-1	2-0	—	Moran 2	3663
6	22	A	Huddersfield T	W	2-0	0-0	8	Senior 2	4689
7	29	A	Rotherham U	W	2-0	0-0	5	Senior, Maskell	4058
8	Oct 2	H	Bournemouth	W	2-1	0-1	—	Senior, Maskell	5300
9	6	H	Birmingham C	D	2-2	2-1	3	McPherson, Senior	5695
10	13	A	Wigan Ath	L	0-1	0-0	4		2576
11	20	A	Bury	L	1-2	1-2	7	McPherson	2807
12	23	H	Brentford	L	1-2	0-1	—	Senior	6562
13	27	H	Leyton Orient	L	1-2	1-0	11	Senior	4513
14	Nov 3	A	Stoke C	W	1-0	1-0	9	Moran	12,245
15	10	A	Bolton W	L	1-3	1-0	14	Gooding	4648
16	24	H	Southend U	L	2-4	0-1	15	Moran, Senior	3927
17	Dec 1	H	Fulham	W	1-0	1-0	11	Lovell	4073
18	14	A	Tranmere R	D	0-0	0-0	—		4691
19	22	A	Swansea C	L	1-3	0-2	14	Lovell	3778
20	26	H	Grimsby T	W	2-0	1-0	11	Gooding 2	3045
21	29	H	Mansfield T	W	2-1	0-0	9	Senior, Jones	4100
22	Jan 12	A	Preston NE	W	2-1	1-0	11	Maskell (pen), Gilkes	4470
23	19	H	Exeter C	W	1-0	0-0	8	Maskell	5123
24	26	H	Wigan Ath	W	3-1	1-0	7	Maskell, Senior 2	3416
25	Feb 1	A	Crewe Alex	L	0-1	0-1	—		3358
26	19	A	Southend U	W	2-1	0-1	—	Moran, Bailey	4588
27	23	H	Bolton W	L	0-1	0-1	11		5997
28	Mar 2	A	Fulham	D	1-1	1-1	11	Gooding	4475
29	5	A	Chester C	L	0-1	0-0	—		631
30	9	H	Tranmere R	W	1-0	0-0	11	Gooding	4440
31	12	A	Bournemouth	L	0-2	0-0	—		5921
32	16	H	Rotherham U	W	2-0	1-0	11	Gooding, McPherson	3250
33	23	A	Birmingham C	D	1-1	0-1	12	Jones	6795
34	26	H	Huddersfield T	L	1-2	1-2	—	Taylor	4231
35	30	A	Grimsby T	L	0-3	0-3	14		7219
36	Apr 1	H	Swansea C	D	0-0	0-0	15		3597
37	6	A	Mansfield T	L	0-2	0-1	16		2498
38	9	A	Cambridge U	L	0-3	0-1	—		5825
39	13	A	Chester C	D	2-2	1-1	16	Conroy, Gooding	2707
40	20	H	Bury	W	1-0	1-0	14	Maskell	3081
41	23	H	Shrewsbury T	L	1-2	1-2	—	Bailey	2422
42	27	A	Brentford	L	0-1	0-0	15		6398
43	30	H	Bradford C	L	1-2	0-1	—	Maskell	1934
44	May 4	A	Leyton Orient	L	0-4	0-1	16		2648
45	7	A	Shrewsbury T	L	1-5	1-4	—	Senior	2425
46	11	H	Stoke C	W	1-0	1-0	15	Senior	4101

Final League Position: 15

GOALSCORERS

League (53): Senior 15, Maskell 10 (1 pen), Moran 8, Gooding 7, McPherson 3, Bailey 2, Jones 2, Lovell 2, Conroy 1, Friel 1, Gilkes 1, Taylor 1.
Rumbelows Cup (1): Hicks 1.
FA Cup (1): Hicks 1.

Francis	Jones	Richardson	McPherson	Hicks	Conroy	Gooding	Seymour	Senior	Maskell	Moran	Friel	Leworthy	Knight	Taylor	Burns	Gilkes	Streete	Lovell	Williams	Bailey	Smith	Morrow	Brooke	Statham	Edwards	Match No.
1	2	3	4	5	6	7	8*	9†	10	11	12	14														1
1		3	4	5	6	7		9	10	11	8	12	2*													2
1	2	3	4	5	6*	7		9	10	11	12		8													3
1	2	3	4	5	6†	7		9	10	11*	8	12	14													4
1	2	3	4	5		7		9	10	11	8			6												5
	2	3	4	5	12	7		9	10†	11	8			6*	1	14										6
	2	3	4	5	6	7		9	12	11†	8*			10	1	14										7
	2	3	4	5	6	7		9	10					8	1	11										8
	2	3	4		6	7	5	9	10					8	1	11										9
	2	3	4	5	6*	7		9	10		12			8	1	11										10
		3	4	5	6*	7	8†	9	10		12		14		1	11	2									11
	2		4	5	12			9	10*	11	7			8	1	3	6†	14								12
			4	5		7	2†	9	12	10	11*	8	14		1	3	6									13
	2		4	5	10	7		9	12	11*				8	1	3		6								14
	2	8	4	5	10*	7		9†	12	11			14		1	3		6								15
1	2		4		10	7	12	9	14	11				8†		3	5*	6								16
1	2		4	5	9	7			10	11				6		3	8									17
1	2	3	4	5	10	7		9						6		11	8									18
1	2	3	4	5	10*	7		9	12					6		11	8									19
1	2	3	4	5		7		9	10							11		8		6						20
1	2	3	4	5		7		9	10							11		12	6	8*						21
1	2	3	4	5		7		9	10							11		12	6	8*						22
1	2		4	5		7		9	10							11		12	6	8*	3					23
1	2		4	5		7		9	10							11		8	6		3					24
1	2		4	5		7		9	10*		12					11		8	6		3					25
1	2		4	5	14	7		9		11				10†		12		8*	6		3					26
1	2		4	5		7		9		11	12			10*				8	6		3					27
1	2†		4	5	10	7		9		11				14				8*	6		3	12				28
1	2		4	5	8†	7		9*	10	11								12	6		3	14				29
1	2		4	5		7			10	11	12							8	6		3	9*				30
1	2		4	5		7			10	11				9*				8	6		3	12				31
1	2	3	4	5		7		12	10*	11				9				8	6			3				32
1	2	3	4	5		7		9	10	11								8	6							33
1		3	4	5	12	7	2†	9	10	14				11				8*	6							34
1		3	4	5	9	7		12	10†					11*				8	6					2	14	35
1		3	4	5	9*	7		12	10					14				8	6					2	11†	36
1		3	4	5	9	7		12	14	10								8*	6					2	11†	37
1		3	4	5	10	7		9										8	6					2	11	38
1	8	3	4	5	10	7		9†	14									12	6					2*	11	39
1	8	3	4	5	9	7		10†	14									12	6					2	11*	40
1	8		4	5	9	7		10†	14		12						3		6					2	11*	41
1			4	5	10	7		9		11				3				8*	6					2	12	42
1			4	5		7	3	14	9	12	11			10				8	2*	6†						43
			4	5	6	7	3		10	11*12	9				1			8	2							44
			4	5		7	3	9	10	11					1			8	2	6						45
1	2		4	5		7*12	3	9	10	11								8		6						46
34	27	32	46	44	29	44	7	35	31	21	8	4	1	25	12	19	4	22	7	26	3	10	1	8	6	
			4s		2s	5s	7s	5s	5s	6s				7s		2s		8s						3s	2s	

Rumbelows Cup First Round Oxford U (h) 0-1
                                                 (a) 1-2

FA Cup First Round Colchester U (a) 1-2

READING

Player and Position	Ht	Wt	Birth Date	Place	Source	Clubs	League App	Gls
Goalkeepers								
Phil Burns*	6 0	12 00	18 12 66	Stockport	Army	Reading	12	—
Steve Francis	5 11	11 05	29 5 64	Billericay	Apprentice	Chelsea	71	—
						Reading	150	—
Defenders								
Martin Hicks	6 3	13 06	27 2 57	Stratford on Avon	Stratford T	Charlton Ath	—	—
						Reading	500	23
Linden Jones	5 6	10 08	5 3 61	Tredegar	Apprentice	Cardiff C	145	2
						Newport Co	142	5
						Reading	123	8
Keith McPherson	5 11	10 11	11 9 63	Greenwich	Apprentice	West Ham U	1	—
						Cambridge U (loan)	11	1
						Northampton T	182	8
						Reading	46	3
Steve Richardson	5 5	10 03	11 2 62	Slough	Apprentice	Southampton	—	—
						Reading	327	2
Chris Seymour	5 10	11 00	14 9 71	Reading	Trainee	Reading	9	—
Floyd Streete	5 11	14 00	5 5 59	Jamaica	Rivet S	Cambridge U	125	19
					Utrecht	Derby Co	35	—
						Wolverhampton W	159	6
						Reading	4	—
Adrian Williams	5 10	11 00	16 8 71	Reading	Trainee	Reading	31	2
Midfield								
Danny Bailey	5 7	12 07	21 5 64	London	Apprentice	Bournemouth	2	—
						Torquay U	1	—
					Wealdstone	Exeter C	64	2
						Reading	26	2
Mick Gooding	5 7	10 08	12 4 59	Newcastle	B Auckland	Rotherham U	102	10
						Chesterfield	12	—
						Rotherham U	156	33
						Peterborough U	47	21
						Wolverhampton W	44	4
						Reading	71	10
Dan Henderson‡			2 5 72	Brighton	Trainee	Reading	—	—
Stuart Lovell	5 10	10 06	9 1 72	Sydney	Trainee	Reading	30	2
Scott Taylor	5 9	11 00	28 11 70	Portsmouth	Trainee	Reading	64	3
Forwards								
Garry Brooke‡	5 7	11 00	24 11 60	Bethnal Green	Apprentice	Tottenham H	73	15
					Groningen	Norwich C	14	2
						Wimbledon	12	—
						Stoke C (loan)	8	—
						Brentford	11	1
						Reading	4	—
Mike Conroy	6 0	11 00	31 12 65	Glasgow	Apprentice	Coventry C	—	—
						Clydebank	114	38
						St Mirren	10	1
						Reading	80	7
George Friel*	5 8	10 11	11 10 70	Reading	Trainee	Reading	16	1
Michael Gilkes	5 8	10 02	20 7 65	Hackney		Reading	180	20
Keith Knight‡	5 8	11 00	16 2 69	Cheltenham	Cheltenham T	Reading	43	8
David Leworthy	5 9	12 00	22 10 62	Portsmouth	Apprentice	Portsmouth	1	—
					Fareham T	Tottenham H	11	3
						Oxford U	37	8
						Shrewsbury T (loan)	6	3
						Reading	38	7

READING

Foundation: Reading was formed as far back as 1871 at a public meeting held at the Bridge Street Rooms. They first entered the FA Cup as early as 1877 when they amalgamated with the Reading Hornets. The club was further strengthened in 1889 when Earley FC joined them. They were the first winners of the Berks and Bucks Cup in 1878–79.

First Football League game: 28 August, 1920, Division 3, v Newport C (a) W 1-0 – Crawford; Smith, Horler; Christie, Mavin, Getgood; Spence, Weston, Yarnell, Bailey (1), Andrews.

Did you know: Although drawn at home to South Norwood for their first ever FA Cup tie in 1877 Reading chose to play the game on the Dolphin Ground at Slough where they won 2-0.

Managers (and Secretary-managers)
Thomas Sefton 1897–1901*, James Sharp 1901–02, Harry Matthews 1902–20, Harry Marshall 1920–22, Arthur Chadwick 1923–25, H. S. Bray 1925–26 (secretary only since 1922 and 26–35), Andrew Wylie 1926–31, Joe Smith 1931–35, Billy Butler 1935–39, John Cochrane 1939, Joe Edelston 1939–47, Ted Drake 1947–52, Jack Smith 1952–55, Harry Johnston 1955–63, Roy Bentley 1963–69, Jack Mansell 1969–71, Charlie Hurley 1972–77, Maurice Evans 1977–84, Ian Branfoot 1984–89, Ian Porterfield 1989–91, Mark McGhee May 1991– .

Player and Position	Ht	Wt	Birth Date	Birth Place	Source	Clubs	League App	Gls
Craig Maskell	5 10	11 04	10 4 68	Aldershot	Apprentice	Southampton	6	1
						Swindon T (loan)	—	—
						Huddersfield T	87	43
						Reading	38	10
Steve Moran*	5 8	11 00	10 1 61	Croydon	Amateur	Southampton	180	78
						Leicester C	43	14
						Reading	116	30
Lee Payne‡	5 10	11 05	12 12 66	Luton	Barnet	Newcastle U	7	—
						Reading	27	3
Trevor Senior	6 1	12 08	28 11 61	Dorchester	Dorchester T	Portsmouth	11	2
						Aldershot (loan)	10	7
						Reading	164	102
						Watford	24	1
						Middlesbrough	10	2
						Reading	112	45

Trainees
Emery, Barry; Fealey, Nathan J; Gardner, Dudley J; Giamattei, Aaron P; Gray, Andrew; Holzman, Mark R; Honey, Daniel W; Liney, Paul; McCance, Daren; McGuigan, Gareth J; Malins, Martin J; Rodgers, Brendan J.K; Schonberger, David P; Silvey, Paul S.

Associated Schoolboys
Brown, Philip R; Champion, Marc G; Clift, David R; Halabi, Karl A; Holzman, Gary R; Hyde, David K; Jupp, Peter R; Lockey, Richard A; Maskell, Gary P; Montgomery, Noel T; Simpson, Derek F; Stowell, Matthew D; Thorpe, Michael S; Topham, Neil R; Vaughan, Christopher A.

Associated Schoolboys who have accepted the club's offer of a Traineeship/Contract
Barkus, Lee P; Bass, David; Ferguson, Gary; Mukabaa, Anthony G; Timothy, David.

ROCHDALE 1990–91 *Back row (left to right):* Willie Burns, Steve Johnson, David Cole, Keith Welch, Gareth Gray, Tony Brown, Andy Milner, Steve O'Shaughnessy.
Centre row: Bernard Ellison (Youth Development Officer), Wayne Goodison, Mick Holmes, Jeff Lee (Assistant Manager), Terry Dolan (Manager), Peter Ward, Jason Dawson, Dave Sutton (Physiotherapist).
Front row: Jon Hill, Mark Hilditch, Steve Elliott, Peter Costello, Zac Hughes, Vinny Chapman, Chris Lee, Jimmy Graham.

Division 4   **ROCHDALE**

Spotland, Willbutts Lane, Rochdale OL11 5DA. Telephone Rochdale (0706) 44648-9. Fax: 0706 48466

Ground capacity: 10,735.

Record attendance: 24,231 v Notts Co, FA Cup 2nd rd, 10 December 1949.

Record receipts: £30,082 v Burnley, Div. 4, 4 May 1991.

Pitch measurements: 113yd × 75yd.

President: Mrs L. Stoney.

Chairman: D. F. Kilpatrick. *Vice-chairman:* G. Morris.

Directors: T. Butterworth, C. Dunphy, L. Hilton, G. R. Brierley, J. Marsh, P. M. Mace, M.CH, FRCS.

Manager: Dave Sutton.

Secretary: F. Hyde AIB. *Asst. Manager:* Mick Docherty.

Commercial Manager: S. Walmsley. *Advertising & Sponsorship Manager:* L. Duckworth.

Physio: P. Stock. *Coach:* J. Lee.

Year Formed: 1907. *Turned Professional:* 1907. *Ltd Co.:* 1910.

Club Nickname: 'The Dale'.

Record League Victory: 8-1 v Chesterfield, Division 3 (N), 18 December 1926 – Hill; Brown, Ward; Hillhouse, Parkes, Braidwood; Hughes, Bertram, Whitehurst (5), Schofield (2), Martin (1).

Record Cup Victory: 8-2 v Crook T, FA Cup, 1st rd, 26 November 1927 – Moody; Hopkins, Ward; Braidwood, Parkes, Barker; Tompkinson, Clennell (3) Whitehurst (4), Hall, Martin (1).

Record Defeat: 0-8 v Wrexham, Division 3 (N), 28 December 1929, 0-8 v Leyton Orient, Division 4, 20 October 1987, and 1-9 v Tranmere R, Division 3 (N), 25 December 1931.

Most League Points (2 for a win): 65, Division 4, 1978–79.

Most League Points (3 for a win): 66, Division 4, 1989–90.

Most League Goals: 105, Division 3 (N), 1926–27.

Highest League Scorer in Season: Albert Whitehurst, 44, Division 3 (N), 1926–27.

Most League Goals in Total Aggregate: Reg Jenkins, 119, 1964–73.

Most Capped Player: None.

Most League Appearances: Graham Smith, 317, 1966–74.

Record Transfer Fee Received: £50,000 from Huddersfield T for Mark Smith, January 1989, and £50,000 from Stockport Co for David Frain, July 1989.

Record Transfer Fee Paid: £25,000 to Bolton W for Mark Gavin, October 1987.

Football League Record: 1921 Elected to Division 3 (N); 1958–59 Division 3; 1959–69 Division 4; 1969–74 Division 3; 1974– Division 4.

Honours: Football League: Division 3 best season: 9th, 1969–70; Division 3 (N) – Runners-up 1923–24, 1926–27. *FA Cup:* best season: 5th rd, 1989–90. *Football League Cup:* Runners-up 1962 (record for 4th Division club).

Colours: All royal blue. **Change colours:** Yellow, black, yellow.

ROCHDALE 1990–91 LEAGUE RECORD

Match No.	Date		Venue	Opponents	Result	H/T Score	Lg. Pos.	Goalscorers	Attendance
1	Aug	25	H	Aldershot	W 4-0	0-0	—	Hilditch, Holmes, Ward 2	1619
2	Sept	1	A	Blackpool	D 0-0	0-0	3		3357
3		8	H	Stockport Co	W 1-0	1-0	3	Elliott	2825
4		15	H	Doncaster R	L 0-3	0-2	5		2607
5		18	A	Hartlepool U	D 2-2	0-1	—	McPhail (og), Costello	5725
6		22	H	Scarborough	D 1-1	1-1	9	Holmes	1715
7		29	H	Walsall	W 3-2	1-0	7	Elliott, Holmes (pen), Costello	1933
8	Oct	2	A	Cardiff C	W 1-0	0-0	—	Milner	3391
9		6	A	Gillingham	D 2-2	0-0	4	Milner, Holmes (pen)	3316
10		13	H	Chesterfield	W 3-0	1-0	2	Costello 2, Ward	2492
11		20	H	Torquay U	D 0-0	0-0	4		3405
12		24	A	Lincoln C	W 2-1	1-1	—	Holmes (pen), Dawson	1974
13		27	A	Burnley	L 0-1	0-1	3		7971
14	Nov	3	H	Darlington	D 1-1	1-1	5	O'Shaughnessy	2881
15		10	A	Scunthorpe U	L 1-2	1-1	7	Elliott	3070
16		24	H	Carlisle U	L 0-1	0-0	8		1733
17	Dec	1	A	Northampton T	L 2-3	2-1	9	Milner, Lee	3809
18		15	H	Wrexham	W 2-0	0-0	9	Costello, Graham	1510
19		21	A	Halifax T	L 0-2	0-1	—		1831
20		29	H	Maidstone U	W 3-2	1-1	8	Burns (pen), Milner, Lee	1778
21	Jan	2	A	Peterborough U	D 1-1	0-1	—	Cole	3687
22		12	A	Blackpool	W 2-1	0-1	7	Costello, Dawson	2621
23		19	A	Aldershot	D 2-2	1-2	8	Dawson 2	1854
24		25	A	Doncaster R	L 0-1	0-1	—		3436
25		30	A	Hereford U	L 0-2	0-0	—		2014
26	Feb	6	A	Scarborough	D 0-0	0-0	—		955
27		16	A	Carlisle U	D 1-1	0-0	12	McInerney	2505
28		23	H	Scunthorpe U	W 2-1	0-1	11	Costello 2	1832
29	Mar	2	H	Northampton T	D 1-1	0-0	13	Costello	1890
30		9	A	Wrexham	L 1-2	1-1	14	Dawson	1323
31		12	H	Cardiff C	D 0-0	0-0	—		1569
32		16	A	Walsall	W 1-0	0-0	13	Costello	2890
33		19	A	Chesterfield	D 1-1	0-0	—	O'Shaughnessy	3048
34		23	H	Gillingham	L 1-3	1-0	14	Ward	1654
35		26	A	Stockport	L 0-3	0-2	—		3697
36		30	A	York C	W 2-0	1-0	15	Morgan 2	2120
37	Apr	1	H	Halifax T	D 1-1	0-1	15	Hilditch	2040
38		6	A	Maidstone U	W 1-0	0-0	12	Milner	1340
39		13	H	Peterborough U	L 0-3	0-1	13		2384
40		16	H	York C	W 2-1	1-0	—	Cole, Hill	1331
41		20	A	Torquay U	L 1-3	1-2	13	Morgan	3049
42		23	H	Hartlepool U	D 0-0	0-0	—		1686
43		27	H	Lincoln C	D 0-0	0-0	12		1481
44		30	H	Hereford U	W 2-1	0-1	—	Chapman, Ward	1166
45	May	4	H	Burnley	D 0-0	0-0	12		7344
46		11	A	Darlington	L 0-2	0-1	12		9160

Final League Position: 12

GOALSCORERS

League (50): Costello 10, Dawson 5, Holmes 5 (3 pens), Milner 5, Ward 5, Elliott 3, Morgan 3, Cole 2, Hilditch 2, Lee 2, O'Shaughnessy 2, Burns 1 (pen), Chapman 1, Graham 1, Hill 1, McInerney 1, own goal 1.
Rumbelows Cup (7): Milner 2, Costello 1, Elliott 1, Goodison 1 (pen), Lee 1, O'Shaughnessy 1.
FA Cup (2): Costello 2.

Welch	Burns	Graham	Brown	O'Shaughnessy	Ward	Milner	Lee	Hilditch	Costello	Holmes	Elliott	Goodison	Cole	Butler	Dawson	Blundell	Hill	Norton	Doyle	Chapman	Lockett	McInerney	Rose	Colleton	Anders	Duggan	Morgan	Herring	Match No.
1	2	3	4	5	6	7	8	9	10*	11	12																		1
1	2	3		5*	6†	7	8	9	10	11	12	4	14																2
1	4*	3				7	8	9	10	11	6†	2	5	12	14														3
1		3†		5	6	7	8	9*	10	12	11	2	14				4												4
1		3	4		6	10	8			7	11	9	2*	5	12														5
1	4	3			6	10	8			7	11	9	2*	5	12														6
1	2*	3		5	6	7	8		10	11		9			12†	14	4												7
1		3		5	6	7	8		10*	11		9	2		12		4												8
1		3		5	6	7*	8		10	11		9	2		12		4												9
1		3		5†		7*	8		10	11		9	2		12		4	14											10
1		3			6	7*	8	12	10	11		9	5				4		2										11
1		3			6		8	7*	10	11		9	5		12		4		2										12
1		3			6		8	7*	10	11		9	5		12		4		2										13
1		3	4		6	7	8		10	11		9*	14	5	12		2†												14
1	14	3	7†	4	6		8		10*	11		9		5	12		2												15
1		3	4		6	7	8*		10			9		5	12		2		11										16
1	5	3	14		6	7*	8		9	10†			12		4		2	11											17
1	5	3		4	9	7	8		10				6				2	11											18
1	5	3		4†	9	7	8		10*	12			6	14			2	11											19
1	2				6	7	8					9	4	5	10			11	3										20
1	2†		14		6	7	8	12				9	4	5	10*			11	3										21
1		3	4		6	7*	8	12				9	2	5	10			11											22
1		3*	4		6		8	7				9	2	5	10			11	12										23
1			4		6	9	8	7			12		2	5	10*	14		11	3†										24
1			4*	6	11		12		10			9	2	5					8	3	7								25
1			6	4	10			12				9	2	5	7*				8	3	11								26
				4†	6	11	12		10*				2	5	9	14			8	3		7	1						27
	4				6	11			10				2	5	9				8	3	7*	1	12						28
	4				6	11	12		10				2	5	9†	14			8	3	7*	1							29
1	4	12			6	11	7*		10†				2	5	9				8	3					14				30
1	4		14		6	11	7*		10				2	5	9†				8	3	12								31
1	4		6	5	11	12†	10*	7				9	2	14					8	3									32
1	4		6	5	11	12		7*				9	2	14	10†				8	3									33
1	4*	12	6	5	11	10†	14	7					2	9					8	3									34
1	7*	4	6		11	12	10†	9					2	5	14				8	3									35
1		3	6	5	11	10		9†					2	12	14		8									4*	7		36
1	12	3	6	5	11	10		9					2	4			8										7*		37
1	5	3	4	7	11	12	10†						2	6	14		8										9*		38
1	5*	3	4	7									2	6	10	11	8						14				9†12		39
1	5	3	4	10†	11	7							2	6	12	14	8										9*		40
1	5	3†	4	10*	11	7							2	6	12	14	8										9		41
1	5	4		6		7		9					2	12		11*	8	3									10		42
1	5	4	14	6		7		9*					2	12	11†		8	3									10		43
1	5	4		6	11	7		9*					2	12			8	3									10		44
1	5	4		6	11	7		9†					2	12	14		8	3									10*		45
1	5	4		6	11	7		10†					2	12	14		8	3									9*		46
43	26	26	24	36	44	30	24	12	31	14	27	33	32	—	12	10	3	9	31	19	1	4	3	—	—	1	11	—	
+	+	+	+		+	+	+	+	+	+		+	+	+	+				+	+		+	+				+		
2s	2s	2s	2s		5s	2s	2s	3s	2s	3s	1s	9s	2s	16s	4s	8s			1s	1s		1s	2s				1s		

Rumbelows Cup First Round   Scarborough (h)   4-0
                               (a)   3-3
             Second Round   Southampton (h)   0-5
                               (a)   0-3
FA Cup   First Round   Scunthorpe U (h)   1-1
                               (a)   1-2

ROCHDALE

Player and Position	Ht	Wt	Birth Date	Place	Source	Clubs	League App	Gls
Goalkeepers								
Gareth Gray	6 0	11 02	24 2 70	Longridge	Darwen	Bolton W	—	—
						Rochdale	—	—
Keith Welch	6 0	12 00	3 10 68	Bolton	Trainee	Bolton W	—	—
						Rochdale	205	—
Defenders								
Chris Blundell*	5 10	10 09	7 12 69	Billlinge	Trainee	Oldham Ath	3	—
						Rochdale	14	—
Tony Brown	6 2	12 07	17 9 58	Bradford	Thackley	Leeds U	24	1
						Doncaster (loan)	14	—
						Doncaster R	73	2
						Scunthorpe U	54	2
						Rochdale	69	—
Willie Burns*	5 11	10 10	10 12 69	Motherwell	Trainee	Manchester C	—	—
						Rochdale	72	2
Vincent Chapman	5 9	11 00	5 12 67	Newcastle	Tow Law T	Huddersfield T	6	—
						York C (loan)	—	—
						Rochdale	24	1
David Cole*	6 0	11 10	28 9 62	Barnsley		Sunderland	—	—
						Swansea C	8	—
						Swindon T	69	3
						Torquay U	110	6
						Rochdale	84	7
Andrew Duggan*	6 3	13 00	19 9 67	Bradford	Apprentice	Barnsley	2	1
						Rochdale (loan)	3	—
						Huddersfield T	29	3
						Hartlepool U (loan)	2	—
						Rochdale	1	—
Wayne Goodison*	5 8	11 07	23 9 64	Wakefield	Apprentice	Barnsley	36	—
						Crewe Alex	94	1
						Rochdale	79	4
Jonathan Hill*	5 10	11 10	20 8 70	Wigan	Trainee	Rochdale	36	1
Zac Hughes	5 11	11 12	6 6 71	Bentley, Australia	Trainee	Rochdale	2	—
Steve O'Shaughnessy	6 2	13 00	13 10 67		Wrexham	Leeds U	—	—
						Bradford C	1	—
						Rochdale	109	16
Midfield								
Steve Doyle	5 9	11 09	2 6 58	Port Talbot	Apprentice	Preston NE	197	8
						Huddersfield T	161	6
						Sunderland	100	2
						Hull C	47	2
						Rochdale	31	—
Jimmy Graham	5 11	11 00	15 11 68	Glasgow	Trainee	Bradford C	7	—
						Rochdale (loan)	11	—
						Rochdale	28	1
Paul Herring§	5 11	11 03	1 7 73	Hyde	Trainee	Rochdale	1	—
Phil Lockett§	5 9	11 02	6 9 72	Stockton	Trainee	Rochdale	3	—
Steve Morgan	5 9	11 05	28 12 70	Wrexham	Trainee	Oldham Ath	2	—
						Wrexham (loan)	7	1
						Rochdale	11	3
Forwards								
Jason Anders§	5 10	10 06	13 3 74	Rochdale	Trainee	Rochdale	2	—
Antony Colleton§	5 8	10 06	17 1 74	Manchester	Trainee	Rochdale	1	—
Jason Dawson*	5 7	11 05	9 2 71	Burslem	Port Vale	Rochdale	55	7
Steve Elliott*	6 0	11 10	15 9 58	Haltwistle	Apprentice	Nottingham F	4	—
						Preston NE	208	70
						Luton T	12	3
						Walsall	69	21
						Bolton W	60	11
						Bury	31	11
						Rochdale	52	9

ROCHDALE

Foundation: Considering the love of rugby in their area, it is not surprising that Rochdale had difficulty in establishing an Association Football club. The earlier Rochdale Town club formed in 1900 went out of existence in 1907 when the present club was immediately established and joined the Manchester League, before graduating to the Lancashire Combination in 1908.

First Football League game: 27 August, 1921, Division 3(N), v Accrington Stanley (h) W 6-3 – Crabtree; Nuttall, Sheehan; Hill, Farrer, Yarwood; Hoad, Sandiford, Dennison (2), Owens (3), Carney (1).

Did you know: In 1919–20 Rochdale drew Arsenal at home in the FA Cup but accepted a £1,000 guarantee to play at Highbury where a crowd numbering 26,596 saw them beaten 4-2.

Managers (and Secretary-managers)
Billy Bradshaw 1920, (run by committee 1920–22), Tom Wilson 1922–23, Jack Peart 1923–30, Will Cameron 1930–31, Herbert Hopkinson 1932–34, Billy Smith 1934–35, Ernest Nixon 1935–37, Sam Jennings 1937–38, Ted Goodier 1938–52, Jack Warner 1952–53, Harry Catterick 1953–58, Jack Marshall 1958–60, Tony Collins 1960–68, Bob Stokoe 1967–68, Len Richley 1968–70, Dick Conner 1970–73, Walter Joyce 1973–76, Brian Green 1976–77, Mike Ferguson 1977–78, Doug Collins 1979, Bob Stokoe 1979–80, Peter Madden 1980–83, Jimmy Greenhoff 1983–84, Vic Halom 1984–86, Eddie Gray 1986–88, Danny Bergara 1988–89, Terry Dolan 1989–91, Dave Sutton February 1991– .

Player and Position	Ht	Wt	Birth Date	Place	Source	Clubs	League App	Gls
Mark Hilditch	6 0	12 01	20 8 60	Royton	Amateur	Rochdale	197	40
						Tranmere R	49	12
						Wigan Ath	103	26
						Rochdale	14	2
Steve Johnson‡	6 0	12 09	23 6 57	Liverpool	Altrincham	Bury	154	52
						Rochdale	19	7
						Wigan Ath	51	18
						Bristol C	21	3
						Rochdale (loan)	6	1
						Chester C (loan)	10	6
						Scunthorpe U	72	20
						Chester C	38	10
					Huskvarna	Rochdale	24	4
Andy Milner	5 11	11 07	10 2 67	Kendal	Netherfield	Manchester C	—	—
						Rochdale	51	9
Kevin Stonehouse‡	5 11	11 01	20 9 59	Bishop Auckland	Shildon	Blackburn R	85	27
						Huddersfield T	22	4
						Blackpool	55	19
						Darlington	72	20
						Carlisle U (loan)	3	—
						Rochdale	14	2
Peter Ward	6 0	11 10	15 10 64	Co Durham	Chester-le-Street	Huddersfield T	37	2
						Rochdale	84	10

Trainees
Anders, Jason S; Barrow, Spencer J; Butler, Paul J; Colleton, Anthony; Gregory, Andrew E; Griffin, Steven W; Grimbaldeston, David A; Herring, Paul J; Lockett, Philip B; Milligan, Stephen J.F; Newsham, Paul J; Smith, Andrew J; Tate, Keith N; Thackra, James.

Associated Schoolboys
Armstrong, Michael; Beaumont, Marcus S; Bentham, Daniel; Davidson, Kevin, Dockray, Martin; Ellis, Christopher; Fothergill, Alan; Frankland, David J; Hoyle, Dominic W; Judd, Christopher; Knaggs, Martin T; Legg, Stuart A; Lenigan, Neil R; McCormick, Matthew P; Owen, Gavin S.B; Pickering, Craig; Taylor, Wayne A; Weston, Daniel B; Winpenny, Richard; Yale, Lee D.

Associated Schoolboys who have accepted the club's offer of a Traineeship/Contract
Beever, Antony M; Clayton, Michael.

ROTHERHAM UNITED 1990-91 *Back row (left to right):* Ronnie Robinson, Andy Barnsley, Paul Haycock, Nigel Johnson, Kevin O'Hanlon, Billy Mercer, Stewart Evans, Nicky Law, Neil Richardson, Steve Spooner.
Centre row: John Breckin (Youth Team Coach), Billy Russell, Bobby Williamson, Mark Dempsey, Phil Henson (Assistant Manager), John Buckley, Andy Pickering, Clive Mendonca, Ian Bailey (Physiotherapist).
Front row: Simon Thompson, Shaun Goater, Gerry Forrest, Billy McEwan (Manager), Martin Scott, Des Hazel, Shaun Goodwin.

Division 4 **ROTHERHAM UNITED**

Millmoor Ground, Rotherham. Telephone Rotherham (0709) 562434.

Ground Capacity: 13,791.

Record attendance: 25,000 v Sheffield U, Division 2, 13 December 1952 and v Sheffield W, Division 2, 26 January 1952.

Record receipts: £44,091 v Manchester U, Littlewoods Cup, 2nd rd 1st leg, 28 September 1989.

Pitch measurements. 115yd × 75yd.

President: Sir J. Layden.

Chairman: K. F. Booth.

Directors: R. Hull (Vice-chairman), C. A. Luckock, J. A. Webb.

Manager: Phil Henson. *Asst. Manager:* John Breckin. *Physio:* Ian Bailey.

Secretary: N. Darnill.

Commercial Manager: D. Nicholls.

Year Formed: 1884. *Turned Professional:* 1905. *Ltd Co.:* 1920.

Club Nickname: 'The Merry Millers'.

Previous Names: 1884, Thornhill United; 1905, Rotherham County; 1925, amalgamated with Rotherham Town under Rotherham United.

Previous Ground: Red House Ground; 1907, Millmoor.

Record League Victory: 8-0 v Oldham Ath, Division 3 (N), 26 May 1947 – Warnes; Selkirk, Ibbotson; Edwards, Horace Williams, Danny Williams; Wilson (2), Shaw (1), Ardron (3), Guest (1), Hainsworth (1).

Record Cup Victory: 6-0 v Spennymoor U, FA Cup, 2nd rd, 17 December 1977 – McAlister; Forrest, Breckin, Womble, Stancliffe, Green, Finney, Phillips (3), Gwyther (2) (Smith), Goodfellow, Crawford (1). 6-0 v Wolverhampton W, FA Cup, 1st rd, 16 November 1985 – O'Hanlon; Forrest, Dungworth, Gooding (1), Smith (1), Pickering, Birch (2), Emerson, Tynan (1), Simmons (1), Pugh.

Record Defeat: 1-11 v Bradford C, Division 3 (N), 25 August 1928.

Most League Points (2 for a win): 71, Division 3 (N), 1950–51.

Most League Points (3 for a win): 82, Division 4, 1988–89.

Most League Goals: 114, Division 3 (N), 1946–47.

Highest League Scorer in Season: Wally Ardron, 38, Division 3 (N), 1946–47.

Most League Goals in Total Aggregate: Gladstone Guest, 130, 1946–56.

Most Capped Player: Harold Millership, 6, Wales.

Most League Appearances: Danny Williams, 459, 1946–62.

Record Transfer Fee Received: £200,000 from Bristol C for Martin Scott, December 1990.

Record Transfer Fee Paid: £100,000 to Cardiff C for Ronnie Moore, August 1980.

Football League Record: 1893 Rotherham Town elected to Division 2; 1896 Failed re-election; 1919 Rotherham County elected to Division 2; 1923–51 Division 3 (N); 1951–68 Division 2; 1968–73 Division 3; 1973–75 Division 4; 1975–81 Division 3; 1981–83 Division 2; 1983–88 Division 3; 1988–89 Division 4; 1989–91 Division 3; 1991– Division 4.

Honours: Football League: Division 2 best season: 3rd, 1954–55 (equal points with champions and runners-up); Division 3 – Champions 1980–81; Division 3 (N) – Champions 1950–51; Runners-up 1946–47, 1947–48, 1948–49; Division 4 – Champions 1988–89. *FA Cup:* best season: 5th rd, 1953, 1968. *Football League Cup:* Runners-up 1961.

Colours: Red shirts, white shorts, red stockings. **Change colours:** White shirts with black collar, black shorts with red and white trim, black stockings with red and white tops.

ROTHERHAM UNITED 1990–91 LEAGUE RECORD

Match No.	Date		Venue	Opponents	Result		H/T Score	Lg. Pos.	Goalscorers	Atten-dance
1	Aug	25	A	Stoke C	L	1-3	0-2	—	Williamson	13,048
2	Sept	1	H	Shrewsbury T	D	2-2	1-0	20	Hazel, Law	4817
3		8	A	Bury	L	1-3	0-2	23	Mendonca	2988
4		15	H	Wigan Ath	W	5-1	1-1	15	Evans 2, Williamson, Mendonca, Griffiths (og)	4100
5		18	H	Brentford	D	2-2	1-0	—	Dempsey, Mendonca	4298
6		22	A	Leyton Orient	L	0-3	0-0	19		3493
7		29	H	Reading	L	0-2	0-0	21		4058
8	Oct	2	A	Grimsby T	L	1-2	0-2	—	Dempsey (pen)	6923
9		6	A	Fulham	L	0-2	0-2	24		3498
10		13	H	Huddersfield T	L	1-3	1-1	24	Buckley	6120
11		20	H	Preston NE	W	1-0	0-0	23	Mendonca	4599
12		23	A	Bolton W	D	0-0	0-0	—		4692
13		27	A	Cambridge U	L	1-4	0-3	24	Williamson (pen)	4142
14	Nov	3	H	Bradford C	L	0-2	0-0	24		6057
15		10	A	Bournemouth	L	2-4	0-2	24	Goater, Scott	5442
16		24	H	Mansfield T	D	1-1	0-1	24	Evans	3729
17	Dec	1	H	Southend U	L	0-1	0-0	24		3465
18		15	A	Birmingham C	L	1-2	0-1	24	Law	4734
19		22	A	Exeter C	L	0-2	0-0	24		3752
20		26	H	Chester C	W	2-1	0-0	24	Evans, Spooner	3547
21		29	H	Tranmere R	D	1-1	1-0	24	Mendonca (pen)	4316
22	Jan	1	A	Swansea C	L	0-5	0-4	24		5938
23		12	A	Shrewsbury T	D	0-0	0-0	24		2800
24		19	H	Stoke C	D	0-0	0-0	24		6236
25	Feb	2	A	Brentford	W	2-1	0-1	24	Dempsey, Cullen	5540
26		5	H	Leyton Orient	D	0-0	0-0	—		4056
27		23	H	Bournemouth	D	1-1	1-0	24	Johnson	4107
28	Mar	1	A	Southend U	L	1-2	0-2	—	Hazel	5622
29		5	H	Bury	L	0-3	0-0	—		3658
30		9	H	Birmingham C	D	1-1	1-0	24	Mendonca	5015
31		12	H	Grimsby T	L	1-4	0-2	—	Mendonca	5542
32		16	A	Reading	L	0-2	0-1	24		3250
33		19	A	Huddersfield T	L	0-4	0-1	—		4576
34		23	H	Fulham	W	3-1	3-0	24	Goodwin, Duffield, Goater	3188
35		26	A	Wigan Ath	L	0-2	0-1	—		1962
36		30	A	Chester C	W	2-1	1-0	24	Pearson, Duffield	1079
37	Apr	1	H	Exeter C	L	2-4	0-0	24	Hathaway, Pearson	3701
38		5	A	Tranmere R	W	2-1	0-1	—	Pearson 2	7398
39		9	H	Crewe Alex	D	1-1	1-1	—	Barrick	4141
40		13	A	Swansea C	L	2-3	2-0	24	Duffield (pen), Richardson	3510
41		20	A	Preston NE	W	2-1	0-0	23	Goodwin, Mendonca	4069
42		23	A	Mansfield T	W	2-1	0-1	—	Pearson, Mendonca	4041
43		27	H	Bolton W	D	2-2	1-0	22	Goodwin, Duffield	8045
44		30	A	Crewe Alex	L	1-3	0-3	—	Barrick	4086
45	May	4	H	Cambridge U	W	3-2	2-2	22	Richardson, Hazel, Mendonca	5402
46		11	A	Bradford C	L	0-1	0-0	23		6354

Final League Position: 23

GOALSCORERS

League (50): Mendonca 10 (1 pen), Pearson 5, Duffield 4 (1 pen), Evans 4, Dempsey 3 (1 pen), Goodwin 3, Hazel 3, Williamson 3 (1 pen), Barrick 2, Goater 2, Law 2, Richardson 2, Buckley 1, Cullen 1, Hathaway 1, Johnson 1, Scott 1, Spooner 1, own goal 1.
Rumbelows Cup (9): Williamson 3 (1 pen), Hazel 2, Dempsey 1, Goodwin 1, own goals 2.
FA Cup (8): Dempsey 2, Goater 2, Mendonca 2, Evans 1, Johnson 1.

Rumbelows Cup	First Round	Doncaster R (a)	6-2
		(h)	2-1
	Second Round	Blackburn R (h)	1-1
		(a)	0-1

O'Hanlon	Forrest	Scott	Goodwin	Law	Robinson	Buckley	Spooner	Williamson	Mendonca	Hazel	Dempsey	Barnsley	Goater	Richardson	Stancliffe	Evans	Jenkinson	Watts	Pickering	Mercer	Russell	Thompson	Howard	Johnson	Cullen	Barrick	Hodges	Duffield	Match No.
1	2	3	4	5	6	7*	8	9	10	11	12																		1
1	2	3	4*	5		12	8	9	10†	11		7		6	14														2
1	2	3	5*	8				9	10	11		7	4	12	6														3
1		3			6		4	9*12		7	8		2		5	10	11												4
1	2	3			6		4	9		7	8				5	10	11												5
1	2	3			6		4	9		7	8				5	10	11												6
1	2	12	14		6		4*			7	8	3	9		5†	10	11												7
1	2	7	5	3	4			9*	14	8	6	12				10	11†												8
1	2	7	5†	3	4			9*	11	8	6	12				10	14												9
1	2*		8		3	7	10			11†			9		5	12	14	4	6										10
	2	3	7		6				9	10	11	8			12			5		1	4*14								11
	2	3	7		6				9	10*11		8						5		1	4	12							12
	2	3	7		6				9	10	11	8						5		1	4*12								13
	2	3	7		6				9	10*11		8				12		5		1	4†14								14
	2	3	7		6		12			14	8*		10		9†			5		1	4	11							15
	2	3	7	5						10*11		8	9				6			1	4	12							16
	2	7	8	5	3		12			11			10†		9			6		1	4*	14							17
	2		7	3			8		9	11		6*10								1	4	12		5					18
		6	7	3			4		9	11*		2	12					10		1†14		8		5					19
1	2		7	6	3		4		9	11								10				8		5					20
1			7	6			4		9	11		2						10				3		8		5			21
1	12		7	6			4		9	14	11	2*		10†								3		8		5			22
1	2		7	6					9	11	8		4									3	10		5				23
1	2		7*	5	6		12		10	11	8			9								3	4						24
1	2		7	14						11	8*	3	9	4		12								5†10					25
1	2			5	6					11	8	3	9	4		12					7*			10					26
1	2				6				10	11	4		9*			12					3			5	7	8			27
1	2				6				10	11	7		9*	4		12					3			5		8			28
1					6				10	11	7		12	4*	9						3			5		8	2		29
1	2				6				9	11	7			4							3			5		8		10	30
1	2*				6				9	11	7			4							3			5		8	12	10	31
1		7	6	3		12			9	11			14	4							2			5		8*	10†		32
1		7	6	3	4			9				2	11											5		8		10	33
		4	6	3						7		2	9						1		12			5		8		10	34
12		4	6	3								2	9						1		7*			5		8		10	35
7		4	6	3						11		2							1							8		10	36
3		4	6	5						11		2	12						1							8		10	37
1	7	4	6	3						11		2												8	5			10	38
1	7	4	6	3						12	11*	2†												8	5			10	39
1	3	7	5	6						10		8		4							2							11	40
1		7	5	6						10				4							2			8				11	41
1		7	5	6						10				4							2			8				11	42
1		7	5	6						10				4							2			8				11	43
1		7*	5	6						10				4							2			8				11	44
1			5	3						10	7			4		6					2			8				11	45
1			5							10	7			4		6					2			8				11	46
33	32	13	33	30	38	2	15	9	32	36	25	19	13	16	5	14	5	10	1	13	25	9	—	17	3	19	3	17	
+2s	+	+1s	+2s		+1s	+4s			+2s	+3s	+1s		+9s					+6s	+2s		+	+	+	+1s	+7s	+1s		+1s	

Hathaway—Match No. 34(11*) 35(11) 37(7*) 39(14) 44(12); Pearson—Match No. 36(9) 37(9) 38(9) 39(9) 40(9) 41(9) 42(9) 43(9) 44(9) 45(9) 46(9); Taylor—Match No. 41(3) 42(3) 43(3) 44(3) 46(3).

FA Cup			
	First Round	Stockport Co (h)	1-0
	Second Round	Halifax T (h)	1-1
		(a)	2-1
	Third Round	Swansea C (a)	0-0
		(h)	4-0
	Fourth Round	Crewe Alex (a)	0-1

440

ROTHERHAM UNITED

Player and Position	Ht	Wt	Birth Date	Place	Source	Clubs	League App	Gls
Goalkeepers								
Stuart Ford*	5 11	11 13	20 7 71	Sheffield	Trainee	Rotherham U	1	—
Billy Mercer	6 1	11 00	22 5 69	Liverpool	Trainee	Liverpool	—	—
						Rotherham U	15	—
Kelham O'Hanlon	6 1	13 03	16 5 62	Saltburn	Apprentice	Middlesbrough	87	—
						Rotherham U	248	—
Defenders								
Andy Barnsley*	6 0	11 11	9 6 62	Sheffield	Denaby U	Rotherham U	28	—
						Sheffield U	77	1
						Rotherham U	83	3
Gerry Forrest*	5 10	10 11	21 1 57	Stockton	South Bank	Rotherham U	357	7
						Southampton	115	—
						Rotherham U	34	—
Mark Hodges	6 0	11 00	24 10 71	Sheffield	Trainee	Rotherham U	4	—
Nigel Johnson	6 2	12 08	23 6 64	Rotherham	Apprentice	Rotherham U	54	1
						Nottingham F (loan)	—	—
						Rotherham U	35	—
						Manchester C	4	—
						Rotherham U	109	5
Nicky Law	6 0	13 05	8 9 61	Greenwich	Apprentice	Arsenal	—	—
						Barnsley	114	1
						Blackpool	66	1
						Plymouth Arg	38	5
						Notts Co	47	4
						Scarborough (loan)	12	—
						Rotherham U	32	2
Ally Pickering	5 9	10 08	22 6 67	Manchester	Buxton	Rotherham U	11	—
Neil Richardson	5 10	10 08	3 6 68	Sunderland		Rotherham U	18	2
Ronnie Robinson	5 9	11 00	22 10 66	Sunderland	Vaux Breweries	Ipswich T	—	—
						Leeds U	27	—
						Doncaster R	78	5
						WBA	1	—
						Rotherham U	81	1
Billy Russell*	5 10	11 04	14 9 59	Glasgow	Apprentice	Everton	—	—
						Celtic	—	—
						Doncaster R	244	15
						Scunthorpe U	117	7
						Rotherham U	99	2
Julian Watts	6 3	12 01	17 3 71	Sheffield		Rotherham U	10	—
Midfield								
Dean Barrick	5 9	11 04	30 9 69	Hemsworth	Trainee	Sheffield W	11	2
						Rotherham U	19	2
Mark Dempsey*	5 8	10 04	14 1 64	Manchester	Apprentice	Manchester U	1	—
						Swindon T (loan)	5	—
						Sheffield U	63	9
						Chesterfield (loan)	3	—
						Rotherham U	75	7
Shaun Goodwin	5 7	8 10	14 6 69	Rotherham	Trainee	Rotherham U	116	13
Simon Thompson	5 8	10 08	27 2 70	Sheffield	Trainee	Rotherham U	28	—
Forwards								
John Buckley (To Partick Th Oct 1990)	5 9	10 07	10 5 62	Glasgow	Queen's Park	Partick Th	45	5
						Doncaster R	84	11
						Leeds U	10	1
						Leicester C (loan)	5	—
						Doncaster R (loan)	6	—
						Rotherham U	105	13

ROTHERHAM UNITED

Foundation: This club traces its history back to the formation of Thornhill United in 1878 (reformed 1884). They changed their name to Rotherham County in 1905. Confusion exists because of the existence of the Rotherham Town club (founded c. 1885) and in the Football League as early as 1893 but this club was not the one previously mentioned. The Town amalgamated with Rotherham County to form Rotherham United in 1925.

First Football League game: 2 September, 1893, Division 2, Rotherham T v Lincoln C (a) D 1-1 – McKay; Thickett, Watson; Barr, Brown, Broadhead; Longden, Cutts, Leatherbarrow, McCormick, Pickering. 1 o.g. 30 August, 1919, Division 2, Rotherham C v Nottingham F (h) W 2-0 – Branston; Alton, Baines; Bailey, Coe, Stanton; Lee (1), Cawley (1), Glennon, Lees, Lamb.

Did you know: In the period between the two world wars Rotherham United was the only club which failed to turn up for a Football League game. Fog prevented them from reaching Hartlepool United's ground, 22 December 1934.

Managers (and Secretary-managers)
Billy Heald 1925–29 (secretary only for long spell), Stanley Davies 1929–30, Billy Heald 1930–33, Reg Freeman 1934–52, Andy Smailes 1952–58, Tom Johnston 1958–62, Danny Williams 1962–65, Jack Mansell 1965–67, Tommy Docherty 1967–68, Jimmy McAnearney 1968–73, Jimmy McGuigan 1973–79, Ian Porterfield 1979–81, Emlyn Hughes 1981–83, George Kerr 1983–85, Norman Hunter 1985–87, Dave Cusack 1987–88, Billy McEwan 1988–91, Phil Henson January 1991– .

Player and Position	Ht	Wt	Birth Date	Birth Place	Source	Clubs	League App	Gls
Stewart Evans	6 4	11 05	15 11 60	Maltby	Apprentice Gainsborough T	Rotherham U	—	
						Sheffield U	—	—
						Wimbledon	175	50
						WBA	14	1
						Plymouth Arg	45	10
						Rotherham U	65	14
						Torquay U (loan)	15	5
Shaun Goater	6 2	12 10	25 2 70	Bermuda		Manchester U	—	
						Rotherham U	34	4
Ian Hathaway	5 8	10 06	22 8 68	Worsley	Bedworth U	Mansfield T	44	2
						Rotherham U	5	1
Paul Haycock‡	6 1	12 00	8 7 62	Sheffield	Burton Alb	Rotherham U	97	22
Desmond Hazel	5 10	10 04	15 7 67	Bradford	Apprentice	Sheffield W	6	—
						Grimsby T (loan)	9	2
						Rotherham U	114	11
Jonathan Howard	5 10	11 07	7 10 71	Sheffield	Trainee	Rotherham U	1	—
Clive Mendonca	5 10	11 07	9 9 68	Tullington	Apprentice	Sheffield U	13	4
						Doncaster R (loan)	2	—
						Rotherham U	84	27
Bobby Williamson (To Kilmarnock Nov 1990)	5 10	11 00	13 8 61	Glasgow	Auchengill	Clydebank	70	28
						Rangers	41	12
						WBA	53	11
						Rotherham U	93	49

Trainees
Anson, Simon D; Clarke, Matthew J; Cox, Darren J; Gleeson, Steven K; Hall, Jason L; Kinnair, Michael R; Lawler, Shane M; McDonagh, Dermot E; Seddons, Darren M; Taylor, Andrew; Tesh, John A; Tompkins, David A.

Associated Schoolboys
Ayrton, Matthew R; Batty, Neil R; Binney, Paul; Brownrigg, Andrew D; Connelly, Ryan J; Curry, Kevin J; Dilkes, Christopher J; Dunleavy, Michael; Embleton, John A; Glossop, Alistair J; Handbury, Lee A; Hoe, Michael J; Kirk, Darren; Partington, Dean J; Ryalls, Scott A; Smeed, Michael E.W; Usher, Colin; Wake, Ryan.

Associated Schoolboys who have accepted the club's offer of a Traineeship/Contract
Bennet, Paul S; Breckin, Ian; Bunting, James R.S; Dolby, Christopher J; Hardwick, Matthew; Hinshelwood, Shane; Hurst, Paul; Jarvis, Steven M.

SCARBOROUGH 1990–91 *Back row (left to right):* Andrew Mockler, Tommy Mooney, Steve Richards, Barry Richardson, Ian Ironside, Lee Hirst, Adrian Meyer, Mick Clarke. *Centre row:* David Logan, Alan Kamara, Mick Matthews, Phil Chambers (Youth Team Coach), Geoffrey Richmond (Chairman), Ray McHale (Manager), John MacDonald, Paul Dobson, Mark Ash.
Front row: George Oghani, Steve Carter, Steve Saunders, Phil Wilson, Lee Slingsby, Steve French, Paul Mudd.

Division 4   SCARBOROUGH

The McCain Stadium, Seamer Road, Scarborough YO12 4HF. Telephone (0723) 375094.

Ground capacity: 7126.

Record Attendance: 11,130 v Luton T, FA Cup 3rd rd, 8 January 1938. Football League: 7314 v Wolverhampton W, Division 4, 15 August 1987.

Record receipts: £19,754 v Wolverhampton W, Division 4, 15 August 1987.

Pitch measurements: 120yd × 75yd.

President: John Birley.

Chairman: G. Richmond.

Directors: M. L. Jones FCA, J. W. Fawcett, A. D. Mollon, M. Bramham, J. Lawrence, A. Jenkinson, J. R. Birley (President and Chief Executive).

Manager: Ray McHale. *Assistant Manager:*

Secretary: E. V. Hall.

Assistant Secretary: Miss S. B. Wright.

Commercial Manager: Shirley Nettleton. *Physio:* K. Warner.

Year Formed: 1879. *Turned Professional:* 1926. *Ltd Co.:* 1933.

Club Nickname: 'The Boro'.

Previous Grounds: 1879–87, Scarborough Cricket Ground; 1887–98, Recreation Ground; 1898– Athletic Ground.

Record League Victory: 4-0 v Bolton W, Division 4, 29 August 1987 – Blackwell; McJannet, Thompson, Bennyworth (Walker), Richards (1) (Cook), Kendall, Hamill (1), Moss, McHale, Mell (1), Graham. (1 og). 4-0 v Newport C, Division 4, 12 April 1988 – Ironside; McJannet, Thompson, Kamara, Richards (1), Short (1), Adams (Cook 1), Brook, Outhart (1), Russell, Graham.

Record Cup Victory: 6-0 v Rhyl Ath, FA Cup, 1st rd, 29 November 1930 – Turner; Severn, Belton; Maskell, Robinson, Wallis; Small (1), Rand (2), Palfreman (2), A. D. Hill (1), Mickman.

Record Defeat: 1-16 v Southbank, Northern League, 15 November 1919.

Most League Points (3 for a win): 77, Division 4, 1988–89.

Most League Goals: 69, Division 4, 1990–91.

Highest League Scorer in Season: George Oghani, 14, Division 4, 1990–91.

Most League Goals in Total Aggregate: Paul Dobson, 22, 1989–91.

Most Capped Player: None.

Most League Appearances: Steve Richards, 119, 1987–90.

Record Transfer Fee Received: £240,000 from Notts Co for Chris Short, September 1990.

Record Transfer Fee Paid: £102,000 to Leicester C for Martin Russell, March 1989.

Football League Record: Promoted to Division 4 1987.

Honours: Football League: Division 4 best season: 5th, 1988–89. *FA Cup:* best seasons: 3rd rd, 1931, 1938, 1976, 1978. *Football League Cup:* best season: 3rd rd 1989.

Colours: Red/black shirts, white shorts, red stockings. **Change colours:** All red.

444

SCARBOROUGH 1990–91 LEAGUE RECORD

Match No.	Date		Venue	Opponents	Result	H/T Score	Lg. Pos.	Goalscorers	Attendance
1	Aug	25	A	Cardiff C	D 0-0	0-0	—		3819
2	Sept	1	H	Chesterfield	W 1-0	0-0	8	Dobson	1990
3		8	A	Burnley	L 1-2	1-0	13	Oghani	4723
4		15	H	Gillingham	W 2-1	1-1	6	Oghani (pen), Dobson	1499
5		18	H	Northampton T	D 1-1	1-0	—	Wilson	1525
6		22	A	Rochdale	D 1-1	1-1	10	Carter	1715
7		29	A	Aldershot	D 2-2	1-0	11	Mockler, Oghani	1857
8	Oct	3	H	Blackpool	L 0-1	0-0	—		1713
9		7	H	Doncaster R	W 2-1	1-0	—	Meyer, Oghani	2156
10		13	A	Wrexham	W 2-1	0-1	10	Carter, MacDonald	2486
11		20	A	Scunthorpe U	L 0-3	0-2	10		2786
12		24	H	Carlisle U	D 1-1	1-0	—	Oghani	1329
13		27	H	Maidstone U	L 0-2	0-0	12		1402
14	Nov	3	A	Hereford U	D 3-3	1-0	13	Carter, Mooney, Richards	3017
15		9	H	Torquay U	W 1-0	1-0	—	Cook (pen)	1447
16		24	A	Hartlepool U	L 0-2	0-1	12		2122
17	Dec	1	A	Lincoln C	L 0-2	0-1	16		2204
18		7	A	Wrexham	W 4-2	4-1	—	Oghani 2 (1 pen), Mockler, Richards	625
19		16	H	Stockport Co	L 0-2	0-0	—		1154
20		21	A	Peterborough U	L 0-2	0-0	—		3237
21		26	H	Halifax T	W 4-1	1-1	13	Mockler, Oghani 2 (1 pen), Hirst	1327
22		29	H	Darlington	D 1-1	0-1	13	Oghani (pen)	2408
23	Jan	1	A	Walsall	D 0-0	0-0	12		4914
24		5	H	York C	D 2-2	0-2	12	Oghani (pen), Hirst	2404
25		12	A	Chesterfield	W 1-0	1-0	10	Mockler	3217
26		25	A	Gillingham	D 1-1	0-0	—	Himsworth	3756
27	Feb	1	A	Northampton T	W 2-0	2-0	—	Reed 2	4058
28		6	H	Rochdale	D 0-0	0-0	—		955
29		16	H	Hartlepool U	W 2-0	0-0	9	Oghani, Mooney	1804
30		19	H	Cardiff C	L 1-2	1-1	—	Mooney	1192
31	Mar	2	H	Lincoln C	W 3-0	2-0	10	Oghani 2 (pen), Mooney	1432
32		8	A	Stockport Co	D 2-2	0-1	—	Mooney, Reed	3172
33		12	A	Blackpool	L 1-3	1-2	—	Reed	3798
34		16	H	Aldershot	W 2-0	2-0	11	Foreman, Mockler (pen)	1195
35		24	A	Doncaster R	W 2-0	1-0	—	Mooney, Foreman	2734
36		26	H	Burnley	L 0-1	0-1	—		2373
37		30	A	Halifax T	W 2-1	1-0	9	Foreman, Mooney	1623
38	Apr	3	H	Peterborough U	W 3-1	3-1	—	Mooney 2, Reed	2141
39		6	A	Darlington	L 1-2	1-0	10	Foreman	3962
40		13	H	Walsall	W 1-0	1-0	9	Mooney	1538
41		20	H	Scunthorpe U	W 3-1	1-1	10	Logan, Richards, Foreman	2046
42		23	A	York C	L 0-2	0-1	—		3017
43		27	A	Carlisle U	L 1-4	0-2	11	Fletcher	1762
44		30	A	Torquay U	L 0-2	0-1	—		2596
45	May	4	A	Maidstone U	W 1-0	0-0	10	Mooney	1277
46		11	H	Hereford U	W 2-1	1-0	9	Mooney 2	1093

Final League Position: 9

GOALSCORERS

League (59): Oghani 14 (7 pens), Mooney 13, Reed 5, Foreman 5, Mockler 5 (1 pen), Carter 3, Richards 3, Dobson 2, Hirst 2, Cook 1 (pen), Fletcher 1, Himsworth 1, Logan 1, MacDonald 1, Meyer 1, Wilson 1.
Rumbelows Cup (3): Oghani 2 (2 pens), Matthews 1.
FA Cup (0).

Richardson	Wilson	Logan	Matthews	Richards	Meyer	Kamara	Mudd	Oghani	MacDonald	Carter	Dobson	Ironside	Mockler	Mooney	Hirst	Clarke	Cook	Brook	Ash	Himsworth	Reed	Lee, R	Foreman	Lee, C	Fletcher	Eshelby	Match No.
1	2	3	4	5	6	7	8	9	10	11*	12																1
	2	3	4	5	6	7	8	9	10	11		1															2
	2	3	4	5	6	7*	8	9	10	11†		1	12	14													3
	2	3	4	5	6		8*	9	10	11	12	1			7												4
	2	3	4	5	6		12	9	10	11*	8†	1		14	7												5
			4	5	6	3		9	10	11	12†	1		7*	14	2	8										6
	2		4	5	6	7	3	9	10	11		1			8												7
	12		4	5	6	2	3	9	10†	11		1	8*	14			7										8
	8		4	5	6	2	3	9	10	11		1					7										9
	8		4	5	6	2	3	9	10	11		1					7										10
1	8	14	4	5	6*	2	3†	9	10	11	12						7										11
	8		4	5	6	2	3	9		11		1					7	10									12
	8*	4†	5			2	3	9	14	11		1	12	6			7	10									13
	8	14	5			2	3	12		11		1	4	9*	6†		7	10									14
	8†	14	5			2	3	12		11		1	4	9*	6		7	10									15
	3	8	5			2	14	12		11		1	4	9*	6		7†	10									16
1	3	4	5		7	12		11				8	9*	6				10	2								17
1	12	3	4	5		9		11				8*		6				10	2	7							18
1	12	3	4	5		14	9	11				8*		6				10	2†	7							19
	10	3	4	5	2	12	9	11				1	8*	6						7							20
	10	3	4	5	2		9	11				1	8	6						7							21
	10*	3	4	5	2		9	11				1	8	12	6					7							22
		3	4	5	2		9	11				1	8	10	6					7							23
		3	4	5	2	10	9	11				1	8		6					7							24
		3	4	5	2		9*	12				1	8		6			10		7	11						25
		3		5	2		9	4				1	8		6			10		7	11						26
		3	4	5	2		9					1	8		6			10		7	11						27
		3	4	5	2		9	10				1	8		6					7	11						28
		3†	4	5	2		9*	10				1	8	12	6					7	11	14					29
			4	5	2	3		12				1	8	9	6*					7	11	10					30
			4	5	2	3	9					1	8	10	6					7	11						31
		3	4	5	10*	2	9					1	8	12	6					7†	11	14					32
		3	4	5	10†	2	9					1	8	12	6						11*	14	7				33
		3	4	5	2		9					1	8		6					7	11*		10	12			34
		3	4	5	2		12					1		9*	6					7†	11	14	10	8			35
1		3*	4	5	2		9†	7					12		6						11	10	8	14			36
		3	4	5	2		7					1		9	6						11		10*	8	12		37
		3	4	5	2		7					1		9	6						11		10	8			38
		3	4	5	2		7*					1		9†	6						11	14	10	8	12		39
		3	4	5	2		12					1	8	9	6					11		14	10			7*	40
		3	4	5	2							1	8	9†	6					11*		14	10	7	12		41
		3	4	5	2							1	8	9	6					11*		12	10	7			42
		3	4	5	2							1	8†	9	6					11*		10	7	12	14		43
		3†	4	5	6	2	8			14		1	12				7					10		9*	11		44
		3	4		6	5	7					1	8	9						2	11	10					45
			4	5	6	3	7					1	8	9						2	11	10					46
6	16	33	43	45	17	40	21	30	10	31	2	40	32	17	32	1	9	8	9	23	14	2	14	8	1	2	
		+	+	+		+	+	+	+	+			+	+						+			+	+	+	+	
		3s	1s	2s		1s	3s	6s	1s	3s			4s							2s	10s		8s	1s	5s	1s	

Rumbelows Cup	First Round	Rochdale (a)	0-4
		(h)	3-3
FA Cup	First Round	Leek T (h)	0-2

SCARBOROUGH

Player and Position	Ht	Wt	Birth Date	Birth Place	Source	Clubs	League App	Gls
Goalkeepers								
Ian Ironside	6 2	13 00	8 3 64	Sheffield	Apprentice N Ferriby U	Barnsley Scarborough	— 88	— —
Barry Richardson‡	6 0	12 00	5 8 69	Willington Key	Trainee	Sunderland Scunthorpe U Scarborough	— — 30	— — —
Defenders								
Mark Ash	5 9	11 04	22 1 68	Sheffield	Apprentice	Rotherham U Scarborough	20 20	— —
Lee Hirst	6 2	12 07	26 1 69	Sheffield		Scarborough	42	2
Alan Kamara	5 9	10 12	15 7 58	Sheffield	Kiveton Park Burton Alb	York C Darlington Scarborough	10 134 159	— 1 2
David Logan	5 9	10 11	5 12 63	Middlesbrough	Whitby	Mansfield T Northampton T Halifax T Stockport Co Scarborough	67 41 3 60 34	1 1 — 4 1
Adrian Meyer	6 0	14 00	22 9 70	Bristol	Trainee	Scarborough	35	3
Paul Mudd	5 8	11 02	13 11 70	Hull	Trainee	Hull C Scarborough	1 24	— 1
Steve Richards	6 0	12 00	24 10 61	Dundee	Apprentice Gainsborough T	Hull C York C Lincoln C Cambridge U Scarborough	58 7 21 4 164	2 — — 2 13
Midfield								
Chris Lee	5 10	11 07	18 6 71	Halifax	Trainee	Bradford C Rochdale Scarborough	— 26 9	— 2 —
Raymond Lee‡	5 8	11 12	19 9 70	Bristol	Trainee	Arsenal Scarborough	— 10	— —
John MacDonald‡	5 9	10 08	15 4 61	Glasgow	Clydebank	Rangers Charlton Ath Barnsley Scarborough	160 2 94 40	44 — 20 6
Mike Matthews	5 8	11 03	25 9 60	Hull	Apprentice	Wolverhampton W Scunthorpe U Halifax T Scarborough Stockport Co Scarborough	76 58 99 7 35 66	7 5 8 1 3 3
Andrew Mockler	5 11	11 13	18 11 70	Stockton	Trainee	Arsenal Scarborough	— 34	— 5
Steve Saunders‡	5 7	10 06	21 9 64	Warrington	Apprentice	Bolton W Crewe Alex Preston NE Grimsby T Scarborough	3 22 — 76 32	— 1 — 13 1
Lee Slingsby‡	5 7	11 04	27 11 70	Doncaster	Doncaster R	Scarborough	1	—
Phil Wilson‡	5 6	11 13	16 10 60	Hemsworth	Apprentice Macclesfield	Bolton W Huddersfield T York C Scarborough	39 233 46 43	4 16 2 2

SCARBOROUGH

Foundation: Scarborough came into being as early as 1879 when they were formed by members of the town's cricket club and went under the name of Scarborough Cricketers' FC with home games played on the North Marine Road Cricket Ground.

First Football League game: 15 August, 1987, Division 4, v Wolverhampton W (h) D 2-2 – Blackwell; McJannet, Thompson, Bennyworth, Richards, Kendall, Hamill, Moss, McHale (1), Mell (1), Graham.

Did you know: The highest aggregate score for an FA Cup tie in which a non-League side beat a League club is 10 – Scarborough 6 Lincoln City 4, 2nd Round, December 13, 1930.

Managers (and Secretary-managers)
B. Chapman 1945–47*, George Hall 1946–47, Harold Taylor 1947–48, Frank Taylor 1948–50, A. C. Bell (Director & Hon. TM) 1950–53, Reg Halton 1953–54, Charles Robson (Hon. TM) 1954–57, George Higgins 1957–58, Andy Smailes 1959–61, Eddie Brown 1961–64, Albert Franks 1964–65, Stuart Myers 1965–66, Graham Shaw 1968–69, Colin Appleton 1969–73, Ken Houghton 1974–75, Colin Appleton 1975–81, Jimmy McAnearney 1981–82, John Cottam 1982–84, Harry Dunn 1984–86, Neil Warnock 1986–88, Colin Morris 1989, Ray McHale November 1989– .

Player and Position	Ht	Wt	Birth Date	Birth Place	Source	Clubs	League App	Gls
Forwards								
Steve Carter	5 8	12 00	13 4 72	Sunderland	Manchester U	Scarborough	34	3
Michael Clarke‡	5 11	11 05	22 12 67	Birmingham		Barnsley	40	3
						Scarborough	37	1
Paul Eshelby	5 9	11 00	29 5 70	Sheffield		Exeter C	19	1
						Scarborough	3	—
Andy Fletcher	6 0	13 00	12 8 71	Cleveland	Trainee	Middlesbrough	—	—
						Scarborough	6	1
Darren Foreman	5 10	10 08	12 2 68	Southampton		Barnsley	47	8
						Crewe Alex	23	4
						Scarborough	14	5
Gary Himsworth	5 7	9 08	19 12 69	Appleton	Trainee	York C	88	8
						Scarborough	23	1
Tommy Mooney	5 10	12 05	11 8 71	Teesside North	Trainee	Aston Villa	—	—
						Scarborough	27	13
George Oghani*	5 11	12 03	2 9 60	Manchester	Hyde U	Bolton W	99	27
						Wrexham (loan)	7	—
						Burnley	74	21
						Stockport Co	8	2
						Hereford U	8	2
						Scarborough	50	18

Trainees
Clarke, Simon J; Hewitt, Stephen; Holmes, David J; Jarman, Matthew J; Kingham, Mark; Manderson, David A; Pollington, Miguel C; Pratt, Jeremy M; Price, Mark A.R.J; Rocca, Jon C; Silk, Matthew; Slade, Paul A; Smith, Lee; Suddes, Lee; Swales, Stephen C; Taylor, Stephen P; Tomlinson, Sean; Townley, Stephen E; Wignall, Adrian; Williams, David J.

Associated Schoolboys
Hudson, Andrew; Lewis, Gareth; Smith, Adam; Stanton, Michael M.

448

SCUNTHORPE UNITED 1990–91 *Back row (left to right):* Mike Buxton (Manager), Bill Green (Assistant Manager), Graham Alexander, Perry Cotton, Gary Marshall, Mark Lillis, Steve Lister, Paul Musselwhite, John Bramhall, Peter Litchfield, Richard Hall, Stuart Hicks, Andy Stevenson, Neil Cox, Paul Ward, Dave Moore (Youth Development Officer), Phil McLoughlin (Physiotherapist).
Centre row: Kevin Taylor, Gordon Tucker, Ian Hamilton, Tony Daws, Andy Founders, David Cowling, Paul Smalley, Paul Longden.
Front row: Allan Evans, Darren Spooner, Andy Godfrey, Paul Gibbs, Stephen Thatcher, Sam Bell, Darren Lelliott, Paul McCullagh, Sean Creaton.

Division 4   **SCUNTHORPE UNITED**

Glanford Park, Scunthorpe, South Humberside. Telephone Scunthorpe (0724) 848077.

Ground capacity: 9200.

Record attendance: Old Showground: 23,935 v Portsmouth, FA Cup 4th rd, 30 January 1954. Glanford Park: 8775 v Rotherham U, Division 4, 1 May 1989.

Record receipts: £30,857 v Grimsby T, Division 4, 26 December 1989.

Pitch measurements: 111yd × 73yd.

President: Sir Reginald Sheffield, Bt.

Vice-presidents: I. T. Botham, G. Johnson, A. Harvey, G. J. Alston, R. Ashman.

Chairman: T. E. Belton.

Directors: R. Garton, J. B. Borrill, C. Plumtree, J. Hayes.

Manager: Bill Green. *Asst. Manager:*   . *Youth Development Officer:* D. Moore.

Physio: Phil McLoughlin.

Chief Executive Secretary: A. D. Rowing. *Commercial Manager:* A. D. Rowing.

Year Formed: 1899. *Turned Professional:* 1912. *Ltd Co.:* 1912.

Club Nickname: 'The Iron'.

Previous Names: Amalgamated with Brumby Hall: North Lindsey United to become Scunthorpe & Lindsey United, 1910; dropped '& Lindsey' in 1958.

Previous ground: Old Showground to 1988.

Record League Victory: 8-1 v Luton T, Division 3, 24 April 1965 – Sidebottom; Horstead, Hemstead; Smith, Neale, Lindsey; Bramley (1), Scott, Thomas (5), Mahy (1), Wilson (1).

Record Cup Victory: 9-0 v Boston U, FA Cup, 1st rd, 21 November 1953 – Malan; Hubbard, Brownsword; Sharpe, White, Bushby; Mosby (1), Haigh (3), Whitfield (2), Gregory (1), Mervyn Jones (2).

Record Defeat: 0-8 v Carlisle U, Division 3 (N), 25 December 1952.

Most League Points (2 for a win): 66, Division 3 (N), 1956–57, 1957–58.

Most League Points (3 for a win): 83, Division 4, 1982–83.

Most League Goals: 88, Division 3 (N), 1957–58.

Highest League Scorer in Season: Barrie Thomas, 31, Division 2, 1961–62.

Most League Goals in Total Aggregate: Steve Cammack, 110, 1979–81, 1981–86.

Most Capped Player: None.

Most League Appearances: Jack Brownsword, 595, 1950–65.

Record Transfer Fee Received: £350,000 from Aston Villa for Neil Cox, February 1991.

Record Transfer Fee Paid: £55,000 to Bristol City for Glenn Humphries, March 1991.

Football League Record: 1950 Elected to Division 3 (N); 1958–64 Division 2; 1964–68 Division 3; 1968–72 Division 4; 1972–73 Division 3; 1973–83 Division 4; 1983–84 Division 3; 1984– Division 4.

Honours: Football League: Division 2 best season: 4th, 1961–62; Division 3 (N) – Champions 1957–58. *FA Cup:* best season: 5th rd, 1957–58, 1969–70. *Football League Cup:* never past 3rd rd.

Colours: Claret and blue striped shirts, blue shorts claret band, blue stockings claret band. **Change colours:** White shirts, claret and blue trim, claret shorts blue band, white stockings claret band.

450

SCUNTHORPE UNITED 1990–91 LEAGUE RECORD

Match No.	Date		Venue	Opponents	Result		H/T Score	Lg. Pos.	Goalscorers	Atten- dance
1	Aug	25	H	Blackpool	W	2-0	1-0	—	Flounders, Hamilton	3024
2	Sept	1	A	Aldershot	L	2-3	0-2	9	Flounders (pen), Daws	2001
3		8	H	Peterborough U	D	1-1	1-0	8	Flounders	3028
4		15	A	Maidstone U	L	1-6	0-3	18	Lillis	1778
5		18	A	Torquay U	D	1-1	0-0	—	Lillis	2811
6		22	H	Lincoln C	W	2-1	1-1	13	Hicks, Hall	2844
7		29	H	Cardiff C	L	0-2	0-0	16		2573
8	Oct	2	A	Walsall	L	0-3	0-3	—		3676
9		6	A	Halifax T	D	0-0	0-0	17		1468
10		13	H	Gillingham	W	1-0	1-0	14	Hall	2357
11		20	H	Scarborough	W	3-0	2-0	11	Daws 2, Taylor	2786
12		23	A	Chesterfield	L	0-1	0-1	—		3371
13		27	A	Darlington	D	0-0	0-0	13		3852
14	Nov	3	A	Stockport Co	W	3-0	0-0	10	Lillis, Flounders (pen), Daws	2826
15		10	H	Rochdale	W	2-1	1-1	10	Flounders, Cotton	3070
16		24	A	Wrexham	L	0-1	0-0	10		1333
17	Dec	1	A	York C	D	2-2	1-2	11	Hall, Powell	2495
18		15	H	Doncaster R	D	1-1	0-1	12	Flounders	3963
19		22	H	Hereford U	L	0-2	0-0	14		2218
20		29	H	Carlisle U	W	2-0	0-0	15	Flounders (pen), Lillis	2971
21	Jan	1	A	Burnley	D	1-1	0-1	15	Lillis	8557
22		12	H	Aldershot	W	6-2	3-1	13	Cowling, Flounders 3 (1 pen), Hamilton, Lillis	2727
23		19	A	Blackpool	L	1-3	0-2	13	Cowling	2494
24		26	H	Maidstone U	D	2-2	1-1	13	Ward, Daws	2703
25	Feb	2	H	Torquay U	W	3-0	0-0	11	Cowling, Cox, Flounders	2502
26		23	A	Rochdale	L	1-2	1-0	16	Daws	1832
27		26	H	Hartlepool U	W	2-1	0-0	—	Taylor, Lillis	2220
28	Mar	2	H	York C	W	2-1	0-0	12	Ward, Daws	2860
29		5	A	Northampton T	W	3-0	3-0	—	Daws, Chard (og), Lillis	2852
30		8	A	Doncaster R	W	3-2	3-1	—	Flounders 2, Daws	4015
31		12	H	Walsall	W	1-0	1-0	—	Daws	3352
32		16	A	Cardiff C	L	0-1	0-0	8		2873
33		19	H	Gillingham	D	1-1	0-0	11	Flounders	2324
34		23	H	Halifax T	D	4-4	1-1	7	Flounders (pen), Taylor, Humphries, Lillis	3134
35		30	A	Northampton T	L	1-2	1-1	10	Taylor	3728
36	Apr	1	H	Hereford U	W	3-0	2-0	9	Flounders 2, Daws	3001
37		6	A	Carlisle U	W	3-0	3-0	9	Hill, Hine, Dalziel (og)	1909
38		9	A	Hartlepool U	L	0-2	0-0	—		2840
39		13	H	Burnley	L	1-3	0-0	11	Hine	4449
40		17	A	Lincoln C	W	2-1	0-0	—	Flounders 2 (1 pen)	3212
41		20	A	Scarborough	L	1-3	1-1	11	Flounders (pen)	2046
42		23	A	Peterborough U	D	0-0	0-0	—		5774
43		27	H	Chesterfield	W	3-0	0-0	9	Daws, Flounders 2	3046
44	May	4	A	Darlington	W	2-1	1-0	8	Flounders, Daws	5769
45		7	H	Wrexham	W	2-0	1-0	—	Daws, Lillis	3572
46		11	A	Stockport Co	L	0-5	0-2	8		6212

Final League Position: 8

GOALSCORERS

League (71): Flounders 23 (7 pens), Daws 14, Lillis 10, Taylor 4, Cowling 3, Hall 3, Hamilton 2, Hine 2, Ward 2, Cotton 1, Cox 1, Hicks 1, Hill 1, Humphries 1, Powell 1, own goals 2.
Rumbelows Cup (1): Lillis 1.
FA Cup (8): Flounders 3 (1 pen), Lillis 2, Bramhall 1, Hicks 1, Ward 1.

Litchfield	Longden	Cowling	Ward	Hicks	Hall	Taylor	Hamilton	Lillis	Flounders	Marshall	Miller	Daws	Smalley	Cotton	Musselwhite	Cox	Bramhall	Powell	Stevenson	Joyce	Humphries	Hill	Hine	Lister	Alexander	Match No.
1	2	3	4	5	6	7	8	9	10	11																1
1	2	3	4	5	6†	7	12		10	11*	8	9	14													2
1	2	3	4	5			8	9	10	11	7	6														3
1	2	3	4	5			11	8	9	10	7	6														4
1	2	3	4	5	6	12	8	9	10†	11	7*		14													5
1	2	3*	4	5	6	12	8	9	10	11	7															6
1	2	3	4	5	6	12	8	9	10	11*	7†		14													7
1	2	3	4	5	6		8		10	11	7	9														8
	2	3*	4	5	6	8	12	9	10						1	7	11									9
	2		4	5	6	8		3	10			9			1	7	11									10
	2		4	5	6	8		3	10			9			1	7	11									11
	2		4	5	6	8		3	10		12	9†	14		1	7	11*									12
	2		4	5	6	8		3	10			9			1	7	11									13
	2		4	5	6	8		3	10			9			1	7	11									14
	2			5	6	8		3	10		12	9*		4	1	7	11									15
	2			5	6	8		3	10					4	1	7	11*	9	12							16
	2	10		5	6	8†		3	12				14	4	1	7	11*	9								17
	2	11	4	5	6	12		3	12			9†		8	1	7*	14									18
	2	11		5	6	4	12	3	10					8	1	7	9*									19
	2	11		5		4	9	3	10					8	1	7	6									20
	2	11	12	5		4	9*	3	10				14	8†	1	7	6									21
	2	11	8	5	6	4	9	3*	10					12	1	7										22
	2	11	8	5	6	4	9		10		12	3*			1	7										23
	2	11	3	5	6	4	9		10					8	1	7										24
	2	4	3	5*	6			9	8	11					1	7			12							25
	2	11	4	5		8		3	10			9			1				6	7						26
	2		4	5	11	8		3	10			9			1				6	7						27
	2		4	5	11	8		3	10			9			1				6	7						28
	2		4	5	11	8		3	10			9			1				6	7						29
	2		4	5	11	8		3	10			9			1					7	6					30
	2		4	5	11	8		3	10			9			1					7	6					31
	2		4	5	11	8		3	10			9			1					7	6					32
	2		4	5	11	8		3	10			9			1					7	6					33
	2		4*	5	11	8		3	10			9	12		1					7	6					34
	2			5	11	8*	12		10			9			1					7	6	3	4			35
	2			5	11	8*	12		10			9			1					7	6	3	4			36
	2			5	11	8			10			9			1					7	6	3	4			37
	2			5	11*	8	12		10			9			1					7	6	3	4			38
	2			5	11*	8†	12		10			9	14		1					7	6	3	4			39
	2			5*	11	8			10			9			1			12		7		3	4	6		40
	2			5	11†	8	14		10			9			1			12		7		3	4	6*	41
	2			5	11	8			10			9			1					7		3	4	6		42
	2			5	11	8		3	10			9			1					7			4*	6	12	43
	2			5	11	8		3	10			9			1					7			4	6		44
	2			5	11	8		3	10			9			1					7			4	6		45
	2			5	11	8		3	10			9			1	12				7†		14	4*	6		46
8	46	18	29	46	21	38	31	35	44	7	8	32	2	10	38	17	11	3	4	21	10	8	12	7	—	
		+				+	+	+	+		+	+	+	+		+	+			+			+		+	
		1s				4s	3s	4s	2s		4s	2s	1s	5s		1s	5s			1s			1s		1s	

Rumbelows Cup   First Round   Carlisle U (a)   0-1
                              (h)   1-1
FA Cup   First Round   Rochdale (a)   1-1
                              (h)   2-1
                Second Round   Tranmere R (h)   3-2
                Third Round   Brighton & HA (a)   2-3

SCUNTHORPE UNITED

Player and Position	Ht	Wt	Birth Date	Place	Source	Clubs	League App	Gls
Goalkeepers								
Peter Litchfield*	6 1	12 12	27 7 56	Manchester	Droylsden	Preston NE	107	—
						Bradford C	88	—
						Oldham Ath (loan)	3	—
						Scunthorpe U	25	—
Paul Musselwhite	6 2	12 07	22 12 68	Portsmouth	Portsmouth†	Scunthorpe U	108	—
Defenders								
Graham Alexander	5 10	11 00	10 10 71	Coventry	Trainee	Scunthorpe U	1	—
John Bramhall*	6 2	13 06	20 11 56	Warrington	Amateur	Tranmere R	170	7
						Bury	167	17
						Chester C (loan)	4	—
						Rochdale	86	13
						Halifax T	62	5
						Scunthorpe U	32	—
Stuart Hicks	6 1	12 06	30 5 67	Peterborough	Apprentice Wisbech	Peterborough U	—	—
						Colchester U	64	—
						Scunthorpe U	46	1
Glenn Humphries	6 0	12 00	11 8 64	Hull	Apprentice	Doncaster R	180	8
						Lincoln C (loan)	9	—
						Bristol C	85	—
						Scunthorpe U	10	1
Joe Joyce	5 9	10 05	18 3 61	Consett	Amateur	Barnsley	334	4
						Scunthorpe U	21	—
Steve Lister	6 1	11 00	18 11 61	Doncaster	Apprentice	Doncaster R	237	30
						Scunthorpe U	163	29
						York C (loan)	4	1
Paul Longden	5 9	11 00	28 9 62	Wakefield	Apprentice	Barnsley	5	—
						Scunthorpe U	307	—
Gordon Tucker*	5 11	11 12	5 1 68	Manchester	Derby Co	Huddersfield T	35	—
						Scunthorpe U	15	1
Midfield								
Perry Cotton*	5 11	11 12	11 11 65	Chislehurst		Scunthorpe U	33	2
David Cowling*	5 7	11 04	27 11 58	Doncaster	Apprentice	Mansfield T	—	—
						Huddersfield T	340	43
						Scunthorpe U (loan)	1	—
						Reading	10	1
						Scunthorpe U	89	5
Ian Hamilton	5 9	11 03	14 12 67	Stevenage	Apprentice	Southampton	—	—
						Cambridge U	24	1
						Scunthorpe U	104	9
Mark Hine	5 8	9 11	18 5 64	Middlesbrough	Local	Grimsby T	22	1
						Darlington	128	8
						Peterborough U	55	8
						Scunthorpe U	12	2
Mark Lillis	6 0	13 06	17 1 60	Manchester	Local	Huddersfield T	206	56
						Manchester C	39	11
						Derby Co	15	1
						Aston Villa	31	4
						Scunthorpe U	68	23
Andy Stevenson	6 0	12 03	29 9 67	Scunthorpe	School	Scunthorpe U	76	1
Kevin Taylor*	5 10	11 00	22 1 61	Sheffield	Apprentice	Sheffield W	125	21
						Derby Co	22	2
						Crystal Palace	87	14
						Scunthorpe U	157	25
Forwards								
Tony Daws	5 9	10 02	10 9 66	Sheffield		Notts Co	8	1
						Sheffield U	11	3
						Scunthorpe U	123	52

SCUNTHORPE UNITED

Foundation: The year of foundation for Scunthorpe United has often been quoted as 1910, but the club can trace its history back to 1899 when Brumby Hall FC, who played on the Old Showground, consolidated their position by amalgamating with some other clubs and changing their name to Scunthorpe United. The year 1910 was when that club amalgamated with North Lindsey United as Scunthorpe and Lindsey United. The link is Mr. W. T. Lockwood whose chairmanship covers both years.

First Football League game: 19 August, 1950, Division 3(N), v Shrewsbury T (h) D 0-0 – Thompson; Barker, Brownsword; Allen, Taylor, McCormick; Mosby, Payne, Gorin, Rees, Boyes.

Did you know: It was this club that initiated the move to extend the size of the Football League by two clubs in each of the two Third Divisions in 1950, persuading Everton to propose the move and Sheffield Wednesday to second it.

Managers (and Secretary-managers)
Harry Allcock 1915–53*, Tom Crilly 1936–37, Bernard Harper 1946–48, Leslie Jones 1950–51, Bill Corkhill 1952–56, Ron Suart 1956–58, Tony McShane 1959, Bill Lambton 1959, Frank Soo 1959–60, Dick Duckworth 1960–64, Fred Goodwin 1964–66, Ron Ashman 1967–73, Ron Bradley 1973–74, Dick Rooks 1974–76, Ron Ashman 1976–81, John Duncan 1981–83, Allan Clarke 1983–84, Frank Barlow 1984–87, Mick Buxton 1987–91, Bill Green February 1991–   .

Player and Position	Ht	Wt	Birth Date	Place	Source	Clubs	League App	Gls
Andy Flounders	5 11	11 06	13 12 63	Hull	Apprentice	Hull C	159	54
						Scunthorpe U	196	87
Ian Miller	5 8	11 12	13 5 55	Perth		Bury	15	—
						Nottingham F	—	—
						Doncaster R	124	14
						Swindon T	127	9
						Blackburn R	268	16
						Port Vale	21	1
						Scunthorpe U	12	—

Trainees
Bell, Stephen J; Clayton, Paul; Evans, Allan; Godfrey, Andrew P; McCullagh, Paul A; Spooner, Darren
**Non-Contract
Moore, David C.
Associated Schoolboys who have accepted the club's offer of a Traineeship/Contract
Hall, James M.
**Non-Contract Players who are retained must be re-signed before they are eligible to play in League matches.

SHEFFIELD UNITED 1990-91 *Back row (left to right):* Simon Webster, Darren Carr, Bob Booker, Brian Deane, John Flower, Phil Kite, Paul Stancliffe, Mark Morris, Billy Whitehurst, Jamie Hoyland, Paul Beesley.

Centre row: Derek French (Physiotherapist), Carl Bradshaw, Richard Lucas, David Barnes, Cliff Powell, John Pemberton, Simon Tracey, Julian Winter, Colin Hill, Tony Agana, Ian Bryson, John Gannon, Geoff Taylor (Assistant Manager).

Front row: Dane Whitehouse, Mitch Ward, Wilf Rostron, Dave Bassett, (Team Manager), Mark Todd, Paul Wood, Peter Duffield.

Division 1   **SHEFFIELD UNITED**

Bramall Lane Ground, Sheffield S2 4SU. Telephone Sheffield (0742) 738955. Bladesline (recorded message): 0898 888650.

Ground capacity: 32,000 (22,000 seats).

Record attendance: 68,287 v Leeds U, FA Cup 5th rd, 15 February 1936.

Record receipts: £178,124 v Tottenham H, Rumbelows Cup 4th rd, 27 November 1990.

Pitch measurements: 110yd × 72yd.

President: R. Wragg M.INST.BM.

Chairman: P. G. Woolhouse. *Managing Director:* D. Dooley.

Directors: D. Dooley, A. H. Laver, M. A. Wragg, R. Wragg.

Team Manager: Dave Bassett. *Team Coach:* Geoff Taylor. *Youth Coach:* Keith Mincher.

Assistant Manager: *Physio:* Derek French.

Secretary: D. Capper AFA. *Commercial Manager:* Andy R. Daykin.

Youth Development Officer: John Dungworth.

Community Programme Organiser: Tony Currie, Tel: 769314.

Year Formed: 1889. *Turned Professional:* 1889. *Ltd Co.:* 1899.

Club Nickname: 'The Blades'.

Record League Victory: 10-0 v Burslem Port Vale, Division 2, 10 December 1892 – Howlett; Witham, Lilley; Howell, Hendry, Needham; Drummond (1), Wallace (1), Hammond (4), Davies (2), Watson (2).

Record Cup Victory: 5-0 v Newcastle U (away), FA Cup, 1st rd, 10 January 1914 – Gough; Cook, English; Brelsford, Howley, Sturgess; Simmons (2), Gillespie (1), Kitchen (1), Fazackerley, Revill (1). 5-0 v Corinthians, FA Cup, 1st rd, 10 January 1925 – Sutcliffe; Cook, Milton; Longworth, King, Green; Partridge, Boyle (1), Johnson 4), Gillespie, Tunstall. 5-0 v Barrow, FA Cup, 3rd rd, 7 January 1956 – Burgin; Coldwell, Mason; Fountain, Johnson, Iley; Hawksworth (1), Hoyland (2), Howitt, Wragg (1), Grainger (1).

Record Defeat: 0-13 v Bolton W, FA Cup 2nd rd, 1 February 1890.

Most League Points (2 for a win): 60, Division 2, 1952–53.

Most League Points (3 for a win): 96, Division 4, 1981–82.

Most League Goals: 102, Division 1, 1925–26.

Highest League Scorer in Season: Jimmy Dunne, 41, Division 1, 1930–31.

Most League Goals in Total Aggregate: Harry Johnson, 205, 1919–30.

Most Capped Player: Billy Gillespie, 25, Northern Ireland.

Most League Appearances: Joe Shaw, 629, 1948–66.

Record Transfer Fee Received: £400,000 from Leeds U for Alex Sabella, May 1980.

Record Transfer Fee Paid: £650,000 to Leeds U for Vinny Jones, September 1990.

Football League Record: 1892 Elected to Division 2; 1893–1934 Division 1; 1934–39 Division 2; 1946–49 Division 1; 1949–53 Division 2; 1953–56 Division 1; 1956–61 Division 2; 1961–68 Division 1; 1968–71 Division 2; 1971–76 Division 1; 1976–79 Division 2; 1979–81 Division 1; 1981–82 Division 4; 1982–84 Division 3; 1984–88 Division 2; 1988–89 Division 3; 1989–90 Division 2; 1990– Division 1.

Honours: *Football League:* Division 1 – Champions 1897–98; Runners-up 1896–97, 1899–1900; Division 2 – Champions 1952–53; Runners-up 1892–93, 1938–39, 1960–61, 1970–71, 1989–90; Division 4 – Champions 1981–82. *FA Cup:* Winners 1899, 1902, 1915, 1925; Runners-up 1901, 1936. *Football League Cup:* best season: 5th rd, 1961–62, 1966–67, 1971–72.

Colours: Colours: Narrow red and white striped shirts with thin black stripe, black shorts, black stockings with red and white trim. *Change colours:* Yellow shirts, red shorts, red stockings.

SHEFFIELD UNITED 1990–91 LEAGUE RECORD

Match No.	Date	Venue	Opponents	Result		H/T Score	Lg. Pos.	Goalscorers	Atten-dance
1	Aug 25	H	Liverpool	L	1-3	0-0	—	Deane	27,009
2	29	A	Derby Co	D	1-1	0-0	—	Deane	18,011
3	Sept 1	A	Crystal Palace	L	0-1	0-1	19		16,831
4	8	H	Manchester C	D	1-1	0-0	18	Deane	21,895
5	15	A	Southampton	L	0-2	0-2	19		15,883
6	23	H	Leeds U	L	0-2	0-0	—		26,078
7	29	A	Chelsea	D	2-2	1-2	19	Jones, Deane	19,873
8	Oct 6	H	Wimbledon	L	1-2	1-1	19	Barnes	17,650
9	20	A	Tottenham H	L	0-4	0-0	20		34,612
10	27	H	Coventry C	L	0-1	0-0	20		17,978
11	Nov 3	A	Norwich C	L	0-3	0-1	20		14,806
12	10	H	Everton	D	0-0	0-0	20		21,447
13	17	A	Manchester U	L	0-2	0-0	20		45,903
14	24	H	Sunderland	L	0-2	0-0	20		19,179
15	Dec 1	A	Aston Villa	L	1-2	0-1	20	Jones	21,713
16	15	A	Liverpool	L	0-2	0-0	20		33,516
17	22	H	Nottingham F	W	3-2	0-0	20	Bryson 2, Deane	20,394
18	26	A	Luton T	W	1-0	0-0	20	Deane	10,004
19	29	A	Arsenal	L	1-4	1-0	20	Bryson	37,866
20	Jan 1	H	QPR	W	1-0	1-0	20	Deane	21,158
21	12	H	Crystal Palace	L	0-1	0-0	20		17,139
22	19	A	Manchester C	L	0-2	0-1	20		25,741
23	26	H	Derby Co	W	1-0	0-0	20	Hodges	18,390
24	Feb 2	H	Southampton	W	4-1	4-0	19	Booker 2, Hodges, Deane	16,887
25	23	A	Everton	W	2-1	1-1	19	Hodges, Marwood	28,148
26	26	H	Manchester U	W	2-1	0-0	—	Deane, Bradshaw	27,570
27	Mar 2	A	Aston Villa	W	2-1	0-0	18	Bryson, Deane	22,074
28	9	A	Sunderland	W	1-0	0-0	14	Bryson	23,238
29	16	H	Chelsea	W	1-0	0-0	12	Bryson	20,581
30	23	A	Wimbledon	D	1-1	0-1	13	Deane (pen)	7031
31	30	H	Luton T	W	2-1	0-0	12	Bryson, Hodges	18,487
32	Apr 1	A	Nottingham F	L	0-2	0-1	14		25,308
33	6	H	Arsenal	L	0-2	0-1	15		26,920
34	13	A	QPR	W	2-1	1-1	16	Deane, Booker	13,801
35	20	H	Tottenham H	D	2-2	0-0	16	Beesley, Deane	25,706
36	May 4	A	Coventry C	D	0-0	0-0	16		17,312
37	8	A	Leeds U	L	1-2	0-1	—	Marwood	28,978
38	11	H	Norwich C	W	2-1	2-1	13	Agana 2	21,019

Final League Position: 13

GOALSCORERS

League (36): Deane 13 (1 pen), Bryson 7, Hodges 4, Booker 3, Agana 2, Jones 2, Marwood 2, Barnes 1, Beesley 1, Bradshaw 1.
Rumbelows Cup (5): Deane 3, Agana 1, Bradshaw 1.
FA Cup (1): Bradshaw 1.

Tracey	Pemberton	Barnes	Booker	Stancliffe	Hill	Hoyland	Rostron	Agana	Deane	Bryson	Morris	Wood	Kite	Beesley	Ward	Gannon	Jones	Whitehurst	Bradshaw	Marwood	Todd	Lake	Whitehouse	Wilder	Lucas	Duffield	Hodges	Sayer	Match No.
1*	2	3	4†	5	6	7	8	9	10	11	12	14																	1
	2	3	4	5	6	7†12		9	10	11*		14	1	8															2
	2	3	4	5†	6		11	9*10		14	12	7	1	8															3
	2	3	4		6		9†		10	11*	5	14	1	8		7	12												4
	2	3	9†		6*				10	14	5		1	8	11	7	4	12											5
	2	14	6†		3				10		5		1	8		12	4		9*	7	11								6
	2	14	6		3		12		10		5		1	8		4			9*	7†11									7
	2	3	6†		7			9*10			5	14	1	8		4	12			11									8
1	2	3	14		8			9	10	11†	5			6		4	12		7*										9
1	2	3			14			9*10		11	5			6		4	12		7	8†									10
1	2	14			11		9	10	12	5*				6	8	4	7			3†									11
1	2	3			12				10	5				6	11	4	9		7*	8									12
1	2	3	14		11†				10	5				6	8*	4	9		7	12									13
1		3†14			11			10	12	5				6	8	4	9		7*			2							14
1		2			11*			10	7	5				6	8	4	9							3	12				15
1		6	14	3				10	7	5				8	4	9*								2†11	12				16
1		6	12	3				10	7	5				8	4*	9								2	11				17
1		6	11					10	7	12	5			8	4	9*								2	3				18
1		6	11					10	7	12	5			8	4	9*								2	3				19
1		6	11					10	7	5*				8	4	12	9†		14					2	3				20
1	2	3	8		6	11			10	7*				5†		4	12		9	14									21
1		3	2		6	11†			10	7*				5		4	8	12						14			9		22
1		3	6		2				10	11*				5		4	12	7						8			9		23
1		3	4		6				10	11				5	14	12			7†	8				2			9*		24
1		3	12		6				10	11				5		8	4*		7†14					2			9		25
1		3*12			6				10	11				5		8	4		7					2			9		26
1		3			6			12	10	11				5		8	4		7					2			9*		27
1		3	14		6			12	10	11				5		8	4		7†					2			9*		28
1		3	4		6				10	11				5		8			7*	12				2			9		29
1		3	8		6				10	11				5		4			7					2			9		30
1	2	3			6	8			10	11				5		4	7	12									9*		31
1	2	3			6†	8			10	11*				5		4	7			14							9	12	32
1	2	3	6						10	11*				5		8	4		7	12							9		33
1	2	3	6			14		12	10	11				5		8†	4		7*	9								12	34
1	2	3	6			11		9	10					5		8	4*		7									12	35
1		3	6			11		9	10					5		4			7†	12	14	2*	8						36
1	2	3	6			11		9	10					5		4			7†	12	14		8*						37
1	6	3	14			11		9	10					5	7†				4	8	2*						12		38
31	21	28	19	3	24	17	9	11	38	25	12	1	7	37	3	19	31	3	24	13	2	3	1	16	8	—	12	—	
		+ 10s			+ 4s	+ 1s		5s		+ 4s	2s			+ 6s			+ 1s	3s		5s	3s	4s	1s	+ 4s	3s		+ 1s	2s	+ 3s	

Rumbelows Cup Second Round Northampton T (a) 1-0
                               (h) 2-1
             Third Round Everton (h) 2-1
             Fourth Round Tottenham H (h) 0-2
FA Cup   Third Round Luton T (h) 1-3

SHEFFIELD UNITED

Player and Position	Ht	Wt	Birth Date	Place	Source	Clubs	League App	Gls
Goalkeepers								
Richard Harrison*			11 1 72	Sheffield	Trainee	Sheffield U	—	—
Phil Kite	6 1	14 07	26 10 62	Bristol	Apprentice	Bristol R	96	—
						Tottenham H (loan)		
						Southampton	4	—
						Middlesbrough (loan)	2	—
						Gillingham	70	—
						Bournemouth	7	—
						Sheffield U	7	—
Simon Tracey	6 0	13 00	9 12 67	Woolwich	Apprentice	Wimbledon	1	—
						Sheffield U	84	—
Defenders								
David Barnes	5 10	11 01	16 11 61	London	Apprentice	Coventry C	9	—
						Ipswich T	17	—
						Wolverhampton W	88	4
						Aldershot	69	1
						Sheffield U	52	1
Paul Beesley	6 1	11 05	21 7 65	Wigan		Wigan Ath	155	3
						Leyton Orient	32	1
						Sheffield U	37	1
Colin Hill	5 11	12 02	12 11 63	Hillingdon	Apprentice	Arsenal	46	1
						Brighton & HA (loan)	—	—
					Maritimo	Colchester U	69	—
						Sheffield U	67	—
Mark Morris	6 0	11 10	26 9 62	Morden	Apprentice	Wimbledon	168	9
						Aldershot (loan)	14	—
						Watford	41	1
						Sheffield U	56	3
John Pemberton	5 11	12 03	11 11 64	Oldham	Chadderton	Rochdale	1	—
						Crewe Alex	121	1
						Crystal Palace	78	2
						Sheffield U	21	—
Cliff Powell	6 0	12 00	21 2 68	Watford	Apprentice	Watford	—	—
						Hereford U (loan)	7	—
						Sheffield U	10	—
						Doncaster R (loan)	4	—
						Cardiff C (loan)	1	—
Brian Smith	5 9	11 02	27 10 66	Sheffield	Local	Sheffield U	84	—
						Scunthorpe U (loan)	6	1
Mitch Ward	5 8	10 07	18 6 71	Sheffield	Trainee	Sheffield U	4	—
						Crewe Alex (loan)	4	1
Chris Wilder	5 10	10 08	23 9 67	Wortley	Apprentice	Southampton	—	—
						Sheffield U	89	1
						Walsall (loan)	4	—
						Charlton Ath (loan)	1	—
Midfield								
Bob Booker	6 2	12 04	25 1 58	Watford	Bedmond Sp	Brentford	251	41
						Sheffield U	97	13
Ian Bryson	5 11	11 11	26 11 62	Kilmarnock		Kilmarnock	215	40
						Sheffield U	105	24
Steve Circuit‡	5 9	10 07	11 4 72	Sheffield	Trainee	Sheffield U	—	—
John Gannon	5 8	10 10	18 12 66	Wimbledon	Apprentice	Wimbledon	16	2
						Crewe Alex (loan)	15	—
						Sheffield U (loan)	16	1
						Sheffield U	61	3
Jamie Hoyland	6 0	12 08	23 1 66	Sheffield	Apprentice	Manchester C	2	—
						Bury	172	35
						Sheffield U	21	—
Vinny Jones	5 11	11 10	5 1 65	Watford	Wealdstone	Wimbledon	77	9
						Leeds U	46	5
						Sheffield U	31	2
Michael Lake	6 1	13 07	16 11 66	Manchester	Macclesfield T	Sheffield U	11	—
Richard Lucas	5 10	11 04	22 9 70	Sheffield	Trainee	Sheffield U	9	—
Brian Marwood	5 7	11 06	5 2 60	Seaham Harbour	Apprentice	Hull C	158	51
						Sheffield W	128	27
						Arsenal	52	16
						Sheffield U	17	2

SHEFFIELD UNITED

Foundation: In March 1889, Yorkshire County Cricket Club formed Sheffield United six days after an FA Cup semi-final between Preston North End and West Bromwich Albion had finally convinced Charles Stokes, a member of the cricket club, that the formation of a professional football club would prove successful at Bramall Lane. The United's first secretary, Mr. J. B. Wostinholm was also secretary of the cricket club.

First Football League game: 3 September, 1892, Division 2, v Lincoln C (h) W 4-2 – Lilley; Witham, Cain; Howell, Hendry, Needham (1); Wallace, Dobson, Hammond (3), Davies, Drummond.

Did you know: United's goalscoring giant Jimmy Dunne once scored four goals in each of two successive First Division games – v Walsall (4-2) January 1, 1930 and v Leicester (7-1) three days later. He followed this by scoring in a 2-1 defeat of Leicester in the FA Cup.

Managers (and Secretary-managers)
J. B. Wostinholm 1889–1899*, John Nicholson 1899–1932, Ted Davison 1932–52, Reg Freeman 1952–55, Joe Mercer 1955–58, Johnny Harris 1959–68 (continued as GM to 1970), Arthur Rowley 1968–69, Johnny Harris (GM resumed TM duties) 1969–73, Ken Furphy 1973–75, Jimmy Sirrel 1975–77, Harry Haslam 1978–81, Martin Peters 1981, Ian Porterfield 1981–86, Billy McEwan 1986–88, Dave Bassett January 1988– .

Player and Position	Ht	Wt	Birth Date	Birth Place	Source	Clubs	League App	Gls
Mark Todd	5 7	10 00	4 12 67	Belfast	Trainee	Manchester U	—	—
						Sheffield U	70	5
						Wolverhampton W (loan)	7	—
Dane Whitehouse	5 8	10 12	14 10 70	Sheffield	Trainee	Sheffield U	21	1
Julian Winter	6 0	11 02	6 9 65	Huddersfield	Local	Huddersfield T	93	5
						Scunthorpe U (loan)	4	—
						Sheffield U	—	—
Forwards								
Tony Agana	5 11	12 02	2 10 63	London	Weymouth	Watford	15	1
						Sheffield U	105	38
Carl Bradshaw	6 0	11 00	2 10 68	Sheffield	Apprentice	Sheffield W	32	4
						Barnsley (loan)	6	1
						Manchester C	5	—
						Sheffield U	57	4
Brian Deane	6 3	12 07	7 2 68	Leeds	Apprentice	Doncaster R	66	12
						Sheffield U	126	56
Peter Duffield	5 6	10 07	4 2 69	Middlesbrough		Middlesbrough		
						Sheffield U	56	14
						Halifax T (loan)	12	6
						Rotherham U (loan)	17	4
Glyn Hodges	6 0	12 03	30 4 63	Streatham	Apprentice	Wimbledon	232	49
						Newcastle U	7	—
						Watford	86	15
						Crystal Palace	7	—
						Sheffield U	12	4
John Reed	5 6	8 11	27 8 72	Rotherham	Trainee	Sheffield U	—	—
						Scarborough (loan)	14	5
Paul Wood	5 9	10 01	1 11 64	Middlesbrough	Apprentice	Portsmouth	47	6
						Brighton & HA	92	8
						Sheffield U	24	3
						Bournemouth (loan)	21	—

Trainees
Atkinson, Timothy; Brocklehurst, David; Cherrill, Matthew G; Evans, James D; Godwin, Jon B; Heywood, Colin L.J; Ingram, Stephen; Jaques, John W; Kent, Shane R; Morris, Lee; Reaney, Andrew; Roberts, Dean E; Stammers, Christopher A.

Associated Schoolboys
Baldwin, Stephen M; Crump, Andrew J; Fowell, Keith M; Harris, Raymond M; Henderson, Dean; Laidlaw, James R; Letts, Simon C; McGovern, Craig P; Quinn, Wayne R; Sampey, Mark P; Taylor, James A; Tee, Jason K; Vine, Darren M; Ward, Timothy M.J; Wright, John D; Zivkovic, Barry L.

Associated Schoolboys who have accepted the club's offer of a Traineeship/Contract
Anthony, Graham J; Battersby, Anthony; Butterfield, Timothy; Cope, Steven G; Dickerson, Ian; Foreman, Matthew B; Myhill, Craig S; Thomson, Martin R; Wainwright, Daniel J; Wainwright, Lee A.

SHEFFIELD WEDNESDAY 1990-91 *Back row (left to right)*: Peter Shirtliff, Chris Turner, Carlton Palmer, Kevin Pressman, Lawrie Madden.
Centre row: Roger Spry (Coach), Richie Barker (Assistant Manager), John Sheridan, Dave Bennett, Philip King, Steve McCall, Nigel Worthington, David Hirst, Alan Smith (Physiotherapist)
Front row: Roland Nilsson, Darren Wood, Paul Williams, Ron Atkinson (Manager), Nigel Pearson, Danny Wilson, Trevor Francis.

Division 1   **SHEFFIELD WEDNESDAY**

Hillsborough, Sheffield, S6 1SW. Telephone Sheffield (0742) 343122. Box Office: Sheffield 337233. Clubcall: 0898 121186.

Ground capacity: 37,323.

Record attendance: 72,841 v Manchester C, FA Cup 5th rd, 17 February 1934.

Record receipts: £398,134, Liverpool v Nottingham F, FA Cup semi-final, 9 April 1988.

Pitch measurements: 115yd × 75yd.

Chairman: D. G. Richards. *Vice-chairman:* K. T. Addy.

Directors: C. Woodward, E. Barron, G. K. Hulley, R. M. Grierson FCA, J. Ashton MP.

Manager: Trevor Francis. *Assistant Manager:* Richie Barker.

Physio: A. Smith.

Secretary: G. H. Mackrell FCCA. *Commercial Manager:* R. Gorrill (Tel. 0742 337235).

Year Formed: 1867 (fifth oldest League club).

Turned Professional: 1887. *Ltd Co.:* 1899.

Club Nickname: 'The Owls'.

Previous Grounds: 1867, Highfield; 1869, Myrtle Road; 1877, Sheaf House; 1887, Olive Grove; 1899, Owlerton (since 1912 known as Hillsborough). Some games were played at Endcliffe in the 1880s. Until 1895 Bramall Lane was used for some games.

Record League Victory: 9-1 v Birmingham, Division 1, 13 December 1930 – Brown; Walker, Blenkinsop; Strange, Leach, Wilson; Hooper (3), Seed (2), Ball (2), Burgess (1), Rimmer (1).

Record Cup Victory: 12-0 v Halliwell, FA Cup, 1st rd, 17 January 1891 – Smith; Thompson, Brayshaw; Harry Brandon (1), Betts, Cawley (2); Winterbottom, Mumford (2), Bob Brandon (1), Woolhouse (5), Ingram (1).

Record Defeat: 0-10 v Aston Villa, Division 1, 5 October 1912.

Most League Points (2 for a win): 62, Division 2, 1958–59.

Most League Points (3 for a win): 88, Division 2, 1983–84.

Most League Goals: 106, Division 2, 1958–59.

Highest League Scorer in Season: Derek Dooley, 46, Division 2, 1951–52.

Most League Goals in Total Aggregate: Andy Wilson, 199, 1900–20.

Most Capped Player: Ron Springett, 33, England.

Most League Appearances: Andy Wilson, 502, 1900–20.

Record Transfer Fee Received: £1,750,000 from Real Sociedad for Dalian Atkinson, July 1990.

Record Transfer Fee Paid: £750,000 to WBA for Carlton Palmer, February 1989.

Football League Record: 1892 Elected to Division 1; 1899–1900 Division 2; 1900–20 Division 1; 1920–26 Division 2; 1926–37 Division 1; 1937–50 Division 2; 1950–51 Division 1; 1951–52 Division 2; 1952–55 Division 1; 1955–56 Division 2; 1956–58 Division 1; 1958–59 Division 2; 1959–70 Division 1; 1970–75 Division 2; 1975–80 Division 3; 1980–84 Division 2; 1984–90 Division 1; 1990–91 Division 2; 1991– Division 1.

Honours: Football League: Division 1 – Champions 1902–03, 1903–04, 1928–29, 1929–30; Runners-up 1960–61; Division 2 – Champions 1899–1900, 1925–26, 1951–52, 1955–56, 1958–59; Runners-up 1949–50, 1983–84. *FA Cup:* Winners 1896, 1907, 1935; Runners-up 1890, 1966. *Football League Cup:* Winners 1990–91. **European Competitions:** *Fairs Cup:* 1961–62, 1963–64.

Colours: Blue and white striped shirts, black shorts, blue stockings. **Change colours:** Yellow shirts, sky blue shorts, sky stockings.

SHEFFIELD WEDNESDAY 1990–91 LEAGUE RECORD

Match No.	Date		Venue	Opponents	Result		H/T Score	Lg. Pos.	Goalscorers	Atten- dance
1	Aug 25		A	Ipswich T	W	2-0	2-0	—	Williams, Shirtliff	17,284
2	Sept	1	H	Hull C	W	5-1	2-1	2	Hirst 4, Williams	23,673
3		8	A	Charlton Ath	W	1-0	0-0	2	Sheridan	7407
4		15	H	Watford	W	2-0	1-0	2	Pearson, Worthington	22,061
5		18	H	Newcastle U	D	2-2	1-1	—	Hirst, McCall	30,628
6		22	A	Leicester C	W	4-2	2-1	2	Hirst 2, Wilson, Williams	16,156
7		29	H	West Ham U	D	1-1	1-0	2	Hirst	28,786
8	Oct	3	A	Brighton & HA	W	4-0	2-0	—	Wilson, Sheridan, Williams, Pearson	10,379
9		6	A	Bristol R	W	1-0	1-0	2	Francis	6413
10		13	H	Plymouth Arg	W	3-0	2-0	1	Wilson, Sheridan 2	23,489
11		20	H	Port Vale	D	1-1	1-0	2	Williams	24,527
12		23	A	Barnsley	D	1-1	0-0	—	Palmer	23,079
13		27	A	Millwall	L	2-4	2-0	3	Hirst 2	12,863
14	Nov	3	H	Oldham Ath	D	2-2	0-2	3	Sheridan 2 (2 pens)	34,845
15		10	A	Blackburn R	L	0-1	0-1	3		13,437
16		17	H	Swindon T	W	2-1	1-0	3	Williams, Pearson	22,715
17		24	A	WBA	W	2-1	0-1	3	Francis, Shirtliff	16,546
18	Dec	1	H	Notts Co	D	2-2	2-0	4	Sheridan (pen), Hirst	23,474
19		8	A	Bristol C	D	1-1	1-1	3	Wilson	11,254
20		15	H	Ipswich T	D	2-2	1-2	3	Francis, Pearson	19,333
21		22	A	Oxford U	D	2-2	2-1	3	Hirst, Wilson	6061
22		26	H	Wolverhampton W	D	2-2	2-0	4	McCall, Palmer	29,686
23		29	H	Portsmouth	W	2-1	1-0	3	Hirst 2	22,885
24	Jan	1	A	Middlesbrough	W	2-0	1-0	3	Hirst, Williams	22,869
25		12	A	Hull C	W	1-0	1-0	3	Williams	10,907
26		19	H	Charlton Ath	D	0-0	0-0	3		22,318
27	Feb	2	A	Watford	D	2-2	0-2	3	Harkes, Williams	10,338
28		19	A	Swindon T	L	1-2	0-0	—	Hirst	8274
29	Mar	2	A	Notts Co	W	2-0	1-0	3	Williams, Thomas (og)	15,546
30		9	H	WBA	W	1-0	0-0	3	Sheridan (pen)	26,934
31		13	H	Brighton & H A	D	1-1	1-0	—	Anderson	23,969
32		16	A	West Ham U	W	3-1	0-0	3	Hirst, Williams 2	26,182
33		19	A	Plymouth Arg	D	1-1	0-0	—	MacKenzie	7806
34		23	H	Bristol R	W	2-1	0-0	3	Clark (og), Williams	25,074
35		30	A	Wolverhampton W	L	2-3	0-2	3	Pearson 2	18,011
36	Apr	1	H	Oxford U	L	0-2	0-0	3		28,682
37		6	A	Portsmouth	L	0-2	0-1	3		10,390
38		10	H	Blackburn R	W	3-1	0-1	—	Anderson, Sheridan 2 (1 pen)	23,139
39		13	H	Middlesbrough	W	2-0	0-0	3	Williams 2	30,598
40		17	A	Newcastle U	L	0-1	0-1	—		18,330
41		24	H	Leicester C	D	0-0	0-0	—		31,308
42		27	H	Barnsley	W	3-1	1-1	3	Hirst, Harkes, MacKenzie	30,693
43	May	4	A	Millwall	W	2-1	1-0	3	Hirst 2	30,278
44		6	A	Port Vale	D	1-1	0-0	—	Hirst	13,317
45		8	H	Bristol C	W	3-1	1-0	—	Hirst 2, Francis	31,706
46		11	A	Oldham Ath	L	2-3	1-0	3	Hirst, Wilson	18,809

Final League Position: 3

GOALSCORERS

League (80): Hirst 24, Williams 15, Sheridan 10 (5 pens), Pearson 6, Wilson 6, Francis 4, Anderson 2, Harkes 2, McCall 2, MacKenzie 2, Palmer 2, Shirtliff 2, Worthington 1, own goals 2.
Rumbelows Cup (15): Pearson 5, Hirst 3, Williams 2, Francis 1, Harkes 1, Sheridan 1, Shirtliff 1, Wilson 1.
FA Cup (8): Hirst 2, Anderson 1, Francis 1, Palmer 1, Pearson 1, Sheridan 1 (pen), Shirtliff 1.

FA Cup			
	Third Round	Mansfield T (a)	2-0
	Fourth Round	Millwall (a)	4-4
		(h)	2-0
	Fifth Round	Cambridge U (a)	0-4

Pressman	Nilsson	King	Palmer	Shirtliff	Pearson	Wilson	Sheridan	Hirst	Williams	Worthington	Francis	McCall	Madden	Whitton	Harkes	Turner	Anderson	Watson	MacKenzie	Newsome	Match No.
1	2	3	4	5	6	7	8	9	10	11											1
1	2	3	4	5	6*	7	8	9	10	11†	12	14									2
1	2	3	4	5	6	7	8	9	10	11											3
1	2	3	4	5	6	7	8	9	10	11											4
1	2	3	4	5	6	7*	8	9	10	11†	12	14									5
1	2	3	4	5	6	7	8	9*	10	11	12										6
1	2	3	4	5	6	7*	8	9	10	11	12										7
1	2	3	4	5	6	7	8†		10*	11	9	14	12								8
1	2	3	4	5	6	7	8		10	11	9*		12								9
1	2	3	4	5	6	7	8		10	11†	9*	14	12								10
1	2	3	4	5	6	7	8	12	10	11	9*										11
1	2	3*	4	5	6	7	8	9	10	11	12										12
1	2*	3	4	5	6†	7	8	9	10	11	12	14									13
1		3*	4	5	6	7	8	9	10	11	12				2						14
1		3	4	5	6	7	8	9	10	11*	12				2						15
1		3	4	5	6	7	8	9*	10	11†	12	14			2						16
1		3	4	5	6	7	8	9	10*	11	12				2						17
1		3	4	5	6	7	8*	9	10	11	12				2						18
1		3	4	5	6	7	8	9	12	11	10*				2						19
1		3*	4	5	6	7	8	9	10	11	12				2						20
1		3	4	5	6	7	8	9	10	11					2						21
1		3	4	5	6	7	8	9	10						2						22
		3	4	5	6	7*	8	9	10	11†	12	14			2	1					23
		3	4	5	6	7	8	9*	10	11	12				2	1					24
		3	4	5	6	7	8	9	10	11*	12					1	2				25
		3	4	5	6	7*	8	9	10	11	12					1	2				26
		3	4		6		8	9	10	11*	12	5			7	1	2				27
		3	4	5	6		8	9	10	11*	12				7	1	2				28
		3	4	5	6		8	9	10*	11†					7	1	2	12	14		29
		3	4	5	6		8	9	10	11					7	1	2				30
		3	4	5	6	7*	8	9	10	11†	12					1	2		14		31
		3	4	5	6	7†	8	9*	10	11	12					1	2		14		32
		3	4	5	6	7*	8	9	10	11†						1	2	12	14		33
		3	4	5	6		8	9	10	11*	12				7	1	2				34
		3	4	5	6		8†	9	10	11*	12	14			7	1	2				35
		3	4	5†	6	7*	8	9	10	11						1	2	12	14		36
	2	3	4		6		8	9	10	11*	12				7	1			5		37
	2	3	4	5			8	9	10	11					7	1	6				38
	2	3	4		6		8	9	10	11					7*	1		12	5		39
	2	3	4	5		7*		9	10	11†	12	14				1	6			8	40
	2	3		5	6†	7	8	9	10	11	12				4*	1			14		41
		3	4	5†		7	8	9	10	11*					2	1	6	12	14		42
	2	3	4				8	9	10	11	12				7	1	6		5*		43
	2	3	4			7	8	9	10		12				11	1	6		5*		44
	2†	3	4	5		7	8	9	10*	11	12				14	1	6				45
1	2	3	4			7	8	9	10*	11	12						6		5		46
23	22	43	45	39	39	35	45	39	40	31	18	13	1	—	22	23	21	1	5	1	

+ + + + + + + + + + + +

1s 1s 2s 6s 2s 20s6s 4s 1s 1s 1s 4s 7s

Rumbelows Cup			
	Second Round	Brentford (h)	2-1
		(a)	2-1
	Third Round	Swindon T (h)	0-0
		(a)	1-0
	Fourth Round	Derby Co (h)	1-1
		(a)	2-1
	Fifth Round	Coventry C (a)	1-0
	Semi-final	Chelsea (a)	2-0
		(h)	3-1
	Final	Manchester U (at Wembley)	1-0

SHEFFIELD WEDNESDAY

Player and Position	Ht	Wt	Birth Date	Birth Place	Source	Clubs	League App	Gls
Goalkeepers								
Marlon Beresford	6 1	10 11	2 9 69	Lincoln	Trainee	Sheffield W	—	—
						Bury (loan)	1	—
						Ipswich T (loan)	—	—
						Northampton T (loan)	13	—
						Crewe Alex (loan)	3	—
Lance Key			13 5 68	Kettering	Histon	Sheffield W	—	—
Kevin Pressman	6 1	13 00	6 11 67	Fareham	Apprentice	Sheffield W	58	—
Chris Turner	6 0	12 04	15 9 58	Sheffield	Apprentice	Sheffield W	91	—
						Lincoln C (loan)	5	—
						Sunderland	195	—
						Manchester U	64	—
						Sheffield W	75	—
						Leeds U (loan)	2	—
Defenders								
Viv Anderson	6 0	11 01	29 8 56	Nottingham	Apprentice	Nottingham F	328	15
						Arsenal	120	9
						Manchester U	54	2
						Sheffield W	22	2
Scott Cam	5 9	10 00	3 5 70	Sheffield	Trainee	Sheffield W	—	—
Mark Dickinson*			24 12 71	Howdershire	Trainee	Sheffield W	—	—
Phil King	5 10	12 00	28 12 67	Bristol		Exeter C	27	—
						Torquay U	24	3
						Swindon T	116	4
						Sheffield W	68	—
Steve McCall	5 11	11 03	15 10 60	Carlisle	Apprentice	Ipswich T	257	7
						Sheffield W	29	2
						Carlisle U (loan)	6	—
Lawrie Madden*	5 11	13 01	28 9 55	London	Amateur Manchester Univ	Arsenal	—	—
						Mansfield T	10	—
						Charlton Ath	113	7
						Millwall	47	2
						Sheffield W	212	2
						Leicester C (loan)	3	—
Jon Newsome	6 2	13 11	6 9 70	Sheffield	Trainee	Sheffield W	7	—
Roland Nilsson	6 0	11 06	27 11 63	Helsingborg	Gothenburg	Sheffield W	42	—
Carlton Palmer	5 10	11 00	5 12 65	West Bromwich	Trainee	WBA	121	4
						Sheffield W	92	3
Nigel Pearson	6 1	13 07	21 8 63	Nottingham	Heanor T	Shrewsbury T	153	5
						Sheffield W	128	11
Peter Shirtliff	6 2	13 04	6 4 61	Barnsley	Apprentice	Sheffield W	188	4
						Charlton Ath	103	7
						Sheffield W	72	4
Shaun Sowden			25 3 68	Blackburn	Histon	Sheffield W	—	—
Mark Taylor	5 10	11 00	22 2 66	Walsall	Local	Walsall	113	4
						Sheffield W	9	—
						Shrewsbury T (loan)	19	2
David Wetherall	6 3	12 00	14 3 71	Sheffield	School	Sheffield W	—	—
Darren Wood	5 10	11 08	9 6 64	Scarborough	Apprentice	Middlesbrough	101	6
						Chelsea	144	3
						Sheffield W	11	—
Nigel Worthington	5 10	12 06	4 11 61	Ballymena	Ballymena U	Notts Co	67	4
						Sheffield W	233	5
Midfield								
John Harkes	5 10	11 10	8 3 67	New Jersey	USSF	Sheffield W	23	2
Graham Hyde	5 7	11 07	10 11 70	Doncaster	Trainee	Sheffield W	—	—
Steve MacKenzie	5 11	12 05	23 11 61	Romford	Apprentice	Crystal Palace	—	—
						Manchester C	58	8
						WBA	148	23
						Charlton Ath	100	7
						Sheffield W	12	2
John Sheridan	5 9	10 08	1 10 64	Stretford	Local	Leeds U	230	47
						Nottingham F	—	—
						Sheffield W	73	12

SHEFFIELD WEDNESDAY

Foundation: Sheffield, being one of the principal centres of early Association Football, this club was formed as long ago as 1867 by the Sheffield Wednesday Cricket Club (formed 1825) and their colours from the start were blue and white. The inaugural meeting was held at the Adelphi Hotel and the original committee included Charles Stokes who was subsequently a founder member of Sheffield United.

First Football League game: 3 September, 1892, Division 1, v Notts C (a) W 1-0 – Allan; T. Brandon (1), Mumford; Hall, Betts, H. Brandon; Spiksley, Brady, Davis, R.N. Brown, Dunlop.

Did you know: No club ever had a more brilliant pair of wingers than Wednesday's Mark Hooper and Ellis Rimmer. For nine seasons 1928–37 they did not miss a single FA Cup tie and were both among the scorers when Wednesday won the Trophy in 1935.

Managers (and Secretary-managers)
Arthur Dickinson 1891–1920*, Robert Brown 1920–33, Billy Walker 1933–37, Jimmy McMullan 1937–42, Eric Taylor 1942–58 (continued as GM to 1974), Harry Catterick 1958–61, Vic Buckingham 1961–64, Alan Brown 1964–68, Jack Marshall 1968–69, Danny Williams 1969–71, Derek Dooley 1971–73, Steve Burtenshaw 1974–75, Len Ashurst 1975–77, Jackie Charlton 1977–83, Howard Wilkinson 1983–88, Peter Eustace 1988–89, Ron Atkinson 1989–91, Trevor Francis June 1991–   .

Player and Position	Ht	Wt	Birth Date	Birth Place	Source	Clubs	League App	Gls
Mike Williams	5 8	10 06	21 11 69	Bradford	Maltby	Sheffield W	—	—
Danny Wilson	5 6	11 04	1 1 60	Wigan	Wigan Ath	Bury	90	8
						Chesterfield	100	13
						Nottingham F	10	1
						Scunthorpe U (loan)	6	3
						Brighton & HA	135	33
						Luton T	110	24
						Sheffield W	36	6
Forwards								
Dalian Atkinson (To Real Sociedad July 1990)	6 1	12 10	21 3 68	Shrewsbury		Ipswich T	60	18
						Sheffield W	38	10
Trevor Francis	5 10	11 07	19 4 54	Plymouth	Apprentice	Birmingham C	280	118
						Nottingham F	70	28
						Manchester C	26	12
						Sampdoria	68	17
						Atalanta	21	1
						Rangers	18	—
						QPR	32	12
						Sheffield W	50	4
Sam Goodacre*	5 10	11 00	1 12 70	Sheffield	School	Sheffield W	—	—
David Hirst	5 11	12 05	7 12 67	Barnsley	Apprentice	Barnsley	28	9
						Sheffield W	156	54
David Johnson	6 2	13 08	29 10 70	Rother Valley	Trainee	Sheffield W	—	—
David Lycett*	5 11	13 08	9 9 70	Sheffield	Trainee	Sheffield W	—	—
Gordon Watson	6 0	12 00	20 3 71	Kent	Trainee	Charlton Ath	31	7
						Sheffield W	5	—
Paul Williams	5 7	10 03	16 8 65	London	Woodford T	Charlton Ath	82	23
						Brentford (loan)	7	3
						Sheffield W	46	15

Trainees
Burton, Paul; Chambers, Leroy D; Curzon, Richard E; Dunn, Gareth T; Flint, Jonathon A; Frank, Ian D; Jones, Ryan A; Linighan, Brian; Linighan, John; Robinson, Nicholas; Robinson, Paul; Rowntree, Michael C; Simpson, Ronald K; Smith, Mark A; Stewart, Simon; Wright, Jeremy H.

Associated Schoolboys
Barker, Richard I; Brookfield, Nicholas; Brown, Steven M; Burkill, Matthew J; Burrows, Marc L; Dey, Brendan S; Faulkner, David P; Gallagher, Richard; Gott, Robert; Harrison, Andrew J; Harrison, Dean L A; Jacks, Daniel M; Ludlam, Craig; McCarthy, Lawrence J; McManus, Steven; McVeigh, Michael B; Nankivell, Lee M; Pass, Steven D; Waring, Phillip.

Associated Schoolboys who have accepted the club's offer of a Traineeship/Contract
Baird, Carl A; Dean, Simon J; Holmes, Darren P; Parker, Scott; Rodgers, Neil.

SHREWSBURY TOWN 1990–91 *Back row (left to right):* Tony Kelly, Tom Lynch, Paul Gorham, Steve Perks, Ken Hughes, Micky Heathcote, Kevin Summerfield, Dean Spink. *Front row:* Kenny Clements, Michael Brown, Mark Blake, Carl Griffiths, Graeme Worsley, Gary Shaw, Billy Askew.

Division 3   **SHREWSBURY TOWN**

Gay Meadow, Shrewsbury. Telephone Shrewsbury (0743) 60111. Commercial Dept: 56316. Clubcall: 0898 121194.

Ground capacity: 15,000.

Record attendance: 18,917 v Walsall, Division 3, 26 April 1961.

Record receipts: £36,240 v Ipswich T, FA Cup 5th rd, 13 February 1982.

Pitch measurements: 116yd × 76yd.

President: *Vice-president:* Dr J. Millard Bryson.

Chairman: K. R. Woodhouse.

Directors: A. C. Williams, F. C. G. Fry, R. Bailey, M. J. Starkey, G. W. Nelson, W. H. Richards.

Manager: John Bond. *Commercial Manager:* M. Thomas.

Physio: L. Helm. *Coach:*

Secretary: M. J. Starkey.

Club Nickname: 'Town' or 'Shrews'.

Year Formed: 1886. *Turned Professional:* 1905 (approx). *Ltd Co.:* 1936.

Previous Ground: Old Shrewsbury Racecourse.

Record League Victory: 7-0 v Swindon T, Division 3 (S), 6 May 1955 – McBride; Bannister, Keech; Wallace, Maloney, Candlin; Price, O'Donnell (1), Weigh (4), Russell, McCue (2).

Record Cup Victory: 7-1 v Banbury Spencer, FA Cup, 1st rd, 4 November 1961 – Gibson; Walters, Skeech; Wallace, Pountney, Harley; Kenning (2), Pragg, Starkey (1), Rowley (2), McLaughlin (2).

Record Defeat: 1-8 v Norwich C, Division 3 (S), 1952–53 and v Coventry C, Division 3, 22 October 1963.

Most League Points (2 for a win): 62, Division 4, 1974–75.

Most League Points (3 for a win): 65, Division 2, 1984–85.

Most League Goals: 101, Division 4, 1958–59.

Highest League Scorer in Season: Arthur Rowley, 38, Division 4, 1958–59.

Most League Goals in Total Aggregate: Arthur Rowley, 152, 1958–65 (thus completing his League record of 434 goals).

Most Capped Player: Jimmy McLaughlin, 5 (12), Northern Ireland and Bernard McNally, 5, Northern Ireland.

Most League Appearances: Colin Griffin, 406, 1975–89.

Record Transfer Fee Received: £385,000 from WBA for Bernard McNally, July 1989.

Record Transfer Fee Paid: £100,000 to Aldershot for John Dungworth, November 1979 and £100,000 to Southampton for Mark Blake, August 1990.

Football League Record: 1950 Elected to Division 3 (N); 1951–58 Division 3 (S); 1958–59 Division 4; 1959–74 Division 3; 1974–75 Division 4; 1975–79 Division 3; 1979–89 Division 2; 1989– Division 3.

Honours: Football League: Division 2 best season: 8th, 1983–84, 1984–85; Division 3 – Champions 1978–79; Division 4 – Runners-up 1974–5. *FA Cup:* best season: 6th rd, 1978–79, 1981–82. *Football League Cup:* Semi-final 1961. *Welsh Cup:* Winners 1891, 1938, 1977, 1979, 1984, 1985; Runners-up 1931, 1948, 1980.

Colours: Amber/blue trim shirts, blue trim, blue shorts, amber stockings, blue trim. **Change colours:** Red shirts, white shorts, red stockings.

SHREWSBURY TOWN 1990–91 LEAGUE RECORD

Match No.	Date	Venue	Opponents	Result	H/T Score	Lg. Pos.	Goalscorers	Attendance
1	Aug 25	H	Bolton W	L	0-1 0-0	—		4608
2	Sept 1	A	Rotherham U	D	2-2 0-1	18	Naughton, Law (og)	4817
3	8	H	Fulham	D	2-2 1-0	19	Spink, Moore	2929
4	14	A	Tranmere R	D	1-1 0-1	—	Weir	7105
5	18	A	Southend U	L	1-2 1-2	—	Clark (og)	5100
6	22	H	Grimsby T	L	1-2 0-0	22	Lynch	2904
7	29	A	Stoke C	W	3-1 2-1	19	Spink, Sandford (og), Worsley	12,672
8	Oct 2	H	Bury	D	1-1 0-0	—	Shaw	3258
9	6	H	Mansfield T	L	0-3 0-1	21		2587
10	13	A	Leyton Orient	L	2-3 1-3	22	Spink, Summerfield	4394
11	20	A	Chester C	L	2-3 0-1	24	Shaw, Clarke (pen)	1431
12	23	H	Swansea C	L	1-2 0-1	—	Summerfield	2589
13	27	H	Birmingham C	W	4-1 2-0	21	Clarke 3, Wimbleton	6050
14	Nov 3	A	Bournemouth	L	2-3 2-2	22	Lynch, Summerfield	5561
15	9	H	Crewe Alex	W	1-0 0-0	—	Clarke	4461
16	24	A	Cambridge U	L	1-3 0-2	21	Clarke	3632
17	Dec 1	A	Preston NE	L	3-4 0-2	22	Summerfield, Blake, Kelly	4515
18	15	H	Wigan Ath	D	0-0 0-0	23		2227
19	22	H	Bradford C	W	4-2 1-2	20	Blake, Shaw 3	5722
20	29	H	Exeter C	D	2-2 1-0	22	Heathcote, Spink	3179
21	Jan 1	A	Brentford	L	0-3 0-1	22		7064
22	12	H	Rotherham U	D	0-0 0-0	21		2800
23	19	A	Bolton W	L	0-1 0-0	22		6164
24	Feb 2	H	Southend U	L	0-1 0-1	23		4377
25	5	A	Grimsby T	L	0-1 0-0	—		5683
26	19	H	Huddersfield T	D	0-0 0-0	—		2821
27	22	A	Crewe Alex	W	2-1 0-0	—	Smart (og), Taylor	3940
28	Mar 2	H	Preston N E	L	0-1 0-1	23		2989
29	9	A	Wigan Ath	D	2-2 1-1	23	Brown, Summerfield	2269
30	12	A	Bury	L	1-2 0-1	—	Kelly	2417
31	16	H	Stoke C	W	2-0 2-0	22	Lyne 2	6210
32	19	H	Leyton Orient	W	3-0 0-0	—	Fee (og), Spink, Taylor	2236
33	23	A	Mansfield T	L	1-2 0-1	21	Lyne	2524
34	26	H	Tranmere R	L	0-1 0-0	—		3949
35	30	A	Huddersfield T	L	1-2 1-2	21	Lyne	5684
36	Apr 2	H	Bradford C	W	1-0 0-0	—	Heathcote	3090
37	9	A	Fulham	L	0-4 0-0	—		3415
38	13	H	Brentford	D	1-1 0-0	22	Spink	2841
39	18	H	Cambridge U	L	1-2 0-1	—	Heathcote	2571
40	20	H	Chester C	W	1-0 1-0	21	Heathcote	2952
41	23	A	Reading	W	2-1 2-1	—	Griffiths 2	2422
42	27	A	Swansea C	W	1-0 0-0	20	Harris (og)	3152
43	30	A	Exeter C	L	0-3 0-1	—		2763
44	May 4	A	Birmingham C	W	1-0 1-0	20	Griffiths	6256
45	7	H	Reading	W	5-1 4-1	—	Kelly 3, Lyne, Griffiths	2425
46	11	H	Bournemouth	W	3-1 0-0	18	Heathcote 2, Lyne	5016

Final League Position: 18

GOALSCORERS

League (61): Clarke 6 (1 pen), Heathcote 6, Lyne 6, Spink 6, Kelly 5, Shaw 5, Summerfield 5, Griffiths 4, Blake 2, Lynch 2, Taylor 2, Brown 1, Moore 1, Naughton 1, Weir 1, Wimbleton 1, Worsley 1, own goals 6.
Rumbelows Cup (3): Griffiths 1, Kelly 1, Moore 1.
FA Cup (8): Shaw 5, Brown 1, Kelly 1 (pen), Spink 1.

Perks	Worsley	Lynch	Kelly	Heathcote	Blake	Griffiths	Wimbleton	Spink	Brown	Gorman	Moore	Naughton	Hartford	Weir	Coughlin	Shaw	Ryan	Summerfield	Parrish	Hughes	Clarke	Clements	Askew	Taylor	Lyne	Burton	O'Toole	Match No.
1	2†	3	4	5	6	7*	8	9	10	11	12	14																1
1	2	3	4	5	6		12	9	10				7		11	8*												2
1	2	3	4†	5	6		12	9	10				7		11*	8	14											3
1	2	12	4*	5	6	11	8	9	10†	3	7		14															4
1	2		4*	5	6	11	8	9	10	3	7					12												5
1	2	12	4	5	6	11		9*	10	3	7					8												6
1	2		4	5	6	11	12	9	10*	3	7					8												7
1	2	12	4	5*	6	11		9	10	3			14		8†	7												8
1	2	12	4	5	6	11*		9†	10	3	7					8		14										9
1	2	12	4	5*	6			9	10	3			14			7†		8	11									10
	2	3	4	5	6				10		12		11*			7		8		1	9							11
	2	3	4	5	6	7	12						11*			9		8		1	10							12
	2	3	4		6	12	14	7	5				11†			9†		8		1	10							13
	2	3	4		6	12		7	5				11			9*		8		1	10							14
	2	3	4		6	11	12	7	5†							9*		8		1	10		14					15
		3	4	5	6	11	12	7	2				14			9†		8*		1	10							16
	2	3	4		6	11	12	7	8							9*		14		1	10		5†					17
	2	3	4		6	10*	11	9	7		12		14					8†		1		5						18
		3	4	11	6			9	7	2						10		8		1		5						19
		3		11	6	12		9	7*	2			14		4†	10		8		1		5						20
		3		11	6	12		9	7	2*			4†		14	10		8		1		5						21
	2	3	4*	11	6	12		9	7				14			10		8†		1		5						22
	2	3		11	6	12		9	7						4*	10		8		1		5						23
14		3	4	11	6	12		9*	7							10		2†		1		5		8				24
		3	4	11	6	12		9	7							10*		2		1		5		8				25
		3	4		6			9	7							10		2		1		5		8	11			26
	2	3	4		6			9	10							7				1		5		8	11			27
	5	3	4	12	2			9	7							8†		14		1		6		11*	10			28
	11	3	4	5	2	12			7							8*		9		1		6		10				29
	11	3	4	5	2	12			7							8*	14	9		1		6		10†				30
		3	4	5	2		8		7									9		1		6		10	11			31
		3	4	5	2		8		7									9		1		6		10	11			32
	12	3	4*	5	2		8		7									9		1		6		10	11			33
		4		5	2		8		7	3	12									1		6		10	11		9*	34
		4†	5	2	14	12			7	3										1		6*		10	11	9	8	35
		4	5	2	9	8			7*	3										1				10	11	12	6	36
		4	5	2	8				7	3						9				1				10	11	12	6*	37
		4	5	2	12	8			7	3						9*				1				10	11		6	38
	6	4	5	2	12	8			7	3										1				10	11		9*	39
	6	4	5	2	9*	12			7	3										1				10	11		8	40
	6	4	5	2	9*	12				3						7				1				10	11		8	41
	6		5	2	4	9†				3*			14			7				1				10	11	12	8	42
	3	6	5	2	9†	14	12		7											1				10	11	4*	8	43
	3	6	5	2	9				4							7				1				10	11		8	44
14	6†	4	5	2	9	12			7	3										1		10			11		8*	45
14	6	4	5	2	9	12			7	3†						8*				1		10			11			46
10	27	34	38	38	46	14	9	30	43	27	7	3	8	—	4	20	1	30	1	36	7	19	5	19	16	3	11	
	+4s	+5s		+1s		+5s	+9s	+13s		+3s	+1s	+3s			+8s	+1s	+2s	+1s	+2s		+1s			+3s				

Rumbelows Cup

Rumbelows Cup	First Round	Gillingham (a)	0-1
		(h)	2-0
	Second Round	Ipswich T (h)	1-1
		(a)	0-3
FA Cup	First Round	Bradford C (a)	0-0
		(h)	2-1
	Second Round	Chorley (h)	1-0
	Third Round	Watford (h)	4-1
	Fourth Round	Wimbledon (h)	1-0
	Fifth Round	Arsenal (h)	0-1

SHREWSBURY TOWN

Player and Position	Ht	Wt	Birth Date	Place	Source	Clubs	League App	Gls
Goalkeepers								
Scott Cooksey‡			24 6 72	Birmingham	Derby Co	Shrewsbury T	—	—
Ken Hughes	6 0	11 08	9 1 66	Barmouth		Crystal Palace	—	—
						Shrewsbury T	51	—
Steve Perks	6 0	12 02	19 4 63	Shrewsbury	Apprentice	Shrewsbury T	221	—
Defenders								
Mark Blake	6 0	12 04	19 12 67	Portsmouth	Apprentice	Southampton	18	2
						Colchester U (loan)	4	1
						Shrewsbury T (loan)	10	—
						Shrewsbury T	46	2
Kenny Clements*	6 1	12 06	9 4 55	Manchester	Amateur	Manchester C	119	—
						Oldham Ath	206	2
						Manchester C (loan)	12	1
						Manchester C	94	—
						Bury	81	1
						Shrewsbury T	20	—
Mike Heathcote	6 2	12 05	10 9 65	Durham		Middlesbrough	—	—
					Spennymoor U	Sunderland	9	—
						Halifax T (loan)	7	1
						York C (loan)	3	—
						Shrewsbury T	39	6
David Moyes (To Dunfermline Ath Aug 1990)	6 1	11 05	25 4 63	Blythswood	Drumchapel A	Celtic	24	—
						Cambridge U	79	1
						Bristol C	83	6
						Shrewsbury T	96	11
Sean Parrish	5 9	10 00	14 3 72	Wrexham	Trainee	Shrewsbury T	3	—
Graeme Worsley	5 10	11 02	4 1 69	Liverpool	Bootle	Shrewsbury T	52	1
Midfield								
Micky Burton‡	5 9	11 03	5 11 69	Birmingham	Trainee	Birmingham C	4	—
						Sheffield W	—	—
						Shrewsbury T	6	—
Paul Gorman	5 10	11 08	6 8 63	Dublin	Apprentice	Arsenal	6	—
						Birmingham C	6	—
						Carlisle U	148	7
						Shelbourne (loan)	—	—
						Shrewsbury T	49	1
Tony Kelly	5 10	11 09	1 10 64	Liverpool	Apprentice	Liverpool	—	—
						Derby Co	—	—
						Wigan Ath	101	15
						Stoke C	36	4
						WBA	26	1
						Chester C (loan)	5	—
						Colchester U (loan)	13	2
						Shrewsbury T	101	15
Tommy Lynch	6 0	12 06	10 10 64	Limerick	Limerick	Sunderland	4	—
						Shrewsbury T	61	2
Patrick O'Toole	5 7	11 00	2 1 65	Dublin	Shelbourne	Leicester C	—	—
						Exeter C (loan)	6	—
						Shrewsbury T	11	—
Darren Ryan			3 7 72	Oswestry	Trainee	Shrewsbury T	2	—
Kevin Summerfield	5 11	11 00	7 1 59	Walsall	Apprentice	WBA	9	4
						Birmingham C	5	1
						Walsall	54	17
						Cardiff C	10	1
						Plymouth Arg	139	26
						Exeter C (loan)	4	—
						Shrewsbury T	32	5

SHREWSBURY TOWN

Foundation: Shrewsbury School having provided a number of the early England and Wales internationals it is not surprising that there was a Town club as early as 1876 which won the Birmingham Senior Cup in 1879. However, the present Shrewsbury Town club was formed in 1886 and won the Welsh FA Cup as early as 1891.

First Football League game: 19 August, 1950, Division 3(N), v Scunthorpe U (a) D 0-0 – Eggleston; Fisher, Lewis; Wheatley, Depear, Robinson; Griffin, Hope, Jackson, Brown, Barker.

Did you know: Shrewsbury Town were unbeaten at home in the FA Cup from 1952 to 1969 during which time they played 22 ties at Gay Meadow winning 14 and drawing eight.

Managers (and Secretary-managers)
W. Adams 1905–12*, A. Weston 1912–34*, Jack Roscamp 1934–35, Sam Ramsey 1935–36, Ted Bousted 1936–40, Leslie Knighton 1945–49, Harry Chapman 1949–50, Sammy Crooks 1950–54, Walter Rowley 1955–57, Harry Potts 1957–58, Johnny Spuhler 1958, Arthur Rowley 1958–68, Harry Gregg 1968–72, Maurice Evans 1972–73, Alan Durban 1974–78, Richie Barker 1978, Graham Turner 1978–84, Chic Bates 1984–87, Ian McNeill 1987–90, Asa Hartford 1990–91, John Bond January 1991– .

Player and Position	Ht	Wt	Birth Date	Place	Source	Clubs	League App	Gls
Paul Wimbleton	5 8	10 06	13 11 64	Havant	Apprentice	Portsmouth	10	—
						Cardiff C	119	17
						Bristol C	16	2
						Shrewsbury T	34	1
						Maidstone U (loan)	2	1
Forwards								
Mike Brown	5 9	10 12	8 2 68	Birmingham		Shrewsbury T	190	9
Carl Griffiths	5 9	10 06	15 7 71	Oswestry	Trainee	Shrewsbury T	65	14
Gary Shaw*	5 9	12 00	21 1 61	Birmingham	Apprentice	Aston Villa	165	59
						Blackpool (loan)	6	—
					Klagenfurt	Walsall	9	3
						Shrewsbury T	22	5
Dean Spink	5 11	13 08	22 1 67	Birmingham	Halesowen T	Aston Villa	—	—
						Scarborough (loan)	3	2
						Bury (loan)	6	1
						Shrewsbury T	56	11
Billy Weir	5 5	9 12	11 4 68	Baillieston	Bailieston J	Shrewsbury T	17	1

Trainees
Atkinson, Neil C; Barton, Michael; Doster, David; Evans, Andrew N; Evans, Jason S; Forster, Nicholas J; Hanmer, Gareth C; Pitman, Jason A; Seabury, Kevin; Steer, James; Thelwell, Kevin D; Williams, Mark.

Associated Schoolboys
Ayton, Paul K; Caudwell, Scott A; Desborough, Mark; Guest, Robert; Maddox, Gareth E; Martin, Lee; Thomas, Neil R.

Associated Schoolboys who have accepted the club's offer of a Traineeship/Contract
Davies, Ashley; Evans, Paul S; Hodgin, Christopher; Jenkins, Sam B; Taylor, Steven D; Yates, Jason.

472

SOUTHAMPTON 1990–91 *Back row (left to right):* Neil Maddison, Tommy Widdrington, Andy Rowland, Dean Radford, Paul Masters.
Third row: Raymond Wallace, Micky Adams, Jason Dodd, Jeff Kenna, Steve Davis, Francis Benali, Andy Cook, Nicky Banger, Sammy Lee, George Horsfall (Coach).
Second row: Don Taylor (Physiotherapist), Dave Merrington (Youth Team Coach), Alex Cherednik, Barry Horne, Ian Andrews, Matthew Le Tissier, Tim Flowers, Neil Ruddock, Gary French, Alan Shearer, Sergei Gotsmanov, Lew Chatterley (Youth Development Officer), Ray Graydon (Reserve Team Coach).
Front row: John Mortimore (Assistant Manager), Paul Rideout, Russell Osman, Kevin Moore, Chris Nicholl (Manager), Jimmy Case, Rodney Wallace, Glen Cockerill, Dennis Rofe (First Team Coach).

Division 1 **SOUTHAMPTON**

The Dell, Milton Road, Southampton SO9 4XX. Telephone Southampton (0703) 220505. Ticket enquiries: (0703) 228575.

Ground capacity: 21,900.

Record attendance: 31,044 v Manchester U, Division 1, 8 October 1969.

Record receipts: £128,730 v Oldham Ath, Littlewoods Cup 5th rd, 24 January 1990.

Pitch measurements: 110yd × 72yd.

Chairman: F. G. L. Askham FCA.

Vice-Chairman: K. St. J. Wiseman.

Directors: J. Corbett, E. T. Bates, I. L. Gordon, B. H. D. Hunt, M. R. Richards FCA.

Manager: Ian Branfoot. ***Assistant Manager:*** John Mortimore.

Coach: Dennis Rofe. ***Physio:*** Don Taylor.

Secretary: Brian Truscott. ***Commercial Manager:*** Bob Russell.

Year Formed: 1885. ***Turned Professional:*** 1894. ***Ltd Co.:*** 1897.

Club Nickname: 'The Saints'.

Previous Name: Southampton St Mary's until 1885.

Previous Grounds: 1885, Antelope Ground; 1897, County Cricket Ground; 1898, The Dell.

Record League Victory: 9-3 v Wolverhampton W, Division 2, 18 September 1965 – Godfrey; Jones, Williams; Walker, Knapp, Huxford; Paine (2), O'Brien (1), Melia, Chivers (4), Sydenham (2).

Record Cup Victory: 7-1 v Ipswich T, FA Cup, 3rd rd, 7 January 1961 – Reynolds; Davies, Traynor; Conner, Page, Huxford; Paine (1), O'Brien (3 incl. 1p), Reeves, Mulgrew (2), Penk (1).

Record Defeat: 0-8 v Tottenham H, Division 2, 28 March 1936 and v Everton, Division 1, 20 November 1971.

Most League Points (2 for a win): 61, Division 3 (S), 1921–22 and Division 3, 1959–60.

Most League Points (3 for a win): 77, Division 1, 1983–84.

Most League Goals: 112, Division 3 (S), 1957–58.

Highest League Scorer in Season: Derek Reeves, 39, Division 3, 1959–60.

Most League Goals in Total Aggregate: Mike Channon, 185, 1966–77, 1979–82.

Most Capped Player: Peter Shilton, 49 (125), England.

Most League Appearances: Terry Paine, 713, 1956–74.

Record Transfer Fee Received: £1,700,000 from Leeds U for Rodney and Ray Wallace, July 1991.

Record Transfer Fee Paid: £1,000,000 to Swindon T for Alan McLoughlin, December 1990.

Football League Record: 1920 Original Member of Division 3; 1921 Division 3 (S); 1922–53 Division 2; 1953–58 Division 3 (S); 1958–60 Division 3; 1960–66 Division 2; 1966–74 Division 1; 1974–78 Division 2; 1978– Division 1.

Honours: *Football League:* Division 1 – Runners-up 1983–84; Division 2 – Runners-up 1965–66, 1977–78; Division 3 (S) – Champions 1921–22; Runners-up 1920–21; Division 3 – Champions 1959–60. *FA Cup:* Winners 1975–76; Runners-up 1900, 1902. *Football League Cup:* Runners-up 1978–79. **European Competitions:** *European Fairs Cup:* 1969–70. *UEFA Cup:* 1971–72, 1981–82, 1982–83, 1984–85. *European Cup-Winners' Cup:* 1976–77.

Colours: Red and white striped shirts, black shorts, white stockings, red trim. **Change colours:** White shirts, Solent green trim, white shorts, white stockings, Solent green trim.

SOUTHAMPTON 1990–91 LEAGUE RECORD

Match No.	Date	Venue	Opponents	Result	H/T Score	Lg. Pos.	Goalscorers	Attendance
1	Aug 25	A	Aston Villa	D 1-1	1-1	—	Le Tissier	29,542
2	28	H	Norwich C	W 1-0	0-0	—	Polston (og)	17,206
3	Sept 1	H	Luton T	L 1-2	1-2	10	Rideout	14,878
4	8	A	Nottingham F	L 1-3	1-1	14	Wallace Rod	18,559
5	15	H	Sheffield U	W 2-0	2-0	10	Le Tissier, Wallace Rod	15,883
6	22	A	Manchester U	L 2-3	1-1	11	Rideout, Wallace Rod	41,228
7	29	A	Everton	L 0-3	0-2	15		23,093
8	Oct 6	H	Chelsea	D 3-3	1-2	15	Shearer, Ruddock, Wallace Rod	16,911
9	20	A	Coventry C	W 2-1	1-1	13	Billing (og), Le Tissier	10,040
10	27	H	Derby Co	L 0-1	0-1	14		16,328
11	Nov 3	A	Wimbledon	D 1-1	0-0	15	Le Tissier (pen)	5485
12	10	H	QPR	W 3-1	1-1	8	Rideout, Le Tissier, Wallace Rod	15,957
13	17	A	Arsenal	L 0-4	0-3	11		36,243
14	24	H	Crystal Palace	L 2-3	2-2	12	Shaw (og), Rideout	15,851
15	Dec 1	A	Leeds U	L 1-2	0-2	15	Rideout	29,341
16	8	A	Norwich C	L 1-3	1-1	17	Le Tissier	11,705
17	15	H	Aston Villa	D 1-1	1-0	14	Le Tissier	16,604
18	22	A	Liverpool	L 2-3	1-2	14	Wallace Rod 2	31,894
19	26	H	Manchester C	W 2-1	1-1	14	Horne, Le Tissier	16,029
20	29	H	Tottenham H	W 3-0	1-0	13	Le Tissier 2, Wallace Rod	21,405
21	Jan 1	A	Sunderland	L 0-1	0-0	15		19,757
22	12	A	Luton T	W 4-3	2-2	12	Wallace Rod 2, Le Tissier 2	9021
23	19	H	Nottingham F	D 1-1	1-1	13	Walker (og)	16,044
24	Feb 2	A	Sheffield U	L 1-4	0-4	14	Moore	16,887
25	23	A	QPR	L 1-2	0-2	14	Le Tissier (pen)	11,009
26	Mar 2	H	Leeds U	W 2-0	1-0	13	Rideout, Cockerill	16,585
27	9	A	Crystal Palace	L 1-2	0-0	15	Cockerill	28,880
28	13	H	Manchester U	D 1-1	1-0	—	Ruddock	15,701
29	16	H	Everton	L 3-4	1-2	18	Ruddock, Newell (og), Shearer	15,410
30	23	A	Chelsea	W 2-0	1-0	16	Shearer, Le Tissier (pen)	13,391
31	30	A	Manchester C	D 3-3	0-0	17	Le Tissier, Osman, McLoughlin	23,163
32	Apr 1	H	Liverpool	W 1-0	1-0	15	Le Tissier	20,255
33	6	A	Tottenham H	L 0-2	0-2	16		24,291
34	9	H	Arsenal	D 1-1	0-0	—	Le Tissier	20,949
35	13	H	Sunderland	W 3-1	1-1	15	Wallace Rod, Le Tissier (pen), Shearer	16,812
36	20	H	Coventry C	W 2-1	2-0	12	Wallace Rod 2	15,461
37	May 4	A	Derby Co	L 2-6	1-3	15	Wallace Rod, Le Tissier (pen)	11,680
38	11	H	Wimbledon	D 1-1	1-0	14	Case	17,052

Final League Position: 14

GOALSCORERS

League (58): Le Tissier 19 (5 pens), Wallace Rod 14, Rideout 6, Shearer 4, Ruddock 3, Cockerill 2, Case 1, Horne 1, McLoughlin 1, Moore 1, Osman 1, own goals 5.
Rumbelows Cup (15): Shearer 6 (1 pen), Banger 3, Le Tissier 2, Wallace Rod 2, Horne 1, Ruddock 1.
FA Cup (8): Le Tissier 2, Shearer 2 (1 pen), Wallace Rod 2, Case 1, Ruddock 1.

Flowers	Cherednik	Adams	Case	Moore	Osman	Le Tissier	Horne	Rideout	Cockerill	Wallace Rod	Shearer	Ruddock	Davis	Cook	Dodd	Gotsmanov	Benali	Banger	McLoughlin	Andrews	Maddison	Gittens	Kenna	Hall	Match No.
1	2	3	4	5	6	7	8	9*	10	11	12														1
1	2	3	4	5	6	7	8	9	10	11															2
1	2	3	4	5	6	7	8	9	10†	11*	12		14												3
1	2	3	4	5		7	8	9	10	11*			14	6†	12										4
1	2	3*	4		6	7	8	9	10	11	12	5													5
1	2†	3	4		6	7	8	9*	10	11	12	5	14												6
1		3	4		6	7*	8		10	11	9	5			12		2								7
1		3†	4		6	7	8		10	11*	9	5	14		12		2								8
1	12		4		6	7	8		10*	11	9	5			3		2								9
1	14		4		6	7	8		10*	11	9	5			12	3†	2								10
1		3	4		6	7	8		10	11	9	5					2								11
1		3	4		6*	7	8		10†	11	9	5	14		12		2								12
1		3	4		6	7	8		10	11†	9*	5	14		12		2								13
1		3	4		6	7	8		10	11*	9	5	14		12		2†								14
1	11	3	4		6	7	8		10*		9	5			12		2								15
1		3	4*		6	7	8		10	11	9	5			12		2								16
1		3	4		6†	7	8		10	11	9*	5	14		12		2		11						17
1		3	4*		6	7	8		10	11	9	5			12		2								18
1		3	4		6	7	8			11	9	5			12		2		10*						19
1	14	3	4		6	7*	8			11	9	5			12		2†		10						20
1	2	3	4		6	7	8			11	9	5							10						21
1	2	3	4		6*	7	8			11	9	5			12				10						22
1	2		4*	5	6	7†	8		10	11	9		14		12		3								23
1			4	5	6*	7	8			11	9				12	2	3		10						24
	14		4†	5	6	7	8			11	9				12	2	3		10*	1					25
1	14		4	5	6	7*	8			11	9				12	2	3		10†						26
1	2		4*		6	7	8		10	11	9	5			12		3								27
1	2		4		6	7	8			11	9	5					3		10*		12				28
1			4		6	7	8†			11	9	5	14		2	3*			10		12				29
1		3	4			7	8			11	9	5			2				10				6		30
1		3	4		6*	7†	8			11	9	5	14		2				10		12				31
1		3	4			7	8			11	9	5			2				10			6			32
1	12	3	4			7†	8*			11	9	5	14		2				10			6			33
1		3	4			7	8			11	9	5			2				10			6			34
1		3	4			7	8			11	9	5			2				10*		12	6			35
1		3	4			7	8*			11	9	5			2				10		12	6			36
1		3	4			7	8			11	9	5†			2*				10		12	6			37
1		3	4			7*	8			11	9	5†	14		2				10		12	6			38
37	12	29	24	19	17	34	38	14	28	35	34	32	1	5	16	2	9	—	22	1	1	7	1	—	
		+3s	+1s	+1s		+3s	+1s	+2s	+4s	+2s	+2s	+3s	+1s	+2s	+3s	+6s	+3s		+6s		+3s	+1s	+1s	+1s	

Rumbelows Cup	Second Round	Rochdale (a)	5-0	
		(h)	3-0	
	Third Round	Ipswich T (a)	2-0	
	Fourth Round	Crystal Palace (h)	2-0	
	Fifth Round	Manchester U (h)	1-1	
		(a)	2-3	
FA Cup	Third Round	Ipswich T (h)	3-2	
	Fourth Round	Coventry C (a)	1-1	
		(h)	2-0	
	Fifth Round	Nottingham F (h)	1-1	
		(a)	1-3	

SOUTHAMPTON

Player and Position	Ht	Wt	Birth Date	Birth Place	Source	Clubs	League App	Gls
Goalkeepers								
Ian Andrews	6 2	12 02	1 12 64	Nottingham	Apprentice	Leicester C	126	—
						Swindon T (loan)	1	—
						Celtic	5	—
						Leeds U (loan)	1	—
						Southampton	4	—
Tim Flowers	6 2	13 04	3 2 67	Kenilworth	Apprentice	Wolverhampton W	63	—
						Southampton (loan)	—	—
						Southampton	97	—
						Swindon T (loan)	2	—
						Swindon T (loan)	5	—
Gary French‡	5 11	11 10	21 11 71	Ilminster	Trainee	Southampton	—	—
Defenders								
Mick Adams	5 7.	10 10	8 11 61	Sheffield	Apprentice	Gillingham	92	5
						Coventry C	90	9
						Leeds U	73	2
						Southampton	53	—
Francis Benali	5 9	11 01	30 12 68	Southampton	Apprentice	Southampton	46	—
Matthew Bound	6 2	14 00	9 11 72	Trowbridge	Trainee	Southampton	—	—
Aleksey Cherednik	5 9	11 07	12 12 60	USSR	Dnepr	Southampton	23	—
Andy Cook	5 9	10 12	10 8 69	Romsey	Apprentice	Southampton	16	1
Steve Davis	6 2	12 08	30 10 68	Hexham	Trainee	Southampton	6	—
						Burnley (loan)	9	—
						Notts Co (loan)	2	—
Jason Dodd	5 10	11 10	2 11 70	Bath		Southampton	41	—
Jon Gittens	5 11	12 06	22 1 64	Moseley	Paget R	Southampton	18	—
						Swindon T	126	6
						Southampton	8	—
Richard Hall	6 1	13 00	14 3 72	Ipswich	Trainee	Scunthorpe U	22	3
						Southampton	1	—
Jeff Kenna	5 11	11 09	27 8 70	Dublin	Trainee	Southampton	2	—
Kevin Moore*	5 11	12 02	29 4 58	Grimsby	Local	Grimsby T	400	27
						Oldham Ath	13	1
						Southampton	100	8
Russell Osman	6 0	11 10	14 2 59	Repton	Apprentice	Ipswich T	294	17
						Leicester C	108	8
						Southampton	91	6
Dean Radford‡	5 11	11 05	14 11 70	London	Trainee	Southampton	—	—
Stephen Roast	5 6	9 04	19 9 72	London	Trainee	Southampton	—	—
Neil Ruddock	6 2	12 06	9 5 68	London	Apprentice	Millwall	—	—
						Tottenham H	9	—
						Millwall	2	1
						Southampton	77	9
Ray Wallace	5 6	10 02	2 10 69	Lewisham	Trainee	Southampton	35	—
Midfield								
Jimmy Case	5 9	12 07	18 5 54	Liverpool	S Liverpool	Liverpool	186	23
						Brighton & HA	127	10
						Southampton	215	10
Glenn Cockerill	6 0	12 04	26 8 50	Grimsby	Louth U	Lincoln C	71	10
						Swindon T	26	1
						Lincoln C	115	25
						Sheffield U	62	10
						Southampton	213	28
Barry Horne	5 10	11 06	18 5 62	St Asaph	Rhyl	Wrexham	136	17
						Portsmouth	70	7
						Southampton	78	5

SOUTHAMPTON

Foundation: Formed largely by players from the Deanery FC, which had been established by school teachers in 1880. Most of the founders were connected with the young men's association of St. Mary's Church. At the inaugural meeting held in November 1885 the club was named Southampton St. Mary's and the church's curate was elected president.

First Football League game: 28 August, 1920, Division 3, v Gillingham (a) D 1-1 – Allen; Parker, Titmuss; Shelley, Campbell, Turner; Barratt, Dominy (1), Rawlings, Moore, Foxall.

Did you know: The season the Saints won the Cup (1975–76) they were only 60 seconds away from being k.o'd in that season's first cup game – home to Aston Villa in the 3rd round when Hugh Fisher got a late equaliser. It was his only first team goal of the season.

Managers (and Secretary-managers)
Cecil Knight 1894–95*, Charles Robson 1895–97, E. Arnfield 1897–1911* (continued as secretary), George Swift 1911–12, E. Arnfield 1912–19, Jimmy McIntyre 1919–24, Arthur Chadwick 1925–31, George Kay 1931–36, George Gross 1936–37, Tom Parker 1937–43, J. R. Sarjantson stepped down from the board to act as secretary-manager 1943–47 with the next two listed being team managers during this period), Arthur Dominy 1943–46, Bill Dodgin Snr 1946–49, Sid Cann 1949–51, George Roughton 1952–55, Ted Bates 1955–73, Lawrie McMenemy 1973–85, Chris Nicholl 1985–91, Ian Branfoot June 1991– .

Player and Position	Ht	Wt	Birth Date	Place	Source	Clubs	League App	Gls
Alan McLoughlin	5 8	10 00	20 4 67	Manchester	Local	Manchester U	—	—
						Swindon T	9	—
						Torquay U	24	4
						Swindon T	97	19
						Southampton	22	1
Neil Maddison	5 9	11 08	2 10 69	Darlington	Trainee	Southampton	11	2
Tommy Widdrington	5 8	11 01	21 11 71	Newcastle	Trainee	Southampton	—	—
Forwards								
Nicky Banger	5 8	10 06	25 2 71	Southampton	Trainee	Southampton	6	—
Sergei Gotsmanov	5 8	11 01	17 3 59	USSR	Dynamo Minsk	Brighton & HA	16	4
						Southampton	8	—
Matthew Le Tissier	6 0	11 06	14 10 68	Guernsey	Vale Recreation	Southampton	141	54
Lee Luscombe	6 0	12 04	16 7 71	Guernsey	Trainee	Southampton	—	—
Lee Powell	5 5	8 10	2 6 73	Newport	Trainee	Southampton	—	—
Paul Rideout	5 11	12 01	14 8 64	Bournemouth	Apprentice	Swindon T	95	38
						Aston Villa	54	19
						Bari	99	23
						Southampton	71	19
						Swindon T (Loan)	9	1
Alan Shearer	5 11	11 03	13 8 70	Newcastle	Trainee	Southampton	77	10
Rodney Wallace	5 7	10 01	2 10 69	Lewisham	Trainee	Southampton	128	45

Trainees
Crowley, Thomas E; Frost, Neil; Good, Nicholas R.J; Hopkins, Colin J; Lamport, David M; MacDonald, Callum; McKilligan, Neil; Peters, Jason G; Phillips, Kevin; Savage, Ian; Selby, Neil S; Taylor, Gareth K; Thomas, Martin R; Thorne, Kevin M; White, Christian J; Whitman, Nathan L; Wright, Scott.

Associated Schoolboys
Allen, Steven; Baker, Jonathan; Barrett, James R; Carr, Neil; Chadkirk, Paul G; Cole, James; Davies, Neil; Eagle, Simon C; Everest, Anthony D; Harper, Paul; Hogarth, Antony C; Hopper, Neil; Joseph, Urias; Kamara, Abdul S; McNally, Aron A; Pitman, Jamie R; Rowe, Damion; Rowe, Richard M; Short, Michael T; Skedd, Antony S; Totten, Alexander; Waters, Jamie S; Winter, Darren; Woodfield, Jamie P.

Associated Schoolboys who have accepted the club's offer of a Traineeship/Contract
Bartlett, Neal; Cleeve, Anthony G; Hughes, David R; Murphy, Kevin; Robinson, Matthew R; Shiers, Benjamin D; Tisdale, Paul R.

478

SOUTHEND UNITED 1990–91 *Back row (left to right):* Dean Austin, Peter Daley, Paul Clark, Mario Walsh, Ian Benjamin, Andy Edwards, Steve Tilson, Paul Smith.
Centre row: David Webb (Manager), Kevin Lock (Coach), Brett Angell, John Cornwell, David Martin, Paul Sansome, Peter Cawley, Spencer Prior, Roy McDonough, Danny Greaves (Coach), Alan Raw (Physiotherapist).
Front row: Adam Locke, Adrian West, Jason Cook, Andy Ansah, Chris Powell, Peter Butler, Christian Hyslop.

Division 2   **SOUTHEND UNITED**

Roots Hall Football Ground, Victoria Avenue, Southend-on-Sea SS2 6NQ. Telephone Southend (0702) 340707. Commercial Dept: (0702) 332113. Soccerline: 0898 700279.

Ground capacity: 11,863.

Record attendance: 31,090 v Liverpool FA Cup 3rd rd, 10 January 1979.

Record receipts: £36,599 v Liverpool, FA Cup 3rd rd, 10 January 1979.

Pitch measurements: 110yd × 74yd.

President: N. J. Woodcock.

Chairman: V. T. Jobson. *Vice-chairman:* J. W. Adams.

Secretary: J. W. Adams.

Directors: J. Bridge, J. N. Foster, D. M. Markscheffel, R. J. Osborne (Company Secretary), F. Van Wezel. *Associate Directors:* R. F. Moore OBE, W. E. Parsons.

Manager: David Webb. *Coaches:* Kevin Lock, Danny Greaves.

Treatment of Injury Officer: Alan Raw. *Stadium Manager:* R. Davy Jnr.

Club Nickname: 'The Blues or The Shrimpers'.

Year Formed: 1906. *Turned Professional:* 1906. *Ltd Co.:* 1919.

Previous Grounds: 1906, Roots Hall, Prittlewell; 1920, Kursaal; 1934, Southend Stadium; 1955, Roots Hall Football Ground.

Record League Victory: 9-2 v Newport Co, Division 3 (S), 5 September 1936 – McKenzie; Nelson, Everest (1); Deacon, Turner, Carr; Bolan, Lane (1), Goddard (4), Dickinson (2), Oswald (1).

Record Cup Victory: 10-1 v Golders Green, FA Cup, 1st rd, 24 November 1934 – Moore; Morfitt, Kelly; Mackay, Joe Wilson, Carr (1); Lane (1), Johnson (5), Cheesmuir (2), Deacon (1), Oswald. 10-1 v Brentwood, FA Cup, 2nd rd, 7 December 1968 – Roberts; Bentley, Birks; McMillan (1) Beesley, Kurila; Clayton, Chisnall, Moore (4), Best (5), Hamilton. 10-1 v Aldershot, Leyland Daf Cup, Pr rd, 6 November 1990 – Sansome; Austin, Powell, Cornwell, Prior (1), Tilson (3), Cawley, Butler, Ansah (1), Benjamin (1), Angell (4).

Record Defeat: 1-9 v Brighton & HA, Division 3, 27 November 1965.

Most League Points (2 for a win): 67, Division 4, 1980–81.

Most League Points (3 for a win): 85, Division 3, 1990–91.

Most League Goals: 92, Division 3 (S), 1950–51.

Highest League Scorer in Season: Jim Shankly, 31, 1928–29 and Sammy McCrory, 1957–58, both in Division 3 (S).

Most League Goals in Total Aggregate: Roy Hollis, 122, 1953–60.

Most Capped Player: George Mackenzie, 9, Eire.

Most League Appearances: Sandy Anderson, 451, 1950–63.

Record Transfer Fee Received: £150,000 from Crystal Palace for Glenn Pennyfather, November 1987, £150,000 from Wolverhampton W for Shane Westley, June 1989 and £150,000 from Tottenham H for Justin Edinburgh, July 1990.

Record Transfer Fee Paid: £111,111 to Blackpool for Derek Spence, December 1979.

Football League Record: 1920 Original Member of Division 3; 1921 Division 3 (S); 1958–66 Division 3; 1966–72 Division 4; 1972–76 Division 3; 1976–78 Division 4; 1978–80 Division 3; 1980–81 Division 4; 1981–84 Division 3; 1984–87 Division 4; 1987–89 Division 3; 1989–90 Division 4; 1990–91 Division 3; 1991– Division 2.

Honours: Football League: Division 3 – Runners-up 1990–91; Division 4 – Champions 1980–81; Runners-up 1971–72, 1977–78. *FA Cup:* best season: old 3rd rd, 1920–21, 5th rd, 1925–26, 1951–52, 1975–76. *Football League Cup:* never past 3rd rd.

Colours: Blue shirts, yellow trim, yellow shorts, blue trim, blue stockings. **Change colours:** All yellow.

SOUTHEND UNITED 1990–91 LEAGUE RECORD

Match No.	Date		Venue	Opponents	Result		H/T Score	Lg. Pos.	Goalscorers	Attendance
1	Aug	25	A	Huddersfield T	W	2-1	1-1	—	Angell, Edwards	5219
2	Sept	1	H	Crewe Alex	W	3-2	1-1	4	Benjamin, Martin (pen), Angell	2994
3		9	A	Cambridge U	W	4-1	1-0	—	Angell 2, Benjamin, Butler	4790
4		14	H	Preston NE	W	3-2	0-1	—	Martin, Benjamin, Cornwell	4614
5		18	H	Shrewsbury T	W	2-1	2-1	—	Tilson, Ansah	5100
6		22	A	Stoke C	L	0-4	0-2	2		11,901
7		29	A	Mansfield T	W	1-0	0-0	1	Benjamin	2120
8	Oct	2	H	Swansea C	W	4-1	1-0	—	Martin 2 (1 pen), Tilson 2	3635
9		5	H	Bournemouth	W	2-1	1-1	—	Martin, Angell	5255
10		13	A	Birmingham C	D	1-1	0-0	2	Ansah	9333
11		20	A	Wigan Ath	L	1-4	0-2	2	Cawley	2691
12		23	H	Exeter C	W	2-1	1-1	—	Powell, Benjamin	4280
13		27	H	Bury	W	2-1	1-1	1	Angell, Tilson	4001
14	Nov	4	A	Brentford	W	1-0	1-0	—	Benjamin	8021
15		10	H	Fulham	D	1-1	1-0	1	Cornwell	5808
16		24	A	Reading	W	4-2	1-0	1	Martin 2, Tilson, Angell	3927
17	Dec	1	A	Rotherham U	W	1-0	0-0	1	Benjamin	3465
18		15	H	Grimsby T	W	2-0	2-0	1	Tilson, Martin	8126
19		22	A	Chester C	L	0-1	0-0	1		1523
20		26	H	Bolton W	D	1-1	0-0	1	Tilson	7539
21		28	H	Bradford C	D	1-1	1-0	—	Tilson	6767
22	Jan	1	A	Tranmere R	L	1-3	1-2	1	Angell	7214
23		12	A	Crewe Alex	W	2-0	1-0	1	Angell 2	3595
24		19	H	Huddersfield T	L	0-1	0-1	1		5509
25		26	A	Preston NE	L	1-2	0-1	2	Ansah	4351
26	Feb	2	A	Shrewsbury T	W	1-0	1-0	1	Angell	4377
27		5	H	Stoke C	W	1-0	1-0	—	Angell	5164
28		19	H	Reading	L	1-2	1-0	—	Benjamin	4588
29		23	A	Fulham	W	3-0	2-0	1	Benjamin, Martin, Ansah	5113
30	Mar	1	H	Rotherham U	W	2-1	2-0	—	Benjamin 2	5622
31		9	A	Grimsby T	L	0-1	0-1	1		9689
32		12	A	Swansea C	W	4-1	1-1	—	Locke 2, Benjamin, Ansah	2712
33		15	H	Mansfield T	W	2-1	0-1	—	Martin, Butler	5400
34		18	H	Birmingham C	W	2-1	0-1	—	Martin, Angell	6328
35		23	A	Bournemouth	L	1-3	1-1	1	Angell	7421
36		30	A	Bolton W	L	0-1	0-0	2		10,666
37	Apr	2	H	Chester C	D	1-1	0-1	—	Ansah	6190
38		6	A	Bradford C	L	1-2	0-1	2	Angell	5846
39		9	A	Leyton Orient	W	1-0	1-0	—	Ansah	6306
40		12	A	Tranmere R	W	1-0	1-0	—	Ansah	8622
41		19	H	Wigan Ath	L	0-2	0-1	—		7550
42		27	A	Exeter C	W	2-1	1-1	1	Ansah, Locke	4941
43		30	H	Cambridge U	D	0-0	0-0	—		10,664
44	May	4	A	Bury	W	1-0	0-0	1	Benjamin	4254
45		7	H	Leyton Orient	D	1-1	0-0	—	Locke	8760
46		11	H	Brentford	L	0-1	0-0	2		9666

Final League Position: 2

GOALSCORERS

League (67): Angell 15, Benjamin 13, Martin 11 (2 pens), Ansah 9, Tilson 8, Locke 4, Butler 2, Cornwell 2, Cawley 1, Edwards 1, Powell 1.
Rumbelows Cup (5): Angell 2, Austin 1, Butler 1, Martin 1.
FA Cup (2): Angell 2.

Sansome	Edwards	Hyslop	Martin	Cornwell	Tilson	Clark	Butler	Ansah	Benjamin	Angell	Powell	Austin	Cook	Prior	Locke	Cawley	Ling	Smith	Scully	Moran	Match No.
1	2	3	4	5	6	7	8	9	10	11											1
1	2		4	5	6	7	8	9	10	11		3									2
1			4	5	6	7	8	9	10	11		3	2								3
1			4	5	6	7	8	9	10	11		3	2								4
1			4	5	6	7	8	9	10	11		3	2								5
1			4	5	6	7	8	9	10	11*		3	2	12							6
1			4		6	7	8	9*	10	11		3	2		5	12					7
1			4		6	7	8	9*	10	11		3	2		5	12					8
1			4		6	7†	8	9*	10	11		3	2		5	12	14				9
1			4	14	6†		8	9	10	11*		3	2		5	12	7				10
1			4†	14	6		8	9*	10	11		3	2		5		7	12			11
1			4*	12	6		8	9	10	11		3	2		5		7				12
1			4		6		8	9	10	11		3	2		5		7				13
1			4		6		8	9	10	11*		3	2		5	12	7				14
1		14	4		6†		8	9	10	11*		3	2		5	12	7				15
1			4		6	7	8		10	11		3	2		5	9					16
1			4		6	7	8		10	11		3	2		5			9			17
1			4		6	7	8		10	11		3	2		5	9					18
1			4		6	7	8		10	11		3	2		5	9					19
1			4		6	7	8		10	11		3	2		5	9					20
1			4		6	7	8	12	10	11		3	2		5	9*					21
1					6	7	8	9	10	11		3	2		5		12	4*			22
1			4		6	7	8	9	10	11		3	2						5		23
1			4		6	7	8	9	10	11*		3	2		12				5		24
1			4	14	6	7	8†	12	10	11		3	2		9*				5		25
1			4		6	7	8	9	10	11		3	2						5		26
1			4		6	7	8	9	10	11		3	2						5		27
1			4	8*	6	7		9	10	11		3	2		12				5		28
1			4		6	7		9	10	11		3	2		8				5		29
1			4		6*	7	8	9	10	12		3	2		11				5		30
1			4		6	7	8	9	10	11*		3	2		12				5		31
1			4		6	7	8	9	10			3	2		11				5		32
1			4		6	7	8	9	10			3	2	5	11						33
1			4		6	7	8	9*	10	12		3	2	5	11						34
1		14	12		6	7*	8		10	11		3	2	5			4			9†	35
1			4		6	7	8	9	10	11		3	2						5		36
1			4		6	7	8	9	10	11		3	2						5		37
1		6	4	8		7		12	10	11		3	2		9*				5		38
1		6	4	8		7		9	10			3	2		11				5		39
1		6	4			7	8	9	10			3	2		11				5		40
1		6	4			7	8	9	10	12		3	2		11*				5		41
1		6	4			7	8	9	10	12		3	2		11*				5		42
1		6	4			7	8	9	10	11		3	2						5		43
1		3	4	14		7	8	9	10	11†	12	2		6*					5		44
1		3	4			7	8	9	10	11*	6	2			12				5		45
1		3†	4	6*		7	8	9	10	12	14	2			11				5		46
46	2	10	40	13	38	40	42	37	46	37	43	44	—	19	18	6	1	2	21	1	

Substitute appearances:
+ + + + + + + + +
1s 1s 6s 3s 5s 2s 1s 10s 1s 2s

Rumbelows Cup First Round Aldershot (h) 2-1
                                                          (a) 2-2
                  Second Round Crystal Palace (a) 0-8
                                                            (h) 1-2
FA Cup First Round Leyton Orient (a) 2-3

SOUTHEND UNITED

Player and Position	Ht	Wt	Birth Date	Place	Source	Clubs	League App	Gls
Goalkeepers								
John Cheesewright*	6 0	11 05	12 1 73		Tottenham H	Southend U	—	—
Paul Sansome	6 0	12 00	6 10 61	N Addington	Apprentice	Crystal Palace	—	—
						Millwall	156	—
						Southend U	142	—
Defenders								
Dean Austin	6 0	12 04	26 4 70	Hemel Hempstead	St Albans	Southend U	51	—
Christian Hyslop	5 11	11 10	14 6 72	Watford	Trainee	Southend U	11	—
Chris Powell	5 8	11 00	8 9 69	Lambeth	Trainee	Crystal Palace	3	—
						Aldershot (loan)	11	—
						Southend U	45	1
Spencer Prior	6 3	12 10	22 4 71	Rochford	Trainee	Southend U	48	2
Pat Scully	6 1	12 07	23 6 70	Dublin	Trainee	Arsenal	—	—
						Preston NE (loan)	13	1
						Northampton T (loan)	15	—
						Southend U	21	—
Midfield								
Peter Butler	5 9	11 01	27 8 66	Halifax	Apprentice	Huddersfield T	5	—
						Cambridge U (loan)	14	1
						Bury	11	—
						Cambridge U	55	9
						Southend U	133	9
Paul Clark	5 10	12 12	14 9 58	Benfleet	Apprentice	Southend U	33	1
						Brighton & HA	79	9
						Reading (loan)	2	—
						Southend U	276	3
Jason Cook*	5 7	10 06	29 12 69	Edmonton	Trainee	Tottenham H	—	—
						Southend U	30	1
John Cornwell	6 0	12 00	13 10 64	Bethnal Green	Apprentice	Orient	202	35
						Newcastle U	33	1
						Swindon T	25	—
						Southend U	19	2
Peter Daley‡	5 10	11 00	14 2 70	Liverpool	Liverpool	Southend U	5	1
Andy Edwards	6 2	12 06	17 9 71	Epping	Trainee	Southend U	11	1
Martin Ling	5 7	9 12	15 7 66	West Ham	Apprentice	Exeter C	116	14
						Swindon T	2	—
						Southend U	138	31
						Mansfield T (loan)	3	—
						Swindon T (loan)	1	—
Adam Locke	5 10	11 10	20 8 70	Croydon	Trainee	Crystal Palace	—	—
						Southend U	28	4
David Martin	6 1	11 08	25 4 63	East Ham	Apprentice	Millwall	140	6
						Wimbledon	35	3
						Southend U	190	17
Paul Smith	5 11	12 00	18 9 71	London	Trainee	Southend U	12	1
Steve Tilson	5 11	11 10	27 7 66	Essex	Burnham	Southend U	70	10
Forwards								
Brett Angell	6 1	12 03	20 8 68	Marlborough		Portsmouth	—	—
					Cheltenham T	Derby Co	—	—
						Stockport Co	70	28
						Southend U	42	15
Andy Ansah	5 10	11 01	19 3 69	Lewisham		Crystal Palace	—	—
						Brentford	8	2
						Southend U	47	10

SOUTHEND UNITED

Foundation: The leading club in Southend around the turn of the century was Southend Athletic, but they were an amateur concern. Southend United was a more ambitious professional club when they were founded in 1906, employing Bob Jack as secretary-manager and immediately joining the Second Division of the Southern League.

First Football League game: 28 August, 1920, Division 3, v Brighton & HA (a) W 2-0 – Capper; Reid, Newton; Wileman, Henderson, Martin; Nicholls, Nuttall, Fairclough (2), Myers, Dorsett.

Did you know: In 1980–81 when United were unbeaten at home goalkeeper Mervyn Cawston kept a clean sheet for one spell of 985 minutes.

Managers (and Secretary-managers)
Bob Jack 1906–10, George Molyneux 1910–11, O. M. Howard 1911–12, Joe Bradshaw 1912–19, Ned Liddell 1919–20, Tom Mather 1920–21, Ted Birnie 1921–34, David Jack 1934–40, Harry Warren 1946–56, Eddie Perry 1956–60, Frank Broome 1960, Ted Fenton 1961–65, Alvan Williams 1965–67, Ernie Shepherd 1967–69, Geoff Hudson 1969–70, Arthur Rowley 1970–76, Dave Smith 1976–83, Peter Morris 1983–84, Bobby Moore 1984–86, Dave Webb 1986–87, Dick Bate 1987, Paul Clark 1987–88, Dave Webb (GM) December 1988– .

Player and Position	Ht	Wt	Birth Date	Birth Place	Source	Clubs	League App	Gls
Ian Benjamin	5 11	12 00	11 12 61	Nottingham	Apprentice	Sheffield U	5	3
						WBA	2	—
						Notts Co	—	—
						Peterborough U	80	14
						Northampton T	150	59
						Cambridge U	25	2
						Chester C	22	2
						Exeter C	32	4
						Southend U	61	17
Steven Heffer			11 1 73	Southend	West Ham U	Southend U	—	—
Roy McDonough‡	6 1	11 11	16 10 58	Solihull	Apprentice	Birmingham C	2	1
						Walsall	82	15
						Chelsea	—	—
						Colchester U	93	24
						Southend U	22	4
						Exeter C	20	1
						Cambridge U	32	5
						Southend U	186	30
Morrys Scott	6 3	12 06	17 12 70	Swansea	Trainee Colchester U	Cardiff C Southend U	9	—
Mario Walsh‡	6 1	11 12	19 1 66	Paddington	Apprentice	Portsmouth	—	—
						Torquay U	100	18
						Colchester U	38	12
						Southend U	11	2
Adrian West‡			6 12 71	Bedford	Trainee	Southend U	—	—

Trainees
Affor, Louis K.J; Brown, Steven R.M; Capleton, Melvin D.R; Furzer, Lee T; Grayburn, Gavin; Grayburn, Marlon S; Hayden, Jason R; Ives, Spencer B; Jones, Antony; Jones, Michael; Jones, Shane N; Matthews, Lee D; Sains, Daniel B; Schneider, Matthew J; Sugrue, Simon.

Associated Schoolboys
Gordon, Christopher; Wellington, Mark A.

STOCKPORT COUNTY 1990–91 *Back row (left to right):* Lee Todd, Steve Bullock, Tony Barras, David Redfern, Paul Cooper, Tony Pennock, Chris Lucketti, David Ritchie, Darren Hope.
Centre row: Rodger Wylde (Physiotherapist), Paul R Williams, Chris Beaumont, Jim Gannon, Alan Finley, Paul A Williams, Neil Matthews, Gary Brabin, Philip Parker, Paul Robertson, John Sainty (Coach), David Jones (Youth Team Coach).
Front row: Malcolm Brown, Ian McInerney, Darren Knowles, Andy Thorpe, Danny Bergara (Manager), Bill Williams, Nick Brookman, David Frain, Mark Payne.

Division 3 STOCKPORT COUNTY

Edgeley Park, Hardcastle Road, Stockport, Cheshire SK3 9DD.
Telephone 061–480 8888. Clubcall: 0898 121638. Promotions
Office: 061-480 8117.

Ground capacity: 8520.

Record attendance: 27,833 v Liverpool, FA Cup 5th rd,
11 February 1950.

Record receipts: £23,515 v Liverpool, Milk Cup 2nd rd, 1st leg,
24 September 1984.

Pitch measurements: 110yd × 71yd.

Hon. Vice-presidents: Mike Yarwood OBE, Freddie Pye,
Andrew Barlow.

Chairman: B. Elwood. *Vice-chairman:* G. White.

Directors: M. Baker, B. Taylor, M. H. Rains, H. T. Stephenson, V. Snell.

Chief Executive/Secretary: J. D. Simpson.

Manager: Danny Bergara. *Assistant. Manager:* John Sainty.

Coach: *Physio:* Rodger Wylde.

Assistant Secretary/Commercial Manager:

General Manager: .*Programme Editors:* Steve Bellis and Todd White.

Year Formed: 1883. *Turned Professional:* 1891. *Ltd Co.:* 1908.

Club Nicknames: 'County' or 'Hatters'.

Previous Names: Heaton Norris Rovers, 1883–88; Heaton Norris, 1888–90.

Previous Grounds: 1883 Heaton Norris Recreation Ground; 1884 Heaton Norris Wanderers
Cricket Ground; 1885 Chorlton's Farm, Chorlton's Lane; 1886 Heaton Norris Cricket
Ground; 1887 Wilkes' Field, Belmont Street; 1889 Nursery Inn, Green Lane; 1902 Edgeley
Park.

Record League Victory: 13-0 v Halifax T, Division 3 (N), 6 January 1934 – McGann;
Vincent (1p), Jenkinson; Robinson, Stevens, Len Jones; Foulkes (1), Hill (3), Lythgoe (2),
Stevenson (2), Downes (4).

Record Cup Victory: 6-2 v West Auckland T (away), FA Cup, 1st rd, 14 November 1959 –
Lea; Betts (1), Webb; Murray, Hodder, Porteous; Wilson (1), Holland, Guy (2), Ritchie (1),
Davock (1).

Record Defeat: 1-8 v Chesterfield, Division 2, 19 April 1902.

Most League Points (2 for a win): 64, Division 4, 1966–67.

Most League Points (3 for a win): 82, Division 4, 1990–91.

Most League Goals: 115, Division 3 (N), 1933–34.

Highest League Scorer in Season: Alf Lythgoe, 46, Division 3 (N), 1933–34.

Most League Goals in Total Aggregate: Jack Connor, 132, 1951–56.

Most Capped Player: Harry Hardy, 1, England.

Most League Appearances: Bob Murray, 465, 1952–63.

Record Transfer Fee Received: £80,000 from Manchester C for Stuart Lee, September 1979.

Record Transfer Fee Paid: £50,000 to Rochdale for David Frain, July 1989 and £50,000 to
Hull C for Keith Edwards, September 1989.

Football League Record: 1900 Elected to Division 2; 1904 Failed re-election; 1905–21
Division 2; 1921–22 Division 3 (N); 1922–26 Division 2; 1926–37 Division 3 (N); 1937–38
Division 2; 1938–58 Division 3 (N); 1958–59 Division 3; 1959–67 Division 4; 1967–70
Division 3; 1970–91 Division 4; 1991– Division 3.

Honours: Football League: Division 2 best season: 10th, 1905–06; Division 3 (N) –
Champions 1921–22, 1936–37; Runners-up 1928–29, 1929-30; Division 4 – Champions
1966–67; Runners-up 1990–91. *FA Cup:* best season: 5th rd, 1935, 1950. *Football League
Cup:* best season: 4th rd, 1972–73.

Colours: Blue with red and white flecked shirts, royal blue shorts, white stockings. **Change
colours:** All red.

STOCKPORT COUNTY 1990–91 LEAGUE RECORD

Match No.	Date		Venue	Opponents	Result	H/T Score	Lg. Pos.	Goalscorers	Attendance
1	Aug 25		A	Halifax T	D	0-0 0-0	—		2362
2	Sept	1	H	Walsall	W	3-0 2-0	4	Beaumont, Payne, Williams PA	2668
3		8	A	Rochdale	L	0-1 0-1	7		2825
4		14	H	Burnley	D	2-2 0-2	—	Payne 2 (1 pen)	3523
5		17	H	Carlisle U	W	3-1 1-0	—	Williams PA 2, Payne	3118
6		22	A	Cardiff C	D	3-3 0-3	7	Matthews, Beaumont, Williams PA	3608
7		29	A	Hereford U	D	0-0 0-0	9		2619
8	Oct	1	H	Maidstone U	W	1-0 0-0	—	Frain	3207
9		6	H	Peterborough U	W	2-1 1-1	3	Beaumont, Payne	2924
10		13	A	Northampton T	L	0-1 0-0	6		3927
11		19	A	Aldershot	D	2-2 0-1	—	Payne 2	2413
12		22	H	Blackpool	D	0-0 0-0	—		4337
13		26	H	York C	W	2-0 2-0	—	Beaumont, Frain	3196
14	Nov	3	A	Scunthorpe U	L	0-3 0-0	8		2826
15		10	H	Lincoln C	W	4-0 2-0	4	Beaumont 2, Payne (pen), Gannon	2644
16	Dec	1	H	Darlington	W	3-1 2-1	5	Williams PA, Gannon, Payne	2938
17		7	A	Torquay U	D	1-1 1-1	—	Beaumont	2370
18		16	A	Scarborough	W	2-0 0-0	—	Williams PR 2	1154
19		21	H	Doncaster R	D	0-0 0-0	—		3347
20		29	A	Chesterfield	D	1-1 1-0	6	Williams PA	4307
21	Jan	1	H	Gillingham	D	1-1 1-1	6	Williams PA	2859
22		4	H	Wrexham	W	2-0 1-0	—	Kilner 2	3021
23		12	A	Walsall	W	2-0 1-0	1	Williams PA 2	4364
24		18	H	Halifax T	W	5-1 3-0	—	Gannon, Kilner, Brown (pen), Beaumont, Williams PA	4030
25		26	A	Burnley	L	2-3 1-2	3	Finley, Williams B	8946
26		29	A	Hartlepool U	L	1-3 1-2	—	Williams PA	2384
27	Feb	2	A	Carlisle U	L	0-1 0-0	4		2750
28		23	A	Lincoln C	W	3-0 1-0	4	Kilner, Beaumont 2	3257
29		26	H	Cardiff C	D	1-1 1-0	—	Gannon	3376
30	Mar	2	A	Darlington	L	0-1 0-0	5		4046
31		8	H	Scarborough	D	2-2 1-0	—	Matthews 2	3172
32		13	A	Maidstone U	W	3-2 1-0	—	Beaumont, Matthews, Williams PA	1412
33		16	H	Hereford U	W	4-2 1-0	4	Beaumont, Williams PA, Kilner 2	2569
34		23	A	Peterborough U	D	0-0 0-0	5		7047
35		26	H	Rochdale	W	3-0 2-0	—	Kilner, Frain, Williams PA	3697
36		29	H	Hartlepool U	L	1-3 0-1	—	Beaumont	5217
37	Apr	1	A	Doncaster R	L	0-1 0-0	5		3372
38		6	H	Chesterfield	W	3-1 3-1	5	Kilner, Beaumont, Matthews	3044
39		9	H	Northampton T	W	2-0 1-0	—	Francis, Matthews	3707
40		13	A	Gillingham	W	3-1 1-1	3	Matthews 2, Gannon	3001
41		16	A	Wrexham	W	3-1 2-0	—	Matthews 2, Francis	1968
42		19	H	Aldershot	W	3-2 2-1	—	Matthews, Francis, Beaumont	4422
43		23	H	Torquay U	W	2-1 0-1	—	Matthews, Kilner	4466
44		27	A	Blackpool	L	2-3 1-2	2	Finley, Gannon	8590
45	May	4	A	York C	W	2-0 0-0	2	Kilner 2 (1 pen)	3441
46		11	H	Scunthorpe U	W	5-0 2-0	2	Matthews 2, Francis 2, Finley	6212

Final League Position: 2

GOALSCORERS

League (84): Beaumont 15, Matthews 14, Williams PA 14, Kilner 11 (1 pen), Payne 9 (2 pens), Gannon 6, Francis 5, Finley 3, Frain 3, Williams PR 2, Brown 1 (pen), Williams B 1.
Rumbelows Cup (1): Williams PA 1.
FA Cup (0).

Cooper	Brown	Robertson	Bullock	Williams B	Finley	Payne	Gannon	Williams PA	Beaumont	Frain	Thorpe	Todd	Maguire	Barras	Matthews	Alexander	McInerney	Redfern	Brabin	Williams PR	Knowles	Kilner	Lee	Francis	Match No.
1	2	3	4	5	6	7	8	9	10	11															1
1	2	3			6	7	4	9	10*	11	5	8	12												2
1	2	3	6			7	4	9*	10	11	5	8†	12	14											3
1	2	3				7	4*	9†	10	11	5	8			6	12	14								4
1	2				6	7		9	10	4	5	11			3	8									5
1	2				6*	7		9	10	4	5	11			3	8	12								6
1	2	3	6†			7	8			4	5	11	14	12		9	10*								7
1	2	3	6			7	8		10	4	5	11				9									8
	2	3	6			7	8*		10	4	5	11		12	9		1								9
1	2	3	6			7	8†		10	4	5	11	14	12		9*									10
1		3	6			7			10	4	5	11		2	8	9									11
1		3	6			7			10	4	5	11		2	8	9*				12					12
1		3	6			7	8		10	4	5			2	11	9									13
1		3	6			7	8		10	4	5			2	11	9									14
1	2	3	6			7	8		10	4	5	11*			9	12									15
1	2	3				7	8	9	10	4	5				6					11					16
1	2	3				7	8	9	10	4	5				6					11					17
	2	3				7*	8	9	10	4	5				6			1		11	12				18
	2	3				7	8	9	10*	4	5				6	12		1		11†14					19
	2	3				7	8	9	10	4	5				6			1		11					20
1	2	3	6			7	8	9	10	4	5									11*	12				21
1	2	3	6			7		9	10	4					5					8	11				22
1	2	3	6					7	9	10	4				5					8	11				23
	2		3	5				7†	9	10	4	14		6	12			1	-	8	11*				24
1			3	2	5			7	9	10	4			6						8	11				25
1	2		3	5				7	9	10	4			6						8	11				26
1	2		5	3	8	7	9*	10	4		12			6						11					27
	2	3	6			7		10		4				5				1	8*	11	9	12			28
	2	3	6			7		10		4				5				1	12	11	9	8*			29
	2	3	6			7	9	10		4				5	12			1	8	11*					30
	2	3				7	9	10	4	5				6	8			1	12	11*					31
	2		6			7	9	10	11	4				5	8			1	3						32
	2	6*				7	9	10	11	4				5	8			1	3		12				33
	2				12	7*	9	10	4	5				6	8			1	3	11					34
	2					7	9	10	4†	5				6	8			1	3	14	11*		12		35
	2					7		10	4	5				6	8			1	3	11		9			36
	2			6		7		10	4	11				5	8†			1	3	14	12	9*			37
	2					7		10	4	5	12			6	8			1	3	11*		9			38
	2†	14*			12	7		10	4	5				6	8			1	3	11		9			39
					2	12	7	10	4	5				6	8			1	3	14	11†	9*			40
					2	12	7	10	4	5				6	8			1	3	11		9*			41
					2		7	10	4	5				6	8			1	3	11		9			42
					2	12	7	10	4	5				6	8			1	3	11		9*			43
					2	9	7	10	4	5				6	8			1	3	11					44
					2	12	7	10	4	5				6	8			1	3	11*		9			45
		14			2	12	7	10	4	5*				6	8			1	3†	11		9			46
22	34	1	29	17	19	24	41	24	45	43	39	12	—	37	22	9	1	24	—	23	6	21	2	11	
	+		+				+		+		+	+		+	+	+	+			+	+	+		+	
	1s	1s		7s			1s	2s	2s		3s	7s	2s	1s						1s	1s	6s	3s	2s	

Rumbelows Cup First Round Burnley (h) 0-2
    (a) 1-0
FA Cup First Round Rotherham U (a) 0-1

STOCKPORT COUNTY

Player and Position	Ht	Wt	Birth Date	Place	Source	Clubs	League App	Gls
Goalkeepers								
Paul Cooper	5 11	13 10	21 12 53	Brierley Hill	Apprentice	Birmingham C	17	—
						Ipswich T	447	—
						Leicester C	56	—
						Manchester C	15	—
						Stockport Co	22	—
Tony Pennock	5 11	10 09	10 4 71	Swansea	School	Stockport Co	—	—
						Wigan Ath (loan)	2	—
David Redfern	6 2	13 08	8 11 62	Sheffield	School	Sheffield W	—	—
						Doncaster R (loan)	—	—
						Rochdale (loan)	19	—
						Rochdale	68	—
					Gainsborough T	Stockport Co	35	—
Defenders								
Tony Barras	6 0	12 03	29 3 71	Teesside	Trainee	Hartlepool U	12	—
						Stockport Co	40	—
Malcolm Brown	6 2	12 06	13 12 56	Salford	Apprentice	Bury	11	—
						Huddersfield T	256	16
						Newcastle U	39	—
						Huddersfield T	96	1
						Rochdale	11	—
						Stockport Co	71	3
Steven Bullock*	5 8	11 01	5 10 66	Stockport	Apprentice	Oldham Ath	18	—
						Tranmere R	30	1
						Stockport Co	120	1
Chris Downes*	5 10	10 08	17 1 69	Sheffield	Trainee	Sheffield U	2	—
						Scarborough (loan)	2	—
						Stockport Co	11	1
Alan Finley	6 3	14 03	10 12 67	Liverpool	Marine	Shrewsbury T	63	2
						Stockport Co	19	3
Jim Gannon	6 2	12 06	7 9 68	London	Dundalk	Sheffield U	—	—
						Halifax T (loan)	2	—
						Stockport Co	48	7
Chris Lucketti*			28 9 71	Littleborough	Trainee	Rochdale	1	—
						Stockport Co	—	—
Paul Robertson*	5 7	11 06	5 2 72	Stockport	York C	Stockport Co	10	—
Andy Thorpe	5 11	12 00	15 9 60	Stockport	Amateur	Stockport Co	314	3
						Tranmere R	53	—
						Stockport Co	141	—
Bill Williams	6 1	12 11	7 10 60	Rochdale	Local	Rochdale	95	2
						Stockport Co	104	1
						Manchester C	1	—
						Stockport Co	83	3
Midfield								
David Bancroft*			20 10 72	Stockport	Trainee	Stockport Co	—	—
Gary Brabin‡			9 12 70	Liverpool	Trainee	Stockport Co	2	—
Nick Brookman‡	5 9	10 07	28 10 68	Manchester	Trainee	Bolton W	57	10
						Stockport Co	6	—
David Frain	5 8	10 05	11 10 62	Sheffield	Rowlinson YC	Sheffield U	44	5
						Rochdale	42	12
						Stockport Co	72	5
Darren Knowles	5 6	10 01	8 10 70	Sheffield	Trainee	Sheffield U	—	—
						Stockport Co	21	—
Philip Parker†			9 12 71	Middleton	Trainee	Stockport Co	—	—
Mark Payne*	5 9	11 09	3 8 60	Cheltenham		Stockport Co	87	16

STOCKPORT COUNTY

Foundation: Formed at a meeting held at Wellington Road South by members of Wycliffe Congregational Chapel in 1883, they called themselves Heaton Norris Rovers until changing to Stockport County in 1890, a year before joining the Football Combination.

First Football League game: 1 September, 1900, Division 2, v Leicester Fosse (a) D 2-2 – Moores; Earp, Wainwright; Pickford, Limond, Harvey; Stansfield, Smith (1), Patterson, Foster, Betteley (1).

Did you know: After losing 2-1 to Bradford PA, 2 April 1927, Stockport were unbeaten at Edgeley Park in either League or Cup until Crewe won there 3-2, 5 October 1929. The summary of that run of home games is P51 W42 D9 L0 F173 A48. Joe Smith of Bolton and Blackpool fame scored 61 of that enormous bag of home goals.

Managers (and Secretary-managers)
Fred Stewart 1894–1911, Harry Lewis 1911–14, David Ashworth 1914–19, Albert Williams 1919–24, Fred Scotchbrook 1924–26, Lincoln Hyde 1926–31, Andrew Wilson 1932–33, Fred Westgarth 1934–36, Bob Kelly 1936–38, George Hunt 1938–39, Bob Marshall 1939–49, Andy Beattie 1949–52, Dick Duckworth 1952–56, Billy Moir 1956–60, Reg Flewin 1960–63, Trevor Porteous 1963–65, Bert Trautmann (GM) 1965–66, Eddie Quigley (TM) 1965–66, Jimmy Meadows 1966–69, Wally Galbraith 1969–70, Matt Woods 1970–71, Brian Doyle 1972–74, Jimmy Meadows 1974–75, Roy Chapman 1975–76, Eddie Quigley 1976–77, Alan Thompson 1977–78, Mike Summerbee 1978–79, Jimmy McGuigan 1979–82, Eric Webster 1982–85, Colin Murphy 1985, Les Chapman 1985–86, Jimmy Melia 1986, Colin Murphy 1986–87, Asa Hartford 1987–89, Danny Bergara April 1989– .

Player and Position	Ht	Wt	Birth Date	Birth Place	Source	Clubs	League App	Gls
Forwards								
Chris Beaumont	5 11	11 07	5 12 65	Sheffield	Denaby	Rochdale	34	7
						Stockport Co	67	20
Kevin Francis	6 7	15 08	6 12 67	Moseley	Mile Oak Rovers			
						Derby Co	10	—
						Stockport Co	13	5
Darren Hope‡	5 6	10 05	3 4 71	Stoke	Trainee	Stoke C	—	—
						Stockport Co	4	—
Andy Kilner			11 10 66	Bolton	Apprentice	Burnley	5	—
						Stockport Co	24	11
Ian McInerney*	5 10	11 08	26 1 64	Liverpool	Blue Star	Huddersfield T	10	1
						Stockport Co	42	8
						Rochdale (loan)	4	1
John Mannion‡			23 7 71	Altrincham	Trainee	Stockport Co	—	—
Neil Matthews	5 11	12 00	19 9 66	Grimsby	Apprentice	Grimsby T	11	1
						Scunthorpe U (loan)	1	—
						Halifax T (loan)	9	2
						Bolton W (loan)	1	—
						Halifax T	105	29
						Stockport Co	29	14
David Ritchie‡	5 11	11 01	20 1 71	Newcastle	Trainee	Stoke C	—	—
						Stockport Co	1	—
Lee Todd	5 5	10 03	7 3 72	Hartlepool	Hartlepool U	Stockport Co	14	—
Paul Williams	5 6	10 07	11 9 69	Leicester	Trainee	Leicester C	—	—
						Stockport Co	31	2

Trainees
Foley, Paul; Holmes, Carl S; Nelson, Michael J; O'Hearns, Stephen; Spofforth, Ian.

Associated Schoolboys
Jordan, Darran M; Kilheeney, Martin J.

Associated Schoolboys who have accepted the club's offer of a Traineeship/Contract
Leigh, Malcolm; Wilks-Wells, Noel J.

STOKE CITY 1990–91. *Back row (left to right)*: Paul Barnes, Mark Higgins, Noel Blake, Lee Sandford, Ian Cranson, Wayne Biggins.
Centre row: Graham Paddon (Coach), David Kevan, John Butler, Danny Noble, Darren Boughey, Peter Fox, Tony Kelly, Derek Statham, Alan Ball (Manager).
Front row: Lee Fowler, Paul Ware, Tony Ellis, Ian Scott, Carl Beeston, Cliff Carr.

Division 3 **STOKE CITY**

Victoria Ground, Stoke-on-Trent. Telephone Stoke-on-Trent (0782) 413511. Commercial Dept: (0782) 45840. Soccerline Information: 0898 700278.

Ground capacity: 35,812.

Record attendance: 51,380 v Arsenal, Division 1, 29 March 1937.

Record receipts: £97,000 v Liverpool, FA Cup 3rd rd, 9 January 1988.

Pitch measurements: 116yd × 75yd.

Vice-president: J. A. M. Humphries.

Chairman: P. Coates. *Vice-chairman:* K. A. Humphreys.

Directors: P. J. Wright, R. D. Kenyon.

Manager: Lou Macari.

Coach: Sammy Chung. *Physio:* Keith Rowley.

Secretary: M. J. Potts.

Sales & Marketing Manager: M. J. Cullerton.

Year Formed: 1863 *(see Foundation).*

Turned Professional: 1885. *Ltd Co.:* 1908.

Club Nickname: 'The Potters'.

Previous Grounds: 1875, Sweeting's Field; 1878, Victoria Ground (previously known as the Athletic Club Ground).

Record League Victory: 10-3 v WBA, Division 1, 4 February 1937 – Doug Westland; Brigham, Harbot; Tutin, Turner (1p), Kirton; Matthews, Antonio (2), Freddie Steele (5), Jimmy Westland, Johnson (2).

Record Cup Victory: 7–1 v Burnley, FA Cup, 2nd rd (replay), 20 February 1896 – Clawley; Clare, Eccles; Turner, Grewe, Robertson; Willie Maxwell, Dickson, A. Maxwell (3), Hyslop (4), Schofield.

Record Defeat: 0–10 v Preston NE, Division 1, 14 September 1889.

Most League Points (2 for a win): 63, Division 3 (N), 1926–27.

Most League Points (3 for a win): 62, Division 2, 1987–88.

Most League Goals: 92, Division 3 (N), 1926–27.

Highest League Scorer in Season: Freddie Steele, 33, Division 1, 1936–37.

Most League Goals in Total Aggregate: Freddie Steele, 142, 1934–49.

Most Capped Player: Gordon Banks, 36 (73), England.

Most League Appearances: Eric Skeels, 506, 1958–76.

Record Transfer Fee Received: £750,000 from Everton for Peter Beagrie, October 1989.

Record Transfer Fee Paid: £480,000 to Sheffield W for Ian Cranson, July 1989.

Football League Record: 1888 Founder Member of Football League; 1890 Not re-elected; 1891 Re-elected; relegated in 1907, and after one year in Division 2, resigned for financial reasons; 1919 re-elected to Division 2; 1922–23 Division 1; 1923–26 Division 2; 1926–27 Division 3 (N); 1927–33 Division 2; 1933–53 Division 1; 1953–63 Division 2; 1963–77 Division 1; 1977–79 Division 2; 1979–85 Division 1; 1985–90 Division 2; 1990– Division 3.

Honours: Football League: Division 1 best season: 4th, 1935–36, 1946–47; Division 2 – Champions 1932–33, 1962–63; Runners-up 1921–22; Promoted 1978–79 (3rd); Division 3 (N) – Champions 1926–27. *FA Cup:* Semi-finals 1899, 1971, 1972. *Football League Cup:* Winners 1971–72. **European Competitions:** *UEFA Cup:* 1972–73, 1974–75.

Colours: Red and white striped shirts, white shorts, white stockings. **Change colours:** Yellow shirts, black shorts, yellow stockings.

STOKE CITY 1990–91 LEAGUE RECORD

Match No.	Date	Venue	Opponents	Result	H/T Score	Lg. Pos.	Goalscorers	Attendance
1	Aug 25	H	Rotherham U	W 3-1	2-0	—	Blake, Kennedy, Thomas	13,048
2	31	A	Tranmere R	W 2-1	2-1	—	Ellis, Kennedy (pen)	10,327
3	Sept 8	H	Birmingham C	L 0-1	0-0	7		16,009
4	15	A	Bournemouth	D 1-1	0-0	6	Statham	6374
5	18	A	Chester C	D 1-1	1-0	—	Thomas	3579
6	22	H	Southend U	W 4-0	2-0	7	Ware, Biggins 2, Cornwell (og)	11,901
7	29	H	Shrewsbury T	L 1-3	1-2	10	Sandford	12,672
8	Oct 2	A	Crewe Alex	W 2-1	1-0	—	Biggins, Ware	7200
9	6	A	Bolton W	W 1-0	0-0	4	Evans	8521
10	13	H	Fulham	W 2-1	1-0	3	Ellis 2	12,394
11	20	H	Cambridge U	D 1-1	0-1	3	Biggins	12,673
12	24	A	Bradford C	W 2-1	0-0	—	Kelly, Thomas	8086
13	27	A	Grimsby T	L 0-2	0-0	3		10,799
14	Nov 3	H	Reading	L 0-1	0-1	3		12,245
15	10	H	Wigan Ath	W 2-0	1-0	3	Biggins, Kennedy (pen)	12,756
16	24	A	Bury	D 1-1	0-0	3	Thomas	5118
17	Dec 1	A	Exeter C	L 0-2	0-0	3		5377
18	16	H	Brentford	D 2-2	1-1	—	Hilaire, Sandford	10,995
19	22	H	Preston NE	L 0-2	0-1	7		7532
20	26	H	Swansea C	D 2-2	1-1	8	Biggins, Thomas	12,534
21	29	H	Huddersfield T	W 2-0	1-0	8	Ellis 2	11,869
22	Jan 1	A	Leyton Orient	W 2-0	1-0	6	Ellis, Thomas	6371
23	12	H	Tranmere R	D 1-1	0-1	7	Butler	13,461
24	19	A	Rotherham U	D 0-0	0-0	7		6236
25	Feb 2	H	Chester C	L 2-3	0-1	10	Kelly, Hilaire	11,037
26	5	A	Southen U	L 0-1	0-1	—		5164
27	16	H	Bury	D 2-2	1-0	13	Biggins 2	9885
28	23	A	Wigan Ath	L 0-4	0-1	14		3728
29	27	H	Bournemouth	L 1-3	0-0	—	Biggins	7797
30	Mar 2	H	Exeter C	W 2-1	1-1	15	Biggins 2	8536
31	5	A	Mansfield T	D 0-0	0-0	—		2941
32	9	A	Brentford	W 4-0	0-0	13	Thomas, Blake, Beeston, Clarke	7249
33	13	H	Crewe Alex	W 1-0	0-0	—	Devlin	15,455
34	16	A	Shrewsbury T	L 0-2	0-2	12		6210
35	19	A	Fulham	W 1-0	0-0	—	Biggins	3131
36	23	H	Bolton W	D 2-2	0-0	10	Devlin, Kelly	13,869
37	26	H	Mansfield T	W 3-1	1-0	—	Clarke 2, Blake	9113
38	30	A	Swansea	L 1-2	0-1	10	Ellis	4418
39	Apr 1	H	Preston NE	L 0-1	0-0	10		11,524
40	6	A	Huddersfield T	L 0-3	0-1	13		6520
41	13	H	Leyton Orient	L 1-2	1-0	13	Beeston	7957
42	16	A	Birmingham C	L 1-2	1-2	—	Ellis	6729
43	20	A	Cambridge U	L 0-3	0-0	15		5743
44	27	H	Bradford C	W 2-1	2-1	13	Ellis, Butler	6946
45	May 4	H	Grimsby T	D 0-0	0-0	14		11,832
46	11	A	Reading	L 0-1	0-1	14		4101

Final League Position: 14

GOALSCORERS

League (55): Biggins 12, Ellis 9, Thomas 7, Blake 3, Clarke 3, Kelly 3, Kennedy 3 (2 pens), Beeston 2, Butler 2, Devlin 2, Hilaire 2, Sandford 2, Ware 2, Evans 1, Statham 1, own goal 1.
Rumbelows Cup (2): Evans 1, Kelly 1.
FA Cup (1): Sandford 1.

Fox	Butler	Statham	Beeston	Blake	Fowler	Kennedy	Ellis	Thomas	Biggins	Kelly	Ware	Sandford	Evans	Cranson	Carr	Kevan	Scott	Barnes	Bright	Whitehurst	Rennie	Hilaire	Gallimore	Devlin	Rice	Clarke	Noble	Baines	Match No.
1	2	3	4	5	6	7	8	9	10	11*12																			1
1	2	3	4	5		7	8	9*10		12	11	6																	2
1	2	3	4*	5		7	8	9	10	11	12	6																	3
1	2	3	4	5	14	7	8*12	10		9†11		6																	4
1	2	3	4	5		7	8	11	10		9	6																	5
1	2	3	4	5		7	8	9*10		12	11	6																	6
1	2	3	4*	5		7	8	12	10		11	6	9†14																7
1	2		5		7	8	11	10		4	6	9		3															8
1	2		5	14	7	8	11*10	12†	4	6	9		3																9
1	2		4	5		7	8	10		11		6	9	3															10
1	2	3	4	5		7	8	12	10		11*	6	9																11
1	2	3	4	5	7†	8	9	10*12	11	6		14																	12
1	2	3	4	5	7*	8	9	10†11		6		14	12																13
1	2	3	4	5		8	9		11	6			7	10*12															14
1	2	3	4	5	7	12	11	10		8*	6							9											15
1		3	4	5†14	7	8	9*10	12		11		6							2										16
1		3	4	5		7	8	12	10		11	6						9*	2										17
1		3	4	5		7	12	8	10		2	6						9*	11										18
1	2	3	4	5		7	8		10	12	9*	6†									11	14							19
1	2	3	4		6	7	8*	9	10	12			5								11								20
1	2		4		3	7	8	9	10			6	5								11								21
1	2		4	5	3		8	9	10		7	6								11									22
1	2	3	4	5		7	8	9*10		12										11									23
1		3		5	2	7	8	9	10*12	4	6									11									24
1	2		5			8	9†	10	4	6		3	14	7*							11	12							25
1	2		5			8		9	4*	6	14	3	12							11†	7	10							26
1	2		4	5		8	12	10	9		6	3									7*11								27
1	2		4	5	6	7	8	10*		9	3										12	11							28
1	2*	3	4	5		7	8†12	10		6									14		11	9							29
1		3	2	5		7		8	10	12	6						11				4*	9							30
1	3†		5		7		8	10	12	2		6	14				11*				4	9							31
1		2	5	6	7		8	10			3										4	11	9						32
1			5	6		8	10	12	14	7	3								2†		4	11*	9						33
1		2	5	6		14	8	10†12		7	3										4	11*	9						34
1		4	5			8	10	2	6		3										7	11	9						35
1		4	5			8		10	2	6		3									7	11	9						36
1		2	5	3	7		8	10		6											4	11	9						37
1		2	5	3	7	14	8	10	12	6*											4†11	9							38
1	4*	5	6	7			10	14	2		3								8†		12	11	9						39
1		4	5		7	12	8	10	6*	2		3									11	9							40
1	2		4	5	6		8	10*	9		3			12						14	7†11								41
	2		4	5	6		8	10	9		3†			12						14	7	11*			1	12			42
	2		5		7	8	10	9		14	12			3	4†					1	11*								43
1	3		5		8	9	10	7		2										6	4	11							44
1	3	4	5	8*	9	12	10	6		2										11	7								45
1	3	4	5	8*	9	12	10	6		2										11	7								46
44	31	22	37	44	14	32	33	32	36	16	29	32	5	7	15	4	1	3	—	3	3	10	4	18	18	9	2	1	
					+	+	+	+	+	+					+	+	+	+		+	+			+	+		+		
		3s			5s	6s	2s	13s	5s						2s	5s	1s	1s		3s	1s			3s	3s		1s		

Wright — Match No. 43(6).

Rumbelows Cup	First Round	Swansea C (h)		0-0
		(a)		1-0
	Second Round	West Ham U (a)		0-3
		(h)		1-2
FA Cup	First Round	Telford U (a)		0-0
		(h)		1-0
	Second Round	Burnley (a)		0-2

STOKE CITY

Player and Position	Ht	Wt	Birth Date	Birth Place	Source	Clubs	League App	Gls
Goalkeepers								
Scott Barrett‡	6 0	12 11	2 4 63	Ilkeston	Amateur	Wolverhampton W	30	—
						Stoke C	51	—
						Colchester U (loan)	13	—
						Stockport Co (loan)	10	—
Peter Fox	5 11	12 10	5 7 57	Scunthorpe	Apprentice	Sheffield W	49	—
						West Ham U (loan)	—	—
						Barnsley (loan)	1	—
						Stoke City	399	—
Daniel Noble*	5 11	12 09	2 9 70	Hull	Trainee	Stoke C	3	—
Defenders								
Noel Blake	6 0	13 05	12 1 62	Kingston, Jamaica	Sutton C T	Walsall	—	—
						Aston Villa	4	—
						Shrewsbury T (loan)	6	—
						Birmingham C	76	5
						Portsmouth	144	10
						Leeds U	51	4
						Stoke C	62	3
John Butler	5 11	11 07	7 2 62	Liverpool	Prescot Cables	Wigan Ath	245	15
						Stoke C	100	3
Cliff Carr*	5 5	10 04	19 6 64	London	Apprentice	Fulham	145	14
						Stoke C	124	1
Ian Cranson	5 11	12 04	2 7 64	Easington	Apprentice	Ipswich T	131	5
						Sheffield W	30	—
						Stoke C	26	2
Lee Fowler	5 7	11 11	26 1 69	Nottingham	Trainee	Stoke C	33	—
Mark Higgins‡	6 1	13 05	29 9 58	Buxton	Apprentice	Everton	152	6
						Manchester U	6	—
						Bury	68	—
						Stoke C	39	1
Scott Reaney‡			15 6 72	Stoke	Trainee	Stoke C	—	—
Paul Rennie	5 9	11 07	26 10 71	Nantwich	Trainee	Crewe Alex	2	—
						Stock C	3	—
Lee Sandford	6 1	12 02	22 4 68	Basingstoke	Apprentice	Portsmouth	72	1
						Stoke C	55	4
Derek Statham*	5 5	11 05	24 3 59	Wolverhampton	Apprentice	WBA	299	8
						Southampton	64	2
						Stoke C	41	1
Ian Wright	5 11	12 02	10 3 72	Lichfield	Trainee	Stoke C	2	—
Midfield								
Paul Baines			15 1 72	Tamworth	Trainee	Stoke C	2	—
Carl Beeston	5 9	10 03	30 6 67	Stoke	Apprentice	Stoke C	116	6
Darren Boughey	5 9	10 13	30 11 70	Stoke	Trainee	Stoke C	7	—
						Wigan Ath (loan)	2	2
						Exeter C (loan)	8	1
David Bright§			5 9 72	Bathavon	School	Stoke C	1	—
Mark Devlin	5 9	11 03	18 1 73	Irvine	Trainee	Stoke C	21	2
Stephen Farrell§			8 3 73	Kilmarnock	Trainee	Stoke C	2	—
Tony Gallimore	5 10	11 10	21 2 72	Crewe	Trainee	Stoke C	8	—
Tony Kelly	5 9	10 12	14 2 66	Meridan	St Albans C	Stoke C	38	3
Mick Kennedy	5 10	10 06	9 4 61	Salford	Apprentice	Halifax T	76	4
						Huddersfield T	81	9
						Middlesbrough	68	5
						Portsmouth	129	4
						Bradford C	45	2
						Leicester C	9	—
						Luton T	32	—
						Stoke C	32	3
David Kevan	5 8	9 10	31 8 68	Wigtown	Apprentice	Notts Co	89	3
						Cardiff C (loan)	7	—
						Stoke C	22	—
						Maidstone U (loan)	3	—
Chris Male	5 9	11 09	16 6 72	Portsmouth		Stoke C	—	—
Ian Scott	5 9	11 04	20 9 67	Radcliffe	Apprentice	Manchester C	24	3
						Stoke C	21	1
						Crewe Alex (loan)	12	1

STOKE CITY

Foundation: The date of the formation of this club has long been in doubt. The year 1863 was claimed, but more recent research by Wade Martin has uncovered nothing earlier than 1868, when a couple of Old Carthusians, who were apprentices at the local works of the old North Staffordshire Railway Company, met with some others from that works, to form Stoke Ramblers. It should also be noted that the old Stoke club went bankrupt in 1908 when a new club was formed.

First Football League game: 8 September, 1888, Football League, v WBA (h) L 0-2 – Rowley; Clare, Underwood; Ramsey, Shutt, Smith; Sayer, McSkimming, Staton, Edge, Tunnicliffe.

Did you know: In the 1930s Arsenal twice broke the ground record at Stoke before helping to create the present record of 51,380 in March 1937. The Gunners were the first side to attract a gate of over 45,000 to the Victoria Ground for a game involving Stoke – 45,348 in 1934 and beat this in 1935 with 45,470.

Managers (and Secretary-managers)
Tom Slaney 1874–83*, Walter Cox 1883–84*, Harry Lockett 1884–90, Joseph Bradshaw 1890–92, Arthur Reeves 1892–95, William Rowley 1895–97, H. D. Austerberry 1897–1908, A. J. Barker 1908–14, Peter Hodge 1914–15, Joe Schofield 1915–19, Arthur Shallcross 1919–23, John "Jock" Rutherford 1923, Tom Mather 1923–35, Bob McGrory 1935–52, Frank Taylor 1952–60, Tony Waddington 1960–77, George Eastham 1977–78, Alan A'Court 1978, Alan Durban 1978–81, Richie Barker 1981–83, Bill Asprey 1984–85, Mick Mills 1985–89, Alan Ball 1989–91, Lou Macari May 1991– .

Player and Position	Ht	Wt	Birth Date	Place	Source	Clubs	League App	Gls
Mickey Thomas*	5 6	10 07	7 7 54	Mochdre	Amateur	Wrexham	230	33
						Manchester U	90	11
						Everton	10	—
						Brighton & HA	20	—
						Stoke C	57	14
						Chelsea	44	9
						WBA	20	—
						Derby Co (loan)	9	—
					Wichita W	Shrewsbury T	40	1
						Leeds U	3	—
						Stoke C (loan)	5	—
						Stoke C	38	7
Paul Ware	5 8	11 02	7 11 70	Congleton	Trainee	Stoke C	62	3
Forwards								
Paul Barnes	5 10	10 02	16 11 67	Leicester	Apprentice	Notts Co	53	14
						Stoke C	11	—
						Chesterfield (loan)	1	—
Wayne Biggins	5 11	11 00	20 11 61	Sheffield	Apprentice Kings Lynn	Lincoln C	8	1
						Burnley	78	29
						Norwich C	79	16
						Manchester C	32	9
						Stoke C	73	22
Tony Ellis	5 11	11 00	20 10 64	Salford	Northwich V	Oldham Ath	8	—
						Preston NE	86	26
						Stoke C	62	15
Vince Hilaire*	5 6	10 00	10 10 59	Forest Hill	Apprentice	Crystal Palace	255	29
						Luton T	6	—
						Portsmouth	146	26
						Leeds U	44	6
						Stoke C (loan)	5	1
						Charlton Ath (loan)	—	—
						Stoke C	10	2
Jason Percival			20 9 73	Nuneaton	Trainee	Stoke C	—	—
Mark Sale*	6 5	13 08	27 2 72	Burton-on-Trent	Trainee	Stoke C	2	—

Trainees
Berks, John A; Berks, Peter R; Bright, David J; Farrell, Stephen; Green, Anthony J; Hobbs, David J; Jennings, Gareth J; Jones, Marcus L; Lees, Ian W; McLeish, Alexander P; Martin, Daniel; Mulligan, James; Potts, Adrian H; Robinson, Jason L; Sutton, Stuart A; Wileman, Matthew L.

Associated Schoolboys
Allerton, Daniel J; Ayres, Timothy; Blair, Scott; Bloor, David; Callan, Aidan J; Coker, Jonathan P; Cullerton, Jamie M; Eyre, Leslie A; Gawthorpe, Kerry J; Hassall, Stephen K; Hawkes, Marc J; Long, Ian G; Meer, Stuart W; Mills, Andrew, J; Prince, Robin J; Woods, Stephen J.

Associated Schoolboys who have accepted the club's offer of a Traineeship/Contract
Baines, Marc; Lovelock, Owen J; Marsh, Christopher T; Mosely, Christopher K; Winstone, Simon J; Woodier, Garry K.

SUNDERLAND AFC 1990-91. *Back row (left to right)*: Warren Hawke, John Cornforth, John MacPhail, Thomas Hauser, Richard Ord, Gary Owers, Paul Williams.
Second row: Denis Smith (Manager), Jim Morrow (Youth Development Officer), Steve Gaughan, Paul Lemon, John Kay, Tony Norman, Tim Carter, Andrew Samms, Gordon
Armstrong, Colin Pascoe, Kieron Brady, Roger Jones (Youth Team Coach), Viv Busby (Assistant Manager).
Seated: Jonathan Trigg, Wayne Walls, Simon Guthrie, David Rush, Brian Atkinson, Ricardo Gabbiadini, Martin Gray, Anthony Smith.
Front row: Steve Smelt (Physiotherapist), Paul Bracewell, Peter Davenport, Marco Gabbiadini, Gary Bennett, Kevin Ball, Paul Hardyman, Reuben Agboola, Malcolm Crosby
(Reserve Team Coach).

Division 2   **SUNDERLAND**

Roker Park Ground, Sunderland. Telephone Sunderland 091-514 0332. Commercial Dept: 091-567 2275.

Ground capacity: 31,887.

Record attendance: 75,118 v Derby Co, FA Cup 6th rd replay, 8 March 1933.

Record receipts: £186,000 v Tottenham H, Division 1, 28 August 1990.

Pitch measurements: 113yd × 74yd.

Chairman: R. S. Murray FCCA.

Directors: G. Davidson FCA, G. S. Wood.

Manager: Denis Smith.

General Manager/Secretary: G. Davidson FCA.

Chief Coach: Viv Busby. *Reserve Coach:* Malcolm Crosby.

Physio: Steve Smelt. *Youth Coach:* Roger Jones.

Commercial Manager: Alec King.

Year Formed: 1879. *Turned Professional:* 1886. *Ltd Co.:* 1906.

Club Nickname: 'Rokermen'.

Previous Name: 1879–80, Sunderland and District Teacher's AFC.

Previous Grounds: 1879, Blue House Field, Hendon; 1882, Groves Field, Ashbrooke; 1883, Horatio Street; 1884, Abbs Field, Fulwell; 1886, Newcastle Road; 1898, Roker Park.

Record League Victory: 9-1 v Newcastle U, Division 1, 5 December 1908 – Roose; Forster, Melton; Daykin, Thomson, Low; Mordue, Hogg (4), Brown, Holley (3), Bridgett (2).

Record Cup Victory: 11-1 v Fairfield, FA Cup, 1st rd, 2 February 1895 – Doig; McNeill, Johnston; Dunlop, McCreadie (1), Wilson; Gillespie (1), Millar (5), Campbell, Hannah (3), Scott (1).

Record Defeat: 0-8 v West Ham U, Division 1, 19 October 1968 and v Watford, Division 1, 25 September 1982.

Most League Points (2 for a win): 61, Division 2, 1963–64.

Most League Points (3 for a win): 93, Division 3, 1987–88.

Most League Goals: 109, Division 1, 1935–36.

Highest League Scorer in Season: Dave Halliday, 43, Division 1, 1928–29.

Most League Goals in Total Aggregate: Charlie Buchan, 209, 1911–25.

Most Capped Player: Martin Harvey, 34, Northern Ireland.

Most League Appearances: Jim Montgomery, 537, 1962–77.

Record Transfer Fee Received: £275,000 from Manchester C for Dennis Tueart, March 1974, from Manchester U for Chris Turner, August 1985 and from Sheffield W for Mark Proctor, September 1987.

Record Transfer Fee Paid: £450,000 to Hull C for Tony Norman, December 1988.

Football League Record: 1890 Elected to Division 1; 1958–64 Division 2; 1964–70 Division 1; 1970–76 Division 2; 1976–77 Division 1; 1977–80 Division 2; 1980–85 Division 1; 1985–87 Division 2; 1987–88 Division 3; 1988–90 Division 2; 1990–91 Division 1; 1991– Division 2.

Honours: Football League: Division 1 – Champions 1891–92, 1892–93, 1894–95, 1901–02, 1912–13, 1935–36; Runners-up 1893–94; 1897–98, 1900–01, 1922–23, 1934–35; Division 2 – Champions 1975–76; Runners-up 1963–64, 1979–80; Division 3 – Champions 1987–88. *FA Cup:* Winners 1937, 1973; Runners-up 1913. *Football League Cup:* Runners-up 1984–85. **European Competitions:** *Cup-Winners' Cup:* 1973–74.

Colours: Red and white striped shirts, black shorts, red stockings, white turnover. **Change colours:** Blue shirts, white shorts, blue stockings, white turnover.

SUNDERLAND 1990–91 LEAGUE RECORD

Match No.	Date		Venue	Opponents	Result	H/T Score	Lg. Pos.	Goalscorers	Atten-dance
1	Aug	25	A	Norwich C	L 2-3	0-2	—	Davenport, Gabbiadini	17,247
2		28	H	Tottenham H	D 0-0	0-0	—		30,214
3	Sept	1	H	Manchester U	W 2-1	1-0	9	Owers, Bennett	26,105
4		8	A	Chelsea	L 2-3	1-2	12	Gabbiadini, Brady	19,424
5		15	H	Everton	D 2-2	2-2	14	Davenport (pen), Gabbiadini	25,004
6		22	A	Wimbledon	D 2-2	1-0	13	Armstrong, Davenport	6143
7		29	H	Liverpool	L 0-1	0-1	16		31,107
8	Oct	6	A	Aston Villa	L 0-3	0-1	16		26,017
9		20	H	Luton T	W 2-0	2-0	15	Gabbiadini, Davenport	20,025
10		27	A	Arsenal	L 0-1	0-0	17		38,539
11	Nov	3	H	Manchester C	D 1-1	1-0	18	Davenport	23,137
12		10	H	Coventry C	D 0-0	0-0	18		20,101
13		17	A	Nottingham F	L 0-2	0-1	18		22,757
14		24	A	Sheffield U	W 2-0	0-0	14	Gabbiadini 2	19,179
15	Dec	1	H	Derby Co	L 1-2	0-1	16	Armstrong	21,212
16		8	A	Tottenham H	D 3-3	2-0	16	Pascoe 2, Davenport	30,431
17		15	H	Norwich C	L 1-2	1-0	17	Armstrong	18,693
18		23	H	Leeds U	L 0-1	0-0	—		23,773
19		26	A	Crystal Palace	L 1-2	0-0	18	Rush	15,560
20		29	A	QPR	L 2-3	1-1	19	Pascoe, Ball (pen)	11,072
21	Jan	1	H	Southampton	W 1-0	0-0	17	Ball (pen)	19,757
22		12	A	Manchester U	L 0-3	0-3	17		45,934
23		19	H	Chelsea	W 1-0	0-0	17	Pascoe	20,038
24	Feb	2	A	Everton	L 0-2	0-0	17		23,124
25		16	H	Nottingham F	W 1-0	1-0	16	Gabbiadini	20,394
26		23	A	Coventry C	D 0-0	0-0	17		10,453
27	Mar	2	A	Derby Co	D 3-3	3-2	19	Armstrong, Gabbiadini, Ball	16,027
28		9	H	Sheffield U	L 0-1	0-0	19		23,238
29		16	A	Liverpool	L 1-2	1-2	19	Armstrong	37,582
30		23	A	Aston Villa	L 1-3	0-1	19	Davenport	21,099
31		30	H	Crystal Palace	W 2-1	1-0	19	Brady, Rush	19,704
32	Apr	2	A	Leeds U	L 0-5	0-3	—		28,132
33		6	H	QPR	L 0-1	0-0	19		17,899
34		13	A	Southampton	L 1-3	1-1	19	Hauser	16,812
35		20	A	Luton T	W 2-1	1-1	19	Armstrong, Pascoe	11,157
36		23	H	Wimbledon	D 0-0	0-0	—		24,036
37	May	4	H	Arsenal	D 0-0	0-0	19		22,606
38		11	A	Manchester C	L 2-3	2-2	19	Gabbiadini, Bennett	39,194

Final League Position: 19

GOALSCORERS

League (38): Gabbiadini 9, Davenport 7 (1 pen), Armstrong 6, Pascoe 5, Ball 3 (2 pens), Bennett 2, Brady 2, Rush 2, Hauser 1, Owers 1.
Rumbelows Cup (6): Gabbiadini 2, Ball 1, Cullen 1, Hauser 1, Owers 1.
FA Cup (1): Own goal 1.

Norman	Kay	Agboola	Bennett	MacPhail	Owers	Bracewell	Armstrong	Davenport	Gabbiadini	Atkinson	Cullen	Hauser	Ball	Hardyman	Brady	Ord	Smith	Carter	Pascoe	Hawke	Rush	Williams	Mooney	Cornforth	Match No.
1	2	3	4	5	6	7	8	9	10†	11*	12	14													1
1	2	3	4		6	7	8	9	10		12		5	11*											2
1	2	3	4		6	7*	8	9	10†			14	5	11	12										3
1	2	3	4		6		8	9	10		7		5	11*	12										4
1	2	3*	4		6	7	8	9	10				5	11	12										5
1	2		4		6	7	8	9	10*		12		5	11		3									6
1	2		4		6	7	8	9	10	11*	12		5			3									7
1	2		4		6	7	8	9	10				5	11			3								8
1	2		4		6	7	8	9	10				5	11			3								9
1	2		4		6	7	8	9	10		12		5	11			3*								10
1	2		4		6	7	8	9	10	11*			5			3	12								11
	2				6	7	8	9	10				5			3		1	11						12
1	2		4		6	7	8	9	10*				5			3			11	12					13
1	2		4		6	7	8	9	10				5			3			11						14
1	2		4		6	7	8	9	10				5			3			11						15
1	2		4		6	7	8	9	10				5			3			11						16
1	2				6	7	8	9	10				5			3	4		11						17
1	2		4		6	7	8		10				5			3	9		11*	12					18
1	2		4		6	7	8		10*				5			3	9		11	12					19
1	2		4		6	7	8	9*					5	14		3			11	12†10					20
1	2		4		6	7	8						5			3			11	9	10				21
1	2†		4		6	7	8		10				5	14		3			11	12	9*				22
1			4		6	7	8	9	10*	2			5			3			11	12					23
1			4		6	7	8	9	10		12		5			3	2		11*						24
1			4		2	7	8	9	10				5			3			11		6				25
1			4		2	7	8	9	10				5			3			11		6				26
1			4		2	7	8	9	10				5			3*	12		11		6				27
1			4		2	7	8	9	10				5		12	3			11		6*				28
1	6†		4		2	7	8		10*				5			3	12		11	9			14		29
1	14		4		2	7	8*	12	10				5			3			11	9			6†		30
1	6		4		2	7	8		10				5			3			11	9					31
1	6		4		2	7	8*	12	10				5			3			11†	9			14		32
1	14		4		2	7	8	9	10†				5			3*			11		6		12		33
1	11		4		2	7	8	9	10*		12		5			3					6				34
1	11†		4		2	7	8	9	10*		12		5			3	14				6				35
1			4		2	7	8	9	10†	11*			5		12	3	14				6				36
1	11		4		2	7		9	10				5			3	12				6			8*	37
1	11		4		2	7		9	10			14	5		12	3*					6			8†	38
37	28	5	37	1	38	37	35	27	30	4	2	5	33	30	4	12	9	1	25	3	8	1	5	1	

Substitute appearances (+):
Kay 2s; Gabbiadini 2s; Atkinson 1s; Cullen 2s; Hauser 3s; Ball 5s; 2s 10s 2s; 4s 3s; 1s 1s

Rumbelows Cup	Second Round	Bristol C (h)	0-1
		(a)	6-1
	Third Round	Derby Co (a)	0-6
FA Cup	Third Round	Arsenal (a)	1-2

SUNDERLAND

Player and Position	Ht	Wt	Birth Date	Birth Place	Source	Clubs	League App	Gls
Goalkeepers								
Tim Carter	6 1	12 00	5 10 67	Bristol	Apprentice	Bristol R	47	—
						Newport Co (loan)	1	—
						Sunderland	22	—
						Carlisle U (loan)	4	—
						Bristol C (loan)	3	—
Tony Norman	6 2	12 08	24 2 58	Mancot	Amateur	Burnley	—	—
						Hull C	372	—
						Sunderland	89	—
Andy Sams‡	6 0	13 01	18 12 70	Bishop Auckland	Trainee	Sunderland	—	—
Defenders								
Reuben Agboola	5 9	11 02	30 5 62	London	Apprentice	Southampton	90	—
						Sunderland	139	—
						Charlton Ath (loan)	1	—
						Port Vale (loan)	9	—
Kevin Ball	5 9	11 06	12 11 64	Hastings	Amateur	Coventry C	—	—
						Portsmouth	105	4
						Sunderland	33	3
Gary Bennett	6 1	12 01	4 12 61	Manchester	Amateur	Manchester C	—	—
						Cardiff C	87	11
						Sunderland	257	20
Paul Hardyman	5 8	11 04	11 3 64	Portsmouth	Fareham	Portsmouth	117	3
						Sunderland	74	7
John Kay	5 10	11 06	29 1 64	Sunderland	Apprentice	Arsenal	14	—
						Wimbledon	63	2
						Middlesbrough (loan)	8	—
						Sunderland	119	—
Richard Ord	6 2	12 08	3 3 70	Easington	Trainee	Sunderland	63	2
						York C (loan)	3	—
Ian Sampson	6 2	12 08	14 11 68	Wakefield	Goole T	Sunderland	—	—
Anthony Smith			22 11 68	Sunderland	Trainee	Sunderland	9	—
Jonathan Trigg	5 8	10 06	8 5 71	Jersey	Trainee	Sunderland	—	—
Wayne Walls			23 7 72	Sunderland	Trainee	Sunderland	—	—
Paul Williams	6 0	12 02	25 9 70	Liverpool	Trainee	Sunderland	3	—
						Swansea C (loan)	12	—
Midfield								
Gordon Armstrong	6 0	11 02	15 7 67	Newcastle	Apprentice	Sunderland	222	34
Paul Bracewell	5 8	10 09	19 7 62	Stoke	Apprentice	Stoke C	129	5
						Sunderland	38	4
						Everton	95	7
						Sunderland	74	2
John Cornforth	6 1	11 05	7 10 67	Whitley Bay	Apprentice	Sunderland	32	2
						Doncaster R (loan)	7	3
						Shrewsbury T (loan)	3	—
						Lincoln C (loan)	9	1
Steven Gaughan	5 11	11 02	14 4 70	Doncaster	Trainee	Doncaster R	67	3
						Sunderland	—	—
Martin Gray	5 9	10 11	17 8 71	Stockton	Trainee	Sunderland	—	—
						Aldershot (loan)	5	—
Brian Mooney	5 11	11 02	2 2 66	Dublin	Home Farm	Liverpool	—	—
						Wrexham (loan)	9	2
						Preston NE	128	20
						Sheffield W (loan)	—	—
						Sunderland	6	—
Gary Owers	5 10	11 10	3 10 68	Newcastle	Apprentice	Sunderland	156	17

SUNDERLAND

Foundation: A Scottish schoolmaster named James Allan, working at Hendon Boarding School, took the initiative in the foundation of Sunderland in 1879 when they were formed as The Sunderland and District Teachers' Association FC at a meeting in the Adults School, Norfolk Street. Because of financial difficulties, they quickly allowed members from outside the teaching profession and so became Sunderland AFC in October 1880.

First Football League game: 13 September, 1890, Football League, v Burnley (h) L 2-3 – Kirtley; Porteous, Oliver; Wilson, Auld, Gibson; Spence (1), Miller, Campbell (1), Scott, D. Hannah.

Did you know: The first time 10 goals were scored in a League game at Roker Park was on 19 January 1907 when Sunderland came back from 4-1 down at half-time to draw 5-5 in a thrilling tussle with Liverpool.

Managers (and Secretary-managers)
Tom Watson 1888–96, Bob Campbell 1896–99, Alex Mackie 1899–1905, Bob Kyle 1905–28, Johnny Cochrane 1928–39, Bill Murray 1939–57, Alan Brown 1957–64, George Hardwick 1964–65, Ian McColl 1965–68, Alan Brown 1968–72, Bob Stokoe 1972–76, Jimmy Adamson 1976–78, Ken Knighton 1979–81, Alan Durban 1981–84, Len Ashurst 1984–85, Lawrie McMenemy 1985–87, Denis Smith May 1987– .

Player and Position	Ht	Wt	Birth Date	Birth Place	Source	Clubs	League App	Gls
Forwards								
Brian Atkinson	5 10	12 00	19 1 71	Darlington	Trainee	Sunderland	22	—
Kieron Brady	5 9	11 13	17 9 71	Glasgow	Trainee	Sunderland	25	4
Tony Cullen	5 6	11 07	30 9 69	Newcastle		Sunderland	28	—
						Carlisle U (loan)	2	1
						Rotherham U (loan)	3	1
Peter Davenport	5 11	11 03	24 3 61	Birkenhead	Amateur Cammel Laird	Everton	—	—
						Nottingham F	118	54
						Manchester U	92	22
						Middlesbrough	59	7
						Sunderland	29	7
Marco Gabbiadini	5 10	11 02	20 1 68	Nottingham	Apprentice	York C	60	14
						Sunderland	148	69
Simon Guthrie			24 6 72	Newcastle	Trainee	Sunderland	—	—
Thomas Hauser	6 3	12 06	10 4 65	West Germany	Berne OB	Sunderland	41	9
Warren Hawke	5 10	10 11	20 9 70	Durham	Trainee	Sunderland	19	1
Colin Pascoe	5 9	10 00	9 4 65	Bridgend	Apprentice	Swansea C	174	39
						Sunderland	106	20
David Rush	5 11	10 10	15 5 71	Sunderland	Trainee	Sunderland	11	2

Trainees
Atkinson, Jonathan; Brodie, Stephen E; Carr, David A; Egen, Jonathan D; Gooding, Robert; Gray, Michael; Harwood, Paul; Jeffrey, Paul E; Maskell, Stuart; Moore, Paul; Morson, David; Patterson, Ian D; Robinson, Anthony; Russell, Craig S; Wales, David J.

Associated Schoolboys
Carmichael, Barry; Coulthard, David; Hails, Stuart A; Lawson, Ian D; Mavin, Simon; Pickering, Steven; Piggott, Craig; Scothern, Andrew; Stoddart, Neil M.

Associated Schoolboys who have accepted the club's offer of a Traineeship/Contract
Ferry, David; McGee, Dean; Musgrave, Sean; Smith, Martin.

SWANSEA CITY 1990–91 *Back row (left to right)*: Simon Davey, David Hough, Des Trick, Chris Coleman, Mark Harris, Jimmy Gilligan, Paul Raynor.
Centre row: Paul Chalmers, Tommy Hutchinson, Mark Kendall, James Heeps, Lee Bracey, Keith Walker, Terry Connors.
Front row: Alan Davies, Steve Thornber, Russell Coughlin, Phil Evans, Clive Freeman, Andy Watson, David D'Auria, Andrew Legg.

Division 3 — SWANSEA CITY

Vetch Field, Swansea SA1 3SU. Telephone Swansea (0792) 474114. Fax: (0792) 646120.

Ground capacity: 16,098.

Record attendance: 32,796 v Arsenal, FA Cup 4th rd, 17 February 1968.

Record receipts: £36,477.42 v Liverpool, Division 1, 18 September 1982.

Pitch measurements: 112yd × 74yd.

President: I. C. Pursey MBE.

Chairman: D. J. Sharpe.

Directors: D. G. Hammond FCA, MBIM (Vice-chairman), M. Griffiths.

Team Manager: Frank Burrows. *Assistant Manager:*

Youth Team Manager: Ron Walton. *Physio:* Ken Davey.

Commercial and Marketing Manager: W. Fleming.

Year Formed: 1912. *Turned Professional:* 1912. *Ltd Co.:* 1912.

Secretary: George Taylor.

Previous Name: Swansea Town until February 1970.

Club Nickname: 'The Swans'.

Record League Victory: 8-0 v Hartlepool U, Division 4, 1 April 1978 – Barber; Evans, Bartley, Lally (1) (Morris), May, Bruton, Kevin Moore, Robbie James (3 incl. 1p), Curtis (3), Toshack (1), Chappell.

Record Cup Victory: 12-0 v Sliema W (Malta), ECWC 1st rd 1st leg, 15 September 1982 – Davies; Marustik, Hadziabdic (1), Irwin (1), Kennedy, Rajkovic (1), Loveridge (2) (Leighton James), Robbie James, Charles (3), Stevenson (1), Latchford (1) (Walsh (3)).

Record Defeat: 1-8 v Fulham, Division 2, 22 January 1938.

Most League Points (2 for a win): 62, Division 3 (S), 1948–49.

Most League Points (3 for a win): 70, Division 4, 1987–88.

Most League Goals: 90, Division 2, 1956–57.

Highest League Scorer in Season: Cyril Pearce, 35, Division 2, 1931–32.

Most League Goals in Total Aggregate: Ivor Allchurch, 166, 1949–58, 1965–68.

Most Capped Player: Ivor Allchurch, 42 (68), Wales.

Most League Appearances: Wilfred Milne, 585, 1919–37.

Record Transfer Fee Received: £370,000 from Leeds U for Alan Curtis, May 1979.

Record Transfer Fee Paid: £340,000 to Liverpool for Colin Irwin, August 1981.

Football League Record: 1920 Original Member of Division 3; 1921–25 Division 3 (S); 1925–47 Division 2; 1947–49 Division 3 (S); 1949–65 Division 2; 1965–67 Division 3; 1967–70 Division 4; 1970–73 Division 3; 1973–78 Division 4; 1978–79 Division 3; 1979–81 Division 2; 1981–83 Division 1; 1983–84 Division 2; 1984–86 Division 3; 1986–88 Division 4; 1988– Division 3.

Honours: Football League: Division 1 best season: 6th, 1981–82; Division 2 – Promoted 1980–81 (3rd); Division 3 (S) – Champions 1924–25, 1948–49; Division 3 – Promoted 1978–79 (3rd); Division 4 – Promoted 1969–70 (3rd), 1977–78 (3rd). *FA Cup:* Semi-finals 1926, 1964. *Football League Cup:* best season: 4th rd, 1964–65, 1976–77. *Welsh Cup:* Winners 9 times; Runners-up 8 times. **European Competitions:** *European Cup-Winners' Cup:* 1961–62, 1966–67, 1981–82, 1982–83, 1983–84.

Colours: White shirts, white shorts, black stockings. **Change colours:** All red.

SWANSEA CITY 1990–91 LEAGUE RECORD

Match No.	Date	Venue	Opponents	Result	H/T Score	Lg. Pos.	Goalscorers	Attendance
1	Aug 25	A	Leyton Orient	L 0-3	0-0	—		4206
2	Sept 1	H	Huddersfield T	W 1-0	0-0	15	Gilligan	4787
3	8	A	Exeter C	L 0-2	0-1	18		4719
4	15	H	Brentford	D 2-2	1-0	17	Davies, Legg	4127
5	18	H	Bury	L 1-2	1-1	—	Davies	3505
6	22	A	Bradford C	W 1-0	0-0	14	D'Auria	7724
7	28	H	Tranmere R	D 1-1	1-0	—	Raynor (pen)	4884
8	Oct 2	A	Southend U	L 1-4	0-1	—	Gilligan	3635
9	6	A	Grimsby T	L 0-1	0-1	19		5974
10	13	H	Crewe Alex	W 3-1	2-1	17	Davies, D'Auria, Raynor (pen)	3888
11	20	H	Fulham	D 2-2	2-0	17	Chalmers, Gilligan	4500
12	23	A	Shrewsbury T	W 2-1	1-0	—	Gilligan, Watson	2589
13	27	A	Bolton W	L 0-1	0-1	17		4158
14	Nov 3	H	Cambridge U	D 0-0	0-0	19		3902
15	10	A	Mansfield T	L 0-2	0-0	19		2200
16	24	H	Chester C	W 1-0	0-0	16	Raynor	3361
17	Dec 1	H	Birmingham C	W 2-0	2-0	16	Connor 2	4896
18	14	A	Bournemouth	L 0-1	0-1	—		5031
19	22	H	Reading	W 3-1	2-0	15	Gilligan 2, Connor	3778
20	26	A	Stoke C	D 2-2	1-1	16	Gilligan 2	12,534
21	29	A	Wigan Ath	W 4-2	0-0	13	Gilligan 3, Raynor	2525
22	Jan 1	H	Rotherham U	W 5-0	4-0	10	Legg 2, Gilligan, Connor, D'Auria	5938
23	12	A	Huddersfield T	W 2-1	1-1	10	Mitchell (og), D'Auria	4052
24	26	A	Brentford	L 0-2	0-0	13		5373
25	Feb 2	A	Bury	L 0-1	0-0	15		2135
26	23	H	Mansfield T	L 1-2	1-1	16	Gilligan	3354
27	26	H	Exeter C	L 0-3	0-0	—		2385
28	Mar 2	A	Birmingham C	L 0-2	0-0	17		6903
29	9	H	Bournemouth	L 1-2	1-0	17	Gilligan	3086
30	12	H	Southend U	L 1-4	1-1	—	Gilligan	2712
31	15	A	Tranmere R	L 1-2	1-1	—	Chalmers	5412
32	19	A	Crewe Alex	L 0-3	0-1	—		2622
33	23	H	Grimsby T	D 0-0	0-0	19		3203
34	26	A	Preston NE	L 0-2	0-0	—		3491
35	30	H	Stoke C	W 2-1	1-0	19	Legg, Harris	4418
36	Apr 1	A	Reading	D 0-0	0-0	18		3597
37	6	H	Wigan Ath	L 1-6	1-3	19	Gilligan	2869
38	13	A	Rotherham U	W 3-2	0-2	19	Penney, Davey 2	3510
39	16	H	Preston NE	W 3-1	1-1	—	Jackson (og), Penney, Connor	2507
40	20	A	Fulham	D 1-1	0-0	18	Legg	4208
41	23	A	Chester C	L 1-2	1-1	—	Raynor	852
42	26	H	Shrewsbury T	L 0-1	0-0	19		3152
43	30	H	Leyton Orient	D 0-0	0-0	—		2132
44	May 4	H	Bolton W	L 1-2	1-1	19	Penney (pen)	4713
45	9	H	Bradford C	L 0-2	0-1	—		2126
46	11	A	Cambridge U	L 0-2	0-2	20		9023

Final League Position: 20

GOALSCORERS

League (49): Gilligan 16, Connor 5, Legg 5, Raynor 5 (2 pens), D'Auria 4, Davies 3, Penney 3 (1 pen), Chalmers 2, Davey 2, Harris 1, Watson 1, own goals 2.
Rumbelows Cup (0).
FA Cup (7): Connor 2, Gilligan 2 (2 pens), Legg 2, Thornber 1.

Bracey	Raynor	Coleman	Hough	Harris	Walker	Thornber	Davies	Gilligan	Connor	Legg	Watson	Trick	Chalmers	D'Auria	Hutchison	Freeman	Davey	Coughlin	Honor	Miller	Bowen	Kendall	Williams	Penney	Jenkins	Match No.
1	2	3	4	5	6*	7	8	9	10	11	12															1
1	2	3		5	6	7	8	9	10	11			4													2
1	2	3		5	6*	7	8†	9		11	10	4	12	14												3
1	2	3	12	5	6	7	8	9		11		4*	10													4
1	2	3		5	12	7	8	9		11	6	4	10*													5
1	2	3		5	12		8	9			7	4	6	10*11												6
1	2	3		5			8	9			7	4	10*	6	11	12										7
1	2	3		5	11		8	9			7*	4	12	6	10†	14										8
1	2	3		5			8	9		11	7	4	10	6												9
1	2	3	4	5			8	9	10*11		7		12	6												10
1	2	3	5				8	9		11	7	4	10		6											11
1	2	3	4	5			8	9		11	12	10*	6				7									12
1	2	3	4	5	14		8	9		11	12	10*	6†				7									13
1	2	3	14	5	4†		8	9	10	11	12		6*				7									14
1	7†	3	2	5			8	6	9*10	11		4	12	14												15
1	12	3	2	5	4		6		10	11	7†		14				9*	8								16
1	7	3	2	5	4	14	6	9*10		11							12	8†								17
1	7	3	2	5	4	9	6	12	10	11*								8								18
1	7	3	2	5	4	12	6	9†10		11*				14				8								19
1	7†	3	2	5	4		6	9	10	11*				14	12			8								20
1	7	3	2	5	4	11*	6	9	10	12								8								21
1	7	3	2	5	4	12	6	9†10		11				14				8*								22
1	7*	3	2	5	4	12	6	9	10	11†				14				8								23
1	12	3		5	4†		6	9	10	11*			7					8		2	14					24
1	10	3		5	4	7*	6	9		12				14				8		2	11†					25
1	7†	3	2	5	4		6	9	10	11*	12	2		14				8								26
1	12	3	2	5	4		6	9	10	11							7*	8								27
1	12	3	2	5	4†		8	9	10*	11			14				7	6								28
1		3	2	5	4	6	9	10		11	12						7*	8								29
1		3	2	5†	4*	6	9	10		11			14				7	8	12							30
		3	2	5	4	6	9	10		11							7	8				1				31
12		3	2	5*	4	6	9	10†		11			14				7	8				1				32
1	7	3	4	5		6	8	9	10	11							2									33
1	7	3	4	5		6	8	9		11*							2	10	12							34
1	7	3	4	5		6	8	9										10					2	11		35
12		3	4	5		6	8	9*10										7				1	2	11		36
12	3*		4	5		6	8†	9	10				14					7				1	2	11		37
	9	3	4	5		6			10								8	7*	12			1	2	11		38
	7	3	4	5		6	8*	9	10									12				1	2	11		39
	8	3	4	5	7*12	6			10									9†	14			1	2	11		40
	8	3	4	5	7 12	6†			10									9*	14			1	2	11		41
	8	3	4	5†14	12	6			10								7*	9				1	2	11		42
	8	3	4	5	7	6			10									9				1	2	11		43
	8	3	4	5	7	6*14	12		10									9				1	2†	11		44
1	8	3	4	5	7†	6			10								12	9*	14				2	11		45
1	8*	3	4	5	6				10		7†						12	9					2	11	14	46
35	36	41	39	41	21	11	35	36	33	37	9	14	12	12	6	2	11	29	2	8	1	11	12	12	—	
	+		+		+	+		+	+		+	+	+	+	+			+		+		+		+		
7s	2s		3s	8s	1s		2s	5s	1s		9s	8s	3s				7s			4s	2s			1s		

Rumbelows Cup First Round Stoke C (a) 0-0
    (h) 0-1
FA Cup First Round Welling (h) 5-2
    Second Round Walsall (h) 2-1
    Third Round Rotherham U (h) 0-0
    (a) 0-4

SWANSEA CITY

Player and Position	Ht	Wt	Birth Date	Birth Place	Source	Clubs	League App	Gls
Goalkeepers								
Lee Bracey	6 1	12 08	11 9 68	Ashford	Trainee	West Ham U	—	—
						Swansea C	96	—
Jimmy Heeps			16 5 71	Luton	Trainee	Swansea C	1	—
Mark Kendall	6 0	12 04	20 9 58	Blackwood	Apprentice	Tottenham H	29	—
						Chesterfield (loan)	9	—
						Newport Co	272	—
						Wolverhampton W	147	—
						Swansea C	11	—
Defenders								
Terry Boyle‡	5 10	12 04	29 10 58	Ammanford	Apprentice	Tottenham H	—	—
						Crystal Palace	26	1
						Wimbledon (loan)	5	1
						Bristol C	37	—
						Newport Co	166	11
						Cardiff C	128	7
						Swansea C	27	1
Chris Coleman	6 2	12 10	10 6 70	Swansea	Apprentice	Swansea C	160	2
Philip Evans*	5 10	11 00	1 3 71	Swansea	Trainee	Swansea C	—	—
Mark Harris	6 1	13 00	15 7 63	Reading	Wokingham	Crystal Palace	2	—
						Burnley (loan)	4	—
						Swansea C	82	3
Paul Miller	6 1	12 02	11 10 59	London	Apprentice	Tottenham H	208	7
						Charlton Ath	42	2
						Watford	20	1
						Bournemouth	47	1
						Brentford (loan)	3	—
						Swansea C	12	—
Des Trick	6 0	12 00	7 11 69	Swansea	Trainee	Swansea C	29	—
Midfield								
Jason Bowen			24 8 72	Merthyr	Trainee	Swansea C	3	—
Russell Coughlin	5 8	11 08	15 2 60	Swansea	Apprentice	Manchester C	—	—
						Blackburn R	24	—
						Carlisle U	130	13
						Plymouth Arg	131	18
						Blackpool	102	8
						Shrewsbury T (loan)	5	—
						Swansea C	29	—
David D'Auria*	5 8	11 00	26 3 70	Swansea	Trainee	Swansea C	45	6
Alan Davies	5 8	11 04	5 12 61	Manchester	Apprentice	Manchester U	7	—
						Newcastle U	21	1
						Charlton Ath (loan)	1	—
						Carlisle U (loan)	4	1
						Swansea C	84	8
						Bradford C	26	1
						Swansea C	35	3
David Hough	5 11	11 02	20 2 66	Crewe	Apprentice	Swansea C	222	9
Tommy Hutchison‡	5 11	11 02	22 9 47	Cardenden	Dundonald B	Alloa	68	4
						Blackpool	165	10
						Coventry C	314	24
					Bulova	Manchester C	46	4
						Burnley	92	4
						Swansea C	178	9
Andy Legg	5 8	10 07	28 7 66	Neath	Briton Ferry	Swansea	71	8
Steve Thornber	5 10	11 02	11 10 65	Dewsbury	Local	Halifax T	104	4
						Swansea C	84	1
Keith Walker	6 0	11 09	17 4 66	Edinburgh	ICI Juveniles	Stirling Alb	91	17
						St Mirren	43	6
						Swansea C	37	—

SWANSEA CITY

Foundation: The earliest Association Football in Wales was played in the Northern part of the country and no international took place in the South until 1894, when a local paper still thought it necessary to publish an outline of the rules and an illustration of the pitch markings. There had been an earlier Swansea club, but this has no connection with Swansea Town (now City) formed at a public meeting in June 1912.

First Football League game: 28 August, 1920, Division 3, v Portsmouth (a) L 0-3 – Crumley; Robson, Evans; Smith, Holdsworth, Williams; Hole, I. Jones, Edmundson, Rigsby, Spottiswood.

Did you know: During their initial First Division season (1981–82) no less than nine of Swansea's players won full international caps – all for Wales.

Managers (and Secretary-managers)
Walter Whittaker 1912–14, William Bartlett 1914–15, Joe Bradshaw 1919–26, Jimmy Thomson 1927–31, Neil Harris 1934–39, Haydn Green 1939–47, Bill McCandless 1947–55, Ron Burgess 1955–58, Trevor Morris 1958–65, Glyn Davies 1965–66, Billy Lucas 1967–69, Roy Bentley 1969–72, Harry Gregg 1972–75, Harry Griffiths 1975–77, John Toshack 1978–83 (resigned October re-appointed in December) 1983–84, Colin Appleton 1984, John Bond 1984–85, Tommy Hutchison 1985–86, Terry Yorath 1986–89, Ian Evans 1989–90, Terry Yorath 1990–91, Frank Burrows March 1991– .

Player and Position	Ht	Wt	Birth Date	Place	Source	Clubs	League App	Gls
Forwards								
Paul Chalmers	5 10	10 03	31 10 63	Glasgow	Eastercraigs	Celtic	4	1
						Bradford C (loan)	2	—
						St Mirren	101	23
						Swansea C	37	6
Terry Connor	5 9	11 08	9 11 62	Leeds	Apprentice	Leeds U	96	19
						Brighton & HA	156	51
						Portsmouth	48	12
						Swansea	33	5
Simon Davey	5 10	11 02	1 10 70	Swansea	Trainee	Swansea C	44	4
Clive Freeman	5	12 12	12 9 62	Leeds		Doncaster R	—	—
					Bridlington	Swansea C	2	—
Jimmy Gilligan	6 2	11 07	24 1 64	Hammersmith	Apprentice	Watford	27	6
						Lincoln C (loan)	3	—
						Grimsby T	25	4
						Swindon T	17	5
						Lincoln C	11	1
						Newport Co (loan)	5	1
						Cardiff C	99	35
						Portsmouth	32	5
						Swansea C	37	16
John Hughes (To Falkirk Aug 1990)	6 0	13 07	9 9 64	Edinburgh	Newtongrange S	Berwick R	41	14
						Swansea C	24	4
Steve Jenkins			16 7 72	Merthyr	Trainee	Swansea C	1	—
Paul Raynor	6 0	11 04	29 4 66	Nottingham	Apprentice	Nottingham F	3	—
						Bristol R (loan)	8	—
						Huddersfield T	50	9
						Swansea C	165	25
						Wrexham (loan)	6	—
Andy Watson	5 9	11 12	1 4 67	Leeds	Harrogate T	Halifax T	83	15
						Swansea	14	1

Trainees
Bishop, Matthew; Brown, Lee J; Chappel, Shaun; Coates, Marc; Davies, Mark; Denham, Martin A; Jones, Neil R; Malsom, David S; Needs, Adrian; Thomas, Christopher; Twose, Geraint C; West, Martyn S.

Associated Schoolboys
Edwards, Christian; James, Rhys; Palser, Christopher R; Thomas, David J.

508

SWINDON TOWN 1990–91 *Back row (left to right):* Liam Dixon, Adrian Viveash, Fraser Digby, Nicky Hammond, Steve White, Tony Galvin (Assistant Manager)
Centre row: Andy Rowland (Reserve Team Coach), Tony Clarke, David Hockaday, Tom Jones, Ross MacLaren, Jon Gittens, Fitzroy Simpson, Paul Bodin, Greg Costello, Chic Bates.
Front row: Neil Tomlinson, Paul Hunt, Steve Foley, David Kerslake, Osvaldo Ardiles (Manager), Colin Calderwood, Alan McLoughlin, Shaun Close, Paul Trollope, Nicky Summerbee.

Division 2   **SWINDON TOWN**

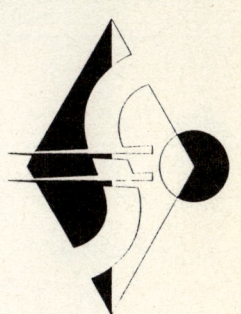

County Ground, Swindon, Wiltshire. Telephone Swindon (0793) 430430. Fax: 0793 536170. Clubcall: 0898 121640.

Ground capacity: 16,153.

Record attendance: 32,000 v Arsenal, FA Cup 3rd rd, 15 January 1972.

Record receipts: £61,053 v Leeds U, Division 2, 4 February 1990.

Pitch measurements: 114yd × 72yd.

President: C. J. Green.

Chairman: K. J. Chapman. *Vice-chairman:* N. H. Arkell.

Directors: P. T. Archer, R. V. Hardman.

Chief Executive: Peter Day.

Manager: Glenn Hoddle. *Assistant. Manager:* Chic Bates.

Coach: Andy Rowland. *Physio:* Kevin Morris.

Secretary: Jon Pollard. *Youth Team Manager:* John Trollope.

Commercial Manager: M. Sullivan.

Year Formed: 1881 *(see Foundation).* *Turned Professional:* 1894. *Ltd Co.:* 1894.

Club Nickname: 'Robins'.

Previous Ground: 1881–96, The Croft.

Record League Victory: 9-1 v Luton T, Division 3 (S), 28 August 1920 – Nash; Kay, Macconachie; Langford, Hawley, Wareing; Jefferson (1), Fleming (4), Rogers, Batty (2), Davies (1). (1og).

Record Cup Victory: 10-1 v Farnham U Breweries (away), FA Cup, 1st rd (replay), 28 November 1925 – Nash; Dickenson, Weston, Archer, Bew, Adey; Denyer (2), Wall (1), Richardson (4), Johnson (3), Davies.

Record Defeat: 1-10 v Manchester C, FA Cup 4th rd (replay), 25 January 1930.

Most League Points (2 for a win): 64, Division 3, 1968–69.

Most League Points (3 for a win): 102, Division 4, 1985–86 (League record).

Most League Goals: 100, Division 3 (S), 1926–27.

Highest League Scorer in Season: Harry Morris, 47, Division 3 (S), 1926–27.

Most League Goals in Total Aggregate: Harry Morris, 216, 1926–33.

Most Capped Player: Rod Thomas, 30 (50), Wales.

Most League Appearances: John Trollope, 770, 1960–80.

Record Transfer Fee Received: £1,000,000 from Southampton for Alan McLoughlin, December 1990.

Record Transfer Fee Paid: £250,000 to Huddersfield T for Duncan Shearer, June 1988.

Football League Record: 1920 Original Member of Division 3; 1921–58 Division 3 (S); 1958–63 Division 3; 1963–65 Division 2; 1965–69 Division 3; 1969–74 Division 2; 1974–82 Division 3; 1982–86 Division 4; 1986–87 Division 3; 1987– Division 2.

Honours: Football League: Division 2 best season; 4th, 1989–90; Division 3 – Runners-up 1962–63, 1968–69; Division 4 – Champions 1985–86 (with record 102 points). *FA Cup:* Semi-finals 1910, 1912. *Football League Cup:* Winners 1968–69. *Anglo-Italian Cup:* Winners 1970.

Colours: Red and white. **Change colours:** White and black.

SWINDON TOWN 1990–91 LEAGUE RECORD

Match No.	Date	Venue	Opponents	Result	H/T Score	Lg. Pos.	Goalscorers	Atten- dance
1	Aug 25	A	Charlton Ath	W 2-1	2-1	—	Bodin, Shearer	7524
2	28	H	Ipswich T	W 1-0	0-0	—	Shearer	10,817
3	Sept 2	H	Bristol C	L 0-1	0-1	—		12,249
4	8	A	Hull C	D 1-1	0-0	6	McLoughlin	5240
5	15	H	Middlesbrough	L 1-3	1-0	11	Shearer	9127
6	18	A	Wolverhampton W	W 1-0	0-0	—	Simpson	12,228
7	22	A	Oxford U	W 4-2	2-2	4	Simpson, Foley, Shearer 2	7961
8	30	H	Millwall	D 0-0	0-0	—		11,667
9	Oct 2	A	Oldham Ath	L 2-3	1-1	—	Hazard, Bodin	12,575
10	6	A	Brighton & HA	D 3-3	1-3	10	McLoughlin 2, White	7940
11	13	H	Bristol R	L 0-2	0-1	10		11,494
12	20	H	West Ham U	L 0-1	0-0	11		13,658
13	24	A	Leicester C	D 2-2	1-0	—	Shearer, White	9592
14	27	A	Barnsley	L 1-5	0-1	15	White	7690
15	Nov 3	H	Port Vale	L 1-2	1-0	18	Beckford (og)	7714
16	10	H	Portsmouth	W 3-0	2-0	15	Lorenzo, Foley, Shearer	8621
17	17	A	Sheffield W	L 1-2	0-1	17	McLoughlin	22,715
18	24	A	Notts Co	D 0-0	0-0	18		6113
19	Dec 1	H	Blackburn R	D 1-1	1-0	18	Shearer	8091
20	8	A	Ipswich T	D 1-1	0-0	15	Shearer	9358
21	15	H	Charlton Ath	D 1-1	0-1	15	Hazard	7396
22	22.	H	WBA	W 2-1	0-1	14	MacLaren, Shearer	7798
23	26	A	Newcastle U	D 1-1	1-1	14	Gittens	17,003
24	29	A	Watford	D 2-2	2-0	14	Shearer, Lorenzo	11,233
25	Jan 1	H	Plymouth Arg	D 1-1	0-0	13	Foley	9736
26	12	A	Bristol C	W 4-0	1-0	12	Hazard, White 2, Shearer	16,169
27	19	H	Hull C	W 3-1	2-0	10	White, Shearer 2	7297
28	Feb 2	A	Middlesbrough	L 0-2	0-2	13		14,588
29	19	H	Sheffield W	W 2-1	0-0	—	Simpson, Foley	8274
30	23	A	Portsmouth	L 1-2	1-2	11	White	8889
31	Mar 2	A	Blackburn R	L 1-2	0-1	14	White	6506
32	5	H	Oxford U	D 0-0	0-0	—		9058
33	12	H	Oldham Ath	D 2-2	0-0	—	Shearer, Calderwood	8193
34	16	A	Millwall	L 0-1	0-0	16		8894
35	20	A	Bristol R	L 1-2	1-1	—	Shearer	6123
36	23	H	Brighton & HA	L 1-3	1-1	18	Shearer	7342
37	30	H	Newcastle U	W 3-2	1-1	17	Hazard (pen), Shearer, Calderwood	9309
38	Apr 1	A	WBA	L 1-2	1-1	17	Rideout	10,415
39	6	A	Watford	L 1-2	0-1	19	White	9699
40	13	A	Plymouth Arg	D 3-3	1-2	20	Hazard, Shearer 2	6712
41	16	A	Wolverhampton W	W 2-1	1-1	—	Shearer, Hazard	9799
42	20	A	West Ham U	L 0-2	0-1	19		25,944
43	23	H	Notts Co	L 1-2	0-1	—	Shearer	7853
44	27	H	Leicester C	W 5-2	3-2	18	Foley 3, Hazard (pen), James (og)	10,404
45	May 4	H	Barnsley	L 1-2	1-2	20	Hazard (pen)	9070
46	11	A	Port Vale	L 1-3	1-2	21	Viveash	7713

Final League Position: 21

GOALSCORERS

League (65): Shearer 22, White 9, Hazard 8 (3 pens), Foley 7, McLoughlin 4, Simpson 3, Bodin 2, Calderwood 2, Lorenzo 2, Gittens 1, MacLaren 1, Rideout 1, Viveash 1, own goals 2.
Rumbelows Cup (4): Close 1, McLo⋯ ⋯ 1, Simpson 1, own goal 1.
FA Cup (3): White 2, Shearer 1.

Digby	Kerslake	Bodin	Simpson	Calderwood	Gittens	Jones	Shearer	Close	MacLaren	Foley	Hockaday	McLoughlin	Summerbee	Buttigieg	Viveash	Hunt	Bennett	White	Tanner	Hazard	Hammond	Lorenzo	Murray	Finnigan	Rideout	Ling	Match No.
1	2	3	4	5	6	7	8	9*	10	11	12																1
1	2	3	4	5	6	7*	8	9	10	11			12														2
1	2	3	4	5	6	7†	8	9*	10	11	14		12														3
1		3	12	5	6	7	8	9†	10	11*	2	4	14														4
1		3	9	5	6	7	8		10	11		4*	14	2	12†												5
1		3	9	5*	6	7	8		10	11		4		2	12												6
1	2	3	9		6	7	8		10	11		4†	14				5*	12									7
1	2	3	9*		6	7†	8		10	11		4						12	5	14							8
1	2	3	9		6		8	12	10			4*						11	5	7							9
1	2	3	11		6		8*12		10			4						9	5	7							10
	2	3	8		14			12	10	11*		4			6†			9	5	7	1						11
1	2	3	8		6	7		12	10	11								9	5	4*							12
1	2	3	4		6	7	8		10	11								9	5								13
1	2	3	11		6	7*	8		10	12	4							9	5								14
1	2	3	11		6	7	8		10	12	4*			5				9									15
1		3	7†		2		8	12	10	11		4			5			9			14*	6					16
1		3	7*		2		8		10	11		4			5			9			12	6					17
1		3	12		2		8		10	11		4			5			9*		7		6					18
1	2	3	12		6	7	8		10	11		4*						9				5					19
	2	3	12		6	7	8		10	11		4			5			9*			1						20
1	2	3	9		6	7	8		10	11*		5			12					4							21
1	2	3			6	7	8		10	11								9		4		5					22
1	2	3			6	7	8		10	11	12							9		4		5*					23
1	2	3			6	7	8		10	11								9		4		5					24
1	2	3			6	7	8		10	11			12					9*		4		5					25
1	2	3			6	7	8		10	11								9		4		5					26
1	2	3			6	7	8		10	11								9		4		5					27
1	2	3			6	7	8		10	11								9		4		5					28
1	2	3	6			7	8	12	10	11				5				9*		4							29
1	2	3	6	12		7*	8		10	11				5				9		4							30
1	2	3†	14	6*		7	8	12	10	11				5				9		4							31
1	2†	3	6			7	8*		10	11				5	12			9		4			14				32
1		7	6	5	2		8		10	11				12	3			9		4*							33
1		7*	6	5	2		8		10	11				12	3†			9		4	14						34
		14	6	5	7		8		10	11				12	3†			9*	4	1	3†		2				35
1	2	14	6	5	7	8		10	11†									9*	4	12		3					36
1	2		6			7	8		10	11					3	12				4		5			9*		37
1	2	12	6			7	8		10*	11					3					4		5			9		38
1	2	10*	6			7	8			11					3†	12				4		5	14		9		39
1	2	12	6			7	8		10	11					3*					4		5			9		40
1	2	12	6			7	8		10	11					3*					4		5			9		41
1	2	5	6			7	8		10	11					3	12				4					9*		42
1	2	5*	6			7	8	12	10	11					3			9		4							43
1	2	14	6			7	8†		10	11					3	12				4		5			9*		44
	2	5*	6			7	8	12	10	11					3					4	1				9		45
	2	5	6			7		8	12	10	11	7			3					4†	1				9*	14	46
41	37	31	27	22	28	42	44	4	45	42	1	15	1	2	23	—	1	28	7	31	5	18	—	2	9	—	

+ + | + | + | + + + + + + + | + | + | + + + | +
11s1s 1s 10s 2s 2s 2s 6s 1s 2s 2s 7s 3s 2s 1s 1s 1s

Rumbelows Cup	Second Round	Darlington (a)	0-3
		(h)	4-0
	Third Round	Sheffield W (a)	0-0
		(h)	0-1
FA Cup	Third Round	Leyton Orient (a)	1-1
		(h)	1-0
	Fourth Round	Norwich C (a)	1-3

SWINDON TOWN

Player and Position	Ht	Wt	Birth Date	Birth Place	Source	Clubs	League App	Gls
Goalkeepers								
Fraser Digby	6 1	12 12	23 4 67	Sheffield	Apprentice	Manchester U	—	—
						Oldham Ath (loan)	—	—
						Swindon T (loan)	—	—
						Swindon T	202	—
Nicky Hammond	6 0	11 13	7 9 67	Hornchurch	Apprentice	Arsenal	—	—
						Bristol R (loan)	3	—
						Peterborough U (loan)	—	—
						Aberdeen (loan)	—	—
						Swindon T	9	—
Defenders								
Colin Calderwood	6 0	11 09	20 1 65	Stranraer	Amateur	Mansfield T	100	1
						Swindon T	238	13
Tony Clarke‡	5 10	11 02	21 9 70	Leamington Spa		Mansfield T	—	—
						Swindon T	—	—
Tony Finnigan‡	6 0	12 00	17 10 62	Wimbledon	Fulham	Crystal Palace	105	10
						Blackburn R	36	—
						Hull C	18	1
						Swindon T	3	—
Richard Green	6 0	11 08	22 11 67	Wolverhampton		Shrewsbury T	125	5
						Swindon T	—	—
Nestor Lorenzo	5 10	12 08	28 2 66	Argentina	Bari	Swindon T	20	2
Ross MacLaren	5 10	12 12	14 4 62	Edinburgh	Rangers	Shrewsbury T	161	18
						Derby Co	122	4
						Swindon T	128	8
Lee Spalding	5 9	11 00	21 8 72	Swindon	Trainee	Swindon T	—	—
Adrian Viveash	6 1	11 12	30 9 69	Swindon	Trainee	Swindon T	25	1
Midfield								
Steve Foley	5 7	10 12	4 10 62	Liverpool	Apprentice	Liverpool	—	—
						Fulham (loan)	3	—
						Grimsby T	31	2
						Sheffield U	66	14
						Swindon T	142	23
Micky Hazard	5 7	10 05	5 2 60	Sunderland	Apprentice	Tottenham H	91	13
						Chelsea	81	9
						Portsmouth	8	1
						Swindon T	34	8
Tommy Jones	5 10	11 07	7 10 64	Aldershot	Weymouth	Aberdeen	28	3
						Swindon T	127	8
David Kerslake	5 8	11 04	19 6 66	London	Apprentice	QPR	58	6
						Swindon T	65	—
Edwin Murray§			31 8 73	Redbridge	Trainee	Swindon T	1	—
Fitzroy Simpson	5 8	10 07	26 2 70	Trowbridge	Trainee	Swindon T	75	5
Paul Trollope	6 0	12 02	3 6 72	Swindon	Trainee	Swindon T	—	—
Paul Willis†	5 11	11 07	24 1 70	Liverpool	Trainee	Halifax T	5	—
						Darlington	2	1
						Swindon T	—	—
Forwards								
Dave Bennett	5 9	10 07	11 7 59	Manchester	Amateur	Manchester C	52	9
						Cardiff C	77	18
						Coventry C	172	25
						Sheffield W	28	—
						Swindon T	1	—

SWINDON TOWN

Foundation: It is generally accepted that Swindon Town came into being in 1881, although there is no firm evidence that the club's founder, Rev. William Pitt, captain of the Spartans (an offshoot of a cricket club) changed his club's name to Swindon Town before 1883, when the Spartans amalgamated with St. Mark's Young Men's Friendly Society.

First Football League game: 28 August, 1920, Division 3, v Luton T (h) W 9-1 – Nash; Kay, Macconachie; Langford, Hawley, Wareing; Jefferson (1), Fleming (4), Rogers, Batty (2), Davies (1). 1 o.g.

Did you know: Local discovery Archie Bown's feat of scoring all six goals for Swindon in a Southern League game with Watford in a Southern League game, 6 April 1915, is still a club record for a first team game.

Managers (and Secretary-managers)
Sam Allen 1902–33, Ted Vizard 1933–39, Neil Harris 1939–41, Louis Page 1945–53, Maurice Lindley 1953–55, Bert Head 1956–65, Danny Williams 1965–69, Fred Ford 1969–71, Dave Mackay 1971–72, Les Allen 1972–74, Danny Williams 1974–78, Bobby Smith 1978–80, John Trollope 1980–83, Ken Beamish 1983–84, Lou Macari 1984–89, Ossie Ardiles 1989–91, Glenn Hoddle April 1991–   .

Player and Position	Ht	Wt	Birth Date	Place	Source	Clubs	League App	Gls
Shaun Close	5 8	10 01	8 9 66	Islington	Trainee	Tottenham H	9	—
						Bournemouth	39	8
						Swindon T	25	—
Liam Dixon‡			28 10 71	Enfield	Trainee	Swindon T	—	—
Paul Hunt	5 5	10 02	8 10 71	Swindon	Trainee	Swindon T	6	—
Duncan Shearer	5 10	10 09	28 8 62	Fort William	Inverness Clach			
						Chelsea	2	1
						Huddersfield T	83	38
						Swindon T	122	56
Nick Summerbee	5 11	11 08	26 8 71	Altrincham	Trainee	Swindon T	8	—
Neil Tomlinson‡	5 11	12 00	14 10 69	Birmingham	Shrewsbury T	Swindon T	—	—
Steve White	5 11	11 04	2 1 59	Chipping	Mangotsfield U			
				Sodbury		Bristol R	50	20
						Luton T	72	25
						Charlton Ath	29	12
						Lincoln C (loan)	3	—
						Luton T (loan)	4	—
						Bristol R	101	24
						Swindon T	181	66

Trainees
Braidwood, Jason P; Fishlock, Murray E; Hall, Darren M; Jones, Glenn P; Murray, Edwin J; O'Sullivan, Wayne S.J; Phillips, Marcus S; Spence, Robert J; Thomson, Andrew J; Williams, Barry J.

Associated Schoolboys
Ballard, Graham; Bates, Andrew; Burry, Scott M; Gee, David G; Jay, Christopher R; Jordan, Mark J; King, Mark D; Meadows, Jonathan; Miles, Wayne; Phillips, James A; Reeves, Stephen J; Richings, Martin J; Underwood, Jamie; Worrall, Benjamin J.

Associated Schoolboys who have accepted the club's offer of a Traineeship/Contract
Lockyer, Mark J; Madden, Andrew A; O'Driscoll, Mark A.

TORQUAY UNITED 1990–91   *Back row (left to right)*: Matthew Elliott, Mark Loram, Phil Lloyd, Wes Saunders, Kenny Veysey, Peter Whiston, Steve Cookson, Steve Kidd.

Centre row: Alan Hay (Youth Development Officer), Ian Bastow, John Morrison, Chris Curran, Paul Holmes, Paul Hall, Paul Smith.

Sean Joyce.

Front row: Dean Edwards, Russell Musker, John James (Chief Scout), John Impey (Assistant Manager), Dave Smith (Manager), Norman Medhurst (Physiotherapist), Tommy

Tynan, John Uzzell.

Division 3   **TORQUAY UNITED**

Plainmoor Ground, Torquay, Devon TQ1 3PS. Telephone Torquay (0803) 328666/7. Clubcall: 0898 121641. Fax: 0803 323976.

Ground capacity: 5539.

Record attendance: 21,908 v Huddersfield T, FA Cup 4th rd, 29 January 1955.

Record receipts: £21,000 v West Ham U, FA Cup, 3rd rd, 6 January 1990.

Pitch measurements: 112yd × 74yd.

President: A. J. Boyce.

Chairman/Managing Director: M. Bateson. *Vice-Chairman:* M. Benney.

Directors: M. Beer, D. Copeland, I. Hayman, F. Mosley, W. Rogers, D. Turner, D. Wilson, C. Olney.

Team Manager: John Impey. *Assistant Manager:*

Physio: Norman Medhurst.

Company Accountant/Company Secretary: C. Olney.

Secretary General Manager: D. F. Turner. *Lottery Administrators:* C. Munslow and A. Sandford.

Year Formed: 1898. *Turned Professional:* 1921. *Ltd Co.:* 1921.

Previous Name: 1910, Torquay Town; 1921, Torquay United,

Nickname: 'The Gulls'.

Previous Grounds: 1898, Teignmouth Road; 1901, Torquay Recreation Ground; 1905, Cricket Field Road; 1907–10, Torquay Cricket Ground.

Record League Victory: 9-0 v Swindon T, Division 3 (S), 8 March 1952 – George Webber; Topping, Ralph Calland; Brown, Eric Webber, Towers; Shaw (1), Marchant (1), Northcott (2), Collins (3), Edds (2).

Record Cup Victory: 7-1 v Northampton T, FA Cup, 1st rd, 14 November 1959 – Gill; Penford, Downs; Bettany, George Northcott, Rawson; Baxter, Cox, Tommy Northcott (1), Bond (3), Pym (3).

Record Defeat: 2-10 v Fulham, Division 3 (S), 7 September 1931 and v Luton T, Division 3 (S), 2 September 1933.

Most League Points (2 for a win): 60, Division 4, 1959–60.

Most League Points (3 for a win): 77, Division 4, 1987–88.

Most League Goals: 89, Division 3 (S), 1956–57.

Highest League Scorer in Season: Sammy Collins, 40, Division 3 (S), 1955–56.

Most League Goals in Total Aggregate: Sammy Collins, 204, 1948–58.

Most Capped Player: None.

Most League Appearances: Dennis Lewis, 443, 1947–59.

Record Transfer Fee Received: £125,000 from Manchester U for Lee Sharpe, May 1988.

Record Transfer Fee Paid: £60,000 to Dundee for Wes Saunders, July 1990.

Football League Record: 1927 Elected to Division 3 (S); 1958–60 Division 4; 1960–62 Division 3; 1962–66 Division 4; 1966–72 Division 3; 1972–91 Division 4; 1991– Division 3.

Honours: Football League: Division 3 best season: 4th, 1967–68; Division 3 (S) – Runners-up 1956–57; Division 4 – Promoted 1959–60 (3rd), 1965–66 (3rd), 1990–91 (Play-offs). *FA Cup:* best season: 4th rd, 1949, 1955, 1971, 1983, 1990. *Football League Cup:* never past 3rd rd. *Sherpa Van Trophy:* Runners-up 1989.

Colours: Yellow and white striped shirts, navy shorts, navy stockings. **Change colours:** Purple shirts, white shorts, purple stockings.

TORQUAY UNITED 1990–91 LEAGUE RECORD

Match No.	Date		Venue	Opponents	Result		H/T Score	Lg. Pos.	Goalscorers	Atten- dance
1	Aug	25	A	Walsall	D	2-2	2-1	—	Bryant (og), Elliott	5219
2		31	H	Gillingham	W	3-1	0-0	—	Saunders, Loram, Tynan	3072
3	Sept	8	A	Cardiff C	D	3-3	2-1	5	Elliott, Edwards, Tynan (pen)	3656
4		15	H	Chesterfield	W	2-0	0-0	3	Loram, Tynan (pen)	2468
5		18	H	Scunthorpe U	D	1-1	0-0	—	Loram	2811
6		21	H	Halifax T	W	1-0	1-0	—	Smith	1447
7		29	A	Peterborough U	W	2-1	0-1	1	Edwards, Tynan	3160
8	Oct	2	H	Doncaster R	W	1-0	1-0	—	Musker	3312
9		6	H	Blackpool	W	2-1	2-0	1	Tynan, Joyce	2854
10		12	A	Aldershot	W	3-2	1-1	—	Edwards 2, Tynan	3289
11		16	H	Wrexham	W	1-0	1-0	—	Tynan (pen)	3577
12		20	A	Rochdale	D	0-0	0-0	1		3405
13		27	A	Carlisle U	W	3-0	0-0	1	Holmes P, Tynan 2	3269
14	Nov	3	A	York C	D	0-0	0-0	1		2412
15		9	A	Scarborough	L	0-1	0-1	—		1447
16	Dec	1	H	Hartlepool U	L	0-1	0-0	2		2835
17		7	H	Stockport Co	D	1-1	1-1	—	Edwards	2370
18		15	A	Darlington	L	0-3	0-1	2		2997
19		22	A	Maidstone U	D	2-2	2-0	3	Elliott, Tynan	2062
20		29	H	Burnley	W	2-0	1-0	2	Edwards, Smith	4210
21	Jan	1	A	Hereford U	D	0-0	0-0	2		3409
22		11	A	Gillingham	D	2-2	1-0	—	Tynan, Loram	4329
23		19	A	Walsall	D	0-0	0-0	5		3191
24		26	A	Chesterfield	D	1-1	0-1	6	Edwards	2921
25	Feb	2	A	Scunthorpe U	L	0-3	0-0	6		2502
26		5	H	Halifax T	W	3-1	1-0	—	Edwards, Tynan, Holmes M	2223
27	Mar	2	A	Hartlepool U	D	0-0	0-0	8		2209
28		5	H	Lincoln C	L	0-1	0-0	—		2330
29		9	H	Darlington	W	2-1	0-0	7	Tynan, Holmes M	3078
30		15	H	Peterborough	D	0-0	0-0	—		2800
31		23	H	Blackpool	L	0-1	0-1	11		4778
32		26	H	Northampton T	D	0-0	0-0	—		2373
33		30	A	Lincoln C	L	2-3	0-0	12	Saunders, Edwards	3315
34	Apr	2	H	Maidstone U	D	1-1	0-1	—	Loram	2456
35		6	A	Burnley	D	1-1	0-0	13	Smith	6661
36		8	H	Aldershot	W	5-0	2-0	—	Smith, Evans 2, Edwards 2	2535
37		10	H	Cardiff C	W	2-1	1-0	—	Saunders, Joyce	3341
38		13	H	Hereford U	D	1-1	1-0	10	Elliott	3238
39		16	A	Northampton T	W	4-1	0-1	—	Loram, Edwards 3 (1 pen)	2678
40		20	A	Rochdale	W	3-1	2-1	8	Evans 2, Myers	3049
41		23	A	Stockport Co	L	1-2	1-0	—	Loram	4466
42		27	A	Wrexham	L	1-2	0-0	8	Elliott	1281
43		30	H	Scarborough	W	2-0	0-0	—	Smith, Edwards	2596
44	May	4	A	Carlisle U	L	1-3	0-1	7	Joyce	2176
45		7	A	Doncaster R	D	1-1	1-1	—	Elliott	1642
46		11	H	York C	W	2-1	2-0	7	Evans, Myers	4337

Final League Position: 7

GOALSCORERS

League (64): Edwards 15 (1 pen), Tynan 13 (3 pens), Loram 7, Elliott 6, Evans 5, Smith 5, Joyce 3, Saunders 3, Holmes M 2, Myers 2, Holmes P 1, Musker 1, own goal 1.
Rumbelows Cup (3): Saunders 1, Tynan 1, Whiston 1.
FA Cup (1): Tynan 1.

Howells	Holmes P	Elliott	Lloyd	Uzzell	Whiston	Musker	Saunders	Loram	Tynan	Edwards	Joyce	Veysey	Smith	Myers	Hall	Curran	Cookson	Holmes M	Hodges	Rowland	Evans	Hay	Match No.
1	2	3	4	5*	6	7	8	9	10	11	12												1
	7	5	4	3	2*	6	10	11	9	8			1	12									2
1	7	5	4	3	2	6	10	11	9	8													3
1	7	5	4	3	2		10	11*	9	8			6	12									4
1	7*	5	4	3	2		10	11	9	8			12	6									5
1	7	5	4	3	2		10	11	9		6		8*	12									6
1	7	5	4	3	2*		10	11	9	12	6		8										7
1	12	5	4	3	2	7*		11	9	10	6		8										8
1	14	5	4	3	2†	7		11*	9	10	6		8	12									9
1	2	5	4	3			12	9	10		6		8*	7†	11	14							10
1	2	5	4	3			11	9	10		6		12	8	7*								11
1	2	5	4	3			11†	9	10		6		7*	8	12	14							12
1	7	5	4	3	2		11	9	10		6		8										13
1	7	5	4	3	2*		8†	12	9	10	6		11	14									14
1	7†	5	4	3	2		8	14	9	10	6		11*	12									15
1	2*	5	4	3	10		8	6	11	9			12	7									16
1	12	5	4	3	2	6	8	9	10	11*			7†	14									17
1	7	5	4	3	11	6	8	12	9†	10			2*	14									18
1		5	4*	3	2	8	6	12	9	10			7	11									19
1		5		3	2	6	4		9	10			7	11				8					20
1	12	5		3	2	6	4		9	10			7	11*				8					21
1	12	5		3	2*	6	4	11	9				7					8	10				22
1	5*			3	2	6	4	11	9	12			7					8	10				23
1	5			3	2	6	4	11	9	12			7					8	10*				24
1	5			3	2	11†	4	12	9	10*			7	14				8	6				25
1	5			3	2		4	11	9	10			7					8	6				26
1	2	5		3		4	6	8	11	9	10		7										27
1	2†	5		3		4	12	8	11	9	10		7	14				6*					28
1	2	5		3		4	7	8	11	9	10							6					29
1	2	5		3		4†	8	12	9*				7	14				6	10	11			30
1	2	5		3			9*						7	11				6	12	10	8	4	31
1	2	5		3		4	9	14					7	11				6†	12	10*	8		32
1	2	5		3		4	11	9	12	8			7					6*	10				33
1		5		3	8†	4	11	9	10*				7	14		2		6	12				34
1		5		3		4	11	10	6				7	8		2	12				9*		35
1		5		3		4	11	10	6†				7	8	14	2	12				9*		36
1		5		3		4	11	10	6				7	8		2					9		37
1		5		3		4	11	10	6†				7	8	14	2	12				9*		38
1		5	12	3		4	11*	10	6				7	8		2					9		39
1		5		3		4	11†	10*	6				7	8	14	2	12				9		40
1		5		3		4	11	10	6				7*	8†	14	2	12				9		41
1	2	5		3		4	11	10*	6†				7	8	14		12				9		42
1	2	5		3		4	11	10	6				7					8			9		43
1	2	5		3		4	11	10†	6				7*	14			8		12		9		44
1	10	5		3		4	11	8					7			2	12				9*	6	45
1	8	5		3†		4	11	12	10		6*		7		14	2					9		46
45	28	45	19	46	27	20	37	34	34	35	23	1	26	24	9	11	—	16	5	4	15	2	

Substitute appearances: Holmes P +5s; Whiston +1s; Musker +1s; Saunders +7s; Loram +1s; Tynan +4s; Edwards +2s; Smith +3s; Myers +5s; Hall +8s; Curran +2s; Cookson +2s; Holmes M +6s; Hodges +5s; Rowland +5s

Rumbelows Cup	First Round	Bristol R (a)		2-1
		(h)		1-1
	Second Round	Manchester C (h)		0-4
		(a)		0-0
FA Cup	First Round	Maidstone U (a)		1-4

TORQUAY UNITED

Player and Position	Ht	Wt	Birth Date	Birth Place	Source	Clubs	League App	Gls
Goalkeepers								
Gareth Howells	6 1	12 08	13 6 70	Guildford	Trainee	Tottenham H	—	—
						Swindon T (loan)	—	—
						Leyton Orient (loan)	—	—
						Torquay U	45	—
Defenders								
Chris Curran	5 11	11 09	17 9 71	Birmingham	Trainee	Torquay U	14	—
Matthew Elliott	6 3	13 06	1 11 68	Surrey	Epsom & Ewell	Charlton Ath	—	—
						Torquay U	91	10
Alan Hay*	6 0	12 06	28 11 58	Dunfermline	Amateur	Bolton W	—	—
						Bristol C	74	1
						St Mirren (loan)	—	—
						York C	150	3
						Tranmere R	28	—
						York C	1	—
						Sunderland	1	—
						Torquay U	10	—
Paul Holmes	5 10	11 00	18 2 68	Sheffield	Apprentice	Doncaster R	47	1
						Torquay U	102	3
Steve Kidd*	6 2	13 13	16 1 72	Harlow	Trainee	Torquay U	—	—
Philip Lloyd	5 11	11 11	26 12 64	Hemsworth	Apprentice	Middlesbrough	—	—
						Barnsley	—	—
						Darlington	127	3
						Torquay U	157	7
John Morrison*	5 6	10 04	27 7 70	Kettering	Trainee	Torquay U	32	—
Wes Saunders	6 0	11 11	23 2 63	Sunderland	School	Newcastle U	79	—
						Bradford C (loan)	4	—
						Carlisle U	97	11
						Dundee	50	2
						Torquay	37	3
John Uzzell	5 10	11 03	31 3 59	Plymouth	Apprentice	Plymouth Arg	302	6
						Torquay U	82	2
Midfield								
Ian Bastow	5 8	9 02	12 8 71	Torquay	Trainee	Torquay U	11	—
David Hodges	5 9	10 02	17 1 70	Hereford		Mansfield T	85	7
						Torquay U	10	—
Sean Joyce	5 8	10 05	15 2 67	Doncaster		Doncaster R	41	2
						Exeter C (loan)	1	—
						Torquay U	96	11
John Matthews‡	6 0	12 06	1 11 55	London	Apprentice	Arsenal	45	2
						Sheffield U	103	14
						Mansfield T	72	6
						Chesterfield	38	1
						Plymouth Arg	135	4
						Torquay U	25	—
Russell Musker*	5 8	11 03	10 7 62	Liverpool	Apprentice	Bristol C	46	1
						Exeter C (loan)	6	—
						Gillingham	64	7
						Torquay U	66	1
Chris Myers	5 11	11 03	1 4 69	Yeovil	Trainee	Torquay U	38	2
Peter Whiston	6 0	11 06	4 1 68	Widnes		Plymouth Arg	10	—
						Torquay U (loan)	8	1
						Torquay U	28	—
Forwards								
Steven Cookson‡	6 1	10 10	19 2 72	Wolverhampton	Trainee	Torquay U	12	1
Dean Edwards	5 11	11 07	25 2 62	Wolverhampton	Apprentice Telford U	Shrewsbury T	13	1
						Wolverhampton W	31	9
						Exeter C	54	17
						Torquay U	109	26

TORQUAY UNITED

Foundation: The idea of establishing a Torquay club was agreed by old boys of Torquay College and Torbay College, while sitting in Princess Gardens listening to the band. A proper meeting was subsequently held at Tor Abbey Hotel at which officers were elected. This was in 1898 and the club's first competition was the Eastern League (later known as the East Devon League).

First Football League game: 27 August, 1927, Division 3(S), v Exeter C (h) D 1–1 – Millsom; Cook, Smith; Wellock, Wragg, Connor, Mackey, Turner (1), Jones, McGovern, Thomson.

Did you know: Beginning 1931–32 with only 15 players injuries soon cut that number to nine and before the season's fifth game (at Mansfield) they had to sign one of the previous season's players. However, the game at Mansfield brought their first win of the season 4-2.

Managers (and Secretary-managers)
Percy Mackrill 1927–29, A. H. Hoskins 1929*, Frank Womack 1929–32, Frank Brown 1932–38, Alf Steward 1938–40, Billy Butler 1945–46, Jack Butler 1946–47, John McNeil 1947–50, Bob John 1950, Alex Massie 1950–51, Eric Webber 1951–65, Frank O'Farrell 1965–68, Alan Brown 1969–71, Jack Edwards 1971–73, Malcolm Musgrove 1973–76, Mike Green 1977–81, Frank O'Farrell 1981–82 (continued as GM to 1983), Bruch Rioch 1982–84, Dave Webb 1984–85, John Sims 1985, Stuart Morgan 1985–87, Cyril Knowles 1987–89, Dave Smith 1989–91, John Impey April 1991– .

Player and Position	Ht	Wt	Birth Date	Place	Source	Clubs	League App	Gls
Paul Hall	5 9	10 02	3 7 72	Manchester	Trainee	Torquay U	27	—
Micky Holmes	5 8	10 12	9 9 65	Blackpool		Bradford C	5	—
						Burnley		
						Wolverhampton W	83	13
						Huddersfield T	7	—
						Cambridge U	11	—
						Rochdale	54	7
						Torquay U	22	2
Mark Loram	6 0	12 00	13 8 67	Paignton	Brixham	Torquay U	52	8
						QPR (loan)	—	—
						QPR	—	—
						Torquay U (loan)	13	4
						Torquay U	165	31
Andy Rowland	6 2	13 10	1 10 65	Taunton		Southampton	—	—
						Torquay U	9	—
Paul Smith	5 8	9 09	5 10 67	London	Apprentice	Arsenal	—	—
						Brentford	17	1
						Bristol R	16	1
						Torquay U	73	12
Tommy Tynan	5 10	12 09	17 11 55	Liverpool	Apprentice	Liverpool	—	—
						Swansea C (loan)	6	2
						Sheffield W	91	31
						Lincoln C	9	1
						Newport Co	183	66
						Plymouth Arg	80	43
						Rotherham U	32	13
						Plymouth Arg (loan)	9	10
						Plymouth Arg	173	74
						Torquay U	35	13

Trainees
Attwood, Darren R; Convey, Alan L; Crook, Alexander L; Darby, Duane A; Gaisford, Darren W; Gardiner, Matthew; Gilbert, Asa J; Henry, Christopher E; Lowe, Matthew I; Moore, Darren M; Nock, Paul A; O'Connor, Christopher J; Poblocki, Dean W; Rose, Peter D; Ryder, Ciaran H; Wadge, Lee K; Whittaker, Matthew J.

Associated Schoolboys
Maloney, Shaun M; Setter, Lee T; Spittle, Neil D; White, Richard.

Associated Schoolboys who have accepted the club's offer of a Traineeship/Contract
Ginter, Anthony; Stamps, Scott.

TOTTENHAM HOTSPUR 1990–91 *Back row (left to right)*: John Moncur, Andy Polston, Gudni Bergsson, Erik Thorstvedt, Mitchell Thomas, Bobby Mimms, Guy Butters, Steve Sedgley, Justin Edinburgh.
Centre row: Doug Livermore (Assistant Manager), Philip Gray, Brian Statham, Pat Van Den Hauwe, Vinny Samways, David Howells, Nayim, Ray Clemence (Reserve Team Manager/Goalkeeping Coach).
Front row: Paul Walsh, Mark Robson, Paul Stewart, Terry Fenwick, Gary Mabbutt, Gary Lineker, Paul Gascoigne, Paul Allen, Paul Moran.

Division 1   **TOTTENHAM HOTSPUR**

748 High Rd, Tottenham, London N17 0AP. Telephone 081-808 8080. Commercial Dept: 081-808 0281. Recorded information: 0898 100515. Dial-a-seat: 081-808 3030. Spurs Line: 0898 100500. Fax: 081-885 1951.

Ground capacity: 33,020.

Record attendance: 75,038 v Sunderland, FA Cup 6th rd, 5 March 1938.

Record receipts: £245,632.10 v Anderlecht, UEFA Cup Final 2nd leg, 23 May 1984.

Pitch measurements: 110yd × 73yd.

Club President: W. Nicholson. *Vice-president:* F. P. Sinclair.

Chairman: A. G. Berry. *Vice-chairman:* D. A. Alexiou.

Holding Company: Tottenham Hotspur plc. *Chief Executive:* T. F. Venables. *Chairman:* A. Sugar. *Vice-chairman:* N. Solomon.

Team Manager: Peter Shreeves.

Assistant Manager: Doug Livermore. *Physios:* John Sheridan and Dave Butler.

Secretary: Peter Barnes. *Commercial Manager:* Mike Rollo. *PRO:* John Fennelly.

Year Formed: 1882. *Turned Professional:* 1895. *Ltd Co.:* 1898. *Chief Scout:* Ted Buxton.

Club Nickname: 'Spurs'.

Previous Name: 1882–85, Hotspur Football Club.

Previous Grounds: 1882, Tottenham Marshes; 1885, Northumberland Park; 1898, White Hart Lane.

Record League Victory: 9-0 v Bristol R, Division 2, 22 October 1977 – Daines; Naylor, Holmes, Hoddle (1), McAllister, Perryman, Pratt, McNab, Moores (3), Lee (4), Taylor (1).

Record Cup Victory: 13-2 v Crewe Alex, FA Cup, 4th rd (replay), 3 February 1960 – Brown; Hills, Henry; Blanchflower, Norman, Mackay; White, Harmer (1), Smith (4), Allen (5), Jones (3 incl. 1p).

Record Defeat: 0-7 v Liverpool, Division 1, 2 September 1978.

Most League Points (2 for a win): 70, Division 2, 1919–20.

Most League Points (3 for a win): 77, Division 1, 1984–85.

Most League Goals: 115, Division 1, 1960-61.

Highest League Scorer in Season: Jimmy Greaves, 37, Division 1, 1962–63.

Most League Goals in Total Aggregate: Jimmy Greaves, 220, 1961–70.

Most Capped Player: Pat Jennings, 74 (119), Northern Ireland.
Most League Appearances: Steve Perryman, 655, 1969–86.

Record Transfer Fee Received: £4,500,000 from Marseille for Chris Waddle, July 1989.

Record Transfer Fee Paid: £2,000,000 to Newcastle U for Paul Gascoigne, July 1988.

Football League Record: 1908 Elected to Division 2; 1909–15 Division 1; 1919–20 Division 2; 1920–28 Division 1; 1928–33 Division 2; 1933–35 Division 1; 1935–50 Division 2; 1950–77 Division 1; 1977–78 Division 2; 1978– Division 1.

Honours: Football League: Division 1 – Champions 1950–51, 1960–61; Runners-up 1921–22, 1951–52, 1956–57, 1962–63; Division 2 – Champions 1919–20, 1949–50; Runners-up 1908–09, 1932–33; Promoted 1977–78 (3rd). *FA Cup:* Winners 1901 (as non-League club), 1921, 1961, 1962, 1967, 1981, 1982, 1991 (8 wins stands as the record); Runners-up 1986–87. *Football League Cup:* Winners 1970–71, 1972–73; Runners-up 1981–82. **European Competitions:** *European Cup:* 1961–62. *European Cup-Winners' Cup:* 1962–63 (winners), 1963–64, 1967–68, 1981–82 (runners-up), 1982–83. *UEFA Cup:* 1971–72 (winners), 1972–73, 1973–74 (runners-up), 1983–84 (winners), 1984–85.

Colours: White shirts, navy blue shorts, navy stockings with white turnovers. **Change colours:** All yellow.

TOTTENHAM HOTSPUR 1990–91 LEAGUE RECORD

Match No.	Date		Venue	Opponents	Result	H/T Score	Lg. Pos.	Goalscorers	Atten-dance
1	Aug	25	H	Manchester C	W 3-1	1-1	—	Lineker 2, Gascoigne	33,501
2		28	A	Sunderland	D 0-0	0-0			30,214
3	Sept	1	A	Arsenal	D 0-0	0-0	5		40,009
4		8	H	Derby Co	W 3-0	1-0	4	Gascoigne 3	29,614
5		15	A	Leeds U	W 2-0	0-0	3	Howells, Lineker	31,342
6		22	H	Crystal Palace	D 1-1	1-0	4	Gascoigne	34,859
7		29	H	Aston Villa	W 2-1	1-1	3	Lineker, Allen	34,939
8	Oct	6	A	QPR	D 0-0	0-0	3		21,405
9		20	H	Sheffield U	W 4-0	0-0	3	Walsh 3, Nayim	34,612
10		27	A	Nottingham F	W 2-1	0-1	3	Howells 2	27,347
11	Nov	4	H	Liverpool	L 1-3	0-1	—	Lineker	35,003
12		10	H	Wimbledon	W 4-2	2-2	3	Stewart, Mabbutt, Walsh, Lineker (pen)	28,769
13		18	A	Everton	D 1-1	1-1	—	Howells	28,716
14		24	H	Norwich C	W 2-1	1-1	3	Lineker 2	33,942
15	Dec	1	A	Chelsea	L 2-3	0-2	4	Gascoigne, Lineker	33,478
16		8	H	Sunderland	D 3-3	0-2	3	Walsh 2, Lineker	30,431
17		15	A	Manchester C	L 1-2	1-0	3	Gascoigne	31,263
18		22	H	Luton T	W 2-1	1-1	4	Stewart 2	27,007
19		26	A	Coventry C	L 0-2	0-0	5		22,731
20		29	A	Southampton	L 0-3	0-1	5		21,405
21	Jan	1	H	Manchester U	L 1-2	1-1	6	Lineker (pen)	29,399
22		12	H	Arsenal	D 0-0	0-0	6		34,753
23		20	A	Derby Co	W 1-0	1-0	—	Lineker	17,747
24	Feb	2	H	Leeds U	D 0-0	0-0	6		32,253
25		23	A	Wimbledon	L 1-5	0-1	7	Bergsson	10,303
26	Mar	2	H	Chelsea	D 1-1	1-1	7	Lineker (pen)	26,168
27		16	A	Aston Villa	L 2-3	0-2	9	Samways, Allen	32,638
28		23	H	QPR	D 0-0	0-0	8		30,860
29		30	H	Coventry C	D 2-2	1-2	8	Nayim 2	29,033
30	Apr	1	A	Luton T	D 0-0	0-0	8		11,322
31		6	H	Southampton	W 2-0	2-0	8	Lineker 2	24,291
32		10	A	Norwich C	L 1-2	1-1	—	Hendry	19,014
33		17	A	Crystal Palace	L 0-1	0-1	—		26,285
34		20	A	Sheffield U	D 2-2	0-0	8	Edinburgh, Walsh	25,706
35		24	H	Everton	D 3-3	1-1	—	Allen, Mabbutt, Nayim	21675
36	May	4	H	Nottingham F	D 1-1	0-1	9	Nayim	30,891
37		11	A	Liverpool	L 0-2	0-1	11		36,192
38		20	A	Manchester U	D 1-1	0-1	—	Hendry	46,791

Final League Position: 10

GOALSCORERS

League (51): Lineker 15 (3 pens), Gascoigne 7, Walsh 7, Nayim 5, Howells 4, Allen 3, Stewart 3, Hendry 2, Mabbutt 2, Bergsson 1, Edinburgh 1, Samways 1.
Rumbelows Cup (11): Gascoigne 6 (1 pen), Stewart 4, Lineker 1.
FA Cup (14): Gascoigne 6, Lineker 3, Stewart 2, Mabbutt 1, own goals 2.

Thorstvedt	Bergsson	Van den Hauwe	Sedgley	Howells	Mabbutt	Stewart	Gascoigne	Nayim	Lineker	Allen	Samways	Walsh	Thomas	Moncur	Edinburgh	Tuttle	Moran	Fenwick	Gray	Hendry	Walker	Hendon	Garland	Match No.
1	2	3	4	5	6	7	8	9	10	11*	12													1
1	2	3	4	5	6	7†	8	9*	10	11	12	14												2
1	2	3	4	5	6	7	8*	9	10	11			12											3
1	2	3	4	5	6	7†	8	9*	10	11	12	14												4
1	2	3	4	5	6	7	8	9	10	11														5
1	2	3	4	5	6	7	8	9	10	11														6
1	2†	3	4	5*	6	7	8	9	10	11			14	12										7
1		3	4	5	6	7*	8	9†10		11		14	2	12										8
1		3	4	5	6	7	8*	9		11		10	2	12										9
1		3	4*	5	6	7	8	9	10	11		12	2											10
1	2*	3	4	5	6	7	8	9†10		11		14		12										11
1		3*	4†	5	6	7	8	9	10	11		14	2		12									12
1		3	4	5	6	7	8	9	10*11			12	2											13
1		3	4	5	6	7	8	9	10	11			2											14
1		3		5	6	7	8	9†10		11		14	2			12		4*						15
1		3		5	6	7*	8	9	10	11	12	14	2					4†						16
1		3	4	5*	6	7	8	9†10		14	12	11	2											17
1		3	4	5	6	7	8	9	10*14		12	11†	2											18
1		3	4*	5	6	7	8	14	10	9	12	11†	2											19
1	14	3	4	5†	6	7		9*	10	11	8	12	2											20
1		3	4*	5	6	7	8	9	10	11			2			12								21
1				5	6	7	8	10	11	9			2		3			4						22
1	14		4	5		7	6*	10†11		8	9	12	3		2									23
1		3	4		6	7	5*	10	11	12	9	8	2											24
1	2		4		6	5*	10	11	7	8	9	3	12											25
1		3	4		6	7	8†	5	10	11	12	14	2						9*					26
1		3	4		6	7	10*	11	8	5	9	2†	12									14		27
1			4		6	7	5*	10	11	8	14	3	12		2				9†					28
1		3	4†		6	7	5	11	8	10	12	14	2						9*					29
1		3			6	7	5	11	8	10			2					4	9					30
1		3	4		6	7	10	11	8†	9	5*	14	2			12								31
		3*	4	2		8†	7	9	5	11	6	10									1	12	14	32
1		3*	4		6	7	8†	5	11	9	10	2	12							14				33
1	12		4	5		7	8	11	9*	10	3	2	6											34
1		14		5	6	7	4	10*	11	9	8†	3	2			12								35
1		3*	4	5	6		8	7	10	11	9	12	2											36
1		3	4	5*	6	7	8	10†11		9	12	2										14		37
1	14		4	5	6†	7	10*	9	8	12	2	3	11											38
37	9	31	33	29	35	35	26	32	32	34	14	16	23	4	14	4	—	4	3	2	1	—	—	

Sub appearances (+): 3s 1s 1s 1s 2s 9s 13s 8s 5s 2s 2s 1s 3s 2s 2s 1s

Rumbelows Cup	Second Round	Hartlepool U (h)	5-0
		(a)	2-1
	Third Round	Bradford C (h)	2-1
	Fourth Round	Sheffield U (a)	2-0
	Fifth Round	Chelsea (a)	0-0
		(h)	0-3
FA Cup	Third Round	Blackpool (a)	1-0
	Fourth Round	Oxford U (h)	4-2
	Fifth Round	Portsmouth (a)	2-1
	Sixth Round	Notts Co (h)	2-1
	Semi-final	Arsenal (at Wembley)	3-1
	Final	Nottingham F (at Wembley)	2-1

TOTTENHAM HOTSPUR

Player and Position	Ht	Wt	Birth Date	Birth Place	Source	Clubs	League App	Gls
Goalkeepers								
Kevin Dearden	5 11	12 08	8 3 70	Luton	Trainee	Tottenham H	—	—
						Cambridge U (loan)	15	—
						Hartlepool U (loan)	10	—
						Oxford U (loan)	—	—
						Swindon T (loan)	1	—
						Peterborough U (loan)	7	—
						Hull C (loan)	3	—
Erik Thorstvedt	6 3	14 04	28 10 62	Stavanger	IFK Gothenburg	Tottenham H	89	—
Ian Walker	6 1	11 09	31 10 71	Watford	Trainee	Tottenham H	1	—
						Oxford U (loan)	2	—
						Ipswich T (loan)	—	—
Defenders								
Gudni Bergsson	5 10	10 07	21 7 65	Iceland	Valur	Tottenham H	38	1
Justin Edinburgh	5 9	11 06	18 12 69	Brentwood	Trainee	Southend U	37	—
						Tottenham H (loan)	—	—
						Tottenham H	16	1
Terry Fenwick	5 11	11 01	17 11 59	Camden, Co. Durham	Apprentice	Crystal Palace	70	—
						QPR	256	33
						Tottenham H	65	8
						Leicester C (loan)	8	1
Ian Hendon	6 0	12 10	5 12 71	Ilford	Trainee	Tottenham H	2	—
Gary Mabbutt	5 9	10 10	23 8 61	Bristol	Apprentice	Bristol R	131	10
						Tottenham H	299	23
David McDonald	5 10	11 00	2 1 71	Dublin	Trainee	Tottenham H	—	—
						Gillingham (loan)	10	—
John Moncur	5 7	9 10	22 9 66	Stepney	Apprentice	Tottenham H	21	1
						Doncaster R (loan)	4	—
						Cambridge U (loan)	4	—
						Portsmouth (loan)	7	—
						Brentford (loan)	5	1
Andy Polston	5 10	11 00	26 7 70	Walthamstow	Trainee	Tottenham H	1	—
						Cambridge U (loan)	3	—
Steve Sedgley	6 1	12 06	26 5 68	Enfield	Apprentice	Coventry C	84	3
						Tottenham H	66	—
Brian Statham	5 11	11 00	21 5 69	Zimbabwe	Apprentice	Tottenham H	24	—
						Reading (loan)	8	—
Mitchell Thomas	6 0	12 00	2 10 64	Luton	Apprentice	Luton T	107	1
						Tottenham H	157	6
David Tuttle	6 1	12 10	6 2 72	Reading	Trainee	Tottenham H	6	—
Pat Van Den Hauwe	6 0	10 08	16 12 60	Dendermonde	Apprentice	Birmingham C	123	1
						Everton	135	2
						Tottenham H	63	—
Midfield								
Paul Allen	5 7	10 10	28 8 62	Aveley	Apprentice	West Ham U	152	6
						Tottenham H	214	17
Nick Barmby	5 6	11 03	11 2 74	Hull	Trainee	Tottenham H	—	—
Matthew Edwards	5 10	9 08	15 6 71	Hammersmith	Trainee	Tottenham H	—	—
						Reading (loan)	8	—
Peter Garland	5 9	12 00	20 1 71	Croydon	Trainee	Tottenham H	1	—
Paul Gascoigne	5 10	11 07	27 5 67	Gateshead	Apprentice	Newcastle U	92	21
						Tottenham H	92	19
Scott Houghton	5 5	11 06	22 10 71	Hitchin	Trainee	Tottenham H	—	—
						Ipswich T (loan)	8	1
Nayim	5 8	11 04	5 11 66	Ceuta	Barcelona	Tottenham H	63	7
Vinny Samways	5 8	9 00	27 10 68	Bethnal Green	Apprentice	Tottenham H	93	7
Kevin Smith	5 9	12 00	25 12 71	Kent	Trainee	Tottenham H	—	—
Neil Smith	5 7	11 10	30 9 71	London	Trainee	Tottenham H	—	—
Forwards								
Ian Gilzean	6 1	12 08	10 12 69	Enfield	Trainee	Tottenham H	—	—
Philip Gray	5 10	11 07	2 10 68	Belfast	Apprentice	Tottenham H	9	—
						Barnsley (loan)	3	—
						Fulham (loan)	3	—

TOTTENHAM HOTSPUR

Foundation: The Hotspur Football Club was formed from an older cricket club in 1882. Most of the founders were old boys St. John's Presbyterian School and Tottenham Grammar School. The Casey brothers were well to the fore as the family provided the club's first goalposts (painted blue and white) and their first ball. They soon adopted the local YMCA as their meeing place, but after a couple of moves settled at the Red House, which is still their headquarters, although now known simply as 748 High Road.

First Football League game: 1 September, 1908, Division 2, v Wolverhampton W (h) W 3-0 – Hewitson; Coquet, Burton; Morris (1), Steel (D), Darnell; Walton, Woodward (2), Macfarlane, R. Steel, Middlemiss.

Did you know: Spurs called on only 17 players for the 49 games when they completed the 'Double' in 1960–61. Three of these made only one appearance each while Henry, Blanchflower and Allen were ever present.

Managers (and Secretary-managers)
Frank Brettell 1897–98, John Cameron 1901–12, Peter McWilliam 1913–27, Billy Minter 1927–30, Percy Smith 1935, Jack Tresadern 1935–38, Peter McWilliam 1938–42, Joe Hulme 1945–49, Arthur Rowe 1949–55, Jimmy Anderson 1955–58, Bill Nicholson 1958–74, Terry Neill 1974–76, Keith Burkinshaw 1976–84, Peter Shreeves 1984–86, David Pleat 1986–87, Terry Venables October 1987– .

Player and Position	Ht	Wt	Birth Date	Birth Place	Source	Clubs	League App	League Gls
John Hendry	5 11	10 00	6 1 70	Glasgow	Hillington YC	Dundee	2	—
						Forfar Ath (loan)	10	6
						Tottenham H	4	2
David Howells	5 11	11 01	15 12 67	Guildford	Trainee	Tottenham H	103	13
Gary Lineker	5 11	12 02	30 11 60	Leicester	Apprentice	Leicester C	194	95
						Everton	41	30
						Barcelona	99	44
						Tottenham H	70	39
Paul Moran	5 10	11 00	22 5 68	Enfield	Trainee	Tottenham H	28	2
						Portsmouth (loan)	3	—
						Leicester C (loan)	10	1
						Newcastle U (loan)	1	—
						Southend U	1	—
Mark Robson	5 7	10 05	22 5 69	Newham	Trainee	Exeter C	26	7
						Tottenham H	8	—
						Reading (loan)	7	—
						Watford (loan)	1	—
						Plymouth Arg (loan)	7	—
Paul Stewart	5 11	11 10	7 10 64	Manchester	Apprentice	Blackpool	201	56
						Manchester C	51	26
						Tottenham H	93	23
Paul Walsh	5 7	10 08	1 10 62	Plumstead	Apprentice	Charlton Ath	87	24
						Luton T	80	24
						Liverpool	77	25
						Tottenham H	99	16

Trainees
Bence, Steven M; Caskey, Darren M; Culverhouse, David P; Deanus, Del; Hall, Mark A; Heath, Michael; Hodges, Lee L; Howell, Gregory C; Jordan, Kevin; Kinnear, Colin B.T; Mahorn, Paul G; Marlow, Andrew D; Morah, Olisa H; Nethercott, Stuart D; Potts, Anthony J; Smart, Lee A; Thompson-Minton, Jeffrey S; Watson, Kevin, E; Wood, Dean B; Young, Neil A.

Associated Schoolboys
Anderson, Ijah M; Archer, Paul L.J; Chandler, Dean A.R; Embleton, Ricky; Foot, Daniel F; Gain, Peter T; Georgiou, Andrew; Haynes, Junior L.A; Hughes, Richard; Hughton, Leon A; Knott, Gareth R; Le Bihan, Neil E.R; McDougall, Alan J; Payne, Ian N; Pinch, Mark C; Pook, Andrew; Reynolds, Andrew; Simpson, Robert A; Slade, Steven A; Smith, Daneal; Williams, Richard I; Wormull, Simon J.

Associated Schoolboys who have accepted the club's offer of a Traineeship/Contract
Binks, Spencer C; Campbell, Sulzeer; Day, Christopher; Hill, Daniel R.L; Landon, Christopher S; McDougald, David; Reynolds, Christopher C; Robinson, Stephen; Turner, Andrew P.

TRANMERE ROVERS 1990–91 *Back row (left to right)*: Kenny Jones (Trainer), Eddie Bishop, Gary Bauress, John McGreal, Scott Taylor, Tony Thomas, Kenny Irons, John Morrissey.
Centre row: Norman Wilson (Secretary), Warwick Rimmer, Steve Vickers, Jim Steel, Chris Malkin, Paul Collings, Eric Nixon, Shaun Garnett, Dave Higgins, Ged Brannan, Ronnie Moore, Ray Mathias (Reserve Coach).
Front row: Dave Martindale, Neil McNab, Mark Hughes, John King (Manager), Jim Harvey, Mark McCarrick, Steve Mungall, Ian Muir.

Division 2   **TRANMERE ROVERS**

Prenton Park, Prenton Road West, Birkenhead. Telephone 051-608 3677. Commercial/Cashline 051-608 0371. Valley Road Training Centre: 051-652 2578. Shop: 051-608 0438.

Ground capacity: 14,200.

Record attendance: 24,424 v Stoke C, FA Cup 4th rd, 5 February 1972.

Record receipts: £48,597 v Tottenham H, Littlewoods Cup 4th rd, 22 November 1989.

Pitch measurements: 112yd × 71yd.

President: H. B. Thomas.

Chairman: P. R. Johnson. *Vice-chairman and Chief Executive:* F. D. Corfe.

Directors: A. J. Adams BDS, G. E. H. Jones LLB, F. J. Williams, J. J. Holsgrove FCA, G. A. Higham MSC TECH LRSC, M INST PI.

Secretary: Norman Wilson FAAI. *Commercial Manager:* Nigel Coates.

Development Manager: Nobby Abbott.

Manager: John King. *Trainer:* Kenny Jones.

Youth Development Manager: Warwick Rimmer.

Coach: Ronnie Moore. *Physio:* Alec McLellaw.

Year Formed: 1885. *Turned Professional:* 1912. *Ltd Co.:* 1920.

Previous Name: Belmont AFC, 1884–85.

Club Nickname: 'The Rovers'.

Previous Grounds: 1884, Steeles Field; 1887, Ravenshaws Field/Old Prenton Park; 1912, Prenton Park.

Record League Victory: 13-4 v Oldham Ath, Division 3 (N), 26 December 1935 – Gray; Platt, Fairhurst; McLaren, Newton, Spencer; Eden, MacDonald (1), Bell (9), Woodward (2), Urmson (1).

Record Cup Victory: 9-0 v AP Leamington, FA Cup, 1st rd, 24 November 1979 – Johnson; Mathias, Flood (Mungall), Bramhall, Edwards, Evans (2), O'Neil (2 incl. 1p), Parry, Peplow, Lumby (3), Beamish (1). (1 og).

Record Defeat: 1-9 v Tottenham H, FA Cup 3rd rd (replay), 14 January 1953.

Most League Points (2 for a win): 60, Division 4, 1964–65.

Most League Points (3 for a win): 80, Division 4, 1988–89 and Division 3, 1989–90.

Most League Goals: 111, Division 3 (N), 1930–31.

Highest League Scorer in Season: Bunny Bell, 35, Division 3 (N), 1933–34.

Most League Goals in Total Aggregate: Ian Muir, 118, 1985–91.

Most Capped Player: Albert Gray, 3 (24), Wales.

Most League Appearances: Harold Bell, 595, 1946–64 (incl. League record 401 consecutive appearances).

Record Transfer Fee Received: £120,000 from Cardiff C for Ronnie Moore, February 1979.

Record Transfer Fee Paid: £250,000 to Real Sociedad for John Aldridge, July 1991.

Football League Record: 1921 Original Member of Division 3 (N): 1938–39 Division 2; 1946–58 Division 3 (N); 1958–61 Division 3; 1961–67 Division 4; 1967–75 Division 3; 1975–76 Division 4; 1976–79 Division 3; 1979–89 Division 4; 1989–91 Division 3; 1991– Division 2.

Honours: Football League Division 2 best season: 22nd, 1938–39; Division 3 (N) – Champions 1937–38; Promotion to 3rd Division: 1966–67, 1975–76; Division 4 – Runners-up 1988–89. *FA Cup:* best season: 5th rd, 1967–68. *Football League Cup:* best season: 4th rd, 1961, 1982, 1989, 1990. *Welsh Cup:* Winners 1935; Runners-up 1934. *Leyland Daf Cup:* Runners-up 1991

Colours: All white. **Change colours:** Claret/sky blue shirts, sky blue shorts and stockings.

TRANMERE ROVERS 1990–91 LEAGUE RECORD

Match No.	Date		Venue	Opponents	Result		H/T Score	Lg. Pos.	Goalscorers	Atten-dance
1	Aug	25	A	Bradford C	W	2-1	1-0	—	Muir 2 (1 pen)	7970
2		31	H	Stoke C	L	1-2	1-2	—	Muir (pen)	10,327
3	Sept	8	A	Preston NE	W	4-0	2-0	4	Morrissey 2, Muir, Steel	5648
4		14	H	Shrewsbury T	D	1-1	1-0	—	Harvey	7105
5		17	H	Leyton Orient	W	3-0	2-0	—	Hughes, Muir 2	5510
6		21	A	Crewe Alex	W	3-2	2-2	—	McNab 2, Muir	4267
7		28	A	Swansea C	D	1-1	0-1	—	Morrissey	4884
8	Oct	1	H	Wigan Ath	D	1-1	1-1	—	McNab	7030
9		6	H	Chester C	L	1-2	0-1	7	Hughes	6642
10		20	A	Exeter C	D	0-0	0-0	10		5045
11		22	H	Mansfield T	W	6-2	1-1	—	Bishop 3, Malkin, Steel, McCarrick	5996
12		26	H	Brentford	W	2-1	0-0	—	Malkin, McCarrick	7173
13		30	A	Bournemouth	L	0-1	0-1	—		6268
14	Nov	3	A	Bury	L	0-3	0-1	5		3766
15		10	H	Grimsby T	L	1-2	1-0	12	Steel	6140
16		24	A	Fulham	W	2-1	1-0	5	Higgins, Harvey	4194
17	Dec	1	A	Bolton W	L	1-2	1-2	7	Harvey	6941
18		14	H	Reading	D	0-0	0-0	—		4691
19		21	H	Birmingham C	W	1-0	1-0	—	Irons	5034
20		26	A	Cambridge U	L	1-3	0-3	9	Steel	4547
21		29	A	Rotherham U	D	1-1	0-1	10	Higgins	4316
22	Jan	1	H	Southend U	W	3-1	2-1	8	Thomas, Muir, Morrissey	7214
23		5	H	Huddersfield T	W	2-0	1-0	6	Steel, Irons	5626
24		12	A	Stoke C	D	1-1	1-0	6	Brannan	13,461
25		18	H	Bradford C	W	2-1	1-0	—	Muir, Irons	6508
26	Feb	2	A	Leyton Orient	L	0-4	0-1	7		4313
27		4	H	Crewe Alex	W	2-0	1-0	—	Muir 2 (1 pen)	5120
28		16	H	Fulham	D	1-1	1-1	6	Nebbeling (og)	5211
29		23	A	Grimsby T	W	1-0	0-0	5	Irons	6375
30		26	A	Huddersfield T	L	1-2	1-0	—	Mungall	4889
31	Mar	1	H	Bolton W	D	1-1	0-0	—	Thomas	10,076
32		9	A	Reading	L	0-1	0-0	9		4440
33		12	A	Wigan Ath	W	1-0	0-0	—	Muir	2912
34		15	H	Swansea C	W	2-1	1-1	—	Muir, Morrissey	5412
35		18	H	Bournemouth	W	1-0	1-0	—	Garnett	5418
36		23	A	Chester C	W	2-0	1-0	5	Morrissey, Malkin	2705
37		26	A	Shrewsbury T	W	1-0	0-0	—	Thomas	3949
38		29	H	Cambridge U	W	2-0	0-0	—	Malkin, Irons	11,079
39	Apr	2	A	Birmingham C	L	0-1	0-0	—		7675
40		5	H	Rotherham U	L	1-2	1-0	—	Morrissey	7398
41		12	A	Southend U	L	0-1	0-1	—		8622
42		20	H	Exeter C	W	1-0	1-0	5	Morrissey	5178
43		27	A	Mansfield T	W	2-0	0-0	5	Steel, Morrissey	2393
44	May	4	A	Brentford	W	2-0	2-0	5	Cooper, Vickers	7341
45		7	H	Preston NE	W	2-1	0-1	—	Flynn (og), Irons (pen)	6006
46		11	H	Bury	L	1-2	1-1	5	Cooper	9081

Final League Position: 5

GOALSCORERS

League (64): Muir 13 (3 pens), Morrissey 9, Irons 6 (1 pen), Steel 6, Malkin 4, Bishop 3, Harvey 3, McNab 3, Thomas 3, Cooper 2, Higgins 2, Hughes 2, McCarrick 2, Brannan 1, Garnett 1, Mungall 1, Vickers 1, own goals 2.
Rumbelows Cup (2): Steel 1, Vickers 1.
FA Cup (4): Irons 1, Morrissey 1, Steel 1, Vickers 1.

Nixon	Mungall	McCarrick	McNab	Hughes	Vickers	Morrissey	Harvey	Steel	Muir	Thomas	Martindale	Irons	Higgins	Malkin	Bishop	Brannan	Cooper	Garnett	Collings	Match No.
1	2	3	4	5	6	7	8*	9	10	11	12									1
1	2	3*	4	5†	6	7	8	9	10	11	12	14								2
1	3		4	5*	6	7	8	9	10	11	12		2							3
1	3		4	5	6	7	8	9	10*	11			2	12						4
1	3		4	5	6	7	8	9	10	11*	12		2							5
1	3		4	5	6	7	8	9	10	11*			2	12						6
1	11	3	4	5	6	7*	8	9	10				2	12						7
1	11	3†	4	5	6	7*	8	9	10		14		2	12						8
1	11	3	4	5*	6	7	8		10		12		2	9						9
1	3			5	6	7*	8	9	10				2	11	12					10
1	3			5	6	7*	8	9	10				2	11	4	12				11
1	3			5	6		8	9	10				2	7	4	11				12
1	3			5*	6	14	8	9	10	11†			2	7	4	12				13
1	3	4			6	14	8*	9	10†		12		2	5	11					14
1	3	4	5	6		7	8*	9	10		14		2†	12	11					15
1			4	5	6	7	8	9	10	11			2	3						16
1			4	5	6	7†	8*	9	10	11		14	2	12	3					17
1			4	5†	6	14	12	9	10*	11		7	2	8	3					18
1			4	5	6		8	9		11		7	2		3	10				19
1			4	5*	6		8	9	12	11		7	2		3	10				20
1	14		4	5†	6		8	9	12	11		7	2		3	10*				21
1			4	5	6	12	8	9	10	11*		7	2		3					22
1			4	5	6	7	8	9	10	11			2		3					23
1	11			5	6	7*	8	9	10			4	2		3	12				24
1	11			5	6	7	8	9	10			4	2		3					25
1	5	4*			6	14	8	9	10	11		7	2		3†12					26
1	3			5	6	7	8	9	10	11		4	2							27
1	3	14	5	6†	7	8	9	10*11				4	12	2						28
1	3	4	5		12	8*	9	10	11			7	2		6					29
1	3	4	5		12	8	9	10	11			7†	2*	14	6					30
1	3	4	5			7*	8	9	10	11	14		2†12		6					31
1	3	4	5	6	7*	8†	9	10	11	14		12	2							32
	3	4	5	6		8*	9	10	11			7	12			2			1	33
	3	4	5	6	14	8	9*10		11†			7	12			2			1	34
	3	4	5	6	7*		9	10	11			8	12			2			1	35
1	3	4	5	6	7		9	10*11				8	12			2				36
1	3	4	5	6	7*12	9†		11				8	10	14	2					37
1	3	4	5	6	7		9		11			8	10		2					38
1	3	4	5*	6	7	12	9		11			8	10†	14	2					39
1	3	4	5*	6	7	12	9†		11			8	10	14	2					40
1	3	4		6	7	8†	9*		11		2		10	12	14	5				41
1	3	4		6	7	8*	9		11	12	2		10	5						42
1	3	4	5	6	7		9		11	8	2	12	10*							43
1	3	4	5	6	7*		9		11	14	8	2	12	10†						44
1	3	4	5	6	7		9*		11	8	2	12	10							45
1	3	4	5†	6	7			11	14	8	2	9*	12	10						46
43	32	11	39	42	42	33	35	43	33	33	2	26	33	12	5	14	9	16	3	

```
        +   +           +   +   +   +           +   +           +   +   +   +
        1s  1s          7s  4s  1s  2s          9s  6s          13s 3s  4s  8s
```

Rumbelows Cup	First Round	Middlesbrough (a)	1-1
		(h)	1-2
FA Cup	First Round	Halesowen (a)	2-1
	Second Round	Scunthorpe U (a)	2-3

TRANMERE ROVERS

Player and Position	Ht	Wt	Birth Date	Place	Source	Clubs	League App	Gls
Goalkeepers								
Paul Collings	6 2	12 00	30 9 68	Liverpool		Tranmere R	4	—
Eric Nixon	6 2	14 03	4 10 62	Manchester	Curzon Ashton	Manchester C	58	—
						Wolverhampton W (loan)	16	—
						Bradford C (loan)	3	—
						Southampton (loan)	4	—
						Carlisle U (loan)	16	—
						Tranmere R (loan)	8	—
						Tranmere R	134	—
Defenders								
Gary Bauress*	6 0	12 00	19 1 71	Liverpool	Trainee	Tranmere R	1	—
Ged Brannan	6 0	13 03	15 1 72	Liverpool	Trainee	Tranmere R	18	1
Mike Foster	5 9	11 06	24 9 73	Portmadoc		Tranmere R	—	—
Dave Higgins	6 0	11 00	19 8 61	Liverpool	Eagle	Tranmere R	28	—
					Caernarfon	Tranmere R	154	5
Mark Hughes	6 1	12 10	3 2 62	Morriston	Apprentice	Bristol R	74	3
						Torquay U (loan)	9	1
						Swansea C	12	—
						Bristol C	22	—
						Tranmere R	214	8
Mark McCarrick*	5 8	10 08	4 2 62	Liverpool	Witton A	Birmingham C	15	—
						Lincoln C	44	—
						Crewe Alex	11	—
					Runcorn	Tranmere R	125	14
John McGreal	5 11	10 08	2 6 72	Birkenhead	Trainee	Tranmere R	—	—
Steve Mungall	5 8	11 02	22 5 58	Bellshill		Motherwell	20	—
						Tranmere R	415	9
Tony Thomas	5 11	12 05	12 7 71	Liverpool	Trainee	Tranmere R	84	7
Steven Vickers	6 2	12 00	13 10 67	B Auckland	Spennymoor U	Tranmere R	215	10
Midfield								
Shaun Garnett	6 2	11 00	22 11 69	Wallasey	Trainee	Tranmere R	21	1
Jimmy Harvey	5 9	11 04	2 5 58	Lurgan	Glenavon	Arsenal	3	—
						Hereford U (loan)	11	—
						Hereford U	267	39
						Bristol C	3	—
						Wrexham (loan)	6	—
						Tranmere R	160	17
Neil McNab	5 7	11 00	4 6 57	Greenock		Morton	14	—
						Tottenham H	72	3
						Bolton W	35	4
						Brighton & HA	103	4
						Leeds U (loan)	5	—
						Portsmouth (loan)	—	—
						Manchester C	221	16
						Tranmere R	62	4
Dave Martindale	5 11	11 10	9 4 64	Liverpool	Apprentice	Liverpool	—	—
					Caernarfon	Tranmere R	96	7
John Smith‡	5 7	10 12	23 7 70	Liverpool		Tranmere R	2	—
Forwards								
Steve Cooper	5 11	10 12	22 6 64	Birmingham		Birmingham C	—	—
						Halifax (loan)	7	1
						Mansfield T (loan)	—	—
						Newport Co	38	11
						Plymouth Arg	73	15
						Barnsley	77	13
						Tranmere R	17	2

TRANMERE ROVERS

Foundation: Formed in 1884 as Belmont they adopted their present title the following year and eventually joined their first league, the West Lancashire League in 1889–90, the same year as their first success in the Wirral Challenge Cup. The club almost folded in 1899–1900 when all the players left en bloc to join a rival club, but they survived the crisis and went from strength to strength winning the 'Combination' title in 1907–08 and the Lancashire Combination in 1913–14. They joined the Football League in 1920 from the Central League.

First Football League game: 27 August, 1921, Division 3(N), v Crewe Alex (h) W 4-1 – Bradshaw; Grainger, Stuart (1); Campbell, Milnes (1), Heslop; Moreton, Groves (1), Hyam, Ford (1), Hughes.

Did you know: On 27 January, 1934, Tranmere Rovers helped create a record for Anfield when they met Liverpool in a 4th Round FA Cup tie. The attendance of 61,036 that day was not exceeded until 1952.

Managers (and Secretary-managers)
Bert Cooke 1912–35, Jackie Carr 1935–36, Jim Knowles 1936–39, Bill Ridding 1939–45, Ernie Blackburn 1946–55, Noel Kelly 1955–57, Peter Farrell 1957–60, Walter Galbraith 1961, Dave Russell 1961–69, Jackie Wright 1969–72, Ron Yeats 1972–75, John King 1975–80, Bryan Hamilton 1980–85, Frank Worthington 1985–87, Ronnie Moore 1987, John King April 1987– .

Player and Position	Ht	Wt	Birth Date	Birth Place	Source	Clubs	League App	Gls
Kenny Irons	5 9	11 00	4 11 70	Liverpool	Trainee	Tranmere R	35	6
Chris Malkin	6 0	10 12	4 6 67	Bebington	Overpool	Tranmere R	90	26
John Morrissey	5 8	11 04	8 3 65	Liverpool	Apprentice	Everton	1	—
						Wolverhampton W	10	1
						Tranmere R	218	33
Ian Muir	5 7	10 10	5 5 63	Coventry	Apprentice	QPR	2	2
						Burnley (loan)	2	1
						Birmingham C	1	—
						Brighton & HA	4	—
						Swindon T (loan)	2	—
						Tranmere R	248	118
Jim Steel	6 3	14 00	4 12 59	Dumfries	Apprentice	Oldham Ath	108	24
						Wigan Ath (loan)	2	2
						Wrexham (loan)	9	6
						Port Vale	28	6
						Wrexham	164	51
						Tranmere R	153	25
Scott Taylor*	6 0	11 00	10 5 72	Birkenhead	Trainee	Tranmere R	—	—

Trainees
Coyne, Daniel; Draper, Anthony J; Dunne, Jamie C; Hardy, Neil J.P; Hill, Christopher P; Hughes, Mark A; James, Scott; Moore, Darren E; Morgan, Alan M; Richardson, Marcus.

Associated Schoolboys
Bate, Christopher J; Deens, Shaun P; Hammond, John E; Lepts, Damien A; McGuiness, Lee; Philips, Andrew.

Associated Schoolboys who have accepted the club's offer of a Traineeship/Contract
Evans, John; Jones, Gary S.

532

WALSALL 1990-91 *Back row (left to right)*: Graeme Forbes, Kenny Mower, Stephen O'Hara, Fred Barber, Paul Cooke, Ron Green, Dave Barnett, Dean Smith. *Centre row*: Ken Gutteridge (Chief Scout), Eric McManus (Youth Development Officer), Darren Riley, John Kelly, Chris Marsh, Martin Goldsmith, Chris Hutchings, Tony Grealish, Tom Bradley (Physiotherapist). *Front row*: Rodney McDonald, Phil Whitehouse, Stuart Rimmer, Paul Taylor (General Manager), Barrie Blower (Chairman), Kenny Hibbitt (Manager), Roy Whalley (Secretary), Peter Skipper, Billy Millen, Alex Taylor, Adrian Littlejohn. The club were unable to name the trainees in the first two rows.

Division 4   **WALSALL**

Bescot Stadium, Bescot Cresent, Walsall ES1 4SA. Telephone Walsall (0922) 22791. Commercial Dept: (0922) 30696. Clubcall: 0898 121104.

Ground capacity: 10,400.

Record attendance: 25,453 v Newcastle U, Division 2, 29 August 1961 (at Fellows Park); 9,551 v Aston Villa, Friendly, 18 August 1990 (at Bescot Stadium).

Record receipts: £50,926.50 v Watford, FA Cup 5th rd, 2nd replay, 2 March 1987 (at Fellows Park); £42,401 v Aston Villa, Friendly, 18 August 1990.

Pitch measurements: 113yd × 73yd.

President: .

Chairman: B. S. Blower.

Managing Director: R. Dox.

Directors: J. Bowser, R. Clift, T. F. Hargreaves, K. R. Whalley.

Manager: John Barnwell. *Assistant Manager:* P. Taylor.

Physio: T. Bradley.

Secretary/Commercial Manager: K. R. Whalley.

Year Formed: 1888. *Turned Professional:* 1888. *Ltd Co.:* 1921.

Club Nickname: 'The Saddlers'.

Previous Names: Walsall Swifts (founded 1877) and Walsall Town (founded 1879) amalgamated in 1888 and were known as Walsall Town Swifts until 1895.

Previous Grounds: Fellows Park to 1990.

Record League Victory: 10-0 v Darwen, Division 2, 4 March 1899 – Tennent; E. Peers (1), Davies; Hickinbotham, Jenkyns, Taggart; Dean (3), Vail (2), Aston (4), Martin, Griffin.

Record Cup Victory: 6-1 v Leytonstone (away), FA Cup, 1st rd, 30 November 1946 – Lewis; Netley, Skidmore; Crutchley, Foulkes, Newman; Maund (1), Talbot, Darby (1), Wilshaw (2), Davies (2). 6–1 v Margate, FA Cup, 1st rd (replay), 24 November 1955 – Davies; Haddington, Vinall; Dorman, McPherson, Crook; Morris, Walsh (3), Richards (2), McLaren (1), Moore.

Record Defeat: 0-12 v Small Heath, 17 December 1892 and v Darwen, 26 December 1896, both Division 2.

Most League Points (2 for a win): 65, Division 4, 1959–60.

Most League Points (3 for a win): 82, Division 3, 1987–88.

Most League Goals: 102, Division 4, 1959–60.

Highest League Scorer in Season: Gilbert Alsop, 40, Division 3 (N), 1933–34 and 1934–35.

Most League Goals in Total Aggregate: Tony Richards, 184, 1954–63, and Colin Taylor, 184, 1958–63, 1964–68, 1969–73.

Most Capped Player: Mick Kearns, 15 (18), Eire.

Most League Appearances: Colin Harrison, 467, 1964–82.

Record Transfer Fee Received: £600,000 from West Ham U for David Kelly, July 1988.

Record Transfer Fee Paid: £175,000 to Birmingham C for Alan Buckley, June 1979.

Football League Record: 1892 Elected to Division 2; 1895 Failed re-election; 1896–1901 Division 2; 1901 Failed re-election; 1921 Original Member of Division 3 (N); 1927–31 Division 3 (S); 1931–36 Division 3 (N); 1936–58 Division 3 (S); 1958–60 Division 4; 1960–61 Division 3; 1961–63 Division 2; 1963–79 Division 3; 1979–80 Division 4; 1980–88 Division 3; 1988–89 Division 2; 1989–90 Division 3; 1990– Division 4.

Honours: Football League: Division 2 best season: 6th, 1898–99; Division 3 – Runners-up 1960–61; Division 4 – Champions 1959–60; Runners-up 1979–80. *FA Cup:* best season: 5th rd, 1939, 1975, 1978, and last 16 1888–89. *Football League Cup:* Semi-final 1983–84.

Colours: Red and white and black, white shorts, red with white hoop stocking. **Change colours:** Blue shirts, white shorts, blue stockings with white hoop.

WALSALL 1990–91 LEAGUE RECORD

Match No.	Date		Venue	Opponents	Result		H/T Score	Lg. Pos.	Goalscorers	Atten- dance
1	Aug	25	H	Torquay U	D	2-2	1-2	—	Rimmer, Goldsmith	5219
2	Sept	1	A	Stockport Co	L	0-3	0-2	22		2668
3		8	H	Darlington	D	2-2	1-2	21	Rimmer, Littlejohn	4348
4		15	A	Peterborough U	D	0-0	0-0	20		4099
5		18	A	Doncaster R	L	0-2	0-1	—		3925
6		22	H	Hereford U	D	0-0	0-0	23		4558
7		29	A	Rochdale	L	2-3	0-1	22	Cecere, Rimmer (pen)	1933
8	Oct	2	H	Scunthorpe U	W	3-0	3-0	—	Cecere, Bodak, Rimmer	3676
9		6	H	Carlisle U	D	1-1	0-1	18	Rimmer (pen)	4284
10		13	A	Maidstone U	W	3-1	1-1	16	Singleton, McDonald, Cecere	2329
11		19	A	Northampton T	L	0-5	0-2	—		4055
12		23	H	York C	D	1-1	0-1	—	Rimmer	3761
13		27	H	Aldershot	D	2-2	2-0	18	Rimmer (pen), Cecere	3567
14	Nov	3	A	Blackpool	W	2-1	2-0	15	Rimmer 2	3233
15		10	H	Burnley	W	1-0	0-0	15	Rimmer	5710
16		25	A	Chesterfield	D	2-2	1-1	—	Brien (og), Methven	3687
17	Dec	1	H	Halifax T	W	3-1	2-1		McDonald, Rimmer 2	4153
18		15	A	Cardiff C	W	2-0	1-0	10	Goldsmith, Rimmer (pen)	2017
19		21	H	Wrexham	W	1-0	1-0	—	Gordon	4420
20		26	A	Gillingham	L	0-1	0-0	9		3695
21	Jan	1	H	Scarborough	D	0-0	0-0	11		4914
22		5	A	Lincoln C	L	1-2	0-1	11	McDonald	2500
23		12	A	Stockport Co	L	0-2	0-1	14		4364
24		19	A	Torquay U	D	0-0	0-0	14		3191
25		26	H	Peterborough U	L	0-1	0-0	17		4438
26	Feb	2	H	Doncaster R	W	1-0	0-0	14	Marsh	3805
27		6	A	Hereford U	D	0-0	0-0	—		1947
28		16	A	Chesterfield	W	3-0	1-0	11	McDonald, Skipper, Ntamark	3995
29		19	H	Lincoln	D	0-0	0-0	—		3582
30		23	A	Burnley	L	0-2	0-0	13		7783
31	Mar	2	A	Halifax T	L	2-5	2-1	15	Naughton (pen), Marsh	1464
32		5	A	Darlington	L	0-1	0-0	—		3971
33		9	H	Cardiff C	D	0-0	0-0	16		3950
34		12	A	Scunthorpe U	L	0-1	0-1	—		3352
35		16	H	Rochdale	L	0-1	0-0	17		2890
36		20	H	Maidstone U	D	0-0	0-0	—		2475
37		23	A	Carlisle U	W	3-0	0-0	15	Cecere 2, McParland (pen)	2433
38		26	A	Hartlepool U	L	1-2	0-2	—	McDonald	2556
39		30	H	Gillingham	D	0-0	0-0	17		3074
40	Apr	1	A	Wrexham	D	1-1	1-0	16	McParland	1588
41		6	H	Hartlepool U	L	0-1	0-0	17		2758
42		13	A	Scarborough	L	0-1	0-1	17		1538
43		20	H	Northampton T	D	3-3	0-1	17	Grealish, Ntamark, McParland	3345
44		26	A	York C	L	0-1	0-1	—		1717
45	May	4	A	Aldershot	W	4-0	0-0	18	Jackson 2, McParland, Ntamark	1826
46		11	H	Blackpool	W	2-0	2-0	16	McParland 2	8051

Final League Position: 16

GOALSCORERS

League (48): Rimmer 13 (4 pens), Cecere 6, McParland 6 (1 pen), McDonald 5, Ntamark 3, Goldsmith 2, Jackson 2, Marsh 2, Bodak 1, Gordon 1, Grealish 1, Littlejohn 1, Methven 1, Naughton 1 (pen), Singleton 1, Skipper 1, own goal 1.
Rumbelows Cup (6): Rimmer 4 (1 pen), Goldsmith 1, Hutchings 1.
FA Cup (2): Hutchings 1, McDonald 1.

Green	Hutchings	Mower	Grealish	Bryant	Skipper	Ntamark	Kelly	Rimmer	Cecere	Marsh	Barnett	Goldsmith	Whitehouse	Smith	Littlejohn	O'Hara	Bodak	Lowery	Singleton	McDonald	Methven	Gordon	Naughton	McParland	Thompson	Barber	Jackson	Match No.
1	2	3	4†	5	6	7	8*	9	10	11	12	14																1
1	2	12		5	6			9	10	11		8†	7*	3	4	14												2
1	2	3	7	5	6			9	10	8					4	11												3
1	2	3	7	5	6			9	10	8					11	4												4
1	2	3	7*	5	6		12	9	10			8†	14		11	4												5
1	2	3	7	5	6*		12	9	10	8					11	4												6
1	2	3		5	6	8		9	10	11					7	4												7
1	2			5	6	8		9	10	11	12				7†	4*			3	14								8
1	2			5	6	8		9	10	11					7*	4			3	12								9
1	2	12	7	5	6	8													4*	3	11							10
1	2		7†	5	6	8*	12	9	10						14				6	4	3	11						11
1	2		7*	5	6	8	12	9	10										12	6	4	3	11					12
1	2	3		5	6	7	4	9	10*	12				8	11													13
1	2				6	11	4	9	10					5	7				3	8								14
1	2				6	11	7	9	10					5					3	8	4							15
1	2				6	8	7	9	10*					5	12				3	11	4							16
1	2				6	8	7	9	10					5	12				3	11*	4							17
1	2				6	8	7	9	10					5	11				3		4							18
1	2	12			6	8	7	9						5	14				3†	11*	4		10					19
1	2		7*		6	8	12	9						5†	14				3	11	4		10					20
1	2				6	8	7	9						5	12				3	11	4		10*					21
1	2				6	8	7	9						5*	12				3	11	4		10					22
1	2				6	8	7	9		12				5	14				3*	11	4		10†					23
1	2		7		6	8		9						5					3	11	4		10					24
1	2		7		6	8	11†	9		12				5*	14				3		4		10					25
1	2	10	7		6	8		9						5						11	4	3						26
1	2	10	7		6	8		9						5						11	4	3						27
1	2	3	7†		6	8	12	9*						5					14	10	4			11				28
1	2*	3			6	8	12	9						5					7	10	4			11				29
1	2†	3	7		6	8	12	9				14		5						10	4			11*				30
1	2	3†	7		6	8	12	9						5					14	10	4			11*				31
1	2	3	7†		6	8	12	9						5					14	10	4			11*				32
1		3	7		6	8		9		2				5	12					10	4			11*				33
1		3*	7		6	8		9		2				5†	11	12			14	10	4							34
1	2		7		6	8	12	9						5*	14				3	10	4			11†				35
1	2				6	8	12	9†						5	14				3*	11	4		10					36
1	2*		7		6	8	12	9						5					3		4	14	10	11*				37
1			7*		6	8		9		2				5†	14	12			3	11	4		10					38
1			7*		6	8†		9		2				5	14	12			3	11	4		10					39
1					6			9		2				5	11*				3		4	7	10	12	8			40
1					6	8		9*		2						12			3	11	4	5	10	7				41
1	2		7		6		12							5					3	11	4	14	9†	10	8*			42
1	2		7		6	8		9							11				3	12	4		5*	10				43
1	2		7		6†	8		9							14	11			3	12	4		5*	10				44
	2		7*		6	8	12								14	11†			3	5	4		10			1	9	45
	2		7†		6	8	12	9							14	11*			3	5	4		10			1		46
44	40	16	29	13	41	40	12	27	26	16	4	2	1	32	15	18	3	6	20	31	32	6	15	11	3	2	1	

Substitute appearances:

```
          +  +           +  +                   +  +  +  +  +  +  +  +              +  +              +
         1s 2s          2s 1s                  6s 7s 1s 2s 2s 1s 18s 2s 1s         8s 5s             1s
```

Rumbelows Cup

	First Round	Cambridge U (h)	4-2
		(a)	1-2
	Second Round	Chelsea (h)	0-5
		(a)	1-4

FA Cup

	First Round	Aylesbury (a)	1-0
	Second Round	Swansea C (a)	1-2

WALSALL

Player and Position	Ht	Wt	Birth Date	Place	Source	Clubs	League App	Gls
Goalkeepers								
Fred Barber	5 11	11 07	28 8 63	Ferryhill	Apprentice	Darlington	135	—
						Everton	—	—
						Walsall	153	—
						Peterborough U (loan)	6	—
						Chester C (loan)	8	—
						Blackpool (loan)	2	—
Ron Green*	6 2	14 00	3 10 56	Birmingham	Alvechurch	Walsall	163	—
						WBA (loan)	—	—
						Shrewsbury T	19	—
						Bristol R (loan)	18	—
						Bristol R	38	—
						Scunthorpe U	78	1
						Wimbledon	4	—
						Shrewsbury T (loan)	17	—
						Manchester C (loan)	—	—
						Walsall	67	—
Defenders								
Graeme Forbes*	6 0	12 00	29 7 58	Forfar	Lochee U	Motherwell	185	16
						Nottingham F (loan)	—	—
						Walsall	173	9
Colin Methven	6 2	12 07	10 12 55	Kirkcaldy	Leven Royals	East Fife	144	14
						Wigan Ath	296	21
						Blackpool	173	11
						Carlisle U (loan)	12	—
						Walsall	32	1
Ken Mower*	6 1	12 04	1 12 60	Walsall	Apprentice	Walsall	415	8
Peter Skipper*	5 11	12 05	11 4 58	Hull	Local	Hull C	23	2
						Scunthorpe U (loan)	1	—
						Darlington	91	4
						Hull C	265	17
						Oldham Ath	27	1
						Walsall	81	2
Dean Smith	6 0	12 01	19 3 71	West Bromwich	Trainee	Walsall	55	—
Phil Whitehouse*	5 6	10 09	23 3 71	Wolverhampton	Trainee	WBA	—	—
						Walsall	12	—
Midfield								
Dave Barnett‡	6 1	12 08	16 4 67	London	Windsor & Eton	Colchester U	20	—
						WBA	—	—
						Walsall	5	—
Peter Bodak‡	5 8	9 10	12 8 61	Birmingham	Apprentice	Coventry C	32	5
						Manchester U	—	—
						Manchester C	14	1
						Walsall	—	—
						Crewe Alex	53	7
						Swansea C	31	4
					Hong Kong	Walsall	4	1
Tony Grealish	5 7	11 08	21 9 56	Paddington	Apprentice	Orient	171	10
						Luton T	78	2
						Brighton & HA	100	6
						WBA	65	5
						Manchester C	11	—
						Rotherham U	110	6
						Walsall	31	1
Chris Hutchings*	5 10	11 00	5 7 57	Winchester	Harrow Bor	Chelsea	87	3
						Brighton & HA	153	4
						Huddersfield T	110	10
						Walsall	40	—
Charlie Ntamark	5 8	11 12	22 7 64	Cameroon		Walsall	42	3
Steve O'Hara	6 1	12 02	21 1 71	Bellshill	Trainee	Walsall	38	—
Martin Singleton	5 10	11 00	2 8 63	Banbury	Apprentice	Coventry C	23	1
						Bradford C	71	3
						WBA	19	1
						Northampton T	50	4
						Walsall	28	1

WALSALL

Foundation: Two of the leading clubs around Walsall in the 1880s were Walsall Swifts (formed 1877) and Walsall Town (formed 1879). The Swifts were winners of the Birmingham Senior Cup in 1881, while the Town reached the 4th round (5th round modern equivalent) of the FA Cup in 1883. These clubs amalgamated as Walsall Town Swifts in 1888, becoming simply Walsall in 1895.

First Football League game: 3 September, 1892, Division 2, v Darwen (h) L 1-2 – Hawkins; Withington, Pinches; Robinson, Whitrick, Forsyth; Marshall, Holmes, Turner, Gray (1), Pangbourn.

Did you know: Centre-forward Gilbert Alsop was the only player to have scored as many as 40 goals[+] in a season in both Division 3(S) and Division 3(N). A feat he achieved in successive seasons 1933–34 – 1934–35.
[+]Some records credit him with 39 goals in that latter season.

Managers (and Secretary-managers)
H. Smallwood 1888–91*, A. G. Burton 1891–93, J. H. Robinson 1893–95, C. H. Ailso 1895–96*, A. E. Parsloe 1896–97*, L. Ford 1897–98*, G. Hughes 1898–99*, L. Ford 1899–1901*, J. E. Shutt 1908–13*, Haydn Price 1914–20, Joe Burchell 1920–26, David Ashworth 1926–27, Jack Torrance 1927–28, James Kerr 1928–29, S. Scholey 1929–30, Peter O'Rourke 1930–32, G. W. Slade 1932–34, Andy Wilson 1934–37, Tommy Lowes 1937–44, Harry Hibbs 1944–51, Tony McPhee 1951, Brough Fletcher 1952–53, Major Frank Buckley 1953–55, John Love 1955–57, Billy Moore 1957–64, Alf Wood 1964, Reg Shaw 1964–68, Dick Graham 1968, Ron Lewin 1968–69, Billy Moore 1969–72, John Smith 1972–73, Doug Fraser 1973–77, Dave Mackay 1977–78, Alan Ashman 1978, Frank Sibley 1979, Alan Buckley 1979–86, Neil Martin (joint manager with Buckley) 1981–82, Tommy Coakley 1986–88, John Barnwell 1989–90, Kenny Hibbitt May 1990– .

Player and Position	Ht	Wt	Birth Date	Place	Source	Clubs	League App	Gls
Forwards								
Michele Cecere	6 0	11 04	4 1 68	Chester	Apprentice	Oldham Ath	52	8
						Huddersfield T	54	8
						Stockport Co (loan)	1	—
						Walsall	32	6
Martin Goldsmith	6 0	11 11	4 11 69	Walsall	Trainee	Walsall	7	2
						Larne (loan)	—	—
Robbie Jackson			9 2 73	Altrincham	Manchester C	Walsall	1	2
Adrian Littlejohn*	5 10	10 04	26 9 70	Wolverhampton	WBA	Walsall	44	1
Chris Marsh	5 10	12 11	14 1 70	Dudley	Trainee	Walsall	48	2
Rod McDonald			20 3 67	London	Colne Dynamoes	Walsall	36	5
Willie Naughton*	6 0	12 08	20 3 62	Catrine	Apprentice	Preston NE	162	10
						Walsall	151	16
						Shrewsbury T	49	4
						Walsall	16	1
Chris Thompson‡	5 11	12 02	24 1 60	Walsall	Apprentice	Bolton W	73	18
						Lincoln C (loan)	6	—
						Blackburn R	85	24
						Wigan Ath	74	14
						Blackpool	39	8
						Cardiff C	2	—
						Walsall	3	—

Trainees
Ayres, Michael; Brown, Richard C; Cooke, Paul J; Demerios, Christakis; Donovan, John D; Edwards, David J; Green, Richard S; Harrison, Seth; Hodges, Christopher J; Knight, Richard; McCall, Gary; Norris, Jonathan D; Read, Paul J; Richardson, Jason P; Tolson, Neil; Turner, Emlyn A; Ward, Anthony.

Associated Schoolboys
Betts, David C; Blackwood, Ian C; Eivors, Gerard; Fullelove, Christopher H; Gough, Paul A; Maddox, Robert J; Oldaker, Andrew J; Pickett, James A; Simcox, Robert S.

Associated Schoolboys who have accepted the club's offer of a Traineeship/Contract
Hodgson, Craig B; Instone, Wayne A; Norman, Karl M; Vaughan, Stephen A.

WATFORD 1990–91 *Back row (left to right):* Alex Inglethorpe, Willie Falconer, Paul Wilkinson, Barry Ashby, Andrew Kennedy, Jason Soloman, Paul Towler, Gary Williams. *Centre row:* Billy Hails (Physiotherapist), Keith Dublin, Jason Drysdale, David Holdsworth, David James, Mel Rees, Gerald Harrison, Alan Devonshire, Gary Penrice, Glenn Roeder (Reserve Team Coach).
Front row: Josh Price, Mark Gavin, Gary Porter, Nigel Gibbs, Colin Lee, David Hay, Joe McLaughlin, Chris Pullan, Rod Thomas, David Evans.

Division 2   WATFORD

Vicarage Road Stadium, Watford WD1 8ER. Telephone Watford (0923) 30933. Answerphone Service: Watford 35133 for information. 0898 700 272 – The 'Hornet Hotline' 24-hour club news service. Ticket Office: 220393. Club shop: 220847. Catering: 221457. Junior Hornets Club: 53836. Marketing: 225761.

Ground capacity: 26,996.

Record attendance: 34,099 v Manchester U, FA Cup 4th rd (replay), 3 February 1969.

Record receipts: £104,347 v Liverpool, FA Cup 6th rd (replay). 17 March 1986.

Pitch measurements: 115yd × 75yd.

Life President: Elton John.

Chairman: J. Petchey. *Vice-chairman:* G. A. Smith.

Directors: Bertie Mee OBE, G. S. Lawson Rogers, C. D. Lissack, DR, S. R. Timperley PHD, M. Winwood.

Chief Executive: Eddie Plumley FAAI.

Team Manager: Steve Perryman MBE. *Assistant Manager:* Peter Shreeves.

Coach: Tom Walley. *Physio:* Billy Hails.

Sales Marketing Manager: C. D. Low. *Public Relations Manager:* Ed Coan.

Year Formed: 1891*(see Foundation). *Turned Professional:* 1897. *Ltd Co.:* 1909.

Club Nickname: 'The Hornets'.

Previous Name: West Herts.

Previous Ground: 1899, Cassio Road; 1922, Vicarage Road.

Record League Victory: 8-0 v Sunderland, Division 1, 25 September 1982 – Sherwood; Rice, Rostron, Taylor, Terry, Bolton, Callaghan (2), Blissett (4), Jenkins (2), Jackett, Barnes.

Record Cup Victory: 10-1 v Lowestoft T, FA Cup, 1st rd, 27 November 1926 – Yates; Prior, Fletcher (1); F. Smith, 'Bert' Smith, Strain; Stephenson, Warner (3), Edmonds (2), Swan (2), Daniels (1). (1 og).

Record Defeat: 0-10 v Wolverhampton W, FA Cup 1st rd (replay), 13 January 1912.

Most League Points (2 for a win): 71, Division 4, 1977–78.

Most League Points (3 for a win): 80, Division 2, 1981–82.

Most League Goals: 92, Division 4, 1959–60.

Highest League Scorer in Season: Cliff Holton, 42, Division 4, 1959–60.

Most League Goals in Total Aggregate: Tommy Barnett, 144, 1928–39.

Most Capped Player: John Barnes, 31 (65), England and Kenny Jackett, 31, Wales.

Most League Appearances: Duncan Welbourne, 411, 1963–74.

Record Transfer Fee Received: £1,000,000 from AC Milan for Luther Blissett, July 1983 and £1,000,000 from Manchester C for Tony Coton, July 1990.

Record Transfer Fee Paid: £550,000 to AC Milan for Luther Blissett, August 1984.

Football League Record: 1920 Original Member of Division 3; 1921–58 Division 3 (S); 1958–60 Division 4; 1960–69 Division 3; 1969–72 Division 2; 1972–75 Division 3; 1975–78 Division 4; 1978–79 Division 3; 1979–82 Division 2; 1982–88 Division 1; 1988– Division 2.

Honours: Football League: Division 1 – Runners-up 1982–83; Division 2 – Runners-up 1981–82; Division 3 – Champions 1968–69; Runners-up 1978–79; Division 4 – Champions 1977–78; Promoted 1959–60 (4th). *FA Cup:* Runners-up 1984. *Football League Cup:* Semi-final 1978–79. **European Competitions:** *UEFA Cup:* 1983–84.

Colours: Yellow shirts (black/red piping), red shorts, yellow trim, red stockings (yellow/black tops). **Change colours:** White shirts (black/red piping), white shorts, white stockings.

WATFORD 1990–91 LEAGUE RECORD

Match No.	Date		Venue	Opponents	Result		H/T Score	Lg. Pos.	Goalscorers	Atten-dance
1	Aug	25	H	Millwall	L	1-2	0-1	—	Kennedy	11,541
2		28	A	Plymouth Arg	D	1-1	0-1	—	McLaughlin	7734
3	Sept	1	A	West Ham U	L	0-1	0-0	22		19,872
4		8	H	Brighton & HA	L	0-1	0-0	22		7847
5		15	A	Sheffield W	L	0-2	0-1	23		22,061
6		22	H	Notts Co	L	1-3	1-3	24	Falconer	7973
7		29	A	Ipswich T	D	1-1	0-0	24	Wilkinson	11,351
8	Oct	2	H	Hull C	L	0-1	0-1	—		6448
9		6	H	Middlesbrough	L	0-3	0-2	24		8057
10		13	A	Blackburn R	W	2-0	1-0	24	Devonshire, Wilkinson	7060
11		20	A	Charlton Ath	W	2-1	0-1	23	Kennedy, Wilkinson	5892
12		23	H	Portsmouth	L	0-1	0-1	—		8274
13		27	H	Oxford U	D	1-1	0-0	24	Wilkinson	7521
14	Nov	3	A	Bristol C	L	2-3	0-1	24	Porter, Holdsworth	11,576
15		10	A	Oldham Ath	L	1-4	1-3	24	Holdsworth	12,410
16		17	H	Bristol R	D	1-1	0-1	24	Kennedy	8285
17		24	A	Newcastle U	L	0-1	0-0	24		13,774
18	Dec	1	H	Barnsley	D	0-0	0-0	24		7839
19		5	A	WBA	D	1-1	1-0	—	Porter (pen)	7657
20		8	H	Plymouth Arg	W	2-0	0-0	24	Wilkinson 2	6361
21		15	A	Millwall	W	2-0	2-0	24	Penrice, Wilkinson	8910
22		23	A	Leicester C	D	0-0	0-0	—		16,920
23		26	H	Port Vale	W	2-1	1-0	21	Penrice, Thomas	8084
24		29	H	Swindon T	D	2-2	0-2	21	Byrne, Penrice	11,233
25	Jan	1	A	Wolverhampton W	D	0-0	0-0	23		18,159
26		12	H	West Ham U	L	0-1	0-0	23		17,172
27		19	A	Brighton & HA	L	0-3	0-2	23		8339
28	Feb	2	H	Sheffield W	D	2-2	2-0	23	Penrice, Wilkinson	10,338
29		16	A	Bristol R	L	1-3	1-1	23	Porter	5736
30		23	H	Oldham Ath	D	1-1	0-1	23	Wilkinson	8230
31	Mar	2	A	Barnsley	L	1-2	0-0	23	Penrice	6755
32		9	H	Newcastle U	L	1-2	0-1	24	Wilkinson	10,018
33		12	A	Hull C	D	1-1	0-0	—	Wilkinson	5815
34		16	H	Ipswich T	D	1-1	1-0	24	Palmer (og)	7732
35		19	A	Blackburn R	L	0-3	0-1	—		6913
36		23	A	Middlesbrough	W	2-1	0-0	24	Porter, Byrne	14,583
37		30	A	Port Vale	D	0-0	0-0	24		6661
38	Apr	1	H	Leicester C	W	1-0	0-0	24	Wilkinson	10,078
39		6	A	Swindon T	W	2-1	1-0	23	Butler, Callaghan	9699
40		13	H	Wolverhampton W	W	3-1	1-0	23	Wilkinson 3	12,014
41		16	A	Notts Co	L	0-1	0-0	—		6168
42		20	H	Charlton Ath	W	2-1	2-0	23	Falconer 2	10,178
43		23	H	WBA	D	1-1	0-0	—	Roeder	15,054
44		27	A	Portsmouth	W	1-0	0-0	21	Falconer	10,074
45	May	4	A	Oxford U	W	1-0	0-0	19	Wilkinson	8437
46		11	H	Bristol C	L	2-3	0-0	20	Wilkinson 2	13,029

Final League Position: 20

GOALSCORERS

League (45): Wilkinson 18, Penrice 5, Falconer 4, Porter 4 (1 pen), Kennedy 3, Byrne 2, Holdsworth 2, Butler 1, Callaghan 1, Devonshire 1, McLaughlin 1, Roeder 1, Thomas 1, own goal 1.
Rumbelows Cup (0).
FA Cup (1): Falconer 1.

James	Gibbs	Dublin	Falconer	McLaughlin	Holdsworth	Thomas	Wilkinson	Kennedy	Devonshire	Williams	Porter	Bazeley	Roeder	Drysdale	Gavin	Harrison	Inglethorpe	Penrice	Ashby	Pullan	Byrne	Denton	Nicholas	Callaghan	Butler	Soloman	Match No.
1	2*	3	4	5	6	7†	8	9	10	11	12	14															1
1		3	10	5	6	7	8	9		2*	11		12	4													2
1		3	10	5	6	7	8	9		2	4		11*	12													3
1		3*	10	5	6	7	8	14	9†	2	4		12	11													4
1	2		10	5	6	9	8	12		11*			4	3		7											5
1	2†		10	5	6	7	8	9	14	11	12		3	4*													6
1	2		10	5	6		8		7	11	4		3					9*	12								7
1	2*		10	5	6	14	8		7	11	4		3†					12	9								8
1		9	5†		6	7	8		10	3	4		12	14				11*	2								9
1		6	4	5		7	8	9	10	3*	12							11	2								10
1		6	4	5		7	8*	9	10	3	12							11	2								11
1		6	4	5†		7	8	9	10*	3	12		14					11	2								12
1	2	3	4		6		8	7	10		12		5					11	9*								13
1	2	6	9	5		7	8		10	3*	4		12					11†	14								14
1	2	6		5		7	8	9	10†	4	14		3					11*	12								15
1	2	6		5			8	9	10	4	12		3					11			7*						16
1	2		4	5	6		8	9	3	10	11										7						17
1	2		4	5	6*		8	9	10	3†	12		14								7						18
1	2		4	5			8	9	6*	3	10		11	12							7						19
1	2		4	14	5		8	9*	6	10	11		3†					12			7						20
1	2		4	5			8	12	6	10	11		3					9*			7						21
1	2		4	5			8	12	6*	10	11		3					9†14			7						22
1	2*		4	7†		14	8		6	12	10		11	3				9	5								23
1	2		4	12	5		14	8	6	11	10		3*					9			7†						24
1	2		4	12	5		14	8	6*	3	10		11					9			7†						25
1	2	11		5		7*	8		6	3	10		12					9	4								26
1	2	11		5		7*	8		6	3†10			14	12				9	4								27
1	2		4	5†		7	8		6	3	10		11	12				9†14									28
1		6		5			8	14		3*10			11†	2	12			9	4		7						29
1	2		5			14	8		6*	10			11	3				9	4		7†12						30
1	2	4	5			14	8		6*12	10			11	3				9			7†						31
1	2	4	9			12	8		6*	10			5	3					7				11				32
1	2	6	4				8		10				5*	3				12			7		11	9			33
1	2	6	4				8		10				5	3							7		11	9			34
1	2	6	4				8	12	10				5	3							7*		11	9			35
1	2	6	4				8		10				5	3*		7		14	12		11			9†			36
1	2	6	4*				8		10				5	3		7					11		12	9†14			37
1	2	6				12	8		10				5	3				4			11		7	9*			38
1	2	6	7				8*		10				5	3				4			11		12	9†14			39
1	2	6	7			12	8		10				5	3				4			11		10*	9			40
1	2	6	7				8		10				5					4			11			9		3	41
1	2	6	7				8		10				5	3†				4			11*12			9		14	42
1	2	6	7				8		10				5					4			11			9		3	43
1	2	6	7				8		10				5					4			11		12	9*		3	44
1	2	6	7				8*		10				5					4			11		12	9		3	45
1	2	6	7				8		10				5*					4			11		12	9		3	46
46	34	43	32	24	15	15	46	13	23	21	40	1	30	25	8	4	1	12	20	1	16	—	15	6	10	5	
	+						+		+	+	+		+	+	+	+	+		+		+	+	+		+	+	
	3s						9s		5s	1s	3s		5s	6s	3s	5s	5s	2s	2s		3s	1s	1s	2s	6s	3s	

Rumbelows Cup Second Round Norwich C (a) 0-2
                                                  (h) 0-3
FA Cup Third Round Shrewsbury T (a) 1-4

WATFORD

Player and Position	Ht	Wt	Birth Date	Birth Place	Source	Clubs	League App	Gls
Goalkeepers								
David James	6 4	14 07	1 8 70	Welwyn	Trainee	Watford	46	—
Tony Meola‡	6 0	14 07	21 2 69	Belleville	USSF	Brighton & HA	1	—
						Watford	—	—
Simon Sheppard			7 8 73	Clevedon	Trainee	Watford		
Keith Waugh	6 1	13 00	27 10 56	Sunderland	Apprentice	Sunderland	—	—
						Peterborough U	195	—
						Sheffield U	99	—
						Cambridge U (loan)	4	—
						Bristol C (loan)	3	—
						Bristol C	167	—
						Coventry C	1	—
						Watford	—	—
Defenders								
Julian Alsford			24 12 72	Poole		Watford	—	—
Barry Ashby	6 2	12 03	21 11 70	London	Trainee	Watford	41	1
Jason Drysdale	5 10	10 07	17 11 70	Bristol	Trainee	Watford	50	—
Keith Dublin	5 11	11 09	29 1 66	Wycombe	Apprentice	Chelsea	51	—
						Brighton & HA	132	5
						Watford	43	—
David Evans‡	5 7	10 02	28 8 72	Bangor	Trainee	Watford	—	—
Willie Falconer	6 1	12 10	5 4 66	Aberdeen	Lewis Utd	Aberdeen	77	13
						Watford	98	12
Nigel Gibbs	5 7	10 02	20 11 65	St Albans	Apprentice	Watford	221	2
David Holdsworth	5 11	11 04	8 11 68	London	Trainee	Watford	92	6
Joe McLaughlin	6 1	12 00	2 6 60	Greenock	School	Morton	134	3
						Chelsea	220	5
						Charlton Ath	31	—
						Watford	24	1
Glenn Roeder	6 0	12 13	13 12 55	Woodford	Apprentice	Orient	115	4
						QPR	157	17
						Notts Co (loan)	4	—
						Newcastle U	193	8
						Watford	78	2
Jason Soloman	6 1	11 09	6 10 70	Welwyn	Trainee	Watford	8	—
Paul Towler‡	5 10	11 10	1 2 72	Bristol	Trainee	Watford	—	—
Gary Williams	5 9	11 01	17 6 60	Wolverhampton	Apprentice	Aston Villa	240	—
						Walsall (loan)	9	—
						Leeds U	39	3
						Watford	42	—
Midfield								
Edward Denton	5 10	11 03	18 5 70	Oxford	Trainee	Oxford U	2	—
						Watford	2	—
Alan Devonshire	5 11	11 00	13 4 56	London	Southall & Ealing	West Ham U	358	29
						Watford	24	1
Gerry Harrison*	5 10	12 02	15 4 72	Lambeth	Trainee	Watford	9	—
Kenny Jackett‡	5 11	11 13	5 1 62	Watford	Apprentice	Watford	335	26
Jim Meara			7 10 72	London	Trainee	Watford		
Peter Nicholas	5 8	11 08	10 11 59	Newport	Apprentice	Crystal Palace	127	7
						Arsenal	60	1
						Crystal Palace	47	7
						Luton T	102	1
						Aberdeen	39	3
						Chelsea	80	2
						Watford	15	—
Gary Porter	5 5	9 10	6 3 66	Sunderland	Apprentice	Watford	204	26
Jonathan Price‡	5 10	11 07	18 9 71	Hemel Hempstead	Trainee	Watford	—	—

WATFORD

Foundation: Tracing this club's foundation proves difficult. Nowadays it is suggested that Watford was formed as Watford Rovers in 1891. Another version is that Watford Rovers were not forerunners of the present club whose history began in 1898 with the amalgamation of West Herts and Watford St. Mary's.

First Football League game: 28 August, 1920, Division 3, v QPR (a) W 2–1 – Williams; Horseman, F. Gregory; Bacon, Toone, Wilkinson; Bassett, Ronald (1), Hoddinott, White (1), Waterall.

Did you know: In the 2nd round of the League Cup in 1980–81 Watford were beaten 4-0 at Southampton but won the 2nd leg 7-1 at Watford.

Managers (and Secretary-managers)
John Goodall 1903–10, Harry Kent 1910–26, Fred Pagnam 1926–29, Neil McBain 1929–37, Bill Findlay 1938–47, Jack Bray 1947–48, Eddie Hapgood 1948–50, Ron Gray 1950–51, Haydn Green 1951–52, Len Goulden 1952–55 (GM to 1956), Johnny Paton 1955–56, Neil McBain 1956–59, Ron Burgess 1959–63, Bill McGarry 1963–64, Ken Furphy 1964–71, George Kirby 1971–73, Mike Keen 1973–77, Graham Taylor 1977–87, Dave Bassett 1987–88, Steve Harrison 1988–90, Colin Lee 1990, Steve Perryman November 1990– .

Player and Position	Ht	Wt	Birth Date	Birth Place	Source	Clubs	League App	Gls
Forwards								
Darren Bazeley			5 10 72	Northampton	Trainee	Watford	8	—
Steve Butler	6 2	11 01	27 1 62	Birmingham	Army	Brentford	21	3
						Maidstone U	76	41
						Watford	10	1
David Byrne	5 8	11 00	5 3 61	London	Kingstonian	Gillingham	23	3
						Millwall	63	6
						Cambridge U (loan)	4	—
						Blackburn R (loan)	4	—
						Plymouth Arg	45	2
						Bristol R (loan)	2	—
						Watford	17	2
Joe Gallen			2 9 72	Hammersmith	Trainee	Watford	—	—
Mark Gavin	5 8	10 07	10 12 63	Bailleston	Apprentice	Leeds U	30	3
						Hartlepool U (loan)	7	—
						Carlisle U	13	1
						Bolton W	49	3
						Rochdale	23	6
						Hearts	9	—
						Bristol C	69	6
						Watford	13	—
Alex Inglethorpe	5 10	11 07	14 11 71	Epsom	School	Watford	1	—
Andy Kennedy	6 1	12 00	8 10 64	Stirling	Sauchie Ath	Rangers	15	3
						Birmingham C	76	18
						Sheffield U (loan)	9	1
						Blackburn R	59	23
						Watford	18	3
Rod Thomas	5 6	10 03	10 10 70	London	Trainee	Watford	78	9
Paul Wilkinson	6 0	11 00	30 10 64	Louth	Apprentice	Grimsby T	71	27
						Everton	31	7
						Nottingham F	34	5
						Watford	134	52

Trainees
Dalli, Marc J; Johnson, Richard M; Lavin, Gerard; Liburd, Marc E; Nwaokolo, Daniel N.P; Procter, Neil S.C; Pugh, Stephen; Snowdon, Trevor; Wild, Matthew J.

Associated Schoolboys
Boachie, Nana; Buoy, Nicholas; Dyer, Bruce A; Georgiou, Jimmy; Hutchins, Neil; McIntosh, Craig; Manners, Andrew C; Merritt, Justin; North, Tyronne L; Page, Robert J; Parkin, Steven C; Riddick, Alexander G; Ross, Jamie M; Seal, Richard; Simpson, Colin R; Simpson, Marc; Slinn, Kevin P; Snell, Ross P; Thirlby, Anthony D; Vier, Matthew P; White, John S; Young, Matthew.

WEST BROMWICH ALBION 1990-91   *Back row (left to right):* Gary Bannister, Colin Anderson, Stacey North, Graham Harbey, Steve Parkin.
Centre row: Sam Allardyce (Coach), Daryl Burgess, Colin West, Paul Raven, Stuart Naylor, Darren Bradley, Craig Shakespeare, Wayne Dobbins, Stuart Pearson (Coach).
Front row: Tony Ford, Gary Robson, Simeon Hodson, Brian Talbot (Manager), Bernard McNally, Don Goodman, Gary Hackett.

Division 3   **WEST BROMWICH ALBION**

The Hawthorns, West Bromwich B71 4LF. Telephone 021-525 8888 (all Depts). Fax: 021-553 6634.

Ground capacity: 31,700 (10,865 seats).

Record attendance: 64,815 v Arsenal, FA Cup 6th rd, 6 March 1937.

Record receipts: £161,632.50 v Aston Villa, FA Cup 5th rd, 17 February 1990.

Pitch measurements: 115yd × 75yd.

President: Sir F. A. Millichip. *Vice-president:*

Chairman: J. G. Silk. *Vice-chairman:* T. J. Summers.

Directors: J. W. Brandrick, J. S. Lucas, M. C. McGinnity, T. J. Summers, A. B. Hale.

Manager: Bobby Gould. *Assistant Manager:* Stuart Pearson.

Coach: Stuart Pearson. *Physio:* John MacGowan MCSP, SRP. *Secretary:* Dr. J. J. Evans.

Club Statistician: Tony Matthews. *Commercial Manager:* Alan Stevenson.

Year Formed: 1879. *Turned Professional:* 1885. *Ltd Co.:* 1892.

Previous Name: 1879–81, West Bromwich Strollers.

Club Nicknames: 'Throstles', 'Baggies', 'Albion'.

Previous Grounds: 1879, Coopers Hill; 1879, Dartmouth Park; 1881, Bunns Field, Walsall Street; 1882, Four Acres (Dartmouth Cricket Club); 1885, Stoney Lane; 1900, The Hawthorns.

Record League Victory: 12-0 v Darwen, Division 1, 4 April 1892 – Reader; Horton, McCulloch; Reynolds (2), Perry, Groves; Bassett (3), McLeod, Nicholls (1), Pearson (4), Geddes (1). (1 og).

Record Cup Victory: 10-1 v Chatham (away), FA Cup, 3rd rd, 2 March 1889 – Roberts; Horton, Green; Timmins (1), Charles Perry, Horton; Bassett (2), Perry (1), Bayliss (2), Pearson, Wilson (3). (1 og).

Record Defeat: 3-10 v Stoke C, Division 1, 4 February 1937.

Most League Points (2 for a win): 60, Division 1, 1919–20.

Most League Points (3 for a win): 72, Division 2, 1988–89.

Most League Goals: 105, Division 2, 1929–30.

Highest League Scorer in Season: William 'Ginger' Richardson, 39, Division 1, 1935–36.

Most League Goals in Total Aggregate: Tony Brown, 218, 1963–79.

Most Capped Player: Stuart Williams, 33 (43), Wales.

Most League Appearances: Tony Brown, 574, 1963–80.

Record Transfer Fee Received: £1,500,000 from Manchester U for Bryan Robson, October 1981.

Record Transfer Fee Paid: £748,000 to Manchester C for Peter Barnes, July 1979.

Football League Record: 1888 Founder Member of Football League; 1901–02 Division 2; 1902–04 Division 1; 1904–11 Division 2; 1911–27 Division 1; 1927–31 Division 2; 1931–38 Division 1; 1938–49 Division 2; 1949–73 Division 1; 1973–76 Division 2; 1976–86 Division 1; 1986–91 Division 2; 1991– Division 3.

Honours: Football League: Division 1 – Champions 1919–20; Runners-up 1924–25, 1953–54; Division 2 – Champions 1901–02, 1910–11; Runners-up 1930–31, 1948–49; Promoted to Division 1 1975–76 (3rd). *FA Cup:* Winners 1888, 1892, 1931, 1954, 1968; Runners-up 1886, 1887, 1895, 1912, 1935. *Football League Cup:* Winners 1965–66; Runners-up 1966–67, 1969–70. **European Competitions:** *European Cup-Winners' Cup:* 1968–69; *European Fairs Cup:* 1966–67; *UEFA Cup:* 1978–79, 1979–80, 1981–82.

Colours: Navy blue and white striped shirts, white shorts, blue and white stockings. **Change colours:** Red and yellow striped shirts, red shorts.

WEST BROMWICH ALBION 1990–91 LEAGUE RECORD

Match No	Date.	Venue	Opponents	Result	H/T Score	Lg. Pos.	Goalscorers	Atten-dance
1	Aug 25	A	Portsmouth	D 1-1	1-0	—	Ford	12,008
2	Sept 1	H	Ipswich T	L 1-2	1-0	21	Bannister	10,318
3	8	A	Oxford U	W 3-1	2-0	13	Bannister, West 2	5225
4	15	H	Bristol C	W 2-1	2-0	8	Bannister, Harbey	12,081
5	22	A	Hull C	D 1-1	1-1	14	McNally	5953
6	29	H	Oldham Ath	D 0-0	0-0	15		13,782
7	Oct 2	A	Plymouth Arg	L 0-2	0-1	—		5617
8	6	A	Millwall	L 1-4	0-2	18	West	10,718
9	13	H	Brighton & HA	D 1-1	0-1	18	Gatting (og)	9833
10	20	H	Barnsley	D 1-1	0-0	19	West (pen)	9577
11	22	A	Port Vale	W 2-1	2-1	—	Bannister, West (pen)	8824
12	27	A	Newcastle U	D 1-1	1-0	16	Anderson	14,774
13	Nov 3	H	Bristol R	W 3-1	2-1	14	West 2, Anderson	10,997
14	6	H	Middlesbrough	L 0-1	0-0	—		10,521
15	10	A	Notts Co	L 3-4	1-3	17	Bannister 2, Bradley	8162
16	17	H	Blackburn R	W 2-0	1-0	13	Bannister, West	6985
17	24	H	Sheffield W	L 1-2	1-0	15	Robson	16,546
18	Dec 1	A	West Ham U	L 1-3	0-2	17	Ford	24,753
19	5	H	Watford	D 1-1	0-1	—	Roberts (pen)	7657
20	15	H	Portsmouth	D 0-0	0-0	14		7856
21	22	A	Swindon T	L 1-2	1-0	18	Roberts (pen)	7798
22	26	H	Charlton Ath	W 1-0	1-0	16	Goodman	9305
23	29	A	Wolverhampton W	D 1-1	0-0	15	Bannister	28,497
24	Jan 1	H	Leicester C	L 1-2	1-0	16	Ford	12,210
25	12	A	Ipswich T	L 0-1	0-0	18		11,036
26	19	H	Oxford U	W 2-0	1-0	16	Bannister, Shakespeare	8017
27	Feb 2	A	Bristol C	L 0-2	0-1	18		11,492
28	16	A	Blackburn R	W 3-0	2-0	15	Robson, Goodman 2	7695
29	19	A	Middlesbrough	L 2-3	0-0	—	Bannister 2	15,334
30	23	H	Notts Co	D 2-2	1-1	16	Bannister 2	11,068
31	Mar 2	H	West Ham U	D 0-0	0-0	17		16,089
32	9	A	Sheffield W	L 0-1	0-0	19		26,934
33	13	H	Plymouth Arg	L 1-2	1-1	—	Palmer	8673
34	16	A	Oldham Ath	L 1-2	1-1	21	Ford	12,584
35	20	A	Brighton & HA	L 0-2	0-1	—		6676
36	23	H	Millwall	L 0-1	0-0	22		9116
37	30	A	Charlton Ath	L 0-2	0-1	22		5686
38	Apr 1	H	Swindon T	W 2-1	1-1	22	Parkin, Roberts (pen)	10,415
39	6	A	Wolverhampton W	D 2-2	1-1	22	Goodman, Ford	22,982
40	10	H	Hull C	D 1-1	1-1	—	Roberts	10,356
41	13	H	Leicester C	W 2-1	1-1	21	White, Goodman	13,991
42	20	A	Barnsley	D 1-1	0-0	22	Strodder	9593
43	23	A	Watford	D 1-1	0-0	—	Goodman	15,054
44	27	H	Port Vale	D 1-1	0-1	23	Goodman	13,650
45	May 4	H	Newcastle U	D 1-1	1-0	22	Goodman	16,706
46	11	A	Bristol R	D 1-1	0-0	23	Ampadu	7595

Final League Position: 23

GOALSCORERS

League (52): Bannister 13, Goodman 8, West 8 (2 pens), Ford 5, Roberts 4 (3 pens), Anderson 2, Robson 2, Ampadu 1, Bradley 1, Harbey 1, McNally 1, Palmer 1, Parkin 1, Shakespeare 1, Strodder 1, White 1, own goal 1.
Rumbelows Cup (2): Bannister 1, Hackett 1.
FA Cup (2): Bradley 1, West 1.

Naylor	Hodson	Harbey	Robson	Burgess	Strodder	Ford	Goodman	Bannister	Bradley	Shakespeare	Hackett	West	McInally	Hawker	Raven	Ehiogu	Anderson	Foster	Dobbins	Palmer	Roberts	Parkin	Rees	Rogers	Williams	White	Ampadu	Match No.
1	2	3	4*	5	6	7	8	9	10	11	12																	1
1	2	3	4	5	6	7		9	10	11*	12	8																2
1	2	3	4	5*	6	7		9	10	11		8	12															3
1	2	3	4*		6	7	12	9	5	11		8	10															4
1	2		4			7	12†	9	5	11		8*10		3	6	14												5
1	2	3	4		6	7		9	5	11		8	10															6
1	2	3	4		6	7		9	5	11*12		8	10															7
1		3	4		6	7*		9	5	11†12		8	10				2	14										8
1		3	4	2	6	7†		9*	5			8	10				11	12	14									9
1		3	4	2	6	7		9	5			8	10				11											10
1		3	4	2	6	7		9	5			8	10				11											11
1		3	4	2	6	7		9	5			8	10				11*	12										12
1		3	4	2	6	7		9	5*14			8	10				11†	12										13
1	12		4*	2	6	7		9	5	11		8	10					3										14
1	12		4	2	6	7		9	5			8	10				11†	3*14										15
1		3		2	6	7	12	9*	5			8	10				11			4								16
1		3	2	14	6	7	12	9*	5			8	10†				11			4								17
1		3	2		6	7	12	9	5			8					11*			4	10							18
1		3	2	6		7	8*	9	5	14		12					11†			4	10							19
1	14	3	2†			7	8*12	5				9	10		6		11*			4								20
1	2	3	9			7	8*12	5					10		6		11†			4	14							21
1		3	11†		6	7	8*	9	5	2		12	10							4	14							22
1		3	11		6	7		9	5	2		8	10							4								23
1		3	11		6	7		9†	5	2		8*10								12	4	14						24
	14				6	7		9		2		12	10	5†	3		11*			4	8	1						25
	2				6	7		10		11	9		5		3					4	8	1						26
	2			5	7	8	9		11		6	3							4	10	1							27
	2	10*	5	14	7	8†	9	6	11		12								4	3	1							28
	2	10	5		7	8*	9	6	11		12								4	3	1							29
	2	10	5	14	7	9	6	3				11†							4	8*	1							30
	2	10	5		7	9	6	3				11							4	8	1							31
	2		5	14	7	9	3*				10†12					11	6	4	8	1								32
	2	3	5		7	9	14				12	11				6†10*	4	8	1									33
	2	14	5		7	9	6	3				12	11	10*	4†	8	1											34
	2†		5	10	7	9	6	3	12			8*	11		4		1	14										35
	2		5	7	9	6	10	8		4†14	12	11*		1	3													36
		5	7	10	6	3		4		8	1	2	9	11*12														37
		5*	7	10	8	2	11	12	3	4	6	1	9															38
	2		5	7	10	8*14	11		3	4	6	1	9†12															39
	2		5	7	10*	8	11	12	3	4	6	1	9															40
	2		5†	7	12	8*	3	11	4	6	1	9	10	14														41
	2		14	7	8*12	3†11	4	6	1	9	10	5																42
1	2		5	7	8	11	3	4	6	9	10*12																	43
1	2	10*	5	7	8	12	3	14	4†	6	9	11																44
1	2		4	5	7	8†12	3	10	6	9	14	11*																45
1			5	7	12	3	11	10*	2	8	6	4†	9	14														46

Naylor	Hodson	Harbey	Robson	Burgess	Strodder	Ford	Goodman	Bannister	Bradley	Shakespeare	Hackett	West	McInally	Hawker	Raven	Ehiogu	Anderson	Foster	Dobbins	Palmer	Roberts	Parkin	Rees	Rogers	Williams	White	Ampadu
28	26	21	30	24	30	46	16	38	38	32	—	24	20	1	11	—	22	2	5	5	27	22	18	3	10	4	3
	+	+	+		+	+	+	+	+	+		+	+		+		+	+	+	+	+		+		+	+	+
	4s	1s	1s		6s	6s	1s	4s	5s	4s		5s	2s		2s		1s	3s	3s	2s	3s		1s		2s	4s	

Rumbelows Cup	First Round	Bristol C (h)	2-2
		(a)	0-1
FA Cup	Third Round	Woking (h)	2-4

WEST BROMWICH ALBION

Player and Position	Ht	Wt	Birth Date	Place	Source	Clubs	League App	Gls
Goalkeepers								
Stuart Naylor	6 4	12 10	6 12 62	Wetherby	Yorkshire A	Lincoln C	49	—
						Peterborough U (loan)	8	—
						Crewe Alex (loan)	55	—
						WBA	200	—
Melvyn Rees	6 2	12 12	25 1 67	Cardiff	Trainee	Cardiff C	31	—
						Watford	3	—
						Crewe Alex (loan)	6	—
						Southampton (loan)	—	—
						Leyton Orient (loan)	9	—
						WBA	18	—
Defenders								
Sam Allardyce‡	6 1	14 00	19 10 54	Dudley	Apprentice	Bolton W	184	21
						Sunderland	25	2
						Millwall	63	2
						Coventry C	28	1
						Huddersfield T	37	—
						Bolton W	14	—
						Preston NE	90	2
						WBA	1	—
Daryl Burgess	5 11	12 03	20 4 71	Birmingham	Trainee	WBA	59	—
Graham Harbey	5 8	10 08	29 8 64	Chesterfield	Apprentice	Derby Co	40	1
						Ipswich T	59	1
						WBA	51	1
Simeon Hodson	5 9	10 02	5 3 66	Lincoln	Apprentice	Notts Co	27	—
						Charlton Ath	5	—
						Lincoln C	56	—
						Newport Co	34	1
						WBA	56	—
Steve Parkin	5 6	10 07	7 11 65	Mansfield	Apprentice	Stoke C	113	5
						WBA	39	2
Paul Raven	6 0	12 03	28 7 70	Salisbury	Schools	Doncaster R	52	4
						WBA	23	—
Graham Roberts	5 11	13 10	3 7 59	Southampton	School	Southampton	—	—
						Bournemouth	—	—
					Sholing S	Portsmouth	—	—
					Dorchester T			
					Weymouth	Tottenham H	209	23
						Rangers	55	3
						Chelsea	70	18
						WBA	27	4
Darren Rogers	5 10	11 04	9 4 71	Birmingham	Trainee	WBA	4	—
Gary Strodder	6 1	11 04	1 4 65	Leeds	Apprentice	Lincoln C	132	6
						West Ham U	65	2
						WBA	34	1
Paul Williams	6 2	12 09	8 9 63	Sheffield	Nuneaton	Preston NE	1	—
						Newport Co	26	3
						Sheffield U	8	—
						Hartlepool U	8	—
						Stockport	24	14
						WBA	10	—
Midfield								
Colin Anderson*	5 9	10 07	26 4 62	Newcastle	Apprentice	Burnley	6	—
						Torquay U	109	11
						QPR (loan)	—	—
						WBA	140	10
Darren Bradley	5 10	11 04	24 11 65	Birmingham	Apprentice	Aston Villa	20	—
						WBA	135	4
Scott Colcombe*	5 6	10 00	15 12 71	West Bromwich	Trainee	WBA	—	—
Wayne Dobbins	5 7	10 08	30 8 68	Bromsgrove	Apprentice	WBA	45	—
Ugo Ehiogu§	6 1	12 00	3 11 72	London	Trainee	WBA	2	—
Phil Hawker‡	6 1	11 07	7 12 62	Solihull	Apprentice	Birmingham C	35	1
						Walsall	177	10
						WBA	1	—
Bernard McNally	5 7	10 11	17 2 63	Shrewsbury	Apprentice	Shrewsbury T	282	23
						WBA	66	6
David Pritchard	5 9	11 05	27 5 72	Wolverhampton	Trainee	WBA	—	—
Gary Robson	5 5	10 10	6 7 65	Co Durham	Apprentice	WBA	164	17
Craig Shakespeare	5 10	11 05	26 10 63	Birmingham	Apprentice	Walsall	284	45
						Sheffield W	17	—
						WBA	54	2

WEST BROMWICH ALBION

Foundation: There is a well known story that when employees of Salter's Spring Works in West Bromwich decided to form a football club in 1879, they had to send someone to the nearby Association Football stronghold of Wednesbury to purchase a football. A weekly subscription of 2d (less than 1p) was imposed and the name of the new club was West Bromwich Strollers.

First Football League game: 8 September, 1888, Football League, v Stoke (a) W 2-0 – Roberts; J. Horton, Green; E. Horton, Perry, Bayliss; Bassett, Woodhall (1), Hendry, Pearson, Wilson (1).

Did you know: In 1973–74 Albion's top scorer Tony Brown netted a total of seven goals in consecutive games at Nottingham. He got a hat-trick against Notts County in a 4-0 FA Cup victory and the following week scored four in a 4-1 League win over Nottingham Forest.

Managers (and Secretary-managers)
Louis Ford 1890–92*, Henry Jackson 1892–94*, Edward Stephenson 1894–95*, Clement Keys 1895–96*, Frank Heaven 1896–1902*, Fred Everiss 1902–48, Jack Smith 1948–52, Jesse Carver 1952, Vic Buckingham 1953–59, Gordon Clark 1959–61, Archie Macaulay 1961–63, Jimmy Hagan 1963–67, Alan Ashman 1967–71, Don Howe 1971–75, Johnny Giles 1975–77, Ronnie Allen 1977, Ron Atkinson 1978–81, Ronnie Allen 1981–82, Ron Wylie 1982–84, Johnny Giles 1984–85, Ron Saunders 1986–87, Ron Atkinson 1987–88, Brian Talbot 1988–91, Bobby Gould February 1991– .

Player and Position	Ht	Wt	Birth Date	Place	Source	Clubs	League App	Gls
Forwards								
Gary Bannister	5 8	11 01	22 7 60	Warrington	Apprentice	Coventry C	22	3
						Sheffield W	118	55
						QPR	136	56
						Coventry C	43	11
						WBA	57	15
Neil Cartwright	5 9	10 13	20 2 71	Stourbridge	Trainee	WBA	8	—
Tony Ford	5 9	12 08	14 5 59	Grimsby	Apprentice	Grimsby T	354	54
						Sunderland (loan)	9	1
						Stoke C	112	13
						WBA	99	14
Adrian Foster	5 9	11 00	20 7 71	Kidderminster	Trainee	WBA	19	1
Donald Goodman	5 10	11 00	9 5 66	Leeds		Bradford C	70	14
						WBA	147	53
Gary Hackett	5 8	10 13	11 10 62	Stourbridge	Bromsgrove R	Shrewsbury T	150	17
						Aberdeen	15	—
						Stoke C	73	7
						WBA	19	2
Les Palmer	5 10	10 10	5 9 71	Birmingham	Trainee	WBA	7	1
Gary Piggott	5 11	12 02	1 4 69	Warley	Dudley T	WBA	—	—
Colin West	6 2	13 11	13 11 62	Wallsend	Apprentice	Sunderland	102	21
						Watford	45	20
						Rangers	10	2
						Sheffield W	45	8
						WBA	66	20
Winston White	5 10	10 12	26 10 58	Leicester	Apprentice	Leicester C	12	1
						Hereford U	175	21
						Chesterfield	1	—
						Port Vale	1	—
						Stockport Co	4	—
						Bury	125	11
						Rochdale (loan)	4	—
						Colchester U	65	8
						Burnley	104	14
						WBA	6	1

Trainees
Bailey, Darren E; Bowen, Stewart A; Coldicott, Stacy; Ehiogu, Ugochuku; Grace, Alexander; Hall, Scott M; Hammond, Kirk; Hollier, Nigel T; Howse, Justin J; Hunter, Roy I; Nelson, Matthew J; Nightingale, Jonathon; Norman, Justin; Price, Lyndon P; Sinfield, Marc R; Treacy, John P; Tymon, Carl L.

Associated Schoolboys
Atkinson, Peter; Berry, Craig S; Cutler, Neil A; Davies, Timothy J; Flint, Richard; Green, Jason K; Hardiker, Paul J; Harnett, David R; Harris, Lee P; Love, Brett A; Mackenzie, Neil D; Marshall, Daniel P; Owen, Darren L; Patson, Ross A; Robinson, Ian; Schofield, Paul B; Skitt, Craig; Stevenson, Ian M; Taylor, Stuart G.

Associated Schoolboys who have accepted the club's offer of a Traineeship/Contract
Darton, Scott R; Harris, Richard J; Hicks, Daniel

WEST HAM UNITED 1990-91. *Back row (left to right):* Tony Gale, Colin Foster, Allen McKnight, Ludek Miklosko, Stephen Banks, Alvin Martin, Jimmy Quinn. *Centre row:* Simon Clarke, Tim Breacker, Trevor Morley, Martin Allen, Ray Stewart, George Parris, Matthew Rush, Stewart Robson, Eamonn Dolan. *Front row:* Kevin Keen, Stuart Slater, Paul Kelly, Frank McAvennie, Julian Dicks, Ian Bishop, Simon Livett, Steve Potts.

Division 1   WEST HAM UNITED

Boleyn Ground, Green Street, Upton Park, London E13. Telephone 081 472-2740. General: 081 472-5756. Commercial: 081 475-0555. Hammer Line: 081 472-3322. Dial-a-seat: 081 472-2422. Football in the Community: 0898 121165 Clubcall.

Ground capacity: 28,863.

Record attendance: 42,322 v Tottenham H, Division 1, 17 October 1970.

Record receipts: £146,074 v Tottenham H, League Cup 5th rd, 27 January 1987.

Pitch measurements: 112yd × 72yd.

Chairman: M. W. Cearns ACIB. *Vice-chairman:* W. F. Cearns.

Directors: L. C. Cearns, W. F. Cearns, T. W. Brown, P. J. Storrie.

Manager: Billy Bonds MBE.

Secretary: T. M. Finn. *Commercial Manager:* Brian Blower.

Year Formed: 1895. *Turned Professional:* 1900. *Ltd Co.:* 1900.

Previous Name: Thames Ironworks FC, 1895–1900.

Club Nickname: 'The Hammers'.

Previous Ground: Memorial Recreation Ground, Canning Town: 1904 Boleyn Ground.

Record League Victory: 8-0 v Rotherham U, Division 2, 8 March 1958 – Gregory; Bond, Wright; Malcolm, Brown, Lansdowne; Grice, Smith (2), Keeble (2), Dick (4), Musgrove. 8-0 v Sunderland, Division 1, 19 October 1968 – Ferguson; Bonds, Charles; Peters, Stephenson, Moore (1); Redknapp, Boyce, Brooking (1), Hurst (6), Sissons.

Record Cup Victory: 10-0 v Bury, League Cup, 2nd rd (2nd leg), 25 October 1983 – Parkes; Stewart (1), Walford, Bonds (Orr), Martin (1), Devonshire (2), Allen, Cottee (4), Swindlehurst, Brooking (2), Pike.

Record Defeat: 2-8 v Blackburn R, Division 1, 26 December 1963.

Most League Points (2 for a win): 66, Division 2, 1980–81.

Most League Points (3 for a win): 87, Division 2, 1990–91.

Most League Goals: 101, Division 2, 1957–58.

Highest League Scorer in Season: Vic Watson, 41, Division 1, 1929–30.

Most League Goals in Total Aggregate: Vic Watson, 306, 1920–35.

Most Capped Player: Bobby Moore, 108, England.

Most League Appearances: Billy Bonds, 663, 1967–88.

Record Transfer Fee Received: £2,000,000 from Everton for Tony Cottee, July 1988.

Record Transfer Fee Paid: £1,250,000 to Celtic for Frank McAvennie, March 1989.

Football League Record: 1919 Elected to Division 2; 1923–32 Division 1; 1932–58 Division 2; 1958–78 Division 1; 1978–81 Division 2; 1981–89 Division 1; 1989–91 Division 2; 1991– Division 1.

Honours: Football League: Division 1 best season: 3rd, 1985–86; Division 2 – Champions 1957–58, 1980–81; Runners-up 1922–23, 1990–91. *FA Cup:* Winners 1964, 1975, 1980; Runners-up 1922–23. *Football League Cup:* Runners-up 1966, 1981. **European Competitions:** *European Cup-Winners' Cup:* 1964–65 (winners), 1965–66, 1975–76 (runners-up), 1980–81.

Colours: Claret and blue shirts, white shorts, white stockings. **Change colours:** White shirts, blue shorts, blue stockings.

WEST HAM UNITED 1990–91 LEAGUE RECORD

Match No.	Date	Venue	Opponents	Result	H/T Score	Lg. Pos.	Goalscorers	Attendance
1	Aug 25	A	Middlesbrough	D 0-0	0-0	—		20,680
2	29	H	Portsmouth	D 1-1	1-1	—	McAvennie	20,835
3	Sept 1	H	Watford	W 1-0	0-0	7	Dicks (pen)	19,872
4	8	A	Leicester C	W 2-1	1-0	4	James (og), Morley	14,605
5	15	H	Wolverhampton W	D 1-1	1-0	6	Martin	23,241
6	19	H	Ipswich T	W 3-1	0-1	—	Bishop, Quinn, Morley	18,764
7	22	A	Newcastle U	D 1-1	1-1	3	Morley	25,462
8	29	A	Sheffield W	D 1-1	0-1	4	Dicks	28,786
9	Oct 3	H	Oxford U	W 2-0	2-0	—	Foster, Morley	18,125
10	6	H	Hull C	W 7-1	2-1	3	Quinn 2, Potts, Dicks 2 (1 pen) Parris, Morley	19,472
11	13	A	Bristol C	D 1-1	0-0	3	McAvennie	16,838
12	20	A	Swindon T	W 1-0	0-0	3	McAvennie	13,658
13	24	H	Blackburn R	W 1-0	1-0		Bishop	20,003
14	27	H	Charlton Ath	W 2-1	0-0	2	Allen 2	24,019
15	Nov 3	A	Notts Co	W 1-0	0-0	2	Morley	10,871
16	10	A	Millwall	D 1-1	0-0	2	McAvennie	20,591
17	17	H	Brighton & HA	W 2-1	0-1	2	Slater, Foster	23,082
18	24	A	Plymouth Arg	W 1-0	0-0	1	McAvennie	11,490
19	Dec 1	H	WBA	W 3-1	2-0	1	Parris, Morley, McAvennie	24,753
20	8	A	Portsmouth	W 1-0	0-0	1	Morley	12,045
21	15	H	Middlesbrough	D 0-0	0-0	1		23,705
22	22	A	Barnsley	L 0-1	0-1	2		10,348
23	26	H	Oldham Ath	W 2-0	1-0	1	Morley, Slater	24,950
24	29	H	Port Vale	D 0-0	0-0	1		23,603
25	Jan 1	A	Bristol R	W 1-0	0-0	1	Quinn	7932
26	12	A	Watford	W 1-0	0-0	1	Morley	17,172
27	19	H	Leicester C	W 1-0	1-0	1	Parris	21,652
28	Feb 2	A	Wolverhampton W	L 1-2	0-1	1	McAvennie	19,454
29	24	H	Millwall	W 3-1	1-1	—	McAvennie 2, Morley	20,503
30	Mar 2	A	WBA	D 0-0	0-0	1		16,089
31	5	H	Plymouth Arg	D 2-2	1-0	—	Marker (og), Breacker	18,933
32	13	A	Oxford U	L 1-2	0-1	—	Quinn	8225
33	16	H	Sheffield W	L 1-3	0-0	2	Quinn	26,182
34	20	H	Bristol C	W 1-0	0-0	—	Gale	22,951
35	23	A	Hull C	D 0-0	0-0	2		9558
36	29	A	Oldham Ath	D 1-1	0-0	—	Bishop (pen)	16,932
37	Apr 1	H	Barnsley	W 3-2	0-2	2	McAvennie, Dowie, Foster	24,607
38	6	A	Port Vale	W 1-0	0-0	1	Bishop	9658
39	10	A	Brighton & HA	L 0-1	0-1	—		11,904
40	17	A	Ipswich T	W 1-0	1-0	—	Morley	20,290
41	20	H	Swindon T	W 2-0	1-0	1	Parris, Dowie	25,944
42	24	H	Newcastle U	D 1-1	0-1	—	Dowie	24,195
43	27	A	Blackburn R	L 1-3	1-3	1	Dowie	10,808
44	May 4	A	Charlton Ath	D 1-1	1-1	1	Allen	16,137
45	8	H	Bristol R	W 1-0	1-0	—	Slater	23,054
46	11	H	Notts Co	L 1-2	0-2	2	Parris	26,551

Final League Position: 2

GOALSCORERS

League (60): Morley 12, McAvennie 10, Quinn 6, Parris 5, Bishop 4 (1 pen), Dicks 4 (2 pens), Dowie 4, Allen 3, Foster 3, Slater 3, Breacker 1, Gale 1, Martin 1, Potts 1, own goals 2.
Rumbelows Cup (6): Allen 2, Dicks 1 (pen), Keen 1, Morley 1, Quinn 1.
FA Cup (15): Morley 4, Parris 3, Bishop 2, Quinn 2, Slater 2, Foster 1, McAvennie 1.

Miklosko	Potts	Dicks	Foster	Martin	Keen	Bishop	McAvennie	Slater	Allen	Morley	Quinn	Parris	Livett	Rush	Gale	Breacker	Hughton	Clarke	Robson	Carr	Rosenior	Dowie	Stewart	Match No.
1	2	3	4	5	6	7	8	9	10	11														1
1	2	3	4	5	6	7	8	9	10	11														2
1	2	3	4	5	6	7	8	9	10†	11*	12	14												3
1	2	3	4	5	6	7	8*	9†	10	11	12	14												4
1	2	3	4	5	6	7	8		10	11	12		9*											5
1	2†	3	4	5	6	7	8*	9	10	11	12	14												6
1	2	3	4	5	6	7	12	9†	10	11	8*	14												7
1	2	3	4	5†	6	7	12	9	10	11	8*	14												8
1	2	3	4	5	6	7		9*	10	11	8	12												9
1	2	3	4	5	6*	7	12		10	11	8†	9			14									10
1	2	3	4	5	6	7	12	9*	10	11	8													11
1	2	3†	4	5	6	7	12		10	11	8*	14			9									12
1		3†	4	5	6	7	12	14	10	11	8*			2	9									13
1			4	5	6	7	8	9*	10	11	12	3		2										14
1			4	5	8	7			10	11		3			9	2	6							15
1			4	5	8	7	9		10*	11		3			12	2	6							16
1			4	5	10	7	8	12		11		3			9*	2	6							17
1			4	5	10	7	8	9		11		3				2	6							18
1			4	5	10*	7	8	9	12	11		3				2	6							19
1			4	5†		7	8*	9	10	11	12	3			14	2	6							20
1	5					7	8	9	10	11*	12	3			4	2	6							21
1	5					7	8*	9	10	11	12	3			4	2	6							22
1	5					7	8	9	10	11		3			4	2	6							23
1	12					7	8	9	10*	11		3			4	2	6							24
1	8					7		9	10	11		3			4	2	6							25
1	10			5†		7	8	9*		11		3			4	2	6			12	14			26
1	10			5		7	8	9*	12	11		3			4	2	6							27
1	10			5		7	8	9*	14	11	12	3†			4	2	6							28
1	10			5		7	8	9	12	11		3			4*	2	6							29
1	10			5		7*	8	9	12	11		3			4	2	6							30
1	10	4		5		7	8	9	12	11		3				2	6*							31
1	10	5		14		7	8		12	11		3			4	2*	6				9†			32
1	2	5	10			7	8	9	12	11†		3			4		6*			14				33
1	2	5	10			7	8	9*	12	11†		3			4		6			14				34
1	2	5	10†			7	8*			11		3			4		6			14	12	9		35
1	2	5				7	8		10	11		3			4		6					9		36
1	2	5	12			7	8		10	11		3			4		6*					9		37
1	2	5				7	10		8	11		3			4		6					9		38
1	2	5				8	7		11	14	10	12			3		6†					9*	4	39
1	2	5†	10			7	12	8	14	11		3			4		6					9*		40
1	2		10*			7	8		12	11		3			4		6					9	5	41
1	2		10			7	8		12	11		3			4		6					9	5*	42
1	2		8			7	10*	12	11†	14		3			4		6					9	5	43
1	2					7	10		8	11	12	3			4		6					9*	5	44
1	4	5	14			7	12	8	10†	11		3			2		6					9*		45
1	2	5	14			7	12	8	10	11		3			4		6†					9*		46
46	36	13	36	20	36	40	24	37	28	38	16	37	1	2	23	23	32	—	—	1	—	12	5	
	+				+	+	+	+			+	+			+	+	+			+	+	+	+	
	1s				4s	10s	3s	12s			10s	7s			3s	1s	1s			1s	1s	2s	2s	

Rumbelows Cup   Second Round   Stoke C (h)   3-0
                                   (a)   2-1
                    Third Round   Oxford U (a) 1-2
FA Cup   Third Round   Aldershot (a) (at West Ham)   0-0
                                   (h)   6-1
                    Fourth Round   Luton T (a)   1-1
                                   (h)   5-0
                    Fifth Round   Crewe Alex (h)   1-0
                    Sixth Round   Everton (h)   2-1
                    Semi-final   Nottingham F (at Villa Park)   0-4

WEST HAM UNITED

Player and Position	Ht	Wt	Birth Date	Birth Place	Source	Clubs	League App	Gls
Goalkeepers								
Steven Banks	5 11	11 04	9 2 72	Hillingdon	Trainee	West Ham U	—	—
Allen McKnight*	6 1	13 07	27 1 64	Antrim	Distillery	Celtic	12	—
						Albion R (loan)	36	—
						West Ham U	23	—
Ludek Miklosko	6 5	14 00	9 12 61	Ostrava	Banik Ostrava	West Ham U	64	—
Defenders								
Tim Breacker	6 0	12 06	2 7 65	Bicester		Luton T	210	3
						West Ham U	24	1
Julian Dicks	5 7	10 08	8 8 68	Bristol	Apprentice	Birmingham C	89	1
						West Ham U	95	15
Colin Foster	6 4	13 10	16 7 64	Chislehurst	Apprentice	Orient	174	10
						Nottingham F	72	5
						West Ham U	58	4
Tony Gale	6 1	13 10	19 11 59	London	Apprentice	Fulham	277	19
						West Ham U	220	4
Chris Harwood‡	5 11	12 00	19 4 70	Hendon	Trainee	West Ham U	—	—
Chris Hughton	5 7	11 05	11 12 58	West Ham	Amateur	Tottenham H	297	12
						West Ham U	32	—
Tommy McQueen (To Falkirk Oct 1990)	5 7	11 01	1 4 63	Bellshill	Gartcosh U	Clyde	112	1
						Aberdeen	53	4
						West Ham U	30	
Alvin Martin	6 1	13 03	29 7 58	Bootle	Apprentice	West Ham U	394	24
George Parris	5 9	12 00	11 9 64	Ilford	Apprentice	West Ham U	202	12
Steven Potts	5 7	10 04	7 5 67	Hartford, USA	Apprentice	West Ham U	115	1
Ray Stewart*	5 11	11 11	7 9 59	Perth	Errol Rovers	Dundee U	44	5
						West Ham U	345	62
Midfield								
Martin Allen	5 10	11 00	14 8 65	Reading	School	QPR	136	16
						West Ham U	79	12
Ian Bishop	5 9	10 06	29 5 65	Liverpool	Apprentice	Everton	1	—
						Crewe Alex (loan)	4	—
						Carlisle U	132	14
						Bournemouth	44	2
						Manchester U	19	2
						West Ham U	57	6
Kevin Keen	5 6	9 08	25 2 67	Amersham	Apprentice	West Ham U	144	14
Paul Kelly*	5 7	10 13	12 10 69	Bexley	Trainee	West Ham U	1	—
Simon Livett	5 10	12 02	8 1 69	Newham	Trainee	West Ham U	1	—
Stewart Robson*	5 11	11 13	6 11 64	Billericay	Apprentice	Arsenal	151	16
						West Ham U	69	4
						Coventry C (loan)	4	—
Matthew Rush	5 11	12 10	6 8 71	Dalston	Trainee	West Ham U	5	—
Forwards								
Simon Clarke	5 11	11 02	23 9 71	Chelmsford	Trainee	West Ham U	1	—
Iain Dowie	6 0	13 03	9 1 65		Hendon	Luton T	66	16
						Fulham (loan)	5	1
						West Ham U	12	4
Frank McAvennie	5 9	11 00	22 11 59	Glasgow	Johnstone B	St Mirren	135	50
						West Ham U	85	33
						Celtic	55	27
						West Ham U	48	10

WEST HAM UNITED

Foundation: Thames Ironworks FC was formed by employees of this shipbuilding yard in 1895 and entered the FA Cup in their initial season at Chatham and the London League in their second. Short of funds, the club was wound up in June 1900 and relaunched a month later as West Ham United. Connection with the Ironworks was not finally broken until four years later.

First Football League game: 30 August, 1919, Division 2, v Lincoln City (h) D 1-1 – Hufton; Cope, Lee; Lane, Fenwick, McCrae; D. Smith, Moyes (1), Puddefoot, Morris, Bradshaw.

Did you know: Centre-forward Vivian Gibbins made more First Division appearances as an amateur than any other player since World War 1 – a total of 129, all for West Ham United—December 1923 until December 1931 when he resigned because he was dropped without warning.

Managers (and Secretary-managers)
Syd King 1902–32, Charlie Paynter 1932–50, Ted Fenton 1950–61, Ron Greenwood 1961–74 (continued as GM to 1977), John Lyall 1974–89, Lou Macari 1989–90, Billy Bonds February 1990–   .

Player and Position	Ht	Wt	Birth Date	Birth Place	Source	Clubs	League App	Gls
Trevor Morley	5 11	12 01	20 3 62	Nottingham	Nuneaton	Northampton T	107	39
						Manchester C	72	18
						West Ham U	57	22
Jimmy Quinn	6 1	12 00	18 11 59	Belfast	Oswestry T	Swindon T	49	10
						Blackburn R	71	17
						Swindon T	64	30
						Leicester C	31	6
						Bradford C	35	14
						West Ham U	47	18
Leroy Rosenior	6 1	11 10	24 3 64	London	School	Fulham	54	16
						QPR	38	7
						Fulham	34	20
						West Ham U	44	14
						Fulham (loan)	11	3
Stuart Slater	5 9	10 04	27 3 69	Sudbury	Apprentice	West Ham U	100	11

Trainees
Basham, Michael; Beard, Simon A; Comerford, Anthony M; Hancock, Darren J; Harriott, Marvin L; Holland, Matthew R; Horlock, Kevin; Lowe, John; Macari, Michael; Marquis, Paul R; Miller, Simon R; Padington, John P; Purdie, John D; Reed, Peter M; Richards, Tony S; Small, Keith P; White, David T; Williamson, Daniel A.

Associated Schoolboys
Bates, Jonathan P; Blaney, Steven D; Fleming, Shaun A; Geraghty, Jason W; Hodson, Benjamin M; Joscelyne, Wayne; Kent, Stuart; Lockwood, Matthew D; Maeer, Darren J; Matthews, Paul C; Oakley, Warren N; Pallecaros, George K; Perkins, Declan O; Rainbow, James R; Richardson, Stuart J; Rose, Christopher A; Shipp, Daniel A; Stone, Damion T; Victory, Jamie C.

Associated Schoolboys who have accepted the club's offer of a Traineeship/Contract
Brunning, John J; Canham, Scott; Johnson, Roy J; Knight, Jason G; Reeve, Mark E.

WIGAN ATHLETIC 1990-91   *Back row (left to right):* Stephen Appleton. Darren Patterson. Phil Daley. Phil Hughes. Nigel Adkins. Ian Hartley. Lee Rogerson. Alan Johnson. John Robertson.

Second row down (left to right): Dave Philpotts. Barry Edwardson. Neil Leyland. David Fairclough. Allen Tankard. Joe Parkinson. Peter Atherton. Don Page. Ray Woods. Lee Hackett. Tyrone Grimes. David Crompton. Alex Cribley.

Third row down (left to right): Paul Musker. Steven Eyre. Andy Pilling. Neill Rimmer. Bryan Hamilton. Bryan Griffiths. Jimmy Carberry. Stuart Phoenix. Lee Hunter.

Front row (left to right): Scott Derbyshire. Philip Alton. Andy Roberts. Chris Woodward. Stephen Nugent. Barry Adkins. Steven Dykes. Paul Johanson. Lee Cunliffe.

Division 3 **WIGAN ATHLETIC**

Springfield Park, Wigan. Telephone Wigan (0942) 44433. Commercial Dept: (0942) 43067. Latics Line: 0898 338308.

Ground capacity: 11,434.

Record attendance: 27,500 v Hereford U, 12 December 1953.

Record receipts: £40,577 v Leeds U, FA Cup 6th rd, 15 March 1987.

Pitch measurements: 117yd × 72yd.

President: T. Hitchen.

Chairman: W. Kenyon. *Vice-chairman:*

Directors: J. A. Bennett, J. D. Fillingham, W. Howard, S. Jackson, W. Pearce.

Chief Executive: Bryan Hamilton. *Vice-president:* J. H. Farrimond.

Secretary: Mark A. Blackbourne. *Commercial Manager:* B. Eccles.

Manager: Bryan Hamilton. *Assistant Manager:* David Philpotts.

Coaches: David Crompton and Mick Lyons. *Physio:* Alex Cribley.

Year Formed: 1932.

Club Nickname: 'The Latics'.

Record League Victory: 7-2 v Scunthorpe U (away), Division 4, 12 March 1982 – Tunks; McMahon, Glenn, Wignall, Cribley, Methven (1), O'Keefe, Barrow (1), Bradd (3), Houghton (2), Evans.

Record Cup Victory: 6-0 v Carlisle U (away), FA Cup, 1st rd, 24 November 1934 – Caunce; Robinson, Talbot; Paterson, Watson, Tufnell; Armes (2), Robson (1), Roberts (2), Felton, Scott (1).

Record Defeat: 1-6 v Bristol R, Division 3, 3 March 1990.

Most League Points (2 for a win): 55, Division 4, 1978–79 and 1979–80.

Most League Points (3 for a win): 91, Division 4, 1981–82.

Most League Goals: 80, Division 4, 1981–82.

Highest League Scorer in Season: Warren Aspinall, 21, Division 3, 1985–86.

Most League Goals in Total Aggregate: Peter Houghton, 62, 1978–84.

Most Capped Player: None.

Most League Appearances: Colin Methven, 296, 1979–86.

Record Transfer Fee Received: £200,000 from Coventry C for Ray Woods, January 1991.

Record Transfer Fee Paid: £65,000 to Everton for Eamon O'Keefe, January 1982.

Football League Record: 1978 Elected to Division 4; 1982 – Division 3.

Honours: Football League: Best season in Division 3: 4th, 1985–86, 1986–87; Division 4 – Promoted (3rd) 1981–82. *FA Cup:* 4th rd 1979–80, 1985–86. *Football League Cup:* best season: 4th rd, 1981–82. *Freight Rover Trophy:* Winners 1984–85.

Colours: Blue shirts red and white trim, blue shorts with red and white trim, blue stockings. **Change colours:** Red shirts with blue and white trim, red shorts with blue and white trim, red stockings.

WIGAN ATHLETIC 1990–91 LEAGUE RECORD

Match No.	Date		Venue	Opponents	Result	H/T Score	Lg. Pos.	Goalscorers	Attendance
1	Aug	25	H	Mansfield T	L 0-2	0-0	—		2032
2	Sept	1	A	Grimsby T	L 3-4	2-1	24	Woods, Page 2	5162
3		8	H	Bournemouth	W 2-0	1-0	14	Page, Patterson	2159
4		15	A	Rotherham U	L 1-5	1-1	22	Page	4100
5		18	A	Fulham	W 2-1	1-1	—	Daley 2	3041
6		22	H	Birmingham C	D 1-1	0-0	13	Page	3907
7		28	H	Bolton W	W 2-1	2-0	—	Patterson, Griffiths B (pen)	4366
8	Oct	1	A	Tranmere R	D 1-1	1-1	—	Page	7030
9		6	A	Crewe Alex	L 0-1	0-0	15		3771
10		13	H	Reading	W 1-0	0-0	13	Daley	2576
11		20	H	Southend U	W 4-1	2-0	9	Page, Daley, Griffiths B 2 (1 pen)	2691
12		23	A	Cambridge U	W 3-2	1-0	—	Johnson, Daley, Page	4626
13		27	A	Bradford C	L 1-2	1-1	8	Woods	6803
14	Nov	3	H	Preston NE	W 2-1	2-1	4	Woods, Page	4728
15		10	A	Stoke C	L 0-2	0-1	11		12,756
16		24	H	Leyton Orient	L 1-2	1-2	14	Johnson	2260
17	Dec	1	H	Bury	L 1-2	0-1	15	Tankard	2861
18		15	A	Shrewsbury T	D 0-0	0-0	15		2227
19		23	A	Brentford	L 0-1	0-1	—		6495
20		26	H	Exeter C	W 4-1	3-0	14	Page, Daley, Griffiths B 2	2045
21		29	H	Swansea C	L 2-4	0-0	15	Page, Patterson	2525
22	Jan	1	A	Huddersfield T	L 0-1	0-0	17		4887
23		12	H	Grimsby T	W 2-0	2-0	16	Griffiths B, Fairclough	2868
24		19	A	Mansfield T	D 1-1	0-1	16	Boughey	2166
25		26	A	Reading	L 1-3	0-1	17	Boughey	3416
26	Feb	2	H	Fulham	W 2-0	1-0	16	Griffiths B, Pilling	2258
27		5	A	Birmingham C	D 0-0	0-0	—		5319
28		23	H	Stoke C	W 4-0	1-0	15	Daley 2, Patterson, Page	3728
29		26	A	Chester C	W 2-1	1-0	—	Johnson, Rimmer	914
30	Mar	2	A	Bury	D 2-2	0-1	14	Johnson 2	2967
31		5	A	Bournemouth	W 3-0	2-0	—	Pilling, Daley, Page	4662
32		9	H	Shrewsbury T	D 2-2	1-1	12	Langley, Pilling	2269
33		12	H	Tranmere R	L 0-1	0-0	—		2912
34		16	A	Bolton W	L 1-2	0-1	14	Griffiths B (pen)	7812
35		23	H	Crewe Alex	W 1-0	0-0	14	Carberry	2426
36		26	H	Rotherham U	W 2-0	1-0	—	Powell, Carberry	1962
37		30	A	Exeter C	L 0-1	0-1	13		4510
38	Apr	1	H	Brentford	W 1-0	0-0	11	Worthington	2160
39		6	A	Swansea C	W 6-1	3-1	10	Carberry, Worthington 2, Daley, Jones, Griffiths B	2869
40		13	H	Huddersfield T	D 1-1	0-1	10	Worthington	4642
41		16	H	Chester C	W 2-0	2-0	—	Griffiths B (pen), Powell	2131
42		19	A	Southend U	W 2-0	1-0	—	Worthington, Rimmer	7550
43		23	A	Leyton Orient	D 1-1	0-0	—	Langley	2613
44		27	H	Cambridge U	L 0-1	0-1	9		3273
45	May	4	H	Bradford C	W 3-0	2-0	9	Griffiths B 2 (1 pen), Powell	3267
46		11	A	Preston N E	L 1-2	1-0	10	Powell	5917

Final League Position: 10

GOALSCORERS

League (71): Page 13, Griffiths B 12 (5 pens), Daley 10, Johnson 5, Worthington 5, Patterson 4, Powell 4, Carberry 3, Pilling 3, Woods 3, Boughey 2, Langley 2, Rimmer 2, Fairclough 1, Jones 1, Tankard 1.
Rumbelows Cup (1): Page 1.
FA Cup (8): Griffiths B 3, Rimmer 2, Page 1, Patterson 1, Woods 1.

Adkins	Parkinson	Tankard	Atherton	Johnson	Hildersley	Woods	Rimmer	Daley	Fairclough	Griffiths B	Patterson	Griffiths I	Page	Appleton	Langley	Rogerson	Carberry	Pilling	Paladino	Pennock	Boughey	Hughes	Jones	Powell	Worthington	Nugent	Match No.
1	2	3	4	5*	6	7	8	9	10	11†12		14															1
1	2	3	4		6†	7	8	9		11*	5	14	10	12													2
1	2	3	4			7	8	9		12	5	11*10	6														3
1	2	3	4	14		7*	8	9†		12	5	11	10	6													4
1	2	3	4	12		7	8	9		11	5	10	6*														5
1	2	3	4	6		7	8	9		11	5	10															6
1	2	3	4			7	8	9†12		11	5	10*	6	14													7
1	2	3	4	5		7	8	9	12	11*		10	6														8
1	2	3	4	5		7	8	9*12		11†	14	10	6														9
1	2	3	4	5		7		9		11		10	6	8													10
1	2	3	4	5		7		9		11	12	10	6	8*													11
1	2	3	4	5		7		9		11	8	10	6														12
1	2*	3	4	5		7	8	9		11	12	10	6†	14													13
1	2*	3	4	5		7	8	9		11†12		10	6	14													14
1	2	3	4	5		7	8	9*		11†12		10	6	14													15
1	2	3	4	5		7†	8	9*14		11		10	6	12													16
1	2	3	4	5			8	9*	7†11		12	14	10	6													17
1	2	3	4	12		7	8			11	5	10*	6	14	9†												18
	2	3	4	6		7	8	9		11*	5	10	12						1								19
	2	3	4	5		7	8	9		11		10	6						1								20
	2	3	4	5	7†		8	9*		11	12	10	6	14					1								21
	2	3	4	5			8	9		11		10	6	7					1								22
	2	3	4	5		7	8	9*11†12				10	6	14					1								23
	2	3	4	5			8	9*11		12		10	6	14					1		7†						24
		3	4	5			8	9		11	2	10	6	12					1		7*						25
		3	4	5	10†		8	9		11*	2	7		6		12				1		14					26
		3	4	5			8	9		11*	2	7		6		12				1		10					27
		3	4	5			8	9		11	2		10	6					1		7						28
		3	4	5			8	9		11*	2		10	6		12				1		7					29
		3	4	5			8	9					10	6	11	2				1		7					30
		3	4	5				9					8	10	6	11	2			1		7					31
		3	4	5				9	14	12		8†10*		6	11	2			1		7						32
		3	4	5				9		11		10*	6	8	2				1		7	12					33
		3	4	5					12	2	10*	6	11	8				1		7	9						34
		3	4	5				9	11	2	6*	12	8†					1		7	10	14					35
		3	4	5				9	11†	2	6	8*12						1		7	10	14					36
		3	4	5				9	12	14	6	8	2†				1		7	10	11*						37
		3	4	5				9	11	12	6	8					1		7	10	2*						38
		3	4	5				9	11†	14	6	8					1		7	10*	2	12					39
		3	4	5			8	9	11*	12	14	6					1		7	10†	2						40
		3	4	5			8	9	11*	6	12						1		7	10	2						41
		3	4	5			8	9	11*	6	12						1		7	10	2						42
		3	4	5			8	9	11	6	12						1		7	10	2*						43
		3	4	5			8	9	11	14	6	12					1		7*10	2†							44
		3	4	5			8	9	11*	14	6	12							7†10	2							45
7		3†	4	5			8	9	12	14	6	11					1		10	2*							46
18	25	46	46	40	4	20	34	41	4	38	18	6	31	3	38	—	14	8	7	2	2	19	19	13	10	—	

Sub appearances: +3s / +3s +5s +10s5s +3s +7s +1s +1s +14s5s / +1s +1s +2s +1s

Rumbelows Cup	First Round	Barnsley (h)	0-1
		(a)	1-0
FA Cup	First Round	Carlisle U (h)	5-0
	Second Round	Hartlepool U (h)	2-0
	Third Round	Coventry (a)	1-1
		(h)	0-1

WIGAN ATHLETIC

Player and Position	Ht	Wt	Birth Date	Place	Source	Clubs	League App	Gls
Goalkeepers								
Nigel Adkins	5 11	12 07	11 3 65	Birkenhead	Apprentice	Tranmere R	86	—
						Wigan Ath	71	—
Philip Hughes*	5 11	12 07	19 11 64	Manchester	Apprentice	Manchester U	—	—
						Leeds U	6	—
						Bury	80	—
						Wigan Ath	99	—
Giuseppe Paladino			29 8 65	Whiston	St Helens	Wigan Ath	7	—
Defenders								
Steve Appleton	5 11	10 09	27 7 73	Liverpool	Trainee	Wigan Ath	10	—
Peter Atherton	5 11	12 03	6 4 70	Orrell	Trainee	Wigan Ath	148	1
Lee Hunter‡	5 10	10 08	5 10 69	Oldham	Trainee	Colchester U	9	—
						Wigan Ath	—	—
Darren Patterson	6 1	12 00	15 10 69	Belfast	Trainee	WBA	—	—
						Wigan Ath	57	5
Stuart Phoenix*	5 4	10 06	3 12 71	Wigan	Trainee	Wigan Ath	—	—
Allen Tankard	5 10	11 07	21 5 69	Fleet	Apprentice	Southampton	5	—
						Wigan Ath	124	3
Midfield								
James Carberry	5 10	11 02	13 10 60	Liverpool	Trainee	Everton	—	—
						Wigan Ath	60	6
Steve Eyre‡	6 0	12 00	9 5 72	Manchester	Burnley	Wigan Ath	—	—
Alan Johnson	5 11	11 12	19 2 71	Ince	Trainee	Wigan Ath	84	7
Philip Jones	5 8	10 09	1 12 69	Liverpool	Trainee	Everton	1	—
						Blackpool (loan)	6	—
						Wigan Ath	20	1
Kevin Langley	6 1	10 03	24 5 64	St Helens	Apprentice	Wigan Ath	160	6
						Everton	16	2
						Manchester C (loan)	9	—
						Manchester C	—	—
						Chester C (loan)	9	—
						Birmingham C	76	2
						Wigan Ath	39	2
Paul Musker‡	5 10	12 00	7 5 72	St Helens	Trainee	Wigan Ath	—	—
Joe Parkinson	5 11	12 02	11 6 71	Eccles	Trainee	Wigan Ath	70	3
Andy Pilling	5 10	11 04	30 6 69	Wigan		Preston NE	1	—
						Wigan Ath	98	14
Neill Rimmer	5 6	10 03	13 11 67	Liverpool	Apprentice	Everton	1	—
						Ipswich T	22	3
						Wigan Ath	97	6
Lee Rogerson‡	6 0	12 00	21 3 67	Darwen	Clitheroe	Wigan Ath	4	—
Forwards								
Simon Andrews‡	5 10	11 00	26 9 70	Macclesfield	Trainee	Manchester U	—	—
						Wigan Ath	—	—
Phil Daley	6 2	12 09	12 4 67	Walton	Newton	Wigan Ath	74	16
David Fairclough‡	5 10	11 00	5 1 57	Liverpool	Apprentice	Liverpool	98	34
						Lucerne	Norwich C	2	—
							Oldham Ath	17	1
							Rochdale	—	—
						Beveren	Tranmere R	14	1
							Wigan Ath	7	1
Bryan Griffiths	5 9	11 00	26 1 65	Prescot	St Helens T	Wigan Ath	117	27

WIGAN ATHLETIC

Foundation: Following the demise of Wigan Borough and their resignation from the Football League in 1931, a public meeting was called in Wigan at the Queen's Hall in May 1932 at which a new club Wigan Athletic, was founded in the hope of carrying on in the Football League. With this in mind, they bought Springfield Park for £2,250, but failed to gain admission to the Football League until 46 years later.

First Football League game: 19 August, 1978, Division 4, v Hereford U (a) D 0–0 – Brown; Hinnigan, Gore, Gillibrand, Ward, Davids, Corrigan, Purdie, Houghton, Wilkie, Wright.

Did you know: In 1979–80 Tony Quinn created a club record that has yet to be beaten by scoring for Wigan Athletic in each of five consecutive Football League games.

Managers (and Secretary-managers)
Charlie Spencer 1932–37, Jimmy Milne 1946–47, Bob Pryde 1949–52, Ted Goodier 1952–54, Walter Crook 1954–55, Ron Suart 1955–56, Billy Cooke 1956, Sam Barkas 1957, Trevor Hitchen 1957–58, Malcolm Barrass 1958–59, Jimmy Shirley 1959, Pat Murphy 1959–60, Allenby Chilton 1960, Johnny Ball 1961–63, Allan Brown 1963–66, Alf Craig 1966–67, Harry Leyland 1967–68, Alan Saunders 1968, Ian McNeill 1968–70, Gordon Milne 1970–72, Les Rigby 1972–74, Brian Tiler 1974–76, Ian McNeill 1976–81, Larry Lloyd 1981–83, Harry McNally 1983–85, Bryan Hamilton 1985–86, Ray Mathias 1986–89, Bryan Hamilton March 1989–   .

Player and Position	Ht	Wt	Birth Date	Birth Place	Source	Clubs	League App	Gls
Ron Hildersley‡	5 4	9 02	6 4 65	Fife	Apprentice	Manchester C	1	—
						Chester (loan)	9	—
						Chester C	9	—
						Rochdale	16	—
						Preston NE	58	3
						Cambridge U (loan)	9	3
						Blackburn R	30	4
						Wigan Ath	4	—
Steve Nugent§			7 5 73	Wigan	Trainee	Wigan Ath	2	—
Don Page	5 10	11 04	18 1 64	Manchester	Runcorn	Wigan Ath	74	15
Gary Worthington	5 10	10 05	10 11 66	Cleethorpes	Apprentice	Manchester U	—	—
						Huddersfield T	—	—
						Darlington	40	15
						Wrexham	72	18
						Wigan Ath	12	5

Trainees
Cunliffe, Lee J; Derbyshire, Scott L; Edwardson, Barry J; Grimes, Tyrone C; Hackett, Lee C; Hartley, Ian M; Johanson, Paul M; Leyland, Neil T; McIlroy, Samuel; Nugent, Stephen; Roberts, Andrew T; Robertson, John N; Woodward, Christopher J.

Associated Schoolboys
Brown, Jason; Curd, Collin D; Dixon, Stephen; Dowds, Scott K; Ellaby, Steven J; Irvine, Kevin; Kirwin, Paul; Merola, Anthony; Ogden, Neil; Pooke, Christopher; Riley, Michael P; Saint, Darren; Strong, Greg; Wallace, Jeffery R.

Associated Schoolboys who have accepted the club's offer of a Traineeship/Contract
Gallagher, Andrew N; Gallagher, Simon K; Harrison, Anthony; O'Brien, Stephen J; Peoples, Martin.

562

WIMBLEDON 1990-91 *Back row (left to right):* Ron Suart (Chief Scout), Detzi Kruszynski, Scott Fitzgerald, Steve Cotterill, Carlton Fairweather, Neil Sullivan, David Hudson, Roger Joseph, Aidan Newhouse, Brian McAllister, Warren Barton, Roger Smith (Youth Development Officer).
Centre row: Syd Neal (Kit Manager), Dean Blackwell, John Scales, John Gayle, Lawrie Sanchez, Steve Anthrobus, Hans Segers, John Fashanu, Alan Cork, Paul Miller, Keith Curle, Clive Goodyear, Steve Allen (Physiotherapist).
Front row: Terry Burton (Youth Team Manager), David Cooper, Gerald Dobbs, Paul McGee, Terry Gibson, Ray Harford (Manager), Matthew Pearson, Vaughan Ryan, Terry Phelan, Mickey Bennett, Joe Kinnear (Reserve Team Manager).

Division 1 WIMBLEDON

Selhurst Park, South Norwood, London SE25. Telephone: 081-771-2233.

Ground capacity: 29,949.

Record attendance: 18,000 v HMS Victory, FA Amateur Cup 3rd rd, 1934–35 (at Plough Lane).

Record receipts: £86,165 v Arsenal, Division 1, 25 August 1990 (at Plough Lane).

Pitch measurements: 110yd × 74yd.

President: Rt Hon Lord Michael Havers of Bury St Edmunds.

Chairman: S. G. Reed. *Vice-chairman:* J. Lelliott.

Managing Director: S. Hammam.

Directors: P. Cork, P. R. Cooper, N. N. Hammam.

Chief Executive: David Barnard.

Manager: Ray Harford.

Coach: Don Howe. *Physio:* Steve Allen.

Secretary: Adrian Cook. *Commercial Manager:* Reg Davis.

Year Formed: 1889. *Turned Professional:* 1964. *Ltd Co.:* 1964.

Previous Name: Wimbledon Old Centrals, 1899–1905.

Club Nickname: 'The Dons'.

Record League Victory: 6-0 v Newport C, Division 3, 3 September 1983 – Beasant; Peters, Winterburn, Galliers, Morris, Hatter, Evans (2), Ketteridge (1), Cork (3 incl. 1p), Downes, Hodges (Driver).

Record Cup Victory: 7-2 v Windsor & Eton, FA Cup, 1st rd, 22 November 1980 – Beasant; Jones, Armstrong, Galliers, Mick Smith (2), Cunningham (1), Ketteridge, Hodges, Leslie, Cork (1), Hubbick (3).

Record Defeat: 0-8 v Everton, League Cup 2nd rd, 29 August 1978.

Most League Points (2 for a win): 61, Division 4, 1978–79.

Most League Points (3 for a win): 98, Division 4, 1982–83.

Most League Goals: 97, Division 3, 1983–84.

Highest League Scorer in Season: Alan Cork, 29, 1983–84.

Most League Goals in Total Aggregate: Alan Cork, 143, 1977–91.

Most Capped Player: Glyn Hodges 5 (13), Wales.

Most League Appearances: Alan Cork, 411, 1977–91.

Record Transfer Fee Received: £1,600,000 from Chelsea for Dennis Wise, July 1990.

Record Transfer Fee Paid: £500,000 to Reading for Keith Curle, October 1988.

Football League Record: 1977 Elected to Division 4; 1979–80 Division 3; 1980–81 Division 4; 1981–82 Division 3; 1982–83 Division 4; 1983–84 Division 3; 1984–86 Division 2; 1986–Division 1.

Honours: Football League: Division 1 best season: 6th, 1986–87; Division 3 – Runners-up 1983–84; Division 4 – Champions 1982–83. *FA Cup:* Winners 1987–88. *Football League Cup:* best season: 4th rd, 1979–80, 1983–84, 1988–89. *League Group Cup:* Runners-up 1981–82.

Colours: Blue shirts yellow trim, blue shorts yellow trim, blue stockings yellow trim. **Change colours:** White shirts, black shorts, white stockings.

WIMBLEDON 1990–91 LEAGUE RECORD

Match No.	Date		Venue	Opponents	Result	H/T Score	Lg. Pos.	Goalscorers	Attendance
1	Aug	25	H	Arsenal	L 0-3	0-0	—		13,733
2		29	A	QPR	W 1-0	0-0	—	Fashanu	9762
3	Sept	1	A	Derby Co	D 1-1	1-0	12	Cotterill	12,469
4		8	H	Liverpool	L 1-2	0-2	16	Cork	12,364
5		15	A	Coventry C	D 0-0	0-0	16		8925
6		22	H	Sunderland	D 2-2	0-1	15	Kruszynski, Scales	6143
7		29	H	Manchester C	D 1-1	0-0	14	Gayle	6158
8	Oct	6	A	Sheffield U	W 2-1	1-1	10	Fairweather, Fashanu	17,650
9		20	H	Aston Villa	D 0-0	0-0	12		6646
10		27	A	Crystal Palace	L 3-4	1-1	13	McGee 2, Fashanu	17,220
11	Nov	3	H	Southampton	D 1-1	0-0	14	Flowers (og)	5485
12		10	A	Tottenham H	L 2-4	2-2	16	Cork, McGee	28,769
13		17	H	Chelsea	W 2-1	1-0	10	Nicholas (og), Gibson	10,773
14		24	H	Everton	W 2-1	1-0	8	Barton, Gibson	6411
15	Dec	1	A	Norwich C	W 4-0	4-0	8	Fashanu 2, Barton, Scales	12,324
16		8	H	QPR	W 3-0	1-0	6	McGee, Fashanu 2	5358
17		15	A	Arsenal	D 2-2	1-2	8	Kruszynski, Fashanu	30,163
18		22	H	Manchester U	L 1-3	1-0	10	Fashanu	9744
19		26	A	Nottingham F	L 1-2	1-2	10	Fashanu	16,221
20		29	A	Leeds U	L 0-3	0-3	10		29,292
21	Jan	1	H	Luton T	W 2-0	1-0	9	Fashanu, Cork	4521
22		12	H	Derby Co	W 3-1	0-0	8	Gibson, Fashanu 2 (1 pen)	4724
23		19	A	Liverpool	D 1-1	0-1	7	Barton	35,030
24	Feb	2	H	Coventry C	W 1-0	0-0	7	Gibson	3981
25		16	A	Chelsea	D 0-0	0-0	8		13,378
26		23	H	Tottenham H	W 5-1	1-0	6	McGee, Curle, Gibson, Fashanu, Cork	10,303
27	Mar	2	H	Norwich C	D 0-0	0-0	6		4041
28		16	A	Manchester C	D 1-1	1-1	7	Fashanu	21,089
29		23	H	Sheffield U	D 1-1	1-0	6	Cork	7031
30		30	H	Nottingham F	W 3-1	1-1	6	Fashanu, McGee, Clarke	6392
31	Apr	2	A	Manchester U	L 1-2	1-0	—	Clarke	36,660
32		6	H	Leeds U	L 0-1	0-1	7		6800
33		10	A	Everton	W 2-1	1-1	—	Fashanu, Clarke	14,590
34		13	A	Luton T	W 1-0	0-0	7	Fashanu	8219
35		20	A	Aston Villa	W 2-1	1-1	7	Fashanu, Newhouse	17,001
36		23	A	Sunderland	D 0-0	0-0	—		24,036
37	May	4	H	Crystal Palace	L 0-3	0-0	7		10,002
38		11	A	Southampton	D 1-1	0-1	7	Fashanu	17,052

Final League Position: 7

GOALSCORERS

League (53): Fashanu 20 (1 pen), McGee 6, Cork 5, Gibson 5, Barton 3, Clarke 3, Kruszynski 2, Scales 2, Cotterill 1, Curle 1, Fairweather 1, Gayle 1, Newhouse 1, own goals 2.
Rumbelows Cup (0).
FA Cup (2): Cork 1, McGee 1.

Segers	Joseph	Phelan	Barton	Scales	Curle	Cork	Miller	Fashanu	Sanchez	Fairweather	Kruszynski	Blackwell	Gayle	McGee	Cotterill	Bennett	Newhouse	Gibson	Elkins	Clarke	Anthrobus	Ryan	Sullivan	Ardley	Match No.
1	2	3	4†	5	6	7	8*	9	10	11	12	14													1
1	2	3	4	5	6			9	10			8	12	7*	11										2
1	2	3	4	5	6	12		9	10			8†	14	7*	11										3
1	2	3	4	5	6	12		9	10			8†	14	7	11*										4
1	2	3	4	5	6	12		9*10				8		7	11										5
1	2	3	4	5	6	12		9†10		11*		8		7	14										6
1	2	3	4		6	9		10				8	5	7	12			11*							7
1	2	3	4		6	9		12	10*11			8	5	7											8
1	2*	3	4	10	6	11†		9			12	8	5	7	14										9
1	2	3*	4	10	6	11†		9	14		12	8	5	7											10
1	2	3	4	10	6			9				8	5	7				11*	12						11
1	2	3†	4*10	6	11			14			8	5	7					12	9						12
1	2		4	10	6	11			14		8	5	7†					12	9*	3					13
1	2	3†	4	10	6	12		9	14		8	5	7				11*								14
1	2	3	4	10	6			9	12		8*	5	7				11								15
1	2	3	4	10	6			9			8	5	7				11								16
1	2	3	4	10	6	12		9			8	5	7*				11								17
1	2	3	4	10	6			9	12		8	5*	7				11								18
1	2	3	4	10	6	12		9			8	5	7				11*								19
1	2	3	4	10	6	12		9	8†			14		7				11*							20
1	2	3	4	10	6	12		9*			8	5	7				11								21
1	2	3	4		6	12		9	10		8	5	7				11*								22
1	2	3	4	10	6	12		9*			8	5	7				11								23
1	2	3	4	10	6			9			8	5	7				11								24
1	2	3	4	10	6			9	12		8*	5	7				11								25
1	2	3	4	10	6	12		9	14		8†	5	7*				11								26
1	2		4	10	6	12		9	5		8		7*				11†		3	14					27
1	2		4*10	6	12			9	8		5		7				11†		3	14					28
1	2		4	10	6	11		9			8	5	7*					12	3						29
1	2		4	10	6	11*		9	8		5		7†	14				12	3						30
1	2		4*10	6	12			9	8		5			14				3	7	11†					31
1	2		4	10	6	12		9*	8		5†			14				3	7	11					32
1	2		4	10	6			9	8*		5	11			14			3†	7		12				33
1	2		4	11	6			9	8		5						12	10*	3	7					34
	2	3		11	6			9			5		10	12			7			4	1	8*			35
1	2	3	4	10	6			9	8		5	11*					12	7							36
1	2	3	4*11	6				9	10		5		7	12			8								37
1	2	3	4	7	6			9	10		5			8			12	11*							38
37	38	29	37	36	37	9	1	34	21	3	25	31	7	26	4	1	1	18	10	7	3	1	1	1	

Substitute appearances: + 16s — + + + + + 1s 8s 2s 2s 4s + 1s + + + 5s 7s 1s + 5s + 1s

Rumbelows Cup	Second Round	Plymouth Arg (a)	0-1
		(h)	0-2
FA Cup	Third Round	Aston Villa (a)	1-1
		(h)	1-0
	Fourth Round	Shrewsbury T (a)	0-1

WIMBLEDON

Player and Position	Ht	Wt	Birth Date	Birth Place	Source	Clubs	League App	Gls
Goalkeepers								
David Hudson*			11 2 72	Dagenham	Trainee	Wimbledon	—	—
Hans Segers	5 11	12 07	30 10 61	Eindhoven	PSV Eindhoven	Nottingham F	58	—
						Stoke C (loan)	1	—
						Sheffield U (loan)	10	—
						Dunfermline Ath (loan)	4	—
						Wimbledon	108	—
Neil Sullivan	6 0	12 01	24 2 70	Sutton	Trainee	Wimbledon	1	—
Defenders								
Warren Barton	6 0	11 00	19 3 69	London	Leytonstone/ Ilford	Maidstone U	42	—
						Wimbledon	37	3
Dean Blackwell	6 1	12 10	5 12 69	London	Trainee	Wimbledon	38	—
						Plymouth Arg (loan)	7	—
Keith Curle	6 0	11 09	14 11 63	Bristol	Bristol	Bristol R	32	4
						Torquay U	16	5
						Bristol C	121	1
						Reading	40	—
						Wimbledon	93	3
Gerald Dobbs	5 8	11 07	24 1 71	London	Trainee	Wimbledon	—	—
Gary Elkins	5 8	10 10	4 5 66	Wallingford	Apprentice	Fulham	104	2
						Exeter C (loan)	5	—
						Wimbledon	10	—
Scott Fitzgerald	6 0	12 02	13 8 69	London	Trainee	Wimbledon	1	—
Roger Joseph	5 11	11 13	24 12 65	Paddington	Juniors	Brentford	104	2
						Wimbledon	88	—
Brian McAllister	5 11	12 05	30 11 70	Glasgow	Trainee	Wimbledon	3	—
						Plymouth Arg (loan)	8	—
Terry Phelan	5 8	10 00	16 3 67	Manchester		Leeds U	14	—
						Swansea C	45	—
						Wimbledon	122	—
John Scales	6 0	12 02	4 7 66	Harrogate		Leeds U		
						Bristol R	72	2
						Wimbledon	127	10
Midfield								
Neil Ardley§			1 9 72	Epsom	Trainee	Wimbledon	1	—
Michael Bennett	5 10	11 11	27 7 69	London	Apprentice	Charlton Ath	35	2
						Wimbledon	13	1
Detsi Kruszynski	6 0	12 12	14 10 61	Divschav	Homburg	Wimbledon	70	4
Paul McGee	5 6	9 10	17 5 68	Dublin	Bohemians	Colchester U	3	—
						Wimbledon	41	7
Aiden Newhouse	6 0	12 00	23 5 72	Wallasey	Trainee	Chester C	44	6
						Wimbledon	10	1
Matthew Pearson*			16 1 72	Aylesbury	Trainee	Wimbledon	—	—
Mark Quamina	5 10	11 07	25 11 69	St Helier	Trainee	Wimbledon	1	—
Vaughan Ryan	5 8	10 12	2 9 68	Westminster		Wimbledon	61	1
						Sheffield U (loan)	3	—
Lawrie Sanchez	5 11	11 07	22 10 59	Lambeth	Amateur	Reading	262	28
						Wimbledon	212	24
Forwards								
Steve Anthrobus	6 2	12 13	10 11 68	Lewisham		Millwall	21	4
						Southend U (loan)	—	—
						Wimbledon	13	—

WIMBLEDON

Foundation: Old boys from Central School formed this club as Wimbledon Old Centrals in 1889. Their earliest successes were in the Clapham League before switching to the Southern Suburban League in 1902.

First Football League game: 20 August, 1978, Division 4, v Halifax T (h) D 3–3 – Guy; Bryant (1), Galvin, Donaldson, Aitken, Davies, Galliers, Smith, Connell (1), Holmes, Leslie (1).

Did you know: When Wimbledon won 1-0 at Burnley in the FA Cup in 1974–75, they were the first non-League club to perform such a feat since Darlington won at Sheffield Wednesday 55 years earlier.

Managers (and Secretary-managers)
Les Henley 1955–71, Mike Everitt 1971–73, Dick Graham 1973–74, Allen Batsford 1974–78, Dario Gradi 1978–81, Dave Bassett 1981–87, Bobby Gould 1987–90, Ray Harford June 1990– .

Player and Position	Ht	Wt	Birth Date	Place	Source	Clubs	League App	Gls
Andy Clarke	5 10	11 07	22 7 67	London	Barnet	Wimbledon	12	3
Alan Cork	6 0	12 00	4 3 59	Derby	Amateur	Derby Co	—	—
						Lincoln C (loan)	5	—
						Wimbledon	411	143
Steve Cotterill	6 1	12 05	20 7 64	Cheltenham	Burton Albion	Wimbledon	10	3
Carlton Fairweather	5 11	11 00	22 9 61	London	Tooting	Wimbledon	132	26
John Fashanu	6 1	11 12	18 9 62	Kensington	Amateur	Cambridge U	—	—
						Norwich C	7	1
						C Palace (loan)	1	—
						Lincoln C	36	10
						Millwall	50	12
						Wimbledon	173	72
Terry Gibson	5 5	10 00	23 12 62	Walthamstow	Apprentice	Tottenham H	18	4
						Coventry C	98	43
						Manchester U	23	1
						Wimbledon	71	21
Paul Miller	6 0	11 00	31 1 68	Bisley	Trainee	Wimbledon	39	7
						Newport Co (loan)	6	2
						Bristol C (loan)	3	—

Trainees
Alexander, Timothy M; Allen, Leighton G; Ardley, Neal C; Bond, Wayne W; Bullen, Michael N.J; Castledine, Stewart M; Fear, Peter S; Jennings, Paul; McCarthy, Jamie; Marchant, Giles R; Orriss, Craig J; Payne, Grant; Perry, Christopher J; Rootes, Michael G; Skinner, Justin J; Taylor, Geoffrey J.

Associated Schoolboys
Adams, Nathan; Archer, Jay; Bassey, Simon J; Bevis, Colin; Bowdery, David J; Bower, Mathew; Bray, Dean M; Brooker, Daniel P; Chapman, Darren P; D'Rubbo, Franco; Evell, Jason J; Fell, Gavin A; Gurr, Paul K; Jones, David G; Jones, Lee; Laidlaw, Iain L; Laker, Barry J; McCormack, David R; Payne, Gary; Phillips, Leon A; Smith, Mathew A; Thompson, Ian; Williams, Christopher J.

Associated Schoolboys who have accepted the club's offer of a Traineeship/Contract
Fairbairn, Neil; Mosley, David; Swift, Kieron; Thomas, Mark.

WOLVERHAMPTON WANDERERS 1990–91 *Back row (left to right):* Steve Bull. Robbie Dennison. Mark Venus. Vince Bartram. Mike Stowell. Tony Lange. Paul Jones. Paul Cook. Andy Mutch.

Centre row: Tim Steele. Rob Hindmarch. Nicky Clarke. Gary Bellamy. John Paskin. Shane Westley. Tom Bennett.

Front row: Andy Thompson. Keith Downing. Garry Pendrey (Coach). Barry Powell (Youth Team Coach). Graham Turner (Coach). Paul Darby (Physiotherapist). Brian Roberts. Paul McLoughlin.

Division 2 **WOLVERHAMPTON WANDERERS**

Molineux Grounds, Wolverhampton WV1 4QR. Telephone Admin office: Wolverhampton (0902) 712181; lottery shop: (0902) 27524. Commercial Office: (0902) 23166.

Ground capacity: 25,000.

Record attendance: 61,315 v Liverpool, FA Cup 5th rd, 11 February 1939.

Record receipts: £110,623 v Sheffield W, FA Cup 3rd rd, 6 January 1990.

Pitch measurements: 115yd × 72yd.

President: Sir Jack Hayward.

Chairman: Jack Harris.

Directors: Jonathan Hayward, Billy Wright, John Harris, Nic Stones.

Team Manager: Graham Turner.

Coaches: Gary Pendrey and Barry Powell. *Physio:* Paul Darby.

Chief Executive:

Secretary: Keither Pearson ACIS. *Commercial Manager:* Keith Butler.

Year Formed: 1877*(see Foundation). *Turned Professional:* 1888. *Ltd Co.:* 1982.

Club Nickname: 'Wolves'.

Previous Grounds: 1877, Goldthorn Hill; 1884, Dudley Road; 1889, Molineux.

Previous Names: 1880, St Luke's, Blakenhall combined with The Wanderers to become Wolverhampton Wanderers (1923) Ltd until 1982.

Record League Victory: 10-1 v Leicester C, Division 1, 15 April 1938 – Sidlow; Morris, Dowen; Galley, Cullis, Gardiner; Maguire (1), Horace Wright, Westcott (4), Jones (1), Dorsett (4).

Record Cup Victory: 14-0 v Cresswell's Brewery, FA Cup, 2nd rd, 13 November 1886 – I. Griffiths; Baugh, Mason; Pearson, Allen (1), Lowder; Hunter (4), Knight (2), Brodie (4), B. Griffiths (2), Wood. Plus one goal 'scrambled through'.

Record Defeat: 1-10 v Newton Heath, Division 1, 15 October 1892.

Most League Points (2 for a win): 64, Division 1, 1957–58.

Most League Points (3 for a win): 92, Division 4, 1988–89.

Most League Goals: 115, Division 2, 1931–32.

Highest League Scorer in Season: Dennis Westcott, 38, Division 1, 1946–47.

Most League Goals in Total Aggregate: Bill Hartill, 164, 1928–35.

Most Capped Player: Billy Wright, 105, England (70 consecutive).

Most League Appearances: Derek Parkin, 501, 1967–82.

Record Transfer Fee Received: £1,150,000 from Manchester C for Steve Daley, September 1979.

Record Transfer Fee Paid: £1,175,000 to Aston Villa for Andy Gray, September 1979.

Football League Record: 1888 Founder Member of Football League: 1906–23 Division 2; 1923–24 Division 3 (N); 1924–32 Division 2; 1932–65 Division 1; 1965–67 Division 2; 1967–76 Division 1; 1976–77 Division 2; 1977–82 Division 1; 1982–83 Division 2; 1983–84 Division 1; 1984–85 Division 2; 1985–86 Division 3; 1986–88 Division 4; 1988–89 Division 3; 1989– Division 2.

Honours: Football League: Division 1 – Champions 1953–54, 1957–58, 1958–59; Runners-up 1937–38, 1938–39, 1949–50, 1954–55, 1959–60; Division 2 – Champions 1931–32, 1976–77; Runners-up 1966–67, 1982–83; Division 3 (N) – Champions 1923–24; Division 3 – Champions 1988–89; Division 4 – Champions 1987–88. *FA Cup:* Winners 1893, 1908, 1949, 1960; Runners-up 1889, 1896, 1921, 1939. *Football League Cup:* Winners 1973–74, 1979–80. *Texaco Cup:* 1970–71. *Sherpa Van Trophy:* Winners 1988. **European Competitions:** *European Cup:* 1958–59, 1959–60. *European Cup-Winners' Cup:* 1960–61. *UEFA Cup:* 1971–72 (runners-up), 1973–74, 1974–75, 1980–81.

Colours: Gold shirts, black shorts, gold stockings. **Change colours:** All sky blue.

WOLVERHAMPTON WANDERERS 1990–91 LEAGUE RECORD

Match No.	Date		Venue	Opponents	Result		H/T Score	Lg. Pos.	Goalscorers	Attendance
1	Aug	25	H	Oldham Ath	L	2-3	1-1	—	Bull 2	20,864
2		28	A	Port Vale	W	2-1	2-1	—	Bellamy, Bull	12,349
3	Sept	1	A	Brighton & HA	D	1-1	1-0	8	Cook	9820
4		8	H	Bristol R	D	1-1	1-1	12	Dennison	17,912
5		15	A	West Ham U	D	1-1	0-1	13	Bull	23,241
6		18	A	Swindon T	L	0-1	0-0	—		12,228
7		22	H	Plymouth Arg	W	3-1	3-1	13	Bull 2, Mutch	15,137
8		29	A	Oxford U	D	1-1	1-1	12	Dennison	7418
9	Oct	2	H	Charlton Ath	W	3-0	1-0	—	Bull 2, Thompson	14,363
10		6	H	Bristol C	W	4-0	2-0	6	Thompson, Bull 3	17,891
11		13	A	Notts Co	D	1-1	1-0	7	Westley	12,833
12		20	A	Hull C	W	2-1	0-1	5	Bull, Dennison	7144
13		23	H	Middlesbrough	W	1-0	0-0	—	Bull	17,285
14		27	H	Blackburn R	L	2-3	0-2	5	Cook, Steele	17,776
15	Nov	3	A	Portsmouth	D	0-0	0-0	6		14,574
16		10	H	Newcastle U	W	2-1	1-1	5	Steele, Bellamy	18,721
17		17	A	Leicester C	L	0-1	0-1	5		16,574
18		24	A	Barnsley	D	1-1	1-1	5	Cook	9267
19	Dec	1	H	Ipswich T	D	2-2	1-2	5	Bull 2	15,803
20		15	A	Oldham Ath	L	1-4	1-1	6	Thompson	11,587
21		22	H	Millwall	W	4-1	2-1	6	Bellamy, Bull, Taylor 2	14,504
22		26	A	Sheffield W	D	2-2	0-2	6	Cook, Bull	29,686
23		29	A	WBA	D	1-1	0-0	6	Hindmarch	28,497
24	Jan	1	H	Watford	D	0-0	0-0	7		18,159
25		12	H	Brighton & HA	L	2-3	1-2	8	Bull, Mutch	12,788
26		19	A	Bristol R	D	1-1	1-1	8	Twentyman (og)	6042
27	Feb	2	H	West Ham U	W	2-1	1-0	8	Birch, Bull	19,454
28		23	A	Newcastle U	D	0-0	0-0	9		18,612
29		26	H	Port Vale	W	3-1	2-1	—	Bull 2, Mutch	15,919
30	Mar	2	A	Ipswich T	D	0-0	0-0	8		13,350
31		5	H	Leicester C	W	2-1	1-1	—	Bull, Mutch	15,707
32		9	H	Barnsley	L	0-5	0-3	7		15,671
33		12	A	Charlton Ath	L	0-1	0-0	—		6853
34		16	H	Oxford U	D	3-3	3-0	9	Bull 3	11,357
35		19	A	Notts Co	L	0-2	0-2	—		12,375
36		23	A	Bristol C	D	1-1	0-0	10	Dennison	15,499
37		30	H	Sheffield W	W	3-2	2-0	10	Mutch 2, Bull	18,011
38	Apr	3	A	Millwall	L	1-2	1-1	—	Cook	13,780
39		6	H	WBA	D	2-2	1-1	10	Dennison, Mutch	22,982
40		9	A	Plymouth Arg	L	0-1	0-0	—		7618
41		13	A	Watford	L	1-3	0-1	12	Cook (pen)	12,014
42		16	H	Swindon T	L	1-2	1-1	—	Hindmarch	9799
43		20	H	Hull C	D	0-0	0-0	13		9313
44		27	A	Middlesbrough	L	0-2	0-1	14		16,447
45	May	4	A	Blackburn R	D	1-1	1-1	15	Paskin	9560
46		11	H	Portsmouth	W	3-1	1-0	12	Birch, Mutch, Downing	12,570

Final League Position: 12

GOALSCORERS

League (63): Bull 26, Mutch 8, Cook 6 (1 pen), Dennison 5, Bellamy 3, Thompson 3, Birch 2, Hindmarch 2, Steele 2, Taylor 2, Downing 1, Paskin 1, Westley 1, own goal 1.
Rumbelows Cup (1): Steele 1.
FA Cup (0).

Stowell	Roberts	Venus	Bellamy	Hindmarch	Downing	Thompson	Cook	Bull	Mutch	Dennison	Paskin	McLoughlin	Ashley	Steele	Westley	Bennett	Jones	Stancliffe	Taylor	Blake	Birch	Clarke	Todd	Burke	Lange	Bartram	Match No.
1	2	3	4	5	6	7	8	9	10	11																	1
1	2	3	4	5	6	7	8	9	10	11																	2
1	2	3	4	5	6	7	8	9*	10	11	12																3
1	2	3	4	5	6	7	8	9	10	11																	4
1	2†	3	4	5	6	7	8	9	10	11*	12	14															5
1		3	4	5	6	7	8	9	10	11			2														6
1			4	5	6	7	8	9	10	11*	12		2	3													7
1			4	5	6	7	8	9		11			2	3	10												8
1			4	5	6	7	8	9		11		12	2	3*	10												9
1			4	5	6	7	8	9		11		12	2†	3*	10	14											10
1			4	5	6	7†	8	9		11		12	2	3*	10	14											11
1	7		4	5	6		8	9		11			2	3	10												12
1	7		4	5	6	12	8	9		11*		10	2	3													13
1			4	5	6	7	8	9		11	12	10*	2	3													14
1			4	5	6	7	8	9		11		10	2	3													15
1			4		6	7	8	9		11		10	2	3				5									16
1			4		6	7	8	9		11		10*	2	3				5	12								17
1			4		6	7	8	9		11		10	2	3				5									18
1	2	3					8	9		11	12			7*		6		5	10								19
1	2		4	10	6	3	8	9		11*				7				5	12								20
1			4	5	6	3	8	9		11		7				2			10								21
1			4	5	6	3	8	9		11		7*	12			2			10								22
1	14		4	5	6	3	8*	9		11		7†	2	12	14												23
1	2		4	5		3		9		11	12			7		8		6	10*								24
1	2		4		6		8	9	10	11			3*	7		12		5									25
1	2		4			3	8	9	10	11						6		5		7							26
1			4			3	8	9	10	11*			12			2		5		6	7						27
1			4			3	8	9	10	11			6			2		5			7						28
1			4		6*	3	8	9	10	11						2		5			7		12				29
1			4			3	8*	9	10	11			6			2		5	12		7						30
1			4			3	8	9	10	11			6			2		5			7						31
1	11		4			3	8*	9	10				6			2		5†	12		7		14				32
1	3		4				8	9	10	11*			6			2		5	12†		7		14				33
1			4			3	8	9	10				12			2		5			7		6		11*		34
1	2		4	11		3	8	9	10				12					5			7			6*			35
1			4		6	3	8	9	10	11						2					7	5					36
1			4		6	3	8	9	10	11						2					7	5					37
1			4		6	3	8	9	10	11*			12			2					7	5					38
1†	14		4		6	3		9	10	11				8*		2					7	5	12				39
	6*		4			3		9	10	11						2					7	5	8	12		1	40
	14		4			3†	8	9	10	11						2*			12		7	5	6			1	41
			4			3	8	9*	10	11						2			12		7	5	6			1	42
			4			3	8	9*	10							2			11		7	5	6	12		1	43
	5		4		6	3	8†		10	11			9*			2					7	14	12			1	44
	14		4		6	3		9	10	11						2†			12		7	5		8*		1	45
			4†		6	3	8	9*	10	14						2			12		7	5			11	1	46
39	17	6	26	40	31	43	42	43	29	41	10	2	15	22	5	24	—	17	6	2	20	10	6	3	3	4	
	+				+						+	+	+	+					+	+		+	+	+	+		
	4s				1s						1s	5s	4s	1s	6s				2s	1s		9s	4s	1s	3s		

Rumbelows Cup Second Round Hull C (a) 0-0
                                 (h) 1-1
FA Cup Third Round Cambridge U (h) 0-1

WOLVERHAMPTON WANDERERS

Player and Position	Ht	Wt	Birth Date	Birth Place	Source	Clubs	League App	Gls
Goalkeepers								
Vincent Bartram	6 2	13 04	7 8 68	Birmingham	Amateur	Wolverhampton W	5	—
						Blackpool (loan)	9	—
						WBA (loan)	—	—
Tony Lange	6 0	12 09	10 12 64	London	Apprentice	Charlton Ath	12	—
						Aldershot (loan)	7	—
						Aldershot	125	—
						Wolverhampton W	8	—
						Aldershot (loan)	2	—
Mike Stowell	6 2	11 10	19 4 65	Preston	Leyland Motors	Preston NE	—	—
						Everton	—	—
						Chester C (loan)	14	—
						York C (loan)	6	—
						Manchester C (loan)	14	—
						Port Vale (loan)	7	—
						Wolverhampton W (loan)	7	—
						Preston NE (loan)	2	—
						Wolverhampton W	39	—
Defenders								
Kevin Ashley	5 7	10 04	31 12 68	Birmingham	Apprentice	Birmingham C	57	1
						Wolverhampton W	16	—
Gary Bellamy	6 2	11 05	4 7 62	Worksop	Apprentice	Chesterfield	184	7
						Wolverhampton W	132	9
Tom Bennett	5 11	11 08	12 12 69	Falkirk	Trainee	Aston Villa	—	—
						Wolverhampton W	58	—
David Butler*	5 11	11 05	19 7 72	Stafford	Trainee	Wolverhampton W	—	—
Nicky Clarke	5 11	12 00	20 8 67	Walsall	Apprentice	Wolverhampton W	80	1
Stuart Evans*	6 2	11 07	1 3 72	Poole	Trainee	Wolverhampton W	—	—
Neville Fennell*	5 09	12 05	21 10 71	Wolverhampton	Trainee	Wolverhampton W	—	—
Rob Hindmarch	6 1	13 4	27 4 61	Stannington	Apprentice	Sunderland	115	2
						Portsmouth (loan)	2	—
						Derby Co	164	9
						Wolverhampton W	40	2
Stuart Leeding	5 8	9 10	6 1 72	Wolverhampton	Trainee	Wolverhampton W	—	—
Brian Roberts	5 8	11 07	6 11 55	Manchester	Apprentice	Coventry C	215	1
						Hereford U (loan)	5	—
						Birmingham C	187	—
						Wolverhampton W	21	—
Paul Stancliffe*	6 2	12 13	5 5 58	Sheffield	Apprentice	Rotherham U	285	8
						Sheffield U	278	12
						Rotherham U (loan)	5	—
						Wolverhampton W	17	—
Mark Venus	6 0	11 08	6 4 67	Hartlepool		Hartlepool U	4	—
						Leicester C	61	1
						Wolverhampton W	89	2
Shane Westley	6 2	12 10	16 6 65	Canterbury	Apprentice	Charlton Ath	8	—
						Southend U	144	10
						Norwich C (loan)	—	—
						Wolverhampton W	42	1
Midfield								
Paul Birch	5 6	10 09	20 11 62	West Bromwich	Apprentice	Aston Villa	173	16
						Wolverhampton W	20	2
Paul Cook	5 11	10 10	22 2 67	Liverpool		Wigan Ath	83	14
						Norwich C	6	—
						Wolverhampton W	70	8
Robert Dennison	5 7	11 00	30 4 63	Banbridge	Glenavon	WBA	16	1
						Wolverhampton W	184	27
Keith Downing	5 8	11 00	23 7 65	Oldbury	Mile Oak	Notts Co	23	1
						Wolverhampton W	128	6
Paul Jones*	5 9	10 04	6 9 65	Walsall	Apprentice	Walsall	143	15
						Wrexham (loan)	5	—
						Wolverhampton W	14	—
Loy Stobart*	5 7	11 02	6 2 72	Wolverhampton	Nottingham F	Wolverhampton W	—	—
Andy Thompson	5 4	10 06	9 11 67	Carnock	Apprentice	WBA	24	1
						Wolverhampton W	194	23

WOLVERHAMPTON WANDERERS

Foundation: Another club where precise details of information are confused, due in part to the existence of an earlier Wolverhampton club which played rugby. However, it is now considered likely that it came into being in 1879 when players from St. Luke's (founded 1877) and Goldthorn (founded 1876) broke away to form Wolverhampton Wanderers Association FC.

First Football League game: 8 September, 1888, Football League, v Aston Villa (h) D 1-1 – Baynton; Baugh, Mason; Fletcher, Allen, Lowder; Hunter, Cooper, Anderson, White, Cannon. Scorer – Cox o.g.

Did you know: But for his international commitments Billy Wright's longest run of consecutive League games for Wolves would have been 88. However, England matches did not interfere with FA Cup ties and he made 44 consecutive appearances for Wolves in this competition 1947–59.

Managers (and Secretary-managers)
George Worrall 1877–85*, John Addenbrooke 1885–1922, George Jobey 1922–24, Albert Hoskins 1924–26 (had been secretary since 1922), Fred Scotchbrook 1926–27, Major Frank Buckley 1927–44, Ted Vizard 1944–48, Stan Cullis 1948–64, Andy Beattie 1964–65, Ronnie Allen 1966–68, Bill McGarry 1968–76, Sammy Chung 1976–78, John Barnwell 1978–81, Ian Greaves 1982, Graham Hawkins 1982–84, Tommy Docherty 1984–85, Bill McGarry 1985, Sammy Chapman 1985–86, Brian Little 1986, Graham Turner October 1986–   .

Player and Position	Ht	Wt	Birth Date	Place	Source	Clubs	League App	Gls
Forwards								
Steve Bull	5 11	11 04	28 3 65	Tipton	Apprentice	WBA	4	2
						Wolverhampton W	204	135
Mark Burke	5 10	11 08	12 2 69	Solihull	Apprentice	Aston Villa	7	—
						Middlesbrough	57	6
						Darlington (loan)	5	1
						Ipswich T (loan)	—	—
						Wolverhampton W	6	—
Paul McLoughlin	5 10	10 07	23 12 63	Bristol	Bristol C	Cardiff C	49	4
					Gisborne C	Hereford U	74	14
						Wolverhampton W	25	4
Andy Mutch	5 10	11 00	28 12 63	Liverpool	Southport	Wolverhampton W	213	78
John Paskin	5 10	11 10	1 2 62	Capetown	Seiko	WBA	25	5
						Wolverhampton W	32	3
Darren Smith	5 11	12 00	29 4 70	Nottingham	Burton Alb	Wolverhampton W	—	—
Tim Steele	5 9	11 00	1 2 67	Coventry	Apprentice	Shrewsbury T	61	5
						Wolverhampton W	54	4
Colin Taylor	6 0	12 07	25 12 71	Liverpool	Trainee	Wolverhampton W	15	2

Trainees
Bradbury, Shaun; Clarke, Mathew L; Collier, Daniel J; Davies, Mark; De Bont, Andrew C; Farrington, Jamie G; Garner, Jamie; Harnett, Andrew J; Howard, Jonathan M; Jones, Warren G; Kelly, Andrew; Morgan, Stephen W; Nicholls, Alan; Owen, John G; Owen, Steven; Read, David L; Scandrett, Raymond P; Tonner, Ian S.; Warmer, Gary R.P.

Associated Schoolboys
Barnett, Jason; Benton, Stuart A; Brodie, Craig K; Chamberlain, Sion; Dale, David A; Dale, Matthew J; Davis, Gari; Graham, Iain; Hanbury, Jay P; Hughes, Stephen; Innes, Michael P; Jones, Samuel O; McCabe, Richard; Macbeth, Andrew M; Male, Neil J; Mills, Shaun; Owen, Adrian J; Owen, Darren W; Rees, Elian W; Robyns, Gethin; Taylor, James M; Taylor, Jamie; Upton, Steven; Warr, John R; Wilkinson, Stephen J; Williams, Eifion W.

Associated Schoolboys who have accepted the club's offer of a Traineeship/Contract
Goode, Mark G; Piearce, Steven; Smith, Jason J; Voice, Scott H.

WREXHAM 1990–91 *Back row (left to right):* Cliff Sear (Youth Team Coach), George Showell (Physiotherapist), Chris Armstrong; Mark Morris, Andy Preece, Vince O'Keefe. Nigel Beaumont, Mark Sertori, Joey Jones (Player Coach), Kevin Reeves (Assistant Manager).

Centre row: Mike Williams, Geoff Hunter, Robbie Barnes, Wayne Phillips, Brian Flynn (Manager). Jon Bowden, Darren Wright, Alan Kennedy, Sean Reck. Mike Rigg (Community Scheme Organiser).

Front row: Gary Worthington, Robert Jones, Graham Cooper, David O'Gorman, Steven Weaver, Gareth Owen, Andy Thackeray.

Division 4 **WREXHAM**

Racecourse Ground, Mold Road, Wrexham. Telephone Wrexham (0978) 262129. Commercial Dept: (0978) 352536. Fax: (0978) 357821. Clubcall: 0898 121642.

Ground capacity: 17,500.

Record attendance: 34,445 v Manchester U, FA Cup 4th rd, 26 January 1957.

Record receipts: £89,036 v Manchester U, European Cup Winners' Cup, 2nd rd, 2nd leg, 7 November 1991.

Pitch measurements: 111yd × 71yd.

President: G. Mytton.

Chairman: W. P. Griffiths.

Vice-chairman/Managing Director: D. L. Rhodes.

Directors: C. Griffiths, S. Mackreth, G. Palletta, B. Williams.

Manager: Brian Flynn. *Assistant Manager:* Kevin Reeves.

Secretary: D. L. Rhodes. *Player-coach:* Joey Jones.

Commercial Manager: P. Stokes. *Physio:* Steve Wade.

Year Formed: 1873 (oldest club in Wales).

Turned Professional: 1912. *Ltd Co.:* 1912.

Previous Ground: Acton Park.

Club Nickname: 'Robins'.

Record League Victory: 10-1 v Hartlepools, Division 4, 3 March 1962 – Keelan; Peter Jones, McGavan; Tecwyn Jones, Fox, Ken Barnes; Ron Barnes (3), Bennion (1), Davies (3), Ambler (3), Ron Roberts.

Record Cup Victory: 6-0 v Gateshead, FA Cup, 1st rd, 20 November 1976 – Lloyd; Evans, Whittle, Davis, Roberts, Thomas (Hill), Shinton (3 incl. 1p), Sutton, Ashcroft (2), Lee (1), Griffiths. 6-0 v Charlton Ath, FA Cup, 3rd rd, 5 January 1980 – Davies; Darracott, Kenworthy, Davis, Jones (Hill), Fox, Vinter (3), Sutton, Edwards (1), McNeil (2), Carrodus.

Record Defeat: 0-9 v Brentford, Division 3, 15 October 1963.

Most League Points (2 for a win): 61, Division 4, 1969–70 and Division 3, 1977–78.

Most League Points (3 for a win): 71, Division 4, 1988–89.

Most League Goals: 106, Division 3 (N), 1932–33.

Highest League Scorer in Season: Tom Bamford, 44, Division 3 (N), 1933–34.

Most League Goals in Total Aggregate: Tom Bamford, 175, 1928–34.

Most Capped Player: Dai Davies, 28 (51), Wales.

Most League Appearances: Arfon Griffiths, 592, 1959–61, 1962–79.

Record Transfer Fee Received: £300,000 from Manchester U for Mickey Thomas, November 1978 and from Manchester C for Bobby Shinton, July 1979.

Record Transfer Fee Paid: £210,000 to Liverpool for Joey Jones, October 1978.

Football League Record: 1921 Original Member of Division 3 (N); 1958–60 Division 3; 1960–62 Division 4; 1962–64 Division 3; 1964–70 Division 4; 1970–78 Division 3; 1978–82 Division 2; 1982–83 Division 3; 1983– Division 4.

Honours: Football League: Division 2 best season: 15th, 1978–79; Division 3 – Champions 1977–78; Division 3 (N) – Runners-up 1932–33; Division 4 – Runners-up 1969–70. *FA Cup:* best season: 6th rd, 1973–74, 1977–78. *Football League Cup:* best season: 5th rd, 1961, 1978. *Welsh Cup:* Winners 21 times. Runners-up 19 times. Record number of victories and appearances in finals. **European Competition:** *European Cup-Winners' Cup:* 1972–73, 1975–76, 1978–79, 1979–80, 1984–85, 1986–87, 1990–91.

Colours: Red shirts, white shorts, red stockings. **Change colours:** Green shirts, yellow shorts, green stockings.

WREXHAM 1990–91 LEAGUE RECORD

Match No.	Date	Venue	Opponents	Result	H/T Score	Lg. Pos.	Goalscorers	Attendance
1	Aug 25	H	Peterborough U	D	0-0	0-0	—	2863
2	Sept 1	A	Doncaster R	L	1-3	1-2	20	Preece	2101
3	8	H	Aldershot	W	4-2	1-1	11	Thackeray, Cooper 2, Worthington	2704
4	15	A	Blackpool	L	1-4	1-2	17	Worthington	3497
5	22	H	Darlington	D	1-1	0-1	18	Armstrong	1908
6	29	H	Chesterfield	D	1-1	0-1	17	Armstrong	2147
7	Oct 5	A	Cardiff C	L	0-1	0-1	—		3452
8	13	H	Scarborough	L	1-2	1-0	23	Reck	2486
9	16	A	Torquay U	L	0-1	0-1	—		3577
10	20	H	Hartlepool U	D	2-2	0-1	23	Beaumont, Worthington	1733
11	27	A	Gillingham	W	3-2	1-1	22	Armstrong, Watkin, Thackeray	3077
12	31	A	Maidstone U	W	2-0	1-0	—	Armstrong, Owen	1668
13	Nov 3	H	Burnley	L	2-4	0-1	21	Armstrong 2	3997
14	9	A	Northampton T	L	0-1	0-0	—		3855
15	24	H	Scunthorpe U	W	1-0	0-0	19	Flynn	1333
16	Dec 1	H	Carlisle U	W	3-0	2-0	19	Worthington 2, Armstrong	1682
17	7	A	Scarborough	L	2-4	1-4	—	Armstrong, Hunter	625
18	15	A	Rochdale	L	0-2	0-0	19		1510
19	21	A	Walsall	L	0-1	0-1	—		4420
20	26	H	Hereford U	L	1-2	1-1	19	Preece	2109
21	29	H	York C	L	0-4	0-1	21		1698
22	Jan 1	A	Lincoln C	D	0-0	0-0	21		2527
23	4	A	Stockport Co	L	0-2	0-1	—		3021
24	12	H	Doncaster R	W	2-1	1-0	21	Ward 2	1850
25	19	A	Peterborough U	D	2-2	0-0	21	Armstrong, Hunter	3208
26	26	H	Blackpool	L	0-1	0-1	22		2393
27	Feb 5	A	Darlington	L	0-1	0-1	—		3279
28	23	H	Northampton T	L	0-2	0-2	22		1790
29	Mar 2	A	Carlisle U	L	0-2	0-0	22		2207
30	5	A	Aldershot	L	2-3	1-2	—	Hunter, Owen	1395
31	9	H	Rochdale	W	2-1	1-1	23	Jones L 2	1323
32	12	H	Halifax T	L	1-2	1-0	—	Jones L	1263
33	16	A	Chesterfield	L	1-2	0-0	24	Worthington	3368
34	22	H	Cardiff C	W	1-0	1-0	—	Bowden	1787
35	26	A	Halifax T	L	0-2	0-0	—		1429
36	30	A	Hereford U	L	0-1	0-0	24		2521
37	Apr 1	H	Walsall	D	1-1	0-1	24	Jones J	1588
38	6	A	York C	D	0-0	0-0	23		1490
39	9	H	Maidstone U	D	2-2	1-1	—	Preece, Bowden (pen)	1020
40	13	A	Lincoln C	D	2-2	0-1	23	Jones J, Bowden (pen)	1269
41	16	H	Stockport Co	L	1-3	0-2	—	Armstrong	1968
42	20	A	Hartlepool U	L	1-2	0-2	23	Jones R	3077
43	27	H	Torquay U	W	2-1	0-0	24	Bowden, Jones L	1281
44	May 4	H	Gillingham	W	3-0	0-0	23	Jones L, Bowden (pen), Preece	1231
45	7	A	Scunthorpe U	L	0-2	0-1	—		3572
46	11	A	Burnley	L	0-2	0-1	24		10,161

Final League Position: 24

GOALSCORERS

League (48): Armstrong 10, Worthington 6, Bowden 5 (3 pens), Jones L 5, Preece 4, Hunter 3, Cooper 2, Jones J 2, Owen 2, Thackeray 2, Ward 2, Beaumont 1, Flynn 1, Jones R 1, Reck 1, Watkin 1.
Rumbelows Cup (3): Worthington 2 (1 pen), Preece 1.
FA Cup (2): Preece 2.

O'Keefe	Phillips	Kennedy	Reck	Beaumont	Sertori	Cooper	Thackeray	Preece	Worthington	Bowden	Armstrong	Owen	Barnes	Morris	Flynn	Hardy	Watkin	Hunter	Jones J	Jones L	O'Gorman	Kelly	Ward	Carey	Jones R	Lunt	Griffiths	Murray	Match No.
1	2	3	4	5	6	7	8	9*	10	11	12																		1
1	2	3	4	5	6	7	8	9	10	11*	12																		2
1	2	3	4*	5	6	7	8	9	10	11		12																	3
1	2	3	4	5	6	7*	8	9	10	11	12																		4
1	2	3	4	5	6	7*	8	9	10	11	12																		5
1	2	3	4	5	6†	12	8	9*	10	11	7	14																	6
	2	3	4	5	6		8	9*	10	11†	7	12		1	14														7
		3	4	5	6	12	2	9*	10	11	7	8		1															8
6			4	5		12	2		10		9	8		1	7	3	11*												9
6			4	5			2	12	10		9	8		1	7	3	11*												10
	6	3†		5			2	12	10	14	9	8		1	7*		11	4											11
6			4	5			2		10		9	8		1		3	11	7											12
6			4	5		14	2	12	10		9	8		1		3	11*	7†											13
	2			5		7	11†	10		9*	8			1	3			4	6	12	14								14
			4*	5			11	10	2	9	8			1	6	3		7		12									15
				5			2	11	10	7	9	8		1	6*	3		4		12									16
				5	14		2	11	10	7	9	8*		1	6†	3		4		12									17
14				5	6		2†11	10	7	9				1	8*	3		4		12									18
2				5	6		8	11	10	7	9			1		3		4											19
2				5*	6		8	11	10	7	9			1		3		4		12									20
2*				5	6		8	11	10	7	9	12		1	4	3													21
				5	4		2	11	10	7		8		1		3			6	9									22
				5	4		2	11	10	7	12	8		1		3			6	9*									23
2				5	6		4		10	7	9*	8		1		3				12		11							24
2					6		4	10*	7	9	8†			1		3			14	12		11	5						25
2					6		4†	10	7	9*	8			1		3			14	12		11	5						26
2					6				7					1	8*	3	11†	4	14	9	12	10	5						27
2				5	6		12		7	11	8			1		3	10*	4†	14	9									28
2				5				10	7	12	8			1	4*	3	11		6	9									29
2				5			11*		7		8			1		3	9	4†	6	10		12		14					30
				5			2	11		7	9*	8		1		3		4	6	10	12								31
				5			2		10	7		8		1		3		4	6	9	11*					12			32
				5			2		10	7	9	8		1			4*	6	11†	12				3	14				33
				5			2			7	9	8		1			4	6	10					3	12	11*			34
				5			2			7	9*	8		1		3		4	6	10†	12				14	11			35
				5			2	10				8†		1		3		4	6	9*12					14	11	7		36
14				5			2	11		7	9*			1		3	4†	6	10	12						8			37
2†				5	14		4	10*		7	9			1		3		6		12					11	8			38
				4			2	10		7	9*			1		3		6		12	5				11	8			39
				4			2	10		7	12			1		3		6	5	9*					11	8			40
12				4			2*10			7	9			1			5	6					3		11	8			41
12				4			2	10		7	9†			1			5*	6	14				3		11	8			42
				4			2	10		7	12			1		3		6	9	5*					11	8			43
				4			2	10		7*	5			1		3		6	9	12				14	11†	8			44
		12		4			2	10		7				1	3*			6	14	9	5				11	8†			45
		3		4			2	10		7				1				6	9	5				12	11	8*			46
6	24	9	13	36	27	5	41	31	29	39	30	24	—	40	10	32	9	22	21	13	8	2	4	3	5	1	11	11	
+			+	+	+		+	+	+	+	+	+		+				+			+	+	+		+	+			
4s			1s	2s	4s		3s	1s	1s	8s	3s	1s		1s				2s			5s	9s	10s		1s	7s			

WREXHAM

Player and Position	Ht	Wt	Birth Date	Place	Source	Clubs	League App	Gls
Goalkeepers								
Mark Morris	5 11	12 00	1 8 68	Chester		Wrexham	55	—
Vince O'Keefe	6 2	13 00	2 4 57	Coleshill	Local	Birmingham C	—	—
						Peterborough U (loan)	—	—
						Walsall	—	—
					AP Leamington	Exeter C	53	—
						Torquay U	108	—
						Blackburn R	68	—
						Bury (loan)	2	—
						Blackpool (loan)	7	—
						Wrexham	49	—
Defenders								
Robert Barnes‡	5 8	10 08	26 11 69	Stoke	Trainee	Manchester C	—	—
						Wrexham	9	—
Nigel Beaumont	6 1	12 07	11 2 67	Pontefract		Bradford C	2	—
						Wrexham	101	4
Phil Hardy			9 4 73	Chester		Wrexham	33	—
Joey Jones	5 10	11 07	4 3 55	Llandudno	Amateur	Wrexham	98	2
						Liverpool	72	3
						Wrexham	146	6
						Chelsea	78	2
						Huddersfield T	68	3
						Wrexham	121	11
Robert Jones*			12 11 71	Liverpool	Crewe Alex	Wrexham	7	1
Alan Kennedy‡	5 9	10 07	31 8 54	Sunderland	Apprentice	Newcastle U	158	9
						Liverpool	251	15
						Sunderland	54	2
						Hartlepool U	5	—
						Wigan Ath	22	—
					Colne Dyn	Wrexham	16	—
Wayne Phillips	5 10	11 00	15 12 70	Bangor	Trainee	Wrexham	33	—
Mark Sertori	6 3	12 00	1 9 67	Manchester		Stockport Co	4	—
						Lincoln C	50	9
						Wrexham	47	2
Steve Weaver*			1 2 72	Chester	Trainee	Wrexham	33	—
Mike Williams	5 10	10 12	6 2 65	Mancot	Apprentice	Chester C	34	4
						Wrexham	178	3
Darren Wright*	5 10	11 04	14 3 68	West Bromwich	Apprentice	Wolverhampton W	1	—
						Wrexham	110	4
Midfield								
John Bowden	6 0	11 07	21 1 63	Stockport	Local	Oldham Ath	82	5
						Port Vale	70	7
						Wrexham	141	17
Brian Flynn	5 4	12 00	12 10 55	Pt Talbot	Limerick	Burnley	120	8
						Leeds U	154	11
						Burnley (loan)	2	—
						Burnley	80	11
						Cardiff C	32	—
						Doncaster R	27	—
					Limerick	Bury	19	—
						Doncaster R	24	1
						Wrexham	92	5
Ian Griffiths	5 6	10 02	17 4 60	Birkenhead	Amateur	Tranmere R	116	5
						Rochdale	42	5
						Port Vale	12	—
						Wigan Ath	82	7
					Bolton W	Wigan Ath	11	—
						Wrexham	11	—

WREXHAM

Foundation: The oldest club still in existence in Wales, Wrexham was founded in 1873 by a group of local businessmen initially to play a 17-a-side game against the Provincial Insurance team. By 1875 their team formation was reduced to 11 men and a year later they were among the founders of the Welsh FA.

First Football League game: 27 August, 1921, Division 3(N), v Hartlepools U (h) L 0-2 – Godding; Ellis, Simpson; Matthias, Foster, Griffiths; Burton, Goode, Cotton, Edwards, Lloyd.

Did you know: Dixie McNeil scored for Wrexham in 10 consecutive Cup ties (total 13 goals) from November 1977 to February 1979. Indeed, around this time he only failed to score in one of 14 actual appearances in this competition.

Managers (and Secretary-managers)
Ted Robinson 1912–25* (continued as secretary to 1930), Charlie Hewitt 1925–29, Jack Baynes 1929–31, Ernest Blackburn 1932–36, Jimmy Logan 1937–38, Arthur Cowell 1938, Tom Morgan 1938–40, Tom Williams 1940–49, Les McDowall 1949–50, Peter Jackson 1951–54, Cliff Lloyd 1954–57, John Love 1957–59, Billy Morris 1960–61, Ken Barnes 1961–65, Billy Morris 1965, Jack Rowley 1966–67, Alvan Williams 1967–68, John Neal 1968–77, Arfon Griffiths 1977–81, Mel Sutton 1981–82, Bobby Roberts 1982–85, Dixie McNeil 1985–89, Brian Flynn November 1989– .

Player and Position	Ht	Wt	Birth Date	Birth Place	Source	Clubs	League App	Gls
Geoff Hunter*	5 10	10 12	27 10 59	Hull	Apprentice	Manchester U	—	
						Crewe Alex	87	8
						Port Vale	221	15
						Wrexham	122	14
Jim Kelly§	5 7	11 10	14 2 73	Liverpool	Trainee	Wrexham	12	—
Robert Lunt§	5 7	10 10	11 12 73	Widnes	Trainee	Wrexham	8	—
Joey Murray†	5 8	10 11	5 11 71	Liverpool	Liverpool	Wrexham	11	—
Gareth Owen	5 9	11 04	21 10 71	Chester	Trainee	Wrexham	40	2
Sean Reck	5 10	12 07	5 5 67	Oxford	Apprentice	Oxford U	14	—
						Newport Co (loan)	15	—
						Reading (loan)	1	—
						Wrexham	45	2
Andy Thackeray	5 9	11 00	13 2 68	Huddersfield		Manchester C	—	
						Huddersfield T	2	—
						Newport Co	54	4
						Wrexham	110	11
Forwards								
Chris Armstrong	6 0	11 00	19 6 71	Newcastle	Local	Wrexham	60	13
Dave O'Gorman*	5 8	11 12	20 6 72	Chester	School	Wrexham	17	—
Andy Preece	6 1	12 00	27 3 67	Evesham		Northampton T	1	—
					Worcester C	Wrexham	41	5
Steve Watkin	5 10	11 00	16 6 71	Wrexham	School	Wrexham	9	1

Trainees
Douglas, Iain S; Durkan, Kieron J; Goss, Alexander J; Jones, Kevin R; Jones, Phillip L; Kelly, James; Knight, Craig; Laughton, Richard J; Lunt, Robert J; Myddleton, Philip J; Smith, Mark A; Williams, Jamie L; Young, Steven J.

**Non-Contract
Connolly, Karl; Murray, Joseph; Tyrrell, Alan H.

Associated Schoolboys
Barnes, Richard I; Davey, Richard W; Futcher, Stephen A; Holman, Matthew J; Jones, Paul; Jones, Richard N; Jones, Scott L; Morgan, Stephen J; Rawlins, Richard; Thomas, David N; Williams, Christopher; Williams, Gavin P.

Associated Schoolboys who have accepted the club's offer of a Traineeship/Contract
Brammer, David; Burke, Damian P.W; Coulthard, Christopher; Cross, Jonathan; Oldfield, Damon M; Sadler, Philip A.

**Non-Contract Players who are retained must be re-signed before they are eligible to play in League matches.

YORK CITY 1990–91 *Back row (left to right):* Richard Crossley, Steve Tutill, Ian Helliwell, Chris Marples, Dan Kiely, Ray Warburton, Andy McMillan, Glenn Naylor, Nigel Pepper.
Centre row: Alan Little (Coach), Ricky Sbragia (Youth Coach), Tony Barrett, Shaun Reid, John Bird (Manager), Gary Howlett, Tony Canham, Jeff Miller (Physiotherapist).
Front row: Dave Longhurst (Deceased), Mark Wood, Wayne Hall, Stuart Ede, Iain Dunn, Gary Himsworth.

Division 4 **YORK CITY**

Bootham Crescent, York. Telephone York (0904) 624447.

Ground capacity: 14,109.

Record attendance: 28,123 v Huddersfield T, FA Cup 6th rd, 5 March 1938.

Record receipts: £38,054 v Liverpool, FA Cup 5th rd, 15 February 1986.

Pitch measurements: 115yd × 75yd.

Chairman: D. M. Craig OBE, JP, BSC, FICE, FI, MUN E, FCI ARB, M CONS E

Directors: B. A. Houghton, C. Webb, M. D. B. Sinclair. E. B. Swallow, J. E. H. Quickfall FCA.

Manager: John Bird. *Assistant Manager:* Alan Little.

Secretary: Keith Usher. *Commercial Manager:* Mrs Sheila Smith.

Physio: Jeff Miller.

Hon. Orthopaedic Surgeon: Mr Peter De Boer MA, FRCS. *Medical Officer:* Dr A. I. MacLeod.

Year Formed: 1922. *Turned Professional:* 1922. *Ltd Co.:* 1922.

Club Nickname: 'Minstermen'.

Previous Ground: 1922, Fulfordgate; 1932, Bootham Crescent.

Record League Victory: 9-1 v Southport, Division 3 (N), 2 February 1957 – Forgan; Phillips, Howe; Brown (1), Cairney, Mollatt; Hill, Bottom (4 incl. 1p), Wilkinson (2), Wragg (1), Fenton (1).

Record Cup Victory: 6-0 v South Shields (away), FA Cup, 1st rd, 16 November 1968 – Widdowson; Baker (1p), Richardson; Carr, Jackson, Burrows; Taylor, Ross (3), MacDougall (2), Hodgson, Boyer.

Record Defeat: 0-12 v Chester, Division 3 (N), 1 February 1936.

Most League Points (2 for a win): 62, Division 4, 1964–65.

Most League Points (3 for a win): 101, Division 4, 1983–84.

Most League Goals: 96, Division 4, 1983–84.

Highest League Scorer in Season: Bill Fenton, 31, Division 3 (N), 1951–52; Arthur Bottom, 31, Division 3 (N), 1954–55 and 1955–56.

Most League Goals in Total Aggregate: Norman Wilkinson, 125, 1954–66.

Most Capped Player: Peter Scott, 7 (10), Northern Ireland.

Most League Appearances: Barry Jackson, 481, 1958–70.

Record Transfer Fee Received: £100,000 from Carlisle U for Gordon Staniforth, October 1979, and from QPR for John Byrne, October 1985.

Record Transfer Fee Paid: £50,000 to Aldershot for Dale Banton, November 1984.

Football League Record: 1929 Elected to Division 3 (N); 1958–59 Division 4; 1959–60 Division 3; 1960–65 Division 4; 1965–66 Division 3; 1966–71 Division 4; 1971–74 Division 3; 1974–76 Division 2; 1976–77 Division 3; 1977–84 Division 4; 1984–88 Division 3; 1988– Division 4.

Honours: Football League: Division 2 best season: 15th, 1974–75; Division 3 – Promoted 1973–74 (3rd); Division 4 – Champions 1983–84. *FA Cup:* Semi-finals 1955, when in Division 3. *Football League Cup:* best season: 5th rd, 1962.

Colours: Red shirts, blue shorts, white stockings. **Change colours:** White shirts, blue shorts, red stockings.

YORK CITY 1990–91 LEAGUE RECORD

Match No.	Date		Venue	Opponents	Result		H/T Score	Lg. Pos.	Goalscorers	Attendance
1	Aug	25	H	Maidstone U	L	0-1	0-1	—		2357
2	Sept	1	A	Hereford U	L	0-2	0-0	24		2422
3		18	A	Darlington	D	0-0	0-0	—		3582
4		22	H	Doncaster R	W	3-1	1-0	21	Warburton, Helliwell, Canham	3742
5		29	H	Gillingham	D	1-1	0-0	21	Howlett (pen)	2259
6	Oct	2	A	Chesterfield	D	2-2	2-0	—	Helliwell, Gunn (og)	3572
7		6	A	Burnley	D	0-0	0-0	21		6808
8		13	H	Cardiff C	L	1-2	0-0	21	Warburton	2596
9		16	A	Hartlepool U	W	1-0	1-0	—	Helliwell	2746
10		20	H	Halifax T	D	3-3	1-0	18	Helliwell, Howlett, Dunn	2601
11		23	A	Walsall	D	1-1	1-0	—	Howlett	3761
12		26	A	Stockport Co	L	0-2	0-2	—		3196
13	Nov	3	H	Torquay U	D	0-0	0-0	20		2412
14		10	A	Carlisle U	L	0-1	0-0	20		2888
15		24	H	Northampton T	L	0-1	0-0	22		2202
16	Dec	1	H	Scunthorpe U	D	2-2	2-1	22	Canham, Naylor	2495
17		15	A	Peterborough U	L	0-2	0-0	23		3335
18		21	H	Aldershot	W	2-0	1-0	—	Helliwell 2	1749
19		29	A	Wrexham	W	4-0	1-0	19	Blackstone 3, Warburton	1698
20	Jan	1	H	Blackpool	L	0-1	0-1	20		3115
21		5	A	Scarborough	D	2-2	2-0	20	Pepper (pen), Canham	2404
22		12	H	Hereford U	W	1-0	0-0	19	Warburton	1942
		19	A	Maidstone U	L	4-5	2-4	19	Pepper (pen), Blackstone, Helliwell, Barratt	1846
		26	H	Hartlepool U	D	0-0	0-0	20		3075
	Feb	2	H	Darlington	L	0-1	0-1	21		2925
26		5	A	Doncaster R	D	2-2	0-0	—	Blackstone, McCarthy	2916
27		15	A	Northampton T	L	1-2	1-1	—	Hall	2685
28		23	H	Carlisle U	W	2-0	0-0	19	Naylor, Dunn	2002
29		26	H	Lincoln C	W	1-0	0-0	—	Dunn	1808
30	Mar	2	A	Scunthorpe U	L	1-2	0-0	19	Blackstone	2860
31		9	H	Peterborough U	L	0-4	0-3	20		2511
32		12	H	Chesterfield	L	0-2	0-1	—		1751
33		16	A	Gillingham	D	0-0	0-0	21		3056
34		19	A	Cardiff C	L	1-2	1-1	—	Canham	2620
35		23	H	Burnley	W	2-0	2-0	20	McMillan, Naylor	4407
36		26	A	Lincoln C	L	1-2	1-1	—	Lister	2564
37		30	H	Rochdale	L	0-2	0-1	21		2120
38	Apr	1	A	Aldershot	W	1-0	0-0	20	Ogley (og)	1904
39		6	H	Wrexham	D	0-0	0-0	19		1490
40		13	A	Blackpool	L	0-1	0-0	20		5086
41		16	A	Rochdale	L	1-2	0-1	—	Naylor	1331
42		19	A	Halifax T	L	1-2	1-1	—	Evans (og)	1421
43		23	H	Scarborough	W	2-0	1-0	—	Canham, McCarthy	3017
44		26	H	Walsall	W	1-0	1-0	—	Naylor	1717
45	May	4	H	Stockport Co	L	0-2	0-0	21		3441
46		11	A	Torquay U	L	1-2	0-2	21	Pepper	4337

Final League Position: 21

GOALSCORERS

League (45): Helliwell 7, Blackstone 6, Canham 5, Naylor 5, Warburton 4, Dunn 3, Howlett 3 (1 pen), Pepper 3 (2 pens), McCarthy 2, Barratt 1, Hall 1, Lister 1, McMillan 1, own goals 3.
Rumbelows Cup (0).
FA Cup (3): Canham 2, Pepper 1.

Marples	McMillan	Hall	Reid	Tutill	Warburton	Barratt	Pepper	Helliwell	Longhurst	Canham	Howlett	Dunn	Himsworth	Weatherhead	McCarthy	Blackstone	Cooper	Naylor	Cook	Kiely	Hart	Bushell	Crossley	Curtis	Lister	Grayson	Bradshaw	Wood	Match No.
1	2	3	4	5	6	7	8*	9	10†	11	12	14																	1
1	2	3	4	5	6	7*12		9	10			8	14	11†															2
1	2	3	4	5		7		9		11		8	10		6														3
1	2	3	4	5	6	7		9		11		8	10															4
1	2	3	4	5	6	7		9		11		8	10*		12													5
1	2	3	4	5*	6			9		11	8	7	12		10													6
1	2	3	4		6	7		9		11	8	10*		5		12												7
1	2	3	4		6	7*		9		11	8	10		5		12												8
1	2	3	4		6	7		9		11	8		5		10													9
1	2	3	4		6	7		9		11	8	12	5		10*													10
1	2	3	4	5	6	7		9		11	8	10																11
1	2	3	4	5	6	7		9		11*	8	10	12															12
1	2	3	4	5	6	7		9		11*	8	10			12													13
1	2	3	4	5	6	7		9		11†14	10*			12	8													14
1	2	3	12	5	6	7		9†		11	8			4	10*14													15
1	2	3	4	5	6			9		11				8	10	7												16
1	2	3	4†	5	6	12		7		11				10	14	8*												17
1	2	3	4	5	6	7		9		11				8	10*12													18
1	2	3	4*	5	6	12	7			11		10		8	9													19
1	2	3	4	5	6	7				11		10		8*	9	12												20
1	2	3	4	5	6	8	7	9		11				10														21
1	2	3	4*	5	6	8	7	9		11	14			10†	12													22
1	2	3		5	6*	8	7	9		11	12			10		4												23
	2	3	4	5	6	7		9		11	8			10					1									24
	2	3	4	5	6	7		9		11	8	12		10*					1									25
	2	3	4	5	6	7		9		11*	12	8		10					1									26
	2	3	4	5		7		9			10†	12	8	11					1		6*14							27
	2	3	4†	5		7		9	12		10*	8	11						1		14	6						28
	2	3	4	5		7		9			10	8*	11						1		12	6						29
	2	3		5		7		9			10	8	12	11					1		4	6*						30
	2	3		5		7		9*			10†	8	12	11					1		4	6	14					31
	2	3	4	5	6	7		9†	12		14	8	10*	11					1									32
1	2	3		5		7	4	9		11	12		8	10*									6					33
1	2	3		5		7	4	9		11			8	10									6					34
1	2	3		5		7	4*	9		11	12		8	10									6					35
1	2	3		5		7	4	9		11	12		8*	10						14	6†						36
1	2†	3		5		7	4	9		11			8	12	10*						14	6						37
1	2	3		5		7	4	9		11		6	10	8*	12									8*	12			38
	2	3		5	4		9	11	14		6	12	10*	1		8	7†											39
	2	3		5	6	4	9	11	12		7	10		1		8*												40
	2	3		5	6	4	9*	11		7	10	12		1		8												41
	2	3		5	6	4		11	12		7†10	9*		1		8								14				42
	2	3		5	6	4		11			7	10	9	1		8												43
	2	3		5	6	4		11	12		7	10	9*	1		8												44
	2	3		5	6	4	9	11		7	10*		1		8	12												45
		3		5	2*	7	6	11		10		8	9†	1		4		12									14	46
29	45	46	28	42	22	27	38	41	2	39	15	18	1	6	26	20	2	17	3	17	1	10	5	2	4	—	—	—	
		+				+	+					+	+	+	+	+	+	+	+			+	+		+	+	+	+	
		1s				2s	1s					2s	2s	15s	1s	2s	1s	8s	3s		3s		5s		3s	1s	1s	1s	

Rumbelows Cup	First Round	Wrexham (h)	0-1
		(a)	0-2
FA Cup	First Round	Darlington (a)	1-1
		(h)	1-0
	Second Round	Mansfield T (a)	1-2

YORK CITY

Player and Position	Ht	Wt	Birth Date	Place	Source	Clubs	League App	Gls
Goalkeepers								
Dean Kiely	5 11	11 08	10 10 70	Manchester	WBA	Coventry C	—	—
						Ipswich T (loan)	—	—
						York C	17	—
Chris Marples	5 11	11 12	3 8 64	Chesterfield		Chesterfield	84	—
						Stockport Co	57	—
						York C	120	—
Defenders								
Tony Barratt	5 8	10 02	18 10 65	Salford	Billingham T	Grimsby T	22	—
						Hartlepool U	98	4
						York C	87	5
Richard Crossley*			5 9 70	Huddersfield	Huddersfield T	York C	6	—
Neil Grayson‡			1 1 64	York	Rowntree M	Doncaster R	129	6
						York C	1	—
Nigel Hart‡	6 0	12 03	1 10 58	Golborne	Local	Wigan Ath	1	—
						Leicester C	—	—
						Blackpool	37	—
						Crewe Alex	142	10
						Bury	45	2
						Stockport Co	39	2
						Chesterfield	46	2
						York C	1	—
Andy McMillan	5 10	10 13	22 6 68	South Africa		York C	94	1
Steve Tutill	6 0	11 10	1 10 69	Derwent	Trainee	York C	127	1
Ray Warburton	6 0	11 05	7 10 67	Rotherham	Apprentice	Rotherham U	4	—
						York C	65	6
Shaun Weatherhead*	5 11	12 03	3 9 70	Halifax				
					Trainee	Huddersfield T	—	—
						York C	8	—
Midfield								
Steve Bushell	5 7	10 05	28 12 72	Manchester	Trainee	York C	15	—
Andy Curtis§	5 10	11 07	2 12 72	Doncaster	Trainee	York C	5	—
Stuart Ede‡	5 7	10 12	19 4 72	Hartlepool	Trainee	York C	—	—
Wayne Hall	5 8	10 04	25 10 68	Rotherham	Darlington†	York C	75	4
Gavin Howell‡			18 3 65	Westow		York C	—	—
Gary Howlett‡	5 8	10 04	2 4 63	Dublin	Home Farm	Coventry C	—	—
						Brighton HA	32	2
						Bournemouth	60	7
						Aldershot (loan)	1	—
						Chester C (loan)	6	1
						York C	101	13
Nigel Pepper	5 10	10 03	25 4 68	Rotherham	Apprentice	Rotherham U	45	1
						York C	39	3
Shaun Reid	5 8	11 08	13 10 65	Huyton	Local	Rochdale	133	4
						Preston NE (loan)	3	—
						York C	78	6
Mark Wood*	5 7	9 12	27 6 72	Scarborough	Trainee	York C	1	—
Forwards								
Ian Blackstone	6 0	13 02	7 8 64	Harrogate	Harrogate	York C	28	6
Tony Canham	5 8	10 07	8 6 60	Leeds	Harrogate R	York C	216	43
Iain Dunn*	5 10	11 07	1 4 70	Derwent	School	York C	77	11
Ian Helliwell	6 3	13 12	7 12 62	Rotherham	Matlock T	York C	160	40

YORK CITY

Foundation: Although there was a York City club formed in 1903 by a soccer enthusiast from Darlington, this has no connection with the modern club because it went out of existence during World War I. Unlike many others of that period who restarted in 1919, York City did not re-form until 1922 and the tendency now is to ignore the modern club's pre-1922 existence.

First Football League game: 31 August, 1929, Division 3(N), v Wigan Borough (a) W 2-0 – Farmery; Archibald, Johnson; Beck, Davis, Thompson; Evans, Gardner, Cowie (1), Smailes, Stockhill (1).

Did you know: Because he wouldn't leave his job in a York chocolate factory Reg Baines restricted his career to Yorkshire clubs – York City(twice), Sheffield United, Doncaster Rovers, Barnsley and Halifax Town. He scored all of City's goals when they beat West Bromwich Albion 3-2 in the FA Cup in 1938.

Managers (and Secretary-managers)
Bill Sherrington 1924–60 (was secretary for most of this time but virtually secretary-manager for a long pre-war spell), John Collier 1929–36, Tom Mitchell 1936–50, Dick Duckworth 1950–52, Charlie Spencer 1952–53, Jimmy McCormick 1953–54, Sam Bartram 1956–60, Tom Lockie 1960–67, Joe Shaw 1967–68, Tom Johnston 1968–75, Wilf McGuinness 1975–77, Charlie Wright 1977–80, Barry Lyons 1980–81, Denis Smith 1982–87, Bobby Saxton 1987–88, John Bird October 1988– .

Player and Position	Ht	Wt	Birth Date	Place	Source	Clubs	League App	Gls
David Longhurst (Deceased)	5 8	10 12	15 1 65	Northampton	Apprentice	Nottingham F	—	—
						Halifax T	85	24
						Northampton T	37	7
						Peterborough U	58	7
						York C	6	2
Jonathan McCarthy	5 9	11 05	18 8 70	Middlesbrough		Hartlepool U	1	—
					Shepshed	York C	27	2
Glenn Naylor	5 9	11 10	11 8 72	York	Trainee	York C	21	5

Trainees
Barlow, Paul D; Cartwright, Mark N; Curtis, Andrew; Dickinson, Justin K; Ellis, Robert J; Hall, Craig; Howard, Michael J; McGarry, Neil; Maynard, Andrew; Pybus, Darren J; Smith, Andrew; Thompson, Geoffrey; Vardy, Richard; Woodward, Simon C.

Associated Schoolboys
Barlow, Stephen M; Brown, Paul A; Davison, Jamie; Duffy, Neil; Hall, Philip A; Medforth, Lee; Mockler, Paul F; Nellies, Murray; Rigby, Ian W; Shephard, Lewis M; Simpson, Elliott; Sturdy, Simon R.

Associated Schoolboys who have accepted the club's offer of a Traineeship/Contract
Dooley, Eammon G; Gosling, Michael; Henry, Craig L; Jordan, Scott; Markwick, Brett; Mennell, Nick.

END OF SEASON PLAY-OFFS 1990–91

The play-off system, which has done as much as anything to increase interest in the Football League competition in recent years, was let down at the final hurdle at Wembley, when the Fourth Division game between Blackpool and Torquay United was settled by that most unsatisfactory of methods — the penalty shoot-out.

This lottery produced a 5-4 win for Torquay following extra time, but such an outcome did nothing to enhance the wretched reputation of this most misguided vehicle for deciding football matches. Nonetheless it enabled Torquay to gain promotion to the Third Division for the first time in 19 years.

They had been the underdogs in the semi-final against Burnley, who threw away their chances at Torquay in the first leg when they lost 2-0 after having David Hamilton sent off. Moreover at Turf Moor, Burnley could only win with a last minute own goal which was not enough over the two legs.

Blackpool had been pushed all the way by Scunthorpe United before emerging as 3-2 winners overall. United had excelled themselves in drawing their home game 1-1 even though Steve Lister had been dismissed for dissent as early as the 19th minute.

Tranmere Rovers needed the aid of extra time to overcome Bolton Wanderers at Wembley with substitute Chris Malkin scoring the only goal in the 98th minute. Rovers were thus promoted to the Second Division for the first time in 52 years.

They had edged out Brentford in the semi-final 3-2, although the West London club had only salvaged a draw with a last gasp effort from Kevin Godfrey at 2-2 in the first leg at Griffin Park. Bolton were given a tough time by fellow Lancastrians Bury before winning 2-1 on aggregate. It was the second time Bolton had failed in the play-offs.

The Division Two winners proved to be Notts County who had ended the regular season's schedule with seven successive victories and were clearly in tip-top form. In the semi-final they held Middlesbrough 1-1 at Ayresome Park, restricting their opponents to a goal four minutes from the final whistle. At home they won 1-0.

Meanwhile Brighton had overcome a heavy injury list and beaten Millwall in convincing fashion. At the Goldstone, they won 4-1 and completed the double with a 2-1 win at The Den. But at Wembley they found Notts County a far more formidable proposition.

Tommy Johnson put Notts in front after half-an-hour and made it 2-0 on the hour. Dave Regis made it 3-0 in the 70th minute and Brighton's only consolation came in the dying seconds when Dean Wilkins scored. It was the second successive season that Notts had gained promotion through the play-offs and put them back in the First Division after an absence of seven years.

PLAY-OFFS

Semi-finals, First Leg

19 MAY

DIVISION 2

Brighton & HA (1) 4 *(Barham, Small, Walker, Codner)*
Millwall (1) 1 *(Stephenson)*   15,390
Brighton & HA: Digweed; Chivers, Gatting, Wilkins, Pates, Bissett, Barham, Iovan, Small, Codner, Walker (Robinson).
Millwall: Horne; Stevens, Dawes, Waddock (Briley) (McCarthy), Thompson, McLeary, Stephenson, Goodman, Sheringham, Rae, Kerr.

Middlesbrough (0) 1 *(Phillips)*
Notts Co (1) 1 *(Turner)*   22,343
Middlesbrough: Dibble; Cooper (Mustoe), Phillips, Kernaghan, Coleman, Putney, Slaven, Proctor, Baird, Hendrie, Ripley (Mowbray).

Notts Co: Cherry; Palmer, Paris, Short Craig, Short Chris, O'Riordan, Harding (Thomas), Turner, Regis, Draper, Johnson.

DIVISION 3

Brentford (1) 2 *(Evans, Godfrey)*
Tranmere R (0) 2 *(Cooper 2)*   9330
Brentford: Benstead; Ratcliffe, Bates, Millen, Evans, Rostron, Jones, Gayle (Peters), Holdsworth, Blissett (Godfrey), Smillie.
Tranmere R: Nixon; Higgins, Mungall (Martindale), Irons, Hughes, Vickers, Morrissey, Harvey, Steel, Cooper, Thomas.

Bury (1) 1 *(Lee (pen))*
Bolton W (0) 1 *(Philliskirk (pen))*   8000
Bury: Kelly; Bishop, Stanislaus, Robinson, Valentine, Greenall, Lee, Sheron, Hulme (Mauge), Parkinson, Kearney.
Bolton W: Felgate; Brown, Cowdrill, Comstive, Seagraves, Stubbs (Green), Storer, Thompson, Cunningham, Philliskirk, Darby.

DIVISION 4

Scunthorpe U (0) 1 *(Lillis)*
Blackpool (0) 1 *(Rodwell)*   6536
Scunthorpe U: Musselwhite; Longden, Lillis, Hine (Hamilton), Hicks, Lister, Joyce, Hill, Daws, Flounders, Taylor.
Blackpool: McIlhargey; Davies, Wright, Groves, Briggs, Gore, Rodwell, Horner, Taylor, Garner, Eyres.

Torquay U (1) 2 *(Edwards, Elliott)*
Burnley (0) 0   5600
Torquay U: Howells; Curran, Holmes P, Saunders, Elliott, Joyce, Myers, Holmes M (Rowland), Evans, Edwards, Loram.
Burnley: Pearce; Measham, Bray, Hamilton, Pender, Davis, Farrell, Deakin, Francis, Jakub, Eli (Sonner).

Semi-finals, Second Leg

22 MAY

DIVISION 2

Millwall (1) 1 *(McGinlay)*
Brighton & HA (0) 2 *(Codner, Robinson)*   17,370
Millwall: Horne; Stevens, Dawes, McGlashan, Thompson, McLeary, Stephenson, McGinlay, Sheringham, Rae, Kerr.
Brighton & HA: Digweed; Chivers, Gatting, Wilkins, Pates, Bissett, Barham (Chapman), Iovan, Small, Codner, Nelson (Robinson).

Notts Co (0) 1 *(Harding)*
Middlesbrough (0) 0   18,249
Notts Co: Cherry; Palmer, Paris, Short Craig, Short Chris, O'Riordan, Harding, Turner (Thomas), Regis, Draper, Johnson (Bartlett).
Middlesbrough: Dibble; Kernaghan, Phillips, Mowbray, Coleman, Putney, Slaven (Russell), Proctor, Baird, Mustoe, Hendrie.

DIVISION 3

Bolton W (1) 1 *(Philliskirk)*

Bury (0) 0   19,198

Bolton W: Felgate; Brown, Cowdrill, Comstive, Seagraves, Stubbs, Storer, Thompson, Cunningham, Philliskirk, Darby.
Bury: Kelly; Bishop, Stanislaus, Robinson, Valentine, Greenall, Lee, Sheron, Hulme, Parkinson, Kearney.

Tranmere R (1) 1 *(Brannan)*

Brentford (0) 0   11,438

Tranmere R: Nixon; Higgins, Brannan, Irons, Hughes, Vickers, Morrissey (Malkin), Martindale (Garnett), Steel, Cooper, Thomas.
Brentford: Benstead; Ratcliffe, Bates, Millen, Evans, Rostron, Jones, Godfrey (Gayle), Holdsworth, Blissett, Smillie.

DIVISION 4

Blackpool (0) 2 *(Eyres 2)*

Scunthorpe U (1) 1 *(Hill)*   7596

Blackpool: McIlhargey; Davies, Wright, Groves, Briggs (Sinclair), Gore, Rodwell, Horner, Taylor, Garner, Eyres.
Scunthorpe U: Musselwhite; Longden, Lillis, Hamilton, Hicks, Stevenson, Joyce, Hill, Daws, Flounders, Taylor (Hine).

Burnley (0) 1 *(Evans (og))*

Torquay U (0) 0   13,620

Burnley: Pearce; Measham, Bray, Deary, Pender (Sonner), Davis, Farrell, Futcher, Francis, Jakub, Eli.
Torquay U: Howells; Curran, Holmes P, Saunders, Elliott, Joyce, Myers, Holmes M, Evans, Edwards, Loram (Rowland).

Finals (at Wembley)

31 MAY

DIVISION 4

Blackpool (1) 2 *(Groves, Curran (og))*

Torquay U (2) 2 *(Saunders, Edwards (pen)) aet*
                                                  21,615

Blackpool: McIlhargey; Davies (Sinclair), Wright, Groves, Horner, Gore, Rodwell, Taylor, Bamber, Garner, Eyres.
Torquay U: Howells; Curran, Holmes P, Saunders, Elliott, Joyce, Myers, Holmes M, Evans (Rowland), Edwards (Hall), Loram.
Torquay U won 5-4 on penalties

1 JUNE

DIVISION 3

Bolton W (0) 0

Tranmere R (0) 1 *(Malkin) aet*   30,217

Bolton W: Felgate; Brown, Cowdrill, Comstive, Seagraves, Stubbs, Storer (Green), Thompson, Cunningham (Reeves), Philliskirk, Darby.
Tranmere R: Nixon; Higgins, Brannan, Irons, Hughes, Garnett, Morrissey, Martindale (Harvey), Steel (Malkin), Cooper, Thomas.

2 JUNE

DIVISION 2

Brighton & HA (0) 1 *(Wilkins)*

Notts Co (1) 3 *(Johnson 2, Regis)*   59,940

Brighton & HA: Digweed; Chivers, Gatting (Byrne), Wilkins, Bissett, Pates, Barham, Iovan (Chapman), Small, Codner, Walker.
Notts Co: Cherry; Palmer, Paris, Short Craig, Yates, O'Riordan, Thomas, Turner, Regis (Bartlett), Draper (Harding), Johnson.

Tommy Johnson shows obvious delight at scoring the first of his two goals for Notts County in their 3-1 play-off success against Brighton at Wembley which put them into the First Division. (Colorsport)

BARCLAYS LEAGUE FINAL TABLES 1990–91

DIVISION 1

		Home			Goals		Away			Goals			
		P	W	D	L	F	A	W	D	L	F	A	Pts	GD
*1	Arsenal	38	15	4	0	51	10	9	9	1	23	8	83	+56
2	Liverpool	38	14	3	2	42	13	9	4	6	35	27	76	+37
3	Crystal Palace	38	11	6	2	26	17	9	3	7	24	24	69	+9
4	Leeds U	38	12	2	5	46	23	7	5	7	19	24	64	+18
5	Manchester C	38	12	3	4	35	25	5	8	6	29	28	62	+11
*6	Manchester U	38	11	4	4	34	17	5	8	6	24	28	59	+13
7	Wimbledon	38	8	6	5	28	22	6	8	5	25	24	56	+7
8	Nottingham F	38	11	4	4	42	21	3	8	8	23	29	54	+15
9	Everton	38	9	5	5	26	15	4	7	8	24	31	51	+4
10	Tottenham H	38	8	9	2	35	22	3	7	9	16	28	49	+1
11	Chelsea	38	10	6	3	33	25	3	4	12	25	44	49	−11
12	QPR	38	8	5	6	27	22	4	5	10	17	31	46	−9
13	Sheffield U	38	9	3	7	23	23	4	4	11	13	32	46	−19
14	Southampton	38	9	6	4	33	22	3	3	13	25	47	45	−11
15	Norwich C	38	9	3	7	27	32	4	3	12	14	32	45	−23
16	Coventry C	38	10	6	3	30	16	1	5	13	12	33	44	−7
17	Aston Villa	38	7	9	3	29	25	2	5	12	17	33	41	−12
18	Luton T	38	7	5	7	22	18	3	2	14	20	43	37	−19
19	Sunderland	38	6	6	7	15	16	2	4	13	23	44	34	−22
20	Derby Co	38	3	8	8	25	36	2	1	16	12	39	24	−38

*Arsenal 2 points deducted.
*Manchester U 1 point deducted.

DIVISION 2

		Home			Goals		Away			Goals			
		P	W	D	L	F	A	W	D	L	F	A	Pts	GD
1	Oldham Ath	46	17	5	1	55	21	8	8	7	28	32	88	+30
2	West Ham U	46	15	6	2	41	18	9	9	5	19	16	87	+26
3	Sheffield W	46	12	10	1	43	23	10	6	7	37	28	82	+29
4	Notts Co	46	14	4	5	45	28	9	7	7	31	27	80	+21
5	Millwall	46	11	6	6	43	28	9	7	7	27	23	73	+19
6	Brighton & HA	46	12	4	7	37	31	9	3	11	26	38	70	−6
7	Middlesbrough	46	12	4	7	36	17	8	5	10	30	30	69	+19
8	Barnsley	46	13	7	3	39	16	6	5	12	24	32	69	+15
9	Bristol C	46	14	5	4	44	28	6	2	15	24	43	67	−3
10	Oxford U	46	10	9	4	41	29	4	10	9	28	37	61	+3
11	Newcastle U	46	8	10	5	24	22	6	7	10	25	34	59	−7
12	Wolverhampton W	46	11	6	6	45	35	2	13	8	18	28	58	0
13	Bristol R	46	11	7	5	29	20	4	6	13	27	39	58	−3
14	Ipswich T	46	9	8	6	32	28	4	10	9	28	40	57	−8
15	Port Vale	46	10	4	9	32	24	5	8	10	24	40	57	−8
16	Charlton Ath	46	8	7	8	27	25	5	10	8	30	36	56	−4
17	Portsmouth	46	10	6	7	34	27	4	5	14	24	43	53	−12
18	Plymouth Arg	46	10	10	3	36	20	2	7	14	18	48	53	−14
19	Blackburn R	46	8	6	9	26	27	6	4	13	25	39	52	−15
20	Watford	46	5	8	10	24	32	7	7	9	21	27	51	−14
21	Swindon T	46	8	6	9	31	30	4	8	11	34	43	50	−8
22	Leicester C	46	12	4	7	41	33	2	4	17	19	50	50	−23
23	WBA	46	7	11	5	26	21	3	7	13	26	40	48	−9
24	Hull C	46	6	10	7	35	32	4	5	14	22	53	45	−28

DIVISION 3

		P	Home W	D	L	Goals F	A	Away W	D	L	Goals F	A	Pts	GD
1	Cambridge U	46	14	5	4	42	22	11	6	6	33	23	86	+30
2	Southend U	46	13	6	4	34	23	13	1	9	33	28	85	+16
3	Grimsby T	46	16	3	4	42	13	8	8	7	24	21	83	+32
4	Bolton W	46	14	5	4	33	18	10	6	7	31	32	83	+14
5	Tranmere R	46	13	5	5	38	21	10	4	9	26	25	78	+18
6	Brentford	46	12	4	7	30	22	9	9	5	29	25	76	+12
7	Bury	46	13	6	4	39	26	7	7	9	28	30	73	+11
8	Bradford C	46	13	3	7	36	22	7	7	9	26	32	70	+8
9	Bournemouth	46	14	6	3	37	20	5	7	11	21	38	70	0
10	Wigan Ath	46	14	3	6	40	20	6	6	11	31	34	69	+17
11	Huddersfield T	46	13	3	7	37	23	5	10	8	20	28	67	+6
12	Birmingham C	46	8	9	6	21	21	8	8	7	24	28	65	−4
13	Leyton Orient	46	15	2	6	35	19	3	8	12	20	39	64	−3
14	Stoke C	46	9	7	7	36	29	7	5	11	19	30	60	−4
15	Reading	46	11	5	7	34	28	6	3	14	19	38	59	−13
16	Exeter C	46	12	6	5	35	16	4	3	16	23	36	57	+6
17	Preston NE	46	11	5	7	33	29	4	6	13	21	38	56	−13
18	Shrewsbury T	46	8	7	8	29	22	6	3	14	32	46	52	−7
19	Chester C	46	10	3	10	27	27	4	6	13	19	31	51	−12
20	Swansea C	46	8	6	9	31	33	5	3	15	18	39	48	−23
21	Fulham	46	8	8	7	27	22	2	8	13	14	34	46	−15
22	Crewe Alex	46	6	9	8	35	35	5	2	16	27	45	44	−18
23	Rotherham U	46	5	10	8	31	38	5	2	16	19	49	42	−37
24	Mansfield T	46	5	8	10	23	27	3	6	14	19	36	38	−21

DIVISION 4

		P	Home W	D	L	Goals F	A	Away W	D	L	Goals F	A	Pts	GD
1	Darlington	46	13	8	2	36	14	9	9	5	32	24	83	+30
2	Stockport Co	46	16	6	1	54	19	7	7	9	30	28	82	+37
3	Hartlepool U	46	15	5	3	35	15	9	5	9	32	33	82	+19
4	Peterborough U	46	13	9	1	38	15	8	8	7	29	30	80	+22
5	Blackpool	46	17	3	3	55	17	6	7	10	23	30	79	+31
6	Burnley	46	17	5	1	46	16	6	5	12	24	35	79	+19
7	Torquay U	46	14	7	2	37	13	4	11	8	27	34	72	+17
8	Scunthorpe U	46	17	4	2	51	20	3	7	13	20	42	71	+9
9	Scarborough	46	13	5	5	36	21	6	7	10	23	35	69	+3
10	Northampton T	46	14	5	4	34	21	4	8	11	23	37	67	−1
11	Doncaster R	46	12	5	6	36	22	5	9	9	20	24	65	+10
12	Rochdale	46	10	9	4	29	22	5	8	10	21	31	62	−3
13	Cardiff C	46	10	6	7	26	23	5	9	9	17	31	60	−11
14	Lincoln C	46	10	7	6	32	27	4	10	9	18	34	59	−11
15	Gillingham	46	9	9	5	35	27	3	9	11	22	33	54	−3
16	Walsall	46	7	12	4	25	17	5	5	13	23	34	53	−3
17	Hereford U	46	9	10	4	32	19	4	4	15	21	39	53	−5
18	Chesterfield	46	8	12	3	33	26	5	2	16	14	36	53	−15
19	Maidstone U	46	9	5	9	42	34	4	7	12	24	37	51	−5
20	Carlisle U	46	12	3	8	30	30	1	6	16	17	59	48	−42
21	York C	46	8	6	9	21	23	3	7	13	24	34	46	−12
22	Halifax T	46	9	6	8	34	29	3	4	16	25	50	46	−20
23	Aldershot	46	8	7	8	38	43	2	4	17	23	58	41	−40
24	Wrexham	46	8	7	8	33	34	2	3	18	15	40	40	−26

FOOTBALL LEAGUE MATCHES
1888–1991

	P	W	D	L	Goals F	A
Aberdare Athletic	252	78	59	115	334	413
Accrington Stanley*	1542	544	298	700	2441	2954
Aldershot	2346	789	605	952	3217	3632
Arsenal	3482	1518	855	1109	5764	4681
Ashington	328	109	71	148	489	650
Aston Villa	3618	1540	816	1262	6199	5412
Barnsley	3458	1256	875	1327	4949	5219
Barrow	1924	624	414	886	2606	3349
Birmingham City	3532	1317	854	1361	5227	5222
Blackburn Rovers	3654	1421	879	1354	5742	5618
Blackpool	3426	1267	845	1314	5019	5087
Bolton Wanderers	3660	1428	846	1386	5548	5360
Bootle	22	8	3	11	49	63
AFC Bournemouth	2724	1026	713	985	3793	3683
Bradford (Park Avenue)	2190	837	476	877	3516	3582
Bradford City	3330	1239	845	1246	4845	4785
Brentford	2836	1085	712	1039	4155	4037
Brighton & Hove Albion	2792	1125	698	969	4193	3843
Bristol City	3326	1301	832	1193	4884	4642
Bristol Rovers	2782	1050	700	1038	4181	4160
Burnley	3660	1426	866	1368	5549	5508
Burton United[1]	484	147	80	257	657	994
Burton Wanderers	90	42	13	35	167	146
Bury	3576	1345	835	1396	5322	5347
Cambridge United	942	337	255	350	1217	1283
Cardiff City	2720	983	676	1061	3763	4107
Carlisle United	2448	893	578	977	3571	3826
Charlton Athletic	2656	956	660	1040	3962	4226
Chelsea	3104	1198	807	1099	4712	4581
Chester City	2386	839	601	946	3398	3553
Chesterfield	3152	1221	741	1190	4614	4468
Colchester United	1838	675	485	678	2647	2679
Coventry City	2764	1014	701	1049	4070	4097
Crewe Alexandra	2908	967	686	1255	3990	4791
Crystal Palace	2754	1016	731	1007	3920	3924
Darlington	2752	947	660	1145	3970	4450
Darwen	232	75	27	130	401	619
Derby County	3622	1431	861	1330	5805	5477
Doncaster Rovers	2792	1009	691	1092	3985	4297
Durham City	286	95	54	137	394	529
Everton	3606	1524	870	1212	5966	5150
Exeter City	2849	973	727	1149	3934	4375
Fulham	3070	1136	752	1182	4593	4555
Gainsborough Trinity	564	175	118	271	718	1029
Gateshead	1466	559	361	546	2292	2335
Gillingham	2640	925	687	1028	3528	3878
Glossop North End	618	197	136	285	829	1026
Grimsby Town	3584	1397	787	1400	5402	5467
Halifax Town	2800	896	726	1178	3615	4409
Hartlepool United	2798	937	619	1242	3776	4674
Hereford United	870	286	247	337	1054	1143
Huddersfield Town	2974	1152	762	1060	4321	4058
Hull City	3186	1228	830	1128	4721	4442
Ipswich Town	1970	807	477	686	2993	2765
Leeds United[2]	3082	1262	770	1050	4687	4251
Leicester City	3482	1290	876	1316	5383	5485
Leyton Orient	3186	1069	814	1303	4098	4679
Lincoln City	3472	1267	808	1397	5242	5500
Liverpool	3482	1634	835	1013	6024	4487
Loughborough Town	158	34	20	104	170	410
Luton Town	2800	1091	692	1017	4414	4115
Maidstone United	92	35	19	38	143	132
Manchester City	3516	1443	840	1233	5868	5226
Manchester United	3514	1547	857	1110	5893	4808
Mansfield Town	2384	871	611	902	3573	3568
Merthyr Town	420	115	106	199	524	779
Middlesbrough	3328	1264	794	1270	5130	4984

	P	W	D	L	Goals F	A
Middlesbrough Ironopolis	28	8	4	16	37	72
Millwall	2776	1097	722	957	4071	3768
Nelson	412	154	73	185	668	796
New Brighton	884	287	187	410	1191	1527
New Brighton Tower	102	48	24	30	194	148
Newcastle United	3498	1430	802	1266	5595	5090
Newport County	2672	888	625	1159	3700	4557
Northampton Town	2836	1108	646	1082	4387	4261
Northwich Victoria	50	12	5	33	72	156
Norwich City	2714	1001	724	989	3941	3963
Nottingham Forest	3518	1322	868	1328	5215	5167
Notts County	3702	1392	897	1413	5465	5546
Oldham Athletic	3138	1177	790	1171	4608	4647
Oxford United	1284	441	376	467	1642	1674
Peterborough United	1426	564	400	462	2130	1865
Plymouth Argyle	2786	1083	716	987	4246	3946
Portsmouth	2730	1009	706	1015	4076	4078
Port Vale[3]	3298	1178	850	1270	4553	4804
Preston North End	3680	1416	911	1353	5568	5337
Queen's Park Rangers	2734	1093	681	960	4128	3796
Reading	2846	1142	697	1007	4380	4067
Rochdale	2798	918	696	1184	3813	4500
Rotherham United[4]	2904	1089	665	1150	4355	4561
Scarborough	184	72	50	62	242	229
Scunthorpe United	1861	657	521	683	2561	2628
Sheffield United	3546	1427	840	1279	5612	5322
Sheffield Wednesday	3542	1401	868	1273	5495	5185
Shrewsbury Town	1852	650	504	698	2557	2641
Southampton	2702	1052	694	956	4208	3950
Southend United	2852	1084	694	1074	4211	4165
Southport	2200	723	568	909	2961	3488
Stalybridge Celtic	76	33	11	32	104	110
Stockport County	3402	1245	812	1345	4802	5009
Stoke City	3346	1202	815	1329	4646	4925
Sunderland	3584	1475	859	1250	5864	5271
Swansea City	2772	1021	657	1094	4021	4288
Swindon Town	2822	1071	729	1022	4217	4080
Thames	84	20	17	47	107	202
Torquay United	2558	908	650	1000	3599	3946
Tottenham Hotspur	2982	1260	728	994	5007	4229
Tranmere Rovers	2798	1072	658	1068	4271	4171
Walsall	3034	1062	726	1246	4498	4825
Watford	2802	1055	718	1029	4079	3955
West Bromwich Albion	3634	1421	876	1337	5780	5471
West Ham United	2732	1051	667	1014	4267	4136
Wigan Athletic	598	247	159	192	845	742
Wigan Borough[5]	412	145	94	173	635	706
Wimbledon	602	252	167	183	908	787
Wolverhampton W	3644	1486	814	1344	6094	5615
Workington	1194	385	310	499	1525	1810
Wrexham	2782	1046	678	1058	4208	4113
York City	2462	870	604	988	3630	3766

The above figures do not include games played at the start of season 1939–40 before the competition was abandoned because of the outbreak of World War II, nor do they include the old end-of-season Test matches or the modern Play-offs.

* Includes the original club known simply as Accrington but none of the games played during season 1961–62 when they resigned from the League.

[1] Includes Burton Swifts who amalgamated with Burton Wanderers to form Burton United in 1901.

[2] Includes Leeds City and the eight games played 1919–20.

[3] Includes only 34 games played 1919–20 when took over from Leeds City.

[4] Including Rotherham County who amalgamated with Rotherham Town to form Rotherham United in 1925.

[5] Games played in season 1931–32 prior to their resignation on 26 October were expunged from the record and therefore not included in these figures.

FOOTBALL LEAGUE 1888–89 to 1990–91

FOOTBALL LEAGUE

	First	Pts	Second	Pts	Third	Pts
1888–89a	Preston NE	40	Aston Villa	29	Wolverhampton W	28
1889–90a	Preston NE	33	Everton	31	Blackburn R	27
1890–91a	Everton	29	Preston NE	27	Notts Co	26
1891–92b	Sunderland	42	Preston NE	37	Bolton W	36

FIRST DIVISION

Maximum points: a 44; b 52; c 60; d 68; e 76; f 84; g 126; h 120; k 114.

	First	Pts	Second	Pts	Third	Pts
1892–93c	Sunderland	48	Preston NE	37	Everton	36
1893–94c	Aston Villa	44	Sunderland	38	Derby Co	36
1894–95c	Sunderland	47	Everton	42	Aston Villa	39
1895–96c	Aston Villa	45	Derby Co	41	Everton	39
1896–97c	Aston Villa	47	Sheffield U*	36	Derby Co	36
1897–98c	Sheffield U	42	Sunderland	37	Wolverhampton W*	35
1898–99d	Aston Villa	45	Liverpool	43	Burnley	39
1899–1900d	Aston Villa	50	Sheffield U	48	Sunderland	41
1900–01d	Liverpool	45	Sunderland	43	Notts Co	40
1901–02d	Sunderland	44	Everton	41	Newcastle U	37
1902–03d	The Wednesday	42	Aston Villa*	41	Sunderland	41
1903–04d	The Wednesday	47	Manchester C	44	Everton	43
1904–05d	Newcastle U	48	Everton	47	Manchester C	46
1905–06e	Liverpool	51	Preston NE	47	The Wednesday	44
1906–07e	Newcastle U	51	Bristol C	48	Everton*	45
1907–08e	Manchester U	52	Aston Villa*	43	Manchester C	43
1908–09e	Newcastle U	53	Everton	46	Sunderland	44
1909–10e	Aston Villa	53	Liverpool	48	Blackburn R*	45
1910–11e	Manchester U	52	Aston Villa	51	Sunderland*	45
1911–12e	Blackburn R	49	Everton	46	Newcastle U	44
1912–13e	Sunderland	54	Aston Villa	50	Sheffield W	49
1913–14e	Blackburn R	51	Aston Villa	44	Middlesbrough*	43
1914–15e	Everton	46	Oldham Ath	45	Blackburn R*	43
1919–20f	WBA	60	Burnley	51	Chelsea	49
1920–21f	Burnley	59	Manchester C	54	Bolton W	52
1921–22f	Liverpool	57	Tottenham H	51	Burnley	49
1922–23f	Liverpool	60	Sunderland	54	Huddersfield T	53
1923–24f	Huddersfield T*	57	Cardiff C	57	Sunderland	53
1924–25f	Huddersfield T	58	WBA	56	Bolton W	55
1925–26f	Huddersfield T	57	Arsenal	52	Sunderland	48
1926–27f	Newcastle U	56	Huddersfield T	51	Sunderland	49
1927–28f	Everton	53	Huddersfield T	51	Leicester C	48
1928–29f	Sheffield W	52	Leicester C	51	Aston Villa	50
1929–30f	Sheffield W	60	Derby Co	50	Manchester C*	47
1930–31f	Arsenal	66	Aston Villa	59	Sheffield W	52
1931–32f	Everton	56	Arsenal	54	Sheffield W	50
1932–33f	Arsenal	58	Aston Villa	54	Sheffield W	51
1933–34f	Arsenal	59	Huddersfield T	56	Tottenham H	49
1934–35f	Arsenal	58	Sunderland	54	Sheffield W	49
1935–36f	Sunderland	56	Derby Co*	48	Huddersfield T	48
1936–37f	Manchester C	57	Charlton Ath	54	Arsenal	52
1937–38f	Arsenal	52	Wolverhampton W	51	Preston NE	49
1938–39f	Everton	59	Wolverhampton W	55	Charlton Ath	50
1946–47f	Liverpool	57	Manchester U*	56	Wolverhampton W	56
1947–48f	Arsenal	59	Manchester U*	52	Burnley	52
1948–49f	Portsmouth	58	Manchester U*	53	Derby Co	53
1949–50f	Portsmouth*	53	Wolverhampton W	53	Sunderland	52
1950–51f	Tottenham H	60	Manchester U	56	Blackpool	50
1951–52f	Manchester U	57	Tottenham H*	53	Arsenal	53
1952–53f	Arsenal*	54	Preston NE	54	Wolverhampton W	51
1953–54f	Wolverhampton W	57	WBA	53	Huddersfield T	51
1954–55f	Chelsea	52	Wolverhampton W*	48	Portsmouth*	48
1955–56f	Manchester U	60	Blackpool*	49	Wolverhampton W	49
1956–57f	Manchester U	64	Tottenham H*	56	Preston NE	56
1957–58f	Wolverhampton W	64	Preston NE	59	Tottenham H	51
1958–59f	Wolverhampton W	61	Manchester U	55	Arsenal*	50
1959–60f	Burnley	55	Wolverhampton W	54	Tottenham H	53
1960–61f	Tottenham H	66	Sheffield W	58	Wolverhampton W	57
1961–62f	Ipswich T	56	Burnley	53	Tottenham H	52
1962–63f	Everton	61	Tottenham H	55	Burnley	54
1963–64f	Liverpool	57	Manchester U	53	Everton	52
1964–65f	Manchester U*	61	Leeds U	61	Chelsea	56
1965–66f	Liverpool	61	Leeds U*	55	Burnley	55
1966–67f	Manchester U	60	Nottingham F*	56	Tottenham H	56

* Won or placed on goal average.

	First	Pts	Second	Pts	Third	Pts
1967–68f	Manchester C	58	Manchester U	56	Liverpool	55
1968–69f	Leeds U	67	Liverpool	61	Everton	57
1969–70f	Everton	66	Leeds U	57	Chelsea	55
1970–71f	Arsenal	65	Leeds U	64	Tottenham H*	52
1971–72f	Derby Co	58	Leeds U*	57	Liverpool*	57
1972–73f	Liverpool	60	Arsenal	57	Leeds U	53
1973–74f	Leeds U	62	Liverpool	57	Derby Co	48
1974–75f	Derby Co	53	Liverpool*	51	Ipswich T	57
1975–76f	Liverpool	60	QPR	59	Manchester U	56
1976–77f	Liverpool	57	Manchester C	56	Ipswich T	52
1977–78f	Nottingham F	64	Liverpool	57	Everton	55
1978–79f	Liverpool	68	Nottingham F	60	WBA	·59
1979–80f	Liverpool	60	Manchester U	58	Ipswich T	53
1980–81f	Aston Villa	60	Ipswich T	56	Arsenal	53
1981–82g	Liverpool	87	Ipswich T	83	Manchester U	78
1982–83g	Liverpool	82	Watford	71	Manchester U	70
1983–84g	Liverpool	80	Southampton	77	Nottingham F*	74
1984–85g	Everton	90	Liverpool*	77	Tottenham H	77
1985–86g	Liverpool	88	Everton	86	West Ham U	84
1986–87g	Everton	86	Liverpool	77	Tottenham H	71
1987–88h	Liverpool	90	Manchester U	81	Nottingham F	73
1988–89k	Arsenal*	76	Liverpool	76	Nottingham F	64
1989–90k	Liverpool	79	Aston Villa	70	Tottenham H	63
1990–91k	Arsenal†	83	Liverpool	76	Crystal Palace	69

No official competition during 1915–19 and 1939–46.
† 2 pts deducted

SECOND DIVISION

Maximum points: a 44; b 56; c 60; d 68; e 76; f 84; g 126; h 132; k 138.

	First	Pts	Second	Pts	Third	Pts
1892–93a	Small Heath	36	Sheffield U	35	Darwen	30
1893–94b	Liverpool	50	Small Heath	42	Notts Co	39
1894–95c	Bury	48	Notts Co	39	Newton Heath*	38
1895–96c	Liverpool*	46	Manchester C	46	Grimsby T*	42
1896–97c	Notts Co	42	Newton Heath	39	Grimsby T	38
1897–98c	Burnley	48	Newcastle U	45	Manchester C	39
1898–99d	Manchester C	52	Glossop NE	46	Leicester Fosse	45
1899–1900d	The Wednesday	54	Bolton W	52	Small Heath	46
1900–01d	Grimsby T	49	Small Heath	48	Burnley	44
1901–02d	WBA	55	Middlesbrough	51	Preston NE*	42
1902–03d	Manchester C	54	Small Heath	51	Woolwich A	48
1903–04d	Preston NE	50	Woolwich A	49	Manchester U	48
1904–05d	Liverpool	58	Bolton W	56	Manchester U	53
1905–06e	Bristol C	66	Manchester U	62	Chelsea	53
1906–07e	Nottingham F	60	Chelsea	57	Leicester Fosse	48
1907–08e	Bradford C	54	Leicester Fosse	52	Oldham Ath	50
1908–09e	Bolton W	52	Tottenham H*	51	WBA	51
1909–10e	Manchester C	54	Oldham Ath*	53	Hull C*	53
1910–11e	WBA	53	Bolton W	51	Chelsea	49
1911–12e	Derby Co*	54	Chelsea	54	Burnley	52
1912–13e	Preston NE	53	Burnley	50	Birmingham	46
1913–14e	Notts Co	53	Bradford PA*	49	Woolwich A	49
1914–15e	Derby Co	53	Preston NE	50	Barnsley	47
1919–20f	Tottenham H	70	Huddersfield T	64	Birmingham	56
1920–21f	Birmingham*	58	Cardiff C	58	Bristol C	51
1921–22f	Nottingham F	56	Stoke C*	52	Barnsley	52
1922–23f	Notts Co	53	West Ham U*	51	Leicester C	51
1923–24f	Leeds U	54	Bury*	51	Derby Co	51
1924–25f	Leicester C	59	Manchester U	57	Derby Co	55
1925–26f	Sheffield W	60	Derby Co	57	Chelsea	52
1926–27f	Middlesbrough	62	Portsmouth*	54	Manchester C	54
1927–28f	Manchester C	59	Leeds U	57	Chelsea	54
1928–29f	Middlesbrough	55	Grimsby T	53	Bradford*	48
1929–30f	Blackpool	58	Chelsea	55	Oldham Ath	53
1930–31f	Everton	61	WBA	54	Tottenham H	51
1931–32f	Wolverhampton W	56	Leeds U	54	Stoke C	52
1932–33f	Stoke C	56	Tottenham H	55	Fulham	50
1933–34f	Grimsby T	59	Preston NE	52	Bolton W*	51
1934–35f	Brentford	61	Bolton W*	56	West Ham U	56
1935–36f	Manchester U	56	Charlton Ath	55	Sheffield U*	52
1936–37f	Leicester C	56	Blackpool	55	Bury	52
1937–38f	Aston Villa	57	Manchester U*	53	Sheffield U	53
1938–39f	Blackburn R	55	Sheffield U	54	Sheffield W	53
1946–47f	Manchester C	62	Burnley	58	Birmingham C	55
1947–48f	Birmingham C	59	Newcastle U	56	Southampton	52
1948–49f	Fulham	57	WBA	56	Southampton	55
1949–50f	Tottenham H	61	Sheffield W*	52	Sheffield U*	52

* Won or placed on goal average/goal difference.

	First	Pts	Second	Pts	Third	Pts
1950–51f	Preston NE	57	Manchester C	52	Cardiff C	50
1951–52f	Sheffield W	53	Cardiff C*	51	Birmingham C	51
1952–53f	Sheffield U	60	Huddersfield T	58	Luton T	52
1953–54f	Leicester C*	56	Everton	56	Blackburn R	55
1954–55f	Birmingham C*	54	Luton T*	54	Rotherham U	54
1955–56f	Sheffield W	55	Leeds U	52	Liverpool*	48
1956–57f	Leicester C	61	Nottingham F	54	Liverpool	53
1957–58f	West Ham U	57	Blackburn R	56	Charlton Ath	55
1958–59f	Sheffield W	62	Fulham	60	Sheffield U*	53
1959–60f	Aston Villa	59	Cardiff C	58	Liverpool*	50
1960–61f	Ipswich T	59	Sheffield U	58	Liverpool	52
1961–62f	Liverpool	62	Leyton O	54	Sunderland	53
1962–63f	Stoke C	53	Chelsea*	52	Sunderland	52
1963–64f	Leeds U	63	Sunderland	61	Preston NE	56
1964–65f	Newcastle U	57	Northampton T	56	Bolton W	50
1965–66f	Manchester C	59	Southampton	54	Coventry C	53
1966–67f	Coventry C	59	Wolverhampton W	58	Carlisle U	52
1967–68f	Ipswich T	59	QPR*	58	Blackpool	58
1968–69f	Derby Co	63	Crystal Palace	56	Charlton Ath	50
1969–70f	Huddersfield T	60	Blackpool	53	Leicester C	51
1970–71f	Leicester C	59	Sheffield U	56	Cardiff C*	53
1971–72f	Norwich C	57	Birmingham C	56	Millwall	55
1972–73f	Burnley	62	QPR	61	Aston Villa	50
1973–74f	Middlesbrough	65	Luton T	50	Carlisle U	49
1974–75f	Manchester U	61	Aston Villa	58	Norwich C	53
1975–76f	Sunderland	56	Bristol C*	53	WBA	53
1976–77f	Wolverhampton W	57	Chelsea	55	Nottingham F	52
1977–78f	Bolton W	58	Southampton	57	Tottenham H*	56
1978–79f	Crystal Palace	57	Brighton*	56	Stoke C	56
1979–80f	Leicester C	55	Sunderland	54	Birmingham C*	53
1980–81f	West Ham U	66	Notts Co	53	Swansea C*	50
1981–82g	Luton T	88	Watford	80	Norwich C	71
1982–83g	QPR	85	Wolverhampton W	75	Leicester C	70
1983–84g	Chelsea*	88	Sheffield W	88	Newcastle U	80
1984–85g	Oxford U	84	Birmingham C	82	Manchester C	74
1985–86g	Norwich C	84	Charlton Ath	77	Wimbledon	76
1986–87g	Derby Co	84	Portsmouth	78	Oldham Ath††	75
1987–88h	Millwall	82	Aston Villa*	78	Middlesbrough	78
1988–89k	Chelsea	99	Manchester C	82	Crystal Palace	81
1989–90k	Leeds U*	85	Sheffield U	85	Newcastle U††	80
1990–91k	Oldham Ath	88	West Ham U	87	Sheffield W	82

No competition during 1915–19 and 1939–46.
††*Not promoted after play-offs.*

THIRD DIVISION

Maximum points: 92; 138 from 1981–82.

1958–59	Plymouth Arg	62	Hull C	61	Brentford*	57
1959–60	Southampton	61	Norwich C	59	Shrewsbury T*	52
1960–61	Bury	68	Walsall	62	QPR	60
1961–62	Portsmouth	65	Grimsby T	62	Bournemouth*	59
1962–63	Northampton T	62	Swindon T	58	Port Vale	54
1963–64	Coventry C*	60	Crystal Palace	60	Watford	58
1964–65	Carlisle U	60	Bristol C*	59	Mansfield T	59
1965–66	Hull C	69	Millwall	65	QPR	57
1966–67	QPR	67	Middlesbrough	55	Watford	54
1967–68	Oxford U	57	Bury	56	Shrewsbury T	55
1968–69	Watford*	64	Swindon T	64	Luton T	61
1969–70	Orient	62	Luton T	60	Bristol R	56
1970–71	Preston NE	61	Fulham	60	Halifax T	56
1971–72	Aston Villa	70	Brighton	65	Bournemouth*	62
1972–73	Bolton W	61	Notts Co	57	Blackburn R	55
1973–74	Oldham Ath	62	Bristol R*	61	York C	61
1974–75	Blackburn R	60	Plymouth Arg	59	Charlton Ath	55
1975–76	Hereford U	63	Cardiff C	57	Millwall	56
1976–77	Mansfield T	64	Brighton & HA	61	Crystal Palace*	59
1977–78	Wrexham	61	Cambridge U	58	Preston NE*	56
1978–79	Shrewsbury T	61	Watford*	60	Swansea C	60
1979–80	Grimsby T	62	Blackburn R	59	Sheffield W	58
1980–81	Rotherham U	61	Barnsley*	59	Charlton Ath	59
1981–82	Burnley*	80	Carlisle U	80	Fulham	78
1982–83	Portsmouth	91	Cardiff C	86	Huddersfield T	82
1983–84	Oxford U	95	Wimbledon	87	Sheffield U*	83
1984–85	Bradford C	94	Millwall	90	Hull C	87
1985–86	Reading	94	Plymouth Arg	87	Derby Co	84
1986–87	Bournemouth	97	Middlesbrough	94	Swindon T	87
1987–88	Sunderland	93	Brighton & HA	84	Walsall	82
1988–89	Wolverhampton W	92	Sheffield U	84	Port Vale	84
1989–90	Bristol R	93	Bristol C	91	Notts Co	87
1990–91	Cambridge U	86	Southend U	85	Grimsby T*	83

*Won or placed on goal average/goal difference.

595

FOURTH DIVISION

Maximum points: 92; 138 from 1981–82.

	First	Pts	Second	Pts	Third	Pts	Fourth	Pts
1958–59	Port Vale	64	Coventry C*	60	York C	60	Shrewsbury T	58
1959–60	Walsall	65	Notts Co*	60	Torquay U	60	Watford	57
1960–61	Peterborough U	66	Crystal Palace	64	Northampton T*	60	Bradford PA	60
1961–62†	Millwall	56	Colchester U	55	Wrexham	53	Carlisle U	52
1962–63	Brentford	62	Oldham Ath*	59	Crewe Alex	59	Mansfield T*	57
1963–64	Gillingham*	60	Carlisle U	60	Workington T	59	Exeter C	58
1964–65	Brighton	63	Millwall*	62	York C	62	Oxford U	61
1965–66	Doncaster R*	59	Darlington	59	Torquay U	58	Colchester U*	56
1966–67	Stockport Co	64	Southport*	59	Barrow	59	Tranmere R	58
1967–68	Luton T	66	Barnsley	61	Hartlepools U	60	Crewe Alex	58
1968–69	Doncaster R	59	Halifax T	57	Rochdale*	56	Bradford C	56
1969–70	Chesterfield	64	Wrexham	61	Swansea C	60	Port Vale	59
1970–71	Notts Co	69	Bournemouth	60	Oldham Ath	59	York C	56
1971–72	Grimsby T	63	Southend U	60	Brentford	59	Scunthorpe U	57
1972–73	Southport	62	Hereford U	58	Cambridge U	57	Aldershot*	56
1973–74	Peterborough U	65	Gillingham	62	Colchester U	60	Bury	59
1974–75	Mansfield T	68	Shrewsbury T	62	Rotherham U	59	Chester*	57
1975–76	Lincoln C	74	Northampton T	68	Reading	60	Tranmere R	58
1976–77	Cambridge U	65	Exeter C	62	Colchester U*	59	Bradford C	59
1977–78	Watford	71	Southend U	60	Swansea C*	56	Brentford	56
1978–79	Reading	65	Grimsby T*	61	Wimbledon*	61	Barnsley	61
1979–80	Huddersfield T	66	Walsall	64	Newport Co	61	Portsmouth*	60
1980–81	Southend U	67	Lincoln C	65	Doncaster R	56	Wimbledon	55
1981–82	Sheffield U	96	Bradford C*	91	Wigan Ath	91	AFC Bournemouth	88
1982–83	Wimbledon	98	Hull C	90	Port Vale	88	Scunthorpe U	83
1983–84	York C	101	Doncaster R	85	Reading*	82	Bristol C	82
1984–85	Chesterfield	91	Blackpool	86	Darlington	85	Bury	84
1985–86	Swindon T	102	Chester C	84	Mansfield T	81	Port Vale	79
1986–87	Northampton T	99	Preston NE	90	Southend U	80	Wolverhampton W††	79
1987–88	Wolverhampton W	90	Cardiff C	85	Bolton W	78	Scunthorpe U††	77
1988–89	Rotherham U	82	Tranmere R	80	Crewe Alex	78	Scunthorpe U††	77
1989–90	Exeter C	89	Grimsby T	79	Southend U	75	Stockport Co††	74
1990–91	Darlington	83	Stockport Co*	82	Hartlepool U	82	Peterborough U	80

†*Maximum points: 88 owing to Accrington Stanley's resignation.*   ††*Not promoted after play-offs.*

THIRD DIVISION—SOUTH (1920–1958)

Maximum points: a 84; b 92.

	First	Pts	Second	Pts	Third	Pts
1920–21a	Crystal Palace	59	Southampton	54	QPR	53
1921–22a	Southampton*	61	Plymouth Arg	61	Portsmouth	53
1922–23a	Bristol C	59	Plymouth Arg*	53	Swansea T	53
1923–24a	Portsmouth	59	Plymouth Arg	55	Millwall	54
1924–25a	Swansea T	57	Plymouth Arg	56	Bristol C	53
1925–26a	Reading	57	Plymouth Arg	56	Millwall	53
1926–27a	Bristol C	62	Plymouth Arg	60	Millwall	56
1927–28a	Millwall	65	Northampton T	55	Plymouth Arg	53
1928–29a	Charlton Ath*	54	Crystal Palace	54	Northampton T*	52
1929–30a	Plymouth Arg	68	Brentford	61	QPR	51
1930–31a	Notts Co	59	Crystal Palace	51	Brentford	50
1931–32a	Fulham	57	Reading	55	Southend U	53
1932–33a	Brentford	62	Exeter C	58	Norwich C	57
1933–34a	Norwich C	61	Coventry C*	54	Reading*	54
1934–35a	Charlton Ath	61	Reading	53	Coventry C	51
1935–36a	Coventry C	57	Luton T	56	Reading	54
1936–37a	Luton T	58	Notts Co	56	Brighton	53
1937–38a	Millwall	56	Bristol C	55	QPR*	53
1938–39a	Newport Co	55	Crystal Palace	52	Brighton	49
1939–46	Competition cancelled owing to war.					
1946–47a	Cardiff C	66	QPR	57	Bristol C	51
1947–48a	QPR	61	Bournemouth	57	Walsall	51
1948–49a	Swansea T	62	Reading	55	Bournemouth	52
1949–50a	Notts Co	58	Northampton T*	51	Southend U	51
1950–51b	Nottingham F	70	Norwich C	64	Reading*	57
1951–52b	Plymouth Arg	66	Reading*	61	Norwich C	61
1952–53b	Bristol R	64	Millwall*	62	Northampton T	62
1953–54b	Ipswich T	64	Brighton	61	Bristol C	56
1954–55b	Bristol C	70	Leyton O	61	Southampton	59
1955–56b	Leyton O	66	Brighton	65	Ipswich T	64
1956–57b	Ipswich T*	59	Torquay U	59	Colchester U	58
1957–58b	Brighton	60	Brentford*	58	Plymouth Arg	58

* *Won or placed on goal average.*

THIRD DIVISION—NORTH (1921–1958)

Maximum points: a 76; b 84; c 80; d 92.

	First	Pts	Second	Pts	Third	Pts
1921–22a	Stockport Co	56	Darlington*	50	Grimsby T	50
1922–23a	Nelson	51	Bradford PA	47	Walsall	46
1923–24b	Wolverhampton W	63	Rochdale	62	Chesterfield	54
1924–25b	Darlington	58	Nelson*	53	New Brighton	53
1925–26b	Grimsby T	61	Bradford PA	60	Rochdale	59
1926–27b	Stoke C	63	Rochdale	58	Bradford PA	55
1927–28b	Bradford PA	63	Lincoln C	55	Stockport Co	54
1928–29g	Bradford C	63	Stockport Co	62	Wrexham	52
1929–30b	Port Vale	67	Stockport Co	63	Darlington*	50
1930–31b	Chesterfield	58	Lincoln C	57	Wrexham*	54
1931–32c	Lincoln C*	57	Gateshead	57	Chester	50
1932–33b	Hull C	59	Wrexham	57	Stockport Co	54
1933–34b	Barnsley	62	Chesterfield	61	Stockport Co	59
1934–35b	Doncaster R	57	Halifax T	55	Chester	54
1935–36b	Chesterfield	60	Chester*	55	Tranmere R	55
1936–37b	Stockport Co	60	Lincoln C	57	Chester	53
1937–38b	Tranmere R	56	Doncaster R	54	Hull C	53
1938–39b	Barnsley	67	Doncaster R	56	Bradford C	52
1939–46	Competition cancelled owing to war.					
1946–47b	Doncaster R	72	Rotherham U	64	Chester	56
1947–48b	Lincoln C	60	Rotherham U	59	Wrexham	50
1948–49b	Hull C	65	Rotherham U	62	Doncaster R	50
1949–50b	Doncaster R	55	Gateshead	53	Rochdale*	51
1950–51d	Rotherham U	71	Mansfield T	64	Carlisle U	62
1951–52d	Lincoln C	69	Grimsby T	66	Stockport Co	59
1952–53d	Oldham Ath	59	Port Vale	58	Wrexham	56
1953–54d	Port Vale	69	Barnsley	58	Scunthorpe U	57
1954–55d	Barnsley	65	Accrington S	61	Scunthorpe U*	58
1955–56d	Grimsby T	68	Derby Co	63	Accrington S	59
1956–57d	Derby Co	63	Hartlepool U	59	Accrington S*	58
1957–58d	Scunthorpe U	66	Accrington S	59	Bradford C	57

* Won or placed on goal average.

PROMOTED AFTER PLAY-OFFS
(Not accounted for in previous section)

1986–87	Aldershot to Division 3.
1987–88	Swansea C to Divison 3.
1988–89	Leyton O to Division 3.
1989–90	Cambridge U to Division 3; Sunderland to Division 1.
1990–91	Notts Co to Division 1; Tranmere R to Division 2; Torquay U to Division 3.

LEAGUE TITLE WINS

LEAGUE DIVISION 1 – Liverpool 18, Arsenal 10, Everton 9, Manchester U 7, Aston Villa 7, Sunderland 6, Newcastle U 4, Sheffield W 4, Huddersfield T 3, Wolverhampton W 3, Blackburn R 2, Portsmouth 2, Preston NE 2, Burnley 2, Manchester C 2, Tottenham H 2, Leeds U 2, Derby Co 2, Chelsea 1, Sheffield U 1, WBA 1, Ipswich T 1, Nottingham F 1 each.

LEAGUE DIVISION 2 – Leicester C 6, Manchester C 6, Sheffield W 5, Birmingham C (one as Small Heath) 4, Derby Co 4, Liverpool 4, Leeds U 3, Notts Co 3, Preston NE 3, Middlesbrough 3, Grimsby T 2, Norwich C 2, Nottingham F 2, Tottenham H 2, WBA 2, Aston Villa 2, Stoke C 2, Ipswich T 2, Burnley 2, Chelsea 2, Manchester U 2, West Ham U 2, Wolverhampton W 2, Bolton W 2, Huddersfield T, Bristol C, Brentford, Bury, Bradford C, Everton, Fulham, Sheffield U, Newcastle U, Coventry C, Blackpool, Blackburn R, Sunderland, Crystal Palace, Luton T, QPR, Oxford U, Millwall, Oldham Ath 1 each.

LEAGUE DIVISION 3 – Portsmouth 2, Oxford U 2, Plymouth Arg, Southampton, Bury, Northampton T, Coventry C, Carlisle U, Hull C, QPR, Watford, Leyton O, Preston NE, Aston Villa, Bolton W, Oldham Ath, Blackburn R, Hereford U, Mansfield T, Wrexham, Shrewsbury T, Grimsby T, Rotherham U, Burnley, Bradford C, Bournemouth, Reading, Sunderland, Wolverhampton W, Bristol R, Cambridge U 1 each.

LEAGUE DIVISION 4 – Chesterfield 2, Doncaster R 2, Peterborough U 2, Port Vale, Walsall, Millwall, Brentford, Gillingham, Brighton, Stockport Co, Luton T, Notts Co, Grimsby T, Southport, Mansfield T, Lincoln C, Cambridge U, Watford, Reading, Huddersfield T, Southend U, Sheffield U, Wimbledon, York C, Swindon T, Northampton T, Wolverhampton W, Rotherham U, Exeter C, Darlington 1 each.

To 1957–58

DIVISION 3 (South) – Bristol C 3; Charlton Ath, Ipswich T, Millwall, Notts Co, Plymouth Arg, Swansea T 2 each; Brentford, Bristol R, Cardiff C, Crystal Palace, Coventry C, Fulham, Leyton O, Luton T, Newport Co, Nottingham F, Norwich C, Portsmouth, QPR, Reading, Southampton, Brighton 1 each.

DIVISION 3 (North) – Barnsley, Doncaster R, Lincoln C 3 each; Chesterfield, Grimsby T, Hull C, Port Vale, Stockport Co 2 each; Bradford PA, Bradford C, Darlington, Derby Co, Nelson, Oldham Ath, Rotherham U, Stoke C, Tranmere R, Wolverhampton W, Scunthorpe U 1 each.

RELEGATED CLUBS

1891–92 League extended. Newton Heath, Sheffield W and Nottingham F admitted. *Second Division formed* including Darwen.

1892–93 In Test matches, Sheffield U and Darwen won promotion in place of Notts Co and Accrington S.

1893–94 In Tests, Liverpool and Small Heath won promotion. Newton Heath and Darwen relegated.

1894–95 After Tests, Bury promoted, Liverpool relegated.

1895–96 After Tests, Liverpool promoted, Small Heath relegated.

1896–97 After Tests, Notts Co promoted, Burnley relegated.

1897–98 Test system abolished after success of Stoke C and Burnley. League extended. Blackburn R and Newcastle U elected to First Division. *Automatic promotion and relegation introduced.*

DIVISION 1 TO DIVISION 2

1898–99 Bolton W and Sheffield W
1899–1900 Burnley and Glossop
1900–01 Preston NE and WBA
1901–02 Small Heath and Manchester C
1902–03 Grimsby T and Bolton W
1903–04 Liverpool and WBA
1904–05 League extended. Bury and Notts Co, two bottom clubs in First Division, re-elected.
1905–06 Nottingham F and Wolverhampton W
1906–07 Derby Co and Stoke C
1907–08 Bolton W and Birmingham C
1908–09 Manchester C and Leicester Fosse
1909–10 Bolton W and Chelsea
1910–11 Bristol C and Nottingham F
1911–12 Preston NE and Bury
1912–13 Notts Co and Woolwich Arsenal
1913–14 Preston NE and Derby Co
1914–15 Tottenham H and Chelsea*
1919–20 Notts Co and Sheffield W
1920–21 Derby Co and Bradford PA
1921–22 Bradford C and Manchester U
1922–23 Stoke C and Oldham Ath
1923–24 Chelsea and Middlesbrough
1924–25 Preston NE and Nottingham F
1925–26 Manchester C and Notts Co
1926–27 Leeds U and WBA
1927–28 Tottenham H and Middlesbrough
1928–29 Bury and Cardiff C
1929–30 Burnley and Everton
1930–31 Leeds U and Manchester U
1931–32 Grimsby T and West Ham U
1932–33 Bolton W and Blackpool
1933–34 Newcastle U and Sheffield U
1934–35 Leicester C and Tottenham H
1935–36 Aston Villa and Blackburn R
1936–37 Manchester U and Sheffield W
1937–38 Manchester C and WBA
1938–39 Birmingham C and Leicester C
1946–47 Brentford and Leeds U
1947–48 Blackburn R and Grimsby T
1948–49 Preston NE and Sheffield U
1949–50 Manchester C and Birmingham C

1950–51 Sheffield W and Everton
1951–52 Huddersfield and Fulham
1952–53 Stoke C and Derby Co
1953–54 Middlesbrough and Liverpool
1954–55 Leicester C and Sheffield W
1955–56 Huddersfield and Sheffield U
1956–57 Charlton Ath and Cardiff C
1957–58 Sheffield W and Sunderland
1958–59 Portsmouth and Aston Villa
1959–60 Luton T and Leeds U
1960–61 Preston NE and Newcastle U
1961–62 Chelsea and Cardiff C
1962–63 Manchester C and Leyton O
1963–64 Bolton W and Ipswich T
1964–65 Wolverhampton W and Birmingham C
1965–66 Northampton T and Blackburn R
1966–67 Aston Villa and Blackpool
1967–68 Fulham and Sheffield U
1968–69 Leicester C and QPR
1969–70 Sunderland and Sheffield W
1970–71 Burnley and Blackpool
1971–72 Huddersfield T and Nottingham F
1972–73 Crystal Palace and WBA
1973–74 Southampton, Manchester U, Norwich C
1974–75 Luton T, Chelsea, Carlisle U
1975–76 Wolverhampton W, Burnley, Sheffield U
1976–77 Sunderland, Stoke C, Tottenham H
1977–78 West Ham U, Newcastle U, Leicester C
1978–79 QPR, Birmingham C, Chelsea
1979–80 Bristol C, Derby Co, Bolton W
1980–81 Norwich C, Leicester C, Crystal Palace
1981–82 Leeds U, Wolverhampton W, Middlesbrough
1982–83 Manchester C, Swansea C, Brighton & HA
1983–84 Birmingham C, Notts Co, Wolverhampton W
1984–85 Norwich C, Sunderland, Stoke C
1985–86 Ipswich T, Birmingham C, WBA
1986–87 Leicester C, Manchester C, Aston Villa
1987–88 Chelsea**, Portsmouth, Watford, Oxford U
1988–89 Middlesbrough, West Ham U, Newcastle U
1989–90 Sheffield W, Charlton Ath, Millwall
1990–91 Sunderland and Derby Co

**Relegated after play-offs.*
Subsequently re-elected to Division 1 when League was extended after the War.

DIVISION 2 TO DIVISION 3

1920–21 Stockport Co
1921–22 Bradford and Bristol C
1922–23 Rotherham C and Wolverhampton W
1923–24 Nelson and Bristol C
1924–25 Crystal Palace and Coventry C
1925–26 Stoke C and Stockport Co
1926–27 Darlington and Bradford C
1927–28 Fulham and South Shields
1928–29 Port Vale and Clapton O
1929–30 Hull C and Notts Co
1930–31 Reading and Cardiff C
1931–32 Barnsley and Bristol C
1932–33 Chesterfield and Charlton Ath
1933–34 Millwall and Lincoln C
1934–35 Oldham Ath and Notts Co
1935–36 Port Vale and Hull C

1936–37 Doncaster R and Bradford C
1937–38 Barnsley and Stockport Co
1938–39 Norwich C and Tranmere R
1946–47 Swansea T and Newport Co
1947–48 Doncaster R and Millwall
1948–49 Nottingham F and Lincoln C
1949–50 Plymouth Arg and Bradford
1950–51 Grimsby T and Chesterfield
1951–52 Coventry C and QPR
1952–53 Southampton and Barnsley
1953–54 Brentford and Oldham Ath
1954–55 Ipswich T and Derby Co
1955–56 Plymouth Arg and Hull C
1956–57 Port Vale and Bury
1957–58 Doncaster R and Notts Co
1958–59 Barnsley and Grimsby T

1959–60 Bristol C and Hull C	1975–76 Oxford U, York C, Portsmouth
1960–61 Lincoln C and Portsmouth	1976–77 Carlisle U, Plymouth Arg, Hereford U
1961–62 Brighton & HA and Bristol R	1977–78 Blackpool, Mansfield T, Hull C
1962–63 Walsall and Luton T	1978–79 Sheffield U, Millwall, Blackburn R
1963–64 Grimsby T and Scunthorpe U	1979–80 Fulham, Burnley, Charlton Ath
1964–65 Swindon T and Swansea T	1980–81 Preston NE, Bristol C, Bristol R
1965–66 Middlesbrough and Leyton O	1981–82 Cardiff C, Wrexham, Orient
1966–67 Northampton T and Bury	1982–83 Rotherham U, Burnley, Bolton W
1967–68 Plymouth Arg and Rotherham U	1983–84 Derby Co, Swansea C, Cambridge U
1968–69 Fulham and Bury	1984–85 Notts Co, Cardiff C, Wolverhampton W
1969–70 Preston NE and Aston Villa	1985–86 Carlisle U, Middlesbrough, Fulham
1970–71 Blackburn R and Bolton W	1986–87 Sunderland**, Grimsby T, Brighton & HA
1971–72 Charlton Ath and Watford	1987–88 Huddersfield T, Reading, Sheffield U**
1972–73 Huddersfield T and Brighton & HA	1988–89 Shrewsbury T, Birmingham C, Walsall
1973–74 Crystal Palace, Preston NE, Swindon T	1989–90 Bournemouth, Bradford, Stoke C
1974–75 Millwall, Cardiff C, Sheffield W	1990–91 WBA and Hull C

DIVISION 3 TO DIVISION 4

1958–59 Rochdale, Notts Co, Doncaster R and Stockport	1973–74 Cambridge U, Shrewsbury T, Southport, Rochdale
1959–60 Accrington S, Wrexham, Mansfield T and York C	1974–75 AFC Bournemouth, Tranmere R, Watford, Huddersfield T
1960–61 Chesterfield, Colchester U, Bradford C and Tranmere R	1975–76 Aldershot, Colchester U, Southend U, Halifax T
1961–62 Newport Co, Brentford, Lincoln C and Torquay U	1976–77 Reading, Northampton T, Grimsby T, York C
1962–63 Bradford PA, Brighton, Carlisle U and Halifax T	1977–78 Port Vale, Bradford C, Hereford U, Portsmouth
1963–64 Millwall, Crewe Alex, Wrexham and Notts Co	1978–79 Peterborough U, Walsall, Tranmere R, Lincoln C
1964–65 Luton T, Port Vale, Colchester U and Barnsley	1979–80 Bury, Southend U, Mansfield T, Wimbledon
1965–66 Southend U, Exeter C, Brentford and York C	1980–81 Sheffield U, Colchester U, Blackpool, Hull C
1966–67 Doncaster R, Workington, Darlington and Swansea T	1981–82 Wimbledon, Swindon T, Bristol C, Chester
1967–68 Scunthorpe U, Colchester U, Grimsby T and Peterborough U (demoted)	1982–83 Reading, Wrexham, Doncaster R, Chesterfield
1968–69 Oldham Ath, Crewe Alex, Hartlepool and Northampton	1983–84 Scunthorpe U, Southend U, Port Vale, Exeter C
1969–70 Bournemouth, Southport, Barrow, Stockport Co	1984–85 Burnley, Orient, Preston NE, Cambridge U
1970–71 Reading, Bury, Doncaster R, Gillingham	1985–86 Lincoln C, Cardiff C, Wolverhampton W, Swansea C
1971–72 Mansfield T, Barnsley, Torquay U, Bradford C	1986–87 Bolton W**, Carlisle U, Darlington, Newport Co
1972–73 Rotherham U, Brentford, Swansea C, Scunthorpe U	1987–88 Doncaster R, York C, Grimsby T, Rotherham U**
	1988–89 Southend U, Chesterfield, Gillingham, Aldershot
	1989–90 Cardiff C, Northampton T, Blackpool, Walsall
	1990–91 Crewe Alex, Rotherham U, Mansfield T

** *Relegated after play-offs.*

APPLICATIONS FOR RE-ELECTION
FOURTH DIVISION

Eleven: Hartlepool U.
Seven: Crewe Alex.
Six: Barrow (lost League place to Hereford U 1972), Halifax T, Rochdale, Southport (lost League place to Wigan Ath 1978), York C.
Five: Chester C, Darlington, Lincoln C, Stockport Co, Workington (lost League place to Wimbledon 1977).
Four: Bradford PA (lost League place to Cambridge U 1970), Newport Co, Northampton T.
Three: Doncaster R, Hereford U.
Two: Bradford C, Exeter C, Oldham Ath, Scunthorpe U, Torquay U.
One: Aldershot, Colchester U, Gateshead (lost League place to Peterborough U 1960), Grimsby T, Swansea C, Tranmere R, Wrexham, Blackpool, Cambridge U, Preston NE.
Accrington S resigned and Oxford U were elected 1962.
Port Vale were forced to re-apply following expulsion in 1968.

THIRD DIVISIONS NORTH & SOUTH

Seven: Walsall.
Six: Exeter C, Halifax T, Newport Co.
Five: Accrington S, Barrow, Gillingham, New Brighton, Southport.
Four: Rochdale, Norwich C.
Three: Crystal Palace, Crewe Alex, Darlington, Hartlepools U, Merthyr T, Swindon T.
Two: Aberdare Ath, Aldershot, Ashington, Bournemouth, Brentford, Chester, Colchester U, Durham C, Millwall, Nelson, QPR, Rotherham U, Southend U, Tranmere R, Watford, Workington.
One: Bradford C, Bradford PA, Brighton, Bristol R, Cardiff C, Carlisle U, Charlton Ath, Gateshead, Grimsby T, Mansfield T, Shrewsbury T, Torquay U, York C.

LEAGUE STATUS FROM 1986–87

RELEGATED FROM LEAGUE		PROMOTED TO LEAGUE
1986–87	Lincoln C	Scarborough
1987–88	Newport Co	Lincoln C
1988–89	Darlington	Maidstone U
1989–90	Colchester U	Darlington
1990–91	—	Barnet

LEADING GOALSCORERS 1990–91

	League	FA Cup	Rumbelows League Cup	Other Cups	Total
DIVISION 1					
Lee Chapman *(Leeds United)*	21	3	4	3	31
Alan Smith *(Arsenal)*	23	2	3	0	28
Ian Rush *(Liverpool)*	16	5	5	0	26
Ian Wright *(Crystal Palace)*	15	1	3	6	25
David Platt *(Aston Villa)*	19	0	3	2	24
Tony Cottee *(Everton)*	10	2	4	8	24
Matthew Le Tissier *(Southampton)*	19	2	2	0	23
Niall Quinn *(Manchester City)*	20	1	0	1	22
Dean Saunders *(Derby County)*	17	0	3	1	21
Mark Hughes *(Manchester United)*	10	2	6	3	21
Brian McClair *(Manchester United)*	13	2	2	4	21
Nigel Clough *(Nottingham Forest)*	14	2	3	1	20
John Fashanu *(Wimbledon)*	20	0	0	0	20
Roy Wegerle *(Queens Park Rangers)*	18	0	1	0	19
Paul Gascoigne *(Tottenham Hotspur)*	7	6	6	0	19
Gary Lineker *(Tottenham Hotspur)*	15	3	1	0	19
Steve Bruce *(Manchester United)*	13	0	2	4	19
Rodney Wallace *(Southampton)*	14	2	2	1	19
DIVISION 2					
Teddy Sheringham *(Millwall)*	33	2	2	1	38
David Hirst *(Sheffield Wednesday)*	24	2	3	3	32
Steve Bull *(Wolverhampton Wanderers)*	26	0	0	1	27
Steve Butler *(Watford) (Including 25 for Maidstone United)*	21	2	2	1	26
Andy Payton *(Hull City)*	25	0	0	0	25
Darren Beckford *(Port Vale)*	22	2	0	0	24
Duncan Shearer *(Swindon Town)*	22	1	0	0	23
Mike Small *(Brighton & Hove Albion)*	15	2	1	2	20
Bernie Slaven *(Middlesbrough)*	16	0	3	1	20
Guy Whittingham *(Portsmouth)*	12	7	1	0	20
Mick Quinn *(Newcastle United)*	18	2	0	0	20
Stuart Rimmer *(Barnsley) (Including 18 for Walsall)*	14	0	4	1	19
Tommy Johnson *(Notts County)*	16	0	3	0	19
Paul Wilkinson *(Watford)*	18	0	0	1	19
Paul Simpson *(Oxford United)*	17	0	1	0	18
Ian Marshall *(Oldham Athletic)*	17	0	0	1	18
DIVISION 3					
Tony Philliskirk *(Bolton Wanderers)*	19	2	5	0	26
Brett Angell *(Southend United)*	15	2	2	7	26
Dion Dublin *(Cambridge United)*	16	4	1	2	23
Luther Blissett *(Bournemouth)*	19	0	2	0	21
Ian Muir *(Tranmere Rovers)*	13	0	0	8	21
John Taylor *(Cambridge United)*	14	5	0	1	20
Jimmy Gilligan *(Swansea City)*	16	2	0	2	20
Don Page *(Wigan Athletic)*	13	1	1	3	18
Steve Castle *(Leyton Orient)*	12	3	3	0	18
Bryan Griffiths *(Wigan Athletic)*	12	3	0	2	17
Sean McCarthy *(Bradford City)*	13	0	2	1	16
Andy Sussex *(Crewe Alexandra)*	11	1	4	0	16
Ian Benjamin *(Southend United)*	13	0	0	3	16
Graham Shaw *(Preston North End)*	10	0	1	5	16
Gary Blissett *(Brentford)*	10	2	0	3	15
David Lee *(Bury)*	15	0	0	0	15
Carl Dale *(Chester City)*	10	4	0	1	15
Craig Hignett *(Crewe Alexandra)*	13	2	0	0	15
Trevor Senior *(Reading)*	15	0	0	0	15
DIVISION 4					
Steve Norris *(Halifax Town) (Including 2 for Carlisle United)*	32	2	0	1	35
Joe Allon *(Hartlepool United)*	28	3	2	2	35
Andy Flounders *(Scunthorpe United)*	23	3	0	1	27
David Puckett *(Aldershot)*	21	2	3	0	26
Steve Lovell *(Gillingham)*	19	0	1	1	21
Ron Futcher *(Burnley)*	18	0	1	1	20
Tommy Tynan *(Torquay United)*	13	1	1	4	19
Dave Bamber *(Blackpool) (Including 2 for Hull City)*	19	0	0	0	19
John Francis *(Burnley)*	14	1	0	1	16
Bobby Barnes *(Northampton Town)*	13	2	1	0	16
George Oghani *(Scarborough)*	14	0	2	0	16
Dean Edwards *(Torquay United)*	15	0	0	1	16
Charlie Henry *(Aldershot)*	13	2	0	0	15
Cohen Griffith *(Cardiff City)*	9	0	5	1	15
Chris Pike *(Cardiff City)*	14	0	1	0	15
John Muir *(Doncaster Rovers)*	13	0	1	1	15
Mark Lillis *(Scunthorpe United)*	10	2	1	2	15
Chris Beaumont *(Stockport County)*	15	0	0	0	15

NB. Other Cups: European Cup-Winners' Cup, UEFA Cup, Zenith Data Systems Cup and Leyland Daf Cup.

FA CHARITY SHIELD WINNERS 1908–90

1908	Manchester U v QPR	4-0 after 1-1 draw	1956	Manchester U v Manchester C		1-0
1909	Newcastle U v Northampton T	2-0	1957	Manchester U v Aston Villa		4-0
1910	Brighton v Aston Villa	1-0	1958	Bolton W v Wolverhampton W		4-1
1911	Manchester U v Swindon T	8-4	1959	Wolverhampton W v Nottingham F		3-1
1912	Blackburn R v QPR	2-1	1960	Burnley v Wolverhampton W		2-2*
1913	Professionals v Amateurs	7-2	1961	Tottenham H v FA XI		3-2
1919	WBA v Tottenham H	2-0	1962	Tottenham H v Ipswich T		5-1
1920	Tottenham H v Burnley	2-0	1963	Everton v Manchester U		4-0
1921	Huddersfield T v Liverpool	1-0	1964	Liverpool v West Ham U		2-2*
1922	Not played		1965	Manchester U v Liverpool		2-2*
1923	Professionals v Amateurs	2-0	1966	Liverpool v Everton		1-0
1924	Professionals v Amateurs	3-1	1967	Manchester U v Tottenham H		3-3*
1925	Amateurs v Professionals	6-1	1968	Manchester C v WBA		6-1
1926	Amateurs v Professionals	6-3	1969	Leeds U v Manchester C		2-1
1927	Cardiff C v Corinthians	2-1	1970	Everton v Chelsea		2-1
1928	Everton v Blackburn R	2-1	1971	Leicester C v Liverpool		1-0
1929	Professionals v Amateurs	3-0	1972	Manchester C v Aston Villa		1-0
1930	Arsenal v Sheffield W	2-1	1973	Burnley v Manchester C		1-0
1931	Arsenal v WBA	1-0	1974	Liverpool† v Leeds U		1-1
1932	Everton v Newcastle U	5-3	1975	Derby Co v West Ham U		2-0
1933	Arsenal v Everton	3-0	1976	Liverpool v Southampton		1-0
1934	Arsenal v Manchester C	4-0	1977	Liverpool v Manchester U		0-0*
1935	Sheffield W v Arsenal	1-0	1978	Nottingham F v Ipswich T		5-0
1936	Sunderland v Arsenal	2-1	1979	Liverpool v Arsenal		3-1
1937	Manchester C v Sunderland	2-0	1980	Liverpool v West Ham U		1-0
1938	Arsenal v Preston NE	2-1	1981	Aston Villa v Tottenham H		2-2*
1948	Arsenal v Manchester U	4-3	1982	Liverpool v Tottenham H		1-0
1949	Portsmouth v Wolverhampton W	1-1*	1983	Manchester U v Liverpool		2-0
1950	World Cup Team v Canadian Touring Team	4-2	1984	Everton v Liverpool		1-0
1951	Tottenham H v Newcastle U	2-1	1985	Everton v Manchester U		2-0
1952	Manchester U v Newcastle U	4-2	1986	Everton v Liverpool		1-1*
1953	Arsenal v Blackpool	3-1	1987	Everton v Coventry C		1-0
1954	Wolverhampton W v WBA	4-4*	1988	Liverpool v Wimbledon		2-1
1955	Chelsea v Newcastle U	3-0	1989	Liverpool v Arsenal		1-0

Each club retained shield for six months. † *Won on penalties.*

FA CHARITY SHIELD 1990

Liverpool (0) 1, Manchester U (1) 1
At Wembley, 18 August 1990, attendance 66,558

Liverpool: Grobbelaar; Hysen, Burrows, Venison, Whelan, Ablett, Beardsley (Rosenthal), Houghton, Rush, Barnes, McMahon.

Scorer: Barnes (pen).

Manchester U: Sealey; Irwin, Donaghy, Bruce, Phelan, Pallister, Blackmore, Ince, McClair, Hughes, Wallace (Robins).

Scorer: Blackmore.

Referee: G. Courtney (Spennymoor).

———

FOOTBALL LEAGUE REPRESENTATIVE GAMES

16 January (in Naples)

Italian League (2) 3 *(Van Basten, Careca, Simeone)*

Football League (0) 0   10,000

Italian League: Galli (Taffarel); Garzya, Aldair (Branco), Pin, Benedetta, Jozic (Minotti), Bianchi (Lentini), Mikhailichenko, Careca, Matthaus (Simeone), Van Basten (Di Canio).
Football League: Southall (Seaman); Dixon, Nicol, Thomas (Bowen), Wright M, Hysen (Curle), Limpar (Saunders), McMahon, Rush (Bull), Davis, Barnes.

13 November (at Windsor Park)

Centenary Match

Irish League (1) 1 *(Murray)*

Football League (0) 1 *(Wegerle)*   3600

Irish League: Keenan; Neill, Scappaticci, Morrison (Quigley), Strain, Byrne, Doolin (McConville), Murphy (Davidson), MacCartney (Douglas), Murray, Burrows.
Football League: Grobbelaar (Spink); Laws, Burrows, Case, Mabbutt, Pallister, Le Tissier, Howells (Barrett), Clough (Gabbiadini), Wegerle, Sinton (Le Saux).

TRANSFERS 1990–91

	From	To	Fee
May 1990			
25 Thompstone, Ian P.	Manchester City	Oldham Athletic	Free
Temporary Transfers			
25 McKinnon, Robert	Hartlepool United	Manchester United	
25 Short, Christian M.	Scarborough	Manchester United	
June 1990			
7 Barton, Warren	Maidstone United	Wimbledon	£300,000
20 Boothroyd, Adrian	Huddersfield Town	Bristol Rovers	£30,000
5 Clarke, Colin J.	Queens Park Rangers	Portsmouth	£450,000
27 Francis, Lee C.	Arsenal	Chesterfield	Free
21 Hindmarch, Robert	Derby County	Wolverhampton Wanderers	£350,000
18 Humphrey, John	Charlton Athletic	Crystal Palace	£450,000
20 Irwin, Denis J.	Oldham Athletic	Manchester United	£650,000
14 Lee, Christopher	Bradford City	Rochdale	Free
14 Lukic, Jovan	Arsenal	Leeds United	£1,000,000
18 McCall, Ian H.	Bradford City	Dunfermline Athletic	£100,000
28 Stowell, Michael	Everton	Wolverhampton Wanderers	£275,000
1 Whiston, Peter M.	Plymouth Argyle	Torquay United	Free
July 1990			
16 Ball, Kevin A.	Portsmouth	Sunderland	£350,000
20 Barnett, Gary L.	Fulham	Huddersfield Town	£27,500
10 Beesley, Paul	Leyton Orient	Sheffield United	£300,000
30 Benstead, Graham M.	Sheffield United	Brentford	£70,000
18 Blades, Paul A.	Derby County	Norwich City	£700,000
27 Bremner, Kevin J.	Brighton & Hove Albion	Peterborough United	£18,000
25 Brennan, Mark R.	Middlesbrough	Manchester City	£500,000
27 Burke, David I.	Crystal Palace	Bolton Wanderers	£60,000
9 Costello, Peter	Bradford City	Rochdale	£10,000
20 Coton, Anthony P.	Watford	Manchester City	£1,000,000
19 Davenport, Peter	Middlesbrough	Sunderland	£300,000
24 Dublin, Keith B. L.	Brighton & Hove Albion	Watford	£275,000
12 Dunphy, Sean	Barnsley	Lincoln City	£30,000
30 Edinburgh, Justin C.	Southend United	Tottenham Hotspur	£150,000
9 Graham, James	Bradford City	Rochdale	£15,000
30 Gray, Gareth	Bolton Wanderers	Rochdale	£5,000
16 Greenall, Colin A.	Oxford United	Bury	£100,000
10 Hayes, Martin	Arsenal	Celtic	£600,000
12 Heathcote, Michael	Sunderland	Shrewsbury Town	£55,000
5 Hendrie, John G.	Leeds United	Middlesbrough	£550,000
31 Hendry, John	Dundee	Tottenham Hotspur	£50,000
1 Henry, Liburd	Watford	Maidstone United	£40,000
17 Hinchcliffe, Andrew, G.	Manchester City	Everton	Exchange + £200,000
16 Hodges, Glyn P.	Watford	Crystal Palace	£410,000
4 Hoyland, Jamie W.	Bury	Sheffield United	£250,000
2 Kelly, Mark D.	Cardiff City	Fulham	£31,000
4 Linighan, Andrew	Norwich City	Arsenal	£1,250,000
2 McAllister, Gary	Leicester City	Leeds United	£1,000,000
4 McCarthy, Sean C.	Plymouth Argyle	Bradford City	£250,000
11 McGinlay, John	Shrewsbury Town	Bury	£175,000
3 Matthews, Neil	Halifax Town	Stockport County	£70,000
30 Mauge, Ronald C.	Fulham	Bury	£40,000
23 Melville, Andrew R.	Swansea City	Oxford United	£275,000
16 Morgan, Stephen A.	Blackpool	Plymouth Argyle	£115,000
25 Mudd, Paul A.	Hull City	Scarborough	£5,000
5 Mustoe, Robbie	Oxford United	Middlesbrough	£375,000
27 Pemberton, John M.	Crystal Palace	Sheffield United	£300,000
18 Pepper, Nigel	Rotherham United	York City	£25,000
17 Pointon, Neil	Everton	Manchester City	Exchange
24 Polston, John D.	Tottenham Hotspur	Norwich City	£300,000
23 Rhodes, Andrew C.	Oldham Athletic	Dunfermline Athletic	£100,000
26 Saunders, Wesley	Dundee	Torquay United	£60,000
31 Simpson, Neil	Aberdeen	Newcastle United	£150,000
31 Sloan, Scott	Berwick Rangers	Newcastle United	£100,000
18 Spooner, Stephen A.	York City	Rotherham United	£45,000
30 Stanislaus, Roger, E. P.	Brentford	Bury	£90,000
3 Swann, Derek A.	Bohemians	Port Vale	£15,000
5 Townsend, Andrew D.	Norwich City	Chelsea	£1,200,000
25 Walter, David W.	Exeter City	Plymouth Argyle	£10,000
31 Watson, Andrew A.	Halifax Town	Swansea City	£40,000
4 Wilson, Clive	Chelsea	Queens Park Rangers	£450,000
3 Wise, Dennis F.	Wimbledon	Chelsea	£1,600,000
17 Woodthorpe, Colin	Chester City	Norwich City	£175,000
Temporary Transfers			
31 Mooney, Brian J.	Preston North End	Sheffield Wednesday	
23 Turner, Robert P.	Bristol City	Plymouth Argyle	

	From	To	Fee
August 1990			
8 Aizlewood, Mark	Bradford City	Bristol City	£125,000
9 Allison, Wayne	Watford	Bristol City	Exchange + £100,000
2 Angell, Brett	Stockport County	Southend United	£100,000
10 Babb, Philip A.	Millwall	Bradford City	Free
24 Balmer, Stuart M.	Celtic	Charlton Athletic	£100,000
10 Blake, Mark C.	Southampton	Shrewsbury Town	£100,000
24 Bromage, Russell	Bristol City	Brighton & Hove Albion	Free
22 Clark, Martin J.	Nottingham Forest	Mansfield Town	£50,000
14 Connor, Terence F.	Portsmouth	Swansea City	£150,000
13 Cooper, Paul D.	Manchester City	Stockport County	Free
16 Cornwell, John A.	Swindon Town	Southend United	£50,000
23 Currie, David N.	Nottingham Forest	Oldham Athletic	£480,000
23 Davies, Alan	Bradford City	Swansea City	Exchange
21 Davies, William M.	St Mirren	Leicester City	£200,000
10 Donowa, Brian L.	Ipswich Town	Bristol City	£55,000
24 Edwards, Keith	Stockport County	Huddersfield Town	£25,000
20 Elkins, Gary	Fulham	Wimbledon	£20,000
2 Evans, David	Bradford City	Halifax Town	Free
3 Finnigan, Anthony	Blackburn Rovers	Hull City	£30,000
9 Gavin, Mark W.	Bristol City	Watford	Exchange
7 Gilligan, James M.	Portsmouth	Swansea City	£125,000
9 Gregory, Anthony G.	Sheffield Wednesday	Halifax Town	Free
15 Hobson, Gordon	Lincoln City	Exeter City	£20,000
22 Hughes, John	Swansea City	Falkirk	£70,000
24 Hurlock, Terence A.	Millwall	Rangers	£325,000
23 James, Robert M.	Swansea City	Bradford City	Exchange
30 Jobson, Richard I.	Hull City	Oldham Athletic	£460,000
13 Keeley, John H.	Brighton & Hove Albion	Oldham Athletic	£240,000
15 Kennedy, Andrew J.	Blackburn Rovers	Watford	Exchange + £60,000
22 Kennedy, Michael F. M.	Luton Town	Stoke City	£180,000
10 Kite, Philip D.	AFC Bournemouth	Sheffield United	£25,000
1 Law, Nicholas	Notts County	Rotherham United	£35,000
22 McGlashan, John	Montrose	Millwall	£50,000
16 McLaughlin, Joseph	Charlton Athletic	Watford	£350,000
24 McPherson, Keith A.	Northampton Town	Reading	Exchange
3 Mail, David	Blackburn Rovers	Hull City	£160,000
2 Maskell, Craig D.	Huddersfield Town	Reading	£250,000
7 May, Andrew M. P.	Huddersfield Town	Bristol City	£90,000
30 Miller, Ian	Port Vale	Scunthorpe United	Free
24 Milligan, Michael	Oldham Athletic	Everton	£1,000,000
21 Moyes, David W.	Shrewsbury Town	Dunfermline Athletic	£42,500
6 Newell, Paul C.	Southend United	Leyton Orient	Nominal
1 O'Dowd, Anthony T.	Shelbourne	Leeds United	£30,000
30 Powell, Christopher G. R.	Crystal Palace	Southend United	Free
21 Pulis, Anthony R.	Gillingham	AFC Bournemouth	£5,000
20 Rae, Alex	Falkirk	Millwall	£100,000
15 Richardson, Lee J.	Watford	Blackburn Rovers	Exchange
2 Roberts, Iwan W.	Watford	Huddersfield Town	£275,000
3 Stuart, Mark R. N.	Plymouth Argyle	Bradford City	£80,000
10 Thomas, Michael R.	Leeds United	Stoke City	Free
1 Thompson, David S.	Wigan Athletic	Preston North End	£77,500
8 Turner, Robert P.	Bristol City	Plymouth Argyle	£150,000
23 Walker, Clive	Fulham	Brighton & Hove Albion	£20,000
3 West, Colin W.	Chelsea	Dundee	£105,000
22 Whitlock, Mark	Reading	Aldershot	Free
6 Wilcox, Russell	Northampton Town	Hull City	£80,000
15 Williams, Paul A.	Charlton Athletic	Sheffield Wednesday	£600,000
1 Wilson, Daniel J.	Luton Town	Sheffield Wednesday	£200,000
24 Wood, Darren	Reading	Northampton Town	Exchange
16 Wood, George	Cardiff City	Hereford United	Free
15 Young, Eric	Wimbledon	Crystal Palace	£850,000

Temporary Transfers		
23 Achampong, Kenneth	Charlton Athletic	Leyton Orient
9 Broddle, Julian R.	Plymouth Argyle	Bradford City
24 Bryant, Matthew	Bristol City	Walsall
23 Cecere, Michele J.	Huddersfield Town	Walsall
24 Dearden, Kevin C.	Tottenham Hotspur	Peterborough United
30 Duggan, Andrew J.	Huddersfield Town	Hartlepool United
17 Edwards, Neil R.	Leeds United	Huddersfield Town
24 Finley, Alan	Shrewsbury Town	Stockport County
23 Howells, Gareth	Tottenham Hotspur	Torquay United
27 Maguire, Peter	Huddersfield Town	Stockport County
1 Parks, Anthony	Brentford	Queens Park Rangers
20 Phillips, Stewart G.	Swansea City	Hereford United
23 Scully, Patrick	Arsenal	Northampton Town
21 Sheffield, Jon	Norwich City	Aldershot
31 Walker, Ian M.	Tottenham Hotspur	Oxford United
30 Watson, Alexander F.	Liverpool	Derby County
16 Webster, Simon P.	Sheffield United	Charlton Athletic
23 Woods, Neil	Bradford City	Grimsby Town
23 Wright, Mark A.	Everton	Blackpool

	From	To	Fee
September 1990			
24 Achampong, Kenneth	Charlton Athletic	Leyton Orient	£25,000
13 Alexander, Keith	Grimsby Town	Stockport County	£8,500
13 Ashley, Kevin M.	Birmingham City	Wolverhampton Wanderers	£500,000
21 Bennett, David	Sheffield Wednesday	Swindon Town	£60,000
28 Butters, Guy	Tottenham Hotspur	Portsmouth	£375,000
19 Byrne, Michael	Huddersfield Town	Shamrock Rovers	Nominal
21 Cecere, Michele	Huddersfield Town	Walsall	£25,000
20 Finley, Alan J.	Shrewsbury Town	Stockport County	£25,000
7 Goddard, Karl E.	Bradford City	Hereford United	Free
28 Hazard, Michael	Portsmouth	Swindon Town	£130,000
14 Hedworth, Christopher	Halifax Town	Blackpool	Comb. fee £80,000
13 Hockaday, David	Swindon Town	Hull City	£50,000
14 Horner, Philip M.	Halifax Town	Blackpool	Comb. fee £80,000
24 Howells, Gareth J.	Tottenham Hotspur	Torquay United	Nominal
1 Jones, Vincent	Leeds United	Sheffield United	£700,000
14 Juryeff, Ian M.	Hereford United	Halifax Town	£50,000
26 Langley, Kevin J.	Birmingham City	Wigan Athletic	£32,500
21 Marwood, Brian	Arsenal	Sheffield United	£350,000
13 Matthews, Neil P.	Blackpool	Cardiff City	£25,000
14 Rammell, Andrew V.	Manchester United	Barnsley	£100,000
19 Rees, Melvyn J.	Watford	West Bromwich Albion	£55,000
24 Seagraves, Mark	Manchester City	Bolton Wanderers	£100,000
5 Short, Christian M.	Scarborough	Notts County	£100,000
13 Webster, Simon P.	Sheffield United	Charlton Athletic	£50,000
27 Woods, Neil	Bradford City	Grimsby Town	£80,000
Temporary Transfers			
27 Beresford, Marlon	Sheffield Wednesday	Northampton Town	
14 Blundell, Christopher K.	Oldham Athletic	Rochdale	
6 Brazil, Gary N.	Newcastle United	Fulham	
5 Brook, Gary	Blackpool	Notts County	
13 Buttigieg, John	Brentford	Swindon Town	
27 Callaghan, Nigel	Aston Villa	Derby County	
18 Carr, Darren J.	Sheffield United	Crewe Alexandra	
13 Cash, Stewart P.	Nottingham Forest	Brentford	
11 Coughlin, Russell J.	Blackpool	Shrewsbury Town	
26 De Graft Rosenior, Leroy	West Ham United	Fulham	
27 Doyle, Maurice	Queens Park Rangers	Wolverhampton Wanderers	
29 Dyer, Alexander C.	Crystal Palace	Charlton Athletic	
25 Evans, Gareth J.	Hibernian	Stoke City	
1 Fee, Gregory P.	Sheffield Wednesday	Preston North End	
27 Gibson, Colin J.	Manchester United	Port Vale	
13 Gordon, Colin K.	Birmingham City	Hereford United	
13 Haylock, Garry A.	Huddersfield Town	Shelbourne	
21 Hooper, Michael D.	Liverpool	Leicester City	
13 Jenkinson, Leigh	Hull City	Rotherham United	
6 Lemon, Paul A.	Sunderland	Chesterfield	
27 Lowery, Anthony W.	Mansfield Town	Walsall	
27 McDonald, David H.	Tottenham Hotspur	Gillingham	
16 MacPhail, John	Sunderland	Hartlepool United	
13 Mardon, Paul J.	Bristol City	Doncaster Rovers	
2 Methven, Colin	Blackpool	Carlisle United	
21 Muggleton, Carl D.	Leicester City	Liverpool	
11 Pender, John P.	Bristol City	Burnley	
6 Powell, Gary	Everton	Lincoln City	
6 Russell, Kevin J.	Leicester City	Peterborough United	
10 Stancliffe, Paul I.	Sheffield United	Rotherham United	
5 Stant, Philip	Notts County	Blackpool	
6 Starbuck, Philip M.	Nottingham Forest	Blackburn Rovers	
28 Tanner, Nicholas	Liverpool	Swindon Town	
20 Warren, Lee A.	Hull City	Lincoln City	
17 Williams, Darren	Leicester City	Chesterfield	
October 1990			
23 Aylott, Trevor K. C.	AFC Bournemouth	Birmingham City	£40,000
12 Breacker, Tim S.	Luton Town	West Ham United	£600,000
19 Buckley, John	Rotherham United	Partick Thistle	£45,000
17 Coughlin, Russell J.	Blackpool	Swansea City	£10,000
18 Cousins, Anthony J.	Dundalk	Liverpool	£70,000
31 Davies, William M.	Leicester City	Dunfermline Athletic	£165,000
12 Fillery, Michael C.	Portsmouth	Oldham Athletic	£30,000
6 Fyfe, Tony	Halifax Town	Carlisle United	Exchange
26 Jones, Andrew M.	Charlton Athletic	AFC Bournemouth	£80,000
3 Lee, Samuel	Southampton	Bolton Wanderers	Free
10 Lowndes, Stephen R.	Barnsley	Hereford United	£10,000
6 McQueen, Thomas F.	West Ham United	Falkirk	£60,000
3 Magilton, James	Liverpool	Oxford United	£100,000
19 Marshall, Gary	Scunthorpe United	Exeter City	£22,000
21 Morgan, Simon C.	Leicester City	Fulham	£100,000
5 Norris, Stephen M.	Carlisle United	Halifax Town	Exchange
4 North, Stacey	West Bromwich Albion	Fulham	£135,000
18 Pender, John P.	Bristol City	Burnley	£70,000
11 Phillips, Stewart G.	Swansea City	Hereford United	£5,000

	From	*To*	*Fee*
10 Summerfield, Kevin	Plymouth Argyle	Shrewsbury Town	Free
20 Taylor, Alex	Walsall	Falkirk	£45,000

Temporary Transfers

	From	*To*	
31 Ampadu, Kwame	Arsenal	Plymouth Argyle	
18 Barber, Frederick	Walsall	Chester City	
11 Beglin, James M.	Leeds United	Blackburn Rovers	
22 Brook, Gary	Blackpool	Scarborough	
3 Burke, Mark S.	Middlesbrough	Darlington	
4 Chapman, Gary A.	Notts County	Mansfield Town	
17 Clarke, Wayne	Manchester City	Shrewsbury Town	
1 Cook, Mitchell	Halifax Town	Scarborough	
8 Dearden, Kevin C.	Peterborough United	Tottenham Hotspur (Tr. Back)	
12 Dibble, Andrew G.	Manchester City	Aberdeen	
31 Dobson, Paul	Scarborough	Halifax Town	
18 Ellis, Mark	Bradford City	Halifax Town	
25 Fenwick, Terence W.	Tottenham Hotspur	Leicester City	
19 Flower, John G.	Sheffield United	Aldershot	
4 Gabbiadini, Ricardo	Sunderland	Crewe Alexandra	
12 Grew, Mark S.	Port Vale	Blackburn Rovers	
12 Jones, Murray	Bristol City	Doncaster Rovers	
18 Kelly, Mark	Portsmouth	Tottenham Hotspur	
22 McGuinness, Paul E.	Manchester United	Brighton & Hove Albion	
11 Miller, Paul W.	Port Vale	Hereford United	
18 Norton, David W.	Notts County	Rochdale	
8 Owen, Gordon	Blackpool	Carlisle United	
5 Pollitt, Michael F.	Manchester United	Oldham Athletic	
4 Smalley, Paul T.	Scunthorpe United	Blackpool	
6 Summerfield, Kevin	Plymouth Argyle	Shrewsbury Town	
29 Veysey, Kenneth	Torquay United	Oxford United	
12 Wilder, Christopher J.	Sheffield United	Charlton Athletic	
18 Withe, Christopher	Bury	Chester City	

November 1990

2 Brazil, Gary N.	Newcastle United	Fulham	£110,000
16 Butcher, Terry I.	Rangers	Coventry City	£500,000
16 Byrne, David S.	Plymouth Argyle	Watford	£50,000
22 Cawley, Peter	Southend United	Exeter City	Free
9 Daniel, Raymond C.	Cardiff City	Portsmouth	£80,000
22 Doyle, Stephen C.	Hull City	Rochdale	Free
30 Dyer, Alexander C.	Crystal Palace	Charlton Athletic	£100,000
16 Ellis, Mark	Bradford City	Halifax Town	Free
30 Fereday, Wayne	Newcastle United	A.F.C. Bournemouth	Exchange
21 Gayle, John	Wimbledon	Birmingham City	£175,000
27 Hutchison, Donald	Hartlepool United	Liverpool	£175,000
8 Lemon, Paul A.	Sunderland	Chesterfield	Nominal
30 Peacock, Gavin K.	AFC Bournemouth	Newcastle United	Exchange + £150,000
15 Roberts, Graham P.	Chelsea	West Bromwich Albion	£250,000
21 Torpey, Stephen	Millwall	Bradford City	£70,000
21 Treacy, Darren	Millwall	Bradford City	£30,000
15 Williamson, Robert	Rotherham United	Kilmarnock	£100,000

Temporary Transfers

21 Agboola, Rueben	Sunderland	Port Vale	
30 Albiston, Arthur R.	Dundee	Chesterfield	
29 Bamber, John D.	Hull City	Blackpool	
14 Barber, Frederick	Chester City	Walsall (Tr. Back)	
29 Barber, Frederick	Walsall	Blackpool	
8 Barnes, Paul L.	Stoke City	Chesterfield	
20 Brazil, Derek M.	Manchester United	Oldham Athletic	
28 Caesar, Gus C.	Arsenal	Queens Park Rangers	
29 Cook, Michael J.	Cambridge United	York City	
8 Cooper, Graham	Wrexham	York City	
28 De Mange, Kenneth J. P. P.	Hull City	Cardiff City	
28 Dobson, Paul	Halifax Town	Scarborough (Tr. Back)	
29 Dobson, Paul	Scarborough	Hereford United	
29 Fee, Gregory P.	Sheffield Wednesday	Northampton Town	
15 Gallacher, Bernard	Aston Villa	Blackburn Rovers	
22 Gaynor, Tommy	Nottingham Forest	Newcastle United	
8 Gray, Philip	Tottenham Hotspur	Fulham	
1 Hughton, Christopher W. G.	Tottenham Hotspur	West Ham United	
8 King, Adam	Plymouth Argyle	Bristol Rovers	
23 Lange, Anthony	Wolverhampton Wanderers	Aldershot	
23 Leonard, Michael C.	Chesterfield	Halifax Town	
8 Nelson, Garry P.	Brighton & Hove Albion	Notts County	
22 Powell, Gary	Everton	Scunthorpe United	
8 Stancliffe, Paul I.	Sheffield United	Wolverhampton Wanderers	
22 Stant, Philip R.	Notts County	Lincoln City	
16 Walker, Ian M.	Tottenham Hotspur	Ipswich Town	
1 Ward, Mitchum D.	Sheffield United	Crewe Alexandra	
2 West, Gary	Port Vale	Gillingham	
9 Whitehurst, William	Sheffield United	Stoke City	
1 Wilson, David G.	Manchester United	Lincoln City	

	From	To	Fee
December 1990			
12 Alexander, Keith	Stockport County	Lincoln City	£7,000
26 Bailey, Danny S.	Exeter City	Reading	£50,000
28 Bishop, Edward M.	Tranmere Rovers	Chester City	£70,000
14 Blundell, Christopher K.	Oldham Athletic	Rochdale	Nominal
21 Broddle, Julian R.	Plymouth Argyle	St Mirren	£50,000
20 Carr, Darren	Sheffield United	Crewe Alexandra	Nominal
13 Cooper, Stephen B.	Barnsley	Tranmere Rovers	£100,000
31 Dolan, Eamonn J.	West Ham United	Birmingham City	£30,000
21 Gibson, Colin J.	Manchester United	Leicester City	£100,000
13 McLoughlin, Alan F.	Swindon Town	Southampton	£1,000,000
13 MacPhail, John	Sunderland	Hartlepool United	Nominal
31 Mimms, Robert A.	Tottenham Hotspur	Blackburn Rovers	£250,000
22 Peacock, Darren	Hereford United	Queens Park Rangers	£200,000
5 Scott, Martin	Rotherham United	Bristol City	£200,000
17 Stancliffe, Paul I.	Sheffield United	Wolverhampton Wanderers	Free
21 Tillson, Andrew	Grimsby Town	Queens Park Rangers	£400,000
Temporary Transfers			
18 Ampadu, Kwame	Plymouth Argyle	Arsenal (Tr. Back)	
21 Baraclough, Ian R.	Leicester City	Grimsby Town	
14 Campbell, David A.	Bradford City	Derry City	
4 Clarke, Wayne	Shrewsbury Town	Manchester City (Tr. Back)	
19 Edwards, Keith	Huddersfield Town	Plymouth Argyle	
24 Evans, Gareth J.	Hibernian	Northampton Town	
24 Fee, Gregory P.	Northampton Town	Sheffield Wednesday (Tr. Back)	
19 Gordon, Colin K.	Birmingham City	Walsall	
7 Gray, Philip	Fulham	Tottenham Hotspur (Tr. Back)	
21 Hill, Andrew R.	Bury	Manchester City	
5 Himsworth, Gary P.	York City	Scarborough	
28 Hitchcock, Kevin	Chelsea	Northampton Town	
24 Holmes, Michael A.	Rochdale	Torquay United	
17 Hooper, Michael D.	Leicester City	Liverpool (Tr. Back)	
17 Leonard, Michael C.	Halifax Town	Chesterfield (Tr. Back)	
5 McAllister, Brian	Wimbledon	Plymouth Argyle	
13 McCarrison, Dugald	Celtic	Ipswich Town	
17 Muggleton, Carl D.	Liverpool	Leicester City (Tr. Back)	
28 Norton, David W.	Rochdale	Notts County (Tr. Back)	
28 O'Toole, Christopher P.	Leicester City	Exeter City	
13 Owen, Gordon	Blackpool	Exeter City	
28 Pennock, Anthony	Stockport County	Wigan Athletic	
4 Rodgerson, Ian	Cardiff City	Birmingham City	
27 Smith, Mark	Nottingham Forest	Reading	
21 Taylor, Peter M. R.	Blackpool	Cardiff City	
28 Walker, Ian M.	Ipswich Town	Tottenham Hotspur (Tr. Back)	
20 Waugh, Keith	Coventry City	Watford	
January 1991			
11 Adcock, Anthony C.	Bradford City	Northampton Town	£75,000
10 Anderson, Vivian A.	Manchester United	Sheffield Wednesday	Free
16 Bamber, John D.	Hull City	Blackpool	£25,000
10 Carter, James W. C.	Millwall	Liverpool	£800,000
18 Crombie, Dean M.	Bolton Wanderers	Lincoln City	Free
17 Dobson, Anthony J.	Coventry City	Blackburn Rovers	£300,000
3 Dobson, Paul	Scarborough	Lincoln City	£40,000
19 Flower, Johannes G.	Sheffield United	Aldershot	£10,000
3 Himsworth, Gary P.	York City	Scarborough	Free
4 Hughton, Christopher W. G.	Tottenham Hotspur	West Ham United	Free
4 Holmes, Michael A.	Rochdale	Torquay United	£10,000
25 Jones, Murray L.	Bristol City	Exeter City	£30,000
22 Kane, Paul	Hibernian	Oldham Athletic	£350,000
17 Livingstone, Stephen	Coventry City	Blackburn Rovers	£450,000
25 Miller, Paul R.	AFC Bournemouth	Swansea City	Free
9 O'Donohue, Fergus	Cork City	Cambridge United	£36,000
18 Paris, Alan D.	Leicester City	Notts County	£80,000
10 Patterson, Mark A.	Bury	Bolton Wanderers	£65,000
15 Redknapp, Jamie F.	AFC Bournemouth	Liverpool	£350,000
3 Rodgerson, Ian	Cardiff City	Birmingham City	£50,000
10 Rostron, John W.	Sheffield United	Brentford	Free
23 Veysey, Kenneth J.	Torquay United	Oxford United	£110,000
18 Watson, Alexander F.	Liverpool	AFC Bournemouth	£150,000
11 Whitton, Stephen P.	Sheffield Wednesday	Ipswich Town	£150,000
30 Woods, Raymond G.	Wigan Athletic	Coventry City	£200,000
Temporary Transfers			
18 Askew, William	Newcastle United	Shrewsbury Town	
17 Blake, Mark A.	Aston Villa	Wolverhampton Wanderers	
17 Boughey, Darren J.	Stoke City	Wigan Athletic	
10 Bromage, Russell	Brighton & Hove Albion	Maidstone United	
29 Burke, Mark S.	Middlesbrough	Ipswich Town	
15 Campbell, David A.	Bradford City	Shamrock Rovers	
17 Carey, Brian P.	Manchester United	Wrexham	
25 Clayton, Gary	Cambridge United	Peterborough United	
29 Cullen, Anthony	Sunderland	Rotherham United	

	From	To	Fee
10 Dearden, Kevin C.	Tottenham Hotspur	Hull City	
3 De Mange, Kenneth J. P. P.	Cardiff City	Hull City (Tr. Back)	
3 Dobson, Paul	Hereford United	Scarborough (Tr. Back)	
17 Doyle, Maurice	Queens Park Rangers	Crewe Alexandra	
4 Edwards, Neil R.	Leeds United	Huddersfield Town	
4 Fee, Gregory P.	Sheffield Wednesday	Preston North End	
17 Futcher, Paul	Halifax Town	Grimsby Town	
23 Gordon, Colin K.	Birmingham City	Bristol Rovers	
9 Gray, Martin D.	Sunderland	Aldershot	
9 Grew, Mark S.	Blackburn Rovers	Port Vale (Tr. Back)	
3 Heaney, Neil A.	Arsenal	Hartlepool United	
4 Hodges, David	Mansfield Town	Torquay United	
17 Hodges, Glynn P.	Crystal Palace	Sheffield United	
23 Honor, Christian R.	Bristol City	Swansea City	
31 Jones, Philip A.	Everton	Wigan Athletic	
24 Kearney, Mark J.	Mansfield Town	Bury	
17 Kernaghan, Alan N.	Middlesbrough	Charlton Athletic	
24 Ling, Martin	Southend United	Mansfield Town	
17 Madden, Lawrence P.	Sheffield Wednesday	Leicester City	
3 McAllister, Brian	Wimbledon	Plymouth Argyle	
21 McGinlay, John	Bury	Millwall	
24 McGugan, Paul J.	Barnsley	Chesterfield	
31 McInerney, Ian D.	Stockport County	Rochdale	
8 Mitchell, David S.	Chelsea	Newcastle United	
16 Morrow, Stephen J.	Arsenal	Reading	
10 Norton, David W.	Notts County	Hull City	
25 O'Dowd, Anthony T.	Leeds United	Kilkerry City	
24 Pennock, Anthony	Wigan Athletic	Stockport Co. (Tr. Back)	
18 Platnauer, Nicholas R.	Notts County	Port Vale	
10 Reed, John P.	Sheffield United	Scarborough	
17 Russell, Kevin J.	Leicester City	Cardiff City	
8 Scully, Patrick J.	Arsenal	Southend United	
3 Stant, Philip R.	Notts County	Huddersfield Town	
17 Walsh, Colin D.	Charlton Athletic	Middlesbrough	
10 Ward, Ashley S.	Manchester City	Wrexham	
31 West, Gary	Port Vale	Lincoln City	
17 Wimbleton, Paul P.	Shrewsbury Town	Maidstone United	
24 Withe, Christopher	Bury	Mansfield Town	
31 Wood, Paul A.	Sheffield United	AFC Bournemouth	

February 1991

	From	To	Fee
14 Barrick, Dean	Sheffield United	Rotherham United	£50,000
1 Birch, Paul	Aston Villa	Wolverhampton Wanderers	£400,000
15 Brevett, Rufus E.	Doncaster Rovers	Queens Park Rangers	£250,000
12 Cox, Neil J.	Scunthorpe United	Aston Villa	£400,000
1 Donegan, John	Kilkenny	Millwall	£30,000
21 Francis, Kevin	Derby County	Stockport County	£60,000
22 Futcher, Paul	Halifax Town	Grimsby Town	£10,000
13 Hall, Richard A.	Scunthorpe United	Southampton	£200,000
5 Hodges, David	Mansfield Town	Torquay United	£15,000
12 Jepson, Ronald F.	Port Vale	Preston North End	£80,000
20 Joyce, Joseph P.	Barnsley	Scunthorpe United	Free
26 McGugan, Paul J.	Barnsley	Chesterfield	£15,000
7 Mooney, Brian J.	Preston North End	Sunderland	£225,000
22 Sandeman, Bradley	Northampton Town	Maidstone United	£10,000
1 Speedie, David R.	Coventry City	Liverpool	£675,000
8 Stant, Philip R.	Notts County	Fulham	£60,000
14 Turnbull, Lee M.	Doncaster Rovers	Chesterfield	£35,000
20 Watson, Gordon	Charlton Athletic	Sheffield Wednesday	£250,000

Temporary Transfers

	From	To	Fee
20 Bartram, Vincent L.	Wolverhampton Wanderers	West Bromwich Albion	
11 Batty, Lawrence W.	Fulham	Brentford	
28 Beresford, Marlon	Sheffield Wednesday	Crewe Alexandra	
21 Brown, Richard A.	Blackburn Rovers	Maidstone United	
6 Carstairs, James W.	Arsenal	Brentford	
20 Dibble, Andrew G.	Manchester City	Middlesbrough	
28 Gleasure, Peter F.	Northampton Town	Gillingham	
7 Gore, Shaun M.	Fulham	Halifax Town	
25 Gray, Martin D.	Aldershot	Sunderland (Tr. Back)	
4 Heritage, Peter M.	Gillingham	Hereford United	
2 Jacobs, Giles W.	Chelsea	Aldershot	
21 Kevan, David J.	Stoke City	Maidstone United	
26 Lancaster, David	Blackpool	Chesterfield	
6 Lee, Jason B.	Charlton Athletic	Stockport County	
28 Lee, Jason B.	Stockport County	Charlton Athletic (Tr. Back)	
28 Lillis, Jason	Maidstone United	Carlisle United	
14 Moran, Paul	Tottenham Hotspur	Newcastle United	
25 O'Toole, Christopher P.	Exeter City	Leicester City (Tr. Back)	
1 Parks, Anthony	Brentford	Fulham	
20 Parsley, Neil R.	Huddersfield Town	Doncaster Rovers	
28 Pates, Colin	Arsenal	Brighton & Hove Albion	
1 Rice, Brian	Nottingham Forest	Stoke City	
25 Robinson, David	Newcastle United	Peterborough United	

		From	To	Fee
14	Rose, Kevin P.	Bolton Wanderers	Rochdale	
3	Stant, Philip R.	Huddersfield Town	Notts County	
1	Sutton, Stephen J.	Nottingham Forest	Coventry City	
7	Taylor, Robert M.	Sheffield Wednesday	Shrewsbury Town	
22	Whitehurst, William	Sheffield United	Doncaster Rovers	
14	Wright, Thomas J.	Newcastle United	Hull City	

March 1991

28	Batty, Lawrence W.	Fulham	Brentford	Exchange
28	Benney, Mark R.	Maidstone United	Brighton & Hove Albion	£30,000
20	Bodin, Paul	Swindon Town	Crystal Palace	£550,000
9	Bullimore, Wayne A.	Manchester United	Barnsley	Free
14	Burke, Mark S.	Middlesbrough	Wolverhampton Wanderers	£15,000
28	Charlery, Kenneth L.	Maidstone United	Peterborough United	£20,000
28	Cooper, Gary	Maidstone United	Peterborough United	£20,000
28	Costello, Peter	Rochdale	Peterborough United	£30,000
28	Cunningham, Anthony	Bury	Bolton Wanderers	£70,000
28	Davis, Darren	Lincoln City	Maidstone United	£27,500
22	Dowie, Iain	Luton Town	West Ham United	£480,000
28	Duggan, Andrew J.	Huddersfield Town	Rochdale	Free
27	Edwards, Robert W.	Carlisle United	Bristol City	£135,000
29	Fee, Gregory P.	Sheffield Wednesday	Mansfield Town	£20,000
22	Ford, Gary	Port Vale	Mansfield Town	Exchange
29	Gavin, Patrick J.	Leicester City	Peterborough United	£15,000
28	Gittens, Jon	Swindon Town	Southampton	£400,000
28	Goodyear, Clive	Wimbledon	Brentford	Free
22	Griffiths, Ian J.	Wigan Athletic	Wrexham	Exchange
22	Hathaway, Ian A.	Mansfield Town	Rotherham United	Exchange
27	Heath, Philip A.	Oxford United	Cardiff City	Free
8	Heritage, Peter M.	Gillingham	Hereford United	£20,000
22	Hill, Andrew	Bury	Manchester City	£200,000
28	Hine, Mark	Peterborough United	Scunthorpe United	£30,000
7	Humphries, Glenn	Bristol City	Scunthorpe United	£55,000
6	Jones, Philip A.	Everton	Wigan Athletic	Free
28	Kearney, Mark J.	Mansfield Town	Bury	Exchange
30	Kelly, Norman	Oldham Athletic	Dunfermline Athletic	Nominal
28	Kent, Kevin J.	Mansfield Town	Port Vale	£80,000 + Exchange
28	Kerr, Paul	Middlesbrough	Millwall	£100,000
14	Lee, Christopher	Rochdale	Scarborough	Free
1	Lee, Jason B.	Charlton Athletic	Lincoln City	£35,000
29	MacKenzie, Stephen	Charlton Athletic	Sheffield Wednesday	£100,000
28	McGinlay, John	Bury	Millwall	£80,000
29	Mahood, Alan S.	Greenock Morton	Nottingham Forest	£300,000
28	Megson, Kevin	Bradford City	Halifax Town	Nominal
28	Morgan, Stephen J.	Oldham Athletic	Rochdale	Free
8	Nicholas, Peter	Chelsea	Watford	£175,000
27	O'Toole, Christopher P.	Leicester City	Shrewsbury Town	Nominal
27	Parks, Anthony	Brentford	Fulham	Exchange
8	Penrice, Gary K.	Watford	Aston Villa	£1,000,000
27	Rosario, Robert M.	Norwich City	Coventry City	£600,000
14	Rowland, Andrew N.	Southampton	Torquay United	£25,000
22	Sansom, Kenneth G.	Queens Park Rangers	Coventry City	£100,000
28	Scully, Patrick J.	Arsenal	Southend United	£100,000
21	Smith, Mark C.	Huddersfield Town	Grimsby Town	£55,000
22	Spooner, Stephen A.	Rotherham United	Mansfield Town	Exchange
28	Swailes, Christopher W.	Ipswich Town	Peterborough United	£10,000
8	Sweeney, Paul	Newcastle United	St Johnstone	£100,000
30	Ward, Paul	Scunthorpe United	Lincoln City	£30,000
28	White, Eric W.	Burnley	West Bromwich Albion	£35,000
21	Whitehurst, William	Sheffield United	Doncaster Rovers	Free
28	Williams, Paul A.	Stockport County	West Bromwich Albion	£250,000
29	Withe, Christopher	Bury	Mansfield Town	Exchange
22	Worthington, Gary L.	Wrexham	Wigan Athletic	Exchange

Temporary Transfers

28	Ampadu, Kwame	Arsenal	West Bromwich Albion	
28	Bailey, Dennis	Birmingham City	Bristol Rovers	
28	Barber, Frederick	Walsall	Chester City	
14	Beckford, Jason	Manchester City	Blackburn Rovers	
28	Boughey, Darren J.	Stoke City	Exeter City	
22	Brightwell, David	Manchester City	Chester City	
18	Butler, Lee S.	Aston Villa	Hull City	
28	Butler, Steven	Maidstone United	Watford	
9	Callaghan, Nigel	Aston Villa	Watford	
11	Carr, Franz	Nottingham Forest	West Ham United	
7	Clarke, Wayne	Manchester City	Stoke City	
21	Clayton, Gary	Peterborough United	Cambridge United (Tr. Back)	
26	Cook, Mitchel	Halifax Town	Darlington	
28	Davis, Stephen M.	Southampton	Notts County	
28	Davison, Aidan	Bury	Blackpool	
28	Day, Mervyn	Leeds United	Coventry City	
28	De Mange, Kenneth J. P. P.	Hull City	Cardiff City	
7	Duffield, Peter	Sheffield United	Rotherham United	
28	Edwards, Mathew	Tottenham Hotspur	Reading	

608

	From	To	Fee
13 Evans, Stewart J.	Rotherham United	Torquay United	
1 Fee, Gregory P.	Sheffield Wednesday	Leyton Orient	
28 Fee, Gregory P.	Leyton Orient	Sheffield Wednesday (Tr. Back)	
21 Fillery, Michael C.	Oldham Athletic	Millwall	
8 Foreman, Darren	Crewe Alexandra	Scarborough	
28 Gardner, Lee	Aberdeen	Oxford United	
28 Hill, David M.	Ipswich Town	Scunthorpe United	
26 Houghton, Scott A.	Tottenham Hotspur	Ipswich Town	
27 Jackson, Mathew	Luton Town	Preston North End	
20 Leighton, James	Manchester United	Arsenal	
28 Ling, Martin	Southend United	Swindon Town	
14 Lister, Stephen H.	Scunthorpe United	York City	
14 Lyne, Neil G. F.	Nottingham Forest	Shrewsbury Town	
28 MacDonald, Kevin	Coventry City	Cardiff City	
18 McParland, Ian J.	Hull City	Walsall	
21 Moran, Paul	Tottenham Hotspur	Southend United	
28 Morgan, Darren	Millwall	Peterborough United	
28 O'Reilly, Gary M.	Crystal Palace	Birmingham City	
28 Owers, Adrian R.	Brighton & Hove Albion	Gillingham	
28 Pearson, John S.	Leeds United	Rotherham United	
28 Penney, David M.	Oxford United	Swansea City	
27 Poole, Kevin	Middlesbrough	Hartlepool United	
10 Powell, Gary	Everton	Wigan Athletic	
27 Quinlan, Philip E.	Everton	Huddersfield Town	
28 Rideout, Paul	Southampton	Swindon Town	
18 Robinson, Philip	Notts County	Birmingham City	
7 Robson, Stewart I.	West Ham United	Coventry City	
26 Sayer, Andrew C.	Leyton Orient	Sheffield United	
27 Scott, Ian	Stoke City	Crewe Alexandra	
18 Sheffield, Johnathan	Norwich City	Cambridge United	
28 Sheron, Michael	Manchester City	Bury	
21 Smith, Mark A.	Nottingham Forest	Mansfield Town	
28 Statham, Brian	Tottenham Hotspur	Reading	
28 Taylor, Robert	Norwich City	Leyton Orient	
8 Thomson, Scott	Dundee United	Barnsley	
14 Todd, Mark K.	Sheffield United	Wolverhampton Wanderers	
7 Whitehead, Philip M.	Barnsley	Halifax Town	
28 Williams, Paul L.	Sunderland	Swansea City	
28 Wilson, David G.	Manchester United	Charlton Athletic	
21 Wright, Mark A.	Everton	Huddersfield Town	

April 1991

12 Butler, Steven	Maidstone United	Watford	
10 Foreman, Darren	Crewe Alexandra	Scarborough	
16 Hodges, Glyn P	Crystal Palace	Sheffield United	£410,000

Temporary Transfers

6 Bartram, Vincent L	West Bromwich Albion	Wolverhampton Wanderers (Tr. Back)	
16 Bradshaw, Mark	Blackpool	York City	
4 Butler, Lee S	Hull City	Aston Villa (Tr. Back)	
3 Kernaghan, Alan N	Charlton Athletic	Middlesbrough (Tr. Back)	
22 Lancaster, David	Chesterfield	Blackpool (Tr. Back)	
15 McIntosh, Martin	St Mirren	Sheffield United	
9 Walsh, Colin D	Middlesbrough	Charlton Athletic (Tr. Back)	

May 1991

28 Cooke, Mitchell	Halifax Town	Darlington	
31 Smalley, Mark	Mansfield Town	Maidstone United	
30 Tiler, Carl	Barnsley	Nottingham Forest	

Temporary Transfers

15 Dryden, Richard A	Exeter City	Manchester City	
13 Morgan, Darren J.	Peterborough United	Millwall (Tr. Back)	

The transfer market boomed in the summer months taking the spending spree to a record level, surpassing the £33 million which changed hands in 1989. Dean Saunders move from Derby County to Liverpool at £2.9 million set a new domestic record and David Platt's £5.5 million transfer from Aston Villa to Bari and the proposed deal involving Paul Gascoigne leaving Tottenham Hotspur for Lazio at the same figure, established a record for British players anywhere.
   Those million or more domestic moves included:

Dean Saunders	Derby County	to Liverpool	£2.9 million
Mark Wright	Derby County	to Liverpool	£2.2 million
Teddy Sheringham	Millwall	to Nottingham F	£2 million
Dalian Atkinson	Real Sociedad	to Aston Villa	£1.6 million
Rodney and Ray Wallace	Southampton	to Leeds United	£1.7 million
Paul Elliott	Celtic	to Chelsea	£1.4 million
Carl Tiler	Barnsley	to Nottingham F	£1.4 million
Tony Dorigo	Chelsea	to Leeds U	£1.3 million
Tony Cascarino	Aston Villa	to Celtic	£1.1 million

Summer moves: Steve Agnew, Barnsley to Blackburn R; Darren Beckford, Port Vale to Norwich C; Tom Boyd, Motherwell to Chelsea; Franz Carr, Nottingham F to Newcastle U; Tony Dorigo, Chelsea to Leeds U; Martin Foyle, Oxford U to Port Vale; Alex Jones, Carlisle U to Rochdale; Billy Manuel, Gillingham to Brentford; Jon Newsome, Sheffield Wednesday to Leeds U; Mark Payne, Stockport Co to Rochdale; Tony Pennock, Stockport Co to Wigan Ath;

Paul Robinson, Plymouth Arg to Hereford U; Rodney Wallace, Southampton to Leeds U; Peter Ward, Rochdale to Stockport Co; Darren Wilson, Manchester C to Bury.

Teddy Sheringham, Millwall to Nottingham F; Phil Barber, Crystal Palace to Millwall; Dalian Atkinson, Real Sociedad to Aston Villa; Shaun Teale, Bournemouth to Aston Villa; Colin Cooper, Middlesbrough to Millwall; Steve Hodge, Nottingham F to Leeds U; Paull Elliott, Celtic to Chelsea; Steve Davis, Burnley to Barnsley; Shaun Taylor, Exeter C to Swindon T; David Mitchell, Chelsea to Swindon T; Tony Cascarino, Aston Villa to Celtic; Vince Bartram, Wolverhampton W to Bournemouth; Steve O'Shaughnessy, Rochdale to Exeter C; Paul Mortimer, Charlton Ath to Aston Villa; Paul Warhurst, Oldham Ath to Sheffield Wednesday; Dennis Bailey, Birmingham C to QPR; John Ryan, Chesterfield to Rochdale; Paul Fitzpatrick, Carlisle U to Leicester C; Tony Shepherd, Carlisle U to Motherwell; Andy Sussex, Crewe Alexandra to Southend U; Paul Fleming, Halifax T to Mansfield T; Gerry Peyton, Bournemouth to Everton; Neil Lyne, Nottingham F to Shrewsbury T; Kwame Ampadu, Arsenal to WBA; David Wetherall, Sheffield W to Leeds U; Mark Wright, Derby Co to Liverpool; Tim Clarke, Coventry C to Huddersfield T; Greg Abbott, Bradford C to Halifax T; Ray Wallace, Southampton to Leeds U; Chris Coleman, Swansea C to Crystal Palace; Mike Conroy, Reading to Burnley; Rob Newman, Bristol C to Norwich C; Dean Saunders, Derby Co to Liverpool; Robbie Earle, Port Vale to Wimbledon; Lee Butler, Aston Villa to Barnsley; Neil Ellis, Chester C to Maidstone U; Jim Dobbin, Barnsley to Grimsby T; Murray Jones, Exeter C to Grimsby T; Mike Milligan, Everton to Oldham Ath; Martin Ling, Southend U to Swindon T; Charlie Bishop, Bury to Barnsley

The Things they said . . .

Irving Scholar (Tottenham Hotspur):
"I have maintained all along that Gary Lineker and Paul Gascoigne would not be sold and nothing has changed." 2 November 1990.

John Major:
"I watched Chelsea long before I got into politics and I will be watching them long after I've left." 30 November 1990.

Joe Jordan, Bristol City manager on turning down the Aston Villa job:
"My reasons for staying are all about what is going on at Bristol City. There is vast potential at Ashton Gate." 17 July 1990.

Joe Jordan on becoming Hearts manager:
"I reached the decision after a sleepless night." 19 September 1990.

John Major after watching Arsenal beat Aston Villa 5-0 on 3 April and on their championship prospects:
"If they keep on playing like that they will win. I was very impressed with them. They looked a super team."

Gordon Taylor, PFA Chief Executive championing the Football League structure:
"When you look at our strength: 92 clubs, 2000 professionals, 1250 trainees, the community programme gaining ground and attendances going up again, the signs are not bad." April 1991.

Gary Lineker looking ahead to whether he will be able to play in the European Championship 1992 and World Cup 1994:
"I don't know really. I would hope Sweden wouldn't be a problem. But you never really know when your legs go in this game, so they say. You're always the first to know."

Graeme Souness after his appointment as Liverpool manager:
"I guarantee we will attempt to play the same kind of football Liverpool have played since a long time before I was a player there."

Bill Fox, Football League President on the Super League:
"We already have a Super League—it's called the First Division and we think that will still be in place in years to come."

Ron Noades, Crystal Palace chairman:
"When I advocated a return to a 22-member First Division last year only two First Division clubs voted against it—Arsenal and Tottenham Hotspur. And Irving Scholar, the Tottenham chairman, only made his decision after tossing a coin."

Glen Kirton, head of external affairs at the Football Association:
"Every World Cup is now a major security headache anyway and who does FIFA come to ask about security? It is us."

Charles Hughes, the FA's director of coaching:
"What we seek to do is to find a circumstance where clubs can be even better. They will be if the stress and strain on those players is reduced. The demands on our players are greater than those on our Continental opponents."

Graham Kelly, Chief Executive of the Football Association:
"It is nonsense to say that clubs will go to the wall. If we get things right at the top of the game there will be plenty of money flowing into the game and I do not see any evidence for the initial fears that have been expressed."

Gordon Taylor, Chief Executive of the Professional Footballers Association:
"The FA is trying to diminish the Football League and, with it, most of the professional clubs in this country. Its blueprint is a way for the leading clubs to seize virtually all the money leaving the remaining clubs to wither and for some die."

Ron Atkinson on changing his mind about not leaving Sheffield Wednesday for Aston Villa:
"I know I have let a lot of Wednesday fans down, but when the dust has settled, I hope they can look back on some memorable days together."

Rick Parry, newly elected chairman of the First Division clubs on the Founder Members Agreement:
"We all trust one another, but it would be foolish to go ahead without protection. The clubs want to know that wherever they are going, they are going together."

David Platt (Aston Villa):
"In Ron Atkinson and Graham Taylor I think I'm playing for the two managers best equipped to help me realise my dream of lifting a trophy with Villa and helping England to victory in the 1992 European Championships."

Arthur Sandford, Chief Executive of the Football League, commenting on the Gallup survey which revealed that 68 per cent of supporters interviewed including 46 per cent of the 'Big Five'—Arsenal, Everton, Liverpool, Manchester United and Tottenham Hotspur—were opposed to the Super League:
"An overwhelming majority of the fans are convinced the Super League idea is a bad thing for English professional football."

Alex Ferguson (Manchester United) after winning the Cup-Winners' Cup:
"It was nerve-racking at the end. But we got there and that is the main thing."

George Graham (Arsenal) after winning the championship:
"Our success is down to all the work we've put in over the last nine months."

BARCLAYS LEAGUE ATTENDANCES 1990–91

	TOTAL ATTENDANCES	AVERAGE ATTENDANCES
TOTAL	19,508,202	9581
DIVISION 1	8,618,709	22,680
DIVISION 2	6,285,068	11,385
DIVISION 3	2,835,759	5137
DIVISION 4	1,768,666	3204

DIVISION ONE STATISTICS

	Average gate			Season 1990/91	
	1989/90	1990/91	+/−%	Highest	Lowest
Arsenal	33,713	36,864	+9.3	42,395	25,558
Aston Villa	25,544	25,663	+0.5	40,026	16,697
Chelsea	21,531	20,738	−3.7	33,478	9416
Coventry City	14,312	13,794	−3.6	22,549	8875
Crystal Palace	17,105	19,660	+14.9	28,131	14,439
Derby County	17,426	16,257	−6.7	31,115	11,680
Everton	26,280	25,028	−4.8	39,808	14,630
Leeds United	28,210	29,312	+3.9	33,699	25,802
Liverpool	36,589	36,038	−1.5	38,463	31,063
Luton Town	9886	10,325	+4.4	12,889	8219
Manchester City	27,975	27,874	−0.36	39,194	20,404
Manchester United	39,077	43,218	+10.6	47,485	32,776
Norwich City	16,737	15,468	−7.6	21,274	11,550
Nottingham Forest	20,606	22,137	+7.4	27,347	16,221
Queens Park Rangers	13,218	13,524	+2.3	21,405	9510
Sheffield United	16,989	21,461	+26.3	27,570	16,887
Southampton	16,463	15,413	−6.4	20,355	13,538
Sunderland	17,728	22,577	+27.4	31,133	17,899
Tottenham Hotspur	26,588	30,632	+15.2	35,003	21,675
Wimbledon	7756	7631	−1.6	13,776	3981

DIVISION TWO STATISTICS

	Average gate			Season 1990/91	
	1989/90	1990/91	+/−%	Highest	Lowest
Barnsley	9033	8937	−1.1	23,079	4921
Blackburn Rovers	9624	8126	−15.6	13,437	5969
Brighton & Hove Albion	8679	8386	−3.4	12,281	5354
Bristol City	11,544	13,495	+16.9	22,269	9346
Bristol Rovers	6202	5929	−4.4	7932	4563
Charlton Athletic	10,748	6548	−39.1	16,086	4455
Hull City	6518	6165	−5.4	10,907	3175
Ipswich Town	12,913	11,772	−8.8	20,451	7570
Leicester City	11,716	11,546	−1.5	19,011	8167
Middlesbrough	16,269	17,023	+4.6	22,869	13,844
Millwall	12,413	10,838	−12.7	20,598	6686
Newcastle United	21,590	16,835	−22.0	25,440	9628
Notts County	6151	8164	+32.7	12,835	5086
Oldham Athletic	9727	13,247	+36.2	18,809	11,296
Oxford United	5820	5780	−0.7	8474	4295
Plymouth Argyle	8749	6851	−21.7	11,490	5039
Portsmouth	8959	9689	+8.1	14,574	6902
Port Vale	8978	8092	−9.9	13,317	5820
Sheffield Wednesday	20,930	26,605	+27.1	34,845	20,431
Swindon Town	9394	9805	+4.4	14,093	7394
Watford	10,353	9576	−7.5	17,172	6361
West Bromwich Albion	11,308	11,993	+6.1	28,310	7657
West Ham United	20,311	22,551	+11.0	26,551	18,125
Wolverhampton Wanderers	17,045	15,837	−7.1	22,982	9313

DIVISION THREE STATISTICS

	Average gate			Season 1990/91	
	1989/90	*1990/91*	*+/−%*	*Highest*	*Lowest*
AFC Bournemouth	7454	6017	−19.3	7421	4662
Birmingham City	8558	7030	−17.9	10,123	4734
Bolton Wanderers	7286	7277	−0.1	12,826	3631
Bradford City	8777	6644	−24.3	9569	4776
Brentford	5662	6144	+8.5	8021	4812
Bury	3450	3572	+3.5	6318	2135
Cambridge United	3359	5503	+63.8	9023	3632
Chester City	2506	1564	−37.6	3759	631
Crewe Alexandra	4008	3748	−6.5	7195	2590
Exeter City	4859	4243	−12.7	6145	2763
Fulham	4484	4057	−9.5	6765	2750
Grimsby Town	5984	7237	+20.9	14,225	5162
Huddersfield Town	5630	5351	−5.0	9697	4052
Leyton Orient	4365	4194	−3.9	6369	2613
Mansfield Town	3129	2683	−14.3	4047	1919
Preston North End	6313	5214	−17.4	9845	3246
Reading	4060	4079	+0.5	6562	1934
Rotherham United	5612	4600	−18.0	8240	3190
Shrewsbury Town	3521	3442	−2.2	6210	2227
Southend United	3836	6174	+60.9	10,665	2982
Stoke City	12,449	11,565	−7.1	16,135	6994
Swansea City	4223	3665	−13.2	5938	2126
Tranmere Rovers	7449	6740	−9.5	11,079	4691
Wigan Athletic	2758	2889	+4.7	4726	1972

DIVISION FOUR STATISTICS

	Average gate			Season 1990/91	
	1989/90	*1990/91*	*+/−%*	*Highest*	*Lowest*
Aldershot	2022	2091	+3.4	3289	1398
Blackpool	4075	4059	−0.4	8590	2065
Burnley	6222	7882	+26.7	18,395	4723
Cardiff City	3642	2946	−19.1	4805	1629
Carlisle United	4740	3006	−36.6	5250	1762
Chesterfield	4181	3712	−11.2	8837	2222
Darlington	3588	4021	+12.1	9160	2882
Doncaster Rovers	2706	2831	+4.6	4244	1642
Gillingham	3887	3523	−9.4	8004	2319
Halifax Town	1895	1699	−10.3	4755	1002
Hartlepool United	2503	3180	+27.0	6957	1916
Hereford United	2676	2599	−2.9	5782	1438
Lincoln City	4071	2967	−27.1	5524	1974
Maidstone United	2427	1854	−23.6	3130	1020
Northampton Town	3187	3710	+16.4	5549	2544
Peterborough United	4804	5211	+8.5	8362	3082
Rochdale	2027	2238	+10.4	7344	1166
Scarborough	2325	1598	−31.3	2408	625
Scunthorpe United	3524	3114	−11.6	5769	2220
Stockport County	3899	3562	−8.6	6212	2569
Torquay United	2147	2986	+39.1	4337	2223
Walsall	4077	4149	+1.8	8051	2575
Wrexham	2368	1885	−20.4	3997	1029
York City	2615	2516	−3.8	4407	1490

LEAGUE ATTENDANCES SINCE 1946–47

Season	Matches	Total	Div. 1	Div. 2	Div. 3 (S)	Div. 3 (N)
1946–47	1848	35,604,606	15,005,316	11,071,572	5,664,004	3,863,714
1947–48	1848	40,259,130	16,732,341	12,286,350	6,653,610	4,586,829
1948–49	1848	41,271,414	17,914,667	11,353,237	6,998,429	5,005,081
1949–50	1848	40,517,865	17,278,625	11,694,158	7,104,155	4,440,927
1950–51	2028	39,584,967	16,679,454	10,780,580	7,367,884	4,757,109
1951–52	2028	39,015,866	16,110,322	11,066,189	6,958,927	4,880,428
1952–53	2028	37,149,966	16,050,278	9,686,654	6,704,299	4,708,735
1953–54	2028	36,174,590	16,154,915	9,510,053	6,311,508	4,198,114
1954–55	2028	34,133,103	15,087,221	8,988,794	5,996,017	4,051,071
1955–56	2028	33,150,809	14,108,961	9,080,002	5,692,479	4,269,367
1956–57	2028	32,744,405	13,803,037	8,718,162	5,622,189	4,601,017
1957–58	2028	33,562,208	14,468,652	8,663,712	6,097,183	4,332,661
					Div. 3	Div. 4
1958–59	2028	33,610,985	14,727,691	8,641,997	5,946,600	4,276,697
1959–60	2028	32,538,611	14,391,227	8,399,627	5,739,707	4,008,050
1960–61	2028	28,619,754	12,926,948	7,033,936	4,784,256	3,874,614
1961–62	2015	27,979,902	12,061,194	7,453,089	5,199,106	3,266,513
1962–63	2028	28,885,852	12,490,239	7,792,770	5,341,362	3,261,481
1963–64	2028	28,535,022	12,486,626	7,594,158	5,419,157	3,035,081
1964–65	2028	27,641,168	12,708,752	6,984,104	4,436,245	3,512,067
1965–66	2028	27,206,980	12,480,644	6,914,757	4,779,150	3,032,429
1966–67	2028	28,902,596	14,242,957	7,253,819	4,421,172	2,984,648
1967–68	2028	30,107,298	15,289,410	7,450,410	4,013,087	3,354,391
1968–69	2028	29,382,172	14,584,851	7,382,390	4,339,656	3,075,275
1969–70	2028	29,600,972	14,868,754	7,581,728	4,223,761	2,926,729
1970–71	2028	28,194,146	13,954,337	7,098,265	4,377,213	2,764,331
1971–72	2028	28,700,729	14,484,603	6,769,308	4,697,392	2,749,426
1972–73	2028	25,448,642	13,998,154	5,631,730	3,737,252	2,081,506
1973–74	2027	24,982,203	13,070,991	6,326,108	3,421,624	2,163,480
1974–75	2028	25,577,977	12,613,178	6,955,970	4,086,145	1,992,684
1975–76	2028	24,896,053	13,089,861	5,798,405	3,948,449	2,059,338
1976–77	2028	26,182,800	13,647,585	6,250,597	4,152,218	2,132,400
1977–78	2028	25,392,872	13,255,677	6,474,763	3,332,042	2,330,390
1978–79	2028	24,540,627	12,704,549	6,153,223	3,374,558	2,308,297
1979–80	2028	24,623,975	12,163,002	6,112,025	3,999,328	2,349,620
1980–81	2028	21,907,569	11,392,894	5,175,442	3,637,854	1,701,379
1981–82	2028	20,006,961	10,420,793	4,750,463	2,836,915	1,998,790
1982–83	2028	18,766,158	9,295,613	4,974,937	2,943,568	1,552,040
1983–84	2028	18,358,631	8,711,448	5,359,757	2,729,942	1,557,484
1984–85	2028	17,849,835	9,761,404	4,030,823	2,667,008	1,390,600
1985–86	2028	16,488,577	9,037,854	3,551,968	2,490,481	1,408,274
1986–87	2028	17,379,218	9,144,676	4,168,131	2,350,970	1,715,441
1987–88	2030	17,959,732	8,094,571	5,341,599	2,751,275	1,772,287
1988–89	2036	18,464,192	7,809,993	5,887,805	3,035,327	1,791,067
1989–90	2036	19,445,442	7,883,039	6,867,674	2,803,551	1,891,178
1990–91	2036	19,508,202	8,618,709	6,285,068	2,835,759	1,768,666

This is the first time since the war that attendances have risen for five consecutive seasons.

THE LITTLEWOODS/MILK/ RUMBELOWS LEAGUE CUP

ZENITH DATA SYSTEMS CUP

LEYLAND DAF CUP

LEAGUE CUP FINALISTS 1961–91

Played as a two-leg final until 1966. All subsequent finals at Wembley.

Year	Winners	Runners-up	Score
1961	Aston Villa	Rotherham U	0-2, 3-0 (aet)
1962	Norwich C	Rochdale	3-0, 1-0
1963	Birmingham C	Aston Villa	3-1, 0-0
1964	Leicester C	Stoke C	1-1, 3-2
1965	Chelsea	Leicester C	3-2, 0-0
1966	WBA	West Ham U	1-2, 4-1
1967	QPR	WBA	3-2
1968	Leeds U	Arsenal	1-0
1969	Swindon T	Arsenal	3-1 (aet)
1970	Manchester C	WBA	2-1 (aet)
1971	Tottenham H	Aston Villa	2-0
1972	Stoke C	Chelsea	2-1
1973	Tottenham H	Norwich C	1-0
1974	Wolverhampton W	Manchester C	2-1
1975	Aston Villa	Norwich C	1-0
1976	Manchester C	Newcastle U	2-1
1977	Aston Villa	Everton	0-0, 1-1 (aet), 3-2 (aet)
1978	Nottingham F	Liverpool	0-0 (aet), 1-0
1979	Nottingham F	Southampton	3-2
1980	Wolverhampton W	Nottingham F	1-0
1981	Liverpool	West Ham U	1-1 (aet), 2-1

MILK CUP

Year	Winners	Runners-up	Score
1982	Liverpool	Tottenham H	3-1 (aet)
1983	Liverpool	Manchester U	2-1 (aet)
1984	Liverpool	Everton	0-0 (aet), 1-0
1985	Norwich C	Sunderland	1-0
1986	Oxford U	QPR	3-0

LITTLEWOODS CUP

Year	Winners	Runners-up	Score
1987	Arsenal	Liverpool	2-1
1988	Luton T	Arsenal	3-2
1989	Nottingham F	Luton T	3-1
1990	Nottingham F	Oldham Ath	1-0

RUMBELOWS LEAGUE CUP

Year	Winners	Runners-up	Score
1991	Sheffield W	Manchester U	1-0

LEAGUE CUP WINS
Liverpool 4, Nottingham F 4, Aston Villa 3, Manchester C 2, Norwich C 2, Tottenham H 2, Wolverhampton W 2, Arsenal 1, Birmingham C 1, Chelsea 1, Leeds U 1, Leicester C 1, Luton T 1, Oxford U 1, QPR 1, Sheffield W 1, Stoke C 1, Swindon T 1, WBA 1.

APPEARANCES IN FINALS
Liverpool 6, Aston Villa 5, Nottingham F 5, Arsenal 4, Norwich C 4, Manchester C 3, Tottenham H 3, WBA 3, Chelsea 2, Everton 2, Leicester C 2, Luton T 2, Manchester U 2, QPR 2, Stoke C 2, West Ham U 2, Wolverhampton W 2, Birmingham C 1, Leeds U 1, Newcastle U 1, Oldham U 1, Oxford U 1, Rochdale 1, Rotherham U 1, Sheffield W 1, Southampton 1, Sunderland 1, Swindon T 1.

APPEARANCES IN SEMI-FINALS
Aston Villa 8, Liverpool 8, Tottenham H 7, West Ham U 7, Arsenal 6, Chelsea 5, Manchester C 5, Manchester U 5, Norwich C 5, Nottingham F 5, Leeds U 4, WBA 4, Burnley 3, Everton 3, QPR 3, Wolverhampton W 3, Birmingham C 2, Bristol C 2, Coventry C 2, Ipswich T 2, Leicester C 2, Luton T 2, Oxford U 2, Plymouth Arg 2, Southampton 2, Stoke C 2, Sunderland 2, Swindon T 2, Blackburn R 1, Blackpool 1, Bolton W 1, Bury 1, Cardiff C 1, Carlisle U 1, Chester C 1, Derby Co 1, Huddersfield T 1, Middlesbrough 1, Newcastle U 1, Oldham Ath 1, Peterborough U 1, Rochdale 1, Rotherham U 1, Sheffield W 1, Shrewsbury T 1, Walsall 1, Watford 1.

RUMBELOWS LEAGUE CUP 1990–91

FIRST ROUND FIRST LEG
27 AUG
Stockport Co (0) 0
Burnley (1) 2 *(Hamilton, Futcher)* 2786
Stockport Co: Cooper; Brown, Robertson (Todd), Bullock, Williams B, Finley, Payne, Gannon (Thorpe), Williams PA, Beaumont, Frain.
Burnley: Pearce; Hamilton, Bray, Deary, Farrell, Davis, White, Francis, Futcher, Jakub, Deakin.

28 AUG
Birmingham C (0) 0
Bournemouth (1) 1 *(Blissett)* 5110
Birmingham C: Thomas; Ashley, Downs, Frain, Overson, Matthewson, Peer, Bailey (Sturridge), Hopkins, Gleghorn, Tait.
Bournemouth: Guthrie; Redknapp, Morrell, Teale, Shearer, Bond, O'Driscoll, Peacock, Aylott, Holmes, Blissett (Ekoku).

Brentford (1) 2 *(Bates, Godfrey)*
Hereford U (0) 0 2993
Brentford: Benstead; Cousins, Fleming, Millen, Bates, Buckle, Jones, May, Holdsworth (Cadette), Godfrey, Smillie.
Hereford U: Wood; Jones MA, Devine, Jones R, Peacock, Pejic, Robinson (Wheeler), Narbett, Juryeff, Bradley, Tester (Phillips).

Carlisle U (1) 1 *(Fitzpatrick)*
Scunthorpe U (0) 0 2531
Carlisle U: Priestley; Miller, Edwards, Graham, Jones, Fitzpatrick, Walsh, Shepherd, Walwyn, Gates, Proudlock (Norris).
Scunthorpe U: Litchfield; Longden, Cowling, Ward, Hicks, Hall, Taylor, Hamilton, Daws, Flounders, Marshall.

Chesterfield (0) 1 *(Morris)*
Hartlepool U (1) 2 *(Allon, Honour)* 2935
Chesterfield: Leonard; Francis, Rogers, Dyche, Brien, Gunn, Plummer, Hewitt, Rolph, Shaw (Williams), Morris.
Hartlepool U: Cox; Olsson, McKinnon, Tinkler, Nobbs, Bennyworth, Allon, Tupling, Baker, Davies (Honour), Dalton.

Darlington (0) 0
Blackpool (0) 0 2254
Darlington: Prudhoe; McJannet, Gray, Gill, Smith, Corner, Emson, Toman, Borthwick (Mardenborough), Cork (Geddis), Tait.
Blackpool: McIlhargey; Wright, Bradshaw, Groves, Briggs, Gore, Sinclair, Brook, Lancaster (Richards), Garner, Eyres.

Doncaster R (2) 2 *(Muir, Jones)* 3665
Rotherham U (3) 6 *(Hazel 2, Williamson 3 (1 pen), Goodwin)*
Doncaster R: Crichton; Rankine, Brevett, Holmes, Ormsby, Douglas, Gormley, Stiles (Turnbull), Muir, Jones, Noteman (Place).
Rotherham U: O'Hanlon; Forrest, Scott, Goodwin, Law, Robinson, Dempsey, Spooner, Williamson, Mendonca (Buckley), Hazel.

Fulham (1) 1 *(Joseph)*
Peterborough U (1) 2 *(Sterling, Bremner)* 2736
Fulham: Batty; Newson, Pike, Scott, Eckhardt, Thomas (Skinner), Baker, Kelly, Cole (Langley), Joseph, Marshall.
Peterborough U: Herbert; Luke, Crosby, Halsall, Robinson (Watkin), McElhinney, Sterling, Oakes, Bremner, Osborne, Butterworth.

Gillingham (0) 1 *(Lovell)*
Shrewsbury T (0) 0 2613
Gillingham: Hillyard; Dunne, Manuel, Haines, Walker, Palmer (Kimble), O'Connor, Trusson, Lovell, Heritage (Beadle), Johnson.
Shrewsbury T: Perks; Worsley, Lynch, Kelly, Heathcote, Blake, Moore, Wimbleton, Spink, Brown, Hartford.

Grimsby T (0) 2 *(Gilbert, Hargreaves)*
Crewe Alex (1) 1 *(Sussex)* 3882
Grimsby T: Sherwood; McDermott, Jobling, Tillson, Knight, Cunnington, Childs, Gilbert, Rees, Cockerill, Hargreaves (Alexander).
Crewe Alex: Greygoose; Jones, Callaghan, Smart, Swain, McKearney, Walters, Hignett (Naylor), Murphy, Gardiner, Sussex (Foreman).

Halifax T (0) 2 *(Fyfe, Richardson)*
Lincoln C (0) 0 1239
Halifax T: Brown; Fleming P, Cook, Evans, Futcher (Gregory), Fleming C, Butler, Richardson, McPhillips, Fyfe, Graham.
Lincoln C: Wallington; Casey, Nicholson, Brown, Stoutt (Dixon), Davis, Schofield (Carmichael), Smith P, Lormor, Smith N, Puttnam.

Mansfield T (0) 1 *(Charles)*
Cardiff C (1) 1 *(Griffith)* 2091
Mansfield T: Beasley; Murray, Kearney, Clark, Foster, Smalley, Kent, Chambers, Wilkinson, Stringfellow, Charles.
Cardiff C: Hansbury; Rodgerson, Daniel, Barnard, Abraham, Perry, Jones, Griffith, Gibbins, Pike (Blake), Heard.

Middlesbrough (1) 1 *(Mowbray)*
Tranmere R (0) 1 *(Vickers)* 10,667
Middlesbrough: Pears; Cooper, Phillips, Mowbray, Kernaghan, Wark, Slaven (Ripley), Mustoe, Baird, Russell, Hendrie.
Tranmere R: Nixon; Mungall, McCarrick, McNab, Hughes, Vickers, Morrissey, Harvey, Steel, Muir, Thomas.

Preston NE (0) 2 *(Shaw, Swann)*
Chester C (0) 0 3503
Preston NE: Farnworth; Senior, Swann, Bogie, Flynn, Wrightson, Williams, Joyce, Thomas, Shaw, James.
Chester C: Stewart; Preece, Lundon, Lightfoot, Abel, Lane, Painter (Ellis), Barrow, Bennett, Dale, Croft.

Reading (0) 0
Oxford U (0) 1 *(Simpson)* 5254
Reading: Francis; Jones, Richardson, McPherson, Hicks, Conroy, Gooding, Williams (Gilkes), Senior, Maskell, Moran (Friel).
Oxford U: Kee; Robinson, Ford, Phillips, Foster, Melville, Evans, Lewis, Foyle, Stein, Simpson.

Rochdale (2) 4 *(Lee, O'Shaughnessy, Milner, Costello)*
Scarborough (0) 0 1448
Rochdale: Welch; Burns, Graham, Brown (Goodison), O'Shaughnessy, Ward, Milner, Lee, Hilditch, Costello, Holmes.
Scarborough: Richardson; Wilson (Mooney), Logan, Matthews, Richards, Meyer, Kamara, Mudd, Oghani, MacDonald, Carter (Dobson).

Southend U (0) 2 *(Butler, Martin)*
Aldershot (1) 1 *(Puckett (pen))* 2254
Southend U: Sansome; Edwards, Hyslop, Martin, Cornwell, Tilson, Clark, Butler, Ansah, Benjamin, Angell.
Aldershot: Coles; Brown, Cooper, Burvill, Whitlock, Wignall, Williams, Puckett, Banton, Henry, Randall.

Walsall (1) 4 *(Goldsmith, Rimmer 2, Hutchings)*
Cambridge U (0) 2 *(Dublin, Leadbitter)* 4085
Walsall: Green; Hutchings, Mower (Whitehouse), Smith, Bryant, Skipper, Goldsmith, Barnett, Rimmer, Cecere, Marsh.
Cambridge U: Vaughan; Fensome, Kimble, Bailie, Chapple, O'Shea, Cheetham (Claridge), Wilkins, Dublin, Taylor, Leadbitter.

Wigan Ath (0) 0
Barnsley (0) 1 *(Cooper)* 2144
Wigan Ath: Adkins; Parkinson, Tankard, Atherton, Patterson, Hildersley, Woods, Rimmer, Daley, Fairclough (Johnson), Griffiths B (Griffiths I).
Barnsley: Baker; Fleming, Taggart, Smith, Tiler, McCord, Banks, Cooper, Saville, Agnew, Archdeacon.

York C (0) 0
Wrexham (0) 1 *(Worthington (pen))* 1428
York C: Marples; McMillan, Hall, Reid, Tutill, Warburton, Barratt, Howlett, Helliwell, Longhurst, Himsworth.
Wrexham: O'Keefe; Phillips, Kennedy, Reck, Beaumont, Sertori, Cooper, Thackeray, Preece, Worthington, Bowden.

29 AUG
Bradford C (2) 2 *(Leonard, Abbott)*
Bury (0) 0 4976
Bradford C: Tomlinson; Mitchell, Tinnion, James, Oliver, Sinnott, Abbott, Duxbury, McCarthy, Leonard, Stuart.
Bury: Kelly; Hill, Stanislaus, Mauge, Valentine, Greenall, Lee (Robinson), Parkinson (Withe), Cunningham, McGinlay, Patterson.

Brighton & HA (0) 0
Northampton T (1) 2 *(Wilkin 2)* 3834
Brighton & HA: Digweed; Crumplin, Bromage, Wilkins, McCarthy, Chivers, Nelson, Robinson (Chapman), Small, Codner, Walker.
Northampton T: Gleasure; Chard, Wilson, Terry, Williams, Wood, Beavon, Wilkin (Campbell), Berry (Thorpe), Barnes, Brown.

Bristol R (0) 1 *(Twentyman)*
Torquay U (0) 2 *(Tynan, Saunders)* 2461
Bristol R: Parkin; Alexander, Twentyman, Yates, Mehew (McClean), Jones, Holloway, Reece, White, Saunders, Pounder.
Torquay U: Howells; Whiston, Uzzell, Lloyd, Elliott, Musker, Holmes, Edwards, Tynan, Saunders (Myers), Loram.

Exeter C (0) 1 *(Dryden)*
Notts Co (1) 1 *(Bartlett)* 3858
Exeter C: Miller; Hiley, Dryden, Rogers, Taylor, Cooper, Hobson, Batty, McDermott (Rowe), Neville, Whitehead.
Notts Co: Cherry; Palmer, Platnauer, Short Craig (Norton), Yates, Robinson, Thomas, Draper, Bartlett, Lund, Johnson.

Huddersfield T (0) 0
Bolton W (2) 3 *(Darby 2, Philliskirk (pen))* 4444
Huddersfield T: Hardwick; Trevitt, Parsley, Marsden, Mitchell, Lewis, O'Regan, Wilson (Edwards), Roberts, Smith, Barnett.
Bolton W: Felgate; Brown, Burke, Cowdrill, Came, Winstanley, Green, Thompson, Reeves, Philliskirk, Darby.

Maidstone U (0) 2 *(Butler 2)*
Leyton Orient (1) 2 *(Berry, Nugent)* 2225
Maidstone U: Johns; Roast, Rumble, Berry, Golley, Madden, Charlery (Gall), Elsey, Pritchard, Butler (Sorrell), Lillis.
Leyton Orient: Heald; Baker, Howard, Sitton, Day (Whitbread), Hales, Harvey, Castle, Nugent, Sayer, Berry (Carter).

Stoke C (0) 0
Swansea C (0) 0 7806
Stoke C: Fox; Butler, Statham, Beeston, Blake, Fowler, Kennedy, Ellis (Boughey), Thomas, Biggins, Kelly.
Swansea C: Bracey; Raynor, Coleman, Hough, Harris, Walker, Thornber, Davies, Gilligan, Connor, Legg.

WBA (1) 2 *(Bannister, Hackett)*
Bristol C (1) 2 *(Morgan 2)* 8721
WBA: Naylor; Hodson, Harbey, Robson, Burgess, Strodder, Ford, Goodman, Bannister, Bradley (Hackett), Shakespeare.
Bristol C: Sinclair; Llewellyn, Aizlewood, May, Shelton, Rennie, Bent, Newman, Taylor (Allison), Morgan, Smith.

FIRST ROUND SECOND LEG
3 SEPT
Tranmere R (0) 1 *(Steel)*
Middlesbrough (0) 2 *(Mustoe, Slaven)* 6135
Tranmere R: Nixon; Mungall, McCarrick, McNab, Hughes (Malkin), Vickers, Morrissey, Harvey, Steel, Muir, Thomas.
Middlesbrough: Pears; Cooper, Phillips, Mowbray, Kernaghan, Wark, Slaven, Mustoe, Ripley (Baird), Russell, Hendrie.
Middlesbrough won 3-2 on aggregate.

4 SEPT
Aldershot (0) 2 *(Puckett 2)*
Southend U (2) 2 *(Austin, Angell)* 2400
Aldershot: Coles; Brown, Cooper, Burvill (Stewart), Whitlock, Wignall, Williams, Puckett, Banton, Henry, Randall.
Southend U: Sansome; Austin, Powell, Martin, Cornwell, Tilson, Clark, Butler, Ansah, Benjamin, Angell.
Southend U won 4-3 on aggregate.

Barnsley (0) 0
Wigan Ath (1) 1 *(Page) aet*   4558
Barnsley: Baker; Fleming, Taggart, McCord, Smith, Tiler, Banks (Robinson), Cooper, Saville, Agnew (O'Connell), Archdeacon.
Wigan Ath: Adkins; Parkinson (Rogerson), Tankard, Atherton, Patterson, Appleton, Woods, Rimmer, Daley, Page, Griffiths I (Griffiths B).
Barnsley won 4-3 on penalties.

Blackpool (1) 1 *(Brook)*
Darlington (0) 1 *(Borthwick) aet*   1696
Blackpool: McIlhargey; Wright, Bradshaw (Rodwell), Groves, Briggs, Gore, Sinclair, Brook, Lancaster (Taylor), Garner, Eyres.
Darlington: Prudhoe; McJannet, Gray, Gill, Smith, Corner, Emson (Geddis), Toman, Borthwick, Cork (Mardenborough), Tait.
Darlington won on away goals.

Bolton W (1) 2 *(Stubbs, Darby)*
Huddersfield T (1) 1 *(O'Regan)*   3101
Bolton W: Felgate; Brown, Burke, Green, Stubbs, Winstanley, Storer, Thompson, Reeves, Philliskirk (Came), Darby.
Huddersfield T: Hardwick; Trevitt, Parsley, Marsden, Mitchell, Lewis, O'Regan, Edwards, Roberts, Smith, Barnett (Onuora).
Bolton W won 5-1 on aggregate.

Bournemouth (1) 1 *(Blissett)*
Birmingham C (0) 1 *(Downs (pen))*   4490
Bournemouth: Guthrie; Mundee, Morrell, Teale, Shearer, Coleman, O'Driscoll, Redknapp, Aylott, Holmes, Blissett.
Birmingham C: Thomas; Ashley, Downs, Frain, Fox (Moran), Matthewson, Peer, Bailey (Sturridge), Hopkins, Gleghorn, Tait.
Bournemouth won 2-1 on aggregate.

Burnley (0) 0
Stockport Co (1) 1 *(Williams PA)*   3912
Burnley: Pearce; Hamilton, Bray, Deary, Farrell, Davis, White, Futcher, Francis, Jakub, Deakin.
Stockport Co: Cooper; Brown, Bullock, Gannon, Thorpe, Finley, Payne, Todd, Williams PA, Beaumont, Frain.
Burnley won 2-1 on aggregate.

Bury (0) 3 *(Mauge, Valentine, Cunningham)*
Bradford C (0) 2 *(McCarthy 2 (1 pen)) aet* 2545
Bury: Kelly; Bishop, Stanislaus (Withe), Mauge, Valentine, Knill, Lee, Parkinson, Cunningham, Robinson (Hulme), Patterson.
Bradford C: Tomlinson; Mitchell, Tinnion, James, Oliver, Sinnott, Abbott, Duxbury, McCarthy, Leonard, Stuart (Babb).
Bradford C won 4-3 on aggregate.

Cambridge U (2) 2 *(Leadbitter, Cheetham)*
Walsall (0) 1 *(Rimmer (pen))*   3517
Cambridge U: Vaughan; Fensome, Kimble, Bailie, Chapple, O'Shea (Taylor), Cheetham, Wilkins, Dublin, Claridge, Leadbitter.
Walsall: Green; Hutchings, Mower, Smith, Bryant, Skipper, Grealish, Barnett, Rimmer, Cecere, Littlejohn.
Walsall won 5-4 on aggregate.

Cardiff C (1) 3 *(Griffith 2, Pike)*
Mansfield T (0) 0   2539
Cardiff C: Hansbury; Rodgerson, Daniel, Blake, Perry, Jones, Griffith, Gibbins, Pike (Chandler), Heard, Martin.

Mansfield T: Beasley; Chambers, Kearney, Clark, Foster, Gray, Kent, Fairclough, Wilkinson (Hodges), Stringfellow, Charles.
Cardiff C won 4-1 on aggregate.

Chester C (2) 5 *(Abel (pen), Croft 2, Ellis, Williams (og))*
Preston NE (0) 1 *(Swann) aet*   1009
Chester C: Stewart; Preece, Pugh, Butler, Abel (Lightfoot), Lane, Bennett, Barrow, Ellis (Painter), Dale Croft.
Preston NE: Farnworth; Senior (Harper), Swann, Bogie, Flynn, Wrightson, Williams, Peel (Hughes), Thomas, Joyce, James.
Chester C won 5-3 on aggregate.

Crewe Alex (1) 1 *(Sussex)*
Grimsby T (0) 0 *aet*   2781
Crewe Alex: Greygoose; Jones, Callaghan, Smart, Swain, McKearney, Walters, Naylor (Foreman), Hignett, Gardiner, Sussex.
Grimsby T: Sherwood; McDermott, Jobling, Tillson, Lever (Watson), Cunnington, Childs, Gilbert, Rees, Cockerill, Hargreaves (Alexander)
Crewe Alex won on away goals.

Leyton Orient (3) 4 *(Harvey, Castle 2, Nugent)*
Maidstone U (0) 1 *(Charlery)*   3429
Leyton Orient: Heald; Baker, Howard, Sitton, Whitbread, Pike, Harvey, Castle, Nugent, Sayer, Berry.
Maidstone U: Beeney; Roast, Cooper (Lillis), Berry, Golley, Madden, Gall (Charlery), Elsey, Pritchard, Butler, Rumble.
Leyton Orient won 6-3 on aggregate.

Northampton T (0) 1 *(Brown)*
Brighton & HA (0) 1 *(Small)*   4760
Northampton T: Gleasure; Chard, Wilson, Terry, Williams, Angus, Beavon, Wilkin, Berry (Thorpe), Barnes, Brown.
Brighton & HA: Meola; Crumplin, Chapman, Wilkins, McCarthy, Chivers, Nelson, Barham, Small, Codner, Walker.
Northampton T won 3-1 on aggregate.

Notts Co (1) 1 *(Johnson)*
Exeter C (0) 0   4204
Notts Co: Cherry; Norton, Platnauer, Palmer, Yates, Robinson, Thomas, Draper, Bartlett, Lund, Johnson (O'Riordan).
Exeter C: Miller; Hiley, Dryden, Rogers (McDermott), Taylor, Cooper, Hobson, Batty, Bailey, Nelville (Rowe), Whitehead.
Notts Co won 2-1 on aggregate.

Peterborough U (1) 2 *(Bremner 2)*
Fulham (0) 0   2968
Peterborough U: Herbert; Luke, Crosby, Halsall, Hine, McElhinney, Sterling, Oakes, Bremner, Culpin, Butterworth.
Fulham: Batty; Newson, Pike, Scott, Thomas, Eckhardt, Kelly, Gore (Baker), Joseph (Haag), Milton, Marshall.
Peterborough U won 4-1 on aggregate.

Rotherham U (1) 2 *(Holmes (og), Dempsey)*
Doncaster R (0) 1 *(Brockie (pen))*   3448
Rotherham U: O'Hanlon; Forrest, Scott, Barnsley, Law, Richardson, Dempsey, Spooner (Goodwin), Williamson, Goater, Hazel (Thompson).
Doncaster R: Crichton; Rankine, Brevett, Holmes, Ormsby, Douglas, Gormley, Stiles (Brockie), Muir, Harle (Adams), Noteman.
Rotherham U won 8-3 on aggregate.

Scunthorpe U (0) 1 *(Lillis)*
Carlisle U (1) 1 *(Walwyn)*   2130
Scunthorpe U: Litchfield; Longden, Cowling, Ward,
Hicks, Hall, Miller, Hamilton (Daws), Lillis,
Flounders, Marshall.
Carlisle U: Priestley; Miller, Edwards, Graham,
Methven, Fitzpatrick, Walsh, Shepherd, Walwyn,
Gates, Proudlock.
Carlisle U won 2-1 on aggregate.

Shrewsbury T (2) 2 *(Moore, Kelly)*
Gillingham (0) 0   2193
Shrewsbury T: Perks; Worsley, Lynch, Kelly, Heath-
cote, Blake, Moore, Hartford, Spink, Brown,
Naughton.
Gillingham: Hillyard; Dunne (Docker), Palmer,
Haines, Walker, O'Shea, O'Connor, Trusson, Lovell,
Heritage (Beadle), Johnson
Shrewsbury T won 2-1 on aggregate.

Swansea C (0) 0
Stoke C (0) 1 *(Kelly)*   4464
Swansea C: Bracey; Raynor, Coleman, Trick, Harris,
Walker (D'Auria), Thornber, Davies, Gilligan,
Connor (Watson), Legg.
Stoke C: Fox; Butler, Statham, Beeston, Blake, Sand-
ford, Kennedy, Ellis, Thomas (Kelly), Biggins, Ware.
Stoke C won 1-0 on aggregate.

Torquay U (1) 1 *(Whiston)*
Bristol R (0) 1 *(Alexander)*   3533
Torquay U: Howells; Whiston, Uzzell, Lloyd, Elliott,
Musker, Holmes, Edwards, Tynan, Saunders (Myers),
Loram.
Bristol R: Parkin; Alexander, Twentyman, Yates,
Mehew, Jones, Bloomer, Reece, White, Saunders,
Pounder.
Torquay U won 3-2 on aggregate.

Wrexham (1) 2 *(Worthington, Preece)*
York C (0) 0   1934
Wrexham: O'Keefe; Phillips, Kennedy, Reck, Beau-
mont, Sertori, Cooper, Thackeray, Preece, Worth-
ington, Bowden.
York C: Marples; McMillan, Hall, Reid, Tutill,
Warburton, Canham, Howlett, Helliwell, Longhurst
(Pepper), Himsworth (Dunn).
Wrexham won 3-0 on aggregate.

5 SEPT
Bristol C (0) 1 *(Smith)*
WBA (0) 0 *aet*   9851
Bristol C: Sinclair; Llewellyn, Aizlewood, May,
Shelton, Rennie, Newman, Bent, Taylor, Morgan
(Allison), Smith.
WBA: Naylor; Hodson, Harbey, Robson (Hackett),
Burgess, Strodder, Ford, West, Bannister (Foster),
Bradley, Shakespeare.
Bristol C won 3-2 on aggregate.

Hereford U (1) 1 *(Phillips)*
Brentford (0) 0   2445
Hereford U: Wood; Jones MA, Devine (Benbow),
Pejic, Peacock, Jones R (Robinson), Bradley, Narbett,
Juryeff, Phillips, Tester.
Brentford: Benstead; Cousins (Evans), Fleming,
Millen, Bates, Buckle (Ratcliffe), Jones, May,
Cadette, Godfrey, Smillie.
Brentford won 2-1 on aggregate.

Lincoln C (1) 1 *(Davis)*
Halifax T (0) 0   2376
Lincoln C: Wallington; Casey, Clarke, Brown,
Nicholson, Davis, Schofield, Smith P, Carmichael
(Scott), Smith N, Puttnam.
Halifax T: Brown; Fleming P, Cook, Evans, Fleming
C, Futcher, Butler, Graham, Richardson, Fyfe
(Broadbent), Hall.
Halifax T won 2-1 on aggregate.

Oxford U (0) 2 *(Foster 2)*
Reading (0) 1 *(Hicks)*   4238
Oxford U: Kee; Robinson, Ford, Phillips, Foster,
Melville, Jackson, Lewis, Foyle, Stein, Simpson.
Reading: Francis; Jones, Richardson, McPherson,
Hicks, Conroy, Gooding, Taylor, Senior, Maskell,
Moran.
Oxford U won 3-1 on aggregate.

Scarborough (1) 3 *(Matthews, Oghani (2 pens))*
Rochdale (1) 3 *(Elliott, Goodison (pen), Milner)* 968
Scarborough: Ironside; Wilson (MacDonald), Logan,
Matthews, Richards, Meyer, Kamara, Mudd
(Mooney), Oghani, Dobson, Carter.
Rochdale: Welch; Goodison, Graham, Burns, Cole,
Elliott, Milner, Lee, Hilditch, Costello, Holmes.
Rochdale won 7-3 on aggregate.

11 SEPT
Hartlepool U (0) 2 *(Allon, Baker)*
Chesterfield (2) 2 *(Morris 2)*   2911
Hartlepool U: Cox; Olsson, McKinnon, Tinkler
(Honour), Harbron (Duggan), Bennyworth, Allon,
Tupling, Baker, Nobbs, Dalton.
Chesterfield: Allison; Rogers, Hart, Lemon, Brien,
Gunn, Rolph, Hewitt (Francis), Morris, Cooke,
Ryan.
Hartlepool U won 4-3 on aggregate.

SECOND ROUND FIRST LEG
24 SEPT
Port Vale (0) 0
Oxford U (0) 2 *(Foyle)*   5265
Port Vale: Wood; Mills, Jeffers, Walker, Aspin,
Glover, Porter, Finney (Jepson), Cross, Beckford,
Ford.
Oxford U: Walker; Robinson, Ford, Phillips, Jackson,
Melville, Penney, Lewis, Foyle, McClaren, Simpson.

25 SEPT
Bournemouth (0) 0
Millwall (0) 0   4911
Bournemouth: Guthrie; Mundee, Coleman, Teale,
O'Driscoll, Bond, Lawrence (Ekoku), Peacock,
Aylott, Holmes, Blissett.
Millwall: Horne; Stevens, Cunningham, Morgan,
Wood, McLeary, Carter, Allen, Sheringham,
Waddock, Stephenson (Rae).

Cardiff C (0) 1 *(Griffith)*
Portsmouth (1) 1 *(Aspinall)*   4224
Cardiff C: Hansbury; Rodgerson, Daniel, Barnard,
Matthews, Perry, Jones, Griffith, Gibbins, Pike,
Heard (Black).
Portsmouth: Gosney; Neill, Beresford, Kuhl, Black,
Maguire, Wigley, Stevens, Clarke, Aspinall, Kelly
(Murray).

Carlisle U (1) 1 *(Proudlock)*
Derby Co (0) 1 *(Saunders)*   7628
Carlisle U: Priestley; Miller, Edwards, Jeffels (Gold-smith), Methven, Fitzpatrick, Walsh, Shepherd, Walwyn (Norris), Gates, Proudlock.
Derby Co: Shilton; Sage, Williams P, Williams G, Wright, Forsyth, Micklewhite, Saunders, Harford, Hebberd, Ramage.

Chester C (0) 0
Arsenal (0) 1 *(Merson)*   4135
Chester C: Stewart; Preece, Pugh, Butler, Abel, Lane, Bennett, Barrow, Ellis, Dale, Croft (Lightfoot).
Arsenal: Seaman; Dixon, Winterburn, Hillier, Bould, Adams, Rocastle (Campbell), Davis, Smith, Merson, Groves.

Crystal Palace (2) 8 *(Bright 3, Wright 3, Hodges, Thompson)*
Southend U (0) 0   9653
Crystal Palace: Martyn; Humphrey (Thompson), Shaw, Pardew, Young, Thorn, McGoldrick, Thomas, Bright, Wright, Barber (Hodges).
Southend U: Sansome; Austin, Powell, Martin, Cornwell (Cook), Tilson, Clark, Butler, Ansah, Benjamin, Angell.

Darlington (0) 3 *(Cork 2, Gray (pen))*
Swindon T (0) 0   4037
Darlington: Prudhoe; McJannet, Gray, Gill, Smith, Corner, Emson, Toman, Borthwick, Cork, Tait.
Swindon T: Digby; Kerslake, Bodin, McLoughlin, Bennett (White), Gittens, Jones, Shearer, Simpson, McLaren, Foley (Buttigieg)

Hull C (0) 0
Wolverhampton W (0) 0   5283
Hull C: Hesford; Hockaday, Thompson (Finnigan), Mail, Buckley, Wilcox, Atkinson, Payton, McParland (Swan), Palin, Doyle.
Wolverhampton W: Stowell; Bennett, Westley, Bellamy, Hindmarch, Downing, Thompson, Cook, Bull, Paskin (Taylor), Steele (Dennison).

Liverpool (2) 5 *(McMahon, Gillespie, Houghton, Rush 2)*
Crewe Alex (1) 1 *(Sussex)*   17,228
Liverpool: Grobbelaar; Hysen, Burrows, Venison, Whelan, Gillespie, Beardsley, Houghton, Rush, Barnes (Rosenthal), McMahon (Molby).
Crewe Alex: Greygoose; Jones, Carr, Smart, Swain, McKearney, Jasper (Lennon), Clayton (Callaghan), Hignett, Gardiner, Sussex.

Luton T (1) 1 *(Harvey)*
Bradford C (0) 1 *(James)*   5120
Luton T: Chamberlain; Breacker, Harvey (James), Rees, Beaumont, Dreyer, Elstrup (Nogan), Preece, Dowie, Hughes, Black.
Bradford C: Tomlinson; Mitchell, Tinnion, James, Oliver, Sinnott, Duxbury, Abbott, McCarthy, Leonard, Stuart.

Middlesbrough (1) 2 *(Mustoe 2)*
Newcastle U (0) 0   15,042
Middlesbrough: Pears; Cooper, Phillips, Mowbray, Kernaghan, Wark, Ripley, Mustoe, Baird, Kerr, Hendrie.
Newcastle U: Burridge; Scott, Sweeney, Aitken, Kristensen, Ranson, Brock, O'Brien, Quinn, McGhee (Simpson), Fereday (Gourlay).

Northampton T (0) 0
Sheffield U (0) 1 *(Deane)*   6714
Northampton T: Gleasure; Chard, Wilson, Terry, Williams, Angus (Sandeman), Beavon, Wilkin (Collins), Bell, Barnes, Brown.
Sheffield U: Kite; Pemberton, Barnes, Jones, Beesley, Booker (Rostron), Bradshaw, Hill, Duffield, Deane, Marwood (Whitehouse).

Notts Co (0) 1 *(Johnson)*
Oldham Ath (0) 0   7089
Notts Co: Cherry; Palmer, Platnauer, Short Craig, Yates, Robinson, Thomas, Draper, Bartlett, Lund, Johnson (Turner).
Oldham Ath: Hallworth; Warhurst, Barlow, Henry, Barrett, Jobson, Palmer, Moulden, Currie (Donachie), Redfearn, Holden.

Plymouth Arg (0) 1 *(Thomas)*
Wimbledon (0) 0   4506
Plymouth Arg: Wilmot; Brown, Morgan, Marker, Burrows, Hodges, Byrne (King), Fiore, Turner, Thomas, Salman.
Wimbledon: Segers; Joseph, Phelan, Barton, Scales, Curle, Fairweather, Kruszynski, Gayle (Cork), Sanchez, Cotterill.

Rochdale (0) 0
Southampton (0) 5 *(Shearer 2, Horne, Wallace Rod, Ruddock)*   3855
Rochdale: Welch; Burns, Graham, Blundell, Cole (Holmes), O'Shaughnessy, Milner (Dawson), Lee, Elliott, Ward, Costello.
Southampton: Flowers; Dodd, Adams, Horne, Ruddock, Osman, Le Tissier, Cockerill, Shearer, Cook, Wallace Rod.

Rotherham U (0) 1 *(Richardson (og))*
Blackburn R (1) 1 *(Johnrose)*   4213
Rotherham: U: O'Hanlon; Forrest (Barnsley), Scott, Spooner, Stancliffe, Robinson, Hazel, Dempsey, Williamson (Goodwin), Evans, Thompson.
Blackburn R: Collier; Atkins, Millar, Reid, Hill, Moran, Irvine, Richardson, Stapleton, Johnrose, Wilcox.

Shrewsbury T (1) 1 *(Griffiths)*
Ipswich T (1) 1 *(Redford)*   2764
Shrewsbury T: Perks; Worsley, Gorman, Kelly, Heathcote, Blake, Moore, Coughlin, Spink, Brown, Griffiths.
Ipswich T: Forrest; Yallop, Hill, Stockwell, Gayle, Linighan, Gregory, Redford, Zondervan (Thompson), Kiwomya, Milton.

Sunderland (0) 0
Bristol C (1) 1 *(Morgan)*   10,358
Sunderland: Norman; Kay, Brady (Ord), Bennett, Ball, Owers (Hauser), Bracewell, Armstrong, Davenport, Gabbiadini, Hardyman.
Bristol C: Sinclair; Llewellyn, Aizlewood, May, Shelton, Rennie, Bent, Newman, Taylor, Morgan, Smith.

Wrexham (0) 0
Everton (2) 5 *(Cottee 3, McDonald, Nevin)*   9072
Wrexham: O'Keefe; Phillips, Kennedy, Reck, Beaumont, Sertori, Armstrong, Thackeray, Preece, Worthington, Bowden.
Everton: Southall; Atteveld, Hinchcliffe, Ratcliffe, Watson, McDonald, Nevin (Newell), McCall, Sharp, Cottee, Ebbrell.

26 SEPT

Aston Villa (0) 1 *(Platt)*
Barnsley (0) 0 14,471
Aston Villa: Spink; Price, Gray, McGrath, Mountfield, Nielsen, Daley, Platt, Olney, Cowans, Ormondroyd (Birch).
Barnsley: Baker; Fleming, Taggart, McCord, Smith, Tiler, Robinson, Cooper (Rammell), Saville, Agnew, Archdeacon.

Charlton Ath (1) 2 *(Watson, Minto)*
Leyton Orient (2) 2 *(Berry, Nugent)* 3238
Charlton Ath: Bolder; Pitcher, Minto, Peake, Webster, Caton, Lee, MacKenzie, Jones, Watson (Crooks), Walsh.
Leyton Orient: Heald; Baker, Howard, Sitton, Whitbread, Pike, Achampong, Castle, Nugent, Carter, Berry.

Coventry C (1) (4) *(Gynn, Gallacher, Livingstone 2)*
Bolton W (1) 2 *(Philliskirk 2)* 6193
Coventry C: Ogrizovic; Borrows, Titterton (McDonald), Perdomo, Kilcline, Peake, Gallacher, Gynn, Regis, Livingstone, Smith.
Bolton W: Felgate; Brown, Burke, Green, Crombie, Seagraves, Storer, Thompson, Reeves, Philliskirk, Darby.

Halifax T (1) 1 *(Evans)*
Manchester U (1) 3 *(Blackmore, McClair, Webb)* 7500
Halifax T: Brown; Fleming P, Cook, Evans, Fleming C, Futcher, Gregory, Butler, McPhillips, Richardson, Martin.
Manchester U: Leighton; Irwin, Blackmore, Donaghy, Phelan, Pallister, Webb, Ince (Martin), McClair, Hughes (Robins), Beardsmore.

Leicester C (1) 1 *(Kelly (pen))*
Leeds U (0) 0 13,744
Leicester C: Hodge; Mauchlen, Paris, Ramsey (Hill), Walsh, James, Wright (Linton), Reid, Oldfield, Mills, Kelly.
Leeds U: Lukic; Sterland, Whitlow (Williams), Batty, Fairclough, Whyte, Strachan, Varadi (Pearson), Chapman, McAllister, Speed.

Norwich C (1) 2 *(Crook, Sherwood)*
Watford (0) 0 7720
Norwich C: Gunn; Culverhouse, Bowen, Butterworth, Blades, Crook, Gordon, Fleck, Sherwood, Fox, Phillips.
Watford: James; Dublin, Drysdale, Roeder, McLoughlin, Holdsworth, Williams, Wilkinson, Inglethorpe (Bazeley), Falconer, Porter.

Nottingham F (1) 4 *(Chettle, Keane, Jemson, Pearce)*
Burnley (0) 1 *(Mumby)* 17,987
Nottingham F: Crossley; Laws, Pearce, Walker, Chettle, Keane, Crosby, Parker, Clough, Jemson, Gaynor.
Burnley: Pearce; Measham, Deakin, Deary, Pender, Davis, White, Mumby (Eli), Francis, Jakub, Hamilton (Farrell).

QPR (0) 3 *(Ferdinand, Maddix, Wegerle)*
Peterborough U (0) 1 *(Culpin)* 8714
QPR: Roberts; Bardsley, Sansom, Parker, McDonald, Maddix, Wilkins, Wilson (Barker), Ferdinand, Wegerle, Sinton.
Peterborough U: Bradshaw; Luke, Crosby, Halsall, Riley, McElhinney, Sterling, Hine, Osborne, Culpin, Butterworth.

Sheffield W (0) 2 *(Hirst, Pearson)*
Brentford (1) 1 *(Evans)* 11,207
Sheffield W: Pressman; Nilsson, King, Palmer, Shirtliff, Pearson, Wilson (McCall), Francis, Hirst, Williams, Worthington.
Brentford: Benstead; Bates, Cash, Millen, Evans, Brooke (Ratcliffe), Jones, May, Holdsworth, Godfrey (Cadette), Smillie.

Torquay U (0) 0
Manchester C (2) 4 *(Hendry, Allen, Harper, Beckford)* 5249
Torquay U: Howells; Whiston, Uzzell, Lloyd, Elliott, Joyce, Holmes, Smith, Tynan, Saunders (Musker), Loram (Edwards).
Manchester C: Coton; Brightwell, Pointon, Harper, Hendry, Redmond, Ward, Allen, Quinn (Beckford), Brennan, Heath.

Tottenham H (2) 5 *(Lineker, Gascoigne 4 (1 pen))*
Hartlepool U (0) 0 19,760
Tottenham H: Thorstvedt; Edinburgh (Thomas), Van Den Hauwe, Sedgley, Howells, Mabbutt, Stewart (Walsh), Gascoigne, Nayim, Lineker, Allen.
Hartlepool U: Cox; Olsson (Honour), McKinnon, Tinkler, Smith (Hutchison), Bennyworth, Allon, Tupling, Baker, Nobbs, Dalton.

Walsall (0) 0
Chelsea (3) 5 *(Townsend 2, Wilson, McAllister, Dixon)* 5666
Walsall: Green; Hutchings, Mower, O'Hara (Grealish), Bryant, Skipper, Bodak (Goldsmith), Ntamark, Rimmer, Cecere, Littlejohn.
Chelsea: Beasant; Clarke, Dorigo, Townsend, Lee, Monkou, McAllister, Nicholas, Dixon, Wilson, Le Saux.

West Ham U (1) 3 *(Dicks (pen), Keen, Quinn)*
Stoke C (0) 0 15,870
West Ham U: Miklosko; Potts, Dicks, Foster, Martin, Keen, Bishop, Quinn, Slater, Allen (Parris), Morley.
Stoke C: Fox; Butler, Statham (Fowler), Beeston, Blake, Sandford, Kennedy, Evans, Kelly (Thomas), Biggins, Ware.

SECOND ROUND SECOND LEG
9 OCT

Arsenal (3) 5 *(Groves 2, Smith, Adams, Merson)*
Chester C (0) 0 22,902
Arsenal: Seaman; Dixon, Winterburn, Hillier, Bould (O'Leary), Adams, Rocastle (Campbell), Davis, Smith, Merson, Groves.
Chester C: Stewart; Preece, Pugh, Butler, Lightfoot, Lane, Bennett, Barrow (Ellis), Morton (Reeves), Dale, Croft.
Arsenal won 6-0 on aggregate.

Barnsley (0) 0
Aston Villa (1) 1 *(Daley)* 13,924
Barnsley: Baker; Banks, Taggart, McCord, Smith (Robinson), Tiler, O'Connell, Rammell, Saville, Agnew, Archdeacon.
Aston Villa: Spink; Price, Gray, McGrath, Mountfield, Comyn, Daley, Platt, Olney (Cascarino), Cowans, Birch.
Aston Villa won 2-0 on aggregate.

Blackburn R (0) 1 *(Stapleton)*
Rotherham U (0) 0   4884
Blackburn R: Collier; Atkins (Oliver), Duxbury, Reid, Dewhurst, Moran, Irvine, Millar, Stapleton, Johnrose, Wilcox.
Rotherham U: O'Hanlon; Forrest, Robinson, Watts, Pickering, Scott, Buckley, Goodwin, Evans (Goater), Spooner, Hazel.
Blackburn R won 2-1 on aggregate.

Bolton W (1) 2 *(Philliskirk 2 (1 pen))*
Coventry C (1) 3 *(Regis 2, Gallacher)*   5222
Bolton W: Felgate; Brown, Cowdrill, Green (Storer), Stubbs, Winstanley, Lee, Thompson, Stevens, Philliskirk, Darby.
Coventry C: Ogrizovic; Borrows, Edwards, Gynn, Kilcline (MacDonald), Peake, Gallacher, Perdomo, Regis, Livingstone, Smith.
Coventry C won 7-4 on aggregate.

Brentford (1) 1 *(Jones (pen))*
Sheffield W (2) 2 *(Francis, Pearson)*   8227
Brentford: Benstead; Cousins, Cash, Millen, Bates, Brooke, Jones, May, Cadette (Blissett), Godfrey, Smillie.
Sheffield W: Pressman; Madden, King, Palmer, Shirtliff, Pearson, Wilson, Sheridan, Francis, Williams, Worthington.
Sheffield W won 4-2 on aggregate.

Bristol C (1) 1 *(Morgan)*
Sunderland (2) 6 *(Hauser, Ball, Owers, Gabbiadini 2, Cullen)*   11,776
Bristol C: Leaning; Llewellyn, Aizlewood, May, Shelton, Rennie, Donowa, Newman, Taylor (Allison), Morgan, Smith.
Sunderland: Norman; Kay, Smith, Bennett, Ball, Owers, Bracewell (Ord), Armstrong, Davenport, Gabbiadini, Hauser (Cullen).
Sunderland won 6-2 on aggregate.

Crewe Alex (0) 1 *(Sussex)*
Liverpool (2) 4 *(Rush 3, Staunton)*   7200
Crewe Alex: Greygoose; Lennon, McKearney (Gardiner), Smart, Swain, Rose, Jasper (Curran), Foreman, Hignett, Jones, Sussex.
Liverpool: Grobbelaar; Ablett, Burrows, Nicol, Venison, Gillespie, Marsh, Houghton, Rush, Barnes (Rosenthal), Staunton.
Liverpool won 9-2 on aggregate.

Everton (3) 6 *(Sharp 3, Cottee, McDonald, Ebbrell)*
Wrexham (0) 0   7415
Everton: Southall; Atteveld, Hinchcliffe, Watson, McDonald, Nevin, McCall (Milligan), Sharp, Cottee (Newell), Ebbrell.
Wrexham: Morris; Phillips, Hardy, Reck, Beaumont, Williams (Owen), Armstrong (Cooper), Thackeray, Preece, Worthington, Bowden.
Everton won 11-0 on aggregate.

Hartlepool U (0) 1 *(Dalton)*
Tottenham H (1) 2 *(Stewart 2)*   9631
Hartlepool U: Cox; Honour (MacDonald), McKinnon, Hutchison, Smith, Bennyworth, Allon, Tupling (Olsson), Baker, Nobbs, Dalton.
Tottenham H: Dearden; Thomas, Edinburgh, Sedgley, Howells (Gascoigne), Mabbutt, Stewart, Moncur (Nayim), Walsh, Samways, Allen.
Tottenham H won 7-1 on aggregate.

Ipswich T (2) 3 *(Redford, Kiwomya, Milton)*
Shrewsbury T (0) 0   7306
Ipswich T: Forrest; Yallop, Zondervan, Stockwell, Gayle, Linighan, Gregory, Redford, Hill, Kiwomya, Milton.
Shrewsbury T: Perks; Worsley, Gorman, Kelly, Heathcote, Lynch, Moore, Summerfield, Shaw (Spink), Brown, Parrish.
Ipswich T won 4-1 on aggregate.

Leyton Orient (0) 1 *(Castle (pen))*
Charlton Ath (0) 0   6811
Leyton Orient: Heald; Zoricich, Howard, Sitton, Whitbread, Pike, Carter, Castle, Nugent, Achampong, Harvey.
Charlton Ath: Salmon; Pitcher, Reid, Peake, Webster, Caton, Lee, MacKenzie, Walsh, Watson, Crooks.
Leyton Orient won 3-2 on aggregate.

Peterborough U (1) 1 *(Sansom (og))*
QPR (0) 1 *(Ferdinand)*   7454
Peterborough U: Bradshaw; Luke, Crosby, Halsall, Berry, McElhinney, Sterling, Hine, Riley (Osborne), Culpin, Butterworth.
QPR: Roberts; Bardsley, Sansom, Parker, McDonald, Maddix, Wilkins, Barker, Ferdinand, Wegerle, Sinton.
QPR won 4-2 on aggregate.

Portsmouth (1) 3 *(Clarke 2, Neill)*
Cardiff C (0) 1 *(Griffith) aet*   6174
Portsmouth: Gosney; Neill, Beresford, Kuhl (Awford), Butters, Maguire, Wigley, Stevens, Clarke, Black, Powell (Anderton).
Cardiff C: Hansbury; Lewis, Daniel, Barnard, Matthews, Perry, Jones (Chandler), Griffith, Gibbins, Blake (Morgan), Heard.
Portsmouth won 4-2 on aggregate.

Southampton (2) 3 *(Banger 3)*
Rochdale (0) 0   6754
Southampton: Flowers; Dodd, Benali, Wallace Ray, Ruddock, Osman, Gotsmanov, Horne, Shearer, Cook (Powell), Banger.
Rochdale: Welch; Cole, Graham, Blundell, O'Shaughnessy, Ward, Dawson, Lee, Elliott, Costello (Hall), Holmes.
Southampton won 8-0 on aggregate.

Southend U (0) 1 *(Angell)*
Crystal Palace (1) 2 *(Young, Salako)*   5199
Southend U: Sansome; Cornwell, Powell, Martin, Prior, Tilson, Cawley, Butler, Locke, Benjamin (Ansah), Angell.
Crystal Palace: Martyn; Humphrey, Shaw, Gray, Young (Southgate), Thorn, Salako, Thomas (Pardew), Bright, Wright, Hodges.
Crystal Palace won 10-1 on aggregate.

Swindon T (3) 4 *(Simpson, Smith (og), Close, McLoughlin)*
Darlington (0) 0   7066
Swindon T: Hammond; Kerslake, Bodin, McLoughlin (Hunt), Viveash, Gittens (Foley), Hazard, Close, White, MacLaren, Simpson.
Darlington: Prudhoe; Trotter, Gray, Gill (Mardenborough), Smith, Corner, Emson (Coatsworth), Toman, Borthwick, Cork, Tait.
Swindon T won 4-3 on aggregate.

Watford (0) 0
Norwich C (1) 3 *(Goss 2, Fleck)* 6148
Watford: James; Ashby (Drysdale), Williams, Porter (Inglethorpe), Roeder, Holdsworth, Thomas, Wilkinson, Falconer, Devonshire, Bazeley.
Norwich C: Gunn; Culverhouse, Goss, Butterworth, Blades, Crook, Gordon (Sutch), Fleck, Sherwood, Fox, Phillips.
Norwich C won 5-0 on aggregate.

Wolverhampton W (1) 1 *(Steele)*
Hull C (1) 1 *(Swan)* aet 14,954
Wolverhampton W: Stowell; Bennett (McLoughlin), Steele (Taylor), Bellamy, Hindmarch, Downing, Thompson, Cook, Bull, Westley, Dennison.
Hull C: Hesford; Brown, Finnigan, Wilcox, Shotton, Doyle, Thomas, Paton, Bamber, Palin, Swan.
Hull C won on away goals.

10 OCT
Bradford C (1) 1 *(James (og))*
Luton T (0) 1 *(Black)* aet 6180
Bradford C: Tomlinson; Mitchell, Tinnion, James, Oliver, Sinnott, Duxbury, Jewell, McCarthy, Leonard, Stuart.
Luton T: Chamberlain; James (Johnson), Harvey, Williams, Beaumont, Dreyer, Nogan, Preece, Dowie, Hughes, Black (Rees).
Bradford C won 5-4 on penalties.

Burnley (0) 0
Nottingham F (0) 1 *(Crosby)* 11,399
Burnley: Pearce; Measham, Deakin, Deary, Farrell, Pender, Mumby, White, Francis, Jakub (Eli), Grewcock.
Nottingham F: Crossley; Laws, Pearce, Walker, Chettle, Hodge (Lyne), Crosby, Parker, Gaynor, Jemson, Keane.
Nottingham F won 5-1 on aggregate.

Chelsea (2) 4 *(Durie, Dixon 2, Le Saux)*
Walsall (0) 1 *(Crosby)* 10,037
Chelsea; Beasant; Clarke, Dorigo, Townsend, Monkou, Lee, Wise, Nicholas (Bumstead), Dixon, Durie, Wilson (Le Saux).
Walsall: Green; Hutchings, Singleton, Lowery, Bryant, O'Hara (Littlejohn), Grealish (Mower), Ntamark, Rimmer, Cecere, McDonald.
Chelsea won 9-1 on aggregate.

Derby Co (1) 1 *(Saunders)*
Carlisle U (0) 0 12,253
Derby Co: Shilton; Sage, Pickering, Williams G, Wright, Forsyth, Micklewhite, Saunders, Harford, Ramage, Briscoe.
Carlisle U: Priestley; Miller, Edwards, Jeffels, Methven, Fitzpatrick, Walsh, Shepherd, Walwyn, Gates (Owen), Proudlock (Goldsmith).
Derby Co won 2-1 on aggregate.

Leeds U (0) 3 *(Walsh (og), Speed, Strachan)*
Leicester C (0) 0 19,090
Leeds U: Day; Sterland, Haddock, Batty, Fairclough, Whyte, Strachan, Pearson (Shutt), Chapman (Kamara), McAllister, Speed.
Leicester C: Hodge; Mauchlen, Paris, Ramsey, Walsh, James, Wright, Reid (Hill), Oldfield (North), Mills, Kelly.
Leeds U won 3-1 on aggregate.

Manchester C (0) 0
Torquay U (0) 0 12,204
Manchester C: Coton (Margetson); Brightwell, Pointon, Harper (Heath), Reid, Redmond, Ward, Megson, Quinn, Allen, Brennan.
Torquay U: Howells; Curran, Holmes, Lloyd, Elliott, Joyce, Myers, Smith (Kidd), Tynan, Edwards, Hall.
Manchester won 4-0 on aggregate.

Manchester U (1) 2 *(Bruce (pen), Anderson)*
Halifax T (0) 1 *(Gregory)* 22,295
Manchester U: Sealey; Anderson, Blackmore (Wallace), Bruce, Phelan, Pallister, Webb, Irwin (Robins), McClair, Hughes, Martin.
Halifax T: Brown; Fleming P, Evans, Fleming C, Futcher, Gregory, Williams, Butler, McPhillips (Patterson), Graham, Butler (Donnelly).
Manchester U won 5-2 on aggregate.

Millwall (1) 2 *(Sheringham 2)*
Bournemouth (0) 1 *(Aylott)* 7702
Millwall: Horne; Stevens, Dawes, Waddock, Wood, McLeary, Carter, Allen, Sheringham, Rae, O'Callaghan.
Bournemouth: Peyton; Miller, Coleman, Teale, O'Driscoll, Bond, Lawrence, Peacock, Aylott, Redknapp, Blissett.
Millwall won 2-1 on aggregate.

Newcastle U (1) 1 *(Anderson)*
Middlesbrough (0) 0 12,778
Newcastle U: Burridge; Scott, Sweeney (Robinson), Aitken, Anderson, Bradshaw, Fereday, Brock, Quinn, McGhee, O'Brien.
Middlesbrough: Pears; Cooper, Phillips, Mowbray, Kernaghan, Wark, Slaven, Mustoe, Baird, Kerr, Hendrie.
Middlesbrough won 2-1 on aggregate.

Oldham Ath (1) 5 *(Holden, Redfearn (pen), Currie 2, Moulden)*
Notts Co (1) 2 *(Johnson (pen), Robinson)* aet 10,757
Oldham Ath: Hallworth; Adams (Currie), Barlow, Henry, Barrett, Jobson, Palmer, Moulden, Marshall, Redfearn, Holden.
Notts Co: Cherry; Palmer, Platnauer, Short Craig, Yates, Robinson, Thomas, Turner, Bartlett, Lund (Regis), Johnson (Draper).
Oldham Ath won 5-3 on aggregate.

Oxford U (0) 0
Port Vale (0) 0 2303
Oxford U: Judge; Robinson, Evans, Phillips, Foster, Melville, Magilton, Durnin (Nogan), Foyle, Beauchamp (Smart), Simpson.
Port Vale: Wood; Mills, Hughes, Walker, Aspin, Glover, Ford, Porter, Jepson, Beckford (Cross), Jeffers.
Oxford U won 2-0 on aggregate.

Sheffield U (0) 2 *(Deane, Agana)*
Northampton T (0) 0 8679
Sheffield U: Kite; Hill, Barnes, Jones, Morris, Beesley, Wood (Duffield), Hoyland, Agana (Booker), Deane, Marwood.
Northampton T: Gleasure; Chard, Wilson, Terry, Williams (Sandeman), Angus, Beavon, Collins, Berry, Barnes, Brown (Bell).
Sheffield U won 3-1 on aggregate.

Stoke C (1) 1 *(Evans)*
West Ham U (0) 2 *(Allen 2)*   8411
Stoke C: Fox; Butler, Carr, Ware, Blake, Sandford, Scott, Ellis, Evans, Biggins, Kevan (Boughey).
West Ham U: Miklosko; Potts, Dicks, Foster, Martin, Keen (Gale), Bishop, Parris, Quinn (McAvennie), Allen, Morley.
West Ham U won 5-1 on aggregate.

Wimbledon (0) 0
Plymouth Arg (1) 2 *(Thomas, Fiore)*   3473
Wimbledon: Segers; Joseph, Phelan, Barton, Blackwell, Curle, Gayle (Newhouse), Kruszynski, Fashanu, Cork, Fairweather (McGee).
Plymouth Arg: Wilmot; Brown, Morgan, Marker, Burrows, Hodges, Byrne (Morrison), Fiore, Turner, Thomas, Salman.
Plymouth Arg won 3-0 on aggregate.

THIRD ROUND
30 OCT
Crystal Palace (0) 0
Leyton Orient (0) 0   12,958
Crystal Palace: Martyn; Humphrey, Shaw, Gray, Young, Thorn, Salako, Thomas, Bright, Wright, Hodges (Barber).
Leyton Orient: Heald; Sitton, Howard, Day, Whitbread, Pike, Carter, Castle, Berry (Nugent), Baker, Harvey.

Ipswich T (0) 0
Southampton (1) 2 *(Le Tissier, Wallace Rod)*   15,573
Ipswich T: Forrest; Yallop, Zondervan, Stockwell, Gayle, Linighan, Gregory (Dozzell), Redford, Hill, Kiwomya, Milton.
Southampton: Flowers; Dodd, Adams, Case, Ruddock, Moore, Le Tissier (Cockerill), Horne, Shearer, Rideout (Benali), Wallace Rod.

Manchester C (0) 1 *(Allen)*
Arsenal (0) 2 *(Groves, Adams)*   26,825
Manchester C: Coton; Harper, Pointon, Reid, Hendry, Redmond, White (Brightwell), Heath, Quinn, Megson (Allen), Ward.
Arsenal: Seaman; Dixon, Winterburn, Thomas, Bould, Adams, Groves, Davis, Smith, Merson, Limpar (Campbell).

Middlesbrough (2) 2 *(Kerr, Hendrie)*
Norwich C (0) 0   17,024
Middlesbrough: Pears; Cooper, Phillips, Mowbray, Kernaghan, Putney, Slaven, Mustoe, Baird, Kerr, Hendrie.
Norwich C: Gunn; Culverhouse, Bowen, Butterworth, Blades, Crook, Gordon, Power, Sherwood, Fox, Phillips.

Sheffield U (0) 2 *(Bradshaw, Deane)*
Everton (0) 1 *(Pemberton (og))*   15,045
Sheffield U: Tracey; Pemberton, Lake, Jones, Morris, Beesley, Marwood, Gannon, Agana (Bradshaw), Deane, Rostron.
Everton: Southall; Atteveld, Keown, Ratcliffe, Watson, McDonald, Newell, McCall, Sharp, Cottee (Nevin), Ebbrell.

Tottenham H (2) 2 *(Gascoigne, Stewart)*
Bradford C (1) 1 *(Oliver)*   25,451
Tottenham H: Thorstvedt; Thomas, Van Den Hauwe, Sedgley, Howells, Mabbutt, Stewart, Gascoigne, Nayim (Walsh), Lineker (Moncur), Allen.

Bradford C: Tomlinson; Mitchell, Babb, James, Oliver, Sinnott, Duxbury, Jewell, McCarthy, Adcock (Jules), Megson (Leonard).

31 OCT
Aston Villa (0) 2 *(Cascarino, Platt (pen))*
Millwall (0) 0   15,117
Aston Villa: Spink; Price, Gray (Birch), Comyn, Mountfield, Nielsen, Daley, Platt, Ormondroyd, Cowans, Cascarino.
Millwall: Branagan; Stevens, Dawes, Waddock, Wood, McLeary, Carter, Allen, Sheringham, Rae, O'Callaghan.

Chelsea (0) 0
Portsmouth (0) 0   16,699
Chelsea: Beasant; Hall, Dorigo, Townsend, Monkou, Lee, McAllister (Le Saux), Nicholas (Bumstead), Wilson, Durie, Wise.
Portsmouth: Gosney; Neill, Beresford, Kuhl, Maguire, Butters, Wigley (Whittingham), Stevens, Clarke, Aspinall, Black.

Coventry C (0) 3 *(Speedie, Livingstone, Regis)*
Hull C (0) 0   7708
Coventry C: Ogrizovic; Borrows, Edwards, Speedie, Billing, Peake, Emerson (Thompson), Gynn, Regis, Livingstone, MacDonald (Drinkell).
Hull C: Hesford; Hockaday, Jacobs, Buckley, Shotton, Doyle, Finnigan, Payton, Bamber (Swan), Palin, McParland.

Derby Co (4) 6 *(Harford 3, Bennett (og), Ramage 2)*
Sunderland (0) 0   16,422
Derby Co: Shilton; Sage, Cross, Williams G, Wright, Forsyth, Micklewhite, Saunders, Harford, Ramage, Pickering.
Sunderland: Norman; Kay, Smith (Cullen), Bennett (Ord), Ball, Owers, Bracewell, Armstrong, Davenport, Gabbiadini, Hardyman.

Leeds U (2) 2 *(Chapman, Speed)*
Oldham Ath (0) 0   26,327
Leeds U: Lukic; Kamara, Snodin, Batty, Fairclough, Whyte, Strachan, Pearson, Chapman, McAllister, Speed.
Oldham Ath: Hallworth; Warhurst (Williams), Barlow, Henry, Barrett, Jobson, Donachie, Ritchie, Currie (Moulden), Redfearn, Holden.

Manchester U (2) 3 *(Bruce (pen), Hughes, Sharpe)*
Liverpool (0) 1 *(Houghton)*   42,033
Manchester U: Sealey; Irwin, Blackmore, Bruce, Phelan (Donaghy), Pallister, Webb, Ince, McClair, Hughes (Wallace), Sharpe.
Liverpool: Grobbelaar; Hysen, Burrows (Rosenthal), Nicol, Staunton, Gillespie, Beardsley, Houghton, Rush, Molby, McMahon.

Oxford U (1) 2 *(Foyle, Magilton)*
West Ham U (1) 1 *(Morley)*   7528
Oxford U: Kee; Robinson, Evans, Lewis, Foster, Melville, Magilton, Stein (Penney), Foyle, Nogan, Simpson.
West Ham U: Miklosko; Rush, Keen, Foster, Martin, Parris, Bishop, Quinn, Slater, Allen, Morley.

Plymouth Arg (0) 1 *(Salman)*
Nottingham F (2) 2 *(Parker, Jemson)*   17,467
Plymouth Arg: Walter; Brown, Morgan, Marker, Burrows, Salman, Barlow, Fiore (Byrne), Turner, Adcock, Morrison.

Nottingham F: Crossley; Laws, Pearce, Walker (Wassall), Chettle, Keane, Crosby, Parker, Clough, Jemson (Starbuck), Gaynor.

QPR (2) 2 *(Falco, Barker)*
Blackburn R (1) 1 *(Hill)*   8396
QPR: Stejskal; Bardsley, Sansom, Parker, McDonald (Law), Maddix, Wilkins, Barker, Falco, Wegerle, Sinton.
Blackburn R: Grew; Dewhurst, Beglin, Reid, Hill, Moran, Gayle, Millar, Stapleton, Garner (Johnrose), Atkins.

Sheffield W (0) 0
Swindon T (0) 0   13,900
Sheffield W: Pressman; Harkes, King, Palmer, Shirtliff, Madden, Wilson, Sheridan, Hirst, Williams (Francis), Worthington (McCall).
Swindon T: Digby; Kerslake, Bodin, Simpson, Viveash, Gittens, Jones, Shearer, White (McLoughlin), McLaren, Foley.

THIRD ROUND REPLAYS
6 NOV
Portsmouth (1) 2 *(Chamberlain, Whittingham)*
Chelsea (0) 3 *(Lee, Wise (pen), Wilson)*   16,085
Portsmouth: Gosney; Neill, Beresford, Kuhl, Butters, Maguire, Chamberlain (Wigley), Stevens, Clarke, Aspinall (Black), Whittingham.
Chelsea: Hitchcock; Hall, Dorigo, Townsend, Cundy, Lee, Wise, Bumstead, Wilson, Durie, Le Saux (Dixon).

Swindon T (0) 0
Sheffield W (1) 1 *(Pearson)*   9043
Swindon T: Digby; Kerslake, Bodin, McLoughlin (Simpson), Viveash, Gittens, Jones, Shearer, White, MacLaren, Foley.
Sheffield W: Pressman; Harkes, McCall (Madden), Palmer, Shirtliff, Pearson, Wilson, Sheridan, Hirst, Williams, Worthington.

7 NOV
Leyton Orient (0) 0
Crystal Palace (0) 1 *(Bright)*   10,158
Leyton Orient: Heald; Baker, Howard, Sitton, Whitbread, Pike, Carter, Castle, Zoricich (Achampong), Harvey, Berry (Nugent).
Crystal Palace: Martyn; Humphrey, Shaw, Gray, Young, Thorn, Salako, Thomas, Bright, Wright, Barber (McGoldrick).

FOURTH ROUND
27 NOV
QPR (0) 0
Leeds U (3) 3 *(McAllister, Fairclough, Chapman)*   15,832
QPR: Roberts; Bardsley, Sansom, Herrera, Wilson, Law, Wilkins, Barker, Iorfa, Wegerle, Sinton.
Leeds U: Lukic; Sterland, Haddock, Batty, Fairclough, Whyte, Strachan (Snodin), Shutt, Chapman, McAllister, Speed.

Sheffield U (0) 0
Tottenham H (0) 2 *(Stewart, Gascoigne)*   25,862
Sheffield U: Tracey; Wilder, Lake, Jones, Morris, Beesley, Bryson, Gannon, Bradshaw, Deane, Rostron (Duffield).

Tottenham H: Thorstvedt; Thomas, Edinburgh, Sedgley (Tuttle), Howells, Mabbutt, Stewart, Gascoigne, Samways (Walsh), Lineker, Allen.

Southampton (1) 2 *(Le Tissier, Shearer)*
Crystal Palace (0) 0   13,765
Southampton: Flowers; Cockerill, Adams, Case, Ruddock, Osman, Le Tissier (Wallace Rod), Horne, Shearer, Rideout, Cherednik (Benali).
Crystal Palace: Martyn; Humphrey, Shaw, Gray, Thorn (Hodges), Young, Salako, Thomas, Bright, Wright, McGoldrick.

28 NOV
Arsenal (0) 2 *(Smith 2)*
Manchester U (3) 6 *(Blackmore, Hughes, Sharp 3, Wallace)*   40,884
Arsenal: Seaman; Dixon, Winterburn, Thomas, Bould, Adams, Groves, Davis, Smith, Merson, Limpar (Campbell).
Manchester U: Sealey; Irwin, Blackmore, Bruce (Donaghy), Phelan, Pallister, Sharpe, Ince, McClair, Hughes, Wallace.

Aston Villa (1) 3 *(Ormondroyd, Daley, Platt (pen))*
Middlesbrough (0) 2 *(Slaven 2)*   17,317
Aston Villa: Spink; Price, Gray, McGrath, Mountfield, Nielsen, Daley, Platt (Birch), Olney, Cowans, Ormondroyd.
Middlesbrough: Pears, Cooper, Phillips, Mowbray, Kernaghan (Ripley), Wark, Slaven, Mustoe, Baird, Kerr, Hendrie.

Coventry C (4) 5 *(Gallacher 3, Livingstone 2)*
Nottingham F (3) 4 *(Clough 3, Parker)*   16,304
Coventry C: Ogrizovic; Borrows, Edwards, Gynn, Billing, Peake, Gallacher, Speedie, Regis, Livingstone, Smith.
Nottingham F: Crossley; Laws, Pearce, Walker, Chettle, Hodge, Crosby, Keane, Clough, Jemson, Parker.

Oxford U (1) 1 *(Melville)*
Chelsea (0) 2 *(Durie 2)*   9789
Oxford U: Veysey; Robinson, Smart, Lewis, Foster, Melville, Magilton, Stein, Foyle, Nogan, Simpson.
Chelsea: Beasant; Hall, Le Saux, Townsend, Cundy, Monkou, Stuart (Wilson), Matthew (Lee), Dixon, Durie, Wise.

Sheffield W (1) 1 *(Hirst)*
Derby Co (1) 1 *(Saunders)*   25,649
Sheffield W: Pressman; Harkes, King (Williams), Palmer, Shirtliff, Pearson, Wilson, Sheridan, Hirst, Francis, Worthington.
Derby Co: Shilton; Patterson, Pickering, Ramage, Wright, Forsyth, Micklewhite, Saunders, Harford, Hebberd, Briscoe.

FOURTH ROUND REPLAY
12 DEC
Derby Co (0) 0 *(Micklewhite)*
Sheffield W (1) 2 *(Harkes, Williams)*   17,050
Derby Co: Shilton; Patterson, Pickering, Ramage (Sage), Wright, Forsyth, Micklewhite, Saunders, Harford, Hebberd, Briscoe (Gee).
Sheffield W: Pressman; Harkes, King, Palmer, Shirtliff, Pearson, Wilson, Sheridan, Hirst, Williams, Worthington.

FIFTH ROUND
16 JAN
Chelsea (0) 0
Totenham H (0) 0   34,178
Chelsea: Beasant; Hall, Dorigo, Townsend, Cundy,
Monkou, Stuart, Matthew, Dixon, Durie, Le Saux.
Tottenham H: Thorstvedt; Thomas (Sedgley),
Edinburgh, Fenwick, Howells, Mabbutt, Stewart,
Samways (Nayim), Walsh, Lineker, Allen.

Leeds U (1) 4 *(Chapman 2, McAllister, Speed)*
Aston Villa (0) 1 *(Ormondroyd)*   28,176
Leeds U: Lukic; Sterland, Snodin (Haddock), Batty,
Fairclough, Whyte, Strachan, Shutt (Pearson),
Chapman, McAllister, Speed.
Aston Villa: Spink; Price, Gray, McGrath, Birch
(Ormondroyd), Nielsen, Yorke, Platt, Cascarino,
Cowans, Callaghan.

Southampton (0) 1 *(Shearer)*
Manchester U (0) 1 *(Hughes)*   21,011
Southampton: Flowers; Cherednik, Adams, Case,
Moore, Osman, Le Tissier, Horne, Shearer, Cockerill,
Wallace Rod.
Manchester U: Sealey; Donaghy, Blackmore, Bruce,
Phelan, Pallister, Robson, Webb (Irwin), McClair,
Hughes, Sharpe.

23 JAN
Coventry C (0) 0
Sheffield W (1) 1 *(Pearson)*   20,712
Coventry C: Ogrizovic; Borrows, Edwards (Drinkell),
McGrath, Butcher, Peake, MacDonald (Emerson),
Gynn, Regis, Speedie, Smith.
Sheffield W: Turner; King, Worthington, Palmer,
Shirtliff, Pearson, Wilson, Sheridan, Hirst, Williams,
McCall.

FIFTH ROUND REPLAYS
Manchester U (0) 3 *(Hughes 3)*
Southampton (0) 2 *(Shearer 2 (1 pen))*   41,093
Manchester U: Sealey; Irwin (Donaghy), Blackmore,
Bruce, Phelan, Pallister, Robson, Webb, McClair,
Hughes, Sharpe (Robins).
Southampton: Flowers; Cherednik, Adams, Case,
Moore, Osman, Gotsmanov, Horne, Shearer,
Cockerill, Wallace Rod.

Tottenham H (0) 0
Chelsea (1) 3 *(Townsend, Dixon, Wise (pen))* 33,861
Tottenham H: Thorstvedt; Fenwick (Sedgley),
Edinburgh, Samways (Nayim), Howells, Mabbutt,
Stewart, Gascoigne, Walsh, Lineker, Allen.
Chelsea: Beasant; Hall, Dorigo, Townsend, Cundy,
Monkou, Stuart, Matthew, Dixon, Durie, Wise.

SEMI-FINALS FIRST LEG
10 FEB
Manchester U (0) 2 *(Sharp, McClair)*
Leeds U (0) 1 *(Whyte)*   34,050
Manchester U: Sealey; Irwin (Donaghy), Martin
(Wallace), Bruce, Blackmore, Pallister, Robson, Ince,
McClair, Hughes, Sharpe.
Leeds U: Lukic; Sterland, Haddock, Whitlow,
Fairclough, Whyte, Strachan, Williams, Chapman,
McAllister, Speed.

24 FEB
Chelsea (0) 0
Sheffield W (0) 2 *(Shirtliff, Hirst)*   34,074
Chelsea: Beasant; Hall, Dorigo, Townsend, Cundy,
Monkou, Stuart, Matthew (Le Saux), Dixon, Durie,
Wise.
Sheffield W: Turner; Harkes, King, Palmer, Shirtliff,
Pearson, Wilson, Sheridan, Hirst, Francis (Williams),
Worthington.

SEMI-FINALS SECOND LEG
Leeds U (0) 0
Manchester U (0) 1 *(Sharpe)*   32,014
Leeds U: Lukic; Sterland, Haddock (Pearson), Batty,
Fairclough, Whyte, Strachan (Whitlow), Shutt,
Chapman, McAllister, Speed.
Manchester U: Sealey; Donaghy, Blackmore, Webb
(Martin), Phelan, Pallister, Robson, Ince, McClair,
Hughes, Sharpe.
Manchester U won 3-1 on aggregate.

27 FEB
Sheffield W (2) 3 *(Pearson, Wilson, Williams)*
Chelsea (0) 1 *(Stuart)*   34,669
Sheffield W: Turner; Harkes, King, Palmer, Shirtliff,
Pearson, Wilson (McCall), Sheridan, Hirst, Francis
(Williams), Worthington.
Chelsea: Beasant; Clarke, Dorigo, Townsend, Cundy,
Monkou, Stuart, Dickens, Dixon, Durie, Wise.
Sheffield W won 5-1 on aggregate.

FINAL at Wembley
21 APR
Sheffield W (1) 1 *(Sheridan)*
Manchester U (0) 0   80,000
Sheffield W: Turner; Nilsson, King, Harkes
(Madden), Shirtliff, Pearson, Wilson, Sheridan, Hirst,
Williams, Worthington.
Manchester U: Sealey; Irwin, Blackmore, Bruce,
Webb (Phelan), Pallister, Robson, Ince, McClair,
Hughes, Sharpe.
Referee: R. Lewis (Gt Bookham)

FOOTBALL TRUST

The Football Trust has approved further grant-aid offers to assist clubs to implement the Taylor Report. The Trust, which was founded through an initiative by Littlewoods, Vernons and Zetters, has announced grant-aid of £7.64m to clubs in the Football League and Scottish Football League towards the cost of proposed safety and improvements projects. The Trust's total allocation of funds to help clubs meet the required standards of safety and comfort, thus far, stands at £16m.

Coventry City are among the major beneficiaries of the Football Trust's latest series of Taylor-related grants. The First Division club have been awarded support of up to £2m towards the construction of a new East Stand and roofing for the North Stand at Highfield Road.

Newcastle United receive £1.4m towards the redevelopment of the North Stand at the Leazes End; Portsmouth, £1m towards the 3,750 seater stand at the Fratton Park End and Scottish First Division side Hamilton Academical receive £500,000 for the construction of a new stadium.

The latest major projects to receive Football Trust approval are detailed below:

MAJOR PROJECTS: GRANTS APPROVED

	Project	Minimum cost of project £	Grant approved £
Football League			
Bradford City	Family stand	600,000	420,000
Coventry City	New stand	4,000,000	2,000,000
Hartlepool United	All-seater stand	300,000	225,000
Newcastle United	Redevelop North Stand	4,000,000	1,400,000
Oldham Athletic	Develop Chadderton Stand	921,000	500,000
Portsmouth	All-seater stand	2,350,000	1,000,000
York City	New covered stand	200,000	100,000
Scottish Football League			
Brechin City	New stand	300,000	210,000
Hamilton Academical	New stadium	7,850,000	500,000
	TOTAL	20,521,000	6,355,000

At its March meeting, the Trust confirmed grant-aid support to 51 clubs assisting safety and improvements projects, the installation of electronic turnstiles and security measures including the provision of police control rooms. The estimated cost of these recently approved projects totals £22.3m.

Peter Lee, Secretary of the Football Trust, commented: "These grants confirm that the Trust is on course to allocate the first year's income from the reduction in pool betting duty. I am sure that the £20 million grant-aid mark will be met when further applications are considered at a special meeting of the Trust next week." He added: "The total cost to football of the latest projects — some £22 million — provides further evidence of the game's commitment to implementing Taylor. The clubs are making an enormous contribution from their own resources to seeing the task through."

The Football Trust has been chosen by the Government as the vehicle through which the proceeds of the 1990 Budget concession on pool betting duty are to be channelled to the game. The Government contributes some £20m annually from this source and a further £12m per annum continues to be donated through the generosity of Littlewoods, Vernons and Zetters from their Spotting-the-Ball competition. The greater part of this money is allocated to assist the professional game implement the Taylor recommendations. Safety work at League grounds remains of paramount importance and will continue to be grant-aided at 75 per cent of eligible approved expenditure. Grants are also available for improvements such as family enclosures, toilets, areas and facilities for people with disabilities and anti-hooligan initiatives such as CCTV and transport improvements. The remainder is spent on helping the game at grass roots level and includes safety and improvements work at clubs outside the full-time professional leagues and a wide variety of community based initiatives.

ROTHMANS FOOTBALL YEARBOOK 1991-92 HB	JACK ROLLIN	£17.95
ROTHMANS RUGBY LEAGUE YEARBOOK 1991-92	D. HOWES/R. FLETCHER	£13.95
ROTHMANS RUGBY UNION YEARBOOK 1991-92	STEPHEN JONES	£13.95
ROTHMANS SNOOKER YEARBOOK 1991-92	JANICE HALE	£13.95
PLAYFAIR FOOTBALL ANNUAL 1991-92	JACK ROLLIN	£2.99
PLAYFAIR NON-LEAGUE FOOTBALL ANNUAL 1991-92	BRUCE SMITH	£3.50
PLAYFAIR WINNERS 1991-92	EDWARD ABELSON	£2.99
BOOKABLE OFFENCE	WHEN SATURDAY COMES	£5.95
LATE TACKLE	WHEN SATURDAY COMES	£5.99
FA COACHING BOOK OF SOCCER TACTICS AND SKILLS	CHARLES HUGHES	£10.99
GAZZA: DAFT AS A BRUSH	PAUL GASCOIGNE	£3.95

Queen Anne Press offers an exciting range of quality titles by both established and new authors. All of the books in this series are available from:

Queen Anne Press Paperbacks
Cash Sales Department,
P.O. Box 11,
Falmouth,
Cornwall TR10 9EN.

Alternatively you may fax your order to the above address. Fax No. 0326 76423.

Payments can be made as follows: Cheque, postal order (payable to Macdonald & Co (Publishers) Ltd) or by credit cards, Visa/Access. Do not send cash or currency. UK customers: please send a cheque or postal order (no currency) and allow 80p for postage and packing for the first book plus 20p for each additional book up to a maximum charge of £2.00.

B.F.P.O. customers please allow 80p for the first book plus 20p for each additional book.

Overseas customers including Ireland, please allow £1.50 for postage and packing for the first book, £1.00 for the second book, and 30p for each additional book.

NAME (Block Letters) ....

ADDRESS ....

....

....

I enclose my remittance for_____

I wish to pay by Access/Visa Card

Number

Card Expiry Date

ZENITH DATA SYSTEMS CUP 1990–91

FIRST ROUND
20 NOV

Middlesbrough (0) 3 *(Baird, Mowbray, Slaven)*
Hull C (0) 1 *(Waites) aet*   8926
Middlesbrough: Pears; Cooper (McGee), Phillips,
Mowbray, Coleman, Proctor, Slaven, Mustoe, Baird,
Kerr, Ripley.
Hull C: Hesford; Brown, Jacobs, Mail, Wilcox,
Waites, Roberts (Jenkinson), Payton, McParland
(Hunter), Palin, Calvert.

Notts Co (1) 1 *(Regis)*
Port Vale (0) 0   2320
Notts Co: Cherry; Palmer, Harding, Short Craig,
Yates, O'Riordan (Johnson), Thomas, Turner,
Bartlett (Chapman), Regis, Draper.
Port Vale: Wood; Mills, Jeffers, Walker, Parkin,
Aspin, Glover, Porter (Webb), Cross, Millar, Ford.

Plymouth Arg (0) 0
Brighton & HA (0) 0 *aet*   3596
Plymouth: Wilmot; Brown, Morgan, Marker,
Burrows, Salman, Barlow, Fiore, Robinson, Ampadu
(Pickard), Hodges.
Brighton & HA: Digweed; Crumplin, Chapman,
Wilkins, Gatting, McCarthy, Barham, Byrne, Small,
Codner, Walker.
Brighton & HA won 3-1 on penalties.

Watford (0) 1 *(Wilkinson)*
Bristol R (2) 2 *(Saunders, Mehew)*   3076
Watford: Meola; Gibbs, Drysdale, Porter,
Holdsworth, Dublin, Byrne, Wilkinson, Kennedy,
Thomas (Bazeley), Harrison.
Bristol R: Parkin; Alexander, Twentyman, Yates,
Mehew, Jones, Holloway (Nixon), Reece, White,
Saunders, Pounder (Purnell).

SECOND ROUND

Southampton (3) 4 *(Shearer 2, Horne, Law (og))*
QPR (0) 0   5071
Southampton: Flowers; Dodd, Adams, Cockerill,
Ruddock, Osman, Le Tissier, Horne, Shearer,
Rideout, Gotsmanov.
QPR: Roberts; Bardsley, Sansom, Parker, Law,
McCarthy, Wilkins, Barker, Allen, Wegerle (Meaker),
Sinton (Wilson).

21 NOV
FIRST ROUND

Oxford U (0) 2 *(Nogan, Magilton (pen))*
Bristol C (0) 2 *(Newman, May (pen)) aet*   1323
Oxford U: Veysey; Robinson, Evans, Lewis (Penney),
Smart, Melville, Magilton, Stein (Beauchamp),
Phillips, Nogan, Simpson.
Bristol C: Sinclair; Llewellyn, Aizlewood, May,
Shelton, Rennie, Bent, Newman, Allison, Taylor,
Honor (Smith).
Oxford U won 3-2 on penalties.

WBA (1) 3 *(Robinson, Bradley, Bannister)*
Barnsley (2) 5 *(Robinson, Smith, Banks 3)*   4452
WBA: Naylor; Dobbins, Harbey (Parkin), Roberts,
Bradley, Strodder, Goodman, West, Bannister,
McNally, Robson (Ford).
Barnsley: Baker; Banks, Smith, Dobbin, Fleming,
Gridelet, Joyce, O'Connell, Marshall (Cross),
Robinson, Archdeacon.

SECOND ROUND

Nottingham F (0) 2 *(Hodge, Clough)*
Newcastle U (1) 1 *(Scott)*   9567
Nottingham F: Crossley; Laws, Pearce, Walker,
Chettle, Hodge, Carr, Wilson (Starbuck), Clough,
Jemson, Parker.
Newcastle U: Burridge; Scott, Anderson, Roche
(Makel), Stimson, Watson, Howey, Brock (Appleby),
Quinn, Sloan, O'Brien.

FIRST ROUND
27 NOV

Leicester C (0) 0
Wolverhampton W (1) 1 *(Bull)*   4705
Leicester C: Hooper; Mauchlen, Spearing (Peake),
Hill, Fenwick, Paris, Wright, North, Reid (Oldfield),
Mills, Kelly.
Wolverhampton W: Stowell; Roberts, Steele, Bellamy,
Stancliffe (Hindmarch), Downing, Thompson, Cook,
Bull, Taylor, Dennison.

SECOND ROUND
11 DEC

Notts Co (1) 2 *(Bartlett, Draper (pen))*
Sunderland (2) 2 *(O'Riordan (og), Armstrong) aet*
                                                          3003
Notts Co: Cherry; Palmer, Harding, Short Craig,
Yates, O'Riordan (Robinson), Thomas, Turner,
Bartlett (Johnson), Regis, Draper.
Sunderland: Norman; Kay, Hardyman, Bennett
(Cornforth), Ball, Owers, Bracewell, Armstrong,
Davenport, Hawke (Ord), Pascoe.
Sunderland won 3-1 on penalties.

Sheffield U (2) 7 *(Bryson 2, Hoyland, Beesley, Deane,
Duffield 2)*
Oldham Ath (2) 2 *(Palmer, Marshall)*   3144
Sheffield U: Treacey; Wilder, Barnes, Hill, Todd,
Beesley, Bryson, Gannon, Bradshaw (Duffield),
Deane (Booker), Hoyland.
Oldham Ath: Hallworth; Warhurst, Barlow, Henry,
Barrett, Jobson, Palmer (Adams), Brazil (Currie),
Marshall, Redfearn, Holden.

12 DEC

Chelsea (0) 1 *(Wise (pen))*
Swindon T (0) 0   5888
Chelsea: Beasant; Hall, Dorigo, Townsend (Stuart),
Cundy, Monkou, Le Saux, Lee, Dixon, Durie, Wise.
Swindon T: Digby; Kerslake, Bodin, Hazard, Viveash,
Gittens, Jones, Shearer, Simpson, MacLaren, Foley.

Oxford U (1) 1 *(Magilton)*
Portsmouth (0) 0   1055
Oxford U: Veysey; Robinson, Evans, Phillips, Foster,
Melville, Magilton, Stein (Lewis), Foyle (Durnin),
Nogan, Simpson.
Portsmouth: Knight; Neill, Beresford, Aspinall,
Butters, Awford, Anderton, Stevens, Clarke (Powell),
Whittingham, Daniel (Wigley).

Wimbledon (0) 0
Ipswich T (1) 2 *(Redford, Kiwomya)*   1787
Wimbledon: Segers; Joseph, Phelan, Barton,
Blackwell, Curle, McGee (Newhouse), Kruszynski,
Cork, Sanchez, Bennett (Elkins).

Ipswich T: Forrest; Yallop, Johnson, Stockwell, Linighan, Dozzell, Lowe, Redford, Palmer, Kiwomya (Gregory), Milton.

18 DEC
Blackburn R (0) 1 *(Skinner)*
Everton (1) 4 *(Newell, Cottee, Watson 2)* 5410
Blackburn R: Reitmaier; Atkins, Sulley, Reid, May, Moran (Duxbury), Skinner, Shepstone, Johnrose, Wilcox, Dewhurst.
Everton: Southall; McDonald, Hinchcliffe, Ratcliffe, Watson, Ebbrell, Nevin, McCall, Newell, Cottee, Beagrie.

Crystal Palace (1) 2 *(Gray, Salako)*
Bristol R (1) 1 *(Pounder)* 5209
Crystal Palace: Martyn; Humphrey, Shaw, Gray, Young, Thorn, Salako, Thomas, Bright, Wright, McGoldrick.
Bristol R: Parkin; Alexander, Twentyman, Yates, Mehew, Jones, Holloway, Reece, White, Saunders, Pounder.

Sheffield W (1) 3 *(Hirst 3)*
Barnsley (0) 3 *(Archdeacon 2, Connelly) aet* 5942
Sheffield W: Pressman; Harkes, Worthington, Palmer, Shirtliff, Pearson, Wilson, Sheridan, Hirst, Francis (McCall), Williams.
Barnsley: Baker; Banks, Taggart, McCord (Smith), Fleming, Tiler, O'Connell, Rammell, Saville, Agnew (Connelly), Archdeacon.
Barnsley won 4-2 on penalties.

19 DEC
Brighton & HA (1) 3 *(Codner, Small 2)*
Charlton Ath (0) 1 *(Walsh)* 2588
Brighton & HA: Digweed; Crumplin, Gatting, Wilkins, McCarthy, Chivers, Barham, Gurinovich, Small, Codner (Chapman), Walker.
Charlton Ath: Bolder; Pitcher (Gritt), Reid, Peake, Balmer, Webster, Minto, Walsh, Dyer, Watson, Mortimer (Leaburn).

Derby Co (0) 1 *(Callaghan)*
Coventry C (0) 0 7270
Derby Co: Taylor; Sage, Pickering, Williams P, Kavanagh, Forsyth, Micklewhite, Saunders, Harford, Hebberd (Ramage), Callaghan.
Coventry C: Ogrizovic; Borrows, Edwards, Emerson, Billing, Peake, Gallacher, McDonald, Regis, Drinkell (Livingstone), Smith.

Luton T (4) 5 *(Farrell 2, Rees, Elstrup, Black)*
West Ham U (0) 1 *(Keen)* 5759
Luton T: Chamberlain; James, Harvey, Williams (Beaumont), McDonough, Dreyer, Elstrup (Nogan), Rees, Farrell, Pembridge, Black.
West Ham U: McKnight; Kelly, Parris, Gale, Potts, Livett, Allen, Quinn, Slater, Keen, Morley.

Manchester C (1) 2 *(White, Quinn)*
Middlesbrough (0) 1 *(Hendrie)* 6406
Manchester C: Coton; Brightwell, Pointon, Harper, Hendry, Redmond, White, Clarke, Quinn, Brennan, Ward.
Middlesbrough: Pears; Cooper, McGee, Mowbray, Coleman, Wark (Proctor), Slaven, Mustoe, Baird, Kerr, Hendrie.

Norwich C (0) 1 *(Rosario)*
Millwall (0) 1 *(Sheringham) aet* 4741
Norwich C: Gunn; Culverhouse, Bowen, Butterworth, Polston, Crook (Smith), Gordon, Sutch (Mortensen), Sherwood, Rosario, Phillips.
Millwall: Horne; Stevens, Dawes, Waddock, Wood, McLeary, Stephenson, Allen, Sheringham, Rae, Briley (Carter).
Norwich C won 6-5 on penalties.

Wolverhampton W (0) 1 *(Cook)*
Leeds U (1) 2 *(Varadi, McAllister)* 11,080
Wolverhampton W: Stowell; Roberts, Thompson, Bellamy, Stancliffe (Bennett), Downing, Steele, Cook, Bull, Taylor, Dennison.
Leeds U: Day; Sterland, Snodin, Beglin, Fairclough, Haddock, Strachan (Williams), Varadi (Kerr), Pearson, McAllister, Speed.

NORTHERN QUARTER-FINALS
22 JAN
Everton (1) 4 *(Cottee 4)*
Sunderland (0) 1 *(Ball)* 4609
Everton: Southall; McDonald, Ebbrell, Ratcliffe, Keown, McCall, Nevin, Cottee, Sharp (Atteveld), Sheedy (Milligan), Beagrie.
Sunderland: Norman; Atkinson, Hardyman, Bennett, Ball, Owers, Bracewell, Armstrong (Cornforth), Davenport (Rush), Gabbiadini, Pascoe.

Leeds U (2) 2 *(Shutt, Chapman)*
Derby Co (0) 1 *(Saunders)* 6334
Leeds U: Lukic; Sterland, Snodin, Batty, Haddock, Whyte, Strachan, Shutt (Varadi), Chapman, Williams, Speed.
Derby Co: Shilton; Sage, Forsyth, Williams G, Wright, Kavanagh, Cross, Saunders, Harford, Hebberd (Patterson), Pickering.

Sheffield U (0) 0
Manchester C (1) 2 *(Ward 2)* 5106
Sheffield U: Tracey; Booker, Barnes, Jones, Beesley, Hill (Lucas), Bryson, Whitehurst, Bradshaw (Duffield), Todd, Wood.
Manchester C: Coton; Hill, Pointon, Harper, Hendry, Redmond, White (Brightwell), Allen (Heath), Quinn, Megson, Ward.

SOUTHERN QUARTER-FINALS
Ipswich T (1) 2 *(Milton, Dozzell)*
Oxford U (1) 1 *(Foster)* 7456
Ipswich T: Forrest; Yallop, Thompson, Stockwell, Johnson, Palmer, Lowe, Zondervan, Whitton, Dozzell, Milton.
Oxford U: Veysey; Robinson, Smart, McClaren (Foyle), Foster, Melville, Magilton, Phillips, Durnin, Nogan, Simpson.

30 JAN
NORTHERN QUARTER-FINAL
Barnsley (1) 2 *(Rammell, O'Connell)*
Nottingham F (1) 1 *(Chettle)* 6692
Barnsley: Baker; Banks, Taggart, Fleming, Smith, Tiler, O'Connell, Rammell, Saville, Agnew, Archdeacon.
Nottingham F: Crossley; Charles, Pearce, Walker, Chettle, Hodge, Crosby, Wilson, Clough, Parker (Gaynor), Woan (Starbuck).

SOUTHERN QUARTER-FINALS
18 FEB
Brighton & HA (0) 0
Crystal Palace (0) 2 *(Bright, Wright) aet*   9633
Brighton & HA: Digweed; Crumplin, Gatting, Wilkins, McCarthy (Chapman), Chivers (Wade), Barham, Byrne, Small, Codner, Walker.
Crystal Palace: Martyn; Humphrey, Shaw, Gray, Young, Pardew, Salako (Osborne), Thomas, Bright, Wright, Barber.

Chelsea (1) 1 *(Stuart)*
Luton T (0) 1 *(Dreyer) aet*   3849
Chelsea: Beasant; Clarke, Dorigo, Dickens, Cundy, Monkou, Stuart (Wilson), Matthew, Dixon, Durie, Le Saux (Hall).
Luton T: Chamberlain; Johnson, Harvey (James), Beaumont, Rodger (Farrell), Dreyer, Elstrup, Preece, Dowie, Pembridge, Rees.
Luton T won 4-1 on penalties.

20 FEB
Norwich C (2) 2 *(Fleck, Goss)*
Southampton (1) 1 *(Wallace Rod)*   5920
Norwich C: Gunn; Culverhouse, Bowen, Blades, Polston, Crook, Gordon, Fleck (Mortensen), Goss, Fox, Phillips.
Southampton: Andrews; Dodd, Cook, Cockerill, Moore (Benali), Ruddock, Gotsmanov (Powell), Horne, Shearer, McLoughlin, Wallace Rod.

NORTHERN SEMI-FINAL
Leeds U (0) 2 *(Williams, Strachan)*
Manchester C (0) 0 *aet*   11,898
Leeds U: Lukic; Sterland, Whitlow, Batty, Fairclough, Whyte, Strachan, Shutt, Chapman, McAllister (Williams), Speed (Davison).
Manchester C: Coton; Brightwell, Pointon, Harper, Hendry, Redmond, White, Allen (Heath), Quinn, Megson, Ward.

SOUTHERN SEMI-FINALS
26 FEB
Crystal Palace (2) 3 *(McGoldrick, Wright 2)*
Luton T (1) 1 *(Rees)*   7170
Crystal Palace: Martyn; Humphrey, Shaw, Gray, Young, Pardew, Salako, Thomas, Bright, Wright, McGoldrick (Barber).
Luton T: Chamberlain; Johnson, James (Jackson), Beaumont, Rodger, Dreyer, Elstrup, Preece, Dowie, Pembridge, Rees (Farrell).

27 FEB
Norwich C (0) 2 *(Fleck, Gordon)*
Ipswich T (0) 0   16,225
Norwich C: Gunn; Culverhouse, Bowen, Blades, Polston, Crook (Fox), Gordon, Fleck, Sherwood, Goss, Phillips.
Ipswich T: Forrest; Yallop, Thompson, Stockwell, Linighan, Humes (Palmer), Zondervan, Goddard, Whitton (Kiwomya), Dozzell, Milton.

SOUTHERN FINAL First Leg
5 MAR
Norwich C (1) 1 *(Sherwood)*
Crystal Palace (1) 1 *(Thomas)*   7554
Norwich C: Gunn; Culverhouse, Bowen, Blades, Polston, Smith (Fox), Gordon, Fleck, Sherwood, Goss, Phillips.
Crystal Palace: Martyn; Humphrey, Shaw, Gray, Southgate, Thorn, Salako, Thomas, Bright, Wright, Pardew (Barber).

NORTHERN SEMI-FINAL
13 MAR
Barnsley (0) 0
Everton (1) 1 *(Cottee)*   10,287
Barnsley: Baker; McCord (Robinson), Fleming, Rimmer, Smith (Banks), Tiler, O'Connell, Rammell, Saville, Agnew, Archdeacon.
Everton: Southall; Keown, Ebbrell, Ratcliffe, Watson, Milligan, Nevin, McCall, Newell, Cottee, Beagrie (McDonald).

19 MAR
NORTHERN FINAL First Leg
Leeds U (2) 3 *(Sterland, Chapman 2)*
Everton (3) 3 *(Beagrie, Warzycha, Milligan)*   13,387
Leeds U: Lukic; Sterland, Whitlow, Batty, Fairclough, Whyte, Strachan, Davison (Shutt), Chapman, McAllister, Williams (Speed).
Everton: Southall: McDonald, Ebbrell, Ratcliffe, Watson, Keown, Warzycha (Nevin), McCall, Newell (Cottee), Milligan, Beagrie.

SOUTHERN FINAL Second Leg
Crystal Palace (1) 2 *(Wright, Bright)*
Norwich C (0) 0   13,857
Crystal Palace: Martyn; Humphrey, Shaw, Gray, Young, Thorn, Salako, Thomas, Bright, Wright, Pardew.
Norwich C: Gunn; Culverhouse, Bowen, Blades (Butterworth), Polston, Crook, Gordon, Fleck, Sherwood, Goss (Fox), Phillips.
Crystal Palace won 3-1 on aggregate.

NORTHERN FINAL Second Leg
21 MAR
Everton (0) 3 *(Cottee 2, Ebbrell)*
Leeds U (1) 1 *(Sterland) aet*   12,603
Everton: Southall; McDonald (Cottee), Ebbrell, Ratcliffe, Watson, Keown, Warzycha, McCall, Newell, Milligan, Beagrie (Nevin).
Leeds U: Lukic; Sterland, Whitlow, Batty, Fairclough, Whyte, Strachan, Shutt (Davison), Chapman, McAllister (Speed), Williams.
Everton won 6-4 on aggregate.

FINAL (at Wembley)
7 APR
Crystal Palace (0) 4 *(Thomas, Wright 2, Salako)*
Everton (0) 1 *(Warzycha) aet*   52,460
Crystal Palace: Martyn; Humphrey, Shaw, Gray (McGoldrick), Young (Thompson), Thorn, Salako, Thomas, Bright, Wright, Pardew.
Everton: Southall; McDonald, Hinchcliffe, Keown (Ratcliffe), Watson, Milligan, Warzycha, McCall, Newell (Nevin), Cottee, Sheedy.
Referee: G. Courtney (Spennymoor).

LEYLAND DAF CUP 1990–91

PRELIMINARY ROUND

5 NOV

Halifax (0) 1 *(Norris (pen))*
Rotherham U (0) 1 *(Thompson)*   956
Halifax T: Gould; Barr, Ellis, Evans, Fleming C, Graham (Fleming P), Gregory, Norris, Juryeff, Dobson, Donnelly.
Rotherham U: Mercer; Forrest, Scott, Pickering, Watts, Robinson, Goodwin, Dempsey, Williamson (Thompson), Spooner, Hazel.

6 NOV

Bolton W (0) 1 *(Reeves)*
Tranmere R (0) 0   3178
Bolton W: Felgate; Brown, Cowdrill, Green, Seagraves, Winstanley, Storer, Thompson, Reeves, Philliskirk, Darby.
Tranmere R: Nixon; Brannan, McCarrick, McNab, Hughes, Vickers, Morrissey, Harvey, Steel, Muir, Malkin.

Bournemouth (0) 0
Gillingham (0) 0   2784
Bournemouth: Peyton; Miller, Morrell, Teale, O'Driscoll, Redknapp, Brooks, Peacock, Jones, Holmes, Blissett.
Gillingham: Lim; McDonald, Manuel, Clarke, West (Dunne), Trusson, O'Connor, Docker, Lovell, Crown (Heritage), Johnson.

Burnley (1) 2 *(White, Francis)*
Crewe Alex (0) 1 *(Clayton)*   3481
Burnley: Pearce; Measham, Deakin, Deary, Pender, Davis, White, Francis, Mumby, Jakub, Grewcock.
Crewe Alex: Greygoose; Lennon, Jones, Carr, McKearney (Edwards R), Rose, Jasper, Ward, Callaghan, Gardiner, Clayton (Gunn).

Carlisle U (1) 1 *(Fyfe)*
Preston NE (1) 1 *(Shaw (pen))*   1826
Carlisle U: Priestley; Edmondson, Bennett, Edwards, Jones, Fitzpatrick, Walsh, Shepherd, Walwyn (Goldsmith), Gates, Fyfe.
Preston NE: Farnworth (Peel); Senior, Rathbone, Joyce, Hughes, Wrightson, James (Easter), Flynn, Greenwood, Shaw, Swann.

Chesterfield (1) 1 *(Lemon)*
Doncaster R (0) 1 *(Grayson)*   2757
Chesterfield: Allison; Francis, Hart, Lemon, Brien, Gunn, Hewitt, Rogers, Caldwell, Cooke, Dyche.
Doncaster R: Crichton; Rankine, Brevett, Ashurst, Ormsby, Harle (Turnbull), Gormley, Stiles, Muir, Jones (Grayson), Noteman.

Grimsby T (0) 1 *(Cockerill)*
York C (2) 3 *(Helliwell, Reid, Blackstone)*   1362
Grimsby T: Sherwood; Watson, Jobling, Tillson, Lever (Knight), Cunnington, Childs (Agnew), Gilbert, Hargreaves, Cockerill, Woods.
York C: Marples; McMillan, Hall, Reid (Wood), Tutill, Warburton, Blackstone, Howlett, Helliwell, Dunn, Canham.

Peterborough U (0) 0
Cambridge U (0) 2 *(Daish, Taylor)*   3279
Peterborough U: Bradshaw; Luke, Crosby, Halsall, Oakes, McElhinney, Sterling, Hine, Bremner, Culpin, Butterworth (Riley).
Cambridge U: Vaughan; Fensome (Claridge), Kimble, Wilkins (Leadbitter), Chapple, Daish, Cook, Bailie, Dublin, Taylor, Philpott.

Southend U (5) 10 *(Benjamin, Tilson 3, Angell 4, Prior, Ansah)*
Aldershot (0) 1 *(Banton)*   1281
Southend U: Sansome; Austin, Powell, Cornwell, Prior, Tilson, Cawley, Butler, Ansah, Benjamin, Angell.
Aldershot: Sheffield; Brown, Cooper, Randall, Wignall (Banton), Flowers, Whitlock, Puckett, Williams, Henry, Stewart.

Stoke C (0) 1 *(Barnes)*
Northampton T (0) 1 *(Beavon (pen))*   4339
Stoke C: Fox; Ware, Carr, Scott, Cranson, Sandford, Kevan (Mail), Ellis, Barnes, Beeston, Boughey.
Northampton T: Beresford; Chard, Wilson, Terry, Scully, Williams (Berry), Beavon, Campbell (Collins), Thorpe, Barnes, Brown.

Torquay U (0) 1 *(Lloyd)*
Swansea C (1) 1 *(Harris)*   2095
Torquay U: Howells; Whiston, Uzzell, Lloyd, Elliott, Joyce, Holmes, Musker, Tynan (Loram), Edwards, Smith (Myers).
Swansea C: Bracey; Hough, Coleman, Trick, Harris, Davies, Raynor, Coughlin (Thornber), Gilligan, Connor, Legg.

Walsall (0) 1 *(Skipper (og))*
Birmingham C (0) 1 *(Skipper (og))*   5053
Walsall: Green; Hutchings, Singleton, Kelly, Skipper, Smith, Littlejohn, McDonald (Bertschin), Rimmer, Cecere, Ntamark.
Birmingham C: Thomas; Hopkins, Downs, Frain, Overson, Matthewson, Peer, Sturridge (Bailey), Aylott (Clarkson), Gleghorn, Tait.

Wigan Ath (3) 4 *(Griffiths B, Page 3)*
Chester C (0) 0   1800
Wigan Ath: Adkins; Tankard, Patterson, Atherton, Johnson, Langley, Woods, Rimmer, Daley, Page, Griffiths B.
Chester C: Stewart; Preece, Pugh, Butler, Abel, Lane, Bennett, Ellis (Painter), Morton, Dale, Croft.

7 NOV

Bradford C (0) 1 *(Abbott)*
Huddersfield T (1) 1 *(O'Regan)*   2941
Bradford C: Tomlinson; Abbott, Babb, James, Oliver, Sinnott, Duxbury, Jewell, McCarthy (Leonard), Adcock, Megson (Tinnion).
Huddersfield T: Hardwick; Trevitt, Charlton, Marsden, Mitchell, Lewis, O'Regan, Wilson, Roberts, Smith, Onuora (Edwards).

12 NOV

Leyton Orient (0) 0
Fulham (0) 2 *(Gray, Haag)*   1359
Leyton Orient: Heald; Baker (Zoricich), Howard, Sitton, Whitbread, Achampong, Carter (Hull), Castle, Nugent, Sayer, Berry.
Fulham: Stannard; Newson, Pike, Skinner, Eckhardt (Haag), Morgan, Thomas, Scott, Gray, Brazil, Davies (Ferney).

13 NOV

Cardiff C (0) 0
Exeter C (1) 1 *(Bailey)*   1024
Cardiff C: Hansbury; Lewis, Searle, Barnard, Matthews, Perry, Stephens (Summers), Griffith, Gibbins, Pike (Blake), Heard.
Exeter C: Miller; Hiley, Dryden, Brown, Taylor, Cooper, Hobson, Bailey, Morgan, Neville, Kelly.

27 NOV

Aldershot (2) 3 *(Randall, Hicks (og), Stewart)*
Reading (0) 1 *(Leworthy)* 2159
Aldershot: Lange; Brown, Cooper, Randall, Ogley, Whitlock, Burvill, Puckett, Williams, Henry (Flower), Stewart (Cornish).
Reading: Francis; Richardson, Gilkes, McPherson, Hicks, Streete (Taylor), Gooding, Williams, Senior, Leworthy, Moran (Lovell).

Birmingham C (2) 2 *(Clarke (og), Sturridge)*
Lincoln C (0) 0 2922
Birmingham C: Thomas; Clarkson, Downs, Frain, Overson, Matthewson, Peer, Bailey, Gayle, Gleghorn, Sturridge.
Lincoln C: Bowling; Casey, Clarke, Brown, Stoutt, Carmichael, Nicholson, Smith P, Scott, Lormor, Puttnam.

Chester C (1) 2 *(Dale, Morton)*
Bury (0) 0 409
Chester C: Stewart; Reeves, Pugh, Butler, Abel, Lane, Bennett, Painter, Morton, Gayle, Croft.
Bury: Kelly; Hill (Withe), Feeley, Mauge, Valentine, Knill, Robinson, Parkinson, Cunningham, McGinlay, Patterson.

Crewe Alex (0) 1 *(Callaghan)*
Stockport Co (0) 1 *(Williams PR)* 1927
Crewe Alex: Edwards; Lennon, McKearney, Callaghan, Carr, Walters, Jasper (Clayton), Rose, Sussex, Gardiner (Smart), Ward.
Stockport Co: Cooper; Brown, Robertson, Frain, Thorpe, Barras, Payne, Knowles, Williams PA, Beaumont, Williams PR (Alexander).

Doncaster R (0) 1 *(Muir)*
Scunthorpe U (0) 0 1394
Doncaster R: Crichton; Rankine, Brevett, Ashurst, Ormsby, Douglas, Stiles (Harle), Turnbull, Muir, Grayson, Noteman.
Scunthorpe U: Musselwhite; Longden, Lillis, Cotton, Hicks, Hall, Cox, Taylor, Powell, Flounders (Ward), Stevenson.

Fulham (0) 1 *(Newson)*
Brentford (1) 1 *(Blissett)* 2761
Fulham: Stannard; Newson, Pike, Skinner, North, Morgan, Thomas (Milton), Scott, Gray, Brazil, Davies.
Brentford: Benstead; Ratcliffe (Cash), Fleming, Millen, Evans, Cockram (Gayle), Jones, May, Godfrey, Blissett, Smillie.

Gillingham (1) 4 *(Walker 2, Crown, Lovell)*
Maidstone U (1) 1 *(Cooper (pen))* 3582
Gillingham: Lim; McDonald, Manuel, Clarke (O'Shea), Walker, Trusson, O'Connor, Docker, Lovell, Crown, Dunne.
Maidstone U: Johns; Berry, Cooper, Stebbing, Golley, Oxbrow (Roast), Gall, Elsey, Osborne, Butler, Charlery (Lillis).

Northampton T (0) 1 *(Beavon (pen))*
Mansfield T (0) 2 *(Stringfellow, Charles)* 2186
Northampton T: Beresford; Chard, Wilson, Terry, Berry, Angus, Beavon, Campbell, Thorpe, Sandeman (Collins), Brown (Johnson).
Mansfield T: Beasley; Murray (Chambers), Kearney, Clark, Foster, Gray, Kent, Charles, Wilkinson, Stringfellow, Fairclough.

Preston NE (1) 3 *(Joyce 2, Harper)*
Rochdale (0) 1 *(Milner)* 1951
Preston NE: Kelly; Senior, Rathbone, Joyce, Hughes, Wrightson, Harper, Bogie, Shaw, Swann, Easter.
Rochdale: Welch; Norton, Graham, Blundell, Burns,
Ward (Dawson), Milner, Lee, Elliott, Costello (Hilditch), Doyle.

Rotherham U (1) 1 *(Scott)*
Scarborough (1) 1 *(Carter)* 1167
Rotherham U: Mercer; Forrest, Robinson, Russell (Thompson), Law, Watts, Hazel, Goodwin, Evans, Mendonca (Goater), Scott.
Scarborough: Richardson; Ash, Logan (Kamara), Matthews, Richards, Hirst, Mudd, Mockler, Mooney (Oghani), MacDonald, Carter.

Swansea C (0) 1 *(Davies)*
Shrewsbury T (1) 1 *(Wimbleton)* 1540
Swansea C: Bracey; Hough, Coleman, Walker, Harris, Davies, Watson (Davey), Coughlin, Raynor, Connor, Legg.
Shrewsbury T: Hughes; Worsley, Lynch, Parrish, Heathcote, Blake, Brown, Gorman, Shaw, Clarke, Wimbleton.

Tranmere R (1) 4 *(Muir 2, Morrissey, Steel)*
Blackpool (0) 0 3901
Tranmere R: Nixon; Higgins, Brannan, McNab, Hughes, Vickers (Irons), Morrissey, Harvey (Martindale), Steel, Muir, Thomas.
Blackpool: McIlhargey; Hedworth (Taylor), Wright, Groves, Briggs, Gore, Rodwell, Horner, Sinclair (Lancaster), Garner, Eyres.

Wrexham (2) 3 *(Armstrong 2, Worthington)*
Peterborough U (2) 3 *(Luke, Culpin, Berry (pen))* 761
Wrexham: Morris; Thackeray, Hardy, Hunter, Beaumont, Flynn (Kelly), Bowden, Owen, Armstrong, Worthington, Preece.
Peterborough U: Herbert; Luke, Berry, Halsall, Oakes (Watkins), McElhinney, Sterling, Hine, Bremner (Osborne), Riley, Culpin.

York C (2) 3 *(McCarthy, Helliwell 2)*
Darlington (1) 2 *(Borthwick 2)* 1339
York C: Marples; McMillan, Hall, Reid, Tutill, Warburton, Pepper, Howlett (Naylor), Helliwell, McCarthy, Canham.
Darlington: Prudhoe; McJannet (Coatsworth), Emson, Gill, Smith, Coverdale, Mardenborough, Toman, Borthwick, Cork (Trotter), Tait.

28 NOV

Exeter C (2) 2 *(Batty, Neville)*
Hereford U (2) 2 *(Lowndes, Narbett (pen))* 1962
Exeter C: Miller; Hiley, Dryden, Brown, Taylor, Cooper (Young), Marshall, Batty, Morgan, Neville, Kelly.
Hereford U: Wood; Jones MA, Bradley (Jones S), Pejic, Peacock, Hemming, Jones R, Narbett, Robinson, Wheeler (Tester), Lowndes.

Huddersfield T (0) 0 *(O'Regan (pen))*
Hartlepool U (1) 4 *(Dalton 2, Allon, Olsson)* 1405
Huddersfield T: Hardwick; Trevitt, Charlton, Marsden, Mitchell, Jackson, O'Regan, Wilson, Roberts, Smith (Barnett), Onuora.
Hartlepool U: Cox; Olsson, McKinnon, Tinkler (Tupling), MacPhail, Davies, Allon, Bennyworth, Baker (Fletcher), Honour, Dalton.

7 DEC

Reading (1) 1 *(Gooding)*
Southend U (1) 4 *(Benjamin 2, Butler, Angell)* 1472
Reading: Francis; Richardson, Gilkes, McPherson, Hicks, Taylor, Gooding, Lovell, Senior, Leworthy, Friel (Conroy).
Southend U: Sansome; Austin, Powell, Martin, Prior, Tilson, Clark, Butler, Locke, Benjamin, Angell.

11 DEC

Bury (0) 2 *(Pilling (og), Parkinson)*
Wigan Ath (0) 1 *(Johnson)* 1070
Bury: Kelly; Feeley, Stanislaus (McGinlay), Mauge, Valentine, Knill, Lee, Parkinson, Cunningham, Robinson, Patterson.
Wigan Ath: Adkins; Parkinson, Tankard, Atherton, Patterson, Langley, Woods, Rimmer (Carberry), Pilling, Page (Johnson), Griffiths.

Darlington (0) 3 *(Toman 3)*
Grimsby T (1) 1 *(Woods)* 1106
Darlington: Prudhoe; Coatsworth, Gray, Willis, Smith, Coverdale, Gill, Toman, Geddis, Cork, Tait.
Grimsby T: Sherwood; McDermott, Agnew, Tillson (Hargreaves), Lever, Cunnington, Watson, Gilbert, Rees, Jobling, Woods.

Hereford U (1) 1 *(Narbett)*
Cardiff C (0) 1 *(Griffith)* 2007
Hereford U: Wood; Jones MA, Tester, Pejic, Peacock, Jones S, Jones R, Narbett, Phillips, Wheeler (Benbow), Lowndes (Mitchell).
Cardiff C: Hansbury; Lewis, Searle, Blake, Matthews, Perry, Jones (Morgan), Griffith (Fry), Gibbins, Pike, Heard.

Maidstone U (2) 3 *(Butler, Elsey, Osborne)*
Bournemouth (0) 1 *(Jones)* 1009
Maidstone U: Beeney; Roast, Henry, Berry, Golley, Stebbing, Gall, Elsey, Osborne, Butler (Lillis), Cooper.
Bournemouth: Peyton; Miller, Morrell, Teale, O'Driscoll, Bond (Mundee), Redknapp, Brooks (Ekoku), Jones, Lawrence, Blissett.

12 DEC

Lincoln C (1) 1 *(Davis)*
Walsall (0) 1 *(Rimmer)* 868
Lincoln C: Bowling; Stoutt, Clark, Brown, Bressington, Davis, Schofield, Smith, Lormor (Scott), Carmichael (Puttnam), Nicholson.
Walsall: Green; Hutchings, Singleton, Methven, Smith, Skipper, Kelly, Ntamark, Rimmer, Cecere (Littlejohn), Grealish.

18 DEC

Blackpool (0) 3 *(Groves, Sinclair, Horner)*
Bolton W (0) 0 2579
Blackpool: McIlhargey; Davies, Wright, Groves, Briggs, Gore, Rodwell, Horner, Sinclair, Garner, Bamber.
Bolton W: Felgate; Brown, Cowdrill, Green (Comstive), Came, Winstanley, Storer, Thompson, Reeves, Philliskirk, Darby.

Cambridge U (1) 1 *(Claridge)*
Wrexham (0) 0 1710
Cambridge U: Vaughan; Kearns, Kimble, Bailie, Chapple, Welsh, Dennis, Wilkins, Claridge, Taylor, Philpott.
Wrexham: Morris; Thackeray, Hardy, Hunter, Beaumont, Sertori, Bowden, Cooper (Kelly), Armstrong, Worthington, Preece.

Hartlepool U (0) 0
Bradford C (1) 4 *(Torpey 3, McCarthy)* 1147
Hartlepool U: Cox; Nobbs, McKinnon, Tinkler (Olsson), MacPhail, Bennyworth, Allon, Tupling, Baker, Honour, Dalton.
Bradford C: Tomlinson; Abbott, Tinnion, James, Oliver, Sinnott, Duxbury, Jewell, McCarthy, Torpey, Treacy.

Rochdale (1) 1 *(Burns (pen))*
Carlisle U (0) 0 718
Rochdale: Gray; Norton, Graham, O'Shaughnessy (Goodison), Burns, Cole, Milner, Lee, Ward, Costello, Blundell.
Carlisle U: Siddall; Edmondson, Edwards, Jeffels, Jones, Miller, Walsh, Shepherd, Walwyn, Gates (Thorpe), Proudlock.

Scunthorpe U (0) 3 *(Lillis 2, Taylor)*
Chesterfield (1) 1 *(Lemon)* 859
Scunthorpe U: Musselwhite; Longden, Lillis, Taylor, Hicks, Hall, Cox, Cotton, Miller (Powell), Flounders, Cowling.
Chesterfield: Leonard; Francis, Albiston, Lemon, Brien, Gunn, Dyche, Ryan (Cordner), Plummer, Cooke, Hart.

Shrewsbury T (0) 1 *(Parrish)*
Torquay U (0) 1 *(Uzzell)* 866
Shrewsbury T: Hughes; Worsley (Wimbleton), Lynch, Kelly, Heathcote, Blake, Brown, Gorman, Spink, Parrish, Weir (Griffiths).
Torquay U: Howells; Weston, Uzzell, Lloyd, Elliott, Saunders, Smith (Loram), Musker, Tynan, Edwards, Hall.

8 JAN

Mansfield T (3) 3 *(Hathaway, Butler (og), Lowery)*
Stoke C (0) 0 1660
Mansfield T: Beasley; Murray, Kearney, Clark, Smalley, Gray, Hathaway, Lowery, Stringfellow, Christie, Fairclough.
Stoke C: Fox; Butler, Fowler, Ware, Blake, Sandford, Kennedy, Ellis, Thomas (Kevan), Biggins, Hilaire (Kelly).

Stockport Co (1) 1 *(Gannon)*
Burnley (1) 1 *(Farrell)* 1707
Stockport Co: Cooper; Brown, Bullock, Frain, Williams PR, Barras, Gannon, Knowles, Williams PA, Matthews, Kilner.
Burnley: Williams; Measham, Deakin, Deary, Pender, Davis, White, Futcher, Francis, Jakub, Farrell.

FIRST ROUND

Gillingham (0) 0
Hereford U (1) 1 *(Wheeler)* 1455
Gillingham: Lim; O'Shea, Harle (Kimble), Clarke, Walker, Trusson, Beadle, Docker, Lovell, Crown, Dunne (Eeles).
Hereford U: Wood; Jones MA, Devine, Pejic, Bradley, Jones R, Robinson, Narbett, Phillips, Wheeler (Jones S), Tester.

Preston NE (1) 2 *(Swann, Joyce (pen))*
Darlington (1) 1 *(Linacre) aet* 2148
Preston NE: Kelly; Senior, Rathbone, Flynn, Fee, Wrightson (Harper), Mooney, Peel (Greenwood), Joyce, Shaw, Swann.
Darlington: Prudhoe; McJannet, Gray, Willis, Smith, Coverdale (Trotter), Gill, Toman, Borthwick, Linacre (Cork), Tait.

Southend U (1) 2 *(Cooper (og), Angell)*
Maidstone U (0) 0 1849
Southend U: Sansome; Austin, Powell, Ling, Prior, Tilson, Clark, Butler, Ansah, Benjamin, Angell.
Maidstone U: Beeney; Roast, Rumble, Berry, Golley, Stebbing, Osborne, Elsey, Charlery, Butler, Cooper (Lillis).

PRELIMINARY ROUND

9 JAN

Scarborough (0) 1 *(Matthews)*
Halifax T (1) 2 *(Broadbent, Cook)*   641
Scarborough: Ironside; Kamara, Logan, Matthews, Richards, Hirst, Himsworth, Mockler, Oghani, Wilson, Carter.
Halifax T: Gould; Fleming P, Barr, Evans, Fleming C, Graham, Butler, Norris, Broadbent, Cook, Ellis.

FIRST ROUND

15 JAN

Doncaster R (0) 0
Scunthorpe U (0) 0 *aet*   1635
Doncaster R: Samways; Rankine, Brevett, Ashurst, Ormsby, Douglas, Turnbull, Gormley, Harle, Grayson (Morrow), Noteman (Adams).
Scunthorpe U: Musselwhite; Longden, Cotton (Daws), Taylor, Hicks, Hall, Cox, Ward, Hamilton, Flounders, Cowling.
Scunthorpe U won 4–3 on penalties.

Tranmere R (2) 3 *(Steel 2, Morrissey)*
Rotherham U (0) 0   2977
Tranmere R: Nixon; Higgins, Brannan, Irons, Hughes, Vickers, Morrissey, Harvey, Steel, Muir, Mungall.
Rotherham U: O'Hanlon; Forrest, Russell, Richardson (Evans), Robinson, Law, Spooner, Dempsey, Mendonca, Thompson, Hazel.

PRELIMINARY ROUND REPLAY

16 JAN

Shrewsbury T (1) 2 *(Shaw, Spink)*
Torquay U (3) 6 *(Tynan 3 (1 pen), Smith, Hodges 2)*   520
Shrewsbury T: Hughes; Worsley, Lynch, Parrish, Heathcote, Blake, Brown (Weir), Summerfield, Spink, Shaw, Naughton.
Torquay U: Howells; Whiston, Uzzell, Saunders, Elliott, Musker, Smith (Edwards), Holmes, Tynan, Hodges, Loram.

FIRST ROUND

22 JAN

Bradford C (1) 3 *(James, Jewell, Sinnott)*
Hartlepool U (1) 2 *(Baker, Allon)*   2308
Bradford C: Tomlinson; Abbott, Tinnion, James, Oliver, Sinnott, Duxbury, Jewell, McCarthy, Torpey, Treacy.
Hartlepool U: Cox; Nobbs, McKinnon, Olsson, MacPhail, Bennyworth, Allon, Tupling, Baker, Davies, Dalton.

Burnley (1) 3 *(Eli, Jakub, White)*
Stockport Co (1) 2 *(Kilner, Williams PR) aet*   3378
Burnley: Pearce; Measham, Deakin, Deary, Pender, Davis, Farrell, Futcher (White), Eli, Jakub, Grewcock.
Stockport Co: Redfern; Thorpe, Bullock (Beaumont), Frain, Barras, Finley, Gannon, Knowles (Williams PR), Williams PA, McInerney, Kilner.

Halifax T (0) 0
Blackpool (0) 1 *(Taylor)*   1267
Halifax T: Gould; Fleming P, Cook, Evans, Fleming C, Graham, Butler, Norris, Juryeff, Martin, Ellis (Broadbent).
Blackpool: McIlhargey; Davies, Wright, Groves, Hedworth, Gore, Rodwell, Horner, Bamber, Garner, Taylor.

Wigan Ath (0) 2 *(Johnson, Griffiths)*
Rochdale (0) 0   1200
Wigan Ath: Paladino; Parkinson, Tankard, Atherton, Johnson, Langley, Carberry, Rimmer, Daley, Page, Griffiths.
Rochdale: Welch; Goodison, Chapman (Blundell), Brown, Cole, O'Shaughnessy, Costello, Lee, Ward, Dawson (Elliott), Doyle.

York C (1) 1 *(Blackstone)*
Bury (0) 2 *(Cunningham 2)*   1397
York C: Kiely; McMillan, Hall, Reid, Tutill, Barratt, Pepper, Howlett, Helliwell, Blackstone, Canham.
Bury: Kelly; Feeley, Stanislaus (Hulme), Atkin, Valentine, Greenall, Lee, Robinson, Cunningham, Price (Bradley), Bishop.

23 JAN

PRELIMINARY ROUND REPLAY

Swansea C (4) 4 *(Gilligan 2 (1 pen), Legg 2)*
Shrewsbury T (2) 2 *(Shaw, Raynor (og))*   1388
Swansea C: Bracey; Raynor, Coleman, Hough, Harris, Davies, D'Auria, Coughlin (Thornber), Gilligan, Connor, Legg (Davey).
Shrewsbury T: Hughes; Worsley, Lynch, Askew, Clements, Blake (Griffiths), Brown, Summerfield, Spink, Shaw, Heathcote.

FIRST ROUND

Exeter C (1) 1 *(Marshall)*
Aldershot (0) 0   2015
Exeter C: Miller; Hiley, Dryden, Brown, Taylor, Cooper, Eshelby, O'Toole, Hobson, Neville, Marshall.
Aldershot: Hucker; Brown, Cooper, Randall, Ogley, Flower, Burvill, Puckett, Gray, Henry (Banton), Stewart.

28 JAN

PRELIMINARY ROUND REPLAY

Torquay U (0) 2 *(Loram, Tynan)*
Swansea C (0) 0   1664
Torquay U: Howells; Whiston (Holmes P), Uzzell, Saunders, Elliott, Hodges, Smith (Hashemi), Holmes M, Tynan, Edwards, Loram.
Swansea C: Bracey; Hough, Honor, Walker, Harris, Davies (Raynor), D'Auria, Coughlin, Gilligan, Connor, Thornber (Legg).

29 JAN

PRELIMINARY ROUND

Brentford (2) 2 *(Blissett 2)*
Leyton Orient (0) 0   2526
Brentford: Benstead; Ratcliffe, Fleming, Millen, Evans, Buckle, Jones, Gayle (Godfrey), Cadette, Blissett, Smillie (Cockram).
Leyton Orient: Heald; Zoricich, Howard, Hoddle, Dickenson (Berry), Pike, Carter, Castle, Bart-Williams, Achampong, Harvey.

FIRST ROUND

Cambridge U (1) 1 *(Dennis)*
Walsall (0) 0   2140
Cambridge U: Vaughan; Fensome, Kimble, Leadbitter, Chapple, Welsh, Dennis, Wilkins, Dublin, Taylor (Claridge), Philpott (Cheetham).
Walsall: Green; Hutchings, Singleton (Kelly), Methven, Smith, Skipper, Grealish, Ntamark, Marsh, Mower, McDonald.

QUARTER-FINALS
Northern Section

Bradford C (0) 0
Burnley (0) 1 *(Futcher)*   5432
Bradford C: Tomlinson; Mitchell (Jewell), Tinnion, James, Oliver, Sinnott, Duxbury, Stuart (Babb), McCarthy, Torpey, Treacy.
Burnley: Pearce; Measham, Deakin, Deary, Pender, Davis, Farrell, Futcher (Francis), Eli, Jakub, Grewcock.

Scunthorpe U (0) 1 *(Flounders)*
Preston NE (3) 4 *(Shaw 2, Mooney 2)*   2155
Scunthorpe U: Musselwhite; Longden, Ward, Taylor, Hicks, Tucker, Cox, Daws, Hamilton, Flounders, Cowling (Cotton).
Preston NE: Farnworth; Joyce, James, Fee, Flynn, Wrightson, Mooney, Harper, Ashcroft, Shaw, Swann.

Tranmere R (0) 2 *(Thomas, Muir (pen))*
Blackpool (0) 0   4129
Tranmere R: Nixon; Higgins, Brannan, Irons, Mungall, Vickers, Morrissey, Harvey, Steel, Muir, Thomas.
Blackpool: McIlhargey; Davies, Wright, Groves, Hedworth, Gore, Rodwell (Eyres), Horner, Bamber, Garner, Taylor (Sinclair).

Wigan Ath (0) 2 *(Langley, Daley)*
Bury (0) 0   1982
Wigan Ath: Hughes; Patterson, Tankard, Atherton, Johnson, Langley, Griffiths B, Rimmer, Daley, Page (Pilling), Griffiths I.
Bury: Kelly; Feeley, Stanislaus, Atkin (Knill), Valentine, Greenall, Lee, Robinson, Cunningham, Parkinson, Bishop (Hulme).

18 FEB
FIRST ROUND

Birmingham C (0) 0
Swansea C (0) 0 *aet*   3555
Birmingham C: Thomas; Clarkson, Rodgerson, Frain, Overson, Matthewson, Peer, Dolan, Aylott (Harris), Gleghorn, Sturridge.
Swansea C: Bracey; Honour, Trick, Harris, Coleman, D'Auria (Watson), Davies, Coughlin, Connor, Raynor, Legg (Thornber).
Birmingham C won 4-2 on penalties.

19 FEB

Mansfield T (2) 2 *(North (og), Wilkinson)*
Fulham (0) 1 *(Milton)*   1511
Mansfield T: Pearcey; Chambers, Smalley, Lowery, Foster, Gray, Kent, Charles, Christie, Wilkinson, Fairclough.
Fulham: Stannard; Eckhardt, Pike, Scott, North, Kearney (Langley), Davies (Milton), Skinner, Stant, Brazil, Marshall.

Torquay U (0) 2 *(Uzzell, Edwards)*
Northampton T (0) 0   2112
Torquay U: Howells; Holmes P, Uzzell, Whiston, Elliott, Hodges (Myers), Smith, Holmes M, Tynan, Edwards, Loram.
Northampton T: Hitchcock; Chard, Wilson, Terry, Williams (Sandeman), Angus, Quow, Bell, Thorpe, Barnes, Brown.

SEMI-FINALS
Northern Section

Preston NE (4) 6 *(Shaw 2, Jepson 3, Ashcroft)*
Burnley (0) 1 *(Bray)*   12,016
Preston NE: Farnworth; James, Joyce (Eaves), Hughes, Flynn, Wrightson, Thompson, Harper, Jepson (Ashcroft), Shaw, Swann.
Burnley: Williams; Measham, Deakin, Deary, Pender, Davis, Farrell, Francis, Eli (White), Jakub, Grewcock (Bray).

Wigan Ath (0) 0
Tranmere R (1) 3 *(Muir 2, Steel)*   4417
Wigan Ath: Hughes; Patterson (Pilling), Tankard, Atherton, Johnson, Langley, Griffiths I (Page), Rimmer, Daley, Jones, Griffiths B.
Tranmere R: Nixon; Higgins, Mungall, McNab, Hughes, Garnett, Irons (Morrissey), Harvey, Steel (Cooper), Muir, Thomas.

QUARTER-FINALS
Southern Section
20 FEB

Exeter C (0) 0
Cambridge U (1) 1 *(Dublin)*   2258
Exeter C: Miller; Hiley, Brown, McNichol, Taylor, Cooper, Morgan (Batty), Hobson, Neville, Dryden, Marshall.
Cambridge U: Vaughan; Fensome, Kimble, Leadbitter (Dennis), Chapple, O'Shea, Cheetham, Wilkins, Dublin, Taylor, Philpott.

FIRST ROUND
21 FEB

Brentford (0) 0
Wrexham (0) 0 *aet*   2247
Brentford: Benstead; Cousins, Carstairs, Bates, Evans, Cockram (Buckle), Jones, Gayle, Holdsworth (Godfrey), Cadette, Smillie.
Wrexham: Morris; Phillips, Hardy, Hunter, Beaumont (Jones L), Sertori, Bowden, Owen, O'Gorman, Ward (Armstrong), Watkins.
Brentford won 3-0 on penalties.

QUARTER-FINALS
Southern Section
26 FEB

Birmingham C (1) 2 *(Matthewson, Gayle)*
Mansfield T (0) 0   5358
Birmingham C: Thomas; Clarkson, Frain, Rodgerson, Overson, Matthewson, Peer, Dolan (Gayle), Gleghorn (Bailey), Sturridge.
Mansfield T: Pearcey; Chambers, Prindiville, Lowery (Hathaway), Foster, Gray, Kent, Charles, Christie, Wilkinson, Fairclough.

Southend U (0) 7 *(Edwards, Martin 2 (1 pen), Ansah 3, Angell)*
Torquay U (0) 0   2273
Southend U: Sansome; Austin, Powell, Martin, Edwards, Tilson, Clark, Butler, Ansah, Benjamin (Angell), Locke.
Torquay U: Howells; Holmes P, Uzzell, Whiston, Elliott, Musker (Myers), Smith, Holmes M (Saunders), Tynan, Edwards, Loram.

28 FEB

Hereford U (0) 0
Brentford (1) 2 *(Smillie, Holdsworth)* 2207
Hereford U: Elliott; Jones MA, Devine, Pejic, Bradley, Jones R (Jones S), Hemming, Narbett, Brain, Wheeler, Tester (Robinson).
Brentford: Benstead; Ratcliffe, Carstairs, Bates, Evans, Buckle, Jones, Cockram, Cadette (Holdsworth), Godfrey, Smillie (Rostron).

5 MAR
SEMI-FINALS
Southern Section

Birmingham C (2) 3 *(Peer, Gleghorn, Overson)*
Cambridge U (0) 1 *(Dublin)* 9429
Birmingham C: Thomas; Clarkson, Rodgerson, Frain, Overson, Matthewson, Peer, Gayle, Aylott, Gleghorn, Sturridge.
Cambridge U: Vaughan; Fensome, Kimble, Leadbitter, Chapple, O'Shea, Cheetham, Wilkins (Bailie), Dublin, Taylor, Philpott.

Southend U (0) 0
Brentford (2) 3 *(Smillie, Jones, Cadette)* 3937
Southend U: Sansome; Austin, Powell, Martin, Edwards, Tilson, Clark, Butler, Locke (Ansah), Benjamin, Angell.
Brentford: Benstead; Ratcliffe (Rostron), Carstairs (Gayle), Millen, Evans, Buckle, Jones, Cockram, Holdsworth, Cadette, Smillie.

Northern Section Final First Leg

Tranmere R (2) 4 *(Muir 3 (1 pen), Harvey)*
Preston NE (0) 0 8633
Tranmere R: Nixon; Garnett, Mungall, McNab, Hughes, Vickers, Morrissey (Malkin), Harvey (Irons), Steel, Muir, Thomas.
Preston NE: Farnworth; Senior, James, Hughes, Flynn, Wrightson, Thompson, Cartwright, Jepson, Shaw, Swann (Ashcroft).

Southern Section Final First Leg
26 MAR

Birmingham C (1) 2 *(Rodgerson, Gayle)*
Brentford (0) 1 *(Gayle)* 16,219
Birmingham C: Thomas; Clarkson, Frain, Yates, Overson, Matthewson, Peer, Gayle, Rodgerson (Robinson), Gleghorn, Sturridge.
Brentford: Benstead; Ratcliffe, Fleming, Bates, Evans, Rostron, Jones, Gayle, Holdsworth, Cadette (Blissett), Godfrey.

9 APR
Northern Section Final Second Leg

Preston NE (1) 1 *(Jepson)*
Tranmere R (0) 0 5763
Preston NE: Kelly; Senior, James, Joyce, Jackson, Flynn, Thompson (Bogie), Cartwright, Jepson, Shaw, Harper.
Tranmere R: Nixon; Higgins, Mungall, McNab, Hughes, Vickers, Morrissey (Irons), Harvey, Steel, Malkin (Cooper), Thomas.

Southern Section Final Second Leg

Brentford (0) 0
Birmingham C (0) 1 *(Sturridge)* 8745
Brentford: Benstead; Ratcliffe, Fleming, Bates, Goodyear, Gayle, Buckle (Cousins), Rostron, Cadette (Cockram), Blissett, Holdsworth.
Birmingham C: Thomas; Clarkson, Frain, Peer, Overson, Matthewson, Robinson, Gayle (Aylott), Yates, Sturridge, Gleghorn.

FINAL (at Wembley)
26 MAY

Birmingham C (2) 3 *(Sturridge, Gayle 2)*
Tranmere R (0) 2 *(Cooper, Steel)* 58,756
Birmingham C: Thomas; Clarkson, Frain, Yates, Overson, Matthewson, Peer, Gayle, Robinson, Gleghorn, Sturridge (Bailey).
Tranmere R: Nixon; Higgins, Brannan, McNab (Martin), Hughes, Vickers (Martindale), Morrissey, Irons, Steel, Cooper, Thomas.
Referee: J. Martin (Alton).

THE FA CUP

THE FOOTBALL ASSOCIATION OFFICIALS

Patron: HER MAJESTY THE QUEEN

President: HRH THE DUKE OF KENT

Honorary Vice-presidents

His Grace the Duke of Marlborough DL; The Rt
Hon The Earl of Derby MC; Air Marshall Michael
Simmons KCB, AFC, RAF; General Sir John
Stibbon KCB, OBE; Admiral of the Fleet Sir John
Fieldhouse GCB, GBE; Right Hon Earl of Harewood
KBE, LLD; Sir Walter Winterbottom CBE; Rt Hon
Lord Westwood FCIS, JP; E. A. Croker CBE

Chairman of the Council

Sir F. A. Millichip (West Bromwich Albion FC)

Vice-chairman of the Council

C. H. Wilcox (Gloucestershire FA)

Life Vice-presidents

A. D. McMullen MBE (Bedfordshire FA)
R. Wragg FInstBM (Sheffield United FC)
R. H. Speake (Kent Co FA)
B. W. Mulrenan (Universities Athletic Union)
Dr J. O'Hara MB, ChB, AMRCGP (Sussex Co FA)
S. A. Rudd (Liverpool Co FA)
E. A. Brown (Suffolk FA)
F. A. Millichip (West Bromwich Albion FC)
L. Smart

Vice-presidents

E. G. Powell FIBA (Herefordshire FA)
W. T. Annable (Nottinghamshire FA)
J. C. Thomas (Durham FA)
P. J. Swales (Manchester City FC)
J. M. Ryder (Cornwall Co FA)
P. Rushton (Worcestershire FA)

Chief Executive

R. H. G. Kelly FCIS, 16 Lancaster Gate, London W2
3LW

FA Challenge Cup Committee

E. A. Brown (Chairman), W. T. Annable, R. I. Burr,
W. G. Halsey, W. G. McKeag, T. Myatt,
Dr J. O'Hara, P. Rushton, S. Seymour,
T. W. Shipman, M. D. B. Sinclair, Sir John Smith

FA CUP FINALS 1872–1991

1872 and 1874–92	Kennington Oval	1911	Replay at Old Trafford
1873	Lillie Bridge	1912	Replay at Bramall Lane
1886	Replay at Derby		
1893	Fallowfield, Manchester	1915	Old Trafford, Manchester
1894	Everton	1920–22	Stamford Bridge
1895–1914	Crystal Palace	1923 to date	Wembley
1901	Replay at Bolton	1970	Replay at Old Trafford
1910	Replay at Everton	1981	Replay at Wembley

Year	Winners	Runners-up	Score
1872	Wanderers	Royal Engineers	1-0
1873	Wanderers	Oxford University	2-0
1874	Oxford University	Royal Engineers	2-0
1875	Royal Engineers	Old Etonians	2-0 (after 1-1 draw aet)
1876	Wanderers	Old Etonians	3-0 (after 1-1 draw aet)
1877	Wanderers	Oxford University	2-1 (aet)
1878	Wanderers*	Royal Engineers	3-1
1879	Old Etonians	Clapham R	1-0
1880	Clapham R	Oxford University	1-0
1881	Old Carthusians	Old Etonians	3-0
1882	Old Etonians	Blackburn R	1-0
1883	Blackburn Olympic	Old Etonians	2-1 (aet)
1884	Blackburn R	Queen's Park, Glasgow	2-1
1885	Blackburn R	Queen's Park, Glasgow	2-0
1886	Blackburn R†	WBA	2-0 (after 0-0 draw)
1887	Aston Villa	WBA	2-0
1888	WBA	Preston NE	2-1
1889	Preston NE	Wolverhampton W	3-0
1890	Blackburn R	Sheffield W	6-1
1891	Blackburn R	Notts Co	3-1
1892	WBA	Aston Villa	3-0
1893	Wolverhampton W	Everton	1-0
1894	Notts Co	Bolton W	4-1
1895	Aston Villa	WBA	1-0
1896	Sheffield W	Wolverhampton W	2-1
1897	Aston Villa	Everton	3-2
1898	Nottingham F	Derby Co	3-1
1899	Sheffield U	Derby Co	4-1
1900	Bury	Southampton	4-0
1901	Tottenham H	Sheffield U	3-1 (after 2-2 draw)
1902	Sheffield U	Southampton	2-1 (after 1-1 draw)
1903	Bury	Derby Co	6-0
1904	Manchester C	Bolton W	1-0
1905	Aston Villa	Newcastle U	2-0
1906	Everton	Newcastle U	1-0
1907	Sheffield W	Everton	2-1
1908	Wolverhampton W	Newcastle U	3-1
1909	Manchester U	Bristol C	1-0
1910	Newcastle U	Barnsley	2-0 (after 1-1 draw)
1911	Bradford C	Newcastle U	1-0 (after 0-0 draw)
1912	Barnsley	WBA	1-0 (aet, after 0-0 draw)
1913	Aston Villa	Sunderland	1-0
1914	Burnley	Liverpool	1-0
1915	Sheffield U	Chelsea	3-0
1920	Aston Villa	Huddersfield T	1-0 (aet)
1921	Tottenham H	Wolverhampton W	1-0
1922	Huddersfield T	Preston NE	1-0
1923	Bolton W	West Ham U	2-0
1924	Newcastle U	Aston Villa	2-0
1925	Sheffield U	Cardiff C	1-0
1926	Bolton W	Manchester C	1-0
1927	Cardiff C	Arsenal	1-0
1928	Blackburn R	Huddersfield T	3-1
1929	Bolton W	Portsmouth	2-0
1930	Arsenal	Huddersfield T	2-0
1931	WBA	Birmingham	2-1
1932	Newcastle U	Arsenal	2-1
1933	Everton	Manchester C	3-0
1934	Manchester C	Portsmouth	2-1
1935	Sheffield W	WBA	4-2
1936	Arsenal	Sheffield U	1-0
1937	Sunderland	Preston NE	3-1
1938	Preston NE	Huddersfield T	1-0 (aet)
1939	Portsmouth	Wolverhampton W	4-1
1946	Derby Co	Charlton Ath	4-1 (aet)
1947	Charlton Ath	Burnley	1-0 (aet)
1948	Manchester U	Blackpool	4-2
1949	Wolverhampton W	Leicester C	3-1
1950	Arsenal	Liverpool	2-0
1951	Newcastle U	Blackpool	2-0
1952	Newcastle U	Arsenal	1-0

Year	Winners	Runners-up	Score
1953	Blackpool	Bolton W	4-3
1954	WBA	Preston NE	3-2
1955	Newcastle U	Manchester C	3-1
1956	Manchester C	Birmingham C	3-1
1957	Aston Villa	Manchester U	2-1
1958	Bolton W	Manchester U	2-0
1959	Nottingham F	Luton T	2-1
1960	Wolverhampton W	Blackburn R	3-0
1961	Tottenham H	Leicester C	2-0
1962	Tottenham H	Burnley	3-1
1963	Manchester U	Leicester C	3-1
1964	West Ham U	Preston NE	3-2
1965	Liverpool	Leeds U	2-1 (aet)
1966	Everton	Sheffield W	3-2
1967	Tottenham H	Chelsea	2-1
1968	WBA	Everton	1-0 (aet)
1969	Manchester C	Leicester C	1-0
1970	Chelsea	Leeds U	2-1 (aet)
	(after 2-2 draw, after extra time, at Wembley)		
1971	Arsenal	Liverpool	2-1 (aet)
1972	Leeds U	Arsenal	1-0
1973	Sunderland	Leeds U	1-0
1974	Liverpool	Newcastle U	3-0
1975	West Ham U	Fulham	2-0
1976	Southampton	Manchester U	1-0
1977	Manchester U	Liverpool	2-1
1978	Ipswich T	Arsenal	1-0
1979	Arsenal	Manchester U	3-2
1980	West Ham U	Arsenal	1-0
1981	Tottenham H	Manchester C	3-2
	(after 1-1 draw, after extra time, at Wembley)		
1982	Tottenham H	QPR	1-0
	(after 1-1 draw, after extra time, at Wembley)		
1983	Manchester U	Brighton & HA	4-0
	(after 2-2 draw, after extra time, at Wembley)		
1984	Everton	Watford	2-0
1985	Manchester U	Everton	1-0 (aet)
1986	Liverpool	Everton	3-1
1987	Coventry C	Tottenham H	3-2 (aet)
1988	Wimbledon	Liverpool	1-0
1989	Liverpool	Everton	3-2 (aet)
1990	Manchester U	Crystal Palace	1-0
	(after 3-3 draw, after extra time, at Wembley)		
1991	Tottenham H	Nottingham F	2-1 (aet)

* *Won outright, but restored to the Football Association.*

† *A special trophy was awarded for third consecutive win.*

FA CUP WINS

Tottenham H 8, Aston Villa 7, Manchester U 7, Blackburn R 6, Newcastle U 6, Arsenal 5, The Wanderers 5, WBA 5, Sheffield U 4, Bolton W 4, Everton 4, Liverpool 4, Wolverhampton W 4, Manchester C 4, Sheffield W 3, West Ham U 3, Bury 2, Old Etonians 2, Preston NE 2, Nottingham F 2, Sunderland 2, Barnsley 1, Blackburn Olympic 1, Blackpool 1, Bradford C 1, Burnley 1, Cardiff C 1, Charlton Ath 1, Chelsea 1, Clapham R 1, Coventry C 1, Derby Co 1, Huddersfield T 1, Ipswich T 1, Leeds U 1, Notts Co 1, Old Carthusians 1, Oxford University 1, Portsmouth 1, Royal Engineers 1, Southampton 1, Wimbledon 1.

APPEARANCES IN FINALS

Arsenal 11, Everton 11, Manchester U 11, Newcastle U 11, WBA 10, Aston Villa 9, Liverpool 9, Tottenham H 9, Blackburn R 8, Manchester C 8, Wolverhampton W 8, Bolton W 7, Preston NE 7, Old Etonians 6, Sheffield U 6, Huddersfield T 5, *The Wanderers 5, Sheffield W 5, Derby Co 4, Leeds U 4, Leicester C 4, Oxford University 4, Royal Engineers 4, West Ham U 4, Blackpool 3, Burnley 3, Chelsea 3, Nottingham F 3, Portsmouth 3, Sunderland 3, Southampton 3, Barnsley 2, Birmingham C 2, *Bury 2, Cardiff C 2, Charlton Ath 2, Clapham R 2, Notts Co 2, Queen's Park (Glasgow) 2, *Blackburn Olympic 1, *Bradford C 1, Brighton & HA 1, Bristol C 1, Coventry C 1, Crystal Palace 1, Fulham 1, *Ipswich T 1, Luton T 1, *Old Carthusians 1, QPR 1, Watford 1, *Wimbledon 1.

* *Denotes undefeated.*

APPEARANCES IN SEMI-FINALS

Everton 22, WBA 19, Liverpool 18, Manchester U 18, Arsenal 17, Aston Villa 17, Blackburn R 16, Sheffield W 15, Derby Co 13, Newcastle U 13, Tottenham H 13, Wolverhampton W 13, Bolton W 12, Nottingham F 12, Southampton 10, Sunderland 10, Preston NE 10, Manchester C 10, Sheffield U 10, Birmingham C 9, Southampton 9, Burnley 8, Leeds U 8, Huddersfield T 7, Leicester C 7, Old Etonians 6, Oxford University 6, West Ham U 6, The Wanderers 5, Notts Co 5, Fulham 5, Portsmouth 4, Queen's Park (Glasgow) 4, Royal Engineers 4, Blackpool 3, Cardiff C 3, Clapham R 3, Millwall 3, Old Carthusians 3, Ipswich T 3, Luton T 3, Stoke C 3, The Swifts 3, Watford 3, Barnsley 2, Blackburn Olympic 2, Bristol C 2, Bury 2, Charlton Ath 2, Crystal Palace (professional club) 2, Grimsby T 2, Norwich C 2, Oldham Ath 2, Swansea T 2, Swindon T 2, Bradford C 1, Brighton & HA 1, Cambridge University 1, Coventry C 1, Crewe Alex 1, Crystal Palace (amateur club) 1, Darwen 1, Derby Junction 1, Glasgow R 1, Hull C 1, Marlow 1, Old Harrovians 1, Orient 1, Plymouth Arg 1, Port Vale 1, QPR 1, Reading 1, Shropshire W 1, Wimbledon 1, York C 1.

640

FA CUP 1990-91

PRELIMINARY AND QUALIFYING ROUNDS

There was an original entry of 563 clubs for the 1990–91 competition. Clubs in the First and Second Divisions of the Football League are exempt to the Third Round Proper, while clubs in the Third and Fourth Divisions are exempt to the First Round Proper. In addition, last season's FA Trophy finalists (Barrow and Leek Town) and two other clubs at the discretion of the FA (Colchester United and Sutton United) are exempt to the First Round Proper. The following 20 clubs are exempt to the Fourth Round Qualifying: Aylesbury United, Basingstoke Town, Bath City, Bishop Auckland, Dartford, Gloucester City, Halesowen Town, Hayes, Kettering Town, Kidderminster Harriers, Macclesfield Town, Merthyr Tydfil, Northwich Victoria, Runcorn, Stafford Rangers, Telford United, Welling United, Whitley Bay, Woking, Yeovil Town.

Preliminary Round

Willington v Cleator Moor Celtic	0-1
Ashington v Prudhoe East End	1-4
Shildon v Garforth Town	3-1
North Shields v Whickham	2-0
West Auckland Town v Annfield Plain	4-2
Bedlington Terriers v Norton & Stockton Ancients	0-4
Blackpool (Wren) Rovers v Accrington Stanley	2-4
Billingham Town v Brandon United	1-0
Netherfield v Murton	0-3
Chester-le-Street Town v Easington Colliery	0-2
Penrith v Harrogate Railway	0-5
Langley Park v Washington	2-0
Ferryhill Athletic v Blackpool Mechanics	3-1
Shotton Comrades v Esh Winning	1-2
Crook Town v Horden CW	1-2
Great Harwood Town v Harrogate Town	2-2, 1-2
Northallerton Town v Clitheroe	4-2
Darwen v Peterlee Newtown	2-0
Darlington CB v Evenwood Town	0-1
Lancaster City v Thackley	2-0
Hebburn v Ryhope CA	0-2
(at Washington FC)	
Whitby Town v Leyland DAF	2-0
Irlam Town v Formby	2-0
Ashton United v Denaby United	0-2
Bridgnorth Town v Vauxhall GM	1-1, 1-4
Knowsley United v Ossett Town	1-1, 3-2
Glossop v Skelmersdale United	1-1, 2-0
Atherton LR v Rossendale United	3-1
Burscough v Maine Road	0-3
Farsley Celtic v Ossett Albion	1-1, 2-0
Prescot AFC v Emley	1-1, 1-2
Bootle v Winsford United	1-0
Chadderton v Radcliffe Borough	1-2
Armthorpe Welfare v Sheffield	3-0
Hednesford Town v Guiseley	2-0
Salford City v Warrington Town	0-3
Newtown v Eastwood Town	1-1, 1-2
Belper Town v St Helens Town	2-3
Oakham United v Long Eaton United	1-1, 1-0
(at Long Eaton United)	
Sutton Town v Rocester	2-2, 0-1
Borrowash Victoria v Gresley Rovers	1-2
North Ferriby United v Leicester United	1-2
Willenhall Town v Brigg Town	1-1, 1-1, 3-1
Louth United v Princes End United	1-1, 0-1
Alfreton Town v Rushall Olympic	2-2, 0-3
Paget Rangers v Boldmere St Michaels	2-0
Nuneaton Borough v Hinckley Town	4-1
Wellingborough Town v Tividale	1-0
Arnold Town v Wednesfield	1-1, 0-1
Alvechurch v Desborough Town	2-1
Stratford Town v Highgate United	3-1
Solihull Borough v Banbury United	0-0, 1-1, 2-2, 4-3
Heanor Town v Halesowen Harriers	0-4

Dudley Town v Corby Town	1-1, 0-1
Hinckley Athletic v Friar Lane OB	3-1
Eastwood Hanley v West Midlands Police	0-2
Irthlingborough Diamonds v Buckingham Town	3-4
Chasetown v Evesham United	0-2
Brackley Town v Walsall-Wood	1-0
Oldbury United v Wolverton	0-0, 1-2
Mile Oak Rovers v Stourbridge	0-5
Sandwell Borough v Northampton Spencer	4-1
Holbeach United v Potton United	1-2
Boston v Kings Lynn	2-0
Malvern Town v Soham Town Rangers	3-0
Rothwell Town v Stamford	7-2
Welwyn GC v Chalfont St Peter	1-2
Wisbech Town v Barton Rovers	1-1, 1-2
Baker Perkins v Letchworth GC	5-2
Lowestoft Town v Mirrless Blackstone	1-0
Boreham Wood v Gorleston	2-0
Haverhill Rovers v Eynesbury Rovers	1-1, 2-0
Leighton Town v Spalding United	0-1
Bourne Town v Ely City	3-0
Great Yarmouth Town v Langford	2-2, 1-0
Wembley v Bury Town	1-0
Newmarket Town v Cheshunt	2-1
Tiptree United v Harlow Town	0-1
Braintree Town v Collier Row	1-0
Rayners Lane v Hoddesdon Town	2-1
Clapton v Felixstowe Town	5-2
Ford United v Kingsbury Town	3-1
Ruislip Manor v Northwood	2-1
Halstead Town v Canvey Island	1-1, 7-1
Cray Wanderers v Waltham Abbey	3-1
Stowmarket Town v Saffron Walden Town	1-1, 1-2
Hemel Hempstead v Metropolitan Police	1-2
Clacton Town v Hertford Town	0-1
Burnham Ramblers v Hornchurch	0-2
Chesham United v Baldock Town	4-1
Arlesey Town v Walthamstow Pennant	0-4
Witham Town v Basildon United	2-3
Harwich & Parkeston v Berkhamsted Town	4-1
Wootton Blue Cross v Hounslow	1-3
Barkingside v Aveley	2-1
East Thurrock United v Stevenage Borough	0-1
Molesey v Vauxhall Motors	1-1, 5-0
Flackwell Heath v Tring Town	5-0
Banstead Athletic v Malden Vale	1-0
Ware v Corinthian Casuals	0-0, 0-1
Alma Swanley v Purfleet	1-2
Billericay Town v Hanwell Town	4-0
Croydon v Egham Town	0-4
Eton Manor v Edgware Town	0-2
Tilbury v Southall	0-0, 3-1
Horsham YMCA v Darenth Heathside	3-2
Harefield United v Merstham	0-1
Croydon Athletic v Andover	2-2, 1-7
Royston Town v Rainham Town	1-1, 2-1
Chertsey Town v Walton & Hersham	0-3
Horsham v Epsom & Ewell	2-0
Slade Green v Ringmer	2-0
Tooting & Mitcham United v Hastings Town	1-1, 2-0
Tonbridge AFC v Shoreham	2-1
Chipstead v Littlehampton Town	2-3
Southwick v Corinthians	1-0
Steyning Town v Whitehawk	1-2
Peacehaven & Telscombe v Selsey	8-1
Ramsgate v Margate	0-1
Camberley Town v Oakwood	0-5
(at Oakwood FC)	
Ashford Town v Leatherhead	3-1
Sheppey United v Pagham	0-2
Sittingbourne v Burgess Hill Town	2-0
Cove v Haywards Heath Town	4-0

Canterbury City v Dorking	0-0, 1-4
Arundel v Chatham Town	2-3
Three Bridges v Wick	1-3
Eastbourne United v Tunbridge Wells	6-5
Langney Sports v Portfield	3-0
Lancing v Lewes	0-3
Havant v Horndean	3-0
Bracknell Town v Hampton	2-3
Hungerford Town v Fareham Town	1-0
Feltham v Thame United	2-0
Salisbury v Uxbridge	1-1, 2-1
Sholing Sports v Abingdon United	1-3
Bournemouth v Thatcham Town	1-0
Newbury Town v Eastleigh	2-1
Chichester City v Lymington AFC	1-5
Trowbridge Town v Clandown	7-1
Totton AFC v Warminster Town	2-3
Calne Town v Paulton Rovers	2-0
Romsey Town v Frome Town	1-0
Melksham Town v Keynsham Town	2-1
Westbury United v Stroud	1-1, 0-3
Clevedon Town v Dawlish Town	3-3, 3-2
Swanage Town & Herston v Devizes Town	4-0
Barry Town v Minehead	2-1
Shortwood United v St Blazey	1-2
Cwmbran Town v Mangotsfield United	0-4
(at Mangotsfield United)	
Maesteg Park v Sharpness	
(Maesteg Park walked over Sharpness—	
Sharpness withdrawn)	
Bridgend Town v Ton Pentre	2-1
Radstock Town v Weston-Super-Mare	0-3
Yate Town v Glastonbury	4-0
Ilfracombe Town v Barnstaple Town	4-0
Wimborne Town v Bideford	3-2
Tiverton Town v Welton Rovers	4-1
St Austell v Falmouth Town	0-4
Saltash United v Torrington	1-1, 5-2

First Qualifying Round

Shildon v Cleator Moor Athletic	2-1
Alnwick Town v Fleetwood Town	0-5
North Shields v Gateshead	1-1, 1-0
Durham City v Prudhoe East End	0-3
Accrington Stanley v West Auckland Town	3-0
Blyth Spartans v Bridlington Town	2-0
Billingham Town v Guisborough Town	1-2
Gretna v Norton & Stockton Ancients	5-1
Harrogate Railway v Murton	2-0
Ferryhill Athletic v South Bank	1-1, 0-1
Langley Park v Tow Law Town	2-1
Colne Dynamoes v Easington Colliery	
(Easington Colliery walked over Colne Dynamoes—	
Colne Dynamoes disbanded)	
Harrogate Town v Esh Winning	1-3
Stockton v Spennymoor United	0-2
(at Spennymoor United)	
Northallerton Town v Billingham Synthonia	2-0
Workington v Horden CW	1-1, 1-2
Lancaster City v Darwen	4-7
Whitby Town v Newcastle Blue Star	4-7
Ryhope CA v Consett	1-2
Seaham Red Star v Evenwood Town	1-1, 1-4
Vauxhall GM v Irlam Town	0-2
Morecambe v Horwich RMI	2-2, 0-3
Knowsley United v Colwyn Bay	0-0, 0-3
Caernarfon Town v Denaby United	
(tie awarded to Caernarfon Town as Denaby United	
unable to fulfil fixture)	
Maine Road v Glossop	1-0
Altrincham v Rhyl	3-2
Farsley Celtic v Bangor City	0-0, 0-3
Harworth CI v Atherton LR	1-2
Radcliffe Borough v Emley	0-0, 0-1
Chorley v Mossley	4-0
Armthorpe Welfare v Southport	1-2
Ilkeston Town v Bootle	2-3
Eastwood Town v Hednesford Town	1-1, 1-1, 1-1, 2-3
Oakham United v Hyde United	1-2

St Helens Town v Curzon Ashton	0-3
South Liverpool v Warrington Town	2-0
Leicester United v Rocester	1-0
Droylsden v Stalybridge Celtic	1-1, 2-1
Willenhall Town v Marine	0-0, 2-2, 1-4
Worksop Town v Gresley Rovers	2-1
Paget Rangers v Princes End United	1-2
Frickley Athletic v Gainsborough Trinity	4-3
Nuneaton Borough v Goole Town	1-0
Blakenall v Rushall Olympic	3-2
Alvechurch v Wellingborough Town	4-1
Witton Albion v Congleton Town	2-0
Stratford Town v Buxton	1-4
Bilston Town v Wednesfield	6-0
Corby Town v Solihull Borough	3-0
West Midlands Police v Matlock Town	0-6
Hinckley Athletic v Grantham Town	2-1
Burton Albion v Halesowen Harriers	2-0
Brackley Town v Buckingham Town	1-1, 1-1, 0-2
Shepshed Charterhouse v Lye Town	3-1
Wolverton AFC v Atherstone United	2-2, 1-4
Racing Club Warwick v Evesham United	0-0, 1-5
Potton United v Stourbridge	1-1, 0-7
Bedworth United v Sutton Coldfield Town	1-5
Boston v Bromsgrove Rovers	0-3
March Town United v Sandwell Borough	1-1, 2-2, 0-1
Chalfont St Peter v Malvern Town	2-6
Moor Green v Tamworth	1-2
Barton Rovers v Redditch United	0-2
Histon v Rothwell Town	2-1
Boreham Wood v Baker Perkins	0-0, 2-1
Spalding United v Rushden Town	0-3
Haverhill Rovers v VS Rugby	1-1, 0-5
Boston United v Lowestoft Town	7-0
Wembley v Bourne Town	4-1
Sudbury Town v Heybridge Swifts	1-3
Newmarket Town v Cambridge City	1-2
Finchley v Great Yarmouth Town	1-2
Rayners Lane v Harlow Town	0-3
Ford United v St Albans City	3-1
Clapton v Barnet *(at Dagenham FC)*	0-2
Hitchin Town v Braintree Town	0-1
Cray Wanderers v Ruislip Manor	2-3
Metropolitan Police v Hendon	1-3
Saffron Walden Town v Wealdstone	0-4
Wivenhoe Town v Halstead Town	3-1
Chesham United v Hertford Town	0-0, 5-1
Enfield v Barking	4-1
Walthamstow Pennant v Chelmsford City	0-3
Biggleswade Town v Hornchurch	2-2, 1-3
Hounslow v Basildon United	4-3
Stevenage Borough v Bishops Stortford	2-3
Barkingside v Redbridge Forest	1-3
Fisher Athletic v Harwich & Parkeston	0-0, 1-2
Banstead Athletic v Molesey	3-3, 0-2
Dagenham v Burnham	1-1, 2-1
Corinthian Casuals v Grays Athletic	1-5
Beckenham Town v Flackwell Heath	0-2
Egham Town v Purfleet	2-1
Tilbury v Witney Town	1-1, 1-2
Edgware Town v Harrow Borough	1-0
Leyton Wingate v Billericay Town	0-0, 0-1
Andover v Horsham YMCA	3-0
Walton & Hersham v Bromley	2-3
Royston Town v Yeading	3-2
Marlow v Merstham	3-0
Tooting & Mitcham United v Horsham	0-0, 2-1
Littlehampton Town v Dulwich Hamlet	2-0
Tonbridge AFC v Hythe Town	3-1
Whyteleafe v Slade Green	2-1
Peacehaven & Telscombe v Southwick	4-1
Folkestone v Bognor Regis Town	1-2
Margate v Gravesend & Northfleet	2-2, 4-1
Redhill v Whitehawk	2-3
Pagham v Oakwood	4-0
Cove v Windsor & Eton	1-3
Sittingbourne v Whitstable Town	1-1, 4-1
Dover Athletic v Ashford Town	1-0
Wick v Dorking	0-3

Carshalton Athletic v Erith & Belvedere	3-0
Eastbourne United v Crawley Town	0-2
Worthing v Chatham Town	3-0
Havant Town v Langney Sports	4-0
Kingstonian v Staines Town	2-1
Hampton v Hailsham Town	0-1
Herne Bay v Lewes	0-1
Salisbury v Hungerford Town	2-0
Bournemouth v Abingdon Town	2-1
Abingdon United v Farnborough Town	0-1
Slough Town v Feltham	8-0
Trowbridge Town v Newbury Town	3-0
Wycombe Wanderers v Maidenhead United	3-0
Warminster Town v Wokingham Town	0-1
Chippenham Town v Lymington AFC	1-1, 0-1
Melksham Town v Calne Town	2-1
Waterlooville v Newport IOW	1-1, 0-3
Stroud v Gosport Borough	4-1
Chard Town v Romsey Town	4-4, 0-3
Barry Town v Clevedon Town	0-0, 3-0
Mangotsfield United v Bashley	2-2, 3-6
St Blazey v Weymouth	0-2
Taunton Town v Swanage Town & Herston	1-2
Weston-Super-Mare v Maesteg Park	2-2, 4-0
Cheltenham Town v Exmouth Town	2-2, 3-3, 3-0
Yate Town v Worcester City	1-3
Bristol Manor Farm v Bridgend Town	1-1, 0-3
Tiverton Town v Ilfracombe Town	5-1
Saltash United v Poole Town	1-1, 2-2, 3-1
Falmouth Town v Dorchester Town	2-4
Liskeard Athletic v Wimborne Town	5-2

Second Qualifying Round

Shildon v Fleetwood Town	0-4
Prudhoe East End v North Shields	0-1
Accrington Stanley v Blyth Spartans	2-1
Gretna v Guisborough Town	2-2, 3-1
Harrogate Railway v South Bank	1-0
Easington Colliery v Langley Park	1-1, 1-0
Esh Winning v Spennymoor United	1-3
Horden CW v Northallerton Town	0-3
Lancaster City v Newcastle Blue Star	2-2, 0-2
Seaham Red Star v Consett	1-1, 0-2
Irlam Town v Horwich RMI	1-3
Caernarfon Town v Colwyn Bay	2-6
Maine Road v Altrincham	0-1
Atherton LR v Bangor City	0-0, 0-4
Emley v Chorley	0-1
Bootle v Southport	2-0
Hednesford Town v Hyde United	2-2, 2-5
South Liverpool v Curzon Ashton	1-0
Leicester United v Droylsden	0-0, 2-2, 4-3
Worksop Town v Marine	1-3
Princes End United v Frickley Athletic	0-4
Blakenall v Nuneaton Borough	3-3, 0-3
Alvechurch v Witton Albion	2-7
Bilston Town v Buxton	2-1
Corby Town v Matlock Town	2-0
Burton Albion v Hinckley Athletic	4-0
Buckingham Town v Shepshed Charterhouse	2-4
Evesham United v Atherstone United	1-2
Stourbridge v Sutton Coldfield Town	1-2
Sandwell Borough v Bromsgrove Rovers	0-2
Malvern Town v Tamworth	3-3, 1-5
Histon v Redditch United	1-1, 0-1
Boreham Wood v Rushden Town	1-0
Boston United v VS Rugby	3-1
Wembley v Heybridge Swifts	2-2, 1-3
Great Yarmouth Town v Cambridge City	0-4
Harlow Town v Ford United	1-0
Braintree Town v Barnet	0-2
Ruislip Manor v Hendon	2-1
Wivenhoe Town v Wealdstone	0-0, 1-2
Chesham United v Enfield	0-3
Hornchurch v Chelmsford City	1-2
Hounslow v Bishops Stortford	1-5
Harwich & Parkeston v Redbridge Forest	1-3
Molesey v Dagenham	1-2
Flackwell Heath v Grays Athletic	2-2, 0-2

Egham Town v Witney Town	1-0
Billericay Town v Edgware Town	1-0
Andover v Bromley	2-0
Marlow v Royston Town	2-2, 2-0
Tooting & Mitcham United v Littlehampton Town	1-2
Whyteleafe v Tonbridge AFC	0-2
Peacehaven & Telscombe v Bognor Regis Town	3-1
Whitehawk v Margate	0-1
Pagham v Windsor & Eton	0-3
Dover Athletic v Sittingbourne	2-0
Dorking v Carshalton Athletic	2-0
Worthing v Crawley Town	3-2
Havant Town v Kingstonian	0-4
Lewes v Hailsham Town	0-3
Salisbury v Bournemouth	4-0
Slough Town v Farnborough Town	2-3
Trowbridge Town v Wycombe Wanderers	0-0, 1-2
Lymington AFC v Wokingham Town	1-1, 1-2
(Replay at Reading FC)	
Melksham Town v Newport IOW	0-2
Romsey Town v Stroud	1-0
Barry Town v Bashley	0-2
Swanage Town & Herston v Weymouth	1-1, 1-2
Weston-Super-Mare v Cheltenham Town	0-2
Bridgend Town v Worcester City	1-7
Tiverton Town v Saltash United	4-2
Liskeard Athletic v Dorchester Town	5-1

Third Round Qualifying

Fleetwood Town v North Shields	2-0
Accrington Stanley v Gretna	2-1
Harrogate Railway v Easington Colliery	2-0
Spennymoor United v Northallerton Town	2-0
Newcastle Blue Star v Consett	3-0
Horwich RMI v Colwyn Bay	1-3
Altrincham v Bangor City	3-0
Chorley v Bootle	6-2
Hyde United v South Liverpool	1-1, 1-3
Leicester United v Marine	0-2
Frickley Athletic v Nuneaton Borough	1-0
Witton Albion v Bilston Town	4-0
Corby Town v Burton Albion	0-1
Shepshed Charterhouse v Atherstone United	2-3
Sutton Coldfield United v Bromsgrove Rovers	0-0, 2-4
Tamworth v Redditch United	2-0
Boreham Wood v Boston United	1-1, 0-4
Heybridge Swifts v Cambridge City	1-0
Harlow Town v Barnet	1-3
Ruislip Manor v Wealdstone	1-0
Enfield v Chelmsford City	1-1, 0-1
Bishops Stortford v Redbridge Forest	2-1
Dagenham v Grays Athletic	3-1
Egham Town v Billericay Town	1-1, 2-1
Andover v Marlow	0-1
Littlehampton Town v Tonbridge AFC	0-0, 3-2
Peacehaven & Telscombe v Margate	1-0
Windsor & Eton v Dover Athletic	1-1, 0-3
Dorking v Worthing	1-1, 4-2
Kingstonian v Hailsham Town	4-0
Salisbury v Farnborough Town	0-3
Wycombe Wanderers v Wokingham Town	4-1
Newport (IOW) v Romsey Town	0-1
Bashley v Weymouth	2-2, 3-2
Cheltenham Town v Worcester City	4-2
Tiverton Town v Liskeard Athletic	1-0

Fourth Round Qualifying

Accrington Stanley v Fleetwood Town	0-2
Marine v Stafford Rangers	1-1, 1-2
Frickley v Witton Albion	0-2
Macclesfield Town v Altrincham	2-2, 0-3
Chorley v Harrogate Railway	3-1
Northwich Victoria v Spennymoor United	1-1, 1-2
Bishop Auckland v South Liverpool	1-0
Colwyn Bay v Whitley Bay	1-4
Runcorn v Newcastle Blue Star	1-0
Dagenham v Aylesbury United	0-2
Burton Albion v Tamworth	0-0, 2-3
Telford United v Egham Town	2-0

Barnet v Heybridge Swifts	3-1	Romsey Town v Littlehampton Town	1-2
Halesowen Town v Ruislip Manor	5-2	Tiverton Town v Peacehaven & Telscombe	3-2
Bishops Stortford v Atherstone United	0-1	Woking v Bath City	2-1
Chelmsford City v Kettering Town	0-0, 2-1	Wycombe Wanderers v Basingstoke Town	6-0
Bromsgrove Rovers v Kidderminster Harriers	1-2	Hayes v Kingstonian	2-0
Dartford v Boston United	1-1, 1-2	Welling United v Bashley	1-0
Yeovil Town v Marlow	3-1	Dover Athletic v Merthyr Tydfil	0-0, 0-2
Farnborough Town v Gloucester City	4-1	Dorking v Cheltenham Town	2-3

FA CUP 1990–91

FIRST ROUND

17 NOV

Aldershot (3) 6 *(Stewart, Henry 2, Williams, Puckett, Randall)*
Tiverton T (1) 2 *(Jones, Durham)*   2706
Aldershot: Coles; Brown, Cornish (Burvill), Randall, Ogley, Whitlock, Banton, Puckett, Williams, Henry, Stewart.
Tiverton T: Knott; Rogers M, Greening, Cadwallader, Short, Jones (Venner), Jarvis (Scott), Saunders, Durham, Rogers P, Steele.

Atherstone (1) 3 *(Parker 3)*
Fleetwood (0) 1 *(Madden)*   1422
Atherstone: Starkey; Abell, Whetton, Jackson, Upton, Parker, Bradder, Olner, Lewis, Green, Gorrie.
Fleetwood: Thornley; Maddox, Lancashire, McCauley (Byron), Gerrard, Haslem (Thomson), Parkinson, Clarkson, Madden, Knowles, Wakenshaw.

Aylesbury (0) 0
Walsall (1) 1 *(McDonald)*   3366
Aylesbury: Garner; Mason, Cox (Wright O), Reed (Cousins), Hutter, Pluckrose, Wright A, Ketteridge, Hercules, Sansom, Lambert.
Walsall: Green; Hutchings, Singleton, Methven, Smith, Skipper, Kelly, Ntamark, Rimmer, Cecere, McDonald.

Barnet (2) 2 *(Bull, Willis)*
Chelmsford C (0) 2 *(Jarvis, Baptiste)*   3217
Barnet: Phillips; Wilson (Richardson), Cooper, Bodley, Howell, Poole, Stein, Clarke, Bull, Willis, Durham.
Chelmsford C: Lewington; Rooke, Lemoine, Stead, May, Jarvis, Kane, Butler, Greene Dennis, Greene David (Baptiste), Jones.

Birmingham C (0) 1 *(Sturridge)*
Cheltenham T (0) 0   7942
Birmingham C: Williams; Hopkins, Downs, Frain, Overson, Matthewson, Peer, Bailey (Gordon), Sturridge, Gleghorn, Tait.
Cheltenham T: Weaver; De Souza (Crouch), Willetts, Brogan, Vircavs, Jordan, Burns, Casey, Tuohy, Buckland, Brain.

Bishop Auckland (0) 0
Barrow (0) 1 *(Burgess)*   1690
Bishop Auckland: Owers; Liddle, Morgan, Linighan, Magee, Healey, Walker, Shaw (Grady), Wiggan, Stonehouse (Fothergill), Deacey.

Barrow: McDonnell; Marsh, Stimpson, Skivington, Messenger, Proctor, Doherty, Gilmour, Cowperthwaite, Lowe, Burgess.

Blackpool (0) 2 *(Groves, Garner)*
Grimsby T (0) 0   4175
Blackpool: McIlhargey; Hedworth, Wright, Groves, Briggs (Davies), Gore, Rodwell, Horner, Sinclair, Garner, Richards.
Grimsby T: Sherwood; Agnew, Jobling, Tillson, Lever (Birtles), Cunnington, Watson, Gilbert, Rees, Cockerill, Woods.

Boston U (1) 1 *(Cavell)*
Wycombe W (1) 1 *(Evans)*   2755
Boston U: McKenna; Shirtliff, Vaughan, Beech, Hardy, Cusack, Tomlinson, McGinley (Mossman), Cavell, Toone, Campbell.
Wycombe W: Granville; Crossley, Walford, Kerr, Creaser, Carroll, Blackler, Stapleton, West, Evans, Hutchinson.

Bournemouth (1) 2 *(Teale, Jones)*
Gillingham (0) 1 *(Crown)*   6113
Bournemouth: Peyton; Miller, Morrell, Teale, O'Driscoll, Bond, Holmes, Peacock, Jones, Redknapp, Blissett.
Gillingham: Lim; Clarke, Manuel, Dunn, Walker, Trusson, O'Conner, Docker, Lovell, Crown, Kimble (Heritage).

Bradford C (0) 0
Shrewsbury T (0) 0   6629
Bradford C: Tomlinson; Abbott, Babb, James, Oliver, Sinnott, Duxbury, Jewell, McCarthy, Leonard, Tinnion.
Shrewsbury T: Hughes; Clements, Lynch, Kelly, Gorman, Blake, Brown, Summerfield (Wimbleton), Spink, Shaw, Heathcote.

Brentford (3) 5 *(Blissett, Holdsworth 2, May, Jones)*
Yeovil (0) 0   4893
Brentford: Benstead; Ratcliffe, Fleming, Millen, Evans, Gayle (Brooke), Jones, May, Holdsworth, Blissett (Godfrey), Cockram.
Yeovil: Fry; Sherewood, Harrower, Shail, Rutter, Jackson, Carroll, Conning (Hirons), Dawkins, Spencer, Lowe.

Cardiff C (0) 0
Hayes (0) 0   1844
Cardiff C: Hansbury; Lewis, Searle, Barnard, Matthews, Perry, Jones, Griffith, Gibbins, Blake, Rodgerson.

Hayes: Hyde; Day, Myers, Court, Leather, Marshall, Clarke (Eaton), Dixon, Benning, Fraser, Walton.

Chester C (1) 2 *(Bennett, Dale)*
Doncaster R (0) 2 *(Gormley, Rankine)* 1749
Chester C: Stewart; Reeves, Lane, Butler, Abel, Lightfoot, Bennett, Pugh, Morton (Painter), Dale, Croft (Ellis).

Doncaster R: Crichton; Rankine, Brevett, Ashurst, Ormsby, Adams, Gormley, Stiles, Grayson, Noteman (Turnbull), Harle.

Chesterfield (3) 3 *(Barnes, Potts (og), Caldwell)*
Spennymoor (1) 2 *(Peattie, Boagey)* 4142
Chesterfield: Leonard; Dyche, Hart, Lemon, Brien, Gunn, Hewitt, Caldwell (Williams), Barnes, Cooke, Rogers.

Spennymoor: Toth; Potts, Blackburn, Robinson, Hartley, Elliott, Ainsley, Peattie (Ross), Boagey, Ord, Storey.

Chorley (2) 2 *(Aspinall, Moss)*
Bury (0) 1 *(Mauge)* 2834
Chorley: Ryan; Jackson, Lampkin, Rutter, Keeley, King, Ward, Aspinall, Ross, Moss (Worrall S) (Barr), Worrall G.

Bury: Kelly; Hill, Stanislaus, Mauge, Cunningham, Knill, Lee, Parkinson (Feeley), Robinson, McGinlay, Patterson.

Colchester U (0) 2 *(Atkins (pen), Marmon)*
Reading (1) 1 *(Hicks)* 3761
Colchester U: Barrett; English, Atkins, Collins, Daniels, Marmon, Donald, Bennett, Yates, Walsh, Smith.

Reading: Francis; Jones, Gilkes, McPherson, Hicks, Williams, Friel (Maskell), Taylor, Senior, Conroy, Moran.

Darlington (0) 1 *(Gill)*
York C (1) 1 *(Canham)* 4638
Darlington: Prudhoe; McJannet, Gray, Gill, Smith, Corner, Mardenborough (Geddis), Toman, Borthwick, Cork (Ellison), Tait.

York C: Marples; McMillan, Hall, McCarthy, Tutill, Warburton, Pepper, Howlett, Helliwell, Dunn, Canham.

Exeter C (0) 1 *(Neville)*
Cambridge U (1) 2 *(Taylor 2)* 4714
Exeter C: Miller; Hiley, Dryden, Brown, Taylor, Cooper, Hobson, Bailey, Morgan, Neville, Kelly.

Cambridge U: Vaughan; Fensome, Kimble, Bailie, Chapple, Daish, Claridge, Leadbitter, Dublin, Taylor, Philpott.

Fulham (1) 2 *(Pike, Brazil (pen))*
Farnborough (0) 1 *(Horton)* 4990
Fulham: Stannard; Newson, Pike, Skinner, North, Morgan, Thomas, Scott, Haag (Milton), Brazil, Cobb (Ferney).

Farnborough: Power; Morris, Rowland, Read (Johnson), Bye, Wigmore, Broome, Horton, Coombs, Docherty, Rogers.

Halesowen (1) 1 *(Flynn)*
Tranmere R (1) 2 *(Morrissey, Steel)* 3690
Halesowen: Scarr; Heywood, Flynn, Smith, Bettles, Hemans, Hazelwood, Edwards, Bourne, Langford (Hunter), Harrison.

Tranmere R: Nixon; Higgins, McCarrick, McNab, Hughes, Vickers, Morrissey, Harvey, Steel, Muir, Brannan.

Halifax T (1) 3 *(Norris, Graham, Juryeff)*
Wrexham (1) 2 *(Preece 2)* 2002
Halifax T: Gould; Butler, Barr, Evans, Fleming, Futcher, Martin, Norris, Juryeff, Graham, Ellis.

Wrexham: Morris; Phillips (Bowden), Hardy, Hunter (Armstrong), Beaumont, Jones, Thackeray, Owens, O'Gorman, Worthington, Preece.

Hereford U (1) 1 *(Narbett)*
Peterborough U (1) 1 *(Riley)* 4209
Hereford U: Wood; Jones MA, Tester, Pejic, Peacock, Hemming, Jones R, Narbett, Robinson, Phillips, Lowndes (Wheeler).

Peterborough U: Bradshaw; Luke, Crosby, Halsall, Oakes, McElhinney, Sterling, Hine, Bremner, Riley, Butterworth.

Leyton Orient (0) 3 *(Castle 2, Nugent)*
Southend U (0) 2 *(Angell 2)* 6095
Leyton Orient: Heald; Baker, Howard, Sitton, Whitbread, Pike, Carter, Castle, Nugent, Harvey, Berry.

Southend U: Sansome; Austin, Powell, Cornwell (Martin), Prior, Tilson, Cawley (Locke), Butler, Ansah, Benjamin, Angell.

Lincoln C (1) 1 *(Lormor)*
Crewe Alex (1) 4 *(Callaghan, Gardiner, McKearney, Ward)* 3596
Lincoln C: Wallington; Bressington, Nicholson, Brown, Thompson (Schofield), Davis, Wilson, Smith P, Lormor, Stoutt, Puttnam.

Crewe Alex: Edwards P; Swain, McKearney, Callaghan, Carr, Lennon, Jasper, Rose, Hignett (Edwards R), Gardiner, Ward.

Littlehampton (0) 0
Northampton T (2) 4 *(Barnes 2, Campbell, Beavon)* 3540
Littlehampton: Phillips; Prees, Skietes, Hammond, Bates, Bicknell, Bennett M, Cox, Bennett P, Withers (Foster), Guille (Horn).

Northampton T: Gleasure; Chard, Wilson, Terry, Gernon, Williams (Collins), Beavon, Campbell, Thorpe, Barnes (Berry), Brown.

Maidstone U (2) 4 *(Butler 2, Osborne, Gall)*
Torquay U (1) 1 *(Tynan)* 2303
Maidstone U: Johns; Berry, Cooper, Stebbing, Golley, Oxbrow (Gall), Lillis, Elsey, Osborne, Butler, Pritchard.

Torquay U: Howells; Whiston, Uzzell, Lloyd, Elliott (Cookson), Joyce (Hall), Loram, Saunders, Tynan, Edwards, Myers.

Merthyr Tydfil (0) 1 *(Sanderson)*
Sutton U (0) 1 *(Gill)* 1279
Merthyr Tydfil: Wager; Tucker, Williams S, Boyle, Stevenson, Rogers, Giles, Webley, Sanderson, Beattie, Williams C.

Sutton U: Sullivan; Thurlow (Dack), Gates, Costello, Golley, Rogers, Jenkins (Seagroatt), Massey, Evans, McKinnon, Gill.

Preston NE (0) 0

Mansfield T (1) 1 *(Kearney)*   5230

Preston NE: Kelly; Senior, Rathbone, Flynn (Harper), Hughes, Wrightson, Swann (Easter), Bogie, Greenwood, Shaw, Joyce.

Mansfield T: Beesley, Murray, Kearney, Clark, Foster, Gray, Kent, Charles, Wilkinson, Christie (Stringfellow), Fairclough.

Rochdale (0) 1 *(Costello)*

Scunthorpe U (0) 1 *(Hicks)*   3259

Rochdale: Welch; Burns, Graham, O'Shaughnessy, Cole, Ward, Dawson, Lee, Elliott, Costello, Holmes.

Scunthorpe U: Musselwhite; Longden, Lillis, Cotton, Hicks, Hall, Cox, Taylor, Miller, Flounders, Bramhall (Tucker).

Rotherham U (0) 1 *(Dempsey)*

Stockport Co (0) 0   4501

Rotherham U: Mercer; Forrest, Scott, Russell, Law, Watts, Goodwin, Dempsey, Evans, Goater (Thompson), Hazel.

Stockport Co: Cooper; Brown, Bullock, Frain, Thorpe, Williams, Payne, Gannon, Alexander, Beaumont, Todd (Matthews).

Runcorn (0) 0

Hartlepool U (1) 3 *(Allon 3)*   1675

Runcorn: Williams; Edwards, Byrne, Carroll, Sang, Harold, Rudge, Brady (Fallon), Withers, Hawtin, Highdale.

Hartlepool U: Cox; Tinkler, McKinnon, Olsson, MacPhail, Bennyworth, Allon, Hutchison, Baker, Honour, Dalton (Fletcher).

Scarborough (0) 0

Leek T (1) 2 *(Sommerville, Sutton)*   1598

Scarborough: Ironside; Kamara, Mudd, Mockler, Richards, Hirst, Cook (Logan), Wilson (Matthews), Mooney, Oghani, Carter.

Leek T: Simpson; Bainbridge, Fisher, McMullan, Norris, Evans, Mellor, Sommerville, Sutton, Camden (Mountford), Jones.

Stafford R (0) 1 *(Anastasi)*

Burnley (2) 3 *(Collymore (og), Mumby, White)* 4117

Stafford R: Price; Turley, Wood R, Simpson (Shelley), Essex, Bremner, Wood F, Anastasi, Palgrave, Collymore, Merchant (Devlin).

Burnley: Pearce; Measham, Deakin, Deary, Pender, Davis, White, Mumby (Futcher), Francis, Jakub, Grewcock.

Swansea C (1) 5 *(Gilligan (pen), Connor, Legg 2, Thornber)*

Welling (1) 2 *(Francis, Robbins)*   3156

Swansea C: Bracey; Hough, Coleman, Walker, Harris, Davies, Raynor (Chappell), Thornber, Gilligan (Davey), Connor, Legg.

Welling: Parsons; Hone (Robinson), Horton, Glover, Ransom, Francis, White, Handford, Abbott (Booker), Robbins, Reynolds.

Tamworth (1) 4 *(Eccleston, Smith 2, Gordon)*

Whitley Bay (2) 6 *(Briggs 2, Chandler, Barker 2, Ferris)*   2600

Tamworth: Whitehead; Llewellyn, Wells, Gethfield, Cartwright, Smith, Gordon, Eccleston, Knight, Green, Morris (Finn).

Whitley Bay: Dickson; Embleton, Teasdale, Briggs, Robinson, Scott (Eagling), Dawson, Johnson, Chandler, Barker, Ferris (Veitch).

Telford U (0) 0

Stoke C (0) 0   3709

Telford U: McDonagh; Salathiel, Dyson, Myers, Brindley, Humphreys, McGinty, Grainger, Crawley, Buxton (Brown), Nelson (Bailey).

Stoke C: Fox; Butler (Fowler), Statham, Beeston, Blake, Cranson, Kennedy, Ellis, Thomas, Biggins, Sandford.

Wigan Ath (3) 5 *(Griffiths 2, Woods, Rimmer 2)*

Carlisle U (0) 0   3947

Wigan Ath: Adkins; Parkinson, Tankard, Atherton, Johnson, Langley, Woods, Rimmer, Daley (Patterson), Page, Griffiths.

Carlisle U: Priestley; Edmondson, Bennett, Edwards, Jones, Fitzpatrick, Walsh, Jeffels (Goldsmith), Walwyn, Gates (Sendall), Fyfe.

Witton A (0) 1 *(Thomas)*

Bolton W (1) 2 *(Darby, Comstive)*   3790

Witton A: Mason; Lee (Ellis), Stewart, McNellis, Cuddy, Anderson, Jarvis, Lodge (Edwards), Thomas, Grimshaw, Connor.

Bolton W: Felgate; Brown, Cowdrill, Henshaw (Comstive), Seagraves, Winstanley, Storer, Thompson, Reeves, Green, Darby.

Woking (0) 0

Kidderminster H (0) 0   3249

Woking: Read; Mitchell, Cowler, Pratt, Baron, Wye S, Brown, Biggins, Mulvaney, Fearon (Clement), Wye L.

Kidderminster H: Jones; Kurila (Attwood), Lowe, Weir, Barnett, Forsyth, Joseph, Howell, Whitehouse, Davies, Lilwall (Benson).

18 NOV

Altrincham (1) 1 *(Rowlands)*

Huddersfield T (2) 2 *(Onuora, Roberts)*   3000

Altrincham: Wealands; Miller, Wiggins, Rowlands, Reid, Anderson, Shaw, Daws, Hughes (Brady), McKenna, Showler.

Huddersfield T: Hardwick; Trevitt, Charlton, Marsden, Mitchell, Jackson, O'Regan, Wilson, Roberts, Smith, Onuora.

FIRST ROUND REPLAYS

19 NOV

York C (1) 1 *(Canham)*

Darlington (0) 0   4035

York C: Marples; McMillan, Hall, McCarthy, Tutill, Warburton, Pepper, Howlett, Helliwell, Dunn, Canham.

Darlington: Prudhoe; McJannet, Gray (Mardenborough), Gill, Smith, Trotter, Geddis, Toman, Borthwick, Ellison, Tait.

20 NOV

Doncaster R (0) 1 *(Noteman)*

Chester C (0) 2 *(Dale, Painter) aet*   3543

Doncaster R: Crichton; Rankine, Brevett, Ashurst, Ormsby, Douglas, Gormley, Stiles, Adams (Grayson), Turnbull, Harle.

Chester C: Stewart; Reeves, Pugh, Butler, Abel, Lane, Bennett, Painter, Ellis, Dale, Croft (Lightfoot).

Peterborough U (2) 2 *(Sterling, Riley)*

Hereford U (0) 1 *(Pejic)*   4179

Peterborough U: Bradshaw; Luke, Crosby, Halsall, Oakes, McElhinney, Sterling, Hine, Bremner, Riley, Butterworth.

Hereford U: Wood; Jones MA, Tester, Pejic, Peacock, Hemming, Jones R, Narbett, Robinson, Phillips, Lowndes (Wheeler).

Scunthorpe U (0) 2 *(Flounders, Lillis)*

Rochdale (1) 1 *(Costello) aet*   3761

Scunthorpe U: Musselwhite; Longden, Lillis, Cotton, Hicks, Hall, Cox, Taylor, Miller (Stevenson), Flounders, Bramhall.

Rochdale: Welch; Burns, Graham, O'Shaughnessy, Cole, Ward, Dawson (Milner), Lee, Elliott (Hilditch), Costello, Holmes.

21 NOV

Chelmsford C (0) 0

Barnet (0) 2 *(Clarke, Willis)*   2612

Chelmsford C: Lewington; Rooke (Greene David), Johnson, Stead, May, Jarvis, Kane, Butler, Greene Dennis, Baptiste, Jones.

Barnet: Phillips; Turner, Cooper, Bodley, Howell, Poole, Stein, Clarke (Murphy), Bull, Willis, Durham (Hayrettin).

Hayes (0) 1 *(Clarke)*

Cardiff C (0) 0 *at Brentford*   4312

Hayes: Hyde; Day (Knight), Myers, Court, Leather, Marshall, Clarke, Dixon, Benning, Fraser (Keen), Walton.

Cardiff C: Hansbury; Lewis, Searle, Barnard, Matthews (Pike), Perry, Jones, Griffith, Gibbins, Blake (Fry), Rodgerson.

Kidderminster H (0) 1 *(Davies)*

Woking (0) 1 *(Baron) aet*   2827

Kidderminster H: Jones; Barton, Lowe, Weir, Benson, Forsyth, Joseph, Howell, Whitehouse (Attwood), Shilvock, Davies.

Woking: Read; Russell, Cowler, Pratt, Baron, Wye S, Brown, Biggins, Mulvaney, Clement, Wye L.

Shrewsbury T (0) 2 *(Shaw 2)*

Bradford C (1) 1 *(Jewell)*   3708

Shrewsbury T: Hughes; Clements, Lynch, Kelly, Gorman, Blake, Brown, Summerfield, Spink, Shaw, Heathcote (Weir).

Bradford C: Tomlinson; Abbott, Tinnion, James, Oliver, Sinnott, Duxbury, Jewell, McCarthy, Leonard, Megson (Adcock).

Stoke C (1) 1 *(Sandford)*

Telford U (0) 0   11,880

Stoke C: Fox; Rennie (Fowler), Statham, Beeston, Blake, Cranson, Kennedy, Whitehurst (Ellis), Thomas, Biggins, Sandford.

Telford U: McDonagh; Salathiel, Dyson, Myers, Brindley, Humphreys, McGinty, Grainger, Crawley, Benbow (Brown), Nelson (Daly).

Sutton U (0) 0

Merthyr Tydfil (1) 1 *(Webley)*   1934

Sutton U: McCann; Gates, Furlong, Costello, Golley, Rogers, Jenkins (Seagroatt), Massey, Evans, McKinnon, Gill.

Merthyr Tydfil: Wager; Tucker, Williams S, Boyle, Lewis, Rogers, Giles, Webley, Sanderson (Stevens), Beattie, Williams C.

Wycombe W (1) 4 *(West 2, Ryan, Creaser)*

Boston U (0) 0   4954

Wycombe W: Granville; Crossley, Walford, Kerr, Creaser, Carroll, Blackler, Stapleton (Smith), West, Evans (Ryan), Hutchinson.

Boston U: McKenna; Shirtliff, Vaughan, Beech (Stephenson), Hardy, Cusack, Tomlinson, Cook, Cavell, Toone (Gilliver), Campbell.

FIRST ROUND SECOND REPLAY
26 NOV

Kidderminster H (1) 1 *(Lilwall)*

Woking (0) 2 *(Clement, Russell)*   3015

Kidderminster H: Jones; Kurila, Lowe, Weir, Barnett, Forsyth, Joseph, Howell, Attwood, Davies (Carroll), Lilwall.

Woking: Read; Russell, Cowler, Pratt, Baron, Clement, Brown, Mitchell, Biggins, Buzaglo, Wye L.

SECOND ROUND
7 DEC

Fulham (0) 0

Cambridge U (0) 0   5929

Fulham: Stannard; Newson, Pike, Skinner, North, Morgan, Thomas, Kelly, Rosenior, Brazil, Davies (Milton).

Cambridge U: Vaughan; Fensome, Kimble, Bailie, Chapple, O'Shea, Cheetham (Dennis), Leadbitter, Dublin, Taylor, Philpott (Wilkins).

8 DEC

Aldershot (1) 2 *(Puckett, Stewart)*

Maidstone U (1) 1 *(Gall)*   3404

Aldershot: Hucker; Brown, Cooper, Randall, Ogley, Whitlock (Flower), Burvill, Puckett, Williams, Henry, Stewart.

Maidstone U: Johns; Roast, Henry, Berry, Golley, Lillis (Charlery), Gall, Elsey, Osborne, Butler, Stebbing.

Barnet (0) 0

Northampton T (0) 0   5002

Barnet: Phillips; Wilson, Cooper, Bodley, Nugent, Richardson, Stein (Durham), Clarke, Bull (Murphy), Willis, Hayrettin.

Northampton T: Gleasure; Chard, Wilson, Terry, Fee, Johnson, Beavon, Campbell, Collins (Scope), Barnes, Brown.

Bournemouth (0) 1 *(Brooks)*

Hayes (0) 0   6510

Bournemouth: Peyton; Miller, Morrell, Teale, O'Driscoll, Bond, Holmes (Lawrence), Redknapp, Jones, Brooks, Blissett.

Hayes: Hyde; Day (Fraser), Myers, Court, Leather, Marshall, Clarke, Dixon, Benning, Keen, Walton.

Scunthorpe U (2) 3 *(Ward, Lillis, Flounders)*

Tranmere R (1) 2 *(Vickers, Irons)*   3576

Scunthorpe U: Musselwhite; Longden, Lillis, Ward, Hicks, Hall, Cox, Cotton, Miller, Flounders, Cowling (Hamilton).

Tranmere R: Nixon; Higgins, Brannan, McNab, Hughes (Harvey), Vickers, Morrissey (Irons), Bishop, Steel, Muir, Thomas.

Swansea C (2) 2 *(Connor, Gilligan (pen))*

Walsall (1) 1 *(Hutchings)*   3744

Swansea C: Bracey; Hough, Coleman, Walker, Harris, Davies, Raynor (Thornber), Coughlin, Gilligan, Connor, Legg.

Walsall: Green; Hutchings, Singleton, Methven, Smith (Grealish), Skipper, Kelly (Littlejohn), Ntamark, Rimmer, Cecere, McDonald.

Wigan Ath (1) 2 *(Page, Griffiths)*

Hartlepool U (0) 0   2492

Wigan Ath: Adkins; Parkinson, Tankard, Atherton, Johnson (Patterson), Langley, Woods, Rimmer, Pilling, Page, Griffiths B.

Hartlepool U: Cox; Olsson, McKinnon, Tinkler, MacPhail, Bennyworth (Nobbs), Allon, Davies, Baker, Honour, Dalton.

Woking (2) 5 *(Wye L, Biggins 3, Buzaglo)*

Merthyr Tydfil (0) 1 *(Haig)*   4000

Woking: Read; Mitchell, Cowler, Pratt, Baron, Clement, Brown, Biggins, Wye S, Buzaglo, Wye L.

Merthyr Tydfil: Wager; Tucker, Williams S, Boyle, Lewis, Rogers, Giles (Mullett), Green (Haig), Sanderson, Beattie, Williams C.

10 DEC

Huddersfield T (0) 0

Blackpool (0) 2 *(Groves, Jackson (og))*   6329

Huddersfield T: Martin; Wilson, Charlton, Marsden, Mitchell, Jackson, O'Regan, Edwards (Smith), Roberts, Barnett, Onuora.

Blackpool: McIlhargey; Hedworth, Wright, Groves, Briggs, Gore, Rodwell, Horner, Richards, Garner, Eyres (Sinclair).

11 DEC

Chesterfield (1) 3 *(Morris, Caldwell, Cooke)*

Bolton W (2) 4 *(Reeves, Philliskirk, Thompson, Storer)*   4833

Chesterfield: Allison; Francis, Albiston, Lemon, Brien, Gunn, Hewitt, Caldwell, Williams (Plummer), Cooke, Morris.

Bolton W: Felgate; Brown, Cowdrill, Green, Came, Winstanley, Storer, Thompson, Reeves, Philliskirk, Darby.

Rotherham U (1) 1 *(Goater)*

Halifax T (0) 1 *(Juryeff)*   2906

Rotherham U: Mercer; Forrest, Robinson, Pickering (Thompson), Law, Watts, Goodwin, Dempsey, Goater, Spooner (Evans), Hazel.

Halifax T: Gould; Fleming P, Barr, Evans, Fleming C, Futcher, Butler, Norris, Juryeff, Graham, Ellis.

Shrewsbury T (1) 1 *(Spink)*

Chorley (0) 0   3380

Shrewsbury T: Hughes; Worsley, Lynch, Kelly, Clements, Blake, Brown (Weir), Gorman (Summerfield), Spink, Shaw, Wimbleton.

Chorley: Ryan; Jackson, Lampkin, Rutter, Keeley, King, Ward (Worrall S), Aspinall (Barr), Ross, Moss, Halliday.

SECOND ROUND REPLAY

Cambridge U (1) 2 *(Kimble (pen), Dublin)*

Fulham (1) 1 *(Davies)*   4966

Cambridge U: Vaughan; Fensome, Kimble, Bailie, Chapple, O'Shea, Cheetham, Wilkins, Dublin, Taylor, Philpott.

Fulham: Batty; Newson, Pike (Eckhardt), Skinner (Marshall), North, Morgan, Thomas, Kelly, Rosenior, Brazil, Davies.

SECOND ROUND

12 DEC

Birmingham C (0) 1 *(Aylott)*

Brentford (2) 3 *(Blissett, Godfrey, Jones)*   5072

Birmingham C: Thomas; Clarkson, Downs, Frain, Overson, Matthewson, Peer (Aylott), Bailey, Gayle, Gleghorn, Sturridge.

Brentford: Benstead; Ratcliffe, Fleming, Millen, Evans, Buckle (Gayle), Jones, Godfrey, Cadette, Blissett (Cockram), Smillie.

Burnley (0) 2 *(Francis, White)*

Stoke C (0) 0   12,949

Burnley: Pearce; Measham, Deakin, Deary, Pender (Farrell), Davis, White, Futcher (Mumby), Francis, Jakub, Grewcock.

Stoke C: Fox; Ware, Statham, Sandford, Blake, Cranson (Beeston), Kennedy, Thomas, Whitehurst, Biggins, Hilaire (Ellis).

Colchester U (0) 0

Leyton Orient (0) 0   6150

Colchester U: Barrett; English, Evans, Atkins, Collins, Daniels, Marmon, Yates (Bennett), McDonough, Walsh, Smith.

Leyton Orient: Heald; Baker, Howard, Zoricich, Whitbread, Pike, Carter, Castle, Nugent, Sitton, Berry.

Crewe Alex (1) 1 *(Sussex)*

Atherstone (0) 0   4113

Crewe Alex: Edwards P; Swain, Lennon, Callaghan, Carr, Smart, Hignett, Rose, Sussex, Gardiner (Edwards R), Clayton (Jasper).

Atherstone: Starkey; Abell, Upton, Whetton, Olner, Randle, Parker (Lewis), Green (Landon), Bradder, Bodkin, Gorrie.

Leek T (0) 1 *(Griffiths)*
Chester C (1) 1 *(Dale)*   3046

Leek T: Simpson; Elsby, Fisher, McMullan, Clowes, Heavens (Griffiths), Mellor, Summerville, Sutton, Camden (Mountford), Norris.

Chester C: Stewart; Butler, Pugh (Lightfoot), Lane, Abel, Painter, Dale, Barrow, Bertschin, Morton, Croft.

Whitley Bay (0) 0
Barrow (0) 1 *(Gilmour)*   3500

Whitley Bay: Young; Embleton, Teasdale, Briggs, Gowans, Scott, Dawson, Johnson, Chandler, Omani, Ferris (Eagling).

Barrow: McDonnell; Marsh, Skivington, Messenger, Stimpson, Lowe, Gilmour, Proctor, Doherty, Cowperthwaite, Wheatley.

Wycombe W (0) 1 *(Blackler)*
Peterborough U (0) 1 *(Culpin)*   5237

Wycombe W: Granville; Whitby (Ryan), Walford, Crossley, Creaser, Carroll, Blackler, Stapleton (Smith), West, Evans, Hutchinson.

Peterborough U: Bradshaw; Luke, Crosby, Halsall, Oakes, McElhinney, Sterling, Hine, Bremner (Culpin), Riley, Butterworth.

SECOND ROUND REPLAY

Northampton T (0) 0
Barnet (0) 1 *(Clarke)*   5837

Northampton T: Gleasure; Chard, Wilson, Terry, Fee (Angus), Johnson, Beavon, Campbell, Thorpe (Scope), Barnes, Brown.

Barnet: Phillips; Wilson, Cooper, Bodley, Nugent, Richardson, Turner (Stein), Clarke, Bull (Murphy), Willis, Durham.

SECOND ROUND
17 DEC

Mansfield T (1) 2 *(Charles, Wilkinson)*
York C (0) 1 *(Pepper)*   3790

Mansfield T: Beasley; Murray, Kearney, Clark, Foster, Gray, Hathaway, Charles, Wilkinson, Christie, Fairclough.

York C: Marples; McMillan, Hall, Reid, Tutill, Warburton, Pepper, McCarthy (Barratt), Helliwell, Naylor (Dunn), Canham.

SECOND ROUND REPLAYS

Chester C (2) 4 *(Bertschin, Dale, Abel (pen), Painter)*
Leek T (0) 0   2420

Chester C: Stewart; Butler, Lane, Lightfoot, Abel, Painter, Bennett (Morton), Barrow, Bertschin, Dale, Croft.

Leek T: Simpson; Elsby, Fisher, McMullan, Clowes, Evans (Griffiths), Mellor, Summerville, Sutton, Camden (Mountford), Norris.

Halifax T (0) 1 *(Norris)*
Rotherham U (2) 2 *(Evans, Johnson)*   2132

Halifax T: Gould; Fleming P, Barr, Evans, Fleming C, Futcher, Butler, Norris, Juryeff, Graham (Richardson), Ellis.

Rotherham U: Mercer; Barnsley, Law, Spooner, Johnson, Forrest, Goodwin, Thompson (Dempsey), Mendonca, Evans, Hazel.

Leyton Orient (2) 4 *(Carter, Howard, Pike, Castle)*
Colchester U (1) 1 *(Masters)*   4615

Leyton Orient: Heald; Baker, Howard, Sitton, Whitbread, Pike, Carter (Hull), Castle (Zoricich), Nugent, Achampong, Berry.

Colchester U: Barrett; English, Atkins, Collins, Daniels (Bruce), Marmon, Donald, Masters (Bennett), Yates, Walsh, Grainger.

Peterborough U (2) 2 *(Halsall, Culpin)*
Wycombe W (0) 0   5692

Peterborough U: Bradshaw; Luke, Crosby, Halsall, Oakes, McElhinney, Sterling, Hine, Riley, Culpin, Butterworth.

Wycombe W: Granville; Whitby (Ryan), Walford, Crossley, Creaser, Carroll, Blackler, Stapleton (Smith), West, Evans, Hutchinson.

THIRD ROUND
5 JAN

Aldershot (0) 0
West Ham U (0) 0 *at West Ham*   22,929

Aldershot: Hucker; Brown, Cooper, Randall, Ogley, Flower, Burvill, Puckett, Williams, Henry, Stewart.

West Ham U: Miklosko; Breacker, Parris, Gale, Foster (Livett), Hughton, Keen, Slater, Quinn, Potts, Morley.

Arsenal (2) 2 *(Smith, Limpar)*
Sunderland (0) 1 *(O'Leary (og))*   35,128

Arsenal: Seaman; Dixon, Winterburn, Thomas, Bould, Linighan, Groves, Davis, Smith, Merson, Limpar (O'Leary).

Sunderland: Norman; Kay, Hardyman, Bennett, Ball, Owers, Bracewell, Armstrong, Hawke (Brady), Rush, Pascoe.

Aston Villa (0) 1 *(Gray)*
Wimbledon (1) 1 *(McGee)*   19,305

Aston Villa: Spink; Price, Gray, McGrath, Comyn (Callaghan), Nielsen, Yorke, Platt, Cascarino, Cowans, Ormondroyd (Birch).

Wimbledon: Segers; Joseph, Phelan, Barton, Blackwell, Kruszynski, McGee, Sanchez, Fashanu, Scales, Gibson.

Barnet (0) 0
Portsmouth (2) 5 *(Aspinall, Whittingham 3, Clarke)*   6209

Barnet: Phillips; Wilson, Poole, Bodley, Cooper (Hayrettin), Turner, Richardson (Stein), Durham, Clarke, Bull, Willis.

Portsmouth: Gosney; Neill, Beresford, Aspinall, Hogg, Stevens, Wigley, Kuhl, Clarke, Whittingham, Chamberlain (Russell).

Blackburn R (0) 1 *(Garner)*
Liverpool (0) 1 *(Atkins (og))*   18,845

Blackburn R: Mimms; Atkins, Duxbury, Reid, May, Moran, Gayle (Johnrose), Millar, Stapleton, Garner, Sellars (Shepstone).

Liverpool: Grobbelaar; Hysen, Burrows, Nicol, Staunton (Molby), Gillespie, Rosenthal, Houghton, Rush, Barnes, McMahon.

Blackpool (0) 0

Tottenham H (0) 1 *(Stewart)* 9100

Blackpool: McIlhargey; Davies, Wright, Groves, Briggs, Gore, Rodwell, Horner, Sinclair, Garner, Bamber.

Tottenham H: Thorstvedt; Fenwick, Edinburgh, Samways, Howells, Mabbutt, Stewart, Gascoigne, Moran, Lineker, Allen.

Bolton W (0) 1 *(Philliskirk)*

Barrow (0) 0 11,475

Bolton W: Felgate; Brown, Cowdrill, Comstive, Came, Winstanley, Storer, Thompson, Reeves, Philliskirk, Darby.

Barrow: McDonnell; Todhunter (Marsh), Chilton, Skivington, Messenger, Proctor, Doherty, Gilmour, Cowperthwaite, Lowe, Wheatley (Stimpson).

Brighton & HA (2) 3 *(Barham 2, Gurinovich)*

Scunthorpe U (1) 2 *(Flounders (pen), Bramhall)* 7785

Brighton & HA: Digweed; Crumplin, Gatting, Wilkins, McCarthy, Chivers, Barham (Robinson), Gurinovich, Small, Codner, Walker.

Scunthorpe U: Musselwhite; Longden, Lillis, Taylor, Hicks (Ward), Bramhall, Cox, Cotton (Miller), Hamilton, Flounders, Cowling.

Bristol R (0) 0

Crewe Alex (1) 2 *(Carr, Hignett)* 6143

Bristol R: Parkin (Nixon); Bloomer, Twentyman, Yates, Mehew, Jones, Holloway, Reece, White, Saunders, Pounder.

Crewe Alex: Greygoose; Swain, McKearney, Smart, Carr, Rose, Murphy, Hignett, Sussex, Gardiner, Clayton.

Charlton Ath (1) 1 *(Dyer)*

Everton (1) 2 *(Ebbrell 2)* 12,234

Charlton Ath: Bolder; Pitcher, Reid, Peake, Webster, Caton, Lee, Curbishley (Minto), Dyer, Leaburn, Mortimer (Watson).

Everton: Southall; McDonald, Hinchcliffe, Ratcliffe, Watson, Ebbrell, Nevin, McCall, Sharp, Sheedy, Beagrie (Newell).

Chelsea (0) 1 *(Dixon)*

Oxford U (1) 3 *(Nogan, Durnin, Magilton)* 14,586

Chelsea: Beasant; Hall, Clarke, Townsend, Cundy, Johnsen (Lee), Stuart, Bumstead (Le Saux), Dixon, Wilson, Wise.

Oxford U: Veysey; Robinson, Smart, McClaren, Foster, Melville, Magilton, Phillips, Durnin, Nogan, Simpson.

Chester C (0) 2 *(Croft 2)*

Bournemouth (2) 3 *(Jones 2, Ekoku)* 1833

Chester C: Stewart; Whelan, Lane, Lightfoot, Abel, Painter, Butler, Barrow, Bertschin, Dale, Croft.

Bournemouth: Peyton; Miller, Fereday, Teale, O'Driscoll, Pulis, Holmes (Mundee), Redknapp, Jones (Ekoku), Lawrence, Blissett.

Coventry C (0) 1 *(Gynn)*

Wigan Ath (0) 1 *(Patterson)* 10,802

Coventry C: Ogrizovic; Borrows, Edwards, Emerson (MacDonald), Billing, Peake, Gallacher, Gynn, Regis, Drinkell, Smith.

Wigan Ath: Pennock; Parkinson, Tankard, Atherton, Johnson, Langley, Woods, Rimmer, Fairclough (Patterson), Griffiths (Carberry), Page.

Hull C (1) 2 *(Buckley, McParland)*

Notts Co (3) 5 *(Buckley (og), Turner, O'Riordan, Bartlett, Lund)* 6655

Hull C: Hesford; Warren (Hunter), Jacobs, Waites, Buckley, Shotton, Thompson, Payton, Swan, Palin, Jenkinson (McParland).

Notts Co: Cherry; Short Chris, Harding, Short Craig, Yates, O'Riordan, Thomas (Robinson), Turner, Bartlett, Lund, Draper.

Leyton Orient (0) 1 *(Pike)*

Swindon T (1) 1 *(Shearer)* 6697

Leyton Orient: Heald; Zoricich, Howard, Sitton, Whitbread, Pike, Carter, Castle (Berry), Nugent, Achampong, Harvey.

Swindon T: Digby; Kerslake, Bodin, Hazard, Lorenzo, Gittens, Jones, Shearer, White, MacLaren, Foley.

Mansfield T (0) 0

Sheffield W (1) 2 *(Shirtliff, Sheridan (pen))* 9076

Mansfield T: Beasley; Murray, Kearney, Clark, Foster, Gray, Kent (Wilkinson), Charles, Stringfellow, Christie (Lowery), Fairclough.

Sheffield W: Turner; Harkes, King, Palmer, Shirtliff, Pearson, Wilson, Sheridan, Hirst, Williams, McCall.

Middlesbrough (0) 0

Plymouth Arg (0) 0 13,042

Middlesbrough: Pears; Cooper, Phillips (McGee), Mowbray, Coleman, Proctor (Ripley), Slaven, Mustoe, Baird, Kerr, Hendrie.

Plymouth Arg: Walter; Brown, Salman, Marker, Burrows, Morgan, Barlow, Hodges, Turner, Adcock (Fiore), Morrison.

Millwall (0) 2 *(Sheringham, Stephenson)*

Leicester C (1) 1 *(James)* 10,766

Millwall: Horne; Stevens, Dawes, Waddock, Wood, McLeary, Stephenson, Goodman, Sheringham, Rae, Briley (McGlashan).

Leicester C: Muggleton; Mauchlen, Gibson, Ramsey, Walsh, James, Wright (Reid), Hill, Oldfield, Mills, Kelly.

Newcastle U (0) 2 *(Quinn, Stimson)*

Derby Co (0) 0 19,748

Newcastle U: Burridge; Ranson, Stimson, Aitken, Anderson, Kristensen, Brock, Dillon, Quinn, Sloan, Watson.

Derby Co: Shilton; Sage, Pickering, Kavanagh, Wright, Forsyth, Ramage (Gee), Saunders, Harford, Francis (Davidson), Cross.

Norwich C (1) 2 *(Rosario, Fleck)*
Bristol C (1) 1 *(Allison)* 12,630
Norwich C: Gunn; Culverhouse, Bowen, Butterworth (Goss), Polston, Crook, Gordon, Fleck, Sherwood, Rosario, Phillips.
Bristol C: Leaning; Llewellyn (Bent), Bailey, May, Shelton, Aizlewood, Rennie, Newman, Allison, Taylor (Donowa), Smith.

Oldham Ath (1) 3 *(Redfearn 2 (2 pens), Adams)*
Brentford (1) 1 *(Holdsworth)* 12,478
Oldham Ath: Hallworth; Warhurst, Barlow, Henry (Donachie), Barrett, Jobson, Adams, Palmer, Currie, Redfearn, Holden.
Brentford: Benstead; Ratcliffe, Fleming, Millen, Evans, Buckle, Jones, Godfrey (Cockram), Holdsworth, Blissett, Gayle.

Port Vale (1) 2 *(Walker (pen), Beckford)*
Peterborough U (1) 1 *(Halsall)* 7490
Port Vale: Wood; Aspin, Webb, Walker, Parkin, Glover, Ford, Earle, Jepson, Beckford, Jeffers.
Peterborough U: Bradshaw; Luke, Crosby, Halsall, McElhinney, Butterworth, Sterling, Hine, Riley, Culpin, Watkins (Osborne).

Sheffield U (0) 1 *(Bradshaw)*
Luton T (0) 3 *(Farrell, Elstrup 2)* 13,897
Sheffield U: Tracey; Wilder, Lucas (Marwood), Jones, Barnes, Hill, Bryson, Gannon, Bradshaw, Deane, Hoyland.
Luton T: Chamberlain; James, Harvey, Pembridge, McDonough, Dreyer, Elstrup, Preece, Farrell, Beaumont, Black.

Shrewsbury T (1) 4 *(Brown, Kelly (pen), Shaw 2)*
Watford (0) 1 *(Falconer)* 5327
Shrewsbury T: Hughes; Worsley, Lynch, Kelly, Clements, Blake, Brown, Summerfield, Spink, Shaw, Heathcote.
Watford: James; Gibbs, Williams (Kennedy), Dublin, McLaughlin, Devonshire (Thomas), Ashby, Wilkinson, Penrice, Porter, Falconer.

Southampton (2) 3 *(Shearer, Le Tissier 2)*
Ipswich T (1) 2 *(Dozzell 2)* 15,101
Southampton: Flowers; Cherednik, Adams, Cockerill, Ruddock, Moore, Le Tissier, Horne, Shearer, McLoughlin, Wallace Rod.
Ipswich T: Forrest; Yallop, Thompson, Stockwell, Linighan, Palmer (Pennyfather), Lowe, Redford, Kiwomya, Dozzell, Milton.

Swansea C (0) 0
Rotherham U (0) 0 6478
Swansea C: Bracey; Hough (Davey), Coleman, Walker, Harris, Davies, Raynor, D'Auria, Gilligan, Connor, Legg.
Rotherham U: O'Hanlon; Forrest, Russell, Richardson, Johnson, Law, Goodwin, Dempsey, Mendonca, Thompson, Hazel.

WBA (1) 2 *(West, Bradley)*
Woking (0) 4 *(Buzaglo 3, Worsfold)* 14,516
WBA: Rees; Shakespeare, Harbey (Palmer), Roberts, Bradley, Strodder, Ford, West, Bannister, McNally, Robson.
Woking: Read; Mitchell, Cowler, Pratt, Baron, Wye S, Brown, Biggins, Franks (Worsfold), Buzaglo, Wye L.

Wolverhampton W (0) 0
Cambridge U (0) 1 *(Leadbitter)* 15,100
Wolverhampton W: Stowell; Roberts, Thompson, Bellamy, Stancliffe, Hindmarch, Steele, Bennett (Ashley), Bull, Paskin (Mutch), Dennison.
Cambridge U: Vaughan; Fensome, Kimble, Bailie (Leadbitter), Chapple, O'Shea, Cheetham, Wilkins, Dublin, Taylor, Philpott.

6 JAN

Barnsley (0) 1 *(Deehan)*
Leeds U (0) 1 *(Sterland)* 22,424
Barnsley: Baker; Banks, Taggart, Fleming, Smith (Deehan), Tiler, O'Connell, Rammell, Saville, Agnew, Archdeacon.
Leeds U: Lukic; Sterland, Snodin, Batty, Fairclough, McClelland, Strachan, Shutt (Pearson), Chapman, McAllister, Speed (Whitlow).

Burnley (0) 0
Manchester C (0) 1 *(Hendry)* 20,331
Burnley: Pearce; Measham, Deakin, Deary, Pender, Davis, White (Hamilton), Futcher, Francis, Jakub, Grewcock (Farrell).
Manchester C: Coton; Brightwell (Allen), Pointon, Reid, Hendry, Redmond, White, Clarke, Harper, Megson, Ward.

Crystal Palace (0) 0
Nottingham F (0) 0 15,396
Crystal Palace: Martyn; Humphrey, Shaw, Gray, Young, Thorn, Salako, Thomas, Bright, Wright, McGoldrick.
Nottingham F: Crossley; Laws, Pearce, Walker, Chettle, Keane, Starbuck, Parker, Clough, Gaynor (Wassall), Crosby.

7 JAN

Manchester U (1) 2 *(Hughes, McClair)*
QPR (1) 1 *(Maddix)* 35,065
Manchester U: Sealey; Irwin, Blackmore, Bruce, Webb, Pallister, Robson, Ince, McClair, Hughes, Sharpe.
QPR: Stejskal; Bardsley, Sansom (Ferdinand), Wilson, Channing (McCarthy), Maddix, Wilkins, Barker, Falco, Wegerle, Sinton.

THIRD ROUND REPLAYS
8 JAN

Liverpool (2) 3 *(Houghton, Rush, Staunton)*
Blackburn R (0) 0 34,175
Liverpool: Grobbelaar; Hysen, Molby, Nicol, Staunton, Gillespie, Rosenthal (McManaman), Houghton (Ablett), Rush, Barnes, McMahon.
Blackburn R: Mimms; Atkins, Duxbury (Johnrose), Reid, May, Moran, Gayle, Millar, Stapleton, Garner, Sellars.

9 JAN

Leeds U (2) 4 *(Smith (og), Chapman, McAllister, Strachan (pen))*

Barnsley (0) 0 19,773

Leeds U: Lukic; Sterland, Snodin, Batty, Fairclough, McClelland, Strachan, Shutt, Chapman (Pearson), McAllister, Speed (Whitlow).

Barnsley: Baker; Banks (Robinson), Taggart, Fleming, Smith (Deehan) Tiler, O'Connell, Rammell, Saville, Agnew, Archdeacon.

Wigan Ath (0) 0

Coventry C (1) 1 *(Gynn)* 7429

Wigan Ath: Pennock; Parkinson, Tankard, Atherton, Johnson, Langley, Woods, Rimmer, Fairclough (Patterson), Page, Griffiths (Carberry).

Coventry C: Ogrizovic; Borrows, Edwards (MacDonald), Billing, Kilcline, Peake, Gallacher (Drinkell), Gynn, Regis, Emerson, Smith.

Wimbledon (0) 1 *(Cork)*

Aston Villa (0) 0 *aet* 7384

Wimbledon: Segers; Joseph, Phelan, Barton, Blackwell, Scales, McGee (Cork), Kruszynski, Fashanu, Sanchez, Gibson.

Aston Villa: Spink; Price, Gray (Birch), Comyn, Nielsen, McGrath, Yorke, Platt, Cascarino, Cowans, Callaghan.

14 JAN

Plymouth Arg (1) 1 *(Marker (pen))*

Middlesbrough (1) 2 *(Baird, Kerr)* 6956

Plymouth Arg: Walter; Brown, Morgan, Marker, Burrows, Salman, Barlow, Hodges, Turner, Adcock, Morrison.

Middlesbrough: Pears; Parkinson, Phillips, Mowbray, Coleman, Putney, Slaven (Hendrie), Wark, Baird, Kerr, Ripley.

Swindon T (0) 1 *(Bodin)*

Leyton Orient (0) 1 *(Dickenson)* 8529

Match abandoned: frozen pitch, after 54 minutes

16 JAN

West Ham U (4) 6 *(Morley 2, Slater, Parris, Bishop, Quinn)*

Aldershot (1) 1 *(Randall)* 21,484

West Ham U: Miklosko; Breacker, Parris, Gale, Robson (Bishop), Hughton, Keen, Slater, Quinn, Potts, Morley.

Aldershot: Hucker; Brown, Cooper, Randall, Ogley, Flower, Burvill, Puckett (Whitlock), Williams, Henry, Stewart.

21 JAN

Nottingham F (0) 2 *(Wilson, Pearce)*

Crystal Palace (1) 2 *(Wright, Salako)* *aet* 23,301

Nottingham F: Crossley; Charles, Pearce, Walker, Chettle, Hodge, Crosby, Keane, Clough, Wilson (Starbuck), Parker.

Crystal Palace: Martyn; Humphrey, Shaw, Gray, Young, Thorn, Salako, Thomas, Bright, Wright, McGoldrick.

Rotherham U (0) 4 *(Dempsey, Mendonca 2, Goater)*

Swansea C (0) 0 4233

Rotherham U: O'Hanlon; Forrest, Russell, Thompson, Johnson, Robinson, Spooner, Dempsey, Goater (Evans), Mendonca, Hazel.

Swansea C: Bracey; Hough, Coleman, Walker, Harris, Davies, Raynor, Coughlin (D'Auria), Gilligan (Thornber), Connor, Legg.

Swindon T (0) 1 *(White)*

Leyton Orient (0) 0 7395

Swindon T: Digby; Kerslake, Bodin, Hazard, Lorenzo, Gittens, Jones, Shearer, White, McLaren, Foley.

Leyton Orient: Heald; Sitton, Howard, Pike, Whitbread (Zoricich), Dickenson, Carter, Castle, Nugent, Berry (Baker), Harvey.

FOURTH ROUND

26 JAN

Cambridge U (0) 2 *(Taylor 2)*

Middlesbrough (0) 0 9531

Cambridge U: Vaughan; Fensome, Kimble, Leadbitter, Chapple, O'Shea, Cheetham, Wilkins, Dublin, Taylor, Philpott (Dennis).

Middlesbrough: Poole; Parkinson, Phillips, Mowbray, Ripley, Putney, Hendrie, Wark, Baird, Mustoe, Walsh (Slaven).

Coventry C (0) 1 *(Kilcline)*

Southampton (0) 1 *(Shearer (pen))* 14,013

Coventry C: Ogrizovic; Borrows, McGrath, Billing, Kilcline, Emerson, MacDonald, Gynn, Regis, Smith, Drinkell.

Southampton: Flowers; Dodd, Adams, Case, Moore, Osman, Gotsmanov, Horne, Shearer, McLoughlin, Wallace Rod.

Crewe Alex (1) 1 *(Hignett)*

Rotherham U (0) 0 6057

Crewe Alex: Greygoose; Swain, McKearney, Smart, Carr, Lennon, Jasper, Hignett (Gardiner), Sussex, Doyle, Clayton.

Rotherham U: O'Hanlon; Forrest, Barnsley, Thompson, Johnson, Robinson, Goodwin, Dempsey, Goater (Evans), Mendonca, Hazel.

Liverpool (0) 2 *(Rush 2)*

Brighton & HA (0) 2 *(Small (pen), Byrne)* 32,670

Liverpool: Grobbelaar; Venison, Burrows, Nicol, Staunton, Ablett, Carter, Molby, Rush, Barnes, Rosenthal (Beardsley).

Brighton & HA: Digweed; Crumplin, Gatting, Wilkins, McCarthy, Chivers, Barham (Chapman), Wade (McGrath), Small, Byrne, Walker.

Luton T (0) 1 *(Black)*

West Ham U (1) 1 *(Parris)* 12,087

Luton T: Chamberlain; James, Harvey, Williams, McDonough, Dreyer, Elstrup, Preece (Rees), Farrell (Dowie), Pembridge, Black.

West Ham U: Miklosko; Breacker, Parris, Gale, Bishop, Hughton, Keen (McAvennie), Slater, Allen, Potts, Morley.

Manchester U (0) 1 *(Hughes)*

Bolton W (0) 0   43,293

Manchester U: Sealey; Irwin, Blackmore, Bruce, Phelan (Robins), Pallister, Robson, Webb, McClair, Hughes, Sharpe.

Bolton W: Felgate; Brown, Cowdrill, Comstive, Seagraves, Winstanley, Storer (Green), Thompson, Reeves, Philliskirk, Darby.

Millwall (2) 4 *(Stephenson, Rae 2, Sheringham)*

Sheffield W (2) 4 *(Hirst, Francis, Pearson, Palmer)*   13,663

Millwall: Horne; Stevens, Dawes, Waddock, Wood, McLeary, Stephenson, Goodman, Sheringham, Rae, O'Callaghan.

Sheffield W: Turner; Anderson, King, Palmer, Shirtliff, Pearson, Harkes, Sheridan, Hirst, Francis (Williams), Worthington.

Norwich C (0) 3 *(Gordon, Mortensen, Fleck)*

Swindon T (0) 1 *(White)*   14,408

Norwich C: Gunn; Culverhouse, Bowen, Butterworth, Polston, Crook, Gordon, Fleck, Sherwood, Smith (Mortensen), Phillips.

Swindon T: Digby; Kerslake, Bodin, Hazard, Lorenzo, Gittens, Jones, Shearer (Summerbee), White (Viveash), MacLaren, Foley.

Notts Co (1) 2 *(Turner, Short Craig)*

Oldham Ath (0) 0   14,002

Notts Co: Cherry; Palmer, Harding, Short Craig, Yates, O'Riordan, Thomas, Turner, Bartlett, Lund, Draper.

Oldham Ath: Hallworth; Warhurst (Adams), Barlow, Henry (Palmer), Barrett, Jobson, Kane, Ritchie, Marshall, Redfearn, Holden.

Portsmouth (1) 5 *(Clarke, Whittingham 4)*

Bournemouth (0) 1 *(Fereday)*   15,800

Portsmouth: Gosney; Neill, Beresford, Aspinall (Murray), Hogg, Stevens, Wigley, Kuhl, Clarke, Whittingham, Chamberlain.

Bournemouth: Peyton; Bond (Fereday), Morrell, Teale, Watson, O'Driscoll, Holmes, Pulis, Jones (Ekoku), Lawrence, Blissett.

Port Vale (1) 1 *(Beckford)*

Manchester C (1) 2 *(Quinn, Allen)*   19,132

Port Vale: Wood; Aspin, Platnauer, Walker, Parkin (Jepson), Glover, Ford (Porter), Earle, Mills, Beckford, Jeffels.

Manchester C: Coton; Brightwell, Pointon, Harper, Brennan, Redmond, White, Heath (Allen), Quinn, Megson, Ward.

Shrewsbury T (1) 1 *(Shaw)*

Wimbledon (0) 0   8269

Shrewsbury T: Hughes; Summerfield, Lynch, Kelly, Clements, Blake, Brown, Askew, Spink, Shaw, Heathcote.

Wimbledon: Segers; Joseph, Phelan, Barton, Blackwell, Curle, McGee (Bennett), Kruszynski (Sanchez), Cork, Scales, Gibson.

Tottenham H (2) 4 *(Mabbutt, Lineker, Gascoigne 2)*

Oxford U (1) 2 *(Foyle 2)*   31,665

Tottenham H: Thorstvedt; Fenwick, Van Den Hauwe, Nayim, Howells (Sedgley), Mabbutt, Stewart, Gascoigne, Walsh, Lineker, Allen.

Oxford U: Veysey; Robinson, Smart, Foyle, Foster, Melville, Magilton, Phillips, Durnin, Nogan (Stein), Simpson.

27 JAN

Arsenal (0) 0

Leeds U (0) 0   30,905

Arsenal: Seaman; Dixon, Winterburn, Thomas, Bould, Groves, O'Leary (Hillier), Davis, Smith, Merson, Limpar (Campbell).

Leeds U: Lukic; Sterland, Haddock, Batty, Fairclough, Whyte, Strachan, Shutt (Pearson), Chapman, McAllister, Speed.

Woking (0) 0

Everton (0) 1 *(Sheedy) at Everton*   34,724

Woking: Read; Mitchell, Cowler, Pratt, Baron, Wye S, Brown, Biggins, Franks (Mulvaney), Buzaglo, Wye L.

Everton: Southall; McDonald, Hinchcliffe, Ratcliffe, Watson, McCall, Nevin, Cottee (Beagrie), Sharp (Keown), Sheedy, Ebbrell.

THIRD ROUND SECOND REPLAY

28 JAN

Nottingham F (0) 3 *(Parker 2, Crosby)*

Crystal Palace (0) 0   22,164

Nottingham F: Crossley; Charles, Pearce, Walker, Chettle, Hodge, Crosby, Wilson, Clough (Gaynor), Keane (Starbuck), Parker.

Crystal Palace: Martyn; Humphrey, Shaw, Gray, Young, Pardew, Salako, Thomas, Bright, Wright, McGoldrick.

FOURTH ROUND REPLAYS

29 JAN

Southampton (1) 2 *(Case, Wallace Rod)*

Coventry C (0) 0   17,001

Southampton: Flowers; Dodd, Cook, Case, Moore, Osman, Gotsmanov, Horne, Shearer, McLoughlin, Wallace Rod.

Coventry C: Ogrizovic; Borrows, McGrath (Hurst), Billing, Kilcline, Emerson, MacDonald, Gynn (Clark), Regis, Thompson, Drinkell.

30 JAN

Brighton & HA (1) 2 *(Small, Byrne)*

Liverpool (1) 3 *(McMahon 2, Rush) aet*   14,392

Brighton & HA: Digweed; Crumplin, Gatting, Wilkins, McCarthy, Chivers, Barham, Byrne, Small, Codner, Walker (Chapman).

Liverpool: Grobbelaar; Venison, Burrows, Nicol, Whelan (Beardsley), Ablett, Carter (Molby), Staunton, Rush, Barnes, McMahon.

Leeds U (0) 1 *(Chapman)*

Arsenal (0) 1 *(Limpar) aet*   27,753

Leeds U: Lukic; Sterland (Snodin), Haddock, Batty, Fairclough, Whyte, Strachan, Pearson, Chapman, McAllister, Speed.

Arsenal: Seaman; Dixon, Winterburn, Thomas, Bould, Hillier, Linighan, Davis, Smith, Merson, Limpar.

Sheffield W (1) 2 *(Anderson, Hirst)*
Millwall (0) 0 25,140

Sheffield W: Turner; Anderson, King, Palmer, Shirtliff, Pearson, Harkes, Sheridan, Hirst, Francis (Williams), Worthington.

Millwall: Horne; Stevens, Dawes, Waddock, Wood, McLeary, Stephenson, Goodman, Sheringham, Rae, O'Callaghan.

West Ham U (1) 5 *(Parris, Bishop, McAvennie, Morley 2)*
Luton T (0) 0 25,659

West Ham U: Miklosko; Breacker, Parris, Gale, Bishop, Hughton, Keen, McAvennie, Slater, Potts, Morley.

Luton T: Chamberlain; James (Johnson), Harvey, Williams, McDonough, Dreyer, Elstrup (Farrell), Preece, Dowie, Pembridge, Black.

FOURTH ROUND
13 FEB

Newcastle U (2) 2 *(Quinn, McGhee)*
Nottingham F (0) 2 *(Pearce, Clough)* 29,231

Newcastle U: Burridge; Ranson, Stimson, Aitken, Anderson, Kristensen, Dillon, Brock, Quinn, McGhee, Watson (O'Brien).

Nottingham F: Crossley; Laws, Pearce, Walker, Chettle, Hodge, Crosby, Wilson, Clough, Keane, Parker.

FOURTH ROUND SECOND REPLAY
Arsenal (0) 0
Leeds U (0) 0 *aet* 30,433

Arsenal: Seaman; Dixon, Winterburn, Thomas, Bould, Groves (Campbell), O'Leary, Davis, Smith, Merson, Limpar (Linighan).

Leeds U: Lukic; Sterland, Haddock (Whitlow), Batty, Fairclough, Whyte, Strachan, Shutt (Davison), Chapman, McAllister, Speed.

FOURTH ROUND THIRD REPLAY
16 FEB

Leeds U (0) 1 *(Chapman)*
Arsenal (2) 2 *(Merson, Dixon)* 27,190

Leeds U: Lukic; Sterland, Whitlow, Batty, Fairclough, Whyte, Strachan, Shutt (Davison), Chapman, McAllister, Speed.

Arsenal: Seaman; Dixon, Winterburn, Thomas, Bould, Linighan, O'Leary, Davis, Smith, Merson, Campbell.

FIFTH ROUND

Cambridge U (1) 4 *(Dublin 2, Philpott, Taylor)*
Sheffield W (0) 0 9624

Cambridge U: Vaughan; Fensome, Kimble, Leadbitter, Chapple, O'Shea, Cheetham, Wilkins, Dublin, Taylor, Philpott.

Sheffield W: Turner; Anderson, King (Francis), Palmer, Shirtliff, Pearson, Wilson, Sheridan, Hirst, Williams (Harkes), Worthington.

Notts Co (0) 1 *(Lund)*
Manchester C (0) 0 18,979

Notts Co: Cherry; Palmer, Harding, Short Craig, Yates, O'Riordan, Paris, Turner, Bartlett, Lund, Draper (Short Chris).

Manchester C: Coton; Brightwell, Pointon, Harper (Heath), Hendry, Redmond, White, Allen, Quinn, Megson, Ward.

Portsmouth (1) 1 *(Chamberlain)*
Tottenham H (0) 2 *(Gascoigne 2)* 26,049

Portsmouth: Gosney; Neill, Beresford, Aspinall (Murray), Hogg, Russell, Wigley, Kuhl, Clarke, Whittingham, Chamberlain (Anderton).

Tottenham H: Thorstvedt; Edinburgh, Van Den Hauwe, Sedgley, Nayim, Mabbutt, Samways (Gray), Gascoigne, Thomas, Lineker, Allen.

West Ham U (0) 1 *(Quinn)*
Crewe Alex (0) 0 25,298

West Ham U: Miklosko; Breacker, Parris, Gale, Bishop, Hughton, Keen, McAvennie (Quinn), Slater, Potts, Morley.

Crewe Alex: Edwards P; Swain, McKearney, Smart, Carr, Lennon, Jasper (Murphy), Hignett (Edwards R), Sussex, Gardiner, Doyle.

17 FEB

Liverpool (0) 0
Everton (0) 0 38,323

Liverpool: Grobbelaar; Hysen, Burrows, Nicol, Molby, Ablett, Speedie (Beardsley), Staunton, Rush, Barnes, McMahon (Venison).

Everton: Southall; McDonald, Ebbrell, Ratcliffe, Watson, Keown, Atteveld, McCall, Sharp, Sheedy (Cottee), Nevin.

FOURTH ROUND REPLAY
18 FEB

Nottingham F (1) 3 *(Clough, Hodge, Parker)*
Newcastle U (0) 0 28,962

Nottingham F: Crossley; Laws, Pearce, Walker, Chettle, Hodge, Crosby, Wilson, Clough, Keane (Starbuck), Parker.

Newcastle U: Burridge; Ranson, Stimson, Aitken, Anderson (Scott), Kristensen, Dillon, Brock, Quinn, McGhee (O'Brien), Watson.

FIFTH ROUND

Norwich C (1) 2 *(Fleck, Gordon)*
Manchester U (1) 1 *(McClair)* 23,058

Norwich C: Gunn; Culverhouse, Bowen, Butterworth, Polston, Crook, Gordon, Fleck, Sherwood, Smith (Fox), Phillips.

Manchester U: Sealey; Irwin, Martin (Wallace), Bruce, Blackmore, Pallister, Robson, Ince, McClair, Hughes, Sharpe.

FIFTH ROUND REPLAY
20 FEB

Everton (0) 4 *(Sharp 2, Cottee 2)*
Liverpool (1) 4 *(Beardsley 2, Rush, Barnes) aet*
37,766

Everton: Southall; Atteveld (McCall), Hinchcliffe, Ratcliffe, Watson, Keown, Nevin (Cottee), McDonald, Sharp, Newell, Ebbrell.

Liverpool: Grobbelaar; Hysen, Burrows, Nicol, Molby, Ablett, Beardsley, Staunton, Rush, Barnes, Venison.

FIFTH ROUND
25 FEB

Southampton (1) 1 *(Ruddock)*
Nottingham F (0) 1 *(Hodge)*
18,512

Southampton: Flowers; Dodd, Benali, Cockerill, Moore, Ruddock, Le Tissier (Maddison), Horne, Rideout, McLoughlin, Wallace Rod.

Nottingham F: Crossley; Laws, Pearce, Walker, Chettle, Hodge (Jemson), Crosby, Wilson, Clough, Keane, Parker.

27 FEB

Shrewsbury T (0) 0
Arsenal (0) 1 *(Thomas)*
12,356

Shrewsbury T: Hughes; Blake, Lynch, Kelly, Heathcote, Clements, Brown, Summerfield (Shaw), Spink, Taylor, Worsley.

Arsenal: Seaman; Dixon, Winterburn, Thomas, Bould, Adams, O'Leary, Hillier, Smith, Merson (Rocastle), Campbell.

FIFTH ROUND REPLAYS
Everton (1) 1 *(Watson)*
Liverpool (0) 0
40,201

Everton: Southall; McDonald, Hinchcliffe, Ratcliffe, Watson, Keown, Atteveld (Nevin), McCall, Sharp, Newell, Ebbrell.

Liverpool: Grobbelaar; Hysen, Venison (Speedie), Nicol, Molby, Ablett, Beardsley, Houghton, Rush, Barnes, Staunton.

4 MAR

Nottingham F (1) 3 *(Jemson 3 (1 pen))*
Southampton (1) 1 *(Wallace Rod)*
26,633

Nottingham F: Crossley; Charles, Pearce, Walker, Chettle, Keane, Crosby, Wilson, Clough, Jemson, Parker.

Southampton: Flowers; Dodd, Benali, Case, Ruddock, Osman, Le Tissier, Horne, Rideout (Shearer), Cockerill, Wallace Rod.

SIXTH ROUND
9 MAR

Arsenal (1) 2 *(Campbell, Adams)*
Cambridge U (0) 1 *(Dublin)*
42,960

Arsenal: Seaman; Dixon, Winterburn, Thomas, Bould, Adams, O'Leary, Hillier (Davis), Smith, Merson, Campbell.

Cambridge U: Vaughan; Fensome, Kimble, Leadbitter, Chapple, O'Shea, Cheetham, Wilkins, Dublin, Taylor, Philpott.

Norwich C (0) 0
Nottingham F (0) 1 *(Keane)*
24,018

Norwich C: Gunn; Culverhouse, Bowen, Blades, Polston, Crook (Fox), Gordon, Fleck, Sherwood, Goss, Phillips.

Nottingham F: Crossley; Charles, Pearce, Walker, Chettle, Keane, Crosby, Wilson, Clough, Jemson, Parker.

10 MAR

Tottenham H (0) 2 *(Short Craig (og), Gascoigne)*
Notts Co (1) 1 *(O'Riordan)*
29,686

Tottenham H: Thorstvedt; Edinburgh, Van Den Hauwe, Sedgley, Nayim (Samways), Mabbutt, Stewart, Gascoigne, Thomas (Walsh), Lineker, Allen.

Notts Co: Cherry; Palmer, Harding, Short Craig, Yates, O'Riordan (Johnson), Thomas, Turner, Bartlett, Lund, Draper.

11 MAR

West Ham U (1) 2 *(Foster, Slater)*
Everton (0) 1 *(Watson)*
28,162

West Ham U: Miklosko; Breacker, Parris, Gale, Foster, Hughton, Bishop, McAvennie (Keen), Slater, Potts, Quinn.

Everton: Southall; McDonald (Cottee), Hinchcliffe, Ratcliffe, Watson, Keown, Nevin, McCall, Sharp, Milligan (Newell), Ebbrell.

SEMI-FINALS
14 APR

Arsenal (1) 1 *(Smith)*
Tottenham H (2) 3 *(Gascoigne, Lineker 2) at Wembley*
77,893

Arsenal: Seaman; Dixon, Winterburn, Thomas, Bould, Adams, Campbell, Davis, Smith, Merson, Limpar (Groves).

Tottenham H: Thorstvedt; Edinburgh, Van Den Hauwe, Sedgley, Howells, Mabbutt, Stewart, Gascoigne (Nayim), Samways (Walsh), Lineker, Allen.

Nottingham F (0) 4 *(Crosby, Keane, Pearce, Charles)*
West Ham U (0) 0 *at Villa Park*
40,041

Nottingham F: Crossley; Charles, Pearce, Walker, Chettle, Parker, Crosby, Keane, Clough (Laws), Glover, Woan.

West Ham U: Miklosko; Potts, Parris, Gale, Foster, Hughton, Bishop, Slater, Allen, Keen, Morley (Quinn).

FINAL at Wembley
18 MAY

Nottingham F (1) 1 *(Pearce)*
Tottenham H (0) 2 *(Stewart, Walker (og)) aet*
80,000

Nottingham F: Crossley; Charles, Pearce, Walker, Chettle, Keane, Crosby, Parker, Clough, Glover (Laws), Woan (Hodge).

Tottenham H: Thorstvedt; Edinburgh, Van Den Hauwe, Sedgley, Howells, Mabbutt, Stewart, Gascoigne (Nayim), Samways (Walsh), Lineker, Allen.
Referee: R. Milford (Bristol).

SCOTTISH FOOTBALL

SCOTTISH LEAGUE CLUB DIRECTORY
SCOTTISH LEAGUE/SKOL CUP
SCOTTISH FA CUP
SCOTTISH CENTENARY CUP

The Scottish Season 1990–91

Once again Scotland stands on the threshold of an international final. Thanks to some stirring performances, we have it in our hands to reach the European finals, but there are tough games ahead. Once again, our international team has done well, and it carries our best wishes for the final games.

In the European club competitions, it was not a successful season. We long for some further success. All four teams fell at the second ditch: the Dons scorned their chances and could have no complaints at losing. Rangers were properly seen off in Belgrade, and although they held on in a good home game, it was not enough; still, Red Star did not do too badly in the subsequent rounds. Dundee United were perhaps the most disappointing: they lost heavily at home, and this was very unlike them. The last of the quartet, Hearts, had a splendid home win against Bologna, but just failed to do enough in the return.

The end of the league season proved to be one of the most interesting, and much was left to the last day to decide. First, however, came the decision to do without relegation from the Premier Division, and to increase the size of it to twelve clubs for the next season. Without going into the rights and wrongs of forty-four league matches in a season together with all the various cup games, the one thing this mid-season decision did was to make a nonsense of the bottom end of the Premier Division.

With the pressure off there might have been some more good games, but there was not much to show for it; the lack of competitive edge inevitably led to a half season when teams were playing for pride – and there seemed little enough of that in some quarters. Even three up and one down would have been better for the one season, but that would never have been agreed to.

At the top of the Premier, the High Noon shoot-out at Ibrox was a magnificent finale, and Rangers won it. They had looked certain winners since Christmas, but Aberdeen had gradually whittled away the lead and it was to their excellent run of performances that this finale owed its tenseness and caused Rangers to pull out all the stops.

For Walter Smith, newly in the hot seat, it must have been a relief. He assumed the mantle when Graeme Souness elected to move south. Souness' contribution to Scottish football must not be underestimated for he gave a new impetus to the Premier and caused other clubs to have a searching look at themselves. Rangers, with their vast resources and superb facilities, have led the field in more ways than one.

It was a different picture for Celtic. Although in the end they managed to filch a place in Europe, the lack of overall success inevitably meant the removal of that great servant to the club and to Scotland, Billy McNeill. It was a pity that the manner of his departure was not handled in the most tactful way; nowadays that does not seem to matter much in business. His successor, Liam Brady, also has a top pedigree as a player, but is so far untried in management: we wish him luck. Scottish football is always the better for a strong challenge at the top of the league.

Falkirk and Airdrie move up to the Premier Division, and Dundee are left to rue important points lost to clubs at the foot of the table in mid-season. These three teams had a battle-royal for the top two places with Partick, Kilmarnock and Hamilton in a supporting role. It was not settled until the final day of the season, though Falkirk had booked their promotion place earlier in the last week; they finished as champions – a far cry from the terrible start to the league season. Jim Jefferies could be proud of his team's success.

The First Division did not confine its interest to the top end. There was a good fight at the lower end of the table to avoid relegation; it looked to be two from Brechin, Clyde and Forfar, though other teams could not breathe safely till the final days of the season. In the end Forfar managed to pull away confidently.

Stirling in the Second Division were run-away champions. At last they had a good start to a season, so that their usual mid-season charge left them well clear at the top. The second place, however, was in doubt until the last game: Montrose had edged up through the field to assume the all important second spot before the final game, and they made no mistake. They had been hotly pursued by Cowdenbeath, who had a fine run, and Stenhousemuir, always there or thereabouts. The early pace setters, East Fife, slipped gradually down the table and ended in tenth place.

In the early rounds of the Skol Cup, Stranraer beat Airdrieonians and Clyde dismissed St Johnstone, newly promoted to the Premier Division. But it was Queen of the South who hit the headlines: after disposing of Montrose in the first round, they beat Dundee at home, and then took the scalp of Dunfermline at East End Park before just losing to Celtic in the quarter-finals.

The semi-finals would have been the 'seeds' – if there had been seeding. The Old Firm took on the New Firm of Aberdeen and Dundee United, and on this occasion it was the Old Firm that won through to the final. There a Richard Gough goal in extra time saw Rangers take the trophy in a game which extended to extra time.

An innovation was the Centenary Cup. This was for the First and Second Divisions only, and proved a popular early-season addition to the calendar. Plenty of games went to extra time and penalties – Cowdenbeath reached the quarter-finals after a thrilling finish against Morton at Cappielow when the decisive penalty gave them an 8-7 win; after extra time the game had been goalless. Dundee beat Ayr United at Fir Park in the final, with the winning goal coming only five minutes before the end of extra time. It was a most successful competition, and well worth its scheduled repeat.

The Scottish Cup had its full quota of excitements: Highland League champions Ross County won away matches against Alloa and Queen of the South before succumbing against Meadowbank, while Inverness Thistle gave a good account of themselves in two games against East Fife. The Fifers nearly brought off the shock of the season in the next round against Dundee United when only a late goal deep into extra time gave United a replay, which itself went into extra time before the subsequent finalists won.

Their passage from there to the final was less stormy than Motherwell's. They had produced a minor shock by winning in the third round at Pittodrie; then they had a comfortable but none the less hard win against Falkirk before two games against Morton, which ended with Morton again losing on penalties. The semi-final was against Celtic who had already beaten Rangers. The first game was goalless, but in the replay Celtic were twice ahead before Motherwell caught them up early in the second half, and then delivered a one-two from which Celtic could not recover.

The final was an excellent family game, with plenty of excitement. United could well have been two ahead early on, but it was Motherwell who took the lead, and although the game went to extra time at three-all, it was Motherwell who took the trophy in the final minute. It was their first cup win since 1952, and a great boost for the town. Theirs was a fine all-round team display – but a mention has to be made of the inspirational performances of the ageless Davie Cooper.

For United there was again disappointment to add to that of losing in the last league game for a place in European competition. It was hard to bear, but they should take considerable satisfaction from a season in which their young team performed well overall and gained much in experience. Their turn must come soon.

Mark Hateley celebrates scoring the first of his two goals for Rangers against Aberdeen on the last day of the season which clinched the title for the Ibrox club. (Colorsport)

ABERDEEN   Premier Division

Year Formed: 1903. *Ground & Address:* Pittodrie Stadium, Pittodrie St, Aberdeen AB2 1QH. *Telephone:* 0224 632328.
Ground Capacity: total: 21,779. seated: All. *Size of Pitch:* 110yd × 72yd.
Chairman: Richard M. Donald. *Secretary:* Ian J. Taggart. *Commercial Manager:* Dave Johnston.
Managers: Alex Smith and Jocky Scott. *Assist. Manager:* Drew Jarvie. *Physio:* David Wylie. *Coach:* Teddy Scott.
Managers since 1975: Ally MacLeod; Billy McNeill; Alex Ferguson; Ian Porterfield; Alex Smith and Jocky Scott.
Club Nickname(s): The Dons. *Previous Grounds:* None.
Record Attendance: 45,061 v Hearts, Scottish Cup 4th rd; 13 Mar, 1954.
Record Transfer Fee received: £800,000 for Steve Archibald to Tottenham Hotspur (1980).
Record Transfer Fee paid: £650,000 for Hans Gillhaus from PSV Eindhoven, November 1989.
Record Victory: 13-0 v Peterhead, Scottish Cup; 9 Feb, 1923.
Record Defeat: 0-8 v Celtic, Division I; 30 Jan, 1965.

ABERDEEN 1990–91 LEAGUE RECORD

Match No.	Date	Venue	Opponents	Result	H/T Score	Lg. Pos.	Goalscorers	Atten- dance
1	Aug 25	H	Hibernian	W 2-0	1-0	—	Gillhaus, Connor	15,500
2	Sept 1	A	Celtic	W 3-0	0-0	1	Mason, Connor, Gillhaus	45,222
3	8	A	Dunfermline Ath	D 1-1	1-1	2	Robertson D	10,200
4	15	H	Dundee U	D 1-1	0-0	2	Bett (pen)	15,500
5	22	H	St Mirren	W 2-1	2-1	2	Irvine, Bett	12,500
6	29	A	St Johnstone	L 0-5	0-3	3		8711
7	Oct 6	H	Rangers	D 0-0	0-0	3		24,000
8	13	A	Motherwell	D 0-0	0-0	3		6602
9	20	H	Hearts	W 3-0	1-0	3	Bett, Grant, Gillhaus	14,800
10	27	A	Hibernian	D 1-1	0-1	2	Gillhaus	10,500
11	Nov 3	H	Celtic	W 3-0	2-0	2	Jess 2, Gillhaus	21,500
12	10	A	St Mirren	W 4-0	2-0	2	Grant, Robertson C, Jess, Gillhaus	7638
13	17	H	St Johnstone	D 0-0	0-0	2		16,000
14	24	A	Dundee U	W 3-2	2-2	1	Jess 3	12,344
15	Dec 1	H	Dunfermline Ath	W 3-2	1-1	2	Irvine, Gillhaus, Mason	12,000
16	8	A	Hearts	L 0-1	0-1	2		9811
17	15	H	Motherwell	D 1-1	1-1	2	Jess	9500
18	22	A	Rangers	D 2-2	0-0	2	Bett 2 (1 pen)	37,998
19	26	H	St Mirren	W 1-0	0-0	—	Jess	8755
20	Jan 1	A	Dundee U	L 0-1	0-1	—		19,000
21	5	A	Dunfermline Ath	W 4-1	2-1	2	Jess 4	7422
22	12	H	Hibernian	W 2-0	1-0	2	Cameron, Booth	13,500
23	19	A	Celtic	L 0-1	0-0	2		28,187
24	Feb 2	H	Hearts	W 5-0	3-0	2	Connor, Booth 2, Mason, Gillhaus	9500
25	13	A	St Johnstone	W 1-0	0-0	2	Booth	7046
26	Mar 2	H	Rangers	W 1-0	0-0	2	Gillhaus	22,500
27	5	A	Motherwell	W 2-0	1-0	—	Wright, Bett	5567
28	13	H	Dunfermline Ath	D 0-0	0-0	—		10,400
29	23	A	Dundee U	W 2-1	1-1	2	Van der Ark, Gillhaus	10,643
30	30	A	Hibernian	W 4-2	3-1	2	Gillhaus 3, Booth	7400
31	Apr 6	H	Celtic	W 1-0	1-0	2	Jess	22,500
32	13	A	Hearts	W 4-1	1-1	2	Gillhaus, McKimmie, Connor 2	16,771
33	20	A	Motherwell	W 3-0	1-0	2	Van der Ark 2, Connor	14,500
34	27	A	St Mirren	W 1-0	0-0	2	Bett	8513
35	May 4	H	St Johnstone	W 2-1	2-1	1	Van der Ark, Booth	18,000
36	11	A	Rangers	L 0-2	0-1	2		37,652

Final League Position: 2

GOALSCORERS
League: (62): Gillhaus 14, Jess 13, Bett 7 (2 pens), Booth 6, Connor 6, Van der Ark 4, Mason 3, Grant 2, Irvine 2, Cameron 1, McKimmie 1, Robertson C 1, Robertson D 1, Wright 1.
Scottish Cup: (0)
Skol Cup: (9): Mason 3, Bett 2 (1 pen), Van de Ven 2, Irvine 1, Jess 1

Most Capped Players: Alex McLeish, 76, Scotland.
Most League Appearances: 556: Willie Miller, 1973–90.
Most League Goals in Season (Individual): 38: Benny Yorston, Division I; 1929–30.
Most Goals Overall (Individual): 199: Joe Harper.

Honours
League Champions: Division I 1954–55. Premier Division 1979–80, 1983–84, 1984–85; *Runners-up:* Division I 1910–11, 1936–37, 1955–56, 1970–71, 1971–72. Premier Division 1977–78, 1980–81, 1981–82, 1988–89, 1989–90, 1990–91.
Scottish Cup Winners: 1947, 1970, 1982, 1983, 1984, 1986, 1990; *Runners-up:* 1937, 1953, 1954, 1959, 1967, 1978.
League Cup Winners: 1955–56, 1976–77, 1985–86, 1989–90; *Runners-up:* 1946–47, 1978–79, 1979–80, 1987–88, 1988–89.
Drybrough Cup Winners: 1971, 1980.
European: *European Cup* 12 matches (1980–81, 1984–85, 1985–86); *Cup Winners Cup Winners:* 1982–83. Semi-finals 1983–84. 35 matches (1967–68, 1970–71, 1978–79, 1982–83, 1983–84, 1986–87, 1990–91; *UEFA Cup* 32 matches (1968–69 *Fairs Cup;* 1971–72, 1972–73, 1973–74, 1977–78, 1979–80, 1981–82, 1987–88, 1988–89, 1989–90).
Club colours: Shirt, Shorts, Stockings: Red with white trim.

Snelders, T	McKimmie, S	Robertson, D	Grant, B	McLeish, A	Irvine, B	Van der Ven, P	Bett, J	Mason, P	Connor, R	Gillhaus, H	Watson Gregg	Jess, E	Booth, S	Wright, S	Robertson, C	Dibble, A	Cameron, I	Robertson, I	Watt, M	Van der Ark, W	Match No.
1	2	3	4	5	6	7	8*	9	10	11	12										1
1	2*	3	4	5	6	7	8	9	10	11	12										2
1	2	3	4	5	6	7	8	9	10	11											3
1	2	3	4	5	6	7*	8	9	10	11†12		14									4
1		3	4	5	6	7	8	9		11	2	10									5
1	2	3	4		6	7*	8	9	10	11†	5	14			12						6
1†	2		4	5	6	3	8	9	10	11	12	7*	14								7
	2	3	4	5	6	7	8	9	10	11						1					8
	2	3	4	5	6	7	8*	9	10	11†	12	14				1					9
	2	3	4	5	6	7*	8	9†10	11		14	12				1					10
	2	3	4	5	6	7	8	10*11		9						1	12				11
	2	3	4†		6*	7	8	10	11	9	5					1	14	12			12
	2	3		5	6	7	8	10	11*	9	4	12				1					13
	2	3		5	6	7	8	9	10	11	4*	12				1					14
	2	3		5	6	7	8	9*10	11		4	12				1					15
		3		5	6	7	8	9	10	11*	4†	2	14			1					16
1	2	3	4			7	8	9*10	11		6†14	12									17
1	2	3	4	5	6	7	8	9		11	10										18
1	2	3	4	5	6	7*	8	9		11†	10	14			12						19
1	2*	3	4	5	6	7	8	9		11†	10	14					12				20
1	2	3	4	5	6		8	9		11	10			7							21
1		3	4	5	6		8	9		11	10*12			2		7					22
1		3	4	5	6	7*	8	9		11	12			2	10						23
1		3	4	5	6	12	8*14	10	11	7		9†	2								24
1		3	4	5	6		8	9	10	11*12			7	2							25
1		3	4*	5	6	12	8	9†10	11		7	2							14		26
1		3	4	5	6	12	8	9†10	11		7*	2							14		27
1		3	4	5	6†		8	9*10	11	12	7		12	7	2				14		28
1		3	4	5	6	12	8	10	11	7†14		2								9*	29
1†	6	3	4	5*		12	8	10	11	14	7	2								9	30
	6	3	4	5	7†	8	10	11	9*14	2									1	12	31
	6	3	4	5	12	8	10	11†	7	14	2*								1	9	32
	6	3	4	5*	12	8	11†10	7	14	2									1	9	33
	6	3	4	5	12	8	10	11	7†14	2									1	9*	34
	6	3	4	5	12	8	10	11	14	7†	2								1	9*	35
	6	3	4	5	7*	8	10	11	9†14	2									1	12	36
21	26	35	32	33	29	23	36	25	29	35	2	20	8	16	2	5	3	—	10	6	
							+9s		+1s			+5s	+7s	+11s	+1s	+6s	+7s	+1s	+5s		

AIRDRIEONIANS   Premier Division

Year Formed: 1878. *Ground & Address:* Broomfield Park, Gartlea Rd, Airdrie ML6 9JL. *Telephone:* 0236 62067.
Ground Capacity: 10,250.   seated: 1350.   *Size of Pitch:* 112yd × 67yd.
Chairman and Secretary: George W. Peat CA. *Commercial Manager:* David McParland.
Manager: Alex MacDonald. *Assistant Manager:* Ian Bird. *Physio:* Harrison Stevenson. *Coach:* Joe Craig.
Managers since 1975: I. McMillan; J. Stewart; R. Watson; W. Munro; A. MacLeod; D. Whiteford; G. McQueen; J. Bone.
Club Nickname(s): The Diamonds or The Waysiders. *Previous Grounds:* Mavisbank.
Record Attendance: 24,000 v Hearts, Scottish Cup; 8 Mar, 1952.
Record Transfer Fee received: £200,000 for Sandy Clark to West Ham U, May 1982.
Record Transfer Fee paid: £175,000 for Owen Coyle from Clydebank, February 1990.

AIRDRIEONIANS 1990–91 LEAGUE RECORD

Match No.	Date	Venue	Opponents	Result	H/T Score	Lg. Pos.	Goalscorers	Atten- dance
1	Aug 25	H	Morton	W 4-0	1-0	—	Coyle 2 (1 pen), Harvey, Watson	1500
2	Sept 1	A	Kilmarnock	W 4-3	3-1	1	Coyle 3, Lawrence	5287
3	8	H	Brechin C	W 3-0	1-0	1	Harvey 3	2000
4	15	A	Forfar Ath	W 4-1	1-0	1	Coyle 3, Lawrence	1293
5	18	H	Meadowbank T	W 2-0	0-0	—	Coyle 2	1500
6	22	H	Ayr U	W 4-0	2-0	1	Harvey, Coyle 3	2700
7	29	A	Clyde	W 4-1	3-0	1	Coyle 4 (1 pen)	1700
8	Oct 6	A	Clydebank	D 2-2	0-0	1	Dawson, Lawrence	2500
9	9	A	Dundee	W 1-0	0-0	—	Lawrence	6360
10	13	A	Hamilton A	W 1-0	0-0	1	Lawrence	3516
11	20	H	Raith R	L 1-5	0-0	1	Lawrence	2500
12	27	H	Falkirk	L 1-3	0-3	1	Watson	5000
13	Nov 3	A	Partick T	D 1-1	0-1	1	Smith J	7225
14	10	H	Kilmarnock	W 2-0	0-0	1	McPhee, Balfour	4400
15	17	A	Morton	L 0-1	0-1	1		2449
16	24	H	Dundee	L 0-1	0-0	—		4718
17	Dec 1	A	Clydebank	L 2-5	2-2	4	Smith A, Lawrence	1610
18	8	H	Clyde	D 2-2	0-1	1	MacDonald J, Crainie	1300
19	15	A	Ayr U	D 2-2	1-0	3	MacDonald J, Lawrence (pen)	2439
20	22	A	Falkirk	D 1-1	1-1	3	Lawrence	6040
21	Jan 2	H	Hamilton A	W 2-1	0-1	—	Watson, Harvey	3200
22	5	A	Raith R	D 1-1	1-1	4	Harvey	2075
23	19	H	Forfar Ath	D 1-1	1-1	2	Harvey	2000
24	Feb 5	A	Brechin C	W 2-1	1-0	—	Coyle, Balfour	700
25	16	A	Brechin C	D 1-1	0-1	3	Smith A	850
26	Mar 2	H	Dundee	L 0-1	0-1	3		4000
27	9	A	Clydebank	W 3-1	1-0	3	Smith A, Lawrence (pen), Conn	1561
28	12	H	Partick T	D 0-0	0-0	—		5400
29	16	A	Kilmarnock	W 2-0	1-0	3	Lawrence, Harvey	5000
30	23	A	Hamilton A	D 1-1	1-0	3	Watson	2546
31	30	H	Falkirk	L 0-3	0-2	3		8200
32	Apr 3	A	Meadowbank T	W 4-2	2-1	—	Belfour, Harvey, Lawrence, Coyle	1200
33	6	A	Meadowbank T	W 1-0	1-0	2	Harvey	1063
34	13	A	Ayr U	W 1-0	0-0	2	Butler	3021
35	20	H	Clyde	D 1-1	0-1	3	Gray (pen)	2500
36	23	H	Morton	W 3-0	2-0	2	Balfour, Butler, Coyle	2100
37	27	H	Forfar Ath	W 2-1	0-0	2	MacDonald J, Balfour	2500
38	May 4	A	Partick T	W 2-0	0-0	1	Butler (pen), Lawrence	5500
39	11	A	Raith R	W 1-0	1-0	2	Balfour	4152

Final League Position: 2

GOALSCORERS

League: (69): Coyle 20 (2 pen), Lawrence 13 (1 Pen), Harvey 11, Balfour 6, Watson 4, Butler 3 (1 pen), MacDonald J 3, Smith A 3, Conn 1, Crainie 1, Dawson 1, Gray 1 (pen), McPhee 1, Smith J 1
Scottish Cup: (2): Jack 1, Watson 1
Skol Cup: (1): Belfour 1

Record Victory: 15-1 v Dundee Wanderers, Division II; 1 Dec, 1894.
Record Defeat; 1-11 v Hibernian, Division I; 24 Oct, 1959.
Most Capped Player; Jimmy Crapnell, 9, Scotland.
Most League Appearances; 523: Paul Jonquin, 1962-79.
Most League Goals in Season (Individual): 52, Hugh Baird, Division II, 1954-55.
Most Goals Overall (Individual): —.

Honours
League Champions: Division II 1902-03, 1954-55, 1973-74; *Runners-up:* Division I 1922-23, 1923-24, 1924-25, 1925-26.
First Division 1979-80, 1989-90, 1990-91. Division II 1900-01, 1946-47, 1949-50, 1965-66.
Scottish Cup Winners: 1924; *Runners-up:* 1975.   *Scottish Spring Cup Winners:* 1976.
League Cup:—.
Club colours: Shirt: White with Red diamond. Shorts: White. Stockings: Red.

Martin, J	Jack, P	McPhee, I	Watson, J	Walsh, R	Smith, A	Lawrence, A	Balfour, E	Harvey, G	Coyle, O	MacDonald, I	Conn, S	Stewart, A	Crainie, D	Hendry, A	Butler, J	Smith, J	Gray, S	Dawson, A	Boyle, J	McAdam, T	Kelly, J	Kirkwood, D	MacDonald, J	Dick, J	Scott, C	Match No.
1	2	3	4	5	6*	7	8	9	10	11†	12	14														1
1	2	3	4		12	7	8	5	9	10		6†	11*	14												2
1	2	3	4		8*	7	6	9	10	14	12	11†				5										3
1	2†	3	4		8*	7	6	9	10	14	12	11				5										4
1	2	3	4†			7	6*	9	10	14	12	11				5	8									5
1	4	3			12	7		9*	10	14	6	11†				5	8	2								6
1	4	3			12	7		9	10	14	6	2*	11			5	8†									7
1		3	4		8*	7	12	9	10		6	11†				5	14	2								8
1	11	3	4		8†	7		9	10		6	12				5	14	2*								9
1	8*	3	4		12	7		9	10	14	6	11†				5		2								10
1	2	3			12	8	9†		10	14	6	11	7		4	5*										11
1	11	3†	4		10	8				14	6	12		9*		5	7	2								12
1	12	3	4		14	7*	9†		10		8	11				5	2		6							13
1		3	4		12	7	9		10		8*	11				5	2		6							14
1	2	3	4		12	7	9*		14	10	8	11†				5			6							15
1		3	4†		14	8	9	11	10*		12					5	7	2	6							16
1	14	3			9	8	4	11	10							5†	7	2	6*	12						17
1	2	3			9	4			8		10†					5			6	7		11	14			18
1		3			14	8	9	6		2	10†					5		4		7*		11	12			19
1	2				10†	8	6	9*		3	12	14				5				7		11				20
1	10	3	4		12	8	6	9			2	14				5†				7		11*				21
1	6	3	4		5†	8		9			2	10								12		7*	11	14		22
1	6*	3	4†		12	8		9	14		2	10				5						7	11			23
1	11	3	4		8†	6	9*		10		2	12				5						7	14			24
	11	3	4		8	6	9†		10		12	2			7*	5							14		1	25
1	11	3	4		8	6		9	10		2					5	7									26
1	11	3	4	7	8	6	14	10†								5	2			12			9*			27
1	11	3	4†	7	8	6	9*	12								5	2			10			14			28
1	11	3	4	7	8	6	9†	12								5	10*	2					14			29
1	11	3	4	7	8*	6		10								5	2			12			9			30
1	11	3	4	7*	8	6	9	10								5	2			12						31
1	2	3	4		8	6	9*	14	10							5	7			12			11†			32
1	2	3	4		8	6	9	11	10*							5†	7			12			14			33
1	2	3	4		8	6	9†	11	10							5	7*			12			14			34
1	2	3	4*		8	6	9	11†	10							5	7			12			14			35
1	4	3			8	6†		10	12						9	5	7	2		14			11*			36
1	4	3*			8	6	14	10	12						9	5	7†	2					11			37
1	4	3*			8	6	14	10·	12	7					9	5		2					11†			38
1	4		12		8	6	11*	10	3	7†					9	5		2		14						39
38	33	36	29	1	17	38	32	24	24	3	18	18	19	2	9	28	13	9	6	9	1	11	10	—	1	
	+	+	+	+	+		+	+	+	+	+	+	+			+		+	+	+		+	+	+		
	2s	1s	1s	11s			1s	3s	4s	9s	3s	7s	9s			1s		2s	1s	5s		5s	4s	3s		

ALBION ROVERS Second Division

Year Formed: 1882.   *Ground & Address:* Cliftonhill Stadium, Main St, Coatbridge ML5 2RB.   *Telephone:* 0236 32350.
Ground Capacity: total: 3496. seated: 538.   *Size of Pitch:* 110yd × 70yd.
Chairman: Jack McGoogan.   *Secretary:* D. Forrester C.A.   *Commercial Manager:* Jacqueline Crawford.
Manager: David Provan.   *Assistant Manager:* Joe Baker.   *Physio:* Jim Maitland.   *Coach:* —.
Managers since 1975: G. Caldwell; S. Goodwin; H. Hood; J. Baker; D. Whiteford; M. Ferguson; W. Wilson; B. Rooney;
A. Ritchie; T. Gemmell; D. Provan.
Club Nickname(s): The Wee Rovers.   *Previous Grounds:* Cowheath Park, Meadow Park, Whifflet.
Record Attendance: 27,381 v Rangers, Scottish Cup 2nd rd; 8 Feb, 1936.
Record Transfer Fee received: £40,000 from Motherwell for Bruce Cleland.

ALBION ROVERS 1990–91 LEAGUE RECORD

Match No.	Date	Venue	Opponents	Result	H/T Score	Lg. Pos.	Goalscorers	Attendance
1	Aug 25	A	Alloa	L	0-1	0-0	—		450
2	Sept 1	H	Cowdenbeath	W	3-1	1-0	6	Cadden, Cougan 2	337
3	8	A	East Fife	D	2-2	2-1	8	Watson, McAnenay	716
4	15	H	Dumbarton	W	3-2	1-1	4	Lauchlan, McKeown, McAnenay	475
5	18	H	Stenhousemuir	L	1-4	1-0	—	Richardson	322
6	22	A	Stirling Albion	L	0-2	0-1	9		730
7	29	H	Stranraer	L	0-1	0-1	10		349
8	Oct 6	A	Berwick R	L	0-3	0-3	13		301
9	9	H	Arbroath	D	1-1	1-1	—	Callaghan	266
10	13	H	Queen's Park	W	1-0	0-0	11	Caven (og)	460
11	20	A	East Stirling	W	3-0	1-0	9	McAnenay 2, Richardson	201
12	27	H	Montrose	L	0-3	0-0	11		320
13	Nov 3	A	Queen of the S	D	1-1	1-1	11	Clark (pen)	569
14	10	A	Cowdenbeath	L	0-2	0-1	12		220
15	17	H	Alloa	W	3-1	1-0	11	McAnenay 2, Cadden	341
16	24	H	East Fife	L	0-2	0-2	11		400
17	Dec 1	A	Dumbarton	D	2-2	1-0	10	Stalker, Henderson	400
18	15	H	Montrose	L	0-5	0-3	11		400
19	22	H	Queen of the S	W	1-0	0-0	11	McAnenay	294
20	Jan 2	A	Queen's Park	D	1-1	0-1	—	Watson	640
21	5	H	East Stirling	W	4-0	4-0	8	Ferguson 2, McAnenay, Watson	220
22	12	A	Arbroath	D	0-0	0-0	9		539
23	19	H	Berwick R	D	1-1	0-0	8	Cadden	600
24	26	A	Stenhousemuir	L	0-2	0-1	8		500
25	Feb 9	A	Stranraer	L	1-2	1-0	12	Clark (pen)	300
26	13	A	Stirling Albion	L	0-3	0-1	—		650
27	16	A	Dumbarton	W	2-0	1-0	10	Cadden, Clark (pen)	500
28	23	H	East Fife	W	3-1	3-0	9	Stalker, McAnenay, Prior (og)	363
29	Mar 2	A	Cowdenbeath	D	2-2	0-1	10	Clark 2 (2 pens)	250
30	9	H	Arbroath	L	1-3	0-0	12	McAnenay	225
31	16	H	Stenhousemuir	D	0-0	0-0	11		258
32	23	H	Stirling Albion	D	2-2	2-2	11	Mitchell (og), Cadden	559
33	30	A	Queen's Park	D	0-0	0-0	11		567
34	Apr 6	H	Queen of the S	D	2-2	0-2	11	Richardson, Henderson	248
35	13	H	Stranraer	L	1-4	1-2	11	Clark (pen)	241
36	20	A	Montrose	L	0-3	0-0	11		480
37	27	H	Berwick R	W	4-2	3-1	11	Clark 2 (2 pens), McAnenay 2	222
38	May 4	A	Alloa	W	2-1	1-0	11	Stalker, Ferguson	386
39	11	A	East Stirling	D	1-1	0-0	11	Stalker	150

Final League Position: 11

GOALSCORERS
League: (48): McAnenay 12, Clark 8 (8 pens), Cadden 5, Stalker 4, Ferguson 3, Richardson 3, Watson 3, Cougan 2, Henderson 2, Callaghan 1, Lauchlan 1, McKeown 1, own goals 3.
Scottish Cup: (0).
Skol Cup: (0).
Centenary Cup: (1): Cougan 1.

Record Transfer Fee paid: £7,000 for Gerry M. Teague to Stirling Albion, September 1989.
Record Victory: 12-0 v Airdriehill, Scottish Cup; 3 Sept, 1887.
Record Defeat: 1-9 v Motherwell, Division I; 2 Jan, 1937.
Most Capped Player: Jock White, 1 (2), Scotland.
Most League Appearances: 399, Murdy Walls, 1921–36.
Most League Goals in Season (Individual): 41: Jim Renwick, Division II; 1932–33.
Most Goals Overall (Individual): 105: Bunty Weir, 1928–31.

Honours
League Champions: Division II 1933–34, Second Division 1988–89; Runners-up: Division II 1913–14, 1937–38, 1947–48.
Scottish Cup Runners-up: 1920.
League Cup:—.
Club colours: Shirt: Yellow with red trim. Shorts: Red with yellow stripes. Stockings: Yellow.

McCulloch, R	Watson, E	Millar, G	Edgar, D	McTeague, G	Clark, R	McAnenay, M	Cadden, S	Henderson, J	McKeown, D	Lauchlan, G	Cougan, C	McDonald, D	Cormack, D	Richardson, A	McGuiness, B	Callaghan, W	McFadzen, J	Quinn, S	Smith, S	McKay, T	Kerr, B	Bettley, I	Cousin, J	Stalker, I	Ferguson, W	Green, J	Match No.
1	2	3	4†	5	6	7	8	9	10	11*	12	14															1
12	3	2*	5	6	7	4	11†	10	9	14				1	8												2
4	2	7	5	6	11*	8	9†	3	12	14				1	10												3
1	4	2	12	5	6	7	10	9*	3	11†	14			8													4
1	4†	2†	12	5	6	7	10	9	3	11	14			8													5
1		2	12	5	8	11	4	14	3*	9	7†			10	6												6
	2	4*	5	6	11	8	9†	10	14	12			1	7	3												7
1	4	3	8†	5	6	7	12			11*	14	9		10	2												8
1	4†			5	6	7	10		3	11	12	2		8	14	9*											9
1		2		5	6	11	4	14	3	7		8*		10	12	9†											10
1				5*	6	11	10	12	3	7†	4			8	2	9	14										11
1	4				6	7	10*	5	3		14	12		8	2	11	9†										12
1	4*	2	7		6†	11	8	5	3		9	12	14	10													13
1	2				6	11	4	8	3			10		5						7†	9	14					14
1	12	2			6	9†	4		10	11	7			5						8	14	3*					15
1	4	2			6	9	8	12	10	11	7			5								3*					16
1	4	2			6	11		14	10	9	7			5								3	8†				17
1	4	2	12		6	11†		9	10		7			5*							14	3	8				18
1	7	2	12		6	11		9	10		8			5									3*			4	19
1	4	3	12		6	7	9†	10*				14	2	5	8										11		20
1	4	3	12		6†	7	8	14	10	11*			2	5											9		21
1	4	3	12		6	7*	8		10	11			2	5											9		22
1	4	3	12		6	7	8	14	10	11			2†	5											9		23
1	4*	2			6	7	8	14	10	11				5									3†	12	9		24
1	4*	2			6	7	8	5	3					10										12	9	11	25
1	12	2			6	11	4	5	3					8†									10		9	7	26
1		2			6	11*	7	5	10				14	12									3	8	9	4†	27
1	12	2			6	9	8	5	10					7									3	11		4†	28
1		2			6	11*	8	5	10				4	12									3	14	9	7†	29
1	12	2			6	11	8	5	10					7†									3	14	9	4*	30
1		2			6	7†	8	5		11			14	10									3	12	9	4*	31
1	4	2			6	9	8	5		11				10									3			7	32
1	4				6	7	8	5		11			2	10									3	12	9*		33
1	4	2			6	9	8	5		11				10									3	12	7*		34
	12	2*		5	6	11	4†	9	3			14	1	10									8	7			35
1	10	2	4	5	6		12	9	3		7			7									8	11*			36
1		3	4	5	6	7	8*	14		11			2										10†	12	9		37
1	4	3	8	5	6	7		14		11			2										10*	12	9†		38
1	4	3†	8		6	7		5		11			2										14	10	9*	12	39
35	24	35	12	15	37	35	32	26	39	7	7	17	4	29	16	1	2	2	—	1	2	—	14	13	17	7	

Substitute appearances: 6s 9s 1s 1s 9s 3s 11s 5s 1s 4s 1s 3s 1s 6s 1s 3s

ALLOA Second Division

Year Formed: 1883. *Ground & Address:* Recreation Park, Clackmannan Rd, Alloa FK10 1RR. *Telephone:* 0259 722695.
Ground Capacity: total: 3100. seated: 180. *Size of Pitch:* 110yd × 75yd.
Chairman: Pat Lawlor. *Secretary:* E. G. Cameron. *Commercial Manager:* William McKie.
Manager: Hugh McCann. *Assistant Manager:* —. *Physio:* —. *Coach:* —.
Managers since 1975: H. Wilson; A Totten; W. Garner; J. Thomson; D. Sullivan; G. Abel; B. Little.
Club Nickname(s): The Wasps. *Previous Grounds:* None.
Record Attendance: 13,000 v Dunfermline Athletic, Scottish Cup 3rd rd replay; 26 Feb, 1939.
Record Transfer Fee received: £30,000 for Martin Nelson to Hamilton A (1988).
Record Transfer Fee paid: —.

ALLOA 1990–91 LEAGUE RECORD

Match No.	Date	Venue	Opponents	Result	H/T Score	Lg. Pos.	Goalscorers	Atten- dance
1	Aug 25	H	Albion R	W 1-0	0-0	—	Irvine	450
2	Sept 1	A	Berwick R	L 0-1	0-1	8		448
3	8	H	Queen of the S	W 4-1	1-1	3	Newbigging, Irvine 2, Ormond	544
4	15	A	Montrose	W 4-2	1-0	2	Irvine 2, Smith, Moffat	450
5	18	H	Arbroath	W 2-1	1-1	—	Newbigging, Moffat	434
6	22	A	Stranraer	L 0-2	0-0	4		670
7	29	H	Stirling Albion	L 0-1	0-1	6		1078
8	Oct 9	A	East Stirling	D 0-0	0-0	—		350
9	13	A	Stenhousemuir	L 0-1	0-1	7		660
10	20	H	Dumbarton	L 0-1	0-1	10		614
11	27	H	Queen's Park	D 1-1	0-1	10	Black	595
12	30	H	Cowdenbeath	L 1-2	1-0	—	Moffat	600
13	Nov 3	A	East Fife	D 2-2	0-2	10	Wilcox 2	761
14	10	H	Berwick R	W 5-0	5-0	9	Moffat, McCulloch, Grant, Irvine, McEntegart	469
15	17	A	Albion R	L 1-3	0-1	9	Irvine	341
16	24	A	Queen of the S	W 3-1	0-0	9	Black, Moffat 2	750
17	Dec 1	H	Montrose	W 1-0	0-0	7	Irvine	594
18	18	A	Queen's Park	L 0-1	0-0	—		400
19	Jan 22	H	Stenhousemuir	W 1-0	0-0	—	Smith	413
20	26	A	Dumbarton	D 0-0	0-0	9		550
21	29	A	Arbroath	D 1-1	0-0	—	Black	250
22	Feb 2	H	Stranraer	L 0-1	0-0	10		399
23	9	A	Stirling Albion	L 0-2	0-1	10		1100
24	19	H	Stenhousemuir	D 1-1	0-0	—	Gibson	354
25	23	A	East Stirling	W 6-1	3-0	10	Grant, Ramsay, McEntegart, Henry, Gibson, Irvine	260
26	26	H	East Stirling	L 0-1	0-1	—		305
27	Mar 2	H	Montrose	W 1-0	0-0	9	Newbigging (pen)	353
28	6	A	Cowdenbeath	D 1-1	0-1	—	Black	220
29	9	A	Queen of the S	D 0-0	0-0	9		476
30	12	H	East Fife	L 3-6	2-2	—	Newbigging, Grant, Irvine	458
31	16	H	Dumbarton	W 2-1	1-0	9	Ormond, Smith	385
32	23	A	Stranraer	D 0-0	0-0	9		350
33	30	A	Stirling Albion	W 2-1	0-1	8	Henry, Irvine	1450
34	Apr 6	A	Arbroath	D 2-2	1-1	8	Newbigging (pen), Henry	314
35	13	A	Queen's Park	L 1-3	1-0	9	McCallum	691
36	20	H	Berwick R	D 1-1	1-0	9	Gibson	306
37	27	A	East Fife	W 3-1	0-0	7	Ramsay, Moffat, Gibson	361
38	May 4	H	Albion R	L 1-2	0-1	9	Wilcox	386
39	11	A	Cowdenbeath	L 0-1	0-0	9		550

Final League Position: 9

GOALSCORERS

League: (51): Irvine 11, Moffat 7, Newbigging 5 (2 pens), Black 4, Gibson 4, Grant 3, Henry 3, Smith 3, Wilcox 3, McEntegart 2, Ormond 2, Ramsay 2, McCallum 1, McCulloch1 .
Scottish Cup: (2): Irvine 1, Newbigging 1 (pen).
Skol Cup: (0).
Centenary Cup: (6): Irvine 2, Moffat 2, McCallum 1, Wilcox 1.

Record Victory: 9-2 v Forfar Ath, Division II; 18 Mar, 1933.
Record Defeat: 0-10 v Dundee, Division II; 8 Mar, 1947: v Third Lanark, League Cup, 8 Aug, 1953.
Most Capped Player: Jock Hepburn, 1, Scotland.
Most League Appearances: —.
Most League Goals in Season (Individual): 49: William 'Wee' Crilley, Division II; 1921–22.
Most Goals Overall (Individual): —.

Honours

League Champions: Division II 1921–22; Runners-up: Division II 1938–39. Second Division 1976–77, 1981–82, 1984–85, 1988–89.
Scottish Cup:—.
League Cup:—.
Club colours: Shirt: Gold with black trim. Shorts: Black. Stockings: Gold.

Lowrie, R	Newbigging, W	Lee, R	Wilcox, D	McCulloch, K	McEntegart, T	Grant, A	Smith, M	Black, I	Irvine, J	Ormond, J	Ramsay, S	Lamont, P	Moffat, B	Thomson, J	McCallum, M	Lee, D	Fenie, M	Campbell, C	Henry, S	McAvoy, N	Butter, J	Gibson, J	Russell, G	Match No.
1	2	3	4	5	6	7	8*	9†	10	11	12	14												1
1	2	3	4	5	6†	7	8*	9	10	11	12	14												2
1	2	3	4	5	6	7	11	9*	10	12	8†	14												3
1	2	3	4	5*	6	7†	11	9	10	12	8	14												4
1	2	3	4	5	6	7	11	9†	10	12	8*	14												5
1	2	3	4	5	6	7†	11	10	14	8	12		9*											6
1	2	3	4	5	6	7†	11	9*	10	14	8	12												7
1	2	3	4†	5	6	7*	11	10	12	14	9	8												8
1	2	3		5	6	7*	11†	10	8	12	9	14	4											9
1	2	3	4	5		7	9†	10	12	11	14		6	8*										10
1	2		4	5	12		9		10		7		3	8	6	11*								11
1	2		4	5	7	10	11*		9				3	8	6	12								12
1	2	6	4	5†	7	10*	12	11	9				3	14	8									13
	2	3	4	5	11	7†	14	10*	12	8	9		6								1			14
	6	3	4	5	11*	7	14	10	12	8	9†		2								1			15
	6	3	4	5		7*	14	10†	12	11	9		2					8			1			16
			4	5	11	7*	14	10	12	8	9†		3	6						2	1			17
	2		4	5	11†	7*	12	10	14	8	9		6	3						3	1			18
	2		4	5		7*	11	10†	14	12	9		3	6							1	8		19
	2		4*	5	11	10	14	7	12	9†			3	6							1	8		20
	2			5	11	9	10	12	4	7*			3	6							1	8		21
1	2			5	11	9	10	7*	4	12			3	6								8		22
1	2			5	12	11	9†	10	4	14			3	6				7				8*		23
1	2		4	5		7*	10	12	8	9			3	6								11		24
1	2		4	5	6	7†	10*	9	12	8			3	14								11		25
1	2*		4	5	6	7†	10	9	12	8			3	14								11		26
1	2		4	5	6	7*	10	12	9	8			3									11		27
1	2†		4	5	6	7*	10	12	9	8			3	14								11		28
1	2		4	5	6	12	10	9†	7	8	14*		3									11		29
1	2	3	4	5	6	7*	11	10	14	12				9†								8		30
	2	6*	5	11	8		9	7					3					4	12		1	10		31
	2		4	5	8		10	9†	7	12			3*					6	14		1	11		32
	2		4	5	3	11		9†	7*	12								6	10		1	8	14	33
	2		4	5	3†	11		9	7*	14	12							6	10		1	8		34
	2		4†	5*	14		10	12	8				3	9				6	7		1	11		35
	2	3		5	12		10	8	7									6	9*	4	1	11		36
	2	3	4	5			10	8	7	9								6			1	11		37
	2	3	4	5			10	8	7*	9								6	12		1	11		38
	2	3	4	5			14	10†	8	7	9							6*	12		1	11		39
22	38	19	34	39	23	24	25	18	31	11	26	—	18	21	11	5	3	11	8	4	17	21	—	
			+2s	+3s		+8s	+6s	+16s	+5s	+2s	+11s	+2s	+2s					+8s	+1s			+1s		

ARBROATH   Second Division

Year Formed: 1878. *Ground & Address;* Gayfield Park, Arbroath DD11 1QB. *Telephone:* 0241 72157.
Ground Capacity; 7,000. seated: 896. *Size of Pitch:* 115yd × 71yd.
President: James King. *Secretary:* Ronald McLeish. *Commercial Manager:* David Kean.
Manager: Walter Borthwick. *Assistant Manager:* Jim Holmes. *Physio:* William Shearer. *Coach:* —.
Managers since 1975: A. Henderson; I. J. Stewart; G. Fleming; J. Bone; J Young.
Club Nickname(s): The Red Lichties. *Previous Grounds:* None.
Record Attendance: 13,510 v Rangers, Scottish Cup 3rd rd; 23 Feb, 1952.
Record Transfer Fee received: £50,000 for Mark McWalter to St Mirren (June 1987).
Record Transfer Fee paid: £20,000 for Douglas Robb from Montrose (1981).

ARBROATH 1990–91 LEAGUE RECORD

Match No.	Date	Venue	Opponents	Result	H/T Score	Lg. Pos.	Goalscorers	Atten- dance
1	Aug 25	H	Berwick R	W 4-2	1-1	—	Marshall, Carlin, Hamilton, Sorbie	439
2	Sept 1	A	Dumbarton	D 1-1	0-0	2	Sorbie	476
3	8	H	Stirling Albion	L 2-3	0-1	7	Hamilton, Powell	612
4	15	A	Stenhousemuir	L 0-2	0-0	9		499
5	18	A	Alloa	L 1-2	1-1	—	Sorbie	434
6	22	H	Cowdenbeath	L 1-2	0-0	12	Bennett	384
7	29	A	East Fife	L 0-2	0-1	13		680
8	Oct 6	H	East Stirling	W 3-0	2-0	10	Sorbie 2, Marshall	231
9	9	A	Albion R	D 1-1	1-1	—	Marshall	266
10	13	A	Montrose	L 0-3	0-1	12		550
11	20	H	Stranraer	W 3-0	1-0	12	Sorbie, Bennett 2	352
12	27	H	Queen of the S	D 1-1	1-0	12	Sorbie	304
13	Nov 3	A	Queen's Park	L 1-2	1-1	12	Sorbie	570
14	10	H	Dumbarton	W 2-1	0-1	11	Bennett 2	411
15	17	A	Berwick R	D 1-1	1-1	12	Bennett	397
16	24	A	Stirling Albion	L 1-3	1-1	12	Bulloch	680
17	Dec 1	H	Stenhousemuir	D 0-0	0-0	12		357
18	15	A	Queen of the S	L 0-1	0-0	12		542
19	22	H	Queen's Park	W 3-0	2-0	12	Morton, Bulloch 2	345
20	Jan 2	H	Montrose	L 0-1	0-0	—		779
21	12	H	Albion R	D 0-0	0-0	12		539
22	16	A	Stranraer	W 3-2	1-1	—	Mitchell, Bennett 2	300
23	19	A	East Stirling	D 1-1	1-1	10	Bennett	150
24	29	H	Alloa	D 1-1	0-0	—	Mitchell	250
25	Feb 2	A	Cowdenbeath	W 1-0	1-0	9	Morton	300
26	9	H	East Fife	D 1-1	0-0	9	Morton	454
27	16	A	Queen's Park	D 0-0	0-0	9		618
28	23	H	Berwick R	L 0-1	0-0	11		333
29	Mar 2	H	Stirling Albion	L 0-1	0-0	12		531
30	9	A	Albion R	W 3-1	0-0	11	Sorbie, Roberts, Morton	225
31	16	H	East Stirling	L 0-1	0-0	12		272
32	23	A	Montrose	L 0-1	0-0	12		400
33	30	H	Stenhousemuir	L 0-2	0-0	12		351
34	Apr 6	A	Alloa	D 2-2	1-1	12	Sorbie, Bulloch	314
35	13	A	Cowdenbeath	L 2-4	1-3	12	Bennett (pen), Morton	300
36	20	H	Dumbarton	L 0-1	0-1	13		257
37	27	A	Queen of the S	L 1-6	1-4	14	Holmes W	406
38	May 4	H	East Fife	L 0-1	0-0	14		264
39	11	A	Stranraer	L 1-5	0-1	14	Thomson B	241

Final League Position: 14

GOALSCORERS
League: (41): Bennett 10 (1 pen), Sorbie 10, Morton 5, Bulloch 4, Marshall 3, Hamilton 2, Mitchell 2, Carlin 1, Holmes W 1, Powell 1, Roberts 1, Thomson B 1.
Scottish Cup: (4): Bennett 1, Bulloch 1, Mitchell 1, Sorbie 1.
Skol Cup: (2): Mitchell 1, Morton 1 (pen).
Centenary Cup: (3): Bennett 1, Bulloch 1, Smith 1.

Record Victory: 36-0 v Bon Accord, Scottish Cup 1st rd; 12 Sept, 1885.
Record Defeat: 0-8 v Kilmarnock, Division II; 3 Jan, 1949.
Most Capped Player: Ned Doig, 2 (5), Scotland.
Most League Appearances: 445: Tom Cargill, 1966–81.
Most League Goals in Season (Individual): 45: Dave Easson, Division II; 1958–59.
Most Goals Overall (Individual): 120: Jimmy Jack; 1966–71.

Honours
League Champions Runners-up: Division II 1934–35, 1958–59, 1967–68, 1971–72.
Scottish Cup:—.
League Cup:—.
Club colours: Shirt: Maroon with white neck & cuffs. Shorts: White. Stockings: Maroon with white hoop tops.

Jackson, D	Mitchell, B	Oliver, M	Bennett, M	Carlin, G	Holmes, J	Hamilton, J	Smith, R	Marshall, J	Sorbie, S	Morton, J	Stewart, I	Gallagher, J	Dewar, G	Powell, D	Farnan, C	Tindall, K	Brand, R	Florence, S	Glennie, R	Gibson, I	Balfour, D	Holmes, W	Bulloch, S	Thompson, G	Kerr, G	Malone, G	Young, J	Campbell, I	Match No.
1	2	3	4	5	6	7	8†	9	10	11*12	14																		1
1	2	3	4	5	6	7	12	9*10			8	11																	2
1	2†	3	4	5	6	7	14		8		12	11*	9	10															3
1		3	4	5	6	7	9†		8			12	10*	2	11	14													4
1		6	10	4	9	2		11*	7				14	12				3	5	8†									5
	1	3	4		6	2			10		12			7			9	11*	5	8									6
1	2	4	8	3	6	7			10		11†14		9*			12	5												7
	6	4	5	2	7*14	9	10			8†11			12				3		1										8
1		6	4	5	2			9	10		8	11*		12			3			7									9
1		6	4	5	2			7	10			11*		12			3				14	9	8†						10
1	11	4	8	5	6	2			10						9		3			7									11
1	8	5	4		6	2				10				12			3			7*	9		11						12
1	14	5	11	4	6	2		12	9		7†						3			8	10*								13
1	2		4	5	6	12		8	9		11						3			7*10									14
	2		4	5	6	8		12	9		11						3			1	7*10								15
1	7		4	5	2	8†14		9			12						3			11*10		6							16
			4	5	6	12		7†	9		2					11	3*			1	14	10	8						17
	2		4	5	6		14		10		8	3				9†				1	7		11						18
	2		4	5	6	8			9	11	14	3								1	7	10†							19
	2		4	5	6	8*			9	11		3				12				1	7	10							20
	2		4	5	6	8			9	11	14	3				7†				1		10							21
	2		4	5	8	9								6			3	7*	1	12	10		11						22
	2		4	5	8	9	12		11	3				6†			14			1	7*10								23
	2		4	5	6	8	7		9	11						10*	3			1	12								24
			5	6	8	7		9	11					4			3			1		10							25
	2	8†	5*	6	12	7		9	11		14			4			3			1		10							26
	2	8†		6	4			9	11		14			5	12		3			1		10*		7					27
	12	8*		6	2	7		9	11†		4			5			3			1		10		14					28
	5			6	2	9†		8	7	11							12			1		10				3	4		29
	4			6	2			9	8	11				5						1	12	10†		14		3			30
	2	9†			6	4	12		8					5						1	11	10*		14		3			31
	11				6	2			10					5						1	12			7*		3			32
	2			6	14	12		8						5						1	7			9*		3†			33
1	2		4		6			11	10					5								12				3			34
1	2		4		6			11	10					5								9				3			35
	8			4	2			9	6					5						1	11					3			36
	4			6	2			10	7					5						1	11					3			37
	4	6*			2			9	7†								14			1	11	10				3			38
	4	6*			2			9	7											1	11	12				3			39
16	30	13	32	24	37	30	7	8	38	18	11	10	1	4	15	1	6	19	2	3	23	17	21	1	4	4	1	11	
	+		+	+	+				+	+	+				+		+	+			+	+				+			
	2s				4s	8s	2s				6s	5s	2s	4s			4s	3s			6s	2s			3s				

Roberts P—Match No. 30(7*) 31(7) 32(9) 33(10) 34(8) 35(8) 36(10) 37(9) 38(5) 39(5); Brown S—Match No. 32(4) 33(4) 34(7) 35(7) 36(7) 37(8) 38(8) 39(8); Thomson B—Match No. 32(8) 33(11) 34(9†) 38(12) 39(10).

AYR UNITED

First Division

Year Formed: 1910. *Ground & Address:* Somerset Park, Tryfield Place, Ayr KA8 9NB. *Telephone:* 0292 263435.
Ground Capacity: total: 15,870. seated: 1593. *Size of Pitch:* 111yd72yd.
Chairman: Robert A. Loudon. *Secretary:* David Quayle. *Commercial Manager:* Mike James.
Manager: George Burley. *Assistant Manager:* David Wells. *Physio:* Robert Pender. *Coach:* David Wells.
Managers since 1975: Alex Stuart; Ally MacLeod; Willie McLean; George Caldwell; Ally MacLeod.
Club Nickname(s): The Honest Men. *Previous Grounds:* None.
Record Attendance: 25,225 v Rangers, Division I; 13 Sept, 1969.
Record Transfer Fee received: £300,000 for Steven Nicol to Liverpool (Oct 1981).
Record Transfer Fee paid: £50,000 for Peter Weir from St Mirren, June 1990.
Record Victory: 11-1 v Dumbarton, League Cup; 13 Aug, 1952.

AYR UNITED 1990–91 LEAGUE RECORD

Match No.	Date		Venue	Opponents	Result	H/T Score	Lg. Pos.	Goalscorers	Atten- dance
1	Aug	25	H	Forfar Ath	D 1-1	0-1	—	Scott	1711
2	Sept	1	A	Hamilton A	D 0-0	0-0	9		1722
3		8	H	Meadowbank T	D 1-1	1-1	9	Bryce	2070
4		15	A	Brechin C	W 2-1	1-1	6	Bryce, Johnston	450
5		18	H	Partick T	L 0-1	0-1	—		2883
6		22	A	Airdrieonians	L 0-4	0-2	10		2700
7		29	H	Raith R	W 2-0	0-0	7	Bryce 2	1888
8	Oct	6	H	Dundee	L 2-4	0-1	9	Johnston, Bryce	2403
9		9	A	Falkirk	W 2-1	1-1	—	Johnston, Graham	2600
10		13	A	Kilmarnock	L 1-3	1-0	9	Bryce	9802
11		20	H	Clyde	W 4-1	1-0	9	McAllister, Bryce, Johnston, Walker	2047
12		27	H	Clydebank	D 1-1	0-1	9	Johnston	2258
13	Nov	3	A	Morton	L 1-2	1-0	10	Graham	2078
14		17	A	Forfar Ath	L 1-3	1-3	12	Johnston	726
15		20	H	Hamilton A	D 2-2	0-1	—	Walker, Weir (pen)	1900
16		24	H	Falkirk	D 1-1	1-0	11	Walker	3673
17	Dec	1	A	Dundee	L 0-1	0-0	11		3416
18		8	A	Raith R	L 0-3	0-2	11		1179
19		15	H	Airdrieonians	D 2-2	0-1	11	Graham, Bryce (pen)	2439
20		22	A	Clydebank	W 2-0	1-0	11	Graham, Johnston	1046
21		29	H	Morton	W 1-0	0-0	10	Hughes	2361
22	Jan	2	H	Kilmarnock	L 1-2	0-2	—	McAllister	9448
23		12	A	Meadowbank T	L 0-1	0-0	11		738
24		19	H	Brechin C	W 4-0	4-0	10	Fraser, Graham, Johnston 2	1778
25	Mar	2	H	Raith R	W 5-3	3-1	9	Fraser 4, Bryce	2386
26		5	A	Dundee	L 0-4	0-4	—		3385
27		9	A	Clyde	L 0-1	0-0	10		1000
28		23	A	Brechin C	D 2-2	0-1	11	Fraser, Bryce	400
29		26	H	Hamilton A	L 1-2	0-1	—	Fraser	2100
30		30	A	Partick T	D 0-0	0-0	11		3826
31	Apr	2	A	Clyde	D 2-2	1-1	—	Graham, Kennedy	1100
32		6	H	Clydebank	L 0-1	0-0	12		1777
33		10	H	Morton	D 1-1	0-0	—	Graham	1659
34		13	H	Airdrieonians	L 0-1	0-0	12		3021
35		20	A	Forfar Ath	D 1-1	1-0	12	Brazil (og)	715
36		23	A	Partick T	L 0-2	0-1	—		1450
37		27	H	Meadowbank T	W 2-0	2-0	11	Graham, Bryce (pen)	1860
38	May	8	A	Falkirk	L 1-4	0-2	—	McAllister	7116
39		11	H	Kilmarnock	W 1-0	1-0	12	Fraser	5884

Final League Position: 12

GOALSCORERS

League: (47): Bryce 11 (2 pens), Johnston 9, Fraser 8, Graham 8, McAllister 3, Walker 3, Hughes 1, Kennedy 1, Scott 1, Weir 1 (pen), own goal 1
Scottish Cup: (6): Bryce 2, Fraser 2, Graham 1, Weir 1
Skol Cup: (0)
Centenary Cup: (14): Graham 3, Walker 3, Bryce 2, Templeton 2, Johnston 1, Kennedy 1, McAllister 1, Smyth 1

Record Defeat: 0-9 in Division I v Rangers (1929); v Hearts (1931); v Third Lanark (1954).
Most Capped Player: Jim Nisbet, 3, Scotland.
Most League Appearances: 371: Ian McAllister, 1977–90.
Most League Goals in Season (Individual): 66: Jimmy Smith, 1927–28.
Most Goals Overall (Individual): —.

Honours
League Champions: Division II 1911–12, 1912–13, 1927–8, 1936–37, 1958–59, 1965–66. Second Division 1987–88;
Runners-up: Division II 1910–11, 1955–56, 1968–69.
Scottish Cup:—.
League Cup:—.
Club colours: Shirt: White with broad black chest panel and pinstripe. Shorts: Black. Stockings: White with black diamond tops.

Purdie, D	Kennedy, D	Love, J	McAllister, I	Gillespie, A	Brown, R	Scott, R	Walker, T	Graham, A	Bryce, T	Weir, P	Evans, S	Smyth, D	Templeton, H	Johnston, S	Furphy, W	Ross, B	Wilson, K	McCann, J	Willock, A	Hughes, J	Fraser, A	Cunningham, W	McIntyre, S	Burley, G	Shaw, G	Duncan, C	George, D	Match No.
1	2	3	4	5*	6	7	8	9	10	11	12																	1
1	2	3	5		4	7	9*	10	8	11	6		12															2
1	2	3	5		4†	7	14	9	8*	11	12		10	6														3
1	2	3	5				12	9	7*	11	6		10	8	4													4
1	2	3	5				12	9	7*	11	6		10	8	4													5
1	2	3	5				6	9†	7	11			10†	8	4	12		14										6
1	2	3		5			10	9	7	11	6			8						4								7
1	2	3		5			9	10	7	12	11	6		8						4								8
1	2	12		5				9	10*	7	11	3	6	8						4								9
1	2	6		5				9	10†	7	11	3	14	8*	4	12												10
1	2	4		5				9	10	7	11*	3	6	12	8													11
1	2	4		5				9	10†	7		3	6	11*	8			14	12									12
1	2	3*		5					10		11		7	8		6		4	9	12								13
1	2*	3	6†	5			12	10		11	7		9	8				4		14								14
1	2	3*	4	5				9	10		11	7	6	12	8													15
1	2			5				9	10	7*	11	3	6	12	8	4												16
	2†	14		5				9	10	7	11	3*	6	12	8	4						1						17
	3			5				9	10	7	11		6	12	8	4		2*				1						18
1				5			8	9	7		6	3	11	10				4						2				19
1				5				9	10	7	6		11	8	4			3						2				20
1				5			8	9	7		6		11	10	4			3						2				21
1		14		5			8†	9	7		6		11	10	4			3						2				22
1				5			12	9	8	11	6		10		4			3			7*			2				23
1		14		5				9	8	11*	6		12	10	4†			3			7			2				24
1		14	3	5				9	8	11	6			10†	4						7			2				25
1		3		5				9	8	11	6			10*	4						7			2	12			26
1	2	11		5				9	8		6			10	4			3*			7				12			27
	6	3	14	5				9	8	11					4						7			2	10†	1		28
10	6	3		5				9	8	11					4						7			2		1		29
	6	3	5*					9	8	11	12				4						7			2		1	10	30
	6	3		5			12	9	8	11					4						7*			2		1	10	31
5		3		5			12	9	8	11					4						7			2		1	10*	32
	2	3		5				9	8	11	6				4						7			10		1		33
	6	3					12		8†	11*		5			4						7		14	2	9	1	10	34
	6	3	4					9		11		5			4						7			2	8	1	10	35
	2	3	6	12				9		11		5		4*							7				8	1	10	36
	2	3	6					9*	8		7	5		4						12					10	1	11	37
1	2	3	6					9	8	11		5*		4							7			12			10	38
	6	3		5			11†	9	8		12				4								7*	2	14	1	10	39
26	30	27	17	27	3	3	18	38	34	28	26	16	11	24	24	3	—	6	2	7	16	2	4	12	5	11	9	
+2s	+1s	+3s	+1s	+8s			+1s	+4s	+8s									+1s	+1s	+1s	+2s	+3s		+1s	+4s			

BERWICK RANGERS Second Division

Year Formed: 1881. *Ground & Address:* Shielfield Park, Tweedmouth, Berwick-upon-Tweed TD15 2EF. *Telephone:* 0289 307424.
Ground Capacity: total: 5235. seated: 1475. *Size of Pitch:* 112yd × 76yd.
Chairman: G. M. Elliott. *Chief Executive:* Alan Bowes. *Secretary:* Mrs Carole Fletcher. *Commercial Manager:* —.
Manager: Ralph Callachan. *Assistant Manager:* J. McNamara. *Physio:* Gordon Roberts. *Coach:* R. Johnson, I Oliver.
Managers since 1975: H. Melrose; G. Haig; D. Smith; F. Connor; J. McSherry; E Tait; J. Thomson; J. Jefferies.
Club Nickname(s): The Borderers. *Previous Grounds:* Bull Stot Close, Pier Field, Meadow Field, Union Park, Old Shielfield.
Record Attendance: 13,365 v Rangers, Scottish Cup 1st rd; 28 Jan, 1967.

BERWICK RANGERS 1990–91 LEAGUE RECORD

Match No.	Date	Venue	Opponents	Result	H/T Score	Lg. Pos.	Goalscorers	Atten- dance
1	Aug 25	A	Arbroath	L	2-4	1-1	—	Sokoluk, Bickmore	439
2	Sept 1	H	Alloa	W	1-0	1-0	9	Sokoluk	448
3	8	H	Montrose	W	2-1	1-1	6	Tait, Bickmore	450
4	15	A	Queen of the S	L	0-2	0-2	8		763
5	18	H	Queen's Park	L	1-2	0-1	—	Sokoluk (pen)	443
6	22	A	East Stirling	W	4-0	1-0	7	Todd 3, Tait	230
7	29	H	Stenhousemuir	L	0-1	0-0	8		417
8	Oct 6	H	Albion R	W	3-0	3-0	6	Todd, Graham, Cass	301
9	10	A	Cowdenbeath	W	1-0	0-0	—	Todd	230
10	13	A	Stirling Albion	L	1-4	1-3	6	Sokoluk	650
11	20	H	East Fife	W	1-0	1-0	6	Tait	430
12	27	A	Dumbarton	D	1-1	1-1	5	Sokoluk	550
13	Nov 3	H	Stranraer	W	3-2	2-0	4	Neil, Sokoluk, Todd	381
14	10	A	Alloa	L	0-5	0-5	7		469
15	17	H	Arbroath	D	1-1	1-1	8	Thorpe	397
16	24	A	Montrose	W	2-1	0-0	6	Ainslie, Todd	400
17	Dec 1	H	Queen of the S	W	2-0	1-0	5	Todd, Graham	407
18	8	H	Stirling Albion	D	1-1	0-0	5	Sokoluk	550
19	15	A	Dumbarton	W	2-1	1-1	2	Ainslie, Todd	322
20	22	A	Stranraer	W	2-1	2-0	2	Todd 2	513
21	Jan 12	H	Cowdenbeath	L	0-1	0-0	3		489
22	19	A	Albion R	D	1-1	0-0	3	Todd	600
23	Feb 2	H	East Stirling	D	2-2	0-1	3	Thorpe 2	459
24	5	A	Queen's Park	L	1-2	0-0	—	Bickmore	506
25	19	A	East Fife	L	1-4	0-1	—	Tait	719
26	23	A	Arbroath	W	1-0	0-0	5	Thorpe	333
27	26	H	Queen of the S	D	3-3	2-3		Graham 2, Garner	466
28	Mar 2	A	Stranraer	L	1-4	1-2	6	Graham	350
29	5	A	Stenhousemuir	L	1-2	1-1	—	Todd	300
30	9	H	Cowdenbeath	D	1-1	1-0	5	Todd	355
31	16	H	Queen's Park	W	2-1	1-0	6	Locke, Graham	473
32	23	A	Dumbarton	L	0-2	0-1	7		620
33	30	H	East Stirling	W	2-0	0-0	7	Graham, Ross	489
34	Apr 6	A	Stenhousemuir	D	1-1	1-0	6	Ross	300
35	13	H	Montrose	L	0-1	0-1	7		442
36	20	A	Alloa	D	1-1	0-1	7	Ross	306
37	27	A	Albion R	L	2-4	1-3	8	Tait, Bickmore	222
38	May 4	H	Stirling Albion	D	0-0	0-0	8		436
39	11	A	East Fife	W	1-0	0-0	8	Thorpe	317

Final League Position: 8

GOALSCORERS

League: (51): Todd 14, Graham 7, Sokoluk 7 (1 pen), Tait 5, Thorpe 5, Bickmore 4, Ross 3, Ainslee 2, Cass 1, Garner 1, Locke 1, Neil 1.
Scottish Cup: (4):Bickmore 1, Garner 1, Graham 1 (pen), Todd 1.
Skol Cup: (3): Graham 2, Todd 1.
Centenary Cup: (0).

Record Transfer Fee received: —.
Record Transfer Fee paid: —.
Record Victory: 8-1 v Forfar Ath, Division II; 25 Dec, 1965; v Vale of Leithen, Scottish Cup; Dec, 1966.
Record Defeat: 1-9 v Hamilton A, First Division; 9 Aug, 1980.
Most Capped Player: —.
Most League Appearances: 435: Eric Tait, 1970–87.
Most League Goals in Season (Individual): 38: Ken Bowron, Division II; 1963–64.
Most Goals Overall (Individual): 115: Eric Tait, 1970–87.

Honours
League Champions: Second Division 1978–79.
Scottish Cup:—.
League Cup: Semi-final 1963–64.
Club colours: Shirt: Black and gold shadow pinstripe. Shorts: Black. Stockings: Black.

Neilson, D	Fraser, S	Holden, D	Smith, R	Marshall, B	Cass, M	Callachan, R	Sokoluk, J	Todd, K	Bickmore, S	Graham, T	Leitch, G	Thorpe, B	Tait, G	O'Donnell, J	Scally, D	Locke, S	Davidson, G	Neil, M	Kerr, N	Garner, W	Ainslie, G	McLaren, P	Ross, A	Match No.
1	2	3	4	5	6	7	8	9	10*	11	12													1
1	2	3	4	5*	6	7	8†	9	10	11		14	12											2
1	2	3	4	5	6	7†	8*			10	11	12	14	9										3
1	2	3	4	5	6	7		9	10*	11		8	12											4
1	2	3	4	5			8	6	9	11		10		7										5
1	14		4	5	6		12	8†		11		2	10	3	7*									6
1	14		4	5	6	12†	8	9		11		2	10	3	7*									7
1	12	3	4				8	9		11		2*	10	6	5	7								8
1	2	3	4				8	9		10		6	11	5	7									9
1	2	3	4	5			8	9		14	12	10†	6	11	7*									10
1		3	4			8*10	14	9		11†	12	5	6	7		2								11
1	12	3*	6			10†	8	9		11		5	4	7		2	14							12
1		3	6			14	8	9		11		5	4	7†		2	10							13
	14	6				7*	8	9		11	12	5	3		2	10†	1	4						14
1	12	3	6					9		11	10	8	4		2	7*		5						15
1	2					10	6	9		14	8		3		4	7†		5	11					16
1	2					10*	6	9	12	14	8		3		4	7		5	11†					17
1	2					6	9	10		8			3		4			5	11	7				18
1	2		14			6	9	12	10	8			3		4			5	11*	7†				19
1	2		7†			6	9	10	11	8			3		4			5		14				20
1	2	14	4†			6	9	10	11	7	8		3		5									21
1	2					6	9	12	14	8	10		3		4			5	11*	7†				22
1	2*		6			12	9	10	11	7	8		3		4			5						23
1		10	5			6	9	11	12	8	2		3		4*	7†				5		14		24
1	2	7	8*			6	9		11			10	3	12	4			5						25
1	2	7	12			6	11		10*	3	8		4					5						26
1	2	6*	12			9	11	10		8	3	7	4					5						27
1		3	8	10†	6	9	11*14	2	12		7		4					5						28
1	2	3	8	10	6	9	11		12	4	7*		5											29
1	2	12†	8	10	6*	9	11		14	3	7		4					5						30
1		5	7	8	12	11		6		3	14	4*	2						9†			10		31
1	14	5	6	8		11		7†		3	10*	4	2					12			9			32
1		4	5	8	6	9*	11		7	12	3		2							10				33
1	6*	5	11†	8	9	14	7	12	3		2	4							10					34
1	2	5		7	9	11*	8†	6	12	3	14		4						10					35
1	2	5	4†14	9	12	8	6	7	3	11*								10						36
1		5		9	8	11	4	7	3		6					2	10							37
1		5		9	8	11*14	4	7	3		6	12				2	10†							38
1		5*	8	14	9†11	12	7	3		6	4					2	10							39
38	22	12	24	16	19	18	28	34	11	30	12	20	18	33	15	4	25	9	1	19	6	6	9	
+	+	+			+	+		+	+	+	+	+		+			+			+	+	+		
6s	2s	2s			4s	6s		4s	6s	5s	5s	8s		3s			1s			1s	1s	2s		

BRECHIN CITY

Second Division

Year Formed: 1906. *Ground & Address:* Glebe Park, Trinity Rd, Brechin, Angus DD9 6BJ. *Telephone:* 03562 2856.
Ground Capacity: total: 3091. seated: 291. *Size of Pitch:* 110yd × 67yd.
Chairman: David H. Will. *Secretary:* George C. Johnston. *Commercial Manager:* —.
Manager: John Ritchie. *Assistant Manager:* Dick Campbell. *Physio:* Jack Sunter. *Coach:* Atholl Henderson.
Managers since 1975: Charlie Dunn; Ian Stewart; Doug Houston; Ian Fleming; John Ritchie.
Club Nickname(s): The City. *Previous Grounds:* Nursery Park.
Record Attendance: 8122 v Aberdeen, Scottish Cup 3rd rd; 3 Feb, 1973.
Record Transfer Fee received: £46,000 for Ken Eadie to Falkirk (1986).
Record Transfer Fee paid: £15,000 for Gerry Lesslie from Dundee U.

BRECHIN CITY 1990–91 LEAGUE RECORD

Match No.	Date	Venue	Opponents	Result	H/T Score	Lg. Pos.	Goalscorers	Attendance
1	Aug 25	H	Raith R	L 0-4	0-1	—		850
2	Sept 1	A	Partick T	D 3-3	2-1	11	Ritchie, Scott, Brown	1800
3	8	A	Airdrieonians	L 0-3	0-1	11		2000
4	15	H	Ayr U	L 1-2	1-1	13	Thomson S	450
5	22	H	Falkirk	L 0-2	0-0	13		1300
6	29	A	Hamilton A	L 1-2	1-1	14	Lees	1102
7	Oct 6	A	Kilmarnock	L 0-2	0-1	14		1299
8	9	A	Morton	D 3-3	1-2	—	Hill, Brown, Wardell	801
9	13	H	Forfar Ath	W 2-1	0-1	14	Brown, Ritchie	600
10	20	A	Meadowbank T	L 1-6	0-5	14	Lees	500
11	27	H	Dundee	L 1-3	1-2	14	Ritchie	2011
12	Nov 3	A	Clydebank	W 4-3	2-0	13	Pryde, Ritchie 2, Lees	637
13	10	H	Partick T	D 2-2	0-1	13	Ritchie, Scott	700
14	13	A	Clyde	D 1-1	1-0	—	Scott	300
15	17	A	Raith R	W 2-1	1-1	13	Ritchie, Lees	1461
16	24	H	Morton	L 0-1	0-1	13		400
17	Dec 1	A	Kilmarnock	L 1-2	1-1	13	Hill	3473
18	11	H	Hamilton A	L 0-1	0-0	—		800
19	15	A	Falkirk	L 0-3	0-2	13		3820
20	22	A	Dundee	W 2-1	0-1	13	Lees, Pryde	3172
21	Jan 5	H	Meadowbank T	L 1-3	1-1	13	Lees	500
22	19	A	Ayr U	L 0-4	0-4	13		1778
23	29	H	Clydebank	W 3-2	1-1	—	Thomson S, Ritchie 2	500
24	Feb 2	H	Clyde	L 0-2	0-0	13		455
25	5	H	Airdrieonians	L 1-2	0-1	—	Pryde	700
26	16	H	Airdrieonians	D 1-1	1-0	13	Thompson S	850
27	19	A	Raith R	L 0-1	0-1	—		1074
28	Mar 2	A	Hamilton A	D 2-2	1-1	13	Pryde, Ritchie	400
29	5	A	Forfar Ath	D 0-0	0-0	—		794
30	9	A	Dundee	W 1-0	1-0	12	Pryde	3051
31	16	A	Clydebank	L 0-1	0-0	12		860
32	23	H	Ayr U	D 2-2	1-0	14	Pryde, Ritchie	400
33	30	H	Clyde	W 2-0	1-0	13	Brown, Lennox	500
34	Apr 6	A	Falkirk	L 1-2	1-1	14	Ritchie	4079
35	13	A	Kilmarnock	D 2-2	0-1	14	Wardell, Ritchie	4543
36	20	H	Morton	L 1-3	0-1	14	Pryde	400
37	27	H	Partick T	L 1-2	0-1	14	Lennox	700
38	May 4	A	Meadowbank T	D 1-1	0-0	14	Paterson I A	200
39	11	A	Forfar Ath	L 1-4	1-1	14	Ritchie	618

Final League Position: 14

GOALSCORERS
League: (44): Ritchie 14, Pryde 7, Lees 6, Brown 4, Scott 3, Thomson S 3, Hill 2, Lennox 2, Wardell 2, Paterson IA 1
Scottish Cup: (0)
Skol Cup: (0)
Centenary Cup: (0)

Record Victory: 12-1 v Thornhill, Scottish Cup 1st rd; 28 Jan, 1926.
Record Defeat: 0-10 v Airdrieonians, Albion R and Cowdenbeath, all in Division II, 1937–38.
Most Capped Player: —.
Most League Appearances: 459: David Watt, 1975–89.
Most League Goals in Season (Individual): 26: W. McIntosh, Division II; 1959–60.
Most Goals Overall (Individual): —.

Honours
League Champions: Second Division 1982–83. C Division 1953–54. Second Division Champions 1989–90. *Runners-up:*—.
Scottish Cup:—.
League Cup:—.
Club colours: Shirt, Shorts, Stockings: Red with white trimmings.

Lawrie, D	Conway, F	Candlish, C	Brown, R	Brash, A	Hutt, G	Wardell, S	Hill, H	Ritchie, P	Sexton, P	Lees, G	Scott, D	Duncan, R	Paterson, IG	Thomson, N	Baillie, R	Thomson, S	Paterson, IA	Kenny, B	Dow, R	McKillop, A	Pryde, I	Smart, B	Lennox, G	Fisher, D	Match No.
1	2*	3	4	5	6	7†	8	9	10	11	12	14													1
1	3		4	5	8†		14	9	10	11*	2	12	6	7											2
1	3		4	5	8		14	9	10	11	2	12		7†	6*										3
1	2		4	5			8	9		12	3		6	11			10*								4
1			4	5	8	11*10	9†		14	3		2	6		7	12									5
1	4	3		5	12		8	9	10	11		2†		6		7									6
1	2	3	4	5			8	12	10†11	14		7*		6		9									7
1	2	8	4	5		7†	8	12	10	11			3	14	9*										8
1		2†	4		14	7*	8	12	10	11	6			3		9	5								9
1	2	3					8	14	10*11	12		6			7	9†	5	4							10
1		3	4		6*		12	9		11	10		8	2	7†				5	14					11
1	3		4			8*	9	10	7	6			12	2	14				5	11†					12
1	3		4			8*	9	10	7	6			12	2	14	5				11†					13
1	3		4			8	9	10*	7†	6			12	2	14				5	11					14
1			4			8	9	6	7	3			12	2	10				5	11*					15
1			4			8*	9	6	10	3			12	2	7				5	11					16
1			4			8	9	6	10	3			12	2*	7				5	11					17
			4			8	9	6	10	3				2	7				5	11	1				18
1	6†	4				8	9		10	3			12	2	7	14			5	11*					19
1	3	4				8	9		10	6			11†	2	7				5	12					20
1	3	4†				8	9*		10	6		14		2	7	12			5	11					21
1	14					8*10		3	11	6				2	7	9†	4		5	12					22
1	8	4					9	6	12	10		3		2	7				5	11*					23
1	8	12	4				9	10	14			3	6*	2	7				5	11†					24
1	8		4			10	9	3	12			6		2	7				5	11*					25
1	10	12	4			14	8	9	3*			6		2	7†				5	11					26
1	10		4			7	8	9	3			6		2		12			5	11*					27
1			4				14	9	3†	10		6		2	7				5	11		8			28
1			4			8				6		3		2	7	9			5	11		10			29
1			4			8	9			6		3		2	7	12			5	11*		10			30
1	14*		4			8	9			6		3		2	7	12			5	11†		10			31
1			4			8	9			10		3		2	7	12			5	11*		6			32
1			4			12	8	9		10†		3	14	2	7*				5	11		6			33
1			4			11	8	9				3	10	2	7				5			6			34
1			4			11*	8	9		10		3		2	7				5	12		6			35
1		4				11*	8	9		10		3		2	7				5	12		6			36
1		4					8*	9		10		3	12	2	7†14				5	11		6			37
1		4				7		9		10		3	2		12				5	11*		6	8		38
1		4				7	8†	9		10*		3	14	2		12			5	11		6			39
38	16	10	36	8	5	10	32	34	21	20	30	—	23	8	34	26	8	4	!	28	23	1	12	1	
+2s	+2s		+2s	+2s	+4s	+4s		+5s	+3s	+3s	+1s		+10s		+4s	+10s				+5s					

CELTIC

Premier Division

Year Formed: 1888. *Ground & Address:* Celtic Park, 95 Kerrydale St, Glasgow G40 3RE. *Telephone:* 041 554 2611.
Ground Capacity: total: 52,000. *Seated:* 9000. *Size of Pitch:* 115yd × 75yd.
Chairman: John C. McGinn. *Chief Executive:* Terry Cassidy. *Financial Consultant:* Peter Lawwell.
Secretary: Chris D. White, CA. *Commercial Manager:* Mike Ryan.
Manager: Liam Brady. *Assistant Manager:* Tommy Craig. Physio: Brian Scott. *Coach:* Bobby Lennox.
Managers since 1975; Jock Stein; Billy McNeill; David Hay; Billy McNeill.
Club Nickname(s): The Bhoys. *Previous Grounds:* None.
Record Attendance: 92,000 v Rangers, Division I; 1 Jan, 1938.
Record Transfer Fee received: £1,250,000 for Frank McAvennie to West Ham United (1989).
Record Transfer Fee paid: £725,000 for Frank McAvennie from West Ham United (1987).
Record Victory: 11-0 v Dundee, Division I; 26 Oct, 1895.
Record Defeat: 0-8 v Motherwell, Division I; 30 Apr, 1937.
Most Capped Player; Danny McGrain, 62, Scotland.
Most League Appearances: 486; Billy McNeill, 1957–75.

CELTIC 1990–91 LEAGUE RECORD

Match No.	Date		Venue	Opponents	Result	H/T Score	Lg. Pos.	Goalscorers	Atten- dance
1	Aug	25	A	Motherwell	L	0-2	0-0	—	17,652
2	Sept	1	H	Aberdeen	L	0-3	0-0	10		45,222
3		8	H	Hibernian	W	2-0	0-0	7	Miller, Dziekanowski	28,068
4		15	A	Rangers	D	1-1	0-0	8	Whyte	38,543
5		22	H	Hearts	W	3-0	1-0	5	Miller 2, Creaney	38,409
6		29	A	St Mirren	W	3-2	0-0	4	McStay, Creaney 2	20,097
7	Oct	6	H	St Johnstone	D	0-0	0-0	4		27,014
8		13	A	Dunfermline Ath	D	1-1	0-1	4	McStay	16,063
9		20	H	Dundee U	D	0-0	0-0	4		34,363
10	Nov	3	A	Aberdeen	L	0-3	0-2	5		21,500
11		6	H	Motherwell	W	2-1	2-0	—	Coyne 2	20,317
12		10	A	Hearts	L	0-1	0-1	5		19,189
13		17	H	St Mirren	W	4-1	1-0	4	Baillie, Miller, Creaney, Coyne	25,686
14		25	H	Rangers	L	1-2	1-1	—	Elliott	52,265
15	Dec	1	A	Hibernian	W	3-0	2-0	5	Coyne 2, Nicholas	16,219
16		8	A	Dundee U	L	1-3	0-1	5	Coyne	16,895
17		15	H	Dunfermline Ath	L	1-2	0-2	5	Nicholas	18,875
18		22	A	St Johnstone	L	2-3	0-2	5	Collins, Coyne	10,260
19		29	H	Hearts	D	1-1	1-0	5	Coyne	28,118
20	Jan	2	A	Rangers	L	0-2	0-1	—		38,398
21		5	H	Hibernian	D	1-1	0-1	5	Coyne	20,521
22		19	A	Aberdeen	W	1-0	0-0	5	Coyne	28,187
23		30	A	Motherwell	D	1-1	1-0	—	Dziekanowski	13,542
24	Feb	2	H	Dundee U	W	1-0	0-0	5	Coyne	26,172
25	Mar	2	H	St Johnstone	W	3-0	1-0	5	Coyne, Elliott, Miller	24,560
26		6	A	Dunfermline Ath	W	1-0	1-0	—	Creaney	12,458
27		9	A	Hibernian	W	2-0	0-0	4	Miller 2	11,500
28		12	A	St Mirren	W	2-0	1-0	—	Creaney 2	11,268
29		24	H	Rangers	W	3-0	1-0	—	Rogan, Miller, Coyne	52,000
30		30	H	Motherwell	L	1-2	1-1	4	Coyne	21,252
31	Apr	6	A	Aberdeen	L	0-1	0-1	4		22,500
32		13	A	Dundee U	L	1-2	0-1	4	Malpas (og)	12,603
33		20	H	Dunfermline Ath	W	5-1	1-0	4	Coyne 2, Nicholas 2, Whyte	14,268
34		27	A	Hearts	W	1-0	0-0	4	Nicholas	17,085
35	May	5	H	St Mirren	W	1-0	1-0	—	Coyne	17,200
36		11	A	St Johnstone	W	3-2	1-1	3	Nicholas, Galloway, Coyne (pen)	9486

Final League Position: 3

GOALSCORERS

League: (52): Coyne 18 (1 pen), Miller 8, Creaney 7, Nicholas 6, Dziekanowski 2, Elliott 2, McStay 2, Whyte 2, Baillie 1, Collins 1, Galloway 1, Rogan 1, own goal 1
Scottish Cup: (9): Creaney 2, Wdowczyk 2, Coyne 1, Miller 1, Rogan 1, own goals 2
Skol Cup: (10): Dziekanowski 4, Elliott 3, Creaney 1, McStay 1, Miller 1

Most League Goals in Season (Individual): 50: James McGrory, Division I; 1935–36.
Most Goals Overall (Individual): 397: James McGrory; 1922–39.

Honours

League Champions: (35 times) Division I 1892–93, 1893–94, 1895–96, 1897–98, 1904–05, 1905–06, 1906–07, 1907–08, 1908–09, 1909–10, 1913–14, 1914–15, 1915–16, 1916–17, 1918–19, 1921–22, 1925–26, 1935–36, 1937–38, 1953–54, 1965–66, 1966–67, 1967–68, 1968–69, 1969–70, 1970–71, 1971–72, 1972–73, 1973–74. Premier Division 1976–77, 1978–79, 1980–81, 1981–82, 1985–86, 1987–88; *Runners-up:* 21 times.
Scottish Cup Winners: (27 times) 1892, 1899, 1900, 1904, 1907, 1908, 1911, 1912, 1914, 1923, 1925, 1927, 1931, 1933, 1937, 1951, 1954, 1965, 1967, 1969, 1971, 1972, 1974, 1975, 1977, 1980, 1985, 1988, 1989; *Runners-up:* 16 times.
League Cup Winners: (9 times) 1956–57, 1957–58, 1965–66, 1966–67, 1967–68, 1968–69, 1969–70, 1974–75, 1982–83; *Runners-up:* 9 times.
European: *European Cup Winners:* 1966–67. 78 matches (1966–67 winners, 1967–68, 1968–69, 1969–70 runners-up, 1970–71, 1971–72 semi-finals, 1972–73, 1973–74 semi-finals, 1974–75, 1977–78, 1979–80, 1981–82, 1982–83, 1986–87, 1988–89); *Cup Winners Cup:* 35 matches (1963–64 semi-finals, 1965–66 semi-finals, 1975–76, 1980–81, 1984–85, 1985–86, 1989–90); *UEFA Cup:* 16 matches (1962–63, 1964–65 *Fairs Cup;* 1976–77, 1983–84, 1987–88).
Club colours: Shirt: Green and white hoops. Shorts: White. Stockings: White.

Bonner, P	Morris, C	Wdowczyk, D	Grant, P	Elliott, D	Whyte, D	Hayes, M	McStay, P	Dziekanowski, D	Walker, A	Collins, J	McLaughlin, P	Miller, J	Nicholas, C	Baillie, L	Fulton, S	McCarrison, D	Creaney, G	Rogan, A	Galloway, M	Hewitt, J	McNally, M	Coyne, T	Britton, G	Mathie, A	Match No.
1	2	3	4	5	6	7†	8	9	10*	11	12	14													1
1	2		4	5	6†	7	8	9	12	11	3	14	10*												2
1			2	5			8	9*	10	11	3	7†			4		6	12	14						3
1	2		4		6		8	9*	10	11		7	5					12	3						4
1			2	5	6		8	9	10†	11		7			4*		14	3	12						5
1			2	5	6		8	9*		11		7			4		10	3	12						6
1	2	8		5	6*			9		11		7			4		10	3	12						7
1	2	3					8	9		11		7*			4		10	6	12						8
1	12	3	2	5		14	8			11		7†			4*		10	6				9			9
1		3	2	5		12	8	9*		11		14			4†		10	6	7						10
1		3					8			11		7	5		4		10	6			2	9			11
1		3	2				8	12		11		7	5		4†		10*	6	14			9			12
1		3					8†	9		11		7*	5		4		10	6	14		2	12			13
1		3*		5	6		8	9		11		7†			4		10		12		2	14			14
1		3		5		12	8	9		11*					4		10	6			2	7			15
1		3	12	5		8		9		11			4*				10†	6			2	7	14		16
1		3	2	5	6		8			11		7*12			10			4				9			17
1	14	3†	2	5		8	12			11		9*	6		4		10					7			18
1	2	3	4	5		8	12			11		9†		14	6		10					7*			19
1	2		4	5	6		8	10*11		14		12			7†	3		9							20
1	2		4	5	6		8	11		12			10		7*	3		9							21
1	2			5	6		8	14	11			7		12	10†	3*		4	9						22
1	2	3		5	6		8	10	12	11		7*			4	9									23
1		3	4	5	6	12	8	10*		11		7						2	9						24
1	4			5	6		8	11				7			10*	3		2	9	12					25
1	4			5	6		8	11				7			10	3		2	9						26
1	4	12	5		6	14	8	11				7			10†	3		2*	9						27
1	2	5	4		6	7*	8	11	12						10	3			9						28
1	2			5	6		8	14	11*			7		12	10†	3		4	9						29
1	4		8	5	6			10†11				7*		12	3			2	9	14					30
1	2*	4	5	6		8	14	11				7			10	3		12	9†						31
1		3	4	5	6		8	11*				7†10			14	12		2	9						32
1	2	4*	5	6		8	11					7†10				3	12		9	14					33
1	12	3			6	8	11					7*10†	4		14	5		2	9						34
1		5	4	6		8	11					7 10†12	3		14			2*	9						35
1		3	4	6		8	11					7*10	5	11	12	8		2	9						36
36	16	23	26	27	24	3	30	11	6	35	6	24	12	8	19	—	22	25	3	1	17	24	—	2	
+3s	+1s	+1s		+4s			+4s	+5s				+1s	+6s	+2s	+1s	+2s	+1s	+9s	+2s	+3s	+3s	+2s	+2s	+2s	

CLYDE   Second Division

Year Formed: 1878.   *Ground & Address:* Douglas Park, Douglas Park Lane, Hamilton ML3 0DF.   *Telephone:* (Mon–
Fri: 041 248 7953), (Match Days Only): 0698 286103.
Ground Capacity: total: 9168. seated: 1595.   *Size of Pitch:* 110yd × 70yd.
Chairman: John F. McBeth F.R.I.C.S.   *Secretary:* John D. Taylor.   *Commercial Manager:* John Donnelly.
Manager: John Clark.   *Assistant Manager:* John Cushley.   *Physio:* J. Watson.   *Coach:* —.
Managers since 1975: S. Anderson; C. Brown; J. Clark.
Club Nickname(s): The Bully Wee.   *Previous Grounds:* None.
Record Attendance: 52,000 v Rangers, Division I; 21 Nov, 1908.
Record Transfer Fee received: £95,000 for Pat Nevin to Chelsea (July 1983).
Record Transfer Fee paid: £14,000 for Harry Hood from Sunderland (1966).

CLYDE 1990–91 LEAGUE RECORD

Match No.	Date	Venue	Opponents	Result	H/T Score	Lg. Pos.	Goalscorers	Attendance
1	Aug 25	H	Clydebank	L	0-1	0-1	—	400
2	Sept 1	A	Raith R	D	1-1	0-1	10	Gilmour	1410
3	8	H	Forfar Ath	D	1-1	0-1	10	Scott	400
4	15	A	Dundee	L	1-3	1-1	10	Gilmour	3518
5	22	A	Meadowbank T	W	2-0	2-0	11	Speirs, Scott	500
6	29	H	Airdrieonians	L	1-4	0-3	12	Gilmour (pen)	1700
7	Oct 6	H	Falkirk	L	1-3	1-0	12	Knox	1000
8	10	A	Hamilton A	L	0-1	0-0	—		1385
9	13	H	Partick T	L	2-4	2-2	13	Scott, Clark G (pen)	3324
10	20	A	Ayr U	L	1-4	0-1	13	McAulay	2047
11	27	H	Morton	L	1-3	1-3	13	McAulay	720
12	Nov 3	A	Kilmarnock	L	1-2	0-0	14	Mallan	3937
13	10	H	Raith R	L	1-2	0-0	14	Mallan	650
14	13	H	Brechin C	D	1-1	0-1	—	Scott	300
15	17	A	Clydebank	L	1-2	0-0	14	Gilmour (pen)	744
16	24	H	Hamilton A	L	0-2	0-1	14		900
17	Dec 1	A	Falkirk	L	0-2	0-0	14		2800
18	8	A	Airdrieonians	D	2-2	1-0	14	Reid, McCoy	1300
19	15	H	Meadowbank T	W	1-0	0-0	14	Mitchell	600
20	Feb 2	A	Brechin C	W	2-0	0-0	14	Mallan 2	455
21	23	A	Forfar Ath	W	3-1	0-0	14	Mallan, Clarke S, Clark G	660
22	26	H	Kilmarnock	D	1-1	0-1	—	McCoy	1000
23	Mar 2	A	Falkirk	L	0-1	0-0	14		3829
24	5	A	Morton	D	0-0	0-0	—		1043
25	9	H	Ayr U	W	1-0	0-0	14	McCoy	1000
26	12	H	Clydebank	W	3-1	1-1	—	Gilmour, Mallan, Clark G	750
27	16	A	Raith R	L	0-1	0-0	14		1013
28	23	A	Dundee	W	4-2	3-2	13	Gilmour, Mallan, Clark G 2	2000
29	26	A	Meadowbank T	D	1-1	0-1	—	Mallan	1100
30	30	A	Brechin C	L	0-2	0-1	14		500
31	Apr 2	H	Ayr U	D	2-2	1-1	—	Thompson, Wilson	1100
32	6	H	Forfar Ath	L	0-1	0-1	13		600
33	13	H	Partick T	W	2-1	0-0	13	Thompson, Tierney (og)	3000
34	16	A	Partick T	L	0-2	0-1	—		2757
35	20	A	Airdrieonians	D	1-1	1-0	13	Speirs	2500
36	27	H	Kilmarnock	W	2-1	1-1	13	Thompson, Scott	1700
37	30	H	Dundee	L	0-1	0-0	—		3100
38	May 4	A	Hamilton A	L	1-3	0-1	13	McCoy	1220
39	11	H	Morton	L	0-1	0-1	13		400

Final League Position: 13

GOALSCORERS

League: (41): Mallan 8, Gilmour 6 (2 pens), Clark G 5 (1 pen), Scott 5, McCoy 4, Thompson 3, McAulay 2, Speirs 2, Clarke S 1, Knox 1, Mitchell 1, Reid 1, Wilson 1, own goal 1.
Scottish Cup: (0).
Skol Cup: (2): Gilmour 1, Scott 1.
Centenary Cup: (8): Gilmour 3 (1 pen), Clarke S 2, Clark G 1, McAuley 1, Reid 1.

Record Victory: 11-1 v Cowdenbeath, Division II; 6 Oct, 1951.
Record Defeat: 0-11 v Dumbarton, Scottish Cup 4th rd, 22 Nov, 1879; v Rangers, Scottish Cup 4th rd, 13 Nov, 1880.
Most Capped Player: Tommy Ring, 12, Scotland.
Most League Appearances: 428: Brian Ahern.
Most League Goals in Season (Individual): 32: Bill Boyd, 1932–33.
Most Goals Overall (Individual): —.

Honours
League Champions: Division II 1904–05, 1951–52, 1956–57, 1961–62, 1972–73. Second Division 1977–78, 1981–82;
Runners-up: Division II 1903–04, 1905–06, 1925–26, 1963–64.
Scottish Cup Winners: 1939, 1955, 1958; *Runners-up:* 1910, 1912, 1949.
League Cup:—.
Club colours: Shirt: White with red and black trim. Shorts: Black. Stockings: White.

Ross, S	Gaughan, M	McVie, G	Reid, W	Speirs, C	McFarlane, B	Thompson, D	Mitchell, J	Scott, M	Clarke, S	Mallan, S	Gilmour, J	Clark, G	Halpin, J	Devlin, J	Knox, K	Nolan, M	McAulay, J	O'Hanlon, S	Brogan, M	O'Hara, F	Wilson, K	McCoy, G	Wylde, G	Match No.
1	2	3	4	5	6	7*	8	9†	10	11	12	14												1
1	2	3	4	5	6		8	9*	10	11	12	7												2
1	2†	3	4	5	6		8	12	10	11*	7	9	14											3
1	2†	3		5	6		8	12	10	11	7	9	4*	14										4
1	2			5	6		8	9	10	11	7	3	4											5
1	2			5	6		8	9†	10	11*14	7	3	4	12										6
1	2			5			8	14	10	12	11	9	6	3*	4	7†								7
	2		4	5	6		8	12	10	7*11	9	3						1						8
	2	3	4	5†	6		8	11	10	12	14	9*	7					1						9
14	6						8	9	10	11	7	5	4*	2†12				1	3					10
	6*	4	5				8	12	14	11	7†	2	10	9				1	3					11
14		4	5				8	9*	7	11	10	6	2	12				1	3†					12
		4	5	6			8	12	9	11	10*	2	7					1	3					13
14		4	5				8	12	9	11	6†	2	7*					1	3	10				14
	2	4	5	6			8	12	14	11	10	7*						1	3	9†				15
		4	5	6	7		8	9*	12	11		2						1	3	10				16
		4	5	6	7†	14	10	9	12	11*		2						1	3	8				17
1			4	5	6	11*	7	12	9			2							3		8	10		18
1			4	5	6	7*	8	14	9	12	11†	2							3			10		19
1		3	4	5	6		8	9	14	12	11*	2									7	10†		20
1		3	4	5	6		8	9	11	12	7	2										10*		21
1		3	4	5	6		8	9	11	7		2										10		22
1		3	4	5	6		8	11	9	2	12	7										10*		23
1		3	4	5	6		8*	11	10	9	2	7	12											24
1		3	4		6		9	11	7	10*	5	2									8	12		25
1		3	4		6		9	10	11*	7	5	2									8†12		14	26
1		3	4	5	6		9	10	11†	7*		2									8	12	14	27
1		3	4	5	6		9	10	11*	7		2									8	12		28
1		3	4		6		9	10	11*	7	5	2									8†12		14	29
1		3	4		6		9	10	11*	7†	5	2									8	12	14	30
1		3	4		6	11*	9	10	7	5		2									8	12		31
1		3	4	5	6	7†	12	11	9	10*		2	14								8			32
1		3*	4	5	6	7†		9	11			2	14								8	12	10	33
1		3	4	5	6	7		9*14	11			2									8†12		10	34
1		3	4	5	6	7		9	11			2	12								10*	8		35
1		3	4	5	6	7*	14	9	11			2									8	12	10†	36
1		3†	4	5	6	7	14	9	11			2									8*12		10	37
1	2	3	4	5	6	7	14	10*	9	11	12											8†		38
1		3	4	5	6	7	14	9	11†			2									12 10		8*	39
29	11	27	34	33	34	14+	22	8+	24+	30+	17+	36+	12	3	32	3	5	10	10+	2	19	7+	7+	
						3s		15s	5s	11s	1s	1s			1s	6s			1s			12s	5s	

CLYDEBANK

First Division

Year Formed: 1965. *Ground & Address:* Kilbowie Park, Arran Place, Clydebank G81 2PB. *Telephone:* 041 952 2887.
Ground Capacity: total: 9950. seated: All. *Size of Pitch:* 110yd × 68yd.
Chairman: C. A. Steedman. *Secretary:* I. C. Steedman. *Commercial Manager:* David Curwood.
Manager: J. S. Steedman. *Managing Director:* J. S. Steedman. *Assistant Manager:* —. *Physio:* John Jolly. *Coach:*
Jim Fallon.
Managers since 1975: William Munro; J. S. Steedman.
Club Nickname(s): The Bankies. *Previous Grounds:* None.
Record Attendance: 14,900 v Hibernian, Scottish Cup 1st rd; 10 Feb, 1965.
Record Transfer Fee received: £175,000 for Owen Coyle from Airdrieonians, February 1990.
Record Transfer Fee paid: £50,000 for Gerry McCabe from Clyde.

CLYDEBANK 1990–91 LEAGUE RECORD

Match No.	Date		Venue	Opponents	Result	H/T Score	Lg. Pos.	Goalscorers	Atten- dance
1	Aug	25	A	Clyde	W 1-0	1-0	—	Eadie (pen)	400
2	Sept	1	H	Falkirk	W 3-1	3-0	2	Eadie 2 (1 pen), Davies	2026
3		8	H	Dundee	L 1-3	1-0	6	Sermanni	1775
4		15	A	Partick T	W 1-0	0-0	5	Eadie	3932
5		18	H	Kilmarnock	L 1-3	1-3	—	Caffrey	2542
6		22	A	Raith R	L 0-2	0-1	6		1535
7		29	H	Meadowbank T	D 2-2	2-0	6	Eadie 2	712
8	Oct	6	A	Airdrieonians	D 2-2	0-0	7	Coyle, Eadie	2500
9		10	H	Forfar Ath	D 2-2	1-1	—	Eadie 2	575
10		13	A	Morton	L 0-2	0-0	8		1609
11		20	H	Hamilton A	W 3-1	1-0	8	Rowe, Kelly, Coyle	1108
12		27	A	Ayr U	D 1-1	1-0	8	Eadie	2258
13	Nov	3	H	Brechin C	L 3-4	0-2	9	Eadie, Rodger, Coyle (pen)	637
14		10	A	Falkirk	L 1-5	0-4	10	Rodger	3600
15		17	H	Clyde	W 2-1	0-0	9	Eadie, Harvey	744
16		24	A	Forfar Ath	W 3-0	1-0	8	Eadie, Kelly, Sermanni	606
17	Dec	1	H	Airdrieonians	W 5-2	2-2	8	Kelly 2, Eadie 2 (1 pen), Sermanni	1610
18		8	A	Meadowbank T	W 3-0	1-0	6	Kelly, Eadie, Sermanni	250
19		15	H	Raith R	D 1-1	1-0	6	Kelly	961
20		22	H	Ayr U	L 0-2	0-1	6		1046
21	Jan	2	H	Morton	L 2-4	2-1	—	Coyle, Kelly	1465
22		5	A	Hamilton A	L 0-2	0-0	9		1086
23		19	H	Partick T	L 2-3	1-1	9	Kelly, Wright (og)	1800
24		29	A	Brechin C	L 2-3	1-1	—	Henry, John Dickson	500
25	Feb	2	A	Kilmarnock	L 0-3	0-2	11		4169
26		5	A	Dundee	L 0-1	0-0	—		2793
27		23	H	Falkirk	D 2-2	1-1	—	Eadie 2	1777
28	Mar	9	H	Airdrieonians	L 1-3	0-1	11	Eadie (pen)	1561
29		12	A	Clyde	L 1-3	1-1	—	Kelly	750
30		16	H	Brechin C	W 1-0	0-0	10	Conway (og)	860
31		23	A	Forfar Ath	D 2-2	2-2	10	Eadie 2	260
32		30	H	Dundee	D 1-1	1-0	10	Rowe	1238
33	Apr	2	A	Morton	D 2-2	0-1	—	John Dickson, Eadie	1200
34		6	A	Ayr U	W 1-0	0-0	10	Eadie	1777
35		13	A	Meadowbank T	W 3-2	1-1	9	Eadie, John Dickson, Templeton	309
36		20	H	Kilmarnock	D 0-0	0-0	10		2205
37		27	H	Hamilton A	L 1-3	1-3	10	Young	767
38	May	4	A	Raith R	W 2-1	0-1	8	Mair, Eadie	875
39		11	A	Partick T	W 7-1	1-1	8	Harvey, John Dickson, Mair, Eadie 4	2106

Final League Position: 8

GOALSCORERS

League: (65): Eadie 29 (4 pens), Kelly 9, Coyle 4 (1 pen), John Dickson 4, Sermanni 4, Harvey 2, Mair 2, Rodger 2, Rowe 2, Caffrey 1, Davies 1, Henry 1, Templeton 1, Wright 1, Young 1, own goal 1
Scottish Cup: (0)
Skol Cup: (2): Eadie 1, Rowe 1
Centenary Cup: (1): Maher 1

Record Victory: 8-1 v Arbroath, First Division; 3 Jan, 1977.
Record Defeat: 1-9 v Gala Fairydean, Scottish Cup qual. rd; 15 Sept, 1965.
Most Capped Player: —.
Most League Appearances: 620: Jim Fallon; 1968–86.
Most League Goals in Season (Individual): 28: Blair Millar, First Division; 1978–79.
Most Goals Overall (Individual): 84, Blair Millar, 1977–83.

Honours
League Champions: Second Division 1975–76; *Runners-up:* First Division 1976–77, 1984–85.
Scottish Cup: Semi-finalists 1990.
League Cup:—.
Club colours: Shirt: White with red shoulders trimmed with black. Shorts: White. Stockings: Red with black tops.

Spence. W	Dickson, Joe	Rodger, J	Maher, J	Sweeney, S	Coyle, T	Harvey, P	Davies, J	Eadie, K	Rowe, G	Kelly, P	Smith, B	Dickson, John	Gallacher, J	Sermanni, P	Caffrey, H	Lansdowne, A	Traynor, J	Ferguson, W	Murdoch, S	Crawford, D	Lamont, P	Wright, B	Duncanson, J	Henry, J	Rossiter, B	Templeton, H	Mair, G	Young, D	Match No.
1	2	3	4	5	6	7	8*	9	10	11		12																	1
	2	3	4	5		7	8	9	10*14		12	11†	1	6															2
	2	3	4	5	12	7	8	9	10			11*	1	6															3
	2*	3	4	5	12	7	8	9	10			14	1	6	11†														4
		3	4	5	10†	7	8	9	2			14	1	6	11*12														5
		3	4	5		7†	8	9	10			12	1	6	11*14	2													6
		3	4	5	6	7	8	9	10†			12	1	14		2	11*												7
		3		5	6	7	8	9	2				1	10			11			4									8
		3	4	5	6	7	8	9				12	1	10		2	11*												9
12			4	5	6	7	8	9	3	11*			1	10		2													10
			4	5	12	7	8	6		11			1	10*14		2					3	9†							11
			4	5	6	7	8	9*	3	11			1	12	14	2						10†							12
12	3	4			6	7	8	9	5*11				1	14		2						10†							13
	2	6*	4			7	8	9	5	11			1	10		12				3									14
	2	3	4			7		9	5	11			1	10		12	8*					6							15
	2	3	4	5		7		9*		11			1	10			8	12				6							16
		3	4	5		7†		9	2	11			1	10			8*12			14		6							17
	2		4	5		7		9	3	11			1	10			8*12					6							18
	2			5		7		9	3	11†	4*14		1	10			8	12				6							19
	2			5		7*		9	3	11	12		1	10			8		4			6							20
	2*	3		5	10	7†		9	8	11	14		1					12	4			6							21
	2	3		5		7		9		11	4	8*	1	10				12				6							22
		3	4	5	10	7		9	2	11*			1					12				6	8						23
1			4	5		7		9	2	14		11				10*				3		6	12	8†					24
	2†	3	4	5	6*	7		9	10	11			1					8					12	14					25
1			4	5		7		9				12						11		8	3	6				10*	2		26
1			4	5		7		9				14					8	12		3	10†	6				2*11			27
1			4	5		7		9				14					8	12		3	10†	6				2*11			28
	2*	3	4	5	11†	7		9					1	10		14	8	12				6							29
1	2	3	4	5		7		9	10								8	12				6				11*			30
1	2*	3	4	5		7		9	8†					10		14		12				6				11			31
1	2	3		5		7		9	8	11	4							12				6				10*			32
1	2	3*		5				9	8		4			10		14	7†12					6				11			33
1	2	3		5		7		9	8		4			10								6				11			34
1	2	3		5		7		9			4			10			8*					6	12			11			35
1	2					7		9	8*		4			10				12		3		6					11	5	36
1	2					7†		9			4			10*				12		3		6	8	14			11	5	37
1		6*				7		9	2		4			10				12		3		6	8				11	5	38
1		3		5		7		9	8		4			12								6				10*11			39
15	20	26	29	33	12	36	14	38	29	17	10	13	24	19	3	14	9	3	3	9	5	21	5	2	3	7	7	3	

```
     +  +        +              +  +        +  +  +  +           +        +  +        +
     1s 1s       3s             3s 1s 13s  10s 3s 2s 12s        2s       2s 1s       2s
```

COWDENBEATH Second Division

Year Formed: 1881. *Ground & Address:* Central Park, Cowdenbeath KY4 9EY. *Telephone:* 0383 511205.
Ground Capacity: total: 4778. seated: 1072. *Size of Pitch:* 110yd × 70yd.
Chairman: Gordon McDougall. *Secretary:* J. Ronald Fairbairn. *Commercial Manager:* James Colvin.
Manager: John Brownlie. *Assistant Manager:* —. *Physio:* James Reekie. *Coach:* John Brownlie.
Managers since 1975: D. McLindon; F. Connor; P. Wilson; A Rolland; H. Wilson; W. McCulloch; J. Clark; J. Craig; R. Campbell; J. Blackley; J. Brownlie.
Club Nickname(s): Cowden. *Previous Grounds:* North End Park, Cowdenbeath.
Record Attendance: 25,586 v Rangers, League Cup quarter final; 21 Sept, 1949.
Record Transfer Fee received: —.
Record Transfer Fee paid: —.

COWDENBEATH 1990–91 LEAGUE RECORD

Match No.	Date		Venue Opponents	Result	H/T Score	Lg. Pos.	Goalscorers	Atten- dance
1	Aug 25	H	Stirling Albion	L 0-2	0-0	—		300
2	Sept 1	A	Albion R	L 1-3	0-1	14	Ross	337
3	8	A	Dumbarton	W 3-1	2-0	11	Malone 2, MacKenzie	500
4	15	A	Queen's Park	L 0-1	0-0	13		540
5	18	H	East Stirling	W 2-1	0-0	—	Wright, Hamill	100
6	22	A	Arbroath	W 2-1	0-0	8	Ross, Scott	384
7	29	H	Queen of the S	W 2-1	0-0	7	Ross, MacKenzie	250
8	Oct 10	A	Berwick R	L 0-1	0-0	—		230
9	13	A	East Fife	D 1-1	1-0	8	Wright	1160
10	20	H	Montrose	L 0-1	0-1	11		212
11	27	A	Stranraer	W 3-1	1-0	9	Buckley, Scott, Ross	700
12	30	A	Alloa	W 2-1	0-1	—	Duffy, Buckley	600
13	Nov 3	H	Stenhousemuir	D 3-3	1-1	6	Wright, Ross 2	245
14	10	H	Albion R	W 2-0	1-0	5	Scott, Ross	220
15	17	A	Stirling Albion	L 1-5	0-2	7	Buckley	650
16	24	H	Dumbarton	W 4-2	3-1	5	Buckley, Malone, Ross, Wright	230
17	Dec 1	H	Queen's Park	L 0-1	0-1	6		250
18	15	H	Stranraer	L 2-3	1-2	7	Malone, MacKenzie	200
19	22	A	Stenhousemuir	W 4-1	1-0	6	Robertson, MacKenzie 3	300
20	Jan 12	A	Berwick R	W 1-0	0-0	6	MacKenzie	489
21	29	A	East Stirling	W 3-1	1-1	—	Ross 2, Scott	200
22	Feb 2	H	Arbroath	L 0-1	0-0	6		300
23	5	A	Montrose	L 0-2	0-1	—		300
24	9	A	Queen of the S	W 4-2	2-0	6	Ross 2, Buckley, MacKenzie	379
25	16	A	Montrose	L 0-1	0-0	8		300
26	27	H	Dumbarton	L 1-3	0-1	—	Ross	150
27	Mar 2	H	Albion R	D 2-2	1-0	8	Syme, Malone (pen)	250
28	6	A	Alloa	D 1-1	1-0	8	Malone	220
29	9	A	Berwick R	D 1-1	0-1	8	Syme	355
30	16	H	Stranraer	W 2-0	1-0	8	Wright, MacKenzie	200
31	23	A	East Stirling	D 0-0	0-0	8		198
32	26	H	East Fife	W 2-0	1-0	—	MacKenzie 2	900
33	30	A	Queen of the S	D 2-2	1-2	5	Wright, Hamill	450
34	Apr 6	A	Queen's Park	W 2-1	0-0	4	MacKenzie, Wright	430
35	13	H	Arbroath	W 4-2	3-1	3	Irvine, Wright, Douglas, MacKenzie	300
36	20	A	East Fife	W 5-0	0-0	2	Malone, Robertson, MacKenzie 2, Wright	618
37	27	A	Stirling Albion	D 0-0	0-0	3		1060
38	May 4	H	Stenhousemuir	D 1-1	0-0	3	Malone (pen)	1000
39	11	H	Alloa	W 1-0	0-0	3	Hamill	550

Final League Position: 3

GOALSCORERS

League: (64): MacKenzie 15, Ross 13, Wright 9, Malone 8 (2 pens), Buckley 5, Hamill 3, Scott 3, Robertson 2, Syme 2, Douglas 1, Duffy 1, Irvine 1, own goal 1.
Scottish Cup: (4): MacKenzie 2, Buckley 1, Wright 1.
Skol Cup: (2): MacKenzie 1, Ross 1.
Centenary Cup: (3): Buckley 1, MacKenzie 1, Ross 1.

Record Victory: 12-0 v St Johnstone, Scottish Cup 1st rd; 21 Jan, 1928.
Record Defeat: 1-11 v Clyde, Division II; 6 Oct, 1951.
Most Capped Player: Jim Paterson, 3, Scotland.
Most League Appearances: —.
Most League Goals in Season (Individual): 40: Willie Devlin, Division II; 1925–26.
Most Goals Overall (Individual): —.

Honours
League Champions: Division II 1913–14, 1914–15, 1938–39; *Runners-up:* Division II 1921–22, 1923–24, 1969–70.
Scottish Cup:—.
League Cup:—.
Club colours: Shirt: Royal blue shadow vertical stripe with white chest band. Shorts: White with blue side stripe. Stockings: Royal blue.

Lamont, W	Watt, D	Robertson, A	McGovern, D	Douglas, H	Thomson, K	Wright, J	Malone, G	MacKenzie, A	Ross, A	Scott, C	Buckley, G	Smith, G	Archibald, E	Abercromby, W	Hamill, K	Dodds, J	Duffy, D	Bennett, W	Dewar, G	Irvine, N	Johnston, P	Paterson, C	Wilson, C	Syme, W	Houston, F	Thomson, C	Match No.
1	2	3	4	5†	6	7	8	9	10*	11	12	14															1
1	2	3	4		6	7*	8	9	10	11†			5	12	14												2
1	2	3	4	5			8	9*	10	11	12	14		7†	6												3
1	2	3	4	5	14		8	9	10†	11			12	7	6*												4
	2	3	4			7	8	9*	10	11			5	6	1	12											5
1	2	4	3	12			8	9	10	11			5	7*						6							6
1	2	12	4	3		7*	8	9	10	11		14	5	6†													7
1	2	12	6	3			8	9	10	11*	7		5						4								8
1	2	11	4	3†		7	8	9	10			14	5							6							9
1	2	3	4*			7	8	9	10	11			5	12						6							10
1	2	3	4	12			8	9	10	11*			5	7						6							11
1		3	4	14		7	8	9	10	11			5	6*	12			2†									12
1	2	3	6	4		7	8	9	10	11*			5†	12	14												13
1	2	3	4*	5	14	7	8	12	9	11	10†									6							14
1	2	3	4*	5		7†	8	14	9	11	10		12							6							15
1	2*	3				7	8	9	10	11			5	12				4		6							16
1		3	2			7	8	12	9	11*	10		5					4		6							17
1		3	14	4†		7	8	10	9	12			5					2	11*	6							18
1		3	4*	12		7	8	10	9				5		14			2	11†	6							19
1		3	4	14		7	10	9	8	12			5					2†	11*	6							20
1	2	3	4	14		7*	10	9	8	11			5					12		6†							21
1	2	3	4†	14		7*	10	9	8	11			5					12		6							22
1	6	4	5			7*	8	10†	9	11			14					2			3	12					23
1		3	4			7	10†	9	8	11			5	12	14			2		6*							24
1		3	4			7	10	9	8	11			5					2		6							25
1		3	4			7	10	9	8	11			5	12				2*		6							26
		3	4			7	14	12	9	11†			5	8				2		6			1	10*			27
		3	4			7	8	14	9	11*			5	12				2		6				10†	1		28
		3	4	5	2*	7	8	9		11			14	12						6				10†	1		29
		3	4	5	2*	7	8	9†		11			14	12						6				10		1	30
		3	4	5	2	7*	8	9		11				12						6				10		1	31
		3		5	2	7	8	9		11								4		6				10		1	32
1		3	4	5	2†	7*	8	9		11				12						6				10			33
1		3	4	5	2	7	8	9	14	11*				12						6				10†			34
1		3	4	5	2*	7	8†	9	10	11				12	14					6							35
1	2*	3	4	5		7	8	9	10	11†				12	14					6							36
1	2	3	4	5		7	8†		10*	11				12	14					6							37
1	2		4	5		7	8	9		11			3	12						6				10*			38
1	2		4	5	3*	7	8	9	10	11				12						6							39
32	21	34	33	19	17	31	35	28	28	35	20	—	23	3	8	1	—	19	3	23	1	—	1	9	2	3	

\+ \+ \+ \+ \+ \+ \+   \+ \+ \+ \+ \+   \+   \+   \+
2s 1s 3s 3s 3s 1s 5s   1s 10s 2s 6s 1s 14s   8s   1s   1s

DUMBARTON Second Division

Year Formed: 1872.   *Ground & Address:* Boghead Park, Miller St, Dumbarton G82 2JA.   *Telephone:* 0389 62569/67864.
Ground Capacity: total: 10,700.   seated: 700.   *Size of Pitch:* 110yd × 75yd.
Chairman: A. Hagen.   *Secretary:* Alistair Paton.   *Company Secretary:* Robert Dawson.   *Commercial Manager:* —.
Manager: Billy Lamont.   *Assistant Manager:* Billy Simpson.   *Physio:* Robert McCallum.   *Coach:* —.
Managers since 1975: A. Wright; D. Wilson; S. Fallon; W. Lamont; D. Wilson; D. Whiteford; A. Totten; M. Clougherty;
R. Auld; J. George.
Club Nickname(s): The Sons.   *Previous Grounds:* None.
Record Attendance: 18,000 v Raith Rovers, Scottish Cup; 2 Mar, 1957.
Record Transfer Fee received: £125,000 for Graeme Sharp to Everton (March 1982).
Record Transfer Fee paid: £50,000 for Charlie Gibson from Stirling Albion 1989.

DUMBARTON 1990–91 LEAGUE RECORD

Match No.	Date	Venue	Opponents	Result	H/T Score	Lg. Pos.	Goalscorers	Atten- dance
1	Aug 25	A	East Fife	L	1-2	0-0	—	McQuade	550
2	Sept 1	H	Arbroath	D	1-1	0-0	10	Morrison (pen)	476
3	8	H	Cowdenbeath	L	1-3	0-2	13	MacIver	500
4	15	A	Albion R	L	2-3	1-1	14	Gibson, Chapman	475
5	18	H	Stranraer	L	0-1	0-1	—		400
6	22	A	Stenhousemuir	D	1-1	1-1	14	Chapman	600
7	29	H	Queen's Park	W	1-0	0-0	12	McQuade	600
8	Oct 6	A	Stirling Albion	D	0-0	0-0	11		600
9	10	A	Queen of the S	W	2-1	2-0	—	Chapman 2	624
10	13	H	East Stirling	W	2-1	0-0	9	Morrison (pen), McQuade	250
11	20	A	Alloa	W	1-0	1-0	7	Morrison	614
12	27	H	Berwick R	D	1-1	1-1	8	McQuade	550
13	Nov 3	A	Montrose	W	2-1	2-1	7	McQuade 2	480
14	10	A	Arbroath	L	1-2	1-0	8	McQuade	411
15	17	H	East Fife	W	3-2	1-1	6	McQuade, Gibson, McGinley	500
16	24	A	Cowdenbeath	L	2-4	1-3	8	McGuire, Boyd	230
17	Dec 1	H	Albion R	D	2-2	0-1	9	Morrison, McQuade	400
18	15	A	Berwick R	L	1-2	1-1	9	Morrison (pen)	322
19	22	H	Montrose	D	1-1	0-0	8	Morrison	476
20	Jan 12	H	Queen of the S	L	0-2	0-2	10		600
21	19	A	Stirling Albion	L	0-2	0-0	11		650
22	22	A	East Stirling	L	1-2	0-2	—	Morrison	214
23	26	H	Alloa	D	0-0	0-0	12		550
24	30	A	Stranraer	L	1-2	1-2	—	McQuade	420
25	Feb 2	H	Stenhousemuir	D	0-0	0-0	12		450
26	9	A	Queen's Park	D	1-1	0-1	11	MacIver	849
27	16	H	Albion R	L	0-2	0-1	12		500
28	27	A	Cowdenbeath	W	3-1	1-0	—	Edgar 2, McQuade	150
29	Mar 2	H	East Fife	W	2-1	1-1	11	MacIver, Meechan	500
30	9	A	Stirling Albion	W	1-0	0-0	10	McQuade	900
31	16	A	Alloa	L	1-2	0-1	10	Martin	385
32	23	H	Berwick R	W	2-0	1-0	10	MacIver, Boyd	620
33	30	H	Montrose	D	2-2	0-0	10	Dempsey, Morrison	600
34	Apr 10	A	Stranraer	W	4-1	1-0	—	Gibson, McQuade, MacIver 2	300
35	13	H	Stenhousemuir	W	2-1	2-1	10	Meechan, Gibson	600
36	20	A	Arbroath	W	1-0	1-0	8	Boyd (pen)	257
37	27	A	East Stirling	L	0-2	0-1	9		254
38	May 4	H	Queen of the S	W	2-0	1-0	6	McQuade, McNair (pen)	700
39	11	H	Queen's Park	W	1-0	0-0	7	McNair	800

Final League Position: 7

GOALSCORERS

League: (49): McQuade 14, Morrison 8 (3 pens), MacIver 6, Chapman 4, Gibson 4, Boyd 3 (1 pen), Edgar 2, McNair 2 (1 pen), Meechan 2, Dempsey 1, McGinley 1, McGuire 1, Martin 1.
Scottish Cup: (1): Morrison (1 pen).
Skol Cup: (2): MacIver 2.
Centenary Cup: (3): Hughes 1, McQuade 1, Morrison 1.

Record Victory: 13-1 v Kirkintilloch Cl. 1st Rd 1 September 1888.
Record defeat; 1-11 v Albion Rovers, Division II; 30 Jan, 1926: v Ayr United, League Cup; 13 Aug, 1952.
Most Capped Player: John Lindsay, 8, Scotland; James McAulay, 8, Scotland.
Most League Appearances: —.
Most Goals in Season (Individual): 38: Kenny Wilson, Division II; 1971–72.
Most Goals Overall (Individual): —.

Honours
League Champions: Division I 1890–91 (shared with Rangers), 1891–92. Division II 1910–11, 1971–72; *Runners-up:* First Division 1983–84. Division II 1907–08.
Scottish Cup Winners: 1883; *Runners-up:* 1881, 1882, 1887, 1891, 1897.
League Cup:—.
Club colours: Shirt: Gold. Shorts: Black. Stockings: Gold and black.

Strachan, HE	Gow, S	Marsland, J	McGarvey, M	McCracken, D	Dempsey, J	McQuade, J	McGinley, J	Gibson, C	MacIver, S	Morrison, S	Quinn, P	Hughes, J	Millar, S	Marshall, S	McKenzie, P	Boyd, J	Chapman, J	Stevenson, H	McGuire, W	McNair, C	Meechan, J	Edgar, D	Graham, P	Melvin, M	Nolan, T	Foster, A	Shearer, G	Martin, P	Match No.
1	2	3	4*	5	6	7	8	9	10	11	12																		1
1	2	3	5*	4	7†			9	12	10		8	11	14	6														2
1	2*	6		5	4	12	14	9	10	11†		7			8	3													3
1	5	2		4	12			9	10†	11		8	14	3	6*		7												4
1	2		14	4	11			9	8†			10	12	5	6*	3	7												5
	2			5	4	12		9		10*	11	6	14	3	8	1	7†												6
	2	4*		5	11			9		12		10		7	3	8	1		6										7
	2			5	4	11		9		14		12		7†	3	8	1	10*	6										8
	2			5	4	7		9	10†			14	12		3	11	1		6	8*									9
	2			5	4†	7		9		11	14	12		10*	3	8	1		6										10
				5	4	7		9	10*	11		12		2	3	8	1		6										11
				5	4	7		9	12	11				2	3	8	1	10*	6										12
	2		4	3	7			9†		11		14		8		6	1	10*	5	12									13
	3			5	7	4*	9			11		14		2	12	8†	1	10	6										14
	2	14			7	10	9			11	12	4		6	3†	1	8*	5											15
	12			5	4	7	10*	9		11		14		2†	3		1	8	6										16
	3	12		5	6	7	11	9†			8	14		2*			1	10	4										17
	2	6		4	7	10	14	11			9				3		1	12	5*	8†									18
	2			5	7	12		9	11			14		8†	3		1	10*			5	14		1	6	4			19
	2			5	7	12		9	11	14			10		12		1	4				6				3*			20
	5	2			7†	8		9	11	14		10		12			1	4			8	10	6				7†		21
	5	2*		14	12			9	11			4	3				1				8	10	6					7†	22
	2			5	7			9	11			12	10	3			1	8*	4				6						23
				5	7			9	11			12			3		1	10†	4*	8	14		2					6	24
	2			5	7	8		9	11*			12			3		1		4				10					6	25
				5	7	14		9	11						3		1		4	8	10†		2					6	26
			10†		6	7	14	9*	11						3		1		4	8	12		2					5	27
	3	2			4	7				11	12	8					1		6	10	9*							5	28
	3	2			4	7		9*	11†	12		10				14	1		6	8								5	29
	6	2			4	7			9*	12		11				3	1		10		8							5	30
	2	12	14		6	7		9		11		10†					1		8*		4							5	31
	2		4	11*	6	7		9†	12	14						3	1		8		10							5	32
			4		6	7		9*	10	11		12				3	1		8		2							5	33
	4	2		5	7			9	10	11*	12					3	1		6	8								5	34
	4*	2	8		7			9	10†	12	14					3	1		6	11								5	35
	2		4		7			9		11	12					3	1		6*	10	8							5	36
	4*	2	6		7			9†		11	14					3	1		12	8	10							5	37
	4	2	8		7			9*	11†	14	12						1		6	10	3							5	38
	5	2	8		7			9		12						3	1	10*	6	11	4								39
5	31	19	3	12	35	35	9	25	19	32	—	5	10	3	18	29	11	33	12	24	19	4	1	17	1	2	1	14	
	+	+	+	+	+	+	+	+	+	+	+	+	+							+	+	+	+						
	4s	1s	1s	1s	4s	4s	1s	2s	5s	10s	4s	16s	2s	1s	3s					1s	1s	2s	2s						

DUNDEE

First Division

Year Formed: 1893.   *Ground & Address:* Dens Park, Sandeman St, Dundee DD3 7JY.   *Telephone:* 0382 826104.
Ground Capacity: 20,136.   seated: 11,516.   *Size of Pitch:* 115yd × 77yd.
Chairman: Angus Cook.   *Secretary:* Ian R. G. Gellatly.   *Commercial manager:* Paul Morris.
Manager: Gordon Wallace.   *Assistant Manager:* John Blackley.   *Physio:* Eric Ferguson.   *Coach:*
Managers since 1975: David White; Tommy Gemmell; Donald Mackay; Archie Knox; Jocky Scott; Dave Smith; Gordon Wallace.
Club Nickname(s): The Dark Blues or The Dee.   *Previous Grounds:* Carolina Port 1893–98.
Record Attendance: 43,024 v Rangers, Scottish Cup; 1953.
Record Transfer Fee received: £500,000 for Tommy Coyne to Celtic, March 1989.
Record Transfer Fee paid: £150,000 for Billy Dodds from Chelsea May 1990.
Record Victory: 10–0 Division II v Alloa; 9 Mar, 1947 and v Dunfermline Ath; 22 Mar, 1947.

DUNDEE 1990–91 LEAGUE RECORD

Match No.	Date	Venue	Opponents	Result	H/T Score	Lg. Pos.	Goalscorers	Atten- dance
1	Aug 25	H	Partick T	D 1-1	0-0	—	Dodds	5040
2	Sept 1	A	Morton	W 1-0	1-0	5	McSkimming	1845
3	8	A	Clydebank	W 3-1	0-1	3	Wright 2, Dodds	1775
4	15	H	Clyde	W 3-1	1-1	2	Wright 2, Dodds (pen)	3518
5	18	A	Hamilton A	L 0-1	0-0	—		1773
6	22	H	Forfar	D 1-1	0-0	4	McQuillan	3053
7	29	H	Kilmarnock	D 1-1	0-0	4	Dodds (pen)	4573
8	Oct 6	A	Ayr U	W 4-2	1-0	4	McLeod, Chisholm, Dodds, Wright	2403
9	9	H	Airdrieonians	L 0-1	0-0	—		6360
10	13	A	Raith R	D 1-1	0-0	4	Campbell S	3494
11	20	H	Falkirk	D 2-2	1-1	4	Wright, Dodds	5531
12	27	A	Brechin C	W 3-1	2-1	4	Wright 2, Dodds	2011
13	Nov 3	H	Meadowbank T	L 1-2	1-1	5	McSkimming	3404
14	17	A	Partick T	W 3-1	1-0	5	McLeod, West, Wright	5476
15	20	H	Morton	W 1-0	1-0	—	McBride	3150
16	24	A	Airdrieonians	W 1-0	0-0	3	Chisholm	4718
17	Dec 1	H	Ayr U	W 1-0	0-0	1	Dodds	3416
18	8	A	Kilmarnock	L 1-2	0-2	2	Wright	4558
19	18	H	Forfar Ath	W 4-1	2-0	2	Wright, Dodds, McBride, Dinnie	2100
20	22	H	Brechin C	L 1-2	1-0	4	Dinnie	3172
21	29	A	Meadowbank T	W 1-0	0-0	2	McSkimming	1000
22	Jan 1	H	Raith R	W 2-1	0-1	2	Chisholm, Jamieson	4815
23	5	A	Falkirk	L 0-1	0-1	2		8500
24	Feb 2	H	Hamilton A	W 3-2	3-1	2	West 2, Shannon	3153
25	5	H	Clydebank	W 1-0	0-0	—	Craig	2793
26	Mar 2	A	Airdrieonians	W 1-0	1-0	2	Dodds (pen)	4000
27	5	A	Ayr U	W 4-0	4-0	2	Wright 3, Dodds	3385
28	9	H	Brechin C	L 0-1	0-1	1		3051
29	16	H	Forfar Ath	W 1-0	0-0	1	Dodds	2618
30	23	A	Clyde	L 2-4	2-3	2	Craig 2	2000
31	26	A	Partick T	L 0-1	0-0	—		3500
32	30	A	Clydebank	D 1-1	1-0	2	Wright	1238
33	Apr 6	H	Morton	W 1-0	1-0	3	Wright	2515
34	13	A	Falkirk	D 0-0	0-0	3		9232
35	20	A	Meadowbank T	W 4-0	3-0	2	Dinnie, Dodds 2, Wright	2716
36	27	H	Raith R	W 2-0	1-0	3	Jamieson, McMartin	3756
37	30	A	Clyde	W 1-0	0-0	—	Wright	3100
38	May 4	A	Kilmarnock	D 0-0	0-0	3		5712
39	11	A	Hamilton A	W 2-1	1-1	3	Shannon (pen), Dodds	3136

Final League Position: 3

GOALSCORERS

League: (59): Wright 18, Dodds 15 (3 pens), Chisholm 3, Craig 3, Dinnie 3, McSkimming 3, West 3, Jamieson 2, McBride 2, McLeod 2, Shannon 2 (1 pen), Campbell S 1, McMartin 1, McQuillan 1
Scottish Cup: (4): Dodds 2, McMartin 1, West 1
Skol Cup: (2): Chisholm 1, Forsyth 1
Centenary Cup: (11): Dodds 6 (1 pen), Wright 3, Campbell S 1, Shannon 1

Record Defeat: 0-11 v Celtic, Division I; 26 Oct, 1895.
Most Capped Player: Alex Hamilton, 24, Scotland.
Most League Appearances: 341: Doug Cowie 1945–61.
Most League Goals in Season (Individual): 38: Dave Halliday, Division I; 1923–24.
Most Goals Overall (individual): 113: Alan Gilzean.

Honours
League Champions: Division I 1961–62. First Division 1978–79. Division II 1946–47; Runners-up: Division I 1902–03, 1906–07, 1908–09, 1948–49, 1980–81.
Scottish Cup Winners: 1910; Runners-up: 1925, 1952, 1964.
League Cup Winners: 1951–52, 1952–53, 1973–74; Runners-up: 1967–68, 1980–81.
European: European Cup: 1962–63 (semi-final). Cup Winners Cup: 1964–65.
UEFA Cup: (Fairs Cup 1967–68 semi-final), 1971–72, 1973–74, 1974–75.
Club colours: Shirt: Dark blue with red and white trim. Shorts: White. Stockings: Blue and White.

Carson, T	McQuillan, J	McSkimming, S	Chisholm, G	Jamieson, W	Forsyth, S	Campbell, D	Shannon, R	Wright, K	Dodds, W	McLeod, G	Craib, M	McBride, J	Mathers, P	West, C	McMartin, G	Campbell, S	Frail, S	Bain, K	Holt, J	Dinnie, A	Craig, A	Beedie, S	Fraser, C	Match No.
1	2	3	4	5	6	7*	8	9	10	11		12												1
	2	11	4	5	6		3	9	10	8		12	1	7*										2
	2	11	4	5	6		3	9	10	8			1	7*	12									3
	2	11	4	5	6		3	9	10	8			1	7*	12									4
	2	11*	4	5	6		3	9	10	8			1	7	12									5
	2	12	4	5	6		3	9	10		14		1	7*	8	11†								6
1	12	11	4	5	2*		3	9	10	8	6	7†			14									7
1	12	11	4	5	2		3	9	10	8	6*					7								8
1	12	11	4*	5	2	14	3	9	10	8						7†	6							9
1	2	11		5	14		3	9		8				10*	12	7†	6	4						10
1		11	6	5			3	9	10	8*	12			14		7	2	4†						11
1				5	14		3	9	10	8*	6	11†		12		7	4			2				12
1		11*	4†	5			3	9	10	8	6			14		7	12			2				13
1			4		8		3	9	10	11*	6			7			5	12		2				14
1			4	5	2		3	9	10	6	14			7†	11	8*	12							15
1			4	5	2		3	9	10	11	6					7*	12	8						16
1			4	5	12		3	9	10	8	6*	11				7		2						17
1	12	11	4	5	2		3	9	10	8†				14		7*	6							18
1			4	5	2	7*	3	9	10	11		12				8		6						19
1	12		4	5	2*	7†	3	9	10	11		14				8		6						20
1	12	11	4	5			3	9	10	8						7*	6	2						21
1		11	4	5			3	9	10	8						7	6	2						22
1		11*	4	5			3	9	10	8			12			7	6	2						23
1			4*	5	12		3	9	10				7	11	8	6	2							24
1			5				3	9	10	11†			7	4	8	6	2		12					25
1		4	5				3	9	10	6	7*	11		8		2	12							26
1		4	5				3	9	10	12	6	7	11†	8*		2	14							27
1		4	5	12			3		10	6	9†	7*	11	8		2	14							28
1		4	5	2	7*		3		10	11	6	14	8†	12				9						29
1		4	5	2*12			9	10		6		11	7				3	8						30
1	2	4	5				10	11		6	14	8*	7				3		9†	12				31
1		5	10	3	9		6			7*			8						2	12	11	4		32
		5	7	3	9	10	6		1		12	8*							2	11	4			33
1		4	5	7*	3	9	10	8											2	12	11	6		34
1		4	5	7*	3	9	10		14	8†									2	12	11	6		35
1		4	5	12	3	9	10	7*		8									2	11	6			36
1		4	5	7	3	9	10*	8											2	12	11	6		37
1		4	5	7†	3	9	10	12	8*										2	14	11	6		38
1		4	5	12	3	9	10	6	7*	8									2	11				39
33	8	15	34	38	18	10	37	36	37	23	17	4	6	16	15	3	25	7	4	25	3	8	7	

```
     +   +          +   +              +   +   +          +   +   +   +            +           +   +
    6s  1s         3s  6s             1s  2s 10s         3s  4s  3s  1s            4s          9s  1s
```

DUNDEE UNITED Premier Division

Year Formed: 1909 (1923). *Ground & Address:* Tannadice Park, Tannadice St, Dundee DD3 7JW. *Telephone:* 0382 833166.
Ground Capacity: total: 20,862. seated: 2562. *Size of Pitch:* 110 × 74yd.
Chairman: James Y. McLean. *Secretary:* Miss Priti Trivedi. *Commercial Manager:* James Connor.
Manager: James Y. McLean. *Assistant Manager:* —. *Physio:* Graham Doig. *Coach:* Paul Sturrock.
Managers since 1975: J. McLean.
Club Nickname(s): The Terrors. *Previous Grounds:* None.
Record Attendance: 28,000 v Barcelona, Fairs Cup; 16 Nov, 1966.
Record Transfer Fee received: £900,000 for Kevin Gallacher to Coventry C (Jan 1990).
Record Transfer Fee paid: £350,000 for Michael O'Neill from Newcastle U, August 1989.
Record Victory: 14-0 v Nithsdale Wanderers, Scottish Cup 1st rd; 17 Jan, 1931.
Record Defeat: 1-12 v Motherwell, Division II; 23 Jan, 1954.
Most Capped Player: Maurice Malpas, 42, Scotland.

DUNDEE UNITED 1990–91 LEAGUE RECORD

Match No.	Date	Venue	Opponents	Result	H/T Score	Lg. Pos.	Goalscorers	Atten-dance
1	Aug 25	A	St Johnstone	W 3-1	2-1	—	Jackson 2, Dailly	7784
2	Sept 1	H	Motherwell	W 1-0	1-0	2	Cleland	7636
3	8	H	St Mirren	W 1-0	0-0	1	Jackson	6968
4	15	A	Aberdeen	D 1-1	0-0	1	McKinnon	15,500
5	22	H	Rangers	W 2-1	1-1	1	McKinlay, Butcher (og)	16,270
6	29	A	Hearts	L 0-1	0-0	1		12,052
7	Oct 10	H	Dunfermline Ath	W 3-0	1-0	—	Bowman, Steinmann, French	9025
8	13	H	Hibernian	W 1-0	0-0	1	Miller (og)	10,289
9	20	A	Celtic	D 0-0	0-0	1		34,363
10	27	H	St Johnstone	L 1-2	0-2	1	Jackson	11,708
11	Nov 3	A	Motherwell	W 2-0	1-0	1	Jackson, Dailly	8117
12	10	A	Rangers	W 2-1	0-0	1	Jackson 2	36,995
13	17	H	Hearts	D 1-1	0-1	1	Jackson	10,821
14	24	H	Aberdeen	L 2-3	2-2	2	McKimmie (og), Malpas (pen)	12,344
15	Dec 1	A	St Mirren	D 1-1	1-1	3	Jackson	4581
16	8	H	Celtic	W 3-1	1-0	3	Dailly, Jackson, Paatelainen	16,895
17	15	A	Hibernian	D 0-0	0-0	3		6000
18	22	A	Dunfermline Ath	L 0-1	0-0	3		8018
19	29	H	Rangers	L 1-2	1-2	3	Jackson	17,564
20	Jan 2	A	Aberdeen	W 1-0	0-0	—	Dailly	19,000
21	5	H	St Mirren	W 3-2	1-1	3	Dailly, Clark, Cleland	6180
22	19	H	Motherwell	W 3-0	0-0	3	Connolly 2, McKinlay	6482
23	Feb 2	A	Celtic	L 0-1	0-0	3		26,172
24	9	H	Hibernian	D 0-0	0-0	3		6114
25	16	A	Hearts	L 1-2	1-0	3	Clark	7216
26	19	A	St Johnstone	W 1-0	0-0	—	Cherry (og)	6190
27	Mar 2	H	Dunfermline Ath	W 1-0	0-0	3	Ferguson	6379
28	9	A	St Mirren	W 1-0	0-0	3	Jackson	3960
29	23	H	Aberdeen	L 1-2	1-1	3	McInally	10,643
30	30	H	St Johnstone	D 0-0	0-0	3		7794
31	Apr 13	H	Celtic	W 2-1	1-0	3	Van der Hoorn, McKinnon	12,603
32	16	A	Motherwell	L 0-1	0-1	—		3531
33	20	A	Hibernian	L 0-1	0-0	3		4000
34	24	A	Rangers	L 0-1	0-1	—		32,397
35	May 4	H	Hearts	W 2-1	1-0	3	French 2	6820
36	11	A	Dunfermline Ath	L 0-1	0-0	4		4894

Final League Position: 4

GOALSCORERS

League: (41): Jackson 12, Dailly 5, French 3, Clark 2, Cleland 2, Connolly 2, McKinlay 2, McKinnon 2, Bowman 1, Ferguson 1, McInally 1, Malpas 1 (pen), Paatelainen 1, Steinmann 1, Van der Hoorn 1, own goals 4
Scottish Cup: (13): Ferguson 3, Clark 2, French 2, Jackson 2, Bowman 1, Connolly 1, McKinnon 1, O'Neil J 1
Skol Cup: (8): Jackson 3, Dailly 2, McInally 1, Van der Hoorn 1, Welsh 1

Most League Appearances: 554, Dave Narey, 1973–91.
Most Appearances in European Matches: 75, Dave Narey (record for Scottish player).
Most League Goals in Season (Individual): 41: John Coyle, Division II; 1955–56.
Most Goals Overall (Individual): 158: Peter McKay.

Honours
League Champions: Premier Division 1982–83. Division II 1924–25, 1928–29; *Runners-up:* Division II 1930–31, 1959–60.
Scottish Cup Runners-up: 1974, 1981, 1985, 1987, 1988, 1991.
League Cup Winners: 1979–80, 1980–81; *Runners-up:* 1981–82, 1984–85.
Summer Cup Runners-up: 1964–65.
Scottish War Cup Runners-up: 1939–40.
European: *European Cup:* 8 matches 1983–84 (semi-finals), 1988–89; *Cup Winners Cup:* 4 matches 1974–75; *UEFA Cup Runners-up:* 1986–87. 78 matches (1966–67, 1969–70, 1970–71 *Fairs Cup;* 1971–72, 1975–76, 1977–78, 1978–79, 1979–80, 1980–81, 1981–82, 1982–83, 1984–85, 1985–86, 1986–87, 1987–88, 1989–90, 1990–91).
Club colours: Tangerine jersey, black shorts. Change colours: all white.

Main, A	Cleland, A	Malpas, M	McInally, J	Krivokapic, M	Welsh, B	Van Der Hoorn, F	McKinlay, W	Dailly, C	Jackson, D	Preston, A	Bowman, D	Paatelainen, M	Thomson, W	O'Neill, M	O'Neill, J	McKinnon, R	Connolly, P	Steinmann, G	French, H	Narey, D	Ferguson, D	Clark, J	Bollan, G	Match No.
1	2	3	4	5	6	7	8	9†10	11*12	14														1
	2	3	4	5	6	7	8	9*10			12	1	11†14											2
	2	3	4*	5	6	7	8	9†10		12	1		11	14										3
	2	3	4		6	7	8	9*10		12	5	1		11										4
	2	3	4		6	7	8	10		9	5	1		11										5
	2†	3	4		6	7	8	10*14		9	5	1		11	12									6
1	2	3			6	7	8	10†		4	12	14		11*	5	9								7
1	2	3			6	7	8	10		4	12	14		11*	5†	9								8
1	2	3	4†		6	7	8	10*		11	12	14			9	5								9
1		3	4*		6		8	14		2	12	10		7†11	9	5								10
1	2	3	4	5		7	8 12	10		9				11*	6									11
1 12		3	4	5	6		8	9†10	7					2*11		14								12
1	2	3	4	5	6		8	9*10			12	7	11											13
1	2*	3	4	5	6	7	8	9					10	12		11								14
1	2	3	4	5	6	7	8	9 10					12 11*											15
1		3	4	5		7	8	9 10	6 11					2										16
1		3	4	5		7	8	9 10	6 11					2										17
1		3	4	5		7	8	9†10	6*14	11				2			12							18
1		3	4	5*		7	8	9 10		11	12			2				6						19
1 12		3	4			7	8	9 10†		11		14		2*	6			5						20
1 12		3	4	5		7	8	9 10†		14	6*			11		14		2						21
1 12		3	4*	5	6	7	8	9 10†						11		14		2						22
1		3	4	5 12		7	8*11	10						14	2†	6		9						23
1		3	4	5		7	8	10		14				12	11*	6		9	2†					24
1		3	4	5		7	8 12	10						6	11*			9	2					25
1		3	4	5		7			6					8	9			11	10	2				26
1		3	4	5		7		12	6					8	9			11*	10	2				27
1		3	4	5		7 12		10	6					8*	9			11		2				28
1		3	4	5		7 12			6	14				8	9*			11	10†	2				29
1		3	4	5		7	6*	10	14	11†				9				12		2				30
1		3	4	5	7 12			11	6					8*	9			10		2				31
1	5	3	4			7 12		11	14	6				8†	9			10*		2				32
1	2*	3	4			7 12		10	6					11	8	9				5				33
1	2*	3	4				8	9						11†	7			10 12	6		5 14			34
1		3		5		7	4	11*						12	8	6		9			2 10			35
1		3	4	5		7	6	12						8*11				9		10	2			36
31	16	36	33	24	16	32	29	16	30	1	17	9	5	17	11	17	7	13	16	4	8	17	1	
			+4s			+1s		+5s	+2s	+3s	+2s	+3s	+11s		+6s	+4s		+3s	+1s	+3s	+1s	+1s	+1s	

DUNFERMLINE ATHLETIC Premier Division

Year Formed: 1885. *Ground & Address:* East End Park, Halbeath Rd, Dunfermline KY12 7RB. *Telephone:* 0383 724295.
Ground Capacity: total: 19,907.   seated: 4014.   *Size of Pitch:* 114yd × 72yd.
Chairman: William M. Rennie. *Secretary and General Manager:* Henry W. Melrose *Commercial Manager:* Audrey Kelly.
Manager: Iain Munro. *Assistant Manager:* —. *Physio:* Philip Yeates, M.C.S.P. *Coach:* Phil Bonnyman.
Managers since 1975: G. Miller; H. Melrose; P. Stanton; T. Forsyth; J. Leishman.
Club Nickname(s): The Pars. *Previous Grounds:* None.
Record Attendance: 27,816 v Celtic, Division I; 30 April 1968.
Record Transfer Fee received: £200,000 for Ian McCall to Rangers (Aug 1987).
Record Transfer Fee paid: £540,000 for Istvan Kozma from Bordeaux, September 1989.

DUNFERMLINE ATHLETIC 1990–91 LEAGUE RECORD

Match No.	Date	Venue	Opponents	Result	H/T Score	Lg. Pos.	Goalscorers	Atten-dance
1	Aug 25	A	Rangers	L	1-3	1-1	—	McCall	39,951
2	Sept 1	H	Hearts	W	2-0	1-0	5	Moyes, McCall	8905
3	8	H	Aberdeen	D	1-1	1-1	5	Moyes	10,200
4	15	A	St Johnstone	L	2-3	1-2	6	Kozma, Moyes	7601
5	22	A	Motherwell	L	0-2	0-2	7		5354
6	29	H	Hibernian	D	1-1	1-0	9	O'Boyle	7704
7	Oct 10	A	Dundee U	L	0-3	0-1	—		9025
8	13	H	Celtic	D	1-1	1-0	9	Jack	16,063
9	20	A	St Mirren	W	1-0	0-0	8	Jack	4488
10	Nov 3	H	Hearts	D	1-1	0-1	8	McCathie	11,897
11	10	H	Motherwell	D	3-3	1-2	8	O'Boyle, Jack, Irons	7100
12	17	A	Hibernian	D	1-1	0-1	7	McCall	7943
13	20	H	Rangers	L	0-1	0-1	—		14,480
14	24	H	St Johnstone	L	1-2	1-2	9	O'Boyle	7822
15	Dec 1	A	Aberdeen	L	2-3	1-1	9	O'Boyle, Irons	12,000
16	11	H	St Mirren	D	0-0	0-0	—		4499
17	15	A	Celtic	W	2-1	2-0	7	Moyes, O'Boyle	18,875
18	22	A	Dundee U	W	1-0	0-0	6	Moyes	8018
19	Jan 2	A	St Johnstone	W	1-0	0-0	—	Jack	9533
20	5	H	Aberdeen	L	1-4	1-2	7	Irons	7422
21	12	A	Rangers	L	0-2	0-1	7		35,120
22	Feb 19	A	St Mirren	D	2-2	1-1		Irons, O'Boyle	2589
23	23	H	Hearts	W	3-1	2-0	7	Jack 2, Leitch	7273
24	27	A	Motherwell	L	0-1	0-1	—		3202
25	Mar 2	A	Dundee U	L	0-1	0-0	7		6379
26	6	H	Celtic	L	0-1	0-1	—		12,458
27	13	A	Aberdeen	D	0-0	0-0	—		10,400
28	16	H	Hibernian	D	1-1	0-0	7	Kozma	4830
29	23	H	St Johnstone	W	3-2	1-1	7	Moyes, Smith, McCall	5696
30	30	H	Rangers	L	0-1	0-0	8		14,256
31	Apr 6	A	Hearts	L	1-4	0-2	8	Smith	8102
32	13	H	St Mirren	D	2-2	2-0	8	Drizic, Jack (pen)	3464
33	20	A	Celtic	L	1-5	0-1	8	Jack	14,268
34	27	H	Motherwell	L	2-5	0-2	8	Leitch 2	3552
35	May 4	A	Hibernian	L	0-3	0-2	8		3500
36	11	H	Dundee U	W	1-0	0-0	8	Moyes	4894

Final League Position: 8

GOALSCORERS

League: (38): Jack 8 (1 pen), Moyes 7, O'Boyle 6, Irons 4, McCall 4, Leitch 3, Kozma 2, Smith 2, Drizic 1, McCathie 1
Scottish Cup: (0)
Skol Cup: (5): Jack (2) (1 pen), Irons 1, O'Brien 1, Smith 1

Record Victory: 11-2 v Stenhousemuir, Division II; 27 Sept, 1930.
Record Defeat: 0-10 v Dundee, Division II; 22 Mar, 1947.
Most Capped Player: Andy Wilson, 6 (12), Scotland.
Most League Appearances: 360: Bobby Robertson; 1977–88.
Most League Goals in Season (Individual): 55: Bobby Skinner, Division II; 1925–26.
Most Goals Overall (Individual): 154: Charles Dickson.

Honours
League Champions: First Division 1988–89. Division II 1925–26. Second Division 1985–86; *Runners-up:* First Division 1986–87. Division II 1912–13, 1933–34, 1954–55, 1957–58, 1972–73. Second Division 1978–79.
Scottish Cup Winners: 1961, 1968; *Runners-up:* 1965.
League Cup Runners-up: 1949–50.
European: *European Cup:*—. *Cup Winners Cup:* 1961–62, 1968–69 (semi-finals). *UEFA Cup:* 1962–63, 1964–65, 1965–66, 1966–67, 1969–70 (*Fairs Cup*).
Club colours: Shirt: Broad black and white vertical stripes. Shorts: Black. Stockings: Black with red diamond tops.

Rhodes, A	Wilson, T	Sharp, R	McCathie, N	Moyes, D	Nicholl, J	Smith, P	Farningham, R	Jack, R	McCall, I	Kosma, I	Rafferty, S	Irons, D	Leitch, S	O'Brien, P	Haro, M	O'Boyle, G	Cunnington, E	Williamson, A	Davies, W	Gallagher, E	McAllister, P	Drizic, M	Gallacher, S	Kelly, N	Sinclair, C	Westwater, I	Match No.
1	2	3*	4	5	6	7	8	9	10†11	12	14																1
1	2	3	4	5	6	7		9	10*11	8	12																2
1	2	3	4	5	6	7		9	10*11†	8	12	14															3
1	2	3	4†	5	6	7		9	10	11	8*12		14														4
1	2	3	4	5	6*	7		9	10	11		12	8														5
1	2	3*	4	5	6			9	10	7		11	12		8												6
1	2	3	4	5	6*	7		9	10			11		8	12												7
1	2	3	4	5		7		9	10	11	8						6										8
1	2	3	4	5		7	14	9	10*11†			8			12		6										9
1	2	3	4	5		7		9	10	11		6						8									10
1	2	3	4	5		7		12	10	11		6		9				8*									11
1	2	3	4	5		7			10	11		6		9				8									12
1	2†		4	5		7		12	10*11			6		14	9	3		8									13
1	2†	3	4	5		7		9*12	11			6		14	10			8									14
1	2	3†	4	5				12	10	11	7	6		14	9*			8									15
1	2	3	4	5		14		12	10*11		7†	6			9			8									16
1	2	3	4	5		14		12	10†11		7	6			9*			8									17
1	2	3	4	5				10		11	7	6			9			8									18
1	2	3	4	5		12		10		11	7*	6			9			8									19
1	2†	3	4	5		9		10		11	7*	6		14				8	12								20
1	2†	3	4	5		7		10		11	12	6		14	9*			8									21
1	2	3	4	5				12	9	11*	7	6			10			8									22
1	2	3	4	5				12	9	10*11		6	7†			3		8		14							23
1	2*		4	5		14	12	9	10	11		6†	7					8									24
1			4	5		12	2	9	10	11		6	7*			3		8									25
1			4	5		12	2	9	10	11		6*	7			3		8									26
1			4	5		8	2*	9†10	11			6				3	12	7	14								27
1	12		4	5			2*	9	10	11		8	7		6	3											28
1	2*	3	4	5		8		9	10	11		12			14			7		6†							29
1	2	3*	4	5†		8			10	11		12	14		9			7		6							30
1		3	4	5		9	2		11		8†12	14			10			7		6*							31
1		3	4	5		2		9	10†11		8	12	14					7*		6							32
1		3	4	5		8	2	9		11		12						7		6†10*14							33
1	2	3	4	5*		8		9	10†12			11						6	7					14			34
1		3	4			8		9		12		6	10†	2*				5	7				11	14			35
	2	3	4	5		8		9	10			6	12					7†11*					14			1	36
35	28	30	36	35	7	25	6	28	28	32	12	24	8	—	2	15	6	4	26	1	—	5	1	1	—	1	
	+																										
	1s	6s	4s	5s	1s	2s	2s	10s	5s	2s	6s	1s	1s	1s			2s	1s				1s	3s				

EAST FIFE

Second Division

Year Formed: 1903. *Ground & Address:* Bayview Park, Methil Fife KY8 3AG. *Telephone:* 0333 26323. *Fax:* 26376.
Ground Capacity: total: 5150. seated: 600. *Size of Pitch:* 110yd × 71yd.
Chairman: James Baxter. *Secretary:* William McPhee. *Commercial Manager:* James Bonthrone.
Manager: Gavin Murray. *Assistant Manager:* —. *Physio:* Bud Porteous. *Coaches:* David Gorman and Brian Fairley.
Managers since 1975: Frank Christie; Roy Barry; David Clarke; Gavin Murray.
Club Nickname(s) The Fifers. *Previous Grounds:* None.
Record Attendance: 22,515 v Raith Rovers, Division I; 2 Jan, 1950.
Record Transfer Fee received: £100,000 for Paul Hunter from Hull C, March 1990.
Record Transfer Fee paid: £29,000 for Ray Charles from Montrose (1987).

EAST FIFE 1990–91 LEAGUE RECORD

Match No.	Date	Venue	Opponents	Result	H/T Score	Lg. Pos.	Goalscorers	Atten- dance
1	Aug 25	H	Dumbarton	W 2-1	0-0	—	Lennox, Taylor P (pen)	550
2	Sept 1	A	Stranraer	D 2-2	0-1	4	Crolla, Lennox	700
3	8	H	Albion R	D 2-2	1-2	4	Brown W, Mitchell	716
4	15	A	Stirling Albion	W 2-1	2-1	3	Mitchell, Brown W	920
5	18	A	Queen of the S	W 2-0	1-0	—	Brown W, Bell	692
6	22	A	Queen's Park	W 2-0	1-0	1	Mitchell, Callan (og)	701
7	29	H	Arbroath	W 2-0	1-0	1	Brown W, Brown I	680
8	Oct 6	H	Stenhousemuir	W 2-1	1-1	1	Crolla, Brown I	731
9	9	A	Montrose	W 2-0	1-0	—	Wilson, Lennox	450
10	13	H	Cowdenbeath	D 1-1	0-1	1	Mitchell	1160
11	20	A	Berwick R	L 0-1	0-1	1		430
12	27	A	East Stirling	L 1-3	0-3	2	Brown W	331
13	Nov 3	H	Alloa	D 2-2	2-0	2	Brown I 2	761
14	10	H	Stranraer	L 1-2	1-0	2	Hope	682
15	17	A	Dumbarton	L 2-3	1-1	3	Brown I (pen), Scott	500
16	24	A	Albion R	W 2-0	2-0	3	Brown I, Mitchell	400
17	Dec 1	H	Stirling Albion	D 1-1	0-0	4	Brown W	1089
18	11	H	East Stirling	D 1-1	1-1	—	Brown I	474
19	Jan 12	H	Montrose	L 1-3	0-2	4	Scott	884
20	Feb 2	H	Queen's Park	W 2-1	2-0	5	Prior, Brown W	643
21	9	A	Arbroath	D 1-1	0-0	8	Scott	454
22	16	A	Stirling Albion	D 2-2	1-1	7	Brown W, Hope	935
23	19	H	Berwick R	W 4-1	1-0	—	Scott 2, Taylor P, Brown W	719
24	23	A	Albion R	L 1-3	0-3	6	Mitchell	363
25	27	A	Stenhousemuir	L 0-2	0-1	—		500
26	Mar 2	A	Dumbarton	L 1-2	1-1	7	Brown I	500
27	6	A	Queen of the S	L 0-3	0-1	—		373
28	9	H	Stenhousemuir	W 1-0	0-0	7	Beaton (pen)	506
29	12	A	Alloa	W 6-3	2-2	—	Scott 3, Beaton, Crolla, Hope	458
30	16	H	Montrose	D 2-2	2-1	5	Scott, Beaton	665
31	23	A	Queen's Park	L 0-2	0-0	5		696
32	26	A	Cowdenbeath	L 0-2	0-1	—		900
33	30	H	Stranraer	L 1-2	0-0	9	Brown W	525
34	Apr 6	A	East Stirling	L 1-5	1-0	9	Hayton	184
35	13	A	Queen of the S	W 3-1	1-1	8	Wilson, Brown I, Mitchell	527
36	20	H	Cowdenbeath	L 0-5	0-0	10		618
37	27	H	Alloa	L 1-3	0-0	10	Scott	361
38	May 4	A	Arbroath	W 1-0	0-0	10	Bennett (og)	264
39	11	H	Berwick R	L 0-1	0-0	10		317

Final League Position: 10

GOALSCORERS
League: (57): Brown W 10, Scott 10, Brown I 9 (1 pen), Mitchell 7, Beaton 3 (1 pen), Crolla 3, Hope 3, Lennox 3, Taylor P 2 (1 pen), Wilson 2, Bell 1, Hayton 1, Prior 1, own goals 2.
Scottish Cup: (8): Hope 3, Wilson 2, Cowell 1, Mitchell 1, Scott 1.
Skol Cup: (3): Mitchell 1, Scott 1, Wilson 1.
Centenary Cup: (5): Brown W 3, Mitchell 2.

Record Victory: 13-2 v Edinburgh City, Division II; 11 Dec, 1937.
Record Defeat: 0-9 v Hearts, Division I; 5 Oct, 1957.
Most Capped Player: George Aitken, 5 (8), Scotland.
Most League Appearances: 517: David Clarke, 1968–86.
Most League Goals in Season (Individual): 41: Jock Wood, Division II; 1926–27 and Henry Morris, Division II; 1947–48.
Most Goals Overall (Individual): 196: George Dewar (149 in League).

Honours

League Champions: Division II 1947–48; *Runners-up:* Division II 1929–30, 1970–71. Second Division 1983–84.
Scottish Cup Winners: 1938; *Runners-up:* 1927, 1950.
League Cup Winners: 1947–48, 1949–50, 1953–54.
Club colours: Shirt: Black and gold stripes. Shorts: Black with gold flashes. Stockings: Black with gold and white tops.

Moffat, J	Hamilton, R	Taylor, P	Lennox, S	Prior, S	Taylor, PH	Mitchell, A	Brown, W	Wilson, S	Scott, R	Crolla, C	Brown, I	Hope, D	Bell, G	Rogerson, S	Hayton, G	Charles, R	Cowell, J	Beaton, D	Halliday, D	Ritchie, I	Match No.
1	2	3	4	5	6	7	8	9	10	11											1
1	2	3	4	5	6	7	8	9*	10†	11	12	14									2
1	2	3	4	5	6	7	8	9	10*	11	12										3
1		3	4	5	6	7	9			11	10*		2	8	12						4
1		3	4	5	6	7	9†	14	10*	11	12		2	8							5
1		3	4	5	6	7†	9	12	14	11	10*		2	8							6
1		3	4	5	6	7	9	12		11	10†		2	8*	14						7
1		3	4	5	6	7	9	12	8*	11	10		2								8
1		3	4	5	6	7	9	8	12	11	10*	14	2†								9
1		3	4	5	6	7	9	8		11	10†		2	14							10
1		3	4	5	6	7	9	8*	14	11	10†		2	12							11
1		3	4	5	6	7	9	8*		11†	10	14	2	12							12
1		3	4	5	6	7	9	8*		11	10		2	12							13
1		3	4*	5†	6	7	9	14	12	11	8	10	2								14
		3			7	9	5	8	6	10	4		2	11	1						15
			5	4	7	9	11	12	8	10*	3†		2	14	1	6					16
			5	6	7	9	8		4*	10†	12		2	14	1	11	3				17
			5	6	7	9	4†	14	11*	10	12		2		1	8	3				18
		3		5	7*	9	4	10		8†		12	2		1	11	6	14			19
		3		5	4	12	9	8	10*	7	14		2		1	11†	6				20
		3		5	4	12	9*	8	10	7	14		2†		1	11	6				21
		3	8	5	4	12	9		7*	10	14	2	6		1	11†					22
		3	4*	5	6	7	9	8	10		12	2	14		1	11†					23
		3†	4	5	6	7	9	8	10*		12	2			1	11	14				24
		3	7	5		9	4	10†	14	12	2*	8			1	11	6				25
		3	7	5	4		8*	10	12	9†			2	14	1	11	6				26
			6	7*	5	4		8	10	2	9†	12		14	1	11	3				27
1		3	8			9	10	4	14	11*	2†	5	7			6	12				28
1		3	8	14		9	10	4	12	11		6	7*			5	2†				29
1		3		5	8	12	9	10	4†	11		2		7*	14	6					30
1		3		14	6	12	9	8	10	4†		2		7*	11	5					31
1		3		5	7	9	8	10†	4	14	11*	2	6	12							32
1		3		6	7	9	10†	4	14	11*	5	8	12	2							33
1		3		5	6	7	9	8	4	12	11*	5	10†	14	2						34
1		3		5	6	7	9	4		10	11	2	8								35
1		3		5	6*	7	9	4	12	10†	11	2	8	14							36
1	14	3†		6	7	9	8	10	4*	2	5	12	11								37
1	2*	3		5	6	7	9	4	11†	12	8	10	14								38
1	2	3		5	6	7	9	8	10	14	4†	11*	12								39
26	5	36	22	32	33	29	34	32	22	30	18	13	28	16	11	13	14	12	3	—	
+1s			+1s	+1s	+5s			+5s	+7s	+2s	+10s	+11s+1s	+1s	+1s	+13s		+4s	+1s	+2s	+2s	

EAST STIRLINGSHIRE Second Division

Year Formed: 1881.   *Ground & Address:* Firs Park, Firs St, Falkirk FK2 7AY.   *Telephone:* 0324 23583.
Ground Capacity: total: 6000. seated: 2000.   *Size of Pitch:* 112yd × 72yd.
Chairman: Peter I. McKay.   *Secretary:* Marshall Paterson.   *Commercial Manager:* —.
Manager: Dom Sullivan.   *Assistant Manager:* Bobby McCulley.   *Physio:* Angus Williamson.   *Coach:* —.
Managers since 1975: I. Ure; D. McLinden; W. P. Lamont; M. Ferguson; W. Little; D. Whiteford; D. Lawson; J. D.
Connell, A. Mackin.
Club Nickname(s): The Shire.   *Previous Grounds:* Burnhouse, Randyford Park, Merchiston Park, New Kilbowie Park.
Record Attendance: 11,500 v Hibernian, Scottish Cup; 10 Feb, 1969.
Record Transfer Fee received: £35,000 for Jim Docherty to Chelsea (1978).

EAST STIRLINGSHIRE 1990–91 LEAGUE RECORD

Match No.	Date		Venue	Opponents	Result		H/T Score	Lg. Pos.	Goalscorers	Atten- dance
1	Aug	25	A	Queen of the S	W	2-1	1-0	—	Derek Walker 2	480
2	Sept	1	H	Stenhousemuir	D	2-2	2-1	5	McNab 2	250
3		8	A	Queen's Park	L	0-4	0-0	10		470
4		15	H	Stranraer	L	0-2	0-0	12		310
5		18	A	Cowdenbeath	L	1-2	0-0	—	McBride	100
6		22	H	Berwick R	L	0-4	0-1	13		230
7		29	H	Montrose	L	0-1	0-0	14		130
8	Oct	6	A	Arbroath	L	0-3	0-2	14		231
9		9	H	Alloa	D	0-0	0-0	—		350
10		13	A	Dumbarton	L	1-2	0-0	14	McDowall	250
11		20	H	Albion R	L	0-3	0-1	14		201
12		27	H	East Fife	W	3-1	3-0	14	Prior (og), Derek Walker 2	331
13	Nov	3	A	Stirling Albion	L	0-3	0-1	14		764
14		10	A	Stenhousemuir	L	1-4	1-2	14	Lytwyn	340
15		17	H	Queen of the S	W	1-0	1-0	14	Lytwyn	308
16		24	H	Queen's Park	L	1-3	0-1	14	Lytwyn	296
17	Dec	1	A	Stranraer	W	2-1	2-0	14	Lytwyn 2	450
18		11	A	East Fife	D	1-1	1-1	—	Lytwyn	474
19	Jan	5	A	Albion R	L	0-4	0-4	14		220
20		19	H	Arbroath	D	1-1	1-1	14	Lytwyn	150
21		22	H	Dumbarton	W	2-1	2-0	—	Lytwyn (pen), Gow (og)	214
22		29	H	Cowdenbeath	L	1-3	1-1	14	Lytwyn	200
23	Feb	2	A	Berwick R	D	2-2	1-0	14	Lytwyn, McBride	459
24		9	A	Montrose	D	2-2	2-1	14	McDowall, Derek Walker	200
25		16	A	Stranraer	L	0-2	0-0	14		300
26		23	H	Alloa	L	1-6	0-3	14	McNally	260
27		26	A	Alloa	W	1-0	1-0	—	Derek Walker	305
28	Mar	2	A	Stenhousemuir	D	0-0	0-0	14		400
29		5	H	Stirling Albion	L	0-1	0-0	—		611
30		9	H	Queen's Park	D	1-1	0-0	14	McNally	340
31		16	A	Arbroath	W	1-0	0-0	14	Derek Walker	272
32		23	H	Cowdenbeath	D	0-0	0-0	14		198
33		30	A	Berwick R	L	0-2	0-0	14		489
34	Apr	6	H	East Fife	W	5-1	0-1	14	Diver 4, Derek Walker (pen)	184
35		13	A	Stirling Albion	L	0-4	0-1	14		1300
36		20	H	Queen of the S	D	1-1	0-0	14	Diver	194
37		27	H	Dumbarton	W	2-0	1-0	13	Diver, Derek Walker (pen)	254
38	May	4	A	Montrose	L	0-2	0-2	13		600
39		11	H	Albion R	D	1-1	0-0	13	Derek Walker	150

Final League Position: 13

GOALSCORERS

League: (36): Lytwyn 10 (1 pen), Derek Walker 10 (2 pens), Diver 6, McBride 2, McDowall 2, McNab 2, McNally 2, own goals 2.
Scottish Cup: (1): Derek Wakler 1.
Skol Cup: (2): Russell 1, Watson P 1.
Centenary Cup: (0).

Record Transfer Fee paid: —.
Record Victory: 10–1 v Stenhousemuir, Scottish Cup 1st rd; 1 Sept, 1888.
Record Defeat: 1–12 v Dundee United, Division II; 13 Apr, 1936.
Most Capped Player: Humphrey Jones, 5 (14), Wales.
Most League Appearances: Gordon Simpson, 1967–79.
Most League Goals in Season (Individual): 36: Malcolm Morrison, Division II; 1938–39.
Most Goals Overall (Individual): —.

Honours
League Champions: Division II 1931–32; *Runners-up:* Division II 1962–63. Second Division 1979–80.
Scottish Cup:—.
League Cup:—.
Club colours: Shirt: White. Shorts: White. Stockings: Black.

Watson, G	Russell, G	Workman, J	Erwin, H	Brannigan, K	Watson, P	Walker, Derek	Rooney, J	Diver, D	Lytwyn, C	McBride, M	McNab, C	McLaren, P	Griffin, J	Hamill, S	Wilson, C	McDowall, P	O'Brien, P	Mackin, A	Lawson, D	Abercromby, W	Clark, J	McCulley, R	McNally, J	Byrne, W	Walker, David	Gray, C	McAleer, E	McKinnon, C	Match No.
1	2	3	4	5	6	7	8	9	10*	11†	12	14																	1
1	2	3	4	5	8	10	6	9	7	11																			2
1	2	3	10	5	8	6	9		7*	11†	12				4	14													3
1	3	6	4	5		10	11	7	9*						2	8	12												4
1	3	6	4	5		10	11	9	7						2	8*	12												5
1	3	6	4	5		8	11*	7	9†						2	14	12												6
1	2	3	10	5	8	6*	4	9	14	7†					11	12													7
1	2	3	10	5	11	8	9	4†	7*						12	6													8
1	2	3	8	5	12	6	11	7	9†	14					10*	4													9
1	2	3	8	5	12	6	11†	9	7	14					10	4*													10
	2	3	6†	5	8	11	9	7	14	10										1	4								11
			4	5	8	9	11	2	12	6					7*					1	10	3							12
			6†	5	8	9	11	2	14	4										1	10	3	7*	12					13
		6		5	7	10	8	9	2	14					4	11†				1	3								14
	2		6†	5	9	4	7	11	14	10										1	8	3							15
	2				9*	7	4†	11	14	12						6				10	1	8	3						16
1	2	3†	4	5	9	7	12	11	10	14						6*					8								17
1	2	3		5	9	6	7	11							4					10	8								18
1	2	3	8	14	9	4	7†	11	12						5					6*	10								19
1	2	6		5	9	12	11	7	14							8*				3	10†				4				20
1	2			5	14	9*	8†	11	7	12						6				3	10				4				21
1	2	12		5	9	8	11	7	14							6*				3†	10				4				22
1	2	6		5	9	11	7	8†								12				14	10*				4	3			23
1	2	12	8*	4	5	9	3	7	11							6					10								24
1	2	12	4	5	9	8	11	7								6					10*				3				25
1	2	6	4†	12	8	11	7	10								9*							14		5	3			26
1				5	9	2	12	11								7*	8				10		6		4	3			27
1		3	4		7	2	8	11	14							6†					9		10*		5	12			28
1	2	6	4		8	7	10	11*								12								9	5	3			29
1	2	8	4		11		7*								12						9			10	5		3	6	30
1	2	7*		5	10	11		9								8				12					4		3	6	31
1	2			5	9	12	7	6								10*					11				4		3	8	32
1	2			5	9	10	11	7*	14							6†					12				4		3	8	33
1	2			5	9	8	10	11												4							3	7	34
1	2	14		5	9	8	10	7†												11*	12				4		3		35
14	3			5	11	4	9	7†							1						12		6*				2	8	36
1	2	3	8	5	11	10	9																		4		7		37
1	2	3	8*	5	11	10	9														12				4		7		38
1	2	3		5	11	8†	9	7*	14												12						4	10	39
32	34	16	25	36	7	35	30	25	26	25	5	2	3	4	4	22	7	1	7	5	15	1	6	10	15	6	10	9	
+	+	+			+	+	+	+	+							+	+	+	+						+	+	+	+	
1s	1s	3s			2s	3s	1s	3s	1s	2s	2s	5s	1s	1s	11s3s	4s									2s	1s	6s 1s	1s	

Ross B—Match No. 34(6) 35(6) 36(10) 37(6) 38(6) 39(6).

FALKIRK Premier Division

Year Formed: 1876. *Ground & Address:* Brockville Park, Hope St, Falkirk FK1 5AX. *Telephone:* 0324
24121/32487. *Fax:* 10324 612418.
Ground Capacity: total: 18,000. seated: 2661. *Size of Pitch:* 110yd × 70yd.
Chairman: David Holmes. *Secretary:* George Deans. *Commercial Manager:* Jim Hendry.
Manager: Jim Jefferies. *Assistant Manager:* W. Brown. *Physio:* D. Hughes. *Coach:* Willie Wilson.
Managers since 1975: J. Prentice; G. Miller; W. Little; J. Hagart; A. Totten; G. Abel; W. Lamont; D. Clarke; J. Duffy.
Club Nickname(s): The Bairns. *Previous Grounds:* Randyford; Blinkbonny Grounds; Hope Street.
Record Attendance: 23,100 v Celtic, Scottish Cup 3rd rd; 21 Feb, 1953.
Record Transfer Fee received: £150,000 for Roddie Manley from St Mirren, 1989.
Record Transfer Fee paid: £70,000 for Gordon Marshall from East Fife, 1987.

FALKIRK 1990–91 LEAGUE RECORD

Match No.	Date	Venue	Opponents	Result	H/T Score	Lg. Pos.	Goalscorers	Atten- dance
1	Aug 25	H	Hamilton A	L	0-1	0-1	—	2800
2	Sept 1	A	Clydebank	L	1-3	0-3	13	Baptie	2026
3	8	H	Partick T	L	0-2	0-0	13		4825
4	15	A	Kilmarnock	D	1-1	1-1	12	Stainrod	4629
5	18	H	Morton	W	2-1	0-0	—	McGivern, Houston	1800
6	22	A	Brechin C	W	2-0	0-0	8	Hughes, Rutherford	1300
7	29	H	Forfar Ath	W	1-0	1-0	5	Beaton	2261
8	Oct 6	A	Clyde	W	3-1	0-1	5	Rutherford 2, McGivern	1000
9	9	H	Ayr U	L	1-2	1-1		Stainrod (pen)	2600
10	13	H	Meadowbank T	D	2-2	2-0	6	Stainrod, McGivern	2200
11	20	A	Dundee	D	2-2	1-1	7	McGivern, Stainrod	5531
12	27	A	Airdrieonians	W	3-1	3-0	5	McGivern 3	5000
13	Nov 3	H	Raith R	W	7-1	2-1	4	McWilliams 2, Hetherston 2, Taylor, McGiven, Cody	3963
14	10	H	Clydebank	W	5-1	4-0	4	Stainrod 3 (1 pen), McGivern 2	3600
15	17	A	Hamilton A	W	2-0	1-0	4	Duffy, Stainrod (pen)	3584
16	24	A	Ayr U	D	1-1	0-1	4	Whittaker	3673
17	Dec 1	H	Clyde	W	2-0	0-0	3	Duffy, Hetherston	2800
18	12	A	Forfar Ath	W	2-1	1-0	—	McGivern, Houston	1273
19	15	H	Brechin C	W	3-0	2-0	1	McGivern 2, Stainrod	3820
20	22	H	Airdrieonians	D	1-1	1-1	1	Stainrod (pen)	6040
21	29	A	Raith R	W	4-1	0-1	1	McWilliams 2, Stainrod 2	3764
22	Jan 5	H	Dundee	W	1-0	1-0	1	Hughes	7672
23	19	H	Kilmarnock	D	1-1	0-1	1	McWilliams	6759
24	Feb 2	A	Morton	D	0-0	0-0	1		3451
25	16	H	Raith R	L	0-2	0-0	1		4197
26	27	A	Clydebank	D	2-2	1-1	—	Stainrod 2	1777
27	Mar 2	H	Clyde	W	1-0	0-0	1	May	3829
28	5	A	Partick T	L	0-2	0-0	—		5257
29	16	H	Hamilton A	W	3-0	1-0	2	May, Hetherston, Taylor	4317
30	20	A	Meadowbank T	W	1-0	1-0	1	McWilliams	1400
31	23	A	Kilmarnock	D	1-1	1-1	1	May	6664
32	30	A	Airdrieonians	W	3-0	2-0	1	McGivern, May, Stainrod	8200
33	Apr 2	A	Forfar Ath	D	0-0	0-0	—		966
34	6	H	Brechin C	W	2-1	1-1	1	McWilliams 2 (1 pen)	4079
35	13	H	Dundee	D	0-0	0-0	1		9232
36	20	A	Partick T	D	1-1	0-1	1	McQueen (pen)	7000
37	27	A	Morton	W	1-0	1-0	1	McQueen (pen)	3708
38	May 8	H	Ayr U	W	4-1	2-0	—	Stainrod, McGivern, May, McWilliams	7116
39	11	H	Meadowbank T	W	4-2	2-0	1	Baptie 2, McWilliams, May	8000

Final League Position: 1

GOALSCORERS

League: (70): Stainrod 16 (4 pens), McGivern 15, McWilliams 10 (1 pen), May 6, Hetherston 4, Baptie 3, Rutherford 3,
Duffy 2, Houston 2, Hughes 2, McQueen 2 (2 pens), Taylor 2, Beaton 1, Cody 1, Whittaker 1
Scottish Cup: (6): McGivern 3, McWilliams 2, Taylor 1
Skol Cup: (1): Houston 1

Record Victory: 12-1 v Laurieston, Scottish Cup 2nd rd; 23 Mar, 1893.
Record Defeat: 1-11 v Airdrieonians, Division I; 28 Apr. 1951.
Most Capped Player: Alex Parker, 14 (15), Scotland.
Most League Appearances: (post-war): John Markie, 349.
Most League Goals in Season (Individual): 43: Evelyn Morrison, Division I; 1928–29.
Most Goals Overall (Individual): Dougie Moran, 86.

Honours
League Champions: Division II 1935–36, 1969–70, 1974–75. First division 1990-91. Second Division 1979–80; Runners-up: Division I 1907–08, 1909–10. First Division 1985–86. Division II 1904–05, 1951–52, 1960–61.
Scottish Cup Winners: 1913, 1957.
League Cup Runners-up: 1947–48.
Club colours: Shirt: Dark blue with white flashings. Shorts: White. Stockings: Red.

Marshall, G	Robertson, J	Whittaker, B	Melvin, M	Beaton, D	Smith, G	Houston, P	Logan, S	McNeill, W	Hughes, J	Rutherford, P	Cowell, J	McGivern, S	Mooney, M	Stainrod, S	Baptie, C	McWilliams, D	Corner, S	McQueen, T	McKinnon, C	Cody, S	McCoy, G	Hetherston, P	Taylor, A	Duffy, N	Nicol, A	May, E	Godfrey, P	Match No.
1	2	3	4	5	6	7	8†	9*10	11	12	14																	1
1	2	3	4	5	6	12		10*	14			7†	8	9	11													2
1	2	3	4	5	6	12		8*	14	7†		10	9	11														3
1	2	3†	8	5	6	12		9	14	7		10*	4	11														4
1	2		3	5	6	7		8		9		10	4	11														5
1	2	3	12	5	6	7*		8	14			9†		10	4	11												6
1	2	3	12	5	6	7*		8	14	9		10†	4	11														7
1		4	2	5†	6		8	9	11		10	7		3	12													8
1	4	2†		6	12		8	9*	11		10	5		3		7	14											9
1	4	2	5				8*		9	10		11†		3	6	7	12	14										10
1	4		6			9	11	10	5			3	12	2			7	8*										11
1	4†	2		9		7	10*	5	11			3		12			6	8	14									12
1	4	2	14	9		7	10	5*11				3		12			6†	8										13
1	4	2		7			10	5	11*			3		9			6	8	12									14
1	4	2	12	7			10	5				3		9*			6	8	11									15
1	4		7	12	10	5	11*			3				6	8	9	2											16
1	4	12		7		10	5	11*	3					6	8	9	2											17
1	12	6		11		10	5			3		9		8*	4	2												18
1		11		7		10	5			3		9		6	8	4	2											19
1		4		7		10	5	11		3				6	8	9	2											20
1	4*		14	7		10	5†11			3		12		6	8	9	2											21
1		4		9		10	5	11		3		7		6	8	2												22
1		4		9	12	10	5	11		3		7		6	8	2*												23
1		9		7		10	5	11		3		4		6	8	2												24
1	12	14	9	7		5	11		3	10*		6	8	4†	2													25
1	2	12	9	7*	10	11		3			6	8	4	5														26
1	2	9†	5	14	10	11		3	6		8	4	12	7*														27
1	4	5	12	10	11		3	9*		8	6	2	7															28
1	6	2		10	11	3			9	8	4		7	5														29
1	6	2		10	11	3			9	8	4		7	5														30
1	6	7		10	11	3			9	8	2		4	5														31
1	6	2	7*	10	11	3		12	8	4		9	5															32
1	6	2	4*	7	10	11	3		12	8		9	5															33
1	6†	2	12	7*	10	11	3		9	8	14	4	5															34
1	6	2	4	7	10	11	3		12	8†14	9*	5																35
1	6	2*	4	7	10		3	11	8	12	9	5																36
1	12	4	7	10	6	3		11	8	2	9*	5																37
1	14	6	7*	10	12	11	3		9	8	2†	4	5															38
1	6	10	9	11	3		12	8	4*	7	5																	39

| 39 | 7 | 25 | 8 | 9 | 27 | 5 | 1 | 2 | 31 | 3 | — | 28 | 1 | 37 | 25 | 29 | 1 | 32 | 2 | 12 | — | 22 | 29 | 20 | 10 | 13 | 11 | |

```
        +        + +      + + + + +      +        + + +      + +
       2s       4s 8s    2s 1s 3s 3s 2s 3s   1s      2s 5s 1s 4s   5s 1s
```

695

FORFAR ATHLETIC
First Division

Year Formed: 1885.   *Ground & Address:* Station Park, Carseview Road, Forfar.   *Telephone:* 0307 63576.
Ground Capacity: total: 8359. seated: 711.   *Size of Pitch:* 115yd × 69yd.
Chairman: George Enston.   *Secretary:* David McGregor.   *Commercial Manager:* —.
Manager: Paul Hegarty.   *Assistant Manager:* Frank Kopel.   *Physio:* Andy Dickson.   *Coach:* John Smith.
Managers since 1975: Jerry Kerr; Archie Knox; Alex Rae; Doug Houston; Henry Hall, Bobby Glennie.
Club Nickname(s): Sky Blues.   *Previous Grounds:* None.
Record Attendance: 10,780 v Rangers, Scottish Cup 2nd rd, 2 Feb, 1970.
Record Transfer Fee received: £44,000 for Kenny Macdonald from Airdrieonians, 1988.
Record Transfer Fee paid: £30,000 for Tom McCafferty from East Fife, 1989.

FORFAR ATHLETIC 1990—91 LEAGUE RECORD

Match No.	Date	Venue	Opponents	Result	H/T Score	Lg. Pos.	Goalscorers	Attendance
1	Aug 25	A	Ayr U	D	1-1	1-0	—	Brewster	1711
2	Sept 1	H	Meadowbank T	W	3-2	1-1	4	Whyte, Brewster, Leslie	688
3	8	A	Clyde	D	1-1	1-0	6	Brazil	400
4	15	H	Airdrieonians	L	1-4	0-1	9	Petrie	1293
5	18	A	Raith R	L	1-2	1-1	—	Whyte	1053
6	22	H	Dundee	D	1-1	0-0	9	Clark	3053
7	29	A	Falkirk	L	0-1	0-1	10		2261
8	Oct 6	H	Partick T	L	0-1	0-0	11		868
9	10	A	Clydebank	D	2-2	1-1	—	Brewster, Clark	575
10	13	A	Brechin C	L	1-2	1-0	11	Kenny (og)	600
11	20	H	Morton	W	5-1	3-1	11	Leslie, Paton 2, Petrie, Reid (og)	701
12	27	H	Kilmarnock	D	2-2	0-2	11	Clinging, Brewster (pen)	1521
13	Nov 3	A	Hamilton A	L	0-2	0-0	12		1125
14	10	A	Meadowbank T	D	2-2	1-1	12	Clark, Paton	250
15	17	A	Ayr U	W	3-1	3-1	11	Paton, Petrie, Brewster	726
16	24	H	Clydebank	L	0-3	0-1	12		606
17	Dec 1	A	Partick T	L	2-3	1-2	12	Whyte 2	2415
18	12	H	Falkirk	L	1-2	0-1	—	Brazil	1273
19	18	A	Dundee	L	1-4	0-2	—	Brewster	2100
20	22	H	Kilmarnock	L	0-1	0-0	12		3224
21	29	H	Hamilton A	D	0-0	0-0	12		606
22	Jan 19	A	Airdrieonians	D	1-1	1-1	12	Whyte	2000
23	Feb 2	H	Raith R	W	3-1	1-0	12	Adam, Brewster, Petrie	826
24	23	H	Clyde	L	1-3	0-0	12	Brewster	660
25	Mar 2	A	Partick T	L	0-2	0-0	12		2554
26	5	H	Brechin C	D	0-0	0-0	—		794
27	12	H	Kilmarnock	D	1-1	1-1	—	Petrie	977
28	16	A	Dundee	L	0-1	0-0	13		2618
29	20	A	Hamilton A	W	1-0	1-0	—	Winter	946
30	23	H	Clydebank	D	2-2	2-2	12	Whyte 2	260
31	26	A	Morton	L	1-1	1-0	—	McKenna I	1120
32	30	H	Meadowbank T	W	2-0	1-0	12	Adam, Whyte	620
33	Apr 2	H	Falkirk	D	0-0	0-0	—		966
34	6	A	Clyde	W	1-0	1-0	11	McKenna I	600
35	13	A	Raith R	W	2-1	0-1	11	Campbell, Petrie	881
36	20	H	Ayr U	D	1-1	0-1	11	Whyte (pen)	715
37	27	A	Airdrieonians	L	1-2	0-0	12	Brewster	2500
38	May 4	H	Morton	D	2-2	1-0	11	Paton, Brewster	637
39	11	H	Brechin C	W	4-1	1-1	10	Whyte 3 (1 pen), Brewster	618

Final League Position: 10

GOALSCORERS
League: (50): Whyte 12 (2 pens), Brewster 11 (1 pen), Petrie 6, Paton 5, Clark 3, Adam 2, Brazil 2, Leslie 2, McKenna I 2, Campbell 1, Clinging 1, Winter 1, own goals 2.
Scottish Cup: (0).
Skol Cup: (1): Brewster 1 (pen).
Centenary Cup: (0).

Record Victory: 14-1 v Lindertis, Scottish Cup 1st rd; 1 Sept 1988.
Record Defeat: 2-12 v King's Park, Division II; 2 Jan, 1930.
Most Capped Player: —.
Most League Appearances: 376: Alex Brash, 1974–86.
Most League Goals in Season (Individual): 45: Dave Kilgour, Division II; 1929–30.
Most Goals Overall (Individual): 124, John Clark.

Honours
League Champions: Second Division 1983–84. C Division 1948–49.
Scottish Cup: Semi-finals 1982.
League Cup: Semi-finals 1977–78.
Club colours: Shirt: Sky blue. Shorts: Navy. Stockings: Sky blue.

Allan, R	Lorimer, R	Hamill, A	Morris, R	Hegarty, P	Smith, P	Paton, P	Brewster, C	Whyte, G	Leslie, A	Petrie, S	Fotheringham, J	Clark, J	Brazil, A	Winter, G	Mearns, G	Clinging, I	McAulay, A	Gardner, S	Feeney, M	McKenna, S	Adam, C	Byrne, J	Holt, J	Campbell, A	McKenna, I	Kennedy, S	Match No.
1	2	3	4	5	6	7†	8	9	10	11*	12	14															1
1	2	3	4	5		7*	8	9	10	11	12	6															2
1	2	-3	4	5	6		8	9	10†	11*	14	7	12														3
1	2	3	4*	5	6		8	9	10	11†	14	7	12														4
1	2†	3		5	6	7*	8	9	12	11		10	4	14													5
1		3	2	5	6	7†	8	9	12	11*		10	14	4		4											6
1	2	3	4†	5			8	9*	12	11		10	7	6	14												7
1		3	2	5	6	7*	8	9	10	11†	14	12	4														8
1	12	3		5†		7	8	9*		11	14	10	2	4	6												9
1	12	3		5*		7	8	11	9			10	2	4	14	6†											10
1		3	2	5	6*	7	8	9	11	10†		4		12	14												11
1		3	2	5	6†	7	8	9	11	10*		4		12	14												12
1		3	2	5	6*		8	9	11†14		4	10	12	7													13
1		3		5		7	8	9	11*	10	2	4†	12	14	6												14
1	6	3	4	5		7	8	9*	11	10	2	12															15
1	6	3	4	5		7	8	9	14	11	10*	2†	12														16
1	6	3†	4	5*12	7	8	9	11		2	14				10												17
1	6	3	4	5	7†	9	11	12	2			8	10*14														18
1	6		4	5	7*10	9	12	11	2		8	3															19
1	6	3	4		10	12		14	9	2	11	7*	8†5														20
1	6	3	4		10	9*		11	7	2	12	8	5														21
1		4	5	6	7	10	9*	11	2	12		8	3														22
1	7	3	4	5	10	9	11	12	2			8*	6														23
1	7	3		5	10	9	11	12	2*	4	8	6															24
1		3	2		10	7	11*	12	4		8	5	6	9													25
1		3	2	5	10	7*	11	12	4		8	6	9														26
1	7	3	2	6	8*	12	10	11	4			5	9														27
1	7*	3	2	6	12	10	11	4	5		8	9†14															28
1	7	3	6	5	8	10†14	12	11	2	4	9*																29
1	7	3	6	5	12	10	9	11	2	4	8*																30
1	7*	3	6	5	11	12	2	8	4	10	9																31
1	7	3	6	5	11	9	2	14	8*	4	10†12																32
1	7	3	6	5	12	9	2	8	4	10	11*																33
1	7	3	6	5	11	12	2	8	4	10	9*																34
	7	3	6	5	2	9	12	8*	4	10	11															1	35
	7	3	6	5	14	12	9	2	8†	4	10	11*														1	36
	7†	3	5	14	8	11	9	2	6*	4	10	12														1	37
	12	3	5	7*	6	11	9	2	8	4	10															1	38
	3†	2		10	7	9	14	8	6	4	5	12	11*													1	39
34	26	37	34	32	14	17	28	31	11	32	—	15	26	22	5	4	1	2	3	1	17	7	14	7	4	5	
	+3s						+3s	+1s	+1s	+4s	+7s	+4s	+1s	+12s	+2s	+4s	+2s	+9s	+4s		+1s			+1s	+1s	+2s	

HAMILTON ACADEMICAL First Division

Year Formed: 1874-75.   *Ground & Address:* Douglas Park, Douglas Park Lane, Hamilton ML3 0DF.   *Telephone:* 0698 286103.
Ground Capacity: total: 9168. seated: 1595.   *Size of Pitch:* 110yd × 70yd.
Chairman: George J. Fulston.   *Secretary:* David S. Morrison.   *Commercial Manager:* George Miller.
Manager: Billy McLaren.   *Assistant Manager:* Willie McLean.   *Physio:* Frank Ness.   *Coach:* Colin Miller.
Managers since 1975: J. Eric Smith; Dave McParland; John Blackley; Bertie Auld; John Lambie; Jim Dempsey, John Lambie.
Club Nickname(s): The Accies.   *Previous Grounds:* Bent Farm, South Avenue, South Haugh.
Record Attendance: 28,690 v Hearts, Scottish Cup 3rd rd, 3 Mar, 1937.
Record Transfer Fee received: £110,000 for Willie Jamieson to Dundee, January 1990.

HAMILTON ACADEMICAL 1990–91 LEAGUE RECORD

Match No.	Date	Venue	Opponents	Result	H/T Score	Lg. Pos.	Goalscorers	Attendance
1	Aug 25	A	Falkirk	W 1-0	1-0	—	Horne	2800
2	Sept 1	H	Ayr U	D 0-0	0-0	6		1722
3	8	H	Kilmarnock	W 3-1	1-1	4	McCluskey, Harris, McDonald	2687
4	15	A	Morton	W 2-0	0-0	3	McCluskey, McDonald	1534
5	18	H	Dundee	W 1-0	0-0		McCluskey	1773
6	22	A	Partick T	W 1-0	0-0	2	Burns	4073
7	29	H	Brechin C	W 2-1	1-1	2	Burns, Harris	1102
8	Oct 6	A	Raith R	L 0-1	0-0	2		1138
9	10	H	Clyde	W 1-0	0-0		McCluskey	1385
10	13	H	Airdrieonians	L 0-1	0-0	2		3516
11	20	A	Clydebank	L 1-3	0-1	3	Napier	1108
12	27	A	Meadowbank T	D 1-1	1-1	3	McCluskey	500
13	Nov 3	H	Forfar Ath	W 2-0	0-0	2	Burns 2	1125
14	10	H	Morton	D 1-1	1-0	2	Napier	1187
15	17	H	Falkirk	L 0-2	0-1	4		3584
16	20	A	Ayr U	D 2-2	1-0	—	Harris, McCluskey	1900
17	24	A	Clyde	W 2-0	1-0	2	O'Hara, Burns	900
18	Dec 1	H	Raith R	D 2-2	2-2	2	McCluskey, Hillcoat	1464
19	11	A	Brechin C	W 1-0	0-0	—	McDonald	800
20	15	H	Partick T	D 2-2	2-1	2	McCluskey, Burns	2519
21	29	A	Forfar Ath	D 0-0	0-0	3		606
22	Jan 2	A	Airdrieonians	L 1-2	1-0	—	McCluskey	3200
23	5	H	Clydebank	W 2-0	0-0	3	McDonald (pen), Lamont (og)	1086
24	12	A	Kilmarnock	L 0-1	0-0	3		4767
25	Feb 2	A	Dundee	L 2-3	1-3	4	McDonald, McGuigan	3153
26	Mar 2	A	Brechin C	D 2-2	1-1	6	McDonald 2 (1 pen)	400
27	9	H	Meadowbank T	D 1-1	0-1	6	Weir	1073
28	13	H	Meadowbank T	W 2-1	1-0	—	Napier 2	1048
29	16	A	Falkirk	L 0-3	0-1	4		4317
30	20	H	Forfar Ath	L 0-1	0-1	—		946
31	23	H	Airdrieonians	D 1-1	0-1	4	Harris (pen)	2546
32	26	A	Ayr U	W 2-1	1-0	—	McCluskey, Weir	2100
33	30	A	Kilmarnock	L 0-1	0-0	6		4449
34	Apr 6	H	Partick T	L 0-1	0-1	6		2627
35	13	A	Morton	W 4-0	2-0	5	Cramb 2, Harris, Napier	1290
36	20	H	Raith R	L 1-2	0-1	6	McCluskey	1140
37	27	A	Clydebank	W 3-1	3-1	6	McCluskey 3	767
38	May 4	H	Clyde	W 3-1	1-0	6	Napier, Harris 2 (1 pen)	1220
39	11	H	Dundee	L 1-2	1-1	6	McGuigan	3136

Final League Position: 6

GOALSCORERS

League: (50): McCluskey 14, Harris 7 (2 pens), McDonald 7 (2 pens), Burns 6, Napier 6, Cramb 2, McGuigan 2, Weir 2, Hillcoat 1, Horne 1, O'Hara 1 (pen), own goal.
Scottish Cup: (2): McCluskey 2, Moore 1.
Skol Cup: (2): Burns 1, McCluskey.
Centenary Cup: (2): Harris 1 (pen), McCluskey 1.

Record Transfer Fee paid: £60,000 for Paul Martin from Kilmarnock, 1988.
Record Victory: 11–1 v Chryston, Lanarkshire Cup, 28 Nov 1885.
Record Defeat: 1–11 v Hibernian, Division I, 6 Nov, 1965.
Most Capped Player: Colin Miller, 5, (16) Canada.
Most League Appearances: 447: Rikki Ferguson, 1974–88.
Most League Goals in Season (Individual): 34: David Wilson, Division I; 1936–37.
Most Goals Overall (Individual): 246: David Wilson, 1928–39.

Honours
League Champions: First Division 1985–86, 1987–88. Division II 1903–04; *Runners-up:* Division II 1952–53, 1964–65.
Scottish Cup Runners-up: 1911, 1935.
League Cup: Semi-finalists three times.
Club colours: Shirt: Red and white hoops. Shorts: White. Stockings: White.

Ferguson, A.	McKee, K.	Napier, C.	Millen, A.	Weir, J	McGinley, M	Harris, C	Horne, J	McCluskey, G	Burns, H	McDonald, P	Moore, S	O'Hara, A	Miller, C	McGuigan, R	McGachie, J	McCabe, G	Hillcoat, C	McQuilter, R	McKenzie, P	Archer, S	MacFarlane, I	Cramb, C	McNeill, N	Match No.
1	2	3	4	5	6	7	8	9*10†11	12	14														1
1	2	10	4	5	14	7	11*	9†	8		12	6	3											2
1	2	6	4	5		7		9	8	11	12	10*	3											3
1	2	10	4	5		7		9	8	11		6*	3	12										4
1	2	10	4	5		7		9	8*11			6	3	12										5
1	2	10	4	5		7	9*	8†11	12			6	3	14										6
1	2	10	4	5		7	9*	8†11	12			6	3	14										7
1	2	10*	4	5		7†		9	11		12	6	3	8	14									8
1	2	10	4	5			14	9	8*11		7†	6	3	12										9
1	2	10	4	5		7	14	9	8†11			6	3*12											10
1	2	10	4	5		7	8	9	11			6*	3	12										11
1	2	10	4	5		7	14	9	11†			6*	3	8	12									12
1	2	6	4	5		7†14	9	10	11		8*	3		12										13
1	2	10	4	5		7	12	9	8	11*		3	14	6†										14
1	2	10	4	5		7	14	9†	8	12		6*	3	11										15
1	2	10	4	5		7		9	8	11		6*	3	12										16
1	2†	6	4	5		7	9*	8	11	10	3		14	12										17
1	2	6	4	5		7*	9	8†11		3	10		14	12										18
1	2	7	4	5			9	8*11	10		12	6	3											19
1	2	7	4	5			9	8*11	12	3	10		6											20
1	2	7	4	5			9	8	12	10*	3	11		6										21
1	2	7	4	5		12	9	8	11†14		3	10		6*										22
1	2	7	4	5			9†	8	11		3	10		12	6*14									23
1	2	7†	4	5			14	8	11		3	10		9*12	6									24
1	2	7*	4	5		12	9	8	11	10†	3	6			14									25
1	2*10	4	5			9	11	7		3	6			12	8									26
1	3	4	5			9	11	7	12	2	6*	8†	10		14									27
1	2	10	4	5			9	11	7†12	3	8		6*		14									28
1	2	10	4	5			9	11	7†12	3	8		6*		14									29
	2	10	4	5	14		9	11	7†12	3	6*		8							1				30
1	2	10	4	5	14		9†	11		6	3	8		12					7*					31
1	2	8	4	5	12		9*	11	7	6	3		10											32
1	2	9	4	5	7*			11	8		3	6	10	12										33
1	2	9	4	5	7*		12	11	8		3		10†	6							14			34
1	2	10	4	5	7*		9†	11	12		3		6								8	14		35
1	2	8*	4	5	7		9	11	12		3		6								10†14			36
1	2	8*	4	5	7		9	11	12		3	10	6											37
1	2	8	4	5	7		9	11			3	10	6											38
	2	8	4	5	7	12	9	11			3	10		6*						1				39

37	38	39	39	39	1	24	4	35	22	36	9	19	37	21	—	9	5	9	1	1	2	2	—	
					+	+	+		+	+	+			+		+	+	+	+	+		+	+	
					1s	3s	10s		1s	2s	11s5s			8s		1s	7s	4s	5s	1s	1s		1s	2s	

HEART OF MIDLOTHIAN Premier Division

Year Formed: 1874. *Ground & Address:* Tynecastle Park, Gorgie Rd, Edinburgh EH11 2NL. *Telephone:* 031 337 6132.
Ground Capacity: total: 25,177. seated: 11,987. *Size of Pitch:* 110yd × 74yd.
Chairman: A. Wallace Mercer. *Secretary:* L. W. Porteous. *Commercial Manager:* Charles Burnett.
Manager: Joe Jordan. *Assistant Manager:* Frank Connor. *Physio:* Alan Rae. *Coach:* (1) Sandy Clark, (2) John Binnie.
Managers since 1975: J. Hagart; W. Ormond; R. Moncur; A. MacDonald; A. MacDonald & W. Jardine; A. MacDonald.
Club Nickname(s): Hearts. *Previous Grounds:* The Meadows 1874, Powderhall 1878, Old Tynecastle 1881, (Tynecastle Park, 1886).
Record Attendance: 53,396 v Rangers, Scottish Cup 3rd rd; 13 Feb, 1932.
Record Transfer Fee received: £700,000 for John Robertson to Newcastle U (April 1988).
Record Transfer Fee paid: £750,000 for Dave McPherson from Rangers (Dec 1988).
Record Victory: 21–0 v Anchor, EFA Cup 1880.

HEART OF MIDLOTHIAN 1990–91 LEAGUE RECORD

Match No.	Date	Venue	Opponents	Result	H/T Score	Lg. Pos.	Goalscorers	Attendance
1	Aug 25	H	St Mirren	D	1-1	0-1	—	Robertson	12,215
2	Sept 1	A	Dunfermline Ath	L	0-2	0-1	8		8905
3	8	H	Rangers	L	1-3	0-2	8	Wright	22,101
4	15	A	Hibernian	W	3-0	3-0	7	Robertson 2, Levein	19,500
5	22	A	Celtic	L	0-3	0-1	8		38,409
6	29	H	Dundee U	W	1-0	0-0	7	Bannon	12,052
7	Oct 6	A	Motherwell	D	1-1	1-0	7	Ferguson I	6780
8	13	H	St Johnstone	L	2-3	1-1	7	Ferguson I, Kirkwood	12,824
9	20	A	Aberdeen	L	0-3	0-1	9		14,800
10	27	A	St Mirren	L	1-2	0-1	9	Colquhoun	5441
11	Nov 3	H	Dunfermline Ath	D	1-1	1-0	10	Colquhoun	11,897
12	10	H	Celtic	W	1-0	1-0	9	Colquhoun	19,189
13	17	A	Dundee U	D	1-1	1-0	8	Levein	10,821
14	24	H	Hibernian	D	1-1	0-0	7	Berry	19,004
15	Dec 1	A	Rangers	L	0-4	0-1	7		37,623
16	8	H	Aberdeen	W	1-0	1-0	6	Colquhoun	9811
17	15	A	St Johnstone	L	1-2	0-1	8	Crabbe	7833
18	22	H	Motherwell	W	3-2	1-1	7	McPherson, Mackay, Robertson (pen)	8625
19	29	A	Celtic	D	1-1	0-1	6	Colquhoun	28,118
20	Jan 2	A	Hibernian	W	4-1	3-0	—	McKinlay, McPherson, Mackay, Levein	13,600
21	5	H	Rangers	L	0-1	0-0	6		20,956
22	22	H	St Mirren	W	2-0	1-0	5	Robertson 2 (1 pen)	10,858
23	Feb 2	A	Aberdeen	L	0-5	0-3	6		9500
24	16	H	Dundee U	W	2-1	0-1	6	Robertson, McLaren	7216
25	23	A	Dunfermline Ath	L	1-3	0-2	6	Wilson (og)	7273
26	Mar 2	A	Motherwell	W	3-1	1-1	6	Foster, Robertson, Sandison	5212
27	6	H	St Johnstone	W	2-1	1-1	—	Ferguson D, Colquhoun	8136
28	9	A	Rangers	L	1-2	1-1	6	Ferguson D	36,128
29	23	H	Hibernian	W	3-1	0-0	5	Levein, Wright, Robertson	14,221
30	30	A	St Mirren	D	0-0	0-0	5		4823
31	Apr 6	H	Dunfermline Ath	W	4-1	2-0	5	Robertson 2, Crabbe, McKinlay	8102
32	13	H	Aberdeen	L	1-4	1-1	5	McKimmie (og)	16,771
33	20	A	St Johnstone	W	2-0	2-0	5	Colquhoun, Mackay	6822
34	27	H	Celtic	L	0-1	0-0	5		17,085
35	May 4	A	Dundee U	L	1-2	0-1	6	Crabbe	6820
36	11	H	Motherwell	W	2-1	1-1	5	Robertson, Bannon	7055

Final League Position: 5

GOALSCORERS

League: (48): Robertson 12 (2 pens), Colquhoun 7, Levein 4, Crabbe 3, Mackay 3, Bannon 2, Ferguson D 2, Ferguson I 2, McKinlay 2, McPherson 2, Wright 2, Berry 1, Foster 1, Kirkwood 1, McLaren 1, Sandison 1, own goals 2.
Scottish Cup: (1): Mackay 1.
Skol Cup: (3): Bannon 1, Crabbe 1, Robertson 1.

Record Defeat: 1–8 v Vale of Leithen, Scottish Cup, 1888.
Most Capped Player: Bobby Walker, 29, Scotland.
Most League Appearances: 394, Jim Cruickshank, 1960–77.
Most League Goals in Season (Individual): 44: Barney Battles.
Most Goals Overall (Individual): 206: Jimmy Wardhaugh, 1946–59.

Honours

League Champions: Division I 1894–95, 1896–97, 1957–58, 1959–60. First Division 1979–80; *Runners-up:* Division I 1893–94, 1898–99, 1903–04, 1905–06, 1914–15, 1937–38, 1953–54, 1956–57, 1958–59, 1964–65. Premier Division 1985–86. First Division 1977–78, 1982–83. *Runners-up:* 1987–88.
Scottish Cup Winners: 1891, 1896, 1901, 1906, 1956; *Runners-up:* 1903, 1907, 1968, 1976, 1986.
League Cup Winners: 1954–55, 1958–59, 1959–60, 1962–63; *Runners-up:* 1961–62.
European: *European Cup* 4 matches (1958–59, 1960–61). *Cup Winners Cup* 4 matches (1976–77). *UEFA Cup:* 27 matches (1961–62, 1963–64, 1965–66, 1988–89, 1990–91) *Fairs Cup;* 1984–85, 1986-87, 1988–89).
Club colours: Shirt: Maroon. Shorts: White. Stockings: Maroon with white tops.

Smith, H	Wright, G	McKinlay, T	Levein, C	McCreery, D	McPherson, D	Colquhoun, J	Ferguson, D	Robertson, J	MacKay, G	Crabbe, S	Bannon, E	Berry, N	McLaren, A	Kidd, W	Foster, W	Kirkwood, D	Sandison, J	Ferguson, I	Walker, N	Harrison, T	Match No.
1	2	3	4	5*	6	7	8†	9	10	11	12	14									1
1		3†	4	5	6	7	8*	9	10	12	14	11	2								2
1	14	3		4	6	7†	8	9	10*		5		2	11	12						3
1	6†	3	4		11		7*	8		5	2	14	9		10	12					4
1	6	3	4	5	11		7*			5	2		9	8	10	12					5
1	8	3	4	5	7	12		11*			2		9†	6	14	10					6
1		3	4†	6	7	14	9*	8	11		2	12	5		10						7
1		3	4	6	7	12	9	8*	11		2		5		10						8
1		3	4	6	7		9*		11	8	2	12	5		10						9
1		3	4	6	7		12	14	11*	8	2		9†	5	10*						10
1		3	4	6	7		2	12	11	8			9	5	10*						11
1		3	4	6	7	10	11*	5		8	12		9†			2	14				12
1		3	4	6	7		11*	5		8			9†10			2	12				13
1		3	4	6	7	10	11	5		8			9*			2	12				14
1	3		4	6	7	10		5	12	8			9*			2	11				15
1		3	4	6	7	10	11	5	12	8			9*			2					16
1		3	4	6	7	10	11	5	12	8			9*			2					17
1		3	4*	6	7	10	11	5	9*	8	14		12			2					18
1		3		6	7	10	11*	5	9	8	4		12			2					19
1		3	4*	6	7	10	11	5	9†	8	12		14			2					20
1		3	4	6	7	10	11†	5	9*12	8	14					2					21
1		3	10	6	7		11	5	9*	8	4		12			2					22
1		3	4 12	6	7	10	11*	5		8			9			2					23
			4*	6	7	10	11	5		8†		3	12	9		2		1	14		24
12	3	4		6*	7	10	11	5		8			9			2		1			25
	3	4		6	7	10	11	5		8			9			2		1			26
12	3	4		6	7	10	11	5		8*			9			2		1			27
	3	4		6	7	10	11	5	8*14				9†			2		1	12		28
	5	3	4	6	7	10	11*		9	8†	14			2				1	12		29
	5	3	4	6	7	10	11		9	8				'2				1			30
	5	3	4	6	7	10	11	12	9	8*				2				1			31
	5	3†	4	6	7	10	11	12	9	8	14			2*				1			32
	5	14	4 12	6	7†10		3	9	8	2	11*							1			33
	5	3	4	6	7*10	11		9	8	2	12							1			34
	5†	3	4 14		7*		9	10	12	8	2	11	6					1			35
	5	14	4	6	7*10		9	3	12	8	2	11†						1			36
23	14	31	33		4	34	36	25	31	27	13	15	18	18	1	21	8	24	7	13 —	
+	+		+			+	+	+	+	+	+	+	+	+	+	+	+			+	
3s	2s		3s			3s	3s	8s	4s	1s	5s	3s	7s	1s	1s	5s				3s	

HIBERNIAN Premier Division

Year formed: 1875. *Ground & Address:* Easter Road Stadium, Albion Rd, Edinburgh EH7 5QG. *Telephone:* 031 661 2159.
Ground Capacity: total: 22,260. seated: 6670. *Size of Pitch:* 112yd × 74yd.
Chairman: David F. Duff. *Managing Director:* James C. Gray. *Secretary:* Cecil F. Graham, F.A.A.I., M.Inst. C.M. *Commercial Manager:* Raymond Sparkes.
Manager: Alex Miller. *Assistant Manager:* Murdo MacLeod. *Physio:* Stewart Collie. *Coach:* Andy Watson.
Manager since: Eddie Turnbull; Willie Ormond; Bertie Auld; Pat Stanton; John Blackley; Alex Miller.
Club Nickname(s): Hibees. *Previous Grounds:* Meadows 1875–78, Powderhall 1878–79, Mayfield 1875–80, First Easter Road 1880–92, Second Easter Road 1892–.
Record Attendance: 65,860 v Hearts, Division I; 2 Jan, 1950.
Record Transfer Fee received: £382,000 for Gordon Durie to Chelsea (May 1986).
Record Transfer Fee paid: £325,000 for Andy Goram from Oldham Ath.

HIBERNIAN 1990–91 LEAGUE RECORD

Match No.	Date	Venue	Opponents	Result	H/T Score	Lg. Pos.	Goalscorers	Atten- dance
1	Aug 25	A	Aberdeen	L	0-2	0-1	—	15,500
2	Sept 1	H	Rangers	D	0-0	0-0	9		17,500
3	8	A	Celtic	L	0-2	0-0	9		28,068
4	15	H	Hearts	L	0-3	0-3	10		19,500
5	22	H	St Johnstone	W	1-0	0-0	10	Hamilton	7000
6	29	A	Dunfermline Ath	D	1-1	0-1	10	Findlay	7704
7	Oct 6	H	St Mirren	W	1-0	1-0	8	Weir	4500
8	13	A	Dundee U	L	0-1	0-0	8		10,289
9	20	H	Motherwell	W	1-0	1-0	7	Burley (og)	5500
10	27	H	Aberdeen	D	1-1	1-0	6	Wright	10,500
11	Nov 3	A	Rangers	L	0-4	0-4	6		33,725
12	10	A	St Johnstone	D	1-1	0-0	6	Wright	7638
13	17	H	Dunfermline Ath	D	1-1	1-0	6	MacLeod	7943
14	24	A	Hearts	D	1-1	0-0	6	Houchen	19,004
15	Dec 1	H	Celtic	L	0-3	0-2	6		16,219
16	11	A	Motherwell	L	1-4	1-1	—	Orr	4121
17	15	H	Dundee U	D	0-0	0-0	9		6000
18	22	A	St Mirren	L	0-1	0-0	10		4478
19	29	H	St Johnstone	L	0-1	0-1	10		5000
20	Jan 2	H	Hearts	L	1-4	0-3	—	Mackay (og)	13,600
21	5	A	Celtic	D	1-1	1-0	10	Wright	20,521
22	12	A	Aberdeen	L	0-2	0-1	10		13,500
23	19	H	Rangers	L	0-2	0-1	10		15,000
24	Feb 2	H	Motherwell	D	1-1	1-0	9	MacLeod	6000
25	9	A	Dundee U	D	0-0	0-0	9		6114
26	Mar 2	H	St Mirren	W	4-3	1-2	9	Wright 2, Hunter, Evans	5500
27	9	H	Celtic	L	0-2	0-0	9		11,500
28	16	A	Dunfermline Ath	D	1-1	0-0	9	Wright (pen)	4830
29	23	A	Hearts	L	1-3	0-0	9	Tortolano	14,221
30	30	H	Aberdeen	L	2-4	1-3	9	Evans, Hamilton	7400
31	Apr 6	A	Rangers	D	0-0	0-0	9		35,507
32	13	A	Motherwell	L	0-1	0-0	9		5012
33	20	H	Dundee U	W	1-0	0-0	9	Fellinger	4000
34	27	A	St Johnstone	D	0-0	0-0	9		5143
35	May 4	H	Dunfermline Ath	W	3-0	2-0	9	McGinlay, Findlay, Miller	3500
36	11	A	St Mirren	L	0-1	0-1	9		3403

Final League Position: 9

GOALSCORERS
League: (24): Wright 6 (1 pen), Evans 2, Findlay 2, Hamilton 2, MacLeod 2, Fellinger 1, Houchen 1, Hunter 1, McGinlay 1, Miller 1, Orr 1, Tortolano 1, Weir 1, own goals 2
Scottish Cup: (3): Hamilton 1, Houchen 1, Miller 1
Skol Cup: (1): Houchen 1.

Record Victory: 22-1 v 42nd Highlanders; 3 Sept, 1881.
Record Defeat: 0-10 v Rangers; 24 Dec, 1898.
Most Capped Player: Lawrie Reilly, 38, Scotland.
Most League Appearances: 446: Arthur Duncan.
Most League Goals in Season (Individual): 42: Joe Baker.
Most Goals Overall (Individual): 364: Gordon Smith.

Honours
League Champions: Division I 1902–03, 1947–48, 1950–51, 1951–52. First Division 1980–81. Division II 1893–94, 1894–95, 1932–33; *Runners-up:* Division I 1896–97, 1946–47, 1949–50, 1952–53, 1973–74.
Scottish Cup Winners: 1887, 1902; *Runners-up:* 1896, 1914, 1923, 1924, 1947, 1958, 1972, 1979.
League Cup Winners: 1972–73; *Runners-up:* 1950–51, 1968–69, 1974–75.
European: *European Cup* 6 matches (1955–56 semi-finals). *Cup Winners Cup* 6 matches (1972–73). *UEFA Cup* 54 matches (1960–61 semi-finals, 1961–62, 1962–63, 1965–66, 1967–68, 1968–69, 1970–71 *Fairs Cup*; 1973–74, 1974–75, 1975–76, 1976–77, 1978–79).
Club colours: Shirt: Green with white sleeves. Shorts: White. Stockings: Green with white trim.

Goram, A.	Miller, W	Mitchell, G	Kane, P	Cooper, N	Farrell, D	Evans, G	McGinlay, P	Findlay, W	Houchen, K	Tortolano, J	McGraw, M	Fellenger, D	Hunter, G	Wright, P	Sneddon, A	Hamilton, B	Milne, C	Weir, M	MacLeod, M	Orr, N	McIntyre, T	Lennon, D	Nicholls, D	Reid, C	Match No.
1	2	3	4	5	6*	7†	8	9	10	11	12	14													1
1	2	3	4	5	12	14	9	10	11	7*	6	8†													2
1	2	3	4*	5	14	8	9	10	11	7†	6	12													3
1	2	4		5*	11	9	10			6	8	3	7	12											4
1	2	3	4		12	10	11	14	6*	8		5	7	9†											5
1	2	6	4		7	12	11*	8	3		5	10	9												6
1	2	3*	4		7	11	12	6	8		5	10	9												7
1	2		4		11	10		6	8	5	3	7	9												8
1	2	12	4		11	14	10	6	8	5	3	7*	9†												9
1	2	12	4		11	7*10		6	8	5	3	9													10
1	3	4			11	10	12	6	8*	5	2	7	9												11
1	3	4			11	6	12	10*	8	5	2	7	9												12
1	3	4			11	6	14	10	8	12	5*	2	7†	9											13
1	4				11	7	9	10*	8	3	5	2	12	6											14
1	4				11	9	10	12	8	3	5*	2	7	6											15
1	3	4			11	9	10	12	8	2		7	6	5*											16
1	3	4			11	8*10	2	9	12		7	6	5												17
1	2	7	4		11	12	10	3	9*		6	5													18
1		5	4		11	7	12	3	10†14	8		9	6	2*											19
1	2	5	4		11	9†14	12		8	10	3	6				7*									20
1		5	4	2		11			8	10	7	6	9	3											21
1	2	10	4	7	11				8	5	3	6													22
1	2	11	4			9			8	10	3	7	6		5										23
1	2	3	4		7	10	11	9				6	8	5											24
1	2	3	4	7*	8	9	10	11	12			6	5												25
1	2		12	11	9			10*	6	8	4	3		14	5	7†									26
1	2	4	11	9			6	8	10	3	12	7*	5												27
1	2		4†	11*	9	10		6	8	12	3	7	14	5											28
1	2	10		12	11	9*	14	6	8	5	3	7	4†												29
1	2			11	9	14	12	4	8	10†3*	7	6	5												30
1	3			11	14	12	4	8*	10	2	9†	6	7	5											31
	2	3		9	11†	12	14	4	8*	10		6	7	5								1			32
1	12	3*		9	10		11	4	8		6	2	5	7											33
1	2		9	3	14	12	11*	4	8	10		6	5	7†											34
1	2	14	11	3	9	12	4	8*	10†	6	5	7													35
1	3*	14	9	7†	11	12	5	8	10	6	2	4													36
35	24	25	21	11	1	11	29	21	17	13	4	8	20	31	5	25	21	17	25	15	9	6	1	1	
	+	+			+	+	+	+	+	+	+	+		+	+	+		+		+					
	1s	3s			1s	4s	3s	5s	4s	5s	9s	4s		2s	1s	1s		3s		2s					

KILMARNOCK First Division

Year Formed: 1869.   *Ground & Address:* Rugby Park, Kilmarnock KA1 2DP.   *Telephone:* 0563 25184.
Ground Capacity: total: 17,528. seated: 5511.   *Size of Pitch:* 115yd × 73yd.
Chairman: Robert Fleeting.   *Secretary:* Walter W. McCrae.   *Commercial Manager:* Dennis Martin.
Manager: Jim Fleeting.   *Assistant Managers:* Jim McSherry and Frank Coulston.   *Physio:* Hugh Allan.   *Coach:* —.
Managers since 1975: W. Fernie; D. Sneddon; J. Clunie; E. Morrison; J. Fleeting.
Club Nickname(s): Killie.   *Previous Grounds:* Rugby Park (Dundonald Rd); The Grange; Holm Quarry; Present ground since 1899.
Record Attendance: 35,995 v Rangers, Scottish Cup 10 March 1962.
Record Transfer Fee received: £120,000 for Davie Provan from Celtic, 1978.
Record Transfer Fee Paid: £100,000 for Bobby Williamson to Rotherham United (Nov 1990).
Record Victory: 11–1 v Paisley Academical, Scottish cup, 18 Jan 1930 (15–0 v Lanemark, Ayrshire Cup, 15 Nov 1890).

KILMARNOCK 1990–91 LEAGUE RECORD

Match No.	Date	Venue	Opponents	Result	H/T Score	Lg. Pos.	Goalscorers	Attendance
1	Aug 25	A	Meadowbank T	L 0-1	0-0	—		1767
2	Sept 1	H	Airdrieonians	L 3-4	1-3	12	Burns, Stark, Sludden	5287
3	8	A	Hamilton A	L 1-3	1-1	12	Tait	2687
4	15	H	Falkirk	D 1-1	1-1	11	Spence	4629
5	18	A	Clydebank	W 3-1	3-1	—	Burns, Reilly, Sludden	2442
6	22	H	Norton	W 3-1	1-0	7	Stark, Watters, Sludden	4322
7	29	A	Dundee	D 1-1	0-0	8	Callaghan	4573
8	Oct 6	A	Brechin C	W 2-0	1-0	6	Callaghan, Sludden	1299
9	9	H	Raith R	D 1-1	1-0	—	Watters	3236
10	13	H	Ayr U	W 3-1	0-1	5	Elliott, Callaghan, Burns	9802
11	20	A	Partick T	L 0-2	0-0	6		4600
12	27	A	Forfar Ath	D 2-2	2-0	7	Sludden, Burns	1521
13	Nov 3	H	Clyde	W 2-1	0-0	6	Sludden, Tait	3937
14	10	A	Airdrieonians	L 0-2	0-0	8		4400
15	17	H	Meadowbank T	L 2-3	2-0	8	Stark, Reilly	4198
16	24	A	Raith R	D 1-1	1-1	9	Burns	2260
17	Dec 1	H	Brechin C	W 2-1	1-1	9	Williamson, Sloan	2473
18	8	H	Dundee	W 2-1	2-0	9	Williamson, Tait	4558
19	15	A	Morton	L 0-3	0-1	9		3724
20	22	H	Forfar Ath	W 1-0	0-0	8	Williamson	3224
21	Jan 2	A	Ayr U	W 2-1	2-0	—	Burns, Sludden	9448
22	5	H	Partick T	L 2-3	2-2	7	Flexney, Callaghan	5588
23	12	H	Hamilton A	W 1-0	0-0	6	Williamson	4767
24	19	A	Falkirk	D 1-1	1-0	5	Sludden	6759
25	Feb 2	H	Clydebank	W 3-0	2-0	5	Williamson 3	4169
26	16	H	Partick T	W 1-0	1-0	4	Williamson	6073
27	26	A	Clyde	D 1-1	1-0	—	Williamson	1000
28	Mar 9	A	Morton	D 1-1	1-0	4	Williamson	4451
29	12	A	Forfar Ath	D 1-1	1-0	—	Williamson	977
30	16	A	Airdrieonians	L 0-2	0-1	5		5000
31	23	H	Falkirk	D 1-1	1-1	5	Stark	6664
32	30	H	Hamilton A	W 1-0	0-0	5	Flexney	4449
33	Apr 6	A	Raith R	W 2-1	1-0	5	Williamson, Campbell	1761
34	10	A	Meadowbank T	W 8-1	6-0	—	Campbell 2, Stark, Williamson 2, Smith, Burns 2	1107
35	13	H	Brechin C	D 2-2	1-0	4	Stark, Campbell	4543
36	20	A	Clydebank	D 0-0	0-0	4		2205
37	27	A	Clyde	L 1-2	1-1	5	Jenkins	1700
38	May 4	H	Dundee	D 0-0	0-0	5		5712
39	11	A	Ayr U	L 0-1	0-1	5		5884

Final League Position: 5

GOALSCORERS

League: (58): Williamson 14, Burns 8, Sludden 8, Stark 6, Callaghan 4, Campbell 4, Tait 3, Flexney 2, Reilly 2, Watters 2, Elliott 1, Jenkins 1, Sloan 1, Smith 1, Spence 1
Scottish Cup: (2): Sludden 2, Burns 1
Skol Cup: (3):Callaghan 1, Spence 1, Stark 1
Centenary Cup: (9): Sludden 5, Burns 1, Elliott 1, Stark 1, Watters 1

Record Defeat: 1–9 v Celtic, Division I, 13 Aug 1938.
Most Capped Player: Joe Nibloe, 11, Scotland.
Most League Appearances: 481: Alan Robertson, 1972–88.
Most League Goals in Season (Individual): 34: Harry 'Peerie' Cunningham 1927–28 and Andy Kerr 1960–61.
Most Goals Overall (Individual): 148: W. Culley; 1912–23.

Honours
League Champions: Division I 1964–65. Division II 1897–98, 1898–99; Runners-up: Division I 1959–60, 1960–61, 1962–63, 1963–64. First Division 1975–76, 1978–79, 1981–82. Division II 1953–54, 1973–74, Second Division 1989–90.
Scottish Cup Winners: 1920, 1929; Runners-up: 1898, 1932, 1938, 1957, 1960.
League Cup Runners-up: 1952–53, 1960–61, 1962–63.
European: European Cup 1965–66. Cup Winners Cup —. UEFA Cup Fairs Cup: 1964–65, 1966–67 (semi-finals), 1969–70, 1970–71.
Club colours: Shirt: Blue and white vertical stripes. Shorts: Blue. Stockings: Blue.

Geddes, R	Montgomerie, R	Spence, T	McStay, W	Flexney, P	MacKinnon, D	Stark, W	Tait, T	Watters, W	Callaghan, T	Shaw, G	Reilly, R	Sludden, J	Jenkins, E	Burns, T	Elliott, D	McKellar, D	Burgess, S	Curran, P	Wylde, G	Williamson, R	Sloan, T	Macpherson, A	Smith, T	Agnew, G	Brayshaw, A	Campbell, C	Match No.
1	2	3	4	5	6	7	8*	9	10	11†12		14															1
1	2	12	5	4		7	8†	9	14	11	10	3*	6														2
1	2	3	4†	5	6	7	8		14	9*10		11	12														3
	2	3	5	4	7*	8		6		9	10	11	12	1													4
1	2	3	5	4	7	8	12	6		9	10*		11														5
1	2	3	5	4	7	8	14	6*		9†10		12	11														6
1	2	3	5	4		8	14	6		9	10†	7*11			12												7
1	2	3	5	4		8	9†	6		7	10		11*14		12												8
1	2	3	5	4		8		6	9	7*10			11	12													9
1	2	3	5	4		8	14	6		9†10		11*	7		12												10
1	2	3	5	4	7	8		6		12	10*		11	9													11
1	2	3	5	4		8	9*	6		12	10		11														12
1	2	3	5	4	7†	8		6		12	10		11	14				9*									13
1	2	3	7	5*	4	7	8	6		9	10								12								14
1	2†	3	5	4	7	8	14			6	10*		11							9	12						15
1	2	3	5	4	7	8	14			6†10*			11							9	12						16
1	2	3	5	4	7*	8		6		12			11							9	10						17
1	2	3	14	5	4		8			6*		12		11	7					9	10†						18
1	2	3	14	5	4†	6	8			12			11	7*						9	10						19
1	2	3*	5			8		6		12	10		11	7		4				9							20
1	2	3	5			8		6		12	10*		11	7		4				9							21
1	2	3	5			8		6			10		11	7		4				9							22
1	2	3†	5	14		8		6		12	10*		11	7		4				9							23
1	2	3	5			8		6			10		11	7		4				9							24
1	2	3	5			8				12	10*		11	7†		4				9	14	6					25
1	2	3	5			8				12	10*		11	7		4				9		6					26
1	2		4	5		8		6					11	7						9		3*10	12				27
1	2		4	5		8		6†		12			11	14						9		7	10*	3			28
1	2		4	5		8		6*		12			11							9		7	10	3			29
1		8	5		7	12		6	10		14		11			4*				9		2		3†			30
1	12	3	4	5	6†	8		7	9	10			11									2*14					31
1		3	4	5		8							11	7						9	12	2	10*	6			32
1	2	3	4	5	6	8		6					11							9		12		7*10			33
1	2	3	4	5†	6*					8	11			14						9		7		12	10		34
1	2	3	4	5	6*		12			8	11			14						9		7†		10			35
1	2	3*	4		6					8	11			5						9		7	12	10			36
1	14	3	4		6†12					8	11	7*		5						2		9		10			37
1	2		4			5		6*		8	11	12								9		3	7		10		38
1	2		4			5		6*		8	11									9		3	12		10		39
38	35	32	19	33	19	21	34	5	26	2	13	23	8	37	14	1	10	1	0	23	3	12	8	3	2	7	

+   +   +   +   + + + + + +   +   +   +   +   +   + +
2s 1s 2s   1s   2s 4s 4s 4s 1s 13s3s 1s 7s 5s 1s 4s 4s 1s 1s

MEADOWBANK THISTLE   First Division

Year Formed: 1974.   *Ground & Address:* Meadowbank Stadium, London Rd, Edinburgh EH7 6AE.   *Telephone:* 031 661 5351.
Ground Capacity: total: : 16,500.   seated: 16,500.   *Size of Pitch:* 105yd × 72yd.
Chairman: John P. Blacklaw.   *Secretary:* William L. Mill.   *Directors:* Terry Christie, Lawrie Glasson.   *Commercial Manager:* Sean Pinkman.
Manager: Terence Christie.   *Assistant Manager:* Michael Lawson.   *Club Doctor:* Dr. M. M. Morrison.   *Physio:* Arthur Duncan.   *Coach:* Tam McLaren.
Managers since 1975: John Bain; Alec Ness; Willie MacFarlane; Terry Christie.
Club Nickname(s) Thistle; Wee Jags.   *Previous Grounds:* None.
Record Attendance: 4000 v Albion Rovers, League Cup 1st rd; 9 Sept, 1974.

MEADOWBANK THISTLE 1990–91 LEAGUE RECORD

Match No.	Date	Venue	Opponents	Result	H/T Score	Lg. Pos.	Goalscorers	Attendance
1	Aug 25	H	Kilmarnock	W 1-0	0-0	—	Perry	1767
2	Sept 1	A	Forfar Ath	L 2-3	1-1	8	Roseburgh, Perry	688
3	8	A	Ayr U	D 1-1	1-1	8	Perry	2070
4	15	H	Raith R	D 1-1	0-0	8	Roseburgh	750
5	18	A	Airdrieonians	L 0-2	0-0	—		1500
6	22	H	Clyde	L 0-2	0-2	12		500
7	29	A	Clydebank	D 2-2	0-2	11	Roseburgh, Little	712
8	Oct 13	A	Falkirk	D 2-2	0-2	10	Little, Irvine W	2200
9	20	H	Brechin C	W 6-1	5-0	10	Irvine W 2, Roseburgh, Sprott 2, Little	500
10	27	H	Hamilton A	D 1-1	1-1	10	Little	500
11	31	H	Morton	D 1-1	0-0	—	Irvine W	350
12	Nov 3	A	Dundee	W 2-1	1-1	8	Boyd, Little	3404
13	6	A	Partick T	D 1-1	0-0	—	Roseburgh	1141
14	10	H	Forfar Ath	D 2-2	1-1	7	Irvine W, Banks	250
15	17	A	Kilmarnock	W 3-2	0-2	6	Roseburgh, Boyd, Little	4198
16	24	H	Partick T	D 1-1	0-1	6	Boyd	1000
17	Dec 1	A	Morton	W 3-0	1-0	6	Forrest 2, Roseburgh	1087
18	8	H	Clydebank	L 0-3	0-1	8		250
19	15	A	Clyde	L 0-1	0-0	8		600
20	29	H	Dundee	L 0-1	0-0	9		1000
21	Jan 5	A	Brechin C	W 3-1	1-1	8	Roseburgh, Forrest, Irvine W	500
22	12	H	Ayr U	W 1-0	0-0	7	Irvine W	738
23	Feb 16	A	Morton	D 1-1	0-1	8	Grant	1182
24	Mar 6	A	Raith R	W 3-1	2-1	—	Prentice 2, Roseburgh	1000
25	9	A	Hamilton A	D 1-1	1-0	8	Roseburgh	1073
26	13	A	Hamilton A	L 1-2	0-1	—	Boyd	1048
27	16	A	Partick T	W 4-2	1-1	8	Forrest 2, Logan, Boyd	3766
28	20	H	Falkirk	L 0-1	0-1	—		1400
29	23	H	Raith R	W 4-1	0-0	8	Little 2, Logan, Roseburgh	300
30	26	H	Clyde	D 1-1	1-0	—	Roseburgh	1100
31	30	A	Forfar Ath	L 0-2	0-1	8		620
32	Apr 3	A	Airdrieonians	L 2-4	1-2	—	Grant, Roseburgh	1200
33	6	H	Airdrieonians	L 0-1	0-1	8		1063
34	10	H	Kilmarnock	L 1-8	0-6	—	Grant	1107
35	13	H	Clydebank	L 2-3	1-1	8	Irvine W, Neil	309
36	20	A	Dundee	L 0-4	0-3	9		2716
37	27	A	Ayr U	L 0-2	0-2	9		1860
38	May 4	H	Brechin C	D 1-1	0-0	10	Forrest	200
39	11	A	Falkirk	L 2-4	0-2	11	Roseburgh 2 (1 pen)	8000

Final League Position: 11

GOALSCORERS

League: (56): Roseburgh 15 (1 pen), Irvine W 8, Little 8, Forrest 6, Boyd 5, Grant 3, Perry 3, Logan 2, Prentice 2, Sprott 2, Banks 1, Neil 1
Scottish Cup: (6): Roseburgh 2 (1 pen), Boyd 1, Forrest 1, Irvine W 1, own goal 1
Skol Cup: (0)
Centenary Cup: (1): Boyd 1

Record Transfer fee received: £??? for John Inglis to St Johnstone (1990).
Record Transfer Fee Paid: £28,000 for Victor Kasule from Albion Rovers (1987).
Record Victory: 6-0 v Raith R, Second Division; 9 Nov, 1985.
Record Defeat: 0-8 v Hamilton A, Division II; 14 Dec, 1974.
Most Capped Player: —.
Most League Appearances: 446: Walter Boyd, 1979–89.
Most League Goals In Season (Individual): 21: John McGachie, 1986–87. *(Team):* 69; Second Division, 1986–87.
Most Goals Overall (Individual): 63: Adrian Sprott, 1980–85.

Honoour
League Champions: Second Division 1986-87; *Runners-up:* Second Division 1982–83. First Division 1987–88.
Scottish Cup: —.
League Cup: Semi-finals 1984–85.
Club colours: Shirt: Amber with black trim. Shorts: Black. Stockings: Amber.

McQueen, J	McCormack, J	Armstrong, G	Grant, D	Williamson, S	Roseburgh, D	Perry, J	Prentice, A	McNaughton, B	Forrest, R	Sprott, A	Banks, A	Graham, T	Irvine, W	Irvine, N	Boyd, W	Little, I	Hendrie, T	Logan, S	Whitehead, D	Bullen, L	Kane, K	Neil, C	Cormack, P	Park, D	Match No.
1	2	3	4	5	6	7	8	9*	10	11		12													1
1	2	3	4	5†	6	7	8		10	11		12	9												2
1	2	3	5		6	7*	8	12	10	11	4		9												3
1	2	3	5		6		8*		10	11	4	12	9			7									4
1	2	3	5		6			12	10	11	4	8*	9			7									5
1	2	3	5		6		8	7†	10*	11	4		9		12	14									6
1	8*	4	5		6					11	3		9		12	14	2	7		10†					7
1		4	5		6*					11	3		9	12	8	10†	2	7	14						8
1		4	5		6					11	3		9	12	8	10	2*	7†	14						9
1		4	5		6				12	11	3		9		8	10*	2	7							10
1		4	5		6					11	3		9		8	10*	2	7	12						11
1		4	5		6					11	3		9		8	10	2	7							12
1		4	5		6				10	11	3		9		8		2	7							13
1		4	5		6			12	14	11	3		9		8	10†	2*	7							14
1		4	5		6				10	11	3		9*		8	12	2	7							15
1		4	5		6				10	11	3		9*		8	12	2	7							16
1		4	5		6			14	10	11	3		12		8	9*	2†	7							17
1		4	5		6			12	10†	11	3		9		8	14	2*	7							18
1		4	5		6			2		11	3		9		8	10		7							19
1		3	5	4	6			2		12	11†	14	9		8	10*		7							20
1		3	5	4	6				10	11		12	9		8		2*	7							21
1		3	5	4	6					11		10	9		8	7†	2	14							22
1		3	5	4†	6			2*	14	10		11	9		8		12	7							23
1		3	5	4	6*		8			11		12	9				2	7			10				24
1		3	5	4	6*		8	14		11		12	9				2	7†			10				25
1		3	5	4	6		8	10*		11†	12	14	9				2	7							26
1	2	3	5		6		8		10	11	4		9					7							27
1	2	3	5		6		8†	12	11		4	10	9*	14				7							28
1		3	5		6			12		11		10*	9		8		2	7							29
1	14	3	5	4†	6				10	11			9		8		2	7*	12						30
1		4	5		6			14	12		3	10	9*		8		2	7†		11					31
1		4	5		6			10*	14		3	12	9		8		2	7		11†					32
1	11	4	5		6			10	9†	3*	14		12		8		2	7							33
1	3	4	5		6			10	11†	12			9		8		2*	7		14					34
1		4	5		6		2			3	10†	12	9*			7	14			11	8				35
1		4	5		6		2†		3	10		8	9	14	7				12	11*					36
1		4	5		6		2†	12		3	10		8*	9	14	7			11						37
1	3		5		6			12		10†			14	9*	2	7		11			4	8			38
1		4	5		6		14		3	9			8	12	2	7		11*					10†		39
39	11	39	39	11	39	3	21	3	18	20	30	2	31	2	27	23	25	32	1	—	8	2	1	2	
				+		+	+	+				+	+	+	+	+	+	+	+	+	+	+			
				1s		6s	4s	8s				3s	4s	3s	2s	7s	7s	4s	1s	1s	3s	3s			

MONTROSE
First Division

Year Formed: 1879.   *Ground & Address:* Links Park, Wellington St, Montrose DD10 8QD.   *Telephone:* 0674 73200.
Ground Capacity: total: 6500. seated: 268.   *Size of Pitch:* 113yd × 70yd.
Chairman: Brian Keith.   *Secretary:* Malcolm J. Watters.   *Commercial Manager:* John Archbold.
Manager: Ian Stewart.   *Assistant Manager:* John Smith.   *Physio:* Andy Bell.   *Coach:* Chic McLelland.
Managers since 1975: A. Stuart; K. Cameron; R. Livingstone; S. Murray; D. D'Arcy; I. Stewart.
Club Nickname(s): The Gable Endies.   *Previous Grounds:* None.
Record Attendance: 8983 v Dundee, Scottish Cup 3rd rd; 17 Mar, 1973.
Record Transfer Fee received: £50,000 for Gary Murray to Hibernian (Dec, 1980).
Record Transfer Fee paid: —.

MONTROSE 1990–91 LEAGUE RECORD

Match No.	Date	Venue	Opponents	Result	H/T Score	Lg. Pos.	Goalscorers	Attendance
1	Aug 25	A	Stenhousemuir	W 1-0	0-0	—	Maver	350
2	Sept 1	H	Queen's Park	W 1-0	1-0	1	Murray	500
3	8	A	Berwick R	L 1-2	1-1	5	Murray	450
4	15	H	Alloa	L 2-4	0-1	7	Dolan, Allan	450
5	22	A	Queen of the S	L 1-2	0-0	11	Allan	615
6	29	A	East Stirling	W 1-0	0-0	9	Fotheringham	130
7	Oct 6	A	Stranraer	L 0-1	0-0	9		450
8	9	H	East Fife	L 0-2	0-1	—		450
9	13	H	Arbroath	W 3-0	1-0	10	Allan, Fotheringham, Stephen	550
10	20	A	Cowdenbeath	W 1-0	1-0	8	Murray (pen)	212
11	23	H	Stirling Albion	L 0-1	0-1	—		811
12	27	A	Albion R	W 3-0	0-0	7	Fotheringham, Dolan, Murray	320
13	Nov 3	H	Dumbarton	L 1-2	1-2	9	Fotheringham	480
14	10	A	Queen's Park	D 0-0	0-0	10		401
15	17	H	Stenhousemuir	L 2-3	1-2	10	Murray, Sheran	387
16	24	H	Berwick R	L 1-2	0-0	10	Murray	400
17	Dec 1	A	Alloa	L 0-1	0-0	11		594
18	15	H	Albion R	W 5-0	3-0	10	Mackay, Kerr 2, Melville 2	400
19	22	A	Dumbarton	D 1-1	0-0	10	Allan	476
20	Jan 2	A	Arbroath	W 1-0	0-0	—	Den Bieman	779
21	12	A	East Fife	W 3-1	2-0	7	Mackay, Dolan 2	884
22	19	H	Stranraer	W 1-0	0-0	4	Dolan	300
23	29	A	Stirling Albion	L 0-3	0-1	—		580
24	Feb 2	H	Queen of the S	D 0-0	0-0	8		300
25	5	H	Cowdenbeath	W 2-0	1-0	—	Murray, Dolan	300
26	9	H	East Stirling	D 2-2	1-2	5	Den Bieman, Dolan	200
27	16	H	Cowdenbeath	W 1-0	0-0	3	Kerr	300
28	23	A	Stenhousemuir	W 1-0	1-0	3	Den Bieman	300
29	Mar 2	A	Alloa	L 0-1	0-0	5		353
30	12	H	Stranraer	W 2-1	1-0	—	Den Bieman, Mackay	250
31	16	A	East Fife	D 2-2	1-2	4	Kerr, Mackay	665
32	23	H	Arbroath	W 1-0	0-0	3	Kerr	400
33	30	A	Dumbarton	D 2-2	0-0	4	Den Bieman, Maver	600
34	Apr 6	H	Stirling Albion	L 0-1	0-0	5		600
35	13	A	Berwick R	W 1-0	1-0	4	Maver	442
36	20	H	Albion R	W 3-0	0-0	3	Rougvie, Dolan, King	480
37	27	A	Queen's Park	W 3-0	3-0	2	Murray, Mackay 2	815
38	May 4	H	East Stirling	W 2-0	2-0	2	Murray, Maver	600
39	11	A	Queen of the S	W 3-0	3-0	2	Rougvie, Murray 2 (1 pen)	606

Final League Position: 2

GOALSCORERS

League: (54): Murray 11 (2 pens), Dolan 8, Mackay 6, Den Bieman 5, Kerr 5, Allan 4, Fotheringham 4, Maver 4, Melville 2, Rougvie 2, King 1, Sheran 1, Stephen 1.
Scottish Cup: (4): Kerr 2 (1 pen), Allan 1, Murray 1.
Skol Cup: (1): Allan 1.
Centenary Cup: (4): Den Bieman 2, Maver 1, Stephen 1.

Record Victory: 12-0 v Vale of Leithen, Scottish Cup 2nd rd; 4 Jan, 1975.
Record Defeat: 0-13 v Aberdeen; 17 Mar, 1951.
Most Capped Player: Alexander Keillor, 2 (6), Scotland.
Most League Appearances: —.
Most League Goals in Season (Individual): 28: Brian Third, Division II; 1972–73.
Most Goals Overall (Individual): —.

Honours
League Champions: Second Division 1984–85, *Runners-up:* 1990–91.
Scottish Cup: Quarter-finals 1973, 1976.
League Cup: Semi-finals 1975–76.
Club colours: Shirt: Blue with white pin stripe. Shorts: White. Stockings: Red.

Larter, D	Morrison, B	King, S	Mackay, H	Rougvie, I	Den Bieman, I	Allan, M	Lyons, A	Powell, D	Feenie, M	Murray, G	Maver, C	Stephen, G	Brown, K	Paterson, D	Fleming, J	Dolan, A	Fotheringham, J	Watt, D	Sheran, J	Price, R	Kerr, B	Melville, D	Chalmers, C	Dornan, A	Match No.
1	2	3	4	5	6*	7	8	9†	10	11	12	14													1
1	2	3		5	6*	7	8		10	11	9		4		12										2
1	2	3		5	12	7	8		6†11		9	14	4			10*									3
1	2	3		5	12	7	8		11*	9			4			10	6								4
1	2	3	4	5	12	7	8		11†	9	14					10*	6								5
1	2		4	5	11	10*	8		14	7	9†				3	6	12								6
1			4	5	6*	7	8		12	14	11†				3	10	9	2							7
1	2		4	5		7	8		9	12					3	10	11*		6						8
1	2		4	5	6*	7	12		14	8	11†				3	10	9								9
1	2	6	4	5		7			9	8*11					3	10	12								10
1	2	14	4	5	6	7	8†		9	11*					3	10	12								11
1	2	6	4	5	8	7			9						3	10	11								12
1	2	6		5	8	7	14		9	12					3	10	11*		4†						13
1	2		4*	5	6	7	8		12	11	9				3	10									14
1	2	3			10*	7	6		9	8	11				4	12			5						15
1	2	3			10	7	8		9	6	12				4	11*			5						16
1	2	3		5	14	7	8†		12	6					4	11					9*10				17
1	2		4	5	11	7*			12	8					3	6	14				9†10				18
1	2	6	5			7*	8		12	11					3	4	14				9†10				19
1	2		4	5	11	7			12	8†					3	6	14				9 10*				20
1	2	6	4	5	11	7	14		12						3	10					9*		8†		21
1	2	6	4	5	11	7									3	10	12				9*		8		22
1	2	6*	4	5	11				12						3	10	7				9			8	23
1	2	4		5	11	8			14	12					3	10	7†				9*		6		24
1	2	4	5		11*				7†12						3	10	14				9		8	6	25
1	2	4	5		11				7*						3	10	12				9		8	6	26
1	2	5	4		11		14		7*	8†					3	10	12				9			6	27
1	2	5	4		11*14				12	7					3	10	8				9†			6	28
1	2	6	4	5	11				12	14					3†10		7*				9		8		29
1	2	6	4	5	11	7*			12	14					3	10					9			8†	30
1	2	5	4		11†	7			12	14					3	10					9	6*	8		31
1	2	5	4		11*	7†	6		12						3	10	14				9		8		32
1	2	5	4†		11*	7	12		8						3	10	14				9		6		33
1	2	6	12	5	11	7*14			8						3	10					9†		4		34
1	2	10		5	11	12			7†	8					3	6	14				9*		4		35
1	2	6		5	11	12			7*	8					3	10	14				9†		4		36
1	2	6	9	5	11*14				7†	8					3	10	12						4		37
1	2	6	9	5	11				7*	8					3	10	12						4		38
1	2	6	9*	5	11	14			7	8†					3	10	12						4		39
39	38	31	28	29	32	27	16	1	3	19	24	7	3	—	34	36	11	1	3	1	20	4	5	17	
	+	+		+	+	+				+	+	+			+						+				
	1s	1s		4s	4s	7s				14s	9s	6s			1s						18s				

MORTON

First Division

Year Formed: 1874. *Ground & Address:* Cappielow Park, Sinclair St, Greenock. *Telephone:* 0475 23511.
Ground Capacity: total: 16,000. seated: 5500. *Size of Pitch:* 110yd × 71yd.
Chairman: John Wilson. *Secretary:* Mrs Jane Rankin. *Commercial Manager:* Iain Baxter.
Manager: Allan McGraw. *Assistant Manager:* John McMaster. *Physio:* John Tierney. *Coach:* Billy Osborne.
Managers since 1975: Joe Gilroy; Benny Rooney; Alex Miller; Tommy McLean; Willie McLean; Allan McGraw.
Club Nickname(s): The Ton. *Previous Grounds:* Grant Street 1874, Garvel Park 1875, Cappielow Park 1879, Ladyburn
Park 1882, (Cappielow Park 1883).
Record Attendance: 23,000 v Celtic; 1922.
Record Transfer Fee received: £350,000 for Neil Orr to West Ham U.
Record Transfer Fee paid: £35,000 for Roddy MacDonald from Hearts.

MORTON 1990–91 LEAGUE RECORD

Match No.	Date		Venue	Opponents	Result		H/T Score	Lg. Pos.	Goalscorers	Atten- dance
1	Aug	25	A	Airdrieonians	L	0-4	0-1	—		1500
2	Sept	1	H	Dundee	L	0-1	0-1	14		1845
3		8	A	Raith R	L	0-1	0-0	14		1395
4		15	H	Hamilton A	L	0-2	0-0	14		1534
5		18	A	Falkirk	L	1-2	0-0	—	Gahagan	1800
6		22	A	Kilmarnock	L	1-3	0-1	14	McInnes	4322
7		29	H	Partick T	W	4-0	2-0	13	MacCabe 3, Alexander	2461
8	Oct	9	H	Brechin C	D	3-3	2-1	—	MacCabe 2, Alexander	801
9		13	H	Clydebank	W	2-0	0-0	12	McInnes, MacCabe	1609
10		20	A	Forfar Ath	L	1-5	1-3	12	Alexander	701
11		27	A	Clyde	W	3-1	3-1	12	Gahagan, Alexander, Collins	720
12		31	A	Meadowbank T	D	1-1	0-0	—	Pickering	350
13	Nov	3	H	Ayr U	W	2-1	0-1	11	MacCabe, Gahagan	2078
14		10	A	Hamilton A	D	1-1	0-1	11	MacCabe	1187
15		17	H	Airdrieonians	W	1-0	1-0	10	Gahagan	2449
16		20	A	Dundee	L	0-1	0-1	—		3150
17		24	A	Brechin C	W	1-0	1-0	10	MacCabe	400
18	Dec	1	H	Meadowbank T	L	0-3	0-1	10		1087
19		8	A	Partick T	D	2-2	0-1	10	Doak, MacCabe	3026
20		15	H	Kilmarnock	W	3-0	1-0	10	MacCabe 2, Pickering	2724
21		29	A	Ayr U	L	0-1	0-0	11		2361
22	Jan	2	A	Clydebank	W	4-2	1-2	—	MacCabe 3, Alexander	1465
23	Feb	2	H	Falkirk	D	0-0	0-0	10		3451
24		16	H	Meadowbank T	D	1-1	1-0	9	MacCabe	1182
25	Mar	5	H	Clyde	D	0-0	0-0	—		1043
26		9	A	Kilmarnock	D	1-1	0-1	9	Gahagan	4451
27		23	H	Partick T	D	1-1	1-0	9	Collins	2854
28		26	H	Forfar Ath	D	1-1	0-0	—	Boag	1120
29		30	H	Raith R	W	4-0	2-0	9	McInnes, Fowler, MacCabe, Deeney	1256
30	Apr	2	H	Clydebank	D	2-2	1-0	—	MacCabe 2	1200
31		6	A	Dundee	L	0-1	0-1	9		2515
32		10	A	Ayr U	D	1-1	0-0	—	MacCabe	1659
33		13	H	Hamilton A	L	0-4	0-2	10		1290
34		16	H	Raith R	L	1-2	0-2	—	Kelly	2453
35		20	A	Brechin C	W	3-1	1-0	8	MacCabe, Gahagan, McDonald	400
36		23	A	Airdrieonians	L	0-3	0-2	—		2100
37		27	H	Falkirk	L	0-1	0-1	8		3708
38	May	4	A	Forfar Ath	D	2-2	0-1	9	Boag, Alexander	637
39		11	A	Clyde	W	1-0	1-0	9	Fowler	400

Final League Position: 9

GOALSCORERS

League: (48): MacCabe 21, Alexander 6, Gahagan 6, McInnes 3, Boag 2, Collins 2, Fowler 2, Pickering 2, Deeney 1, Doak
1, Kelly 1, McDonald 1
Scottish Cup: (5): Gahagan 2, MacCabe 2, Alexander 1
Skol Cup: (3): Hopkin 2, Fowler 1
Centenary Cup: (2): Alexander 1, Reid 1

Record Victory: 11-0 v Carfin Shamrock, Scottish Cup 1st rd; 13 Nov, 1886.
Record Defeat: 1-10 v Port Glasgow Ath, Division II; 5 May, 1894: v St Bernards, Division II; 14 Oct, 1933.
Most Capped Player: Jimmy Cowan, 25, Scotland.
Most League Appearances: 358: David Hayes, 1969–84.
Most League Goals in Season (Individual): 58: Allan McGraw, Division II; 1963–64.
Most Goals Overall (Individual): —.

Honours

League Champions: First Division 1977–78, 1983–84, 1986–87. Division II 1949–50, 1963–64, 1966–67.
Scottish Cup Winners: 1922; *Runners-up:* 1948.
League Cup Runners-up: 1963–64.
European: *European Cup —. Cup Winners Cup —. UEFA Cup (Fairs):* 1968–69.
Club colours: Shirt: Blue and white hoops. Shorts: White. Stockings: Blue.

Wylie, D	Collins, D	Pickering, M	Doak, M	Boag, J	Cowie, G	McNeil, J	McDonald, I	Alexander, R	Fowler, J	Hopkin, D	McInnes, D	Hamilton, D	Hunter, J	McGoldrick, K	Reid, B	Gahagan, J	MacCabe, D	Deeney, M	Mahood, A	Kelly, G	Brown, C	McArthur, S	Graham, P	Match No.
1	2	3	4	5	6	7†	8*	9	10	11	12	14												1
1	2		4	5	3	7†	8*	9	10		12	14	6			11								2
1	14	3†	5	11	2*	10	8	9			12		6			4	7							3
1		3	5	8		2†	12	9	14	11	10*		6			4	7							4
1	2	3	4				8*	9	12		10		6		5	11	7							5
1	2	3*	4		12		8	9			10		6		5	11	7							6
1	2	3*	4		14		8†	9	12		10		6		5	11	7							7
1	2	3	4*		14		8†	9	12		10		6		5	11	7							8
1	2	3	4		14		8†	9	12		10*		6		5	11	7							9
1	2		4	3*			8†	9	12	14	10		6		5	11	7							10
1	2	3	4				8*	9	12	14	10		6		5	11	7†							11
1	2	3		4	14		8*	9	12		10		6		5	11	7†							12
1	2	3†		4	14		8	9	12		10*		6		5	11	7							13
1	2		4		3		8*	9	10		12		6		5	11	7							14
1	2		4		3		8	9	10		12		6		5	11*	7							15
1	2		4				8†	9	3		10		6		5	11	7*	12	14					16
1	2	14	4	3†			8	9			10		6		5	11*	7	12						17
1	2	3	4	10†			8	9*	5				6	14		11	7	12						18
1	2	3	4	5			8	9	12		10*		6			11†	7		14					19
1	2	3*	4	5				9			10		6	14		11	7	8†						20
1	2	3	4*	5	12			9			10		6			11	7†	14	8					21
1	2	3	4	5	12		8*	9			10		6			11†	7	14						22
1	2	3†	4		12		8	9			10		6		5	11*	7	14						23
1	2	3*	4				8	9	12				6		5	11	7	10						24
1	2		4		10		8	9	3†			14	6		5	11*	7	12						25
1	2	3	4				8*	9	12			14	6		5	11	7†	10						26
1	2	3	4	5			8*	9	12		10		6			11	7†	14						27
1	2	3	4	5			8	9*			10		6			11	7	12						28
1	2	3	4	5			8*			12	10	14	6			11†	7	9						29
1	2		4	5			8*			12	10	3	6			11	7	9†						30
1	2	3	4	5*			8			12	10	14	6			11	7	9†						31
1	2	3	4				8*		11		10		6	14			7	9†		5		12		32
1		3	4				8	9*		12	10	2	6			11	7			5				33
1	2	3	4				8*		12	9†	10		6			11	7	14		5				34
1	2	3	4				12	9	8		10*		6			11	7			5				35
1	2	3*	4				8	9	10				6	12		11	7			5†		14		36
1	2	3		5			8	9	11	10†			6	12			7					14	4*	37
1	2	3*		5			8†	9	11			10	6			12	7					14	4	38
	2		4	5			8	9	3†		10		6			11	7*	12				14	1	39
38	36	30	33	20	10	3	34	34	18	4	24	2	38	1	19	34	35	4	4	5	—	2	1	

+ +   +   +   + + +   +   +   + +   + +

1s 1s   9s   2s   17s 6s   7s 2s   5s   1s   10s 4s   3s 2s

MOTHERWELL Premier Division

Year Formed: 1886. *Ground & Address:* Fir Park, Motherwell ML1 2QN. *Telephone:* 0698 61437/8/9.
Ground Capacity: total: 18,000. seated: 3500. *Size of Pitch:* 110yd × 75yd.
Chairman: John C. Chapman. *Secretary:* Alan C. Dick. *Commercial Manager:* John Swinburne.
Manager: Tommy McLean. *Assistant Manager:* Tom Forsyth. *Physio:* Bobby Holmes. *Coach:* Cameron Murray.
Managers since 1975: Ian St John; Willie McLean; Rodger Hynd; Ally MacLeod; David Hay; Jock Wallace; Bobby Watson; Tommy McLean.
Club Nickname(s): The 'Well. *Previous Grounds:* Roman Road, Dalziel Park.
Record Attendance: 35,632 v Rangers, Scottish Cup 4th rd replay; 12 Mar, 1952.
Record Transfer Fee received: £375,000 for Andy Walker to Celtic (Aug 1987).
Record Transfer Fee paid: £110,000 for Iain Ferguson from Hearts (Dec 1990).
Record Victory: 12-1 v Dundee U, Division II; 23 Jan, 1954.

MOTHERWELL 1990–91 LEAGUE RECORD

Match No.	Date		Venue	Opponents	Result	H/T Score	Lg. Pos.	Goalscorers	Atten-dance
1	Aug	25	H	Celtic	W 2-0	0-0	—	Russell, Arnott	17,652
2	Sept	1	A	Dundee U	L 0-1	0-1	4		7636
3		8	H	St Johnstone	W 3-0	2-0	4	O'Neill, Cusack, Kirk	5069
4		15	A	St Mirren	L 0-1	0-0	4		4678
5		22	H	Dunfermline Ath	W 2-0	2-0	3	Arnott, Cooper	5354
6		29	A	Rangers	L 0-1	0-0	5		34,863
7	Oct	6	A	Hearts	D 1-1	0-1	5	Cusack	6780
8		13	H	Aberdeen	D 0-0	0-0	5		6602
9		20	A	Hibernian	L 0-1	0-1	6		5500
10	Nov	3	H	Dundee U	L 0-2	0-1	7		8117
11		6	A	Celtic	L 1-2	0-2	—	Russell	20,317
12		10	A	Dunfermline Ath	D 3-3	2-1	7	Arnott, Cusack, Cooper	7100
13		17	H	Rangers	L 2-4	0-1	9	Cooper, Bryce	16,457
14		24	H	St Mirren	D 1-1	0-1	8	Dolan	4720
15	Dec	1	A	St Johnstone	L 1-2	0-0	8	Griffin	6784
16		11	H	Hibernian	W 4-1	1-1	—	Griffin 2, Arnott, Boyd	4121
17		15	A	Aberdeen	D 1-1	1-1	6	Arnott	9500
18		22	A	Hearts	L 2-3	1-1	9	Arnott 2	8625
19	Jan	2	A	St Mirren	D 2-2	1-1	—	Cusack, Paterson	6683
20		5	H	St Johnstone	D 2-2	1-0	8	Cooper, Arnott	5338
21		19	A	Dundee U	L 0-3	0-0	8		6482
22		30	H	Celtic	D 1-1	0-1	—	Angus	13,542
23	Feb	2	A	Hibernian	D 1-1	0-1	7	Ferguson	6000
24		16	A	Rangers	L 0-2	0-1	7		32,192
25		27	H	Dunfermline Ath	W 1-0	1-0	—	Cooper	3202
26	Mar	2	H	Hearts	L 1-3	1-1	8	Griffin	5212
27		5	A	Aberdeen	L 0-2	0-1	—		5567
28		9	A	St Johnstone	W 4-1	2-0	7	Arnott 2, McLeod, Ferguson	5079
29		23	H	St Mirren	W 3-1	1-1	8	Arnott, Cooper, Ferguson	6207
30		30	A	Celtic	W 2-1	1-1	7	Boyd, Ferguson	21,252
31	Apr	13	H	Hibernian	W 1-0	0-0	7	Arnott	5012
32		16	A	Dundee U	W 1-0	1-0	—	Ferguson	3531
33		20	A	Aberdeen	L 0-3	0-1	7		14,500
34		27	A	Dunfermline Ath	W 5-2	2-0	6	Ferguson 3, Kirk, Paterson	3552
35	May	4	H	Rangers	W 3-0	1-0	5	Philliben, Arnott 2	17,672
36		11	A	Hearts	L 1-2	1-1	6	Angus	7055

Final League Position: 6

GOALSCORERS

League: (51): Arnott 14, Ferguson 8, Cooper 6, Cusack 4, Griffin 4, Angus 2, Boyd 2, Kirk 2, Paterson 2, Russell 2, Bryce 1, Dolan 1, McLeod 1, O'Neill 1, Philliben 1
Scottish Cup: (14): Kirk 4, Arnott 2, Cusack 2, Angus 1, Boyd 1, Ferguson 1, McLeod 1, O'Donnell 1, O'Neill 1
Skol Cup: (6): Cusack 2, O'Neill 2, Arnott 1, Burley 1

Record Defeat: 0-8 v Aberdeen, Premier Division; 26 Mar, 1979.
Most Capped Player: George Stevenson, 12, Scotland.
Most League Appearances: 626: Bobby Ferrier, 1918–37.
Most League Goals in Season (Individual): 52: Willie McFadyen, Division I; 1931–32.
Most Goals Overall (Individual): 283: Hugh Ferguson, 1916–25.

Honours

League Champions: Division I 1931–32. First Division 1981–82, 1984–85. Division II 1953–54, 1968–69; *Runners-up:* Division I 1926–27, 1929–30, 1932–33, 1933–34. Division II 1894–95, 1902–03.
Scottish Cup: 1952, 1991; *Runners-up:* 1931, 1933, 1939, 1951.
League Cup: 1950–51; *Runners-up:* 1954–55.
Scottish Summer Cup: 1944, 1965.
Club colours: Shirt: Amber with claret trimmings. Shorts: Claret. Stockings: Amber.

Maxwell, A	Burley, G	Boyd, T	Paterson, C	Nijholt, L	McCart, C	Russell, R	O'Neill, C	Arnott, D	Kirk, S	Gahagan, J	Cusack, N	Griffin, J	Philliben, J	Cooper, D	Angus, I	McLeod, J	Bryce, S	Dolan, J	O'Donnell, P	Mair, G	McLean, P	McGrillen, P	Ferguson, I	Match No.
1	2	3	4*	5	6	7	8	9	10	11	12													1
1	2	3		5	6	7*	8†	9	10		12			4	11	14								2
1	2	3	5	12	6		8*	4	7†10		9			11	14									3
1	2	3	5		6		8	4	7*10		9			11	12									4
1	2	3	12	5	6		8*	4	7†10		9			11	14									5
1	2	3	4	5	6	7	8*	9	10†		12			11	14									6
1	2	3		5	6		8	4	7	10	9			11										7
1	2	3	12	5	6*			4	7†10		9			11	8	14								8
1	2	3	14	5*	6	8		4	12		9			11	10†	7								9
1	2*	3	12	5	6	8		7	10†		9	4		11	14									10
1	2	3	4	5*	6	12	8†		14		9	10		11	7									11
1	2	3	5		6	8		7	10†		9	4*		11	14	12								12
1	2	3	5		6	8†			10*		9			11	4	7	12	14						13
1	2	3	5		6			9					7	12	8	4*10†14								14
1	2	3	5		6			9	12	4	11		7	8†	10*	14								15
1	2	3	5		6	10	4*	7†			9	8		11	12	14								16
1	2	3	5		6	10*	4	7†			9	8		11	14	12								17
1	2	3	5		6	10*	4	7			9	8		11	12									18
1	2	3	5		6		4	7			9	10		11	12							8*		19
1	2	3	5		6		4	7	12		9*10			11								8		20
1		3	5		6	12	4	7	14		9†	2		11	10*							8		21
1		3	5	14	6		4†	7	8*		12			2	11	10						9		22
1		3	5	4†	6			12	14		9*	8	2	11	10							7		23
1		3	5		6			7†12			9*	8	2	11	10	14		4						24
1		3	5	2	6	12		10			8			11	7			4				9*		25
1		3	5	2	6		4*	10			8			11	12	7						9		26
1		3	5	2	6	12	4	14			9	8		11	10*	7†								27
1		3	5	2		6		9	12		8			11†10	7*			4				14		28
1		3	5†	2	6	10*		9	12		14			4	11			8				7		29
1		3		2	6		4	7†12			8	5		11	14			10				9*		30
1		3		2	6		4*	7†10			9	8	5	11				12		14				31
1		5†	2	6			12	10			8			11	3	7	14	4				9*		32
1		4	2	6			7	14			8	5†11*	3	9		10						12		33
1		5	2	6			7†	8			4*	11	12		14	3	10					9		34
1		5		6			7	12			14	4	2	11†	3		8	10				9*		35
1			2	6			7	8†			12	4	5	11	3		14	10				9*		36
36	20	30	28	21	36	15	21	26	18	1	22	22	11	34	14	10	1	4	11	2	—	—	13	

+4s 2s (Burley) +4s (Paterson) +3s 11s (McCart/Russell) +7s 1s (Arnott/Kirk) +6s 12s 3s (Cusack/Griffin/Philliben) +4s 1s (Cooper/Angus) +1s 2s 2s (O'Donnell/Mair/McLean)

PARTICK THISTLE First Division

Year Formed: 1876.   *Ground & Address:* Firhill Park, 90 Firhill Rd, Glasgow G20 7AL.   *Telephone:* 041 945 4811.
Ground Capacity: total: 17,393. seated: 2966.   *Size of Pitch:* 106yd × 72yd.
Chairman: James Oliver.   *Company Secretary:* Robert Reid.   *Secretary:* —.   *Commercial Manager:* Gez Mozey.
Manager: John Lambie.   *Assistant Manager:* Gerry Collins.   *Physio:* Jim Martin.   *Coach:* Ian Jardine.
Managers since 1975: R. Auld; P. Cormack; B. Rooney; R. Auld; D. Johnstone; W. Lamont, S. Clark, J. Lambie.
Club Nickname(s): The Jags.   *Previous Grounds:* Jordanvale Park; Muirpark; Inchview; Meadowside Park.
Record Attendance: 49,838 v Rangers, Division I; 18 Feb, 1922.
Record Transfer Fee received: £100,000 for Mo Johnston from Watford.
Record Transfer Fee paid: £60,000 for Cammy Duncan from Motherwell, October 1989.

PARTICK THISTLE 1990–91 LEAGUE RECORD

Match No.	Date		Venue	Opponents	Result	H/T Score	Lg. Pos.	Goalscorers	Atten- dance
1	Aug 25	A	Dundee		D 1-1	0-0	—	Charnley	5040
2	Sept 1	H	Brechin C		D 3-3	1-2	7	Flood, Charnley, English	1800
3	8	A	Falkirk		W 2-0	0-0	5	Charnley, Elliot	4825
4	15	H	Clydebank		L 0-1	0-0	7		3932
5	18	A	Ayr U		W 1-0	1-0	—	McGlashan	2883
6	22	H	Hamilton A		L 0-1	0-0	5		4073
7	29	A	Morton		L 0-4	0-2	9		2461
8	Oct 6	A	Forfar Ath		W 1-0	0-0	8	Peebles	868
9	13	A	Clyde		W 4-2	2-2	7	McGovern 2, Charnley, Gallagher	3224
10	20	H	Kilmarnock		W 2-0	0-0	5	Charnley, McGovern	4600
11	27	A	Raith R		D 0-0	0-0	6		3052
12	Nov 3	H	Airdrieonians		D 1-1	1-0	7	Peebles (pen)	7225
13	6	H	Meadowbank T		D 1-1	0-0	—	McGlashan	1141
14	10	A	Brechin C		D 2-2	1-0	5	McGlashan, Elliot	700
15	17	H	Dundee		L 1-3	0-1	7	McGlashan	5476
16	24	A	Meadowbank T		D 1-1	1-0	7	Charnley	1000
17	Dec 1	H	Forfar Ath		W 3-2	2-1	7	Elliot 3	2415
18	8	H	Morton		D 2-2	1-0	7	McGlashan 2	3026
19	15	A	Hamilton A		D 2-2	1-2	7	McGlashan, Peebles	2519
20	Jan 5	A	Kilmarnock		W 3-2	2-2	6	Campbell 3	5588
21	19	A	Clydebank		W 3-2	1-1	7	Duffy 2 (2 pen), Elliot	1800
22	Feb 16	A	Kilmarnock		L 0-1	0-1	7		6073
23	23	H	Raith R		L 0-3	0-2	7		3600
24	Mar 2	H	Forfar Ath		W 2-0	0-0	7	Buckley, Elliot	2554
25	5	H	Falkirk		W 2-0	0-0	—	Buckley 2	5257
26	9	A	Raith R		W 5-1	3-1	5	Roche, Elliot, Charnley, Buckley, McGlashan	2255
27	12	A	Airdrieonians		D 0-0	0-0	—		5400
28	16	H	Meadowbank T		L 2-4	1-1	7	McGlashan, Campbell	3766
29	23	A	Morton		D 1-1	0-1	6	English	2854
30	26	H	Dundee		W 1-0	0-0	—	Buckley	3500
31	30	H	Ayr U		D 0-0	0-0	4		3826
32	Apr 6	A	Hamilton A		W 1-0	1-0	4	Elliot	2627
33	13	A	Clyde		L 1-2	0-0	6	Elliot	3000
34	16	H	Clyde		W 2-0	1-0	—	McGovern, Elliot	2757
35	20	H	Falkirk		D 1-1	1-0	5	McGlashan	7000
36	23	H	Ayr U		W 2-0	1-0	—	Love (og), Elliot	1450
37	27	A	Brechin C		W 2-1	1-0	4	Tierney, Elliot	700
38	May 4	H	Airdrieonians		L 0-2	0-0	4		5500
39	11	A	Clydebank		L 1-7	1-1	4	Johnston	2106

Final League Position: 4

GOALSCORERS

League: (56): Elliot 13, McGlashan 10, Charnley 7, Buckley 5, Campbell 4, McGovern 4, Peebles 3 (1 pen), Duffy 2 (2 pens), English 2, Flood 1, Gallagher 1, Johnston 1, Roche 1, Tierney 1, own goal 1
Scottish Cup: (3): Duffy 1 (pen), McGlashan 1, Roche 1
Skol Cup: (2): Charnley 1, Peebles 1
Centenary Cup: (1): Campbell 1 (pen)

Record Victory: 16-0 v Royal Albert, Scottish Cup 1st rd; 17 Jan, 1931.
Record Defeat: 0-10 v Queen's Park, Scottish Cup; 3 Dec, 1881.
Most Capped Player: Alan Rough, 51 (53), Scotland.
Most League Appearances: 410: Alan Rough, 1969–82.
Most League Goals in Season (Individual): 41: Alec Hair, Division I; 1926–27.
Most Goals Overall (Individual): —.

Honours
League Champions: First Division 1975–76. Division II 1896–97, 1899–1900, 1970–71; *Runners-up:* Division II 1901–02.
Scottish Cup Winners: 1921; *Runners-up:* 1930.
League Cup Winners: 1971–72; *Runners-up:* 1953–54, 1956–57, 1958–59.
European: *European Cup* —. *Cup Winners Cup* —. *UEFA Cup* 6 matches (1963–64 *Fairs Cup*; 1972–73).
Club colours: Shirts: Amber with red shoulders and sleeves. Shorts: Red with amber stripe. Stockings: Red.

Duncan, C	Robertson, G	Elliot, D	Duffy, J	Peebles, G	Tierney, G	Law, R	Campbell, C	McGlashan, C	Flood, J	Charnley, C	Gallagher, B	English, I	Nelson, C	Wright, B	Rae, G	McGovern, P	Buckley, J	Craig, D	Roche, D	Murdoch, A	McLaughlin, P	Johnston, S	McConville, A	Kennedy, A	Smith, T	Match No.
1	2	3	4	5	6	7	8*	9†	10	11	12	14														1
	2*	3	5	12	6	4	9†	7	10	11		14	1		8											2
1	2	3	4		6	7			9	10	11			8	5											3
1	2*	3	4		6	7	12		9	10	11			8	5											4
1	2	3	4	12	6	7			9	10	11			8	5*											5
1	2	3	4	12	6	7*14			9	10	11			8†	5											6
1	2	3	4	12	6	7*14			9	10†11				8	5											7
1	2	3	4	5	6	7	10				11			8	9											8
1	2	3	4	5	6	7	10†14		12	11				8*	9											9
1	2	3	4	5	6	7	10			11					9	8										10
1	2	3		5	6	7	10			11				4	9	8										11
1	2	3*	4	5	6	7	10	12		11					9	8										12
1	2	3	4	5	6	7	10	9		11						8										13
1	2	3	4*	5	6	7	10	9		11			8	12												14
1	2	3		5*	6	7	10	9		11	14			4	12	8†										15
1	2	3		5	6	7	10*	9		11†				4	12	8	14									16
1	2	11	4		6	3	12	8		10				5	9	7*										17
1	2	11	4	8	6	3	12	7		10				5	9*											18
1	2	11	4	14	6	3	9*	8		10				5		7†12										19
1	2	11	4		6	3	8	9		10				5		7										20
1	2	11	4	8*	6	3	10	9						5		7	12									21
	2	11	4	12	6		10*	9		7†14				5				8	1	3						22
	2	11	4	12	6*			9			14			5	10	7		8†	1	3						23
		11	4	2				9		6	10			5		7*14		8	1	3						24
		11	4	2			12	9		6	10			5		7		8*	1	3						25
		11	4	2			12	9		6	10			5		7*		8	1	3						26
		11	4	2		14	12	9†		6	10*			5		7		8	1	3						27
14		11	4	2			12	9		6	10*			5		7		8†	1	3						28
	2	11	4	8			14	9†			10*			5	12	7			1	3	6					29
	2	10	4	8				9		11				5		7			1	3	6					30
	2	10	4	8			12	9		11				5		7			1	3	6*					31
	2	10	4	8				9*		11	12			5		7			1	3	6					32
	2	10	4	8*	5			9		11	12					7			1	3	6					33
	2	11	4	8	5	12		9		10						7*			1	3	6					34
	2	11	4	8				9		6				5	12	7*			1	3	10					35
	2	11	4	8		6		9			10*			5	12	7†			1	3		14				36
	2	11		8†	6	7		9						5	12	10*		14	1	3			4			37
	2				6	8		9						5	10	7		12	1	3		11†	4*14			38
	2		4		6	10		9						5	12	11		8*	1	3	7					39
20	34	37	34	26	28	25	15	34	7	29	3	7	1	9	29	10	26	—	8	18	18	8	1	2	—	
	+			+	+	+		+		+	+	+			+	+		+	+			+		+		
	1s			7s			2s	11s	2s	1s	2s	6s			1s	7s		3s	3s			1s		1s		

QUEEN OF THE SOUTH   Second Division

Year Formed: 1919.   *Ground & Address:* Palmerston Park, Terregles St, Dumfries DG2 9BA.   *Telephone:* 0387 54853.
Ground Capacity: total: 6750. seated: 1300.   *Size of Pitch:* 112yd × 72yd.
Chairman: W. J. Harkness C.B.E.   *Secretary:* Mrs Doreen Alcorn.   *Commercial Manager:* W. J. Harkness.
Manager: Ally MacLeod.   *Assistant Manager:* —.   *Physio:* —.   *Coach:* I. McChesney.
Managers since 1975: M. Jackson; G. Herd; A. Busby; R. Clark; M. Jackson; D. Wilson; W. McLaren.
Club Nickname(s): The Doonhamers.   *Previous Grounds:* None.
Record Attendance: 24,500 v Hearts, Scottish Cup 3rd rd; 23 Feb, 1952.
Record Transfer Fee received: £100,000 for K. McMinn from Rangers, 1985.
Record Transfer Fee paid: —.
Record Victory: 11-1 v Stranraer, Scottish Cup 1st rd; 16 Jan, 1932.

QUEEN OF THE SOUTH 1990–91 LEAGUE RECORD

Match No.	Date	Venue	Opponents	Result	H/T Score	Lg. Pos.	Goalscorers	Atten- dance
1	Aug 25	H	East Stirling	L	1-2	0-1	—	Thomson A	480
2	Sept 1	A	Stirling Albion	D	0-0	0-0	12		700
3	8	A	Alloa	L	1-4	1-1	14	Robertson	544
4	15	H	Berwick R	W	2-0	2-0	11	McGarvey 2	763
5	18	A	East Fife	L	0-2	0-1	—		692
6	22	H	Montrose	W	2-1	0-0	10	Fraser, Robertson	615
7	29	A	Cowdenbeath	L	1-2	0-0	11	McGuire	250
8	Oct 6	A	Queen's Park	L	1-3	0-1	12	Sloan	478
9	10	H	Dumbarton	L	1-2	0-2	—	Sim	624
10	13	A	Stranraer	L	1-4	1-2	13	Sloan	950
11	20	H	Stenhousemuir	W	3-2	2-1	13	Gordon 2, Adams	698
12	27	A	Arbroath	D	1-1	0-1	13	Robertson	304
13	Nov 3	H	Albion R	D	1-1	1-1	13	Gordon	569
14	10	A	Stirling Albion	D	0-0	0-0	13		931
15	17	A	East Stirling	L	0-1	0-1	13		308
16	24	H	Alloa	L	1-3	0-0	13	Watters	750
17	Dec 1	A	Berwick R	L	0-2	0-1	13		407
18	15	H	Arbroath	W	1-0	0-0	13	Thomson A	542
19	22	H	Albion R	L	0-1	0-0	13		294
20	Jan 2	H	Stranraer	D	1-1	0-1	—	Thomson I	1041
21	12	A	Dumbarton	W	2-0	2-0	13	Gordon, Robertson	600
22	26	H	Queen's Park	W	3-2	1-0	13	Gordon, McGuire, Thomson A	537
23	Feb 2	A	Montrose	D	0-0	0-0	13		300
24	5	A	Stenhousemuir	L	1-2	1-2	—	Anderson (og)	318
25	9	H	Cowdenbeath	L	2-4	0-2	13	Gordon, Thomson A	379
26	23	H	Stranraer	L	1-2	0-1	13	Thomson A	568
27	26	A	Berwick R	D	3-3	3-2	—	Thomson A, MacDonald 2	466
28	Mar 2	A	Queen's Park	L	0-3	0-2	13		587
29	6	H	East Fife	W	3-0	1-0	—	Watters 2, McGuire	373
30	9	H	Alloa	D	0-0	0-0	13		476
31	16	H	Stirling Albion	D	0-0	0-0	13		472
32	23	A	Stenhousemuir	W	1-0	1-0	13	Fraser	400
33	30	H	Cowdenbeath	D	2-2	2-1	13	McGhie, Thomson A	450
34	Apr 6	A	Albion R	D	2-2	2-0	13	Fraser, Watters	248
35	13	A	East Fife	L	1-3	1-1	13	McGuire	527
36	20	A	East Stirling	D	1-1	0-0	12	Gordon	194
37	27	H	Arbroath	W	6-1	4-1	12	Thomson I, Thomson A 4, Hetherington	406
38	May 4	A	Dumbarton	L	0-2	0-1	12		700
39	11	H	Montrose	L	0-3	0-3	12		606

Final League Position: 12

GOALSCORERS

League: (46): Thomson A 11, Gordon 7, McGuire 4, Roberston 4, Watters 4, Fraser 3, MacDonald 2, McGarvey 2, Sloan 2, Thomson I 2, Adams 1, Hetherington 1, McGhie 1, Sim 1, own goal 1.
Scottish Cup: (7): Watters 2, Gordon 1, McGhie 1, McGuire 1, Sim 1, Thomson A 1.
Skol Cup: (7): Thomson A 3, McGuire 2, Fraser 1, McGhie.
Centenary Cup: (6): Gordon 2, Fraser 1, McGarvey 1, Robertson 1, Sloan 1.

Record Defeat: 2-10 v Dundee, Division I; 1 Dec, 1962.
Most Capped Player: Billy Houliston, 3, Scotland.
Most League Appearances: 619: Allan Ball; 1962–83.
Most League Goals in Season (Individual): 33: Jimmy Gray, Division II; 1927–28.
Most Goals Overall (Individual): —.

Honours
League Champions: Division II 1950–51; *Runners-up:* Division II 1932–33, 1961–62, 1974–75. Second Division 1980–81, 1985–86.
Scottish Cup:—.
League Cup:—.
Club colours: Shirt: Royal blue. Shorts: White. Stockings: Royal blue with white tops.

Davidson, A	McCafferty, T	Thomson, I	Fraser, G	Hetherington, K	McGhie, W	Andrews, G	Thomson, A	Gordon, S	Sim, W	Robertson, J	McGarvey, F	Sloan, T	McCulloch, D	McGuire, J	Mills, D	Johnston, G	Thomson, M	Adams, S	Rennie, A	Campbell, K	Moffat, I	McFarlane, A	McKeown, B	Watters, W	MacDonald, R	Wylde, G	Possee, M	McCulloch, D	Match No.
1	2	3	4	5	6	7†	8	9*10	11	12	14																		1
1	5	3	4†		6	14	8	9	10	12		7	2	11*															2
	2	3	4	5	6	14	9	12	11	8	7*	10†		1															3
1	2	3			6	12	9	10	14	8*	4	11†	5	7*															4
1	2	3	14	12	6		9	10		8	4†	11	5	7*															5
1	2	3	10	4	6	14	9	7	12	8†		11*	5																6
1	3	7	4	6	14		9	12	10*	8	11†	5		2															7
1	3	4			8	10	11	7	9	5		2	6																8
	3	4*		6	9	7	10	11	8			5†		1	2		12	14											9
1	6	4	5			7	3	10	8†	9	11*			2			14	12											10
	6	5	14	7	3	11	8*	9	4†			1	2	10	12														11
1		6†12	7*	4	10	11		9	5	2		14	8	3															12
1	14	12	6		7	4	10	11	9	5	2*	8†	3																13
1	2		14	4	8	7	10†11*12	9		5		3	6																14
1	12		4	2	8	7	14	11†	9*	5		3	6	10															15
1	10*		4	2	8	7	12	11	5			3	6	9															16
1	10		4	6	8	7	14	12	11*		2	3†		9	5														17
1	2	4		5	12	7	10	8†	11*14			3	6	9															18
1	2	4		5	8	7	10	11*14	12	3	6	9†																	19
1	2	3		5	9	7*	11	8	12	4	10	6																	20
1	3	4 14	2	8	7	11*12	9†			10	6		5																21
1	2	3	4	5	8	7	11	12	9*	10	6																		22
1	2	3	4	8	7	11*12	9			10	6	5																	23
1	2	3 12	8*	7	9	11		10	6	5	4																		24
1	2*	3	12	8	7	11		10	6	9	5	4																	25
	3	4*	2	7	8	10	12		1	6	9	5	11																26
	3	2	8	7†10	12	11*	1	14	6	9	5	4																	27
	3 12	2*	8	7	10	14	1	11†	6	9	5	4																	28
1	3†	2	4	7	8	11*	14	10	5	9	6 12																		29
1	8	6	2	4	7*12	10	11	3	5	9																			30
1	8	6*	2	5	7	12	10	14	11†	3	4	9																	31
1	8	6	2	5	7	12	10†14	11*	3	4	9																		32
1	8	6	7	10	11	3	4	9	2																				33
1	8	6*	2	5	7†10	12	11	14	3	4	9																		34
1	8	6*	2	5	7	10	12	11	3	4	9																		35
1	8	5	2	7	6	10	11	3	4	9																			36
1	8	5	2	7	6	10	11	3	4	9																			37
1	8	12	5*	2	7	6	10	11	3	4	9																		38
	8	6	5	7	9	10	11	1	2	3	4																		39
32	20	29	22	13	35	2	34	32	24	17	12	11	2	25	12	2	7	8	1	2	2	26	25	19	8	6	—	1	
+2s					+6s	+2s	+1s	+5s	+3s	+4s	+6s	+5s	+7s	+1s			+4s	+2s			+2s	+3s	+4s			+1s			

QUEEN'S PARK Second Division

Year Formed: 1867. *Ground & Address:* Hampden Park, Mount Florida, Glasgow G42 9BA. *Telephone:* 041 632 1275.
Ground Capacity: total: 64,110. seated: 10,000. *Size of Pitch:* 115yd × 75yd.
President: Martin B. Smith. *Chairman:* —. *Secretary:* James C. Rutherford. *Commercial Manager:* —.
Physio: A. P. McEwan. *Coach:* Edward Hunter.
Coaches since 1975: D. McParland, J. Gilroy, E. Hunter.
Club Nickname(s): The Spiders. *Previous Grounds:* 1st Hampden (Titwood Park), 2nd Hampden, 3rd Hampden.
Record Attendance: 95,772 v Rangers, Scottish Cup; 18 Jan, 1930.
Record for ground: 149,547, Scotland v England, 1937.
Record Transfer Fee received: —.
Record Transfer Fee paid: —.

QUEEN'S PARK 1990–91 LEAGUE RECORD

Match No.	Date		Venue	Opponents	Result	H/T Score	Lg. Pos.	Goalscorers	Atten-dance
1	Aug 25	H	Stranraer	W	3-1	1-0	—	Crooks, Hendry, Greig	340
2	Sept 1	A	Montrose	L	0-1	0-1	7		500
3	8	H	East Stirling	W	4-0	0-0	2	Hendry 3, Ogg	470
4	15	H	Cowdenbeath	W	1-0	0-0	1	Hendry	540
5	18	A	Berwick R	W	2-1	1-0	—	Ogg, Greig	443
6	22	H	East Fife	L	0-2	0-1	3		701
7	29	A	Dumbarton	L	0-1	0-0	5		600
8	Oct 6	H	Queen of the S	W	3-1	1-0	3	Morton, Caven, Ogg	478
9	9	A	Stenhousemuir	W	2-1	1-0	—	Hendry 2	500
10	13	A	Albion R	L	0-1	0-0	7		460
11	20	H	Stirling Albion	D	0-0	0-0	3		858
12	27	A	Alloa	D	1-1	1-0	3	Hendry	595
13	Nov 3	H	Arbroath	W	2-1	1-1	3	Caven 2	570
14	10	H	Montrose	D	0-0	0-0	3		401
15	17	A	Stranraer	L	1-2	0-0	4	Elder	750
16	24	A	East Stirling	W	3-1	1-0	4	Hendry 2, Elder	296
17	Dec 1	A	Cowdenbeath	W	1-0	1-0	3	Hendry (pen)	250
18	18	H	Alloa	W	1-0	0-0	—	Hendry	400
19	22	A	Arbroath	L	0-3	0-2	3		345
20	Jan 2	H	Albion R	D	1-1	1-0	—	Caven	640
21	5	A	Stirling Albion	W	1-0	0-0	2	Caven	840
22	12	H	Stenhousemuir	W	1-0	0-0	2	Greig	954
23	26	A	Queen of the S	L	2-3	0-1	2	Elder, Hendry	537
24	Feb 2	A	East Fife	L	1-2	0-2	2	Elder	643
25	5	H	Berwick R	W	2-1	0-0	—	Hendry, Elder	506
26	9	H	Dumbarton	D	1-1	1-0	2	McNamee	849
27	16	A	Arboath	D	0-0	0-0	2		618
28	23	A	Stirling Albion	L	0-2	0-1	2		785
29	Mar 2	H	Queen of the S	W	3-0	2-0	2	Hendry (pen), McEntegart, Greig	587
30	9	A	East Stirling	D	1-1	0-0	2	O'Brien	340
31	16	A	Berwick R	L	1-2	0-1	2	Greig	473
32	23	H	East Fife	W	2-0	0-0	2	Hendry, James McFadyen	696
33	30	H	Albion R	D	0-0	0-0	2		567
34	Apr 6	A	Cowdenbeath	L	1-2	0-0	2	Caven	430
35	13	H	Alloa	W	3-1	0-1	2	Elder, Joe McFadyen, O'Brien	691
36	20	A	Stenhousemuir	L	1-4	1-0	4	O'Brien	500
37	27	H	Montrose	L	0-3	0-3	5		815
38	May 4	A	Stranraer	W	3-1	0-0	5	Greig, O'Brien, Hendry	400
39	11	A	Dumbarton	L	0-1	0-0	5		800

Final League Position: 5

GOALSCORERS

League: (48): Hendry 17 (2 pens), Caven 6, Elder 6, Greig 6, O'Brien 4, Ogg 3, Crooks 1, McEntegart 1, James McFadyen 1, Joe McFadyen 1, McNamee 1, Morton 1.
Scottish Cup: (1): own goal 1.
Skol Cup: (4): Hendry 2, McEntegart, O'Brien 1.
Centenary Cup: (1): McEntegart 1.

Record Victory: 16-0 v St Peters, Scottish Cup 1st rd; 29 Aug, 1885.
Record Defeat: 0-9 v Motherwell, Division I; 26 Apr, 1930.
Most Capped Player: Walter Arnott, 14, Scotland.
Most League Appearances: 473: J. B. McAlpine.
Most League Goals in Season (Individual): 30: William Martin, Division 1; 1937–38.
Most Goals Overall (Individual): 163: J. B. McAlpine.

Honours

League Champions: Division II 1922–23. B Division 1955–56. Second Division 1980–81.
Scottish Cup Winners: 1874, 1875, 1876, 1880, 1881, 1882, 1884, 1886, 1890, 1893; *Runners-up:* 1892, 1900.
League Cup:—.
FA Cup runners-up: 1884, 1885.
Club colours: Shirt: White and black hoops. Shorts: White. Stockings: White with black hoops.

Monaghan. M	Callan. D	Ogg. G	Jack. S	McNamee. P	McEntegart. S	Caven. R	O'Brien. J	Hendry. M	MacKenzie. K	Crooks	Graig. D	Morris. S	McFadyen. Joe	Elder. G	Morton. C	McFadyen. James	Millar. G	McKay. M	Rodden. J	McKeever. R	Match No.
1	2	3	4	5	6	7	8	9	10*	11	12										1
1	2	3	4	5	6	7	8	9	11*	10	12										2
1	2	3	5	7*	6	10	8	9	12		11			4							3
1	2	3	5	7	6	10	8	9	12		11			4*							4
1	2	3	5	7	6	10	8*	9	12		11			4							5
1	2	3	5	7*	6	10	8	9	12		11†			4	14						6
1	2	3	5	7	6*	10	8	11	9†		12			4	14						7
1	2	3	5	12	7*	8	6	10†	9		11		14	4							8
1	2	3	5	12	7	8	6	10*	9		11			4							9
1	2*	3	5	6	12	7	8†	9	10		11		14	4							10
1	2	3	4	6	7	8	10	12	9*		11			5							11
1	2	3	4	6*	12	7	8	9	10		11†		14	5							12
1	2	3	5	7*	6	10	8	11	12		9†			4	14						13
1	2		4	7	6	10	8†	11			9		14	5	3						14
1	2		4	7†	6	10	11	9	12			8*	14	5	3						15
1	2	3	5	7	6	10	8†	9			11			4	14						16
1	2	3	5	7	6	10	8	9			11			4							17
1	2*	3	5	7	6	10	8	9†			11		14	4	12						18
1		3	5	7	6†	10	8*	9			11		14	4	12				2			19
1		3	5	6	7	8	9	12	10†		11			4		14*			2			20
1		3	5	6	7	8	9†	10	12		11*			4	14				2			21
1			5	6	7	8	9*	10	12					4	3				2	11		22
1			5	8	7	6	10	9	12					4	3				2	11*		23
1		3*	5	12	6	7	11	10			9†		14	4	8				2			24
1		3	5	7*	6	8	9	10	12		11			4					2			25
1		3	5	8*	6	7	9	10†	12		11			4	14				2			26
1		3*	5†	6	7	10	11		12		9		14	4	8				2		9	27
1	2		5	6	7	8	11	10						4	3						9	28
1	2		5	7	6	10	8†	11	12				14	4	3						9*	29
1	2	3	5	7	6	10	8*	9			11			4	12							30
1	2	3	5	7*	6	10	11	9			8			4	12							31
1	2	3	5	7*	6	10	9	11†			8			4	12	14						32
1	2	3	5	6	7	9	10*	11			8			4	12							33
1	2	3*	5	6	7	11	9	10			8			4	12							34
1	2	3	5	7*	6	10	8	9	12		11†			4	14							35
1	2	3	5	7†	6	10	8	9*	12		11			4	14							36
1	2	3	5	7†	6	10	8	9	12		11*			4	14							37
1	2	3	5	7	6	10	8	9*			11†		14	4	12							38
1	2	3	6	7*	8	9	10	11	5					4	12						39
39	29	33	38	30	33	39	31	38	15	2	19	1	2	37	28	—	—	10	2	3	
		+	+		+		+				+		+		+			+			
		1s	5s		1s		7s				14s2s		11s		4s	8s	1s	3s			

RAITH ROVERS First Division

Year Formed: 1883. *Ground & Address:* Stark's Park, Pratt St, Kirkcaldy KY1 1SA. *Telephone:* 0592 263514.
Ground Capacity: total: 8500. seated: 3040. *Size of Pitch:* 113yd × 67yd.
Chairman: John Urquhart. *Secretary:* P. J. Campsie. *Commercial Manager:* P. Rodger.
Manager: James Nicholl. *Assistant Manager:* Murray Cheyne. *Physio:* T. Healey. *Coach:* M. Cheyne. *Reserve Coach:* Andy Harrow.
Managers since 1975: R. Paton; A. Matthew; W. McLean; G. Wallace; R. Wilson; F. Connor.
Club Nickname(s): Rovers. *Previous Grounds:* Robbie's Park.
Record Attendance: 31,306 v Hearts, Scottish Cup 2nd rd; 7 Feb, 1953.
Record Transfer Fee received: £85,000 for Andy Harrow to Luton T (Oct 1980).
Record Transfer Fee paid: £70,000 for Kenny Macdonald from Airdrieonians (Oct 1989).

RAITH ROVERS 1990–91 LEAGUE RECORD

Match No.	Date	Venue	Opponents	Result	H/T Score	Lg. Pos.	Goalscorers	Atten-dance
1	Aug 25	A	Brechin C	W 4-0	1-0	—	Dalziel 2, Nelson, Logan	850
2	Sept 1	H	Clyde	D 1-1	1-0	3	Dalziel	1410
3	8	H	Morton	W 1-0	0-0	2	Dalziel	1395
4	15	A	Meadowbank T	D 1-1	0-0	4	Dalziel	750
5	18	H	Forfar Ath	W 2-1	1-1	—	Macdonald, Lorimer (og)	1053
6	22	H	Clydebank	W 2-0	1-0	3	Dalziel, Macdonald (pen)	1535
7	29	A	Ayr U	L 0-2	0-0	3		1888
8	Oct 6	H	Hamilton A	W 1-0	0-0	3	Ferguson	1138
9	9	A	Kilmarnock	D 1-1	0-1	—	Dalziel	3236
10	13	H	Dundee	D 1-1	0-0	3	Coyle	3494
11	20	A	Airdrieonians	W 5-1	0-0	2	Conn (og), Ferguson 2, Logan 2	2500
12	27	H	Partick T	D 0-0	0-0	2		3052
13	Nov 3	A	Falkirk	L 1-7	1-2	3	Dalziel	3963
14	10	A	Clyde	W 2-1	0-0	3	Dalziel 2	650
15	17	H	Brechin C	L 1-2	1-1	3	Logan	1461
16	24	H	Kilmarnock	D 1-1	1-1	5	Simpson	2260
17	Dec 1	A	Hamilton A	D 2-2	2-2	5	Dalziel 2	1464
18	8	A	Ayr U	W 3-0	2-0	3	Romaines, Sinclair, Ferguson	1179
19	15	A	Clydebank	D 1-1	0-1	4	Dalziel	961
20	29	H	Falkirk	L 1-4	1-0	5	Dalziel	3764
21	Jan 1	A	Dundee	L 1-2	1-0	—	Nelson	4815
22	5	H	Airdrieonians	D 1-1	1-1	5	Nelson	2075
23	Feb 2	A	Forfar Ath	L 1-3	0-1	7	Dalziel	826
24	16	A	Falkirk	W 2-0	1-0	6	Nelson, Ferguson	4197
25	19	H	Brechin C	W 1-0	1-0	—	Dalziel	1074
26	23	A	Partick T	W 3-0	2-0	4	Dalziel 2, Ferguson	3600
27	Mar 2	A	Ayr U	L 3-5	1-3	4	Ferguson 2, Dalziel	2386
28	6	A	Meadowbank T	L 1-3	1-2	—	Dalziel	1000
29	9	H	Partick T	L 1-5	1-3	7	Dalziel	2255
30	16	H	Clyde	W 1-0	0-0	6	Dalziel	1013
31	23	A	Meadowbank T	L 1-4	0-0	7	Dunleavy	300
32	30	A	Morton	L 0-4	0-2	7		1256
33	Apr 6	H	Kilmarnock	L 1-2	0-1	7	McStay	1761
34	13	H	Forfar Ath	L 1-2	1-0	7	Dunleavy	881
35	16	A	Morton	W 2-1	2-0	—	Dennis, Dalziel	2453
36	20	A	Hamilton A	W 2-1	1-0	7	Dalziel, MacLeod	1140
37	27	A	Dundee	L 0-2	0-1	7		3756
38	May 4	H	Clydebank	L 1-2	1-0	7	Dalziel	875
39	11	H	Airdrieonians	L 0-1	0-1	7		4152

Final League Position: 7

GOALSCORERS

League: (54): Dalziel 25, Ferguson 8, Logan 4, Nelson 4, Dunleavy 2, MacDonald 2 (1 pen), Coyle 1, Dennis 1, MacLeod 1, McStay 1, Romaines 1, Simpson 1, Sinclair 1, own goals 2
Scottish Cup: (0).
Skol Cup: (5): McGeachie 2, Coyle 1, Dalziel 1, own goal 1.
Centenary Cup: (6): Burn 2, Dalziel 2, Macdonald 1, own goal 1.

Record Victory: 10-1 v Coldstream, Scottish Cup 2nd rd; 13 Feb, 1954.
Record Defeat: 2-11 v Morton, Division II; 18 Mar, 1936.
Most Capped Player: Dave Morris, 6, Scotland.
Most League Appearances: 430: Willie McNaught.
Most League Goals in Season (Individual): 38: Norman Haywood, Division II; 1937–38.
Most Goals Overall (Individual): 105: Ernie Copland *(League).*

Honours
League Champions: Division II 1907–08, 1909–10 (shared), 1937–38, 1948–49; *Runners-up:* Division II 1908–09, 1926–27, 1966–67. Second Division 1975–76, 1977–78, 1986–87.
Scottish Runners-up: 1913.
League Cup Runners-up: 1948–49.
Club colours: Shirt: Royal blue. Shorts: White. Stockings: Royal blue; all with red/white trimmings.

Arthur, G	McStay, J	MacLeod, I	Fraser, C	Dennis, S	McGeachie, G	Simpson, S	Dalziel, G	Macdonald, K	Coyle, R	Nelson, M	Logan, A	Ferguson, I	Murray, D	Burn, P	Romaines, S	Sinclair, D	Strang, S	Nicholl, J	Raeside, R	Dunleavy, D	Henderson, N	Banner, A	Young, D	Match No.
1	2	3	4	5	6†	7*	8	9	10	11	12	14												1
1	2	3	4	5	6		8		10	11	7	9*	12											2
1	2	3*	4	5	6†	7	8		10	11	14	9	12											3
1	2		4	5	6	7	8	9*	10†	11	12				14	3								4
1	2		4	5	6	7*	8	9	10†	11	12				14	3								5
1	2		4	5	6†	7*	8	9	10	11	12				14	3								6
1	2		4†	5	6	7*	8	9	10	11	12				14	3								7
1	2			5		12	8	9	4		7*10			3	11	6†14								8
1	2			5	6		8†	9	4	11	7*12	3			10	14								9
1	2		4	5	6†		8	9*10	11	7	12				14	3								10
1	2	3		5†	6		8*	9	4	11	7	12	14	10										11
1	2	3		5		12	8	9*	4	11	7	10	6†			14								12
1	2	3		5	6†12		8		4	11	7*	9			10	14								13
1	2	3		5	6	7	8		4	11	9	10												14
1	2	3	4	5		7*	8		10	11	9	6				12								15
1	2	3*		5		7	8†14	4		9	10	11			6	12								16
1	2			5	6	7*	8		4		9	10	3		11	12								17
1	2			5	6*		8		4		9	7	3		10	11	12							18
1	2			5	6		8		4		9	7	3		10	11								19
1	2	6	10	5			8		4	11	12	9	3			7*								20
1	2	6	10†	5			8		4	11	12	9	3			7*14								21
1	2	3	10	5	6*		8		4	11	7	9			12									22
1	4	3		5	7*		8			11		9	12			10			2	6				23
1	2	3		5*			8			11		9	12			10			4	6	7			24
1	2	3	6	5*			8			11		9				10			4	12	7			25
1	2	3		5			8			11		9			12	10*			4	6	7			26
1	2	3		5			8		10	11		9							4	6	7			27
1	2	3		5	6		8		10	11	12	9							4		7*			28
1	2	3	7	5	6		8		10*11	12			14						4†		9			29
1		3*		5	12		8			4	11	9				10			2	6	7			30
1				5	3		8			2	11	9				10			6	4	7			31
	2			5	3		8			4	11	12	9		14	10†			6*	7			1	32
	2	3		5	10		8			4	11	9				12			6	7*			1	33
	2	3†		5	10		8			4	11	9*12			14				6	7			1	34
	2			5			8			6	11	9*12				10			4	3	7		1	35
1	2	3		5			8			4	11	9				10				6	7			36
1	2	3		5*	6		8			4	11	9				10	12				7			37
1*		3		5	6		8	12			9	11†			10	14			4	7			2	38
	2*	3		5†	6		8			4	11	12	9			10			14	7			1	39
34	36	26	13	35	30	11	39	10	34	33	17	27	14	3	8	15	—	10	12	15	1	5	1	

+ + + + + + + + +
1s 3s 1s 1s 12s 6s 3s 7s 5s 8s 4s +
2s

RANGERS

Premier Division

Year Formed: 1873. *Ground & Address:* Ibrox Stadium, Edminston Drive, Glasgow G51 2XD. *Telephone:* 041 427 5232/041 427 1117 (Information Service).
Ground Capacity: total: 44,500. seated: 36,500. *Size of Pitch:* 115yd × 75yd.
Chairman: David Murray. *Secretary:* R. C. Ogilvie. *Commercial Manager:* Bob Reilly.
Manager: Walter Smith. *Assistant Manager:* Archie Knox. *Physio:* . *Coach:* Billy Kirkwood.
Managers since 1975: Jock Wallace; John Greig; Jock Wallace; Graeme Souness.
Club Nickname(s): The Gers. *Previous Grounds:* None.
Record Attendance: 118,567 v Celtic, Division I; 2 Jan, 1939.
Record Transfer Fee received: £580,000 for Robert Fleck to Norwich C (Dec. 1987).
Record Transfer Fee paid: £2,000,000 for Alexei Mikhailichenko from Sampdoria, June 1991.
Record Victory: 14-2 v Blairgowrie, Scottish Cup 1st rd; 20 Jan, 1934.
Record Defeat: 2-10 v Airdrieonians, 1886.
Most Capped Player: George Young, 53, Scotland.
Most League Appearances: 496: John Greig, 1962–78.
Most League Goals in Season (Individual): 44: Sam English, Division I; 1931–32.

RANGERS 1990–91 LEAGUE RECORD

Match No.	Date		Venue	Opponents	Result	H/T Score	Lg. Pos.	Goalscorers	Atten- dance
1	Aug	25	H	Dunfermline Ath	W 3-1	1-1	—	Hateley, Johnston, Walters (pen)	39,951
2	Sept	1	A	Hibernian	D 0-0	0-0	3		17,500
3		8	A	Hearts	W 3-1	2-0	3	Huistra, McCoist 2	22,101
4		15	H	Celtic	D 1-1	0-0	3	Hurlock	38,543
5		22	A	Dundee U	L 1-2	1-1	4	Johnston	16,270
6		29	A	Motherwell	W 1-0	0-0	2	Brown	34,863
7	Oct	6	A	Aberdeen	D 0-0	0-0	1		24,000
8		13	H	St Mirren	W 5-0	2-0	2	McCoist 2 (1 pen), Walters 2, Johnston	38,031
9		20	A	St Johnstone	D 0-0	0-0	2		10,504
10	Nov	3	H	Hibernian	W 4-0	4-0	3	Hateley 2, Walters, Steven T	33,725
11		10	A	Dundee U	L 1-2	0-0	3	McCoist	36,995
12		17	A	Motherwell	W 4-2	1-0	3	Walters, Johnston, Stevens G 2	16,457
13		20	A	Dunfermline Ath	W 1-0	1-0	—	Hateley	14,480
14		25	A	Celtic	W 2-1	1-1		Johnston, McCoist	52,265
15	Dec	1	H	Hearts	W 4-0	1-0	1	Johnston, Hurlock, McCoist, Walters (pen)	37,623
16		8	H	St Johnstone	W 4-1	2-0	1	Walters 2, Johnston (pen), Stevens G	34,610
17		15	A	St Mirren	W 3-0	1-0	1	Walters, Johnston, Hateley	15,197
18		22	H	Aberdeen	D 2-2	0-0	1	McCoist 2	37,998
19		29	A	Dundee U	W 2-1	2-1	1	Johnston, Walters	17,564
20	Jan	2	H	Celtic	W 2-0	1-0	—	Walters, Hateley	38,398
21		5	A	Hearts	W 1-0	0-0	1	Hateley	20,956
22		12	A	Dunfermline Ath	W 2-0	1-0	1	Huistra, Johnston	35,120
23		19	A	Hibernian	W 2-0	1-0	1	Johnston, Vinnicombe	15,000
24	Feb	9	H	St Mirren	W 1-0	0-0	1	McCoist	31,769
25		16	H	Motherwell	W 2-0	1-0	1	McCoist, Hateley	32,192
26		26	A	St Johnstone	D 1-1	0-0	—	Huistra	10,721
27	Mar	2	A	Aberdeen	L 0-1	0-0	1		22,500
28		9	H	Hearts	W 2-1	1-1	1	Steven T, Walters	36,128
29		24	A	Celtic	L 0-3	0-1	—		52,000
30		30	A	Dunfermline Ath	W 1-0	0-0	1	Stevens G	14,256
31	Apr	6	H	Hibernian	D 0-0	0-0	1		35,507
32		13	H	St Johnstone	W 3-0	2-0	1	Durrant, Spencer, Huistra	35,930
33		20	A	St Mirren	W 1-0	0-0	1	Robertson	18,473
34		24	H	Dundee U	W 1-0	1-0	—	Ferguson	32,397
35	May	4	A	Motherwell	L 0-3	0-1	2		17,672
36		11	H	Aberdeen	W 2-0	1-0	1	Hateley 2	37,652

Final League Position: 1

GOALSCORERS

League: (62): Walters 12 (2 pens), Johnston 11 (1 pen), McCoist 11 (1 pen), Hateley 10, Huistra 4, Stevens G 4, Hurlock 2, Steven T 2, Brown 1, Durrant 1, Ferguson 1, Robertson 1, Spencer 1, Vinnicombe 1
Scottish Cup: (7): Hateley 2, Huistra 1, McCoist 1, Nisbet 1, Spackman 1, Walters 1 (pen)
Skol Cup: (15): Johnston 3, McCoist 3, Steven T 3, Hateley 2, Walters 2, Butcher 1, Gough 1

Most Goals Overall (Individual): 233: Bob McPhail; 1927–39.

Honours
League Champions: (41 times) Division I 1890–91 (shared), 1898–99, 1899–1900, 1900–01, 1901–02, 1910–11, 1911–12, 1912–13, 1917–18, 1919–20, 1920–21, 1922–23, 1923–24, 1924–25, 1926–27, 1927–28, 1928–29, 1929–30, 1930–31, 1932–33, 1933–34, 1934–35, 1936–37, 1938–39, 1946–47, 1948–49, 1949–50, 1952–53, 1955–56, 1956–57, 1958–59, 1960–61, 1962–63, 1963–64, 1974–75. Premier Division 1975–76, 1977–78, 1986–87, 1988–89, 1989–90, 1990–91; *Runners-up:* 23 times.
Scottish Cup Winners: (24 times) 1894, 1897, 1898, 1903, 1928, 1930, 1932, 1934, 1935, 1936, 1948, 1949, 1950, 1953, 1960, 1962, 1963, 1964, 1966, 1973, 1976, 1978, 1979, 1981; *Runners-up:* 15 times.
League Cup Winners: (17 times) 1946–47, 1948–49, 1960–61, 1961–62, 1963–64, 1964–65, 1970–71, 1975–76, 1977–78, 1978–79, 1981–82, 1983–84, 1984–85, 1986–87, 1987–88, 1988–89, 1990–91; *Runners-up:* 7 times.
European: *European Cup:* 57 matches (1956–57, 1957–58, 1959–60 semi-finals, 1961–62, 1963–64, 1964–65, 1975–76, 1976–77, 1978–79, 1987–88, 1989–90, 1990–91).
Cup Winners Cup Winners: 1971–72. 50 matches (1960–61 runners-up, 1962–63, 1966–67 runners-up, 1969–70, 1971–72 winners, 1973–74, 1977–78, 1979–80, 1981–82, 1983–84). *UEFA Cup:* 38 matches (1967–68, 1968–69 semi-finals, 1970–71 *Fairs Cup*; 1982–83, 1984–85, 1985–86, 1986–87, 1988–89).
Club colours: Shirt: Royal blue with red and white trim. Shorts: White. Stockings: Red.

Woods, C	Stevens, G	Brown, J	Gough, R	Spackman, N	Butcher, T	Steven, T	Ferguson, I	Hateley, M	Johnston, M	Walters, M	McCoist, A	Huistra, P	Hurlock, T	Munro, S	Kuznetzov, O	Nisbet, S	Robertson, A	McSwegan, G	Vinnicombe, C	Dodds, D	Spencer, J	Reid, B	Durrant, I	Cowan, T	Match No.
1	2	3	4	5	6	7	8†	9	10	11*12	14														1
1	2	3	4	5	6	7	8	9*10		12	11														2
1	2		4	5	6	7		9	10	12	8	11*	3												3
1	2	12	4	5	6	7		9†10	14		8	11*	3												4
1	2	12	4	5	6	7		9†10	14		8	11*	3												5
1	2	6	4	5		7		12	10	8	9*11			3											6
1	2	6	4	5		7		12	10	11*	9		8	3											7
1	2		4	5		7			10	11	9	12	8	3*	6										8
1	2		4	5		7		14	10	11	9†12		8	3	6*										9
1	2		4	5		7*12	10		11†	9	14	8	3		6										10
1	2	6		5		7*			10	11	9		8	3†			4	12	14						11
1	2	6		5				9	10	11*12						4	8		3	7					12
1	2	6		5				8	10		9		7			4			3	11					13
1	2	6*		5				9	10†11	14	12	7	3			4	8								14
1	2	6		5				9	10*11	12		7	3			4	8								15
1	2	6		5		7*		9	10	11†14	12	8	3			4									16
1	2	6	4	5		7		9	10	11*12		8	3												17
1	2	6	4			7†		9	10	11	14	12	8	3			5*								18
1	2	6	4	5				9	10†11	14	12		3			8		7*							19
1	2	6	4	5				9	10	7		11*	8	3		12									20
1	2	6	4	5				9	10	7		11*	8	3		12									21
1	2	6*	4	5				9	10	7		11	8			12		3							22
1	2		4	5				9	10	7*14	11	8†				6		3					12		23
1	2	6	4	5		7			8	9	11*					12		3	10						24
1	2	6*	4	5		7			11	10	12	8				3									25
1	2	6	4	5		7		9	8	14	10†12	11				3*									26
1	2	5	6	4		7		9	10	11*		12	8			3									27
1	2		4	5		7	6*	9		11	10	12	8			3									28
1	2		4	5			8*	10		9						6	12			7	11		3		29
1	2		4	5				8	9	10*11†		14	7				3			12	6				30
1	2		4	5				9	8			11	7				3*			12	6	10			31
1	2	4		5				8	9			12	7					14	3	11†	6	10*			32
1	2	6		5				8	9			12	7			4	14	11*	3			10†			33
1	2	6	4	5				8	9	10	7*	12				11							3		34
1	2†	6		5				8*	9	10	11		12	7		4	14						3		35
1	2	6†		5				8	9	10	11	14		7		4						12	3*		36
36	36	25	26	35	5	19	10	30	29	26	15	10	29	14	2	15	7	1	10	3	3	3	3	4	
		+					+	+		+	+	+					+	+			+		+	+	
		2s					1s	3s		4s	11s	17s					8s	2s			2s		1s	1s	

ST JOHNSTONE · Premier Division

Year Formed: 1884. *Ground & Address:* McDiarmid Park, Crieff Road, Perth PH1 2SJ. *Telephone:* 0738 26961. *Clubcall:* 0898 121559. *Ground Capacity:* 10,721 seated: all. *Size of Pitch:* 115yd × 75yd.
Chairman: G. S. Brown. *Secretary and General Manager:* John Litster. *Commercial Manager* —.
Manager: Alex Totten. *Assistant Manager:* Bert Paton. *Physio:* J. Peacock. *Coach:* T. Campbell.
Managers since 1975: J. Stewart, J. Storrie; A. Stuart; A. Rennie; I. Gibson; A. Totten.
Club Nickname(s): Saints. *Previous Grounds:* Recreation Grounds, Muirton Park.
Record Attendance: 29,972 v Dundee, Scottish Cup 2nd rd; 10 Feb, 1952.
Record Transfer Fee received: £400,000 for Ally McCoist to Sunderland (1982).
Record Transfer Fee paid: £160,000 for John Davies from Clydebank (Nov 1990).
Record Victory: 8-1 v Partick Th, League Cup; 16 Aug, 1969.

St JOHNSTONE 1990–91 LEAGUE RECORD

Match No.	Date		Venue	Opponents	Result		H/T Score	Lg. Pos.	Goalscorers	Atten-dance
1	Aug 25		H	Dundee U	L	1-3	1-2	—	Curran	7784
2	Sept	1	A	St Mirren	D	2-2	2-1	7	Curran, Turner	4116
3		8	A	Motherwell	L	0-3	0-2	10		5069
4		15	H	Dunfermline Ath	W	3-2	2-1	9	Curran, Moore, Grant	7601
5		22	A	Hibernian	L	0-1	0-0	9		7000
6		29	H	Aberdeen	W	5-0	3-0	6	Grant 2, Treanor 2, Maskrey	8711
7	Oct	6	A	Celtic	D	0-0	0-0	6		27,014
8		13	A	Hearts	W	3-2	1-1	6	Turner, Grant, Curran	12,824
9		20	H	Rangers	D	0-0	0-0	5		10,504
10		27	A	Dundee U	W	2-1	2-0	4	Inglis, Maskrey	11,708
11	Nov	3	H	St Mirren	L	0-1	0-0	4		7349
12		10	H	Hibernian	D	1-1	0-0	4	Curran	9233
13		17	A	Aberdeen	D	0-0	0-0	5		16,000
14		24	A	Dunfermline Ath	W	2-1	2-1	4	Grant, Maskrey	7822
15	Dec	1	H	Motherwell	W	2-1	0-0	4	Curran, Moore	6784
16		8	A	Rangers	L	1-4	0-2	4	Grant	34,610
17		15	H	Hearts	W	2-1	1-0	4	Davies, Maskrey	7833
18		22	A	Celtic	W	3-2	2-0	4	Maskrey, Curran, Turner	10,260
19		29	A	Hibernian	W	1-0	1-0	4	Curran	5000
20	Jan	2	H	Dunfermline Ath	L	0-1	0-0	—		9533
21		5	A	Motherwell	D	2-2	0-1	4	Maskrey, Ward	5338
22		19	A	St Mirren	W	1-0	1-0	4	Curran	5715
23	Feb	13	A	Aberdeen	L	0-1	0-0	—		7046
24		19	H	Dundee U	L	0-1	0-0	—		6190
25		26	H	Rangers	D	1-1	0-0	—	Moore	10,721
26	Mar	2	A	Celtic	L	0-3	0-1	4		24,560
27		6	A	Hearts	L	1-2	1-1	—	Moore	8136
28		9	H	Motherwell	L	1-4	0-2	5	Treanor (pen)	5079
29		23	A	Dunfermline Ath	L	2-3	1-1	6	McVicar, Moore	5696
30		30	A	Dundee U	D	0-0	0-0	6		7794
31	Apr	9	H	St Mirren	W	2-1	0-0	—	Bingham, Treanor (pen)	4300
32		13	A	Rangers	L	0-3	0-2	6		35,930
33		20	H	Hearts	L	0-2	0-2	6		6822
34		27	H	Hibernian	D	0-0	0-0	7		5143
35	May	4	A	Aberdeen	L	1-2	1-2	7	Maskrey	18,000
36		11	H	Celtic	L	2-3	1-1	7	Grant, Bingham	9486

Final League Position: 7

GOALSCORERS

League: (41): Curran 9, Grant 7, Maskrey 7, Moore 5, Treanor 4 (2 pens), Turner 3, Bingham 2, Davies 1, Inglis 1, McVicar 1, Ward 1
Scottish Cup: (12): Moore 4, Grant 3, Maskrey 3, Curran 2
Skol Cup: (0)

Record Defeat: 0-12 v Cowdenbeath, Scottish Cup, 21 January 1928.
Most Capped Player: Sandy McLaren, 5, Scotland.
Most League Appearances: 298: Drew Rutherford.
Most League Goals in Season (Individual): 36: Jimmy Benson, Division II; 1931–32.
Most Goals Overall (Individual): 114: John Brogan, 1977–83.

Honours
League Champions: First Division 1982–83, 1989–90. Division II 1923–24, 1959–60, 1962–63; *Runners-up:* Division II 1931–32. Second Division 1987–88.
Scottish Cup: Semi-finals 1934, 1968, 1989.
League Cup Runners-up: 1969.
European: *European Cup*—. *Cup Winners Cup*—. *UEFA Cup:* 1971–72.
Club colours: Shirt: Royal blue with white semi-circular chest panel. Shorts: Royal blue. Stockings: Royal blue.

Balavage, J	Treanor, M	McVicar, D	Baltacha, S	Inglis, J	McGinnis, G	Moore, A	Turner, T	Maskrey, S	Grant, R	Curran, H	Johnston, S	Cherry, P	Heddle, I	Hamilton, L	Lee, I	Deas, P	Barron, D	Ward, K	Davies, J	Macdonald, K	Nicolson, K	Sweeney, P	Bingham, D	Match No.
1	2	3	4	5	6	7	8*	9	10	11†	12		14											1
1	2	3	4	5	6	8	9*	7	10		12	11		1										2
	2	3	4	5	6		8	9*	7	10		12	11	1										3
	2		3	5	6*	7†11		9	10	8		4	12	1	14									4
	2	12	3	5	6	7	11	9	10	8*		4		1										5
	2		3	5	6	7	8*	9	10	11†		4		1		12	14							6
	2		3	5	6	7	8*	9	10	11		4		1	.	12								7
	2		3	5	6	7	8†	9*10	11			4	12	1	14									8
	2		3	5	6	7	8	9	10	11		4		1										9
	2		3	5	6†	7	8	9*10	11			4		1	14	12								10
	2		3	5	6†	7	8	9	10	11*		4		1	14	12								11
	2	12	3	5	6	7		9	10	11		4		1	8*									12
	2†11		3	5	6	7		9	10*	8		4		1	14	12								13
	11		3	5		7		9	10	8		4*	1	14	2	12	6†							14
	11		3	5	2	7	12	9	10†	8		4*		1		6*14								15
	11		3	5	2	7	6	9†10	8			4*		1	12	14								16
	4		3	5	2	7	8†	9	10*11					1	14	6	12							17
	2	12	3	5	6	7	8	9	10†11*			4		1	14									18
	2	4	3	5	6	7	8	9*10	11					1	12									19
	2	12	3	5	6	7	8	9*10†11						1	4	14								20
	2		3	5	6	7		9	11			4		1	12	8*10								21
	2		3	5	6	7	8	9	11			4		1	12	10*								22
	2		3	5		7	8	9	10	11		4		1	6									23
	2		3	5*	6	7	8	9	10†11			4		1	14	12								24
	2	4	3		6	7	8	9*12	11					1	10				5					25
	2	12	3		4	7	8	9*10	11					1	14	6†			5					26
	2	4	3		6	7		10	11	12				1	9†	8*14			5					27
	2		3	4		7	8	9	10†11					1	14	12			5*	6				28
	2	11	3	5†	6	7	12	10	8			14		1	9*				4					29
	2	3		5		8		10	12			12		1	4	14	7	9*		6	11†			30
	2	4	3	5	6	7	8	9		11*				1	12				10					31
	2	10	3	5	6	7	8	9		11				1*	12				4†14					32
	2	4	3	5		7	8	9		11				1	10				6*12					33
	2*	4	3	5		8		9	10	11†				1	12		7		6	14				34
		3*	5	6		9		10	11					1	12		8	2	4	7				35
	6		5	2		9		10	11			1	12		4	14	8		3*	7†				36
2	30	18	34	31	32	31	27	33	29	35	—	18	2	34	1	—	3	1	13	5	5	8	4	
	+					+	+	+			+	+	+			+	+		+	+	+	+	+	
	5s					1s	1s	1s			1s	2s	5s			4s	1s	8s	9s	8s	6s		3s	

ST MIRREN
Premier Division

Year Formed: 1877.   *Ground & Address:* St Mirren Park, Love St, Paisley PA3 2EJ.   *Telephone:* 041 889 2558/041 840 1337.
Ground Capacity: total: 21,800. seated: 2420.   *Size of Pitch:* 112yd × 73yd.
Chairman: Allan W. Marshall.   *Secretary:* George N. Pratt.   *Commercial Manager:* Jack Copland.
Manager: David Hay.   *Assistant Manager:* Gordon Smith.   *Physio:* Bob Pender   *Coach:* Gordon McQueen.
Managers since 1975: Alex Ferguson; Jim Clunie; Rikki MacFarlane; Alex Miller; Alex Smith; Tony Fitzpatrick.
Club Nickname(s): The Buddies.   *Previous Grounds:* Short Roods 1877–79, Thistle Park Greenhill 1879–83, Westmarch 1883–94.
Record Attendance: 47,428 v Celtic, Scottish Cup 4th rd; 7 Mar, 1925.
Record Transfer Fee received: £850,000 for Ian Ferguson to Rangers (1988).
Record Transfer Fee paid: £400,000 for Thomas Stickroth from Bayer Uerdingen, 1990.
Record Victory: 15-0 v Glasgow University, Scottish Cup 1st rd; 30 Jan, 1960.

St MIRREN 1990–91 LEAGUE RECORD

Match No.	Date	Venue	Opponents	Result	H/T Score	Lg. Pos.	Goalscorers	Atten- dance
1	Aug 25	A	Hearts	D	1-1	1-0	—	Kinnaird	12,215
2	Sept 1	H	St Johnstone	D	2-2	1-2	5	McWalter, Lambert	4116
3	8	A	Dundee U	L	0-1	0-0	6		6968
4	15	H	Motherwell	W	1-0	0-0	5	Stickroth	4678
5	22	A	Aberdeen	L	1-2	1-2	6	Kinnaird	12,500
6	29	H	Celtic	L	2-3	0-0	8	McWalter, Kinnaird	20,097
7	Oct 6	A	Hibernian	L	0-1	0-1	10		4500
8	13	A	Rangers	L	0-5	0-2	10		38,031
9	20	H	Dunfermline Ath	L	0-1	0-0	10		4488
10	27	H	Hearts	W	2-1	1-0	10	Lambert, Torfason	5441
11	Nov 3	A	St Johnstone	W	1-0	0-0	9	Torfason	3749
12	10	H	Aberdeen	L	0-4	0-2	10		7638
13	17	A	Celtic	L	1-4	0-1	10	McDowall	25,686
14	24	A	Motherwell	D	1-1	1-0	10	Torfason	4720
15	Dec 1	H	Dundee U	D	1-1	1-1	10	McDowall	4581
16	11	A	Dunfermline Ath	D	0-0	0-0	—		4499
17	15	H	Rangers	L	0-3	0-1	10		15,197
18	22	H	Hibernian	W	1-0	0-0	9	Black	4478
19	26	A	Aberdeen	L	0-1	0-0	—		8755
20	Jan 2	H	Motherwell	D	2-2	1-1	—	McDowall, Archibald	6683
21	5	A	Dundee U	L	2-3	1-1	9	McDowall, Archibald	6180
22	12	A	Hearts	L	0-2	0-1	9		10,858
23	19	H	St Johnstone	L	0-1	0-1	9		5715
24	Feb 9	A	Rangers	L	0-1	0-0	10		31,769
25	19	H	Dunfermline Ath	D	2-2	1-1	10	Victor, Black	2589
26	Mar 2	A	Hibernian	L	3-4	2-1	10	Kinnaird, Martin, Torfason	5500
27	9	H	Dundee U	L	0-1	0-0	10		3960
28	12	H	Celtic	L	0-2	0-1	—		11,268
29	23	A	Motherwell	L	1-3	1-1	10	Shaw	6207
30	30	H	Hearts	D	0-0	0-0	10		4823
31	Apr 9	A	St Johnstone	L	1-2	0-0	—	McWalter	4300
32	13	A	Dunfermline Ath	D	2-2	0-2	10	Martin, McIntyre	3464
33	20	H	Rangers	L	0-1	0-0	10		18,473
34	27	H	Aberdeen	L	0-1	0-0	10		8513
35	May 5	A	Celtic	L	0-1	0-1	—		17,200
36	11	H	Hibernian	W	1-0	1-0	10	McEwan	3403

Final League Position: 10

GOALSCORERS
League: (28): Kinnaird 4, McDowall 4, Torfason 4, McWalter 3, Archibald 2, Black 2, Lambert 2, Martin 2, McEwan 1, McIntyre 1, Shaw 1, Stickroth 1, Victor 1
Scottish Cup: (5): Torfason 2, Kinnaird 1, McDowall 1, Victor 1
Skol Cup: (1): Stickroth 1

Record Defeat: 0-9 v Rangers, Division I; 4 Dec, 1897.
Most Capped Player: Godmundor Torfason, 29, Iceland.
Most League Appearances: 287: Billy Abercromby, 1976–87.
Most League Goals in Season (Individual): 45: Dunky Walker, Division I; 1921–22.
Most Goals Overall (Individual): —.

Honours
League Champions: First Division 1976–77. Division II 1967–68; *Runners-up* 1935–36.
Scottish Cup Winners: 1926, 1959, 1987; *Runners-up:* 1908, 1934, 1962.
League Cup Runners-up: 1955–56.
Victory Cup: 1919–20.
Summer Cup: 1943–44.
Anglo-Scottish Cup: 1979–80.
European: *European Cup*—. *Cup Winners Cup:* 1987–88. *UEFA Cup:* 1980–81, 1983–84, 1985–86.
Club colours: Shirt: Black and white vertical stripes. Shorts: White with black side panel. Stockings: White with black hoop. Change colours: All red.

Money. C	Wishart. F	Black. T	Lambert. P	Godfrey. P	Manley. R	Shaw. G	Martin. B	Stickroth. T	McWalter. M	Kinnaird. P	McDowall. K	Dawson. R	McGill. D	Thiele. G	Torfason. G	McWhirter. N	Winnie. D	Fridge. L	Archibald. S	Victor. Munoz	Irvine. A	Broddie. J	McGowne. K	Hutchinson. T	McIntyre. P	McEwan. A	Match No.
1	2	3	4*	5	6	7	8	9	10	11	12																1
1	2	3	4		6	7	5	9	10	11	8																2
1	2	3	4	5	6	7	10	11*	8			12															3
1	2	3	4*	5	6	7†	8	9	10	11	12	14															4
1	2	3	4		6	12	8	9	10*11	7	5																5
1	2	3	4*	5	6	7†	8	9	10	11	12	14															6
1	2	3	4*	5	6	14	8	9	7	11†12					10												7
1		3	4	5	6	7	8*	9		11	12				10	2											8
1		3	4		6	7	8	9		11*12	2				10	5											9
1		3	4	5		7	8	9		11	12	2			10		6*										10
14		3	4†	5		7	8	9		11	12	2			10*	6		1									11
	3*	4	5		14	7	9		11†12	2				10	6		1	8									12
1	3		4*		6	14	7	9		12	2			10	11				8†	5							13
1		3	4		6	12	2	9		7				10*11				8	5								14
1	12	3	4		6	14	2	9		7				10†11				8	5*								15
	12	3	4*		6	10	2		14	7				11			1	8	5	9†							16
		3	4		6	10*	2	9	12	7				11			1	8	5								17
7		3	4*	2		8	6	12	9†	14				11			1	10	5								18
7		3	4*	2	11	8	6	10	9†	12							1		5	14							19
	2	3		6	11	12		8	9†14	7					4		1	10*	5								20
	2	3		6*	8	4		9	11	7							1†10		5	12	14						21
	2	3		6	8		12	9	14	7							1	10*	5†		11	4					22
1	2	3*		6	14		8	9†12							11			10	5		7	4					23
1	2	3		6		7		12	11	8				10*	4			5		9							24
1	2	3	12	6*		14	4			7†				10	11			8	5	9							25
1	2*	3	4		14	7	8		11					10	6			5	9†		12						26
1		3	8		7	6	12	14	11*	2				10†	4			9	5								27
1		3	8†		7	4	12	10	14	2				11*				5	9	6							28
1	12	8		7	6		14	11*	2					4		10	5	9†	3								29
1		3	8		14	6	7		11*	2				9	4		10	5†	12								30
1		3	8		6	7	12			2				10*	4			5	9	11							31
1	2		8		11	5	9							10	4			12	3	6		7*					32
1	2*	3	8		12	6	7							9	4		10†	14	5		11						33
	3	10		7*	6	9	12		2					4	1		11		5	8							34
1		3	8		6	7	11	12		2				4				9*	5		10						35
	3	8†		6	7*		14			9	4			1	10				5	2	12	11					36
25	19	33	30	14	19	21	31	26	16	18	11	13	1	—	18	25	1	11	16	18	8	7	10	—	4	1	
+	+	+		+		+	+	+	+	+	+	+							+	+		+					
3s	1s	1s		12s		5s	6s	5s	12s1s	2s	1s								3s	3s		2s					

STENHOUSEMUIR Second Division

Year Formed: 1884. *Ground & Address:* Ochilview Park, Gladstone Rd, Stenhousemuir FK5 5QL. *Telephone:* 0324 562992.
Ground Capacity: total: 3480. seated: 340. *Size of Pitch:* 113yd × 78yd.
Chairman: John Cook. *Secretary:* A. T. Bulloch. *Commercial Manager:* Greig Thomson. (*Vice-Chairman*)
Manager: Dennis Lawson. *Assistant Manager:* David Connell. *Physio:* Garry Binnie. *Coach:* David Connell.
Managers since 1975: H. Glasgow; J. Black; A. Rose; W. Henderson; A. Rennie; J. Meakin.
Club Nickname(s): The Warriors. *Previous Grounds:* Tryst Ground 1884–86, Goschen Park 1886–90.
Record Attendance: 12,500 v East Fife, Scottish Cup 4th rd; 11 Mar, 1950.
Record Transfer Fee received: £30,000 for David Beaton to Falkirk (June 1989).
Record Transfer Fee paid: £7,000 to Meadowbank Th for Lee Bullen (Nov 1990).

STENHOUSEMUIR 1990–91 LEAGUE RECORD

Match No.	Date	Venue	Opponents	Result	H/T Score	Lg. Pos.	Goalscorers	Atten- dance
1	Aug 25	H	Montrose	L 0-1	0-0	—		350
2	Sept 1	A	East Stirling	D 2-2	1-2	11	McCormick (pen), Speirs	250
3	8	A	Stranraer	W 2-1	0-0	9	Speirs, Elliott	550
4	15	A	Arbroath	W 2-0	0-0	5	McCormick 2	499
5	18	A	Albion R	W 4-1	0-1	—	Speirs 2, McCormick 2	322
6	22	H	Dumbarton	D 1-1	1-1	2	McCormick	600
7	29	A	Berwick R	W 1-0	0-0	2	Speirs	417
8	Oct 6	A	East Fife	L 1-2	1-1	4	Walker	731
9	9	H	Queen's Park	L 1-2	0-1	—	Clouston	500
10	13	H	Alloa	W 1-0	1-0	5	Aitken	660
11	20	A	Queen of the S	L 2-3	1-2	5	Speirs, Anderson	698
12	27	H	Stirling Albion	D 2-2	0-0	4	Hallford, McCormick	1050
13	Nov 3	A	Cowdenbeath	D 3-3	1-1	5	Speirs 2, McAvoy	245
14	10	H	East Stirling	W 4-1	2-1	4	Speirs, McCormick, McAvoy 2	340
15	17	A	Montrose	W 3-2	2-1	2	Speirs, Bullen, McCormick	387
16	24	H	Stranraer	W 3-2	1-2	2	McCormick, Bullen, Walker	300
17	Dec 1	A	Arbroath	D 0-0	0-0	2		357
18	15	A	Stirling Albion	D 1-1	1-0	3	McAvoy	1080
19	22	H	Cowdenbeath	L 1-4	0-1	5	Bullen	300
20	Jan 12	A	Queen's Park	L 0-1	0-0	5		954
21	22	A	Alloa	L 0-1	0-0	—		214
22	26	H	Albion R	W 2-0	1-0	4	Bell, Speirs (pen)	500
23	Feb 2	A	Dumbarton	D 0-0	0-0	4		450
24	5	H	Queen of the S	W 2-1	2-1	—	Bell 2	318
25	19	A	Alloa	D 1-1	0-0	—	Walker	354
26	23	H	Montrose	L 0-1	0-1	7		300
27	27	H	East Fife	W 2-0	1-0	—	Bullen, Speirs	500
28	Mar 2	H	East Stirling	D 0-0	0-0	4		400
29	5	H	Berwick R	W 2-1	1-1	—	Walker, McCormick	300
30	9	A	East Fife	L 0-1	0-0	3		506
31	16	A	Albion R	D 0-0	0-0	3		258
32	23	H	Queen of the S	L 0-1	0-1	4		400
33	30	A	Arbroath	W 2-0	0-0	3	Gardiner, Donald	351
34	Apr 6	H	Berwick R	D 1-1	0-1	3	Cairney	300
35	13	A	Dumbarton	L 1-2	0-2	5	Speirs (pen)	600
36	20	A	Queen's Park	W 4-1	0-1	5	Speirs 2 (1 pen), Quinton, McCormick	500
37	27	A	Stranraer	W 2-0	1-0	4	Speirs, Cairney	637
38	May 4	A	Cowdenbeath	D 1-1	0-0	4	Speirs	1000
39	11	H	Stirling Albion	W 2-1	0-1	4	McCormick, Quinton	1000

Final League Position: 4

GOALSCORERS

League: (56): Speirs 17 (3 pens), McCormick 13 (1 pen), Bullen 4, McAvoy 4, Walker 4, Bell 3, Cairney 2, Quinton 2, Aitken 1, Anderson 1, Clouston 1, Donald 1, Elliott 1, Gardiner 1, Hallford 1.
Scottish Cup: (0).
Skol Cup: (0).
Centenary Cup: (0).

Record Victory: 9-2 v Dundee U, Division II; 19 Apr, 1937.
Record Defeat: 2-11 v Dunfermline Ath, Division II; 27 Sept, 1930.
Most Capped Player: —.
Most League Appearances: 298: Harry Cairney.
Most League Goals in Season (Individual): 32, Robert Taylor, Division II, 1925–26.
Most Goals Overall (Individual): —.

Honours
League Champions:—.
Scottish Cup: Semi-finals 1902–03.
League Cup: Quarter-finals 1947–48, 1960–61, 1975–76.
Club colours: Shirt: Maroon with white pinstripe. Shorts: White. Stockings: Maroon with three white hoops.

Kelly, C	Nelson, M	Kemp, B	Cairney, H	Tracey, K	Speirs, A	Clouston, B	Aitken, N	McCormick, S	Hallford, E	Walker, C	Bell, A	McGurn, J	Anderson, P	Quinton, I	Elliott, T	McNab, J	McAvoy, M	Rennie, S	Bullen, L	Gardiner, J	Donald, G	Joyce, A	Match No.
1	2†	3	4	5	6*	7	8	9	10	11	12		14										1
1	10*	4	5	11	8	2†	9	3	7		12		6	14									2
1		4	5	11	8	2†	9	3	7*				6	10	12	14							3
1	12	10	4		11	5	2	9	3	7	14		6*	8†									4
1		10	4	5	11	8	2	9	3	7*			6	12									5
1	12	10	4	5†11*	8		2	9	3	7			6	14									6
1	12	10	4	5	11*	8		9†	3	7			6	2			14						7
1		10	4	5	11	8		9†	3	7			6	2	14								8
1	11*	4	5		7	2	8	9†	3	10	12		6	14									9
1		10	4*	14	8	2	9	3	11				6	12		7†	5						10
1		10	4		7†	8	2	9	3	11			6	14	12	5*							11
1	8		6	4	11	7	2	9	3	10			5										12
1	2	8	6*	4	11†	7		9	3	10	14		5					12					13
1	12	6*	8		11		2	9	3	10	7†		5			14	4						14
1		6	8		11		2	9	3	7			5			12	4	10*					15
1		6	8		11*		2	9	3	7			5			12	4	10					16
1		6	8	4†11			2	9	3	7			5			14		10					17
1	14	6	8	4	11	3		9		7†			5	12		10*		2					18
1		6	8	12	4	2†	9	3	11				5	14		10*		7					19
1	8†10	4	5	14		2		9*	3	7			6	11			12						20
1		10	4	5	11*12		2	9†	3	7	14		6				8						21
1		10	4	5	14	12	2	9†	3	11		7	6				8*						22
1		10	4	5	11†	8	2*14	3		9		7	6				12						23
1		10	4	5*11†	8		2	14	3	9	7		6				12						24
1		10	4		8†	5	2	9*	3	11	7		6	14			12						25
1	14	10	4		12	5	2		3	11	7		6			8*		9†					26
1		10	4	11*		5	2	9	3	7	12		6				8						27
1		10	4	11*	5†	2	9	3	7	12			6			14		8					28
1		10	4		11	8	2	9	3	7			6	12				5*					29
1		10	4		11†	8	2	9	3	7	12		6	14				5*					30
1	2	10	4		11†	5		9	3	8	12		6			14		7*					31
1	2	10†	4		12	5		9	3	7			6	14		11		8*					32
1	6†	4		7	10	2		9	3				5	12						8	11		33
	10*	4	5	11		7	2†	9	3	8	14		6	12						1			34
1		8	5	14	4	2	9*	3	7	12			6	11					10†				35
1	2†	8	5	11	4		9	3	10	7*			6	12			14						36
1	2		4	5	11		9	3	10	7*			6	8			12						37
1	2		8	5*11			9	3	10	7			6	4			12						38
1	2		8	5	11		9	3	10*	7			6	4			12						39
38	10	33	39	22	32	30	28	36	38	38	10	0	38	9	0	1	6	3	14	1	2	1	
+				+	+		+				+	+	+	+	+		+		+				
6s				7s	2s		2s				11s2s		15s1s	3s	9s		7s						

STIRLING ALBION First Division

Year Formed: 1945. *Ground & Address:* Annfield Park, St Ninians Rd, Stirling FK8 2HE. *Telephone:* 0786 50399.
Ground Capacity: total: 12,000. seated: 643. *Size of Pitch:* 110yd × 74yd.
Chairman: Peter McKenzie. *Secretary:* Duncan McCallum. *Commercial Manager:* —.
Manager: John Brogan. *Assistant Manager:* Tom O'Neill, Jimmy Sinclair. *Physio:* Fred Rae. *Coach:* Jim McSherry.
Managers since 1975: A. Smith; G. Peebles; J. Fleeting; J. Brogan.
Club Nickname(s): The Binos. *Previous Grounds:* None.
Record Attendance: 26,400 v Celtic, Scottish Cup 4th rd; 14 Mar, 1959.
Record Transfer Fee received: £70,000 for John Philliben to Doncaster R (Mar 1984).
Record Transfer Fee paid: £17,000 for Douglas Lawrie from Airdrieonians, December 1989.
Record Victory: 20-0 v Selkirk, Scottish Cup, 1st rd; 8 Dec, 1984.

STIRLING ALBION 1990–91 LEAGUE RECORD

Match No.	Date	Venue	Opponents	Result	H/T Score	Lg. Pos.	Goalscorers	Atten- dance
1	Aug 25	A	Cowdenbeath	W 2-0	0-0	—	Shanks, Mailer	300
2	Sept 1	H	Queen of the S	D 0-0	0-0	3		700
3	8	A	Arbroath	W 3-2	1-0	1	Reid 2, Lawrie	612
4	15	H	East Fife	L 1-2	1-2	5	Reid	920
5	22	H	Albion R	W 2-0	1-0	5	Lloyd 2	730
6	29	A	Alloa	W 1-0	1-0	3	Reid	1078
7	Oct 6	A	Dumbarton	D 0-0	0-0	5		600
8	9	H	Stranraer	W 3-1	0-1	—	Moore, Reid, Docherty	440
9	13	H	Berwick R	W 4-1	3-1	2	Lawrie, Reid, Kerr, Robertson	650
10	20	A	Queen's Park	D 0-0	0-0	2		858
11	23	A	Montrose	W 1-0	1-0	—	Lloyd	811
12	27	A	Stenhousemuir	D 2-2	0-0	1	Moore, Mitchell	1050
13	Nov 3	H	East Stirling	W 3-0	1-0	1	Conway, Lloyd, McInnes	764
14	10	A	Queen of the S	D 0-0	0-0	1		931
15	17	H	Cowdenbeath	W 5-1	2-0	1	Lloyd 3, Shanks, Moore	650
16	24	H	Arbroath	W 3-1	1-1	1	Docherty, Lawrie, Conway	680
17	Dec 1	A	East Fife	D 1-1	0-0	1	Reid	1089
18	8	A	Berwick R	D 1-1	0-0	1	Reid	550
19	15	H	Stenhousemuir	D 1-1	0-1	1	Moore	1080
20	Jan 5	H	Queen's Park	L 0-1	0-0	1		840
21	12	A	Stranraer	W 4-1	2-0	1	McGachie 3, Reid	450
22	19	H	Dumbarton	W 2-0	0-0	1	Lloyd, Moore	650
23	29	H	Montrose	W 3-0	1-0	—	Reid, Docherty, McGachie	580
24	Feb 9	H	Alloa	W 2-0	1-0	1	McInnes, Moore	1100
25	13	H	Albion R	W 3-0	1-0	—	Moore 3	650
26	16	A	East Fife	D 2-2	1-1	1	Lawrie, Moore	935
27	23	H	Queen's Park	W 2-0	1-0	1	Lloyd, Moore	785
28	Mar 2	A	Arbroath	W 1-0	0-0	1	Lloyd	531
29	5	A	East Stirling	W 1-0	0-0	—	Lloyd	611
30	9	H	Dumbarton	L 0-1	0-0	1		900
31	16	A	Queen of the S	D 0-0	0-0	1		472
32	23	A	Albion R	D 2-2	2-2	1	Moore, Lloyd	559
33	30	H	Alloa	L 1-2	1-0	1	Docherty	1450
34	Apr 6	A	Montrose	W 1-0	0-0	1	McGachie	600
35	13	H	East Stirling	W 4-0	1-0	1	McInnes, Reid, Moore (pen), Lloyd	1300
36	20	A	Stranraer	D 0-0	0-0	1		450
37	27	H	Cowdenbeath	D 0-0	0-0	1		1060
38	May 4	A	Berwick R	D 0-0	0-0	1		436
39	11	A	Stenhousemuir	L 1-2	1-0	1	Lloyd	1000

Final League Position: 1

GOALSCORERS

League: (62): Lloyd 14, Moore 13 (1 pen), Reid 11, McGachie 5, Docherty 4, Lawrie 4, McInnes 3, Conway 2, Shanks 2, Kerr 1, Mailer 1, Mitchell 1, Robertson 1.
Scottish Cup: (2): Docherty 1, Lloyd 1.
Skol Cup: (1): Reid 1.
Centenary Cup: (1): McConville 1.

Record Defeat: 0-9 v Dundee U, Division I; 30 Dec, 1967.
Most Capped Player: —.
Most League Appearances: 504: Matt McPhee, 1967–81.
Most League Goals in Season (Individual): 29: Joe Hughes, Division II; 1969–70.
Most Goals Overall (Individual): 129: Billy Steele, 1971–83.

Honours
League Champions: Division II 1952–53, 1957–58, 1960–61, 1964–65. Second Division 1976–77, 1990–91; *Runners-up:* Division II 1948–49, 1950–51.
Scottish Cup—.
League Cup—.
Club colours: Shirt: Red with white sleeves. Shorts: White. Stockings: White.

McGeown, M	Mitchell, C	Hay, G	Shanks, D	Lawrie, D	Kerr, J	McInnes, I	Moore, W	Mailer, J	McConville, R	Docherty, R	Robertson, S	Reid, J	Lloyd, D	Haggart, L	Colquhoun, J	Conway, M	Watson, P	McGachie, J	Pew, D	Match No.
1	2	3	4	5	6	7†	8	9	10*	11	12		14							1
1	2	3	4	5	6	7†	8	9	10*	11	12		14							2
1	2	3	4	5	6		8	9*	10	11†	14	7	12							3
1	2*	3	4†	5	6	12	8	9	10	11	14	7								4
1	2	3	4	5	6	12	14	8†	11	10	7	9*								5
1	2	3	4	5†	6	12	14	8	11	10	7	9*								6
1		3	4	5	6	7	12	9†	8*	11	10			2	14					7
1	2	3	4	5	6	12	8	14	10	7*	9				11†					8
1	2	3	4	5	6		8		11	10	7	9								9
1	2	3	4*	5	6	12	8†	14	11	10	7	9								10
1	2	3	4	5	6	12	8		11	10	7*	9								11
1	2	3	4	5	6	12	8	14	11	10†	7	9*								12
1	2	3	4	5	6	7			10	11	9					8				13
1	2	3	4	5	6	11	8	14		12	7†	9				10*				14
1	2	3	4	5	6	12	8		11		7	9				10*				15
1	2	3	4	5	6	10	12		11†		7*	9				8	14			16
1	2	3	4	5	6	12			11	10	7	9*				8				17
1	2	3	4*	5	6	10†14			11	12	7	9				8				18
1	2	3	4*	5	6	12	8		11	10	7†	9				14				19
1	2	3	4*	5	6	12	8		11	10	7†	9				14				20
1	2	3	5	6	4	8†			11	10	12	9	14				7*			21
1	2	3	4	5	6	11†	8			10	12	9	14				7*			22
1	2	3	4	5	6		8		11	10	7*	9				12				23
1	2	3	5	6	4	8			11	10†	7*	9				14	12			24
1	2	3	4*	5	6	10	8		11			9				12	7			25
1	2	3	4†	5	6	10	8		11	12		9				14	7*			26
1	2	3	5	6	4	8			11	10	7	9								27
1	2	3	6	5	4	8	14	11†10			7*	9				12				28
1	2	3	5	6	4	8		14	11	10†12		9					7*			29
1	2	3	4	5	6	10	8	14	11*		7†	9				12				30
1	2		4	5	6	10	8†12	14	11			9*					3	7		31
1	2		4	5	6	10	8		11*12			9					3	7		32
1	2		4*	5	6	10	8†	12	11			9					3	7	14	33
1	2	3	4	5	6	11	8	14		10	7*	9†						12		34
1	2*	3	4	5	6	11†	8	14		10	7	9						12		35
1	2	3	4	5	6	11†	8	14		10	7*	9						12		36
1	2	3	4	5	6	11*	8†	14		10	7	9						12		37
1	2	3	4	5	6	11				10	7*	9				8		12		38
1	2	3	4	5	6	11	8	14		10†	7	9*						12		39
39	38	36	35	39	38	25	31	6	10	27	24	27	34	1	—	8	3	8	—	

+ + + + + + + +   + + + +
11s4s 3s 10s3s 7s 6s 1s   1s 6s 1s 11s1s

STRANRAER Second Division

Year Formed: 1870. *Ground & Address:* Stair Park, London Rd, Stranraer DG9 8BS. *Telephone:* 0776 3271.
Ground Capacity: total: 4000. seated: 250. *Size of Pitch:* 110 × 70yd.
Chairman: T. Rice. *Secretary:* Graham Rodgers. *Commercial Manager:* —.
Manager: Alex McAnespie. *Assistant Manager:* —. *Physio:* —. *Coach:* John McNiven.
Managers since 1975: J. Hughes; N. Hood; G. Hamilton; D. Sneddon; J. Clark; R. Clark; A. McAnespie.
Club Nickname(s): The Blues. *Previous Grounds:* None.
Record Attendance: 6500 v Rangers, Scottish Cup 1st rd; 24 Jan, 1948.
Record Transfer Fee received: —.
Record Transfer Fee paid: £15,000 for Colin Harkness from Kilmarnock, August 1989.

STRANRAER 1990–91 LEAGUE RECORD

Match No.	Date	Venue	Opponents	Result	H/T Score	Lg. Pos.	Goalscorers	Atten- dance
1	Aug 25	A	Queen's Park	L	1-3	0-1	—	Duncan	340
2	Sept 1	H	East Fife	D	2-2	1-0	13	Harkness, Henderson	700
3	8	H	Stenhousemuir	L	1-2	0-0	12	Harkness	550
4	15	A	East Stirling	W	2-0	0-0	10	McMillan, George	310
5	18	A	Dumbarton	W	1-0	1-0	—	McMillan	400
6	22	H	Alloa	W	2-0	0-0	6	Cook, Henderson	670
7	29	A	Albion R	W	1-0	1-0	4	Cook	349
8	Oct 6	H	Montrose	W	1-0	0-0	2	Cook	450
9	9	A	Stirling Albion	L	1-3	1-0	—	Cook	440
10	13	H	Queen of the S	W	4-1	2-1	3	George, Cook 2, Henderson	950
11	20	A	Arbroath	L	0-3	0-1	4		352
12	27	H	Cowdenbeath	L	1-3	0-1	6	Harkness	700
13	Nov 3	A	Berwick R	L	2-3	0-2	8	McMillan, Cook	381
14	10	A	East Fife	W	2-1	0-1	6	McNiven, McCutcheon (pen)	682
15	17	H	Queen's Park	W	2-1	0-0	5	McMillan, Shirkie	750
16	24	A	Stenhousemuir	L	2-3	2-1	7	Harkness, Walker (pen)	300
17	Dec 1	H	East Stirling	L	1-2	0-2	8	Thompson	450
18	15	A	Cowdenbeath	W	3-2	2-1	6	George, Cook 2	200
19	22	A	Berwick R	L	1-2	0-2	—	Grant	513
20	Jan 2	A	Queen of the S	D	1-1	1-0	—	Cook	1041
21	12	H	Stirling Albion	L	1-4	0-2	8	McCutcheon	450
22	16	H	Arbroath	L	2-3	1-1	—	Thompson, McNiven	300
23	19	A	Montrose	L	0-1	0-0	9		300
24	30	H	Dumbarton	W	2-1	2-1	—	Harkness 2	420
25	Feb 2	A	Alloa	W	1-0	0-0	7	McNiven	399
26	9	H	Albion R	W	2-1	0-1	7	Harkness, McNiven	300
27	16	H	East Stirling	W	2-0	0-0	4	McMillan, Harkness	300
28	23	A	Queen of the S	W	2-1	1-0	4	Grant, McMillan	568
29	Mar 2	H	Berwick R	W	4-1	2-1	3	Harkness 2 (1 pen), Gallagher, Henderson	350
30	12	A	Montrose	L	1-2	0-1	—	Grant	250
31	16	A	Cowdenbeath	L	0-2	0-1	7		200
32	23	H	Alloa	D	0-0	0-0	6		350
33	30	A	East Fife	W	2-1	0-0	6	Spittal 2	525
34	Apr 10	H	Dumbarton	L	1-4	0-1	—	McNiven	300
35	13	A	Albion R	W	4-1	2-1	6	Harkness 4 (1 pen)	241
36	20	H	Stirling Albion	D	0-0	0-0	6		450
37	27	H	Stenhousemuir	L	0-2	0-1	6		637
38	May 4	H	Queen's Park	L	1-3	0-0	7	Henderson	400
39	11	A	Arbroath	W	5-1	1-0	6	Ewing, Grant, Cook 2, Gallagher	241

Final League Position: 6

GOALSCORERS

League: (61): Harkness 14 (2 pens), Cook 12, McMillan 6, Henderson 5, McNiven 5, Grant 4, George 3, Gallagher 2, McCutcheon 2 (1 pen), Spittal 2, Thompson 2, Duncan 1, Ewing 1, Shirkie 1, Walker 1 (pen).
Scottish Cup: (3): George 1, Grant 1, Henderson.
Skol Cup: (6): George 2, Cook 1, Henderson 1, McMillan 1, Spittal 1.
Centenary Cup: (1): Harkness 1.

Record Victory: 7-0 v Brechin C, Division II; 6 Feb, 1965.
Record Defeat: 1-11 v Queen of the South, Scottish Cup 1st rd; 16 Jan, 1932.
Most Capped Player: —.
Most League Appearances: 256: Dan McDonald.
Most League Goals in Season (Individual): 27: Derek Frye, Second Division; 1977–78.
Most Goals Overall (Individual): —.

Honours
League Champions:—.
Scottish Cup:—.
League Cup:—.
Club colours: Shirt: Royal blue with amber chest band. Shorts: Royal blue. Stockings: Royal blue.

Duffy, B	Corrie, T	Lindsay, C	McNiven, J	Gallagher, A	McCutcheon, D	George, D	McMillan, G	Harkness, C	Duncan, G	Henderson, D	Cook, D	Spittal, I	Walke, Dr	Lowe, L	Shirkie, S	Grant, A	Thompson, H	Scott, R	Holland, B	Kyle, M	Atkins, D	Muir, W	Tierney, M	McCann, J	Hughes, J	Ewing, A	Match No.
1	2†	3	4	5	6	7	8	9*10	11	12	14																1
1	2	3	4	5		7†	8	9*10	11	12	6	14															2
1		3	4	5	6	7	8	9*		11†12	10	14	2														3
1			4	5		7	10	9†14	11*12			3	2		6	8											4
1	14		4*			12	7		6	11		9	10	3	2†	5	8										5
1						12	7*		6	11		9	10	3	2	5	8										6
1			4	12		7*	14		6	11		9†10	3	2	5	8											7
1			4	12		7*	14		6	11		9†10	3	2	5	8											8
1			4	12		7	14		6	11		9†10	3	2*	5	8											9
1			4		6	7	12			11		9	10	3	2*	5	8†14										10
1	2		4†	6		7	14	12	10	11		9*	5	3		8											11
1	2		4			7	8	9	6	11	12	3		5*10													12
1	2*		4	5	10	7	11	9	3	12	14		6†	8													13
1			4		6	7	10	8*	3		9	2	11		5	12											14
1			4	14		7	10	12		11		9*	6†	3	2	5	8										15
1			4*	12		7		9†10	11	14		6	3	2	5	8											16
1			4			7	10	9	6†11	12		3	2*	5	8	14											17
1			4*	5	14	7†		12	6	11	9		3	2	8	10											18
			4			7	14	12	5	11†	9	6	3*	2	8	10	1										19
			4	5		7		12		11	9†14	3	2	6	8	10*	1										20
	14		4		6		12	7		11	9	5	3†	2*	8	10	1										21
	12		4		6		7			11	9	5	3*	2†	8	10	1	14									22
	3		4*		6	7	12	9	10	11		5		8	14	2†	1										23
	3†		4		6	7*12	9	8		14	5	11	2	10			1										24
	3	4	5			7	11	9*10		6		2	8		1		12										25
	3	4	5			7	11	9†10	14	12	6		2	8*		1											26
	3	4	5			7	2	9	10*11†		6		8	12		1		14									27
1	3	4	5			7	2	9	10†11*		6		8	14				12									28
1	3	4	5			7	2*	9†10	11	12	6		8	14													29
1	3	4	5			7	2	9*10†11	12	6			8	14													30
1	3*	4	5			7	14	9	10	11†12	6		8	2													31
1	12		4*			7	9	2		8	6	11	5†	10					14	3							32
1			4†	5			9	12	8*	6	7	11		2					14	10	3						33
1			4	5†			9	7*14	12	2	11	6	8						10	3							34
1			4				9	14	11†12	6	10	5	8*	7					2	3							35
1			4				9	12	11	14	6†	7	5	8	10*				2	3							36
1			4†12				9	7	11	10*	6	5	8				14	2	3								37
1				5			9	12	11	14	4	10	6*	8				7†	2	3							38
1			14				9	7	12	10	6	11	2	5†	8					3	4*						39
30	5	12	37	17	10	28	18	27	28	30	18	33	25	20	22	33	1	10	8	—	1	—	1	7	7	1	
+	+		+	+	+	+	+	+	+	+	+		+	+	+			+	+		+		+	+			
1s	3s		2s	6s	2s	6s	9s	5s	4s	17s2s	2s		1s	4s	3s			1s	1s		5s						

B & Q SCOTTISH LEAGUE FINAL TABLES
1990–91

PREMIER DIVISION

		Home		Goals			Away		Goals			
	P	W	D	L	F	A	W	D	L	F	A	GD	Pts
Rangers	36	14	3	1	40	8	10	4	4	22	15	+39	55
Aberdeen	36	12	5	1	30	7	10	4	4	32	20	+35	53
Celtic	36	10	4	4	30	14	7	3	8	22	24	+14	41
Dundee U	36	11	3	4	28	16	6	4	8	13	13	+12	41
Hearts	36	10	3	5	28	22	4	4	10	20	33	−7	35
Motherwell	36	9	5	4	28	18	3	4	11	23	32	+1	33
St Johnstone	36	6	4	8	23	25	5	5	8	18	29	−13	31
Dunfermline Ath	36	5	7	6	23	26	3	4	11	15	35	−23	27
Hibernian	36	6	5	7	17	25	0	8	10	7	26	−27	25
St Mirren	36	4	5	9	14	25	1	4	13	14	34	−31	19

FIRST DIVISION

		Home		Goals			Away		Goals			
	P	W	D	L	F	A	W	D	L	F	A	GD	Pts
Falkirk	39	12	4	4	40	18	9	8	2	30	17	+35	54
Airdrieonians	39	9	5	5	32	21	12	6	2	37	22	+26	53
Dundee	39	12	3	4	33	15	10	5	5	26	18	+26	52
Partick T	39	7	6	6	25	24	9	7	4	31	29	+3	45
Kilmarnock	39	10	6	3	32	21	5	7	8	26	27	+10	43
Hamilton A	39	8	6	6	25	20	8	4	7	25	21	+9	42
Raith R	39	7	5	8	22	26	7	4	8	32	38	−10	37
Clydebank	39	6	6	8	40	39	7	4	8	25	31	−5	36
Morton	39	6	7	6	25	22	5	6	9	23	33	−7	35
Forfar Ath	39	6	9	5	32	28	3	6	10	18	29	−7	33
Meadowbank T	39	4	7	8	25	33	6	6	8	31	35	−12	33
Ayr U	39	7	7	6	32	24	3	5	11	15	35	−12	32
Clyde	39	6	4	10	24	32	3	5	11	17	29	−20	27
Brechin C	39	3	4	12	20	37	4	6	10	24	43	−36	24

SECOND DIVISION

		Home		Goals			Away		Goals			
	P	W	D	L	F	A	W	D	L	F	A	GD	Pts
Stirling Albion	39	12	3	4	39	11	8	11	1	23	13	+38	54
Montrose	39	10	2	7	29	18	10	4	6	25	16	+20	46
Cowdenbeath	39	9	4	7	31	26	9	5	5	33	24	+14	45
Stenhousemuir	39	11	4	5	32	20	5	8	6	24	22	+14	44
Queen's Park	39	11	6	2	27	12	6	2	12	21	30	+6	42
Stranraer	39	8	3	8	30	30	10	1	9	31	30	+1	40
Dumbarton	39	8	8	4	23	20	7	2	10	26	29	0	40
Berwick R	39	9	6	4	27	18	6	4	10	24	39	−6	40
Alloa	39	8	4	7	27	22	5	7	8	24	24	+5	37
East Fife	39	7	7	6	30	31	7	2	10	27	34	−8	37
Albion R	39	8	5	6	31	30	3	8	9	17	33	−15	35
Queen of the S	39	7	6	7	31	29	2	6	11	15	33	−16	30
East Stirling	39	5	7	8	22	32	4	4	11	14	39	−35	29
Arbroath	39	5	5	10	22	24	3	6	10	19	35	−18	27

SCOTTISH LEAGUE 1890–91 to 1990–91

*On goal average/difference.   †Held jointly after indecisive play-off.   ‡Won on deciding match.
††Held jointly.   ¶Two points deducted for fielding ineligible player.
Competition suspended 1940–45 during war.   ‡‡Two points deducted for registration irregularities.

PREMIER DIVISION
Maximum points: 72

	First	Pts	Second	Pts	Third	Pts
1975–76	Rangers	54	Celtic	48	Hibernian	43
1976–77	Celtic	55	Rangers	46	Aberdeen	43
1977–78	Rangers	55	Aberdeen	53	Dundee U	40
1978–79	Celtic	48	Rangers	45	Dundee U	44
1979–80	Aberdeen	48	Celtic	47	St Mirren	42
1980–81	Celtic	56	Aberdeen	49	Rangers*	44
1981–82	Celtic	55	Aberdeen	53	Rangers	43
1982–83	Dundee U	56	Celtic*	55	Aberdeen	55
1983–84	Aberdeen	57	Celtic	50	Dundee U	47
1984–85	Aberdeen	59	Celtic	52	Dundee U	47
1985–86	Celtic*	50	Hearts	50	Dundee U	47

Maximum points: 88

	First	Pts	Second	Pts	Third	Pts
1986–87	Rangers	69	Celtic	63	Dundee U	60
1987–88	Celtic	72	Hearts	62	Rangers	60

Maximum points: 72

	First	Pts	Second	Pts	Third	Pts
1988–89	Rangers	56	Aberdeen	50	Celtic	46
1989–90	Rangers	51	Aberdeen*	44	Hearts	44
1990–91	Rangers	55	Aberdeen	53	Celtic*	41

FIRST DIVISION
Maximum points: 52

	First	Pts	Second	Pts	Third	Pts
1975–76	Partick T	41	Kilmarnock	35	Montrose	30

Maximum points: 78

	First	Pts	Second	Pts	Third	Pts
1976–77	St Mirren	62	Clydebank	58	Dundee	51
1977–78	Morton*	58	Hearts	58	Dundee	57
1978–79	Dundee	55	Kilmarnock*	54	Clydebank	54
1979–80	Hearts	53	Airdrieonians	51	Ayr U	44
1980–81	Hibernian	57	Dundee	52	St Johnstone	51
1981–82	Motherwell	61	Kilmarnock	51	Hearts	50
1982–83	St Johnstone	55	Hearts	54	Clydebank	50
1983–84	Morton	54	Dumbarton	51	Partick T	46
1984–85	Motherwell	50	Clydebank	48	Falkirk	45
1985–86	Hamilton A	56	Falkirk	45	Kilmarnock	44

Maximum points: 88

	First	Pts	Second	Pts	Third	Pts
1986–87	Morton	57	Dunfermline Ath	56	Dumbarton	53
1987–88	Hamilton A	56	Meadowbank T	52	Clydebank	49

Maximum points: 78

	First	Pts	Second	Pts	Third	Pts
1988–89	Dunfermline Ath	54	Falkirk	52	Clydebank	48
1989–90	St Johnstone	58	Airdrieonians	54	Clydebank	44
1990–91	Falkirk	54	Airdrieonians	53	Dundee	52

SECOND DIVISION
Maximum points: 52

	First	Pts	Second	Pts	Third	Pts
1975–77	Clydebank*	40	Raith R	40	Alloa	35

Maximum points: 78

	First	Pts	Second	Pts	Third	Pts
1976–77	Stirling A	55	Alloa	51	Dunfermline Ath	50
1977–78	Clyde*	53	Raith R	53	Dunfermline Ath	48
1978–79	Berwick R	54	Dunfermline Ath	52	Falkirk	50
1979–80	Falkirk	50	East Stirling	49	Forfar Ath	46
1980–81	Queen's Park	50	Queen of the S	46	Cowdenbeath	45
1981–82	Clyde	59	Alloa*	50	Arbroath	50
1982–83	Brechin C	55	Meadowbank T	54	Arbroath	49
1983–84	Forfar Ath	63	East Fife	47	Berwick R	43
1984–85	Montrose	53	Alloa	50	Dunfermline Ath	49
1985–86	Dunfermline Ath	57	Queen of the S	55	Meadowbank T	49
1986–87	Meadowbank T	55	Raith R*	52	Stirling A	52
1987–88	Ayr U	61	St Johnstone	59	Queen's Park	51
1988–89	Albion R	50	Alloa	45	Brechin C	43
1989–90	Brechin C	49	Kilmarnock	48	Stirling A	47
1990–91	Stirling A	54	Montrose	46	Cowdenbeath	45

FIRST DIVISION to 1974–75

Maximum points: a 36; b 44; c 40; d 52; e 60; f 68; g 76; h 84.

	First	Pts	Second	Pts	Third	Pts
1890–91a††	Dumbarton	29	Rangers	29	Celtic	24
1891–92b	Dumbarton	37	Celtic	35	Hearts	30
1892–93a	Celtic	29	Rangers	28	St Mirren	23
1893–94a	Celtic	29	Hearts	26	St Bernard's	22
1894–95a	Hearts	31	Celtic	26	Rangers	21
1895–96a	Celtic	30	Rangers	26	Hibernian	24
1896–97a	Hearts	28	Hibernian	26	Rangers	25
1897–98a	Celtic	33	Rangers	29	Hibernian	22
1898–99a	Rangers	36	Hearts	26	Celtic	24
1899–1900a	Rangers	32	Celtic	25	Hibernian	24
1900–01c	Rangers	35	Celtic	29	Hibernian	25
1901–02a	Rangers	28	Celtic	26	Hearts	22
1902–03b	Hibernian	37	Dundee	31	Rangers	29
1903–04d	Third Lanark	43	Hearts	39	Rangers*	38
1904–05d	Celtic‡	41	Rangers	41	Third Lanark	35
1905–06e	Celtic	49	Hearts	43	Airdrieonians	38
1906–07f	Celtic	55	Dundee	48	Rangers	45
1907–08f	Celtic	55	Falkirk	51	Rangers	50
1908–09f	Celtic	51	Dundee	50	Clyde	48
1909–10f	Celtic	54	Falkirk	52	Rangers	46
1910–11f	Rangers	52	Aberdeen	48	Falkirk	44
1911–12f	Rangers	51	Celtic	45	Clyde	42
1912–13f	Rangers	53	Celtic	49	Hearts*	41
1913–14g	Celtic	65	Rangers	59	Hearts*	54
1914–15g	Celtic	65	Hearts	61	Rangers	50
1915–16g	Celtic	67	Rangers	56	Morton	51
1916–17g	Celtic	64	Morton	54	Rangers	53
1917–18f	Rangers	56	Celtic	55	Kilmarnock	43
1918–19f	Celtic	58	Rangers	57	Morton	47
1919–20h	Rangers	71	Celtic	68	Motherwell	57
1920–21h	Rangers	76	Celtic	66	Hearts	56
1921–22h	Celtic	67	Rangers	66	Raith R	56
1922–23g	Rangers	55	Airdrieonians	50	Celtic	46
1923–24g	Rangers	59	Airdrieonians	50	Celtic	41
1924–25g	Rangers	60	Airdrieonians	57	Hibernian	52
1925–26g	Celtic	58	Airdrieonians*	50	Hearts	50
1926–27g	Rangers	56	Motherwell	51	Celtic	49
1927–28g	Rangers	60	Celtic*	55	Motherwell	55
1928–29g	Rangers	67	Celtic	51	Motherwell	50
1929–30g	Rangers	60	Motherwell	55	Aberdeen	53
1930–31g	Rangers	60	Celtic	58	Motherwell	56
1931–32g	Motherwell	66	Rangers	61	Celtic	48
1932–33g	Rangers	62	Motherwell	59	Hearts	50
1933–34g	Rangers	66	Motherwell	62	Celtic	47
1934–35g	Rangers	55	Celtic	52	Hearts	50
1935–36g	Celtic	66	Rangers*	61	Aberdeen	61
1936–37g	Rangers	61	Aberdeen	54	Celtic	52
1937–38g	Celtic	61	Hearts	58	Rangers	49
1938–39g	Rangers	59	Celtic	48	Aberdeen	46
1946–47e	Rangers	46	Hibernian	44	Aberdeen	39
1947–48e	Hibernian	48	Rangers	46	Partick T	36
1948–49e	Rangers	46	Dundee	45	Hibernian	39
1949–50e	Rangers	50	Hibernian	49	Hearts	43
1950–51e	Hibernian	48	Rangers*	38	Dundee	38
1951–52e	Hibernian	45	Rangers	41	East Fife	37
1952–53e	Rangers*	43	Hibernian	43	East Fife	39
1953–54e	Celtic	43	Hearts	38	Partick T	35
1954–55e	Aberdeen	49	Celtic	46	Rangers	41
1955–56f	Rangers	52	Aberdeen	46	Hearts*	45
1956–57f	Rangers	55	Hearts	53	Kilmarnock	42
1957–58f	Hearts	62	Rangers	49	Celtic	46
1958–59f	Rangers	50	Hearts	48	Motherwell	44
1959–60f	Hearts	54	Kilmarnock	50	Rangers*	42
1960–61f	Rangers	51	Kilmarnock	50	Third Lanark	42
1961–62f	Dundee	54	Rangers	51	Celtic	46
1962–63f	Rangers	57	Kilmarnock	48	Partick T	46
1963–64f	Rangers	55	Kilmarnock	49	Celtic*	47
1964–65f	Kilmarnock*	50	Hearts	50	Dunfermline Ath	49
1965–66f	Celtic	57	Rangers	55	Kilmarnock	45
1966–67f	Celtic	58	Rangers	55	Clyde	46

	First	Pts	Second	Pts	Third	Pts
1967–68f	Celtic	63	Rangers	61	Hibernian	45
1968–69f	Celtic	54	Rangers	49	Dunfermline Ath	45
1969–70f	Celtic	57	Rangers	45	Hibernian	44
1970–71f	Celtic	56	Aberdeen	54	St Johnstone	44
1971–72f	Celtic	60	Aberdeen	50	Rangers	44
1972–73f	Celtic	57	Rangers	56	Hibernian	45
1973–74f	Celtic	53	Hibernian	49	Rangers	48
1974–75f	Rangers	56	Hibernian	49	Celtic	45

SECOND DIVISION to 1974–75

Maximum points: a 76; b 72; c 68; d 52; e 60; f 36; g 44; h 52.

	First	Pts	Second	Pts	Third	Pts
1893–94f	Hibernian	29	Cowlairs	27	Clyde	24
1894–95f	Hibernian	30	Motherwell	22	Port Glasgow	20
1895–96f	Abercorn	27	Leith Ath	23	Renton	21
1896–97f	Partick T	31	Leith Ath	27	Kilmarnock	21
1897–98f	Kilmarnock	29	Port Glasgow	25	Morton	22
1898–99f	Kilmarnock	32	Leith Ath	27	Port Glasgow	25
1899–1900f	Partick T	29	Morton	26	Port Glasgow	20
1900–01f	St Bernard's	26	Airdrieonians	23	Abercorn	21
1901–02g	Port Glasgow	32	Partick T	31	Motherwell	26
1902–03g	Airdrieonians	35	Motherwell	28	Ayr U	27
1903–04g	Hamilton A	37	Clyde	29	Ayr U	28
1904–05g	Clyde	32	Falkirk	28	Hamilton A	27
1905–06g	Leith Ath	34	Clyde	31	Albion R	27
1906–07g	St Bernard's	32	Vale of Leven*	27	Arthurlie	27
1907–08g	Raith R	30	Dumbarton	‡‡27	Ayr U	27
1908–09g	Abercorn	31	Raith R*	28	Vale of Leven	28
1909–10g‡	Leith Ath	33	Raith R	33	St Bernard's	27
1910–11g	Dumbarton	31	Ayr U	27	Albion R	25
1911–12g	Ayr U	35	Abercorn	30	Dumbarton	27
1912–13h	Ayr U	34	Dunfermline Ath	33	East Stirling	32
1913–14g	Cowdenbeath	31	Albion R	27	Dunfermline Ath	26
1914–15h	Cowdenbeath*	37	St Bernard's*	37	Leith Ath	37
1921–22a	Alloa	60	Cowdenbeath	47	Armadale	45
1922–23a	Queen's Park	57	Clydebank	¶50	St Johnstone	¶45
1923–24a	St Johnstone	56	Cowdenbeath	55	Bathgate	44
1924–25a	Dundee U	50	Clydebank	48	Clyde	47
1925–26a	Dunfermline Ath	59	Clyde	53	Ayr U	52
1926–27a	Bo'ness	56	Raith R	49	Clydebank	45
1927–28a	Ayr U	54	Third Lanark	45	King's Park	44
1928–29b	Dundee U	51	Morton	50	Arbroath	47
1929–30a	Leith Ath*	57	East Fife	57	Albion R	54
1930–31a	Third Lanark	61	Dundee U	50	Dunfermline Ath	47
1931–32a	East Stirling*	55	St Johnstone	55	Raith Rovers*	46
1932–33c	Hibernian	54	Queen of the S	49	Dunfermline Ath	47
1933–34c	Albion R	45	Dunfermline Ath*	44	Arbroath	44
1934–35c	Third Lanark	52	Arbroath	50	St Bernard's	47
1935–36c	Falkirk	59	St Mirren	52	Morton	48
1936–37c	Ayr U	54	Morton	51	St Bernard's	48
1937–38c	Raith R	59	Albion R	48	Airdrieonians	47
1938–39c	Cowdenbeath	60	Alloa*	48	East Fife	48
1946–47d	Dundee	45	Airdrieonians	42	East Fife	31
1947–48e	East Fife	53	Albion R	42	Hamilton A	40
1948–49e	Raith R*	42	Stirling Albion	42	Airdrieonians*	41
1949–50e	Morton	47	Airdrieonians	44	St Johnstone*	36
1950–51e	Queen of the S*	45	Stirling Albion	45	Ayr U	36
1951–52e	Clyde	44	Falkirk	43	Ayr U	39
1952–53e	Stirling Albion	44	Hamilton A	43	Queen's Park	37
1953–54e	Motherwell	45	Kilmarnock	42	Third Lanark*	36
1954–55e	Airdrieonians	46	Dunfermline Ath	42	Hamilton A	39
1955–56b	Queen's Park	54	Ayr U	51	St Johnstone	49
1956–57b	Clyde	64	Third Lanark	51	Cowdenbeath	45
1957–58b	Stirling Albion	55	Dunfermline Ath	53	Arbroath	47
1958–59b	Ayr U	60	Arbroath	51	Stenhousemuir	40
1959–60b	St Johnstone	53	Dundee U	50	Queen of the S	49
1960–61b	Stirling Albion	55	Falkirk	54	Stenhousemuir	50
1961–62b	Clyde	54	Queen of the S	53	Morton	44
1962–63b	St Johnstone	55	East Stirling	49	Morton	48
1963–64b	Morton	67	Clyde	53	Arbroath	46
1964–65b	Stirling Albion	59	Hamilton A	50	Queen of the S	45
1965–66b	Ayr U	53	Airdrieonians	50	Queen of the S	49
1966–67b	Morton	69	Raith R	58	Arbroath	57

738

	First	Pts	Second	Pts	Third	Pts
1967–68b	St Mirren	62	Arbroath	53	East Fife	40
1968–69b	Motherwell	64	Ayr U	53	East Fife*	47
1969–70b	Falkirk	56	Cowdenbeath	55	Queen of the S	50
1970–71b	Partick T	56	East Fife	51	Arbroath	46
1971–72b	Dumbarton*	52	Arbroath	52	Stirling Albion	50
1972–73b	Clyde	56	Dumfermline Ath	52	Raith R*	47
1973–74b	Airdrieonians	60	Kilmarnock	59	Hamilton A	55
1974–75a	Falkirk	54	Queen of the S	53	Montrose	53

Elected to First Division: 1894 Clyde; 1897 Partick T; 1899 Kilmarnock; 1900 Partick T; 1902 Partick T; 1903 Airdrieonians; 1905 Falkirk, Aberdeen and Hamilton A; 1906 Clyde; 1910 Raith R; 1913 Ayr U.

RELEGATED FROM PREMIER DIVISION

1975–76 Dundee, St Johnstone
1976–77 Hearts, Kilmarnock
1977–78 Ayr U, Clydebank
1978–79 Hearts, Motherwell
1979–80 Dundee, Hibernian
1980–81 Kilmarnock, Hearts
1981–82 Partick T, Airdrieonians
1982–83 Morton, Kilmarnock
1983–84 St Johnstone, Motherwell
1984–85 Dumbarton, Morton
1985–86 *No relegation due to League reorganisation*
1986–87 Clydebank, Hamilton A
1987–88 Falkirk, Dunfermline Ath, Morton
1988–89 Hamilton A
1989–90 Dundee
1990–91 None

RELEGATED FROM DIVISION 1

1975–76 Dunfermline Ath, Clyde
1976–77 Raith R, Falkirk
1977–78 Alloa Ath, East Fife
1978–79 Montrose, Queen of the S
1979–80 Arbroath, Clyde
1980–81 Stirling A, Berwick R
1981–82 East Stirling, Queen of the S
1982–83 Dunfermline Ath, Queen's Park
1983–84 Raith R, Alloa
1984–85 Meadowbank T, St Johnstone
1985–86 Ayr U, Alloa
1986–87 Brechin C, Montrose
1987–88 East Fife, Dumbarton
1988–89 Kilmarnock, Queen of the S
1989–90 Albion R, Alloa
1990–91 Clyde, Brechin C

RELEGATED FROM DIVISION 1 (TO 1973–74)

1921–22 *Queen's Park, Dumbarton, Clydebank
1922–23 Albion R, Alloa Ath
1923–24 Clyde, Clydebank
1924–25 Third Lanark, Ayr U
1925–26 Raith R, Clydebank
1926–27 Morton, Dundee U
1927–28 Dunfermline Ath, Bo'ness
1928–29 Third Lanark, Raith R
1929–30 St Johnstone, Dundee U
1930–31 Hibernian, East Fife
1931–32 Dundee U, Leith Ath
1932–33 Morton, East Stirling
1933–34 Third Lanark, Cowdenbeath
1934–35 St Mirren, Falkirk
1935–36 Airdrieonians, Ayr U
1936–37 Dunfermline Ath, Albion R
1937–38 Dundee, Morton
1938–39 Queen's Park, Raith R
1946–47 Kilmarnock, Hamilton A
1947–48 Airdrieonians, Queen's Park
1948–49 Morton, Albion R
1949–50 Queen of the S, Stirling Albion
1950–51 Clyde, Falkirk

1951–52 Morton, Stirling Albion
1952–53 Motherwell, Third Lanark
1953–54 Airdrieonians, Hamilton A
1954–55 No clubs relegated
1955–56 Stirling Albion, Clyde
1956–57 Dunfermline Ath, Ayr U
1957–58 East Fife, Queen's Park
1958–59 Queen of the S, Falkirk
1959–60 Arbroath, Stirling Albion
1960–61 Ayr U, Clyde
1961–62 St Johnstone, Stirling Albion
1962–63 Clyde, Raith R
1963–64 Queen of the S, East Stirling
1964–65 Airdrieonians, Third Lanark
1965–66 Morton, Hamilton A
1966–67 St Mirren, Ayr U
1967–68 Motherwell, Stirling Albion
1968–69 Falkirk, Arbroath
1969–70 Raith R, Partick T
1970–71 St Mirren, Cowdenbeath
1971–72 Clyde, Dunfermline Ath
1972–73 Kilmarnock, Airdrieonians
1973–74 East Fife, Falkirk

*Season 1921–22 – only 1 club promoted, 3 clubs relegated.

The Scottish Football League was reconstructed into three divisions at the end of the 1974–75 season, so the usual relegation statistics do not apply. Further reorganisation took place at the end of the 1985–86 season. From 1986–87, the Premier and First Division had 12 teams each. The Second Division remains at 14. From 1988–89, the Premier Division reverted to 10 teams, and the First Division to 14 teams.

SCOTTISH LEAGUE SKOL CUP FINALS 1946–91

Season	Winners	Runners-up	Score
1946–47	Rangers	Aberdeen	4-0
1947–48	East Fife	Falkirk	4-1 after 0-0 draw
1948–49	Rangers	Raith R	2-0
1949–50	East Fife	Dunfermline Ath	3-0
1950–51	Motherwell	Hibernian	3-0
1951–52	Dundee	Rangers	3-2
1952–53	Dundee	Kilmarnock	2-0
1953–54	East Fife	Partick T	3-2
1954–55	Hearts	Motherwell	4-2
1955–56	Aberdeen	St Mirren	2-1
1956–57	Celtic	Partick T	3-0 after 0-0 draw
1957–58	Celtic	Rangers	7-1
1958–59	Hearts	Partick T	5-1
1959–60	Hearts	Third Lanark	2-1
1960–61	Rangers	Kilmarnock	2-0
1961–62	Rangers	Hearts	3-1 after 1-1 draw
1962–63	Hearts	Kilmarnock	1-0
1963–64	Rangers	Morton	5-0
1964–65	Rangers	Celtic	2-1
1965–66	Celtic	Rangers	2-1
1966–67	Celtic	Rangers	1-0
1967–68	Celtic	Dundee	5-3
1968–69	Celtic	Hibernian	6-2
1969–70	Celtic	St Johnstone	1-0
1970–71	Rangers	Celtic	1-0
1971–72	Partick T	Celtic	4-1
1972–73	Hibernian	Celtic	2-1
1973–74	Dundee	Celtic	1-0
1974–75	Celtic	Hibernian	6-3
1975–76	Rangers	Celtic	1-0
1976–77	Aberdeen	Celtic	2-1
1977–78	Rangers	Celtic	2-1
1978–79	Rangers	Aberdeen	2-1
1979–80	Dundee U	Aberdeen	3-0 after 0-0 draw
1980–81	Dundee U	Dundee	3-0
1981–82	Rangers	Dundee U	2-1
1982–83	Celtic	Rangers	2-1
1983–84	Rangers	Celtic	3-2
1984–85	Rangers	Dundee U	1-0
1985–86	Aberdeen	Hibernian	3-0
1986–87	Rangers	Celtic	2-1
1987–88	Rangers	Aberdeen	3-3
		(Rangers won 5-3 on penalties)	
1988–89	Rangers	Aberdeen	3-2
1989–90	Aberdeen	Rangers	2-1
1990–91	Rangers	Celtic	2-1

SCOTTISH LEAGUE CUP WINS

Rangers 17, Celtic 9, Hearts 4, Aberdeen 4, Dundee 3, East Fife 3, Dundee U 2, Hibernian 1, Motherwell 1, Partick T 1.

APPEARANCES IN FINALS

Rangers 23, Celtic 20, Aberdeen 9, Dundee 5, Hearts 5, Hibernian 5, Dundee U 4, Partick T 4, East Fife 3, Kilmarnock 3, Motherwell 2, Dunfermline Ath 1, Falkirk 1, Morton 1, Raith R 1, St Johnstone 1, St Mirren 1, Third Lanark 1.

SKOL CUP 1990–91

FIRST ROUND

14 AUG

East Stirling (0) 2 *(Russell, Watson P (pen))*
Dumbarton (1) 2 *(MacIver 2)* 350
after extra time
East Stirling: Watson G; Russell, Workman, Walker, Brannigan, Erwin, Rooney, Watson P, Diver, McNab (McBride), Lytwyn.
Dumbarton: Strachan; Gow, Boyd, McGinley, McCracken, Dempsey, McQuade, McGuire (Marsland), Gibson, Morrison, MacIver.
(East Stirling won 4–1 on penalties)

Queen's Park (2) 3 *(O'Brien, McEntegart, Hendry)*
East Fife (0) 3 *(Scott, Mitchell, Wilson)* 400
after extra time
Queen's Park: Monaghan; Callan, Ogg, Elder, McLean (Crooks), McEntegart, Jack, O'Brien (Morris), Greig, Caven, Hendry.
East Fife: Moffat; Hamilton, Taylor P, Crolla, Prior, Taylor P H, Mitchell, Brown W (Brown I), Wilson, Scott, Hope (Lennox).
(Queen's Park won 5–4 on penalties)

Stenhousemuir (0) 0
Cowdenbeath (2) 2 *(Ross, MacKenzie)* 300
Stenhousemuir: Paterno; Clouston, Hallford, Cairney, Tracey, Kemp, Nelson, McGurn, McCormick, Walker (McNab) McAvoy (Speirs).
Cowdenbeath: Lamont; Watt, Robertson, Hamill, Douglas, McGovern, Wright (Buckley), Malone, McKenzie, Ross, Scott (Thomson).

15 AUG

Montrose (0) 1 *(Allan)*
Queen of the S (0) 2 *(Thomson A, McGuire)* 400
after extra time
Montrose: Larter; Morrison, King, McKay, Rougvie, Den Bieman, Maver, Lyons, Murray, Dolan (Watt), Stephen (Allan).
Queen of the S: Davidson; McCafferty, Thomson I, Fraser (Anderson), Hetherington, McGhie, Thomson A, McGarvey (Sloan), Gordon, Sim, McGuire.

Stirling Albion (1) 1 *(Reid) at Firs Park*
Arbroath (1) 2 *(Morton (pen), Mitchell]* 300
Stirling Albion: McGeown; Mitchell, Hay, Shanks (McConville), Lawrie, Kerr, Reid, Moore (McInnes), Mailer, Robertson, Docherty.
Arbroath: Jackson; Carlin, Florence, Mitchell, Oliver, Holmes J, Hamilton, Bennett, Sorbie, Morton, Marshall.

Stranraer (2) 4 *(McMillan, Henderson, George, Spittal) at Somerset Park*
Berwick R (1) 3 *(Graham 2, Todd)* 350
after extra time
Stranraer: Duffy; Corrie (Cook), Lindsay, McNiven, Gallagher, McCutcheon, George, McMillan, Grant, Duncan, Henderson (Spittal).
Berwick R: Neilson; Fraser, Holden, Smith, Marshall, Cass (Thorpe), Sokoluk, Graham, Todd (Leitch), Callachan, Bickmore.

SECOND ROUND

21 AUG

Airdrieonians (0) 1 *(Balfour)*
Stranraer (0) 2 *(George, Cook)* 1000
Airdrieonians: Martin; Stewart (Boyle), Conn (Smith A), Watson, Walsh, McPhee, Jack, Balfour, Harvey, Coyle, MacDonald.
Stranraer: Duffy; Corrie, Lindsay, McNiven, Gallagher, McCutcheon, George, McMillan, Grant (Cook), Duncan, Henderson (Spittal).

Alloa (0) 0
Dundee U (3) 3 *(Jackson, Dailly, Welsh)* 1835
Alloa: Lowrie; Newbigging, Lee R, Wilcox, McCulloch (Ormond), McEntegart, Grant, Ramsay, Black, Lamont (Irvine), Smith.
Dundee U: Main; Cleland, Malpas, McInally, Krivokapic, Welsh, Van der Hoorn, McKinlay, Dailly (O'Neill M), Jackson, Preston (Connolly).

Brechin C (0) 0
Hamilton A (0) 2 *(Burns, McCluskey)* 500
Brechin C: Lawrie; Baillie (Duncan), Scott, Conway, Brash, Hutt, Wardell, Hill, Ritchie, Sexton, Lees.
Hamilton A: Ferguson; McKee, Miller, Millen, Archer (Moore), Burns, Harris, Weir, McCluskey, McGinley, Donaghy (Horne).

Dunfermline Ath (1) 4 *(Jack 2, Smith P, O'Brien)*
Albion R (0) 0 3239
Dunfermline Ath: Westwater; Wilson, Nicholl (Sharp), McCathie, Moyes, Farningham, Smith P, Rafferty (O'Brien), Jack, McCall, Kozma.
Albion R: McCulloch; Watson (Cougan), Millar, Edgar, McTeague, Clark, Richardson (King), Cadden, Henderson, McKeown, Lauchlan.

Forfar Ath (1) 1 *(Brewster (pen))*
Raith R (0) 2 *(McGeachie, Dalziel)* 1114
Forfar Ath: Allan; Lorimer, Hamill, Morris, Hegarty, Smith, Paton, Brewster, Whyte, Leslie, Petrie.
Raith R: Arthur; McStay, MacLeod, Fraser, Dennis, McGeachie, Simpson (Logan), Dalziel, Macdonald, Ferguson, Burn.

Kilmarnock (1) 3 *(Spence, Stark, Callaghan)*
Clydebank (2) 2 *(Rowe, Eadie)* 4777
Kilmarnock: Geddes; Montgomerie, Spence, McStay (Reilly), Jenkins, MacKinnon, Stark, Tait, Watters, Burns, Shaw (Callaghan).
Clydebank: Gallacher; Joe Dickson, Rodger (Smith), Maher, Sweeney, Coyle, Harvey, Davies, Eadie, Rowe, Kelly (John Dickson).

Motherwell (1) 4 *(O'Neill 2, Arnott, Burley)*
Morton (1) 3 *(Hopkin 2, Fowler)* 3189
Motherwell: Maxwell; Burley, Boyd, Paterson, Nijholt, McCart, Russell (Mair), O'Neill, Arnott, Kirk, Cusack (Philliben).
Morton: Wylie; Collins, Cowie, Doak, Boag, Hunter, McNeil (Fowler), McDonald (McInnes), Alexander, Turner, Hopkin.

Queen of the S (1) 2 *(Fraser, McGhie)*
Dundee (0) 2 *(Chisholm, Forsyth)* 1000
after extra time
Queen of the S: Davidson; McCafferty, Thomson I, Fraser, Hetherington, McGhie, McGuire (Sloan), Thomson A, Gordon (Anderson), Sim, Robertson.
Dundee: Carson; McQuillan, McSkimming, Shannon (Craib), Jamieson, Chisholm, West, Forsyth, Wright, Dodds, McLeod (McBride).
(Queen of the S won 4–1 on penalties)

Queen's Park (1) 1 *(Hendry)*
Aberdeen (1) 2 *(Jess, Bett)* 2201
Queen's Park: Monaghan; Callan, Ogg, Jack, McNamee, McEntegart, Caven, O'Brien (Morris), Crooks, Mackenzie (Greig), Hendry.
Aberdeen: Snelders; McKimmie, Robertson D, Grant, Irvine, Miller, Jess (Van de Ven), Bett (Booth), Mason, Connor, Gillhaus.

Rangers (1) 5 *(Steven T, Hateley 2, Walters, Johnston)*
East Stirling (0) 0 25,595
Rangers: Woods; Stevens G, Brown, Gough, Spackman, Butcher, Steven T, Walters, Hateley, Johnston, Huistra.
East Stirling: Watson G; Russell, Workman, Walker, Brannigan, Erwin, Rooney, Watson P, Diver (McNab), Lytwyn (McNally), McBride.

St Johnstone (0) 0
Clyde (1) 2 *(Scott, Gilmour)* 3550
St Johnstone: Balavage; Treanor (Heddle), McVicar, Baltacha, Inglis, Johnston (Cherry), Moore, McGinnis, Bingham, Grant, Curran.
Clyde: Ross; Gaughan, Graeme McVie, Reid, Speirs, McFarlane, Thompson (Clark G), Mitchell, Scott (Gilmour), Clarke S, Mallan.

22 AUG

Celtic (3) 4 *(Elliott 2, Dziekanowski 2)*
Ayr U (0) 0 21,462
Celtic: Bonner; Morris, Wdowczyk, Grant (Hewitt), Elliott, Whyte, Hayes (Miller), McStay, Dziekanowski, Walker, Collins.
Ayr U: Purdie; Kennedy, Love, McAllister, Gillespie, Brown, Templeton (Walker), Scott, Graham (Evans), Bryce, Weir.

Cowdenbeath (0) 0
Hearts (1) 2 *(Robertson, Bannon)* 5133
Cowdenbeath: Lamont; Watt, Robertson (Thomson), Hamill, Douglas, McGovern, Wright, Malone, MacKenzie, Ross, Scott.
Hearts: Smith; Kidd, McKinlay, Levein, McCreery, McPherson, Ferguson, Mackay, Robertson, Crabbe, Foster (Bannon).

Falkirk (0) 1 *(Houston)*
Partick T (0) 1 *(Peebles)* 5200
after extra time
Falkirk: Marshall; Robertson, Whittaker, Melvin, Beaton, Smith, Houston (Cowell), McWilliams, Baptie, Hughes, Rutherford (McNeill).
Partick T: Duncan; Robertson, Elliot, Duffy, Rae, Tierney, Peebles, (McGovern), Law (Campbell), McGlashan, Flood, Charnley.
(Partick won 4–1 on penalties)

Meadowbank T (0) 0 *at Starks Park*
Hibernian (0) 1 *(Houchen)* 3849
after extra time
Meadowbank T: McQueen; McCormack, Armstrong, Grant, Williamson, Roseburgh, Perry, Irvine, McNaughton, Forrest, Sprott.
Hibernian: Goram; Miller, Mitchell, Kane, Cooper, Sneddon, Evans, McGinlay, Findlay, Houchen, Tortolano.

St Mirren (1) 1 *(Stickroth)*
Arbroath (0) 0 2600
St Mirren: Money; Wishart, Black, Lambert, Martin, Manley, Shaw, McDowall, Stickroth, Torfason, Kinnaird.
Arbroath: Jackson; Mitchell, Florence, Oliver, Carlin, Holmes, Hamilton, Bennett, Marshall, Sorbie, Morton.

THIRD ROUND

28 AUG

Dunfermline Ath (0) 1 *(Irons)*
Queen of the S (1) 2 *(McGuire, Thomson A)* 3923
after extra time
Dunfermline Ath: Rhodes; Wilson, Nicholl, McCathie, Moyes, Farningham, Smith P, Rafferty (O'Brien), Jack, McCall, Kozma (Irons).
Queen of the S: Davidson; McCafferty, Thomson I, Fraser, Hetherington, McGhie, Sloan, Thomson A, McGarvey (Gordon), Sim, McGuire (Robertson).

Motherwell (1) 2 *(Cusack 2)*
Clyde (0) 0 3535
Motherwell: Maxwell; Burley, Boyd (Griffin), O'Neill, Nijholt, McCart, Arnott, Russell, Cusack, Kirk, Cooper.
Clyde: Ross; Gaughan, Graeme McVie, Reid, Speirs, McFarlane, Clark G, Nolan, Scott (Gilmour), Clarke S, Mallan.

Partick T (0) 1 *(Charnley)*
Dundee U (1) 3 *(Dailly, Jackson, Van der Hoorn)* 4000
Partick T: Duncan; Robertson, Elliot, Duffy, Peebles (Rae), Tierney, Law, Campbell (Gallagher), McGlashan, Flood, Charnley.
Dundee U: Thomson W; Cleland, Malpas, McInally (Connolly), Krivokapic, Welsh, Van der Hoorn, McKinlay, Dailly, Jackson, Bowman (O'Neill M).

Rangers (0) 1 *(Johnston)*
Kilmarnock (0) 0 32,671
Rangers: Woods; Stevens G, Brown, Gough, Spackman, Butcher, Steven T, Ferguson (Hurlock), McCoist (Hateley), Johnston, Huistra.
Kilmarnock: Geddes; Jenkins, Spence (Callaghan), Montgomerie, Flexney, MacKinnon, Stark, Tait (Shaw), Watters, Burns, Reilly.

29 AUG

Aberdeen (2) 4 *(Mason 2, Van de Ven, Irvine)*
Stranraer (0) 0   10,000
Aberdeen: Snelders; McKimmie (Gregg Watson), Robertson D, Grant, McLeish, Irvine, Van de Ven, Jess, Mason (Cameron), Connor, Gillhaus.
Stranraer: Duffy; Corrie, Lindsay (Harkness), McNiven, Duncan, McCutcheon, George, McMillan, Grant (Cook), Spittal, Henderson.

Hamilton A (0) 0
Celtic (0) 1 *(Dziekanowski)*   9168
Hamilton A: Ferguson; McKee, Napier, Millen, Weir, O'Hara, Harris (McGinley), Burns (McDonald), McCluskey, Miller, Moore.
Celtic: Bonner; Morris, McLaughlin, Grant, Elliott, Whyte, Hayes, McStay, Dziekanowski, Walker, Collins.

Raith R (1) 1 *(McGeachie)*
Hibernian (0) 0   4631
Raith R: Arthur; McStay, MacLeod, Fraser, Dennis, McGeachie, Logan, Dalziel, Macdonald (Ferguson), Coyle, Nelson (Burn).
Hibernian: Goram; Miller, Mitchell, Kane, Cooper, Farrell (Evans), McGinlay, Wright (McGraw), Findlay, Houchen, Tortolano.

St Mirren (0) 0
Hearts (0) 1 *(Crabbe)*   6860
after extra time
St Mirren: Money; Wishart, Black, Lambert, Godfrey, Manley, Shaw, Martin, Stickroth, McWalter (McDowall), Kinnaird.
Hearts: Smith; MacLaren, McKinlay, Levein, McCreery (Bannon), McPherson, Colquhoun (Crabbe), Ferguson D, Robertson, Mackay, Berry.

QUARTER-FINALS

4 SEPT

Dundee U (2) 2 *(McInally, Jackson)*
Motherwell (0) 0   8475
Dundee U: Thomson W; Cleland, Malpas, McInally, Krivokapic, Welsh, Van der Hoorn, McKinlay, Dailly (Paatelainen), Jackson, McKinnon.
Motherwell: Maxwell; Burley, Boyd, Paterson, Nijholt, McCart, Arnott, O'Neill (Russell), Cusack, Kirk, Cooper.

Rangers (1) 6 *(McCoist 3, Johnston, Butcher, Steven T)*
Raith R (1) 2 *(Coyle, Butcher(og))*   31,230
Rangers: Woods; Stevens G, Hurlock, Gough, Spackman, Butcher, Steven T, McCoist, Hateley, Johnston, Huistra.
Raith R: Arthur; McStay, MacLeod, Fraser, Dennis, McGeachie, Coyle, Dalziel, Logan (Ferguson), Burn (Murray), Nelson.

5 SEPT

Aberdeen (2) 3 *(Van de Ven, Mason, Bett (pen))*
Hearts (0) 0   15,500
Aberdeen: Snelders; McKimmie, Robertson D, Grant, McLeish, Irvine, Van de Ven, Bett, Mason, Connor, Gillhaus (Jess).
Hearts: Smith; Berry, McKinlay, Levein, McCreery (Kidd), McPherson, Colquhoun, Mackay, Robertson, Foster, Bannon.

Celtic (1) 2 *(Dziekanowski, Miller)*
Queen of the S (0) 1 *(Thomson A)*   18,699
Celtic: Bonner; Morris, McLaughlin, Grant, Elliott, Whyte, Hayes (Miller), McStay, Dziekanowski, Nicholas (Walker), Collins.
Queen of the S: Davidson; McCafferty, Thomson I, Fraser, Hetherington, McGhie, Sloan, McGarvey (Gordon), Thomson A, Sim, McGuire (Robertson).

SEMI-FINALS

25 SEPT

Celtic (1) 2 *(Creaney, McStay) at Hampden Park*
Dundee U (0) 0   49,975
Celtic: Bonner; Grant, Rogan, Fulton (Galloway), Elliott, Whyte, Miller, McStay, Dziekanowski (Walker), Creaney, Collins.
Dundee U: Thomson W; Cleland, Malpas, McInally, Preston, Welsh, Van der Hoorn, McKinlay, Dailly (Paatelainen), Jackson, McKinnon.

26 SEPT

Aberdeen (0) 0 *at Hampden Park*
Rangers (1) 1 *(Steven T)*   40,855
Aberdeen: Snelders; McKimmie, Robertson D, Grant, McLeish, Irvine, Van de Ven, Bett, Mason, Connor, Jess (Robertson C).
Rangers: Woods; Stevens G, Munro, Gough, Spackman, Brown, Steven T, Hurlock, McCoist, Johnston, Walters.

FINAL

28 OCT

Rangers (0) 2 *(Walters, Gough) at Hampden Park*
Celtic (0) 1 *(Elliott)*   62,817
after extra time
Rangers: Woods; Stevens G, Munro, Gough, Spackman, Brown, Steven T, Hurlock (Huistra), McCoist (Ferguson), Hateley, Walters.
Celtic: Bonner; Grant, Wdowczyk, Fulton (Hewitt), Elliott, Rogan, Miller (Morris), McStay, Dziekanowski, Creaney, Collins.
Referee: J McCluskey (Stewarton).

SCOTTISH CUP FINALS 1874–1991

Year	Winners	Runners-up	Score
1874	Queen's Park	Clydesdale	2-0
1875	Queen's Park	Renton	3-0
1876	Queen's Park	Third Lanark	2-0 after 1-1 draw
1877	Vale of Leven	Rangers	3-2 after 0-0 and 1-1 draws
1878	Vale of Leven	Third Lanark	1-0
1879	Vale of Leven*	Rangers	
1880	Queen's Park	Thornlibank	3-0
1881	Queen's Park†	Dumbarton	3-1
1882	Queen's Park	Dumbarton	4-1 after 2-2 draw
1883	Dumbarton	Vale of Leven	2-1 after 2-2 draw
1884	Queen's Park‡	Vale of Leven	
1885	Renton	Vale of Leven	3-1 after 0-0 draw
1886	Queen's Park	Renton	3-1
1887	Hibernian	Dumbarton	2-1
1888	Renton	Cambuslang	6-1
1889	Third Lanark§	Celtic	2-1
1890	Queen's Park	Vale of Leven	2-1 after 1-1 draw
1891	Hearts	Dumbarton	1-0
1892	Celtic¶	Queen's Park	5-1
1893	Queen's Park	Celtic	2-1
1894	Rangers	Celtic	3-1
1895	St Bernard's	Renton	2-1
1896	Hearts	Hibernian	3-1
1897	Rangers	Dumbarton	5-1
1898	Rangers	Kilmarnock	2-0
1899	Celtic	Rangers	2-0
1900	Celtic	Queen's Park	4-3
1901	Hearts	Celtic	4-3
1902	Hibernian	Celtic	1-0
1903	Rangers	Hearts	2-0 after 1-1 and 0-0 draws
1904	Celtic	Rangers	3-2
1905	Third Lanark	Rangers	3-1 after 0-0 draw
1906	Hearts	Third Lanark	1-0
1907	Celtic	Hearts	3-0
1908	Celtic	St Mirren	5-1
1909	●●		
1910	Dundee	Clyde	2-1 after 2-2 and 0-0 draws
1911	Celtic	Hamilton A	2-0 after 0-0 draw
1912	Celtic	Clyde	2-0
1913	Falkirk	Raith R	2-0
1914	Celtic	Hibernian	4-1 after 0-0 draw
1920	Kilmarnock	Albion R	3-2
1921	Partick T	Rangers	1-0
1922	Morton	Rangers	1-0
1923	Celtic	Hibernian	1-0
1924	Airdrieonians	Hibernian	2-0
1925	Celtic	Dundee	2-1
1926	St Mirren	Celtic	2-0
1927	Celtic	East Fife	3-1
1928	Rangers	Celtic	4-0
1929	Kilmarnock	Rangers	2-0
1930	Rangers	Partick T	2-1 after 0-0 draw
1931	Celtic	Motherwell	4-2 after 2-2 draw
1932	Rangers	Kilmarnock	3-0 after 1-1 draw
1933	Celtic	Motherwell	1-0
1934	Rangers	St Mirren	5-0
1935	Rangers	Hamilton A	2-1
1936	Rangers	Third Lanark	1-0
1937	Celtic	Aberdeen	2-1
1938	East Fife	Kilmarnock	4-2 after 1-1 draw
1939	Clyde	Motherwell	4-0
1947	Aberdeen	Hibernian	2-1
1948	Rangers	Morton	1-0 after 1-1 draw
1949	Rangers	Clyde	4-1
1950	Rangers	East Fife	3-0
1951	Celtic	Motherwell	1-0
1952	Motherwell	Dundee	4-0
1953	Rangers	Aberdeen	1-0 after 1-1 draw
1954	Celtic	Aberdeen	2-1
1955	Clyde	Celtic	1-0 after 1-1 draw
1956	Hearts	Celtic	3-1
1957	Falkirk	Kilmarnock	2-1 after 1-1 draw
1958	Clyde	Hibernian	1-0
1959	St Mirren	Aberdeen	3-1
1960	Rangers	Kilmarnock	2-0
1961	Dunfermline Ath	Celtic	2-0 after 0-0 draw
1962	Rangers	St Mirren	2-0
1963	Rangers	Celtic	3-0 after 1-1 draw
1964	Rangers	Dundee	3-1

Year	Winners	Runners-up	Score
1965	Celtic	Dunfermline Ath	3-2
1966	Rangers	Celtic	1-0 after 0-0 draw
1967	Celtic	Aberdeen	2-0
1968	Dunfermline Ath	Hearts	3-1
1969	Celtic	Rangers	4-0
1970	Aberdeen	Celtic	3-1
1971	Celtic	Rangers	2-1 after 1-1 draw
1972	Celtic	Hibernian	6-1
1973	Rangers	Celtic	3-2
1974	Celtic	Dundee U	3-0
1975	Celtic	Airdrieonians	3-1
1976	Rangers	Hearts	3-1
1977	Celtic	Rangers	1-0
1978	Rangers	Aberdeen	2-1
1979	Rangers	Hibernian	3-2 after 0-0 and 0-0 draws
1980	Celtic	Rangers	1-0
1981	Rangers	Dundee U	4-1 after 0-0 draw
1982	Aberdeen	Rangers	4-1 (aet)
1983	Aberdeen	Rangers	1-0 (aet)
1984	Aberdeen	Celtic	2-1 (aet)
1985	Celtic	Dundee U	2-1
1986	Aberdeen	Hearts	3-0
1987	St Mirren	Dundee U	1-0 (aet)
1988	Celtic	Dundee U	2-1
1989	Celtic	Rangers	1-0
1990	Aberdeen	Celtic	0-0 (aet)
		(Aberdeen won 9-8 on penalties)	
1991	Motherwell	Dundee U	4-3 (aet)

*Vale of Leven awarded cup, Rangers failing to appear for replay after 1-1 draw.
†After Dumbarton protested the first game, which Queen's Park won 2-1.
‡Queen's Park awarded cup, Vale of Leven failing to appear.
§Replay by order of Scottish FA because of playing conditions in first match, won 3-0 by Third Lanark.
¶After mutually protested game which Celtic won 1-0.
●●Owing to riot, the cup was withheld after two drawn games – Celtic 2-1, Rangers 2-1.

SCOTTISH CUP WINS

Celtic 29, Rangers 24, Queen's Park 10, Aberdeen 7, Hearts 5, Clyde 3, St Mirren 3, Vale of Leven 3, Dunfermline Ath 2, Falkirk 2, Hibernian 2, Kilmarnock 2, Motherwell 2, Renton 2, Third Lanark 2, Airdrieonians 1, Dumbarton 1, Dundee 1, East Fife 1, Morton 1, Partick Th 1, St Bernard's 1.

APPEARANCES IN FINAL

Celtic 46, Rangers 40, Aberdeen 13, Queen's Park 12, Hearts 10, Hibernian 10, Kilmarnock 7, Vale of Leven 7, Clyde 6, Dumbarton 6, St Mirren 6, Third Lanark 6, Dundee U 6, Motherwell 6, Renton 5, Dundee 4, Dunfermline Ath 3, East Fife 3, Airdrieonians 2, Falkirk 2, Hamilton A 2, Morton 2, Partick Th 2, Albion R 1, Cambuslang 1, Clydesdale 1, Raith R 1, St Bernard's 1 Thornlibank 1.

Iain Ferguson (Motherwell) starts off the seven-goal thriller with Dundee United. His team went on to win 4-3 after extra time in the 1991 final. (Bob Thomas)

SCOTTISH CUP 1990–91

FIRST ROUND

8 DEC

East Stirling (0) 1 (*Byrne*)
Queen of the S (2) 3 (*Gordon, Watters 2*)   465

East Stirling: Watson G; McDowall, Workman, Rooney, Brannigan, Watson P, McBride, Erwin, Derek Walker, Clark, Lytwyn (Byrne).
Queen of the S: Davidson; McCafferty, McFarlane, Fraser, McGhie, McKeown, Gordon, McGarvey, Watters, Sim, McGuire (Thomson A).

Fraserburgh (1) 3 (*McCafferty, Lavelle 2*)
Vale of Leithen (1) 1 (*Hogarth*)   812
Fraserburgh: Gordon W; Gordon R, Sim, Young, Duthie, Thomson A, McCafferty, McCredie, Keith, Lavelle, Thomson J (Smith).
Vale of Leithen: McDermott; Ross, Graham, Bird, McNaughton, Taylor, Thorpe, Mitchell, Spence, Hogarth (Selkirk), Lynch (Waddell).

Ross County (1) 1 (*Williamson*)
Alloa (1) 1 (*Irvine*)   2300
Ross County: Ure; Somerville, Campbell, Williamson, Bellshaw, Lemmon, Ferries, Grant, Duff (Wilson), Connelly, Allan.
Alloa: Butter; Newbigging, Thomson (Ormond), Wilcox, McCulloch, Lee D, Grant, Ramsay, Moffat, Irvine, McEntegart.

11 DEC

Montrose (0) 0
Dumbarton (0) 0   365
Montrose: Larter; Morrison, Fleming, Mackay, Rougvie, Dolan, Allan, Maver, Kerr (Murray), Melville, Fotheringham.
Dumbarton: Stevenson; Gow, Boyd, Dempsey, McCracken (Marsland), Meechan, McQuade, McGuire (Quinn), Gibson, McGinley, Morrison.

15 DEC

Threave Rovers (1) 1 (*McKie*)
Spartans (2) 2 (*Treagus, Egan*)   550
Threave Rovers: Shanks; Smith, Cravens, O'Mara, Findlay, Jardine, Houston, McGinlay, Maxwell, Rudd (Middleton), McKie (Green).
Spartans: Houston; Carney, MacDonald, Lynch, Lennox, Smith, Egan, Goran, Campbell, Galbraith (Burns), Treagus (Binnie).

Whitehill Welfare (0) 0
East Fife (2) 4 (*Mitchell, Hope 2, Wilson*)   600
Whitehill Welfare: Stewart; D'Angelo, Robertson, Millar, Docherty, Krawiec, Anthony McKenna, Innes, Alan McKenna, Connachan (Aitchison), Curran (Brydon).
East Fife: Charles; Bell, Beaton, Wilson, Prior, Taylor PH, Mitchell, Cowell, Brown W, Brown I (Scott), Hope (Hayton).

FIRST ROUND REPLAYS

15 DEC

Alloa 0 (1) (*Newbigging (pen)*)
Ross County (2) 3 (*Campbell, Duff, Wilson*)   1051
Alloa: Butter; Newbigging, Lee D, Wilcox, McCulloch, McAvoy, Ormond, Ramsay, Moffat, Irvine (Black), McEntegart (Grant).
Ross County: Ure; Somerville, Campbell, Williamson, Bellshaw, Lemmon, Ferries, Grant, Duff, Connelly (Robertson), Allan (Wilson).

17 DEC

Dumbarton (0) 1 (*Morrison (pen)*)
Montrose (1) 4 (*Kerr 2 (1 pen), Murray, Allan*)   500
Dumbarton: Stevenson; Gow, Boyd, Dempsey, McNair, Meechan, McQuade, McGinley, Gibson, Morrison (McGuire), Millar (Quinn).
Montrose: Larter; Morrison, Fleming, Dolan, Rougvie, King, Allan, Maver, Kerr, Melville (Murray), Den Bieman (Fotheringham).

SECOND ROUND

29 DEC

Berwick R (0) 1 (*Graham (pen)*)
Albion R (0) 0   656
Berwick R: Neilson; Fraser, O'Donnell, Davidson, Garner, Sokoluk, Smith, Leitch, Todd, Bickmore, Graham.
Albion R: McCulloch; Stalker, Henderson (Cougan), McKeown, Richardson (Edgar), Millar, McGuiness, Clark, Cadden, McDonald, Watson.

Fraserburgh (0) 1 (*Keith*)
Cove Rangers (2) 4 (*Baxter, Smith, Megginson 2*)   2500
Fraserburgh: Gordon W; Gordon R, Sutherland, Young, Thomson A, Sim S (Sim B), McCafferty (Duthie), McCredie, Keith, Lavelle, Thomson J.
Cove Rangers: Beckett; Forbes, Whyte, Brown, Paterson, Cormack, Park, Yule, Smith D (Smith G), Baxter (King), Megginson.

Montrose (0) 0
Arbroath (1) 2 (*Bulloch, Bennett*)   650
Montrose: Larter; Morrison, Fleming, Dolan, Rougvie, King, Allan, Maver, Kerr, Melville, Den Bieman.
Arbroath: Balfour; Mitchell, Gallagher, Bennett, Carlin, Holmes J, Holmes W, Hamilton, Sorbie, Bulloch, Morton.

Queen's Park (0) 1 (*Henderson (og)*)
Stranraer (1) 2 (*Henderson, Grant*)   2013
Queen's Park: Monaghan; Mackay, Ogg, Elder, Jack, McEntegart, McNamee (James McFadyen), O'Brien, Hendry (Joe McFadyen), Caven, Morton.
Stranraer: Holland; Lowe, Walker (Spittal), McNiven, Gallagher, Shirkie, George, Grant, Cook, Scott, Henderson (Harkness).

Stirling Albion (0) 2 (*Docherty, Lloyd*)
Stenhousemuir (0) 0   900
Stirling Albion: McGeown; Mitchell, Hay, Shanks, Lawrie, Kerr, Reid (McInnes), Moore, Lloyd, Robertson, Docherty.

Stenhousemuir: Kelly; Aitken, Hallford, Anderson, Rennie, Cairney, Bullen (Walker), Clouston, McCormick, Kemp, Speirs (Quinton).

5 JAN

Inverness Thistle (1) 1 *(Noble)*
East Fife (1) 1 *(Hope)*   2500
Inverness Thistle: Calder; Skinner, Stevenson, Wilson, Milroy, Christie (Sutherland), MacDonald (Clark), Noble, Taylor, Robertson, Docherty.
East Fife: Charles; Bell, Beaton, Wilson, Prior, Taylor PH, Mitchell, Hope, Brown W, Brown I, Cowell.

9 JAN

Spartans (0) 0
Cowdenbeath (0) 0   350
Spartans: Houston; Carney (Burns), MacDonald, Lynch, Lennox, Smith, Egan, McKinnon, Goran, Galbraith, Treagus.
Cowdenbeath: Lamont; Bennett, Robertson, McGovern, Archibald, Irvine, Wright, Scott, Ross, MacKenzie, Dewar (Duffy).

23 JAN

Ross County (1) 2 *(Duff, Somerville)*
Queen of the S (1) 2 *(Sim, Thomson A)*   5500
Ross County: Ure; Somerville, Campbell, Williamson, Bellshaw, Lemmon, Ferries, Grant, Duff, Connelly (Robertson), Allan (Wilson).
Queen of the S: Davidson; McCafferty, McFarlane, Fraser, MacDonald, Hetherington, Thomson A, McGarvey, McGuire, Sim (Moffat), Robertson (Campbell).

SECOND ROUND REPLAYS

7 JAN

East Fife (0) 1 *(Scott)*
Inverness Thistle (0) 0   400
East Fife: Moffat; Bell, Beaton, Wilson, Prior, Taylor PH (Taylor P), Mitchell, Hope, Brown I (Brown W), Scott, Cowell.
Inverness Thistle: Calder; Skinner, Stevenson, Wilson, Milroy, Christie, Sutherland, Noble, Taylor, Robertson, Docherty (Hill).

21 JAN

Cowdenbeath (1) 2 *(MacKenzie 2)*
Spartans (0) 0   480
Cowdenbeath: Lamont; Bennett, Robertson, McGovern, Archibald, Irvine, Wright, Scott, Ross (Buckley), MacKenzie, Dewar.
Spartans: Houston; Burns (McKinnon), MacDonald, Lynch, Lennox, Smith, Egan, Goran (Binnie), Campbell, Galbraith, Treagus.

28 JAN

Queen of the S (0) 2 *(McGuire, McGhie)*
Ross County (1) 6 *(Williamson, Grant 3, Duff, Ferries)*   2121
Queen of the S: Davidson; McCafferty, Thomson I, Fraser, McGhie, McKeown, McFarlane (McGarvey), Thomson A, McGuire, Sim, Robertson.
Ross County: Cathcart; Somerville, Campbell, Williamson, Bellshaw, Lemmon, Ferries (Wilson), Grant, Duff (Robertson), Connelly, Allan.

THIRD ROUND

26 JAN

Aberdeen (0) 0
Motherwell (0) 1 *(Kirk)*   15,000
Aberdeen: Snelders; Wright, Robertson D, Jess, McLeish, Irvine, Van de Ven, Bett, Mason (Cameron), Connor, Gillhaus (Booth).
Motherwell: Maxwell; Philliben, Boyd, O'Neill, Paterson, McCart, Arnott, Dolan, Ferguson (Kirk), Angus, Cooper.

Airdrieonians (0) 2 *(Jack, Watson)*
Hearts (1) 1 *(Mackay)*   10,000
Airdrieonians: Martin; Stewart, McPhee, Watson, Smith J, Balfour, Kirkwood, Lawrence (MacDonald J) (Crainie), Harvey, Coyle, Jack.
Hearts: Smith; Sandison, McKinlay, McLaren, Mackay, McPherson, Colquhoun, Berry, Crabbe (Foster), Ferguson D, Robertson.

Clydebank (0) 0
Ayr U (0) 1 *(Bryce)*   2316
Clydebank: Spence; Joe Dickson, Rodger (John Dickson), Maher, Sweeney, Rowe, Harvey, Sermanni, Eadie, Duncanson, Kelly.
Ayr U: Purdie; Burley, Hughes, Furphy, Gillespie, Evans, Fraser, Bryce, Graham, Johnston, Weir.

Cove Rangers (1) 1 *(Smith)*
Cowdenbeath (0) 2 *(Wright, Buckley)*   1400
Cove Rangers: Beckett; Forbes (Paterson S), Whyte, Brown (King), Paterson A, Cormack, Park, Yule, Smith, Baxter, Megginson.
Cowdenbeath: Lamont; Bennett (Watt), Robertson, McGovern, Archibald, Irvine, Wright, Scott, Ross, MacKenzie, Dewar (Buckley).

Dundee (1) 1 *(West)*
Brechin C (0) 0   3446
Dundee: Carson; Forsyth, Shannon, Dinnie, Jamieson, Bain, West, Frail, Wright, Dodds, Campbell S.
Brechin C: Lawrie; Baillie, Paterson IG, Brown, McKillop, Sexton, Thomson S, Conway, Ritchie, Scott, Pryde (Lees).

East Fife (1) 1 *(Cowell)*
Dundee U (0) 1 *(Connolly)*   4947
East Fife: Charles; Bell, Taylor P, Taylor PH, Prior, Beaton, Hope (Crolla), Wilson, Brown W, Scott, Cowell.
Dundee U: Main; Clark (Paatelainen), Malpas, McInally, Krivokapic, Welsh, Van der Hoorn, McKinlay, Dailly (O'Neill M), Jackson, Connolly.

Forfar Ath (0) 0
Celtic (2) 2 *(Coyne, Wdowczyk)*   8359
Forfar Ath: Allan; Brazil (Winter), Hamill, Morris, Hegarty, Holt, Paton (Clark), Lorimer, Whyte, Brewster, Petrie.
Celtic: Bonner; Morris, Wdowczyk, McNally, Baillie, Whyte, Miller (Fulton), McStay, Coyne, Dziekanowski, Collins.

Kilmarnock (1) 3 *(Sludden 2, Burns)*
Arbroath (1) 2 *(Sorbie, Mitchell)*   4991
Kilmarnock: Geddes; MacKinnon, Spence, Burgess, Flexney, Callaghan (Reilly), Elliott, Tait, Williamson, Sludden, Burns.
Arbroath: Balfour; Mitchell, Florence, Bennett, Carlin, Holmes J, Smith, Hamilton, Sorbie, Bulloch, Morton.

Partick T (0) 0
Falkirk (0) 0 9552

Partick T: Duncan; Robertson, Law, Duffy, Rae, Tierney, Buckley, Campbell (McGovern), McGlashan, Roche, Elliot.
Falkirk: Marshall; Cody (Duffy), McQueen, Smith, Baptie, Hetherston, McGivern, Taylor, Hughes, Stainrod, McWilliams.

Raith R (0) 0
Hamilton A (0) 1 (*McCluskey*) 2226

Raith R: Arthur; McStay, MacLeod, Fraser (Sinclair), McGeachie, Romaines, Simpson (Logan), Dalziel, Ferguson, Murray, Nelson.
Hamilton A: Ferguson; McKee, Miller, Millen, Weir, O'Hara (Horne), Napier, Burns, McCluskey, McGuigan (McCabe), McDonald.

St Johnstone (0) 0
Berwick R (0) 0 5495

St Johnstone: Hamilton; Treanor, Baltacha, McVicar (Ward), Inglis, McGinnis, Moore, Turner, Maskrey (Grant), Macdonald, Curran.
Berwick R: Neilson; Fraser, O'Donnell, Davidson, Garner, Sokoluk, Neil (Thorpe), Leitch, Todd, Bickmore, Graham (Smith).

Stirling Albion (0) 0
Morton (0) 1 (*MacCabe*) 1898

Stirling Albion: McGeown; Mitchell, Hay, Shanks, Lawrie, Kerr, Reid, Moore (Conway), Lloyd (McGachie), Robertson, Docherty.
Morton: Wylie; Collins, Pickering, Doak, Reid, Hunter, MacCabe (Deeney), McDonald I, Alexander, Fowler (Cowie), Gahagan.

Stranraer (0) 1 (*George*)
St Mirren (2) 5 (*Torfason 2, Kinnaird, McDowall, Victor*) 4500

Stranraer: Holland; Lowe, Lindsay, McNiven, Spittal, McCutcheon (Harkness), George, Grant, McMillan, Duncan, Henderson (Cook).
St Mirren: Money; Wishart, Black, McWhirter, Victor, Godfrey, Shaw, McDowall, Broddle (McWalter), Torfason (Stickroth), Kinnaird.

28 JAN

Clyde (0) 0
Hibernian (0) 2 (*Houchen, Miller*) 4000

Clyde: Ross; Knox, McVie, Reid, Speirs, McFarlane, Wilson, Mitchell, Clarke S, McCoy, Clark G (Mallan).
Hibernian: Goram; Miller, Tortolano, Cooper, McIntyre, MacLeod, Findlay, Orr, Weir, Houchen, Mitchell (Fellinger).

29 JAN

Rangers (2) 2 (*Huistra, Spackman*)
Dunfermline Ath (0) 0 29,003

Rangers: Woods; Stevens G, Vinnicombe (Dodds), Gough, Spackman, Nisbet, Steven T, Robertson, Hateley, Johnston, Huistra (McCoist).
Dunfermline Ath: Rhodes; Wilson (Farningham), Sharp, McCathie, Moyes, Irons (Smith T), Smith P, Davies, Jack, O'Boyle, Kozma.

23 FEB

Ross County (0) 1 (*Duff*)
Meadowbank T (2) 6 (*Bellshaw (og), Forrest, Roseburgh 2 (1 pen), Irvine, Boyd*) 4374

Ross County: Cathcart; Somerville, Campbell, Williamson (Robertson), Bellshaw, Allan R, Ferries (Wilson), Grant, Duff, Connelly, Allan A.

Meadowbank T: McQueen; Hendrie, Armstrong, Williamson, Grant, Roseburgh, Logan, Boyd (Banks), Irvine, Forrest (McNaughton), Prentice.

THIRD ROUND REPLAYS
29 JAN

Dundee U (1) 2 (*Clark, Ferguson*)
East Fife (1) 1 (*Wilson*) *after extra time* 7190

Dundee U: Main; Clark (Welsh), Malpas, McInally, Krivokapic, O'Neill M (Dailly), Van der Hoorn, McKinlay, Ferguson, Jackson, Connolly.
East Fife: Charles; Bell, Taylor P (Halliday), Taylor PH, Prior, Beaton, Crolla (Hope), Wilson, Brown W, Scott, Cowell.

30 JAN

Berwick R (1) 3 (*Todd, Garner, Bickmore*)
St Johnstone (3) 4 (*Maskrey, Grant, Curran, Moore*) *aet* 3053

Berwick R: Neilson; Fraser, O'Donnell, Davidson, Garner, Sokoluk (Smith), Neil (Thorpe), Leitch, Todd, Bickmore, Graham.
St Johnstone: Hamilton; Treanor, Baltacha, McVicar (Davies), Inglis, McGinnis, Moore, Turner, Maskrey, Grant (Ward), Curran.

Falkirk (1) 4 (*McGivern 2, McWilliams 2*)
Partick T (1) 3 (*Duffy (pen), McGlashan, Roche*) 10,000

Falkirk: Marshall; Cody, McQueen, Smith, Baptie, Hetherston, McGivern, Taylor, Hughes, Stainrod, McWilliams.
Partick T: Duncan; Robertson, Law, Duffy, Rae, Tierney, Buckley (McGovern), Campbell, McGlashan, Roche, Elliot.

FOURTH ROUND
23 FEB

Ayr U (0) 0
Hamilton A (0) 0 4524

Ayr U: Purdie; Burley, Hughes, Furphy, Gillespie, Evans, Bryce, Shaw, Graham, Johnston, Weir.
Hamilton A: Ferguson; McKee, Miller, Millen, Weir, Napier (Moore), McGuigan, Burns (McQuilter), McCluskey, McCabe, McDonald.

Dundee (2) 2 (*McMartin, Dodds*)
Kilmarnock (0) 0 7195

Dundee: Carson; Dinnie, Shannon, Chisholm, Jamieson, Craib, West (Craig), Frail, Wright, Dodds, McMartin.
Kilmarnock: Geddes; Montgomerie, Spence, Burgess (Callaghan), Flexney, MacPherson (Reilly), Elliott, Tait, Williamson, Sludden, Burns.

Dundee U (0) 2 (*French 2*)
Airdrieonians (0) 0 8648

Dundee U: Main; Clark, Malpas, McInally, Krivokapic, Bowman, Van der Hoorn, O'Neil J, McKinnon (McKinlay), Ferguson (Jackson), French.
Airdrieonians: Martin; Stewart, McPhee, Watson, Smith J (Crainie), Jack, Kirkwood, Lawrence, Harvey (MacDonald J), Coyle, Balfour.

Motherwell (1) 4 (*Cusack 2, McLeod, Kirk*)
Falkirk (1) 2 (*McGivern, Taylor*) 10,271

Motherwell: Maxwell; Philliben, Boyd, O'Donnell (Kirk), Paterson, McCart, McLeod, Ferguson (Russell), Cusack, Angus, Cooper.
Falkirk: Marshall; Duffy, McQueen, Smith, Baptie (Nicol), Hetherston, McGivern, Taylor (Cody), Hughes, Stainrod, McWilliams.

Rangers (3) 5 (*Hateley 2, Nisbet, McCoist, Walters (pen)*)

Cowdenbeath (0) 0   29,527

Rangers: Woods; Stevens G, Nisbet, Gough, Spackman, Brown (Huistra), Steven T, Hurlock, Hateley (Johnston), McCoist, Walters.
Cowdenbeath: Lamont; Bennett (Hamill), Robertson, McGovern, Archibald, Irvine, Wright (Buckley), Malone, Ross, MacKenzie, Scott.

St Johnstone (0) 2 (*Maskrey, Grant*)

Hibernian (1) 1 (*Hamilton*)   9153

St Johnstone: Hamilton; Treanor (Ward), Baltacha, McVicar (Heddle), McGinnis, Davies, Moore, Turner, Maskrey, Grant, Curran.
Hibernian: Goram; Miller, McIntyre, Cooper, Hunter, MacLeod, Hamilton, Mitchell (Findlay), McGinlay, Houchen, Tortolano.

26 FEB

Celtic (3) 3 (*McWhirter (og), Creaney, Miller*)

St Mirren (0) 0   27,189

Celtic: Bonner; McNally, Rogan, Morris, Elliott, Whyte, Miller, McStay, Coyne, Creaney, Collins.
St Mirren: Fridge; Martin, Black, McWhirter, Victor, Godfrey, Shaw, Achibald, Broddle (Lambert), Torfason (Stickroth), Kinnaird.

2 MAR

Morton (3) 3 (*MacCabe, Gahagan, Alexander*)

Meadowbank T (0) 0   2427

Morton: Wylie; Collins, Pickering (McInnes), Doak, Reid, Hunter, MacCabe, McDonald (Fowler), Alexander, Mahood, Gahagan.
Meadowbank T: McQueen; Hendrie (Banks), Armstrong, Williamson, Grant, Roseburgh, Logan, Boyd, Irvine, Forrest (McNaughton), Prentice.

FOURTH ROUND REPLAY

27 FEB

Hamilton A (1) 2 (*McCluskey, Moore*)

Ayr U (1) 3 (*Graham, Weir, Fraser*)   2749

Hamilton A: Ferguson; McKee, Miller, Millen, Weir, McGuigan, Moore, Burns (McCabe), McCluskey, Napier, McDonald.
Ayr U: Purdie; Burley, Hughes, Furphy, Gillespie, Evans, Fraser, Bryce, Graham, Johnston, Weir.

QUARTER-FINALS

13 MAR

Dundee U (1) 3 (*McKinnon, Jackson, Ferguson*)

Dundee (1) 1 (*Dodds*)   16,228

Dundee U: Main; Clark, Malpas, Krivokapic, Bowman, Van der Hoorn, O'Neil J, McKinnon (McKinlay), Ferguson, Jackson.
Dundee: Carson; Dinnie, Shannon, Chisholm, Jamieson, Craib, Frail, McMartin, Craig, Dodds, McSkimming (Campbell D).

16 MAR

Motherwell (0) 0

Morton (0) 0   9005

Motherwell: Maxwell; Nijholt, Boyd, O'Donnell, Paterson, McCart, McLeod (Ferguson), Griffin, Arnott, Angus (Kirk), Cooper.
Morton: Wylie; Collins, Pickering (McInnes), Doak, Reid, Hunter, MacCabe, McDonald (Fowler), Alexander, Mahood, Gahagan.

St Johnstone (2) 5 (*Grant, Maskrey, Moore 3*)

Ayr U (0) 2 (*Fraser, Bryce*)   7697

St Johnstone: Hamilton; Treanor, Baltacha, McGinnis, Inglis, Davies, Moore, Turner, Maskrey, Grant (Macdonald), Curran (McVicar).
Ayr U: Purdie; Burley, Love, Furphy, Gillespie, Evans, Fraser, Bryce, Shaw (Walker), Johnston, Weir.

17 MAR

Celtic (2) 2 (Creaney, Wdowczyk)

Rangers (0) 0   52,000

Celtic: Bonner; Wdowczyk, Rogan, Grant, Elliott, Whyte, Miller, McStay, Coyne, Creaney, Collins.
Rangers: Woods; Stevens G, Munro (Cowan), Gough, Nisbet, Hurlock, Steven T (Huistra), Ferguson, Hateley, Johnston, Walters.

QUARTER-FINAL REPLAY

19 MAR

Morton (0) 1 (*Gahagan*)

Motherwell (1) 1 (*Boyd*)   5400

Morton: Wylie; Collins, Pickering, Doak, Reid, Hunter, MacCabe, McDonald, Alexander, Fowler, Gahagan (McInnes).
Motherwell: Maxwell; Nijholt (O'Donnell), Boyd, O'Neill, Paterson, McCart, Arnott, Russell, Cusack (Ferguson), Kirk, Cooper.
aet; Motherwell won 5-4 on penalties

SEMI-FINALS

3 APR *at Hampden Park*

Celtic (0) 0

Motherwell (0) 0   41,765

Celtic: Bonner; Morris, Rogan, Wdowczyk, Elliott, Whyte, Miller, McStay, Coyne, Creaney (Britton), Collins.
Motherwell: Maxwell; Nijholt, Boyd, O'Neill, Philliben, McCart, Arnott (Kirk), Griffin, Ferguson, O'Donnell, Angus.

6 APR *at East End Park*

Dundee U (1) 2 (*Clark, Ferguson*)

St Johnstone (1) 1 (*Curran*)   16,560

Dundee: Main; Clark, Malpas, McInally, Krivokapic, Bowman, Van der Hoorn, O'Neil J, McKinnon (French), Ferguson, Jackson.
St Johnstone: Hamilton; Treanor (Davies), Baltacha, McVicar, Inglis, McGinnis, Moore, Turner, Maskrey, Grant, Curran.

SEMI-FINAL REPLAY

9 APR *at Hampden Park*

Celtic (2) 2 (*Boyd (og), Rogan*)

Motherwell (1) 4 (*Arnott 2, O'Neill, Kirk*)   31,371

Celtic: Bonner; McNally, Rogan, Wdowczyk, Elliott, Whyte, Miller, McStay, Coyne, Creaney (Britton), Collins.
Motherwell: Maxwell; Nijholt, Boyd (Cusack), O'Neill, Philliben, McCart, Arnott, Griffin, Ferguson, O'Donnell, Angus (Kirk).

FINAL

18 MAY *at Hampden Park*

Motherwell (1) 4 (*Ferguson, O'Donnell, Angus, Kirk*)

Dundee U (0) 3 (*Bowman, O'Neil J, Jackson*) *aet*   57,319

Motherwell: Maxwell; Nijholt, Boyd, Griffin, Paterson, McCart, Arnott, Angus, Ferguson (Kirk), O'Donnell, Cooper (O'Neill).
Dundee U: Main; Clark, Malpas, McInally, Krivokapic, Bowman, Van der Hoorn, McKinnon (McKinlay), French, Ferguson (O'Neil J), Jackson.
Referee: D. Syme (Rutherglen).

B & Q CENTENARY CUP 1990–91

FIRST ROUND

2 OCT

Airdrieonians (1) 2 *(McPhee, Smith A)*
Partick T (0) 1 *(Campbell (pen))*   3200
after extra time
Airdrieonians: Martin; Jack, McPhee, Watson, Smith J, Conn, Lawrence, Balfour (Harvey), Smith A, Coyle, MacDonald (Crainie).
Partick T: Duncan; Robertson, Elliot, Duffy, Peebles, Tierney, Law, Wright, McGovern (McConville), Campbell, Gallagher (English).

Alloa (0) 3 *(Moffat 2, McCallum)*
Forfar Ath (0) 0   347
Alloa: Butter; Newbigging, Lee R, Wilcox, Lee D, McEntegart, Moffat, Henry (Thomson), McCallum, Ormond (Irvine), Smith.
Forfar Ath: Allan; Morris, Hamill, Brazil, Winter, Lorimer, Paton, Brewster, Whyte, Leslie (Clinging), Petrie.

Arbroath (0) 2 *(Bennett, Smith)*
Queen's Park (0) 1 *(McEntegart)*   221
after extra time
Arbroath: Jackson; Holmes J, Florence, Bennett, Carlin, Oliver, Hamilton, Stewart (Smith), Marshall (Powell), Sorbie, Gallacher.
Queen's Park: Monaghan; Callan, Ogg, Elder, Jack, McEntegart, McNamee, O'Brien (Morton), Hendry, Mackenzie (Joe McFadyen), Greig.

Ayr U (2) 3 *(Walker, Kennedy, Graham)*
Brechin C (0) 0   1300
Ayr U: Cunningham; Kennedy, Love, McCann, Gillespie, Smyth, Bryce, Evans, Graham, Walker, Johnston.
Brechin C: Lawrie; Baillie, Candlish, Brown, Kenny, Hutt (Paterson I G), Lees, Scott, Ritchie (Thomson), Sexton, Paterson I A.

Clydebank (0) 1 *(Maher)*
East Fife (1) 2 *(Brown W, Mitchell)*   528
Clydebank: Gallacher; Maher, Rodger, Smith, Sweeney, Sermanni, Harvey, Davies, Eadie, Coyle (Caffrey), Ferguson.
East Fife: Moffat; Hamilton, Taylor P, Lennox, Prior, Taylor P H, Hayton, Wilson, Brown W, Scott (Crolla), Hope (Mitchell).

Cowdenbeath (1) 2 *(Buckley, MacKenzie)*
Albion R (0) 1 *(Cougan)*   200
Cowdenbeath: Lamont; Watt, Robertson, Bennett, Archibald, McGovern, Duffy, Malone, MacKenzie, Buckley, Scott.
Albion R: Cormack (Watson); Miller, McDonald, Cadden (Cougan), McTeague, Clark, Richardson, Edgar, McAnenay, McKeown, Lauchlan.

Falkirk (0) 0
Raith R (1) 3 *(Whittaker(og), Macdonald, Burn)*
     2000
Falkirk: Marshall; Robertson, Whittaker, Baptie, Beaton, Smith, Houston, Hughes, Rutherford (Cody), McNeill (Cowell), McWilliams.

Raith R: Arthur; McStay, Murray, Coyle, Dennis, Romaines (Sinclair), Logan, Dalziel, Macdonald, Ferguson (Burn), Nelson.

Kilmarnock (1) 4 *(Burns, Sludden 3)*
Stirling Albion (0) 1 *(McConville)*   2612
Kilmarnock: Geddes; Montgomerie, Spence, MacKinnon, Flexney, Callaghan (Elliott), Reilly, Tait, Watters, Sludden, Burns (Burgess).
Stirling Albion: McGeown; Mitchell, Hay, Shanks, Moore, Kerr, Reid, McConville, Mailer (McInnes), Robertson, Docherty (Conway).

Montrose (0) 2 *(Stephen, Den Bieman)*
Berwick R (0) 0   150
Montrose: Larter; Morrison, Fleming, Mackay, Rougvie, Den Bieman, Allan, Lyons, Fotheringham, Stephen, Dolan.
Berwick R: Neilson; Leitch, O'Donnell, Smith, Marshall, Cass, Fraser, Tait, Todd (Sokoluk), Bickmore, Graham.

Stenhousemuir (0) 0
Queen of the S (0) 0   150
after extra time
Stenhousemuir: Kelly; Nelson, Elliott (McNab), Cairney, Tracey, Quinton, Walker, Clouston, McAvoy, Kemp, McGurn (Speirs).
Queen of the S: Davidson; Adams, McCafferty, Fraser, Mills, McGhie, Gordon, McGarvey, Andrews (Thomson A), Campbell, McGuire.
(Stenhousemuir won 4–3 on penalties)

Clyde (1) 4 *(McAulay, Clarke S 2, Gilmour (pen))*
Dumbarton (1) 3 *(Morrison, Hughes, McQuade)* 262
Clyde: Ross; Knox, Brogan, Nolan (Gaughan), Speirs, McFarlane, McAulay, Mitchell, Clark G, Clarke S, Gilmour (Mallan).
Dumbarton: Stevenson; Marsland, Chapman, Dempsey, McCracken, McNair, McQuade, McKenzie, Gibson (Boyd), Morrison, Miller (Hughes).

Meadowbank T (0) 1 *(Boyd)*
Morton (0) 2 *(Alexander, Reid)*   470
after extra time
Meadowbank T: McQueen; Prentice, Banks, Armstrong, Grant, Boyd, Park (Graham), Irvine N, Irvine W, Whitehead (Bullen), Sprott.
Morton: Wylie; Collins (Fowler), Pickering, Doak, Reid, Hunter, MacCabe, McDonald (Cowie), Alexander, McInnes, Gahagan.

SECOND ROUND

16 OCT

Airdrieonians (0) 0
Clyde (1) 2 *(Clark G, Gilmour)*   2700
Airdrieonians: Martin; Jack, McPhee (MacDonald), Watson, Smith J, Conn, Lawrence, Gray, Balfour, Coyle, Crainie (Smith A).
Clyde: O'Hanlon; Nolan, Graeme McVie, Reid, Halpin, McFarlane, Clark G, Mitchell, Scott (McAulay), Clark S, Gilmour.

Alloa (0) 3 *(Wilcox, Irvine 2)*
Dundee (2) 5 *(Dodds 2 (2 pens), Campbell, Wright, Shannon)* 915
Alloa: Butter; Newbigging, Lee R, Wilcox, McCulloch, Lee D, Grant, Feenie (Moffat), Black, Irvine, Henry (Ormond).
Dundee: Carson; Frail, Shannon, Holt, Jamieson, Bain, Campbell D (Lennox), McLeod (McSkimming), Wright, Dodds, Campell S.

East Fife (1) 2 *(Brown W 2)*
Stranraer (0) 1 *(Harkness)* 778
East Fife: Moffat; Bell, Taylor P, Lennox, Prior, Taylor P H, Mitchell, Wilson, Brown W, Hope (Hayton), Crolla.
Stranraer: Duffy; Corrie, Walker (Harkness), McNiven, Shirkie, Duncan, George (McCutcheon), Grant, Cook, Spittal, Henderson.

Kilmarnock (2) 3 *(Sludden, Elliott, Stark)*
Arbroath (0) 1 *(Bulloch)* 3437
Kilmarnock: Geddes; Montgomerie, Spence, MacKinnon, Flexney, Callaghan (Stark), Elliott, Tait, Reilly (Watters), Sludden, Burns.
Arbroath: Jackson; Hamilton, Florence (Gallacher), Carlin, Oliver, Holmes J, Mitchell, Bennett, Bulloch, Sorbie, Holmes W.

Montrose (0) 2 *(Den Bieman, Maver)*
Ayr U (0) 3 *(Walker, Graham, Templeton)* 550
after extra time
Montrose: Larter; Morrison, Fleming, Mackay, Rougvie, Den Bieman, Allan (Murray), Maver, Stephen, Dolan, Fotheringham (Lyons).
Ayr U: Purdie; Kennedy, Evans (Templeton), Smyth, Gillespie, McAllister, Bryce, Johnston, Walker, Graham, Weir.

Morton (0) 0
Cowdenbeath (0) 0 1123
after extra time
Morton: Wylie; Collins, Pickering (Cowie), Doak (Fowler), Reid, Hunter, MacCabe, McDonald, Alexander, McInnes, Gahagan.
Cowdenbeath: Lamont; Watt, Robertson, McGovern, Archibald, Bennett, Wright, Malone, MacKenzie, Ross (Duffy), Scott (Hamill).
(Cowdenbeath won 8–7 on penalties)

Queen of the S (2) 5 *(Robertson, Fraser, Gordon 2, McGarvey)*
East Stirling (0) 0 631
Queen of the S: Davidson; Adams, Sim, Fraser, McGhie, McCafferty, Gordon, McGarvey, Sloan, Campbell, Robertson.
East Stirling: Lawson; Hamill, Workman, Walker, Brannigan, Erwin, O'Brien, McDowall, Wilson (McBride), Rooney (McNab), McNally.

Raith R (2) 3 *(Dalziel 2, Burn)*
Hamilton A (1) 2 *(Harris (pen), McCluskey)* 1416
Raith R: Arthur; McStay, MacLeod, Coyle, Dennis, Burn, Logan, Dalziel, Macdonald, Ferguson (Murray), Nelson.
Hamilton A: Ferguson; McKee, McGuigan, Millen, Weir, O'Hara, Harris, McGinley (Moore), McCluskey (Horne), Napier, McDonald.

QUARTER-FINALS

23 OCT

Ayr U (2) 4 *(Walker, Bryce 2, Templeton)*
Queen of the S (0) 1 *(Sloan)* 2100
Ayr U: Purdie; Kennedy, Evans, Smyth, Gillespie, McAllister, Bryce, Johnston, Walker, Graham, Templeton.
Queen of the S: Davidson; Adams, Sim, Fraser, Mills, McCafferty, Gordon, Thomson A, Sloan, Campbell (Moffat), Robertson.

Clyde (2) 2 *(Reid, Gilmour)*
Cowdenbeath (0) 1 *(Ross)* 600
Clyde: O'Hanlon; Halpin, Graeme McVie, Reid, Speirs (Scott), McFarlane, Clark G, Mitchell, McAulay, Clarke S (Brogan), Gilmour.
Cowdenbeath: Lamont; Watt, Robertson, Dewar (Hamill), Archibald, Bennett, Wright, Malone, MacKenzie (Buckley), Ross, Scott.

East Fife (0) 1 *(Mitchell)*
Kilmarnock (1) 2 *(Sludden, Watters)* 2101
East Fife: Moffat; Bell, Taylor P, Lennox, Prior, Taylor P H, Mitchell, Hayton, Brown W, Scott (Brown I), Crolla (Hope).
Kilmarnock: Geddes; Montgomerie, Spence, MacKinnon, Flexney, Burgess, Stark, Tait, Watters, Sludden (Callaghan), Burns.

Raith R (0) 0
Dundee (0) 1 *(Dodds)* 4061
after extra time
Raith R: Arthur; McStay, MacLeod, Coyle, Dennis, Murray, Ferguson, Dalziel, Macdonald (Logan), Burn (Sinclair), Nelson.
Dundee: Carson, Dinnie, Shannon, Chisholm (Campbell S), Jamieson, Craib, Frail, McLeod, Wright, Dodds, McSkimming.

SEMI-FINALS

30 OCT

Ayr U (0) 2 *(Graham, Johnston)*
Clyde (0) 0 3482
Ayr U: Purdie; Kennedy, McAllister, McCann, Gillespie, Smyth, Bryce (Fraser), Johnston, Willock, Graham, Templeton.
Clyde: O'Hanlon; Knox, Brogan, Reid, Speirs, McFarlane, Clark G, Mitchell, McAulay (Scott), Clarke S (Mallan), Gilmour.

Kilmarnock (0) 0
Dundee (1) 2 *(Wright 2)* 7933
Kilmarnock: Geddes; Montgomerie, Spence, MacKinnon, Flexney, Callaghan, Stark, Tait, Reilly (Elliott), Sludden, Burns.
Dundee: Carson; Dinnie, Shannon, Chisholm (Holt), Jamieson, Craib, Frail, Forsyth, Wright, Dodds, McSkimming.

FINAL

11 NOV *at Fir Park*

Dundee (0) 3 *(Dodds 3 (1 pen)*
Ayr U (1) 2 *(McAllister, Smyth)* 11,506
after extra time
Dundee: Carson; Dinnie, Shannon, Chisholm, Jamieson, Craib, West (McBride), Forsyth, Wright, Dodds, McLeod (Frail).
Ayr U: Purdie; Kennedy, Smyth, McAllister, Gillespie, McCann, Bryce (Evans), Johnston, Graham, Templeton, Weir.
Referee: K. J. Hope (Clarkston).

WELSH
and
NORTHERN IRISH
FOOTBALL

LEAGUE TABLES, CUP WINNERS
AND HONOURS PAST AND PRESENT

WELSH FOOTBALL 1990–91

THE ABACUS LEAGUE

National Division

	P	W	D	L	F	A	Pts
Abergavenny	30	21	6	3	68	23	69
Aberystwyth Town	30	18	5	7	68	35	59
Haverfordwest	30	16	6	8	56	34	54
Ton Pentre	30	15	8	7	51	30	53
Maesteg Park	30	15	5	10	50	41	50
Inter Cardiff	30	12	8	10	58	46	44
Briton Ferry Athletic	30	12	6	12	63	67	42
Brecon Corries	30	10	10	10	47	49	40
Cwmbran Town	30	11	6	13	63	58	39
Pembroke	30	10	9	11	49	51	39
Bridgend Town	30	11	6	13	50	56	39
Afan Lido	30	9	8	13	44	62	35
Ferndale	30	9	7	14	39	54	34
Llanelli	30	8	5	17	48	57	29
Port Talbot	30	8	5	17	31	56	29
Ammanford	30	2	6	22	20	86	12

Division One

	P	W	D	L	F	A	Pts
Morriston Town	32	16	12	4	58	37	60
Caldicot	32	17	9	6	50	30	60
Ebbw Vale	32	16	11	5	72	29	59
Llanwern	32	17	5	10	67	40	56
Aberaman	32	16	7	9	63	46	55
BP	32	13	5	14	55	61	44
Blaenrhondda	32	12	8	12	49	56	44
Seven Sisters	32	12	7	13	57	56	43
Newport YMCA	32	11	10	11	43	50	43
Garw	32	11	7	14	43	59	40
Ynysybwl	32	11	4	17	55	60	37
Caerleon	32	9	9	14	39	51	36
Merthyr Tydfil	32	10	6	16	53	67	36
Pontllanfraith	32	11	3	18	39	60	36
Cardiff Corries	32	9	8	15	44	57	35
Panteg	32	9	8	15	47	64	35
Milford*	32	8	9	15	51	62	22

*11 points deducted

Division Two

	P	W	D	L	F	A	Pts
Cardiff Civil Service	32	25	3	4	100	36	78
Risca Utd	32	24	3	5	77	34	75
Taffs Well	32	20	6	6	76	25	66
Caerau	32	17	6	9	41	30	57
Carmarthen	32	17	5	10	82	57	56
Treharris	32	16	3	13	65	68	51
Skewen	32	13	10	9	54	43	49
AFC Tondu	32	13	6	13	36	48	45
South Wales Police	32	12	5	15	48	55	41
Pontardawe	32	11	5	16	45	55	38
Blaenavon	32	9	9	14	56	58	36

	P	W	D	L	F	A	Pts
Cardiff Institute	32	11	3	18	40	70	36
Tonyrefail	32	8	11	13	38	44	35
Pontyclun	32	9	5	18	35	62	32
Abercynon	32	7	9	16	43	74	30
Trelewis	32	7	8	17	42	64	29
Pontlottyn	32	2	5	25	32	87	11

MANWEB CYMRU ALLIANCE

	P	W	D	L	F	A	Pts
Flint Town United	26	22	1	3	77	24	67
Caersws	26	19	3	4	66	26	60
Connah's Quay Nomads	26	16	3	7	54	36	51
Lex XI	26	14	6	6	59	41	48
Conwy United	26	12	6	8	54	34	42
Porthmadog	26	12	5	9	65	40	41
Welshpool	26	11	7	8	54	40	40
Mostyn	26	8	7	11	37	60	31
Holywell Town	26	6	6	14	29	40	24
Llanidloes Town	26	6	6	14	24	51	24
Carno	26	7	2	17	26	56	23
Mold Alexandra	26	6	5	15	27	66	23
Gresford Athletic	26	4	8	14	28	53	20
Penrhyncoch	26	4	5	17	27	59	17

In the League Cup Final Lex XI beat Caersws 2-1 at Llanidloes.

Football Association of Wales Challenge Cup – Flint Town United 2, Abergavenny Thursdays 1.
South Wales Senior Cup – Winners: Maesteg Park; Runners-up: Barry Town.
Saturday Intermediate – Winners: Llwydcoed Welfare; Runners-up: Bridgend Street.
Youth – Winners: Inter Cardiff; Runners-up: Cadoxton Imps.
Junior – Winners: Inter Cardiff; Runners-up: Cascade YC.
North-East Wales FC Goodwins Challenge Cup – Winners: Lex XI; Runners-up: Wrexham.
Wrexham Lager Sunday Cup – Winners: Broughton Crusaders; Runners-up: Red Lion.
Horace Wynne Challenge Cup – Winners: Penley; Runners-up: Castell Alun.
Under-18 Youth Cup – Winners: Hawarden Rangers Youth; Runners-up: Johnstown.
Under-16 Challenge Cup – Buckley and Bistre; Runners-up: RAFA.
Presidents Cup – Winners: Lex XI; Runners-up: Broughton Crusaders.
Central Wales Challenge Cup – Winners: Caersws; Runners-up: Morda.
J. Emrys Morgan Cup – Winners: Llanfair Caereinion; Runners-up: Vale of Arrow.
Youth Cup – Newtown Youth; Runners-up: Penrhyncoch Youth.

WELSH INTERMEDIATE CUP 1990–91

First Round

Bala Town v Rubery Owen Rockwell	2-3
Caldicot Town v Llantwit Major	2-0
Cardiff Civil Service v AFC Porth	0-1
Carmarthen Town v Albion Rovers	2-0
Carno v Llansantffraid	0-2
Corwen Amateurs v New Broughton	0-4
Croesyceiliog v Bryntirion Athletic	1-2
Fields Park Athletic v Llantwit Fardre	2-1
Goytre United v Cardiff Inst. Higher Education	1-4
Johnstown Athletic v Druids United	2-0
Knighton Town v Builth Wells	3-0
Llanfairpwll PG v Blaenau Ffestiniog Amateurs	4-0
Llanrug United v Llandudno	0-0, 2-1
Llanrwst United v Pwllheli Borough	3-0
Llwydcoed Welfare v Dinas Powys	1-2
Mostyn v Mochdre	3-0
Nefyn United v Locomotive Llanberis	2-4
Penparcau v Tywyn & Bryncrug	4-3
Penycae v Penley	1-3
Pilkington (St Asaph) v Llandyrnog United	5-2
Rhos Aelwyd v Rhostyllen MV	1-1, 2-0
Rhyl Victory Club v Deeside	2-0
Ruthin Town v Buckley	1-3
Tredomen v BSC Port Talbot	0-5
Treharris v Trelewis Welfare	3-1

Second Round

Afan Lido v Morriston Town	5-0
BSC Port Talbot v Pontyclun	2-0
Bethesda Athletic v Llanrug United	3-1
Brecon Corinthians v Morda United	0-1
Brymbo Steel Works v Buckley	3-3, 3-0
Bryntirion Athletic v Caldicot Town	1-0
Caermarthen Town v Cardiff Inst. Higher Education	3-2
Cefn Albion v Llay Royal British Legion	2-2, 3-4
Connah's Quay Nomads v Rhyl Victory Club	5-1
Felinheli v Nantlle Vale	4-0
Flint Town United v Conwy United	2-2, 3-1
Gresford Athletic v Chirk AAA	0-0, 0-3
Johnston Town v Marchwiel Villa	2-3
Kenfig Hill v AFC Porth	0-3
Knighton Town v Caersws	2-1
Llanfairpwll PG v Llanrwst United	4-1
Llanidloes Town v Aberystwyth Town	0-3
Llay Welfare v Lex XI	3-2
Locomotive Llanberis v Porthmadog	0-1
Mostyn v Holywell Town	1-1, 5-2
New Broughton v Rhos Aelwyd	1-1, 1-0
Newport Corinthians v Dinas Powys	1-3
Penley v Rubery Owen Rockwell	3-2
Penparcau v Penrhyncoch	1-1, 1-3
Risca United v Cardiff Corinthians	3-0

Taffs Well v Abergavenny Thursdays	1-7
Tondu v Fields Park Athletic	3-1
Treharris Athletic v Hirwaun Welfare	2-2, 1-2
Welshpool Town v Llansantffraid	0-2

Third Round

Chirk AAA v Marchwiel Villa	1-0

Fourth Round

AFC Porth v Afan Lido	1-3
Aberystwyth Town v Mold Alexandra	4-1
BSC Port Talbot v Abergavenny Thursdays	0-1
Brymbo Steelworks v Penrhyncoch	1-0
Bryntirion Athletic v Carmarthen Town	2-0
Chirk AAA v Llay Royal British Legion	1-0
Connah's Quay Nomads v Porthmadog	0-0, 2-3
Felinheli v Bethesda Athletic	2-1
Flint Town United v Mostyn	1-2
Hirwaun Welfare v Porthcawl Town	0-3
Llanfairpwll PG v Pilkington (St Asaph)	3-5
Llansantffraid v Knighton Town	2-3
Morda United v Llay Welfare	1-1, 3-2
Penley v New Broughton	2-2, 2-3
Ragged School v Dinas Powys	3-1
AFC Tondu v Risca United	3-0

Fifth Round

AFC Tondu v Felinheli	2-2, 0-3
Afan Lido v Porthmadog	3-1
Brymbo Steelworks v Porthcawl Town	1-3
Bryntirion Athletic v Abergavenny Thursdays	1-6
Chirk AAA v Morda United	2-0
Knighton Town v Mostyn	0-1
Pilkington (St Asaph) v Aberystwyth Town	1-4
Ragged School v New Broughton	1-2

Quarter-finals

Aberystwyth Town v Felinheli	4-1
Chirk AAA v Abergavenny Thursdays	0-4
Mostyn v Afan Lido	4-1
Porthcawl Town v New Broughton	1-1, 3-1

Semi-finals

Aberystwyth Town v Abergavenny Thursdays	0-0
(at Llanelli FC – abandoned 23 minutes)	
(at Aberystwyth Town FC)	1-3
Porthcawl Town v Mostyn	0-1
(at Caersws FC – abandoned 52 minutes)	
(at Welshpool Town FC)	2-3

Final

Abergavenny Thursdays v Mostyn	2-0
(at Llanidloes Town FC)	

ALLBRIGHT BITTER WELSH CUP 1990–91

First Round

Ammanford Town v Skewen Athletic	1-1, 7-6
BP Llandarcy v South Wales Constabulary	1-0
Bala Town v Rubery Owen Rockwell	5-0
Brecon Corinthians v Carmarthen Town	1-2
Bridgend Town v Seven Sisters	4-1
British Aerospace v Mochdre	1-8
Briton Ferry Athletic v Afan Lido	1-0
Brymbo Steel Works v Llay Welfare	2-0
Buckley v Lex XI	1-1
(aet, Lex won 3-0 on pens)	
Builth Wells v Llansantffraid	2-1
Caerleon v Caldicot Town	0-1
Caersws v Tywyn & Bryncrug	2-1
Cardiff Inst. Higher Education v Pontllanfraith	0-3
Carno v Worcester City	0-1
Chirk AAA v New Broughton	1-1, 1-0
Colwyn Bay v Bethesda Athletic	2-0
Connah's Quay Nomads v Pilkington (St Asaph)	5-2
Conwy United v Llanrwst United	3-2
Corwen Amateurs v Llay Royal British Legion	1-2
Ebbw Vale v Tonyrefail Welfare	3-0

Ferndale Athletic v Cheltenham Town	1-1, 0-4
Flint Town United v Ruthin Town	2-1
Knighton Town v Llanidloes Town	3-1
Llandudno v Llanfairpwll PG	1-1, 0-1
Llangefni Town v Pwllheli Borough	5-1
Locomotive Llanberis v Porthmadog	1-1, 1-4
Morda United v Hednesford Town	0-2
Mostyn v Rhyl Victory Club	4-2
Newport YMCA v Inter Cardiff	2-2, 2-4
Newtown v Penrhyncoch	5-0
Penycae v Gresford Athletic	1-1, 1-2
Pontardawe Athletic v Pembroke Borough	1-2
Pontllotyn Blast Furnace v AFC Newport	0-9
Pontyclun v Morriston Town	1-2
Port Talbot Athletic v Caerau	2-0
Rhos Aelwyd v Cefn Albion	3-5
Rhyl v Holywell Town	9-0
Risca United v Cardiff Civil Service	1-1, 3-7
Stourbridge v Welshpool Town	4-1
Stroud v Llanwern	3-0
Taffs Well v Abercynon Athletic	8-0
Trelewis v Cardiff Corinthians	0-2

Second Round

Abergavenny Thursdays v Carmarthen Town	4-0
Aberystwyth Town v Knighton Town	5-1
Ammanford Town v Cardiff Civil Service	3-0
Builth Wells v Cheltenham Town	1-5
(played at Cheltenham)	
Caldicot Town v Cardiff Corinthians	0-0, 0-2
Chirk AAA v Brymbo Steel Works	5-0
Connah's Quay Nomads v Colwyn Bay	0-1
Conwy United v Llangefni Town	0-3
Cwmbran Town v Maesteg Park Athletic	1-1, 1-0
Haverfordwest County v Ebbw Vale	3-0
Hednesford Town v Stourbridge	1-3
Inter Cardiff v Ton Pentre	0-2
Lex XI v Bala Town	3-0
Llanelli v Morriston Town	2-1
Llanfairpwll PG v Caernarfon Town	1-4
Llay Royal British Legion v Gresford Athletic	2-0
Mochdre v Flint Town United	0-3
AFC Newport v Pembroke Borough	3-0
Newtown v Cefn Albion	6-2
Pontllanfraith v Bridgend Town	0-3
Port Talbot Athletic v Briton Ferry Athletic	1-1
(aet, Briton Ferry Athletic won 7-6 on pens)	
Porthmadog v Bangor City	0-4
Rhyl v Mostyn	2-0
Stroud v Kidderminster Harriers	3-3, 3-2
Taffs Well v BP Llandarcy	0-2
Worcester City v Caersws	4-1

Third Round

Ammanford Town v Haverfordwest County	2-1
Bangor v Stourbridge	2-1
Bridgend Town v Abergavenny Thursdays	1-1
(Abergavenny Thursdays went through by default, Bridgend Town unable to field a team for replay)	

Briton Ferry Athletic v BP Llandarcy	0-1
Cardiff City v Merthyr Tydfil	1-4
Cardiff Corinthians v AFC Newport	0-3
(played at Newport)	
Chirk AAA v Stroud	0-3
Colwyn Bay v Rhyl	3-1
Cwmbran Town v Cheltenham Town	1-7
Flint Town United v Aberystwyth Town	1-2
Hereford United v Newtown	1-1
(aet, Newton won 5-4 on pens)	
Lex XI v Llangefni Town	4-3
Llay Royal British Legion v Caernarfon Town	0-2
Swansea City v Llanelli	8-1
Ton Pentre v Barry Town	0-1
Wrexham v Worcester City	3-1

Fourth Round

Aberystwyth Town v Hereford United	1-3
Ammanford Town v Wrexham	0-5
BP Llandarcy v Stroud	0-3
Bangor City v Lex XI	4-1
Barry Town v Cheltenham Town	3-1
Caernarfon Town v Abergavenny Thursdays	1-2
Merthyr Tydfil v Swansea City	1-2
AFC Newport v Colwyn Bay	0-1

Quarter-finals

Barry Town v Abergavenny Thursdays	1-1, 1-0
Colwyn Bay v Swansea City	1-1, 1-2
Hereford United v Bangor City	1-1
(Hereford United won 5-4 on pens)	
Stroud v Wrexham	1-2

Semi-finals

Barry Town v Swansea City	2-2, 0-1
Wrexham v Hereford United	1-1, 2-1

Final: Swansea City 2, Wrexham 0
(at Cardiff, 19 May 1991) Att: 5046

Swansea City: Kendall; Williams, Coleman, Hough, Trick, Legg, Watson (Chalmers), Raynor, Coughlin, Connor, Penney.
Scorers: Penney (pen), Raynor.

Wrexham: Morris; Thackeray (Owen), Hardy, Sertori, Phillips, Jones J, Bowden, Murray (Beaumont), Jones L, Preece, Griffiths.

Referee: K. Burge.

WELSH YOUTH CUP 1990–91

First Round

Abergavenny Thursdays v Worcester City	0-5
Cardiff Corinthians v South Wales Constabulary	1-5
Holyhead United v Bethesda Athletic *(Withdrawn)*	
Llanidloes v Caersws	1-6
Newport v Cardiff Civil Service	3-1
Penparcau v Aberystwyth Town	0-3
Penyffordd v Deeside	4-2
Pontlottyn Blast Furnace v Merthyr Tydfil	3-2
Pontyclun v Llantwit Fardre	1-4
Pwllheli v Caernarfon Town	1-2
Rhayader v Penrhyncoch	0-6
Rhyl v Lex XI *(Withdrawn)*	

Second Round

Aberystwyth Town v Newton	2-1
Briton Ferry v South Wales Constabulary	5-6
Caernarfon Town v Porthmadog	3-1
Caersws v Worcester City	
(Caersws withdrew; tie awarded to Worcester City)	
Caldicot Town v Cogan Coronation	4-0
Cwmbran Town v Newport	0-2
Hereford United v Penrhyncoch	2-0
Holyhead United v Llanrwst	6-0
Llantwit Fardre v Pontlottyn Blast Furnace	
(Pontlottyn Blast Furnace withdrew; tie awarded to Llantwit Fardre)	

Penyffordd v Mynydd Isa Youth	1-0
Rhyl v Wrexham Schools	0-1
Tregaron v Caerau	
(Caerau withdrew; tie awarded to Tregaron)	

Third Round

Caernarfon Town v Hawarden Rangers	0-9
Cardiff City v Llantwit Fardre	9-0
Newport v Hereford United	0-4
Penyffordd v Wrexham	2-5
South Wales Constabulary v Aberystwyth Town	3-1
Tregaron v Swansea City	0-12
Worcester City v Caldicot Town	2-2, 2-3
Wrexham Schools v Holyhead United	5-0

Quarter-finals

Caldicot Town v South Wales Constabulary	0-3
Hereford United v Hawarden Rangers	1-3
Swansea City v Cardiff City	3-1
Wrexham Schools v Wrexham	2-3

Semi-finals

Hawarden Rangers v Wrexham	0-4
Swansea City v South Wales Constabulary	1-0

Final

Swansea City v Wrexham	0-1

NORTHERN IRISH FOOTBALL 1990–91

Mid-Ulster clubs dominated Northern Ireland domestic football in the 1990–91 season with Portadown retaining the Smirnoff Irish League championship and winning the Bass Irish Cup for the first time in their history. It was a remarkable and deserved double by a team which revealed skill, flair, goal-scoring power and consistency.

Portadown also won the Lombard Ulster Cup, Budweiser Cup and Ronnie McFall was named Manager of the Year, while arch rivals Glenavon, beaten Cup finalists, collected three trophies. Bangor finished runners-up and gained a UEFA Cup place.

For the second successive year Linfield, so long the dominant club of Irish football, failed to qualify for Europe and so, too, did Glentoran, although they were constant championship challengers to Portadown throughout the season.

Yet again the Irish League, completing a successful centenary season, have had all competitions commercially backed with the Football Trust announcing there would be a substantial increase in the £300,000 grant aid allocated to the 16 clubs over the next two years for ground improvements.

Internationally, it was a season of mixed fortunes, some promising results by a team which, under manager Billy Bingham, has revealed signs of maturing and development. But then came the let down in the 1-1 draw against the fledgling Faroe Islands at Windsor Park on a night when forwards should have scored half a dozen goals. Good build-up and 90 per cent possession, however, came to nothing.

The Irish FA hit the jackpot with a £200,000 three year sponsorship by Vauxhall for internationals at all levels. The package also includes marketing and promotional incentives in an attempt to regenerate interest in and awareness of the game in the build-up to the 1994 World Cup finals. The cash input has also enabled the IFA to appoint a commercial manager.

There were some surprise managerial changes. Bertie McMinn quit Ards, Roy Coyle, formerly with Linfield, took over but left Castlereagh Park in early May to join League of Ireland side Derry City.

Alex McKee resigned from Ballymena United with Jim Hagan, ex-Coventry City and Birmingham centre-half, taking over; Paul Malone moved from Larne to Ards; Paul McAnea departed from Omagh Town with Roy McCreadie (Portadown) nominated as his successor.

Belfast Celtic, who withdrew from football in 1949, but still function as a limited company, held their centenary dinner at the Europa Hotel, Belfast, in April — a glittering, nostalgic affair attended by more than 400 including many ex-players from all parts of the world, officials of the various Football Associations' all Irish League clubs and Jack McGinn, Glasgow Celtic chairman. It was presided over by Harry Walker, last captain of Celtic who also unveiled a plaque at the Park Shopping Complex on the Donegal Road — the site of Celtic Park or Paradise as it was known to the fans.

The Intermediate League side Donegal Celtic were again unable to play their Irish Cup matches against a senior side at home. They were scheduled to meet Ards in a replay but police refused them permission on the grounds of security and public order and, after consultations with the IFA, the club decided to withdraw from the competition for the second successive season.

MALCOLM BRODIE

SMIRNOFF IRISH LEAGUE CHAMPIONSHIP
FINAL TABLE

	P	W	D	L	F	A	Pts
Portadown	30	22	5	3	61	22	77
Bangor	30	19	4	7	52	29	61
Glentoran	30	18	6	6	50	32	60
Glenavon	30	17	6	7	63	38	57
Newry Town	30	15	5	10	50	42	50
Cliftonville	30	14	7	9	59	41	49
Linfield	30	12	10	8	40	34	46
Ballymena	30	12	8	10	49	46	44
Ards	30	12	7	11	47	40	43
Crusaders	30	11	9	10	53	46	42
Distillery	30	10	5	15	47	57	35
Omagh Town	30	10	4	16	48	66	34
Larne	30	8	6	16	41	59	30
Ballyclare	30	5	6	19	33	68	21
Carrick	30	4	5	21	30	58	17
Coleraine	30	2	5	23	25	70	11

BUDWEISER CUP

Final

(Windsor Park, 11 December 1990)

Glenavon 0
Portadown 2 *(Davidson, Cowan)*

Glenavon: Robson C; McKeown, Scappiticci, McCullough, Byrne, Russell (Robson B), McConville, McCoy, Ferguson, McBride, Ferris (Cochrane).

Portadown: Keenan; Major, Curliss, Cunningham, Strain, Stewart (McKeever), Doolin, Mills, Magee, Cowan, Davidson.

Referee: D Magill (Belfast).

Semi-finals Glenavon 3 Omagh Town 0 *(at Shamrock Park)*
Portadown 2 Ballymena United 2 *(Portadown won 5-3 after penalties) at Seaview, Belfast).*

Previous winners: 1988: Glentoran; 1989: Glenavon; 1990: Glentoran

IRISH LEAGUE CHAMPIONSHIP WINNERS

1891 Linfield	1909 Linfield	1931 Glentoran	1956 Linfield	1974 Coleraine
1892 Linfield	1910 Cliftonville	1932 Glentoran	1957 Glentoran	1975 Linfield
1893 Linfield	1911 Linfield	1933 Belfast Celtic	1958 Ards	1976 Crusaders
1894 Glentoran	1912 Glentoran	1934 Linfield	1959 Linfield	1977 Glentoran
1895 Linfield	1913 Glentoran	1935 Linfield	1960 Glenavon	1978 Linfield
1896 Distillery	1914 Linfield	1936 Belfast Celtic	1961 Linfield	1979 Linfield
1897 Glentoran	1915 Belfast Celtic	1937 Belfast Celtic	1962 Linfield	1980 Linfield
1898 Linfield	1920 Belfast Celtic	1938 Belfast Celtic	1963 Distillery	1981 Glentoran
1899 Distillery	1921 Glentoran	1939 Belfast Celtic	1964 Glentoran	1982 Linfield
1900 Belfast Celtic	1922 Linfield	1940 Belfast Celtic	1965 Derry City	1983 Linfield
1901 Distillery	1923 Linfield	1948 Belfast Celtic	1966 Linfield	1984 Linfield
1902 Linfield	1924 Queen's Island	1949 Linfield	1967 Glentoran	1985 Linfield
1903 Distillery	1925 Glentoran	1950 Linfield	1968 Glentoran	1986 Linfield
1904 Linfield	1926 Belfast Celtic	1951 Glentoran	1969 Linfield	1987 Linfield
1905 Glentoran	1927 Belfast Celtic	1952 Glenavon	1970 Glentoran	1988 Glentoran
1906 Cliftonville/Dist	1928 Belfast Celtic	1953 Glentoran	1971 Linfield	1989 Linfield
1907 Linfield	1929 Belfast Celtic	1954 Linfield	1972 Glentoran	1990 Portadown
1908 Linfield	1930 Linfield	1955 Linfield	1973 Crusaders	1991 Portadown

LOMBARD ULSTER CUP

SECTIONAL TABLES

Section A	P	W	D	L	F	A	Pts
Portadown	3	3	0	0	8	2	9
Ballymena Utd	3	1	0	2	6	0	0
Larne	3	1	0	2	4	8	3
Crusaders	3	1	0	2	5	6	3

Section B	P	W	D	L	F	A	Pts
Glenavon	3	3	0	0	12	2	9
Bangor	3	2	0	1	6	2	6
Carrick Rangers	3	0	1	2	4	11	1
Distillery	3	0	1	2	3	10	1

Section C	P	W	D	L	F	A	Pts
Glentoran	3	2	1	0	6	1	7
Coleraine	3	2	0	1	4	3	6
Newry Town	3	1	1	1	4	2	4
Ballyclare Comrades	3	0	0	3	2	6	0

Section D	P	W	D	L	F	A	Pts
Cliftonville	3	1	2	0	3	2	5
Linfield	3	1	2	0	2	1	5
Ards	3	1	1	1	3	3	4
Omagh Town	3	0	1	2	1	3	1

Quarter-finals
Glentoran 0 Linfield 1; Cliftonville 1 Coleraine 1 (Coleraine won 5-4 on penalties)
Portadown 2 Bangor 1; Glenavon 4 Ballymena United 0.

Semi-finals
Portadown 4 Linfield 2 (Oval); Glenavon 5 Coleraine 1

Final
(at the Oval, 25 September 1990)
Glenavon 1 *(Ferguson)*
Portadown 1 *(Cunningham)*
Glenavon: Beck; McCullough, Scappaticci, McCann, Byrne, McLoughlin, McConville, Ferguson, Blackledge, McBride, Conville.
Portadown: Keenan; Major, Curliss, McKeever, Strain, Stewart, Doolin, (Davidson), McCreadie, Fraser, Cowan, Cunningham.
Referee: F. McKnight (Newtownards). Attendance 4,600

Replay
(The Oval, 23 October 1990).
Portadown 1 *(Cunningham)*
Glenavon 1 *(Ferris) (aet)*
Portadown won 3-2 on penalties
Portadown: Kennan; Major, Curliss, Cunningham (McKeever), Strain, Stewart, Doolin, McCreadie, Fraser (Williamson), Cowan, Davidson.
Glenavon: Beck; McCullough, Scappaticci, Russell (Campbell), Byrne, McLaughlin (Ferris), McConville, Ferguson, Blackledge, McBride, Conville.
Referee: R. Stewart (Dunmurry).
Attendance 7,000

Winners

1949	Linfield	1960	Linfield	1971	Linfield	1982	Glentoran
1950	Larne	1961	Ballymena U	1972	Coleraine	1983	Glentoran
1951	Glentoran	1962	Linfield	1973	Ards	1984	Linfield
1952		1963	Crusaders	1974	Linfield	1985	Coleraine
1953	Glentoran	1964	Linfield	1975	Coleraine	1986	Coleraine
1954	Crusaders	1965	Coleraine	1976	Glentoran	1987	Larne
1955	Glenavon	1966	Glentoran	1977	Linfield	1988	Glentoran
1956	Linfield	1967	Linfield	1978	Linfield	1989	Glentoran
1957	Linfield	1968	Coleraine	1979	Linfield	1990	Portadown
1958	Distillery	1969	Coleraine	1980	Ballymena U		
1959	Glenavon	1970	Linfield	1981	Glentoran		

TNT GOLD CUP

FINAL SECTIONAL TABLES

Section A	P	W	D	L	F	A	Pts
Portadown	3	1	2	0	4	3	5
Distillery	3	1	1	1	4	3	4
Carrick Rangers	3	1	1	1	2	4	4
Newry	3	1	0	2	5	5	3

Section B	P	W	D	L	F	A	Pts
Cliftonville	3	2	1	0	6	2	7
Ballymena Utd	3	1	1	1	4	4	4
Coleraine	3	1	1	1	2	2	4
Ards	3	0	1	2	4	8	1

Section C	P	W	D	L	F	A	Pts
Bangor	3	2	1	0	6	3	7
Larne	3	1	2	0	5	4	5
Ballyclare Comrades	3	0	2	1	1	2	2
Linfield	3	0	1	2	2	5	1

Section D	P	W	D	L	F	A	Pts
Glenavon	3	2	0	1	10	8	6
Omagh	3	2	0	1	8	7	6
Crusaders	3	1	0	2	8	9	3
Glentoran	3	1	0	2	3	5	3

Quarter-finals
Cliftonville 3 Distillery 1; Portadown 3 Ballymena Utd 1; Bangor 1 Omagh Town 0; Glenavon 1 Larne 0.

Semi-finals
Glenavon 2 Cliftonville 1 *(Windsor Park)*
Portadown 1 Bangor 0 *(The Oval) aet*

Final
(at Windsor Park, Belfast, 20 November 1990)
Portadown 1 *(Cunningham)*
Glenavon 2 *(McCullough, McBride pen)*
Portadown: Keenan; Major, Curliss (Magee), Cunningham, Strain, Stewart, Doolin, McCreadie (McKeever), Cowan, Fraser, Davidson.
Glenavon: Beck; Davies, Scappaticci, McCullough, Byrne, Ferguson (Russell), McConville, McCoy, Ferris, McBride, Conville.
Referee: N. Loughins (Belfast).

Winners

1946	Belfast Celtic	1958	Coleraine	1970	Linfield	1982	Linfield
1947	Belfast Celtic	1959	Linfield	1971	Linfield	1983	Glentoran
1948	Linfield	1960	Glentoran	1972	Portadown	1984	Linfield
1949	Linfield	1961	Linfield	1973	Linfield	1985	Linfield
1950	Linfield	1962	Glentoran	1974	Ards	1986	Crusaders
1951	Glentoran	1963	Linfield	1975	Ballymena U	1987	Glentoran
1952	Portadown	1964	Derry City	1976	Coleraine	1988	Linfield
1953	Ards	1965	Linfield	1977	Glentoran	1989	Linfield
1954	Glenavon	1966	Glentoran	1978	Glentoran	1990	Linfield
1955	Glenavon	1967	Linfield	1979	Portadown	1991	Glenavon
1956	Glenavon	1968	Linfield	1980	Linfield		
1957	Linfield	1969	Coleraine	1981	Cliftonville		

BASS IRISH CUP 1990–91

First Round

Ballynahinch Utd v East Belfast	1-4
GEC (Larne) v Comber Rec	1-2
Dundela v H & W Sport	2-0
Downshire v Cullybackey	0-2
Dromara Village v Annalong Swifts	1-4
Dervock Utd v Connor	4-4, 2-5
Mosside Utd v Bangor Amateurs	2-4
Fisher Body v STC	0-3
Newtownabbey Town v Jordanstown	1-0
Shorts v Bridgend Utd	2-0
Institute v H & W Welders	1-6
RUC v Oxford Utd Stars	2-1
Armagh Thistle v Roe Valley	1-0
UU Coleraine v Killymoon Rangers	1-2
Islandmagee v AFC	0-2
Killyleagh v Drumaness Mills	4-2
Loughgall v Donard Hospital	3-1
Queen's University v 1st Bangor	1-1, 1-0
Barn Utd v Cromac Albion	1-1, 0-3
Larne Tech OB v Moyola Park	2-2, 3-3
(Larne Tech won 7-6 on penalties)	
Orangefield OB v Annagh Utd	3-2
FC Enkalon v Civil Service	3-0
Tandragee Rovers v Magherafelt	5-2
Macosquin v 1st Liverpool	6-3
Glebe Rangers v Dromore Amateurs	3-2
Armoy Utd v Portstewart	3-0
British Telecom v Hanover	3-2

Byes
Crumlin Utd, Armagh City, Portglenone, Ards Rangers, Nitos Athletic, Kilmore Rec, Sirocco Works, Ballymoney Utd, Star of the Sea, Limavady Utd, Magherafelt Sky Blues, Saintfield Utd, Rathfriland Rangers.

Second Round

Ards Rangers v Magherafelt Sky Blues	5-4
Sirocco Works v Star of the Sea	5-1
Crumlin Utd v Comber Res	0-1
Larne Tech OB v British Telecom	0-1
Cullybackey v Glebe Rangers	1-1, 1-3
Queen's University v Killymoon Rangers	1-0
Killyleagh v H & W Welders	1-3
Connor v Cromac Albion	0-0, 3-2
Nitos Athletic v Armagh Thistle	0-2
Dundela v Kilmore Rec	5-1
Orangefield OB v Armoy Utd	5-1
STC v RUC	1-1, 0-1
Saintfield v Macosquin	0-0, 2-2
(Saintfield won 6-4 on penalties)	
Portglenone v Shorts	1-3
Loughgall v AFC	3-1
Bangor Amateurs v Newtownabbey Town	3-0
East Belfast v Limavady Utd	3-1
Tandragee Rovers v FC Enkalon	2-4
Armagh City v Rathfriland Rangers	2-1
Annalong Swifts v Ballymoney Utd	3-2

Third Round

Bangor Amateurs v Saintfield Utd	4-2
Shorts v FC Enkalon	2-0
Comber Rec v Ards Rangers	5-1
British Telecom v Connor	2-1
RUC v East Belfast	1-2
Armagh Thistle v Loughgall	0-2

Orangefield OB v Dundela	0-3
H & W Welders v Glebe Rangers	5-3
Sirocco Works v Armagh City	1-1, 0-3
Annalong Swifts v Queen's University	1-0

Fourth Round

H & W Welders v Bangor Amateurs	2-1
British Telecom v Dundela	2-2, 0-2
Annalong Swifts v Loughgall	1-3
Comber Rec v East Belfast	0-0, 0-4
Armagh City v Shorts	1-2

Fifth Round

Portadown v Newry Town	0-0, 2-0
Cliftonville v Dundela	2-1
Distillery v Crusaders	0-1
Brantwood v Glenavon	0-2
Omagh Town v Ballymena Utd	3-2
Dunmurry Rec v Bangor	1-3
Linfield v H & W Welders	1-1, 4-1
Crewe Utd v Coagh Utd	0-3
Larne v East Belfast	4-1
Coleraine v Banbridge Town	3-1
Cookstown Utd v Donegal Celtic	0-1
Carrick Rangers v Shorts	2-1
Chimney Corner v Ballyclare Comrades	1-5
Tobermore Utd v Loughgall	2-1
Ballinamallard Utd v Glentoran	0-4
Dungannon Swifts v Ards	1-3

Sixth Round

Coagh Utd v Ballyclare Comrades	0-7
Linfield v Coleraine	2-0
Portadown v Omagh Town	3-1
Glentoran v Tobermore Utd	9-1
Glenavon v Bangor	2-0
Ards v Donegal Celtic	0-0
Carrick Rangers v Larne	1-3
Cliftonville v Crusaders	0-0, 2-3

NB: Police vetoed the Donegal Celtic v Ards replay at Celtic Park because of security implications and public order. The Irish FA Senior Clubs Committee then instructed that it be played at Castlereagh Park under Irish Cup rules but Donegal Celtic decided to withdraw from the competition.

Quarter-finals

Larne v Glentoran	1-1, 1-4
Crusaders v Portadown	2-4
Ards v Linfield	3-2
Glenavon v Ballyclare Comrades	4-0

Semi-finals

Ards v Portadown *(Oval)*	0-2
Glenavon v Glentoran *(Windsor Park)*	3-1

Final
(at Windsor Park, 4 May 1991)
Portadown 2 *(Cowan 2)*
Glenavon 1 *(Ferguson)* — *attendance 12,000*
Portadown: Keenan; Major, Curliss, Cunningham, Strain, Stewart, Doolin, Rafferty, Fraser, Cowan, Davidson.
Glenavon: Beck; McKeown, Scappaticci, McCullough, Byrne, Russell (McCann), McDermott (Davies), McCoy, Ferguson, McBride, McConville.
Referee: L. Irvine (Limavady).

IRISH CUP FINALS (from 1946–47)

1946–47	Belfast Celtic 1, Glentoran 0	1962–63	Linfield 2, Distillery 1	1977–78	Linfield 3, Ballymena U 1
1947–48	Linfield 3, Coleraine 0	1963–64	Derry City 2, Glentoran 0	1978–79	Cliftonville 3, Portadown 2
1948–49	Derry City 3, Glentoran 1	1964–65	Coleraine 2, Glenavon 1	1979–80	Linfield 2, Crusaders 0
1949–50	Linfield 2, Distillery 1	1965–66	Glentoran 2, Linfield 0	1980–81	Ballymena U 1, Glenavon 0
1950–51	Glentoran 3, Ballymena U 1	1966–67	Crusaders 3, Glentoran 1	1981–82	Linfield 2, Coleraine 1
1951–52	Ards 1, Glentoran 0	1967–68	Crusaders 2, Linfield 0	1982–83	Glentoran 1 : 2, Linfield 1 : 1
1952–53	Linfield 5, Coleraine 0	1968–69	Ards 4, Distillery 2	1983–84	Ballymena U 4,
1953–54	Derry City 1, Glentoran 0	1969–70	Linfield 2, Ballymena U 1		Carrick Rangers 1
1954–55	Dundela 3, Glenavon 0	1970–71	Distillery 3, Derry City 0	1984–85	Glentoran 2, Coleraine 1
1955–56	Distillery 1, Glentoran 0	1971–72	Coleraine 2, Portadown 1	1984–85	Glentoran 1 : 1, Linfield 1 : 0
1956–57	Glenavon 2, Derry City 0	1972–73	Glentoran 3, Linfield 2	1985–86	Glentoran 2, Coleraine 1
1957–58	Ballymena U 2, Linfield 0	1973–74	Ards 2, Ballymena U 1	1986–87	Glentoran 1, Larne 0
1958–59	Glenavon 2, Ballymena U 0	1974–75	Coleraine 1 : 0 : 1,	1987–88	Glentoran 1, Glenavon 0
1959–60	Linfield 5, Ards 1		Linfield 1 : 0 : 0	1988–89	Ballymena U 1, Larne 0
1960–61	Glenavon 5, Linfield 1	1975–76	Carrick Rangers 2, Linfield 1	1989–90	Glentoran 3, Portadown 0
1961–62	Linfield 4, Portadown 0	1976–77	Coleraine 4, Linfield 1	1990–91	Portadown 2, Glenavon 1

FOOTBALL AND THE LAW

Football and the law hardly could avoid each other during season 1990–91, both on and off the field, in the Council Chamber and in Court.

The domestic dimension peaked with the public order conflict between Manchester United and Arsenal at Old Trafford before Christmas 1990. The police were content to let the punishment fit the crime within the FA's jurisdiction, and this produced two original dimensions.

Each club was fined substantially by the FA, who also deducted Football League points. More significantly, Arsenal's directorate fined its manager. After the Championship had been won, Arsenal's chairman was reported in the London *Evening Standard* to have called the potentially destructive penalty, 'a silly decision'. Perhaps it was not so silly if it had the desired effect to warn everyone at Highbury, Old Trafford and beyond, of the consequences of field misconduct and, indeed, ultimately shaped the season's ultimate success.

A more permanent domestic sanction within the game was FIFA's decision belatedly to accept the FA's proposal and operate a mandatory red card for the so-called professional foul. Sadly, the consequences of uniform or consistent interpretation was never thought through, and Keith Hackett's debatable application of it to the tackle by West Ham United's Tony Gale in the FA Cup semi-final against Nottingham Forest highlighted the problem.

Elsewhere Tottenham Hotspur were never far away from the legal columns. The Stock Exchange suspended share dealings in its holding company Tottenham Hotspur Plc, and Paul Gascoigne suffered a set-back when he failed in the Chancery Division of the High Court to injunct publication of an unauthorised biography.

Finally, since the law also stems from Parliament in addition to the Courts the Home Affairs Committee of the House of Commons published a Report on Policing Football Hooliganism and also a Bill which will become law before season 1991–92 to outlaw disorderly conduct including throwing missiles.

If it had existed in 1984, Reading Football Club might have been able to avoid the disorderly conduct which ended in the High Court with a substantial damages award to police officers who had been injured with materials picked up by spectators from within the ground, for which the club was held responsible.

As Parliament extends its control, and clubs become responsible in the manner manifested by the Arsenal directorate, football will perhaps need less of the law than it has this season and in the past. Only time and the conduct of all involved within the game can tell how far this could ever be possible.

EDWARD GRAYSON

Barclays Bank Manager of the Year George Graham of Arsenal receives his award—the Barclays trophy and a Barclays Higher Rate Deposit Account Cheque for £5,000—from Barclays Chairman, Sir John Quinton. It was George's second Manager of the Year award in three seasons.

INTERNATIONAL
FOOTBALL

INTERNATIONAL DIRECTORY

EUROPEAN CHAMPIONSHIP

EUROPEAN CLUB RESULTS

BRITISH AND IRISH INTERNATIONAL RESULTS
AND APPEARANCES

UNDER-21, UNDER-18 AND UNDER-16

WOMEN'S EUROPEAN CHAMPIONSHIP

SCHOOLS AND YOUTH FOOTBALL

SOUTH AMERICA AND OTHER
INTERNATIONAL FOOTBALL

OLYMPICS

INTERNATIONAL DIRECTORY

The latest available information has been given regarding numbers of clubs and players registered with FIFA, the world governing body. Where known, official colours are listed. With European countries, League tables show a number of signs. * indicates relegated teams, + play-offs, * + relegated after play-offs. In Yugoslavia, drawn matches result in penalty shoot-outs, the winners receiving a point.

There are 165 FIFA members. These include the four home countries, England, Scotland, Northern Ireland and Wales, dealt with elsewhere in the Yearbook; but basic details appear in this directory.

EUROPE

ALBANIA

Federation Albanaise De Football, Rruga Dervish Hima Nr. 31, Tirana.
Founded: 1930; *Number of Clubs:* 49; *Number of Players:* 3,757; *National Colours:* Red shirts, black shorts, red stockings.
Telephone: 72-56; *Cable:* ALBSPORT TIRANA; *Telex:* 2142.

International matches 1990

Iceland (a) 0-2, Greece (a) 0-1, France (h) 0-1, Spain (a) 0-9.

League Championship wins (1945–91)

Dinamo Tirana 15; Partizan Tirana 14; 17 Nentori 8; Vlaznia 6; Flamurtari 1; Labinoti 1.

Cup wins (1948–91)

Dinamo Tirana 12; Partizan Tirana 12; 17 Nentori 6; Vllaznia 5; Flamurtari 2; Labinoti 1.

Final League Table 1990–91

	P	W	D	L	F	A	Pts
Flamurtari	39	24	6	9	63	32	54
Partizan Tirana	39	18	12	9	52	35	48
Vllaznia	39	16	13	10	58	49	45
17 Nentori	39	16	12	11	52	40	44
Tomori	39	13	14	12	62	46	40
Dinamo	39	13	14	12	53	44	40
Apolonia	39	13	12	14	49	47	38
Lokomotiva	39	12	15	12	30	38	36
Labinoti	39	11	14	14	29	37	36
Skenderbeu	39	10	15	14	45	55	35
Besa	39	11	12	16	45	50	34
Kastrioti	39	12	10	17	41	62	34
Traktori	39	12	10	17	41	62	32
Luftetari*	39	12	6	21	31	55	30

Top scorer: Bozgo (Tomori) 29
Cup Final: Partizan 1, Flamurtari 1
Partizan won 5–3 on penalties

AUSTRIA

Oesterreichischer Fussball-Bund, Wiener Stadion, Sektor A/F, Meierestrasse, A-1020 Wien.
Founded: 1904; *Number of Clubs:* 1,992; *Number of Players:* 253,576; *National Colours:* White shirts, black shorts, black stockings.
Telephone: 0043-1-217 18; *Cable:* FOOTBALL WIEN; *Telex:* 111919 OEFB A; *Fax:* 0043-1-218 16 32.

International matches 1990

Egypt (a) 0-0, Spain (a) 3-2, Hungary (h) 3-0, Argentina (h) 1-1, Holland (h) 3-2, Italy (n) 0-1, Czechoslovakia (n) 0-1, USA (n) 2-1, Switzerland (h) 1-3, Faeroes (a) 0-1, Yugoslavia (a) 1-4, Northern Ireland (h) 0-0.
Goalscorers: Ogris 4, Rodax 2, Zsak 2, Artner 1, Hortnagl 1, Keglevits 1, Pecl 1, Pfeffer 1, Polster 1.

League Championship wins (1912–91)

Rapid Vienna 29; Austria/Vienna (prev. Austria/WAC, FK Austria and WAC) 20; Admira-Energie-Wacker (prev. Sportklub Admira & Admira-Energie) 8; First Vienna 6; Tirol-Svarowski-Innsbruck (prev. Wacker Innsbruck) 7; Wiener Sportklub 3; FAC 1; Hakoah 1; Linz ASK 1; Wacker Vienna 1; WAF 1; Voest Linz 1.

Cup wins (1919–91)

Austria/WAC 23; Rapid Vienna 13; TS Innsbruck (prev. Wacker Innsbruck) 6; Admira-Energie-Wacker (prev. Sportklub Admira & Admira-Energie) 5; First Vienna 3; Linz ASK 1; Wacker Vienna 1; WAF 1; Wiener Sportklub 1; Graz 1; Stockerau 1.

Qualifying Table

	P	W	D	L	F	A	Pts
Tirol	22	13	6	3	49	18	32
FK Austria	22	12	6	4	48	21	30
Rapid	22	13	3	6	47	21	29
Sturm Graz	22	11	5	6	42	25	27
Austria Salzburg	22	12	2	8	38	28	26
Vorwaerts	22	8	6	8	32	33	22
Alpine	22	6	9	7	25	33	21
Admira Wacker	22	6	7	9	17	29	19
Wiener SC	22	7	3	12	25	42	17
Vienna	22	6	5	11	29	48	17
Krems SC	22	3	7	12	18	40	13
St Polten	22	3	5	14	18	50	11

Final League Table 1990–91

	P	W	D	L	F	A	Pts
FK Austria	36	22	6	7	73	30	36
Tirol	36	21	9	6	78	35	35
Sturm Graz	36	18	10	9	60	37	32
Rapid	36	18	5	13	67	41	27
Austria Salzburg	36	16	8	13	58	37	24
Admira Wacker	36	9	14	13	30	47	23
Vorwaerts	36	10	11	15	46	62	21
Alpine	36	8	11	16	38	63	19

Top scorer: Danek (Tirol) 29
Cup Final: Stockerau 2, Rapid 1
Promotion: Voest Linz, Krems, St Polten, Vienna
Relegation: Modling, Linz ASK, Stockerau, Wiener SC

BELGIUM

Union Royale Belge Des Societes De Football; Eturl, Association, Rue De La Loi 43, Boite 1, B-1040 Bruxelles.
Founded: 1895; *Number of Clubs:* 3,362; *Number of Players:* 289,770; *National Colours:* Red shirts with tri-coloured trim, red shorts, red stockings with trim.
Telephone: 32 2 477 1211; *Cable:* UBSFA BRUXELLES; *Telex:* 23257 BVBFBF B; *Fax:* 32 2 2147 82391.

International matches 1990

Greece (a) 0-2, Sweden (h) 0-0, Romania (h) 2-2, Mexico (h) 3-0, Poland (h) 1-1, South Korea (n) 2-0, Uruguay (n) 3-1, Spain (n) 1-2, England (n) 0-1, East Germany (h) 0-2, Wales (a) 1-3.
Goalscorers: Degryse 3, Clijsters 2, Scifo 2, Versavel 2, Ceulemans 1, Dewolf 1, Emmers 1, Vervoort 1.

League Championship wins (1896–1991)

Anderlecht 21; Union St Gilloise 11; Standard Liège 8; Beerschot 7; FC Brugge 8; RC Brussels 6; FC Liège 5; Daring Brussels 5; Antwerp 4; Mechelen 4; Lierse SK 3; SV Brugge 3; Beveren 2; RWD Molenbeek 1.

Cup wins (1954–91)

Anderlecht 7; FC Brugge 5; Standard Liège 4; Beerschot 2; Waterschei 2; Beveren 2; Gent 2; Antwerp 1; Lierse SK 1; Racing Doornik 1; Waregem 1; SV Brugge 1; Mechelen 1; FC Liège 1.

Final League Table 1990–91

	P	W	D	L	F	A	Pts
Anderlecht	34	23	7	4	74	22	53
Mechelen	34	20	10	4	59	24	50
FC Brugge	34	18	11	5	61	27	47
Gent	34	20	7	7	67	37	47
Ekeren	34	17	8	9	55	41	42
Standard Liège	34	16	10	8	51	42	42
Antwerp	34	11	14	9	54	45	36
Charleroi	34	9	15	10	36	36	33
FC Liège	34	11	10	13	42	45	32
Lokeren	34	12	8	14	41	45	32
RWD Molenbeek	34	10	8	16	40	45	28
Waregem	34	8	12	14	33	45	28
Genk	34	10	8	16	33	64	28
Lierse SK	34	8	11	15	24	43	27
Kortrijk	34	10	5	19	41	57	25
CS Brugge	34	9	7	18	40	73	25
St Truiden*	34	6	10	18	30	51	22
Beerschot*	34	5	5	24	33	72	15

Top scorer: Vandenbergh (Gent) 23
Cup Final: FC Brugge 3, Mechelen 1

BULGARIA

Bulgarian Football Union, Gotcho Gopin 19, 1000 Sofia.
Founded: 1923; *Number of Clubs:* 4,328; *Number of Players:* 442,829. *National Colours:* White shirts, green shorts, red stockings.
Telephone: 87 74 90; *Cable:* BULFUTBOL; *Telex:* 23145 BFS BG; *Fax:* 87 74 90.

International matches 1990

Brazil (a) 1-2, Switzerland (a) 0-2, Sweden (a) 0-2, Romania (a) 3-0, Scotland (h) 1-1.
Goalscorers: Todorov 3, Kostadinov 1, Sirakov 1.

League Championship wins (1925–91)

CFKA Sredets (prev. CSKA Sofia, CDNA) 26; Levski Spartak (prev. Levski Sofia) 16; Slavia Sofia 6; Vladislav Varna 3; Lokomotiv Sofia 3; Trakia Plovdiv 2; AS 23 Sofia 1; Botev Plovdiv 1; SC Sofia 1; Sokol Varna 1; Spartak Plovdiv 1; Tichka Varna 1; ZSK Sofia 1; Beroe Stara Zagora 1; Etur 1.

Cup wins (1946–91)

Levski Spartak (prev. Levski Sofia) 16; CFKA Sredets (prev. CSKA Sofia, CDNA) 13; Slavia Sofia 6; Lokomotiv Sofia 3; Botev Plovdiv 1; Spartak Plovdiv 1; Spartak Sofia 1; Marek Stanke 1; Trakia Plovdiv 1; Spartak Varna 1; Sliven 1.

Final League Table 1990–91

	P	W	D	L	F	A	Pts
Etur	30	18	8	4	49	21	44
Slavia Sofia	30	15	8	7	53	31	38
CSKA Sofia	30	14	8	8	53	33	36
Botev Plovdiv	30	13	10	7	49	41	36
Lokomotiv Sofia	30	12	11	7	46	35	35
Levski Sofia	30	12	9	9	50	37	33
Tschernomoretz	30	11	8	11	41	50	30
Lokomotiv Gorna	30	13	3	14	42	39	29
Mineur	30	10	8	12	35	40	28
Beroe	30	10	7	13	37	40	27
Lokomotiv Plovdiv	30	9	9	12	34	42	27
Pirin	30	11	4	15	38	40	26
Sliven	30	9	8	13	39	49	26
Yantra	30	9	8	13	31	44	26
Dounav*	30	8	6	16	23	42	22
Haskovo*	30	7	3	20	27	63	17

Top scorer: Yordanov (Lokomotiv Gorna) 21
Cup Final: Levski 2, Botev Plovdiv 1

CYPRUS

Cyprus Football Association, Stasinos Str. 1, Engomi 152, P.O. Box 5071, Nicosia.
Founded: 1934; *Number of Clubs:* 87; *Number of Players:* 23,000; *National Colours:* Sky blue shirts, white shorts, blue and white stockings.
Telephone: (2) 44 53 41, 44 53 42, 45 99 59; *Cable:* FOOTBALL NICOSIA; *Telex:* 3880 FOOTBALL CY; *Fax:* (2) 47 25 44.

International matches 1990

Hungary (a) 2-4, Norway (h) 0-3, Italy (h) 0-4.
Goalscorers: Tsolakis 1, Xiourouppas 1.

League Championship wins (1935–91)

Omonia 16; Apoel 14; Anorthosis 6; AEL 5; EPA 3; Olympiakos 3; Pezoporikos 2; Chetin Kayal 1; Trast 1; Apollon 1.

Cup wins (1935–91)

Apoel 12; Omonia 9; AEL 6; EPA 5; Anorthosis 4; Apollon 3; Trast 3; Chetin Kayal 2; Olympiakos 1; Pezoporikos; Salamina 1.

Final League Table 1990–91

	P	W	D	L	F	A	Pts
Apollon	26	19	6	1	60	20	44
Anorthosis	26	18	5	3	42	14	41
Apoel	26	13	9	4	48	23	35
Omonia	26	12	7	7	41	22	31
AEL	26	10	8	8	36	36	28
Salamina	26	9	9	8	38	31	27
Pezoporikos	26	8	11	7	35	28	27
Aris	26	9	6	11	33	40	24
Alki	26	8	8	10	32	40	24
EPA	26	7	10	9	29	37	24
Olympiakos	26	7	9	10	36	37	23
Paralimni	26	7	7	12	33	45	21
APEP*	26	3	3	20	19	65	9
APOP*	26	1	4	21	20	63	6

Top scorers: Xiourouppas (Omonia) and Pesirovic (Apollon) 19
Cup Final: Omonia 1, Olympiakos 0

CZECHOSLOVAKIA

Ceskoslovensky Fotbalovy Svaz, Na Porici 12, 11530 Praha 1.
Founded: 1906; *Number of Clubs:* 5,972; *Number of Players:* 374,421; *National Colours:* Red shirts, white shorts, blue stockings.
Telephone: 225836/2350065; *Cable:* SPORTSVAZ PRAHA; *Telex:* 122650 CSTV C.

International matches 1990

Spain (a) 0-1, Egypt (h) 0-1, England (a) 2-4, West Germany (a) 0-1, USA (n) 5-1, Austria (n) 1-0, Italy (n) 0-2, Costa Rica (h) 4-1, West Germany (a) 0-1, Finland (a) 1-1, Iceland (h) 1-0, France (a) 1-2, Spain (h) 3-2.
Goalscorers: Skuhravy 7, Danek 3, Bilek 2 (2 pens), Kubik 2, Hasek 1, Kuka 1, Luhovy 1, Moravcik 1.

League Championship wins (1926–91)

Sparta Prague 20; Slavia Prague 12; Dukla Prague (prev. UDA) 11; Slovan Bratislava 6; Spartak Trnava 5; Banik Ostrava 3; Inter-Bratislava 1; Spartak Hradec Kralove 1; Viktoria Zizkov 1; Zbrojovka Brno 1; Bohemians 1; Vitkovice 1.

Cup wins (1961–91)

Dukla Prague 8; Sparta Prague 7; Slovan Bratislava 5; Spartak Trnava 4; Banik Ostrava 3; Lokomotiv Kosice 2; TJ Gottwaldov 1; Dunajska Streda 1.

Final League Table 1990–91

	P	W	D	L	F	A	Pts
Sparta Prague	30	15	9	6	58	28	39
Slovan Bratislava	30	16	6	8	47	27	38
Sigma Olomouc	30	16	5	9	52	34	37
DAC Dunajska	30	12	11	7	39	36	35
Banik Ostrava	30	14	4	12	50	34	32
RH Cheb	30	13	6	11	44	36	32
Inter Bratislava	30	10	10	10	41	42	30
Dukla Bystrica	30	11	8	11	35	37	30
Slavia Prague	30	10	10	10	44	48	30
Tatran Presov	30	10	9	11	42	40	29
Dukla Prague	30	12	5	13	38	52	29
Vitkovice	30	12	4	14	47	52	28
Bohemians	30	10	7	13	35	50	27
Hradec Kralove	30	10	7	13	33	52	27
Plastika Nitra*	30	9	7	14	30	35	25
Zbrojovka Brno*	30	2	8	20	20	52	12

Top scorer: Kukleta (Sparta Prague) 17
Cup Final: Banik Ostrava 6, Trnava 1

DENMARK

Dansk Boldspil Union, Ved Amagerbanen 15, DK-2300, Copenhagen S.
Founded: 1889; *Number of Clubs:* 1,510; *Number of Players:* 323,605; *National Colours:* Red shirts, white shorts, red stockings.
Telephone: (45) 3195 0511; *Cable:* DANSKBOLDSPIL COPENHAGEN; *Telex:* 15545 DBU DK; *Fax:* (45) 3195 0588.

International matches 1990

UAE (a) 1-1, UAE (a) 5-0, Bahrain (a) 2-1, Egypt (a) 0-0, Turkey (h) 1-0, England (a) 0-1, West Germany (a) 0-1, Norway (a) 2-1, Sweden (a) 1-0, Wales (h) 1-0, Faeroes (h) 4-1, Northern Ireland (a) 1-1, Yugoslavia (h) 0-2.
Goalscorers: Jacobsen 4, Laudrup M 3, Larsen 2, Povlsen 2, Bartram 1 (pen), Christensen 1, Elstrup 1, Hogh 1, Laudrup B 1, Risom 1, Svinggard 1.

League Championship wins (1913–90)

KB Copenhagen 15; B 93 Copenhagen 9; AB (Akademisk) 9; B 1903 Copenhagen 7; Frem 6; Esbjerg BK 5; Vejle BK 5; AGF Aarhus 5; Brondby 4; Hvidovre 3; Odense BK 3; B 1909 Odense 2; Koge BK 2; Lyngby 1.

Cup wins (1955–90)

Aarhus GF 7; Vejle BK 6; Randers Freja 3; Lyngby 3; BK 09 Odense 2; Aalborg BK 2; Esbjerg BK 2; Frem 2; B 1903 Copenhagen 2; B 93 Copenhagen 1; KB Copenhagen 1; Vanlose 1; Hvidovre 1; Odense BK 1; Brondby 1.

Final League Table 1990

	P	W	D	L	F	A	Pts
Brondby	26	17	8	1	50	16	42
B 1903	26	10	12	4	44	26	32
Ikast	26	11	8	7	38	27	30
Silkeborg	26	10	9	7	34	26	29
Frem	26	7	15	4	33	25	29
Lyngby	26	10	8	8	44	30	28
Aarhus	26	9	10	7	31	25	28
Odense	26	9	9	8	32	28	27
Vejle	26	8	10	8	32	32	26
Aalborg	26	8	10	8	32	34	26
Naestved*	26	6	10	10	20	34	22
Herfolge*	26	4	9	13	21	47	17
KB*	26	4	6	16	24	52	14
Viborg*	26	5	4	17	19	52	14

Top scorer: Christensen (Brondby) 17
Cup Final: Aarhus 0,1 Lyngby 0,6

Extra League 1991

	P	W	D	L	F	A	Pts
Brondby	18	10	6	2	26	15	26
Lyngby	18	10	4	4	35	18	24
Frem	18	6	7	5	25	24	19
B 1903	18	7	4	7	19	16	18
Aarhus	18	5	8	5	27	26	18
Odense	18	3	11	4	21	20	17
Aalborg	18	6	5	7	29	33	17
Vejle	18	5	6	7	20	22	16
Silkeborg	18	4	7	7	23	33	15
Ikast	18	3	4	11	9	27	10

ENGLAND

The Football Association, 16 Lancaster Gate, London W2 3LW.
Founded: 1863; *Number of Clubs:* 41,750; *Number of Players:* 1,005,000; *National Colours:* White shirts, navy blue shorts, white stockings.
Telephone: 071/262 4542; *Cable:* FOOTBALL ASSOCIATION LONDON W2; *Telex:* 261110; *Fax:* 071/402 0486.

FAEROE ISLANDS

Fotboltssamband Foroya, The Faeroes' Football Assn., Gundalur, P.O. Box 1028, FR-110, Torshavn.
Founded: 1979; *Number of Clubs:* 22; *Number of Players:* 4694.
Telephone: 298 12606; *Telex:* 81332 ITROTT FA; *Fax:* 298 12421.

International matches 1990

Iceland (h) 2-3, Austria (h) 1-0, Denmark (a) 1-4.
Goalscorers: Morkore K 2, Hansen 1, Nielsen 1.

Final League Table 1990

	P	W	D	L	F	A	Pts
HB	18	9	6	3	37	22	24
MB	18	7	6	5	30	25	20
B36	18	9	2	7	30	27	20
VB	18	7	4	7	27	27	18
B68	18	6	6	6	19	21	18
GI	18	7	3	8	28	22	17
KI	18	6	5	7	30	36	17
TB	18	7	2	9	21	26	16
SIF*	18	7	2	9	22	29	16
B71*	18	4	6	8	17	26	14

Top scorer: Rasmussen (MB) 10
Cup Final: KI 6, GI 1

FINLAND

Suomen Palloliitto Finlands Bollfoerbund, Kuparitie 1, P.O. Box 29, SF-00441 Helsinki.
Founded: 1907; *Number of Clubs:* 1,140; *Number of Players:* 57,732; *National Colours:* White shirts, blue shorts, white stockings.
Telephone: 90-56 26 233; *Cable:* SUOMIFOTBOLL HELSINKI; *Telex:* 1001438 SPL SF; *Fax:* 5626413.

International matches 1990

UAE (a) 1-1, Kuwait (a) 1-0, USA (a) 1-2, Rep of Ireland (a) 1-1, Sweden (a) 0-6, Czechoslovakia (h) 1-1, Portugal (h) 0-0, Tunisia (a) 2-1, Malta (a) 1-1.
Goalscorers: Aaltonen 1, Holmgren 1, Jarvinen 1, Paatelainen 1, Tarkkio 1, Tauriainen 1, Tegelberg 1, Tiainen 1.

League Championship wins (1949–90)

Helsinki JK 8; Turun Palloseura 5; Kuopion Palloseura 5; Valkeakosken Haka 4; Lahden Reipas 3; Kuusysi 3; Ilves-Kissat 2; IF Kamraterna 2; Kotkan TP 2; OPS Oulu 2; Torun Pyrkivä 1; IF Kronohagens 1; Helsinki PS 1; Kokkolan PV 1; IF Kamraterna 1; Vasa 1.

Cup wins (1955–90)

Valkeakosken Haka 9; Lahden Reipas 7; Kotkan TP 4; Helsinki JK 3; Mikkelin 2; Kuusysi 2; Kuopion Palloseura 2; Ilves Tampere 1; IFK Abo 1; Drott 1; Helsinki PS 1; Pallo-Peikot 1; Rovaniemi PS 1.

Final League Table 1990

	P	W	D	L	F	A	Pts
Kuusysi	22	14	5	3	34	12	33
Rops Rovaniemi	22	12	5	5	29	17	29
HJK Helsinki	22	11	6	5	40	29	28
Kups Kuopio	22	8	8	6	24	22	24
Reipas Lahti	22	7	9	6	35	21	23
TPS Turku	22	7	9	6	27	20	23
MP Mikkeli	22	6	11	5	20	22	23
Haka Valkeakosken	22	8	6	8	27	34	22
Ilves Tampere	22	6	8	8	37	33	20
OTP Oulu	22	4	7	11	16	32	15
KPV Kokkola*	22	6	3	13	15	32	15
Kuusankoski*	22	1	7	14	13	43	9

Quarter-finals: Kuusysi–Haka 3-1, 0-0; Rops–MP 1-1, 2-1, 0-0; TPS–HJK 0-0, 1-2, 1-3; Kups–Reipas 1-1, 0-2
Semi-finals: Kuusysi–MP 3-1, 1-0; HJK–Reipas 3-2, 1-0
Final: Kusysi–HJK 1-1, 0-1
Top scorers: Czakon (Ilves) and Tarkkio (HJK) 16
Cup Final: Ilves Tampere 2, HJK Helsinki 1

FRANCE

Federation Francaise De Football, 60 Bis Avenue D'Iena, F-75783 Paris, Cedex 16.
Founded: 1919; *Number of Clubs:* 22,829; *Number of Players:* 1,608,470; *National Colours:* Blue shirts, white shorts, red stockings.
Telephone: 44 31 73 00; *Cable:* CEFI PARIS 034; *Telex:* 640000; *Fax:* (1) 4720 8296.

International matches 1990

Kuwait (a) 1-0, East Germany (h) 3-0, West Germany (h) 2-1, Hungary (a) 3-1, Poland (h) 0-0, Iceland (a) 2-1, Czechoslovakia (h) 2-1, Albania (a) 1-0.
Goalscorers: Cantona 6, Papin 4, Blanc 1, Boli 1, Deschamps 1, Sauzee 1.

League Championship wins (1933–91)

Saint Etienne 10; Olympique Marseille 7; Stade de Reims 6; Nantes 6; AS Monaco 5; OGC Nice 4; Girondins Bordeaux 4; Lille OSC 3; FC Sete 2; Sochaux 2; Racing Club Paris 1; Roubaix-Tourcoing 1; Strasbourg 1; Paris St Germain 1.

Cup wins (1918–91)

Olympique Marseille 10; Saint Etienne 6; Lille OSC 5; Racing Club Paris 5; Red Star 5; AS Monaco 5; Olympique Lyon 3; Girondins Bordeaux 3; CAS Genereaux 2; Nancy 2; OGC Nice 2; Racing Club Strasbourg 2; Sedan 2; FC Sete 2; Stade de Reims 2; SO Montpellier 2; Stade Rennes 2; Paris St Germain 2; AS Cannes 1; Club Français 1; Excelsior Roubaix 1; Le Havre 1; Olympique de Pantin 1; CA Paris 1; Sochaux 1; Toulouse 1; Bastia 1; Nantes 1; Metz 1.

Final League Table 1990–91

	P	W	D	L	F	A	Pts
Marseille	38	22	11	5	67	28	55
Monaco	38	20	11	7	51	30	51
Auxerre	38	19	10	9	63	36	48
Cannes	38	12	17	9	32	26	41
Lyon	38	15	11	12	39	44	41
Lille	38	11	17	10	39	37	39
Montpellier	38	12	14	12	44	35	38
Caen	38	13	12	13	38	36	38
Paris St Germain	38	13	12	13	40	42	38
Bordeaux	38	11	15	12	34	32	37
Brest	38	11	15	12	45	46	37
Metz	38	12	12	14	44	51	36
St Etienne	38	13	9	16	40	46	35
Nice	38	10	14	14	40	42	34
Nantes	38	9	16	13	34	44	34
Toulon	38	9	16	13	31	41	34
Nancy	38	11	11	16	38	58	33
Sochaux	38	8	16	14	24	33	32
Toulouse*	38	8	15	15	33	45	31
Rennes*	38	7	14	17	29	51	28

Top scorer: Papin (Marseille) 23
Cup Final: Monaco 1, Marseille 0

EAST GERMANY (now part of the new Germany)

International matches 1990

France (a) 0-3, Kuwait (a) 2-1, USA (h) 3-2, Egypt (h) 2-0, Scotland (a) 1-0, Brazil (a) 3-3, USA (a) 2-1, Belgium (a) 2-0.
Goalscorers: Kirsten 3, Sammer 3, Doll 2 (1 pen), Wuckel 2, Ernst 1, Gerlach 1, Peschke 1, Rische 1, Steinmann 1.

League Championship wins (1950–91)

Dynamo Berlin 10; Dynamo Dresden 7; ASK Vorwaerts 6; Wismut Karl-Marx-Stadt 4; FC Magdeburg 4; Carl Zeiss Jena (prev. Motor Jena) 3; Chemie Leipzig 2; Turbine Erfurt 2; Turbine Halle 1; Zwickau Horch 1; Empor Rostock 1; ZSG Halle 1; Planitz 1; Hansa Rostock 1.

Cup wins (1949–91)

Dynamo Dresden 7; Carl Zeiss Jena (prev. Motor Jena) 5; Lokomotiv Leipzig 5; FC Magdeburg 4; Dynamo Berlin 3; Chemie Leipzig 2; Magdeburg Aufbau 2; Motor Zwickau 2; ASK Vorwaerts 2; Dresden Einheit SC 1; Dresden VP 1; Chemie Halle SC 1; North Dessau Waggonworks 1; Thale EHW 1; Union East Berlin 1; Wismut Karl-Marx-Stadt 1; Sachsenring Zwickau 1; Hansa Rostock 1.

Final League Table 1990–91

	P	W	D	L	F	A	Pts
Hansa Rostock†	26	13	9	4	44	25	35
Dynamo Dresden†	26	12	8	6	48	28	32
Rot-Weiss Erfurt	26	11	9	6	30	26	31
Chemie Halle	26	10	9	7	40	31	29
Chemnitz	26	9	11	6	24	23	29
Carl Zeiss Jena	26	12	4	10	40	36	28
Lokomotiv Leipzig	26	10	8	8	37	33	28
Brandenburg	26	9	9	8	34	31	27
Eisenhuttenstadt	26	7	12	7	29	25	26
FC Magdeburg	26	9	8	9	34	32	26
FC Berlin	26	7	8	11	25	39	22
Sachsen Leipzig	26	6	10	10	23	37	22
Cottbus	26	3	10	13	21	38	16
Viktoria Frankfurt	26	3	4	17	29	54	13

Top scorer: Gutschow (Dynamo Dresden) 20
Cup Final: Hansa Rostock 1, Eisenhuttenstadt 1
†promoted to West German Bundesliga

GERMANY (West German details given)

Deutsche Fussball-Bund, Otto-Fleck-Schneise 6, Postfach 710265, D-6000, Frankfurt (Main) 71.
Founded: 1900; *Number of Clubs:* 21,510; *Number of Players:* 4,765,146; *National Colours:* White shirts, black shorts, white stockings.
Telephone: (069) 67 880; *Cable:* FUSSBALL FRANKFURT; *Telex:* 4 168 15; *Fax:* (69) 67 88 266.

International matches 1990

France (a) 1-2, Uruguay (h) 3-3, Czechoslovakia (h) 1-0, Denmark (h) 1-0, Yugoslavia (h) 4-1, UAE (n) 5-1, Colombia (n) 1-1, Holland (n) 2-1, Czechoslovakia (n) 1-0, England (n) 1-1, Argentina (n) 1-0, Portugal (a) 1-1, Sweden (a) 3-1, Luxembourg (a) 3-2, Switzerland (h) 4-0.
Goalscorers: Voller 8, Matthaus 7 (1 pen), Klinsmann 6, Brehme 4 (1 pen), Bein 3, Littbarski 1, Moller 1, Riedle 1, Thon 1.

League Championship wins (1903–91)

Bayern Munich 12; IFC Nuremberg 9; Schalke 04 7; SV Hamburg 6; Borussia Moenchengladbach 5; VfB Leipzig 3; VfB Stuttgart 3; Sp Vgg Furth 3; Borussia Dortmund 3; IFC Cologne 3; IFC Kaiserslautern 3; Viktoria Berlin 2; Hertha Berlin 2; Hanover 96 2; Dresden SC 2; Werder Bremen 2; Munich 1860 1; Union Berlin 1; FC Freiburg 1; Phoenix Karlsruhe 1; Karlsruher FV 1; Holstein Kiel 1; Fortuna Dusseldorf 1; Rapid Vienna 1; VfB Mannheim 1; Rot-Weiss Essen 1; Eintracht Frankfurt 1; Eintracht Brunswick 1.

Cup wins (1935–91)

Bayern Munich 8; IFC Cologne 4; Eintracht Frankfurt 4; IFC Nuremberg 3; SV Hamburg 3; Dresden SC 2; Fortuna Dusseldorf 2; Karlsruhe SC 2; Munich 1860 2; Schalke 04 2; VfB Stuttgart 2; Borussia Moenchengladbach 2; Werder Bremen 2; First Vienna 1; VfB Leipzig 1; Kickers Offenbach 1; Rapid Vienna 1; Rot-Weiss Essen 1; SW Essen 1; Bayer Uerdingen 1; IFC Kaiserslautern 1.

Final League Table 1990–91

	P	W	D	L	F	A	Pts
Kaiserslautern	34	19	10	5	72	45	48
Bayern Munich	34	18	9	7	74	41	45
Werder Bremen	34	14	14	6	46	29	42
Eintracht Frankfurt	34	15	10	9	63	40	40
Hamburg	34	16	8	10	60	38	40
Stuttgart	34	14	10	10	57	44	38
Cologne	34	13	11	10	50	43	37
Leverkusen	34	11	13	10	47	46	35
Moenchengladbach	34	9	17	8	49	54	35
Borussia Dortmund	34	10	14	10	46	57	34
Wattenscheid	34	9	15	10	42	51	33
Fortuna Dusseldorf	34	11	10	13	40	49	32
Karlsruhe	34	8	15	11	46	52	31
Bochum	34	9	11	14	50	52	29
Nuremberg	34	10	9	15	40	54	29
St Pauli*†	34	6	15	13	33	53	27
Bayer Uerdingen*	34	5	13	16	34	54	23
Hertha Berlin*	34	3	8	23	37	84	14

Top scorer: Wohlfarth (Bayern Munich) 21
Cup Final: Werder Bremen 1, Cologne 1 aet, Werder Bremen won 5–4 on penalties

GREECE

Federation Hellenique De Football, Singrou Avenue 137, Athens.
Founded: 1926; *Number of Clubs:* 3,678; *Number of Players:* 282,550; *National Colours:* White shirts, blue shorts, white stockings.
Telephone: 9338850; *Cable:* FOOTBALL ATHENES; *Telex:* 215328; *Fax:* 9359666.

International matches 1990

Belgium (h) 2-0, Israel (h) 2-1, Italy (a) 0-0, Albania (h) 1-0, Egypt (h) 6-1, Malta (h) 4-0, Holland (a) 0-2, Poland (a) 1-2.
Goalscorers: Saravakos 6 (3 pens), Tsalouhidis 3, Manolas 2, Apostolakis 1, Borbokis 1, Dimitriadis 1, Karapialis 1, Tsiantakis 1.

League Championship wins (1928–91)

Olympiakos 25; Panathinaikos 16; AEK Athens 8; Aris Salonika 3; PAOK Salonika 2; Larissa 1.

Cup wins (1932–91)

Olympiakos 19; Panathinaikos 12; AEK Athens 9; PAOK Salonika 2; Aris Salonika 1; Ethnikos 1; Iraklis 1; Panionios 1; Kastoria 1; Larissa 1; Ofi Crete 1.

Final League Table 1990–91

	P	W	D	L	F	A	Pts
Panathinaikos	34	23	8	3	77	22	54
Olympiakos	34	19	10	5	77	28	48
AEK Athens	34	18	6	10	59	33	42
PAOK Salonika	34	16	9	9	56	39	38
Athinaikos	34	16	5	13	40	33	37
Iraklis	34	14	9	11	40	36	37
Ofi Crete	34	11	12	11	37	38	34
Doxa Drama	34	14	6	14	42	44	34
Aris Salonika	34	11	12	11	34	38	33
Panionios	34	9	12	13	38	54	30
Apollon	34	10	10	14	41	62	30
Larissa	34	10	9	15	38	46	29
Panachaiki	34	9	10	15	36	48	28
Panserraikos	34	9	10	15	30	42	28
Xanthi	34	9	10	15	35	53	28
Ionikos*	34	9	9	16	36	50	27
Levadiakos*	34	10	7	17	35	51	27
Iannina*	34	8	9	17	20	54	25

Top scorer: Saravakos (Panathinaikos) 23
Cup Final: Panathinaikos 3, 2 Athinaikos 0, 1

HOLLAND

Koninklijke Nederlandsche Voetbalbond,
Woudenbergseweg 56, Postbus 515, NL-3700 AM, Zeist.
Founded: 1889; *Number of Clubs:* 7,912; *Number of Players:* 978,324; *National Colours:* Orange shirts, white shorts, orange stockings.
Telephone: 3429 9211/1268; *Cable:* VOETBAL ZEIST; *Telex:* 40497; *Fax:* 03439 1397.

International matches 1990

Italy (h) 0-0, USSR (a) 1-2, Austria (a) 2-3, Yugoslavia (a) 2-0, Egypt (n) 1-1, England (n) 0-0, Rep of Ireland (n) 1-1, West Germany (n) 1-2, Italy (a) 0-1, Portugal (a) 0-1, Greece (h) 2-0, Malta (a) 8-0.
Goalscorers: Van Basten 8 (1 pen), Bergkamp 3, Koeman R 3 (2 pens), Gullit 1, Kieft 1, Rijkaard 1, Winter 1.

League Championship wins (1898–1991)

Ajax Amsterdam 23; Feyenoord 13; PSV Eindhoven 12; HVV The Hague 8; Sparta Rotterdam 6; Go Ahead Deventer 4; HBS The Hague 3; Willem II Tilburg 3; RCH Haarlem 2; RAP 2; Heracles 2; ADO The Hague 2; Quick The Hague 1; BVV Schiedam 1; NAC Breda 1; Eindhoven 1; Enschede 1; Volewijckers Amsterdam 1; Limburgia 1; Rapid JC Haarlem 1; DOS Utrecht 1; DWS Amsterdam 1; Haarlem 1; Be Quick Groningen 1; SVV Schiedam 1; AZ 67 Alkmaar 1.

Cup wins (1899–1991)

Ajax Amsterdam 11; PSV Eindhoven 7; Feyenoord 7; Quick The Hague 4; AZ 67 Alkmaar 3; HEC 3; Sparta Rotterdam 3; DFC 2; Fortuna Geleen 2; Haarlem 2; HBS The Hague 2; RCH 2; VOC 2; Wageningen 2; Willem II Tilburg 2; FC Den Haag 2; Concordia Rotterdam 1; CVV 1; Eindhoven 1; HVV The Hague 1; Longa 1; Quick Nijmegen 1; RAP 1; Roermond 1; Schoten 1; Velocitas Breda 1; Velocitas Groningen 1; VSV 1; VUC 1; VVV Groningen 1; ZFC 1; NAC Breda 1; Twente Enschede 1; Utrecht 1.

Final League Table 1990–91

	P	W	D	L	F	A	Pts
PSV Eindhoven	34	23	7	4	84	28	53
Ajax	34	22	9	3	75	21	53
Groningen	34	18	10	6	62	38	46
Utrecht	34	16	10	8	42	29	42
Vitesse	34	11	15	8	39	32	37
Twente	34	13	10	11	58	48	36
RKC	34	11	13	10	51	49	35
Feyenoord	34	8	16	10	39	40	32
Volendam	34	10	12	12	37	45	32
Roda	34	12	7	15	39	52	31
Willem II	34	13	4	17	53	50	30
Fortuna Sittard	34	9	12	13	33	47	30
Sparta	34	7	15	12	39	56	29
Den Haag	34	10	8	16	40	60	28
Maastricht	34	9	9	16	38	56	27
SVV	34	8	8	18	31	52	24
Heerenveen	34	9	6	19	41	63	24
NEC	34	6	11	17	27	62	23

Top scorer: Romario (PSV Eindhoven) and Bergkamp (Ajax) 25
Cup Final: Feyenoord 1, Den Bosch 0

HUNGARY

Magyar Labdarugo Szovetseg, Hungarian Football Federation, Nepkoztarsasag Utja 47, H-1061 Budapest VI.
Founded: 1901; *Number of Clubs:* 2,503; *Number of Players:* 129,087; *National Colours:* Red shirts, white shorts, green stockings.
Telephone: 36-1-1225 817, 36-1-1420 704; 36-1-1425 103, 36-1-1421 556; *Cable:* MLSZ BUDAPEST; *Telex:* 225782 MLSZ H; *Fax:* 36-1-1425 103.

International matches 1990

USA (h) 2-0, France (h) 1-3, Austria (a) 0-3, UAE (h) 3-0, Colombia (h) 3-1, Turkey (h) 4-1, England (a) 0-1, Norway (a) 0-0, Italy (h) 1-1, Cyprus (h) 4-2.
Goalscorers: Kovacs 6, Kiprich 4 (1 pen), Bognar 1, Disztl 1, Kozma 1, Limperger 1, Lorincz 1, Petres 1, Pinter 1 (pen), own goal 1.

League Championship wins (1901–91)

Ferencvaros (prev. FRC) 23; MTK-VM Budapest (prev. Hungaria, Bastay and Vörös Lobogo) 19; Ujpest Dozsa 19; Honved 12; Vasas Budapest 6; Csepel 3; Raba Györ (prev. Vasas Györ) 3; BTC 2; Nagyvarad 1.

Cup wins (1910–91)

Ferencvaros (prev. FRC) 15; MTK-VM Budapest (prev. Hungaria, Bastay and Vörös Lobogo) 9; Ujpest Dozsa 7; Raba Györ (prev. Vasas Györ) 4; Vasas Budapest 3; Honved 3; Diösgyör 2; Bocskai 1; III Ker 1; Kispesti AC 1; Soroksar 1; Szolnoki MAV 1; Siofok Banyasz 1; Bekescsaba 1; Pecs 1.

Cup not regularly held until 1964

Final League Table 1990–91

	P	W	D	L	F	A	Pts
Honved	30	19	7	4	50	20	64
Ferencvaros	30	15	10	5	47	22	55
Pecsi Munkas	30	15	7	8	32	20	52
Vac Izzo	30	14	8	8	38	29	50
Veszprem	30	11	12	7	34	25	45
Tatabanya	30	12	9	9	37	32	45
Ujpest Dozsa	30	13	4	13	36	39	43
Siofok	30	10	11	9	25	28	41
Videoton	30	10	9	11	32	39	39
MTK VM	30	10	7	13	38	36	37
Raba Györ	30	8	10	12	35	41	34
Szeged	30	9	6	15	26	37	33
Vasas	30	8	8	14	32	43	32
Debrecen	30	7	8	15	25	38	29
Volan	30	8	5	17	28	50	29
Bekescsaba	30	7	7	16	24	40	28

Top scorer: Gregor (Honved) 15
Cup Final: Ferencvaros 1, Vac Izzo 0

ICELAND

Knattspyrnusamband Island, P.O. Box 8511, 128 Reykjavik.
Founded: 1929; *Number of Clubs:* 82; *Number of Players:* 19,400; *National Colours:* Blue shirts, white shorts, blue stockings.
Telephone: 84 444; *Cable:* KSI REYKJAVIK; *Telex:* 2314 ISI IS; *Fax:* 1 68 97 66.

International matches 1990

Luxembourg (a) 2-1, Bermuda (a) 4-0, USA (a) 1-4, Albania (h) 2-0, Faeroes (a) 3-2, France (h) 1-2, Spain (a) 1-2.
Goalscorers: Petursson 4, Edvaldsson 2, Gregory 2, Gudjohnsen 2, Einarsson 1, Jonsson Siggi 1, Ormslev 1, Thordarsson 1.

League Championship wins (1912–90)

KR 20; Valur 19; Fram 18; IA Akranes 12; Vikingur 4; IBK Keflavik 3; IBV Vestmann 2; KA Akureyri 1.

Cup wins (1960–90)

KR 7; Fram 7; Valur 6; IA Akranes 5; IBV Vestmann 3; IBA Akureyri 1; Vikingur 1; IBK Keflavik 1.

Final League Table 1990

	P	W	D	L	F	A	Pts
Fram	18	12	2	4	39	16	38
KR	18	12	2	4	31	17	38
IBV	18	11	4	3	39	32	37
Valur	18	10	3	5	29	21	33
Stjarnam	18	8	2	8	25	27	26
Hafnafjordur	18	7	2	9	24	29	23
Vikingur	18	4	7	7	17	24	19
KA	18	5	1	12	18	28	16
Thor*	18	4	3	11	13	24	15
IA Akranes*	18	3	2	13	19	36	11

Top scorer: Magnusson (Hafnafjordur) 13
Cup Final: Valur 1, KR 1 aet; Valur won 5–4 on penalties

REPUBLIC OF IRELAND

The Football Association of Ireland, (Cumann Peile Na H-Eireann), 80 Merrion Square, South Dublin 2.
Founded: 1921; *Number of Clubs:* 3,503; *Number of Players:* 33,028; *National Colours:* Green shirts, white shorts, green stockings.
Telephone: 76 68 64; *Cable:* SOCCER DUBLIN; *Telex:* 91397 FAI EI; *Fax:* (01) 610 931.

League Championship wins (1922–91)

Shamrock Rovers 14; Dundalk 8; Shelbourne 7;
Bohemians 7; Waterford 6; Cork United 5; Drumcondra
5; St Patrick's Athletic 4; St James's Gate 2; Cork
Athletic 2; Sligo Rovers 2; Limerick 2; Athlone Town 2;
Dolphin 1; Cork Hibernians 1; Cork Celtic 1; Derry City
1.

Cup wins (1922–91)

Shamrock Rovers 23; Dundalk 8, Drumcondra 5;
Bohemians 4; Shelbourne 3; Cork Athletic 2; Cork
United 2; St James's Gate 2; St Patrick's Athletic 2;
Cork Hibernians 2; Limerick 2; Waterford 2; Alton
United 1; Athlone Town 1; Cork 1; Fordsons 1;
Transport 1; Finn Harps 1; Home Farm 1; Sligo 1;
UCD 1; Derry City 1; Bray Wanderers 1; Galway
United 1.

Final League Table 1990–91

	P	W	D	L	F	A	Pts
Dundalk	33	22	8	3	52	16	52
Cork City	33	19	12	2	45	17	50
St Patrick's Ath	33	17	10	6	46	21	44
Shelbourne	33	18	6	9	57	30	42
Sligo Rovers	33	13	12	8	34	22	38
Shamrock Rovers	33	14	9	10	51	37	37
Derry City	33	13	9	11	50	47	35
Galway United	33	9	5	20	35	61	23
Bohemians	33	7	8	18	26	41	22
Athlone Town	33	6	7	20	22	53	19
Limerick*	33	6	5	22	20	53	17
Waterford*	33	6	5	22	22	63	17

Top scorer: Hanrahan (Dundalk) 18
Cup Final: Galway United 1, Shamrock Rovers 0

ITALY

Federazione Italiana Giuoco Calcio, Via Gregorio Allegri
14, C.P. 2450, I-00198, Roma.
Founded: 1898; *Number of Clubs:* 20,117; *Number of
Players:* 1,129,667; *National Colours:* Blue shirts, white
shorts, blue stockings, white trim.
Telephone: 84 911; *Cable:* FEDERCALCIO ROMA;
Telex: 611438 CALCIO; *Fax:* 06 849 1239.

International matches 1990

Holland (a) 0-0, Switzerland (a) 1-0, Greece (h) 0-0,
Austria (n) 1-0, USA (n) 1-0, Czechoslovakia (n) 2-0,
Uruguay (n) 2-0, Rep of Ireland (n) 1-0, Argentina (n)
1-1, England (n) 2-1, Holland (h) 1-0, Hungary (a) 1-1,
USSR (h) 0-0, Cyprus (a) 4-0.
Goalscorers: Schillaci 6 (1 pen), Baggio 4 (1 pen), Serena
3, De Agostini 1, Giannini 1, Lombardo 1, Vierchowod
1.

League Championship wins (1898–1991)

Juventus 22; Inter-Milan 13; AC Milan 11; Genoa 9;
Torino 8; Pro Vercelli 7; Bologna 7; Fiorentina 2;
Napoli 2; AS Roma 2; Casale 1; Novese 1; Cagliari 1;
Lazio 1; Verona 1; Sampdoria 1.

Cup wins (1922–91)

Juventus 8; AS Roma 7; Torino 4; Fiorentina 4; AC
Milan 4; Inter-Milan 3; Napoli 3; Sampdoria 3; Bologna
2; Atalanta 1; Genoa 1; Lazio 1; Vado 1; Venezia 1.

Final League Table 1990–91

	P	W	D	L	F	A	Pts
Sampdoria	34	20	11	3	57	24	51
AC Milan	34	18	10	6	46	19	46
Internazionale	34	18	10	6	56	31	46
Genoa	34	14	12	8	51	36	40
Torino	34	12	14	8	40	29	38
Parma	34	13	12	9	35	34	38
Juventus	34	13	11	10	45	32	37
Napoli	34	11	15	8	37	37	37
Roma	34	11	14	9	43	37	36
Atalanta	34	11	13	10	38	37	35
Lazio	34	8	19	7	33	36	35
Fiorentina	34	8	15	11	40	34	31
Bari	34	9	11	14	41	47	29
Cagliari	34	6	17	11	29	44	29
Lecce*	34	6	13	15	20	47	25
Pisa*	34	8	6	20	34	60	22
Cesena*	34	5	9	20	28	58	19
Bologna*	34	4	10	20	29	63	18

Top scorer: Vialli (Sampdoria) 19
Cup Final: Roma 3, 1 Sampdoria 1, 1

LIECHTENSTEIN

Liechtensteiner Fussball-Verband, Postfach 165, FL-9490,
Vaduz.
Founded: 1933; *Number of Clubs:* 7; *Number of Players:*
1,300; *National Colours:* Blue & red shirts, red shorts,
blue stockings.
Telephone: 075 23344; *Cable:* FUSSBALLVERBAND
VADUZ; *Telex:* 889 261; *Fax:* 075 28265.

International matches 1990

USA (h) 1-4.
Goalscorer: Marxer 1.

Liechtenstein has no national league. Teams compete in
Swiss regional leagues.

LUXEMBOURG

Federation Luxembourgeoise De Football, (F.L.F),
50, Rue De Strasbourg, L-2560, Luxembourg.
Founded: 1908; *Number of Clubs:* 199; *Number of
Players:* 23,252; *National Colours:* Red shirts, white
shorts, blue stockings.
Telephone: 48 86 65; *Cable:* FOOTBALL
LUXEMBOURG; *Telex:* 2426 FLF LU; *Fax:* 400 201.

International matches 1990

Iceland (h) 1-2, West Germany (h) 2-3, Wales (h) 0-1.
Goalscorers: Girres 1, Langers 1, Malget 1.

League Championship wins (1910–91)

Jeunesse Esch 21; Spora Luxembourg 11; Stade
Dudelange 10; Red Boys Differdange 6; US Hollerich-
Bonnevoie 5; Fola Esch 5; US Luxembourg 5; Avenir
Beggen 4; Aris Bonnevoie 3; Progres Niedercorn 3.

Cup wins (1922–91)

Red Boys Differdange 16; Jeunesse Esch 9; US
Luxembourg 9; Spora Luxembourg 8; Stade Dudelange
4; Progres Niedercorn 4; Fola Esch 3; Avenir Beggen 3;
Alliance Dudelange 2; US Rumelange 2; Aris Bonnevoie
1; US Dudelange 1; Jeunesse Hautcharage 1; National
Schiffige 1; Racing Luxembourg 1; SC Tetange 1;
Hesperange 1.

Final League Table 1990–91

	P	W	D	L	F	A	Pts
Union	10	5	3	2	12	8	28
Jeunesse Esch	10	5	3	2	16	9	25
Spora	10	4	3	3	17	11	22
Avenir Beggen	10	8	0	4	19	14	22
Grevenmacher	10	2	2	6	18	24	16
Hesperange	10	2	1	7	12	23	14

N.B. Points include those from qualifying table
Top scorer: Marocutti (Union) 23
Cup Final: Union 3, Jeunesse Esch 0

MALTA

Malta Football Association, 280 St. Paul Street, Valletta.
Founded: 1900; *Number of Clubs:* 242; *Number of Players:* 4,024; *National Colours:* Red shirts, white shorts, red stockings.
Telephone: 22 26 97; *Cable:* FOOTBALL MALTA VALLETTA; *Telex:* 1752 MALFA MW; *Fax:* 24 51 36.

International matches 1990

Norway (h) 1-1, South Korea (h) 1-2, USA (a) 0-1, Scotland (h) 1-2, Rep of Ireland (h) 0-3, Greece (a) 0-4, Finland (h) 1-1, Holland (h) 0-8.
Goalscorers: Degiorgio 1, Laferla 1, Scerri 1, Suda 1.

League Championship wins (1910–91)

Floriana 24; Sliema Wanderers 22; Valletta 13; Hibernians 6; Hamrun Spartans 6; Rabat Ajax 2; St George's 1; KOMR 1.

Cup wins (1935–91)

Sliema Wanderers 17; Floriana 16; Valletta 6; Hibernians 5; Hamrun Spartans 5; Gzira United 1; Melita 1; Zurrieq 1; Rabat Ajax 1.

Final League Table 1990–91

	P	W	D	L	F	A	Pts
Hamrun Spartans	16	10	4	2	31	18	24
Valletta	16	8	3	5	28	17	19
Floriana	16	6	6	4	15	11	18
Hibernians	16	5	7	4	18	15	17
Sliema Wanderers	16	4	7	5	24	20	15
Rabat Ajax	16	4	6	6	19	20	14
Zurrieq	16	4	6	6	12	19	14
Birkirkara	16	3	7	6	14	23	13
Naxxar Lions	16	3	4	9	11	29	10

Top scorer: Zarb (Valletta) 12
Cup Final: Valletta 2, Sliema Wanderers 1

NORTHERN IRELAND

Irish Football Association Ltd, 20 Windsor Avenue, Belfast BT9 6EG
Founded: 1880; *Number of Clubs:* 1,555; *Number of Players:* 24,558; *National Colours:* Green shirts, white shorts, green stockings.
Telephone: (0232) 66 94 58; *Cable:* FOOTBALL BELFAST; *Telex:* 747317; *Fax:* (0232) 667620.

NORWAY

Norges Fotballforbund Ulleval Stadion, Postboks 3823, Ulleval Hageby, 0805 Oslo 8.
Founded: 1902; *Number of Clubs:* 3,449; *Number of Players:* 298,400; *National Colours:* Red shirts, white shorts, blue & white stockings.
Telephone: 02 46 98 30; *Cable:* FOTBALLFORBUND OSLO; *Telex:* 71722 NFF N; *Fax:* 02 60 82 22.

International matches 1990

South Korea (h) 3-2, Malta (a) 1-1, Northern Ireland (a) 3-2, Denmark (h) 1-2, Sweden (h) 1-2, USSR (a) 0-2, Hungary (h) 0-0, Cameroon (h) 6-1, Tunisia (a) 3-1, Cyprus (a) 3-0.
Goalscorers: Dahlum 3, Fjortoft 3, Andersen 2, Bohinen 2, Skammelsrud 2, Sorloth 2, Ahlsen 1 (pen), Berg 1, Brandhaug 1, Bratseth 1, Ingebrigtsen 1, Johnsen 1, Tangen 1.

League Championship wins (1938–90)

Fredrikstad 9; Viking Stavanger 7; Lillestroem 6; Rosenborg Trondheim 6; Valerengen 4; Larvik Turn 3; Brann Bergen 2; Lyn Oslo 2; IK Start 2; Friedig 1; Fram 1; Skeid Oslo 1; Strömsgodset Drammen 1; Moss 1.

Cup wins (1902–90)

Odds Bk, Skien 11; Fredrikstad 10; Lyn Oslo 8; Skeid Oslo 8; Sarpsborg FK 6; Brann Bergen 5; Rosenborg Trondheim 5; Orn F Horten 4; Lillestroem 4; Viking Stavanger 4; Frigg 3; Strömsgodset Drammen 3; Mjondalens F 3; Mercantile 2; Grane Nordstrand 1; Kvik Halden 1; Sparta 1; Gjovik 1; Bodo-Glimt 1; Valerengen 1; Moss 1; Tromso 1; Byrne 1.
(Until 1937 the cup-winners were regarded as champions.)

Final League Table 1990–91

	P	W	D	L	F	A	Pts
Rosenborg	22	13	5	4	60	24	44
Tromso	22	12	6	4	36	21	42
Molde	22	12	4	6	34	29	40
Brann	22	11	6	5	34	25	39
Viking	22	10	5	7	41	30	35
Start	22	9	4	9	39	34	31
Fylingen	22	7	7	8	23	30	28
Kongsvinger	22	7	6	9	24	32	27
Strömsgodset	22	8	3	11	29	45	27
Lillestroem	22	7	4	11	30	30	25
Valerengen*	22	4	4	14	26	53	16
Moss*	22	3	4	15	24	47	13

Top scorer: Dahlum (Start) 20
Cup Final: Rosenborg 5, Fylingen 1

POLAND

Federation Polonaise De Foot-Ball, Al. Ujazdowskie 22, 00-478 Warszawa.
Founded: 1923; *Number of Clubs:* 5,881; *Number of Players:* 317,442; *National Colours:* White shirts, red shorts, white & red stockings.
Telephone: 48-22-28 93 44; 48-22-28 58 21; *Cable:* PEZETPEEN WARSZAWA; *Telex:* 825320 PZPN PL; *Fax:* 48 22 219175.

International matches 1990

Iran (a) 2-0, Iran (a) 1-0, Kuwait (a) 1-1, Yugoslavia (h) 0-0, Colombia (a) 1-2, Costa Rica (a) 2-0, USA (a) 1-3, Scotland (a) 1-1, Belgium (a) 1-1, France (a) 0-0, Romania (a) 1-2, USA (h) 2-3, England (a) 0-2, Turkey (a) 1-0, Greece (h) 2-1.
Goalscorers: Ziober 5, Kosecki 4, Kosrenski 1, Nowak 1, Pisz 1, Szewczyk 1, Szoczywski 1, Warzycha 1, own goal 1.

League Championship wins (1921–91)

Gornik Zabrze 14; Ruch Chorzow 13; Wisla Krakow 6; Cracovia 3; Pogon Lwow 4; Legia Warsaw 4; Lech Poznan 3; Warta Poznan 2; Polonia Bytom 2; Stal Mielec 2; Widzew Lodz 2; Garbarnia Krakow 1; Polonia Warsaw 1; LKS Lodz 1; Slask Wroclaw 1; Szombierki Bytom 1; Zaglebie Lubin 1.

Cup wins (1951–91)

Legia Warsaw 9, Gornik Zabrze 6; Zaglebie Sosnowiec 4; Lech Poznan 3; Ruch Chorzow 2; Slask Wroclaw 2; GKS Katowice 2; Gwardia Warsaw 1; LKS Lodz 1; Polonia Warsaw 1; Wisla Krakow 1; Stal Rzeszow 1; Arka Gdynia 1; Lechia Gdansk 1; Widzew Lodz 1.

Final League Table 1990–91

	P	W	D	L	F	A	Pts
Zaglebie Lubin	30	18	8	4	49	25	44
Gornik Zabrze	30	15	10	5	55	24	40
Wisla	30	13	14	3	52	26	40
Katowice	30	16	7	7	33	26	39
Hutnik	30	14	9	7	53	34	37
Lech	30	10	13	7	49	28	33
Slask	30	12	9	9	41	37	33
Olimpia	30	9	12	9	37	41	30
Legia	30	8	12	10	34	24	28
Motor Lublin	30	10	8	12	33	38	28
LKS Lodz	30	11	6	13	25	36	28
Debica	30	7	12	11	29	45	26
Ruch	30	7	11	12	25	35	25
Bydgoszcz	30	8	7	15	27	41	23
Stal*	30	3	10	17	25	49	16
Sosnowiec*	30	2	6	22	21	69	10

Top scorer: Dziubinski (Wisla Krakow) 21
Cup Final: Katowice 1, Legia Warsaw 0

PORTUGAL

Federacao Portuguesa De Futebol, Praca Da Alegria
N.25, Apartado 21.100, P-1128, Lisboa Codex.
Founded: 1914; *Number of Clubs:* 1,605; *Number of Players:* 55,499; *National Colours:* Red shirts, white shorts, red stockings.
Telephone: 328207/08/09; *Cable:* FUTEBOL LISBOA;
Telex: 13489 FPF P; *Fax:* 346 7231.

International matches 1990

West Germany (h) 1-1, Finland (a) 0-0, Holland (h) 1-0, USA (h) 1-0.
Goalscorers: Rui Aguas 2, Domingos 1.

League Championship wins (1935–91)

Benfica 29; Sporting Lisbon 16; FC Porto 11; Belenenses 1.

Cup wins (1939–91)

Benfica 21; Sporting Lisbon 11; FC Porto 7; Boavista 3; Belenenses 3; Vitoria Setubal 2; Academica Coimbra 1; Leixoes Porto 1; Sporting Braga 1; Amadora 1.

Final League Table 1990–91

	P	W	D	L	F	A	Pts
Benfica	38	32	5	1	89	18	69
Porto	38	31	5	2	77	22	67
Sporting	38	24	8	6	58	23	56
Boavista	38	15	11	12	53	46	41
Salgueiros	38	12	12	14	32	48	36
Beira Mar	38	12	12	14	40	49	36
Farense	38	14	6	18	46	47	34
Chaves	38	10	14	14	49	52	34
Braga	38	13	8	17	42	45	34
Guimaraes	38	12	10	16	31	40	34
Maritimo	38	12	10	16	37	48	34
Famalicao	38	11	11	16	33	41	33
Tirsense*	38	10	13	15	39	50	33
Gil Vicente	38	11	11	16	34	46	33
Penafiel	38	12	9	17	34	51	33
Uniao Madeira	38	9	15	14	30	51	33
Setubal*	38	9	14	15	37	53	32
Amadora*	38	9	14	15	37	46	32
Belenenses*	38	10	9	19	27	38	29
Nacional*	38	8	11	19	33	60	27

Top scorer: Rui Aguas (Benfica) 25
Cup Final: Porto 3, Beira Mar 1

ROMANIA

Federatia Romana De Fotbal, Vasile Conta 16, Bucharest 70130.
Founded: 1908; *Number of Clubs:* 5,453; *Number of Players:* 179,987; *National Colours:* Yellow shirts, blue shorts, red stockings.
Telephone: 10 70 90; *Cable:* SPORTROM
BUCURESTI-FOTBAL; *Telex:* 11180; *Fax:* 11 70 75 and 11 98 69.

International matches 1990

Egypt (a) 3-1, Algeria (a) 0-0, Switzerland (a) 1-2, Israel (a) 4-1, Egypt (h) 1-0, Belgium (a) 2-2, USSR (n) 2-0, Cameroon (n) 1-2, Argentina (n) 1-1, Rep of Ireland (n) 0-0, USSR (a) 2-1, Scotland (a) 1-2, Poland (h) 2-1, Bulgaria (h) 0-3, San Marino (h) 6-0.
Goalscorers: Balint 4, Lacatus 4 (3 pens), Camataru 2, Hagi 2 (1 pen), Lupescu 2, Raducioiu 2, Sabau 2, Timofte 2, Badea 1, Lazar 1, Mateut 1, Petrescu 1, Rednic 1, Rotariu 1.

League Championship wins (1910–91)

Steaua Bucharest (prev. CCA) 14; Dinamo Bucharest 13; Venus Bucharest 7; CSC Temesvar 6; UT Arad 6; Ripensia Temesvar 4; Uni Craiova 4; Petrolul Ploesti 3; Rapid Bucharest 2; Olimpia Bucharest 2; CAC Bucharest 2; Arges Pitesti 2; Soc RA Bucharest 1; Prahova Ploesti 1; CSC Brasov 1; Juventus Bucharest 1; SSUD Reita 1; Craiova Bucharest 1; Progresul 1; Ploesti United 1; Unirea Tricolor 1.

Cup wins (1934–91)

Steaua Bucharest (prev. CCA) 17; Rapid Bucharest 9; Dinamo Bucharest 7; Uni Craiova 5; UT Arad 2; Progresul 2; Ripensia Temesvar 2; ICO Oradeo 1; Metal Ochimia Resita 1; Petrolul Ploesti 1; Stinta Cluj 1; Stinta Timisoara 1; Turnu Severin 1; Chimia Rannicu 1; Jiul Petroseni 1; Poli Timisoara 1.

Final League Table 1990–91

	P	W	D	L	F	A	Pts
Uni Craiova	34	22	6	6	74	25	50
Steaua	34	20	10	4	67	28	50
Dinamo	34	16	11	7	54	27	43
Inter Sibiu	34	18	2	14	56	46	38
Gloria	34	15	7	12	51	38	37
Timisoara	34	14	7	13	45	45	35
Petrolul	34	15	5	14	48	49	35
Arges	34	13	8	13	49	42	34
Brasov	34	14	6	14	47	45	34
Farul	34	12	10	12	40	40	34
Rapid	34	13	6	15	45	45	32
Sportul	34	10	12	12	43	54	32
Corvinul[1]	34	15	2	17	47	62	31
Progresul	34	13	5	16	33	49	31
Bacau	34	11	7	16	32	42	29
Petrosani*	34	11	6	17	47	65	28
Oradea[2]*	34	7	8	19	40	75	20
Uni Cluj*	34	5	6	23	26	67	16

Top scorer: Hanganu (Corvinul) 22
Cup Final: Uni Craiova 2, Bacau 1
[1] two points deducted; [2] four points deducted

SAN MARINO

Federazione Sammarinese Giuoco Calcio, Palazzo C.O.N.S., Via Del Bando 28, 47031 Borgo Maggiore.
Founded: 1931; *Number of Clubs:* 17; *Number of Players:* 920; *Colours:* Blue and white.
Telephone: (0549) 90 22 28 and 90 25 08; *Cable:* FEDERCALCIO SAN MARINO; *Telex:* 0505 284 CONSMAR SO; *Fax:* 0549 902516.

International matches 1990

Switzerland (h) 0-4, Romania (a) 0-6.

SCOTLAND

The Scottish Football Association Ltd, 6 Park Gardens, Glasgow G3 7YF.
Founded: 1873; *Number of Clubs:* 6,148; *Number of Players:* 139,000; *National Colours:* Dark blue shirts, white shorts, red stockings.
Telephone: 41 332 6372; *Cable:* EXECUTIVE GLASGOW; *Telex:* 778904 SFA G; *Fax:* 41 332 7559.

SPAIN

Real Federacion Espanola De Futbol, Calle Alberto Bosch 13, Apartado Postal 347, E-28014 Madrid.
Founded: 1913; *Number of Clubs:* 30,920; *Number of Players:* 343,657; *National Colours:* Red shirts, dark blue shorts, black stockings, yellow trim.
Telephone: 420 13 62; *Cable:* FUTBOL MADRID; *Telex:* 42420 RFEF; *Fax:* 420 20 94.

International matches 1990

Czechoslovakia (h) 1-0, Austria (h) 2-3, Yugoslavia (a) 1-0, Uruguay (n) 0-0, South Korea (n) 3-1, Belgium (n) 2-1, Yugoslavia (n) 1-2, Brazil (h) 3-0, Iceland (h) 2-1, Czechoslovakia (a) 2-3, Albania (h) 9-0.
Goalscorers: Butragueno 8, Michel 5 (1 pen), Carlos 5, Manolo 2, Amor 1, Bakero 1, Fernando 1, Gorriz 1, Hierro 1, Salinas 1.

League Championship wins (1945–91)

Real Madrid 25; Barcelona 11; Atletico Madrid 8; Athletic Bilbao 8; Valencia 4; Real Sociedad 2; Real Betis 1; Seville 1.

Cup wins (1902–91)

Athletic Bilbao 23; Barcelona 22; Real Madrid 16; Atletico Madrid 7; Valencia 6; Real Union de Irun 3; Seville 3; Real Zaragoza 3; Espanol 2; Arenas 1; Ciclista Sebastian 1; Racing de Irun 1; Vizcaya Bilbao 1; Real Betis 1; Real Sociedad 1.

Final League Table 1990–91

	P	W	D	L	F	A	Pts
Barcelona	38	25	7	6	74	33	57
Atletico Madrid	38	17	13	8	52	28	47
Real Madrid	38	20	6	12	63	37	46
Osasuna	38	15	15	8	43	34	45
Sporting Gijon	38	16	12	10	50	37	44
Oviedo	38	13	16	9	36	35	42
Valencia	38	15	10	13	44	40	40
Seville	38	15	8	15	45	47	38
Burgos	38	10	17	11	32	27	37
Valladolid	38	12	13	13	38	40	37
Logrones	38	13	11	14	28	35	37
Real Sociedad	38	11	14	13	39	45	36
Athletic Bilbao	38	15	6	17	41	50	36
Tenerife	38	14	7	17	37	53	35
Espanol	38	12	10	16	39	47	34
Mallorca	38	9	16	13	32	40	34
Zaragoza	38	11	11	16	36	40	33
Cadiz	38	7	15	16	29	41	29
Castellon*	38	8	12	18	27	48	28
Betis*	38	6	13	19	37	65	25

Top scorer: Butragueno (Real Madrid) 19
Cup Final: Atletico Madrid 1, Mallorca 0

SWEDEN

Svenska Fotbollfoerbundet, Box 1216, S-17123 Solna.
Founded: 1904; *Number of Clubs:* 3,400; *Number of Players:* 437,000; *National Colours:* Yellow shirts, blue shorts, yellow and blue stockings.
Telephone: 8-735 0900; *Cable:* FOOTBALL-S; *Telex:* 17711 FOTBOL S; *Fax:* 8-27 51 47.

International matches 1990

UAE (a) 1-2, UAE (a) 2-0, Belgium (a) 0-0, Algeria (a) 1-1, Wales (h) 4-2, Finland (h) 6-0, Brazil (n) 1-2, Scotland (n) 1-2, Costa Rica (n) 1-2, Norway (a) 2-1, Denmark (h) 0-1, Bulgaria (h) 2-0, West Germany (h) 1-3.
Goalscorers: Brolin 5, Ingesson 3, Rehn 2 (1 pen), Schwarz 2, Andersson 1, Corneliusson 1, Ekstrom 1, Engqvist 1, Fjellstrom 1, Larsson 1, Limpar 1, Magnusson 1, Stromberg 1, Thern 1.

League Championship wins (1896–1990)

Oergryte IS Gothenburg 14; Malmo FF 13; IFK Norrköping 12; IFK Gothenburg 12; Djurgaarden 8; AIK Stockholm 8; GAIS Gothenburg 6; IF Halsingborg 5; Boras IF Elfsborg 4; Oster Vaxjo 4; Halmstad 2; Atvidaberg 2; IFK Ekilstune 1; IF Gavic Brynas 1; IF Gothenburg 1; Fassbergs 1; Norrköping IK Sleipner 1.

Cup wins (1941–90)

Malmo FF 13; IFK Norrköping 5; AIK Stockholm 4; IFK Gothenburg 3; Atvidaberg 2; Kalmar 2; GAIS Gothenburg 1; IF Halsingborg 1; Raa 1; Landskrona 1; Oster Vaxjo 1; Djurgaarden 1.

Final League Table 1990

	P	W	D	L	F	A	Pts
IFK Gothenburg	22	14	3	5	39	21	45
Norrköping	22	12	4	6	41	23	40
Orebro	22	10	6	6	23	17	36
Osters	22	10	6	6	28	27	36
Djurgaarden	22	9	6	7	36	23	33
Malmo	22	6	10	6	20	15	28
GAIS Gothenburg	22	7	7	8	17	17	28
AIK	22	8	3	11	25	39	27
Halmstad	22	7	5	10	27	34	26
Brage*	22	5	9	8	23	26	24
Oergryte*	22	6	3	13	22	40	21
Hammarby*	22	5	4	13	32	51	19

Semi-finals: Orebro–IFK Gothenburg 1–1, 0–2; Osters–Norrköping 4–3, 1–2
Final: Norrköping 0, IFK Gothenburg 3
Top scorer: Eskelinen (IFK Gothenburg) 10
Cup Final: Norrköping 4, Osters 1

SWITZERLAND

Association Suisse De Football, Laubeggstrasse 70, B.P. CH-3000, Berne 32.
Founded: 1895; *Number of Clubs:* 1,480; *Number of Players:* 182,953; *National Colours:* Red shirts, white shorts, red stockings.
Telephone: 031-43 51 11; *Cable:* SWISSFOOT BERNE; *Telex:* 912910 SFV CH; *Fax:* (031) 44 33 80.

International matches 1990

Italy (h) 0-1, Romania (h) 2-1, Argentina (h) 1-1, USA (h) 2-1, Austria (a) 3-1, Bulgaria (h) 2-0, Scotland (a) 1-2, San Marino (a) 4-0, West Germany (a) 0-4.
Goalscorers: Knup 4, Turkyilmaz 3, Chassot 2, Bickel 1, Chapuisat 1, Hermann 1, Hottiger 1, Schepull 1, Sutter A 1.

League Championship wins (1898–1991)

Grasshoppers 22; Servette 15; Young Boys Berne 11; FC Zurich 9; FC Basle 8; Lausanne 7; La Chaux-de-Fonds 3; FC Lugano 3; Winterthur 3; FX Aarau 2; Neuchatel Xamax 2; FC Anglo-American 1; St Gallen 1; FC Brühl 1; Cantonal-Neuchatel 1; Biel 1; Bellinzona 1; FC Etoile La Chaux-de-Fonds 1; Lucerne 1.

Cup wins (1926–91)

Grasshoppers 17; Lausanne 7; La Chaux-de-Fonds 6; Young Boys Berne 6; Servette 6; FC Sion 6; FC Basle 5; FC Zurich 5; FC Lugano 1; FC Granges 1; Lucerne 1; St Gallen 1; Urania Geneva 1; Young Fellows Zurich 1; Aarau 1.

Qualifying Table

	P	W	D	L	F	A	Pts
Sion	22	10	10	2	31	20	30
Grasshoppers	22	9	9	4	29	17	27
Neuchatel Xamax	22	8	10	4	25	15	26
Lausanne	22	9	8	5	39	30	26
Lugano	22	8	9	5	27	22	25
Servette	22	9	6	7	30	27	24
Young Boys	22	6	11	5	35	26	23
Lucerne	22	8	7	7	30	28	23
St Gallen††	22	7	8	7	26	26	22
Aarau††	22	3	9	10	19	30	15
Zurich††	22	3	6	13	21	45	12
Wettingen††	22	3	5	14	24	50	11

††had to play-off in promotion/relegation section

Final League Table 1990–91

	P	W	D	L	F	A	Pts
Grasshoppers	14	7	5	2	27	15	33
Sion	14	3	8	3	14	15	29
Neuchatel Xamax	14	5	6	3	16	13	29
Lausanne	14	5	6	3	15	13	29
Lugano	14	5	4	5	16	15	27
Young Boys	14	3	6	5	21	26	24
Servette	14	1	9	4	16	24	23
Lucerne	14	3	4	7	16	20	22

N.B. Teams take half points from qualifying table
Top scorer: Zuffi (Young Boys) 17
Cup Final: Sion 3, Young Boys 2

TURKEY

Federation Turque De Football, Konur Sokak No. 10, Ankara — Kizilay.
Founded: 1923; *Number of Clubs:* 3,754; *Number of Players:* 87,200; *National Colours:* White shirts, white shorts, red and white stockings.
Telephone: 1259182/1259189; *Cable:* FUTBOLSPOR ANKARA; *Telex:* 46308; *Fax:* (4) 117 1090.

International matches 1990

Denmark (a) 0-1, Rep of Ireland (h) 0-0, Hungary (a) 1-4, Rep of Ireland (a) 0-5, Poland (h) 0-1
Goalscorers: Tanju 1.

League Championship wins (1960–91)

Fenerbahce 12; Galatasaray 8; Besiktas 8; Trabzonspor 6.

Cup wins (1963–91)

Galatasaray 9; Fenerbahce 4; Besiktas 4; Trabzonspor 3; Goztepe Izmir 2; Atay Ismir 2; Ankaragucu 2; Eskisehirspor 1; Bursapor 1; Genclerbirligi 1; Sakaryaspor 1.

Final League Table 1990–91

	P	W	D	L	F	A	Pts
Besiktas	30	20	9	1	63	24	69
Galatasaray	30	19	7	4	63	31	64
Trabzonspor	30	14	9	7	55	37	51
Sariyer	30	11	12	7	39	34	45
Fenerbahce	30	12	8	10	53	53	44
Barkiroy	30	12	7	11	53	42	43
Ankaragucu	30	11	8	11	46	43	41
Bursaspor	30	11	5	14	31	36	38
Boluspor	30	8	13	9	36	36	37
Genclerbirligi	30	9	9	12	36	47	36
Aydinspor	30	7	13	10	44	51	34
Konyaspor	30	10	4	16	33	45	34
Gaziantep	30	9	6	15	28	45	33
Zeytinburnu*	30	6	11	13	26	40	29
Karsiyaka*	30	6	8	16	32	50	26
Adana*	30	5	11	14	34	58	26

Top scorer: Tanju (Galatasaray) 31
Cup Final: Galatasaray 3, Ankaragucu 1

USSR

USSR Football Federation, Luzhnetskaja Naberezhnaja 8, 119270 Moscow.
Founded: 1912; *Number of Clubs:* 50,198; *Number of Players:* 4,800,300; *National Colours:* Red shirts, white shorts, red stockings.
Telephone: 201 08 34; *Cable:* SPORTKOMITET SSSR MOSCOW; *Telex:* 411287 PRIZ SU; *Fax:* 2480814.

International matches 1990

Colombia (n) 0-0, Costa Rica (n) 2-1, USA (a) 3-1, Holland (h) 2-1, Rep of Ireland (a) 0-1, Israel (a) 2-3, Romania (n) 0-2, Argentina (n) 0-2, Cameroon (n) 4-0, Romania (h) 1-2, Norway (h) 2-0, Israel (h) 3-0, Italy (a) 0-0, USA (a) 0-0, Trinidad & Tobago (a) 2-0, Guatemala (h) 3-0
Goalscorers: Litovchenko 3, Protasov 3 (1 pen), Dobrovolski 2, Mikhailichenko 2, Tcherenkov 2, Youran 2, Bessonov 1, Kolivanov 1, Kontchelskis 1, Kuznetsov 1, Liuti 1, Mostovoi 1, Shalimov 1, Tsvelba 1, Zavarov 1, Zygmantovich 1.

League Championship wins (1936–90)

Dynamo Kiev 13; Spartak Moscow 12; Dynamo Moscow 11; CSKA Moscow 6; Torpedo Moscow 3; Dynamo Tbilisi 2; Dnepr Dnepropetrovsk 2; Saria Voroshilovgrad 1; Ararat Erevan 1; Dynamo Minsk 1; Zenit Leningrad 1.

Cup wins (1936–90)

Dynamo Kiev 10; Spartak Moscow 9; Torpedo Moscow 6; Dynamo Moscow 6; CSKA Moscow 4; Donetsk Shaktyor 4; Lokomotiv Moscow 2; Dynamo Tbilisi 2; Ararat Erevan 2; Karpaty Lvov 1; SKA Rostov 1; Zenit Leningrad 1; Metalist Kharkov 1; Dnepr 1.

Final League Table 1990

	P	W	D	L	F	A	Pts
Dynamo Kiev	24	14	6	4	44	20	34
CSKA Moscow	24	13	5	6	43	26	31
Dynamo Moscow	24	12	7	5	27	24	31
Torpedo Moscow	24	13	4	7	28	24	30
Spartak Moscow	24	12	5	7	39	26	29
Dnepr	24	11	6	7	39	26	28
Ararat Erevan	24	8	7	9	25	23	23
Donetsk	24	6	10	8	23	31	22
Chernomorets	24	8	3	13	23	29	19
Douchambe	24	7	4	13	26	34	18
Kharkov	24	5	8	11	13	28	18
Dynamo Minsk	24	6	3	15	20	34	15
Rotor Volgograd*	24	4	6	14	14	39	14

Top scorers: Protasov (Dynamo Kiev) and Chmarov (Spartak Moscow) 12
Cup Final: Dynamo Kiev 6, Lokomotive Moscow 1

WALES

The Football Association of Wales Limited, Plymouth Chambers, 3 Westgate Street, Cardiff. *Founded:* 1876; *Number of Clubs:* 1,923; *Number of Players:* 51,578; *National Colours:* All red. *Telephone:* 0222 372325; *Telex:* 497 363 FAW G.

YUGOSLAVIA

Yugoslav Football Association, P.O. Box 263, Terazije 35, 11000 Beograd.
Founded: 1919; *Number of Clubs:* 7,455; *Number of Players:* 270,229; *National Colours:* Blue shirts, white shorts, red stockings.
Telephone: 333-433 and 11/334-253; *Cable:* JUGOFUDBAL BEOGRAD; *Telex:* 11666 FSJ YU; *Fax:* 0038-11-33 34 33.

International matches 1990

Poland (a) 0-0, Spain (h) 0-1, Holland (h) 0-2, West Germany (n) 1-4, Colombia (n) 1-0, UAE (n) 4-1, Spain (n) 2-1, Argentina (n) 0-0, Northern Ireland (a) 2-0, Austria (h) 4-1, Denmark (a) 2-0
Goalscorers: Pancev 6, Josic 2, Prosinecki 2, Stojkovic 2, Bazdarevic 1, Jarni 1, Katanec 1, Susic 1.

League Championship wins (1923–91)

Red Star Belgrade 18; Partizan Belgrade 11; Hajduk Split 9; Gradjanski Zagreb 5; BSK Belgrade 5; Dynamo Zagreb 4; Jugoslavija Belgrade 2; Concordia Zagreb 2; FC Sarajevo 2; Vojvodina Novi Sad 2; HASK Zagreb 1; Zeljeznicar 1.

Cup wins (1947–91)

Red Star Belgrade 12; Hajduk Split 9; Dynamo Zagreb 8; Partizan Belgrade 5; BSK Belgrade 2; OFK Belgrade 2; Rejeka 2; Velez Mostar 2; Vardar Skopje 1; Borac Banjaluka 1.

Final League Table 1990–91

	P	W	D=	L	F	A	Pts
Red Star Belgrade	36	25	6	5	88	35	54
Dynamo Zagreb	36	20	10	6	72	36	46
Partizan Belgrade	36	18	8	10	62	36	41
Hajduk Split	36	16	9	11	50	39	36
Borac	36	14	11	11	42	37	35
Proleter	36	17	4	15	49	49	35
Vojvodina	36	14	9	13	47	52	34
Rad	36	14	7	15	42	34	32
Radnicki	36	14	5	17	36	49	32
Sarajevo	36	13	10	13	36	47	31
Velez	36	12	10	14	53	54	30
Zeljeznicar	36	11	13	12	34	40	30
Osijek	36	13	6	17	51	58	30
Zemun	36	12	10	14	40	52	30
Olimpia	36	14	3	19	42	59	30
Rijeka	36	13	10	13	33	25	29
Buducnost*	36	13	6	17	43	48	28
Sloboda*	36	11	7	18	36	56	24
Spartak*	36	1	10	25	24	74	4

* = penalty shoot-outs after drawn games with one point for winners
Top scorer: Pancev (Red Star Belgrade) 34
Cup Final: Hajduk Split 1, Red Star Belgrade 0

SOUTH AMERICA

ARGENTINA

Asociacion Del Futbol Argentina, Viamonte 1366/76, 1053 Buenos Aires.
Founded: 1893; *Number of Clubs:* 3,035; *Number of Players:* 306,365; *National Colours:* Blue & white shirts, black shorts, white stockings.
Telephone: 40-4276; *Cable:* FUTBOL BUENOS AIRES; *Telex:* 22710 AFA AR; *Fax:* 953 3469 AFA.

BOLIVIA

Federacion Boliviana De Futbol, Av. 16 De Julio No. N. 0782, Casilla Postal No. 484, Cochabamba.
Founded: 1925; *Number of Clubs:* 305; *Number of Players:* 15,290; *National Colours:* Green shirts, white shorts, green stockings.
Telephone: 4-5064; *Cable:* FEDFUTBOL COCHABAMBA; *Telex:* 6239 FEDBOL; *Fax:* 4-7951.

BRAZIL

Confederacao Brasileira De Futebol, Rua Da Alfandega, 70, P.O. Box 1078, 20.070 Rio De Janeiro.
Founded: 1914; *Number of Clubs:* 12,987; *Number of Players:* 551,358; *National Colours:* Yellow shirts, blue shorts, white stockings, green trim.
Telephone: 221/5937; *Cable:* DESPORTOS RIO DE JANEIRO; *Telex:* 2121509 CBDS BR; *Fax:* (021) 252 9294.

CHILE

Federacion De Futbol De Chile, Calle Erasmo Escala No. 1872, Casilla No. 3733, Santiago De Chile.
Founded: 1895; *Number of Clubs:* 4,598; *Number of Players:* 609,724; *National Colours:* Red shirts, blue shorts, white stockings.
Telephone: 696 5381; *Cable:* FEDFUTBOL SANTIAGO DE CHILE; *Telex:* 440474 FEBOL CZ; *Fax:* 698 7082.

COLOMBIA

Federacion Colombiana De Futbol, Avenida 32, No. 16-22, Apartado Aereo No. 17.602, Bogota, D.E.
Founded: 1925; *Number of Clubs:* 3,685; *Number of Players:* 188,050; *National Colours:* Red shirts, blue shorts, tricolour stockings.
Telephone: 245 5370; *Cable:* COLFUTBOL BOGOTA; *Telex:* 45598 COLFU CO.

ECUADOR

Federacion Ecuatoriana De Futbol, Calle Jose Mascote 1.103 (Piso 2), Luque, Casilla 7447, Guayaquil.
Founded: 1906; *Number of Clubs:* 170; *Number of Players:* 15,700; *National Colours:* Yellow shirts, blue shorts, red stockings.
Telephone: 37 16 74; *Cable:* ECUAFUTBOL GUAYAQUIL; *Telex:* 42970 FEECFU ED; *Fax:* (593-4) 373-320.

PARAGUAY

Liga Paraguaya De Futbol, Estadio De Sajonia, Calles Mayor Martinez Y Alejo Garcia, Asuncion.
Founded: 1906; *Number of Clubs:* 1,500; *Number of Players:* 140,000; *National Colours:* Red & white shirts, blue shorts, blue stockings.
Telephone: 81743; *Telex:* 627 PY FUTBOL; *Fax:* 595 21 81743.

PERU

Federacion Peruana De Futbol, Estadio Nacional/Puerto No. 4, Calle Jose Diaz, Lima.
Founded: 1922; *Number of Clubs:* 10,000; *Number of Players:* 325,650; *National Colours:* White shirts, red trim, white shorts, white stockings.
Telephone: 32 05 17; *Cable:* FEPEFUTBOL LIMA; *Telex:* 20066 FEPEFUT PE.

URUGUAY

Asociacion Uruguaya De Futbol, Guayabo 1531, Montevideo.
Founded: 1900; *Number of Clubs:* 1,091; *Number of Players:* 134,310; *National Colours:* Light blue shirts, black shorts, black stockings.
Telephone: 40 71 01/06; *Cable:* FUTBOL MONTEVIDEO; *Telex:* AUF UY 22607.

VENEZUELA

Federacion Venezolana De Futbol, Avda Este Estadio Nacional, El Paraiso Apdo. Postal 14160, Candelaria, Caracas.
Founded: 1926; *Number of Clubs:* 1,753; *Number of Players:* 63,175; *National Colours:* Magenta shirts, white shorts, white stockings.
Telephone: 461 80 10; *Cable:* FEVEFUTBOL CARACAS; *Telex:* 26 140 FVFCS VC.

ASIA

AFGHANISTAN

The Football Federation of National Olympic Committee, Kabul.
Founded: 1922; *Number of Clubs:* 30; *Number of Players:* 3,300; *National Colours:* White shirts, white shorts, white stockings.
Telephone: 20579; *Cable:* OLYMPIC KABUL.

BAHRAIN

Bahrain Football Association, P.O. Box 5464, Bahrain.
Founded: 1951; *Number of Clubs:* 25; *Number of Players:* 2,030; *National Colours:* White shirts, red shorts, white stockings.
Telephone: 72 95 63; *Cable:* BAHKORA BAHRAIN; *Telex:* 9040 FAB BN; *Fax:* 729361.

BANGLADESH

Bangladesh Football Federation, Stadium, Dhaka 2.
Founded: 1972; *Number of Clubs:* 1,265; *Number of Players:* 30,385; *National Colours:* Orange shirts, white shorts, green stockings.
Telephone: 23 60 72/23 59 28; *Cable:* FOOTBALFED DHAKA; *Telex:* 642460 BHL BJ.

BRUNEI

Brunei Amateur Football Association, P.O. Box 2010, Bandar Seri Begawan 1920, Brunei Darussalam.
Founded: 1959; *Number of Clubs:* 22; *Number of Players:* 830; *National Colours:* Gold shirts, black shorts, gold stockings.
Telephone: 673-02-24 22 83, 24 31 71; *Cable:* BAFA BRUNEI; *Telex:* dirwyas BU 2575 Attn: BAFA; *Fax:* 673-02-24 23 00.

BURMA (now Myanmar)

Myanmar Football Federation, Aung San Memorial Stadium, Kandawgalay Post Office, Yangon.
Founded: 1947; *Number of Clubs:* 600; *Number of Players:* 21,000; *National Colours:* Red shirts, white shorts, red stockings.
Telephone: 75 249; *Cable:* YANGON MYANMAR; *Telex:* 21218 BRCROS BRN.

CHINA PR

Football Association of The People's Republic of China, 9 Tiyuguan Road, Beijing.
Founded: 1924; *Number of Clubs:* 1,045; *Number of Players:* 2,250,000; *National Colours:* Red shirts, white shorts, red stockings.
Telephone: 5112533; *Cable:* SPORTSCHINE BEIJING; *Telex:* 22034 ACSF CN.

HONG KONG

The Hong Kong Football Association Ltd. 55 Fat Kwong Street, Homantin, Kowloon, Hong Kong.
Founded: 1914; *Number of Clubs:* 69; *Number of Players:* 3,274; *National Colours:* Red shirts, white shorts, red stockings.
Telephone: 3-712 9122-5; *Cable:* FOOTBALL HONG KONG; *Telex:* 40518 FAHKG HX; *Fax:* 3-760 4303.

INDIA

All India Football Federation. Netaji Indoor Stadium, Eden Gardens, Calcutta 700 021.
Founded: 1937; *Number of Clubs:* 2,000; *Number of Players:* 56,000; *National Colours:* Light blue shirts, white shorts, dark blue stockings.
Telephone: 28 8484; *Cable:* SOCCER CALCUTTA; *Telex:* 212216 MCPL IN.

INDONESIA

All Indonesia Football Federation, Main Stadium Senayan, Gate VII, P.O. Box 2305, Jakarta.
Founded: 1930; *Number of Clubs:* 2,880; *Number of Players:* 97,000; *National Colours:* Red shirts, white shorts, red stockings.
Telephone: 581541/584386; *Cable:* PSSI JAKARTA; *Telex:* 44439 PSSI IA; *Fax:* (021) 584386.

IRAN

Football Federation of The Islamic Republic of Iran, Ave Varzandeh No. 10, P.O. Box 11/1642, Tehran.
Founded: 1920; *Number of Clubs:* 6,326; *Number of Players:* 306,000; *National Colours:* Green shirts, white shorts, red stockings.
Telephone: (021) 825534; *Cable:* FOOTBALL IRAN — TEHRAN; *Telex:* 212691 VARZ IR.

IRAQ

Iraqi Football Association, Youth City, P.O. Box 484, Baghdad.
Founded: 1948; *Number of Clubs:* 155; *Number of Players:* 4,400; *National Colours:* White shirts, white shorts, white stockings.
Telephone: 772 8430; *Cable:* BALL BAGHDAD; *Telex:* 214074 IRFA IK.

ISRAEL

Israel Football Association, 12 Carlibach Street, P.O. Box 20188, Tel Aviv 61201.
Founded: 1928; *Number of Clubs:* 544; *Number of Players:* 30,449; *National Colours:* White shirts, blue shorts, white stockings.
Telephone: 56 10 888; *Cable:* CADUREGEL TEL AVIV; *Telex:* 361353 FA; *Fax:* 03 5610838.

JAPAN

The Football Association of Japan, 1-1-1 Jinnan, Shibuya-Ku, Tokyo.
Founded: 1921; *Number of Clubs:* 13,047; *Number of Players:* 358,989; *National Colours:* Blue shirts, white shorts, blue stockings.
Telephone: 03-481-2311; *Cable:* SOCCERJAPAN TOKYO; *Telex:* 2422975 FOTJPN J; *Fax:* 81 3 481 0976.

JORDAN

Jordan Football Association, P.O. Box 1954, Amman.
Founded: 1949; *Number of Clubs:* 98; *Number of Players:* 4,305; *National Colours:* White shirts, white shorts, white stockings.
Telephone: 62 59 93; *Cable:* JORDAN FOOTBALL ASSOCIATION AM; *Telex:* 22415 FOBALL JO.

KAMPUCHEA

Federation Khmere De Football Association, C.P. 101, Complex Sportif National, Phnom-Penh.
Founded: 1933; *Number of Clubs:* 30; *Number of Players:* 650; *National Colours:* Red shirts, white shorts, red stockings.
Telephone: 22 469; *Cable:* FKFA PHNOMPENH.

KOREA, NORTH

Football Association of The Democratic People's Rep. of Korea, Munsin-Dong 2, Dongdaewon Distr, Pyongyang.
Founded: 1928; *Number of Clubs:* 90; *Number of Players:* 3,420; *National Colours:* Red shirts, white shorts, red stockings.
Telephone: 6-3998; *Cable:* DPR KOREA FOOTBALL PYONGYANG; *Telex:* 5472 KP.

KOREA, SOUTH

Korea Football Association, 110-39, Kyeonji-Dong, Chongro-Ku, Seoul.
Founded: 1928; *Number of Clubs:* 476; *Number of Players:* 2,047; *National Colours:* Red shirts, red shorts, red stockings.
Telephone: 02-733-6764; *Cable:* FOOTBALLKOREA SEOUL; *Telex:* KFASEL K 25373; *Fax:* 02 735 2755.

KUWAIT

Kuwait Football Association, Udailiyya, BL. 4, Al-Ittihad St, P.O. Box 2029 (Safat), 13021 Safat.
Founded: 1952; *Number of Clubs:* 14 (senior); *Number of Players:* 1,526; *National Colours:* Blue shirts, white shorts, blue stockings.
Telephone: 254 9955; *Cable:* FOOTKUWAIT; *Telex:* FOOTKUW 22600 KT; *Fax:* 2555939.

LAOS

Federation De Foot-Ball Lao, c/o Dir. Des Sports, Education, Physique Et Artistique, Vientiane.
Founded: 1951; *Number of Clubs:* 76; *Number of Players:* 2,060; *National Colours:* Red shirts, white shorts, blue stockings.
Telephone: 27 41; *Cable:* FOOTBALL VIENTIANE.

LEBANON

Federation Libanaise De Football Association, P.O. Box 4732, Omar Ibn Khattab Street, Beirut.
Founded: 1933; *Number of Clubs:* 105; *Number of Players:* 8,125; *National Colours:* Red shirts, white shorts, red stockings.
Telephone: (1) 30 07 60; *Cable:* FOOTBALL BEIRUT; *Telex:* 23001 ALABAL.

MACAO

Associacao De Futebol De Macau (AFM), P.O. Box 920, Macau.
Founded: 1939; *Number of Clubs:* 52; *Number of Players:* 800; *National Colours:* Green shirts, white shorts, green and white stockings.
Telephone: 71 996 (559315); *Cable:* FOOTBALL MACAU.

MALDIVES REPUBLIC

Football Association of Maldives, Attn. Mr. Bandhu Ahamed Saleem, Sports Divison, Male.
Founded: 1986; *Number of Clubs:* —; *Number of Players:* —; *National Colours:* Green shirts, white shorts, green and white stockings.
Telephone: 3432; *Telex:* 77039 MINHOM MF; *Fax:* (960) 32 47 39.

MALAYSIA

Football Association of Malaysia, Wisma Fam, Tingkat 4, Jalan SS5A/9, Kelana Jaya, 47301 Petaling, Jaya Selangor.
Founded: 1933; *Number of Clubs:* 450; *Number of Players:* 11,250; *National Colours:* Black and gold shirts, white shorts, black and gold stockings.
Telephone: 03-776 3766; *Cable:* FOOTBALL PETALING JAYA SELANGO; *Telex:* FAM PJ MA 36701; *Fax:* 03-775 7984.

NEPAL

All-Nepal Football Association, Dasharath Rangashala, Tripureshwor, Kathmandu.
Founded: 1951; *Number of Clubs:* 85; *Number of Players:* 2,550; *National Colours:* Red shirts, blue shorts, blue and white stockings.
Telephone: 2-15 703; *Cable:* ANFA KATHMANDU; *Telex:* 2390 NSC NP.

OMAN

Oman Football Association, P.O. Box 6462, Ruwi-Muscat.
Founded: 1978; *Number of Clubs:* 47; *Number of Players:* 2,340; *National Colours:* White shirts, red shorts, white stockings.
Telephone: 70 78 85; *Cable:* FOOTBALL MUSCAT; *Telex:* 3760 FOOTBALL ON; *Fax:* 707829.

PAKISTAN

Pakistan Football Federation, Mohd. Saeed Kahn, Gen. Secr. Deputy Inspector of Police, Peshawar-Central Police Office
Founded: 1948; *Number of Clubs:* 882; *Number of Players:* 21,000; *National Colours:* Green shirts, white shorts, green stockings.
Telephone: 79 725, 70 013; *Cable:* FOOTBALL QUETTA; *Telex:* 52369 PCOPE PK; *Fax:* 92 081-73 979.

PHILIPPINES

Philippine Football Federation, Room 207, Administration Building, Rizal Memorial Sports Complex, Vito Cruz, Metro Manila.
Founded: 1907; *Number of Clubs:* 650; *Number of Players:* 45,000; *National Colours:* Blue shirts, white shorts, blue stockings.
Telephone: 58 83 17; *Cable:* FOOTBALL MANILA; *Telex:* 63539 ANSCOR PN.

QATAR

Qatar Football Association, P.O. Box 5333, Doha.
Founded: 1960; *Number of Clubs:* 8 (senior); *Number of Players:* 1,380; *National Colours:* White shirts, maroon shorts, white stockings.
Telephone: 351641, 454444; *Cable:* FOOTQATAR DOHA; *Telex:* 4749 QATFOT DH; *Fax:* (0974) 411660.

SAUDI ARABIA

Saudi Arabian Football Federation, North Al-Morabbaa' Quarter, P.O. Box 5844, Riyadh 11432.
Founded: 1959; *Number of Clubs:* 120; *Number of Players:* 9,600; *National Colours:* White shirts, white shorts, white stockings.
Telephone: 402 2699; *Cable:* KORA RIYADH; *Telex:* 404300 SAFOTB SJ; *Fax:* 01 402 1276.

SINGAPORE

Football Association of Singapore, Jalan Besar Stadium, Tyrwhitt Road, Singapore 0820
Founded: 1892; *Number of Clubs:* 250; *Number of Players:* 8,000; *National Colours:* Sky blue shirts, sky blue shorts, sky blue stockings.
Telephone: 293 1477; *Cable:* SOCCER SINGAPORE; *Telex:* SINFA RS 37683.

SRI LANKA

Football Federation of Sri Lanka, No. 2, Old Grand Stand, Race Course — Reid Avenue, Colombo 7.
Founded: 1939; *Number of Clubs:* 600; *Number of Players:* 18,825; *National Colours:* Maroon shirts, white shorts, white stockings.
Telephone: 596179; *Cable:* SOCCER COLOMBO; *Telex:* 21537 METALIX CE; *Fax:* 94-1-580721.

SYRIA

Association Arabe Syrienne De Football, General Sport Fed. Building, October Stadium, Damascus — Baremke.
Founded: 1936; *Number of Clubs:* 102; *Number of Players:* 30,600; *National Colours:* White shirts, white shorts, white stockings.
Telephone: 33 15 11; *Cable:* FOOTBALL DAMASCUS; *Telex:* HOTECH 41 19 35.

THAILAND

The Football Association of Thailand, c/o National Stadium, Rama 1 Road, Bangkok.
Founded: 1916; *Number of Clubs:* 168; *Number of Players:* 15,000; *National Colours:* Crimson shirts, white shorts, crimson stockings.
Telephone: 02 214 1058; *Cable:* FOOTBALL BANGKOK; *Telex:* 20211 FAT TH; *Fax:* 2154494.

UNITED ARAB EMIRATES

United Arab Emirates Football Association, Post Box 5458, Dubai.
Founded: 1971; *Number of Clubs:* 23 (senior); *Number of Players:* 1,787; *National Colours:* White shirts, white shorts, white stockings.
Telephone: 245 636; *Cable:* FOOTBALL EMIRATES DUBAI; *Telex:* 47623 UAEFA EM; *Fax:* 245 559.

VIETNAM

Association De Football De La Republique Du Viet-Nam, No. 36, Boulevard Tran-Phu, Hanoi. *Founded:* 1962; *Number of Clubs:* 55 (senior); *Number of Players:* 16,000; *National Colours:* Red shirts, white shorts, red stockings.
Telephone: 5/48 67; *Cable:* AFBVN, 36, TRAN-PHU-HANOI.

YEMEN

Yemen Football Association. (Amalgamation of Yemen AR and PDR Yemen, May 1990.) No new details available.

CONCACAF

ANTIGUA

The Antigua Football Association, P.O. Box 773, St. Johns.
Founded: 1928; *Number of Clubs:* 60; *Number of Players:* 1,008; *National Colours:* Gold shirts, black shorts, black stockings.
Telephone: 809 462 3945; *Cable:* AFA ANTIGUA; *Telex:* 2177 SIDAN AK; *Fax:* 809 462 2649.

BAHAMAS

Bahamas Football Association, P.O. Box N 8434, Nassau, N.P.
Founded: 1967; *Number of Clubs:* 14; *Number of Players:* 700; *National Colours:* Yellow shirts, black shorts, yellow stockings.
Telephone: 809 32 47099; *Cable:* BAHSOCA NASSAU; *Fax:* 809 324 6484.

BARBADOS

Barbados Football Association, P.O. Box 833E, Bridgetown.
Founded: 1910; *Number of Clubs:* 92; *Number of Players:* 1,100; *National Colours:* Royal blue shirts, gold shorts, royal blue stockings.
Telephone: 809 424 4413; *Cable:* FOOTBALL BRIDGETOWN; *Telex:* 2306 SHAMROCK WB; *Fax:* (809) 436 0130.

BELIZE

Belize National Football Association, P.O. Box 1742, Belize City.
Founded: 1986; *National Colours:* Blue shirts, red & white trim, white shorts, blue stockings.
Telephone: 08-2609 or 08 2637; 02 77031 32; 08-2200; *Telex:* 102 FOREIGN BZ.

BERMUDA

The Bermuda Football Association, P.O. Box HM 745, Hamilton 5 HM CX.
Founded: 1928; *Number of Clubs:* 30; *Number of Players:* 1,947; *National Colours:* Blue shirts, white shorts, white stockings.
Telephone: (809) 295 2199; *Cable:* FOOTBALL BERMUDA; *Telex:* 3441 BFA BA; *Fax:* (809) 295 0773.

CANADA

The Canadian Soccer Association, 1600 James Naismith Drive, Gloucester, Ont. K1B 5N4.
Founded: 1912; *Number of Clubs:* 1600; *Number of Players:* 224,290; *National Colours:* Red shirts, red shorts, red stockings.
Telephone: (613) 748-5667; *Cable:* SOCCANADA OTTAWA; *Telex:* 053-3350; *Fax:* (613) 745-1938.

COSTA RICA

Federacion Costarricense De Futbol, Calle 40-Ave, CTL1, San Jose.
Founded: 1921; *Number of Clubs:* 431; *Number of Players:* 12,429; *National Colours:* Red shirts, blue shorts, white stockings.
Telephone: 22 15 44; *Cable:* FEDEFUTBOL SAN JOSE; *Telex:* 3394 DIDER CR.

CUBA

Asociacion De Futbol De Cuba, c/o Comite Olimpico Cubano, Calle 13 No. 601, Esq. C. Vedado, La Habana, ZP 4.
Founded: 1924; *Number of Clubs:* 70; *Number of Players:* 12,900; *National Colours:* White shirts, blue shorts, white stockings.
Telephone: 40 35 81; *Cable:* FOOTBALL HABANA; *Telex:* 511332 INDER CU.

DOMINICAN REPUBLIC

Federacion Dominicana de Futbol, Apartado De Correos No. 1953, Santo Domingo.
Founded: 1953; *Number of Clubs:* 128; *Number of Players:* 10,706; *National Colours:* Blue shirts, white shorts, red stockings.
Telephone: 542-6923; *Cable:* FEDOFUTBOL SANTO DOMINGO.

EL SALVADOR

Federacion Salvadorena De Futbol, Av. Jm. Delgado, Col. Escalon, Centro Espanol, Apartado 1029, San Salvador.
Founded: 1936; *Number of Clubs:* 944; *Number of Players:* 21,294; *National Colours:* Blue shirts, blue shorts, blue stockings.
Telephone: 23 73 62; *Cable:* FESFUT SAN SALVADOR; *Telex:* 20484 FESFUT SAL.

GRENADA

Grenada Football Association, No. 2 Hillsborough Street, P.O. Box 326, Grenada.
Founded: 1924; *Number of Clubs:* 15; *Number of Players:* 200; *National Colours:* Green & yellow shirts, red shorts, green & yellow stockings.
Telephone: 809-440-1986; *Cable:* GRENBALL GRENADA; *Telex:* 3431 CW BUR; *Fax:* 809-440-2123.

GUATEMALA

Federacion Nacional De Futbol De Guatemala C.A.
Palacio De Los Deportes, 2 Piso, Zona 4, Guatemala C.A.
Founded: 1933; *Number of Clubs:* 1,611; *Number of Players:* 43,516; *National Colours:* White/blue diagonal striped shirts, blue shorts, white stockings.
Telephone: 362211; *Cable:* FEDFUTBOL GUATEMALA.

GUYANA

Guyana Football Association, P.O. Box 10727 Georgetown.
Founded: 1902; *Number of Clubs:* 103; *Number of Players:* 1,665; *National Colours:* Green & yellow shirts, black shorts, white & green stockings.
Telephone: 02-59458/9; *Cable:* FOOTBALL GUYANA; *Telex:* 2266 RICEBRD GY; *Fax:* (005922) 52169.

HAITI

Federation Haitienne De Football, Stade Sylvio-Cator, Port-Au-Prince.
Founded: 1904; *Number of Clubs:* 40; *Number of Players:* 4,000; *National Colours:* Red shirts, black shorts, red stockings.
Telephone: 2/3237; *Cable:* FEDHAFOOB PORT-AU-PRINCE.

HONDURAS

Federacion Nacional Autonoma De Futbol De Honduras, Apartado Postal 827, Costa Oeste Del Est. Nac, Tegucigalpa, De. C.
Founded: 1951; *Number of Clubs:* 1,050; *Number of Players:* 15,300; *National Colours:* Blue shirts, blue shorts, blue stockings.
Telephone: 32-1897; *Cable:* FENAFUTH TEGUCIGALPA; *Telex:* 1209 FENEFUTH; *Fax:* 31 14 28.

JAMAICA

Jamaica Football Federation, Room 9, National Stadium, Kingston 6.
Founded: 1910; *Number of Clubs:* 266; *Number of Players:* 45,200; *National Colours:* Green shirts, black shorts, green & gold stockings.
Cable: FOOTBALL JAMAICA KINGSTON.

MEXICO

Federacion Mexicana De Futbol Asociacion, A.C., Abraham Gonzales 74, C.P. 06600, Col. Juarez, Mexico 6, D.F.
Founded: 1927; *Number of Clubs:* 77 (senior); *Number of Players:* 1,402,270; *National Colours:* Green shirts, white shorts, green stockings.
Telephone: 566 21 55; *Cable:* MEXFUTBOL MEXICO; *Telex:* 1771678 MSUTME; *Fax:* (915) 566 7580.

NETHERLANDS ANTILLES

Nederlands Antiliaanse Voetbal Unie, P.O. Box 341, Curacao, N.A.
Founded: 1921; *Number of Clubs:* 85; *Number of Players:* 4,500; *National Colours:* white shirts, white shorts, red stockings.
Telephone: —; *Cable:* NAVU CURACAO; *Telex:* 1046 ennia na; *Fax:* (599-9) 611173 ennia caribe.

NICARAGUA

Federacion Nicaraguense De Futbol, Inst. Nicaraguense De Deportes, Apartado Postal 976 0 383, Managua. *Founded:* 1968; *Number of Clubs:* 31; *Number of Players:* 160 (senior); *National Colours:* Blue shirts, blue shorts, blue stockings. *Telephone:* 52 271; *Cable:* FEDEFOOT MANAGUA; *Telex:* 2156 IND NK.

PANAMA

Federacion Nacional De Futbol De Panama, Apdo 1436, Balboa, Ancon, Panama. *Founded:* 1937; *Number of Clubs:* 65; *Number of Players:* 4,225; *National Colours:* Red & white shirts, blue shorts, red stockings. *Telephone:* 60 50 32; *Cable:* PANAOLIMPIC PANAMA; *Telex:* 2534 INDE PG; *Fax:* (507) 60 41 66.

PUERTO RICO

Federacion Puertorriquena De Futbol, Coliseo Roberto Clemente, P.O. Box 4355, Hato Rey, 00919-4355. *Founded:* 1940; *Number of Clubs:* 175; *Number of Players:* 4,200; *National Colours:* White & red shirts, blue shorts, white & blue stockings. *Telephone:* 766 1461; *Cable:* BORIKENFPF; *Telex:* 3450296; *Fax:* 8660489, 764-2025.

SURINAM

Surinaamse Voetbal Bond, Cultuuruinlaan 7, P.O. Box 1223, Paramaribo.

Founded: 1920; *Number of Clubs:* 168; *Number of Players:* 4,430; *National Colours:* Red shirts, white shorts, white stockings. *Telephone:* 73112; *Cable:* SVB Paramaribo.

TRINIDAD & TOBAGO

Trinidad & Tobago Football Association, Cor. Duke & Scott-Bushe Street, Port of Spain, Trinidad, P.O. Box 400. *Founded:* 1906; *Number of Clubs:* 124; *Number of Players:* 5,050; *National Colours:* Red shirts, black shorts, red stockings. *Telephone:* 624 5183; *Cable:* TRAFA PORT OF SPAIN; *Telex:* 22652 TRAFA; *Fax:* 627-7661.

USA

United States Soccer Federation, 1750 East Boulder Street, Colorado Springs, CO 80909. *Founded:* 1913; *Number of Clubs:* 7,000; *Number of Players:* 1,411,500; *National Colours:* White shirts, blue shorts, red stockings. *Telephone:* (719) 578-4678; *Cable:* SOCCERUSA COLORADOSPRINGS; *Telex:* 450024 US SOCCER FED; *Fax:* (719) 578-4636.

Recent additions: ARUBA, SANTA LUCIA, ST. VINCENT and the GRENADINES. Aruba is an island in the Caribbean with 1,500 registered players. St. Lucia is another island in the same area with 4,000 players. St. Vincent and the Grenadines is similarly situated and has 5,000 players.

OCEANIA

AUSTRALIA

Australian Soccer Federation, First Floor, 23-25 Frederick Street, Rockdale, NSW 2216. *Founded:* 1961; *Number of Clubs:* 6,816; *Number of Players:* 433,957; *National Colours:* Gold shirts, green shorts, white stockings. *Telephone:* 29 7026; *Cable:* FOOTBALL SYDNEY; *Telex:* AA 170512; *Fax:* 02 296 556.

FIJI

Fiji Football Association, Mr. J. D. Maharaj, Hon. Secretary Government Bldgs, P.O.B. 2514 Suva. *Founded:* 1946; *Number of Clubs:* 140; *Number of Players:* 21,300; *National Colours:* White shirts, black shorts, black stockings. *Telephone:* 300453; *Cable:* FOOTSOCCER SUVA; *Telex:* 2366 FJ; *Fax:* 304642.

NEW ZEALAND

New Zealand Football Association, Inc. P.O. Box 62-532, Central Park, Green Lane, Auckland 6; *Founded:* 1891; *Number of Clubs:* 312; *Number of Players:* 52,969; *National Colours:* White shirts, black shorts, white stockings. *Telephone:* 0-9-525-6120; *Fax:* 0-9-525-6123.

PAPUA-NEW-GUINEA

Papua New Guinea Football (Soccer) Association Inc., P.O. Box 1716, Boroko. *Founded:* 1962; *Number of Clubs:* 350; *Number of Players:* 8,250; *National Colours:* Red shirts, black shorts, red stockings. *Telephone:* 25 41 09; *Telex:* TOTOTRA NE 23436.

WESTERN SAMOA

Western Samoa Football (Soccer) Association, Min. of Youth, Sports Culture, Private Bag, Apia. *Founded:* 1986; *National Colours:* Blue shirts, white shorts, blue and white stockings. *Telephone:* 23315; *Telex:* 230 SAMGAMES SX.

Recent additions: SOLOMON ISLANDS, TAHITI and VANUATU. The Solomon Islands are situated in the South Pacific to the south-east of Papua New Guinea. There are 4,000 registered players. Vanuatu was formerly known as the New Hebrides and is a double chain of islands to the south-east of the Solomons.

AFRICA

ALGERIA

Federation Algerienne De Futbol, Route Ahmed Ouaked, Boite Postale No. 39, Alger — Dely Ibrahim.
Founded: 1962; *Number of Clubs:* 780; *Number of Players:* 58,567; *National Colours:* Green shirts, white shorts, red stockings.
Telephone: 799443/796733; *Cable:* FAFOOT ALGER; *Telex:* 61378.

ANGOLA

Federation Angolaise De Football, B.P. 3449, Luanda.
Founded: 1977; *Number of Clubs:* 276; *Number of Players:* 4,269; *National Colours:* Red shirts, black shorts, red stockings.
Telephone: 338635/338233; *Cable:* FUTANGOLA; *Telex:* 4072 CIAM AN.

BENIN

Federation Beninoise De Football, B.P. 965, Cotonou.
Founded: 1968; *Number of Clubs:* 117; *Number of Players:* 6,700; *National Colours:* Green shirts, green shorts, green stockings.
Telephone: 33 05 37; *Cable:* FEBEFOOT COTONOU; *Telex:* 5033 BIMEX COTONOU: *Fax:* 30 02 14.

BOTSWANA

Botswana Football Association, P.O. Box 1396, Gabarone.
Founded: 1976; *National Colours:* Sky blue shirts, white shorts, sky blue stockings. *Cable:* BOTSBALL GABARONE; *Telex:* 2977 BD; *Fax:* (267) 372 911.

BURKINA FASO

Federation Burkinabe De Foot-Ball, B.P. 57, Ouagadougou.
Founded: 1960; *Number of Clubs:* 57; *Number of Players:* 4,672; *National Colours:* Black shirts, white shorts, red stockings.
Telephone: 33 58 20; *Cable:* FEDEFOOT OUAGADOUGOU.

BURUNDI

Federation De Football Du Burundi, B.P. 3426, Bujumbura.
Founded: 1948; *Number of Clubs:* 132; *Number of Players:* 3,930; *National Colours:* Red shirts, white shorts, green stockings.
Telephone: 2 3078; *Cable:* FFB BUJA.

CAMEROON

Federation Camerounaise De Football, B.P. 1116, Yaounde.
Founded: 1960; *Number of Clubs:* 200; *Number of Players:* 9,328; *National Colours:* Green shirts, red shorts, yellow stockings.
Telephone: 22 25 38; *Cable:* FECAFOOT YAOUNDE; *Telex:* JEUNESPO 8568 KN

CAPE VERDE ISLANDS

Federacao Cabo-Verdiana De Futebol, C.P. 234, PRAIA.
Founded: 1986; *National Colours:* Green shirts, green shorts, green stockings.
Telephone: 611362; *Cable:* FCF–CV; *Telex:* 6030 MICD–CV.

CENTRAL AFRICAN REPUBLIC

Federation Centrafricaine De Football, B.P. 344, Bangui.
Founded: 1937; *Number of Clubs:* 256; *Number of Players:* 7,200; *National Colours:* Grey & blue shirts, white shorts, red stockings.
Telephone: 2141; *Cable:* FOOTBANGUI BANGUI.

CONGO

Federation Congolaise De Football, B.P. 4041, Brazzaville.
Founded: 1962; *Number of Clubs:* 250; *Number of Players:* 5,940; *National Colours:* Red shirts, red shorts, white stockings.
Telephone: 81 51 01; *Cable:* FECOFOOT BRAZZAVILLE; *Telex:* 5210 KG.

EGYPT

Egyptian Football Association, 5, Shareh Gabalaya, Gueziza, Al Borg Post Office, Cairo.
Founded: 1921; *Number of Clubs:* 247; *Number of Players:* 19,735; *National Colours:* Red shirts, white shorts, black stockings.
Telephone: 340 1793; *Cable:* KORA CAIRO; *Telex:* 23504 KORA.

ETHIOPIA

Ethiopia Football Federation, Addis Ababa Stadium, P.O. Box 1080, Addis Ababa.
Founded: 1943; *Number of Clubs:* 767; *Number of Players:* 20,594; *National Colours:* Green shirts, yellow shorts, red stockings.
Telephone: 51 44 53 and 51 43 21. *Cable:* FOOTBALL ADDIS ABABA; *Telex:* 21377 NESCO ET.

GABON

Federation Gabonaise De Football, B.P. 181, Libreville.
Founded: 1962; *Number of Clubs:* 320; *Number of Players:* 10,000; *National Colours:* Blue shirts, white shorts, white stockings.
Telephone: 72 22 37; *Cable:* FEGAFOOT LIBREVILLE; *Telex:* 5642 GO.

GAMBIA

Gambia Football Association, P.O. Box 523, Banjul.
Founded: 1952; *Number of Clubs:* 30; *Number of Players:* 860; *National Colours:* White & red shirts, white shorts, white stockings.
Telephone: 958 34; *Cable:* SPORTS GAMBIA BANJUL; *Fax:* GNOSC 220/96270.

GHANA

Ghana Football Association, P.O. Box 1272, Accra.
Founded: 1957; *Number of Clubs:* 347; *Number of Players:* 11,275; *National Colours:* White shirts, white shorts, white stockings.
Telephone: 63 924/7; *Cable:* GFA ACCRA; *Telex:* 2519 SPORTS GH.

GUINEA

Federation Guineenne De Football, P.O. Box 3645, Conakry.
Founded: 1959; *Number of Clubs:* 351; *Number of Players:* 10,000; *National Colours:* Red shirts, yellow shorts, green stockings.
Telephone: 445041; *Cable:* GUINEFOOT CONAKRY; *Telex:* 22302 MJ.

GUINEA-BISSAU

Federacao De Football Da Guinea-Bissau, Apartado 375, 1035 Bissau–Codex, Rua 4 no 10c.
Founded: 1986; *National Colours:* Green shirts, green shorts, green stockings.
Telephone: 21 25 45; *Cable:* FUTEBOL BISSAU; *Telex:* PAIGC 230 BI.

GUINEA, EQUATORIAL

Federacion Ecuatoguineana De Futbol, Malabo.
Founded: 1986; *National Colours:* All red.
Telephone: 2732; *Cable:* FEGUIFUT/MALABO.

IVORY COAST

Federation Ivoirienne De Football, Stade Felix Houphouet Boigny, B.P. 1202, Abidjan.
Founded: 1960; *Number of Clubs:* 84 (senior); *Number of Players:* 3,655; *National Colours:* Orange shirts, white shorts, green stockings.
Telephone: 22 22 82; *Cable:* FIF ABIDJAN; *Telex:* 22722 FIF CI.

KENYA

Kenya Football Federation, Nyayo National Stadium, P.O. Box 40234, Nairobi.
Founded: 1960; *Number of Clubs:* 351; *Number of Players:* 8,880; *National Colours:* Red shirts, red shorts, red stockings.
Telephone: 340382/339761/9; *Cable:* KEFF NAIROBI; *Telex:* 25784 KFF.

LESOTHO

Lesotho Sports Council, P.O. Box 138, Maseru 100.
Founded: 1932; *Number of Clubs:* 88; *Number of Players:* 2,076; *National Colours:* White shirts, blue shorts, white stockings.
Telephone: 311 291 MASERU; *Cable:* LIPAPALI MASERU; *Telex:* 4493.

LIBERIA

The Liberia Football Association, P.O. Box 1066, Monrovia.
Founded: 1962; *National Colours:* Blue & white shirts, white shorts, blue & white stockings.
Telephone: 22 21 77; *Cable:* LIBFOTASS MONROVIA; *Telex:* 44508 LFA LI.

LIBYA

Libyan Arab Jamahiriya Football Federation, P.O. Box 5137, Tripoli.
Founded: 1963; *Number of Clubs:* 89; *Number of Players:* 2,941; *National Colours:* Green shirts, white shorts, green stockings.
Telephone: 46 610; *Telex:* 20896 KURATP LY.

MADAGASCAR

Federation Malagasy De Football, c/o Comite Nat. De Coordination De Football, B.P. 4409, Antananarivo 101.
Founded: 1961; *Number of Clubs:* 775; *Number of Players:* 23,536; *National Colours:* Red shirts, white shorts, green stockings.
Telephone: 21373; *Telex:* 22264.

MALAWI

Football Association of Malawi, P.O. Box 865, Blantyre.
Founded: 1966; *Number of Clubs:* 465; *Number of Players:* 12,500; *National Colours:* Red shirts, red shorts, red stockings.
Telephone: 636686; *Cable:* FOOTBALL BLANTYRE; *Telex:* 4526 SPORTS MI.

MALI

Federation Malienne De Football, Stade Mamdou Konate, B.P. 1020, Bamako.
Founded: 1960; *Number of Clubs:* 128; *Number of Players:* 5,480; *National Colours:* Green shirts, yellow shorts, red stockings.
Telephone: 22 41 52; *Cable:* MALIFOOT BAMAKO; *Telex:* 0985 1200/1202.

MAURITANIA

Federation De Foot-Ball De La Rep. Isl. De Mauritanie, B.P. 566, Nouakshott.
Founded: 1961; *Number of Clubs:* 59; *Number of Players:* 1,930; *National Colours:* Green and yellow shirts, blue shorts, green stockings.
Telephone: 536 09; *Cable:* FOOTRIM NOUAKSHOTT.

MAURITIUS

Mauritius Football Association, Chancery House, 14 Lislet Geoffroy Street, (2nd Floor, Nos. 303–305), Port Louis.
Founded: 1952; *Number of Clubs:* 397; *Number of Players:* 29,375; *National Colours:* Red shirts, white shorts, red stockings.
Telephone: 212 1418, 212 5771; *Cable:* MFA PORT LOUIS; *Telex:* 4427 MSA IW; *Fax:* (230) 208 41 00.

MOROCCO

Federation Royale Marocaine De Football, Av. Ibn Sina, C.N.S. Bellevue, B.P. 51, Rabat.
Founded: 1955; *Number of Clubs:* 350; *Number of Players:* 19,768; *National Colours:* Red shirts, green shorts, red stockings.
Telephone: 727 06/08; *Cable:* FERMAFOOT RABAT; *Telex:* 32940 FERMFOOT M.

MOZAMBIQUE

Federacao Mocambicana De Futebol, Av. Samora Machel, 11-2, Caixa Postal 1467, Maputo.
Founded: 1978; *Number of Clubs:* 144; *National Colours:* Red shirts, red shorts, red stockings.
Telephone: 26 475; *Cable:* MOCAMBOLA MAPUTO; *Telex:* 6-221/2.

NIGER

Federation Nigerienne De Football, Stade National Niamey, B.P. 10299, Niamey.
Founded: 1967; *Number of Clubs:* 64; *Number of Players:* 1,525; *National Colours:* Orange shirts, white shorts, green stockings.
Telephone: 73 31 97; *Cable:* FEDERFOOT NIGER NIAMEY.

NIGERIA

Nigeria Football Association National Sports Commission, National Stadium, P.O. Box 466, Lagos.
Founded: 1945; *Number of Clubs:* 326; *Number of Players:* 80,190; *National Colours:* Green shirts, white shorts, green stockings.
Telephone: 234-1-83 52 65; *Cable:* FOOTBALL LAGOS; *Telex:* 26570 NFA NG; *Fax:* 234-1-82 49 12.

RWANDA

Federation Rwandaise De Foot-Ball Amateur, B.P. 2000, Kigali.
Founded: 1972; *Number of Clubs:* 167; *National Colours:* Red shirts, red shorts, red stockings.
Telephone: 75811 ext. 223; *Cable:* MIJENCOOP KIGALI; *Telex:* 22504 PUBLIC RW; *Fax:* (250) 76574.

SENEGAL

Federation Senegalaise De Football, Stade De L'Amitie, Route De L'Aeroport De Yoff, Dakar.
Founded: 1960; *Number of Clubs:* 75 (senior); *Number of Players:* 3,977; *National Colours:* Green shirts, yellow shorts, red stockings.
Telephone: 25 00 57; *Cable:* SENEFOOT DAKAR.

SEYCHELLES

Seychelles Football Federation, P.O. Box 580, Mont Fleuri, Victoria.
Founded: 1986; *National Colours:* Green shirts, yellow shorts, red stockings.
Telephone: 24 126; *Telex:* 2271 SZ; *Fax:* 23 518.

ST. THOMAS AND PRINCIPE

Federation Santomense De Fut., P.O. Box 42, Sao Tome.
Founded: 1986; *National Colours:* Green shirts, green shorts, green stockings.
Telephone: 22320; *Telex:* 213 PUBLICO STP.

SIERRA LEONE

Sierra Leone Amateur Football Association, S. Stevens Stadium, Brookfields, P.O. Box 672, Freetown.
Founded: 1967; *Number of Clubs:* 104; *Number of Players:* 8,120; *National Colours:* Green shirts, white shorts, blue stockings.
Telephone: 41872; *Cable:* SLAFA FREETOWN; *Telex:* 3210 BOOTH SL.

SOMALIA

Somali Football Federation, Ministry of Sports, C.P. 247, Mogadishu.
Founded: 1951; *Number of Clubs:* 46 (senior); *Number of Players:* 1,150; *National Colours:* Sky blue shirts, white shorts, white stockings.
Telephone: 22 273; *Cable:* SOMALIA FOOTBALL MOGADISHU; *Telex:* 3061 SONOC SM.

SUDAN

Sudan Football Association, P.O. Box 437, Khartoum.
Founded: 1936; *Number of Clubs:* 750; *Number of Players:* 42,200; *National Colours:* White shirts, white shorts, white stockings.
Telephone: 76 633; *Cable:* ALKOURA, KHARTOUM; *Telex:* 23007 KOR SD.

SWAZILAND

National Football Association of Swaziland, P.O. Box 641, Mbabane.
Founded: 1976; *Number of Clubs:* 136; *National Colours:* Blue and gold shirts, white shorts, blue and gold stockings.
Telephone: 46 852; *Telex:* 2245 EXP WD.

TANZANIA

Football Association of Tanzania, P.O. Box 1574, Dar Es Salaam.
Founded: 1930; *Number of Clubs:* 51; *National Colours:* Yellow shirts, yellow shorts, yellow stockings.
Telephone: 32 334; *Cable:* FAT DAR ES SALAAM.

TOGO

Federation Togolaise De Football, C.P. 5, Lome.
Founded: 1960; *Number of Clubs:* 144; *Number of Players:* 4,346; *National Colours:* Red shirts, white shorts, red stockings.
Telephone: 21 26 98; *Cable:* TOGOFOOT LOME; *Telex:* 5015 CNOT TG.

TUNISIA

Federation Tunisienne De Football, 2, Rue Hamza Abdelmottaleb, El Menzah VI, Tunis.
Founded: 1957; *Number of Clubs:* 215; *Number of Players:* 18,300; *National Colours:* Red shirts, white shorts, red stockings.
Telephone: 23 33 03, 23 35 44; *Cable:* FOOTBALL TUNIS; *Telex:* 14783 FTFOOT TN.

UGANDA

Federation of Uganda Football Associations, P.O. Box 20077, Kampala.
Founded: 1924; *Number of Clubs:* 400; *Number of Players:* 1,518; *National Colours:* Yellow shirts, black shorts, yellow stockings.
Telephone: 254478/77; *Cable:* FUFA KAMPALA.

ZAIRE

Federation Zairoise De Football-Association, B.P. 1284, Rue Dima No. 10, Kinshasa 1.
Founded: 1919; *Number of Clubs:* 3,800; *Number of Players:* 64,627; *National Colours:* Green shirts, yellow shorts, yellow stockings. *Cable:* FEZAFA KINSHASA; *Telex:* 221 605.

ZAMBIA

Football Association of Zambia, P.O. Box 33474, Lusaka.
Founded: 1929; *Number of Clubs:* 20 (senior); *Number of Players:* 4,100; *National Colours:* Green shirts, white shorts, black stockings.
Telephone: 21 11 45; *Cable:* FOOTBALL LUSAKA; *Telex:* 40204.

ZIMBABWE

Zimbabwe Football Association, P.O. Box 8343, Causeway, Harare.
Founded: 1965; *National Colours:* White shirts, black shorts, black stockings.
Telephone: 79 12 75/6/7; *Cable:* SOCCER HARARE; *Telex:* 22299 SOCCER ZW; *Fax:* 793 320.

Recent addition: CHAD (readmitted). This landlocked country was once a FIFA member up to 1974 and has now been reaffiliated.

EUROPEAN CHAMPIONSHIP 1990–92

Qualifying Tournament
GROUP 1
Reykjavik, 30 May 1990, 5250
Iceland (1) 2 *(Gudjohnsen 42, Edvaldsson 88)*
Albania (0) 0
Iceland: Kristinsson B; Thordarsson, Edvaldsson, Orlygsson T (Jonsson K 46), Gretarson, Jonsson Saevar, Berg, Ormslev, Torfarson (Orlyggson O 67), Petursson, Gudjohnsen.
Albania: Strakosha; Noga (Illiadhe 75), Lekbello, Kovi, Vapa, Jeri, Shehu (Arbete 46), Josa, Millo, Abazi, Demollari.

Reykjavik, 5 September 1990, 8388
Iceland (0) 1 *(Edvaldsson 85)*
France (1) 2 *(Papin 12, Cantona 74)*
Iceland: Sigurdsson; Thrainsson, Edvaldsson, Bergsson, Jonsson Saevar, Orlygsson T (Margeirsson 63), Gretarson, Thordarsson, Ormslev (Kristinsson 63), Gudjohnsen, Petursson.
France: Martini; Amoros, Boli, Sauzee, Casoni, Blanc (Durand 75), Pardo, Deschamps, Perez, Papin, Cantona (Fernandez 83).

Kosice, 26 September 1990, 30,184
Czechoslovakia (1) 1 *(Danek 43)*
Iceland (0) 0
Czechoslovakia: Stejskal; Kadlec, Kocian, Hipp, Hasek, Bilek (Weiss 67), Kubik, Kula, Moravcik, Skuhravy, Danek.
Iceland: Sigurdsson; Thrainsson, Bergsson, Edvaldsson, Jonsson Saevar, Kristinsson (Jonsson K 61), Gretarson, Thordarsson, Jonsson Siggi, Gudjohnsen, Margeirsson (Ormslev 76).

Seville, 10 October 1990, 18,399
Spain (1) 2 *(Butragueno 63, Munoz 66)*
Iceland (0) 1 *(Jonsson Siggi 66)*
Spain: Zubizarreta; Nando, Serna, Rafa Paz (Beguiristain 62), Sanchis, Fernando, Goicoechea, Michel, Butragueno, Martin Vazquez, Carlos (Valverde 71).
Iceland: Sigurdsson; Thrainsson, Edvaldsson, Jonsson K (Gregory 80), Gretarson, Jonsson Saevar, Bergsson, Jonsson Siggi (Ormslev 72), Gudjohnsen, Thordarsson, Margeirsson.

Paris, 13 October 1990, 38,249
France (0) 2 *(Papin 60, 83)*
Czechoslovakia (0) 1 *(Skuhravy 89)*
France: Martini; Boli, Blanc, Casoni, Angloma (Fernandez 52), Deschamps, Sauzee, Durand, Papin, Cantona, Vahirua (Silvestre 85).
Czechoslovakia: Stejskal; Kula, Kadlec, Kocian, Hipp, Moravcik, Chovanec, Kubik (Tittel 85), Bilek (Pecko 82), Skuhravy, Knoflicek.

Prague, 14 November 1990, 21,980
Czechoslovakia (1) 3 *(Danek 16, 67, Moravcik 77)*
Spain (1) 2 *(Roberto 30, Carlos 54)*
Czechoslovakia: Miklosko; Kocian, Kadlec, Hipp, Hasek, Tittel, Moravcik, Kula, Bilek (Bielik 80), Danek (Kuka 89), Skuhravy.
Spain: Zubizarreta; Quique, Sanchis, Nando, Serna, Michel (Amor 85), Martin Vazquez, Roberto, Goicoechea, Butragueno, Carlos (Bakero 62).

Tirana, 17 November 1990, 12,972
Albania (0) 0
France (1) 1 *(Boli 25)*
Albania: Arapi; Leskaj (Ferko 46), Stafa, Ibro, Hodja, Lekbello, Zmijani, Demollari, Josa, Kushta, Majaci (Kacasi 56).
France: Martini; Boli, Durand, Casoni, Blanc, Pardo, Deschamps, Sauzee, Tibeuf (Ginola 66), Ferreri, Vahirua (Angloma 82).

Seville, 19 December 1990, 12,625
Spain (4) 9 *(Amor 21, Carlos 24, 65, Butragueno 31, 57, 68, 88, Hierro 40, Bakero 76)*
Albania (0) 0
Spain: Zubizarreta; Sanchis, Alcorta, Goicoechea (Bakero 75), Amor, Hierro, Manolo, Michel (Quique 62), Butragueno, Martin Vazquez, Carlos.

Albania: Arapi; Ibro, Lekbello, Stafa, Kola (Demollari 39), Kushta, Millo, Zmijani, Ferko (Josa 55), Dema, Tahiri.

Paris, 20 February 1991, 45,000
France (1) 3 *(Sauzee 15, Papin 58, Blanc 77)*
Spain (1) 1 *(Bakero 11)*
France: Martini; Amoros, Boli, Casoni, Blanc, Pardo (Fernandez 50), Durand, Sauzee, Papin, Cantona, Vahirua (Deschamps 83).
Spain: Zubizarreta; Quique, Nando, Juanito, Sanchis, Michel, Amor, Vizcaino (Soler 61), Goicoechea, Bakero, Butragueno (Manolo 75).

Paris, 30 March 1991, 25,000
France (4) 5 *(Sauzee 1, 19, Papin 34 (pen), 43, Lekbello 79(og))*
Albania (0) 0
France: Martini; Amoros, Boli, Blanc, Durand, Fernandez, Sauzee (Deschamps 73), Cocard, Cantona, Papin, Vahirua (Baills 57).
Albania: Nallbani; Zmijani, Lekbello, Vata, Gjergi, Ocelli, Dume, Canaj, Demollari, Tahiri, Kepa.

Tirana, 1 May 1991, 10,000
Albania (0) 0
Czechoslovakia (0) 2 *(Kubik 47, Kuka 67)*
Albania: Nallbani; Zmijani, Dema (Kola 73), Daja, Ocelli, Shpuza, Kushta, Memushi, Barbullushi (Dosti 63), Dume (Kole 70), Milori.
Czechoslovakia: Miklosko; Kula, Kadlec, Hasek (Hapal 19), Grussmann, Tittel, Nemec, Kubik, Kuka, Kukleta (Chylek 84), Moravcik.

Tirana, 26 May 1991, 5000
Albania (0) 1 *(Abazi 56)*
Iceland (0) 0
Albania: Nallbani; Memushi (Josa 17), Ocelli, Lekbello, Shpuza, Daja, Millo, Demollari, Milori, Kushta, Abazi.
Iceland: Sigurdsson; Jonsson Saevar, Bergsson, Gislason, Kristiansson, Kristinsson (Stefansson 62), Orlygsson T, Thordarsson, Gretarson, Sverrison, Gregory (Marteinsson 75).

Reykjavik, 5 June 1991, 5000
Iceland (0) 0
Czechoslovakia (1) 1 *(Hasek 15)*
Iceland: Sigurdsson; Jonsson Saever, Bergsson, Edvaldsson, Gislason, Thordarsson, Gretarson, Orlygsson T, Kristinsson, Gudjohnsen, Sverrison (Stefansson 70).
Czechoslovakia: Miklosko; Grussmann, Kocian, Tittel, Hasek, Hapal, Kubik, Kula, Nemec, Danek (Pecko 89), Skuhravy.

	P	W	D	L	F	A	Pts
France	5	5	0	0	13	3	10
Czechoslovakia	5	4	0	1	8	4	8
Spain	4	2	0	2	14	7	4
Iceland	6	1	0	5	4	7	2
Albania	6	1	0	5	1	19	2

Remaining fixtures: 4.9.91. Czechoslovakia v France; 25.9.91. Iceland v Spain; 12.10.91. Spain v France; 16.10.91. Czechoslovakia v Albania; 13.11.91. Spain v Czechoslovakia, France v Iceland; 18.12.91. Albania v Spain.

GROUP 2
Geneva, 12 September 1990, 12,000
Switzerland (1) 2 *(Hottiger 19, Bickel 63)*
Bulgaria (0) 0
Switzerland: Walker; Geiger, Herr, Schepull, Hottiger, Koller, Bickel, Hermann, Sutter A (Piffaretti 88), Knup (Chapuisat 64), Turkyilmaz.
Bulgaria: Valov; Dochev, Zhelev, Iliev, Ivanov, Vassev (Bankov 14), Yanchev, Yordanov, Balakov (Todorov 65), Kostadinov, Stoichkov.

Hampden Park, 12 September 1990, 12,081
Scotland (1) 2 *(Robertson 37, McCoist 76)*
Romania (1) 1 *(Camataru 13)*
Scotland: Goram; McKimmie, Malpas, McAllister (Nevin 73), Irvine, McLeish, Robertson, McStay, McCoist, MacLeod, Connor (Boyd 59).

Romania: Lung; Petrescu, Klein, Sandoi, Rotariu, Popescu, Lacatus, Mateut (Sabau 79), Camataru (Raducioiu 62), Hagi, Lupescu.

Bucharest, 17 October 1990, 15,350

Romania (0) 0

Bulgaria (1) 3 *(Sirakov 28, Todorov 48, 76)*

Romania: Stelea; Petrescu, Klein (Sandoi 46), Andone, Rotariu, Popescu, Lacatus, Sabau, Raducioiu (Balint 46), Hagi, Lupescu.

Bulgaria: Mikhailov; Dochev, Ivanov, Vassev, Iliev, Yankov, Yanchev, Stoichkov, Balakov, Sirakov (Kostadinov 75), Yordanov (Todorov 46).

Hampden Park, 17 October 1990, 20,740

Scotland (1) 2 *(Robertson 34, McAllister 53)*

Switzerland (0) 1 *(Knup 66)*

Scotland: Goram; McKimmie, Nicol, McCall, McPherson, McLeish, Robertson, McAllister (Collins 79), McCoist, MacLeod, Boyd (Durie 68).

Switzerland: Walker; Piffaretti (Sutter B 80), Schepull (Chassot 73), Herr, Egli, Bickel, Knup, Hermann, Turkyilmaz, Sutter A, Chapuisat.

Sofia, 14 November 1990, 40,000

Bulgaria (0) 1 *(Todorov 74)*

Scotland (1) 1 *(McCoist 9)*

Bulgaria: Mikhailov; Dochev, Mladenov, Yankov, Bankov, Yanchev (Todorov 52), Yordanov, Stoichkov, Penev, Sirakov, Balakov (Kostadinov 80).

Scotland: Goram; McKimmie, Malpas, McInally, McPherson, Gillespie, Durie (Nevin 67), McAllister, McCoist, McClair, Boyd.

Serravalle, 14 November 1990, 931

San Marino (0) 0

Switzerland (3) 4 *(Sutter A 7, Chapuisat 27, Knup 43, Chassot 87)*

San Marino: Benedettini; Montironi, Guerra, Gobbi, Muccioli (Toccaceli 46), Bonini (Matteoni 46), Zanotti L, Francini, Ceccoli, Pasolini, Macina.

Switzerland: Walker; Hottiger, Geiger, Herr, Sutter B, Bickel (Piffaretti 59), Chapuisat, Hermann, Sutter A, Turkyilmaz (Chassot 46), Knup.

Bucharest, 5 December 1990, 6380

Romania (3) 6 *(Sabau 2, Mateut 18, Raducioiu 43, Lupescu 56, Badea 77, Petrescu 85)*

San Marino (0) 0

Romania: Prunea; Petrescu, Iovan, Popescu, Rednic, Sabau, Mateut, Lupescu (Stanici 65), Dumitrescu (Badea 46), Lacatus, Raducioiu.

San Marino: Benedettini; Montironi, Conti, Guerra, Zanotti L, Toccaceli, Matteoni, Ceccoli, Francini, Pasolini (Zanotti P 72), Macina (Bacciocchi 46).

Hampden Park, 27 March 1991, 33,119

Scotland (0) 1 *(Collins 84)*

Bulgaria (0) 1 *(Kostadinov 89)*

Scotland: Goram; McPherson, Malpas, McInally, Gough, McLeish, Strachan (Collins 80), McClair, McCoist, McStay, Durie (Robertson 80).

Bulgaria: Mikhailov; Dochev, Ivanov, Kiryakov, Iliev, Yankov, Kostadinov, Yordanov, Penev, Sirakov (Alexandrov 86), Balakov (Tanev 86).

Serravalle, 27 March 1991, 745

San Marino (1) 1 *(Pasolini 30 (pen))*

Romania (2) 3 *(Hagi 17 (pen), Raducioiu 45, Matteoni (og) 86)*

San Marino: Benedettini; Canti, Guerra, Gobbi (Toccaceli 74), Muccioli, Matteoni, Francini, Pasolini (Mularoni 89), Ceccoli, Mazza M, Mazza P.

Romania: Prunea; Petrescu, Popescu (Timofte D 46), Lupescu, Klein, Sandoi, Sabau, Mateut (Timofte J 65), Hagi, Lacatus, Raducioiu.

Neuchatel, 3 April 1991, 15,700

Switzerland (0) 0

Romania (0) 0

Switzerland: Huber; Geiger, Hottiger, Ohrel, Herr, Koller, Bonvin (Bickel 33), Hermann, Aeby, Turkyilmaz (Sutter B 75), Knup.

Romania: Prunea; Petrescu, Klein, Sandoi, Lupescu, Popescu, Sabau, Hagi (Mateut 85), Lacatus, Raducioiu (Timofte J 89), Timofte D.

Sofia, 1 May 1991, 40,000

Bulgaria (2) 2 *(Kostadinov 11, Sirakov 25)*

Switzerland (0) 3 *(Knup 58, 85, Turkyilmaz 90)*

Bulgaria: Mikhailov; Dochev (Todorov 75), Kiriakov, Yankov, Iliev, Ivanov, Yordanov, Penev, Sirakov (Tanev 65), Balakov, Kostadinov.

Switzerland: Huber; Egli, Herr, Hottiger, Ohrel, Bonvin, Hermann, Knup (Schepull 87), Koller (Chapuisat 75), Sutter B, Turkyilmaz.

Serravalle, 1 May 1991, 3512

San Marino (0) 0

Scotland (0) 2 *(Strachan 63 (pen), Durie 66)*

San Marino: Benedettini; Canti, Muccioli, Zanotti (Toccaceli 60), Gobbi, Guerra, Ceccoli, Mazza M, Mazza P, Francini, Pasolini (Matteoni 79).

Scotland: Goram; McKimmie, Nicol (Robertson 74), McCall, McPherson, Malpas, Gallacher, Strachan, McClair (Nevin 57), McAllister, Durie.

Serravalle, 22 May 1991, 612

San Marino (0) 0

Bulgaria (2) 3 *(Ivanov Z 12, Sirakov 19, Penev 59)*

San Marino: Benedettini; Canti, Montironi, Muccioli, Gobbi, Guerra, Ceccoli (Matteoni 82), Mazza M, Mazza P, Francini, Pasolini (Bacciocchi 64).

Bulgaria: Mikhailov; Dimitrov, Ivanov I, Kiriakov, Anghelov, Ivanov Z (Todorov 76), Kostadinov E, Gheorghiev, Penev, Sirakov, Yotov (Metkov 56).

St Gallen, 5 June 1991, 12,000

Switzerland (3) 7 *(Knup 2, 86, Hottiger 12, Sutter B 28, Hermann 54, Ohrel 77, Turkyilmaz 89)*

San Marino (0) 0

Switzerland: Huber; Egli (Schepull 74), Herr, Hottiger (Ohrel 74), Hermann, Koller, Sutter A, Sutter B, Turkyilmaz, Knup, Chapuisat.

San Marino: Benedettini; Muccioli, Guerra, Gobbi, Canti, Matteoni (Valentini 46), Mazza M, Francini, Zanotti, Pasolini, Bacciocchi (Malaroni 65).

	P	W	D	L	F	A	Pts
Switzerland	6	4	1	1	17	4	9
Scotland	5	3	2	0	8	4	8
Bulgaria	6	2	2	2	10	7	6
Romania	5	2	1	2	10	6	5
San Marino	6	0	0	6	1	25	0

Remaining fixtures: 11.9.91. Switzerland v Scotland; 16.10.91. Bulgaria v San Marino, Romania v Scotland; 13.11.91. Scotland v San Marino, Romania v Switzerland; 20.11.91. Bulgaria v Romania.

GROUP 3

Moscow, 12 September 1990, 23,000

USSR (1) 2 *(Kontchelskis 22, Kuznetsov 60)*

Norway (0) 0

USSR: Uvarov; Chernishev, Gorlukovich, Kuznetsov, Tishenko (Kulkov 79), Shalimov, Mikhailichenko, Kontchelskis, Getsko (Kolivanov 70), Protasov, Dobrovolski.

Norway: Thorstvedt; Lydersen, Pedersen T, Bratseth, Halle, Berg (Pedersen E 61), Ahlsen, Gulbrandsen, Jakobsen, Andersen A, Fjortoft (Dahlum 66).

Bergen, 10 October 1990, 6300

Norway (0) 0

Hungary (0) 0

Norway: Thorstvedt; Halle, Pedersen T, Bratseth, Lydersen, Pedersen E, Ahlsen, Brandhaug, Jakobsen (Andersen A 72), Sorloth, Fjortoft (Dahlum 76).

Hungary: Petry; Monos, Pinter, Szalma, Kovacs E, Limperger, Kiprich (Fodor 79), Kozma, Bognar, Lorincz, Kovacs K (Urbanyi 89).

Budapest, 17 October 1990, 24,600

Hungary (1) 1 *(Disztl L 16)*

Italy (0) 1 *(Baggio 54)*

Hungary: Petry; Monos, Disztl L, Garaba (Fodor 60), Szalma, Bognar, Limperger, Kiprich, Kozma (Urbanyi 87), Lorincz, Kovacs K.

Italy: Zenga; Bergomi, De Agostini, Baresi, Ferri, Marocchi, Donadoni, De Napoli, Schillaci (Serena 80), Giannini (Berti 87), Baggio.

Budapest, 31 October 1990, 2300
Hungary (3) 4 *(Lorincz 1, 19, Kiprich 20 (pen), 67 (pen))*
Cyprus (1) 2 *(Xiourouppas 13, Tsolakis 89)*
Hungary: Petry; Disztl L, Monos, Garaba, Limperger, Szalma, Kozma (Discher 56), Bognar, Lorincz, Kiprich (Rugovics 75), Kovacs K.
Cyprus: Onisforu; Kalotheou, Miamiliotis, Christodolou, Socratous, Yiangudakis, Andreou (Tsolakis 59), Savva, Kastanas, Constantinou (Orthanides 73), Xiourouppas.

Rome, 3 November 1990, 52,208
Italy (0) 0
USSR (0) 0
Italy: Zenga; Ferrara, Baresi, Ferri, Maldini, De Napoli, Crippa, De Agostini, Mancini, Schillaci (Serena 70), Baggio.
USSR: Uvarov; Chernishev, Kulkov, Tsvelba, Shalimov, Aleinikov, Mikhailichenko, Kontchelskis, Getsko (Protasov 67), Mostovoi (Tatarchuk 85), Dobrovolski.

Nicosia, 14 November 1990, 2123
Cyprus (0) 0
Norway (1) 3 *(Sorloth 39, Bohinen 50, Brandhaug 64)*
Cyprus: Charitou; Kalotheou (Kantilos 49), Miamiliotis, Kastanas, Socratous, Yiangudakis, Christodolou, Savva, Tsolakis (Constantinou 74), Nicolau, Xiourouppas.
Norway: Thorstvedt; Lydersen, Pedersen T, Bratseth, Lohen (Pedersen E 64), Halle, Brandhaug, Leonhardsen, Bohinen, Sorloth, Dahlum (Fjortoft 80).

Nicosia, 22 December 1990, 9185
Cyprus (0) 0
Italy (3) 4 *(Vierchowod 15, Serena 22, 50, Lombardo 44)*
Cyprus: Onisforu; Kalotheou, Miamiliotis, Christodolou, Socratous, Yiangudakis, Punnas, Savva (Constantinou 56), Tsolakis, Nicolau, Papavasiliu (Xiourouppas 64).
Italy: Zenga; Bergomi, Ferrara, Eranio, Vierchowod, Crippa, Lombardo, Berti, Schillaci, Morocchi, Serena.

Limassol, 3 April 1991, 3000
Cyprus (0) 0
Hungary (2) 2 *(Kiprich 40, Szalma 15)*
Cyprus: Marangos; Constantinou G, Pittas (Kasianos 75), Ioannou, Constantinou C, Yiangudakis, Christofi, Savva (Sotiriu 83), Savvidis, Nicolau, Tsolakis.
Hungary: Petry; Monos, Disztl L, Szalma, Nagy, Limperger, Kiprich, Bognar, Fischer (Maroszan 72), Lorincz, Kovacs K.

Budapest, 17 April 1991, 40,000
Hungary (0) 0
USSR (1) 1 *(Mikhailichenko 30)*
Hungary: Petry; Disztl L, Garaba, Limperger, Monos, Kozma (Detari 63), Bognar (Vincze 71), Lorincz, Szalma, Kiprich, Kovacs K.
USSR: Uvarov; Chernishev, Kulkov, Tsvelba, Galiamin, Shalimov, Mikhailichenko, Kontchelskis, Youran (Kuznetsov D 86), Kolivanov, Aleinikov.

Salerno, 1 May 1991, 45,000
Italy (2) 3 *(Donadoni 4, 16, Vialli 56)*
Hungary (0) 1 *(Bognar 66)*
Italy: Zenga; Ferrara (Vierchowod 65), Ferri, Baresi, Maldini, Crippa, De Napoli, Giannini, Donadoni (Eranio 36), Vialli, Mancini.
Hungary: Petry; Monos, Disztl L, Palaczky (Kozma 33), Limperger, Garaba, Kiprich (Gregor 46), Lorincz, Bognar, Detari, Kovacs K.

Oslo, 1 May 1991, 7833
Norway (0) 3 *(Lydersen 49 (pen), Dahlum 65, Sorloth 90)*
Cyprus (0) 0
Norway: Thorstvedt; Pedersen T, Bratseth (Ingebritsen 46), Lydersen, Halle (Pedersen E), Ahlsen, Brandhaug, Leonhardsen, Bjornbyre, Sorloth, Dahlum.
Cyprus: Charitou; Nicolau (Sotiriu 89), Constantinou G, Ioannou, Costa, Kalotheou (Constantinou C 84), Savva, Yiangudakis, Pittas, Savvidis, Xiourouppas.

Moscow, 29 May 1991, 20,000
USSR (1) 4 *(Mostovoi 20, Mikhailichenko 51, Korneyev 83, Aleinikov 89)*
Cyprus (0) 0
USSR: Uvarov; Chernishev, Kulkov, Mostovoi (Kuznetsov D 74), Galamin, Shalimov, Mikhailichenko,

Kontchelskis, Aleinikov, Kolivanov, Youran (Korneyev 46).
Cyprus: Charitou; Kalotheou, Pittas, Ioannou, Nicolau, Yiangudakis, Costa, Christofi, Savvidis, Christodolou (Constantinou 88), Xiourouppas (Savva 89).

Oslo, 5 June 1991, 27,500
Norway (2) 2 *(Dahlum 4, Bohinen 24)*
Italy (0) 1 *(Schillaci 79)*
Norway: Thorstvedt; Pedersen T, Ahlsen, Bratseth, Lydersen, Dahlum (Pedersen E 46), Bohinen, Lokken, Ingebritsen, Jakobsen, Sorloth.
Italy: Zenga; Baresi, Ferrara, Ferri (Bergomi 89), Maldini, Lombardo, Eranio, De Napoli (Schillaci 53), Crippa, Vialli, Mancini.

	P	W	D	L	F	A	Pts
USSR	4	3	1	0	7	0	7
Norway	5	3	1	1	8	3	7
Italy	5	2	2	1	9	4	6
Hungary	6	2	2	2	8	7	6
Cyprus	6	0	0	6	2	20	0

Remaining fixtures: 28.8.91. Norway v USSR; 25.9.91. USSR v Hungary; 12.10.91. USSR v Italy; 30.10.91. Hungary v Norway; 13.11.91. Italy v Norway, Cyprus v USSR; 21.12.91. Italy v Cyprus.

GROUP 4
Windsor Park, 12 September 1990, 9008
Northern Ireland (0) 0
Yugoslavia (1) 2 *(Pancev 36, Prosinecki 86)*
Northern Ireland: Kee; Donaghy, Worthington, Taggart, McDonald, Rogan, Dennison (Clarke 66), Wilson D, Dowie, Wilson K, Black.
Yugoslavia: Ivkovic; Spasic, Jozic, Vulic, Hadzibegic, Najdoski, Prosinecki, Savicevic, Pancev (Petrovic 87) Stojkovic, Binic (Stosic 87).

Landskrona, Sweden, 12 September 1990, 1544
Faeroes (0) 1 *(Nielsen 61)*
Austria (0) 0
Faeroes: Knudsen; Jakobsen, Hansen TE, Danielsen, Hansen J, Morkore A, Nielsen, Dam, Hansen A, Reynheim, Morkore K.
Austria: Konsel; Russ, Pecl, Hartmann, Streiter, Peischl, Rodax, Linzmaier, Polster, Herzog (Pacult 63), Reisinger (Wilfurth 63).

Copenhagen, 10 October 1990, 38,500
Denmark (2) 4 *(Laudrup M 8, 48, Elstrup 37, Povlsen 89)*
Faeroes (1) 1 *(Morkore A 21)*
Denmark: Schmeichel; Sivebaek, Nielsen K, Olsen L, Heintze, Bartram, Vilfort, Elstrup (Rasmussen E 73), Povlsen, Laudrup M, Laudrup B.
Faeroes: Knudsen; Jakobsen, Hansen TE, Danielsen, Hansen J, Morkore A (Jarnskor 88), Nielsen T, Dam, Hansen A, Reynheim, Morkore K (Mohr 76).

Windsor Park, 17 October 1990, 9079
Northern Ireland (0) 1 *(Clarke 58)*
Denmark (1) 1 *(Bartram 11)*
Northern Ireland: Kee; Donaghy, Worthington, Taggart, McDonald, Rogan, Wilson D, O'Neill C (McBride), Dowie, Clarke, Black.
Denmark: Schmeichel; Sivebaek, Nielsen K, Olsen L, Heintze, Bartram, Larsen, Vilfort, Povlsen, Laudrup B (Helt 80), Laudrup B (Elstrup 70).

Belgrade, 31 October 1990, 11,422
Yugoslavia (2) 4 *(Pancev 32, 52, 85, Katanec 43)*
Austria (1) 1 *(Ogris A 15)*
Yugoslavia: Ivkovic; Vulic, Spasic, Katanec (Jarni 86), Hadzibegic, Josic, Prosinecki, Susic (Boban 63), Bazdarevic, Pancev, Vujovic.
Austria: Konsel; Artner, Aigner, Pecl, Streiter, Hortnagl, Schottel, Herzog (Linzmaier 46), Reisinger, Ogris A (Pacult 52), Polster.

Copenhagen, 14 November 1990, 40,000
Denmark (0) 0
Yugoslavia (0) 2 *(Bazdarevic 77, Jarni 84)*
Denmark: Schmeichel; Sivebaek, Nielsen K, Olsen L, Heintze, Vilfort, Molby (Elstrup 72), Laudrup M, Bartram, Laudrup B, Povlsen (Jensen 46).
Yugoslavia: Ivkovic; Vulic, Spasic, Hadzibegic, Jarni,

Katanec, Jozic, Susic, Bazdarevic, Pancev (Boban 12), Vujovic (Najdoski 89).

Vienna, 14 November 1990, 7062
Austria (0) 0
Northern Ireland (0) 0
Austria: Konsel; Schottel, Pecl, Polger, Artner, Willfurth, Reischl, Linzmaier, Hortnagl, Ogris A, Polster (Pacult 67).
Northern Ireland: Kee; Donaghy, Worthington, Taggart, McDonald, Rogan, Dennison, Wilson D, Clarke (Dowie 62), Wilson K, Black (Morrow 82).

Belgrade, 27 March 1991, 10,000
Yugoslavia (1) 4 *(Binic 35, Pancev 46, 60, 61)*
Northern Ireland (1) 1 *(Hill 45)*
Yugoslavia: Ivkovic; Vulic (Najdoski 85), Jozic, Jarni, Bazdarevic, Spasic, Hadzibegic, Prosinecki, Savicevic, Pancev, Binic.
Northern Ireland: Kee; Fleming, Rogan, Donaghy, Morrow, Hill, Dennison (Quinn 70), Magilton, Dowie, Wilson K (Clarke 60), Black.

Belgrade, 1 May 1991, 26,000
Yugoslavia (0) 1 *(Pancev 50)*
Denmark (1) 2 *(Christensen 31, 62)*
Yugoslavia: Ivkovic; Vulic, Jarni (Najdoski 84), Spasic, Hadzibegic, Jozic, Prosinecki, Savicevic, Pancev, Bazdarevic, Binic.
Denmark: Schmeichel; Sivebaek (Larsen 54), Nielsen K, Olsen L, Kristensen, Bartram, Jensen (Goldbaek 82), Christofte, Povlsen, Vilfort, Christensen.

Windsor Park, 1 May 1991, 10,000
Northern Ireland (1) 1 *(Clarke 44)*
Faeroes (0) 1 *(Reynheim 65)*
Northern Ireland: Kee; Donaghy, Worthington, Taggart, McDonald, Magilton, Wilson D (Dennison 83), Clarke, Dowie (Williams 83), Wilson K, Black.
Faeroes: Knudsen; Jakobsen, Hansen TE, Danielsen, Muller, Morkore A, Nielsen, Dam, Hansen A, Reynheim (Thomassen 74), Morkore K (Rasmussen 85).

Belgrade, 16 May 1991, 8000
Yugoslavia (2) 7 *(Najdoski 20, Prosinecki 24, Pancev 50, 74, Vulic 66, Boban 70, Suker 86)*
Faeroes (0) 0
Yugoslavia: Ivkovic (Lazic 80); Stanojkovic, Jarni (Suker 67), Vulic, Najdoski, Spasic, Prosinecki, Boban, Pancev, Savicevic, Mihajlovic.
Faeroes: Knudsen; Jakobsen, Hansen TE, Danielsen, Jarnskor, Morkore A, Nielsen, Dam, Hansen A, Reynheim, Morkore K (Muller 49).

Vienna, 22 May 1991, 13,000
Austria (1) 3 *(Pfeifenberger 13, Streiter 48, Wetl 63)*
Faeroes (0) 0
Austria: Konsel (Wohlfahrt 86); Baur, Russ, Pfeifenberger (Hortnagl 24), Hartmann, Stoger, Schottel, Herzog, Streuter, Wetl, Ogris A.
Faeroes: Knudsen; Jakobsen, Morkore A, Danielsen, Hansen TE, Simonsen, Nielsen, Hansen A, Dam (Thomassen 71), Reynheim, Rasmussen (Mohr 85).

Copenhagen, 5 June 1991, 12,521
Denmark (1) 2 *(Christensen 2, 77)*
Austria (0) 1 *(Ogris E 83)*
Denmark: Schmeichel; Hansen, Nielsen K, Olsen L, Bruun, Vilfort, Larsen, Nielsen BS, Nielsen C (Goldbaek 46), Povlsen (Rasmussen E 78), Christensen.
Austria: Konrad; Russ (Prosenik 72), Baur, Hartmann, Pfeifenberger, Streiter, Ogris E, Schottel (Hortnagl 66), Herzog, Stoger, Westerhaler.

	P	W	D	L	F	A	Pts
Yugoslavia	6	5	0	1	20	4	10
Denmark	5	3	1	1	9	6	7
Austria	5	1	1	3	5	7	3
Northern Ireland	5	0	3	2	3	8	3
Faeroes	5	1	1	3	3	15	3

Remaining fixtures: 11.9.91. Faeroes v Northern Ireland; 25.9.91. Faeroes v Denmark; 9.10.91. Austria v Denmark; 16.10.91. Faeroes v Yugoslavia, Northern Ireland v Austria; 13.11.91. Denmark v Northern Ireland, Austria v Yugoslavia.

GROUP 5

Ninian Park, 17 October 1990, 12,000
Wales (1) 3 *(Rush 29, Saunders 86, Hughes 88)*
Belgium (1) 1 *(Versavel 24)*
Wales: Southall; Ratcliffe, Blackmore, Young, Aizlewood, Bodin, Horne, Nicholas, Hughes, Rush, Saunders.
Belgium: Preud'homme; Gerets, Grun, Demol, De Wolf, Versavel, Van der Elst, Scifo, Emmers, Ceulemans, Nilis (Wilmots 75).

Luxembourg, 31 October 1990, 9512
Luxembourg (0) 2 *(Girres 57, Langers 65)*
West Germany (2) 3 *(Klinsmann 16, Bein 30, Voller 49)*
Luxembourg: Van Rijswick; Malgret, Petry, Bossi, Birsens, Groff, Hellers, Girres, Salbene (Jeitz 85), Weis, Langers.
West Germany: Illgner; Binz, Berthold, Kohler, Strunz, Hassler, Matthaus, Bein (Reinhardt 73), Brehme, Klinsmann, Voller.

Luxembourg, 14 November 1990, 6800
Luxembourg (0) 0
Wales (1) 1 *(Rush 15)*
Luxembourg: Van Rijswick; Malget, Bossi, Birsens, Petry, Morocutti (Krings 60), Hellers, Girres, Salbene, Weis, Langers.
Wales: Southall; Blackmore, Bodin, Aizlewood, Young, Hughes, Ratcliffe, Horne, Nicholas, Rush (Speed 83), Saunders (Allen 88).

Brussels, 27 February 1991, 24,505
Belgium (3) 3 *(Vandenbergh 7, Ceulemans 17, Scifo 36)*
Luxembourg (0) 0
Belgium: Preud'homme; Grun, Albert, Emmers, Versavel, Dauwen, Scifo, Ceulemans, Degryse, Vandenbergh, Wilmots.
Luxembourg: Koch; Malget (Jeitz 46), Bossi, Birsens, Patry, Groff (Scuto 75), Hellers, Girres, Salbene, Weis, Krings.

Brussels, 27 March 1991, 25,000
Belgium (0) 1 *(Degryse 47)*
Wales (0) 1 *(Saunders 58)*
Belgium: Preud'homme; Gerets, Albert, Grun, Clijsters, Versavel, Van der Elst, Scifo, Degryse, Vandenbergh, Wilmots.
Wales: Southall; Phillips, Ratcliffe, Young, Aizlewood, Bodin, Horne, Nicholas, Hughes, Rush, Saunders.

Hanover, 1 May 1991, 56,000
West Germany (1) 1 *(Matthaus 3)*
Belgium (0) 0
West Germany: Illgner; Berthold, Reuter, Beiersdorfer, Brehme, Hassler, Sammer, Matthaus, Doll, Klinsmann (Helmer 77), Voller (Riedle 88).
Belgium: Preud'homme; Emmers, Crasson, Grun, Albert, Van der Elst, Scifo, Vervoort, Versavel, Degryse, Wilmots (Nilis 77).

Cardiff (Arms Park), 5 June 1991, 38,000
Wales (0) 1 *(Rush 69)*
West Germany (0) 0
Wales: Southall; Phillips, Melville, Bodin, Aizlewood, Ratcliffe, Nicholas, Saunders (Speed 89), Rush, Hughes, Horne.
West Germany: Illgner; Reuter, Brehme, Kohler, Berthold, Buchwald, Helmer, Sammer (Effenberg 76), Matthaus (Doll 46), Klinsmann, Voller.

	P	W	D	L	F	A	Pts
Wales	4	3	1	0	6	2	7
West Germany	3	2	0	1	4	3	4
Belgium	4	1	1	2	5	5	3
Luxembourg	3	0	0	3	2	7	0

Remaining fixtures: 11.9.91. Luxembourg v Belgium; 16.10.91. West Germany v Wales; 13.11.91. Wales v Luxembourg; 20.11.91. Belgium v West Germany; 17.12.91. West Germany v Luxembourg.

GROUP 6

Helsinki, 12 September 1990, 10,242
Finland (0) 0
Portugal (0) 0
Finland: Huttunen; Rinne, Holmgren, Europaeus, Heikkinen, Petaja, Tarkkio (Paavola 73), Litmanen, Jarvinen (Myyry 84), Hjelm, Paatelainen.

Portugal: Silvino; Joao Pinto, Veloso, Ferreira, Venancio, Fonseca (Pacheco 63), Paneira, Andre, Jaime Pacheco, Rui Barros, Rui Aguas (Cadete 46).

Porto, 17 October 1990, 17,198
Portugal (0) 1 *(Rui Aguas 54)*
Holland (0) 0
Portugal: Silvino; Joao Pinto, Veloso, Venancio, Leal, Paneira, Oceano, Semedo (Ferreira 89), Nelo (Carlos Xavier 87), Rui Aguas, Cadete.
Holland: Van Breukelen; De Boer (Gillhaus 75), Blind, Van Tiggelen (Van't Schip 58), Valckx, Rutjes, Vanenburg, Witschge, Bergkamp, Van Basten, Gullit.

Athens, 31 October 1990, 7768
Greece (2) 4 *(Tsiantakis 37, Karapialis 40, Saravakos 59, Borbokis 88)*
Malta (0) 0
Greece: Papadopoulos T; Apostolakis, Papadopoulos G, Manolas, Kalitzakis, Tsiantakis, Tsalouhidis, Karapialis, Kofidis, Saravakos, Dimitriadis (Borbokis 31).
Malta: Cini; Carabott, Vella S, Galea, Scerri, Buttigieg, Vella R, Suda (Degiorgio 46), Laferla, Zerafa, Busuttil.

Rotterdam, 21 November 1990, 25,430
Holland (2) 2 *(Bergkamp 7, Van Basten 18)*
Greece (0) 0
Holland: Van Breukelen; De Jong, Blind, Rutjes, Vanenburg, Wouters, Bergkamp (Winter 80), Witschge, Van't Schip, Van Basten, Roy.
Greece: Papadopoulos T; Apostolakis, Papadopoulos G, Manolas, Kalitzakis, Tsalouhidis, Kofidis (Karageorgiou 53), Karapialis, Tsiantakis, Saravakos, Bormpokis.

Ta'Qali, 25 November 1990, 7200
Malta (0) 1 *(Suda 74)*
Finland (0) 1 *(Holmgren 87)*
Malta: Cluett; Buttigieg, Vella S, Galea, Scerri, Vella R, Laferla, Degiorgio, Carabott, Busuttil, Zarb (Suda 71).
Finland: Huttunen; Europaeus, Rinne (Petaja 46), Heikkinen, Holmgren, Myyry, Litmanen, Hjelm, Tauriainen, Tarkkio (Tegelberg 79), Paatelainen.

Ta'Qali, 19 December 1990, 10,254
Malta (0) 0
Holland (3) 8 *(Van Basten 9, 20, 23, 64, 80 (pen), Winter 53, Bergkamp 60, 66)*
Malta: Cluett; Camilleri E (Suda 46), Camilleri J, Galea, Laferla, Vella S, Carabott, Degiorgio, Scerri, Busuttil, Vella R.
Holland: Van Breukelen; Blind, De Jong, De Boer, Wouters, Koeman E (Winter 46), Bergkamp (Van den Brom 71), Van't Schip, Gullit, Van Basten, Roy.

Athens, 23 January 1991, 20,000
Greece (1) 3 *(Borbokis 7, Manolas 68, Tsalouhidis 85)*
Portugal (1) 2 *(Rui Aguas 18, Futre 62)*
Greece: Sarganis; Apostolakis, Papadopoulos G, Manolas, Kalitzakis, Tsalouhidis, Kofidis (Athanasiadis 69), Tursunides, Tsiantakis, Borbokis (Dimitriadis 65), Saravakos.
Portugal: Vitor Baia; Joao Pinto, Veloso, Leal, Venancio, Paneira, Oceano, Rui Barros (Cadete 71), Futre, Rui Aguas, Sousa.

Ta'Qali, 9 February 1991, 5000
Malta (0) 0
Portugal (1) 1 *(Futre 27)*
Malta: Cluett; Vella S, Azzopardi, Galea, Laferla, Buttigieg, Busuttil, Vella R, Suda, Degiorgio, Zerafa.
Portugal: Vitor Baia; Joao Pinto, Leal, Venancio, Veloso, Oceano, Paneira, Rui Barros (Cadete 67), Rui Aguas, Futre (Sousa 63), Semedo.

Porto, 20 February 1991, 5303
Portugal (3) 5 *(Rui Aguas 5, Leal 33, Paneira 41 (pen), Futre 48, Cadete 81)*
Malta (0) 0
Portugal: Vitor Baia; Joao Pinto (Cadete 46), Leal, Venancio (Madeira 67), Veloso, Oceano, Peneira, Sousa, Rui Aguas, Futre, Semedo.
Malta: Cluett; Vella S, Azzopardi, Camilleri J (Scerri 38), Laferla, Buttigieg, Busuttil, Vella R, Suda (Carabott 51), Degiorgio, Zerafa.

Rotterdam, 13 March 1991, 40,000
Holland (1) 1 *(Van Basten 31 (pen))*
Malta (0) 0
Holland: Van Breukelen; Blind, Vink, De Boer (Kieft 46), Van't Schip, Wouters, Witschge, Gullit, Bergkamp, Van Basten, Roy (Vanenburg 69).
Malta: Cini; Laferla, Camilleri E, Vella S, Brincat (Suda 86), Camilleri J, Azzopardi (Saliba 89), Scerri, Vella R, Degiorgio, Zerafa.

Rotterdam, 17 April 1991, 25,000
Holland (1) 2 *(Van Basten 9, Gullit 75)*
Finland (0) 0
Holland: Van Breukelen; Blind, Vink, De Jong, Gullit, Wouters, Bergkamp (Kieft 72), Witschge, Van't Schip, Van Basten (Rutjes 76), Huistra.
Finland: Huttunen; Kanerva, Heikkinen, Europaeus, Holmgren, Ukkonen, Petaja, Litmanen (Tegelberg 46), Myyry, Tauriainen (Nyssonen 83), Paatelainen.

Helsinki, 16 May 1991, 5150
Finland (0) 2 *(Jarvinen 51, Litmanen 88)*
Malta (0) 0
Finland: Huttunen; Petaja, Holmgren, Heikkinen, Kanerva, Myyry, Litmanen, Ukkonen, Tarkkio (Tauriainen 87), Paatelainen (Paavola 63), Jarvinen.
Malta: Cini; Buttigieg, Brincat, Vella S, Camilleri J (Zerafa 70), Laferla, Busuttil, Vella R, Degiorgio, Scerri, Suda.

Helsinki, 5 June 1991, 21,207
Finland (0) 1 *(Holmgren 78)*
Holland (0) 1 *(De Boer 60)*
Finland: Huttunen; Petaja, Heikkinen, Ukkonen (Hjelm 81), Holmgren, Paavola, Myyry, Litmanen, Jarvinen, Tarkkio, Paatelainen (Tegelberg 66).
Holland: Hiele; Rutjes, Blind, Wouters, De Boer, Koeman R, Winter, Witschge, Van't Schip, Van Basten, Huistra (Kieft 75).

	P	W	D	L	F	A	Pts
Holland	6	4	1	1	14	2	9
Portugal	5	3	1	1	9	3	7
Finland	5	1	3	1	4	4	5
Greece	3	2	0	1	7	4	4
Malta	7	0	1	6	1	22	1

Remaining fixtures: 11.9.91. Portugal v Finland; 9.10.91. Finland v Greece; 16.10.91. Holland v Portugal; 30.10.91. Greece v Finland; 20.11.91. Portugal v Greece; 4.12.91. Greece v Holland; 22.12.91. Malta v Greece.

GROUP 7
Wembley, 17 October 1990, 77,040
England (1) 2 *(Lineker 39 (pen), Beardsley 89)*
Poland (0) 0
England: Woods; Dixon, Pearce, Parker, Walker, Wright M, Platt, Gascoigne, Bull (Waddle 56), Lineker (Beardsley 56), Barnes.
Poland: Wandzik; Czachowski, Wdowczyk, Szewczyk, Kaczmarek, Nawrocki, Tarasiewicz, Warzycha R, Furtok (Warzycha K 75), Ziober, Kosecki (Kubicki 85).

Dublin, 17 October 1990, 46,000
Republic of Ireland (2) 5 *(Aldridge 15, 58, 73 (pen), O'Leary 40, Quinn 66)*
Turkey (0) 0
Republic of Ireland: Bonner; Irwin, Staunton, McCarthy, O'Leary, Hughton, Townsend (Moran 73), Houghton, Quinn (Cascarino 66), Aldridge, Sheridan.
Turkey: Engin; Riza, Tugay, Kemal, Gokhan, Erkan (Tanju 46), Bulent, Oguz, Mehmet, Hami, Sercan (Metin 46).

Dublin, 14 November 1990, 45,000
Republic of Ireland (0) 1 *(Cascarino 79)*
England (0) 1 *(Platt 67)*
Republic of Ireland: Bonner; Morris, Staunton, McCarthy, O'Leary, Whelan (McLoughlin 74), McGrath, Houghton, Quinn (Cascarino 62), Aldridge, Townsend.
England: Woods; Dixon, Pearce, Adams, Walker, Wright M, Platt, Cowans, Beardsley, Lineker, McMahon.

Istanbul, 14 November 1990, 4868
Turkey (0) 0
Poland (1) 1 *(Dziekanowski 37)*
Turkey: Engin; Riza, Uiken (Mehmet 67), Bulent, Gokhan, Yusuf, Muhmmed (Sercan 67), Unal, Oguz, Tanju, Hami.
Poland: Wandzik; Kubicki, Kaczmarek, Wdowczyk, Warzycha R, Nawrocki, Tarasiewicz, Prusik, Warzycha K, Dziekanowski (Ziober 74), Kosecki.

Wembley, 27 March 1991, 77,753
England (1) 1 *(Dixon 9)*
Republic of Ireland (1) 1 *(Quinn 27)*
England: Seaman; Dixon, Pearce, Adams (Sharpe 46), Walker, Wright M, Robson, Platt, Beardsley, Lineker (Wright I 75), Barnes.
Republic of Ireland: Bonner; Irwin, Staunton, O'Leary, Moran, Townsend, McGrath, Houghton, Quinn, Aldridge (Cascarino 70), Sheedy.

Warsaw, 17 April 1991, 1000
Poland (0) 3 *(Tarasiewicz 75, Urban 81, Kosecki 88)*
Turkey (0) 0
Poland: Wandzik; Kubicki, Kaczmarek (Czachowski 62), Wdowczyk, Jakolcewicz, Warzycha K, Warzycha R, Tarasiewicz, Urban, Kosecki, Ziober (Soczynski 70).
Turkey: Engin; Riza, Tayfun, Gokhan, Kemal, Bulent, Feyyaz, Ucar (Faruk 80), Muhammed Mehmet, Tanju, Osman (Abdullah 70).

Dublin, 1 May 1991, 48,000
Republic of Ireland (0) 0
Poland (0) 0
Republic of Ireland: Bonner; Irwin, Staunton, O'Leary, Moran, Townsend, McGrath, Houghton, Quinn (Slaven 70), Aldridge (Cascarino 70), Sheedy.
Poland: Wandzik; Kubicki, Jakolcewicz, Wdowczyk, Soczynski, Warzycha R, Tarasiewicz, Czachowski, Furtok (Kosecki 89), Urban (Warzycha K 88), Szewczyk.

Izmir, 1 May 1991, 20,000
Turkey (0) 0
England (1) 1 *(Wise 32)*
Turkey: Hayrettin; Riza, Ogun, Gokhan, Recap, Muhammed, Unal, Ridvan, Mehmet, Tanju, Ali (Feyyaz 72).
England: Seaman; Dixon, Pearce, Wise, Walker, Pallister, Platt, Thomas G (Hodge 46), Smith, Lineker, Barnes.

	P	W	D	L	F	A	Pts
England	4	2	2	0	5	2	6
Republic of Ireland	4	1	3	0	7	2	5
Poland	4	2	1	1	4	2	5
Turkey	4	0	0	4	0	10	0

Remaining fixtures: 16.10.91. Poland v Republic of Ireland, England v Turkey; 13.11.91. Turkey v Republic of Ireland, Poland v England.

THE WORLD CUP 1930–1990

Year	Winners		Runners-up		Venue	Attendance	Referee
1930	Uruguay	4	Argentina	2	Montevideo	90,000	Langenus (B)
1934	Italy	2	Czechoslovakia	1	Rome	50,000	Eklind (Se)
	(after extra time)						
1938	Italy	4	Hungary	2	Paris	45,000	Capdeville (F)
1950	Uruguay	2	Brazil	1	Rio de Janeiro	199,854	Reader (E)
1954	West Germany	3	Hungary	2	Berne	60,000	Ling (E)
1958	Brazil	5	Sweden	2	Stockholm	49,737	Guigue (F)
1962	Brazil	3	Czechoslovakia	1	Santiago	68,679	Latychev (USSR)
1966	England	4	West Germany	2	Wembley	93,802	Dienst (Sw)
	(after extra time)						
1970	Brazil	4	Italy	1	Mexico City	107,412	Glockner (EG)
1974	West Germany	2	Holland	1	Munich	77,833	Taylor (E)
1978	Argentina	3	Holland	1	Buenos Aires	77,000	Gonella (I)
	(after extra time)						
1982	Italy	3	West Germany	1	Madrid	90,080	Coelho (Br)
1986	Argentina	3	West Germany	2	Mexico City	114,580	Filho (Br)
1990	West Germany	1	Argentina	0	Rome	73,603	Codesal (Mex)

GOALSCORING AND ATTENDANCES IN WORLD CUP FINAL ROUNDS

	Matches	Goals (avge)	Attendance (avge)
1930, Uruguay	18	70 (3.8)	434,500 (24,138)
1934, Italy	17	70 (4.1)	395,000 (23,235)
1938, France	18	84 (4.6)	483,000 (26,833)
1950, Brazil	22	88 (4.0)	1,337,000 (60,772)
1954, Switzerland	26	140 (5.3)	943,000 (36,270)
1958, Sweden	35	126 (3.6)	868,000 (24,800)
1962, Chile	32	89 (2.7)	776,000 (24,250)
1966, England	32	89 (2.7)	1,614,677 (50,458)
1970, Mexico	32	95 (2.9)	1,673,975 (52,311)
1974, West Germany	38	97 (2.5)	1,774,022 (46,684)
1978, Argentina	38	102 (2.6)	1,610,215 (42,374)
1982, Spain	52	146 (2.8)	1,766,277 (33,967)
1986, Mexico	52	132 (2.5)	2,199,941 (42,307)
1990, West Germany	52	115 (2.21)	2,510,686* (48,282)

International Records

MOST GOALS IN AN INTERNATIONAL

England	Malcolm Macdonald (Newcastle U) 5 goals v Cyprus, at Wembley	16.4.1975
	Willie Hall (Tottenham H) 5 goals v Ireland, at Old Trafford	16.11.1938
	G. O. Smith (Corinthians) 5 goals v Ireland, at Sunderland	18.2.1899
	Steve Bloomer (Derby Co) 5 goals* v Wales, at Cardiff	16.3.1896
	Oliver Vaughton (Aston Villa) 5 goals v Ireland, at Belfast	18.2.82
Scotland	Charles Heggie (Rangers) 5 goals v Ireland, at Belfast	20.3.1886
Ireland	Joe Bambrick (Linfield) 6 goals v Wales, at Belfast	1.2.1930
Wales	James Price (Wrexham) 4 goals v Ireland, at Wrexham	25.2.1882
	Mel Charles (Cardiff C) 4 goals v Ireland, at Cardiff	11.4.1962
	Ian Edwards (Chester) 4 goals v Malta, at Wrexham	25.10.1978

* There are conflicting reports which make it uncertain whether Bloomer scored four or five goals in this game.

MOST GOALS IN AN INTERNATIONAL CAREER

		Goals	Games
England	Bobby Charlton (Manchester U)	49	106
Scotland	Denis Law (Huddersfield T, Manchester C, Torino, Manchester U)	30	55
	Kenny Dalglish (Celtic, Liverpool)	30	102
Ireland	Billy Gillespie (Sheffield U)	12	25
	Joe Bambrick (Linfield, Chelsea)	12	11
	Gerry Armstrong (Tottenham H, Watford, Real Mallorca, WBA, Chesterfield)	12	63
Wales	Trevor Ford (Swansea T, Aston Villa, Sunderland, Cardiff C)	23	38
	Ivor Allchurch (Swansea T, Newcastle U, Cardiff C)	23	68
Republic of Ireland	Frank Stapleton (Arsenal, Manchester U, Ajax, Derby Co, Le Havre, Blackburn R)	20	70

HIGHEST SCORES

World Cup Match	New Zealand	13	Fiji	0	1981
Olympic Games	Denmark	17	France	1	1908
	Germany	16	USSR	0	1912
International Match	Germany	13	Finland	0	1940
	Spain	13	Bulgaria	0	1933
European Cup	Feyenoord	12	K R Reykjavik	2	1969
European Cup-Winners' Cup	Sporting Lisbon	16	Apoel Nicosia	1	1963
Fairs & UEFA Cups	Ajax	14	Red Boys	0	1984

GOALSCORING RECORDS

World Cup Final	Geoff Hurst (England) 3 goals v West Germany	1966
World Cup Final tournament	Just Fontaine (France) 13 goals	1958
Major European Cup game	Lothar Emmerich (Borussia Dortmund) v Floriana in Cup-Winners' Cup – 6 goals	1965
Career	Arthur Friedenreich (Brazil) 1329 goals	1910–30
	Pelé (Brazil) 1281 goals	*1956–78
	Franz 'Bimbo' Binder (Austria, Germany) 1006 goals	1930–50

*Pelé has since scored two goals in Testimonial matches making his total 1283.

MOST CAPPED INTERNATIONALS IN BRITISH ISLES

England	Bobby Moore	108 appearances	1962–73
Northern Ireland	Pat Jennings	119 appearances	1964–86
Scotland	Kenny Dalglish	102 appearances	1971–86
Wales	Joey Jones	72 appearances	1975–87
Republic of Ireland	Liam Brady	67 appearances	1974–90

TRANSFERS

British players £2 million and over

£3,200,000 Ian Rush, Liverpool to Juventus, June 1987
£2,900,000 Dean Saunders, Derby Co to Liverpool, July 1991
£2,800,000 Ian Rush, Juventus to Liverpool, August 1988
£2,750,000 Gary Lineker, Everton to Barcelona, June 1986
£2,300,000 Mark Hughes, Manchester U to Barcelona, May 1986
£2,300,000 Gary Pallister, Middlesbrough to Manchester U, August 1989
£2,200,000 Tony Cottee, West Ham to Everton, July 1988
£2,200,000 Mark Wright, Derby Co to Liverpool, July 1991
£2,000,000 Paul Gascoigne, Newcastle U to Tottenham H, July 1988
£2,000,000 Teddy Sheringham, Millwall to Nottingham Forest, July 1991

World records

£7,700,000 Roberto Baggio, Fiorentina to Juventus, June 1990
£6,900,000 Diego Maradona, Barcelona to Napoli, June 1984
£5,500,000 Ruud Gullit, PSV Eindhoven to AC Milan, June 1987
£5,500,000 Karl-Heinz Riedle, Werder Bremen to Lazio, June 1990
£5,500,000 Thomas Hassler, Cologne to Juventus, June 1990
£5,500,000 David Platt, Aston Villa to Bari, July 1991
£4,800,000 Diego Maradona, Argentinos Juniors to Barcelona, June 1982
£4,800,000 Lajos Detari, Eintracht Frankfurt to Olympiakos, July 1988
£4,800,000 Dragan Stojkovic, Red Star Belgrade to Marseille, June 1990
£4,500,000 Chris Waddle, Tottenham H to Marseille, July 1989

EUROPEAN FOOTBALL CHAMPIONSHIP

(formerly EUROPEAN NATIONS' CUP)

Year	Winners		Runners-up		Venue
1960	USSR	2	Yugoslavia	1	Paris
1964	Spain	2	USSR	1	Madrid
1968	Italy	2	Yugoslavia	0	Rome
			After 1-1 draw		
1972	West Germany	3	USSR	0	Brussels
1976	Czechoslovakia	2	West Germany	2	Belgrade
	(Czechoslovakia won on penalties)				
1980	West Germany	2	Belgium	1	Rome
1984	France	2	Spain	0	Paris
1988	Holland	2	USSR	0	Munich

EUROPEAN NATIONS' CUP 1958–60

Preliminary Round

Eire 2, Czechoslovakia 0
Czechoslovakia 4, Eire 0

First Round

France 7, Greece 1
Greece 1, France 1
USSR 3, Hungary 1
Hungary 0, USSR 1
Romania 3, Turkey 0
Turkey 2, Romania 0
Norway 0, Austria 1
Austria 5, Norway 2
Yugoslavia 2, Bulgaria 0
Bulgaria 1, Yugoslavia 1
Portugal 3, East Germany 2
East Germany 0, Portugal 2
Denmark 2, Czechoslovakia 2
Czechoslovakia 5, Denmark 1
Poland 2, Spain 4
Spain 3, Poland 0

Quarter-Finals

Portugal 2, Yugoslavia 1
Yugoslavia 5, Portugal 1
France 5, Austria 2
Austria 2, France 4
Romania 0, Czechoslovakia 2
Czechoslovakia 3, Romania 0
USSR w.o. Spain withdrew

Semi-Finals

Yugoslavia 5, France 4 (in Paris)
USSR 3, Czechoslovakia 0 (in Marseilles)

Third Place Match (Marseilles)

Czechoslovakia 2, France 0

Final (Paris, 10 July 1960)

USSR (0) 2, Yugoslavia (1) 1 after extra time

USSR: Yachin; Tchekeli, Kroutikov; Voinov, Maslenkin, Netto; Metreveli, Ivanov, Ponedelnik, Bubukin, Meshki.
Yugoslavia: Vidinic; Durkovic, Jusufi; Zanetic, Miladinovic, Perusic; Sekularac, Jerkovic, Galic, Matus, Kostic.
Scorers: Metreveli, Ponedelnik for USSR; Netto og for Yugoslavia.

EUROPEAN NATIONS' CUP 1962–64

First Round

Spain 6, Romania 0
Romania 3, Spain 1
Poland 0, Northern Ireland 2

Northern Ireland 2, Poland 0
Denmark 6, Malta 1
Malta 1, Denmark 3
Eire 4, Iceland 2
Iceland 1, Eire 1
Greece withdrew against Albania
East Germany 2, Czechoslovakia 1
Czechoslovakia 1, East Germany 1
Hungary 3, Wales 1
Wales 1, Hungary 1
Italy 6, Turkey 0
Turkey 0, Italy 1
Holland 3, Switzerland 1
Switzerland 1, Holland 1
Norway 0, Sweden 2
Sweden 1, Norway 1
Yugoslavia 3, Belgium 2
Belgium 0, Yugoslavia 1
Bulgaria 3, Portugal 1
Portugal 3, Bulgaria 1
Bulgaria 1, Portugal 0
England 1, France 1
France 5, England 2

Second Round

Spain 1, Northern Ireland 1
Northern Ireland 0, Spain 1
Denmark 4, Albania 0
Albania 1, Denmark 0
Austria 0, Eire 0
Eire 3, Austria 2
East Germany 1, Hungary 2
Hungary 3, East Germany 3
USSR 2, Italy 0
Italy 1, USSR 1
Holland 1, Luxembourg 1
Luxembourg 2, Holland 1
Yugoslavia 0, Sweden 0
Sweden 3, Yugoslavia 2
Bulgaria 1, France 0
France 3, Bulgaria 1

Quarter-Finals

Luxembourg 2, Denmark 2
Denmark 3, Luxembourg 3
Denmark 1, Luxembourg 0
Spain 5, Eire 1
Eire 0, Spain 2
France 1, Hungary 3
Hungary 2, France 1
Sweden 1, USSR 1
USSR 3, Sweden 1

Semi-Finals

USSR 3, Denmark 0 (in Barcelona)
Spain 2, Hungary 1 (in Madrid)

Third Place Match (Barcelona)

Hungary 3, Denmark 1 after extra time

Final (Madrid, 21 June 1964)

Spain (1) 2, USSR (1) 1

Spain: Iribar; Rivilla, Calleja; Fuste, Olivella, Zoco; Amancio, Pereda, Marcellino, Suarez, Lapetra.
USSR: Yachin; Chustikov, Mudrik, Voronin, Shesternjev, Anitchkin; Chislenko, Ivanov, Ponedelnik, Kornaev, Khusainov.
Scorers: Pereda, Marcellino for Spain; Khusainov for USSR.

EUROPEAN CHAMPIONSHIP 1966–68

Group 1
Eire 0, Spain 0
Eire 2, Turkey 1
Spain 2, Eire 0
Turkey 0, Spain 0
Turkey 2, Eire 1
Eire 0, Czechoslovakia 2
Spain 2, Turkey 0
Czechoslovakia 1, Spain 0
Spain 2, Czechoslovakia 1
Czechoslovakia 3, Turkey 0
Turkey 0, Czechoslovakia 0
Czechoslovakia 1, Eire 2

Group 2
Norway 0, Bulgaria 0
Portugal 1, Sweden 2
Bulgaria 4, Norway 2
Sweden 1, Portugal 1
Norway 1, Portugal 2
Sweden 0, Bulgaria 2
Norway 3, Sweden 1
Sweden 5, Norway 2
Bulgaria 3, Sweden 0
Portugal 2, Norway 1
Bulgaria 1, Portugal 0
Portugal 0, Bulgaria 0

Group 3
Finland 0, Austria 0
Austria 2, Finland 1
Greece 2, Finland 1
Greece 4, Austria 1
Finland 1, Greece 1
Austria 1, USSR 0
USSR 4, Austria 3
Greece 0, USSR 1
USSR 2, Finland 0
Austria 1, Greece 1
Finland 2, USSR 5
USSR 4, Greece 0

Group 4
Albania 0, Yugoslavia 2
West Germany 6, Albania 0
Yugoslavia 1, West Germany 0
West Germany 3, Yugoslavia 1
Yugoslavia 4, Albania 0
Albania 0, West Germany 0

Group 5
Holland 2, Hungary 2
Hungary 6, Denmark 0
Holland 2, Denmark 0
East Germany 4, Holland 3
Hungary 2, Holland 1
Denmark 0, Hungary 2
Denmark 1, East Germany 1
Holland 1, East Germany 0
Hungary 3, East Germany 1
Denmark 3, Holland 2
East Germany 3, Denmark 2
East Germany 1, Hungary 0

Group 6
Cyprus 1, Romania 5
Romania 4, Switzerland 2
Italy 3, Romania 1
Cyprus 0, Italy 2
Romania 7, Cyprus 0

Switzerland 7, Romania 1
Italy 5, Cyprus 0
Switzerland 5, Cyprus 0
Switzerland 2, Italy 2
Italy 4, Switzerland 0
Cyprus 2, Switzerland 1
Romania 0, Italy 1

Group 7
Poland 4, Luxembourg 0
France 2, Poland 1
Luxembourg 0, France 3
Luxembourg 0, Bulgaria 5
Luxembourg 0, Poland 0
Poland 3, Belgium 1
Belgium 2, France 1
Poland 1, France 4
Belgium 2, Poland 4
France 1, Belgium 1
Belgium 3, Luxembourg 0
France 3, Luxembourg 1

Group 8
Northern Ireland 0, England 2
Wales 1, Scotland 1
England 5, Wales 1
Scotland 2, Northern Ireland 1
Northern Ireland 0 Wales 0
England 2, Scotland 3
Wales 0, England 3
Northern Ireland 1, Scotland 0
England 2, Northern Ireland 0
Scotland 3, Wales 2
Scotland 1, England 1
Wales 2, Northern Ireland 0

Quarter-Finals
England 1, Spain 0
Spain 1, England 2
Bulgaria 3, Italy 2
Italy 2, Bulgaria 0
France 1, Yugoslavia 1
Yugoslavia 5, France 1
Hungary 2, USSR 0
USSR 3, Hungary 0

Semi-Finals
Yugoslavia 1, England 0 (in Florence)
Italy 0, USSR 0 (Italy won toss) (in Naples)

Third Place Match (Rome)
England 2, USSR 0

Final (Rome, 8 June 1968)
Italy (0) 1, Yugoslavia (1) 1
Italy: Zoff; Burgnich, Facchetti; Ferrini, Guarneri, Castano; Domenghini, Juliano, Anastasi, Lodetti, Prati.
Yugoslavia: Pantelic; Fazlagic, Damjanovic; Pavlovic, Paunovic, Holcer; Petkovic, Acimovic, Musemic, Trivic, Dzajic.
Scorers: Domenghini for Italy; Dzajic for Yugoslavia.

Final Replay (Rome, 10 June 1968)
Italy (2) 2, Yugoslavia (0) 0
Italy: Zoff; Burgnich, Facchetti; Rosato, Guarneri, Salvadore; Domenghini, Mazzola, Anastasi, De Sisti, Riva.
Yugoslavia: Pantelic; Fazlagic, Damjanovic; Pavlovic, Paunovic, Holcer; Hosic, Acimovic, Musemic, Trivic, Dzajic.
Scorers: Riva, Anastasi for Italy.

EUROPEAN CHAMPIONSHIP 1970–72

Group 1

Czechoslovakia 1, Finland 1
Romania 3, Finland 0
Wales 0, Romania 0
Wales 1, Czechoslovakia 3
Finland 0, Wales 1
Czechoslovakia 1, Romania 0
Finland 0, Czechoslovakia 4
Finland 0, Romania 4
Wales 3, Finland 0
Czechoslovakia 1, Wales 0
Romania 2, Czechoslovakia 1
Romania 2, Wales 0

Group 2

Norway 1, Hungary 3
France 3, Norway 1
Bulgaria 1, Norway 1
Hungary 1, France 1
Bulgaria 3, Hungary 0
Norway 1, Bulgaria 4
Norway 1, France 3
Hungary 2, Bulgaria 0
France 0, Hungary 2
Hungary 4, Norway 0
France 2, Bulgaria 1
Bulgaria 2, France 1

Group 3

Greece 0, Switzerland 1
Malta 1, Switzerland 2
Malta 0, England 1
England 3, Greece 0
Switzerland 5, Malta 0
England 5, Malta 0
Malta 1, Greece 1
Switzerland 1, Greece 0
Greece 2, Malta 0
Switzerland 2, England 3
England 1, Switzerland 1
Greece 0, England 2

Group 4

Spain 3, Northern Ireland 0
Cyprus 0, Northern Ireland 3
Northern Ireland 5, Cyprus 0
Cyprus 1, USSR 3
Cyprus 0, Spain 2
USSR 2, Spain 1
USSR 6, Cyprus 1
USSR 1, Northern Ireland 0
Northern Ireland 1, USSR 1
Spain 0, USSR 0
Spain 7, Cyprus 0
Northern Ireland 1, Spain 1

Group 5

Denmark 0, Portugal 1
Scotland 1, Denmark 0
Belgium 2, Denmark 0
Belgium 3, Scotland 0
Belgium 3, Portugal 0
Portugal 2, Scotland 0
Denmark 1, Scotland 0
Portugal 5, Denmark 0
Denmark 1, Belgium 2
Scotland 2, Portugal 1
Scotland 1, Belgium 0
Portugal 1, Belgium 1

Group 6

Eire 1, Sweden 1
Sweden 1, Eire 0
Austria 1, Italy 2

Italy 3, Eire 0
Eire 1, Italy 2
Eire 1, Austria 4
Sweden 1, Austria 0
Sweden 0, Italy 0
Austria 1, Sweden 0
Italy 3, Sweden 0
Austria 6, Eire 0
Italy 2, Austria 2

Group 7

Holland 1, Yugoslavia 1
East Germany 1, Holland 0
Luxembourg 0, East Germany 5
Yugoslavia 2, Holland 0
East Germany 2, Luxembourg 1
Luxembourg 0, Yugoslavia 2
Holland 6, Luxembourg 0
East Germany 1, Yugoslavia 2
Holland 3, East Germany 2
Yugoslavia 0, East Germany 0
Yugoslavia 0, Luxembourg 0
Luxembourg 0, Holland 8

Group 8

Poland 3, Albania 0
West Germany 1, Turkey 1
Turkey 2, Albania 1
Albania 0, West Germany 1
Turkey 0, West Germany 3
Albania 1, Poland 1
West Germany 2, Albania 0
Poland 5, Turkey 1
Poland 1, West Germany 3
Albania 3, Turkey 0
West Germany 0, Poland 0
Turkey 1, Poland 0

Quarter-Finals

England 1, West Germany 3
Italy 0, Belgium 0
Hungary 1, Romania 1
Yugoslavia 0, USSR 0
West Germany 0, England 0
Belgium 2, Italy 1
USSR 3, Yugoslavia 0
Romania 2, Hungary 2
Play-off: Hungary 2, Romania 1

Semi-Finals

USSR 1, Hungary 0 (in Brussels)
West Germany 2, Belgium 1 (in Antwerp)

Third Place Match (Liège)

Belgium 2, Hungary 1

Final (Brussels, 18 June 1972)

West Germany (1) 3, USSR (0) 0

West Germany: Maier; Hottges, Schwarzenbeck, Beckenbauer, Breitner, Hoeness, Wimmer, Netzer, Heynckes, Müller, Kremers.
USSR: Rudakov; Dzodzuashvili, Khurtsilava, Kaplichny, Istomin, Troshkin, Kolotov, Baidachni, Konkov (Dolmatov), Banishevski (Kozinkievits), Onishenko.
Scorers: Müller 2, Wimmer for West Germany.

EUROPEAN CHAMPIONSHIP 1974–76

Group 1

England 3, Czechoslovakia 0
England 0, Portugal 0
England 5, Cyprus 0
Czechoslovakia 4, Cyprus 0
Czechoslovakia 5, Portugal 0

Cyprus 0, England 1
Cyprus 0, Portugal 2
Czechoslovakia 2, England 1
Portugal 1, Czechoslovakia 1
Portugal 1, England 1
Cyprus 0, Czechoslovakia 3
Portugal 1, Cyprus 0

Group 2

Austria 2, Wales 1
Luxembourg 2, Hungary 4
Wales 2, Hungary 0
Wales 5, Luxembourg 0
Luxembourg 1, Austria 2
Austria 0, Hungary 0
Hungary 1, Wales 2
Luxembourg 1, Wales 3
Hungary 2, Austria 1
Austria 6, Luxembourg 2
Hungary 8, Luxembourg 1
Wales 1, Austria 0

Group 3

Norway 2, Northern Ireland 1
Yugoslavia 3, Norway 1
Sweden 0, Northern Ireland 2
Northern Ireland 1, Yugoslavia 0
Sweden 1, Yugoslavia 2
Norway 1, Yugoslavia 3
Sweden 3, Norway 1
Norway 0, Sweden 2
Northern Ireland 1, Sweden 2
Yugoslavia 3, Sweden 0
Northern Ireland 3, Norway 0
Yugoslavia 1, Northern Ireland 0

Group 4

Denmark 1, Spain 2
Denmark 0, Romania 0
Scotland 1, Spain 2
Spain 1, Scotland 1
Spain 1, Romania 1
Romania 6, Denmark 1
Romania 1, Scotland 1
Denmark 0, Scotland 1
Spain 2, Denmark 0
Scotland 3, Denmark 1
Romania 2, Spain 2
Scotland 1, Romania 1

Group 5

Finland 1, Poland 2
Finland 1, Holland 3
Poland 3, Finland 0
Holland 3, Italy 1
Italy 0, Poland 0
Finland 0, Italy 1
Holland 4, Finland 1
Poland 4, Holland 1
Italy 0, Finland 0
Holland 3, Poland 0
Poland 0, Italy 0
Italy 1, Holland 0

Group 6

Eire 3, USSR 0
Turkey 1, Eire 1
Turkey 2, Switzerland 1
USSR 3, Turkey 0
Switzerland 1, Turkey 1
Eire 2, Switzerland 1
USSR 2, Eire 1
Switzerland 1, Eire 0
Switzerland 0, USSR 1
Eire 4, Turkey 0
USSR 4, Switzerland 1
Turkey 1, USSR 0

Group 7

Iceland 0, Belgium 2
East Germany 1, Iceland 1
Belgium 2, France 1
France 2, East Germany 2
East Germany 0, Belgium 0
Iceland 0, France 0
Iceland 2, East Germany 1
France 3, Iceland 0
Belgium 1, Iceland 0
Belgium 1, East Germany 2
East Germany 2, France 1
France 0, Belgium 0

Group 8

Bulgaria 3, Greece 3
Greece 2, West Germany 2
Greece 2, Bulgaria 1
Malta 0, West Germany 1
Malta 2, Greece 0
Bulgaria 1, West Germany 1
Greece 4, Malta 0
Bulgaria 5, Malta 0
West Germany 1, Greece 1
West Germany 1, Bulgaria 0
Malta 0, Bulgaria 2
West Germany 8, Malta 0

Quarter-Finals

Spain 1, West Germany 1
Yugoslavia 2, Wales 0
Czechoslovakia 2, USSR 0
Holland 5, Belgium 0
West Germany 2, Spain 0
USSR 2, Czechoslovakia 2
Wales 1, Yugoslavia 1
Belgium 1, Holland 2

Semi-Finals

Czechoslovakia 3, Holland 1 after extra time (in Zagreb)
West Germany 4, Yugoslavia 2 after extra time (in Belgrade)

Third Place Match (Zagreb)

Holland 3, Yugoslavia 2 after extra time

Final (Belgrade, 20 June 1976)

Czechoslovakia (2) 2, West Germany (1) 2 (aet)
(*Czechoslovakia won 5-3 on penalties*)
Czechoslovakia: Viktor; Dobias (Vesely F), Pivarnik, Ondrus, Capkovic, Gogh, Moder, Panenka, Svehlic (Jurkemik), Masny, Nehoda.
West Germany: Maier; Vogts, Beckenbauer, Schwarzenbeck, Dietz, Bonhof, Wimmer (Flohe), Müller D, Beer (Bongartz), Hoeness, Holzenbein.
Scorers: Svehlic, Dobias for Czechoslovakia; Müller, Holzenbein for West Germany.

EUROPEAN CHAMPIONSHIP 1978–80

Group 1

Denmark 3, Eire 3
Denmark 3, England 4
Eire 0, Northern Ireland 0
Denmark 2, Bulgaria 2
Eire 1, England 1
Northern Ireland 2, Denmark 1
Bulgaria 0, Northern Ireland 2
England 4, Northern Ireland 0
Northern Ireland 2, Bulgaria 0
Eire 2, Denmark 0
Bulgaria 1, Eire 0
Denmark 4, Northern Ireland 0
Bulgaria 0, England 3
England 1, Denmark 0

Eire 3, Bulgaria 0
Northern Ireland 1, England 5
Bulgaria 3, Denmark 0
Northern Ireland 1, Eire 0
England 2, Bulgaria 0
England 2, Eire 0

Group 2

Norway 0, Austria 2
Belgium 1, Norway 1
Austria 3, Scotland 2
Portugal 1, Belgium 1
Scotland 3, Norway 2
Austria 1, Portugal 2
Portugal 1, Scotland 0
Belgium 1, Austria 1
Austria 0, Belgium 0
Norway 0, Portugal 1
Norway 0, Scotland 4
Austria 4, Norway 0
Norway 1, Belgium 2
Belgium 2, Portugal 0
Scotland 1, Austria 1
Portugal 3, Norway 1
Belgium 2, Scotland 0
Portugal 1, Austria 2
Scotland 1, Belgium 3
Scotland 4, Portugal 1

Group 3

Yugoslavia 1, Spain 2
Romania 3, Yugoslavia 2
Spain 1, Romania 0
Spain 5, Cyprus 0
Cyprus 0, Yugoslavia 3
Romania 2, Spain 2
Cyprus 1, Romania 1
Spain 0, Yugoslavia 1
Yugoslavia 2, Romania 1
Yugoslavia 5, Cyprus 0
Romania 2, Cyprus 0
Cyprus 1, Spain 3

Group 4

Iceland 0, Poland 2
Holland 3, Iceland 0
East Germany 3, Iceland 1
Switzerland 1, Holland 3
Holland 3, East Germany 0
Poland 2, Switzerland 0
Holland 3, Switzerland 0
East Germany 2, Poland 1
Poland 2, Holland 0
Switzerland 0, East Germany 2
Switzerland 2, Iceland 0
Iceland 1, Switzerland 2
Iceland 0, Holland 4
Switzerland 0, Poland 2
Iceland 0, East Germany 3
Poland 1, East Germany 1
Poland 2, Iceland 0
East Germany 5, Switzerland 2
Holland 1, Portugal 1
East Germany 2, Holland 3

Group 5

France 2, Sweden 2
Sweden 1, Czechoslovakia 3
Luxembourg 1, France 3
France 3, Luxembourg 0
Czechoslovakia 2, France 0
Luxembourg 0, Czechoslovakia 3
Sweden 3, Luxembourg 0
Sweden 1, France 3
Czechoslovakia 4, Sweden 1
Luxembourg 1, Sweden 1
France 2, Czechoslovakia 0
Czechoslovakia 4, Luxembourg 0

Group 6

Finland 3, Greece 0
Finland 2, Hungary 1
USSR 2, Greece 0
Hungary 2, USSR 0
Greece 8, Finland 1
Greece 4, Hungary 1
Hungary 0, Greece 0
USSR 2, Hungary 2
Finland 1, USSR 1
Greece 1, USSR 0
Hungary 3, Finland 1
USSR 2, Finland 2

Group 7

Wales 7, Malta 0
Wales 1, Turkey 0
Malta 0, West Germany 0
Turkey 2, Malta 1
Turkey 0, West Germany 0
Wales 0, West Germany 2
Malta 0, Wales 2
West Germany 5, Wales 1
Malta 1, Turkey 2
Turkey 1, Wales 0
West Germany 2, Turkey 0
West Germany 8, Malta 0

Final Tournament
Group 1

West Germany 1, Czechoslovakia 0
Greece 0, Holland 1
West Germany 3, Holland 2
Czechoslovakia 3, Greece 1
Czechoslovakia 1, Holland 1
West Germany 0, Greece 0

Group 2

Belgium 1, England 1
Spain 0, Italy 0
Spain 1, Belgium 2
Italy 1, England 0
England 2, Spain 1
Italy 0, Belgium 0

Third Place Match (Naples)

Italy 1, Czechoslovakia 1 after extra time
(*Czechoslovakia won 9-8 on penalties*)

Final (Rome, 22 June 1980)

West Germany (1) 2, Belgium (0) 1

West Germany: Schumacher; Briegel, Forster K,
Dietz, Schuster, Rummenigge, Hrubesch, Müller,
Aloffs, Stielike, Kaltz.
Belgium: Pfaff; Gerets, Millecamps, Meeuws,
Renquin, Cools, Van der Eycken, Van Moer,
Mommens, Van der Elst, Ceulemans.
Scorers: Hrubesch 2 for West Germany; Van der
Eycken for Belgium.

EUROPEAN CHAMPIONSHIP 1982–84
Group 1

Belgium 3, Switzerland 0
Scotland 2, East Germany 0
Switzerland 2, Scotland 0
Belgium 3, Scotland 2
East Germany 1, Belgium 2
Scotland 2, Switzerland 2
Belgium 2, East Germany 1
Switzerland 0, East Germany 0
East Germany 3, Switzerland 0
Scotland 1, Belgium 1
Switzerland 3, Belgium 1
East Germany 2, Scotland 1

Group 2

Finland 2, Poland 3
Finland 0, Portugal 2

Portugal 2, Poland 1
USSR 2, Finland 0
Poland 1, Finland 1
USSR 5, Portugal 0
Poland 1, USSR 1
Finland 0, USSR 0
Portugal 5, Finland 0
USSR 2, Poland 0
Poland 0, Portugal 1
Portugal 1, USSR 0

Group 3

Denmark 2, England 2
Luxembourg 0, Greece 2
Luxembourg 1, Denmark 2
Greece 0, England 3
England 9, Luxembourg 0
Luxembourg 2, Hungary 6
England 0, Greece 0
Hungary 6, Luxembourg 2
Denmark 1, Greece 0
England 2, Hungary 0
Hungary 2, Greece 3
Denmark 3, Hungary 1
England 0, Denmark 1
Denmark 6, Luxembourg 0
Hungary 0, England 3
Hungary 1, Denmark 0
Greece 0, Denmark 2
Luxembourg 0, England 4
Greece 2, Hungary 2
Greece 1, Luxembourg 0

Group 4

Wales 1, Norway 0
Norway 3, Yugoslavia 1
Bulgaria 2, Norway 1
Bulgaria 0, Yugoslavia 1
Yugoslavia 4, Wales 4
Wales 1, Bulgaria 0
Norway 1, Bulgaria 2
Norway 0, Wales 0
Yugoslavia 2, Norway 1
Bulgaria 1, Wales 0
Wales 1, Yugoslavia 1
Yugoslavia 3, Bulgaria 2

Group 5

Romania 3, Cyprus 1
Romania 2, Sweden 0
Czechoslovakia 2, Sweden 2
Cyprus 0, Sweden 1
Italy 2, Czechoslovakia 2
Italy 0, Romania 0
Cyprus 1, Italy 1
Cyprus 1, Czechoslovakia 1
Czechoslovakia 6, Cyprus 0
Romania 1, Italy 0
Sweden 5, Cyprus 0
Romania 0, Czechoslovakia 1
Sweden 2, Italy 0
Sweden 0, Romania 1
Sweden 1, Czechoslovakia 0
Italy 0, Sweden 3
Cyprus 0, Romania 1
Czechoslovakia 2, Italy 0
Czechoslovakia 1, Romania 1
Italy 3, Cyprus 1

Group 6

Austria 5, Albania 0
Austria 2, Northern Ireland 0
Turkey 1, Albania 0
Austria 4, Turkey 0
Northern Ireland 1, West Germany 0
Albania 0, Northern Ireland 0
Albania 1, West Germany 2
Northern Ireland 2, Turkey 1

Turkey 0, West Germany 3
Austria 0, West Germany 0
Northern Ireland 1, Albania 0
Albania 1, Turkey 1
Albania 1, Austria 2
Northern Ireland 3, Austria 1
West Germany 3, Austria 0
Turkey 1, Northern Ireland 0
West Germany 5, Turkey 1
Turkey 3, Austria 1
West Germany 0, Northern Ireland 1
West Germany 2, Albania 1

Group 7

Malta 2, Iceland 1
Iceland 1, Holland 1
Holland 2, Eire 1
Eire 2, Iceland 0
Spain 1, Iceland 0
Eire 3, Spain 3
Malta 0, Holland 6
Spain 1, Holland 0
Malta 0, Eire 1
Spain 2, Eire 0
Malta 2, Spain 3
Iceland 0, Spain 1
Iceland 1, Malta 0
Holland 3, Iceland 0
Iceland 0, Eire 3
Eire 2, Holland 3
Holland 2, Spain 1
Eire 8, Malta 0
Holland 5, Malta 0
Spain 12, Malta 1

Final Tournament

Group 1

France 1, Denmark 0
Belgium 2, Yugoslavia 0
France 5, Belgium 0
Denmark 5, Yugoslavia 0
France 3, Yugoslavia 2
Denmark 3, Belgium 2

Group 2

West Germany 0, Portugal 0
Spain 1, Romania 1
Spain 1, Portugal 1
West Germany 2, Romania 1
West Germany 0, Spain 1
Portugal 1, Romania 0

Semi-Finals

France 3, Portugal 2
Denmark 1, Spain 1 after extra time
(*Spain won 5-4 on penalties*)

Final (Paris, 27 June 1984, 80,000)

France (0) 2, Spain (0) 0

France: Bats; Battiston (Amoros), Le Roux, Bossis, Domergue, Giresse, Platini, Tigana, Fernandez, Lacombe (Genghini), Bellone.
Spain: Arconada; Urquiaga, Salva (Roberto), Gallego, Camacho, Francisco, Julio Alberto (Sarabia), Senor, Victor, Carrasco, Santillana.
Scorers: Platini, Bellone for France.

EUROPEAN CHAMPIONSHIP 1986-88

Group 1

Romania 4, Austria 0
Austria 3, Albania 0
Spain 1, Romania 0
Albania 1, Spain 2
Romania 5, Albania 1
Austria 2, Spain 3

Albania 0, Austria 1
Romania 3, Spain 1
Spain 2, Austria 0
Albania 0, Romania 1
Spain 5, Albania 0
Austria 0, Romania 0

Group 2

Sweden 2, Switzerland 0
Portugal 1, Sweden 1
Switzerland 1, Portugal 1
Italy 3, Switzerland 2
Malta 0, Sweden 5
Malta 0, Italy 2
Italy 5, Malta 0
Portugal 0, Italy 1
Portugal 2, Malta 2
Switzerland 4, Malta 1
Sweden 1, Malta 0
Sweden 1, Italy 0
Switzerland 1, Sweden 1
Sweden 0, Portugal 1
Switzerland 0, Italy 0
Portugal 0, Switzerland 0
Italy 2, Sweden 1
Malta 1, Switzerland 1
Italy 3, Portugal 0
Malta 0, Portugal 1

Group 3

Iceland 0, France 0
Iceland 1, USSR 1
Norway 0, East Germany 0
France 0, USSR 2
USSR 4, Norway 0
East Germany 2, Iceland 0
East Germany 0, France 0
France 2, Iceland 0
USSR 2, East Germany 0
Norway 0, USSR 1
Iceland 0, East Germany 6
Norway 2, France 0
USSR 1, France 1
Iceland 2, Norway 1
Norway 0, Iceland 1
East Germany 1, USSR 1
France 1, Norway 1
USSR 2, Iceland 0
East Germany 3, Norway 1
France 0, East Germany 1

Group 4

England 3, Northern Ireland 0
Yugoslavia 4, Turkey 0
England 2, Yugoslavia 0
Turkey 0, Northern Ireland 0
Northern Ireland 0, England 2
Northern Ireland 1, Yugoslavia 2
Turkey 0, England 0
Yugoslavia 3, Northern Ireland 0
England 8, Turkey 0
Yugoslavia 1, England 4
Northern Ireland 1, Turkey 0
Turkey 2, Yugoslavia 3

Group 5

Hungary 0, Holland 1
Poland 2, Greece 1
Greece 2, Hungary 1
Holland 0, Poland 0
Cyprus 2, Greece 4
Cyprus 0, Holland 2
Greece 3, Cyprus 1
Cyprus 0, Hungary 1
Holland 1, Greece 1
Poland 0, Cyprus 0
Greece 1, Poland 0
Holland 2, Hungary 0

Hungary 5, Poland 3
Poland 3, Hungary 2
Hungary 3, Greece 0
Poland 0, Holland 2
Holland 8, Cyprus 0
Cyprus 0, Poland 1
Hungary 1, Cyprus 0
Holland 4, Cyprus 0
Greece 0, Holland 3

Group 6

Finland 1, Wales 1
Czechoslovakia 3, Finland 0
Denmark 1, Finland 0
Czechoslovakia 0, Denmark 0
Wales 4, Finland 0
Finland 0, Denmark 1
Wales 1, Czechoslovakia 1
Denmark 1, Czechoslovakia 1
Wales 1, Denmark 0
Finland 3, Czechoslovakia 0
Denmark 1, Wales 0
Czechoslovakia 2, Wales 0

Group 7

Scotland 0, Bulgaria 0
Belgium 2, Eire 2
Luxembourg 0, Belgium 6
Eire 0, Scotland 0
Scotland 3, Luxembourg 0
Belgium 1, Bulgaria 1
Scotland 0, Eire 1
Belgium 4, Scotland 1
Bulgaria 2, Eire 1
Eire 0, Belgium 0
Luxembourg 1, Bulgaria 4
Bulgaria 3, Luxembourg 0
Luxembourg 0, Eire 2
Eire 2, Luxembourg 1
Bulgaria 2, Belgium 0
Scotland 2, Belgium 0
Eire 2, Bulgaria 0
Belgium 3, Luxembourg 0
Bulgaria 0, Scotland 1
Luxembourg 0, Scotland 0

Final Tournament
Group 1

West Germany 1, Italy 1
Spain 3, Denmark 2
West Germany 2, Denmark 0
Italy 1, Spain 0
West Germany 2, Spain 0
Italy 2, Denmark 0

Group 2

England 0, Eire 1
Holland 0, USSR 1
Holland 3, England 1
Eire 1, USSR 1
England 1, USSR 3
Holland 1, Eire 0

Semi-Finals

West Germany 1, Holland 2
USSR 2, Italy 0

Final (Munich, 25 June 1988, 72,308)

Holland (1) 2, USSR (0) 0

Holland: Van Breukelen; Van Aerle, Van Tiggelen,
Wouters, Koeman R, Rijkaard, Vanenburg, Gullit,
Van Basten, Muhren, Koeman E.
USSR: Dassayev; Khidiatulin, Aleinikov,
Mikhailichenko, Litovchenko, Demianenko, Belanov,
Gotsmanov (Baltacha 68), Protasov (Pasulko 71),
Zavarov, Rats.
Scorers: Gullit, Van Basten for Holland.

BRITISH AND IRISH INTERNATIONAL RESULTS 1872–1991

BRITISH INTERNATIONAL CHAMPIONSHIP 1883–1984

Year	Champions	Pts	Year	Champions	Pts	Year	Champions	Pts
1883–84	Scotland	6	1920–21	Scotland	6	1956–57	England	5
1884–85	Scotland	5	1921–22	Scotland	4	1957–58	England	4
1885–86	England	5	1922–23	Scotland	5		N. Ireland	4
	Scotland	5	1923–24	Wales	6	1958–59	N. Ireland	4
1886–87	Scotland	6	1924–25	Scotland	6		England	4
1887–88	England	6	1925–26	Scotland	6		England	4
1888–89	Scotland	5	1926–27	Scotland	4	1959–60	Scotland	4
1889–90	Scotland	5		England	4		Wales	4
	England	5	1927–28	Wales	5	1960–61	England	6
1890–91	England	6	1928–29	Scotland	6	1961–62	Scotland	6
1891–92	England	6	1929–30	England	6	1962–63	Scotland	6
1892–93	England	6	1930–31	Scotland	4	1963–64	Scotland	4
1893–94	Scotland	5		England	4		England	4
1894–95	England	5	1931–32	England	6		N. Ireland	4
1895–96	Scotland	5	1932–33	Wales	5	1964–65	England	5
1896–97	Scotland	5	1933–34	Wales	5	1965–66	England	5
1897–98	England	6	1934–35	England	4	1966–67	Scotland	5
1898–99	England	6		Scotland	4	1967–68	England	5
1899–1900	Scotland	6	1935–36	Scotland	4	1968–69	England	6
1900–01	England	5	1936–37	Wales	6	1969–70	England	4
1901–02	Scotland	5	1937–38	England	4		Scotland	4
1902–03	England	4	1938–39	England	4		Wales	4
	Ireland	4		Scotland	4	1970–71	England	5
	Scotland	4		Wales	4	1971–72	England	4
1903–04	England	5	1946–47	England	5		Scotland	4
1904–05	England	5	1947–48	England	5	1972–73	England	6
1905–06	England	4	1948–49	Scotland	6	1973–74	England	4
	Scotland	4	1949–50	England	6		Scotland	4
1906–07	Wales	5	1950–51	Scotland	6	1974–75	England	4
1907–08	Scotland	5	1951–52	Wales	5	1975–76	Scotland	6
	England	5		England	5	1976–77	Scotland	5
1908–09	England	6	1952–53	England	4	1977–78	England	6
1909–10	Scotland	4		Scotland	4	1978–79	England	5
1910–11	England	5	1953–54	England	6	1979–80	N. Ireland	5
1911–12	England	5	1954–55	England	6	1980–81	Not completed	
	Scotland	5	1955–56	England	3	1981–82	England	6
1912–13	England	4		Scotland	3	1982–83	England	5
1913–14	Ireland	5		Wales	3	1983–84	N. Ireland	3
1919–20	Wales	4		N. Ireland	3			

Note: In the results that follow, wc = World Cup, ec = European Championship. For Ireland, read Northern Ireland from 1921.

ENGLAND v SCOTLAND

Played: 107; England won 43, Scotland won 40, Drawn 24. *Goals:* England 188, Scotland 168.

Year	Venue	E	S	Year	Venue	E	S	Year	Venue	E	S
1872	Glasgow	0	0	1887	Blackburn	2	3	1902	Birmingham	2	2
1873	Kennington Oval	4	2	1888	Glasgow	5	0	1903	Sheffield	1	2
1874	Glasgow	1	2	1889	Kennington Oval	2	3	1904	Glasgow	1	0
1875	Kennington Oval	2	2	1890	Glasgow	1	1	1905	Crystal Palace	1	0
1876	Glasgow	0	3	1891	Blackburn	2	1	1906	Glasgow	1	2
1877	Kennington Oval	1	3	1892	Glasgow	4	1	1907	Newcastle	1	1
1878	Glasgow	2	7	1893	Richmond	5	2	1908	Glasgow	1	1
1879	Kennington Oval	5	4	1894	Glasgow	2	2	1909	Crystal Palace	2	0
1880	Glasgow	4	5	1895	Everton	3	0	1910	Glasgow	0	2
1881	Kennington Oval	1	6	1896	Glasgow	1	2	1911	Everton	1	1
1882	Glasgow	1	5	1897	Crystal Palace	1	2	1912	Glasgow	1	1
1883	Sheffield	2	3	1898	Glasgow	3	1	1913	Chelsea	1	0
1884	Glasgow	0	1	1899	Birmingham	2	1	1914	Glasgow	1	3
1885	Kennington Oval	1	1	1900	Glasgow	1	4	1920	Sheffield	5	4
1886	Glasgow	1	1	1901	Crystal Palace	2	2	1921	Glasgow	0	3

		E	S				E	S				E	S
1922	Aston Villa	0	1	wc1950	Glasgow	1	0	1971	Wembley	3	1
1923	Glasgow	2	2	1951	Wembley	2	3	1972	Glasgow	1	0
1924	Wembley	1	1	1952	Glasgow	2	1	1973	Wembley	5	0
1925	Glasgow	0	2	1953	Wembley	2	2	1973	Glasgow	1	0
1926	Manchester	0	1	wc1954	Glasgow	4	2	1974	Wembley	0	2
1927	Glasgow	2	1	1955	Wembley	7	2	1975	Wembley	5	1
1928	Wembley	1	5	1956	Glasgow	1	1	1976	Glasgow	1	2
1929	Glasgow	0	1	1957	Wembley	2	1	1977	Wembley	1	2
1930	Wembley	5	2	1958	Glasgow	4	0	1978	Glasgow	1	0
1931	Glasgow	0	2	1959	Wembley	1	0	1979	Wembley	3	1
1932	Wembley	3	0	1960	Glasgow	1	1	1980	Glasgow	2	0
1933	Glasgow	1	2	1961	Wembley	9	3	1981	Wembley	0	1
1934	Wembley	3	0	1962	Glasgow	0	2	1982	Glasgow	1	0
1935	Glasgow	0	2	1963	Wembley	1	2	1983	Wembley	2	0
1936	Wembley	1	1	1964	Glasgow	0	1	1984	Glasgow	1	1
1937	Glasgow	1	3	1965	Wembley	2	2	1985	Glasgow	0	1
1938	Wembley	0	1	1966	Glasgow	4	3	1986	Wembley	2	1
1939	Glasgow	2	1	EC1967	Wembley	2	3	1987	Glasgow	0	0
1947	Wembley	1	1	EC1968	Glasgow	1	1	1988	Wembley	1	0
1948	Glasgow	2	0	1969	Wembley	4	1	1989	Glasgow	2	0
1949	Wembley	1	3	1970	Glasgow	0	0				

ENGLAND v WALES

Played: 97; England won 62, Wales won 14, Drawn 21. *Goals:* England 239, Scotland 90.

		E	W				E	W				E	W
1879	Kennington Oval	2	1	1911	Millwall	3	0	1955	Cardiff	1	2
1880	Wrexham	3	2	1912	Wrexham	2	0	1956	Wembley	3	1
1881	Blackburn	0	1	1913	Bristol	4	3	1957	Cardiff	4	0
1882	Wrexham	3	5	1914	Cardiff	2	0	1958	Aston Villa	2	2
1883	Kennington Oval	5	0	1920	Highbury	1	2	1959	Cardiff	1	1
1884	Wrexham	4	0	1921	Cardiff	0	0	1960	Wembley	5	1
1885	Blackburn	1	1	1922	Liverpool	1	0	1961	Cardiff	1	1
1886	Wrexham	3	1	1923	Cardiff	2	2	1962	Wembley	4	0
1887	Kennington Oval	4	0	1924	Blackburn	1	2	1963	Cardiff	4	0
1888	Crewe	5	1	1925	Swansea	2	1	1964	Wembley	2	1
1889	Stoke	4	1	1926	Crystal Palace	1	3	1965	Cardiff	0	0
1890	Wrexham	3	1	1927	Wrexham	3	3	EC1966	Wembley	5	1
1891	Sunderland	4	1	1927	Burnley	1	2	EC1967	Cardiff	3	0
1892	Wrexham	2	0	1928	Swansea	3	2	1969	Wembley	2	1
1893	Stoke	6	0	1929	Chelsea	6	0	1970	Cardiff	1	1
1894	Wrexham	5	1	1930	Wrexham	4	0	1971	Wembley	0	0
1894	Queen's Club,			1931	Liverpool	3	1	1972	Cardiff	3	0
	Kensington	1	1	1932	Wrexham	0	0	wc1972	Cardiff	1	0
1896	Cardiff	9	1	1933	Newcastle	1	2	wc1973	Wembley	1	1
1897	Sheffield	4	0	1934	Cardiff	4	0	1973	Wembley	3	0
1898	Wrexham	3	0	1935	Wolverhampton	1	2	1974	Cardiff	2	0
1899	Bristol	4	0	1936	Cardiff	1	2	1975	Wembley	2	2
1900	Cardiff	1	1	1937	Middlesbrough	2	1	1976	Wrexham	2	1
1901	Newcastle	6	0	1938	Cardiff	2	4	1976	Cardiff	1	0
1902	Wrexham	0	0	1946	Manchester	3	0	1977	Wembley	0	1
1903	Portsmouth	2	1	1947	Cardiff	3	0	1978	Cardiff	3	1
1904	Wrexham	2	2	1948	Aston Villa	1	0	1979	Wembley	0	0
1905	Liverpool	3	1	wc1949	Cardiff	4	1	1980	Wrexham	1	4
1906	Cardiff	1	0	1950	Sunderland	4	2	1981	Wembley	0	0
1907	Fulham	1	1	1951	Cardiff	1	1	1982	Cardiff	1	0
1908	Wrexham	7	1	1952	Wembley	5	2	1983	Wembley	2	1
1909	Nottingham	2	0	wc1953	Cardiff	4	1	1984	Wrexham	0	1
1910	Cardiff	1	0	1954	Wembley	3	2				

ENGLAND v IRELAND

Played: 96; England won 74, Ireland won 6, Drawn 16. *Goals:* England 319, Ireland 80.

Year	Venue	E	I	Year	Venue	E	I	Year	Venue	E	I
1882	Belfast	13	0	1914	Middlesbrough	0	3	1957	Wembley	2	3
1883	Liverpool	7	0	1919	Belfast	1	1	1958	Belfast	3	3
1884	Belfast	8	1	1920	Sunderland	2	0	1959	Wembley	2	1
1885	Manchester	4	0	1921	Belfast	1	1	1960	Belfast	5	2
1886	Belfast	6	1	1922	West Bromwich	2	0	1961	Wembley	1	1
1887	Sheffield	7	0	1923	Belfast	1	2	1962	Belfast	3	1
1888	Belfast	5	1	1924	Everton	3	1	1963	Wembley	8	3
1889	Everton	6	1	1925	Belfast	0	0	1964	Belfast	4	3
1890	Belfast	9	1	1926	Liverpool	3	3	1965	Wembley	2	1
1891	Wolverhampton	6	1	1927	Belfast	0	2	EC1966	Belfast	2	0
1892	Belfast	2	0	1928	Everton	2	1	EC1967	Wembley	2	0
1893	Birmingham	6	1	1929	Belfast	3	0	1969	Belfast	3	1
1894	Belfast	2	2	1930	Sheffield	5	1	1970	Wembley	3	1
1895	Derby	9	0	1931	Belfast	6	2	1971	Belfast	1	0
1896	Belfast	2	0	1932	Blackpool	1	0	1972	Wembley	0	1
1897	Nottingham	6	0	1933	Belfast	3	0	1973	Everton	2	1
1898	Belfast	3	2	1935	Everton	2	1	1974	Wembley	1	0
1899	Sunderland	13	2	1935	Belfast	3	1	1975	Belfast	0	0
1900	Dublin	2	0	1936	Stoke	3	1	1976	Wembley	4	0
1901	Southampton	3	0	1937	Belfast	5	1	1977	Belfast	2	1
1902	Belfast	1	0	1938	Manchester	7	0	1978	Wembley	1	0
1903	Wolverhampton	4	0	1946	Belfast	7	2	EC1979	Wembley	4	0
1904	Belfast	3	1	1947	Everton	2	2	1979	Belfast	2	0
1905	Middlesbrough	1	1	1948	Belfast	6	2	EC1979	Belfast	5	1
1906	Belfast	5	0	wc1949	Manchester	9	2	1980	Wembley	1	1
1907	Everton	1	0	1950	Belfast	4	1	1982	Wembley	4	0
1908	Belfast	3	1	1951	Aston Villa	2	0	1983	Belfast	0	0
1909	Bradford	4	0	1952	Belfast	2	2	1984	Wembley	1	0
1910	Belfast	1	1	wc1953	Everton	3	1	wc1985	Belfast	1	0
1911	Derby	2	1	1954	Belfast	2	0	wc1985	Wembley	0	0
1912	Dublin	6	1	1955	Wembley	3	0	EC1986	Wembley	3	0
1913	Belfast	1	2	1956	Belfast	1	1	EC1987	Belfast	2	0

SCOTLAND v WALES

Played: 101; Scotland won 60, Wales won 18, Drawn 23. *Goals:* Scotland 238, Wales 111.

Year	Venue	S	W	Year	Venue	S	W	Year	Venue	S	W
1876	Glasgow	4	0	1910	Kilmarnock	1	0	1955	Glasgow	2	0
1877	Wrexham	2	0	1911	Cardiff	2	2	1956	Cardiff	2	2
1878	Glasgow	9	0	1912	Tynecastle	1	0	1957	Glasgow	1	1
1879	Wrexham	3	0	1913	Wrexham	0	0	1958	Cardiff	3	0
1880	Glasgow	5	1	1914	Glasgow	0	0	1959	Glasgow	1	1
1881	Wrexham	5	1	1920	Cardiff	1	1	1960	Cardiff	0	2
1882	Glasgow	5	0	1921	Aberdeen	2	1	1961	Glasgow	2	0
1883	Wrexham	4	1	1922	Wrexham	1	2	1962	Cardiff	3	2
1884	Glasgow	4	1	1923	Paisley	2	0	1963	Glasgow	2	1
1885	Wrexham	8	1	1924	Cardiff	0	2	1964	Cardiff	2	3
1886	Glasgow	4	1	1925	Tynecastle	3	1	EC1965	Glasgow	4	1
1887	Wrexham	2	0	1926	Cardiff	3	0	EC1966	Cardiff	1	1
1888	Edinburgh	5	1	1927	Glasgow	3	0	1967	Glasgow	3	2
1889	Wrexham	0	0	1928	Wrexham	2	2	1969	Wrexham	5	3
1890	Paisley	5	0	1929	Glasgow	4	2	1970	Glasgow	0	0
1891	Wrexham	4	3	1930	Cardiff	4	2	1971	Cardiff	0	0
1892	Edinburgh	6	1	1931	Glasgow	1	1	1972	Glasgow	1	0
1893	Wrexham	8	0	1932	Wrexham	3	2	1973	Wrexham	2	0
1894	Kilmarnock	5	2	1933	Edinburgh	2	5	1974	Glasgow	2	0
1894	Wrexham	2	2	1934	Cardiff	2	3	1975	Cardiff	2	2
1896	Dundee	4	0	1935	Aberdeen	3	2	1976	Glasgow	3	1
1895	Wrexham	2	2	1936	Cardiff	1	1	wc1977	Glasgow	1	0
1898	Motherwell	5	2	1937	Dundee	1	2	1977	Wrexham	0	0
1899	Wrexham	6	0	1938	Cardiff	1	2	wc1977	Liverpool	2	0
1900	Aberdeen	5	2	1939	Edinburgh	3	2	1978	Glasgow	1	1
1901	Wrexham	1	1	1946	Wrexham	1	3	1979	Cardiff	0	3
1902	Greenock	5	1	1947	Glasgow	1	2	1980	Glasgow	1	0
1903	Cardiff	1	0	wc1948	Cardiff	3	1	1981	Swansea	0	2
1904	Dundee	1	1	1949	Glasgow	2	0	1982	Glasgow	1	0
1905	Wrexham	1	3	1950	Cardiff	3	1	1983	Cardiff	2	0
1906	Edinburgh	0	2	1951	Glasgow	0	1	1984	Glasgow	2	1
1907	Wrexham	0	1	wc1952	Cardiff	2	1	wc1985	Glasgow	0	1
1908	Dundee	2	1	1953	Glasgow	3	3	wc1985	Cardiff	1	1
1909	Wrexham	2	3	1954	Cardiff	1	0				

SCOTLAND v IRELAND

Played: 91; Scotland won 60, Ireland won 15, Drawn 16. *Goals:* Scotland 253, Ireland 81.

Year	Venue	S	I	Year	Venue	S	I	Year	Venue	S	I
1884	Belfast	5	0	1920	Glasgow	3	0	1957	Belfast	1	1
1885	Glasgow	8	2	1921	Belfast	2	0	1958	Glasgow	2	2
1886	Belfast	7	2	1922	Glasgow	2	1	1959	Belfast	4	0
1887	Glasgow	4	1	1923	Belfast	1	0	1960	Glasgow	5	2
1888	Belfast	10	2	1924	Glasgow	2	0	1961	Belfast	6	1
1889	Glasgow	7	0	1925	Belfast	3	0	1962	Glasgow	5	1
1890	Belfast	4	1	1926	Glasgow	4	0	1963	Belfast	1	2
1891	Glasgow	2	1	1927	Belfast	2	0	1964	Glasgow	3	2
1892	Belfast	3	2	1928	Glasgow	0	1	1965	Belfast	2	3
1893	Glasgow	6	1	1929	Belfast	7	3	1966	Glasgow	2	1
1894	Belfast	2	1	1930	Glasgow	3	1	1967	Belfast	0	1
1895	Glasgow	3	1	1931	Belfast	0	0	1969	Glasgow	1	1
1896	Belfast	3	3	1932	Glasgow	3	1	1970	Belfast	1	0
1897	Glasgow	5	1	1933	Belfast	4	0	1971	Glasgow	0	1
1898	Belfast	3	0	1934	Glasgow	1	2	1972	Glasgow	2	0
1899	Glasgow	9	1	1935	Belfast	1	2	1973	Glasgow	1	2
1900	Belfast	3	0	1936	Edinburgh	2	1	1974	Glasgow	0	1
1901	Glasgow	11	0	1937	Belfast	3	1	1975	Glasgow	3	0
1902	Belfast	5	1	1938	Aberdeen	1	1	1976	Glasgow	3	0
1903	Glasgow	0	2	1939	Belfast	2	0	1977	Glasgow	3	0
1904	Dublin	1	1	1946	Glasgow	0	0	1978	Glasgow	1	1
1905	Glasgow	4	0	1947	Belfast	0	2	1979	Glasgow	1	0
1906	Dublin	1	0	1948	Glasgow	3	2	1980	Belfast	0	1
1907	Glasgow	3	0	1949	Belfast	8	2	wc1981	Glasgow	1	1
1908	Dublin	5	0	1950	Glasgow	6	1	1981	Glasgow	2	0
1909	Glasgow	5	0	1951	Belfast	3	0	wc1981	Belfast	0	0
1910	Belfast	0	1	1952	Glasgow	1	1	1982	Belfast	1	1
1911	Glasgow	2	0	1953	Belfast	3	1	1983	Glasgow	0	0
1912	Belfast	4	1	1954	Glasgow	2	2	1984	Belfast	0	2
1913	Dublin	2	1	1955	Belfast	1	2				
1914	Belfast	1	1	1956	Glasgow	1	0				

WALES v IRELAND

Played: 90; Wales won 42, Ireland won 27, Drawn 21. *Goals:* Wales 181, Ireland 126.

Year	Venue	W	I	Year	Venue	W	I	Year	Venue	W	I
1882	Wrexham	7	1	1912	Cardiff	2	3	wc1954	Wrexham	1	2
1883	Belfast	1	1	1913	Belfast	1	0	1955	Belfast	3	2
1884	Wrexham	6	0	1914	Wrexham	1	2	1956	Cardiff	1	1
1885	Belfast	8	2	1920	Belfast	2	2	1957	Belfast	0	0
1886	Wrexham	5	0	1921	Swansea	2	1	1958	Cardiff	1	1
1887	Belfast	1	4	1922	Belfast	1	1	1959	Belfast	1	4
1888	Wrexham	11	0	1923	Wrexham	0	3	1960	Wrexham	3	2
1889	Belfast	3	1	1924	Belfast	1	0	1961	Belfast	5	1
1890	Shrewsbury	5	2	1925	Wrexham	0	0	1962	Cardiff	4	0
1891	Belfast	2	7	1926	Belfast	0	3	1963	Belfast	4	1
1892	Bangor	1	1	1927	Cardiff	2	2	1964	Cardiff	2	3
1893	Belfast	3	4	1928	Belfast	2	1	1965	Belfast	5	0
1894	Swansea	4	1	1929	Wrexham	2	2	1966	Cardiff	1	4
1895	Belfast	2	2	1930	Belfast	0	7	ec1967	Belfast	0	0
1896	Wrexham	6	1	1931	Wrexham	3	2	ec1968	Wrexham	2	0
1897	Belfast	3	4	1932	Belfast	0	4	1969	Belfast	0	0
1898	Llandudno	0	1	1933	Wrexham	4	1	1970	Swansea	1	0
1899	Belfast	0	1	1934	Belfast	1	1	1971	Belfast	0	1
1900	Llandudno	2	0	1935	Wrexham	3	1	1972	Wrexham	0	0
1901	Belfast	1	0	1936	Belfast	2	3	1973	Everton	0	1
1902	Cardiff	0	3	1937	Wrexham	4	1	1974	Wrexham	1	0
1903	Belfast	0	2	1938	Belfast	0	1	1975	Belfast	0	1
1904	Bangor	0	1	1939	Wrexham	3	1	1976	Swansea	1	0
1905	Belfast	2	2	1947	Belfast	1	2	1977	Belfast	1	1
1906	Wrexham	4	4	1948	Wrexham	2	0	1978	Wrexham	1	0
1907	Belfast	3	2	1949	Belfast	2	0	1979	Belfast	1	1
1908	Aberdare	0	1	wc1950	Wrexham	0	0	1980	Cardiff	0	1
1909	Belfast	3	2	1951	Belfast	2	1	1982	Wrexham	3	0
1910	Wrexham	4	1	1952	Swansea	3	0	1983	Belfast	1	0
1911	Belfast	2	1	1953	Belfast	3	2	1984	Swansea	1	1

OTHER BRITISH INTERNATIONAL RESULTS 1908–90
ENGLAND

		v ALBANIA	E	A
wc1989	8 Mar	Tirana	2	0
wc1989	26 Apr	Wembley	5	0

		v ARGENTINA	E	A
1951	9 May	Wembley	2	1
1953	17 May	Buenos Aires	0	0
(abandoned after 21 mins)				
wc1962	2 June	Rancagua	3	1
1964	6 June	Rio de Janeiro	0	1
wc1966	23 July	Wembley	1	0
1974	22 May	Wembley	2	2
1977	12 June	Buenos Aires	1	1
1980	13 May	Wembley	3	1
wc1986	22 June	Mexico City	1	2
1991	25 May	Wembley	2	2

		v AUSTRALIA	E	A
1980	31 May	Sydney	2	1
1983	11 June	Sydney	0	0
1983	15 June	Brisbane	1	0
1983	18 June	Melbourne	1	1
1991	1 June	Sydney	1	0

		v AUSTRIA	E	A
1908	6 June	Vienna	6	1
1908	8 June	Vienna	11	1
1909	1 June	Vienna	8	1
1930	14 May	Vienna	0	0
1932	7 Dec	Chelsea	4	3
1936	6 May	Vienna	1	2
1951	28 Nov	Wembley	2	2
1952	25 May	Vienna	3	2
wc1958	15 June	Boras	2	2
1961	27 May	Vienna	1	3
1962	4 Apr	Wembley	3	1
1965	20 Oct	Wembley	2	3
1967	27 May	Vienna	1	0
1973	26 Sept	Wembley	7	0
1979	13 June	Vienna	3	4

		v BELGIUM	E	B
1921	21 May	Brussels	2	0
1923	19 Mar	Highbury	6	1
1923	1 Nov	Antwerp	2	2
1924	8 Dec	West Bromwich	4	0
1926	24 May	Antwerp	5	3
1927	11 May	Brussels	9	1
1928	19 May	Antwerp	3	1
1929	11 May	Brussels	5	1
1931	16 May	Brussels	4	1
1936	9 May	Brussels	2	3
1947	21 Sept	Brussels	5	2
1950	18 May	Brussels	4	1
1952	26 Nov	Wembley	5	0
wc1954	17 June	Basle	4	4*
1964	21 Oct	Wembley	2	2
1970	25 Feb	Brussels	3	1
EC1980	12 June	Turin	1	1
wc1990	27 June	Bologna	1	0
*After extra time				

		v BOHEMIA	E	B
1908	13 June	Prague	4	0

		v BRAZIL	E	B
1956	9 May	Wembley	4	2
wc1958	11 June	Gothenburg	0	0
1959	13 May	Rio de Janeiro	0	2

			E	B
wc1962	10 June	Vina del Mar	1	3
1963	8 May	Wembley	1	1
1964	30 May	Rio de Janeiro	1	5
1969	12 June	Rio de Janeiro	1	2
wc1970	7 June	Guadalajara	0	1
1976	23 May	Los Angeles	0	1
1977	8 June	Rio de Janeiro	0	0
1978	19 Apr	Wembley	1	1
1981	12 May	Wembley	0	1
1984	10 June	Rio de Janeiro	2	0
1987	19 May	Wembley	1	1
1990	28 Mar	Wembley	1	0

		v BULGARIA	E	B
wc1962	7 June	Rancagua	0	0
1968	11 Dec	Wembley	1	1
1974	1 June	Sofia	1	0
EC1979	6 June	Sofia	3	0
EC1979	22 Nov	Wembley	2	0

		v CAMEROON	E	C
wc1990	1 July	Naples	3	2
1991	6 Feb	Wembley	2	0

		v CANADA	E	C
1986	24 May	Burnaby	1	0

		v CHILE	E	C
wc1950	25 June	Rio de Janeiro	2	0
1953	24 May	Santiago	2	1
1984	17 June	Santiago	0	0
1989	23 May	Wembley	0	0

		v COLOMBIA	E	C
1970	20 May	Bogota	4	0
1988	24 May	Wembley	1	1

		v CYPRUS	E	C
EC1975	16 Apr	Wembley	5	0
EC1975	11 May	Limassol	1	0

		v CZECHOSLOVAKIA	E	C
1934	16 May	Prague	1	2
1937	1 Dec	Tottenham	5	4
1963	29 May	Bratislava	4	2
1966	2 Nov	Wembley	0	0
wc1970	11 June	Guadalajara	1	0
1973	27 May	Prague	1	1
EC1974	30 Oct	Wembley	3	0
EC1975	30 Oct	Bratislava	1	2
1978	29 Nov	Wembley	1	0
wc1982	20 June	Bilbao	2	0
1990	25 Apr	Wembley	4	2

		v DENMARK	E	D
1948	26 Sept	Copenhagen	0	0
1955	2 Oct	Copenhagen	5	1
wc1956	5 Dec	Wolverhampton	5	2
wc1957	15 May	Copenhagen	4	1
1966	3 July	Copenhagen	2	0
EC1978	20 Sept	Copenhagen	4	3
EC1979	12 Sept	Wembley	1	0
EC1982	22 Sept	Copenhagen	2	2
EC1983	21 Sept	Wembley	0	1
1988	14 Sept	Wembley	1	0
1989	7 June	Copenhagen	1	1
1990	15 May	Wembley	1	0

v ECUADOR

			E	Ec
1970	24 May	Quito	2	0

v EGYPT

			E	Eg
1986	29 Jan	Cairo	4	0
wc1990	21 June	Cagliari	1	0

v FIFA

			E	FIFA
1938	26 Oct	Highbury	3	0
1953	21 Oct	Wembley	4	4
1963	23 Oct	Wembley	2	1

v FINLAND

			E	F
1937	20 May	Helsinki	8	0
1956	20 May	Helsinki	5	1
1966	26 June	Helsinki	3	0
wc1976	13 June	Helsinki	4	1
wc1976	13 Oct	Wembley	2	1
1982	3 June	Helsinki	4	1
wc1984	17 Oct	Wembley	5	0
wc1985	22 May	Helsinki	1	1

v FRANCE

			E	F
1923	10 May	Paris	4	1
1924	17 May	Paris	3	1
1925	21 May	Paris	3	2
1927	26 May	Paris	6	0
1928	17 May	Paris	5	1
1929	9 May	Paris	4	1
1931	14 May	Paris	2	5
1933	6 Dec	Tottenham	4	1
1938	26 May	Paris	4	2
1947	3 May	Highbury	3	0
1949	22 May	Paris	3	1
1951	3 Oct	Highbury	2	2
1955	15 May	Paris	0	1
1957	27 Nov	Wembley	4	0
EC1962	3 Oct	Sheffield	1	1
EC1963	27 Feb	Paris	2	5
wc1966	20 July	Wembley	2	0
1969	12 Mar	Wembley	5	0
wc1982	16 June	Bilbao	3	1
1984	29 Feb	Paris	0	2

v GERMANY

			E	G
1930	10 May	Berlin	3	3
1935	4 Dec	Tottenham	3	0
1938	14 May	Berlin	6	3

v EAST GERMANY

			E	EG
1963	2 June	Leipzig	2	1
1970	25 Nov	Wembley	3	1
1974	29 May	Leipzig	1	1
1984	12 Sept	Wembley	1	0

v WEST GERMANY

			E	WG
1954	1 Dec	Wembley	3	1
1956	26 May	Berlin	3	1
1965	12 May	Nuremberg	1	0
1966	23 Feb	Wembley	1	0
wc1966	30 July	Wembley	4	2*
1968	1 June	Hanover	0	1
wc1970	14 June	Leon	2	3*
EC1972	29 Apr	Wembley	1	3
EC1972	13 May	Berlin	0	0
1975	12 Mar	Wembley	2	0
1978	22 Feb	Munich	1	2
wc1982	29 June	Madrid	0	0
1982	13 Oct	Wembley	1	2
1985	12 June	Mexico City	3	0
1987	9 Sept	Dusseldorf	1	3
wc1990	4 July	Turin	1	1*

*After extra time

v GREECE

			E	G
EC1971	21 Apr	Wembley	3	0
EC1971	1 Dec	Athens	2	0
EC1982	17 Nov	Athens	3	0
EC1983	30 Mar	Wembley	0	0
1989	8 Feb	Athens	2	1

v HOLLAND

			E	N
1935	18 May	Amsterdam	1	0
1946	27 Nov	Huddersfield	8	2
1964	9 Dec	Amsterdam	1	1
1969	5 Nov	Amsterdam	1	0
1970	14 Jun	Wembley	0	0
1977	9 Feb	Wembley	0	2
1982	25 May	Wembley	2	0
1988	23 Mar	Wembley	2	2
EC1988	15 June	Dusseldorf	1	3
wc1990	16 June	Cagliari	0	0

v HUNGARY

			E	H
1908	10 June	Budapest	7	0
1909	29 May	Budapest	4	2
1909	31 May	Budapest	8	2
1934	10 May	Budapest	1	2
1936	2 Dec	Highbury	6	2
1953	25 Nov	Wembley	3	6
1954	23 May	Budapest	1	7
1960	22 May	Budapest	0	2
wc1962	31 May	Rancagua	1	2
1965	5 May	Wembley	1	0
1978	24 May	Wembley	4	1
wc1981	6 June	Budapest	3	1
wc1982	18 Nov	Wembley	1	0
EC1983	27 Apr	Wembley	2	0
EC1983	12 Oct	Budapest	3	0
1988	27 Apr	Budapest	0	0
1990	12 Sept	Wembley	1	0

v ICELAND

			E	I
1982	2 June	Reykjavik	1	1

v REPUBLIC OF IRELAND

			E	RI
1946	30 Sept	Dublin	1	0
1949	21 Sept	Everton	0	2
wc1957	8 May	Wembley	5	1
wc1957	19 May	Dublin	1	1
1964	24 May	Dublin	3	1
1976	8 Sept	Wembley	1	1
EC1978	25 Oct	Dublin	1	1
EC1980	6 Feb	Wembley	2	0
1985	26 Mar	Wembley	2	1
EC1988	12 June	Stuttgart	0	1
wc1990	11 June	Cagliari	1	1
EC1990	14 Nov	Dublin	1	1
EC1991	27 Mar	Wembley	1	1

v ISRAEL

			E	I
1986	26 Feb	Ramat Gan	2	1
1988	17 Feb	Tel Aviv	0	0

v ITALY

			E	I
1933	13 May	Rome	1	1
1934	14 Nov	Highbury	3	2
1939	13 May	Milan	2	2
1948	16 May	Turin	4	0
1949	30 Nov	Tottenham	2	0
1952	18 May	Florence	1	1
1959	6 May	Wembley	2	2
1961	24 May	Rome	3	2
1973	14 June	Turin	0	2
1973	14 Nov	Wembley	0	1
1976	28 May	New York	3	2
wc1976	17 Nov	Rome	0	2

			E	I
wc1977	16 Nov	Wembley	2	0
EC1980	15 June	Turin	0	1
1985	6 June	Mexico City	1	2
1989	15 Nov	Wembley	0	0
wc1990	7 July	Bari	1	2

		v KUWAIT	E	K
wc1982	25 June	Bilbao	1	0

		v LUXEMBOURG	E	L
1927	21 May	Luxembourg	5	2
wc1960	19 Oct	Luxembourg	9	0
wc1961	28 Sept	Highbury	4	1
wc1977	30 Mar	Wembley	5	0
wc1977	12 Oct	Luxembourg	2	0
EC1982	15 Dec	Wembley	9	0
EC1983	16 Nov	Luxembourg	4	0

		v MALAYSIA	E	M
1991	12 June	Kuala Lumpur	4	2

		v MALTA	E	M
EC1971	3 Feb	Valletta	1	0
EC1971	12 May	Wembley	5	0

		v MEXICO	E	M
1959	24 May	Mexico City	1	2
1961	10 May	Wembley	8	0
wc1966	16 July	Wembley	2	0
1969	1 June	Mexico City	0	0
1985	9 June	Mexico City	0	1
1986	17 May	Los Angeles	3	0

		v MOROCCO	E	M
wc1986	6 June	Monterrey	0	0

		v NEW ZEALAND	E	NZ
1991	3 June	Auckland	1	0
1991	8 June	Wellington	2	0

		v NORWAY	E	N
1937	14 May	Oslo	6	0
1938	9 Nov	Newcastle	4	0
1949	18 May	Oslo	4	1
1966	29 June	Oslo	6	1
wc1980	10 Sept	Wembley	4	0
wc1981	9 Sept	Oslo	1	2

		v PARAGUAY	E	P
wc1986	18 June	Mexico City	3	0

		v PERU	E	P
1959	17 May	Lima	1	4
1962	20 May	Lima	4	0

		v POLAND	E	P
1966	5 Jan	Everton	1	1
1966	5 July	Chorzow	1	0
wc1973	6 June	Chorzow	0	2
wc1973	17 Oct	Wembley	1	1
wc1986	11 June	Monterrey	3	0
wc1989	3 June	Wembley	3	0
wc1989	11 Oct	Katowice	0	0
EC1990	17 Oct	Wembley	2	0

		v PORTUGAL	E	P
1947	25 May	Lisbon	10	0
1950	14 May	Lisbon	5	3
1951	19 May	Everton	5	2
1955	22 May	Oporto	1	3
1958	7 May	Wembley	2	1
wc1961	21 May	Lisbon	1	1

			E	P
wc1961	25 Oct	Wembley	2	0
1964	17 May	Lisbon	4	3
1964	4 June	São Paulo	1	1
wc1966	26 July	Wembley	2	'1
1969	10 Dec	Wembley	1	0
1974	3 Apr	Lisbon	0	0
EC1974	20 Nov	Wembley	0	0
EC1975	19 Nov	Lisbon	1	1
wc1986	3 June	Monterrey	0	1

		v ROMANIA	E	R
1939	24 May	Bucharest	2	0
1968	6 Nov	Bucharest	0	0
1969	15 Jan	Wembley	1	1
wc1970	2 June	Guadalajara	1	0
wc1980	15 Oct	Bucharest	1	2
wc1981	29 April	Wembley	0	0
wc1985	1 May	Bucharest	0	0
wc1985	11 Sept	Wembley	1	1

		v SAUDI ARABIA	E	SA
1988	16 Nov	Riyadh	1	1

		v SPAIN	E	S
1929	15 May	Madrid	3	4
1931	9 Dec	Highbury	7	1
wc1950	2 July	Rio de Janeiro	0	1
1955	18 May	Madrid	1	1
1955	30 Nov	Wembley	4	1
1960	15 May	Madrid	0	3
1960	26 Oct	Wembley	4	2
1965	8 Dec	Madrid	2	0
1967	24 May	Wembley	2	0
EC1968	3 Apr	Wembley	1	0
EC1968	8 May	Madrid	2	1
1980	26 Mar	Barcelona	2	0
EC1980	18 June	Naples	2	1
1981	25 Mar	Wembley	1	2
wc1982	5 July	Madrid	0	0
1987	18 Feb	Madrid	4	2

		v SWEDEN	E	S
1923	21 May	Stockholm	4	2
1923	24 May	Stockholm	3	1
1937	17 May	Stockholm	4	0
1947	19 Nov	Highbury	4	2
1949	13 May	Stockholm	1	3
1956	16 May	Stockholm	0	0
1959	28 Oct	Wembley	2	3
1965	16 May	Gothenburg	2	1
1968	22 May	Wembley	3	1
1979	10 June	Stockholm	0	0
1986	10 Sept	Stockholm	0	1
wc1988	19 Oct	Wembley	0	0
wc1989	6 Sept	Stockholm	0	0

		v SWITZERLAND	E	S
1933	20 May	Berne	4	0
1938	21 May	Zurich	1	2
1947	18 May	Zurich	0	1
1948	2 Dec	Highbury	6	0
1952	28 May	Zurich	3	0
wc1954	20 June	Berne	2	0
1962	9 May	Wembley	3	1
1963	5 June	Basle	8	1
EC1971	13 Oct	Basle	3	2
EC1971	10 Nov	Wembley	1	1
1975	3 Sept	Basle	2	1
1977	7 Sept	Wembley	0	0
wc1980	19 Nov	Wembley	2	1
wc1981	30 May	Basle	1	2
1988	28 May	Lausanne	1	0

		v TUNISIA	E	T
1990	2 June	Tunis	1	1

		v TURKEY	E	T
wc1984	14 Nov	Istanbul	8	0
wc1985	16 Oct	Wembley	5	0
EC1987	29 Apr	Izmir	0	0
EC1987	14 Oct	Wembley	8	0
EC1991	1 May	Izmir	1	0

		v URUGUAY	E	U
1953	31 May	Montevideo	1	2
wc1954	26 June	Basle	2	4
1964	6 May	Wembley	2	1
wc1966	11 July	Wembley	0	0
1969	8 June	Montevideo	2	1
1977	15 June	Montevideo	0	0
1984	13 June	Montevideo	0	2
1990	22 May	Wembley	1	2

		v USA	E	USA
wc1950	29 June	Belo Horizonte	0	1
1953	8 June	New York	6	3
1959	28 May	Los Angeles	8	1
1964	27 May	New York	10	0
1985	16 June	Los Angeles	5	0

		v USSR	E	USSR
1958	18 May	Moscow	1	1
wc1958	8 June	Gothenburg	2	2
wc1958	17 June	Gothenburg	0	1
1958	22 Oct	Wembley	5	0
1967	6 Dec	Wembley	2	2
EC1968	8 June	Rome	2	0
1973	10 June	Moscow	2	1
1984	2 June	Wembley	0	2
1986	26 Mar	Tbilisi	1	0
EC1988	18 June	Frankfurt	1	3
1991	21 May	Wembley	3	1

		v YUGOSLAVIA	E	Y
1939	18 May	Belgrade	1	2
1950	22 Nov	Highbury	2	2
1954	16 May	Belgrade	0	1
1956	28 Nov	Wembley	3	0
1958	11 May	Belgrade	0	5
1960	11 May	Wembley	3	3
1965	9 May	Belgrade	1	1
1966	4 May	Wembley	2	0
EC1968	5 June	Florence	0	1
1972	11 Oct	Wembley	1	1
1974	5 June	Belgrade	2	2
EC1986	12 Nov	Wembley	2	0
EC1987	11 Nov	Belgrade	4	1
1989	13 Dec	Wembley	2	1

SCOTLAND

		v ARGENTINA	S	A
1977	18 June	Buenos Aires	1	1
1979	2 June	Glasgow	1	3
1990	28 Mar	Glasgow	1	0

		v AUSTRALIA	S	A
wc1985	20 Nov	Glasgow	2	0
wc1985	4 Dec	Melbourne	0	0

		v AUSTRIA	S	A
1931	16 May	Vienna	0	5
1933	29 Nov	Glasgow	2	2
1937	9 May	Vienna	1	1
1950	13 Dec	Glasgow	0	1
1951	27 May	Vienna	0	4
wc1954	16 June	Zurich	0	1
1955	19 May	Vienna	4	1
1956	2 May	Glasgow	1	1
1960	29 May	Vienna	1	4
1963	8 May	Glasgow	4	1
(abandoned after 79 mins)				
wc1968	6 Nov	Glasgow	2	1
wc1969	5 Nov	Vienna	0	2
EC1978	20 Sept	Vienna	2	3
EC1979	17 Oct	Glasgow	1	1

		v BELGIUM	S	B
1947	18 May	Brussels	1	2
1948	28 Apr	Glasgow	2	0
1951	20 May	Brussels	5	0
EC1971	3 Feb	Liège	0	3
EC1971	10 Nov	Aberdeen	1	0
1974	2 June	Brussels	1	2
EC1979	21 Nov	Brussels	0	2
EC1979	19 Dec	Glasgow	1	3
EC1982	15 Dec	Brussels	2	3
EC1983	12 Oct	Glasgow	1	1
EC1987	1 Apr	Brussels	1	4
EC1987	14 Oct	Glasgow	2	0

		v BRAZIL	S	B
1966	25 June	Glasgow	1	1
1972	5 July	Rio de Janeiro	0	1
1973	30 June	Glasgow	0	1
wc1974	18 June	Frankfurt	0	0
1977	23 June	Rio de Janeiro	0	2
wc1982	18 June	Seville	1	4
1987	26 May	Glasgow	0	2
wc1990	20 June	Turin	0	1

		v BULGARIA	S	B
1978	22 Feb	Glasgow	2	1
EC1986	10 Sept	Glasgow	0	0
EC1987	11 Nov	Sofia	1	0
EC1990	14 Nov	Sofia	1	1
EC1991	27 Mar	Glasgow	1	1

		v CANADA	S	C
1983	12 June	Vancouver	2	0
1983	16 June	Edmonton	3	0
1983	20 June	Toronto	2	0

		v CHILE	S	C
1977	15 June	Santiago	4	2
1989	30 May	Glasgow	2	0

		v COLOMBIA	S	C
1988	17 May	Glasgow	0	0

		v COSTA RICA	S	CR
wc1990	11 June	Genoa	0	1

		v CYPRUS	S	C
wc1968	17 Dec	Nicosia	5	0
wc1969	11 May	Glasgow	8	0
wc1989	8 Feb	Limassol	3	2
wc1989	26 Apr	Glasgow	2	1

v CZECHOSLOVAKIA

			S	C
1937	22 May	Prague	3	1
1937	8 Dec	Glasgow	5	0
wc1961	14 May	Bratislava	0	4
wc1961	26 Sept	Glasgow	3	2
wc1961	29 Nov	Brussels	2	4*
1972	2 July	Porto Alegre	0	0
wc1973	26 Sept	Glasgow	2	1
wc1973	17 Oct	Prague	0	1
wc1976	13 Oct	Prague	0	2
wc1977	21 Sept	Glasgow	3	1

*After extra time

v DENMARK

			S	D
1951	12 May	Glasgow	3	1
1952	25 May	Copenhagen	2	1
1968	16 Oct	Copenhagen	1	0
EC1970	11 Nov	Glasgow	1	0
EC1971	9 June	Copenhagen	0	1
wc1972	18 Oct	Copenhagen	4	1
wc1972	15 Nov	Glasgow	2	0
EC1975	3 Sept	Copenhagen	1	0
EC1975	29 Oct	Glasgow	3	1
wc1986	4 June	Nezahualcayotl	0	1

v EGYPT

			S	E
1990	16 May	Aberdeen	1	3

v FINLAND

			S	F
1954	25 May	Helsinki	2	1
wc1964	21 Oct	Glasgow	3	1
wc1965	27 May	Helsinki	2	1
1976	8 Sept	Glasgow	6	0

v FRANCE

			S	F
1930	18 May	Paris	2	0
1932	8 May	Paris	3	1
1948	23 May	Paris	0	3
1949	27 Apr	Glasgow	2	0
1950	27 May	Paris	1	0
1951	16 May	Glasgow	1	0
wc1958	15 June	Orebro	1	2
1984	1 June	Marseilles	0	2
wc1989	8 Mar	Glasgow	2	0
wc1989	11 Oct	Paris	0	3

v GERMANY

			S	G
1929	1 June	Berlin	1	1
1936	14 Oct	Glasgow	2	0

v EAST GERMANY

			S	EG
1974	30 Oct	Glasgow	3	0
1977	7 Sept	East Berlin	0	1
EC1982	13 Oct	Glasgow	2	0
EC1983	16 Nov	Halle	1	2
1985	16 Oct	Glasgow	0	0
1990	25 Apr	Glasgow	0	1

v WEST GERMANY

			S	WG
1957	22 May	Stuttgart	3	1
1959	6 May	Glasgow	3	2
1964	12 May	Hanover	2	2
wc1969	16 Apr	Glasgow	1	1
wc1969	22 Oct	Hamburg	2	3
1973	14 Nov	Glasgow	1	1
1974	27 Mar	Frankfurt	1	2
1986	8 June	Queretaro	1	2

v HOLLAND

			S	N
1929	4 June	Amsterdam	2	0
1938	21 May	Amsterdam	3	1
1959	27 May	Amsterdam	2	1
1966	11 May	Glasgow	0	3
			S	N
1968	30 May	Amsterdam	0	0
1971	1 Dec	Rotterdam	1	2
wc1978	11 June	Mendoza	3	2
1982	23 Mar	Glasgow	2	1
1986	29 Apr	Eindhoven	0	0

v HUNGARY

			S	H
1938	7 Dec	Glasgow	3	1
1954	8 Dec	Glasgow	2	4
1955	29 May	Budapest	1	3
1958	7 May	Glasgow	1	1
1960	5 June	Budapest	3	3
1980	31 May	Budapest	1	3
1987	9 Sept	Glasgow	2	0

v ICELAND

			S	I
wc1984	17 Oct	Glasgow	3	0
wc1985	28 May	Reykjavik	1	0

v IRAN

			S	I
wc1978	7 June	Cordoba	1	1

v REPUBLIC OF IRELAND

			S	RI
wc1961	3 May	Glasgow	4	1
wc1961	7 May	Dublin	3	0
1963	9 June	Dublin	0	1
1969	21 Sept	Dublin	1	1
EC1986	15 Oct	Dublin	0	0
EC1987	18 Feb	Glasgow	0	1

v ISRAEL

			S	I
wc1981	25 Feb	Tel Aviv	1	0
wc1981	28 Apr	Glasgow	3	1
1986	28 Jan	Tel Aviv	1	0

v ITALY

			S	I
1931	20 May	Rome	0	3
wc1965	9 Nov	Glasgow	1	0
wc1965	7 Dec	Naples	0	3
1988	22 Dec	Perugia	0	2

v LUXEMBOURG

			S	L
1947	24 May	Luxembourg	6	0
EC1986	12 Nov	Glasgow	3	0
1987	2 Dec	Esch	0	0

v MALTA

			S	M
1988	22 Mar	Valletta	1	1
1990	28 May	Valletta	2	1

v NEW ZEALAND

			S	NZ
wc1982	15 June	Malaga	5	2

v NORWAY

			S	N
1929	28 May	Oslo	7	3
1954	5 May	Glasgow	1	0
1954	19 May	Oslo	1	1
1963	4 June	Bergen	3	4
1963	7 Nov	Glasgow	6	1
1974	6 June	Oslo	2	1
EC1978	25 Oct	Glasgow	3	2
EC1979	7 June	Oslo	4	0
wc1988	14 Sept	Oslo	2	1
wc1989	15 Nov	Glasgow	1	1

v PARAGUAY

			S	P
wc1958	11 June	Norrkoping	2	3

v PERU

			S	P
1972	26 Apr	Glasgow	2	0
wc1978	3 June	Cordoba	1	3
1979	12 Sept	Glasgow	1	1

		v POLAND	S	P
1958	1 June	Warsaw	2	1
1960	4 June	Glasgow	2	3
wc1965	23 May	Chorzow	1	1
wc1965	13 Oct	Glasgow	1	2
1980	28 May	Poznan	0	1
wc1990	19 May	Glasgow	1	1

		v PORTUGAL	S	P
1950	21 May	Lisbon	2	2
1955	4 May	Glasgow	3	0
1959	3 June	Lisbon	0	1
1966	18 June	Glasgow	0	1
EC1971	21 Apr	Lisbon	0	2
EC1971	13 Oct	Glasgow	2	1
1975	13 May	Glasgow	1	0
EC1978	29 Nov	Lisbon	0	1
EC1980	26 Mar	Glasgow	4	1
wc1980	15 Oct	Glasgow	0	0
wc1981	18 Nov	Lisbon	1	2

		v ROMANIA	S	R
EC1975	1 June	Bucharest	1	1
EC1975	17 Dec	Glasgow	1	1
1986	26 Mar	Glasgow	3	0
EC1990	12 Sept	Glasgow	2	1

		v SAN MARINO	S	S
EC1991	1 May	Serravalle	2	0

		v SAUDI ARABIA	S	SA
1988	17 Feb	Riyadh	2	2

		v SPAIN	S	Sp
wc1957	8 May	Glasgow	4	2
wc1957	26 May	Madrid	1	4
1963	13 June	Madrid	6	2
1965	8 May	Glasgow	0	0
EC1974	20 Nov	Glasgow	1	2
EC1975	5 Feb	Valencia	1	1
1982	24 Feb	Valencia	0	3
wc1984	14 Nov	Glasgow	3	1
wc1985	27 Feb	Seville	0	1
1988	27 Apr	Madrid	0	0

		v SWEDEN	S	Sw
1952	30 May	Stockholm	1	3
1953	6 May	Glasgow	1	2

			S	Sw
1975	16 Apr	Gothenburg	1	1
1977	27 Apr	Glasgow	3	1
wc1980	10 Sept	Stockholm	1	0
wc1981	9 Sept	Glasgow	2	0
wc1990	16 June	Genoa	2	1

		v SWITZERLAND	S	Sw
1931	24 May	Geneva	3	2
1948	17 May	Berne	1	2
1950	26 Apr	Glasgow	3	1
wc1957	19 May	Basle	2	1
wc1957	6 Nov	Glasgow	3	2
1973	22 June	Berne	0	1
1976	7 Apr	Glasgow	1	0
EC1982	17 Nov	Berne	0	2
EC1983	30 May	Glasgow	2	2
EC1990	17 Oct	Glasgow	2	1

		v TURKEY	S	T
1960	8 June	Ankara	2	4

		v URUGUAY	S	U
wc1954	19 June	Basle	0	7
1962	2 May	Glasgow	2	3
1983	21 Sept	Glasgow	2	0
wc1986	13 June	Nezahualcoyotl	0	0

		v USA	S	USA
1952	30 Apr	Glasgow	6	0

		v USSR	S	USSR
1967	10 May	Glasgow	0	2
1971	14 June	Moscow	0	1
wc1982	22 June	Malaga	2	2
1991	6 Feb	Glasgow	0	1

		v YUGOSLAVIA	S	Y
1955	15 May	Belgrade	2	2
1956	21 Nov	Glasgow	2	0
wc1958	8 June	Vasteras	1	1
1972	29 June	Belo Horizonte	2	2
wc1974	22 June	Frankfurt	1	1
1984	12 Sept	Glasgow	6	1
wc1988	19 Oct	Glasgow	1	1
wc1989	6 Sept	Zagreb	1	3

		v ZAIRE	S	Z
wc1974	14 June	Dortmund	2	0

WALES

		v AUSTRIA	W	A
1954	9 May	Vienna	0	2
EC1955	23 Nov	Wrexham	1	2
EC1974	4 Sept	Vienna	1	2
1975	19 Nov	Wrexham	1	0

		v BELGIUM	W	B
1949	22 May	Liège	1	3
1949	23 Nov	Cardiff	5	1
EC1990	17 Oct	Cardiff	3	1
EC1991	27 Mar	Brussels	1	1

		v BRAZIL	W	B
wc1958	19 June	Gothenburg	0	1
1962	12 May	Rio de Janeiro	1	3
1962	16 May	São Paulo	1	3
1966	14 May	Rio de Janeiro	1	3
1966	18 May	Belo Horizonte	0	1
1983	12 June	Cardiff	1	1

		v BULGARIA	W	B
EC1983	27 Apr	Wrexham	1	0
EC1983	16 Nov	Sofia	0	1

		v CANADA	W	C
1986	10 May	Toronto	0	2
1986	20 May	Vancouver	3	0

		v CHILE	W	C
1966	22 May	Santiago	0	2

		v COSTA RICA	W	CR
1990	20 May	Cardiff	1	0

		v CZECHOSLOVAKIA	W	C
wc1957	1 May	Cardiff	1	0
wc1957	26 May	Prague	0	2
EC1971	21 Apr	Swansea	1	3
EC1971	27 Oct	Prague	0	1

			W	C
wc1977	30 Mar	Wrexham	3	0
wc1977	16 Nov	Prague	0	1
wc1980	19 Nov	Cardiff	1	0
wc1981	9 Sept	Prague	0	2
EC1987	29 Apr	Wrexham	1	1
EC1987	11 Nov	Prague	0	2

v DENMARK

			W	D
wc1964	21 Oct	Copenhagen	0	1
wc1965	1 Dec	Wrexham	4	2
EC1987	9 Sept	Cardiff	1	0
EC1987	14 Oct	Copenhagen	0	1
1990	11 Sept	Copenhagen	0	1

v FINLAND

			W	F
EC1971	26 May	Helsinki	1	0
EC1971	13 Oct	Swansea	3	0
EC1987	10 Sept	Helsinki	1	1
EC1987	1 Apr	Wrexham	4	0
wc1988	19 Oct	Swansea	2	2
wc1989	6 Sept	Helsinki	0	1

v FRANCE

			W	F
1933	25 May	Paris	1	1
1939	20 May	Paris	1	2
1953	14 May	Paris	1	6
1982	2 June	Toulouse	1	0

v EAST GERMANY

			W	EG
wc1957	19 May	Leipzig	1	2
wc1957	25 Sept	Cardiff	4	1
wc1969	16 Apr	Dresden	1	2
wc1969	22 Oct	Cardiff	1	3

v WEST GERMANY

			W	WG
1968	8 May	Cardiff	1	1
1969	26 Mar	Frankfurt	1	1
1976	6 Oct	Cardiff	0	2
1977	14 Dec	Dortmund	1	1
EC1979	2 May	Wrexham	0	2
EC1979	17 Oct	Cologne	1	5
wc1989	31 May	Cardiff	0	0
wc1989	15 Nov	Cologne	1	2
EC1991	5 June	Cardiff	1	0

v GREECE

			W	G
wc1964	9 Dec	Athens	0	2
wc1965	17 Mar	Cardiff	4	1

v HOLLAND

			W	H
wc1988	14 Sept	Amsterdam	0	1
wc1989	11 Oct	Wrexham	1	2

v HUNGARY

			W	H
wc1958	8 June	Sanviken	1	1
wc1958	17 June	Stockholm	2	1
1961	28 May	Budapest	2	3
EC1962	7 Nov	Budapest	1	3
EC1963	20 Mar	Cardiff	1	1
EC1974	30 Oct	Cardiff	2	0
EC1975	16 Apr	Budapest	2	1
1985	16 Oct	Cardiff	0	3

v ICELAND

			W	I
wc1980	2 June	Reykjavik	4	0
wc1981	14 Oct	Swansea	2	2
wc1984	12 Sept	Reykjavik	0	1
wc1984	14 Nov	Cardiff	2	1
1991	1 May	Cardiff	1	0

v IRAN

			W	I
1978	18 Apr	Teheran	1	0

v REPUBLIC OF IRELAND

			W	RI
1960	28 Sept	Dublin	3	2
1979	11 Sept	Swansea	2	1
1981	24 Feb	Dublin	3	1
1986	26 Mar	Dublin	1	0
1990	28 Mar	Dublin	0	1
1991	6 Feb	Wrexham	0	3

v ISRAEL

			W	I
wc1958	15 Jan	Tel Aviv	2	0
wc1958	5 Feb	Cardiff	2	0
1984	10 June	Tel Aviv	0	0
1989	8 Feb	Tel Aviv	3	3

v ITALY

			W	I
1965	1 May	Florence	1	4
wc1968	23 Oct	Cardiff	0	1
wc1969	4 Nov	Rome	1	4
1988	4 June	Brescia	1	0

v KUWAIT

			W	K
1977	6 Sept	Wrexham	0	0
1977	20 Sept	Kuwait	0	0

v LUXEMBOURG

			W	L
EC1974	20 Nov	Swansea	5	0
EC1975	1 May	Luxembourg	3	1
EC1990	14 Nov	Luxembourg	1	0

v MALTA

			W	M
EC1978	25 Oct	Wrexham	7	0
EC1979	2 June	Valletta	2	0
1988	1 June	Valletta	3	2

v MEXICO

			W	M
wc1958	11 June	Stockholm	1	1
1962	22 May	Mexico City	1	2

v NORWAY

			W	M
EC1982	22 Sept	Swansea	1	0
EC1983	21 Sept	Oslo	0	0
1984	6 June	Trondheim	0	1
1985	26 Feb	Wrexham	1	1
1985	5 June	Bergen	2	4

v POLAND

			W	P
wc1973	28 Mar	Cardiff	2	0
wc1973	26 Sept	Katowice	0	3
1991	29 May	Radom	0	0

v PORTUGAL

			W	P
1949	15 May	Lisbon	2	3
1951	12 May	Cardiff	2	1

v ROMANIA

			W	R
EC1970	11 Nov	Cardiff	0	0
EC1971	24 Nov	Bucharest	0	2
1983	12 Oct	Wrexham	5	0

v SAUDI ARABIA

			W	SA
1986	25 Feb	Dahran	2	1

v SPAIN

			W	S
wc1961	19 Apr	Cardiff	1	2
wc1961	18 May	Madrid	1	1
1982	24 Mar	Valencia	1	1
wc1984	17 Oct	Seville	0	3
wc1985	30 Apr	Wrexham	3	0

v SWEDEN

			W	S
wc1958	15 June	Stockholm	0	0
1988	27 Apr	Stockholm	1	4
1989	26 Apr	Wrexham	0	2
1990	25 Apr	Stockholm	2	4

		v SWITZERLAND	W	S
1949	26 May	Berne	0	4
1951	16 May	Wrexham	3	2

		v TURKEY	W	T
EC1978	29 Nov	Wrexham	1	0
EC1979	21 Nov	Izmir	0	1
wc1980	15 Oct	Cardiff	4	0
wc1981	25 Mar	Ankara	1	0

		v REST OF UNITED KINGDOM	W	UK
1951	5 Dec	Cardiff	3	2
1969	28 July	Cardiff	0	1

		v URUGUAY	W	U
1986	21 Apr	Wrexham	0	0

		v USSR	W	USSR
wc1965	30 May	Moscow	1	2
wc1965	27 Oct	Cardiff	2	1
wc1981	30 May	Wrexham	0	0
wc1981	18 Nov	Tbilisi	0	3
1987	18 Feb	Swansea	0	0

		v YUGOSLAVIA	W	Y
1953	21 May	Belgrade	2	5
1954	22 Nov	Cardiff	1	3
EC1976	24 Apr	Zagreb	0	2
EC1976	22 May	Cardiff	1	1
EC1982	15 Dec	Titograd	4	4
EC1983	14 Dec	Cardiff	1	1
1988	23 Mar	Swansea	1	2

NORTHERN IRELAND

		v ALBANIA	NI	A
wc1965	7 May	Belfast	4	1
wc1965	24 Nov	Tirana	1	1
EC1982	15 Dec	Tirana	0	0
EC1983	27 Apr	Belfast	1	0

		v ALGERIA	NI	A
wc1986	3 June	Guadalajara	1	1

		v ARGENTINA	NI	A
wc1958	11 June	Halmstad	1	3

		v AUSTRALIA	NI	A
1980	11 June	Sydney	2	1
1980	15 June	Melbourne	1	1
1980	18 June	Adelaide	2	1

		v AUSTRIA	NI	A
wc1982	1 July	Madrid	2	2
EC1982	13 Oct	Vienna	0	2
EC1983	21 Sept	Belfast	3	1
EC1991	14 Nov	Vienna	0	0

		v BELGIUM	NI	B
wc1976	10 Nov	Liège	0	2
wc1977	16 Nov	Belfast	3	0

		v BRAZIL	NI	B
wc1986	12 June	Guadalajara	0	3

		v BULGARIA	NI	B
wc1972	18 Oct	Sofia	0	3
wc1973	26 Sept	Sheffield	0	0
EC1978	29 Nov	Sofia	2	0
EC1979	2 May	Belfast	2	0

		v CHILE	NI	C
1989	26 May	Belfast	0	1

		v CYPRUS	NI	C
EC1971	3 Feb	Nicosia	3	0
EC1971	21 Apr	Belfast	5	0
wc1973	14 Feb	Nicosia	0	1
wc1973	8 May	London	3	0

		v CZECHOSLOVAKIA	NI	C
wc1958	8 June	Halmstad	1	0
wc1958	17 June	Malmo	2	1*

*After extra time

		v DENMARK	NI	D
EC1978	25 Oct	Belfast	2	1
EC1979	6 June	Copenhagen	0	4
1986	26 Mar	Belfast	1	1
EC1990	17 Oct	Belfast	1	1

		v FAEROES	NI	F
EC1991	1 May	Belfast	1	1

		v FINLAND	NI	F
wc1984	27 May	Pori	0	1
wc1984	14 Nov	Belfast	2	1

		v FRANCE	NI	F
1951	12 May	Belfast	2	2
1952	11 Nov	Paris	1	3
wc1958	19 June	Norrkoping	0	4
1982	24 Mar	Paris	0	4
wc1982	4 July	Madrid	1	4
1986	26 Feb	Paris	0	0
1988	27 Apr	Belfast	0	0

		v WEST GERMANY	NI	WG
wc1958	15 June	Malmo	2	2
wc1960	26 Oct	Belfast	3	4
wc1961	10 May	Hamburg	1	2
1966	7 May	Belfast	0	2
1977	27 Apr	Cologne	0	5
EC1982	17 Nov	Belfast	1	0
EC1983	16 Nov	Hamburg	1	0

		v GREECE	NI	G
wc1961	3 May	Athens	1	2
wc1961	17 Oct	Belfast	2	0
1988	17 Feb	Athens	2	3

		v HOLLAND	NI	N
1962	9 May	Rotterdam	0	4
wc1965	17 Mar	Belfast	2	1
wc1965	7 Apr	Rotterdam	0	0
wc1976	13 Oct	Rotterdam	2	2
wc1977	12 Oct	Belfast	0	1

		v HONDURAS	NI	H
wc1982	21 June	Zaragoza	1	1

		v HUNGARY	NI	H
wc1988	19 Oct	Budapest	0	1
wc1989	6 Sept	Belfast	1	2

		v ICELAND	NI	I
wc1977	11 June	Reykjavik	0	1
wc1977	21 Sept	Belfast	2	0

		v REPUBLIC OF IRELAND	NI	RI
EC1978	20 Sept	Bublin	0	0
EC1979	21 Nov	Belfast	1	0
wc1988	14 Sept	Belfast	0	0
wc1989	11 Oct	Dublin	0	3

		v ISRAEL	NI	I
1968	10 Sept	Jaffa	3	2
1976	3 Mar	Tel Aviv	1	1
wc1980	26 Mar	Tel Aviv	0	0
wc1981	18 Nov	Belfast	1	0
1984	16 Oct	Belfast	3	0
1987	18 Feb	Tel Aviv	1	1

		v ITALY	NI	I
wc1957	25 Apr	Rome	0	1
1957	4 Dec	Belfast	2	2
wc1958	15 Jan	Belfast	2	1
1961	25 Apr	Bologna	2	3

		v MALTA	NI	M
1988	21 May	Belfast	3	0
wc1989	26 Apr	Valletta	2	0

		v MEXICO	NI	M
1966	22 June	Belfast	4	1

		v MOROCCO	NI	M
1986	23 Apr	Belfast	2	1

		v NORWAY	NI	N
EC1974	4 Sept	Oslo	1	2
EC1975	29 Oct	Belfast	3	0
1990	27 Mar	Belfast	2	3

		v POLAND	NI	P
EC1962	10 Oct	Katowice	2	0
EC1962	28 Nov	Belfast	2	0
1988	23 Mar	Belfast	1	1
1991	5 Feb	Belfast	3	1

		v PORTUGAL	NI	P
wc1957	16 Jan	Lisbon	1	1
wc1957	1 May	Belfast	3	0
wc1973	28 Mar	Coventry	1	1
wc1973	14 Nov	Lisbon	1	1
wc1980	19 Nov	Lisbon	0	1
wc1981	29 Apr	Belfast	1	0

		v ROMANIA	NI	R
wc1984	12 Sept	Belfast	3	2
wc1985	16 Oct	Bucharest	1	0

		v SPAIN	NI	S
1958	15 Oct	Madrid	2	6
1963	30 May	Bilbao	1	1
1963	30 Oct	Belfast	0	1
EC1970	11 Nov	Seville	0	3
EC1972	16 Feb	Hull	1	1
wc1982	25 June	Valencia	1	0
1985	27 Mar	Palma	0	0
wc1986	7 June	Guadalajara	1	2
wc1988	21 Dec	Seville	0	4
wc1989	8 Feb	Belfast	0	2

		v SWEDEN	NI	S
EC1974	30 Oct	Solna	2	0
EC1975	3 Sept	Belfast	1	2
wc1980	15 Oct	Belfast	3	0
wc1981	3 June	Solna	0	1

		v SWITZERLAND	NI	S
wc1964	14 Oct	Belfast	1	0
wc1964	14 Nov	Lausanne	1	2

		v TURKEY	NI	T
wc1968	23 Oct	Belfast	4	1
wc1968	11 Dec	Istanbul	3	0
EC1983	30 Mar	Belfast	2	1
EC1983	12 Oct	Ankara	0	1
wc1985	1 May	Belfast	2	0
wc1985	11 Sept	Izmir	0	0
EC1986	12 Nov	Izmir	0	0
EC1987	11 Nov	Belfast	1	0

		v URUGUAY	NI	U
1964	29 Apr	Belfast	3	0
1990	18 May	Belfast	1	0

		v USSR	NI	USSR
wc1969	19 Sept	Belfast	0	0
wc1969	22 Oct	Moscow	0	2
EC1971	22 Sept	Moscow	0	1
EC1971	13 Oct	Belfast	1	1

		v YUGOSLAVIA	NI	Y
EC1975	16 Mar	Belfast	1	0
EC1975	19 Nov	Belgrade	0	1
wc1982	17 June	Zaragoza	0	0
EC1987	29 Apr	Belfast	1	2
EC1987	14 Oct	Sarajevo	0	3
EC1990	12 Sept	Belfast	0	2
EC1991	27 Mar	Belgrade	1	4

REPUBLIC OF IRELAND

		v ALGERIA	RI	A
1982	28 Apr	Algiers	0	2

		v ARGENTINA	RI	A
1951	13 May	Dublin	0	1
1979	29 May	Dublin	0	0*
1980	16 May	Dublin	0	1

* Not considered a full international

		v AUSTRIA	RI	A
1952	7 May	Vienna	0	6
1953	25 Mar	Dublin	4	0
1958	14 Mar	Vienna	1	3
1962	8 Apr	Dublin	2	3
EC1963	25 Sept	Vienna	0	0
EC1963	13 Oct	Dublin	3	2
1966	22 May	Vienna	0	1
1968	10 Nov	Dublin	2	2
EC1971	30 May	Dublin	1	4
EC1971	10 Oct	Linz	0	6

		v BELGIUM	RI	B
1928	12 Feb	Liège	4	2
1929	30 Apr	Dublin	4	0
1930	11 May	Brussels	3	1
wc1934	25 Feb	Dublin	4	4
1949	24 Apr	Dublin	0	4
1950	10 May	Brussels	1	5
1965	24 Mar	Dublin	0	2
1966	25 May	Liège	3	2
wc1980	15 Oct	Dublin	1	1
wc1981	25 Mar	Brussels	0	1
EC1986	10 Sept	Brussels	2	2
EC1987	29 Apr	Dublin	0	0

		v BRAZIL	RI	B
1974	5 May	Rio de Janeiro	1	2
1982	27 May	Uberlandia	0	7
1987	23 May	Dublin	1	0

		v BULGARIA	RI	B
wc1977	1 June	Sofia	1	2
wc1977	12 Oct	Dublin	0	0
EC1979	19 May	Sofia	0	1
EC1979	17 Oct	Dublin	3	0
EC1987	1 Apr	Sofia	1	2
wc1987	14 Oct	Dublin	2	0

		v CHILE	RI	C
1960	30 Mar	Dublin	2	0
1972	21 June	Recife	1	2
1974	12 May	Santiago	2	1
1982	22 May	Santiago	0	1
1991	22 May	Dublin	1	1

		v CYPRUS	RI	C
wc1980	26 Mar	Nicosia	3	2
wc1980	19 Nov	Dublin	6	0

		v CZECHOSLOVAKIA	RI	C
1938	18 May	Prague	2	2
EC1959	5 Apr	Dublin	2	0
EC1959	10 May	Bratislava	0	4
wc1961	8 Oct	Dublin	1	3
wc1961	29 Oct	Prague	1	7
EC1967	21 May	Dublin	0	2
EC1967	22 Nov	Prague	2	1
wc1969	4 May	Dublin	1	2
wc1969	7 Oct	Prague	0	3
1979	26 Sept	Prague	1	4
1981	29 Apr	Dublin	3	1
1986	27 May	Reykjavik	1	0

		v DENMARK	RI	D
wc1956	3 Oct	Dublin	2	1
wc1957	2 Oct	Copenhagen	2	0
wc1968	4 Dec	Dublin	1	1
(abandoned after 51 mins)				
wc1969	27 May	Copenhagen	0	2
wc1969	15 Oct	Dublin	1	1
EC1978	24 May	Copenhagen	3	3
EC1979	2 May	Dublin	2	0
wc1984	14 Nov	Copenhagen	0	3
wc1985	13 Nov	Dublin	1	4

		v ECUADOR	RI	E
1972	19 June	Natal	3	2

		v EGYPT	RI	E
wc1990	17 June	Palermo	0	0

		v ENGLAND	RI	E
1946	30 Sept	Dublin	0	1
1949	21 Sept	Everton	2	0

			RI	E
wc1957	8 May	Wembley	1	5
wc1957	19 May	Dublin	1	1
1964	24 May	Dublin	1	3
1976	8 Sept	Wembley	1	1
EC1978	25 Oct	Dublin	1	1
EC1980	6 Feb	Wembley	0	2
1985	26 Mar	Wembley	1	2
EC1988	12 June	Stuttgart	1	0
wc1990	11 June	Cagliari	1	1
EC1990	14 Nov	Dublin	1	1
EC1991	27 Mar	Wembley	1	1

		v FINLAND	RI	F
wc1949	8 Sept	Dublin	3	0
wc1949	9 Oct	Helsinki	1	1
1990	16 May	Dublin	1	1

		v FRANCE	RI	F
1937	23 May	Paris	2	0
1952	16 Nov	Dublin	1	1
wc1953	4 Oct	Dublin	3	5
wc1953	25 Nov	Paris	0	1
wc1972	15 Nov	Dublin	2	1
wc1973	19 May	Paris	1	1
wc1976	17 Nov	Paris	0	2
wc1977	30 Mar	Dublin	1	0
wc1980	28 Oct	Paris	0	2
wc1981	14 Oct	Dublin	3	2
1989	7 Feb	Dublin	0	0

		v GERMANY	RI	G
1935	8 May	Dortmund	1	3
1936	17 Oct	Dublin	5	2
1939	23 May	Bremen	1	1

		v WEST GERMANY	RI	WG
1951	17 Oct	Dublin	3	2
1952	4 May	Cologne	0	3
1955	28 May	Hamburg	1	2
1956	25 Nov	Dublin	3	0
1960	11 May	Dusseldorf	1	0
1966	4 May	Dublin	0	4
1970	9 May	Berlin	1	2
1975	1 Mar	Dublin	1	0†
1979	22 May	Dublin	1	3
1981	21 May	Bremen	0	3†
1989	6 Sept	Dublin	1	1
†v West Germany 'B'				

		v HOLLAND	RI	N
1932	8 May	Amsterdam	2	0
1934	8 Apr	Amsterdam	2	5
1935	8 Dec	Dublin	3	5
1955	1 May	Dublin	1	0
1956	10 May	Rotterdam	4	1
wc1980	10 Sept	Dublin	2	1
wc1981	9 Sept	Rotterdam	2	2
EC1982	22 Sept	Rotterdam	1	2
EC1983	12 Oct	Dublin	2	3
EC1988	18 June	Gelsenkirchen	0	1
wc1990	21 June	Palermo	1	1

		v HUNGARY	RI	H
1934	15 Dec	Dublin	2	4
1936	3 May	Budapest	3	3
1936	6 Dec	Dublin	2	3
1939	19 Mar	Cork	2	2
1939	18 May	Budapest	2	2
wc1969	8 June	Dublin	1	2
wc1969	5 Nov	Budapest	0	4
wc1989	8 Mar	Budapest	0	2
wc1989	4 June	Dublin	2	0

808

v ICELAND

			RI	I
EC1962	12 Aug	Dublin	4	2
EC1962	2 Sept	Reykjavik	1	1
EC1982	13 Oct	Dublin	2	0
EC1983	21 Sept	Reykjavik	3	0
1986	25 May	Reykjavik	2	1

v IRAN

			RI	I
1972	18 June	Recife	2	1

v N. IRELAND

			RI	NI
EC1978	20 Sept	Dublin	0	0
EC1979	21 Nov	Belfast	0	1
WC1988	14 Sept	Belfast	0	0
WC1989	11 Oct	Dublin	3	0

v ISRAEL

			RI	I
1984	4 Apr	Tel Aviv	0	3
1985	27 May	Tel Aviv	0	0
1987	10 Nov	Dublin	5	0

v ITALY

			RI	I
1926	21 Mar	Turin	0	3
1927	23 Apr	Dublin	1	2
EC1970	8 Dec	Rome	0	3
EC1971	10 May	Dublin	1	2
1985	5 Feb	Dublin	1	2
WC1990	30 June	Rome	0	1

v LUXEMBOURG

			RI	I
1936	9 May	Luxembourg	5	1
WC1953	28 Oct	Dublin	4	0
WC1954	7 Mar	Luxembourg	1	0
EC1987	28 May	Luxembourg	2	0
EC1987	9 Sept	Dublin	2	1

v MALTA

			RI	M
EC1983	30 Mar	Valletta	1	0
EC1983	16 Nov	Dublin	8	0
WC1989	28 May	Dublin	2	0
WC1989	15 Nov	Valletta	2	0
1990	2 June	Valletta	3	0

v MEXICO

			RI	M
1984	8 Aug	Dublin	0	0

v MOROCCO

			RI	M
1990	12 Sept	Dublin	1	0

v NORWAY

			RI	N
WC1937	10 Oct	Oslo	2	3
WC1937	7 Nov	Dublin	3	3
1950	26 Nov	Dublin	2	2
1951	30 May	Oslo	3	2
1954	8 Nov	Dublin	2	1
1955	25 May	Oslo	3	1
1960	6 Nov	Dublin	3	1
1964	13 May	Oslo	4	1
1973	6 June	Oslo	1	1
1976	24 Mar	Dublin	3	0
1978	21 May	Oslo	0	0
WC1984	17 Oct	Oslo	0	1
WC1985	1 May	Dublin	0	0
1988	1 June	Oslo	0	0

v POLAND

			RI	P
1938	22 May	Warsaw	0	6
1938	13 Nov	Dublin	3	2
1958	11 May	Katowice	2	2
1958	5 Oct	Dublin	2	2
1964	10 May	Cracow	1	3
1964	25 Oct	Dublin	3	2
1968	15 May	Dublin	2	2
1968	30 Oct	Katowice	0	1
1970	6 May	Dublin	1	2
1970	23 Sept	Dublin	0	2
1973	16 May	Wroclaw	0	2
1973	21 Oct	Dublin	1	0
1976	26 May	Posnan	2	0
1977	24 Apr	Dublin	0	0
1978	12 Apr	Lodz	0	3
1981	23 May	Bydgoszcz	0	3
1984	23 May	Dublin	0	0
1986	12 Nov	Warsaw	0	1
1988	22 May	Dublin	3	1
EC1991	1 May	Dublin	0	0

v PORTUGAL

			RI	P
1946	16 June	Lisbon	1	3
1947	4 May	Dublin	0	2
1948	23 May	Lisbon	0	2
1949	22 May	Dublin	1	0
1972	25 June	Recife	1	2

v ROMANIA

			RI	R
1988	23 Mar	Dublin	2	0
WC1990	25 June	Genoa	0	0

v SCOTLAND

			RI	S
WC1961	3 May	Glasgow	1	4
WC1961	7 May	Dublin	0	3
1963	9 June	Dublin	1	0
1969	21 Sept	Dublin	1	1
EC1986	15 Oct	Dublin	0	0
EC1987	18 Feb	Glasgow	1	0

v SPAIN

			RI	S
1931	26 Apr	Barcelona	1	1
1931	13 Dec	Dublin	0	5
1946	23 June	Madrid	1	0
1947	2 Mar	Dublin	3	2
1948	30 May	Barcelona	1	2
1949	12 June	Dublin	1	4
1952	1 June	Madrid	0	6
1955	27 Nov	Dublin	2	2
EC1964	11 Mar	Seville	1	5
EC1964	8 Apr	Dublin	1	0
WC1965	5 May	Dublin	1	0
WC1965	27 Oct	Seville	1	4
WC1965	10 Nov	Paris	0	1
EC1966	23 Oct	Dublin	0	0
EC1966	7 Dec	Valencia	0	2
1977	9 Feb	Dublin	0	1
EC1982	17 Nov	Dublin	3	3
EC1983	27 Apr	Zaragoza	0	2
WC1985	26 May	Cork	0	0
WC1988	16 Nov	Seville	0	2
WC1989	26 Apr	Dublin	1	0

v SWEDEN

			RI	S
WC1949	2 June	Stockholm	1	3
WC1949	13 Nov	Dublin	1	3
1959	1 Nov	Dublin	3	2
1960	18 May	Malmo	1	4
EC1970	14 Oct	Dublin	1	1
EC1970	28 Oct	Malmo	0	1

v SWITZERLAND

			RI	S
1935	5 May	Basle	0	1
1936	17 Mar	Dublin	1	0
1937	17 May	Berne	1	0
1938	18 Sept	Dublin	4	0
1948	5 Dec	Dublin	0	1
EC1975	11 May	Dublin	2	1
EC1975	21 May	Berne	0	1

809

			RI	S
1980	30 Apr	Dublin	2	0
wc1985	2 June	Dublin	3	0
wc1985	11 Sept	Berne	0	0

v TRINIDAD & TOBAGO			RI	TT
1982	30 May	Port of Spain	1	2

v TUNISIA			RI	T
1988	19 Oct	Dublin	4	0

v TURKEY			RI	T
EC1966	16 Nov	Dublin	2	1
EC1967	22 Feb	Ankara	1	2
EC1974	20 Nov	Izmir	1	1
EC1975	29 Oct	Dublin	4	0
1976	13 Oct	Ankara	3	3
1978	5 Apr	Dublin	4	2
1990	26 May	Izmir	0	0
EC1990	17 Oct	Dublin	5	0

v URUGUAY			RI	U
1974	8 May	Montevideo	0	2
1986	23 Apr	Dublin	1	1

v USA			RI	USA
1979	29 Oct	Dublin	3	2
1991	1 June	Boston	1	1

v USSR			RI	USSR
wc1972	18 Oct	Dublin	1	2
wc1973	13 May	Moscow	0	1
EC1974	30 Oct	Dublin	3	0
EC1975	18 May	Kiev	1	2
wc1984	12 Sept	Dublin	1	0
wc1985	16 Oct	Moscow	0	2
EC1988	15 June	Hanover	1	1
1990	25 Apr	Dublin	1	0

v WALES			RI	W
1960	28 Sept	Dublin	2	3
1979	11 Sept	Swansea	1	2
1981	24 Feb	Dublin	1	3
1986	26 Mar	Dublin	0	1
1990	28 Mar	Dublin	1	0
1991	6 Feb	Wrexham	3	0

v YUGOSLAVIA			RI	Y
1955	19 Sept	Dublin	1	4
1988	27 Apr	Dublin	2	0

OTHER BRITISH AND IRISH INTERNATIONAL MATCHES 1990–91

Copenhagen, 11 September 1990, 8700

Denmark (0) 1 *(Laudrup B 64)*

Wales (0) 0

Denmark: Schmeichel; Sivebaek, Nielsen K, Olsen L, Andersen, Larsen, Larsen (Olsen J 73), Vilfort, Povlsen, Christensen (Molby 46), Laudrup B.
Wales: Southall; Phillips, Bodin, Aizlewood, Young, Ratcliffe, Saunders, Horne, Rush, Hughes, Speed (Nicholas 69).

Wembley, 12 September 1990, 51,459

England (1) 1 *(Lineker 44)*

Hungary (0) 0

England: Woods; Dixon, Pearce (Dorigo 46), Parker, Walker, Wright M, Platt, Gascoigne, Bull (Waddle 73), Lineker, Barnes.
Hungary: Petry; Monos (Simon 68), Disztl, Keller, Limperger, Garaba (Aczel 71), Kozma, Bucs (Balog 80), Gregor, Berczy, Kovacs K.

Dublin, 12 September 1990, 19,450

Republic of Ireland (0) 1 *(Kelly D 74)*

Morocco (0) 0

Republic of Ireland: Bonner; Irwin, McCarthy, O'Leary, Staunton, Houghton, Whelan, Townsend (Sheridan 65), Kelly M (McLoughlin 69), Quinn (Cascarino 58), Kelly D.
Morocco: Brazi; Benabicha, Naybat, Mouhcine, Jbilou (Tahar 76), Raghib, El Ghrissi, Majid, Daoudi, Khairi, Nader.

Wembley, 6 February 1991, 61,075

England (1) 2 *(Lineker 20 (pen), 61)*

Cameroon (0) 0

England: Seaman; Dixon, Pearce, Steven, Walker, Wright M, Robson (Pallister 70), Gascoigne (Hodge 67), Wright I, Lineker, Barnes.
Cameroon: Bell; Ebwelle, Onana, Kunde, Tataw, M'Fede, Mbouh-Mbouh, Pagel, Kana-Biyik (Libiih 42), Omam-Biyik, Ekeke (Tapoko 78).

Hampden Park, 6 February 1991, 20,763

Scotland (0) 0

USSR (0) 1 *(Kuznetsov 89)*

Scotland: Goram; Malpas, Nicol, McCall (McAllister 69), Gough, McLeish (McPherson 46), Strachan, Fleck (Durie 75) McCoist, McStay, Boyd (MacLeod 46).
USSR: Uvarov; Chernishev, Kulkov, Tsvelba, Gorlukovich, Shalimov, Aleinikov, Kontchelskis, Youran (Kolyvanov 62), Mostovoi (Kuznetsov 69), Dobrovolski.

Racecourse Ground, 6 February 1991, 9168

Wales (0) 0

Republic of Ireland (1) 3 *(Quinn 24, 67, Byrne 87)*

Wales: Southall; Hall, Bodin, Aizlewood, Young (Speed 46), Ratcliffe, Horne, Nicholas, Rush (Allen 51), Saunders, Pascoe.
Republic of Ireland: Bonner; Irwin, Staunton, McGrath, Moran, McLoughlin, Townsend, Byrne, Quinn, Slaven (Kelly D 68), Sheedy.

Ninian Park, 1 May 1991, 3656

Wales (1) 1 *(Bodin 35 (pen))*

Iceland (0) 0

Wales: Southall; Phillips, Bodin, Aizlewood, Melville, Ratcliffe, Goss, Horne, Saunders, Hughes (Pascoe 69), Speed.
Iceland: Sigurdsson; Gislasson, Edvaldsson, Kristinsson, Gretarsson, Jonsson, Bergsson, Orlygsson (Stefansson 79), Gudjohnsen, Thordarsson, Gregory (Kristgannsson 73).

Wembley, 21 May 1991, 23,789

England (2) 3 *(Smith 16, Platt 4 (pen), 89)*

USSR (1) 1 *(Wright (og))*

England: Woods; Stevens, Dorigo, Wise (Batty 70), Parker, Wright M, Platt, Thomas, Smith, Wright I (Beardsley 70), Barnes.
USSR: Uvarov; Chernishev, Kulkov, Tsvelba, Galiamin, Shalimov, Mikhailichenko, Kontchelskis, Kolianov, Tatarchuk (Mostovoi 50), Kuznetsov D.

Dublin, 22 May 1991, 32,230

Republic of Ireland (0) 1 *(Kelly D 82)*

Chile (0) 1 *(Estay 64)*

Republic of Ireland: Peyton; Hughton, Staunton, O'Leary (McGrath 6), Moran, Townsend, Keane, Houghton (McLoughlin 64), Sheridan, Kelly D, Sheedy (Cascarino 71).
Chile: Toledo; Romero, Fuentes, Guevara (Miranda 15), Barca, Parraguez, Rubio, Gomez, Vera (Contreras 64), Estay, Guarda (Gonzales 79).

Wembley, 25 May 1991, 44,497

England (1) 2 *(Lineker 15, Platt 50)*

Argentina (0) (2) *(Garcia 66, Franco 70)*

England: Seaman; Dixon, Pearce, Batty, Walker, Wright M, Platt, Thomas, Smith, Lineker, Barnes (Clough 63).
Argentina: Goycochea; Vazquez, Enrique, Basualdo, Gamboa, Ruggeri, Garcia, Franco, Simeone, Martellotto (Mohammed 60), Boldrini.

Radom, 29 May 1991 11,000

Poland (0) 0

Wales (0) 0

Poland: Bako (Wandzik 46); Kubicki, Jakolcewicz, Wdowczyk, Soczynski, Nawrocki, Tarasiewicz, Warzycha K, Furtok, Kosecki, Ziober.
Wales: Southall; Phillips, Bodin, Aizlewood, Melville, Ratcliffe, Nicholas (Goss), Saunders, Rush, Hughes, Horne.

Boston, 1 June 1991, 51,273

USA (0) 1 *(Wynalda 68)*

Republic of Ireland (0) 1 *(Cascarino 56)*

USA: Meola; Balboa, Trittschuh, Michalik, Quinn (Snyder 85), Henderson, Agoos, Savage, Murray, Vermes (Perez 54), Wynalda.
Republic of Ireland: Bonner; Irwin, Staunton, McCarthy, Moran, Townsend, McGrath, Houghton (Sheridan 72), Cascarino, Kelly D, Sheedy.

Sydney, 1 June 1991, 35,472

Australia (0) 0

England (1) 1 *(Gray 40 (og))*

Australia: Zabica; Gray, Durakovic, Zelic, Tobin, Vidmar T, Wade, Petersen, Arnold, Tapai (Brown 76), Vidmar A.
England: Woods; Parker, Pearce, Batty, Walker, Wright M, Platt, Thomas, Clough, Lineker (Wise 81), Hirst (Salako 46).

Auckland, 3 June 1991, 17,500

New Zealand (0) 0

England (0) 1 *(Lineker 90)*

New Zealand: Gosling; Ridenton, Gray, Dunford, Evans, Ironside, McGarry, Halligan, Edge D, De Jong, Ferris.
England: Woods; Parker, Pearce, Batty (Deane 46), Walker, Barrett, Platt, Thomas, Wise, Lineker, Walters (Salako 70).

Wellington, 8 June 1991, 25,000

New Zealand (0) 0

England (1) 2 *(Pearce 12, Hirst 50)*

New Zealand: Schofield; Ridenton, Gray, Dunford, Evans, Ironside, McGarry, Halligan, Edge D (Edge T 62), De Jong, Ferris.
England: Woods; Charles, Pearce, Wise, Walker, Wright M, Platt, Thomas, Deane (Hirst 46), Wright I, Salako.

Kuala Lumpur, 12 June 1991, 45,000

Malaysia (0) 2 *(Matian 52, 76)*

England (3) 4 *(Lineker 1, 23, 30, 70)*

Malaysia: Hassan (Khairul 66); Serbegeth, Lee, Zaid (Azizol 46), Jayakanthan, Chow, Ahmad, Nasir, Matian, Sainal, Dollah.
England: Woods; Charles, Pearce, Batty, Walker, Wright M, Platt, Thomas, Clough, Lineker, Salako.

John Sheridan (No. 8) scores for Sheffield Wednesday in the 1991 Rumbelows Cup Final. He also played in the Republic of Ireland's national team during the season. (Bob Thomas)

812

INTERNATIONAL APPEARANCES

This is a list of full international appearances by Englishmen, Irishmen, Scotsmen and Welshmen in matches against the Home Countries and against foreign nations. It does not include unofficial matches against Commonwealth and Empire countries. The year indicated refers to the season; ie 1991 is the 1990-91 season.

Explanatory code for matches played by all five countries: A represents Austria; Alb, Albania; Alg, Algeria; Arg, Argentina; Aus, Australia; B, Bohemia; Bel, Belgium; Br, Brazil; Bul, Bulgaria; Ca, Canada; Cam, Cameroon; Ch, Chile; Chn, China; Co, Colombia; Cr, Costa Rica; Cy, Cyprus; Cz, Czechoslovakia; D, Denmark; E, England; Ec, Ecuador; Ei, Eire; EG, East Germany; Eg, Egypt; F, France; Fa, Faeroes; Fi, Finland; G, Germany (pre-war); Gr, Greece; H, Hungary; Ho, Holland; Hon, Honduras; I, Italy; Ic, Iceland; Ir, Iran; Is, Israel; K, Kuwait; L, Luxembourg; M, Mexico; Ma, Malta; Mal, Malaysia; Mor, Morocco; N, Norway; Ni, Northern Ireland; Nz, New Zealand; P, Portugal; Para, Paraguay; Pe, Peru; Pol, Poland; R, Romania; R of E, Rest of Europe; R of UK, Rest of United Kingdom; R of W, Rest of World; S.Ar, Saudi Arabia; S, Scotland; Se, Sweden; Sm, San Marino; Sp, Spain; Sw, Switzerland; T, Turkey; Tr, Trinidad & Tobago; Tun, Tunisia; U, Uruguay; UK, Rest of United Kingdom; US, United States of America; USSR, Soviet Union; W, Wales; WG, West Germany; Y, Yugoslavia; Z, Zaire.
As at 12 June 1991.

ENGLAND

Abbott, W. (Everton), 1902 v W (1)
A'Court, A. (Liverpool), 1958 v Ni, Br, A, USSR; 1959 v W (5)
Adams, T. A. (Arsenal), 1987 v Sp, T, Br; 1988 v WG, T, Y, Ho, H, S, Co, Sw, Ei, Ho, USSR; 1989 v D, Se, S.Ar.; 1991 v Ei (2) (19)
Adcock, H. (Leicester C), 1929 v F, Bel, Sp; 1930 v Ni, W (5)
Alcock, C. W. (Wanderers), 1875 v S (1)
Alderson, J. T. (C Palace), 1923 v F (1)
Aldridge, A. (WBA), 1888 v Ni; (with Walsall Town Swifts), 1889 v Ni (2)
Allen, A. (Stoke C) 1960 v Se, W, Ni (3)
Allen, A. (Aston Villa), 1888 v Ni (1)
Allen, C. (QPR), 1984 v Br (sub), U, Ch; (with Tottenham H), 1987 v T; 1988 v Is (5)
Allen, H. (Wolverhampton W), 1888 v S, W, Ni; 1889 v S; 1890 v S (5)
Allen, J. P. (Portsmouth), 1934 v Ni, W (2)
Allen, R. (WBA), 1952 v Sw; 1954 v Y, S; 1955 v WG, W (5)
Alsford, W. J. (Tottenham H), 1935 v S (1)
Amos, A. (Old Carthusians), 1885 v S; 1886 v W (2)
Anderson, R. D. (Old Etonians), 1879 v W (1)
Anderson, S. (Sunderland), 1962, v A, S (2)
Anderson, V. (Nottingham F), 1979 v Cz, Se; 1980 v Bul, Sp; 1981 v N, R, W, S; 1982 v Ni, Ic; 1984 v Ni; (with Arsenal), 1985 v T, Ni, Ei, R, Fi, S, M, US; 1986 v USSR, M; 1987 v Se, Ni (2), Y, Sp, T; (with Manchester U), 1988 v WG, H, Co (30)
Angus, J. (Burnley), 1961 v A (1)
Armfield, J. C. (Blackpool), 1959 v Br, Pe, M, US; 1960 v Y, Sp, H, S; 1961 v L, P, Sp, M, I, A, W, Ni, S; 1962 v A, Sw, Pe, W, Ni, S, L, P, H, Arg, Bul, Br; 1963 v F (2), Br, EG, Sw, Ni, W, S; 1964 v R of W, W, Ni, S; 1966 v Y, Fi (43)
Armitage, G. H. (Charlton Ath), 1926 v Ni (1)
Armstrong, D. (Middlesbrough), 1980 v Aus; (with Southampton), 1983 v WG; 1984 v W (3)
Armstrong, K. (Chelsea), 1955 v S (1)
Arnold, J. (Fulham), 1933 v S (1)
Arthur, J. W. H. (Blackburn R), 1885 v S, W, Ni; 1886 v S, W; 1887 v W, Ni (7)
Ashcroft, J. (Woolwich Arsenal), 1906 v Ni, W, S (3)
Ashmore, G. S. (WBA), 1926 v Bel (1)
Ashton, C. T. (Corinthians), 1926 v Ni (1)
Ashurst, W. (Notts Co), 1923 v Se (2); 1925 v S, W, Bel (5)
Astall, G. (Birmingham C), 1956 v Fi, WG (2)
Astle, J. (WBA), 1969 v W; 1970 v S, P, Br (sub), Cz (5)
Aston, J. (Manchester U), 1949 v S, W, D, Sw, Se, N, F; 1950 v S, W, Ni, Ei, I, P, Bel, Ch, US; 1951 v Ni (17)
Athersmith, W. C. (Aston Villa), 1892 v Ni, 1897 v S, W, Ni; 1898 v S, W, Ni; 1899 v S, W, Ni; 1900 v S, W (12)

Atyeo, P. J. W. (Bristol C), 1956 v Br, Se, Sp; 1957 v D, Ei (2) (6)
Austin, S. W. (Manchester C), 1926 v Ni (1)

Bach, P. (Sunderland), 1899 v Ni (1)
Bache, J. W. (Aston Villa), 1903 v W; 1904 v W, Ni; 1905 v S; 1907 v Ni; 1910 v Ni; 1911 v S (7)
Baddeley, T. (Wolverhampton W), 1903 v S, Ni; 1904 v S, W, Ni (5)
Bagshaw, J. J. (Derby Co), 1920 v Ni (1)
Bailey, G. R. (Manchester U), 1985 v Ei, M (2)
Bailey, H. P. (Leicester Fosse), 1908 v W, A (2), H, B (5)
Bailey, M. A. (Charlton Ath), 1964 v US; 1965 v W (2)
Bailey, N. C. (Clapham Rovers), 1878 v S; 1879 v S, W; 1880 v S; 1881 v S; 1882 v S, W; 1883 v S, W; 1884 v S, W, Ni; 1885 v S, W; 1886 v S, W; 1887 v S, W (19)
Baily, E. F. (Tottenham H), 1950 v Sp; 1951 v Y, Ni, W; 1952 v A (2), Sw, W; 1953 v Ni (9)
Bain, J. (Oxford University), 1887 v S (1)
Baker, A. (Arsenal), 1928 v W (1)
Baker, B. H. (Everton), 1921 v Bel; (with Chelsea), 1926 v Ni (2)
Baker, J. H. (Hibernian), 1960 v Y, Sp, H, Ni, S; (with Arsenal) 1966 v Sp, Pol, Ni (8)
Ball, A. J. (Blackpool), 1965 v Y, WG, Se; 1966 v S, Sp, Fi, D, U, Arg, P, WG (2), Pol (2); (with Everton), 1967 v W, S, Ni, A, Cz, Sp; 1968 v W, S, USSR, Sp (2), Y, WG; 1969 v Ni, W, S, R (2), M, Br, U; 1970 v P, Co, Ec, R, Br, Cz (sub), WG, W, S, Bel; 1971 v Ma, EG, Gr, Ma (sub), Ni, S; 1972 v Sw, Gr; (with Arsenal) WG (2), S; 1973 v W (3), Y, S (2), Cz, Ni, Pol; 1974 v P (sub); 1975 v WG, Cy (2), Ni, W, S (72)
Ball, J. (Bury), 1928 v Ni (1)
Balmer, W. (Everton), 1905 v Ni (1)
Bamber, J. (Liverpool), 1921 v W (1)
Bambridge, A. L. (Swifts), 1881 v W; 1883 v W; 1884 v Ni (3)
Bambridge, E. C. (Swifts), 1879 v S; 1880 v S; 1881 v S; 1882 v S, W, Ni; 1883 v W; 1884 v S, W, Ni; 1885 v S, W, Ni; 1886 v S, W; 1887 v S, W, Ni (18)
Bambridge, E. H. (Swifts), 1876 v S (1)
Banks, G. (Leicester C), 1963 v S, Br, Cz, EG; 1964 v W, Ni, S, R of W, U, P (2), US, Arg; 1965 v Ni, S, H, Y, WG, Se; 1966 v Ni, S, Sp, Pol (2), WG (2), Y, Fi, U, M, F, Arg, P; 1967 v Ni, W, S, Cz; (with Stoke C), 1968 v W, Ni, S, USSR (2), Sp, WG, Y; 1969 v Ni, S, R (2), F, U, Br; 1970 v W, Ni, S, Ho, Bel, Co, Ec, R, Br, Cz; 1971 v Gr, Ma (2), Ni, S; 1972 v Sw, Gr, WG (2), W, S (73)
Banks, H. E. (Millwall), 1901 v Ni (1)
Banks, T. (Bolton W), 1958 v USSR (3), Br, A; 1959 v Ni (6)
Bannister, W. (Burnley), 1901 v W; (with Bolton W), 1902 v Ni (2)

Barclay, R. (Sheffield W), 1932 v S; 1933 v Ni; 1936 v S (3)
Barham, M. (Norwich C), 1983 v Aus (2) (2)
Barkas, S. (Manchester C), 1936 v Bel; 1937 v S; 1938 v W, Ni, Cz (5)
Barker, J. (Derby Co), 1935 v I, Ho, S, W, Ni; 1936 v G, A, S, W, Ni; 1937 v W (11)
Barker, R. (Herts Rangers), 1872 v S (1)
Barker, R. R. (Casuals), 1895 v W (1)
Barlow, R. J. (WBA), 1955 v Ni (1)
Barnes, J. (Watford), 1983 v Ni (sub), Aus (sub), Aus (2); 1984 v D, L (sub), F (sub), S, USSR, Br, U, Ch; 1985 v EG, Fi, T, Ni, R, Fi, S, I (sub), M, WG (sub), US (sub); 1986 v R (sub), Is (sub), M (sub), Ca (sub), Arg (sub); 1987 v Se, T (sub), Br; (with Liverpool), 1988 v WG, T, Y, Is, Ho, S, Co, Sw, Ei, Ho, USSR; 1989 v Se, Gr, Alb, Pol, D; 1990 v Se, I, Br, D, U, Tun, Ei, Ho, Eg, Bel, Cam; 1991 v H, Pol, Cam, Ei, T, USSR, Arg (65)
Barnes, P. S. (Manchester C), 1978 v I, WG, Br, W, S, H; 1979 v D, Ei, Cz, Ni (2), S, Bul, A; (with WBA), 1980 v D, W; 1981 v Sp (sub), Br, W, Sw (sub); (with Leeds U), 1982 v N (sub), Ho (sub) (22)
Barnet, H. H. (Royal Engineers), 1882 v Ni (1)
Barrass, M. W. (Bolton W), 1952 v W, Ni; 1953 v S (3)
Barrett, A. F. (Fulham), 1930 v Ni (1)
Barrett, E. D. (Oldham Ath), 1991 v Nz (1)
Barrett, J. W. (West Ham U), 1929 v Ni (1)
Barry, L. (Leicester C), 1928 v F, Bel; 1929 v F, Bel, Sp (5)
Barson, F. (Aston Villa), 1920 v W (1)
Barton, J. (Blackburn R), 1890 v Ni (1)
Barton, P. H. (Birmingham), 1921 v Bel; 1922 v Ni; 1923 v F; 1924 v Bel, S, W; 1925 v Ni (7)
Bassett, W. I. (WBA), 1888 v Ni, 1889 v S, W; 1890 v S, W; 1891 v S, Ni; 1892 v S; 1893 v S, W; 1894 v S; 1895 v S, Ni; 1896 v S, W, Ni (16)
Bastard, S. R. (Upton Park), 1880 v S (1)
Bastin, C. S. (Arsenal), 1932 v W; 1933 v I, Sw; 1934 v S, Ni, W, H, Cz; 1935 v S, Ni, I; 1936 v S, W, G, A; 1937 v W, Ni; 1938 v S, G, Sw, F (21)
Batty, D. (Leeds U), 1991 v USSR (sub), Arg, Aus, Nz, Mal (5)
Baugh, R. (Stafford Road), 1886 v Ni; (with Wolverhampton W) 1890 v Ni (2)
Bayliss, A. E. J. M. (WBA), 1891 v Ni (1)
Baynham, R. L. (Luton T), 1956 v Ni, D, Sp (3)
Beardsley, P. A. (Newcastle U), 1986 v Eg (sub), Is, USSR, M, Ca (sub), P (sub), Pol, Para, Arg; 1987 v Ni (2), Y, Sp, Br, S; (with Liverpool), 1988 v WG, T, Y, Is, Ho, H, S, Co, Sw, Ei, Ho; 1989 v D, Se, S.Ar, Gr (sub), Alb (sub + 1), Pol, D; 1990 v Se, Pol, I, Br, U (sub), Tun (sub), Ei, Eg (sub), Cam (sub), WG, I; 1991 v Pol (sub), Ei (2), USSR (sub) (49)
Beasant, D. J. (Chelsea), 1990 v I (sub), Y (sub) (2)
Beasley, A. (Huddersfield T), 1939 v S (1)
Beats, W. E. (Wolverhampton W), 1901 v W; 1902 v S (2)
Beattie, T. K. (Ipswich T), 1975 v Cy (2), S; 1976 v Sw, P; 1977 v Fi, I (sub), Ho; 1978 v L (sub) (9)
Becton, F. (Preston NE), 1895 v Ni; (with Liverpool), 1897 v W (2)
Bedford, H. (Blackpool), 1923 v Se; 1925 v Ni (2)
Bell, C. (Manchester C), 1968 v Se, WG; 1969 v W, Buf, F, U, Br; 1970 v Ni (sub), Ho (2), P, Br (sub), Cz, WG (sub); 1972 v Gr, WG (2), W, Ni, S; 1973 v W (3), Y, S (2), Ni, Cz, Pol; 1974 v A, Pol, I, W, Ni, S, Arg, EG, Bul, Y; 1975 v Cz, P, WG, Cy (2), Ni, S; 1976 v Sw, Cy (48)
Bennett, W. (Sheffield U), 1901 v S, W (2)
Benson, R. W. (Sheffield U), 1913 v Ni (1)
Bentley, R. T. F. (Chelsea), 1949 v Se; 1950 v S, P, Bel, Ch, USA; 1953 v W, Bel; 1955 v W, WG, Sp, P (12)
Beresford, J. (Aston Villa), 1934 v Cz (1)
Berry, A. (Oxford University), 1909 v Ni (1)
Berry, J. J. (Manchester U), 1953 v Arg, Ch, U; 1956 v Se (4)

Bestall, J. G. (Grimsby T), 1935 v Ni (1)
Betmead, H. A. (Grimsby T), 1937 v Fi (1)
Betts, M. P. (Old Harrovians), 1877 v S (1)
Betts, W. (Sheffield W), 1889 v W (1)
Beverley, J. (Blackburn R), 1884 v S, W, Ni (3)
Birkett, R. H. (Clapham Rovers), 1879 v S (1)
Birkett, R. J. E. (Middlesbrough), 1936 v Ni (1)
Birley, F. H. (Oxford University), 1874 v S; (with Wanderers), 1875 v S (2)
Birtles, G. (Nottingham F), 1980 v Arg (sub), I; 1981 v R (3)
Bishop, S. M. (Leicester C), 1927 v S, Bel, L, F (4)
Blackburn, F. (Blackburn R), 1901 v S; 1902 v Ni; 1904 v S (3)
Blackburn, G. F. (Aston Villa), 1924 v F (1)
Blenkinsop, E. (Sheffield W), 1928 v F, Bel; 1929 v S, W, Ni, F, Bel, Sp; 1930 v S, W, Ni, G, A; 1931 v S, W, Ni, F, Bel; 1932 v S, W, Ni, Sp; 1933 v S, W, Ni, A (26)
Bliss, H. (Tottenham H), 1921 v S (1)
Blissett, L. (Watford), 1983 v WG (sub), L, W, Gr (sub), H, Ni, S (sub), Aus (1 + 1 sub); 1984 v D (sub), H, W (sub), S, USSR (14)
Blockley, J. P. (Arsenal), 1973 v Y (1)
Bloomer, S. (Derby Co), 1895 v S, Ni; 1896 v W, Ni; 1897 v S, W, Ni; 1898 v S; 1899 v S, W, Ni; 1900 v S; 1901 v S, W; 1902 v S, W, Ni; 1904 v S; 1905 v S, W, Ni; (with Middlesbrough), 1907 v S, W (23)
Blunstone, F. (Chelsea), 1955 v W, S, F, P; 1957 v Y (5)
Bond, R. (Preston NE), 1905 v Ni, W; 1906 v S, W, Ni; (with Bradford C), 1910 v S, W, Ni (8)
Bonetti, P. P. (Chelsea), 1966 v D; 1967 v Sp, A; 1968 v Sp; 1970 v Ho, P, WG (7)
Bonsor, A. G. (Wanderers), 1873 v S; 1875 v S (2)
Booth, F. (Manchester C), 1905 v Ni (1)
Booth, T. (Blackburn R), 1898 v W; (with Everton), 1903 v S (2)
Bowden, E. R. (Arsenal), 1935 v W, I; 1936 v W, Ni, A; 1937 v H (6)
Bower, A. G. (Corinthians), 1924 v Ni, Bel; 1925 v W, Bel; 1927 v W (5)
Bowers, J. W. (Derby Co), 1934 v S, Ni, W (3)
Bowles, S. (QPR), 1974 v P, W, Ni; 1977 v I, Ho (5)
Bowser, S. (WBA), 1920 v Ni (1)
Boyer, P. J. (Norwich C), 1976 v W (1)
Boyes, W. (WBA), 1935 v Ho; (with Everton), 1939 v W, R of E (3)
Boyle, T. W. (Burnley), 1913 v Ni (1)
Brabrook, P. (Chelsea), 1958 v USSR; 1959 v Ni; 1960 v Sp (3)
Bracewell, P. W. (Everton), 1985 v WG (sub), US; 1986 v Ni (3)
Bradford, G. R. W. (Bristol R), 1956 v D (1)
Bradford, J. (Birmingham), 1924 v Ni; 1925 v Bel; 1928 v S; 1929 v Ni, W, F, Sp; 1930 v S, Ni, G, A; 1931 v W (12)
Bradley, W. (Manchester U), 1959 v I, US, M (sub) (3)
Bradshaw, F. (Sheffield W), 1908 v A (1)
Bradshaw, T. H. (Liverpool), 1897 v Ni (1)
Bradshaw, W. (Blackburn R), 1910 v W, Ni; 1912 v Ni; 1913 v W (4)
Brann, G. (Swifts), 1886 v S, W; 1891 v W (3)
Brawn, W. F. (Aston Villa), 1904 v W, Ni (2)
Bray, J. (Manchester C), 1935 v W; 1936 v S, W, Ni, G; 1937 v S (6)
Brayshaw, E. (Sheffield W), 1887 v Ni (1)
Bridges, B. J. (Chelsea), 1965 v S, H, Y; 1966 v A (4)
Bridgett, A. (Sunderland), 1905 v S; 1908 v S, A (2), H, B; 1909 v Ni, W, H (2), A (11)
Brindle, T. (Darwen), 1880 v S, W (2)
Brittleton, J. T. (Sheffield W), 1912 v S, W, Ni; 1913 v S; 1914 v W (5)
Britton, C. S. (Everton), 1935 v S, W, Ni, I; 1937 v S, Ni, H, N, Se (9)

Broadbent, P. F. (Wolverhampton W), 1958 v USSR; 1959 v S, W, Ni, I, Br; 1960 v S (7)

Broadis, I. A. (Manchester C), 1952 v S, A, I; 1953 v S, Arg, Ch, U, US; (with Newcastle U) 1954 v S, H, Y, Bel, Sw, U (14)

Brockbank, J. (Cambridge University), 1872 v S (1)

Brodie, J. B. (Wolverhampton W), 1889 v S, Ni; 1891 v Ni (3)

Bromilow, T. G. (Liverpool), 1921 v W; 1922 v S, W; 1923 v Bel; 1926 v Ni (5)

Bromley-Davenport, W. E. (Oxford University), 1884 v S, W (2)

Brook, E. F. (Manchester C), 1930 v Ni; 1933 v Sw: 1934 v S, W, Ni, F, H, Cz; 1935 v S, W, Ni, I; 1936 v S, W, Ni; 1937 v H; 1938 v W, Ni (18)

Brooking, T. D. (West Ham U), 1974 v P, Arg, EG, Bul, Y; 1975 v Cz (sub), P; 1976 v P, W, Br, I, Fi; 1977 v Ei, Fi, I, Ho, Ni, W; 1978 v I, WG, W, S (sub), H; 1979 v D, Ei, Ni, W (sub), S, Bul, Se (sub), A; 1980 v D, Ni, Arg (sub), W, Ni, S, Bel, Sp; 1981 v Sw, Sp, R, H; 1982 v H, S, Fi, Sp (sub) (47)

Brooks, J. (Tottenham H), 1957 v W, Y, D (3)

Broome, F. H. (Aston Villa), 1938 v G, Sw, F; 1939 v N, I, R, Y (7)

Brown, A. (Aston Villa), 1882 v S, W, Ni (3)

Brown, A. S. (Sheffield U), 1904 v W; 1906 v Ni (2)

Brown, A. (WBA), 1971 v W (1)

Brown, G. (Huddersfield T), 1927 v S, W, Ni, Bel, L, F; 1928 v W; 1929 v S; (with Aston Villa), 1933 v W (9)

Brown, J. (Blackburn R), 1881 v W; 1882 v Ni; 1885 v S, W, Ni (5)

Brown, J. H. (Sheffield W), 1927 v S, W, Bel, L, F; 1930 v Ni (6)

Brown, K. (West Ham U), 1960 v Ni (1)

Brown, W. (West Ham U), 1924 v Ni (1)

Bruton, J. (Burnley), 1928 v F, Bel; 1929 v S (3)

Bryant, W. I. (Clapton), 1925 v F (1)

Buchan, C. M. (Sunderland), 1913 v Ni; 1920 v W; 1921 v W, Bel; 1923 v F; 1924 v S (6)

Buchanan, W. S. (Clapham R), 1876 v S (1)

Buckley, F. C. (Derby Co), 1914 v Ni (1)

Bull, S. G. (Wolverhampton W), 1989 v S (sub), D (sub); 1990 v Y, Cz, D (sub), U (sub), Tun (sub), Ei (sub), Ho (sub), Eg, Bel (sub); 1991 v H, Pol (13)

Bullock, F. E. (Huddersfield T), 1921 v Ni (1)

Bullock, N. (Bury), 1923 v Bel; 1926 v W; 1927 v Ni (3)

Burgess, H. (Manchester C), 1904 v S, W, Ni; 1906 v S (4)

Burgess, H. (Sheffield W), 1931 v S, Ni, F, Bel (4)

Burnup, C. J. (Cambridge University), 1896 v S (1)

Burrows, H. (Sheffield W), 1934 v H, Cz; 1935 v Ho (3)

Burton, F. E. (Nottingham F), 1889 v Ni (1)

Bury, L. (Cambridge University), 1877 v S; (with Old Etonians), 1879 v W (2)

Butcher, T. (Ipswich T), 1980 v Aus; 1981 v Sp; 1982 v W, S, F, Cz, WG, Sp; 1983 v D, WG, L, W, Gr, H, Ni, S, Aus (3); 1984 v D, H, L, F, Ni; 1985 v EG, Fi, T, Ni, Ei, R, Fi, S, I, WG, US; 1986 v Is, USSR, S, M, Ca, P, Mor, Pol, Para, Arg; (with Rangers), 1987 v Se, Ni (2), Y, Sp, Br, S; 1988 v T, Y; 1989 v D, Se, Gr, Alb (2), Ch, S, Pol, D; 1990 v Se, Pol, I, Y, Br, Cz, D, U, Tun, Ei, Ho, Bel, Cam, WG (77)

Butler, J. D. (Arsenal), 1925 v Bel (1)

Butler, W. (Bolton W), 1924 v S (1)

Byrne, G. (Liverpool), 1963 v S; 1966 v N (2)

Byrne, J. J. (C Palace), 1962 v Ni; (with West Ham U), 1963 v Sw; 1964 v S, U, P (2), Ei, Br, Arg; 1965 v W, S (11)

Byrne, R. W. (Manchester U), 1954 v S, H, Y, Bel, Sw, U; 1955 v S, W, Ni, WG, F, Sp, P; 1956 v S, W, Ni, Br, Se, Fi, WG, D, Sp; 1957 v S, W, Ni, Y, D (2), Ei (2); 1958 v W, Ni, F (33)

Callaghan, I. R. (Liverpool), 1966 v Fi, F; 1978 v Sw, L (4)

Calvey, J. (Nottingham F), 1902 v Ni (1)

Campbell, A. F. (Blackburn R), 1929 v W, Ni; (with Huddersfield T), 1931 v W, S, Ni; 1932 v W, Ni, Sp (8)

Camsell, G. H. (Middlesbrough), 1929 v F, Bel; 1930 v Ni, W; 1934 v F; 1936 v S, G, A, Bel (9)

Capes, A. J. (Stoke C), 1903 v S (1)

Carr, J. (Middlesbrough), 1920 v Ni; 1923 v W (2)

Carr, J. (Newcastle U), 1905 v Ni; 1907 v Ni (2)

Carr, W. H. (Owlerton, Sheffield), 1875 v S (1)

Carter, H. S. (Sunderland), 1934 v S, H; 1936 v G; 1937 v S, Ni, H; (with Derby Co), 1947 v S, W, Ni, Ei, Ho, F, Sw (13)

Carter, J. H. (WBA), 1926 v Bel; 1929 v Bel, Sp (3)

Catlin, A. E. (Sheffield W), 1937 v W, Ni, H, N, Se (5)

Chadwick, A. (Southampton), 1900 v S, W (2)

Chadwick, E. (Everton), 1891 v S, W; 1892 v S; 1893 v S; 1894 v S; 1896 v Ni; 1897 v S (7)

Chamberlain, M (Stoke C), 1983 v L (sub); 1984 v D (sub), S, USSR, Br, U, Ch; 1985 v Fi (sub) (8)

Chambers, H. (Liverpool), 1921 v S, W, Bel; 1923 v S, W, Ni, Bel; 1924 v Ni (8)

Channon, M. R. (Southampton), 1973 v Y, S (2), Ni, W, Cz, USSR, I; 1974 v A, Pol, I, P, W, Ni, S, Arg, EG, Bul, Y; 1975 v Cz, P, WG, Cy (2), Ni (sub), W, S; 1976 v Sw, Cz, P, W, Ni, S, Br, I, Fi; 1977 v Fi, I, L, Ni, W, S, Br (sub), Arg, U; (with Manchester C), 1978 v Sw (46)

Charles, G. A. (Nottingham F), 1991 v Nz, Mal (2)

Charlton, J. (Leeds U), 1965 v S, H, Y, WG, Se; 1966 v W, Ni, S, A, Sp, Pol (2), WG (2), Y, Fi, D, U, M, F, Arg, P; 1967 v W, S, Ni, Cz; 1968 v W, Sp; 1969 v W, R, F; 1970 v Ho (2), P, Cz (35)

Charlton, R. (Manchester U), 1958 v S, P, Y; 1959 v S, W, Ni, USSR, I, Br, Pe, M, US; 1960 v S, W, Se, Y, Sp, H; 1961 v Ni, W, S, L, P, Sp, M, I, A; 1962 v W, Ni, S, A, Sw, Pe, L, P, H, Arg, Bul, Br; 1963 v S, F, Br, Cz, EG, Sw; 1964 v S, W, Ni, R of W, U, P, Ei, Br, Arg, US (sub); 1965 v Ni, S, Ho; 1966 v W, Ni, S, A, Sp, WG (2), Y, Fi, N, Pol, U, M, F, Arg, P; 1967 v Ni, W, S, Cz; 1968 v W, Ni, S, USSR, USSR (2), Sp (2), Se, Y; 1969 v S, W, Ni, R (2), Bul, M, Br; 1970 v W, Ni, Ho (2), P, Co, Ec, Cz, R, Br, WG (106)

Charnley, R. O. (Blackpool), 1963 v F (1)

Charsley, C. C. (Small Heath), 1893 v Ni (1)

Chedgzoy, S. (Everton), 1920 v W; 1921 v W, S, Ni; 1922 v Ni; 1923 v S; 1924 v W; 1925 v Ni (8)

Chenery, C. J. (C Palace), 1872 v S; 1873 v S; 1874 v S (3)

Cherry, T. J. (Leeds U), 1976 v W, S (sub), Br, Fi; 1977 v Ei, I, L, Ni, S (sub), Br, Arg, U; 1978 v Sw, L, I, Br, W; 1979 v Cz, W, Se; 1980 v Ei, Arg (sub), W, Ni, S, Aus, Sp (sub) (27)

Chilton, A. (Manchester U), 1951 v Ni; 1952 v F (2)

Chippendale, H. (Blackburn R), 1894 v Ni (1)

Chivers, M. (Tottenham H), 1971 v Ma (2), Gr, Ni, S; 1972 v Sw (1+1 sub), Gr, WG (2), Ni (sub), S; 1973 v W (3), S (2), Ni, Cz, Pol, USSR, I; 1974 v A, Pol (24)

Christian, E. (Old Etonians), 1879 v S (1)

Clamp, E. (Wolverhampton W), 1958 v USSR (2), Br, A (4)

Clapton, D. R. (Arsenal), 1959 v W (1)

Clare, T. (Stoke C), 1889 v Ni; 1892 v Ni; 1893 v W; 1894 v S (4)

Clarke, A. J. (Leeds U), 1970 v Cz; 1971 v EG, Ma, Ni, W (sub), S (sub); 1973 v S (2), W, Cz, Pol, USSR, I; 1974 v A, Pol, I; 1975 v P; 1976 v Cz, P (sub) (19)

Clarke, H. A. (Tottenham H), 1954 v S (1)

Clay, T. (Tottenham H), 1920 v W; 1922 v W, S, Ni (4)

Clayton, R. (Blackburn R), 1956 v Ni, Br, Se, Fi, WG, Sp; 1957 v S, W, Ni, Y, D (2), Ei (2); 1958 v S, W, Ni, F, P, Y, USSR; 1959 v S, W, Ni, USSR, I, Br, Pe, M, US; 1960 v W, Ni, S, Se, Y (35)

Clegg, J. C. (Sheffield W), 1872 v S (1)

Clegg, W. E. (Sheffield W), 1873 v S; (with Sheffield Albion), 1879 v W (2)

Clemence, R. N. (Liverpool), 1973 v W (2); 1974 v EG, Bul, Y; 1975 v Cz, P, WG, Cy, Ni, W, S; 1976 v Sw, Cz, P, W (2), Ni, S, Br, Fi; 1977 v Ei, Fi, I, Ho, L, S, Br, Arg, U; 1978 v Sw, L, I, WG, Ni, S; 1979 v D, Ei, Ni (2), S, Bul, A (sub); 1980 v D, Bul, Ei, Arg, W, S, Bel, Sp; 1981 v R, Sp, Br, Sw, H; (with Tottenham H), 1982 v N, Ni, Fi; 1983 v L; 1984 v L (61)

Clement, D. T. (QPR), 1976 v W (sub + 1), I; 1977 v I, Ho (5)

Clough, B. H. (Middlesbrough), 1960 v W, Se (2)

Clough, N. H. (Nottingham F), 1989 v Ch; 1991 v Arg (sub), Aus, Mal (4)

Coates, R. (Burnley), 1970 v Ni; 1971 v Gr (sub); (with Tottenham H), Ma, W (4)

Cobbold, W. N. (Cambridge University), 1883 v S, Ni; 1885 v S, Ni; 1886 v S, W; (with Old Carthusians), 1887 v S, W, Ni (9)

Cock, J. G. (Huddersfield T), 1920 v Ni; (with Chelsea), v S (2)

Cockburn, H. (Manchester U), 1947 v W, Ni, Ei; 1948 v S, I; 1949 v S, Ni, D, Sw, Se; 1951 v Arg, P; 1952 v F (13)

Cohen, G. R. (Fulham), 1964 v U, P, Ei, US, Br; 1965 v W, S, Ni, Bel, H, Ho, Y, WG, Se; 1966 v W, S, Ni, A, Sp, Pol (2), WG (2), N, D, U, M, F, Arg, P; 1967 v W, S, Ni, Cz, Sp; 1968 v W, Ni (37)

Coleclough, H. (C Palace), 1914 v W (1)

Coleman, E. H. (Dulwich Hamlet), 1921 v W (1)

Coleman, J. (Woolwich Arsenal), 1907 v Ni (1)

Common, A. (Sheffield U), 1904 v W, Ni; (with Middlesbrough), 1906 v W (3)

Compton, L. H. (Arsenal), 1951 v W, Y (2)

Conlin, J. (Bradford C), 1906 v S (1)

Connelly, J. M. (Burnley), 1960 v W, N, S, Se; 1962 v W, A, Sw, P; 1963 v W, F; (with Manchester U), 1965 v H, Y, Se; 1966 v W, Ni, S, A, N, D, U (20)

Cook, T. E. R. (Brighton), 1925 v W (1)

Cooper, N. C. (Cambridge University), 1893 v Ni (1)

Cooper, T. (Derby Co), 1928 v Ni; 1929 v W, Ni, S, F, Bel, Sp; 1931 v F; 1932 v W, Sp; 1933 v S; 1934 v S, H, Cz; 1935 v W (15)

Cooper, T. (Leeds U), 1969 v W, S, F, M; 1970 v Ho, Bel, Co, Ec, R, Cz, Br, WG; 1971 v EG, Ma, Ni, W, S; 1972 v Sw (2); 1975 v P (20)

Coppell, S. J. (Manchester U), 1978 v I, WG, Br, W, Ni, S, H; 1979 v D, Ei, Cz, Ni (2), W (sub), S, Bul, A; 1980 v D, Ni, Ei (sub), Sp, Arg, W, S, Bel, I; 1981 v R (sub), Sw, R, Br, W, S, Sw, H; 1982 v H, S, Fi, F, Cz, K, WG; 1983 v L, Gr (42)

Copping, W. (Leeds U), 1933 v I, Sw; 1934 v S, Ni, W, F; (with Arsenal), 1935 v Ni, I; 1936 v A, Bel; 1937 v N, Se, Fi; 1938 v S, W, Ni, Cz; 1939 v W, R of E; (with Leeds U), R (20)

Corbett, B. O. (Corinthians), 1901 v W (1)

Corbett, R. (Old Malvernians), 1903 v W (1)

Corbett, W. S. (Birmingham), 1908 v A, H, B (3)

Corrigan, J. T. (Manchester C), 1976 v I (sub), Br; 1979 v W; 1980 v Ni, Aus; 1981 v W, S; 1982 v W, Ic (9)

Cottee, A. R. (West Ham U), 1987 v Se (sub), Ni (sub); 1988 v H (sub); (with Everton) 1989 v D (sub), Se (sub), Ch (sub), S (7)

Cotterill, G. H. (Cambridge University), 1891 v Ni; (with Old Brightonians), 1892 v W; 1893 v S, Ni (4)

Cottle, J. R. (Bristol C), 1909 v Ni (1)

Cowan, S. (Manchester C), 1926 v Bel; 1930 v A; 1931 v Bel (3)

Cowans, G. (Aston Villa), 1983 v W, H, Ni, S, Aus (3); (with Bari), 1986 v Eg, USSR; (with Aston Villa), 1991 v Ei (10)

Cowell, A. (Blackburn R), 1910 v Ni (1)

Cox, J. (Liverpool), 1901 v Ni; 1902 v S; 1903 v S (3)

Cox, J. D. (Derby Co), 1892 v Ni (1)

Crabtree, J. W. (Burnley), 1894 v Ni; 1895 v Ni, S; (with

Aston Villa), 1896 v W, S, Ni; 1899 v S, W, Ni; 1900 v S, W, Ni; 1901 v W; 1902 v W (14)

Crawford, J. F. (Chelsea), 1931 v S (1)

Crawford, R. (Ipswich T), 1962 v Ni, A (2)

Crawshaw, T. H. (Sheffield W), 1895 v Ni; 1896 v S, W, Ni; 1897 v S, W, Ni; 1901 v Ni; 1904 v W, Ni (10)

Crayston, W. J. (Arsenal), 1936 v S, W, G, A, Bel; 1938 v W, Ni, Cz (8)

Creek, F. N. S. (Corinthians), 1923 v F (1)

Cresswell, W. (South Shields), 1921 v W; (with Sunderland), 1923 v F; 1924 v Bel; 1925 v Ni; 1926 v W; 1927 v Ni; (with Everton), 1930 v Ni (7)

Crompton, R. (Blackburn R), 1902 v S, W, Ni; 1903 v S, W; 1904 v S, W, Ni; 1906 v S, W, Ni; 1907 v S, W, Ni; 1908 v S, W, Ni, A (2), H, B; 1909 v S, W, Ni, H (2), A; 1910 v S, W; 1911 v S, W, Ni; 1912 v S, W, Ni; 1913 v S, W, Ni; 1914 v S, W, Ni (41)

Crooks, S. D. (Derby Co), 1930 v S, G, A; 1931 v S, W, Ni, F, Bel; 1932 v S, W, Ni, Sp; 1933 v Ni, W, A; 1934 v S, Ni, W, F, H, Cz; 1935 v Ni; 1936 v S, W; 1937 v W, H (26)

Crowe, C. (Wolverhampton W), 1963 v F (1)

Cuggy, F. (Sunderland), 1913 v Ni; 1914 v Ni (2)

Cullis, S. (Wolverhampton W), 1938 v S, W, Ni, F, Cz; 1939 v S, Ni, R of E, N, I, R, Y (12)

Cunliffe, A. (Blackburn R), 1933 v Ni, W (2)

Cunliffe, D. (Portsmouth), 1900 v Ni (1)

Cunliffe, J. N. (Everton), 1936 v Bel (1)

Cunningham, L. (WBA), 1979 v W, Se, A (sub); (with Real Madrid), 1980 v Ei, Sp (sub); 1981 v R (sub) (6)

Currey, E. S. (Oxford University), 1890 v S, W (2)

Currie, A. W. (Sheffield U), 1972 v Ni; 1973 v USSR, I; 1974 v A, Pol, I; 1976 v Sw; (with Leeds U), 1978 v Br, W (sub), Ni, S, H (sub); 1979 v Cz, Ni (2), W, Se (17)

Cursham, A. W. (Notts Co), 1876 v S; 1877 v S; 1878 v S; 1879 v W; 1883 v S, W (6)

Cursham, H. A. (Notts Co), 1880 v W; 1882 v S, W, Ni; 1883 v S, W, Ni; 1884 v Ni (8)

Daft, H. B. (Notts Co), 1889 v Ni; 1890 v S, W; 1891 v Ni; 1892 v Ni (5)

Danks, T. (Nottingham F), 1885 v S (1)

Davenport, P. (Nottingham F), 1985 v Ei (sub) (1)

Davenport, J. K. (Bolton W), 1885 v W; 1890 v Ni (2)

Davis, G. (Derby Co), 1904 v W, Ni (2)

Davis, H. (Sheffield W), 1903 v S, W, Ni (3)

Davison, J. E. (Sheffield W), 1922 v W (1)

Dawson, J. (Burnley), 1922 v S, Ni (2)

Day, S. H. (Old Malvernians), 1906 v Ni, W, S (3)

Dean, W. R. (Everton), 1927 v S, W, F, Bel, L; 1928 v S, W, Ni, F, Bel; 1929 v S, W, Ni; 1931 v S; 1932 v Sp; 1933 v Ni (16)

Deane, B. C. (Sheffield U), 1991 v Nz (sub + 1) (2)

Deeley, N. V. (Wolverhampton W), 1959 v Br, Pe (2)

Devey, J. H. G. (Aston Villa), 1892 v Ni; 1894 v Ni (2)

Devonshire, A. (West Ham U), 1980 v Aus (sub), Ni; 1982 v Ho, Ic; 1983 v WG, W, Gr; 1984 v L (8)

Dewhurst, F. (Preston NE), 1886 v W, Ni; 1887 v S, W, Ni; 1888 v S, W, Ni; 1889 v W (9)

Dewhurst, G. P. (Liverpool Ramblers), 1895 v W (1)

Dickinson, J. W. (Portsmouth), 1949 v N, F; 1950 v S, W, Ei, P, Bel, Ch, US, Sp; 1951 v Ni, W, Y; 1952 v W, Ni, S, A (2), I, Sw; 1953 v W, Ni, S, Bel, Arg, Ch, U, US; 1954 v W, Ni, S, R of E, H (2), Y, Bel, Sw, U; 1955 v Sp, P; 1956 v W, Ni, S, D, Sp; 1957 v W, Y, D (48)

Dimmock, J. H. (Tottenham H), 1921 v S; 1926 v W, Bel (3)

Ditchburn, E. G. (Tottenham H), 1949 v Sw, Se; 1953 v US; 1957 v W, Y, D (6)

Dix, R. W. (Derby Co), 1939 v N (1)

Dixon, J. A. (Notts Co), 1885 v W (1)

Dixon, K. M. (Chelsea), 1985 v M (sub), WG, US; 1986 v Ni, Is, M (sub), Pol (sub); 1987 v Se (8)

Dixon, L. M. (Arsenal), 1990 v Cz; 1991 v H, Pol, Ei (2), Cam, T, Arg (8)

Dobson, A. T. C. (Notts Co), 1882 v Ni; 1884 v S, W, Ni (4)

Dobson, C. F. (Notts Co), 1886 v Ni (1)

Dobson, J. M. (Burnley), 1974 v P, EG, Bul, Y; (with Everton), 1975 v Cz (5)

Doggart, A. G. (Corinthians), 1924 v Bel (1)

Dorigo, A. R. (Chelsea), 1990 v Y (sub), Cz (sub), D (sub), I; 1991 v H (sub), USSR (6)

Dorrell, A. R. (Aston Villa), 1925 v W, Bel, F; 1926 v Ni (4)

Douglas, B. (Blackburn R), 1958 v S, W, Ni, F, P, Y, USSR (2), Br, A; 1959 v S, USSR; 1960 v Y, H; 1961 v Ni, W, S, L, P, Sp, M, I, A; 1962 v W, Ni, S, Pe, L, P, H, Arg, Bul, Br; 1963 v S, Br, Sw (36)

Downs, R. W. (Everton), 1921 v Ni (1)

Doyle, M. (Manchester C), 1976 v W, S (sub), Br, I; 1977 v Ho (5)

Drake, E. J. (Arsenal), 1935 v Ni, I; 1936 v W; 1937 v H; 1938 v F (5)

Ducat, A. (Woolwich Arsenal), 1910 v S, W, Ni; (with Aston Villa), 1920 v S, W; 1921 v Ni (6)

Dunn, A. T. B. (Cambridge University), 1883 v Ni; 1884 v Ni; (with Old Etonians), 1892 v S, W (4)

Duxbury, M. (Manchester U), 1984 v L, F, W, S, USSR, Br, U, Ch; 1985 v EG, Fi (10)

Earle, S. G. J. (Clapton), 1924 v F; (with West Ham U), 1928 v Ni (2)

Eastham, G. (Arsenal), 1963 v Br, Cz, EG; 1964 v W, Ni, S, R of W, U, P, Ei, US, Br, Arg; 1965 v H, WG, Se; 1966 v Sp, Pol, D (19)

Eastham, G. R. (Bolton W), 1935 v Ho (1)

Eckersley, W. (Blackburn R), 1950 v Sp; 1951 v S, Y, Arg, P; 1952 v A (2), Sw; 1953 v Ni, Arg, Ch, U, US; 1954 v W, Ni, R of E, H (17)

Edwards, D. (Manchester U), 1955 v S, F, Sp, P; 1956 v S, Br, Se, Fi, WG; 1957 v S, Ni, Ei (2), D (2); 1958 v W, Ni, F (18)

Edwards, J. H. (Shropshire Wanderers), 1874 v S (1)

Edwards, W. (Leeds U), 1926 v S, W; 1927 v W, Ni, S, F, Bel, L; 1928 v S, F, Bel; 1929 v S, W, Ni; 1930 v W, Ni (16)

Ellerington, W. (Southampton), 1949 v N, F (2)

Elliott, G. W. (Middlesbrough), 1913 v Ni; 1914 v Ni; 1920 v W (3)

Elliott, W. H. (Burnley), 1952 v I, A; 1953 v Ni, W, Bel (5)

Evans, R. E. (Sheffield U), 1911 v S, W, Ni; 1912 v W (4)

Ewer, F. H. (Casuals), 1924 v F; 1925 v Bel (2)

Fairclough, P. (Old Foresters), 1878 v S (1)

Fairhurst, D. (Newcastle U), 1934 v F (1)

Fantham, J. (Sheffield W), 1962 v L (1)

Fashanu, J. (Wimbledon), 1989 v Ch, S (2)

Felton, W. (Sheffield W), 1925 v F (1)

Fenton, M. (Middlesbrough), 1938 v S (1)

Fenwick, T. (QPR), 1984 v W (sub), S, USSR, Br, U, Ch; 1985 v Fi, S, M, US; 1986 v R, T, Ni, Eg, M, P, Mor, Pol, Arg; (with Tottenham H), 1988 v Is (sub) (20)

Field, E. (Clapham Rovers), 1876 v S; 1881 v S (2)

Finney, T. (Preston NE), 1947 v W, Ni, Ei, Ho, F, P; 1948 v S, W, Ni, Bel, Se, I; 1949 v S, W, Ni, Se, N, F; 1950 v S, W, Ni, Ei, I, P, Bel, Ch, US, Sp; 1951 v S, Arg, P; 1952 v W, Ni, S, F, I, Sw, A; 1953 v W, Ni, S, Bel, Arg, Ch, U, US; 1954 v W, S, Bel, Sw, U, H, Y; 1955 v WG; 1956 v S, W, Ni, D, Sp; 1957 v S, W, Y, D (2), Ei (2); 1958 v W, S, F, P, Y, USSR (76)

Fleming, H. J. (Swindon T), 1909 v S, H (2); 1910 v W, Ni; 1911 v W, Ni; 1912 v Ni; 1913 v S, W; 1914 v S (11)

Fletcher, A. (Wolverhampton W), 1889 v W; 1890 v W (2)

Flowers, R. (Wolverhampton W), 1955 v F; 1959 v S, W, I, Br, Pe, US, M (sub); 1960 v W, Ni, S, Se, Y, Sp, H;

1961 v Ni, W, S, L, P, Sp, M, I, A; 1962 v W, Ni, S, A, Sw, Pe, L, P, H, Arg, Bul, Br; 1963 v Ni, W, S, F (2), Sw; 1964 v Ei, US, P; 1965 v W, Ho, WG; 1966 v N (49)

Forman, Frank (Nottingham F), 1898 v S, Ni; 1899 v S, W, Ni; 1901 v S; 1902 v S, Ni; 1903 v W (9)

Forman, F. R. (Nottingham F), 1899 v S, W, Ni (3)

Forrest, J. H. (Blackburn R), 1884 v W; 1885 v S, W, Ni; 1886 v S, W; 1887 v S, W, Ni; 1889 v S; 1890 v Ni (11)

Fort, J. (Millwall), 1921 v Bel (1)

Foster, R. E. (Oxford University), 1900 v W; (with Corinthians), 1901 v W, Ni, S; 1902 v W (5)

Foster, S. (Brighton & HA), 1982 v Ni, Ho, K (3)

Foulke, W. J. (Sheffield U), 1897 v W (1)

Foulkes, W. A. (Manchester U), 1955 v Ni (1)

Fox, F. S. (Gillingham), 1925 v F (1)

Francis, G. C. J. (QPR), 1975 v Cz, P, W, S; 1976 v Sw, Cz, P, W, Ni, S, Br, Fi (12)

Francis, T. (Birmingham C), 1977 v Ho, L, S, Br; 1978 v Sw, L, I (sub), WG (sub), Br, W, S, H; (with Nottingham F), 1979 v Bul (sub), Se, A (sub); 1980 v Ni, Bul, Sp; 1981 v Sp, R, S (sub), Sw; (with Manchester C), 1982 v N, Ni, W, S (sub), Fi (sub), F, Cz, K, WG, Sp; (with Sampdoria), 1983 v D, Gr, H, Ni, S, Aus (3); 1984 v D, Ni, USSR; 1985 v EG (sub), T (sub), Ni (sub), R, Fi, S, I, M; 1986 v S (52)

Franklin, C. F. (Stoke C), 1947 v S, W, Ni, Ei, Ho, F, Sw, P; 1948 v S, W, Ni, Bel, Se, I; 1949 v S, W, Ni, D, Sw, N, F, Se; 1950 v W, S, Ni, Ei, I (27)

Freeman, B. C. (Everton), 1909 v S, W; (with Burnley), 1912 v S, W, Ni (5)

Froggatt, J. (Portsmouth), 1950 v Ni, I; 1951 v S; 1952 v S, A (2), I, Sw; 1953 v Ni, W, S, Bel, US (13)

Froggatt, R. (Sheffield W), 1953 v W, S, Bel, US (4)

Fry, C. B. (Corinthians), 1901 v Ni (1)

Furness, W. I. (Leeds U), 1933 v I (1)

Galley, T. (Wolverhampton W), 1937 v N, Se (2)

Gardner, T. (Aston Villa), 1934 v Cz; 1935 v Ho (2)

Garfield, B. (WBA), 1898 v W (1)

Garratty, W. (Aston Villa), 1903 v W (1)

Garrett, T. (Blackpool), 1952 v S, I; 1954 v W (3)

Gascoigne, P. J. (Tottenham H), 1989 v D (sub), S.Ar (sub), Alb (sub), Ch, S (sub); 1990 v Se (sub), Br (sub), Cz, D, U, Tun, Ei, Ho, Eg, Bel, Cam, WG; 1991 v H, Pol, Cam (20)

Gates, E. (Ipswich T), 1981 v N, R (2)

Gay, L. H. (Cambridge University), 1893 v S; (with Old Brightonians), 1894 v S, W (3)

Geary, F. (Everton), 1890 v Ni; 1891 v S (2)

Geaves, R. L. (Clapham Rovers), 1875 v S (1)

Gee, C. W. (Everton), 1932 v W, Sp; 1937 v Ni (3)

Geldard, A. (Everton), 1933 v I, Sw; 1935 v S; 1938 v Ni (4)

George, C. (Derby Co), 1977 v Ei (1)

George, W. (Aston Villa), 1902 v S, W, Ni (3)

Gibbins, W. V. T. (Clapton), 1924 v F; 1925 v F (2)

Gidman, J. (Aston Villa), 1977 v L (1)

Gillard, I. T. (QPR), 1975 v WG, W; 1976 v Cz (3)

Gilliat, W. E. (Old Carthusians), 1893 v Ni (1)

Goddard, P. (West Ham U), 1982 v Ic (sub) (1)

Goodall, F. R. (Huddersfield T), 1926 v S; 1927 v S, F, Bel, L; 1928 v S, W, F, Bel; 1930 v S, G, A; 1931 v S, W, Ni, Bel; 1932 v Ni; 1933 v W, Ni, A, I, Sw; 1934 v W, Ni, F (25)

Goodall, J. (Preston NE), 1888 v S, W; 1889 v S, W; (with Derby Co), 1891 v S, W; 1892 v S; 1893 v W; 1894 v S; 1895 v S, Ni; 1896 v S, W; 1898 v W (14)

Goodhart, H. C. (Old Etonians), 1883 v S, W, Ni (3)

Goodwyn, A. G. (Royal Engineers), 1873 v S (1)

Goodyer, A. C. (Nottingham F), 1879 v S (1)

Gosling, R. C. (Old Etonians), 1892 v W; 1893 v S; 1894 v W; 1895 v W, S (5)

Gosnell, A. A. (Newcastle U), 1906 v Ni (1)

Gough, H. C. (Sheffield U), 1921 v S (1)

Goulden, L. A. (West Ham U), 1937 v Se, N; 1938 v W, Ni, Cz, G, Sw, F; 1939 v S, W, R of E, I, R, Y (14)

Graham, L. (Millwall), 1925 v S, W (2)

Graham, T. (Nottingham F), 1931 v F; 1932 v Ni (2)

Grainger, C. (Sheffield U), 1956 v Br, Se, Fi, WG; 1957 v W, Ni; (with Sunderland), 1957 v S (7)

Greaves, J. (Chelsea), 1959 v Pe, M, US; 1960 v W, Se, Y, Sp; 1961 v Ni, W, S, L, P, Sp, I, A; (with Tottenham H), 1962 v S, Sw, Pe, H, Arg, Bul, Br; 1963 v Ni, W, S, F (2), Br, Cz, Sw; 1964 v W, Ni, R of W, P (2), Ei, Br, U, Arg; 1965 v Ni, S, Bel, Ho, H, Y; 1966 v W, A, Y, N, D, Pol, U, M, F; 1967 v S, Sp, A (57)

Green, F. T. (Wanderers), 1876 v S (1)

Green, G. H. (Sheffield U), 1925 v F; 1926 v S, Bel, W; 1927 v W, Ni; 1928 v F, Bel (8)

Greenhalgh, E. H. (Notts Co), 1872 v S; 1873 v S (2)

Greenhoff, B. (Manchester U), 1976 v W, Ni; 1977 v Ei, Fi, I, Ho, Ni, W, S, Br, Arg, U; 1978 v Br, W, Ni, S (sub); (with Leeds U), 1980 v Aus (sub) (18)

Greenwood, D. H. (Blackburn R), 1882 v S, Ni (2)

Gregory, J. (QPR), 1983 v Aus (3); 1984 v D, H, W (6)

Grimsdell, A. (Tottenham H), 1920 v S, W; 1921 v S, Ni; 1923 v W, Ni (6)

Grosvenor, A. T. (Birmingham), 1934 v Ni, W, F (3)

Gunn, M. (Notts Co), 1884 v S, W (2)

Gurney, R. (Sunderland), 1935 v S (1)

Hacking, J. (Oldham Ath), 1929 v S, W, Ni (3)

Hadley, N. (WBA), 1903 v Ni (1)

Hagan, J. (Sheffield U), 1949 v D (1)

Haines, J. T. W. (WBA), 1949 v Sw (1)

Hall, A. E. (Aston Villa), 1910 v Ni (1)

Hall, G. W. (Tottenham H), 1934 v F; 1938 v S, W, Ni, Cz; 1939 v S, Ni, R of E, I, Y (10)

Hall, J. (Birmingham C), 1956 v S, W, Ni, Br, Se, Fi, WG, D, Sp; 1957 v S, W, Ni, Y, D (2), Ei (2) (17)

Halse, H. J. (Manchester U), 1909 v A (1)

Hammond, H. E. D. (Oxford University), 1889 v S (1)

Hampson, J. (Blackpool), 1931 v Ni, W; 1933 v A (3)

Hampton, H. (Aston Villa), 1913 v S, W; 1914 v S, W (4)

Hancocks, J. (Wolverhampton W), 1949 v Sw; 1950 v W; 1951 v Y (3)

Hapgood, E. (Arsenal), 1933 v I, Sw; 1934 v S, Ni, W, H, Cz; 1935 v S, Ni, W, I, Ho; 1936 v S, Ni, W, G, A, Bel; 1937 v Fi; 1938 v S, G, Sw, F; 1939 v S, W, Ni, R of E, N, I, Y (30)

Hardinge, H. T. W. (Sheffield U), 1910 v S (1)

Hardman, H. P. (Everton), 1905 v W; 1907 v S, Ni; 1908 v W (4)

Hardwick, G. F. M. (Middlesbrough), 1947 v S, W, Ni, Ei, Ho, F, Sw, P; 1948 v S, W, Ni, Bel, Se (13)

Hardy, H. (Stockport Co), 1925 v Bel (1)

Hardy, S. (Liverpool), 1907 v S, W, Ni; 1908 v S; 1909 v S, W, Ni, H (2), A; 1910 v S, W, Ni; 1912 v Ni; (with Aston Villa), 1913 v S; 1914 v Ni, W, S; 1920 v S, W, Ni (21)

Harford, M. G. (Luton T), 1988 v Is (sub); 1989 v D (2)

Hargreaves, F. W. (Blackburn R), 1880 v W; 1881 v W; 1882 v Ni (3)

Hargreaves, J. (Blackburn R), 1881 v S, W (2)

Harper, E. C. (Blackburn R), 1926 v S (1)

Harris, G. (Burnley), 1966 v Pol (1)

Harris, P. P. (Portsmouth), 1950 v Ei; 1954 v H (2)

Harris, S. S. (Cambridge University), 1904 v S; (with Old Westminsters), 1905 v Ni, W; 1906 v S, W, Ni (6)

Harrison, A. H. (Old Westminsters), 1893 v S, Ni (2)

Harrison, G. (Everton), 1921 v Bel; 1922 v Ni (2)

Harrow, J. H. (Chelsea), 1923 v Ni, Se (2)

Hart, E. (Leeds U), 1929 v W; 1930 v W, Ni; 1933 v S, A; 1934 v S, H, Cz (8)

Hartley, F. (Oxford C), 1923 v F (1)

Harvey, A. (Wednesbury Strollers), 1881 v W (1)

Harvey, J. C. (Everton), 1971 v Ma (1)

Hassall, H. W. (Huddersfield T), 1951 v S, Arg, P; 1952 v F; (with Bolton W), 1954 v Ni (5)

Hateley, M. (Portsmouth), 1984 v USSR (sub), Br, U, Ch; (with AC Milan), 1985 v EG (sub), Fi, Ni, Ei, Fi, S, I, M; 1986 v R, T, Eg, S, M, Ca, P, Mor, Para (sub); 1987 v T (sub), Br (sub), S; (with Monaco), 1988 v WG (sub), Ho (sub), H (sub), Co (sub), Ei (sub), Ho (sub), USSR (sub) (31)

Haworth, G. (Accrington), 1887 v Ni, W, S; 1888 v S; 1890 v S (5)

Hawtrey, J. P. (Old Etonians), 1881 v S, W (2)

Hawkes, R. M. (Luton T), 1907 v Ni; 1908 v A (2), H, B (5)

Haygarth, E. B. (Swifts), 1875 v S (1)

Haynes, J. N. (Fulham), 1955 v Ni; 1956 v S, Ni, Br, Se, Fi, WG, Sp; 1957 v W, Y, D, Ei (2); 1958 v W, Ni, S, F, P, Y, USSR (3), Br, A; 1959 v S, Ni, USSR, I, Br, Pe, M, US; 1960 v Ni, Y, Sp, H; 1961 v Ni, W, S, L, P, Sp, M, I, A; 1962 v W, Ni, S, A, Sw, Pe, P, H, Arg, Bul, Br (56)

Healless, H. (Blackburn R), 1925 v Ni; 1928 v S (2)

Hector, K. J. (Derby Co), 1974 v Pol (sub), I (sub) (2)

Hedley, G. A. (Sheffield U), 1901 v Ni (1)

Hegan, K. E. (Corinthians), 1923 v Bel, F; 1924 v Ni, Bel (4)

Hellawell, M. S. (Birmingham C), 1963 v Ni, F (2)

Henfrey, A. G. (Cambridge University), 1891 v Ni; (with Corinthians), 1892 v W; 1895 v W; 1896 v S, W (5)

Henry, R. P. (Tottenham H), 1963 v F (1)

Heron, F. (Wanderers), 1876 v S (1)

Heron, G. H. H. (Uxbridge), 1873 v S; 1874 v S; (with Wanderers), 1875 v S; 1876 v S; 1878 v S (5)

Hibbert, W. (Bury), 1910 v S (1)

Hibbs, H. E. (Birmingham), 1930 v S, W, A, G; 1931 v S, W, Ni; 1932 v W, Ni, Sp; 1933 v S, W, Ni, A, I, Sw; 1934 v Ni, W, F; 1935 v S, W, Ni, Ho; 1936 v G, W (25)

Hill, F. (Bolton W), 1963 v Ni, W (2)

Hill, G. A. (Manchester U), 1976 v I; 1977 v Ei (sub), Fi (sub), L; 1978 v Sw (sub), L (6)

Hill, J. H. (Burnley), 1925 v W; 1926 v S; 1927 v S, Ni, Bel, F; 1928 v Ni, W; 1929 v F, Bel, Sp (11)

Hill, R. (Luton T), 1983 v D (sub), WG; 1986 v Eg (sub) (3)

Hill, R. H. (Millwall), 1926 v Bel (1)

Hillman, J. (Burnley), 1899 v Ni (1)

Hills, A. F. (Old Harrovians), 1879 v S (1)

Hilsdon, G. R. (Chelsea), 1907 v Ni; 1908 v S, W, Ni, A, H, B; 1909 v Ni (8)

Hine, E. W. (Leicester C), 1929 v W, Ni; 1930 v W, Ni; 1932 v W, Ni (6)

Hinton, A. T. (Wolverhampton W), 1963 v F; (with Nottingham F), 1965 v W, Bel (3)

Hirst, D. E. (Sheffield W), 1991 v Aus, Nz (sub) (2)

Hitchens, G. A. (Aston Villa), 1961 v M, I, A; (with Inter-Milan), 1962 v Sw, Pe, H, Br (7)

Hobbis, H. H. F. (Charlton Ath), 1936 v A, Bel (2)

Hoddle, G. (Tottenham H), 1980 v Bul, W, Aus, Sp; 1981 v Sp, W, S; 1982 v N, Ni, W, Ic, Cz (sub), K; 1983 v L (sub), Ni, S; 1984 v H, L, F; 1985 v Ei (sub), S, I (sub), M, WG, US; 1986 v R, T, Ni, Is, USSR, S, M, Ca, P, Mor, Pol, Para, Arg; 1987 v Se, Ni, Y; (with Monaco), 1988 v WG, T (sub), Y (sub), Ho (sub), H (sub), Co (sub), Ei (sub), Ho, USSR (53)

Hodge, S. B. (Aston Villa), 1986 v USSR (sub), S, Ca, P (sub), Mor (sub), Pol, Para, Arg; 1987 v Se, Ni, Y; (with Tottenham H), Sp, Ni, T, S; (with Nottingham F), 1989 v D; 1990 v I (sub), Y (sub), Cz, D, U, Tun; 1991 v Cam (sub), T (sub) (24)

Hodgetts, D. (Aston Villa), 1888 v S, W, Ni; 1892 v S, Ni; 1894 v Ni (6)

Hodgkinson, A. (Sheffield U), 1957 v S, Ei (2), D; 1961 v W (5)

1948 v Se; (with Preston NE), 1949 v D, Se; (with Bolton W), 1950 v S; 1951 v Ni (11)

Latchford, R. D. (Everton), 1978 v I, Br, W; 1979 v D, Ei, Cz (sub), Ni (2), W, S, Bul, A (12)

Latheron, E. G. (Blackburn R), 1913 v W; 1914 v Ni (2)

Lawler, C. (Liverpool), 1971 v Ma, W, S; 1972 v Sw (4)

Lawton, T. (Everton), 1939 v S, W, Ni, R of E, N, I, R, Y; (with Chelsea), 1947 v S, W, Ni, Ei, Ho, F, Sw, P; 1948 v W, Ni, Bel; (with Notts Co), 1948 v S, Se, I; 1949 v D (23)

Leach, T. (Sheffield W), 1931 v W, Ni (2)

Leake, A. (Aston Villa), 1904 v S, Ni; 1905 v S, W, Ni (5)

Lee, E. A. (Southampton), 1904 v W (1)

Lee, F. H. (Manchester C), 1969 v Ni, W, S, Bul, F, M, U; 1970 v W, Ho (2), P, Bel, Co, Ec, R, Br, WG; 1971 v EG, Gr, Ma, Ni, W, S; 1972 v Sw (2), Gr, WG (27)

Lee, J. (Derby Co), 1951 v Ni (1)

Lee, S. (Liverpool), 1983 v Gr, L, W, Gr, H, S, Aus; 1984 v D, H, L, F, Ni, W, Ch (sub) (14)

Leighton, J. E. (Nottingham F), 1886 v Ni (1)

Lilley, H. E. (Sheffield U), 1892 v W (1)

Linacre, H. J. (Nottingham F), 1905 v W, S (2)

Lindley, T. (Cambridge University), 1886 v S, W, Ni; 1887 v S, W, Ni; 1888 v S, W, Ni; (with Nottingham F), 1889 v S; 1890 v S, W; 1891 v Ni (13)

Lindsay, A. (Liverpool), 1974 v Arg, EG, Bul, Y (4)

Lindsay, W. (Wanderers), 1877 v S (1)

Lineker, G. (Leicester C), 1984 v S (sub); 1985 v Ei, R (sub), S (sub), I (sub), WG, US; (with Everton), 1986 v R, T, Ni, Eg, USSR, Ca, P, Mor, Pol, Para, Arg; (with Barcelona), 1987 v Ni (2), Y, Sp, T, Br; 1988 v WG, T, Y, Ho, H, S, Co, Sw, Ei, Ho, USSR; 1989 v Se, S.Ar, Gr, Alb (2), Pol, D; (with Tottenham H) 1990 v Se, Pol, I, Y, Br, Cz, D, U, Tun, Ei, Ho, Eg, Bel, Cam, WG, I; 1991 v H, Pol, Ei (2), Cam, T, Arg, Aus, Nz, Mal (68)

Lintott, E. H. (QPR), 1908 v S, W, Ni; (with Bradford C), 1909 v S, Ni, H (2) (7)

Lipsham, H. B. (Sheffield U), 1902 v W (1)

Little, B. (Aston Villa), 1975 v W (sub) (1)

Lloyd, L. V. (Liverpool), 1971 v W; 1972 v Sw, Ni; (with Nottingham F), 1980 v W (4)

Lockett, A. (Stoke C), 1903 v Ni (1)

Lodge, L. V. (Cambridge University), 1894 v W; 1895 v S, W; (with Corinthians), 1896 v S, Ni (5)

Lofthouse, J. M. (Blackburn R), 1885 v S, W, Ni; 1887 v S, W; (with Accrington), 1889 v Ni; (with Blackburn R), 1890 v Ni (7)

Lofthouse, N. (Bolton W), 1951 v Y; 1952 v W, Ni, S, A (2), I, Sw; 1953 v W, Ni, S, Bel, Arg, Ch, U, US; 1954 v W, Ni, R of E, Bel, U; 1955 v Ni, S, F, Sp, P; 1956 v W, S, Sp, D, Fi (sub); 1959 v W, USSR (33)

Longworth, E. (Liverpool), 1920 v S; 1921 v Bel; 1923 v S, W, Bel (5)

Lowder, A. (Wolverhampton W), 1889 v W (1)

Lowe, E. (Aston Villa), 1947 v F, Sw, P (3)

Lucas, T. (Liverpool), 1922 v Ni; 1924 v F; 1926 v Bel (3)

Luntley, E. (Nottingham F), 1880 v S, W (2)

Lyttelton, Hon. A. (Cambridge University), 1877 v S (1)

Lyttelton, Hon. E. (Cambridge University), 1878 v S (1)

McCall, J. (Preston NE), 1913 v S, W; 1914 v S; 1920 v S; 1921 v Ni (5)

McDermott, T. (Liverpool), 1978 v Sw, L; 1979 v Ni, W, Se; 1980 v D, Ni (sub), Ei, Ni, S, Bel (sub), Sp; 1981 v N, R, Sw, R (sub), Br, Sw (sub), H; 1982 v N, H, W (sub), Ho, S (sub), Ic (25)

McDonald, C. A. (Burnley), 1958 v USSR (3), Br, A; 1959 v W, Ni, USSR (8)

McFarland, R. L. (Derby Co), 1971 v Gr, Ma (2), Ni, S; 1972 v Sw, Gr, WG, W, S; 1973 v W (3), Ni, S, Cz, Pol, USSR, I; 1974 v A, Pol, I, W, Ni; 1976 v Cz, S; 1977 v Ei, I (28)

McGarry, W. H. (Huddersfield T), 1954 v Sw, U; 1956 v W, D (4)

McGuinness, W. (Manchester U), 1959 v Ni, M (2)

McInroy, A. (Sunderland), 1927 v Ni (1)

McMahon, S. (Liverpool), 1988 v Is, H, Co, USSR; 1989 v D (sub); 1990 v Se, Pol, I, Y (sub), Br, Cz (sub), D, Ei (sub), Eg, Bel, I; 1991 v Ei (17)

McNab, R. (Arsenal), 1969 v Ni, Bul, R (1 + 1 sub) (4)

McNeal, R. (WBA), 1914 v S, W (2)

McNeil, M. (Middlesbrough), 1961 v W, Ni, S, L, P, Sp, M, I; 1962 v L (9)

Mabbutt, G. (Tottenham H), 1983 v WG, Gr, L, W, Gr, H, Ni, S (sub); 1984 v H; 1987 v Y, Ni, T; 1988 v WG (13)

Macaulay, R. H. (Cambridge University), 1881 v S (1)

Macdonald, M. (Newcastle U), 1972 v W, Ni, S (sub); 1973 v USSR (sub); 1974 v P, S (sub), Y (sub); 1975 v WG, Cy (2), Ni; 1976 v Sw (sub), Cz, P (14)

Macrae, S. (Notts Co), 1883 v S, W, Ni; 1884 v S, W, Ni (6)

Maddison, F. B. (Oxford University), 1872 v S (1)

Madeley, P. E. (Leeds U), 1971 v Ni; 1972 v Sw (2), Gr, WG (2), W, S; 1973 v S, Cz, Pol, USSR, I; 1974 v A, Pol, I; 1975 v Cz, P, Cy; 1976 v Cz, P, Fi; 1977 v Ei, Ho (24)

Magee, T. P. (WBA), 1923 v W, Se; 1925 v S, Bel, F (5)

Makepeace, H. (Everton), 1906 v S; 1910 v S; 1912 v S, W (4)

Male, C. G. (Arsenal), 1935 v S, Ni, I, Ho; 1936 v S, W, Ni, G, A, Bel; 1937 v S, Ni, H, N, Se, Fi; 1939 v I, R, Y (19)

Mannion, W. J. (Middlesbrough), 1947 v S, W, Ni, Ei, Ho, F, Sw, P; 1948 v W, Ni, Bel, Se, I; 1949 v N, F; 1950 v S, Ei, P, Bel, Ch, US; 1951 v Ni, W, S, Y; 1952 v F (26)

Mariner, P. (Ipswich T), 1977 v L (sub), Ni; 1978 v L, W (sub), S; 1980 v W, Ni (sub), S, Aus, I (sub), Sp (sub); 1981 v N, Sw, Sp, Sw, H; 1982 v N, H, Ho, S, Fi, F, Cz, K, WG, Sp; 1983 v D, WG, Gr, W; 1984 v D, H, L; (with Arsenal), 1985 v EG, R (35)

Marsden, J. T. (Darwen), 1891 v Ni (1)

Marsden, W. (Sheffield W), 1930 v W, S, G (3)

Marsh, R. W. (QPR), 1972 v Sw (sub); (with Manchester C), WG (sub + 1), W, Ni, S; 1973 v W (2), Y (9)

Marshall, T. (Darwen), 1880 v W; 1881 v W (2)

Martin, A. (West Ham U), 1981 v Br, S (sub); 1982 v H, Fi; 1983 v Gr, L, W, Gr, H; 1984 v H, L, W; 1985 v Ni; 1986 v Is, Ca, Para; 1987 v Se (17)

Martin, H. (Sunderland), 1914 v Ni (1)

Marwood, B. (Arsenal), 1989 v S.Ar (sub) (1)

Maskrey, H. M. (Derby Co), 1908 v Ni (1)

Mason, C. (Wolverhampton W), 1887 v Ni; 1888 v W; 1890 v Ni (3)

Matthews, R. D. (Coventry C), 1956 v S, Br, Se, WG; 1957 v Ni (5)

Matthews, S. (Stoke C), 1935 v W, I; 1936 v G; 1937 v S; 1938 v S, W, Cz, G, Sw, F; 1939 v S, W, Ni, R of E, N, I, Y; 1947 v S; (with Blackpool), 1947 v Sw, P; 1948 v S, W, Ni, Bel, I; 1949 v S, W, Ni, D, Sw; 1950 v Sp; 1951 v Ni, S; 1954 v Ni, R of E, H, Bel, U; 1955 v Ni, W, S, F, WG, Sp, P; 1956 v W, Br; 1957 v S, W, Ni, Y, D (2), Ei (54)

Matthews, V. (Sheffield U), 1928 v F, Bel (2)

Maynard, W. J. (1st Surrey Rifles), 1872 v S; 1876 v S (2)

Meadows, J. (Manchester C), 1955 v S (1)

Medley, L. D. (Tottenham H), 1951 v Y, W; 1952 v F, A, W, Ni (6)

Meehan, T. (Chelsea), 1924 v Ni (1)

Melia, J. (Liverpool), 1963 v S, Sw (2)

Mercer, D. W. (Sheffield U), 1923 v Ni, Bel (2)

Mercer, J. (Everton), 1939 v S, Ni, I, R, Y (5)

Merrick, G. H. (Birmingham C), 1952 v Ni, S, A (2), I, Sw; 1953 v Ni, W, S, Bel, Arg, Ch, U; 1954 v W, Ni, S, R of E, H (2), Y, Bel, Sw, U (23)

Metcalfe, V. (Huddersfield T), 1951 v Arg, P (2)

Mew, J. W. (Manchester U), 1921 v Ni (1)

Middleditch, B. (Corinthians), 1897 v Ni (1)

Milburn, J. E. T. (Newcastle U), 1949 v S, W, Ni, Sw; 1950 v W, P, Bel, Sp; 1951 v W, Arg, P; 1952 v F; 1956 v D (13)

Miller, B. G. (Burnley), 1961 v A (1)

Miller, H. S. (Charlton Ath), 1923 v Se (1)

Mills, G. R. (Chelsea), 1938 v W, Ni, Cz (3)

Mills, M. D. (Ipswich T), 1973 v Y; 1976 v W (2), Ni, S, Br, I (sub), Fi; 1977 v Fi (sub), I, Ni, W, S; 1978 v WG, Br, W, Ni, S, H; 1979 v D, Ei, Ni (2), S, Bul, A; 1980 v D, Ni, Sp (2); 1981 v Sw (2), H; 1982 v N, H, S, Fi, F, Cz, K, WG, Sp (42)

Milne, G. (Liverpool), 1963 v Br, Cz, EG; 1964 v W, Ni, S, R of W, U, P, Ei, Br, Arg; 1965 v Ni, Bel (14)

Milton, C. A. (Arsenal), 1952 v A (1)

Milward, A. (Everton), 1891 v S, W; 1897 v S, W (4)

Mitchell, C. (Upton Park), 1880 v W; 1881 v S; 1883 v S, W; 1885 v W (5)

Mitchell, J. F. (Manchester C), 1925 v Ni (1)

Moffat, H. (Oldham Ath), 1913 v W (1)

Molyneux, G. (Southampton), 1902 v S; 1903 v S, W, Ni (4)

Moon, W. R. (Old Westminsters), 1888 v S, W; 1889 v S, W; 1890 v S, W; 1891 v S (7)

Moore, H. T. (Notts Co), 1883 v Ni; 1885 v W (2)

Moore, J. (Derby Co), 1923 v Se (1)

Moore, R. F. (West Ham U), 1962 v Pe, H, Arg, Bul, Br; 1963 v W, Ni, S, F (2), Br, Cz, EG, Sw; 1964 v W, Ni, S, R of W, U, P (2), Ei, Br, Arg; 1965 v Ni, S, Bel, H, Y, WG, Se; 1966 v W, Ni, S, A, Sp, Pol (2), WG (2), N, D, U, M, F, Arg, P; 1967 v W, Ni, S, Cz, Sp, A; 1968 v W, Ni, S, USSR (2), Sp (2), Se, Y, WG; 1969 v Ni, W, S, R, Bul, F, M, U, Br; 1970 v W, Ni, S, Ho, P, Bel, Co, Ec, R, Br, Cz, WG; 1971 v EG, Gr, Ma, Ni, S; 1972 v Sw (2), Gr, WG (2), W, S; 1973 v W (3), Y, S (2), Ni, Cz, Pol, USSR, I; 1974 v I (108)

Moore, W. G. B. (West Ham U), 1923 v Se (1)

Mordue, J. (Sunderland), 1912 v Ni; 1913 v Ni (2)

Morice, C. J. (Barnes), 1872 v S (1)

Morley, A. (Aston Villa), 1982 v H (sub), Ni, W, Ic; 1983 v D, Gr (6)

Morley, H. (Notts Co), 1910 v Ni (1)

Morren, T. (Sheffield U), 1898 v Ni (1)

Morris, F. (WBA), 1920 v S; 1921 v Ni (2)

Morris, J. (Derby Co), 1949 v N, F; 1950 v Ei (3)

Morris, W. W. (Wolverhampton W), 1939 v S, Ni, R (3)

Morse, H. (Notts Co), 1879 v S (1)

Mort, T. (Aston Villa), 1924 v W, F; 1926 v S (3)

Morten, A. (C Palace), 1873 v S (1)

Mortensen, S. H. (Blackpool), 1947 v P; 1948 v W, S, Ni, Bel, Se, I; 1949 v S, W, Ni, Se, N; 1950 v S, W, Ni, I, P, Bel, Ch, US, Sp; 1951 v S, Arg; 1954 v R of E, H (25)

Morton, J. R. (West Ham U), 1938 v Cz (1)

Mosforth, W. (Sheffield W), 1877 v S; (with Sheffield Albion), 1878 v S; 1879 v S, W; 1880 v S, W; (with Sheffield W), 1881 v W; 1882 v S, W (9)

Moss, F. (Arsenal), 1934 v S, H, Cz; 1935 v I (4)

Moss, F. (Aston Villa), 1922 v S, Ni; 1923 v Ni; 1924 v S, Bel (5)

Mosscrop, E. (Burnley), 1914 v S, W (2)

Mozley, B. (Derby Co), 1950 v W, Ni, Ei (3)

Mullen, J. (Wolverhampton W), 1947 v S; 1949 v N, F; 1950 v Bel (sub), Ch, US; 1954 v W, Ni, S, R of E, Y, Sw (12)

Mullery, A. P. (Tottenham H), 1965 v Ho; 1967 v Sp, A; 1968 v W, Ni, WG, S, USSR, Sp (2), Se, Y; 1969 v Ni, S, R, Bul, F, M, U, Br; 1970 v W, Ni, S (sub), Ho (sub), Bel, P, Co, Ec, R, Cz, WG, Br; 1971 v Ma, EG, Gr; 1972 v Sw (35)

Neal, P. G. (Liverpool), 1976 v W, I; 1977 v W, S, Br, Arg.

U; 1978 v Sw, I, WG, Ni, S, H; 1979 v D, Ei, Ni (2), S, Bul, A; 1980 v D, Ni, Sp, Arg, W, Bel, I; 1981 v R, Sw, Sp, Br, H; 1982 v N, H, W, Ho, Ic, F (sub), K; 1983 v D, Gr, L, W, Gr, H, Ni, S, Aus (2); 1984 v D (50)

Needham, E. (Sheffield U), 1894 v S; 1895 v S; 1897 v S, W, Ni; 1898 v S, W; 1899 v S, W, Ni; 1900 v S, Ni; 1901 v S, W, Ni; 1902 v W (16)

Newton, K. R. (Blackburn R), 1966 v S, WG; 1967 v Sp, A; 1968 v W, S, Sp, Se, Y, WG; 1969 v Ni, W, S, R, Bul, M, U, Br, F; (with Everton), 1970 v Ni, S, Ho, Co, Ec, R, Cz, WG (27)

Nicholls, J. (WBA), 1954 v S, Y (2)

Nicholson, W. E. (Tottenham H), 1951 v P (1)

Nish, D. J. (Derby Co), 1973 v Ni; 1974 v P, W, Ni, S (5)

Norman, M. (Tottenham H), 1962 v Pe, H, Arg, Bul, Br; 1963 v S, F, Br, Cz, EG; 1964 v W, Ni, S, R of W, U, P (2), US, Br, Arg; 1965 v Ni, Bel, Ho (23)

Nuttall, H. (Bolton W), 1928 v W, Ni; 1929 v S (3)

Oakley, W. J. (Oxford University), 1895 v W; 1896 v S, W, Ni; (with Corinthians), 1897 v S, W, Ni; 1898 v S, W, Ni; 1900 v S, W, Ni; 1901 v S, W, Ni (16)

O'Dowd, J. P. (Chelsea), 1932 v S; 1933 v Ni, Sw (3)

O'Grady, M. (Huddersfield T), 1963 v Ni; (with Leeds U), 1969 v F (2)

Ogilvie, R. A. M. M. (Clapham R), 1874 v S (1)

Oliver, L. F. (Fulham), 1929 v Bel (1)

Olney, B. A. (Aston Villa), 1928 v F, Bel (2)

Osborne, F. R. (Fulham), 1923 v Ni, F; (with Tottenham H), 1925 v Bel; 1926 v Bel (4)

Osborne, R. (Leicester C), 1928 v W (1)

Osgood, P. L. (Chelsea), 1970 v Bel, R (sub), Cz (sub); 1974 v I (4)

Osman, R. (Ipswich T), 1980 v Aus; 1981 v Sp, R, Sw; 1982 v N, Ic; 1983 v D, Aus (3); 1984 v D (11)

Ottaway, C. J. (Oxford University), 1872 v S; 1874 v S (2)

Owen, J. R. B. (Sheffield), 1874 v S (1)

Owen, S. W. (Luton T), 1954 v H, Y, Bel (3)

Page, L. A. (Burnley), 1927 v S, W, Bel, L, F; 1928 v W, Ni (7)

Paine, T. L. (Southampton), 1963 v Cz, EG; 1964 v W, Ni, S, R of W, U, US, P; 1965 v Ni, H, Y, WG, Se; 1966 v W, A, Y, N, M (19)

Pallister, G. A. (Middlesbrough), 1988 v H; 1989 v S.Ar; (with Manchester U), 1991 v Cam (sub), T (4)

Pantling, H. H. (Sheffield U), 1924 v Ni (1)

Paravacini, P. J. de (Cambridge University), 1883 v S, W, Ni (3)

Parker, P. A. (QPR), 1989 v Alb (sub), Ch, D; 1990 v Y, U, Ho, Eg, Bel, Cam, WG, I; 1991 v H, Pol, USSR, Aus, Nz (16)

Parker, T. R. (Southampton), 1925 v F (1)

Parkes, P. B. (QPR), 1974 v P (1)

Parkinson, J. (Liverpool), 1910 v S, W (2)

Parr, P. C. (Oxford University), 1882 v W (1)

Parry, E. H. (Old Carthusians), 1879 v W; 1882 v W, S (3)

Parry, R. A. (Bolton W), 1960 v Ni, S (2)

Patchitt, B. C. A. (Corinthians), 1923 v Se (2) (2)

Pawson, F. W. (Cambridge University), 1883 v Ni; (with Swifts), 1885 v Ni (2)

Payne, J. (Luton T), 1937 v Fi (1)

Peacock, A. (Middlesbrough), 1962 v Arg, Bul; 1963 v Ni, W; (with Leeds U), 1966 v W, Ni (6)

Peacock, J. (Middlesbrough), 1929 v F, Bel, Sp (3)

Pearce, S. (Nottingham F), 1987 v Br, S; 1988 v WG (sub), Is, H; 1989 v D, Se, S.Ar, Gr, Alb (2), Ch, S, Pol, D; 1990 v Se, Pol, I, Y, Br, Cz, D, U, Tun, Ei, Ho, Eg, Bel, Cam, WG; 1991 v H, Pol, Ei (2), Cam, T, Arg, Aus, Nz (2), Mal (41)

Pearson, H. F. (WBA), 1932 v S (1)

Pearson, J. H. (Crewe Alex), 1892 v Ni (1)

Pearson, J. S. (Manchester U), 1976 v W, Ni, S, Br, Fi;

R, Br, W, S, Sw; 1982 v Ni, W, Ho, S, Fi, F, Cz, WG, Sp; 1983 v D, WG, Gr, L, Gr, H, Ni, S; 1984 v D, H, L, F, S, USSR, Br, U, Ch; 1985 v EG, Fi, T, Ni, Ei, R, Fi, S, I, M, WG, US; 1986 v R, T, Ni, Eg, Is, USSR, S, M, Ca, P, Mor, Pol, Para, Arg; 1987 v Se, Ni (2), Y, Sp, T; 1988 v WG, T, Y, Ho, S, Co, Sw, Ei, Ho, USSR (86)

Saunders, F. E. (Swifts), 1888 v W (1)

Savage, A. H. (C Palace), 1876 v S (1)

Sayer, J. (Stoke C), 1887 v Ni (1)

Scattergood, E. (Derby Co), 1913 v W (1)

Schofield, J. (Stoke C), 1892 v W; 1893 v W; 1895 v Ni (3)

Scott, L. (Arsenal), 1947 v S, W, Ni, Ei, Ho, F, Sw, P; 1948 v S, W, Ni, Bel, Se, I; 1949 v W, Ni, D (17)

Scott, W. R. (Brentford), 1937 v W (1)

Seaman, D. A. (QPR), 1989 v S.Ar, D (sub); 1990 v Cz (sub); (with Arsenal), 1991 v Cam, Ei, T, Arg (7)

Seddon, J. (Bolton W), 1923 v F, Se (2); 1924 v Bel; 1927 v W; 1929 v S (6)

Seed, J. M. (Tottenham H), 1921 v Bel: 1923 v W, Ni, Bel; 1925 v S (5)

Settle, J. (Bury), 1899 v S, W, Ni; (with Everton), 1902 v S, Ni; 1903 v Ni (6)

Sewell, J. (Sheffield W), 1952 v Ni, A, Sw; 1953 v Ni; 1954 v H (2) (6)

Sewell, W. R. (Blackburn R), 1924 v W (1)

Shackleton, L. F. (Sunderland), 1949 v W, D; 1950 v W; 1955 v W, WG (5)

Sharp, J. (Everton), 1903 v Ni; 1905 v S (2)

Sharpe, L. S. (Manchester U), 1991 v Ei (sub) (1)

Shaw, G. E. (WBA), 1932 v S (1)

Shaw, G. L. (Sheffield U), 1959 v S, W, USSR, I; 1963 v W (5)

Shea, D. (Blackburn R), 1914 v W, Ni (2)

Shellito, K. J. (Chelsea), 1963 v Cz (1)

Shelton A. (Notts Co), 1889 v Ni; 1890 v S, W; 1891 v S, W; 1892 v S (6)

Shelton, C. (Notts Rangers), 1888 v Ni (1)

Shepherd, A. (Bolton W), 1906 v S; (with Newcastle U), 1911 v Ni (2)

Shilton, P. L. (Leicester C), 1971 v EG, W; 1972 v Sw, Ni; 1973 v Y, S (2), Ni, W, Cz, Pol, USSR, I; 1974 v A, Pol, I, W, Ni, S, Arg; (with Stoke C), 1975 v Cy; 1977 v Ni, W; (with Nottingham F), 1978 v W, H; 1979 v Cz, Se, A; 1980 v Ni, Sp, I; 1981 v N, Sw, R; 1982 v H, Ho, S, F, Cz, K, WG, Sp; (with Southampton), 1983 v D, WG, Gr, W, Gr, H, Ni, S, Aus (3); 1984 v D, H, F, Ni, W, S, USSR, Br, U, Ch; 1985 v EG, Fi, T, Ni, R, Fi, S, I, WG; 1986 v R, T, Ni, Eg, Is, USSR, S, M, Ca, P, Mor, Pol, Para, Arg; 1987 v Se, Ni (2), Sp, Br; (with Derby Co), 1988 v WG, T, Y, Ho, S, Co, Sw, Ei, Ho; 1989 v D, Se, Gr, Alb (2), Ch, S, Pol, D; 1990 v Se, Pol, I, Y, Br, Cz, D, U, Tun, Ei, Ho, Eg, Bel, Cam, WG, I (125)

Shimwell, E. (Blackpool), 1949 v Se (1)

Shutt, G. (Stoke C), 1886 v Ni (1)

Silcock, J. (Manchester U), 1921 v S, W; 1923 v Se (3)

Sillett, R. P. (Chelsea), 1955 v F, Sp, P (3)

Simms, E. (Luton T), 1922 v Ni (1)

Simpson, J. (Blackburn R), 1911 v S, W, Ni; 1912 v S, W, Ni; 1913 v S; 1914 v W (8)

Slater, W. J. (Wolverhampton W), 1955 v W, WG; 1958 v S, P, Y, USSR (3), Br, A; 1959 v USSR; 1960 v S (12)

Smalley, T. (Wolverhampton W), 1937 v W (1)

Smart, T. (Aston Villa), 1921 v S; 1924 v S, W; 1926 v Ni; 1930 v W (5)

Smith, A. (Nottingham F), 1891 v S, W; 1893 v Ni (3)

Smith, A. K. (Oxford University), 1872 v S (1)

Smith, A. M. (Arsenal), 1989 v S.Ar (sub), Gr, Alb (sub), Pol (sub); 1991 v T, USSR, Arg (7)

Smith, B. (Tottenham H), 1921 v S; 1922 v W (2)

Smith, C. E. (C Palace), 1876 v S (1)

Smith, G. O. (Oxford University), 1893 v Ni; 1894 v W, S; 1895 v W; 1896 v Ni, W, S; (with Old Carthusians) 1897

v Ni, W, S; 1898 v Ni, W, S; (with Corinthians), 1899 v Ni, W, S; 1899 v Ni, W, S; 1901 v S (20)

Smith, H. (Reading), 1905 v W, S; 1906 v W, Ni (4)

Smith, J. (WBA), 1920 v Ni; 1923 v Ni (2)

Smith, Joe (Bolton W), 1913 v Ni; 1914 v S, W; 1920 v W, Ni (5)

Smith, J. C. R. (Millwall), 1939 v Ni, N (2)

Smith, J. W. (Portsmouth), 1932 v Ni, W, Sp (3)

Smith, Leslie (Brentford), 1939 v R (1)

Smith, Lionel (Arsenal), 1951 v W; 1952 v W, Ni; 1953 v W, S, Bel (6)

Smith, R. A. (Tottenham H), 1961 v Ni, W, S, L, P, Sp; 1962 v S; 1963 v S, F, Br, Cz, EG; 1964 v W, Ni, R of W (15)

Smith, S. (Aston Villa), 1895 v S (1)

Smith, S. C. (Leicester C), 1936 v Ni (1)

Smith, T. (Birmingham C), 1960 v W, Se (2)

Smith, T. (Liverpool), 1971 v W (1)

Smith, W. H. (Huddersfield T), 1922 v W, S; 1928 v S (3)

Sorby, T. H. (Thursday Wanderers, Sheffield), 1879 v W (1)

Southworth, J. (Blackburn R), 1889 v W; 1891 v W; 1892 v S (3)

Sparks, F. J. (Herts Rangers), 1879 v S; (with Clapham Rovers), 1880 v S, W (3)

Spence, J. W. (Manchester U), 1926 v Bel; 1927 v Ni (2)

Spence, R. (Chelsea), 1936 v A, Bel (2)

Spencer, C. W. (Newcastle U), 1924 v S; 1925 v W (2)

Spencer, H. (Aston Villa), 1897 v S, W; 1900 v W; 1903 v Ni; 1905 v W, S (6)

Spiksley, F. (Sheffield W), 1893 v S, W; 1894 v S, Ni; 1896 v Ni; 1898 v S, W (7)

Spilsbury, B. W. (Cambridge University), 1885 v Ni; 1886 v Ni, S (3)

Spink, N. (Aston Villa), 1983 v Aus (sub) (1)

Spouncer, W. A. (Nottingham F), 1900 v W (1)

Springett, R. D. G. (Sheffield W), 1960 v Ni, S, Y, Sp, H; 1961 v Ni, S, L, P, Sp, M, I, A; 1962 v W, Ni, S, A, Sw, Pe, L, P, H, Arg, Bul, Br; 1963 v Ni, W, F (2), Sw; 1966 v W, A, N (33)

Sproston, B. (Leeds U), 1937 v W; 1938 v S, W, Ni, Cz, G, Sw, F; (with Tottenham H), 1939 v W, R of E; (with Manchester C), N (11)

Squire, R. T. (Cambridge University), 1886 v S, W, Ni (3)

Stanbrough, M. H. (Old Carthusians), 1895 v W (1)

Staniforth, R. (Huddersfield T), 1954 v S, H, Y, Bel, Sw, U; 1955 v W, WG (8)

Starling, R. W. (Sheffield W), 1933 v S; (with Aston Villa), 1937 v S (2)

Statham, D. (WBA), 1983 v W, Aus (2) (3)

Steele, F. C. (Stoke C), 1937 v S, W, Ni, N, Se, Fi (6)

Stein, B. (Luton T), 1984 v F (1)

Stephenson, C. (Huddersfield T), 1924 v W (1)

Stephenson, G. T. (Derby Co), 1928 v F, Bel; (with Sheffield W), 1931 v F (3)

Stephenson, J. E. (Leeds U), 1938 v S; 1939 v Ni (2)

Stepney, A. C. (Manchester U), 1968 v Se (1)

Sterland, M. (Sheffield W), 1989 v S.Ar (1)

Steven, T. M. (Everton), 1985 v Ni, Ei, R, Fi, I, US (sub); 1986 v T (sub), Eg, USSR (sub), M (sub), Pol, Para, Arg; 1987 v Se, Y (sub), Sp (sub); 1988 v T, Y, Ho, H, S, Sw, Ho, USSR; 1989 v S; (with Rangers), 1990 v Cz, Cam (sub), WG (sub), I; 1991 v Cam (30)

Stevens, G. A. (Tottenham H), 1985 v Fi (sub), T (sub), Ni; 1986 v S (sub), M (sub), Mor (sub), Para (sub) (7)

Stevens, M. G. (Everton), 1985 v I, WG; 1986 v R, T, Ni, Eg, Is, S, Ca, P, Mor, Pol, Para, Arg; 1987 v Br, S; 1988 v T, Y, Is, Ho, H (sub), S, Sw, Ei, Ho, USSR; (with Rangers), 1989 v D, Se, Gr, Alb (2), S, Pol; 1990 v Se, Pol, I, Br, D, Tun, Ei, I; 1991 v USSR (42)

Stewart, J. (Sheffield W), 1907 v S, W; (with Newcastle U), 1911 v S (3)

Stiles, N. P. (Manchester U), 1965 v S, H, Y, Se; 1966 v W,

Ni, S, A, Sp, Pol (2), WG (2), N, D, U, M, F, Arg, P; 1967 v Ni, W, S, Cz; 1968 v USSR; 1969 v R; 1970 v Ni, S (28)

Stoker, J. (Birmingham), 1933 v W; 1934 v S, H (3)

Storer, H. (Derby Co), 1924 v F; 1928 v Ni (2)

Storey, P. E. (Arsenal), 1971 v Gr, Ni, S; 1972 v Sw, WG, W, Ni, S; 1973 v W (3), Y, S (2), Ni, Cz, Pol, USSR, I (19)

Storey-Moore, I. (Nottingham F), 1970 v Ho (1)

Strange, A. H. (Sheffield W), 1930 v S, A, G; 1931 v S, W, Ni, F, Bel; 1932 v S, W, Ni, Sp; 1933 v S, Ni, A, I, Sw; 1934 v Ni, W, F (20)

Stratford, A. H. (Wanderers), 1874 v S (1)

Streten, B. (Luton T), 1950 v Ni (1)

Sturgess, A. (Sheffield U), 1911 v Ni; 1914 v S (2)

Summerbee, M. G. (Manchester C), 1968 v S, Sp, WG; 1972 v Sw, WG (sub), W, Ni; 1973 v USSR (sub) (8)

Sunderland, A. (Arsenal), 1980 v Aus (1)

Sutcliffe, J. W. (Bolton W), 1893 v W; 1895 v S, Ni; 1901 v S; (with Millwall), 1903 v W (5)

Swan, P. (Sheffield W), 1960 v Y, Sp, H; 1961 v Ni, W, S, L, P, Sp, M, I, A; 1962 v W, Ni, S, A, Sw, L, P (19)

Swepstone, H. A. (Pilgrims), 1880 v S; 1882 v S, W; 1883 v S, W, Ni (6)

Swift, F. V. (Manchester C), 1947 v S, W, Ni, Ei, Ho, F, Sw, P; 1948 v S, W, Ni, Bel, Se, I; 1949 v S, W, Ni, D, N (19)

Tait, G. (Birmingham Excelsior), 1881 v W (1)

Talbot, B. (Ipswich T), 1977 v Ni (sub), S, Br, Arg, U; (with Arsenal), 1980 v Aus (6)

Tambling, R. V. (Chelsea), 1963 v W, F; 1966 v Y (3)

Tate, J. T. (Aston Villa), 1931 v F, Bel; 1933 v W (3)

Taylor, E. (Blackpool), 1954 v H (1)

Taylor, E. H. (Huddersfield T), 1923 v S, W, Ni, Bel; 1924 v S, Ni, F; 1926 v S (8)

Taylor, J. G. (Fulham), 1951 v Arg, P (2)

Taylor, P. H. (Liverpool), 1948 v W, Ni, Se (3)

Taylor, P. J. (C Palace), 1976 v W (sub+1), Ni, S (4)

Taylor, T. (Manchester U), 1953 v Arg, Ch, U; 1954 v Bel, Sw; 1956 v S, Br, Se, Fi, WG; 1957 v Ni, Y (sub), D (2), Ei (2); 1958 v W, Ni, F (19)

Temple, D. W. (Everton), 1965 v WG (1)

Thickett, H. (Sheffield U), 1899 v S, W (2)

Thomas, D. (Coventry C), 1983 v Aus (1+1 sub) (2)

Thomas, D. (QPR), 1975 v Cz (sub), P, Cy (sub+1), W, S (sub); 1976 v Cz (sub), P (sub) (8)

Thomas, G. R. (C Palace), 1991 v T, USSR, Arg, Aus, Nz (2), Mal (7)

Thomas, M. L. (Arsenal), 1989 v S.Ar; 1990 v Y (2)

Thompson, P. (Liverpool), 1964 v P (2), Ei, US, Br, Arg; 1965 v Ni, W, S, Bel, Ho; 1966 v Ni; 1968 v Ni, WG; 1970 v S, Ho (sub) (16)

Thompson, P. B. (Liverpool), 1976 v W (2), Ni, S, Br, I, Fi; 1977 v Fi; 1979 v Ei (sub), Cz, Ni, S, Bul, Se (sub), A; 1980 v D, Ni, Bul, Ei, Sp (2), Arg, W, S, Bel, I; 1981 v N, R, H; 1982 v N, H, W, Ho, S, Fi, F, Cz, K, WG, Sp; 1983 v WG, Gr (42)

Thompson T. (Aston Villa), 1952 v W; (with Preston NE), 1957 v S (2)

Thomson, R. A. (Wolverhampton W), 1964 v Ni, US, P, Arg; 1965 v Bel, Ho, Ni, W (8)

Thornewell, G. (Derby Co), 1923 v Se (2); 1924 v F; 1925 v F (4)

Thornley, I. (Manchester C), 1907 v W (1)

Tilson, S. F. (Manchester C), 1934 v H, Cz; 1935 v W; 1936 v Ni (4)

Titmuss, F. (Southampton), 1922 v W; 1923 v W (2)

Todd, C. (Derby Co), 1972 v Ni; 1974 v P, W, Ni, S, Arg, EG, Bul, Y; 1975 v P (sub), WG, Cy (2), Ni, W, S; 1976 v Sw, Cz, P, Ni, S, Br, Fi; 1977 v Ei, Fi, Ho (sub), Ni (27)

Toone, G. (Notts Co), 1892 v S, W (2)

Topham, A. G. (Casuals), 1894 v W (1)

Topham, R. (Wolverhampton W), 1893 v Ni; (with Casuals) 1894 v W (2)

Towers, M. A. (Sunderland), 1976 v W, Ni (sub), I (3)

Townley, W. J. (Blackburn R), 1889 v W; 1890 v Ni (2)

Townrow, J. E. (Clapton Orient), 1925 v S; 1926 v W (2)

Tremelling, D. R. (Birmingham), 1928 v W (1)

Tresadern, J. (West Ham U), 1923 v S, Se (2)

Tueart, D. (Manchester C), 1975 v Cy (sub), Ni; 1977 v Fi, Ni, W (sub), S (sub) (6)

Tunstall, F. E. (Sheffield U), 1923 v S; 1924 v S, W, Ni, F; 1925 v Ni, S (7)

Turnbull, R. J. (Bradford), 1920 v Ni (1)

Turner, A. (Southampton), 1900 v Ni; 1901 v Ni (2)

Turner, H. (Huddersfield T), 1931 v F, Bel (2)

Turner, J. A. (Bolton W), 1893 v W; (with Stoke C) 1895 v Ni; (with Derby Co) 1898 v Ni (3)

Tweedy, G. J. (Grimsby T), 1937 v H (1)

Ufton, D. G. (Charlton Ath), 1954 v R of E (1)

Underwood A. (Stoke C), 1891 v Ni; 1892 v Ni (2)

Urwin, T. (Middlesbrough), 1923 v Se (2); (with Newcastle U), 1924 v Bel; 1926 v W (4)

Utley, G. (Barnsley), 1913 v Ni (1)

Vaughton, O. H. (Aston Villa), 1882 v S, W, Ni; 1884 v S, W (5)

Veitch, C. C. M. (Newcastle U), 1906 v S, W, Ni; 1907 v S, W; 1909 v W (6)

Veitch, J. G. (Old Westminsters), 1894 v W (1)

Venables, T. F. (Chelsea), 1965 v Ho, Bel (2)

Vidal, R. W. S. (Oxford University), 1873 v S (1)

Viljoen, C. (Ipswich T), 1975 v Ni, W (2)

Viollet, D. S. (Manchester U), 1960 v H; 1962 v L (2)

Von Donop (Royal Engineers), 1873 v S; 1875 v S (2)

Wace, H. (Wanderers), 1878 v S; 1879 v S, W (3)

Waddle, C. R. (Newcastle U), 1985 v Ei, R (sub), Fi (sub), S (sub), I, M (sub), WG, US; (with Tottenham H), 1986 v R, T, Ni, Is, USSR, S, M, Ca, P, Mor, Pol (sub), Arg (sub); 1987 v Se (sub), Ni (2), Y, Sp, T, Br, S; 1988 v WG, Is, H, S (sub), Co, Sw (sub), Ei, Ho (sub); 1989 v Se, S.Ar, Alb (2), Ch, S, Pol, D (sub); (with Marseille), 1990 v Se, Pol, I, Y, Br, D, U, Tun, Ei, Ho, Eg, Bel, Cam, WG, I (sub); 1991 v H (sub), Pol (sub) (61)

Wadsworth, S. J. (Huddersfield T), 1922 v S; 1923 v S, Bel; 1924 v S, Ni; 1925 v S, Ni; 1926 v W; 1927 v Ni (9)

Wainscoat, W. R. (Leeds U), 1929 v S (1)

Waiters, A. K. (Blackpool), 1964 v Ei, Br; 1965 v W, Bel, Ho (5)

Walker, D. S. (Nottingham F), 1989 v D (sub), Se (sub), Gr, Alb (2), Ch, S, Pol, D; 1990 v Se, Pol, I, Y, Br, Cz, D, U, Tun, Ei, Ho, Eg, Bel, Cam, WG, I; 1991 v H, Pol, Ei (2), Cam, T, Arg, Aus, Nz (2), Mal (36)

Walden, F. I. (Tottenham H), 1914 v S; 1922 v W (2)

Walker, W. H. (Aston Villa), 1921 v Ni; 1922 v Ni, W, S; 1923 v Se (2); 1924 v S; 1925 v Ni, W, S, Bel, F; 1926 v Ni, W, S; 1927 v Ni, W; 1933 v A (18)

Wall, G. (Manchester U), 1907 v W; 1908 v Ni; 1909 v S; 1910 v W, S; 1912 v S; 1913 v Ni (7)

Wallace, C. W. (Aston Villa), 1913 v W; 1914 v Ni; 1920 v S (3)

Wallace, D. L. (Southampton), 1986 v Eg (1)

Walsh, P. (Luton T), 1983 v Aus (2+1 sub) (3)

Walters, A. M. (Cambridge University), 1885 v S, N; 1886 v S; 1887 v S, W; (with Old Carthusians), 1889 v S, W; 1890 v S, W (9)

Walters, K. M. (Rangers), 1991 v Nz (1)

Walters, P. M. (Oxford University), 1885 v S, Ni; (with Old Carthusians), 1886 v S, W, Ni; 1887 v S, W; 1888 v S, Ni; 1889 v S, W; 1890 v S, W (13)

Walton, N. (Blackburn R), 1890 v Ni (1)

Ward, J. T. (Blackburn Olympic), 1885 v W (1)

Ward, P. (Brighton & HA), 1980 v Aus (sub) (1)

Ward, T. V. (Derby Co), 1948 v Bel; 1949 v W (2)

Waring, T. (Aston Villa), 1931 v F, Bel; 1932 v S, W, Ni (5)

Warner, C. (Upton Park), 1878 v S (1)

Warren, B. (Derby Co), 1906 v S, W, Ni; 1907 v S, W, Ni; 1908 v S, W, Ni, A (2), H, B; (with Chelsea), 1909 v S, Ni, W, H (2), A; 1911 v S, Ni, W (22)

Waterfield, G. S. (Burnley), 1927 v W (1)

Watson, D. (Norwich C), 1984 v Br, U, Ch; 1985 v M, US (sub); 1986 v S; (with Everton), 1987 v Ni; 1988 v Is, Ho, S, Sw (sub), USSR (12)

Watson, D. V. (Sunderland), 1974 v P, S (sub), Arg, EG, Bul, Y; 1975 v Cz, P, WG, Cy (2), Ni, W, S; (with Manchester C), 1976 v Sw, Cz (sub), P; 1977 v Ho, L, Ni, W, S, Br, Arg, U; 1978 v Sw, L, I, WG, Br, W, Ni, S, H; 1979 v D, Ei, Cz, Ni (2), W, S, Bul, Se, A; (with Werder Bremen), 1980 v D; (with Southampton), Ni, Bul, Ei, Sp (2), Arg, Ni, S, Bel, I; 1981 v N, R, Sw, R, W, S, Sw, H; (with Stoke C), 1982 v Ni, Ic (65)

Watson, V. M. (West Ham U), 1923 v W, S; 1930 v S, G, A (5)

Watson, W. (Burnley), 1913 v S; 1914 v Ni; 1920 v Ni (3)

Watson, W. (Sunderland), 1950 v Ni, I; 1951 v W, Y (4)

Weaver, S. (Newcastle U), 1932 v S, 1933 v S, Ni (3)

Webb, G. W. (West Ham U), 1911 v S, W (2)

Webb, N. J. (Nottingham F), 1988 v WG (sub), T, Y, Is, Ho, S, Sw, Ei, USSR (sub); 1989 v D, Se, Gr, Alb (2), Ch, S, Pol, D; (with Manchester U), 1990 v Se, I (sub) (20)

Webster, M. (Middlesbrough), 1930 v S, A, G (3)

Wedlock, W. J. (Bristol C), 1907 v S, Ni, W; 1908 v S, Ni, W, A (2), H, B; 1909 v S, W, Ni, H (2), A; 1910 v S, W, Ni; 1911 v S, W, Ni; 1912 v S, W, Ni; 1914 v W (26)

Weir, D. (Bolton W), 1889 v S, Ni (2)

Welch, R. de C. (Wanderers), 1872 v S; (with Harrow Chequers), 1874 v S (2)

Weller, K. (Leicester C), 1974 v W, Ni, S, Arg (4)

Welsh, D. (Charlton Ath), 1938 v G, Sw; 1939 v R (3)

West, G. (Everton), 1969 v W, Bul, M (3)

Westwood, R. W. (Bolton W), 1935 v S, W, Ho; 1936 v Ni, G; 1937 v W (6)

Whateley, O. (Aston Villa), 1883 v S, Ni (2)

Wheeler, J. E. (Bolton W), 1955 v Ni (1)

Wheldon, G. F. (Aston Villa), 1897 v Ni; 1898 v S, W, Ni (4)

White, T. A. (Everton), 1933 v I (1)

Whitehead, J. (Accrington), 1893 v W; (with Blackburn R), 1894 v Ni (2)

Whitfeld, H. (Old Etonians), 1879 v W (1)

Witham, M. (Sheffield U), 1892 v Ni (1)

Whitworth, S. (Leicester C), 1975 v WG, Cy, Ni, W, S; 1976 v Sw, P (7)

Whymark, T. J. (Ipswich T), 1978 v L (sub) (1)

Widdowson, S. W. (Nottingham F), 1880 v S (1)

Wignall, F. (Nottingham F), 1965 v W, Ho (2)

Wilkes, A. (Aston Villa), 1901 v S, W; 1902 v S, W, Ni (5)

Wilkins, R. G. (Chelsea), 1976 v I; 1977 v Ei, Fi, Ni, Br, Arg, U; 1978 v Sw (sub), L, I, WG, W, Ni, S, H; 1979 v D, Ei, Cz, Ni, W, S, Bul, Se (sub), A; (with Manchester U), 1980 v D, Ni, Bul, Sp (2), Arg, W (sub), Ni, S, Bel, I; 1981 v Sp (sub), R, Br, W, S, Sw, H (sub); 1982 v Ni, W, Ho, S, Fi, F, Cz, K, WG, Sp; 1983 v D, WG; 1984 v D, Ni, W, S, USSR, Br, U, Ch; (with AC Milan), 1985 v EG, Fi, T, Ni, Ei, R, Fi, S, I, M; 1986 v T, Ni, Is, Eg, USSR, S, M, Ca, P, Mor; 1987 v Se, Y (sub) (84)

Wilkinson, B. (Sheffield U), 1904 v S (1)

Wilkinson, L. R. (Oxford University), 1891 v W (1)

Williams, B. F. (Wolverhampton W), 1949 v F; 1950 v S, W, Ei, I, P, Bel, Ch, US, Sp; 1951 v Ni, S, Y, Arg, P; 1952 v W, F; 1955 v S, WG, F, Sp, P; 1956 v W (24)

Williams, O. (Clapton Orient), 1923 v W, Ni (2)

Williams, S. (Southampton), 1983 v Aus (1 + 1 sub); 1984 v F; 1985 v EG, Fi, T (6)

Williams, W. (WBA), 1897 v Ni; 1898 v W, Ni, S; 1899 v W, Ni (6)

Williamson, E. C. (Arsenal), 1923 v Se (2) (2)

Williamson, R. G. (Middlesbrough), 1905 v Ni; 1911 v Ni, S, W; 1912 v S, W; 1913 v Ni (7)

Willingham, C. K. (Huddersfield T), 1937 v Fi; 1938 v S, G, Sw, F; 1939 v S, W, Ni, R of E, N, I, Y (12)

Willis, A. (Tottenham H), 1952 v F (1)

Wilshaw, D. J. (Wolverhampton W), 1954 v W, Sw, U; 1955 v S, F, Sp, P; 1956 v W, Ni, Fi, WG; 1957 v Ni (12)

Wilson, C. P. (Hendon), 1884 v S, W (2)

Wilson, C. W. (Oxford University), 1879 v W; 1881 v S (2)

Wilson, G. (Sheffield W), 1921 v S, W, Bel; 1922 v S, Ni; 1923 v S, W, Ni, Bel; 1924 v W, Ni, F (12)

Wilson, G. P. (Corinthians), 1900 v S, W (2)

Wilson, R. (Huddersfield T), 1960 v S, Y, Sp, H; 1962 v W, Ni, S, A, Sw, Pe, P, H, Arg, Bul, Br; 1963 v Ni, F, Br, Cz, EG, Sw; 1964 v W, S, R of W, U, P (2), Ei, Br, Arg; (with Everton), 1965 v S, H, Y, WG, Se; 1966 v WG (sub), W, Ni, A, Sp, Pol (2), Y, Fi, D, U, M, F, Arg, P, WG; 1967 v Ni, W, S, Cz, A; 1968 v Ni, S, USSR (2), Sp (2), Y (63)

Wilson, T. (Huddersfield T), 1928 v S (1)

Winckworth, W. N. (Old Westminsters), 1892 v W; 1893 v Ni (2)

Windridge, J. E. (Chelsea), 1908 v S, W, Ni, A (2), H, B; 1909 v Ni (8)

Wingfield-Stratford, C. V. (Royal Engineers), 1877 v S (1)

Winterburn, N. (Arsenal), 1990 v I (sub) (1)

Wise, D. F. (Chelsea), 1991 v T, USSR, Aus (sub), Nz (2) (5)

Withe, P. (Aston Villa), 1981 v Br, W, S; 1982 v N (sub), W, Ic; 1983 v H, Ni, S; 1984 v H (sub); 1985 v T (11)

Wollaston, C. H. R. (Wanderers), 1874 v S; 1875 v S; 1877 v S; 1880 v S (4)

Wolstenholme, S. (Everton), 1904 v S; (with Blackburn R), 1905 v W, Ni (3)

Wood, H. (Wolverhampton W), 1890 v S, W; 1896 v S (3)

Wood, R. E. (Manchester U), 1955 v Ni, W; 1956 v Fi (3)

Woodcock, A. S. (Nottingham F), 1978 v Ni; 1979 v Ei (sub), Cz, Bul (sub), Se; 1980 v Ni; (with Cologne), Bul, Ei, Sp (2), Arg, Bel, I; 1981 v N, R, Sw, R, W (sub), S; 1982 v Ni (sub), Ho, Fi, WG (sub), Sp; (with Arsenal), 1983 v WG (sub), Gr, L, Gr; 1984 v L, F (sub), Ni, W, S, Br, U (sub); 1985 v EG, Fi, T, Ni; 1986 v R (sub), T (sub), Is (sub) (42)

Woodger, G. (Oldham Ath), 1911 v Ni (1)

Woodhall, G. (WBA), 1888 v S, W (2)

Woodley, V. R. (Chelsea), 1937 v S, N, Se, Fi; 1938 v S, W, Ni, Cz, G, Sw, F; 1939 v S, W, Ni, R of E, N, I, R, Y (19)

Woods, C. C. E. (Norwich C), 1985 v US; 1986 v Eg (sub), Is (sub), Ca (sub); (with Rangers), 1987 v Y, Sp (sub), Ni (sub), T, S; 1988 v Is, H, Sw (sub), USSR; 1989 v D (sub); 1990 v Br (sub), D (sub); 1991 v H, Pol, Ei, USSR, Aus, Nz (2), Mal (24)

Woodward, V. J. (Tottenham H), 1903 v S, W, Ni; 1904 v S, Ni; 1905 v S, W, Ni; 1907 v S; 1908 v S, W, Ni, A (2), H, B; 1909 v W, Ni, H (2), A; (with Chelsea), 1910 v Ni; 1911 v W (23)

Woosnam, M. (Manchester C), 1922 v W (1)

Worrall, F. (Portsmouth), 1935 v Ho; 1937 v Ni (2)

Worthington, F. S. (Leicester C), 1974 v Ni (sub), S, Arg, EG, Bul, Y; 1975 v Cz, P (sub) (8)

Wreford-Brown, C. (Oxford University), 1889 v Ni; (with Old Carthusians), 1894 v W; 1895 v W; 1898 v S (4)

Wright, E. G. D. (Cambridge University), 1906 v W (1)

Wright, I. E. (C Palace), 1991 v Cam, Ei (sub), USSR, Nz (4)

Wright, J. D. (Newcastle U), 1939 v N (1)

Wright, M. (Southampton), 1984 v W; 1985 v EG, Fi, T,

Ei, R, I, WG; 1986 v R, T, Ni, Eg, USSR; 1987 v Y, Ni, S; (with Derby Co), 1988 v Is, Ho (sub), Co, Sw, Ei, Ho; 1990 v Cz (sub), Tun (sub), Ho, Eg, Bel, Cam, WG, I; 1991 v H, Pol, Ei (2), Cam, USSR, Arg, Aus, Nz, Mal (40)

Wright, T. J. (Everton), 1968 v USSR; 1969 v R (2), M (sub), U, Br; 1970 v W, Ho, Bel, R (sub), Br (11)

Wright, W. A. (Wolverhampton W), 1947 v S, W, Ni, Ei, Ho, F, Sw, P; 1948 v S, W, Ni, Bel, Se, I; 1949 v S, W, Ni, D, Sw, Se, N, F; 1950 v S, W, Ni, Ei, I, P, Bel, Ch, US, Sp; 1951 v Ni, S, Arg; 1952 v W, Ni, S, F, A (2), I, Sw; 1953 v Ni, W, S, Bel, Arg, Ch, U, US; 1954 v W, Ni, S, R of E, H (2), Y, Bel, Sw, U; 1955 v W, Ni, S, WG, F, Sp, P; 1956 v Ni, W, S, Br, Se, Fi, WG, D, Sp; 1957 v S,

W, Ni, Y, D (2), Ei (2); 1958 v W, Ni, S, P, Y, USSR (3), Br, A, F; 1959 v W, Ni, S, USSR, I, Br, Pe, M, US (105)

Wylie, J. G. (Wanderers), 1878 v S (1)

Yates, J. (Burnley), 1889 v Ni (1)

York, R. E. (Aston Villa), 1922 v S; 1926 v S (2)

Young, A. (Huddersfield T), 1933 v W; 1937 v S, H, N, Se; 1938 v G, Sw, F; 1939 v W (9)

Young, G. M. (Sheffield W), 1965 v W (1)

R. E. Evans also played for Wales against E, Ni, S; J. Reynolds also played for Ireland against E, W, S.

NORTHERN IRELAND

Aherne, T. (Belfast C), 1947 v E; 1948 v S; 1949 v W; (with Luton T), 1950 v W (4)

Alexander, A. (Cliftonville), 1895 v S (1)

Allen, C. A. (Cliftonville), 1936 v E (1)

Allen, J. (Limavady), 1887 v E (1)

Anderson, T. (Manchester U), 1973 v Cy, E, S, W; 1974 v Bul, P; (with Swindon T), 1975 v S (sub); 1976 v Is; 1977 v Ho, Bel, WG, E, S, W, Ic; 1978 v Ic, Ho, Bel; (with Peterborough U), S, E, W; 1979 v D (22)

Anderson, W. (Linfield), 1898 v W, E, S; 1899 v S (4)

Andrews, W. (Glentoran), 1908 v S; (with Grimsby T), 1913 v E, S (3)

Armstrong, G. (Tottenham H), 1977 v WG, E, W (sub), Ic (sub); 1978 v Bel, S, E, W; 1979 v Ei, D, Bul, E, Bul, E, S, W, D; 1980 v E, Ei, Is, S, E, W, Aus (3); 1981 v Se; (with Watford), P, S, P, S, Se; 1982 v S, Is, E, F, W, Y, Hon, Sp, A, F; 1983 v A, T, Alb, S, E, W; (with Real Mallorca), 1984 v A, WG, E, W, Fi; 1985 v R, Fi, E, Sp; (with WBA), 1986 v T, R (sub), E (sub), F (sub); (with Chesterfield), D (sub), Br (sub) (63)

Baird, G. (Distillery), 1896 v S, E, W (3)

Baird, H. (Huddersfield T), 1939 v E (1)

Balfe, J. (Shelbourne), 1909 v E; 1910 v W (2)

Bambrick, J. (Linfield), 1929 v W, S, E; 1930 v W, S, E; 1932 v W; (with Chelsea), 1935 v W; 1936 v E, S; 1938 v W (11)

Banks, S. J. (Cliftonville), 1937 v W (1)

Barr, H. H. (Linfield), 1962 v E; (with Coventry C), 1963 v E, Pol (3)

Barron, H. (Cliftonville), 1894 v E, W, S; 1895 v S; 1896 v S; 1897 v E, W (7)

Barry, H. (Bohemians), 1900 v S (1)

Baxter, R. A. (Cliftonville), 1887 v S, W (2)

Bennett, L. V. (Dublin University), 1889 v W (1)

Berry, J. (Cliftonville), 1888 v S, W; 1889 v E (3)

Best, G. (Manchester U), 1964 v W, U; 1965 v E, Ho (2), S, Sw (2), Alb; 1966 v S, E, Alb; 1967 v E; 1968 v S; 1969 v E, S, W, T; 1970 v S, E, W, USSR; 1971 v Cy (2), Sp, E, S, W; 1972 v USSR, Sp; 1973 v Bul; 1974 v P; (with Fulham), 1977 v Ho, Bel, WG; 1978 v Ic, Ho (37)

Bingham, W. L. (Sunderland), 1951 v F; 1952 v E, S, W; 1953 v E, S, F, W; 1954 v E, S, W; 1955 v E, S, W; 1956 v E, S, W; 1957 v E, S, W, P (2), I; 1958 v S, E, W, I (2), Arg, Cz (2), WG, F; (with Luton T), 1959 v E, S, W, Sp; 1960 v S, E, W; (with Everton), 1961 v E, S, WG (2), Gr, I; 1962 v E, Gr; 1963 v E, S, Pol (2), Sp; (with Port Vale), 1964 v S, E, Sp (56)

Black, J. (Glentoran), 1901 v E (1)

Black, K. (Luton T), 1988 v Fr (sub), Ma (sub); 1989 v Ei, H, Sp (2), Ch (sub); 1990 v H, N, U; 1991 v Y (2), D, A, Pol, Fa (16)

Blair, H. (Portadown), 1931 v S; 1932 v S; (with Swansea), 1934 v S (3)

Blair, J. (Cliftonville), 1907 v W, E, S; 1908 v E, S (5)

Blair, R. V. (Oldham Ath), 1975 v Se (sub), S (sub), W; 1976 v Se, Is (5)

Blanchflower, R. D. (Barnsley), 1950 v S, W; 1951 v E, S; (with Aston Villa), F; 1952 v W; 1953 v E, S, W, F; 1954 v E, S, W; (with Tottenham H), 1955 v E, S, W; 1956 v E, S, W; 1957 v E, S, W, I, P (2); 1958 v E, S, W, I (2), Cz (2), Arg, F, WG; 1959 v E, S, W, Sp; 1960 v E, S, W; 1961 v E, S, W, WG (2); 1962 v E, S, W, Gr, Ho; 1963 v E, S, Pol (2) (56)

Blanchflower, J. (Manchester U), 1954 v W; 1955 v E, S; 1956 v S, W; 1957 v S, E, P; 1958 v S, E, I (2) (12)

Bookman, L. O. (Bradford C), 1914 v W; (with Luton T), 1921 v S, W; 1922 v E (4)

Bothwell, A. W. (Ards), 1926 v S, E, W; 1927 v E, W (5)

Bowler, G. C. (Hull C), 1950 v E, S, W (3)

Boyle, P. (Sheffield U), 1901 v E; 1902 v E; 1903 v S, W; 1904 v E (5)

Braithwaite, R. S. (Linfield), 1962 v W; 1963 v P, Sp; (with Middlesbrough), 1964 v W, U; 1965 v E, S, Sw (2), Ho (10)

Breen, T. (Belfast C), 1935 v E, W; 1937 v E, S; (with Manchester U), 1937 v W; 1938 v E, S; 1939 v W, S (9)

Brennan, B. (Bohemians), 1912 v W (1)

Brennan, R. A. (Luton T), 1949 v W; (with Birmingham C), 1950 v E, S, W; (with Fulham), 1951 v E (5)

Briggs, W. R. (Manchester U), 1962 v W; (with Swansea T), 1965 v Ho (2)

Brisby, D. (Distillery), 1891 v S (1)

Brolly, T. (Millwall), 1937 v W; 1938 v W; 1939 v E, W (4)

Brookes, E. A. (Shelbourne), 1920 v S (1)

Brotherston, N. (Blackburn R), 1980 v S, E, W, Aus (3); 1981 v Se, P; 1982 v S, Is, E, F, S, W, Hon (sub), A (sub); 1983 v A (sub), WG, Alb, T, Alb, S (sub), E (sub), W; 1984 v T; 1985 v Is (sub), T (27)

Brown, J. (Glenavon), 1921 v W; (with Tranmere R), 1924 v E, W (3)

Brown, J. (Wolverhampton W), 1935 v E, W; 1936 v E; (with Coventry C), 1937 v E, W; 1938 v S, W; (with Birmingham C), 1939 v E, S, W (10)

Brown, W. G. (Glenavon), 1926 v W (1)

Brown, W. M. (Limavady), 1887 v E (1)

Browne, F. (Cliftonville), 1887 v E, S, W; 1888 v E, S (5)

Browne, R. J. (Leeds U), 1936 v E, W; 1938 v E, W; 1939 v E, S (6)

Bruce, W. (Glentoran), 1961 v S; 1967 v W (2)

Buckle, H. (Cliftonville), 1882 v E (1)

Buckle, H. R. (Sunderland), 1904 v E; (with Bristol R), 1908 v W (2)

Burnett, J. (Distillery), 1894 v E, W, S; (with Glentoran), 1895 v E, W (5)

Burnison, J. (Distillery), 1901 v E, W (2)

Burnison, S. (Distillery), 1908 v E; 1910 v E, S; (with Bradford), 1911 v E, S, W; (with Distillery), 1912 v E; 1913 v W (8)

Burns, J. (Glenavon), 1923 v E (1)

Butler, M. P. (Blackpool), 1939 v W (1)

Campbell, A. C. (Crusaders), 1963 v W; 1965 v Sw (2)
Campbell, D. A. (Nottingham F), 1986 v Mor (sub), Br; 1987 v E (2), T, Y; 1988 v Y (with Charlton Ath), T (sub), Gr (sub), Pol (sub) (10)
Campbell, J. (Cliftonville), 1896 v W; 1897 v E, S, W; (with Distillery), 1898 v E, S, W; (with Cliftonville), 1899 v E; 1900 v E, S; 1901 v S, W; 1902 v S; 1903 v E; 1904 v S (15)
Campbell, J. P. (Fulham), 1951 v E, S (2)
Campbell, R. (Bradford C), 1982 v S, W (sub) (2)
Campbell, W. G. (Dundee), 1968 v S, E; 1969 v T; 1970 v S, W, USSR (6)
Carey, J. J. (Manchester U), 1947 v E, S, W; 1948 v E; 1949 v E, S, W (7)
Carroll, E. (Glenavon), 1925 v S (1)
Casey, T. (Newcastle U), 1955 v W; 1956 v W; 1957 v E, S, W, I, P (2); 1958 v WG, F; (with Portsmouth), 1959 v E, Sp (12)
Cashin, M. (Cliftonville), 1898 v S (1)
Caskey, W. (Derby Co), 1979 v Bul, E, Bul, E, D (sub); 1980 v E (sub); (with Tulsa R), 1982 v F (sub) (7)
Cassidy, T. (Newcastle U), 1971 v E (sub); 1972 v USSR (sub); 1974 v Bul (sub), S, E, W; 1975 v N; 1976 v S, E, W; 1977 v WG (sub); 1980 v E, Ei (sub), Is, S, E, W, Aus (3); (with Burnley), 1981 v Se, P; 1982 v Is, Sp (sub) (24)
Caughey, M. (Linfield), 1986 v F (sub), D (sub) (2)
Chambers, J. (Distillery), 1921 v W; (with Bury), 1928 v E, S, W; 1929 v E, S, W; 1930 v S, W; (with Nottingham F), 1932 v E, S, W (12)
Chatton, H. A. (Partick T), 1925 v E, S; 1926 v E (3)
Christian, J. (Linfield), 1889 v S (1)
Clarke, C. J. (Bournemouth), 1986 v F, D, Mor, Alg (sub), Sp, Br; (with Southampton), 1987 v E, T, Y; 1988 v Y, T, Gr, Pol, F, Ma; 1989 v Ei, H, Sp (1 + 1 sub); (with QPR), Ma, Ch; 1990 v H, Ei, N; (with Portsmouth), 1991 v Y (sub), D, A, Pol, Y (sub), Fa (30)
Clarke, R. (Belfast C), 1901 v E, S (2)
Cleary, J. (Glentoran), 1982 v S, W; 1983 v W (sub); 1984 v T (sub); 1985 v Is (5)
Clements, D. (Coventry C), 1965 v W, Ho; 1966 v M; 1967 v S, W; 1968 v S, E; 1969 v T (2), S, W; 1970 v S, E, W, USSR; 1971 v Sp, E, S, W, Cy; (with Sheffield W), 1972 v USSR (2), Sp, E, S, W; 1973 v Bul, Cy (2), P, E, S, W; (with Everton), 1974 v Bul, P, S, E, W; 1975 v N, Y, E, S, W; 1976 v Se, Y; (with New York Cosmos), E, W (48)
Clugston, J. (Cliftonville), 1888 v W; 1889 v W, S, E; 1890 v E, S; 1891 v E, W; 1892 v E, S, W; 1893 v E, S, W (14)
Cochrane, D. (Leeds U), 1939 v E, W; 1947 v E, S, W; 1948 v E, S, W; 1949 v S, W; 1950 v S, E (12)
Cochrane, M. (Distillery), 1898 v S, W, E; 1899 v E; 1900 v E, S, W; (with Leicester Fosse), 1901 v S (8)
Cochrane, T. (Coleraine), 1976 v N; (with Burnley), 1978 v S (sub), E (sub), W (sub); 1979 v Ei (sub); (with Middlesbrough), D, Bul, E, Bul, E; 1980 v Is, E (sub), W (sub), Aus (1 + 2 sub); 1981 v Se (sub), P (sub), S, P, S, Se; 1982 v E (sub), F; (with Gillingham), 1984 v S, Fi (sub) (26)
Collins, F. (Celtic), 1922 v S (1)
Condy, J. (Distillery), 1882 v W; 1886 v E, S (3)
Connell, T. (Coleraine), 1978 v W (sub) (1)
Connor, J. (Glentoran), 1901 v S, E; (with Belfast C), 1905 v E, S, W; 1907 v E, S; 1908 v E, S; 1909 v W; 1911 v S, E, W (13)
Connor, M. J. (Brentford), 1903 v S, W; (with Fulham), 1904 v E (3)
Cook, W. (Celtic), 1933 v E, W, S; (with Everton), 1935 v E; 1936 v S, W; 1937 v E, S, W; 1938 v E, S, W; 1939 v E, S, W (15)

Cooke, S. (Belfast YMCA), 1889 v E; (with Cliftonville), 1890 v E, S (3)
Coulter, J. (Belfast C), 1934 v E, S, W; (with Everton), 1935 v E, S, W; 1937 v S, W; (with Grimsby T), 1938 v S, W; (with Chelmsford C), 1939 v S (11)
Cowan, J. (Newcastle U), 1970 v E (sub) (1)
Cowan, T. S. (Queen's Island), 1925 v W (1)
Coyle, F. (Coleraine), 1956 v E, S; 1957 v P; (with Nottingham F), 1958 v Arg (4)
Coyle, L. (Derry C), 1989 v Ch (sub) (1)
Coyle, R. I. (Sheffield W), 1973 v P, Cy (sub), W (sub); 1974 v Bul (sub), P (sub) (5)
Craig, A. B. (Rangers), 1908 v E, S, W; 1909 v S; (with Morton), 1912 v S, W; 1914 v E, S, W (9)
Craig, D. J. (Newcastle U), 1967 v W; 1968 v W; 1969 v T (2), E, S, W; 1970 v E, S, W, USSR; 1971 v Cy (2), S (1 + 1 sub); 1972 v USSR, S (sub); 1973 v Cy (2), E, S, W; 1974 v Bul, P; 1975 v N (25)
Crawford, S. (Distillery), 1889 v E, W; (with Cliftonville), 1891 v E, S, W; 1893 v E, W (7)
Croft, T. (Queen's Island), 1924 v E (1)
Crone, R. (Distillery), 1889 v S; 1890 v E, S, W (4)
Crone, W. (Distillery), 1882 v W; 1884 v E, S, W; 1886 v E, S, W; 1887 v E; 1888 v E, W; 1889 v S; 1890 v W (12)
Crooks, W. (Manchester U), 1922 v W (1)
Crossan, E. (Blackburn R), 1950 v S; 1951 v E; 1955 v W (3)
Crossan, J. A. (Sparta-Rotterdam), 1960 v E; (with Sunderland), 1963 v W, P, Sp; 1964 v E, S, W, U, Sp; 1965 v E, S, Sw (2); (with Manchester C), W, Ho (2), Alb; 1966 v S, E, Alb, WG; 1967 v S; (with Middlesbrough), 1968 v S (24)
Crothers, C. (Distillery), 1907 v W (1)
Cumming, L. (Huddersfield T), 1929 v W, S; (with Oldham Ath), 1930 v E (3)
Cunningham, R. (Ulster), 1892 v S, E, W; 1893 v E (4)
Cunningham, W. E. (St Mirren), 1951 v W; 1953 v E; 1954 v S; 1955 v S; (with Leicester C), 1956 v E, S, W; 1957 v E, S, W, I, P (2); 1958 v S, W, I, Cz (2), Arg, WG, F; 1959 v E, S, W; 1960 v E, S, W; (with Dunfermline Ath), 1961 v W; 1962 v W, Ho (30)
Curran, S. (Belfast C), 1926 v S, W; 1928 v S (3)
Curran, J. J. (Glenavon), 1922 v W; (with Pontypridd), 1923 v E, S; (with Glenavon), 1924 v E (4)
Cush, W. W. (Glenavon), 1951 v E, S; 1954 v S, E; 1957 v W, I, P (2); (with Leeds U), 1958 v I (2), W, Cz (2), Arg, WG, F; 1959 v E, S, W, Sp; 1960 v E, S, W; (with Portadown), 1961 v WG, Gr; 1962 v Gr (26)

Dalton, W. (YMCA), 1888 v S; (with Linfield), 1890 v S, W; 1891 v S, W; 1892 v E, S, W; 1894 v E, S, W (11)
D'Arcy, S. D. (Chelsea), 1952 v W; 1953 v E; (with Brentford), 1953 v S, W, F (5)
Darling, J. (Linfield), 1897 v S; 1900 v S; 1902 v E, S, W; 1903 v E, S, W; 1905 v E, S, W; 1906 v E, S, W; 1908 v W; 1909 v E; 1910 v E, S, W; 1912 v S (21)
Davey, H. H. (Reading), 1926 v E; 1927 v E, S; 1928 v E; (with Portsmouth), 1928 v W (5)
Davis, T. L. (Oldham Ath), 1937 v E (1)
Davison, J. R. (Cliftonville), 1882 v E, W; 1883 v E, W; 1884 v E, W, S; 1885 v E (8)
Dennison, R. (Wolverhampton W), 1988 v F, Ma; 1989 v H, Sp Ch (sub); 1990 v Ei, U; 1991 v Y (2), A. Pol, Fa (sub) (12)
Devine, J. (Glentoran), 1990 v U (sub) (1)
Devine, W. (Limavady), 1886 v E, W; 1887 v W; 1888 v W (4)
Dickson, D. (Coleraine), 1970 v S (sub), W; 1973 v Cy, P (4)
Dickson, T. A. (Linfield), 1957 v S (1)
Dickson, W. (Chelsea), 1951 v W, F; 1952 v E, S, W; 1953 v E, S, W, F; (with Arsenal), 1954 v E, W; 1955 v E (12)
Diffin, W. (Belfast C), 1931 v W (1)

Dill, A. H. (Knock and Down Ath), 1882 v E, W; (with Cliftonville), 1883 v W; 1884 v E, S, W; 1885 v E, S, W (9)
Doherty, I. (Belfast C), 1901 v E (1)
Doherty, J. (Cliftonville), 1933 v E, W (2)
Doherty, L. (Linfield), 1985 v Is; 1988 v T (sub) (2)
Doherty, M. (Derry C), 1938 v S (1)
Doherty, P. D. (Blackpool), 1935 v E, W; 1936 v E, S; (with Manchester C), 1937 v E, W; 1938 v E, S; 1939 v E, W; (with Derby Co), 1947 v E; (with Huddersfield T), 1947 v W; 1948 v E, W; 1949 v S; (with Doncaster R), 1951 v S (16)
Donaghy, M. (Luton T), 1980 v S, E, W; 1981 v Se, P, S (sub); 1982 v S, Is, E, F, S, W, Y, Hon, Sp, F; 1983 v A, WG, Alb, T, Alb, S, E, W; 1984 v A, T, WG, S, E, W, Fi; 1985 v R, Fi, E, Sp, T; 1986 v T, R, E, F, D, Mor, Alg, Sp, Br; 1987 v E (2), T, Is, Y; 1988 v Y, T, Gr, Pol, F, Ma; 1989 v Ei, H; (with Manchester U), Sp (2), Ma, Ch; 1990 v Ei, N; 1991 v Y (2), D, A, Pol, Fa (70)
Donnelly, L. (Distillery), 1913 v W (1)
Doran, J. F. (Brighton), 1921 v E; 1922 v E, W (3)
Dougan, A. D. (Portsmouth), 1958 v Cz; (with Blackburn R), 1960 v S; 1961 v E, W, I, Gr; (with Aston Villa), 1963 v S, P (2); (with Leicester C), 1966 v S, E, W, M, Alb, WG; 1967 v E, S; (with Wolverhampton W), 1967 v W; 1968 v S, W, Is; 1969 v T (2), E, S, W; 1970 v S, E, USSR (2); 1971 v Cy (2), Sp, E, S, W; 1972 v USSR (2), E, S, W; 1973 v Bul, Cy (43)
Douglas, J. P. (Belfast C), 1947 v E (1)
Dowd, H. O. (Glenavon), 1974 v W; 1975 v N (sub), Se (3)
Dowie, I. (Luton T), 1990 v N (sub), U; 1991 v Y, D, A (sub), (with West Ham U), Y, Fa (7)
Duggan, H. A. (Leeds U), 1930 v E; 1931 v E, W; 1933 v E; 1934 v E; 1935 v S, W; 1936 v S (8)
Dunlop, G. (Linfield), 1985 v Is; 1987 v E, Y; 1990 v Ei (4)
Dunne, J. (Sheffield U), 1928 v W; 1931 v W, E; 1932 v E, S; 1933 v E, W (7)

Eames, W. L. E. (Dublin U), 1885 v E, S, W (3)
Eglington, T. J. (Everton), 1947 v S, W; 1948 v E, S, W; 1949 v E (6)
Elder, A. R. (Burnley), 1960 v W; 1961 v S, E, W, WG (2), Gr; 1962 v E, S, Gr; 1963 v E, S, W, P (2), Sp; 1964 v W, U; 1965 v E, S, W, Sw (2), Ho (2), Alb; 1966 v E, S, W, M, Alb; 1967 v E, S, W; (with Stoke C), 1968 v E, W; 1969 v E (sub), S, W; 1970 v USSR (40)
Elleman, A. R. (Cliftonville), 1889 v W; 1890 v E (2)
Elwood, J. H. (Bradford), 1929 v W; 1930 v E (2)
Emerson, W. (Glentoran), 1920 v E, S, W; 1921 v E; 1922 v E, S; (with Burnley), 1922 v W; 1923 v E, S, W; 1924 v E (11)
English, S. (Rangers), 1933 v W, S (2)
Enright, J. (Leeds C), 1912 v S (1)

Falloon, E. (Aberdeen), 1931 v S; 1933 v S (2)
Farquharson, T. G. (Cardiff C), 1923 v S, W; 1924 v E, S, W; 1925 v E, S (7)
Farrell, P. (Distillery), 1901 v S, W (2)
Farrell, P. (Hibernian), 1938 v W (1)
Farrell, P. D. (Everton), 1947 v S, W; 1948 v E, S, W; 1949 v E, W (7)
Feeney, J. M. (Linfield), 1947 v S; (with Swansea T), 1950 v E (2)
Feeney, W. (Glentoran), 1976 v Is (1)
Ferguson, W. (Linfield), 1966 v M; 1967 v E (2)
Ferris, J. (Belfast C), 1920 v E, W; (with Chelsea), 1921 v S, E; (with Belfast C), 1928 v S (5)
Ferris, R. O. (Birmingham C), 1950 v S; 1951 v F; 1952 v S (3)
Finney, T. (Sunderland), 1975 v N, E (sub), S, W; 1976 v N, Y, S; (with Cambridge U), 1980 v E, Is, S, E, W, Aus (2) (14)
Fitzpatrick, J. C. (Bohemians), 1896 v E, S (2)

Flack, H. (Burnley), 1929 v S (1)
Fleming, J. J. G. (Nottingham F), 1987 v E (2), Is, Y; 1988 v T, Gr, Pol; 1989 v Ma, Ch; (with Manchester C), 1990 v H, Ei; (with Barnsley), 1991 v Y (12)
Forbes, G. (Limavady), 1888 v W; (with Distillery), 1891 v E, S (3)
Forde, J. T. (Ards), 1959 v Sp; 1961 v E, S, WG (4)
Foreman, T. A. (Cliftonville), 1899 v S (1)
Forsyth, J. (YMCA), 1888 v E, S (2)
Fox, W. (Ulster), 1887 v E, S (2)
Fulton, R. P. (Belfast C), 1930 v W; 1931 v E, S, W; 1932 v W, E; 1933 v E, S; 1934 v E, W, S; 1935 v E, W, S; 1936 v S, W; 1937 v E, S, W; 1938 v W (20)

Gaffikin, J. (Linfield Ath), 1890 v S, W; 1891 v S, W; 1892 v E, S, W; 1893 v E, S, W; 1894 v E, S, W; 1895 v E, W (15)
Galbraith, W. (Distillery), 1890 v W (1)
Gallagher, P. (Celtic), 1920 v E, S; 1922 v S; 1923 v S, W; 1924 v S, W; 1925 v S, W, E; (with Falkirk), 1927 v S (11)
Gallogly, C. (Huddersfield T), 1951 v E, S (2)
Gara, A. (Preston NE), 1902 v E, S, W (3)
Gardiner, A. (Cliftonville), 1930 v S, W; 1931 v S; 1932 v E, S (5)
Garrett, J. (Distillery), 1925 v W (1)
Gaston, R. (Oxford U), 1969 v Is (sub) (1)
Gaukrodger, G. (Linfield), 1895 v W (1)
Gaussen, A. W. (Moyola Park), 1884 v E, S; 1888 v E, W; 1889 v E, W (6)
Geary, J. (Glentoran), 1931 v S; 1932 v S (2)
Gibb, J. T. (Wellington Park) 1884 v S, W; 1885 v S, E, W; 1886 v S; 1887 v S, E, W; 1889 v S (10)
Gibb, T. J. (Cliftonville), 1936 v W (1)
Gibson W. K. (Cliftonville), 1894 v S, W, E; 1895 v S; 1897 v W; 1898 v S, W, E; 1901 v S, W, E; 1902 v S, W (13)
Gillespie, R. (Hertford), 1886 v E, S, W; 1887 v E, S, W (6)
Gillespie, W. (Sheffield U), 1913 v E, S; 1914 v E, W; 1920 v S, W; 1921 v E; 1922 v E, S, W; 1923 v E, S, W; 1924 v E, S, W; 1925 v E, S; 1926 v S, W; 1927 v E, W; 1928 v E; 1929 v E; 1931 v E (25)
Gillespie, W. (West Down), 1889 v W (1)
Goodall, A. L. (Derby Co), 1899 v S, W; 1900 v E, W; 1901 v E; 1902 v S; 1903 v E, W; (with Glossop), 1904 v E, W (10)
Goodbody, M. F. (Dublin University), 1889 v E; 1891 v W (2)
Gordon, H. (Linfield), 1891 v S; 1892 v E, S, W; 1893 v E, S, W; 1895 v E, W; 1896 v E, S (11)
Gordon, T. (Linfield), 1894 v W; 1895 v E (2)
Gorman, W. C. (Brentford), 1947 v E, S, W; 1948 v W (4)
Gowdy, J. (Glentoran), 1920 v E; (with Queen's Island), 1924 v W; (with Falkirk), 1926 v E, S; 1927 v E, S (6)
Gowdy, W. A. (Hull C), 1932 v S; (with Sheffield W), 1933 v S; (with Linfield), 1935 v E, S, W; (with Hibernian), 1936 v W (6)
Graham, W. G. L. (Doncaster R), 1951 v W, F; 1952 v E, S, W; 1953 v S, F; 1954 v E, W; 1955 v S, W; 1956 v E, S; 1959 v E (14)
Greer, W. (QPR), 1909 v E, S, W (3)
Gregg, H. (Doncaster R), 1954 v W; 1957 v E, S, W, I, P (2); 1958 v E, I; (with Manchester U), 1958 v Cz, Arg, WG, F, W; 1959 v E, W; 1960 v S, E, W; 1961 v E, S; 1962 v S, Gr; 1964 v S, E (25)

Hall, G. (Distillery), 1897 v E (1)
Halligan, W. (Derby Co), 1911 v W; (with Wolverhampton W), 1912 v E (2)
Hamill, M. (Manchester U), 1912 v E; 1914 v E, S; (with Belfast C), 1920 v E, S, W; (with Manchester C), 1921 v S (7)

Hamilton, B. (Linfield), 1969 v T; 1971 v Cy (2), E, S, W; (with Ipswich T), 1972 v USSR (1 + 1 sub), Sp; 1973 v Bul, Cy (2), P, E, S, W; 1974 v Bul, S, E, W; 1975 v N, Se, Y, E; 1976 v Se, N, Y; (with Everton), Is, S, E, W; 1977 v Ho, Bel, WG, E, S, W, Ic; (with Millwall), 1978 v S, E, W; 1979 v Ei (sub); (with Swindon T), Bul (2). E, S, W, D; 1980 v Aus (2 sub) (50)

Hamilton, J. (Knock), 1882 v E, W (2)

Hamilton, R. (Distillery), 1908 v W (1)

Hamilton, R. (Rangers), 1928 v S; 1929 v E; 1930 v S, E; 1932 v S (5)

Hamilton, W. (QPR), 1978 v S (sub); (with Burnley), 1980 v S, E, Aus (2); 1981 v Se, P, S, P, S, Se; 1982 v S, Is, E, W, Y, Hon, Sp, A, F; 1983 v A, WG, Alb (2), S, E, W; 1984 v A, T, WG, S, E, W, Fi; (with Oxford U), 1985 v R, Sp; 1986 v Mor (sub), Alg, Sp (sub), Br (sub), (41)

Hamilton, W. D. (Dublin Association), 1885 v W (1)

Hamilton, W. J. (Dublin Association), 1885 v W (1)

Hampton, H. (Bradford C), 1911 v E, S, W; 1912 v E, W; 1913 v E, S, W; 1914 v E (9)

Hanna, D. R. A. (Portsmouth), 1899 v W (1)

Hanna, J. (Nottingham F), 1912 v S, W (2)

Hannon, D. J. (Bohemians), 1908 v E, S; 1911 v E, S; 1912 v W; 1913 v E (6)

Harkin, J. T. (Southport), 1968 v W; 1969 v T; (with Shrewsbury T), W (sub); 1970 v USSR; 1971 v Sp (5)

Harland, A. I. (Linfield), 1923 v E (1)

Harris, J. (Cliftonville), 1921 v W (1)

Harris, V. (Shelbourne), 1906 v E; 1907 v E, W; 1908 v E, W, S; (with Everton), 1909 v E, W, S; 1910 v E, S, W; 1911 v E, S, W; 1912 v E; 1913 v E, S; 1914 v S, W (20)

Harvey, M. (Sunderland), 1961 v I; 1962 v Ho; 1963 v W, Sp; 1964 v S, E, W, U, Sp; 1965 v E, S, W, Sw (2), Ho (2), Alb; 1966 v S, E, W, M, Alb, WG; 1967 v E, S; 1968 v E, W; 1969 v Is, T (2), E; 1970 v USSR; 1971 v Cy, W (sub) (34)

Hastings, J. (Knock), 1882 v E, W; (with Ulster), 1883 v W; 1884 v E, S; 1886 v E, S (7)

Hatton, S. (Linfield), 1963 v S, Pol (2)

Hayes, W. E. (Huddersfield T), 1938 v E, S; 1939 v E, S (4)

Healy, F. (Coleraine), 1982 v S, W, Hon (sub); (with Glentoran), 1983 v A (sub) (4)

Hegan, D. (WBA), 1970 v USSR; (with Wolverhampton W), 1972 v USSR, E, S, W; 1973 v Bul, Cy (7)

Henderson, A. W. (Ulster), 1885 v E, S, W (3)

Hewison, G. (Moyola Park), 1885 v E, S (2)

Hill, C. F. (Sheffield U, 1990 v N, U; 1991 v Pol, Y (4)

Hill, M. J. (Norwich C), 1959 v W; 1960 v W; 1961 v WG; 1962 v S; (with Everton), 1964 v S, E, Sp (7)

Hinton, E. (Fulham), 1947 v S, W; 1948 v S, E, W; (with Millwall), 1951 v W, F (7)

Hopkins, J. (Brighton), 1926 v E (1)

Houston, J. (Linfield), 1912 v S, W; 1913 v W; (with Everton), 1913 v E, S; 1914 v S (6)

Houston, W. (Linfield), 1933 v W (1)

Houston, W. G. (Moyola Park), 1885 v E, S (2)

Hughes, P. (Bury), 1987 v E, T, Is (3)

Hughes, W. (Bolton W), 1951 v W (1)

Humphries, W. (Ards), 1962 v W; (with Coventry C), 1962 v Ho; 1963 v E, S, W, Pol, Sp; 1964 v S, E, Sp; 1965 v S; (with Swansea T), 1965 v W, Ho, Alb (14)

Hunter, A. (Distillery), 1905 v W; 1906 v W, E, S; (with Belfast C), 1908 v W; 1909 v W, E, S (8)

Hunter, A. (Blackburn R), 1970 v USSR; 1971 v Cy (2), E, S, W; (with Ipswich T), 1972 v USSR (2), Sp, E, S, W; 1973 v Bul, Cy (2), P, E, S, W; 1974 v Bul, S, E, W; 1975 v N, Se, Y, E, S, W; 1976 v Se, N, Y, Is, S, E, W; 1977 v Ho, Bel, WG, E, S, W, Ic; 1978 v Ic, Ho, Bel; 1979 v Ei, D, S, W, D; 1980 v E, Ei (53)

Hunter, J. (Cliftonville), 1884 v E, S, W (3)

Hunter, V. (Coleraine), 1962 v E; 1964 v Sp (2)

Irvine, R. J. (Linfield), 1962 v Ho; 1963 v E, S, W, Pol (2), Sp; (with Stoke C), 1965 v W (8)

Irvine, R. W. (Everton), 1922 v S; 1923 v E, W; 1924 v E, S; 1925 v E; 1926 v E; 1927 v E, W; 1928 v E, S; (with Portsmouth), 1929 v E; 1930 v S; (with Connah's Quay), 1931 v E; (with Derry C), 1932 v W (15)

Irvine, W. J. (Burnley), 1963 v W, Sp; 1965 v S, W, Sw, Ho (2), Alb; 1966 v S, E, W, M, Alb; 1967 v E, S; 1968 v E, W; (with Preston NE), 1969 v Is, T, E; (with Brighton), 1972 v E, S, W (23)

Irving, S. J. (Dundee), 1923 v S, W; 1924 v S, E, W; 1925 v S, E, W; 1926 v S, W; (with Cardiff C), 1927 v S, E, W; 1928 v S, E, W; (with Chelsea), 1929 v E; 1931 v S, W (18)

Jackson, T. (Everton), 1969 v Is, E, S, W; 1970 v USSR (1 + 1 sub); (with Nottingham F), 1971 v Sp; 1972 v E, S, W; 1973 v Cy, E, S, W; 1974 v Bul, P, S (sub), E (sub), W (sub); 1975 v N (sub), Se, Y, E, S, W; (with Manchester U); 1976 v Se, N, Y; 1977 v Ho, Bel, WG, E, S, W, Ic (35)

Jamison, J. (Glentoran), 1976 v N (1)

Jennings, P. A. (Watford), 1964 v W, U; (with Tottenham H), 1965 v E, S, Sw (2), Ho, Alb; 1966 v S, E, W, Alb, WG; 1967 v E, S; 1968 v S, E, W; 1969 v Is, T (2), E, S, W; 1970 v S, E, USSR; 1971 v Cy (2), E, S, W; 1972 v USSR, Sp, S, E, W; 1973 v Bul, Cy, P, E, S, W; 1974 v P, S, E, W; 1975 v N, Se, Y, E, S, W; 1976 v Se, N, Y, Is, S, E, W; 1977 v Ho, Bel, WG, E, S, W, Ic; (with Arsenal), 1978 v Ic, Ho, Bel; 1979 v Ei, D, Bul, E, Bul, E, S, W, D; 1980 v E, Ei, Is; 1981 v S, P, S, Se; 1982 v S, Is, E, W, Y, Hon, Sp, F; 1983 v Alb, S, E, W; 1984 v A, T, WG, S, W, Fi; 1985 v R, Fi, E, Sp, T; (with Tottenham H); 1986 v T, R, E, F, D; (with Everton), Mor; (with Tottenham H), Alg, Sp, Br (119)

Johnston, H. (Portadown), 1927 v W (1)

Johnston, R. (Old Park), 1885 v S, W (2)

Johnston, S. (Distillery), 1882 v W; 1884 v E; 1886 v E, S (4)

Johnston, S. (Linfield), 1890 v W; 1893 v S, W; 1894 v E (4)

Johnston, S. (Distillery), 1905 v W (1)

Johnston, W. C. (Glenavon), 1962 v W; (with Oldham Ath), 1966 v M (sub) (2)

Jones, J. (Linfield), 1930 v S, W; 1931 v S, W, E; 1932 v S, E; 1933 v S, E, W; 1934 v S, E, W; 1935 v S, E, W; 1936 v E, S; (with Hibernian), 1936 v W; 1937 v E, W, S; (with Glenavon), 1938 v E (23)

Jones, J. (Glenavon), 1956 v W; 1957 v E, W (3)

Jones, S. (Distillery), 1934 v E; (with Blackpool), 1934 v W (2)

Jordan, T. (Linfield), 1895 v E, W (2)

Kavanagh, P. J. (Celtic), 1930 v E (1)

Keane, T. R. (Swansea T), 1949 v S (1)

Kearns, A. (Distillery), 1900 v E, S, W; 1902 v E, S, W (6)

Kee, P. V. (Oxford U), 1990 v N; 1991 v Y (2), D, A, Pol, Fa (7)

Keith, R, M. (Newcastle U), 1958 v E, W, Cz (2), Arg, I, WG, F; 1959 v E, S, W, Sp; 1960 v S, E; 1961 v S, E, W, I, WG (2), Gr; 1962 v W, Ho (23)

Kelly, H. R. (Fulham), 1950 v E, W; (with Southampton), 1951 v E, S (4)

Kelly, J. (Glentoran), 1896 v E (1)

Kelly, J. (Derry C), 1932 v E, W; 1933 v E, W, S; 1934 v W; 1936 v E, S, W; 1937 v S, E (11)

Kelly, P. (Manchester C), 1921 v E (1)

Kelly, P. M. (Barnsley), 1950 v S (1)

Kennedy, A. L. (Arsenal), 1923 v W; 1925 v E (2)

Kernaghan, N. (Belfast C), 1936 v W; 1937 v S; 1938 v E (3)

Kirkwood, H. (Cliftonville), 1904 v W (1)

Kirwan, J. (Tottenham H), 1900 v W; 1902 v E, W; 1903 v E, S, W; 1904 v E, S, W; 1905 v E, S, W; (with Chelsea), 1906 v E, S, W; 1907 v W; (with Clyde), 1909 v S (17)

Lacey, W. (Everton), 1909 v E, S, W; 1910 v E, S, W; 1911 v E, S, W; 1912 v E; (with Liverpool), 1913 v W; 1914 v E, S, W; 1920 v E, S, W; 1921 v E, S, W; 1922 v E, S; (with New Brighton), 1925 v E (23)

Lawther, W. I. (Sunderland), 1960 v W; 1961 v I; (with Blackburn R), 1962 v S, Ho (4)

Leatham, J. (Belfast C), 1939 v W (1)

Ledwidge, J. J. (Shelbourne), 1906 v S, W (2)

Lemon, J. (Glentoran), 1886 v W; 1888 v S; (with Belfast YMCA), 1889 v W (3)

Leslie, W. (YMCA), 1887 v E (1)

Lewis, J. (Glentoran), 1899 v S, E, W; (with Distillery), 1900 v S (4)

Little, J. (Glentoran), 1898 v W (1)

Lockhart, H. (Rossall School), 1884 v W (1)

Lockhart, N. (Linfield), 1947 v E; (with Coventry C), 1950 v W; 1951 v W; 1952 v W; (with Aston Villa), 1954 v S, E; 1955 v W; 1956 v W (8)

Lowther, R. (Glentoran), 1888 v E, S (2)

Loyal, J. (Clarence), 1891 v S (1)

Lutton, R. J. (Wolverhampton W), 1970 v S, E; (with West Ham U), 1973 v Cy (sub), S (sub), W (sub); 1974 v P (6)

Lyner, D. (Glentoran), 1920 v E, W; 1922 v S, W; (with Manchester U), 1923 v E; (with Kilmarnock), 1923 v W (6)

McAdams, W. J. (Manchester C), 1954 v W; 1955 v S; 1957 v E; 1958 v S, I; (with Bolton W), 1961 v E, S, W, I, WG (2), Gr; 1962 v E, Gr; (with Leeds U), Ho (15)

McAlery, J. M. (Cliftonville), 1882 v E, W (2)

McAlinden, J. (Belfast C), 1938 v S; 1939 v S; (with Portsmouth), 1947 v E; (with Southend U), 1949 v E (4)

McAllen, J. (Linfield), 1898 v E; 1899 v E, S, W; 1900 v E, S, W; 1901 v W; 1902 v S (9)

McAlpine, W. J. (Cliftonville), 1901 v S (1)

McArthur, A. (Distillery), 1886 v W (1)

McAuley, J. L. (Huddersfield T), 1911 v E, W; 1912 v E, S; 1913 v E, S (6)

McAuley, P. (Belfast C), 1900 v S (1)

McBride, S. (Glenavon), 1991 v D (sub), Pol (sub) (2)

McCabe, J. J. (Leeds U), 1949 v S, W; 1950 v E; 1951 v W; 1953 v W; 1954 v S (6)

McCabe, W. (Ulster), 1891 v E (1)

McCambridge, J. (Ballymena), 1930 v S, W; (with Cardiff C), 1931 v W; 1932 v E (4)

McCandless, J. (Bradford), 1912 v W; 1913 v W; 1920 v W, S; 1921 v E (5)

McCandless, W. (Linfield), 1920 v E, W; 1921 v E; (with Rangers), 1921 v W; 1922 v S; 1924 v W, S; 1925 v S; 1929 v W (9)

McCann, P. (Belfast C), 1910 v E, S, W; 1911 v E; (with Glentoran), 1911 v S; 1912 v E; 1913 v W (7)

McCashin, J. (Cliftonville), 1896 v W; 1898 v S, W; 1899 v S (4)

McCavana, W. T. (Coleraine), 1955 v S; 1956 v E, S (3)

McCaw, D. (Distillery), 1882 v E (1)

McCaw, J. H. (Linfield), 1927 v W; 1930 v S; 1931 v E, S, W (5)

McClatchey, J. (Distillery), 1886 v E, S, W (3)

McClatchey, R. (Distillery), 1895 v S (1)

McCleary, J. W. (Cliftonville), 1955 v W (1)

McCleery, W. (Cliftonville), 1922 v N; 1930 v E, W; 1931 v E, S, W; 1932 v S, W; 1933 v E, W (10)

McClelland, J. (Arsenal), 1961 v W, I, WG (2), Gr; (with Fulham), 1967 v M (6)

McClelland, J. (Mansfield T), 1980 v S (sub), Aus (3); 1981 v Se, S; (with Rangers), S, Se; 1982 v S, W, Y, Hon, Sp, A, F; 1983 v A, WG, Alb, T, Alb, S, E, W; 1984 v A, T,

WG, S, E, W, Fi; 1985 v R, (with Watford), Fi, Is, E, Sp, T; 1986 v T, F (sub); 1987 v E (2), T, Is, Y; 1988 v T, Gr, F, Ma; 1989 v Ei, H, Sp (2), Ma; (with Leeds U), 1990 v N (53)

McCluggage, A. (Bradford), 1924 v E; (with Burnley), 1927 v S, W; 1928 v S, E, W; 1929 v S, E, W; 1930 v W; 1931 v E, W (12)

McClure, G. (Cliftonville), 1907 v S, W; 1908 v E; (with Distillery), 1909 v E (4)

McConnell, E. (Cliftonville), 1904 v S, W; (with Glentoran), 1905 v S; (with Sunderland), 1906 v E; 1907 v E; 1908 v S, W; (with Sheffield W), 1909 v S, W; 1910 v S, W, E (12)

McConnell, P. (Doncaster R), 1928 v W; (with Southport), 1932 v E (2)

McConnell, W. G. (Bohemians), 1912 v W; 1913 v E, S; 1914 v E, S, W (6)

McConnell, W. H. (Reading), 1925 v W; 1926 v E, W; 1927 v E, S, W; 1928 v E, W (8)

McCourt, F. J. (Manchester C), 1952 v E, W; 1953 v E, S, W, F (6)

McCoy, J. (Distillery), 1896 v W (1)

McCoy, R. (Coleraine), 1987 v T (sub) (1)

McCracken, R. (C Palace), 1921 v E; 1922 v E, S, W (4)

McCracken, W. (Distillery), 1902 v E, W; 1903 v E; 1904 v E, S, W; (with Newcastle U), 1905 v E, S, W; 1907 v E; 1920 v E; 1922 v E, S, W; (with Hull C), 1923 v S (15)

McCreery, D. (Manchester U), 1976 v S (sub), E, W; 1977 v Ho, Bel, WG, E, S, W, Ic; 1978 v Ic, Ho, Bel, S, E, W; 1979 v Ei, D, Bul, E, Bul, W, D; (with QPR), 1980 v E, Ei, S (sub), E (sub), W (sub), Aus (1+1 sub); 1981 v Se (sub), P (sub); (with Tulsa R), S, P, Se; 1982 v S, Is, E (sub), F, Y, Hon, Sp, A, F; (with Newcastle U), v A; 1984 v T (sub); 1985 v R, Sp (sub); 1986 v T (sub), R, E, F, D, Alg, Sp, Br; 1987 v T, E, Y; 1988 v Y; 1989 v Sp, Ma, Ch; (with Hearts), 1990 v H, Ei, N, U (67)

McCrory, S. (Southend U), 1958 v E (1)

McCullough, K. (Belfast C), 1935 v W; 1936 v E; (with Manchester C), 1936 v S; 1937 v E, S (5)

McCullough, W. J. (Arsenal), 1961 v I; 1963 v Sp; 1964 v S, E, W, U, Sp; 1965 v E, Sw; (with Millwall), 1967 v E (10)

McCurdy, C. (Linfield), 1980 v Aus (sub) (1)

McDonald, A. (QPR), 1986 v R, E, F, D, Mor, Alg, Sp, Br; 1987 v E (2), T, Is, Y; 1988 v Y, T, Pol, F, Ma; 1989 v Ei, H, Sp, Ch; 1990 v H, Ei, U; 1991 v Y, D, A, Fa (29)

McDonald, R. (Rangers), 1930 v S; 1932 v E (2)

McDonnell, J. (Bohemians), 1911 v E, S; 1912 v W; 1913 v W (4)

McElhinney, G. (Bolton W), 1984 v WG, S, E, W, Fi; 1985 v R (6)

McFaul, W. S. (Linfield), 1967 v E (sub); (with Newcastle U), 1970 v W; 1971 v Sp; 1972 v USSR; 1973 v Cy; 1974 v Bul (6)

McGarry, J. K. (Cliftonville), 1951 v W, F, S (3)

McGaughey, M. (Linfield), 1985 v Is (sub) (1)

McGee, G. (Wellington Park), 1885 v E, S, W (3)

McGrath, R. C. (Tottenham H), 1974 v S, E, W; 1975 v N; 1976 v Is (sub); 1977 v Ho; (with Manchester U), Bel, WG, E, S, W, Ic; 1978 v Ic, Ho, Bel, S, E, W; 1979 v Bul (sub), E (2 sub) (21)

McGregor, S. (Glentoran), 1921 v S (1)

McGrillen, J. (Clyde), 1924 v S; (with Belfast C), 1927 v S (2)

McGuire, E. (Distillery), 1907 v S (1)

McIlroy, H. (Cliftonville), 1906 v E (1)

McIlroy, J. (Burnley), 1952 v E, S, W; 1953 v E, S, W; 1954 v E, W; 1955 v E, S, W; 1956 v E, S, W; 1957 v E, S, W, I, P (2); 1958 v E, S, W, I (2), Cz (2), Arg, WG, F; 1959 v E, S, W, Sp; 1960 v E, S, W; 1961 v E, W, WG (2), Gr; 1962 v E, S, Gr, Ho; 1963 v E, S, Pol (2); (with Stoke C), 1963 v W; 1966 v S, E, Alb (55)

McIlroy, S. B. (Manchester U), 1972 v Sp, S (sub); 1974 v S, E, W; 1975 v N, Se, Y, E, S, W; 1976 v Se, N, Y, S, E, W; 1977 v Ho, Bel, E, S, W, Ic; 1978 v Ic, Ho, Bel, S, E, W; 1979 v Ei, D, Bul, E, Bul, E, S, W, D; 1980 v E, Ei, Is, S, E, W; 1981 v Se, P, S, P, S, Se; 1982 v S, Is; (with Stoke C), E, F, S, W, Y, Hon, Sp, A, F; 1983 v A, WG, Alb, T, Alb, S, E, W; 1984 v A, T, S, E, W, Fi; 1985 v Fi, E, T; (with Manchester C), 1986 v T, R, E, F, D, Mor, Alg, Sp, Br; 1987 v E (sub) (88)

McIlvenny, J. (Distillery), 1890 v E; 1891 v E (2)

McIlvenny, P. (Distillery), 1924 v W (1)

McKeag, W. (Glentoran), 1968 v S, W (2)

McKee, F. W. (Cliftonville), 1906 v S, W; (with Belfast C), 1914 v E, S, W (5)

McKelvie, H. (Glentoran), 1901 v W (1)

McKenna, J. (Huddersfield), 1950 v E, S, W; 1951 v E, S, F; 1952 v E (7)

McKenzie, H. (Distillery), 1923 v S (1)

McKenzie, R. (Airdrie), 1967 v W (1)

McKeown, H. (Linfield), 1892 v E, S, W; 1893 v S, W; 1894 v S, W (7)

McKie, H. (Cliftonville), 1895 v E, S, W (3)

McKinney, D. (Hull C), 1921 v S; (with Bradford C), 1924 v S (2)

McKinney, V. J. (Falkirk), 1966 v WG (1)

McKnight, A. (Celtic), 1988 v Y, T, Gr, Pol, F, Ma; (with West Ham U) 1989 v Ei, H, Sp (2) (10)

McKnight, J. (Preston NE), 1912 v E; (with Glentoran), 1913 v S (2)

McLaughlin, J. C. (Shrewsbury T), 1962 v E, S, W, Gr; 1963 v W; (with Swansea T), 1964 v W, U; 1965 v E, W, Sw (2); 1966 v W (12)

McLean, T. (Limavady), 1885 v S (1)

McMahon, J. (Bohemians), 1934 v S (1)

McMaster, G. (Glentoran), 1897 v E, S, W (3)

McMichael, A. (Newcastle U), 1950 v E, S; 1951 v E, S, F; 1952 v E, S, W; 1953 v E, S, W, F; 1954 v E, S, W; 1955 v E, W; 1956 v W; 1957 v E, S, W, I, P (2); 1958 v E, S, W, I (2), Cz (2), Arg, WG, F; 1959 v S, W, Sp; 1960 v E, S, W (40)

McMillan, G. (Distillery), 1903 v E; 1905 v W (2)

McMillan, S. (Manchester U), 1963 v E, S (2)

McMillen, W. S. (Manchester U), 1934 v E; 1935 v S; 1937 v S; (with Chesterfield), 1938 v S, W; 1939 v E, S (7)

McMordie, A. S. (Middlesbrough), 1969 v Is, T (2), E, S, W; 1970 v E, S, W, USSR; 1971 v Cy (2), E, S, W; 1972 v USSR, Sp, E, S, W; 1973 v Bul (21)

McMorran, E. J. (Belfast C), 1947 v E; (with Barnsley), 1951 v E, S, W; 1952 v E, S, W; 1953 v E, S, F; (with Doncaster R), 1953 v W; 1954 v E; 1956 v W; 1957 v I, P (15)

McMullan, D. (Liverpool), 1926 v E, W; 1927 v S (3)

McNally, B. A. (Shrewsbury T), 1986 v Mor; 1987 v T (sub); 1988 v Y, Gr, Ma (sub) (5)

McNinch, J. (Ballymena), 1931 v S; 1932 v S, W (3)

McParland, P. J. (Aston Villa), 1954 v W; 1955 v E, S; 1956 v E, S; 1957 v E, S, W, P; 1958 v E, S, W, I (2), Cz (2), Arg, WG, F; 1959 v E, S, W, Sp; 1960 v E, S, W; 1961 v E, S, W, I, WG (2), Gr; (with Wolverhampton W), 1962 v Ho (34)

McShane, J. (Cliftonville), 1899 v S; 1900 v E, S, W (4)

McVickers, J. (Glentoran), 1888 v E; 1889 v S (2)

McWha, W. B. R. (Knock), 1882 v E, W; (with Cliftonville), 1883 v E, W; 1884 v E; 1885 v E, W (7)

Macartney, A. (Ulster), 1903 v S, W; (with Linfield), 1904 v S, W; (with Everton), 1905 v E, S; (with Belfast C), 1907 v E, S, W; 1908 v E, S, W; (with Glentoran), 1909 v E, S, W (15)

Mackie, J. (Arsenal), 1923 v W; (with Portsmouth), 1935 v S, W (3)

Madden, O. (Norwich C), 1938 v E (1)

Magill, E. J. (Arsenal), 1962 v E, S, Gr; 1963 v E, S, W, Pol (2), Sp; 1964 v E, S, W, U, Sp; 1965 v E, S, Sw (2),

Ho, Alb; 1966 v S, E; (with Brighton), 1966 v Alb, W, WG, M (26)

Magilton, J. (Oxford U), 1991 v Pol, Y, Fa (3)

Maginnis, H. (Linfield), 1900 v E, S, W; 1903 v S, W; 1904 v E, S, W (8)

Maguire, E. (Distillery), 1907 v S (1)

Mahood, J. (Belfast C), 1926 v S; 1928 v E, S, W; 1929 v E, S, W; 1930 v W; (with Ballymena), 1934 v S (9)

Manderson, R. (Rangers), 1920 v W, S; 1925 v S, E; 1926 v S (5)

Mansfield, J. (Dublin Freebooters), 1901 v E (1)

Martin, C. J. (Glentoran), 1947 v S; (with Leeds U), 1948 v E, S, W; (with Aston Villa), 1949 v E; 1950 v W (6)

Martin, D. (Bo'ness), 1925 v S (1)

Martin, D. C. (Cliftonville), 1882 v E, W; 1883 v E (3)

Martin, D. K. (Belfast C), 1934 v E, S, W; 1935 v S; (with Wolverhampton W), 1935 v E; 1936 v W; (with Nottingham F), 1937 v S; 1938 v S; 1939 v S (10)

Mathieson, A. (Luton T), 1921 v W; 1922 v E (2)

Maxwell, J. (Linfield), 1902 v W; 1903 v W, E; (with Glentoran), 1905 v W, S; (with Belfast C), 1906 v W; 1907 v S (7)

Meek, H. L. (Glentoran), 1925 v W (1)

Mehaffy, J. A. C. (Queen's Island), 1922 v W (1)

Meldon, J. (Dublin Freebooters), 1899 v S, W (2)

Mercer, H. V. A. (Linfield), 1908 v E (1)

Mercer, J. T. (Distillery), 1898 v E, S, W; 1899 v E; (with Linfield), 1902 v E, W; (with Distillery), 1903 v S, W; (with Derby Co), 1904 v E, W; 1905 v E; 1905 v S (11)

Millar, W. (Barrow), 1932 v W; 1933 v S (2)

Miller, J. (Middlesbrough), 1929 v W, S; 1930 v E (3)

Milligan, D. (Chesterfield), 1939 v W (1)

Milne, R. G. (Linfield), 1894 v E, S, W; 1895 v E, W; 1896 v E, S, W; 1897 v E, S; 1898 v E, S, W; 1899 v E, W; 1901 v W; 1902 v E, S, W; 1903 v E, S; 1904 v E, S, W; 1906 v E, S, W (27)

Mitchell, C. (Glentoran), 1934 v W (1)

Mitchell, E. J. (Cliftonville), 1933 v S (1)

Mitchell, W. (Distillery), 1932 v E, W; 1933 v E, W; (with Chelsea), 1934 v W; 1935 v S, E; 1936 v S, E; 1937 v E, S, W; 1938 v E, S (15)

Molyneux, T. B. (Ligoniel), 1883 v E, W; (with Cliftonville), 1884 v E, W, S; 1885 v E, W; 1886 v E, W, S; 1888 v S (11)

Montgomery, F. J. (Coleraine), 1955 v E (1)

Moore, C. (Glentoran), 1949 v W (1)

Moore, J. (Linfield Ath), 1891 v E, S, W (3)

Moore, P. (Aberdeen), 1933 v E (1)

Moore, T. (Ulster), 1887 v S, W (2)

Moore, W. (Falkirk), 1923 v S (1)

Moorhead, F. W. (Dublin University), 1885 v E (1)

Moorhead, G. (Linfield), 1923 v S; 1928 v S; 1929 v S (3)

Moran, J. (Leeds C), 1912 v S (1)

Moreland, W. (Derby Co), 1979 v Bul (2 sub), E, S; 1980 v E, Ei (6)

Morgan, F. G. (Linfield), 1923 v E; (with Nottingham F), 1924 v S; 1927 v E; 1928 v E, S, W; 1929 v E (7)

Morgan, S. (Port Vale), 1972 v Sp; 1973 v Bul (sub), P, Cy, E, S, W; (with Aston Villa), 1974 v Bul, P, S, E; 1975 v Se; 1976 v Se (sub), N, Y; (with Brighton & HA), S, W (sub); (with Sparta Rotterdam), 1979 v D (18)

Morrison, J. (Linfield Ath), 1891 v E, W (2)

Morrison, T. (Glentoran), 1895 v E, S, W; (with Burnley), 1899 v W; 1900 v W; 1902 v E, S (7)

Morrogh, E. (Bohemians), 1896 v S (1)

Morrow, S. J. (Arsenal), 1990 v U (sub); 1991 v A (sub), Pol, Y (4)

Morrow, W. J. (Moyola Park), 1883 v E, W; 1884 v S (3)

Muir, R. (Oldpark), 1885 v S, W (2)

Mullan, G. (Glentoran), 1983 v S, E, W, Alb (sub) (4)

Mulholland, S. (Celtic), 1906 v S, E (2)

Mulligan, J. (Manchester C), 1921 v S (1)

Murphy, J. (Bradford C), 1910 v E, S, W (3)

Murphy, N. (QPR), 1905 v E, S, W (3)

Murray, J. M. (Motherwell), 1910 v E, S; (with Sheffield W), 1910 v W (3)

Napier, R. J. (Bolton W), 1966 v WG (1)

Neill, W. J. T. (Arsenal), 1961 v I, Gr, WG; 1962 v E, S, W, Gr; 1963 v E, W, Pol, Sp; 1964 v S, E, W, U, Sp; 1965 v E, S, W, Sw, Ho (2), Alb; 1966 v S, E, W, Alb, WG, M; 1967 v S, W; 1968 v S, E; 1969 v E, S, W, Is, T (2); 1970 v S, E, W, USSR (2); (with Hull C), 1971 v Cy, Sp; 1972 v USSR (2), Sp, S, E, W; 1973 v Bul, Cy (2), P, E, S, W (59)

Nelis, P. (Nottingham F), 1923 v E (1)

Nelson, S. (Arsenal), 1970 v W, E (sub); 1971 v Cy, Sp, E, S, W; 1972 v USSR (2), Sp, E, S, W; 1973 v Bul, Cy, P; 1974 v S, E; 1975 v Se, Y; 1976 v Se, N, Is, E; 1977 v Bel (sub), WG, W, Ic; 1978 v Ic, Ho, Bel; 1979 v Ei, D, Bul, E, Bul, E, S, W, D; 1980 v E, Ei, Is; 1981 v S, P, S, Se; (with Brighton & HA), 1982 v E, S, Sp (sub), A (51)

Nicholl, C. J. (Aston Villa), 1975 v Se, Y, E, S, W; 1976 v Se, N, Y, S, E, W; 1977 v W; (with Southampton), 1978 v Bel (sub), S, E, W; 1979 v Ei, Bul, E, Bul, E, W; 1980 v Ei, Is, S, E, W, Aus (3); 1981 v Se, P, S, P, S, Se; 1982 v S, Is, E, F, W, Y, Hon, Sp, A, F; 1983 v S (sub), E, W; (with Grimsby T), 1984 v A, T (51)

Nicholl, H. (Belfast C), 1902 v E, W; 1905 v E (3)

Nicholl, J. M. (Manchester U), 1976 v Is, W (sub); 1977 v Ho, Bel, E, S, W, Ic; 1978 v Ic, Ho, Bel, S, E, W; 1979 v Ei, D, Bul, E, Bul, E, S, W, D; 1980 v E, Ei, Is, S, E, W, Aus (3); 1981 v Se, P, S, P, S, Se; 1982 v S, Is, E; (with Toronto B), F, W, Y, Hon, Sp, A, F; (with Sunderland), 1983 v A, WG, Alb, T, Alb; (with Toronto B), S, E, W; (with Rangers), 1984 v T, WG, S, E; (with Toronto B), Fi; 1985 v R; (with WBA), Fi, E, Sp, T; 1986 v T, R, E, F, Alg, Sp, Br (73)

Nicholson, J. J. (Manchester U), 1961 v S, W; 1962 v E, W, Gr, Ho; 1963 v E, S, Pol (2); (with Huddersfield T), 1965 v W, Ho (2), Alb; 1966 v S, E, W, Alb, M; 1967 v S, W; 1968 v S, E, W; 1969 v S, E, W, T (2); 1970 v S, E, W, USSR (2); 1971 v Cy (2), E, S, W; 1972 v USSR (2) (41)

Nixon, R. (Linfield), 1914 v S (1)

Nolan-Whelan, J. V. (Dublin Freebooters), 1901 v E, W; 1902 v S, W (4)

O'Brien, M. T. (QPR), 1921 v S; (with Leicester C), 1922 v S, W; 1924 v S, W; (with Hull C), 1925 v S, E, W; 1926 v W; (with Derby Co), 1927 v W (10)

O'Connell, P. (Sheffield W), 1912 v E, S; (with Hull C), 1914 v E, S, W (5)

O'Doherty, A. (Coleraine), 1970 v E, W (sub) (2)

O'Driscoll, J. F. (Swansea T), 1949 v E, S, W (3)

O'Hagan, C. (Tottenham H), 1905 v S, W; 1906 v S, W, E; (with Aberdeen), 1907 v E, S, W; 1908 v S, W; 1909 v E (11)

O'Hagan, W. (St Mirren), 1920 v E, W (2)

O'Hehir, J. C. (Bohemians), 1910 v W (1)

O'Kane, W. J. (Nottingham F), 1970 v E, W, S (sub); 1971 v Sp, E, S, W; 1972 v USSR (2); 1973 v P, Cy; 1974 v Bul, P, S, E, W; 1975 v N, Se, E, S (20)

O'Mahoney, M. T. (Bristol R), 1939 v S (1)

O'Neill, C. (Motherwell), 1989 v Ch (sub); 1990 v Ei (sub); 1991 v D (3)

O'Neill, J. (Leicester C), 1980 v Is, S, E, W, Aus (3); 1981 v P, S, P, S, Se; 1982 v S, Is, E, F, S, F (sub); 1983 v A, WG, Alb, T, Alb; S; 1984 v S (sub); 1985 v Is, Fi, E, Sp, T; 1986 v T, R, E, F, D, Mor, Alg, Sp, Br (39)

O'Neill, J. (Sunderland), 1962 v W (1)

O'Neill, M. A. (Newcastle U), 1988 v Gr, Pol, F, Ma; 1989 v Ei, H, Sp (sub), Ma (sub), Ch; (with Dundee U), 1990 v H (sub), Ei; 1991 v Pol (13)

O'Neill, M. H. (Distillery), 1972 v USSR (sub), (with Nottingham F), Sp (sub), W (sub); 1973 v P, Cy, E, S,

W; 1974 v Bul, P, E (sub), W; 1975 v Se, Y, E, S; 1976 v Y; 1977 v E (sub), S; 1978 v Ic, Ho, S, E, W; 1979 v Ei, D, Bul, E, Bul, D; 1980 v Ei, Is, Aus (3); 1981 v Se, P; (with Norwich C), P, S, Se; (with Manchester C), 1982 v S; (with Norwich C), E, F, S, Y, Hon, Sp, A, F; 1983 v A, WG, Alb, T, Alb, S, E; (with Notts Co), 1984 v A, T, WG, E, W, Fi; 1985 v R, Fi (64)

O'Reilly, H. (Dublin Freebooters), 1901 v S, W; 1904 v S (3)

Parke, J. (Linfield), 1964 v S; (with Hibernian), 1964 v E, Sp; (with Sunderland), 1965 v Sw, S, W, Ho (2), Alb; 1966 v WG; 1967 v E, S; 1968 v S, E (14)

Peacock, R. (Celtic), 1952 v S; 1953 v F; 1954 v W; 1955 v E, S; 1956 v E, S; 1957 v W, I, P; 1958 v S, E, W, I (2), Arg, Cz (2), WG; 1959 v E, S, W; 1960 v S, E; 1961 v E, S, I, WG (2), Gr; (with Coleraine), 1962 v S (31)

Peden, J. (Linfield), 1887 v S, W; 1888 v W, E; 1889 v S, E; 1890 v W, S; 1891 v W, E; 1892 v W, E; 1893 v E, S, W; (with Distillery), 1896 v W, E, S; 1897 v W, S; 1898 v W, E, S; (with Linfield), 1899 v W (24)

Penney, S. (Brighton & HA), 1985 v Is; 1986 v T, R, E, F, D, Mor, Alg, Sp; 1987 v E, T, Is; 1988 v Pol, F, Ma; 1989 v Ei, Sp (17)

Percy, J. C. (Belfast YMCA), 1889 v W (1)

Platt, J. A. (Middlesbrough), 1976 v Is (sub); 1978 v S, E, W; 1980 v S, E, W, Aus (3); 1981 v Se, P; 1982 v F, S, W (sub), A; 1983 v A, WG, Alb, T; (with Ballymena U), 1984 v E, W (sub); (with Coleraine), 1986 v Mor (sub) (23)

Ponsonby, J. (Distillery), 1895 v S; 1896 v E, S, W; 1897 v E, S, W; 1899 v E (8)

Potts, R. M. C. (Cliftonville), 1883 v E, W (2)

Priestley, T. J. (Coleraine), 1933 v S; (with Chelsea), 1934 v E (2)

Pyper, Jas. (Cliftonville), 1897 v S, W; 1898 v S, E, W; 1899 v S; 1900 v E (7)

Pyper, John (Cliftonville), 1897 v E, S, W; 1899 v E, W; 1900 v E, W, S; 1902 v S (9)

Pyper, M. (Linfield), 1932 v W (1)

Quinn, J. M. (Blackburn R), 1985 v Is, Fi, E, Sp, T; 1986 v T, R, E, F, D (sub), Mor (sub); 1987 v E (sub), T; (with Swindon T), 1988 v Y (sub), T, Gr, Pol, F (sub), Ma; (with Leicester C), 1989 v Ei, H (sub), Sp (sub+1); (with Bradford C), Ma, Ch; 1990 v H, (with West Ham U), N; 1991 v Y (sub) (28)

Rafferty, P. (Linfield), 1980 v E (sub) (1)

Ramsey, P. (Leicester C), 1984 v A, WG, S; 1985 v Is, E, Sp, T; 1986 v T, Mor; 1987 v Is, E, Y (sub); 1988 v Y; 1989 v Sp (14)

Rankine, J. (Alexander), 1883 v E, W (2)

Raper, E. O. (Dublin University), 1886 v W (1)

Rattray, D. (Avoniel), 1882 v E; 1883 v E, W (3)

Rea, B. (Glentoran), 1901 v E (1)

Redmond, J. (Cliftonville), 1884 v W (1)

Reid, G. H. (Cardiff C), 1923 v S (1)

Reid, J. (Ulster), 1883 v E; 1884 v W; 1887 v S; 1889 v W; 1890 v S, W (6)

Reid, S. E. (Derby Co), 1934 v E, W; 1936 v E (3)

Reid, W. (Hearts), 1931 v E (1)

Reilly, J. (Portsmouth), 1900 v E; 1902 v E (2)

Renneville, W. T. (Leyton), 1910 v S, E, W; (with Aston Villa), 1911 v W (4)

Reynolds, J. (Distillery), 1890 v E, W; (with Ulster), 1891 v E, S, W (5)

Reynolds, R. (Bohemians), 1905 v W (1)

Rice, P. J. (Arsenal), 1969 v Is; 1970 v USSR; 1971 v E, S, W; 1972 v USSR, Sp, E, S, W; 1973 v Bul, Cy, E, S, W; 1974 v Bul, P, S, E, W; 1975 v N, Y, E, S, W; 1976 v Se, N, Y, Is, S, E, W; 1977 v Ho, Bel, WG, E, S, Ic; 1978 v Ic, Ho, Bel; 1979 v Ei, D, E (2), S, W, D; 1980 v E (49)

Roberts, F. C. (Glentoran), 1931 v S (1)

Robinson, P. (Distillery), 1920 v S; (with Blackburn R), 1921 v W (2)

Rogan, A. (Celtic), 1988 v Y (sub), Gr, Pol (sub); 1989 v Ei (sub), H, Sp (2), Ma (sub), Ch; 1990 v H, N (sub), U; 1991 v Y (2), D, A (16)

Rollo, D. (Linfield), 1912 v W; 1913 v W; 1914 v W, E; (with Blackburn R), 1920 v S, W; 1921 v E, S, W; 1922 v E; 1923 v E; 1924 v S, W; 1925 v W; 1926 v E; 1927 v E (16)

Rosbotham, A. (Cliftonville), 1887 v E, S, W; 1888 v E, S, W; 1889 v E (7)

Ross, W. E. (Newcastle U), 1969 v Is (1)

Rowley, R. W. M. (Southampton), 1929 v S, W; 1930 v W, E; (with Tottenham H), 1931 v W; 1932 v S (6)

Russell, A. (Linfield), 1947 v E (1)

Russell, S. R. (Bradford C), 1930 v E, S; (with Derry C), 1932 v E (3)

Ryan, R. A. (WBA), 1950 v W (1)

Sanchez, L. P. (Wimbledon), 1987 v T (sub); 1989 v Sp, Ma (3)

Scott, E. (Liverpool), 1920 v S; 1921 v E, S, W; 1922 v E; 1925 v W; 1926 v E, S, W; 1927 v E, S, W; 1928 v E, S, W; 1929 v E, S, W; 1930 v E; 1931 v E; 1932 v W; 1933 v E, S, W; 1934 v E, S, W; (with Belfast C), 1935 v S; 1936 v E, S, W (31)

Scott, J. (Grimsby), 1958 v Cz, F (2)

Scott, J. E. (Cliftonville), 1901 v S (1)

Scott, L. J. (Dublin University), 1895 v S, W (2)

Scott, P. W. (Everton), 1975 v W; 1976 v Y; (with York C), Is, S, E (sub), W; 1978 v S, E, W; (with Aldershot), 1979 v S (sub) (10)

Scott, T. (Cliftonville), 1894 v E, S; 1895 v S, W; 1896 v S, E, W; 1897 v E, W; 1898 v E, S, W; 1900 v W (13)

Scott, W. (Linfield), 1903 v E, S, W; 1904 v E, S, W; (with Everton), 1905 v E, S; 1907 v E, S; 1908 v E, S, W; 1909 v E, S, W; 1910 v E, S; 1911 v E, S, W; 1912 v E; (with Leeds City), 1913 v E, S, W (25)

Scraggs, M. J. (Glentoran), 1921 v W; 1922 v E (2)

Seymour, H. C. (Bohemians), 1914 v W (1)

Seymour, J. (Cliftonville), 1907 v W; 1909 v W (2)

Shanks, T. (Woolwich Arsenal), 1903 v S; 1904 v W; (with Brentford), 1905 v E (3)

Sharkey, P. (Ipswich T), 1976 v S (1)

Sheehan, Dr G. (Bohemians), 1899 v S; 1900 v E, W (3)

Sheridan, J. (Everton), 1903 v W, E, S; 1904 v E, S; (with Stoke C), 1905 v E (6)

Sherrard, J. (Limavady), 1885 v S; 1887 v W; 1888 v W (3)

Sherrard, W. (Cliftonville), 1895 v E, W, S (3)

Sherry, J. J. (Bohemians), 1906 v E; 1907 v W (2)

Shields, J. (Southampton), 1957 v S (1)

Silo, M. (Belfast YMCA), 1888 v E (1)

Simpson, W. J. (Rangers), 1951 v W, F; 1954 v E, S; 1955 v E; 1957 v I, P; 1958 v S, E, W, I; 1959 v S (12)

Sinclair, J. (Knock), 1882 v E, W (2)

Slemin, J. C. (Bohemians), 1909 v W (1)

Sloan, A. S. (London Caledonians), 1925 v W (1)

Sloan, D. (Oxford U), 1969 v Is; 1971 v Sp (2)

Sloan, H. A. de B. (Bohemians), 1903 v E; 1904 v S; 1905 v E; 1906 v W; 1907 v E, W; 1908 v W; 1909 v S (8)

Sloan, J. W. (Arsenal), 1947 v W (1)

Sloan, T. (Cardiff C), 1926 v S, W, E; 1927 v W, S; 1928 v E, W; 1929 v E; (with Linfield), 1930 v W, S; 1931 v S (11)

Sloan, T. (Manchester U), 1979 v S, W (sub), D (sub) (3)

Small, J. (Clarence), 1887 v E (1)

Small, J. M. (Cliftonville), 1893 v E, S, W (3)

Smith, E. E. (Cardiff C), 1921 v S; 1923 v W, E; 1924 v E (4)

Smith, J. (Distillery), 1901 v S, W (2)

Smyth, R. H. (Dublin University), 1886 v W (1)

Smyth, S. (Wolverhampton W), 1948 v E, S, W; 1949 v S, W; 1950 v E, S, W; (with Stoke C), 1952 v E (9)

Smyth, W. (Distillery), 1949 v E, S; 1954 v S, E (4)

Snape, A. (Airdrie), 1920 v E (1)

Spence, D. W. (Bury), 1975 v Y, E, S, W; 1976 v Se, Is, E, W, S (sub); (with Blackpool), 1977 v Ho (sub), WG (sub), E (sub), S (sub), W (sub), Ic (sub); 1979 v Ei, D (sub), E (sub), Bul (sub), E (sub), S, W, D; 1980 v Ei; (with Southend U), Is (sub), Aus (sub); 1981 v S (sub), Se (sub); 1982 v F (sub) (29)

Spencer, S. (Distillery), 1890 v E, S; 1892 v E, S, W; 1893 v E (6)

Spiller, E. A. (Cliftonville), 1883 v E, W; 1884 v E, W, S (5)

Stanfield, O. M. (Distillery), 1887 v E, S, W; 1888 v E, S, W; 1889 v E, S, W; 1890 v E, S; 1891 v E, S, W; 1892 v E, S, W; 1893 v E, W; 1894 v E, S, W; 1895 v E, S; 1896 v E, S, W; 1897 v E, S, W (30)

Steele, A. (Charlton Ath), 1926 v W, S; (with Fulham), 1929 v W, S (4)

Stevenson, A. E. (Rangers), 1934 v E, S, W; (with Everton), 1935 v E, S; 1936 v S, W; 1937 v E, W; 1938 v E, W; 1939 v E, S, W; 1947 v S, W; 1948 v S (17)

Stewart, A. (Glentoran), 1967 v W; 1968 v S, E; (with Derby Co), 1968 v W; 1969 v Is, T (1+1 sub) (7)

Stewart, D. C. (Hull C), 1978 v Bel (1)

Stewart, I. (QPR), 1982 v F (sub); 1983 v A, WG, Alb, T, Alb, S, E, W; 1984 v A, T, WG, S, E, W, Fi; 1985 v R, Fi, Is, E, Sp, T; (with Newcastle U), 1986 v R, E, D, Mor, Alg (sub), Sp (sub), Br; 1987 v E, Is (sub) (31)

Stewart, R. H. (St Columb's Court), 1890 v E, S, W; (with Cliftonville), 1892 v E, S, W; 1893 v E, W; 1894 v E, S, W (11)

Stewart, T. C. (Linfield), 1961 v W (1)

Swan, S. (Linfield), 1899 v S (1)

Taggart, G. P. (Barnsley), 1990 v N, U; 1991 v Y, D, A, Pol, Fa (7)

Taggart, J. (Walsall), 1899 v W (1)

Thompson, F. W. (Cliftonville), 1910 v E, S, W; (with Bradford C), 1911 v E; (with Linfield), v W; 1912 v E, W; 1913 v E, S, W; 1914 v E, S (12)

Thompson, J. (Belfast Ath), 1889 v S (1)

Thompson, J. (Distillery), 1897 v S (1)

Thunder, P. J. (Bohemians), 1911 v W (1)

Todd, S. J. (Burnley), 1966 v M (sub); 1967 v E; 1968 v W; 1969 v E, S, W; 1970 v S, USSR; (with Sheffield W), 1971 v Cy (2), Sp (sub) (11)

Toner, J. (Arsenal), 1922 v W; 1923 v W; 1924 v W, E; 1925 v E, S; (with St Johnstone), 1927 v E, S (8)

Torrans, R. (Linfield), 1893 v S (1)

Torrans, S. (Linfield), 1889 v S; 1890 v S, W; 1891 v S, W; 1892 v E, S, W; 1893 v E, S; 1894 v E, S, W; 1895 v E; 1896 v E, S, W; 1897 v E, S, W; 1898 v E, S, W; 1899 v E, W; 1901 v S, W (26)

Trainor, D. (Crusaders), 1967 v W (1)

Tully, C. P. (Celtic), 1949 v E; 1950 v E; 1952 v S; 1953 v E, S, W, F; 1954 v S; 1956 v E; 1959 v Sp (10)

Turner, E. (Cliftonville), 1896 v E, W (2)

Turner, W. (Cliftonville), 1886 v E; 1886 v S; 1888 v S (3)

Twoomey, J. F. (Leeds U), 1938 v W; 1939 v E (2)

Uprichard, W. N. M. C. (Swindon T), 1952 v E, S, W; 1953 v E, S; (with Portsmouth), 1953 v W, F; 1955 v E, S, W; 1956 v E, S, W; 1958 v S, I, Cz; 1959 v S, Sp (18)

Vernon, J. (Belfast C), 1947 v E, S; (with WBA), 1947 v W; 1948 v E, S, W; 1949 v E, S, W; 1950 v E, S; 1951 v E, S, W, F; 1952 v S, E (17)

Waddell, T. M. R. (Cliftonville), 1906 v S (1)

Walker, J. (Doncaster R), 1955 v W (1)

Walker, T. (Bury), 1911 v S (1)

Walsh, D. J. (WBA), 1947 v S, W; 1948 v E, S, W; 1949 v E, S, W; 1950 v W (9)

Walsh, W. (Manchester C), 1948 v E, S, W; 1949 v E, S (5)

Waring, R. (Distillery), 1899 v E (1)

Warren, P. (Shelbourne), 1913 v E, S (2)

Watson, J. (Ulster), 1883 v E, W; 1886 v E, S, W; 1887 v S, W; 1889 v E, W (9)

Watson, P. (Distillery), 1971 v Cy (sub) (1)

Watson, T. (Cardiff C), 1926 v S (1)

Wattle, J. (Distillery), 1899 v E (1)

Webb, C. G. (Brighton), 1909 v S, W; 1911 v S (3)

Weir, E. (Clyde), 1939 v W (1)

Welsh, E. (Carlisle U), 1966 v W, WG, M; 1967 v W (4)

Whiteside, N. (Manchester U), 1982 v Y, Hon, Sp, A, F; 1983 v WG, Alb, T; 1984 v A, T, WG, S, E, W, Fi; 1985 v R, Fi, Is, E, Sp, T; 1986 v R, E, F, D, Mor, Alg, Sp, Br; 1987 v E (2), Is, Y; 1988 v T, Pol, F; (with Everton), 1990 v H, Ei (38)

Whiteside, T. (Distillery), 1891 v E (1)

Whitfield, E. R. (Dublin University), 1886 v W (1)

Williams, J. R. (Ulster), 1886 v E, S (2)

Williams, P. A. (WBA), 1991 v Fa (sub) (1)

Williamson, J. (Cliftonville), 1890 v E; 1892 v S; 1893 v S (3)

Willigham, T. (Burnley), 1933 v W; 1934 v S (2)

Willis, G. (Linfield), 1906 v S, W; 1907 v S; 1912 v S (4)

Wilson, D. J. (Brighton & HA), 1987 v T, Is, E (sub); (with Luton T), 1988 v Y, T, Gr, Pol, F, Ma; 1989 v Ei, H, Sp, Ma, Ch; 1990 v H, Ei, N, U; (with Sheffield W), 1991 v Y, D, A, Fa (22)

Wilson, H. (Linfield), 1925 v W (1)

Wilson, K. J. (Ipswich T), 1987 v Is, E, Y; (with Chelsea), 1988 v Y, T, Gr (sub), Pol (sub), F (sub); 1989 v H (sub), Sp (2), Ma, Ch; 1990 v Ei (sub), N, U; 1991 v Y (2), A, Pol, Fa (21)

Wilson, M. (Distillery), 1884 v E, S, W (3)

Wilson, R. (Cliftonville), 1888 v S (1)

Wilson, S. J. (Glenavon), 1962 v S; 1964 v S; (with Falkirk), 1964 v E, W, U, Sp; 1965 v E, Sw; (with Dundee), 1966 v W, WG; 1967 v S; 1968 v E (12)

Wilton, J. M. (St Columb's Court), 1888 v E, W; 1889 v S, E; (with Cliftonville), 1890 v E; (with St Columb's Court), 1892 v W; 1893 v S (7)

Worthington, N. (Sheffield W), 1984 v W, Fi (sub); 1985 v Is, Sp (sub); 1986 v T, R (sub), E (sub), D, Alg, Sp; 1987 v E (2), T, Is, Y; 1988 v Y, T, Gr, Pol, F, Ma; 1989 v Ei, H, Sp, Ma; 1990 v H, Ei, U; 1991 v Y, D, A, Fa (32)

Wright, J. (Cliftonville), 1906 v E, S, W; 1907 v E, S, W (6)

Wright, T. J. (Newcastle U), 1989 v Ma, Ch; 1990 v H, U (4)

Young, S. (Linfield), 1907 v E, S; 1908 v E, S; (with Airdrie), 1909 v E; 1912 v S; (with Linfield), 1914 v E, S, W (9)

SCOTLAND

Adams, J. (Hearts), 1889 v Ni; 1892 v W; 1893 v Ni (3)

Agnew, W. B. (Kilmarnock), 1907 v Ni; 1908 v W, Ni (3)

Aird, J. (Burnley), 1954 v N (2), A, U (4)

Aitken, A. (Newcastle U), 1901 v E; 1902 v E; 1903 v E, W; 1904 v E; 1905 v E, W; 1906 v E; (with Middlesbrough), 1907 v E, W; 1908 v E; (with Leicester Fosse), 1910 v E; 1911 v E, Ni (14)

Aitken, G. G. (East Fife), 1949 v E, F; 1950 v W, Ni, Sw; (with Sunderland), 1953 v W, Ni; 1954 v E (8)

Aitken, R. (Dumbarton), 1886 v E; 1888 v Ni (2)

Aitken, R. (Celtic), 1980 v Pe (sub), Bel, W (sub), E, Pol; 1983 v Bel, Ca (1 + 1 sub); 1984 v Bel (sub), Ni, W (sub); 1985 v E, Ic; 1986 v W, EG, Aus (2), Is, R, E, D, WG, U; 1987 v Bul, Ei (2), L, Bel, E, Br; 1988 v H, Bel, Bul, L, S.Ar, Ma, Sp, Co, E; 1989 v N, Y, I, Cy, F, Cy, E, Ch; 1990 v Y, F, N; (with Newcastle U), Arg (sub), Pol, Ma, Cr, Se, Br (56)

Aitkenhead, W. A. C. (Blackburn R), 1912 v Ni (1)

Albiston, A. (Manchester U), 1982 v Ni; 1984 v U, Bel, EG, W, E; 1985 v Y, Ic, Sp (2), W; 1986 v EG, Ho, U (14)

Alexander, D. (East Stirlingshire), 1894 v W, Ni (2)

Allan, D. S. (Queen's Park), 1885 v E, W; 1886 v W (3)

Allan, G. (Liverpool), 1897 v E (1)

Allan, H. (Hearts), 1902 v W (1)

Allan, J. (Queen's Park), 1887 v E, W (2)

Allan, T. (Dundee), 1974 v WG, N (2)

Ancell, R. F. D. (Newcastle U), 1937 v W, Ni (2)

Anderson, A. (Hearts), 1933 v E; 1934 v A, E, W, Ni; 1935 v E, W, Ni; 1936 v E, W, Ni; 1937 v G, E, W, Ni, A; 1938 v E, W, Ni, Cz, Ho; 1939 v W, H (23)

Anderson, F. (Clydesdale), 1874 v E (1)

Anderson, G. (Kilmarnock), 1901 v Ni (1)

Anderson, H. A. (Raith R), 1914 v W (1)

Anderson, J. (Leicester C), 1954 v Fi (1)

Anderson, K. (Queen's Park), 1896 v Ni; 1898 v E, Ni (3)

Anderson, W. (Queen's Park), 1882 v E; 1883 v E, W; 1884 v E; 1885 v E, W (6)

Andrews, P. (Eastern), 1875 v E (1)

Archibald, A. (Rangers), 1921 v W; 1922 v W, E; 1923 v Ni; 1924 v E, W; 1931 v E; 1932 v E (8)

Archibald, S. (Aberdeen), 1980 v P (sub); (with Tottenham H), Ni, Pol, H; 1981 v Se (sub), Is, Ni, Is, Ni, E; 1982 v Ni, P, Sp (sub), Ho, Nz (sub), Br, USSR; 1983 v EG, Sw (sub), Bel; 1984 v EG, E, F; (with Barcelona), 1985 v Sp, E, Ic (sub); 1986 v WG (27)

Armstrong, M. W. (Aberdeen), 1936 v W, Ni; 1937 v G (3)

Arnott, W. (Queen's Park), 1883 v W; 1884 v E, Ni; 1885 v E, W; 1886 v E; 1887 v E, W; 1888 v E; 1889 v E; 1890 v E; 1891 v E; 1892 v E; 1893 v E (14)

Auld, J. R. (Third Lanark), 1887 v E, W; 1889 v W (3)

Auld, R. (Celtic), 1959 v H, P; 1960 v W (3)

Baird, A. (Queen's Park), 1892 v Ni; 1894 v W (2)

Baird, D. (Hearts), 1890 v Ni; 1891 v E; 1892 v W (3)

Baird, H. (Airdrieonians), 1956 v A (1)

Baird, J. C. (Vale of Leven), 1876 v E; 1878 v W; 1880 v E (3)

Baird, S. (Rangers), 1957 v Y, Sp (2), Sw, WG; 1958 v F, Ni (7)

Baird, W. U. (St Bernard), 1897 v Ni (1)

Bannon, E. (Dundee U), 1980 v Bel; 1983 v Ni, W, E, Ca; 1984 v EG; 1986 v Is, R, E, D (sub), WG (11)

Barbour, A. (Renton), 1885 v Ni (1)

Barker, J. B. (Rangers), 1893 v W; 1894 v W (2)

Barrett, F. (Dundee), 1894 v Ni; 1895 v W (2)

Battles, B. (Celtic), 1901 v E, W, Ni (3)

Battles, B. jun. (Hearts), 1931 v W (1)

Bauld, W. (Hearts), 1950 v E, Sw, P (3)

Baxter, J. C. (Rangers), 1961 v Ni, Ei (2), Cz; 1962 v Ni, W, E, Cz (2), U; 1963 v W, Ni, E, A, N, Ei, Sp; 1964 v W, E, N, WG; 1965 v W, Ni, Fi; (with Sunderland), 1966 v P, Br, Ni, W, E, I; 1967 v W, E, USSR; 1968 v W (34)

Baxter, R. D. (Middlesbrough), 1939 v E, W, H (3)

Beattie, A. (Preston NE), 1937 v E, A, Cz; 1938 v E; 1939 v W, Ni, H (7)

Beattie, R. (Preston NE), 1939 v W (1)

Begbie, I. (Hearts), 1890 v Ni; 1891 v E; 1892 v W; 1894 v E (4)

Bell, A. (Manchester U), 1912 v Ni (1)

Bell, J. (Dumbarton), 1890 v Ni; 1892 v E; (with Everton),

1896 v E; 1897 v E; 1898 v E; (with Celtic), 1899 v E, W, Ni; 1900 v E, W (10)

Bell, M. (Hearts), 1901 v W (1)

Bell, W. J. (Leeds U), 1966 v P, Br (2)

Bennett, A. (Celtic), 1904 v W; 1907 v Ni; 1908 v W; (with Rangers), 1909 v W, Ni, E; 1910 v E, W; 1911 v E, W; 1913 v Ni (11)

Bennie, R. (Airdrieonians), 1925 v W, Ni; 1926 v Ni (3)

Berry, D. (Queen's Park), 1894 v W; 1899 v W, Ni (3)

Berry, W. H. (Queen's Park), 1888 v E; 1889 v E; 1890 v E; 1891 v E (4)

Bett, J. (Rangers), 1982 v Ho; 1983 v Bel; (with Lokeren), 1984 v Bel, W, E, F; 1985 v Y, Ic, Sp (2), W, E, Ic; (with Aberdeen), 1986 v W, Is, Ho; 1987 v Bel; 1988 v H (sub); 1989 v Y; 1990 v F (sub), N, Arg, Eg, Ma, Cr (25)

Beveridge, W. W. (Glasgow University), 1879 v E, W; 1880 v W (3)

Black, A. (Hearts), 1938 v Cz, Ho; 1939 v H (3)

Black, D. (Hurlford), 1889 v Ni (1)

Black, E. (Metz), 1988 v H (sub), L (sub) (2)

Black, I. H. (Southampton), 1948 v E (1)

Blackburn, J. E. (Royal Engineers), 1873 v E (1)

Blacklaw, A. S. (Burnley), 1963 v N, Sp; 1966 v I (3)

Blackley, J. (Hibernian), 1974 v Cz, E, Bel, Z; 1976 v Sw; 1977 v W, Se (7)

Blair, D. (Clyde), 1929 v W, Ni; 1931 v E, A, I; 1932 v W, Ni; (with Aston Villa), 1933 v W (8)

Blair, J. (Sheffield W), 1920 v E, Ni; (with Cardiff C), 1921 v E; 1922 v E; 1923 v E, W, Ni; 1924 v W (8)

Blair, J. (Motherwell), 1934 v W (1)

Blair, J. A. (Blackpool), 1947 v W (1)

Blair, W. (Third Lanark), 1896 v W (1)

Blessington, J. (Celtic), 1894 v E, Ni; 1896 v E, Ni (4)

Blyth, J. A. (Coventry C), 1978 v Bul, W (2)

Bone, J. (Norwich C), 1972 v Y (sub); 1973 v D (2)

Bowie, J. (Rangers), 1920 v E, Ni (2)

Bowie, W. (Linthouse), 1891 v Ni (1)

Bowman, G. A. (Montrose), 1892 v Ni (1)

Boyd, J. M. (Newcastle U), 1934 v Ni (1)

Boyd, R. (Mossend Swifts), 1889 v Ni; 1891 v W (2)

Boyd, T. (Motherwell), 1991 v R (sub), Sw, Bul, USSR (4)

Boyd, W. G. (Clyde), 1931 v I, Sw (2)

Brackenbridge, T. (Hearts), 1888 v Ni (1)

Bradshaw, T. (Bury), 1928 v E (1)

Brand, R. (Rangers), 1961 v Ni, Cz, Ei (2); 1962 v Ni, W, Cz, U (8)

Branden, T. (Blackburn R), 1896 v E (1)

Brazil, A. (Ipswich T), 1980 v Pol (sub), H; 1982 v Sp, Ho (sub), Ni, W, E, Nz, USSR (sub); 1983 v EG, Sw, W, E (sub) (13)

Bremner, D. (Hibernian), 1976 v Sw (sub) (1)

Bremner, W. J. (Leeds U), 1965 v Sp; 1966 v E, Pol, P, Br, I (2); 1967 v W, Ni, E; 1968 v W, E; 1969 v W, E, Ni, D, A, WG, Cy (2); 1970 v Ei, WG, A; 1971 v W, E; 1972 v P, Bel, Ho, Ni, W, E, Y, Cz, Br; 1973 v D (2), E (2), Ni (sub), Sw, Br; 1974 v Cz, WG, Ni, W, E, Bel, N, Z, Br, Y; 1975 v Sp (2); 1976 v D (54)

Brennan, F. (Newcastle U), 1947 v W, Ni; 1953 v W, Ni, E; 1954 v Ni, E (7)

Breslin, B. (Hibernian), 1897 v W (1)

Brewster, G. (Everton), 1921 v E (1)

Brogan, J. (Celtic), 1971 v W, Ni, P, E (4)

Brown, A. (Middlesbrough), 1904 v E (1)

Brown, A. (St Mirren), 1890 v W; 1891 v W (2)

Brown, A. D. (East Fife), 1950 v Sw, P, F; (with Blackpool), 1952 v USA, D, Se; 1953 v W; 1954 v W, E, N (2), Fi, A, U (14)

Brown, G. C. P. (Rangers), 1931 v W; 1932 v E, W, Ni; 1933 v E; 1935 v A, E, W; 1936 v E, W; 1937 v G, E, W, Ni, Cz; 1938 v E, W, Cz, Ho (19)

Brown, H. (Partick T), 1947 v W, Bel, L (3)

Brown, J. (Cambuslang), 1890 v W (1)

Brown, J. B. (Clyde), 1939 v W (1)

Brown, J. G. (Sheffield U), 1975 v R (1)

Brown, R. (Dumbarton), 1884 v W, Ni (2)

Brown, R. (Rangers), 1947 v Ni; 1949 v Ni; 1952 v E (3)

Brown, R. jun. (Dumbarton), 1885 v W (1)

Brown, W. D. F. (Dundee), 1958 v F; 1959 v E, W, Ni; (with Tottenham H), 1960 v W, Ni, Pol, A, H, T; 1962 v Ni, W, E, Cz; 1963 v W, Ni, E, A; 1964 v Ni, W, N; 1965 v E, Fi, Pol, Sp; 1966 v Ni, Pol, I (28)

Browning, J. (Celtic), 1914 v W (1)

Brownlie, J. (Hibernian), 1971 v USSR; 1972 v Pe, Ni, E; 1973 v D (2); 1976 v R (7)

Brownlie, J. (Third Lanark), 1909 v E, Ni; 1910 v E, W, Ni; 1911 v W, Ni; 1912 v W, Ni, E; 1913 v W, Ni, E; 1914 v W, Ni, E (16)

Bruce, D. (Vale of Leven), 1890 v W (1)

Bruce, R. F. (Middlesbrough), 1934 v A (1)

Buchan, M. M. (Aberdeen), 1972 v P (sub), Bel; (with Manchester U), W, Y, Cz, Br; 1973 v D (2), E; 1974 v WG, Ni, W, N, Br, Y; 1975 v EG, Sp, P; 1976 v D, R; 1977 v Fi, Cz, Ch, Arg, Br; 1978 v EG, W (sub), Ni, Pe, Ir, Ho; 1979 v A, N, P (34)

Buchanan, J. (Cambuslang), 1889 v Ni (1)

Buchanan, J. (Rangers), 1929 v E; 1930 v E (2)

Buchanan, P. S. (Chelsea), 1938 v Cz (1)

Buchanan, R. (Abercorn), 1891 v W (1)

Buckley, P. (Aberdeen), 1954 v Ni; 1955 v W, Ni (3)

Buick, A. (Hearts), 1902 v W, Ni (2)

Burley, G. (Ipswich T), 1979 v W, Ni, E, Arg, N; 1980 v P, Ni, E (sub), Pol; 1982 v W (sub), E (11)

Burns, F. (Manchester U), 1970 v A (1)

Burns, K. (Birmingham C), 1974 v WG; 1975 v EG (sub), Sp (2); 1977 v Cz (sub), W, Se, W (sub); (with Nottingham F), 1978 v Ni (sub), W, E, Pe, Ir; 1979 v N; 1980 v Pe, A, Bel; 1981 v Is, Ni, W (20)

Burns, T. (Celtic), 1981 v Ni; 1982 v Ho (sub), W; 1983 v Bel (sub), Ni, Ca (1 + 1 sub); 1988 v E (sub) (8)

Busby, M. W. (Manchester C), 1934 v W (1)

Cairns, T. (Rangers), 1920 v W; 1922 v E; 1923 v E, W; 1924 v Ni; 1925 v W, E, Ni (8)

Calderhead, D. (Queen of the South), 1889 v Ni (1)

Calderwood, R. (Cartvale), 1885 v Ni, E, W (3)

Caldow, E. (Rangers), 1957 v Sp (2), Sw, WG, E; 1958 v Ni, W, Sw, Par, H, Pol, Y, F; 1959 v E, W, Ni, WG, Ho, P; 1960 v E, W, Ni, A, H, T; 1961 v E, W, Ni, Ei (2), Cz; 1962 v Ni, W, E, Cz (2), U; 1963 v W, Ni, E (40)

Callaghan, P. (Hibernian), 1900 v Ni (1)

Callaghan, W. (Dunfermline Ath), 1970 v Ei (sub), W (2)

Cameron, J. (Rangers), 1886 v Ni (1)

Cameron, J. (Queen's Park), 1896 v Ni (1)

Cameron, J. (St Mirren), 1904 v Ni; (with Chelsea), 1909 v E (2)

Campbell, C. (Queen's Park), 1874 v E; 1876 v W; 1877 v E, W; 1878 v E; 1879 v E; 1880 v E; 1881 v E; 1882 v E, W; 1884 v E; 1885 v E; 1886 v E (13)

Campbell, H. (Renton), 1889 v W (1)

Campbell, Jas (Sheffield W), 1913 v W (1)

Campbell, J. (South Western), 1880 v W (1)

Campbell, J. (Kilmarnock), 1891 v Ni; 1892 v W (2)

Campbell, John (Celtic), 1893 v E, Ni; 1898 v E, Ni; 1900 v E, Ni; 1901 v E, W, Ni; 1902 v W, Ni; 1903 v W (12)

Campbell, John (Rangers), 1899 v E, W, Ni; 1901 v Ni (4)

Campbell, K. (Liverpool), 1920 v E, W, Ni; (with Partick T), 1921 v W, Ni; 1922 v W, Ni, E (8)

Campbell, P. (Rangers), 1878 v W; 1879 v W (2)

Campbell, P. (Morton), 1898 v W (1)

Campbell, R. (Falkirk), 1947 v Bel, L; (with Chelsea), 1950 v Sw, P, F (5)

Campbell, W. (Morton), 1947 v Ni; 1948 v E, Bel, Sw, F (5)

Carabine, J. (Third Lanark), 1938 v Ho; 1939 v E, Ni (3)

Carr, W. M. (Coventry C), 1970 v Ni, W, E; 1971 v D; 1972 v Pe; 1973 v D (sub) (6)

Cassidy, J. (Celtic), 1921 v W, Ni; 1923 v Ni; 1924 v W (4)

Chalmers, S. (Celtic), 1965 v W, Fi; 1966 v P (sub), Br; 1967 v Ni (5)

Chalmers, W. (Rangers), 1885 v Ni (1)

Chalmers, W. S. (Queen's Park), 1929 v Ni (1)

Chambers, T. (Hearts), 1894 v W (1)

Chaplin, G. D. (Dundee), 1908 v W (1)

Cheyne, A. G. (Aberdeen), 1929 v E, N, G, Ho; 1930 v F (5)

Christie, A. J. (Queen's Park), 1898 v W; 1899 v E, Ni (3)

Christie, R. M. (Queen's Park), 1884 v E (1)

Clark, J. (Celtic), 1966 v Br; 1967 v W, Ni, USSR (4)

Clark, R. B. (Aberdeen), 1968 v W, Ho; 1970 v Ni; 1971 v W, Ni, E, D, P, USSR; 1972 v Bel, Ni, W, E, Cz, Br; 1973 v D, E (17)

Clarke, S. (Chelsea), 1988 v H, Bel, Bul, S.Ar, Ma (5)

Cleland, J. (Royal Albert), 1891 v Ni (1)

Clements, R. (Leith Ath), 1891 v Ni (1)

Clunas, W. L. (Sunderland), 1924 v E; 1926 v W (2)

Collier, W. (Raith R), 1922 v W (1)

Collins, J. (Hibernian), 1988 v S.Ar; 1990 v EG, Pol (sub), Ma (sub); (with Celtic), 1991 v Sw (sub), Bul (sub) (6)

Collins, R. Y. (Celtic), 1951 v W, Ni, A; 1955 v Y, A, H; 1956 v Ni, W; 1957 v E, W, Sp (2), Sw, WG; 1958 v Ni, W, Sw, H, Pol, Y, F, Par; (with Everton), 1959 v E, W, Ni, WG, Ho, P; (with Leeds U), 1965 v E, Pol, Sp (31)

Collins, T. (Hearts), 1909 v W (1)

Colman, D. (Aberdeen), 1911 v E, W, Ni; 1913 v Ni (4)

Colquhoun, E. P. (Sheffield U), 1972 v P, Ho, Pe, Y, Cz, Br; 1973 v D (2), E (9)

Colquhoun, J. (Hearts), 1988 v S.Ar (sub) (1)

Combe, J. R. (Hibernian), 1948 v E, Bel, Sw (3)

Conn, A. (Hearts), 1956 v A (1)

Conn, A. (Tottenham H), 1975 v Ni (sub), E (2)

Connachan, E. D. (Dunfermline Ath), 1962 v Cz, U (2)

Connelly, G. (Celtic), 1974 v Cz, WG (2)

Connolly, J. (Everton), 1973 v Sw (1)

Connor, J. (Airdrieonians), 1886 v Ni (1)

Connor, J. (Sunderland), 1930 v F; 1932 v Ni; 1934 v E; 1935 v Ni (4)

Connor, R. (Dundee), 1986 v Ho; (with Aberdeen), 1988 v S.Ar (sub); 1989 v E; 1991 v R (4)

Cook, W. L. (Bolton W), 1934 v E; 1935 v W, Ni (3)

Cooke, C. (Dundee), 1966 v W, I; (with Chelsea), P, Br; 1968 v E, Ho; 1969 v W, Ni, A, WG (sub), Cy (2); 1970 v A; 1971 v Bel; 1975 v Sp, P (16)

Cooper, D. (Rangers), 1980 v Pe, A (sub); 1984 v W, E; 1985 v Y, Ic, Sp (2), W; 1986 v W (sub), EG, Aus (2), Ho, WG (sub), U (sub); 1987 v Bul, L, Ei, Br; (with Motherwell), 1990 v N, Eg (22)

Cormack, P. B. (Hibernian), 1966 v Br; 1969 v D (sub); 1970 v Ei, WG; (with Nottingham F), 1971 v D (sub), W, P, E; 1972 v Ho (sub) (9)

Cowan, J. (Aston Villa), 1896 v E; 1897 v E; 1898 v E (3)

Cowan, J. (Morton), 1948 v Bel, Sw; F; 1949 v E, W, F; 1950 v E, W, Ni, Sw, P, F; 1951 v E, W, Ni, A (2), D, F, Bel; 1952 v Ni, W, USA, D, Se (25)

Cowan, W. D. (Newcastle U), 1924 v E (1)

Cowie, D. (Dundee), 1953 v E, Se; 1954 v Ni, W, Fi, N, A, U; 1955 v W, Ni, A, H; 1956 v W, A; 1957 v Ni, W; 1958 v H, Pol, Y, Par (20)

Cox, C. J. (Hearts), 1948 v F (1)

Cox, S. (Rangers), 1948 v F; 1949 v E, F; 1950 v E, F, W, Ni, Sw, P; 1951 v E, D, F, Bel, A; 1952 v Ni, W, USA, D, Se; 1953 v W, Ni, E; 1954 v W, Ni, E (25)

Craig, A. (Motherwell), 1929 v N, Ho; 1932 v E (3)

Craig, J. (Celtic), 1977 v Se (sub) (1)

Craig, J. P. (Celtic), 1968 v W (1)

Craig, T. (Rangers), 1927 v Ni; 1928 v Ni; 1929 v N, G, Ho; 1930 v Ni, E, W (8)

Craig, T. B. (Newcastle U), 1976 v Sw (1)

Crapnell, J. (Airdrieonians), 1929 v E, N, G; 1930 v F; 1931 v Ni, Sw; 1932 v E, F; 1933 v Ni (9)

Crawford, D. (St Mirren), 1894 v W, Ni; 1900 v W (3)

Crawford, J. (Queen's Park), 1932 v F, Ni; 1933 v E, W, Ni (5)

Crerand, P. T. (Celtic), 1961 v Ei (2), Cz; 1962 v Ni, W, E, Cz (2), U; 1963 v W, Ni; (with Manchester U), 1964 v Ni; 1965 v E, Pol, Fi; 1966 v Pol (16)

Cringan, W. (Celtic), 1920 v W; 1922 v E, Ni; 1923 v W, E (5)

Crosbie, J. A. (Ayr U), 1920 v W; (with Birmingham), 1922 v E (2)

Croal, J. A. (Falkirk), 1913 v Ni; 1914 v E, W (3)

Cropley, A. J. (Hibernian), 1972 v P, Bel (2)

Cross, J. H. (Third Lanark), 1903 v Ni (1)

Cruickshank, J. (Hearts), 1964 v WG; 1970 v W, E; 1971 v D, Bel; 1976 v R (6)

Crum, J. (Celtic), 1936 v E; 1939 v Ni (2)

Cullen, M. J. (Luton T), 1956 v A (1)

Cumming, D. S. (Middlesbrough), 1938 v E (1)

Cumming, J. (Hearts), 1955 v E, H, P, Y; 1960 v E, Pol, A, H, T (9)

Cummings, G. (Partick T), 1935 v E; 1936 v W, Ni; (with Aston Villa), E; 1937 v G; 1938 v W, Ni, Cz; 1939 v E (9)

Cunningham, A. N. (Rangers), 1920 v Ni; 1921 v W, E; 1922 v Ni; 1923 v E, W; 1924 v E, Ni; 1926 v E, Ni; 1927 v E, W (12)

Cunningham, W. C. (Preston NE), 1954 v N (2), U, Fi, A; 1955 v W, E, H (8)

Curran, H. P. (Wolverhampton W), 1970 v A; 1971 v Ni, E, D, USSR (sub) (5)

Dalglish, K. (Celtic), 1972 v Bel (sub), Ho; 1973 v D (1+1 sub), E (2), W, Ni, Sw, Br; 1974 v Cz (2), WG (2), Ni, W, E, Bel, N (sub), Z, Br, Y; 1975 v EG, Sp (sub+1), Se, P, W, Ni, E, R; 1976 v D (2), R, Sw, Ni, E; 1977 v Fi, Cz, W (2), Se, Ni, E, Ch, Arg, Br; (with Liverpool), 1978 v EG, Cz, W, Bul, Ni (sub), W, E, Pe, Ir, Ho; 1979 v A, N, P, W, Ni, E, Arg, N; 1980 v Pe, A, Bel (2), P, Ni, W, E, Pol, H; 1981 v Se, P, Is; 1982 v Se, Ni, P (sub), Sp, Ho, Ni, W, E, Nz, Br (sub); 1983 v Bel, Sw; 1984 v U, Bel, EG; 1985 v Y, Ic, Sp, W; 1986 v EG, Aus, R; 1987 v Bul (sub), L (102)

Davidson, D. (Queen's Park), 1878 v W; 1879 v W; 1880 v W; 1881 v E, W (5)

Davidson, J. A. (Partick T), 1954 v N (2), A, U; 1955 v W, Ni, E, H (8)

Davidson, S. (Middlesbrough), 1921 v E (1)

Dawson, A. (Rangers), 1980 v Pol (sub), H; 1983 v Ni, Ca (2) (5)

Dawson, J. (Rangers), 1935 v Ni; 1936 v E; 1937 v G, E, W, Ni, A, Cz; 1938 v W, Ho, Ni; 1939 v E, Ni, H (14)

Deans, J. (Celtic), 1975 v EG, Sp (2)

Delaney, J. (Celtic), 1936 v W, Ni; 1937 v G, E, A, Cz; 1938 v Ni; 1939 v W, Ni; (with Manchester U), 1947 v E; 1948 v E, W, Ni (13)

Devine, A. (Falkirk), 1910 v W (1)

Dewar, G. (Dumbarton), 1888 v Ni; 1889 v E (2)

Dewar, N. (Third Lanark), 1932 v E, F; 1933 v W (3)

Dick, J. (West Ham U), 1959 v E (1)

Dickie, M. (Rangers), 1897 v Ni; 1899 v Ni; 1900 v W (3)

Dickson, W. (Dumbarton), 1888 v Ni (1)

Dickson, W. (Kilmarnock), 1970 v Ni, W, E; 1971 v D, USSR (5)

Divers, J. (Celtic), 1895 v W (1)

Divers, J. (Celtic), 1939 v Ni (1)

Docherty, T. H. (Preston NE), 1952 v W; 1953 v E, Se; 1954 v N (2), A, U; 1955 v W, E, H (2), A; 1957 v E, Y, Sp (2), Sw, WG; 1958 v Ni, W, E, Sw; (with Arsenal), 1959 v W, E, Ni (25)

Dodds, D. (Dundee U), 1984 v U (sub), Ni (2)

Dodds, J. (Celtic), 1914 v E, W, Ni (3)

Doig, J. E. (Arbroath), 1887 v Ni; 1889 v Ni; (with Sunderland), 1896 v E; 1899 v E; 1903 v E (5)

Donachie, W. (Manchester C), 1972 v Pe, Ni, E, Y, Cz, Br; 1973 v D, E, W, Ni; 1974 v Ni; 1976 v R, Ni, W, E; 1977 v Fi, Cz, W (2), Se, Ni, E, Ch, Arg, Br; 1978 v EG, W, Bul, W, E, Ir, Ho; 1979 v A, N, P (sub) (35)

Donaldson, A. (Bolton W), 1914 v E, Ni, W; 1920 v E, Ni; 1922 v Ni (6)

Donnachie, J. (Oldham Ath), 1913 v E; 1914 v E, Ni (3)

Dougall, C. (Birmingham C), 1947 v W (1)

Dougall, J. (Preston NE), 1939 v E (1)

Dougan, R. (Hearts), 1950 v Sw (1)

Douglas, A. (Chelsea), 1911 v Ni (1)

Douglas, J. (Renfrew), 1880 v W (1)

Dowds, P. (Celtic), 1892 v Ni (1)

Downie, R. (Third Lanark), 1892 v W (1)

Doyle, D. (Celtic), 1892 v E; 1893 v W; 1894 v E; 1895 v E, Ni; 1897 v E; 1898 v E, Ni (8)

Doyle, J. (Ayr U), 1976 v R (1)

Drummond, J. (Falkirk), 1892 v Ni; (with Rangers), 1894 v Ni; 1895 v Ni, E; 1896 v E, Ni; 1897 v Ni; 1898 v E; 1900 v E; 1901 v E; 1902 v E, W, Ni; 1903 v Ni (14)

Dunbar, M. (Cartvale), 1886 v Ni (1)

Duncan, A. (Hibernian), 1975 v P (sub), W, Ni, E, R; 1976 v D (6)

Duncan, D. (Derby Co), 1933 v E, W; 1934 v A, W; 1935 v E, W; 1936 v E, W, Ni; 1937 v G, E, W, Ni; 1938 v W (14)

Duncan, D. M. (East Fife), 1948 v Bel, Sw, F (3)

Duncan, J. (Alexandra Ath), 1878 v W; 1882 v W (2)

Duncan, J. (Leicester C), 1926 v W (1)

Duncanson, J. (Rangers), 1947 v Ni (1)

Dunlop, J. (St Mirren), 1890 v W (1)

Dunlop, W. (Liverpool), 1906 v E (1)

Dunn, J. (Hibernian), 1925 v W, Ni; 1927 v Ni; 1928 v Ni, E; (with Everton), 1929 v W (6)

Durie, G. S. (Chelsea), 1988 v Bul (sub); 1989 v I (sub), Cy; 1990 v Y, EG, Eg, Se; 1991 v Sw (sub), Bul (2), USSR (sub), Sm (12)

Durrant, I. (Rangers), 1988 v H, Bel, Ma, Sp; 1989 v N (sub) (5)

Dykes, J. (Hearts), 1938 v Ho; 1939 v Ni (2)

Easson, J. F. (Portsmouth), 1931 v A, Sw; 1934 v W (3)

Ellis, J. (Mossend Swifts), 1892 v Ni (1)

Evans, A. (Aston Villa), 1982 v Ho, Ni, E, Nz (4)

Evans, R. (Celtic), 1949 v E, W, Ni, F; 1950 v W, Ni, Sw, P; 1951 v E, A; 1952 v Ni; 1953 v Se; 1954 v Ni, W, E, N, Fi; 1955 v Ni, P, Y, A, H; 1956 v E, Ni, W, A; 1957 v WG, Sp; 1958 v Ni, W, E, Sw, H, Pol, Y, Par, F; 1959 v E, WG, Ho, P; 1960 v E, Ni, W, Pol; (with Chelsea), 1960 v A, H, T (48)

Ewart, J. (Bradford C), 1921 v E (1)

Ewing, T. (Partick T), 1958 v W, E (2)

Farm, G. N. (Blackpool), 1953 v W, Ni, E, Se; 1954 v Ni, W, E; 1959 v WG, Ho, P (10)

Ferguson, D. (Rangers), 1988 v Ma, Co (sub) (2)

Ferguson, I. (Rangers), 1989 v I, Cy (sub), F (3)

Ferguson, J. (Vale of Leven), 1874 v E; 1876 v E, W; 1877 v E, W; 1878 v W (6)

Ferguson, R. (Kilmarnock), 1966 v W, E, Ho, P, Br; 1967 v W, Ni (7)

Fernie, W. (Celtic), 1954 v Fi, A, U; 1955 v W, Ni; 1957 v E, Ni, W, Y; 1958 v W, Sw, Par (12)

Findlay, R. (Kilmarnock), 1898 v W (1)

Fitchie, T. T. (Woolwich Arsenal), 1905 v W; 1906 v W, Ni; (with Queen's Park), 1907 v W (4)

Flavell, R. (Airdrieonians), 1947 v Bel, L (2)

Fleck, R. (Norwich C), 1990 v Arg, Se, Br (sub); 1991 v USSR (4)

Fleming, C. (East Fife), 1954 v Ni (1)

Fleming, J. W. (Rangers), 1929 v G, Ho; 1930 v E (3)

Fleming, J. (Morton), 1886 v Ni (1)

Forbes, A. R. (Sheffield U), 1947 v Bel, L, E; 1948 v W,

Ni; (with Arsenal), 1950 v E, P, F; 1951 v W, Ni, A; 1952 v W, D, Se (14)

Forbes, J. (Vale of Leven), 1884 v E, W, Ni; 1887 v W, E (5)

Ford, D. (Hearts), 1974 v Cz (sub), WG (sub), W (3)

Forrest, J. (Rangers), 1966 v W, I; (with Aberdeen), 1971 v Bel (sub), D, USSR (5)

Forrest, J. (Motherwell), 1958 v E (1)

Forsyth, A. (Partick T), 1972 v Y, Cz, Br; 1973 v D; (with Manchester U), E; 1975 v Sp, Ni (sub), R, EG; 1976 v D (10)

Forsyth, C. (Kilmarnock), 1964 v E; 1965 v W, Ni, Fi (4)

Forsyth, T. (Motherwell), 1971 v D; (with Rangers), 1974 v Cz; 1976 v Sw, Ni, W, E; 1977 v Fi, Se, W, Ni, E, Ch, Arg, Br; 1978 v Cz, W, Ni, W (sub), E, Pe, Ir (sub), Ho (22)

Foyers, R. (St Bernards), 1893 v W; 1894 v W (2)

Fraser, D. M. (WBA), 1968 v Ho; 1969 v Cy (2)

Fraser, J. (Moffat), 1891 v Ni (1)

Fraser, M. J. E. (Queen's Park), 1880 v W; 1882 v W, E; 1883 v W, E (5)

Fraser, J. (Dundee), 1907 v Ni (1)

Fraser, W. (Sunderland), 1955 v W, Ni (2)

Fulton, W. (Abercorn), 1884 v Ni (1)

Fyfe, J. H. (Third Lanark), 1895 v W (1)

Gabriel, J. (Everton), 1961 v W; 1964 v N (sub) (2)

Gallacher, H. K. (Airdrieonians), 1924 v Ni; 1925 v E, W, Ni; 1926 v W; (with Newcastle U), 1926 v E, Ni; 1927 v E, W, Ni; 1928 v E, W; 1929 v E, W, Ni; 1930 v W, Ni, F; (with Chelsea), 1934 v E; (with Derby Co), 1935 v E (20)

Gallacher, K. W. (Dundee U), 1988 v Co, E (sub); 1989 v N, I (4); (with Coventry C), 1991 v Sm (5)

Gallacher, P. (Sunderland), 1935 v Ni (1)

Galt, J. H. (Rangers), 1908 v W, Ni (2)

Gardiner, I. (Motherwell), 1958 v W (1)

Gardner, D. R. (Third Lanark), 1897 v W (1)

Gardner, R. (Queen's Park), 1872 v E; 1873 v E; (with Clydesdale), 1874 v E; 1875 v E; 1878 v E (5)

Gemmell, T. (St Mirren), 1955 v P, Y (2)

Gemmell, T. (Celtic), 1966 v E; 1967 v W, Ni, E, USSR; 1968 v Ni, E; 1969 v W, Ni, E, D, A, WG, Cy; 1970 v E, Ei, WG; 1971 v Bel (18)

Gemmill, A. (Derby Co), 1971 v Bel; 1972 v P, Ho, Pe, Ni, W, E; 1976 v D, R, Ni, W, E; 1977 v Fi, Cz, W (2), Ni (sub), E (sub), Ch (sub), Arg, Br; 1978 v EG (sub); (with Nottingham F), Bul, Ni, W, E (sub), Pe (sub), Ir, Ho; 1979 v A, N, P, N; (with Birmingham C), 1980 v A, P, Ni, W, E, H; 1981 v Se, P, Is, Ni (43)

Gibb, W. (Clydesdale), 1873 v E (1)

Gibson, D. W. (Leicester C), 1963 v A, N, Ei, Sp; 1964 v Ni; 1965 v W, Fi (7)

Gibson, J. D. (Partick T), 1926 v E; 1927 v E, W, Ni; (with Aston Villa), 1928 v E, W; 1930 v W, Ni (8)

Gibson, N. (Rangers), 1895 v E, Ni; 1896 v E, Ni; 1897 v E, Ni; 1898 v E; 1899 v E, W, Ni; 1900 v E, Ni; 1901 v W; (with Partick T), 1905 v Ni (14)

Gilchrist, J. E. (Celtic), 1922 v E (1)

Gilhooley, M. (Hull C), 1922 v W (1)

Gillespie, G. (Rangers), 1880 v W; 1881 v E, W; 1882 v E; (with Queen's Park), 1886 v W; 1890 v W; 1891 v Ni (7)

Gillespie, G. T. (Liverpool), 1988 v Bel, Bul, Sp; 1989 v N, F, Ch; 1990 v Y, EG, Eg, Pol, Ma, Br (sub); 1991 v Bul (13)

Gillespie. Jas (Third Lanark), 1898 v W (1)

Gillespie. John (Queen's Park), 1896 v W (1)

Gillespie, R. (Queen's Park), 1927 v W; 1931 v W; 1932 v F; 1933 v E (4)

Gillick, T. (Everton), 1937 v A, Cz; 1939 v W, Ni, H (5)

Gilmour, J. (Dundee), 1931 v W (1)

Gilzean, A. J. (Dundee), 1964 v W, E, N, WG; 1965 v Ni, (with Tottenham H), Sp; 1966 v Ni, W, Pol, I; 1968 v W;

1969 v W, E, WG, Cy (2), A (sub); 1970 v Ni, E (sub), WG, A; 1971 v P (22)

Glavin, R. (Celtic), 1977 v Se (1)

Glen, A. (Aberdeen), 1956 v E, Ni (2)

Glen, R. (Renton), 1895 v W; 1896 v W; (with Hibernian), 1900 v Ni (3)

Goram, A. L. (Oldham Ath), 1986 v EG (sub), R, Ho; 1987 v Br; (with Hibernian) 1989 v Y,I; 1990 v EG, Pol, Ma; 1991 v R, Sw, Bul (2), USSR, Sm (15)

Gordon, J. E. (Rangers), 1912 v E, Ni; 1913 v E, Ni, W; 1914 v E, Ni; 1920 v W, E, Ni (10)

Gossland, J. (Rangers), 1884 v Ni (1)

Goudle, J. (Abercorn), 1884 v Ni (1)

Gough, C. R. (Dundee U), 1983 v Sw, Ni, W, E, Ca (3); 1984 v U, Bel, EG, Ni, W, E, F; 1985 v Sp, E, Ic; 1986 v W, EG, Aus, Is, R, E, D, WG, U; (with Tottenham H), 1987 v Bul, L, Ei (2), Bel, E, Br; 1988 v H; (with Rangers), S.Ar, Sp, Co, E; 1989 v Y, I, Cy, F, Cy; 1990 v F, Arg, EG, Eg, Pol, Ma, Cr; 1991 v USSR, Bul (52)

Gourlay, J. (Cambuslang), 1886 v Ni; 1888 v W (2)

Govan, J. (Hibernian), 1948 v E, W, Bel, Sw, F; 1949 v Ni (6)

Gow, D. R. (Rangers), 1888 v E (1)

Gow, J. J. (Queen's Park), 1885 v E (1)

Gow, J. R. (Rangers), 1888 v Ni (1)

Graham, A. (Leeds U), 1978 v EG (sub); 1979 v A (sub), N, W, Ni, E, Arg, N; 1980 v A; 1981 v W (10)

Graham, G. (Arsenal), 1972 v P, SW (sub), Ho, Ni, Y, Cz, Br; 1973 v D (2); (with Manchester U), E, W, Ni, Br (sub) (13)

Graham, J. (Annbank), 1884 v Ni (1)

Graham, J. A. (Arsenal), 1921 v Ni (1)

Grant, J. (Hibernian), 1959 v W, Ni (2)

Grant, P. (Celtic), 1989 v E (sub), Ch (2)

Gray, A. (Hibernian), 1903 v Ni (1)

Gray, A. M. (Aston Villa), 1976 v R, Sw; 1977 v Fi, Cz; 1979 v A, N; (with Wolverhampton W), 1980 v P, E (sub); 1981 v Se, P, Is (sub), Ni; 1982 v Se (sub), Ni (sub); 1983 v Ni, W, E, Ca (1 + 1 sub); (with Everton), 1985 v Ic (20)

Gray, D. (Rangers), 1929 v W, Ni, G, Ho; 1930 v W, E, Ni; 1931 v W; 1933 v W, Ni (10)

Gray, E. (Leeds U), 1969 v E, Cy; 1970 v WG, A; 1971 v W, Ni; 1972 v Bel, Ho; 1976 v W, E; 1977 v Fi, W (12)

Gray, F. T. (Leeds U), 1976 v Sw; 1979 v N, P, W, Ni, E, Arg (sub); (with Nottingham F), 1980 v Bel (sub); 1981 v Se, P, Is, Ni, Is, W; (with Leeds U), Ni, E; 1982 v Se, Ni, P, Sp, Ho, W, Nz, Br, USSR; 1983 v EG, Sw, Bel, Sw, W, E, Ca (32)

Gray, W. (Pollokshields Ath), 1886 v E (1)

Green, A. (Blackpool), 1971 v Bel (sub), P (sub), Ni, E; 1972 v W, E (sub) (6)

Greig, J. (Rangers), 1964 v E, WG; 1965 v W, Ni, E, Fi (2), Sp, Pol; 1966 v Ni, W, E, Pol, I (2), P, Ho, Br; 1967 v W, Ni, E; 1968 v Ni, W, E, Ho; 1969 v W, Ni, E, D, A, WG, Cy (2); 1970 v W, E, Ei, WG, A; 1971 v D, Bel (sub), Ni, E; 1976 v D (44)

Groves, W. (Hibernian), 1888 v W; (with Celtic), 1889 v Ni; 1890 v E (3)

Guilliland, W. (Queen's Park), 1891 v W; 1892 v Ni; 1894 v E; 1895 v E (4)

Gunn, B. (Norwich C), 1990 v Eg (1)

Haddock, H. (Clyde), 1955 v E, H (2), P, Y; 1958 v E (6)

Haddow, D. (Rangers), 1894 v E (1)

Haffey, F. (Celtic), 1960 v E; 1961 v E (2)

Hamilton, A. (Queen's Park), 1885 v E, W; 1886 v E; 1888 v E (4)

Hamilton, A. W. (Dundee), 1962 v Cz, U, W, E; 1963 v W, Ni, E, A, N, Ei; 1964 v Ni, W, E, N, WG; 1965 v Ni, W, E, Fi (2), Pol, Sp; 1966 v Pol, Ni (24)

Hamilton, G. (Aberdeen), 1947 v Ni; 1951 v Bel, A; 1954 v N (2) (5)

Hamilton, G. (Port Glasgow Ath), 1906 v Ni (1)

Hamilton, J. (Queen's Park), 1892 v W; 1893 v E, Ni (3)

Hamilton, J. (St Mirren), 1924 v Ni (1)

Hamilton, R. C. (Rangers), 1899 v E, W, Ni; 1900 v W; 1901 v E, Ni; 1902 v W, Ni; 1903 v E; 1904 v Ni; (with Dundee), 1911 v W (11)

Hamilton, T. (Hurlford), 1891 v Ni (1)

Hamilton, T. (Rangers), 1932 v E (1)

Hamilton, W. M. (Hibernian), 1965 v Fi (1)

Hannah, A. B. (Renton), 1888 v W (1)

Hannah, J. (Third Lanark), 1889 v W (1)

Hansen, A. D. (Liverpool), 1979 v W, Arg; 1980 v Bel, P; 1981 v Se, P, Is; 1982 v Se, Ni, P, Sp, Ni (sub), W, E, Nz, Br, USSR; 1983 v EG, Sw, Bel, Sw; 1985 v W (sub); 1986 v R (sub); 1987 v Ei (2), L (26)

Hansen, J. (Partick T), 1972 v Bel (sub), Y (sub) (2)

Harkness, J. D. (Queen's Park), 1927 v E, Ni; 1928 v E; (with Hearts), 1929 v W, E, Ni; 1930 v E, W; 1932 v W, F; 1934 v Ni, W (12)

Harper, J. M. (Aberdeen), 1973 v D (1 + 1 sub); (with Hibernian), 1976 v D; (with Aberdeen), 1978 v Ir (sub) (4)

Harper, W. (Hibernian), 1923 v E, Ni, W; 1924 v E, Ni, W; 1925 v E, Ni, W; (with Arsenal), 1926 v E, Ni (11)

Harris, J. (Partick T), 1921 v W, Ni (2)

Harris, N. (Newcastle U), 1924 v E (1)

Harrower, W. (Queen's Park), 1882 v E; 1884 v Ni; 1886 v W (3)

Hartford, R. A. (WBA), 1972 v Pe, W (sub), E, Y, Cz, Br; (with Manchester C), 1976 v D, R, Ni (sub); 1977 v Cz (sub), W (sub), Se, W, Ni, E, Ch, Arg, Br; 1978 v EG, Cz, W, Bul, W, E, Pe, Ir, Ho; 1979 v A, N, P, W, Ni, E, Arg, N; (with Everton), 1980 v Pe, Bel; 1981 v Ni (sub), Is, W, Nz, E; 1982 v Se; (with Manchester C), Ni, P, Sp, Ni, W, E, Br (50)

Harvey, D. (Leeds U), 1973 v D; 1974 v Cz, WG, Ni, W, E, Bel, Z, Br, Y; 1975 v EG, Sp (2); 1976 v D (2); 1977 v Fi (sub) (16)

Hastings, A. C. (Sunderland), 1936 v Ni; 1938 v Ni (2)

Haughney, M. (Celtic), 1954 v E (1)

Hay, D. (Celtic), 1970 v Ni, W, E; 1971 v D, Bel, W, P, Ni; 1972 v P, Bel, Ho; 1973 v W, Ni, E, Sw, Br; 1974 v Cz (2), WG, Ni, W, E, Bel, N, Z, Br, Y (27)

Hay, J. (Celtic), 1905 v Ni; 1909 v Ni; 1910 v W, Ni, E; 1911 v Ni, E; (with Newcastle U), 1912 v E, W; 1914 v E, Ni (11)

Hegarty, P. (Dundee U), 1979 v W, Ni, E, Arg, N (sub); 1980 v W, E; 1983 v Ni (8)

Heggie, C. (Rangers), 1886 v Ni (1)

Henderson, G. H. (Rangers), 1904 v Ni (1)

Henderson, J. G. (Portsmouth), 1953 v Se; 1954 v Ni, E, N; 1956 v W; (with Arsenal), 1959 v W, Ni (7)

Henderson, W. (Rangers), 1963 v W, Ni, E, A, N, Ei, Sp; 1964 v W, Ni, E, N, WG; 1965 v Fi, Pol, E, Sp; 1966 v Ni, W, Pol, I, Ho; 1967 v W, Ni; 1968 v Ho; 1969 v Ni, E, Cy; 1970 v Ei; 1971 v P (29)

Hepburn, J. (Alloa Ath), 1891 v W (1)

Hepburn, R. (Ayr U), 1932 v Ni (1)

Herd, A. C. (Hearts), 1935 v Ni (1)

Herd, D. G. (Arsenal), 1959 v E, W, Ni; 1961 v E, Cz (5)

Herd, G. (Clyde), 1958 v E; 1960 v H, T; 1961 v W, Ni (5)

Herriot, J. (Birmingham C), 1969 v Ni, E, D, Cy (2), W (sub); 1970 v Ei (sub), WG (8)

Hewie, J. D. (Charlton Ath), 1956 v E, A; 1957 v E, Ni, W, Y, Sp (2), Sw, WG; 1958 v H, Pol, Y, F; 1959 v Ho, P; 1960 v Ni, W, Pol (19)

Higgins, A. (Kilmarnock), 1885 v Ni (1)

Higgins, A. (Newcastle U), 1910 v E, Ni; 1911 v E, Ni (4)

Highet, T. C. (Queen's Park), 1875 v E; 1876 v E, W; 1878 v E (4)

Hill, D. (Rangers), 1881 v E, W; 1882 v W (3)

Hill, D. A. (Third Lanark), 1906 v Ni (1)

Hill, F. R. (Aberdeen), 1930 v F; 1931 v W, Ni (3)

Lang, J. J. (Clydesdale), 1876 v W; (with Third Lanark), 1878 v W (2)

Latta, A. (Dumbarton), 1888 v W; 1889 v E (2)

Law, D. (Huddersfield T), 1959 v W, Ni, Ho, P; 1960 v Ni, W; (with Manchester C), 1960 v E, Pol, A; 1961 v E, Ni; (with Torino), 1962 v Cz (2), E; (with Manchester U), 1963 v W, Ni, E, A, N, Ei, Sp; 1964 v W, E, N, WG; 1965 v W, Ni, E, Fi (2), Pol, Sp; 1966 v Ni, E, Pol; 1967 v W, E, USSR; 1968 v Ni; 1969 v Ni, A, WG; 1972 v Pe, Ni, W, E, Y, Cz, Br; (with Manchester C), 1974 v Cz (2), WG (2), Ni, Z (55)

Law, G. (Rangers), 1910 v E, Ni, W (3)

Law, T. (Chelsea), 1928 v E; 1930 v E (2)

Lawrence, J. (Newcastle U), 1911 v E (1)

Lawrence, T. (Liverpool), 1963 v Ei; 1969 v W, WG (3)

Lawson, D. (St Mirren), 1923 v E (1)

Leckie, R. (Queen's Park), 1872 v E (1)

Leggat, G. (Aberdeen), 1956 v E; 1957 v W; 1958 v Ni, H, Pol, Y, Par; (with Fulham), 1959 v E, W, Ni, WG, Ho; 1960 v E, Ni, W, Pol, A, H (18)

Leighton, J. (Aberdeen), 1983 v EG, Sw, Bel, Sw, W, E, Ca (2); 1984 v U, Bel, Ni, W, E, F; 1985 v Y, Ic, Sp (2), W, E, Ic; 1986 v W, EG, Aus (2), Is, D, WG, U; 1987 v Bul, Ei (2), L, Bel, E; 1988 v H, Bel, Bul, L, S.Ar, Ma, Sp; (with Manchester U), Co, E; 1989 v N, Cy, F, Cy, E, Ch; 1990 v Y, F, N, Arg, Ma (sub, Cr, Se, Br (58)

Lennie, W. (Aberdeen), 1908 v W, Ni (2)

Lennox, R. (Celtic), 1967 v Ni, E, USSR; 1968 v W, L; 1969 v D, A, WG, Cy (sub); 1970 v W (sub) (10)

Leslie, L. G. (Airdrieonians), 1961 v W, Ni, Ei (2), Cz (5)

Levein, C. (Hearts), 1990 v Arg, EG, Eg (sub), Pol, Ma (sub), Se (6)

Liddell, W. (Liverpool), 1947 v W, Ni; 1948 v E, W, Ni; 1950 v E, W, P, F; 1951 v W, Ni, E, A; 1952 v W, Ni, E, USA, D, Se; 1953 v W, Ni, E; 1954 v W; 1955 v P, Y, A, H; 1956 v Ni (28)

Liddle, D. (East Fife), 1931 v A, I, Sw (3)

Lindsay, D. (St Mirren), 1903 v Ni (1)

Lindsay, J. (Dumbarton), 1880 v W; 1881 v W, E; 1884 v W, E; 1885 v W, E; 1886 v E (8)

Lindsay, J. (Renton), 1888 v E; 1893 v E, Ni (3)

Linwood, A. B. (Clyde), 1950 v W (1)

Little, R. J. (Rangers), 1953 v Se (1)

Livingstone, G. T. (Manchester C), 1906 v E; (with Rangers), 1907 v W (2)

Lochhead, A. (Third Lanark), 1889 v W (1)

Logan, J. (Ayr U), 1891 v W (1)

Logan, T. (Falkirk), 1913 v Ni (1)

Logie, J. T. (Arsenal), 1953 v Ni (1)

Loney, W. (Celtic), 1910 v W, Ni (2)

Long, H. (Clyde), 1947 v Ni (1)

Longair, W. (Dundee), 1894 v Ni (1)

Lorimer, P. (Leeds U), 1970 v A (sub); 1971 v W, Ni; 1972 v Ni (sub), W, E; 1973 v D (2), E (2); 1974 v WG (sub), E, Bel, N, Z, Br, Y; 1975 v Sp (sub); 1976 v D (2), R (sub) (21)

Love, A. (Aberdeen), 1931 v A, I, Sw (3)

Low, A. (Falkirk), 1934 v Ni (1)

Low, T. P. (Rangers), 1897 v Ni (1)

Low, W. L. (Newcastle U), 1911 v E, W; 1912 v Ni; 1920 v E, Ni (5)

Lowe, J. (Cambuslang), 1891 v Ni (1)

Lowe, J. (St Bernards), 1887 v Ni (1)

Lundie, J. (Hibernian), 1886 v W (1)

Lyall, J. (Sheffield W), 1905 v E (1)

McAdam, J. (Third Lanark), 1880 v W (1)

McAllister, G. (Leicester C), 1990 v EG, Pol, Ma (sub); (with Leeds U), 1991 v R, Sw, Bul, USSR (sub), Sm (8)

McArthur, D. (Celtic), 1895 v E, Ni; 1899 v W (3)

McAtee, A. (Celtic), 1913 v W (1)

McAulay, J. (Dumbarton), 1882 v W; (with Arthurlie), 1884 v Ni (2)

McAulay, J. (Dumbarton), 1883 v E, W; 1884 v E; 1885 v E, W; 1886 v E; 1887 v E, W (8)

McAuley, R. (Rangers), 1932 v Ni, W (2)

McAvennie, F. (West Ham U), 1986 v Aus (2), D (sub), WG (sub); (with Celtic), 1988 v S.Ar (5)

McBain, E. (St Mirren), 1894 v W (1)

McBain, N. (Manchester U), 1922 v E; (with Everton), 1923 v Ni; 1924 v W (3)

McBride, J. (Celtic), 1967 v W, Ni (2)

McBride, P. (Preston NE), 1904 v E; 1906 v E; 1907 v E, W; 1908 v E; 1909 v W (6)

McCall, J. (Renton), 1886 v W; 1887 v E, W; 1888 v E; 1890 v E (5)

McCall, S. M. (Everton), 1990 v Arg, EG, Eg (sub), Pol, Ma, Cr, Se, Br; 1991 v Sw, USSR, Sm (11)

McCalliog, J. (Sheffield W), 1967 v E, USSR; 1968 v Ni; 1969 v D; (with Wolverhampton W), 1971 v P (5)

McCallum, N. (Renton), 1888 v Ni (1)

McCann, R. J. (Motherwell), 1959 v WG; 1960 v E, Ni, W; 1961 v E (5)

McCartney, W. (Hibernian), 1902 v Ni (1)

McClair, B. (Celtic), 1987 v L, Ei, E, Br (sub); (with Manchester U), 1988 v Bul, Ma (sub), Sp (sub); 1989 v N, Y, I (sub), Cy, F (sub); 1990 v N (sub), Arg (sub); 1991 v Bul (2), Sm (17)

McClory, A. (Motherwell), 1927 v W; 1928 v Ni; 1935 v W; 1908 v E; 1909 v W (6)

McCloy, P. (Ayr U), 1924 v E; 1925 v E (2)

McCloy, P. (Rangers), 1973 v W, Ni, Sw, Br (4)

McCoist, A. (Rangers), 1986 v Ho; 1987 v L (sub), Ei (sub), Bel, E, Br; 1988 v H, Bel, Ma, Sp, Co, E; 1989 v Y (sub), F, Cy, E; 1990 v Y, F, N, EG (sub), Eg, Pol, Ma (sub), Cr (sub), Se (sub), Br; 1991 v R, Sw, Bul (2), USSR (31)

McColl, A. (Renton), 1888 v Ni (1)

McColl, I. M. (Rangers), 1950 v E, F; 1951 v W, Ni, Bel; 1957 v E, Ni, W, Y, Sp, Sw, WG; 1958 v Ni, E (14)

McColl, R. S. (Queen's Park), 1896 v W, Ni; 1897 v Ni; 1898 v Ni; 1899 v Ni, E, W; 1900 v E, W; 1901 v E, W; (with Newcastle U), 1902 v E; (with Queen's Park), 1908 v Ni (13)

McColl, W. (Renton), 1895 v W (1)

McCombie, A. (Sunderland), 1903 v E, W; (with Newcastle U), 1905 v E, W (4)

McCorkindale, J. (Partick T), 1891 v W (1)

McCormick, R. (Abercorn), 1886 v W (1)

McCrae, D. (St Mirren), 1929 v N, G (2)

McCreadie, A. (Rangers), 1893 v Ni; 1894 v E (2)

McCreadie, E. G. (Chelsea), 1965 v E, Sp, Fi, Pol; 1966 v P, Ni, W, Pol, I; 1967 v E, USSR; 1968 v Ni, W, E, Ho; 1969 v W, Ni, E, D, A, WG, Cy (2) (23)

McCulloch, D. (Hearts), 1935 v W; (with Brentford), 1936 v E; 1937 v W, Ni; 1938 v Cz; (with Derby Co), 1939 v H, W (7)

MacDonald, A. (Rangers), 1976 v Sw (1)

McDonald, J. (Edinburgh University), 1886 v E (1)

McDonald, J. (Sunderland), 1956 v W, Ni (2)

MacDougall, E. J. (Norwich C) 1975 v Se, P, W, Ni, E; 1976 v D, R (7)

McDougall, J. (Liverpool), 1931 v I, A (2)

McDougall, J. (Airdrieonians), 1926 v Ni (1)

McDougall, J. (Vale of Leven), 1877 v E, W; 1878 v E; 1879 v E, W (5)

McFadyen, W. (Motherwell), 1934 v A, W (2)

Macfarlane, A. (Dundee), 1904 v W; 1906 v W; 1908 v W; 1909 v Ni; 1911 v W (5)

McFarlane, R. (Greenock Morton), 1896 v W (1)

Macfarlane, W. (Hearts), 1947 v L (1)

McGarr, E. (Aberdeen), 1970 v Ei, A (2)

McGarvey, F. P. (Liverpool), 1979 v Ni (sub), Arg; (with Celtic), 1984 v U, Bel, EG (sub), Ni, W (7)

McGeoch, A. (Dumbreck), 1876 v E, W; 1877 v E, W (4)

McGhee, J. (Hibernian), 1886 v W (1)

McGhee, M. (Aberdeen), 1983 v Ca (1 + 1 sub); 1984 v Ni (sub), E (4)

McGonagle, W. (Celtic), 1933 v E; 1934 v A, E, Ni; 1935 v Ni, W (6)

McGrain, D. (Celtic), 1973 v W, Ni, E, Sw, Br; 1974 v Cz (2), WG, W (sub), E, Bel, N, Z, Br, Y; 1975 v Sp, Se, P, W, Ni, E, R; 1976 v D (2), Sw, Ni, W, E; 1977 v Fi, Cz, W (2), Se, Ni, E, Ch, Arg, Br; 1978 v EG, Cz; 1980 v Bel, P, Ni, W, E, Pol, H; 1981 v Se, P, Is, Ni, Is, W (sub), Ni, E; 1982 v Se, Sp, Ho, Ni, E, Nz, USSR (sub) (62)

McGregor, J. C. (Vale of Leven), 1877 v E, W; 1878 v E; 1880 v E (4)

McGrory, J. E. (Kilmarnock), 1965 v Ni, Fi; 1966 v P (3)

McGrory, J. (Celtic), 1928 v Ni; 1931 v E; 1932 v Ni, W; 1933 v E, Ni; 1934 v Ni (7)

McGuire, W. (Beith), 1881 v E, W (2)

McGurk, F. (Birmingham), 1934 v W (1)

McHardy, H. (Rangers), 1885 v Ni (1)

McInally, A. (Aston Villa), 1989 v Cy (sub), Ch; (with Bayern Munich), 1990 v Y (sub), F (sub), Arg, Pol (sub), Ma, Cr (8)

McInally, J. (Dundee U), 1987 v Bel, Br; 1988 v Ma (sub); 1991 v Bul (2) (5)

McInally, T. B. (Celtic), 1926 v Ni; 1927 v W (2)

McInnes, T. (Cowlairs), 1889 v Ni (1)

McIntosh, W. (Third Lanark), 1905 v Ni (1)

McIntyre, A. (Vale of Leven), 1878 v E; 1882 v E (2)

McIntyre, H. (Rangers), 1880 v W (1)

McIntyre, J. (Rangers), 1884 v W (1)

McKay, D. (Celtic), 1959 v E, WG, Ho, P; 1960 v E, Pol, A, H, T; 1961 v W, Ni; 1962 v Ni, Cz, U (sub) (14)

Mackay, D. C. (Hearts), 1957 v Sp; 1958 v F; 1959 v W, Ni; (with Tottenham H), 1959 v WG, E; 1960 v W, Ni, A, Pol, H, T; 1961 v W, Ni, E; 1963 v E, A, N; 1964 v Ni, W, N; 1966 v Ni (22)

Mackay, G. (Hearts), 1988 v Bul (sub), L (sub), S.Ar (sub), Ma (4)

McKay, J. (Blackburn R), 1924 v W (1)

McKay, R. (Newcastle U), 1928 v W (1)

McKean, R. (Rangers), 1976 v Sw (1)

McKenzie, D. (Brentford), 1938 v Ni (1)

Mackenzie, J. A. (Partick T), 1954 v W, E, N, Fi, A, U; 1955 v E, H; 1956 v A (9)

McKeown, M. (Celtic), 1889 v Ni; 1890 v E (2)

McKie, J. (East Stirling), 1898 v W (1)

McKillop, T. R. (Rangers), 1938 v Ho (1)

McKimmie, S. (Aberdeen), 1989 v E, Ch; 1990 v Arg, Eg, Cr (sub); Br; 1991 v R, Sw, Bul, Sm (10)

McKinlay, D. (Liverpool), 1922 v W, Ni (2)

McKinnon, A. (Queen's Park), 1874 v E (1)

McKinnon, R. (Rangers), 1966 v W, E, I (2), Ho, Br; 1967 v W, Ni, E; 1968 v Ni, W, E, Ho; 1969 v D, A, WG, Cy; 1970 v Ni, W, E, Ei, WG, A; 1971 v D, Bel, P, USSR, D (28)

MacKinnon, W. (Dumbarton), 1883 v E, W; 1884 v E, W (4)

McKinnon, W. W. (Queen's Park), 1872 v E; 1873 v E; 1874 v E; 1875 v E; 1876 v E, W; 1877 v E; 1878 v E; 1879 v E (9)

McLaren, A. (St Johnstone), 1929 v N, G, Ho; 1933 v W, Ni (5)

McLaren, A. (Preston NE), 1947 v E, Bel, L; 1948 v W (4)

McLaren, J. (Hibernian), 1888 v W; (with Celtic), 1889 v E; 1890 v E (3)

McLean, A. (Celtic), 1926 v W, Ni; 1927 v W, E (4)

McLean, D. (St Bernards), 1896 v W; 1897 v Ni (2)

McLean, D. (Sheffield W), 1912 v E (1)

McLean, G. (Dundee), 1968 v Ho (1)

McLean, T. (Kilmarnock), 1969 v D, Cy, W; 1970 v Ni, W; 1971 v D (6)

McLeish, A. (Aberdeen), 1980 v F, Ni, W, E, Pol, H; 1981 v Se, Is, Ni, Is, Ni, E; 1982 v Se, Sp, Ni, Br (sub); 1983 v

Bel, Sw (sub), W, E, Ca (3); 1984 v U, Bel, EG, Ni, W, E, F; 1985 v Y, Ic, Sp (2), W, E, Ic; 1986 v W, EG, Aus (2), E, Ho, D; 1987 v Bel, E, Br; 1988 v Bel, Bul, L, S.Ar (sub), Ma, Sp, Co, E; 1989 v N, Y, I, Cy, F, Cy, E, Ch; 1990 v Y, F, N, Arg, EG, Eg, Cr, Se, Br; 1991 v R, Sw, USSR, Bul (76)

McLeod, D. (Celtic), 1905 v Ni; 1906 v E, W, Ni (4)

McLeod, J. (Dumbarton), 1888 v Ni; 1889 v W; 1890 v Ni; 1892 v E; 1893 v W (5)

MacLeod, J. M. (Hibernian), 1961 v E, Ei (2), Cz (4)

MacLeod, M. (Celtic), 1985 v E (sub); 1987 v Ei, L, E, Br; (with Borussia Dortmund), 1988 v Co, E; 1989 v I, Ch; 1990 v Y, F, N (sub), Arg, EG, Pol, Se Br; (with Hibernian), 1991 v R, Sw, USSR (sub) (20)

McLeod, W. (Cowlairs), 1886 v Ni (1)

McLintock, A. (Vale of Leven), 1875 v E; 1876 v E; 1880 v E (3)

McLintock, F. (Leicester C), 1963 v N (sub), Ei, Sp; (with Arsenal), 1965 v Ni; 1967 v USSR; 1970 v Ni; 1971 v W, Ni, E (9)

McLuckie, J. S. (Manchester C), 1934 v W (1)

McMahon, A. (Celtic), 1892 v E; 1893 v E, Ni; 1894 v E; 1901 v Ni; 1902 v W (6)

McMenemy, J. (Celtic), 1905 v Ni; 1909 v Ni; 1910 v E, W; 1911 v Ni, W, E; 1912 v W; 1914 v W, Ni, E; 1920 v Ni (12)

McMenemy, J. (Motherwell), 1934 v W (1)

McMillan, J. (St Bernards), 1897 v W (1)

McMillan, I. L. (Airdrieonians), 1952 v E, USA, D; 1955 v E; 1956 v E; (with Rangers), 1961 v Cz (6)

McMillan, T. (Dumbarton), 1887 v Ni (1)

McMullan, J. (Partick T), 1920 v W; 1921 v W, Ni, E; 1924 v E, Ni; 1925 v E; 1926 v W; (with Manchester C), 1926 v E; 1927 v E, W; 1928 v E, W; 1929 v W, E, Ni (16)

McNab, A. (Morton), 1921 v E, Ni (2)

McNab, A. (Sunderland), 1937 v A; (with WBA), 1939 v E (2)

McNab, C. D. (Dundee), 1931 v E, W, A, I, Sw; 1932 v E (6)

McNab, J. S. (Liverpool), 1923 v W (1)

McNair, A. (Celtic), 1906 v W; 1907 v Ni; 1908 v E, W; 1909 v; 1910 v W; 1912 v E, W, Ni; 1913 v E; 1914 v E, Ni; 1920 v E, W, Ni (15)

McNaught, W. (Raith R), 1951 v A, W, Ni; 1952 v E; 1955 v Ni (5)

McNeil, H. (Queen's Park), 1874 v E; 1875 v E; 1876 v E, W; 1877 v W; 1878 v E; 1879 v E, W; 1881 v E, W (10)

McNeil, M. (Rangers), 1876 v W; 1880 v E (2)

McNeill, W. (Celtic), 1961 v E, Ei (2), Cz; 1962 v Ni, E, Cz, U; 1963 v Ei, Sp; 1964 v W, E, WG; 1965 v E, Fi, Pol, Sp; 1966 v Ni, Pol; 1967 v USSR; 1968 v E; 1969 v Cy, W, E, Cy (sub); 1970 v WG; 1972 v Ni, W, E (29)

McPhail, J. (Celtic), 1950 v W; 1951 v W, Ni, A; 1954 v Ni (5)

McPhail, R. (Airdrieonians), 1927 v E; (with Rangers), 1929 v W; 1931 v E, Ni; 1932 v W, Ni, F; 1933 v E, Ni; 1934 v A, Ni; 1935 v E; 1937 v G, E, Cz; 1938 v W, Ni (17)

McPherson, D. (Kilmarnock), 1892 v Ni (1)

McPherson, D. (Hearts), 1989 v Cy, E; 1990 v N, Ma, Cr, Se, Br; 1991 v Sw, Bul (2), USSR (sub), Sm (12)

McPherson, J. (Clydesdale), 1875 v E (1)

McPherson, J. (Vale of Leven), 1879 v E, W; 1880 v E; 1881 v W; 1883 v E, W; 1884 v E; 1885 v Ni (8)

McPherson, J. (Kilmarnock), 1888 v W; (with Cowlairs), 1889 v E; 1890 v Ni, E; (with Rangers), 1892 v W; 1894 v E; 1895 v E, Ni; 1897 v Ni (9)

McPherson, J. (Hearts), 1891 v E (1)

McPherson, R. (Arthurlie), 1882 v E (1)

McQueen, G. (Leeds U), 1974 v Bel; 1975 v Sp (2), P, W, Ni, E, R; 1976 v D; 1977 v Cz, W (2), Ni, E; 1978 v EG,

Cz, W; (with Manchester U), Bul, Ni, W; 1979 v A, N, P, Ni, E, N; 1980 v Pe, A, Bel; 1981 v W (30)

McQueen, M. (Leith Ath), 1890 v W; 1891 v W (2)

McRorie, D. M. (Morton), 1931 v W (1)

McSpadyen, A. (Partick T), 1939 v E, H (2)

McStay, P. (Celtic), 1984 v U, Bel, EG, Ni, W, E (sub); 1985 v Ic, Sp (2), W; 1986 v EG (sub), Aus, Is, U; 1987 v Bul, Ei (1 + 1 sub), L (sub), Bel, E, Br; 1988 v H, Bel, Bul, L, S.Ar, Sp, Co, E; 1989 v N, Y, I, Cy, F, Cy, E, Ch; 1990 v Y, F, N, Arg, EG (sub), Eg, Pol (sub), Ma, Cr, Se (sub); Br; 1991 v R, USSR, Bul (51)

McStay, W. (Celtic), 1921 v W, Ni; 1925 v E, Ni, W; 1926 v E, Ni, W; 1927 v E, Ni, W; 1928 v W, Ni (13)

McTavish, J. (Falkirk), 1910 v Ni (1)

McWhattie, G. C. (Queen's Park), 1901 v W, Ni (2)

McWilliam, P. (Newcastle U), 1905 v E; 1906 v E; 1907 v E, W; 1909 v E, W; 1910 v E; 1911 v W (8)

Macari, L. (Celtic), 1972 v W (sub), E, Y, Cz, Br; 1973 v D; (with Manchester U), E (2), W (sub), Ni (sub); 1975 v Se, P (sub), W, E (sub), R; 1977 v Ni (sub), E (sub), Ch, Arg; 1978 v EG, W, Bul, Pe (sub), Ir (24)

Macauley, A. R. (Brentford), 1947 v E; (with Arsenal), 1948 v E, W, Ni, Bel, Sw, F (7)

Madden, J. (Celtic), 1893 v W; 1895 v W (2)

Main, F. R. (Rangers), 1938 v W (1)

Main, J. (Hibernian), 1909 v Ni (1)

Maley, W. (Celtic), 1893 v E, Ni (2)

Malpas, M. (Dundee U), 1984 v F; 1985 v E, Ic; 1986 v W, Aus (2), Is, R, E, Ho, D, WG; 1987 v Bul, Ei, Bel; 1988 v Bel, Bul, L, S.Ar, Ma; 1989 v N, Y, I, Cy, F, Cy, E, Ch; 1990 v Y, F, N, Eg, Pol, Ma, Cr, Se, Br; 1991 v R, Bul (2), USSR, Sm (42)

Marshall, H. (Celtic), 1899 v W; 1900 v Ni (2)

Marshall, J. (Middlesbrough), 1921 v E, W, Ni; 1922 v E, W, Ni; (with Llanelly), 1924 v W (7)

Marshall, J. (Third Lanark), 1885 v Ni; 1886 v W; 1887 v E, W (4)

Marshall, J. (Rangers), 1932 v E; 1933 v E; 1934 v E (3)

Marshall, R. W. (Rangers), 1892 v Ni; 1894 v Ni (2)

Martin, F. (Aberdeen), 1954 v N (2), A, U; 1955 v E, H (6)

Martin, N. (Hibernian), 1965 v Fi, Pol; (with Sunderland), 1966 v I (3)

Martis, J. (Motherwell), 1961 v W (1)

Mason, J. (Third Lanark), 1949 v E, W, Ni; 1950 v Ni; 1951 v Ni, Bel, A (7)

Massie, A. (Hearts), 1932 v Ni, W, F; 1933 v Ni; 1934 v E, Ni; 1935 v E, Ni, W; 1936 v W, Ni; (with Aston Villa), 1936 v E; 1937 v G, E, W, Ni, A; 1938 v W (18)

Masson, D. S. (QPR), 1976 v Ni, W, E; 1977 v Fi, Cz, W, Ni, E, Ch, Arg, Br; 1978 v EG, Cz, W; (with Derby Co), Ni, E, Pe (17)

Mathers, D. (Partick T), 1954 v Fi (1)

Maxwell, W. S. (Stoke C), 1898 v E (1)

May, J. (Rangers), 1906 v W, Ni; 1908 v E, Ni; 1909 v W (5)

Meechan, P. (Celtic), 1896 v Ni (1)

Meiklejohn, D. D. (Rangers), 1922 v W; 1924 v W; 1925 v W, Ni, E; 1928 v W, Ni; 1929 v E, Ni; 1930 v E, Ni; 1931 v E; 1932 v W, Ni; 1934 v A (15)

Menzies, A. (Hearts), 1906 v E (1)

Mercer, R. (Hearts), 1912 v W; 1913 v Ni (2)

Middleton, R. (Cowdenbeath), 1930 v Ni (1)

Millar, A. (Hearts), 1939 v W (1)

Millar, J. (Rangers), 1897 v E; 1898 v E, W (3)

Millar, J. (Rangers), 1963 v A, Ei (2)

Miller, J. (St Mirren), 1931 v E, I, Sw; 1932 v F; 1934 v E (5)

Miller, P. (Dumbarton), 1882 v E; 1883 v E, W (3)

Miller, T. (Liverpool), 1920 v E; (with Manchester U), 1921 v E, Ni (3)

Miller, W. (Third Lanark), 1876 v E (1)

Miller, W. (Celtic), 1947 v E, W, Bel, L; 1948 v W, Ni (6)

Miller, W. (Aberdeen), 1975 v R; 1978 v Bul; 1980 v Bel,

W, E, Pol, H; 1981 v Se, P, Is (sub), Ni, W, Ni, E; 1982 v Ni, P, Ho, Br, USSR; 1983 v EG, Sw (2), W, E, Ca (3); 1984 v U, Bel, EG, W, E, F; 1985 v Y, Ic, Sp (2), W, E, Ic; 1986 v W, EG, Aus (2), Is, R, E, Ho, D, WG, U; 1987 v Bul, E, Br; 1988 v H, L, S.Ar, Ma, Sp, Co, E; 1989 v N, Y; 1990 v Y, N (65)

Mills, W. (Aberdeen), 1936 v W, Ni; 1937 v W (3)

Milne, J. V. (Middlesbrough), 1938 v E; 1939 v E (2)

Mitchell, D. (Rangers), 1890 v Ni; 1892 v E; 1893 v E, Ni; 1894 v E (5)

Mitchell, J. (Kilmarnock), 1908 v Ni; 1910 v Ni, W (3)

Mitchell, R. C. (Newcastle U), 1951 v D, F (2)

Mochan, N. (Celtic), 1954 v N, A, U (3)

Moir, W. (Bolton W), 1950 v E (1)

Moncur, R. (Newcastle U), 1968 v Ho; 1970 v Ni, W, E, Ei; 1971 v D, Bel, W, P, Ni, E, D; 1972 v Pe, Ni, W, E (16)

Morgan, H. (St Mirren), 1898 v W; (with Liverpool), 1899 v E (2)

Morgan, W. (Burnley), 1968 v Ni; (with Manchester U), 1972 v Pe, Y, Cz, Br; 1973 v D (2), E (2), W, Ni, Sw, Br; 1974 v Cz (2), WG (2), Ni, Bel (sub), Br, Y (21)

Morris, D. (Raith R), 1923 v Ni; 1924 v E, Ni; 1925 v E, W, Ni (6)

Morris, H. (East Fife), 1950 v Ni (1)

Morrison, T. (St Mirren), 1927 v E (1)

Morton, A. L. (Queen's Park), 1920 v W, Ni; (with Rangers), 1921 v E; 1922 v E, W; 1923 v E, W, Ni; 1924 v E, W, Ni; 1925 v E, W, Ni; 1927 v E, Ni; 1928 v E, W, Ni; 1929 v E, W, Ni; 1930 v E, W, Ni; 1931 v E, W, Ni; 1932 v E, W, F (31)

Morton, H. A. (Kilmarnock), 1929 v G, Ho (2)

Mudie, J. K. (Blackpool), 1957 v W, Ni, E, Y, Sw, Sp (2), WG; 1958 v Ni, E, W, Sw, H, Pol, Y, Par, F (17)

Muir, W. (Dundee), 1907 v Ni (1)

Muirhead, T. A. (Rangers), 1922 v Ni; 1923 v E; 1924 v W; 1927 v Ni; 1928 v Ni; 1929 v W, Ni; 1930 v W (8)

Mulhall, G. (Aberdeen), 1960 v Ni; (with Sunderland), 1963 v Ni; 1964 v Ni (3)

Munro, A. D. (Hearts), 1937 v W, Ni; (with Blackpool), 1938 v Ho (3)

Munro, F. M. (Wolverhampton W), 1971 v Ni (sub), E (sub), D, USSR; 1975 v Se, W (sub), Ni, E, R (9)

Munro, I. (St Mirren), 1979 v Arg, N; 1980 v Pe, A, Bel, W, E (7)

Munro, N. (Abercorn), 1888 v W; 1889 v E (2)

Murdoch, J. (Motherwell), 1931 v Ni (1)

Murdoch, R. (Celtic), 1966 v W, E, I (2); 1967 v Ni; 1968 v Ni; 1969 v W, Ni, E, WG, Cy; 1970 v A (12)

Murphy, F. (Celtic), 1938 v Ho (1)

Murray, J. (Renton), 1895 v W (1)

Murray, J. (Hearts), 1958 v E, H, Pol, Y, F (5)

Murray, J. W. (Vale of Leven), 1890 v W (1)

Murray, P. (Hibernian), 1896 v Ni; 1897 v W (2)

Murray, S. (Aberdeen), 1972 v Bel (1)

Mutch, G. (Preston NE), 1938 v E (1)

Napier, C. E. (Celtic), 1932 v E; 1935 v E, W; (with Derby Co), 1937 v Ni, A (5)

Narey, D. (Dundee U), 1977 v Se (sub); 1979 v P, Ni (sub), Arg; 1980 v P, Ni, Pol, H; 1981 v W, E (sub); 1982 v Ho, W, E, Nz (sub), Br, USSR; 1983 v EG, Sw, Bel, Ni, W, E, Ca (3); 1986 v Is, R, Ho, WG, U; 1987 v Bul, E, Bel; 1989 v I, Cy (35)

Neil, R. G. (Hibernian), 1896 v W; (with Rangers), 1900 v W (2)

Neill, R. W. (Queen's Park), 1876 v W; 1877 v E, W; 1878 v W; 1880 v E (5)

Neilles, P. (Hearts), 1914 v W, Ni (2)

Nelson, J. (Cardiff C), 1925 v W, Ni; 1928 v E; 1930 v F (4)

Nevin, P. K. F. (Chelsea), 1986 v R (sub), E (sub); 1987 v

L. Ei, Bel (sub); 1988 v L; (with Everton), 1989 v Cy, E; 1991 v R (sub), Bul (sub), Sm (sub) (11)

Niblo, T. D. (Aston Villa), 1904 v E (1)

Nibloe, J. (Kilmarnock), 1929 v E, N, Ho; 1930 v W; 1931 v E, Ni, A, I, Sw; 1932 v E, F (11)

Nicholas, C. (Celtic), 1983 v Sw, Ni, E, Ca (3); (with Arsenal), 1984 v Bel, F (sub); 1985 v Y (sub), Ic (sub), Sp (sub), W (sub); 1986 v Is, R (sub), E, D, U (sub); 1987 v Bul, E (sub); (with Aberdeen), 1989 v Cy (sub) (20)

Nicol, S. (Liverpool), 1985 v Y, Ic, Sp, W; 1986 v W, EG, Aus, E, D, WG, U; 1988 v H, Bul, S.Ar, Sp, Co, E; 1989 v N, Y, Cy, F; 1990 v Y, F; 1991 v Sw, USSR, Sm (26)

Nisbet, J. (Ayr U), 1929 v N, G, Ho (3)

Niven, J. B. (Moffatt), 1885 v Ni (1)

O'Donnell, F. (Preston NE), 1937 v E, A, Cz; 1938 v E, W; (with Blackpool), Ho (6)

Ogilvie, D. H. (Motherwell), 1934 v A (1)

O'Hare, J. (Derby Co), 1970 v W, Ni, E; 1971 v D, Bel, W, Ni; 1972 v P, Bel, Ho (sub), Pe, Ni, W (13)

Ormond, W. E. (Hibernian), 1954 v E, N, Fi, A, U; 1959 v E (6)

O'Rourke, F. (Airdrieonians), 1907 v Ni (1)

Orr, J. (Kilmarnock), 1892 v W (1)

Orr, R. (Newcastle U), 1902 v E; 1904 v E (2)

Orr, T. (Morton), 1952 v Ni, W (2)

Orr, W. (Celtic), 1900 v Ni; 1903 v Ni; 1904 v W (3)

Orrock, R. (Falkirk), 1913 v W (1)

Oswald, J. (Third Lanark), 1889 v E; (with St Bernards), 1895 v E; (with Rangers), 1897 v W (3)

Parker, A. H. (Falkirk), 1955 v P, Y, A; 1956 v E, Ni, W, A; 1957 v Ni, W, Y; 1958 v Ni, W, E, Sw; (with Everton), Par (15)

Parlane, D. (Rangers), 1973 v W, Sw, Br; 1975 v Sp (sub), Se, P, W, Ni, E, R; 1976 v D (sub); 1977 v W (12)

Parlane, R. (Vale of Leven), 1878 v W; 1879 v E, W (3)

Paterson, G. D. (Celtic), 1939 v Ni (1)

Paterson, J. (Leicester C), 1920 v E (1)

Paterson, J. (Cowdenbeath), 1931 v A, I, Sw (3)

Paton, A. (Motherwell), 1952 v D, Se (2)

Paton, D. (St Bernards), 1896 v W (1)

Paton, M. (Dumbarton), 1883 v E; 1884 v W; 1885 v W, E; 1886 v E (5)

Paton, R. (Vale of Leven), 1879 v E, W (2)

Patrick, J. (St Mirren), 1897 v E, W (2)

Paul, H. McD. (Queen's Park), 1909 v E, W, Ni (3)

Paul, W. (Partick T), 1888 v W; 1889 v W; 1890 v W (3)

Paul, W. (Dykebar), 1891 v Ni (1)

Pearson, T. (Newcastle U), 1947 v E, Bel (2)

Penman, A. (Dundee), 1966 v Ho (1)

Pettigrew, W. (Motherwell), 1976 v Sw, Ni, W; 1977 v W (sub), Se (5)

Phillips, J. (Queen's Park), 1877 v E, W; 1878 v W (3)

Plenderleith, J. B. (Manchester C), 1961 v Ni (1)

Porteous, W. (Hearts), 1903 v Ni (1)

Pringle, C. (St Mirren), 1921 v W (1)

Provan, D. (Rangers), 1964 v Ni, N; 1966 v I (2), Ho (5)

Provan, D. (Celtic), 1980 v Bel (2 sub), P (sub), Ni (sub); 1981 v Is, W, E; 1982 v Se, P, Ni (10)

Pursell, P. (Queen's Park), 1914 v W (1)

Quinn, J. (Celtic), 1905 v Ni; 1906 v Ni, W; 1908 v Ni, E; 1909 v E; 1910 v E, Ni, W; 1912 v E, W (11)

Quinn, P. (Motherwell), 1961 v E, Ei (2); 1962 v U (4)

Rae, J. (Third Lanark), 1889 v W; 1890 v Ni (2)

Raeside, J. S. (Third Lanark), 1906 v W (1)

Raisbeck, A. G. (Liverpool), 1900 v E; 1901 v E; 1902 v E; 1903 v E, W; 1904 v E; 1906 v E; 1907 v E (8)

Rankin, G. (Vale of Leven), 1890 v Ni; 1891 v E (2)

Rankin, R. (St Mirren), 1929 v N, G, Ho (3)

Redpath, W. (Motherwell), 1949 v W, Ni; 1951 v E, D, F, Bel, A; 1952 v Ni, E (9)

Reid, J. G. (Airdrieonians), 1914 v W; 1920 v W; 1924 v Ni (3)

Reid, R. (Brentford), 1938 v E, Ni (2)

Reid, W. (Rangers), 1911 v E, W, Ni; 1912 v Ni; 1913 v E, W, Ni; 1914 v E, Ni (9)

Reilly, L. (Hibernian), 1949 v E, W, F; 1950 v W, Ni, Sw, F; 1951 v W, E, D, F, Bel, A; 1952 v Ni, W, E, USA, D, Se; 1953 v Ni, W, E, Se; 1954 v W; 1955 v H (2), P, Y, A, E; 1956 v E, W, Ni, A; 1957 v E, Ni, W, Y (38)

Rennie, H. G. (Hearts), 1900 v E, Ni; (with Hibernian), 1901 v E; 1902 v E, Ni, W; 1903 v Ni, W; 1904 v Ni; 1905 v W; 1906 v Ni; 1908 v Ni, W (13)

Renny-Tailyour, H. W. (Royal Engineers), 1873 v E (1)

Rhind, A. (Queen's Park), 1872 v E (1)

Richmond, A. (Queen's Park), 1906 v W (1)

Richmond, J. T. (Clydesdale), 1877 v E; (with Queen's Park), 1878 v E; 1882 v W (3)

Ring, T. (Clyde), 1953 v Se; 1955 v W, Ni, E, H; 1957 v E, Sp (2), Sw, WG; 1958 v Ni, Sw (12)

Rioch, B. D. (Derby Co), 1975 v P, W, Ni, E, R; 1976 v D (2), R, Ni, W, E; 1977 v Fi, Cz, W; (with Everton), W, Ni, E, Ch, Br; 1978 v Cz; (with Derby Co), Ni, E, Pe, Ho (24)

Ritchie, A. (East Stirlingshire), 1891 v W (1)

Ritchie, H. (Hibernian), 1923 v W; 1928 v Ni (2)

Ritchie, J. (Queen's Park), 1897 v W (1)

Ritchie, W. (Rangers), 1962 v U (sub) (1)

Robb, D. T. (Aberdeen), 1971 v W, E, P, D (sub), USSR (5)

Robb, W. (Rangers), 1926 v W; (with Hibernian), 1928 v W (2)

Robertson, A. (Clyde), 1955 v P, A, H; 1958 v Sw, Par (5)

Robertson, G. (Motherwell), 1910 v W; (with Sheffield W), 1912 v W; 1913 v E, Ni (4)

Robertson, G. (Kilmarnock), 1938 v Cz (1)

Robertson, H. (Dundee), 1962 v Cz (1)

Robertson, J. (Dundee), 1931 v A, I (2)

Robertson, J. (Hearts), 1991 v R, Sw, Bul (sub), Sm (sub) (4)

Robertson, J. N. (Nottingham F), 1978 v Ni, W (sub), Ir; 1979 v P, N; 1980 v Pe, A, Bel (2), P; 1981 v Se, P, Is, Ni, Is, Ni, E; 1982 v Se, Ni (2), E (sub), Nz, Br, USSR; 1983 v EG, Sw; (with Derby Co), 1984 v U, Bel (28)

Robertson, J. G. (Tottenham H), 1965 v W (1)

Robertson, J. T. (Everton), 1898 v E; (with Southampton), 1899 v E; (with Rangers), 1900 v E; 1901 v W, Ni, E; 1902 v W, Ni, E; 1903 v E, W; 1904 v E, W, Ni; 1905 v W (16)

Robertson, P. (Dundee), 1903 v Ni (1)

Robertson, T. (Queen's Park), 1889 v Ni; 1890 v E; 1891 v W; 1892 v Ni (4)

Robertson, T. (Hearts), 1898 v Ni (1)

Robertson, W. (Dumbarton), 1887 v E, W (2)

Robinson, R. (Dundee), 1974 v WG (sub); 1975 v Se, Ni, R (sub) (4)

Rough, A. (Partick T), 1976 v Sw, Ni, W, E; 1977 v Fi, Cz, W (2), Se, Ni, E, Ch, Arg, Br; 1978 v Cz, W, Ni, E, Pe, Ir, Ho; 1979 v A, P, W, Arg, N; 1980 v Pe, A, Bel (2), P, W, E, Pol, H; 1981 v Se, P, Is, Ni, Is, W, E; 1982 v Se, Ni, Sp, Ho, W, E, Nz, Br, USSR; (with Hibernian), 1986 v W (sub), E (53)

Rougvie, D. (Aberdeen), 1984 v Ni (1)

Rowan, A. (Caledonian), 1880 v E; (with Queen's Park), 1882 v W (2)

Russell, D. (Hearts), 1895 v E, Ni; (with Celtic), 1897 v W; 1898 v Ni; 1901 v W, Ni (6)

Russell, J. (Cambuslang), 1890 v Ni (1)

Russell, W. F. (Airdrieonians), 1924 v W; 1925 v E (2)

Rutherford, E. (Rangers), 1948 v F (1)

St John, I. (Motherwell), 1959 v WG; 1960 v E, Ni, W, Pol, A; 1961 v E; (with Liverpool), 1962 v Ni, W, E, Cz (2), U; 1963 v W, Ni, E, N, Ei (sub), Sp; 1964 v Ni; 1965 v E (21)

Sawers, W. (Dundee), 1895 v W (1)

Scarff, P. (Celtic), 1931 v Ni (1)

Schaedler, E. (Hibernian), 1974 v WG (1)

Scott, A. S. (Rangers), 1957 v Ni, Y, WG; 1958 v W, Sw; 1959 v P; 1962 v Ni, W, E, Cz, U; (with Everton), 1964 v W, N; 1965 v Fi; 1966 v P, Br (16)

Scott, J. (Hibernian), 1966 v Ho (1)

Scott, J. (Dundee), 1971 v D (sub), USSR (2)

Scott, M. (Airdrieonians), 1898 v W (1)

Scott, R. (Airdrieonians), 1894 v Ni (1)

Scoular, J. (Portsmouth), 1951 v D, F, A; 1952 v E, USA, D, Se; 1953 v W, Ni (9)

Sellar, W. (Battlefield), 1885 v E; 1886 v E; 1887 v E, W; 1888 v E; (with Queen's Park), 1891 v E; 1892 v E; 1893 v E, Ni (9)

Semple, W. (Cambuslang), 1886 v W (1)

Shankly, W. (Preston NE), 1938 v E; 1939 v E, W, Ni, H (5)

Sharp, G. M. (Everton), 1985 v Ic; 1986 v W, Aus (2 sub), Is, R, U; 1987 v Ei; 1988 v Bel (sub), Bul, L, Ma (12)

Sharp, J. (Dundee), 1904 v W; (with Woolwich Arsenal), 1907 v W, E; 1908 v E; (with Fulham), 1909 v W (5)

Shaw, D. (Hibernian), 1947 v W, Ni; 1948 v E, Bel, Sw, F; 1949 v W, Ni (8)

Shaw, F. W. (Pollokshields Ath), 1884 v E, W (2)

Shaw, J. (Rangers), 1947 v E, Bel, L; 1948 v Ni (4)

Shearer, R. (Rangers), 1961 v E, Ei (2), Cz (4)

Sillars, D. C. (Queen's Park), 1891 v Ni; 1892 v E; 1893 v W; 1894 v E; 1895 v W (5)

Simpson, J. (Third Lanark), 1895 v E, W, Ni (3)

Simpson, J. (Rangers), 1935 v E, W, Ni; 1936 v E, W, Ni; 1937 v G, E, W, Ni, A, Cz; 1938 v W, Ni (14)

Simpson, N. (Aberdeen), 1983 v Ni; 1984 v F (sub); 1987 v E; 1988 v E (4)

Simpson, R. C. (Celtic), 1967 v E, USSR; 1968 v Ni, E; 1969 v A (5)

Sinclair, G. L. (Hearts), 1910 v Ni; 1912 v W, Ni (3)

Sinclair, J. W. E. (Leicester C), 1966 v P (1)

Skene, L. H. (Queen's Park), 1904 v W (1)

Sloan, T. (Third Lanark), 1904 v W (1)

Smellie, R. (Queen's Park), 1887 v Ni; 1888 v W; 1889 v E; 1891 v E; 1893 v E, Ni (6)

Smith, A. (Rangers), 1898 v E; 1900 v E, Ni, W; 1901 v E, Ni, W; 1902 v E, Ni, W; 1903 v E, Ni, W; 1904 v Ni; 1905 v W; 1906 v E, Ni; 1907 v W; 1911 v E, Ni (20)

Smith, D. (Aberdeen), 1966 v Ho; (with Rangers), 1968 v Ho (2)

Smith, G. (Hibernian), 1947 v E, Ni; 1948 v W, Bel, Sw, F; 1952 v E, USA; 1955 v P, Y, A, H; 1956 v E, Ni, W; 1957 v Sp (2), Sw (18)

Smith, H. G. (Hearts), 1988 v S.Ar (sub) (1)

Smith, J. (Rangers), 1935 v Ni; 1938 v Ni (2)

Smith, J. (Ayr U), 1924 v E (1)

Smith, J. (Aberdeen), 1968 v Ho (sub); (with Newcastle U), 1974 v WG, Ni (sub), W (sub) (4)

Smith, J. E. (Celtic), 1959 v H, P (2)

Smith, Jas (Queen's Park), 1872 v E (1)

Smith, John (Mauchline), 1877 v E, W; 1879 v E, W; (with Edinburgh University), 1880 v E; (with Queen's Park), 1881 v W, E; 1883 v E, W; 1884 v E (10)

Smith, N. (Rangers), 1897 v E; 1898 v W; 1899 v E, W, Ni; 1900 v E, W, Ni; 1901 v Ni, W; 1902 v E, Ni (12)

Smith, R. (Queen's Park), 1872 v E; 1873 v E (2)

Smith, T. M. (Kilmarnock), 1934 v E; (with Preston NE), 1938 v E (2)

Somers, P. (Celtic), 1905 v E, Ni; 1907 v Ni; 1909 v W (4)

Somers, W. S. (Third Lanark), 1879 v E, W; (with Queen's Park), 1880 v W (3)

Somerville, G. (Queen's Park), 1886 v E (1)

Souness, G. J. (Middlesbrough), 1975 v EG, Sp, Se; (with Liverpool), 1978 v Bul, W, E (sub), Ho; 1979 v A, N, W, Ni, E; 1980 v Pe, A, Bel, P, Ni; 1981 v P, Is (2); 1982 v Ni, P, Sp, W, E, Nz, Br, USSR; 1983 v EG, Sw, Bel, Sw, W, E, Ca (2 + 1 sub); 1984 v U, Ni, W; (with Sampdoria), 1985 v Y, Ic, Sp (2), W, E, Ic; 1986 v EG, Aus (2), R, E, D, WG (54)

Speedie, D. R. (Chelsea), 1985 v E; 1986 v W, EG (sub), Aus, E; (with Coventry C), 1989 v Y (sub), I (sub), Cy (1+1 sub), Ch (10)

Speedie, F. (Rangers), 1903 v E, W, Ni (3)

Speirs, J. H. (Rangers), 1908 v W (1)

Stanton, P. (Hibernian), 1966 v Ho; 1969 v Ni; 1970 v Ei, A; 1971 v D, Bel, P, USSR, D; 1972 v P, Bel, Ho, W; 1973 v W, Ni; 1974 v WG (16)

Stark, J. (Rangers), 1909 v E, Ni (2)

Steel, W. (Morton), 1947 v E, Bel, L; (with Derby Co), 1948 v F, E, W, Ni; 1949 v E, W, Ni, F; 1950 v E, W, Ni, Sw, P, F; (with Dundee), 1951 v W, Ni, E, A (2), D, F, Bel; 1952 v W; 1953 v W, E, Ni, Se (30)

Steele, D. M. (Huddersfield), 1923 v E, W, Ni (3)

Stein, C. (Rangers), 1969 v W, Ni, D, E, Cy (2); 1970 v A (sub), Ni (sub), W, E, Ei, WG; 1971 v D, USSR, Bel, D; 1972 v Cz (sub); (with Coventry C), 1973 v E (2 sub), W (sub), Ni (21)

Stephen, J. F. (Bradford), 1947 v W; 1948 v W (2)

Stevenson, G. (Motherwell), 1928 v W, Ni; 1930 v Ni, E, F; 1931 v E, W; 1932 v W, Ni; 1933 v Ni; 1934 v E; 1935 v Ni (12)

Stewart, A. (Queen's Park), 1888 v Ni; 1889 v W (2)

Stewart, A. (Third Lanark), 1894 v W (1)

Stewart, D. (Dumbarton), 1888 v Ni (1)

Stewart, D. (Queen's Park), 1893 v W; 1894 v Ni; 1897 v Ni (3)

Stewart, D. S. (Leeds U), 1978 v EG (1)

Stewart, G. (Hibernian), 1906 v W, E; (with Manchester C), 1907 v E, W (4)

Stewart, J. (Kilmarnock), 1977 v Ch (sub); (with Middlesbrough), 1979 v N (2)

Stewart, R. (West Ham U), 1981 v W, Ni, E; 1982 v Ni, P, W; 1984 v F; 1987 v Ei (2), L (10)

Stewart, W. E. (Queen's Park), 1898 v Ni; 1900 v Ni (2)

Storrier, D. (Celtic), 1899 v E, W, Ni (3)

Strachan, G. (Aberdeen), 1980 v Ni, W, E, Pol, H (sub); 1981 v Se, P; 1982 v Ni, P, Sp, Ho (sub), Nz, Br, USSR; 1983 v EG, Sw, Bel, Sw, Ni (sub), W, E, Ca (2+1 sub); 1984 v EG, Ni, E, F; (with Manchester U), 1985 v Sp (sub), E, Ic; 1986 v W, Aus, R, D, WG, U; 1987 v Bul, Ei (2); 1988 v H; 1989 v F (sub); (with Leeds U), 1990 v F; 1991 v USSR, Bul, Sm (46)

Sturrock, P. (Dundee U), 1981 v W (sub), Ni, E (sub); 1982 v P, Ni (sub), W (sub), E (sub); 1983 v EG (sub), Sw, Bel (sub), Ca (3); 1984 v W; 1985 v Y (sub); 1986 v Is (sub), Ho, D, U; 1987 v Bel (20)

Summers, W. (St Mirren), 1926 v E (1)

Symon, J. S. (Rangers), 1939 v H (1)

Tait, T. S. (Sunderland), 1911 v W (1)

Taylor, J. (Queen's Park), 1872 v E; 1873 v E; 1874 v E; 1875 v E; 1876 v E, W (6)

Taylor, J. D. (Dumbarton), 1892 v W; 1893 v W; 1894 v Ni; (with St Mirren), 1895 v Ni (4)

Taylor, W. (Hearts), 1892 v E (1)

Telfer, W. (Motherwell), 1933 v Ni; 1934 v Ni (2)

Telfer, W. D. (St Mirren), 1954 v W (1)

Templeton, R. (Aston Villa), 1902 v E; (with Newcastle U), 1903 v W; 1904 v E; (with Woolwich Arsenal), 1905 v W; (with Kilmarnock), 1908 v Ni; 1910 v E, Ni; 1912 v E, Ni; 1913 v W (11)

Thomson, A. (Arthurlie), 1886 v Ni (1)

Thomson, A. (Third Lanark), 1889 v W (1)

Thomson, A. (Airdrieonians), 1909 v Ni (1)

Thomson, A. (Celtic), 1926 v E; 1932 v F; 1933 v W (3)

Thomson, C. (Hearts), 1904 v Ni; 1905 v E, Ni, W; 1906 v W, Ni; 1907 v E, W, Ni; 1908 v E, W, Ni; (with Sunderland), 1909 v W; 1910 v E; 1911 v Ni; 1912 v E, W; 1913 v E, W; 1914 v E, Ni (21)

Thomson, C. (Sunderland), 1937 v Cz (1)

Thomson, D. (Dundee), 1920 v W (1)

Thomson, J. (Celtic), 1930 v F; 1931 v E, W, Ni (4)

Thomson, J. J. (Queen's Park), 1872 v E; 1873 v E; 1874 v E (3)

Thomson, J. R. (Everton), 1933 v W (1)

Thomson, R. (Celtic), 1932 v W (1)

Thomson, R. W. (Falkirk), 1927 v E (1)

Thomson, S. (Rangers), 1884 v W, Ni (2)

Thomson, W. (Dumbarton), 1892 v W; 1893 v W; 1898 v Ni, W (4)

Thomson, W. (Dundee), 1896 v W (1)

Thornton, W. (Rangers), 1947 v W, Ni; 1948 v E, Ni; 1949 v F; 1952 v D, Se (7)

Thomson, W. (St Mirren), 1980 v Ni; 1981 v Ni (sub+1) 1982 v P; 1983 v Ni, Ca; 1984 v EG (7)

Toner, W. (Kilmarnock), 1959 v W, Ni (2)

Townsley, T. (Falkirk), 1926 v W (1)

Troup, A. (Dundee), 1920 v E; 1921 v W, Ni; 1922 v Ni; (with Everton), 1926 v E (5)

Turnbull, E. (Hibernian), 1948 v Bel, Sw; 1951 v A; 1958 v H, Pol, Y, Par, F (8)

Turner, T. (Arthurlie), 1884 v W (1)

Turner, W. (Pollokshields Ath), 1885 v Ni; 1886 v Ni (2)

Ure, J. F. (Dundee), 1962 v W, Cz; 1963 v W, Ni, E, A, N, Sp; (with Arsenal), 1964 v Ni, N; 1968 v Ni (11)

Urquhart, D. (Hibernian), 1934 v W (1)

Vallance, T. (Rangers), 1877 v E, W; 1878 v E; 1879 v E, W; 1881 v E, W (7)

Venters, A. (Cowdenbeath), 1934 v Ni; (with Rangers), 1936 v E; 1939 v E (3)

Waddell, T. S. (Queen's Park), 1891 v Ni; 1892 v E; 1893 v E, Ni; 1895 v E, Ni (6)

Waddell, W. (Rangers), 1947 v W; 1949 v E, W, Ni, F; 1950 v E, Ni; 1951 v E, D, F, Bel, A; 1952 v Ni, W; 1954 v Ni; 1955 v W, Ni (17)

Wales, H. M. (Motherwell), 1933 v W (1)

Walker, A. (Celtic), 1988 v Co (sub) (1)

Walker, F. (Third Lanark), 1922 v W (1)

Walker, G. (St Mirren), 1930 v F; 1931 v Ni, A, Sw (4)

Walker, J. (Hearts), 1895 v Ni; 1897 v W; 1898 v Ni; (with Rangers), 1904 v W, Ni (5)

Walker, J. (Swindon T), 1911 v E, W, Ni; 1912 v E, W, Ni; 1913 v E, W, Ni (9)

Walker, R. (Hearts), 1900 v E, Ni; 1901 v E, W; 1902 v E, W, Ni; 1903 v E, W, Ni; 1904 v E, W, Ni; 1905 v E, W, Ni; 1906 v Ni; 1907 v E, Ni; 1908 v E, W, Ni; 1909 v E, W; 1912 v E, W, Ni; 1913 v E, W (29)

Walker, T. (Hearts), 1935 v E, W; 1936 v E, W, Ni; 1937 v G, E, W, Ni, A, Cz; 1938 v E, W, Ni, Cz, Ho; 1939 v E, W, Ni, H (20)

Walker, W. (Clyde), 1909 v Ni; 1910 v Ni (2)

Wallace, I. A. (Coventry C), 1978 v Bul (sub); 1979 v P (sub), W (3)

Wallace, W. S. B. (Hearts), 1965 v Ni; 1966 v E, Ho; (with Celtic), 1967 v E, USSR (sub); 1968 v Ni; 1969 v E (sub) (7)

Wardhaugh, J. (Hearts), 1955 v H; 1957 v Ni (2)

Wark, J. (Ipswich T), 1979 v W, Ni, E, Arg, N (sub); 1980 v Pe, A, Bel (2); 1981 v Is, Ni; 1982 v Se, Sp, Ho, Ni, Nz, Br, USSR; 1983 v EG, Sw (2), Ni, E (sub); 1984 v U, Bel, EG; (with Liverpool), E, F; 1985 v Y (29)

Watson, A. (Queen's Park), 1881 v E, W; 1882 v E (3)

Watson, J. (Sunderland), 1903 v E, W; 1904 v E; 1905 v E; (with Middlesbrough), 1909 v E, Ni (6)

Watson, J. (Motherwell), 1948 v Ni; (with Huddersfield T), 1954 v Ni (2)

Watson, J. A. K. (Rangers), 1878 v W (1)

Watson, P. R. (Blackpool), 1934 v A (1)

Watson, R. (Motherwell), 1971 v USSR (1)

Watson, W. (Falkirk), 1898 v W (1)

Watt, F. (Kilbirnie), 1889 v W, Ni; 1890 v W; 1891 v E (4)

Watt, W. W. (Queen's Park), 1887 v Ni (1)

Waugh, W. (Hearts), 1938 v Cz (1)

Weir, A. (Motherwell), 1959 v WG; 1960 v E, P, A, H, T (6)

Weir, J. (Third Lanark), 1887 v Ni (1)

Weir, J. B. (Queen's Park), 1872 v E; 1874 v E; 1875 v E; 1878 v W (4)

Weir, P. (St Mirren), 1980 v N (sub), W, Pol (sub), H; (with Aberdeen), 1983 v Sw; 1984 v Ni (6)

White, John (Albion R), 1922 v W; (with Hearts), 1923 v Ni (2)

White, J. A. (Falkirk), 1959 v WG, Ho, P; 1960 v Ni; (with Tottenham H), 1960 v W, Pol, A, T; 1961 v W; 1962 v Ni, W, E, Cz (2); 1963 v W, Ni, E; 1964 v Ni, W, E, N, WG (22)

White, W. (Bolton W), 1907 v E; 1908 v E (2)

Whitelaw, A. (Vale of Leven), 1887 v Ni; 1890 v W (2)

Whyte, D. (Celtic), 1988 v Bel (sub), L; 1989 v Ch (sub) (3)

Wilson, A. (Sheffield W), 1907 v E; 1908 v E; 1912 v E; 1913 v E, W; 1914 v Ni (6)

Wilson, A. (Portsmouth), 1954 v Fi (1)

Wilson, A. N. (Dunfermline), 1920 v E, W, Ni; 1921 v E, W, Ni; (with Middlesbrough), 1922 v E, W, Ni; 1923 v E, W, Ni (12)

Wilson, D. (Queen's Park), 1900 v W (1)

Wilson, D. (Oldham Ath), 1913 v E (1)

Wilson, D. (Rangers), 1961 v E, W, Ni, Ei (2), Cz; 1962 v Ni, W, E, Cz, U; 1963 v W, E, A, N, Ei, Sp; 1964 v E, WG; 1965 v Ni, E, Fi (22)

Wilson, G. W. (Hearts), 1904 v W; 1905 v E, Ni; 1906 v W; (with Everton), 1907 v E; (with Newcastle U), 1909 v E (6)

Wilson, Hugh, (Newmilns), 1890 v W; (with Sunderland), 1897 v E; (with Third Lanark), 1902 v W; 1904 v Ni (4)

Wilson, I. A. (Leicester C), 1987 v E, Br; (with Everton), 1988 v Bel, Bul, L (5)

Wilson, J. (Vale of Leven), 1888 v W; 1889 v E; 1890 v E; 1891 v E (4)

Wilson, P. (Celtic), 1926 v Ni; 1930 v F; 1931 v Ni; 1933 v E (4)

Wilson, P. (Celtic), 1975 v Sp (sub) (1)

Wilson, R. P. (Arsenal), 1972 v P, Ho (2)

Wiseman, W. (Queen's Park), 1927 v W; 1930 v Ni (2)

Wood, G. (Everton), 1979 v Ni, E, Arg (sub); (with Arsenal), 1982 v Ni (4)

Woodburn, W. A. (Rangers), 1947 v E, Bel, L; 1948 v W, Ni; 1949 v E, F; 1950 v E, W, Ni, P, F; 1951 v E, W, Ni, A (2), D, F, Bel; 1952 v E, W, Ni, USA (24)

Wotherspoon, D. N. (Queen's Park), 1872 v E; 1873 v E (2)

Wright, T. (Sunderland), 1953 v W, Ni, E (3)

Wylie, T. G. (Rangers), 1890 v Ni (1)

Yeats, R. (Liverpool), 1965 v W; 1966 v I (2)

Yorston, B. C. (Aberdeen), 1931 v Ni (1)

Yorston, H. (Aberdeen), 1955 v W (1)

Young, A. (Hearts), 1960 v E, A (sub), H, T; 1961 v W, Ni; (with Everton), Ei; 1966 v P (8)

Young, A. (Everton), 1905 v E; 1907 v W (2)

Young, G. L. (Rangers), 1947 v E, Ni, Bel, L; 1948 v E, Ni, Bel, Sw, F; 1949 v E, W, Ni, F; 1950 v E, W, Ni, Sw, P, F; 1951 v E, W, Ni, A (2), D, F, Bel; 1952 v E, W, Ni, USA, D, Se; 1953 v W, E, Ni, Se; 1954 v Ni, W; 1955 v W, Ni, P, Y; 1956 v Ni, W, E, A; 1957 v E, Ni, W, Y, Sp, Sw (53)

Young, J. (Celtic), 1906 v Ni (1)

Younger, T. (Hibernian), 1955 v P, Y, A, H; 1956 v E, Ni, W, A; (with Liverpool), 1957 v E, Ni, W, Y, Sp (2), Sw, WG; 1958 v Ni, W, E, Sw, H, Pol, Y, Par (24)

WALES

Adams, H. (Berwyn R), 1882 v Ni, E; (with Druids), 1883 v Ni, E (4)

Aizlewood, M. (Charlton Ath), 1986 v S.Ar, Ca (2); 1987 v Fi; (with Leeds U), USSR, Fi (sub); 1988 v D (sub), Se, Ma, I; 1989 v Ho, Se (sub), WG; (with Bradford C), 1990 v Fi, WG, Ei, Cr; (with Bristol C), 1991 v D, Bel (2), L, Ei, Ic, Pol, WG (25)

Allchurch, I. J. (Swansea T), 1951 v E, Ni, P, Sw; 1952 v E, S, Ni, R of UK; 1953 v S, E, Ni, F, Y; 1954 v S, E, Ni, A; 1955 v S, E, Ni, Y; 1956 v E, S, Ni, A; 1957 v E, S; 1958 v Ni, Is (2), H (2), M, Sw, Br; (with Newcastle U), 1959 v E, S, Ni; 1960 v S, E; 1961 v Ni, H, Sp (2); 1962 v E, S, Br (2), M; (with Cardiff C), 1963 v S, E, Ni, H (2); 1964 v E; 1965 v S, E, Ni, Gr, I, USSR; 1966 (with Swansea T), v USSR, E, S, D, Br (2), Ch (68)

Allchurch, L. (Swansea T), 1955 v Ni; 1956 v A; 1958 v S, Ni, EG, Is; 1959 v S; (with Sheffield U), 1962 v S, Ni, Br; 1964 v E (11)

Allen, B. W. (Coventry C), 1951 v S, E (2)

Allen, M. (Watford), 1986 v S.Ar (sub), Ca (1 + 1 sub); (with Norwich C), 1989 v Is (sub); 1990 v Ho, WG; (with Millwall), Ei, Se, Cr (sub); 1991 v L (sub), Ei (sub) (11)

Arridge, S. (Bootle), 1892 v S, Ni; (with Everton), 1894 v Ni; 1895 v Ni; 1896 v E; (with New Brighton Tower), 1898 v E, Ni; 1899 v E (8)

Astley, D. J. (Charlton Ath), 1931 v Ni; (with Aston Villa), 1932 v E; 1933 v E, S, Ni; 1934 v E, S; 1935 v S; 1936 v E, Ni; (with Derby Co), 1939 v E, S; (with Blackpool), F (13)

Atherton, R. W. (Hibernian), 1899 v E, Ni; 1903 v E, S, Ni; (with Middlesbrough), 1904 v E, S, Ni; 1905 v Ni (9)

Bailiff, W. E. (Llanelly), 1913 v E, S, Ni; 1920 v Ni (4)

Baker, C. W. (Cardiff C), 1958 v M; 1960 v S, Ni; 1961 v S, E, Ei; 1962 v S (7)

Baker, W. G. (Cardiff C), 1948 v Ni (1)

Bamford, T. (Wrexham), 1931 v E, S, Ni; 1932 v Ni; 1933 v F (5)

Barnes, W. (Arsenal), 1948 v E, S, Ni; 1949 v E, S, Ni; 1950 v E, S, Ni, Bel; 1951 v E, S, Ni, P; 1952 v E, S, Ni, R of UK; 1954 v E, S; 1955 v S, Y (22)

Bartley, T. (Glossop NE), 1898 v E (1)

Beadles, G. H. (Cardiff C), 1925 v E, S (2)

Bell, W. S. (Shrewsbury Engineers), 1881 v E, S; (with Crewe Alex), 1886 v E, S, Ni (5)

Bennion, S. R. (Manchester U), 1926 v S; 1927 v S; 1928 v S, E, Ni; 1929 v S, E, Ni; 1930 v S; 1932 v Ni (10)

Berry, G. F. (Wolverhampton W), 1979 v WG; 1980 v Ei, WG (sub), T; (with Stoke C), 1983 v E (sub) (5)

Blackmore, C. G. (Manchester U), 1985 v N (sub); 1986 v S (sub), H (sub), S.Ar, Ei, U; 1987 v Fi (2), USSR, Cz; 1988 v D (2), Cz, Y, Se, Ma, I; 1989 v Ho, Fi, Is, WG; 1990 v F; Ho, WG, Cr; 1991 v Bel, L (27)

Blew, H. (Wrexham), 1899 v E, S, Ni; 1902 v S, Ni; 1903 v E, S; 1904 v E, S, Ni; 1905 v S, Ni; 1906 v E, S, Ni; 1907 v S; 1908 v E, S, Ni; 1909 v E, S; 1910 v E (22)

Boden, T. (Wrexham), 1880 v E (1)

Bodin, P. J. (Swindon T), 1990 v Cr; 1991 v D, Bel, L, Ei; (with C Palace), Bel, Ic, Pol, WG (9)

Bostock, A. M. (Shrewsbury), 1892 v Ni (1)

Boulter, L. M. (Brentford), 1939 v Ni (1)

Bowdler, H. E. (Shrewsbury), 1893 v S (1)

Bowdler, J. C. H. (Shrewsbury), 1890 v Ni; (with Wolverhampton W), 1891 v S; 1892 v Ni; (with Shrewsbury), 1894 v E (4)

Bowen, D. L. (Arsenal), 1955 v S, Y; 1957 v Ni, Cz, EG; 1958 v S, Ni, EG, Is (2), H (2), M, Se, Br; 1959 v E, S, Ni (19)

Bowen, E. (Druids), 1880 v S; 1883 v S (2)

Bowen, M. R. (Tottenham H), 1986 v Ca (2 sub); (with Norwich C), 1988 v Y (sub); 1989 v Fi (sub), Is, Se, WG (sub); 1990 v Fi (sub), Ho, WG, Se (11)

Bowsher, S. J. (Burnley), 1929 v Ni (1)

Boyle, T. (C Palace), 1981 v Ei, S (sub) (2)

Britten, T. J. (Parkgrove), 1878 v S; (with Presteigne), 1880 v S (2)

Brookes, S. J. (Llandudno), 1900 v E, Ni (2)

Brown, A. I. (Aberdare Ath), 1926 v Ni (1)

Bryan, T. (Oswestry), 1886 v E, Ni (2)

Buckland, T. (Bangor), 1899 v E (1)

Burgess, W. A. R. (Tottenham H), 1947 v E, S, Ni; 1948 v E, S; 1949 v E, S, Ni, P, Bel, Sw; 1950 v E, S, Ni, Bel; 1951 v S, Ni, P, Sw; 1952 v E, S, Ni, R of UK; 1953 v S, E, Ni, F, Y; 1954 v S, E, Ni, A (32)

Burke, T. (Wrexham), 1883 v E; 1884 v S; 1885 v E, S, Ni; (with Newton Heath), 1887 v E, S; 1888 v S (8)

Burnett, T. B. (Ruabon), 1877 v S (1)

Burton, A. D. (Norwich C), 1963 v Ni, H; (with Newcastle U), 1964 v E; 1969 v S, E, Ni, I, EG; 1972 v Cz (9)

Butler, A. (Druids), 1900 v S, Ni (2)

Butler, J. (Chirk), 1893 v E, S, Ni (3)

Cartwright, L. (Coventry C), 1974 v E (sub), S, Ni; 1976 v S (sub); 1977 v WG (sub); (with Wrexham), 1978 v Ir (sub); 1979 v Ma (7)

Carty, T. (Wrexham), 1889 v Ni (1)

Challen, J. B. (Corinthians), 1887 v E, S; 1888 v E; (with Wellingborough GS), 1890 v E (4)

Chapman, T. (Newtown), 1894 v E, S, Ni; 1895 v S, Ni; (with Manchester C), 1896 v E; 1897 v E (7)

Charles, J. M. (Swansea C), 1981 v Cz, T (sub), S (sub), USSR (sub); 1982 v Ic; 1983 v N (sub), Y (sub), Bul (sub), S, Ni, Br; 1984 v Bul (sub); (with QPR), Y (sub), S; (with Oxford U), 1985 v Ic (sub), Sp, Ic; 1986 v Ei; 1987 v Fi (19)

Charles, M. (Swansea T), 1955 v Ni; 1956 v E, S, A; 1957 v E, Ni, Cz (2), EG; 1958 v E, S, EG, Is (2), H (2), M, Se, Br; 1959 v E, S; (with Arsenal), 1961 v Ni, H, Sp (2); 1962 v E, S; (with Cardiff C), 1962 v Br, Ni; 1963 v S, H (31)

Charles, W. J. (Leeds U), 1950 v Ni; 1951 v Sw; 1953 v Ni, F, Y; 1954 v E, S, A; 1955 v S, E, Ni, Y; 1956 v E, S, A, Ni; 1957 v S, Ni, Cz (2), EG; (with Juventus), 1958 v Is (2), H (2) M, Se; 1960 v S; 1962 v E, Br (2), M; (with Leeds U), 1963 v S; (with Cardiff C), 1964 v S; 1965 v S, USSR (38)

Clarke, R. J. (Manchester C), 1949 v E; 1950 v S, Ni, Bel; 1951 v E, S, Ni, P, Sw; 1952 v S, E, Ni, R of UK; 1953 v S, E; 1954 v E, S, Ni; 1955 v Y, S, E; 1956 v Ni (22)

Collier, D. J. (Grimsby T), 1921 v S (1)

Collins, W. S. (Llanelly), 1931 v S (1)

Conde, C. (Chirk), 1884 v E, S, Ni (3)

Cook, F. C. (Newport Co), 1925 v E, S; (with Portsmouth), 1928 v E, S; 1930 v E, S, Ni; 1932 v E (8)

Crompton, W. (Wrexham), 1931 v E, S, Ni (3)

Cross, E. A. (Wrexham), 1876 v S; 1877 v S (2)

Cross, K. (Druids), 1879 v S; 1881 v E, S (3)

Crowe, V. H. (Aston Villa), 1959 v E, Ni; 1960 v E, Ni; 1961 v S, E, Ni, Ei, H, Sp (2); 1962 v E, S, Br, M; 1963 v H (16)

Cumner, R. H. (Arsenal), 1939 v E, S, Ni (3)

Curtis, A. (Swansea C), 1976 v E, Y (sub), S, Ni, Y (sub), E; 1977 v WG, S (sub), Ni (sub); 1978 v WG, E, S; 1979 v WG, S; (with Leeds U), E, Ni, Ma; 1980 v Ei, WG, T; (with Swansea C), 1982 v Cz, Ic, USSR, Sp, E, S, Ni; 1983 v N; 1984 v R (sub); (with Southampton), S; 1985 v Sp, N (1 + 1 sub); 1986 v H; (with Cardiff C), 1987 v USSR (35)

Curtis, E. R. (Cardiff C), 1928 v S; (with Birmingham), 1932 v S; 1934 v Ni (3)

Daniel, R. W. (Arsenal), 1951 v E, Ni, P; 1952 v E, S, Ni, R of UK; 1953 v S, E, Ni, F, Y; (with Sunderland), 1954 v E, S, Ni; 1955 v E, Ni; 1957 v S, E, Ni, Cz (21)

Darvell, S. (Oxford University), 1897 v S, Ni (2)

Davies, A. (Manchester U), 1983 v Ni, Br; 1984 v E, Ni; 1985 v Ic; (with Newcastle U), 1986 v H; (with Swansea C), 1988 v Ma, I; 1989 v Ho; (with Bradford C), 1990 v Fi, Ei (11)

Davies, A. (Wrexham), 1876 v S; 1877 v S (2)

Davies, A. (Shrewsbury), 1891 v Ni (1)

Davies, A. (Druids), 1904 v S; (with Middlesbrough), 1905 v S (2)

Davies, A. O. (Barmouth), 1885 v Ni; 1886 v E, S; (with Swifts), 1887 v E, S; 1888 v E, Ni; (with Wrexham), 1889 v S; (with Crewe Alex), 1890 v E (9)

Davies, C. (Brecon), 1899 v Ni; (with Hereford), 1900 v Ni (2)

Davies, C. (Charlton Ath), 1972 v R (sub) (1)

Davies, D. (Bolton W), 1904 v S, Ni; 1908 v E (sub) (3)

Davies, D. W. (Treharris), 1912 v Ni; (with Oldham Ath), 1913 v Ni (2)

Davies, E. Lloyd (Stoke C), 1904 v E; 1907 v E, S, Ni; (with Northampton T), 1908 v S; 1909 v Ni; 1910 v Ni; 1911 v E, S; 1912 v E, S; 1913 v E, S; 1914 v Ni, E, S (16)

Davies, E. R. (Newcastle U), 1953 v S, E; 1954 v E, S; 1958 v E, EG (6)

Davies, G. (Fulham), 1980 v T, Ic; 1982 v Sp (sub), F (sub); 1983 v E, Bul, S, Ni, Br; 1984 v R (sub), S (sub), E, Ni; 1985 v Ic (2); (with Chelsea), N; (with Manchester C), 1986 v S.Ar, Ei (18)

Davies, Rev. H. (Wrexham), 1928 v Ni (1)

Davies, Idwal (Liverpool Marine), 1923 v S (1)

Davies, J. E. (Oswestry), 1885 v E (1)

Davies, Jas (Wrexham), 1878 v S (1)

Davies, John (Wrexham), 1879 v S (1)

Davies, Jos (Newton Heath), 1888 v E, S, Ni; 1889 v S; 1890 v E; (with Wolverhampton W), 1892 v E; 1893 v E (7)

Davies, Jos (Everton), 1889 v S, Ni; (with Chirk), 1891 v Ni; (with Ardwick), v E, S; (with Sheffield U), 1895 v E, S, Ni; (with Manchester C), 1896 v E; (with Millwall), 1897 v E; (with Reading), 1900 v E (11)

Davies, J. P. (Druids), 1883 v E, Ni (2)

Davies, Ll. (Wrexham), 1907 v Ni; 1910 v Ni, S, E; (with Everton), 1911 v S, Ni; 1912 v Ni, S, E; 1913 v Ni, S, E; 1914 v Ni (13)

Davies, L. S. (Cardiff C), 1922 v E, S, Ni; 1923 v E, S, Ni; 1924 v E, S, Ni; 1925 v S, Ni; 1926 v E, Ni; 1927 v E, Ni; 1928 v S, Ni, E; 1929 v S, Ni, E; 1930 v E, S (23)

Davies, O. (Wrexham), 1890 v S (1)

Davies, R. (Wrexham), 1883 v Ni; 1884 v Ni; 1885 v Ni (3)

Davies, R. (Druids), 1885 v E (1)

Davies, R. O. (Wrexham), 1892 v Ni, E (2)

Davies, R. T. (Norwich C), 1964 v Ni; 1965 v E; 1966 v Br (2), Ch; (with Southampton), 1967 v S, E, Ni; 1968 v S, Ni, WG; 1969 v S, E, Ni, I, WG, R of UK; 1970 v E, S, Ni; 1971 v Cz, S, E, Ni; 1972 v R, E, S, N; (with Portsmouth), 1974 v E (29)

Davies, R. W. (Bolton W), 1964 v E; 1965 v E, S, Ni, D, Gr, USSR; 1966 v E, S, Ni, USSR, D, Br (2), Ch (sub); 1967 v S; (with Newcastle U), E; 1968 v S, Ni, WG; 1969 v S, E, Ni, I; 1970 v EG; 1971 v R, Cz; (with Manchester C), 1972 v E, S, Ni; (with Manchester U), 1973 v E, S (sub), Ni; (with Blackpool), 1974 v Pol (34)

Davies, Stanley (Preston NE), 1920 v E, S, Ni; (with Everton), 1921 v E, S, Ni; (with WBA), 1922 v E, S, Ni; 1923 v S; 1925 v S, Ni, Ni; 1926 v S, E, Ni; 1927 v S; 1928 v S; (with Rotherham U), 1930 v Ni (18)

Davies, T. (Oswestry), 1886 v E (1)

Davies, T. (Druids), 1903 v E, Ni, S; 1904 v S (4)

Davies, W. (Wrexham), 1884 v Ni (1)

Davies, W. (Swansea T), 1924 v E, S, Ni; (with Cardiff C), 1925 v E, S, Ni; 1926 v E, S, Ni; 1927 v S; 1928 v Ni; (with Notts Co), 1929 v E, S, Ni; 1930 v E, S, Ni (17)

Davies, William (Wrexham), 1903 v Ni; 1905 v Ni; (with Blackburn R), 1908 v E, S; 1909 v E, S, Ni; 1911 v E, S, Ni; 1912 v Ni (11)

Davies, W. C. (C Palace), 1908 v S; (with WBA), 1909 v E; 1910 v S; (with C Palace), 1914 v E (4)

Davies, W. D. (Everton), 1975 v H, L, S, E, Ni; 1976 v Y (2), E, Ni; 1977 v WG, S (2), Cz, E, Ni; 1978 v K; (with Wrexham), S, Cz, WG, Ir, E, S, Ni; 1979 v Ma, T, WG, S, E, Ni, Ma; 1980 v Ei, WG, T, E, S, Ni, Ic; 1981 v T, Cz, Ei, T, S, E, USSR; (with Swansea C), 1982 v Cz, Ic, USSR, Sp, E, S, F; 1983 v Y (52)

Davies, W. H. (Oswestry), 1876 v S; 1877 v S; 1879 v E; 1880 v E (4)

Davies, W. O. (Millwall Ath), 1913 v E, S, Ni; 1914 v S, Ni (5)

Davis, G. (Wrexham), 1978 v Ir, E (sub), Ni (3)

Day, A. (Tottenham H), 1934 v Ni (1)

Deacy, N. (PSV Eindhoven), 1977 v Cz, S, E, Ni; 1978 v K (sub), S (sub), Cz (sub), WG, Ir, S (sub), Ni; (with Beringen), 1979 v T (12)

Dearson, D. J. (Birmingham), 1939 v S, Ni, F (3)

Derrett, S. C. (Cardiff C), 1969 v S, WG; 1970 v I; 1971 v Fi (4)

Dewey, F. T. (Cardiff Corinthians), 1931 v E, S (2)

Dibble, A. (Luton T), 1986 v Ca (1 + 1 sub); (with Manchester C), 1989 v Is (3)

Doughty, J. (Druids), 1886 v S; (with Newton Heath), 1887 v S, Ni; 1888 v E, S, Ni; 1889 v S; 1890 v E (8)

Doughty, R. (Newton Heath and Druids), 1888 v S, Ni (2)

Durban, A. (Derby Co), 1966 v Br (sub); 1967 v Ni; 1968 v E, S, Ni, WG; 1969 v EG, S, E, Ni, WG; 1970 v E, S, Ni, EG, I; 1971 v R, S, E, Ni, Cz, Fi; 1972 v Fi, Cz, E, S, Ni (27)

Dwyer, P. (Cardiff C), 1978 v Ir, E, S, Ni; 1979 v T, S, E, Ni, Ma (sub); 1980 v WG (10)

Edwards, C. (Wrexham), 1878 v S (1)

Edwards, G. (Birmingham), 1947 v E, S, Ni; 1948 v E, S, Ni; (with Cardiff C), 1949 v Ni, P, Bel, Sw; 1950 v E, S (12)

Edwards, H. (Wrexham Civil Service), 1878 v S; 1880 v E; 1882 v E, S; 1883 v S; 1884 v Ni; 1887 v Ni (7)

Edwards, J. H. (Wanderers), 1876 v S (1)

Edwards, J. H. (Oswestry), 1895 v Ni; 1897 v E, Ni; (with Aberystwyth), 1898 v Ni (4)

Edwards, L. T. (Charlton Ath), 1957 v Ni, EG (2)

Edwards, R. I. (Chester), 1978 v K (sub); 1979 v Ma, WG; (with Wrexham), 1980 v T (sub) (4)

Edwards, T. (Linfield), 1932 v S (1)

Egan, W. (Chirk), 1892 v S (1)

Ellis, B. (Motherwell), 1932 v E; 1933 v E, S; 1934 v S; 1936 v E; 1937 v S (6)

Ellis, E. (Nunhead), 1931 v E; (with Oswestry), S; 1932 v Ni (3)

Emanuel, W. J. (Bristol C), 1973 v E (sub), Ni (sub) (2)

England, H. M. (Blackburn R), 1962 v Ni, Br, M; 1963 v Ni, H; 1964 v E, S, Ni; 1965 v E, D, Gr (2), USSR, Ni, I; 1966 v E, S, Ni, USSR, D; (with Tottenham H), 1967 v S, E; 1968 v E, Ni, WG; 1969 v EG; 1970 v R of UK, EG, E, S, Ni, I; 1971 v R; 1972 v Fi, E, S, Ni; 1973 v E (3), S; 1974 v Pol; 1975 v H, L (44)

Evans, B. C. (Swansea C), 1972 v Fi, Cz; 1973 v E (2), Pol, S; (with Hereford U), 1974 v Pol (7)

Evans, D. G. (Reading), 1926 v Ni; 1927 v Ni, E; (with Huddersfield T), 1929 v S (4)

Evans, H. P. (Cardiff C), 1922 v E, S, Ni; 1924 v E, S, Ni (6)

Evans, I. (Crystal Palace), 1976 v A, E, Y (2), E, Ni; 1977 v WG, S (2), Cz, E, Ni; 1978 v K (13)

Evans, J. (Oswestry), 1893 v Ni; 1894 v E, Ni (3)

Evans, J. (Cardiff C), 1912 v Ni; 1913 v Ni; 1914 v S; 1920 v S, Ni; 1922 v Ni; 1923 v E, Ni (8)

Evans, J. H. (Southend U), 1922 v E, S, Ni; 1923 v S (4)

Evans, Len (Cardiff C), 1931 v E, S; (with Birmingham), 1934 v Ni (3)

Evans, L. H. (Aberdare Ath), 1927 v Ni (1)

Evans, M. (Oswestry), 1884 v E (1)

Evans, R. (Clapton), 1902 v Ni (1)

Evans, R. E. (Wrexham), 1906 v E, S; (with Aston Villa), Ni; 1907 v E; 1908 v E, S; (with Sheffield U), 1909 v S; 1910 v E, S, Ni (10)

Evans, R. O. (Wrexham), 1902 v Ni; 1903 v E, S, Ni; (with Blackburn R), 1908 v Ni; (with Coventry C), 1911 v E, Ni; 1912 v E, S, Ni (10)

Evans, R. S. (Swansea T), 1964 v Ni (1)

Evans T. J. (Clapton Orient), 1927 v S; 1928 v E, S; (with Newcastle U), Ni (4)

Evans, W. (Tottenham H), 1933 v Ni; 1934 v E, S; 1935 v E; 1936 v E, Ni (6)

Evans, W. A. W. (Oxford University), 1876 v S; 1877 v S (2)

Evans, W. G. (Bootle), 1890 v E; 1891 v E; (with Aston Villa), 1892 v E (3)

Evelyn, E. C. (Crusaders), 1887 v E (1)

Eyton-Jones, J. A. (Wrexham), 1883 v Ni; 1884 v Ni, E, S (4)

Farmer, G. (Oswestry), 1885 v E, S (2)

Felgate, D. (Lincoln C), 1984 v R (sub) (1)

Finnigan, R. J. (Wrexham), 1930 v Ni (1)

Flynn, B. (Burnley), 1975 v L (2 sub), H (sub), S, E, Ni; 1976 v A, E, Y (2), E, Ni; 1977 v WG (sub), S (2), Cz, E, Ni; 1978 v K (2), S; (with Leeds U), Cz, WG, Ir (sub), E, S, Ni; 1979 v Ma, T, S, E, Ni, Ma; 1980 v Ei, WG, E, S, Ni, Ic; 1981 v T, Cz, Ei, T, S, E, USSR; 1982 v Cz, USSR, E, S, Ni, F; 1983 v N; (with Burnley), v Y, E, Bul, S, Ni, Br; 1984 v N, R, Bul, Y, S, N, Is (66)

Ford, T. (Swansea T), 1947 v S; (with Aston Villa), 1947 v Ni; 1948 v S, Ni; 1949 v E, S, Ni, P, Bel, Sw; 1950 v E, S, Ni, Bel; 1951 v S; (with Sunderland), 1951 v E, Ni, P, Sw; 1952 v E, S, Ni, R of UK; 1953 v S, E, Ni, F, Y; (with Cardiff C), 1954 v A; 1955 v S, E, Ni, Y; 1956 v S, Ni, E, A; 1957 v S (38)

Foulkes, H. E. (WBA), 1932 v Ni (1)

Foulkes, W. I. (Newcastle U), 1952 v E, S, Ni, R of UK; 1953 v E, S, F, Y; 1954 v E, S, Ni (11)

Foulkes, W. T. (Oswestry), 1884 v Ni; 1885 v S (2)

Fowler, J. (Swansea T), 1925 v E; 1926 v E, Ni; 1927 v S; 1928 v S; 1929 v E (6)

Garner, J. (Aberystwyth), 1896 v S (1)

Giles, D. (Swansea C), 1980 v E, S, Ni, Ic; 1981 v T, Cz, T (sub), E (sub), USSR (sub); (with C Palace), 1982 v Sp (sub); 1983 v Ni (sub), Br (12)

Gillam, S. G. (Wrexham), 1889 v S, Ni; (with Shrewsbury), 1890 v E, Ni; (with Clapton), 1894 v S (5)

Glascodine, G. (Wrexham), 1879 v E (1)

Glover, E. M. (Grimsby T), 1932 v S; 1934 v Ni; 1936 v S; 1937 v E, S, Ni; 1939 v Ni (7)

Godding, G. (Wrexham), 1923 v S, Ni (2)

Godfrey, B. C. (Preston NE), 1964 v Ni; 1965 v D, I (3)

Goodwin, U. (Ruthin), 1881 v E (1)

Goss, J. (Norwich C), 1991 v Ic, Pol (sub) (2)

Gough, R. T. (Oswestry White Star), 1883 v S (1)

Gray, A. (Oldham Ath), 1924 v E, S, Ni; 1925 v E, S, Ni; 1926 v E, S; 1927 v S; (with Manchester C), 1928 v E, S; 1929 v E, S, Ni; (with Manchester Central), 1930 v S; (with Tranmere R), 1932 v E, S, Ni; (with Chester), 1937 v E, S, Ni; 1938 v E, S, Ni (24)

Green, A. W. (Aston Villa), 1901 v Ni; (with Notts Co), 1903 v E; 1904 v S, Ni; 1906 v Ni, E; (with Nottingham F), 1907 v E; 1908 v S (8)

Green, C. R. (Birmingham C), 1965 v USSR, I; 1966 v E, S, USSR, Br (2); 1967 v E; 1968 v E, S, Ni, WG; 1969 v S, I, Ni (sub) (15)

Green, G. H. (Charlton Ath), 1938 v Ni; 1939 v E, Ni, F (4)

Grey, Dr W. (Druids), 1876 v S; 1878 v S (2)

Griffiths, A. T. (Wrexham), 1971 v Cz (sub); 1975 v A, H (2), L (2), E, Ni; 1976 v A, E, S, E (sub), Ni, Y (2); 1977 v WG, S (17)

Griffiths, F. J. (Blackpool), 1900 v E, S (2)

Griffiths, G. (Chirk), 1887 v Ni (1)

Griffiths, J. H. (Swansea T), 1953 v Ni (1)

Griffiths, M. W. (Leicester C), 1947 v Ni; 1949 v P, Bel; 1950 v E, S, Bel; 1951 v E, Ni, P, Sw; 1954 v A (11)

Griffiths, P. (Chirk), 1884 v E, Ni; 1888 v E; 1890 v S, Ni; 1891 v Ni (6)

Griffiths, S. (Wrexham), 1902 v S (1)

Griffiths, T. P. (Everton), 1927 v E, Ni; 1929 v E; 1930 v E; 1931 v Ni; 1932 v Ni, S, E; (with Bolton W), 1933 v F, E, S, Ni; (with Middlesbrough), 1934 v E, S; 1935 v E, Ni; 1936 v S; (with Aston Villa), Ni; 1937 v E, S, Ni (21)

Hall, G. D. (Chelsea), 1988 v Y (sub), Ma, I; 1989 v Ho, Fi, Is; 1990 v Ei; 1991 v Ei (8)

Hallam, J. (Oswestry), 1889 v E (1)

Hanford, H. (Swansea T), 1934 v Ni; 1935 v S; 1936 v E; (with Sheffield W), 1936 v Ni; 1938 v E, S; 1939 v F (7)

Harrington, A. C. (Cardiff C), 1956 v Ni; 1957 v E, S; 1958 v S, Ni, Is (2); 1961 v S, E; 1962 v E, S (11)

Harris, C. S. (Leeds U), 1976 v E, S; 1978 v WG, Ir, E, S, Ni; 1979 v Ma, T, WG, E (sub), Ma; 1980 v Ni (sub), Ic (sub); 1981 v T, Cz (sub), Ei, T, S, E, USSR; 1982 v Cz, Ic, E (sub) (24)

Harris, W. C. (Middlesbrough), 1954 v A; 1957 v EG, Cz; 1958 v E, S, EG (6)

Harrison, W. C. (Wrexham), 1899 v E; 1900 v E, S, Ni; 1901 v Ni v (5)

Hayes, A. (Wrexham), 1890 v Ni; 1894 v Ni (2)

Hennessey, W. T. (Birmingham C), 1962 v Ni, Br (2); 1963 v S, E, H (2); 1964 v E, S; 1965 v S, E, D, Gr, USSR; 1966 v E, USSR; (with Nottingham F), 1966 v S, Ni, D, Br (2), Ch; 1967 v S, E; 1968 v E, S, Ni; 1969 v WG, EG, R of UK, EG; (with Derby Co), 1970 v E, S, Ni; 1972 v Fi, Cz, E, S; 1973 v E (39)

Hersee, A. M. (Bangor), 1886 v S, Ni (2)

Hersee, R. (Llandudno), 1886 v Ni (1)

Hewitt, R. (Cardiff C), 1958 v Ni, Is, Se, H, Br (5)

Hewitt, T. J. (Wrexham), 1911 v E, S, Ni; (with Chelsea), 1913 v E, S, Ni; (with South Liverpool), 1914 v E, S (8)

Heywood, D. (Druids), 1879 v E (1)

Hibbott, H. (Newtown Excelsior), 1880 v E, S (2)

Hibbott, R. (Newtown), 1885 v S (1)

Higham, G. G. (Oswestry), 1878 v S; 1879 v E (2)

Hill, M. R. (Ipswich T), 1972 v Cz, R (2)

Hockey, S. (Sheffield U), 1972 v Fi, R; 1973 v E (2); (with Norwich C), Pol, S, E, Ni; (with Aston Villa), 1974 v Pol (9)

Hoddinott, T. F. (Watford), 1921 v E, S (2)

Hodges, G. (Wimbledon), 1984 v N (sub), Is (sub); 1987 v USSR, Fi, Cz; (with Newcastle U), 1988 v D (with Watford), D (sub), Cz (sub), Se, Ma, I (sub); 1990 v Se, Cr (13)

Hodgkinson, A. V. (Southampton), 1908 v Ni (1)

Holden, A. (Chester C), 1984 v Is (sub) (1)

Hole, B. G. (Cardiff C), 1963 v Ni; 1964 v Ni; 1965 v S, E, Ni, D, Gr (2), USSR, I; 1966 v E, S, Ni, USSR, D, Br (2), Ch; (with Blackburn R), 1967 v S, E, Ni; 1968 v E, S, Ni, WG; (with Aston Villa), 1969 v I, WG, EG; 1970 v I; (with Swansea C), 1971 v R (30)

Hole, W. J. (Swansea T), 1921 v Ni; 1922 v E; 1923 v E, Ni; 1928 v E, S, Ni; 1929 v E, S (9)

Hollins, D. M. (Newcastle U), 1962 v Br (sub), M; 1963 v Ni, H; 1964 v E; 1965 v Ni, Gr, I; 1966 v S, D, Br (11)

Hopkins, I. J. (Brentford), 1935 v S, Ni; 1936 v E, Ni; 1937 v E, S, Ni; 1938 v E, Ni; 1939 v E, S, Ni (12)

Hopkins, J. (Fulham), 1983 v Ni, Br; 1984 v N, R, Bul, Y, S, E, Ni, N, Is; 1985 v Ic (1 + 1 sub), N (14)

Hopkins, M. (Tottenham H), 1956 v Ni; 1957 v Ni, S, E, Cz (2), EG; 1958 v E, S, Ni, EG, Is (2), H (2), M, Se, Br; 1959 v E, S, Ni; 1960 v E, S; 1961 v Ni, H, Sp (2); 1962 v Ni, Br (2), M; 1963 v S, Ni, H (34)

Horne, B. (Portsmouth), 1988 v D (sub), Y, Se (sub), Ma, I; 1989 v Ho, Fi, Is; (with Southampton), Se, WG; 1990 v WG (sub), Ei, Se, Cr; 1991 v D, Bel (2), L, Ei, Ic, Pol, WG (22)

Howell, E. G. (Builth), 1888 v Ni; 1890 v E; 1891 v E (3)

Howells, R. G. (Cardiff C), 1954 v E, S (2)

Hugh, A. R. (Newport Co), 1930 v Ni (1)

Hughes, A. (Rhos), 1894 v E, S (2)

Hughes, A. (Chirk), 1907 v Ni (1)

Hughes, A. J. (Aberystwyth), 1879 v S (1)

Hughes, E. (Everton), 1899 v S, Ni; (with Tottenham H), 1901 v E, S; 1902 v Ni; 1904 v E, Ni, S; 1905 v E, Ni, S; 1906 v E, Ni; 1907 v E (14)

Hughes, E. (Wrexham), 1906 v S; (with Nottingham F), 1906 v Ni; 1908 v S, E; 1910 v Ni, E, S; 1911 v Ni, E, S; (with Wrexham), 1912 v Ni, E, S; (with Manchester C), 1913 v E, S; 1914 v N (16)

Hughes, F. W. (Northwich Victoria), 1882 v E, Ni; 1883 v E, Ni, S; 1884 v S (6)

Hughes, I. (Luton T), 1951 v E, Ni, P, Sw (4)

Hughes, J. (Cambridge University), 1877 v S (1)

Hughes, J. (Liverpool), 1905 v E, S, Ni (3)

Hughes, J. I. (Blackburn R), 1935 v Ni (1)

Hughes, L. M. (Manchester U), 1984 v E, Ni; 1985 v Ic, Sp, Ic, N, S, Sp, N; 1986 v S, H, U; (with Barcelona), 1987 v USSR, Cz; 1988 v D (2), Cz, Se, Ma, I; (with Manchester U), 1989 v Ho, Fi, Is, Se, WG; 1990 v Fi, WG, Cr; 1991 v D, Bel (2), L, Ic, Pol, WG (35)

Hughes, P. W. (Bangor), 1887 v Ni; 1889 v Ni, E (3)

Hughes, W. (Bootle), 1891 v E; 1892 v S, Ni (3)

Hughes, W. A. (Blackburn R), 1949 v E, Ni, P, Bel, Sw (5)

Hughes, W. M. (Birmingham), 1938 v E, Ni, S; 1939 v E, Ni, S, F; 1947 v E, S, Ni (10)

Humphreys, J. V. (Everton), 1947 v Ni (1)

Humphreys, R. (Druids), 1888 v Ni (1)

Hunter, W. H. (North End, Belfast), 1887 v Ni (1)

Jackett, K. (Watford), 1983 v N, Y, E, Bul, S; 1984 v N, R, Y, S, Ni, N, Is; 1985 v Ic, Sp, Ic, N, S, Sp, N; 1986 v S, H, S.Ar, Ei, Ca (2); 1987 v Fi (2); 1988 v D, Cz, Y, Se (31)

Jackson, W. (St Helens Rec), 1899 v Ni (1)

James, C. (Chirk), 1893 v E, Ni; 1894 v E, S, Ni; 1898 v E; 1899 v Ni (7)

James, E. G. (Blackpool), 1966 v Br (2), Ch; 1967 v Ni; 1968 v S; 1971 v Cz, S, E, Ni (9)

James, L. (Burnley), 1972 v Cz, R, S (sub); 1973 v E (3), Pol, S, Ni; 1974 v Pol, E, S, Ni; 1975 v A, H (2), L (2), S, E, Ni; 1976 v A; (with Derby Co), S, E, Y (2), Ni; 1977 v WG, S (2), Cz, E, Ni; 1978 v K (2); (with QPR), WG; (with Burnley), 1979 v T; (with Swansea C), 1980 v E, S, Ni, Ic; 1981 v T, Ei, T, S, E; 1982 v Cz, Ic, USSR, E (sub); (with Sunderland), 1983 v E (sub) (54)

James, R. M. (Swansea C), 1979 v Ma, WG (sub), S, E, Ni, Ma; 1980 v WG; 1982 v Cz (sub), Ic, Sp, E, S, Ni, F; 1983 v N, Y, E, Bul; (with Stoke C), 1984 v N, R, Bul, Y, S, E, Ni, N, Is; 1985 v Ic, Sp, Ic; (with QPR), N, S, Sp, N; 1986 v S, S.Ar, Ei, U, Ca (2); 1987 v Fi (2), USSR, Cz; (with Leicester C), 1988 v D (2); (with Swansea C), Y (47)

James, W. (West Ham U), 1931 v Ni; 1932 v Ni (2)

Jarrett, R. H. (Ruthin), 1889 v Ni; 1890 v S (2)

Jarvis, A. L. (Hull C), 1967 v S, E, Ni (3)

Jenkins, E. (Lovell's Ath), 1925 v E (1)

Jenkins, J. (Brighton), 1924 v Ni, E, S; 1925 v S, Ni; 1926 v E, S; 1927 v S (8)

Jenkins, R. W. (Rhyl), 1902 v Ni (1)

Jenkyns, C. A. L. (Small Heath), 1892 v E, S, Ni; 1895 v E; (with Woolwich Arsenal), 1896 v S; (with Newton Heath), 1897 v Ni; (with Walsall), 1898 v S, E (8)

Jennings, W. (Bolton W), 1914 v E, S; 1920 v S; 1923 v Ni, E; 1924 v E, S, Ni; 1927 v S, Ni; 1929 v S (11)

John, R. F. (Arsenal), 1923 v S, Ni; 1925 v Ni; 1926 v E; 1927 v E; 1928 v E, Ni; 1930 v E, S; 1932 v E; 1933 v F, Ni; 1935 v Ni; 1936 v S; 1937 v E (15)

John, W. R. (Walsall), 1931 v Ni; (with Stoke C), 1933 v E, S, Ni, F; 1934 v E, S; (with Preston NE), 1935 v E, S; (with Sheffield U), 1936 v E, S, Ni; (with Swansea T), 1939 v E, S (14)

Johnson, M. G. (Swansea T), 1964 v Ni (1)

Jones, A. (Port Vale), 1987 v Fi, Cz (sub); 1988 v D, (with Charlton Ath), D (sub), Cz (sub); 1990 v Hol (sub) (6)

Jones, A. F. (Oxford University), 1877 v S (1)

Jones, A. T. (Nottingham F), 1905 v E; (with Notts Co), 1906 v E (2)

Jones, Bryn (Wolverhampton W), 1935 v Ni; 1936 v E, S, Ni; 1937 v E, S, Ni; 1938 v E, S, Ni; (with Arsenal), 1939 v E, S, Ni; 1947 v S, Ni; 1948 v E; 1949 v S (17)

Jones, B. S. (Swansea T), 1963 v S, E, Ni, H (2); 1964 v S, Ni; (with Plymouth Arg), 1965 v D; (with Cardiff C), 1969 v S, E, Ni, I (sub), WG, EG, R of UK (15)

Jones, Charlie (Nottingham F), 1926 v E; 1927 v S, Ni; 1928 v E; (with Arsenal), 1930 v E, S; 1932 v E; 1933 v F (8)

Jones, Cliff (Swansea T), 1954 v A; 1956 v E, Ni, S, A; 1957 v E, S, Ni, Cz (2), EG; 1958 v EG, E, S, Is (2); (with Tottenham H), 1958 v Ni, H (2), M, Se, Br; 1959 v Ni; 1960 v E, S; 1961 v S, E, Ni, Sp, H, Ei; 1962 v E, Ni, S, Br (2), M; 1963 v S, Ni, H; 1964 v E, S, Ni; 1965 v E, S, Ni, D, Gr (2), USSR, I; 1967 v S, E; 1968 v E, S, WG; (with Fulham), 1969 v I, R of UK (59)

Jones, C. W. (Birmingham), 1935 v Ni; 1939 v F (2)

Jones, D. (Chirk), 1888 v S, Ni; (with Bolton W), 1889 v E, S, Ni; 1890 v E, Ni; 1891 v S; 1892 v Ni; 1893 v E; 1894 v E; 1895 v E; 1898 v S; (with Manchester C), 1900 v E, Ni (15)

Jones, D. E. (Norwich C), 1976 v S, E (sub); 1978 v S, Cz, WG, Ir, E; 1980 v E (8)

Jones, D. O. (Leicester C), 1934 v E, Ni; 1935 v E, S; 1936 v E, Ni; 1937 v Ni (7)

Jones, Evan (Chelsea), 1910 v S, Ni; (with Oldham Ath), 1911 v E, S; 1912 v E, S; (with Bolton W), 1914 v Ni (7)

Jones, F. R. (Bangor), 1885 v E, Ni; 1886 v S (3)

Jones, F. W. (Small Heath), 1893 v S (1)

Jones, G. P. (Wrexham), 1907 v S, Ni (2)

Jones, H. (Aberaman), 1902 v Ni (1)

Jones, Humphrey (Bangor), 1885 v E, Ni, S; 1886 v E, Ni, S; (with Queen's Park), 1887 v E; (with East Stirlingshire), 1889 v E, Ni; 1890 v E, S, Ni; (with Queen's Park), 1891 v E, S (14)

Jones, Ivor (Swansea T), 1920 v S, Ni; 1921 v Ni, E; 1922 v S, Ni; (with WBA), 1923 v E, Ni; 1924 v S; 1926 v Ni (10)

Jones, Jeffrey (Llandrindod Wells), 1908 v Ni; 1909 v Ni; 1910 v S (3)

Jones, J. (Druids), 1876 v S (1)

Jones, J. (Berwyn Rangers), 1883 v S, Ni; 1884 v S (3)

Jones, J. (Wrexham), 1925 v Ni (1)

Jones, J. L. (Sheffield U), 1895 v E, S, Ni; 1896 v Ni, S, E; 1897 v Ni, S, E; (with Tottenham H), 1898 v Ni, E, S; 1899 v S, Ni; 1900 v S; 1902 v E, S, Ni; 1904 v E, S, Ni (21)

Jones, J. Love (Stoke C), 1906 v S; (with Middlesbrough), 1910 v Ni (2)

Jones, J. O. (Bangor), 1901 v S, Ni (2)

Jones, J. P. (Liverpool), 1976 v A, E, S; 1977 v WG, S (2),

Cz, E, Ni; 1978 v K (2), S, Cz, WG, Ir, E, S, Ni; (with Wrexham), 1979 v Ma, T, WG, S, E, Ni, Ma; 1980 v Ei, WG, T, E, S, Ni, Ic; 1981 v T, Ei, T, S, E, USSR; 1982 v Cz, Ic, USSR, Sp, E, S, Ni, F; 1983 v N; (with Chelsea), v Y, E, Bul, S, Ni, Br; 1984 v N, R, Bul, Y, S, E, Ni, N, Is; 1985 v Ic, N, S, N; (with Huddersfield T), 1986 v S, H, Ei, U, Ca (2) (72)

Jones, J. T. (Stoke C), 1912 v E, S, Ni; 1913 v E, Ni; 1914 v S, Ni; 1920 v E, S, Ni; (with C Palace), 1921 v E, S; 1922 v E, S, Ni (15)

Jones, K. (Aston Villa), 1950 v S (1)

Jones, Leslie J. (Cardiff C), 1933 v F; (with Coventry C), 1935 v Ni; 1936 v S; 1937 v E, S, Ni; (with Arsenal), 1938 v E, S, Ni; 1939 v E, S (11)

Jones, P. W. (Bristol R), 1971 v Fi (1)

Jones, R. (Bangor), 1887 v S; 1889 v E; (with Crewe Alex), 1890 v E (3)

Jones, R. (Druids), 1899 v S; (with Millwall), 1906 v S, Ni (3)

Jones, R. (Bangor), 1900 v S, Ni (2)

Jones, R. A. (Druids), 1884 v E, Ni, S; 1885 v S (4)

Jones, R. S. (Everton), 1894 v Ni; (with Leicester Fosse), 1898 v S (2)

Jones, S. (Wrexham), 1887 v Ni; (with Chester), 1890 v S (2)

Jones, S. (Wrexham), 1893 v S, Ni; (with Burton Swifts), 1895 v S; 1896 v E, Ni (5)

Jones, T. (Manchester U), 1926 v Ni; 1927 v E, Ni; 1930 v Ni (4)

Jones, T. D. (Aberdare), 1908 v Ni (1)

Jones, T. G. (Everton), 1938 v Ni; 1939 v E, S, Ni; 1947 v E, S; 1948 v E, S, Ni; 1949 v E, Ni, P, Bel, Sw; 1950 v E, S, Bel (17)

Jones, T. J. (Sheffield W), 1932 v Ni; 1933 v F (2)

Jones, W. (Druids), 1899 v E (1)

Jones, W. E. A. (Swansea T), 1947 v E, S; (with Tottenham H), 1949 v E, S (4)

Jones, W. J. (Aberdare), 1901 v E, S; (with West Ham U), 1902 v E, S (4)

Jones, W. Lot (Manchester C), 1905 v E, Ni; 1906 v E, S, Ni; 1907 v E, S, Ni; 1908 v S; 1909 v E, S, Ni; 1910 v E; 1911 v E; 1913 v E, S; 1914 v S, Ni; (with Southend U), 1920 v E, Ni (20)

Jones, W. P. (Druids), 1889 v E, Ni; (with Wynstay), 1890 v S, Ni (4)

Jones, W. R. (Aberystwyth), 1897 v S (1)

Keenor, F. C. (Cardiff C), 1920 v E, Ni; 1921 v E, Ni, S; 1922 v Ni; 1923 v E, Ni, S; 1924 v E, Ni, S; 1925 v E, Ni, S; 1926 v S; 1927 v E, Ni, S; 1928 v E, Ni, S; 1929 v E, Ni, S; 1930 v E, Ni, S; 1931 v E, Ni, S; (with Crewe Alex), 1933 v S (32)

Kelly, F. C. (Wrexham), 1899 v S, Ni; (with Druids), 1902 v Ni (3)

Kelsey, A. J. (Arsenal), 1954 v Ni, A; 1955 v S, Ni, Y; 1956 v E, Ni, S, A; 1957 v E, Ni, S, Cz (2), EG; 1958 v E, S, Ni, Is (2), H (2), M, Se, Br; 1959 v E, S; 1960 v E, Ni, S; 1961 v E, Ni, S, H, Sp (2); 1962 v E, S, Ni, Br (2) (41)

Kenrick, S. L. (Druids), 1876 v S; 1877 v S; (with Oswestry), 1879 v E, S; (with Shropshire Wanderers), 1881 v E (5)

Ketley, C. F. (Druids), 1882 v Ni (1)

King, J. (Swansea T), 1955 v E (1)

Kinsey, N. (Norwich C), 1951 v Ni, P, Sw; 1952 v E; (with Birmingham C), 1954 v Ni; 1956 v E, S (7)

Knill, A. R. (Swansea C), 1989 v Ho (1)

Krzywicki, R. L. (Huddersfield T), 1970 v E, S; (with WBA), Ni, EG, I; 1971 v R, Fi; 1972 v Cz (sub) (8)

Lambert, R. (Liverpool), 1947 v S; 1948 v E; 1949 v P, Bel, Sw (5)

Lathom, G. (Liverpool), 1905 v E, S; 1906 v S; 1907 v E,

S, Ni; 1908 v E; 1909 v Ni; (with Southport Central), 1910 v E; (with Cardiff C), 1913 v Ni (10)

Law, B. J. (QPR), 1990 v Se (1)

Lawrence, E. (Clapton Orient), 1930 v Ni; (with Notts Co), 1932 v S (2)

Lawrence, S. (Swansea T), 1932 v Ni; 1933 v F; 1934 v S, E, Ni; 1935 v E, S; 1936 v S (8)

Lea, A. (Wrexham), 1889 v E; 1891 v S, Ni; 1893 v Ni (4)

Lea, C. (Ipswich T), 1965 v Ni, I (2)

Leary, P. (Bangor), 1889 v Ni (1)

Leek, K. (Leicester C), 1961 v S, E, Ni, H, Sp (2); (with Newcastle U), 1962 v S; (with Birmingham C), v Br (sub), M; 1963 v E; 1965 v S, Gr; (with Northampton T), 1965 v Gr (13)

Lever, A. R. (Leicester C), 1953 v S (1)

Lewis, B. (Wrexham), 1891 v Ni; 1892 v S, E, Ni; (with Middlesbrough), 1893 v S, E; (with Wrexham), 1894 v S, E, Ni; 1895 v S (10)

Lewis, D. (Arsenal), 1927 v E; 1928 v Ni; 1930 v E (3)

Lewis, D. (Swansea C), 1983 v Br (sub) (1)

Lewis, D. J. (Swansea T), 1933 v E, S (2)

Lewis, J. (Bristol R), 1906 v E (1)

Lewis, J. (Cardiff C), 1926 v S (1)

Lewis, T. (Wrexham), 1881 v E, S (2)

Lewis, W. (Bangor), 1885 v E; 1886 v S; 1887 v E, S; 1888 v E; 1889 v E, Ni, S; (with Crewe Alex), 1890 v E, Ni, S; 1891 v E, Ni, S; 1892 v E, S, Ni; 1894 v E, S, Ni; (with Chester), 1895 v S, Ni, E; 1896 v E, S, Ni; (with Manchester C), 1897 v E, S; (with Chester), 1898 v Ni (30)

Lewis, W. L. (Swansea T), 1927 v E, Ni; 1928 v E, Ni; 1929 v S; (with Huddersfield T), 1930 v E (6)

Lloyd, B. W. (Wrexham), 1976 v A, E, S (3)

Lloyd, J. W. (Wrexham), 1879 v S; (with Newtown), 1885 v S (2)

Lloyd, R. A. (Ruthin), 1891 v Ni; 1895 v S (2)

Lockley, A. (Chirk), 1898 v Ni (1)

Lovell, S. (C Palace), 1982 v USSR (sub); (with Millwall), 1985 v N; 1986 v S (sub), H (sub), Ca (1 + 1 sub) (6)

Lowrie, G. (Coventry C), 1948 v E, S, Ni; (with Newcastle U), 1949 v P (4)

Lowndes, S. (Newport Co), 1983 v S (sub), Br (sub); (with Millwall), 1985 v N (sub); 1986 v S.Ar (sub), Ei, U, Ca (2); (with Barnsley), 1987 v Fi (sub); 1988 v Se (sub) (10)

Lucas, P. M. (Leyton Orient), 1962 v Ni, M; 1963 v S, E (4)

Lucas, W. H. (Swansea T), 1949 v S, Ni, P, Bel, Sw; 1950 v E; 1951 v E (7)

Lumberg, A. (Wrexham), 1929 v Ni; 1930 v E, S; (with Wolverhampton W), 1932 v S (4)

McMillan, R. (Shrewsbury Engineers), 1881 v E, S (2)

Maguire, G. T. (Portsmouth), 1990 v Fi (sub), Ho, WG, Ei, Se (5)

Mahoney, J. F. (Stoke C), 1968 v E; 1969 v EG; 1971 v Cz; 1973 v E (3), Pol, S, Ni; 1974 v Pol, E, S, Ni; 1975 v A, H (2), L (2), S, E, Ni; 1976 v A, Y (2), E, Ni; 1977 v WG, Cz, S, E, Ni; (with Middlesbrough), 1978 v K (2), S, Cz, Ir, E (sub), S, Ni; 1979 v WG, S, E, Ni, Ma; (with Swansea C), 1980 v Ei, WG, T (sub); 1982 v Ic, USSR; 1983 v Y, E (51)

Martin, T. J. (Newport Co), 1930 v Ni (1)

Marustik, C. (Swansea C), 1982 v Sp, E, S, Ni, F; 1983 v N (6)

Mates, J. (Chirk), 1891 v Ni; 1897 v E, S (3)

Mathews, R. W. (Liverpool), 1921 v Ni; (with Bristol C), 1923 v E; (with Bradford), 1926 v Ni (3)

Matthews, W. (Chester), 1905 v Ni; 1908 v E (2)

Matthias, J. S. (Brymbo), 1896 v S, Ni; (with Shrewsbury), 1897 v S; (with Wolverhampton W), 1899 v S (5)

Matthias, T. J. (Wrexham), 1914 v S, E; 1920 v Ni, S, E; 1921 v S, E, Ni; 1922 v S, E, Ni; 1923 v S (12)

Mays, A. W. (Wrexham), 1929 v Ni (1)

Medwin, T. C. (Swansea T), 1953 v Ni, F, Y; (with Tottenham H), 1957 v E, S, Ni, Cz (2), EG; 1958 v E, S, Ni, Is (2), H (2), M, Br; 1959 v E, S, Ni; 1960 v E, S, Ni; 1961 v S, Ei, Sp; 1963 v E, H (29)

Melville, A. K. (Swansea C), 1990 v WG, Ei, Se, Cr (sub); (with Oxford U), 1991 v Ic, Pol, WG (7)

Meredith, S. (Chirk), 1900 v S; 1901 v S, E, Ni; (with Stoke C), 1902 v E; 1903 v Ni; 1904 v E; (with Leyton), 1907 v E (8)

Meredith, W. H. (Manchester C), 1895 v E, Ni; 1896 v E, Ni; 1897 v E, Ni, S; 1898 v E, Ni; 1899 v E; 1900 v E, Ni; 1901 v E, Ni; 1902 v E, S; 1903 v E, S, Ni; 1904 v E; 1905 v E, S; (with Manchester U), 1907 v E, S, Ni; 1908 v E, Ni; 1909 v E, S, Ni; 1910 v E, S, Ni; 1911 v E, S, Ni; 1912 v E, S, Ni; 1913 v E, S, Ni; 1914 v E, S, Ni; 1920 v E, S, Ni (48)

Mielczarek, R. (Rotherham U), 1971 v Fi (1)

Millership, H. (Rotherham Co), 1920 v E, S, Ni; 1921 v E, S, Ni (6)

Millington, A. H. (WBA), 1963 v S, E, H; (with C Palace), 1965 v E, USSR; (with Peterborough U), 1966 v Ch, Br; 1967 v E, Ni; 1968 v Ni, WG; 1969 v I, EG; (with Swansea T), 1970 v E, S, Ni; 1971 v Cz, Fi; 1972 v Fi (sub), Cz, R (21)

Mills, T. J. (Clapton Orient), 1934 v E, Ni; (with Leicester C), 1935 v E, S (4)

Mills-Roberts, R. H. (St Thomas' Hospital), 1885 v E, S, Ni; 1886 v E; 1887 v E; (with Preston NE), 1888 v E, Ni; (with Llanberis), 1892 v E (8)

Moore, G. (Cardiff C), 1960 v S, Ni; 1961 v Ei, Sp; (with Chelsea), 1962 v Br; 1963 v Ni, H; (with Manchester U), 1964 v S, Ni; (with Northampton T), 1966 v Ni, Ch; (with Charlton Ath), 1969 v S, E, Ni, R of UK; 1970 v E, S, Ni, I; 1971 v R (21)

Morgan, J. R. (Cambridge University), 1877 v S; (with Swansea T), 1879 v S; (with Derby School Staff), 1880 v E, S; 1881 v E, S; 1882 v E, S, Ni; (with Swansea T), 1883 v E (10)

Morgan, J. T. (Wrexham), 1905 v Ni (1)

Morgan-Owen, H. (Oxford University), 1901 v E, S; 1902 v S; 1906 v E, Ni; (with Welshpool), 1907 v S (6)

Morgan-Owen, M. M. (Oxford University), 1897 v S, Ni; 1898 v E, S; 1899 v S; 1900 v E; (with Corinthians), 1903 v S; 1906 v S, E, Ni; 1907 v E (11)

Morley, E. J. (Swansea T), 1925 v E; (with Clapton Orient), 1929 v E, S, Ni (4)

Morris, A. G. (Aberystwyth), 1896 v E, Ni, S; (with Swindon T), 1897 v E; 1898 v S; (with Nottingham F), 1899 v E, S; 1903 v E, S; 1905 v E, S; 1907 v E, S; 1908 v E; 1910 v E, S, Ni; 1911 v E, S, Ni; 1912 v E (21)

Morris, C. (Chirk), 1900 v E, S, Ni; (with Derby Co), 1901 v E, Ni; 1902 v E, S; 1903 v E, S, Ni; 1904 v Ni; 1905 v E, S, Ni; 1906 v S; 1907 v S; 1908 v E, S; 1909 v E, S, Ni; 1910 v E, S, Ni; (with Huddersfield T), 1911 v E, S, Ni (28)

Morris, E. (Chirk), 1893 v E, S, Ni (3)

Morris, H. (Sheffield U), 1894 v S; (with Manchester C), 1896 v E; (with Grimsby T), 1897 v E (3)

Morris, J. (Oswestry), 1887 v S (1)

Morris, J. (Chirk), 1898 v Ni (1)

Morris, R. (Chirk), 1900 v E, Ni; 1901 v Ni; 1902 v S; (with Shrewsbury T), 1903 v E, Ni (6)

Morris, R. (Druids), 1902 v E, S; (with Newtown), Ni; (with Liverpool), 1903 v S, Ni; 1904 v E, S, Ni; (with Leeds C), 1906 v S; (with Grimsby T), 1907 v Ni; (with Plymouth Arg), 1908 v Ni (11)

Morris, S. (Birmingham), 1937 v E, S; 1938 v E, S; 1939 v F (5)

Morris, W. (Burnley), 1947 v Ni; 1949 v E; 1952 v S, Ni, R of UK (5)

Moulsdale, J. R. B. (Corinthians), 1925 v Ni (1)

Murphy, J. P. (WBA), 1933 v F, E, Ni; 1934 v E, S; 1935 v E, S, Ni; 1936 v E, S, Ni; 1937 v S, Ni; 1938 v E, S (15)

Nardiello, D. (Coventry C), 1978 v Cz, WG (sub) (2)

Neal, J. E. (Colwyn Bay), 1931 v E, S (2)

Newnes, J. (Nelson), 1926 v Ni (1)

Newton, L. F. (Cardiff Corinthians), 1912 v Ni (1)

Nicholas, D. S. (Stoke C), 1923 v S; (with Swansea T), 1927 v E, Ni (3)

Nicholas, P. (C Palace), 1979 v S (sub), Ni (sub); Ma; 1980 v Ei, WG, T, E, S, Ni, Ma; 1981 v T, Cz, E; (with Arsenal), T, S, E, USSR; 1982 v Cz, Ic, USSR, Sp, E, S, Ni, F; 1983 v Y, Bul, S (sub), Ni; 1984 v N, Bul, N, Is; (with C Palace), 1985 v Sp; (with Luton T), N, S, Sp, N; 1986 v S, H, S.Ar, Ei, U, Ca (2); 1987 v Fi (2) USSR, Cz; (with Aberdeen), 1988 v D (2), Cz, Y, Se; (with Chelsea), 1989 v Ho, Fi, Is, Se, WG; 1990 v Fi, Ho, WG, Ei, Se, Cr; 1991 v D (sub), Bel, L, Ei; (with Watford), Bel, Pol, WG (72)

Nicholls, J. (Newport Co), 1924 v E, Ni; (with Cardiff C), 1925 v E, S (4)

Niedzwiecki, E. A. (Chelsea), 1985 v N (sub); 1988 v D (2)

Nock, W. (Newtown), 1897 v Ni (1)

Norman, A. J. (Hull C), 1986 v Ei (sub), U, Ca; 1988 v Ma, I (5)

Nurse, M. T. G. (Swansea T), 1960 v E, Ni; 1961 v S, E, H, Ni, Ei, Sp (2); (with Middlesbrough), 1963 v E, H; 1964 v S (12)

O'Callaghan, E. (Tottenham H), 1929 v Ni; 1930 v S; 1932 v S, E; 1933 v Ni, S, E; 1934 v Ni, S, E; 1935 v E (11)

Oliver, A. (Blackburn R), 1905 v E; (with Bangor), S (2)

O'Sullivan, P. A. (Brighton), 1973 v S (sub); 1976 v S; 1979 v Ma (sub) (3)

Owen, D. (Oswestry), 1879 v E (1)

Owen, E. (Ruthin Grammar School), 1884 v E, Ni, S (3)

Owen, G. (Chirk), 1888 v S; (with Newton Heath), 1889 v S, Ni; 1892 v E; 1893 v Ni (5)

Owen, Trevor (Crewe Alex), 1899 v E, S (2)

Owen, T. (Oswestry), 1879 v E (1)

Owen, W. (Chirk), 1884 v E; 1885 v Ni; 1887 v E; 1888 v E; 1889 v E, Ni, S; 1890 v S, Ni; 1891 v E, S, Ni; 1892 v E, S; 1893 v S, Ni (16)

Owen, W. P. (Ruthin), 1880 v E, S; 1881 v E, S; 1882 v E, S, Ni; 1883 v E, S; 1884 v E, S, Ni (12)

Owens, J. (Wrexham), 1902 v S (1)

Page, M. E. (Birmingham C), 1971 v Fi; 1972 v S, Ni; 1973 v E (1 + 1 sub), Ni; 1974 v S, Ni; 1975 v H, L, S, E, Ni; 1976 v E, Y (2), E, Ni; 1977 v WG, S; 1978 v K (sub + 1), WG, Ir, S; 1979 v Ma, WG (28)

Palmer, D. (Swansea T), 1957 v Cz; 1958 v E, EG (3)

Parris, J. E. (Bradford), 1932 v Ni (1)

Parry, B. J. (Swansea T), 1951 v S (1)

Parry, C. (Everton), 1891 v E, S; 1893 v E; 1894 v E; 1895 v E, S; (with Newtown), 1896 v E, S, Ni; 1897 v Ni; 1898 v E, S, Ni (13)

Parry, E. (Liverpool), 1922 v S; 1923 v E, Ni; 1925 v Ni; 1926 v Ni (5)

Parry, H. (Newtown), 1895 v Ni (1)

Parry, M. (Liverpool), 1901 v E, S, Ni; 1902 v E, S, Ni; 1903 v E, S; 1904 v E, Ni; 1906 v E; 1908 v E, S, Ni; 1909 v E, S (16)

Parry, T. D. (Oswestry), 1900 v E, S, Ni; 1901 v E, S, Ni; 1902 v E (7)

Pascoe, C. (Swansea C), 1984 v N, Is; (with Sunderland), 1989 v Fi, Is, WG (sub); 1990 v Ho (sub), WG (sub); 1991 v Ei, Ic (sub) (9)

Paul, R. (Swansea T), 1949 v E, S, Ni, P, Sw; 1950 v E, S, Ni, Bel; (with Manchester C), 1951 v S, E, Ni, P, Sw; 1952 v E, S, Ni, R of UK; 1953 v S, E, Ni, F, Y; 1954 v E, S, Ni; 1955 v S, E, Y; 1956 v E, Ni, S, A (33)

Peake, E. (Aberystwyth), 1908 v Ni; (with Liverpool), 1909 v Ni, S, E; 1910 v S, Ni; 1911 v Ni; 1912 v E; 1913 v E, Ni; 1914 v Ni (11)

Peers, E. J. (Wolverhampton W), 1914 v Ni, S, E; 1920 v

E, S; 1921 v S, Ni, E; (with Port Vale), 1922 v E, S, Ni; 1923 v E (12)

Perry, E. (Doncaster R), 1938 v E, S, Ni (3)

Phennah, E. (Civil Service), 1878 v S (1)

Phillips, C. (Wolverhampton W), 1931 v Ni; 1932 v E; 1933 v S; 1934 v E, S, Ni; 1935 v E, S, Ni; 1936 v S; (with Aston Villa), 1936 v E, Ni; 1938 v S (13)

Phillips, D. (Plymouth Arg), 1984 v E, Ni, N; (with Manchester C), 1985 v Sp, Ic, S, Sp, N; 1986 v S, H, S.Ar, Ei, U; (with Coventry C), 1987 v Fi, Cz; 1988 v D (2), Cz, Y, Se; 1989 v Se, WG; (with Norwich C), 1990 v Fi, Ho, WG, Ei, Se; 1991 v D, Bel, Ic, Pol, WG (32)

Phillips, L. (Cardiff C), 1971 v Cz, S, E, Ni; 1972 v Cz, R, S, Ni; 1973 v E; 1974 v Pol (sub), Ni; 1975 v A; (with Aston Villa), H (2), L (2), S, E, Ni; 1976 v A, E, Y (2), E, Ni; 1977 v WG, S (2), Cz, E; 1978 v K (2), S, Cz, WG, E, S; 1979 v Ma; (with Swansea C), T, WG, S, E, Ni, Ma; 1980 v Ei, WG, T, S (sub), Ni, Ic; 1981 v T, Cz, T, S, E, USSR; (with Charlton Ath), 1982 v Cz, USSR (58)

Phillips, T. J. S. (Chelsea), 1973 v E; 1974 v E; 1975 v H (sub); 1978 v K (4)

Phoenix, H. (Wrexham), 1882 v S (1)

Poland, G. (Wrexham), 1939 v Ni, F (2)

Pontin, K. (Cardiff C), 1980 v E (sub), S (2)

Powell, A. (Leeds U), 1947 v E, S; 1948 v E, S, Ni; (with Everton), 1949 v E; 1950 v Bel; (with Birmingham C), 1951 v S (8)

Powell, D. (Wrexham), 1968 v WG; (with Sheffield U), 1969 v S, E, Ni, I, WG; 1970 v E, S, Ni, EG; 1971 v R (11)

Powell, I. V. (QPR), 1947 v E; 1948 v E, S, Ni; (with Aston Villa), 1949 v Bel; 1950 v S, Bel; 1951 v S (8)

Powell, J. (Druids), 1878 v S; 1880 v E, S; 1882 v E, S, Ni; 1883 v E, S, Ni; (with Bolton W), 1884 v E; (with Newton Heath), 1887 v S; 1888 v E, S, Ni (15)

Powell, Seth (WBA), 1885 v S; 1886 v E, Ni; 1891 v E, S; 1892 v E, S (7)

Price, H. (Aston Villa), 1907 v S; (with Burton U), 1908 v Ni; (with Wrexham), 1909 v S, E, Ni (5)

Price, J. (Wrexham), 1877 v S; 1878 v S; 1879 v E; 1880 v E, S; 1881 v E, S; (with Druids), 1882 v S, E, Ni; 1883 v S, Ni (12)

Price, P. (Luton T), 1980 v E, S, Ni, Ic; 1981 v T, Cz, Ei, T, S, E, USSR; (with Tottenham H), 1982 v USSR, Sp, F; 1983 v N, Y, E, Bul, S, Ni; 1984 v N, R, Bul, Y, S (sub) (25)

Pring, K. D. (Rotherham U), 1966 v Ch, D; 1967 v Ni (3)

Pritchard, H. K. (Bristol C), 1985 v N (sub) (1)

Pryce-Jones, A. W. (Newtown), 1895 v E (1)

Pryce-Jones, W. E. (Cambridge University), 1887 v S; 1888 v S, E, Ni; 1890 v Ni (5)

Pugh, A. (Rhostyllen), 1889 v S (sub) (1)

Pugh, D. H. (Wrexham), 1896 v S, Ni; 1897 v S, Ni; (with Lincoln C), 1900 v S; 1901 v S, E (7)

Pugsley, J. (Charlton Ath), 1930 v Ni (1)

Pullen, W. J. (Plymouth Arg), 1926 v E (1)

Rankmore, F. E. J. (Peterborough), 1966 v Ch (sub) (1)

Ratcliffe, K. (Everton), 1981 v Cz, Ei, T, S, E, USSR; 1982 v Cz, Ic, USSR, Sp, E; 1983 v Y, E, Bul, S, Ni, Br; 1984 v N, R, Bul, Y, S, E, Ni, N, Is; 1985 v Ic, Sp, Ic, N, S, Sp; 1986 v S, H, S.Ar, U; 1987 v Fi (2), USSR, Cz; 1988 v D (2), Cz; 1989 v Fi, Is, Se, WG; 1990 v Fi; 1991 v D, Bel (2), L, Ei, Ic, Pol, WG (56)

Rea, J. C. (Aberystwyth), 1894 v Ni, S, E; 1895 v S; 1896 v Ni; 1897 v S, Ni; 1898 v Ni (9)

Reece, G. I. (Sheffield U), 1966 v E, S, Ni, USSR; 1967 v S; 1969 v R of UK (sub); 1970 v I (sub); 1971 v S, E, Ni, Fi; 1972 v Fi, R, E (sub), S, Ni; (with Cardiff C), 1973 v E (sub), Ni; 1974 v Pol (sub), E, S, Ni; 1975 v A, H (2), L (2), S, Ni (29)

Reed, W. G. (Ipswich T), 1955 v S, Y (2)

Rees, A. (Birmingham C), 1984 v N (sub) (1)

Rees, R. R. (Coventry C), 1965 v S, E, Ni, D, Gr (2), I, R; 1966 v E, S, Ni, R, D, Br (2), Ch; 1967 v E, Ni; 1968 v E, S, Ni; (with WBA), WG; 1969 v I; (with Nottingham F), 1969 v WG, EG, S (sub), R of UK; 1970 v E, S, Ni, EG, I; 1971 v Cz, R, E (sub), Ni (sub), Fi; 1972 v Cz (sub), R (39)

Rees, W. (Cardiff C), 1949 v Ni, Bel, Sw; (with Tottenham H), 1950 v Ni (4)

Richards, A. (Barnsley), 1932 v S (1)

Richards, D. (Wolverhampton W), 1931 v Ni; 1933 v E, S, Ni; 1934 v E, S, Ni; 1935 v E, S, Ni; 1936 v S; (with Brentford), 1936 v E, Ni; 1937 v S, E; (with Birmingham), Ni; 1938 v E, S, Ni; 1939 v E, S (21)

Richards, G. (Druids), 1899 v E, S, Ni; (with Oswestry), 1903 v Ni; (with Shrewsbury), 1904 v S; 1905 v Ni (6)

Richards, R. W. (Wolverhampton W), 1920 v E, S; 1921 v Ni; 1922 v E, S; (with West Ham U), 1924 v E, S, Ni; (with Mold), 1926 v S (9)

Richards, S. V. (Cardiff C), 1947 v E (1)

Richards, W. E. (Fulham), 1933 v Ni (1)

Roach, J. (Oswestry), 1885 v Ni (1)

Robbins, W. W. (Cardiff C), 1931 v E, S; 1932 v Ni, E, S; (with WBA), 1933 v F, E, S, Ni; 1934 v S; 1936 v S (11)

Roberts, D. F. (Oxford U), 1973 v Pol, E (sub), Ni; 1974 v E, S; 1975 v A; (with Hull C), L, Ni; 1976 v S, Ni, Y; 1977 v E (sub), Ni; 1978 v K (1 + 1 sub), S, Ni (17)

Roberts, I. W. (Watford), 1990 v Ho (1)

Roberts, Jas (Chirk), 1898 v S (1)

Roberts, Jas (Wrexham), 1913 v S, Ni (2)

Roberts, J. (Corwen), 1879 v S; 1880 v E, S; 1882 v E, S, Ni; (with Berwyn R), 1883 v E (7)

Roberts, J. (Ruthin), 1881 v S; 1882 v S (2)

Roberts, J. (Bradford C), 1906 v Ni; 1907 v Ni (2)

Roberts, J. G. (Arsenal), 1971 v S, E, Ni, Fi; 1972 v Fi, E, Ni; (with Birmingham C), 1973 v E (2), Pol, S, Ni; 1974 v Pol, E, S, Ni; 1975 v A, H, S, E; 1976 v E, S (22)

Roberts, J. H. (Bolton), 1949 v Bel (1)

Roberts, P. S. (Portsmouth), 1974 v E; 1975 v A, H, L (4)

Roberts, R. (Druids), 1884 v S; (with Bolton W), 1887 v S; 1888 v S, E; 1889 v S, E; 1890 v S; 1892 v Ni; (with Preston NE), S (9)

Roberts, R. (Wrexham), 1886 v Ni; 1887 v Ni; 1891 v Ni (3)

Roberts, R. (Rhos), 1891 v Ni; (with Crewe Alex), 1893 v E (2)

Roberts, W. (Llangollen), 1879 v E, S; 1880 v E, S; (with Berwyn R), 1881 v S; 1883 v E, S (7)

Roberts, W. (Wrexham), 1886 v E, S, Ni; 1887 v Ni (4)

Roberts, W. H. (Ruthin), 1882 v E, S; 1883 v E, S, Ni; (with Rhyl), 1884 v S (6)

Rodrigues, P. J. (Cardiff C), 1965 v Ni, Gr (2); 1966 v USSR, E, S, D; (with Leicester C), v Ni, Br (2), Ch; 1967 v S; 1968 v E, S, Ni; 1969 v E, Ni, EG, R of UK; 1970 v E, S, Ni, EG; (with Sheffield W), 1971 v R, E, S, Cz, Ni; 1972 v Fi, Cz, R, E, Ni (sub); 1973 v E (3), Pol, S, Ni; 1974 v Pol (40)

Rogers, J. P. (Wrexham), 1896 v E, S, Ni (3)

Rogers, W. (Wrexham), 1931 v E, S (2)

Roose, L. R. (Aberystwyth), 1900 v Ni; (with London Welsh), 1901 v E, S, Ni; (with Stoke C), 1902 v E, S; 1904 v E; (with Everton), 1905 v S, E; (with Stoke C), 1906 v E, S, Ni; 1907 v E, S, Ni; (with Sunderland), 1908 v E, S; 1909 v E, S, Ni; 1910 v E, S, Ni; 1911 v S (24)

Rouse, R. V. (C Palace), 1959 v Ni (1)

Rowlands, A. C. (Tranmere R), 1914 v E (1)

Rowley, T. (Tranmere R), 1959 v Ni (1)

Rush, I. (Liverpool), 1980 v S (sub), Ni; 1981 v E (sub); 1982 v Ic (sub), USSR, E, S, Ni, F; 1983 v N, Y, E, Bul; 1984 v N, R, Bul, Y, S, E, Ni; 1985 v Ic, N, S, Sp; 1986 v S, S.Ar, Ei, U; 1987 v Fi (2), USSR, Cz; (with Juventus), 1988 v D, Cz, Y, Se, Ma, I; (with Liverpool), 1989 v Ho,

Fi, Se, WG; 1990 v Fi, Ei; 1991 v D, Bel (2), L, Ei, Pol, WG (51)

Russell, M. R. (Merthyr T), 1912 v S, Ni; 1914 v E; (with Plymouth Arg) 1920 v E, S, Ni; 1921 v E, S, Ni; 1922 v E, Ni; 1923 v E, S, Ni; 1924 v E, S, Ni; 1925 v E, S; 1926 v E, S; 1928 v S; 1929 v E (23)

Sabine, H. W. (Oswestry), 1887 v Ni (1)

Saunders, D. (Brighton & HA), 1986 v Ei (sub), Ca (2); 1987 v Fi, USSR (sub); (with Oxford U), 1988 v Y, Se, Ma, I (sub); 1989 v Ho (sub), Fi, Is; (with Derby Co), Se, WG; 1990 v Fi, Ho, WG, Se, Cr; 1991 v D, Bel (2), L, Ei, Ic, Pol, WG (27)

Savin, G. (Oswestry), 1878 v S (1)

Sayer, P. (Cardiff C), 1977 v Cz, S, E, Ni; 1978 v K (2), S (7)

Scrine, F. H. (Swansea T), 1950 v E, Ni (2)

Sear, C. R. (Manchester C), 1963 v E (1)

Shaw, E. G. (Oswestry), 1882 v Ni; 1884 v S, Ni (3)

Sherwood, A. T. (Cardiff C), 1947 v E, Ni; 1948 v S, Ni; 1949 v E, S, Ni, P, Sw; 1950 v E, S, Ni, Bel; 1951 v E, S, Ni, P, Sw; 1952 v E, S, Ni, R of UK; 1953 v S, E, Ni, F, Y; 1954 v E, S, Ni, A; 1955 v S, E, Y, Ni; 1956 v E, S, Ni, A; (with Newport Co), 1957 v E, S (41)

Shone, W. W. (Oswestry), 1879 v E (1)

Shortt, W. W. (Plymouth Arg), 1947 v Ni; 1950 v Ni, Bel; 1952 v E, S, Ni, R of UK; 1953 v S, E, Ni, F, Y (12)

Showers, D. (Cardiff C), 1975 v E (sub), Ni (2)

Sidlow, C. (Liverpool), 1947 v E, S; 1948 v E, S, Ni; 1949 v S; 1950 v E (7)

Sisson, H. (Wrexham Olympic), 1885 v Ni; 1886 v S, Ni (3)

Slatter, N. (Bristol R), 1983 v S; 1984 v N (sub), Is; 1985 v Ic, Sp, Ic, N, S, Sp, N; (with Oxford U), 1986 v H (sub), S.Ar, Ca (2); 1987 v Fi (sub), Cz; 1988 v D (2), Cz, Ma, I; 1989 v Is (sub) (22)

Smallman, D. P. (Wrexham), 1974 v E (sub), S (sub), Ni; (with Everton), 1975 v H (sub), E, Ni (sub); 1976 v A (7)

Southall, N. (Everton), 1982 v Ni; 1983 v N, E, Bul, S, Ni, Br; 1984 v N, R, Bul, Y, S, E, Ni, N, Is; 1985 v Ic, Sp, Ic, N, S, Sp, N; 1986 v S, H, S.Ar, Ei; 1987 v USSR, Fi, Cz; 1988 v D, Cz, Y, Se; 1989 v Ho, Fi, Se, WG; 1990 v Fi, Ho, WG, Ei, Se, Cr; 1991 v D, Bel (2), L, Ei, Ic, Pol, WG (52)

Speed, G. A. (Leeds U), 1990 v Cr (sub); 1991 v D, L (sub), Ei (sub), Ic, WG (sub) (6)

Sprake, G. (Leeds U), 1964 v S, Ni; 1965 v S, D, Gr; 1966 v E, Ni, USSR; 1967 v S; 1968 v E, S; 1969 v S, E, Ni, WG, R of UK; 1970 v EG, I; 1971 v R, S, E, Ni; 1972 v Fi, E, S, Ni; 1973 v E (2), Pol, S, Ni; 1974 v Pol; (with Birmingham C), S, Ni; 1975 v A, H, L (37)

Stansfield, F. (Cardiff C), 1949 v S (1)

Stevenson, B. (Leeds U), 1978 v Ni; 1979 v Ma, T, S, E, Ni, Ma; 1980 v WG, T, Ic (sub); 1982 v Cz; (with Birmingham C), Sp, S, Ni, F (15)

Stevenson, N. (Swansea C), 1982 v E, S, Ni; 1983 v N (4)

Stitfall, R. F. (Cardiff C), 1953 v E; 1957 v Cz (2)

Sullivan, D. (Cardiff C), 1953 v Ni, F, Y; 1954 v Ni; 1955 v E, Ni; 1957 v E, S; 1958 v Ni, H (2), Se, Br; 1959 v S, Ni; 1960 v E, S (17)

Tapscott, D. R. (Arsenal), 1954 v A; 1955 v S, E, Ni, Y; 1956 v E, Ni, S, A; 1957 v Ni, Cz, EG; (with Cardiff C), 1959 v E, Ni (14)

Taylor, J. (Wrexham), 1898 v E (1)

Taylor, O. D. S. (Newtown), 1893 v S, Ni; 1894 v S, Ni (4)

Thomas, C. (Druids), 1899 v Ni; 1900 v S (2)

Thomas, D. A. (Swansea T), 1957 v Cz; 1958 v EG (2)

Thomas, D. S. (Fulham), 1948 v E, S, Ni; 1949 v S (4)

Thomas, E. (Cardiff Corinthians), 1925 v E (1)

Thomas, G. (Wrexham), 1885 v E, S (2)

Thomas, H. (Manchester U), 1927 v E (1)

Thomas, M. (Wrexham), 1977 v WG, S (1+1 sub), Ni

(sub); 1978 v K (sub), S, Cz, Ir, E, Ni (sub); 1979 v Ma; (with Manchester U), T, WG, Ma (sub); 1980 v Ei, WG (sub), T, E, S, Ni; 1981 v Cz, S, E, USSR; (with Everton), 1982 v Cz; (with Brighton & HA), USSR (sub), Sp, E, S (sub), Ni (sub); 1983 (with Stoke C), v N, Y, E, Bul, S, Ni, Br; 1984 v R, Bul, Y; (with Chelsea), S, E; 1985 v Ic, Sp, Ic, S, Sp, N; 1986 v S; (with WBA), H, S.Ar (sub) (51)

Thomas, M. R. (Newcastle U), 1987 v Fi (1)

Thomas, R. J. (Swindon T), 1967 v Ni; 1968 v WG; 1969 v E, Ni, I, WG, R of UK; 1970 v E, S, Ni, EG, I; 1971 v S, E, Ni, R, Cz; 1972 v Fi, Cz, R, E, S, Ni; 1973 v E (3), Pol, S, Ni; 1974 v Pol; (with Derby Co), E, S, Ni; 1975 v H (2), L (2), S, E, Ni; 1976 v A, Y, E; 1977 v Cz, S, E, Ni; 1978 v K, S; (with Cardiff C), Cz (50)

Thomas, T. (Bangor), 1898 v S, Ni (2)

Thomas, W. R. (Newport Co), 1931 v E, S (2)

Thomson, D. (Druids), 1876 v S (1)

Thomson, G. F. (Druids), 1876 v S; 1877 v S (2)

Toshack, J. B. (Cardiff C), 1969 v S, E, Ni, WG, EG, R of UK; 1970 v EG, I; (with Liverpool), 1971 v S, E, Ni, Fi; 1972 v Fi, E; 1973 v E (3), Pol, S; 1975 v A, H (2), L (2), S, E; 1976 v Y (2), E; 1977 v S; 1978 v K (2), S, Cz; (with Swansea C), 1979 v WG (sub), S, E, Ni, Ma; 1980 v WG (40)

Townsend, W. (Newtown), 1887 v Ni; 1893 v Ni (2)

Trainer, H. (Wrexham), 1895 v E, S, Ni (3)

Trainer, J. (Bolton W), 1887 v S; (with Preston NE), 1888 v S; 1889 v E; 1890 v S; 1891 v S; 1892 v Ni, S; 1893 v E; 1894 v Ni, E; 1895 v Ni, E; 1896 v S; 1897 v Ni, S, E; 1898 v S, E; 1899 v Ni, S (20)

Turner, H. G. (Charlton Ath), 1937 v E, S, Ni; 1938 v E, S, Ni; 1939 v Ni, F (8)

Turner, J. (Wrexham), 1892 v E (1)

Turner, R. E. (Wrexham), 1891 v E, Ni (2)

Turner, W. H. (Wrexham), 1887 v E, Ni; 1890 v S; 1891 v E, S (5)

Van Den Hauwe, P. W. R. (Everton), 1985 v Sp; 1986 v S, H; 1987 v USSR, Fi, Cz; 1988 v D (2), Cz, Y, I; 1989 v Fi, Se (13)

Vaughan, Jas (Druids), 1893 v E, S, Ni; 1899 v E (4)

Vaughan, John (Oswestry), 1879 v S; 1880 v S; 1881 v E, S; 1882 v E, S, Ni; 1883 v E, S, Ni; (with Bolton W), 1884 v E (11)

Vaughan, J. O. (Rhyl), 1885 v Ni; 1886 v Ni, E, S (4)

Vaughan, N. (Newport Co), 1983 v Y (sub), Br; 1984 v N; (with Cardiff C), R, Bul, Y, Ni (sub), N, Is; 1985 v Sp (sub) (10)

Vaughan, T. (Rhyl), 1885 v E (1)

Vearncombe, G. (Cardiff C), 1958 v EG; 1961 v Ei (2)

Vernon, T. R. (Blackburn R), 1957 v Ni, Cz (2), EG; 1958 v E, S, EG, Se; 1959 v S; (with Everton), 1960 v Ni; 1961 v S, E, Ei; 1962 v Ni, Br (2), M; 1963 v S, E, H; 1964 v E, S; (with Stoke C), 1965 v Ni, Gr, I; 1966 v E, S, Ni, USSR, D; 1967 v Ni; 1968 v E (32)

Villars, A. K. (Cardiff C), 1974 v E, S, Ni (sub) (3)

Vizard, E. T. (Bolton W), 1911 v E, S, Ni; 1912 v E, S; 1913 v S; 1914 v E, Ni; 1920 v E; 1921 v E, S, Ni; 1922 v E, S; 1923 v E, Ni; 1924 v E, S, Ni; 1926 v E, S; 1927 v S (22)

Walley, J. T. (Watford), 1971 v Cz (1)

Walsh, I. (C Palace), 1980 v Ei, T, E, S, Ic; 1981 v T, Cz, Ei, T, S, E, USSR; 1982 v Cz (sub), Ic; (with Swansea C), Sp, S (sub), Ni (sub), F (18)

Ward, D. (Bristol R), 1959 v E; (with Cardiff C), 1962 v E (2)

Warner, J. (Swansea T), 1937 v E; (with Manchester U), 1939 v F (2)

Warren, F. W. (Cardiff C), 1929 v Ni; (with Middlesbrough), 1931 v Ni; 1933 v F, E; (with Hearts), 1937 v Ni; 1938 v Ni (6)

Watkins, A. E. (Leicester Fosse), 1898 v E, S; (with Aston Villa), 1900 v E, S; (with Millwall), 1904 v Ni (5)

Watkins, W. M. (Stoke C), 1902 v E; 1903 v E, S; (with Aston Villa); 1904 v E, S, Ni; (with Sunderland), 1905 v E, S, Ni; (with Stoke C), 1908 v Ni (10)

Webster, C (Manchester U), 1957 v Cz; 1958 v H, M, Br (4)

Whatley, W. J. (Tottenham H), 1939 v E, S (2)

White, P. F. (London Welsh), 1896 v Ni (1)

Wilcocks, A. R. (Oswestry), 1890 v Ni (1)

Wilding, J. (Wrexham Olympians), 1885 v E, S, Ni; 1886 v E, Ni; (with Bootle), 1887 v E; 1888 v S, Ni; (with Wrexham), 1892 v S (9)

Williams, A. L. (Wrexham), 1931 v E (1)

Williams, B. (Bristol C), 1930 v Ni (1)

Williams, B. D. (Swansea T), 1928 v Ni, E; 1930 v E, S; (with Everton), 1931 v Ni; 1932 v E; 1933 v E, S, Ni; 1935 v Ni (10)

Williams, D. G. (Derby Co), 1988 v Cz, Y, Se, Ma, I; 1989 v Ho, Is, Se, WG; 1990 v Fi, Ho (11)

Williams, D. M. (Norwich C), 1986 v S.Ar (sub), U, Ca (2); 1987 v Fi (5)

Williams, D. R. (Merthyr T), 1921 v E, S; (with Sheffield W), 1923 v S; 1926 v S; 1927 v E, Ni; (with Manchester U), 1929 v E, S (8)

Williams, E. (Crewe Alex), 1893 v E, S (2)

Williams, E. (Druids), 1901 v E, Ni, S; 1902 v E, Ni (5)

Williams, G. (Chirk), 1893 v S; 1894 v S; 1895 v E, S, Ni; 1898 v Ni (6)

Williams, G. E. (WBA), 1960 v Ni; 1961 v S, E, Ei; 1963 v Ni, H; 1964 v E, S, Ni; 1965 v S, E, Ni, D, Gr (2), USSR, I; 1966 v Ni, Br (2), Ch; 1967 v S, E, Ni; 1968 v Ni; 1969 v I (26)

Williams, G. G. (Swansea T), 1961 v Ni, H, Sp (2); 1962 v E (5)

Williams, G. J. J. (Cardiff C), 1951 v Sw (1)

Williams, G. O. (Wrexham), 1907 v Ni (1)

Williams, H. J. (Swansea), 1965 v Gr (2); 1972 v R (3)

Williams, H. T. (Newport Co), 1949 v Ni, Sw; (with Leeds U), 1950 v Ni; 1951 v S (4)

Williams, J. H. (Oswestry), 1884 v E (1)

Williams, J. T. (Middlesbrough), 1925 v Ni (1)

Williams, J. T. (Wrexham), 1939 v F (1)

Williams, J. W. (C Palace), 1912 v S, Ni (2)

Williams, R. (Newcastle U), 1935 v S, E (2)

Williams, R. P. (Caernarvon), 1886 v S (1)

Williams, S. G. (WBA), 1954 v A; 1955 v E, Ni; 1956 v E, S, A; 1958 v E, S, Ni, Is (2), H (2), M, Se, Br; 1959 v E, S, Ni; 1960 v E, S, Ni; 1961 v Ni, Ei, H, Sp (2); 1962 v E, S, Ni, Br (2), M; (with Southampton), 1963 v S, E, H (2); 1964 v E, S; 1965 v S, E, D; 1966 v D (43)

Williams, W. (Druids), 1876 v S; 1878 v S; (with Oswestry), 1879 v E, S; (with Druids), 1880 v E, S; 1881 v E, S; 1882 v E, S, Ni; 1883 v Ni (12)

Williams, W. (Northampton T), 1925 v S (1)

Witcomb, D. F. (WBA), 1947 v E, S; (with Sheffield W), 1947 v Ni (3)

Woosnam, A. P. (Leyton Orient), 1959 v S; (with West Ham U), E; 1960 v E, S, Ni; 1961 v S, E, Ni, Ei, Sp, H; 1962 v E, S, Ni, Br; (with Aston Villa), 1963 v Ni, H (17)

Woosnam, G. (Newton White Star), 1879 v S (1)

Worthington, T. (Newtown), 1894 v S (1)

Wynn, G. A. (Chirk), 1903 v Ni; (with Wrexham), 1909 v E, S, Ni; (with Manchester C), 1910 v E; 1911 v Ni; 1912 v E, S; 1913 v E, S; 1914 v E, S (12)

Yorath, T. C. (Leeds U), 1970 v I; 1971 v S, E, Ni; 1972 v Cz, E, S, Ni; 1973 v E, Pol, S; 1974 v Pol, E, S, Ni; 1975 v A, H (2), L (2), S; 1976 v A, E, S, Y (2), E, Ni; (with Coventry C), 1977 v WG, S (2), Cz, E, Ni; 1978 v K (2), S, Cz, WG, Ir, E, S, Ni; 1979 v T, WG, S, E, Ni; (with Tottenham H), 1980 v Ei, T, E, S, Ni, Ic; 1981 v T, Cz; (with Vancouver W), Ei, T, USSR (59)

Young, E. (Wimbledon), 1990 v Cr; (with C Palace), 1991 v D, Bel (2), L, Ei (6)

REPUBLIC OF IRELAND

Aherne, T. (Belfast C), 1946 v P, Sp; (with Luton T), 1950 v Fi, E, Fi, Se, Bel; 1951 v N, Arg, N; 1952 v WG (2), A, Sp; 1953 v F; 1954 v F (16)

Aldridge, J. W. (Oxford U), 1986 v W, U, Ic, Cz; 1987 v Bel, S, Pol; (with Liverpool), S, Bul, Bel, Br, L; 1988 v Bul, Pol, N, E, USSR, Ho; 1989 v Ni, Tun, Sp, F, H, Ma (sub), H; 1990 v WG; (with Real Sociedad), Ni, Ma, Fi (sub). T, E, Eg, Ho, R, I; 1991 v T, E (2), Pol (39)

Ambrose, P. (Shamrock R), 1955 v N, Ho; 1964 v Pol, N, E (5)

Anderson, J. (Preston NE), 1980 v Cz (sub), US (sub); 1982 v Ch, Br, Tr; (with Newcastle U), 1984 v Chn; 1986 v W, Ic, Cz; 1987 v Bul, Bel, Br, L; 1988 v R (sub), Y (sub); 1989 v Tun (16)

Andrews, P. (Bohemians), 1936 v Ho (1)

Arrigan, T. (Waterford), 1938 v N (1)

Bailham, E. (Shamrock R), 1964 v E (1)

Barber, E. (Shelbourne), 1966 v Sp; (with Birmingham C), 1966 v Bel (2)

Barry, P. (Fordsons), 1928 v Bel; 1929 v Bel (2)

Beglin, J. (Liverpool), 1984 v Chn; 1985 v M, D, I, Is, E, N, Sw; 1986 v Sw, USSR, D, W; 1987 v Bel (sub), S, Pol (15)

Bermingham, J. (Bohemians), 1929 v Bel (1)

Bermingham, P. (St James' Gate), 1935 v H (1)

Braddish, S. (Dundalk), 1978 v Pol (1)

Bonner, P. (Celtic), 1981 v Pol; 1982 v Alg; 1984 v Ma, Is, Chn; 1985 v I, Is, E, N; 1986 v U, Ic; 1987 v Bel (2), S (2), Pol, Bul, Br, L; 1988 v Bul, R, Y, N, E, USSR, Ho;

1989 v Sp, F, H, Sp, Ma, H; 1990 v WG, Ni, Ma, W, Fi, T, E, Eg, Ho, R, I; 1991 v Mor, T, E (2), W, Pol, US (50)

Bradshaw, P. (St James' Gate), 1939 v Sw, Pol, H (2), G (5)

Brady, F. (Fordsons), 1926 v I; 1927 v I (2)

Brady, T. R. (QPR), 1964 v A (2), Sp (2), Pol, N (6)

Brady, W. L. (Arsenal), 1975 v USSR, T, Sw, USSR, Sw, WG; 1976 v T, N, Pol; 1977 v E, T, F (2), Sp, Bul; 1978 v Bul, N; 1979 v Ni, E, D, Bul, WG; 1980 v W, Bul, E, Cy; (with Juventus), 1981 v Ho, Bel, F, Cy, Bel; 1982 v Ho, F, Ch, Br, Tr; 1983 (with Sampdoria), v Ho, Sp, Ic, Ma; 1984 v Ic, Ho, Ma, Pol, Is; (with Internazionale), 1985 v USSR, N, D, I, E, N, Sp, Sw; 1986 v Sw, USSR, D, W; (with Ascoli), 1987 v Bel, S (2), Pol; (with West Ham U), Bul, Bel, Br, L; 1988 v L, Bul; 1989 v F, H (sub), H (sub); 1990 v WG, Fi (72)

Breen, T. (Manchester U), 1937 v Sw, F; (with Shamrock R), 1947 v E, Sp, P (5)

Brennan, F. (Drumcondra), 1965 v Bel (1)

Brennan, S. A. (Manchester U), 1965 v Sp; 1966 v Sp, A, Bel; 1967 v Sp, T, Sp; 1969 v Cz, D, H; 1970 v S, Cz, D, H, Pol (sub), WG; (with Waterford), 1971 v Pol, Se, I (19)

Brown, J. (Coventry C), 1937 v Sw, F (2)

Browne, W. (Bohemians), 1964 v A, Sp, E (3)

Buckley, L. (Shamrock R), 1984 v Pol (sub); (with Waregem), 1985 v M (2)

Burke, F. (Cork), 1934 v Bel (1)

Burke, F. (Cork Ath), 1952 v WG (1)

Burke, J. (Shamrock R), 1929 v Bel (1)

Byrne, A. B. (Southampton), 1970 v D, Pol, WG; 1971 v Pol, Se (2), I (2), A; 1973 v F, USSR (sub), F, N; 1974 v Pol (14)

Byrne, D. (Shelbourne), 1929 v Bel; (with Shamrock R), 1932 v Sp; (with Coleraine), 1934 v Bel (3)

Byrne, J. (Bray Unknowns), 1928 v Bel (1)

Byrne, J. (QPR), 1985 v I, Is (sub), E (sub), Sp (sub); 1987 v S (sub), Bel (sub), Br, L (sub); 1988 v L, Bul (sub), Is, R, Y (sub), Pol (sub); (with Le Havre), 1990 v WG (sub), W, Fi, T (sub), Ma; (with Brighton & HA), 1991 v W (20)

Byrne, P. (Shamrock R), 1984 v Pol, Chn; 1985 v M, I; 1986 v D (sub), W (sub), U (sub), Ic (sub), Cz (9)

Byrne, P. (Shelbourne), 1931 v Sp; 1932 v Ho; (with Drumcondra), 1934 v Ho (3)

Byrne, S. (Bohemians) 1931 v Sp (1)

Campbell, A. (Santander), 1985 v I (sub), Is, Sp (3)

Campbell, N. (St Patrick's Ath), 1971 v A (sub); (with Fortuna, Cologne), 1972 v Ir, Ec, Ch, P; 1973 v USSR, F (sub); 1975 v WG; 1976 v N; 1977 v Sp, Bul (sub) (11)

Cannon, H. (Bohemians), 1926 v I; 1928 v Bel (2)

Cantwell, N. (West Ham U), 1954 v L; 1956 v Sp, Ho; 1957 v D, WG, E (2); 1958 v D, Pol, A; 1959 v Pol, Cz (2); 1960 v Se, Ch, Se; 1961 v N; (with Manchester U), S (2); 1962 v Cz (2), A; 1963 v Ic (2), S; 1964 v A, Sp, E; 1965 v Pol, Sp; 1966 v Sp (2), A, Bel; 1967 v Sp, T (36)

Carey, J. J. (Manchester U), 1938 v N, Cz, Pol; 1939 v Sw, Pol, H (2), G; 1946 v P, Sp; 1947 v E, Sp, P; 1948 v P, Sp; 1949 v Sw, Bel, P, Se, Sp; 1950 v Fi, E, Fi, Se; 1951 v N, Arg, N; 1953 v F, A (29)

Carolan, J. (Manchester U), 1960 v Se, Ch (2)

Carroll, B. (Shelbourne), 1949 v Bel; 1950 v Fi (2)

Carroll, T. R. (Ipswich T), 1968 v Pol; 1969 v Pol, A, D; 1970 v Cz, Pol, WG; 1971 v Se; (with Birmingham C), 1972 v Ir, Ec, Ch, P; 1973 v USSR (2), Pol, F, N (17)

Cascarino, A. G. (Gillingham), 1986 v Sw, USSR, D; (with Millwall), 1988 v Pol, N (sub), USSR (sub), Ho (sub); 1989 v Ni, Tun, Sp, F, H, Sp, Ma, H; 1990 v WG (sub), Ni, Ma; (with Aston Villa), W, Fi, T, E, Eg, Ho (sub), R (sub), I (sub); 1991 v Mor (sub), T (sub), E (2 sub), Pol (sub), Ch (sub), US (33)

Chandler, J. (Leeds U), 1980 v Cz (sub), US (2)

Chatton, H. A. (Shelbourne), 1931 v Sp; (with Dumbarton), 1932 v Sp; (with Cork), 1934 v Ho (3)

Clarke, J. (Drogheda U), 1978 v Pol (sub) (1)

Clarke, K. (Drumcondra), 1948 v P, Sp (2)

Clarke, M. (Shamrock R), 1950 v Bel (1)

Clinton, T. J. (Everton), 1951 v N; 1954 v F, L (3)

Coad, P. (Shamrock R), 1947 v E, Sp, P; 1948 v P, Sp; 1949 v Sw, Bel, P, Se; 1951 v N (sub); 1952 v Sp (11)

Coffey, T. (Drumcondra), 1950 v Fi (1)

Colfer, M. D. (Shelbourne), 1950 v Bel; 1951 v N (2)

Collins, F. (Jacobs), 1927 v I (1)

Conmy, O. M. (Peterborough U), 1965 v Bel; 1967 v Cz; 1968 v Cz, Pol; 1970 v Cz (5)

Connolly, J. (Fordsons), 1926 v I (1)

Connolly, N. (Cork), 1937 v G (1)

Conroy, G. A. (Stoke C), 1970 v Cz, D, H, Pol, WG; 1971 v Pol, Se (2), I; 1973 v USSR, F, USSR, N; 1974 v Pol, Br, U, Ch; 1975 v T, Sw, USSR, Sw, WG; 1976 v T (sub), Pol; 1977 v E, T, Pol (27)

Conway, J. P. (Fulham), 1967 v Sp, T, Sp; 1968 v Cz; 1969 v A (sub), H; 1970 v S, Cz, D, H, Pol, WG; 1971 v I, A; 1974 v U, Ch; 1975 v WG (sub); 1976 v N, Pol; (with Manchester C), 1977 v Pol (20)

Corr, P. J. (Everton), 1949 v P, Sp; 1950 v E, Se (4)

Courtney, E. (Cork Unknowns), 1946 v P (1)

Cummins, G. P. (Luton T), 1954 v L (2); 1955 v N (2), WG; 1956 v Y, Sp; 1958 v D, Pol, A; 1959 v Pol, Cz (2); 1960 v Se, Ch, WG, Se; 1961 v S (2) (19)

Cuneen, T. (Limerick), 1951 v N (1)

Curtis, D. P. (Shelbourne), 1957 v D, WG; (with Bristol C), 1957 v E (2); 1958 v D, Pol, A; (with Ipswich T), 1959 v Pol; 1960 v Se, Ch, WG, Se; 1961 v N, S; 1962 v A; 1963 v Ic; (with Exeter C), 1964 v A (17)

Cusack, S. (Limerick), 1953 v F (1)

Daly, G. A. (Manchester U), 1973 v Pol (sub), N; 1974 v Br (sub), U (sub); 1975 v Sw (sub), WG; 1977 v E, T, F; (with Derby Co), F, Bul; 1978 v Bul, T, D; 1979 v Ni, E, D, Bul; 1980 v Ni, E, Cy, Sw, Arg; (with Coventry C), 1981 v Ho, Bel, Cy, W, Bel, Cz, Pol (sub); 1982 v Alg, Ch, Br, Tr; 1983 v Ho, Sp (sub), Ma; 1984 v Is (sub); (with Birmingham C), 1985 v M (sub), N, Sp, Sw; 1986 v Sw; (with Shrewsbury T), U, Ic (sub), Cz (sub); 1987 v S (sub) (47)

Daly, J. (Shamrock R), 1932 v Ho; 1935 v Sw (2)

Daly, M. (Wolverhampton W), 1978 v T, Pol (2)

Daly, P. (Shamrock R), 1950 v Fi (sub) (1)

Davis, T. L. (Oldham Ath), 1937 v G, H; (with Tranmere R), 1938 v Cz, Pol (4)

Deacy, E. (Aston Villa), 1982 v Alg (sub), Ch, Br, Tr (4)

De Mange, K. J. P. P. (Liverpool), 1987 v Br (sub); (with Hull C), 1989 v Tun (sub) (2)

Dempsey, J. T. (Fulham), 1967 v Sp, Cz; 1968 v Cz, Pol; 1969 v Pol, A, D; (with Chelsea), 1969 v Cz, D; 1970 v H, WG; 1971 v Pol, Se (2), I; 1972 v Ir, Ec, Ch, P (19)

Dennehy, J. (Cork Hibernians), 1972 v Ec (sub), Ch; (with Nottingham F), 1973 v USSR (sub), Pol, F, N; 1974 v Pol (sub); 1975 v T (sub), WG (sub); (with Walsall), 1976 v Pol (sub); 1977 v Pol (sub) (11)

Desmond, P. (Middlesbrough), 1950 v Fi, E, Fi, Se (4)

Devine, J. (Arsenal), 1980 v Cz, Ni; 1981 v Cz; 1982 v Ho, Alg; 1983 v Sp, Ma; (with Norwich C), 1984 v Ic, Ho, Is; 1985 v USSR, N (12)

Donnelly, J. (Dundalk), 1935 v H, Sw, G; 1936 v Ho, Sw, H, L; 1937 v G, H; 1938 v N (10)

Donnelly, T. (Drumcondra), 1938 v N; (Shamrock R), 1939 v Sw (2)

Donovan, D. C. (Everton), 1955 v N, Ho, N, WG; 1957 v E (5)

Donovan, T. (Aston Villa), 1980 v Cz (1)

Dowdall, C. (Fordsons), 1928 v Bel; (with Barnsley), 1929 v Bel; (with Cork), 1931 v Sp (3)

Doyle, C. (Shelbourne), 1959 v Cz (1)

Doyle, D. (Shamrock R), 1926 v I (1)

Doyle, L. (Dolphin), 1932 v Sp (1)

Duffy, B. (Shamrock R), 1950 v Bel (1)

Duggan, H. A. (Leeds U), 1927 v I; 1930 v Bel; 1936 v H, L; (with Newport Co), 1938 v N (5)

Dunne, A. P. (Manchester U), 1962 v A; 1963 v Ic, S; 1964 v A, Sp, Pol, N, E; 1965 v Pol, Sp; 1966 v Sp (2), A, Bel; 1967 v Sp, T, Sp; 1969 v Pol, D, H; 1970 v H; 1971 v Se, I, A; (with Bolton W), 1974 v Br (sub), U, Ch; 1975 v T, Sw, USSR, Sw, WG; 1976 v T (33)

Dunne, J. (Sheffield U), 1930 v Bel; (with Arsenal), 1936 v Sw, H, L; (with Southampton), 1937 v Sw, F; (with Shamrock R), 1938 v N (2), Cz, Pol; 1939 v Sw, Pol, H (2), G (15)

Dunne, J. C. (Fulham), 1971 v A (1)

Dunne, L. (Manchester C), 1935 v Sw, G (2)

Dunne, P. A. J. (Manchester U), 1965 v Sp; 1966 v Sp (2), WG; 1967 v T (5)

Dunne, S. (Luton T), 1953 v F, A; 1954 v F, L; 1956 v Sp, Ho; 1957 v D, WG, E; 1958 v D, Pol, A; 1959 v Pol; 1960 v WG, Se (15)

Dunne, T. (St Patrick's Ath), 1956 v Ho; 1957 v D, WG (3)

Dunning, P. (Shelbourne), 1971 v Se, I (2)

Dunphy, E. M. (York C), 1966 v Sp; (with Millwall), 1966 v WG; 1967 v T, Sp, T, Cz; 1968 v Cz, Pol; 1969 v Pol, A, D (2), H; 1970 v D, H, Pol, WG (sub); 1971 v Pol, Se (2), I (2), A (23)

Dwyer, N. M. (West Ham U), 1960 v Se, Ch, WG, Se;

(with Swansea T), 1961 v W, N, S (2); 1962 v Cz (2); 1964 v Pol (sub), N, E; 1965 v Pol (14)

Eccles, P. (Shamrock R), 1986 v U (sub) (1)

Egan, R. (Dundalk), 1929 v Bel (1)

Eglington, T. J. (Shamrock R), 1946 v P, Sp; (with Everton), 1947 v E, Sp, P; 1948 v P; 1949 v Sw, P, Se; 1951 v N, Arg; 1952 v WG (2), A, Sp; 1953 v F, A; 1954 v F, L, F; 1955 v N, Ho, WG; 1956 v Sp (24)

Ellis, P. (Bohemians), 1935 v Sw, G; 1936 v Ho, Sw, L; 1937 v G, H (7)

Fagan, E. (Shamrock R), 1973 v N (sub) (1)

Fagan, F. (Manchester C), 1955 v N; 1960 v Se; (with Derby Co), 1960 v Ch, WG, Se; 1961 v W, N, S (8)

Fagan, K. (Shamrock R), 1926 v I (1)

Fairclough, M. (Dundalk), 1982 v Ch (sub), Tr (sub) (2)

Fallon, S. (Celtic), 1951 v N; 1952 v WG (2), A, Sp; 1953 v F; 1955 v N, WG (8)

Fallon, W. J. (Notts Co), 1935 v H; 1936 v H; 1937 v H, Sw, F; 1939 v Sw, Pol; (with Sheffield W), 1939 v H, G (9)

Farquharson, T. G. (Cardiff C), 1929 v Bel; 1930 v Bel; 1931 v Sp; 1932 v Sp (4)

Farrell, P. (Hibernian), 1937 v Sw, F (2)

Farrell, P. D. (Shamrock R), 1946 v P, Sp; (with Everton), 1947 v Sp, P; 1948 v P, Se; 1949 v Sw, P (sub), Sp; 1950 v E, Fi, Se; 1951 v Arg, N; 1952 v WG (2), A, Sp; 1953 v F, A; 1954 v F (2); 1955 v N, Ho, WG; 1956 v Y, Sp; 1957 v E (28)

Feenan, J. J. (Sunderland), 1937 v Sw, F (2)

Finucane, A. (Limerick), 1967 v T, Cz; 1969 v Cz, D, H; 1970 v S, Cz; 1971 v Se, I (1 + 1 sub); 1972 v A (11)

Fitzgerald, F. J. (Waterford), 1955 v Ho; 1956 v Ho (2)

Fitzgerald, P. J. (Leeds U), 1961 v W, N, S; 1962 v Cz (2) (5)

Fitzpatrick, K. (Limerick), 1970 v Cz (1)

Fitzsimons, A. G. (Middlesbrough), 1950 v Fi, Bel; 1952 v WG (2), A, Sp; 1953 v F, A; 1954 v F, L, F; 1955 v Ho, N, WG; 1956 v Y, Sp, Ho; 1957 v D, WG, E (2); 1958 v D, Pol, A; 1959 v Pol; (with Lincoln C), 1959 v Cz (26)

Flood, J. J. (Shamrock R), 1926 v I; 1929 v Bel; 1930 v Bel; 1931 v Sp; 1932 v Sp (5)

Fogarty, A. (Sunderland), 1960 v WG, Se; 1961 v S; 1962 v Cz (2); 1963 v Ic (2), S (sub); 1964 v A (2); (with Hartlepools U), Sp (11)

Foley, J. (Cork), 1934 v Bel, Ho; (with Celtic), 1935 v H, Sw, G; 1937 v G, H (7)

Foley, M. (Shelbourne), 1926 v I (1)

Foley, T. C. (Northampton T), 1964 v Sp, Pol, N; 1965 v Pol, Bel; 1966 v Sp (2), WG; 1967 v Cz (9)

Foy, T. (Shamrock R), 1938 v N; 1939 v H (2)

Fullam, J. (Preston NE), 1961 v N; (with Shamrock R), 1964 v Sp, Pol, N; 1966 v A, Bel; 1968 v Pol; 1969 v Pol, A, D; 1970 v Cz (sub) (11)

Fullam, R. (Shamrock R), 1926 v I; 1927 v I (2)

Gallagher, C. (Celtic), 1967 v T, Cz (2)

Gallagher, M. (Hibernian), 1954 v L (1)

Gallagher, P. (Falkirk), 1932 v Sp (1)

Galvin, A. (Tottenham H), 1983 v Ho, Ma; 1984 v Ho (sub), Is (sub); 1985 v M, USSR, N, D, I, N, Sp; 1986 v U, Ic, Cz; 1987 v Bel (2), S, Bul, L; (with Sheffield W), 1988 v L, Bul, R, Pol, N, E, USSR, Ho; 1989 v Sp; (with Swindon T), 1990 v WG (29)

Gannon, E. (Notts Co), 1949 v Sw; (with Sheffield W), 1949 v Bel, P, Se, Sp; 1950 v Fi; 1951 v N; 1952 v G, A; 1954 v L, F; 1955 v N; (with Shelbourne), 1955 v N, WG (14)

Gannon, M. (Shelbourne), 1972 v A (1)

Gaskins, P. (Shamrock R), 1934 v Bel, Ho; 1935 v H, Sw, G; (with St James' Gate), 1938 v Cz, Pol (7)

Gavin, J. T. (Norwich C), 1950 v Fi (2); 1953 v F; 1954 v

L; (with Tottenham H), 1955 v Ho, WG; (with Norwich C), 1957 v D (7)

Geoghegan, M. (St James' Gate), 1937 v G; 1938 v N (2)

Gibbons, A. (St Patrick's Ath), 1952 v WG; 1954 v L; 1956 v Y, Sp (4)

Gilbert, R. (Shamrock R), 1966 v WG (1)

Giles, C. (Doncaster R), 1951 v N (1)

Giles, M. J. (Manchester U), 1960 v Se, Ch; 1961 v W, N, S (2); 1962 v Cz (2), A; 1963 v Ic, S; (with Leeds U), 1964 v A (2), Sp (2), Pol, N, E; 1965 v Sp; 1966 v Sp (2), A, Bel; 1967 v Sp, T (2); 1969 v A, D, Cz; 1970 v S, Pol, WG; 1971 v I; 1973 v F, USSR; 1974 v Br, U, Ch; 1975 v USSR, T, Sw, USSR, Sw; (with WBA), 1976 v T; 1977 v E, T, F (2), Pol, Bul; (with Shamrock R), 1978 v Bul, T, Pol, N, D; 1979 v Ni, D, Bul, WG (60)

Givens, D. J. (Manchester U), 1969 v D, H; 1970 v S, Cz, D, H; (with Luton T), 1970 v Pol, WG; 1971 v Se, I (2), A; 1972 v Ir, Ec, P; (with QPR), 1973 v F, USSR, Pol, F, N; 1974 v Pol, Br, U, Ch; 1975 v USSR, T, Sw, USSR, Sw, WG; 1976 v T, N, Pol; 1977 v E, T, F (2), Sp, Bul; 1978 v Bul, N, D; (with Birmingham C), 1979 v Ni (sub), E, D, Bul, WG; 1980 v US (sub), Ni (sub), Sw, Arg; 1981 v Ho, Bel, Cy (sub), W; (with Neuchatel X), 1982 v F (sub) (56)

Glen, W. (Shamrock R), 1927 v I; 1929 v Bel; 1930 v Bel; 1932 v Sp; 1936 v Ho, Sw, H, L (8)

Glynn, D. (Drumcondra), 1952 v WG; 1955 v N (2)

Godwin, T. F. (Shamrock R), 1949 v P, Se, Sp; 1950 v Fi, E; (with Leicester C), 1950 v Fi, Se, Bel; 1951 v N; (with Bournemouth), 1956 v Ho; 1957 v E; 1958 v D, Pol (13)

Golding, L. (Shamrock R), 1928 v Bel; 1930 v Bel (2)

Gorman, W. C. (Bury), 1936 v Sw, H, L; 1937 v G, H; 1938 v N, Cz, Pol; 1939 v Sw, Pol, H; (with Brentford), 1947 v E, P (13)

Grace, J. (Drumcondra), 1926 v I (1)

Grealish, A. (Orient), 1976 v N, Pol, D; 1979 v Ni, E, WG; (with Luton T), 1980 v W, Cz, Bul, US, Ni, E, Cy, Sw, Arg; 1981 v Ho, Bel, F, Cy, W, Bel, Pol; (with Brighton & HA), 1982 v Ho, Alg, Ch, Br, Tr; 1983 v Ho, Sp, Ic, Sp; 1984 v Ic, Ho; (with WBA), Pol, Chn; 1985 v M, USSR, N, D, Sp (sub), Sw; 1986 v USSR, D (44)

Gregg, E. (Bohemians), 1978 v Pol, D (sub); 1979 v E (sub), D, Bul, WG; 1980 v W, Cz (9)

Griffith, R. (Walsall), 1935 v H (1)

Grimes, A. A. (Manchester U), 1978 v T, Pol, N (sub); 1980 v Bul, US, Ni, E, Cy; 1981 v Cz, Pol; 1982 v Alg; 1983 v Sp (2); (with Coventry C), 1984 v Pol, Is; (with Luton T), 1988 v L, R (17)

Hale, A. (Aston Villa), 1962 v A; (with Doncaster R), 1963 v Ic; 1964 v Sp (2); (with Waterford), 1967 v Sp; 1968 v Pol (sub); 1969 v Pol, A, D; 1970 v S, Cz; 1971 v Pol (sub); 1972 v A (sub) (13)

Hamilton, T. (Shamrock R), 1959 v Cz (2) (2)

Hand, E. K. (Portsmouth), 1969 v Cz (sub); 1970 v Pol, WG; 1971 v Pol, A; 1973 v USSR, F, USSR, Pol, F; 1974 v Pol, Br, U, Ch; 1975 v T, Sw, USSR, Sw, WG; 1976 v T (20)

Harrington, W. (Cork), 1936 v Ho, Sw, H, L (4)

Hartnett, J. B. (Middlesbrough), 1949 v Sp; 1954 v L (2)

Haverty, J. (Arsenal), 1956 v Ho; 1957 v D, WG, E (2); 1958 v D, Pol, A; 1959 v Pol; 1960 v Se, Ch; 1961 v W, N, S (2); (with Blackburn R), 1962 v Cz (2); (with Millwall), 1963 v S; 1964 v A, Sp, Pol, N, E; (with Celtic), 1965 v Pol; (with Bristol R), 1965 v Sp; (with Shelbourne), 1966 v Sp (2), WG, A, Bel; 1967 v T, Sp (32)

Hayes, A. W. P. (Southampton), 1979 v D (1)

Hayes, W. E. (Huddersfield T), 1947 v E, P (2)

Hayes, W. J. (Limerick), 1949 v Bel (1)

Healey, R. (Cardiff C), 1977 v Pol; 1980 v E (sub) (2)

Heighway, S. D. (Liverpool), 1971 v Pol, Se (2), I, A; 1973 v USSR; 1975 v USSR, T, USSR, WG; 1976 v T, N;

1977 v E, F (2), Sp, Bul; 1978 v Bul, N, D; 1979 v Ni, Bul; 1980 v Bul, US, Ni, E, Cy, Arg; 1981 v Bel, F, Cy, W, Bel; (with Minnesota K), 1982 v Ho (34)

Henderson, B. (Drumcondra), 1948 v P, Sp (2)

Hennessy, J. (Shelbourne), 1956 v Pol, B, Sp; 1966 v WG; (with St Patrick's Ath), 1969 v A (5)

Herrick, J. (Cork Hibernians), 1972 v A, Ch (sub); (with Shamrock R), 1973 v F (sub) (3)

Higgins, J. (Birmingham C), 1951 v Arg (1)

Holmes, J. (Coventry C), 1971 v A (sub); 1973 v F, USSR, Pol, F, N; 1974 v Pol, Br; 1975 v USSR, Sw; 1976 v T, N, Pol; 1977 v E, T, F, Sp; (with Tottenham H), F, Pol, Bul; 1978 v Bul, T, Pol, N, D; 1979 v Ni, E, D, Bul; (with Vancouver W), 1981 v W (30)

Horlecher, A. F. (Bohemians), 1930 v Bel; 1932 v Sp, Ho; 1935 v H; 1936 v Ho, Sw (6)

Houghton, R. J. (Oxford U), 1986 v W, U, Ic, Cz; 1987 v Bel (2), S (2), Pol, L; 1988 v L, Bul, F, Cy, W, Bel, Y, N, E, USSR, Ho; 1989 v Ni, Tun, Sp, F, H, Sp, Ma, H; 1990 v Ni, Ma, Fi, E, Eg, Ho, R, I; 1991 v Mor, T, E (2), Pol, Ch, US (41)

Howlett, G. (Brighton & HA), 1984 v Chn (sub) (1)

Hoy, M. (Dundalk), 1938 v N; 1939 v Sw, Pol, H (2), G (6)

Hughton, C. (Tottenham H), 1980 v US, E, Sw, Arg; 1981 v Ho, Bel, F, Cy, W, Bel, Pol; 1982 v F; 1983 v Ho, Sp, Ma, Sp; 1984 v Ic, Ho, Ma; 1985 v M (sub), USSR, N, I, Is, E, Sp; 1986 v Sw, USSR, U, Ic; 1987 v Bel, Bul; 1988 v Is, Y, Pol, N, E, USSR, Ho; 1989 v Ni, F, H, Sp, Ma, H; 1990 v W (sub), USSR (sub), Fi, T (sub), Ma (sub); 1991 v T; (with West Ham U), Ch (18)

Hurley, C. J. (Millwall), 1957 v E; 1958 v D, Pol, A; (with Sunderland), 1959 v Cz (2); 1960 v Se, Ch, WG, Se; 1961 v W, N, S (2); 1962 v Cz (2), A; 1963 v Ic (2), S; 1964 v A (2), Sp (2), Pol, N; 1965 v Sp; 1966 v WG, A, Bel; 1967 v T, Sp, T, Cz; 1968 v Cz, Pol (2); (with Bolton W), 1969 v D, Cz, H (40)

Hutchinson, F. (Drumcondra), 1935 v Sw, G (2)

Irwin, D. J. (Manchester U), 1991 v Mor, T, W, E, Pol, US (6)

Jordan, D. (Wolverhampton W), 1937 v Sw, F (2)

Jordan, W. (Bohemians), 1934 v Ho; 1938 v N (2)

Kavanagh, P. J. (Celtic), 1931 v Sp; 1932 v Sp (2)

Keane, R. M. (Nottingham F), 1991 v Ch (1)

Keane, T. R. (Swansea T), 1949 v Sw, P, Se, Sp (4)

Kearin, M. (Shamrock R), 1972 v A (1)

Kearns, F. T. (West Ham U), 1954 v L (1)

Kearns, M. (Oxford U), 1970 v Pol (sub); (with Walsall), 1974 v Pol (sub), U, Ch; 1976 v N, Pol; 1977 v E, T, F (2), Sp, Bul; 1978 v N, D; 1979 v Ni, E; (with Wolverhampton W), 1980 v US, Ni (18)

Kelly, D. T. (Walsall), 1988 v Is, R, Y; (with West Ham U), 1989 v Tun (sub); (with Leicester C), 1990 v USSR, Ma; 1991 v Mor, W (sub), Ch, US (10)

Kelly, J. (Derry C), 1932 v Ho; 1934 v Bel; 1936 v Sw, L (4)

Kelly, J. A. (Drumcondra), 1957 v WG, E; (with Preston NE), 1962 v A; 1963 v Ic (2), S; 1964 v A (2), Sp (2), Pol; 1965 v Bel; 1966 v A, Bel; 1967 v Sp (2), T, Cz (2), Pol; 1968 v Pol, A, D, Cz, D, H; 1970 v S, D, H, Pol, WG; 1971 v Pol, Se (2), I (2), A; 1972 v Ir, Ec, Ch, P; 1973 v USSR, F, USSR, Pol, F, N (47)

Kelly, J. P. V. (Wolverhampton W), 1961 v W, N, S; 1962 v Cz (2) (5)

Kelly, M. J. (Portsmouth), 1988 v Y, Pol (sub); 1989 v Tun; 1991 v Mor (4)

Kelly, N. (Nottingham F), 1954 v L (1)

Kendrick, J. (Everton), 1927 v I; 1934 v Bel, Ho; 1936 v Ho (4)

Kennedy, M. F. (Portsmouth), 1986 v Ic, Cz (sub) (2)

Kennedy, W. (St James' Gate), 1932 v Ho; 1934 v Bel, Ho (3)

Keogh, J. (Shamrock R), 1966 v WG (sub) (1)

Keogh, S. (Shamrock R), 1959 v Pol (1)

Kiernan, F. W. (Shamrock R), 1951 v Arg, N; (with Southampton), 1952 v WG (2), A (5)

Kinnear, J. P. (Tottenham H), 1967 v T; 1968 v Cz, Pol; 1969 v A; 1970 v Cz, D, H, Pol; 1971 v Se (sub), I; 1972 v Ir, Ec, Ch, P; 1973 v USSR, F; 1974 v Pol, Br, U, Ch; 1975 v USSR, T, Sw, USSR, WG; (with Brighton & HA), 1976 v T (sub) (26)

Kinsella, J. (Shelbourne), 1928 v Bel (1)

Kinsella, P. (Shamrock R), 1932 v Ho; 1938 v N (2)

Kirkland, A. (Shamrock R), 1927 v I (1)

Lacey, W. (Shelbourne), 1927 v I; 1928 v Bel; 1930 v Bel (3)

Langan, D. (Derby Co), 1978 v T, N; 1980 v Sw, Arg; (with Birmingham C), 1981 v Ho, Bel, F, Cy, W, Bel, Cz, Pol; 1982 v Ho, F; (with Oxford U), 1985 v N, Sp, Sw; 1986 v W, U; 1987 v Bel, S, Pol, Br (sub), L (sub); 1988 v L (25)

Lawler, J. F. (Fulham), 1953 v A; 1954 v L, F; 1955 v N, H, N, WG; 1956 v Y (8)

Lawlor, J. C. (Drumcondra), 1949 v Bel; (with Doncaster R), 1951 v N, Arg (3)

Lawlor, M. (Shamrock R), 1971 v Pol, Se (2), I (sub); 1973 v Pol (5)

Lawrenson, M. (Preston NE), 1977 v Pol; (with Brighton), 1978 v Bul, Pol, N (sub); 1979 v Ni, E; 1980 v E, Cy, Sw; 1981 v Ho, Bel, F, Cy, Pol; (with Liverpool), 1982 v Ho, F; 1983 v Ho, Sp, Ic, Ma, Sp; 1984 v Ic, Ho, Ma, Is; 1985 v USSR, N, D, I, E, N; 1986 v Sw, USSR, D; 1987 v Bel, S; 1988 v Bul, Is (38)

Leech, M. (Shamrock R), 1969 v Cz, D, H; 1972 v A, Ir, Ec, P; 1973 v USSR (sub) (8)

Lennon, C. (St James' Gate), 1935 v H, Sw, G (3)

Lennox, G. (Dolphin), 1931 v Sp; 1932 v Sp (2)

Lowry, D. (St Patrick's Ath), 1962 v A (sub) (1)

Lunn, R. (Dundalk), 1939 v Sw, Pol (2)

Lynch, J. (Cork Bohemians), 1934 v Bel (1)

McAlinden, J. (Portsmouth), 1946 v P, Sp (2)

McCann, J. (Shamrock R), 1957 v WG (1)

McCarthy, J. (Bohemians), 1926 v I; 1928 v Bel; 1930 v Bel (3)

McCarthy, M. (Manchester C), 1984 v Pol, Chn; 1985 v M, D, I, Is, E, Sp, Sw; 1986 v Sw, USSR, W (sub), U, Ic, Cz; 1987 v S (2), Pol, Bul, Bel, Br, L; (with Celtic), 1988 v Bul, Is, R, Y, N, E, USSR, Ho; 1989 v Ni, Tun, Sp, F, H, Sp; (with Lyon), 1990 v WG, Ni, W, USSR, Fi, T, E, Eg, Ho, R, I; (with Millwall), 1991 v Mor, T, E, US (51)

McCarthy, M. (Shamrock R), 1932 v Ho (1)

McConville, T. (Dundalk), 1972 v A; (with Waterford), 1973 v USSR, F, USSR, Pol, F (6)

McDonagh, Joe (Shamrock R), 1984 v Pol (sub), Ma; 1985 v M (sub) (3)

McDonagh, J. (Everton), 1981 v W, Bel, Cz; (with Bolton W), 1982 v Ho, F, Ch, Br; 1983 v Ho, Sp, Ic, Ma, Sp; (with Notts Co), 1984 v Ic, Ho, Pol; 1985 v M, USSR, N, D, Sp, Sw; 1986 v Sw, USSR, D (24)

McEvoy, M. A. (Blackburn R), 1961 v S (2); 1963 v S; 1964 v A, Sp (2), Pol, N, E; 1965 v Pol, Bel, Sp; 1966 v Sp (2); 1967 v Sp, T, Cz (17)

McGee, P. (QPR), 1978 v T, N (sub), D (sub); 1979 v Ni, E, D (sub), Bul (sub); 1980 v Cz, Bul; (with Preston NE), US, Ni, Cy, Sw, Arg; 1981 v Bel (sub) (15)

McGowan, D. (West Ham U), 1949 v P, Se, Sp (3)

McGowan, J. (Cork U), 1947 v Sp (1)

McGrath, M. (Blackburn R), 1958 v A; 1959 v Pol, Cz (2); 1960 v Se, WG, Se; 1961 v W; 1962 v Cz (2); 1963 v S;

1964 v A (2), E; 1965 v Pol, Bel, Sp; 1966 v Sp; (with Bradford), 1966 v WG, A, Bel; 1967 v T (22)

McGrath, P. (Manchester U), 1985 v I (sub), Is, E, N (sub), Sw (sub); 1986 v Sw (sub), D, W, Ic, Cz; 1987 v Bel (2), S (2), Pol, Bul, Br, L; 1988 v L, Bul, Y, Pol, N, E, Ho; 1989 v Ni, F, H, Sp, Ma, H; (with Aston Villa), 1990 v WG, Ma, USSR, Fi, T, E, Eg, Ho, R, I; 1991 v E (2), W, Pol, Ch (sub), US (47)

McGuire, W. (Bohemians), 1936 v Ho (1)

McKenzie, G. (Southend U), 1938 v N (2), Cz, Pol; 1939 v Sw, Pol, H (2), G (9)

Mackey, G. (Shamrock R), 1957 v D, WG, E (3)

McLoughlin, A. F. (Swindon T), 1990 v Ma, E (sub), Eg (sub); 1991 v Mor (sub), E (sub); (with Southampton), W, Ch (sub) (7)

McLoughlin, F. (Fordsons), 1930 v Bel; (with Cork), 1932 v Sp (2)

McMillan, W. (Belfast Celtic), 1946 v P, Sp (2)

McNally, J. B. (Luton T), 1959 v Cz; 1961 v Sp; 1963 v Ic (3)

Macken, A. (Derby Co), 1977 v Sp (1)

Madden, O. (Cork), 1936 v H (1)

Maguire, J. (Shamrock R), 1929 v Bel (1)

Malone, G. (Shelbourne), 1949 v Bel (1)

Mancini, T. J. (QPR), 1974 v Pol, Br, U, Ch; (with Arsenal), 1975 v USSR (5)

Martin, C. (Bo'ness), 1927 v I (1)

Martin, C. J. (Glentoran), 1946 v P (sub), Sp; 1947 v E; (with Leeds U), 1947 v Sp; 1948 v P, Sp; (with Aston Villa), 1949 v Sw, Bel, P, Se, Sp; 1950 v Fi, E, Fi, Se, Bel; 1951 v Arg; 1952 v WG, A, Sp; 1954 v F (2), L; 1955 v N, Ho, N, WG; 1956 v Y, Sp, Ho (30)

Martin, M. P. (Bohemians), 1972 v A, Ir, Ec, Ch, P; 1973 v USSR; (with Manchester U), 1973 v USSR, Pol, F, N; 1974 v Pol, Br, U, Ch; 1975 v USSR, T, Sw, USSR, Sw, WG; (with WBA), 1976 v T, N, Pol; 1977 v E, T, F (2), Sp, Pol, Bul; (with Newcastle U), 1979 v D, Bul, WG; 1980 v W, Cz, Bul, US, Ni; 1981 v F, Bel, Cz; 1982 v Ho, F, Alg, Ch, Br, Tr; 1983 v Ho, Sp, Ma, Sp (51)

Meagan, M. K. (Everton), 1961 v S; 1962 v A; 1963 v Ic; 1964 v Sp; (with Huddersfield T), 1965 v Bel; 1966 v Sp (2), A, Bel; 1967 v Sp, T, Sp, T, Cz; 1968 v Cz, Pol; (with Drogheda), 1970 v S (17)

Meehan, P. (Drumcondra), 1934 v Ho (1)

Monahan, P. (Sligo R), 1935 v Sw, G (2)

Mooney, J. (Shamrock R), 1965 v Pol, Bel (2)

Moore, P. (Shamrock R), 1931 v Sp; 1932 v Ho; (with Aberdeen), 1934 v Bel, Ho; 1935 v H, G; (with Shamrock R), 1936 v Ho; 1937 v G, H (9)

Moran, K. (Manchester U), 1980 v Sw, Arg; 1981 v Bel, F, Cy, W (sub), Bel, Cz, Pol; 1982 v F, Alg; 1983 v Ic; 1984 v Ic, Ho, Ma, Is; 1985 v M; 1986 v D, Ic, Cz; 1987 v Bel (2), S (2), Pol, Bul, Br, L; 1988 v L, Bul, Is, R, Y, Pol, N, E, USSR, Ho; (with Sporting Gijon), 1989 v Ni, Sp, H, Sp, Ma, H; (with Blackburn R), 1990 v Ni, Ma, W, USSR (sub), Ma, E, Eg, Ho, R, I; 1991 v T (sub), W, E, Pol, Ch, US (60)

Moroney, T. (West Ham U), 1948 v Sp; 1949 v P, Se, Sp; 1950 v Fi, E, Fi, Bel; 1951 v N (2); 1952 v WG; 1954 v F (12)

Morris, C. B. (Celtic), 1988 v Is, R, Y, Pol, N, E, USSR, Ho; 1989 v Ni, Tun, Sp, F, H (1+1 sub); 1990 v WG, Ni, Ma (sub), W, USSR, Fi (sub), T, E, Eg, Ho, R, I; 1991 v E (27)

Moulson, C. (Lincoln C), 1936 v H, L; (with Notts Co), 1937 v H, Sw, F (5)

Moulson, G. B. (Lincoln C), 1948 v P, Sp; 1949 v Sw (3)

Mucklan, C. (Drogheda U), 1978 v Pol (1)

Muldoon, T. (Aston Villa), 1927 v I (1)

Mulligan, P. M. (Shamrock R), 1969 v Cz, D, H; 1970 v S, Cz, D; (with Chelsea), 1973 v Pol, WG; 1971 v Pol, Se, I; 1972 v A, Ir, Ec, Ch, P; (with C Palace), 1973 v F, USSR, Pol, F, N; 1974 v Pol, Br, U, Ch; 1975 v USSR, T, Sw, USSR, Sw; (with WBA), 1976 v T, Pol; 1977 v E, T, F (2), Pol, Bul; 1978 v Bul, N, D; 1979 v E, D, Bul (sub), WG; (with Shamrock R), 1980 v W, Cz, Bul, US (sub) (50)

Munroe, L. (Shamrock R), 1954 v L (1)

Murphy, A. (Clyde), 1956 v Y (1)

Murphy, B. (Bohemians), 1986 v U (1)

Murphy, J. (C Palace), 1980 v W, US, Cy (3)

Murray, T. (Dundalk), 1950 v Bel (1)

Newman, W. (Shelbourne), 1969 v D (1)

Nolan, R. (Shamrock R), 1957 v D, WG, E; 1958 v Pol; 1960 v Ch, WG, Se; 1962 v Cz (2); 1963 v Ic (10)

O'Brien, F. (Philadelphia F), 1980 v Cz, E, Cy (sub), Arg (4)

O'Brien, L. (Shamrock R), 1986 v U; (with Manchester U), 1987 v Br; 1988 v Is (sub), R (sub), Y (sub), Pol (sub); 1989 v Tun; (with Newcastle U), Sp (sub) (8)

O'Brien, M. T. (Derby Co), 1927 v I; (with Walsall), 1929 v Bel; (with Norwich C), 1930 v Bel; (with Watford), 1932 v Ho (4)

O'Brien, R. (Notts Co), 1976 v N, Pol; 1977 v Sp, Pol (4)

O'Byrne, L. B. (Shamrock R), 1949 v Bel (1)

O'Callaghan, B. R. (Stoke C), 1979 v WG (sub); 1980 v W, US; 1981 v W; 1982 v Br, Tr (6)

O'Callaghan, K. (Ipswich T), 1981 v Cz, Pol; 1982 v Alg, Ch, Br, Tr (sub); 1983 v Sp, Ic (sub), Ma (sub), Sp (sub); 1984 v Ic, Ho, Ma; 1985 v M (sub), N (sub), D (sub), E (sub); (with Portsmouth), 1986 v Sw (sub), USSR (sub); 1987 v Br (20)

O'Connell, A. (Dundalk), 1967 v Sp; (with Bohemians), 1971 v Pol (sub) (2)

O'Connor, T. (Shamrock R), 1950 v Fi, E, Fi, Se (4)

O'Connor, T. (Fulham), 1968 v Cz; (with Dundalk), 1972 v A, Ir (sub), Ec (sub), Ch; (with Bohemians), 1973 v F (sub), Pol (sub) (7)

O'Driscoll, J. F. (Swansea T), 1949 v Sw, Bel, Se (3)

O'Driscoll, S. (Fulham), 1982 v Ch, Br, Tr (sub) (3)

O'Farrell, F. (West Ham U), 1952 v A; 1953 v A; 1954 v F; 1955 v Ho, N; 1956 v Y, Ho; (with Preston NE), 1958 v D; 1959 v Cz (9)

O'Flanagan, K. P. (Bohemians), 1938 v N, Cz, Pol (2), H (2), G; (with Arsenal), 1947 v E, Sp, P (10)

O'Flanagan, M. (Bohemians), 1947 v E (1)

O'Hanlon, K. G. (Rotherham U), 1988 v Is (1)

O'Kane, P. (Bohemians), 1935 v H, Sw, G (3)

O'Keefe, E. (Everton), 1981 v W; (with Port Vale), 1984 v Chn; 1985 v M, USSR (sub), E (5)

O'Keefe, T. (Cork), 1934 v Bel; (with Waterford), 1938 v Cz, Pol (3)

O'Leary, D. (Arsenal), 1977 v E, F (2), Sp, Bul; 1978 v Bul, N, D; 1979 v E, Bul, WG; 1980 v W, Bul, Ni, E, Cy; 1981 v Ho, Cz, Pol; 1982 v Ho, F; 1983 v Ho, Ic, Sp; 1984 v Pol, Is, Chn; 1985 v USSR, N, D, Is, E (sub), N, Sp, Sw; 1986 v Sw, USSR, D, W; 1989 v Sp, Ma, H; 1990 v WG, Ni (sub), Ma, W (sub), USSR, Fi, T, Ma, R (sub); 1991 v Mor, T, E (2), Pol, Ch (57)

O'Leary, P. (Shamrock R), 1980 v Bul, US, Ni, E (sub), Cz, Arg; 1981 v Ho (7)

O'Mahoney, M. T. (Bristol R), 1938 v Cz, Pol; 1939 v Sw, Pol, H, G (6)

O'Neill, F. S. (Shamrock R), 1962 v Cz (2); 1965 v Pol, Bel, Sp; 1966 v Sp (2), WG, A; 1967 v Sp, T, Sp, T; 1969 v Pol, A, D, Cz, D (sub), H (sub); 1972 v A (20)

O'Neill, J. (Everton), 1952 v Sp; 1953 v F, A; 1954 v F, L, F; 1955 v N, Ho, N, WG; 1956 v Y, Sp; 1957 v D; 1958 v M; 1959 v Pol, Cz (2) (17)

O'Neill, J. (Preston NE), 1961 v W (1)

O'Neill, W. (Dundalk), 1936 v Ho, Sw, H, L; 1937 v G, H, Sw, F; 1938 v N; 1939 v H, G (11)

O'Regan, K. (Brighton & HA), 1984 v Ma, Pol; 1985 v M, Sp (sub) (4)

O'Reilly, J. (Brideville), 1932 v Ho; (with Aberdeen), 1934 v Bel, Ho; (with Brideville), 1936 v Ho; Sw, H, L; (with St James' Gate), 1937 v G, H, Sw, F; 1938 v N (2), Cz, Pol; 1939 v Sw, Pol, H (2), G (20)

O'Reilly, J. (Cork U), 1946 v P, Sp (2)

Peyton, G. (Fulham), 1977 v Sp (sub); 1978 v Bul, T, Pol; 1979 v D, Bul, WG; 1980 v W, Cz, Bul, E, Cy, Sw, Arg; 1981 v Ho, Bel, F, Cy; 1982 v Tr; 1985 v M (sub); 1986 v W, Cz; (with Bournemouth), 1988 v L, Pol; 1989 v Ni, Tun; 1990 v USSR, Ma; 1991 v Ch (29)

Peyton, N. (Shamrock R), 1957 v WG; (with Leeds U), 1960 v WG, Se (sub); 1961 v W; 1963 v Ic, S (6)

Quinn, N. J. (Arsenal), 1986 v Ic (sub), Cz; 1987 v Bul (sub); 1988 v L (sub), Bul (sub), Is, R (sub), Pol (sub), E (sub); 1989 v Tun (sub), Sp (sub), H (sub); (with Manchester C), 1990 v USSR, Ma, Eg (sub), Ho, R, I; 1991 v Mor, T, E, (2) W, Pol (24)

Reid, C. (Brideville), 1931 v Sp (1)
Richardson, D. J. (Shamrock R), 1972 v A (sub); (with Gillingham), 1973 v N (sub); 1980 v Cz (3)
Rigby, A. (St James' Gate), 1935 v H, Sw, G (3)
Ringstead, A. (Sheffield U), 1951 v Arg, N; 1952 v WG (2), A, Sp; 1953 v A; 1954 v F; 1955 v N; 1956 v Y, Sp, Ho; 1957 v E (2); 1958 v D, Pol, A; 1959 v Pol, Cz (2) (20)
Robinson, J. (Bohemians), 1928 v Bel; (with Dolphin), 1931 v Sp (2)
Robinson, M. (Brighton & HA), 1981 v F, Cy, Bel, Pol; 1982 v Ho, F, Alg, Ch; 1983 v Ho, Sp, Ic, Ma; (with Liverpool), 1984 v Ic, Ho, Is; 1985 v USSR, N; (with QPR), N, Sp, Sw; 1986 v D (sub), W, Cz (23)
Roche, P. J. (Shelbourne), 1972 v A; (with Manchester U), 1975 v USSR, T, Sw, USSR, Sw, WG; 1976 v T (8)
Rogers, E. (Blackburn R), 1968 v Cz, Pol; 1969 v Pol, A, D, Cz, D, H; 1970 v S, D, H; 1971 v I (2), A; (with Charlton Ath), 1972 v Ir, Ec, Ch, P; 1973 v USSR (19)
Ryan, G. (Derby Co), 1978 v T; (with Brighton & HA), 1979 v E, WG; 1980 v W, Cy (sub), Sw, Arg (sub); 1981 v F (sub), Pol (sub); 1982 v Ho (sub), Alg (sub), Ch (sub), Tr; 1984 v Pol, Chn; 1985 v M (16)
Ryan, R. A. (WBA), 1950 v Se, Bel; 1951 v N, Arg, N; 1952 v WG (2), A, Sp; 1953 v F, A; 1954 v F, L, F; 1955 v N; (with Derby Co), 1956 v Sp (16)

Saward, P. (Millwall), 1954 v L; (with Aston Villa), 1957 v E (2); 1958 v D, Pol, A; 1959 v Pol, Cz; 1960 v Se, Ch, WG, Se; 1961 v W, N; (with Huddersfield T), 1961 v S; 1962 v A; 1963 v Ic (2) (18)
Scannell, T. (Southend U), 1954 v L (1)
Scully, P. J. (Arsenal), 1989 v Tun (sub) (1)
Sheedy, K. (Everton), 1984 v Ho (sub), Ma; 1985 v D, I, Is, Sw; 1986 v Sw, D; 1987 v S, Pol; 1988 v Is, R, Pol, E (sub), USSR; 1989 v Ni, Tun, H, Sp, Ma, H; 1990 v Ni, Ma, W (sub), USSR, Fi (sub), T, E, Eg, Ho, R, I; 1991 v W, E, Pol, Ch, US (37)
Sheridan, J. J. (Leeds U), 1988 v R, Y, Pol, N (sub); 1989 v Sp; (with Sheffield W), 1990 v W, T (sub), Ma, I (sub); 1991 v Mor (sub), T, Ch, US (sub) (13)
Slaven, B. (Middlesbrough), 1990 v W, Fi, T (sub), Ma; 1991 v W, Pol (sub) (6)
Sloan, J. W. (Arsenal), 1946 v P, Sp (2)
Smyth, M. (Shamrock R), 1969 v Pol (sub) (1)
Squires, J. (Shelbourne), 1934 v Ho (1)
Stapleton, F. (Arsenal), 1977 v T, F, Sp, Bul; 1978 v Bul, N, D; 1979 v Ni, E (sub), D, WG; 1980 v W, Bul, Ni, E, Cy; 1981 v Ho, Bel, F, Cy, Bel, Cz, Pol; (with Manchester U), 1982 v Ho, F, Alg; 1983 v Ho, Sp, Ic, Ma, Sp; 1984 v Ic, Ho, Ma, Pol, Is, Chn; 1985 v N, D, I, Is, E, N, Sw; 1986 v Sw, USSR, D, U, Ic, Cz (sub); 1987 v Bel (2), S (2), Pol, Bul, L; (with Ajax), 1988 v L, Bul,

R; (with Derby Co), Y, N, E, USSR, Ho; (with Le Havre), 1989 v F, Sp, Ma; (with Blackburn R), 1990 v WG, Ma (sub) (70)
Staunton, S. (Liverpool), 1989 v Tun, Sp (2), Ma, H; 1990 v WG, Ni, Ma, W, USSR, Fi, T, Ma, E, Eg, Ho, R, I; 1991 v Mor, T, E (2), W, Pol, Ch, US (26)
Stevenson, A. E. (Dolphin), 1932 v Ho; (with Everton), 1947 v E, Sp, P; 1948 v P, Sp; 1949 v Sw (7)
Strahan, F. (Shelbourne), 1964 v Pol, N, E; 1965 v Pol; 1966 v WG (5)
Sullivan, J. (Fordsons), 1928 v Bel (1)
Swan, M. M. G. (Drumcondra), 1960 v Se (sub) (1)
Synnott, N. (Shamrock R), 1978 v T, Pol; 1979 v Ni (3)

Thomas, P. (Waterford), 1974 v Pol, Br (2)
Townsend, A. D. (Norwich C), 1989 v F, Sp (sub), Ma (sub), H; 1990 v WG (sub), Ni, Ma, W, USSR, Fi (sub), T, Ma (sub), E, Eg, Ho, R, I; (with Chelsea), 1991 v Mor, T, E (2), W, Pol, Ch, US (25)
Traynor, T. J. (Southampton), 1954 v L; 1962 v A; 1963 v Ic (2), S; 1964 v A (2), Sp (8)
Treacy, R. C. P. (WBA), 1966 v WG; 1967 v Sp, Cz; 1968 v Cz; (with Charlton Ath), 1968 v Pol; 1969 v Pol, Cz, D; 1970 v S, D, H (sub), Pol (sub), WG (sub); 1971 v Pol, Se (sub + 1), I, A; (with Swindon T), 1972 v Ir, Ec, Ch, P; 1973 v USSR, F, USSR, Pol, F, N; 1974 v Pol; (with Preston NE), Br; 1975 v USSR, Sw (2), WG; 1976 v T, N (sub), Pol (sub); (with WBA), 1977 v F, Pol; (with Shamrock R), 1978 v T, Pol (2); 1980 v Cz (sub) (43)
Tuohy, L. (Shamrock R), 1956 v Y; 1959 v Cz (2); (with Newcastle U), 1962 v A; 1963 v Ic (2); (with Shamrock R), 1964 v A; 1965 v Bel (8)
Turner, A. (Celtic), 1963 v S; 1964 v Sp (2)
Turner, C. J. (Southend U), 1936 v Sw; 1937 v G, H, Sw, F; (with West Ham U), 1938 v N (2), Cz, Pol; 1939 v H (10)

Vernon, J. (Belfast C), 1946 v P, Sp (2)

Waddock, G. (QPR), 1980 v Sw, Arg; 1981 v W, Pol (sub); 1982 v Alg; 1983 v Ic, Ma, Sp, Ho (sub); 1984 v Ic, Ho, Is; 1985 v I, Is, E, N, Sp; 1986 v USSR; (with Millwall), 1990 v USSR, T (20)
Walsh, D. J. (WBA), 1946 v P, Sp; 1947 v Sp, P; 1948 v P, Sp; 1949 v Sw, P, Se, Sp; 1950 v E, Fi, Se; 1951 v N; (with Aston Villa), v Arg, N; 1952 v Sp; 1953 v A; 1954 v F (2) (20)
Walsh, J. (Limerick), 1982 v Tr (1)
Walsh, M. (Blackpool), 1976 v N, Pol; 1977 v F (sub), Pol; (with Everton), 1979 v Ni (sub); (with QPR), D (sub), Bul, WG (sub); (with Porto), 1981 v Bel (sub), Cz; 1982 v Alg (sub); 1983 v Sp, Ho (sub), Sp (sub); 1984 v Ic (sub), Ma, Pol, Chn; 1985 v USSR, N (sub), D (22)
Walsh, M. (Everton), 1982 v Ch, Br, Tr; 1983 v Sp; (with Norwich C), Ic (5)
Walsh, W. (Manchester C), 1947 v E, Sp, P; 1948 v P, Sp; 1949 v Bel; 1950 v E, Se, Bel (9)
Waters, J. (Grimsby T), 1977 v T; 1980 v Ni (sub) (2)
Watters, F. (Shelbourne), 1926 v I (1)
Weir, E. (Clyde), 1939 v H (2), G (3)
Whelan, R. (St Patrick's Ath), 1964 v A, E (sub) (2)
Whelan, R. (Liverpool), 1981 v Cz (sub); 1982 v Ho (sub), F; 1983 v Ic, Ma, Sp; 1984 v Is; 1985 v USSR, N, I (sub), Is, E, N (sub), Sw (sub); 1986 v USSR (sub), W; 1987 v Bel (sub), S, Bul, Bel, Br, L; 1988 v L, Bul, Pol, N, E, USSR, Ho; 1989 v Ni, F, H, Sp, Ma; 1990 v WG, Ni, Ma, W, Ho (sub); 1991 v Mor, E (41)
Whelan, W. (Manchester U), 1956 v Ho; 1957 v D, E (2) (4)
White, J. J. (Bohemians), 1928 v Bel (1)
Whittaker, R. (Chelsea), 1959 v Cz (1)
Williams, J. (Shamrock R), 1938 v N (1)

BRITISH AND IRISH INTERNATIONAL GOALSCORERS SINCE 1872

Where two players with the same surname and initials have appeared for the same country, and one or both have scored, they have been distinguished by reference to the club which appears *first* against their name in the international appearances section (pages 812–859). Unfortunately, four of the scorers in Scotland's 10-2 victory v Ireland in 1888 are unknown, as is the scorer of one of their nine goals v Wales in March 1878.

ENGLAND

Name		Name		Name		Name	
A'Court, A.	1	Carter, J. H.	4	Greaves, J.	44	Mariner, P.	13
Adams, T. A.	4	Chadwick, E.	3	Grovesnor, A. T.	2	Marsh, R. W.	1
Adcock, H.	1	Chamberlain, M.	1	Gunn, W.	1	Matthews, S.	11
Alcock, C. W.	1	Chambers, H.	5			Matthews, V.	1
Allen, A.	3	Channon, M. R.	21	Haines, J. T. W.	2	McCall, J.	1
Allen, R.	2	Charlton, J.	6	Hall, G. W.	9	McDermott, T.	3
Anderson, V.	2	Charlton, R.	49	Halse, H. J.	2	Medley, L. D.	1
Astall, G.	1	Chenery, C. J.	1	Hampson, J.	5	Melia, J.	1
Athersmith, W. C.	3	Chivers, M.	13	Hampton, H.	2	Mercer, D. W.	1
Atyeo, P. J. W.	5	Clarke, A. J.	10	Hancocks, J.	2	Milburn, J. E. T.	10
		Cobbold, W. N.	7	Hardman, H. P.	1	Miller, H. S.	1
Bache, J. W.	4	Cock, J. G.	2	Harris, S. S.	2	Mills, G. R.	3
Bailey, N. C.	2	Common, A.	2	Hassall, H. W.	4	Milward, A.	3
Baily, E. F.	5	Connelly, J. M.	7	Hateley, M.	9	Mitchell, C.	5
Baker, J. H.	3	Coppell, S. J.	7	Haynes, J. N.	18	Moore, J.	1
Ball, A. J.	8	Cotterill, G. H.	2	Hegan, K. E.	4	Moore, R. F.	2
Bambridge, A. L.	1	Cowans, G.	2	Henfrey, A. G.	2	Moore, W. G. B.	2
Bambridge, E. C.	12	Crawford, A.	1	Hilsdon, G. R.	14	Morren, T.	1
Barclay, R.	2	Crawshaw, T. H.	1	Hine, E. W.	4	Morris, F.	1
Barnes, J.	10	Crayston, W. J.	1	Hirst, D. E.	1	Morris, J.	3
Barnes, P. S.	4	Creek, F. N. S.	1	Hitchens, G. A.	5	Mortensen, S. H.	23
Barton, J.	1	Crooks, S. D.	7	Hobbis, H. H. F.	1	Morton, J. R.	1
Bassett, W. I.	7	Currey, E. S.	2	Hoddle, G.	8	Mosforth, W.	3
Bastin, C. S.	12	Currie, A. W.	3	Hodgetts, D.	1	Mullen, J.	6
Beardsley, P. A.	8	Cursham, A. W.	2	Hodgson, G.	1	Mullery, A. P.	1
Beasley, A.	1	Cursham, H. A.	5	Holley, G. H.	8		
Beattie, T. K.	1			Houghton, W. E.	5	Neal, P. G.	5
Becton, F.	2	Daft, H. B.	3	Howell, R.	1	Needham, E.	3
Bedford, H.	1	Davenport, J. K.	2	Hughes, E. W.	1	Nicholls, J.	1
Bell, C.	9	Davis, G.	1	Hulme, J. H. A.	4	Nicholson, W. E.	1
Bentley, R. T. F.	9	Davis, H.	1	Hunt, G. S.	1		
Bishop, S. M.	1	Day, S. H.	2	Hunt, R.	18	O'Grady, M.	3
Blackburn, F.	1	Dean, W. R.	18	Hunter, N.	2	Osborne, F. R.	3
Blissett, L.	3	Devey, J. H. G.	1	Hurst, G. C.	24	Own goals	22
Bloomer, S.	28	Dewhurst, F.	11				
Bond, R.	2	Dix, W. R.	1	Jack, D. N. B.	3	Page, L. A.	1
Bonsor, A. G.	1	Dixon, K. M.	4	Johnson, D. E.	6	Paine, T. L.	7
Bowden, E. R.	1	Dixon, L. M.	1	Johnson, E.	2	Parry, E. H.	1
Bowers, J. W.	2	Douglas, B.	11	Johnson, J. A.	2	Parry, R. A.	1
Bowles, S.	1	Drake, E. J.	6	Johnson, T. C. F.	5	Pawson, F. W.	1
Bradford, G. R. W.	1	Ducat, A.	1	Johnson, W. H.	1	Payne, J.	2
Bradford, J.	7	Dunn, A. T. B.	2			Peacock, A.	3
Bradley, W.	2			Kail, E. I. L.	2	Pearce, S.	2
Bradshaw, F.	3	Eastham, G.	2	Kay, A. H.	1	Pearson, J. S.	5
Bridges, B. J.	1	Edwards, D.	5	Keegan, J. K.	21	Pearson, S. C.	5
Bridgett, A.	3	Elliott, W. H.	3	Kelly, R.	8	Perry, W.	2
Brindle, T.	1	Evans, R. E.	1	Kennedy, R.	3	Peters, M.	20
Britton, C. S.	1			Kenyon-Slaney, W. S.	2	Pickering, F.	5
Broadbent, P. F.	2	Finney, T.	30	Kevan, D. T.	8	Platt, D.	7
Broadis, I. A.	8	Fleming, H. J.	9	Kidd, B.	1	Pointer, R.	2
Brodie, J. B.	1	Flowers, R.	10	Kingsford, R. K.	1		
Bromley-Davenport, W.	2	Forman, Frank	1	Kirchen, A. J.	2	Quantrill, A.	1
Brook, E. F.	10	Forman, Fred	3	Kirton, W. J.	1		
Brooking, T. D.	5	Foster, R. E.	3			Ramsay, A. E.	3
Brooks, J.	2	Francis, G. C. J.	3	Langton, R.	1	Revie, D. G.	4
Broome, F. H.	3	Francis, T.	12	Latchford, R. D.	5	Reynolds, J.	3
Brown, A.	4	Freeman, B. C.	3	Latherton, E. G.	1	Richardson, J. R.	2
Brown, A. S.	1	Froggatt, J.	2	Lawler, C.	1	Rigby, A.	3
Brown, G.	5	Froggatt, R.	2	Lawton, T.	22	Rimmer, E. J.	2
Brown, J.	3			Lee, F.	10	Roberts, H.	1
Brown, W.	1	Galley, T.	1	Lee, J.	1	Roberts, W. T.	4
Buchan, C. M.	4	Gascoigne, P. J.	2	Lee, S.	2	Robinson, J.	3
Bull, S. G.	4	Geary, F.	3	Lindley, T.	15	Robson, B.	26
Bullock, N.	2	Gibbins, W. V. T.	3	Lineker, G.	45	Robson, R.	4
Burgess, H.	4	Gilliatt, W. E.	3	Lofthouse, J. M.	3	Rowley, J. F.	6
Butcher, T.	3	Goddard, P.	1	Lofthouse, N.	30	Royle, J.	2
Byrne, J. J.	8	Goodall, J.	12	Hon. A. Lyttelton	1	Rutherford, J.	3
		Goodyer, A. C.	1				
Camsell, G. H.	18	Gosling, R. C.	2	Mabbutt, G.	1	Sagar, C.	1
Carter, H. S.	7	Goulden, L. A.	4	Macdonald, M.	6	Sandilands, R. R.	2
		Grainger, C.	3	Mannion, W. J.	11	Sansom, K.	1

Delaney, J. 3
Devine, A. 1
Dewar, G. 1
Dewar, N. 4
Dickson, W. 4
Divers, J. 1
Docherty, T. H. 1
Dodds, D. 1
Donaldson, A. 1
Donnachie, J. 1
Dougall, J. 1
Drummond, J. 2
Dunbar, M. 1
Duncan, D. 7
Duncan, D. M. 1
Duncan, J. 1
Dunn, J. 2
Durie, G. S. 2

Easson, J. F. 1
Ellis, J. 1

Ferguson, J. 6
Fernie, W. 1
Fitchie, T. T. 1
Flavell, R. 2
Fleming, C. 2
Fleming, J. W. 3
Fraser, M. J. E. 4

Gallacher, H. K. 23
Gallacher, P. 1
Galt, J. H. 1
Gemmell, T. (St Mirren) 1
Gemmell, T. (Celtic) 1
Gemmill, A. 8
Gibb, W. 1
Gibson, D. W. 3
Gibson, J. D. 2
Gibson, N. 1
Gillespie, Jas. 3
Gillick, T. 3
Gilzean, A. J. 10
Gossland, J. 2
Goudie, J. 1
Gough, C. R. 5
Gourlay, J. 1
Graham, A. 2
Graham, G. 1
Gray, A. 7
Gray, E. 3
Gray, F. 1
Greig, J. 3
Groves, W. 5

Hamilton, G. 4
Hamilton, J. 3
(Queen's Park)
Hamilton, R. C. 14
Harper, J. M. 2
Harrower, W. 5
Hartford, R. A. 3
Heggie, C. 1
Henderson, J. G. 1
Henderson, W. 5
Herd, D. G. 4
Hewie, J. D. 2
Higgins, A. 1
(Newcastle U)
Higgins, A. (Kilmarnock) 4
Highet, T. C. 1
Holton, J. A. 2
Houliston, W. 2
Howie, H. 1
Howie, J. 2
Hughes, J. 1
Hunter, W. 1
Hutchison, T. 1
Hutton, J. 2
Hyslop, T. 1

Imrie, W. N. 1

Jackson, A. 8
Jackson, C. 1

James, A. W. 3
Jardine, A. 1
Jenkinson, T. 1
Johnston, L. H. 1
Johnston, M. 14
Johnstone, D. 2
Johnstone, J. 4
Johnstone, Jas. 1
Johnstone, R. 9
Johnstone, W. 1
Jordan, J. 11

Kay, J. L. 5
Keillor, A. 3
Kelly, J. 1
Kelso, J. 1
Ker, G. 10
King, A. 1
King, J. 1
Kinnear, D. 1

Lambie, W. A. 5
Lang, J. J. 1
Law, D. 30
Leggat, J. 8
Lennie, W. 1
Lennnox, R. 3
Liddell, W. 6
Lindsay, J. 6
Linwood, A. B. 1
Logan, J. 1
Lorimer, P. 4
Love, A. 1
Lowe, J. (Cambuslang) 1
Lowe, J. (St Bernards) 1

Macari, L. 5
MacDougall, E. J. 3
MacLeod, M. 1
Mackay, D. C. 4
Mackay, G. 1
MacKenzie, J. A. 1
Madden, J. 5
Marshall, H. 1
Marshall, J. 1
Mason, J. 4
Massie, A. 1
Masson, D. S. 5
McAdam, J. 1
McAllister, G. 1
McAulay, J. 1
McAvennie, F. 1
McCall, J. 1
McCall, S. M. 1
McCalliog, J. 1
McCallum, N. 1
McCoist, A. 8
McColl, R. S. 13
McCulloch, D. 3
McDougall, J. 4
McFarlane, A. 1
McFadyen, W. 2
McGhee, M. 2
McGregor, J. C. 1
McGrory, J. 6
McGuire, W. 1
McInally, A. 3
McInnes, T. 2
McKie, J. 2
McKimmie, S. 1
McKinnon, A. 1
McKinnon, R. 1
McKinnon, W. W. 5
McLaren, A. 4
McLaren, J. 1
McLean, A. 1
McLean, T. 1
McLintock, F. 1
McMahon, A. 6
McMenemy, J. 5
McMillan, I. L. 2
McNeil, H. 5
McNeill, W. 3
McPhail, J. 3
McPhail, R. 7

McPherson, J. 8
McPherson, R. 1
McQueen, G. 5
McStay, P. 6
Meiklejohn, D. D. 3
Millar, J. 2
Miller, T. 2
Miller, W. 1
Mitchell, R. C. 1
Morgan, W. 1
Morris, D. 1
Morris, H. 3
Morton, A. L. 5
Mudie, J. K. 9
Mulhall, G. 1
Munro, A. D. 1
Munro, N. 1
Murdoch, R. 5
Murphy, F. 1
Murray, J. 1

Napier, C. E. 3
Narey, D. 1
Neil, R. G. 2
Nicholas, C. 5
Nisbet, J. 1

O'Donnell, F. 2
O'Hare, J. 5
Ormond, W. E. 1
O'Rourke, F. 1
Orr, R. 1
Orr, T. 1
Oswald, J. 1
Own goals 14

Parlane, D. 1
Paul, H. McD. 2
Paul, W. 6
Pettigrew, W. 2
Provan, D. 1

Quinn, J. 7
Quinn, P. 1

Rankin, G. 2
Rankin, R. 2
Reid, W. 4
Reilly, L. 22
Renny-Tailyour, H. W. 1
Richmond, J. T. 1
Ring, T. 2
Rioch, B. D. 6
Ritchie, J. 1
Robertson, A. 2
Robertson, J. 2
Robertson, J. N. 8
Robertson, J. T. 2
Robertson, T. 1
Robertson, W. 1
Russell, D. 1

Scott, A. S. 5
Sellar, W. 4
Sharp, G. 1
Shaw, F. W. 1
Simpson, J. 1
Smith, A. 5
Smith, G. 4
Smith, J. 1
Smith, John 12
Somerville, G. 1
Souness, G. J. 3
Speedie, F. 2
St John, I. 9
Steel, W. 12
Stein, C. 10
Stevenson, G. 4
Stewart, R. 1
Stewart, W. E. 1
Strachan, G. 5
Sturrock, P. 3

Taylor, J. D. 1
Templeton, R. 1

Thomson, A. 1
Thomson, C. 4
Thomson, R. 1
Thomson, W. 1
Thornton, W. 1

Waddell, T. S. 1
Waddell, W. 6
Walker, J. 2
Walker, R. 7
Walker, T. 9
Wallace, I. A. 1
Wark, J. 7
Watson, J. A. K. 1
Watt, F. 2
Watt, W. W. 1
Weir, A. 1
Weir, J. B. 2
White, J. A. 3
Wilson, A. 2
Wilson, A. N. 13
Wilson, D. 2
(Queen's Park)
Wilson, D. (Rangers) 9
Wilson, H. 1
Wylie, T. G. 1

Young, A. 5

WALES

Allchurch, I. J. 23
Allen, M. 3
Astley, D. J. 12
Atherton, R. W. 2

Bamford, T. 1
Barnes, W. 1
Bodin, P. J. 1
Boulter, L. M. 1
Bowdler, J. C. H. 3
Bowen, D. L. 1
Bowen, M. 1
Boyle, T. 1
Bryan, T. 1
Burgess, W. A. R. 1
Burke, T. 1
Butler, A. 1

Chapman, T. 2
Charles, J. 1
Charles, M. 6
Charles, W. J. 15
Clarke, R. J. 5
Collier, D. J. 1
Cross, K. 1
Cumner, R. H. 1
Curtis, A. 6
Curtis, E. R. 3

Davies, D. W. 1
Davies, E. Lloyd 1
Davies, G. 2
Davies, L. S. 6
Davies, R. T. 8
Davies, R. W. 7
Davies, S. 5
Davies, W. 6
Davies, W. H. 1
Davies, William 5
Davies, W. O. 1
Deacy, N. 4
Doughty, J. 6
Doughty, R. 2
Durban, A. 2
Dwyer, P. 2

Edwards, G. 2
Edwards, R. I. 5
England, H. M. 3
Evans, I. 1
Evans, J. 1
Evans, R. E. 2
Evans, W. 1
Eyton-Jones, J. A. 1

Flynn, B. — 6
Ford, T. — 23
Foulkes, W. I. — 1
Fowler, J. — 3

Giles, D. — 2
Glover, E. M. — 7
Godfrey, B. C. — 2
Green, A. W. — 3
Griffiths, A. T. — 6
Griffiths, M. W. — 2
Griffiths, T. P. — 3
Harris, C. S. — 1
Hersee, R. — 1
Hewitt, R. — 1
Hockey, T. — 1
Hodges, G. — 2
Hole, W. J. — 1
Hopkins, I. J. — 2
Horne, B. — 2
Howell, E. G. — 3
Hughes, L. M. — 9

James, E. — 2
James, L. — 10
James, R. — 7
Jarrett, R. H. — 3
Jenkyns, C. A. — 1
Jones, A. — 1
Jones, Bryn — 6
Jones, B. S. — 2
Jones, Cliff — 15
Jones, C. W. — 1
Jones, D. E. — 1
Jones, Evan — 1
Jones, H. — 1
Jones, I. — 1
Jones, J. O. — 1
Jones, J. P. — 1
Jones, Leslie J. — 1
Jones, R. A. — 2
Jones, W. L. — 6

Keenor, F. C. — 2
Krzywicki, R. L. — 1

Leek, K. — 5
Lewis, B. — 3
Lewis, J. — 1
Lewis, W. — 10
Lewis, W. L. — 2
Lovell, S. — 1
Lowrie, G. — 2

Mahoney, J. F. — 1
Mays, A. W. — 1
Medwin, T. C. — 6
Meredith, W. H. — 11
Mills, T. J. — 1
Moore, G. — 1
Morgan, J. R. — 2
Morgan-Owen, H. — 1
Morgan-Owen, M. M. — 2
Morris, A. G. — 9
Morris, H. — 2
Morris, R. — 1

Nicholas, P. — 2

O'Callaghan, E. — 3
O'Sullivan, P. A. — 1
Owen, G. — 2
Owen, W. — 4
Owen, W. P. — 6
Own goals — 12

Palmer, D. — 3
Parry, T. D. — 3
Paul, R. — 1
Peake, E. — 1
Perry, E. — 1
Phillips, C. — 5
Phillips, D. — 1
Powell, A. — 1
Powell, D. — 1
Price, J. — 4
Price, P. — 1
Pryce-Jones, W. E. — 3
Pugh, D. H. — 2
Reece, G. I. — 2
Rees, R. R. — 3
Richards, R. W. — 1
Roach, J. — 2
Robbins, W. W. — 4
Roberts, J. (*Corwen*) — 1
Roberts, Jas. — 1
Roberts, P. S. — 1
Roberts, R. (*Druids*) — 1
Roberts, W. (*Llangollen*) — 2
Roberts, W. (*Wrexham*) — 1
Roberts, W. H. — 1
Rush, I. — 19
Russell, M. R. — 1

Sabine, H. W. — 1
Saunders, D. — 9
Shaw, E. G. — 2
Sisson, H. — 4
Slatter, N. — 2
Smallman, D. P. — 1

Tapscott, D. R. — 4
Thomas, M. — 4
Thomas, T. — 1
Toshack, J. B. — 13
Trainer, H. — 2

Vaughan, John — 2
Vernon, T. R. — 8
Vizard, E. T. — 1

Walsh, I. — 7
Warren, F. W. — 3
Watkins, W. M. — 4
Wilding, J. — 4
Wiliams, G. E. — 2
Williams, W. — 1
Woosnam, A. P. — 4
Wynn, G. A. — 1

Yorath, T. C. — 2

EIRE

Aldridge, J. — 6
Ambrose, P. — 1
Anderson, J. — 1
Bermingham, P. — 1
Bradshaw, P. — 4
Brady, L. — 9
Brown, D. — 1
Byrne, J. (*Bray*) — 1
Byrne, J. (*QPR*) — 3

Cantwell, J. — 14
Carey, J. — 3
Carroll, T. — 1
Cascarino, A. — 7
Coad, P. — 3
Conroy, T. — 2
Conway, J. — 3
Cummings, G. — 5
Curtis, D. — 8

Daly, G. — 13
Davis, T. — 4
Dempsey, J. — 1
Dennehy, M. — 2
Donnelly, J. — 3
Donnelly, J. — 1
Duffy, B. — 1
Duggan, H. — 1
Dunne, J. — 12
Dunne, L. — 1

Eglington, T. — 2
Ellis, P. — 1

Fagan, F. — 5
Fallon, S. — 2
Fallon, W. — 2
Farrell, P. — 3
Fitzgerald, P. — 2
Fitzgerald, J. — 1
Fitzsimmons, A. — 7
Flood, J. J. — 4
Fogarty, A. — 3
Fullam, J. — 1
Fullam, R. — 1

Galvin, A. — 1
Gavin, J. — 2
Geoghegan, M. — 2
Giles, J. — 5
Givens, D. — 19
Glynn, D. — 1
Grealish, T. — 8
Grimes, A. A. — 1

Hale, A. — 2
Hand, E. — 2
Haverty, J. — 3
Holmes, J. — 1
Horlacher, A. — 2
Houghton, R. — 2
Hughton, C. — 1
Hurley, C. — 2

Jordan, D. — 1

Kelly, D. — 6
Kelly, J. — 2
Lacey, W. — 1
Lawrenson, M. — 5
Leech, M. — 2

McCann, J. — 1
McCarthy, M. — 1
McEvoy, A. — 6
McGee, P. — 4
McGrath, P. — 4
Madden, O. — 1
Mancini, T. — 1
Martin, C. — 6
Martin, M. — 4
Mooney, J. — 1
Moore, P. — 7
Moran, K. — 6
Moroney, T. — 1
Mulligan, P. — 1

O'Callaghan, K. — 1
O'Connor, T. — 2
O'Farrell, F. — 2
O'Flanagan, K. — 3
O'Keefe, E. — 1
O'Leary, D. A. — 1
O'Neill, F. — 1
O'Reilly, J. — 2
O'Reilly, J. — 1

Own goals — 5

Quinn, N. — 7

Ringstead, A. — 7
Robinson, M. — 4
Rogers, E. — 5
Ryan, G. — 1
Ryan, R. — 3

Sheedy, K. — 6
Sheridan, J. — 1
Slaven, B. — 1
Sloan, W. — 1
Squires, J. — 1
Stapleton, F. — 20
Sheridan, J.
Strahan, J. — 1
Sullivan, J. — 1

Townsend, A. D. — 1
Treacy, R. — 5
Touhy, L. — 4

Waddock, G. — 3
Walsh, D. — 5
Walsh, M. — 3
Waters, J. — 1
White, J. J. — 2
Whelan, R. — 3

OTHER INTERNATIONAL MATCHES 1990

February
Uganda 4, Mauritius 1
Bermuda 0, USA 1
Egypt 0, South Korea 0

April
Barbados 2, Trinidad & Tobago 0
Bermuda 3, Barbados 0

July
Malawi 2, Tanzania 0
Malawi 1, Tanzania 1
Malawi 0, Tanzania 0

August
Malawi 0, Zaire 0
Tunisia 0, Morocco 0
Zambia 0, Zaire 0
New Zealand 2, China 1
New Zealand 1, China 0

September
Comores 1, Seychelles 2
South Korea 1, Australia 0
Malaysia 0, Yemen 1
South Korea 1, Australia 0
Singapore 3, Malaysia 0
USA 3 Trinidad & Tobago 1
Aruba 1, Netherlands Antilles 3

October
South Korea 1, North Korea 0

November
Trinidad & Tobago 0, USA 0
Tanzania 1, Uganda 1

December
Morocco 0, Senegal 0

CONCACAF GOLD CUP
Final Tournament (*in Los Angeles*)

Group A
Honduras 4, Canada 2

Mexico 4, Jamaica 1
Honduras 5, Jamaica 0
Mexico 3, Canada 1
Canada 3, Jamaica 2
Mexico 1, Honduras 1

Group B
Costa Rica 2, Guatemala 0
USA 2, Trinidad & Tobago 1
Trinidad & Tobago 2, Costa Rica 1
USA 3, Guatemala 0
Guatemala 1, Trinidad & Tobago 0
USA 3, Costa Rica 2

Third place: Mexico 2, Costa Rica 0

Final
USA 0, Honduras 0
    (*USA won 4-3 on penalties*)

African Champions Cup
Final: JS Kabylie (Algeria) 1, 0, Nkana Red Devils (Zambia) 0, 1

African Cup-Winners' Cup
Final: BCC Lions (Nigeria) 3, 1, Club Africain (Tunisia) 1, 1

Africa UDEAC Cup
Final: Congo 2, Cameroon 1

East and Central African Cup
Final: Uganda 2, Sudan 0

Shell Caribbean Cup
Final: Jamaica 2, Trinidad & Tobago 0

World Military Championships
Final: Italy 3, Germany 3
    (*Italy won on penalties*)

Central American Championship
Final: Costa Rica 1, Guatemala 0

8th UEFA UNDER-21 TOURNAMENT 1990–92

Group 1 *(Czechoslovakia, Spain, France, Albania, Iceland)*
Iceland (0) 0, Albania (0) 0 — Kopavoqur, 29 May 1990
Iceland (0) 0, France (0) 1 — Reykjavik, 4 September 1990
Czechoslovakia (5) 7, Iceland (0) 0 — Michalovc, 25 September 1990
Spain (2) 2, Iceland (0) 0 — Puerto Sa, 9 October 1990
France (1) 1, Czechoslovakia (1) 2 — Le Mans, 12 October 1990
Czechoslovakia (3) 3, Spain (0) 1 — Ceske Bud, 13 November 1990
Albania (0) 0, France (0) 0 — Berati, 16 November 1990
Spain (0) 1, Albania (0) 0 — Huelva, 18 December 1990
France (0) 0, Spain (0) 1 — Tours, 19 February 1991
France (0) 3, Albania (0) 0 — 29 March 1991
Albania (1) 1, Czechoslovakia (2) 5 — 30 April 1991
Albania (0) 2, Iceland (0) 1 — 25 May 1991

Group 2 *(Bulgaria, Scotland, Romania, Switzerland)*
Scotland (1) 2, Romania (0) 0 — Edinburgh, 11 September 1990
Switzerland (0) 0, Bulgaria (0) 2 — Yverdon, 11 September 1990
Romania (0) 0, Bulgaria (1) 1 — Ploiesti, 16 October 1990
Scotland (2) 4, Switzerland (1) 2 — Dunfermline, 16 October 1990
Bulgaria (2) 2, Scotland (0) 0 — Sofia, 13 November 1990
Scotland (1) 1, Bulgaria (0) 0 — 26 March 1991
Switzerland (0) 0, Romania (1) 2 — 2 April 1991
Bulgaria (1) 1, Switzerland (0) 0 — 30 April 1991

Group 3 *(Norway, Italy, USSR, Hungary)*
USSR (1) 2, Norway (0) 2 — Moscow, 11 September 1990
Norway (2) 3, Hungary (0) 1 — Kristiansand, 9 October 1990
Italy (0) 1, Hungary (0) 0 — Ferrara, 19 October 1990
Hungary (0) 0, USSR (0) 0 — 18 April 1991
Hungary (0) 0, Italy (0) 1 — 2 May 1991

Group 4 *(Denmark, Austria, Yugoslavia, San Marino, Liechtenstein)*
Leichtenstein (0) 0, Austria (3) 6 — Balzers, 11 September 1990
Austria (6) 10, Liechtenstein (0) 0 — Wien-Neud, 16 October 1990
San Marino (0) 0, Denmark (1) 3 — San Marin, 17 October 1990
Yugoslavia (0) 1, Austria (0) 0 — Maribor, 30 October 1990
Denmark (1) 3, Yugoslavia (0) 0 — Aalborg, 13 November 1990
San Marino (0) 0, Austria (2) 2 — San Marin, 21 November 1990
Yugoslavia (4) 5, San Marino (0) 0 — 13 March 1991
Austria (0) 3, San Marino (0) 0 — Schwechat, 3 April 1991
Denmark (4) 7, San Marino (0) 0 — 17 April 1991
Yugoslavia (0) 2, Denmark (1) 6 — 30 April 1991

Group 5 *(Germany, Luxembourg, Belgium)*
Luxembourg (0) 0, Germany (0) 3 — Lux.-Verl, 30 October 1990
Belgium (0) 2, Luxembourg (0) 0 — Charleroi, 26 February 1991
Germany (1) 3, Belgium (1) 1 — Osnabruck, 30 April 1991

Group 6 *(Portugal, Holland, Finland, Malta)*
Finland (0) 0, Portugal (1) 1 — Lahti, 11 September 1990
Portugal (0) 0, Holland (0) 0 — Porto, 16 October 1990
Malta (1) 1, Holland (2) 4 — Ta'Qali, 18 December 1990
Malta (0) 1, Portugal (1) 3 — Ta'Qali, 8 February 1991
Portugal (2) 2, Malta (0) 0 — Porto, 19 February 1991
Holland (3) 7, Malta (0) 1 — Utrecht, 12 March 1991
Holland (0) 1, Finland (0) 0 — 16 April 1991

Group 7 *(Poland, England, Republic of Ireland, Turkey)*
England (0) 0, Poland (0) 1 — Tottenham, 16 October 1990
Republic of Ireland (1) 3, Turkey (1) 2 — Dublin, 16 October 1990
Republic of Ireland (0) 0, England (1) 3 — Cork, 13 November 1990
Turkey (0) 0, Poland (0) 1 — Istanbul, 13 November 1990
England (1) 3, Republic of Ireland (0) 0 — 26 March 1991
Poland (1) 2, Turkey (0) 0 — 16 April 1991
Republic of Ireland (0) 1, Poland (0) 2 — Dundalk, 30 April 1991
Turkey (1) 2, England (1) 2 — 30 April 1991

Group 8 *(Sweden, Israel, Cyprus, Greece)*
Sweden (2) 5, Greece (0) 0 — Malmo, 31 October 1990
Cyprus (0) 1, Sweden (0) 1 — Paphos, 21 November 1990
Greece (2) 2, Israel (1) 2 — Xanthi, 21 November 1990
Israel (1) 4, Cyprus (0) 0 — Haifa, 20 March 1991
Cyprus (1) 1, Greece (0) 0 — Limassol, 17 April 1991
Sweden (2) 6, Cyprus (0) 0 — Halsingborg, 1 May 1991

7th UEFA UNDER-21 TOURNAMENT 1988–90

Final
First leg
Yugoslavia (1) 2, USSR (2) 4 — Sarajevo, 5 September 1990

Second leg
USSR (1) 3, Yugoslavia (0) 1 — Simferopol, 17 October 1990

8th UEFA UNDER-18 CHAMPIONSHIP 1990-92

Group 1 *(Israel, Greece, Turkey, Switzerland)*
Greece (1) 1, Switzerland (0) 1   Rhodes, 10 October 1990
Israel (2) 2, Switzerland (0) 0   Herzelia, 16 October 1990
Turkey (1) 1, Israel (1) 1   Istanbul, 18 November 1990

Group 2 *(Cyprus, Romania, Hungary, Bulgaria)*
Hungary (0) 1, Romania (0) 0   Debrecen, 26 September 1990
Hungary (0) 0, Cyprus (0) 1   Budapest, 31 October 1990
Cyprus (1) 3, Bulgaria (1) 1   Lymbia, 14 November 1990
Rumonia (0) 3, Cyprus (0) 2   Tirgovist, 5 December 1990

Group 3 *(Portugal, France, Denmark, Luxembourg)*
Denmark (2) 7, Luxembourg (0) 0   Slagelse, 31 October 1990
Portugal (0) 0, France (0) 0   Lisbon, 31 October 1990
France (0) 2, Denmark (0) 0   Istres, 13 November 1990
Luxembourg (0) 0, Portugal (3) 5   Dudelange, 1 December 1990
France (0) 0, Portugal (2) 3   Sedan, 5 December 1990

Group 4 *(Italy, Spain, Malta, FR Germany)*
Italy (2) 9, Malta (0) 0   Siderno, 21 November 1990
Spain (0) 0, Italy (1) 2   Murcia, 20 December 1990
Malta (0) 1, Spain (0) 1   Ta'Qali, 13 February 1991

Group 5 *(England, Belgium, Iceland, Wales)*
Iceland (1) 2, England (1) 3   Varmarvol, 12 September 1990
Belgium (1) 1, Iceland (1) 1   Marche-en, 3 October 1990
England (0) 0, Belgium (0) 0   Sunderland, 16 October 1990

Group 6 *(Poland, Republic of Ireland, Scotland, Northern Ireland)*
Northern Ireland (0) 0, Republic of Ireland (1) 2 Lurgan, 9 October 1990
Poland (0) 1, Scotland (0) 0   Warjaw, 10 October 1990
Republic Ireland (2) 2, Scotland (0) 1   Dublin, 6 November 1990
Poland (1) 3, Northern Ireland (0) 0   Warjaw, 7 November 1990

Group 7 *(Norway, Finland, Holland, Austria)*
Finland (0) 0, Norway (2) 2   Valkeakos, 18 September 1990
Norway (2) 4, Holland (0) 1   Stavanger, 10 October 1990

Group 8 *(Yugoslavia, USSR, Sweden, Czechoslovakia)*
Yugoslavia (2) 3, USSR (1) 2   Bogatic, 20 September 1990
Czechoslovakia (0) 2, Sweden (2) 2   Turnov, 26 September 1990
USSR (2) 3, Czechoslovakia (0) 0   Ternobol, 17 October 1990
Sweden (1) 1, Yugoslavia (0) 1   Kalmar, 18 October 1990

7th UEFA UNDER-18 CHAMPIONSHIP 1988-90

Final tournament (in Hungary)
Quarter-finals

Sweden (0) 0, USSR (2) 3		Debrecen, 24 July 1990
Republic of Ireland (0) 0, Spain (0) 3		Gyula, 24 July 1990
Belgium (1) 1, England (0) 1		Nyiregyha, 24 July 1990
England won on penalties		
Portugal (0) 1, Hungary (1) 1		Bekescsaba, 24 July 1990
Portugal won on penalties		

Matches for 5th/6th place

Republic of Ireland (1) 1, Hungary (0) 0	Szarvas, 26 July 1990
Sweden (2) 6, Belgium (0) 0	Nyiregyha, 26 July 1990

Semi-finals

Spain (1) 1, Portugal (2) 2	Gyula, 26 July 1990
USSR (2) 3, England (1) 1	Debrecen, 26 July 1990

Match for Third place

Spain (1) 1, England (0) 0	Bekescsaba, 29 July 1990

Final

USSR (0) 0, Portugal (0) 0	Bekescsaba, 29 July 1990
USSR won 4-2 on penalties	

UEFA YOUTH TOURNAMENT FINALS 1948–90

Year	Winners		Runners-up		Venue
1948	England	3	Netherlands	2	London
1949	France	4	Netherlands	1	Rotterdam
1950	Austria	3	France	2	Vienna
1951	Yugoslavia	3	Austria	2	Cannes
1952	Spain*	0	Belgium	0	Barcelona
1953	Hungary	2	Yugoslavia	0	Brussels
1954	Spain*	2	West Germany	2	Cologne
1955–56 Played in groups only					
1957	Austria	3	Spain	2	Madrid
1958	Italy	1	England	0	Luxembourg
1959	Bulgaria	1	Italy	0	Sofia
1960	Hungary	2	Romania	1	Vienna
1961	Portugal	4	Poland	0	Lisbon
1962	Romania	4	Yugoslavia	1	Bucharest
1963	England	4	Northern Ireland	0	London
1964	England	4	Spain	0	Amsterdam
1965	East Germany	3	England	2	Essen
1966	Italy†	0	USSR	0	Belgrade
1967	USSR	1	England	0	Istanbul
1968	Czechoslovakia	2	France	1	Cannes
1969	Bulgaria*	1	East Germany	1	Leipzig
1970	East Germany*	1	Netherlands	1	Glasgow
1971	England	3	Portugal	0	Prague
1972	England	2	West Germany	0	Barcelona
1973	England	3	East Germany	2	Florence
1974	Bulgaria	1	Yugoslavia	0	Malmo
1975	England	1	Finland	0	Berne
1976	USSR	1	Hungary	0	Budapest
1977	Belgium	2	Bulgaria	1	Brussels
1978	USSR	3	Yugoslavia	0	Krakow
1979	Yugoslavia	1	Bulgaria	0	Vienna
1980	England	2	Poland	1	Leipzig

UEFA YOUTH CHAMPIONSHIPS

Year	Winners		Runners-up		Venue
1981	West Germany	1	Poland	0	Dusseldorf
1982	Scotland	3	Czechoslovakia	1	Helsinki
1983	France	1	Czechoslovakia	0	London
1984	Hungary**	0	USSR	0	Moscow
1986	East Germany	3	Italy	1	Subotica
1988	USSR	3	Portugal	1	Prague
1990	USSR**	0	Portugal	0	Bekescsaba

*Won on toss of a coin. †Joint holders. ** Won on penalty kicks.

9th UEFA UNDER-16 CHAMPIONSHIP 1991

Group 1: Greece 1, Turkey 1; Turkey 0, Greece 2. Greece qualified.
Group 2: Cyprus 1, Yugoslavia 5; Yugoslavia 1, Cyprus 0. Yugoslavia qualified.
Group 3: Romania 2, Czechoslovakia 0; Czechoslovakia 2, Romania 1. Romania qualified.
Group 4: Malta 1, Spain 1; Spain 5, Malta 0. Spain qualified.
Group 5: Albania 1, Bulgaria 2; Bulgaria 1, Albania 0. Bulgaria qualified.
Group 6: Liechtenstein 1, France 7; France 5, Liechtenstein 0. France qualified.
Group 7: Finland 4, Belgium 1; Belgium 0, Finland 0. Finland qualified.
Group 8: Wales 1, Iceland 0; Iceland 6, Wales 0. Iceland qualified.
Group 9: Sweden 4, Luxembourg 0; Luxembourg 1, Sweden 1. Sweden qualified.
Group 10: West Germany 3, Northern Ireland 0; Northern Ireland 0, West Germany 1. West Germany qualified.
Group 11: Italy 0, Portugal 0; Portugal 0, Italy 0. Portugal qualified.
Group 12: Holland 0, Austria 1; Austria 1, Holland 1. Austria qualified.
Group 13: Poland 4, Scotland 0; Scotland 0, Poland 1. Poland qualified.
Group 14: Norway 1, Denmark 3; Norway 1, Republic of Ireland 1; Denmark 3, Norway 0; Denmark 1, Republic of Ireland 0; Republic of Ireland 2, Denmark 3; Republic of Ireland 1, Norway 0. Denmark qualified.
Group 15: Hungary 1, USSR 1; USSR 2, Hungary 1; USSR 1, Israel 1; Israel 1, Hungary 0; Hungary 0, Israel 1; Israel 0, USSR 1. USSR qualified.

FINAL TOURNAMENT IN SWITZERLAND

GROUP A

Austria (0) 3, West Germany (1) 1		St Gallen, 8 May 1991
Bulgaria (0) 0, Sweden (0) 1		Frauenfeld, 8 May 1991
Bulgaria (0) 1, Austria (0) 2		Wil, 10 May 1991
Sweden (0) 0, West Germany (0) 1		Weinfelden, 10 May 1991
Bulgaria (0) 0, West Germany (2) 5		Kreuzlingen, 12 May 1991
Sweden (0) 1, Austria (0) 0		St Gallen, 12 May 1991

	P	W	D	L	F	A	Pts
West Germany	3	2	0	1	7	3	4
Austria	3	2	0	1	5	3	4
Sweden	3	2	0	1	2	1	4
Bulgaria	3	0	0	3	1	8	0

GROUP B

Greece (1) 1, Poland (0) 0		Lenzburg, 8 May 1991
Portugal (0) 2, Switzerland (0) 0		Muri, 8 May 1991
Portugal (1) 1, Greece (0) 1		Baden, 10 May 1991
Switzerland (0) 1, Poland (0) 1		Zofingen, 10 May 1991
Portugal (1) 1, Poland (0) 0		Wettingen, 12 May 1991
Switzerland (0) 0, Greece (0) 4		Aarau, 12 May 1991

	P	W	D	L	F	A	Pts
Greece	3	2	1	0	6	1	5
Portugal	3	2	1	0	4	1	5
Poland	3	0	1	2	1	3	1
Switzerland	3	0	1	2	1	7	1

GROUP C

France (0) 0, Finland (0) 0		Vevey, 8 May 1991
Romania (0) 1, Denmark (0) 1		Yverdon, 8 May 1991
Finland (1) 2, Denmark (1) 1		Renens, 10 May 1991
France (2) 3, Romania (0) 0		Yverdon, 10 May 1991
Finland (1) 1, Romania (1) 2		Vevey, 12 May 1991
France (1) 4, Denmark (0) 1		Renens, 12 May 1991

	P	W	D	L	F	A	Pts
France	3	2	1	0	7	1	5
Finland	3	1	1	1	3	3	3
Romania	3	1	1	1	3	5	3
Denmark	3	0	1	2	3	7	1

GROUP D

USSR (1) 1, Spain (2) 4		Baar, 8 May 1991
Yugoslavia (1) 1, Iceland (1) 2		Surse, 8 May 1991
Iceland (0) 1, Spain (1) 2		Hochdorf, 10 May 1991
Yugoslavia (0) 1, USSR (0) 3		Kussnacht, 10 May 1991
Iceland (0) 0, USSR (1) 2		Entlebuch, 12 May 1991
Yugoslavia (2) 3, Spain (2) 2		Menzingen, 12 May 1991

	P	W	D	L	F	A	Pts
Spain	3	2	0	1	8	5	4
USSR	3	2	0	1	6	5	4
Yugoslavia	3	1	0	2	5	7	2
Iceland	3	1	0	2	3	5	2

Semi-finals

West Germany (0) 1, France (0) 1 *aet*		Bulle, 15 May 1991
West Germany won on penalties		
Greece (0) 0, Spain (0) 1		Langenthal, 15 May 1991

Third-place match

France (1) 1, Greece (1) 1 *aet*		Berne, 18 May 1991
Greece won on penalties		

Final

West Germany (0) 0, Spain (2) 2		Berne, 18 May 1991

ENGLAND UNDER-21 RESULTS 1976–91

EC UEFA Competition for Under-21 Teams

v ALBANIA

Year	Date		Venue	Eng	Alb
EC1989	Mar	7	Shkroda	2	1
EC1989	April	25	Ipswich	2	0

v BULGARIA

				Eng	Bulg
EC1979	June	5	Pernik	3	1
EC1979	Nov	20	Leicester	5	0
1989	June	5	Toulon	2	3

v CZECHOSLOVAKIA

				Eng	Cz
1990	May	28	Toulon	2	1

v DENMARK

				Eng	Den
EC1978	Sept	19	Hvidovre	2	1
EC1979	Sept	11	Watford	1	0
EC1982	Sept	21	Hvidovre	4	1
EC1983	Sept	20	Norwich	4	1
EC1986	Mar	12	Copenhagen	1	0
EC1986	Mar	26	Manchester	1	1
1988	Sept	13	Watford	0	0

v EAST GERMANY

				Eng	EG
EC1980	April	16	Sheffield	1	2
EC1980	April	23	Jena	0	1

v FINLAND

				Eng	Fin
EC1977	May	26	Helsinki	1	0
EC1977	Oct	12	Hull	8	1
EC1984	Oct	16	Southampton	2	0
EC1985	May	21	Mikkeli	1	3

v FRANCE

				Eng	Fra
EC1984	Feb	28	Sheffield	6	1
EC1984	Mar	28	Rouen	1	0
1987	June	11	Toulon	0	2
EC1988	April	13	Besancon	2	4
EC1988	April	27	Highbury	2	2
1988	June	12	Toulon	2	4
1990	May	23	Toulon	7	3
1991	June	3	Toulon	1	0

v GREECE

				Eng	Gre
EC1982	Nov	16	Piraeus	0	1
EC1983	Mar	29	Portsmouth	2	1
1989	Feb	7	Patras	0	1

v HUNGARY

				Eng	Hun
EC1981	June	5	Keszthely	2	1
EC1981	Nov	17	Nottingham	2	0
EC1983	April	26	Newcastle	1	0
EC1983	Oct	11	Nyiregyhaza	2	0
1990	Sept	11	Southampton	3	1

v ITALY

				Eng	Italy
EC1978	Mar	8	Manchester	2	1
EC1978	April	5	Rome	0	0
EC1984	April	18	Manchester	3	1
EC1984	May	2	Florence	0	1
EC1986	April	9	Pisa	0	2
EC1986	April	23	Swindon	1	1

v ISRAEL

				Eng	Isr
1985	Feb	27	Tel Aviv	2	1

v MEXICO

				Eng	Mex
1988	June	5	Toulon	2	1
1991	May	29	Toulon	6	0

v MOROCCO

				Eng	Mor
1987	June	7	Toulon	2	0
1988	June	9	Toulon	1	0

v NORWAY

				Eng	Nor
EC1977	June	1	Bergen	2	1
EC1977	Sept	6	Brighton	6	0
1980	Sept	9	Southampton	3	0
1981	Sept	8	Drammen	0	0

v POLAND

				Eng	Pol
EC1982	Mar	17	Warsaw	2	1
EC1982	April	7	West Ham	2	2
EC1989	June	2	Plymouth	2	1
EC1989	Oct	10	Jastrzebie	3	1
EC1990	Oct	16	Tottenham	0	1

v PORTUGAL

				Eng	Por
1987	June	13	Toulon	0	0
1990	May	21	Toulon	0	1

v REPUBLIC OF IRELAND

				Eng	Rep Ire
1981	Feb	25	Liverpool	1	0
1985	Mar	25	Portsmouth	3	2
1989	June	9	Toulon	0	0
EC1990	Nov	13	Cork	3	0
EC1991	Mar	26	Brentford	3	0

v ROMANIA

				Eng	Rom
EC1980	Oct	14	Ploesti	0	4
EC1981	April	28	Swindon	3	0
EC1985	April	30	Brasov	0	0
EC1985	Sept	10	Ipswich	3	0

v SENEGAL

				Eng	Sen
1989	June	7	Toulon	6	1
1991	May	27	Toulon	2	1

v SCOTLAND

				Eng	Scot
1977	April	27	Sheffield	1	0
EC1980	Feb	12	Coventry	2	1
EC1980	Mar	4	Aberdeen	0	0
EC1982	April	19	Glasgow	1	0
EC1982	April	28	Manchester	1	1
EC1988	Feb	16	Aberdeen	1	0
EC1988	Mar	22	Nottingham	1	0

v SPAIN

				Eng	Spa
EC1984	May	17	Seville	1	0
EC1984	May	24	Sheffield	2	0
1987	Feb	18	Burgos	2	1

v SWEDEN

				Eng	Swe
1979	June	9	Vasteras	2	1
1986	Sept	9	Ostersund	1	1
EC1988	Oct	18	Coventry	1	1
EC1989	Sept	5	Uppsala	0	1

v SWITZERLAND

				Eng	Swit
EC1980	Nov	18	Ipswich	5	0
EC1981	May	31	Neuenburg	0	0
1988	May	28	Lausanne	1	1

v USA

				Eng	USA
1989	June	11	Toulon	0	2

v TURKEY

				Eng	Tur
EC1984	Nov	13	Bursa	0	0
EC1985	Oct	15	Bristol	3	0
EC1987	April	28	Izmir	0	0
EC1987	Oct	13	Sheffield	1	1
EC1991	April	30	Izmir	2	2

v USSR

				Eng	USSR
1987	June	9	Toulon	0	0
1988	June	7	Toulon	1	0
1990	May	25	Toulon	2	1
1991	May	31	Toulon	2	1

v WALES

				Eng	Wales
1976	Dec	15	Wolverhampton	0	0
1979	Feb	6	Swansea	1	0
1990	Dec	5	Tranmere	0	0

v WEST GERMANY

				Eng	WG
EC1982	Sept	21	Sheffield	3	1
EC1982	Oct	12	Bremen	2	3
1987	Sept	8	Ludenscheid	0	2

v YUGOSLAVIA

				Eng	Yugo
EC1978	April	19	Novi Sad	1	2
EC1978	May	2	Manchester	1	1
EC1986	Nov	11	Peterborough	1	1
EC1987	Nov	10	Zemun	5	1

BRITISH AND IRISH UNDER-21 TEAMS 1990-91

England Under-21 Internationals

11 Sept
England (0) 3 *(Robins, Blake, Johnson)*
Hungary (1) 1 *(Jarsas (pen))*　　　　9534
England: Miller; Charles, Sharpe (Vinnicombe), Warhurst, Lee, Tiler, Ebbrell, Campbell (Robins), Olney, Blake, Wallace (Johnson).

16 Oct
England (0) 0
Poland (0) 1 *(Adamczyk)*　　　　2146
England: Miller; Dodd, Vinnicombe, Warhurst, Lee, Tiler (Sharpe), Ebbrell, Robins, Olney (Ramage), Blake, Wallace.

13 Nov
Republic of Ireland (0) 0
England (1) 3 *(Shearer 2, Olney)*　　　　3000
Republic of Ireland: O'Dowd; Cunningham, O'Donoghue, Scully, McCarthy P, Poutch, Keane, Roche (Arkins), Power, Cousins, Kelly M (Brady K).
England: James; Dodd, Vinnicombe, Lee, Cundy, Tiler, Ebbrell, Blake, Olney, Shearer, Sharpe.

5 Dec
England (0) 0
Wales (0) 0　　　　6288
England: Walker; Warhurst (Charles), Minto, Blackwell, Ord, Ebbrell, Ramage, Shearer, Jemson, McManaman, Blake (Atkinson).
Wales: Roberts; Perry, Coleman, Melville, Law, Symons, Rees, Nogan L, Nogan K (Graham), Speed, Ebdon (Owen).

26 Mar
England (1) 3 *(Wallace, Shearer, Cundy)*
Republic of Ireland (0) 0　　　　9120
England: James; Charles, Vinnicombe, Lee, Cundy, Tiler, Blake, Matthew (Draper), Shearer, Olney, Wallace (Johnson).
Republic of Ireland: Gough; Cunningham, Kenna, Scully, Fitzgerald, McGrath, Keane, Collins (Roach), Power, Arkins, O'Donoghue (McCarthy P).

30 Apr
Turkey (1) 2 *(Cam, Hakam)*
England (1) 2 *(Shearer, Campbell)*　　　　2000
England: James; Dodd, Vinnicombe, Lee, Blackwell, Tiler, Hillier (Stuart), Ebrell, Shearer, Olney (Campbell), Wallace.

27 May
England (0) 2 *(Shearer 2)*
Senegal (1) 1 *(Warhurst (og))*　　　　1000
England: James; Dodd, Vinnicombe, Lee (Blackwell), Warhurst, Tiler, Wallace, Watson (Kitson), Shearer, Williams P, Atkinson.

29 May
England (4) 6 *(Shearer 3 (2 pens), Kitson, Wallace, Matthew)*
Mexico (0) 0　　　　1000
England: James; Dodd, Blackwell, Ord, Vinnicombe, Wallace (Warhurst), Matthew, Williams P, Atkinson, Kitson, Shearer (McManaman).

31 May
England (1) 2 *(Watson, Shearer)*
USSR (1) 1 *(Sharan)*　　　　2000
England: James; Warhurst, Blackwell, Tiler, Ord, Matthew, Lee, Williams P (Atkinson), Wallace, Shearer, Watson (Vinnicombe).

3 June
France (0) 0
England (0) 1 *(Shearer)*　　　　6000
England: James; Dodd, Blackwell, Tiler, Vinnicombe, Matthew, Lee (Warhurst), Atkinson, Kitson, Shearer, Wallace.

Scotland Under 21 Internationals

11 Sept
Scotland (1) 2 *(Jess, Booth)*
Romania (0) 0　　　　1900
Scotland: Watt; Miller, Sharp, Cleland, Sweeney, Fulton (Connelly), McKinnon, Findlay, Jess, Lambert, Dailly (Booth).

16 Oct
Scotland (2) 4 *(Creaney, Findlay 2, Connelly)*
Switzerland (1) 2 *(Walker, Fink)*　　　　5483
Scotland: Watt; Miller, Sharp, Cleland, McLaren (Sweeney), Fulton, Connelly, Findlay, Creaney, Lambert, Jess (Spencer).

13 Nov
Bulgaria (2) 2 *(Dimitrov, Yotov)*
Scotland (0) 0　　　　3000
Scotland: Watt; McNally, Sharp (Rae), Cleland, Sweeney, Fulton, Findlay, Connelly (Booth), Creaney, Lambert, Jess.

26 Mar
Scotland (1) 1 *(Findlay)*
Bulgaria (0) 0　　　　3722
Scotland: Watt; Miller, Sweeney, Wright, McLaren, Lambert (McWhirter), Findlay, Rae, Creaney (O'Neil), Jess, Booth.

28 May
Poland (0) 0
Scotland (0) 1 *(Jess)*
Scotland: Watt; Wright, Sweeney, McLaren, Miller (McKinnon), Findlay, Lambert, Fulton, Booth, Creaney, Jess.

30 May
France (0) 1 *(Loko (pen))*
Scotland (0) 1 *(Rae)*　　　　2000
Scotland: Watt; Wright, McLaren, Reid, Fulton (Rae), Miller, Robertson, Jess, Spencer (Booth), Creaney, Lambert.

Other Under-21 Internationals (Wales and Republic of Ireland

16 Oct
Republic of Ireland (1) 3 *(Cousins 2 (1 pen), Arkins)*
Turkey (1) 2 *(Emin 2)*　　　　3500
Republic of Ireland: O'Dowd; O'Donoghue, Cunningham, McCarthy T, Scully, Keane, Ampadu (Poutch), Brady P, Arkins, Cousins, Kelly M (Power).

30 Apr
Republic of Ireland (0) 1 *(Fitzgerald)*
Poland (1) 2 *(Kowalczyk, Waldoch)*　　　　2000
Republic of Ireland: Gough; McDonald, McCarthy P (McCarthy T), Kenna, Fitzgerald, Keane, McGrath, O'Donoghue, Power, Cousins, Brady K (Arkins).

Continued on Page 876

UNDER-21 APPEARANCES 1976–1991

ENGLAND

Ablett, G. (Liverpool), 1988 v Fr (1)

Adams, A. (Arsenal). 1985 v Ei, Fi; 1986 v D; 1987 v Se, Y (5)

Adams, N. (Everton), 1987 v Se (1)

Allen, C. (QPR), 1980 v EG (sub); (with C Palace), 1981 v N, R (3)

Allen, M. (QPR), 1987 v Se (sub); 1988 v Y (sub) (2)

Allen, P. (West Ham U), 1985 v Ei, R; (with Tottenham H, 1986 v R (3)

Anderson, V. A. (Nottingham F), 1978 v I (1)

Andrews, I. (Leicester C), 1987 v Se (1)

Atkinson, B. (Sunderland), 1991 v W (sub), Sen, M, USSR (sub), F (5)

Bailey, G. R. (Manchester U), 1979 v W, Bul; 1980 v D, S (2), EG; 1982 v N; 1983 v D, Gr; 1984 v H, F (2), I, Sp (14)

Baker, G. E. (Southampton), 1981 v N, R (2)

Barker, S. (Blackburn R), 1985 v Is (sub), Ei, R; 1986 v I (4)

Bannister, G. (Sheffield W), 1982 v Pol (1)

Barnes, J. (Watford), 1983 v D, Gr (2)

Barnes, P. S. (Manchester C), 1977 v W (sub), S, Fi, N; 1978 v N, Fi, I (2), Y (9)

Barrett, E. D. (Oldham Ath), 1990 v P, F, USSR, Cz (4)

Batty, D. (Leeds U), 1988 v Sw (sub); 1989 v Gr (sub), Bul, Sen, Ei, US; 1990 v Pol (7)

Beagrie, P. (Sheffield U), 1988 v WG, T (2)

Beardsmore, R. (Manchester U), 1989 v Gr, Alb (sub), Pol, Bul, USA (5)

Beeston, C (Stoke C), 1988 v USSR (1)

Bertschin, K. E. (Birmingham C), 1977 v S; 1978 v Y (2) (3)

Birtles, G. (Nottingham F), 1980 v Bul, EG (sub) (2)

Blackwell, D. R. (Wimbledon), 1991 v W, T, Sen (sub), M, USSR, F (6)

Blake, M. A. (Aston Villa), 1990 v F (sub), Cz (sub); 1991 v H, Pol, Ei (2), W (7)

Blissett, L. L. (Watford), 1979 v W, Bul (sub), Se; 1980 v D (4)

Bracewell, P. (Stoke C), 1983 v D, Gr (1 + 1 sub), H; 1984 v D, H, F (2), I (2), Sp (2); 1985 v T (13)

Bradshaw, P. W. (Wolverhampton W), 1977 v W, S; 1978 v Fi, Y (4)

Breacker, T. (Luton T), 1986 v I (2) (2)

Brennan, M. (Ipswich T), 1987 v Y, Sp, T, Mor, F (5)

Brightwell, I. (Manchester C), 1989 v D, Alb; 1990 v Se (sub), Pol (4)

Brock, K. (Oxford U), 1984 v I, Sp (2); 1986 v I (4)

Bull, S. G. (Wolverhampton W), 1989 v Alb (2) Pol; 1990 v Se, Pol (5)

Burrows, D. (WBA), 1989 v Se (sub); (with Liverpool), Gr, Alb (2) Pol; 1990 v Se, Pol (7)

Butcher, T. I. (Ipswich T), 1979 v Se; 1980 v D, Bul, S (2), EG (2) (7)

Butters, G. (Tottenham H), 1989 v Bul, Sen (sub), Ei (sub) (3)

Butterworth, I. (Coventry C), 1985 v T, R; (with Nottingham F), 1986 v R, T, D (2), I (2) (8)

Caesar, G. (Arsenal), 1987 v Mor, USSR (sub), F (3)

Callaghan, N. (Watford), 1983 v D, Gr (sub), H (sub); 1984 v D, H, F (2), I, Sp (9)

Campbell, K. J. (Arsenal), 1991 v H, T (sub) (2)

Carr, C. (Fulham), 1985 v Ei (sub) (1)

Carr, F. (Nottingham F), 1987 v Se, Y, Sp (sub), Mor, USSR; 1988 v WG (sub), T, Y, F (9)

Caton, T. (Manchester C), 1982 v N, H (sub), Pol (2), S; 1983 v WG (2), Gr; 1984 v D, H, F (2), I (2) (14)

Chamberlain, M. (Stoke C), 1983 v Gr; 1984 v F (sub), I, Sp (4)

Chapman, L. (Stoke C), 1981 v Ei (1)

Charles, G. A. (Nottingham F), 1991 v H, W (sub), Ei (3)

Chettle, S. (Nottingham F), 1988 v M, USSR, Mor, F; 1989 v D, Se, Gr, Alb (2), Bul; 1990 v Se, Pol (12)

Clough, N. (Nottingham F), 1986 v D (sub); 1987 v Se, Y, T, USSR, F (sub). P; 1988 v WG, T, Y, S (2), M, Mor, F (15)

Coney, D. (Fulham), 1985 v T (sub); 1986 v R; 1988 v T, WG (8)

Connor, T. (Brighton & H A), 1987 v Y (1)

Cooke, R. (Tottenham H), 1986 v D (sub) (1)

Cooper, C. (Middlesbrough), 1988 v F (2), M, USSR, Mor; 1989 v D, Se, Gr (8)

Corrigan, J. T. (Manchester C), 1978 v I (2), Y (3)

Cottee, A. (West Ham U), 1985 v Fi (sub), Is (sub), Ei, R, Fi; 1987 v Sp, P; 1988 v WG (8)

Cowans, G. S. (Aston Villa), 1979 v W, Se; 1980 v Bul, EG; 1981 v R (5)

Cranson, I. (Ipswich T), 1985 v Fi, Is, R; 1986 v R, I (5)

Crooks, G. (Stoke C), 1980 v Bul, S (2), EG (sub) (4)

Crossley, M. G. (Nottingham F), 1990 v P, USSR, Cz (3)

Cundy, J. V. (Chelsea), 1991 v Ei (2) (2)

Cunningham, L. (WBA), 1977 v S, Fi, N (sub); 1978 v N, Fi, I (6)

Curbishley, L. C. (Birmingham C), 1981 v Sw (1)

Daniel, P. W. (Hull C), 1977 v S, Fi, N; 1978 v Fi, I, Y (2) (7)

Davis, P. (Arsenal), 1982 v Pol, S; 1983 v D, Gr (1 + 1 sub), H (sub); 1987 v T; 1988 v WG, T, Y, Fr (11)

D'Avray, M. (Ipswich T), 1984 v I, Sp (sub) (2)

Deehan, J. M. (Aston Villa), 1977 v N; 1978 v N, Fi, I; 1979 v Bul, Se (sub); 1980 v D (7)

Dennis, M. E. (Birmingham C), 1980 v Bul; 1981 v N, R (3)

Dickens, A. (West Ham U), 1985 v Fi (sub) (1)

Dicks, J. (West Ham U), 1988 v Sw (sub), M, Mor, F (4)

Digby, F. (Swindon T), 1987 v Sp (sub), USSR, P; 1988 v T; 1990 v Pol (5)

Dillon, K. P. (Birmingham C), 1981 v R (1)

Dixon, K. (Chelsea), 1985 v Fi (1)

Dobson, A. (Coventry C), 1989 v Bul, Sen, Ei, US (4)

Dodd, J. R. (Southampton), 1991 v Pol, Ei, T, Sen, M, F (6)

Donowa, L. (Norwich C), 1985 v Is, R (sub), Fi (sub) (3)

Dorigo, A. (Aston Villa), 1987 v Se, Sp, T, Mor, USSR, F, P; 1988 v WG, Y, S (2) (11)

Dozzell, J. (Ipswich T), 1987 v Se, Y (sub), Sp, USSR, F, P; 1989 v Se, Gr (sub); 1990 v Se (sub) (9)

Draper, M. A. (Notts Co), 1991 v Ei (sub) (1)

Duxbury, M. (Manchester U), 1981 v Sw (sub), Ei (sub), R (sub), Sw; 1982 v N; 1983 v WG (2) (7)

Dyson, P. I. (Coventy C), 1981 v N, R, Sw, Ei (4)

Ebbrell, J. (Everton), 1989 v Sen, Ei, US (sub); 1990 v P, F, USSR, Cz; 1991 v H, Pol, Ei, W, T (12)

Elliott, P. (Luton T), 1985 v Fi; 1986 v T, D (3)

Fairclough, C. (Nottingham F), 1985 v T, Is, Ei; 1987 v Sp, T; (with Tottenham H), 1988 v Y, F (7)

Fairclough, D. (Liverpool), 1977 v W (1)

Fashanu, J. (Norwich C), 1980 v EG; 1981 v N (sub), R, Sw, Ei (sub), H; (with Nottingham F), 1982 v N, H, Pol. S; 1983 v WG (sub) (11)

Fenwick, T. W. (C Palace), 1981 v N, R, Sw, Ei; (with QPR), R; 1982 v N, H, S (2); 1983 v WG (2) (11)

Fereday, W. (QPR), 1985 v T, Ei (sub), Fi; 1986 v T (sub), I (5)

Williams, S. C. (Southampton), 1977 v S, Fi, N; 1978 v N, I (1 + sub), Y (2); 1979 v D, Bul, Se (sub); 1980 v D, EG (2) (14)

Winterburn, N. (Wimbledon), 1986 v I (1)

Wise, D. (Wimbledon), 1988 v Sw (1)

Woodcock, A. S. (Nottingham F), 1978 v Fi, I (2)

Woods, C. C. E. (Nottingham F), 1979 v W (sub). Se; (with QPR), 1980 v Bul, EG; 1981 v Sw; (with Norwich C), 1984 v D (6)

Wright, M. (Southampton), 1983 v Gr, H; 1984 v D, H (4)

Wright, W. (Everton), 1979 v D, W, Bul; 1980 v D, S (2) (6)

Yates, D. (Notts Co), 1989 v D (sub), Bul, Sen, Ei, US (5)

SCOTLAND

Aitken, R. (Celtic), 1977 v Cz, W, Sw; 1978 v Cz, W; 1979 v P, N (2); 1980 v Bel, E; 1984 v EG, Y (2); 1985 v WG, Ic, Sp (16)

Albiston, A. (Manchester U), 1977 v Cz, W, Sw; 1978 v Sw, Cz (5)

Archdeacon, O. (Celtic), 1987 v WG (sub) (1)

Archibald, S. (Aberdeen), 1980 v B, E (2), WG; (with Tottenham H), 1981 v D (5)

Bannon, E. J. P. (Hearts), 1979 v US, (with Chelsea), P, N (2); (with Dundee U), 1980 v Bel, WG, E (7)

Beaumont, D. (Dundee U), 1985 v Ic (1)

Bell, D. (Aberdeen), 1981 v D; 1984 v Y (2)

Bett, J. (Rangers), 1981 v Se, D; 1982 v Se, D, I, E (2) (7)

Black, E. (Aberdeen), 1983 v EG, Sw (2), Bel; 1985 v Ic, Sp (2), Ic (8)

Blair, A. (Coventry C), 1980 v E; 1981 v Se; (with Aston Villa), 1982 v Se, D, I (5)

Booth, S. (Aberdeen), 1991 v R (sub), Bul (sub + 1) Pol, F (sub) (5)

Bowman, D. (Hearts), 1985 v WG (sub) (1)

Boyd, T. (Motherwell), 1987 v WG, Ei (2), Bel; 1988 v Bel (5)

Brazil, A. (Hibernian), 1978 v W (1)

Brazil, A. (Ipswich T), 1979 v N; 1980 v Bel (2), E (2), WG; 1981 v Se; 1982 v Se (8)

Brough, J. (Hearts), 1981 v D (1)

Burley, G. E. (Ipswich T), 1977 v Cz, W, Sw; 1978 v Sw, Cz (5)

Burns, H. (Rangers), 1985 v Sp, Ic (sub) (2)

Burns, T. (Celtic), 1977 v Cz, W, E; 1978 v Sw; 1982 v E (5)

Campbell, S. (Dundee), 1989 v N (sub), Y, F (3)

Casey, J. (Celtic), 1978 v W (1)

Clark, R. (Aberdeen), 1977 v Cz, W, Sw (3)

Clarke, S. (St Mirren), 1984 v Bel, EG, Y; 1985 v WG, Ic, Sp (2), Ic (8)

Cleland, A. (Dundee U), 1990 v F, N (2); 1991 v R, Sw, Bul (6)

Collins, J. (Hibernian), 1988 v Bel, E; 1989 v N, Y, F; 1990 v Y, F, N (8)

Connolly, P. (Dundee U), 1991 v R (sub), Sw, Bul (3)

Connor, R. (Ayr U), 1981 v Se; 1982 v Se (2)

Cooper, D. (Clydebank), 1977 v Cz, W, Sw, E; (with Rangers), 1978 v Sw, Cz (6)

Cooper, N. (Aberdeen), 1982 v D, E (2); 1983 v Bel, EG, Sw (2); 1984 v Bel, EG, Y; 1985 v Ic, Sp, Ic (13)

Crabbe, S. (Hearts), 1990 v Y (sub), F (2)

Craig, T. (Newcastle U), 1977 v E (1)

Crainie, D. (Celtic), 1983 v Sw (sub) (1)

Creaney, G. (Celtic), 1991 v Sw, Bul (2), Pol, F (5)

Dailly, C. (Dundee U), 1991 v R (1)

Dawson, A. (Rangers), 1979 v P, N (2); 1980 v B (2), E (2) WG (8)

Dodds, D. (Dundee U), 1978 v W (1)

Duffy, J. (Dundee), 1987 v Ei (1)

Durie, G. S. (Chelsea), 1987 v WG, Ei, Bel; 1988 v Bel (4)

Durrant, I. (Rangers), 1987 v WG, Ei, Bel; 1988 v E (4)

Doyle, J. (Partick Th), 1981 v D, I (sub) (2)

Ferguson, D. (Rangers), 1987 v WG, Ei, Bel; 1988 v E; 1990 v Y (5)

Ferguson, J. (Dundee), 1983 v EG (sub), Sw (sub); 1984 v Bel (sub), EG (4)

Ferguson, I. (Clyde), 1987 v WG (sub), Ei (with St Mirren), Ei, Bel; 1988 v Bel; (with Rangers), E (sub) (6)

Ferguson, R. (Hamilton A), 1977 v E (1)

Findlay, W. (Hibernian), 1991 v R, Pol, Bul (2), Pol (5)

Fitzpatrick, A. (St Mirren), 1977 v W (sub), Sw (sub), E; 1978 v Sw, Cz (5)

Fleck, R. (Rangers), 1987 v WG (sub), Ei, Bel; (with Norwich C), 1988 v E (2); 1989 v Y (6)

Fridge, L. (St Mirren), 1989 v F; 1990 v Y (2)

Fulton, M. (St Mirren), 1980 v Bel, WG, E; 1981 v Se, D (Sub) (5)

Fulton, S. (Celtic), 1991 v R, Sw, Bul, Pol, F (5)

Gallacher, K. (Dundee U), 1987 v WG, Ei (2), Bel (sub); 1988 v E (2); 1990 v Y (7)

Galloway, M. (Hearts), 1989 v F; (with Celtic), 1990 v N (2)

Geddes, R. (Dundee), 1982 v Se, D, E (2); 1988 v E (5)

Gillespie, G. (Coventry C), 1979 v US; 1980 v E; 1981 v D; 1982 v Se, D, I (2), E (8)

Glover, L. (Nottingham F), 1988 v Bel (sub); 1989 v N; 1990 v Y (3)

Goram, A. (Oldham Ath), 1987 v Ei (1)

Gough, C. R. (Dundee U), 1983 v EG, Sw, Bel; 1984 v Y (2) (5)

Grant, P. (Celtic), 1985 v WG, Ic, Sp; 1987 v WG, Ei (2), Bel; 1988 v Bel, E (2) (10)

Gray, S. (Aberdeen), 1987 v WG (1)

Gunn, B. (Aberdeen), 1984 v EG, Y (2); 1985 v WG, Ic, Sp (2), Ic; 1990 v F (9)

Hamilton, B. (St Mirren), 1989 v Y, F (sub); 1990 v F, N (4)

Hartford, R. A. (Manchester C), 1977 v Sw (1)

Hegarty, P. (Dundee U), 1987 v WG, Bel; 1988 v E (2); 1990 v F, N (4)

Hewitt, J. (Aberdeen), 1982 v I; 1983 v EG, Sw (2); 1984 v Bel, Y (sub) (6)

Hogg, G. (Manchester U), 1984 v Y; 1985 v WG, Ic, Sp (4)

Hunter, G. (Hibernian), 1987 v Ei (sub); 1988 v Bel, E (3)

Hunter, P. (East Fife), 1989 v N (sub), F (sub); 1990 v F (sub) (3)

Jardine, I. (Kilmarnock), 1979 v US (1)

Jess, E. (Aberdeen), 1990 v F (sub), N (sub); 1991 v R, Sw, Bul (2), Pol, F (8)

Johnston, M. (Partick Th), 1984 v EG (sub); (with Watford), v Y (2) (3)

Kirkwood, D. (Hearts), 1990 v Y (1)

Lambert, P. (St Mirren), 1991 v R, Sw, Bul (2), Pol, F (6)

Leighton, J. (Aberdeen), 1982 v I (1)

Levein, C. (Hearts), 1985 v Sp, Ic (2)

Lindsey, J. (Motherwell), 1979 v US (1)

McAllister, G. (Leicester C), 1990 v N (1)

McAlpine, H. (Dundee U), 1983 v EG, Sw (2), Bel; 1984 v Bel (5)

McAvennie, F. (St Mirren), 1982 v I, E; 1985 v Is, Ei, R (5)

McBride, J. (Everton), 1981 v D (1)

McCall, S. (Bradford C), 1988 v E; (with Everton), 1990 v F (2)

McClair, B. (Celtic), 1984 v Bel (sub), EG, Y (1 + sub); 1985 v WG, Ic, Sp, Ic (8)

McCluskey, G. (Celtic), 1979 v US, P; 1980 v Bel, (2); 1982 v D, I (6)

McCoist, A. (Rangers), 1984 v Bel (1)

continued on page 895

FA SCHOOLS AND YOUTH GAMES
1990–91

Under-15 Nordic Tournament
28 July 1990 (at Maalahti)
England (3) 4 *(Campbell, McDougald 2, Forrester)*
Iceland (0) 0   350
England: Rust (Cousin); Cotterell, Gray, Binks, Blyth, Sharp, Campbell, Hill (Dean), McDougald, Forrester (Darkoh), Turner (Daly)

29 July 1990 (at Kauhajoki)
England (1) 1 *(McDougald)*
Denmark (2) 2   150
England: Cousin; Cotterell, Gray (Campbell St), Hill, Binks, Sharp, Turner, Forrester, McDougald (Darkoh), Dean, Daly.

31 July 1990 (at Pietarsaari)
England (2) 4 *(McDougald 2, Darkoh, Campbell)*
Norway (0) 0   250
England: Rust (Cousin); Cotterell, Campbell St, Binks (Blyth), Sharp, Hill, Campbell S, Dean, McDougald, Darkoh (Forrester), Turner (Daly).

1 Aug 1990 (at Seinajoki)
England (2) 3 *(Turner, Campbell, McDougald)*
Finland (0) 0   450
England: Cousin (Rust); Cotterell, Campbell St, Blyth, Sharp, Hill, Dean (Daly), Campbell S, McDougald, Darkoh (Forrester), Turner.

3 Aug 1990 (at Narpio)
England (0) 1 *(Campbell)*
Sweden (1) 2   387
England: Rust; Cotterell, Campbell St, Blyth, Sharp, Dean, Campbell S, Hill, McDougald, Forrester (Darkoh), Daly (Turner).

European Youth Championship Finals 1988–90
Third Place play-off
29 July 1990 (at Gyula)
England (0) 0
Spain (1) 1
England: Livingstone; Hendon, Wright, Hayward, Tuttle, Awford, Harkness (Houghton), Rouse, Cole, Newhouse, Clark (Small).

Semi-final
26 July 1990 (at Debrecen)
England (1) 1 *(Newhouse)*
USSR (2) 3
England: Walker; Hendon, Wright, Hayward, Tuttle, Awford, Harkness, Rouse, Cole, Newhouse (Clark), Allen.

Quarter-final (at Nyiregyhaza)
24 July 1990
England (0) 1 *(Allen)*
Belgium (1) 1
England won 5–4 on penalties
England: Walker; Kavanagh, Wright, Hayward, Tuttle, Awford, Harkness (Small), Rouse, Cole, Newhouse, (Allen), Houghton.

Youth Championship 1990–92
12 Sept (at Reykjavik)
Iceland (1) 2
England (1) 3 *(Hall, Caskey, Barmby)*
England: Thomson; Marlowe, Hughes, Harriott, Hall, Unsworth, Howe (Myers), Caskey, Barmby, Hodges, Lee.

16 Oct 1990 (at Sunderland)
England (0) 0
Belgium (0) 0   4119
England: Thomson; Marlowe, Hughes, Harriott, Hall, Unsworth, Myers, Caskey, Barmby, Hodges, Lee (Nguyen).

30 Apr 1991 (at Wrexham)
Wales (0) 0
England (0) 1 *(Howe)*   870
England: Sheppard; Watson, Unsworth, Harriott, Basham, Hughes, Caskey, Bart-Williams, Barmby, Myers, Howe.

22 May 1991 (at Yeovil)
England (0) 3 *(Barmby 2 (1 pen), Unsworth)*
Wales (0) 0   6153
England: Sheppard; Watson, Unsworth, Harriott, Jackson, Hughes, Bart-Williams, Caskey, Barmby, Myers, Howe.

Under-16 tour to Italy
9 Oct 1990 (at Chiavari)
England (0) 0
Spain (2) 3
England: Rust; Cotterell, Campbell St, Hill (Daly), Binks, Sharp, Campbell S, Dean, McDougald, Forrester (Darkoh), Turner.

10 Oct 1990 (at Sestri)
England (1) 1 *(Sharp)*
France (0) 3
England: Cousin; Blyth, Gray, Binks, Sharp, Cotterell, Hill (Dean), Daly, McDougald, Forrester (Darkoh), Turner.

11 Oct 1990 (at Chiavari)
England (0) 0
Austria (0) 1
England: Rust (Cousin); Campbell St, Blyth (Campbell S), Binks, Sharp, Cotterell, Hill, Dean (Gray), McDougald, Forrester (Darkoh), Turner.

Under-19 Internationals
25 May 1991 (at Wembley)
England (1) 1 *(Awford)*
Spain (1) 1   44,000
England: Walker (Livingstone); Watson (Kavanagh), Minto, Tuttle, Hendon (Phillips), Awford, Hayward, Rouse, Cole (McManaman), Bart-Williams (Houghton) (Anderton), Harkness (Myers).

6 Feb 1991 (at Oxford)
England (0) 1 *(Harkness (pen))*
Denmark (3) 5   1819
England: Walker; Sutch, Minto, Hendon, Tuttle, Whitworth, Kavanagh, Cole, McManaman (Taylor), Newhouse (Peake), Small (Harkness).

25 Mar 1991 (at Port of Spain)
Trinidad & Tobago (0) 0
England (3) 4 *(Newhouse, Cole 2, Hendon)*
England: Winters; Hendon, Wright (Smith), Minto, Kavanagh (Whitworth), Awford, Hayward, Rouse, Cole (Houghton), Newhouse (Clark), Harkness (Redknapp).

27 Mar 1991 (at Port of Spain)
Mexico (2) 3
England (0) 1 *(Hayward)*
England: Winters (Bayes); Hendon (Smith), Wright, Minto (Houghton), Kavanagh (Whitworth), Awford, Hayward, Rouse, Cole, Newhouse, Harkness (Heaney).

Under-17 XI
13 Nov 1990 (at Lilleshall)
England (3) 4 *(Myers 2, Barmby, Hughes)*
Aston Villa Youth (0) 0
England: Sheppard (Watson D); Watson S, Unsworth (Lee), Hall (Jackson), Harriott, Hughes, Shaw (Marlowe), Caskey, Barmby, Mike, Myers.

World Youth Cup
15 June 1991 (at Faro)
England (0) 0
Spain (0) 1   11,000

England: Walker; Hendon, Wright, Watson (Minto), Tuttle, Awford, Hayward (Houghton), Rouse, Cole, Harkness, Allen.

18 June 1991 (at Faro)
England (1) 3 *(Allen, Awford 2)*
Syria (2) 3   4000
England: Walker: Hendon, Wright, Watson, Tuttle, Awford, Hayward (Houghton), Rouse, Cole, Allen (Kavanagh), Minto.

20 June 1991 (at Faro)
England (0) 0
Uruguay (0) 0   4000
England: Walker; Hendon, Wright, Kavanagh, Houghton, Hayward, Watson, Rouse, Allen (Clark), Mills (Cole), Minto.

6TH WORLD YOUTH CUP (in Portugal)

Group A
Portugal 2, Republic of Ireland 0
Argentina 0, Korea 1
Republic of Ireland 1, Korea 1
Portugal 3, Argentina 0
Republic of Ireland 2, Argentina 2
Portugal 1, Korea 0

Group B
Mexico 3, Sweden 0
Brazil 2, Ivory Coast 1
Brazil 2, Mexico 2
Ivory Coast 1, Sweden 4
Ivory Coast 1, Mexico 1
Brazil 2, Sweden 0

Group C
Trinidad & Tobago 0, Australia 2
Australia 1, USSR 0
Egypt 6, Trinidad & Tobago 0
Egypt 0, USSR 1
Australia 1, Egypt 0
USSR 4, Trinidad & Tobago 0

Group D
England 0, Spain 1
Syria 1, Uruguay 0
Uruguay 0, Spain 6
England 3, Syria 3
Spain 0, Syria 0
England 0, Uruguay 0

Quarter-finals
Portugal 2, Mexico 1 *aet*
Australia 1, Syria 1 *aet*
Australia won 4-3 on penalties

Brazil 5, Korea 1
Spain 1, USSR 3

Semi-finals
Brazil 3, USSR 0
Portugal 1, Australia 0

Third Place
USSR 1, Australia 1 *aet*
USSR won 5-4 on penalties

Final (in Lisbon)
Portugal 0, Brazil 0 *aet* (att: 130,000)
Portugal won 4-2 on penalties

BRITISH AND IRISH UNDER-21 TEAMS 1990-91

Continued from Page 869

30 May
Poland (0) 1
Wales (1) 2 *(Speed 2)*
Wales: Roberts (Walton); Edwards (Searle), Perry, Symons, Blake, Coleman, Rees (Griffiths), Owen (Powell), Pembridge, Speed, Giggs.

England B Internationals
11 Dec
Algeria (0) 0
England (0) 0   1000
England: Martyn (Lukic); Sterland (Thomas M), Burrows, Webb, Mabbutt, Pallister (Ablett), Robson, Clough, Smith (Wallace), Wright I, Thomas G.

5 Feb
Wales (0) 0
England (1) 1 *(Davies)*   4618
Wales: Norman; Blake, Pembridge, Maguire, Perry, Melville, Rees, Morgan (Nogan L), McCarthy, Allen, Hodges.
England: Spink (Beasant); Laws, Burrows, Thomas M, Mabbutt, Barrett, Gordon, Beardsley, Bull, Davis (Thomas G), Walters.

27 Apr
England (0) 1 *(Clough)*
Iceland (0) 0   3814
England: Spink; Joseph, Dorigo, Batty, Mabbutt, Pallister (Curle), White, Clough, Chapman (Deane), Hodge, Barton (Stewart).

20 May
England (1) 2 *(Hirst 2)*
Switzerland (1) 1 *(Chassot)*   10,628
England: Martyn; Joseph (Curle), King, Bishop (Ebbrell), Elliott, Barrett, Gordon (Slater), Hirst, Deane, Palmer, Le Saux.

ENGLAND YOUTH INTERNATIONAL MATCHES 1947–91

*Professionals.   †Abandoned.   UYT *UEFA Youth Tournament.*   WYT *World Youth Tournament.*

v SCOTLAND

			E	S
1947	25 Oct	Doncaster	4	2
1948	30 Oct	Aberdeen	1	3
UYT1949	21 Apr	Utrecht	0	1
1950	4 Feb	Carlisle	7	1
1951	3 Feb	Kilmarnock	6	1
1952	15 Mar	Sunderland	3	1
1953	7 Feb	Glasgow	4	3
1954	6 Feb	Middlesbrough	2	1
1955	5 Mar	Kilmarnock	3	4
1956	3 Mar	Preston	2	2
1957	9 Mar	Aberdeen	3	1
1958	1 Mar	Hull	2	0
1959	28 Feb	Aberdeen	1	1
1960	27 Feb	Newcastle	1	1
1961	25 Feb	Elgin	3	2
1962	24 Feb	Peterborough	4	2
UYT1963	19 Apr	White City	1	0
1963	18 May	Dumfries	3	1
1964	22 Feb	Middlesbrough	1	1
1965	27 Feb	Inverness	1	2
1966	5 Feb	Hereford	5	3
1967	4 Feb	Aberdeen	0	1
UYT1967	1 Mar	Southampton	1	0
UYT1967	15 Mar	Dundee	0	0
1968	3 Feb	Walsall	0	5
1969	1 Feb	Stranraer	1	1
1970	31 Jan	Derby	1	2
1971	30 Jan	Greenock	1	2
1972	30 Jan	Bournemouth	2	0
1973	20 Jan	Kilmarnock	3	2
1974	26 Jan	Brighton	2	2
UYT1981	27 May	Aachen	0	1
UYT1982	23 Feb	Glasgow	0	1
UYT1982	23 Mar	Coventry	2	2
UYT1983	15 May	Birmingham	4	2
U16 1983	5 Oct	Middlesbrough	3	1
U16 1983	19 Oct	Motherwell	4	0
UYT1984	27 Nov	Craven Cottage	1	2
1985	8 Apr	Cannes	1	0
1985	25 Mar	Aberdeen	1	4

v WALES

			E	W
1948	28 Feb	High Wycombe	4	2
UYT1948	15 Apr	Shepherds Bush	4	0
1949	26 Feb	Swansea	0	0
1950	25 Feb	Worcester	1	0
1951	17 Feb	Wrexham	1	1
1952	23 Feb	Plymouth	6	0
1953	21 Feb	Swansea	4	2
1954	20 Feb	Derby	2	1
1955	19 Feb	Milford Haven	7	2
1956	18 Feb	Shrewsbury	5	1
1957	9 Feb	Cardiff	7	1
1958	15 Feb	Reading	8	2
1959	14 Feb	Portmadoc	3	0
1960	19 Mar	Canterbury	1	1
1961	18 Mar	Newtown	4	0
1962	17 Mar	Swindon	4	0
1963	16 Mar	Haverfordwest	1	0
1964	15 Mar	Leeds	2	1
1965	20 Mar	Newport	2	2
1966	19 Mar	Northampton	4	1
1967	18 Mar	Cwmbran	3	3
1968	16 Mar	Watford	2	3
1969	15 Mar	Haverfordwest	3	1
UYT1970	25 Feb	Newport	0	0
UYT1970	18 Mar	Leyton	1	2
1970	20 Apr	Reading	0	0
1971	20 Feb	Aberystwyth	1	2
1972	19 Feb	Swindon	4	0
1973	24 Feb	Portmadoc	4	1
UYT1974	9 Jan	West Bromwich	1	0
1974	2 Mar	Shrewsbury	2	1
UYT1974	13 Mar	Cardiff	0	1
UYT1976	11 Feb	Cardiff	1	0
UYT1976	3 Mar	Maine Road	2	3
UYT1977	9 Mar	West Bromwich	1	0
UYT1977	23 Mar	Cardiff	1	1

v NORTHERN IRELAND

			E	S
1948	15 May	Belfast	2	2
UYT1949	18 Apr	Haarlem	3	3
1949	14 May	Hull	4	2
1950	6 May	Belfast	0	1
1951	5 May	Liverpool	5	2
1952	19 Apr	Belfast	0	2
1953	11 Apr	Wolverhampton	0	0
UYT1954	10 Apr	Bruehl	5	0
1954	8 May	Newtownards	2	2
1955	14 May	Watford	3	0
1956	12 May	Belfast	0	1
1957	11 May	Leyton	6	2
1958	10 May	Bangor	2	4
1959	9 May	Liverpool	5	0
1960	14 May	Portadown	5	2
1961	13 May	Manchester	2	0
1962	12 May	Londonderry	1	2
UYT1963	23 Apr	Wembley	4	0
1963	11 May	Oldham	1	1
1964	25 Jan	Belfast	3	1
1965	22 Jan	Birkenhead	2	3
1966	26 Feb	Belfast	4	0
1967	25 Feb	Stockport	3	0
1968	23 Feb	Belfast	0	2
1969	28 Feb	Birkenhead	0	2
1970	28 Feb	Lurgan	1	3
1971	6 Mar	Blackpool	1	1
1972	11 Mar	Chester	1	1
UYT1972	17 May	Sabadell	4	0
1973	24 Mar	Telford	3	0
1974	19 Apr	Birkenhead	1	2
UYT1975	13 May	Kriens	3	0
UYT1980	16 May	Arnstadt	1	0
UYT1981	11 Feb	Walsall	1	0
UYT1981	11 Mar	Belfast	3	0

v ALGERIA

			E	A
1984	22 Apr	Cannes	3	0

v ARGENTINA

			E	A
*WYT1981	5 Oct	Sydney	1	1

v AUSTRIA

			E	A
UYT1949	19 Apr	Zeist	4	2
UYT1952	17 Apr	Barcelona	5	5
UYT1957	16 Apr	Barcelona	0	3
1958	4 Mar	Highbury	3	2
1958	1 June	Graz	4	3
UYT1960	20 Apr	Vienna	0	1
UYT1964	1 Apr	Rotterdam	2	1
1980	6 Sept	Pazin	0	1
UYT1981	29 May	Bonn	7	0
1981	3 Sept	Umag	3	0
1984	6 Sept	Izola	2	2

v AUSTRALIA

			E	A
*WYT1981	8 Oct	Sydney	1	1

v BELGIUM

			E	B
UYT1948	16 Apr	West Ham	3	1
UYT1951	22 Mar	Cannes	1	1
UYT1953	31 Mar	Brussels	2	0
†1956	7 Nov	Brussels	3	2
1957	13 Nov	Sheffield	2	0
UYT1965	15 Apr	Ludwigshafen	3	0
UYT1969	11 Mar	West Ham	1	0
UYT1969	26 Mar	Waregem	2	0
UYT1972	13 May	Palma	0	0
UYT1973	4 June	Viareggio	0	0
UYT1977	19 May	Lokeren	1	0
1979	17 Jan	Brussels	4	0
1980	8 Sept	Labia	6	1
1983	13 Apr	Birmingham	1	1
1988	20 May	Chatel	0	0
UYT1990	24 July	Nyiregyhaza	1	1
UYT1990	16 Oct	Sunderland	0	0

v BRAZIL

			E	B
1986	29 Mar	Cannes	0	0
1986	13 May	Peking	1	2

<table>

v BULGARIA

			E	B
UYT1956	28 Mar	Salgotarjan	1	2
UYT1960	16 Apr	Graz	0	1
UYT1962	24 Apr	Ploesti	0	0
UYT1968	7 Apr	Nimes	0	0
UYT1979	31 May	Vienna	0	1

v CAMEROON

			E	C
*WYT1981	3 Oct	Sydney	2	0

v CHINA

			E	C
1983	13 Mar	Cannes	5	1
1985	26 Aug	Baku	0	2
1986	5 May	Peking	1	0

v CZECHOSLOVAKIA

			E	C
UYT1955	7 Apr	Lucca	0	1
UYT1966	21 May	Rijeka	2	3
UYT1969	20 May	Leipzig	3	1
UYT1979	24 May	Bischofshofen	3	0
1979	8 Sept	Pula	1	2
1982	11 Apr	Cannes	0	1
UYT1983	20 May	Highbury	1	1
UYT1989	26 Apr	Bystrica	0	1
UYT1989	14 Nov	Portsmouth	1	0
1989	25 Apr	Wembley	1	1

v DENMARK

			E	D
*1955	1 Oct	Plymouth	9	2
1956	20 May	Esbjerg	2	1
UYT1979	31 Oct	Esbjerg	3	1
UYT1980	26 Mar	Coventry	4	0
*1982	15 July	Stjordal	5	2
1983	16 July	Holbeck	0	1
1987	16 Feb	Maine Road	2	1
1990	28 Mar	Wembley	0	0
1991	6 Feb	Oxford	1	5

v EGYPT

			E	Eg
*WYT1981	11 Oct	Sydney	4	2

v FINLAND

			E	F
UYT1975	19 May	Berne	1	1

v FRANCE

			E	F
1957	24 Mar	Fontainebleau	1	0
1958	22 Mar	Eastbourne	0	1
UYT1966	23 May	Rijeka	1	2
UYT1967	11 May	Istanbul	2	0
*1968	25 Jan	Paris	0	1
UYT1978	8 Feb	Selhurst Park	3	1
UYT1978	1 Mar	Paris	0	0
UYT1979	2 June	Vienna	0	0
1982	12 Apr	Cannes	0	1
1983	2 Apr	Cannes	0	2
UI61984	1 Mar	Watford	4	0
UI61984	21 Mar	Bourg en Bresse	1	1
1984	23 Apr	Cannes	1	2
1986	31 Mar	Cannes	1	2
1986	11 May	Peking	1	1
1988	22 May	Monthey	1	2
UYT1988	15 Nov	Bradford	1	1
UYT1989	11 Oct	Martigues	0	0

v EAST GERMANY

			E	EG
UYT1958	7 Apr	Neunkirchen	1	0
1959	8 Mar	Zwickau	3	4
1960	2 Apr	Portsmouth	1	1
UYT1965	25 Apr	Essen	2	3
UYT1969	22 May	Magdeburg	0	4
UYT1973	10 June	Florence	3	2
UYT1984	25 May	Moscow	1	1
1988	21 May	Monthey	1	0

v WEST GERMANY

			E	WG
UYT1953	4 Apr	Boom	3	1
UYT1954	15 Apr	Gelsenkirchen	2	2
UYT1956	1 Apr	Sztalinvaros	2	1
1957	31 Mar	Oberhausen	4	1
1958	12 Mar	Bolton	1	2
1961	12 Mar	Flensburg	0	2
*1962	31 Mar	Northampton	1	0
*1967	14 Feb	Moenchengladbach	1	0
UYT1972	22 May	Barcelona	2	0
1975	25 Jan	Las Palmas	4	2

(v West Germany continued)

1976	14 Nov	Monte Carlo	1	1
UYT1979	28 May	Salzburg	2	0
1979	1 Sept	Pula	1	1
1983	5 Sept	Pazin	2	0

v GREECE

			E	G
UYT1957	18 Apr	Barcelona	2	3
UYT1959	2 Apr	Dimitrovo	4	0
UYT1977	23 May	Beveren	1	1
UI61983	28 July	Puspokladany	1	0
UYT1988	26 Oct	Tranmere	5	0
UYT1989	8 Mar	Xanthi	3	0

v HOLLAND

			E	N
UYT1948	17 Apr	Tottenham	3	2
UYT1951	26 Mar	Cannes	2	1
*1954	21 Nov	Arnhem	2	3
*1955	5 Nov	Norwich	3	1
1957	2 Mar	Brentford	5	5
UYT1957	14 Apr	Barcelona	1	2
1957	2 Oct	Amsterdam	3	1
1961	9 Mar	Utrecht	0	1
*1962	31 Jan	Brighton	4	0
UYT1962	22 Apr	Ploesti	0	3
1963	13 Apr	Wimbledon	5	0
UYT1968	9 Apr	Nimes	1	0
UYT1974	13 Feb	West Bromwich	1	1
UYT1974	27 Feb	The Hague	1	0
UYT1979	23 May	Halle	1	0
1982	9 Apr	Cannes	1	0
1985	7 Apr	Cannes	1	3
1987	1 Aug	Wembley	3	1

v HUNGARY

			E	H
UYT1954	11 Apr	Dusseldorf	1	3
UYT1956	31 Mar	Tatabanya	2	4
*1956	23 Oct	Tottenham	2	1
*1956	25 Oct	Sunderland	2	1
UYT1965	21 Apr	Wuppertal	5	0
UYT1975	16 May	Olten	3	1
UYT1977	10 Oct	Las Palmas	3	0
1979	5 Sept	Pula	2	0
1980	11 Sept	Pula	1	2
1981	7 Sept	Porec	4	0
UI61983	29 July	Debrecen	1	2
1983	3 Sept	Umag	3	2
1986	30 Mar	Cannes	2	0

v ICELAND

			E	I
UYT1973	31 May	Viareggio	2	0
UYT1977	21 May	Turnhout	0	0
UI61983	17 Sept	Reykjavik	2	1
UI61983	19 Sept	Blackburn	4	0
1983	12 Oct	Reykjavik	3	0
1983	1 Nov	Selhurst Park	3	0
UYT1984	16 Oct	Maine Road	5	3
1985	11 Sept	Reykjavik	5	0
UYT1990	12 Sept	Reykjavik	3	2

v REPUBLIC OF IRELAND

			E	RI
UYT1953	5 Apr	Leuven	2	0
UYT1964	30 Mar	Middleburg	6	0
UYT1968	7 Feb	Dublin	0	0
UYT1968	28 Feb	Portsmouth	4	1
UYT1970	14 Jan	Dublin	4	1
UYT1970	4 Feb	Luton	10	0
UYT1975	9 May	Brunnen	1	0
UYT1985	26 Feb	Dublin	1	0
1986	25 Feb	Leeds	2	0
1987	17 Feb	Stoke	2	0
1988	20 Sept	Dublin	2	0

v ISRAEL

			E	I
*1962	20 May	Tel Aviv	3	1
*1962	22 May	Haifa	1	2

v ITALY

			E	I
UYT1958	13 Apr	Luxembourg	0	1
UYT1959	25 Mar	Sofia	0	3
UYT1961	4 Apr	Braga	2	3
UYT1965	23 Apr	Marl-Huels	3	1
UYT1966	25 May	Rijeka	1	1
UYT1967	5 May	Izmir	1	0
1973	14 Feb	Cava dei Tirreni	0	1
1973	14 Mar	Highbury	1	0
</table>

			E	
UYT1973	6 June	Viareggio	1	0
1978	19 Nov	Monte Carlo	1	2
UYT1979	28 Feb	Rome	1	0
UYT1979	4 Apr	Villa Park	2	0
UYT1983	22 May	Watford	1	1
1983	20 Apr	Cannes	1	0
1985	5 Apr	Cannes	2	2

v LUXEMBOURG

			E	L
UYT1950	25 May	Vienna	1	2
UYT1954	17 Apr	Bad Neuenahr	0	2
1957	2 Feb	West Ham	7	1
1957	17 Nov	Luxembourg	3	0
UYT1958	9 Apr	Esch sur Alzette	5	0
UYT1984	29 May	Moscow	2	0

v MALTA

			E	M
UYT1969	18 May	Wolfen	6	0
UYT1979	26 May	Salzburg	3	0

v MEXICO

			E	M
1983	18 Apr	Cannes	4	0
1985	29 Aug	Baku	0	1
1991	27 Mar	Port of Spain	1	3

v NORWAY

			E	N
*1982	13 July	Levanger	1	4
1983	14 July	Korsor	1	0

v PARAGUAY

			E	P
1985	24 Aug	Baku	2	2

v POLAND

			E	P
UYT1960	18 Apr	Graz	4	2
UYT1964	26 Mar	Breda	1	1
UYT1971	26 May	Presov	0	0
UYT1972	20 May	Valencia	1	0
1975	21 Jan	Las Palmas	1	1
UYT1978	9 May	Chorzow	0	2
1979	3 Sept	Porac	0	1
UYT1980	25 May	Leipzig	2	1
*1982	17 July	Steinkver	3	2
1983	12 July	Slagelse	1	0
1990	15 May	Wembley	3	0

v PORTUGAL

			E	P
UYT1954	18 Apr	Bonn	0	2
UYT1961	2 Apr	Lisbon	0	4
UYT1964	3 Apr	The Hague	4	0
UYT1971	30 May	Prague	3	0
1978	13 Nov	Monte Carlo	2	0
UYT1980	18 May	Rosslau	1	1
1982	7 Apr	Cannes	3	0

v QATAR

			E	Q
*WYT1981	14 Oct	Sydney	1	2
1983	4 Apr	Cannes	1	1

v ROMANIA

			E	R
1957	15 Oct	Tottenham	4	2
UYT1958	11 Apr	Luxembourg	1	0
UYT1959	31 Mar	Pazardjic	1	2
UYT1963	15 Apr	Highbury	3	0
*WYT1981	17 Oct	Adelaide	0	1

v SAAR

			E	S
UYT1954	13 Apr	Dortmund	1	1
UYT1955	9 Apr	Prato	3	1

v SPAIN

			E	S
UYT1952	15 Apr	Barcelona	1	4
1957	26 Sept	Birmingham	4	4
UYT1958	5 Apr	Saarbrucken	2	2
*1958	8 Oct	Madrid	4	2
UYT1961	30 Mar	Lisbon	0	0
*1964	27 Feb	Murcia	2	1
UYT1964	5 Apr	Amsterdam	4	0
UYT1965	17 Apr	Heilbronn	0	0
*1966	30 Mar	Swindon	3	0
UYT1967	7 May	Manisa	2	1
*1971	31 Mar	Pamplona	2	3
*1971	20 Apr	Luton	1	1
1972	9 Feb	Alicante	0	0
1972	15 Mar	Sheffield	4	1
UYT1975	25 Feb	Bristol	1	1
UYT1975	18 Mar	Madrid	1	0
1976	12 Nov	Monte Carlo	3	0

			E	
UYT1978	7 May	Bukowno	1	0
1978	17 Nov	Monte Carlo	1	1
UYT1981	25 May	Siegen	1	2
UYT1983	13 May	Stoke	1	0
UYT1990	29 July	Gyula	0	1
1991	25 May	Wembley	1	1
WYT1991	15 June	Faro	0	1

v SWEDEN

			E	S
UYT1971	24 May	Poprad	1	0
1981	5 Sept	Pazin	3	2
1984	10 Sept	Rovinj	1	1
1986	10 Nov	West Bromwich	3	3

v SWITZERLAND

			E	S
UYT1950	26 May	Stockerau	2	1
UYT1951	27 Mar	Nice	3	1
UYT1952	13 Apr	Barcelona	4	0
UYT1955	11 Apr	Florence	0	0
1956	11 Mar	Schaffhausen	2	0
1956	13 Oct	Brighton	2	2
1958	26 May	Zurich	3	0
*1960	8 Oct	Leyton	4	3
*†1962	22 Nov	Coventry	1	0
*1963	21 Mar	Bienne	7	1
UYT1973	2 June	Forte dei Marmi	2	0
UYT1975	11 May	Buochs	4	0
1980	4 Sept	Rovini	3	0
*1982	6 Sept	Porec	2	0
UI61983	26 July	Hajduboszormeny	4	0
1983	1 Sept	Porec	4	2
1988	19 May	Sion	2	0

v SYRIA

			E	S
WYT1991	18 June	Faro	3	3

v THAILAND

			E	T
1986	7 May	Peking	1	2

v TRINIDAD & TOBAGO

			E	T
1991	25 Mar	Port of Spain	4	0

v TURKEY

			E	T
UYT1959	29 May	Dimitrovo	1	1
UYT1978	5 May	Wodzislaw	1	1

v URUGUAY

			E	U
1977	9 Oct	Las Palmas	1	1
WYT1991	20 June	Faro	0	0

v USSR

			E	U
UYT1963	17 Apr	Tottenham	2	0
UYT1967	13 May	Istanbul	0	1
UYT1968	11 Apr	Nimes	1	1
UYT1971	28 May	Prague	1	1
1978	10 Oct	Las Palmas	1	0
*1982	4 Sept	Umag	1	0
1983	29 Mar	Cannes	0	0
UYT1983	17 May	Aston Villa	0	2
UI61984	3 May	Ludwigsburg	0	2
UYT1984	27 May	Moscow	1	1
1984	8 Sept	Porec	1	0
1985	3 Apr	Cannes	2	1
UYT1990	26 July	Debrecen	1	3

v WALES

			E	W
WYT1991	30 Apr	Wrexham	1	0
UYT1991	22 May	Yeovil	3	0

v YUGOSLAVIA

			E	Y
UYT1953	2 Apr	Liège	1	1
1958	4 Feb	Chelsea	2	2
UYT1962	20 Apr	Ploesti	0	5
UYT1967	9 May	Izmir	1	1
UYT1971	22 May	Bardejor	1	0
UYT1972	18 May	Barcelona	1	0
1976	16 Nov	Monte Carlo	0	3
1978	15 Nov	Monte Carlo	1	1
UYT1980	20 May	Altenburg	2	0
1981	10 Sept	Pula	5	0
*1982	9 Sept	Pula	1	0
UI61983	25 July	Debrecen	4	4
**1983	8 Sept	Pula	2	2
UI61984	5 May	Boblingen	1	0
1984	12 Sept	Buje	1	4

SCHOOLS FOOTBALL 1990–91

ESFA INTER-ASSOCIATION TROPHY COMPETITION 1990–91

Fourth Round

Vale of White Horse v Luton	1-2
Salisbury v Aldershot	2-3
Sefton v Hull	3-2
Leeds v Stafford	4-0
Brierley Hill/Dudley v Wigan	2-4
Sunderland v South Notts	1-0
Kirby/Knowsley v Wirral	0-0, 2-1
Newcastle v Derby	1-1, 1-1, 1-1, 1-4
Barking v Torbay	5-0
South London v Plymouth	5-1
North Kent v Exeter	2-2, 1-3
Havering v South East Sussex	1-0
Langbaurgh v Barnsley	0-3
South Cheshire v Trafford	6-2
Islington & Camden v Mansfield	7-1
Nottingham v Southampton	1-1, 2-0

Fifth Round

Luton v Aldershot	3-3, 2-0
Sefton v Leeds	2-1

Wigan v Sunderland	0-1
Kirby/Knowsley v Derby	0-1
Barking v South London	3-2
Exeter v Havering	2-1
Barnsley v South Cheshire	2-0
Islington & Camden v Nottingham	3-1

Sixth Round

Luton v Sefton	0-4
Sunderland v Derby	2-0
Barking v Exeter	0-1
Barnsley v Islington	3-1

Semi-finals

Sefton v Sunderland	1-1, 2-1
Exeter v Barnsley	1-2

Final

Sefton v Barnsley	0-3, 1-0

ESFA DIAMIK U.16 1990–91

Second Round

Merseyside A v West Midlands A	4-1
Shropshire v West Midlands B	0-1
West Yorkshire A v Lincolnshire	3-2
Derbyshire v South Yorkshire B	1-6
Humberside B v Durham A	1-1, 0-2
Durham B v Cleveland B	2-1
Lancashire A v Cheshire B	4-1
Merseyside B v Lancashire B	1-1, 0-1
Cambridgeshire A v Suffolk	3-1
Kent A v Hertfordshire	1-0
Kent B v Hampshire A	3-1
Surrey v Wiltshire	5-1
Northants v Cambridgeshire B	3-1
Buckinghamshire v Middlesex B	0-1
Gloucestershire v Devon A	2-1
Dorset v Devon B	4-2

Third Round

Merseyside A v West Midlands B	3-0
West Yorkshire A v South Yorkshire B	2-3
Durham A v Durham B	3-6

Lancashire A v Lancashire B	0-4
Cambridgeshire A v Kent A	0-5
Kent B v Surrey	4-3
Northants v Middlesex B	3-2
Gloucestershire v Dorset	1-3

Fourth Round

Merseyside A v South Yorkshire B	5-3
Durham B v Lancashire B	2-1
Kent A v Kent B	5-1
Northants v Dorset	4-3

Semi-finals

Merseyside A (De La Salle School Liverpool) v Durham B (Hewarth Grange, Gateshead)	3-0
Kent A (Erith School) v Northants (Kingsthorpe Upper School, Northampton)	2-2, 1-2

Final

Merseyside A v Northants	2-1

ESFA BARCLAYS BANK COMPETITION 1990–91

Second Round

Somerset v Devon	2-1
Dorset v Avon	2-1
Gloucestershire v Middlesex A	0-1
Bedfordshire v Essex A	3-1
Inner London A v Kent A	3-1
Sussex v Hampshire B	0-1
Cambridgeshire v Suffolk A	4-1
Essex B v Inner London B	1-2
Greater Manchester A v Lancashire	4-1
Greater Manchester B v Merseyside B	4-0
Northumberland A v Cleveland	1-2
Northumberland B v North Yorkshire A	3-1
West Midlands A v Derbyshire	4-1
West Midlands B v Hereford & Worcestershire	1-7
South Yorkshire A v Humberside A	4-1
Humberside B v Nottinghamshire	2-1

Third Round

Somerset v Dorset	9-1
Middlesex A v Bedfordshire	2-3
Inner London A v Hampshire B	0-1

Cambridgeshire v Inner London B	1-0
Greater Manchester A v Greater Manchester B	0-2
Cleveland v Northumberland B	1-0
West Midlands A v Hereford & Worcestershire	3-2
South Yorkshire A v Humberside B	4-1

Quarter-finals

Somerset v Bedfordshire	7-0
Hampshire B v Cambridgeshire	3-1
Greater Manchester B v Cleveland	3-2
West Midlands A v South Yorkshire A	3-4

Semi-finals

Merseyside A (De La Salle School Liverpool) v Durham B (Hewarth Grange, Gateshead)	3-0
Kent A (Erith School) v Northants (Kingsthorpe Upper School, Northampton)	2-2, 1-2

Final

Somerset v Greater Manchester B	2-1

ESFA ADIDAS U.19 INTER-COUNTY COMPETITION 1990–91

Round 1:
Somerset (Reg. V) v Essex (Reg. IV)   0-3

Round 2:
Cheshire (Reg. II) v Essex (Reg. IV)   1-1, 1-2
Lincolnshire (Reg. III) v
   Northumberland (Reg. I)   1-2

Final:
Northumberland (Reg. I) v Essex (Reg. IV)   1-1
*(at St. James' Park, Newcastle United FC
on Saturday, 11 May 1991)*

Joint Winners:
Northumberland CSFA and Essex CSFA

CENTENARY SHIELD 1990–91 (Under 18)

England 2, Wales 2 – 16 March, Gloucester
England 1, Switzerland 1 – 19 March, Norwich
Wales 1, Switzerland 3 – 21 March, Caernarfon

	P	W	D	L	F	A	Pts
Switzerland	2	1	1	0	4	2	3
England	2	0	2	0	3	3	2
Wales	2	0	1	1	3	5	1

ESFA INTER-COUNTY COMPETITION HONOURS LIST

	Winners	*Runners-up*
1978	Devon and South Yorkshire	Joint Holders
1979	Berkshire	Essex
1980	Berkshire	Durham
1981	Merseyside	Middlesex
1982	Humberside	Merseyside
1983	Greater Manchester	Humberside
1984	Hampshire	Durham
1985	Middlesex	Hampshire
1986	Merseyside	Bedfordshire
1987	Northumberland	Hertfordshire
1988	Northumberland	Avon
1989	West Midlands	Lincolnshire
1990	Greater Manchester	Northumberland
1991	Northumberland and Essex	Joint Holders

VICTORY SHIELD 1990–91 (Under-15)

Northern Ireland 1, England 3 – 23 February, Bangor
Scotland 2, Northern Ireland 0 – 2 March, Glasgow
England 2, Scotland 1 – 9 March, Wembley
Northern Ireland 1, Wales 4 – 14 March, Ballinam'd
Scotland 2, Wales 0 – 20 April, Shotts

Wales 1, England 0 – 3 May, Newport

	P	W	D	L	F	A	Pts
England	3	2	0	1	5	3	4
Scotland	3	2	0	1	5	2	4
Wales	3	2	0	1	5	3	4
Northern Ireland	3	0	0	3	2	9	0

ENGLAND'S INTERNATIONAL PROGRAMME 1991

Under-15
Northern Ireland 1, England 3 *(Gallen 2, Murray)* – 23
   February, Bangor
England 2 *(Murray, Irving)*, Scotland 1 – 9 March,
   Wembley
England 2 *(Gallen 2)*, Switzerland 0 – 27 March,
   Chesterfield
Wales 1, England 0 – 3 May, Newport
Belgium 1, England 5 *(Gallen 2, Johnson, Irving, Vaughan)*
   – 22 May, Waregem

Holland 1, England 1 *(Irving)* – 25 May, Utrecht
England 1 *(Gallen)*, Germany 3 – 8 June, Wembley
England 2 *(Gallen 2)*, Germany 2 – 10 June, Bradford

Under-18
Holland 2, England 0 – 5 March, Gouda
England 2 *(Robinson, Holland)*, Wales 2 – 16 March,
   Gloucester
England 1 *(Hughes)*, Switzerland 1 — 19 March, Norwich
Eire 0, England 1 *(Price)* – 12 April, Dublin

OLYMPIC FOOTBALL

Previous medallists

1896 Athens*	1 Denmark	1928 Amsterdam	1 Uruguay	1964 Tokyo	1 Hungary	
	2 Greece		2 Argentina		2 Czechoslovakia	
1990 Paris*	1 Great Britain		3 Italy		3 East Germany	
	2 France	1932 Los Angeles	no tournament	1968 Mexico City	1 Hungary	
1904 St Louis**	1 Canada	1936 Berlin	1 Italy		2 Bulgaria	
	2 USA		2 Austria		3 Japan	
1908 London	1 Great Britain		3 Norway	1972 Munich	1 Poland	
	2 Denmark	1948 London	1 Sweden		2 Hungary	
	3 Holland		2 Yugoslavia		3 E Germany/USSR	
1912 Stockholm	1 England		3 Denmark	1976 Montreal	1 East Germany	
	2 Denmark	1952 Helsinki	1 Hungary		2 Poland	
	3 Holland		2 Yugoslavia		3 USSR	
1920 Antwerp	1 Belgium		3 Sweden	1980 Moscow	1 Czechoslovakia	
	2 Spain	1956 Melbourne	1 USSR		2 East Germany	
	3 Holland		2 Yugoslavia		3 USSR	
1924 Paris	1 Uruguay		3 Bulgaria	1984 Los Angeles	1 France	
	2 Switzerland	1960 Rome	1 Yugoslavia		2 Brazil	
	3 Sweden		2 Denmark		3 Yugoslavia	
			3 Hungary	1988 Seoul	1 USSR	
					2 Brazil	
					3 West Germany	

* No official tournament
** No official tournament but gold medal later awarded by IOC

1992 Olympics (in Spain)

1992 OLYMPICS in Spain

Qualifying tournament (European zone as Under-21 European Championship)

Concacaf

Group: Caribbean Zone, First Round

Puerto Rico 0, Jamaica 3
Jamaica 2, Puerto Rico 0
Haiti 1, Cuba 1
Cuba 2, Haiti 2
Aruba 3, Santa Lucia 3

Santa Lucia 9 Aruba 0
Antigua 0, Barbados 0
Barbados 5, Antigua 0
Netherlands Antilles 0, Surinam 1
Surinam 0, Netherlands Antilles 0

Second Round

Barbados 0, Surinam 0
Surinam 2, Barbados 1
Deciding Match: Trinidad & Tobago 2, Jamaica 1 (*in Puerto Rico*)
St Lucia 1, Haiti 1

Trinidad & Tobago 1, Jamaica 0
Jamaica 1, Trinidad & Tobago 0

Haiti 2, St Lucia 1

Group: Central Zone

Guatemala 2, Honduras 2
Honduras 2, Guatemala 0
Panama v Costa Rica (suspended for all FIFA competitions with age limit)

Belize 0, El Salvador 2
El Salvador 3, Belize 0

Africa
First Round

Mauritius 1, Somalia 0
Somalia 2, Mauritius 1
Mozambique 0, Swaziland 0
Swaziland 0, Mozambique 1
Ethiopia v Libya (withdrew)
Botswana 0, Gabon 0

Gabon 2, Botswana 1
Senegal v Burkino Faso (withdrew)
Sierra Leone v Mali (withdrew)
Mauritania v Gambia (withdrew)
Congo , Togo
Togo , Congo

Asia
First Round First Leg (*in Seoul*)

South Korea 10, Philippines 0
Bangladesh 2, Thailand 3
Malaysia v Philippines 0
Bangladesh 0, South Korea 6
Bangladesh 0, Malaysia 1

Thailand 1, South Korea 2
Thailand 4, Malaysia 1
Philippines 0, Bangladesh 8
Philippines 1, Thailand 7
South Korea 0, Malaysia 0

Oceania
First Round

Australia 4, Papua New Guinea 0
Australia 2, New Zealand 0

Australia 7, Fiji 0

EUROPEAN
CLUB
FOOTBALL

EUROPEAN CHAMPION CLUBS CUP

EUROPEAN CUP-WINNERS' CUP

FAIRS CUP AND UEFA CUP

BRITISH AND IRISH CLUBS IN EUROPE

WORLD CLUB CHAMPIONSHIP

EUROPEAN SUPER CUP

EUROPEAN CUP

EUROPEAN CUP FINALS 1956–90

Year	Winners		Runners-up		Venue	Attendance	Referee
1956	Real Madrid	4	Reims	3	Paris	38,000	Ellis (E)
1957	Real Madrid	2	Fiorentina	0	Madrid	124,000	Horn (Ho)
1958	Real Madrid	3	AC Milan	2 *(aet)*	Brussels	67,000	Alsteen (Bel)
1959	Real Madrid	2	Reims	0	Stuttgart	80,000	Dutsch (WG)
1960	Real Madrid	7	Eintracht Frankfurt	3	Glasgow	135,000	Mowat (S)
1961	Benfica	3	Barcelona	2	Berne	28,000	Dienst (Sw)
1962	Benfica	5	Real Madrid	3	Amsterdam	65,000	Horn (Ho)
1963	AC Milan	2	Benfica	1	Wembley	45,000	Holland (E)
1964	Internazionale	3	Real Madrid	1	Vienna	74,000	Stoll (A)
1965	Internazionale	1	Benfica	0	Milan	80,000	Dienst (Sw)
1966	Real Madrid	2	Partizan Belgrade	1	Brussels	55,000	Kreitlein (WG)
1967	Celtic	2	Internazionale	1	Lisbon	56,000	Tschenscher (WG)
1968	Manchester U	4	Benfica	1 *(aet)*	Wembley	100,000	Lo Bello (I)
1969	AC Milan	4	Ajax	1	Madrid	50,000	Ortiz (Sp)
1970	Feyenoord	2	Celtic	1 *(aet)*	Milan	50,000	Lo Bello (I)
1971	Ajax	2	Panathinaikos	0	Wembley	90,000	Taylor (E)
1972	Ajax	2	Internazionale	0	Rotterdam	67,000	Helies (F)
1973	Ajax	1	Juventus	0	Belgrade	93,500	Guglovic (Y)
1974	Bayern Munich	1	Atletico Madrid	1	Brussels	65,000	Loraux (Bel)
Replay	Bayern Munich	4	Atletico Madrid	0	Brussels	65,000	Delcourt (Bel)
1975	Bayern Munich	2	Leeds U	0	Paris	50,000	Kitabdjian (F)
1976	Bayern Munich	1	St Etienne	0	Glasgow	54,864	Palotai (H)
1977	Liverpool	3	Moenchengladbach	1	Rome	57,000	Wurtz (F)
1978	Liverpool	1	FC Brugge	0	Wembley	92,000	Corver (Ho)
1979	Nottingham F	1	Malmo	0	Munich	57,500	Linemayr (A)
1980	Nottingham F	1	Hamburg	0	Madrid	50,000	Garrido (P)
1981	Liverpool	1	Real Madrid	0	Paris	48,360	Palotai (H)
1982	Aston Villa	1	Bayern Munich	0	Rotterdam	46,000	Konrath (F)
1983	Hamburg	1	Juventus	0	Athens	75,000	Rainea (R)
1984	Liverpool	1	Roma	1	Rome	69,693	Fredriksson (Se)
	(aet; Liverpool won 4–2 on penalties)						
1985	Juventus	1	Liverpool	0	Brussels	58,000	Daina (Sw)
1986	Steaua Bucharest	0	Barcelona	0	Seville	70,000	Vautrot (F)
	(aet; Steaua won 2–0 on penalties)						
1987	Porto	2	Bayern Munich	1	Vienna	59,000	Ponnet (Bel)
1988	PSV Eindhoven	0	Benfica	0	Stuttgart	70,000	Agnolin (I)
	(aet; PSV won 6–5 on penalties)						
1989	AC Milan	4	Steaua Bucharest	0	Barcelona	97,000	Tritschler (WG)
1990	AC Milan	1	Benfica	0	Vienna	57,500	Kohl (A)

Marseille defender Manuel Amoros, seen here avoiding the tackle of the striped-shirted Red Star Belgrade forward Sinisa Mihajlovic, had the misfortune to miss from the penalty spot in the disappointing 1991 final. (Allsport)

EUROPEAN CUP 1990–91

First Round, First Leg

Apoel (1) 2 (*Gogic 4, Pantziaras 77*), Bayern Munich (0) 3 (*Reuter 70, McInally 86, Strunz 88*) 11,000
Akureyri (1) 1 (*Bragason 12*), CSKA Sofia (0) 0 1208
Dinamo Bucharest (3) 4 (*Dobos 3, Damaschin 20, Mateut 40, Cheregi 82*), St Patrick's Athletic (0) 0 13,000
Lech Poznan (2) 3 (*Jakolcewicz 1, 19, Rzepka 61*), Panathinaikos (0) 0 13,063
Lillestrom (0) 1 (*Halle 78*) FC Brugge (1) 1 (*Staelens 2*) 1939
Malmo (1) 3 (*Lindmann 29, Sundstrom 58, Cetin Recep og 62*), Besiktas (0) 2 (*Ucar 52, 60*) 5580
Marseille (1) 5 (*Papin 44 pen, 69, 75, Cantona 72, Vercruysse 89*), Dinamo Tirana (0) 1 (*Tahiri 88 pen*) 20,000
Napoli (0) 3 (*Baroni 35, Maradona 43, 77*), Ujpest Dozsa (0) 0 60,000
Odense (1) 1 (*Pedersen 22*), Real Madrid (2) 4 (*Aldana 18, Sanchez 27, Villaroya 83, Maqueda 88*) 8200
Porto (3) 5 (*Geraldao 7, Paille 16, 75, Kostadinov 32, Branco 48*), Portadown (0) 0 5000 (in Setubal)
Red Star Belgrade (1) 1 (*Binic 44*), Grasshoppers (1) 1 (*Koezle 14*) 50,000
Sparta Prague (0) 0, Spartak Moscow (1) 2 (*Shalimov 25, Shmarov 58*) 7000
Tirol (3) 5 (*Pacult 41, 58, 80, Gorosito 29, Prudio 35*), Kuusysi (0) 0 7250
Union Luxembourg (0) 0, Dynamo Dresden (0) 500
Valetta (0) 0, Rangers (1) 4 (*McCoist 16 pen, Hateley 67, Johnston 75, 79*) 8000
AC Milan *bye*

First Round, Second Leg

Bayern Munich (0) 4 (*Augenthaler 48, Mihajlovic 63, 88, 89*), Apoel (0) 0 8000
Besiktas (2) 2 (*Ali 30, Feyyaz 43*), Malmo (0) 2 (*Ekheim 53, Skammelsrup 63*) 40,000
FC Brugge (1) 2 (*Booy 2, Farina 85*), Lillestrom (0) 0 14,000
CSKA Sofia (1) 3 (*Marashliev 19, 80, Georgiev 48*), Akureyri (0) 0 12,000
Dinamo Tirana (0) 0, Marseille (0) 0 10,000
Dynamo Dresden (3) 3, (*Jahnig 18, 44, Gutschow 34*), Union Luxembourg (0) 0 6250
Grasshoppers (0) 1 (*Koezle 62 pen*), Red Star Belgrade (1) 4 (*Pancev 12, Prosinecki 48 pen, Savicevic 59*) 25,500
Kuusysi (0) 1 (*Vehkakoski 71 pen*), Tirol (1) 2 (*Pacult 5, 50 pen*) 430
Panathinaikos (1) 1 (*Saravakos 44*), Lech Poznan (0) 2 (*Pahelski 68, Moscal 85*) 30,000
Portadown (1) 1 (*Fraser 36*), Porto (4) 8 (*Madjer 9, 15, 33, 55, Semedo 40, Paille 50, 79, Couto 68*) 5000
Rangers (4) 6 (*Dodds 5, Spencer 6, Johnston 23, 37, 79 pen, McCoist 75*), Valetta (0) 0 20,627
Real Madrid (2) 6 (*Losada 13, 52, 73, Michel 34 pen, Aldana 46, 85*), Odense (0) 0 40,000
St Patrick's Athletic (1) 1 (*Fenlon 36*), Dinamo Bucharest (0) 1 (*Mateut 76*) 1500
Spartak Moscow (1) 2 (*Perepadenko 33, Ivanov 49*), Sparta Prague (0) 0 35,000
Ujpest Dozsa (0) 0, Napoli (2) 2 (*Incocciati 13, Alemao 35*) 24,000

Second Round, First Leg

Bayern Munich (2) 4 (*Reuter 3, 62 pen, Wohlfarth 28, Augenthaler 54*), CSKA Sofia (0) 0 12,000
Dinamo Bucharest (0) 0, Porto (0) 0 7500
Dynamo Dresden (1) 1 (*Gutschow 44*), Malmo (1) 1 (*Engqvist 18*) 6870
Lech Poznan (2) 3 (*Lukasik 30, Pachelski 41, Juskowiak 58*), Marseille (1) 2 (*Fournier 7, Waddle 64*) 23,000
AC Milan (0) 0, FC Brugge (0) 0 71,300
Napoli (0) 0, Spartak Moscow (0) 0 71,000
Real Madrid (5) 9 (*Butragueno 4, 31, 48, Sanchez 7, 12, 72, 85, Hierro 37, Tendillo 79*), Tirol (1) 1 (*Pacult 15*) 40,000
Red Star Belgrade (1) 3 (*Brown og 8, Prosinecki 65, Pancev 74*), Rangers (0) 0 82,000

Second Round, Second Leg

FC Brugge (0) 0, AC Milan (0) 1 (*Carbone 46*) 23,500
CSKA Sofia (0) 0, Bayern Munich (1) 3 (*Wohlfarth 16, Effenberg 73, McInally 82*) 15,000
Malmo (0) 1 (*Persson 72 pen*), Dynamo Dresden (1) 1 (*Gutschow 19 pen*) 8112 *Dynamo Dresden won 5–4 on penalties*
Marseille (3) 6 (*Papin 19, Vercruysse 33, 44, 83, Tigana 88, Boli 90*), Lech Poznan (1) 1 (*Jakolcewicz 59 pen*) 40,000
Porto (2) 4 (*Kostadinov 2, 25, Geraldao 48 pen, Domingos 63*), Dinamo Bucharest (0) 0 45,000
Rangers (0) 1 (*McCoist 76*), Red Star Belgrade (0) 1 (*Pancev 52*) 23,821
Spartak Moscow (0) 0, Napoli (0) 0 102,000 *Spartak Moscow won 5–3 on penalties*
Tirol (1) 2 (*Hortnagl 14, Linzmaier 89*), Real Madrid (2) 2 (*Losada 34, 44*) 14,000

Quarter-finals, First Leg

Bayern Munich (1) 1 (*Bender 30*), Porto (0) 1 (*Domingos 66*) 40,000
AC Milan (1) 1 (*Gullit 16*), Marseille (1) 1 (*Papin 27*) 82,500
Red Star Belgrade (2) 3 (*Prosinecki 21, Binic 42, Savicevic 56*), Dynamo Dresden (0) 0 82,500
Spartak Moscow (0) 0, Real Madrid (0) 0 100,000

Quarter-finals, Second Leg

Dynamo Dresden (1) 1 (*Gutschow 2 pen*), Red Star Belgrade (0) 2 (*Savicevic 52, Pancev 69*) 10,761
Marseille (0) 1 (*Waddle 74*), AC Milan (0) 0 37,603
Porto (0) 0, Bayern Munich (1) 2 (*Ziege 18, Bender 67*) 90,000
Real Madrid (1) 1 (*Butragueno 9*), Spartak Moscow (2) 3 (*Radchenko 19, 37, Shmarov 63*) 91,800

Semi-finals, First Leg

Bayern Munich (1) 1 (*Wohlfarth 24*), Red Star Belgrade (1) 2 (*Pancev 44, Savicevic 70*) 66,000
Spartak Moscow (0) 1 (*Shalimov 65*), Marseille (2) 3 (*Pele 27, Papin 32, Vercruysse 88*) 95,000

Semi-finals, Second Leg

Marseille (1) 2 (*Pele 33, Boli 48*), Spartak Moscow (0) 1 (*Mostovoi 58 pen*) 37,500
Red Star Belgrade (1) 2 (*Mihajlovic 26, Augenthaler og 89*), Bayern Munich (0) 2 (*Augenthaler 62, Wohlfarth 66*) 76,500

Final: Red Star Belgrade (0) 0, Marseille (0) 0 *aet*

(Red Star Belgrade won 5–3 on penalties)

(in Bari, 29 May 1991, 56,000)

Red Star Belgrade: Stojanovic; Yugovic, Marovic, Sabanadzovic, Belodedic, Najdovski, Prosinecki, Mihajlovic, Pancev, Savicevic (Dodic 84), Binic.
Marseille: Olmeta; Amoros, Di Meco (Stojkovic 112), Boli, Mozer, Germain, Casoni, Waddle, Papin, Pele, Fournier (Vercruysse 75).
Referee: Lanese (Italy).
Penalty shoot-out: Red Star Belgrade: Prosinecki, Binic, Belodedic, Mihajlovic and Pancev scored; *Marseille*: Amoros (shot saved), Casoni, Papin and Mozer scored.

EUROPEAN CUP 1990–91 – BRITISH AND IRISH CLUBS

FIRST ROUND, FIRST LEG

19 SEPT

Dinamo Bucharest (3) 4 *(Dobos, Damaschin, Mateut, Cheregi)*
St Patrick's Athletic (0) 0   13,000

Dinamo Bucharest: Stelea; Mihaescu, Rednic, Mateit, Selymesi, Dobos, Mateut, Zamfir (Cheregi), Timofte, Damaschin, Marcu (Radacanu).
St Patrick's Athletic: Devlin; Fleming, McDonnell, Byrne, Kelch, Fenlon, Tracey, O'Connor, Moody, Ennis (Lawless), O'Driscoll.

Porto (3) 5 *(Geraldao, Paille 2, Kostadinov, Branco)*
Portadown (0) 0   5000

Porto: Victor Baia; Joao Pinto, Branco, Aloisio, Geraldao, Kiki, Semedo, Couto, Domingos (Placido), Paille, Kostadinov.
Portadown: Keenan; Major, Curtiss, McKeeger, Strain, Stewart, Doolin, Cullingham, Magee (Fraser), Couran, Davidson (McCreadle).

Valletta (0) 0   8000
Rangers (1) 4 *(McCoist (pen), Hateley, Johnston 2)*

Valletta: Cini; Briffa, McKay, Laferla, Sciberras, Camilleri, Saliba (Gilbent), Giorev, Busuttil (Agius), Zarb, Zerafa.
Rangers: Woods; Stevens G, Munro (Brown), Gough, Spackman, Butcher, Steven T, McCoist, Hateley, Johnston, Walters.

FIRST ROUND, SECOND LEG

2 OCT

Rangers (4) 6 *(Dodds, Spencer, Johnston 3 (1 pen), McCoist)*
Valletta (0) 0   20,627

Rangers: Woods; Stevens G, Munro, Cowan (Robertson), Dodds (McCoist), Brown, Steven T, Walters, Spencer, Johnson, Huistra.
Valletta: Cini; Briffa, McKay, Laferla, Sciberras, Camilleri, Saliba (Maujaon), Giorev, Agius (Busuttil), Zarb, Zerafa.
Rangers won 10–0 on aggregate

3 OCT

Portadown (1) 1 *(Fraser)*
Porto (4) 8 *(Madjer 4, Semedo, Paille 2, Couto)* 5000

Portadown: Keenan (Magee); Major, Curtiss, McKeever (Davidson), Strain, Stewart, Doolin, McCreadle, Fraser, Cowan, Cunningham.
Porto: Victor Baia; Joao Pinto, Branco, Aloisio, Geraldao, Kiki, Couto, Madjer, Paille, Semedo (Morgado), Andre (Magalhaes).
Porto won 13–1 on aggregate

St Patrick's Athletic (1) 1 *(Fenlon)*
Dinamo Bucharest (0) 1 *(Mateut)*   1500

St Patrick's Athletic: Devlin; Fleming, McDonnell, Byrne (O'Driscoll), Kelch, Fenlon, Tracey, Moody, Gaffney, Lawless (Kelly), O'Connor.
Dinamo Bucharest: Stelea; Mihaescu, Rednic, Marcu, Timofte, Dobos, Mateut, Zamfir, Cheregi, Eduard, Selymesi (Damasch).
Dinamo Bucharest won 5–1 on aggregate

SECOND ROUND, FIRST LEG

24 OCT

Red Star Belgrade (1) 3 *(Brown (og), Prosinecki, Pancev)*
Rangers (0) 0   82,000

Red Star Belgrade: Stojanovic; Radinovic, Sarovic, Sadanadzovic, Belodedic, Najdovski, Prosinecki, Stosic, Pancev, Yugovic (Momcilovic), Binic (Ratkovic).
Rangers: Woods; Stevens G, Munro, Gough, Spackman, Brown, Steven T, Ferguson, Walters, Johnston, Huistra (McCoist).

SECOND ROUND, SECOND LEG

7 NOV

Rangers (0) 1 *(McCoist)*
Red Star Belgrade (0) 1 *(Pancev)*   23,821

Rangers: Woods; Stevens G, Munro, Gough (Nisbet), Spackman, Brown, Steven T, Dodds (Robertson), McCoist, Hateley, Walters.
Red Star Belgrade: Stojanovic (Kaludjerovic); Radinovic, Sarovic, Sabanadzovic, Belodedic, Najdovski, Prosinecki, Stosic, Pancev, Yugovic (Juric), Binic.
Red Star Belgrade won 4–1 on aggregate

EUROPEAN CUP-WINNERS' CUP

EUROPEAN CUP-WINNERS' CUP FINALS 1961–90

Year	Winners	Runners-up	Venue	Attendance	Referee
1961	Fiorentina 2	Rangers 0 *(1st Leg)*	Glasgow	80,000	Steiner (A)
	Fiorentina 2	Rangers 1 *(2nd Leg)*	Florence	50,000	Hernadi (H)
1962	Atletico Madrid 1	Fiorentina 1	Glasgow	27,389	Wharton (S)
Replay	Atletico Madrid 3	Fiorentina 0	Stuttgart	45,000	Tschenscher (WG)
1963	Tottenham Hotspur 5	Atletico Madrid 1	Rotterdam	25,000	Van Leuwen (Ho)
1964	Sporting Lisbon 3	MTK Budapest 3 *(aet)*	Brussels	9000	Van Nuffel (Bel)
Replay	Sporting Lisbon 1	MTK Budapest 0	Antwerp	18,000	Versyp (Bel)
1965	West Ham U 2	Munich 1860 0	Wembley	100,000	Szolt (H)
1966	Borussia Dortmund 2	Liverpool 1 *(aet)*	Glasgow	41,657	Schwinte (F)
1967	Bayern Munich 1	Rangers 0 *(aet)*	Nuremberg	69,480	Lo Bello (I)
1968	AC Milan 2	Hamburg 0	Rotterdam	60,000	Ortiz (Sp)
1969	Slovan Bratislava 3	Barcelona 2	Basle	40,000	Van Ravens (Ho)
1970	Manchester C 2	Gornik Zabrze 1	Vienna	10,000	Schiller (A)
1971	Chelsea 1	Real Madrid 1 *(aet)*	Athens	42,000	Scheurer (Sw)
Replay	Chelsea 2	Real Madrid 1 *(aet)*	Athens	24,000	Bucheli (Sw)
1972	Rangers 3	Moscow Dynamo 2	Barcelona	35,000	Ortiz (Sp)
1973	AC Milan 1	Leeds U 0	Salonika	45,000	Mihas (Gr)
1974	Magdeburg 2	AC Milan 0	Rotterdam	5000	Van Gemert (Ho)
1975	Dynamo Kiev 3	Ferencvaros 0	Basle	13,000	Davidson (S)
1976	Anderlecht 4	West Ham U 2	Brussels	58,000	Wurtz (F)
1977	Hamburg 2	Anderlecht 0	Amsterdam	65,000	Partridge (E)
1978	Anderlecht 4	Austria/WAC 0	Amsterdam	48,679	Adlinger (WG)
1979	Barcelona 4	Fortuna Dusseldorf 3 *(aet)*	Basle	58,000	Palotai (H)
1980	Valencia 0	Arsenal 0	Brussels	40,000	Christov (Cz)
	(aet; Valencia won 5-4 on penalties)				
1981	Dynamo Tbilisi 2	Carl Zeiss Jena 1	Dusseldorf	9000	Lattanzi (I)
1982	Barcelona 2	Standard Liege 1	Barcelona	100,000	Eschweiler (WG)
1983	Aberdeen 2	Real Madrid 1 *(aet)*	Gothenburg	17,804	Menegali (I)
1984	Juventus 2	Porto 1	Basle	60,000	Prokop (EG)
1985	Everton 3	Rapid Vienna 1	Rotterdam	30,000	Casarin (I)
1986	Dynamo Kiev 3	Atletico Madrid 0	Lyon	39,300	Wohrer (A)
1987	Ajax 1	Lokomotiv Leipzig 0	Athens	35,000	Agnolin (I)
1988	Mechelen 1	Ajax 0	Strasbourg	39,446	Pauly (WG)
1989	Barcelona 2	Sampdoria 0	Berne	45,000	Courtney (E)
1990	Sampdoria 2	Anderlecht 0	Gothenburg	20,103	Galler (Sw)

Steve Bruce (4) wheels away in elation after heading in the ball which was followed up on the line by Mark Hughes during Manchester United's 2-1 European Cup Final victory over Barcelona in 1991. (Allsport)

EUROPEAN CUP-WINNERS CUP 1990–91

Preliminary Round, First Leg

Bray Wanderers (0) 1 (*Nugent 52*), Trabzonspor (1) 1 (*Djukic 12*) 5000

Preliminary Round, Second Leg

Trabzonspor (0) 2 (*Djukic 47, Hamdi 60*), Bray Wanderers (0) 0 17,000

First Round, First Leg

Amadora (1) 1 (*Owuburiki 26*), Neuchatel (0) 1 (*Sutter B 56*) 5000

Famagusta (0) 0, Aberdeen (0) 2 (*Mason 62, Gillhaus 81*) 7000

Fram (0) 3 (*Ragnarsson 56, 58, Ormslev 85*), Djurgaarden (0) 0 637

Glentoran (0) 1 (*Douglas 84*), Steaua Bucharest (0) 1 (*Stan 47 pen*) 8000

Kaiserslautern (0) 1 (*Kuntz 77*), Sampdoria (0) 0 33,000

KuPS (0) 2 (*Hyssonen 38, Gayle 89*), Kiev Dynamo (1) 2 (*Salenkov 11, Youran 67*) 2460

Legia Warsaw (0) 3 (*Kosecki 48, 79, Pisz 89*), Hesperange (0) 0 4172

Manchester U (0) 2 (*Blackmore 8, Webb 16*), Pecsi Munkas (0) 0 26,411

Montpellier (0) 1 (*Ziober 54*), PSV Eindhoven (0) 0 12,000

Olympiakos (2) 3 (*Anastopoulos 9, 69, Hadjidis 26*), Flamurtari (0) 1 (*Ziu 75*) 25,000

Schwerin (0) 0, FK Austria (2) 2 (*Milewski 34, Zsak 36*) 835

Sliema Wanderers (1) 1 (*Walker 49*), Dukla Prague (0) 2 (*Rada 33, Kostelnik 87*) 2500

Sliven (0) 0, Juventus (1) 2 (*Schillaci 26, Baggio 88 pen*) 17,600

Trabzonspor (0) 1 (*Hamdi 68*), Barcelona (0) 0 27,500

Viking (0) 0, Liege (1) 2 (*Boffin 15, Hernes 82*) 1845

Wrexham (0) 0, Lyngby (0) 0 3417

First Round, Second Leg

Aberdeen (2) 3 (*Robertson 13, Andreou og 33, Jess 67*), Famagusta (0) 0 7,000

Barcelona (5) 7 (*Beguiristain 13, Amor 29, Koeman 32, 41, 76 pen, Stoichkov 44, 87*), Trabzonspor (1) 2 (*Hami 7, Soner 68*) 35,000

Djurgaarden (0) 1 (*Martinsson 83*), Fram (1) 1 (*Ormslev 9*) 956

Dukla Prague (0) 2 (*Rada 47, Zalesky 72*), Sliema Wanderers (0) 0 677

FK Austria (0) 0, Schwerin (0) 0 1500

Flamurtari (0) 0, Olympiakos (0) 2 (*Christodoulu 84, Mitropoulos 87*) 5000

Hesperange (0) 0, Legia Warsaw (0) 3 (*Jozwiak 61, Latka 74, Kosecki 88*) 800

Juventus (3) 6 (*Baggio 15 pen, 18, Schillaci 25, Corini 49, Bonetti 53, Julio Cesar 55*), Sliven (0) 1 (*Kelepov 84*) 10,000

Kiev Dynamo (2) 4 (*Salenko 14, Litovchenko 25, 54, Youran 85*), KuPS (0) 0 28,500

Liege (2) 3 (*Boffin 22, 35, 88*), Viking (0) 0 5000

Lyngby (0) 0, Wrexham (1) 1 (*Armstrong 11*) 1515

Neuchatel (0) 1 (*Sutter B 49*), Amadora (0) 1 (*Valerio 83*) *Amadora won 4–3 on penalties*

Pecsi Munkas (0) 0, Manchester U (0) 1 (*McClair 77*) 15,000

PSV Eindhoven (0) 0, Montpellier (0) 0 24,500

Sampdoria (1) 2 (*Mancini 7 pen, Branca 74*), Kaiserslautern (0) 0 40,000

Steaua (3) 5 (*Stan 21, Dumitrescu 38, 44, Petrescu 80, 88*), Glentoran (0) 0 5000

Second Round, First Leg

Aberdeen (0) 0, Legia Warsaw (0) 0 16,000

Fram (0) 1 (*Dadason 54*), Barcelona (1) 2 (*Salinas 36, Stoichkov 86*) 1700

FK Austria (0) 0, Juventus (2) 4 (*Casiraghi 30, De Agostini 44, Baggio 48, Schillaci 69 pen*) 12,000

Kiev Dynamo (0) 1 (*Litovchenko 65 pen*), Dukla Prague (0) 0 42,500

Liege (1) 2 (*Malbasa 7, Milosevic 86*), Amadora (0) 0 7000

Manchester U (2) 3 (*McClair 40, Bruce 42 pen, Pallister 59*), Wrexham (0) 0 29,405

Montpellier (0) 5 (*Ziober 27, 75, Xuereb 51, Blanc 56 pen, Castro 85*), Steaua Bucharest (0) 0 16,000

Olympiakos (0) 0, Sampdoria (0) 1 (*Katanec 52*) 13,000

Second Round, Second Leg

Amadora (0) 1 (*Dias 33*), Liege (0) 0, 10,000

Barcelona (2) 3 (*Eusebio 17, Beguiristain 33, Pinilla 69*), Fram (0) 0 19,000

Dukla Prague (0) 2 (*Foldyna 51, Bittengel 72*), Kiev Dynamo (1) 2 (*Youran 6, 60*) 2191

Juventus (2) 4 (*Alessio 3, Baggio 25 pen, 46, 52*), FK Austria (0) 0 19,000

Legia Warsaw (0) 1 (*Iwanicki 85*), Aberdeen (0) 0 5665

Sampdoria (2) 3 (*Lombardo 16, Branca 28, 66*), Olympiakos (0) 1 (*Nentidis 61*) 25,000

Steaua Bucharest (0) 0, Montpellier (0) 3 (*Colleter 52, Garande 72, Guerin 81*) 5000

Wrexham (0) 0, Manchester U (2) 2 (*Robins 31, Bruce 35*) 13,327

Quarter-finals, First Leg

Kiev Dynamo (1) 2 (*Zayets 33, Salenko 81 pen*), Barcelona (2) 3 (*Bakero 5, Urbano 44, Stoichkov 63 pen*) 98,000

Legia Warsaw (1) 1 (*Czykier 44*), Sampdoria (0) 0 12,000

Liege (0) 1 (*Houben 83*), Juventus (2) 3 (*Marocchi 32, Baggio 42, Julio Cesar 47*) 23,000

Manchester U (1) 1 (*McClair 1*), Montpellier (1) 1 (*Martin og 7*) 41,942

Quarter-finals, Second Leg

Barcelona (0) 1 (*Amor 89*), Kiev Dynamo (0) 1 (*Youran 61*) 61,500

Juventus (3) 3 (*Casiraghi 9, Wegria og 18, Hassler 22*), Liege (0) 0 33,500

Montpellier (0) 0, Manchester U (1) 2 (*Blackmore 45, Bruce 48 pen*) 20,500

Sampdoria (0) 2 (*Mancini 67, Vialli 88*), Legia Warsaw (1) 2 (*Kowalczyk 19, 54*) 30,000

Semi-finals, First Leg

Barcelona (0) 3 (*Stoichkov 55, 59, Goicoechea 74*), Juventus (1) 1 (*Casiraghi 12*) 110,000

Legia Warsaw (1) 1 (*Cyzio 35*), Manchester U (1) 3 (*McClair 36, Hughes 57, Bruce, 67*) 17,500

Semi-finals, Second Leg

Juventus (0) 1 (*Baggio 60*), Barcelona (0) 0 70,000

Manchester U (1) 1 (*Sharpe 28*), Legia Warsaw (0) 1 (*Kowalczyk 57*) 44,269

Final: Manchester U (0) 2, Barcelona (0) 1

(in Rotterdam, 15 May 1991, 45,000)

Manchester U: Sealey; Irwin, Blackmore, Bruce, Phelan, Pallister, Robson, Ince, McClair, Hughes, Sharpe. *Scorer*: Hughes 68, 74.

Barcelona: Busquets; Nando, Alexanco (Pinilla 73), Koeman, Ferrer, Bakero, Goicoechea, Eusebio, Salinas, Laudrup, Beguiristain. *Scorer*: Koeman 80.

Referee: Karlsson (Sweden).

EUROPEAN CUP-WINNERS' CUP 1990–91 – BRITISH AND IRISH CLUBS

PRELIMINARY ROUND, FIRST LEG

22 AUG

Bray Wanderers (0) 1 *(Nugent)*
Trabzonspor (1) 1 *(Djukic)*   5000
Bray Wanderers: Moran; McKeever, Cosgrave, Doohan, Judge, Philips, Nugent, MacAuley (Parsons), Smith, Ryan, Corcoran (Lynch).
Trabzonspor: Petranovic; Ogun, Hamdi, Kemal, Sehmuz, Orhan, Unal (Tyrgut), Ivanovic, Soner, Hami, Djukic.

PRELIMINARY ROUND, SECOND LEG

5 SEPT

Trabzonspor (0) 2 *(Djukic, Hamdi)*
Bray Wanderers (0) 0   17,000
Trabzonspor: Levent; Sehmuz, Ogun, Kemal, Mehmet, Unal, Soner, Lemi (Orhan), Hami, Djukic (Tyrgut), Hamdi.
Bray Wanderers: Moran; McKeever, Doohan, Philips, Cosgrave, Smith, Reynolds (Parsons), Judge, Lynch (Cairns), Nugent, Ryan.

FIRST ROUND, FIRST LEG

19 SEPT

Famagusta (0) 0
Aberdeen (0) (2) *(Mason, Gillhaus)*   7000
Famagusta: Christofi; Andreou A, Tsikelis, Yiannaki, Nicolaou, Dyer, Andreou G, David, McNeill, Elia, Adamou.
Aberdeen: Snelders; McKimmie, Robertson D, Grant, McLeish, Irvine, Van de Ven, Bett, Mason (Jess), Booth (Watson), Gillhaus.

Glentoran (0) 1 *(Douglas)*
Steaua Bucharest (0) 1 *(Stan (pen))*   8000
Glentoran: Smyth; Neill, McCaffrey, Devine, Moore, Bowers (Totten), Campbell, Jameson, Douglas, Manley (McCartney), Morrison.
Steaua Bucharest: Stingaciu; Petrescu, Ungureanu, Bumbescu, Minea D, Iovan, Sedecaru, Dumitrescu, Minea N (Pistol), Lazar (Saviou), Istvan.

Manchester U (2) 2 *(Blackmore, Webb)*
Pecsi Munkas (0) 0   26,411
Manchester U: Sealey; Irwin, Blackmore, Bruce, Phelan, Pallister, Webb, Ince (Sharpe), McClair, Robins (Hughes), Beardsmore.
Pecsi Munkas: Bodnar; Konya, Braun, Palaczki (Czerna), Berczy, Balogh, Czeh, Tomka, Lovasz (Bojas), Megyeri, Lehota.

Wrexham (0) 0
Lyngby (0) 0   3417
Wrexham: Morris; Phillips, Beaumont, Owen, Williams M, Sertori, Cooper, Flynn (Hunter), Preece, Worthington, Bowden.

Lyngby: Rindom; Kuhn H, Wieghorst, Gothernborg, Christiansen C, Larsen, Rode (Andersen V), Kuhn A, Holt, Schafer, Christiansen F.

FIRST ROUND, SECOND LEG

3 OCT

Aberdeen (2) 3 *(Robertson C, Andreou A (og), Jess)*
Famagusta (0) 0   7000
Aberdeen: Snelders; McKimmie, Robertson D, Robertson C, McLeish (Van de Ven), Irvine, Jess, Bett, Mason (Gardner), Connor, Gillhaus.
Famagusta: Ioannou; Andreou A, Tsikelis, Yiannaki, Nicolaou (David), Dyer, Adamou, Mavrou, McNeill (Andreou C), Elia, Georgiou.
Aberdeen won 5–0 on aggregate

Lyngby (0) 0
Wrexham (1) 1 *(Armstrong)*   1515
Lyngby: Rindom; Kuhn H, Wieghorst, Gothernborg, Christiansen C, Larsen, Helt, Rode (Clem), Christiansen F, Kirchhoff (Rasmussen), Kuhn A.
Wrexham: Morris; Phillips, Kennedy, Owen, Williams M, Sertori, Cooper (Wright), Flynn, Armstrong, Worthington, Bowden.
Wrexham won 1–0 on aggregate

Pecsi Munkas (0) 0
Manchester U (0) 1 *(McClair)*   15,000
Pecsi Munkas: Bodnar; Konya, Czerna, Palaczki, Balogh, Berczy, Lovasz, Braun, Czeh, Megyeri, Lehota (Bajos).
Manchester U: Sealey; Anderson, Donaghy, Bruce, Pallister, Phelan, Webb, Blackmore, McClair, Hughes, Martin (Sharpe).
Manchester U won 3–0 on aggregate

Steaua Bucharest (3) 5 *(Stan, Dumitrescu 2, Petrescu 2)*
Glentoran (0) 0   5000
Steaua Bucharest: Stingaciu; Petrescu, Ungureanu, Bumbescu, Saviou, Iovan, Stan (Pistol), Sedecaru, Dumitrescu, Minea D, Lazar.
Glentoran: Smyth; Neill, McCaffrey, Devine, Moore, Bowers (Jameson), Campbell, Caskey, McCartney, Manley, Morrison.
Steaua Bucharest won 6–1 on aggregate

SECOND ROUND, FIRST LEG

23 OCT

Manchester U (2) 3 *(McClair, Bruce (pen), Pallister)*
Wrexham (0) 0   29,405
Manchester U: Sealey; Blackmore, Martin, Bruce, Sharpe, Pallister, Webb, Ince (Beardsmore), McClair, Hughes, Wallace (Robins).
Wrexham: Morris; Phillips, Kennedy, Reck, Beaumont, Williams (Hunter), Flynn, Owen, Armstrong, Cooper, Bowden.

24 OCT

Aberdeen (0) 0
Legia Warsaw (0) 0   16,000

Aberdeen: Watt; McKimmie, Robertson D, Grant,
McLeish, Irvine, Van de Ven (Robertson C), Bett,
Mason, Connor, Gillhaus.
Legia Warsaw: Szczesny; Kubicki, Gmur, Wiak,
Budka, Czykier, Pisz (Modzelewski), Iwanicki, Latka,
Kosecki, Cyzio.

SECOND ROUND, SECOND LEG

7 NOV

Legia Warsaw (0) 1 *(Iwanicki)*
Aberdeen (0) 0   5665

Legia Warsaw: Szczesny; Kubicki, Gmur, Wiak,
Budka, Czykier, Bak, Iwanicki, Modzelewski,
Kosecki, Cyzio.
Aberdeen: Watt; McKimmie, Robertson D, Grant,
McLeish, Irvine, Van de Ven, Bett, Mason (Jess),
Connor, Gillhaus.
Legia Warsaw won 1–0 on aggregate

Wrexham (0) 0
Manchester U (2) 2 *(Robins, Bruce)*   13,327

Wrexham: Morris; Thackeray, Hardy, Hunter,
Beaumont, Phillips, Flynn (Jones J), Owen,
Armstrong (Jones K), Jones L, Cooper.
Manchester U: Sealey; Irwin, Blackmore, Bruce,
Phelan, Pallister, Webb, Ince (Donaghy), McClair
(Martin), Robins, Wallace.
Manchester U won 5–0 on aggregate

QUARTER-FINALS, FIRST LEG

6 MAR

Manchester U (1) 1 *(McClair)*
Montpellier (1) 1 *(Martin (og))*   41.942

Manchester U: Sealey; Blackmore, Martin (Wallace),
Donaghy, Phelan, Pallister, Robson, Ince, McClair,
Hughes, Sharpe.
Montpellier: Barrabe; Baills, Lucchesi, Der-Zakarian,
Blanc, Lemoult, Suvrijn (Brouard), Guerin, Garcia
(Xuereb), Colleter, Ziober.

QUARTER-FINALS, SECOND LEG

19 MAR

Montpellier (0) 0
Manchester U (1) 2 *(Blackmore, Bruce (pen))* 20,500

Montpellier: Barrabe; Brouard (Xuereb), Lucchesi,
Thetis, Blanc, Lemoult, Suvrijn, Colleter, Garcia,
Valderrama, Ziober.
Manchester U: Sealey; Irwin, Blackmore, Bruce,
Phelan, Pallister, Robson, Ince (Martin), McClair,
Hughes, Sharpe.
Manchester U won 3–1 on aggregate

SEMI-FINALS, FIRST LEG

10 APR

Legia Warsaw (1) 1 *(Cyzio)*
Manchester U (1) 3 *(McClair, Hughes, Bruce)* 17,500

Legia Warsaw: Robakiewicz; Bak, Gmur (Wojcik),
Jozwiak, Czachowski, Czykier, Pisz, Iwanicki,
Kowalczyk, Modzelewski, Cyzio.
Manchester U: Sealey; Irwin, Blackmore, Bruce,
Phelan (Donaghy), Pallister, Webb, Ince, McClair,
Hughes, Sharpe.

SEMI-FINALS, SECOND LEG

24 APR

Manchester U (1) 1 *(Sharpe)*
Legia Warsaw (0) 1 *(Kowalczyk)*   44,269

Manchester U: Walsh; Irwin, Blackmore (Donaghy),
Bruce, Phelan, Pallister, Robson, Webb, McClair,
Hughes, Sharpe.
Legia Warsaw: Robakiewicz; Kubicki, Gmur, Bak,
Czachowski, Czykier, Pisz, Iwanicki, Kowalczyk,
Sobczak (Latka), Cyzio.
Manchester U won 4–2 on aggregate

EUROPEAN CUPS DRAW 1991–92

EUROPEAN CUP
First Round: Union Luxembourg v Marseille; Brondby v
Zaglebie Lubin; Honved v Dundalk; Sparta Prague v
Rangers; Barcelona v Hansa Rostock; Red Star Belgrade v
Portadown; Uni Craiova v Apollon; IFK Gothenburg v
Flamurtari; Sampdoria v Rosenborg; Hamrun v Benfica;
Arsenal v FK Austria; Dynamo Kiev v HJK Helsinki;
Besiktas v PSV Eindhoven; Fram v Panathinaikos;
Anderlecht v Grasshoppers; Kaiserslautern v Etur
Tarnovo

CUP-WINNERS' CUP
Preliminary Round: Odense v Galway; Stockerau v
Tottenham H
First Round: Omonia v Brugge; Stockerau or Tottenham v
Hajduk Split; Norrkoping v Jeunesse Esch; Glenavon v
Ilves Tampere; Katowice v Motherwell; Odense or Galway
v Banik Ostrava; Swansea C v Monaco; Sion v Valur
Reykjavik; Levski v Ferencvaros; PAE Athinaikos v
Manchester U; Eisenhuttenstadt v Galatasaray; Bacau v

Werder Bremen; Valleta v Porto; Fylingen v Atletico
Madrid; Partizani Tirana v Feyenoord; CSKA Moscow v
Roma

UEFA CUP
First Round: Cork C v Bayern Munich; Vaci Izzo v
Dynamo Moscow; Aberdeen v B 1903 Copenhagen; Gent
v Lausanne; Eintracht Frankfurt v Spora Luxembourg;
Real Madrid v Slovan Bratislava; Sturm Graz v Utrecht;
Cannes v Salgueiros; Stuttgart v Pecs; Reykjavik v Torino;
Celtic v Ekeren; Lyon v Osters; Chemie Halle v Torpedo
Moscow; Auxerre v Ikast; Bangor v Olomouc; Liverpool v
Kuusysi; Hamburg v Gornik Zabrze; Ajax v Orebro;
Spartak Moscow v MP Mikkeli; Tirol v Tromso; PAOK
Salonika v Mechelen; Steaua v Anorthosis; CSKA Sofia v
Parma; Gijon v Partizan Belgrade; Groningen v Enfurt;
Sporting Lisbon v Dinamo Bucharest; Vllaznia v AEK
Athens; Oviedo v Genoa; Boavista v Internazionale;
Neuchatel Xamax v Floriana; Osasuna v Slavia Sofia;
Hask Gradjanski v Trabzonspor

INTER-CITIES FAIRS & UEFA CUP

FAIRS CUP FINALS 1958–71

(Winners in italics)

Year	First Leg	Attendance	Second Leg	Attendance
1958	London 2 Barcelona 2	45,466	*Barcelona* 6 London 0	62,000
1960	Birmingham C 0 Barcelona 0	40,500	*Barcelona* 4 Birmingham C 1	70,000
1961	Birmingham C 2 Roma 2	21,005	*Roma* 2 Birmingham C 0	60,000
1962	Valencia 6 Barcelona 2	65,000	Barcelona 1 *Valencia* 1	60,000
1963	Dynamo Zagreb 1 Valencia 2	40,000	*Valencia* 2 Dynamo Zagreb 0	55,000
1964	*Zaragoza* 2 Valencia 1	50,000	(in Barcelona)	
1965	*Ferencvaros* 1 Juventus 0	25,000	(in Turin)	
1966	Barcelona 0 Zaragoza 1	70,000	Zaragoza 2 *Barcelona* 4	70,000
1967	Dynamo Zagreb 2 Leeds U 0	40,000	Leeds U 0 *Dynamo Zagreb* 0	35,604
1968	Leeds U 1 Ferencvaros 0	25,368	Ferencvaros 0 *Leeds U* 0	70,000
1969	Newcastle U 3 Ujpest Dozsa 0	60,000	Ujpest Dozsa 2 *Newcastle U* 3	37,000
1970	Anderlecht 1 Arsenal 1	37,000	*Arsenal* 3 Anderlecht 0	51,612
1971	Juventus 0 Leeds U 0 *(abandoned 51 minutes)*	42,000		
	Juventus 2 Leeds U 2	42,000	*Leeds U* 1* Juventus 1	42,483

UEFA CUP FINALS 1972–90

(Winners in italics)

Year	First Leg	Attendance	Second Leg	Attendance
1972	Wolverhampton W 1 Tottenham H 2	45,000	*Tottenham H* 1 Wolverhampton W 1	48,000
1973	Liverpool 0 Moenchengladbach 0 *(abandoned 27 minutes)*	44,967		
	Liverpool 3 Moenchengladbach 0	41,169	Moenchengladbach 0 *Liverpool* 2	35,000
1974	Tottenham H 2 Feyenoord 2	46,281	*Feyenoord* 2 Tottenham 0	68,000
1975	Moenchengladbach 0 Twente 0	45,000	Twente 1 *Moenchengladbach* 5	24,500
1976	Liverpool 3 FC Brugge 2	56,000	FC Brugge 1 *Liverpool* 1	32,000
1977	Juventus 1 Athletic Bilbao 0	75,000	Athletic Bilbao 2 *Juventus* 1*	43,000
1978	Bastia 0 PSV Eindhoven 0	15,000	*PSV Eindhoven* 3 Bastia 0	27,000
1979	Red Star Belgrade 1 Moenchengladbach 1	87,500	*Moenchengladbach* 1 Red Star Belgrade 0	45,000
1980	Moenchengladbach 3 Eintracht Frankfurt 2	25,000	*Eintracht Frankfurt* 1* Moenchengladbach 0	60,000
1981	Ipswich T 3 AZ 67 Alkmaar 0	27,532	AZ 67 Alkmaar 4 *Ipswich T* 2	28,500
1982	Gothenburg 1 Hamburg 0	42,548	Hamburg 0 *Gothenburg* 3	60,000
1983	Anderlecht 1 Benfica 0	45,000	Benfica 1 *Anderlecht* 1	80,000
1984	Anderlecht 1 Tottenham H 1	40,000	*Tottenham H* 1[1] Anderlecht 1	46,258
1985	Videoton 0 Real Madrid 3	30,000	*Real Madrid* 0 Videoton 1	98,300
1986	Real Madrid 5 Cologne 1	80,000	Cologne 2 *Real Madrid* 0	15,000
1987	Gothenburg 1 Dundee U 0	50,023	Dundee U 1 *Gothenburg* 1	20,911
1988	Espanol 3 Bayer Leverkusen 0	42,000	*Bayer Leverkusen* 3[2] Espanol 0	22,000
1989	Napoli 2 Stuttgart 1	83,000	Stuttgart 3 *Napoli* 3	67,000
1990	Juventus 3 Fiorentina 1	45,000	Fiorentina 0 *Juventus* 0	32,000

* won on away goals   [1] *Tottenham H won 4-3 on penalties aet*   [2] *Bayer Leverkusen won 3-2 on penalties aet*

The 1991 UEFA Cup Final was another all-Italian affair. Inter-Milan's Jurgen Klinsmann (striped shirt) outpaces the Roma rearguard in the second leg. Although his team lost the game 1-0, they won 2-1 on aggregate. (Bob Thomas)

UEFA CUP 1990–91

First Round, First Leg

Anderlecht (0) 2 (*Verheyen 64, Nilis 85 pen*), Petrolul (0) 0 7000

Antwerp (0) 0, Ferencvaros (0) 0 4500

Aston Villa (1) 3 (*Platt 31, Mountfield 58, Olney 59*), Banik Ostrava (1) 1 (*Chyiek 30*) 27,317

Atalanta (0) 0, Dinamo Zagreb (0) 0 25,000

Avenir Beggen (2) 2 (*Krahn 36, 41*), Inter Bratislava (1) 1 (*Stojka 4*) 4000

Bayer Leverkusen (1) 1 (*Kirsten 41*), Twente (0) 0 8000

Borussia Dortmund (1) 2 (*Helmer 20, Mill 89*), Chemnitz (0) 0 30,000

Brondby (1) 5 (*Christensen 54, 83, Chukwu 9, Christofte 63 pen, Madsen 80*), Eintracht Frankfurt (0) 0 12,400

Chernomorets Odessa (1) 3 (*Tsymbalar 3, Getsko 48, Kondratiev 58*), Rosenborg (0) 1 (*Serlos 79*) 15,500

Derry (0) 0, Vitesse (1) 1 (*Loffen 18*) 3500

Dnepr (0) 1 (*Gudimenko 56*), Hearts (1) 1 (*Robertson 22*) 15,500

Fenerbahce (2) 3 (*Vokri 34, Turan 40, Senol 62*), Guimaraes (0) 0 30,000

Glenavon (0) 0, Bordeaux (0) 0 4000

Hafnarfjordur (1) 1 (*Jonsson 2*), Dundee U (1) 3 (*Jackson 32, Cleland 77, Jonsson og 89*) 213

Hibernians Malta (0) 0, Partizan Belgrade (1) 3 (*Djurdjevic 15, Djordjevic 81, Mijatovic 90*) 5000

Iraklis (0) 0, Valencia (0) 0 15,000

Katowice (1) 3 (*Heikkinen og 18, Strojek 54, Prabucki 81*), Turun (0) 0 15,000

Lausanne (0) 3 (*Hottigen 50, 89, Chapuisat 78*), Real Sociedad (2) 2 (*Lumbreras 17, Gajate 28*) 20,600

Magdeburg (0) 0, Rovanenmi (0) 0 3250

MTK VM (1) 1 (*Cservenkai 44*), Lucerne (1) 1 (*Knupp 17*) 2000

Norrkoping (0) 0, Cologne (0) 0 10,403

Partizani (0) 0, Uni Craiova (0) 1 (*Ciurea 88*) 9200

Rapid (0) 2 (*Pfeifenberger 56, Weber 72*), Internazionale (1) 1 (*Matthaus 5*) 15,000

Roda (1) 1 (*Arnold 40*), Monaco (2) 3 (*Weah 27, Passi 44, Dib 88*) 10,000

Roma (1) 1 (*Carnevale 1*), Benfica (0) 0 59,000

Seville (0) 0, PAOK (0) 0 40,000

Slavia Sofia (1) 2 (*Petkov 5, Ignatov 82*), Omonia (0) 1 (*Micinec 68*) 12,000

Sporting Lisbon (1) 1 (*Cadete 37*), Mechelen (0) 0 50,000

Timisoara (1) 2 (*Bungau 43 pen, Popescu 65*), Atletico Madrid (0) 0 23,000

Torpedo Moscow (4) 4 (*Gitselov 15, Tishkov 26, 32, Grishin 44*), GAIS Gothenburg (0) 1 (*Geransson 76*) 2000

Vejle (0) 0, Admira Wacker (0) 1 (*Binder 65*) 2400

Zaglebie Lubin (0) 0, Bologna (0) 1 (*Bonini 80*) 20,000

First Round, Second Leg

Admira Wacker (3) 3 (*Binder 18, Marschall 27, Ogris 44*), Vejle (0) 0 2000

Atletico Madrid (0) 1 (*Rodriguez 88*), Timisoara (0) 0 58,200

Banik Ostrava (1) 1 (*Necas 41*), Aston Villa (0) 2 (*Mountfield 52, Stas og 60*), 20,000

Benfica (0) 0, Roma (0) 1 (*Giannini 27*) 70,000

Bologna (0) 1 (*Di Gia 89*), Zaglebie Lubin (0) 0 15,000

Bordeaux (2) 2 (*Dugarry 6, Ferreri 10*), Glenavon (0) 0 12,000

Chemnitz (0) 0, Borussia Dortmund (1) 2 (*Helmer 24, Rummenigge 50*) 15,000

Cologne (0) 3 (*Higl 49, Banach 72, Ordenewitz 78*), Norrkoping (1) 1 (*Hellstrom 20*) 8000

Dinamo Zagreb (0) 1 (*Boban 54*), Atalanta (0) 1 (*Evair 62*) 25,000

Dundee United (0) 2 (*Connolly 63, Hilmarsson og 80*), Hafnarfjordur (1) 2 (*Magnusson 19, Gislason 28*) 5475

Eintracht Frankfurt (3) 4 (*Yeboah 5, Eckstein 22, Bein 37, Moller 86 pen*), Brondby (1) 1 (*Christensen 28*) 10,000

Ferencvaros (0) 3 (*Kereszturi 93, Topor 102, Fischer 117*), Antwerp (0) 1 (*Van Rooy 107 pen*) 20,000

GAIS Gothenburg (0) 1 (*Kohl 67*), Torpedo Moscow (1) 1 (*Tishkov 41*) 3725

Guimaraes (1) 2 (*Soeiro 32, Basaula 77*), Fenerbahce (3) 3 (*Vokri 6, Mujdet 10, Aykut 25*) 24,000

Hearts (3) 3 (*McKinlay 20, Robertson 21 pen, 41*), Dnepr (1) 1 (*Shakhov 40*) 23,000

Internazionale (2) 3 (*Berti 67, 82, Klinsmann 101*), Rapid (1) 1 (*Weber 88*) 30,000 *in Verona*

Inter Bratislava (2) 5 (*Kubica 5, Stojka 15, Jurasko 50 pen, 59 pen, Weiss 83*), Avenir Beggen (0) 0 1089

Lucerne (0) 2 (*Van Eck 54, Nadig 80*), MTK VM (0) 1 (*Kardos 70*) 10,350

Mechelen (2) 2 (*Albert 8, Xavier og 55*), Sporting Lisbon (1) 2 (*Gomes 28, Cadete 81*) 6800

Monaco (1) 3 (*Weah 34, Passi 64, Diaz 83*), Roda (0) 1 (*Jansen 87*) 2500

Omonia (1) 4 (*Micinec 3 pen, Xiouruppas 52, Kalotheos 109, 118*), Slavia Sofia (1) 2 (*Kirov 10, Dermendiev 107*) 18,000

PAOK (0) 0, Seville (0) 0 20,000 *Seville won 4–3 on penalties*

Partizan Belgrade (1) 2 (*Stevanovic 26, Scepanovic 80*), Hibernians Malta (0) 0 12,000

Petrolul (0) 0, Anderlecht (1) 2 (*Nilis 21, 88*) 6000

Real Sociedad (0) 1 (*Aldridge 55*), Lausanne (0) 0 18,000

Rovanenmi (0) 0, Magdeburg (1) 1 (*Lassig 4*) 3294

Rosenborg (1) 2 (*Jakobsen 28, Sollied 76*), Chernomorets Odessa (1) 1 (*Sheltnytski 39*) 14,440

Turun (0) 0, Katowice (1) 1 (*Szewczyk 26*) 1171

Twente (0) 1 (*Paus 83*), Bayer Leverkusen (0) 1 (*Kirsten 97*) 18,000

Uni Craiova (0) 1 (*Zamfir 75*), Partizani (0) 0 25,000

Valencia (0) 2 (*Fernando 101, Luxart 104*), Iraklis (0) 0 35,000

Vitesse (0) 0, Derry (0) 0 5742

Second Round, First Leg

Aston Villa (1) 2 (*Nielsen 14, Platt 67*), Internazionale (0) 0 36,461

Brondby (1) 3 (*Christofte 29, Chukwu 80, Vilfort 89*), Ferencvaros (0) 0 14,200

Chernomorets Odessa (0) 0, Monaco (0) 0 28,000

Cologne (0) 0, Inter Bratislava (0) 1 (*Obsitnik 64*) 8000

Fenerbahce (0) 0, Atalanta (1) 1 (*Bonacina 44*) 30,000

Hearts (3) 3 (*Foster 7, 24, Ferguson I 38*), Bologna (0) 1 (*Notaristefano 61*) 11,155

Katowice (0) 1 (*Szierczewski 84*), Bayer Leverkusen (1) 2 (*Thom 27, Buncol 48*) 6000

Lucerne (0) 0, Admira Wacker (0) 1 (*Binder 72*) 10,500

Magdeburg (0) 0, Bordeaux (1) 1 (*Ferreri 44 pen*) 5500

Omonia (0) 1 (*Mavrotis 83*), Anderlecht (0) 1 (*Kalotheou og 51*) 12,000

Real Sociedad (0) 1 (*Larranaga 89*), Partizan Belgrade (0) 0 21,000

Sporting Lisbon (2) 7 (*Cadete 30, 50, 64, Gomes 36, 61, Souza 79, Bozinovski 89*), Timisoara (0) 0 35,000

Torpedo Moscow (0) 3 (*Tishkov 58, Zhukov 84 pen, Shirinbekov 89*), Seville (0) 1 (*Polster 71*) 15,000

Uni Craiova (0) 0, Borussia Dortmund (0) 3 (*Zorc 59, Mill 69, 76*) 25,000

Valencia (1) 1 (*Roberto 25*), Roma (0) 1 (*Rizzitelli 73*) 37,400

Vitesse (1) 1 (*Eijer 28*), Dundee U (0) 0 8331

Second Round, Second Leg

Admira Wacker (0) 1 (*Marschall 53*), Lucerne (0) 1 (*Marini 89*) 4000

Anderlecht (3) 3 (*Verheyen 6, Oliveira 38, Rutjes 60 pen*), Omonia (0) 0 20,000

Atalanta (1) 4 (*Evair 2, Perrone 56, Nicolini 57, Bonacini 62*), Fenerbahce (0) 1 (*Ismail 89*) 18,000

Bayer Leverkusen (1) 4 (*Lesniak 28, Jorginho 78, Herrlich 81, Schreier 88*), Katowice (0) 0 8700

Bologna (1) 3 (*Detari 19, Villa 73, Mariani 84*), Hearts (0) 0 15,000

Bordeaux (0) 1 (*Ferreri 58*), Magdeburg (0) 0 20,000

Borussia Dortmund (0) 1 (*Zorc 39*), Uni Craiova (0) 0 20,117

Dundee U (0) 0, Vitesse (2) 4 (*Latuheru 10, 37, Van den Brom 62 pen, Eijer 73*) 10,261

Ferencvaros (0) 0, Brondby (0) 1 (*Christensen 75*) *Behind closed doors*
Inter Bratislava (0) 0, Cologne (1) 2 (*Gotz 11, Janssen 62*) 8000
Internazionale (1) 3 (*Klinsmann 6, Berti 62, Bianchi 74*), Aston Villa (0) 0 80,000
Monaco (1) 1 (*Weah 14*), Chernomorets Odessa (0) 0 5000
Partizan Belgrade (0) 1 (*Stevanovic 48*), Real Sociedad (0) 0 40,000 *Partizan Belgrade won 5–4 on penalties*
Roma (1) 2 (*Giannini 36, Völler 63 pen*), Valencia (0) 1 (*Fernando 71 pen*) 35,000
Seville (1) 2 (*Bengoechea 25, Ramon 62*), Torpedo Moscow (1) 1 (*Savichev 10*) 26,700
Timisoara (1) 2 (*Vlaicu 44, Varga 52 pen*), Sporting Lisbon (0) 0 20,000

Third Round, First Leg

Admira Wacker (2) 3 (*Gretschnig 31, 55, Muller 36*), Bologna (0) 0 8000
Anderlecht (0) 1 (*Van der Linden 74*), Borussia Dortmund (0) 0 18,000
Brondby (1) 3 (*Frank 6, 66, Christensen 60*), Bayer Leverkusen (0) 0 23,000
Cologne (0) 1 (*Progna og 50*), Atalanta (0) 1 (*Bordin 55*) 24,000
Internazionale (1) 3 (*Matthaus 32, Mandorlini 48, Bianchi 70*), Partizan Belgrade (0) 0 65,000
Roma (2) 5 (*Völler 10, 44 pen, 50, Gerolin 60, 75*), Bordeaux (0) 0 50,000
Torpedo Moscow (2) 2 (*Tishkov 19, Savichev 44*), Monaco (0) 1 (*Passi 56*) 10,000
Vitesse (0) 0, Sporting Lisbon (2) 2 (*Xavier 23, Gomes 36*) 10,000

Third Round, Second Leg

Atalanta (1) 1 (*Nicolini 15*), Cologne (0) 0 18,000
Bayer Leverkusen (0) 0, Brondby (^) 0 10,000
Bologna (1) 3 (*Waas 6, Cabrini 5ʋ Negro 70*), Admira Wacker (0) 10,500 *Bologna won 6–. 'n penalties*

Bordeaux (0) 0, Roma (0) 2 (*Voller 72 pen, Desideri 89*) 10,000
Borussia Dortmund (0) 2 (*Gorlukovich 49, Schulz 79*), Anderlecht (1) 1 (*Van Baekel 36*) 40,100
Monaco (0) 1 (*Diaz 83*), Torpedo Moscow (0) 2 (*Tishkov 70, Gichelov 86*) 10,000
Partizan Belgrade (0) 1 (*Stevanovic 63*), Internazionale (0) 1 (*Matthaus 64*) 37,000
Sporting Lisbon (1) 2 (*Douglas 26, 67*), Vitesse (0) 1 (*Van Arum 78*) 44,000

Quarter-finals, First Leg

Atalanta (0) 0, Internazionale (0) 0 35,000
Bologna (0) 1 (*Turkyilmaz 50*), Sporting Lisbon (0) 1 (*Luizinho 89*) 32,500
Brondby (0) 1 (*Madsen 59*), Torpedo Moscow (0) 0 15,600
Roma (1) 3 (*Comi 44, Voller 73, Rizzitelli 75*) Anderlecht (0) 0 55,000

Quarter-finals, Second Leg

Anderlecht (0) 2 (*Kooiman 76, Lamptey 82*), Roma (1) 3 (*Voller 22, 55, 70*) 26,000
Internazionale (0) 2 (*Serena 60, Matthaus 63*), Atalanta (0) 0 45,000
Sporting Lisbon (1) 2 (*Cadete 20, Gomes 80 pen*), Bologna (0) 0 70,000
Torpedo Moscow (0) 1 (*Shirinbekov 87*), Brondby (0) 0 30,000 *Brondby won 4–2 on penalties*

Semi-finals, First Leg

Brondby (0) 0, Roma (0) 18,000
Sporting Lisbon (0) 0, Internazionale (0) 80,000

Semi-finals, Second Leg

Internazionale (2) 2 (*Matthaus 15 pen, Klinsmann 35*), Sporting Lisbon (0) 0, 72,500
Roma (1) 2 (*Rizzitelli 34, Voller 89*), Brondby (0) 1 (*Nela og 51*) 54,000

Final

First Leg: Internazionale (0) 2, Roma (0) 0

(in Milan, 8 May 1991, 68,887)

Internazionale: Zenga; Bergomi, Brehme, Battistini, Ferri, Paganin (Baresi 65), Bianchi, Berti, Matthaus, Klinsmann, Serena (Pizzi 90).
Scorers: Matthaus 55 pen, Berti 65.
Roma: Cervone; Tempestilli, Nela, Berthold, Aldair (Carboni 72), Comi (Muzzi 75), Gerolin, Di Mauro, Giannini, Voller, Rizzitelli.
Referee: Spirin (USSR).

Second Leg: Roma (0) 1 Internazionale (0) 0

(in Rome, 22 May 1991, 70,901)

Roma: Cervone; Tempestilli (Salsano 57), Aldair, Nela, Berthold, Gerolin, Desideri (Muzzi 69), Di Mauro, Giannini, Voller, Rizzitelli.
Scorer: Rizzitelli 81.
Internazionale: Zenga; Paganin, Bergomi, Ferri, Brehme, Battistini, Bianchi, Matthaus, Berti, Klinsmann, Pizzi (Mandorlini 67).
Referee: Quiniou (France).

UEFA CUP 1990–91 – BRITISH AND IRISH CLUBS

FIRST ROUND, FIRST LEG

18 SEPT

Glenavon (0) 0
Bordeaux (0) 0   4000

Glenavon: Beck; Davies, Scappaticci, McCann, Byrne, McLoughlin, McConville, Ferguson, Blackledge, McBride, Conville.
Bordeaux: Bell; Dogon, Lizarazu, Senac, Battiston, Deschamps, Durand, Vervoort, Fargeon, Ferreri, Dugarry.

Hafnarfjordur (1) 1 *(Jonsson)*
Dundee U (1) 3 *(Jackson, Cleland, Jonsson (og))* 213

Hafnarfjordur: Halldorsson; Skulason, Marteinsson, Hilmarsson G, Jonsson B, Sigurdsson, Gislason, Vikingsson, Magnusson, Palsson, Kristiansson.
Dundee U: Thomson; Cleland, Malpas, McInally, Paatelainen, Welsh, Van der Hoorn, McKinlay, Preston, Jackson, McKinnon.

19 SEPT

Aston Villa (1) 3 *(Platt, Mountfield, Olney)*
Banik Ostrava (1) 1 *(Chyiek)*   27,317

Aston Villa: Spink; Price, Gray, McGrath, Mountfield, Nielsen, Daley, Platt, Gage (Ormondroyd), Cowans, Cascarino (Olney).
Banik Ostrava: Smicek; Horvath, Kubanek, Kula, Skarabela, Stalini, Chyiek, Stas, Ollender, Necas, Palinek.

Derry (0) 0
Vitesse (1) 1 *(Loffen)*   3500

Derry: Dalton; Curran, Brady, Healy, McCarthy, Coady, Carlyle, McGee, Speak, Gauld, Hanrahan.
Vitesse: Van der Gouw; Sturing, Straal, Bos, Vermeulen, Laamers, Van den Brom, Eijer, Latuheru, Van Arum, Loffen (Van Breemen).

Dnepr (0) 1 *(Gudimenko)*
Hearts (1) 1 *(Robertson)*   15,500

Dnepr: Gorodov; Yudin, Guerschenko, Beshenar, Sidainikov, Kudritsky, Bagmut, Benko (Yaravenko), Sonn, Gudimenko, Shakhov.
Hearts: Smith; McLaren, McKinlay, Levein, Berry (Kirkwood), Wright, Robertson, McCreery (Kidd), Foster, Sandison, Colquhoun.

FIRST ROUND, SECOND LEG

2 OCT

Bordeaux (0) 2 *(Dugarry, Ferreri)*
Glenavon (0) 0   12,000

Bordeaux: Bell; Dogon, Lizarazu (Fargeon), Senac, Battiston, Deschamps, Durand, Plancque (Ben Mabrouk), Bade, Ferreri, Dugarry.
Glenavon: Beck; McCullough, Scappaticci, McCann (Cochrane), McLoughlin, McConville (Campbell), Ferguson, Blackledge, McBride, Conville, Byrne.

Vitesse (0) 0
Derry (0) 0   5742

Vitesse: Van der Gouw; Van Breemen, Straal, Bos, Vermeulen, Laamers, Van den Brom, Eijer, Latuheru, Van Arum, Loffen (Visser).
Derry: Dalton; Curran, Brady, Healy, Hegarty T, Coady, Carlyle, McGee, Speak, Gauld, Hegarty P.
Vitesse won 1–0 on aggregate

3 OCT

Banik Ostrava (1) 1 *(Necas)*
Aston Villa (0) 2 *(Mountfield, Stas (og))*   20,000

Banik Ostrava: Kubanek; Horvath, Kula, Skarabela, Stalini, Chyiek (Basta), Stas, Ollender, Necas, Vrto.
Aston Villa: Spink; Price, Gray, McGrath, Mountfield, Nielsen, Daley, Platt, Olney, Cowans, Ormondroyd.
Aston Villa won 5–2 on aggregate

Dundee U (0) 2 *(Connolly, Hilmarsson (og))*
Hafnarfjordur (2) 2 *(Magnusson, Gislason)*   5475

Dundee U: Thomson; Kopel, Malpas, McInally, Clark, Welsh, Bowman, McKinlay, Dailly (Connolly), O'Neill M, Preston (Cleland).
Hafnarfjordur: Halldorsson; Skulason, Marteinsson, Hilmarsson G, Jonsson, Sigurdsson, Gislason (Gardarsson), Vikingsson (Amarson), Magnusson, Palsson, Jansson.
Dundee U won 5–3 on aggregate

Hearts (3) 3 *(McKinlay, Robertson 2 (1 pen))*
Dnepr (1) 1 *(Shakhov (pen))*   18,760

Hearts: Smith; McLaren, McKinlay, Levein, Kirkwood, McPherson, Colquhoun (Ferguson D), Wright (Mackay), Robertson, Ferguson I, Bannon.
Dnepr: Gorodov; Yudin (Benko), Guerschenko, Sidainikov, Beshenar, Kudritsky, Bagmut, Mamtchyr, Sonn, Gudimenko (Yaravenko), Shakhov.
Hearts won 4–2 on aggregate

SECOND ROUND, FIRST LEG

24 OCT

Aston Villa (1) 2 *(Nielsen, Platt)*
Internazionale (0) 0   36,461

Aston Villa: Spink; Price, Gray, Comyn, Mountfield, Nielsen, Daley, Platt, Birch, Cowans, Cascarino.
Internazionale: Zenga; Bergomi, Brehme, Berti, Ferri, Battistini, Stringara, Pizzi (Baresi), Klinsmann, Matthaus, Serena.

Hearts (3) 3 *(Foster 2, Ferguson I)*
Bologna (0) 1 *(Notaristefano)*   11,155

Hearts: Smith; McLaren, McKinlay, Levein, Kirkwood (Ferguson D), McPherson, Colquhoun, Berry, Foster, Ferguson I, Bannon.
Bologna: Cusin; Mariani, Villa, Di Gia, Iliev, Tricella, Verga, Bonini (Biondo), Waas, Notaristefano, Lorenzo (Campione).

Vitesse (1) 1 *(Eijer)*
Dundee U (0) 0   8331

Vitesse: Van der Gouw; Sturing (Loffen), Thijssen, Bos, Vermeulen, Laamers, Van den Brom, Eijer, Latuheru, Van Arum (Hilgers), Straal.
Dundee U: Main; Cleland, Malpas, McInally, Narey, Welsh, Van der Hoorn, McKinlay, French, Jackson (Paatelainen), Bowman.

Dundee U (0) 0   10,261
Vitesse (2) 4 *(Latuheru 2, Van den Brom (pen), Eijer)*

Dundee: Main; Cleland, Malpas, McInally (Connolly). Krivokapic, Narey (Dailly), Van der Hoorn, McKinlay, Paatelainen, Jackson, French.
Vitesse: Van der Gouw; Sturing (Vermeulen), Thijssen, Bos (Van Breemen), Straal, Laamers, Van den Brom, Eijer, Latuheru, Van Arum, Hilgers.
Vitesse won 5–0 on aggregate

SECOND ROUND, SECOND LEG
7 NOV

Bologna (1) 3 *(Detari, Villa, Mariani)*
Hearts (0) 0   15,000

Bologna: Cusin; Biondo, Cabrini, Bonini, Tricella, Villa, Mariani, Verga, Campioni (Poli), Detari (Lorenzo), Notaristefano.
Hearts: Smith; Mackay, McKinlay, Levein, Kirkwood, McPherson, Colquhoun, Berry, Robertson (Crabbe), Ferguson I, Bannon (McLaren).
Bologna won 4–3 on aggregate

Internazionale (1) 3 *(Klinsmann, Berti, Bianchi)*
Aston Villa (0) 0   80,000

Internazionale: Zenga; Bergomi, Brehme, Berti (Mandorlini), Ferri, Battistini (Paganin), Bianchi, Pizzi, Klinsmann, Matthaus, Serena.
Aston Villa: Spink; Price, Gray, McGrath, Mountfield (Olney), Nielsen, Daley, Platt, Birch, Cowans, Cascarino.
Internazionale won 3–2 on aggregate

Wales Under-21 appearances continued from page 874

Coleman, C. (Swansea C), 1990 v Pol; 1991 v E, Pol (3)
Curtis, A. T. (Swansea C), 1977 v E (1)

Davies, A. (Manchester U), 1982 v F (2) Ho; 1983 v N, Y, Bul (6)
Davies, I. C. (Norwich C), 1978 v S (sub) (1)
Deacy, N. (PSV Eindhoven), 1977 v S (1)
Dibble, A. (Cardiff C), 1983 v Bul; 1984 v N, Bul (3)
Doyle, S. C. (Preston NE), 1979 v E (sub); (with Huddersfield T), 1984 v N (2)
Dwyer, P. J. (Cardiff C), 1979 v E (1)

Ebdon, M. (Everton), 1990 v Pol; 1991 v E (2)
Edwards, R. (Bristol C.), 1991 v Pol (1)
Edwards, R. I. (Chester), 1977 v S; 1978 v W (2)
Evans, A. (Bristol R), 1977 v E (1)

Freestone, R. (Chelsea), 1990 v Pol (1)
Gale, D. (Swansea C), 1983 v Bul; 1984 v N (sub) (2)
Giggs, R. (Manchester U), 1991 v Pol (1)
Giles, D. C. (Cardiff C), 1977 v S; 1978 v S; (with Swansea C), 1981 v Ho; (with C. Palace), 1983 v Y (4)
Giles, P. (Cardiff C), 1982 v F (2), Ho (3)
Graham, D. (Manchester U.), 1991 v E (1)
Griffith, C. (Cardiff C), 1990 v Pol (1)
Griffiths, C. (Shrewsbury T), 1991 v Pol (sub) (1)

Hall, G. D. (Chelsea), 1990 v Pol (1)
Hodges, G. (Wimbledon), 1983 v Y (sub), Bul (sub); 1984 v N, Bul, Y (5)
Holden, A. (Chester C), 1984 v Y (sub) (1)
Hopkins, J. (Fulham), 1982 v F (sub), Ho; 1983 v N, Y, Bul (5)
Hughes, M. (Manchester U), 1983 v N, Y; 1984 v N. Bul, Y (5)
Hughes, W. (WBA), 1977 v E, S; 1978 v S (3)

Jackett, K. (Watford), 1981 v Ho; 1982 v F (2)
James, R. M. (Swansea C), 1977 v E, S; 1978 v S (3)
Jones, F. (Wrexham), 1981 v Ho (1)
Jones, L. (Cardiff C), 1982 v F (2), Ho (3)
Jones, V. (Bristol R), 1979 v E; 1981 v Ho (2)

Kendall, M. (Tottenham H), 1978 v S (1)

Law, B. J. (QPR), 1990 v Pol; 1991 v E (2)
Letheran, G. (Leeds U), 1977 v E, S (2)
Lewis, D. (Swansea C), 1982 v F (2), Ho; 1983 v N, Y, Bul; 1984 v N, Bul, Y (9)
Lewis, J. (Cardiff C), 1983 v N (1)
Loveridge, J. (Swansea C), 1982 v Ho; 1983 v N, Bul (3)
Lowndes, S. R. (Newport Co), 1979 v E; 1981 v Ho; (with Millwall), 1984 v Bul, Y (4)

Maddy, P. (Cardiff C), 1982 v Ho; 1983 v N (sub) (2)

Marustik, C. (Swansea C), 1982 v F (2); 1983 v Y, Bul; 1984 v N, Bul, Y (7)
Melville, A. K. (Swansea C), 1990 v Pol; (with Oxford U), 1991 v E (2)
Micallef, C. (Cardiff C), 1982 v F, Ho; 1983 v N (3)
Nardiello, D. (Coventry C), 1978 v S (1)
Nicholas, P. (C Palace), 1978 v S; 1979 v E; (with Arsenal), 1982 v F (3)
Nogan, K. (Luton T), 1990 v Pol; 1991 v E (2)
Nogan, L. (Oxford U.) 1991 v E (1)

Owen, G. (Wrexham), 1991 v E (sub), Pol (2)

Pascoe, C. (Swansea C), 1983 v Bul (sub); 1984 v N (sub), Bul, Y (4)
Pembridge, M. (Luton T), 1991 v Pol (1)
Perry, J. (Cardiff C), 1990 v Pol; 1991 v E, Pol (3)
Phillips, D. (Plymouth Arg), 1984 v N, Bul, Y (3)
Phillips, L. (Swansea C), 1979 v E; (with Charlton Ath), 1983 v N (2)
Pontin, K. (Cardiff C), 1978 v S (1)
Powell, L. (Southampton), 1991 v Pol (sub) (1)
Price, P. (Luton T), 1981 v Ho (1)
Pugh, D. (Doncaster R), 1982 v F (2) (2)

Ratcliffe, K. (Everton), 1981 v Ho; 1982 v F (2)
Rees, A. (Birmingham C), 1984 v N (1)
Rees, J. (Luton T), 1990 v Pol; 1991 v E, Pol (3)
Roberts, A. (QPR), 1991 v E, Pol (2)
Roberts, G. (Hull C), 1983 v Bul (1)
Roberts, J. G. (Wrexham), 1977 v E (1)
Rush, I. (Liverpool), 1981 v Ho; 1982 v F (2)

Sayer, P. A. (Cardiff C), 1977 v E, S (2)
Searle, D. (Cardiff C), 1991 v Pol (sub) (1)
Slatter, N. (Bristol R), 1983 v N, Y, Bul; 1984 v N, Bul, Y (6)
Speed, G. A. (Leeds U), 1990 v Pol; 1991 v E, Pol (3)
Stevenson, N. (Swansea C), 1982 v F, Ho (2)
Stevenson, W. B. (Leeds U), 1977 v E, S; 1978 v S (3)
Symons, K. (Portsmouth), 1991 v E, Pol (2)

Thomas, Martin R. (Bristol R), 1979 v E; 1981 v Ho (2)
Thomas, Mickey R. (Wrexham), 1977 v E; 1978 v S (2)
Thomas, D. G. (Leeds U), 1977 v E; 1979 v E; 1984 v N (3)
Tibbott, L. (Ipswich T), 1977 v E, S (2)

Vaughan, N. (Newport Co), 1982 v F, Ho (2)

Walsh, I. P. (C Palace), 1979 v E; (with Swansea C), 1983 v Bul (2)
Walton, M. (Norwich C.), 1991 v Pol (sub) (1)
Williams, D. (Bristol R), 1983 v Y (1)
Williams, G. (Bristol R), 1983 v Y, Bul (2)
Wilmot, R. (Arsenal), 1982 v F (2), Ho; 1983 v N, Y; 1984 v Y (6)

Summary of Appearances

EUROPEAN CUP (1955–91)

English clubs
12 Liverpool
5 Manchester U
3 Nottingham F
2 Derby Co, Wolverhampton W, Everton, Leeds U, Aston Villa
1 Burnley, Tottenham H, Ipswich T, Manchester C, Arsenal

Scottish clubs
15 Celtic
12 Rangers
3 Aberdeen
2 Hearts
1 Dundee, Dundee U, Kilmarnock, Hibernian

Clubs for Northern Ireland
17 Linfield
7 Glentoran
2 Crusaders
1 Glenavon, Ards, Distillery, Derry C, Coleraine, Portadown

Clubs for Eire
7 Shamrock R
6 Waterford, Dundalk
3 Drumcondra
2 Bohemians, Limerick, Athlone T
1 Shelbourne, Cork Hibs, Cork Celtic, Derry C*, Sligo Rovers, St Patrick's Ath

Winners: Celtic 1966–67; Manchester U 1967–68; Liverpool 1976–77, 1977–78, 1980–81, 1983–84; Nottingham F 1978–79, 1979–80; Aston Villa 1981–82

Finalists: Celtic 1969–70; Leeds U 1974–75; Liverpool 1984–85

EUROPEAN CUP-WINNERS' CUP (1960–91)

English clubs
5 Tottenham H
4 West Ham U, Manchester U
3 Liverpool
2 Chelsea, Everton, Manchester C
1 Wolverhampton W, Leicester C, WBA, Leeds U, Sunderland, Southampton, Ipswich T, Arsenal

Scottish clubs
10 Rangers
7 Celtic, Aberdeen
2 Dunfermline Ath, Dundee U
1 Dundee, Hibernian, Hearts, St Mirren

Welsh clubs
12 Cardiff C
7 Wrexham
6 Swansea C
2 Bangor C
1 Borough U, Newport Co, Merthyr Tydfil

Clubs from Northern Ireland
7 Glentoran
4 Ballymena U, Coleraine
3 Crusaders
2 Ards, Glenavon, Linfield
1 Derry C, Distillery, Portadown, Carrick Rangers, Cliftonville

Clubs from Eire
6 Shamrock R
3 Limerick, Waterford, Dundalk
2 Cork Hibs, Bohemians
1 Shelbourne, Cork Celtic, St Patrick's Ath, Finn Harps, Home Farm, Sligo Rovers, University College Dublin, Galway U, Derry C*, Cork City, Bray Wanderers

Winners: Tottenham H 1962–63; West Ham U 1964–65; Manchester C 1969–70; Chelsea 1970–71; Rangers 1971–72; Aberdeen 1982–83; Everton 1984–85; Manchester U 1990–91

Finalists: Liverpool 1965–66; Rangers 1960–61, 1966–67; Leeds U 1972–73; West Ham U 1975–76; Arsenal 1979–80

EUROPEAN FAIRS CUP & UEFA CUP (1955–91)

English clubs
8 Leeds U, Ipswich T
6 Liverpool, Everton, Arsenal
5 Manchester U, Southampton, Tottenham H
4 Manchester C, Birmingham C, Newcastle U, Nottingham F, Wolverhampton W, WBA, Aston Villa
3 Chelsea
2 Sheffield W, Stoke C, Derby Co, QPR
1 Burnley, Coventry C, London Rep XI, Watford

Scottish clubs
16 Dundee U
13 Hibernian
10 Aberdeen
8 Rangers
7 Hearts
5 Dunfermline Ath, Celtic
4 Dundee
3 St Mirren, Kilmarnock
2 Partick Th
1 Morton, St Johnstone

Clubs from Northern Ireland
11 Glentoran
6 Coleraine
4 Linfield
3 Glenavon
1 Ards, Portadown, Ballymena U

Clubs from Eire
7 Bohemians
4 Dundalk
3 Finn Harps, Shamrock R
2 Shelbourne, Drumcondra, St Patrick's Ath
1 Cork Hibs, Athlone T, Limerick, Drogheda U, Galway U, Derry*

Winners: Leeds U 1967–68, 1970–71; Newcastle U 1968–69; Arsenal 1969–70; Tottenham H 1971–72, 1983–84; Liverpool 1972–73, 1975–76; Ipswich T 1980–81

Finalists: London 1955–58, Birmingham C 1958–60, 1960–61; Leeds U 1966–67; Wolverhampton W 1971–72; Tottenham H 1973–74; Dundee U 1986–87

Now playing in League of Ireland.

4th WOMEN'S EUROPEAN TOURNAMENT

Group 1
Holland 2, Rep of Ireland 0; Northern Ireland 1, Rep of Ireland 2; Northern Ireland 0, Holland 6; Rep of Ireland 0, Holland 0; Holland 9, Northern Ireland 0; Rep of Ireland 4, Northern Ireland 0.

Group 2
Poland 1, France 3; Sweden 4, Poland 1; France 0, Sweden 2; Poland 0, Sweden 2; France 2, Poland 0; Sweden 4, France 1.

Group 3
Finland 0, Norway 1; England 0, Finland 0; Norway 4, Belgium 0; Belgium 0, England 3; England 1, Belgium 0; Finland 3, Belgium 0; Norway 2, England 0; Norway 4, Finland 0; England 0, Norway 0; Belgium 0, Norway 1; Finland 0, England 0; Belgium 1, Finland 0.

Group 4
West Germany 0, Hungary 0; Czechoslovakia 2, Bulgaria 0; Bulgaria 0, Hungary 3; West Germany 5, Czechoslovakia 0; Bulgaria 1, West Germany 4; Czechoslovakia 0, West Germany 1; Hungary 2, Czechoslovakia 0, Hungary 2, Bulgaria 0; West Germany 4, Bulgaria 0; Czechoslovakia 3; Hungary 0; Bulgaria 2, Czechoslovakia 3; Hungary 0, West Germany 4.

Group 5
Switzerland 0, Denmark 4; Spain 0, Switzerland 0; Spain 1, Denmark 3; Italy 4, Switzerland 1; Italy 3, Spain 1; Switzerland 0, Italy 4; Denmark 1, Italy 0; Switzerland 2, Spain 1; Denmark 4, Switzerland 0; Denmark 5, Spain 0; Italy 1, Denmark 1; Spain 0, Italy 0.

Quarter-finals
Norway 2, Hungary 1; Sweden 1, Italy 1; Denmark 0, Holland 0; England 1, West Germany 4; Hungary 0, Norway 2; Italy 0, Sweden 0; Holland 0, Denmark 1; West Germany 2, England 0.

Semi-finals
Norway 0, Denmark 0 *aet*; *Norway won 8–7 on penalties*; Germany 3, Italy 0.

Match for third place
Denmark 2, Italy 1 *aet*.

Final
Germany 3, Norway 1 *aet*.

WORLD CLUB CHAMPIONSHIP

Played annually up to 1974 and intermittently since then between the winners of the European Cup and the winners of the South American Champions Cup — known as the Copa Libertadores. In 1980 the winners were decided by one match arranged in Tokyo in February 1981 and the venue has been the same since.

1960 Real Madrid beat Penarol 0-0, 5-1	1976 Bayern Munich beat Cruzeiro 2-0, 0-0
1961 Penarol beat Benfica 0-1, 5-0, 2-1	1977 Boca Juniors beat Borussia Moenchengladbach* 2-2, 3-0
1962 Santos beat Benfica 3-2, 5-2	1978 Not contested
1963 Santos beat AC Milan 2-4, 4-2, 1-0	1979 Olimpia beat Malmö* 1-0, 2-1
1964 Inter-Milan beat Independiente 0-1, 2-0, 1-0	1980 Nacional beat Nottingham Forest 1-0
1965 Inter-Milan beat Independiente 3-0, 0-0	1981 Flamengo beat Liverpool 3-0
1966 Penarol beat Real Madrid 2-0, 2-0	1982 Penarol beat Aston Villa 2-0
1967 Racing Club beat Celtic 0-1, 2-1, 1-0	1983 Gremio Porto Alegre beat SV Hamburg 2-1
1968 Estudiantes beat Manchester United 1-0, 1-1	1984 Independiente beat Liverpool 1-0
1969 AC Milan beat Estudiantes 3-0, 1-2	1985 Juventus beat Argentinos Juniors 4-2 on penalties after a 2-2 draw
1970 Feyenoord beat Estudiantes 2-2, 1-0	1986 River Plate beat Steaua Bucharest 1-0
1971 Nacional beat Panathinaikos* 1-1, 2-1	1987 FC Porto beat Penarol 2-1 after extra time
1972 Ajax beat Independiente 1-1, 3-0	1988 Nacional (Uru) beat PSV Eindhoven 7-6 on penalties after 1-1 draw
1973 Independiente beat Juventus* 1-0	1989 AC Milan beat Atletico Nacional (Col) 1-0 after extra time
1974 Atlético Madrid* beat Independiente 0-1, 2-0	
1975 Independiente and Bayern Munich could not agree dates; no matches.	

*European Cup runners-up; winners declined to take part.

1990

9 December in Tokyo

AC Milan (1) 3 *(Rijkaard 43, 65, Stroppa 62)*

Olimpia (0) 0 62,228

AC Milan: Pazzagli; Tassotti, Baresi, Costacurta, Maldini (Galli F 22), Carbone, Donadoni (Guerreiri 82), Rijkaard, Van Basten, Gullit, Stroppa.
Olimpia: Almeida; Fernandez, Caceres, Guasch, Ramirez (Chamac 48), Suarez, Hoyn (Cubilla 68), Balbuena, Monzon, Amarilla, Samaniego.
Referee: Wright (Brazil).

EUROPEAN SUPER CUP

Played annually between the winners of the European Champions' Cup and the European Cup-Winners' Cup.

Previous Matches

1972 Ajax beat Rangers 3-1, 3-2
1973 Ajax beat AC Milan 0-1, 6-0
1974 Not contested
1975 Dynamo Kiev beat Bayern Munich 1-0, 2-0
1976 Anderlecht beat Bayern Munich 4-1, 1-2
1977 Liverpool beat Hamburg 1-1, 6-0
1978 Anderlecht beat Liverpool 3-1, 1-2
1979 Nottingham F beat Barcelona 1-0, 1-1
1980 Valencia beat Nottingham F 1-0, 1-2
1981 Not contested
1982 Aston Villa beat Barcelona 0-1, 3-0
1983 Aberdeen beat Hamburg 0-0, 2-0
1984 Juventus beat Liverpool 2-0
1985 Juventus v Everton not contested due to UEFA ban on English clubs
1986 Steaua Bucharest beat Dynamo Kiev 1-0
1987 FC Porto beat Ajax 1-0, 1-0
1988 KV Mechelen beat PSV Eindhoven 3-0, 0-1
1989 AC Milan beat Barcelona 1-1, 1-0

1990

First Leg, 10 October 1990, Genoa

Sampdoria (1) 1 *(Mikhailichenko 31)*

AC Milan (1) 1 *(Evani 39)* 25,000

Sampdoria: Pagliuca; Mannini, Invernizzi, Pari, Lanna, Pellegrini, Mikhailichenko, Lombardo, Branca, Mancini, Dossena.
AC Milan: Pazzagli; Tassotti, Costacurta, Gaudenzi, Galli F, Baresi, Donadoni (Rijkaard 59), Ancelotti, Massaro, Gullit, Evani (Stroppa 70).
Referee: Dos Santos (Portugal).

Second Leg, 29 November 1990, Bologna

AC Milan (1) 2 *(Gullit 44, Rijkaard 76)*

Sampdoria (0) 0 25,000

AC Milan: Pazzagli; Tassotti, Baresi, Costacurta (Galli F 78), Maldini, Carbone, Ancelotti, Rijkaard, Evani, Gullit (Donadoni 73), Agostini.
Sampdoria: Pagliuca; Lanna, Pellegrini, Vierchowod, Bonetti, Pari, Mikhailichenko (Dossena 67), Katanec (Branca 83), Lombardo, Vialli, Mancini.
Referee: Petrovic (Yugoslavia).

SOUTH AMERICA

COPA LIBERTADORES
(South American Cup) 1991

Group 1

	P	W	D	L	F	A	Pts
Bolivar (Bol)	6	3	1	2	9	5	7
Boca Juniors (Arg)	6	2	2	2	6	6	6
Oriente (Bol)	6	2	3	1	5	7	6
River Plate (Arg)	6	2	1	3	10	12	5

Group 2

	P	W	D	L	F	A	Pts
Colo Colo (Chi)	6	3	3	0	10	3	9
Liga Deportivo (Ecu)	6	2	2	2	5	6	6
Dep Concepcion (Chi)	6	2	2	2	6	8	6
Barcelona (Ecu)	6	0	3	3	5	9	3

Group 3

	P	W	D	L	F	A	Pts
Flamengo (Br)	6	3	3	0	11	4	9
Corinthians (Br)	6	1	4	1	7	6	6
Nacional (Uru)	6	2	2	2	7	6	6
Bella Vista (Uru)	6	0	3	3	5	14	3

Group 4

	P	W	D	L	F	A	Pts
Colegiales (Para)	6	2	4	0	10	5	8
Cerro Porteno (Para)	6	2	4	0	9	4	8
Universitario (Per)	6	1	3	2	4	6	5
Sport Boys (Per)	6	1	1	4	7	15	3

Play-off: Colegiales 0, Cerro Porteno 1.

Group 5

	P	W	D	L	F	A	Pts
America (Col)	6	5	1	0	10	3	11
Nacional (Col)	6	2	2	2	7	7	6
Tachira (Ven)	6	1	3	2	6	7	5
Maritimo (Ven)	6	0	2	4	4	10	2

Second Round First Leg
Dep Concepcion 0, America 3
Nacional (Uruguay) 4, Bolivar 1
Universitario 0, Colo Colo 0
Boca Juniors 3, Corinthians 1
Colegiales 1, Olimpia 1
Liga Deportivo 2, Nacional (Colombia) 2
Tachira 2, Flamengo 3
Oriente 1, Cerro Porteno 1

Second Round Second Leg
Bolivar 1, Nacional 1
Colo Colo 2, Universitario 1
Flamengo 5, Tachira 0
Corinthians 1, Boca Juniors 1
Cerro Porteno 2, Oriente 0
Nacional 2, Liga Deportivo 0
(at San Cristobal, Venezuela)
America 3, Concepcion 3
(at San Cristobal, Venezuela)
Olimpia 3, Colegiales 1

Quarter-finals First Leg
Flamengo 2, Boca Juniors 1
Cerro Porteno 1, Olimpia 0
Colo Colo 4, Nacional (Uruguay) 0
America 0, Nacional (Colombia) 0
(at Miami, Florida)

Quarter-finals Second Leg
Nacional 2, Colo Colo 0
Boca Juniors 3, Flamengo 0
Olimpia 3, Cerro Porteno 0
Nacional 2, America 0
(at San Cristobal, Venezuela)

Semi-finals First Leg
Boca Juniors 1, Colo Colo 0
Nacional (Colombia) 0, Olimpia 0

Semi-finals Second Leg
Colo Colo 3, Boca Juniors 1
Olimpia 1, Nacional 0

Final First Leg
Olimpia 0, Colo Colo 0

Final Second Leg
Colo Colo 3, Olimpia 0

COPA LIBERTADORES
(South American Cup) 1990

continued from last year's edition

Second Round First Leg
Pepeganga 0, Independiente 6
Defensor 1, River Plate 2
Univ Catolica 3, The Strongest 1
Vasco da Gama 0, Colo Colo 0
Barcelona 2, Progreso 0
Union Huaral 1, Emelec 0
Cerro Porteno 0, Nacional (Colombia) 0

Second Round Second Leg
River Plate 2, Defensor 1
Independiente 3, Pepeganga 0
Colo Colo 3, Vasco da Gama 3
The Strongest 1, Univ Catolica 1
Emelec 2, Union Huaral 0
Nacional 1, Cerro Porteno 0
Progreso 2, Barcelona 2

Quarter-finals First Leg
Olimpia 2, Univ Catolica 0
River Plate 2, Independiente 0
Emelec 0, Barcelona 0
Vasco da Gama 0, Nacional (Colombia) 0

Quarter-finals Second Leg
Independiente 1, River Plate 1
Colo Colo 4, Olimpia 4
Barcelona 1, Emelec 0
Nacional 2, Vasco da Gama 0
(game ordered to be replayed because of death threats to Vasco players and alleged bribery of referee!)
Replay: Nacional 1, Vasco da Gama 0
(at Santiago, Chile)

Semi-finals First Leg
River Plate 1, Barcelona 0
Nacional (Colombia)1, Olimpia 2
(played in Santiago, Chile)

Semi-finals Second Leg
Barcelona 1, River Plate 0
(aggregate 1-1; Barcelona won 4-3 on penalties)
Olimpia 2, Nacional 3
(aggregate 4-4; Olimpia won 2-1 on penalties)

Final First Leg
Olimpia 2, Barcelona 0

Final Second Leg
Barcelona 1, Olimpia 1

Champions:
Argentina: River Plate
Bolivia: Oriente
Brazil: Corinthians
Chile: Colo Colo
Colombia: America
Ecuador: LDU Quito
Paraguay: Cerro Porteno
Peru: Universitario
Uruguay: Bella Vista
Venezuela: Maritimo

Inter-American Cup
Nacional (Colombia) 2, 4, UNAM (Mexico) 0, 1

Cup-Winners' Cup
Boca Juniors 1, Nacional (Colombia) 0

South American Super Cup

First Round First Leg
Penarol 0, Santos 0
Independiente 1, Nacional (Uruguay) 1
Argentinos Juniors 3, Flamengo 1
Cruzeiro 1, Racing 0
River Plate 3, Olimpia 0
Gremio 1, Estudiantes 0
Nacional (Colombia) declared forfeit

First Round Second Leg
Santos 2, Penarol 2
Penarol won 4-2 on penalties
Olimpia 3, River Plate 0
Olimpia won 4-3 on penalties
Racing 1, Cruzeiro 0
Racing won 4-2 on penalties
Nacional 2, Independiente 1
Estudiantes 2, Gremio 1
Flamengo 3, Argentinos Juniors 1
Argentinos Juniors won 4-3 on penalties

Second Round First Leg
Penarol 0, Boca Juniors 1
Olimpia 1, Racing 1
Argentinos Juniors 2, Nacional (Uruguay) 1

Second Round Second Leg
Nacional 3, Argentinos Juniors 1
Boca Juniors 0, Penarol 2
Racing 0, Olimpia 3

Semi-finals First Leg
Penarol 2, Olimpia 1
Estudiantes 0, Nacional (Uruguay) 0

Semi-finals Second Leg
Nacional 0, Estudiantes 0
Nacional won 5-3 on penalties
Olimpia 6, Penarol 0

Final First Leg
Nacional (Uruguay) 0, Olimpia 3

Final Second Leg
Olimpia 3, Nacional 3

International matches 1990
Argentina
Guatemala (a) 0-0; Mexico (a) 0-2; Scotland (a) 0-1;
Austria (a) 1-1; Switzerland (a) 1-1; Israel (a) 2-1;
Cameroon (n) 0-1; USSR (n) 2-0; Romania (n) 1-1; Brazil
(n) 1-0; Yugoslavia (n) 0-0; Italy (n) 1-1; West Germany
(n) 0-1
Goalscorers: Caniggia 3, Burruchaga 2, Balboa 1,
Maradona 1, Monzon 1, Troglio 1.

Bolivia
no matches

Brazil
England (a) 0-1; Bulgaria (h) 2-1; East Germany (h) 3-3;
Sweden (n) 2-1; Costa Rica (n) 1-0; Scotland (n) 1-0;
Argentina (n) 0-1; Spain (a) 0-3; Chile (a) 0-0; Chile (h) 0-
0; Mexico (a) 0-0
Goalscorers: Careca 3, Muller 3, Aldair 1, Alemao 1,
Dunga 1.

Chile
Brazil (h) 0-0; Brazil (a) 0-0

Colombia
Uruguay (h) 0-2; USA (a) 1-1; USSR (h) 0-0; Mexico (a)
0-2; USA (a) 1-0; Poland (h) 2-1; Egypt (a) 1-1; Hungary
(a) 1-3; UAE (n) 2-0; Yugoslavia (n) 0-1; West Germany
(h) 1-1; Cameroon (n) 1-2.
Goalscorers: Rincon 3, Redin 2, Estrada 1, Fajardo 1,
Guerrero 1, Iguaran 1, Valderrama 1.

Ecuador
no matches

Paraguay
no matches

Peru
no matches

Uruguay
Colombia (h) 2-0; Costa Rica (h) 2-0; Mexico (a) 1-2; West
Germany (a) 3-3; Northern Ireland (a) 0-1; England (a)
2-1; Spain (n) 0-0; Belgium (n) 1-3; South Korea (n) 1-0;
Italy (n) 0-2
Goalscorers: Castro 2, Ostolaza 2, Aguilera 1, Bengoechea
1, Fonseca 1, Martinez 1, Pedrucci 1, Perdomo 1, Revelez
1, Suarez 1.

Venezuela
no matches

Copa America (South American Championship in Chile)
Group A
Chile 2, Venezuela 0
Paraguay 1, Peru 0
Chile 4, Peru 2
Argentina 3, Venezuela 0
Chile 0, Argentina 1
Paraguay 5, Venezuela 0
Peru 5, Venezuela 1
Argentina 3, Peru 2
Argentina 4, Paraguay 1
Chile 4, Paraguay 0

Group B
Bolivia 1, Uruguay 1
Colombia 1, Ecuador 0
Ecuador 1, Uruguay 1
Brazil 2, Bolivia 1
Ecuador 4, Bolivia 0
Brazil 1, Uruguay 1
Colombia 0, Bolivia 0
Colombia 2, Brazil 0
Colombia 0, Uruguay 1
Brazil 3, Ecuador 1

Final round
Argentina 3, Brazil 2
Chile 1, Colombia 1
Brazil 2, Colombia 0
Argentina 0, Chile 0
Brazil 2, Chile 0
Argentina 2, Colombia 1

NON-LEAGUE FOOTBALL

FA CHALLENGE TROPHY

FA CHALLENGE VASE

FA SUNDAY CUP

FA YOUTH CUP AND COUNTY YOUTH CUP

GM VAUXHALL CONFERENCE

HFS LOANS LEAGUE

BEAZER HOMES LEAGUE

VAUXHALL FOOTBALL LEAGUE

AC DELCO CUP

PREMIER INTER-LEAGUE CHALLENGE CUP

LOCTITE TROPHY

LOCTITE CUP

LOCTITE YOUTH CUP

AFA, SCHOOLS AND UNIVERSITIES

GM VAUXHALL CONFERENCE 1990–91

Barnet secured the championship on the last Saturday of the season with a 4-2 win at Fisher Athletic. They only had to avoid defeat as they had a vastly superior goal difference to Colchester United, who thus just failed to return to the Football League after one season.

It was an outstanding season for the competition which saw Kettering Town emerge as the favourites for many months only to be overshadowed by Altrincham's undefeated run of 28 matches. But a backlog of fixtures eventually took their toll of Altrincham who finished third.

Barnet's success ended a five year wait for promotion during which they had finished runners-up on three occasions. They scored 103 goals and averaged crowds of 2,918 at Underhill.

GM VAUXHALL CONFERENCE TABLE 1990–91

	P	Home W	D	L	Goals F	A	W	Away D	L	Goals F	A	Pts
Barnet	42	13	4	4	50	23	13	5	3	53	29	87
Colchester United	42	16	4	1	41	13	9	6	6	27	22	85
Altrincham	42	12	6	3	48	22	11	7	3	39	24	82
Kettering Town	42	12	6	3	38	19	11	5	5	29	26	80
Wycombe Wanderers	42	15	3	3	46	17	6	8	7	29	29	74
Telford United	42	11	3	7	30	21	9	4	8	32	31	67
Macclesfield Town	42	11	4	6	38	22	6	8	7	25	30	63
Runcorn	42	12	4	5	44	29	4	6	11	25	38	58
Merthyr Tydfil	42	9	5	7	37	24	7	4	10	25	37	57
Barrow	42	10	8	3	34	24	5	4	12	25	41	57
Welling United	42	7	10	4	33	27	6	5	10	22	30	54
Northwich Victoria	42	8	7	6	33	30	5	6	10	32	45	52
Kidderminster Harriers	42	8	5	8	33	30	6	5	10	23	37	52
Yeovil Town	42	9	5	7	38	29	4	6	11	20	29	50
Stafford Rangers	42	7	9	5	30	26	5	5	11	18	25	50
Cheltenham Town	42	8	6	7	29	25	4	6	11	25	47	48
Gateshead	42	10	3	8	32	38	4	3	14	20	54	48
Boston United	42	9	4	8	40	31	3	7	11	15	38	47
Slough Town	42	9	4	8	31	29	4	2	15	20	51	45
Bath City	42	9	4	8	39	27	1	8	12	16	34	42
Sutton United	42	6	6	9	29	33	4	3	14	33	49	39
Fisher Athletic	42	3	9	9	22	30	2	6	13	16	49	30

GM VAUXHALL CONFERENCE ATTENDANCES 1990–91

Aggregate 1990–91	Average Gate	% Inc	Gates over 1000	Gates over 2000	Clubs with % Inc
653,860	1415	−0.09	57%	21%	11

GM VAUXHALL CONFERENCE ATTENDANCES BY CLUB 1990–91

Club	Aggregate Attendance 1990/91	Average Gate 1990/91	% Inc or Dec	Average Gate 1989/90	Gates over 1000
Colchester United	63,068	3003	− 5	3159	21
Barnet	61,280	2918	+ 2	2869	21
Wycombe Wanderers	58,794	2800	+48	1890	21
Yeovil Town	55,321	2634	+17	2253	21
Kettering Town	53,831	2563	+16	2208	20
Barrow	29,958	1427	+10	1292	21
Altrincham	29,085	1385	+76	789	14
Boston United	28,820	1372	−13	1579	19
Kidderminster Harriers	25,132	1197	−15	1415	17
Telford United	24,924	1186	− 3	1219	16
Stafford Rangers	24,626	1174	− 1	1188	13
Cheltenham Town	21,619	1029	−27	1423	11
Macclesfield Town	21,027	1001	−29	1422	11
Slough Town	24,537	1168	+83	640	8
Welling United	20,696	985	−11	1108	8
Bath City	18,555	883	+14	776	7
Sutton United	18,365	874	− 4	915	4
Merthyr Tydfil	17,309	824	−49	1645	5
Northwich Victoria	15,706	748	+ 3	726	3
Runcorn	15,316	729	−10	809	2
Fisher Athletic	13,663	651	+16	562	2
Gateshead	12,318	586	+93	303	0

HIGHEST ATTENDANCES 1990–91

7221	Colchester United v Altrincham	20.4.91	
5105	Barnet v Colchester United	1.1.91	
5048	Colchester United v Kettering Town	17.4.91	
5020	Kettering Town v Colchester United	10.11.90	
4579	Barnet v Wycombe Wanderers	18.9.90	
4540	Kettering Town v Barnet	23.3.91	
4402	Wycombe Wanderers v Barnet	29.4.91	
4283	Fisher Athletic v Barnet	4.4.91	
4261	Barnet v Kettering Town	4.9.90	
4169	Yeovil Town v Colchester United	18.8.90	

GM VAUXHALL CONFERENCE LEADING GOALSCORERS 1990–91

GMVC			FA	BL	FT
30	Gary Bull (Barnet	+	2	—	
24	Mark West (Wycombe Wanderers)	+	6	—	3
22	Ken McKenna (Altrincham	+	3	2	3
19	Mark Carter (Barnet)	+	—	1	1
	Paul Randall (Bath City)	+	—	—	3
18	Colin Cowperthwaite (Barrow)	+	—	2	1
	Terry Robbins (Welling United)	+	2	1	
17	Mario Walsh (Colchester United)	+	—	—	1
16	Paul Cavell (Boston United)	+	5	1	2
	Nicky Evans (Barnet)	+	5	—	
15	Charlie Butler (Gateshead)	+	—	1	—
	Peter Howell (Kidderminster Harriers)	+	—	1	4
14	John Askey (Macclesfield Town)	+	—	—	
	John Brady (Altrincham)	+	1	—	2
	Kim Casey (Cheltenham Town)	+	2	—	1

FA: FA Cup. *BL:* Bob Lord Trophy. *FT:* FA Challenge Trophy.

GM VAUXHALL CONFERENCE SPONSORSHIP AWARDS 1990–91

	Vauxhall Motors Sponsorship	Vauxhall Goals Jackpot	Title Award	Sportscast	PPA	Total
Barnet	4000	1000	8000	4450	2000	19,450
Colchester United	4000	—	4000	4700	2000	14,700
Altrincham	4000	1000	3000	2750	2000	12,750
Kettering Town	4000	—	—	3225	2000	9225
Northwich Victoria	4000	500	—	2075	2000	8575
Wycombe Wanderers	4000	500	—	1825	2000	8325
Macclesfield Town	4000	—	—	2075	2000	8075
Runcorn	4000	—	—	2075	2000	8075
Slough Town	4000	—	—	2075	2000	8075
Stafford Rangers	4000	—	—	2075	2000	8075
Telford United	4000	—	—	2075	2000	8075
Barrow	4000	—	—	1825	2000	7825
Fisher Athletic	4000	—	—	1825	2000	7825
Kidderminster Harriers	4000	—	—	1825	2000	7825
Sutton United	4000	—	—	1825	2000	7825
Yeovil Town	4000	500	—	1200	2000	7700
Bath City	4000	—	—	1200	2000	7200
Boston United	4000	—	—	1200	2000	7200
Cheltenham Town	4000	—	—	1200	2000	7200
Gateshead	4000	—	—	1200	2000	7200
Merthyr Tydfil	4000	—	—	1200	2000	7200
Welling United	4000	—	—	1200	2000	7200

HIGHEST SCORERS

4   Ian Benbow Kettering Town v *TELFORD UNITED* (GM Vauxhall Conference 6.4.91)
Gary Bull *BARNET* v Slough Town (GM Vauxhall Conference 21.8.90)
BARNET v Fisher Athletic (GM Vauxhall Conference 16.10.90)
Chris Burton *CHELTENHAM TOWN* v Boston United (GM Vauxhall Conference 1.5.91)
Mark Carter *RUNCORN* v Kidderminster Harriers (GM Vauxhall Conference 15.9.90)
Chris Cook *BOSTON UNITED* v Lowestoft Town (FA Cup First Qualifying Round 15.9.90)
Malcolm O'Connor *NORTHWICH VICTORIA* v Cheltenham Town (GM Vauxhall Conference 4.5.91)
Chris Townsend *BATH CITY* v Northwich Victoria (GM Vauxhall Conference 16.4.91)
Mark West *WYCOMBE WANDERERS* v Kettering Town (GM Vauxhall Conference 3.11.90)
WYCOMBE WANDERERS v Sutton United (GM Vauxhall Conference 15.12.90)

HIGHEST AGGREGATE SCORES

Altrincham 9-2 Merthyr Tydfil 16.2.91
Barnet 8-1 Fisher Athletic 16.10.90
Welling United 4-5 Northwich Victoria 29.9.90
Gateshead 0-9 Sutton United 22.9.90
Yeovil Town 7-2 Slough Town 6.4.91

LARGEST HOME WINS

Altrincham 9-2 Merthyr Tydfil 16.2.91
Barnet 8-1 Fisher Athletic 16.10.90
Merthyr Tydfil 7-0 Fisher Athletic 24.11.90
Welling United 6-0 Gateshead 30.3.91

LARGEST AWAY WINS

Gateshead 0-9 Sutton United 22.9.90
Boston United 2-6 Altrincham 16.2.91
Gateshead 0-4 Northwich Victoria 1.12.90

MATCHES WITHOUT DEFEAT

28   Altrincham
15   Kettering Town
12   Colchester United
10   Barnet, Stafford Rangers
9   Kettering Town

MATCHES WITHOUT A WIN

13   Fisher Athletic
12   Kidderminster Harriers, Welling United
10   Bath City, Cheltenham Town, Northwich Victoria
9   Cheltenham Town, Sutton United
8   Kidderminster Harriers, Stafford Rangers (twice), Sutton United, Yeovil Town (twice)

CONSECUTIVE CONFERENCE VICTORIES

7   Barnet, Kettering Town
5   Altrincham, Merthyr Tydfil, Northwich Victoria, Telford United
4   Barrow, Colchester United (3 times), Macclesfield Town, Wycombe Wanderers (twice)

CONSECUTIVE CONFERENCE DEFEATS

7   Yeovil Town
6   Kidderminster Harriers
5   Bath City, Boston United, Runcorn, Slough Town (twice), Sutton United

GM VAUXHALL CONFERENCE 1990–91

APPEARANCES AND GOALSCORERS

Altrincham
Anderson 26; Baker 1; Brady 30(2); Byrne 4(5); Daws 42; Gamble 8; Hughes 12(13); Kelly (6); Lewis 9(5); McCarrick 12; McKenna 39; Miller 25; Nisbett 3(1); Reid 29(2); Roberts 4; Rooney 15(1); Rowlands 40; Shaw 40; Showler 41; Simpson 2; Staunton 2(2); Wealands 38; Wiggins 40; Young (3).
Goals (87): McKenna 22, Brady 14, Shaw 12, Hughes 8, Showler 8, Daws 6, Anderson 5, Rowlands 5, McCarrick 2, Reid 1, Rooney 1, Wiggins 1, Young 1, own goal 1.

Barnet
Bodley 32; Bull 30(3); Carter 7(4); Clarke 26; Cooper 24(1); Culpin 4; Durham 29(2); Evans 15; Gipp 1; Harding 10; Hayrettin 3(6); Howell 19(2); Lowe 18; Lynch 3(11); Murphy 3(7); Nugent 33; Payne 3(2); Phillips 42; Poole 31(2); Regis 6(3); Richardson 22(4); Steine 24(3); Sugrue (1); Tomlinson 7(3); Turner 11(3); Welsh 3(1); Willis 27(10); Willis 29(4).
Goals (103): Bull 30, Clarke 12, Willis 10, Evans 9, Lynch 7, Bodley 6, Regis 5, Murphy 4, Durham 3, Culpin 3, Harding 2, Lowe 2, Nugent 2, Poole 2, Richardson 2, Carter 1, Cooper 1, Howell 1, Steine 1, own goal 1.

Barrow
Brown 4(1); Burgess 4(5); Butler 13; Capstick 17(1); Chilton 36(2); Copeland 1; Cowperthwaite 33; Doherty 42; Farrell 12(8); Gilmour 29(1); King 15; Lowe 5; McDonnell 41; Marsh 18; Messenger 34(3); Proctor 31(1); Robinson 2(1); Skivington 34; Slater 6; Stimpson 13(6); Todhunter 27(5); Vincent 1(5); Wheatley 24; Wood (3).
Goals (59): Cowperthwaite 18, Doherty 12, Gilmour 8, Messenger 5, Wheatley 5, Butler 3, Proctor 3, Capstick 2, King 1, Stimpson 1, Todhunter 1.

Bath City
Banks 39; Brown 30; Churchward 33; Clark 1; Crowley 31; Cousins 24(6); Freegard 22(1); Gamble 1; Gill 6; Gocan (3); Hedges 7; Hirons 1(4); Lowe 8; Lunden 22(1); Mellon 3; Mings 17(9); Painter 1; Palmer 23; Payne 23(4); Preston 9; Radford (3); Randall 38(4); Ricketts 16(1); Singleton 31(3); Smith 10(5); Stevens 6; Tanner 5(1); Townsend 6(7); Underhill 25(2); Weston 11(1); Whitehouse 2; Withy 11.
Goals (55): Randall 19, Freegard 7, Lunden 4, Mings 4, Townsend 4, Brown 3, Withy 3, Crowley 2, Lowe 2, Smith 2, Cousins 1, Palmer 1, Ricketts 1, own goals 2.

Boston United
Adams 13; Beech 33(3); Bennett 1; Buckley 1(1); Campbell 31(2); Cavell 31; Cook, C. 10(2); Cook, M. 9(1); Cusack 29(2); Danzey 1; Deane 10(2); Fraser 2; Gilliver (2); Hardy 32; Hamill 1; Hartford 15; McGinley 20(3); McKenna 42; Morris 1(6); Mossman 6(7); Nesbitt 12(2); Raffell 25(5); Richardson 4; Scott 2; Shirtliff 36; Stephenson 16(1); Tomlinson 16(1); Toone 15(3); Vaughan 20(1); Wharton 28(1).
Goals (55): Cavell 16, Hardy 5, McGinley 5, Deane 4, Tomlinson 4, Wharton 4, Cook, C. 3, Beech 2, Adams 2, Campbell 2, Nesbitt 2, Scott 2, Vaughan 2, Cook, M. 1, Mossman 1.

Cheltenham Town
Adams (1); Barrett 31; Barron 5; Bartram 4; Bloomfield 26(2); Brain 12(1); Brogan 40; Brooks 22(3); Brown 4; Buckland 35(2); Burns 19(4); Burton 16(3); Camden 12(3); Casey 31(2); Crouch 19(4); Dougherty 12; Gennard 10(2); Hancox 2; Howarth (1); Jordan 32(6); Knight 3; Lynch 3; Nuttell 7(1); Payne 23; Sissons 1(3); Stuart 7; Tucker (1); Tuohy 3(5); Vircavs 27; Upshall 3; Weaver 2; Willetts 42; Williams 19(6).
Goals (54): Casey 14, Burton 8, Buckland 6, Brain 4, Burns 4, Payne 4, Willetts 4, Brooks 3, Brogan 2, Jordan 2, Vircavs 2, own goal 1.

Colchester United
Atkins 41; Barrett 42; Bennett 34(2); Bruce 2(2); Collins 35; Daniels 40; Donald 33(5); Elliott 14(5); English 39(1); Grainger 3(2); Hedman 10; Kinsella 6(5); Leworthy 9; McDonough 17(7); McGavin 2(6); Marmon 36(1); Masters 2(9); Osbourne 5(1); Radford 1(3); Rees (1); Ryan 3(10); Scott 1(3); Smith 34; Walsh 31(1); Yates 22(3).
Goals (68): Walsh 17, Bennett 9, McDonough 8, Atkins 7, English 7, Yates 6, Leworthy 4, Ryan 3, Collins 2, Marmon 2, Daniels 1, Donald 1, Masters 1.

Fisher Athletic
Bastock 28; Barton 3; Biley 3; Blackford 24(3); Bright 4; Collins 33; Cormack (1); Docker 15(2); Dryden 3(1); Edwards 11(6); Foley (1); Friar 18; Gorman 30; Hamill 1; Jacobs 3(1); Jolly 11; Kelleher 1(3); Latigo 8(2); Little 41; Mann 13(4); Marks 3(2); Martin 29(7); Mehmet 21; Mitchell 7(4); Mummary 2(2); Murphy 6; Norman 3; Nunes 2; O'Brien 2(2); Parry 2(1); Pearson 16; Pollard, J. 1; Pollard, K. 4; Quinn 27; Restarick 11; Riley 1; Roberts 24; Smart 17; Sweales 21; Tagoe 5(1); Victor 11; Ward 16.
Goals (38): Gorman 12, Martin 5, Little 4, Mehmet 4, Blackford 2, Mann 2, Foley 1, Jacobs 1, Biley 1, Mitchell 1, Pearson 1, Quinn 1, Restarick 1, Riley 1, own goal 1.

Gateshead
Allen 21(1); Arnott 1(1); Atkinson, Pat 11(4); Atkinson, Paul 3(2); Baxter 8; Bell 40; Brabin 10; Butler 26; Carter 2; Davies (3); Dixon 24(7); Doolan 4(2); Emmerson (2); Farrey 16(7); Gowens 25(1); Graham (2); Granycombe 26; Hall 30(2); Halliday 20; Harrison 15; Hulse 9(1); Leonard 8(2); McNall 12(8); Nicholson 10(9); O'Brien 31; Plaskett 7(4); Robinson 3(4); Scott 2; Sharkey 20(6); Silver (1); Smith, SI 42; Smith, S2 1; Statham 10(1); Stokes 7; Toone 10; Trewick 8.
Goals (52): Butler 12, Allen 10, Granycombe 5, Bell 4, Sharkey 4, Statham 3, McNall 2, Nicholson 2, Scott 2, Smith, S2 2, Atkinson, Pat 1, Gowens 1, Hall 1, Halliday 1, Harrison 1, O'Brien 1.

Kettering Town
Bancroft 40; Bastock 3; Blackwell 24; Brook 1; Brown 27(7); Browne 1; Collins 18(1); Cooke 23(2); Emson 10(2); Goodwin 30(3); Graham 11(29); Hunt 23(1); Huxford 35(2); Jones 19(7); Kearns 31; Keast 40(1); Moran 1; Moss 5(1); Neville 3; Nicol 40; Phillips 34(1); Quow 13(4); Ritchie 1; Shoemake 12; Slack 40; Walwyn 7; Wright (1).
Goals (67): Graham 13, Bancroft 10, Cooke 9, Hunt 6, Brown 5, Goodwin 5, Jones 4, Keast 4, Huxford 2, Moss 2, Slack 2, Emson 1, Nicol 1, Ritchie 1, Walwyn 1, own goal 1.

Kidderminster Harriers
Attwood 4(5); Barnett 19; Barton 1; Benton 28(4); Burton 5(3); Carroll 10(7); Congrave 1(1); Davies 29(3); Forsyth 32(3); Hadley 16(1); Hawker 3; Howell 31(3); Humphreys 23; Jones 41; Joseph 39(1); Kurila 36(1); Lilwal 35(1); Lowe 8; McGrath 27(2); Shilvock 7(3); Steadman 1; Taylor (2); Weir 38; Whitehouse 15(3); Wilcox 12(4); Wolsey 2.
Goals (56): Howell 15, Forsyth 9, Davies 6, Weir 5, Humphreys 4, Whitehouse 4, Hadley 3, McGrath 2, Wilcox 2, Burton 1, Carroll 1, Congrave 1, Lilwal 1, Shilvock 1, own goal 1.

Macclesfield Town
Askey 39; Burr 28(2); Camden 6(4); Connor 12(1); Cutler 2(1); Edey 2(4); Edwards 37; Ellis 25(8); Farrelly, M. 16(8); Farrelly, S. 13; Hanlon 42; Heesom 21(5); Imrie 25(2); Johnson 26(2); Kelsey (1); Kendall 25(6); Lambert 31(5); Melrose 2(4); Pollitt 1; Ridings 1; Ridler 3; Shepherd 21; Timmons 17; Tobin 36(2); Tomlinson 6(2); Zelem 25.
Goals (63): Askey 15, Burr 10, Timmons 8, Hanlon 7,

Heesom 5, Ellis 4, Lambert 4, Edwards 3, Camden 1, Cutler 1, Imrie 1, Johnson 1, Tobin 1, own goals 2.

Merthyr Tydfil

Beattie 38; Boyle 38(1); Evans 6(3); Giles 21(9); Green 12(7); Haig 1; Hemming 11; Holvey 4; Hutchison 8(3); Jarrett (1); Lewis 35; Lissaman 13(4); Marsh 2; Morris 2; Mullen, Richard 3; Mullen, Roger 10; Rogers 41(1); Sanderson 31(9); Stevens (2); Stevenson 3(1); Thompson 7; Tucker 39; Wager 37; Webley 32; Williams, C. 30(2); Williams, M. 8(1); Williams, S. 30(1).
Goals (62): Green 10, Webley 9, Williams, C. 8, Rogers 7, Sanderson 7, Tucker 7, Boyle 2, Giles 2, Lewis 2, Thompson 2, Williams, S. 2, Lissaman 1, Williams, M. 1, own goals 2.

Northwich Victoria

Anderton 8(1); Atkinson 6(3); Ball 41; Barnes, P. 2(5); Barnes, R. 5(1); Blain 36(3); Bullock 1; Buxton 13(2); Callaghan 33(6); Clarke 4; Cooper 1; Cutler (1); Doran 2(1); Easter 4(2); Graham 16; Griffiths 1; Hanchard 19; Hancock 25(2); Hemmings 12; Holland 2(1); Johnson 1(2); Jones 32; Lucketti 2; Maguire 35(5); Mills 3; Morton 9(1); O'Connor 37; O'Gorman 3; Parker, D. 3(7); Parker, J. 16(1); Ritchie (1); Salathiel 14(1); Senior (1); Shaw 2(3); Sproson 11(1); Stringer 16(3); Williams 1; Wrench 31(1); Young 16.
Goals (65): O'Connor 12, Maguire 9, Hanchard 8, Blain 4, Callaghan 4, Graham 4, Parker, D. 4, Buxton 3, Morton 3, Hemmings 3, Mills 2, O'Gorman 2, Stringer 2, Anderton 1, Holland 1, Johnson 1, own goals 2.

Runcorn

Brady 27(2); Byrne, C. 1; Byrne, S. 31(1); Carroll 35; Carter 26; Dooner 3(3); Edwards 34(1); Fallon 1(1); Harold 41; Hawtin 27(3); Henshaw 8(3); Highdale 15(1); Hill 10; Hodgett 1; Hopley 6(1); Houghton 1; Hughes 9(1); King 1(3); McBride 11; Miller 2; Murphy 2(6); Pacey 2; Rudge 34(1); Sang 8(2); Saunders 34; Seasman 2; Shaughnessy 14(1); Williams, A. 29; Williams, D. 4; Willis 1(3); Wilson 15; Withers 29(11).
Goals (69): Carter 18, Saunders 14, Brady 12, Shaughnessy 6, Withers 4, Harold 4, Carroll 2, Hawtin 2, Byrne 1, Edwards 1, Highdale 1, Hill 1, Hopley 1, Murphy 1, Rudge 1.

Slough Town

Adams 3(2); Anderson 34(1); Bashir 7(7); Brown (2); Bunting 2; Dell 28(1); Dennis 2; Dodd 3; Donnellan 20; Hill 27; How 33(1); Howell 3; Hunt 4(3); Johnson 3; Knight 41; Lahiff 10; Langley 23(4); Mallinson 28(2); Murphy 4; Pratt 7(2); Rake 10(11); Rowe 5; Sissons 20(3); Stacey 28; Stanley 29(2); Thompson 38; Turkington 11(2); Wilson 9.
Goals (51): Thompson 14, Sissons 8, Stanley 7, Langley 4, Donnellan 3, How 3, Bashir 2, Anderson 1, Dennis 1, Hill 1, Knight 1, Mallinson 1, Murphy 1, Pratt 1, Rake 1, Turkington 1, Wilson 1.

Stafford Rangers

Anastasi 24(11); Barnes 4(1); Bradshaw 13; Bremner 32(1); Butterworth 19; Collymore 17; Devlin 19(5); Dunne 1; Essex 39; Garner 1; Griffiths 3; Hendry 6; Henley 1(3); Jones 11; Khan 11(9); Lloyd 2; Love (1); Maskrey 2; Merchant 2(7); Meyer (3); Morrison 4(1); Palgrave 37; Pearson 26; Price 42; Sadler 1; Shelley 5; Shepherd 2; Simpson 39; Sproson 2; Tuohy 24(1); Turley 25(5);

Whitehouse 4; Wilkinson 1(1); Wood, F. 39(1); Wood, R. 4.
Goals (48): Anastasi 11, Collymore 7, Tuohy 7, Devlin 4, Wood, F. 4, Simpson 3, Essex 2, Butterworth 1, Jones 1, Khan 1, Lloyd 1, Merchant 1, Meyer 1, Palgrave 1, Turley 1, Wood, R. 1, own goal 1.

Sutton United

Adam 14(1); Anderson 3(4); Barnes 26; Berry 34(1); Costello 16(1); Dack 5(8); Dawson 19; Dennis 15(1); Elliott 13(3); Evans 18(3); Gates 34(2); Gill 19(1); Golley 36(1); Hawkins (1); Hemsley 6(1); Hopkins 7; Howell 2; Jenkins 3(5); McCann 11; McKinnon 34(5); Massey 36(3); Newman 4(7); Rains 21; Rogers 41(1); Scott (2); Seagroatt 11(6); Sullivan 31; Thurlow 3(1).
Goals (62): Barnes 12, McKinnon 12, Massey 9, Dennis 7, Seagroatt 6, Gill 4, Newman 3, Rogers 3, Evans 2, Golley 2, Elliott 1, own goal 1.

Telford United

Acton 3; Benbow 28; Bridge 1; Brindley 40; Brown 17(8); Buxton 14; Charlton 11; Clarke 4; Crawley 16(4); Daly 7(4); Davidson, ?. 7; Davidson, M. 3; Dyson 35(1); Grainger 34(1); Humphreys 41; Humphries 22; Hurst 1(3); Lancaster 1(1); Langford 11(3); Lynex 3(1); McDonough 6; McGinty 38; Myers 39; Nelson 35; Osbourne 7(4); Richards 5; Salathiel 5; Thompson 3; Worrall 18(1).
Goals (62): Benbow 13, Myers 9, Crawley 5, Humphreys 4, Langford 4, McGinty 4, Dyson 3, Grainger 3, Nelson 3, Worrall 3, Brown 2, Buxton 2, Daly 2, Brindley 1, Hurst 1, Salathiel 1, own goals 2.

Welling United

Abbott 38(3); Barron 25; Berry 3; Booker 29(6); Brown 2; Burgess 1(2); Clemmence 30(5); Francis 15(13); Glover 38(1); Handford 39; Hone 32; Horton 27; Humphries 14; Parsons 3; Ransom 41; Reynolds 34(1); Robbins 40(1); Robinson 18(3); White 33(6).
Goals (55): Robbins 18, Abbott 11, Glover 7, Booker 5, Ransom 3, Clemmence 2, Hone 2, Reynolds 2, Francis 1, Handford 1, own goals 3.

Wycombe Wanderers

Blackler 12(2); Carroll 28(2); Cash 11(1); Cook 1(1); Creaser 39; Crossley 33; Durham (2); Evans 13; Granville 33; Guppy 26(4); Hanlan 2; Hutchinson 22(9); Kerr 33; Lambert (4); Moussaddik 9; Nuttell 7(5); Price 3; Robinson 19(11); Ryan 24(6); Scope 1(2); Scott 11(1); Smith 19(5); Stapleton 34(2); Walford 22; West 36; Whitby 24(2).
Goals (75): West 24, Carroll 8, Evans 7, Ryan 6, Scott 6, Creaser 4, Kerr 4, Nuttell 3, Stapleton 2, Hutchinson 2, Robinson 2, Blackler 1, Guppy 1, Scope 1, Smith 1, own goals 3.

Yeovil Town

Batty 11; Bond 8; Boulton 1(1); Carroll 28(2); Conning 33(3); Cooper 21(1); Cordice 7(1); Dawkins 8(1); Dent 7(4); De Souza 22; Fry 34; Gardener (1); Gowans 9(6); Harrower 26(1); Hirons 9(8); Housely 1(1); Jackson 17(1); Lowe 14(2); McDermott 27(1); McEvoy 1(1); Pritchard 12(5); Rutter 30(4); Sale 2(1); Shail 33(1); Sherewood 14; Spencer 19(2); Stevenson 19; Wallace 9; Whitehead 1; Willmott 8; Wilson 31(1).
Goals (58): Carroll 9, Wilson 8, McDermott 8, Conning 6, Dent 6, Spencer 5, Hirons 4, Batty 3, Wallace 3, Fry 1, Rutter 1, Sherewood 1, Stevenson 1, own goal 2.

GM VAUXHALL CONFERENCE: MEMBER CLUBS SEASON 1991–1992

Club: ALTRINCHAM
Colours: Red and black striped shirts,
  black shorts
Ground: Moss Lane, Altrincham, Cheshire
  WA15 8AP
Tel: 061-928 1045
Year Formed: 1903
Record Gate: 10,275 (1925 v Sunderland
  Boys)
Nickname: The Robins
Manager: John King
Secretary: Jean Baldwin

Club: BARROW
Colours: White shirts, blue shorts
Ground: Holker Street,
  Barrow-in-Furness, Cumbria
Tel: 0229 820346
Year Formed: 1901
Record Gate: 16,840 (1954 v Swansea
  City)
Nickname: The Bluebirds
Manager: Ray Wilkie
Secretary: Cyril Whiteside

Club: BATH CITY
Colours: Black and white striped shirts,
  black shorts
Ground: Twerton Park, Bath BA2 1DB
Telephone: 0225 423087 and 313247
Year Formed: 1889
Record Gate: 18,020 (1960 v Brighton)
Nickname: City
Manager: George Rooney
Secretary: Paul Britton

Club: BOSTON UNITED
Colours: Wolves gold shirts, black shorts
Ground: York Street Ground, York
  Street, Boston, Lincs
Tel: 0205 365524/5
Year Formed: 1934
Record Gate: 10,086 (v Corby Town)
Nickname: The Pilgrims
Manager: Dave Cusack
Secretary: John Blackwell

Club: CHELTENHAM TOWN
Colours: Red and white shirts, white shorts
Ground: Whaddon Road, Cheltenham,
  Glos. GL52 5NA
Tel: 0242 573558
Year Formed: 1892
Record Gate: 8326 (1956 v Reading)
Nickname: The Robins
Manager: Ally Robertson
Secretary: Keith Astbury

Club: COLCHESTER UNITED
Colours: Royal blue and white shirts,
  royal blue shorts
Ground: Layer Road, Colchester
Tel: 0206 574042
Year Formed: 1937

Record Gate: 19,072 (1948 v Reading)
Nickname: The U's
Manager: Ian Atkins
Executive Director: Trevor Spall

Club: FARNBOROUGH TOWN
Colours: Yellow shirts and blue trim,
  yellow shorts and blue trim
Ground: John Roberts Ground,
  Cherrywood Road, Farnborough, Hants
  GU14 8UD
Tel: 0252 541469
Year Formed: 1967
Record Gate: 3000 (1977 v Billericay Town)
Nickname: The Boro
Manager: Ted Pearce
Secretary: Paul Johnstone

Club: GATESHEAD
Colours: White shirts, black shorts
Ground: International Stadium, Neilson
  Road, Gateshead NE10 0EF
Telephone: 091-478 3883
Year Formed: 1977 (Reformed)
Record Gate: 20,752 (1937 v Lincoln City)
Nickname: Tynesiders
Manager: Tony Lee
Secretary: Jason Davies

Club: KETTERING TOWN
Colours: All red
Ground: Rockingham Road, Kettering,
  Northants NN16 9AW
Tel: 0536 83028
Year Formed: 1875
Record Gate: 11,536 (1947 v
  Peterborough)
Nickname: The Poppies
Manager: Peter Morris
Secretary: George Ellitson

Club: KIDDERMINSTER HARRIERS
Colours: Red/white halved shirts, white
  shorts
Ground: Aggborough, Hoo Road,
  Kidderminster
Tel: 0562 823931
Year Formed: 1886
Record Gate: 9155 (1948 v Hereford)
Nickname: The Harriers
Manager: Graham Allner
Secretary: Ray Mercer

Club: MACCLESFIELD TOWN
Colours: Royal blue shirts, white shorts
Ground: Moss Rose Ground, London
  Road, Macclesfield, Cheshire SK11 7SP
Tel: 0625 424324
Year Formed: 1875
Record Gate: 8900 (1968 v Stockport
  County)
Nickname: The Silkmen
Manager: Peter Wragg
Secretary: Barry Lingard

Club: MERTHYR TYDFIL
Colours: White shirts, black shorts
Ground: Penydarren Park, Merthyr Tydfil
Tel: 0685 4102
Year Formed: 1945
Record Gate: 21,000 (1949 v Reading)
Nickname: The Martyrs
Manager: Wynford Hopkins
Secretary: Phil Dauncey

Club: NORTHWICH VICTORIA
Cololurs: Green and white shirts, white
    shorts
Ground: The Drill Field, Northwich,
    Cheshire CW9 5HN
Tel: 0606 41450
Year Formed: 1874
Record Gate: 11,290 (1949 v Witton
    Albion)
Nickname: The Vics
Manager: Sammy McIlroy
Secretary: Derek Nuttall

Club: REDBRIDGE FOREST
Colours: Red/blue stripe shirts, royal blue
    shorts
Ground: Victoria Road Ground, Victoria
    Road, Dagenham, Essex RM10 7XL
Tel: 081-592 7194, 081-593 3864
Year formed: 1979
Record gate: 1052 (1991 v Dagenham)
Nickname: The Stones or The Fords
Manager: John Still
Secretary: K. H. Mizen

Club: RUNCORN
Colours: Yellow shirts, green shorts
Ground: Canal Street, Runcorn, Cheshire
Tel: 09285 60076
Year Formed: 1919
Record Gate: 10,011 (1939 v Preston NE)
Nickname: The Linnets
Manager: Peter O'Brien
Secretary: Dave Bignall

Club: SLOUGH TOWN
Colours: Amber and navy broad hoops,
    navy blue shorts
Ground: Wexham Park Stadium, Wexham
    Road, Slough SL2 5QR
Tel: 0753 523358
Year Formed: 1890
Record Gate: 8940 (1953 v Pegasus at
    Dolphin Stadium); 5000 (1982 v
    Millwall at Wexham Stadium)
Nickname: The Rebels
Manager: Alan Davies
Secretary: Richard Hayward

Club: STAFFORD RANGERS
Colours: Black and white shirts, white
    shorts
Ground: Marston Road, Stafford
    ST16 3BX
Tel: 0785 42750

Year Formed: 1876
Record Gate: 8536 (1975 v Rotherham)
Nickname: The Boro
Manager: Chris Wright
Secretary: Angela Meddings

Club: TELFORD UNITED
Colours: White shirts, blue shorts
Ground: Bucks Head, Watling Street,
    Telford TF1 2NJ
Tel: 0952 223838
Year Formed: 1877
Record Gate: 13,000 (1935 v Shrewsbury)
Nickname: The Lillywhites
Manager: Derek Mann
Secretary: Mike Ferriday

Club: WELLING UNITED
Colours: Red shirts, red shorts
Ground: Park View Road Ground,
    Welling, Kent
Tel: 081-301 1196
Year Formed: 1963
Record Gate: 4020 (1989 v Gillingham)
Nickname: The Wings
Manager: Nicky Brigden
Secretary: Barrie Hobbins

Club: WITTON ALBION
Colours: Red and white striped shirts,
    black shorts
Ground: Wincham Park, Chapel Street,
    Wincham, Northwich, Cheshire
    CW9 6DA
Tel: 0606 43008
Year Formed: 1890
Record Gate: 10,000 (1948 v Northwich
    Victoria)
Nickname: The Albion
Manager: Stan Allan
Secretary: David Leather

Club: WYCOMBE WANDERERS
Colours: Light blue and dark blue
    quarters, navy blue shorts
Ground: Adams Park, Hillbottom Road,
    Sands, High Wycombe HP12 4HJ
Tel: 0494 472100
Year Formed: 1884
Record Gate: 16,000 (1950 v St Albans)
Nickname: The Blues
Manager: Martin O'Neill
Secretary: John Goldsworthy

Club: YEOVIL TOWN
Colours: Green/white striped shirts, white
    shorts
Ground: Huish Park, Lufton Way, Yeovil
    BA22 8YF
Tel: 0935 23663
Year Formed: 1923
Record Gate: 17,200 (1949 v Sunderland)
Nickname: The Glovers
Manager: Steve Rutter
Secretary: Roger Brinsford

GM VAUXHALL CONFERENCE RESULTS 1990–91

	Altrincham	Barnet	Barrow	Bath City	Boston United	Cheltenham Town	Colchester United	Fisher Athletic	Gateshead	Kettering Town	Kidderminster Harriers	Macclesfield Town	Merthyr Tydfil	Northwich Victoria	Runcorn	Slough Town	Stafford Rangers	Sutton United	Telford United	Welling United	Wycombe Wanderers	Yeovil Town
Altrincham	—	4-1	1-1	2-0	1-1	3-0	2-2	0-0	4-1	3-2	1-2	5-2	9-2	0-2	1-0	3-0	0-0	4-1	2-1	0-1	1-0	2-2
Barnet	0-0	—	3-1	2-0	5-0	2-1	1-3	8-1	1-1	0-1	2-3	3-1	2-3	1-1	2-0	6-1	2-0	1-0	0-0	3-2	3-2	3-2
Barrow	1-0	4-2	—	1-1	1-1	0-0	2-2	3-1	3-1	0-1	1-3	1-1	0-2	2-2	2-1	2-1	0-1	3-1	2-1	1-1	2-2	1-0
Bath City	2-3	1-4	1-1	—	1-0	2-0	1-2	0-1	3-0	3-3	4-1	0-2	0-0	4-1	6-1	4-0	0-2	2-2	0-1	2-1	1-2	2-1
Boston United	2-6	1-3	0-2	3-0	—	2-1	1-3	4-1	5-1	1-2	3-1	1-1	3-0	4-1	2-2	0-1	0-2	3-2	2-1	0-0	0-1	4-0
Cheltenham Town	1-4	1-4	3-1	0-0	5-0	—	1-2	0-0	1-0	1-2	0-0	2-2	0-1	1-1	1-3	2-0	2-0	1-0	0-1	3-0	1-0	1-0
Colchester United	1-1	0-0	1-0	2-0	3-1	3-1	—	2-1	3-0	3-1	2-0	1-0	3-1	4-0	2-1	2-1	2-0	1-0	2-0	2-1	2-2	0-1
Fisher Athletic	0-0	2-4	1-2	0-3	1-2	1-1	0-0	—	0-2	0-0	1-1	1-2	0-0	5-2	0-1	1-3	1-3	1-1	2-0	1-1	2-3	0-1
Gateshead	0-3	1-3	5-1	2-0	0-1	3-3	1-2	1-0	—	1-2	2-1	1-1	1-0	0-4	3-1	1-1	1-3	0-9	5-1	0-3	2-3	2-1
Kettering Town	1-1	1-3	2-0	1-1	1-1	5-1	1-2	3-2	1-0	—	4-1	2-0	1-0	5-2	3-1	0-0	2-1	5-2	2-5	0-3	0-1	1-1
Kidderminster Harriers	0-1	0-3	3-1	3-2	3-3	2-0	0-0	3-3	2-3	3-0	—	0-0	1-2	3-1	3-1	1-2	2-1	1-0	1-3	1-2	1-2	0-0
Macclesfield Town	0-1	3-2	3-0	3-1	2-0	5-1	1-0	7-0	4-0	1-2	0-0	—	0-1	3-2	0-0	1-2	2-1	1-0	1-2	2-1	0-0	2-1
Merthyr Tydfil	0-2	1-1	0-0	0-0	3-0	5-2	3-1	0-0	3-1	1-3	1-2	0-2	—	0-3	1-4	2-0	2-0	3-0	2-3	1-0	2-4	3-3
Northwich Victoria	1-1	0-2	2-2	1-1	3-1	1-1	2-2	0-0	3-2	2-1	1-1	4-1	0-1	—	1-4	3-1	1-1	1-0	2-4	2-3	1-1	2-1
Runcorn	1-3	3-2	3-1	1-1	2-1	1-3	0-3	5-1	2-0	2-1	5-1	1-2	2-1	2-1	—	3-1	1-0	5-1	0-0	2-3	1-1	2-0
Slough Town	3-3	1-3	3-0	2-0	2-0	0-3	0-2	1-0	1-1	0-3	0-0	0-1	2-0	2-4	1-1	—	2-1	1-2	2-0	3-0	3-3	2-0
Stafford Rangers	2-1	2-2	2-2	2-1	1-2	2-2	0-2	2-0	0-1	0-0	3-1	2-2	2-0	0-0	1-1	3-4	—	1-2	1-1	1-0	3-0	1-1
Sutton United	1-2	0-1	2-1	1-1	0-0	2-3	0-1	3-1	1-3	1-2	1-2	3-1	1-1	2-2	1-3	5-2	0-3	—	0-3	1-1	1-0	1-0
Telford United	1-2	1-1	0-1	2-2	1-0	1-2	2-0	3-1	1-2	0-1	1-0	1-2	3-1	1-0	2-0	2-1	0-0	4-2	—	2-1	1-0	1-2
Welling United	2-2	1-4	4-2	2-1	0-0	0-0	1-1	1-1	6-0	1-0	0-0	0-0	4-5	3-0	2-2	2-0	4-1	1-2	1-1	—	1-1	0-3
Wycombe Wanderers	3-0	1-3	2-1	0-0	3-0	0-2	1-0	2-0	4-0	5-1	2-3	2-1	2-1	3-0	1-1	2-1	3-0	4-1	3-2	4-1	—	2-0
Yeovil Town	2-3	1-4	0-3	3-2	1-1	4-0	2-0	0-1	4-1	0-1	2-0	2-1	3-3	1-1	1-0	7-2	0-0	2-1	1-2	0-1	2-2	—

THE BOB LORD CHALLENGE TROPHY 1990–91

First Round *(two legs)*

Altrincham 2 *(Hughes, McKenna)*
Barrow 2 *(Gilmour, Butler)* — 589

Barrow 3 *(Marsh, Chilton, Doherty N)*
Altrincham 2 *(Reid, McKenna)* — 1566

Northwich Victoria 3 *(O'Connor 2, Morton)*
Gateshead 0 — 360

Gateshead 1 *(Hulse)*
Northwich Victoria 3 *(Maguire, O'Connor 2)* — 174

Telford United 5 *(Grainger, Crawley 3, Buxton)*
Cheltenham Town 2 *(Crouch, Tuohy)* — 773

Cheltenham Town 4 *(Brogan, Gennard, Buckland 2)*
Telford United 2 *(Crawley, Benbow)* — 412

Stafford Rangers 1 *(Collymore)*
Boston United 0 — 811

Boston United 3 *(Tomlinson (pen), Cavell, Campbell)*
Stafford Rangers 3 *(Anastasi, Collymore 2)* — 1151

Slough Town 2 *(Dodd, Rake)*
Fisher Athletic 4 *(Gorman, Mann 2, Kelleher)* — 503

Fisher Athletic 2 *(Little, Mann)*
Slough Town 1 *(Stanley)* — 250

Bath City 0
Wycombe Wanderers 1 *(Kerr A)* — 445

Wycombe Wanderers 0
Bath City 0 — 1167

Byes to Second Round
Colchester United, Barnet, Runcorn, Macclesfield Town, Kettering Town, Welling United, Yeovil Town, Sutton United, Merthyr Tydfil and Kidderminster Harriers

Second Round

Merthyr Tydfil 1 *(Giles)*
Sutton United 2 *(Seagroatt, McKinnon)* — 431

Kettering Town 1 *(Moss E)*
Wycombe Wanderers 0 — 1435

Kidderminster Harriers 3 *(Forsyth, Howell, Hadley)*
Yeovil Town 2 *(Carroll 2)* — 672

Fisher Athletic 2 *(Mehmet, Gorman)*
Colchester United 3 *(Marmon, Restarick 2) aet* — 293

Welling United 1 *(Robbins (pen))*
Barnet 0 — 705

Northwich Victoria 1 *(Essex (og))*
Stafford Rangers 2 *(Anastasi 2)* — 429

Barrow 2 *(Cowperthwaite, Wheatley)*
Macclesfield Town 1 *(Burr)* — 1011

Telford United 0
Runcorn 2 *(Saunders, Withers)* — 443

Third Round

Runcorn 1 *(Carter)*
Kidderminster Harriers 2 *(Benton, Humphreys) aet* — 522

Barrow 2 *(Ballantyne, Proctor)*
Stafford Rangers 1 *(Simpson (pen))* — 1330

Kettering Town 1 *(Emson)*
Welling United 0 — 1145

Sutton United 2 *(Dennis, Massey)*
Colchester United 0 — 582

Semi-finals *(two legs)*

Kettering Town 0
Sutton United 2 *(Barnes, Dennis)* — 1104

Sutton United 4 *(Barnes 2, McKinnon, Massey)*
Kettering Town 1 *(Graham)* — 707

Barrow 2 *(Gilmour, Proctor)*
Kidderminster Harriers 0 — 1504

Kidderminster Harriers 2 *(Wilcox, Carroll)*
Barrow 4 *(Gilmour 3, Doherty N)* — 808

Final: First Leg: Barrow 1, Sutton United 1, attendance 1502

Barrow: McDonnell; Messenger, Slater, Skivington, Capstick, King, Doherty, Farrell, Cowperthwaite, Proctor, Wheatley. *Substitutes:* Robinson (67), Vincent (82). *Scorer:* Cowperthwaite.

Sutton United: Sullivan; Golley, Berry, Gates, Massey, McKinnon, Dack, Rogers, Elliott, Barnes, Hemsley. *Scorer:* Barnes.

Final: Second Leg: Sutton United 5, Barrow 0, attendance 855

Sutton United: Sullivan; Rains, Gill, Gates, Massey, Rogers, Adam, Elliott, Seagroatt, Barnes, Hemsley. *Substitutes:* McKinnon (80), Evans (80). *Scorers:* Elliott, Barnes, Seagroatt, Massey, own goal.

Barrow: McDonnell; Slater, Chilton, Farrell, Capstick, King, Doherty, Vincent, Cowperthwaite, Proctor, Wheatley. *Substitutes:* Brown (62), McDonald (73).

HFS LOANS LEAGUE 1990-91

HFS LOANS LEAGUE – PREMIER DIVISION

		Home			Goals		Away			Goals		
	P	W	D	L	F	A	W	D	L	F	A	Pts
Witton Albion	40	15	4	1	48	16	13	5	2	33	15	93
Stalybridge Celtic	40	14	5	1	29	8	8	6	6	15	18	77
Morecambe	40	12	7	1	49	26	7	9	4	23	18	73
Fleetwood Town	40	9	6	5	33	20	11	3	6	36	24	69
Southport	40	11	5	4	32	20	7	9	4	34	28	68
Marine	40	11	3	6	36	20	7	8	5	20	19	65
Bishop Auckland	40	10	3	7	28	22	7	7	6	34	34	61
Buxton	40	10	7	3	36	22	7	4	9	30	39	59
Leek Town	40	7	8	5	27	23	8	3	9	21	21	56
Frickley Athletic	40	9	2	9	36	33	7	4	9	28	29	54
Hyde United	40	10	4	6	52	29	4	7	9	21	34	53
Goole Town	40	9	4	7	34	27	5	6	9	34	47	52
Droylsden	40	7	7	6	40	33	5	4	11	27	37	47
Chorley	40	8	4	8	32	27	4	6	10	23	28	46
Mossley	40	9	7	4	31	25	4	3	13	24	43	45
Horwich	40	7	6	7	35	29	6	0	14	27	52	45
Matlock Town	40	6	5	9	29	31	6	2	12	23	39	43
Bangor City	40	6	4	10	21	28	3	8	9	31	42	39
South Liverpool	40	5	4	11	29	44	5	5	10	29	48	39
Gainsborough Trinity	40	6	7	7	35	38	3	4	13	22	46	38
Shepshed Charterhouse	40	3	4	13	18	34	3	3	14	20	49	25

Leading scorers (*HFS Loans League and HFS cups only*)

Premier Division

32	Coleman (Morecambe)
30	Thomas (Witton Albion)
29	Clarke (Buxton)
28	Holden (Southport)
19	Blackhurst (Southport)
	Kirkham (Hyde United)
	Whitehall (Southport)
18	Green (South Liverpool)
	Lutkevitch (Hyde United)
	Wakenshaw (Fleetwood Town)
17	Clarkson (Fleetwood Town)
	Ross (Chorley)
16	Collier (Goole Town)
15	Grimshaw (Witton Albion)
14	Cain (Morecambe)
	Hurlstone (Goole Town)
	Shaw (Bishop Auckland)

First Division

33	Barker (Whitley Bay)
29	Chandler (Whitley Bay)
	Clark (Worksop Town)
27	Fleming (Netherfield)
26	Richardson (Eastwood Town)
25	Beck (Accrington Stanley)
24	Biddle (Congleton Town)
	Lloyd (Rhyl)
	Wylie (Rossendale United)
19	Archer (Bridlington Town)
	Priest (Curzon Ashton)
18	Edwards (Newtown)
	Gascoigne (Bridlington)
	Moss (Worksop Town)
17	Downing (Harrogate Town)
	Dunn (Warrington Town)
16	Curley (Radcliffe Borough)
	McDonald (Radcliffe Borough)
	Nicholson (Workington)

HFS LOANS LEAGUE – FIRST DIVISION

		Home			Goals		Away			Goals		
	P	W	D	L	F	A	W	D	L	F	A	Pts
Whitley Bay	42	17	4	0	67	15	8	6	7	28	23	85
Emley	42	13	5	3	47	20	11	7	3	31	17	84
Worksop Town	42	15	3	3	49	20	10	4	7	36	36	82
Accrington Stanley	42	12	6	3	46	22	9	7	5	37	35	76
Rhyl	42	15	2	4	38	24	6	5	10	24	39	70
Eastwood Town	42	10	5	6	37	25	7	6	8	33	35	62
Warrington Town	42	12	5	4	43	15	5	5	11	25	37	61
Lancaster City	42	13	4	4	38	17	6	4	11	20	40	61
Bridlington Town	42	9	5	7	43	26	6	10	5	29	26	60
Curzon Ashton	42	7	7	7	28	29	7	7	7	21	28	56
Congleton Town	42	10	8	3	36	28	4	4	13	21	43	54
Netherfield	42	8	7	6	36	26	6	4	11	31	40	53
Newtown	42	8	8	5	39	30	5	4	12	29	45	51
Caernarfon Town	42	12	3	6	41	25	1	7	13	10	39	49
Rossendale United	42	8	5	8	42	33	4	8	9	25	34	48
Radcliffe Borough	42	8	6	7	32	31	4	6	11	18	38	48
Irlam Town	42	6	7	8	27	31	6	4	11	28	45	47
Winsford United	42	5	10	6	23	27	6	3	12	28	39	46
Harrogate Town	42	7	9	5	27	23	4	4	13	28	50	46
Workington	42	9	7	5	31	19	2	4	15	23	48	41
Farsley Celtic	42	6	3	12	28	37	5	6	10	21	41	39
Alfreton Town	42	6	4	11	24	40	1	8	12	17	44	33

HFS LOANS LEAGUE – PREMIER DIVISION RESULTS 1990-91

Home \ Away	Bangor City	Bishop Auckland	Buxton	Chorley	Droylsden	Fleetwood Town	Frickley Athletic	Gainsborough Trinity	Goole Town	Horwich	Hyde United	Leek Town	Marine	Matlock Town	Morecambe	Mossley	Shepshed Charterhouse	South Liverpool	Southport	Stalybridge Celtic	Witton Albion
Bangor City	—	0-1	1-3	1-3	1-3	2-4	1-0	0-0	2-3	3-1	1-0	1-1	1-1	1-0	1-1	2-1	1-2	1-1	2-1	0-1	0-1
Bishop Auckland	3-0	—	2-2	1-0	2-1	0-1	1-0	3-1	3-0	1-2	2-0	0-3	0-0	1-1	3-3	1-0	3-1	2-0	3-4	0-1	0-4
Buxton	1-1	1-2	—	4-3	1-1	1-2	2-1	4-3	3-1	5-1	0-0	0-2	0-3	2-1	2-1	2-1	4-0	1-0	0-0	1-1	4-0
Chorley	1-3	1-0	4-3	—	3-0	2-2	1-3	5-3	2-2	1-2	4-0	0-0	1-0	1-0	3-1	1-2	1-1	3-1	1-2	2-0	0-1
Droylsden	2-2	3-4	3-0	0-0	—	1-3	2-2	3-0	4-2	3-1	2-0	1-1	4-0	2-1	6-1	0-0	4-2	3-2	2-2	2-2	1-4
Fleetwood Town	3-1	0-1	2-2	1-0	1-3	—	5-0	2-0	1-1	3-2	4-1	1-1	4-1	1-3	3-2	2-3	1-1	1-2	0-0	3-1	0-2
Frickley Athletic	2-2	0-1	2-1	1-4	3-2	2-0	—	3-1	3-2	0-1	3-1	4-1	0-0	1-2	2-1	4-2	2-3	5-1	1-4	3-1	0-1
Gainsborough Trinity	1-1	2-1	5-3	2-1	5-4	0-4	3-1	—	4-2	4-1	2-1	2-1	2-3	2-4	4-4	3-1	3-2	3-1	1-3	0-0	0-0
Goole Town	4-3	0-3	2-2	2-1	0-0	0-1	4-3	2-2	—	4-1	4-2	1-3	0-1	1-2	5-3	2-4	2-1	2-4	0-1	0-1	1-2
Horwich	4-1	3-2	5-0	1-1	2-0	0-2	1-1	2-1	1-3	—	0-0	0-3	0-0	5-0	3-1	6-2	3-0	9-1	2-2	0-1	1-2
Hyde United	4-5	3-2	4-0	3-1	1-0	1-1	2-0	1-2	1-2	2-0	—	2-0	1-1	5-3	1-3	7-0	2-0	1-1	1-3	1-1	1-1
Leek Town	0-2	0-2	0-2	0-0	2-1	1-2	2-1	4-0	1-1	0-3	2-0	—	2-3	2-0	3-1	3-3	3-1	2-1	1-1	1-0	0-0
Marine	1-1	1-2	0-3	3-1	1-1	1-0	1-3	3-0	2-0	2-1	1-3	4-1	—	2-0	0-0	3-1	3-0	3-1	2-3	0-1	1-1
Matlock Town	2-2	3-1	2-1	1-2	0-1	1-1	1-3	2-3	1-2	2-1	1-3	2-0	2-0	—	4-1	4-0	1-0	1-1	0-0	0-1	1-3
Morecambe	1-1	3-3	0-0	1-1	6-1	3-2	2-1	4-4	5-3	5-2	1-1	1-2	1-2	4-1	—	0-2	3-0	2-1	2-1	0-0	1-2
Mossley	2-0	2-3	2-1	1-1	3-3	2-1	0-0	1-0	2-0	5-3	2-2	0-2	1-3	0-1	0-2	—	1-0	0-2	2-2	0-1	2-1
Shepshed Charterhouse	1-1	2-2	4-0	1-2	0-2	1-4	0-1	1-0	2-2	1-2	1-4	1-0	0-2	0-1	3-0	1-0	—	1-2	0-3	0-2	1-2
South Liverpool	2-1	2-0	1-0	2-1	3-4	2-4	1-4	1-1	2-4	3-0	2-3	0-1	0-1	0-1	2-1	4-0	0-3	—	3-4	2-0	1-1
Southport	3-2	3-4	0-0	2-1	0-2	2-1	0-1	1-0	3-3	2-0	2-1	1-1	0-1	0-0	2-1	1-0	1-0	3-4	—	2-2	2-1
Stalybridge Celtic	3-1	0-1	1-1	1-0	1-0	2-0	0-0	1-0	1-1	3-0	3-1	1-0	1-0	1-0	0-0	3-2	3-1	1-1	2-0	—	0-1
Witton Albion	2-1	0-4	4-0	1-0	1-0	0-1	2-1	4-0	4-0	4-1	1-1	2-0	0-0	2-0	1-1	2-1	1-1	4-1	2-1	3-0	—

HFS LOANS LEAGUE – FIRST DIVISION RESULTS 1990-91

	Accrington Stanley	Alfreton Town	Bridlington Town	Caernarfon Town	Congleton Town	Curzon Ashton	Eastwood Town	Emley	Farsley Celtic	Harrogate Town	Irlam Town	Lancaster City	Netherfield	Newtown	Radcliffe Borough	Rhyl	Rossendale United	Warrington Town	Whitley Bay	Winsford United	Workington	Worksop Town
Accrington Stanley	—	2-2	0-0	3-0	5-2	0-1	2-1	0-0	2-0	4-1	2-3	2-1	1-1	5-3	3-3	3-0	4-0	0-0	0-2	4-1	2-1	2-0
Alfreton Town	1-1	—	0-1	1-1	1-1	3-1	0-5	0-3	1-2	1-4	3-2	0-2	0-1	2-6	1-0	2-1	3-1	0-2	0-0	0-1	4-3	1-2
Bridlington Town	5-1	0-2	—	0-1	4-1	4-1	2-2	1-2	4-0	4-0	2-3	1-1	2-3	0-0	1-1	3-0	0-1	2-2	2-1	1-2	2-1	3-1
Caernarfon Town	3-0	6-3	1-1	—	1-2	0-1	3-1	1-0	0-3	1-4	5-1	4-0	4-0	1-0	1-0	2-0	1-2	3-1	1-4	1-1	3-1	0-0
Congleton Town	3-3	2-2	1-1	1-0	—	3-3	0-0	1-0	0-0	2-2	2-1	1-1	3-1	1-2	2-1	2-4	2-1	3-1	1-1	0-2	3-1	3-4
Curzon Ashton	1-1	1-1	0-3	1-0	1-1	—	0-0	0-1	3-1	0-1	0-2	1-1	3-1	4-1	0-0	2-4	1-1	0-0	1-1	3-2	3-2	1-3
Eastwood Town	0-2	1-0	2-0	2-1	2-0	0-3	—	2-3	5-0	5-2	2-0	1-0	1-2	1-2	0-0	2-2	1-1	4-1	1-0	3-0	2-3	1-2
Emley	0-3	1-1	2-0	5-1	6-0	0-0	4-2	—	3-1	1-0	0-0	0-0	1-3	3-4	3-1	3-0	2-2	0-3	2-3	1-2	1-1	1-1
Farsley Celtic	0-3	4-0	0-3	1-1	1-0	0-2	1-1	0-3	—	4-1	0-0	0-1	0-0	4-1	1-2	0-2	3-2	2-1	1-0	2-0	4-0	0-2
Harrogate Town	1-2	0-0	1-5	2-1	2-0	1-1	0-1	2-2	1-1	—	0-0	0-1	0-1	4-1	3-3	1-1	1-1	0-1	1-3	2-2	4-1	2-0
Irlam Town	1-2	2-0	2-2	3-2	2-1	0-0	0-2	1-1	1-1	2-1	—	1-1	2-3	4-1	3-1	4-0	2-1	3-1	2-0	2-0	0-1	0-3
Lancaster City	1-2	4-0	4-0	1-1	0-0	1-0	2-2	0-1	1-2	2-1	2-1	—	2-3	2-1	3-1	4-0	1-1	0-1	1-1	2-0	3-0	2-1
Netherfield	2-2	5-1	2-2	2-1	2-0	1-1	1-3	1-1	1-2	1-1	2-0	2-0	—	4-0	4-0	0-2	0-0	0-2	1-1	1-3	1-0	3-3
Newtown	1-2	2-1	0-2	0-0	4-2	2-2	0-0	1-1	3-3	4-1	5-0	2-2	4-3	—	1-2	1-1	2-0	1-0	2-3	2-1	0-0	2-4
Radcliffe Borough	2-1	1-1	2-2	3-0	2-0	1-0	1-2	1-3	0-0	4-2	1-2	0-1	1-4	1-1	—	1-2	1-1	2-1	0-2	4-3	2-1	2-3
Rhyl	2-3	3-1	1-0	0-0	3-1	2-1	3-2	1-1	2-1	2-1	1-2	2-0	2-1	2-0	3-0	—	0-6	2-0	0-2	3-1	3-1	2-0
Rossendale United	2-2	1-1	5-1	1-0	1-3	1-2	2-3	0-3	7-1	0-2	2-2	3-2	2-0	1-1	1-0	0-1	—	4-1	2-2	2-4	5-1	0-1
Warrington Town	2-0	2-0	1-1	0-0	2-2	0-0	3-1	1-2	2-0	4-0	6-1	5-0	3-2	2-2	1-0	2-0	0-1	—	2-0	3-0	2-2	1-2
Whitley Bay	2-0	3-1	1-0	7-0	3-0	4-2	2-0	0-0	3-1	3-0	1-0	6-0	1-1	2-0	6-0	2-2	4-1	5-1	—	1-1	2-2	6-1
Winsford United	2-2	2-0	0-0	0-0	0-3	0-1	1-2	0-0	1-2	1-1	4-3	2-3	1-1	2-1	2-0	0-0	2-2	0-4	0-0	—	1-0	2-2
Workington	2-2	4-0	0-2	3-0	1-2	0-1	3-1	0-0	1-1	2-2	3-1	0-2	2-2	0-1	0-0	2-0	3-0	1-1	1-0	1-0	—	2-1
Worksop Town	2-3	2-0	2-2	2-0	1-0	6-0	4-1	0-1	1-0	3-1	0-3	3-1	2-1	2-1	0-0	6-2	1-0	5-1	1-2	2-1	2-1	—

BEAZER HOMES LEAGUE 1990–91

PREMIER DIVISION

	P	W	D	L	F	A	W	D	L	F	A	Pts
			Home		Goals			Away		Goals		
Farnborough Town	42	13	3	5	47	26	13	4	4	32	17	85
Gloucester City	42	15	6	0	56	24	8	8	5	30	25	83
Cambridge City	42	14	4	3	41	20	7	10	4	22	23	77
Dover Athletic	42	10	7	4	27	16	11	4	6	29	21	74
Bromsgrove Rovers	42	14	4	3	45	21	6	7	8	23	28	71
Worcester City	42	10	7	4	32	17	8	5	8	23	25	66
Burton Albion	42	11	6	4	31	15	4	9	8	28	33	60
Halesowen Town	42	8	6	7	35	28	9	3	9	38	39	60
V.S. Rugby	42	10	3	8	35	22	6	8	7	21	24	59
Bashley	42	8	5	8	30	27	7	7	7	26	25	57
Dorchester Town	42	12	4	5	29	23	3	8	10	18	31	57
Wealdstone	42	9	4	8	31	29	7	4	10	26	29	56
Dartford	42	13	4	4	45	22	2	5	14	16	42	54
Rushden Town	42	10	6	5	42	23	4	5	12	22	43	53
Atherstone United	42	7	5	9	27	27	7	5	9	28	31	52
Moor Green	42	10	2	9	38	34	5	4	12	26	41	51
Poole Town	42	8	4	9	29	33	4	9	8	27	36	49
Chelmsford City	42	3	11	7	23	31	8	4	9	34	37	48
Crawley Town	42	7	9	5	28	27	5	3	13	17	40	48
Waterlooville	42	5	8	8	25	29	6	5	10	26	41	46
Gravesend & Northfleet	42	7	6	8	28	31	2	1	18	18	60	34
Weymouth	42	3	8	10	25	30	1	4	16	25	58	24

MIDLAND DIVISION

	P	W	D	L	F	A	W	D	L	F	A	Pts
			Home		Goals			Away		Goals		
Stourbridge	42	18	2	1	45	17	10	4	7	35	31	90
Corby Town	42	16	2	3	54	16	11	2	8	45	32	85
Hednesford Town	42	13	3	5	40	23	12	4	5	39	24	82
Tamworth	42	14	1	6	43	24	11	4	6	41	21	80
Nuneaton Borough	42	13	6	2	42	23	8	5	8	32	28	70*4
Barry Town	42	13	3	5	38	21	7	4	10	23	27	67
Newport A.F.C.	42	10	3	8	28	24	9	3	9	26	22	63
King's Lynn	42	11	4	6	27	25	6	5	10	26	37	60
Grantham Town	42	8	4	9	28	27	9	3	9	34	29	58
Redditch United	42	9	6	6	35	34	7	4	10	31	41	58
Hinckley Town	42	8	6	7	43	34	8	3	10	29	34	57
Sutton Coldfield Town	42	9	5	7	28	29	6	6	9	28	36	56
Bedworth United	42	10	4	7	30	31	5	5	11	27	42	54
Bilston Town	42	9	5	7	47	37	5	4	12	22	42	51
Leicester United	42	9	7	5	33	32	5	3	13	32	45	51*1
Racing Club Warwick	42	7	6	8	32	32	5	7	9	24	39	49
Bridgnorth Town	42	8	4	9	36	35	5	5	11	26	39	48
Stroud	42	8	5	8	27	27	3	9	9	24	37	47
Dudley Town	42	6	7	8	24	37	5	6	10	24	36	46
Alvechurch	42	6	5	10	32	44	4	3	14	22	48	38
Willenhall Town	42	6	6	9	31	32	4	4	13	27	37	37*3
Spalding United	42	5	4	12	16	32	3	5	13	19	38	33

*1, *3, *4 denotes points deducted

SOUTHERN DIVISION

	P	W	D	L	F	A	W	D	L	F	A	Pts
			Home		Goals			Away		Goals		
Buckingham Town	40	14	2	4	35	18	11	6	3	38	20	83
Trowbridge Town	40	14	6	0	43	11	8	6	6	24	20	78
Salisbury	40	14	5	1	39	14	8	6	6	24	25	77
Baldock Town	40	14	3	3	40	20	7	6	7	26	32	72
Ashford Town	40	14	3	3	51	19	8	2	10	31	33	71
Yate Town	40	12	3	5	42	23	9	5	6	34	25	71
Hastings Town	40	13	3	4	39	16	5	8	7	27	30	65
Hythe Town	40	10	5	5	32	18	7	4	9	23	26	59*1
Andover	40	9	4	7	40	37	7	2	11	29	39	54
Margate	40	9	5	6	30	25	5	6	9	22	30	53
Burnham	40	10	6	4	35	17	2	10	8	22	32	52
Bury Town	40	10	2	8	34	33	5	3	12	24	41	50
Sudbury Town	40	7	6	7	34	29	6	4	10	26	39	49
Newport I.O.W.	40	6	5	9	20	26	7	4	9	36	36	48
Gosport Borough	40	4	7	9	20	26	8	4	8	27	32	47
Witney Town	40	8	6	6	36	35	4	5	11	21	40	47
Dunstable	40	2	10	8	22	29	7	5	8	26	34	42
Canterbury City	40	8	2	10	37	41	4	4	12	23	42	42
Erith & Belvedere	40	6	4	10	26	31	4	2	14	20	42	36
Fareham Town	40	7	5	8	26	35	2	4	14	20	39	36
Corinthian	40	4	8	8	21	33	1	4	15	13	45	27

*1 denotes point deducted

BEAZER HOMES SOUTHERN LEAGUE – PREMIER DIVISION RESULTS 1990-91

Home \ Away	Atherstone United	Bashley	Bromsgrove Rovers	Burton Albion	Cambridge City	Chelmsford City	Crawley Town	Dartford	Dorchester Town	Dover Athletic	Farnborough Town	Gloucester City	Gravesend & Northfleet	Halesowen Town	Moor Green	Poole Town	Rushden Town	VS Rugby	Waterlooville	Wealdstone	Weymouth	Worcester City
Atherstone United	—	1-0	0-1	1-1	1-1	0-1	1-0	3-0	0-3	3-2	1-2	2-2	3-4	2-0	0-2	1-1	4-0	0-1	1-1	1-2	1-0	1-3
Bashley	0-0	—	1-1	2-1	2-2	2-1	0-1	0-1	2-2	0-3	1-1	0-1	3-1	1-2	4-1	1-0	3-1	0-2	5-1	0-1	3-2	0-2
Bromsgrove Rovers	2-0	2-4	—	3-3	2-2	1-0	3-2	4-0	4-0	1-2	3-2	0-1	3-0	2-1	0-0	1-1	2-0	4-1	3-0	1-0	2-1	1-0
Burton Albion	1-0	0-0	1-0	—	2-0	1-1	2-0	1-0	1-0	1-2	2-0	3-3	1-1	1-2	3-4	1-0	0-1	0-0	1-0	3-2	3-2	0-0
Cambridge City	4-3	2-2	0-0	2-1	—	4-0	4-1	2-1	3-1	0-0	0-0	0-2	1-0	1-3	2-1	1-1	1-4	2-0	3-0	2-1	5-0	1-0
Chelmsford City	3-4	2-2	1-2	2-2	0-0	—	1-4	1-1	0-0	1-1	1-2	3-3	1-0	2-2	3-4	1-1	0-3	1-0	1-1	0-0	2-0	0-0
Crawley Town	1-0	1-0	3-2	1-1	1-1	2-3	—	2-2	3-0	0-1	1-3	1-0	2-1	2-2	1-0	1-0	1-2	2-0	1-0	1-0	2-2	1-1
Dartford	1-1	1-0	2-1	2-0	0-2	1-1	6-1	—	3-0	1-0	1-2	2-1	3-0	3-3	2-1	0-0	0-0	0-3	5-1	1-2	5-3	1-3
Dorchester Town	1-2	2-1	1-0	1-0	0-1	3-2	2-0	1-1	—	1-0	2-1	3-0	2-1	2-1	1-2	2-4	1-2	2-0	0-3	5-1	1-3	3-2
Dover Athletic	1-0	0-1	4-2	0-0	0-1	1-1	1-1	0-2	1-0	—	1-0	1-0	4-1	2-1	0-2	1-0	0-0	0-0	0-3	2-3	2-2	1-1
Farnborough Town	3-1	1-3	0-2	1-0	1-1	3-2	2-0	2-2	1-1	1-3	—	3-0	3-1	2-1	2-1	0-0	1-0	1-3	3-1	2-1	3-2	2-0
Gloucester City	2-2	3-0	3-1	2-1	2-2	0-2	5-0	2-0	1-3	4-1	1-0	—	5-0	2-1	3-2	2-1	4-0	2-2	0-3	1-0	1-1	3-1
Gravesend & Northfleet	4-1	2-1	1-1	1-1	3-0	1-4	0-1	3-1	2-0	2-2	6-3	5-0	—	3-1	2-1	3-2	3-2	0-1	3-1	2-3	3-1	2-1
Halesowen Town	0-1	2-4	1-2	1-3	0-1	1-0	1-2	1-1	2-0	0-1	1-2	2-1	3-1	—	3-1	4-0	0-0	3-0	0-1	2-0	1-1	2-0
Moor Green	1-2	0-1	0-0	1-2	1-2	1-2	2-1	3-1	1-3	1-1	2-1	3-2	3-0	1-2	—	2-4	3-0	2-2	0-3	3-2	5-0	1-1
Poole Town	1-4	2-2	2-3	2-3	0-0	6-1	2-0	1-0	1-0	1-1	3-1	1-1	3-3	4-3	1-0	—	4-0	1-1	3-1	0-1	4-2	1-2
Rushden Town	2-1	1-1	4-1	1-1	4-1	0-1	3-1	4-2	1-0	0-1	4-0	1-1	3-1	3-1	2-2	5-4	—	4-2	3-1	2-2	3-0	0-1
VS Rugby	2-0	1-1	2-2	2-3	0-1	0-1	0-1	1-0	3-0	0-1	1-1	2-2	4-0	2-3	2-3	0-1	4-2	—	1-2	2-1	1-1	3-0
Waterlooville	1-1	0-1	0-1	2-0	0-1	3-3	0-0	2-1	1-1	0-4	1-0	2-2	2-0	1-2	2-1	4-1	2-1	1-0	—	2-2	3-0	2-3
Wealdstone	1-3	1-1	1-1	0-0	1-1	0-3	2-0	2-1	2-1	0-1	2-1	2-1	3-0	2-3	4-1	2-1	1-1	1-1	1-3	—	2-1	0-1
Weymouth	0-2	0-1	1-1	0-0	1-1	2-5	1-1	0-0	2-0	0-1	1-1	2-2	1-2	1-2	4-1	4-2	2-1	3-0	1-1	4-2	—	0-1
Worcester City	0-0	1-0	2-1	4-1	0-1	2-0	2-0	3-0	1-1	2-0	1-2	1-1	1-1	1-2	1-1	0-0	1-1	1-2	2-1	3-2	3-0	—

LEADING GOALSCORERS

Premier Division

S. Fergusson (Gloucester City)	25
P. Moody (Waterlooville)	25
C. Hanks (Bromsgrove Rovers)	22
L. Whale (Bashley)	21
A. Diaz (Dorchester Town)	20
Dennis Greene (Chelmsford City)	20

BEAZER HOMES SOUTHERN LEAGUE – SOUTHERN DIVISION RESULTS 1990–91

	Andover	Ashford Town	Baldock Town	Buckingham Town	Burnham	Bury Town	Canterbury City	Corinthian	Dunstable	Erith & Belvedere	Fareham Town	Gosport Borough	Hastings Town	Hythe Town	Margate	Newport I.O.W.	Salisbury	Sudbury Town	Trowbridge Town	Witney Town	Yate Town
Andover	—	1-4	2-2	0-5	2-1	2-0	4-2	0-0	3-2	0-1	2-0	8-1	2-2	3-3	2-1	1-3	0-1	2-1	0-2	4-1	2-5
Ashford Town	5-1	—	1-1	5-1	2-3	3-1	3-1	5-0	3-0	1-4	4-0	1-0	1-1	1-0	2-1	3-0	2-2	4-1	0-1	3-1	2-0
Baldock Town	2-1	1-0	—	1-2	5-1	4-0	2-0	2-0	1-3	2-3	2-1	2-2	2-1	2-1	1-0	3-2	0-0	2-0	2-1	1-1	3-1
Buckingham Town	1-0	0-2	0-0	—	1-1	4-1	4-2	2-1	3-0	2-3	2-0	2-2	2-0	1-0	4-1	2-1	0-1	0-2	2-1	1-1	2-1
Burnham	3-0	2-0	0-1	1-1	—	2-1	4-2	2-1	5-0	3-0	2-0	0-0	2-0	1-0	0-1	2-1	0-1	0-2	0-1	1-0	0-2
Bury Town	1-5	4-1	3-3	0-3	3-0	—	3-1	2-1	0-1	4-1	0-2	0-0	2-1	1-2	1-0	1-1	2-0	1-2	3-1	1-0	1-1
Canterbury City	1-2	4-1	0-2	5-3	1-1	2-4	—	2-1	1-2	2-0	4-2	2-0	0-3	1-2	1-0	2-1	3-1	0-3	2-1	3-4	1-1
Corinthian	0-4	0-0	1-1	0-0	1-1	2-4	3-1	—	1-2	2-0	1-0	1-0	3-3	1-3	0-3	3-1	3-1	3-4	2-1	0-3	1-4
Dunstable	0-1	0-0	2-2	2-2	0-0	2-0	0-0	—	—	1-5	1-0	1-2	1-2	2-2	0-0	1-2	2-3	0-1	2-3	0-0	1-1
Erith & Belvedere	4-1	1-2	2-1	0-1	1-1	2-1	1-0	1-1	—	—	2-1	1-3	1-2	0-4	3-0	1-2	2-3	0-0	2-3	0-1	2-2
Fareham Town	2-1	1-0	3-1	2-0	2-1	2-1	0-1	2-1	0-1	2-1	—	—	1-2	0-4	3-0	0-5	0-1	2-1	1-2	4-2	1-4
Gosport Borough	0-1	4-2	0-1	0-2	1-1	1-1	2-3	1-0	0-2	0-0	0-2	—	2-1	0-1	1-2	0-5	1-1	5-2	0-3	0-2	1-2
Hastings Town	3-0	2-0	4-1	2-0	2-0	2-1	1-1	4-0	4-0	4-2	2-1	2-1	—	5-0	1-1	2-4	0-0	3-0	0-0	4-0	0-1
Hythe Town	1-2	3-2	0-1	0-2	3-2	2-1	1-0	2-0	1-1	4-2	2-1	0-1	1-3	—	—	1-2	2-1	3-0	0-0	4-0	2-0
Margate	2-1	1-3	2-1	0-2	2-2	1-0	3-1	4-0	4-0	0-1	2-1	3-0	3-1	1-0	—	2-4	0-1	2-0	1-0	1-1	2-1
Newport I.O.W.	1-1	3-1	2-1	0-2	0-1	1-3	4-0	3-1	1-2	4-2	2-1	1-2	1-1	1-0	0-0	—	1-2	3-2	2-2	3-1	1-2
Salisbury	3-1	1-0	2-1	2-0	3-1	4-0	6-2	0-1	0-0	2-1	1-1	0-4	4-1	0-1	2-2	0-0	—	0-1	1-0	0-0	0-1
Sudbury Town	4-1	2-3	5-1	0-3	1-1	2-2	3-2	1-0	3-3	4-1	3-1	1-1	0-0	3-1	0-3	2-1	2-2	—	1-1	2-0	1-0
Trowbridge Town	1-1	1-0	3-1	0-0	2-2	2-0	3-0	1-0	1-0	3-1	3-1	2-1	0-0	0-0	3-0	2-0	3-0	5-1	—	3-0	0-3
Witney Town	1-3	2-5	0-2	0-2	1-0	5-1	1-2	5-2	2-1	1-1	3-3	3-1	1-1	5-0	2-2	3-2	1-4	5-1	1-1	—	1-1
Yate Town	4-2	1-2	2-3	1-4	1-1	4-1	3-0	2-1	1-1	2-0	2-0	1-2	3-0	1-0	2-0	1-2	3-0	2-1	1-1	3-2	—

LEADING GOALSCORERS

Midland Division

J. O'Connor (Hednesford Town)	34
P. Whitehurst (Grantham Town)	32
S. Diver (Corby Town)	31
M. Twigger (Nuneaton Borough)	31
M. Hallam (Leicester United)	28
D. Morris (Tamworth)	25
M. Richards (Bilston Town)	23
H. Wright (Stourbridge)	22
M. Smith (Tamworth)	21

BEAZER HOMES SOUTHERN LEAGUE – MIDLAND DIVISION RESULTS 1990–91

	Alvechurch	Barry Town	Bedworth United	Bilston Town	Bridgnorth Town	Corby Town	Dudley Town	Grantham Town	Hednesford Town	Hinckley Town	King's Lynn	Leicester United	Newport A.F.C.	Nuneaton Borough	Racing Club Warwick	Redditch United	Spalding United	Stourbridge	Stroud	Sutton Coldfield Town	Tamworth	Willenhall Town
Alvechurch	—	1-0	2-1	3-0	1-0	0-4	2-2	1-2	1-1	0-2	2-4	1-5	0-0	1-2	1-1	7-2	2-1	1-2	1-3	2-4	0-5	3-3
Barry Town	4-2	—	0-1	5-1	0-2	3-2	4-1	2-1	3-2	3-0	0-0	1-0	1-0	1-1	1-1	1-3	2-0	1-3	2-0	1-2	1-0	3-0
Bedworth United	3-0	0-1	—	5-0	3-1	6-2	2-2	1-2	0-2	1-1	3-2	2-0	2-1	1-0	2-1	1-0	0-2	1-1	2-2	2-2	3-0	3-1
Bilston Town	2-2	5-1	5-3	—	5-0	1-1	2-1	0-2	2-0	3-3	1-2	3-2	0-2	4-0	1-0	2-2	5-2	2-3	4-4	2-2	1-2	2-1
Bridgnorth Town	3-0	1-2	2-1	3-1	—	1-1	2-3	0-2	2-0	3-2	2-0	3-2	0-2	1-3	4-0	3-1	3-3	0-1	2-2	2-2	1-2	1-0
Corby Town	2-1	3-2	6-0	6-2	1-1	—	2-3	1-1	2-3	2-1	5-0	6-0	1-0	0-1	4-0	0-2	3-3	3-0	1-1	0-3	1-0	1-0
Dudley Town	2-1	1-0	2-2	2-1	0-2	1-4	—	1-1	2-0	3-3	1-1	2-2	1-0	2-2	2-1	0-2	0-2	1-2	1-1	0-1	0-4	2-2
Grantham Town	1-1	0-1	1-2	2-0	0-0	0-2	5-0	—	2-0	1-0	3-2	2-0	0-2	0-3	0-0	2-3	5-1	2-2	3-0	2-0	0-3	0-1
Hednesford Town	3-4	1-3	0-2	0-0	2-0	2-0	0-2	2-0	—	3-3	3-1	2-0	3-1	3-2	2-2	6-0	0-0	1-1	2-2	1-1	3-2	0-2
Hinckley Town	3-1	4-1	1-2	3-3	2-1	1-3	3-0	—	3-0	—	0-0	2-4	0-1	2-0	2-2	3-2	1-0	1-1	2-2	1-1	0-2	1-0
King's Lynn	2-0	2-1	1-1	1-2	1-0	0-6	1-0	1-0	0-0	1-0	—	2-3	2-1	0-3	2-0	4-2	1-1	0-3	3-1	2-0	0-4	2-1
Leicester United	5-0	0-2	2-0	3-2	4-1	1-2	0-3	2-3	2-4	2-3	1-0	—	0-2	4-1	1-2	0-1	2-0	1-0	2-2	2-1	1-1	3-2
Newport A.F.C.	1-1	2-0	1-0	3-2	4-1	1-2	0-0	0-0	2-3	1-4	2-0	2-1	—	4-1	1-2	2-1	2-0	4-1	2-2	2-1	0-0	1-0
Nuneaton Borough	4-0	2-0	1-0	3-0	3-2	3-2	1-1	3-1	1-1	0-3	4-1	4-2	1-0	—	3-3	0-2	0-0	3-2	1-1	3-1	2-3	2-2
Racing Club Warwick	3-2	1-1	2-1	3-4	0-1	1-2	2-3	3-2	2-3	4-2	1-1	4-2	1-1	1-0	—	0-2	2-1	3-3	1-3	1-3	2-4	2-2
Redditch United	0-1	0-1	1-0	0-0	1-1	0-1	1-3	1-3	0-1	2-3	0-0	4-2	1-1	1-1	2-2	—	2-1	0-2	0-0	2-1	0-0	2-1
Spalding United	1-0	2-3	0-2	0-2	0-1	0-1	1-3	1-5	1-3	1-3	1-2	2-1	0-0	0-0	2-1	1-4	—	0-2	2-0	3-0	2-0	2-0
Stourbridge	3-0	2-0	0-2	3-2	0-1	0-1	3-1	1-0	1-1	1-0	4-2	2-0	4-1	3-2	1-3	0-2	1-0	—	0-0	0-2	3-3	1-3
Stroud	0-1	2-2	2-3	3-0	3-0	2-0	3-1	4-3	3-1	4-1	3-0	2-1	2-0	0-3	3-2	1-4	2-3	0-2	—	2-0	0-0	3-2
Sutton Coldfield Town	3-2	2-2	1-1	1-1	3-2	1-0	1-0	1-2	1-0	1-0	4-0	2-4	0-1	3-2	1-2	2-4	0-0	0-1	2-0	—	2-1	2-1
Tamworth	2-0	0-1	3-0	3-4	3-2	3-1	3-1	2-0	1-0	1-0	4-0	2-4	1-4	2-2	2-0	3-0	2-0	2-1	1-0	1-2	—	0-2
Willenhall Town	1-3	1-1	3-1	0-1	2-2	1-3	1-0	0-1	2-3	3-2	3-3	3-1	1-1	0-1	1-2	2-0	1-0	2-2	5-1	2-2	0-2	—

LEADING GOALSCORERS

Southern Division

35	J. Smith (Salisbury)	22	D. Iddles (Yate Town)
29	D. Arter (Hythe Town)	21	K. Clarke (Witney Town)
25	P. Odey (Andover)	21	P. Underwood (Margate)
24	K. Maddock (Fareham Town)	20	D. Tilley (Yate Town)
22	S. Greening (Newport I.O.W.)		

VAUXHALL LEAGUE 1990–91

Premier Division

	P	W	D	L	W	D	L	F	A	GD	Pts
		Home			*Away*			*Goals*			
Redbridge Forest	42	17	1	3	12	5	4	74	43	31	93
Enfield	42	14	6	1	12	5	4	83	30	53	89
Aylesbury United	42	17	1	3	7	10	4	90	47	43	83
Woking	42	13	6	2	11	4	6	84	39	45	82
Kingstonian	42	14	6	1	7	6	8	86	57	29	75
Grays Athletic	42	12	3	6	8	5	8	66	53	13	68
Marlow	42	10	7	4	8	6	7	72	49	23	67
Hayes	42	11	5	5	9	0	12	60	57	3	65
Carshalton Athletic	42	10	5	6	9	2	10	80	67	13	64
Wivenhoe Town	42	6	8	7	10	3	8	69	66	3	59
Wokingham Town	42	9	6	6	6	7	8	58	54	4	58
Windsor & Eton	42	12	0	9	3	10	8	48	63	−15	55
Bishops Stortford	42	9	5	7	5	7	9	54	49	5	54
Dagenham	42	6	9	6	7	2	12	62	68	−6	50
Hendon	42	5	7	9	7	3	11	48	62	−14	46
St Albans City	42	5	4	12	6	8	7	60	74	−14	45
Bognor Regis Town	42	4	6	11	8	2	11	44	71	−27	44
Basingstoke Town	42	6	4	11	6	3	12	57	95	−38	43
Staines Town	42	6	5	10	4	5	12	46	79	−33	39
Harrow Borough	42	5	4	12	5	4	12	57	84	−27	38
Barking	42	3	7	11	5	3	13	41	85	−44	34
Leyton-Wingate	42	5	1	15	2	6	13	44	91	−47	28

Staines deducted 1 point by order of the League

Division One

	P	W	D	L	W	D	L	F	A	GD	Pts
		Home			*Away*			*Goals*			
Chesham United	42	13	4	4	14	4	3	102	37	65	89
Bromley	42	13	6	2	9	8	4	62	37	25	80
Yeading	42	14	3	4	9	5	7	75	45	30	77
Aveley	42	9	7	5	12	2	7	76	43	33	72
Hitchin Town	42	13	2	6	8	7	6	78	50	28	72
Tooting & Mitcham	42	8	8	5	12	4	5	71	48	23	72
Walton & Hersham	42	12	5	4	9	3	9	73	48	25	71
Molesey	42	13	3	5	9	2	10	65	46	19	71
Whyteleafe	42	10	4	7	11	3	8	62	53	9	69
Dorking	42	11	3	7	9	2	10	78	67	11	65
Chalfont St Peter	42	12	3	6	7	2	12	56	63	−7	62
Dulwich Hamlet	42	7	5	9	9	6	6	67	54	13	59
Harlow Town	42	10	4	7	7	4	10	73	64	9	59
Boreham Wood	42	10	3	8	5	5	11	46	53	−7	53
Wembley	42	6	5	10	7	7	7	62	59	3	51
Uxbridge	42	5	3	13	10	2	9	45	61	−16	50
Croydon	42	8	2	11	7	3	11	44	85	−41	50
Heybridge Swifts	42	6	5	10	7	5	9	46	59	−13	49
Southwick	42	10	3	8	3	5	13	49	75	−26	47
Lewes	42	5	4	12	5	4	12	49	82	−33	38
Metropolitan Police	42	5	2	14	4	4	13	55	76	−21	33
Worthing	42	2	3	16	0	1	20	28	157	−129	10

Division Two (North)

	P	W	D	L	W	D	L	F	A	GD	Pts
		Home			*Away*			*Goals*			
Stevenage Borough	42	21	0	0	13	5	3	122	29	93	107
Vauxhall Motors	42	14	4	3	10	6	5	82	50	32	82
Billericay	42	12	3	6	10	5	6	70	41	29	74
Ware	42	13	3	5	9	5	7	78	51	27	74
Berkhamsted	42	10	9	2	9	2	10	60	51	9	68
Witham Town	42	12	3	6	7	7	7	70	59	11	67
Purfleet	42	8	7	6	9	7	5	68	57	11	65
Rainham Town	42	11	4	6	8	3	10	57	46	11	64
Hemel Hempstead	42	7	10	4	9	4	8	62	56	6	62
Barton Rovers	42	10	6	5	7	4	10	61	58	3	61
Saffron Walden	42	10	7	4	6	6	9	72	77	−5	61
Collier Row	42	8	5	8	8	6	7	63	63	0	59
Kingsbury Town	42	10	4	7	7	4	10	64	72	−8	59
Edgware Town	42	12	2	7	5	5	11	73	65	8	58
Hertford Town	42	8	4	9	8	6	7	69	70	−1	58
Royston Town	42	8	7	6	6	8	7	78	62	16	57
Tilbury	42	6	5	10	8	1	12	70	79	−9	48
Basildon United	42	6	7	8	5	3	13	61	90	−29	43
Hornchurch	42	6	5	10	4	4	13	53	87	−34	39
Clapton	42	5	6	10	4	4	13	54	93	−39	34
Finchley	42	2	2	17	4	5	12	50	112	−62	24
Tring Town	42	1	3	17	0	6	15	30	99	−69	12

Clapton deducted 3 points by order of the League
Finchley deducted 1 point by order of the League

Division Two (South)

	P	W	D	L	W	D	L	F	A	GD	Pts
			Home			Away			Goals		
Abingdon Town	42	15	2	4	14	5	2	95	28	67	94
Maidenhead United	42	16	2	3	12	6	3	85	33	52	92
Egham Town	42	13	4	4	14	2	5	100	46	54	87
Malden Vale	42	13	3	5	13	2	6	72	44	28	83
Ruislip Manor	42	14	2	5	11	3	7	93	44	49	80
Southall	42	14	4	3	9	6	6	84	43	41	79
Harefield United	42	14	5	2	9	5	7	81	56	25	79
Newbury Town	42	10	5	6	13	3	5	71	45	26	77
Hungerford Town	42	10	4	7	6	9	6	84	69	15	61
Leatherhead	42	9	6	6	8	3	10	82	55	27	60
Banstead Athletic	42	8	6	7	7	7	7	58	62	−4	58
Hampton	42	6	9	6	8	6	7	62	43	19	57
Epsom & Ewell	42	9	5	7	6	7	8	49	50	−1	57
Chertsey Town	42	8	6	7	7	3	11	76	72	4	54
Horsham	42	8	4	9	6	3	12	58	67	−9	49
Flackwell Heath	42	5	8	8	6	3	12	56	78	−22	44
Bracknell Town	42	5	4	12	6	3	12	60	97	−37	40
Feltham	42	8	4	9	2	4	15	45	80	−35	38
Cove	42	6	2	13	4	5	12	51	94	−43	37
Eastbourne United	42	9	3	9	1	4	16	53	109	−56	37
Petersfield	42	3	3	15	3	0	18	35	119	−84	21
Camberley Town	42	1	2	18	0	4	17	27	143	−116	9

LEADING GOALSCORERS

Premier Division		VL	ACD	LOC	PIL				VL	AVD	LOC	PIL
47	Jim Bolton	28	7	8	4	21	Mario Russo		18	3		
	(Carshalton Ath)						(Metropolitan Police)					
27	Francis Vines	26	1			20	Andy Cosby		17	1	2	
	(Kingstonian)						(Chesham U)					
25	Dave Pearce	24	1				*(includes 5 League and 1 AC Delco for St Albans C)*					
	(Kingstonian)											
	Glen Donegal	18	1	6		**Second Division North**						
	(Aylesbury U)					30	David Matthews		27	1	2	
24	Cliff Hercules	20	1	3			(Purfleet)					
	(Aylesbury U)					29	Paddy Butcher		28		1	
	Richard Cherry	22	1		1		(Royston T)					
	(Grays Ath)					28	Steve Jones		23	4	1	
	Steve Clark	19	2	1	2		(Billericay T)					
	(Wivenhoe T)						*(includes 11 League, 4 AC Delco and 1 Loctite Trophy*					
21	Richard Smart	21					*for Basildon U)*					
	(Woking)						Jimmy Hughes		26	1	1	
	(includes 14 League for Whyteleafe)						(Stevenage Bor)					
20	John Warner	16	2	1	1	25	Lee McLean		22		3	
	(Dagenham)						(Tilbury)					
	Eamon O'Connor	16			4	22	Mark Phillips		21	1		
	(Harrow Bor)						(Tilbury)					
First Division						**Second Division South**						
31	Paul Battram	28	3			35	Benny Laryea		31	2	2	
	(Harlow T)						(Maidenhead U)					
27	Michael Rose	20	5	2		31	Micky Havermars		28	1	2	
	(Molesey)						(Bracknell T)					
26	John Collins	26				30	Kevin Quinn		22		5	
	(Tooting & Mitcham U)						(Ruislip Manor)					
24	Phil Grainger	23		1		29	Mark Butler		28		1	
	(Dorking)						(Egham T)					
23	Michael Banton	19		4			Carlton Walcott		28		1	
	(Chesham U)						(Chertsey T)					
22	Byron Walton	21	1				Steve Lawrence		27		2	
	(Chesham U)						(Ruislip Manor)					

LEADING CLUB GOALSCORERS

Premier Division	VL	ACD	LOC	PIL		VL	ACD	LOC	PIL
Aylesbury U (Glen Donegal)	18	1	6		Hendon (Uche Egbe)	7		2	2
Barking (Jimmy Tibbs)	11				Kingstonian (Francis Vines)	26	1		
Basingstoke T (Chris Lawrence)	16				Leyton-Wingate	10			3
B Stortford (Devon Gayle)	8	1		1	(Tommy Williams)				
(Leo West)	6	1	1	2	Marlow (Kevin Davies)	12	4		
(Pat Ryan)	5	1	2	2	Redbridge For (Kurt Davidson)	17		2	
Bognor Regis T (Lee Cormack)	10				St Albans C (Andy Cox)	7			
Carshalton Ath (Jim Bolton)	28	7	8	4	Staines T (Simon Pentland)	6			
Dagenham (John Warner)	16	2	1	1	Windsor & Eton (Sean Gilman)	14	2		2
Enfield (Gary Britnell)	16	1		1	Wivenhoe (Steve Clark)	19	2	1	2
Grays Ath (Richard Cherry)	22	1		1	Woking (Tim Buzaglo)	9	2		
Harrow Bor (Eamon O'Connor)	16			4	(Bradley Pratt)	11			
Hayes (Chris Walton)	9				Wokingham T (Phil Alexander)	9	1		1

VL: Vauxhall League. *ACD*: AC Delco Cup. *LOC*: Loctite Trophy. *PIL*: Premier Inter-League Cup.

VAUXHALL FOOTBALL LEAGUE PREMIER DIVISION RESULTS 1990-91

	Aylesbury United	Barking	Basingstoke Town	Bishops Stortford	Bognor Regis Town	Carshalton Athletic	Dagenham	Enfield	Grays Athletic	Harrow Borough	Hayes	Hendon	Kingstonian	Leyton-Wingate	Marlow	Redbridge Forest	St Albans City	Staines Town	Windsor & Eton	Wivenhoe Town	Woking	Wokingham Town
Aylesbury United	—	2-1	1-1	0-2	1-1	3-5	3-2	1-1	4-1	2-2	2-2	1-1	0-0	0-4	3-3	0-4	1-2	0-1	1-2	1-2	2-3	3-1
Barking	3-2	—	4-2	0-5	0-2	0-2	0-2	2-2	5-3	3-4	2-1	1-1	0-2	0-0	3-1	0-1	3-3	1-1	1-1	0-1	0-1	0-0
Basingstoke Town	1-1	3-2	—	3-2	2-5	0-4	4-0	2-0	0-1	2-3	2-4	2-4	2-0	0-1	0-0	1-2	0-1	1-0	1-1	0-1	0-6	2-2
Bishops Stortford	0-2	3-2	1-1	—	0-2	3-2	1-0	0-0	1-1	2-0	4-2	0-0	1-1	3-1	1-4	1-2	0-1	3-0	1-3	1-2	2-0	1-0
Bognor Regis Town	1-1	0-1	3-1	1-0	—	1-1	2-0	0-2	0-3	1-1	0-1	1-0	1-3	0-0	1-2	2-4	1-2	2-0	1-1	0-2	0-2	1-0
Carshalton Athletic	3-5	4-0	2-4	3-1	4-0	—	0-3	1-3	2-2	1-3	4-0	1-0	1-3	2-2	0-2	2-4	2-2	2-0	1-0	2-2	2-2	1-0
Dagenham	3-2	0-0	5-2	0-0	0-2	1-3	—	1-3	3-0	3-0	4-0	3-2	2-2	1-0	1-2	1-1	1-1	4-0	2-2	2-0	0-2	1-0
Enfield	3-2	2-2	2-0	0-0	4-0	2-0	1-1	—	3-0	6-1	3-1	4-0	3-0	3-1	3-0	1-1	1-1	0-0	1-0	2-0	0-1	1-1
Grays Athletic	4-1	5-1	5-3	1-2	0-2	2-0	3-2	0-2	—	0-2	1-0	2-0	2-1	1-1	3-1	1-1	3-0	1-3	1-0	2-2	1-1	2-1
Harrow Borough	2-2	3-4	0-1	2-1	1-3	1-3	4-1	2-4	0-2	—	1-2	1-3	0-2	2-1	2-0	2-3	1-1	2-1	3-3	1-3	0-1	3-3
Hayes	1-1	2-1	2-3	2-0	0-0	1-1	1-0	0-3	2-0	2-0	—	3-1	0-0	3-0	0-0	2-0	1-2	2-0	3-0	0-1	4-1	4-1
Hendon	0-0	5-1	1-2	1-1	0-3	0-2	1-2	4-1	0-1	1-1	1-0	—	3-1	3-3	1-1	2-2	2-2	0-1	0-0	2-3	3-1	1-0
Kingstonian	0-4	2-0	1-2	0-3	4-1	3-1	2-0	4-1	5-1	—	1-0	2-1	3-1	—	0-2	1-2	5-2	1-2	2-0	3-1	4-2	1-1
Leyton-Wingate	3-3	3-1	2-0	3-1	5-0	1-3	3-0	1-1	1-2	1-0	1-0	1-3	1-1	—	0-2	1-2	3-0	1-2	2-0	1-2	0-4	1-4
Marlow	0-4	2-0	2-0	5-0	1-0	5-1	1-0	2-1	1-0	1-0	1-2	3-0	3-4	7-4	—	2-1	0-0	2-0	3-0	1-2	1-1	0-1
Redbridge Forest	0-4	2-0	1-1	1-1	1-0	2-4	2-4	0-1	0-3	1-0	1-2	3-0	3-4	2-1	0-4	—	2-1	2-2	3-0	1-0	0-1	2-2
St Albans City	1-2	1-2	1-1	0-0	0-4	0-4	5-1	1-3	1-3	2-0	2-3	1-2	0-3	2-1	2-2	1-2	—	2-2	0-1	1-0	1-2	1-1
Staines Town	0-1	1-2	2-1	0-0	1-2	0-4	5-1	1-1	1-3	0-5	2-3	1-3	0-3	2-1	2-2	2-1	3-3	—	1-0	1-0	0-7	1-1
Windsor & Eton	1-2	2-1	1-0	1-0	2-0	3-2	1-2	0-3	0-5	0-5	1-4	1-3	1-3	6-2	1-0	0-1	2-0	2-1	—	3-2	2-1	3-2
Wivenhoe Town	1-1	2-1	3-3	0-4	1-2	1-3	1-1	0-1	3-1	2-3	3-0	1-3	6-1	1-1	1-1	0-2	1-1	3-0	2-2	—	4-4	2-1
Woking	3-1	0-0	0-2	0-0	3-0	2-4	1-0	2-1	1-1	4-0	4-0	2-0	0-0	3-0	4-1	0-0	2-0	5-1	0-0	1-0	—	4-0
Wokingham Town	0-0	1-0	3-0	0-0	3-0	3-2	0-2	0-2	1-1	1-0	2-1	3-0	0-1	0-1	2-2	1-1	1-4	1-1	5-0	4-0	0-2	—

VAUXHALL FOOTBALL LEAGUE DIVISION ONE RESULTS 1990-91

	Aveley	Boreham Wood	Bromley	Chalfont St Peter	Chesham United	Croydon	Dorking	Dulwich Hamlet	Harlow Town	Heybridge Swifts	Hitchin Town	Lewes	Metropolitan Police	Molesey	Southwick	Tooting & Mitcham	Uxbridge	Walton & Hersham	Wembley	Whyteleafe	Worthing	Yeading
Aveley	—	0-0	1-1	4-1	1-1	1-2	4-1	2-2	2-2	2-1	1-1	1-2	2-1	0-1	2-0	0-1	3-0	2-0	1-1	1-2	5-1	1-0
Boreham Wood	0-2	—	1-2	1-0	2-3	0-1	1-2	2-2	0-0	3-1	1-2	3-1	3-0	3-2	0-0	1-0	4-1	2-1	0-2	0-2	3-2	2-1
Bromley	2-4	3-0	—	1-1	2-0	3-0	0-3	0-0	3-2	0-0	3-1	5-1	2-0	1-0	1-1	1-1	2-1	1-0	3-0	1-1	3-0	1-0
Chalfont St Peter	1-0	3-1	0-0	—	1-0	2-1	4-2	1-0	2-1	1-1	0-3	3-0	2-0	0-1	1-0	1-1	0-2	0-1	2-1	0-1	3-1	1-4
Chesham United	3-1	2-1	0-1	3-2	—	4-0	2-0	2-0	2-1	5-1	0-0	5-2	1-3	0-2	8-1	0-0	0-1	1-3	1-1	7-2	8-0	2-2
Croydon	0-5	1-2	0-0	2-1	0-4	—	2-0	1-3	2-4	4-0	1-1	1-0	0-5	4-3	1-0	0-4	0-2	2-2	0-2	0-1	2-1	1-3
Dorking	0-3	1-0	0-1	5-0	0-3	0-0	—	2-4	1-0	1-2	5-2	3-0	4-2	0-0	2-1	2-4	0-1	0-2	0-2	0-1	4-0	3-2
Dulwich Hamlet	1-1	1-0	0-1	1-0	1-3	1-2	4-1	—	1-3	1-1	0-2	0-0	2-1	4-1	4-0	0-1	3-0	3-1	3-3	0-2	9-0	0-0
Harlow Town	4-1	2-0	3-0	0-1	0-3	2-2	0-3	1-1	—	1-1	1-3	3-2	2-0	1-0	1-0	1-1	1-1	0-2	0-4	3-1	6-2	0-1
Heybridge Swifts	0-2	0-0	0-2	2-1	0-2	2-2	1-2	0-1	0-4	—	1-4	5-0	1-1	1-2	0-0	3-0	1-2	1-0	0-1	2-0	0-0	2-1
Hitchin Town	2-0	1-2	0-0	2-0	1-1	6-3	1-4	2-3	1-0	3-1	—	2-0	2-1	2-0	6-1	0-2	4-0	0-1	2-1	2-0	9-1	0-1
Lewes	1-2	0-1	3-4	1-2	1-4	5-1	3-2	5-2	1-0	0-2	1-1	—	1-3	2-1	0-0	1-2	1-2	2-3	0-1	0-2	4-1	1-5
Metropolitan Police	0-4	0-1	3-1	1-2	0-3	1-0	3-0	0-1	4-2	1-0	0-2	2-0	—	1-1	4-0	1-0	1-0	0-3	2-3	0-2	2-0	4-1
Molesey	0-1	3-1	1-2	2-0	1-3	2-0	3-5	1-1	0-0	2-0	0-0	0-0	1-0	—	4-1	1-3	1-0	0-2	5-2	0-1	3-0	1-1
Southwick	0-2	2-0	1-0	2-1	1-1	2-0	1-1	2-1	2-1	0-2	2-1	0-0	2-2	2-4	—	5-1	5-0	4-4	0-1	8-3	5-1	0-2
Tooting & Mitcham	0-0	0-0	2-2	2-5	1-0	3-0	1-1	0-1	0-0	0-2	2-1	1-2	1-1	1-3	5-1	—	1-3	1-0	1-2	0-1	4-1	0-1
Uxbridge	0-3	0-1	0-1	0-2	0-3	3-0	1-4	0-1	1-0	3-3	1-0	1-2	1-1	1-2	0-1	1-3	—	1-0	1-2	0-1	4-1	0-1
Walton & Hersham	3-1	2-1	1-1	2-0	0-0	4-0	2-1	2-2	3-1	0-2	4-0	3-1	3-0	3-1	0-1	1-3	0-2	—	3-3	0-2	4-0	1-1
Wembley	1-2	0-1	0-1	2-3	3-4	3-0	0-0	3-1	1-3	0-0	0-2	1-3	1-1	2-1	0-1	1-3	0-2	3-0	—	2-2	4-0	1-1
Whyteleafe	2-1	1-1	3-0	2-4	0-2	1-0	1-0	1-2	3-1	1-3	1-1	1-0	2-1	2-1	1-1	0-2	2-1	1-0	1-1	—	10-0	1-3
Worthing	0-4	1-1	0-2	2-2	0-4	0-4	1-2	0-5	0-3	1-3	0-0	1-3	2-3	0-4	0-1	0-2	0-6	0-3	3-2	0-2	—	0-3
Yeading	2-1	2-1	1-2	5-0	0-1	1-1	1-0	2-0	4-3	4-1	3-4	2-2	1-1	1-0	3-1	2-0	0-1	1-0	1-0	2-1	4-1	—

VAUXHALL FOOTBALL LEAGUE DIVISION TWO NORTH RESULTS 1990–91

	Barton Rovers	Basildon United	Berkhamsted	Billericay	Clapton	Collier Row	Edgware Town	Finchley	Hemel Hempstead	Hertford Town	Hornchurch	Kingsbury Town	Purfleet	Rainham Town	Royston Town	Saffron Walden	Stevenage Borough	Tilbury	Tring Town	Vauxhall Motors	Ware	Witham Town
Barton Rovers	—	5-0	1-2	0-1	2-0	0-0	3-1	5-1	2-1	0-0	0-1	3-0	1-1	2-1	1-1	2-1	0-2	2-2	0-0	0-1	2-0	2-1
Basildon United	1-1	—	0-4	0-0	3-2	0-0	1-3	3-2	1-1	1-1	2-0	3-4	2-2	2-0	1-5	0-1	0-0	2-3	3-2	2-2	0-4	0-1
Berkhamsted	2-0	3-0	—	1-0	1-1	2-1	1-2	2-1	2-1	0-1	0-0	1-0	2-2	1-0	1-2	7-1	1-0	1-0	1-0	1-1	1-1	1-1
Billericay	3-0	2-0	0-5	—	1-0	0-1	4-2	1-2	1-1	1-3	0-1	2-2	1-3	2-1	0-1	3-1	2-1	3-1	3-1	1-1	1-0	2-1
Clapton	2-1	2-0	0-3	7-1	—	3-0	0-0	1-0	1-1	3-1	0-2	2-2	4-3	6-3	1-0	4-2	0-3	1-2	1-1	0-1	1-2	2-0
Collier Row	0-1	—	2-0	0-2	1-2	2-1	4-4	2-1	2-1	3-1	0-1	0-4	0-2	1-1	6-1	1-0	0-1	1-1	2-1	0-0	3-3	3-3
Edgware Town	3-1	4-0	2-1	1-0	3-0	6-1	—	1-0	3-1	0-1	3-2	1-0	0-3	3-1	0-3	0-1	1-0	2-3	1-2	3-1	1-0	2-0
Finchley	5-1	3-1	4-0	1-0	2-2	2-2	7-0	—	3-1	0-0	1-0	1-0	2-2	0-0	2-2	1-0	6-3	4-2	0-1	4-2	1-3	0-1
Hemel Hempstead	1-3	1-1	2-1	2-1	1-0	1-3	3-1	0-3	—	1-2	3-2	1-0	1-2	4-3	2-3	3-1	0-3	1-4	2-1	3-1	1-0	2-3
Hertford Town	2-4	3-1	2-2	2-1	2-1	2-1	1-2	1-1	0-3	—	1-2	7-0	1-0	3-3	4-3	2-4	2-3	0-3	4-2	0-1	1-1	0-0
Hornchurch	3-0	3-0	2-0	2-0	2-1	1-1	2-1	4-2	1-1	1-1	—	3-1	1-3	1-0	4-2	4-2	0-1	3-2	3-2	0-0	2-2	4-4
Kingsbury Town	3-0	1-0	1-0	1-0	3-1	0-0	1-2	2-0	2-5	0-1	4-2	—	2-0	1-2	1-2	3-1	0-1	1-0	5-0	1-2	2-1	4-1
Purfleet	1-1	0-1	1-2	1-3	0-2	3-1	0-2	1-1	0-0	2-1	1-1	3-1	—	1-0	2-2	3-2	1-3	5-2	1-3	1-3	2-2	2-1
Rainham Town	2-0	3-2	2-0	4-1	3-2	4-1	2-1	7-0	6-0	3-3	1-0	4-4	1-0	—	1-0	1-0	2-3	3-1	5-0	1-2	0-1	1-0
Royston Town	3-0	0-3	1-3	1-1	1-2	2-2	2-1	1-0	0-1	0-1	4-2	2-0	0-2	1-4	—	1-1	0-3	5-3	1-0	1-2	2-1	1-1
Saffron Walden	4-0	2-3	2-0	5-0	4-1	2-3	3-0	3-1	1-2	0-0	4-2	1-1	3-2	1-0	1-5	—	1-4	1-3	4-2	1-3	2-0	0-1
Stevenage Borough	0-2	2-2	1-1	5-1	4-1	2-3	0-2	1-3	1-4	1-3	0-0	1-3	2-3	0-6	2-3	0-1	—	0-0	0-1	0-3	3-3	2-0
Tilbury	4-1	1-0	1-0	1-0	1-3	2-3	3-0	5-1	5-2	5-3	1-2	1-0	5-2	0-2	2-1	0-2	2-3	—	3-1	3-1	2-3	0-1
Tring Town	5-2	1-0	1-0	1-0	0-1	3-1	1-0	3-0	3-3	1-0	3-2	0-1	0-3	3-1	5-0	5-0	1-3	5-2	—	3-3	3-4	1-3
Vauxhall Motors	2-1	0-2	1-1	1-0	4-1	0-2	1-2	0-3	3-3	0-2	1-4	0-1	1-3	0-2	3-3	1-4	0-3	1-2	1-1	—	2-2	1-2
Ware	3-4	0-1	1-2	2-0	2-3	3-3	2-0	2-1	0-1	2-5	2-1	2-2	2-4	1-0	1-3	1-0	3-3	1-2	1-0	1-1	—	2-0
Witham Town	2-1	1-1	2-1	3-1	1-0	2-0	0-1	1-0	2-3	1-1	2-1	4-4	0-1	2-3	0-1	2-1	3-3	0-1	0-1	1-2	1-3	—

VAUXHALL FOOTBALL LEAGUE DIVISION TWO SOUTH RESULTS 1990-91

	Abingdon Town	Banstead Athletic	Bracknell Town	Camberley Town	Chertsey Town	Cove	Eastbourne United	Egham Town	Epsom & Ewell	Feltham	Flackwell Heath	Hampton	Harefield United	Horsham	Hungerford Town	Leatherhead	Maidenhead United	Malden Vale	Newbury Town	Petersfield	Ruislip Manor	Southall
Abingdon Town	—	2-0	0-1	11-0	1-0	4-0	3-0	2-1	4-0	4-0	2-1	2-0	3-0	3-0	6-1	1-1	0-1	0-0	2-1	2-0	0-1	1-2
Banstead Athletic	3-3	—	5-1	3-0	2-0	3-1	0-0	1-5	0-2	2-1	0-0	1-1	1-2	0-3	2-5	2-0	0-0	2-1	0-2	4-1	0-4	0-0
Bracknell Town	1-2	0-2	—	3-0	0-3	2-2	1-0	0-2	1-5	0-0	3-1	0-1	2-2	4-0	1-1	1-2	0-3	0-1	1-3	3-1	3-6	0-1
Camberley Town	0-4	0-1	3-0	—	0-8	2-1	0-3	1-3	2-0	3-1	1-2	0-5	1-4	2-2	0-5	0-7	1-4	1-4	0-6	2-1	2-3	1-3
Chertsey Town	0-1	2-2	2-4	0-8	—	5-2	1-1	0-4	0-1	1-0	1-1	1-0	2-2	0-1	2-2	4-3	4-3	1-2	1-3	0-3	0-1	2-0
Cove	1-2	1-3	4-1	5-2	5-2	—	1-0	0-4	2-0	3-1	3-5	1-3	4-1	2-0	2-3	0-5	1-1	0-2	1-2	2-1	1-1	0-2
Eastbourne United	1-1	1-1	4-3	1-1	1-0	3-2	—	0-4	3-0	1-0	4-2	0-2	0-4	2-0	2-2	2-4	0-2	0-1	1-2	4-0	3-1	1-3
Egham Town	1-1	1-3	0-1	8-1	1-7	4-0	0-4	—	3-0	1-0	3-2	1-2	1-0	2-0	2-1	2-0	1-2	2-4	1-1	3-1	1-0	1-1
Epsom & Ewell	0-1	3-2	4-0	0-0	1-0	2-2	2-2	3-0	—	1-1	1-0	3-2	2-0	1-3	2-1	2-0	3-4	2-0	0-1	7-0	1-0	0-0
Feltham	2-3	0-0	2-2	2-1	1-4	0-2	4-0	1-3	0-0	—	3-2	1-0	2-3	1-1	1-1	2-1	1-1	1-2	1-2	3-0	1-1	2-0
Flackwell Heath	1-3	1-1	7-1	1-0	2-2	0-1	3-1	3-4	0-0	3-2	—	0-0	0-1	0-2	2-2	2-2	0-3	0-1	2-1	2-0	1-5	0-0
Hampton	1-4	2-0	3-2	2-0	3-1	5-0	5-1	1-4	0-0	1-0	1-1	—	0-2	0-1	1-1	2-1	1-1	1-0	0-0	5-0	0-2	2-1
Harefield United	2-2	0-0	4-1	5-0	2-2	5-0	11-1	4-2	1-1	4-1	4-1	0-3	—	3-0	2-1	0-2	0-2	2-1	2-1	1-2	2-2	2-2
Horsham	0-3	2-2	3-2	5-0	3-1	6-1	3-1	2-3	4-0	4-2	4-1	1-1	1-2	—	1-2	2-1	1-1	1-4	1-0	1-3	2-0	1-1
Hungerford Town	1-2	1-2	4-0	3-2	1-1	1-1	5-0	1-2	1-1	4-0	0-1	2-1	2-2	5-2	—	1-0	1-1	1-3	1-3	1-3	2-3	0-3
Leatherhead	1-2	2-2	2-1	4-1	5-0	5-0	3-0	2-1	4-0	5-0	5-0	0-0	1-1	2-0	3-2	—	1-2	1-1	1-0	5-1	2-0	1-4
Maidenhead United	1-3	2-0	2-1	5-1	1-0	1-0	2-0	0-3	2-0	1-0	1-0	1-2	2-1	2-0	3-1	1-2	—	3-0	0-0	3-0	1-0	1-0
Malden Vale	1-0	2-2	2-1	2-0	3-1	5-0	3-1	2-0	0-2	3-0	0-4	2-1	1-1	3-0	2-3	3-3	3-2	—	1-2	2-0	1-3	2-3
Newbury Town	0-0	1-2	1-2	1-2	4-2	2-0	2-2	1-2	0-1	1-1	2-1	0-0	2-1	1-3	0-0	2-0	2-0	2-0	—	3-1	0-6	4-3
Petersfield	0-3	1-3	2-2	5-1	2-3	0-1	5-3	2-0	2-0	1-0	0-4	0-4	3-2	3-2	0-3	0-2	2-0	1-2	0-1	—	7-0	0-4
Ruislip Manor	0-2	4-0	3-1	3-1	4-1	1-1	2-0	2-3	2-0	7-1	3-0	2-0	1-0	4-0	0-0	0-1	2-0	2-3	1-2	7-0	—	2-1
Southall	1-0	2-1	5-1	2-2	2-1	1-0	7-1	3-1	1-1	1-0	6-1	2-2	2-2	4-0	2-1	2-5	0-0	0-1	1-2	5-0	2-0	—

PREMIER INTER-LEAGUE CHALLENGE CUP 1990–91

Preliminary Round
Halesowen Town 3 (*Harrison, Hemans, Langford*)
Rushden Town 0   858
Woking 0
Wivenhoe Town 2 (*Gittings 2*)   921

First Round
Bognor Regis Town 0
Bishops Stortford 1 (*West*)   190
Dagenham 1 (*Warner*)
Wealdstone 0   428
Horwich 4 (*Warmsley, McLacklan 3*)
Marine 5 (*Gautrey, Rowlands, Meachin 2, Beales*) (*aet*)   148
Worcester City 4 (*Carter, Fergusson 3*)
Gloucester City 0   1491
Barking 1 (*Benstock*)
Carshalton Athletic 4 (*Gale, Bolton, Beste*)   60
Chorley 2 (*Roberts, Worrall*)
Morecambe 1 (*Cain*)   330
Crawley Town 5 (*Cant 3, O'Sullivan, Gallagher*)
Basingstoke Town 3 (*Devereux, Webb, Lucas*) (*aet*)   340
Dover Athletic 2 (*Dixon, Rogers*)
Farnborough Town 1 (*Johnson*)   801
Enfield 2 (*Turner, Donnalan*)
Grays Athletic 1 (*Cherry*) (*aet*)   327
Fleetwood Town 1 (*Clarkson*)
Southport 2 (*Holden*)   317
Gainsborough Trinity 1 (*Crapper*)
Bromsgrove Rovers 1 (*Cooper*) (*aet*)   341
Goole Town 2 (*Hurlestone, Collier*)
Frickley Athletic 1 (*Rolph*)   335
Gravesend & Northfleet 1 (*Blewden*)
St Albans City 0   302
Halesowen Town 1 (*Langford*)
Shepshed Charterhouse 2 (*Deane 2*)   674
Harrow Borough 4 (*O'Connor, James, Ripley, Hopson*)
Chelmsford City 2 (*Engwell, Young*)   239
Hayes 0
Wivenhoe Town 3 (*Coleman, Clark 2*)   158
Hendon 2 (*Shirt, Egbe*)
Leyton-Wingate 2 (*Williams 2*) (*aet*)   161
Kingstonian 3 (*Westly, Griffith, Lewis*)
Aylesbury United 2 (*Mason, Pert*)   641
Leek Town 1 (*Pearce*)
Burton Albion 4 (*Canning 3, McLaren*)   587
Marlow 1 (*Lay*)
Dartford 3 (*Brown, Sowerby 2*)   263
Matlock Town 2 (*Hoyland, Tilley*)   410
Atherstone United 0
Moor Green 1 (*Taylor*)
Witton Albion 4 (*Jarvis, Thomas 2, Edwards*) (*aet*)   268
Staines Town 1 (*Colwill*)
Cambridge City 4 (*Lockhart, McLean 2, Genovese*)   196
Stalybridge Celtic 1 (*Diamond*)
Hyde United 2 (*McCluskie 2*)   756
Windsor & Eton 1 (*Woods*)
Wokingham Town 1 (*Pearce*) (*aet*)   348
Bashley 1 (*Whale*)
Dorchester Town 1 (*Thorpe*) (*aet*)   355
Poole Town 2 (*Funnell, Manson*)
Weymouth 8 (*Compton, Smith 2, Evans 2, McGory, Ferns (og), Copelin (og)*)   230
Redbridge Forest 5 (*Pamphlett, Simmonds, Dingwall, Gurney, Quail*)
Waterlooville 0   159
South Liverpool 0
Bangor City 2 (*Powell, Jones*)   131
VS Rugby 3 (*Shearer, Smith, Geddes*)
Buxton 2 (*Johnson, Clarke 2*) (*aet*)   527
Bishop Auckland 4 (*Stonehouse 3, Shaw*)
Droylsden 2 (*Kershaw*)   253
Colne Dynamos withdrew. Mossley received walk-over.

Replays
Bromsgrove Rovers 2 (*O'Connor, Stott*)
Gainsborough Trinity 1 (*Lowe*)   718
Leyton-Wingate 1 (*Williams*)
Hendon 3 (*Holmes, Egbe 2*)   162

Wokingham Town 1 (*Alexander*)
Windsor & Eton 2 (*Gilman 2*)   157
Dorchester Town 2 (*Green, Townsend*)
Bashley 0   500

Second Round
Cambridge City 2 (*Lockhart, Grogan*)
Shepshed Charterhouse 0   162
Carshalton Athletic 3 (*Warden, Bolton, Beste*)
Gravesend & Northfleet 2 (*Day, Schweiso*)   250
Hyde United 3 (*Lutkevitch 2, Chadwick*)
Bishop Auckland 2 (*Healey, Wiggan*)   368
Bishops Stortford 2 (*Ryan, Gayle*)
Dagenham 0   365
Bromsgrove Rovers 1 (*O'Meara*)
Burton Albion 3 (*Harbottle, Redfern, Canning*)   707
Dartford 0
Dover Athletic 3 (*Bartlett, Davis, Ambrose*)   463
Enfield 1 (*Salmon*)
Wivenhoe Town 0   265
Hendon 2 (*Holmes, Shirt*)
Kingstonian 1 (*Dear*)   252
Marine 1 (*Murray*)
Witton Albion 2 (*Jarvis, Edwards*)   277
Mossley 2 (*Joynes 2*)
Bangor City 1 (*Johnson*)   242
Redbridge Forest 1 (*Pamphlett*)
Harrow Borough 3 (*O'Connor 3 (2 pens)*)   100
Southport 2 (*Holden, Whitehall*)
Chorley 0   382
VS Rugby 4 (*Boyland 3, Smith*)
Goole Town 0   345
Worcester City 0
Matlock Town 1 (*Marsh*)   981
Weymouth 2 (*Diaz, Vessey (og)*)
Crawley Town 2 (*Vessey, Gallagher*) (*aet*)   412
Windsor & Eton 1 (*Woods*)
Dorchester Town 0   222

Replay
Crawley Town 0
Weymouth 1 (*Wickins (og)*)   378

Third Round
Dover Athletic 3 (*Davis, Lee, Shea (og)*)
Harrow Borough 1 (*Payne*)   529
Enfield 1 (*Britnell*)
Weymouth 3 (*Fullbrook 2, Docherty*) (*aet*)   310
Hendon 0
Carshalton 3 (*Warden, Jacobs, Bolton*)   196
Matlock Town 2 (*Hunter, Hoyland*)
Cambridge City 1 (*Genovese*)   350
Mossley 0
Witton Albion 2 (*Thomas, Grimshaw*)   363
VS Rugby 0
Burton Albion 3 (*Elliot, Jones, Niblett (og)*)   392
Windsor & Eton 1 (*White*)
Bishops Stortford 2 (*Ryan, West*)   218
Southport 2 (*Holden, Whitehall*)
Hyde United 1 (*Hodgert*)   287

Semi-finals (2 legs)
Dover Athletic 2 (*Ambrose, Davis*)
Bishops Stortford 1 (*Hardwick*) (*aet*)   859
Weymouth 1 (*Wilson*)
Carshalton Athletic 3 (*Beste, Kane*)   423
Southport 3 (*Mitchell, Whitehall 2*)
Matlock Town 1 (*Gee*)   343
Burton Albion 0
Witton Albion 3 (*Antrobus, Senior 2*)   501
Dover Athletic 3 (*Ambrose, Lynch 2*)
Carshalton Athletic 0   910
Southport 4 (*McDonald, Blackhurst, Mitchell, Whitehall*)
Witton Albion 1 (*McNeilis*)   511

Final (2 May 1991 at Aylesbury United FC)
Dover Athletic 3 (*Jackson 43, Ambrose 60, Tim Dickson 87*)
Southport 2 (*Whitehall 58, McDonald 65*)   466

924

THE LOCTITE CUP COMPETITION 1990–91

First Round
Basingstoke Town 1, Molesey 2
Tooting & Mitcham United 4, Bromley 3 (aet)
Dorking 1, Harrow Borough 4
Hayes 2, Wembley 1
Uxbridge 2, Aylesbury United 3
Barking 0, Leyton-Wingate 1
Woking 4, Bognor Regis Town 1
Lewes 2, Whyteleafe 1
Chesham United 2, Enfield 1 (aet)
Staines Town 1, Walton & Hersham 5
St Albans City 0, Dagenham 1
Aveley 1, Wokingham Town 2

Second Round
Molesey 0, Carshalton Athletic 2
Worthing 2, Southwick 0
Tooting & Mitcham United 3, Harlow Town 2
Redbridge Forest 1, Chalfont St Peter 0
Harrow Borough 0, Bishop's Stortford 2
Yeading 0, Windsor & Eton 2
Hitchin Town 2, Marlow 2 (aet)
Heybridge Swifts 0, Wivenhoe Town 1 (aet)
Hayes 2, Aylesbury United 3 (aet)
Croydon 0, Dulwich Hamlet 3
Leyton-Wingate 1, Woking 0
Metropolitan Police 0, Hendon 1
Lewes 1, Boreham Wood 1 (aet)
Chesham United 1, Walton & Hersham 0
Kingstonian 0, Dagenham 1 (aet)
Grays Athletic 0, Wokingham Town 0 (aet)

Replays
Marlow 2, Hitchin Town 4
Boreham Wood 1, Lewes 2
Wokingham Town 0, Grays Athletic 1

Third Round
Carshalton Athletic 13, Worthing 0
Tooting & Mitcham 1, Redbridge Forest 8
Bishop's Stortford 1, Windsor & Eton 0
Hitchin Town 1, Wivenhoe Town 3 (aet)
Aylesbury United 1, Dulwich Hamlet 0 (aet)
Leyton-Wingate 1, Hendon 2
Lewes 0, Chesham United 1
Dagenham 3, Grays Athletic 2

Fourth Round
Carshalton Athletic 0, Redbridge Forest 1
Bishop's Stortford 2, Wivenhoe Town 1
Aylesbury United 4, Hendon 1
Chesham United 5, Dagenham 1

Semi-finals First Leg
Redbridge Forest 2, Bishop's Stortford 0
Aylesbury United 1, Chesham United 2

Semi-finals Second Leg
Bishop's Stortford 3, Redbridge Forest 0,
Chesham United 1, Aylesbury United 1

Final
Bishop's Stortford 2, Chesham United 2 (aet)
(Bishop's Stortford won 5–4 on penalties)

THE LOCTITE TROPHY 1990–91

First Round
Berkhamsted Town 2, Chertsey Town 1
Hampton 2, Epsom & Ewell 0
Tring Town 0, Witham Town 3
Edgware Town 2, Maidenhead United 4
Barton Rovers 3, Feltham 1
Bracknell Town 4, Malden Vale 4
Ware 6, Tilbury 6
Billericay Town 0, Abingdon Town 1
Ruislip Manor 2, Rainham Town 0
Saffron Walden Town 3, Royston Town 4
Hornchurch 3, Kingsbury Town 3
Newbury Town 3, Hemel Hempstead 1

Replays
Malden Vale 2, Bracknell Town 0
Tilbury 1, Ware 1 (aet)
Kingsbury Town 1, Hornchurch 2

Second Round
Petersfield United 2, Harefield United 5
Berkhamsted Town 1, Hampton 2
Egham Town 1, Witham Town 2
Collier Row 1, Vauxhall Motors 2
Hungerford Town 1, Maidenhead United 0
Barton Rovers 0, Malden Vale 5
Ware 1, Abingdon Town 1
Stevenage Borough 4, Southall 2
Eastbourne United 3, Cove 5
Purfleet 3, Camberley Town 1
Ruislip Manor 2, Basildon United 1
Leatherhead 3, Royston Town 0
Hornchurch 0, Finchley 1
Horsham 2, Clapton 0
Flackwell Heath 7, Hertford Town 0
Newbury Town 1, Banstead Athletic 0

Replay
Abingdon Town 2, Ware 1

Third Round
Harefield United 0, Hampton 1
Witham Town 1, Vauxhall Motors 0
Hungerford Town 0, Malden Vale 0
Abingdon Town 1, Stevenage Borough 0
Cove 2, Purfleet 1
Ruislip Manor 5, Leatherhead 1
Finchley 0, Horsham 2
Flackwell Heath 0, Newbury Town 0

Replays
Malden Vale 0, Hungerford Town 3
Newbury Town 3, Flackwell Heath 0

Fourth Round
Hampton 0, Witham Town 1
Hungerford Town 0, Abingdon Town 2
Cove 0, Ruislip Manor 2
Horsham 3, Newbury Town 0

Semi-finals First Leg
Witham Town 0, Abingdon Town 1
Ruislip Manor 3, Horsham 1

Semi-finals Second Leg
Abingdon Town 1, Witham Town 1
Horsham 1, Ruislip Manor 1

Final
Ruislip Manor 2, Abingdon Town 1
(At Chesham)

THE LOCTITE YOUTH CUP 1990–91

First Round
Staines Town 3, Feltham 2
Purfleet 2, Walton & Hersham 0
Aylesbury United 2, Uxbridge 2 (aet)
Whyteleafe received a walkover from Croydon
Basingstoke Town 3, Bracknell Town 1
Maidenhead United 6, Leatherhead 0
Epsom & Ewell 3, Flackwell Heath 1
Horsham 1, Enfield 8
Marlow received a walkover from Basildon United

Southall 4, Harefield United 0
Rainham Town 0, Petersfield United 2
Dulwich Hamlet 3, Hemel Hempstead 1
Berkhamsted Town 1, Dorking 0
Malden Vale 5, Edgware Town 0
Wokingham Town 0, St Albans City 2 (aet)
Hertford Town 1, Billericay Town 2
Harrow Borough 0, Abingdon Town 6
Carshalton Athletic 5, Wembley 0

Replays
Uxbridge 2, Aylesbury United 0

Second Round
Staines Town 2, Windsor & Eton 1
Witham Town 3, Purfleet 1
Uxbridge 4, Kingstonian 2
Chesham United 1, Barton Rovers 2
Whyteleafe 4, Basingstoke Town 0
Maidenhead United 0, Wivenhoe Town 1
Clapton 0, Epsom & Ewell 1
Enfield 2, Yeading 1
Marlow 0, Bognor Regis Town 2
Newbury Town 0, Bromley 5
Southall 2, Ruislip Manor 0 (aet)
Petersfield United 1, Dulwich Hamlet 1 (aet)
Berkhamsted Town 4, Hendon 2
Malden Vale 1, St Albans City 3 (aet)
Billericay Town 1, Abingdon Town 3 (aet)
Carshalton Athletic 5, Hitchin Town 1

Replays
Dulwich Hamlet 4, Petersfield United 1

Third Round
Staines Town 2, Witham Town 5
Uxbridge 4, Barton Rovers 1

Whyteleafe 5, Wivenhoe Town 1
Epsom & Ewell 2, Enfield 0
Bognor Regis Town 1, Bromley 5
Southall 3, Dulwich Hamlet 4
Berkhamsted Town 1, St Albans City 0
Abingdon Town 0, Carshalton Athletic 6

Fourth Round
Witham Town 2, Uxbridge 4
Whyteleafe 2, Epsom & Ewell 2 (aet)
Bromley 3, Dulwich Hamlet 1
Berkhamsted Town 1, Carshalton Athletic 3

Replays
Epsom & Ewell 2, Whyteleafe 1

Semi-finals First Leg
Epsom & Ewell 3, Uxbridge 2
Bromley 2, Carshalton Athletic 1

Semi-finals Second Leg
Uxbridge 1, Epsom & Ewell 3
Carshalton Athletic 2, Bromley 2

Final
Epsom & Ewell 4, Bromley 1
 (At Carshalton)

AC DELCO CUP 1990–91

Preliminary Round
Kingsbury Town 0, Yeading 4
Royston Town 0, Southall 1
Harefield United 2, Hungerford Town 1
Abingdon Town 0, Flackwell Heath 0 (aet)
Malden Vale 4, Eastbourne United 1
Hertford Town 0, Witham Town 3
Tring Town 2, Leatherhead 0
Berkhamsted Town 2, Cove 0
Purfleet 3, Epsom & Ewell 2
Hampton 3, Rainham Town 1 (aet)
Bracknell Town 2, Horsham 3 (aet)
Heybridge Swifts 3, Vauxhall Motors 1
Tilbury 1, Basildon United 3 (aet)
Newbury Town 4, Clapton 1
Chertsey Town 0, Hemel Hempstead 3 (aet)
Saffron Walden Town 3, Collier Row 4
Banstead Athletic 1, Billericay Town 0
Barton Rovers 0, Ware 3
Feltham 1, Molesey 2
Stevenage Borough 2, Hornchurch 1
Ruislip Manor 1, Aveley 2
Edgware Town 5, Maidenhead United 2
Camberley Town 0, Petersfield United 1
Finchley 0, Egham Town 2
Replays
Flackwell Heath 0, Abingdon Town 1 (aet)
First Round
Wokingham Town 1, Enfield 3
Bromley 2, Leyton-Wingate 0
Yeading 3, St Albans City 2 (aet)
Southall 1, Carshalton Athletic 2
Harlow Town 2, Aylesbury United 2
Harefield United 1, Abingdon Town 2
Kingstonian 3, Whyteleafe 1
Malden Vale 1, Southwick 0
Witham Town 1, Barking 3 (aet)
Staines Town 0, Redbridge Forest 2
Wembley 5, Tring Town 0
Windsor & Eton 5, Bognor Regis Town 1
Uxbridge 3, Hitchin Town 2
Croydon 2, Berkhamsted Town 2 (aet)
Purfleet 2, Walton & Hersham 1
Boreham Wood 2, Hampton 2 (aet)
Harrow Borough 3, Metropolitan Police 4 (aet)
Dulwich Hamlet 1, Horsham 0
Wivenhoe Town 2, Tooting & Mitcham United 1 (aet)
Chalfont St Peter 1, Lewes 2
Hayes 3, Heybridge Swifts 4
Basildon United 2, Newbury Town 1
Dagenham 4, Hemel Hempstead 1
Collier Row 2, Banstead Athletic 1
Ware 1, Molesey 3
Hendon 1, Chesham United 1 (aet)
Stevenage Borough 1, Grays Athletic 2

Basingstoke Town 0, Aveley 2
Edgware Town 0, Marlow 3
Worthing 3, Petersfield United 4 (aet)
Bishop's Stortford 3, Dorking 0
Egham Town 0, Woking 2
Replays
Aylesbury United 1, Harlow Town 2
Berkhamsted Town 0, Croydon 2
Hampton 1, Boreham Wood 0
Chesham United 1, Hendon 2
Second Round
Enfield 0, Bromley 1
Yeading 0, Carshalton Athletic 1
Harlow Town 3, Abingdon Town 0
Kingstonian 3, Malden Vale 1
Barking 0, Redbridge Forest 2
Wembley 0, Windsor & Eton 0 (aet)
Uxbridge 4, Croydon 1 (aet)
Purfleet 0, Hampton 1
Metropolitan Police 0, Dulwich Hamlet 2
Wivenhoe Town 3, Lewes 2
Heybridge Swifts 3, Basildon United 1
Dagenham 1, Collier Row 0
Molesey 2, Hendon 0
Grays Athletic 3, Aveley 2
Marlow 5, Petersfield Utd 2
Bishop's Stortford 3, Woking 3 (aet)
Replays
Windsor & Eton 2, Wembley 3
Woking 2, Bishop's Stortford 1
Third Round
Bromley 0, Carshalton Athletic 3
Harlow Town 1, Kingstonian 0
Redbridge Forest 4, Wembley 1 (aet)
Uxbridge 2, Hampton 1
Dulwich Hamlet 0, Wivenhoe Town 1
Heybridge Swifts 0, Dagenham 2
Molesey 1, Grays Athletic 0
Marlow 1, Woking 3
Fourth Round
Carshalton Athletic 3, Harlow Town 0
Redbridge Forest 3, Uxbridge 0
Wivenhoe Town 1, Dagenham 2
Molesey 1, Woking 2 (aet)
Semi-finals First Leg
Carshalton 4, Redbridge Forest 1
Dagenham 1, Woking 2
Semi-finals Second Leg
Carshalton Athletic 0, Redbridge Forest 2
Dagenham 1, Woking 1
Final
Woking 2, Carshalton Athletic 1

FA CHALLENGE TROPHY 1990–91

The following 32 clubs were exempted to the First Round Proper: Altrincham, Aylesbury United, Barnet, Barrow, Bath City, Billingham Synthonia, Cheltenham Town, Colchester United, Colne Dynamoes, Dartford, Dover Athletic, Farnborough Town, Gateshead, Gretna, Hyde United, Kettering Town, Kidderminster Harriers, Leek Town, Macclesfield Town, Merthyr Tydfil, Northwich Victoria, Redbridge Forest, Runcorn, Slough Town, Stafford Rangers, Sutton United, Telford United, Welling United, Woking, Wokingham Town, Wycombe Wanderers, Yeovil Town.

The following 32 clubs were exempted to the Third Round Qualifying: Bangor City, Bishop Auckland, Blyth Spartans, Boston United, Bromsgrove Rovers, Burton Albion, Carshalton Athletic, Chorley, Dagenham, Enfield, Fisher Athletic, Frickley Athletic, Gravesend & Northfleet, Guisborough Town, Harrow Borough, Hendon, Kingstonian, Leyton-Wingate, Marine, Metropolitan Police, Newcastle Blue Star, Nuneaton Borough, Seaham Red Star, South Bank, Spennymoor United, Tow Law Town, Wealdstone, Weymouth, Windsor & Eton, Witton Albion, Wivenhoe Town, Worcester City.

First Round Qualifying

Easington Colliery v Durham City	4-1
Accrington Stanley v Whitley Bay	3-2
Ferryhill Athletic v North Shields	0-0, 2-0
Stockton v Fleetwood Town	1-4
Emley v Southport	2-1
Consett v Whitby Town	2-1
South Liverpool v Brandon United	3-1
Whickham v Alnwick Town	0-1
Morecambe v Workington	3-0
Horwich RMI v Alfreton Town	1-0
Congleton Town v Newtown	3-1
Moor Green v Hednesford Town	1-0
Winsford United v Droylsden	1-4
Alvechurch v Mossley	0-1
Halesowen Town v Colwyn Bay	1-3
Gainsborough Trinity v Worksop Town	2-0
Rhyl v Goole Town	1-0
Stalybridge Celtic v Shepshed Charterhouse	1-0
Grantham Town v Atherstone United	0-1
Redditch United v Eastwood Town	1-0
Bedworth Town v Willenhall Town	4-0
Matlock Town v Buxton	3-2
Caernarfon Town v Leicester United	0-1
Cambridge City v Chalfont St Peter	3-0
Sutton Coldfield Town v Boreham Wood	2-2, 1-1, 1-1, 1-0
Burnham v Wembley	2-2, 1-3
Bishops Stortford v Rushden Town	2-1
Chelmsford City v Tamworth	0-1
Uxbridge v Stourbridge	1-1, 2-0
Marlow v Aveley	2-1
Yeading v Bury Town	3-1
Barking v Witney Town	4-1
St Albans City v Chesham United	0-4
Banbury United v VS Rugby	1-5
Grays Athletic v Heybridge Swifts	1-0
Staines Town v Harlow Town	0-3
Corby Town v Hayes	0-1
Whyteleafe v Tooting & Mitcham United	3-0
Fareham Town v Worthing	1-1, 0-1
Basingstoke Town v Molesey	0-0, 2-2, 4-2
Crawley Town v Hampton	2-0
Walton & Hersham v Lewes	1-1, 3-2
Andover v Canterbury City	0-0, 1-4
Dulwich Hamlet v Bromley	2-1
Gosport Borough v Bashley	5-2
Bognor Regis Town v Erith & Belvedere	2-1
Dorking v Waterlooville	5-3
Ashford Town v Southwick	1-1, 0-1
Croydon v Folkestone	2-2, 2-0
Bridgend Town v Bideford	3-0
Dorchester Town v Taunton Town	5-0
Barry Town v Saltash United	1-0
Cwmbran Town v Maesteg Park	0-0, 1-3
Weston-Super-Mare v Newport AFC	2-2, 2-0
Gloucester City v Ton Pentre	3-0
Stroud v Poole Town	

Second Round Qualifying

Accrington Stanley v Easington Colliery	2-1
Consett v Alnwick Town	1-1, 0-1
Shildon v Morecambe	0-3
Ferryhill Athletic v Emley	0-0, 1-4
South Liverpool v Fleetwood Town	0-1
(at Marine)	
Congleton Town v Radcliffe Borough	1-0
Redditch United v Bedworth United	1-2
Stalybridge Celtic v Colwyn Bay	0-1
Droylsden v Matlock Town	3-3, 2-0
Gainsborough Trinity v Moor Green	1-3

Horwich RMI v Rhyl	3-2
Leicester United v Dudley Town	5-2
Mossley v Atherstone United	1-3
Sutton Coldfield Town v Baldock Town	2-1
VS Rugby v Grays Athletic	1-1, 2-1
Barking v Uxbridge	1-2
Bishops Stortford v Harlow Town	2-3
Marlow v Wembley	5-0
Cambridge City v Yeading	1-1, 1-2
Hayes v Hitchin Town	1-1, 2-1
Tamworth v Chesham United	1-2
Gosport Borough v Crawley Town	1-1, 1-0
Andover v Salisbury	1-2
Dorking v Tooting & Mitcham United	2-2, 1-0
Fareham Town v Bognor Regis Town	0-2
Walton & Hersham v Croydon	6-0
Margate v Bromley	2-1
Southwick v Molesey	0-3
Gloucester City v Llanelli	3-0
Cwmbran Town v Dorchester Town	1-1, 1-4
Barry Town v Bridgend Town	4-0
Newport AFC v Stroud	0-3

Third Round Qualifying

Emley v Morecambe	2-1
Spennymoor United v Chorley	0-0, 0-1
Frickley Athletic v Seaham Red Star	2-0
South Bank v Blyth Spartans	2-2, 1-1, 2-0
Bishop Auckland v Newcastle Blue Star	3-1
Tow Law Town v Alnwick Town	2-1
Fleetwood Town v Marine	2-0
Guisborough Town v Accrington Stanley	4-1
Colwyn Bay v Witton Albion	1-3
Boston United v Leicester United	3-0
Droylsden v Bromsgrove Rovers	3-3, 3-1
Nuneaton Borough v Burton Albion	1-2
Sutton Coldfield Town v Horwich RMI	1-3
Congleton Town v Moor Green	0-3
Bedworth United v Bangor City	1-1, 2-1
Dagenham v Enfield	0-1
Margate v VS Rugby	1-1, 0-5
Leyton-Wingate v Wealdstone	0-2
Harrow Borough v Fisher Athletic	3-2
Hayes v Kingstonian	3-2
Metropolitan Police v Harlow Town	0-1
Yeading v Molesey	0-2
Atherstone United v Wivenhoe Town	3-0
Gravesend & Northfleet v Hendon	1-2
Marlow v Chesham United	3-0
Bognor Regis Town v Worcester City	3-1
Stroud v Uxbridge	0-1
Walton & Hersham v Windsor & Eton	1-1, 0-3
Weymouth v Gloucester City	2-1
Dorking v Gosport Borough	5-0
Carshalton Athletic v Dorchester Town	0-0, 0-1
Barry Town v Salisbury	

First Round Proper

Northwich Victoria v Tow Law Town	2-1
South Bank v Bishop Auckland	1-0
Horwich RMI v Bedworth United	2-0
Guisborough Town v Witton Albion	2-2, 1-2
Runcorn v Boston United	2-0
Droylsden v Fleetwood Town	2-1
Hyde United v Stafford Rangers	1-2
Burton Albion v Moor Green	3-0
Barrow v Chorley	2-0
Macclesfield Town v Gretna	0-2
Gateshead v Billingham Synthonia	2-2, 3-0
Leek Town v Altrincham	0-4
Telford United v Emley	0-0, 0-1

Barnet v Farnborough Town	2-3
Slough Town v Bath City	2-4
Wokingham Town v Wivenhoe Town	1-2
Kidderminster Harriers v Sutton United	4-2
Carshalton Athletic v Dartford	0-0, 1-1, 2-3
Enfield v Chesham United	1-0
Dover Athletic v Dorking	1-0
Gloucester City v Yeovil Town	1-0
Gravesend & Northfleet v Cheltenham Town	2-2, 1-5
Fisher Athletic v Redbridge Forest	1-2
Salisbury v VS Rugby	1-4
Wycombe Wanderers v Wealdstone	1-0
Windsor & Eton v Colchester United	0-1
Bognor Regis Town v Aylesbury United	2-4
Molesey v Merthyr Tydfil	1-1, 1-0
Welling United v Hayes	3-1
Kettering Town v Woking	2-0
Stroud v Metropolitan Police	2-2, 2-0

Second Round Proper

Dartford v Cheltenham Town	0-2
Colchester United v Runcorn	2-0
Kidderminster Harriers v Dover Athletic	1-0
Merthyr Tydfil v Gloucester City	1-3
Hyde United v Emley	0-0, 2-3
Welling United v Aylesbury United	2-1
Farnborough Town v Bath City	1-3
Barrow v Kettering Town	0-0, 1-2
VS Rugby v Wycombe Wanderers	0-1
Northwich Victoria v Droylsden	4-1
Horwich RMI v Gretna	2-1
Enfield v Wivenhoe Town	0-2
Witton Albion v South Bank	3-2
Redbridge Forest v Frickley Athletic	2-1
Altrincham v Gateshead	3-1
Stroud v Burton Albion	3-2

Third Round Proper

Horwich RMI v Redbridge Forest	2-1
Witton Albion v Gloucester City	3-0
Welling United v Altrincham	1-2
Colchester United v Wivenhoe Town	3-0
Emley v Kettering Town	3-2
Kidderminster Harriers v Bath City	3-1
Northwich Victoria v Stroud	2-0
Wycombe Wanderers v Cheltenham Town	2-1

Fourth Round Proper

Colchester United v Witton Albion	0-2
Kidderminster Harriers v Emley	3-0
Altrincham v Horwich RMI	5-0
Northwich Victoria v Wycombe Wanderers	2-3

Semi-finals first leg

Kidderminster Harriers v Witton Albion	1-0
Wycombe Wanderers v Altrincham	2-1

Second leg

Witton Albion v Kidderminster Harriers	4-3
Altrincham v Wycombe Wanderers	0-2

FINAL at Wembley

11 MAY

Kidderminster Harriers (0) 1 *(Hadley)*

Wycombe Wanderers (1) 2 *(Scott, West)*   34,842

Kidderminster Harriers: Jones; Kurila, McGrath, Weir, Barnett, Forsyth, Joseph (Wilcox) Howell (Whitehouse), Hadley, Lilwall, Humphreys.
Wycombe Wanderers: Granville; Crossley, Cash, Kerr, Creaser, Carroll, Bryan, Stapleton, West, Scott, Guppy (Hutchinson).
Referee: J. Watson.

FA COUNTY YOUTH CUP 1990–91

First Round

Northumberland v Westmorland	10-0
Cumberland v North Riding	3-1
West Riding v Derbyshire	4-1
Liverpool v Shropshire	2-3
Cheshire v Leicestershire & Rutland	2-3
Birmingham v Oxfordshire	6-3
Norfolk v Suffolk	4-2
Huntingdonshire v Essex	3-2
London v Middlesex	2-0
Kent v Sussex	2-1
Army v Dorset	1-4
Devon v Herefordshire	5-2
Somerset & Avon (South) v Wiltshire	0-5

Second Round

Northumberland v Durham	1-2
Cumberland v Lancashire	0-2
West Riding v East Riding	4-2
Shropshire v Manchester	2-0
Leicestershire & Rutland v Nottinghamshire	1-0
Staffordshire v Sheffield & Hallamshire	2-3
Lincolnshire v Northamptonshire	1-3
Birmingham v Worcestershire	4-4, 3-5
Norfolk v Cambridgeshire	1-2
Huntingdonshire v Bedfordshire	3-1
London v Hertfordshire	4-2
Kent v Surrey	2-4
Berks & Bucks v Hampshire	2-3

Dorset v Royal Navy	1-1, 2-3
Devon v Gloucestershire	4-2
Wiltshire v Cornwall	3-5

Third Round

Durham v Lancashire	1-2
Shropshire v Leicestershire & Rutland	1-1, 2-1
West Riding v Sheffield & Hallamshire	4-1
Worcestershire v Cambridgeshire	3-1
Northamptonshire v Huntingdonshire	3-1
Surrey v Hampshire	8-3
London v Royal Navy	2-0
Devon v Cornwall	2-0

Fourth Round

West Riding v Northamptonshire	2-1
Lancashire v Shropshire	3-2
Worcestershire v Devon	5-2
Surrey v London	2-0

Semi-finals

Lancashire v West Riding	2-0
Surrey v Worcestershire	3-2

Final

Lancashire v Surrey	6-0
(at Bolton Wanderers FC)	

FA CHALLENGE VASE 1990–91

The following 32 clubs were exempted to the Second Round: Abingdon Town, Billericay Town, Braintree Town, Bridlington Town, Bridport, Burnham Ramblers, Chertsey Town, East Thurrock United, Eastwood Hanley, Falmouth Town, Farsley Athletic, Great Yarmouth Town, Guiseley, Hastings Town, Harefield United, Harrogate RA, Haverhill Rovers, Heanor Town, Holbeach United, Hucknall Town, Hungerford Town, Hythe Town, North Ferriby United, Ossett Town, Paget Rangers, Paulton Rovers, Potton United, Rossendale United, Spalding United, Sudbury Town, Thatcham Town, Wisbech Town.

The following 32 clubs were exempted to the First Round: Berkhamsted Town, Boldmere St Michaels, Borrowash Victoria, Bourne Town, Bridgnorth Town, Camberley Town, Chard Town, Clevedon Town, Collier Row, Corinthians, Dawlish Town, Epsom & Ewell, Exmouth Town, Garforth Town, Greenwich Borough, Gresley Rovers, Harrogate Town, Hailsham Town, Havant Town, Horsham, Hounslow, March Town United, Merstham, Old Georgians, Rainworth MW, Raunds Town, St Helens Town, Sholing Sports, Tilbury, Warrington Town, Whitstable Town, Yate Town.

Extra Preliminary Round

Pickering Town v Newton Aycliffe	0-3
Heaton Stannington v Boldon CA	0-1
Yorkshire Amateurs v Sunderland Roker	3-1
Eppleton CW v Darlington RA	3-1
Dunston FB v Seaton Delaval Amateurs	1-0
Whitehaven Miners Social v Marchon	1-2
Coundon TT v South Shields	3-4
Prudhoe East End v Marske United	1-0
Annfield Plain v Sunderland Vaux Ryhope	1-0
Cleator Moor Celtic v Ponteland United	4-1
Knowsley United v Flixton	3-1
Padiham v Poulton Victoria	2-1
Westhoughton Town v Maghull	1-5
St Dominics v Christleton	2-0
Nantwich Town v Newton (WC)	2-0
Great Harwood Town v Atherton LR	3-1
General Chemicals v Cheadle Town	3-1
Prestwich Heys v Ashville	2-3
Newton v Newcastle Town	1-2
Knypersley Victoria v Rylands	2-1
Cammell Laird v Redgate Clayton	3-0
Hanley Town v Waterloo Dock	0-1
Heswall v Vauxhall GM	1-6
Salford City v Atherton Collieries	2-4
Merseyside Police v Rocester	2-1
Hatfield Main v Gainsborough Town	1-0
Oakham United v Pontefract Collieries	0-0, 0-0, 2-0*, 1-1 (aet), 3-4
(abandoned after 45 minutes — floodlight failure)	
Yorkshire Main v Kimberley Town	2-0
Skegness Town v Eccleshill United	3-4
Liversedge v Nettleham	2-1
Grimethorpe MW v Bradley Rangers	0-5
Glasshoughton Welfare v Clipstone Welfare	0-1
Priory (Eastwood) v Brodsworth MW	5-1
Mickleover RBL v Maltby MW	1-5
Immingham Town v Selby Town	2-5
Derby Prims v Rossington Main	
(Rossington Main walked over Derby Prims—Derby Prims expelled)	
Hallam v Worsboro Bridge MW	0-3
Hall Road Rangers v Winterton Rangers	1-5
Stocksbridge Park Steels v Blidworth MW	3-1
Radford v Bacup Borough	1-1, 0-3
Hinckley v Coleshill Town	2-4
Northfield Town v Norton United	2-1
Wolverhampton Casuals v Kings Heath	2-1
Solihull Borough v Chelmsley Town (9.9.90)	3-1
Long Buckby v Melton Town	2-3
Hamlet S & L v Blakenhall	2-1
Eccleshall v Bolehall Swifts	3-0
Oadby Town v Bloxwich Town	3-4
Meir KA v Lutterworth Town	1-2
Holwell Sports v St Andrews	2-1
Burton Park Wanderers v Pegasus Juniors	2-3
Heath Hayes v Westfields	3-2
Highfield Rangers v Stourport Swifts	0-0, 0-3
Stapenhill v Anstey Nomads	1-0
Knowle v Oldswinford	0-1
Norwich United v Chatteris Town	2-0
LBC Ortonians v Sawbridge Town	2-1
Clarksteel Yaxley v Long Sutton Athletic	2-1
Cornard United v Ramsey Town	1-2
Brantham Athletic v Clacton Town	2-0
Diss Town v Stanstead	0-1
Ispwich Wanderers v Thetford Town	1-3
Huntingdon United v Watton United	0-8
Downham Town v Wroxham	2-3
Brightlingsea United v Somersham Town	1-1, 4-1
Ely City v St Ives Town	0-1

Pirton v The 61	3-0
Viking Sports v Stotfold	0-2
Brimsdown Rovers v Electrolux	2-0
Beaconsfield United v Langford	1-2
Rayners Lane v Beckton United	
(Rayners Lane walked over Beckton United—Beckton United expelled)	
Waltham Abbey v Cockfosters	1-2
Amersham Town v Shillington	3-2
Ford United v Elliott Star	1-2
London Colney v Wolverton	0-3
Totternhoe v Wingate	4-4, 2-3
Mount Grace (Potters Bar) v Winslow United (at Elliott Star)	3-2
Walthamstow Pennant v Biggleswade Town	3-0
Brook House v Kempston Rovers	2-2, 0-0, 1-0
Milton Keynes Borough v Haringey Borough	0-3
Godalming Town v Farleigh Rovers	2-2, 2-0
Eastbourne Town v Bedfont	1-0
West Wickham v Selsey (at Selsey)	2-0
Danson (Bexley Boro) v Cove	1-1, 0-2
Crockenhill v Oakwood	2-1
Thomas Polytechnic v Farnham Town	0-3
Cobham v Old Salesians	2-1
Horley Town v Faversham Town	0-4
Ash United v Slade Green	0-4
Broadbridge Heath v Hartley Wintney	2-3
Christchurch v Brockenhurst	2-1
Wallingford Town v Kintbury Rangers	1-2
Bemerton Heath Harlequins v Chipping Norton Town	4-0
Swindon Athletic v Bishops Cleve	2-4
Sherborne Town v AFC Lymington	0-4
Bicester Town v Folland Sports	3-0
Didcot Town v Easington Sports	1-0
Wantage Town v Flight Refuelling	1-7
Highworth Town v DRG(FP)	2-0
Clanfield v Backwell United	1-2
Wotton Rovers v Portishead	1-1, 3-3
Clandown v Cinderford Town	0-2
Cirencester Town v Hallen	1-3
Sharpness v Fairford Town	
(Fairford Town walked over Sharpness—Sharpness withdrawn)	
Bridgwater Town v Odd Down	1-0
Larkhall Athletic v Harrow Hill	2-2, 2-0
Almondsbury Picksons v Port of Bristol	2-1
Brislington v Keynsham Town	0-0, 0-3
Ottery St Mary v St Austell	2-0

Preliminary Round

Chester-le-Street Town v Marchon	5-3
Langley Park v Washington	2-1
Penrith v Shotton Comrades	0-3
Horden CW v Norton & Stockton Ancients	0-0, 2-1
Peterlee Newtown v Ryhope CA	2-0
Willington v Darlington CB	1-2
West Auckland Town v Eppleton CW	2-2, 0-7
Esh Winning v West Allotment Celtic	2-2, 2-5
Annfield Plain v Newton Aycliffe	1-1, 0-1
(abandoned after 90 mins—high winds)	
Yorkshire Amateurs v Prudhoe East End	2-3
Netherfield v Northallerton Town	1-0
Bolden CA v Hebburn	0-1
Ashington v Cleator Moor Celtic	3-1
Crook Town v Murton	1-3
Billingham Town v South Shields	1-0
Dunston FB v Evenwood Town	3-1
Irlam Town v Lancaster City	0-1
Bootle v Clitheroe	1-1, 2-3

Nantwich Town v Chadderton	2-0
Thackley v Leyland Motors	0-1
Prescot AFC v Darwen	4-3
Maine Road v Atherton Collieries	3-1
Ashton United v Formby	6-3
Wythenshawe Amateurs v Curzon Ashton	0-1
Merseyside Police v Knypersley Victoria	2-3
Blackpool (Wren) Rovers v Ashville	4-2
St Dominics v Blackpool Mechanics	1-2
Knowsley United v General Chemicals	3-1
Douglas High School OB v Skelmersdale United	0-2
Newcastle Town v Padiham	2-1
Maghull v Vauxhall GM	0-1
Oldham Town v Cammell Laird	0-2
Glossop v Waterloo Dock	2-1
Great Harwood Town v Burscough	4-0
Liversedge v Maltby MW	1-6
Rossington Main v Priory (Eastwood)	0-2
Denaby United v Louth United	2-0
Arnold Town v Friar Lane OB	2-0
Bradley Rangers v Belper Town	4-4, 2-2, 1-2
Worsboro Bridge MW v Ilkeston Town	2-0
Armthorpe Welfare v Clipstone Welfare	1-0
Ossett Albion v Long Eaton United	2-0
Hatfield Main v Yorkshire Main	0-2
Selby Town v Bacup Borough	2-0
Eccleshill United v Stocksbridge Park Steels	2-0
Winterton Rangers v Brigg Town	2-1
Harworth CI v Sutton Town	4-2
Pontefract Collieries v Sheffield	0-3
Brackley Town v Northampton Spencer	1-0
Wednesfield v Bloxwich Town	2-0
Stratford Town v Wolverhampton Casuals	5-0
Melton Town v Stapenhill	2-1
Baker Perkins v Halesowen Harriers	4-3
Mile Oak Rovers v Eccleshall	2-0
Lye Town v Lincoln United	0-1
Desborough Town v Lutterworth Town	3-3, 1-1, 2-1
Pegasus Juniors v Chasetown	0-3
Heath Hayes v Evesham United	0-3
Northfield v Solihull Borough	2-0
Oldbury United v Irthlingborough Diamonds	0-2
Holwell Sports v Malvern Town	8-1
Highgate United v Rushall Olympic	0-1
Walsall Wood v Stourport Swifts	2-1
Hinckley Athletic v Bilston Town	1-0
Wellingborough Town v Hinckley Town	1-2
Rothwell Town v West Midlands Police	4-3
Boston v Sandwell Borough	1-0
Coleshill Town v Hamlet S & L	0-2
Racing Club Warwick v Oldswinford	3-1
Princes End United v Tividale	2-3
Canvey Island v Thetford Town	0-2
Kings Lynn v Stowmarket Town	2-0
Royston Town v Stamford	3-0
Histon v Rainham Town	4-3
Saffron Walden Town v Soham Town Rangers	2-1
Norwich United v Felixstowe Town	2-3
Witham Athletic v Brantham Athletic	1-0
Gorleston v Tiptree United	3-1
Brightlingsea United v LBC Ortonians	2-1
Ramsey Town v Wroxham	3-1
Mirrless Blackstone v Newmarket Town	1-1, 2-0
Clarksteel Yaxley v Harwich & Parkeston	0-3
Barton Rovers v St Ives Town	0-1
Eynesbury Town v Lowestoft Town	1-2
Basildon United v Watton United	0-1
Stanstead v Halstead Town	1-5
Bracknell Town v Hoddesdon Town	4-0
Vauxhall Motors v Amersham Town	4-2
Southall v Stotfold	1-2
Langford v Brook House	2-0
Arlesey Town v Edgware Town	0-2
Hertford Town v Cockfosters	2-0
Hanwell Town v Ruislip Manor	0-5
Cheshunt v Elliott Star	1-2
Wingate v Buckingham Town	1-4
Mount Grace (Potters Bar) v Clapton	1-0
Pirton v Brimsdown Rovers	1-2
Hornchurch v Flackwell Heath	0-1
Wolverton AFC v Hemel Hempstead	1-1, 1-6
Eton Manor v Northwood	0-1
Tring Town v Walthamstow Pennant	0-0, 0-2
Feltham v Barkingside	0-5
Ware v Finchley	2-2, 1-2
Letchworth GC v Welwyn GC	3-3, 1-1, 5-3
Cray Wanderers v Purfleet	2-4
Wootton Blue Cross v Rayners Lane	1-0
Leighton Town v Haringey Borough	1-0
Kingsbury Town v Stevenage Borough	0-1
West Wickham v Alma Swanley	1-3
Corinthian Casuals v Littlehampton Town	3-3, 2-7
Sheppey United v Croydon Athletic	1-3
Lancing v Langney Sports	0-6
Tonbridge v Beckenham Town	1-1, 2-2, 0-3
Herne Bay v Tunbridge Wells	1-2
Cobham v Faversham Town	1-2
Farnham Town v Steyning Town	3-0
Egham Town v Eastbourne Town	3-1
Ringmer v Chipstead	3-1
Godalming Town v Redhill	3-0
Whitehawk v Peacehaven & Telscombe	1-0
Maidenhead United v Sittingbourne	0-1
Horsham YMCA v Darenth Heathside	1-4
Haywards Heath Town v Chatham Town	3-0
Slade Green v Three Bridges	1-0
Eastbourne United v Chichester City	2-1
Pagham v Leatherhead	2-1
Ramsgate v Hartley Wintney	2-0
Shoreham v Arundel	3-2
Banstead Athletic v Horndean	3-1
Wick v Burgess Hill Town	1-2
Portfield v Crockenhill	3-4
Malden Vale v Cove	3-3, 3-2
AFC Totton v Bicester Town	4-1
AFC Lymington v First Tower United	0-1
Kintbury Rovers v Abingdon United	1-3
Newbury Town v Bishops Cleeve	0-1
Westbury United v Flight Refuelling	2-1
Thame United v East Cowes Victoria Athletic	3-0
Romsey Town v Didcot Town	2-4
Vale Recreation v Bournemouth	0-1
Swanage Town & Herston v Newport IOW	4-6
Eastleigh v Bemerton Heath Harlequins	2-1
Christchurch v Trowbridge Town	0-2
Warminster v Wimborne Town	0-2
Shortwood United v Larkhall Athletic	3-1
Bridgwater Town v Frome Town	0-1
Cinderford Town v Bristol Manor Farm	2-0
Mangotsfield United v Fairford Town	3-0
Highworth Town v Keynsham Town	2-4
Radstock Town v Chippenham Town	3-3, 0-2
Minehead v Almondsbury Picksons	1-1, 3-5
Wellington v Calne Town	3-1
Moreton Town v Melksham Town	1-3
Devizes Town v Hallen	2-4
Wotton Rovers v Glastonbury	3-1
Welton Rovers v Blackwell United	1-0
Ilfracombe Town v Barnstaple Town	0-2
Newquay v Ottery St Mary	5-0
Torrington v St Blazey	2-1
Tiverton Town v Liskeard Athletic	2-1

First Round

Darlington CB v Horden CW	1-2
Billingham Town v Netherfield	2-0
Chester-le-Street Town v Peterlee Newtown	1-0
Murton v Shotton Comrades	1-0
Ashington v Hebburn (Subject to protest)	1-0, 3-0*
*(match ordered to be replayed)	
Langley Park v Prudhoe East End	1-0
Eppleton CW v West Allotment Celtic	5-1
Dunston FB v Newton Aycliffe	3-1
Blackpool (Wren) Rovers v Ashton United	3-0
Maine Road v Warrington Town	0-2
Great Harwood Town v Vauxhall GM	2-0
Prescot AFC v Nantwich Town	4-5
Leyland Motors v Skelmersdale United	0-2
Glossop v Curzon Ashton	6-1
Clitheroe v Newcastle Town	3-2
Knowsley United v Knypersley Victoria	5-0
St Helens Town v Cammell Laird	1-2
Lancaster City v Blackpool Mechanics	1-0
Selby Town v Harrogate Town	0-2
Belper Town v Harworth CI	3-1
Garforth Town v Ossett Albion	3-1
Yorkshire Main v Sheffield	1-2
Denaby United v Worsboro Bridge MW	0-4
Winterton Rangers v Arnold Town	1-0
Rainworth MW v Armthorpe Welfare	2-1
Eccleshill United v Priory (Eastwood)	1-2
Borrowash Victoria v Maltby MW	2-0

Stratford Town v Hamlet S & L — 0-3
Boldmere St Michaels v Bridgnorth Town — 1-2
Rothwell Town v Wednesfield — 2-0
Racing Club Warwick v Tividale — 6-1
Hinckley Athletic v Desborough Town — 3-1
Chasetown v Walsall Wood — 1-1, 0-1
Raunds Town v Irthlingborough Diamonds — 2-0
Brackley Town v Northfield — 1-2
Hinckley Town v Holwell Sports — 0-1
Melton Town v Rushall Olympic — 0-2
Boston v Lincoln United — 1-6
Baker Perkins v Evesham United — 4-3
Mile Oak Rovers v Gresley Rovers — 2-1*
(tie awarded to Gresley Rovers as Mile Oak Rovers fielded an ineligible player)
Gorleston v Saffron Walden Town — 2-4
Histon v Bourne Town — 5-0
Halstead Town v St Ives Town — 3-1
Royston Town v Thetford Town — 1-2
Kings Lynn v Mirrless Blackstone — 2-0
Watton United v Felixstowe Town — 0-1
Tilbury v Harwich & Parkeston — 4-6
Ramsey Town v Witham Town — 2-2, 2-3
Berkhamsted Town v Lowestoft Town — 3-5
March Town United v Brightlingsea United — 3-0
Mount Grace (Potters Bar) v Wootton Blue Cross — 1-0
Purfleet v Stotfold — 2-0
Barkingside v Collier Row — 2-1
Edgware Town v Letchworth GC — 1-0
Hemel Hempstead v Stevenage Borough — 1-0
Buckingham Town v Bracknell Town — 4-1
Ruislip Manor v Leighton Town — 4-3
Brimsdown Rovers v Hounslow — 3-0
Elliott Star v Hertford Town — 5-4
Vauxhall Motors v Finchley — 3-2
Walthamstow Pennant v Langford — 1-0
Flackwell Heath v Northwood — 0-2
Epsom & Ewell v Shoreham — 2-3
Littlehampton Town v Godalming Town — 5-0
Faversham Town v Ringmer — 1-0
Alma Swanley v Tunbridge Wells — 1-2
Farnham Town v Egham Town — 4-0
Darenth Heathside v Hailsham Town — 1-0
Sittingbourne v Pagham — 1-2
Horsham v Whitehawk — 2-1
Crockenhill v Haywards Heath Town — 0-3
Eastbourne United v Burgess Hill Town — 1-2
Langney Sports v Beckenham Town — 3-1
Slade Green v Whitstable Town — 2-0
Camberley Town v Malden Vale — 1-1*, 0-3
(abandoned in extra time—floodlight failure 110 mins)
Greenwich Borough v Croydon Athletic — 2-1
Corinthians v Banstead Athletic — 2-2, 1-2
Ramsgate v Merstham — 1-1, 1-1, 0-2
Wimborne Town v Newport IOW — 1-0
AFC Totton v Trowbridge Town — 1-4
Abingdon United v Didcot Town — 0-3
Havant Town v Bishops Cleeve — 4-0
Sholing Sports v First Tower United — 2-1
Thame United v Bournemouth — 0-1
Eastleigh v Westbury United — 1-0
Frome Town v Yate Town — 2-2, 0-3
Wotton Rovers v Almondsbury Picksons — 0-2
Chard Town v Shortwood United — 1-2
Hallen v Old Georgians — 1-2
Melksham Town v Wellington — 0-1
Clevedon Town v Chippenham Town — 3-1
Cinderford Town v Mangotsfield United — 1-3
Welton Rovers v Keynsham Town — 2-0
Newquay v Torrington — 2-1
Tiverton Town v Dawlish Town — 3-4
Barnstaple Town v Exmouth Town — 5-1

Second Round

Bridlington Town v Blackpool (Wren) Rovers — 1-0
Horden CW v Great Harwood Town — 1-2
Harrogate RA v Chester-le-Street Town — 2-1
Rossendale United v Ossett Town — 0-2
Lancaster City v Eppleton CW — 1-2
North Ferriby United v Murton — 5-3
Langley Park v Ashington — 1-0
Farsley Celtic v Clitheroe — 1-0
Dunston FB v Billingham Town — 2-3
Rainworth MW v Harrogate Town — 2-1
Knowsley United v Eastwood Hanley — 5-3
Glossop v Winterton Rangers — 4-0

Cammell Laird v Sheffield — 4-1
Borrowash Victoria v Belper Town — 5-3
Warrington Town v Guiseley — 2-2, 1-1, 1-3
Skelmersdale United v Garforth Town — 1-4
Lincoln United v Priory (Eastwood) — 1-2
Worsboro Bridge MW v Heanor Town — 4-1
Hucknall Town v Nantwich Town — 2-2, 2-1
Holbeach United v Raunds Town — 2-2, 0-3
Hinckley Athletic v March Town United — 3-0
Racing Club Warwick v Gresley Rovers — 1-3
Walsall Wood v Rushall Olympic — 1-2
Spalding United v Northfield — 1-0
Hamlet S & L v Wisbech Town — 1-3
Rothwell Town v Holwell Sports — 3-2
Potton United v Paget Rangers — 1-3
Baker Perkins v Histon — 1-3
Kings Lynn v Bridgnorth Town — 4-0
Sudbury Town v Ruislip Manor — 0-0, 2-1
Harwich & Parkeston v Burnham Ramblers — 6-1
Braintree Town v Barkingside — 2-2, 2-3
Northwood v Felixstowe Town — 2-1
Elliott Star v Mount Grace (Potters Bar) — 1-3
Halstead Town v Great Yarmouth Town — 5-1
Thetford Town v Billericay Town — 4-1
Vauxhall Motors v Purfleet — 0-1
Walthamstow Pennant v Edgware Town — 2-1
Saffron Walden Town v Witham Town — 5-2
Brimsdown Rovers v East Thurrock United — 0-1
Buckingham Town v Lowestoft Town — 2-1
Haverhill Rovers v Hemel Hempstead — 1-0
Pagham v Hythe Town — 3-4
Slade Green v Faversham Town — 1-0
Littlehampton Town v Abingdon Town — 2-0
Eastleigh v Langney Sports — 1-0
Didcot Town v Banstead Athletic — 2-0
Haywards Heath Town v Farnham Town — 3-1
Burgess Hill Town v Shoreham — 2-0
Havant Town v Merstham — 2-0
Hungerford Town v Chertsey Town — 1-0
Whitehawk v Malden Vale — 1-2
Thatcham Town v Tunbridge Wells — 4-5
Harefield United v Greenwich Borough — 2-0
Darenth Heathside v Hastings Town — 2-3
Old Georgians v Almondsbury Picksons — 0-2
Bridport v Shortwood United — 2-0
Clevedon Town v Paulton Rovers — 0-0, 0-3
Dawlish Town v Barnstaple Town — 3-3, 1-0
Newquay v Bournemouth — 1-0
Mangotsfield United v Wimborne Town — 1-4
Sholing Sports v Trowbridge Town — 1-2
Wellington v Welton Rovers — 3-1
Yate Town v Falmouth Town — 2-1

Third Round

Glossop v North Ferriby United — 1-0
Cammell Laird v Ashington — 1-1, 3-0
Garforth Town v Borrowash Victoria — 2-6
Farsley Celtic v Guiseley — 0-1
Bridlington Town v Eppleton CW — 4-0
Knowsley United v Ossett Town — 4-2
Billingham Town v Harrogate RA — 3-1
Worsboro Bridge MW v Great Harwood Town — 1-2
Kings Lynn v Rushall Olympic — 2-1
Paget Rangers v Hinckley Athletic — 0-4
Rainworth MW v Hucknall Town — 1-2
Gresley Rovers v Raunds Town — 2-1
Spalding United v Wisbech Town — 1-0
Rothwell Town v Priory (Eastwood) — 2-2, 1-0
East Thurrock United v Eastleigh — 1-2
Saffron Walden Town v Burgess Hill Town — 4-3
Haywards Heath Town v Thetford Town — 1-2
Hythe Town v Haverhill Rovers — 4-0
Halstead Town v Histon — 0-1
Harefield United v Havant Town — 3-1
Hastings Town v Tunbridge Wells — 5-0
Buckingham Town v Mount Grace (Potters Bar) — 2-1
Sudbury Town v Harwich & Parkeston — 3-3, 1-2
Walthamstow Pennant v Barkingside — 5-2
Littlehampton Town v Slade Green — 5-0
Malden Vale v Didcot Town — 1-1, 1-2
Northwood v Purfleet — 0-1
Almondsbury Picksons v Trowbridge Town — 1-2
Hungerford Town v Newquay — 0-2
Dawlish Town v Wellington — 4-1
Paulton Rovers v Bridport — 0-1
Yate Town v Wimborne Town — 5-3

Fourth Round

Bridlington Town v Borrowash Victoria	3-1
Knowsley United v Spalding United	3-0
Glossop v Cammell Laird	2-2, 1-2
Gresley Rovers v Billingham Town	2-1
Great Harwood Town v Rothwell Town	1-1, 1-0
Kings Lynn v Guiseley	1-4
Hinckley Athletic v Hucknall Town	2-1
Harefield United v Hythe Town	0-5
Trowbridge Town v Yate Town	5-0
Eastleigh v Littlehampton Town	0-1
Didcot Town v Dawlish Town	0-1
Harwich & Parkeston v Purfleet	2-1
Hastings Town v Histon	4-0
Buckingham Town v Bridport	0-0, 2-0
Newquay v Saffron Walden Town	2-2, 0-1
Walthamstow Pennant v Thetford Town	5-1

Fifth Round

Cammell Laird v Harwich & Parkeston	2-3
Great Harwood Town v Bridlington Town	1-1, 1-0
Hinckley Athletic v Guiseley	1-4
Knowsley United v Gresley Rovers	4-5
Littlehampton Town v Walthamstow Pennant	3-2
Hastings Town v Hythe Town	0-0, 1-3
Saffron Walden Town v Buckingham Town	1-2
Trowbridge Town v Dawlish Town	1-0

Sixth Round

Buckingham Town v Guiseley	0-1
Hythe Town v Trowbridge Town	0-0, 1-1, 1-3
Littlehampton Town v Great Harwood Town	2-1
Harwich & Parkeston v Gresley Rovers	0-2

Semi-final first leg

Gresley Rovers v Littlehampton Town	3-1
Trowbridge Town v Guiseley	1-2

Second leg

Littlehampton Town v Gresley Rovers	1-2
Guiseley v Trowbridge Town	1-1

FINAL at Wembley

4 MAY

Gresley Rovers (1) 4 *(Rathbone, Smith 2, Stokes (pen))*

Guiseley (3) 4 *(Tennison 2, Walling, Roberts A) aet*

11,314

Gresley Rovers: Aston; Barry, Elliott (Adcock), Denby, Land, Astley, Stokes, Smith, Acklam, Rathbone, Lovell (Weston).
Guiseley: Maxted; Bottomley, Hogarth, Tetley, Morgan, McKenzie, Atkinson (Adams), Tennison, Walling, Roberts A, Roberts B (Annan).
Referee: C. Trussell.

Replay at Bramall Lane

7 MAY

Gresley Rovers (1) 1 *(Tennison)*

Guiseley (1) 3 *(Astley, Walling, Atkinson)*

7585

Gresley Rovers: Aston; Barry, Elliott, Denby, Land, Astley, Stokes (Weston), Smith, Acklam, Rathbone, Lovell (Adcock).
Guiseley: Maxted; Atkinson, Hogarth, Tetley, Morgan, McKenzie (Bottomley), Roberts A, Tennison (Noteman), Walling, Annan, Roberts B.
Referee: C. Trussell.

WOMEN'S NATIONAL LEAGUE

Just twenty-one years after the establishment of the Women's Football Association, the organisation has initiated a far reaching restructuring programme which has resulted in the formation of the first ever Women's National League. The National League will consist of a Premier Division supported by divisions one north and south; each will comprise eight clubs.

The restructuring, which follows closely the pyramid model established by the leading non-league clubs in 1979, is designed to provide a focus for the game as it attempts to build upon the successes of recent years.

Membership of the Women's Football Association has grown by over 50 per cent in two years, and the sport has achieved consistently high viewing figures following the first television coverage by Channel 4 in 1989. Indeed April's England v Scotland match attracted an audience of 2.4 million, knocking "Gazza's Soccer School" from its number one position in the Channel 4 sports ratings.

MYCIL WOMEN'S FA CUP 1990–91

Quarter-finals

Nottingham Rangers 1, Millwall Lionesses 2
Doncaster Belles 11, Ipswich 1
Leasowe Pacific 2, Friends of Fulham 1
Davis Argyle 2, Arsenal Ladies 2

Replay

Arsenal Ladies 3, Davis Argyle 0 *aet*

Semi-finals *(at Watford)*

Arsenal Ladies 1, Millwall Lionesses 2
Doncaster Belles 8, Leasowe Pacific 1

Final *(at Tranmere Rovers)*

Millwall Lionesses 1, Doncaster Belles 0

England's Women's Internationals 1990–91

England 0, Norway 0
Finland 0, England 0
England 1, Germany 4
Germany 2, England 0
England 5, Scotland 0
USA 3, England 1

FA SUNDAY CUP 1990–91

First Round

Baildon Athletic v Croxteth & Gilmoss RBL	1-0
Royal Oak v Toshiba Sharples	3-0
Woodlands Hotel 84 v A3	1-3
Blyth Waterloo SC v Western Approaches	3-2
Dudley & Weetslade v Carnforth	2-3
Blue Union v Chesterfield Park	2-5
East Bowling Unity v Hartlepool Lion Hotel	2-0
Iron Bridge v Airedale Magnet	0-2
AC Sparks v Kebroyd Rovers	6-3
Dock v Carlisle United Supporters	2-1
Green Man 88 v Lynemouth Inn	2-3
Hope Farm Metro v West Wideopen	0-4
Netherley RBL v Framwellgate Moor & Pity Me	3-1
Eagle-Knowsley v Oakenshaw	2-1
Nenthead v Littlewoods AFC	3-0
Deborah United v Clubmoor Nalgo	1-2
Railway Hotel v Stanton Dale	3-1
Whetley Lane v St Josephs (Wallasey)	2-0
Overpool United v Queens Arms	0-4
FC Coachman v Radford Park Rangers	1-1, 1-0
Ansells Stockland Star v Altone Steels	1-3
Kenwick Dynamo v Brookvale Athletic	2-1
Hanham Sunday v Inter Volante	1-4
Birmingham Celtic v Kettering Odyssey	0-0, 0-1
(Replay at Burton Latimer FC)	
St Josephs (Luton) v Chequers	5-0
Rolls Royce v Olympic Star	3-2
Cork & Bottle v Beaufort	4-1
Elliott Star v St Josephs (South Oxhey)	1-2
Grosvenor Park v Phoenix	2-1
Chequers (Hunts) v Dereham Hobbies	4-1
Fryerns Community v Trinity	2-1
Watford Labour Club v Shouldham Sunday	1-3
Ely City v Ouzavich	0-3
Trax v Sawston Keys	4-3
Merton Admiral v Oxford Road Social	3-2
Shakespeare v St Clements Hospital	2-7
Whittingham v Chapel United	
(Chapel United walked over Whittingham—	
Whittingham withdrawn)	
Concord Rangers v Inter Royalle	2-0
Priory Sports v Essex Sports	2-0
Collier Row Supporters v Santogee 66	1-5
Ranelagh Sports v Theale	1-0
Biddestone v Broad Plain House	2-4
Lebeq Tavern v Bishopstoke AFC	3-0
Brimsdown Rovers v Old Paludians	3-0

Second Round

AC Sparks v Baildon Athletic	1-3
Almithak v A3	1-2
West Wideopen v Nenthead	1-2
Dock v East Bowling Unity	3-2
Railway Hotel v East Levenshulme	1-4
Royal Oak v Humbledon Plains Farm	0-3
Blyth Waterloo SC v East & West Toxteth	3-1
Morrison Sports v Eagle-Knowsley	2-5
Lynemouth Inn v Netherley RBL	1-4
Nicosia v Whetley Lane	3-2
Queens Arms v Airedale Magnet	0-0, 3-2
(Replay at Marley Stadium, Keighley)	

Chesterfield Park v Northwood	2-3
Avenue Victoria Lodge v Carnforth	2-1
Concord Rangers v Slade Celtic	1-1, 1-2
(Replay at Boldmere St Michaels FC)	
Brereton Town v Newey Goodman	3-0
Priory Sports v Poringland Wanderers	0-1
FC Coachman v Chequers (Hunts)	0-1
Lodge Cottrell v Brimsdown Rovers	2-1
Marston Sports v St Clements Hospital	2-0
Rolls Royce v Fryerns Community	0-1
Shouldham Sunday v Ford Basildon	2-5
Chapel United v Altone Steels	2-2, 0-0, 2-4
(Replay at Sutton Coldfield Town FC)	
Grovesnor Park v Ouzavich	1-3
St Josephs (South Oxhey) v Trax	0-1
Cork & Bottle v Santogee 66	1-2
Lee Chapel North v Merton Admiral	3-1
Ranelagh Sports v Inter Volante	2-1
Broad Plain House v St Josephs (Luton)	2-0
Leyton Argyle v Sandwell	4-3
Lebeq Tavern v Kenwick Dynamo	0-2

Third Round

Brereton Town v Netherley RBL	2-3
Nenthead v East Levenshulme	1-2
Dock v A3	0-1
Clubmoor Nalgo v Nicosia	0-1
Baildon Athletic v Northwood	3-0
Eagle-Knowsley v Queens Arms	2-0
Blyth Waterloo SC v Avenue Victoria Lodge	2-1
Humbledon Plains Farm v Marston Sports	0-3
Kenwick Dynamo v Kettering Odyssey	3-0
Chequers (Hunts) v Slade Celtic	0-2
Leyton Argyle v Altone Steels	3-2
Ranelagh Sports v Santogee 66	5-0
Ouzavich v Fryerns Community	0-0, 3-2
Lodge Cottrell v Lee Chapel North	1-0
Ford Basildon v Trax	6-4
Broad Plain House v Poringland Wanderers	0-4

Fourth Round

A3 v Baildon Athletic	4-0
Nertherley RBL v Nicosia	0-1
East Levenshulme v Blyth Waterloo SC	3-2
Marston Sports v Eagle-Knowsley	2-3
Leyton Argyle v Ouzavich	0-1
Kenwick Dynamo v Ranelagh Sports	1-2
Slade Celtic v Ford Basildon	1-0
Poringland Wanderers v Lodge Cottrell	0-3

Fifth Round

Nicosia v East Levenshulme	2-1
Eagle Knowsley v A3	3-1
Ranelagh Sports v Lodge Cottrell	0-0, 3-0
Slade Celtic v Ouzavich	0-2

Semi-final

Nicosia v Eagle-Knowsley	1-0
Ranelagh Sports v Ouzavich	0-2

Final

Nicosia v Ouzavich	3-2

FA CHALLENGE YOUTH CUP 1990–91

The following 30 clubs were exempted to the Second Round: Arsenal, Birmingham City, Brentford, Charlton Athletic, Chelsea, Coventry City, Crystal Palace, Doncaster Rovers, Everton, Ipswich Town, Leeds United, Leicester City, Leyton Orient, Liverpool, Luton Town, Manchester City, Manchester United, Middlesbrough, Newcastle United, Plymouth Argyle, Portsmouth, Queens Park Rangers, Reading, Sheffield United, Sheffield Wednesday, Southend United, Stoke City, Tottenham Hotspur, Watford, West Bromwich Albion.

The following 50 clubs were exempted to the First Round: Aston Villa, Barnsley, Blackburn Rovers, Blackpool, AFC Bournemouth, Bradford City, Brighton & Hove Albion, Bristol City, Burnley, Cambridge United, Cardiff City, Carlisle United, Colchester United, Crewe Alexandra, Darlington, Derby County, Epson & Ewell, Fulham, Gillingham, Grimsby Town, Hartlepool United, Hednesford United, Hendon, Hereford United, Horndean, Hull City, Mansfield Town, Millwall, Newbury Town, Northampton Town, Nottingham Forest, Notts County, Oldham Athletic, Oxford United, Peterborough United, Port Vale, Scunthorpe United, Southampton, Sunderland, Sutton United, Swansea City, Swindon Town, Tranmere Rovers, Walsall, West Ham United, Whyteleafe, Wigan Athletic, Wimbledon, Wokingham Town, Wolverhampton Wanderers.

Preliminary Round

Murton v Southbank	3-2
Stockton v Chester-le-Street Town	1-0
Billingham Synthonia v Ashington	
(Billingham Synthonia walked over Ashington—	
Ashington withdrawn)	
Marske United v Guisborough Town	0-2
Yorkshire Amateurs v Scarborough	1-2
Rotherham United v Chesterfield	3-1
Halifax Town v Huddersfield Town	2-3
Marine v Skelmersdale United	3-1
Atherton Collieries v Accrington Stanley	3-5
Blackpool Mechanics v Lancaster City	2-0
Bolton Wanderers v Preston North End	4-1
Chester City v Chadderton	4-1
(at Chadderton)	
Bury v Stockport County	3-0
Shrewsbury Town v Wrexham	4-2
Irlam Town v Rochdale	0-5
Walsall Wood v Telford United	1-3
Hinckley Athletic v Lye Town	2-3
Willenhall Town v Tamworth	3-0
Oldswinford v Kidderminster Harriers	1-6
Alvechurch v Hinckley Town	2-1
Burton Albion v Radford	14-0
Moor Green v Mile Oak Rovers	3-1
Nuneaton Borough v Corby Town	2-1
Cambridge City v Ely City	5-1
Rothwell Town v Wellingborough Town	2-1
Rainham Town v Basildon United	0-5
Bishops Stortford v Wivenhoe Town	2-0
Witham Town v Braintree Town	3-1
Billericay Town v Canvey Island	1-2
Boreham Wood v Letchworth Garden City	4-0
East Thurrock United v Stevenage Borough	5-3
St Albans City v Royston Town	7-0
Enfield v Welwyn Garden City	8-1
Edgware Town v Clapton	1-7
Fisher Athletic v Erith & Belvedere	
(Fisher Athletic walked over Erith & Belvedere—	
Erith & Belvedere withdrawn)	
Berkhamsted Town v Kinsbury Town	1-1, 4-5
Hillingdon Borough v Hounslow	1-1, 2-1
Slough Town v Staines Town	10-1
Wycombe Wanderers v Southall	3-2
Windsor & Eton v Egham Town	0-2
Chertsey Town v Northwood	1-4
Marlow v Maidenhead United	2-5
Thatcham Town v Uxbridge	2-4
Ramsgate v Dover Athletic	2-2, 1-4
Ringmer v Worthing United	0-1
Chatham Town v Whitehawk	2-1
Horsham YMCA v Dorking	4-4, 3-1
Croydon v Three Bridges	2-4 (aet)
Steyning Town v Worthing	0-6
Redhill v Shoreham	3-3, 0-3
Farnborough Town v Carshalton Athletic	1-1, 0-1
Banstead Athletic v Malden Vale	0-1
Walton & Hersham v Wick	3-3, 2-1*
(Replay at Littlehampton FC)	
Feltham v Havant Town	3-1
Bracknell Town v Aldershot	1-8
Abingdon Town v Bicester Town	0-3
Hungerford Town v Witney Town	3-1
Exeter City v Bournemouth	4-1
Warminster Town v Frome Town	1-2
(at Frome Town)	
Dorchester Town v Torquay United	0-4
Worcester City v Wotton Rovers	4-0

Yate Town v Gloucester City	3-3, 0-5
Cheltenham Town v Bristol Rovers	1-5
Weston-Super-Mare v Trowbridge Town	0-0, 2-4

First Round Qualifying

Stockton v Billingham Synthonia	2-0
Guisborough Town v Murton	4-1
Rotherham United v Huddersfield Town	2-1
York City v Scarborough	1-0
Accrington Stanley v Blackpool Mechanics	3-1
Bolton Wanderers v Marine	5-1
Bury v Shrewsbury Town	2-0
Rochdale v Chester City	2-2, 2-1*
(Replay at Rochdale)	
Lye Town v Willenhall Town	1-2
Leek Town v Telford United	0-3
Alvechurch v Burton Albion	4-0
Moor Green v Kidderminster Harriers	0-3
Cambridge City v Rothwell Town	9-1
Norwich City v Nuneaton Borough	9-0
Bishops Stortford v Witham Town	5-1
Canvey Island v Basildon United	3-4
(at Basildon United)	
East Thurrock United v St Albans City	0-5
Enfield v Boreham Wood	5-0
Fisher Athletic v Kingsbury Town	1-1, 5-0
Finchley v Clapton	0-1
Slough Town v Wycombe Wanderers	2-6
Bedfont Town v Hillingdon Borough	2-1
Northwood v Maidenhead United	3-5
Uxbridge v Egham Town	0-3
Ringmer v Chatham Town	0-6
Herne Bay v Dover Athletic	0-2
Three Bridges v Worthing	1-3
Shoreham v Horsham YMCA	4-2
Malden Vale v Walton & Hersham	1-10
Feltham v Carshalton Athletic	1-2
Bicester Town v Hungerford Town	1-1, 5-1
(at Witney Town)	
Basingstoke Town v Aldershot	0-7
Frome Town v Torquay United	0-7
Romsey Town v Exeter City	0-3
Gloucester City v Bristol Rovers	2-4
Trowbridge Town v Worcester City	3-3, 0-3

Second Round Qualifying

Stockton v Guisborough Town	1-5
Rotherham United v York City	1-2
Accrington Stanley v Bolton Wanderers	0-3
Bury v Rochdale	4-1
Willenhall Town v Telford United	1-2
Alvechurch v Kidderminster Harriers	4-3
Cambridge City v Norwich City	3-3, 1-2
Bishops Stortford v Basildon United	1-2
St Albans City v Enfield	0-3
Fisher Athletic v Clapton	0-1
Wycombe Wanderers v Bedfont Town	3-1
Maidenhead United v Egham Town	2-6
Chatham Town v Dover Athletic	0-1
Worthing v Shoreham	2-2, 0-4
Walton & Hersham v Carshalton Athletic	2-2, 0-6
Bicester Town v Aldershot	1-3
(at Witney Town)	
Torquay United v Exeter City	1-1, 1-2
Bristol Rovers v Worcester City	11-0

First Round Proper

Oldham Athletic v Bolton Wanderers	2-0
Wigan Athletic v Burnley	0-3

Bury v Tranmere Rovers	3-0
York City v Sunderland	3-0
Port Vale v Wolverhampton Wanderers	0-1
Oxford United v Hendon	3-0
Wokingham Town v Egham Town	1-1, 1-3
Epsom & Ewell v Dover Athletic	4-0
Basildon United v Carshalton Athletic	0-0, 2-5
Whyteleafe v Enfield	3-3, 2-1
Clapton v Gillingham	1-4
Bristol City v Exeter City	1-2
Newbury Town v Swansea City	1-9

Second Round Proper

Bradford City v Sheffield United	3-0
Everton v Scunthorpe United	1-0
Hull City v York City	1-1, 2-1
Liverpool v Middlesbrough	3-0
Sheffield Wednesday v Bury	4-1
Newcastle United v Oldham Athletic	2-0
Darlington v Manchester United	0-6
Manchester City v Barnsley	0-1
Doncaster Rovers v Burnley	4-0
Blackburn Rovers v Leeds United	1-1, 1-3
Leyton Orient v Ipswich Town	2-1
West Bromwich Albion v Peterborough United	3-2
Wolverhampton Wanderers v Walsall	0-2
Notts County v Arsenal	0-0, 1-1, 2-1
Leicester City v Coventry City	2-3
Birmingham City v Tottenham Hotspur	1-0
Alvechurch v Crewe Alexandra	0-4
Watford v Luton Town	1-0
Southend United v Stoke City	0-0, 3-2
Derby County v Aston Villa	0-3
Colchester United v Carshalton Athletic	3-2
Whyteleafe v Epsom & Ewell	2-3
Egham Town v Exeter City	0-0, 0-2
Charlton Athletic v Plymouth Argyle	1-2
Portsmouth v Hereford United	2-1
Wimbledon v Oxford United	3-0
Reading v Swansea City	1-1, 1-2
Brentford v Chelsea	2-2, 1-1, 4-7
Swindon Town v Millwall	0-1
Aldershot v West Ham United	1-1, 0-4
Crystal Palace v Queens Park Rangers	3-3, 1-0
Gillingham v Southampton	2-3

Third Round Proper

Bradford City v Barnsley	2-1
Aston Villa v Sheffield Wednesday	2-3
Doncaster Rovers v Leeds United	0-3
Walsall v Liverpool	2-2, 1-4
Manchester United v Everton	1-1, 2-1
Newcastle United v West Bromwich Albion	1-2
Crewe Alexandra v Hull City	0-2
Millwall v Portsmouth	3-1

Leyton Orient v Birmingham City	1-2
Swansea City v Colchester United	1-3
Plymouth Argyle v Epsom & Ewell	2-0
Wimbledon v Coventry City	2-0
Watford v Notts County	0-0, 1-2
Southend United v West Ham United	1-5
Southampton v Exeter City	6-0
Chelsea v Crystal Palace	4-0

Fourth Round Proper

Plymouth Argyle v Millwall	0-1
Liverpool v Manchester United	1-3
Chelsea v Wimbledon	2-2, 0-2
Sheffield Wednesday v West Bromwich Albion	2-1
West Ham United v Birmingham City	2-0
Southampton v Bradford City	4-0
Leeds United v Hull City	1-2
Notts County v Colchester United	2-0

Fifth Round Proper

Sheffield Wednesday v Hull City	1-1, 1-1, 5-1
Southampton v Manchester United	0-2
West Ham United v Notts County	3-1
Millwall v Wimbledon	1-1, 3-2

Semi-final first leg

West Ham United v Millwall	1-2
Sheffield Wednesday v Manchester United	1-1

Second leg

Millwall v West Ham United	2-0
Manchester United v Sheffield Wednesday	0-1

FINAL First Leg
1 May
Sheffield Wednesday (0) 0
Millwall (1) 3 (*Lee, Devine, Walker*)   1666
Sheffield Wednesday: Robinson P; Linighan, Dunn, Simpson, Stewart, Burton, Rowntree, Jones, Robinson N, Chambers, Curzon.
Millwall: Emberson; McArthur, Dolby, Roberts, Foran, Lee, Dickson, Devine, Walker, Manning, Smith.
Referee: I. Borrett

Second Leg
7 May
Millwall (0) 0
Sheffield Wednesday (0) 0   4271
Millwall: Emberson; McArthur, Dolby, Roberts, Foran, Lee, Dickson, Devine, Walker, Manning, Smith.
Sheffield Wednesday: Robinson P; Linighan, Dunn, Simpson, Stewart, Burton, Rowntree, Jones, Robinson N, Chambers, Curzon.
Referee: I. Borrett

FA CHALLENGE TROPHY FINALS 1970–90

1970	Macclesfield T	2	Telford U	0	1981	Bishop's Stortford	1	Sutton U	0
1971	Telford U	3	Hillingdon B	2	1982	Enfield	1	Altrincham	aet 0
1972	Stafford R	3	Barnet	0	1983	Telford U	2	Northwich V	1
1973	Scarborough	2	Wigan Ath	aet 2	1984	Northwich V	2	Bangor C (after 1-1 draw)	1
1974	Morecambe	2	Dartford	1	1985	Wealdstone	2	Boston U	1
1975	Matlock	4	Scarborough	0	1986	Altrincham	1	Runcorn	0
1976	Scarborough	3	Stafford R	aet 2	1987	Kidderminster H	2	Burton A (after 0-0 draw)	1
1977	Scarborough	2	Dagenham	1	1988	Enfield	3	Telford U (after 0-0 draw)	2
1978	Altrincham	3	Leatherhead	1	1989	Telford U	1	Macclesfield T	aet 0
1979	Stafford R	2	Kettering T	0	1990	Barrow	3	Leek T	0
1980	Dagenham	2	Mossley	1					

FA CHALLENGE VASE FINALS 1975–90

1975	Hoddesdon T	2	Epsom & Ewell	1	1983	VS Rugby	1	Halesowen T	0
1976	Billericay T	1	Stamford	aet 0	1984	Stansted	3	Stamford	2
1977	Billericay T	2	Sheffield (after 1-1 draw)	1	1985	Halesowen T	3	Fleetwood T	1
1978	Blue Star	2	Barton R	1	1986	Halesowen T	3	Southall	0
1979	Billericay T	4	Almondsbury G	1	1987	St Helens T	3	Warrington T	2
1980	Stamford	2	Guisborough T	0	1988	Colne D	1	Emley	0
1981	Whickham	3	Willenhall T	aet 2	1989	Tamworth	3	Sudbury (after 1-1 draw)	0
1982	Forest Green R	3	Rainworth MW	1	1990	Yeading	1	Bridlington T (after 0-0 draw)	0

FA YOUTH CHALLENGE CUP FINALS 1953–90 (aggregate scores)

1953	Wolverhampton W	3	Wolverhampton W	3	1972	Aston Villa	5	Liverpool	2
1954	Manchester U	5	Wolverhampton W	4	1973	Ipswich T	4	Bristol C	1
1955	Manchester U	7	WBA	1	1974	Tottenham H	2	Huddersfield T	1
1956	Manchester U	4	Chesterfield	3	1975	Ipswich T	5	West Ham U	1
1957	Manchester U	8	West Ham U	2	1976	WBA	5	Wolverhampton W	0
1958	Wolverhampton W	7	Chelsea	6	1977	C Palace	1	Everton	0
1959	Blackburn R	2	West Ham U	1	1978	C Palace	1	Aston Villa (one game only)	0
1960	Chelsea	5	Preston NE	2	1979	Millwall	2	Manchester C	0
1961	Chelsea	5	Everton	3	1980	Aston Villa	3	Manchester C	2
1962	Newcastle U	2	Wolverhampton W	1	1981	West Ham U	2	Tottenham H	1
1963	West Ham U	6	Liverpool	5	1982	Watford	7	Manchester U	6
1964	Manchester U	5	West Ham U	2	1983	Norwich C	6	Everton (inc replay)	5
1965	Everton	3	Arsenal	2	1984	Everton	4	Stoke C	2
1966	Arsenal	5	Sunderland	3	1985	Newcastle U	4	Watford	1
1967	Sunderland	2	Birmingham C	0	1986	Manchester C	3	Manchester U	1
1968	Burnley	3	Coventry C	2	1987	Coventry C	2	Charlton Ath	1
1969	Sunderland	6	WBA	3	1988	Arsenal	6	Doncaster R	1
1970	Tottenham H	4	Coventry C	3	1989	Watford	2	Manchester C	1
1971	Arsenal	2	Cardiff C	0	1990	Tottenham H	3	Middlesbrough	2

FA COUNTY YOUTH CHALLENGE CUP FINALS 1945–90 (aggregate scores)

1945	Staffordshire	3	Wiltshire	2	1969	Northumberland	1	Sussex	0
1946	Berks & Bucks	4	Durham	3		(one game only from here)			
1947	Durham	4	Essex	2	1970	Hertfordshire	2	Cheshire	1
1948	Essex	5	Liverpool	3	1971	Lancashire	2	Gloucestershire	0
1949	Liverpool	4	Middlesex	3	1972	Middlesex	2	Liverpool	0
1950	Essex	4	Middlesex	3	1973	Hertfordshire	3	Northumberland	0
1951	Middlesex	3	Leics. & Rutland	1	1974	Nottinghamshire	2	London	0
1952	Sussex	3	Liverpool	1	1975	Durham	2	Bedfordshire	1
1953	Sheffield & Hallam	5	Hampshire	3	1976	Northamptonshire	7	Surrey	1
1954	Liverpool	4	Gloucestershire	1	1977	Liverpool	3	Surrey	0
1955	Bedfordshire	2	Sheffield & Hallam	0	1978	Liverpool	3	Kent	1
1956	Middlesex	3	Staffordshire	2	1979	Hertfordshire	4	Liverpool	1
1957	Hampshire	4	Cheshire	3	1980	Liverpool	2	Lancashire	0
1958	Staffordshire	8	London	0	1981	Lancashire	3	East Riding	2
1959	Birmingham	7	London	5	1982	Devon	3	Kent (after 0-0 draw)	2
1960	London	6	Birmingham	4	1983	London	3	Gloucestershire	0
1961	Lancashire	6	Nottinghamshire	3	1984	Cheshire	2	Manchester	1
1962	Middlesex	6	Nottinghamshire	3	1985	East Riding	2	Middlesex	1
1963	Durham	3	Essex	2	1986	Hertfordshire	4	Manchester	0
1964	Sheffield & Hallam	1	Birmingham	0	1987	North Riding	3	Gloucestershire	1
1965	Northumberland	4	Middlesex	4	1988	East Riding	5	Middlesex (after 0-0 draw)	3
1966	Leics. & Rutland	6	London	5	1989	Liverpool	2	Hertfordshire	0
1967	Northamptonshire	5	Hertfordshire	4	1990	Staffordshire	2	Hampshire (after 1-1 draw)	1
1968	North Riding	7	Devon	4					

FA SUNDAY CUP FINALS 1965–90

1965	London	6	Staffordshire (on aggregate)	2	1978	Arras	2	Lion R (after 2-2 draw)	1
1966	Unique U	1	Aldridge F	0	1979	Lobster	3	Carlton U	2
1967	Carlton U	2	Stoke W	0	1980	Fantail	1	Twin Foxes	0
1968	Drovers	2	Brook U	0	1981	Fantail	1	Mackintosh	0
1969	Leigh Park	3	Loke U	1	1982	Dingle Rail	2	Twin Foxes	1
1970	Vention U	1	Unique U	0	1983	Eagle	2	Lee Chapel N (after 1-1 draw)	1
1971	Beacontree R	2	Saltley U	1	1984	Lee Chapel N	4	Eagle	3
1972	Newton Unity	4	Springfield C	1	1985	Hobbies	2	Avenue (after 1-1, 2-2 draws)	0
1973	Carlton U	2	Wear Valley	aet 1	1986	Avenue	1	Glenn Sports	0
1974	Newtown Unity	2	Brentford E	0	1987	Lodge Cottrell	1	Avenue	0
1975	Fareham T Cent	1	Players Ath E	0	1988	Nexday	2	Sunderland HP	0
1976	Brandon U	2	Evergreen	1	1989	Almethak	3	East Levenshulme	1
1977	Langley Park RH	2	Newton Unity	0	1990	Humbledon PF	2	Marston SP	1

OVENDEN PAPERS FOOTBALL COMBINATION

	P	W	D	L	F	A	Pts
Chelsea	38	24	7	7	93	43	79
Tottenham Hotspur	38	24	6	8	79	37	78
Crystal Palace	38	21	10	7	90	44	73
Wimbledon	38	22	7	9	64	36	73
Southampton	38	20	8	10	68	50	68
Portsmouth	38	19	8	11	67	46	65
Arsenal	38	19	8	11	65	54	65
Norwich City	38	15	12	11	61	52	57
Luton Town	38	15	9	14	66	52	54
QPR	38	14	8	16	60	62	50
Charlton Athletic	38	14	7	17	66	65	49
Oxford Utd	38	14	6	18	57	57	48
Millwall	38	11	11	16	63	69	44
West Ham Utd	38	12	8	18	57	90	44
Swindon Town	38	12	7	19	60	77	43
Ipswich Town	38	11	7	20	40	66	40
Brighton & Hove Albion	38	11	6	21	48	69	39
Fulham	38	11	6	21	42	75	39
Watford	38	9	9	20	46	84	36
Reading	38	4	6	28	24	88	18

PONTIN'S CENTRAL LEAGUE

Division One

	P	W	D	L	F	A	Pts
Sheffield Wednesday	34	23	6	5	69	36	75
Nottingham Forest	34	21	6	7	92	51	69
Manchester United	34	20	5	9	55	35	65
Liverpool	34	17	5	12	60	39	56
Everton	34	16	5	13	59	51	53
Rotherham United	34	14	9	11	56	51	51
Aston Villa	34	12	11	11	39	48	47
Sunderland	34	13	7	14	63	60	46
Leeds United	34	11	12	11	44	47	45
Blackburn Rovers	34	12	8	14	56	51	44
Coventry City	34	10	13	11	46	48	43
Sheffield United	34	12	6	16	58	72	42
Newcastle United	34	12	5	17	46	52	41
Manchester City	34	11	6	17	47	59	39
Derby County	34	9	10	15	30	42	37
Huddersfield Town	34	8	10	16	36	66	34
Wolverhampton Wanderers	34	8	8	18	42	73	32
Leicester City	34	7	8	19	41	62	29

Division Two

	P	W	D	L	F	A	Pts
West Bromwich Albion	34	23	7	4	77	27	76
Barnsley	34	23	7	4	84	39	76
Bolton Wanderers	34	17	9	8	70	42	60
Bradford City	34	19	3	12	71	52	60
Hull City	34	18	5	11	61	49	59
Notts County	34	16	6	12	56	46	54
Middlesbrough	34	15	8	11	62	50	53
Burnley	34	13	11	10	53	48	50
Port Vale	34	14	5	15	61	72	47
Oldham Athletic	34	12	7	15	81	79	43
Stoke City	34	12	5	17	51	67	41
Scunthorpe United	34	10	10	14	45	60	40
Mansfield Town	34	10	8	16	45	49	38
York City	34	11	5	18	53	78	38
Grimsby Town	34	10	5	19	28	56	35
Blackpool	34	9	6	19	62	84	33
Wigan Athletic	34	9	3	22	56	94	30
Preston North End	34	6	8	20	59	83	26

SKOL NORTHERN LEAGUE

Division One

	P	W	D	L	F	A	Pts
Gretna	38	30	5	3	86	23	95
Guisborough Town	38	21	12	5	79	43	75
Blyth Spartans	38	20	8	10	80	50	68
Billingham Synthonia	38	20	8	10	72	43	68
Consett	38	19	11	8	67	43	68
Whitby Town	38	16	13	9	66	49	61
Tow Law Town	38	16	10	12	65	64	58
Ferryhill Athletic*	38	16	9	13	55	50	54
Northallerton Town	38	14	11	13	50	46	53
Newcastle Blue Star	38	13	13	12	59	48	52
Seaham Red Star	38	12	12	14	44	46	48
South Bank	38	9	16	13	40	43	43
Murton	38	10	11	17	47	59	41
Shildon	38	10	9	19	49	75	39
Whickham	38	10	9	19	44	71	39
Peterlee Newtown	38	7	17	14	57	65	38
Brandon United	38	9	11	18	44	70	38
Stockton	38	10	6	22	40	79	36
Alnwick Town	38	7	10	21	40	78	31
Durham City	38	6	9	23	47	86	27

Division Two

	P	W	D	L	F	A	Pts
West Auckland	36	24	7	5	72	39	79
Langley Park	36	24	4	8	83	40	76
Easington	36	20	8	8	80	42	68
Hebburn*	36	22	5	9	89	56	68
Billingham Town	36	21	5	10	69	39	68
Evenwood Town*	36	20	8	8	69	40	65
Esh Winning	36	19	6	11	77	57	63
Prudhoe East End	36	16	10	10	71	46	58
Norton & Stockton Ancients	36	16	3	17	60	67	51
Darlington CB	36	14	7	15	53	60	49
Bedlington Terriers	36	14	6	16	60	73	48
Ashington	36	14	6	16	47	68	48
Crook Town	36	13	8	15	57	64	47
Ryhope CA	36	13	4	19	54	57	43
Shotton Comrades	36	7	9	20	43	73	30
Chester-le-Street Town	36	6	11	19	45	68	29
Washington	36	7	6	23	44	79	27
Willington	36	4	9	23	34	77	21
Horden CW	36	2	10	24	37	99	16

*Denotes three points deducted.

T.S.W. PRINTERS (SCUNTHORPE) LINCOLNSHIRE FOOTBALL LEAGUE

	P	W	D	L	F	A	Pts
Bottesford Town	32	21	10	1	85	31	73
Grimsby Borough	32	23	4	5	90	38	73
Sleaford Town	32	15	14	3	55	37	59
Barton Town*	32	18	5	9	85	55	55
Skegness Town	32	16	8	8	76	58	55
Immingham Athletic	32	14	9	9	63	48	51
Ruston Sports	32	15	5	12	67	51	50
Louth United Reserves	32	14	8	10	51	39	50
Louth Old Boys	32	14	5	13	51	50	47
Appleby Frodingham Athletic	32	13	4	15	66	79	43
Lincoln United Colts	32	13	8	13	67	63	41
Spilsby Town	32	12	3	17	49	64	39
Grimsby Ross Amateurs	32	10	8	14	45	46	38
Nettleham Mulsanne	32	6	8	18	50	76	26
Brigg Town Reserves	32	5	9	18	44	67	24
Eaton Hall College	32	5	6	21	41	91	21
Mablethorpe Athletic	31	1	4	27	24	116	7

*Four points deducted—ineligible player.

MIDLAND COMBINATION

Premier Division

	P	W	D	L	F	A	Pts
West Midlands Police	40	22	14	4	84	41	80
Solihull Borough	40	24	6	10	74	35	78
Evesham United	40	21	11	8	83	46	74
Sandwell Borough	40	20	14	6	63	31	74
Stratford Town	40	19	12	9	81	43	69
Northfield Town	40	18	13	9	63	37	67
Stapenhill	40	18	12	10	60	50	66
Coleshill Town	40	18	11	11	57	42	65
Highgate United	40	18	11	11	48	35	65
Hinckley FC	40	18	9	13	56	47	63
Walsall Wood	40	17	8	15	53	48	59
Boldmere St Michaels	40	14	11	15	51	56	53
Kings Heath	40	12	14	14	65	62	50
Knowle	40	14	7	19	47	66	49
Bloxwich Town	40	11	11	18	64	73	44
Bolehall Swifts	40	12	5	23	41	79	41
Mile Oak Rovers	40	9	10	21	40	73	37
Chelmsley Town	40	9	9	22	43	77	36
Princes End United	40	10	6	24	34	71	36
Polesworth North Warwick	40	5	12	23	39	86	27
Kings Norton Ex-service	40	4	8	28	32	80	20

Division One

	P	W	D	L	F	A	Pts
Alcester Town	28	20	4	4	85	28	64
Wilmcote	28	19	3	6	47	20	60
Pershore Town	28	17	6	5	63	20	57
Studley BKL	28	16	8	4	56	27	56
Stapenhill Reserves	28	12	7	9	58	57	43
Wellesbourne	28	11	7	10	57	52	40
Dudley Sports	28	11	5	12	42	45	38
Handrahan Timbers	28	10	7	11	43	52	37
Triplex	28	9	8	11	33	41	35
Southam United	28	9	7	12	39	48	34
Kings Heath Reserves	28	7	7	14	41	54	28
West Midlands Fire Services	28	8	4	16	37	63	28
West Heath United	28	6	5	17	39	65	23
Upton Town	28	5	7	16	31	57	22
Wythall	28	5	5	18	28	70	20

Resigned Streetly Celtic—all records expunged.

BASS NORTH WEST COUNTIES LEAGUE

First Division

	P	W	D	L	F	A	Pts
Knowsley United	36	25	8	3	95	37	83
Colwyn Bay	36	22	10	4	85	32	76
Ashton United	36	20	7	9	80	45	67
Eastwood Hanley	36	16	12	8	42	29	60
Vauxhall GM	36	15	10	11	42	36	55
Prescot	36	13	12	11	57	55	51
Flixton	36	14	7	15	48	72	49
St Helens Town	36	13	9	14	52	47	48
Maine Road	36	13	9	14	58	61	48
Skelmersdale United	36	12	11	13	56	49	47
Nantwich Town	36	13	8	15	43	56	47
Leyland DAF	36	12	10	14	51	53	46
Bootle	36	10	9	17	55	64	39
Bacup Borough	36	9	12	15	38	47	39
Clitheroe	36	10	8	18	50	63	38
Darwen	36	9	11	16	44	62	38
Penrith	36	10	8	18	41	65	38
Atherton LR	36	9	11	16	42	68	38
Salford City	36	6	10	20	30	68	28

Second Division

	P	W	D	L	F	A	Pts
Great Harwood Town	34	27	5	2	81	22	86
Blackpool (Wren) Rovers*	34	25	4	5	84	33	78
Bradford Park Avenue	34	20	9	5	72	41	69
Bamber Bridge	34	20	6	8	78	46	66
Blackpool Mechanics	34	18	7	9	51	30	61
Newcastle Town	34	16	12	6	48	30	60
Cheadle Town	34	17	3	14	55	54	54
Glossop	34	12	10	12	47	42	46
Burscough	34	12	8	14	39	51	44
Westhoughton Town	34	11	10	13	50	64	43
Castleton Gabriels	34	11	9	14	42	47	42
Chadderton	34	10	6	18	51	61	36
Maghull	34	9	8	17	37	54	35
Kidsgrove Athletic	34	7	10	17	37	65	31
Ashton Town	34	9	2	23	43	86	29
Oldham Town*	34	8	4	22	35	66	27
Formby	34	5	9	20	46	63	24
Atherton Collieries	34	6	4	24	37	78	22

*1 point deducted for breach of rule.

VAUX WEARSIDE LEAGUE

Division One

	P	W	D	L	F	A	Pts
Eppleton CW	32	29	1	2	126	27	88
Boldon CA	32	19	6	7	78	43	63
Annfield Plain	32	19	5	8	76	40	62
Dunston FB*	30	18	6	6	89	41	60
South Shields	32	17	4	11	72	49	55
Marske Utd	33	16	5	12	82	55	53
Roker	34	15	8	11	65	47	53
Cleator Moor	31	17	1	13	54	63	52
Dawdon CW*	34	13	8	13	64	64	47
Vaux Ryhope	34	14	5	15	79	82	47
Newton Aycliffe	32	12	10	10	58	40	46
Greatham	34	14	2	18	48	55	44
NEI Bohemians	34	11	3	20	40	76	36
Coundon TT*	31	9	5	17	45	60	32
Wolviston	34	9	2	23	55	90	29
Herrington CW	34	8	4	21	48	101	28
Hartlepool BWOB	34	9	3	22	62	142	27
Nissan	34	4	6	24	40	90	18

Division Two

	P	W	D	L	F	A	Pts
Cleadon SC	32	19	7	6	63	30	64
Usworth Vill	32	17	8	7	49	31	59
Darlington RA	32	16	9	7	68	37	57
Windscale	30	14	8	8	75	45	50
Thornley	32	15	5	12	65	56	50
Blackhall CW	32	13	9	10	53	72	48
Stanley Utd	32	13	8	11	57	47	47
Silksworth	33	11	7	15	48	52	40
Marchon	30	10	7	13	49	52	37
Lambton St	32	8	7	17	50	61	31
Wingate	31	7	5	19	45	75	26
RSH Pineapple	30	2	8	20	20	84	14

*resigned.

JEWSON SOUTH-WESTERN LEAGUE

	P	W	D	L	F	A	Pts
Bodmin Town	32	25	5	2	87	31	55
St Blazey	32	22	8	2	105	29	52
Falmouth Town	32	18	9	5	82	39	45
Newquay	32	20	5	7	73	40	45
St Austell	32	17	7	8	83	46	41
Torpoint Athletic	32	16	8	8	66	37	40
Truro	32	16	6	10	67	44	38
Bugle	32	16	6	10	57	37	38
Appledore/BAAC	32	13	5	14	66	59	31
Wadebridge Town	32	10	8	14	47	52	28
Millbrook	32	12	3	17	69	79	27
Tavistock	32	8	9	15	46	67	25
Porthleven	32	11	2	19	52	72	24
Clyst Rovers	32	10	1	21	43	100	21
Launceston	32	6	8	18	46	75	20
Holsworthy	32	3	4	25	32	110	10
Penzance	32	1	2	29	31	136	4

McEWAN'S NORTHERN ALLIANCE

Premier Division

	P	W	D	L	F	A	Pts
West Allotment	28	20	2	6	82	35	62
Seaton Terrace	28	17	3	8	65	34	54
Heaton Stannington	28	13	10	5	57	37	49
Seaton Delaval	28	13	7	8	50	42	46
Forest Hall	28	13	4	11	50	44	43
Swalwell	28	11	9	8	56	54	42
Walker	28	10	9	9	47	43	39
Newbiggin	28	12	3	13	52	65	39
Ponteland United	28	10	7	11	44	47	37
Westerhope	28	9	6	13	52	53	33
Gillford Park	28	9	6	13	59	64	33
Morpeth Town	28	10	2	16	49	70	32
Haltwhistle	28	8	6	14	38	55	30
Wark	28	8	5	15	43	68	29
Percy Main	28	3	9	16	33	66	18

BANKS'S BREWERY LEAGUE

Premier Division

	P	W	D	L	F	A	Pts
Gresley Rovers	42	32	5	5	104	36	101
Chasetown	42	24	13	5	79	32	85
Oldbury United	42	23	14	5	75	37	83
Darlaston	42	20	11	11	89	67	71
Hinckley Athletic	42	20	10	12	75	51	70
Wednesfield	42	21	7	14	76	59	70
Ilkeston Town	42	19	12	11	75	49	69
West Bromwich Town	42	19	11	12	76	51	68
Lye Town	42	19	19	13	53	41	67
Halesowen Harriers	42	19	9	14	84	54	66
Rocester	42	18	12	12	72	44	66
Rushall Olympic	42	17	12	13	67	51	63
Stourport Swifts	42	15	13	14	74	56	58
Blakenall	42	14	16	12	56	59	58
Pelsall Villa	42	14	10	18	49	64	44
Wolverhampton Casuals	42	11	10	21	50	98	43
Paget Rangers	42	10	8	24	50	94	38
Oldswinford	42	9	10	23	60	89	37
Tividale	42	9	15	28	45	100	32
Westfields*	42	9	11	22	49	87	32
Malvern Town	42	6	7	29	36	106	25
Tipton Town	42	4	8	30	27	97	20

*6 points deducted.

Derbyshire Senior Cup
Gresley Rovers 7 Borrowash 1 (on aggregate)

Birmingham County FA Vase
Darlaston 6 Chelmsley Wood 2

Walsall Senior Cup
Blakenall 0 Chasetown 1 (aet)

League Cup
Chasetown 1 Oldbury United 0

Division 1

	P	W	D	L	F	A	Pts
Cradley Town	28	20	6	2	75	27	66
Ludlow Town	28	17	6	5	53	20	57
Cannock Chase	28	16	4	8	62	47	52
Moxley Rangers	28	15	5	8	37	31	50
Great Wyrley	28	13	5	10	45	38	44
Wolverhampton United	28	12	4	12	38	36	40
Donnington Wood	28	11	7	10	41	39	40
Ettingshall HT	28	12	4	12	42	57	40
Newport Town	28	10	6	12	41	40	36
Broseley Athletic	28	9	7	12	34	39	34
Lichfield	28	11	1	16	37	47	34
Wem Town	28	9	5	14	38	46	32
Gornal Athletic	28	7	7	14	30	49	28
Hill Top Rangers	28	7	5	16	45	65	26
Chasetown Reserves	28	3	4	21	25	62	13

League Cup
Ludlow Town 2 Broseley Athletic 1

WINSTONLEAD KENT LEAGUE

Division One

	P	W	D	L	F	A	Pts
Sittingbourne	40	32	8	0	87	19	104
Cray Wanderers	40	27	11	2	91	33	92
Herne Bay	40	24	11	5	83	28	83
Tonbridge AFC*	40	24	8	8	72	34	79
Deal Town	40	23	8	9	88	43	77
Faversham Town	40	20	10	10	62	33	70
Whitstable Town	40	20	8	12	67	44	68
Alma Swanley	40	18	9	13	60	53	63
Slade Green	40	16	10	14	65	49	58
Ramsgate	40	16	9	15	60	63	57
Tunbridge Wells	40	16	6	18	71	79	54
Chatham Town	40	13	9	18	61	71	48
Darenth Heathside**	40	12	9	19	44	68	45
Beckenham Town	40	12	7	21	37	54	43
Crockenhill*	40	10	11	19	47	89	40
Thames Poly	40	10	7	23	49	76	37
Greenwich Borough	40	10	5	25	49	77	35
Danson	40	7	13	20	41	80	34
Kent Police	40	8	9	23	51	77	33
Met. Police (Hayes)	40	5	10	25	37	89	25
Sheppey United	40	6	4	30	39	105	22

*1 goal and 1 point deducted.
**1 goal deducted.

GREAT MILLS LEAGUE

Premier Division

	P	W	D	L	F	A	Pts
Mangotsfield United	40	28	8	4	113	39	92
Torrington	40	25	7	8	91	41	82
Plymouth Argyle*	40	25	8	7	100	28	79
Tiverton Town	40	22	11	7	85	45	77
Weston Super Mare	40	20	10	10	74	57	70
Saltash United	40	20	6	14	67	46	66
Taunton Town	40	18	9	13	62	49	63
Liskeard Athletic	40	18	7	15	85	69	61
Dawlish Town	40	15	16	9	58	49	61
Paulton Rovers	40	16	11	13	74	60	59
Clevedon Town	40	16	10	14	52	55	58
Bideford	40	13	10	17	61	76	49
Frome Town	40	14	6	20	56	78	48
Bristol Manor Farm	40	12	9	19	52	66	45
Welton Rovers	40	11	11	18	40	61	44
Chard Town	40	11	10	19	48	86	43
Chippenham Town	40	10	12	19	42	64	42
Ottery St Mary	40	11	4	25	43	88	37
Exmouth Town	40	9	8	23	59	93	35
Barnstaple Town	40	8	10	22	44	86	34
Radstock Town	40	4	5	31	46	116	17

*4 points deducted.

First Division

	P	W	D	L	F	A	Pts
Minehead	40	28	9	3	102	42	93
Elmore	40	24	6	10	89	47	78
Calne Town	40	25	2	13	85	55	77
Odd Down	40	22	10	8	59	36	76
Westbury United	40	21	9	10	60	44	72
Bridport	40	18	11	11	65	48	65
Torquay United	40	17	10	13	62	52	61
Devizes Town	40	17	10	13	68	66	61
Ilfracombe Town	40	15	12	13	62	54	57
Crediton United	40	14	13	13	55	48	55
Wellington	40	15	10	15	58	55	55
Bath City	40	14	11	15	67	64	53
Keynsham Town	40	14	9	17	59	58	51
Clandown	40	14	8	18	43	71	50
Melksham Town	40	13	10	17	54	60	49
Backwell United	40	11	9	20	56	70	42
Yeovil Town	40	10	6	24	59	91	36
Warminster Town	40	9	9	22	39	74	36
Larkhall Athletic	40	9	8	23	38	70	35
Heavitree United	40	6	12	22	32	81	30
Glastonbury	40	5	14	21	39	65	29

JEWSON LEAGUE

Premier Division

	P	W	D	L	F	A	Pts
Wisbech Town	40	27	10	3	97	39	91
Braintree Town	40	25	10	5	85	38	85
Halstead Town	40	26	4	10	105	52	82
Haverhill Rovers	40	24	8	8	82	45	80
Harwich & Parkeston	40	23	4	13	85	51	73
Watton United	40	20	10	10	62	50	70
Wroxham	40	17	13	10	63	64	64
Cornard United	40	16	12	12	73	59	60
Lowestoft Town	40	16	12	12	56	51	60
Histon	40	17	7	16	55	53	58
Stowmarket Town	40	15	11	14	51	52	56
Clacton Town	40	15	9	16	64	56	54
Felixstowe Town	40	14	11	15	59	58	53
Thetford Town	40	14	10	16	65	81	52
March Town United	40	12	9	19	48	62	45
Tiptree United	40	12	6	22	45	65	42
Gorleston	40	11	5	24	53	74	38
Great Yarmouth Town*	40	9	6	25	43	90	32
Brantham Athletic	40	6	9	25	41	74	27
Newmarket Town	40	6	8	26	32	87	26
Chatteris Town	40	5	6	29	29	92	21

*1 point deducted.

Division One

	P	W	D	L	F	A	Pts
Norwich United	36	26	6	4	65	19	84
Brightlingsea United	36	24	5	7	77	38	77
Fakenham Town	36	22	8	6	70	35	74
Diss Town	36	19	11	6	74	32	68
Downham Town	36	21	5	10	89	52	68
Soham Town Rangers	36	20	7	9	66	46	67
Long Sutton Athletic	36	16	9	11	54	43	57
Woodbridge Town	36	17	6	13	54	45	57
Ely City	36	16	7	13	54	44	55
Clarksteel Yaxley	36	15	7	14	46	51	52
Somersham Town	36	14	4	18	64	59	46
Sudbury Town Reserves	36	10	14	12	61	57	44
Ipswich Wanderers	36	11	10	15	56	57	43
King's Lynn Reserves	36	13	4	19	59	74	43
Swaffham Town*	36	10	6	20	42	65	35
Huntingdon United	36	8	9	19	42	70	33
Mildenhall Town	36	5	7	24	39	100	22
Bury Town Reserves	36	3	8	25	25	78	17
Warboys Town	36	4	3	29	39	111	15

*1 point deducted.

CENTRAL MIDLANDS LEAGUE

Supreme Division

	P	W	D	L	F	A	Pts
Hucknall Town	31	22	6	3	75	29	72
Heanor Town	32	21	4	7	70	33	67
Lincoln Town	32	20	6	6	70	25	66
Arnold Town*	32	18	11	3	59	22	64
Nettleham	32	15	6	11	43	40	51
Harworth CI	31	13	9	9	45	33	48
Rossington Main	32	11	9	12	43	45	42
Boston	32	12	6	14	50	65	42
Sheffield Aurora	29	11	8	10	64	42	41
Louth United	32	11	8	13	47	55	41
Oakham United	31	9	10	12	39	42	37
Borrowash Victoria	32	11	1	20	46	66	34
Gainsborough Town	32	8	6	18	36	66	30
Wombwell Town	32	7	6	19	37	75	27
Priory (Eastwood)	30	5	11	14	33	53	26
Melton Town	30	6	8	16	42	74	26
Blidworth	32	6	7	19	40	76	25

*1 point deducted.

Premier Division

	P	W	D	L	F	A	Pts
Mickleover RBL	33	24	3	6	103	42	75
Highfield Rangers	33	22	7	4	66	29	73
Blackwell MW	33	22	6	5	67	33	72
Glapwell	33	19	8	6	80	43	65
Shirebrook Colliery	34	17	9	8	68	42	60
Bulwell United	34	14	9	11	65	56	51
Derby Rolls Royce	33	14	7	12	64	54	49
Lincoln Moorlands	33	12	7	14	52	61	44
Radford	34	12	5	17	37	56	41
Brailsford	33	12	4	17	51	78	40
Rossington	34	9	12	13	48	51	39
Long Eaton United	34	11	6	17	41	72	39
Kilburn MW	34	11	4	19	39	57	37
West Hallam	33	11	4	18	42	62	37
Stanton	34	8	9	17	39	48	33
Newhall United	34	8	6	20	53	74	30
Kimberley Town	33	7	8	18	37	60	29
Slack & Parr	33	6	10	17	42	76	28

GREENE KING SPARTAN LEAGUE

Premier Division

	P	W	D	L	F	A	Pts
Walthamstow Pennant	36	24	9	3	77	30	81
Barkingside	36	24	8	4	77	32	80
Northwood	36	23	9	4	85	33	78
Cheshunt	36	20	7	9	56	38	67
Corinthian Casuals*	36	22	3	11	78	40	66
Haringey Borough	36	18	8	10	67	44	62
Brimsdown Rovers	36	18	6	12	54	47	60
Hanwell Town	36	15	7	14	58	56	52
Waltham Abbey*	36	14	8	14	49	47	47
Amersham Town	36	13	6	17	62	67	45
Southgate Athletic	36	13	6	17	55	67	45
Brook House	36	12	8	16	52	60	44
Beaconsfield United	36	12	6	18	48	65	42
Beckton United	36	12	5	19	61	71	41
Croydon Athletic	36	12	3	21	60	76	39
Hillingdon Borough	36	8	7	21	47	73	31
North Greenford United	36	7	7	22	44	76	28
Eltham Town	36	7	5	24	39	93	26
Thamesmead Town	36	6	6	24	43	97	24

*3 points deducted.

Division One

	P	W	D	L	F	A	Pts
Sangley Sports	28	22	3	3	94	21	69
AFC Millwall	28	17	7	4	64	27	58
Royal George	28	18	3	7	76	35	57
KPG Tipples	28	17	3	8	68	39	54
Walthamstow Trojans	28	17	2	9	80	46	53
Metrogas	28	14	6	8	64	52	48
Leyton County	28	13	6	9	67	51	45
Ilford*	28	11	6	11	78	58	36
Old Roan	29	9	8	11	57	54	35
Swanley Town	28	8	8	12	46	55	32
Catford Wanderers	28	8	8	12	38	54	32
Met Police (Chigwell)	28	6	9	13	49	77	27
Ulysses	28	6	7	15	38	66	25
Phoenix Sports	28	4	2	22	27	112	14
Penhill Standard	28	0	2	26	15	114	2

*3 points deducted.

ESSEX SENIOR LEAGUE

	P	W	D	L	F	A	Pts
Southend Manor	28	20	4	4	52	20	64
Brentwood	28	18	6	4	66	30	60
Burnham Ramblers	28	17	8	3	57	30	59
Sawbridgeworth Town	28	15	5	8	47	26	50
Bowers United	28	14	7	7	50	32	49
Stambridge	28	13	5	10	50	38	44
Ford United	28	13	4	11	47	33	43
East Thurrock United	28	11	9	8	46	38	42
Canvey Island	28	9	7	12	34	47	34
Stansted	28	7	8	13	40	42	29
Eton Manor	28	6	9	13	35	45	27
Hullbridge Sports	28	5	8	15	16	38	23
Maldon United	28	6	5	17	27	57	23
East Ham United	28	5	4	19	35	95	19
Woodford Town	28	5	3	20	33	64	18

940

EVERARDS BREWERY LEICESTERSHIRE SENIOR LEAGUE

Premier Division

	P	W	D	L	F	A	Pts
Lutterworth Town	30	17	6	7	60	30	57
Anstey Nomads	30	16	9	5	67	38	57
Oadby Town	30	16	8	6	53	33	56
Syston St Peters	30	15	10	5	56	36	55
Pedigree Petfoods	30	16	5	9	51	40	53
Barlestone St Giles	30	14	7	9	49	37	49
Holwell Sports	30	12	5	13	68	43	41
Newfoundpool WMC	30	11	7	12	38	42	40
Friar Lane OB	30	11	6	13	39	43	39
Birstall United	30	10	8	12	51	47	38
St Andrews SC	30	10	6	14	37	45	36
Narborough & Lit/trpe	30	9	7	14	39	54	34
Barwell Athletic*	30	10	7	13	48	65	34
Hillcroft	30	7	6	17	26	42	27
Rolls Royce (M'sorrel)	30	6	8	16	35	54	26
Thringstone	30	5	5	20	25	93	20

*3 points deducted.

Division One

	P	W	D	L	F	A	Pts
Houghton Rangers	32	26	5	1	107	33	83
Ibstock Welfare	32	26	2	4	84	32	80
Leics. Constabulary	32	23	4	5	88	35	73
Kirby Muxloe SC	32	19	6	7	74	49	63
Aylestone Park OB	32	12	10	10	64	55	46
Anstey Town	32	12	10	10	65	57	46
Wigston Fields	32	12	9	11	54	46	45
Sileby Town	32	14	3	15	56	56	45
Downes Sports	32	10	10	12	38	54	40
Whetstone Athletic	32	10	7	15	43	57	37
Barrow Town	32	10	6	16	60	66	36
Harborough Town	32	9	9	14	62	73	36
Loughborough Dynamo	32	10	4	18	50	66	34
Earl Shilton Albion*	32	10	5	17	60	70	32
Quorn	32	8	7	17	40	55	31
Leicester YMCA	32	4	8	20	43	89	20
North Kilworth	32	2	5	25	44	139	11

*3 points deducted.

WEEKLY WINNER NORTHERN COUNTIES EAST LEAGUE

Premier Division

	P	W	D	L	F	A	Pts
Guiseley	30	24	4	2	78	25	76
North Shields	29	22	2	5	74	29	68
Spennymoor United	30	19	4	7	55	29	61
North Ferriby United	30	14	8	8	55	42	50
Brigg Town	30	13	8	9	40	40	47
Maltby MW	30	13	7	10	44	46	46
Harrogate Railway	30	12	9	9	49	40	45
Ossett Town	29	9	10	10	35	38	37
Armthorpe Welfare	30	10	6	14	52	55	36
Winterton Regulars	29	9	9	11	49	58	36
Thackley	30	9	7	14	43	46	34
Sutton Town	29	9	6	14	53	59	33
Belper Town	30	7	10	13	37	52	31
Ossett Albion	30	3	12	15	34	51	21
Denaby United	30	5	6	19	33	81	21
Pontefact Collieries	30	4	4	22	34	74	16

Division One

	P	W	D	L	F	A	Pts
Sheffield	24	21	1	2	60	16	64
Hallam	24	18	1	5	61	27	55
Liversedge	24	15	2	7	61	35	47
Pickering Town	24	15	2	7	54	41	47
Eccleshill United	24	14	2	8	58	36	44
Garforth Town	24	11	7	6	45	33	40
Selby Town	24	10	3	11	60	41	33
Hatfield Main	24	9	5	10	38	42	32
RES Parkgate	24	7	6	11	40	49	27
York RI	24	7	3	14	32	47	24
Glasshoughton Welfare	24	4	5	15	18	50	17
Yorkshire Main	24	2	3	19	16	61	9
Mexborough Town	24	3	0	21	16	81	9

SOUTH EAST COUNTIES LEAGUE

Division One

	P	W	D	L	F	A	Pts
Arsenal	30	24	4	2	84	30	52
Tottenham Hotspur	30	20	7	3	82	36	47
West Ham Utd	30	20	5	5	82	43	45
Gillingham	30	15	6	9	59	50	36
Leyton Orient	30	12	8	10	52	42	32
Millwall	30	13	6	11	50	49	32
Watford	30	12	6	12	53	35	30
Norwich	30	10	8	12	48	44	28
Chelsea	30	11	5	14	47	49	27
Charlton Athletic	30	9	9	12	52	62	27
QPR	30	10	6	14	39	53	26
Fulham	30	8	8	14	31	47	24
Southend Utd	30	9	6	15	38	61	24
Portsmouth	30	6	7	17	36	56	19
Ipswich Town	30	7	4	19	40	78	18
Cambridge Utd	30	4	5	21	41	99	13

Division 2

	P	W	D	L	F	A	Pts
Wimbledon	30	21	8	1	76	23	50
Bristol Rovers	30	18	5	7	66	41	41
Crystal Palace	30	18	3	9	79	54	39
Oxford Utd	30	16	7	7	63	44	39
Aldershot	30	16	4	10	60	51	36
Southampton	30	13	7	10	64	46	33
Colchester Utd	30	13	5	12	43	44	31
AFC Bournemouth	30	12	5	13	59	68	29
Reading	30	10	9	11	52	62	29
Brighton & HA	30	7	11	12	43	52	25
Tottenham Hotspur	30	7	10	13	49	57	24
Brentford	30	7	9	14	44	62	23
Bristol City	30	7	8	15	63	79	22
Luton Town	30	8	4	18	53	68	20
Swindon Town	30	6	8	16	40	68	20
Maidstone Utd	30	7	5	18	42	77	19

HELLENIC LEAGUE

Premier Division

	P	W	D	L	F	A	Pts
Milton Utd	34	20	11	3	66	26	71
Fairford Town	34	22	5	7	69	38	71
Bicester Town	34	19	6	9	70	37	63
Didcot Town	34	18	8	8	65	30	62
Headington Amateurs	34	18	8	8	54	34	62
Shortwood Utd	34	18	5	11	77	60	59
Abingdon Utd	34	17	6	11	57	37	57
Banbury Utd	34	17	4	13	58	51	55
Hounslow	34	16	5	13	63	47	53
Almondsbury Picksons	34	13	9	12	57	58	48
Kintbury Rangers	34	12	8	14	54	57	44
Carterton Town	34	10	7	17	49	62	37
Rayners Lane	34	10	6	18	34	63	36
Bishops Cleeve	34	9	8	17	43	79	35
Pegasus Juniors	34	8	7	19	46	68	31
Swindon Athletic	34	6	10	18	31	64	28
Moreton Town	34	5	7	22	30	73	22
Wantage Town	34	4	8	22	31	70	20

Division One

	P	W	D	L	F	A	Pts
Cinderford Town	30	24	3	3	94	22	75
Cirencester Town	30	22	5	3	66	21	71
Purton	30	18	6	6	66	28	60
North Leigh	30	18	3	9	83	43	57
Wallingford Town	30	17	5	8	61	35	56
Viking Sports	30	15	10	5	53	20	55
Highworth Town	30	15	4	11	45	49	49
Wootton Bassett	30	11	8	11	32	36	41
Cirencester United	30	11	7	12	48	51	40
Easington Sports	30	10	7	13	52	51	37
Clanfield	30	9	8	13	43	44	35
Kidlington	30	6	16	18	36	56	26
Supermarine	30	7	5	18	29	53	26
Cheltenham Saracens	30	6	7	17	31	44	25
Chipping Norton	30	4	1	25	12	122	13
Lambourn Sports	30	2	3	25	27	103	9

SOUTH MIDLANDS FOOTBALL LEAGUE

Premier Division

	P	W	D	L	F	A	Pts
Thame United	38	25	5	8	76	28	80
Wolverton AFC	38	24	8	6	98	51	80
Biggleswade Town	38	22	9	7	77	43	75
Leighton Town	38	22	8	8	77	38	74
Shillington	38	21	10	7	77	40	73
Letchworth GC	38	19	10	9	65	45	67
Harpenden Town	38	19	8	11	64	53	65
Wingate	38	18	8	12	71	62	62
Hoddesdon Town	38	16	8	14	74	60	56
Electrolux	38	13	16	9	50	38	55
Totternhoe	38	13	12	13	74	64	51
Welwyn Garden City	38	13	9	16	51	57	48
Langford	38	13	8	17	45	54	47
Pirton	38	12	9	17	56	54	45
The 61 FC	38	11	5	22	54	84	38
Pitstone & Ivinghoe	38	10	3	25	43	77	33
New Bradwell	38	9	6	23	42	87	33
Brache Sparta	38	8	7	23	37	84	31
MK Borough	38	7	7	24	40	84	28
Winslow Utd	38	3	8	27	27	95	17

Division One

	P	W	D	L	F	A	Pts
Buckingham A	34	25	7	2	99	26	82
Shenley & Loughton	34	25	3	6	101	42	78
Oxford City	34	20	9	5	79	47	69
Potters Bar C	34	20	4	10	89	56	64
Ashcroft	34	17	12	5	77	39	63
Caddington	34	17	7	10	49	39	58
Delco Products	34	16	7	11	57	52	55
Flamstead	34	14	8	12	70	52	50
Walden Rangers	34	13	8	13	59	64	47
Bedford Utd	34	12	6	16	57	56	42
Ickleford	34	13	2	19	44	71	41
Tring Athletic	34	12	4	18	51	57	40
Shefford Town	34	11	6	17	40	64	39
Cranfield Utd	34	10	8	16	45	69	38
Toddington R	34	7	9	18	39	61	30
Stony Stratford Town	34	8	4	22	44	84	28
Risborough R	34	7	1	26	37	97	22
Sandy Albion	34	4	5	25	37	98	17

HEREWARD SPORTS UNITED COUNTIES LEAGUE

Premier Division

	P	W	D	L	F	A	Pts
Bourne	42	29	6	7	83	45	93
Rothwell	42	25	10	7	75	37	85
Eynesbury	42	24	9	9	68	42	81
Potton	42	23	7	12	64	46	76
Northampton Spencer	42	22	8	12	84	59	74
Raunds	42	21	8	13	72	43	71
Desborough	42	19	13	10	62	40	70
Cogenhoe	42	17	12	13	68	58	63
Long Buckby	42	18	8	16	60	64	62
Stotfold	42	18	5	19	71	59	59
Baker Perkins	42	17	8	17	56	59	59
Mirrless Blackstone	42	16	10	16	61	59	58
Holbeach	42	17	6	19	75	77	57
Irthlingborough	42	13	10	19	80	81	49
Kempston	42	11	16	15	56	61	49
Wellingborough	42	11	16	15	54	65	49
Hamlet S & L	42	11	14	17	49	53	47
Arlesey	42	11	13	18	57	75	46
Wootton	42	11	7	24	42	81	40
Brackley	42	9	10	23	50	83	37
Stamford	42	9	6	27	54	106	33
Burton PW	42	5	8	29	38	86	23

Division One

	P	W	D	L	F	A	Pts
Daventry	36	30	5	1	95	20	95
Ramsey	36	30	3	3	119	23	93
Harrowby	36	25	3	8	74	37	78
Newport Pagnell	36	17	11	8	57	40	62
Higham	36	17	10	9	53	36	61
Bugbrooke	36	15	8	13	78	60	53
Olney	36	16	5	15	60	50	53
St Ives	36	15	5	15	55	48	50
Thrapston	36	14	7	15	67	64	49
O N Chenecks	36	13	8	15	48	53	47
Ampthill	36	13	7	16	62	73	46
Timken Duston	36	12	9	15	71	55	45
Ford Sports	36	13	6	17	50	80	45
Whitworths	36	12	8	16	62	79	44
Cottingham	36	11	10	15	39	62	43
Towcester	36	6	9	21	36	83	27
Blisworth	36	5	8	23	32	78	23
Sharnbrook	36	6	5	25	37	93	23
Irchester	36	6	5	25	30	91	23

HIGHLAND LEAGUE

	P	W	D	L	F	A	Pts
Ross County	34	24	4	6	91	37	76
Inverness Caledonian	34	23	4	7	87	40	73
Cove Rangers	34	23	2	9	95	52	71
Forres Mechanics	34	22	3	9	77	49	69
Inverness Thistle	34	20	5	9	55	38	65
Huntly	34	17	10	7	79	52	61
Elgin City	34	17	6	11	84	53	57
Peterhead	34	13	11	10	50	45	50
Brora Rangers	34	13	10	11	66	54	49
Lossiemouth	34	14	5	15	69	61	47
Buckie Thistle	34	12	7	15	47	52	43
Fort William	34	11	10	13	76	85	43
Fraserburgh	34	11	8	15	54	56	41
Keith	34	11	4	19	37	55	37
Deveronvale	34	7	9	18	37	91	30
Clachnacuddin	34	8	2	24	42	92	26
Nairn County	34	4	3	27	36	104	15
Rothes	34	2	5	27	36	102	11

SOUTH WEST COUNTIES LEAGUE

	P	W	D	L	F	A	Pts
Bristol C	22	16	1	5	73	21	53
Bristol R	22	15	4	3	71	30	48
Bournemouth	22	14	4	4	50	21	46
Torquay U	22	11	6	5	35	31	38
Swansea C	22	10	9	3	52	31	33
Plymouth Arg	22	10	9	3	49	41	33
Cardiff C	22	10	11	1	40	31	31
Hereford U	22	6	11	5	41	49	23
Exeter C	22	5	11	6	37	41	21
Merthyr Tydfil	22	6	14	2	22	81	20
Cheltenham T	22	5	13	4	32	56	19
Yeovil T	22	2	17	3	14	83	9

AMATEUR FOOTBALL ALLIANCE
SEASON 1990–91

CUP COMPETITION FINALS

Senior
Norsemen v Carshalton — 1-0

Greenland Memorial
O. Parmiterians v West Wickham — 2-0

Essex Senior
Old Parkonians v Old Chigwellians — 4-2

Middlesex Senior
Norsemen v Old Ignatians — 4-0

Surrey Senior
Fulham Compton Old Boys v Nottsborough — 0-5

Intermediate
Corinthian-Casuals 'A' v Old Dorkinians — 0-1

Essex Intermediate
Old Chigwellians 2nd v Old Bealonians 2nd — 3-2

Kent Intermediate
West Wickham 2nd v Old Addeyans 2nd — 3-0

Middlesex Intermediate
Civil Service 2nd v Southgate Olympic 2nd — 0-1

Surrey Intermediate
Nottsborough 2nd v Old Tenisonians 2nd — 1-4

Junior
Southgate Olympic 3rd v Wake Green 3rd — 3-1

Minor
E. Barnet Old Grammarians 4th v Old Stationers 4th — 3-2

Senior Novets
Old Camdenians 5th v National Westminster Bank 5th — 1-0

Intermediate Novets
Alexandra Park 6th v Old Bromleians 6th — 2-1

Junior Novets
Old Parmiterians 10th v Midland Bank 7th — 3-1

Veterans'
William Fitt Veterans v Winchmore Hill Veterans — 2-0

Open Veterans'
William Fitt Veterans v Corinthian-Casuals Veterans — *2-2, 0-1

* after extra time

AMATEUR FOOTBALL ALLIANCE SENIOR CUP 1990–91

1st Round Proper
Hale End Athletic v Mill Hill Village — 2-3
Witan v O. Finchleians — 3-1
O. Actonians Assn. v Royal Bank of Scotland — 8-2
O. Elizabethans v O. Malvernians — 4-0
O. Tiffinians v O. Hamptonians — 1-3
Carshalton v O. Isleworthians — 2-1
O. Monovians v O. Owens — 0-1
O. Salesians v Liverpool Victoria — 5-0
Leyton County OB v Enfield O. Grammarians — 1-5
O. Ignatians v O. Danes — 4-0
Winchmore Hill v Inland Revenue — 6-2
O. Esthameians v O. Parkonians — 3-0
Broomfield v O. Meadonians — 0-1
Merton v Polytechnic — *3-2
Kew Association v O. Bromleians — 0-2
O. Westhamians v O. Edmontonians — 3-1
Crouch End Vampires v O. Greenfordians — 3-2
Wandsworth Borough v O. Chigwellians — 1-6
Barclays Bank v Glyn Old Boys — 1-1, 0-4
O. Uxonians v Midland Bank — 6-2
Colposa v Chertsey O. Salesians — 3-2
National Westminster Bank v Hassocks — 2-1
O. Tollingtonians v Norsemen — 0-4
Parkfield v Reigate Priory — 7-0
O. Parmiterians v O. Salopians — 5-0
Nottsborough v O. Vaughanians — 2-1
O. Bealonians v Civil Service — *2-2, 1-4
O. Salvatorians v Fulham Compton OB — *4-4, 0-2
British Petroleum v O. Manorians — 6-0
West Wickham v Wake Green — 3-0
South Bank Polytechnic v O. Kingsburians — 7-0
O. Brentwoods v London Airways — 0-1

2nd Round Proper
Mill Hill Village v Witan — 2-4
O. Actonians Assn. v O. Elizabethans — 1-0
O. Hamptonians v Carshalton — 2-4

O. Owens v O. Salesians — 0-4
Enfield O. Grammarians v O. Ignatians — 2-1
Winchmore Hill v O. Esthameians — *2-2, 0-2
O. Meadonians v Merton — 1-0
O. Bromleians v O. Westhamians — 3-0
Crouch End Vampires v O. Chigwellians — 6-3
Glyn Old Boys v Midland Bank — 1-0
Colposa v National Westminster Bank — 4-2
Norsemen v Parkfield — 7-2
O. Parmiterians v Nottsborough — 0-2
Fulham Compton OB v Civil Service — 5-2
British Petroleum v West Wickham — 1-7
South Bank Polytechnic v London Airways — 8-0

3rd Round Proper
Witan v O. Actonians Assn. — 1-4
Carshalton v O. Salesians — 3-1
Enfield O. Grammarians v O. Esthameians — 3-1
O. Meadonians v O. Bromleians — *0-0, 1-0
Crouch End Vampires v Glyn Old Boys — 0-1
Colposa v Norsemen — 0-3
Nottsborough v Fulham Compton OB — *4-3
West Wickham v South Bank Polytechnic — *3-3, 1-0

4th Round Proper
O. Actonians Assn. v Carshalton — 1-2
Enfield O. Grammarians v O. Meadonians — 1-0
Glyn O. Boys v Norsemen — 0-1
Nottsborough v West Wickham — 1-2

Semi-finals
Carshalton v Enfield O. Grammarians — *5-3
Norsemen v West Wickham — 1-0

Final
Norsemen v Carshalton — 1-0

* after extra time

REPRESENTATIVE MATCHES

v Army FA	Won 3-0	v Royal Navy FA	Won 1-0
v Cambridge University	Won 2-1	v Sussex County FA	Lost 1-3
v Oxford University	Won 1-0	v London University	Won 2-0
v Royal Air Force	Cancelled		

ARTHUR DUNN CUP

Final Tie: Old Carthusians v Old Reptonians *1-1, 0-4

ARTHURIAN LEAGUE

Premier Division

	P	W	D	L	F	A	Pts
Lancing Old Boys	16	8	4	4	30	25	20
Old Foresters	16	8	3	5	43	34	19
Old Carthusians	16	6	7	3	23	19	19
Old Chigwellians	16	6	5	5	31	27	17
Old Reptonians	16	7	2	7	33	29	16
Old Brentwoods	16	6	3	7	27	31	15
Old Malvernians	16	5	4	7	23	27	14
Old Wellingburians	16	5	4	7	26	32	14
Old Salopians	16	4	2	10	25	37	10

Division One

	P	W	D	L	F	A	Pts
Old Cholmeleians	16	13	1	2	47	11	27
Old Etonians	16	11	1	4	40	16	23
Old Wykehamists	16	9	2	5	41	30	20
Old Aldenhamians	16	8	2	6	36	24	18
Old Haileyburians	16	6	3	7	32	36	15
Old Harrovians	16	6	2	8	27	33	14
Old Bradfieldians	16	6	1	9	28	28	13
Old Ardinians	16	5	1	10	28	47	11
Old Westminsters	16	1	1	14	12	66	3

Division Two

	P	W	D	L	F	A	Pts
Old Chigwellians 2nd	16	13	2	1	55	15	28
Old Carthusians 2nd	16	9	2	5	34	24	20
Old Aldenhamians 2nd	16	9	1	6	52	31	19
Old Harrovians 2nd	16	7	3	6	23	32	17
Lancing Old Boys 2nd	16	7	1	8	24	37	15
Old Chigwellians 3rd	16	5	4	7	24	38	14
Old Witleians	16	4	5	7	28	28	13
Old Malvernians 2nd	16	5	1	10	29	37	11
Old Brentwoods 2nd	16	2	3	11	19	46	7

Division Three

	P	W	D	L	F	A	Pts
Old Cholmeleians 2nd	16	15	1	0	52	13	31
Old Etonians 2nd	16	12	1	3	44	18	25
Old Reptonians 2nd	16	7	4	5	51	43	18
Old Salopians 2nd	16	8	2	6	42	37	18
Old Foresters 2nd	16	7	2	7	47	38	16
Old Cholmeleians 3rd	16	7	1	8	35	36	15
Old Chigwellians 4th	16	4	2	10	33	53	10
Old Bradfieldians 2nd	16	2	4	10	29	45	8
Old Brentwoods 3rd	16	1	1	14	17	67	3

Division Four – 9 Teams – won by Old Foresters 3rd
Division Five – 6 Teams – won by Old Westminsters 2nd

Junior League Cup
Old Aldenhamians 2nd v O. Etonians 2nd 1-0
Jim Dixson VI-a-Side
O. Chigwellians v O. Wellingburians 2-0

LONDON LEGAL LEAGUE 1990–91

Division One

	P	W	D	L	F	A	Pts
Gray's Inn	22	18	2	2	73	22	38
Freshfields	22	18	1	3	66	24	37
Pegasus	22	16	2	4	54	23	34
Slaughter & May	22	11	5	6	41	22	27
Cameron Markby Hewitt	22	11	3	8	52	43	25
Clifford Chance	22	8	5	9	41	43	21
Wilde Sapte	22	9	2	11	34	53	20
Linklaters & Paines	22	6	5	11	37	56	17
Nabarro Nathanson	22	5	5	12	43	50	15
Titmuss Sainer & Webb	22	4	5	13	24	54	13
Boodle Hatfield	22	3	3	16	19	55	9
Taylor Joynson Garret	22	3	2	17	26	65	8

Division Two

	P	W	D	L	F	A	Pts
Lovell White Durrant	20	18	0	2	77	24	36
Norton Rose	20	14	2	4	55	32	30
Macfarlanes	20	12	4	4	56	29	28
Allen & Overy	20	11	1	8	62	36	23
D. J. Freeman & Co	20	9	4	7	45	34	22
Baker McKenzie	20	7	4	9	32	46	18
McKenna & Co	20	5	8	7	32	48	18
Denton Hall Burgin & Warrens	20	8	1	11	38	50	17
Gouldens	20	5	2	13	38	66	12
Beachcroft Stanleys	20	2	5	13	25	47	9
Bristows	20	3	1	16	20	68	7
Goddard Mitchell	withdrew and record expunged

League Challenge Cup
Freshfields v Gray's Inn 3-2 (aet)
Weavers Arms Cup
Pegasus v Wilde Sapte 1-0

LONDON INSURANCE FA 1990–91

Division One

	P	W	D	L	F	A	Pts
Liverpool Victoria	16	13	2	1	56	21	28
Gaflac	16	8	6	2	62	33	22
Eagle Star	16	9	2	5	46	42	20
Granby	16	7	3	6	47	48	17
Temple Bar	16	7	1	8	53	40	15
Sun Alliance	16	7	1	8	36	37	15
Bowring	16	2	5	9	38	56	9
Sedgwick	16	3	3	10	30	56	9
Bardhill	16	4	1	11	36	71	9

Division Two

	P	W	D	L	F	A	Pts
Sun Alliance 2nd	18	15	2	1	87	16	32
Colonial Mutual	18	14	3	1	50	16	31
Medical Sickness	18	10	3	5	57	41	23
Temple Bar 2nd	17	9	1	7	58	31	19
Liverpool Victoria 2nd	18	8	3	7	40	39	19
Granby 2nd	18	7	2	9	39	58	16
Noble Lowndes*	18	6	2	10	36	40	14
Eagle Star 2nd	18	5	3	10	32	45	13
Guardian Royal Exchange	18	4	0	14	35	81	8
Sedgwick 2nd	17	1	1	15	23	90	3

Division Three

	P	W	D	L	F	A	Pts
Asphalia	20	16	1	3	71	24	33
Norwich Union (London)	20	14	4	2	81	33	32
Gaflac 2nd	20	11	6	3	57	29	28
Sun Alliance 3rd	20	10	6	4	63	36	26
Temple Bar 3rd	20	11	3	6	80	44	25
Gaflac 3rd	20	8	3	9	44	49	19
Nobel Lowndes 2nd*	20	7	4	9	58	55	18
Bowring 2nd	20	8	2	10	45	49	18
Liverpool Victoria 3rd	20	4	0	16	17	73	8
Eagle Star 3rd	20	3	1	16	36	92	7
Temple Bar 4th	20	3	0	17	23	71	6

* formerly Hill Samuel IS

Charity Cup – Gaflac 1 Cuaco 0
Challenge Cup – Liverpool Victoria 2*:3 Gaflac 2*:1
Junior Cup – Temple Bar 1*:2* Granby 2nd 1*:1*
Minor Cup – Asphalia 1*:6 Gaflac 2nd 1*:1
W. A. Jewell Memorial Trophy
Granby (5-a-Side): Runners-up – Bowring
Sportsmanship Trophy – Eagle Star

* after extra time

Representative Matches
Southern Olympian League v London Insurance FA 3-0
Bristol Insurance Institute v London Insurance FA 3-2
London Insurance FA v Southern Amateur League 'B' 4-3
London Insurance FA v United Hospitals 4-0
London Banks FA v London Insurance FA 'A' 1-3

LONDON BANKS FA 1990–91

Division One

	P	W	D	L	F	A	Pts
Coutts & Co	16	9	4	3	42	22	22
Hill Samuel & Co	16	10	0	6	36	26	20
Kleinwort Benson	16	8	2	6	33	29	18
Allied Irish Banks	16	7	4	5	28	27	18
Midland Montagu	16	7	3	6	29	23	17
Bank of America	16	6	4	6	30	27	16
Morgan Guaranty Trust Co	16	6	3	7	25	32	15
Chase Manhattan Bank	16	4	2	10	22	41	10
Citibank	16	2	4	10	25	43	8

Division Two

	P	W	D	L	F	A	Pts
Salomon Brothers	18	12	4	2	58	33	28
Credit Suisse	18	10	3	5	49	27	23
National Westminster Bank 'A'	18	10	3	5	52	35	23
Coutts & Co 2nd	18	8	6	4	45	34	22
Banque National de Paris	18	6	6	6	32	36	18
Manufacturers Hanover Trust	18	6	6	6	43	48	18
Hong Kong & Shanghai Bank	18	7	2	9	39	40	16

	P	W	D	L	F	A	Pts
Bank of Scotland	18	6	3	9	36	39	15
Standard Chartered Bank	18	4	1	13	27	64	9
Westpac	18	3	2	13	30	55	8

Division Three	P	W	D	L	F	A	Pts
Union Bank of Switzerland	18	11	5	2	43	23	27
Polytechnic	18	8	9	1	39	21	25
Morgan Stanley	18	8	8	2	41	17	24
Bank of America 2nd	18	8	5	5	34	19	21
C. Hoare & Co	18	6	6	6	44	45	18
Chase Manhattan Bank 2nd	18	6	5	7	35	40	17
National Westminster Bank 'B'	18	5	2	11	29	39	15
National Westminster Bank 'C'	18	5	2	11	29	45	12
Citibank 2nd	18	3	6	9	25	44	12
Bank of Ireland	18	3	3	12	17	43	9

Division Four	P	W	D	L	F	A	Pts
Bank Credit & Commerce Intl	16	14	1	1	53	13	29
Bankers Trust Co	16	12	1	3	45	24	25
National Westminster Bank 'D'	16	9	3	4	34	24	21
Austral & N.Z. Banking Group	16	5	5	6	24	25	15
Banque Indosuez	16	6	1	9	27	36	13
First Chicago	16	5	2	9	36	38	12
Morgan Guaranty Trust Co 2nd	16	5	2	9	28	52	12
Swiss Bank Corpn	16	4	2	10	27	41	10
Trustee Savings Bank	16	2	3	11	18	39	7

Division Five	P	W	D	L	F	A	Pts
Nikko Securities	18	18	0	0	88	16	36
Abbey National	18	14	2	2	64	19	30
Manufact'rs Hanover Trust 2nd	18	11	0	7	51	29	22
National Westminster Bank 'E'	18	9	3	6	56	40	21
Midland Bank 'B'	18	9	1	8	28	56	19
Midland Bank 'A'	18	7	3	8	47	43	17
Coutts & Co 3rd	18	8	0	10	51	45	16
Standard Chartered Bank 2nd	18	5	2	11	47	59	12
Lloyds Bank 10th	18	2	0	16	25	83	4
Royal Bank of Scotland 7th	18	1	1	16	27	94	3

Challenge Cup – 18 Entries
National Westminster v Midland ... 1-2
Senior Cup – 43 Entries
Hill Samuel & Co v BCCI ... 4-1
Senior Plate – 16 Entries
Chase Manhattan v Midland Montagu ... 1-0
Minor Cup – 23 Entries
Manufacturers Hanover Trust v Barclays ... 4-0
Junior Cup – 46 Entries
Union Bank of Switzerland v BCCI ... 1-2
Junior Plate – 16 Entries
National Westminster v Morgan Gty Trust ... 0-0, 5p-3p
Veterans' Cup – 13 Entries
National Westminster v Polytechnic ... 0-4
Sportsman's Cup – National Westminster v C. Hoare & Co ... 2-0

Representative Matches:
United Banks v Stock Exchange ... 1-2
United Banks v Royal Marines ... 4-3
United Banks v Southern Olympian League ... 2-0
United Banks v London University ... 5-2
United Banks v Old Boys' League 'A' ... 2-1
United Banks v London Banks ... 3-1
London Banks v Old Boys' League 'B' ... 2-2
London Banks v Royal Marines ... 4-1
London Banks v London Legal League ... 2-2
London Banks v Southern Amateur League 'B' ... 2-4
London Banks v London Insurance ... 1-3

LONDON OLD BOYS' CUP
1990–91

Senior Cup (73 Entries)
Cardinal Manning OB v O. Tenisonians ... 1-0
Intermediate Cup (73)
O. Alpertonian 2nd v O. Chigwellians 2nd ... 0-1
Junior Cup (72)
O. Bealonians 3rd v O. Grammarians ... *1-3
Minor Cup (61)
O. Parmiterians 4th v O. Suttonians 4th ... 0-0, 3-0
Novets Cup (54)
O. Minchendenians 5th v O. Suttonians 5th ... 3-2
Drummond Cup (33)
O. Bromleians 6th v O. Parmiterians 6th ... 2-7
Nemean Cup (37)
O. Parmiterians 7th v O. Parmiterians 8th ... 2-0
Veterans' Cup (33)
O. Owens Veterans v William Fitt Veterans ... *1-3

THE OLD BOYS' FOOTBALL LEAGUE
1990–91

Premier Division	P	W	D	L	F	A	Pts
Old Ignatians	20	17	0	3	49	23	34
Glyn OB	20	11	4	5	40	21	26
Old Meadonians	19	11	3	5	45	33	25
Cardinal Manning OB	19	7	6	6	28	27	20
Latymer OB	20	7	6	7	36	37	20
Enfield Old Grammarians	19	8	3	8	34	31	19
Chertsey O. Salesians	19	7	4	8	24	33	18
Old Danes	20	7	3	10	40	42	17
Old Aloysians	20	6	3	11	35	35	15
Old Suttonians	20	5	2	13	34	41	12
Old Kingsburians	20	4	2	14	25	63	10

Senior Division Two	P	W	D	L	F	A	Pts
Old Tenisonians	20	15	3	2	54	17	33
Old Isleworthians	20	13	5	2	41	24	31
Old Wilsonians	20	11	3	6	33	27	25
Old Minchendenians	20	7	8	5	29	27	22
Old Westhamians	20	7	5	8	41	41	19
Old Wokingians	20	7	5	8	33	35	19
Old Salvatorians	20	6	6	8	34	39	18
Phoenix OB	20	6	5	9	26	29	17
Mill Hill County OB	20	7	2	11	28	37	16
Old Greenfordians	20	4	5	11	32	44	13
Old Josephians	20	1	5	14	21	52	7

Senior Division Two	P	W	D	L	F	A	Pts
Old Tiffinians	22	16	5	1	58	29	37
Old Edmontonians	22	14	2	6	51	26	30
Old Tollingtonians	22	12	4	6	47	28	28
Old Sinjuns	22	10	6	6	43	27	26
Old Ignatians 2nd	22	9	5	8	35	40	23
Old Southallians	22	7	7	8	40	34	21
Clapham O. Xaverians	22	6	6	10	40	55	18
Old Alpertonians	22	7	3	12	30	48	17
Shene Old Grammarians	22	6	5	11	23	47	17
John Fisher OB	22	5	6	11	32	47	16
Old Vaughanians	22	4	7	11	21	34	15
Strand Hollingtonian OB	22	6	4	12	40	45	*14

* two points deducted for breach of rule

Senior Division 3 (A) – 12 Teams – won by O. Buckwellians
Senior Division 3 (B) – 12 Teams – won by O. Tenisonians 2nd
Senior Division 4 (North) – 11 Teams – won by O. Aloysians 2nd
Senior Division 4 (South) – 11 Teams – won by O. Wilsonians 2nd
Senior Division 4 (West) – 11 Teams – won by O. Southallians 2nd
Intermediate Division North – 11 Teams – won by O. Highburians 2nd
Intermediate Division South – 11 Teams – won by O. Dorkinians 2nd

Intermediate Division West – 11 Teams – won by O. Manorians 2nd
Division One North – 10 Teams – won by London Hospital OB
Division One South – 11 Teams – won by O. Wilsonians 3rd
Division One West – 11 Teams – won by O. Salvatorians 3rd
Division Two North – 11 Teams – won by O. Grocers 2nd
Division Two South – 12 Teams – won by O. Dorkinians 3rd
Division Two West – 11 Teams – won by O. Danes 3rd
Division Three North – 12 Teams – won by O. Minchendenians 5th
Division Three South – 12 Teams – won by O. Thorntonians 3rd
Division Three West – 11 Teams – won by O. Salvatorians 5th
Division Four North – 12 Teams – won by O. Elysians 4th
Division Four South – 11 Teams – won by O. Dorkinians 4th
Division Four West – 11 Teams – won by Mill Hill County OB 5th
Division Five North – 11 Teams – won by O. Camdenians 7th
Division Five South – 11 Teams – won by O. St Mary's 2nd
Division Five West – 10 Teams – won by O. Tiffinians 5th
Division Six South – 10 Teams – won by O. Sinjuns 6th
Division Six West – 10 Teams – won by O. Uffingtonians 6th

SOUTHERN AMATEUR LEAGUE
1990–91

SENIOR SECTION

Division One	P	W	D	L	F	A	Pts
West Wickham	22	14	4	4	47	21	32
Norsemen	22	13	4	5	47	21	30
Carshalton	22	11	4	7	40	31	26
Civil Service	22	10	6	6	37	34	26
Old Actonians Asso.	22	8	8	6	37	29	24
Midland Bank	22	10	3	9	34	27	23
National Westminster Bank	22	9	4	9	32	30	22
Old Esthameians	22	7	7	8	24	29	21
Winchmore Hill	22	8	4	10	27	34	20
Old Parkonians	22	6	7	9	25	36	19
Old Stationers	22	4	4	14	25	53	12
Old Salesians	22	2	5	15	34	64	9

Division Two	P	W	D	L	F	A	Pts
Old Bromleians	22	14	5	3	55	20	33
British Petroleum	22	14	5	3	53	23	33
Southgate Olympic	22	13	6	3	50	19	32
Barclays Bank	22	8	7	7	33	36	23
East Barnet Old Grammarians	22	8	6	8	38	45	22
Polytechnic	22	8	5	9	33	32	21
Crouch End Vampires	22	7	6	9	27	28	20
Broomfield	22	7	6	9	35	45	20
South Bank Polytechnic	22	7	5	10	27	35	19
Ibis	22	7	4	11	35	49	18
Merton	22	5	5	12	30	46	15
Old Lyonians	22	3	2	17	24	62	8

Division Three	P	W	D	L	F	A	Pts
Alexandra Park	22	17	3	2	58	21	37
Lloyds Bank	22	13	5	4	46	20	31
Royal Bank of Scotland	22	11	6	5	48	29	28
Old Latymerians	22	10	4	8	32	27	24
Lensbury	22	9	6	7	30	36	24
Bank of England	22	11	1	10	32	35	23
Kew Association	22	9	3	10	36	36	21
Alleyn Old Boys	22	8	5	9	44	45	21
Old Westminster Citizens	22	5	6	11	33	47	16
Cuaco	22	7	1	14	41	47	15
Reigate Priory	22	3	6	13	25	51	12
Brentham	20	5	2	15	22	53	12

RESERVE TEAM SECTION

Division One – 12 Teams – won by Southgate Olympic 2nd
Division Two – 12 Teams – won by National Westminster Bank 2nd

Division Three – 12 Teams – won by Royal Bank of Scotland 2nd

THIRD TEAM SECTION
Division One – 12 Teams – won by Southgate Olympic 3rd
Division Two – 12 Teams – won by Old Latymerians 3rd
Division Three – 12 Teams – won by West Wickham 3rd

FOURTH TEAM SECTION
Division One – 12 Teams – won by Carshalton 4th
Division Two – 12 Teams – won by Old Actonians Association 4th
Division Three – 12 Teams – won by Old Latymerians 4th

FIFTH TEAM SECTION
Division One – 12 Teams – won by National Westminster Bank 5th
Division Two – 11 Teams – won by Old Actonians Association 5th
Division Three – 11 Teams – won by East Barnet Old Grammarians 5th

SIXTH TEAM SECTION
Division One – 11 Teams – won by Winchmore Hill 6th
Division Two – 10 Teams – won by Old Latymerians 6th
Division Three – 9 Teams – won by Old Stationers 6th

SEVENTH TEAM SECTION
Division One – 10 Teams – won by Old Esthameians 7th
Division Two – 9 Teams – won by Lloyds Bank 7th

EIGHTH TEAM SECTION
Division One – 10 Teams – won by Winchmore Hill 8th
Division Two – 10 Teams – won by Norsemen 8th

SOUTHERN OLYMPIAN LEAGUE
1990–91

SENIOR SECTION

Division One	P	W	D	L	F	A	Pts
Old Parmiterians	18	12	4	2	62	25	28
Witan	18	7	5	6	33	31	19
Parkfield	18	7	5	6	27	32	19
Mill Hill Village	18	8	2	8	39	36	18
Old Finchleians	18	7	4	7	40	42	18
Old Bealonians	18	7	4	7	40	43	18
St Mary's College	18	7	2	9	33	30	16
Southgate County	18	7	1	10	29	40	15
Old Grammarians	18	6	2	10	25	40	14
Colposa	18	6	3	9	29	38	*13

Division Two	P	W	D	L	F	A	Pts
Old Owens	20	15	5	0	71	32	35
Nottsborough	19	14	2	3	64	21	30
Hadley	20	11	7	2	41	26	29
Fulham Compton OB	20	10	1	9	53	40	21
Albanian	20	5	8	7	34	39	18
Old Fairlopians	19	7	5	7	26	32	*17
Old Monovians	20	6	5	9	29	42	17
Hale End Athletic	20	6	4	10	27	41	16
Pollygons	20	5	3	12	39	58	13
Old Colfeians	20	4	4	12	27	51	12
Inland Revenue	20	2	4	14	25	54	8

Division Three	P	W	D	L	F	A	Pts
Hampstead Heathens	18	11	6	1	50	27	28
Wandsworth Borough	18	9	5	4	38	29	23
Academicals	18	8	6	4	48	31	22
BBC	18	9	3	6	35	30	21
Birkbeck College	18	6	7	5	35	32	19
Ealing Association	18	7	3	8	39	42	17
Electrosport	18	6	5	7	49	52	17
Old Woodhousians	18	4	8	6	42	39	16
Mayfield Athletic	18	3	4	11	28	41	10
Cent YMCA	18	2	3	13	17	58	7

Division Four	P	W	D	L	F	A	Pts
Duncombe Sports	18	14	3	1	74	20	31
Corinthian-Casuals 'A'	18	12	4	2	55	20	28
Brent	18	11	3	4	40	17	25
Westerns	18	10	2	6	59	32	22
Tansley	18	9	2	7	39	39	20

London Airways   18 9 1 8 44 29 19
Pegasus   18 8 2 8 47 39 18
London Welsh   18 3 1 14 21 57   7
Economicals   18 1 3 14 15 61   5
Distillers   18 1 3 14 20 100   5

* points deducted for breach of rule

Intermediate Division One – 10 Teams – won by Mill Hill Village 2nd
Intermediate Division Two – 10 Teams – won by Colposa 2nd
Intermediate Division Three – 10 Teams – won by Old Woodhouseians 2nd
Intermediate Division Four – 10 Teams – won by Corinthian-Casuals 'B'
Junior Division One – 10 Teams – won by Old Parmiterians 3rd
Junior Division Two – 10 Teams – won by Old Parmiterians 4th
Junior Division Three – 10 Teams – won by Old Finchleians 4th
Junior Division Four – 10 Teams – won by Old Parmiterians 6th
Minor Division 'A' – 10 Teams – won by Tansley 3rd
Minor Division 'B' – 8 Teams – won by Parkfield 6th
Minor Division 'C' – 9 Teams – won by Duncombe Sports 2nd

Minor Division 'D' – 9 Teams – won by Fulham Compton OB 4th
Minor Division 'E' – 8 Teams – won by Old Owens 4th
Minor Division 'F' – 10 Teams – won by Ealing Association 6th
Minor Division 'G' – 10 Teams – won by Hale End Athletic 5th
Veterans' Section – 7 Teams – won by Tansley Veterans
Challenge Bowl – won by St Mary's College
Challenge Shield – won by Old Finchleians
Intermediate Challenge Cup – won by Albanian 2nd
Intermediate Challenge Shield – won by Mill Hill Village 2nd
Junior Challenge Cup – won by Old Owens 3rd
Junior Challenge Shield – won by Hampstead Heathens 3rd
Mander Challenge Cup – won by Old Finchleians 4th
Mander Challenge Shield – won by Mill Hill Village 4th
Burntwood Trophy – won by Mill Hill Village 5th
Burntwood Challenge Shield – won by Hale End Athletic 5th
Thomas Parmiter Cup – won by Old Parmiterians 6th
Thomas Parmiter Challenge Shield – won by Old Parmiterians 8th
Veterans' Cup – won by Old Fairlopians Vets
Veterans' Challenge Shield – won by Albanian Vets
Ken Elbourne Memorial Award – won by Wandsworth Borough

MIDLAND AMATEUR ALLIANCE
1990–91

Division One	P	W	D	L	F	A	Pts
Brunts Old Boys	22	17	2	3	68	28	36
Sherwood Amateurs	22	17	1	4	79	39	35
Magdala Amateurs	22	11	5	6	63	42	27
Wollaton	22	11	5	6	49	38	27
Kirton BW	22	13	1	8	46	39	27
Derbyshire Amateurs	22	10	4	8	62	48	24
Old Elizabethans	22	8	6	8	43	38	22
Tibshelf Old Boys	22	9	3	10	43	59	21
Bassingfield	22	9	2	11	48	52	20
Beeston OBA	22	4	1	17	31	81	9
FC Toton	22	4	0	18	33	66	8
Nottinghamshire	22	2	4	16	24	59	8

Division Two	P	W	D	L	F	A	Pts
Wollaton 2nd	22	15	6	1	59	25	36
Lady Bay	22	14	3	5	86	36	31
Old Elizabethans 2nd	22	12	7	3	67	21	31
Peoples College	22	11	5	6	48	35	27
Brunts OB 2nd	22	12	3	7	45	27	27
Old Bemrosians	22	9	6	7	56	34	24
Nottingham Univ PG's	22	8	5	9	50	50	21
Heanor Amateurs	22	7	5	10	36	48	19
Nottingham Spartan	22	6	6	10	42	43	18
Nottinghamshire 2nd	22	4	8	10	35	63	16
Chilwell	22	2	6	14	30	62	10
Mapperley Park	22	0	4	18	18	118	4

Division Three	P	W	D	L	F	A	Pts
Nottingham Cougars	26	22	2	2	105	31	46
Magdala Amateurs 2nd	26	16	3	7	73	45	35
Old Elizabethans 3rd	26	14	6	6	52	38	34
Lady Bay 2nd	26	14	4	8	69	49	32
Derbyshire Amateurs 2nd	26	14	2	10	77	50	30
Sherwood Amateurs 2nd	26	11	5	10	60	48	27
Wollaton 3rd	26	11	4	11	52	56	26
Tibshelf Old Boys 2nd	26	10	5	11	54	45	25
Bassingfield 2nd	26	9	7	10	58	57	25
Old Bemrosians 2nd	26	9	5	12	57	68	23
W. Bridgford Casuals	26	8	5	13	56	83	21
Peoples College 2nd	26	7	3	16	42	73	17
Heanor Amateurs 2nd	26	4	5	17	46	99	13
Beeston OB Assn 2nd	26	3	4	19	42	101	10

Division Four	P	W	D	L	F	A	Pts
County Nalgo	22	15	5	2	90	25	35
Charnos	22	15	5	2	81	27	35
Magdala Amateurs 3rd	22	12	4	6	63	49	28
Old Elizabethans 4th	22	12	4	6	52	39	28
Nottinghamshire 3rd	22	11	4	7	75	61	26
Monty Hind OB	22	10	3	9	55	50	23
Woodborough United	22	10	1	11	48	56	21
Derbyshire Amateurs 3rd	22	7	5	10	56	54	19
Tibshelf Old Boys 3rd	22	7	3	12	34	65	17
Old Bemrosians 3rd	22	3	6	13	21	56	12
Lady Bay 3rd	22	4	3	15	30	71	11
Peoples College 3rd	22	3	3	16	31	83	9

Senior Cup – won by Old Elizabethans
Intermediate Cup – won by Old Elizabethans 2nd
Minor Cup – won by Old Elizabethans 3rd
1st Division Challenge Trophy – won by Sherwood Amateurs
2nd Division Challenge Cup – won by Old Elizabethans 2nd
3rd Division Challenge Cup – won by Lady Bay 2nd
4th Division Challenge Cup – won by County Nalgo
H B Poole Trophy – won by Wollaton

THE OLD BOYS' INVITATION CUP
1990–1991

Senior Cup
O. Tenisonians 2nd v E. Barnet O. Grammarians   2-0
Junior Cup
O. Tenisonians 2nd v O. Latymerians 2nd   3-0
Minor Cup
O. Salesians 3rd v O. Tenisonians 3rd   1-0
4th XI Cup
E. Barnet O. Grammarians 4th v O. Stationers 4th   3-1
5th XI Cup
O. Bromleians 5th v O. Esthameians 5th   4-1
6th XI Cup
O. Minchendenians 6th v O. Wilsonians 6th   2-0
7th XI Cup
O. Finchleians 9th v O. Finchleians 7th   3 : pw-3 : pl
Veterans' Cup
O. Finchleians Veterans v O. Bromleians Veterans   1 : pw-1 : pl

UNIVERSITY FOOTBALL 1990–91

UNIVERSITY OF LONDON INTER-COLLEGIATE LEAGUE 1990–91

Premier Division

	P	W	D	L	F	A	Pts
King's College	16	12	2	2	43	18	26
University College	16	8	1	7	27	24	17
Queen Mary Westfield College	16	7	3	6	25	23	17
Goldsmiths' College	16	6	4	6	31	31	16
London School of Economics	16	7	2	7	25	25	16
R. Holloway & Bedford New College	16	7	1	8	35	37	15
Imperial College	16	6	3	7	24	31	15
King's College M. S.	16	5	3	8	29	33	13
Untd. Med. & Dent. Schs Guys–St. Thomas's.	16	2	5	9	27	44	9

Division One

	P	W	D	L	F	A	Pts
St George's Hospital M. S.	18	13	1	4	64	33	27
Imperial College 2nd	18	11	4	3	52	26	26
School of Pharmacy	18	10	2	6	45	40	22
University College 2nd	18	9	1	8	40	25	19
King's College 2nd	18	8	3	7	41	31	19
Queen Mary Westfield College 2nd	18	8	2	8	39	48	18
Royal Free Hospital Sch. Medicine	18	6	5	7	39	35	17
Middlesex & Univ. Coll. Hosp's M.S.	18	5	2	11	23	50	12
United Med. & Dental Schools 2nd	18	4	3	11	21	68	11
The Royal London Hosp. Med. College	18	4	1	13	38	46	9

Division Two

	P	W	D	L	F	A	Pts
St Mary's Hospital Med. Sch.	18	11	3	4	39	16	25
R. Holloway & Bedford New College 2nd	18	11	3	4	43	25	25
Royal School of Mines (Imperial College)	18	10	1	7	36	27	21
London School of Economics 2nd	18	10	1	7	39	33	21
St Bartholomew's Hospital Med. Coll.	18	9	2	7	46	31	20
Charing Cross & W'min Hospital M.S.	18	7	5	6	27	31	19
University College 3rd	18	7	3	8	47	38	17
Imperial College 3rd	18	6	5	7	32	39	17
SOAS & SSEES	18	3	7	8	27	48	13
London School of Economics 3rd	18	0	2	16	14	62	2

Division 3 – 9 Teams – won by Goldsmiths' College 2nd
Division 4 – 9 Teams – won by Westfield College
Division 5 – 9 Teams – won by King's College 6th

Challenge Cup – R. Holloway & Bedford New College 1
Queen Mary Westfield College 0

Upper Reserves Cup – R. Holloway & Bedford New College 2nd 1 University College 3rd 0

Lower Reserves Cup – Goldsmiths' College 3rd 5 Imperial College 6th 1

UNIVERSITY MATCH
(30 March 1991, at Craven Cottage, Fulham)
Oxford 0, Cambridge 0

Oxford: A. Weaver; M. Ramsey, P. Sullivan, S. Lang, P. Dowie, M. Kachingwe, S. Moorley, J. Keeble, A. Mitchell, A. Dechet, D. Westgate. *Subs:* D. O'Brien, D. Goldie.
Cambridge: S. Taylor; G. Luff, S. Ainsworth, B. Bennett, D. Pickup, P. Harris, B. Buchinleck, M. Yates, A. Thompson, C. Jones, J. Beeby. *Subs:* S. Finnigan, M. Morris.
(This match was also part of the BUSF Tournament to decide 3/4th place, which the teams thus shared.)

COMMERCIAL UNION/UAU 1990–91
First team championship

NORTH EAST GROUP

Durham 0, Hull 2   Newcastle 1, Durham 4
Newcastle 2, Leeds 1   Durham 1, York 3
Leeds 3, Durham 0   Hull 0, Newcastle 1
Hull 5, York 0   Leeds 2, Hull 3
York 3, Leeds 3   York 0, Newcastle 0

	P	W	D	L	F	A	Pts
Hull	4	3	0	1	10	3	6
Newcastle	4	2	1	1	4	5	5
York	4	1	2	1	6	9	4
Leeds	4	1	1	2	9	8	3
Durham	4	1	0	3	5	9	2

Hull qualified for Challenge Round; Newcastle for Play-off Round; York and Leeds for East Play-off Round.

NORTH WEST GROUP

Manchester 1, Liverpool 3   UMIST 2, Salford 0
Salford 3, Lancaster 1   Manchester 2, Salford 0
Liverpool 2, UMIST 1   Lancaster 0, UMIST 1
Lancaster 5, Manchester 0   UMIST 0, Manchester 2
Liverpool 3, Lancaster 0   Salford 0, Liverpool 1

	P	W	D	L	F	A	Pts
Liverpool	4	4	0	0	9	2	8
UMIST	4	2	0	2	4	4	4
Manchester	4	2	0	2	5	8	4
Lancaster	4	1	0	3	6	7	2
Salford	4	1	0	3	3	6	2

Liverpool qualified for Challenge Round; UMIST and Manchester for Play-off Round.

EAST MIDLANDS GROUP

Sheffield 1, Loughborough 7
Bradford 2, Nottingham 2
Loughborough 6, Nottingham 2
Sheffield 4, Bradford 1
Bradford 0 Loughborough 2
Nottingham 0, Sheffield 0

	P	W	D	L	F	A	Pts
Loughborough	3	3	0	0	15	3	6
Sheffield	3	1	1	1	5	8	3
Nottingham	3	0	2	1	4	8	2
Bradford	3	0	1	2	3	8	1

Loughborough qualified for Challenge Round; Sheffield for Play-off Round; Nottingham and Bradford for East Play-off Round.

WEST MIDLANDS GROUP

Aston 2, Warwick 2   Warwick 1, Leicester 0
Leicester 0, Birmingham 0   Warwick 2, Keele 0
Birmingham 1, Warwick 1   Leicester 2, Aston 0
Aston 4, Keele 0   Birmingham 0, Aston 1
Keele 1, Birmingham 1

	P	W	D	L	F	A	Pts
Warwick	4	2	2	0	6	3	6
Aston	4	2	1	1	7	4	5
Leicester	4	1	2	1	3	2	4
Birmingham	4	0	3	1	2	3	3
Keele	4	0	2	2	2	8	2

Warwick qualified for Challenge Round; Aston and Leicester for Play-off Round.

SOUTH EAST (NORTH) GROUP

Kings 1, Essex 3
Brunel 0, East Anglia 1
UCL 2, Buckingham 1
City 1, Kings 7
UCL 0, East Anglia 5
Buckingham 2, Essex 2
East Anglia 1, City 1
Essex 3, Brunel 2
Kings 3, Buckingham 1
East Anglia 3, Kings 1
City 4, UCL 4
Buckingham 2, Brunel 2
Essex 8, City 1
Brunel 5, UCL 2
Brunel 1, Kings 3
Essex 8, UCL 0
Buckingham 2, City 0
City 1, Brunel 2
East Anglia 0, Essex 0
UCL 1, Kings 1
N.B. Buckingham w.o. East Anglia scratched

	P	W	D	L	F	A	Pts
Essex	6	4	2	0	24	6	10
East Anglia	6	3	2	1	10	2	8
Kings	6	3	1	2	16	10	7
Buckingham	6	2	2	2	8	9	6
Brunel	6	2	1	3	12	12	5
UCL	6	1	2	3	9	24	4
City	6	0	2	4	8	24	2

Essex qualified for Challenge Round; East Anglia and Kings for Play-off Round.

SOUTH EAST (SOUTH) GROUP

Surrey 5, Sussex 0　　　　RHBNC 1, Surrey 3
Imperial 1, Kent 2　　　　LSE 3, Sussex 1
RHBNC 0, LSE 1　　　　Imperial 0, Surrey 3
Sussex 0, Kent 4　　　　Kent 5, RHBNC 0
LSE 1, Surrey 7　　　　Surrey 2, Kent 0
Imperial 1, RHBNC 2　　LSE 4, Imperial 0
Kent 0, LSE 0　　　　Sussex 2, RHBNC 2
Sussex 1, Imperial 1

	P	W	D	L	F	A	Pts
Surrey	5	5	0	0	20	2	10
Kent	5	3	1	1	11	3	7
LSE	5	3	1	1	9	8	7
RHBNC	5	1	1	3	5	12	3
Sussex	5	0	2	3	4	15	2
Imperial	5	0	1	4	3	12	1

Surrey qualified for Challenge Round; Kent and LSE for Play-off Round

SOUTH WEST GROUP

Reading 1, Southampton 1　　Southampton 1, Exeter 3
Bristol 0, Exeter 1　　　　Cranfield 0, Reading 1
Cranfield 1, Bath 0　　　　Southampton 0, Bath 3
Bristol 0, Southampton 1　　Exeter 0, Reading 0
Bath 1, Reading 3　　　　Bristol 1, Cranfield 3
Exeter 1, Cranfield 1　　　　Reading 5, Bristol 1
Bath 2, Bristol 0　　　　Exeter 1, Bath 1
　　　　　　　　　Cranfield 1, Southampton 5

	P	W	D	L	F	A	Pts
Reading	5	3	2	0	10	3	8
Exeter	5	2	3	0	6	3	7
Bath	5	2	1	2	7	5	5
Southampton	5	2	1	2	8	8	5
Cranfield	5	2	1	2	6	8	5
Bristol	5	0	0	5	2	12	0

Reading qualified for Challenge Round; Exeter and Bath for Play-off Round.

WELSH GROUP

Aberystwyth 2, UWCC 3
UCNW (Bangor) 0, Swansea 5
Lampeter 2, Swansea 10
UCNW (Bangor) 1, Aberystwyth 0
UWCC 3, Lampeter 0
Aberystwyth 2, Swansea 2
Lampeter 2, Aberystwyth 2
UWCC 2, UCNW (Bangor) 1
Lampeter 0, UCNW (Bangor) 0
Swansea 1, UWCC 2

	P	W	D	L	F	A	Pts
UWCC	4	4	0	0	10	4	8
Swansea	4	2	1	1	18	6	5
UCNW (Bangor)	4	1	1	2	2	7	3
Aberystwyth	4	0	2	2	6	8	2
Lampeter	4	0	2	2	4	15	2

UWCC qualified for Challenge Round; Swansea and UCNW (Bangor) for Play-off Round.

Play-offs (Eastern Division)

Nottingham 1, Leeds 4
York 2, Bradford 3

Play-off Round

East Anglia 1, Bath 0
Exeter 4, LSE 1
Newcastle 2, Manchester 1
Surrey 1, Leicester 0
Kent 1, Kings 2
Sheffield 1, Bradford 1
Aston 1, UCNW (Bangor) 2
UMIST 2, Leeds 6 aet

Challenge Round

UWCC 1, East Anglia 0
Warwick 2, Exeter 0
Hull 3, Newcastle 2
Essex 4, Swansea 1
Loughborough 6, Kings 1
Liverpool 8, Bradford 0
Surrey 2, UCNW (Bangor) 0
Reading 2, Leeds 1 aet

Quarter-finals

UWCC 0, Warwick 1
Hull 0, Essex 0 aet
Essex won 4–2 on penalties
Loughborough 6, Liverpool 1
Surrey 2, Reading 1 aet

Semi-finals

Warwick 2, Essex 0
Loughborough 1, Surrey 1
Replay: Loughborough 2, Surrey 0

Final *at Walsall FC*

Warwick 2, Loughborough 5

REPRESENTATIVE MATCHES

East UAU 5, Bradford City 1
South UAU 1, Royal Navy 1
West UAU 0, Marine 1
West UAU 1, Tranmere Rovers 2
UAU I 5, Stoke City 1
UAU II 2, Latvian Select XI 2
UAU I 5, BCSA 1
UAU I 1, Bradford City 4
UAU II 0, Tranmere Rovers Youth team 1
UAU II 1, Irish Technical Colleges 1

BUSF TOURNAMENT (IN EDINBURGH)

Group A

UAU I 2, Cambridge 2
Scotland 2, Northern Ireland 1
Scotland 1, UAU I 2
Northern Ireland 1, Cambridge 1
Cambridge 2, Scotland 0
UAU I 5, Northern Ireland 1
Positions: 1, UAU I; 2, Cambridge; 3, Scotland; 4, Northern Ireland.

Group B

UAU II 5, London 3
Oxford 2, Wales 1
Oxford 0, UAU II 0
Wales 3, London 2
London 1, Oxford 1
UAU II 4, Wales 0
Positions: 1, UAU II; 2, Oxford; 3, Wales; 4, London
Play-offs: 7/8th Northern Ireland 4, London 1.
5/6th Scotland 6, Wales 0
3/4th Oxford v Cambridge held over for University Match
(see previous page)
Final: UAU I 5, UAU II 0

INFORMATION
AND
RECORDS

LAWS OF THE GAME

OBITUARIES

AWARDS

RECORDS

IMPORTANT ADDRESSES

FOOTBALL LEAGUE FIXTURES

INTERNATIONAL AND CUP DATES

ADDRESSES

The Football Association: R. H. G. Kelly, F.C.I.S., 16 Lancaster Gate, London W2 3LW

Scotland: J. Farry, 6 Park Gardens, Glasgow G3 7YE. *041-332 6372*
Northern Ireland (Irish FA): D. I. Bowen, 20 Windsor Avenue, Belfast BT9 6EG. *0232-669458*
Wales: A. Evans, 3 Westgate Street, Cardiff, South Glamorgan CF1 1JF. *0222-372325*
Republic of Ireland (FA of Ireland): S. Connolly, 80 Merrion Square South, Dublin 2. *0001-766864*

International Federation (FIFA): S. Blatter, FIFA House, Hitzigweg 11, CH-8032 Zurich, Switzerland. *1-384-9595. Fax: 1-384-9696*
Union of European Football Associations: G. Aigner, PO Box 16, CH-3000 Berne 15, Switzerland. *031-321735. Fax: 031-321838.*

THE LEAGUES

The Football League: J. D. Dent, F.C.I.S., The Football League, Lytham St Annes, Lancs FY8 1JG. *0253-729421. Telex 67675*
The Scottish League: P. Donald, 188 West Regent Street, Glasgow G2 4RY. *041-248 384415*
The Irish League: M. Brown, 87 University Street, Belfast BT7 1HP. *0232-242888*
Football League of Ireland: E. Morris, 80 Merrion Square South, Dublin 2. *0001-765120*
GM Vauxhall Conference: P. D. Hunter, 24 Barnehurst Road, Bexleyheath, Kent DA7 6EZ. *0322-521116*
Central League: D. J. Grimshaw, 118 St Stephens Road, Deepdale, Preston, Lancs PR1 6TD. *0772-795386*
North West Counties League: N. A. Rowles, 845 Liverpool Road, Peel Green, Eccles, Manchester M30 7LJ. *061-962 4623*
Eastern Counties League: M. E. Davis, Ely House, 158 Lynn Road, Wisbech, Cambs PE13 3EB. *0945-583567*
Football Combination: N. Chamberlain, 2 Vicarage Close, Old Costessey, Norwich NR8 5DL. *0603-743998*
Hellenic League: T. Cuss, 7 Blenheim Road, Kidlington, Oxford OX5 2HP. *08675-5920*
Kent League: R. Vintner, The Smithy, The Square, Chilham, Canterbury, Kent CT4 8BY
Lancashire Amateur League: R. G. Bowker, 13 Shores Green Drive, Wincham, Northwich, Cheshire CW9 6EE. *061-480 7723*
Lancashire Football League: J. W. Howarth, 465 Whalley Road, Clapton-le-Moors, Accrington, Lancs BB5 5RP. *0254-398957*
Leicestershire Senior League: P. Henwood, 450 London Road, Leicester LE2 2PP. *Leicester 704121*
London Spartan: D. Cordell, 44 Greenleas, Waltham Abbey, Essex. *Lea Valley 712428*
Manchester League: F. J. Fitzpatrick, 102 Victoria Road, Stretford, Manchester. *061-865 2726*
Midland Combination: L. W. James, 175 Barnet Lane, Kingswinford, Brierley Hill, West Midlands. *Kingswinford 3459*
Mid-Week Football League: N. A. S. Matthews, Cedar Court, Steeple Aston, Oxford. *0869-40347*

Northern Premier: R. D. Bayley, 22 Woburn Drive, Hale, Altrincham, Cheshire. *061-980 7007*
Northern Intermediate League: G. Thompson, Clegg House, 253 Pitsmoor Road, Sheffield S3 9AQ. *0742-27817*
Northern League: J. Ritchie, 17 Netherton Close, Langley Park, Co. Durham DH7 9FB. *091-373 2612*
North Midlands League: G. Thompson, 7 Wren Park Close, Ridgway, Sheffield.
Peterborough and District League: M. J. Croson, 44 Storrington Way, Werrington, Peterborough, Cambs PE4 6QP.
Vauxhall League: N. Robinson, 226 Rye Lane, Peckham SE15 4NL. *081-653 3903*
Southern Amateur League: S. J. Lucas, 23 Beaufort Close, North Weald Bassett, Epping, Essex CM16 6JZ. *037882-3932*
South-East Counties League: R. A. Bailey, 10 Highlands Road, New Barnet, Herts EN5 5AB. *081-449 5131*
Southern League: D. J. Strudwick, 11 Welland Close, Durrington, Worthing, West Sussex BN13 3NR. *0903-67788*
South Midlands League: M. Mitchell, 26 Leighton Court, Dunstable, Beds LU6 1EW. *0582-67291*
South Western League: R. Lowe, Panorama, Lamerton, Tavistock, Devon PL19 8SD. *0822-61376*
United Counties League: R. Gamble, 8 Bostock Avenue, Northampton. *0604-37766*
Wearside League: B. Robson, 12 Deneside, Howden-le-Wear, Crook, Co. Durham DL15 8JR. *0388-762034*
Western League: M. E. Washer, 126 Chessel Street, Bristol BS3 3DQ. *0272-638308*
The Welsh League: K. J. Tucker, 16 The Parade, Merthyr Tydfil, Mid Glamorgan CF47 0ET. *0685-723884*
West Midlands Regional League: K. H. Goodfellow, 11 Emsworth Grove, Kings Heath, Birmingham B14 6HY. *021-444 3056*
West Yorkshire League: W. Keyworth, 2 Hill Court Grove, Bramley, Yorks L13 2AP. *Pudsey 74465*
Northern Counties (East): B. Wood, 6 Restmore Avenue, Guiseley, Nr Leeds LS20 9DG. *0943-874558 (home); Bradford 29595 (9 a.m. to 5 p.m.)*

COUNTY FOOTBALL ASSOCIATIONS

Bedfordshire: R. G. Berridge, The Limes, 14 Bedford Road, Sandy, Beds SG19 1EL. *0767-680417*
Berks and Bucks: W. S. Gosling, 15a London Street, Faringdon, Oxon SN7 8AG. *0367-242099*
Birmingham County: M. Pennick, County FA Offices, Rayhall Lane, Great Barr, Birmingham B43 6JE. *021-357 4278*
Cambridgeshire: R. E. Rogers, 20 Aingers Road, Histon, Cambridge CB4 4JP. *022023-2803*
Cheshire: A. Collins, 50 Ash Grove, Timperley, Altrincham WA15 6JX. *061-980 4706*
Cornwall: J. M. Ryder, Penare, 16 Gloweth View, Truro, Cornwall TR1 3JZ.
Cumberland: R. Johnson, 72 Victoria Road, Workington, Cumbria CA14 2QT. *0900-3979*
Derbyshire: K. Compton, The Grandstand, Moorways Stadium, Moor Lane, Derby DE2 8FB. *0332-361422*
Devon County: C. Squirrel, 51a Wolborough Street, Newton Abbot, Devon TQ12 1JQ. *0626 332077*

Dorset County: P. Hough, 9 Parkstone Road, Poole, Dorset BH15 2NN. *0202-746244*
Durham: J. R. Walsh, 'Codeslaw', Ferens Park, Durham DH1 1JZ. *0385-48653*
East Riding County: D. R. Johnson, 52 Bethune Ave, Hull HU4 7EJ. *0482-641458*
Essex County: T. Alexander, 31 Mildmay Road, Chelmsford, Essex CM2 0DN. *0245-357727*
Gloucestershire: E. J. Marsh, 46 Douglas Road, Horfield, Bristol BS7 0JD. *0272-519435*
Guernsey: G. R. Skuse, Ar-Hyd-Y-Nos, Courtil Olivier Castel, Guernsey CI. *0481-26241*
Hampshire: R. G. Barnes, 8 Ashwood Gardens, off Winchester Road, Southampton SO9 2UA. *0703-766884*
Herefordshire: E. R. Prescott, 7 Kirkland Close, Hampton Park, Hereford HR1 1XP. *0432-51134*
Hertfordshire: E. R. Brown, 21 Hawthorn Crescent, Caddington, Luton, Beds LU1 4EQ. *082-423094*

Huntingdonshire: M. M. Armstrong, 1 Chapel End, Great Giddings, Huntingdon. Cambs PE17 5NP. *08323-262*

Isle of Man: Mrs A. Garrett, 120 Bucks Road, Douglas, IOM. *0624-6349*

Jersey: C. Tostevin, Wellesley, Greve Dazette St Clement

Kent County: K. T. Masters, 69 Maidstone Road, Chatham, Kent ME4 6DT. *0634-43824*

Lancashire: J. Kenyon, 31a Wellington St, St John's, Blackburn, Lancs BB1 8AU. *0254-64333*

Leicestershire and Rutland: R. E. Barston, Holmes Park, Dog and Gun Lane, Whetstone, Leicester LE8 3LJ. *0533-867828*

Lincolnshire: F. S. Richardson, PO Box 26, 12 Dean Road, Lincoln LN2 4DP. *0522-24917*

Liverpool County: P. Oldcorn, 23 Greenfield Road, Old Swann, Liverpool L13 3EN. *051-526 9515*

London: R. S. Ashford, 4 Aldworth Grove, London SE13 6HY. *081-690 9626*

Manchester County: F. Brocklehurst, Sports Complex, Brantingham Road, Chorlton, Manchester M21 1TG. *061-881 0299*

Middlesex County: P. J. Clayton, 30 Rowland Avenue, Kenton, Harrow, Middx HA3 9AF.

Norfolk County: R. Kiddell, 39 Beaumont Road, Costessey, Norwich NR5 0HG. *0603-742421*

Northamptonshire: B. Walden, 37 Harding Terrace, Northampton NN1 2PF. *0604-39584*

North Riding County: P. Kirby, 284 Linthorpe Road, Middlesbrough TS1 3QU. *0642-224585*

Northumberland: R. E. Maughan 3, Osborne Terrace, Jesmond, Newcastle upon Tyne NE2 1NE. *091-297 0101*

Nottinghamshire: W. T. Annable, 7 Clarendon Street, Nottingham NG1 5HS. *0602-418954*

Oxfordshire: P. J. Ladbrook, 3 Wilkins Road, Cowley, Oxford OX4 2HY. *0865-775432*

Sheffield and Hallamshire: G. Thompson, Clegg House, 5 Onslow Road, Sheffield S11 7AF. *0742-670068*

Shropshire: A. W. Brett, High Street Chambers, 10–11 High Street, Shrewsbury SY1 1SG. *0743-56066*

Somerset & Avon (South): Mrs H. Marchment, 30 North Road, Midsomer Norton, Bath BA3 2QQ. *0761-413176*

Staffordshire: G. S. Brookes, 2 Miller Street, Newcastle, Staffs ST5 1HB. *0782-622585*

Suffolk County: W. M. Steward, 2 Millfields, Haughley, Suffolk IP14 3PU. *0449-673481*

Surrey County: L. F. J. Smith, 2 Fairfield Avenue, Horley, Surrey RH6 7PD. *0293-784445*

Sussex County: D. M. Worsfold, County Office, Culver Road, Lancing, Sussex BN15 9AX. *0903-753547*

Westmorland: J. B. Fleming, 101, Burneside Road, Kendal, Cumbria LA9 4RZ. *0539-722915*

West Riding County: R. Carter, Unit 3, Low Mills Road, Wortley, Leeds LS12 4UY. *0532-310101*

Wiltshire: E. M. Parry, 44 Kennet Avenue, Swindon SN2 3LG. *0793-29036*

Worcestershire: P. Rushton, 84 Windermere Drive, Warndon, Worcester WR4 9IB. *0905-51166*

OTHER USEFUL ADDRESSES

Amateur Football Alliance: W. P. Goss, 55 Islington Park Street, London N1 1QB. *071-359 3493*

English Schools FA: C. S. Allatt, 4a Eastgate Street, Stafford ST16 2NN. *0785-51142*

Oxford University: S. Morley, The Queen's College, Oxford OX1 4AW.

Cambridge University: Dr A. J. Little, St Catherine's College, Cambridge CB2 1RL.

Army: Major T. C. Knight, Clayton Barracks, Aldershot, Hants GU11 2BG. *0252-24431 Ext 3571*

Royal Air Force: Group Capt P. W. Hilton, Ministry of Defence (Block 10) St, Georges Road, Harrogate, N. Yorks HG2 9DB. *0423-793295*

Royal Navy: Lt-Cdr J. Danks, R.N. Sports Office, H.M.S. Temeraire, Portsmouth, Hants PO1 4QS. *0705-822351 Ext 22671*

Universities Athletic Union: G. Gregory-Jones, Suite 36, London Fruit Exchange, Brushfield Street, London E1 6EU. *071-247 3066*

Central Council of Physical Recreation: General Secretary, 70 Brompton Road, London SW3 1HE. *071-584 6651*

British Olympic Association: 6 John Prince's Street, London W1M 0DH. *071-408 2029*

National Federation of Football Supporters' Clubs: Lottery Office: 1 Saville Row, Bath, Avon BA1 2QP. *0224-312247.* General Secretary: Malcolm Gamlen, 69 Fourth Avenue, Chelmsford, Essex. *0245-263305*

National Playing Fields Association: Col R. Satterthwaite, O.B.E., 25b Catherine Place, London, SW1.

The Scottish Football Commercial Managers Association: J. E. Hillier (Chairman), c/o Keith FC Promotions Office, 60 Union Street, Keith, Banffshire, Scotland.

Professional Footballers' Association: G. Taylor, 2 Oxford Court, Bishopsgate, Off Lower Mosley Street, Manchester M2 3W2. *061-236 0575*

Referees' Association: W. J. Taylor, Cross Offices, Summerhill, Kingswinford, West Midlands DY6 9JE. *0384-288386*

Women's Football Association: Miss L. Whitehead, 448/450 Hanging Ditch, The Corn Exchange, Manchester M4 3ES. *061-832 5911*

The Association of Football League Commercial Managers: G. H. Dimbleby, Secretary WBA FC, The Hawthorns, Halford Lane, West Bromwich B71 4LF.

The Association of Football Statisticians: R. J. Spiller, 22 Bretons, Basildon, Essex SS15 5BY. *0268-416020*

The Football Programme Directory: David Stacey, 'The Beeches', 66 Southend Road, Wickford, Essex SS11 8EN.

England Football Supporters Association: Publicity Officer, David Stacey, 66 Southend Road, Wickford, Essex SS11 8EN.

The Football League Executive Staffs Association: PO Box 52, Leamington Spa, Warwickshire.

The Ninety-Two Club: 104 Gilda Crescent, Whitchurch, Bristol BS14 9LD.

The Football Trust: Second Floor, Walkden House, 10 Melton Street, London NW1 2EJ. *071-388 4504*

The Football Supporters Association: PO Box 11, Liverpool L26 1XP. *051-709-2594.*

Association of Provincial Football Supporters' Clubs in London: Miss Sallyann Watson, Secretary APFSCIL. 6 Bradshaws Close, Kings Road, London SE25 4ES. *081-676 8390 (home)*

OTHER AWARDS 1990–91

FOOTBALLER OF THE YEAR

The Football Writers' Association Award for the Footballer of the Year went to Gordon Strachan of Leeds United and Scotland.

Past Winners
1947–48 Stanley Matthews (Blackpool), 1948–49 Johnny Carey (Manchester U), 1949–50 Joe Mercer (Arsenal), 1950–51 Harry Johnston (Blackpool), 1951–52 Billy Wright (Wolverhampton W), 1952–53 Nat Lofthouse (Bolton W), 1953–54 Tom Finney (Preston NE), 1954–55 Don Revie (Manchester C), 1955–56 Bert Trautmann (Manchester C), 1956–57 Tom Finney (Preston NE), 1957–58 Danny Blanchflower (Tottenham H), 1958–59 Syd Owen (Luton T), 1959–60 Bill Slater (Wolverhampton W), 1960–61 Danny Blanchflower (Tottenham H), 1961–62 Jimmy Adamson (Burnley), 1962–63 Stanley Matthews (Stoke C), 1963–64 Bobby Moore (West Ham U), 1964–65 Bobby Collins (Leeds U), 1965–66 Bobby Charlton (Manchester U), 1966–67 Jackie Charlton (Leeds U), 1967–68 George Best (Manchester U), 1968–69 Dave Mackay (Derby Co) shared with Tony Book (Manchester C), 1969–70 Billy Bremner (Leeds U), 1970–71 Frank McLintock (Arsenal), 1971–72 Gordon Banks (Stoke C), 1972–73 Pat Jennings (Tottenham H), 1973–74 Ian Callaghan (Liverpool), 1974–75 Alan Mullery (Fulham), 1975–76 Kevin Keegan (Liverpool), 1976–77 Emlyn Hughes (Liverpool), 1977–78 Kenny Burns (Nottingham F), 1978–79 Kenny Dalglish (Liverpool), 1979–80 Terry McDermott (Liverpool), 1980–81 Frans Thijssen (Ipswich T), 1981–82 Steve Perryman (Tottenham H), 1982–83 Kenny Dalglish (Liverpool), 1983–84 Ian Rush (Liverpool), 1984–85 Neville Southall (Everton), 1985–86 Gary Lineker (Everton), 1986–87 Clive Allen (Tottenham H), 1987–88 John Barnes (Liverpool), 1988–89 Steve Nicol (Liverpool), 1989–90 John Barnes (Liverpool).

THE PFA AWARDS 1991

Player of the Year: Mark Hughes (Manchester U).
Previous Winners: 1974 Norman Hunter (Leeds U); 1975 Colin Todd (Derby Co); 1976 Pat Jennings (Tottenham H); 1977 Andy Gray (Aston Villa); 1978 Peter Shilton (Nottingham F); 1979 Liam Brady (Arsenal); 1980 Terry McDermott (Liverpool); 1981 John Wark (Ipswich T); 1982 Kevin Keegan (Southampton); 1983 Kenny Dalglish (Liverpool); 1984 Ian Rush (Liverpool); 1985 Peter Reid (Everton); 1986 Gary Lineker (Everton); 1987 Clive Allen (Tottenham H); 1988 John Barnes (Liverpool); 1989 Mark Hughes (Manchester U); 1990 David Platt (Aston Villa).
Young Player of the Year: Lee Sharpe (Manchester U).
Previous Winners: 1974 Kevin Beattie (Ipswich T); 1975 Mervyn Day (West Ham U); 1976 Peter Barnes (Manchester C); 1977 Andy Gray (Aston Villa); 1978 Tony Woodcock (Nottingham F); 1979 Cyrille Regis (WBA); 1980 Glenn Hoddle (Tottenham H); 1981 Gary Shaw (Aston Villa); 1982 Steve Moran (Southampton); 1983 Ian Rush (Liverpool); 1984 Paul Walsh (Luton T); 1985 Mark Hughes (Manchester U); 1986 Tony Cottee (West Ham U); 1987 Tony Adams (Arsenal); 1988 Paul Gascoigne (Tottenham H); 1989 Paul Merson (Arsenal); 1990 Matthew Le Tissier (Southampton).
Merit Award: Tommy Hutchison.
Previous Winners: 1974 Bobby Charlton CBE, Cliff Lloyd OBE; 1975 Denis Law; 1976 George Eastham OBE; 1977 Jack Taylor OBE; 1978 Bill Shankly OBE; 1979 Tom Finney OBE; 1980 Sir Matt Busby CBE; 1981 John Trollope MBE; 1982 Joe Mercer OBE; 1983 Bob Paisley OBE; 1984 Bill Nicholson; 1985 Ron Greenwood; 1986 The 1966 England World Cup team, Sir Alf Ramsey, Harold Shepherdson; 1987 Sir Stanley Matthews; 1988 Billy Bonds MBE; 1989 Nat Lofthouse; 1990 Peter Shilton.

BARCLAYS BANK MANAGER OF THE YEAR 1990–91

George Graham of Barclays League Champions Arsenal, was named Barclays Bank Manager of the Year for the second time in three years by a panel of 30 leading football journalists and commentators. He received the Barclays trophy and a Barclays Higher Rate Deposit Account cheque for £5,000 prior to the Gunners last home match of the seasons. The presentation was made by Sir John Quinton, chairman of Barclays Bank.

It was Graham's twelfth managerial award in eight years – his eighth in the past five years since being appointed at Arsenal: the first four were at Millwall.

It is the fifth time a Scot has won the award in the past six years – Kenny Dalglish, having received the accolade in 1986, 1988 and 1990; and the ninth time a Scot has taken the top manager title in 26 years (Jock Stein in 1966 and 1967, Matt Busby in 1968 and Bill Shankly in 1973).

BARCLAYS BANK DIVISIONAL MANAGERS OF THE SEASON 1990–91

Barclays Bank Managers of the Season 1990–91 – each manager of the winning Barclays League Championship club in Divisions Two, Three and Four – received their awards at the Barclays Bank Managers Awards Luncheon at the Savoy Hotel in London.

Joe Royle (Oldham Athletic) in Division Two, John Beck (Cambridge United) and Brian Little (Darlington) each received a Silver Eagle trophy and a cheque for £1,000 from Mr Alastair Robinson, executive director of Barclays Bank.

Alex Ferguson, European Cup Winners' Cup-winning manager for a second time when Manchester United triumphed in Rotterdam, was named for a Barclays Bank Special Award – a Silver Eagle and a cheque for £1,000; and Ron Atkinson of Sheffield Wednesday, promoted to Division One and League Cup victors, was nominated for a Barclays Bank Special Award (a Silver Eagle plus a cheque for £1,000) by The football League.

BARCLAYS YOUNG EAGLE OF THE YEAR 1991

Lee Sharpe of Manchester United, whose exciting wing play helped take the Old Trafford club to their second major final, was named Barclays Young Eagle of the Year 1991 by a panel, chaired by England team manager Graham Taylor, which includes Jack Charlton, Jimmy Armfield, Ron Greenwood, Bill Nicholson, Stan Cullis, Trevor Cherry and Terry Yorath.

Nineteen-year-old Lee – named PFA Young Player of the Year by his fellow professionals in March – received a Silver Eagle trophy and a Barclays Higher Rate Deposit Account cheque for £5,000.

BARCLAYS YOUNG EAGLES AWARDS 1990–91

September	**Mark Crossley** (Nottingham Forest)
October	**David Batty** (Leeds United)
November	**Lee Sharpe** (Manchester United)
December	**Roy Keane** (Nottingham Forest)
January	**Alan Shearer** (Southampton)
February	**John Ebbrell** (Everton)
March	**Kevin Campbell** (Arsenal)

THE SCOTTISH PFA AWARDS 1990

Player of the Year: Premier Division: Paul Elliott (Celtic); First Division: Simon Stainrod (Falkirk); Second Division: Kevin Todd (Berwick R).
Previous Winners: 1978 Derek Johnstone (Rangers); 1979 Paul Hegarty (Dundee U); 1980 Davie Provan (Celtic); 1981 Sandy Clark (Airdrieonians); 1982 Mark McGhee (Aberdeen); 1983 Charlie Nicholas (Celtic); 1984 Willie Miller (Aberdeen); 1985 Jim Duffy (Morton); 1986 Richard Gough (Dundee U); 1987 Brian McClair (Celtic); 1988 Paul McStay (Celtic); 1989 Theo Snelders (Aberdeen); 1989 Jim Bett (Aberdeen).
Young Player of the Year: Eoin Jess (Aberdeen).
Previous Winners: 1978 Graeme Payne (Dundee U); 1979 Graham Stewart (Dundee U); 1980 John MacDonald (Rangers); 1981 Francis McAvennie (St Mirren); 1982 Charlie Nicholas (Celtic); 1983 Pat Nevin (Clyde); 1984 John Robertson (Hearts); 1985 Craig Levein (Hearts); 1986 Craig Levein (Hearts); 1987 Robert Fleck (Rangers); 1988 John Collins (Hibernian); 1989 Bill McKinlay (Dundee U); 1990 Scott Crabbe (Hearts).

SCOTTISH FOOTBALL WRITERS' ASSOCIATION

Player of the Year 1991 – Maurice Malpas (Dundee U)

1965 **Billy McNeill** (Celtic)	1972 **Dave Smith** (Rangers)
1966 **John Greig** (Rangers)	1973 **George Connelly** (Celtic)
1967 **Ronnie Simpson** (Celtic)	1974 **Scotland's World Cup Squad**
1968 **Gordon Wallace** (Raith R)	1975 **Sandy Jardine** (Rangers)
1969 **Bobby Murdoch** (Celtic)	1976 **John Greig** (Rangers)
1970 **Pat Stanton** (Hibernian)	1977 **Danny McGrain** (Celtic)
1971 **Martin Buchan** (Aberdeen)	1978 **Derek Johnstone** (Rangers)

1979 **Andy Ritchie** (Morton)
1980 **Gordon Strachan** (Aberdeen)
1981 **Alan Rough** (Partick Th)
1982 **Paul Sturrock** (Dundee U)
1983 **Charlie Nicholas** (Celtic)
1984 **Willie Miller** (Aberdeen)

1985 **Hamish McAlpine** (Dundee U)
1986 **Sandy Jardine** (Hearts)
1987 **Brian McClair** (Celtic)
1988 **Paul McStay** (Celtic)
1989 **Richard Gough** (Rangers)
1990 **Alex McLeish** (Aberdeen)

EUROPEAN FOOTBALLER OF THE YEAR 1990

In World Cup year, the country which provides the winner of the tournament can expect to have one of its players chosen in the poll carried out by *France Football* magazine. Thus Lothar Matthaus, captain of West Germany, became the fourth from that country to win the award following in the wake of Gerd Muller, Franz Beckenbauer and Karl-Heinz Rummenigge. Beckenbauer was the successful manager of the German team in 1990.

Past winners

1956 **Stanley Matthews** (Blackpool
1957 **Alfredo Di Stefano** (Real Madrid)
1958 **Raymond Kopa** (Real Madrid)
1959 **Alfredo Di Stefano** (Real Madrid)
1960 **Luis Suarez** (Barcelona)
1961 **Omar Sivori** (Juventus)
1962 **Josef Masopust** (Dukla Prague)
1963 **Lev Yashin** (Moscow Dynamo)
1964 **Denis Law** (Manchester United)
1965 **Eusebio** (Benfica)
1966 **Bobby Charlton** (Manchester United)
1967 **Florian Albert** (Ferencvaros)
1968 **George Best** (Manchester United)
1969 **Gianni Rivera** (AC Milan)
1970 **Gerd Muller** (Bayern Munich)
1971 **Johan Cruyff** (Ajax)
1972 **Franz Beckenbauer** (Bayern Munich)
1973 **Johan Cruyff** (Barcelona)

1974 **Johan Cruyff** (Barcelona)
1975 **Oleg Blokhin** (Dynamo Kiev)
1976 **Franz Beckenbauer** (Bayern Munich)
1977 **Allan Simonsen** (Borussia Moenchengladbach)
1978 **Kevin Keegan** (SV Hamburg)
1979 **Kevin Keegan** (SV Hamburg)
1980 **Karl-Heinz Rummenigge** (Bayern Munich)
1981 **Karl-Heinz Rummenigge** (Bayern Munich)
1982 **Paolo Rossi** (Juventus)
1983 **Michel Platini** (Juventus)
1984 **Michel Platini** (Juventus)
1985 **Michel Platini** (Juventus)
1986 **Igor Belanov** (Dynamo Kiev)
1987 **Ruud Gullit** (AC Milan)
1988 **Marco Van Basten** (AC Milan)
1989 **Marco Van Basten** (AC Milan)

BARCLAYS BANK MANAGER AWARDS 1990–91

AUGUST/SEPTEMBER
Division 1 – **Kenny Dalglish** (Liverpool); *Division 2* – **Ron Atkinson** (Sheffield Wednesday); *Division 3* – **David Webb** (Southend United); *Division 4* – **Dave Smith** (Torquay United).

OCTOBER
Division 1 – **Dr Jozef Venglos** (Aston Villa); *Division 2* – **Billy Bonds** (West Ham United); *Division 3* – **Alan Buckley** (Grimsby Town); *Division 4* – **Dave Smith** (Torquay United).

NOVEMBER
Division 1 – **Howard Wilkinson** (Leeds United); *Division 2* – **Billy Bonds** (West Ham United); *Division 3* – **Phil Neal** (Bolton Wanderers); *Division 4* – **Theo Foley** (Northampton Town).

DECEMBER
Division 1 – **Steve Coppell** (Crystal Palace); *Division 2* – **Neil Warnock** (Notts County); *Division 3* – **Phil Holder** (Brentford); *Division 4* – **Billy Bremner** (Doncaster Rovers).

JANUARY
Division 1 – **Alex Ferguson** (Manchester United); *Division 2* – **Billy Bonds** (West Ham United); *Division 3* – **John Beck** (Cambridge United); *Division 4* – **Theo Foley** (Northampton Town).

FEBRUARY
Division 1 – **George Graham** (Arsenal); *Division 2* – **Ron Atkinson** (Sheffield Wednesday); *Division 3* – **Phil Neal** (Bolton Wanderers); *Division 4* – **Brian Little** (Darlington).

MARCH
Division 1 – **Dave Bassett** (Sheffield United); *Division 2* – **Lennie Lawrence** (Charlton Athletic); **Alan Buckley** (Grimsby Town); *Division 4* – **Chris McMenemy** (Chesterfield).

APRIL
Division 1 – **Brian Clough** (Nottingham Forest); *Division 2* – **Ron Atkinson** (Sheffield Wed); *Division 3* – **John Beck** (Cambridge United); *Division 4* – **Billy Ayre** (Blackpool).

RECORDS

Major British Records

HIGHEST WINS

First-Class Match		Arbroath	36	Bon Accord	0	12 Sept 1885
		(*Scottish Cup 1st Round*)				
International Match		England	13	Ireland	0	18 Feb 1882
FA Cup		Preston NE	26	Hyde U	0	15 Oct 1887
		(*1st Round*)				
League Cup		West Ham U	10	Bury	0	25 Oct 1983
		(*2nd Round, 2nd Leg*)				
		Liverpool	10	Fulham	0	23 Sept 1986
		(*2nd Round, 1st Leg*)				

FOOTBALL LEAGUE						
Division 1	(*Home*)	WBA	12	Darwen	0	4 April 1892
		Nottingham F	12	Leicester Fosse	0	21 April 1909
	(*Away*)	Newcastle U	1	Sunderland	9	5 Dec 1908
		Cardiff C	1	Wolverhampton W	9	3 Sept 1955
Division 2	(*Home*)	Newcastle U	13	Newport Co	0	5 Oct 1946
	(*Away*)	Burslem PV	0	Sheffield U	10	10 Dec 1892
Division 3	(*Home*)	Gillingham	10	Chesterfield	0	5 Sept 1987
	(*Away*)	Halifax T	0	Fulham	8	16 Sept 1969
Division 3(S)	(*Home*)	Luton T	12	Bristol R	0	13 April 1936
	(*Away*)	Northampton T	0	Walsall	8	2 Feb 1947
Division 3(N)	(*Home*)	Stockport Co	13	Halifax T	0	6 Jan 1934
	(*Away*)	Accrington S	0	Barnsley	9	3 Feb 1934
Division 4	(*Home*)	Oldham Ath	11	Southport	0	26 Dec 1962
	(*Away*)	Crewe Alex	1	Rotherham U	8	8 Sept 1973
Aggregate Division 3(N)		Tranmere R	13	Oldham Ath	4	26 Dec 1935

SCOTTISH LEAGUE						
Premier	(*Home*)	Aberdeen	8	Motherwell	0	26 March 1979
Division	(*Away*)	Hamilton A	0	Celtic	8	5 Nov 1988
Division 1	(*Home*)	Celtic	11	Dundee	0	26 Oct 1895
	(*Away*)	Airdrieonians	1	Hibernian	11	24 Oct 1950
Division 2	(*Home*)	Airdrieonians	15	Dundee Wanderers	1	1 Dec 1894
	(*Away*)	Alloa Ath	0	Dundee	10	8 March 1947

LEAGUE CHAMPIONSHIP HAT-TRICKS

Huddersfield T	1923–24 to 1925–26
Arsenal	1932–33 to 1934–35
Liverpool	1981–82 to 1983–84

MOST GOALS FOR IN A SEASON

		Goals	Games	Season
FOOTBALL LEAGUE				
Division 1	Aston V	128	42	1930–31
Division 2	Middlesbrough	122	42	1926–27
Division 3(S)	Millwall	127	42	1927–28
Division 3(N)	Bradford C	128	42	1928–29
Division 3	QPR	111	46	1961–62
Division 4	Peterborough U	134	46	1960–61
SCOTTISH LEAGUE				
Premier Division	Dundee U	90	36	1982–83
	Celtic	90	36	1982–83
	Celtic	90	44	1986–87
Division 1	Hearts	132	34	1957–58
Division 2	Raith R	142	34	1937–38
New Division 1	Motherwell	92	39	1981–82
New Division 2	Ayr U	95	39	1987–88

FEWEST GOALS FOR IN A SEASON

	(minimum 42 games)	Goals	Games	Season
FOOTBALL LEAGUE				
Division 1	Stoke C	24	42	1984–85
Division 2	Watford	24	42	1971–72
Division 3(S)	Crystal Palace	33	42	1950–51
Division 3(N)	Crewe Alex	32	42	1923–24
Division 3	Stockport Co	27	46	1969–70
Division 4	Crewe Alex	29	46	1981–82

SCOTTISH LEAGUE	(minimum 30 games)			
Premier Division	Hamilton A	19	36	1988–89
Division 1	Stirling Alb	18	39	1980–81
	Ayr U	20	34	1966–67
Division 2	Lochgelly U	20	38	1923–24
New Division 1	Stirling Alb	18	39	1980–81
New Division 2	Berwick R	32	39	1987–88

MOST GOALS AGAINST IN A SEASON

FOOTBALL LEAGUE		Goals	Games	Season
Division 1	Blackpool	125	42	1930–31
Division 2	Darwen	141	34	1898–99
Division 3(S)	Merthyr T	135	42	1929–30
Division 3(N)	Nelson	136	42	1927–28
Division 3	Accrington S	123	46	1959–60
Division 4	Hartlepools U	109	46	1959–60

SCOTTISH LEAGUE				
Premier Division	Morton	100	36	1984–85
	Morton	100	44	1987–88
Division 1	Leith Ath	137	38	1931–32
Division 2	Edinburgh C	146	38	1931–32
New Division 1	Queen of the S	99	39	1988–89
New Division 2	Meadowbank Th	89	39	1977–78

FEWEST GOALS AGAINST IN A SEASON

FOOTBALL LEAGUE	(minimum 42 games)	Goals	Games	Season
Division 1	Liverpool	16	42	1978–79
Division 2	Manchester U	23	42	1924–25
Division 3(S)	Southampton	21	42	1921–22
Division 3(N)	Port Vale	21	46	1953–54
Division 3	Middlesbrough	30	46	1986–87
Division 4	Lincoln C	25	46	1980–81

SCOTTISH LEAGUE	(minimum 30 games)			
Premier Division	Rangers	19	36	1989–90
Division 1	Celtic	14	38	1913–14
Division 2	Morton	20	38	1966–67
New Division 1	Hibernian	24	39	1980–81
New Division 2	St Johnstone	24	39	1987–88
	Stirling Alb	24	39	1990–91

MOST POINTS IN A SEASON

FOOTBALL LEAGUE	(under old system)	Points	Games	Season
Division 1	Liverpool	68	42	1978–79
Division 2	Tottenham H	70	42	1919–20
Division 3	Aston V	70	46	1971–72
Division 3(S)	Nottingham F	70	46	1950–51
	Bristol C	70	46	1954–55
Division 3(N)	Doncaster R	72	42	1946–47
Division 4	Lincoln C	74	46	1975–76

FOOTBALL LEAGUE	(three points for a win)	Points	Games	Season
Division 1	Everton	90	42	1984–85
	Liverpool	90	40	1987–88
Division 2	Chelsea	99	46	1988–89
Division 3	Bournemouth	97	46	1986–87
Division 4	Swindon T	102	46	1985–86

SCOTTISH LEAGUE				
Premier Division	Celtic	72	44	1987–88
Division 1	Rangers	76	42	1920–21
Division 2	Morton	69	38	1966–67
New Division 1	St Mirren	62	39	1976–77
New Division 2	Forfar Ath	63	39	1983–84

FEWEST POINTS IN A SEASON

FOOTBALL LEAGUE	(minimum 34 games)	Points	Games	Season
Division 1	Stoke C	17	42	1984–85
Division 2	Doncaster R	8	34	1904–05
	Loughborough T	8	34	1899–1900
Division 3	Rochdale	21	46	1973–74
	Cambridge U	21	46	1984–85

Division 3(S)	Merthyr T	21	42	1924–25
				& 1929–30
	QPR	21	42	1925–26
Division 3(N)	Rochdale	11	40	1931–32
Division 4	Workington	19	46	1976–77

SCOTTISH LEAGUE (minimum 30 games)

Premier Division	St Johnstone	11	36	1975–76
Division 1	Stirling Alb	6	30	1954–55
Division 2	Edinburgh C	7	34	1936–37
New Division 1	Queen of the S	10	39	1988–89
New Division 2	Berwick R	16	39	1987–88
	Stranraer	16	39	1987–88

MOST WINS IN A SEASON

FOOTBALL LEAGUE		Wins	Games	Season
Division 1	Tottenham H	31	42	1960–61
Division 2	Tottenham H	32	42	1919–20
Division 3(S)	Millwall	30	42	1927–28
	Plymouth Arg	30	42	1929–30
	Cardiff C	30	42	1946–47
	Nottingham F	30	46	1950–51
	Bristol C	30	46	1954–55
Division 3(N)	Doncaster R	33	42	1946–47
Division 3	Aston Villa	32	46	1971–72
Division 4	Lincoln C	32	46	1975–76
	Swindon T	32	46	1985–86

SCOTTISH LEAGUE				
Premier Division	Aberdeen	27	36	1984–85
	Rangers	31	44	1986–87
	Celtic	31	44	1987–88
Division 1	Rangers	35	42	1920–21
Division 2	Morton	33	38	1966–67
New Division 1	Motherwell	26	39	1981–82
New Division 2	Forfar Ath	27	39	1983–84
	Ayr U	27	39	1987–88

RECORD HOME WINS IN A SEASON

Brentford won all 21 games in Division 3(S), 1929–30

UNDEFEATED AT HOME

Liverpool 85 games (63 League, 9 League Cup, 7 European, 6 FA Cup), Jan 1978–Jan 1981

RECORD AWAY WINS IN A SEASON

Doncaster R won 18 of 21 games in Division 3(N), 1946–47

FEWEST WINS IN A SEASON

FOOTBALL LEAGUE		Wins	Games	Season
Division 1	Stoke	3	22	1889–90
	Woolwich Arsenal	3	38	1912–13
	Stoke C	3	42	1984–85
Division 2	Loughborough T	1	34	1899–1900
Division 3(S)	Merthyr T	6	42	1929–30
	QPR	6	42	1925–26
Division 3(N)	Rochdale	4	40	1931–32
Division 3	Rochdale	2	46	1973–74
Division 4	Southport	3	46	1976–77

SCOTTISH LEAGUE				
Premier Division	St Johnstone	3	36	1975–76
	Kilmarnock	3	36	1982–83
Division 1	Vale of Leven	0	22	1891–92
Division 2	East Stirlingshire	1	22	1905–06
	Forfar Ath	1	38	1974–75
New Division 1	Queen of the S	2	39	1988–89
New Division 2	Forfar Ath	4	26	1975–76
	Stranraer	4	39	1987–88

MOST DEFEATS IN A SEASON

FOOTBALL LEAGUE		Defeats	Games	Season
Division 1	Stoke C	31	42	1984–85
Division 2	Tranmere R	31	42	1938–39
Division 3	Cambridge U	33	46	1984–85
Division 3(S)	Merthyr T	29	42	1924–25
	Walsall	29	46	1952–53
	Walsall	29	46	1953–54
Division 3(N)	Rochdale	33	40	1931–32
Division 4	Newport Co	33	46	1987–88
SCOTTISH LEAGUE				
Premier Division	Morton	29	36	1984–85
Division 1	St Mirren	31	42	1920–21
Division 2	Brechin C	30	36	1962–63
	Lochgelly	30	38	1923–24
New Division 1	Queen of the S	29	39	1988–89
New Division 2	Berwick R	29	39	1987–88

HAT-TRICKS

Career 34 Dixie Dean (Tranmere R, Everton, Notts Co, England)
Division 1 (one season post-war) 6 Jimmy Greaves (Chelsea), 1960–61
Three for one team one match
West, Spouncer, Hooper, Nottingham F v Leicester Fosse, Division 1, 21 April 1909
Barnes, Ambler, Davies, Wrexham v Hartlepools U, Division 4, 3 March 1962
Adcock, Stewart, White, Manchester C v Huddersfield T, Division 2, 7 Nov 1987
Loasby, Smith, Wells, Northampton T v Walsall, Division 3S, 5 Nov 1927
Bowater, Hoyland, Readman, Mansfield T v Rotherham U, Division 3N, 27 Dec 1932

FEWEST DEFEATS IN A SEASON
(Minimum 20 games)

FOOTBALL LEAGUE		Defeats	Games	Season
Division 1	Preston NE	0	22	1888–89
	Arsenal	1	38	1990–91
	Liverpool	2	40	1987–88
	Leeds U	2	42	1968–69
Division 2	Liverpool	0	28	1893–94
	Burnley	2	30	1897–98
	Bristol C	2	38	1905–06
	Leeds U	3	42	1963–64
Division 3	QPR	5	46	1966–67
	Bristol R	5	46	1989–90
Division 3(S)	Southampton	4	42	1921–22
	Plymouth Arg	4	42	1929–30
Division 3(N)	Port Vale	3	46	1953–54
	Doncaster R	3	42	1946–47
	Wolverhampton W	3	42	1923–24
Division 4	Lincoln C	4	46	1975–76
	Sheffield U	4	46	1981–82
	Bournemouth	4	46	1981–82
SCOTTISH LEAGUE				
Premier Division	Celtic	3	44	1987–88
Division 1	Rangers	1	42	1920–21
Division 2	Clyde	1	36	1956–57
	Morton	1	36	1962–63
	St Mirren	1	36	1967–68
New Division 1	Partick Th	2	26	1975–76
	St Mirren	2	39	1976–77
New Division 2	Raith R	1	26	1975–76
	Clydebank	3	26	1975–76
	Forfar Ath	3	39	1983–84
	Raith R	3	39	1986–87

MOST DRAWN GAMES IN A SEASON

FOOTBALL LEAGUE		Draws	Games	Season
Division 1	Norwich C	23	42	1978–79
Division 4	Exeter C	23	46	1986–87
SCOTTISH LEAGUE				
Premier Division	Hibernian	19	44	1987–88

MOST GOALS IN A GAME

FOOTBALL LEAGUE

Division 1	Ted Drake (Arsenal) 7 goals v Aston Villa	14 Dec 1935
	James Ross (Preston NE) 7 goals v Stoke	6 Oct 1888
Division 2	Tommy Briggs (Blackburn R) 7 goals v Bristol R	5 Feb 1955
	Neville Coleman (Stoke C) 7 goals v Lincoln C (away)	23 Feb 1957
Division 3(S)	Joe Payne (Luton T) 10 goals v Bristol R	13 April 1936
Division 3(N)	Bunny Bell (Tranmere R) 9 goals v Oldham Ath	26 Dec 1935
Division 3	Steve Earle (Fulham) 5 goals v Halifax T	16 Sept 1969
	Barrie Thomas (Scunthorpe U) 5 goals v Luton T	24 April 1965
	Keith East (Swindon T) 5 goals v Mansfield T	20 Nov 1965
	Alf Wood (Shrewsbury T) 5 goals v Blackburn R	2 Oct 1971
	Tony Caldwell (Bolton W) 5 goals v Walsall	10 Sept 1983
	Andy Jones (Port Vale) 5 goals v Newport Co	4 May 1987
	Steve Wilkinson (Mansfield T) 5 goals v Birmingham C	3 April 1990
Division 4	Bert Lister (Oldham Ath) 6 goals v Southport	26 Dec 1962
FA CUP	Ted MacDougall (Bournemouth) 9 goals v Margate (*1st Round*)	20 Nov 1971
LEAGUE CUP	Frankie Bunn (Oldham Ath) 6 goals v Scarborough	25 Oct 1989
SCOTTISH LEAGUE CUP	Jim Fraser (Ayr U) 5 goals v Dumbarton	13 Aug 1952

SCOTTISH LEAGUE

Premier Division	Paul Sturrock (Dundee U) 5 goals v Morton	17 Nov 1984
Division 1	Jimmy McGrory (Celtic) 8 goals v Dunfermline Ath	14 Sept 1928
Division 2	Owen McNally (Arthurlie) 8 goals v Armadale	1 Oct 1927
	Jim Dyet (King's Park) 8 goals v Forfar Ath	2 Jan 1930
	John Calder (Morton) 8 goals v Raith R	18 April 1936
	Norman Hayward (Raith R) 8 goals v Brechin C	20 Aug 1937
SCOTTISH CUP	John Petrie (Arbroath) 13 goals v Bon Accord (*1st Round*)	12 Sept 1885

MOST LEAGUE GOALS IN A SEASON

FOOTBALL LEAGUE

		Goals	Games	Season
Division 1	Dixie Dean (Everton)	60	39	1927–28
Division 2	George Camsell (Middlesbrough)	59	37	1926–27
Division 3(S)	Joe Payne (Luton T)	55	39	1936–37
Division 3(N)	Ted Harston (Mansfield T)	55	41	1936–37
Division 3	Derek Reeves (Southampton)	39	46	1959–60
Division 4	Terry Bly (Peterborough U)	52	46	1960–61
FA CUP	Sandy Brown (Tottenham H)	15		1900–01
LEAGUE CUP	Clive Allen (Tottenham H)	12		1986–87

SCOTTISH LEAGUE

		Goals	Games	Season
Division 1	William McFadyen (Motherwell)	52	34	1931–32
Division 2	Jim Smith (Ayr U)	66	38	1927–28

MOST LEAGUE GOALS IN A CAREER

FOOTBALL LEAGUE

		Goals	Games	Season
Arthur Rowley	WBA	4	24	1946–48
	Fulham	27	56	1948–50
	Leicester C	251	303	1950–58
	Shrewsbury T	152	236	1958–65
		434	619	

SCOTTISH LEAGUE

Jimmy McGrory	Celtic	1	3	1922–23
	Clydebank	13	30	1923–24
	Celtic	396	375	1924–38
		410	408	

MOST CUP GOALS IN A CAREER

FA CUP
Denis Law 41 (Huddersfield T, Manchester C, Manchester U)

A CENTURY OF LEAGUE AND CUP GOALS IN CONSECUTIVE SEASONS

George Camsell	Middlesbrough	59 Lge	5 Cup	1926–27
(101 goals)		33	4	1927–28
Steve Bull	Wolverhampton W	34 Lge	18 Cup	1987–88
(102 goals)		37	13	1988–89

(Camsell's cup goals were all scored in the FA Cup; Bull had 12 in the Sherpa Van Trophy, 3 Littlewoods Cup, 3 FA Cup in 1987–88; 11 Sherpa Van Trophy, 2 Littlewoods Cup in 1988–89.)

LONGEST WINNING SEQUENCE

FOOTBALL LEAGUE		Games	Season
Division 1	Everton	12	1893–94 (4) and 1894–95 (8)
Division 2	Manchester U	14	1904–05
	Bristol C	14	1905–06
	Preston NE	14	1950–51
Division 3	Reading	13	1985–86
From season's start			
Division 1	Tottenham H	11	1960–61

LONGEST SEQUENCE WITHOUT A WIN FROM SEASON'S START

Division 1	Manchester U	12	1930–31

LONGEST SEQUENCE OF CONSECUTIVE SCORING (Individual)

FOOTBALL LEAGUE RECORD		
Bill Pendergast (Chester)	15 in 12 games	1938–39

LONGEST WINNING SEQUENCE IN A SEASON

FOOTBALL LEAGUE		Games	Season
Division 1	Tottenham H	11	1960–61
Division 2	Manchester U	14	1904–05
Division 2	Bristol C	14	1905–06
Division 2	Preston NE	14	1950–51
SCOTTISH LEAGUE			
Division 2	Morton	23	1963–64

LONGEST UNBEATEN SEQUENCE

FOOTBALL LEAGUE		Games	Seasons
Division 1	Nottingham F	42	Nov 1977–Dec 1978

LONGEST UNBEATEN CUP SEQUENCE

Liverpool   25 rounds   League/Milk Cup   1980–84

LONGEST UNBEATEN SEQUENCE IN A SEASON

FOOTBALL LEAGUE		Games	Season
Division 1	Burnley	30	1920–21

LONGEST UNBEATEN START TO A SEASON

FOOTBALL LEAGUE		Games	Season
Division 1	Leeds U	29	1973–74
Division 1	Liverpool	29	1987–88

LONGEST SEQUENCE WITHOUT A WIN IN A SEASON

FOOTBALL LEAGUE		Games	Season
Division 2	Cambridge U	31	1983–84

LONGEST SEQUENCE OF CONSECUTIVE DEFEATS

FOOTBALL LEAGUE		Games	Season
Division 2	Darwen	18	1898–99

GOALKEEPING RECORDS (without conceding a goal)

British record *(all competitive games)*
Chris Woods, Rangers, in 1196 minutes from 26 November 1986 to 31 January 1987.

Football League
Steve Death, Reading, 1103 minutes from 24 March to 18 August 1979.

PENALTIES

Most in a season (individual)		*Goals*	*Season*
Division 1	Francis Lee (Manchester C)	13	1971–72
Most awarded in one game			
Five	Crystal Palace (4 – 1 scored, 3 missed) v Brighton & HA (1 scored), Div 2		1988–89
Most saved in a season			
Division 1	Paul Cooper (Ipswich T)	8 (of 10)	1979–80

MOST LEAGUE APPEARANCES

FOOTBALL LEAGUE

930 Peter Shilton (286 Leicester City, 110 Stoke City, 202 Nottingham Forest, 188 Southampton, 144 Derby County) 1966–91
824 Terry Paine (713 Southampton, 111 Hereford United) 1957–77
795 Tommy Hutchison (165 Blackpool, 314 Coventry City, 46 Manchester City, 92 Burnley 178 Swansea City, also 68 Alloa 1965–68) 1968–91
777 Alan Oakes (565 Manchester City, 211 Chester City, 1 Port Vale) 1959–84
770 John Trollope (all for Swindon Town) 1960–80†
764 Jimmy Dickinson (all for Portsmouth) 1946–65
761 Roy Sproson (all for Port Vale) 1950–72
758 Ray Clemence (48 Scunthorpe United, 470 Liverpool, 240 Tottenham Hotspur) 1966–87
757 Pat Jennings (48 Watford, 472 Tottenham Hotspur, 237 Arsenal) 1963–86
† record for one club

Consecutive
401 Harold Bell (401 Tranmere R; 459 in all games) 1946–55

FA CUP
88 Ian Callaghan (79 Liverpool, 7 Swansea C, 2 Crewe Alex)

Most Senior Matches
1271 Peter Shilton (930 League, 82 FA Cup, 93 League Cup, 125 Internationals, 13 Under-23, 4 Football League XI, 53 others including European Cup, UEFA Cup, World Club Championship, various domestic cup competitions)

MOST CUP WINNERS' MEDALS

FA CUP – 5 medals each

James Forrest (Blackburn R) 1884, 1885, 1886, 1890, 1891.
Hon. A. F. Kinnaird (Wanderers) 1873, 1877, 1878, (Old Etonians) 1879, 1882.
C. H. R. Wollaston (Wanderers) 1872, 1873, 1876, 1877, 1878.

SCOTTISH CUP – 7 medals each

Jimmy McMenemy (Celtic) 1904, 1907, 1908, 1911, 1912, 1914, (Partick Th) 1921.
Bob McPhail (Airdieonians) 1924, (Rangers) 1928, 1930, 1932, 1934, 1935, 1936.
Billy McNeill (Celtic) 1965, 1967, 1969, 1971, 1972, 1974, 1975.

MOST LEAGUE MEDALS

Phil Neal (Liverpool) 8: 1976, 1977, 1979, 1980, 1982, 1983, 1984, 1986

RECORD ATTENDANCES

Football League	83,260	Manchester U v Arsenal, Maine Road	17.1.1948
Scottish League	118,567	Rangers v Celtic, Ibrox Stadium	2.1.1939
FA Cup Final	126,047*	Bolton W v West Ham U, Wembley	28.4.1923
European Cup	135,826	Celtic v Leeds U, semi-final at Hampden Park	15.4.1970
Scottish Cup	146,433	Celtic v Aberdeen, Hampden Park	24.4.37
World Cup	199,854†	Brazil v Uruguay, Maracana, Rio	16.7.50

* It has been estimated that as many as 70,000 more broke in without paying.
† 173,830 paid.

OTHER RECORDS

YOUNGEST PLAYERS
Football League Albert Geldard, 15 years 158 days, Bradford Park Avenue v Millwall, Division 2, 16.9.29; and Ken Roberts, 15 years 158 days, Wrexham v Bradford Park Avenue, Division 3N, 1.9.51
Football League scorer
Ronnie Dix, 15 years 180 days, Bristol Rovers v Norwich City, Division 3S, 3.3.28.
Division 1
Derek Forster, 15 years 185 days, Sunderland v Leicester City, 22.8.84.
Division 1 scorer
Jason Dozzell, 16 years 57 days as substitute Ipswich Town v Coventry City, 4.2.84
Division 1 hat-tricks
Alan Shearer, 17 years 240 days, Southampton v Arsenal, 9.4.88
Jimmy Greaves, 17 years 10 months, Chelsea v Portsmouth, 25.12.57
FA Cup (any round)
Andy Awford, 15 years 88 days as substitute Worcester City v Borehamwood, 3rd Qual. rd, 10.10.87
FA Cup proper
Scott Endersby, 15 years 288 days, Kettering v Tilbury, 1st rd, 26.11.77

FA Cup Final
   Paul Allen, 17 years 256 days, West Ham United v Arsenal, 1980
FA Cup Final scorer
   Norman Whiteside, 18 years 18 days, Manchester United v Brighton & Hove Albion, 1983
FA Cup Final captain
   David Nish, 21 years 212 days, Leicester City v Manchester City, 1969
League Cup Final scorer
   Norman Whiteside, 17 years 324 days, Manchester United v Liverpool, 1983
League Cup Final captain
   Barry Venison, 20 years 7 months, 8 days, Sunderland v Norwich City, 1985

INTERNATIONALS
England
   Pre-war: James Prinsep (Clapham Rovers) 17 years 252 days, v Scotland, 5.4.1879
   Post-war; Duncan Edwards (Manchester United), 18 years 183 days, v Scotland, 2.4.55
Northern Ireland
   Norman Whiteside (Manchester United), 17 years 42 days, v Yugoslavia, 17.6.82
Scotland
   Johnny Lambie (Queen's Park), 17 years 92 days, v Ireland, 20.3.1886
Wales
   John Charles (Leeds United), 18 years 71 days, v Ireland, 8.3.50
Republic of Ireland
   Jimmy Holmes, 17 years 200 days, v Austria, 30.5.71

OLDEST PLAYERS
Football League
   Neil McBain, 52 years 4 months, New Brighton v Hartlepools United, Div 3N, 15.3.47 (McBain was New Brighton's manager and had to play in an emergency)
Division 1
   Stanley Matthews, 50 years 5 days, Stoke City v Fulham, 6.2.65
FA Cup Final
   Walter Hampson, 41 years 8 months, Newcastle United v Aston Villa, 1924
FA Cup
   Billy Meredith, 49 years 8 months, Manchester City v Newcastle United, 29.3.24
International debutant
   Leslie Compton, 38 years 2 months, England v Wales, 15.11.50
International
   Billy Meredith, 45 years 229 days, Wales v England, 15.3.20

SENDINGS-OFF

Season	242 (211 League, 19 FA Cup, 12 Milk Cup)	1982–83
Day	15 (3 League, 12 FA Cup*)	20 Nov 1982
	worst overall FA Cup total	
League	13	14 Dec 1985
FA Cup Final	Kevin Moran, Manchester U v Everton	1985
Wembley	Boris Stankovic, Yugoslavia v Sweden (Olympics)	1948
	Antonio Rattin, Argentina v England (World Cup)	1966
	Billy Bremner (Leeds U) and Kevin Keegan (Liverpool), Charity Shield	1974
	Gilbert Dresch, Luxembourg v England (World Cup)	1977
	Mike Henry, Sudbury T v Tamworth (FA Vase)	1989
Quickest	Ambrose Brown, Wrexham v Hull C (away) Div 3N: 20 secs	25 Dec 1936
Division 1	Liam O'Brien, Manchester U v Southampton (away): 85 secs	3 Jan 1987
World Cup	Jose Batista, Uruguay v Scotland, Neza, Mexico (World Cup): 55 secs	13 June 1986
Most one game	Four: Crewe Alex (2) v Bradford PA (2) Div 3N	8 Jan 1955
	Four: Sheffield U (1) v Portsmouth (3) Div 2	13 Dec 1986
	Four: Port Vale (2) v Northampton T (2) Littlewoods Cup	18 Aug 1987
	Four: Brentford (2) v Mansfield T (2) Div 3	12 Dec 1987

LAWS OF THE GAME

The Laws of the Game and Decisions of the International Board that follow are reproduced with the special permission of FIFA, and the text is the official text as published by FIFA.

LAW I

THE FIELD OF PLAY

The Field of Play and appurtenances shall be as shown in the following plan:

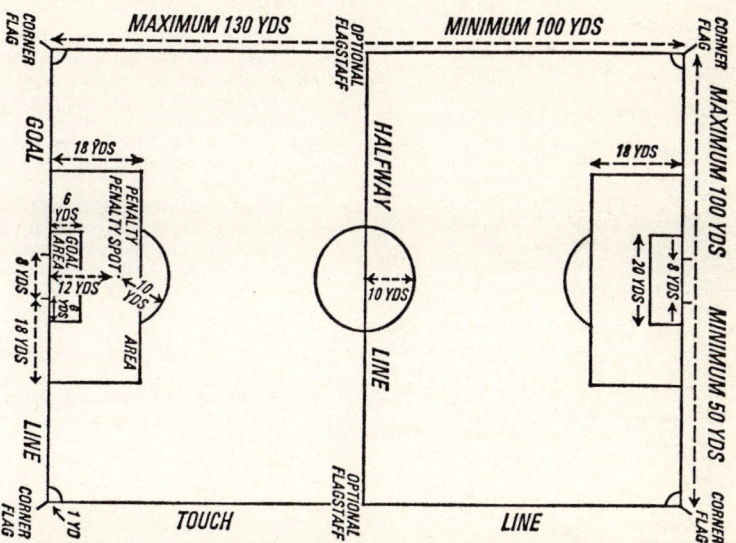

(1) **Dimensions.** The field of play shall be rectangular, its length being not more that 130 yards nor less than 100 yards, and its breadth not more than 100 yards nor less than 50 yards. (In International Matches the length shall be not more than 120 yards nor less than 110 yards and the breadth not more than 80 yards nor less than 70 yards.) The length shall in all cases exceed the breadth.

(2) **Marking.** The field of play shall be marked with distinctive lines, not more than 5 inches in width, not by a V-shaped rut, in accordance with the plan, the longer boundary lines being called the touch-lines and the shorter the goal-lines. A flag on a post not less than 5ft high and having a non-pointed top, shall be placed at each corner; a similar flag-post may be placed opposite the half-way-line on each side of the field of play, not less than 1 yard outside the touch-line. A half-way-line shall be marked out across the field of play. The centre of the field of play shall be indicated by a suitable mark and a circle with a 10 yards radius shall be marked around it.

(3) **The Goal-Area.** At each end of the field of play two lines shall be drawn at right-angles to the goal-line, 6 yards from each goal-post. These shall extend into the field of play for a distance of 6

yards and shall be joined by a line drawn parallel with the goal-line. Each of the spaces enclosed by these goal-lines and the goal-line shall be called a goal-area.

(4) **The Penalty-Area.** At each end of the field of play two lines shall be drawn at right angles to the goal-line, 18 yards from each goal-post. These shall extend into the field of play for a distance of 18 yards and shall be joined by a line drawn parallel with the goal-line. Each of the spaces enclosed by these lines and the goal-line shall be called a penalty-area. A suitable mark shall be made within each penalty area, 12 yards from the mid-point of the goal-line, measured along an undrawn line at right-angles thereto. These shall be the penalty-kick marks. From each penalty-kick mark an arc of a circle, having a radius of 10 yards, shall be drawn outside the penalty-area.

(5) **The Corner Area.** From each corner-flag post a quarter circle, having a radius of 1 yard, shall be drawn inside the field of play.

(6) **The Goals.** The goals shall be placed on the centre of each goal-line and shall consist of two upright posts, equidistant from the corner-flags and 8 yards apart (inside measurement), joined by a horizontal cross-bar the lower edge of which shall be 8ft from the ground. The width and depth

of the goal-posts and the width and depth of the cross-bars shall not exceed 5 inches (12cm). The goal-posts and the cross-bars shall have the same width.

Nets may be attached to the posts, cross-bars and ground behind the goals. They should be appropriately supported and be so placed as to allow the goal-keeper ample room.

Footnote

Goal nets. The use of nets made of hemp, jute or nylon is permitted. The nylon strings may, however, not be thinner than those made of hemp or jute.

Decisions of the International Board

---

(1) In International Matches the dimensions of the field of play shall be: maximum 110×75 metres; minimum 100×64 metres.

(2) National Associations must adhere strictly to these dimensions. Each National Association organising an International Match must advise the visiting Association, before the match, of the place and the dimensions of the field of play.

(3) The Board has approved this table of measurements for the laws of the Game:

130 yards	. . . 120 metres
120 yards	. . . 110
110 yards	. . . 100
100 yards	. . . 90
80 yards	. . . 75
70 yards	. . . 64
50 yards	. . . 45
18 yards	. . . 16.50
12 yards	. . . 11
10 yards	. . . 9.15
8 yards	. . . 7.32
6 yards	. . . 5.50
1 yard	. . . 1
8 feet	. . . 2.44
5 feet	. . . 1.50
28 inches	. . . 0.71
27 inches	. . . 0.68
9 inches	. . . 0.22
5 inches	. . . 0.12
$\frac{3}{4}$ inch	. . . 0.019
$\frac{1}{2}$ inch	. . . 0.0127
$\frac{3}{8}$ inch	. . . 0.010
14 ounces	. . . 396 grams
16 ounces	. . . 453 grams
15 lb/sq in	. . . 1 kg/cm^2

(4) The goal-line shall be marked the same width as the depth of the goal-posts and the cross-bar, so that the goal-line and goal-post will conform to the same interior and exterior edges.

(5) The 6 yards (for the outline of the goal-area) and the 18 yards (for the outline of the penalty-area) which have to be measured along the goal-line, must start from the inner sides of the goal-posts.

(6) The space within the inside areas of the field of play includes the width of the lines marking these areas.

(7) All Associations shall provide standard equipment, particularly in International Matches, when the laws of the Game must be complied with in every respect and especially with regard to the size of the ball and other equipment which must conform to the regulations. All cases of failure to provide standard equipment must be reported to FIFA.

(8) In a match played under the Rules of a Competition, if the cross-bar becomes displaced or broken, play shall be stopped and the match abandoned unless the cross-bar has been repaired and replaced in position or a new one provided without such being a danger to the players. A rope is not considered to be a satisfactory substitute for a cross-bar.

In a Friendly Match, by mutual consent, play may be resumed without the cross-bar provided it has been removed and no longer constitutes a danger to the players. In these circumstances, a rope may be used as a substitute for a cross-bar. If a rope is not used and the ball crosses the goal-line at a point which in the opinion of the Referee is below where the cross-bar should have been, he shall award a goal.

The game shall be restarted by the Referee dropping the ball at the place where it was when play was stopped.

(9) National Associations may specify such maximum and minimum dimensions for the cross-bars and goal-posts, within the limits laid down in Law I, as they consider appropriate.

(10) Goal-posts and cross-bars must be made of wood, metal or other approved material as decided from time to time by the International FA Board. They may be square, rectangular, round, half-round or elliptical in shape. Goal-posts and cross-bars made of other materials and in other shapes are not permitted. The goal-posts must be of white colour.

(11) 'Curtain-raisers' to International Matches should only be played following agreement on the day of the match, and taking into account the condition of the field of play, between representatives of the two Associations and the Referee (of the International Match).

(12) National Associations, particularly in International Matches, should
— restrict the number of photographers around the field of play.
— have a line ('photographers' line') marked behind the goal-lines at least 2 metres from the corner flag going through a point situated at least 3.5 metres behind the intersection of the goal-line with the line marking the goal area to a point situated at least 6 metres behind the goal-posts.
— prohibit photographers from passing over these lines.
— forbid the use of artificial lighting in the form of 'flashlights'.

LAW II – THE BALL

The ball shall be spherical; the outer casing shall be of leather or other approved materials. No material shall be used in its construction which might prove dangerous to the players.

The circumference of the ball shall not be more than 28in and not less than 27in. The weight of the ball at the start of the game shall not be more than 16oz nor less than 14oz. The pressure shall be equal to 0.6–1.1 atmosphere ($=600$ –1100 g/ cm^2) at sea level. The ball shall not be changed during the game unless authorised by the Referee.

Decisions of the International Board

(1) The ball used in any match shall be considered the property of the Association or Club on whose ground the match is played, and at the close of play it must be returned to the Referee.

(2) The International Board, from time to time, shall decide what constitutes approved materials. Any approved material shall be certified as such by the International Board.

(3) The Board has approved these equivalents of the weights specified in the Law: 14 to 16 ounces $=396$ to 453 grams.

(4) If the ball bursts or becomes deflated during the course of a match, the game shall be stopped and restarted by dropping the new ball at the place where the first ball became defective.

(5) If this happens during a stoppage of the game (place-kick, goal-kick, corner-kick, free-kick, penalty-kick or throw-in) the game shall be restarted accordingly.

LAW III – NUMBER OF PLAYERS

(1) A match shall be played by two teams, each consisting of not more than eleven players, one of whom shall be the goalkeeper.

(2) Substitutes may be used in any match played under the rules of an official competition under the jurisdiction of FIFA, Confederations or National Associations, subject to the following conditions:

(a) that the authority of the international association(s) or national association(s) concerned, has been obtained.

(b) that, subject to the restriction contained in the following paragraph (c), the rules of a competition shall state how many, if any, substitutes may be nominated and how many of those nominated may be used.

(c) that a team shall not be permitted to use more than two substitutes in any match, who must be chosen from not more than five players whose names may (subject to the rules of competition) be required to be given to the referee prior to the commencement of the match.

(3) Substitutes may be used in any other match, provided that the two teams concerned reach agreement on a maximum number, not exceeding five, and that the terms of such agreement are intimated to the Referee, before the match. If the Referee is not informed, or if the teams fail to reach agreement, no more than two substitutes shall be permitted. In all cases, the substitutes must be chosen from not more than five players whose names may be required to be given to the Referee prior to the commencement of the match.

(4) Any of the other players may change places with the goalkeeper, provided that the Referee is informed before the change is made, and provided also, that the change is made during a stoppage in the game.

(5) When a goalkeeper or any other player is to be replaced by a substitute, the following conditions shall be observed.

(a) the Referee shall be informed of the proposed substitution, before it is made.

(b) the substitute shall not enter the field of play until the player he is replacing has left, and then only after having received a signal from the Referee.

(c) he shall enter the field during a stoppage in the game, and at the half-way line.

(d) a player who has been replaced shall not take any further part in the game.

(e) a substitute shall be subject to the authority and jurisdiction of the Referee whether called upon to play or not.

(f) the substitution is completed when the substitute enters the field of play, from which moment he becomes a player and the player whom he is replacing ceases to be a player.

Punishment:

(a) Play shall not be stopped for an infringement of paragraph 4. The players concerned shall be cautioned immediately the ball goes out of play.

(b) If a substitute enters the field of play without the authority of the Referee, play shall be stopped. The substitute shall be cautioned or sent off according to the circumstances. The game shall be restarted by the Referee dropping the ball at the place where it was when play was stopped, unless it was within the goal-area at that time, in which case it shall be dropped on the part of the goal-area line which runs parallel to the goal-line, at the point nearest to where the ball was when play was stopped.

(c) For any other infringement of the Law, the player concerned shall be cautioned, and if the game is stopped by the Referee, to administer the caution, it shall be restarted by an indirect free-kick, to be taken by a player of the opposing team from the place where the ball was when play was stopped. If the free-kick is awarded to a team within its own goal-area, it may be taken from any point within that half of the goal-area in which the ball was when play was stopped.

(d) If a competition's rules require the names of substitutes to be given to the Referee prior to the commencement of the match, then failure to do so will mean no substitutes can be permitted.

(1) The minimum number of players in a team is left to the discretion of National Associations.

(2) The Board is of the opinion that a match should not be considered valid if there are fewer than seven players in either of the teams.

(3) A player who has been ordered off before play begins may be replaced only by one of the named substitutes. The kick-off must not be delayed to allow the substitute to join his team.

A player who has been ordered off after play has started may not be replaced.

A named substitute who has been ordered off, either before or after play has started, may not be replaced (this decision relates only to players who are ordered off under Law XII. It does not apply to players who have infringed Law IV).

(4) A player who has been replaced shall not take any further part in the game.

(5) For any offence committed on the field of play a substitute shall be subject to the same punishment as any other player whether called upon or not.

LAW IV – PLAYERS' EQUIPMENT

(1) (a) The basic compulsory equipment of a player shall consist of a jersey or shirt, shorts, stockings, shinguards and footwear.

(b) A player shall not wear anything which is dangerous to another player.

(2) Shinguards, which must be covered entirely by the stocking, shall be made of a suitable material (rubber, plastic, polyurethane or similar substance) and shall afford a reasonable degree of protection.

(3) Footwear (boots or shoes) must conform to the following standard.

(a) Bars shall be made of leather or rubber and shall be transverse and flat, not less than half an inch in width and shall extend the total width of the sole and be rounded at the corners.

(b) Studs which are independently mounted on the sole and are replaceable shall be made of leather, rubber, aluminium, plastic or similar material and shall be solid. With the exception of that part of the stud forming the base, which shall not protrude from the sole more than one quarter of an inch, studs shall be round in plan and not less than half an inch in diameter. Where studs are tapered, the minimum diameter of any section of the stud must not be less than half an inch. Where metal seating for the screw type is used, this seating must be embedded in the sole of the footwear and any attachment screw shall be part of the stud. Other than the metal seating for the screw type of stud, no metal plates even though covered with leather or rubber shall be worn, neither studs which are threaded to allow them to be screwed on to a base screw that is fixed by nails or otherwise to the soles of footwear, nor studs which, apart from the base, have any form of protruding edge rim or relief marking or ornament should be allowed.

(c) Studs which are moulded as an integral part of the sole and are not replaceable shall be made of rubber, plastic, polyurethene or similar soft materials. Provided that there are no fewer than ten studs on the sole, they shall have a minimum diameter of three-eighths of an inch (10mm). Additional supporting material to stabilise studs of soft materials, and ridges which shall not protrude more than 5mm from the sole and moulded to strengthen it, shall be permitted provided that they are in no way dangerous to other players. In all other respects they shall conform to the general requirements of this Law.

(d) Combined bars and studs may be worn, provided the whole conforms to the general requirements of this Law. Neither bars not studs on the soles or heels shall project more than three-quarters of an inch. If nails are used they shall be driven in flush with the surface.

The goalkeeper shall wear colours which distinguish him from the other players and from the Referee.

Punishment: For any infringement of this Law, the player at fault shall be sent off the field of play to adjust his equipment and he shall not return without first reporting to the Referee, who shall satisfy himself that the player's equipment is in order; the player shall only re-enter the game at a moment when the ball has ceased to be in play.

(1) In International Matches, International Competitions, International Club Competitions and friendly matches between clubs of different National Associations, the Referee, prior to the start of the game, shall inspect the players' equipment and prevent any player whose equipment does not conform to the requirements of this Law from playing until such time as it does comply. The rules of any competition may include a similar provision.

(2) If the Referee finds that a player is wearing articles not permitted by the Laws and which may constitute a danger to other players, he shall order him to take them off. If he fails to carry out the Referee's instruction, the player shall not take part in the match.

(3) A player who has been prevented from taking part in the game or a player who has been sent off the field for infringing Law IV must report to the Referee during a stoppage of the game and may not enter or re-enter the field of play unless and until the Referee has satisfied himself that the player is no longer infringing Law IV.

(4) A player who has been prevented from taking part in a game or who has been sent off because of an infringement of Law IV, and who enters or re-enters the field of play to join or rejoin his team, in breach of the conditions of Law XII(j), shall be cautioned. If the Referee stops the

game to administer the caution, the game shall be restarted by an indirect free-kick, taken by a player of the opposing side, from the place where the ball was when the Referee stopped the game. If the free-kick is awarded to a side within its own goal-area, it may be taken from any point within that half of the goal-area in which the ball was when play was stopped.

LAW V – REFEREES

A Referee shall be appointed to officiate in each game. The authority and the exercise of the powers granted to him by the Laws of the Game commence as soon as he enters the field of play.

His power of penalising shall extend to offences committed when play has been temporarily suspended, or when the ball is out of play. His decision on points of fact connected with the play shall be final, so far as the result of the game is concerned. He shall:

(a) Enforce the Laws.

(b) Refrain from penalising in cases where he is satisfied that, by doing so, he would be giving an advantage to the offending team.

(c) Keep a record of the game, act as time-keeper and allow the full or agreed time, adding thereto all time lost through accident or other cause.

(d) Have discretionary power to stop the game for any infringement of the Laws and to suspend or terminate the game whenever, by reason of the elements, interference by spectators, or other cause, he deems such stoppage necessary. In such a case he shall submit a detailed report to the competent authority, within the stipulated time, and in accordance with the provisions set up by the National Association under whose jurisdiction the match was played. Reports will be deemed to be made when received in the ordinary course of post.

(e) From the time he enters the field of play, caution any player guilty of misconduct or ungentlemanly behaviour and, if he persists, suspend him from further participation in the game. In such cases the Referee shall send the name of the offender to the competent authority, within the stipulated time, and in accordance with the provisions set up by the National Association under whose jurisdiction the match was played. Reports will be deemed to be made when received in the ordinary course of post.

(f) Allow no person other than the players and linesmen to enter the field of play without his permission.

(g) Stop the game if, in his opinion, a player has been seriously injured, have the player removed as soon as possible from the field of play, and immediately resume the game. If a player is slightly injured, the game shall not be stopped until the ball has ceased to be in play. A player who is able to go to the touch or goal-line for attention of any kind, shall not be treated on the field of play.

(h) Send off the field of play, any player who, in his opinion, is guilty of violent conduct, serious foul play, or the use of foul or abusive language.

(i) Signal for recommencement of the game after all stoppages.

(j) Decide that the ball provided for a match meets with the requirement of Law II.

Decisions of the International Board

(1) Referees in International Matches shall wear a blazer or blouse the colour of which is distinct from the colours worn by the contesting teams.

(2) Referees for International Matches will be selected from a neutral country unless the countries concerned agree to appoint their own officials.

(3) The Referee must be chosen from the official list of International Referees. This need not apply to Amateur and Youth International Matches.

(4) The Referee shall report to the appropriate authority misconduct or any misdemeanour on the part of spectators, officials, players, named substitutes or other persons which take place either on the field of play or in its vicinity at any time prior to, during, or after the match in question so that appropriate action can be taken by the authority concerned.

(5) Linesmen are assistants of the Referee. In no case shall the Referee consider the intervention of a Linesman if he himself has seen the incident and from his position on the field, is better able to judge. With this reserve, and the Linesman neutral, the Referee can consider the intervention and if the information of the Linesman applies to that phase of the game immediately before the scoring of a goal, the Referee may act thereon and cancel the goal.

(6) The Referee, however, can only reverse his first decision so long as the game has not been restarted.

(7) If the Referee has decided to apply the advantage clause and to let the game proceed, he cannot revoke his decision if the presumed advantage has not been realised, even though he has not, by any gesture, indicated his decision. This does not exempt the offending player from being dealt with by the Referee.

(8) The Laws of the Game are intended to provide that games should be played with as little interference as possible, and in this view it is the duty of Referees to penalise only deliberate breaches of the Law. Constant whistling for trifling and doubtful breaches produces bad feeling and loss of temper on the part of the players and spoils the pleasure of spectators.

(9) By para. (d) of Law V the Referee is empowered to terminate a match in the event of grave disorder, but he has no power or right to decide, in such event, that either team is disqualified and thereby the loser of the match. He must send a detailed report to the proper

968

authority who alone has power to deal further with the matter.

(10) If a player commits two infringements of a different nature at the same time, the Referee shall punish the more serious offence.

(11) It is the duty of the Referee to act upon the information of neutral Linesmen with regard to incidents that do not come under the personal notice of the Referee.

(12) The Referee shall not allow any person to enter the field until play has stopped, and only then, if he has given him a signal to do so, nor shall he allow coaching from the boundary lines.

LAW VI – LINESMEN

Two Linesmen shall be appointed, whose duty (subject to the decision of the Referee) shall be to indicate when the ball is out of play, which side is entitled to the corner-kick, goal-kick or throw-in, and when a substitute is desired. They shall also assist the Referee to control the game in accordance with the Laws. In the event of undue interference or improper conduct by a Linesman, the Referee shall dispense with his services and arrange a substitute to be appointed. (The matter shall be reported by the Referee to the competent authority.) The Linesmen should be equipped with flags by the Club on whose ground the match is played.

LAW VII – DURATION OF THE GAME

The duration of the game shall be two equal periods of 45 minutes, unless otherwise mutually agreed upon, subject to the following: (a) Allowance shall be made in either period for all time lost through substitution, the transport from the field of injured players, time-wasting or other cause, the amount of which shall be a matter for the discretion of the Referee; (b) Time shall be extended to permit a penalty-kick being taken at or after the expiration of the normal period in either half.

At half-time the interval shall not exceed five minutes except by consent of the Referee.

LAW VIII – THE START OF PLAY

(a) **At the beginning of the game,** choice of ends and the kick-off shall be decided by the toss of a coin. The team winning the toss shall have the option of choice of ends or the kick-off. The Referee having given a signal, the game shall be started by a player taking a place-kick (i.e. a kick at the ball while it is stationary on the ground in the centre of the field of play) into his opponents' half of the field of play. Every player shall be in his own half of the field and every player of the team opposing that of the kicker shall remain not less than 10 yards from the ball until it is kicked-off; it shall not be deemed in play until it has travelled the distance of its own circumference. The kicker shall not play the ball a second time until it has been touched or played by another player.

(b) **After a goal is scored,** the game shall be restarted in like manner by a player of the team losing the goal.

(c) **After half-time:** when restarting after half-time, ends shall be changed and the kick-off shall be taken by a player of the opposite team to that of the player who started the game.

Punishment: For any infringement of this Law, the kick-off shall be retaken, except in the case of the kicker playing the ball again before it has been touched or played by another player; for this offence, an indirect free-kick shall be taken by a player of the opposing team from the place where the infringement occurred, unless the offence is committed by a player in his opponents' goal-area, in which case the free-kick shall be taken from a point anywhere within that half of the goal-area in which the offence occurred. A goal shall not be scored direct from a kick-off.

(d) **After any other temporary suspension:** when restarting the game after a temporary suspension of play from any cause not mentioned elsewhere in these Laws, provided that immediately prior to the suspension the ball has not passed over the touch or goal-lines, the Referee shall drop the ball at the place where it was when play was suspended, unless it was within the goal area at that time, in which case it shall be dropped on that part of the goal area line which runs parallel to the goal-line, at the point nearest to where the ball was when play was stopped. It shall be deemed in play when it has touched the ground; if, however, it goes over the touch or goal-lines after it has been dropped by the Referee, but before it is touched by a player, the Referee shall again drop it. A player shall not play the ball until it has touched the ground. If this section of the Law is not complied with the Referee shall again drop the ball.

(1) If, when the Referee drops the ball, a player infringes any of the Laws before the ball has touched the ground, the player concerned shall be cautioned or sent off the field according to the seriousness of the offence, but a free-kick cannot be awarded to the opposing team because the ball was not in play at the time of the offence. The ball shall therefore be again dropped by the Referee.

(2) Kicking-off by persons other than the players competing in a match is prohibited.

LAW IX – BALL IN AND OUT OF PLAY

The ball is out of play:

(a) When it has wholly crossed the goal-line or touch-line, whether on the ground or in the air.

(b) When the game has been stopped by the Referee.

The ball is in play at all other times from the start of the match to the finish including:

(a) If it rebounds from a goal-post, cross-bar or corner-flag post into the field of play.

(b) If it rebounds off either the Referee or Linesmen when they are in the field of play.

(c) In the event of a supposed infringement of the Laws, until a decision is given.

Decisions of the International Board

(1) The lines belong to the area of which they are the boundaries. In consequence, the touch-lines and the goal-lines belong to the field of play.

LAW X – METHOD OF SCORING

Except as otherwise provided by these Laws, a goal is scored when the whole of the ball has passed over the goal-line, between the goal-posts and under the cross-bar, provided it has not been thrown, carried or intentionally propelled by hand or arm, by a player of the attacking side, except in the case of a goalkeeper, who is within his own penalty-area.

The team scoring the greater number of goals during a game shall be the winner; if no goals, or an equal number of goals are scored, the game shall be termed a 'draw'.

Decisions of the International Board

(1) Law X defines the only method according to which a match is won or drawn; no variation whatsoever can be authorised.

(2) A goal cannot in any case be allowed if the ball has been prevented by some outside agent from passing over the goal-line. If this happens in the normal course of play, other than at the taking of a penalty-kick, the game must be stopped and restarted where the ball came into contact with the interference.

(3) If, when the ball is going into goal, a spectator enters the field before it passes wholly over the goal-line, and tries to prevent a score, a goal shall be allowed if the ball goes into goal unless the spectator has made contact with the ball or has interfered with play, in which case the Referee shall stop the game and restart it by dropping the ball at the place where the contact or interference occurred.

LAW XI – OFF-SIDE

(1) A player is in an off-side position if he is nearer to his opponents' goal-line than the ball, unless:

(a) he is in his own half of the field of play, or

(b) he is not nearer to his opponents' goal-line than at least two of his opponents.

(2) A player shall only be declared off-side and penalised for being in an off-side position, if, at the moment the ball touches, or is played by, one of his team, he is, in the opinion of the Referee:

(a) interfering with play or with an opponent, or

(b) seeking to gain an advantage by being in that position.

(3) A player shall not be declared off-side by the referee

(a) merely because of his being in an off-side position, or

(b) if he receives the ball, direct from a goal-kick, a corner-kick or a throw-in.

(4) If a player is declared off-side, the Referee shall award an indirect free-kick, which shall be taken by a player of the opposing team from the place where the infringement occurred, unless the offence is committed by a player in his opponents' goal-area, in which case, the free-kick shall be taken from a point anywhere within that half of the goal-area in which the offence occurred.

Decisions of the International Board

(1) Off-side shall not be judged at the moment the player in question receives the ball, but at the moment when the ball is passed to him by one of his own side. A player who is not in an off-side position when one of his colleagues passes the ball to him or takes a free-kick, does not therefore become off-side if he goes forward during the flight of the ball.

(2) A player who is level with the second last opponent or with the last two opponents is not in an off-side position.

LAW XII – FOULS AND MISCONDUCT

A player who intentionally commits any of the following nine offences:

(a) Kicks or attempts to kick an opponent;

(b) Trips an opponent, i.e. throwing or

attempting to throw him by the use of the legs or by stooping in front of or behind him;

(c) Jumps at an opponent;

(d) Charges an opponent in a violent or dangerous manner;

(e) Charges an opponent from behind unless the latter be obstructing;

(f) Strikes or attempts to strike an opponent;

(g) Holds an opponent;

(h) Pushes an opponent;

(i) Handles the ball, i.e. carries, strikes or propels the ball with his hand or arm. (This does not apply to the goalkeeper within his own penalty-area);

shall be penalised by the award of a **direct free-kick** to be taken by the opposing side from the place where the offence occurred, unless the offence is committed by a player in his opponents' goal-area in which case, the free-kick shall be taken from a point anywhere within that half of the goal-area in which the offence occurred.

Should a player of the defending side intentionally commit one of the above nine offences within the penalty-area he shall be penalised by a **penalty-kick.**

A penalty-kick can be awarded irrespective of the position of the ball, if in play, at the time an offence within the penalty-area is committed.

A player committing any of the five following offences:

(1) Playing in a manner considered by the Referee to be dangerous, e.g. attempting to kick the ball while held by the goalkeeper.

(2) Charging fairly, i.e. with the shoulder, when the ball is not within playing distance of the players concerned and they are definitely not trying to play it.

(3) When not playing the ball, intentionally obstructing an opponent, i.e. running between the opponent and the ball, or interposing the body so as to form an obstacle to an opponent.

(4) Charging the goalkeeper except when he

(a) is holding the ball;

(b) is obstructing an opponent;

(c) has passed outside the goal-area.

(5) When playing as goalkeeper and within his own penalty-area

(a) from the moment he takes control of the ball with his hands, he takes more than four steps in any direction whilst holding, bouncing or throwing the ball in the air and catching it again, without releasing it into play, or, having released the ball into play before, during or after the four steps, he touches it again with his hands, before it has been touched or played by another player of the same team outside of the penalty-area or by a player of the opposing team either inside or outside of the penalty-area, or

(b) indulges in tactics which, in the opinion of the Referee, are designed merely to hold up the game and thus waste time and so give an unfair advantage to his own team—shall be penalised by the award of an **indirect free-kick** to be taken by the opposing side from the place where the

infringement occurred, unless the offence is committed by a player in his opponents' goal-area, in which case the free-kick shall be taken from a point anywhere within that half of the goal-area in which the offence occurred.

A player shall be **cautioned** if:

(j) he enters or re-enters the field of play to join or rejoin his team after the game has commenced, or leaves the field of play during the progress of the game (except through accident) without, in either case, first having received a signal from the Referee showing him that he may do so. If the Referee stops the game to administer the caution the game shall be restarted by an indirect free-kick taken by a player of the opposing team from the place where the ball was when the Referee stopped the game. If the free-kick is awarded to a side within its own goal-area it may be taken from any point within the half of the goal-area in which the ball was when play was stopped. If, however, the offending player has committed a more serious offence he shall be penalised according to that section of the law he infringed.

(k) he persistently infringes the Laws of the Game;

(l) he shows by word or action, dissent from any decision given by the Referee;

(m) he is guilty of ungentlemanly conduct.

For any of these last three offences, in addition to the caution, an **indirect free-kick** shall also be awarded to the opposing side from the place where the offence occurred unless a more serious infringement of the Laws of the Game was committed. If the offence is committed by a player in his opponents' goal-area, a free-kick shall be taken from a point anywhere within that half of the goal-area in which the offence occurred.

A player shall be **sent off** the field of play, if:

(n) in the opinion of the Referee he is guilty of violent conduct or serious foul play;

(o) he uses foul or abusive language;

(p) he persists in misconduct after having received a caution.

If play be stopped by reason of a player being ordered from the field for an offence without a separate breach of the Law having been committed, the game shall be resumed by an **indirect free-kick** awarded to the opposing side from the place where the infringement occurred, unless the offence is committed by a player in his opponents' goal-area, in which case the free-kick shall be taken from a point anywhere within that half of the goal-area in which the offence occurred.

Decisions of the International Board

If, in the opinion of the referee, a player who is moving towards his opponents' goal with an obvious opportunity to score a goal is intentionally and physically impeded by unlawful means, i.e. an offence punishable by a free-kick (or a penalty-kick), thus denying the attacking player's team the aforesaid goal-scoring opportunity, the offending player shall be sent off the field of play for serious foul play in accordance with Law XII (n).

(1) If the goalkeeper either intentionally strikes an opponent by throwing the ball vigorously at him or pushes him with the ball while holding it, the Referee shall award a penalty-kick, if the offence took place within the penalty-area.

(2) If a player deliberately turns his back to an opponent when he is about to be tackled, he may be charged but not in a dangerous manner.

(3) In case of body-contact in the goal-area between an attacking player and the opposing goalkeeper not in possession of the ball, the Referee, as sole judge of intention, shall stop the game if, in his opinion, the action of the attacking player was intentional, and award an indirect free-kick.

(4) If a player leans on the shoulders of another player of his own team in order to head the ball, the Referee shall stop the game, caution the player for ungentlemanly conduct and award an indirect free-kick to the opposing side.

(5) A player's obligation when joining or rejoining his team after the start of the match to 'report to the Referee' must be interpreted as meaning 'to draw the attention of the Referee from the touch-line'. The signal from the Referee shall be made by a definite gesture which makes the player understand that he may come into the field of play; it is not necessary for the Referee to wait until the game is stopped (this does not apply in respect of an infringement of Law IV), but the Referee is the sole judge of the moment in which he gives his signal of acknowledgement.

(6) The letter and spirit of Law XII do not oblige the Referee to stop a game to administer a caution. He may, if he chooses, apply the advantage. If he does apply the advantage, he shall caution the player when play stops.

(7) If a player covers up the ball without touching it in an endeavour not to have it played by an opponent, he obstructs but does not infringe Law XII para. 3 because he is already in possession of the ball and covers it for tactical reasons whilst the ball remains within playing distance. In fact, he is actually playing the ball and does not commit an infringement; in this case, the player may be charged because he is in fact playing the ball.

(8) If a player intentionally stretches his arms to obstruct an opponent and steps from one side to the other moving his arms up and down to delay his opponent, forcing him to change course, but does not make 'bodily contact' the Referee shall caution the player for ungentlemanly conduct and award an indirect free-kick.

(9) If a player intentionally obstructs the opposing goalkeeper, in an attempt to prevent him from putting the ball into play in accordance with Law XII, 5(a), the Referee shall award an indirect free-kick.

(10) If, after a Referee has awarded a free-kick a player protests violently by using abusive or foul language and is sent off the field, the free-kick should not be taken until the player has left the field.

(11) Any player, whether he is within or outside the field of play, whose conduct is ungentlemanly or violent, whether or not it is directed towards an opponent, a colleague, the Referee, a Linesman or other person, or who uses foul or abusive language, is guilty of an offence, and shall be dealt with according to the nature of the offence committed.

(12) If, in the opinion of the Referee a goal-keeper intentionally lies on the ball longer than is necessary, he shall be penalised for ungentlemanly conduct and

(a) be cautioned and an indirect free-kick awarded to the opposing team;

(b) in case of repetition of the offence, be sent off the field.

(13) The offence of spitting at opponents, officials or other persons, or similar unseemly behaviour shall be considered as violent conduct within the meaning of section (n) of Law XII.

(14) If, when a Referee is about to caution a player, and before he has done so, the player commits another offence which merits a caution, the player shall be sent off the field of play.

LAW XIII – FREE-KICK

Free-kicks shall be classified under two headings: 'Direct' (from which a goal can be scored direct against the offending side), and 'Indirect' (from which a goal cannot be scored unless the ball has been played or touched by a player other than the kicker before passing through the goal).

When a player is taking a direct or an indirect free-kick inside his own penalty-area, all of the opposing players shall be at least 10 yards (9.15m) from the ball and shall remain outside the penalty area until the ball has been kicked out of the area. The ball shall be in play immediately it has travelled the distance of its own circumference and is beyond the penalty-area. The goalkeeper shall not receive the ball into his hands, in order that he may thereafter kick it into play. If the ball is not kicked direct into play, beyond the penalty-area, the kick shall be retaken.

When a player is taking a direct or an indirect free-kick outside his own penalty-area, all of the opposing players shall be at least ten yards from the ball, until it is in play, unless they are standing on their own goal-line, between the goal-posts. The ball shall be in play when it has travelled the distance of its own circumference.

If a player of the opposing side encroaches into the penalty-area, or within ten yards of the ball, as the case may be, before a free-kick is taken, the Referee shall delay the taking of the kick, until the Law is complied with.

The ball must be stationary when a free-kick is taken, and the kicker shall not play the ball a second time, until it has been touched or played by another player.

Notwithstanding any other reference in these Laws to the point from which a free-kick is to be taken:

1. Any free-kick awarded to the defending team, within its own goal-area, may be taken from any point within that half of the goal-area in which the free-kick has been awarded.

2. Any indirect free-kick awarded to the attacking team within its opponents' goal-area shall be taken from that part of the goal-area line which runs parallel to the goal-line, at the point nearest to where the offence was committed.

Punishment: If the kicker, after taking the free-kick, plays the ball a second time before it has been touched or played by another player an indirect free-kick shall be taken by a player of the opposing team from the spot where the infringement occurred, unless the offence is committed by a player in his opponents' goal-area, in which case the free-kick shall be taken from a point anywhere within that half of the goal-area in which the offence occurred.

course of play, or when time has been extended at half-time or full-time to allow a penalty-kick to be taken or retaken, a goal shall not be nullified if, before passing between the posts and under the cross-bar, the ball touches either or both of the goal-posts or the cross-bar, or the goal-keeper, or any combination of these agencies, providing that no other infringement has occurred.

Punishment: For any infringement of this Law:

(a) by the defending team, the kick shall be retaken if a goal has not resulted.

(b) by the attacking team other than by the player taking the kick, if a goal is scored it shall be disallowed and the kick retaken.

(c) by the player taking the penalty-kick, committed after the ball is in play, a player of the opposing team shall take an indirect free-kick from the spot where the infringement occurred. If, in the case of paragraph (c), the offence is committed by the player in his opponents' goal-area, the free-kick shall be taken from a point anywhere within that half of the goal-area in which the offence occurred.

Decisions of the International Board

(1) In order to distinguish between a direct and indirect free-kick, the Referee, when he awards an indirect free-kick, shall indicate accordingly by raising an arm above his head. He shall keep his arm in that position until the kick has been taken and retain the signal until the ball has been played or touched by another player or goes out of play.

(2) Players who do not retire to the proper distance when a free-kick is taken must be cautioned and on any repetition be ordered off. It is particularly requested of Referees that attempts to delay the taking of a free-kick by encroaching should be treated as serious misconduct.

(3) If, when a free-kick is being taken, any of the players dance about or gesticulate in a way calculated to distract their opponents, it shall be deemed ungentlemanly conduct for which the offender(s) shall be cautioned.

LAW XIV – PENALTY-KICK

A penalty-kick shall be taken from the penalty-mark and, when it is being taken, all players with the exception of the player taking the kick, properly identified, and the opposing goalkeeper, shall be within the field of play but outside the penalty-area, and at least 10 yards from the penalty-mark. The opposing goalkeeper must stand (without moving his feet) on his own goal-line, between the goal-posts, until the ball is kicked. The player taking the kick must kick the ball forward; he shall not play the ball a second time until it has been touched or played by another player. The ball shall be deemed in play directly it is kicked, i.e. when it has travelled the distance of its circumference. A goal may be scored directly from a penalty-kick. When a penalty-kick is being taken during the normal

---

Decisions of the International Board

(1) When the Referee has awarded a penalty-kick, he shall not signal for it to be taken, until the players have taken up position in accordance with the Law.

(2) (a) If, after the kick has been taken, the ball is stopped in its course towards goal, by an outside agent, the kick shall be retaken.

(b) If, after the kick has been taken, the ball rebounds into play, from the goalkeeper, the cross-bar or a goal-post, and is then stopped in its course by an outside agent, the Referee shall stop play and restart it by dropping the ball at the place where it came into contact with the outside agent.

(3) (a) If, after having given the signal for a penalty-kick to be taken, the Referee sees that the goalkeeper is not in his right place on the goal-line, he shall, nevertheless, allow the kick to proceed. It shall be retaken, if a goal is not scored.

(b) If, after the Referee has given the signal for a penalty-kick to be taken, and before the ball has been kicked, the goalkeeper moves his feet, the Referee shall, nevertheless, allow the kick to proceed. It shall be retaken, if a goal is not scored.

(c) If, after the Referee has given the signal for a penalty-kick to be taken, and before the ball is in play, a player of the defending team encroaches into the penalty-area, or within 10 yards of the penalty-mark, the Referee shall, nevertheless, allow the kick to proceed. It shall be retaken, if a goal is not scored.

The player concerned shall be cautioned.

(4) (a) If, when a penalty-kick is being taken, the player taking the kick is guilty of ungentlemanly conduct, the kick, if already taken, shall be retaken, if a goal is scored.

The player concerned shall be cautioned.

(b) If, after the Referee has given the signal for a penalty-kick to be taken, and before the ball is in play, a colleague of the player taking the kick encroaches into the penalty-area or within ten yards of the penalty-mark, the Referee shall, nevertheless, allow the kick to proceed. If a goal is scored, it shall be disallowed, and the kick retaken.

The player concerned shall be cautioned.

(c) If, in the circumstances described in the foregoing paragraph, the ball rebounds into play from the goalkeeper, the cross-bar or a goal-post and a goal has not been scored, the Referee shall stop the game, caution the player and award an indirect free-kick to the opposing team from the place where the infringement occurred, subject to the over-riding conditions imposed in Law XIII.

(5) (a) If, after the referee has given the signal for a penalty-kick to be taken, and before the ball is in play, the goalkeeper moves from his position on the goal-line, or moves his feet, and a colleague of the kicker encroaches into the penalty-area or within 10 yards of the penalty mark, the kick, if taken, shall be retaken.

The colleague of the kicker shall be cautioned.

(b) If, after the Referee has given the signal for a penalty-kick to be taken, and before the ball is in play, a player of each team encroaches into the penalty area, or within 10 yards of the penalty-mark, the kick if taken, shall be retaken.

The players concerned shall be cautioned.

(6) When a match is extended, at half-time or full-time, to allow a penalty-kick to be taken or retaken, the extension shall last until the moment that the penalty-kick has been completed, i.e. until the Referee has decided whether or not a goal is scored, and the game shall terminate immediately the Referee has made his decision. After the player taking the penalty-kick has put the ball into play, no player other than the defending goalkeeper may play or touch the ball before the kick is completed.

A goal is scored when the ball passes wholly over the goal-line.

(a) direct from the penalty-kick.

(b) having rebounded from either goal-post or the cross-bar, or

(c) having touched or been played by the goalkeeper.

The game shall terminate immediately the Referee has made his decision.

(7) When a penalty-kick is being taken in extended time:

(a) the provisions of all of the foregoing paragraphs, except paragraphs (2)(b) and (4)(c) shall apply in the usual way, and

(b) in the circumstances described in paragraphs (2)(b) and (4)(c) the game shall terminate immediately the ball rebounds from the goalkeeper, the cross-bar or the goal-post.

LAW XV – THROW-IN

When the whole of the ball passes over a touch-line, either on the ground or in the air, it shall be thrown in from the point where it crossed the line, in any direction, by a player of the team opposite to that of the player who last touched it. The thrower at the moment of delivering the ball must face the field of play and part of each foot shall be either on the touch-line or on the ground outside the touch-line. The thrower shall use both hands and shall deliver the ball from behind and over his head. The ball shall be in play immediately it enters the field of play, but the thrower shall not again play the ball until it has been touched or played by another player. A goal shall be scored direct from a throw-in.

Punishment:

(a) If the ball is improperly thrown in, the throw-in shall be taken by a player of the opposing team.

(b) If the thrower plays the ball a second time before it has been touched or played by another player, an indirect free-kick shall be taken by a player of the opposing team from the place where the infringement occurred, unless the offence is committed by a player in his opponents' goal-area, in which case the free-kick shall be taken from a point anywhere within that half of the goal-area in which the offence occurred.

Decisions of the International Board

---

(1) If a player taking a throw-in, plays the ball a second time by handling it within the field of play before it has been touched or played by another player, the Referee shall award a direct free-kick.

(2) A player taking a throw-in must face the field of play with some part of his body.

(3) If, when a throw-in is being taken, any of the opposing players dance about or gesticulate in a way calculated to distract or impede the thrower, it shall be deemed ungentlemanly conduct for which the offender(s) shall be cautioned.

(4) A throw-in taken from any position other than the point where the ball passed over the touch-line shall be considered to have been improperly thrown.

LAW XVI – GOAL-KICK

When the whole of the ball passes over the goal-line excluding that portion between the goal-posts, either in the air or on the ground, having last been played by one of the attacking team, it shall be kicked direct into play beyond the penalty-area from a point within that half of the goal-area nearest to where it crossed the line, by a player of the defending team. A goalkeeper shall not receive the ball into his hands from a goal-kick in order that he may thereafter kick it into play. If the ball is not kicked beyond the penalty-area, i.e. direct into play, the kick shall be retaken. The kicker shall not play the ball a second time until it has touched—or been played by—another player. A goal shall not be scored direct from such a kick. Players of the team opposing that of the player taking the goal-kick shall remain outside the penalty-area whilst the kick is being taken.

Punishment: If a player taking a goal-kick plays the ball a second time after it has passed beyond the penalty-area, but before it has touched or been played by another player, an indirect free-kick shall be awarded to the opposing team, to be taken from the place where the infringement occurred, unless the offence is committed by a player in his opponents' goal-area, in which case the free-kick shall be taken from a point anywhere within that half of the goal-area in which the offence occurred.

Decisions of the International Board

(1) When a goal-kick has been taken and the player who has kicked the ball touches it again before it has left the penalty-area, the kick has not been taken in accordance with the Laws and must be retaken.

LAW XVII – CORNER-KICK

When the whole of the ball passes over the goal-line, excluding that portion between the goal-posts, either in the air or on the ground, having last been played by one of the defending team, a member of the attacking team shall take a corner-kick, i.e. the whole of the ball shall be placed within the quarter circle at the nearest corner-flag post, which must not be moved, and it shall be kicked from that position. A goal may be scored direct from such a kick. Players of the team opposing that of the player taking the corner-kick shall not approach within 10 yards of the ball until it is in play, i.e. it has travelled the distance of its own circumference, nor shall the kicker play the ball a second time until it has been touched or played by another player.

Punishment:

(a) If the player who takes the kick plays the ball a second time before it has been touched or played by another player, the Referee shall award

an indirect free-kick to the opposing team, to be taken from the place where the infringement occurred, unless the offence is committed by a player in his opponents' goal-area, in which case the free-kick shall be taken from a point anywhere within that half of the goal-area in which the offence occurred.

(b) For any other infringement the kick shall be retaken.

1991 AMENDMENTS

LAW XII – FOULS AND MISCONDUCT

Three new decisions:

Decision No (15): If, in the opinion of the referee, a player who is moving toward his opponents' goal with an obvious opportunity to score a goal is intentionally impeded by an opponent, through unlawful means, i.e. an offence punishable by a free kick (or a penalty kick), thus denying the attacking player's team the aforesaid goal-scoring opportunity, the offending player shall be sent off the field of play for serious foul play in accordance with Law XII (n).

Decision No (16): If, in the opinion of the referee, a player, other than the goalkeeper within his own penalty area, denies his opponents a goal, or an obvious goal-scoring opportunity, by intentionally handling the ball, he shall be sent off the field of play for serious foul play in accordance with Law XII (n).

Decision No (17): The International FA Board is of the opinion that a goalkeeper, in the circumstances described in Law XII 5(a), will be considered to be in control of the ball when he takes possession of the ball by touching it with any part of his hands or arms. Possession of the ball would include the goalkeeper intentionally playing the ball, but would not include circumstances where, in the opinion of the referee, the ball rebounds accidentally from the goalkeeper, for example after he has made a save.

OBITUARIES

Alderman, Albert (b. Alvaston, Derbyshire 30.10.1907; d. 6.6.1990). Perhaps better known as a cricketer (scoring 12,376 runs for Derbyshire) than a footballer, he did, nevertheless, make 21 League appearances for Derby County 1928–34 and 19 in one season with Burnley 1934–35, principally as an inside-right. Also played cricket for Berkshire and became a first-class umpire.

Boyd, Jimmy (b. Glasgow 29.4.1907; d. March 1991). A fast-moving right winger who made his name with Newcastle United helping them win the FA Cup in 1932. Joined from Edinburgh St. Bernard's in 1925 and played over 200 League and Cup games before moving to Derby County in 1935. During this period he won one Scottish cap. Noted for his accurate corners he subsequently served Bury, Dundee and Grimsby Town before retiring during the war.

Clamp, Eddie (b. Burton 13.11.22; d. Swadlincote June 1990). Not to be confused with the Wolves star this player was a goalkeeper with Derby County and Oldham Athletic between 1947 and 1949 with only one and three League appearances for each respectively. Joined Buxton 1950.

Connelly, Eddie (b. Dumbarton 9.12.1916; d. Luton 16.2.1990). A typical Scottish ball-playing inside-forward. Newcastle United signed him from Rosslyn Park in 1935, but he did not establish himself until going to Luton in 1938. West Bromwich signed him just before the outbreak of war but he was so highly regarded by Luton that they took him back in 1946. A cartilage injury cost him his place but he recovered enough to make appearances with Orient and Brighton before retiring in 1950.

Corbett, Norman (b. Falkirk 23.6.1919; d. Derbyshire June 1990). Joined West Ham United from Hearts in 1937 and after making his League debut as a winger settled at wing-half. Became a Sgt. Major PTI during the war but still managed to play fairly regularly for the Hammers. When he left Upton Park for Clapton FC in 1950 he had totalled 174 peace-time League and Cup appearances plus well over 100 war-time games.

Curry, Bill (b. Newcastle-u-Tyne 12.10.35; d. Mansfield 20 August 1990). A colourful striker who scored 184 goals in 393 League appearances. Began with Newcastle United in 1954 and won an England U-23 cap before transfer to Brighton for £12,000 in July 1959. Moved to Derby County in October 1960 and was later with Mansfield Town and Chesterfield before leaving the League in 1968 and finishing his playing career with Boston United.

Dearson, Don (b. Ynysybwl, nr. Pontypridd 13.5.1914; d. Birmingham 24.12.1990). Capped for Wales as an amateur with Barry Town before joining Birmingham City in April 1934. Gained three full Welsh caps prior to the outbreak of war and added 15 wartime international appearances. Tall and well-built he could play almost anywhere and cost Coventry City a club record £6,000 fee when they signed him in 1947. Inside-forward, wing-half or full-back he was always reliable. Finished League career with a season at Walsall 1950–51.

Friday, Robin (b. London 27.7.52; d. London December 1990). Seemed destined for an outstanding footballing career when he made his name with Reading, scoring 46 goals in 121 League appearances 1973–76. However, soon after moving to Cardiff City for a £28,000 fee he began to run into trouble on and off the field and his contract was terminated in 1978. Tragically found dead in his London flat.

Gee, Harry (b. Haydock 25.12.1894; d. Cheshire 3.10.90). A left-half who first turned professional with Burnley making five First Division appearances in 1922–23. Had four seasons with New Brighton 1923–27 and joined Exeter City in August 1927. Established a regular first-team position until a broken ankle ended his playing career in March 1928. Later became New Brighton Supporters' Club chairman.

Guy, Jimmy (b. Swansea 29.1.21; d. Gt. Yarmouth 29.11.1990). Played as an amateur for Wolves, Swansea and Norwich City before turning professional with the Canaries in August 1946. Turned out in several positions but was unable to establish a permanent place and went to Yarmouth Town 1948 after making only a dozen League appearances. Joined Gorleston 1950.

Handysides, Ian (b. Jarrow 14.12.62; d. August 1990). Made League debut with Birmingham City in January 1981. Generally recognised as a midfield player he joined Walsall three years later. Birmingham re-signed him in March 1986 when they were struggling to avoid relegation from the First Division and he extended his appearances for the Blues to a total of over 100 before ill-health forced his retirement in 1988. He died tragically at the age of only 27 following a brain tumour operation.

Kerrigan, Don (b. Seamill 7.5.41; d. December 1990). Could play in any forward position and led St Mirren's attack in the Scottish Cup Final of 1962, but generally preferred to be on the wing. Played for Johnstone Burgh, St Mirren, Aberdeen, Hearts, and Dunfermline before Fulham introduced him to the Football League in February 1968. They loaned him to Lincoln City in March 1969 but after only 16 League appearances for both clubs he returned to Scotland.

Longhurst, David (b. Northampton 15.1.65; d. York 8.9.90). Died while playing for York City against Lincoln City at Bootham Crescent, the first player to die on the field in a Football League game for 63 years. An apprentice with Nottingham Forest he made his name as a striker with Halifax Town 1985–87 and then had spells with Northampton Town and Peterborough before his transfer to York City in January 1990.

Martin, David "Boy" (b. Belfast 25.7.14, d. 9.1.1991), Irish international centre-forward (10 caps) who was signed by Wolves from Belfast Celtic in 1934. Went to Nottingham Forest for a big fee in 1936 and saved them from relegation to the Third Division by breaking the club scoring record with 31 goals (including two in the Cup). Transferred to Notts County in November 1938 and remained with them until the war. Indeed, he played a small number of war-time games up to and including 1945–46. Known as "Boy" because he had been a boy soldier in the Royal Ulster Rifles.

STAN MORTENSEN
Blackpool

Mercer OBE, Joe (b. Ellesmere Port 9.8.14; d. Merseyside August 1990). One of soccer's best loved characters who began his brilliant career as a 15-year-old with Everton and blossomed into an outstanding wing-half, making 184 peace-time League and Cup appearances (one Championship medal) before his surprise transfer to Arsenal in November 1946. Leg injuries had slowed him down but the move to Highbury rejuvenated him and he captained the Gunners to two League Championships and an FA Cup Final victory. Continued to play into his 40th year until a leg fracture ended his career in 1954 after 293 Arsenal appearances. Subsequently managed Sheffield United, Aston Villa and Manchester City. He was also general manager of Coventry City and had two spells as temporary manager of England. Five England caps plus 27 war-time and Victory games.

Moody, Ken (b. Grimsby 12.11.24; d. Sheffield 14.9.90). Signed for Grimsby Town in 1943 but first attracted attention as a powerful full-back while guesting for Arsenal in 1945. Returned to Grimsby after leaving the Services and made 114 League appearances. Joined Peterborough 1951.

Mortensen, Stanley (b. South Shields 26.5.21; d. 22.5.91), recovered from head injuries sustained in a war-time bomber crash to become one of England's most exciting forwards in the early post-war period. A great favourite with Blackpool whom he joined in 1938 and played in 320 League games, scoring 197 goals before ending his career with Hull City (1955–57) and Southport (1957–58). He returned to Blackpool as manager 1967–69. Noted for his speed and marksmanship he played in three Cup Finals including the "Matthews Final" in which he scored a hat-trick. Made international debut as substitute for Wales in a war-time game and scored four goals when playing in the first of 25 peace-time England games (24 goals).

Stevenson, George (b. Kilbirnie, Ayrshire 4.4.1905; d. May 1990). Devoted his career to Motherwell—as a player from 1923 until the war and as manager from 1946 to 1955. Made over 500 League appearances, generally as inside-left, gaining a Championship medal in 1932 and appearing in three Scottish Cup Finals. He was capped 12 times.

Continued on Page 992

BARCLAYS LEAGUE FIXTURES 1991–92

Saturday 17 August

Division One
Arsenal v QPR
Chelsea v Wimbledon
Coventry C v Manchester C
Crystal Palace v Leeds U
Liverpool v Oldham Ath
Manchester U v Notts Co
Norwich C v Sheffield U
Nottingham F v Everton
Sheffield W v Aston Villa
Southampton v Tottenham H
West Ham U v Luton T

Division Two
Blackburn R v Portsmouth
Brighton & HA v Tranmere R
Bristol R v Ipswich T
Charlton Ath v Newcastle U
Grimsby T v Cambridge U
Middlesbrough v Millwall
Plymouth Arg v Barnsley
Port Vale v Oxford U
Southend U v Bristol C
Sunderland v Derby Co
Swindon T v Leicester C
Watford v Wolverhampton W

Division Three
AFC Bournemouth v Darlington
Birmingham C v Bury
Bolton W v Huddersfield T
Bradford C v Stoke C
Brentford v Leyton O
Chester C v Fulham
Peterborough U v Preston NE
Reading v Hull C
Stockport Co v Swansea C
Torquay U v Hartlepool U
WBA v Exeter C

Division Four
Barnet v Crewe Alex
Blackpool v Walsall
Cardiff C v Lincoln C
Chesterfield v Maidstone U
Doncaster R v Carlisle U
Gillingham v Scunthorpe U
Halifax T v Northampton T
Rochdale v York C
Rotherham U v Burnley
Scarborough v Mansfield T
Wrexham v Hereford U

Sunday 18 August
Division Three
Shrewsbury T v Wigan Ath (1.00)

Tuesday 20 August
Division One
Everton v Arsenal
Leeds U v Nottingham F (7.45)
Notts Co v Southampton (7.45)
Sheffield U v West Ham U (7.45)
Wimbledon v Sheffield W (7.45)

Division Two
Barnsley v Sunderland (7.45)
Bristol C v Brighton & HA (7.45)
Ipswich T v Port Vale (7.45)

Wednesday 21 August
Division One
Aston Villa v Manchester U
Coventry C v Luton T (7.45)
Manchester C v Liverpool (7.45)
Oldham Ath v Chelsea
QPR v Norwich C (7.45)

Division Two
Derby Co v Middlesbrough

Friday 23 August
Division Two
Tranmere R v Bristol R

Division Three
Wigan Ath v Chester C

Saturday 24 August
Division One
Aston Villa v Arsenal
Everton v Manchester U
Leeds U v Sheffield W
Luton T v Liverpool
Manchester C v Crystal Palace
Notts Co v Nottingham F
Oldham Ath v Norwich C
QPR v Coventry C
Sheffield U v Southampton
Tottenham H v Chelsea
Wimbledon v West Ham U

Division Two
Barnsley v Brighton & HA
Bristol C v Blackburn R
Cambridge U v Swindon T
Derby Co v Southend U
Ipswich T v Middlesbrough
Leicester C v Plymouth Arg
Millwall v Sunderland
Newcastle U v Watford
Oxford U v Grimsby T
Portsmouth v Port Vale
Wolverhampton W v Charlton Ath

Division Three
Bury v Shrewsbury T
Darlington v WBA
Exeter C v Brentford
Fulham v Birmingham C
Hartlepool U v Reading
Hull C v Peterborough U
Leyton O v Stockport Co
Preston NE v Torquay U
Stoke C v AFC Bournemouth
Swansea C v Bolton W

Division Four
Burnley v Aldershot
Carlisle U v Blackpool
Crewe Alex v Cardiff C
Hereford v Scarborough
Lincoln C v Rotherham U
Maidstone U v Halifax T
Mansfield T v Barnet
Scunthorpe U v Doncaster R
Walsall v Wrexham
York C v Gillingham

Sunday 25 August
Division Three
Huddersfield T v Bradford C (12.30)

Tuesday 27 August
Division One
Arsenal v Luton T (7.45)
Crystal Palace v Wimbledon (7.45)
Liverpool v QPR

Division Two
Middlesbrough v Newcastle U
Port Vale v Barnsley

Wednesday 28 August
Division One
Chelsea v Notts Co

Coventry C v Sheffield U (7.45)
Manchester U v Oldham Ath (8.00)
Norwich C v Manchester C (7.45)
Nottingham F v Tottenham H
Sheffield W v Everton (7.45)
Southampton v Leeds U
West Ham U v Aston Villa (7.45)

Friday 30 August
Division Three
Stockport Co v Preston NE

Division Four
Halifax T v York C
Wrexham v Northampton T

Saturday 31 August
Diviision One
Arsenal v Manchester C
Chelsea v Luton T
Coventry C v Wimbledon
Crystal Palace v Sheffield U
Liverpool v Everton
Manchester U v Leeds U
Norwich C v Tottenham H
Nottingham F v Oldham Ath
Sheffield W v QPR
Southampton v Aston Villa
West Ham U v Notts Co

Division Two
Blackburn R v Ipswich T
Brighton & HA v Wolverhampton W
Bristol R v Newcastle U
Charlton Ath v Derby Co
Grimsby T v Tranmere R
Middlesbrough v Portsmouth
Plymouth Arg v Millwall
Port Vale v Bristol C
Southend U v Leicester C
Sunderland v Oxford U
Swindon T v Barnsley
Watford v Cambridge U

Division Three
AFC Bournemouth v Hull C
Birmingham C v Darlington
Bolton W v Leyton O
Bradford C v Hartlepool U
Brentford v Huddersfield T
Chester C v Swansea C
Peterborough U v Stoke C
Reading v Bury
Shrewsbury T v Exeter C
Torquay U v Fulham
WBA v Wigan Ath

Division Four
Aldershot v Maidstone U
Barnet v Hereford U
Blackpool v Scunthorpe U
Cardiff C v Carlisle U
Chesterfield v Mansfield T
Doncaster R v Burnley
Rochdale v Lincoln C
Rotherham U v Crewe Alex
Scarborough v Walsall

Tuesday 3 September
Division One
Everton v Norwich C
Leeds U v Arsenal (7.45)
Notts Co v Sheffield W (7.45)
Oldham Ath v Coventry C
Sheffield U v Chelsea
Wimbledon v Manchester U (7.45)

Division Two
Barnsley v Watford (7.45)

Bristol C v Bristol R (7.45)
Cambridge U v Southend U (7.45)
Ipswich T v Swindon T (7.45)
Portsmouth v Sunderland (7.45)
Tranmere R v Charlton Ath
Wolverhampton W v PortVale

Division Three
Bury v Peterborough U
Darlington v Bolton W
Fulham v WBA
Hartlepool U v Brentford
Hull C v Birmingham C
Leyton O v Bradford C (7.45)
Preston NE v AFC Bournemouth
Swansea C v Reading
Wigan Ath v Stockport Co

Division Four
Burnley v Chesterfield
Carlisle U v Rotherham U
Crewe Alex v Aldershot
Mansfield T v Wrexham
Northampton T v Doncaster R
Scunthorpe U v Scarborough
Walsall v Rochdale (7.45)
York C v Blackpool

Wednesday 4 September
Division One
Aston Villa v Crystal Palace
Luton T v Southampton (7.45)
Manchester C v Nottingham F (7.45)
QPR v West Ham U (7.45)

Division Two
Derby Co v Blackburn R (7.45)
Leicester C v Grimsby T (7.45)
Millwall v Brighton & HA (7.45)
Newcastle U v Plymouth Arg
Oxford U v Middlesbrough

Division Three
Exeter C v Torquay U
Huddersfield T v Chester C
Stoke C v Shrewsbury T
Hereford U v Gillingham
Lincoln C v Barnet (7.45)
Maidstone U v Cardiff C (8.00)

Friday 6 September
Division Three
Stockport Co v Torquay U

Division Four
Aldershot v Carlisle

Saturday 7 September
Division One
Arsenal v Coventry C
Aston Villa v Tottenham H
Everton v Crystal Palace
Leeds U v Manchester C
Manchester U v Norwich C
Notts Co v Liverpool
Oldham Ath v Sheffield U
QPR v Southampton
Sheffield W v Nottingham F
West Ham U v Chelsea
Wimbledon v Luton T

Division Two
Bristol R v Grimsby T
Derby Co v Barnsley
Ipswich T v Southend U
Leicester C v Bristol C
Millwall v Cambridge U
Plymouth Arg v Charlton Ath
Port Vale v Swindon T
Portsmouth v Brighton & HA
Sunderland v Blackburn R
Tranmere R v Newcastle U
Watford v Middlesbrough
Wolverhampton W v Oxford U

Division Three
Bolton W v WBA
Chester C v AFC Bournemouth
Darlington v Stoke C
Fulham v Swansea C
Hartlepool U v Leyton O
Huddersfield T v Exeter C
Hull C v Bury
Peterborough U v Wigan Ath
Preston NE v Bradford C
Reading v Birmingham C
Shrewsbury T v Brentford

Division Four
Burnley v Crewe Alex
Cardiff C v Rochdale
Doncaster R v Wrexham
Gillingham v Scarborough
Mansfield T v Blackpool
Northampton T v Barnet
Rotherham U v Hereford U
Scunthorpe U v Maidstone U
Walsall v Halifax T
York C v Chesterfield

Friday 13 September
Division Two
Cambridge U v Derby Co (7.45)

Division Four
Crewe Alex v Mansfield T
Halifax v Rotherham U

Saturday 14 September
Division One
Chelsea v Leeds U
Coventry C v Notts Co
Crystal Palace v Arsenal
Liverpool v Aston Villa
Luton T v Oldham Ath
Manchester C v Sheffield W
Norwich C v West Ham U
Nottingham F v Wimbledon
Sheffield U v Everton
Southampton v Manchester U
Tottenham H v QPR

Division Two
Barnsley v Ipswich T
Blackburn R v Port Vale
Brighton & HA v Watford
Bristol C v Tranmere R
Charlton Ath v Portsmouth
Grimsby T v Plymouth Arg
Middlesbrough v Leicester C
Newcastle U v Wolverhampton W
Oxford U v Millwall
Southend U v Bristol R
Swindon T v Sunderland

Division Three
AFC Bournemouth v Bolton W
Birmingham C v Peterborough U
Bradford C v Chester C
Brentford v Reading
Bury v Huddersfield T
Exeter C v Hartlepool U
Leyton O v Darlington
Stoke C v Fulham
Swansea C v Preston NE
Torquay U v Shrewsbury T
WBA v Stockport Co
Wigan Ath v Hull C

Division Four
Barnet v Doncaster R
Blackpool v Cardiff C
Carlisle U v Lincoln C
Chesterfield v Scunthorpe U
Hereford U v Burnley
Maidstone U v Walsall
Rochdale v Northampton T
Scarborough v Aldershot
Wrexham v Gillingham

Tuesday 17 September
Division One
Crystal Palace v West Ham U (7.45)
Manchester C v Everton (7.45)
Sheffield U v Notts Co

Division Two
Barnsley v Leicester C (7.45)
Blackburn R v Watford (7.45)
Bristol C v Millwall (7.45)
Cambridge U v Wolverhampton W
(7.45)
Charlton Ath v Sunderland (7.45)
Grimsby T v Portsmouth
Middlesbrough v Tranmere R
Southend U v Plymouth Arg (7.45)
Swindon v Bristol R (7.45)

Division Three
AFC Bournemouth v Shrewsbury T
(7.45)
Birmingham C v Chester C (8.00)
Bradford C v Bolton W
Brentford v Hull C (7.45)
Bury v Fulham
Leyton O v Preston NE (7.45)
Torquay U v Reading
Wigan Ath v Huddersfield T

Division Four
Barnet v Scunthorpe U (7.45)
Blackpool v Gillingham
Carlisle U v Mansfield T
Chesterfield v Walsall
Crewe Alex v Northampton T
Halifax v Cardiff C
Rochdale v Rotherham U
Wrexham v Aldershot

Wednesday 18 September
Division One
Chelsea v Aston Villa
Coventry C v Leeds U (7.45)
Luton T v QPR (7.45)
Norwich C v Sheffield W (7.45)
Southampton v Wimbledon

Division Two
Brighton & HA v Port Vale
Newcastle U v Ipswich T
Oxford U v Derby Co

Division Three
Exeter C v Stockport Co
Stoke C v Hartlepool U
WBA v Peterborough U

Division Four
Hereford U v York C
Maidstone U v Lincoln C (8.00)
Scarborough v Doncaster R

Friday 20 September
Division Four
Aldershot v Halifax T
Doncaster R v Blackpool

Saturday 21 September
Division One
Arsenal v Sheffield U
Aston Villa v Nottingham F
Everton v Coventry C
Leeds U v Liverpool
Manchester U v Luton T
Notts Co v Norwich C
Oldham Ath v Crystal Palace
QPR v Chelsea
Sheffield W v Southampton
West Ham U v Manchester C
Wimbledon v Tottenham H

Division Two
Bristol R v Oxford U
Derby C v Brighton & HA
Ipswich T v Bristol C
Leicester C v Blackburn R

Millwall v Newcastle U
Plymouth Arg v Middlesbrough
Port Vale v Southend U
Portsmouth v Cambridge U
Sunderland v Grimsby T
Tranmere R v Barnsley
Watford v Charlton Ath
Wolverhampton W v Swindon T

Division Three
Bolton W v Wigan Ath
Chester C v WBA
Darlington v Brentford
Fulham v Leyton O
Hartlepool U v Birmingham C
Huddersfield T v AFC Bournemouth
Hull C v Torquay U
Peterborough U v Exeter C
Preston NE v Stoke C
Reading v Bradford C
Shrewsbury T v Swansea C
Stockport Co v Bury

Division Three
Burnley v Rochdale
Cardiff C v Scarborough
Gillingham v Barnet
Lincoln C v Chesterfield
Northampton T v Carlisle U
Rotherham U v Maidstone U
Scunthorpe U v Crewe Alex
Walsall v Hereford U
York C v Wrexham

Friday 27 September
Division Three
AFC Bournemouth v Fulham (7.45)

Division Four
Halifax T v Mansfield T

Saturday 28 September
Division One
Chelsea v Everton
Coventry C v Aston Villa
Crystal Palace v QPR
Liverpool v Shefield W
Luton T v Notts Co
Manchester C v Oldham Ath
Norwich C v Leeds U
Nottingham F v West Ham U
Sheffield U v Wimbledon
Southampton v Arsenal
Tottenham H v Manchester U

Division Two
Barnsley v Millwall
Blackburn R v Tranmere R
Brighton & HA v Bristol R
Bristol C v Portsmouth
Charlton Ath v Port Vale
Grimsby T v Ipswich T
Middlesbrough v Sunderland
Newcastle U v Derby Co
Oxford U v Plymouth Arg
Southend U Wolverhampton W
Swindon T v Watford

Division Three
Birmingham C v Preston NE
Bradford C v Shrewsbury T
Brentford v Bolton W
Bury v Hartlepool U
Exeter C v Reading
Leyton O v Huddersfield T
Stoke C v Stockport Co
Swansea C v Peterborough U
Torquay U v Chester C
WBA v Hull C
Wigan Ath v Darlington

Division Four
Barnet v Cardiff C
Blackpool v Rotherham U
Carlisle U v Walsall
Chesterfield v Aldershot
Crewe Alex v Gillingham

Hereford U v Lincoln C
Maidstone U v York C
Rochdale v Doncaster R
Scarborough v Burnley
Wrexham v Scunthorpe U

Sunday 29 September
Division Two
Cambridge U v Leicester C

Friday 4 October
Division Two
Tranmere R v Southend U

Division Four
Aldershot v Rochdale

Saturday 5 October
Division One
Arsenal v Chelsea
Aston Villa v Luton T
Everton v Tottenham H
Leeds U v Sheffield U
Manchester U v Liverpool
Oldham Ath v Southampton
QPR v Nottingham F
Sheffield W v Crystal Palace
West Ham U v Coventry C
Wimbledon v Norwich C

Division Two
Bristol R v Middlesbrough
Derby Co v Bristol C
Ipswich T v Oxford U
Leicester C v Charlton Ath
Millwall v Blackburn R
Plymouth Arg v Swindon T
Port Vale v Cambridge U
Portsmouth v Newcastle U
Sunderland v Brighton & HA
Watford v Grimsby T
Wolverhampton W v Barnsley

Division Three
Bolton W v Torquay U
Chester C v Stoke C
Darlington v Bury
Fulham v Brentford
Hartlepool U v Wigan Ath
Huddersfield T v Swansea C
Hull C v Exeter C
Peterborough U v Leyton O
Preston NE v WBA
Reading v AFC Bournemouth
Shrewsbury T v Birmingham C
Stockport Co v Bradford C

Division Four
Burnley v Carlisle U
Cardiff C v Wrexham
Doncaster R v Crewe Alex
Gillingham v Chesterfield
Lincoln C v Halifax T
Mansfield T v Maidstone U
Northampton T v Blackpool
Scunthorpe U v Hereford U
Walsall v Barnet
York C v Scarborough

Sunday 6 October
Division One
Notts Co v Manchester C

Friday 11 October
Division Three
Wigan Ath v Reading

Division Four
Crewe Alex v Walsall

Saturday 12 October
Division Two
Barnsley v Portsmouth
Blackburn R v Plymouth Arg
Brighton & HA v Ipswich T

Bristol C v Watford
Cambridge U v Sunderland
Charlton Ath v Bristol R
Grimsby T v Port Vale
Middlesbrough v Wolverhampton W
Newcastle U v Leicester C
Oxford U v Tranmere R
Southend U v Millwall
Swindon T v Derby Co

Division Three
AFC Bournemouth v Hartlepool U
Birmingham C v Stockport Co
Bradford C v Fulham
Brentford v Peterborough U
Bury v Preston NE
Exeter C v Darlington
Leyton O v Chester C
Stoke C v Bolton W
Swansea C v Hull C
Torquay U v Huddersfield T
WBA v Shrewsbury T

Division Four
Barnet v York C
Carlisle U v Scunthorpe U
Chesterfield v Rotherham U
Halifax T v Gillingham
Hereford U v Aldershot
Maidstone U v Doncaster R
Rochdale v Mansfield T
Scarborough v Northampton T
Wrexham v Burnley

Sunday 13 October
Division Four
Blackpool v Lincoln C

Tuesday 15 October
Division Four
Northampton T v Chesterfield

Friday 18 October
Division Two
Tranmere R v Cambridge U

Division Three
Stockport Co v Chester C

Division Four
Aldershot v Rotherham U

Saturday 19 October
Division One
Chelsea v Liverpool
Coventry C v Crystal Palace
Everton v Aston Villa
Luton T v Sheffield W
Manchester U v Arsenal
Notts Co v Leeds U
Oldham Ath v West Ham U
Sheffield U v Nottingham F
Southampton v Norwich C
Tottenham H v Manchester C
Wimbledon v QPR

Division Two
Barnsley v Bristol C
Bristol R v Plymouth Arg
Charlton Ath v Brighton & HA
Derby Co v Portsmouth
Grimsby T v Middlesbrough
Ipswich T v Millwall
Leicester C v Wolverhampton W
Newcastle U v Oxford U
Port Vale v Sunderland
Swindon T v Blackburn R
Watford v Southend U

Division Three
Birmingham C v Wigan Ath
Bolton W v Fulham
Bradford C v Torquay U
Brentford v WBA
Darlington v Shrewsbury T
Exeter C v Bury

Hartlepool U v Hull C
Leyton O v AFC Bournemouth
Preston NE v Huddersfield T
Reading v Peterborough U
Swansea C v Stoke C

Division Four
Barnet v Blackpool
Burnley v Walsall
Crewe Alex v Scarborough
Doncaster R v Gillingham
Halifax T v Chesterfield
Maidstone U v Rochdale
Mansfield T v Cardiff C
Northampton T v Scunthorpe U
Wrexham v Carlisle U
York C v Lincoln C

Tuesday 22 October
Division Two
Cambridge U v Blackburn R (7.45)
Portsmouth v Plymouth Arg (7.45)
Tranmere R v Watford
Wolverhampton W v Grimsby T

Wednesday 23 October
Division Two
Leicester C v Bristol R (7.45)
Millwall v Swindon T (7.45)
Newcastle U v Southend U
Oxford U v Charlton Ath

Friday 25 October
Division Three
Huddersfield T v Stockport Co

Division Four
Rotherham U v York C

Saturday 26 October
Division One
Arsenal v Notts Co
Aston Villa v Wimbledon
Crystal Palace v Chelsea
Leeds U v Oldham Ath
Liverpool v Coventry C
Manchester C v Sheffield U
Norwich C v Luton T
Nottingham F v Southampton
QPR v Everton
Sheffield W v Manchester U
West Ham U v Tottenham H

Division Two
Blackburn R v Grimsby T
Brighton & HA v Swindon T
Bristol C v Newcastle U
Cambridge U v Barnsley
Middlesbrough v Port Vale
Millwall v Derby Co
Oxford U v Leicester C
Plymouth Arg v Watford
Portsmouth v Ipswich T
Southend U v Charlton Ath
Sunderland v Bristol R
Wolverhampton W v Tranmere R

Division Three
AFC Bournemouth v Bradford C
Bury v Brentford
Chester C v Bolton W
Fulham v Preston NE
Hull C v Darlington
Peterborough U v Hartlepool U
Shrewsbury T v Reading
Stoke C v Leyton O
Torquay U v Swansea C
WBA v Birmingham C
Wigan Ath v Exeter C

Division Four
Blackpool v Wrexham
Cardiff C v Doncaster R
Carlisle U v Crewe Alex
Chesterfield v Hereford U
Gillingham v Northampton T

Lincoln C v Burnley
Rochdale v Halifax
Scarborough v Barnet
Scunthorpe U v Mansfield T
Walsall v Aldershot

Tuesday 29 October
Division Two
Blackburn R v Wolverhampton W (7.45)
Charlton Ath v Ipswich T (7.45)
Grimsby T v Derby Co
Plymouth Arg v Cambridge U (7.45)
Southend U v Oxford U (7.45)
Sunderland v Tranmere R (7.45)
Swindon T v Bristol C (7.45)
Watford v Millwall

Wednesday 30 October
Division Two
Brighton & HA v Leicester C
Bristol R v Portsmouth (8.00)

Friday 1 November
Division Three
AFC Bournemouth v Stockport Co (7.45)
Wigan Ath v Swansea C

Saturday 2 November
Division One
Arsenal v West Ham U
Coventry C v Chelsea
Liverpool v Crystal Palace
Luton T v Everton
Manchester U v Sheffield U
Norwich C v Nottingham F
Notts Co v Oldham Ath
QPR v Aston Villa
Sheffield W v Tottenham H
Southampton v Manchester C
Wimbledon v Leeds U

Division Two
Blackburn R v Brighton & HA
Bristol R v Port Vale
Cambridge U v Bristol C
Derby Co v Tranmere R
Grimsby T v Charlton Ath
Leicester C v Ipswich T
Middlesbrough v Southend U
Millwall v Portsmouth
Oxford U v Barnsley
Plymouth Arg v Wolverhampton W
Sunderland v Watford
Swindon T v Newcastle U

Division Three
Birmingham C v Torquay U
Bolton W v Reading
Bradford C v Brentford
Chester C v Preston NE
Darlington v Hartlepool U
Fulham v Hull C
Leyton O v Exeter C
Shrewsbury T v Peterborough U
Stoke C v Huddersfield T
WBA v Bury

Division Four
Blackpool v Scarborough
Cardiff C v Scunthorpe U
Carlisle U v Gillingham
Halifax T v Burnley
Lincoln C v Aldershot
Maidstone U v Hereford U
Mansfield T v Doncaster R
Rochdale v Chesterfield
Rotherham U v Northampton T
Wrexham v Barnet
York C v Walsall

Tuesday 5 November
Division Two
Barnsley v Middlesbrough (7.45)
Bristol C v Plymouth Arg (7.45)

Charlton Ath v Swindon T (7.45)
Ipswich T v Sunderland (7.45)
Port Vale v Derby Co
Portsmouth v Leicester C (7.45)
Southend U v Blackburn R (7.45)
Tranmere R v Millwall
Wolverhampton W v Bristol R

Division Three
Brentford v Birmingham C (7.45)
Bury v Stoke C
Hartlepool U v WBA
Hull C v Shrewsbury T
Peterborough U v Chester C
Preston NE v Wigan Ath
Stockport Co v Bolton W
Swansea C v Leyton O

Division Four
Aldershot v Blackpool
Barnet v Carlisle U (7.45)
Burnley v York C
Crewe Alex v Maidstone U
Doncaster R v Rotherham U
Gillingham v Cardiff C (7.45)
Northampton T v Mansfield T
Scarborough v Wrexham
Scunthorpe U v Rochdale
Walsall v Lincoln C (7.45)

Wednesday 6 November
Division Two
Brighton & HA v Grimsby T
Newcastle U v Cambridge U
Watford v Oxford U (7.45)

Division Three
Exeter C v Bradford C
Huddersfield T v Fulham
Reading v Darlington (7.45)
Torquay U v AFC Bournemouth

Division Four
Hereford U v Halifax T

Friday 8 November
Division Two
Tranmere R v Plymouth Arg

Division Three
Stockport Co v Shrewsbury T
Swansea C v AFC Bournemouth

Division Four
Aldershot v Cardiff C
Doncaster R v York C

Saturday 9 November
Division Two
Barnsley v Bristol R
Brighton & HA v Middlesbrough
Bristol C v Sunderland
Charlton Ath v Blackburn R
Ipswich T v Cambridge U
Newcastle U v Grimsby T
Port Vale v Millwall
Portsmouth v Oxford U
Southend U v Swindon T
Watford v Leicester C
Wolverhampton W v Derby Co

Division Three
Brentford v Wigan Ath
Bury v Bolton W
Exeter C v Stoke C
Hartlepool U v Fulham
Huddersfield T v Birmingham C
Hull C v Chester C
Peterborough U v Bradford C
Preston NE v Darlington
Reading v WBA
Torquay U v Leyton O

Division Four
Barnet v Halifax T
Burnley v Mansfield T

Chesterfield v Blackpool
Crewe Alex v Wrexham
Gillingham v Maidstone U
Hereford U v Rochdale
Northampton T v Lincoln C
Scarborough v Carlisle U
Scunthorpe U v Rotherham U

Saturday 16 November
Division One
Aston Villa v Notts Co
Chelsea v Norwich C
Crystal Palace v Southampton
Everton v Wimbledon
Leeds U v QPR
Manchester C v Manchester U
Nottingham F v Coventry C
Oldham Ath v Arsenal
Tottenham H v Luton T
West Ham U v Liverpool

Division Two
Blackburn R v Barnsley
Bristol R v Watford
Cambridge U v Brighton & HA
Derby Co v Ipswich T
Middlesbrough v Charlton Ath
Millwall v Wolverhampton W
Oxford U v Bristol C
Plymouth Arg v Port Vale
Swindon T v Portsmouth

Sunday 17 November
Division One
Sheffield U v Sheffield W (12.00)

Friday 22 November
Division Two
Tranmere R v Swindon T

Division Three
AFC Bournemouth v Brentford (7.45)
Wigan Ath v Bury

Division Four
Halifax T v Scarborough (7.45)
Rotherham U v Walsall

Saturday 23 November
Division One
Aston Villa v Leeds U
Everton v Notts Co
Luton T v Manchester C
Manchester U v West Ham U
Norwich C v Coventry C
Nottingham F v Crystal Palace
QPR v Oldham Ath
Sheffield W v Arsenal
Southampton v Chelsea
Tottenham H v Sheffield U
Wimbledon v Liverpool

Division Two
Bristol R v Derby Co
Charlton Ath v Cambridge U
Grimsby T v Millwall
Leicester C v Port Vale
Middlesbrough v Bristol C
Newcastle U v Blackburn R
Oxford U v Brighton & HA
Plymouth Arg v Sunderland
Southend U v Barnsley
Watford v Portsmouth
Wolverhampton W v Ipswich T

Division Three
Birmingham C v Exeter C
Bolton W v Preston NE
Bradford C v Swansea C
Chester C v Reading
Darlington v Peterborough U
Fulham v Stockport Co
Leyton O v Hull C

Shrewsbury T v Hartlepool U
Stoke C v Torquay U
WBA v Huddersfield T

Division Four
Blackpool v Crewe Alex
Cardiff C v Northampton T
Carlisle U v Hereford U
Lincoln C v Scunthorpe U
Maidstone U v Burnley
Mansfield T v Gillingham
Rochdale v Barnet
Wrexham v Chesterfield
York C v Aldershot

Tuesday 26 November
Division One
Tottenham H v Crystal Palace (7.45)

Saturday 30 November
Division One
Arsenal v Tottenham H
Chelsea v Nottingham F
Coventry C v Southampton
Crystal Palace v Manchester U
Leeds U v Everton
Liverpool v Norwich C
Manchester C v Wimbledon
Notts Co v QPR
Oldham Ath v Aston Villa
Sheffield U v Luton T
West Ham U v Sheffield W

Division Two
Barnsley v Newcastle U
Blackburn R v Middlesbrough
Brighton & HA v Plymouth Arg
Bristol C v Charlton Ath
Cambridge U v Oxford U
Derby Co v Leicester C
Ipswich T v Tranmere R
Millwall v Bristol R
Port Vale v Watford
Portsmouth v Wolverhampton W
Sunderland v Southend U
Swindon T v Grimsby T

Division Three
Birmingham C v Bradford C
Brentford v Swansea C
Bury v AFC Bournemouth
Darlington v Fulham
Exeter C v Chester C
Hartlepool U v Huddersfield T
Hull C v Preston NE
Peterborough U v Torquay U
Reading v Stockport Co
Shrewsbury T v Bolton W
WBA v Stoke C
Wigan Ath v Leyton O

Division Four
Barnet v Chesterfield
Blackpool v Halifax T
Cardiff C v Rotherham U
Carlisle U v Maidstone U
Crewe Alex v Hereford U
Doncaster R v Lincoln C
Gillingham v Aldershot
Mansfield T v Walsall
Northampton T v Burnley
Scarborough v Rochdale
Scunthorpe U v York C

Friday 6 December
Division Two
Tranmere R v Portsmouth

Saturday 7 December
Division One
Aston Villa v Manchester C
Everton v West Ham U
Luton T v Leeds U
Manchester U v Coventry C
Norwich C v Crystal Palace
Nottingham F v Arsenal

QPR v Sheffield U
Sheffield W v Chelsea
Southampton v Liverpool
Tottenham H v Notts Co
Wimbledon v Oldham Ath

Division Two
Bristol R v Cambridge U
Charlton Ath v Barnsley
Grimsby T v Bristol C
Leicester C v Millwall
Middlesbrough v Swindon T
Newcastle U v Port Vale
Oxford U v Blackburn R
Plymouth Arg v Ipswich T
Southend U v Brighton & HA
Watford v Derby Co
Wolverhampton W v Sunderland

Friday 13 December
Division Two
Port Vale v Tranmere R (7.45)

Division Three
Fulham v Reading
Stockport Co v Peterborough U

Division Four
Halifax T v Wrexham

Saturday 14 December
Division One
Arsenal v Norwich C
Chelsea v Manchester U
Coventry C v Sheffield W
Leeds U v Tottenham H
Liverpool v Nottingham F
Manchester C v QPR
Notts Co v Wimbledon
Oldham Ath v Everton
Sheffield U v Aston Villa
West Ham U v Southampton

Division Two
Barnsley v Grimsby T
Blackburn R v Bristol R
Brighton & HA v Newcastle U
Bristol C v Wolverhampton W
Cambridge U v Middlesbrough
Derby Co v Plymouth Arg
Ipswich T v Watford
Millwall v Charlton Ath
Portsmouth v Southend U
Sunderland v Leicester C
Swindon T v Oxford U

Division Three
AFC Bournemouth v Birmingham C
Bolton W v Hull C
Bradford C v WBA
Chester C v Shrewsbury T
Huddersfield T v Darlington
Leyton O v Bury
Preston NE v Hartlepool U
Stoke C v Wigan Ath
Swansea C v Exter C
Torquay U v Brentford

Division Four
Aldershot v Doncaster R
Burnley v Scunthorpe U
Chesterfield v Crewe Alex
Hereford U v Mansfield T
Lincoln C v Scarborough
Maidstone U v Barnet
Rochdale v Blackpool
Rotherham U v Gillingham
Walsall v Northampton T
York C v Cardiff C

Sunday 15 December
Division One
Crystal Palace v Luton T

Wednesday 18 December
Division One
Tottenham H v Liverpool (7.45)

Friday 20 December
Division One
Luton T v Coventry C (7.45)
Southampton v Notts Co

Division Two
Port Vale v Wolverhampton W (7.45)
Swindon T v Ipswich T (7.45)

Division Three
Birmingham C v Fulham (7.45)
Peterborough U v Hull C
Reading v Hartlepool U (7.45)
Torquay U v Preston NE

Division Four
Doncaster R v Scunthorpe U
Wrexham v Walsall

Saturday 21 December
Division One
Arsenal v Everton
Chelsea v Oldham Ath
Liverpool v Manchester C
Manchester U v Aston Villa
Norwich C v QPR
Sheffield W v Wimbledon
West Ham U v Shefield U

Division Two
Blackburn R v Derby Co
Brighton & HA v Millwall
Bristol R v Bristol C
Charlton Ath v Tranmere R
Grimsby T v Leicester C
Middlesbrough v Oxford U
Plymouth Arg v Newcastle U
Southend U v Cambridge U
Sunderland v Portsmouth

Division Three
AFC Bournemouth v Stoke C
Bolton W v Swansea C
Chester C v Wigan Ath
Shrewsbury T v Bury
Stockport Co v Leyton O

Division Four
Aldershot v Burnley
Barnet v Mansfield T
Blackpool v Carlisle U
Cardiff C v Crewe Alex
Chesterfield v Northampton T
Gillingham v York C
Halifax T v Maidstone U
Rotherham U v Lincoln C
Scarborough v Hereford U

Sunday 22 December
Division One
Crystal Palace v Tottenham H
Nottingham F v Leeds U

Division Two
Watford v Barnsley

Division Three
Bradford C v Huddersfield T (12.00)
Brentford v Exeter C (11.30)
WBA v Darlington

Thursday 26 December
Division One
Aston Villa v West Ham U
Everton v Sheffield W
Leeds U v Southampton
Luton T v Arsenal (11.30)
Manchester C v Norwich C
Notts C v Chelsea
Oldham Ath v Manchester U
QPR v Liverpool
Sheffield U v Coventry C
Tottenham H v Nottingham F
Wimbledon v Crystal Palace

Division Two
Barnsley v Port Vale
Bristol C v Swindon T
Cambridge U v Plymouth Arg
Derby Co v Grimsby T
Ipswich T v Charlton Ath
Leicester C v Brighton & HA (11.30)
Millwall v Watford
Newcastle U v Middlesbrough (12.00)
Oxford U v Southend U
Portsmouth v Bristol R
Tranmere R v Sunderland
Wolverhampton W v Blackburn R

Division Three
Bury v Reading
Darlington v Birmingham C
Exeter C v Shrewsbury T
Fulham v Torquay U
Hartlepool U v Bradford C
Huddersfield T v Brentford
Hull C v AFC Bournemouth
Leyton O v Bolton W
Preston NE v Stockport Co (12.00)
Stoke C v Peterborough U
Swansea C v Chester C
Wigan Ath v WBA (12.00)

Division Four
Burnley v Rotherham U
Carlisle U v Doncaster R
Crewe Alex v Barnet
Hereford U v Wrexham
Lincoln C v Cardiff C
Maidstone U v Chesterfield
Mansfield T v Scarborough
Northampton T v Halifax T
Scunthorpe U v Gillingham
Walsall v Blackpool
York C v Rochdale

Saturday 28 December
Division One
Aston Villa v Southampton
Everton v Liverpool
Leeds U v Manchester U
Luton T v Chelsea
Manchester C v Arsenal
Notts Co v West Ham U
Oldham Ath v Nottingham F
QPR v Sheffield W
Sheffield U v Crystal Palace
Tottenham H v Norwich C
Wimbledon v Coventry C

Division Two
Barnsley v Swindon T
Bristol C v Port Vale
Derby Co v Charlton Ath
Ipswich T v Blackburn R
Leicester C v Southend U
Millwall v Plymouth Arg
Newcastle U v Bristol R
Oxford U v Sunderland
Portsmouth v Middlesbrough
Tranmere R v Grimsby T
Wolverhampton W v Brighton & HA

Division Three
Bury v Birmingham C
Darlington v AFC Bournemouth
Exeter C v WBA
Fulham v Chester C
Hartlepool U v Torquay U
Huddersfield T v Bolton W
Hull C v Reading
Leyton O v Brentford
Preston NE v Peterborough U
Stoke C v Bradford C
Swansea C v Stockport Co
Wigan Ath v Shreswbury T

Division Four
Burnley v Doncaster R
Carlisle U v Cardiff C
Crewe Alex v Rotherham U
Hereford U v Barnet

Lincoln C v Rochdale
Maidstone U v Aldershot
Mansfield T v Chesterfield
Northampton T v Wrexham
Scunthorpe U v Blackpool
Walsall v Scarborough
York C v Halifax T

Sunday 29 December
Division Two
Cambridge U v Watford

Wednesday 1 January 1992
Division One
Arsenal v Wimbledon
Chelsea v Manchester C
Coventry C v Tottenham H
Crystal Palace v Notts Co
Liverpool v Sheffield U
Manchester U v QPR
Norwich C v Aston Villa
Nottingham F v Luton T
Sheffield W v Oldham Ath
Southampton v Everton
West Ham U v Leeds U

Division Two
Blackburn R v Cambridge U
Brighton & HA v Bristol C
Bristol R v Leicester C
Charlton Ath v Oxford U
Grimsby T v Wolverhampton W
Middlesbrough v Derby Co
Plymouth Arg v Portsmouth
Port Vale v Ipswich T
Southend U v Newcastle U
Sunderland v Barnsley
Swindon T v Millwall
Watford v Tranmere R

Division Three
AFC Bournemouth v Preston NE
Birmingham C v Hull C
Bolton W v Darlington
Bradford C v Leyton O
Brentford v Hartlepool U
Chester C v Huddersfield T
Peterborough U v Bury
Reading v Swansea C
Shrewsbury T v Stoke C
Stockport Co v Wigan Ath
Torquay U v Exeter C
WBA v Fulham

Division Four
Aldershot v Crewe Alex
Barnet v Lincoln C
Blackpool v York C
Cardiff C v Maidstone U
Chesterfield v Burnley
Doncaster R v Northampton T
Gillingham v Hereford U
Rochdale v Walsall
Rotherham U v Carlisle U
Scarborough v Scunthorpe U
Wrexham v Mansfield T

Friday 3 January
Division Four
Aldershot v Scunthorpe U

Saturday 4 January
Division Three
AFC Bournemouth v Exeter C
Bolton W v Peterborough U
Bradford C v Bury
Chester C v Darlington
Fulham v Wigan Ath
Huddersfield T v Hull C
Leyton O v Shrewsbury T
Preston NE v Reading
Stockport Co v Brentford
Stoke C v Birmingham C
Swansea C v Hartlepool U
Torquay U v WBA

Division Four
Burnley v Cardiff C
Chesterfield v Carlisle U
Halifax T v Crewe Alex
Hereford U v Northampton T
Lincoln C v Gillingham
Maidstone U v Blackpool
Rochdale v Wrexham
Rotherham U v Scarborough
Walsall v Doncaster R
York V v Mansfield T

Saturday 11 January
Division One
Arsenal v Aston Villa
Chelsea v Tottenham H
Coventry C v QPR
Crystal Palace v Manchester C
Liverpool v Luton T
Manchester U v Everton
Norwich C v Oldham Ath
Nottingham F v Notts C
Sheffield W v Leeds U
Southampton v Sheffield U
West Ham U v Wimbledon

Division Two
Blackburn R v Bristol C
Brighton & HA v Barnsley
Bristol R v Tranmere R
Charlton Ath v Wolverhampton W
Grimsby T v Oxford U
Middlesbrough v Ipswich T
Plymouth Arg v Leicester C
Port Vale v Portsmouth
Southend U v Derby Co
Sunderland v Millwall
Swindon T v Cambridge U
Watford v Newcastle U

Division Three
Birmingham C v Leyton O
Brentford v Stoke C
Bury v Swansea C
Darlington v Torquay U
Exeter C v Bolton W
Hartlepool U v Chester C
Hull C v Stockport Co
Peterborough U v Fulham
Reading v Huddersfield T
Shrewsbury T v Preston NE
WBA v AFC Bournemouth
Wigan Ath v Bradford C

Division Four
Barnet v Rotherham U
Blackpool v Burnley
Cardiff C v Hereford U
Carlisle U v Rochdale
Crewe Alex v Lincoln C
Doncaster R v Halifax T
Gillingham v Walsall
Mansfield T v Aldershot
Northampton T v York C
Scarborough v Chesterfield
Wrexham v Maidstone U

Friday 17 January
Division Two
Tranmere R v Brighton & HA

Division Four
Aldershot v Barnet

Saturday 18 January
Division One
Aston Villa v Sheffield W
Everton v Nottingham F
Leeds U v Crystal Palace
Luton T v West Ham U
Manchester C v Coventry C
Notts Co v Manchester U
Oldham Ath v Liverpool
QPR v Arsenal
Shefield U v Norwich C
Tottenham H v Southampton
Wimbledon v Chelsea

Division Two
Barnsley v Plymouth Arg
Bristol C v Southend U
Cambridge U v Grimsby T
Derby Co v Sunderland
Ipswich T v Bristol R
Leicester C v Swindon T
Millwall v Middlesbrough
Newcastle U v Charlton Ath
Oxford U v Port Vale
Portsmouth v Blackburn R
Wolverhampton W v Watford

Division Three
AFC Bournemouth v Wigan Ath
Bolton W v Hartlepool U
Bradford C v Hull C
Chester C v Brentford
Fulham v Shrewsbury T
Huddersfield T v Peterborough U
Leyton O v WBA
Preston NE v Exeter C
Stockport Co v Darlington
Stoke C v Reading
Swansea C v Birmingham C
Torquay U v Bury

Division Four
Burnley v Gillingham
Chesterfield v Doncaster R
Halifax T v Scunthorpe U
Hereford U v Blackpool
Lincoln C v Wrexham
Maidstone U v Northampton T
Rochdale v Crewe Alex
Rotherham U v Mansfield T
Walsall v Cardiff C
York C v Carlisle U

Friday 24 January
Division Three
Wigan Ath v Torquay U

Division Four
Doncaster R v Hereford U

Saturday 25 January
Division Three
Birmingham C v Bolton W
Brentford v Preston NE
Bury v Chester C
Darlington v Bradford C
Exeter C v Fulham
Hartlepool U v Stockport Co
Hull C v Stoke C
Peterborough U v AFC Bournemouth
Reading v Leyton O
Shrewsbury T v Huddersfield T
WBA v Swansea C

Division Four
Barnet v Burnley
Cardiff C v Chesterfield
Carlisle U v Halifax T
Crewe Alex v York C
Gillingham v Rochdale
Mansfield T v Lincoln C
Northampton T v Aldershot
Scarborough v Maidstone U
Scunthorpe U v Walsall
Wrexham v Rotherham U

Tuesday 28 January
Dvision One
Liverpool v Arsenal
Tottenham H v Oldham Ath (7.45)

Division Two
Grimsby T v Southend U

Division Three
Swansea C v Darlington

Wednesday 29 January
Division One
Nottingham F v Manchester U

Division Two
Leicester C v Tranmere R (7.45)

Friday 31 January
Division Two
Cambridge U v Tranmere R (7.45)

Division Three
Wigan Ath v Birmingham C

Division Four
Cardiff C v Mansfield T

Saturday 1 February
Division One
Arsenal v Manchester U
Aston Villa v Everton
Crystal Palace v Coventry C
Leeds U v Notts Co
Liverpool v Chelsea
Manchester C v Tottenham H
Norwich C v Southampton
Nottingham F v Sheffield U
QPR v Wimbledon
Sheffield W v Luton T
West Ham U v Oldham Ath

Division Two
Blackburn R v Swindon T
Brighton & HA v Charlton Ath
Bristol C v Barnsley
Middlesbrough v Grimsby T
Millwall v Ipswich T
Oxford U v Newcastle U
Plymouth Arg v Bristol R
Portsmouth v Derby Co
Southend U v Watford
Sunderland v Port Vale
Wolverhampton W v Leicester C

Division Three
AFC Bournemouth v Leyton O
Bury v Exeter C
Chester C v Stockport Co
Fulham v Bolton W
Huddersfield T v Preston NE
Hull C v Hartlepool U
Peterborough U v Reading
Shrewsbury T v Darlington
Stoke C v Swansea C
Torquay U v Bradford C
WBA v Brentford

Division Four
Blackpool v Barnet
Carlisle U v Wrexham
Chesterfield v Halifax T
Gillingham v Doncaster R
Lincoln C v York C
Rochdale v Maidstone U
Rotherham U v Aldershot
Scarborough v Crewe Alex
Scunthorpe U v Northampton T
Walsall v Burnley

Friday 7 February
Division Three
Stockport Co v Huddersfield T

Division Four
Crewe Alex v Carlisle U

Saturday 8 February
Division One
Chelsea v Crystal Palace
Coventry C v Liverpool
Everton v QPR
Luton T v Norwich C
Manchester U v Sheffield W
Notts Co v Arsenal
Oldham Ath v Leeds U
Sheffield U v Manchester C
Southampton v Nottingham F
Tottenham H v West Ham U
Wimbledon v Aston Villa

Division Two
Barnsley v Cambridge U
Bristol R v Sunderland
Charlton Ath v Southend U
Derby Co v Millwall
Grimsby T v Blackburn R
Ipswich T v Portsmouth
Leicester C v Oxford U
Newcastle U v Bristol C
Port Vale v Middlesbrough
Swindon T v Brighton & HA
Tranmere R v Wolverhampton W
Watford v Plymouth Arg

Division Three
Birmingham C v WBA
Bolton W v Chester C
Bradford C v AFC Bournemouth
Brentford v Bury
Darlington v Hull C
Exeter C v Wigan Ath
Hartlepool U v Peterborough U
Leyton O v Stoke C
Preston NE v Fulham
Reading v Shrewsbury T
Swansea C v Torquay U

Division Four
Aldershot v Walsall
Barnet v Scarborough
Burnley v Lincoln C
Doncaster R v Cardiff C
Halifax T v Rochdale
Hereford U v Chesterfield
Mansfield T v Scunthorpe U
Northampton T v Gillingham
Wrexham v Blackpool
York C v Rotherham U

Tuesday 11 February
Division Three
AFC Bournemouth v Bury (7.45)
Bolton W v Shrewsbury T
Bradford C v Birmingham C
Chester C v Exeter C
Fulham v Darlington
Huddersfield T v Hartlepool U
Leyton O v Wigan Ath (7.45)
Preston NE v Hull C
Stockport Co v Reading
Swansea C v Brentford
Torquay U v Peterborough U

Division Four
Aldershot v Gillingham
Burnley v Northampton T
Chesterfield v Barnet
Rochdale v Scarborough
Rotherham U v Cardiff C
Walsall v Mansfield T (7.45)
York C v Scunthorpe U

Wednesday 12 February
Division Three
Stoke C v WBA

Division Four
Halifax T v Blackpool
Hereford U v Crewe Alex
Lincoln C v Doncaster R (7.45)
Maidstone U v Carlisle U (8.00)

Saturday 15 February
Division One
Arsenal v Sheffield W
Chelsea v Southampton
Coventry C v Norwich C
Crystal Palace v Nottingham F
Leeds U v Aston Villa
Liverpool v Wimbledon
Manchester C v Luton T
Notts Co v Everton
Oldham Ath v QPR
Sheffield U v Tottenham H
West Ham U v Manchester U

Division Two
Barnsley v Southend U
Blackburn R v Newcastle U
Brighton & HA v Oxford U
Bristol C v Middlesbrough
Cambridge U v Charlton Ath
Derby Co v Bristol R
Ipswich T v Wolverhampton W
Millwall v Grimsby T
Port Vale v Leicester C
Portsmouth v Watford
Sunderland v Plymouth Arg
Swindon T v Tranmere R

Division Three
Birmingham C v AFC Bournemouth
Brentford v Torquay U
Bury v Leyton O
Darlington v Huddersfield T
Exeter C v Swansea C
Hartlepool U v Preston NE
Hull C v Bolton W
Peterborough v Stockport Co
Reading v Fulham
Shrewsbury T v Chester C
WBA v Bradford C
Wigan Ath v Stoke C

Division Four
Barnet v Maidstone U
Blackpool v Rochdale
Cardiff C v York C
Crewe Alex v Chesterfield
Doncaster R v Aldershot
Gillingham v Rotherham U
Mansfield T v Hereford U
Northampton T v Walsall
Scarborough v Lincoln C
Scunthorpe U v Burnley (11.00)
Wrexham v Halifax T

Friday 21 February
Division Two
Tranmere R v Ipswich T

Division Four
Aldershot v Mansfield T

Saturday 22 February
Division One
Aston Villa v Oldham Ath
Everton v Leeds U
Luton T v Sheffield U
Manchester U v Crystal Palace
Norwich C v Liverpool
Nottingham F v Chelsea
QPR v Notts Co
Sheffield W v West Ham U
Southampton v Coventry C
Tottenham H v Arsenal
Wimbledon v Manchester C

Division Two
Bristol R v Millwall
Charlton Ath v Bristol C
Grimsby T v Swindon T
Leicester C v Derby Co
Middlesbrough v Blackburn R
Newcastle U v Barnsley
Oxford U v Cambridge U
Plymouth Arg v Brighton & HA
Southend U v Sunderland
Watford v Port Vale
Wolverhampton W v Portsmouth

Division Three
AFC Bournemouth v WBA
Bolton W v Exeter C
Bradford C v Wigan Ath
Chester C v Hartlepool U
Fulham v Peterborough U
Huddersfield T v Reading
Leyton O v Birmingham C
Preston NE v Shrewsbury T
Stockport Co v Hull C
Stoke C v Brentford

Swansea C v Bury
Torquay U v Darlington

Division Four
Burnley v Blackpool
Chesterfield v Scarborough
Halifax T v Doncaster R
Hereford U v Cardiff C
Lincoln C v Crewe Alex
Maidstone U v Wrexham
Rochdale v Carlisle U
Rotherham U v Barnet
Walsall v Gillingham
York C v Northampton T

Friday 28 February
Division Two
Cambridge U v Bristol R (7.45)

Division Three
Wigan Ath v Fulham

Division Four
Crewe Alex v Halifax T

Saturday 29 February
Division One
Arsenal v Nottingham F
Chelsea v Sheffield W
Coventry C v Manchester U
Crystal Palace v Norwich C
Leeds U v Luton T
Liverpool v Southampton
Manchester C v Aston Villa
Notts Co v Tottenham H
Oldham Ath v Wimbledon
Sheffield U v QPR
West Ham U v Everton

Division Two
Barnsley v Charlton Ath
Blackburn R v Oxford U
Brighton & HA v Southend U
Bristol C v Grimsby T
Derby Co v Watford
Ipswich T v Plymouth Arg
Millwall v Leicester C
Port Vale v Newcastle U
Portsmouth v Tranmere R
Sunderland v Wolverhampton W
Swindon T v Middlesbrough

Division Three
Birmingham C v Stoke C
Brentford v Stockport Co
Bury v Bradford C
Darlington v Chester C
Exeter C v AFC Bournemouth
Hartlepool U v Swansea C
Hull C v Huddersfield T
Peterborough U v Bolton W
Reading v Preston NE
Shrewsbury T v Leyton O
WBA v Torquay U

Division Four
Blackpool v Maidstone U
Cardiff C v Burnley
Carlisle U v Chesterfield
Doncaster R v Walsall
Gillingham v Lincoln C
Mansfield T v York C
Northampton T v Hereford U
Scarborough v Rotherham U
Scunthorpe U v Aldershot
Wrexham v Rochdale

Tuesday 3 March
Division Three
Birmingham C v Swansea C (8.00)
Brentford v Chester C (7.45)
Bury v Torquay U
Darlington v Stockport Co
Hartlepool U v Bolton W
Hull C v Bradford C
Peterborough U v Huddersfield T

Shrewsbury T v Fulham
Wigan Ath v AFC Bournemouth

Division Four
Barnet v Aldershot (7.45)
Blackpool v Hereford U
Cardiff C v Walsall
Carlisle U v York C
Crewe Alex v Rochdale
Doncaster R v Chesterfield
Gillingham v Burnley (7.45)
Mansfield T v Rotherham U
Northampton T v Maidstone U
Scunthorpe U v Halifax T
Wrexham v Lincoln C

Wednesday 4 March
Division Three
Exeter C v Preston NE
Reading v Stoke C (7.45)
WBA v Leyton O

Friday 6 March
Division Two
Tranmere R v Port Vale

Division Three
Stockport Co v Hartlepool U

Division Four
Halifax T v Carlisle U

Saturday 7 March
Division One
Aston Villa v Sheffield U
Everton v Oldham Ath
Luton T v Crystal Palace
Manchester U v Chelsea
Norwich C v Arsenal
Nottingham F v Liverpool
QPR v Manchester C
Sheffield W v Coventry C
Southampton v West Ham U
Tottenham H v Leeds U
Wimbledon v Notts Co

Division Two
Bristol R v Blackburn R
Charlton Ath v Millwall
Grimsby T v Barnsley
Leicester C v Sunderland
Middlesbrough v Cambridge U
Newcastle U v Brighton & HA
Oxford U v Swindon T
Plymouth Arg v Derby Co
Southend U v Portsmouth
Watford v Ipswich T
Wolverhampton W v Bristol C

Division Three
AFC Bournemouth v Peterborough U
Bolton W v Birmingham C
Bradford C v Darlington
Chester C v Bury
Fulham v Exeter C
Huddersfield T v Shrewsbury T
Leyton O v Reading
Preston NE v Brentford
Stoke C v Hull C
Swansea C v WBA
Torquay U v Wigan Ath

Division Four
Aldershot v Northampton T
Burnley v Barnet
Chesterfield v Cardiff C
Hereford U v Doncaster R
Lincoln C v Mansfield T
Maidstone U v Scarborough
Rochdale v Gillingham
Rotherham U v Wrexham
Walsall v Scunthorpe U
York C v Crewe Alex

Tuesday 10 March
Division One
Arsenal v Oldham Ath (7.45)
Liverpool v West Ham U
Notts Co v Aston Villa (7.45)
Wimbledon v Everton (7.45)

Division Two
Blackburn R v Southend U (7.45)
Cambridge U v Newcastle U (7.45)
Grimsby T v Brighton & HA
Middlesbrough v Barnsley
Plymouth Arg v Bristol C (7.45)
Sunderland v Ipswich T (7.45)
Swindon T v Charlton Ath (7.45)

Division Three
AFC Bournemouth v Torquay U
(7.45)
Birmingham C v Brentford (8.00)
Bolton W v Stockport Co
Bradford C v Exeter C
Chester C v Peterborough U
Darlington v Reading
Fulham v Huddersfield T
Leyton O v Swansea C (7.45)
Shrewsbury T v Hull C
Wigan Ath v Preston NE

Division Four
Blackpool v Aldershot
Cardiff C v Gillingham
Carlisle U v Barnet
Mansfield T v Northampton T
Rochdale v Scunthorpe U
Rotherham U v Doncaster R
Wrexham v Scarborough
York C v Burnley

Wednesday 11 March
Division One
Coventry C v Nottingham F (7.45)
Luton T v Tottenham H (7.45)
Manchester U v Manchester C (8.00)
Norwich C v Chelsea (7.45)
QPR v Leeds U (7.45)
Sheffield W v Sheffield U (7.45)
Southampton v Crystal Palace

Divsion Two
Bristol R v Wolverhampton W (8.00)
Derby Co v Port Vale
Leicester C v Portsmouth (7.45)
Millwall v Tranmere R (7.45)
Oxford U v Watford

Division Three
Stoke C v Bury
WBA v Hartlepool U

Division Four
Halifax T v Hereford U
Lincoln C v Walsall
Maidstone U v Crewe Alex (8.00)

Friday 13 March
Division Three
Stockport Co v AFC Bournemouth

Saturday 14 March
Division One
Aston Villa v QPR
Chelsea v Coventry C
Crystal Palace v Liverpool
Everton v Luton T
Leeds U v Wimbledon
Manchester C v Southampton
Nottingham F v Norwich C
Oldham Ath v Notts Co
Sheffield U v Manchester U
Tottenham H v Sheffield W
West Ham U v Arsenal

Division Two
Barnsley v Oxford U
Brighton & HA v Blackburn R

Bristol C v Cambridge U
Charlton Ath v Crimsby T
Ipswich T v Leicester C
Newcastle U v Swindon T
Port Vale v Bristol R
Portsmouth v Millwall
Southend U v Middlesbrough
Tranmere R v Derby Co
Watford v Sunderland
Wolverhampton W v Plymouth Arg

Division Three
Brentford v Bradford C
Bury v WBA
Exeter C v Leyton O
Hartlepool U v Darlington
Huddersfield T v Stoke C
Hull C v Fulham
Peterborough U v Shrewsbury T
Preston NE v Chester C
Reading v Bolton W
Swansea C v Wigan Ath
Torquay U v Birmingham C

Division Four
Aldershot v Lincoln C
Barnet v Wrexham
Burnley v Halifax T
Chesterfield v Rochdale
Doncaster R v Mansfield T
Gillingham v Carlisle U
Hereford U v Maidstone U
Northampton T v Rotherham U
Scarborough v Blackpool
Scunthorpe U v Cardiff C
Walsall v York C

Friday 20 March
Division Three
AFC Bournemouth v Swansea C
(7.45)
Fulham v Hartlepool U
Shrewsbury T v Stockport Co
Wigan Ath v Brentford

Division Four
Cardiff C v Aldershot

Saturday 21 March
Division One
Arsenal v Leeds U
Chelsea v Sheffield U
Coventry C v Oldham Ath
Crystal Palace v Aston Villa
Liverpool v Tottenham H
Manchester U v Wimbledon
Norwich C v Everton
Nottingham F v Manchester C
Sheffield W v Notts Co
Southampton v Luton T
West Ham U v QPR

Division Two
Blackburn R v Charlton Ath
Bristol R v Barnsley
Cambridge U v Ipswich T
Derby Co v Wolverhampton W
Grimsby T v Newcastle U
Leicester C v Watford
Middlesbrough v Brighton & HA
Millwall v Port Vale
Oxford U v Portsmouth
Plymouth Arg v Tranmere R
Sunderland v Bristol C
Swindon T v Southend U

Division Three
Birmingham C v Huddersfield T
Bolton W v Bury
Bradford C v Peterborough U
Chester C v Hull C
Darlington v Preston NE
Leyton O v Torquay U
Stoke C v Exeter C
WBA v Reading

Division Four
Blackpool v Chesterfield
Carlisle U v Scarborough
Halifax T v Barnet
Lincoln C v Northampton T
Maidstone U v Gillingham
Mansfield T v Burnley
Rochdale v Hereford U
Rotherham U v Scunthorpe U
Wrexham v Crewe Alex
York C v Doncaster R

Friday 27 March
Division Two
Tranmere R v Leicester C

Division Three
Stockport Co v Fulham

Division Four
Aldershot v York C

Saturday 28 March
Division One
Aston Villa v Norwich C
Everton v Southampton
Leeds U v West Ham U
Luton T v Nottingham F
Manchester C v Chelsea
Notts Co v Crystal Palace
Oldham Ath v Sheffield W
QPR v Manchester U
Sheffield U v Liverpool
Tottenham H v Coventry C
Wimbledon v Arsenal

Division Two
Barnsley v Blackburn R
Brighton & HA v Cambridge U
Bristol C v Oxford U
Charlton Ath v Middlesbrough
Ipswich T v Derby Co
Port Vale v Plymouth Arg
Portsmouth v Swindon T
Southend U v Grimsby T
Watford v Bristol R
Wolverhampton W v Millwall

Division Three
Bury v Wigan Ath
Exeter C v Birmingham C
Hartlepool U v Shrewsbury T
Huddersfield T v WBA
Hull C v Leyton O
Peterborough U v Darlington
Preston NE v Bolton W
Reading v Chester C
Swansea C v Bradford C
Torquay U v Stoke C

Division Four
Barnet v Rochdale
Burnley v Maidstone U
Chesterfield v Wrexham
Crewe Alex v Blackpool
Gillingham v Mansfield T
Hereford U v Carlisle U
Northampton T v Cardiff C
Scarborough v Halifax T
Scunthorpe U v Lincoln C
Walsall v Rotherham U

Sunday 29 March
Division Two
Newcastle U v Sunderland (12.00)

Division Three
Brentford v AFC Bournemouth
(11.30)

Tuesday 31 March
Division Two
Ipswich T v Barnsley (7.45)
Plymouth Arg v Grimsby T (7.45)
Port Vale v Blackburn R
Portsmouth v Charlton Ath (7.45)

Tranmere R v Bristol C
Watford v Brighton & HA (7.45)
Wolverhampton W v Newcastle U

Division Three
Bolton W v AFC Bournemouth
Chester C v Bradford C
Darlington v Leyton O
Fulham v Stoke C
Hartlepool U v Exeter C
Huddersfield T v Bury
Hull C v Wigan Ath
Peterborough U v Birmingham C
Preston NE v Swansea C
Shrewsbury T v Torquay U
Stockport Co v WBA

Division Four
Aldershot v Scarborough
Burnley v Hereford U
Cardiff C v Blackpool
Doncaster R v Barnet
Gillingham v Wrexham (7.45)
Mansfield T v Crewe Alex
Northampton T v Rochdale
Rotherham U v Halifax T
Scunthorpe U v Chesterfield
Walsall v Maidstone U (7.45)

Wednesday 1 April
Division Two
Bristol R v Southend U (8.00)
Derby Co v Cambridge U
Leicester C v Middlesbrough (7.45)
Millwall v Oxford U (7.45)
Sunderland v Swindon T

Division Three
Reading v Brentford (7.45)

Division Four
Lincoln C v Carlisle U

Friday 3 April
Division Three
AFC Bournemouth v Chester C
(7.45)
Wigan Ath v Peterborough U

Division Four
Halifax T v Walsall
Wrexham v Doncaster R

Saturday 4 April
Division One
Chelsea v West Ham U
Coventry C v Arsenal
Crystal Palace v Everton
Liverpool v Notts Co (11.30)
Luton T v Wimbledon
Manchester C v Leeds U
Norwich C v Manchester U
Nottingham F v Sheffield W
Sheffield U v Oldham Ath
Southampton v QPR
Tottenham H v Aston Villa

Division Two
Barnsley v Derby Co
Blackburn R v Sunderland
Brighton & HA v Portsmouth
Bristol C v Leicester C
Cambridge U v Millwall
Charlton Ath v Plymouth Arg
Grimsby T v Bristol R
Middlesbrough v Watford
Newcastle U v Tranmere R
Oxford U v Wolverhampton W
Southend U v Ipswich T
Swindon T v Port Vale

Division Three
Birmingham C v Reading
Bradford C v Preston NE
Brentford v Shrewsbury T
Bury v Hull C

Exeter C v Huddersfield T
Leyton O v Hartlepool U
Stoke C v Darlington
Swansea C v Fulham
Torquay U v Stockport Co
WBA v Bolton W

Division Four
Barnet v Northampton T
Blackpool v Mansfield T
Carlisle U v Aldershot
Chesterfield v York C
Crewe Alex v Burnley
Hereford U v Rotherham U
Maidstone U v Scunthorpe U
Rochdale v Cardiff C
Scarborough v Gillingham

Friday 10 April
Division Two
Tranmere R v Middlesbrough

Division Four
Aldershot v Wrexham

Saturday 11 April
Division One
Arsenal v Crystal Palace
Aston Villa v Liverpool
Everton v Sheffield U
Leeds U v Chelsea
Manchester U v Southampton
Notts Co v Coventry C
Oldham Ath v Luton T
QPR v Tottenham H
Sheffield W v Manchester C
West Ham U v Norwich C
Wimbledon v Nottingham F

Division Two
Bristol R v Swindon T
Derby Co v Oxford U
Ipswich T v Newcastle U
Leicester C v Barnsley
Millwall v Bristol C
Plymouth Arg v Southend U
Port Vale v Brighton & HA
Portsmouth v Grimsby T
Sunderland v Charlton Ath
Watford v Blackburn R
Wolverhampton W v Cambridge U

Division Three
Bolton W v Bradford C
Chester C v Birmingham C
Darlington v Swansea C
Fulham v Bury
Hartlepool U v Stoke C
Huddersfield T v Wigan Ath
Hull C v Brentford
Peterborough U v WBA
Preston NE v Leyton O
Reading v Torquay U
Shrewsbury T v AFC Bournemouth
Stockport Co v Exeter C

Division Four
Cardiff C v Halifax T
Doncaster R v Scarborough
Gillingham v Blackpool
Lincoln C v Maidstone U
Mansfield T v Carlisle U
Northampton T v Crewe Alex
Rotherham U v Rochdale
Scunthorpe U v Barnet
Walsall v Chesterfield
York C v Hereford U

Tuesday 14 April
Division Two
Southend U v Port Vale (7.45)

Division Three
AFC Bournemouth v Huddersfield T
(7.45)
Torquay U v Hull C

Division Four
Blackpool v Doncaster R
Scarborough v Cardiff C

Wednesday 15 April
Division Two
Brighton & HA v Derby Co

Friday 17 April
Division Two
Cambridge U v Portsmouth

Division Three
Brentford v Darlington (12.00)
Swansea C v Shrewsbury T

Division Four
Halifax T v Aldershot

Saturday 18 April
Division One
Chelsea v QPR
Coventry C v Everton
Crystal Palace v Oldham Ath
Liverpool v Leeds U
Luton v Manchester U
Manchester C v West Ham U
Norwich C v Notts Co
Nottingham F v Aston Villa
Sheffield U v Arsenal
Southampton v Sheffield W
Tottenham H v Wimbledon

Division Two
Barnsley v Tranmere R
Blackburn R v Leicester C
Bristol C v Ipswich T
Charlton Ath v Watford
Grimsby T v Sunderland
Middlesbrough v Plymouth Arg
Newcastle U v Millwall
Oxford U v Bristol R
Swindon T v Wolverhampton W

Division Three
Birmingham C v Hartlepool U
Bradford C v Reading
Bury v Stockport Co
Exeter C v Peterborough U
Leyton O v Fulham
Stoke C v Preston NE
WBA v Chester C
Wigan Ath v Bolton W

Division Four
Barnet v Gillingham
Carlisle U v Northampton T
Chesterfield v Lincoln C
Crewe Alex v Scunthorpe U
Hereford U v Walsall
Maidstone U v Rotherham U
Rochdale v Burnley
Wrexham v York C

Monday 20 April
Division One
Arsenal v Liverpool
Aston Villa v Chelsea
Everton v Manchester C
Manchester U v Nottingham F
Notts Co v Sheffield U (7.45)
Oldham Ath v Tottenham H
QPR v Luton T
Shefield W v Norwich C
West Ham U v Crystal Palace
Wimbledon v Southampton

Division Two
Bristol R v Brighton & HA
Derby Co v Newcastle U
Plymouth Arg v Oxford U
Port Vale v Charlton Ath
Portsmouth v Bristol C

Sunderland v Middlesbrough
Tranmere R v Blackburn R (7.30)
Watford v Swindon T
Wolverhampton W v Southend U

Division Three
Bolton W v Brentford
Chester C v Torquay U
Darlington v Wigan Ath
Fulham v AFC Bournemouth
Hartlepool U v Bury
Huddersfield T v Leyton O
Hull C v WBA
Preston NE v Birmingham C
Reading v Exeter C
Shrewsbury T v Bradford C
Stockport Co v Stoke C (7.30)

Division Four
Aldershot v Chesterfield
Burnley v Scarborough
Cardiff C v Barnet
Doncaster R v Rochdale
Gillingham v Crewe Alex
Lincoln C v Hereford U
Rotherham U v Blackpool
Scunthorpe U v Wrexham
York C v Maidstone U

Tuesday 21 April
Division One
Leeds U v Coventry C (7.45)

Division Two
Ipswich T v Grimsby T (7.45)
Leicester C v Cambridge U (7.45)

Division Three
Peterborough U v Swansea C

Division Four
Mansfield T v Halifax T
Walsall v Carlisle U (7.45)

Wednesday 22 April
Division Two
Millwall v Barnsley (7.45)

Friday 24 April
Division Three
Wigan Ath v Hartlepool U

Division Four
Crewe Alex v Doncaster R

Saturday 25 April
Division One
Chelsea v Arsenal
Coventry C v West Ham U
Crystal Palace v Sheffield W
Liverpool v Manchester U
Luton v Aston Villa
Manchester C v Notts Co
Norwich C v Wimbledon
Nottingham F v QPR
Sheffield U v Leeds U
Southampton v Oldham Ath
Tottenham H v Everton

Division Two
Barnsley v Wolverhampton W
Blackburn R v Millwall
Brighton & HA v Sunderland
Bristol C v Derby Co
Cambridge U v Port Vale
Charlton Ath v Leicester C
Grimsby T v Watford
Middlesbrough v Bristol R
Newcastle U v Portsmouth
Oxford U v Ipswich T
Southend U v Tranmere R
Swindon T v Plymouth Arg

Division Three
AFC Bournemouth v Reading
Birmingham C v Shrewsbury T
Bradford C v Stockport Co
Bury v Darlington
Exeter C v Hull C
Leyton O v Peterborough U
Stoke C v Chester C
Swansea C v Huddersfield T
Torquay U v Bolton W
WBA v Preston NE

Division Four
Barnet v Walsall
Blackpool v Northampton T
Carlisle U v Burnley
Chesterfield v Gillingham
Halifax T v Lincoln C
Hereford U v Scunthorpe U
Maidstone U v Mansfield T
Rochdale v Aldershot
Scarborough v York C
Wrexham v Cardiff C

Sunday 26 April
Division Three
Brentford v Fulham

Saturday 2 May
Division One
Arsenal v Southampton
Aston Villa v Coventry C
Everton v Chelsea
Leeds U v Norwich C
Manchester U v Tottenham H
Notts Co v Luton T
Oldham Ath v Manchester C
QPR v Crystal Palace
Sheffield W v Liverpool
West Ham U v Nottingham F
Wimbledon v Sheffield U

Division Two
Bristol R v Charlton Ath
Derby Co v Swindon T
Ipswich T v Brighton & HA
Leicester C v Newcastle U
Millwall v Southend U
Plymouth Arg v Blackburn R
Port Vale v Grimsby T
Portsmouth v Barnsley
Sunderland v Cambridge U
Tranmere R v Oxford U
Watford v Bristol C
Wolverhampton W v Middlesbrough

Division Three
Bolton W v Stoke C
Chester C v Leyton O
Darlington v Exeter C
Fulham v Bradford C
Hartlepool U v AFC Bournemouth
Huddersfield T v Torquay U
Hull C v Swansea C
Peterborough U v Brentford
Preston NE v Bury
Reading v Wigan Ath
Shrewsbury T v WBA
Stockport Co v Birmingham C

Division Four
Aldershot v Hereford U
Burnley v Wrexham
Doncaster R v Maidstone U
Gillingham v Halifax T
Lincoln C v Blackpool
Mansfield T v Rochdale
Northampton T v Scarborough
Rotherham U v Chesterfield
Scunthorpe U v Carlisle U
Walsall v Crewe Alex
York C v Barnet

BARCLAYS LEAGUE FIXTURES 1991–92

DIVISION ONE

	Arsenal	Aston Villa	Chelsea	Coventry C	Crystal Palace	Everton	Leeds U	Liverpool	Luton T	Manchester C	Manchester U	Norwich C	Nottingham F	Notts Co	Oldham Ath	QPR	Sheffield U	Sheffield W	Southampton	Tottenham H	West Ham U	Wimbledon
Arsenal	—	11.1	5.10	7.9	11.4	21.12	21.3	20.4	27.8	31.8	1.2	14.12	29.2	26.10	10.3	17.8	21.9	15.2	2.5	30.11	2.11	1.1
Aston Villa	24.8	—	20.4	2.5	4.9	1.2	21.12	11.4	5.10	7.12	21.8	28.3	21.9	16.11	22.2	14.3	7.3	18.1	28.12	7.9	26.12	26.10
Chelsea	25.4	18.9	—	14.3	8.2	28.9	14.9	19.10	31.8	1.1	14.12	16.11	30.11	28.8	21.12	18.4	21.3	29.2	15.2	11.1	4.4	17.8
Coventry C	4.4	28.9	2.11	—	19.10	18.4	18.9	8.2	21.8	17.8	29.2	15.2	11.3	14.9	21.3	11.1	28.8	14.12	30.11	1.1	25.4	31.8
Crystal Palace	14.9	21.3	26.10	1.2	—	4.4	17.8	14.3	15.12	1.11	30.11	29.2	15.2	1.1	18.4	28.9	31.8	25.4	16.11	22.12	17.9	27.8
Everton	18.8	19.10	2.5	21.9	7.9	—	22.2	28.12	14.3	20.4	24.8	3.9	18.1	23.11	7.3	8.2	11.4	26.12	28.3	5.10	7.12	16.11
Leeds U	3.9	15.2	11.4	21.4	18.1	30.11	—	21.9	29.2	7.9	28.12	2.5	18.8	1.2	26.10	16.11	5.10	24.8	26.12	14.12	28.3	14.3
Liverpool	28.1	14.9	1.2	26.10	2.11	31.8	18.4	—	1.11	21.12	25.4	30.11	14.12	4.4	17.8	27.8	1.1	28.9	29.2	19.10	10.3	15.2
Luton T	26.12	25.4	28.12	20.12	7.3	2.11	7.12	24.8	—	15.2	23.11	8.2	28.3	28.9	14.9	18.9	22.2	19.10	4.9	1.2	18.1	4.4
Manchester C	28.12	29.2	28.3	18.1	24.8	17.9	4.4	21.8	15.2	—	16.11	26.12	4.9	25.4	28.9	14.9	26.10	14.9	14.3	1.2	18.4	30.11
Manchester U	19.10	21.12	7.3	7.12	22.2	21.3	31.8	28.9	21.9	11.3	—	4.4	18.1	29.1	24.8	15.2	2.11	14.3	11.3	17.8	21.9	25.4
Norwich C	7.3	1.1	11.3	7.12	29.2	3.9	2.5	30.11	8.2	26.12	7.9	—	2.11	18.4	11.1	21.12	17.8	18.9	26.10	31.8	24.8	5.10
Nottingham F	7.12	21.9	30.11	11.3	15.2	18.1	18.8	14.12	28.3	4.9	2.11	2.11	—	24.8	5.10	19.10	18.9	1.2	22.2	28.12	14.12	25.4
Notts Co	8.2	18.4	22.2	11.4	1.1	23.11	1.2	4.4	28.9	25.4	18.1	19.10	10.11	—	2.11	7.9	28.3	3.9	5.10	18.8	19.10	29.2
Oldham Ath	16.11	30.11	3.9	2.5	18.4	7.3	26.10	17.8	14.9	28.9	2.11	4.4	2.11	23.11	—	15.2	7.9	28.3	7.9	28.8	5.10	18.8
QPR	18.1	2.11	21.9	11.1	28.9	8.2	16.11	27.8	18.9	14.9	24.8	19.10	5.10	7.9	15.2	—	7.12	28.12	7.9	11.4	4.9	1.2
Sheffield U	18.4	14.12	21.3	28.8	31.8	11.4	5.10	1.1	22.2	26.10	2.11	21.3	19.10	28.12	7.9	7.12	—	17.11	24.8	15.2	18.8	28.9
Sheffield W	23.11	7.12	29.2	14.12	25.4	26.12	24.8	28.9	19.10	14.9	28.8	18.9	18.4	3.9	28.3	28.12	17.11	—	21.9	2.11	21.9	21.12
Southampton	28.9	31.8	15.2	30.11	16.11	28.3	26.12	29.2	4.9	14.3	26.10	2.11	1.2	2.11	7.9	7.9	24.8	18.4	—	17.8	7.3	18.9
Tottenham H	22.2	4.4	11.1	26.11	22.12	5.10	14.12	19.10	1.2	21.12	28.12	26.12	7.12	28.1	14.9	23.11	14.3	18.1	18.1	—	14.12	11.1
West Ham U	14.3	28.8	7.9	20.4	17.9	7.12	28.3	10.3	18.1	15.2	14.12	28.9	26.12	1.2	5.10	4.9	18.8	21.9	7.3	8.2	—	11.1
Wimbledon	28.3	8.2	18.1	28.12	26.12	10.3	14.3	7.3	5.10	11.4	7.3	7.12	19.10	2.5	18.8	20.4	21.9	18.8	20.4	21.9	24.8	—

DIVISION TWO

	Barnsley	Blackburn R	Brighton & HA	Bristol C	Bristol R	Cambridge	Charlton Ath	Derby Co	Grimsby T	Ipswich T	Leicester C	Middlesbrough	Millwall	Newcastle U	Oxford U	Plymouth Arg	Portsmouth	Port Vale	Southend U	Sunderland	Swindon T	Tranmere R	Watford	Wolverhampton W
Barnsley	—	16.11	11.1	1.2	21.3	26.10	7.12	7.9	7.3	31.3	11.4	10.3	22.4	2.11	17.8	2.5	27.8	23.11	31.8	21.9	1.1	22.12	5.10	5.10
Blackburn R	16.11	—	14.3	11.1	7.3	9.11	5.11	4.9	8.2	31.8	21.9	30.11	25.4	15.2	29.2	12.10	2.5	14.9	10.3	5.11	7.9	28.9	17.9	29.10
Brighton & HA	24.8	2.11	—	1.1	28.9	28.3	23.11	19.10	10.3	2.5	26.12	2.2	19.10	1.1	28.3	7.3	25.4	14.9	29.2	5.10	8.2	20.4	17.1	28.12
Bristol C	19.10	1.1	1.1	—	21.12	23.11	10.3	22.2	10.3	17.8	21.9	7.9	11.4	31.8	21.9	19.10	21.3	16.11	2.11	9.2	26.10	17.8	12.10	28.12
Bristol R	21.3	7.3	20.4	21.12	—	3.9	31.8	31.8	14.3	21.3	21.9	25.4	17.9	26.10	28.3	19.10	31.8	28.12	28.12	25.4	26.10	17.8	12.10	31.8
Cambridge	8.2	1.1	28.3	14.3	3.9	—	15.2	1.4	17.8	9.11	21.4	7.3	7.9	6.11	7.9	6.11	29.10	21.9	5.10	20.4	2.5	18.10	1.1	8.2
Charlton Ath	7.12	9.11	19.10	2.5	10.3	31.8	—	31.8	14.3	29.10	29.9	28.3	4.4	10.3	21.9	18.1	17.4	25.4	3.9	12.10	24.8	31.1	29.12	17.9
Derby Co	4.4	21.3	21.9	22.2	5.10	13.9	31.8	—	4.9	21.3	25.4	28.3	7.3	10.3	11.4	7.9	21.3	25.4	3.9	12.10	24.8	31.1	1.2	21.3
Grimsby T	14.12	26.10	4.4	17.8	9.11	21.9	31.3	14.3	—	26.12	21.4	19.10	1.2	14.12	1.2	28.9	21.9	16.11	30.11	7.3	31.8	21.3	29.2	1.1
Ipswich T	14.9	31.8	29.10	18.4	11.1	29.10	7.9	7.12	26.12	—	28.9	19.10	7.12	26.10	21.9	4.9	26.10	16.11	3.9	22.2	26.12	2.11	29.12	15.2
Leicester C	17.9	18.4	2.5	21.9	21.9	4.4	1.1	25.4	30.11	28.9	—	14.3	14.9	2.5	14.3	12.10	26.10	12.10	28.1	13.12	1.4	31.8	25.4	1.2
Middlesbrough	5.11	30.11	28.9	3.9	15.2	14.12	28.3	21.8	19.10	16.11	24.8	—	1.4	4.9	21.12	18.4	21.9	16.11	28.12	14.3	4.9	13.12	21.3	2.5
Millwall	5.11	25.4	21.12	29.2	3.9	17.9	14.12	7.3	8.2	28.9	23.11	1.4	—	7.12	8.2	28.12	21.3	26.10	2.5	11.4	9.11	29.10	4.4	16.11
Newcastle U	30.11	15.2	1.1	21.12	26.10	31.8	10.3	20.4	17.8	7.12	21.3	1.4	2.5	—	19.10	4.9	21.12	1.2	23.10	29.2	1.1	2.11	26.12	12.10
Oxford U	14.3	29.2	28.3	21.12	21.9	21.9	1.1	11.4	1.1	5.10	8.2	21.12	1.4	19.10	—	4.9	20.4	9.11	2.5	21.3	17.8	14.3	4.4	7.9
Plymouth Arg	18.1	12.10	12.10	5.11	19.10	26.12	26.12	14.12	4.4	14.9	11.1	1.4	28.12	21.12	28.12	—	1.1	16.11	26.12	28.12	7.3	7.3	4.4	18.1
Portsmouth	12.10	17.8	14.9	28.9	30.10	17.4	25.4	14.9	19.10	17.9	17.9	11.3	31.8	25.4	21.3	1.1	—	11.3	26.12	19.10	7.3	23.11	22.2	22.2
Port Vale	26.12	14.9	18.9	3.9	2.11	25.4	4.9	14.9	11.3	12.10	20.8	23.11	26.10	21.3	21.3	18.1	1.1	—	7.9	19.10	14.4	6.3	2.2	3.9
Southend U	15.2	10.3	29.2	23.11	1.4	23.11	3.9	8.2	24.8	28.1	5.11	28.12	2.5	23.10	9.11	28.9	26.12	16.11	—	21.9	30.11	4.10	19.10	20.4
Sunderland	20.8	4.4	25.4	14.3	8.2	12.10	3.9	8.2	17.9	8.2	14.3	20.4	28.9	24.8	14.3	4.9	28.12	16.11	23.11	—	22.2	13.12	30.11	7.12
Swindon T	28.12	1.2	26.10	26.10	2.5	11.4	24.8	2.5	22.2	7.12	23.10	14.3	7.12	23.10	9.11	28.12	5.10	16.11	21.3	9.11	—	1.4	15.2	26.10
Tranmere R	18.4	28.9	17.8	11.1	11.1	31.1	31.1	2.11	31.8	22.2	3.9	29.1	17.9	11.3	14.3	12.10	21.3	29.2	13.12	25.4	15.2	—	22.10	26.10
Watford	3.9	17.9	14.9	16.11	16.11	29.12	18.4	1.2	29.2	25.4	14.12	21.3	4.4	26.12	12.10	14.12	26.12	3.12	2.11	30.11	1.2	22.10	—	18.1
Wolverhampton W	25.4	29.10	31.8	14.12	11.3	17.9	1.1	21.3	1.1	15.2	12.0	16.11	14.9	4.4	2.11	30.11	20.12	28.9	29.2	18.4	11.3	17.8	18.1	—

DIVISION THREE

	Birmingham C	Bolton W	Bournemouth	Bradford C	Brentford	Bury	Chester C	Darlington	Exeter C	Fulham	Hartlepool U	Huddersfield T	Hull C	Leyton O	Peterborough U	Preston NE	Reading	Shrewsbury T	Stockport Co	Stoke C	Swansea C	Torquay U	WBA	Wigan Ath
Birmingham C	—	25.1	15.2	30.11	10.3	17.8	17.9	31.8	23.11	20.12	18.4	21.3	1.1	1.1	14.9	28.9	4.4	25.4	12.10	29.2	3.3	2.11	8.2	19.10
Bolton W	7.3	—	31.3	11.4	20.4	21.3	17.9	9.11	1.2	2.11	3.3	15.2	26.12	29.2	25.1	23.11	2.11	11.2	5.11	2.5	21.12	5.10	7.9	21.9
Bournemouth	14.12	14.9	—	26.10	22.11	30.11	14.3	28.12	29.2	12.10	2.5	14.4	31.8	1.2	7.3	1.1	25.4	17.9	1.11	21.12	20.3	10.3	22.2	18.1
Bradford C	11.2	17.9	26.10	—	2.11	4.1	14.9	25.1	10.3	12.10	21.3	22.12	18.1	1.1	21.3	4.4	18.4	28.9	25.4	17.8	30.11	15.2	14.12	22.2
Brentford	5.11	28.9	3.3	2.11	—	8.2	3.3	4.1	22.12	26.4	9.11	14.9	17.9	5.10	3.9	12.10	26.12	24.8	18.4	5.10	31.8	15.2	14.3	28.3
Bury	28.12	9.11	30.11	29.2	26.10	—	25.1	19.10	1.2	17.8	26.12	14.9	4.4	21.4	3.9	2.11	26.12	24.8	18.4	5.10	31.8	20.4	14.3	21.12
Chester C	11.4	26.10	7.9	31.3	18.1	7.3	—	3.3	11.2	17.8	8.2	1.1	2.5	31.3	10.3	21.3	14.3	14.2	3.3	5.10	31.8	11.1	11.4	20.4
Darlington	26.12	3.9	28.12	25.1	21.9	6.11	24.8	—	2.5	30.11	31.3	15.2	8.2	31.3	18.4	13.12	10.3	19.10	18.9	9.11	15.2	26.12	28.12	8.2
Exeter C	28.3	1.2	29.2		2.5				—	25.1	4.4	10.3	2.11	21.9	2.2	4.3	28.9	26.12	22.11	9.11	7.9	4.9	28.12	4.1
Fulham	24.8	1.2	20.4	2.5	5.10	24.8	7.3	2.5	—	30.11	4.1	30.11	19.10	7.9	8.2	26.10	13.12	18.1	25.1	31.3	7.9	26.12	5.11	5.10
Hartlepool U	21.9	3.3	2.5	26.12	26.12	19.10	31.3	14.9	31.3	9.11	—	4.1	19.10	28.3	2.2	1.2	24.8	28.3	25.1	11.4	2.5	28.12	28.3	11.4
Huddersfield T	9.11	15.2	21.9	25.8	26.12	14.12	11.4	12.10	11.4	15.2	28.12	—	23.11	28.3	25.4	17.9	28.12	5.11	14.3	25.1	2.5	21.3	28.3	31.3
Hull C	22.2	26.12	2.5	3.9	28.12	14.12	12.10	14.9	7.9	30.12	11.4	23.11	—	20.12	25.4	7.3	1.2	4.1	25.1	5.11	10.3	21.3	20.4	11.2
Leyton O	3.9	29.2	3.9	11.4	1.4	2.5	14.3	12.10	2.11	1.2	7.9	29.2	23.11	—	25.4	17.9	1.2	14.3	15.2	31.8	21.4	30.11	18.1	7.9
Peterborough U	31.3	29.2	25.1	9.11	2.5	1.1	14.3	28.32	18.1	8.2	14.12	3.3	10.11	20.12	—	30.8	22.2	22.2	26.12	21.9	31.3	24.8	9.11	5.11
Preston NE	20.4	28.3	3.9	5.10	14.3	21.9	21.3	6.11	20.4	14.12	7.9	11.1	11.2	11.4	28.12	—	4.1	8.2	19.10	21.9	11.4	11.4	9.11	2.5
Reading	7.9	14.3	5.10	21.9	7.9	21.12	15.2	1.2	31.8	3.3	25.1	17.8	10.3	29.2	1.1	10.3	—	20.3	1.1	21.9	31.3	13.3	2.5	18.8
Shrewsbury T	5.10	30.11	11.4	20.4	1.2	21.12	18.10	18.1	31.8	6.3	7.2	2.11	7.3	21.12	11.1	30.8	11.2	—	8.11	21.4	17.8	6.9	31.3	1.1
Stockport Co	2.5	5.11	13.3	4.1	31.8	11.3	25.4	18.1	21.3	14.9	18.9	2.11	7.3	7.3	29.2	18.4	39	4.9	—	20.4	1.2	22.11	12.2	14.12
Stoke C	4.1	12.10	24.8	28.12	1.1	25.4	4.4	21.3	14.12	4.4	4.1	12.10	12.10	5.11	11.1	18.4	39	17.4	28.9	—	1.2	19.10	19.10	14.3
Swansea C	18.1	24.8	28.12	22.2	11.2	26.12	4.4	22.2	1.1	31.8	17.8	1.1	29.2	21.4	8.2	20.12	17.9	14.9	4.4	28.3	—	17.8	2.5	7.3
Torquay U	26.10	25.4	11.1	28.12	1.2	14.12	21.3	17.8	31.8	1.1	2.11	12.10	28.9	4.3	18.9	25.4	21.3	14.9	4.4	30.11	25.1	—	29.2	14.3
WBA	26.10	4.4	11.1	15.2	1.2	22.11	17.8	11.3	1.1	3.4	18.9	2.11	14.9	18.9	3.4	20.12	11.10	28.12	3.9	30.11	1.11	24.1	—	31.8
Wigan Ath	31.1	18.4	—	20.3	23.8	28.9	23.8	8.2	26.10	28.2	15.2	17.9	14.9	30.11	3.4	10.3	11.10	28.12	3.9	15.2	1.11	24.1	26.12	—

DIVISION FOUR

	Aldershot	Barnet	Blackpool	Burnley	Cardiff C	Carlisle U	Chesterfield	Crewe Alex	Doncaster R	Gillingham	Halifax T	Hereford U	Lincoln C	Maidstone	Mansfield T	Northampton T	Rochdale	Rotherham U	Scarborough	Scunthorpe U	Walsall	Wrexham	York C
Aldershot	—	17.1	5.11	21.12	8.11	6.9	20.4	1.1	14.12	11.2	18.10	31.3	3.1	8.2	10.4	27.3							
Barnet	3.3	—	19.10	25.1	28.9	5.11	30.11	17.8	14.9	18.4	14.12	11.2	8.2	25.4	14.3	12.10							
Blackpool	10.3	1.2	—	11.1	14.9	21.12	21.3	23.11	14.4	17.9	30.11	31.8	11.1	17.8	26.10	1.1							
Burnley	24.8	7.3	22.2	—	4.1	5.10	3.9	7.9	28.12	18.1	10.3	14.3	31.3	8.2	28.3	2.5	5.11						
Cardiff C	20.3	20.4	31.3	29.2	—	31.8	25.1	21.12	26.10	10.3	11.4	31.3	8.2	28.3	14.12	19.10	2.11	3.3					
Carlisle U	4.4	10.3	24.8	28.12	28.12	—	29.2	26.10	26.12	18.1	25.1	17.8	30.11	14.9	23.11	21.9	7.9	3.9	1.2	12.10	28.9	1.2	3.3
Chesterfield	28.9	11.2	9.11	1.1	7.3	4.1	—	14.12	18.1	25.4	12.10	26.10	30.11	30.11	21.12	14.3	14.3	3.9	26.12	14.9	28.9	28.3	4.4
Crewe Alex	3.9	26.12	28.3	7.3	24.8	7.2	15.2	—	14.12	18.1	18.4	18.4	11.1	17.9	12.10	21.12	11.1	3.9	19.10	14.9	17.9	28.3	25.1
Doncaster R	15.2	31.3	20.9	31.8	8.2	7.2	15.2	—	—	24.4	28.9	30.11	24.1	13.9	21.12	14.3	3.3	28.12	22.2	18.4	17.9	7.9	9.11
Gillingham	30.11	21.9	11.4	3.3	17.8	7.8	3.3	5.10	24.4	—	1.1	24.1	30.11	14.3	5.11	1.1	20.4	5.11	19.10	20.12	29.2	7.9	25.1
Halifax T	17.4	21.3	12.2	5.11	8.2	6.3	5.10	20.4	—	2.5	—	11.3	29.2	2.5	28.3	26.10	25.1	15.2	7.9	17.8	11.1	31.3	8.11
Hereford U	12.10	11.4	18.1	17.9	17.9	19.10	19.10	4.1	1.2	22.2	2.5	—	25.4	21.12	27.9	17.8	8.2	13.9	7.9	22.11	3.4	13.12	30.8
Lincoln C	2.11	4.9	2.5	26.12	28.12	6.3	8.2	22.2	22.2	12.10	14.3	11.3	—	14.12	14.12	4.1	9.11	4.4	24.8	25.4	18.4	26.12	18.9
Maidstone	28.12	23.11	26.10	11.4	11.4	28.3	26.12	21.3	12.10	22.2	4.1	28.9	11.4	—	7.3	21.3	28.12	24.8	14.12	23.11	11.3	18.1	1.2
Mansfield T	11.1	4.4	4.1	4.9	4.9	12.2	28.12	31.3	2.11	23.11	5.10	11.4	7.3	25.4	—	7.3	19.10	24.8	7.3	23.11	14.9	22.2	28.9
Northampton T	25.1	7.9	7.9	21.3	19.10	19.10	28.12	31.3	3.9	8.2	6.11	20.4	21.3	18.1	25.4	—	10.3	3.3	26.12	4.4	30.11	3.9	29.2
Rochdale	1.2	23.11	21.3	14.12	15.10	11.4	2.11	11.4	8.2	7.3	5.10	2.11	25.1	3.3	18.1	10.3	—	14.3	2.5	19.10	15.2	28.12	11.1
Rotherham U	14.9	14.12	18.4	28.3	10.3	21.9	1.1	18.1	7.3	29.2	3.3	29.2	9.11	3.3	5.11	14.9	31.3	—	17.9	10.3	1.1	4.1	17.8
Scarborough	29.2	12.12	14.2	11.2	2.5	1.1	31.8	18.1	10.3	14.12	31.3	21.12	21.12	21.9	12.10	14.9	11.4	17.9	—	4.1	21.3	22.11	7.3	25.10
Scunthorpe U	14.9	26.10	14.3	28.9	14.4	9.11	1.2	18.9	4.4	28.3	28.3	21.12	15.2	25.1	17.8	12.10	30.11	29.2		1.1	31.8	5.11	25.4
Walsall	29.2	11.4	28.12	15.2	14.3	31.3	21.9	24.8	26.12	3.3	5.10	28.3	7.9	26.10	26.10	1.2	5.11	9.11	3.9		25.1	20.4	30.11
Wrexham	26.10	5.10	26.12	12.2	18.1	21.4	11.4	2.5	4.1	22.2	7.9	21.9	5.11	31.3	11.2	14.12	3.9	28.3	28.12	7.3	25.1	—	24.8	14.3
York C	23.11	2.5	3.9	10.3	14.12	18.1	7.9	21.3	21.3	3.4	14.9	15.2	17.8	28.12	11.4	24.8	29.2	26.12	8.2	5.10	11.2	2.11	21.9

THE FOOTBALL ASSOCIATION
FIXTURE PROGRAMME—SEASON 1991–92

August
3 Sat   Official Opening Season
10 Sat   FA Charity Shield
17 Sat   Football League Season Commences
26 Mon   Bank Holiday
31 Sat   FA Challenge Cup Preliminary Round

September
7 Sat   FA Challenge Vase Extra Preliminary Round
        FA Youth Challenge Cup Preliminary Round*
10 Tue   England v Germany (U21)
11 Wed   England v Germany (F)
14 Sat   FA Challenge Cup 1st Round Qualifying
18 Wed   EC/ECWC/UEFA 1st Round (1st Leg)
21 Sat   FA Challenge Trophy 1st Round Qualifying
28 Sat   FA Challenge Cup 2nd Round Qualifying
        FA Youth Challenge Cup 1st Round
        Qualifying*

October
2 Wed   EC/ECWC/UEFA 1st Round (2nd Leg)
5 Sat   FA Challenge Vase Preliminary Round
12 Sat   FA Challenge Cup 3rd Round Qualifying
        FA Youth Challenge Cup 2nd Round
        Qualifying*
13 Sun   FA Sunday Cup 1st Round
15 Tue   England v Turkey (U21)
16 Wed   England v Turkey (EC)
19 Sat   FA Challenge Trophy 2nd Round Qualifying
        FA County Youth Challenge Cup 1st Round*
23 Wed   EC/ECWC/UEFA 2nd Round (1st Leg)
26 Sat   FA Challenge Cup 4th Round Qualifying

November
2 Sat   FA Challenge Vase 1st Round
6 Wed   EC/ECWC/UEFA 2nd Round (2nd Leg)
9 Sat   FA Youth Challenge Cup 1st Round Proper*
10 Sun   FA Sunday Cup 2nd Round
12 Tue   Poland v England (U21)
13 Wed   Poland v England (EC)
16 Sat   FA Challenge Cup 1st Round Proper
23 Sat   FA Challenge Vase 2nd Round
27 Wed   EC Quarter-Final Round In Groups
        UEFA 3rd Round (1st Leg)
30 Sat   FA Challenge Trophy 3rd Round Qualifying
        FA County Youth Challenge Cup 2nd Round*

December
7 Sat   FA Challenge Cup 2nd Round Proper
        FA Youth Challenge Cup 2nd Round Proper*
8 Sun   FA Sunday Cup 3rd Round
11 Wed   EC Quarter-Final Round in Groups
        UEFA 3rd Round (2nd Leg)

14 Sat   FA Challenge Vase 3rd Round
26 Thu   Boxing Day

January
1 Wed   New Years Day
4 Sat   FA Challenge Cup 3rd Round Proper
11 Sat   FA Challenge Trophy 1st Round Proper
        FA Youth Challenge Cup 3rd Round Proper*
18 Sat   FA Challenge Vase 4th Round
        FA County Youth Challenge Cup 3rd Round*
19 Sun   FA Sunday Cup 4th Round
25 Sat   FA Challenge Cup 4th Round Proper

February
1 Sat   FA Challenge Trophy 2nd Round Proper
8 Sat   FA Challenge Vase 5th Round
        FA Youth Challenge Cup 4th Round Proper*
15 Sat   FA Challenge Cup 5th Round Proper
16 Sun   FA Sunday Cup 5th Round
19 Wed   England v France (F)
22 Sat   FA Challenge Trophy 3rd Round Proper
        FA County Youth Challenge Cup 4th Round*
29 Sat   FA Challenge Vase 6th Round

March
4 Wed   EC Quarter-Final Round in Groups
        ECWC/UEFA Quarter-Final (1st Leg)
7 Sat   FA Challenge Cup 6th Round Proper
        FA Youth Challenge Cup 5th Round Proper*
14 Sat   FA Challenge Trophy 4th Round Proper
18 Wed   EC Quarter-Final Round in Groups
        ECWC/UEFA Quarter-Final (2nd Leg)
21 Sat   FA Challenge Vase Semi-Final (1st Leg)
        FA County Youth Challenge Cup Semi-Final*
22 Sun   FA Sunday Cup Semi-Final
25 Wed   Czechoslovakia v England (F)
28 Sat   FA Challenge Vase Semi-Final (2nd Leg)

April
1 Wed   EC Quarter-Final Round in Groups
        ECWC/UEFA Semi-Final (1st Leg)
4 Sat   FA Challenge Trophy Semi-Final (1st Leg)
        FA Youth Challenge Cup Semi-Final*
5 Sun   FA Challenge Cup Semi-Final
11 Sat   FA Challenge Trophy Semi-Final (2nd Leg)
15 Wed   EC Quarter-Final Round in Groups
        ECWC/UEFA Semi-Final (2nd Leg)
20 Mon   Bank Holiday
25 Sat   FA Challenge Vase Final (Wembley Stadium)
29 Wed   USSR v England (F)
        UEFA Final (1st Leg)

Continued from page 976
Taylor, Peter (b. Nottingham 2.7.28; d. Majorca 4.10.90). A goalkeeper with Coventry City 1946–55, Middlesbrough 1955–61 and Port Vale 1961, he made over 200 appearances. It was, however, as managerial assistant to Brian Clough at Derby County and Nottingham Forest that he found fame with so much success in the 1970s. His managerial experience had begun with Burton Albion before he teamed up with Clough at Derby. They moved together to Brighton and Taylor stayed behind to manage that club alone 1974–76 before resuming his partnership with Clough at Nottingham Forest. They finally split in 1982 and Taylor had a brief spell in charge at Derby before retiring in 1984.

Tiler, Brian (b. Whiston 15.3.43; d. Italy July 1990). A clever half-back who played in over 350 League games 1962–73 with Rotherham, Aston Villa and Carlisle United. Subsequently in America with Atlanta Chiefs and Portland Timbers before becoming assistant manager of Wigan Athletic. Was National Coach in Zambia 1979–82, and held an administrative position with Bournemouth for a short while in 1983. Was in the Villa team that regained Second Division status in 1971–72.

Wyles, Cecil (b. Dunsby Fen 1.11.1919; d. October 1990). Capped for England as a schoolboy he developed with Peterborough before joining Everton in 1938. After a number of war-time games moved to Blackburn Rovers in 1945. As a centre-forward he scored four goals in one game against Burnley in October 1945, and was the club's penalty expert. Transferred to Bury in May 1946 and on to Southport before the year was out. Enjoyed much adulation with Southport for whom he scored 54 goals in 143 appearances. Finished his career with Bangor and Spalding.